Karl Devenport

211,

Sandy, Utah 84093

((801)-943-5033)

October 1992

Expedition to Amazon Basin
Iquitos, Peru → Explorama Camp
+ Napo Camp

1994

A GUIDE TO THE BIRDS OF COLOMBIA

A GUITDE TO THE

# Birds of Colombia

By Steven L. Hilty and
William L. Brown

SIXTY-NINE COLOR AND
BLACK AND WHITE PLATES BY

Guy Tudor

AND H. WAYNE TRIMM, JOHN GWYNNE,
LARRY MCQUEEN, JOHN YRIZARRY,
AND P. PRALL

LINE DRAWINGS BY
MICHEL KLEINBAUM
AND JOHN GWYNNE

PRINCETON UNIVERSITY PRESS

DEDICATED TO THE MEMORY OF
DR. F. CARLOS LEHMANN V.

*Colombian ornithologist and*
*pioneering conservationist.*
*This book was one of his goals,*
*and its inception is owed*
*in no small way to his legacy.*

# CONTENTS

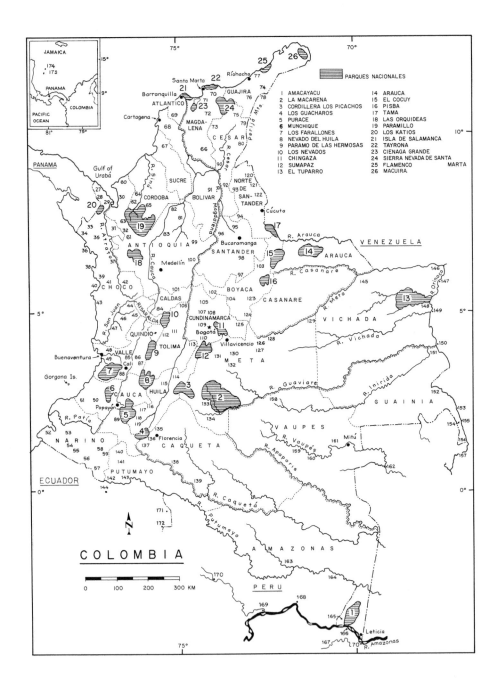

PARQUES NACIONALES

| 1 | AMACAYACU | 14 | ARAUCA |
|---|---|---|---|
| 2 | LA MACARENA | 15 | EL COCUY |
| 3 | CORDILLERA LOS PICACHOS | 16 | PISBA |
| 4 | LOS GUACHAROS | 17 | TAMA |
| 5 | PURACE | 18 | LAS ORQUIDEAS |
| 6 | MUNCHIQUE | 19 | PARAMILLO |
| 7 | LOS FARALLONES | 20 | LOS KATIOS |
| 8 | NEVADO DEL HUILA | 21 | ISLA DE SALAMANCA |
| 9 | PARAMO DE LAS HERMOSAS | 22 | TAYRONA |
| 10 | LOS NEVADOS | 23 | CIENAGA GRANDE |
| 11 | CHINGAZA | 24 | SIERRA NEVADA DE SANTA MARTA |
| 12 | SUMAPAZ | 25 | FLAMENCO |
| 13 | EL TUPARRO | 26 | MACUIRA |

COLOMBIA

0   100   200   300 KM

PACIFIC COLOMBIA AND
URABÁ REGION
27. Acandí 0-100m
28. Cerro Tacarcuna 1900m
29. Unguí 15m
30. Turbo 0 m
31. Río Sucio
32. Mutatá 200m
33. Río Salaquí 100-300m
34. Río Juradó
35. Río Truandó
36. Bahía Octavia
37. Río Napipí
38. Bahía Solano
39. Baudó Mts. 1070m
40. Nuquí 30m
41. Río Uva
42. Quibdó 50m
43. Río Baudó 100-1100m
44. Tadó 90m
45. Cerro Tatamá 3950m
46. Novita 70m
47. Noanamá 50m
48. Dagua Val. 0-1800m
49. Río Anchicayá 0-1250m
50. Cerro Munchique 1800-
    3000m
51. Guapí 50m
52. Tumaco 0 m
53. Barbacoas 50m
54. Junín 1100m
55. Ricaurte 1400m
56. Volcán Cumbal 4750m
57. Ipiales 2900m
58. Pasto 2600m
59. Laguna La Cocha 2800m

CARIBBEAN REGION TO
PERIJA MTS.
60. Río Mulatos
61. Frontino
62. Quimarí (Snía. Abibe) 1000m
63. Río Verde del Sinú
64. Tierralta 120m
65. Cerro Murrucucú 1270m
66. El Difícil 100m
67. Snía. de San Jacinto 800m
68. Turbaco 200m
69. Laguna Luruaco 20m
70. Cuchilla de San Lorenzo
    1600-2800m
71. Río Frío 30m
72. Fundación 50m
73. Caracolicito 200-250m
74. Carraipía 150m
75. Valledupar 200m
76. Río Ranchería

77. Manaure 0 m
78. Montes de Oca 150-600m
79. Codazzi 200m
80. Casacará 100m

CAUCA VALLEY
81. Río Nechí
82. Caucasia 100m
83. Pto. Valdivia 200m; Valdivia
    1200m
84. Manizales 2000m
85. Bosque Yotoco 1400m
86. Lago de Sonso 1000m
87. Palmira 1000m
88. Pichindé Val. 1500-1800m
89. Coconuco 2500m

MAGDALENA VALLEY
90. El Banco; Cga. de Zapatosa
    50m
91. Snía. San Lucas (Volador)
    800m
92. Gamarra 70m
93. Ocaña 1200m
94. Cáchira 2000m
95. Río Lebrija 50-1000m
96. Barrancabermeja (El Cen-
    tro) 100m
97. Virolín 2000m
98. San Gil 1100m
99. Remedios 1000m
100. Pto. Berrío 150m
101. Río Samaná 1200m (Pá-
     ramo Sonsón 3000m)
102. Muzo
103. Soatá 2600m
104. Laguna Fúquene 2600m
105. Yacopí 1400m
106. Honda 250m
107. Sasaima 1200m
108. Represa Neusa 3000m
109. Sabana de Bogotá 2600m
110. Fusagasugá 1750m
111. Ibagué 1300m
112. Río Toche 2000-2500m
113. Melgar 430m
114. Villavieja 400m
115. Neiva 430m
116. Río Moscopán 2000-2900m
117. Finca Merenberg 2300m
118. Isnos 1700m
119. San Agustín 1600m

EAST OF THE ANDES
120. Catatumbo lowlands
121. Petrólea 100m
122. Zulia Val.

123. Lago Tota 3000m
124. Río Upía
125. Río Guavio
126. Pto. López 200m
127. Mozambique 100m
128. Remolino 200m
129. Carimagua 300m
130. Hacienda La Corocora
     400m
131. Guamal
132. San Martín
133. Macarena Mts.
134. Río Guayabero
135. Pto. Venecia 300m
136. Morelia; Río Bodoquiera;
     300m
137. Belén 400-450m
138. Tres Esquinas 200m
139. Tres Troncos 150m
140. Mocoa 600m
141. Pto. Umbría 400-500m
142. Río San Miguel
143. Pto. Asís 250m
144. Limoncocha, Ecuador 250m
145. Hato El Tigre
146. Pto. Carreño 100m
147. Pto. Ayacucho, Venez. 100m
148. Maipures 150m
149. Munduapo, Venez.
150. San Fernando de Atabapo,
     Venez.
151. Pto. Inírida
152. Río Guainía
153. Río Ventuari, Venez.
154. San Felipe 100-150m
155. San Carlos 100-150m
156. Río Macacuní 100-150m
157. Río Negro 100m
158. San José del Guaviare
159. El Dorado 300m
160. Miraflores 275m
161. Caño Cubiyú 100m
162. Tahuapunto
163. Río Igara-Paraná 200m
164. San Martín, Peru
165. Pto. Nariño 100m
166. Monkey Isl. (Isla San So-
     phia III) and Isla Corea
     100m
167. Río Javarí, Brazil-Peru
168. Pebas, Peru
169. Pto. Indiana, Peru
170. Mouth of Río Curaray, Peru
171. Zancudocha, Ecuador
172. Jatuncocha, Ecuador
173. San Andrés
174. Providencia

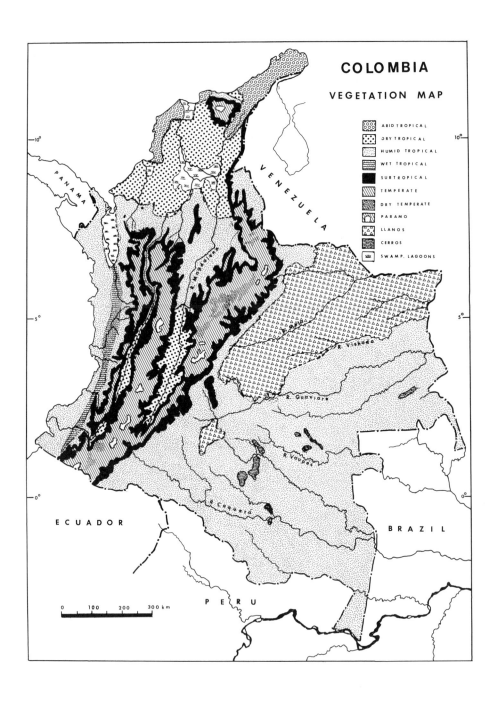

COLOMBIA

VEGETATION MAP

ARID TROPICAL
DRY TROPICAL
HUMID TROPICAL
WET TROPICAL
SUBTROPICAL
TEMPERATE
DRY TEMPERATE
PARAMO
LLANOS
CERROS
SWAMP, LAGOONS

PANAMA

VENEZUELA

ECUADOR

BRAZIL

PERU

R. Magdalena

R. Meta

R. Vichada

R. Guaviare

R. Vaupes

R. Caqueta

0    100    200    300 km

# ACKNOWLEDGMENTS

THIS BOOK could not have been completed without the help of many persons. Our greatest debt is to collaborator Robert S. Ridgely, who read most of the text and contributed extensively to many species accounts. The late Eugene Eisenmann provided a wealth of ideas and encouragement and gave us much valuable advice on taxonomic matters. Guy Tudor, through his ideas, criticisms, and painstaking attention to detail, has improved the species descriptions and comparisons immeasurably and given insight into many taxonomic problems. Others (in alphabetical order) that have contributed substantially to the manuscript include, Peter Alden, Jon Barlow, Charles T. Collins, Thomas H. Davis, John Fitzpatrick, Sean Furniss, Alan Gast, Paul Gertler, Steve Gniadek, Michael Gochfeld, Jorge I. Hernández C., Terry B. Johnson, Kenn Kaufman, the late Wallace McKay, William J. Mader, J. Van Remsen, the late Hernando Romero Z., Stephen M. Russell, Theodore A. Parker III, Thomas S. Schulenberg, the late James R. Silliman, Phil Silverstone, and François Vuilleumier. James Gulledge permitted us to use the Laboratory of Ornithology's Library of Natural Sounds at Cornell University, including the extensive tape recordings of the late Paul Schwartz. Ben Coffee also made available taped sound recordings. The late Eugene Eisenmann and Wesley Lanyon (American Museum of Natural History, New York), Storrs Olson (United States National Museum, Washington), John P. O'Neill (Louisiana State University Museum of Zoology), the late Padre Olivares (Museo del Universidad Nacional, Bogotá), the late F. Carlos Lehmann V. (Museo de Ciencias Natural, Cali), and José Ignacio Borrero (Museo del Universidad del Valle, Cali), allowed us to use the bird collections in their care. We acknowledge the contribution of J. W. Fitzpatrick and D. E. Willard in reviewing the collection of Colombian birds in the Field Museum of Natural History, Chicago, and providing new information in time to be included in this volume. The names of many other contributors can be found with their data in the text and are gratefully acknowledged.

The late Rodolphe Meyer de Schauensee and William H. Phelps, Jr., generously granted us permission to use plates from *A Guide to the Birds of Venezuela* (1978), and Robert S. Ridgely has kindly allowed us to use plates from *A Guide to the Birds of Panama* (3d ed., 1981). Species or subspecies of birds not occurring in Colombia in the above plates were replaced with ones from Colombia. These plates and many new plates have made it possible to portray most of the resident birds of Colombia.

Guy Tudor, one of the most talented living bird illustrators, planned and supervised all of the art work. The thirty-eight color plates and nine black and white plates that he painted amply display his commitment to accurate detail and artistic perfection. Other excellent plates were painted by H. Wayne Trimm, John Gwynne, Larry McQueen, John Yrizarry and P. Prell. Michel Kleinbaum is responsible for the many beautiful line drawings and one black and white plate.

Special thanks for the loan of museum specimens to the artists is hereby acknowledged to the following: American Museum of Natural History, New York; Academy of Natural Sciences, Philadelphia; Museum of Zoology, Louisiana State University; and the Field Museum of Natural History, Chicago.

Hilty's work in Colombia began in 1971. It has been aided by a University of Arizona/Peace Corps graduate program, the Instituto Nacional de los Recursos Naturales Renovables y del Ambiente (INDERENA), the Corporación Autónoma y Regional para el Desarrolla del Valle (CVC), Ira Joel Abramson of Bird Bonanzas, Inc., Eliécer Solarte N. and Hector Perdomo of the CVC, the late F. Carlos Lehmann V. in Cali, and the hospitality of Pic and the late Donald S. Bailey and also Peter Jennings in Cali, Daniel Margolis in Bogotá, Tim and Bunny Cain at Puerto Inírida, and many Colombians throughout the country. His greatest debt is owed Beverly Hilty for her support throughout field work and writing and for suffering much neglect during this period.

Brown's work in Colombia began in 1960. On early visits the late Dr. F. Carlos Lehmann V. arranged many trips to various parts of Colombia, and it was at this time that a book on the birds of Colombia was first conceived. Special thanks are due to Dr. José Borrero of Cali, Professor Leo Garcia of Pasto and Popayán, Emma and Nick Ponomareff for their hospitality on several visits to their ranch in the llanos, Dr. Reinaldo Diaz and the staff at Museo de Ciencias Natural in Cali. Great credit is due Carmel Brown who often cheerfully endured rather-primitive accommodation in the field and typed many versions of the manuscript and seemingly endless revisions.

*Steven L. Hilty, Tucson, Arizona*
*William L. Brown, Toronto, Canada*
*May 30, 1984*

A GUIDE TO THE BIRDS OF COLOMBIA

# PLAN OF THE BOOK

THIS BOOK treats all of the 1695 species of resident and migrant birds known to have been reliably recorded in Colombia and on its island possessions of Gorgona and Malpelo prior to 1984. A number of additional species reported for the Colombian islands of San Andrés and Providencia in the Caribbean are listed in Appendix II. An additional 133 species described in the notes to the species accounts probably occur in Colombia but have not been recorded within its boundaries as yet. A few of these can be found on the south bank of the Amazon opposite Colombia but are not known to cross the Amazon.

In general we follow the scientific nomenclature and order of species set out by Meyer de Schauensee in *The Species of Birds of South America with their Distribution* (1966) and by the *American Ornithologists' Union Checklist* (1957). Where we differ, the sources are noted in the text. Through notes we attempt to point out taxonomic questions or existing controversy when it applies to Colombian populations. English names are generally those standardized by Eisenmann in "The Species of Middle American Birds" (1955) and by Meyer de Schauensee (*Birds of South America*), although some alternative English names are mentioned. Spanish names are not given because of their lack of standardization.

## FAMILY ACCOUNTS

The sequence of families described is taken from Wetmore's "A Classification for the Birds of the World" (1960), with a few exceptions, which are so identified in the text. The family summary preceding the species accounts assumes a relatively standard plan: the general distribution of the family is followed by some broad comments on physical appearance, habitat, habits, breeding behavior, and sometimes taxonomic problems. The total number of Colombian species in the family is shown in the heading.

## SPECIES ACCOUNTS

Each species account is divided into a maximum of eight sections, although one or more sections may be omitted when not applicable or when information is lacking.

### IDENTIFICATION

The species' average length from bill tip to tail tip is given first, in both inches and centimeters. Key features—for instance, bill size, bill shape, soft part colors—or additional measurements may follow. Then the species is described; if sexually dimorphic, males are described first, distinguishing marks for immatures or juveniles are given last. For migrants that are most likely seen in Colombia in their nonbreeding plumage, this plumage is described first. If racial variation is slight, the extent is described—for example, olive to olive green, without mentioning the subspecies—but when differences are clearly observable in the field, subspecies are described separately and followed by the subspecific name. Subspecies names are also used when a taxonomic problem exists.

## SIMILAR SPECIES

This section gives field marks separating similar species that overlap in range. Species whose ranges are not likely to overlap are not discussed even though they may be similar in appearance. For quick reference, the species number of each similar species in the family is given in parentheses. Similar species in other families are referenced with a page number.

## VOICE

Onomatopoeic transcriptions of songs, calls, and mechanical sounds are given when known and believed useful. A number of transcriptions were recorded outside of Colombia. If they accurately describe the bird's notes in Colombia, the country of origin is not given. When doubt exists, the source location is given. Similarly, one or more source locations within Colombia may be cited if the notes differ between populations. Published or unpublished transcriptions or tape recordings other than our own are acknowledged.

## BEHAVIOR

The emphasis in this paragraph varies with the family—for instance, flight characteristics in parrots, display in manakins, or foraging in flycatchers—but the data is intended to be, in part, an aid in finding and identifying the species.

## BREEDING

Colombian breeding dates are emphasized but may be supplemented by data from adjacent countries. Data on nests, nest sites, and eggs follow when available. In the shorthand used, the abbreviation "BC" denotes "breeding condition," thus "5 BC males May" means five breeding condition males were collected in May.

## STATUS AND HABITAT

This section gives the relative abundance of a species, major habitat preference(s), and sometimes places where the species can be seen or where specimens have been collected, as well as comments on species replacement or zones of contact and overlap with congeners.

### Abundance

Because most birds are "common" in the proper habitat, their apparent abundance is often more a function of observer ability or improper habitat, and so forth, than of actual disposition of the species. Notwithstanding, sightings of some birds are recorded more often than others, and an estimate of abundance can lend some reality to one's expectations of finding a bird. A few caveats should be kept in mind however. First, our relative abundance estimates may be biased by the localities we have visited, by the information we have had at hand, and by the habitats we have visited. Second, birds of the forest floor and undergrowth (e.g., tinamous and antpittas) may be heard frequently but are rarely seen; our abundance estimates in these cases are based on vocalizations. Third, some birds are vocal during their breeding period, especially nightjars, and thus seem common at such times, but at other times are silent and very difficult to find. Fourth, birds found near the periphery of their range, elevationally or geographically, are likely to be rarer than in the center of their range. Last, because small birds are, in an absolute sense, usually more numerous than large birds, one must compare abundance estimates for birds of similar sizes, similar habitats, and so on.

In defining abundance, we will use the following terms:

*Common.* Recorded on virtually all field trips, often in numbers in proper habitat and season.

*Fairly common.* Recorded on at least half of the trips, in proper habitat and season.

*Uncommon.* Recorded on about a quarter of the trips.

*Rare.* Recorded on fewer than a quarter of the trips; often few records in Colombia.

*Local.* Denotes a species' real or apparent absence from habitat that seems to be suitable.

*Irregular* or *erratic.* Used interchangeably to denote a migrant or wanderer with strong and unpredictable fluctuations in numbers.

*Hypothetical.* Unless a record is supported by a specimen collected or a photograph from Colombia, it is considered hypothetical. The data for hypothetical species are given in the status and habitat section, the English name is placed in square brackets.

RANGE AND MAPS

Our indications of the highest and lowest elevations at which a species can be found are based on specimens unless noted. If only one elevation is given, it may be assumed that the species occurs from sea level or the lowlands up to the stated elevation. Because species commonly occur at lower elevation in humid mountain zones than in corresponding drier zones, a second set of elevations may be given if these differences are pronounced. Other factors mostly beyond the scope of this book also locally affect the elevations we describe. These may include the size of the mountain mass (Massenerhebungeffekt), prevailing winds, fog cover, historical factors and of course, recent human activity.

Elevational zones are usually not given in the text because of space limitations but they are a valuable means of categorizing the large number of species, and students of Colombian birds should be familiar with them. As defined by Chapman (1917) their limits are: Tropical Zone, sea level to 1400-1600m; Subtropical Zone, 1400-1600 to 2300-2600m; Temperate Zone, 2300-2600 to 3100-3400m; and Paramo Zone, 3100-3400m to snow line.

Elevation data are followed by definition of the Colombian range and then the extralimital range of the species. All range data in the text are based on specimens or published sources unless noted otherwise. Subspecies ranges are described when one or more forms differ markedly, or when a taxonomic question exists.

In late 1982 a new department or political unit called Guaviare was created from northwestern Vaupés. However, in the text we use the old boundary of Vaupés, extending to the Río Guaviare. For range localities not on the cover map see Paynter and Traylor (1981).

*Maps*

Range maps for most species are at the back of the book. When the number of records is small, black dots are used to mark the location of each record. Unverified but presumed ranges are marked by dots showing the known records and a heavy dashed line showing the probable range boundary. A question mark is used on the maps when gaps between the records are large and when information is insufficient to determine if a species is found there. The locations of extralimital records near the Colombian border are also marked by dots. Within the range limits, which are the broadest we can verify, gaps in the range may occur because of unsuitable habitat or because human activity has altered the environment. Therefore some species may no longer be as widespread as indicated on the maps, and the text should be consulted for details.

NOTE

This paragraph includes comments on taxonomy or brief descriptions and information on allied species likely but not yet reported in Colombia.

ABBREVIATIONS

| | |
|---|---|
| ad. | adult |
| AMNH | American Museum of Natural History, New York |
| ANSP | Academy of Natural Sciences, Philadelphia |
| BC | breeding condition |
| c | central |
| conspic. | conspicuous |
| e, s, w, n | east or eastward, south or southward, etc. |
| FMNH | Field Museum of Natural History, Chicago |
| imm. | immature |
| juv. | juvenile or juvenal (plumage) |
| MCN | Museo de Ciencias Natural, Cali |
| MM | Medellin Museum |
| MUNB | Museo de Historia Natural, Universidad Nacional de Colombia, Bogotá |
| MVZ | Museum of Vertebrate Zoology, Berkeley |
| opp. | opposite |
| PN | Parque Nacional |
| poss. | possible or possibly |
| presum. | presumed or presumably |
| prob. | probable or probably |
| prom. | prominent(ly) |
| Pto. | Puerto |
| rec. | record or recorded |
| reg. | regular(ly) |
| sim. | similar(ly) |
| Snía. | Serranía |
| subad. | subadult |
| USNM | United States National Museum, Washington, D.C. |
| val. | valley |

# TOPOGRAPHY

COLOMBIA stretches from the Caribbean Sea to the Río Amazon (12°31'N to 04°14'S) and from the Ríos Orinoco and Negro to the Pacific Ocean (66°51'W to 79°13'W), encompassing an area of slightly over 1,100,000 square kilometers. The eastern half of the country is flat, but the topography of the western half is the most complicated in South America, due mainly to the fact that in Colombia the Andes split into a complex series of three more or less parallel and north-south oriented mountain ranges, the Eastern, Central, and Western Andes. Near the Ecuadorian border all three ranges merge into a single larger range, topped by two volcanic cones that exceed 4700m elevation.

The three Andean ranges are separated by two large, deep valleys: the Cauca between the Western and Central Andes, and the Magdalena between the Central and Eastern Andes. The Cauca Valley is higher and narrower than the Magdalena but has a broad, flat, and fertile flood plain extending from the Cauca-Valle border north to Cartago. The Magdalena Valley is rather broad throughout its length.

The Western Andes are the lowest of the three ranges, with an average ridge line of about 2000m and an average width at the 1000-meter contour of 40 kilometers. There are no snow-capped peaks in the Western Andes and little paramo. The Central Andes, the highest range, have a prominent ridge line at an elevation of 3000-3500m. A few peaks, notably the nevados of the Caldas-Quindío region and the Nevado de Huila, exceed 5400m elevation and are capped by glaciers. The average width of the Central Andes at their base is about 80-100 kilometers. The Eastern Andes are the widest of the three ranges, averaging 100-200 kilometers. With an average ridge line of 2500m, the Eastern Andes are lower than the Central Andes, but higher than the Western. Much of the northern half of the Eastern Andes, from about 4° to 8°N, consists of a broad, high plateau. The Sabana de Bogotá, site of the capital city, forms the southern end of this plateau. The Eastern Andes contain extensive areas of paramo and the largest snowfield in the Colombian Andes, the latter in the Sierra Nevada del Cocuy. At about 7°30'N the Eastern Andes bifurcate. The main range continues eastward into Venezuela and a narrow high spine, the Perijá Mountains, extends northward along the Venezuelan boundary. The highest peak in the Perijás, Cerro de las Tetas, exceeds 3600m.

Both the Western and Central Andes terminate rather abruptly in tropical foothills at about 7°30'N. The northern end of the Western Andes divides into two northward projecting spurs, the Serranía de Abibe on the west, and Cerro Murucucú on the east. The Río Sinú flows between these two ridges. Alto de Quimarí, the highest point in the Abibe range is below 1000m, while Cerro Murrucucú reaches 1250m. Extensions of both ridges can be traced as low lines of hills well to the north of the Western Andes, those of Cerro Murrucucú eventually resurfacing near the Caribbean coast as the Serranía de San Jacinto, which reaches 600-800m.

The Central Andes end in a long northward projecting spur called the Serranía San Lucas, which has an average ridge line elevation of about 600-800m. According to Haffer (1974), a geological continuation of the Central Andes can be traced northward through the isolated Sierra Nevada de Santa Marta massif, the low Serranía de Macuira on the outer Guajira Peninsula, and the island chain of the Netherlands Antilles. The Macuira hills reach a maximum height of about 850m.

The isolated Sierra Nevada de Santa Marta forms a pyramid-shaped massif that springs abruptly from the flat Caribbean plain to permanent snowfields at nearly 5800m. These snowfields, the most extensive in Colombia, encompass Pico Simon Bolívar and Pico Cristobal, the highest peaks in Colombia.

West of the Gulf of Urabá and along the Panama boundary the Serranía del Darién reaches 1900m on Cerro Tacarcuna. A geological link between the Serranía del Darién and the Western Andes is indicated by the Cerro Cuchillo, a low ridge rising a little over 500 meters above the Atrato swamps on the east side of the Río Atrato. Farther west on the Panama border a rugged basalt range reaches 1550m on Cerro Pirre and continues south for about 200 kilometers along the Pacific coast as a series of low hills to the Serranía del Baudó. Alto del Buey, at 1070m, is the highest peak in the Baudó range, according to Haffer (1974). A low saddle between the Baudó Mountains and the Western Andes separates the Río Atrato, which drains north to the Caribbean, from the Río San Juan, the only Colombian river of importance that empties into the Pacific.

The eastern half of Colombia may be divided into two parts, both flat. The northern half, the llanos, is a vast plains area that declines almost imperceptibly toward the Orinoco. The monotonous topography of the llanos, which varies from about 500m near the Andes to 200m along the Orinoco, is interrupted by several long, east-flowing rivers. The most important of these rivers—the Arauca, Casanare, Meta, and Guaviare—all arise from sources high on the eastern wall of the Andes and cross the piedmont grasslands in straight lines to the Orinoco. North of the llanos, the Río Catatumbo arises from the bifurcation of the Eastern Andes and flows northeastward to the Maracaibo Basin in Venezuela.

The southern half of eastern Colombia, which lies generally south of the Río Guaviare, is a flat sea of forest stretching to the Amazon. It is also topographically featureless except for several large rivers, the Macarena Mountains, and a broad belt of isolated cerros scattered in an arc from the headwaters of the Río Apaporis to the Venezuela border. The most important rivers include the Guainía and Vaupés, tributaries of the Río Negro, and the Caquetá and Putumayo, which flow into the Río Amazon in Brazil. The Putumayo forms most of the long boundary with Peru, while the Amazon itself forms the south-ernmost boundary at Leticia.

The isolated Macarena Mountains rise in a southeastward trending line in southern Meta and are geologically distinct from the Andes. Over 100 kilometers in length and between 15 and 25 kilometers in width, they reach an estimated elevation of 1800m. The west-facing slope is a precipitous cliff towering above the humid forest, while the eastern slope rises gently from the forest floor. Geologically, the Ma-carena Mountains are related to the isolated table mountains and cerros scattered eastward, and to the tepuis of the Guiana Shield. The Macarenas and other table mountains of Colombia are more or less

1. Sandstone cerro along Río Inírida ca. 40km south of Puerto Inírida, Intendencia de Guainía. Similar cerros dot the landscape from the Río Orinoco in eastern Vichada south to eastern and central Vaupés. El. at base of cerro is ca. 150m. Sept 1978.

isolated erosional remnants of sandstone and conglomerate with relatively flat, mesa-like tops. Their forested lower slopes are usually
overshadowed by sheer cliffs rising high above the forest. Their summits are heavily weathered and covered by low xerophytic vegetation
that grows where thin sandy and bouldery soil accumulates in cracks
or depressions. Most soil on the summits is rapidly washed away by
frequent rains (Haffer 1974).

About 150 kilometers southeast of the Macarena Mountains, a number of rather large table mountains extend from the headwaters of
the Río Apaporis to the Río Caquetá. They attain elevations of between
700 and 900m, and rise 200-500 meters above the forested lowlands.
Most of these cerros, including Cerro Campana, Cerro Chiribiquete,
and the Mesas de Iguaje, have not been explored by ornithologists.
Eastward, many of the cerros are characteristically dome-shaped (fig.
1) and rise like great humpbacked monoliths above a flat landscape.
Their smoothly weathered and blackened surfaces are devoid of vegetation.

# CLIMATE

COLOMBIA is a land of climatic extremes, although with more than 70 percent of the land surface lying below 500m elevation, it enjoys a warm tropical climate for the most part. The dominant influences on Colombia's climate are the movement of the sun and the general atmospheric circulation of the tropics. Regionally, the coastlines, mountains, and the vegetation also play a significant role. These various factors often produce marked climatic changes over very short distances as well as significant seasonal differences in rainfall and wind speed.

The major *seasonal* change in Colombia's weather is rainfall. This is brought about by the north-south shifting of the sun's declination as it moves between the two tropics. As the sun's declination changes, there is a corresponding north-south shifting and subsequent strengthening and weakening of the high pressure areas in the trade wind belts on either side of the equator in the Atlantic and the Pacific. Ideally, these shifting high-pressure zones result in two rainy and two dry seasons each year in regions near the equator, but in Colombia this pattern is often complicated by various regional factors.

The Andes themselves are the most important regional factor. They exert their influence by altering existing atmospheric flows, by acting as important elevated heat sources and heat sinks, and by their elevational gradient. Vegetation is also an important regional factor affecting the climate of southeastern Colombia. The vast Amazonian forests lose moisture through evapotranspiration and create a daily cycle of cooling that plays an important role in the generation of afternoon rain showers.

Temperature and the length of days show relatively little variation through the year. Differences in the length of a day are minor because of Colombia's equatorial position. Temperature normally varies more during the course of a day than between months. But temperature varies with elevation, decreasing about 6°C with each 1000-meter increase in elevation, and it is the dominant climatic factor that produces the dramatic change one observes in the flora and fauna when ascending mountain slopes. Air temperatures on the north coast are the highest in Colombia, averaging 28-30°C (83-87°F), with less than 2°C difference between the coolest and warmest months. Cali, at 1000m elevation, has warm daytime temperatures and balmy evenings (annual average 24-26°C, or 75-79°F), while Bogotá, at 2600m, is chilly (12-14°C, or 54-58°F) and a city of sweaters. Temperatures below freezing are common in the upper paramo zone.

*Caribbean lowlands.* The climate of northern Colombia is strongly affected by the southward shifting of the northern trade wind belt during the temperate winter. From mid-December to mid-April dry northeastern trade winds buffet the Caribbean lowlands and produce a severe dry season. At this time trees drop their leaves, grass becomes brown and parched, and only a few species of birds breed. After mid-April the winds abate.

Average rainfall over most of the northern coastal zone is less than 850 millimeters (33.5″) per year (fig. 2), increasing to 1500 millimeters (59″) inland and 3000 millimeters (118″) at the northern base of the Andes. Rain falls principally from mid-May to October, peaking in May–June and September–October. The least rain falls on the desertlike Guajira Peninsula. Here the driest zones receive less than 300 millimeters (11.5″) a year.

Average annual temperature at sea level is 28°-30°C (83-87°F), with less than 2°C difference between the warmest and coolest months. The major exceptions to the climatic pattern described above occur on the steep, verdant, north- and west-facing slopes of the Sierra Nevada de Santa Marta and in a narrow humid zone extending down to sea level at the northeastern base of the Santa Marta Mountains. For much of the year these slopes are bathed by moisture-laden trade winds that precipitate over cool forests and help buffer the zone from the desiccating conditions of the surrounding lowlands. Rainfall is highest on the western (lee) side of the massif, presumably due to atmospheric movement around rather than over the mountains. In this zone, in a narrow band just below 2000m elevation, total annual rainfall may reach 4000 millimeters (157″).

*The Pacific region.* On the Pacific coast climatic conditions are very different. The dry trade wind dominated climate of the Gulf of Urabá in northern Chocó rapidly gives way southward to a hot, humid, and very rainy climate. Rainfall here is the heaviest and most nonseasonal in the Americas, varying from about 3000 millimeters (118″) at the northern and southern extremes to more than 10,000 millimeters (394″) annually in the vicinity of the upper Atrato-San Juan river divide. The annual average at Andagoya, south of Quibdó, is about 13,300 millimeters (524″), the highest in the Western Hemisphere. The highest single year total, reported in 1936 at Quibdó, was a remarkable 19,839 millimeters (781″) (Schmidt *in* Schwerdtfeger 1976).

Rain falls mainly in the late afternoon or at night, in many areas on 250 to 300 days per year. Mornings are usually clear with brilliant sunlight over steamy, forest-clad hills, but by noon on most days clouds cover the Pacific slope in a thick white blanket. The heaviest rainfall occurs in a narrow belt of the foothills between about 50-250m elevation. Rainfall diminishes gradually at higher elevations but is augmented by condensation from clouds. Month-to-month variation in

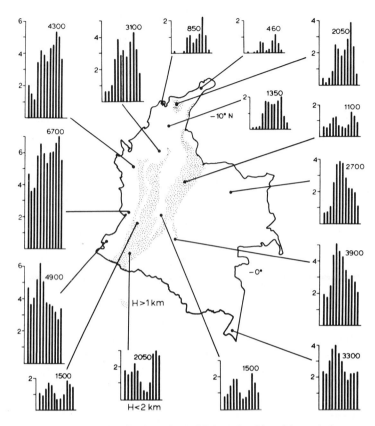

2. Annual distribution of rainfall in Colombia, with vertical
lines in mm/100, annual totals in mm. Based on period
between 1931 and 1960. Certain data are subject to reduction.
Reproduced with permission from Schwerdtfeger, ed., 1976
(above fig. adapted from J. W. Snow, author of chap. 6).

total rainfall is small, but May–June and October–November are usually rainier periods. Northward near the Gulf of Urabá and southward
in Nariño rainfall is more strongly seasonal.

*The Andes.* Throughout most of the Colombian Andes there are two
wet and two dry seasons each year. The rainiest periods are mid-
March to mid-June and October to mid-December. The longer and
true "dry season" in the Colombian Andes lasts from June through
September. Annual rainfall varies from about 1500 to 4000 millimeters (59-157″) due to the complex topography. Many valleys lie in
"rain shadows" that occur when surrounding higher ridges block in-
coming and moisture-filled clouds. Consequently, rain precipitates on
the high slopes but rarely on the hot dry valley floors below. Mountain
breezes that descend into rain shadow valleys are warmed and cause

even more drying. Some of these dry interior valleys are covered by thorn scrub and cactus. The most important rain shadow valleys are the middle and upper Magdalena and Cauca. The Cauca Valley floor is slightly higher and narrower and is also the drier, receiving about 1500 millimeters (59″) yearly over its floor and 2000 millimeters (79″) on its slopes. Corresponding figures for the Magdalena Valley are 1700 millimeters (67″) on the valley floor and 3000 (118″) on its slopes, but its upper end in Huila gets less than 1200 millimeters (47″) and is drier than the Cauca Valley. On the Pacific slope the small, arid, upper ends of the Río Sucio, Río Dagua, and Río Patía are surrounded by a sea of dripping cloud forest.

A similar situation at higher elevation occurs over the broadest part of the Eastern Andes, from Santander and southern Norte de Santander south to Cundinamarca. Moisture from the eastern lowlands precipitates on the foothills and the east-facing slopes, leaving the broad temperate zone *altiplano* with only about 800-1200 millimeters (31.5-47″) of rainfall annually. The same is true also of the deep Río Guáitara and Río Carchi valleys south of Pasto in Nariño.

*The llanos and Amazonian region.* The vast grasslands east of the Andes comprise the llanos. The climate is monsoonal with a severe dry season from late November to March and a single long wet season from April to mid-November. Over 90 percent of the annual precipitation in the llanos falls during the wet season, averaging 1600 millimeters (63″) in the north, 2000 millimeters (79″) in the south, and increasing to 3000 millimeters (118″) or more along the eastern base of the Andes.

South of the Río Guaviare, which roughly forms the southern boundary of the llanos, the climate is dominated by a large, more or less stationary equatorial air mass, resulting in almost daily afternoon rains. Rain usually falls in brief, hard showers that are quite local. The daily weather cycle in Amazonia is typical of that of many humid tropical regions—a morning cloud build-up, followed by an afternoon downpour, and then clearing skies and spectacular sunsets. Rainfall across most of Amazonian Colombia averages nearly 3500 millimeters (138″) a year, increasing to 3900 millimeters (154″) or more in the vicinity of the Macarena Mountains. There is no well-marked dry season, although April, May, and June are rainer than other months. South of the equator, in southern Amazonas, more rain falls between November and May, the first hint of the Southern Hemisphere climatic pattern. Although humidity is high in Amazonia, temperatures are moderate because of the cooling effect of the vast forests.

# VEGETATION

THE MAJOR vegetational formations in Colombia correspond closely to prevailing climate, although they may be modified by soil, fire, wind, or other factors locally. Our designations for principal plant formations, based on Holdridge (1967, *Life Zone Ecology*, San José: Trop. Sci. Center), are, (1) desert scrub, thorn woodland, and dry forest of the Caribbean, (2) tropical humid forest (called Tropical Moist Forest by Holdridge) of the humid lowlands east and west of the Andes, (3) tropical wet forest (includes Tropical Rain Forest in Holdridge) of the Pacific lowlands, (4) humid premontane and montane forest of the mountains, (5) paramo, and (6) tropical savanna of the llanos orientales. Below we describe each of these formations. Twenty-two habitat types used frequently in the text are discussed in the habitat descriptions that follow this section.

*Desert scrub to dry forest.* Rainfall 200-2000mm. The vegetation of the Caribbean coast from the lower Río Sinú to Guajira and south into the Cesar Valley consists of xerophytic scrub with stunted bushes, columnar cactus (fig. 3), and in the driest zones, terrestrial spiny bromeliads (*Bromelia*). The most frequently encountered small bushes include *Acacia*, *Calotropis*, *Mimosa*, and *Prosopis*. Commoner cactus in-

3. Thorn woodland with columnar cactus (*Lemaireocereus*), south of Santa Marta during rainy season. Dept. Magdalena, 5m el. June 1980.

clude *Lemaireocereus* (columnar), *Pereskia*, and *Opuntia*. The driest portions of the Guajira Peninsula are open and desertlike, but where precipitation increases, as along the northern and western bases of the Santa Marta Mountains, desert scrub gives way to a thorny woodland, and eventually to tropical dry forest or even tropical moist forest (fig. 4).

Most of the tropical dry forest has been removed by man except in Tayrona National Park and in the vicinity of Santa Marta; there are scattered remains in the Serranía San Jacinto and in Guajira and the Cesar Valley. Xerophytic scrub with spiny cactus also occurs on the Pacific slope in the upper Río Sucio near Dabeiba, the upper Dagua Valley, and the upper Patía Valley; in the middle Magdalena Valley near Aguachica and the upper Magdalena Valley from extreme southern Tolima to central Huila; and east of the Andes in the Zulia Valley around Cúcuta.

*Tropical humid forest.* Rainfall 2000-4000mm. This is the dominant forest of the humid middle Magdalena Valley west to the Gulf of Urabá and of forested zones east of the Andes. Much forest in the Urabá region has been destroyed, and significant inroads have been made locally into forestland along the northern base of the Western and Central Andes. East of the Andes extensive clearing has occurred along the base of the Andes, in the Macarena and San José del Guaviare region, and in western Caquetá and western Putumayo. Much

4. Caribbean coast east of Santa Marta at Cañaveral, Tayrona National Park, Dept. Magdalena. Coconut Palms line the beach. Feb 1972.

of the forest from the eastern half of Vaupés to Vichada along the Orinoco grows on a white sand soil and is somewhat lower in height and less diverse than in Amazonia. The diversity of trees, palms, and lianas in the humid lowland forests of Colombia is immense. Typically there is no dominant species or species group, although legumes of many species are common. Some common emergent trees, often reaching heights of 40-50 meters or more, include *Cedrela, Ceiba, Lecythis,* and *Terminalia.* Important genera of the canopy and edge include *Cecropia, Erythrina, Ficus, Hura, Inga, Jacaranda, Nectandra, Ochroma, Pentaclethra, Spondias, Tabebuia,* and *Virola.* In *várzea* forest *Calophyllum spruceanum, Ficus insipida,* and *Ogcodela,* are important trees, as well as many of the above genera. Some of the trees in the humid tropical forests may lose their leaves in the dry season, but deciduousness is usually not prominent. Forests, probably transitional between dry forest and moist forest, formerly occurred in the middle and upper Cauca Valley but are now completely destroyed except for two small remnants.

*Tropical wet forest.* Rainfall 4000-10,000mm. This is the dominant forest of the Pacific lowlands and is broadly connected with the humid forests of the Urabá region. Wet forest also occurs in limited bands along the northern base of the Western and Central Andes, the eastern base of the Andes, and in the Macarena Mountains. True tropical rain forest, where rainfall exceeds 8000 millimeters annually, occurs only in limited zones of the Pacific lowlands. The diversity of trees, palms, lianas, and epiphytic growth on trees in these forests is very high. A few commoner broadleaf genera include *Ardisia, Brosimum, Calophyllum, Cecropia, Cedrela, Cespedesia, Dussia, Gustavia, Gutteria, Hieronyma, Hirtella, Inga, Isertia, Jacaranda, Miconia, Nectandra, Parkia, Tapirira, Virola, Vismia,* and *Vochysia.* Destruction of tropical wet forest in Colombia is much less extensive than of the other forest formations.

*Humid premontane and montane forest.* Rainfall 1000-4000mm. These are the mature and usually humid or very humid forests of the mountain slopes (figs. 5 and 6). Because of the great variation in climate, mountain forests in Colombia include many plant formations ranging from dry to wet. Forests of the middle elevations are often called "subtropical" (or "premontane"). The trees are usually tall and are festooned with bromeliads, ferns, moss, and other arboreal epiphytes. Tree ferns are a characteristic component of these forests. The dominant families of trees include Lauraceae, Moraceae, and Myrtaceae. Locally, oaks (*Quercus*) are common. Other frequent genera include *Cassia, Cecropia, Clusia, Coussapoa, Croton, Erythrina, Ficus, Inga, Isertia, Juglans, Miconia* spp., *Myrcia, Ochroma, Persea, Tecoma, Trema, Vismia,* and *Weinmannia.* With increasing elevation the character of the forest changes to that of a temperate or "montane," forest. The trees are

5. Premontane wet forest in upper Anchicayá Valley, 1000m el., Pacific slope, Dept. Valle. The emergent trees on the left are *Cassia*. Mar 1973.

6. Two trees completely enveloped by moss and epiphytes in premontane rain forest ("cloud forest"), upper Río Verde/Río Anchicayá watershed divide, 1250m el., Pacific slope, Dept. Valle. In this very wet, foggy region most trees carry heavy burdens of epiphytes. Nov 1972.

7. *Espeletia* (Compositae) in paramo on Volcán Galeras, Dept. Nariño.
3800m el. May 1981.

short, notably gnarled, and heavily burdened with arboreal epiphytes
in humid regions. The undergrowth is typically cluttered and impenetrable. Mountain Bamboo (*Chusquea*) is an important component of
temperate forest zones. Locally, Colombia's national tree, the Wax
Palm (*Ceroxylon* spp.), is common. Higher still, at tree line, the woody
vegetation consists of stunted trees and shrubs that form an ecotone
between the temperate forest and the paramo. Common woody plants
in this zone include *Baccharis, Escallonia, Hedsomum, Podocarpus, Polylepis, Rubus, Senecio, Vaccinium, Viburnum,* and *Weinmannia.*

The natural vegetation of the arid temperate zone of Colombia,
especially in the northern half of the Eastern Andes and in the central
mountains of Nariño, is now almost wholly destroyed. *Agave, Eu-
phorbia, Spartium, Opuntia,* and other native plants occur locally, but
many areas are now extensively planted with introduced species such
as eucalyptus, cypress, and pine.

Above 3100-3400m temperate forest gives way to paramo, (fig. 7)
a wet grassland that extends from tree line to the upper limits of
vegetation. In the Western Andes the paramo occurs only at the extreme northern end, and perhaps in the Farallones above Cali. Paramo
is more extensive along the ridge line of the Central and Eastern
Andes but comprises less than 2 percent of Colombia's total land
surface. The lower paramo is characterized by *Espeletia*, a tall com-

posite that is responsible for the distinctive physiognomic appearance of the paramo. Patches of *Polylepis* woodland persist to 3900 meters, and in ravines one finds other shrubs such as *Alchemilla, Buddleia, Escallonia, Gynoxys, Libonathamus,* and *Senecio.* At higher elevations the slopes are open, and the typical vegetation includes *Agrostis, Calamagrostis, Carex, Festuca,* and other grasses and sedges mixed with *Espeletia* and bryophytes. Small lagoons and acid bogs, often filled with *Spaghum* spp., are scattered throughout. Above 4600-4800m, and near snow line, the slopes are bare and rocky.

*Tropical savanna.* Rainfall 1700-4000mm. This is the grassland that covers the vast llanos orientales from the eastern base of the Andes east to the Orinoco and south to about the Río Guaviare (fig. 8). An isolated savanna south of the Macarena Mountains and along the Río Guaviare extends for over 100 kilometers southward. Savanna formation in eastern Colombia is the result of several environmental factors, such as fire and soil condition, that deter forest development; it is not due to climate.

Relict forests are mixed with tropical savanna near the base of the Andes and on the higher dissected plains, and there is a border of gallery forest along all of the major rivers. Otherwise, the predominant vegetation is grasses, ranging from low bunch grass *Axonopus, Leptocoryphirum, Paspalum,* and *Trachypogon* in the drier zones to tall bunch grass (*Andropogon* and *Mesosetum*) in areas that are seasonally inundated. Scattered trees and scrubs occur locally throughout the savanna, either as well-separated individuals or in small groves. In the drier zones the common tree genera are *Brysonima, Curatella, Mauritia* (palm), *Palicourea, Pavonia,* and *Psidium,* and in tree groves *Acrocomia* (palm), *Jacaranda,* and *Miconia.* In seasonally inundated areas *Caraipa* is dominant. In low-lying areas small ponds remain throughout the year, but in the rainy season extensive areas of the llanos are covered by shallow pools that remain for months. South of the Río Guaviare the grasslands abruptly give way to the vast Amazonian forests discussed earlier (and see next section). Figures 9 and 10 depict this vegetation zone in Amazonia.

8. Aerial photo of gallery forest in llanos of eastern Vichada, about 4km west of Puerto Careño. Dept. Vichada, 100m el. Note sandstone cerros in background. Sept 1978.

9. Amazon River, Dept. Amazonas. Two large river islands of *várzea* forest divide the river into several channels. River width is ca. 3km. Leticia is in background. 100m el. July 1976.

10. Interior of humid *terra firme* forest in Amazonian
lowlands near Leticia, Amazonas. 100m el. Understory
is thicker than in *várzea* forest. July 1975.

# HABITAT DESCRIPTIONS

WET FOREST. The "super wet" forest of the Pacific lowlands and, to a limited extent, of the north end and east base of the Andes. Mature, canopied, tall, often exceeding 30m high, with emergent trees higher, the wet forest includes "rain forests," a term not used here because of its ambiguity in popular usage. The true tropical rain forest (Holdridge 1967) is very limited in extent.

HUMID FOREST. The luxuriant, largely evergreen forest found throughout the majority of Colombia's humid lowlands. It resembles the wet forest, but rainfall is lower, though still abundant. There are usually one or two dry seasons of varying length. Holdridge calls this the tropical moist forest.

CLOUD FOREST. A term of popular though ambiguous usage, which refers to any *very* humid mountain forest that is frequently enveloped in clouds and whose trees are heavily moss- and epiphyte-laden.

ELFIN FOREST AND ELFIN WOODLAND. An elfin forest is a stunted or dwarf forest growing on an exposed ridge top, usually at high elevation. Formed under constant exposure to wind and fog, it is characteristically gnarled, mossy, and miniature in size (around 2-5m high). Elfin woodland is similar but refers to regions where trees and shrubs are more widely spaced.

TERRA FIRME FOREST. Humid lowland forests that are not subject to inundation. Designation is applied mainly to Amazonian forests to distinguish them from *várzea* forests (fig. 10).

VÁRZEA FOREST. Forest that is seasonally flooded, often for several months, one or more times each year and to depths of about 2-6m. It is floristically less complex than *terra firme* forest, and it occurs extensively along the Amazon and along its major tributaries (fig. 9).

SWAMP FOREST. Forest in low, more or less permanently flooded zones; these forests are often dominated by palms. They occur extensively in the lower Atrato and lower Magdalena valleys, and to a lesser extent in the Amazon basin, chiefly on river islands, near oxbow lakes, or as extensions of *várzea* forest in low-lying areas.

RIVER EDGE FOREST. This is a zone of *Cecropia, Erythrina, Ficus,* and tall grass along the banks of the Amazon. It may or may not flood seasonally.

SANDY-BELT FOREST. A humid forest growing on white sand soil. Like *terra firme* forest it is not seasonally flooded, but it differs in being less luxuriant, usually having a lower canopy, and containing a high proportion of trees with tannins, phenols, and strong defensive chemicals in their leaves. Rivers flowing through sandy-belt forests are always black. This is the predominant forest in the upper Río Orinoco and Río Negro drainage of eastern Vaupés, Guainía, and Vichada (fig. 11).

SAVANNA WOODLAND. Resembles sandy-belt forest but is scrubbier, shorter (about 3-15m), and more open. In its extreme form it resembles cerrado, with well-spaced, shrublike trees. In appearance, it is intermediate between sandy-belt forest and savanna.

DRY FOREST. Rather open forest that grows where the dry season is longer and more severe than in humid forest zones. Most of the trees lose their leaves for up to six months. This type of forest was formerly widespread in northern Colombia.

GALLERY FOREST. Gallery forest or riparian woodland is a strip of trees confined to and dependent upon watercourses in otherwise largely open or

11. White sand savanna and sandy-belt forest near Puerto Inirida,
Guainía, Sept 1978.

scrubby country. It borders virtually all rivers in the llanos (unless removed by man).

LIGHTER WOODLAND AND THINNED WOODLAND. These habitats include parklike areas. They are forests thinned by human activity—e.g., for coffee
plantations or by lumbering—where a more or less continuous canopy
is maintained but much undergrowth is removed. An important habitat
for wintering North American migrants.

SECOND GROWTH WOODLAND. A relatively advanced regrowth stage of forest
that in time will become mature forest. It differs from the latter in species
composition, absence of emergent trees, usually lower canopy height,
and more open canopy (older stages largely closed) with well-lighted,
bushy undergrowth.

FOREST OR WOODLAND BORDER. The edge of a forest or woodland along a
road, stream, around a treefall, etc., is usually dense and shrubby; older
stages become a solid wall of vegetation. Common plants include *Cecropia*,
*Heliconia*, *Miconia*, *Piper*, and vines. This is the most frequently "birded"
habitat in most tropical areas, and it usually contains a mixture of both
forest and nonforest species.

SHRUBBY AREAS AND CLEARINGS (with or without scattered trees). This represents any regrowth stage that follows deforestation but precedes woodland. Its dominant vegetation is low shrubs, thickets, grass, and small
trees. Later stages give way to larger trees.

RIVER ISLAND SHRUBBERY. Essentially the same as the preceding, but these
areas are seasonally inundated, hence a shrubby forerunner of *várzea*.
They are found only on Amazon river islands and immediately follow
sand-bar deposition on downstream ends of the islands. This habitat
contains a few highly characteristic birds.

SCRUBBY AREAS. A relatively permanent plant community (not a regrowth stage) found chiefly in drier regions. It is characterized by scraggly bushes and small trees, often *Acacia*. In some cases, shrubby areas become so permanently altered as a result of human activity (erosion, overgrazing, fuel wood cutting, etc.) that forest regeneration is unlikely and they become scrubby areas. Examples of the latter occur in parts of the upper Dagua Valley and the eroded hills west of the Bogotá savanna.

ARID SCRUB (OR DESERT SCRUB). The permanent scrub zone of the arid Caribbean coast and, locally inland, of rain shadow valleys. They are characterized by low, often thorny bushes, small drought resistant trees, and several cacti.

MARSHES. Marshes are areas with more or less permanent standing water and emergent vegetation but not trees; the water can be fresh or brackish. In Amazonia, marshes occur at the edges of oxbow lakes, around lagoons on river islands, and at the mouths of sluggish streams.

MANGROVES. A forest community of a few species of evergreen trees and shrubs that grow within the tidal zone; the trees are characterized by shiny, dark green foliage and a tangle of aerial or stiltlike roots. On the Caribbean, mangroves occur from the Magdalena Delta to Ciénaga and in Guajira; on the Pacific, from central Chocó southward.

COASTAL, OFFSHORE, AND PELAGIC. These habitats are within sight of land, beyond sight of land but over the continental shelf, and in open ocean beyond the continental shelf, respectively.

SAVANNA (or grassland). A tropical grassland with or without trees. Where the scattered trees are extensive stands of Moriche Palms (*Mauritia*), these zones are called Morichales. The Colombian-Venezuelan llanos comprise the largest savanna in northern South America.

PARAMO. The paramo is a wet, tropical, alpine grassland or shrubland that is found from tree line to about snow line. It is characterized by large expanses of bunch grass mixed with rosette shrubs (*Espeletia* spp.). Quaking bogs and cold lakes dot the lower areas.

CULTIVATED AREAS, RESIDENTIAL AREAS, PARKS, GARDENS, AND RANCHLANDS. These are more or less self-descriptive terms, all man-maintained.

# MIGRANTS

DUE IN large part to its geographical position, Colombia is host to a considerable influx of long-distance migrants each year, the greatest number being north temperate breeders that spend the northern winter in Colombia (Table 1). In addition, populations of several species that breed in Colombia are augmented by populations that breed in Central America during the dry season and migrate to Colombia during the wet season (Table 2). The extent of movement of many of the latter species is not fully known because of the difficulties of recognizing migratory and resident subspecies in the field. Examples of Central American breeders that migrate to Colombia and elsewhere in South America include the American Swallow-tailed Kite, Plumbeous Kite, Piratic Flycatcher, Gray-breasted Martin, and Red-eyed Vireo (*flavoviridis*).

More surprising is the extent of movement of south temperate breeders northward to Colombia (Table 3). Accumulating evidence suggests that this phenomenon has been greatly overlooked, particularly in Amazonia, where a number of south temperate breeders are regular trans-Amazonian migrants to southern Colombia. Unlike their long-distance north temperate counterparts, these austral migrants form a rather inconspicuous part of the avifauna, even in disturbed areas, and are easily overlooked. Further, most of them occur chiefly east of the Andes where much less ornithological work has been done. Consequently, documentation of the nature and extent of movements of austral migrants to Colombia has barely begun.

For some species the breeding population in Colombia is augmented by an influx of austral(?) migrants from May to September. For example, in Amazonas the number of Tropical Kingbirds doubles or triples along the banks of the Amazon and along channels and lagoons on river islands during the austral winter.

Many long-distance northern migrants are relatively conspicuous and comprise a significant proportion of the total avifauna. For example, shorebirds of many species are numerous on both coasts, especially during periods of migratory movement. And substantial numbers of north temperate breeding shorebirds remain in Colombia even during the "summer" breeding months. Many of the latter may be first-year birds that are not yet in breeding condition, and some may remain several years. Small north temperate passerine migrants—for instance, the Blackburnian Warbler—may be numerous in forest edges and disturbed areas in the foothills and mountains, but few are common in the lowlands (e.g., below 500 meters). Numbers of northern migrants rapidly diminish eastward and southward in Amazonia as well.

TABLE 1

NORTH TEMPERATE BREEDING BIRDS THAT REACH COLOMBIA AS LONG-DISTANCE MIGRANTS (those with an asterisk may also have populations that breed in Colombia. A question mark (?) denotes a species whose status in Colombia as a northern migrant is not proven.)

| | | |
|---|---|---|
| Great Blue Heron | Whimbrel | Gray Catbird |
| Green Heron | Hudsonian Godwit | Veery |
| Least Bittern | Marbled Godwit | Wood Thrush |
| Glossy Ibis | Long-billed Dowitcher | Gray-cheeked Thrush |
| American Wigeon | Short-billed Dowitcher | Swainson's Thrush |
| Common Pintail | Common Snipe | Cedar Waxwing |
| Blue-winged Teal | Wilson's Phalarope | Yellow-throated Vireo |
| Cinnamon Teal | Red Phalarope | Philadelphia Vireo |
| Northern Shoveler | Ring-billed Gull | Red-eyed Vireo |
| Lesser Scaup | Herring Gull | Orchard Oriole |
| Turkey Vulture | Laughing Gull | Northern (Baltimore) Oriole |
| American Swallow-tailed Kite (?) | Franklin's Gull | Bobolink |
| Mississippi Kite | Sabine's Gull | Black-and-white Warbler |
| Cooper's Hawk | Black Tern | Golden-winged Warbler |
| Swainson's Hawk | Gull-billed Tern | Blue-winged Warbler |
| Broad-winged Hawk | Caspian Tern | Tennessee Warbler |
| Northern Harrier | Common Tern | Yellow Warbler |
| Osprey | Arctic Tern | Chestnut-sided Warbler |
| Peregrine Falcon | Roseate Tern | Cerulean Warbler |
| Merlin | Bridled Tern | Black-throated |
| American Kestrel (?) | Least Tern | Blue-Warbler |
| Sora | Royal Tern | Yellow-throated Warbler |
| Common Gallinule (?) | Elegant Tern | Townsend's Warbler |
| American Coot | Cayenne Tern | Black-throated |
| Black-bellied Plover | Sandwich Tern | Green Warbler |
| Golden Plover | Black Skimmer (?) | Prairie Warbler |
| Semipalmated Plover | Mourning Dove | Blackburnian Warbler |
| Snowy Plover (?) | Black-billed Cuckoo | Magnolia Warbler |
| Killdeer | Yellow-billed Cuckoo | Yellow-rumped Warbler |
| Thick-billed Plover | Lesser Nighthawk* | Cape May Warbler |
| Solitary Sandpiper | Common Nighthawk | Black-poll Warbler |
| Lesser Yellowlegs | Chuck-will's-widow | Bay-breasted Warbler |
| Greater Yellowlegs | Chimney Swift | American Redstart |
| Spotted Sandpiper | Belted Kingfisher | Ovenbird |
| Willet | Traill's Flycatcher | Northern Waterthrush |
| Ruddy Turnstone | Acadian Flycatcher | Louisiana Waterthrush |
| Wandering Tattler | Eastern Wood-Pewee | Prothonotary Warbler |
| Red Knot | Western Wood-Pewee | Common Yellowthroat |
| Least Sandpiper | Olive-sided Flycatcher | Kentucky Warbler |
| Baird's Sandpiper | Great Crested | Connecticut Warbler |
| White-rumped Sandpiper | Flycatcher | Mourning Warbler |
| Pectoral Sandpiper | Sulphur-bellied | Hooded Warbler |
| Semipalmated Sandpiper | Flycatcher | Canada Warbler |
| Western Sandpiper | Eastern Kingbird | Summer Tanager |
| Sanderling | Tree Swallow | Scarlet Tanager |
| Stilt Sandpiper | Purple Martin | Dickcissel |
| Buff-breasted Sandpiper | Bank Swallow | Indigo Bunting |
| Ruff | Barn Swallow | Blue Grosbeak |
| Upland Sandpiper | Cliff Swallow | Rose-breasted Grosbeak |

TABLE 2
MIDDLE AMERICAN OR CARIBBEAN BREEDING MIGRANTS TO COLOMBIA
(all also breed in Colombia except those with an asterisk)

| | |
|---|---|
| Turkey Vulture | Common Nighthawk* |
| Lesser Yellow-headed Vulture (?) | Piratic Flycatcher |
| Black Vulture | Streaked Flycatcher |
| American Swallow-tailed Kite | Fork-tailed Flycatcher |
| Plumbeous Kite | Gray Kingbird |
| Reddish Egret | Gray-breasted Martin |
| Snowy Plover | Red-eyed Vireo (*flavoviridis*) |
| Lesser Nighthawk | Black-whiskered Vireo* |

Many resident breeders also undergo some form of seasonal movement within Colombia. Relatively little is known about most of these movements, but for some species it may take the form of postbreeding dispersal, dispersal of juveniles, or seasonal movements in relation to food supply, or even in response to severe weather at very high elevations. For example, postbreeding dispersal of many waders doubtless accounts for the occasional presence of ibises, spoonbills, and other large waders far into the upper Magdalena and Cauca valleys where they no longer breed. In the mountains movements of Bronze-winged and Scaly-naped Parrots (both notably erratic in occurrence) are more likely due to shifting food supplies, as are movements of large macaws in eastern Guainía and Vaupés and of Mealy Parrots up the Pacific slope when *Pourouma* fruits are ripe. It is widely known that hummingbirds move seasonally up and down mountain slopes, but the phenomenon is poorly understood. Shifts of the hummingbird

TABLE 3
SOUTH TEMPERATE BREEDING MIGRANTS TO COLOMBIA
(those with an asterisk may also breed in Colombia)

| | |
|---|---|
| Gray-bellied Hawk (?)* | Scrub Flycatcher* |
| Red-backed Hawk | Euler's Flycatcher* |
| Peregrine Falcon (?) | Pied Water-Tyrant* |
| Speckled Crake (?) | Crowned Slaty-Flycatcher |
| Black Skimmer (?)* | Variegated Flycatcher |
| Gray Gull | Swainson's Flycatcher |
| Picui Ground-Dove | Vermilion Flycatcher* |
| Ash-colored Cuckoo | Dusky-chested Flycatcher* |
| Pearly-breasted Cuckoo | Streaked Flycatcher* |
| Dark-billed Cuckoo* | Fork-tailed Flycatcher* |
| Short-tailed Nighthawk* | Tropical Kingbird* |
| Lesser Nighthawk* | White-throated Kingbird |
| Nacunda Nighthawk* | Brown-chested Martin* |
| Chapman's Swift | Southern Martin |
| Ashy-tailed Swift | Gray-chested Martin (?)* |
| Large Elaenia | Blue-and-white Swallow* |
| Brownish Elaenia | Tawny-headed Swallow (?) |
| Small-billed Elaenia | Lined Seedeater |
| Slaty Elaenia | Double-collared Seedeater |
| Mottle-backed Elaenia | |

populations can frequently be swift and dramatic, an entire population virtually disappearing overnight. Such movements are attributed to changing availability of nectar in most cases. Less well known but no less remarkable is the postbreeding dispersal of oilbirds from centuries-old breeding caves to new food supplies in valleys far away. Some movements are common, but usually go unnoticed, such as the large "floating" populations of young manakins in humid forest undergrowth. Postbreeding dispersal of seedeaters out of grassland breeding areas during the dry season is well documented in Panama and probably occurs locally in Colombia as well, although it is not yet reported.

East of the Andes many large waders, most of which breed in Colombia, undergo some local or even long-distance migratory movement on a seasonal basis. An indication of the extent of this phenomenon, documented independently by Furniss and McKay (unpubl.), can be gained from the following list of species which apparently show a marked increase in numbers during the latter half of the dry season and first half of the wet season but thereafter are widely dispersed or even absent for several months. Some examples include the Common Egret, Whistling Heron, Stripe-backed and Pinnated bitterns, Wood Stork, Maguari Stork, Jabiru, Buff-necked, Whispering, White, and Scarlet ibises, Roseate Spoonbill, White-faced Whistling-Duck, Brazilian Duck, Masked Duck, Ash-throated and Yellow-breasted crakes, Purple and Azure gallinules, Wattled Jacana, and Collared Plover. Population shifts of this magnitude clearly will have important bearing on agriculture and on faunal reserve planning.

Several species that breed and forage on or over sand bars on the Amazon and its tributaries are adversely affected by the twice annual flooding and appear to vacate the region during these periods. This group includes Pied Lapwing, Collared Plover, Sand-colored Nighthawk, and Nacunda Nighthawk. It is uncertain where these species are found during the flood periods.

Finally, although many north temperate migrants establish permanent winter territories in Colombia and elsewhere—for instance, the Northern Waterthrush—others may abandon a location, or reappear elsewhere, apparently in response to changing food resources. For example, several north temperate migrants, including Yellow-billed Cuckoo, Swainson's Thrush, Red-eyed Vireo, Prothonotary Warbler, and Black-poll Warbler, are present in desert scrub near Santa Marta during the October–November wet months but disappear at the onset of the dry season in December (Russell 1980). Similar movements into or out of the Cauca Valley, Anchicayá Valley, and Santa Marta highlands are also reported.

Increasingly, migratory birds of all kinds are coming into conflict with human activities. The oilbirds mentioned above provide a poignant example. In a cycle established over millenia, they disperse across the once forested Cauca Valley after breeding to search for fruit. But now the valley is filled with agricultural crops, highways, and cities, and the birds find little food. They often wander aimlessly, becoming so emaciated and weakened they can be picked up by hand. The conflict also assumes a more global aspect as north temperate migrants compete for space each winter in tropical forests that are shrinking in area at an alarming rate. There seems little doubt that the world of the future for many migrants will be a good deal less certain than the one today.

# CONSERVATION AND NATIONAL PARKS

DEPENDING upon the locality that one visits in Colombia, one can come away with two very different views of the state of the Colombian environment. Large portions of the Pacific slope, the eastern slope of the Eastern Andes, and the lowlands east of the Andes are still largely undisturbed. Conversely, the extent of exploitation and environmental degradation in the central mountain region between the east slope of the Western Andes and the west slope of the Eastern Andes is alarming; a large portion of this once forested region now consists of bare, eroding hillsides, silt-laden streams, and subsistence agricultural efforts. Similarly, deforestation across most of northern Colombia, including the Urabá region, is extensive and locally expanding along the northern base of the Andes as well as along the eastern base of the Eastern Andes. Thus, whereas some portions of Colombia remain very much in a natural state, the environmental situation in most of the northern and intermontane region is of concern.

The environmental problems that plague Colombia are similar to the ones that many developing and industrialized nations face today. Fundamentally, the problems stem from two sources: a failure of the agricultural and industrial sectors to view land as a renewable natural resource, and the inability of regulating agencies to enforce environmental policies. The basic problems are familiar. The major ones are (1) forest destruction, (2) inappropriate land use leading to massive soil erosion, soil deterioration, and deficient water quality, and (3) environmental poisoning through the use of toxic chemicals by both agriculture and industry. These problems are aggravated by a rapidly expanding population forced to seek short-term and often inappropriate solutions to long-term problems. The result in Colombia is a large rural population that practices desperate agriculture on marginal or unsuitable lands, and a burgeoning urban population that places ever greater strains on rational planning and public services.

Within the central Andean region environmental changes during the past 40 or 50 years have resulted in major documented changes in the distribution of bird life. For example, several species are now established in central and southern Colombia that were unknown there before clearing. Examples include the Ruddy Ground-Dove, Dwarf Cuckoo, Red-breasted Blackbird, and Eastern Meadowlark. Others, such as the Eared Dove, Blue-and-white Swallow, Scrub Tanager, and the ubiquitous Rufous-collared Sparrow, were doubtless present but have obviously profited from the clearing of land. According to Lehmann (1970), many species have been completely eliminated from the plateau of the middle Cauca Valley, which was formerly tropical moist forest but is now wholly converted to agriculture. Some of the species that are no longer present there include the Little Tinamou, Jabiru, Roseate Spoonbill, Muscovy Duck, King Vulture, several *Accipiters*, Great Black-Hawk, Bat Falcon, and Chestnut-fronted Macaw. Throughout Colombia the species most vulnerable to expanding human pressure are the large cracids. These unwary forest-dwellers do not survive even slight hunting.

The conservation picture, however, is not altogether bleak. Colombia presently has a network of about thirty-four national parks established and largely administered by the Instituto Nacional de los Recursos Naturales Renovables y del Ambiente (INDERENA). This park system, as fine as any existing in Latin America, encompasses portions of virtually all of the major biogeographical provinces in Colombia. Twenty-six of the parks are shown on the map on p. viii and all are listed at the end of this section. INDERENA has identified up to seventy additional areas for study, and some of these may eventually be given status as parks or protected areas.

Several other agencies have been active in Colombian environmental matters. The Corporación Autónoma y Regional para el Desarrolla del Valle (CVC), a leading development corporation in Colombia, is primarily concerned with hydropower projects but has been instrumental in protecting numerous major watersheds (e.g., Anchicayá) and has jurisdiction over conservation matters and some national parks in Valle and Cauca. The large and prestigious Instituto Geográfico, "Agustín Codazzi," the national geographical institution, employs many foresters as well as other professionals and is developing a forest map through remote sensing techniques. The Instituto Vallecaucano de Investigaciónes Científicas (INCIVA), a new organization, oversees the activities of the natural history museum in Cali and the botanical garden in Tuluá and coordinates the activities of the Smithsonian Institution in Colombia.

There have also been a few notable successes in land management and reforestation in the private sector. One of the best examples is Finca Merenberg, a private and self-supporting farm located in the Central Andes in Huila. Owned by Gunther Buch, it is an enviable model of the successful integration of agriculture and conservation through sound land management. The farm has one of the few remaining tracts of subtropical forest left anywhere in the region. In 1980 Gunther Buch and friends formed Fundación Merenberg, which has ties with the World Wildlife Fund (WWF-US) and La Asociación para la Naturaleza (ACUA), a private and nonprofit Colombian conservation organization. Fundación Merenberg is planning a variety of reforestation and special training projects as well as other innovative conservation activities and will seek MAB (Man and the Biosphere)

Reserve status for the property. It is hoped that this important pioneering project will ultimately receive public acceptance and stimulate others with undisturbed private holdings to take similar action.

The protection and maintenance of Colombia's vast park system and other public and private reserves is of overriding concern. Two national parks, the Sierra Nevada de Santa Marta and the Serranía de la Macarena, had to be decreased in size because of the invasion of the park boundaries by settlers and the subsequent forest destruction. A third park, Isla de Salamanca, has been threatened by plans for an industrial port complex within its boundaries. The integrity of others is being threatened by the activities of guerrilla forces and/or drug-related activities that present serious obstacles to management or public use. The owners of the Merenberg property have suffered great personal tragedy and resisted intense opposing pressure in their efforts to establish and maintain Merenberg as a biological preserve. Clearly, there is no room for complacency and the chief administerial agency, INDERENA, faces a formidable task. They, and all others involved in conservation in Colombia urgently need support from both private and public sectors, and ultimately the acceptance of their efforts by the Colombian people.

## NATIONAL PARKS

1960. Cueva de los Guácharos (Cave of the Oilbirds). 15,000 hectares. 1900-3600m el. Se Huila. Largest Colombian oilbird colony. Black Tinamou, Wattled Guan, Andean Cock-of-the-Rock. Unique geological formations.

1964. Tayrona. 11,600 hectares. To 350m el. N coast Santa Marta Mts. Thorn woodland to humid forest. Over three hundred species of birds, numerous sandy beaches, sea turtle breeding area, immense wealth of archeological remains of Tayrona culture.

1964. Isla de Salamanca. 21,000 hectares. To 10m. N coast e of Barranquilla. Extensive mangroves, beaches, estuaries, large concentrations of water and shore birds, many northern migrants, only known population of Bronze-brown Cowbird.

1967. Sierra Nevada de Santa Marta. 50,000 hectares. Paramo and permanent snowfields above 4000m contour. Protects only two of twelve endemic Santa Marta Mts. species. A forest reserve borders the n and w sides. Formerly included 383,000 ha.

1968. Puracé. 83,000 hectares. 1500-4700m. E of Popayán in C Andes of Cauca and Huila. Subtropical and temperate forest, paramo and snowfields. Seven volcanic craters, hot springs, 175-200 species of birds, great scenic beauty.

1968. Los Farallones. 150,000 hectares. 400-3800m. W Andes in Valle. Under jurisdiction of CVC. Protects watershed of Río Anchicayá hydropower plant. Vast Pacific slope avifauna. Spectacled Bear, marmosets. One of only two paramo zones in W Andes.

1970. El Tuparro. 290,000 hectares. 100-200m. E Vichada between Río Tomo and Río Tuparrito, bordered on e by Río Orinoco. Very remote. Mainly savanna and gallery forest, diverse llanos flora and fauna.

1971. La Macarena. 600,000 hectares. 350-1800m. Macarena Mts. of Meta, s to Río Guaviare. Largest park in Colombia. A transition zone between Andean, Orinoco, and Amazonian habitats. Great scenic beauty, spectacular waterfalls; of archaeological importance because of native engravings.

1972. Munchique. 44,000 hectares. 500-3000m. W Andes in Cauca. Includes Cerro Munchique. Protects habitat of Golden-headed Quetzal. Wet subtropical forest.

1973. Los Nevados. 38,000 hectares. 2600-5400m in portions of Tolima, Risaralda, Quindío, and Caldas in C Andes. Three snow-covered peaks: Ruiz, Santa Isabel, and Tolima. Up to eleven endemic species may occur in park, also Colombia's national tree (Wax Palm) and hot mineral springs.

1973. Las Orquídeas. 32,000 hectares. Tropical to paramo zone, 300-3850m. W Andes in sw Antioquia. Rich flora, at least twenty-two genera of orchids, many birds, one endemic hummingbird. Spectacled bear.

1973. Los Kátios. 52,000 hectares. 50-800m. On Panama border in nw Chocó. Highly endemic flora, many birds of restricted range, including perhaps Sooty-capped Puffbird and Chestnut-mantled Oropendola. Katios, Cuna, and Chocó Indians.

1975. Los Estoraques. 450 hectares. Norte de Santander. Spectacular rock formations recall Bryce Canyon in w U.S.A.

1975. Iguaqua. 6700 hectares. Sanctuary in E Andes, about 30km nw of Tunjá, Boyacá.

1975. Amacayacú. 170,000 hectares. S Amazonas. Large representative tract of Amazonian flora and fauna.

1975. Los Flamencos. 7000 hectares. Two areas on arid n coast of Guajira. Xerophytic scrub surrounding saline lagoons. Feeding and possible breeding areas of Greater Flamingo. Many water birds, sea turtle breeding beaches.

1977. Nevado de Huila. 150,000 hectares. Both slopes C Andes in Cauca, Tolima, and Huila. Subtropical to paramo zone, reaching 5750m el. on Nevado de Huila. Important watershed for agricultural communities below. Andean Condor, Spectacled Bear.

1977. Las Hermosas. 125,000 hectares. Both slopes C Andes in Tolima and Cauca. Temperate forest and paramo. Numerous highland lakes.

1977. Isla Coroto. 2600m. Flora and fauna island sanctuary in Laguna La Cocha, Nariño.

1977. Isla Rosario. 18,000 hectares. Coral island off coast of Bolívar. Important reefs, mangroves, breeding colony of pelicans and frigatebirds.

1977. Arauca. 90,000 hectares. Savanna, gallery forest, lagoons, and foothill forest, n Arauca. Representative llanos flora and fauna.

1977. Sierra Nevado del Cocuy. 706,000 hectares. 500-5400m. Boyacá-Arauca boundary near n end of E Andes. Foothills to paramo and permanent snowfields. Small Andean Condor population.

1977. Sanquianga. 89,000 hectares. Sw Nariño. Wet lowland and hill forest. Mangroves.

1977. Paramillo. 460,000 hectares. 1000-3850m. N end W Andes in n Antioquia. Important highland forest and paramo.

1977. Chingaza. 20,000 hectares. 2700-4000m. Cundinamarca-Meta boundary. Diverse East Andean slope flora and fauna. Spectacled Bear.

1977. Tamá. 48,000 hectares. Norte de Santander on Venezuelan border. Humid forest to paramo. Important watershed.

1977. Sumapaz. 154,000 hectares. 500-4600m. Upper tropical zone to paramo. Representative flora and fauna of e Andean slope.

1977. Cordillera de los Picachos. 286,000 hectares. 300-3500m. Forested wilderness on Meta-Huila-Caquetá border. A narrow extension of E Andes, important as future recreation area.

1977. Pisba. 45,000 hectares. Subtropical forest to paramo on Boyacá-Casanare border, ne of Lago de Tota. Protects broad range of rapidly disappearing habitats.

1977. Macuira. 25,000 hectares. To 800m. Macuira Hills region of e Guajira. Xerophytic scrub and humid valleys, abundant epiphytes on fog-covered hilltops. Important primate population.

1977. Los Colorados. 1000 hectares. Lowlands near San Juan Nepomuceno, n Bolívar. Dry to humid forest. Important primate population.

1977. Ciénega Grande. 23,000 hectares. Alluvial plain of former Magdalena delta. Mangroves, swamps, marshes. Important for fisheries, many water birds.

1977. Manaure. N Guajira. Similar to Los Flamencos. Water birds.

1977. Báhia Portete. Ne Guajira. Similar to Los Flamencos.

# REVIEW OF COLOMBIAN ORNITHOLOGY

COLOMBIAN birds first became known to science in the early 1800s through trade skins labeled "Bogotá" or "Nouvelle Grenada" that were sent to Europe for millinery purposes. Most of these birds were secured by native hunters, probably trained by J. Goudot as early as 1825. Since that date hundreds of thousands of birds have been shipped from Bogotá for the millinery trade, which peaked about 1885. Most probably came from the general area of Bogotá, the Magdalena Valley, or the eastern llanos, but none are known by date or specific locality. A few of these species are still known in Colombia only from "Bogotá."

The first Colombian birds recorded from a definite locality were collected by the Frenchman Delattre in 1849, between Buenaventura and Pasto. During the later 1800s and early 1900s several collections were made. In the Andes the most important was T. K. Salmon's 3500 specimens along with nests and eggs from Antioquia in 1872-78. Prior to 1910 the most important collections in western Colombia were made by W. S. Wood, Jr., and C. J. Wood for the Micheler expedition during a canal survey up the Atrato in 1858 and by M. G. Palmer, who worked in the vicinity of Buenaventura, Cali, and the upper Río San Juan from 1907 to 1909. Other collections were those of C. Wyatt in Santander in 1870, Wheeler and Detwiler, Count Von Berlepsch, and W. Robinson in the Magdalena Valley, and W. F. Rosenberg, G. Hopke, E. Andre, and Kerr west of the West Andes.

The first Santa Marta collection was made by F. A. Simons who ascended both slopes to snow line in 1878-79. In the late 1800s W. W. Brown and H. Smith, working independently, secured Santa Marta material for the Museum of Comparative Zoology and the American Museum of Natural History, respectively. M. A. Carriker's notes and large Santa Marta collection, obtained between 1911 and 1920 for the Carnegie Museum, formed the basis for Todd and Carriker's subsequent *Birds of the Santa Marta Region of Colombia*, published in 1922.

Eight expeditions sponsored by the American Museum of Natural History between 1910 and 1915 sampled birdlife along transects from the lowlands to the paramos in all three ranges and in the Serranía del Darién. These expeditions resulted in Chapman's synthesis of the Andean avifauna on a zoogeographical basis (1917). From 1938 to 1952 K. Von Sneidern collected about 12,500 specimens in various parts of Colombia for the Academy of Natural Science. This work, along with that of A. Dugand, J. I. Borrero, M. Nicéforo, and the Mena brothers, formed the basis for Meyer de Schauensee's catalogues published in 1948-52.

The first Macarena collection was assembled by E. T. Gilliard for the American Museum of Natural History in 1942. This was followed by C. C. Doncaster's small collection for the British Museum in 1949. Von Sneidern took an additional 1100 Macarena birds in 1957 (Blake 1962). Brother Olivares directed further collecting in Macarena in 1959 as well as in many other parts of Colombia from the early 1950s to mid-1970s. Collections and field work were carried out by F. C. Lehmann during a similar time span. Carriker, working throughout the western half of Colombia, took about 23,000 specimens between 1941 and 1953 for the United States National Museum. In the early 1970s Von Sneidern collected in southeast Nariño and west Putumayo near the Ecuador boundary for the Field Museum of Natural History.

Seabirds of Colombia's Pacific waters were studied by Murphy in the 1930s but have received little attention since. Brown and Thayer were the first ornithologists to visit Gorgona Island. Since their 1904 visit the island has been visited by several groups. Isla Malpelo was visited by the Vanderbilt expedition in 1937 (Bond and Meyer de Schauensee 1938). Islas San Andrés and Providencia have been visited at least six times by ornithological expeditions and during the past decade by several ornithologists (see Appendix II).

During the past two decades an increasing number of ornithologists have studied Colombian birds, and their findings appear in this book, acknowledged either in the text or in the literature cited at the end. Of these, Haffer and Meyer de Schauensee have made the most significant contributions. Between 1958 and 1967 Haffer collected and studied birds mainly in northwestern Colombia. This added to our understanding of speciation and zoogeography in Colombia as well as throughout South America. Meyer de Schauensee's prolific syntheses of the distribution of birds in Colombia and South America, as well as his role in the standardization of names, has been of inestimable value to workers in ornithology. The work of these two men has placed our knowledge of the distribution of Colombian birds on firm footing.

Events of the past several decades such as deforestation and rapid environmental degradation have accelerated the need for information on behavior, breeding, voice, and the status and habitat of Colombian birds. This data, together with a solid taxonomic base, are the tools of biologists, conservationists, and political decision makers. Unfortunately, this information along with modern field identification criteria have been widely scattered and not readily available, or did not exist at the onset of this project. This volume brings together for the first time a base of ecological field data for each species of bird in Colombia, along with diagnostic criteria for distinguishing them. It is, in a sense, the product of all those who have gone before us, and the kind of guide we would like to have had when we first visited Colombia.

# THE BIRDS OF COLOMBIA

# PENGUINS: Spheniscidae

Penguins are a well-known group of flightless seabirds of colder south temperate and antarctic waters. Two species might wander to Colombian waters (unconfirmed sightings off Isla Gorgona—H. Von Prahl).

## 1. [GALAPAGOS PENGUIN]
*Spheniscus mendiculus*
**Identification:** 20″. Head, throat, and upperparts black; below white; face bordered above and behind by narrow white line; chest crossed by 2 blackish bands. Worn plumage more brownish, imm. much duller but pattern recognizable.

## 2. [HUMBOLDT PENGUIN]
*S. humboldti*
**Identification:** Sim. to Galapagos Penguin but larger (27″), and with 1, not 2, slaty chest bands.

# TINAMOUS: Tinamidae (16)

Tinamous are plump, slender-necked, small-headed birds found from western Mexico to southern Argentina. They have very short tails and short rounded wings. In Colombia they are furtive terrestrial birds of forested or wooded regions. All are cryptically patterned and when alarmed prefer to slip quietly away by walking. In those species studied, the sex role is reversed and the ♂ incubates the eggs and cares for the young. ♀♀ may lay in several nests for different ♂♂ or two or more may lay in one nest. Their beautiful eggs, satiny and porcelainlike in texture, are usually unmarked greenish, turquoise, or vinaceous. The taxonomy of several forms, especially of the genus *Crypturellus*, is complex and poorly understood.

[*Tinamus*: Med. to large size; mostly lowlands or lower el.; roost lengthwise on low branch, presum. aided by rasplike posterior tarsal surface.]

## 1. GRAY TINAMOU
*Tinamus tao*    Pl. 1, Map 1
**Identification:** 18″ (46cm). *Large and mostly grayish.* Crown and hindneck black; *sides of head freckled black and white*, indistinct blackish band across sides of head and down neck; otherwise grayish olive above more or less barred black; below grayish brown; *throat whitish;* flanks and under tail coverts barred blackish and buff; bill and legs dusky.
**Similar species:** Most likely confused with Great Tinamou (3), which is browner or buffier (not grayish olive) and lacks the speckling and stripe on head and neck. Highland Tinamou (5) is much more rufescent with cinnamon throat.
**Voice:** ♂ in s Amazonian Brazil an abrupt single hoot with quality sim. to that of Great Tinamou and often answered by shorter, higher-pitched hoot of ♀ (R. Ridgely; H. Sick).
**Behavior:** Sim. to Great Tinamou.
**Breeding:** Jan nests, sw Cauca (Olivares 1957b), Feb–Mar in Macarena Mts. (Nicéforo and Olivares 1964); BC ♂, 19 Mar, w base Perijá Mts. (Carriker). June nest, Rancho Grande, Venez. (Hilty); 2-9 shiny greenish blue eggs, in depression on ground, at base of tree, or slightly above ground, in rotten stump or palm clump.
**Status and habitat:** Rare and local. Well-shaded floor of humid *terra firme* forest. Most recs. in hill country or lower mt. el.
**Range:** To 1900m. Pacific coast in sw Cauca (Guapí), perhaps Cauca Val. above Cali (formerly), Perijá Mts., and upper Cesar Val. near Fonseca; e base E Andes from Arauca to Macarena Mts. Guyana, and n Venez. to e Ecuador, Bolivia, and Amazonian Brazil.

## 2. BLACK TINAMOU
*Tinamus osgoodi*    Map 2
**Identification:** 18″ (46cm). *Large. Uniform black above and slaty black below, with dark gray throat;* lower breast and belly dusky brown; under tail coverts chestnut barred black; bill blackish above, pale below, legs bluish gray.
**Similar species:** Large and mostly black. Likely confused only with Highland or Tawny-breasted Tinamous (5, 6), both smaller and mostly rufescent (not black), or Gray Tinamou (1), which is mainly gray (not blackish).
**Breeding:** 1 nest, Peru; 2 nearly spherical, glossy blue eggs (Traylor 1952).
**Status and habitat:** Very rare. Colombian form (*hershkovitzi*) is known from 3 specimens and 1 recent sight rec., all in regions of humid forest.

Range: 1500-2100m. Head of Magdalena Val. in Huila (San Adolfo; Río Aguas Claras; Acevedo; and sighting in PN Cueva de los Guácharos, 1976—P. Gertler). Colombia and Peru.

## 3. GREAT TINAMOU
*Tinamus major*                    Pl. 1, Map 3
Identification: 18″ (46cm). *Large.* Crown chestnut, otherwise *light to dark olive brown above with rather indistinct broken black bars*; underparts grayish brown; *distinctly whitish on throat and center of belly*; flanks and under tail coverts barred dusky. Or with distinct crest (*saturatus*); or with distinct crest and slaty crown (*latifrons*); or sometimes a paler color phase with yellowish olive upperparts (*zuliensis*).
Similar species: Much larger than other lowland tinamous that occur with it. Highland and Tawny-breasted tinamous (5, 6), both usually at higher el., are smaller; Highland has cinnamon (not whitish) throat, Tawny-breasted has rich rufescent to tawny underparts.
Voice: Learn the call; dozens will be heard for every bird glimpsed. Most common call is 2-3 resonant tremulous whistles, last slightly higher and sometimes sliding downward (Eisenmann 1952). At dawn and dusk a ser. of 6 or more tremulous whistles, each gaining a little in pitch and vol. Latter is one of the most haunting and beautiful sounds of the neotropics. *Caution:* most calls of Great Tinamou are duplicated by Little Tinamou, but latter's are weaker, flatter, and lack the full-bodied resonance.
Behavior: A shy terrestrial bird usually encountered accidentally. Almost always attempts to avoid detection by quietly walking away, but if surprised, 1 or a pair may flush a short distance with a loud roar of wings.
Breeding: 16 BC birds, Jan–June, n Colombia (Carriker; Blake 1955); 1 nest, Chocó, Feb (Haffer 1959); 1 nest in Santa Marta, May (Todd and Carriker 1922); Feb chick in Putumayo (Blake 1955); leaf-filled nest depression on ground, usually betw. buttress roots of large tree; 6-7 glossy turquoise eggs (Wetmore 1965a).
Status and habitat: Fairly common (by voice) where not persecuted; floor of humid and wet forest.
Range: To 1000m. Pacific coast from Baudó Mts. s to Nariño (*latifrons*); Panama border (Río Juradó) e to mid. Magdalena Val. and s to Remedios, Antioquia (*saturatus*); w base of Santa Marta Mts. e to w base Perijá Mts. (*zuliensis*); e of Andes from nw Meta and Vaupés (Mitú) southward (*peruvianus*). Se Mexico to n Bolivia and Amazonian Brazil.

## 4. WHITE-THROATED TINAMOU
*Tinamus guttatus*                  Pl. 1, Map 4
Identification: 14.5″ (37cm). Crown slaty; otherwise dark rufescent brown above inconspic. vermiculated black; *lower back and inner remiges spotted buffy white*; sides of head and neck dusky brown finely speckled ochraceous; throat whitish; rest of underparts rufescent brown (paler than upperparts), becoming buffy on lower underparts; flanks barred black; legs greenish.
Similar species: Much like Great Tinamou (3) but smaller and with buffy white spotting on posterior upperparts. Also cf. 7, 9, 11, 15, and 16, all of which *could* overlap in portions of range.
Voice: Melancholy song a long mellow whistle followed by a short whistle a half tone lower, then a pause, a ser. of accelerating whistles, and the 1st 2 notes repeated again (Meyer de Schauensee and Phelps 1978).
Breeding: 4 BC birds, Mar–Apr, upper Orinoco, Venez. (Friedmann 1948).
Status and habitat: Floor of humid forest. Fairly common in Mitú area well away from habitations.
Range: To 500m. E of Andes where known from w Caquetá, w Putumayo, and Vaupés (Mitú). Prob. also Guainía and Amazonas. S Venez. (Amazonas) and e Ecuador to n Bolivia and Amazonian Brazil.

[*Nothocercus*: Med. size; mostly highlands.]

## 5. HIGHLAND TINAMOU
*Nothocercus bonapartei*            Pl. 1, Map 5
Identification: 15″ (38cm). Crown and nape blackish slate; otherwise *deep rufescent brown above* vermiculated black; *wing coverts and rump with small buffy white spots; throat bright cinnamon ochraceous*; rest of underparts rufous brown becoming cinnamon on belly; lower underparts with fine wavy black bars and pale spots; legs dark gray.
Similar species: Tawny-breasted Tinamou (6) has chestnut (not slaty) crown and white throat. Gray Tinamou (1) is larger and grayish (not refescent).
Voice: Loud *quok* alarm (McKay 1980); in Venez. repeats a loud, deep, slightly nasal *cawoh* or *kooyoo* (Eisenmann).
Breeding: 9 BC birds, Mar–June and Nov, Perijá Mts., W and C Andes (Carriker; Miller 1963); ground depression nest at base of tree root, in stump, etc. (Schäfer 1954); 1 nest, PN Cueva de los Guácharos, 2 aqua blue eggs, hatched 11 Mar (McKay 1980).
Status and habitat: Floor of humid and wet forest and dense second growth, sometimes

near forest openings; foothills and lower highlands. Generally at lower el. than allied Tawny-breasted Tinamou.
**Range:** Mostly 1500-2200m (to 700m on Pacific slope; to 500m at e base of E Andes). Spottily, in Perijá Mts. and the Andes. Costa Rica and w Panama; n Venez. s in mts. to Peru.

## 6. TAWNY-BREASTED TINAMOU
*Nothocercus julius*                                      Pl. 1, Map 6
**Identification:** 15″ (38cm). *Forecrown bright chestnut;* rest of upperparts olive brown finely waved and barred black; *throat white* becoming olive brown (paler than above) on chest and *bright cinnamon rufous on lower breast and rest of underparts;* legs bluish gray.
**Similar species:** Only tinamou in upper part of its range. Most likely confused with Highland Tinamou (5), which has cinnamon throat and slaty crown.
**Voice:** Apparently a loud, 2-noted whistle (Hilty).
**Breeding:** 5 BC birds, June–Aug, E Andes (Carriker; Blake 1955).
**Status and habitat:** Floor of humid and wet forest and small forest openings. Presumed to replace Highland Tinamou (5) at higher el. Range now highly fragmented because of deforestation.
**Range:** 1700-3100m. All 3 Andean ranges (no Nariño recs.). Nw Venez. to e Ecuador and e Peru.

[*Crypturellus*: Small size; mostly lowlands; no specialized tarsus; roost on ground.]

## 7. CINEREOUS TINAMOU
*Crypturellus cinereus*                                   Pl. 1, Map 7
**Identification:** 12″ (30cm). *Almost uniform grayish brown above and below,* only slightly paler on underparts; throat finely streaked whitish, appearing pale gray; crown and nape tinged rufescent; legs pale dull orange.
**Similar species:** A small, essentially uniform tinamou without contrasting throat or abdomen. Little Tinamou (9) has contrasting whitish throat and in area of overlap a slaty crown. Brown Tinamou (10) is darker and browner above, much more rufescent below. Also cf. 4, 11, 15, and 16, all of which could overlap in range (but not necessarily in habitat).
**Voice:** Song a single tremulous whistle (about 1.5 sec. duration), rarely a ser. of faintly tremulous whistles on same pitch (at a distance tremulous sound inaudible); the single whistle much like that of Sunbittern but richer, less penetrating.
**Behavior:** Like others of the genus, notably

furtive and difficult to see. Prefers to walk or run when surprised rather than fly.
**Breeding:** 4 BC birds, June, w Caquetá (Carriker); nest on forest floor, in thick vegetation; 2 salmon violet eggs (Haverschmidt 1968).
**Status and habitat:** Floor of second growth, esp. near streams, also *várzea* forest and damp or swampy woods with thickets.
**Range:** To 500m. From e base of E Andes in n Meta and e Vichada (Maipures) s to Putumayo; no Vaupés or Amazonas recs. Guianas and s Venez. to n Bolivia and Amazonian Brazil.
**Note:** Does not incl. Berlepsch's Tinamou of Pac. coast, often treated as a race of this sp.

## 8. BERLEPSCH'S TINAMOU
*Crypturellus berlepschi*                                 Pl. 1, Map 8
**Identification:** 11″ (28cm). *Mostly dark dusky brown above and below; head and neck blackish;* bill blackish above, *red below;* legs dull dark reddish; eyes yellow.
**Similar species:** A very dark tinamou with a blackish head; in the hand, note red lower mandible. Little Tinamou (9) is grayish brown with whitish throat; Choco Tinamou (14) is indistinctly barred dusky above, has gray throat, ruddy underparts, and strong barring on flanks and belly.
**Breeding:** BC ♂, Feb, Chocó (Carriker).
**Status and habitat:** Widespread on floor of wet forest, esp. denser mid. age second growth; mostly coastal lowlands and hill country; perhaps replaced in upper foothills by Choco Tinamou. Does not enter the drier more seasonal forests of Gulf of Urabá region (Haffer 1975).
**Range:** To 500m (once to 900m in Anchicayá Val.). Pacific coast from Baudó Mts. and base of W Andes near Mutatá (nw Antioquia) southward. W Colombia and nw Ecuador.
**Note:** Sometimes treated as a race of Cinereous Tinamou of e of Andes.

## 9. LITTLE TINAMOU
*Crypturellus soui*                                       Pl. 1, Map 9
**Identification:** 9″ (23cm). *Smallest Colombian tinamou.* Grayish brown to rufescent brown above, head slightly grayer; *throat whitish,* rest of underparts ruddy brown to buffy brown, chest often darker; flanks faintly barred blackish. Or as above but crown and sides of head sooty or blackish (*mustelinus, caquetae, soui*). ♀: head usually darker and underparts brighter rufous than ♂ (or crown and sides of head brownish—*mustelinus;* or blackish to sooty—*caquetae, soui*).
**Similar species:** Small with virtually unbarred lower underparts. Several tinamous are rather

sim. (all slightly larger). E of Andes see White-throated, Cinereous, Brown, Undulated, and Variegated tinamous (4, 7, 10, 11, 15); w of Andes Berlepsch's, Red-legged, and Choco Tinamou (8, 13, 14).

**Voice:** In much of Colombia the most frequently heard tinamou and everywhere heard far more than seen. Two main calls: a ser. of tremulous whistles, each a little higher in pitch than the preceding and increasing in vol. and speed, then ending suddenly; the 2d, 2 tremulous whistles, the 1st rising a half-tone, the 2d falling a full tone (Eisenmann). There are other var. and all calls flatter, weaker, and less resonant than corresponding but very sim. calls of Great Tinamou.

**Behaviour:** As with other *Crypturellus*, shy and very difficult to see. Feeds and roosts on the ground and even more difficult to flush than larger *Tinamus*.

**Breeding:** 12 BC birds, Feb–May, n Colombia (Carriker); a Mar nest, Leticia (Brown), an Aug nest near Santa Marta (Todd and Carriker 1922); in Panama, 2 eggs, uniform brownish drab (Wetmore 1965a).

**Status and habitat:** Common in forest borders and younger stages of second growth with dense undergrowth; dry to humid areas.

**Range:** To 2000m. Pacific coast (*harterti*), upper Río Sinú e to mid. Magdalena Val. (s to latitude of Bogotá) and formerly entire Cauca Val. (*caucae*); n Sucre (Snía. San Jacinto) e to Santa Marta and Perijá Mts. and e of Andes s to Río Casanare (*mustelinus*); nw Meta and Vaupés s to Amazonas (*soui*), sw Meta (Macarena Mts.) s to Putumayo (*caquetae*) s Mexico to n Bolivia and s Brazil.

## 10. BROWN TINAMOU
*Crypturellus obsoletus*               Pl. 1, Map 10
**Identification:** 11″ (28cm). Crown and nape sooty black; otherwise *rich rufous chestnut above* becoming paler on rump; sides of head and neck brownish gray, *throat grayer*; rest of underparts deep rufous (paler than above); *flanks and under tail coverts marked black*; legs olive gray.

**Similar species:** Much like darker, ruddier forms of Little Tinamou (9) but slightly larger, throat gray (not whitish), and flanks definitely barred. Also see Highland and Tawny-breasted tinamous (5, 6).

**Voice:** In Brazil, loud, forceful, and very tremulous whistled *eEEeert*, repeated at short intervals, or in long faster ser. (up to 40 notes in 30sec), swelling to a crescendo, sometimes falling slightly at end (P. Schwartz recording). At a distance sounds like a loud cricket. In e Peru same whistle trebled, last note higher (T. Parker).

**Breeding:** Nest, w Brazil, depression on ground; 4 dark glossy brown eggs (Frisch and Frisch 1964).

**Status and habitat:** Known only from "Bogotá"; no recent recs. In Venez. 1300-2200m in forest (Meyer de Schauensee and Phelps 1978); in Ecuador also mainly in subtropics; e of Río Amazon extensively in lowlands.

**Range:** Prob. e slope of E Andes (no definite localities known). N Venez. e Ecuador (Río Suno) to n Argentina and Brazil s of Río Amazon.

## 11. UNDULATED TINAMOU
*Crypturellus undulatus*               Pl. 1, Map 11
**Identification:** 11″ (28cm). Crown dusky brown; otherwise dull dark brown above finely vermiculated black (not obvious in field); wings tinged olivaceous; *throat white*; foreneck and breast grayish brown becoming *buffy white on center of belly*; flanks and under tail coverts barred ochraceous and black. Legs greenish gray.

**Similar species:** Despite its name, appears uniform grayish olive brown with a white throat and blackish flank barring in the field. Little Tinamou (9) is slightly smaller with less obvious white throat and more rufescent underparts (none of this easy to see in field).

**Voice:** Learn its distinctive often heard song: a melancholy whistled *whoo, who-who-uh?*, last note higher or sliding upscale; less often *whoo, ho, who-uh?* 2d and 4th whistles higher; most vocal Jan–July (J. V. Remsen).

**Behavior:** Notably vocal day or night and less furtive than many others of the genus. Often attracted to a whistled imitation of its call.

**Breeding:** BC birds, Feb, e Putumayo (Blake 1955), 2 BC birds Mar, Macarena Mts.; 1 nest on ground, 3 glossy vinaceous pink eggs, 17 Mar (Olivares 1962); 2 nests, May, w Caquetá (Nicéforo and Olivares 1964).

**Status and habitat:** Common on floor of *várzea* forest and swampy river isl. forest; also in wet young second growth in pastures and clearings, but usually near seasonally flooded areas. Absent, or nearly so, from Amazonian river isls. during twice annual flooding and has been noted flying across smaller Amazon channels and river isl. lagoons (J. V. Remsen; Hilty).

**Range:** To 500m. E of Andes from Meta (Villavicencio; Macarena Mts.) and Vaupés (Mitú) s to Putumayo and Amazonas (Leticia). Guyana and s Venez. to Bolivia, Amazonian Brazil, and w Argentina.

## 12. GRAY-LEGGED TINAMOU
*Crypturellus duidae*                         Map 12
**Identification:** 12″ (30cm). ♂: crown rufous

brown; rest of upperparts dark brown indistinctly barred black on rump and tail; *throat white, sides of head, neck, and entire breast rufous,* fading to pale cinnamon buff on belly; *flanks coarsely barred black*; legs gray to bluish gray. ♀: sim. but inner remiges and lower back darker brown with *narrow yellowish buff bars.*
**Similar species:** ♂ much like Undulated Tinamou (11), but breast rufous (not gray brown), and like Little Tinamou (9) but larger and flanks conspic. barred. ♀ unique in known range. Also cf. Cinereous Tinamou (7).
**Status and habitat:** Little known even in its Venez. range. Apparently humid forest and scrubby open woodland.
**Range:** 400-500m. Known only from s Meta on e side of Macarena Mts. (San Juan de Arama; Caño Guapayá; Los Micos) undoubtedly e Vichada (on Venez. bank of Orinoco at Caño Cuao and Sanariapo). Perhaps table mts. of Vaupés. Venez. (Amazonas, 100-200m) and e Colombia.
**Note:** By some treated as a subsp. of *C. noctivagus* (Yellow-legged Tinamou) of Brazil.

### 13. RED-LEGGED TINAMOU
*Crypturellus erythropus*       Pl. 1, Map 13
**Identification:** 12″ (30cm). *Legs reddish pink.* ♂: forecrown dusky becoming dull brown on rest of upperparts; wing coverts and lower back more or less finely barred and vermiculated black; throat white; *sides of head rufescent; foreneck and chest gray contrasting with cinnamon to buff breast;* belly paler cinnamon; flanks and under tail coverts barred blackish. Or as above but crown brown (*idoneus*), or crown light gray (*cursitans*), or belly whitish (*saltuarius*). ♀: sim. but *lower back, rump, and entire wings prom. barred black and buff.*
**Similar species:** A widespread med.-small tinamou *and the only one in its range with pink legs*; normally shows barring above (much stronger in ♀), and white throat contrasting with cinnamon breast and rufescent sides of head. Little Tinamou (9) is essentially unbarred. Also cf. Cinereous Tinamou (7).
**Voice:** Song a hollow tremulous whistle, *whooohoooa*, repeated at intervals of about half a min (P. Schwartz recording).
**Behavior:** Sim. to Little Tinamou.
**Breeding:** 1 Santa Marta nest, Sept; 3 eggs, light glossy pinkish brown—*idoneus* (Darlington 1931). BC pair, the ♀ laying, Mar, Río Nechí; BC ♂, Apr, upper Sinú—*columbianus*; 3 BC ♂♂ and laying ♀, Jan–July, s Magdalena and n Cesar—*idoneus* (Carriker).
**Status and habitat:** Status of var. forms uncertain. Floor of drier thickets, second growth, and dry to moist deciduous forest.

**Range:** To 600m (to 1300m in n Venez.). Upper Sinú and Nechí vals. and Snía. San Jacinto se of Cartagena (*columbianus*); lower Magdalena Val. e across Santa Marta region (absent from n slope?) to w Guajira and base of Perijá Mts. (*idoneus*); mid. Magdalena Val. (1 specimen) at w base of E Andes near La Mata, 8°37′N, s Cesar (*saltuarius*); e base of E Andes in Arauca and n Boyacá (*cursitans*). N Colombia and n Venez. to the Guianas and n Brazil n of Río Amazon.
**Note 1:** Blake (1977) and recent unpublished proposals of P. Schwartz and Eisenmann are followed in provisionally considering *C. idoneus* (Santa Marta Tinamou), *C. columbianus* (Colombian Tinamou), and *C. saltuarius* (Magdalena Tinamou) as subspp. of *C. erythropus* of n Amazonian Venez. and the Guianas. Based on mallophagan studies, Carriker (1955) reached a sim. conclusion; but further work is warranted. *C. columbianus* has been considered a race of *C. boucardi* (Slaty-breasted Tinamou) or a separate sp. *C. saltuarius* has been considered a separate sp. or a subsp. of *C. kerriae* (Choco Tinamou). *C. idoneus* has been variously treated as a subsp. of *C. cinnamomeus* (Thicket Tinamou) or of *C. noctivagus* (Redfooted Tinamou) or a separate sp. **Note 2:** Some incl. *C. erythropus* and its subspp. as races of *C. atrocapillus* of e Peru and n Bolivia.

### 14. CHOCO TINAMOU
*Crypturellus kerriae*          Map 14
**Identification:** 12″ (30cm). *Legs reddish.* ♂: *crown blackish*, otherwise dark umber brown above inconspic. barred black; *sides of head slate gray;* upper throat white becoming gray on lower throat; *dusky chestnut* on foreneck and chest, and dull cinnamon brown on rest of underparts; flanks and crissum barred black. ♀: like ♂ but upperparts darker, more chestnut; *wing coverts prom. barred black; breast and sides slate gray.*
**Similar species:** Berlepsch's Tinamou (8) is even darker, unbarred, and has dark (not red) legs. Little Tinamou (9) is also virtually unbarred.
**Voice:** In e Panama a low, tremulous, and very resonant whistle lasting about 1 sec; heard reg. Feb–Mar (Wetmore and Galindo 1972) and July (R. Ridgely).
**Status and habitat:** Very little known. Described from 2 specimens from Baudó Mts.; more recently found in e Panama "in heavy forest" in foothills (300-800m) of Cerro Quía near Colombian border (Wetmore and Galindo 1972).
**Range:** Baudó Mts. (Rió Baudó, 450m). E Panama and w Colombia.
**Note:** May be closely allied or conspecific with

*C. boucardi* (Slaty-breasted Tinamou) from s
Mexico to Costa Rica (Eisenmann).

### 15. VARIEGATED TINAMOU
*Crypturellus variegatus*          Pl. 1, Map 15
**Identification:** 13″ (33cm). Distinctive. *Crown
and sides of head black*; throat white; *neck, upper
mantle,* and *breast bright rufous* becoming pale
buff on lower underparts; *entire back and wings
black boldly barred ochraceous*; legs dull greenish.
**Similar species:** Not likely confused if seen
clearly. Black head, bold barring above, and
rufous neck and breast are the marks. Barred
Tinamou (16) lacks black cap and bright rufous breast. Also cf. 4, 7, 9, 11, and 16, all of
which could overlap in portions of range.
**Voice:** Distinctive song a long, melancholy,
tremulous whistle rising at end, then after a
pause, 5 short faster whistles, each sliding upscale slightly, *wuuuuuuuh . . . wuu, wuu, wuu,
wuu, wu*, from Guyana to Ecuador (Beebe 1925;
P. Schwartz; R. Ridgely).
**Breeding:** BC ♂, 9 Apr, Amazonas, Venez.
(Friedmann 1948). Guyana nests mostly May–
July (rainy season); 1 egg, light glossy purplish
vinaceous; in depression on ground (Beebe
1925).
**Status and habitat:** Floor of humid forest and
overgrown clearings; not well known in Colombia but common eastward.
**Range:** To 500m. W Caquetá (Morelia) and
Vaupés (Mitú); prob. also to e Vichada (on
Venez. side of Río Orinoco). The Guianas, s
Venez., and e Ecuador to e central Peru and
n Amazonian and e Brazil.
**Note 1:** Rather sim. Rusty Tinamou (*C. brevi-
rostris*) of w Amazonian Brazil (Río Uaupés

near Colombian border), Fr. Guiana, and e
Peru may occur in e Vaupés. Like Variegated,
but crown rufous chestnut, abdomen whitish
(not pale buff), and bill shorter (18-22mm vs
23-28mm). **Note 2:** Bartlett's Tinamou (*C.
bartletti*) of w Amazonian Brazil and e Peru
may occur near Leticia (s bank only). Barely
distinct from Rusty Tinamou, it has sooty (not
rufous chestnut) crown.

### 16. BARRED TINAMOU
*Crypturellus casiquiare*          Pl. 1, Map 16
**Identification:** 10″ (25cm). Small. Head and
hindneck chestnut; *remaining upperparts boldly
barred black and rufous*; throat white; *foreneck
and breast gray* becoming whitish on lower underparts; flanks barred pale buff and black;
legs greenish yellow. Imm.: speckled rufous
on chest.
**Similar species:** Most like Variegated Tinamou (15) but gray (not bright rufous) below
and no black cap.
**Voice:** Easily recognized. A single whistled
*wooooa*, then a long ser. of about 30 shorter
whistles (in 40 sec), rising slightly, then falling,
and more widely spaced at end; quality of Little Tinamou (P. Schwartz recording).
**Status and habitat:** Little known. Apparently
confined to sandy-belt forests of upper Río
Negro-Río Orinoco drainage basins.
**Range:** To 300m. Known only from Vaupés
(Río Vaupés near Brazilian border); prob. also
extreme e Guainía (rec. on Caño Casiquiare,
Venez., opp. San Felipe, Guainía, and on Yavita-Pimichín Trail). S Venez. (Amazonas) and
e Colombia.

# GREBES: Podicipedidae (4)

Colombian grebes live in fresh water ponds and lakes from the tropical lowlands to the cool
temperate zone. They have lobed toes and swim and dive expertly but are seldom on land except
when nesting. Their nests are floating rafts of reeds and vegetation anchored to emergent water
plants. All Colombian species are resident.

### 1. LEAST GREBE
*Podiceps dominicus*          Ill. 1, Map 17
**Identification:** 9″ (23cm). *Tiny. Slender black bill
and orange yellow eyes.* Head and neck slaty gray;
throat white, otherwise mainly dark grayish
brown, paler below, with small white wing
speculum (visible in flight). Breeding birds have
crown and throat black.
**Similar species:** From Pied-billed Grebe (4) by
smaller size, slender pointed black bill (not
thick and whitish), pale eye, and blacker head.
**Voice:** Rather quiet; occas. a musical reedy *hoot*
(ffrench 1973).

**Behavior:** Usually alone or in pairs swimming
in small pools; infrequently gathers in small
loose groups when not breeding. Often with
Pied-billed Grebe but also on pools too shallow
for the latter.
**Breeding:** Downy young, 4 Feb, upper Patía
Val., Cauca (Wallace 1958); BC ♂, 3 Jan, coastal
Bolívar (Carriker). Nests reported Jan–July in
Panama; floating platforms of weeds an-
chored to live or dead plants (Wetmore 1965a);
Feb–June nests in arid w Ecuador; 4-6 dirty
white eggs (Marchant 1960).
**Status and habitat:** Locally common. Resident

1.  PIED-BILLED GREBE (left), LEAST GREBE (right)

2.  COLOMBIAN GREBE (left), SILVERY GREBE (right)

on freshwater lakes, ponds, and marshes with aquatic vegetation.
**Range:** To 2600m (mostly below 2000m). Carib. region, in Atlántico and n Magdalena (Ciénaga), Cauca Val. (Valle and Cauca), E Andes and e base of them in Meta and Caquetá. Perhaps locally throughout. S Texas and Mexico to c Argentina. W Indies.
**Note:** Placed in the genus *Tachybaptus* by some.

## 2. SILVERY GREBE
*Podiceps occipitalis*          Ill. 2, Map 18
**Identification:** 11″ (28cm). Slender pointed black bill. Eyes red. Crown and sides of head gray with tuft of silvery buff feathers springing from ear coverts; flattish crest and hindneck black; otherwise gray above; wings blackish; *throat, foreneck, and underparts white.* In flight shows white patch on secondaries. Nonbreeding birds are duller and lack plumes on ear coverts.
**Similar species:** Nonbreeding birds much like Colombian Grebe (3) but lack the white patch on ear coverts.
**Behavior:** Breed in colonies but at other times seen singly, in 2's, or small groups, usually in deeper water and on larger lakes than Pied-billed or Least grebes. Like other grebes, patters over water or dives on alarm and reluctant to fly.
**Breeding:** Feb breeding colony, Lago La Cocha (Borrero 1952b); also on Laguna de Cusiyaco, se Cauca (Borrero and Hernández 1961); in n Chile up to 400 in breeding colonies in Feb; 2 pale blue eggs, quickly staining brown as they are covered before the ads. leave (Johnson 1965).
**Status and habitat:** Uncommon. Large freshwater lakes, esp. with bordering aquatic vegetation.
**Range:** 2800-3600m. S part of C Andes in Cauca (Laguna de Cusiyaco; Laguna San Rafael, PN Puracé) s through Nariño (Lago La Cocha). S Colombia s to Falkland Isls. S birds migrate n to c Argentina.

## 3. COLOMBIAN GREBE
*Podiceps andinus*          Ill. 2, Map 19
**Identification:** 12″ (30cm). Slender black bill slightly upturned. Eyes red. Breeding plumage: crown, nape, and throat blackish brown; tuft of plumes on sides of head golden buff to chestnut; rest of upperparts dark brownish black; *foreneck and sides of body chestnut;* center of lower underparts white. In flight a white

patch on secondaries. Nonbreeding plumage: duller, more brownish gray above; *entire underparts white inc. throat, forehead, and distinct patch extending up onto ear coverts* (no plumes).
**Similar species:** Nonbreeding Pied-billed Grebe (4) sim. but lacks whitish on forehead and ear coverts. Also see Silvery Grebe (2).
**Behavior:** Like others of the genus and with Pied-billed Grebe at Lago Tota, Feb 1977 (R. Ridgely).
**Breeding:** Several ♀♀ ready to lay, Aug, Lago Tota, Boyacá (Borrero 1947).
**Status and habitat:** Rare and endangered. Resident on med. to large freshwater lakes with reeds. Only recent rec. is 2-3 on Lago Tota, Feb 1977 (R. Ridgely). Formerly numerous.
**Range:** ENDEMIC. 2500-3100m. E Andes from s Boyacá (Lago Tota) s to Sabana de Bogotá.
**Note:** By some considered a subsp. of *P. nigricollis* (Eared Grebe) but differs from all forms of latter in having chestnut (not black) foreneck and chest.

## 4. PIED-BILLED GREBE
*Podilymbus podiceps*          Ill. 1, Map 20
**Identification:** 12-14″ (30-36cm). *Whitish chicken-like bill with black ring.* Eyes dark. Breeding plumage: throat black, rest of plumage mostly grayish brown, paler below, and with white central abdomen and under tail coverts. Nonbreeding plumage: black ring on bill indistinct or lacking and throat grayish white. Juv.: white stripes on sides of head and neck.
**Similar species:** See Colombian Grebe (3) and smaller Least Grebe (1).
**Voice:** Call, in breeding season, a loud *cuk-cuk, cuk-cuk, cou-cou-cou* (Ridgely 1976).
**Behavior:** Sim. to Least Grebe though usually in deeper water.
**Breeding:** Pairs with downy chicks, 7 July and 14 Aug (Hilty); nests, Jan–Mar, near Bogotá; 1 BC ♀, 7 Mar, Cauca Val. (Borrero 1952b); 3 white eggs, in floating platform of vegetation.
**Status and habitat:** Locally common resident (no migrants) in freshwater ponds and lakes with emergent vegetation. Most numerous on Sabana de Bogotá and in Cauca and lower Magdalena vals.
**Range:** To 3100m. W of Andes, rarely e of them. Breeds from N America to Tierra del Fuego. W Indies. N birds winter s to w Panama.

# ALBATROSSES: Diomedeidae (1)

Albatrosses, often known as gooneys or mollymawks, are famous for their remarkable powers of gliding flight. All are very large, tube-nosed seabirds with long narrow wings, webbed feet, and heavy hooked bills. Most are found in the Southern Hemisphere and remain at sea for extended periods except when breeding on islands. They feed on cuttlefish and other marine organisms. Probably none occurs regularly in Colombian waters.

## 1. GALAPAGOS (WAVED) ALBATROSS
*Diomedea irrorata*
**Identification:** 35″ (89cm). Very large with long narrow wings (wingspan about 7-9 ft. or 213-274 cm). *Heavy yellow bill. Head and neck white* tinged yellow; *rest of body sooty* very narrowly vermiculated white; rump white sparsely barred sooty; wings and tail mostly sooty; under wing coverts mottled grayish white. Imm.: uniform dark brown with grayish white under wing coverts.
**Similar species:** A med.-large albatross with white head, dark body, and yellow bill.
**Behavior:** On windy days glides and banks swiftly on motionless extended wings for long periods of time; follows updrafts near waves and troughs.
**Status and habitat:** Prob. casual, but only rec. is 1 on 8 Mar 1941, betw. Octavia Rocks and Bahía de Aguacate off extreme nw Chocó coast. Most likely in pelagic waters off Colombia's Pacific coast Jan–late Mar. Breeds Apr–Dec in Galapagos.
**Range:** Pacific coast. Breeds on Hood Isl. in the Galapagos and Isla de La Plata off coast of Ecuador (small population). Wanders to Peru, Colombia, and Panama waters.

# SHEARWATERS, PETRELS: Procellariidae (7)

Shearwaters and petrels are tube-nosed birds of the open sea. They are somewhat gull-like in appearance, but their flight is very different. Shearwaters skim rapidly just above the water, alternating a few fast stiff flaps with long directional glides. Food is taken directly from the surface or in shallow dives. Gadfly-petrels flap and glide like shearwaters but hold their wings slightly bent at the wrist, not straight, and often bank and swing erratically, sometimes arcing high above the water. Their food is mostly squid taken from the surface of the water. Most members of the family spend up to five or six months each year nesting in burrows or holes in sea cliffs on small oceanic islands. They are mainly nocturnal around the breeding colony. When not breeding they migrate or wander widely.

## 1. CAPE (PINTADO) PETREL
*Daption capense*
**Identification:** 14-16″ (36-41cm); wing span 3′ (90cm). Unmistakable. Upper surface of wing dark brown with *2 large white patches on each wing* (conspic. in flight); back and rump checkered black and white; head black and underparts white; underwing white edged blackish; short tail tipped blackish.
**Behavior:** Flies with alternating stiff-winged flapping and short glides; often follows ships at sea.
**Status and habitat:** Only Colombian rec. is a sighting (with photo) along the coast of Gorgona Isl. (w of Cauca), 12 Oct 1981 (Borrero 1981).
**Range:** Breeds in Antarctica and outlying isls. When not breeding, occurs off Pacific coast; yr.-round in Chile and reg. to Peru, sometimes to Ecuador and s Colombia (Gorgona Isl.), accidentally to Mexico and California. On Atlantic coast n to Uruguay and Rio de Janeiro.

## 2. BLACK-CAPPED PETREL
*Pterodroma hasitata*
**Identification:** 14-16″ (36-41cm). Short black bill. Flesh-colored feet. Light phase: *cap black; forehead and entire neck and underparts white*; rest of upperparts grayish brown; lower back and tail black with *conspic. V-shaped white rump patch*; underwing white bordered black all around. Dark phase: sooty brown with white rump.
**Similar species:** Large gadfly-petrel with black cap, white collar and white rump. The nearly extinct Cahow (*P. cahow*), unrec. though poss. anywhere in Carib., is sim. but lacks white collar and shows only a very small pale patch (not a broad band) at base of tail.
**Behavior:** Flies close to water; short ser. of fast fluttering wing beats alternate with graceful arcing glides (Watson 1966).
**Status and habitat:** Accidental. Once betw. Guajira Peninsula and Aruba. To be looked for in pelagic waters.
**Range:** Carib. coast. Breeds on Haiti (mt. tops); wanders to n Atlantic from Florida to Ontario; also off coastal Brazil.

## 3. DARK-RUMPED PETREL
*Pterodroma phaeopygia*
**Identification:** 16-17″ (41-43cm). Short stout black bill. Rather short wedge-shaped tail. Legs pinkish. *Crown and wings blackish*; otherwise

brown above; *forecrown, cheeks, and entire underparts white* (incl. sides of rump and under tail coverts); underwings white with broad dusky edges and tip.
**Similar species:** From other Colombian procellarids by white forecrown and cheeks. Light phase Wedge-tailed Shearwater (4) is paler above and has dark under tail coverts and darker forecrown.
**Behavior:** Swerving flight much like that of sim.-sized *Puffinus* (R. Ridgely); on windy days often curves high above the water in steeply banked arcs followed by long glides. Holds wings bent at wrist, slow flapping alternates with long glides. Wing beats slower than smaller spp. of *Pterodroma*.
**Status and habitat:** Rec. off Malpelo Isl. and may be a reg. migrant or visitant to pelagic Pacific waters; most likely in 1st half of yr.; breeds June–Dec in Galapagos.
**Range:** Malpelo Isl. off Pacific coast. Breeds in Galapagos and Hawaiian Isls. (poss. endangered on both). Galapagos form wanders to coast of C and S America from Mexico to Peru.
**Note:** Parkinson's Petrel (*Procellaria parkinsoni*) is known from scattered rec. in Pacific waters of Mid. and S America incl. Guatemala, Costa Rica, Ecuador, Peru, and sightings off Panama and Galapagos. It should eventually be found in Colombian waters. Large (18″), and entirely sooty black with pale bluish gray to greenish yellow bill, tip and culmen black; underside of primary shafts white, *legs black*. Poss. a reg. visitant. Breeds in New Zealand where considered endangered.

### 4. WEDGE-TAILED SHEARWATER
*Puffinus pacificus*
**Identification:** 16-17″ (41-43cm). Long slender bill *pinkish to dark gray. Legs and feet flesh color.* Dark phase: entirely sooty brown incl. entire wing lining. Light phase: dark brown above, cheeks grayer; otherwise mostly white below with dark under tail coverts; wing linings white; tip and broad trailing edge dusky. Rather long wedge-shaped tail (not always obvious in field) extends beyond wing tips when at rest.
**Similar species:** From dark phase Sooty Shearwater by dark (not grayish white) wing linings, sometimes also by pale bill. Light phase easily confused with Pink-footed Shearwater (see 5). Also see note below.
**Status and habitat:** Few recs. To be looked for in pelagic waters. Panama sightings and a single specimen are scattered from late Feb–mid-June (Ridgely 1976).
**Range:** Pacific coast. Breeds in Revilla Gigedo Isls. off w Mexico and most isls. in sw Pacific and in Indian Ocean. Wanders e to coasts from Mexico s to Ecuador.

**Note:** Flesh-footed Shearwater (*P. carneipes*) is unrec. but poss. off Pacific Colombian coast. Very like dark phase Wedge-tail but with short, rounded tail and always with pale bill.

### 5. [PINK-FOOTED SHEARWATER]
*Puffinus creatopus*
**Identification:** 19-20″ (48-51cm). Bill and feet pale yellowish flesh. Grayish brown above, mainly *white below* mottled gray on sides of breast and flanks, *under wing linings mottled gray and white*.
**Similar species:** Much like light phase Wedge-tailed (4) but larger with rounded tail, pale bill (never dark), paler and grayer upperparts, and this extending much lower to sides of breast and flanks; wing linings mottled gray and white (not white), and a broader dusky trailing edge on wing. Audubon's (7) is much smaller with more blackish upperparts.
**Status and habitat:** Hypothetical. Sight recs. of 6 birds off coast of Chocó, 7 Dec 1977, betw. 5°58′N, 79°53′W, and 6°22′N, 79°43′W (R.G.B. Brown).
**Range:** Pacific coast. Breeds on the Juan Fernández Isls. and Mocha Isl. Chile, ranging n to coast of Peru, Ecuador, Colombia, Pacific US, casually to Alaska.
**Note:** Sometimes considered a pale subsp. of Flesh-footed Shearwater (*P. carneipes*).

### 6. SOOTY SHEARWATER
*Puffinus griseus*
**Identification:** 19″ (48cm). Short rounded tail. *Dark slender bill.* Feet dark. *Entirely sooty brown*, slightly paler below; *under wing linings pale gray to silvery* (conspic. as bird banks).
**Similar species:** See dark phase Wedge-tailed Shearwater (4). Several other shearwaters, poss. but unrec., closely resemble Sooty Shearwater (see note).
**Behavior:** Often in flocks. Flies stiffly and very rapidly, skimming close to the water, then banking or arcing sharply to change direction. A few stiff rapid wing beats alternate with long glides. Dives readily and during calm periods frequently rests on the water.
**Status and habitat:** Prob. fairly common off Pacific coast in cold offshore or pelagic waters. Rec. 18 May at Octavia Rocks off Chocó coast but may occur sporadically yr.-round (Murphy 1936). In Panama mainly June–Sept. (Ridgely 1976). Only Carib. recs. are 1 seen 17 Jan 1979, Cañaveral, PN Tayrona (J. Hernández *in* Naranjo 1979b), and 1 seen 10 miles to sea off Galerazamba (n of Barranquilla), 2 Feb 1979 (Naranjo 1979b). Breeds mostly Oct–May in s S America.
**Range:** Pacific and Carib. coasts. Breeds on isls. of entire Cape Horn Archipelago, Staten Isl.,

Argentina, and New Zealand; migrates n (esp. on Pacific side of S America) in a broad front, some reaching the arctic.

**Note:** Short-tailed Shearwater (*P. tenuirostris*), poss. in colder Pacific coast waters, resembles Sooty Shearwater but usually has dark under wing linings (occas. pale like Sooty) and short thick bill (not long and slender). Sight identifications, except for flocks of birds with predom. dark under wings, would be risky. Flesh-footed Shearwater (*P. carneipes*) also poss. off Pacific coast, differs from Sooty in yellow bill and dark underwings.

**7. AUDUBON'S (DUSKY-BACKED) SHEARWATER**

*Puffinus lherminieri*                                    Ill. 3

**Identification:** 11″ (28cm). *Very small shearwater.* Slender black bill. Pink Feet. *Blackish brown above and pure white below*; under tail coverts black or partly black; dark of head reaching to below eyes (a capped appearance) *sharply set off from underparts*; under wing linings white (occas. grayish), flight feathers dusky.

**Similar species:** Much smaller and more clean-cut than other shearwaters likely to occur in Colombian waters.

**Status and habitat:** One specimen, that of the Galapagos race, off Gulf of Cupica, n Chocó. Also breeds and taken on Crab Cay off Isla Providencia. In Panama, occas. on entire Carib. coast and fairly common in Gulf of Panama from s of Pearl Isls. to e Darién (Ridgely 1976); doubtelss reg. off n Chocó.

**Range:** Pacific coast (prob. also Carib.). Breeds in Bermuda, the W Indies, isls. off Carib. coast of Panama and Venez., Tobago, Galapagos and many isls. in warmer parts of Pacific and Indian oceans.

# STORM-PETRELS: Hydrobatidae (7)

Storm-petrels are a worldwide group of small swallowlike seabirds. Some flutter close to the water, especially those of the genus *Oceanites*, pattering or skipping across the water on dangling webbed feet and constantly beating wings. Others swoop and dive more like gadfly-petrels. All

3. BLACK STORM-PETREL (left), AUDUBON'S (DUSKY-BACKED) SHEARWATER (right)

differ anatomically from the gadfly-petrels in having the tube nostrils united into one opening. They eat planktonic crustaceans, small fish, squid and oil from surface films. Most follow ships and are sometimes attracted to lights on shipboard at night. Nesting is colonial in burrows or rock crevices on oceanic islands. Field identification is notably difficult for many species, even with the aid of flight and feeding characters.

### 1. WHITE-VENTED STORM-PETREL
*Oceanites gracilis*
**Identification:** 6″ (15cm). Small. Legs black, *webs on feet yellow*. In flight feet project beyond *square or slightly forked tail*. Mainly sooty black with pale diagonal band on upper wing coverts and *white band across rump; mid. of belly to vent mixed black and white* (sometimes white extends to midbreast).
**Similar species:** Very sim. to Wilson's Storm-Petrel, which is poss. but unrec. (see note). Also see Wedge-rumped (3) and Band-rumped storm-petrels (4).
**Behavior:** Flies with rapid wing beats and a rather direct level flight (Harris 1974). Feeds by pattering across the surface of water, "walking on the water," with dangling legs.
**Status and habitat:** The race (breeding?) in the Galapagos is prob. reg. in Pacific Colombian waters; reported abundant off the Nariño coast in late Sept. (Murphy 1941). Presumed to breed Apr–Sept in the Galapagos (Harris 1974).
**Range:** S Pacific coast of Colombia s in cooler waters to c Chile (about 33°S). Sight recs. attributed to Panama. Breeding area unknown but presum. Galapagos Isls. and coastal deserts of Chile and Peru.
**Note:** Wilson's Storm-Petrel (*Oceanites oceanicus*) is poss. but unrec. in Colombia. Prob. vagrant to Pacific waters, also to Carib. waters. Breeds in cold antarctic and subantarctic water, winters (austral winter) to both the Atlantic and Pacific, and is very like White-vented Storm-Petrel (doubtfully separable in field). It differs in slightly larger size (7-7.5″) and no white on belly (or only a few feathers edged white). Like White-vented Storm-Petrel, it feeds by fluttering with dangling legs on the surface of water.

### 2. LEAST STORM-PETREL
*Oceanodroma (Halocyptena) microsoma*
**Identification:** 5-6″ (13-15cm). *Smallest storm-petrel*. Bill, legs, and feet black. Feet do not extend beyond tail. *Sooty black* with pale upper wing coverts forming a diagonal band; tail wedge-shaped (*appears relatively short in flight*).
**Similar species:** A tiny storm-petrel that appears almost tailless at a distance, the short wedge-shaped tail is apparent only at close range (D. Roberson). Other "black" storm-petrels have square or slightly forked tails.
**Behavior:** Flight is fairly direct with rather deep wing beats, reminiscent of Black Storm-Petrel but more rapid (Stallcup 1976). Usually flies close to the water's surface.
**Status and habitat:** Prob. reg. in offshore or pelagic waters of Pacific coast; rec. in Mar at Octavia Rocks, Chocó; during most mos. in Gulf of Panama.
**Range:** Breeds on San Benito Isls off Baja California and in the Gulf of California July–Oct; wanders at sea s to Peru.

### 3. WEDGE-RUMPED (GALAPAGOS) STORM-PETREL
*Oceanodroma tethys*                          Ill. 4
**Identification:** 6-7″ (15-18cm). *Legs and feet black*, not extending beyond tail. Mostly sooty black with *large triangular white rump patch*, the apex almost reaching notch in slightly forked tail (tail appears squarish in field); upper wing coverts pale forming a diagonal band.
**Similar species:** Under favorable conditions may be told from all other dark storm-petrels with white rumps by the large triangular (not rectangular) rump patch. Best told from Leach's (see note under 5) by much smaller size, darker color, relatively shorter wings, and bright white triangular rump patch; from very sim. Wilson's (see note under 1) by somewhat smaller size, black feet, deliberate flight, and

4. WEDGE-RUMPED (GALAPAGOS) STORM-PETREL

triangular rump patch (Stallcup 1976); from White-vented (1) by larger size, black (not yellow) feet, and uniform dark belly; from Band-rumped (4) by noticeably smaller size and more fluttering twisting flight (not reg. horizontal zigzags).

**Behavior:** In calm weather flight is deliberate and rather direct, more like that of Least or Black storm-petrels and unlike the fluttering nighthawklike flight of Leach's (D. Roberson). May patter across surface but less so than White-vented.

**Status and habitat:** Rec. only Mar, July, and Aug (July rec. at Gorgona Isl., 1979—R. A. Silverstone) but prob. reg. to offshore and pelagic waters of Pacific coast; most numerous in Gulf of Panama May–Nov, rare or absent Jan–Feb (Ridgely 1976); Galapagos birds breed May–Aug (Harris 1974).

**Range:** Pacific coast. Breeds in the Galapagos; also San Gallán and Pescadores Isls. off Peru; wanders s to c Chile, n casually to California.

### 4. [BAND-RUMPED (HARCOURT'S) STORM-PETREL]
*Oceanodroma castro*
**Identification:** 7.5-9″ (19-23cm). Sooty brown with a diagonal pale band across upper wing coverts; *white band across rump extending well onto flanks*; slightly forked tail; black legs and feet.

**Similar species:** Almost identical to Leach's Storm-Petrel (see note under 5) but slightly larger and more robust, rump band narrower and crisper (never any dark mottling in center), tail nearly square (not decidedly forked). Perhaps *best told by flight pattern*, banking left with ca. 6 shallow wing beats, then back to the right about 6 beats, producing a ser. of horizontal zigzags very unlike erratic side to side and vertically bounding flight of Leach's (R.G.B. Brown). Also cf. smaller Wedge-rumped (3), White-vented (1), and Wilson's storm-petrels (note under 1).

**Status and habitat:** Hypothetical. Sight rec. of 2 with a flock of 11 Wedge-rumped Storm-Petrels on the water at 2°6′N, 80°33′W, off the coast of Nariño, 6 Dec 1977 (R.G.B. Brown). Usually at sea near the breeding grounds all yr. but wanders to Pacic coast.

**Range:** Pacific coast. Breeds in the n Atlantic, the Galapagos, Hawaii, and Japan.

### 5. BLACK STORM-PETREL
*Oceanodroma melania*          Ill. 3
**Identification:** 9″ (23cm). Large for a storm-petrel. *Tail deeply forked.* Legs rather long and black. *Entirely sooty black* with a paler band across upper wing coverts.

**Similar species:** Large size, forked tail, all dark plumage, and smoother, slow, very deep wing beats separate it from other storm-petrels rec. in Colombia (cf. Sooty Storm-Petrel, 6). Dark-rumped forms of Leach's Storm-Petrel, poss. but as yet unrec., are quite sim. (see note below).

**Behavior:** Sometimes solitary. Flight is direct, graceful, and deliberate with slower wing beats than Leach's Storm-Petrel (note below). Wing beats are fairly deep (wings raised above the horizontal), spaced, and reminiscent of flight of Black Tern (Stallcup 1976).

**Status and habitat:** Reg. visitant, though apparently in small nos.; 20 seen in Buenaventura harbor, 7-9 Jan 1983 (R. Ridgely and B. Whitney).

**Range:** Pacific coast. Breeds off Baja California and w Mexico, May–Oct; disperses n to c California and s to s Peru.

**Note 1:** Sometimes placed in the genus *Loomelania* because of relatively long legs. **Note 2:** Although unrec., 1 or more dark-rumped races of Leach's Storm-Petrel (*O. leucorhoa*) should be found in Pacific Colombian waters. The race *chapmani*, breeding off Baja California, disperses at sea s to coastal Ecuador and prob. the Galapagos and is the most likely. It is usually not safely separated in the field from the Black Storm-Petrel but is smaller, has only notched (not deeply forked) tail, and more fluttery erratic flight.

### 6. [SOOTY (MARKHAM'S) STORM-PETREL]
*Oceanodroma markhami*
**Identification:** 9.5″ (24cm). A large, dark, fork-tailed storm-petrel sim. to Black Storm-Petrel (4) but a little larger, mainly sooty brown, slightly paler below (normally appears all black), legs slightly shorter.

**Similar species:** Essentially inseparable in field from Black Storm-Petrel. Reportedly differs in shallower wing beats, broken by glides (Black Storm-Petrel has deep wing beats, may or may not glide) as confirmed by specimens off Peru (R.G.B. Brown).

**Status and habitat:** Hypothetical. Sight recs. off coast of Nariño, Colombia, Dec 1980 at 03°16′N, 80°21′W, but in Nov was not found north of 03°00′S (R.G.B. Brown).

**Range:** A Humboldt Current sp. found commonly off coastal Peru and Chile (breeding area unknown) and rec. n to Galapagos, Cocos, and Clipperton isls.

### 7. RINGED STORM-PETREL
*Oceanodroma hornbyi*
**Identification:** 8.5-9″ (22-23cm). Dusky brown

above; *white foreface, white underparts with dusky chest band*; pale band on hindneck. Tail deeply forked.
**Similar species:** No other S American petrel is white below with a dark chest band.
**Status and habitat:** One specimen, July 1979,

Isla Gorgona (P. A. Silverstone). Colder off-shore waters, perhaps also coastal waters. A Humboldt Current sp.
**Range:** Sw Colombia and Ecuador to n Chile; may breed in Andes of Peru.

# TROPICBIRDS: Phaethontidae (2)

Tropicbirds are a very small group of highly pelagic seabirds found in warmer oceans throughout the world. The adults are lovely white birds best known for their two greatly elongated, stream-erlike central tail feathers. Strong and dovelike on the wing, they typically fly high, and on sighting fish or squid, hover momentarily like terns before diving. They nest in colonies on ledges or in crevices on rocky sea cliffs. After nesting they disperse alone or in pairs at sea.

**1. RED-BILLED TROPICBIRD**
*Phaethon aethereus*                                    Ill. 5
**Identification:** 20-24″ (51-61cm), with *long central tail feathers up to 40″ (102 cm)*. Ternlike. Heavy red bill. *Mostly white with black primaries,*

black stripe through eye, and *back and rump finely barred black*. Imm.: lacks long tail feathers, *bill yellow*, barring on back coarser and eyestripes meet on nape forming indistinct nuchal crest.

5. Brown Pelican (left), Magnificent Frigatebird (♂ upper right),
Red-billed Tropicbird (lower right)

**Similar species:** See White-tailed Tropicbird (2). Imm. from all other tropicbirds by black stripe encircling nape.

**Behavior:** Feeds alone or in pairs, not in flocks. Flight is strong and direct with rowing pigeonlike wing beats. Swims well, holding tail cocked up out of the water but cannot stand or walk on land

**Breeding:** Reported on Malpelo Isl. (Wetmore 1965a); Colonies breed almost yr.-round in the Galapagos (Harris 1974).

**Status and habitat:** Only recs. are Malpelo Isl. and 1 seen near Buenaventura 3 May 1976 (R. Ridgely); prob. wanders reg. to rocky Pacific coast isls.

**Range:** Breeds on isls. of Baja California, Malpelo Isl., the Galapagos, and isls. off coast of Venez., Tobago, Ecuador, and Peru; also in Red Sea and Indian Ocean.

## 2. [WHITE-TAILED TROPICBIRD]
*Phaethon lepturus*

**Identification:** 16″ (41cm); incl. long central tail feathers 30″ (76cm). Ternlike. Bill orange. *All white with small black stripe through eye, outer primaries black, diagonal black band from bend of wing to scapulars.* Imm.: sim. but lacks tail streamers, has yellow bill, and hindneck and mantle finely barred dusky; short rounded tail tipped black.

**Similar species:** Red-billed Tropicbird (1) is decidedly larger and stockier with black barring on back and shoulders (no bands). Imm. resembles Red-billed but is smaller and lacks the nape band.

**Behavior:** Flight sim. to but more buoyant than Red-billed Tropicbird, and wing beats snappier. Like Red-billed, hovers and dives ternlike, often from great hts.

**Status and habitat:** Hypothetical. Two old sight recs.; no specimens. Prob. wanders reg. to offshore and pelagic waters.

**Range:** Carib. coast. Breeds from Bermuda s through Antilles as well as isls. in tropical s Atlantic, c Pacific, and Indian oceans; disperses to many areas away from breeding isls.

# PELICANS: Pelecanidae (1)

Pelicans are very large, social birds, well known to all for their large bills and huge extensible gular pouches. They commonly fly in stately formation with slow, heavy wing beats and short sails. In flight or at rest the head is drawn back with the bill resting on the neck. They capture fish by short awkward dives or by swimming, submerging the head and neck.

## 1. BROWN PELICAN
*Pelecanus occidentalis*　　　　Ill. 5

**Identification:** 45-54″; (114-137cm). Large and bulky with hunchbacked appearance. *Huge pouched bill.* Breeding plumage: mainly gray above; neck and underparts brown, head and stripe on sides of neck white. Nonbreeding adults have neck white like head. Imm.: brownish above incl. head and neck; whitish below.

**Behavior:** Their familiar formations scaling low over the water are a common sight on beaches and coastlines of the Carib. and Pacific In deeper water they feed by diving, in shallower water by swimming, sometimes in cooperative groups.

**Breeding:** Nest on rocky sea cliffs e of PN Tayrona, perhaps also Pacific coast (no colonies known). In Trinidad Feb–Apr in colonies up to 150 pairs; rough stick nest usually in low bush; 2-3 white eggs (ffrench 1973).

**Status and habitat:** Common in coastal waters; stray inland. Populations appear not to have suffered declines sim. to those of birds in the s US that were exposed to excessive pesticide contamination.

**Range:** Carib. and Pacific coastlines. Rec. inland near Popayán, and Bogotá (Laguna de Fúquene; sighting Represa Neusa 3000m— A. Gast). Coasts of s and w US s to nw Brazil and s Chile. W Indies.

# BOOBIES: Sulidae (5)

Boobies and gannets are large sociable seabirds, rather angular in appearance and with pointed bill, narrow pointed wings, and wedge-shaped tail. Boobies occur mainly in warm tropical oceans, and gannets replace them in cooler temperate oceans. Boobies differ from gannets chiefly in having a bare rather than mostly feathered distensible throat pouch. Both feed by plunging obliquely into the sea from considerable heights for fish that they sometimes pursue and swallow under the surface. Boobies breed colonially, either on the ground or in low trees.

6. BLUE-FOOTED BOOBY

## 1. BLUE-FOOTED BOOBY
*Sula nebouxii*                                   Ill. 6

**Identification:** 32-36″ (81-91cm). *Feet and legs bright blue* (grayer in imm.). Bill dull greenish or grayish. *Head and neck white heavily streaked cinnamon brown*; upperparts and underwing brown with large *white patch on mantle and rump*; underparts white; tail brown. In flight looks white on both ends. Imm.: sim. but browner on head and neck; white patches on mantle and rump mottled brown.

**Similar species:** Peruvian Booby (2) very sim. in flight, but head and neck whiter (no streaks) and rump mottled brown (but may look white at a distance). Imm. resembles imm. Masked Booby (3) but underwings brown (not mostly white). Imm. Peruvian Booby may not be separable in field.

**Voice:** Ad. ♂ a plaintive whistle; ♀ and imm. a hoarse, ducklike note (Harris 1974).

**Behavior:** Social in loose groups, sometimes numbering in the hundreds. Flight is strong and direct, several flaps followed by a short glide; when foraging, flies with bill pointing downward. Dives from a considerable ht. for prey, mostly fish.

**Breeding:** On Gorgonilla Isl. peak egg laying reportedly Nov–Mar; breeding ends before mid-June (Thayer and Bangs 1905). Nests colonially; 2-3 chalky white eggs.

**Status and habitat:** When not breeding, resident in offshore waters, seldom pelagic.
**Range:** Pacific coast. Breeds off Baja California and from Panama to n Peru and the Galapagos.

## 2. PERUVIAN BOOBY
*Sula variegata*

**Identification:** 28-30″ (71-76cm). Legs bluish gray. Bill purplish blue. *Head, neck, and entire underparts pure white; wings, back, and rump brown mottled white*; flight feathers and tail brown; upper tail coverts and base of tail with some white. Imm.: sim., but white areas mottled or tinged buffy.

**Similar species:** Smaller than Blue-footed Booby (1) and with pure white head and neck (not streaked), and in flight rump streaked, only upper tail coverts and base of tail with white.

**Behavior:** Likely to be seen as straggling individuals or pairs in Colombian waters. In colder s waters usually in flocks. Flight and feeding habits much as in other boobies.

**Status and habitat:** Prob. vagrant. Rec. at Bahía de Málaga n of Buenaventura in Mar. A guano bird of the cold Humboldt Current that may enter Colombian waters mainly when warm waters shift southward. Coastal and offshore waters, rarely pelagic.

**Range:** Breeds from s Peru to s Chile; wanders n to sw Colombia.

## 3. MASKED (BLUE-FACED) BOOBY
*Sula dactylatra*                              Ill. 7

**Identification:** 32-36″ (81-91cm). Bill orange yellow (♂) or pinkish yellow (♀), darker at tip. Bare facial skin slaty blue. Legs olive or slaty. *Mostly white with blackish flight feathers and tail* (central tail feathers white). Imm.: mostly mottled grayish brown, sharply demarcated white breast and belly; *whitish collar on upper back, and pale rump*. Bill yellowish gray, feet slaty.

**Similar species:** White plumage and black flight feathers and tail set it apart from other boobies rec. in Colombia, but see Red-footed Booby (4). Imm. resembles ad. Brown Booby (5) but is decidedly paler on upper back and rump (not uniform dark brown), has whiter lower underparts, and dark (not yellow) feet. Imm. Blue-footed Booby (1) has all dark wings below and pale head and rump. Imm. Peruvian Booby also has pale (not dark) head.

**Voice:** ♂♂ whistle, ♀♀ trumpet (Harris 1974).

**Behavior:** Small groups in flight or perched on debris or swimming far at sea.

**Breeding:** Large colony breeding early Feb,

7. MASKED BOOBY (left), BROWN BOOBY (center), RED-FOOTED BOOBY,
white phase (right), brown phase flying

Malpelo Isl. (Bond and Meyer de Schauensee 1938); reported to breed on Isla San Andrés (J. Hernández); 2 chalky white eggs.
**Status and habitat:** Prob. reg. off both coasts; at times quite numerous in Gulf of Panama s of Pearl Isls. and off Darién, Panama; 2 ads. off Buenaventura, 3 May 1976 (R. Ridgely). More pelagic than most boobies.
**Range:** Breeds on Malpelo Isl. off Pacific coast, Los Monjes Isl. off the Carib., and throughout warmer parts of Atlantic, Pacific, and Indian oceans; sites near Colombia incl. the Galapagos, and off coasts of Ecuador, Peru, and Venez.

## 4. [RED-FOOTED BOOBY]
*Sula sula*                                      Ill. 7
**Identification:** 26-29″ (66-74cm). Bill and facial skin pale blue. Feet and legs red. Light phase ad.: *mostly white with black flight feathers and white tail*; head tinged yellowish. Dark phase ad.: entirely grayish brown with a *white belly, rump, and tail* (white tail conspic.). Intermed. phase ad.: like dark phase bird but paler. Imm.: uni-

form brown with dark breast band, dull yellow feet, and bluish bill.
**Similar species:** Resembles Masked Booby but smaller with white or sometimes grayish tail (but never black). Imm. Brown Booby (5) is sim. to young Red-footed Booby but larger with contrasting underparts.
**Status and habitat:** Hypothetical. Sight rec. of 3 light phase birds, 31 Oct 1980, off Pacific Colombian coast betw. 04°23′N, 80°10′W, and 04°11′N, 80°13′W (R.G.D. Brown). Even more pelagic than Blue-faced Booby and rarely seen near coastlines.
**Range:** Pacific coast of Colombia and almost certainly off Carib. coast. Breeds on isls. of Carib. and s Atlantic, w coast of Mexico, and isls. of Indian and Pacific oceans. Closest known colonies breed in Lesser Antilles, coastal Venez., Galapagos, and Cocos Isls.

## 5. BROWN BOOBY
*Sula leucogaster*                               Ill. 7
**Identification:** 26-30″ (66-76cm). Bill and feet yellowish; bare facial skin pale yellow (or gray-

ish; nonbreeding?). Ad. entirely dark brown with *contrasting white lower breast and belly* and white wing linings (or ad. ♂ with forecrown grayish distinctly paler than back—*etesiaca*). Imm.: patterned like ad. but white of underparts replaced by grayish brown; bill gunmetal gray.

**Similar species:** Imm. Blue-footed and Masked Boobies (1, 3) show some whitish on upperparts (not all dark); imm. Red-footed Booby (4) is all dark (both ad. and imm. Brown Booby show contrasting underparts).

**Behavior:** Often rather gregarious. In flight alternates flapping with long rather stiff glides from well above water to near surface.

**Breeding:** Breeds on Gorgona Isl. (Murphy 1936) and Tonel Isl. on w side of Gulf of Urabá; unconfirmed reports on Islas del Rosario, Bolívar. In Panama (*etesiaca*) egg-laying early Dec–late Apr; leaf- or twig-lined nest depression on ground (Wetmore 1965a).

**Status and habitat:** The most common booby on either coast and the only one likely to be seen from shore, often even in harbors. Most numerous in Gulf of Urabá region and Pacific coast of n Chocó.

**Range:** Carib. coast (*leucogaster*) and Pacific coast (*etesiaca*). Throughout tropical waters of Atlantic, Pacific, and Indian oceans.

# CORMORANTS: Phalacrocoracidae (2)

Cormorants are a widespread and ancient group of totipalmate swimmers that are found in coastal waters and along most inland lakes and rivers. They eat mostly fish taken in an underwater chase. They are sociable and nest colonially, often in tremendous aggregations on sea cliffs, on the ground, or in small trees. The Guanay Cormorant, economically important to man, is the chief producer of guano on the Peruvian coast. Other species are well-known servants of man, being trained for fishing in the Orient.

## 1. OLIVACEOUS (NEOTROPIC) CORMORANT

*Phalacrocorax olivaceus*                    Ill. 8

**Identification:** 25-28″ (64-71cm). Long narrow black bill hooked at tip. Legs black. *Oily black; gular pouch and facial skin dull yellow* (color varies somewhat with season) outlined behind by narrow white band. Imm.: grayish brown to dusky brown above; pale brown below becoming whitish on breast in younger birds.

**Similar species:** Anhinga has longer and thinner neck and tail and pointed stiletto-like bill (not hooked); in flight gray wing patches.

**Voice:** Usually silent, occas. low croaking or grunting.

**Behavior:** A sociable bird often seen in straggling lines or V-shaped wedges flying low over water, although more often alone or in pairs along forested rivers. Like all cormorants, floats low in the water and sometimes submerges until only the head, neck and uptilted bill remain visible. When not swimming usually perches on dead snags or bushes with wings and tail held spread to dry.

**Breeding:** Nearly complete by late June in mangroves near Manaure, Guajira (A. Sprunt IV). Large untidy nest 1-10m up over water; in Panama some nesting begins in Apr; about 6 eggs (Wetmore 1965a).

**Status and habitat:** Common on freshwater lakes and rivers and salt and estuarine habitats on both coasts; chiefly lowlands, occas. (usually imms.) to temperate zone lakes. Imms. wander widely, some movements may be seasonal.

**Range:** To 2600m. Throughout. Breeds from s US to s S America; also the Bahamas, Cuba, Trinidad, and Dutch Leeward Isls.

## 2. GUANAY CORMORANT

*Phalacrocorax bougainvillii*

**Identification:** 30″ (76cm). Long narrow bill horn gray. Legs and feet pinkish red. Glossy greenish black with gular pouch and bare facial skin red; *patch on upper throat* and *lower foreneck to belly immaculate white*. Imm.: brownish with entire foreneck and underparts white.

**Status and habitat:** Casual. Rec. 19 Mar at Bahía de Málaga and 20 Apr on Gorgona Isl.; flock of about 100 seen 21 May flying n off Ensenada de Guayabo Chiquito off s coast of Darién, Panama, very near Colombia (Murphy 1941). A Humboldt Current endemic; may or may not straggle n with shifts in El Niño current.

**Range:** Pacific coast. Breeds on coastal isls. of Peru and n Chile; wanders mostly in Humboldt Current n to Ecuador (rarely to Panama) and s to s Chile.

8. OLIVACEOUS (NEOTROPIC) CORMORANT (left), ANHINGA (♂ right)

# DARTERS: Anhingidae (1)

The darters are a small but widespread group of aquatic birds closely related to cormorants. They are found mainly on freshwater lakes and rivers in warmer parts of the world. Superficially they resemble cormorants, but they differ in having a longer broader tail and much slimmer neck, among other things. Anhingas fly well and often soar, but alight and take off with difficulty. They swim underwater, propelled by their short, fully webbed feet, and spear fish with their pointed bill rather than grasp them. At the surface they often swim submerged with only their long thin head and neck visible, for which habit they are called "snakebirds."

## 1. ANHINGA

*Anhinga anhinga*                Ill. 8

**Identification:** 32-36″ (81-91cm). *Long rapier-like bill.* Small head, long slender neck, and long fanshaped tail. ♂: glossy greenish black with numerous small spots and *large silvery gray band across upper wing.* ♀: sim. but *head, neck and chest buffy brown.*

**Similar species:** Resembles a cormorant but with a much longer snakelike neck, longer tail, and pale wing patches.

**Voice:** Usually quiet; infrequently a rapid clicking or cluttering or harsh *cruk-cruk-cruk* repeated rapidly (Friedmann and Smith 1950).

**Behavior:** The plumage, like that of cormo-rants, is not water repellent, and birds are frequently seen perched on low bushes near water with wings and tail spread to dry. Occur alone or in pairs; swim well, often with only head and neck above the surface, and frequently soar.

**Breeding:** A BC ♀, Aug, Vaupés (Olivares and Hernández 1962), another 22 Feb, and a nestling early Mar, Macarena Mts. (Olivares 1962). Often nests in small colonies, sometimes with herons and other waders. Stick and dead-leaf nests usually 1-4 m above water; 3 pale blue eggs.

**Status and habitat:** Fairly common locally in sluggish freshwater rivers, swamps and for-

ested streams, occas. brackish water. Most numerous in forest zones n and e of Andes.
**Range:** Tropical zone throughout. Breeds from se US to w Ecuador, n Argentina, and Uruguay; also Cuba, Grenada, Trinidad, and Tobago.

# FRIGATEBIRDS: Fregatidae (1)

Frigatebirds or "Man-o'-War Birds" are a small and interesting group of marine birds that ply the warmer oceans of the world. Remarkably, they are the only seabirds that do not ever intentionally settle on the water. They have the largest wingspread of any bird in proportion to their weight and are exceptionally buoyant and agile in the air. They feed on flying fish and squid or by aerially pirating prey of other seabirds. Nesting is colonial on oceanic islands; there the ♂♂ inflate and display a spectacular balloonlike red gular pouch.

## MAGNIFICENT FRIGATEBIRD
*Fregata magnificens*
**Identification:** 38-42″ (97-107cm). Large, with prom. crook in *long narrow pointed wings* (wingspan up to 7.5 ft.; 225cm). *Long, deeply forked tail.* ♂: *all black* with bare red throat pouch (usually not visible except during courtship). ♀: black with *white breast* (no throat pouch). Imm.: like ♀ but head also white.
**Voice:** At nesting colony a continuous nasal cackling, sharp and whining (Eisenmann); aggressive call a rapid rattle descending in pitch and accelerating (Nelson 1975).
**Behavior:** Spends most of day soaring lazily and effortlessly, either alone or in loosely composed groups. Roosts in groups in small bushes or trees near the ocean.
**Breeding:** Feb on Malpelo Isl. (Bond and Meyer de Schauensee 1938) prob. during 1st of yr. on Gorgonilla Isl. (Thayer and Bangs 1905); 40 nests with eggs or young, May 1979, Islas de Rosario near Cartagena, colony active Apr–

Ill. 5

July (Naranjo 1979b); stick nests in low bush or on rocks; 1-2 white eggs.
**Status and habitat:** Common along coastal waters, bays and offshore isls.; usually within sight of land.
**Range:** Pacific and Carib. coasts. Occas. strays inland. Breed on small isls. or coast from w Mexico to Galapagos and in tropical Atlantic Ocean; disperses n to California, gulf coast of US, and s to n Peru and Uruguay.
**Note:** Great Frigatebird (*F. minor*), unrec. in Colombia, prob. wanders into its Pacific waters. In e Pacific breeds as close as the Galapagos and Cocos Isls. (presumed sights from Malpelo Isl.). Very like Magnificent Frigatebird (about same size) and easily overlooked. ♂ differs by having upper wing coverts brown forming a diagonal band across wing. ♀ differs by also having pale diagonal band on upper wing, and the upper throat and foreneck grayish white (not throat and foreneck black). Imm. has underparts tinged rusty.

# HERONS, EGRETS, BITTERNS: Ardeidae (22)

Herons and bitterns form a well-known and cosmopolitan family of notably ancient origin. They are characterized by, among other things, long legs, long necks, usually a straight pointed bill, and concealed powder downs. Most are found in or near fresh or salt water, where they stand patiently or wade in shallows. Prey is animal food, especially fish and other aquatic organisms. Two Colombian species, the Cattle Egret and Whistling Heron, are regularly found in dry grassy areas. Many herons roost and nest communally, often in mixed species heronries, very few of which have yet been located in Colombia. The tiger-herons, bitterns, "green" herons, and perhaps also the Zig-zag Heron, nest solitarily or in small groups. For alternate classifications of the family, see Hancock and Elliott (1978).

## 1. GREAT BLUE HERON
*Ardea herodias*          Ill. 9, Map 21
**Identification:** 40-50″ (102-130cm). Very large, slender and long-necked. Bill dull yellow; legs dusky greenish yellow. *Head and throat white with sides of crown and occipital area black* (also long pointed black occipital crest in breeding

plumage); neck grayish, streaked black and white in front, rest of upperparts and *wings bluish gray*; underparts more or less streaked black and white; *thighs chestnut*. Imm.: duller with top of head blackish and no occipital plumes. White phase not reported in Colombia.

**Similar species:** See Cocoi (White-necked) Heron (2)

**Behavior:** Usually solitary; stands and waits or wades in shallow water.

**Status and habitat:** Winter resident, rec. Oct–mid-Apr, in very small nos. in estuaries, mangroves, and freshwater marshes and lakes; most recs. on Carib. coast from Barranquilla to Santa Marta. Three "summer" sight recs.: late Aug 1976, ne Meta—S. Furniss; 28 June 1974, Manaure, Guajira; 29 June 1974 near Barranquilla (A. Sprunt IV).

**Range:** To 2600m. N Colombia s to upper Cauca Val., Sabana de Bogotá and e of the Andes in ne Meta (3 sightings, Carimagua, 1975, 1976—S. Furniss). Breeds in N America s to s Mexico, Greater Antilles, isls. off coastal Venez. and on the Galapagos; winters s to n Colombia, n Venez. Trinidad and Tobago. W Ecuador (sight).

## 2. COCOI (WHITE-NECKED) HERON
*Ardea cocoi*                   Ill. 9, Map 22

**Identification:** 40-50″ (102-130cm). Resembles Great Blue Heron but shows much more white. Differs mainly in *crown as well as sides of head black* (when breeding has long black occipital plumes with white tips); *neck and upper breast white* (not gray) with a few black streaks on foreneck; *lower underparts black, thighs white.* In flight *upper wing surface mostly white with blackish flight feathers* (not gray with slaty flight feathers).

**Voice:** A guttural *gawk uk, guk uk, guk uck uck* (Brown), higher-pitched than Great Blue Heron (Hancock and Elliott 1978).

**Behavior:** Usually solitary and wary except when nesting. Stands and waits or wades in shallow water; flight rather slow and labored.

**Breeding:** Colonial. In Cauca Val. (Río Bolo near Palmira) 8 nests with fledged or nearly fledged young, 25 Aug (Lehmann 1960b).

9. GREAT BLUE HERON (left), COCOI (WHITE-NECKED) HERON (right)

**Status and habitat:** Common in estuaries and mangroves on Carib. coast (esp. PN Salamanca and Ciénaga Grande), slightly less numerous in freshwater lakes, marshes, and sluggish rivers elsewhere.
**Range:** To 1500m. Throughout. E Panama to s Chile and Falkland Isls. Trinidad.

### 3. GREAT (COMMON) EGRET

*Casmerodius albus*　　　　Ill. 10, Map 23
**Identification:** 36-40″ (91-102cm). Large, slender long-necked egret. *All white with yellow bill and long black legs.* Breeding birds have long conspic. scapular plumes.
**Similar species:** White phase Reddish Egret (6) has blue gray (not black) legs and bicolored bill; Snowy Egret and imm. Little Blue Heron (4, 5) are smaller with black or bicolored bills. Cattle Egret (11) is much smaller, stockier, and shorter-legged.
**Voice:** A harsh *cáw-ca* or rasping *ca-aa-a-uw* (Friedmann and Smith 1950).
**Behavior:** Solitary or well-spaced individuals feed by standing motionless for long periods in shallow water; often rests in mixed groups during midday. Roosts gregariously.

**Breeding:** Jan–July, birds had nuptial plumes (Nicéforo and Olivares 1964); breeds colonially, prob. on both coasts, and in lower Magdalena Val., but no Colombian colonies yet reported; active colony mid-Feb, Panama Bay (Wetmore 1965a); colonies with up to 140 nests July–Nov, Guárico, Venez. (Thomas 1979b); twiggy platform nest about 2m up in mangroves, cactus, or broadleaf tree; 2-3 blue gray eggs.
**Status and habitat:** Common resident in mangroves, estuaries, freshwater marshes, ponds, and rivers; mostly lowlands. At Carimagua, ne Meta, peak nos. Feb–Mar, few and irreg. May–Aug (S. Furniss); in w Meta (Hacienda Corocora) present late Dec–June, peaking Mar–mid-May (W. McKay). Some n migrants reach n Colombia; individuals banded in US have been recovered in Sept. and Nov.
**Range:** To 2600m (Sabana de Bogotá); mainly below 1000m. Throughout. Virtually worldwide from tropical to temperate latitudes. In Western Hemisphere from s Canada to s Chile.
**Note 1:** Often placed in the genus *Egretta*. **Note 2:** Called Great White Egret in Old World.

10. Great (Common) Egret (left), Snowy Egret (center), Little Blue Heron (juv. upper right), Cattle Egret (lower right)

## 4. SNOWY EGRET

*Egretta thula*                    Ill. 10, Map 24

**Identification:** 20-24″ (51-61cm). *Entirely pure white with black bill and legs; feet bright yellow;* lores yellow. Breeding birds have long, lacey, recurved aigrettes arising from the crown, breast, and back.

**Similar species:** Great Egret (3) is much larger with longer neck and yellow bill. Imm. Little Blue Heron has bicolored bill and greenish legs.

**Voice:** Usually silent; a hoarse *aah* or *a-wah-wah-wah*, esp. at breeding colony (ffrench 1973).

**Behavior:** Feeds rather actively, sometimes stirring the water with a foot as it walks elegantly in shallow water; usually in loose groups.

**Breeding:** BC ♂, 7 Mar, near Cali (Borrero 1952b); pair displaying, 24 Apr, in Cattle Egret colony n of Cali (Lehmann 1959a); up to 4 nests in colonies, Aug–Oct, sw Guárico, Venez. (Thomas 1979b). Trinidad nests May–Oct, stick platforms in mixed colonies in mangroves; 2-4 pale blue green eggs (ffrench 1973).

**Status and habitat:** Fairly common in mangroves, estuaries, and coastal mudflats; less numerous and local inland in freshwater marshes and ponds; esp. numerous in lower Magdalena Val. and adj. Ciénaga Grande. In w Meta seen only late Feb–mid-May (W. McKay). Nos. may be augmented during n winter by migrants.

**Range:** To about 1000m; occas. to 2600m (Sabana de Bogotá). Throughout. S. US to c Chile and n Argentina; the Antilles and Trinidad.

## 5. LITTLE BLUE HERON

*Florida caerulea*              Ills. 10, 11, Map 25

**Identification:** 20-25″ (51-64cm). *Bill blue gray, distal two-thirds black.* Legs greenish. Dark slate blue with head and neck deep maroon (subadults lack the maroon). Imm.: pure white, usually with dusky tips on flight feathers, or pied and mottled dusky to varying degrees; bill as in adult; legs dull greenish,

**Similar species:** All white imm. easily confused with white phase adult Reddish Egret (6), which has basal half of bill pinkish (not basal third blue gray) and slate blue legs (not greenish). Reddish Egret's shaggy head and erratic behavior is often helpful. Cf. imm. with other white egrets (3, 4, 11).

**Behavior:** Usually found alone or in scattered

11. Reddish Egret (dark phase, top), Little Blue Heron (ad. bottom)

2's or 3's; sometimes feeds rather actively but normally less so than Reddish Egret.

**Breeding:** In Venez. llanos, July–Oct, up to 5 nests in heronry (Thomas 1979b). Trinidad colonies Feb–Aug, usually in mangroves; stick platforms 1-3m above water; 2-5 blue eggs (ffrench 1973).

**Status and habitat:** Fairly common resident (though thinly spread) in both fresh and brackish water; more numerous in coastal areas. Seen only late Feb–late May at Hacienda Corocora, w Meta (W. McKay). Banded N American migrants rec. Nov–Mar.

**Range:** To 2600m (Sabana de Bogotá); usually much lower. Throughout. S US s to w Peru, n Chile, Uruguay, and se Brazil. Dutch Antilles; Trinidad and Tobago.

**Note:** Sometimes placed in the genus *Egretta*.

## 6. REDDISH EGRET
*Dichromanassa rufescens*          Ill. 11, Map 26

**Identification:** 29-31″ (74-79cm). *Bill pinkish flesh, distal third black. Legs slaty blue.* Dark phase: *reddish brown head and neck shaggy and dishevelled;* rest of plumage reddish brown to slaty gray. Light phase: all white; otherwise sim. Imm. white phase birds have *blackish bills;* dark phase imms. are grayish brown, usually with a suggestion of ad.'s reddish brown head and neck; *bill, legs, and feet dark.*

**Similar species:** See imm. Little Blue Heron (5). Imm. light phase birds from other white waders by uniformly dark bill, legs, and feet, and shaggy appearance; erratic behavior helpful but not diagnostic.

**Behavior:** Usually, but not always, forages very actively in shallow water, customarily running, hopping, and staggering erratically about; sometimes flicks open wings or holds wings outstretched when foraging. Alone or with other waders.

**Status and habitat:** Shallow brackish pools on ne coast. First rec. 4 and 12 July 1963, Mayapo, Guajira (Nicéforo and Olivares 1964), and since at several localities w to Barranquilla (Donahue 1977) though notably erratic (seasonal?). Largest group is 70 dark and 34 light phase ads. with some juvs. still with down on head (prob. breeding) at Manaure, Guajira, 27 June 1974 (Sprunt 1976).

**Range:** Coastal lagoons from Barranquilla (sightings, Los Cocos, PN Salamanca) e to Guajira; once on Pacific coast at Buenaventura Bay (1 dark phase ad. seen 19 June 1975–Hilty). Breeds on coast of s US, Mexico, the Bahamas, Greater Antilles, Bonaire in Lesser Antilles, and presum. ne Colombia. Winters s to El Salvador, the Dutch Antilles, and coastal Venez. Vagrant to Pacific coast of C America.

**Note:** Sometimes placed in the genus *Egretta*.

## 7. TRICOLORED (LOUISIANA) HERON
*Hydranassa tricolor*          Pl. 2, Map 27

**Identification:** 22-26″ (56-66cm). Slender long-necked heron. Bill bluish with black tip; legs salmon (or bill and legs greenish yellow—nonbreeding). *Mostly bluish slate with contrasting white belly, under wing coverts, and rump;* long white stripe down front of neck mixed maroon, base of neck maroon; long white occipital plumes when breeding. Imm.: browner above and no occipital plumes.

**Similar species:** In flight, contrasting white belly and under wing coverts are diagnostic. Ad. Little Blue Heron (5) lacks the white belly. Cf. rare Agami Heron (10).

**Behavior:** Usually solitary except when breeding.

**Breeding:** Colonial. Nesting in mangroves, late June, Manaure, Guajira (A. Sprunt IV); in Trinidad Feb–Aug in mixed heronries, stick platform nest; 2-4 eggs (ffrench 1973).

**Status and habitat:** Uncommon to fairly common resident in brackish water, much less numerous inland in fresh water where prob. a wanderer. N breeders reported s to Panama (Hancock and Elliott 1978).

**Range:** Pacific and Carib. coasts, occas. inland; mostly in lowlands below 1000m. Breeds from se US to coastal n S America; coastal s Peru and e Brazil. Bahamas, Greater Antilles, and Trinidad.

**Note:** Sometimes placed in the genus *Egretta*.

## 8. GREEN HERON
*Butorides virescens*          Map 28

**Identification:** 15-17″ (38-43cm). *Small, chunky, and dark.* Short legs orange yellow. Crown and bushy crest (not always apparent) black, *sides of head, neck, and chest maroon chestnut* with a narrow black line bordered white down front of neck; otherwise mainly greenish black above, brownish gray below. Imm.: greenish brown above, white heavily streaked brown below; legs dull yellow.

**Similar species:** See Striated Heron (9).

**Voice:** Indistinguishable from that of Striated Heron.

**Behavior:** As in Striated Heron (9).

**Status and habitat:** Apparently a migrant and winter resident in very small nos. to both fresh and salt water. Not known to breed in Colombia although several have been taken in June and July. Most recs. are from Santa Marta area; 2 near Villavicencio, Jan (Nicéforo and Olivares 1964) and 29 Apr 1977 (sighting—W. McKay).

**Range:** To 2600m (Sabana de Bogotá). N Colombia s to Río Baudó on the Pacific, the Sabana de Bogotá, and w Meta. Breeds from s Canada to c Panama, W Indies, and Tobago; migrants reach n Colombia and n Venez.; and e Ecuador (Napo).
**Note:** Prob. conspecific with Striated Heron (*B. striatus*). In Colombia intermeds. are known from Guajira, Cauca Val., and upper Magdalena Val. in Huila (Payne 1974).

### 9. STRIATED HERON

*Butorides striatus* Pl. 2, Map 29
**Identification:** 15-17″ (38-43cm). Resembles Green Heron but *sides of head, neck, and chest gray* (not chestnut); white stripe down front of throat wider on chest. Imm.: may not be safely separable in field from imm. Green Heron, but sides of head and neck grayer.
**Voice:** A sharp *keoup* when flushed.
**Behavior:** Normally alone. Stands on a perch just above or at the edge of water to hunt but seldom wades. Often perches in trees and when alarmed flicks tail and raises and lowers bushy crest.
**Breeding:** Solitary. 2 BC ♂♂, Mar and Aug, Chocó and n Antioquia (Carriker); in Guárico, Venez., Jul–Oct (Thomas 1979b); in Venez. Orinoco, platform nest 8 July, 1 m above water in tree on river bank; 3 pale greenish gray eggs (Cherrie 1916).
**Status and habitat:** Common in all kinds of freshwater and saltwater habitats; mostly lowlands. Abundant along *várzea* streams in Amazonia.
**Range:** To 2600m. Throughout. C Panama to n Chile, n Argentina, and Uruguay. Trinidad and Tobago. Warmer parts of Old World, Australia, and many w Pacific isls.
**Note:** Some incl. *B. virescens* (Green Heron) with the above, calling the enlarged sp. Greenbacked Heron. All *Butorides* ("green herons") are sometimes placed in the genus *Ardeola*.

### 10. AGAMI (GHESTNUT-BELLIED) HERON

*Agamia agami* Pl. 2, Map 30
**Identification:** 26-30″ (65-76cm). Long neck and *very long slender greenish bill.* Rather short yellow legs. Mainly deep glossy green above; head black with long blue gray occipital crest; *neck and underparts deep chestnut*; throat and median line on foreneck white; patch on chest blue gray. Imm.: deep brown above, blackish on crown and flight feathers; throat and median line on foreneck white; lowere underparts streaked brown and white.
**Similar species:** Imm. Tricolored Heron (7) is

superficially sim. but has white belly, white wing linings, and shorter bill.
**Voice:** A low *kookookookook* and rattling piglike *krurr* in Costa Rica (Slud 1964); flight call *squok* (Herklots 1961).
**Behavior:** A shy, solitary, and infrequently seen heron. Crouches in well-shaded wet places or streams with thickets and overhanging vegetation and when alarmed flies or attempts to creep away by slowly climbing into a low thicket or tree. Rarely or never wades in shallow water in the open.
**Breeding:** In Barinas, nw Venez., 6 nests with 2 chicks each were placed 1.5-2m above water in bushes in a small seasonal marsh surrounded by forest. This colony was active in the rainy season, June–Sept (Ramo and Busto 1982).
**Status and habitat:** Rare. Smaller forested streams, wet and muddy areas inside forest and in mangroves; mostly lowlands.
**Range:** To 500m. Spotty. Santa Marta area w to lower Magdalena Val. (Atlántico) and n Chocó (surely s); n Cundinamarca (Laguna Cucunubá; Lago de Fúquene, 2600m); e of Andes from Meta (e of Villavicencio) s to Amazonas; prob. to e Guainía (rec. at El Carmen, Venez. opp. se Guainía). Se Mexico to nw Ecuador, n Bolivia, and Mato Grosso, Brazil. Trinidad.

### 11. CATTLE EGRET

*Bubulcus ibis* Ill. 10, Map 31
**Identification:** 18-20″ (46-51cm). A small, chunky, *white* heron with a thick neck. *Bill yellow and legs dull greenish.* Breeding birds have buff tinge on crown, back, and breast and reddish bill and legs. Imm.: like nonbreeding ad., but legs black.
**Similar species:** Smaller and stockier than other white herons or egrets in Colombia and the only one with a yellow or reddish bill.
**Voice:** Rather quiet except at nest site; greet with *rick-rack* at nest; in courtship a harsh *roo* and muffled *thonk* (Lancaster 1970).
**Behavior:** Gregarious flocks customarily assoc. with cattle, other grazing animals, or follow farm implements in search of disturbed insects and smaller vertebrates. Their long lines streaming to and from roosts are now a familiar sight in warmer rural Colombia.
**Breeding:** Nests colonially though usually not with other herons or egrets; some breeding spread over entire year (Lehmann 1959a; Lancaster 1970); in Guárico, Venez., mainly July–Oct (Thomas 1979b).
**Status and habitat:** Common in open country wherever there are cattle and agricultural activity; notably adaptable and wanders widely.

In w Meta most numerous late Nov–late May (W. McKay) First reported in Colombia in 1917 (1st specimen in 1937). Now widespread and still spreading into suitable areas.
**Range:** To 2600m. W of Andes and e of them s to w Caquetá and Vaupés (Mitú), prob. to w Putumayo. An invader from the Old World; now found from e and s US and Canada to n Chile, n Argentina, and se Brazil. W Indies.

## 12. WHISTLING HERON
*Syrigma sibilatrix* Pl. 2, Map 32
**Identification:** 21-23″ (53-58cm). Relatively thick, blunt *bill pink with black tip. Large bare facial area encircling eye bright blue.* Short greenish legs. Crown and long loose occipital crest black; *sides of head, neck, breast, and broad scapular area golden buff;* upperparts blue gray; *lower back, belly, and tail white.* Imm.: dull gray above, darker on crown and flight feathers; wing coverts faintly streaked tawny, below light gray, *rump, belly, and tail white.*
**Similar species:** Not likely confused. In flight dark back contrasting with white rearparts is conspic.
**Voice:** Frequent call a loud, flutelike, whistled *kleeer-er*, repeated rapidly on ground or in flight (Brown); harsh alarm *quah-h-h* (Wetmore 1926).
**Behavior:** Feeds alone or in small to large loosely composed groups by walking in dry pastures, tall grass, or shallow water with emergent vegetation. Eats grasshoppers, snakes, amphibians, and other smaller prey.
**Breeding:** As yet unreported in Colombia; prob. May–Sept in Venez. (Meyer de Schauensee 1948); 1 solitary nest of loose sticks 4 m up in eucalyptus in ne Argentina (Zapata 1965); 2 eggs (Hudson 1920), or 4 eggs, pale blue and speckled (Devincenizi *in* Hancock and Elliott 1978).
**Status and habitat:** Common seasonally in dry to marshy pastures, flooded fields, and drainage ditches. In ne Meta at Carimagua, present Oct–Mar with peak nos. Mar (S. Furniss); in w Meta at Hacienda La Corocora mostly Jan–May, occas. in loose groups of 100 or more (W. McKay).
**Range:** To 500m. E of Andes s to Río Guaviare e to nw Vichada (sighting—P. Silverstone). C. Venez. and adj. Colombian llanos. N Bolivia and s Brazil to c Argentina and Uruguay.

## 13. CAPPED HERON
*Pilherodius pileatus* Pl. 2, Map 33
**Identification:** 22-24″ (56-61cm). *Bare lores and facial skin cobalt blue,* bill gray blue. Legs gray. *Crown black with white forehead;* plumage otherwise entirely white; long occipital plumes white.

Breeding birds (nonbreeders?) tinged *creamy buff on neck and breast.* Imm.: crown steaked with white, no buff on neck or breast.
**Similar species:** Easily mistaken for an egret, but note the black crown. In flight chunky shape recalls a night-heron.
**Voice:** Usually silent: occas. a short croak when flushed (Friedmann and Smith 1950).
**Behavior:** Rather wary and often seen alone, less frequently in 2's or 3's, feeding on muddy banks, in shallow flooded areas, or even wading belly deep. Rather inactive though sometimes takes a few quick steps to lunge at prey.
**Breeding:** Surely breeds in Colombia, though no definite recs.; Schomburgk (in Wetmore 1965a) reports low tree nests with 2 eggs.
**Status and habitat:** Usually uncommon and thinly spread along muddy, grassy, or rocky river banks, less frequently freshwater marshes and ponds.
**Range:** To 500m. Sinú drainage (Río Uré; Río Sinú) e across the n lowlands to Santa Marta area, s to upper Magdalena Val. (once—Ataco, Tolima), and generally e of the Andes from Zulia Val. southward. C Panama to n Bolivia, n Paraguay, and se Brazil.

## 14. BLACK-CROWNED NIGHT-HERON
*Nycticorax nycticorax* Pl. 2, Map 34
**Identification:** 24-27″ (61-69cm). Chunky with short neck and heavy black bill. Legs greenish yellow (reddish when breeding). *Crown and back glossy black;* long occipital plumes white; *wings and tail gray;* forehead, sides of head, and *underparts whitish;* eyes red. Imm.; brown above streaked and spotted throughout; below dull white streaked light brown; bill and legs dull greenish, bill with dusky tip. In flight feet (but not legs) protrude beyond tail.
**Similar species:** Ad. resembles Boat-billed Heron but has black (not gray) back, all white underparts, and less massive bill. Imm. easily confused with imm. Yellow-crowned Night-Heron (see 15).
**Voice:** A sharp *guck* or *quok*, often in flight.
**Behavior:** Groups roost by day in swampy woodland or mangroves and are rarely abroad before dark, then often seen silhouetted in flight on their way to feeding areas. Imms. are more frequently active by day.
**Breeding:** Colonial; large young 1 Aug, Santa Marta (Todd and Carriker 1922); active nests at Manaure, Guajira, late June (A. Sprunt IV); and Guárico, Venez., July–Oct (Thomas 1979b); bulky twig nest 1-7m up in mangroves; 2-3 pale bluish green eggs (ffrench 1973).
**Status and habitat:** Locally common resident

in mangroves and swampy and marshy freshwater areas.
**Range:** To 1000 m; smaller nos. to 2600m (Sabana de Bogotá). Spottily w of E Andes from Carib. n Sucre e to Santa Marta, s in Magdalena Val. to s Bolívar, the Cauca Val. to Popayán, E Andes from Boyacá to Sabana de Bogotá and prob. mt. lakes of Nariño (rec. near Otavalo, Ecuador); e of Andes throughout (no recs. in Vichada or Guainía). S Canada to Tierra del Fuego. Virtually worldwide except holoarctic regions and Australia.

## 15. YELLOW-CROWNED NIGHT-HERON
*Nyctanassa violacea* Pl. 2, Map 35
**Identification:** 24-28″ (61-71cm). Shape of Black-crowned Night-Heron but bill thicker and legs longer; in flight feet and part of legs protrude behind tail (only feet in Black-crowned). Bill black; legs orange yellow. *Head black with broad white crown and long white stripe behind eye* (yellow forehead rarely visible), *otherwise light bluish gray;* back blackish; the feathers edged whitish. Imm.: like imm. Black-crowned Night-Heron but bill thicker, legs longer, upperparts darker, more slaty brown, and spots and streaks finer. On the ground, stands taller and slimmer without Black-crown's stocky, hunched appearance.
**Voice:** Sim. to Black-crowned Night-Heron but higher-pitched.
**Behavior:** Less nocturnal than Black-crowned Night-Heron and can be found feeding by day or by night. More often seen alone than Black-crowned. Diet varied, but specializes to some extent on crustaceans.
**Breeding:** On Isla Punta Arenas near Buenaventura, 10 active nests, late Mar (Ralph and Chaplin 1973); Santa Marta young, Jan–May (Todd and Carriker 1922); Oct breeding, Guárico, Venez. (Thomas 1979b). 3 pale green eggs (Wetmore 1965a).
**Status and habitat:** Chiefly coastal in mangroves, estuaries, and tidal flats, infrequently inland along rivers and freshwater ponds; prob. common in Pacific coast mangroves, though seldom seem because of difficult access to habitat (common in coastal Pacific Panama; Ridgely 1976).
**Range:** To 500m. Mainly Pacific and Carib. coasts and extreme lower Magdalena Val. (once on Río Magdalena in n Tolima and lower Cauca in n Antioquia); e of Andes in Meta (few rec.). E and c US to nw Peru and e Brazil (mainly coastal throughout). W Indies and the Galapagos.
**Note:** Sometimes placed in the genus *Nycticorax.*

## 16. RUFESCENT TIGER-HERON
*Tigrisoma lineatum* Pl. 2, Map 36
**Identification:** 26-30′7 (66-76cm). *Long thick neck.* Strong yellowish bill. Legs dull green. *Head, neck, and chest deept reddish chestnut;* median white stripe on foreneck; rest of underparts buffy brown, flanks banded black and white; back, wings, and tail buffy brown vermiculated black. Juv.: *mainly cinnamon buff broadly barred black;* throat, median underparts, and abdomen whitish. Reach ad. plumage in about 5 yrs.
**Similar species:** Other ad. tiger-herons (17, 18) are mainly grayish (not reddish chestnut) on head and neck. Juv. Bare-throated (18) has fairly obvious bare yellow throat. Juv. Fasciated (17), however, differs from juv. Rufescent mainly in shorter thicker bill, and less barring on flanks (not obvious even in the hand) and is doubtfully separable in the field. Also see Pinnated Bittern (22).
**Voice:** A fast series, *wok-wok-wok . . . ,* winding down and fading (P. Schwartz recording); or sim. ser. of paired hoots, *hoo-hoo, hoo-hoo. . . .* Also a prolonged hoot rising sharply at end *ooooooo-ooh* (J. V. Remsen).
**Behavior:** Rather furtive and inconspic., customarily freezing without elevating the bill when disturbed. Normally hunts alone and inactively in shallow water at the edge of pools or damp areas inside forest. Flight is labored, and if flushed bird often perches well up in a tree.
**Breeding:** 3 BC ♀♀, Mar–Nov, Meta and n Colombia (Carriker; Olivares 1974b). Nests July–Sept, Guárico, Venez. (Thomas 1979b); solitary frail stick platform high in tree; 1 egg, bluish white blotched pale violet (Haverschmidt 1968).
**Status and habitat:** Banks of forest streams, vegetation-choked lagoons, and freshwater ponds and lakes. Thinly spread (easily overlooked) in wooded areas; more common in llanos.
**Range:** To 500m (once to 1600m—Santa Marta Mts.) Pacific coast in n Chocó (Juradó) and Gulf of Urabá e across n lowlands to Guajira, Magdalena Val. s to Antioquia (Pto. Berrío); 1 old rec. near Cali; and generally e of Andes. Se Mexico; Honduras to w Ecuador, n Argentina, Uruguay, and s Brazil.

## 17. FASCIATED TIGER-HERON
*Tigrisoma fasciatum* Pl. 2, Map 37
**Identification:** 23-26″ (58-66cm). Dusky bill shorter and heavier than other tiger-herons and with *slightly arched culmen.* Crown black, sides of head slaty; neck and upperparts slaty black *finely vermiculated pale buff;* medial line down foreneck white, lower underparts ru-

fous, flanks slaty. Juv.: not safely separated from juv. Rufescent Tiger-Heron but whiter below, less distinctly barred on flanks and under wing coverts, and with shorter thicker bill. In the hand has concealed interscapular powder downs (lacking in 16). Imm. and subadult resemble adults but duller and with buff barring on crown.

**Similar species:** See Rufescent and Bare-throated tiger-herons (16, 18).

**Behavior:** A forested hill country replacement of lowland Rufescent Tiger-Heron. Usually perch on boulders in turbulent streams where conspic. but wary and flush rapidly up or down stream (R. Ridgely).

**Breeding:** 2 BC ♀♀, Mar, Chocó (Carriker).

**Status and habitat:** Rare and spotty; gravel bars and boulders along fast-flowing foothill and lower el. mt. streams; usually, but not always, in humid areas.

**Range:** 120-1800m (mostly above 600m). Pacific slope in Chocó and Cauca, spottily on both slopes above entire Cauca Val. (now mostly deforested), nw slope of Santa Marta Mts. and lower Cauca and mid. Magdalena vals. in s Bolívar; e base of E Andes in Macarena Mts., and w Caquetá. Locally from Costa Rica to nw Argentina and se Brazil.

## 18. BARE-THROATED TIGER-HERON
*Tigrisoma mexicanum*                    Map 38

**Identification:** 28-32″ (71-81cm). *Bare throat greenish yellow to bright yellow.* Legs dull greenish gray. Crown black, sides of head light gray, *neck and upper surface blackish finely barred buff,* broad median stripe down foreneck white with black border, rest of underparts dull cinnamon brown. Juv.: coarsely barred buff and black above and below, lower underparts paler; *bare yellow throat as in adult.*

**Similar species:** Separable from other tiger-herons (16, 17) in any plumage by large bare yellow throat instead of feathered white throat (but juv. of all *Tigrisoma* may have some bare yellow on throat). Ad. otherwise much like ad. Fasciated Tiger-Heron but with longer thinner bill and wider buff barring on neck and back (not so blackish).

**Voice:** A harsh croaking *wok wok wok* when flushed; in late afternoon or at night a froglike barking, var. to a loud froglike *tr'r'r'r'uk-tr'r'r'r'uk* rapidly repeated and at times becoming louder and louder (Wetmore 1965a; Hilty).

**Behavior:** Rather solitary and at times remarkably unwary. Feed on ground along streams, mudflats, or other wet areas and at rest often perch high in a tree. Partially nocturnal.

**Breeding:** Nests solitarily. Well-feathered young, early Apr, in nw Costa Rica nest (Hilty); Pan-

ama ♀ ready to lay and 2 nests with young, 9 Feb–18 Mar; stick platform nest, larger than for most herons, 4-15m up, sometimes over water; 2-3 eggs (from Mexico), pale glaucous green sparsely dotted pinkish buff (Wetmore 1965a).

**Status and habitat:** Forested streams, swampy woodland, marshes, and mangroves. Observed on several streams in Urabá region (Haffer 1975).

**Range:** To 200m. The extreme nw in lower Atrato and Gulf of Urabá region. Mexico to nw Colombia.

## 19. ZIGZAG HERON
*Zebrilus undulatus*             Pl. 2, Map 39

**Identification:** 12-13″ (30-33cm). *Very small and chunky with heavy-headed appearance.* Bill blackish; legs grayish horn, toes yellowish. Crown and bushy occipital crest black, *sides of head and upperparts dusky black finely barred with narrow wavy buff bands;* flight feathers and tail unbarred dusky; *below buff vermiculated black on foreneck and chest,* vaguely on lower underparts. Imm.: above black vermiculated rufous; sides of head, neck, and sometimes breast rufous chestnut, with or without sparse blackish vermiculations and streaks. A presumed rufous ad. phase is prob. an imm. plumage.

**Similar species:** Suggests a minature imm. tiger-heron with a distinctly dark back. No other barred heron or bittern in Colombia is so small, although barring inconspic. See Striated Heron (9), Stripe-backed and Least bitterns (20, 21).

**Behavior:** Secretive and little known. Forages in moist soil and leaf litter inside forest (Pearson 1975), on ground around shallow pools in swampy forest (R. Ridgely) or at creeks inside forest (Davis et al. 1980).

**Status and habitat:** Rare and local; known from swamps or grass-choked borders of small pools or stream channels inside forest or along forested rivers. Several reported in Mitú region (Olivares and Hernández 1962).

**Range:** To 400m. E of Andes where known from Arauca (Río Arauca) and Vaupés (Mitú). Likely in e Guainía as rec. at El Carmen, Venez. (opp. se Guainía) on Río Negro. Doubtless more widespread. Spottily from Guianas and e and s Venez. s to Peru (incl. mouth of Río Curaray), n Bolivia, Paraguay, and w and c Brazil.

## 20. STRIPE-BACKED BITTERN
*Ixobrychus involucris*          Pl. 2, Map 40

**Identification:** 12-13″ (30-33cm). Tiny heron. Bill yellowish green; legs pale green. *Mostly pale ochraceous yellow with broad black coronal streak and bold black stripes on back;* throat white, rest of underparts more or less steaked white;

primaries cinnamon rufous with black patch at base.

**Similar species:** Like Least Bittern (21) but paler and without latter's solid black (or chestnut— ♀) back and contrasting rufous on sides of head and hindneck. In flight Least shows conspic. pale cinnamon shoulder patch. Also cf. Zigzag Heron (19); in flight from rails by slower, labored wing beats.

**Behavior:** As in Least Bittern.

**Status and habitat:** Not well known; fresh and brackish water marshes (breeding?); recently reported fairly common late Mar–June (absent rest of yr.) in emergent marsh vegetation and rice fields in w Meta at Hacienda Corocora; some pairs but no breeding evidence (W. McKay).

**Range:** To 500m. Known from marshes along lower Magdalena Val. in Atlántico, adj. Ciénaga Grande, and e of Andes in w Meta (sightings 1978–W. McKay). N Venez. (May–Oct), Trinidad (May; July–Sept). Guyana, and Surinam (Dec–Mar). A s population is resident in se Bolivia and c Chile e to se Brazil; e Peru (sight). Migratory movements between n and s populations not proved.

## 21. LEAST BITTERN
*Ixobrychus exilis* Pl. 2, Map 41

**Identification:** 10-11″ (25-28cm), or 13-14″ (33-35cm)—*bogotensis*. Tiny. ♂: *crown, entire back, and tail black* with a narrow pale stripe ("suspenders") on each side of back: *sides of head and hindneck rufous*; foreneck and underparts buffy white (or sides of head ochraceous and underparts deep buff—*bogotensis*); wings rufous with *large pale buff shoulder patch* (prom. in flight). ♀: sim. but crown and back dark brown. Imm.: like ♀ but buffy edgings above and vaguely streaked below.

**Similar species:** See Stripe-backed Bittern (20) and Zigzag Heron (19).

**Voice:** Call, mostly in breeding season, a low drawling *kwuh-h-h-h*, often repeated (Wetmore 1965a); loud *knock* alarm (ffrench 1973).

**Behavior:** Shy and inconspic. and usually attempts to hide by "freezing" in marsh vegetation with elongated neck and bill pointing skyward. Runs or climbs among reeds and usually difficult to flush, but may fly strongly for some distance.

**Breeding:** A Santa Marta ♀ nearly ready to lay, 13 Oct (Todd and Carriker 1922). Trinidad breeding July–Oct; twig nest low in reeds or mangroves; 3 buffy white eggs (ffrench 1973).

**Status and habitat:** Common locally in fresh-water marshes with taller emergent vegetation. N migrant (*exilis?*) once reported in Sept from Cauca Val.

**Range:** Spottily distributed. To 1000m at w base of Santa Marta Mts., mid. Cauca Val. (Cali to Buga), and e of Andes in Norte de Santander (*erythromelas*); 2600-3100m in C Andes in Antioquia, and E Andes from s Boyacá (Lago Tota) to Sabana de Bogotá (*bogotensis*). May occur in Putumayo as rec. at Limoncocha, ne Ecuador (*limoncochae*); sight recs. on Isla Corea, Amazonas; 17-22 Feb 1984 (Hilty; Ridgely). N America s to ne Argentina and se Brazil.

## 22. PINNATED BITTERN
*Botaurus pinnatus* Pl. 2, Map 42

**Identification:** 25″ (64cm). *Resembles a juv. tiger-heron*. Bill and legs dull yellowish. Forecrown dark brown, hindcrown and sides and back of neck buff finely barred black; *rest of upperparts buff streaked and variegated blackish; flight feathers black* tipped tawny (forms band on rear of wing in flight); throat white, foreneck and underparts buffy white streaked light brown. Imm.: sim. but paler.

**Similar species:** From juv. tiger-herons by streaked wings and back (not barred), neck mostly buff with fine black bars (not vice versa), and in flight blackish flight feathers (not barred black and white). If in doubt flush the bird.

**Voice:** Sim. to the deep pumping *oong-ka-choonk* of American Bittern (*B. lentiginosus*) but higher and less hollow (Birkenholz and Jenni 1964).

**Behavior:** Solitary and secretive in tall marshy vegetation; usually attempts to escape notice by "freezing" with bill pointed upward but may also stalk away slowly. Unlike tiger-herons, if flushed, rarely or never alights in a tree.

**Breeding:** Not rec. in Colombia. In Trinidad July–Oct; nest in marsh just above water; 2-3 olive eggs (ffrench 1973).

**Status and habitat:** Very local in freshwater marshes with taller emergent vegetation; also drainage ditches and flooded fields (esp. rice fields). Present only late Mar–late May in w Meta at Hacienda Corocora (W. McKay).

**Range:** Spottily to 2600m. Known from mid. Cauca Val. (Cali to Buga area), upper Patía Val. (Río Timbío); s Boyacá (Lago de Fúquene) s to Sabana de Bogotá, and e of Andes in n Arauca (1 seen Nov 1978—W. McKay and J. Jorgenson) and w Meta (photo, Mar 1961—Brown). Se Mexico to Costa Rica; Colombia to w Ecuador, n Argentina, se Brazil, and the Guianas. Trinidad.

# BOAT-BILLED HERONS: Cochleariidae (1)

The Boat-billed Heron is a poorly known neotropical species most closely related to the Black-crowned Night-Heron. Although some have suggested placing it in the Ardeidae, it differs in several aspects, most notably the remarkable shovel-like bill that is thought to be sensitive to touch. It eats small shrimp, fish, insects, mud, mud-inhabiting organisms, and other small prey much like true herons.

## 1. BOAT-BILLED HERON

*Cochlearius cochlearius*          Pl. 2, Map 43

**Identification:** 18-20" (46-51cm). Chunky hunched heron with *very broad heavy bill*. Forehead white; rest of crown, broad occipital crest, and upper back black; *lower back and wings light gray*; sides of head and breast white; *lower underparts rufous with black flanks*; very large dark eyes. Birds from nw Chocó (*panamensis*) are darker gray above and tinged pinkish buff on cheeks, foreneck, and chest. Imm.: cinnamon to rufous above, whitish tinged buff below, no crest.

**Similar species:** See Black-crowned Night-Heron (p 66).

**Voice:** Low *qua, qua, qua*, when disturbed (Wetmore 1965a); variable chanting *on-on-ah-an-an*, also bill clapping in territorial defence (Mock 1975).

**Behavior:** Roosts by day in groups of its own in thicker trees and at dusk flies to feeding sites on gravel bars, shallow ripples, or muddy areas. Feeds mostly alone, apparently with a scooping rather than spearing motion of the bill.

**Breeding:** No colonies reported in Colombia, though they will surely be found. Breeding (in mixed heronries) perhaps triggered by seasonal flooding of lagoons in w Mexico (Mock 1975); 13 nests in colony (not mixed) Aug–Sept, Guárico, Venez. (Thomas 1979b). In Trinidad June–Oct; frail twig nest 2-7m up in mangroves; 1-3 bluish white eggs, sometimes faintly spotted reddish at large end (ffrench 1973).

**Status and habitat:** Local, though easily overlooked because of nocturnal habits. Mangroves, brackish lagoons, freshwater marshes, and forested rivers; mostly lowlands.

**Range:** Mainly below 800m. Pacific coast (no recs. s of Chocó), n lowlands e to Santa Marta area, s to mid. Magdalena Val. in ne Antioquia; throughout e of Andes; wanders to Sabana de Bogotá (2600m). W Mexico locally to n Argentina and se Brazil. Trinidad.

**Note:** The Mid. American group (*C. zeledoni* incl. *panamensis*) s to extreme nw Colombia (Acandí) has been considered a separate sp.

# STORKS: Ciconiidae (3)

Storks are a small though ancient family distributed throughout most warmer parts of the world. The three New World species occur in Colombia. All are large long-legged birds resembling herons, although they are less dependent on water and differ from herons in having a heavier bill, flying with the neck fully extended, and often soaring to great heights, among other things. They feed in shallow water or in grassy areas on fish, amphibians, snakes, insects, and other smaller prey.

## 1. WOOD STORK

*Mycteria americana*          Ill. 12, Map 44

**Identification:** 34-39" (86-100cm). Blackish bill thick at base and decurved. Legs black. A large *white* stork with a *bare black neck and head and black flight feathers*. Imm.: sim. but dingier; head and neck partially feathered brownish, bill yellow.

**Similar species:** Maguari Stork (2) has white head and neck (not black) and less white in wings. Soaring birds recall King Vultures (p 88).

**Behavior:** Notably gregarious. Perches on the ground or in trees, flies with slow wing beats alternating with glides, and often soars effortlessly to great hts. Known to feed cooperatively, wading together in shallow water and stirring the bottom with a foot.

**Breeding:** All age groups late June, Manaure, Guajira (A. Sprunt IV); a juv., 25 Jan, e of Villavicencio (Olivares 1974b). Nests colonially.

**Status and habitat:** Widespread but local in mangroves, tidal pools, and freshwater marshes and swamps. Most numerous on Carib. coast; thinly spread elsewhere but wanders widely. Formerly reported in nos. to upper Cauca Val. (Nicéforo and Olivares 1964) but few recent

12. MAGUARI STORK (left), JABIRU (center), WOOD STORK (right)

recs. Groups of 10-14 frequently noted crossing e Andes (above 2000m) from upper Magdalena Val. to w Caquetá in June–July (P. Gertler).

**Range:** To about 2200m (prob. higher). Northernmost Chocó (Gulf of Urabá) and upper Río Sinú e across Carib. lowlands to Guajira, s to upper Cauca and Magdalena vals.; throughout e of Andes (no recs. in Amazonas). S US to s Argentina. Greater Antilles; Trinidad.

## 2. MAGUARI STORK

*Ciconia maguari*                Ill. 12, Map 45
**Identification:** 38-40″ (97-102cm). *Straight* bill gray with dark reddish tip; *base of bill and bare facial skin orange red. Legs orange red*; iris cream white. A large *white* stork with *black greater wing coverts and tail; outer half of flight feathers black.* Juv.: entirely black for first 3 mos. Fledglings like ad. but soft parts duller, eyes brown.
**Similar species:** See Wood Stork (1). The red

facial skin and legs are conspic. In flight see King Vulture (p 88).
**Voice:** Occas. a wheezy bisyllabic whistling note (Kahl 1971).
**Behavior:** When not breeding found alone, in pairs, or in groups; may assoc. with other storks around ponds. Soars well and sometimes found far from water. Like Wood Stork may feed cooperatively in shallow water (W. McKay).
**Breeding:** 1 flightless young, late Mar, Carimagua, ne Meta (S. Furniss). Nests colonially, in Venez. llanos mostly June–Nov; stick nest in low bush or reeds, near or over water; 2-4 white eggs (Zahl 1950; Kahl 1971; Thomas 1979b).
**Status and habitat:** Local. Savanna and ranchland with ponds and temporary lagoons. Mostly in remote c or e llanos, rarely w to base of Andes. At Carimagua, ne Meta, scattered pairs, Dec–Apr, a group of about 180 late May (S. Furniss); 7 at Hacienda La Corocora, late May (W. McKay).

**Range:** To 500m. E of Andes s to s Meta and Río Guaviare. Colombia to the Guianas, and e Brazil; s Bolivar to s Chile Argentina and s Brazil.

**Note:** Sometimes placed in the genus *Euxenura*.

**3. JABIRU**
*Jabiru mycteria* Ill. 12, Map 46
**Identification:** 48-55″ (122-140cm). *Huge Pleistocenelike bird with grotesquely large black bill.* Legs black. *Entirely white with bare head and swollen bare black neck*; basal third of neck red. Imm.: mostly brownish gray, becoming whiter with age.

**Behavior:** As in Maguari Stork. When not breeding wander widely and sometimes gather in groups of several hundred to loaf. Stalk prey in dry grassy or marshy areas.

**Breeding:** Pair at nest 8 Nov, Arauca (W. McKay and J. Jorgenson); 2 downy nestlings in Dec nest on Río San Jorge, lower Magdalena Val. (Chapman 1917); up to 6 nests alone or near heronry, and on top of palms, Guárico, Venez.; July–Dec; 2-5 white eggs (Thomas 1979b, 1981).

**Status and habitat:** Local. Freshwater marshes, savanna, and ranchland with ponds and lagoons; wanders to coastal estuaries and larger forested rivers. Individuals and groups of var. size, Jan–Mar, once in Apr ne Meta (S. Furniss); groups of 75-100 in n Arauca in late dry season, Mar–Apr (J. Jorgenson).

**Range:** To 500m. Extreme lower Cauca Val., lower and mid. Magdalena Val. (s to Pto. Berrío, Antioquia); e of Andes s to Río Guaviare and s Meta, occas. to w Caquetá. S Mexico (accidental in s Texas) s locally to n Argentina and Uruguay.

# IBISES, SPOONBILLS: Threskiornithidae (8)

Ibises and spoonbills are a well-known group of long-legged waders found almost worldwide in warmer tropical to temperate regions. Ibises are notable for their long, slender decurved bills, spoonbills for their broad flat bills. All are characterized by bare facial skin. Like storks but unlike herons, they fly with the neck outstretched, typically in V's or lines. Ibises probe soft mud for crustaceans, insects, and other small prey; spoonbills sift shallow water with a sweeping motion of the bill. Nesting is colonial or solitary.

**1. BUFF-NECKED IBIS**
*Theristicus caudatus* Pl. 3, Map 47
**Identification:** 28-32″ (71-81cm). Long decurved bill; bare face black. Legs pinkish red. *Head, neck, and chest pale creamy buff* stained rusty on crown and lower chest; otherwise dark gray above, *wings black with slivery white upper wing coverts* (conspic. in flight); lower underparts and tail black. Imm.: head and neck streaked brown.

**Similar species:** Rather gooselike at a distance, though can always be told by long bill. See Orinoco Goose (p 80). Superficially resembles several imm. ibises, but none have black underparts.

**Voice:** A reedy, bugled *tur-tút*, often repeated in flight or on ground.

**Behavior:** Loose groups or occas. solitary birds walk, probing in grassy pastures and wetlands.

**Breeding:** BC ♀, 10 Apr, sw Huila (Carriker). In Chile 10-30 pairs nest colonially in trees or on ground near water; 2-3 greenish eggs spotted brown (Johnson 1965).

**Status and habitat:** Savanna, ranchland, and open terrain with wet grassy fields, ponds, and marshy lagoons. Mostly in remoter c and e llanos where resident in small nos. throughout year. Wanders widely (breeds?) w of Andes where rare.

**Range:** To 1000m; once to 1600m. Cauca Val. s to w slope Patía Val. (Río Pasto), entire Magdalena Val. (s to Villavieja, n Huila), upper Cesar Val. and e of Andes s to Meta and Río Guaviare. E Panama spottily s to Tierra del Fuego. S birds migratory.

**Note:** Birds from the Andes of Ecuador to Chile and in Patagonia may be a separate sp., *T. melanopis* (Black-faced Ibis).

**2. SHARP-TAILED IBIS**
*Cercibis oxycerca* Pl. 3, Map 48
**Identification:** 28-32″ (71-81cm). *Large and robust with decurved bill. Bare facial skin red*, bare throat orange. *Legs pinkish red.* Glossy greenish black with slight bushy nuchal crest; forehead and short malar stripe whitish gray. In flight legs do not protrude beyond *notably long tail.*

**Similar species:** Much larger and stockier than Whispering Ibis (4) and with longer tail, and dark (not pinkish) bill. At close range orange throat more obvious than malar stripe. Green Ibis (3) has dark face and legs.

**Voice:** A loud nasal bugled *tur-dee*, or *tur-dur*, often repeated in flight, paired notes sometimes doubled or with other var. such as *tur-cut cáuda.* A local name "Tarotaro" suggests the call.

**Behavior:** Single birds, pairs, or a few birds

(not large flocks) walk and probe in soft muddy areas. Flight slower and more labored than other Colombian ibises; usually do not fly far.
**Status and habitat:** Open country along muddy shores of ponds and rivers, muddy rice fields, damp grass, and other open wet areas. The least numerous Colombian ibis.
**Range:** To 500m. E of Andes in Arauca, Casanare, ne Meta (Carimagua—S. Furniss) and Vichada (Tuparro—INDERENA). Guyana, Venez., w Amazonian and Mato Grosso Brazil.

### 3. GREEN IBIS
*Mesembrinibis cayennensis*     Pl. 3, Map 49
**Identification:** 22″ (56cm). *Short legs and decurved bill jade green. Bare face slaty. Dark bronzy green*, brighter on hindneck; inconspic. bushy nuchal crest.
**Similar species:** More numerous Whispering Ibis (4) is slightly smaller, with pinkish bill and legs and faster, smoother wing beats in flight, and is normally in groups. Rare Glossy Ibis (7) is bronzy maroon though at a distance or in poor light looks blackish; then best told from Green by less robust appearance, proportionally longer legs, and lack of green on neck.
**Voice:** Easily recognized call, often heard at dawn and dusk, a mellow, rolling *clu-clu-clu-clu-clu* (P. Schwartz recording); also a fast gobbling *kullakulla* (Snyder 1966), often several times in ser., on ground or in flight.
**Behavior:** Usually alone or in pairs, occas. in groups of 6-8. Probes in muddy or gravelly areas or in shallow water along wooded streams, ponds, and lagoon edges. Normally rather wary. Flight is jerky and limpkinlike with quick upflick of stiff wings.
**Breeding:** Laying ♀, 26 Apr, n Antioquia (Carriker). Solitary. July nest, Venez. (Thomas 1979b); frail twig platform high in Surinam swamp (Haverschmidt 1968).
**Status and habitat:** Uncommon and local in swamp and gallery forest, and along forested streams; less often in open marshy or muddy areas near woodland. Spottily distributed in Amazonia.
**Range:** To 500m. From Panama boundary (s in lower Atrato Val. to Río Truandó), e across n Colombia to w base of Santa Marta Mts. (Ciénaga area), s to mid. Magdalena Val. (Pto. Berrío, Antioquia) and locally throughout e of Andes. Costa Rica to n Argentina and Paraguay.

### 4. WHISPERING (BARE-FACED) IBIS
*Phimosus infuscatus*     Pl. 3, Map 50
**Identification:** 19-20″ (48-51cm). *Decurved bill pinkish to reddish brown; bare face and legs pinkish*

*red*. Plumage entirely bronzy greenish black.
**Similar species:** No other all dark Colombian ibis has a pink to reddish bill, facial skin and legs, but this often hard to see, hence bird easily confused with Glossy Ibis (7). Sharptailed Ibis (2) bulks considerably larger and has distinctly long tail and slow labored flight; up close an orange throat and whitish malar.
**Voice:** A very fast gobbling *cucucucucu . . . or cocococo . . .* (P. Schwartz recording). Usually silent away from nest (P. Alden).
**Behavior:** Typically in groups of var. size, from a few individuals to several dozen or more that walk, probing soft ground in grassy pastures, wetlands, or along edges of lagoons. Fly with rather fast steady wing beats, less gliding than Glossy Ibis, and often in straggling lines or V's like cormorants.
**Breeding:** Incubating ♀, 27 Dec, Magdalena (Carriker). Small colonies. Near Ciénaga Grande Aug–Oct (early wet season); small twig platform in bush or low tree; 1-6 light greenish blue eggs (Todd and Carriker 1922); active heronry near *C. maguari* colony July–Oct, Guárico, Venez. (Thomas 1979b).
**Status and habitat:** Most common Colombian ibis e and w of Andes. Pastures, marshes, rice fields, and muddy or vegetation-choked borders of lagoons, ponds, and rivers; present Oct–late Apr. peaking early Apr in ne Meta (S. Furniss); Feb–early May, small nos. lingering to late June, Hacienda La Corocora, w Meta (W. McKay).
**Range:** To 1000 m (once, 2600m, sight rec. La Florida Park, Bogotá, 24 Feb 1984 (R. Ridgely). Sinú Val. e to w base of Santa Marta Mts. and w Guajira, s in Cauca Val. to Valle, Magdalena Val. to nw Santander, and e of Andes s to w Caquetá and Vaupés. N Colombia and generally e of Andes (except Amazon basin) s to c Argentina and Paraguay. E Ecuador (once).

### 5. WHITE IBIS
*Eudocimus albus*     Ill. 13, Map 51
**Identification:** 23-25″ (58-64cm). *Decurved bill and bare facial skin red* (bill black when breeding). *Legs pink.* White with black wing tips. Imm.: *upperparts dark brown*, head and neck light brown streaked whitish, *sharply separated from white lower underparts and rump*; bill pinkish tipped dark, legs pinkish to dusky.
**Similar species:** Black wing tips, decurved bill and red face separate the adult from other white waders. Much larger Maguari Stork (p 71) and Wood Stork (p 70) have all the flight feathers black. Imm.: often not safely told from imm. Scarlet Ibis (6); older Scarlet's usually show pink tinge on rump, sometimes also on back, wings, and underparts.

13. WHITE IBIS (left), SCARLET IBIS (right)

**Voice:** Occas. nasal grunting, *urnk* . . . , in flight.
**Behavior:** Notably gregarious. Probes soft mud like many other ibises and when not breeding congregates at communal roosts, often commuting considerable distance between feeding areas and roosts. E of Andes almost always with Scarlet Ibis (W. McKay).
**Breeding:** Not reported in Colombia although likely. In c Venez. in colonies with Scarlet Ibis, June–Oct (Zahl 1950); a June colony with eggs off Pacific Canal Zone entrance; shallow twig and leaf platform in small tree or cactus; 2 eggs, white to buffy white blotched and finely speckled brown (Wetmore 1965a).
**Status and habitat:** Uncommon resident in mangroves and tidal areas of Carib. coast; scattered individuals in flooded fields e of Andes; Nov–Apr in n Arauca (W. McKay and J. Jorgenson), Jan–mid-May at Hacienda La Corocora, w Meta (W. McKay); only Mar at Carimagua, ne Meta (S. Furniss).
**Range:** To 500m. Carib. coast from Río Sinú locally e to Guajira; e of Andes s to s Meta (incl. Macarena Mts.) and e to Carimagua, ne Meta (sightings 1976—S. Furniss). Se US and Mexico s to Pacific coast of e Panama (poss. mangroves of Pacific Colombia); w Ecuador, nw Peru, and coastal and inland Venez. (breeds in llanos). Greater Antilles.

## 6. SCARLET IBIS

*Eudocimus ruber*          Pl. 3, Ill. 13, Map 52
**Identification:** 22-24″ (56-61cm). *Ad. unmistakable.* Decurved bill, facial skin, and legs pink (bill usually black when breeding). Plumage *entirely brilliant scarlet with black wing tips.* Imm.: sim. to imm. White Ibis (often not separable) but sometimes rump tinged pink. Older birds may show pink tinge on back, wings, or underparts as well.
**Behavior:** As in White Ibis and often with it. A flock of ads. in flight is one of the most spectacular and impressionable sights in the avian world.
**Breeding:** Not reported in Colombia but likely. In Apure, Venez., large breeding colony, Sept (Zahl 1950). In Trinidad, frail stick platforms 2-12m up in mangroves; 2-3 dull grayish olive eggs spotted and blotched brown (ffrench 1973).
**Status and habitat:** Common nonbreeding resident (groups up to several hundred) e of Andes in Meta from Dec or Jan to May or June (W. McKay; S. Furniss), rare stragglers later (once Aug, Florencia, Caquetá—Hilty; once Oct, w Meta—W. McKay); freshwater marshes, shallow lakes, wetlands, and rice fields. Rare in lower Magdalena Val., mainly in mangroves and tidal areas.

**Range:** To 500m. Extreme lower Magdalena Val. from sw Atlántico e to Ciénaga Grande, Guajira at Bahía Manaure, and doubtless eastward; e of Andes from Arauca s to Meta (prob. e to Vichada) and w Caquetá (Florencia). Colombia, Venez., the Guianas, and e Brazil; Trinidad. Stragglers to e Ecuador, Panama, W Indies, and poss. se US.

### 7. GLOSSY IBIS
*Plegadis falcinellus*                    Pl. 3, Map 53
**Identification:** 20-22″ (51-56cm). Decurved bill slaty; bare facial skin slaty. Legs dusky. Breeding plumage: *mainly bronzy chestnut to bronzy maroon* with more or less purplish reflections; lower back and wings greener; only breeding birds have *whitish border to bare facial skin.* Nonbreeding plumage: head and neck streaked whitish. Imm.: like nonbreeding adult but duller, esp. on head and neck; foreneck and underparts dingy grayish white.
**Similar species:** Usually appears blackish in poor light or at a distance. See larger and more robust Green Ibis (3). Whispering Ibis (4) has pinkish bill and legs. Imm. White and Scarlet Ibis (5, 6) have contrasting white lower underparts and rump.
**Breeding:** Not reported in Colombia; recently found breeding in Aragua, Venez. (P. Schwartz).
**Status and habitat:** Casual. One specimen and a very few sight recs.; freshwater marshes and wetlands. Most recent is 2 seen w of Pivijay, Magdalena, 8 Feb 1977 (R. Ridgely).
**Range:** Known only from Laguna de Guájaro, sw Atlántico (100m), and sight recs. in lower Magdalena Val. Breeds in s coastal US, Greater Antilles, and locally in warmer parts of Old World and Australia. Mid. American and some Colombian sight recs. may refer to this sp. or to White-faced Ibis (see note).

**Note:** White-faced Ibis (*P. chihi*) of w N America and s S America may wander to n Colombia. Almost identical to Glossy Ibis, ads. differ in red eye, reddish bill and legs, and bare red facial skin, and when breeding, latter outlined by a *feathered white* border. Nonbreeders lack Glossy's pale line from bill to eye. Imms. inseparable in field.

### 8. ROSEATE SPOONBILL
*Ajaia ajaja*                    Ill. 14, Map 54
**Identification:** 28-32″ (71-81cm). Long flat *"spoonbill"* unmistakable in any plumage. Bald head grayish; neck and upper back white; *otherwise pink with bloody red shoulders*; legs red. Imm.: white incl. feathered head; bill yellow, legs dusky red. Ad. plumage attained gradually in about 3 yrs.
**Behavior:** Small groups wade in shallow water and sift for plankton-sized organisms by swinging the bill from side to side. Flight is steady without gliding.
**Breeding:** Laying ♀, 31 Mar, s Bolívar (Carriker).
**Status and habitat:** Common in brackish water, mangroves, and on tidal flats of the Carib. (breeding?); rare on Pacific; wander inland to ponds, rice fields, and other freshwater areas, mainly Dec–early June in Meta (W. McKay; S. Furniss).
**Range:** To 1000m. Carib. region from Cartagena area e to Guajira; wanders up Cauca Val. to Cali (now very rare), lower Magdalena Val., and e of Andes from Arauca to w Caquetá, rarely to Vaupés and n Amazonas; once on Pacific coast s to Guapí, Cauca. Coastal se US and Mexico s locally to Uruguay and c Chile. Greater Antilles; Trinidad and Tobago; Dutch Leewards.

# FLAMINGOS: Phoenicopteridae (1)

Flamingos are pinkish wading birds with extraordinarily long necks, long legs, and webbed toes. The various species are scattered in discontinuous populations in parts of both the New and Old World, and all show a distinct preference for brackish or alkaline water. Their remarkable bill is thick and bent sharply downward at the midpoint. When feeding the bill is held in an inverted position with the head immersed in shallow water. Their food, obtained by sifting and straining water, is mostly minute crustaceans, algae, diatoms, salt fly larvae and occasionally small fish.

### 1. GREATER (AMERICAN) FLAMINGO
*Phoenicopterus ruber*                    Ill. 15, Map 55
**Identification:** 40-48″ (102-122cm). *Unmistakable.* Bent bill pink with black tip; long pink legs. Rosy pink with black-tipped wings. Imm.:

mostly dull grayish white, uppersurface and flight feathers washed pale brown.
**Voice:** A nasal gabbling honk in flight; in courtship an incessantly repeated *eep-eep cak-cak* (Palmer 1962).

14. ROSEATE SPOONBILL (juv. left, ad. right)

15. GREATER (AMERICAN) FLAMINGO

**Behavior:** Breeds, forages, and loafs in groups of var. size, often large, although individuals wander alone. When feeding, wades actively in shallow water. Flight is remarkably swift and direct with fast steady wing beats and neck and legs outstretched.

**Breeding:** Formerly reported to breed on shores of Ciénaga Grande. Known to breed (recently?) in Guajira at Carrizal and Bahía Portete (Sprunt 1976), also Musiche, Bahía Honda, and Playones del Descocotado (J. Hernández *in* Naranjo 1979b). On Bonaire breeds Apr–Sept; nest a large truncated mud cone with saucerlike top; 1 white egg.

**Status and habitat:** Very rare in lower Magdalena Val. in fresh or brackish water; recent recs. in PN Salamanca are prob. wandering individuals, rarely groups (30 seen 23 Aug

1972 is largest recent report—T. B. Johnson). Near Manaure, Guajira, apparently present yr.-round in flocks of 10-1000 or more in coastal lagoons. Groups of 400 and 600 on 24 June 1974 contained all age groups with about 10% young of the yr., some prob. from Bonaire colony (Sprunt 1976).

**Range:** To 200m. Mouth of Magdalena River and locally on coastal Guajira; at least formerly inland along Magdalena River to El Banco (9°N) and Ciénaga de Zapatosa near nw base of E Andes. Bahamas, Greater Antilles, Yucatan, Netherland Antilles (Bonaire), and locally from coastal ne Colombia to ne Brazil; the Galapagos. Casually to Gulf coast US.

**Note:** Many now incl. Chilean Flamingo (*P. chilensis*) of Peru s as a subsp. of *P. ruber*.

# SCREAMERS: Anhimidae (2)

Screamers are a small group of peculiar aquatic birds found only in South America. They are heavy-bodied, gooselike birds related to waterfowl but anatomically unique. Among other things, they lack feather tracts, have a crest or long horny frontal spike on top of the head, and sharp spurs on the bend of the wing. With heavy legs and very large unwebbed feet they walk readily over floating marshy vegetation. Their voices, more a gargled hoot than a scream, are among the loudest of all birds.

## 1. HORNED SCREAMER
*Anhima cornuta*     Ill. 16, Map 56

**Identification:** 34-37" (86-94cm). Huge corpulent bird with short fowllike bill. Long bare quill protruding from forecrown. *Mainly greenish black*; crown and entire neck glazed and dappled white; *large silvery white shoulder patch* conspic. in flight; under wing coverts and *belly white*.

**Voice:** Powerful and far carrying call unlike any other; typically several throaty *U-who*'s, 1 to several gulping *gulp-hoo*'s and a more raucous *quuk-quoo, quuk-quoo, yoik-yok, yoik-yok* ending, or with var. in the sequence. Not forgotten once heard.

**Behavior:** A sedate vegetarian that feeds in marshy grass or in floating vegetation. When not feeding, single birds, pairs, or several loosely assoc. individuals loaf on tops of the highest nearby vegetation, usually a low bush or tree, though if alarmed readily seek the tops of tall trees. Fly ponderously though buoyantly and soar well.

**Breeding:** Flightless young, 29 May (J. V. Remsen), and Aug nest with eggs (Hilty), Leticia; 3 nests with eggs in Aug, another early Dec at Mozambique e of Villavicencio (Gill et al. 1974); 3 downy young, Macarena Mts., 5 Feb (T. O. Lemke and P. Gertler). Nest a large

pile of floating marsh vegetation partially anchored to brush or grass in shallow water; 2-3 olive brown eggs.

**Status and habitat:** Local. Swampy backwaters and vegetation-choked shores of lagoons and lakes in open or forested zones. Numerous in suitable habitat in Amazonia where not persecuted by man, but rare or absent from low productivity blackwater rivers and lakes of Vaupés and Guainía region. About 12 pairs remain at Lago de Sonso near Cali.

**Range:** To 1000m. Cauca Val. (now confined to Lago de Sonso, Valle), mid. Magdalena Val. (extent of range unknown, but rec. at Barrancabermeja w of Bucaramanga), Catatumbo lowlands and generally e of Andes (except e Guainía and e Vaupés). Colombia, Venez., and the Guianas s to e Bolivia and Amazonian Brazil; w Ecuador.

## 2. NORTHERN SCREAMER
*Chauna chavaria*     Ill. 16, Map 57

**Identification:** 30-36" (76-91cm). Large and heavy-bodied like previous sp. *Bare orbital skin and legs reddish pink*. Crown and ragged occipital crest gray; *throat and sides of head to behind eye white* forming a broad "chinstrap"; neck black; otherwise dark gray, upperparts darker and glossed green.

16. Horned Screamer (left), Northern Screamer (right)

**Voice:** Powerful bugled *kleer-a-ruk, cherio.*
**Behavior:** Much like Horned Screamer but more often in loose groups rather than alone or pairs (R. Ridgely).
**Breeding:** Several nests early May near Lake Maracaibo, Venez.; large mass of marsh vegetation built up from the water and concealed in marsh; 2-7 soiled white eggs (Osgood and Conover 1922).
**Status and habitat:** Swampy backwaters, marshes and vegetation-choked lagoons and lakes in forested or open country. Common in lower Magdalena, Sinú and Atrato vals. (Haffer 1975). Suffers from loss of habitat in some settled areas; small nos. and widely scattered in PN Salamanca.
**Range:** To 200 m. Wetlands from lower Atrato Val. e to w base of Santa Marta Mts. and upper Cesar Val., and s in mid. Magdalena Val. to s Bolívar. N Colombia and nw Venez.

## DUCKS, GEESE: Anatidae (21)

Birds of this family are familiar the world over. The various Colombian species, including a few migrants, are distributed from sea level to treeline but do not usually comprise a significant proportion of the avifauna. Whistling-ducks, numerically the most abundant ducks in Colombia, are best known for their gangly appearance, whistling calls, and in some cases, habit of perching in trees. The Orinoco Goose is the only "shelduck" in Colombia, and like other shelducks, the ♂ has no courtship display but instead fights for a mate. Dabbling ducks such as *Anas* have metallic wing speculums, feed by "tipping up" at the surface, and spring directly into the air. In contrast, pochards and divers such as *Aythya* and *Oxyura* lack iridescent speculums, dive expertly, and patter to get airborne. Tree or perching ducks like Muscovies and Comb Ducks are notably arboreal, whereas the little Torrent Duck, often placed with the dabblers, is the only member of the family to spend its entire life amid raging mountain torrents.

## 1. FULVOUS WHISTLING-DUCK (TREE-DUCK)

*Dendrocygna bicolor*        Pl. 3, Map 58
**Identification:** 18-21″ (46-53cm). Long-legged and gooselike. Bill and legs gray. *Mostly cinnamon brown*; crown and line down hindneck dark brown; back and wings blackish broadly scaled buff; patch of whitish streaks on neck and *creamy white stripes on sides*. In flight *wings blackish*, linings brown; *conspic. white band across base of tail*. Flies with head and neck slightly drooped and legs trailing behind tail.
**Similar species:** See other whistling-ducks (2, 3). In flight look for the diagnostic white ring at base of tail. ♀ Northern Pintail (9) shows a white border behind wing speculum in flight and lacks the white at base of tail.
**Voice:** Call a high reedy *kur-dúr*, mostly in flight and constantly repeated.
**Behavior:** Pairs or flocks of var. size, often mixed with Black-bellied Whistling-Ducks, are active by day or night. Seldom perch in trees.
**Breeding:** Jan–Feb Cauca Val. nests (F. C. Lehmann), and groups of 2-week-old young, early Mar (Borrero 1952b). In Trinidad, leafy nest on ground in marsh; up to 6 white eggs (ffrench 1973).
**Status and habitat:** Fairly common in freshwater marshes, grassy lagoons, wet pastures, and occas. brackish water.
**Range:** Lowlands along Carib. coast from Sinú Val. e to w base of Santa Marta Mts., Cauca Val. to Valle, lower Magdalena Val. and to 2600m in E Andes (rare) from s Boyacá to Sabana de Bogotá; wander to lowlands e of Andes from Arauca to w Meta (small groups seen, Hacienda La Corocora, May–June 1978—W. McKay). S US locally to Honduras; c Panama (accidental) s spottily to Bolivia and c Argentina, occas. Chile. Trinidad. E Africa and se Asia.

## 2. WHITE-FACED WHISTLING-DUCK (TREE-DUCK)

*Dendrocygna viduata*        Pl. 3, Map 59
**Identification:** 16-18″ (41-46cm). Bill slaty; legs gray. *Forepart of head and large patch on foreneck white*, rest of head and neck black; otherwise brown above with black wings, rump and tail; lower neck and chest rich rufous chestnut becoming black on center of underparts; sides and flanks narrowly barred black and white. In flight *wings, rump, and tail all dark*. Imm.: crown and hindneck dusky; sides of head and all of underparts grayish; older birds with some barring on sides.
**Similar species:** The white face is diagnostic.
**Voice:** High, reedy whistle a hurried *wee-te-de*, often repeated in flight.

**Behavior:** Sim. to Black-bellied Whistling-Duck and often with them, though seldom perches in trees. Like other whistling-ducks, wary, and when flushed circle and call incessantly.
**Breeding:** 5 BC birds, May, Ciénaga de Ayapel, e Córdoba (Borrero 1955); in Venez. llanos breeds June–July (Friedmann and Smith 1950; Thomas 1979b). In Trinidad, leafy nest on ground in marsh; up to 9 creamy white eggs (ffrench 1973; also in hollow trees (Delacour 1954).
**Status and habitat:** Freshwater marshes, grassy lagoons, and flooded fields, occas. brackish water. Large nos. Feb–late July at Hacienda La Corocora, w Meta, absent remainder of yr. (W. McKay); fairly common locally in n Colombia but the least numerous *Dendrocygna* in PN Salamanca (T. B. Johnson).
**Range:** Carib. lowlands from Sinú Val. e to Ciénaga Grande, occas. to Guajira; Magdalena Val. s to Santander, to 2600m in E Andes (rare) from n Boyacá to Sabana de Bogotá; lowlands e of Andes from Norte de Santander to w Caquetá, Vaupés, and n Amazonas. Costa Rica spottily to n Argentina and Uruguay. Trinidad. Tropical Africa and Madagascar.

## 3. BLACK-BELLIED WHISTLING-DUCK (TREE-DUCK)

*Dendrocygna autumnalis*        Pl. 3, Map 60
**Identification:** 20-22″ (51-56cm). *Bill orange red*; long legs pinkish orange. Mostly rufescent brown, sides of head and upper foreneck and chest grayish brown; *breast and belly black*. In flight, wings black above and below with *large white shoulder patch*. Imm.: much duller and grayer though always with a suggestion of ad. pattern; bill and legs dusky. Flies with long neck slightly drooped and legs protruding behind tail.
**Similar species:** Only whistling-duck with white in wing. From other ducks in flight by slower wing beats and gangly shape. Head and legs dangle downward when landing.
**Voice:** Call, mostly in flight, a reedy, whistled *wee-ree*.
**Behavior:** Usually in small groups active by day or night. The only Colombian whistling-duck that readily perches and roosts in trees, esp. on large high dead branches.
**Breeding:** Ads. with young, Apr–Aug and Dec–Feb near Cali (Lehmann 1957); BC ♀, Oct, Santa Marta (Todd and Carriker 1922); Sept–Oct breeding, Guárico, Venez. (Thomas 1979b). Nest in hollow tree, marsh, or flooded field; in Trinidad up to 14 eggs (ffrench 1973).
**Status and habitat:** Locally fairly common in freshwater ponds, marshes, and flooded fields, occas. brackish water and mangroves. W of

Andes generally the most numerous whistling-duck; e of Andes at Hacienda La Corocora, w Meta only Feb–early Aug and much less numerous than White-faced Whistling-Duck (W. McKay).
**Range:** Lowlands over most of n Colombia, up Cauca Val. to Valle, to 2600m in E Andes from s Boyacá to Sabana de Bogotá and lowlands e of Andes to s Meta and Vaupés (Mitú); locally along Pacific coast. S Texas and Mexico to n Argentina, Paraguay, and se Brazil. Trinidad.

### 4. ORINOCO GOOSE
*Neochen jubata*                    Pl. 3, Map 61
**Identification:** 24-30″ (61-76cm). *Large.* Upper mandible black, lower red; legs reddish. *Head, neck, chest, and center of breast pale creamy buff;* otherwise mostly chestnut becoming dark green on lower back and tail; under tail coverts white; wings dark green with a *broad white band across secondaries* (conspic. in flight).
**Similar species:** Larger and more robust than Black-bellied Whistling-Duck (3) and with entire forepart of body creamy white. In flight Black-bellied has white on forepart of wing, not the secondaries. Also see Buff-necked Ibis (p 72).
**Voice:** ♂ a high whistle, ♀ a loud cackle; loud guttural honking by ♂ in breeding season.
**Behavior:** Gather in flocks during eclipse molt; otherwise in family groups or pairs (Delacour 1954). ♂♂ fight fiercely with wings and honk constantly when breeding (Cherrie 1916).
**Breeding:** 12 young, 2-3 weeks old, late Jan, n Arauca (W. McKay and J. Jorgenson); Jan–Feb breeding in Venez. Orinoco; down-lined tree cavity nest; 6-10 eggs, pale brownish cream (Delacour 1954).
**Status and habitat:** Local and uncommon though once more widespread; river banks, freshwater marshes, and lakes in forested and open country. Wanders widely along tributaries of Ríos Amazon and Orinoco.
**Range:** To 500m. E of Andes from Arauca s to Meta; once at 2600m in E Andes (Laguna de Fúquene, n Cundinamarca); once on Río Amazon near Leticia (sighting 21 July 1976—Hilty et al.). Spottily throughout e of Andes s to n Argentina and Paraguay.

### 5. SPECKLED TEAL
*Anas flavirostris*                    Pl. 3, Map 62
**Identification:** 15-17″ (38-43cm). A small brownish "♀-plumaged" duck with speckles. *Bill blue gray,* darker above. Head and neck light grayish buff finely speckled black; otherwise dark brown above with paler edgings, wing speculum green (more conspic. in flight) bordered buffy white behind; underparts buffy

white, *usually conspic. spotted brown on foreneck and breast.* Imm.: has less spotting.
**Similar species:** ♀ Blue-winged Teal (10) has light blue upper wing coverts. ♀ Yellow-billed and Northern pintails (8, 9) are both much larger and have pointed tails; Yellow-billed also has yellow bill (not gray).
**Voice:** ♂ a mellow whistle like that of Yellow-billed Pintail; ♀ cackles (Borrero 1952b).
**Behavior:** Pairs dabble and "up end" in shallow water or stand in wet boggy areas. Sometimes in flocks or with other ducks.
**Breeding:** BC birds, Feb, Lago de Cumbal, Nariño (Borrero 1952b); 3-week-old young and ready-to-lay ♀, mid-Mar, and BC pair, 30 Sept (4300m), n Boyacá (Carriker). Breed in marshes or near shores of lakes in paramo.
**Status and habitat:** Sparse resident on ponds, lakes, and cold wet bogs. Occas. at sulphur springs in PN Puracé; reported "abundant" at Lago de Cumbal, Nariño (Borrero 1952b).
**Range:** 2600-4300m (usually above 3000m). E Andes, and in C Andes from nevados in Caldas-Quindío area s through Nariño. Nw Venez. to Tierra del Fuego. S birds migratory.
**Note:** Dark-billed birds from Venez. to Ecuador may be a separate sp., *A. andinus* (Andean Teal), from birds of Peru southward.

### 6. AMERICAN WIDGEON
*Anas americana*
**Identification:** 17-20″ (43-51cm). Bill blue gray. ♂: *crown white* with green mask behind eyes; throat and neck light buff speckled black (looks gray at a distance); otherwise brown above; chest and flanks pinkish brown contrasting with white central underparts; *white flank patch bordered behind by black rear end.* ♀: mostly russet brown with *grayish head and neck;* below like ♂ but duller. In flight both show conspic. white wing coverts (above and below) and green speculum.
**Similar species:** ♂ is easily picked out by white crown, but in flight Blue-winged and Cinnamon teals (10, 12) and Northern Shoveler (13) have sim. placed light wing patches. Speckled Teal (5) has no white on front of wing.
**Voice:** ♂ whistles *whee whee whew,* ♀ *qua-ack* (Peterson 1980).
**Status and habitat:** Uncommon and erratic winter visitant or resident (Oct–Apr) on freshwater marshes, ponds, and lakes, less frequently salt water. Occas. concentrates in nos. (about 300 in PN Salamanca, 16 Feb 1972—Hilty and T. B. Johnson), but usually small groups.
**Range:** Lowlands of n Colombia (mainly lower Magdalena Val.), up Cauca Val. to Valle and casually to 2600m in E Andes from s Boyacá

to Sabana de Bogotá. Breeds in nw N America; winters mostly from s and coastal US s to n Colombia, rarely nw Venez. W Indies and Trinidad.

## 7. WHITE-CHEEKED (BAHAMA) PINTAIL
*Anas bahamensis*    Pl. 3, Map 63
**Identification:** 16-17″ (41-43cm). Bill blue gray, red basally. A small brown duck with large white cheeks. Mostly fulvous brown with *sides of head, throat, and foreneck white*; underparts speckled black. In flight shows buff-bordered green speculum and *pale buff rear end contrasting with darker back.*
**Voice:** ♂ a low squeaking, ♀ a quack (Bond 1961).
**Behavior:** Pairs or small flocks dabble in shallow brackish water or rest on mudflats.
**Breeding:** 6 BC birds, July–Aug, Atlántico (Borrero 1961). In W Indies nest concealed in grass or under mangrove root; 5-12 buff eggs (Bond 1961).
**Status and habitat:** Uncommon to fairly common resident (presumed to breed) in brackish water, tidal regions, and mangroves; less frequently inland to shallow freshwater ponds and marshes.
**Range:** To 100m. Carib. coastal region from Cartagena e to Ciénaga Grande. Prob. also coastal Guajira. Bahamas (casual in s Florida and s Texas), W Indies, Dutch Antilles, most of coastal S America (except Pacific coast s to w Ecuador and the extreme s), and e Brazil w to ne Argentina. Galapagos.

## 8. YELLOW-BILLED PINTAIL
*Anas georgica*    Ill. 17
**Identification:** 24-28″ (61-71cm). Bill yellow, ridge and tip slaty. Nondescript with *rather long pointed tail.* Brown above with prom. buffy edgings on back; otherwise mostly pale fulvous; sides of head finely speckled blackish; chest, breast, and sides more coarsely spotted black, center of belly white. In flight shows *greenish black speculum bordered buff in front and*

17. Yellow-billed Pintail

*behind.* Or sim. but somewhat smaller and darker (*niceforoi*).
**Similar species:** Much like ♀ Northern Pintail (9) but bill yellow (not dark gray). Also see much smaller and dark-billed Speckled Teal (5).
**Voice:** ♂ a mellow trilled whistle, ♀ a low *ka-ack* or *qua-ack* in Argentina (Wetmore 1926), both apparently much like those of Northern Pintail.
**Behavior:** Colombian populations poorly known. Dabbles and tips up like other *Anas* (Wetmore 1926; Weller 1975).
**Breeding:** BC birds, Mar–Apr and Oct–Nov in Nariño and w Putumayo (Borrero 1952b); in Chile grass- and down-lined nest on high ground near water; 4-10 eggs (Johnson 1965).
**Status and habitat:** Freshwater marshes, ponds, and lakes. Small flocks reported on Laguna La Cocha, larger ones on Lago de Cumbal, Nariño, and in Sibundoy Val., Putumayo. A pair repeatedly seen on Laguna La Cocha, 1 June 1981 (Hilty). No recent recs. of *niceforoi* and this subsp. perhaps extinct (Borrero 1952b; J. Hernández).
**Range:** 2200-3300m. Nariño and w Putumayo (*spinicauda*); E Andes from s Boyacá (Lago Tota and Laguna de Fúquene) s to Sabana de Bogotá; once in Cauca Val. (1000m) near Cali (*niceforoi*). Colombia s in Andes to Tierra del Fuego. S birds migratory.
**Note:** Both *spinicauda* and *niceforoi* have been considered distinct spp.

## 9. NORTHERN PINTAIL
*Anas acuta*
**Identification:** 22-26″ (56-66cm). Long slender neck; *pointed tail with needlelike central tail feathers* (much shorter in ♀). Bill gray. ♂: *head brown; underparts white extending up on foreneck to a point behind eye*; upperparts and sides gray; white patch on flanks in front of black rear end. ♀: all brown, lighter below, mottled throughout with dark brown. In flight both sexes show a green speculum with white rear border.
**Similar species:** ♀ very like Yellow-billed Pintail (8) but bill gray (not yellow). In the hand, rear border of speculum white (not pale buff) and throat brown (not whitish buff). Speckled Teal (5) is much smaller.
**Voice:** ♂ an infrequently heard, low, double-noted whistle; ♀ quacks.
**Behavior:** Fast-flying, streamlined duck most likely seen in flocks in Colombia.
**Status and habitat:** Very erratic and local winter visitant and resident (Oct–late Apr; once 2 June) in freshwater marshes, ponds, and

lakes, occas. brackish water. Apparently no recent recs. from Colombia.

**Range:** To 2600m. Lower Magdalena Val., Cauca Val., and W and E Andes. Breeds throughout N Hemisphere; winter s in New World to n Colombia and Venez., rarely e to Surinam.

## 10. BLUE-WINGED TEAL
*Anas discors*                                    Pl. 3, Map 64
**Identification:** 14-16″ (36-41cm). Bill gray; eyes dark. ♂: head gray blue, crown blackish and with *prom. white crescent on foreface*; otherwise brown, underparts lighter and thickly spotted black; white rear flank patch in front of black rear end. ♀: all buffy brown spotted and mottled dark brown. In flight both sexes show *large light blue patch on front of wing* and small green speculum.
**Similar species:** ♂ with crescent face is distinctive, but this sometimes faint or lacking in fall birds. ♂ Cinnamon Teal (12) looks "dark bodied," Shoveller (13) is larger with big "spoonbill," but in flight both show blue wing patches like Blue-winged Teal. ♀ prob. not separable in field from ♀ Cinnamon Teal; latter is darker (all subspp.), has more spatulate bill, more sloping forecrown, less distinct pale loral spot and fainter dark eyeline. Nonbreeding ♂ Cinnamon Teal from ♀ by red eyes.
**Behavior:** Gregarious and often with other spp. of ducks. Like other teals, fast-flying in tight compact flocks.
**Status and habitat:** The most abundant and widespread migrant and winter resident duck in Colombia (early Sept–late Apr, rarely to early June); coastal estuaries, freshwater marshes, ponds, and lakes.
**Range:** To 3600m. Throughout w of Andes, a few e of Andes s to s Meta, once to Vaupés (Mitú). Breeds in N America; winters from s US to n S America, rarely to c Argentina and Uruguay.

## 11. GREEN-WINGED TEAL
*Anas crecca*
**Identification:** 13-16″ (33-41cm). Pint-sized duck with dark wings. ♂: mostly gray with *chestnut head and green mask from eyes to nape*; breast buffy white, spotted black; *vertical white stripe on sides in front of wing*; under tail coverts creamy buff. ♀: sim. to ♀ Blue-winged Teal, but forewing dark (not light blue). In flight both sexes show green speculum (in good light) with light borders, and from below, white bellies. Legs *dark* in both sexes.
**Similar species:** Cf. other teals (10, 12). Both differ in having yellow legs.
**Status and habitat:** Accidental. One old rec.

Laguna de Fúquene, n Cundinamarca (2600m), 24 Jan.
**Range:** Breeds in N Hemisphere; in New World winters s to Honduras and W Indies. Once to Colombia and Tobago.

## 12. CINNAMON TEAL
*Anas cyanoptera*
**Identification:** 15-17″ (38-43cm). Small. Bill blackish. ♂: eyes red; *mostly bright reddish chestnut*; back mottled blackish; breast and sides spotted black (or unspotted below—*septentrionalium*); rump and tail black. ♀: almost identical to ♀ Blue-winged Teal and prob. not separable in field. In flight both sexes show *pale blue upper wing coverts* and green speculum as in Blue-winged Teal. Resident subadult ♂♂ resemble ♀♀ but underparts spotted (not mottled) black. In hand, smallest-billed individuals of *tropicus* and largest of *septentrionalium* and *borreroi* could be told from ♀ Blue-winged Teals by bill length (35.5-45 vs 37-41.5mm).
**Similar species:** In breeding plumage ♂♂ easily picked out, but at other seasons resemble ♀♀; then can be told from ♀ Blue-winged Teal (10) only by red (not dark) eyes; perhaps also by flatter head, more spatulate bill. N migrants acquire breeding dress by Dec or Jan.
**Behavior:** As in Blue-winged Teal.
**Breeding:** May and Oct recs. on Sabana de Bogotá; BC ♂♂ and ready-to-lay ♀, Feb. Sibundoy Val. (2200m), w Putumayo; BC ♀, early Mar, Cauca Val. (Borrero 1952b); grass and aquatic vegetation nest in marsh.
**Status and habitat:** Local in freshwater marshes and lakes; small nos. present yr.-round on Sabana de Bogotá and in Cauca Val. where presum. breed. N migrants (very rare) rec. Oct– Apr.
**Range:** To 1000m w of Andes and once on Pacific coast (migrant *septentrionalium*); lower Magdalena Val. and entire (now only Valle?) Cauca Val. (resident *tropicus*); 2100-3100m in E Andes from s Boyacá (Lago Tota) to Sabana de Bogotá and mts. of e Nariño and w Putumayo at Lago La Cocha and Sibundoy Val. (resident *borreroi*). Breeds in w N America s to c Mexico, spottily in Colombia, and generally from s Peru and se Brazil to Tierra del Fuego; n and s populations migratory, n ones s casually to n S America.

## 13. NORTHERN SHOVELER
*Anas clypeata*
**Identification:** 17-20″ (43-51cm). *Long wide spatulate bill*. ♂: *head and neck dark glossy green*; center of back black, chest and breast white; *belly and sides chestnut* bordered behind by white

patch on rear flank. ♀: mottled brownish. In flight both sexes show large light blue patch on front of wing and small green speculum. **Similar species:** Best mark is the big bill ("spoonbill"). In flight looks long-necked. See Blue-winged and Cinnamon teals (10, 12).
**Behavior:** Pairs or flocks float low with bill angled downward and usually dabble and sift in shallow water. Flies very fast and directly.
**Status and habitat:** Usually reg. winter resident in small nos. (mostly Oct–Mar) to shallow marshy freshwater and saltwater areas.
**Range:** Lowlands of lower and mid. Magdalena Val., Cauca Val. (mainly in Valle) and occas. to 2600m in E Andes (Sabana de Bogotá). Breeds in n part of N Hemisphere; in New World winters s to n Colombia, twice to n Venez. (sightings Mar 1970, Jan 1976—P. Alden).

### 14. TORRENT DUCK
*Merganetta armata*                    Pl. 3, Map 65
**Identification:** 14-16″ (36-41cm). Small streamlined duck with rubbery *red bill* and long stiff tail. ♂: *head and neck white; crown and stripe down hindneck black; black line from eye down side of neck,* rest of upperparts blackish more or less streaked tawny and gray, underparts white lightly streaked gray; green wing speculum bordered white (hard to see). ♀ very different: crown and hindneck blue gray, rest of upperparts like ♂; *sides of head and entire underparts orange cinnamon.* Imm.: above like ♀, below white barred gray on sides, bill dusky.
**Similar species:** Only duck likely in raging mt. torrents.
**Voice:** Loud high-pitched *wheek wheek* in flight, softer in display (Moffett 1970).
**Behavior:** Pairs or families rest on slippery wet boulders in swift cold-water streams or swim and dive expertly in fast-flowing turbulent water, though they often take advantage of eddies behind boulders or slower currents near the bank where they can be easily overlooked. Eat mostly stonefly larvae.
**Breeding:** 6 BC birds, Feb–Oct, W and C Andes (Carriker; Chapman 1917). Feb young with ads., Boyacá, 2800m (Borrero 1952b). E of Cali in C Andes a down-lined nest on rock ledge near torrent 30 Nov; 2, dull buff eggs (Phillips 1926); 43- 44-day incubation may be longest in family (Moffett 1970).
**Status and habitat:** Local in cascading mt. streams. Maximum density about 1 pair per km (Borrero 1952b; Moffett 1970). Deforestation and resulting siltation has threatened or eliminated populations in many areas. Most easily seen on Río Bedón in PN Puracé; occas. Río Pichindé.

**Range:** Mainly 1500-3500m; a few wander lower (1 sighting to 300m in Río Anchicayá—F. C. Lehmann and J. Haffer). All 3 Andean ranges. Nw Venez. s in Andes to Tierra del Fuego.

### 15. SOUTHERN POCHARD
*Netta erythrophthalma*                    Ill. 18, Map 66
**Identification:** 19-20″ (48-51cm). Bill blue gray. Eyes red. ♂: mostly dark brownish black; *head, neck, and breast black glossed purple;* upperparts vermiculated black (hard to see in field). ♀: uniform brown with *whitish throat, patch at base of bill, and patch behind cheeks.* In flight both sexes show white band on secondaries.
**Similar species:** All black-looking ♂ lacks the whitish sides of Lesser Scaup (16). Patchy-faced ♀ nearest ♀ Lesser Scaup but latter has white confined to area around bill. Also cf. ♀ Brazilian Duck (17).
**Behavior:** Usually in pairs or small parties, seldom large groups. Floats high in water, springs directly into air, and feeds mostly at the surface or by "up ending," or sometimes by diving.
**Breeding:** Not reported in Colombia but likely, at least formerly; many flightless and in eclipse plumage, Jan–Feb, Cauca Val. in Valle (Lehmann 1957). Elsewhere, grass and reed nest; 5-9 creamy white eggs (Delacour 1959).
**Status and habitat:** Very rare and notably erratic in freshwater ponds and marshes, usually where there is an abundance of reeds and emergent vegetation; a ♀ seen 16 Feb 1977 at Engativá near Bogotá is only recent rec. (R. Ridgely).
**Range:** Known from lower Magdalena Val. (s of Barranquilla) and Cauca Val. (Valle); to 2600m in E Andes from s Boyacá (Laguna de Fúquene) to Sabana de Bogotá; lowlands e of Andes in w Caquetá (sight—Tres Esquinas). Spottily from nw Venez. to s Chile, mostly in or near Andes; also e Brazil. E and s Africa.

### 16. LESSER SCAUP
*Aythya affinis*                    Ill. 18
**Identification:** 15-18″ (38-46cm). Bill bluish. ♂: head, neck, and chest black (head glossed purple in sun); otherwise gray above, white below, and with black rear end. ♀: all brown with *distinct white patch encircling base of bill.* In flight both sexes show a white stripe on secondaries.
**Similar species:** See Southern Pochard (15).
**Behavior:** Usually in small flocks in or near open deeper water. Dives when feeding.
**Status and habitat:** Prob. rare and sporadic winter visitant or winter resident (rec. Jan–Mar) to larger freshwater lakes.
**Range:** To 1000m in mid. Cauca Val. (esp. Lago de Sonso, Valle); to 2600m in E Andes from

18. SOUTHERN POCHARD (top) (♂ left; ♀ right),
LESSER SCAUP (bottom) (♂ left; ♀ right)

s Boyacá (Laguna de Fúquene) to Sabana de Bogotá. Prob. lower Magdalena Val. Breeds in nw N America; winters from coastal and c US s to Colombia and n Venez., accidental to w Ecuador and Surinam. Trinidad.

**Note:** Ring-necked Duck (*A. collaris*), a N American breeder wintering in very small nos. to Panama (once Venez.), may show up in Colombia. ♂ like Lesser Scaup but white ring on bill, black back, and conspic. white mark on sides in front of wing. ♀: brown with diffused whitish area at base of bill and white eyering.

### 17. BRAZILIAN DUCK
*Amazonetta brasiliensis*         Pl. 3, Map 67
**Identification:** 14-16″ (36-41cm). *Bill and legs orange red* (or bill gray—♀). ♂: mostly brown; crown and hindneck darker with a *conspic. pale gray area on rear cheeks and sides of upper neck*; rump and tail black with pale brown band across upper tail coverts; sides spotted black. ♀: sim. but with *large white spot on sides of forecrown, behind eye, at base of bill, and on throat.* In flight, wings of both sexes *blackish green with white patch on inner secondaries and axillaries.*

**Similar species:** A brown duck with iridescent black wings. Good marks for "hen-plumaged" ♂ are red bill and pale sides of head and neck (see Black-bellied Whistling-Duck, 3). ♀ resembles ♀ Southern Pochard (15) but has more white spots on obviously pale head.

**Voice:** ♂ a strong piercing whistle, ♀ a deep

quack (Delacour 1959). Also a conversational, soft *uuk uuk . . .* or *tuck tuck . . .* and a whistling flight call *tuwee tuwee . . .* in fast ser. (P. Schwartz recording).

**Behavior:** Pairs or small groups dabble in shallow water near shore and cover or stand on the bank; sometimes with other water birds such as ibises and whistling-ducks.

**Breeding:** Half-grown young, Nov, Guyana (Davis 1935); nest in Brazil, a floating mass of leaves in rushes; about 6 white eggs tinged yellow (Frisch and Frisch 1964).

**Status and habitat:** Var. nos. in shallow ponds, marshes, flooded fields, and wet grassy areas. In e and w Meta reported only Dec–early Apr (S. Furniss; W. McKay); many near Arauca in Arauca, Nov (W. McKay and J. Jorgenson).

**Range:** To 500m. E of Andes from Arauca to s Meta and e to Vichada. E Colombia, c Venez., and Guyana; e Bolivia and s Brazil s to c Argentina. A few birds from s population may winter n to Venez. (Blake 1977) and Colombia(?).

### 18. COMB DUCK
*Sarkidiornis melanotos*         Ill. 19, Map 68
**Identification:** ♂ 30″ (76cm); ♀ 22″ (56 cm). Gooselike. ♂ has *large fleshy round comb on upper mandible;* ♂: line down center of crown and hindneck black; the feathers slightly curly; *rest of head, neck, and most of underparts white*; head and neck irreg. *spotted black*; rest of upperparts

19. Comb Duck (upper left) (♀ left; ♂ right),
Muscovy Duck (lower right), (♂ left; ♀ right)

and wings black glossed green and purple. ♀: sim. but smaller, more profusely spotted on head, and no comb. Imm.: crown and upperparts dark brown, white of ad. replaced by buffy brown; dark eyeline and spots on flanks.
**Similar species:** A large (esp. ♂) homely duck that looks white-headed at a distance. Might be mistaken for a domesticated Muscovy (some show much white below) but all ad. Muscovies (19) have white patch on front of wing.
**Behavior:** Scattered individuals, pairs, or small groups are notably wary; in Venez. llanos often consort with larger concentrations of whistling-ducks around grassy lagoons. Also occas. perch in trees. Usually silent.
**Breeding:** A BC bird, 4 July, Venez. (Friedmann and Smith 1950); apparently pairs not formed, the sexes forming separate groups as in Old World. Old World birds nest in tree cavities (Delacour 1959).
**Status and habitat:** Spotty and very sporadic (presumed to breed but no rec.) in freshwater marshes and lakes. Likely on swampy or forested rivers of extreme nw Chocó (known from adj. Panama) and larger lagoons e of Andes

in llanos (common Jan–June in Guárico, Venez. (Thomas 1979b).
**Range:** To 3500m. Mid. and upper Cauca Val. (at least formerly), C Andes (Laguna San Rafael, PN Puracé), E Andes from s Boyacá (Laguna de Fúquene) to Sabana de Bogotá; s Nariño (Lago Cumbal) and once at Manaure, Guajira. E Panama very locally s (mostly e of Andes) to central Argentina. Africa, se Asia.
**Note:** American birds, *S. sylvicola* (South American Comb Duck), have been considered a separate sp. by some.

### 19. MUSCOVY DUCK
*Cairina moschata*                     Ill. 19, Map 69
**Identification:** ♂ 33″ (84cm); ♀ 26″ (66cm). Ad. ♂ has gray bill with broad diagonal black band around center; red caruncles around bare black ocular region and at base of bill; ♂: glossy greenish black with slightly bushy crest, *large white shoulder patches* and white wing linings. ♀: smaller, no caruncles or crest, less white. Imm.: dark brown with *white on wing reduced or often absent.*
**Similar species:** Ad.'s white wing patches are

conspic. in flight. Cf. Black-bellied Whistling-Duck (3). Dark imms. could be mistaken for Olivaceous (Neotropic) Cormorant (p 58) or even Anhinga (p 59).

**Behavior:** Usually in pairs or small groups up to a doz.; large groups up to 100 now rare; reg. perch and roost high in trees (occas. in large nos.). Feral birds are notably wary and rarely assoc. with other spp. of ducks in contrast to domesticated ones.

**Breeding:** Apparently promiscuous. Panama ♀ with 11 downy young, 28 June (Wetmore 1965a); juvs., July and Nov, Guárico, Venez. (Thomas 1979b); nests in tree cavities; eggs cream color (Haverschmidt 1968).

**Status and habitat:** Uncommon and rather local. Forest streams, swamps, mangroves, and freshwater ponds and marshes near wooded areas. Now extirpated from most of Cauca and mid. Magdalena Vals.; elsewhere often persecuted by hunting and in low nos.

**Range:** Mostly below 500m. Throughout in suitable habitat; stragglers to 2600m in E Andes from s Boyacá (Laguna de Fúquene) to Sabana de Bogotá. On Pacific slope rec. only from n Chocó and Nariño. W Mexico locally to sw Ecuador, n Argentina, and Uruguay.

## 20. RUDDY DUCK

*Oxyura jamaicensis*　　　　Ill. 20, Map 70

**Identification:** 15-17″ (38-43cm). Chunky with *bright blue bill* (esp. ♂) and *stiff fan-shaped tail often cocked up.* Breeding plumage ♂: head and neck black with cheeks more or less heavily spotted white (or cheeks black, only chin white—*ferruginea*); otherwise *bright reddish chestnut.* ♀ and nonbreeding ♂: grayish brown above; sides of head buffy white, *crown and stripe below eye dark brown*; underparts buffy brown narrowly barred blackish on sides. In flight both sexes show *all dark wings* and tail.

20. RUDDY DUCK (*Andean* race)
(♀ top; ♂ bottom)

**Similar species:** ♀ and nonbreeding ♂♂ easily confused with ♀ Masked Duck (21), which has 2 stripes on sides of head (not 1); ♂ Masked has only forepart of head black. In flight all Masked Ducks have large white patch on rear of wing.

**Voice:** Displaying N American ♂♂ chuckle, *chuck-uck-uck-uck-ur-r-r* (Peterson 1961).

**Behavior:** Pairs or small groups float low in water, dive expertly, and are alarmed often dive rather than fly. Flight is fast and unsteady with buzzy wing beats. ♀-plumaged birds usually outnumber breeding plumage ♂♂.

**Breeding:** Apparently yr.-round on Sabana de Bogotá; downy chicks Dec, Mar, May, and Sept, and ads. in all stages of sexual development (Borrero 1952b). Nest a floating mass of vegetation in reeds; 7-12 eggs, large for size of bird, esp. in *ferruginea.*

**Status and habitat:** Locally common breeding resident in freshwater marshes and lakes with dense rushes and reeds; no migrants.

**Range:** 2500-4000m. E Andes (Boyacá to s Cundinamarca on Paramo de Sumapaz), and C Andes in PN Puracé (*andina*); mts. of Nariño (*ferruginea*). Breeds in w N America and from Colombia s in Andes to Tierra del Fuego. N birds winter s to Honduras.

**Note:** Some regard S American birds, *O. ferruginea* (Andean Duck), incl. the more intermed. *andina,* a separate sp.

## 21. MASKED DUCK

*Oxyura dominica*　　　　Pl. 3, Map 71

**Identification:** 12-14″ (30-36cm). Chunky with *bright blue bill* (duller in ♀); stiff spiky tail held depressed or elevated. Breeding plumage ♂: *forepart of head black; otherwise mostly rufous chestnut* becoming more buffy on breast and belly; back and sides spotted black. ♀ and nonbreeding ♂: dark brown above; sides of head buffy white with *dusky stripe through eye, another below eye*; underparts buffy white spotted and mottled dark brown. In flight both sexes show *large white patch on rear of wing.*

**Similar species:** See Ruddy Duck (20).

**Voice:** ♂ a repeated *kuri-kirro* (Delacour 1959).

**Behavior:** Pairs or small groups of its own, infrequently up to 20 or more (W. McKay) or with Ruddy Ducks (R. Ridgely). Normally retiring and hard to see. Swim low in water or partially submerged with only head and neck visible and often escape by diving or by swimming and pushing into dense marsh vegetation. Tip up or dive for vegetable matter. As in Ruddy Duck there is apparently an eclipse plumage as ♀-plumaged birds far outnumber breeding plumage ♂♂.

**Breeding:** 3 Trinidad nests (Sept; Nov) in

marshes; 3-4 buffy white eggs with granular shells (ffrench 1973).

**Status and habitat:** Local in freshwater marshes and ponds with dense rushes or emergent vegetation (esp. Water Hyacinth). Fairly common (hard to see) on Sabana de Bogotá; at Hacienda La Corocora, w Meta, only Mar–June in 2 successive yrs. (W. McKay).

**Range:** Spottily in tropical zone of nw Chocó (Juradó near Panama; sighting, May 1972, Bahía Solano—R. Chipley and J. Silliman). Cauca Val. (local) and lower and mid. Magdalena Val.; to 2600m in E Andes from s Boyacá (Laguna de Fúquene) to Sabana de Bogotá; e of Andes at Hacienda La Corocora, w Meta (sightings 1977, 1978—W. McKay) and w Putumayo (Pto. Asís); Isla Gorgona, July 1979 (P. A. Silverstone). S Texas and Mexico to s Argentina. W Indies, Trinidad.

# AMERICAN VULTURES: Cathartidae (6)

The American vultures are a small group of primarily carrion feeders found from southern Canada to Tierra del Fuego and the Falkland Islands. Related to hawks and eagles, they differ in having, among other things, an unfeathered head, slit nostrils, and much weaker bills and feet. All soar with great proficiency and find most of their food through keen eyesight, although at least in the Turkey Vulture, olfaction is also suspected to be of some importance. The family contains the two largest flying birds in the world, the Andean Condor and the California Condor. The Andean Condor still thrives in portions of its range but is now greatly reduced throughout Colombia and survives only in remote areas or in national parks. Without increased protection, even the remaining populations of these magnificent soaring birds may eventually be threatened in Colombia.

[*Cathartes*: From other New World vultures by longer tail, narrower wings, no ruff or collar on neck, and teetering flight with wings held in dihedral. Always appear neckless.]

## 1. TURKEY VULTURE

*Cathartes aura*          Pl. I, Map 72

**Identification:** 26-30″ (66-76cm). Bare head and neck reddish. Rather long tail. Plumage brownish black, wings 2-toned with dark under wing linings and pale gray flight feathers. Resident *ruficollis* (e of Andes) has whitish band across nape. Imm.: browner with bare brown head and neck. In flight tilts unevenly from side to side, wings held well above horizontal.

**Similar species:** Shares 2-toned under wing with other *Cathartes* (2, 3) but latter have yellow heads (not red) and show prom. pale area at base of primaries from above, due to white (not brownish) primary quills. Greater Yellowhead is more robust, blacker, and innermost primaries distinctly blacker than other flight feathers from below.

**Voice:** Usually silent, rarely weak hisses and grunts.

**Behavior:** Single birds or a few loosely assoc. individuals scatter widely and soar high with unequaled mastery of the air as they tilt and teeter to take advantage of the slightest thermal. Mainly a carrion feeder and may concentrate in large milling groups with Black Vulture over suitable carcasses.

**Breeding:** Nest with egg, 18 Jan, upper Magdalena Val. (Miller 1947), another, 8 Mar, Meta (S. Furniss). 1-2 creamy white eggs dotted red brown (Sclater and Salvin 1879); in stump, under boulder, cave entrance, even abandoned hawk nests.

**Status and habitat:** Common and widespread in open country, less so in heavily forested areas where partially replaced by *C. melambrotus*. Nos. augmented by n migrants during n winter; this most noticeable in nw Colombia where a few presumed migrating flocks have been reported in Mar (Haffer 1959; 1975).

**Range:** To 3000m (usually much lower). Resident E Andes westward (*jota*); resident e of Andes (*ruficollis*); n migrant and winter resident (*meridionalis*). S Canada to Falkland Isls. Greater Antilles; Trinidad.

## 2. LESSER YELLOW-HEADED (SAVANNA) VULTURE

*Cathartes burrovianus*          Pl. I, Map 73

**Identification:** 23-26″ (58-66cm). Much like better-known Turkey Vulture (incl. 2-toned underwings) but slightly smaller and *with distinct pale area* (due to white quills) *at base of primaries from above*; up close has bare *yellow head* with reddish forecrown and nape, and blue gray central crown. Imm.: sim. but browner, head dusky, and nape white.

**Similar species:** See more widespread Turkey Vulture (1) also Greater Yellow-headed Vulture (3).

**Behavior:** Single birds or well-separated individuals tilt and teeter with wings held in dihedral, but unlike Turkey Vulture usually glide low over marshes or wet fields, very infrequently soar high and are more often seen perched on fence posts or other low sites. Takes mostly small prey or carrion and is less attracted to large animals than Black and Turkey Vulture.

**Breeding:** Ready-to-lay ♀, 5 Aug, ne Meta (S. Furniss); Feb Surinam nests in large tree cavities; eggs dirty white blotched brown, esp. at larger end (Haverschmidt 1968).

**Status and habitat:** Fairly common to common over open marshy terrain and wet grassland; wanders over dry fields and clearings. Outnumbers Turkey Vulture at Carimagua, Meta (S. Furniss). Limited migratory movement poss. Nos. thought to vary seasonally in Panama (Ridgely 1976); in Venez. Friedmann and Smith (1950) reported higher nos. Oct–Mar.

**Range:** To 1000m. Locally in Cauca Val. (at least formerly), upper Patía Val., lower Magdalena Val. e to Guajira and locally s to mid. Magdalena Val.; e of Andes known only in sw and ne Meta, but poss. throughout *in suitable habitat* (Amazonian recs. need confirmation). E Mexico locally s to n Bolivia, n Argentina and Uruguay.

## 3. GREATER YELLOW-HEADED VULTURE

*Cathartes melambrotus*          Pl. I, Map 74

**Identification:** 29-32″ (74-81cm). *Bare head rich yellow*, crown tinged blue. Plumage deep black, wings 2-toned with under wing linings black and flight feathers paler; *inner primaries blackish* (from below) *producing a conspic. dark patch that contrasts with rest of flight feathers*; primary quills white from above.

**Similar species:** Once learned, easily told from other vultures in the field. Compared with Turkey and Lesser Yellow-headed Vulture (1, 2), Greater is larger, much blacker (almost velvety black), and has broader wings and distinctly dark inner primaries contrasting with rest of flight feathers. Flight is heavier, steadier (less teetering), and wings held nearly flat or only slightly above horizontal. At close range deep yellow head diagnostic.

**Behavior:** Much like Turkey Vulture and sometimes roosts with it; when soaring mainly solitary or in pairs; rarely gathers in groups.

**Status and habitat:** Common over extensively forested regions, there greatly outnumbering or virtually replacing Turkey Vulture; wanders over grassland, but seldom far from forest. Most common vulture away from settled areas in Amazonia.

**Range:** To 700m. E of Andes from s Meta (Ma-

carena Mts.) and Vaupés s (perhaps n to Río Guaviare). Surinam, Guyana, and s Venez. s to e Ecuador, e Peru, n Bolivia, and Amazonian Brazil.

## 4. BLACK VULTURE

*Coragyps atratus*          Pl. I, Map 75

**Identification:** 22-26″ (56-66cm). *Entirely black* incl. bare head and neck; whitish patch at base of primaries conspic. in flight from below (white quills only from above).

**Similar species:** One of the most common soaring birds over w half of Colombia. Learn the flight profile well. Soars with wings flat (not uptilted), often alternates flapping with sailing (instead of mostly soaring), and does not teeter. In profile rear edge of wings angle forward markedly; short, square tail barely protrudes beyond wings and at closer range shows white patch at base of primaries.

**Behavior:** Mainly a carrion feeder and widespread in settled areas; often roosts in trees or on buildings in towns and sometimes becomes assertive and bold around garbage dumps. Roosts and usually soars in groups and the only vulture likely to be abroad at or before dawn.

**Breeding:** Nest with 2 young, e Meta, 8 Apr (S. Furniss). In Panama Jan–May; 2 bluish white eggs heavily spotted brown, in hollow log, cavity at base of tree, betw. rocks etc., usually in woods (Wetmore 1965a).

**Status and habitat:** Very common in towns and all kinds of settled, partially cleared, and open country. Largely absent from extensively forested zones. Presumed migratory movements reported in Panama (R. Ridgely).

**Range:** To 2700m (usually much lower). In suitable habitat throughout. Central US to c Chile, and s Argentina. Trinidad.

## 5. KING VULTURE

*Sarcoramphus papa*          Ill. 21, Map 76

**Identification:** 28-32″ (71-81cm). Large with wingspread to 6.5 ft. (198cm). Bare head and neck sculptured and wattled orange, yellow, and purple. *A white vulture with black flight feathers, rump, and tail*; neck ruff dusky. Imm.: sooty brown; under wing linings usually paler reflecting pattern of ad. and becoming increasingly white with age. In flight, wings broad and flat (no dihedral), almost squarish at tips, tail very short, and head rather small.

**Similar species:** Soaring ad. likely confused only with Wood Stork (p 70). Imm.: resembles Turkey Vulture (1) but soars with flat wings and usually shows "echo" of ad. pattern.

**Behavior:** Soars alone or in pairs, rarely several, often very high and seldom assoc. for prolonged periods with other vultures. Soar-

21. KING VULTURE (ad.)

ing is steady and sustained without teetering or flapping. Seldom seen perched, then usually inside forest.

**Breeding:** BC ♂, 29 Apr, lower Cauca Val. (Carriker); Panama nest, Mar, in rotted low stump in humid forest; 1 white egg; Jan downy young, Panama (Brown and Amadon 1968).

**Status and habitat:** Fairly common in small nos. over dry to humid forest or partially cleared areas though usually well away from settled areas.

**Range:** To 1500m; occas. wanders to 3300m. Nw Chocó (Juradó and Urabá area) e across n Colombia to Santa Marta region spottily s to upper Magdalena Val. (Villavieja, n Huila) and e of Andes from Norte de Santander southward. Formerly in mid. and upper Cauca Val. S Mexico s to nw Peru (absent from wet belt on Pacific Colombian coast), n Argentina, and Uruguay.

## 6. ANDEAN CONDOR

*Vultur gryphus*                    Ill. 22, Map 77

**Identification:** 40-50″ (102-130cm). *Very large* with long broad wings (spread to about 10 ft.; 300cm). Bare wrinkled head dull reddish, ♂ with prom. comb on forehead and dewlap on throat. Black with *large silvery white patch on upper surface of wing* and conspic. white neck ruff. Imm.: entirely dusky brown incl. ruff; no caruncles on lightly feathered brown head. Soars on flat wings; fingerlike primaries bend up noticeably at tip.

**Similar species:** Ad. recognized by size, neck ruff, and silvery white patches on upper wing; imm. by size and shape.

**Voice:** Normally silent. *Tok-tok-tok* by displaying captive bird (Brown and Amadon 1968); poss. a croak (Norton 1975).

**Behavior:** Single birds, pairs or 3's soar effortlessly and magnificently, sometimes following canyon walls or climbing to great hts. Larger groups now very rare in Colombia. Roost on cliffs and seldom aloft until well after dawn or even midmorning.

**Breeding:** Near Pasto presumed nuptial display early Apr (Brown); downy chick following July (F. C. Lehmann). One pair still breed on cliff opp. Pilimbalá, PN Puracé. 1 white egg (Johnson 1965); young fly in 6 mos.

**Status and habitat:** Very local (once widespread) in steep canyons and mt. terrain; require rocky cliffs for roosting or nesting. Formerly 1800-5200m, now rarely below 3000m except Santa Marta Mts., where often down to 1800-2000m (T. B. Johnson; Norton 1975); 3 at carcass with other vultures, 29 Apr 1973, near Valledupar (200m) is lowest recent rec. (T. B. Johnson). Present Colombian population thought to be about 40 in Santa Marta Mts., 6 in Puracé, 6 near Pasto and an undetermined no. in the Nevados de Cocuy (Boyacá), Huila and n Tolima, perhaps scattered birds elsewhere (J. Hernández).

**Range:** Temperate and paramo zone of Santa Marta Mts. and spottily near nevados in C Andes and Nariño (poss. still in E Andes). Nw Venez. (sightings w of Mérida, 7 July 1976— Zonfrillo 1977) s in Andes to Tierra del Fuego.

22. ANDEAN CONDOR (♂ top; ♀ bottom)

# OSPREY: Pandionidae (1)

The Osprey is a large, nearly cosmopolitan raptor closely allied to hawks, eagles, and kites (Accipitridae), but differing from them in leg musculature, more compact plumage, equal length toes, a reversible outer toe (like owls), and sharp spines (spicules) on the soles of the feet.

## 1. OSPREY
*Pandion haliaetus*          Pl. I, Map 78
**Identification:** 21-24″ (53-61cm). *Long slender wings bent at "wrist"* (carpal area). Dark brown above; *head and underparts white; broad stripe through eye black;* hindcrown streaked brown; tail with several narrow brown bands. Underside of wings mostly white with prom. black patch on "wrist." Imm.: crown streaked brown; some white edging above and brownish streaking below.
**Voice:** A ser. of high-pitched whistles.
**Behavior:** Typically seen either flying, or perched alone on a high exposed branch near water. Feeds mostly on fish taken by flying out rather high over water, hovering momentarily, then plunging feet first. Flies with deep measured wing beats, usually flapping more than gliding.
**Status and habitat:** Fairly common nonbreeding resident on both coasts and inland around larger rivers and lakes; wanders widely from lowlands to treeline. "Summering" birds (n summer) are presum. imms.
**Range:** To 3300m. Throughout. Breeds virtually worldwide except in S America; New World birds breed s to Guatemala and Belize; winter (some oversummer) to s S America.

# HAWKS, EAGLES, KITES: Accipitridae (50)

Members of this large cosmopolitan family of diurnal predators all possess a strong hooked bill and gripping feet but are otherwise notably heterogeneous in appearance and behavior. English names for many members are particularly misleading and unfortunately do not always reflect natural groups. Kites, in particular, are an artificial collection of pointed-winged and broad-winged genera with diverse habits and appearance. The Buteonine subfamily, including the buteos, black-hawks, hawk-eagles, etc., are mostly broad-winged, but many do not soar, and hunting behavior, diet, and habits vary widely. *Accipiters* and harriers, by contrast, are well-defined natural assemblages. *Accipiters* are short-winged, long-tailed woodland hawks notable for speedy maneuverable pursuit of prey, often birds. Harriers are best known for their lanky shape, facial ruffs, and quartering flight over open country. As elsewhere, Colombia's raptors have been affected by man's activities. This is particularly true in portions of the Cauca and Magdalena valleys and in some other settled areas where deforestation and extensive use of pesticides, their two most serious threats, have virtually eliminated some populations. The systematic order is that of Brown and Amadon (1968) except 24-25.

## 1. GRAY-HEADED KITE
*Leptodon cayanensis*          Pls. III, V, Map 79
**Identification:** 18-21″ (46-53cm). *Broad, bluntly rounded wings* and long *Accipiter*-like tail. Bare lores and legs blue gray. Head pale gray in contrast to slaty upperparts blending into white throat and underparts; tail black with 2 visible white bands (sometimes 3 from above) and narrow white tip; *under wing coverts black; flight feathers boldly barred black and white.* Light phase imm.: head, neck, and underparts white, or head mostly white with brownish central crown patch and streak over eye; otherwise brown above, tail blackish banded grayish brown; *under wing coverts white;* flight feathers barred dusky; cere, lores, and legs yellow. Dark phase imm.: quite variable but usually brownish black above incl. sides of head; below whitish, lightly to heavily streaked blackish; streaking ranges from breast nearly solid black to breast nearly white with only a few fine dusky marks on center of throat and chest; wings, tail, and soft parts as in pale phase imm.
**Similar species:** Ad. is distinctive (note black wing linings in flight). Pale phase imm. very sim. to ad. Black-and-white Hawk-Eagle (47) but smaller, browner above, lores and cere yellow (not black lores and orange cere), legs much shorter and weaker, and banding broader on primaries. Also see Crested Eagle (45), imm. Ornate Hawk-Eagle (49), and imm. Hook-billed Kite (2), all with different flight profile, last 2 with some barring below. Dark imm. difficult to identify (learn the flight profile), but most look black-headed; cf. smaller imm. Double-toothed Kite (8), also imm. Gray and Roadside hawks and Common Black-Hawk (34, 35, 27), and larger *Spizaetus* (47-49).

**Voice:** Loud *kek kek kek kek* at short intervals (Wetmore 1965a); when soaring a gull-like *aaaaahh-yál*, 1st note rising, 2d dropping (J. V. Remsen).

**Behavior:** Usually perch partly concealed in crown of trees where easily overlooked, though sometimes in open in early morning or evening. Soar occas. with *Accipiter*-like flapping and gliding, but seldom stay aloft long or soar high. Notably catholic diet incl. wasp larvae, insects, honeycomb, bird eggs, small vertebrates, even mollusks.

**Breeding:** 3 BC birds, Jan–Mar, s Córdoba, n Antioquia, and s Magdalena (Carriker); 3 eggs, presum. this sp., grayish white dotted and scrawled reddish brown, from high twig nest (Brown and Amadon 1968).

**Status and habitat:** Uncommon and in small nos. in humid forest and forest borders, particularly along rivers; more numerous in Amazonian region than elsewhere.

**Range:** To 1000m. Pacific coast, eastward n of Andes in upper Sinú and Nechí vals. and Carib. area from Atlántico to w and nw base of Santa Marta Mts.; s in Magdalena Val. to nw Santander (near Bucaramanga); e of Andes from w Caquetá (s of Florencia) and Vaupés (sight, El Dorado, June 1976—R. Ridgely) southward. E Mexico to w Ecuador, n Argentina, and s Brazil.

## 2. HOOK-BILLED KITE
*Chondrohierax uncinatus*     Pls. 4, II, III, V, Map 80

**Identification:** 16-18″ (41-46cm). Rather long tail (usually held closed). Broad lanky wings *obviously narrower at base*. Notably var., but in any plumage has heavy *conspic. hooked bill, greenish facial skin with orange spots in front of white eye*, and short yellow legs. Normal (light phase) ad. ♂: slaty gray, underparts paler and usually narrowly barred whitish, sometimes barred rusty, or uniform gray; upper tail coverts whitish; tail with 2 broad white to grayish bands and narrow white tip. In flight from below, wing linings grayish, flight feathers barred black and white (or occas. more or less uniform below). Normal (light phase) ad. ♀: dark brown above with rusty nuchal collar and gray sides of head; underparts rusty to brownish narrowly barred white, tail as in ♂. In flight from below, wing linings grayish white, flight feathers barred black and white. Rare melanistic phase (both sexes): entirely brownish black, incl. unbarred underwings; tail with 1 broad white band. Imm.: brownish black above with narrow whitish nuchal collar; underparts creamy white becoming progressively barred with age; 3 or 4 narrow grayish (or brownish—

♀) bands on tail. Melanistic imm.: all black with white tail bands.

**Similar species:** Normal ads. (barred) can be confused with several buteos (cf. Gray Hawk, 34) but are rangier in profile, and have heavier bill, and bolder, coarser pattern on underparts and flight feathers. Relatively uncommon melanistic ad. can be difficult; chunkier Slate-colored Hawk (21) has orange cere and legs, ♂ Snail Kite (6) has very broad white band at base of tail, ad. black-hawks (27, 28) have broader rounded wings and tail and whitish at base of primaries. Cf. imm. with imms. of Collared Forest-Falcon (p 118), Gray-headed Kite (1) and Bicolored Hawk (19).

**Voice:** A musical oriolelike whistle and loud shrill scream (Brown and Amadon 1968). A rapid chuckling, *wi-i-i-i-i-i-i-i-uh!* (Willis and Eisenmann 1979).

**Behavior:** Rather sedentary and sluggish, usually perching inside canopy foliage. Soar occas. with some flapping, but seldom aloft very long or very high. Eat mostly arboreal or terrestrial land snails.

**Breeding:** 3 BC birds, Mar–Apr, Santa Marta Mts. (Carriker).

**Status and habitat:** Thinly spread in humid forest, swampy areas, second growth, and gallery woodland; also occas. thorn scrub (e.g., Santa Marta area).

**Range:** Mostly lowlands to 1000m, rarely to 2700m. Carib. region from Atlántico e to base of Santa Marta Mts. and w Guajira; upper Sinú Val. and formerly (no recent rec.) in mid. and upper Cauca and Magdalena vals.; e of Andes from Boyacá and w Meta, prob. e Vichada (rec. in adj. Venez. on Orinoco), s to Amazonas. Mexico (rarely s Texas) to n Argentina and se Brazil. Trinidad. Cuba and Grenada.

## 3. AMERICAN SWALLOW-TAILED KITE
*Elanoides forficatus*     Ill. 23, Map 81

**Identification:** 22-26″ (56-66cm). Unmistakable. Pointed wings. Head, neck, and entire underparts white; back wings and *long deeply forked tail* black; upper back and shoulders somewhat glossed greenish.

**Voice:** Usually silent; *klee-klee-klee* or occas. *kees-a-we* at nest or in display.

**Behavior:** Notably gregarious. Pairs or several, occas. groups of 30 or more, drift with elegant and symmetrical grace along mt. ridges or above lowland forest in sunny weather. Infrequently seen perched, but when perched or roosting, usually in groups on exposed high bare branches. Eat large canopy insects and var. small vertebrates snatched and devoured in flight. Recently reported eating fruit.

23. American Swallow-tailed Kite

**Breeding:** Usually in loose groups; 2 BC birds, 5 Mar, Macarena Mts. (Olivares 1962). In Costa Rica Jan–May, nest high and exposed (Skutch 1965); in Panama 2 nests in Mar, tall forest trees in foothills (R. Ridgely; Eisenmann).

**Status and habitat:** Fairly common in humid forested regions but often local (or seasonal) and wanders widely. Some Mid. American birds (*yetapa*) are almost certainly transients or seasonal nonbreeding residents to Colombia as marked movements in Panama rec. late Jan–Feb, and late July–early Sept (Ridgely 1976). Migrant *forficatus* of se US may also reach Colombia, as it is reported in w Ecuador. It differs in having upperparts glossed dark purplish blue (not glossed dark green), but is doubtfully separable in field.

**Range:** Mostly lowlands and foothills; wanders to 2600m. Throughout *except* dry Carib. region from Atlántico (Cartagena) eastward, drier inter-Andean vals. (upper Dagua, upper Patía, mid. and upper Cauca, parts of Magdalena), and llanos e of Andes. Se US to n Argentina, Uruguay, and se Brazil. N birds s apparently to Panama (Colombia?) are migratory. Transients or wanderers reported in Cuba, Jamaica, and elsewhere.

## 4. PEARL KITE
*Gampsonyx swainsonii*     Pls. 5, VII, Map 82

**Identification:** 8″ (20cm). *Pygmy-sized kite* with pointed wings and square-tipped tail. *Mostly blackish above and white below*; forehead and cheeks creamy yellow, narrow rufous-edged white nuchal collar (inconspic.), *blackish patch on sides of chest and rufous thighs*. In flight posterior edge of wing prom. edged white.

**Similar species:** Likely confused only with Aplomado Falcon (p 120) or American Kestrel (p 119). In flight neither has white trailing edge on wing. Aplomado has black lower underparts; both have prom. "sideburns."

**Voice:** High-pitched scolding *kitt-y, kitt-y, kitt-y* (Friedmann and Smith 1955).

**Behavior:** A confiding little hawk usually seen perched in open on utility wires, poles, or tops of scrubby trees. Hunts mainly from a perch, and in flight is dashing and falconlike but occas. hovers momentarily before stooping on lizards, insects, and other small prey, seldom birds.

**Breeding:** Pair incubating, 30 Nov, near downtown Santa Marta (Hilty). 3 BC birds, Apr–May, nw Antioquia and base Perijá Mts. (Carriker); 2 nestlings, Apr, Venez, Orinoco; frail dead twig platform about 4-7m up; 3 white eggs irreg. blotched chestnut (Cherrie 1916). **Status and habitat:** Fairly common in drier open country with scattered trees, sparsely wooded savanna, and dry to arid scrub; often in vacant lots in towns where there are a few trees. Numerous in humid partially deforested regions of s Córdoba where doubtless a recent invader. **Range:** To about 1000m. Gulf of Urabá (Turbo) e across Carib. lowlands to Guajira and Cesar Val., s to n base of Andes (s Córdoba; Río Nechí) and drier parts of mid. Magdalena Val. s to Cundinamarca-Tolima boundary (sw of Bogotá); e of Andes in Norte de Santander and sightings in w Meta (9 June 1978, Hacienda La Corocora—W. McKay), Tuparro, e Vichada (seen Mar–Apr 1977, T. O. Lemke); and Leticia, Amazonas (several sightings, 17-22 Feb 1984—Hilty and R. Ridgely). Nicaragua; w Ecuador, nw Peru; e of Andes locally (drier areas mainly) from the Guianas and Venez. to ne Ecuador (recent sightings, Río Napo), e Peru (incl. Pebas) and s to nw Argentina and Paraguay. Trinidad.

### 5. BLACK-SHOULDERED KITE

*Elanus caeruleus*       Pl. VII, Ill, 24, Map 83
**Identification:** 15-17″ (38-43cm). Long pointed wings and rather long square tail. *Mostly pearl gray above and white below with white tail; prom. black shoulders*; and from below, small black "wrists." Imm.: sim. but more or less streaked and tinged brown on upperparts, breast, and tail. Note habitual hovering.
**Similar species:** No other med.-sized white hawk has sim. shape. ♂ Cinereous Harrier (13) is larger with black wing tips and black on tail.
**Voice:** Rather quiet; greet with whistled or chirped *kewp*; also *eee-grack*, the 1st note whistled, 2d guttural and raspy (Brown and Amadon 1968).
**Behavior:** Often seen perched exposed in tops of scattered trees in open country. Flies with graceful fluid motion frequently interrupted by extended periods of hovering with body angled upward; sometimes then drops to ground in controlled fall with wings held up in V.
**Breeding:** Laying ♀, May, Santa Marta Mts., BC ♂, Apr, s Huila (Carriker); Feb nest, Venez. (Meyer de Schauensee and Phelps 1978). Panama nests in Dec (eggs), fledged juvs., June; small twig platform in top of small tree in open (R. Ridgely).
**Status and habitat:** Drier open grassland or ranchland with scattered trees or gallery woodland. Fairly common in Carib. region and

24. BLACK-SHOULDERED KITE

e of Andes. First reported in new clearings and pastures in Urabá region (Turbo) in 1959 (Haffer 1975) and then in adj. Panama in 1967 (Eisenmann 1971).
**Range:** Mainly below 1000m (to 1800m near Popayán; to 2600m on Sabana de Bogotá). Gulf of Urabá region e across n Colombia, s to upper Cauca Val. (few recent recs.), drier parts of Magdalena Val. and e of Andes from Norte de Santander to Río Guaviare and along base of Andes to w Caquetá (should spread to w Putumayo with deforestation); occas. to Sabana de Bogotá. Sw Costa Rica to c Panama; n Colombia e to Surinam; c and e Brazil, Uruguay, n Argentina, e Bolivia, and Chile. Trinidad.

### 6. SNAIL (EVERGLADE) KITE

*Rostrhamus sociabilis*       Pls. 4, III, Map 84
**Identification:** 16-18″ (41-46cm). Med.-long wings broadest at tip; square-tipped tail. *Slender black bill strongly hooked; cere, facial skin, and legs orange red.* Ad. ♂: uniform slaty black, *upper and under tail coverts and basal half of tail white*, narrow tip white; eyes red. Ad. ♀: dusky brown above with whitish forehead and eyestripe, below (incl. underwings) creamy buff mottled and streaked brown, throat paler; *tail like ♂.* Imm.: like ♀ but browner above, more distinctly streaked below, and soft parts more orange. In flight, wings *bend down* at tip.
**Similar species:** Any sex or age by combination of red facial skin, thin hooked bill, and white on base of tail. Slender-billed Kite (7) lacks white (imm. with narrow tail bands); harriers (12-14) have only rump white.
**Voice:** A raspy, clicking *crik-ik-ik-ik, ik, ik, ik; kor-ee-ee-a.* A sheeplike bleating in courtship.
**Behavior:** Sociable; usually several are seen

beating low over open wetlands in characteristic floppy, disconnected flight, with body or head angled slightly sideways. Occas. soars; eat freshwater *Pomacea* snails.
**Breeding:** Usually colonial. In Guárico, Venez., 4 nests with eggs, 1 with downy chicks, in palms, 19 Sept (Mader 1981); Surinam breeding Jan–July, in deeper freshwater marshes; frail platforms 1-4m up in bush or tree over water; 2-3 whitish eggs spotted and blotched brown (Haverschmidt 1968).
**Status and habitat:** Locally fairly common in freshwater marshes; mostly lowlands. Nos. peak with Apr–June flooding and snail emergence in PN Salamanca (T. B. Johnson). Replaced in swampy regions by next sp.
**Range:** Mainly below 1000m. W side of Gulf of Urabá (Unguía) e across n Colombia to w base of Santa Marta Mts., up Cauca Val. to Valle (Lago de Sonso where may breed), Magdalena Val., rarely straggling s to Sabana de Bogotá (2600m). Prob. spottily e of Andes in suitable habitat but rec. only in w Caquetá; also Venez. side of Río Arauca. S Florida, Cuba, Mexico locally s to w Ecuador, n Argentina, and Uruguay.

## 7. SLENDER-BILLED KITE
*Helicolestes hamatus*          Pls. 4, III, Map 85
**Identification:** 14-16″ (36-41cm). Broad wings; *very short square tail, and slender sharply hooked black bill.* Cere, facial skin, and legs orange red. *Uniform slaty gray* with yellowish white eyes. Imm.: sim. but vague whitish or buff bars on underparts; *2-3 narrow white bands and white tip on tail;* flight feathers lightly and obscurely mottled grayish and rusty. Flight profile very chunky with short tail barely protruding beyond rear of wings.
**Similar species:** Broader-beamed and shorter-tailed than Snail Kite (6) and without white at base of tail. Larger Slate-colored Hawk (21, same habitat but seldom soars), has roundish tail, a single white tail band, and heavier bill. Black phase Hook-billed Kite (2) has greenish facial skin (not orange red) and white tail band.
**Voice:** Call a nasal, buzzy, kazoolike *wheeeaaaaah,* rising, then falling (Hilty); not unlike a small *Buteo* and very unlike rachetlike or cackling call of Snail Kite (G. Tudor).
**Behavior:** Single birds or several loosely assoc. individuals hunt from low to med.-high perches around shallow pools and swampy lagoons. Reg. soar in groups but usually not high. Eat, as far as known, freshwater *Pomacea* snails, as does Snail Kite.
**Breeding:** Small twig nest high in Ceiba tree, 20 July, 1 chick, Surinam (Haverschmidt 1968); in Guárico, Venez., 2 nests with chicks in tall

trees, mid-Aug–mid-Sept; 2 brownish cinnamon eggs splotched darker (Mader 1981).
**Status and habitat:** Uncommon to fairly common locally in swampy forest, and around shallow stagnant lagoons and drying pools in *várzea* forest. Replaced in open marshland by preceding sp.
**Range:** To 700m. From Panama boundary (Río Truandó) and Gulf of Urabá (Unguía) e spottily along n base of Andes to mid. Magdalena Val. s to Remedios; e of Andes near Leticia, Amazonas. Surely more widespread e of Andes (rec. at El Amparo, on Venez. side of Río Arauca and "common" at Limoncocha, Ecuador). E Panama locally to Surinam and s to n Bolivia and Amazonian Brazil.

## 8. DOUBLE-TOOTHED KITE
*Harpagus bidentatus*          Pls. 5, II, Map 86
**Identification:** 13-15″ (33-38cm). *Accipiter*-like with rather long tail but shorter-legged; fairly *short rounded wings beveled inward on trailing edge near body.* Cere greenish yellow, eyes red, legs yellow. Head bluish gray, remaining upper surface more brownish gray; throat white with *dusky center stripe;* chest rufous; breast and belly rufous thickly barred gray and white; tail dusky with 3 whitish bands and narrow white tip. In flight from below under wing linings whitish contrasting with dark body and barred flight feathers; *prom. fluffy white under tail coverts puff out on sides slightly* (visible from above). Imm.: sim. but browner above; breast and belly creamy white to heavily streaked brown; retains throat stripe.
**Similar species:** Resembles an *Accipiter* or short-winged buteo in the air but can be told at any distance by beveled wings and *conspic.* puffy white under tail coverts; at closer range by diagnostic throat stripe; in the hand by blunt bill and "double tooth." Combination of gray head and rufous chest often useful even in flight. See Roadside, Broad-winged and Sharp-shinned hawks (35, 37, 15).
**Voice:** In flight a high thin ser. of *peeeawe*'s, slightly tremulous (Hilty); a thin *tsip-tsip-tsip-tsip-wheeeooooip* and long, drawn, flycatcherlike *wheeeooo* (Brown and Amadon 1968).
**Behavior:** Rather tame and unobtrusive. Usually perches at midlevel just inside or well inside forest. Eats lizards and large insects snatched from limbs or foliage, and commonly "shadows" monkey troops taking prey disturbed by their activities. Soars for short periods during midday, either low or sometimes riding thermals to great hts.
**Breeding:** 8 BC birds, Jan–Apr, Santa Marta, n Antioquia, and Chocó (Carriker), and Feb, Macarena Mts. (Olivares 1962). Nest building,

e Costa Rica, early Apr (Hilty et al.), and in Panama late June; shallow twig saucer about 10-23m up; 1 white egg speckled brown (Laughlin 1952).
**Status and habitat:** Fairly common in humid and wet forest and taller second growth woodland.
**Range:** To about 1200m. The Santa Marta region, Pacific coast, and n base of Andes from upper Sinú and Nechí vals. to mid. Magdalena Val. (s to nw Cundinamarca); e base of Andes from n Boyacá, s Meta, and e Guainía southward (sight recs. but no specimens in Amazonas); no Putumayo recs. S Mexico to w Ecuador (to 2100m—R. Ridgely), e Bolivia, and se Brazil. Trinidad.

## 9. PLUMBEOUS KITE

*Ictinia plumbea*                     Pls. 4, VII, Map 87
**Identification:** 14″ (36cm). *Unusually long pointed wings*; square-tipped tail. Eyes red. *Short legs orange. Mostly slate gray*, slightly paler on head and underparts; 2-3 narrow white bands on tail from below. In flight shows *rufous patch at base of primaries*. At rest *folded wings extend beyond tip of tail.* Imm.: mostly slate gray above, edged and streaked white; below white, streaked dusky on breast and belly; tail with 3 whitish bands; wings usually show some rufous at base of primaries.
**Similar species:** Easily confused with Mississippi Kite (see 10). No other Colombian hawks have such long curving wings in flight, or wings that project beyond the tail at rest. Note short-legged posture when perched.
**Voice:** Usually silent. A soft, mournful, whistled *swee-zeeeew*, falling at end (J. V. Remsen).
**Behavior:** A highly visible bird, usually seen soaring, either alone, in pairs, or often in flocks of its own or with other birds of prey, often quite high. Perches high on exposed branch where rather unsuspicious. Catches insects in the air or smaller prey from the canopy.
**Breeding:** 3 BC ♀♀, Mar–May, n Antioquia (Carriker); w Meta nest about 16m up in isolated tree held a nearly grown young, 16 Mar (Brown); building another nest, same ht., edge of clearing near Leticia, late July–mid-Sept (J. V. Remsen); eggs bluish white (Brown and Amadon 1968).
**Status and habitat:** Fairly common to common resident in humid forest, forest borders, taller second growth, and more extensive gallery woodland; wanders over open areas. Mid. American birds notably migratory; flocks up to several hundred early Feb–mid-Mar and early Aug–late Sept in Panama, and apparently absent there mid-Oct–Jan (Ridgely 1976).

A few small migrating groups noted in Colombia including 60 + over PN Puracé, 16 July 1975 (R. Ridgely), and 8 on 11 Aug 1978 (Hilty).
**Range:** To 2600m. Throughout at least as wanderer or migrant (scarce or absent in drier open regions). Breeds from e Mexico to w Ecuador, n Argentina, and se Brazil. Some or all Mid. American birds migratory.

## 10. MISSISSIPPI KITE

*Ictinia mississippiensis*
**Identification:** 14″ (36cm). Unusually long pointed wings; rather long, square-tipped tail. *Short legs blackish.* Dark gray above, plain gray below; *head paler, more pearl gray* (looks whitish at a distance); tail black (no bands). In flight *wings dark gray with contrasting pale gray inner secondaries.* Imm.: slaty above, more or less streaked whitish; below whitish, *heavily streaked rusty brown*; under wing coverts usually with some rufous edging; tail black with 3 whitish bands and narrow white tip.
**Similar species:** Under ideal conditions ad. in flight could be told from more numerous Plumbeous Kite (9) by absence of rufous in wings, pale inner secondaries, and all-black tail (these marks seldom unequivocal in flight). When perched, look for blackish (not orange) legs and paler head in contrast to back. Imm.: may not be separable in field, but Mississippi has wide rufous brown (not dusky) streaks below and is browner above.
**Status and habitat:** Apparently a rare migrant; 2 specimens: 1 an imm. from a flock of about 30, 17 Oct 1972, 30 km nw Bogotá (Torres 1975); 1 an imm. without data (Blake 1977). Flock of about 200 seen in Nov at edge of Barranquilla (Dugand *in* Meyer de Schauensee and Phelps 1978). In Panama reliable sightings of flocks and individuals, suggest s movement in Oct, n movement mid-Mar–mid-Apr, in both periods migrating later than Plumbeous Kite (Ridgely 1976).
**Range:** Breeds in c and s US; winters to Paraguay (Oct–Feb) and n Argentina (Jan). Wintering range and migratory routes not well known, but some known to move through C America and Colombia.

## 11. CRANE-HAWK

*Geranospiza caerulescens*     Pls. 4, III, Map 88
**Identification:** 17-20″ (43-51cm). Lanky with rounded wings, long tail, and *very long reddish orange legs.* Bill weak; cere and lores slaty; eyes red. *Mostly bluish slate with prom. white crescent on outer primaries* (mostly visible from below in flight); lower underparts often barred with white or buff; tail black with 2 broad white

bands and narrow white tip. In flight from below, wing linings gray finely barred white. Imm.: sim. to ad. but brownish; head more or less streaked white; underparts extensively mottled and barred chamois and white; white tail bands slightly wider. Double-jointed legs (tarsus) can bend 30° behind vertical. **Similar species:** When flying, in any plumage, note conspic. white crescent on primaries and very long reddish legs. Perched birds look small-headed and long-legged, then most resembling a black-hawk (27, 28), or Slate-colored Hawk (21). All of latter are more squat and robust; black-hawks have yellow cere and legs, Slate-colored has reddish cere and pale eyes. Also see Zone-tailed Hawk (44) and Slender-billed Kite (7), esp. imm. of latter. **Voice:** Usually quiet. Rarely a repeated whistle, *wheeoo* (J. V. Remsen). **Behavior:** Versatile. Active, agile, usually solitary, and notably catholic in diet. In woodland, perch mostly at midlevel or higher, where they scramble clumsily among branches, examine tree cavities, bromeliads, and even hang upside down momentarily. The long legs facilitate reaching into holes and crevices for prey. In more open terrain, beat with flap-and-glide flight over marshes and wetlands, perch on fence posts, or walk on ground. Ocas. soar like a buteo. **Breeding:** BC ♂, 7 July, se base Santa Marta Mts. (Carriker); 1 Panama nest, Jan (R. Ridgely); 7 in Guárico, Venez., 23 July–28 Sept (4 with eggs, 3 with downy chick; 2 eggs (Mader 1981). **Status and habitat:** Local but found in a wide var. of habitats from dry deciduous woodland to humid forest, tall second growth, swampy woodland, gallery forest, and savanna with marshes and pools. Often near water. Seldom common, though found in nos. w and s of Fundación, Magdalena (R. Ridgely). **Range:** To about 500m. Pacific coast s to Baudó Mts., (southward?), lower Magdalena Val. (Atlántico) e to w Guajira (Ríohacha), and s to lower Cauca Val. (Río Nechí); formerly to upper Cauca and upper Magdalena Vals.; e of Andes from Norte de Santander (Cúcuta) and n Arauca (sight, Nov 1978—W. McKay and J. Jorgenson) s to s Meta (Macarena Mts.), Vaupés (sight 1976—R. Ridgely), and Amazonas (Leticia); also Venez. bank of Río Meta opp. Vichada. Prob. spottily throughout e of Andes. W Mexico to w Ecuador and nw Peru; e of Andes s to n Argentina and Uruguay. **Note:** Incl. *G. nigra* (Blackish Crane-Hawk) of w Mexico to w Ecuador and nw Peru, and *G. caerulescens* (Gray Crane-Hawk) of n and e Colombia s to Amazonia.

[*Circus*: Harriers. Slender body, long narrow wings held above horizontal when gliding; long tail, small head, owllike facial ruff, and low buoyant quartering flight. Most with complicated plumages.]

## 12. NORTHERN HARRIER (MARSH HAWK)
*Circus cyaneus*

**Identification:** 18-21″ (46-53cm). Typical harrier shape. *Conspic. white rump* in both sexes. ♂: *mostly light gray with black wing tips*; lower breast and belly white lightly spotted and barred buff; tail light gray with broad black subterminal band and several narrow indistinct bars. In flight underside of wing white, primaries tipped black. ♀: mostly dark brown, *paler more buff on breast and belly*, and streaked darker on breast. In flight underside of wings and tail barred buff and dusky. Imm.: like ♀ but more uniform rufous below. **Similar species:** Note numerous confusing plumages of Colombian harriers. This sp. and Cinereous Harrier (the 2 most sim.) are sympatric in Bogotá area in n winter (poss. elsewhere). ♂ from ♂ Cinereous Harrier (13) thus: slightly paler overall, breast and belly mainly white (not boldly barred rufous and white). ♀ essentially like normal phase imm. and ♀ Long-winged Harrier (14) but buff (not whitish) below, underwing ground color buff (not brownish gray), and flight feathers (from above) uniformly barred dusky and brown *without gray areas*. Field separation of the various imm. harriers is difficult or often impossible. Imm. Northern on average is darker and more rufescent below than imm. Cinereous and lacks latter's rufescent nuchal collar. From imm. Long-winged by *lack* of contrasting gray areas on flight feathers from above. **Behavior:** Industrious quartering flight, usually close to ground, is characterized by short buoyant glides and much tilting. In N America flies higher in migration, often soaring. Essentially silent on wintering grounds. **Status and habitat:** Very rare winter resident or visitant, Nov–Mar. Most records Nov–Dec (but none recent) to open grassy or marshy areas. **Range:** To 2600m. Scattered recs. from n Chocó (lower Atrato Val.), mid. and upper Cauca Val., and Sabana de Bogotá. Breeds in N America and Old World; American birds winter mostly from s US to Panama; casually to Colombia, once Venez.

## 13. CINEREOUS HARRIER
*Circus cinereus*                    Pl. III, Map 89

**Identification:** 17-20″ (43-50cm). Typical harrier shape. *Conspic. white rump* in both sexes. ♂ very like ♂ Northern Harrier but differs as follows: *lower breast and belly boldly and coarsely barred rufous* (instead of a few faint buff spots and bars). ♀: upperparts, head, throat, and upper breast blackish brown, sometimes with some white mottling from crown to shoulders; *lower underparts and tail as in ♂*, latter more prom. barred. Underwings barred dusky. Imm.: sim. to ♀ above but darker, prom. buff to rufescent nuchal collar; below whitish heavily streaked dusky or rufous.

**Similar species:** Ad. of either sex from other Colombian harriers by bold rufous and white barring on lower breast and belly. Imm. much like other imm. and ♀ harriers (12, 14) but with buff or rufous collar.

**Behavior:** As in other harriers.

**Breeding:** In Chile, nest in grass or on platform in marsh; 3-4 pale blue eggs (Johnson 1965).

**Status and habitat:** Uncertain. Apparently very local in open grassland and marshy terrain in highlands.

**Range:** 1700-2600m in E Andes from s Boyacá to Sabana de Bogotá in Cundinamarca. 2200-3000m in mts. of Nariño and w Putumayo (Volcán Cumbal; Lago La Cocha; Sibundoy Val.). Colombia s in Andes to Tierra del Fuego; se Brazil. Paraguay, and Argentina.

## 14. LONG-WINGED HARRIER
*Circus buffoni*                    Pl. III, Map 90

**Identification:** 18-24″ (46-61cm). Typical harrier shape. Plumage notably var.: *all show white rump and gray primaries barred dusky from above.* Light phase ♂: *upperparts and sides of head black with white forehead and eyestripe; below white with contrasting black chest band;* lower underparts faintly spotted black; tail with several light gray and black bands and narrow white tip. In flight, underwing pale brownish gray barred black, primaries tipped black. Light phase ♀: like ♂ but brownish above; facial markings and throat buff; breast and abdomen lightly streaked brown; thighs tawny. Dark phase (both sexes): body sooty black, browner below; rump barred white; *facial markings, underwings, and tail as in respective sex of light phase.* Imm.: like light phase ♀ but more broadly streaked below. Dark phase imm. like dark phase ad., but *thighs and under tail coverts rufous;* rest of underparts sooty streaked whitish.

**Similar species:** Ad. ♂ (either phase) and dark phase ♀ are distinctive. Light phase ♀ and light phase imm. would be very difficult to separate with certainty from other harriers, but *ranges not known to overlap*, and all phases show *distinct grayish areas on flight feathers from*

*above* (lacking in ♀ and imm. Northern Harrier and imm. Cinereous Harrier, 12, 13). Heavily streaked dark phase imm. best told by rufous on lower underparts.

**Voice:** Usually quiet. Alarm a fairly rapid ser. of high sandpiperlike notes (ffrench 1973).

**Behavior:** Like other harriers, quarters low and buoyantly over savannas, pastures, and wetlands; frequently hovers before pouncing on prey.

**Breeding:** One carrying grass in Aug, ne Meta (Carimagua), may have been building nest (S. Furniss). June nest, Trinidad; 2 bluish white eggs (ffrench 1973).

**Status and habitat:** Local in grassland, wet pastures, and marshy areas. Fairly common in ne Meta (S. Furniss), less numerous in w Meta, rare in Cauca Val.

**Range:** 300-1000m. W of Andes in mid. Cauca Val. (1000m) in Valle; e of Andes from Arauca to s Meta (Macarena Mts.) and e to extreme ne Meta (Carimagua—S. Furniss). Doubtless Vichada. Colombia and n Venez. e to Guianas; Trinidad and Tobago; e Brazil s of Amazon s to e Bolivia and s Argentina, rarely c Chile.

## 15. SHARP-SHINNED HAWK
*Accipiter striatus*              Pls. 5, II, Map 91

**Identification:** ♂ 11-12″ (28-30cm); ♀ 12-13″ (30-33cm). Typical *Accipiter* shape, but plumage var. Uniform dark gray above; tail blackish with 4 gray bands (usually 3 visible); *thighs rufous* (except melanistic phase); underparts var., but usually with whitish throat finely streaked darker, and remaining underparts cinnamon rufous more or less barred and spotted white, but var. to almost completely white with only a few dusky shaft streaks, to faintly barred on sides, to largely chestnut barred grayish white (latter mostly e of Andes). A melanistic phase (known from Cauca Val.) is mostly slate gray with paler abdomen and thighs. Imm.: dark brown above, streaked brown and white below, and with *rufous thighs.* Melanistic imm.: dark brown above, heavily streaked chestnut and brown below.

**Similar species:** Pale individuals closely resemble larger Bicolored Hawk (19) but are almost always whitish below (not gray) with some streaking or barring. Also see Double-toothed Kite (8, different shape), Tiny Hawk (17, smaller, no rufous thighs), and imm. Semicollared Hawk (16, cinnamon collar). Melanistic birds are smaller than other all "gray" hawks in Colombia. Imm. is only "streaked" *Accipiter* other than rare imm. Cooper's Hawk.

**Voice:** Sometimes noisy; a high-pitched (esp. ♂) cackling *qui qui qui* like other *Accipiter*, rapidly repeated.

**Behavior:** An inconspic. woodland hawk. Perches concealed in foliage, then dashes through dense cover in pursuit of small birds. Occas. soars briefly.

**Breeding:** BC ♀, 13 June, se Antioquia (Carriker).

**Status and habitat:** Uncommon to fairly common resident of humid forest borders, woodlots, and brushy second growth with openings. More numerous at higher el.

**Range:** 900-2700m (sightings to 3400m, PN Puracé—Hilty; J. Silliman). Santa Marta Mts., all 3 Andean ranges and Macarena Mts. (*ventralis*). Breeds from N America to Nicaragua (*velox*); winters to w Panama. All S American forms are resident; nw Venez. s in Andes to n Argentina; Paraguay to se Brazil.

## 16. SEMICOLLARED HAWK
*Accipiter collaris*  Map 92

**Identification:** 12-14″ (30-36cm). Rare. Closely resembles Tiny Hawk. Eyes yellow. Brownish black above, *broken whitish collar on hindneck* (not always conspic.); sides of head *crisply mottled* black and white; throat white; *rest of underparts conspic. barred brownish black* (bars rather wide); tail dusky brown with 4-5 broad gray bands. Brown phase imm. Like ad. above but duller and with incomplete rufous collar (indistinct); throat white, rest of underparts buffy white coarsely barred pale rufous. Rufous phase imm.: dark rufous above with conspic. cinnamon nuchal collar; throat whitish, rest of underparts tawny coarsely barred rufous brown (bars broad).

**Similar species:** From similar Tiny Hawk (17) by decidedly larger size, whitish or tawny collar on hindneck, wider barring below, and sharply mottled black and white cheeks (instead of pale gray). Also see other larger forest-falcons (pp 117 and 118). Imm. from Sharp-shinned Hawk (15) in any phase by rufous or cinnamon nuchal collar.

**Breeding:** BC ♂, 28 Jan, Puracé, Cauca (Carriker).

**Status and habitat:** Little known anywhere in range. Specimens are from regions of humid or wet forest averaging higher in el. than allied Tiny Hawk.

**Range:** 600-1800m. Known from Pacific slope in Antioquia, Valle, and Cauca, C Andes in Tolima and Cauca (Puracé), E Andes in n Norte de Santander, Santa Marta Mts., and e slope E Andes in w Meta (Río Guatiquía). Venez. (once), w Ecuador, and Peru (once).

## 17. TINY HAWK
*Accipiter superciliosus*  Pl. 5, Map 93

**Identification:** ♂ 8-9″ (20-23cm); ♀ 10-11″ (25-28cm). *Pint-sized forest Accipiter* with usual shape of genus. Eyes red; cere and legs yellow. Slaty gray above, crown blacker; *underparts white finely barred throughout with dark gray except on throat*; tail blackish with 3-4 (usually 3 visible) grayish bands. Rufous phase: sim. but rufous brown above, indistinctly barred dusky, reddish buff barred reddish brown below. Normal phase imm.: dusky brown above; buff below finely barred cinnamon; tail with 6-7 dusky brown and ashy brown bands. Rufous phase imm.: chestnut barred black above, tail brighter rufous, duskier on head, buff barred rufous brown below.

**Similar species:** Closely resembles its slightly larger and rarer upper el. replacement, the Semicollared Hawk (16), but latter has white or tawny nuchal collar and is more coarsely barred below. Also see much larger Lined (p 117) and Barred Forest Falcon (p 116).

**Voice:** High, thin, weak *krie-rie-rie-rie* (Brown and Amadon 1968); seldom heard.

**Behavior:** Rather secretive and infrequently seen little predator that "still hunts" on perch from undergrowth to the canopy and occas. even perches fairly exposed high in canopy; at times changes perches in quick succession working through thicker lower growth (Hilty). Thought to specialize on hummingbirds to some extent (Stiles 1978).

**Breeding:** 2 BC ♂♂, Feb, Chocó, BC ♀, 3 Oct, Norte de Santander (Carriker); 1 breaking off small dead twigs at forest edge, early Apr, Anchicayá Val., 800m (Hilty); Feb, Panama nest (R. Ridgely); usurped abandoned *Busarellus* nest in Venez.; 1 white egg (Hewitt *in* Wetmore 1965a).

**Status and habitat:** Uncommon to rare (easily overlooked) in humid and wet forest, forest borders of young to old second growth, and younger *várzea*.

**Range:** To 1500m. Prob. forested areas throughout. Rec. from entire Pacific coast, e in humid lowlands n of Andes to mid. Magdalena Val. in ne Antioquia (Remedios); n slope Santa Marta Mts. (to 1500m); e of Andes from w Meta (Villavicencio; Macarena Mts.) and the Orinoco (Maipures) s to w Caquetá and Leticia (sightings—J. V. Remsen; Hilty). Nicaragua spottily to w Ecuador, e Peru, n Bolivia, n Argentina, Paraguay, and s Brazil.

## 18. COOPER'S HAWK
*Accipiter cooperi*

**Identification:** ♂ 15-17″ (38-43cm); ♀ 17-20″ (43-51cm). Cere and legs yellow; eyes red. Dark bluish gray above (cap darker—♂), cinnamon buff below more or less evenly barred white; under tail coverts white; tail crossed by 3-4 black bands and tipped white; closed tail *usually* slightly rounded at tip. Imm.: brown above, dull white below, heavily streaked brown; otherwise as in ad.

**Similar species:** Resident *ventralis* subsp. of Sharp-shinned Hawk (15) is smaller and var. below but always with solid rufous (not barred) thighs; tail *usually* more square-tipped.

**Status and habitat:** Accidental; 1 old rec. of a bird banded at Charleswood, Manitoba, Canada, and taken in E Andes in s Cundinamarca (Colonia Agricola de Sumapaz), 1 Feb.

**Range:** Breeds from s Canada to n Mexico; winters s rarely to Costa Rica.

## 19. BICOLORED HAWK
*Accipiter bicolor*          Pl. 5, Map 94
**Identification:** ♂ 14″ (36cm); ♀ 17″ (43cm). Rather long tail, roundish at tip. Cere and legs yellow, eyes orange. *Slate gray above*, blacker on head, wings, and tail; latter with 3 narrow ashy white bands and tip; *below light gray* (occas. dark gray) *with conspic. rufous thighs.* Imm.: blackish brown above, usually with narrow indistinct buff or whitish collar, underparts usually buffy white, but varying from whitish to occas. rufous, thighs normally darker or mottled rufous.

**Similar species:** Distinctive ad. likely confused only with pale individuals of *ventralis* subsp. of Sharp-shinned Hawk (15), almost all of which usually show some barring below. Caution should be used in identifying the notably var. imm.; imm. Sharp-shinned (*ventralis*) is smaller, faintly barred below, and has solid rufous thighs (rufous absent or mottled on imm. Bicolored); ad. Gray-bellied Hawk (20) is larger (esp. ♀), usually paler (whitish or pale gray below), cheeks usually darker and thighs never rufous; buffy and pale phase ad. Collared Forest-Falcons (p 118) have longer graduated tails and a black mark protruding onto cheek; Slaty-backed Forest-Falcon (p 117) is always whitish below (never rufous on thighs) and lacks collar.

**Voice:** Scolding *cak-cak-cak-cak* near nest (Friedmann and Smith 1955); unbirdlike, long throat-clearing groan (Slud 1964).

**Behavior:** Not well known. Apparently rather secretive but reported bold and rapacious in pursuit of prey, chiefly birds. "Still hunt" from perch on inner branches, then dash out after prey, or fly low and quietly through lower growth.

**Breeding:** BC ♀, 10 May, sw Huila; BC ♂ and laying ♀ 19 Feb, lower Cauca Val. (Carriker). Tree nest, eggs, Guárico, Venez., 9 May (Mader 1981); small leaf-lined, cup-shaped nest near

end of branch 12m up; 2 white eggs with slight rusty streaks (Wetmore 1965a).

**Status and habitat:** Apparently rare (few recs.). Dry to humid regions in open or thinned forest, forest borders, gallery woodland, and second growth. More recs. from drier parts of Santa Marta area and Magdalena Val. (lowlands) than elsewhere.

**Range:** To 2000m. Prob. throughout; known from nw Chocó (Río Juradó) spottily ne to Santa Marta region and s to n end C Andes, s Tolima, and n Huila in Magdalena Val., and once in upper Cauca Val. (Popayán); e base of Andes from Arauca to Caquetá e to ne Guainía (Pto. Inírida) and Vaupés (Mitú). E Mexico spottily to Tierra del Fuego.

## 20. GRAY-BELLIED HAWK
*Accipiter poliogaster*          Pl. 5, Map 95
**Identification:** 17-20″ (43-51cm). Large *Accipiter* with contrasting upper and underparts. Cere and legs yellow, eyes reddish orange. Cap blackish; sides of head and upperparts slaty black (varying to gray on cheeks); below light gray to grayish white incl. unbarred under wings; throat and under tail coverts white; tail blackish with 3 broad gray bars and narrow white tip. Very different imm. looks like a miniature of Ornate Hawk-Eagle; *crown black*; rest of upperparts blackish with *broad chestnut nuchal collar continuing onto sides of head and to sides of chest*; white throat bordered by *black malar stripe*; remaining underparts white with coarse *broken black barring*; tail as in ad.; eyes yellow.

**Similar species:** Ad. much like Slaty-backed Forest-Falcon (p 117), but tail shorter and squarish (not graduated), more distinct dark-capped appearance, sides of head usually much darker, the blackish reaching to sides of throat, no extensive bare yellow facial area, and legs shorter. In flight, wing linings and flight feathers more or less unbarred (not conspic. barred on flight feathers). Imm. is a half-sized version of Ornate Hawk-Eagle (49) but lacks latter's pointed crest and has bare (not feathered) legs.

**Behavior:** In Vaupés 1 bird about 12m up inside forest near a clearing allowed close approach (R. Ridgely).

**Status and habitat:** Rare and little known throughout its extensive range; known from humid lowland forest, riparian forest borders, and isolated patches of dense woodland. Poss. migrant from s; all Colombian recs. are in early austral winter, as follows: 7 and 10 Mar, 26 Apr, and sight rec. early June. Thought to be migratory, at least in s part of range (Wattel 1973).

**Range:** To 500m. Once from Santa Marta area

(near Bonda), once in Cesar Val.; e of Andes in s Meta (Macarena Mts.) and El Dorado, Vaupés (sight, June 1976—R. Ridgely). Venez. (Burgua, Táchira, Río Orinoco opp. Vichada) e to Guyana; e Ecuador, ne Peru (Pasco), Amazonian Brazil e of Ríos Negro and Madeira, and s to ne Bolivia, n Argentina, and Paraguay.

[*Leucopternis*: Buteonine with broad wings and usually broad tails. Unlike buteos, "still hunt," seldom soar (except 23 and 26), and prey mostly on reptiles and amphibians.]

### 21. SLATE-COLORED HAWK
*Leucopternis schistacea*      Pls. 4, III, Map 96
**Identification:** 16-17″ (41-43cm). Chunky med.-sized hawk with *conspic. reddish orange cere and legs.* Eyes yellow. Entirely *dark bluish slate,* incl. underside of wings; tail slaty black with a *single median white band* and narrow white tip. Imm.: sim. but lower underparts and underwings barred white; tail sometimes with a 2d white band.
**Similar species:** Slender-billed Kite (7) has very slender sharply hooked bill and squarish tail with no bands; rare black phase Hook-billed Kite (2) is black (not bluish slate), with heavier bill and greenish facial skin; larger black-hawks (27, 28) are black with yellow ceres and legs.
**Voice:** Call a loud, piercing whistle, *wheeeeeeeeer,* minor key and downslurred (J. V. Remsen).
**Behavior:** A bird of flooded backwaters, swamps, and forested streams. Usually very unsuspicious and perches in open along borders of watercourses from fairly high to low (sometimes very low or even on stream banks). Drops on prey at edge of water, but avoids diving directly into water. Apparently seldom or never soars.
**Status and habitat:** Common along sluggish *várzea* forest streams, swampy lagoons, and rivers, occas. swampy gallery forest or tree-bordered ponds in the s portions of llanos. Thinly spread along blackwater rivers of Guainía and Vaupés.
**Range:** To 500m. E of Andes from w Meta (e of Villavicencio) and the Orinoco region (sight, Pto. Inírida, Sept 1978—Hilty and M. Robbins; also rec. just across Orinoco at San Fernando de Atabapo, Amazonas, Venez.) southward. Sw Venez. and e Colombia s to n Bolivia and Amazonian Brazil. Explorama Camp, Peru

### 22. PLUMBEOUS HAWK
*Leucopternis plumbea*      Pl. 4, Map 97
**Identification:** 14-15″ (36-38cm). Small and chunky with short, broad, rounded wings. Cere, lores, and legs orange; eyes orange to red.

*Entirely dark bluish slate;* wings and tail blackish; *1 median white tail band.* Imm.: flanks, belly, and thighs barred and spotted white, wing linings with black barring, tail often with a 2d or partial 2d band.
**Similar species:** From any other all dark Pacific coast raptor by combination of orange cere and legs and white under wing coverts; cf. esp. dark phase Hook-billed Kite (2), Slender-billed Kite (7), Plumbeous Kite (9), much larger Crane-Hawk (11), and black-hawks (27, 28).
**Behavior:** Not well known in Colombia though apparently much like Semiplumbeous Hawk. May perch on high exposed branch in early morning but otherwise mainly at low to mod. hts. inside forest; does not soar (R. Ridgely).
**Status and habitat:** Apparently rare; known from a few scattered humid and wet forest localities. Mostly lowlands and foothills; in nw Ecuador favors foothills 200-800 m (R. Ridgely)
**Range:** To 700-800m. Pacific coast (no Valle recs.) and n end of W Andes in upper Sinú region (Sniá. de Abibe). W Panama to extreme nw Peru.

### 23. BARRED (PRINCE OR BLACK-CHESTED) HAWK
*Leucopternis princeps*      Pls. 4, VII, Map 98
**Identification:** 21-23″ (53-58cm). Buteonine shape with very broad wings and noticeably short tail. Base of bill, cere and legs yellow. *Entire upperparts, head, throat, and chest slaty black; breast and lower underparts white finely barred black* (at a distance looks unbarred grayish white); tail black with 1 median white band, traces of others on underside. In flight black head and chest contrast sharply with pale underparts and underwings.
**Similar species:** A large stately hawk easily told by contrasting underparts. At high el. see Black-chested Buzzard-Eagle (32; no known overlap).
**Voice:** Often noisy when soaring; a screaming *Spizaetus*-like *wheeyoor* 1 to several times, sometimes followed by a rapid ser. of *weep*'s, often given during playful looping dives (Slud 1964; Hilty).
**Behavior:** Solitary birds or groups of 3-4 soar majestically; most frequently aloft midmorning on sunny days. "Still hunt" from perches within forest, sometimes low. Apparently eat mainly reptiles.
**Status and habitat:** Local. Humid or wet heavily forested foothills and lower slopes. Seldom on coastal plain. Can be found reg. in Anchicayá Val.
**Range:** 50-1800m (mostly 300-1200m). Spot-

tily on Pacific slope from near Quibdó, Chocó southward; mid. Magdalena Val. (w slope E Andes in Santander) and head of Magdalena Val. in Huila (photo, PN Cueva de los Guácharos—P. Gertler). Prob. e slope E Andes at s end. Costa Rica to n Ecuador (both w and e of Andes).

### 24. SEMIPLUMBEOUS HAWK
*Leucopternis semiplumbea*          Pl. 4, Map 99
**Identification:** 13-14″ (33-36cm). Small and chunky with short rounded wings. *Cere, base of bill, and legs reddish orange*; eyes yellow. *Entire upperparts slaty gray*, incl. sides of head to well below eyes; *white below, tail blackish with 1 median white tail band* (2d semiconcealed at base). Underside of wings mostly white. Imm.: sim. but breast with a few dusky streaks, tail with 2-3 white bands.
**Similar species:** Superficially like Slaty-backed Forest-Falcon (p 117) and pale phase Short-tailed Hawk (38); the former with much longer broader tail, 3 narrow tail bands (not 1), and yellow cere; the latter, also with yellow cere, has paler, obscurely barred tail and is almost always seen soaring. Also see much larger Gray-headed Kite (1).
**Voice:** *Spizaetus*-like *ooeé ooeé ooeé ooeé*, but thinner (Slud 1964); a long clear whistled *kiak er-eeeeeeeeeeer*, 1st note faint (Brown and Amadon 1968).
**Behavior:** A sedentary forest hawk that is usually seen perched low to high inside forest; frequently on high exposed branches in early morning, well below canopy level at other times. Remarkably tame though usually alone, unobtrusive, and easily overlooked. Like several others of the genus, rarely or never soars. Flies with rapid shallow wing beats, occas. a short glide.
**Breeding:** BC ♂, 19 Feb, Chocó (Carriker). In Costa Rica, building nest in Jan, forest canopy (Slud 1964).
**Status and habitat:** Fairly common in wet forest, forest borders, and tall second growth. Reg. along Río Calima road e of Buenaventura.
**Range:** To 1000m (usually lowlands). Pacific coast, e along humid n base of W and C Andes, and s in mid. Magdalena Val. to Santander (w of Bucaramanga). Honduras to nw Ecuador.

### 25. BLACK-FACED HAWK
*Leucopternis melanops*          Pl. V, Map 100
**Identification:** 15-17″ (38-43cm). Miniature replica of White Hawk. *Cere orange.* Head, neck, and entire underparts white; *crown and hindneck finely streaked black*; lores black; remaining upperparts black; upper back and scapulars

broadly edged and spotted white; *tail black with a single median white band* and narrow white tip. Imm.: white of ad. tinged buffy, streaks on head reduced; tail with 2 white bands and narrow tip.
**Similar species:** Smaller than White Hawk (26) with much more crown streaking (usually), orange (not gray) cere, and tail black with a single median white band, not broad white tip and base (cf. *albicollis* race of White Hawk).
**Behavior:** Unlike White Hawk, rarely or never soars. In Guyana reported to frequent mangroves and river border thickets where usually perches low and seldom in open (Smooker). Rec. food mostly reptiles.
**Breeding:** BC ♂, 28 Apr, upper Orinoco, Venez. (Friedmann 1948).
**Status and habitat:** Known from only 2 humid forest localities in Colombia; apparently favors dense cover along river banks and watercourses.
**Range:** To 500m. Known from w Caquetá (Río Bodoquero s of Florencia) and w Putumayo (Pto. Umbría). E Peru, e Ecuador, and e Colombia e to s Venez. (incl. upper Orinoco opp. Guainía, Colombia), the Guianas, and Amazonian Brazil mostly n of Río Amazon (incl. Cucuhy near se tip of Guainía, Colombia).

### 26. WHITE HAWK
*Leucopternis albicollis*          Pl. V, Ill. 25, Map 101
**Identification:** 18-22″ (46-56cm). Ample rounded wings and broad tail. *Cere gray.* 3 Colombian subspp. (amt. of white var.). Entirely *white*; wings from above mostly black with white edgings and *white shoulders*; *broad black subterminal tail band* (*costaricensis*). Or sim., but shoulders and upper back also black with white edgings; crown and nape spotted black (*williaminae*). Or entirely white; wings (from above) and upper back solid black, only shoul-

25. WHITE HAWK (*costaricensis* race)

ders edged white; *tail mostly black, base and terminal band white (albicollis)*. In flight from below in all plumages mostly white with black lores, black wing tips, and black tail band. Imm.: much like ad.; crown often streaked dark.

**Similar species:** See smaller but very sim. Black-faced Hawk (25). Other "black and white" hawks are differently proportioned, all with longer tails and several black and white tail bands.

**Voice:** When soaring a loud, husky scream *shreeeeerr*.

**Behavior:** A strikingly patterned hawk, usually seen alone or in pairs wheeling low over humid forest, less often high. Perch low or high but frequently near or along forest borders, where they "still hunt" for reptilian prey, mainly snakes. Often lethargic and easily approached.

**Breeding:** Panama nest, 9 Mar (Chapman *in* Willis and Eisenmann 1979). A Mar nest, atop bromeliad high in tree, Trinidad; 1 bluish white egg marked brown (Herklots 1961).

**Status and habitat:** Apparently very local in humid forest and forest borders, perhaps occas. drier forest of Carib. region; mostly lowlands and foothills. Fairly common in Orinoco region of ne Guainía. Status elsewhere uncertain.

**Range:** To 1400m. Panama border s on Pacific coast to Anchicayá Val. (few recs.; *costaricensis*); upper Sinú Val. e to Atlántico, Santa Marta region (rare), and Perijá Mts. E base of E Andes in Casanare, prob. s to Meta (*williaminae*); s Meta (Macarena Mts.) to w Caquetá, ne Guainía (sightings, Pto. Inírida, Sept 1978— Hilty and M. Robbins), and presum. southward (*albicollis*). S Mexico locally to e Bolivia and Amazonian Brazil. Trinidad.

**Note:** Gray-mantled Hawk (*L. occidentalis*), of w Ecuador (Pichincha) to Peruvian border, may occur n to w Nariño, or allied White Hawk may occur s to this region. Formerly considered a race of White Hawk, it differs from Pacific coast race (*costaricensis*) of latter in entire upperparts plumbeous black incl. crown, sides of head, hindneck, and back; hindneck marked with white, white rump dotted black.

### 27. COMMON BLACK-HAWK
*Buteogallus anthracinus*     Pl. IV, Map 102
**Identification:** 17-21″ (43-53cm). Very broad wings and short tail. *Cere, lores, and legs yellow.* Mostly black with *1 median white tail band and narrow white tip.* In flight from below shows a small whitish patch at base of primaries (more conspic. on Pacific coast birds, some of which show rufous patch). Imm.: blackish brown above with some buff markings on head and

indistinct buff eyestripe; below deep buff streaked and blotched dusky (streaks formed by tear-shaped spots); thighs barred black; tail buff crossed by about 5-8 narrow dark bars and broader subterminal band. An occas. pale subad. plumage occurs, which is mostly clay to buffy clay, esp. on head, which is finely and faintly streaked darker.

**Similar species:** Much like Great Black-Hawk (28), which differs as follows: somewhat larger size (broader-winged), basal half of tail white, less yellow on bill (base of bill black), and legs noticeably longer (in hand tarsus longer than 110mm vs less than 100mm). Imm. even more sim. and often not separable: Great Black-Hawk usually has more tail bars (10-14 vs 5-8). Also compare ad. with dark phase Hook-billed Kite (2), Plumbeous Hawk (22), Slate-colored Hawk (21), Crane-Hawk (11), dark phase Short-tailed Hawk (38), and Solitary Eagle (29).

**Voice:** The call, quite unlike the harsh scream of Great Black-Hawk, is a rapid ser. of "spinking," whistled notes (Slud 1964) often given when soaring.

**Behavior:** single birds or pairs, occas. 3's are more often seen aloft soaring than perched. Often hunt from a small tree or low perch. esp. for crabs. Walk on ground frequently.

**Breeding:** BC ♀, Jan, n Antioquia (Carriker); brancher, 4 Aug, PN Tayrona (Hilty). Nesting in Panama Jan–Mar; bulky stick structures usually high in mangroves (Wetmore 1965a); normally 1 pale blue egg, some marked dark (ffrench 1973).

**Status and habitat:** Fairly common in mangroves, tidal flats, riparian woodland, and along larger streams and rivers of the Carib.; only mangroves on Pacific coast (few recs.).

**Range:** To 500m. Gulf of Urabá e on Carib. coast and in lowlands to Guajira and s to n end of Snía. San Lucas to n Huila; Pacific coast (Nuquí; Guapí), and Gorgona Isl.; locally along e base of Andes(?) from Norte de Santander to s Meta (Macarena Mts.). Sw US to nw Peru and coastal Guyana. Trinidad, Lesser Antilles.

**Note:** Pacific coast birds from Mexico to Peru are sometimes regarded as a distinct sp. *B. subtilus* (Mangrove Black-Hawk). Differ in virtual confinement to beach scrub and mangroves and in rufous markings at base of secondaries and inner primaries.

### 28. GREAT BLACK-HAWK
*Buteogallus urubitinga*     Pl. IV, Map 103
**Identification:** 22-25″ (56-64cm). Very broad wings and rather short tail. *Cere and legs yellow;* lores yellow (usually) or slaty. Entirely black with *basal half of tail and upper tail coverts white,*

narrow tail tip white; thighs uniform black. In flight from below shows small whitish patch at base of outer primaries (less obvious than on Common Black-Hawk). Imm.: sim. to imm. Common Black-Hawk but larger and tail with more dusky bands (10-14 vs 5-8).

**Similar species:** Very sim. to smaller Common Black-Hawk (see 27). Much larger and rarer Solitary Eagle (29) can be difficult to separate. It differs as follows: greater size, proportionally broader and longer wings, longer attenuated primaries (usually bend up at tips when soaring like those of condor), shorter tail (barely protrudes in flight), single median white tail band, overall bluish slate plumage (obvious from above at a distance), and more projecting aquiline head in flight; up close an inconspic. bushy crest and no whitish area at base of outer primaries.

**Voice:** Perched or soaring a high-pitched whistled scream *wheeeeeeeuur.*

**Behavior:** Much like Common Black-Hawk. Soars frequently though seen perched more often.

**Breeding:** Juv., 4 June, Carraipía, Guajira (Carriker). In Guárico, Venez., 1 nest with egg in palm, 28 Aug (Mader 1981). Panama nests Mar–Apr, well up in trees near rivers or marshes (Wetmore 1965a).

**Status and habitat:** Uncommon in forest borders, riparian and swampy woodland, mangroves, and savanna with patches of forest. Often but not invariably near water and much more a bird of interior than mainly coastal Common Black-Hawk.

**Range:** To 1000m. From Panama border s on Pacific to Baudó Mts. (Río Baudó), and from Gulf of Urabá region e across Carib. lowlands and Santa Marta region to Guajira; formerly Cauca Val. in Valle (no recent recs.); throughout e of Andes (*urubitinga*). N Mexico s to Bolivia, n Argentina, and Uruguay; w Ecuador and nw Peru. Trinidad.

**Note:** The n subsp. of Great Black-Hawk (*B. u. ridgwayi*) from n Mexico s to c Darien, Panama, may wander to extreme nw Chocó. It differs in having tail black with white upper tail coverts, 2 *white bands*, and narrow white tip; white barred thighs and slaty lores.

## 29. SOLITARY EAGLE
*Harpyhaliaetus solitarius*     Pl. IV, Map 104

**Identification:** 26-28″ (66-71cm). Large. *Very long broad wings and extremely short tail* (when soaring fanned tail hardly protrudes beyond trailing edge of wing). Cere, lores, and legs yellow. *Entirely dark slate gray to bluish slate with 1 median white tail band* and narrow white tip; inconspic. bushy occipital crest may be no-

ticeable at rest. In flight underwings all dark. Imm.: brownish black above with rufous edgings; sides of head and underparts buffy, heavily streaked, blotched, and mottled black, becoming *almost solid black on chest and thighs;* tail buffy gray mottled dusky and becoming blacker on terminal half. In flight from below wing linings mottled yellowish buff and dusky, flight feathers dark.

**Similar species:** Ad. easily confused with Great Black-Hawk (see 28). Imm. from imm. Great Black by greater size, more extensive black mottling below, esp. on chest and thighs (not spotted), and lack of prom. narrow tail barring.

**Voice:** When soaring, a piercing *pipipipipip* like Barred Hawk, and an arresting *yeep . yeep . yeep . yeep . yeep . yeep,* unlike screams of Great Black-Hawk (Slud 1964).

**Behavior:** As its name implies, usually alone, occas. in pairs, soaring heavily on flat wings at var. hts. over hill or mt. forest or in long glides down steep mt. vals. When seen perched, has been on rather high exposed bare branches.

**Breeding:** Juv., 28 June, Perijá Mts. (Carriker). Nests in w Mexico were very high in tall trees; prob. 1 egg (Harrison and Kiff 1977).

**Status and habitat:** Very local. Small nos. in dry to very humid forested foothills and lower slopes. Several sightings are from n slope of Santa Marta Mts. (Pueblito at 200m in PN Tayrona; Minca; San Lorenzo), and e slope E Andes at s end.

**Range:** 750-2200m (sighting at 200m). N slope of Santa Marta Mts., Perijá Mts., W Andes in Cauca (Munchique area), E Andes in w Caquetá above Florencia (sightings June 1975, Sept 1978—Hilty and M. Robbins). Presumed sightings away from Andean region (i.e., Leticia) will require specimen confirmation. Nw Mexico very locally s to n Venez. and in mts. s to Bolivia and nw Argentina.

## 30. SAVANNA HAWK
*Heterospizias meridionalis*     Pls. 4, IV, Map 105

**Identification:** 18-24″ (46-61cm). *Very long broad wings* (almost too large for size of bird) and short tail. Long yellow legs. *Mostly dull cinnamon rufous;* back tinged grayish; underparts narrowly and rather indistinctly barred dusky; rump and tail black, *single median white tail band* and white tip. In flight *wings mostly rufous* above and below; flight feathers tipped black. Imm.: dusky brown above with buff eyestripe and buff or white mottling on back and wings; below deep buff heavily mottled and marked dusky; shoulders and thighs usually with some rufous edging suggesting ad. pattern; tail barred but var. Older birds gradually acquire the rufous of ad.

**Similar species:** A large handsome hawk likely confused only with Black-collared Hawk (see 31).

**Voice:** A shrill *keeeeeeru*, infrequent.

**Behavior:** Soar reg., stoop on prey in flight or more frequently "still hunt" from low perch on tree, fence post, shrub, even the ground, and often walk on ground. Usually one of the most conspic. open country raptors; sometimes groups of several doz. (up to about 100 reported in w Meta—W. McKay) follow grass fires or agricultural implements, esp. plows.

**Breeding:** Nest, 8 Feb (R. Ridgely), 1 building nest, 6 Mar, w of Santa Marta Mts.; another incubating near Cartagena, 30 Mar (Brown). In Guárico, Venez., mainly Apr–Oct (79 nests), peaking in early wet season, June–Aug; nest usually low in top of small tree or palm; 1, rarely 2, white eggs (W. Mader).

**Status and habitat:** Drier ranchland and savanna with scattered trees. Common e of Andes, less numerous and local in Carib. region where sometimes even along seashore.

**Range:** Mainly below 1000m; rarely to 1800m. From e side of Gulf of Urabá e to Guajira, s formerly to upper Cauca Val. (no recent Cauca Val. recs.), to upper Magdalena Val. (Villavieja, n Huila), and e of Andes s to s Meta (Macarena Mts.) and Río Guaviare (s of Guaviare locally in pockets of savanna in e Guainía). W Panama s to n Argentina and Brazil.

### 31. BLACK-COLLARED HAWK

*Busarellus nigricollis*      Pls. 4, IV, Map 106

**Identification:** 18-20″ (46-51cm). Aquiline with long broad wings and very short fanned tail in flight. Heavy feet and legs bluish white. *Mostly bright cinnamon rufous with buffy white head and black crescent on upper chest*; tail narrowly barred rufous and black with broad black band near tip. In flight from below wing linings rufous, primaries and broad tips on secondaries black. Imm.: upperparts mottled rufous brown and dusky; head, neck, and throat whitish more or less streaked dusky; rest of underparts buffy white streaked and mottled blackish; *usually with traces of black crescent on chest*; tail as in ad. but duller. In flight from below outer third of wing blackish, remainder paler and mottled.

**Similar species:** Savanna Hawk (30) is mostly rufous, incl. head and underwing, but lacks black chest patch, and tail shows 1 or more prom. white bands. Imm.: usually shows enough ad. markings for recognition.

**Voice:** Ads. a protracted guttural croak, imm.

and ads. a reedy whistled scream, *wheeeeeah*, rising, then falling (J. V. Remsen).

**Behavior:** A rather unsuspicious "fishing hawk" usually seen perched stolidly in the open at med. hts. on a stub, bush, or tree overlooking water, esp. where there is floating vegetation. Fishes by dropping feet first into midst of floating vegetation or into shallow water near edges. A fine soarer and often seen cruising low over swampy or marshy terrain.

**Breeding:** BC ♀, Apr, Meta (Borrero 1955); Surinam nests, June–Sept; large stick platform 12-15m up in mangrove or tree at edge of swamp; 1 grayish white egg blotched brown (Haverschmidt 1968).

**Status and habitat:** Common but somewhat local in mangroves, freshwater marshes, swampy lagoons, and lakes with emergent or floating vegetation; in the llanos mostly around small pools with trees. Absent or very local in blackwater regions of the extreme east. Notably common in swampy, lagoon-filled river isls. on Río Amazon.

**Range:** To 500m. Lower Río Atrato (Río Truandó near Panama border) e locally across Carib. lowlands to Guajira; generally throughout e of Andes from Norte de Santander and Arauca s to Amazonas in suitable habitat (no Putumayo or Orinoco recs.). W and s Mexico s locally to e Bolivia and s Brazil.

### 32. BLACK-CHESTED BUZZARD-EAGLE

*Geranoaëtus melanoleucus*      Pls. IV, VII, Map 107

**Identification:** 24-27″ (61-69cm). Large chunky eagle-sized hawk. Wings long and extremely broad; tail short, wedge-shaped, scarcely protruding beyond wings in flight. Cere and legs yellow. *Entire upperparts slaty black with pale gray shoulders*; throat light gray *becoming slaty on chest*; remaining underparts white very finely barred black (barring not visible at a distance); tail black narrowly tipped white. In flight from below wing linings white, flight feathers blackish. Imm.: above like ad. but browner, somewhat mottled, no gray on shoulders and with pale superciliaries; below tawny buff spotted and streaked black on throat and chest, more barred on lower underparts; tail decidedly longer than in ad. and more prom. wedgeshaped, gray with numerous blackish bars. In flight from above base of primaries sometimes pale.

**Similar species:** Ad. easily told in cold highlands by broad-beamed shape, gray shoulders, and short tail. Dark chest and flight feathers recall Swainson's Hawk (40) but size and shape differ; imm. best told by wing and tail shape. See imm. Black-and-chestnut Eagle (50, bigger; protruding head), imm. Solitary Eagle (29, usually lower el.) and smaller Red-backed and Variable hawks (42, 43).

**Voice:** High reedy whistle.

**Behavior:** Almost always seen soaring high over rugged terrain, frequently in pairs. Soaring is graceful, heavy, and with much wheeling; wings held flat. Perch on rocks, ledges, or on ground, seldom in trees. Eat a var. of prey incl. carrion.

**Breeding:** Bulky twig nest on rock ledge or cliff; 2 white eggs (Johnson 1965).

**Status and habitat:** Local over humid mt. canyons, temperate forest, and lower paramo.

**Range:** 1600-3500m (mostly well above 2500m). E Andes s to s Cundinamarca; C Andes from Puracé area (Cauca and Huila) s through Nariño. Nw Venez. s in Andes to Tierra del Fuego. N Argentina, Paraguay, and e Brazil (Bahia) s to c Argentina.

**Note:** One seen over cactus scrub on Río Chama (600m), Lagunilla, Venez. (P. Alden), and may occas. descend low in arid habitat in Colombia. Normally found in dry regions in s Peru and Chile.

### 33. HARRIS' (BAY-WINGED) HAWK

*Parabuteo unicinctus*          Pl. 4, Map 108

**Identification:** 19-22″ (48-56cm). Rangier than *Buteo* and with longer, narrower tail. Mostly sooty brown with *prom. chestnut shoulders* and thighs; tail blackish; *rump, basal half of tail, and narrow tip white*. In flight from below *wing linings chestnut*, flight feathers black. Imm.: *resembles ad. above* but somewhat edged and streaked buff and white, chestnut shoulders fainter; below buffy white with var. amts. of dusky streaking and spotting, heaviest on breast and belly; from below tail grayish, much dingier than ad. and narrowly barred. In flight from below, wing linings pale rufous, base of primaries whitish.

**Similar species:** Lanky blackish appearance, chestnut shoulders, and white at base of tail are the marks. Imm. usually enough like ad. to be recognized; in flight from below resembles imm. Snail Kite, but wing linings pale rufous (not creamy buff mottled brown), less white shows at base of tail, and bill not strongly hooked.

**Behavior:** Usually "still hunts," stooping suddenly on prey from a perch; occas. pairs or 3's hunt cooperatively (W. Mader). Soars frequently, usually rather low; often perches low, sometimes on ground. Has been reported eating carrion.

**Breeding:** W of Popayán 2 nearly flying young in rock ledge nest, July; tree nest in upper Patía Val., late June (Lehmann 1960a).

**Status and habitat:** Dry to arid semiopen coun-

try and grassland with scattered trees; often near lagoons in arid regions. Common in Guajira, and locally in small nos. e across dry Carib. region.

**Range:** To 1500m. Carib. region from Cartagena area e to Guajira, s in drier open regions to upper Cauca Val. (no recent recs.), upper Patía Val. (status?), and the mid. Magdalena Val. to nw Santander; e Norte de Santander (sight, June 1980—Hilty and P. Hall). Prob. e of Andes in n llanos. Sw US spottily s to s Chile and central Argentina.

### 34. GRAY HAWK

*Buteo nitidus*          Pls. 4, 5, II, Map 109

**Identification:** 15-17″ (38-43cm). Small and compact. Light gray above, very obscurely barred darker gray; *white below, narrowly and closely barred gray; tail black, usually with 2 white bands* (sometimes a 3d concealed at base) and narrow white tip. In flight from below wing linings light gray barred darker gray, flight feathers paler. Imm.: dark brown above with var. amts. of buff and whitish edging; *head and underparts whitish to buffy white*; head mottled dusky; *chest and breast with numerous dropshaped dusky spots*, sometimes also with a suggestion of dusky malar; tail blackish with 4-6 narrow pale bands. In flight from above shows *prom. pale patches at base of primaries*.

**Similar species:** Ad. likely confused only with somewhat smaller Roadside Hawk (35), which is usually tinged brownish (Carib. birds can be very light gray), and has unbarred throat and chest and rufous wings. Imm. closely resembles several other streaked imms. but is generally the buffiest, esp. on the head, more spotted (less streaked) below; in flight has light wing patches; cf. especially imm. Broad-winged (37) and Roadside Hawk (35), larger, chunkier black-hawks with more tail bars (27, 28), and imm. Yellow-headed Caracara (p 115).

**Voice:** Loud clear descending *schweeeeer*.

**Behavior:** Rather active buteo sometimes even pursuing prey through trees. Frequently soars for short periods but usually not high. Often "still hunts" from partially exposed perch.

**Breeding:** Copulation, 30 Mar, w Meta (W. McKay); BC ♀, Jan, Acandí, n Chocó (Carriker); early Feb nest, e Panama (Wetmore 1965a); incubating bird, May, Venez. (Friedmann and Smith 1950). Nest well up in trees; 1-3 whitish or pale bluish eggs.

**Status and habitat:** Uncommon to fairly common; forest borders, semiopen or lightly wooded areas, and riparian woodland (shows some fondness for vicinity of water) in dry to humid zones.

**Range:** To 600m. Lower Atrato Val. (s to Mutatá), e across n Colombia to Santa Marta Mts. and Guajira, s to mid. Magdalena Val. in Tolima (Melgar), and spottily e of Andes (w Meta; Norte de Santander) s to Leticia (many sight recs.). Sw US s to w Peru, c Argentina, and se Brazil. Trinidad.

## 35. ROADSIDE HAWK
*Buteo magnirostris*            Pls. 5, II, Map 110
**Identification:** 13-15″ (33-38cm). *Common.* Small buteo, proportionally longer-tailed and shorter-winged than others of the genus. Eyes yellow. Upperparts, throat and chest brownish gray (or light gray—*insidiatrix*); *breast and lower underparts thickly barred cinnamon and white*; tail dusky with 4 or 5 gray (or cinnamon brown—*ecuadoriensis*) bars. In flight *always shows conspic. rufous patch at base of primaries.* Imm.: dull brown above; buffy white below, throat and breast more or less streaked brown, sometimes also with indistinct dusky malar; lower underparts with some tawny barring (more prom. in older birds, which gradually acquire ad. dress).
**Similar species:** Rather nondescript grayish plumage with unbarred throat and chest. Rufous in wings can be hard to see at rest. If in doubt flush this widespread open country hawk. See Gray Hawk and imm. Broad-winged Hawk (34, 37).
**Voice:** Often heard call, a slightly buzzy *kzweeeeooo* (Ridgely 1976), also a ser. of rather nasal annoying *kee*'s in flight or at rest.
**Behavior:** A sluggish and rather guileless hawk, usually seen perching on open lower branches, fence posts, or in other exposed places. Flies weakly, and seldom far, rapid flapping alternating with a glide. Soars infrequently and then usually not very well. Eats insects, small vertebrates, and occas. even stoops on unwary birds.
**Breeding:** 2 Santa Marta nests with eggs, Apr (Todd and Carriker 1922); 1 nest in May, Venez. Orinoco (Cherrie 1916); 8 nests (6 with eggs) in trees, early May–mid-Aug, Guárico, Venez.; 1-2 largely white eggs, speckled or lightly streaked brown (Mader 1981).
**Status and habitat:** The most frequently seen hawk in Colombia in almost all kinds of dry to wet forest and river borders, and open or shrubby areas with trees. Scarce in arid parts of Carib. lowlands.
**Range:** To 2500m. Guajira and Santa Marta region s to mid. Magdalena Val. near Bucaramanga, w to upper Sinú Val. and Pacific coast s to mid. Río San Juan (*insidiatrix*); Pacific coast s of above, Cauca Val. and both slopes of Nariño (*ecuadoriensis*); Magdalena Val. from e slope E Andes, Antioquia, and s Santander southward, and e of Andes throughout (*mag-*

*nirostris*). E Mexico to c Argentina and se Brazil.

## 36. WHITE-RUMPED HAWK
*Buteo leucorrhous*            Pl. II, Map 111
**Identification:** 13-15″ (33-38cm). Small black buteo; somewhat *short-winged. Mainly black with white rump* and under tail coverts; black tail with a single grayish brown band above, 2-3 white bands from below; thighs inconscpic. barred rufous. In flight from below *wing linings white, flight feathers blackish.* Imm.: dark brown mottled rufous above; head, neck, and underparts creamy buff heavily streaked dark brown; *upper and under tail coverts white*; tail blackish with 1 ashy band above, 2 below; *thighs barred rufous.* In flight from below underwing shows more white than in ad.; *primaries barred black.*
**Similar species:** In any plumage a small very dark buteo with white wing linings. When soaring the white rump is usually conspic.
**Voice:** A short whistled scream, sometimes tirelessly repeated on perch as wags tail (T. B. Johnson).
**Behavior:** Single birds or less frequently pairs soar often but usually not high and mostly over forest. At times perches on exposed branches in canopy or subcanopy (T. B. Johnson).
**Breeding:** 1 active nest, Feb–Mar, PN Cueva de los Guácharos (P. Gertler).
**Status and habitat:** Local in humid forest and forest borders, esp. near clearings and broken forest on steep hillsides. Reg. on Cuchilla de San Lorenzo in Santa Marta Mts.
**Range:** 1700-2900m. Santa Marta and Perijá mts. and spottily in all 3 Andean ranges (W Andes only near Cerro Munchique, Cauca, and no recs. n of Caldas in C Andes). N Venez. s through mts. to n Argentina; se Brazil and Paraguay.

## 37. BROAD-WINGED HAWK
*Buteo platypterus*            Pls. 5, II, Map 112
**Identification:** 15-18″ (38-46cm). A stocky med.-sized buteo. Dark grayish brown above; throat white bordered dusky; *rest of underparts white rather thickly barred and spotted brownish rufous*; broad tail black with *2 wide white bands and narrow white tip* (sometimes a 3d band shows at base). In flight from below wings mostly white with dark border. Imm.: brown above; whitish below broadly streaked dark brown; tail narrowly and evenly banded dusky and whitish.
**Similar species:** Grayer Roadside Hawk (35) shows rufous wing patches in flight. Imm. could

be confused with several smaller imm. buteos, esp. Gray Hawk (34), which is creamier below and more sparsely and obviously spotted (less streaked), and Roadside Hawk (35), which is browner below with barred (not streaked) lower underparts. Also see Double-toothed Kite (8). **Behavior:** Scattered individuals reg. circle over partially wooded terrain; also are commonly seen perched in semiopen areas. **Status and habitat:** Common transient and winter resident (Oct–Mar or early Apr, stragglers to late Apr) to forest borders, second growth woodland, and clearings. No large migratory flocks yet reported as in C America. **Range:** To 2800m. W of Andes and e slope of E Andes (no rec. e away from Andes). Breeds in N America and W Indies; winters from s Florida and s Mexico to Bolivia and n Brazil.

## 38. SHORT-TAILED HAWK

*Buteo brachyurus*                    Pl. II, Map 113
**Identification:** 15-18″ (38-46cm). Usual broad-winged, short-tailed buteo shape. Frequently confused. Light phase: slaty black above *incl. sides of head to well below eyes* (looks "hooded"); forehead and *underparts pure white*; tail grayish brown above, whitish below with several narrow black bands and a broader black subterminal band. In flight from below *underwings mostly white*, flight feathers slightly grayish, primaries tipped black. Dark phase (rather rare): entirely sooty black with white forehead; tail as in light phase. In flight from below *under wing linings black contrasting sharply with pale flight feathers*. Imm.: above rather like respective ad. phase, but tail with more numerous bars: pale phase imm. with some white edging above, head and underparts creamy buff to whitish lightly to heavily streaked and spotted brown, esp. on head and neck; dark phase imm. boldly spotted white below. **Similar species:** Widespread. Good marks are rather small compact proportions, absence of prom. tail bands, and in light phase the dark cheeks, contrasting upper and underparts, and wing linings in slight (not strong) contrast to grayer flight feathers (cf. esp. Semiplumbeous, White-throated, Swainson's, and White-tailed hawks, 24, 39, 40, 41). More difficult dark phase resembles several others, but shape, size, and strongly 2-toned underwings are helpful. See esp. imm. and dark phase White-tailed and Swainson's hawks. Ad. Zone-tailed (44) and the black-hawks (27, 28) have 1 or more tail bands. Underwing pattern of White-rumped and Plumbeous hawks (36, 22) is reverse of dark phase Short-tailed. **Behavior:** Seldom seen except when soaring, then normally quite high and at a distance.

Usually alone, occas. in pairs; stoop like other buteos. **Breeding:** 1 active Feb nest, c Panama (Eisenmann), another in Trinidad, Mar (ffrench 1973). **Status and habitat:** Uncommon and thinly spread over partially open or lightly wooded terrain; e of Andes also over humid forested zones. **Range:** To 1800m (once to 2500m). W of Andes (no Pacific coast recs.; none recent in Cauca Val.); e of Andes so far known only from sight recs. in w Meta (Hilty; W. McKay), and near Leticia (P. Alden, Hilty et al.) but common at Limoncocha, Ecuador, near Putumayo (Pearson et al. 1977) and sightings from many areas in llanos of Venez. (P. Alden). S Florida. Mexico s to n Argentina, Paraguay, and se Brazil. Trinidad.

## 39. WHITE-THROATED HAWK

*Buteo albigula*                    Pl. II, Map 114
**Identification:** 16-19″ (41-48cm). Upper el. ally of Short-tailed Hawk. *Blackish brown above and on sides of head to below eyes* (looks "hooded"); *sides of neck and sides of breast chestnut brown*; rest of underparts white with a *necklace of brown streaks across chest*; rest of underparts usually more or less *streaked, esp. flanks*; thighs barred amber and white; tail dark brown above, grayish below, and with numerous indistinct dark bars. Imm.: sim. but also with large dark brown spots on breast and flanks. **Similar species:** Proportions like those of Short-tailed Hawk (38), but usually appears somewhat longer-tailed in flight and in any plumage more heavily and obviously streaked on sides and flanks than corresponding plumage of Short-tailed (cf. esp. imm. and subad.). Imm. also near imm. Broad-winged Hawk (37), but sides and flanks darker and more streaked; older birds show "hood." **Behavior:** Not well known. A single bird at PN Puracé soared in rather small circles at low to mod. hts. over steep forest. **Status and habitat:** Apparently rare and local in humid mt. forest; esp. low or stunted forest above 2500m. **Range:** 1700-3500m. Known from C Andes in Quindío area w of Ibaque (3500m), e of Popayán (1800m), Peñablanca (2900m), and Curaré on nw side PN Puracé (3200m), a sighting on ne side (3400m, 18 Aug 1979—Hilty et al.), and W Andes at Munchique and El Tambo (1700-1900m). Spottily from n Venez. s in mts. to nw Argentina. **Note:** By some considered a subsp. of *B. brachyurus* (Short-tailed Hawk), but ranges may

overlap and no integration is known (Lehmann and Haffer 1960).

## 40. SWAINSON'S HAWK
*Buteo swainsoni*

**Identification:** 19-22″ (48-56cm). Fairly large rangy buteo. Pale phase: dark brown above, *whitish below with broad reddish brown chest band; tail whitish basally* (looks pale-rumped) becoming grayer toward tip and crossed by numerous faint black bands and a broader subterminal band. In flight from below *whitish under wing coverts contrast with dark flight feathers.* Dark phase (rare): *entirely brownish black, incl. underwings;* tail as in pale phase. Intermediates resembling light phase birds but with var. amts. of brown on lower underparts also occur. Imm.: dark brown above, hindcrown, mantle, and sides of head mottled whitish; underparts buffy white streaked and spotted brown.

**Similar species:** Pale phase birds are distinctive and are usually the ones seen. Dark phase birds are very confusing, but most other dark, or dark phase, or imm. Colombian buteos show some contrast between wing lining and flight feathers, often also white on forehead or underparts (cf. Zone-tailed, imm. White-tailed, and dark phase Short-tailed Hawk, 44, 41, 38), or are var., sometimes with rufous on back, or with white tail with black subterminal band (Red-backed and Variable hawks, 42, 43). In all plumages Swainson's usually looks decidedly pale-rumped.

**Status and habitat:** Uncommon migrant and rare winter resident, mainly in E and C Andes. Flocks of var.-size reported Feb–Mar and Sept–early Nov, stragglers and occas. large flocks in early Aug (several groups totaling about 150 birds over PN Puracé is earliest—Lehmann 1959b). Enormous flocks sim. to ones reported in C America are rare (largest reported is several thousand, 24 Oct 1963, at Bogotá—Nicéforo and Olivares 1964). Only recs. away from Andes are a single bird, and flocks of 40 and 60 near Leticia, 7, 8, and 9 Mar, respectively (P. Alden, S. Hilty).

**Range:** To 2600m. W of Andes, once e of them (Leticia). Breeds in w N America; migrates mostly through C America and n S America and winters to s S America.

## 41. WHITE-TAILED HAWK
*Buteo albicaudatus*                    Pl. IV, Map 115

**Identification:** 20-24″ (51-61cm). A large buteo with broad wings (primaries long and attenuated) and shortish rounded tail. Slaty above, incl. sides of head; *conspic. rufous shoulders; underparts, rump, and tail white; tail with broad black band near tip;* throat sometimes black (esp. in Meta). In flight from below wing linings white, flight feathers grayish. Dark phase (uncommon and mainly e of Andes): entirely slate gray with white-barred under tail coverts, *usually some rufous on shoulders, tail as in normal ad.* Imm.: brownish black with var. amts. of white mottling and streaking below; shoulders often tinged rufous; rump whitish barred brown; tail brownish to light gray crossed by numerous fine darker bars and often with ill-defined black subterminal band; tail becomes whiter with age. From below wing linings blackish, darker than flight feathers.

**Similar species:** In flight from below resembles Short-tailed Hawk (38, both show dark "hood" over sides of head), which is smaller, lacks the strongly contrasting underwings, and at closer range has several narrow black tail bands. White Hawk (26), sim. from below, very different above and forest-based. Red-backed and Variable hawks (42, 43) may or may not have rufous backs but never have rufous shoulders. Dark phase White-tailed lacking rufous on shoulders probably cannot be safely separated from 42 or 43 except by range. Imm. can present even more problems but most show enough whitish on rump and tail or rufous tinge on shoulders to be recognized. See dark phases of Short-tailed (38) and Swainson's (40).

**Voice:** Several high whistled *klee*'s.

**Behavior:** Often in pairs soaring to hts. over open or scrubby country and along with high el. Red-backed (and Variable?) Hawk is the only Colombian buteo that reg. hovers. Frequently perches on ground or low bush.

**Breeding:** Near Yumbo, Valle, 1 flightless young in nest Aug (Lehmann 1957); near Bosque Yotoco, Valle, ad. pair (1 light, 1 dark phase) on nest atop large boulder, 21 Apr 1973 (G. Tudor); 4 nests Jan–May, ne Meta near Carimagua (S. Furniss). 1-2 dull white eggs (ffrench 1973).

**Status and habitat:** Drier savanna, semiopen country, and ranchland, occas. broken partially wooded terrain. Fairly common to locally common in Guajira and e of Andes.

**Range:** To 1800m. Santa Marta region e across Guajira, drier regions s to upper Cauca Val. (formerly but now rare or absent), upper Magdalena Val. (very spotty), and e of Andes from Arauca to Meta, Macarena Mts., and Río Guaviare. Sw US to se Peru, c Argentina, s Brazil, and Fr. Guiana. Dutch Antilles; Trinidad.

## 42. RED-BACKED HAWK
*Buteo polyosoma*                    Pl. VII, Map 116

**Identification:** 18-21″ (46-53cm). Typical bu-

teo shape. Notably var., but *all ads. have white tail with broad black subterminal band.* About 5 ad. color phases: 1. *Head, thighs, and under tail coverts dark brown; upper surface mostly dark gray; upper back and most of underparts rufous, esp. abdomen.* 2. Dark gray above, head browner, upper back rufous; underparts white finely barred gray on sides. 3. Above like 1 and 2 but throat and chest dark gray; center of breast more or less mixed rufous; thighs and lower underparts boldly barred black and white. 4. Above gray, below white incl. under wing coverts. 5. Almost entirely dark gray to slaty black above and below. Birds with rufous backs are usually (but not always) ♀♀; gray birds or those gray above and white below are apparently ♂♂. Imm. (light phase): var. but usually dark brown above, sometimes with rufous on back; below buff, streaked on throat and chest and irreg. barred on lower underparts with brown. Imm. (dark phase): mostly dark brownish black, with some white mottling. Wings and tail proportionally longer than in ad.
**Similar species:** Essentially inseparable, from Variable Hawk (see 43) in field. In hand Red-backed has 3d primary from outside usually longer than 5th (the reverse in Variable) and is smaller than Variable; flat wing (sexes combined) 350-436 vs 418-483mm; tail 173-243 vs 213-263mm; tarsus 70-87 vs 80-91mm (Blake 1977). Imm. not safely told in field from imm. Variable but is larger and sootier on average; and often has large areas of solid dark brown on sides and lower underparts. Light phase imm. most common in Red-backed Hawk; dark phase most common in Variable Hawk. Cf. White-tailed Hawk (41).
**Voice:** Shrill *yeeak-yeeak* or *kyeah-kyeah* (Brown and Amadon 1968).
**Behavior:** A handsome, graceful hawk of open mt. slopes, usually seen near or above treeline. Like White-tailed Hawk, characteristically hovers, often on nearly motionless wings. Reg. perches on rock ledges or on ground.
**Breeding:** Not known to breed in Colombia. In Ecuador, late Mar–early May; bulky stick nest in tree, large cactus, or rock ledge; 1-2 grayish or greenish white eggs (Marchant 1960).
**Status and habitat:** Uncertain; perhaps only a migrant to Colombia. Most recs. are May–Sept (austral winter) to s Colombian highlands from Puracé southward.
**Range:** 1800-3200m (prob. higher). C Andes from Nevado de Santa Isabel (Quindío area) and upper Cauca Val. from e and w of Popayán s through mts. of Nariño. S Colombia s in Andes to Tierra del Fuego.

**Note:** Relationship to *B. poecilochrous* (Variable Hawk) unclear.

### 43. VARIABLE HAWK
*Buteo poecilochrous*                    Map 117
**Identification:** 20-24″ (51-61cm). Larger than Red-backed Hawk, but largest individuals of latter found in Andes in regions where likely confused with Variable Hawk. *Every plumage of Red-backed Hawk (42) is prob. duplicated in Variable Hawk,* but 1st plumage phase apparently not reported in Variable. The plumages of Red-backed where the back is rufous and the underparts barred slaty gray and white, with or without rufous on breast (plumages 2 and 3) are the most frequent in Variable, least in Red-backed.
**Similar species:** See discussion under Red-backed Hawk (42). Over most of range found at somewhat higher el. (on average) than Red-backed Hawk, but most Colombian specimens have been taken at lower el.
**Breeding:** May or may not breed in Colombia.
**Status and habitat:** Perhaps a migrant from the s to open highlands. From Ecuador s found mostly at or above treeline.
**Range:** 900-2000m (prob. higher). S end of W Andes in Valle and Cauca (rec. only on e slope in Cauca). S Colombia s in Andes to n Chile and nw Argentina.
**Note:** Relationship to *B. polyosoma* (Red-backed Hawk) unclear.

### 44. ZONE-TAILED HAWK
*Buteo albonotatus*          Pls. II, III, Map 118
**Identification:** 18-22″ (46-56cm). Long wings of uniform width; rather long tail. A mimic of Turkey Vulture. *All black with 3 grayish (dorsal) or white (ventral) tail bands* (2 always visible), outer 1 broadest. In flight from below *wings 2-toned* with black wing linings and grayish flight feathers; tail proportionally longer and narrower than most buteos. Imm.: sim. but browner overall; *underparts mottled or spotted white;* tail grayish brown above, grayish white below with several narrow black bands.
**Similar species:** Two-toned wings and tilting and teetering flight with wings held in dihedral suggest a Turkey Vulture (p 87), but latter is larger, lacks white tail bands, and has smaller bare red head. Dark phase Short-tailed Hawk (38) is smaller with broader more typical buteo-shaped wings and tail. Black-hawks (27, 28) are much stockier and with fewer tail bands. See dark phase Swainson's and imm. White-tailed hawks (40, 41).
**Behavior:** Single birds or occas. well-spaced pairs soar at low to mod. hts. over open country or forest. The remarkable convergence with

Turkey Vulture's flight profile presum. elicits little alarm from potential prey (Willis 1963).
**Breeding:** Pair presumed incubating, Aug, 2 consecutive yrs. in emergent *várzea* tree near Leticia (Hilty); 1 downy chick, May, Venez. (Friedmann and Smith 1955); 2 pale bluish white eggs (ffrench 1973).
**Status and habitat:** Dry deciduous forest, open or semiopen scrub, and riparian woodland in n Colombia; mainly humid forest e of Andes, but wanders over ranchland. Apparently local.
**Range:** To 500m. Santa Marta region to s Magdalena (prob. both w along Carib. lowlands and e through Guajira); e of Andes from w Meta, w Caquetá, and Amazonas (Leticia). Sw US spottily to n Venez., the Guianas, Ecuador e and w Peru, e Brazil, Bolivia, and Paraguay.

## 45. CRESTED EAGLE

*Morphnus guianensis* Pl. VI, Ill. 26, Map 119
**Identification:** 31-35″ (79-89cm). Large *slender* eagle. Broad rounded wings, *decidedly long tail*; pointed black occipital crest. Cere and lores slaty. Light phase: brownish black above; *head, neck, and chest pale gray tinged brown*, contrasting with white breast and belly, latter sometimes with faint brownish barring; tail black

with 3 broad gray bands. In flight from below wing linings creamy white, flight feathers broadly banded black and gray. Dark phase (or banded): sim., but *head, neck, and chest dark gray, remaining underparts and wing linings whitish boldly barred with black.* Intermediate plumages and an almost wholly black plumage are known. Imm.: entire head, neck, and underparts white, lores slaty; crest tipped black; upperparts blackish with white mottling; tail grayish with 7-8 narrow dusky bands. Several yrs. required to attain full ad. plumage.
**Similar species:** Ad. not unlike Harpy Eagle (46) but somewhat smaller and slighter and has proportionally longer tail. Additionally differs as follows: smaller weaker bill, longer and much weaker tarsi, undivided crest, and in light phase, immaculate wing linings, and no black chest band; banded phase easily recognized. Also cf. smaller Gray-headed Kite (1). Imm. much like imm. Harpy but of slighter proportions (as above) and with single pointed crest. Also compare much smaller imm. Ornate Hawk-Eagle (49), ad. Black-and-white Hawk Eagle (47), and imm. Black-and-chestnut Eagle (50; only highlands), all of which have feathered legs.
**Behavior:** Little known. Soars frequently (Wet-

26. Crested Eagle (left), Harpy Eagle (right)

more 1965a) and reported to perch immobile for long periods high in trees; call resembles that of Great Black-Hawk (Lehmann 1943).

**Breeding:** Adult adding green sprigs to large stick platform 20m up in tall forest tree, Mar 1981, Bolívar, Venez. (R. Ridgely, G. Tudor et al.).

**Status and habitat:** Rare. Scattered recs. in humid forest and more extensive gallery forest in s llanos. There are more recs. from n Chocó and w Caquetá (now extensively deforested) than elsewhere.

**Range:** To 600m. Prob. throughout in lowland forest. Known from n Chocó s to Baudó Mts. and Anchicayá Val. (sight presum. this sp., 1000m, 1973—Hilty); upper Sinú Val. of sw Córdoba; e end Perijá Mts., Guajira (Carraipía), e of Andes in w Meta (e of Villavicencio), and w Caquetá. Honduras to w Ecuador, Bolivia, ne Argentina, Paraguay, and se Brazil.

## 46. HARPY EAGLE
*Harpia harpyja*       Pl. VI, Ill. 26, Map 120
**Identification:** 35-40″ (89-102cm). The world's most powerful bird of prey. Broad rounded wings, long tail, and enormously thick yellow tarsi. Cere and heavy bill black. Head and upper throat gray with *conspic. bifurcated black crest*; upperparts black, feathers indistinctly edged gray; *entire chest black*; rest of underparts white; thighs barred black; tail black with 3 broad gray bands and narrow gray tip. In flight from below wing linings barred black and white, flight feathers *boldly banded* black and white. Imm.: *head and entire underparts white* (incl. divided crest); brownish gray to light gray above; tail gray with several narrow dusky bands; underwing much as in ad. There are several intermed. plumages leading to fully ad. plumage; older imm. shows gray chest much like ad. Crested Eagle. Acquires dark crest early.

**Similar species:** Ad. or imm. likely confused only with Crested Eagle (see 45).

**Voice:** Ad. a loud, wailing *wheeeeeeee*; imm. a weaker version of same (Rettig 1977).

**Behavior:** Occas. soars low over canopy but normally keeps within tree crowns where it displays considerable agility as it glides and dodges through branches very rapidly. Despite its enormous size it is not conspic. and usually seen only when crossing rivers or other forest openings. Preys on a var. of large arboreal mammals, incl. monkeys, sloths, coatis, also large birds and snakes as well as terrestrial mammals.

**Breeding:** Large stick nest usually in crown of emergent *Ceiba* tree; 1-2 white eggs, mid-June at 1 nest in s Guyana; incubation about 8 wks.,

young fly by 5th mo. (Fowler and Cope 1964; Rettig 1977).

**Status and habitat:** Rare and undoubtedly local but perhaps more widespread in humid forested regions than recs. indicate. Favors relatively undisturbed lowland forest of large areal extent well away from human settlement, where monkeys, sloths, and other large arboreal mammals exist.

**Range:** Mainly below 800m, once to 1600m. W of Andes known from n Chocó (Río Salaquí) and sight in Baudó Mts. (Von Sneidern), mid. Magdalena Val. (s of Bucaramanga, now deforested), upper Magdalena Val. (Tolima), and numerous localities e of Andes from nw Meta and Vaupés southward. Se Mexico to n Argentina and s Brazil.

## 47. BLACK-AND-WHITE HAWK-EAGLE
*Spizastur melanoleucus*       Pl. V, Map 121
**Identification:** 22-24″ (56-61cm). Smaller chunky eagle; wings and tail mod. long. *Cere red orange*; eyes yellow. *Head, entire underparts, and feathered legs white; small mask; short bushy crest and entire upperparts black;* tail black with at least 3 broad grayish bands and narrow tip. In flight from below mostly white with a few blackish bars on tips of primaries. Imm.: sim. but back and uppersurface of wings brownish gray with white edgings.

**Similar species:** *Often confused* with more numerous imm. Ornate Hawk-Eagle (49), which is brownish (not black) above, lacks black lores, and is barred black on flanks, thighs, and usually somewhat on underwings. Pale phase imm. Gray-headed Kite (1) is quite sim. but slighter with proportionally shorter wings, longer tail, and more crisply barred outer primaries; nearby has browner back, lacks black mask and crest, and has short *bare* legs. Also see White Hawk (26).

**Voice:** Shrill *kree-ówow* unlike Ornate Hawk-Eagle.

**Behavior:** Soars frequently and sometimes perches on high exposed limbs.

**Breeding:** Building nest, 24 Sept, 40m up in large tree, e Panama, copulation in Oct (Strauch 1975). Guyana eggs, Mar–Apr (Brown and Amadon 1968).

**Status and habitat:** Rare and very local in humid and wet forest, mostly near borders or openings.

**Range:** To 1700m (1 sighting at 2900m, Moscopán, Huila). Known from Perijá Mts. of Guajira and Cesar, w slope E Andes in nw Cundinamarca (near Paime) and e slope (Gachetá), upper Magdalena Val. (Río Moscopán, Huila), and Pacific coast in Valle; e of Andes in Casanare, Meta (e of Villavicencio;

Macarena Mts.), w Caquetá (near Florencia), and Amazonas (sightings near Leticia, Aug 1974—J. V. Remsen; Aug 1979—Hilty). S Mexico locally s to Bolivia, n Argentina, Paraguay, and s Brazil.

## 48. BLACK HAWK-EAGLE
*Spizaetus tyrannus*          Pl. VI, Map 122
**Identification:** 25-28″ (64-71cm). Bluntly rounded wings slightly swept forward and *conspic. indented at rear base*; long tail; cere slaty. *Mostly black* with short bushy occipital crest, latter spotted white at base; *thighs sharply barred black and white*; under tail coverts black barred white, tail with 3 broad grayish bars (whitish from below). In flight from below wing linings mottled black and white; *flight feathers boldly checkered black and white*. Imm.: upperparts brownish black with var. amts. of whitish mottling; *eyestripe, and throat white, cheeks blackish*; below buffy white heavily streaked blackish; almost solid blackish on sides and flanks; *thighs and abdomen barred with black*.
**Similar species:** Flight profile as in Ornate Hawk-Eagle (49), but all plumages much darker (note imm.'s black cheeks separating white eyestripe and throat). No other dark raptor has such boldly banded or checkered flight feathers and such obviously rounded wings swept forward and narrowing at rear base.
**Voice:** Often vocal when aloft, uttering a rhythmically whistled *whit, whit whit wheeéeeeer*, or *whet, whet, witwheéeear*, with last note downslurred (the reverse of Ornate Hawk-Eagle); occas. only last note given.
**Behavior:** Reg. soars, often to great hts., during midmorning or midday. Like Ornate Hawk-Eagle usually perches within canopy or lower and infrequently seen except when soaring. Apparently hunts mostly from perches rather than stooping.
**Breeding:** Mar nest 14m up in tree, Panama; 1 or more young (Brown and Amadon 1968).
**Status and habitat:** Locally fairly common in humid forest borders, second growth woodland, and along natural openings and rivers in extensively forested zones. May favor or tolerate more open woodland than Ornate Hawk-Eagle and not found in "super wet" Pacific lowlands. The most frequently seen hawk-eagle within its range; reg. in Cañaveral area of PN Tayrona.
**Range:** To 500m. From Panama boundary s on Pacific coast to Baudó Mts., e in humid region n of Andes to lower Cauca Val. (Pto. Valdivia) and mid. Magdalena Val. (e slope Snía. de San Lucas); n slope of Santa Marta Mts. and w slope Perijá Mts.; e of Andes in Norte de Santander (Petrólea) and from w

Meta (s of Villavicencio) to Amazonas (Leticia) and sight at Pto. Inírida, Guainía (Hilty and Robbins). E Mexico s to ne Argentina, Paraguay, and se Brazil. Trinidad.

## 49. ORNATE HAWK-EAGLE
*Spizaetus ornatus*          Pls. V, VI, Map 123
**Identification:** 23-25″ (58-64cm). Lanky eagle with bluntly rounded *wings narrowing at base*; long tail. Cere yellow, lores gray; legs feathered. Crown and long pointed crest black (crest usually held flat unless excited); *sides of head, hindneck, and sides of chest rufous*; back and wings black; throat and center of chest white bordered by *black malar, rest of underparts including thighs white coarsely barred black*; tail black with 3 broad grayish bands. In flight undersurface of wings white, wing linings spotted, and flight feathers banded black. Imm.: head and underparts white, thighs and flanks barred black (mostly white in younger birds); upperparts dusky brown; tail blackish with broad grayish brown bands. Underwings sim. to ad. but less spotted and banded (nearly white in youngest birds). Soars with flat wings angled slightly forward, aquiline head protruding prom.
**Similar species:** Handsome ad. not likely confused; plumage (but not shape) mimicked by imm. Gray-bellied Hawk (20), an *Accipiter* that differs as follows: decidedly smaller, no crest, bare legs, slighter build, and short rounded wings (not likely to be seen soaring). Imm. from imm. Black-and-white Hawk-Eagle (47) by black flank and thigh barring, usually spotted wing linings (nearly white in youngest birds), yellow (not red orange) cere, no prom. black "mask" around eyes, longer crest (turning black only on older birds), and browner upperparts. See Crested Eagle (45), Black Hawk-Eagle (48) and pale phase imm. Grayheaded Kite (1).
**Voice:** Often noisy when soaring; a loud whistled, *whit, wheéeuuu, whep whep, whep whep*, 1st note faint or lacking, next emphasized and down-slurred (cf. with Black Hawk-Eagle).
**Behavior:** Reg. aloft on sunny mornings but usually soars closer to canopy than Black Hawk-Eagle and seldom is up as long. Wheels in leisurely circles, occas. broken by short "butterflylike" wing flutters. May terrorize potential canopy prey by stooping but normally hunts by moving from 1 inconspic. perch to the next at med.-hts. or higher along forest borders or inside forest.
**Breeding:** In Panama a bulky stick nest about 27m up in tree, late Dec, had at least 1 young that left late May (Willis *in* Brown and Amadon 1968).
**Status and habitat:** Uncommon in humid for-

est, forest borders, and gallery woodland. Usually along or near natural forest openings or in broken hill forest rather than deep inside unbroken forest. Outnumbered by Black Hawk-Eagle where found together.

**Range:** To 1200m, rarely to 1800m. Pacific coast (s to upper Anchicayá Val.), e in humid regions n of Andes to lower Cauca Val. (Pto. Valdivia) and mid. Magdalena Val. (Remedios), and Atlántico e to Santa Marta area (where rare) and w Guajira; e of Andes from extreme e Cundinamarca, Macarena Mts., w Caquetá, the Río Orinoco (on Venez. side opp. Vichada) s to Vaupés and Amazonas (sight only in latter 2 areas, 1978—Hilty); no Putumayo recs. E Mexico to w Ecuador, n Argentina, and s Brazil. Trinidad.

## 50. BLACK-AND-CHESTNUT EAGLE
*Oroaetus isidori*     Pls. VI, VII, Map 124
**Identification:** 25-29″ (64-74cm). Large and robust. Broad wings resemble *Spizaetus* but are proportionally longer; tail shorter. Legs feathered. *Mainly black* incl. spikelike crest (often held elevated in flight); *breast and lower underparts chestnut streaked black;* thighs black; feathered tarsi chestnut; *tail pale grayish with a broad black band near tip.* In flight from below wing linings chestnut, flight feathers grayish, with a few dusky bars and black tips, *outer primaries with large light patch at base.* Imm.: brown above with buff edgings, crest tipped black; forehead and eyestripe buffy white; sides of head and underparts whitish stained and streaked dusky and chestnut, mostly on sides of head, chest, and sides; tail brownish gray with 3 or 4 narrower black bands. In flight from below wing linings mottled, flight feathers banded,

base of primaries show light patch (above or below). Young birds become progressively darker with maturity; subads. are quite dark but blotchy and mottled (rusty coloration becoming obvious).

**Similar species:** Handsome ad. is distinctive. Undistinguished imm. is confusing. Latter from *Spizaetus* hawk-eagles (48-49) by larger more robust proportions, longer less "oval" wings, shorter tail, and more ponderous flight. Imm. Black Hawk-Eagle is much darker below, imm. Ornate whiter without the mottled "dirty" appearance. Imm. Solitary Eagle (29) shows more contrast between black chest and striped lower underparts.

**Voice:** Rather quiet. Ads. near nest a loud *pe-e-e-eo*; alarm *chee-chee-chee* (Lehmann 1959b).

**Behavior:** Reg. soar low to mod. high over mt. forest but seldom seen perched. Fly less buoyantly than *Spizaetus* and seemingly without occas. "wing flutters" of latter. Reported to prey on arboreal birds and mammals ranging in size from squirrels to guans.

**Breeding:** Building nest high in emergent tree in Huila (Moscopán), Feb–Mar, 1 young hatched in May, nearly full grown late July (Lehmann 1959b); 1 Bolivian egg, white washed and spotted brown (L. E. Miller).

**Status and habitat:** Local. Relatively undisturbed humid and wet mt. forest. Can be found fairly reg. on highest slopes of Cuchilla de San Lorenzo (usually above 2200m) at nw end of Santa Marta Mts., the mts. above Florencia, Caquetá (above 1800m), and in W Andes around Cerro Munchique, Cauca.

**Range:** Mostly 1600-2800m (rec. 150-3300m). Spottily in Santa Marta and Perijá Mts. and all 3 Andean ranges. N. Venez. and Andes s to nw Argentina.

# FALCONS, CARACARAS: Falconidae (18)

The members of this family form a rather heterogeneous group of Old and New World species. In addition to anatomical characters, they differ most obviously from hawks, eagles, and kites (Accipitridae) in having a "tooth" or notch on the upper mandible. The caracaras, a New World group, have rather long wings and tails and, with the exception of the Red-throated Caracara, are notably omnivorous and opportunistic in behavior, often scavenging. The Laughing Falcon and forest-falcons are also strictly American groups, the former rather large-headed and notably vocal, the latter rather slender-bodied and almost accipiterlike in appearance. Nidification has been reported only a few times for the Laughing Falcon, and for only one species of forest-falcon. True falcons (*Falco*) are a cosmopolitan group of streamlined, pointed-winged predators capable of fast flight and tremendous speed when stooping. They seldom soar, although open country species often hover. The systematic order is that of Brown and Amadon (1968) except 15-16.

## 1. BLACK CARACARA
*Daptrius ater* Pl. I, Map 125
**Identification:** 17-19″ (43-48cm). Rather long narrow wings and tail. Bill black; *extensive bare facial skin bright orange becoming yellow on throat*; legs yellow. *Glossy black with broad white band across base of tail.* Imm.: facial skin and legs duller, more lemon yellow; underparts indistinctly barred and spotted buff, basal two-thirds of tail white with 3-4 black bars.
**Similar species:** Orange face and white at base of tail is diagnostic. See Red-throated Caracara (2), mainly a forest bird of different (more eaglelike) proportions.
**Voice:** A harsh, scratchy scream, *kra-a-a-a-a-a-a*, descending somewhat, hoarser than respective call of Yellow-headed Caracara; in flight sim. harsh screams, *cheeoow, chew-chew-chew.*
**Behavior:** Often in family groups of 3-4. Perch exposed on sand bars or high in trees along rivers or forest borders. Fly direct with almost continuous flapping; rarely soar but may glide short distances. Eat a var. of food from carrion and nestlings to insects and palm fruits.
**Breeding:** BC ♀, 3 Aug, Petrólea, e Norte de Santander (Carriker). Mar–June in Guyana; 2-3 buff eggs spotted brown (Brown and Amadon 1968).
**Status and habitat:** Usually fairly common in gallery forest, and forest borders, esp. along larger rivers, sandbars, or in other semiopen areas in forested zones.
**Range:** To 600m. E of Andes from Norte de Santander (Petrólea), w Meta, and e Vichada (Tuparro—INDERENA) southward. Prob. throughout llanos in or near gallery forest. The Guianas and Venez. s to n Bolivia and Amazonian Brazil.

## 2. RED-THROATED CARACARA
*Daptrius americanus* Pl. I, Map 126
**Identification:** 19-22″ (48-56cm). Distinctive plumage. Fowllike bill and longish tail suggest a cracid. Mostly glossy black with belly and under tail coverts white; *bare red facial skin, throat, and legs*; bill yellow, base gray.
**Similar species:** Black Caracara (1) has bare orange face, white base of tail, and very different habits and voice.
**Voice:** Often very noisy, uttering an incredibly loud, raucous *ah-ah-ah-áou* (hence common Spanish name "Come Cacao") or sim. var.; often a quarrelsome cacaphony, at a distance suggesting a group of macaws.
**Behavior:** A social forest caracara often seen traveling in small noisy groups. Perch in tree crowns along river edge or forest borders but sometimes much lower inside forest, even on the ground. Often prey on wasp and bee larvae, apparently raiding nests of even the most vicious sp. with impunity; also notably frugivorous. Flight is slow and labored, usually with much flapping, occas. a short sail; does not soar.
**Breeding:** Reportedly a twig nest in trees; 2-3 white or buff eggs spotted brown (Brown and Amadon 1968); BC pair, 11 July, se base Santa Marta Mts. (Carriker); Panama ♀ nearly ready to lay, late Mar (Wetmore 1965a).
**Status and habitat:** Uncommon in humid *terra firme* and *várzea* forest, forest borders, and clearings with scattered trees. Least numerous on Pacific coast and blackwater region of extreme east.
**Range:** To 1400m. Pacific coast (not rec. from s Chocó or Valle), e in humid regions n of Andes to w base of Santa Marta Mts. (Ciénaga Grande) and s through lower and mid. Magdalena to n Antioquia and w Santander; e of Andes from w Meta (Villavicencio area) and e Vichada (Maipures on Orinoco) southward. Se Mexico to w Ecuador, e Peru, and Amazonian Brazil.

## 3. CARUNCULATED CARACARA
*Phalcoboenus carunculatus* Pl. I, Map 127
**Identification:** 20-22″ (51-56cm). Bold pattern. Long wings narrowing at tip; long rounded tail and curly crest. Bare wrinkled skin of face and throat orange red; bill and legs yellow. *Mostly black*, breast broadly streaked white; thighs, lower underparts, upper tail coverts, and tip of tail white. In flight from below *wing linings and base of flight feathers white; flight feathers otherwise black tipped white.* Imm.: dark brown above; head, rump, and underparts indistinctly mottled whitish; tail with narrow white tip; bare face and legs dusky. In flight shows light patch at base of primaries.
**Similar species:** Distinctive curly-headed ad. the only Colombian caracara with an all-black head and the only one likely in the paramo. Imm. from Crested Caracara (4) by solid buffy brown head (no blackish crown) and brown tail.
**Behavior:** Single birds, occas. pairs, are usually conspic. where they do occur but are rarely in nos. except near cattle. Spend most of time walking on the ground scavenging almost anything edible. Fly strongly and often soar, frequently into strong gusty mt. winds where they are swept along great distances on half-closed wings. In general seem to fill the role of crows or ravens (*Corvus*) of n latitudes.
**Status and habitat:** Uncommon to locally fairly

common in drier treeless highlands, esp. grassy pastures and windswept paramo. Most numerous in Cumbal area of s Nariño, less so northward.
**Range:** 3000-4000m. From s C Andes in Cauca (PN Puracé) s through mts. of Nariño. S Colombia and Ecuador.
**Note:** Perhaps a subsp. of Mountain Caracara (*P. megalopterus*) of n Peru to Chile and nw Argentina.

## 4. CRESTED CARACARA
*Polyborus plancus*                    Pl. I, Map 128
**Identification:** 20-24″ (51-61cm). Long-legged and bushy-crested; powerful bill. *Bare facial skin and base of bill red. Crown black; rest of head, neck, and throat white*; mantle barred black and white; otherwise black above; breast white barred black, becoming solid black on thighs and belly; *rump and tail whitish* with narrow wavy black bars (fainter at base) and broad black subterminal band. In flight shows *conspic. white patches on outer primaries.* Imm.: much browner, duller, and streaked below.
**Similar species:** See Yellow-headed Caracara (5), also Carunculated Caracara (3); latter, mostly in treeless highlands, has all black head, white wing linings, and black flight feathers tipped white.
**Voice:** Rather quiet, a grating rattle; a harsh *quick quick-quick quick querr.*
**Behavior:** A conspic. bird of ranchland. Perches on fence posts or tops of small or large trees and often seen on the ground, esp. along roads. Pairs or several walk almost gallinelike, are opportunistic scavengers and predators, and often given to piracy. Fly strongly, occas. soar on strong updrafts in the mts. but rarely in lowlands.
**Breeding:** Mostly dry season. Building nest, late Jan, PN Tayrona (Hilty); 3 nests, mid-Feb–early May in Meta (Brown; S. Furniss); 6 nests (5 with nestlings), mid-Mar (Mader 1981); and other nests, Sept–Dec, Guárico, Venez. (Thomas 1979b). Nest usually atop palm. Usually 2 white eggs freckled reddish brown (Brown and Amadon 1968).
**Status and habitat:** Fairly common to common in drier open or semiopen country, esp. grassland or scrub with scattered trees. Usually less numerous than Yellow-headed Caracara and mostly a recent invader to deforested highlands.
**Range:** To 3000m. Throughout *except* Pacific coast, Urabá area, and forested regions s of the Río Guaviare (no recs. in Vichada or Guainía). S Florida and sw US to Tierra del Fuego. Cuba, Dutch Antilles, and Trinidad.

## 5. YELLOW-HEADED CARACARA
*Milvago chimachima*              Pls. 4, I, Map 129
**Identification:** 16-18″ (41-46cm). Rather long wings and tail, latter rounded at tip. Bill and feet weak. *Head, neck, and underparts creamy white to pale buff with blackish streak behind eye*; above mostly blackish brown; tail with numerous narrow wavy dark bars (fainter at base) and broad subterminal band. In flight shows *conspic. large whitish patch on base of outer primaries.* Imm.: sim., but upperparts dull brown; head, neck, and underparts buffy with a profusion of blurred brown streaks; wings and tail as in ad.
**Similar species:** Smaller and slighter than Crested Caracara (4) with all pale head and underparts. Imm. can be confused with several imm. hawks, esp. Gray Hawk (p 105).
**Voice:** Occas. a rough, growling *kraa-kraa-kraa* or thin, hissing whistle.
**Behavior:** A conspic. open country bird often seen perched in tops of trees or afoot along roads and river banks, which it patrols with great diligence. Scavenges carrion, almost any edible plant or animal matter, and often perches on backs of cattle to look for ticks. Flight is buoyant with even wing beats and occas. sweeping glides but not sustained soaring.
**Breeding:** Near Leticia, building nest, 24 Jan and 24 Aug, and carrying food, 30 Aug (Hilty); 2 feathered nestlings, 16 Aug, Guárico, Venez. (Mader 1981). Stick nest in tree, esp. palm, usually high; 1-2 buff eggs marked rufous brown (Brown and Amadon 1968).
**Status and habitat:** Common in open country with scattered trees, agricultural areas, ranchland, and along edges of larger rivers in forested zones.
**Range:** To about 1800m, rarely 2600m (Sabana de Bogotá). Throughout except Nariño; w of W Andes only in upper Dagua Val. and recently following larger clearings into forested regions of Gulf of Urabá region (Turbo), Anchicayá Val., and elsewhere. S of Río Guaviare, mainly along larger Amazonian rivers (i.e., at Leticia) and in cattelands of w Caquetá and w Putumayo. Sw Costa Rica to n Argentina and Uruguay. Trinidad.

## 6. LAUGHING FALCON
*Herpetotheres cachinnans*        Ill. 27, Map 130
**Identification:** 18-22″ (46-56cm). Big-headed with short rounded wings and long tail. Head and entire underparts creamy white to pale buff with a *conspic. broad black mask extending from eyes around hindneck*; upperparts dark brown, tail blackish with several narrow white

27. Laughing Falcon

bands and pale tip. In flight shows buffy patch on primaries.

**Similar species:** The "Panda Bear" of the bird world and not likely confused if seen well. Smaller ad. Yellow-headed Caracara (5) lacks the erect posture and broad black mask (shows only a narrow black line through eye).

**Voice:** Calls tirelessly, mostly in early morning or late evening, sometimes even after dark, typically a long, far-carrying, lamenting, ti-rade *gúa-co, gúa-co* . . . or sim. var. lasting several min., often increasing in tempo and becoming more rhythmic as it goes along. Less frequently a shorter ser. of chuckling *gwa* or *hah* notes suggesting muffled laughter. Well-separated members of a pair often call simultaneously, their notes alternately syncopated, simultaneous, or out of sequence, but not antiphonal.

**Behavior:** Normally sluggish and confiding; perch for long periods at med. hts. in rather open trees that afford good visibility. Characteristically perch erect with head slightly bowed. Fly slowly with stiff rapid wing beats, than a short glide. Do not soar. Often eat snakes, also other small prey.

**Breeding:** Not well known. Usually tree cavity, less frequently old hawk's nest; BC ♂, 17 May, sw Huila (Carriker); 1 incubating, Feb, Costa Rica (R. Ridgely); 1 nest, Guárico, Venez., 19 Sept; 1 egg (Mader 1981).

**Status and habitat:** Uncommon to fairly common in forest borders, clearings with scattered trees, riparian woodland, and semiopen areas with scattered trees. Dry to humid regions, most numerous in latter, esp. where partially wooded.

**Range:** To 2400m (usually much lower). Throughout but not yet rec. in Vichada and Guainía. Mexico to w Peru, n Argentina, and s Brazil.

## 7. BARRED FOREST-FALCON
*Micrastur ruficollis* Pl. 5, Map 131

**Identification:** 13-15″ (33-38cm). Small with usual *Micrastur* shape. *Cere, lores, and orbital area yellow orange*; legs yellow; eyes yellow ochre to brown. Ad. with 2 color phases w of Andes (only gray phase known e of Andes). Gray phase: dark slaty gray above, entirely white below very *narrowly and evenly barred black*; tail black with 3 (occas. 2 or 4) narrow white bars and white tip (bars on central tail feathers sometimes obsolete—*concentricus*). Rufous phase: sim., but sides of head, nape, back, throat, and chest cinnamon rufous (sometimes cinnamon on lowerparts confined to chest band). Imm. (no phases): dark brown above, buffy white below with *widely spaced narrow black bars, usually with whitish nuchal collar*; less frequently underparts uniform deep buff without bars; tail as in ad.; rump speckled white.

**Similar species:** Dapper ad. with crisply barred underparts likely confused only with Lined Forest-Falcon (8) of extreme e Colombia and Plumbeous Forest-Falcon (9) of sw Nariño (see under those species). Rare Semicollared Hawk (p 98) of mts. lacks orange yellow orbital skin, usually shows broken pale nuchal collar, has 4 broad ashy bands on tail (not 3 narrow ones), and has ungraduated tail. Typical imms. with barring below should be recognizable (cf. imm. Collared, 11, and Slaty-backed Forest-Falcon, 10) and much smaller imm. Tiny Hawk (p 98). Less numerous buffy imm. from imm. Bicolored Hawk (p 99) by orange yellow facial skin, narrow white tail bars, and smaller size; buffy adults of Collared Forest-Falcon are much larger with black cheek mark and greenish cere and lores.

**Voice:** Usual call, heard frequently, mostly before dawn or in late evening, a ser. of distinct sharp barks resembling that of a distant small dog, *ow* or *our* (Slud 1964); often tirelessly repeated at short intervals but difficult to locate. Excited birds cackle with short bursts of *kuop* notes, slowing and dropping in pitch. In upper Anchicayá Val. calling strongly seasonal, mostly Nov–May (Hilty).

**Behavior:** Like others of the genus, furtive and usually keep concealed in mid. or lower forest levels and seldom detected except by voice. A rapacious predator, mostly on smaller birds (up to trogon size—G. Tudor et al.); it relies on stealth, surprise, and agile pursuit and has been reported at army ant swarms and on the ground. Avoids crossing openings.

**Breeding:** BC ♀, 3 Oct, Norte de Santander (Carriker).

**Status and habitat:** Fairly common at least locally (seldom seen) in humid and wet forest and advanced second growth woodland; seems most numerous in foothills and on lower slopes.

**Range:** To 2500m. Pacific slope, n end of W Andes (Snía. de Abibe), both slopes above Cauca Val., but only Quindío area on w slope C Andes (*interstes*); Perijá Mts. and Santa Marta Mts. (*zonothorax*); n end E Andes on e slope, Norte de Santander (poss. new subsp.— A. Wetmore); e of Andes only Macarena Mts. (2 specimens) in s Meta (*concentricus*). S Mexico s to w Ecuador, nw Argentina, and s Brazil.

**Note:** Does not incl. *M. gilvicollis* (Lined Forest-Falcon) of e of Andes, by some treated as a subsp. of Barred Forest-Falcon, but see Schwartz (1972b).

## 8. LINED FOREST-FALCON

*Micrastur gilvicollis*          Pl. 5, Map 132

**Identification:** 12-14″ (30-36cm). Closely resembles Barred Forest-Falcon but lacks rufous phase. *Cere, lores, and bare ocular area reddish orange*; legs yellow; *eyes white*. Slaty gray above, white below finely and reg. barred blackish; *flanks weakly barred; belly and under tail coverts usually pure white*; tail blackish with *2 narrow white bars* and narrow tip. Imm.: almost identical to imm. Barred Forest-Falcon. In hand usually told by uniformly dark upper tail coverts (lacks white spotting of latter).

**Similar species:** From ad. Barred Forest-Falcon (7) as follows: shorter tail, proportionally longer wings, white eyes, orange red facial skin, 2 (occas. only 1) white tail bars, and weaker barring or unbarred lower underparts. See discussion of other sp. under 7. Occas. birds with little barring (restricted to sides of upper breast—imms.) might be confused with Slaty-backed Forest-Falcon (10) which is unbarred below.

**Voice:** Typically a lamenting 2-note rather than 1-note bark of Barred Forest-Falcon (Schwartz 1972b).

**Behavior:** Presum. sim. to Barred Forest-Falcon. A pair in e Vaupés were at med. hts. well inside unbroken forest (Hilty).

**Status and habitat:** Humid *terra firme* forest. Not well known.

**Range:** To 1500m (Macarena Mts.). E of Andes in Macarena Mts. and Vaupés (sight and tape recording, 18 Feb 1978, e of Mitú—Hilty) but certainly more widespread (rec. on Venez. side

of Orinoco at Sanariapo and elsewhere opp. s Vichada). E Colombia, s Venez., and the Guianas s to n Bolivia and Amazonian Brazil.

**Note:** Often treated as a race of *M. ruficollis* (Barred Forest-Falcon) but found to be sympatric with latter in parts of Amazonian region (Schwartz 1972b).

## 9. PLUMBEOUS FOREST-FALCON

*Micrastur plumbeus*          Map 133

**Identification:** 12-14″ (30-36cm). Shorter-tailed and proportionally longer-winged than subsp. of Barred Forest-Falcon (*interstes*) found with it. Cere and legs as in Barred Forest-Falcon. Above slate gray; throat light gray, rest of underparts whitish finely barred blackish; barring sometimes becoming indistinct (or absent) on lower underparts; tail blackish with *1 central white bar and narrow tip*. Imm.: mostly white below with a few scattered dusky bars on breast and sides; tail as in ad.

**Similar species:** From Barred Forest-Falcon (7) by single white tail bar (*interstes* subsp. of Barred presum. always with at least 2, usually 3 white bars). In hand unsexed birds have shorter tails, 123-140 vs 146-170mm, and greater wing/tail ratio, 1.23-1.34 vs 1.02-1.12mm than *interstes* (Schwartz 1972b).

**Status and habitat:** Rare and few specimens. Colombian birds are from foothills and lower slopes in wet forest.

**Range:** 600-900m. Pacific slope of sw Colombia from Cauca (Río Munchique) and Nariño (Guayacana) s to nw Ecuador (Carondelet, 20km s of Nariño).

**Note:** Often treated as an isolated subsp. of *M. gilvicollis* (Lined Forest-Falcon) of e of Andes.

## 10. SLATY-BACKED FOREST-FALCON

*Micrastur mirandollei*          Pl. 5, Map 134

**Identification:** 16-18″ (41-46cm). Typical *Micrastur* shape. Tail proportionally shorter and less graduated than larger Collared Forest-Falcon. *Cere and facial skin yellowish, eyes yellowish brown. Crown and upperparts dark slaty gray (no collar); cheeks pale gray*; below white or white tinged buff; tail black with 3 narrow white or gray bands and narrow white tip; wing linings white, flight feathers barred dusky and whitish. Imm.: browner above, but mostly yellow, underparts white *broadly scaled dusky*.

**Similar species:** A difficult sp. to identify even under favorable conditions. Ad. Gray-bellied Hawk (p 99) has shorter legs, usually blackish gray (not pale gray) cheeks, the gray extending well down to sides of throat, and only cere and lores yellow (not larger facial area). Imm. Barred Forest-Falcons (7) that lack bars below (older birds usually with some barring) resemble buffier ads. (most ads. white below) but are smaller, paler on sides of head and with less graduated tails. Sim.-sized imm. Bicolored Hawk (p 99) resembles buffiest ads. but is shorter-legged and usually has buffy nuchal collar. Imm. is only one of the genus with scaling, mottling, or streaking below, *never barring.*

**Voice:** A nasal subdued *aah* repeated 5-8 times, weaker than Collared Forest-Falcon (Ridgely 1976), sometimes last 2 notes var. to *how-au, how-au,* at dawn (P. Schwartz).

**Behavior:** Occurs mainly in mid. or lower forest levels occas. even on ground (Wetmore 1965a), and more a bird of forest interior than Collared Forest-Falcon. Like others of the genus, can be attracted by squeaking.

**Status and habitat:** Relatively undisturbed humid forest or taller second growth. Several recs. in n Chocó where reportedly more frequent, elsewhere presum. rare.

**Range:** Below 500m. From Panama border s on Pacific coast to sw Nariño (Río Guiza) and e to n end of W Andes (Snía. de Abibe); e of Andes in w Meta (near Villavicencio) and w Caquetá (s of Florencia). Doubtless more widespread. Costa Rica to Bolivia and Amazonian Brazil.

## 11. COLLARED FOREST–FALCON
*Micrastur semitorquatus*  Pls. 4, 5, VI,
Map 135

**Identification:** 19-24″ (38-61cm). Long-tailed; largest of the genus. *Lores and cere dull green.* 3 phases in ad. plumage. Light phase: blackish above, the black of hindcrown continuing diagonally forward across cheeks *as a narrow black crescent; narrow collar on hindneck, cheeks, and entire underparts white*; tail black with several narrow white bands. Tawny phase: sim. but white replaced by buff to tawny. Dark phase (rare): mostly sooty black (no nuchal collar) with grayish white tail bands and usually minor white barring on rump, flanks, and abdomen. Imm. var.: like ad. above but brownish, the feathers scaled buff, and with whitish to tawny nuchal collar (sometimes indistinct or lacking); below white to tawny, coarsely barred brown or black; chest conspic. washed cinnamon or chestnut; tail blackish banded buffy brown to white. Older imms. gradually lose buff scaling above. Dark phase imm.: entirely dark brown with white barring on thighs and belly, tail as in ad.

**Similar species:** Combination of pale collar and dark crescent on cheek is diagnostic in light and tawny phase ads. except for rare Buckley's Forest-Falcon (see 12). Cf. smaller imm. Bicolored Hawk (p 99), which has pale nu-

chal collar (usually), dark cheeks (no crescent), shorter legs, shorter ungraduated tail, and yellow lores. Dark phase ads. best told by shape, ventral barring, and green lores. Lighter imms. are much larger than imm. Barred Forest-Falcon (7), more coarsely barred below, and usually with tawny or buff collar (white or lacking in Barred) and dull green lores. Cf. imm. of 5.

**Voice:** Call, mostly at dusk from higher perch along forest or river edge, a slowly repeated loud hollow, *cow . . . cow . . . cow . . .* , quality of Laughing Falcon but slower, and does not accelerate into repetitious syncopated rhythm of latter. Also cf. call of Slaty-backed Forest-Falcon.

**Behavior:** A furtive forest hawk that generally perches concealed in lower or mid. levels of vegetation, usually avoids crossing openings and is difficult to see. Often more easily seen from late afternoon to twilight when takes a prom. forest edge perch to call or moves into open. Flies from perch to perch hunting by stealth, then a bold pursuit, often through dense cover. Reported even to run on ground. Eats a var. of mostly vertebrate prey, often birds.

**Breeding:** BC ♀, 16 May, upper Magdalena Val. (Carriker); 1 ready-to-lay ♀, w Amazonas, Venez., 5 Apr (Friedmann 1948). 1 nearly fledged chick in tree cavity nest (no nest material) 12m up in tall gallery forest tree, 20 Aug, Guárico, Venez., is 1st described nest of the genus (Mader 1979).

**Status and habitat:** Rare or uncommon (or seldom seen) in moist to humid forest, forest borders, and second growth woodland, esp. with well-developed understory.

**Range:** To 1000m. Prob. throughout in forested regions. Pacific coast s to Cauca (Río Munchique), eastward n of Andes to mid. Magdalena Val. in Cesar. Atlántico, w base of Santa Marta Mts., and s to head of Magdalena Val. (near San Agustín); e base of E Andes from n Boyacá s to Putumayo and Amazonas (Leticia). Mexico to extreme nw Peru, n Argentina, and s Brazil.

## 12. [BUCKLEY'S FOREST-FALCON]
*Micrastur buckleyi*  Map 136

**Identification:** 16-20″ (41-51cm). A miniature of Collared Forest-Falcon (11) but *tail with 4 (instead of 6) white bars* on outer tail feathers. ♀ sim. to ♂ but with *distinct white spots on scapulars and secondaries.* Imm. resembles imm. Collared Forest-Falcon, but breast is *uniform cinnamon buff* with no black markings. In the hand flat wing of unsexed birds 219 mm or

less vs 244 mm or larger for Collared (Blake 1977).
**Similar species:** Ad. from Collared Forest-Falcon (11) by smaller size and fewer tail bands; white wing spots of ♀ also diagnostic. Imm. by unmarked breast, 4 tail bands, and smaller size.
**Status and habitat:** Hypothetical. One sight rec., 24 May 1976, at edge of forest on lower Río Amacayacú, near Leticia, Amazonas (R. Ridgely and D. Gardner). Rare; only about a doz. specimens known.
**Range:** Se Amazonas. E Ecuador (Sarayacú; Río Suno; San José); ne Peru (Yarinacocha; Orosa; Perico) to se Peru (Cuzco).
**Note:** Sometimes considered a subsp. of Collared Forest-Falcon (*M. semitorquatus*).

### 13. AMERICAN KESTREL
*Falco sparverius*          Pls. 5, VII, Map 137
**Identification:** 9-11″ (23-28cm). Small with pointed wings. ♂: mostly rufous above with black bars and bluish crown and wings; throat and sides of head white with *vertical black stripe below eye, another behind eye,* and black spot on sides of nape; sides of neck and underparts whitish buff to pinkish cinnamon (or cinnamon to orange cinnamon—*ochraceus*; or deeper cinnamon rufous, sides spotted black—*aequatorialis*); tail rufous with broad black subterminal band and white tip. ♀: head like ♂, otherwise entirely rufous brown barred black above, incl. wings and tail; underparts buff streaked brown.
**Similar species:** Told by small size, *rufous back and tail,* and distinctive facial pattern.
**Voice:** Vocal, esp. near nest; a high, thin *killy-killy-killy* or *kleé-kleé-kleé.*
**Behavior:** Familiar little open country falcon. Sits alert and erect on fence posts, utility poles, wires, or tops of trees, flies out over grassy areas, hovers frequently, then stoops on mostly insect prey. Always alone except when breeding.
**Breeding:** 4 BC birds, Jan–May, n Bolivar, n Antioquia, sw Huila (Carriker); copulation, 28 Apr; fed fledgling, 21 May, Finca Merenberg, w Huila (R. Ridgely and S. Gaulin 1980). Cavity nest in tree, termite nest, or building. Jan–Apr in Venez.; 3-4 buffy eggs mottled rufous brown (Friedmann and Smith 1950).
**Status and habitat:** Fairly common resident in grassland, roadsides, and other open or semiopen terrain with scattered trees; follows clearings into forested regions. N temperate migrants poss. but as yet unrec.
**Range:** To 3200m. Gulf of Urabá region e to Guajira and lower Cauca Val.; e of Andes at Maipures, e Vichada (*isabellinus*); Pacific slope,

Cauca Val. and mts. of Nariño (*aequatorialis*); mid. and upper Magdalena Val., E Andes, and e of Andes from Norte de Santander s to Meta and w Caquetá (*ochraceus*). Breeds from n N America s to Tierra del Fuego. N temperate birds winter s to easternmost Panama, prob. n S America.

### 14. MERLIN (PIGEON HAWK)
*Falco columbarius*          Pl. VII, Map 138
**Identification:** 10-13″ (25-33cm). Small and compact. ♂: *dark grayish above;* forehead and eyestripe buffy white; *sides of head and underparts whitish* to buffy white streaked dark brown; slight indication of dark "sideburns"; tail dusky with *3 broad gray bands* and pale tip. ♀ and imm.: sim. but brown above.
**Similar species:** Small falcon with streaked underparts, evenly banded tail, and no obvious black facial pattern. See American Kestrel (13).
**Behavior:** Perch rather exposed but usually low, hence inconspic., and often overlooked. More often seen in swift low flight; often preys on small birds.
**Status and habitat:** Uncommon transient and winter resident (Oct–early May; once July) in open or partially open terrain.
**Range:** To 3400m. Spottily throughout w of Andes. Breeds in n N America and the Old World; N American birds winter from s US to n Peru and Venez., and in W Indies and Trinidad.

### 15. BAT FALCON
*Falco rufigularis*          Pls. 5, VII, Map 139
**Identification:** 9-12″ (23-30cm). Small dark falcon with long pointed wings. Cere, orbit, and legs yellow. Upperparts and sides of head black; *throat, chest, and crescent on sides of neck white* sometimes tinged rufescent; *breast and upper belly black very finely barred white;* lower underparts rufous; tail black with several narrow white bars. Imm.: sim. but throat buffier; under tail coverts barred with black.
**Similar species:** See very rare Orange-breasted Falcon (16). Paler Aplomado Falcon (17) has white band encircling crown, whitish sides of head, and prom. black "sideburns" below eye.
**Voice:** Shrill, high-pitched *ke-ke-ke-ke* in flight or perched.
**Behavior:** Single birds or pairs spend most of time perched on high exposed dead branches and reg. return to favorite ones. Hunt in little sorties from perch and take prey, mostly bats, birds, and insects, in swift fluid flight; somewhat crepuscular. Often confiding.
**Breeding:** 3 BC birds, Feb–Mar, Gulf of Urabá; n Cesar (Carriker). Feb nest, Trinidad (ffrench 1973); Mar (eggs), n Venez. (Beebe 1950); Apr

(eggs), Guyana. Hole nest in tree or building; 2-3 umber brown eggs speckled darker (Brown and Amadon 1968).

**Status and habitat:** Uncommon to fairly common in dry to humid zones; forest edge and clearings with scattered large trees.

**Range:** To 1600m. Throughout. S Mexico to n Argentina and se Brazil. Trinidad.

## 16. ORANGE-BREASTED FALCON
*Falco deiroleucus*                    Pl. 5, Map 140

**Identification:** 13-15″ (33-38cm). Much like more numerous Bat Falcon but larger. Aside from greater size (large ♀ Bat Falcon nearly as big as small ♂ Orange-breasted), differ as follows: black vest narrower (usually), crossing only lower breast and upper belly (not entire breast); rufous wash on chest and upper breast (rufous also often present to some extent on chest of Bat Falcon); *definite coarse buff barring on black vest* not fine white edging; and proportionally much stronger larger feet.

**Similar species:** Also see Aplomado Falco (17).

**Voice:** Peregrinelike; a rasping *aczeek-aczeek* (Haverschmidt 1968).

**Behavior:** Presum. much like Bat or Peregrine Falcon. The reasons for its scarcity are obscure.

**Breeding:** Nest on cliffs or rock ledges. Nests attributed to this sp. in other sites need confirmation.

**Status and habitat:** Very rare. A forest-based sp. usually found near openings or borders. The few known localities are humid forest in foothills or mts.

**Range:** 100-2400m (or higher). Spotty. Pacific slope in Cauca, w base of Perijá Mts., upper Magdalena Val. (Purificación, Tolima; Río Moscopán, Cauca); e base of E Andes in Casanare (Río Upía) and recent sightings at Macarena Mts. (23 Oct 1975 near Caño Duda; 13 Feb 1976, 5 km e El Pueblo La Macarena—T. Lemke). Se Mexico very locally s to Bolivia, n Argentina, and s Brazil.

## 17. APLOMADO FALCON
*Falco femoralis*                    Pls. 5, VII, Map 141

**Identification:** 14-17″ (36-43cm). Slender; "faded" plumage, and with proportionally longer tail than other *Falco*. Cere, orbit, and legs yellow. *Pale bluish slate above with conspic. buffy white eyestripe from forehead encircling crown*; lower cheeks, sides of neck, and chest whitish to pale buff with *prom. black "sideburns" below eye*; sides and band across upper belly black very finely barred white; lower underparts pale rufous; tail dull slate with several narrow white bars. In flight underwings blackish checkered

white. Imm.: sim. but duller, browner above, and breast coarsely streaked brown.

**Similar species:** Bat and Orange-breasted falcons (15, 16) are shorter-tailed, darker, and lack the white headband and black "sideburns."

**Voice:** Scolding *ee-ee-ee-ee-ee* (Friedmann and Smith 1955).

**Behavior:** More an open country bird than related Bat Falcon. Usually alone, perched rather low atop smaller trees, fence posts, or utility poles. Hunts from a perch flying out low and fast, sometimes hovering for prey incl. insects, small birds, and bats; often follows grass fires.

**Breeding:** BC ♀ and imm., 5 July, se base Santa Marta Mts. (Carriker). Nest, 17 Mar, Guárico, Venez., 3 chicks (Mader 1981); another nest, Apr, Trinidad; occupy old stick nest of other birds; 1-3 bluish or cream eggs with red brown blotches (ffrench 1973).

**Status and habitat:** Uncommon and local in grassland, scrub, and dry to arid semiopen areas with scattered trees.

**Range:** To 1000m, rarely to 1700m. Carib. region from Río Sinú e to Guajira, formerly s to upper Cauca Val. (recent recs. ?), upper Dagua Val. (pair seen above Queremal, Jan 1983, Feb 1984—R. Ridgely), and upper Patía Val.; Magdalena Val. (Gamarra, s Cesar; n Huila); e of Andes s to w Meta (Villavicencio; sightings in Macarena Mts. 1975-1976—T. Lemke; P. Gertler), and ne Vichada (Río Tomo). Sw US (now rare) s locally to Tierra del Fuego.

## 18. PEREGRINE FALCON
*Falco peregrinus*                    Pl. VII, Map 142

**Identification:** 15-20″ (38-51cm). *Long pointed wings* and tapered tail. Cere, orbit and legs yellow. *Dark bluish slate above; crown, nape, and broad "sideburns" extending below eye black;* auricular area, sides of neck, and underparts white; breast and belly washed buff and coarsely barred dusky; tail pale blue gray barred dusky. In flight from below underwings barred black and grayish white (*anatum*). Or darker gray above; sides of head entirely black, incl. auriculars; and ventral plumage buffier (*cassini*). Or like *cassini* (inseparable in field) but paler, longer-winged, and less spotted and barred below (*tundrius*). Imm.: sim. but brownish above, buffy white streaked dusky below, soft parts bluish gray.

**Similar species:** Best marks are large size, facial pattern, and dark crown. See Aplomado Falcon (17).

**Voice:** Occas. sharp repeated *hek* notes.

**Behavior:** Usually alone, either in the air or

perched in rather open areas. Flight is swift, graceful, and coordinated with short quick wing beats, sometimes short glides. Stoops on prey at tremendous speeds and gives aerial chase. N temperate populations have declined alarmingly.

**Status and habitat:** Uncommon migrant and n winter resident (Oct–Apr). Mostly coastal (incl. Malpelo Isl.) or high in mts. Presence of s *cassini* or arctic *tundrius* needs confirmation. Sight recs., Apr–Aug, in Canyon of Río Pasto,

upper Magdalena Val. and Puracé area are presum. s temperate migrants; breeding poss., as recently reported breeding n to Peru and n Ecuador (Ellis and Glinski 1980; Jenny et al. 1981).

**Range:** To at least 2800m. W of Andes (no recs. e of Andes). Virtually cosmopolitan. N American breeders (*anatum*) and nearctic breeders (*tundrius*) winter s to Chile and Argentina; s breeders (*cassini*) winter n from Argentina and Chile to sw Colombia.

# CHACHALACAS, GUANS, CURASSOWS: Cracidae (23)

Cracids are a rather homogeneous group of gallinelike birds found chiefly in the New World tropics. They have large strong legs and feet, fowllike bills, and are predominantly arboreal, although some, especially curassows, spend much time on the ground. They eat mostly vegetable matter, especially fruits, seeds, and young shoots. The majority live in forested regions in the humid lowlands, smaller numbers occur in drier habitats or cooler highland forests, and only one normally reaches cold temperate forests near treeline. In most of Colombia at least two species coexist, in the Amazonian region up to four may occur together. All are considered game birds. The chachalacas, despite noisy and rather conspicuous habits, flourish near man and often expand into brushy regrowth areas following deforestation. In contrast, most curassows require undisturbed forest and do not survive even under light hunting pressure. The sequence and taxonomy follow Delacour and Amadon (1973).

[*Ortalis* (Chachalacas): Small, slender, and dull-colored with bare red throat skin (no knobs, wattles, or dewlaps). Dwell in brush, thickets, or forest borders at lower el.; on ground more than guans, much less so than curassows. Loud raucous chorus; no flight display.]

## 1. GRAY-HEADED CHACHALACA

*Ortalis cinereiceps*          Ill. 28, Map 143

**Identification:** 18″ (46cm). Long-tailed. Bare red malar; facial skin and legs slaty. Head and upper neck slaty gray; *otherwise mostly olive brown* becoming grayish brown on lower underparts; *primaries bright chestnut* (conspic. in flight); tail greenish black, outer feathers tipped white.

**Similar species:** Only chachalaca in its range; Chestnut-winged Chachalaca (2), also with chestnut primaries, has rufous head and white lower underparts.

**Voice:** Loud dawn chorus sim. to others of the genus (R. Ridgely) but weaker and less often heard; also a var. of harsh cackling, clucking, and soft notes.

**Behavior:** Typical of the genus. A social bird usually in groups of 6-12 or more; in pairs only when breeding. Mostly arboreal but often in bushes or lower trees; frequently come to the ground. Walk along branches, hop nimbly among twigs, and thread easily through dense

thickets. Not notably shy but become extremely suspicious and wary when hunted.

**Breeding:** BC ♂, Mar, Antioquia (Carriker); 5 Costa Rican nests, Feb–May; low in dense tangle; 3 white eggs (Skutch 1963c).

**Status and habitat:** Common in thickets, second growth in clearings, and forest and river borders.

**Range:** To 300m. Chocó w of Gulf of Urabá and Río Atrato, and s to Quibdó (several seen near Yuto on upper Río Atrato, 10 Mar 1978—Hilty). Honduras to extreme nw Colombia.

**Note:** Sometimes considered a subsp. of Chestnut-winged Chachalaca. Latter differs in voice and plumage and is separated by the swampy lower Río Atrato, a region prob. unsuitable to any chachalaca. Deforestation could bring these populations in contact.

## 2. CHESTNUT-WINGED CHACHALACA

*Ortalis garrula*          Pl. 6, Map 144

**Identification:** 21″ (53cm). Slender and long-tailed. Bare red malar; facial skin and legs slaty. *Head and upper neck chestnut*; rest of upperparts and chest olive brown; *lower underparts white; primaries chestnut* (conspic. in flight); tail greenish black, outer feathers tipped white.

**Similar species:** Only Colombian chachalaca with a chestnut head and white belly. Rufous-

28. CRESTED GUAN (top left, two views), GREAT CURASSOW (bottom center, (♀ left, ♂ right), GRAY-HEADED CHACHALACA (top right, two views)

vented Chachalaca (3), which it may meet or overlap in Guajira, has gray head and no chestnut in wings. In extreme nw Colombia see Gray-headed Chachalaca (1; no known overlap).

**Voice:** Song, typical of the genus, a reverberating chorus (many individuals) with a pronounced "beat" or rhythm. The individual *chá-cha-lac* phrases usually hopelessly lost in an ear-splitting cacaphony recognizable simply as chachalacas. Also a squealing *whooeeell* and *OOEE-chu'uck* in chorus.

**Behavior:** As in Gray-headed Chachalaca.

**Breeding:** BC ♂, Apr, n Antioquia (Carriker); Santa Marta nest, Apr; 3 creamy white eggs, rough-textured (Delacour and Amadon 1973).

**Status and habitat:** Common in scrubby deciduous forest, thickety second growth, arid scrub, riparian borders, and mangroves of n coastal region; humid forest borders at n base of Andes.

**Range:** ENDEMIC. To 800m. Carib. region from upper Río Sinú e to nw, w and sw foothills of Santa Marta Mts., and s to lower Cauca Val. (Río Nechí area) and mid. Magdalena Val. (El Banco, 9°N, s Magdalena). A specimen from Macuira Hills, e Guajira (Marinkelle 1970), may refer to Rufous-vented Chachalaca. Sight recs. of chachalacas (*Ortalis* sp.) from e side of Gulf of Urabá near Turbo may refer to this or previous sp. (Haffer 1975).

**Note 1:** Does not incl. *O. cinereiceps* (Gray-headed Chachalaca) of Mid. America s to nw Colombia, often considered a race of this sp. **Note 2:** Rufous-headed Chachalaca (*O. erythroptera*) from nw Ecuador to nw Peru may occur in sw Nariño, Colombia. Much like Chestnut-winged Chachalaca, but lower underparts buffy and tail tipped chestnut. Humid to drier brushy areas.

### 3. RUFOUS-VENTED CHACHALACA

*Ortalis ruficauda*                   Pl. 6, Map 145

**Identification:** 21" (53cm). Slender and long-tailed. Bare red malar; facial skin and legs slaty. *Head and upper neck slate gray*; upperparts and breast olive brown; belly grayish buff becoming *rufous on under tail coverts*; tail greenish black, outer feathers *broadly tipped white* (or *chestnut—ruficauda*).

**Similar species:** From Variable Chachalaca (4) of s llanos by unmarked breast (no spots), and rufous under tail coverts. From Chestnut-winged Chachalaca (2) in e Santa Marta region by plain olive primaries, gray head, and buff to rufous lower underparts.

**Voice:** Like most chachalacas, greets the dawn with a loud chorus (see under 2); also clucking notes, a low rising whistle, and a harsh squawk when alarmed (Lapham 1970).

**Behavior:** Like others of the genus (see 1).

**Breeding:** 4 BC birds, July, n Cesar (Carriker);

4 shallow twig and leaf nests, May–June, Venez., 1-3 m up (occas. on ground or quite high); 3-4 white eggs, rough-shelled (Friedmann and Smith 1955).
**Status and habitat:** Common in thorny deciduous brushland, dry thickets, and gallery woodland in Guajira.
**Range:** To about 900m. The ne and se foothills of Santa Marta Mts. (w to Río Dibulla and 70km sw of Valledupar) e across Guajira (*ruficrissa*); Nazareth Mts. e tip Guajira (*lamprophonia*); e of Andes in Norte de Santander and n Arauca (*ruficauda*) with intermed. forms *ruficrissa* x *ruficauda* n of Cúcuta. Ne Colombia and n Venez. Lesser Antilles and Tobago.

## 4. VARIABLE (SPECKLED) CHACHALACA
*Ortalis motmot*                    Pl. 6, Map 146
**Identification:** 21″ (53cm). Slender and longtailed. Bare red malar; bare facial skin slaty, legs rosy red. W of Andes (*columbiana*): head pale gray with whitish forehead (or gray—Cauca Val.); otherwise grayish brown above and *brown scaled white on foreneck and breast*; lower underparts buffy white; tail grayish brown, outer feathers mostly *chestnut*. E of Andes (*guttata*): rufescent brown above; head, neck, and breast dark brown; *foreneck and breast conspic. spotted white*; lower underparts rufescent; tail as above.
**Similar species:** In field the 2 races look rather different: *columbiana* is pale-headed and palebellied; *guttata* of e of Andes is darker, more rufescent, and conspic. spotted below. Along n base of Andes may meet Chestnut-winged Chachalaca (2), e of Andes poss. Rufous-vented Chachalaca (3) but as yet no known range overlap. Cf. Andean Guan (see 6).
**Voice:** Loud sunrise chorus sim. to others of the genus (see 2); also quieter chuckling notes and a soft, clear whistle (J. V. Remsen).
**Behavior:** Much like other chachalacas (see 1), though at least in humid Amazonia often in midlevel or canopy at forest edge. Fond of *Cecropia* catkins.
**Breeding:** BC ♂, 10 June, w Caquetá (Carriker); 2 BC birds and imm., Feb, n Huila (Miller 1952).
**Status and habitat:** Fairly common e of Andes in humid forest borders, gallery forest, and clearings with second growth and scattered trees; less often canopy of tall forest. Local w of Andes (largely extirpated) in pockets of humid forest and scrubby woodland. Accessible populations remain w of Buga at Bosque Yotoco (Cauca Val.) and Finca Merenberg, Huila (Magdalena Val.).
**Range:** 100-2500m. Slopes above Cauca Val.

from n Antioquia s to Cauca, and Magdalena Val. from Cundinamarca to Huila (*columbiana*); e of Andes from w Casanare, ne Meta, and Vaupés region (*guttata*) southward. Venez. s of Orinoco and the Guianas s to e Bolivia and most of Amazonia and e Brazil.
**Note 1:** Variable Chachalaca here incl. the forms *O. m. motmot* (Little Chachalaca) of the Guianas and s Venez. s to Río Amazon; *O. m. superciliaris* (Buff-browed Chachalaca) of se Brazil; *O. m. columbiana* (Colombian Chachalaca) w of E Andes; and *O. m. guttata* (Speckled Chachalaca) of Amazonian Colombia to Bolivia. Each has been considered a separate sp. and the present treatment (Delacour and Amadon 1973) may be an oversimplification. **Note 2:** The form *O. m. motmot* (Little Chachalaca) has not been rec. in Colombia but may occur in e Vichada and Guainía (rec. in several places on Venez. side of Orinoco). From *guttata* thus: rufous chestnut head and upper neck contrast with browner lower neck; no white scaling or spotting on foreneck and breast.

[*Penelope* (typical guans): Med. to large size; less robust than curassows; red dewlap and bare blue facial skin conspic.; dark plumage often edged white; prom. flight display with drumming; lowlands and mts.]

## 5. BAND-TAILED GUAN
*Penelope argyrotis*                 Pl. 6, Map 147
**Identification:** 26″ (66cm). Rather long neck and tail; bare ocular area dull blue; dewlap and legs red. *Sides of head frosty white forming a prom. pale eyestripe and cheek patch*; otherwise mainly brown to rufescent brown; mantle and breast conspic. streaked or daubed white (sides of feathers edged white); *tail broadly tipped rufous* (or buffy white—*albicauda*).
**Similar species:** Only guan with pale tail band (not always easy to see). Closely resembles Andean Guan (6), which lacks frosty head pattern and pale tail band and has little or no visible dewlap. Also see Crested and Sicklewinged guans (10, 13).
**Voice:** Noisy during territory establishment (Feb–Apr in n Venez.); otherwise quiet. Wing rattle display, two 1- to 2-sec bursts ("canvas ripping" sound) in flight (P. Schwartz); ♂'s territorial song a low *kuak*, mostly early mornings; alarm a loud grating *gi-gi-gigigi-gik* and ventriloquial rolling *gu-rr-urr-urrrr* (Schäfer 1953b).
**Behavior:** Travel in small families or bands of 3-5; quiet and secretive except during breeding season. Primarily arboreal and wary, seldom on ground except for fallen fruits or to drink.

**Breeding:** 9 BC birds, Jan–Sept, chicks Apr and June, Santa Marta Mts. (Carriker; Todd and Carriker 1922); loose nest 1-7m up in dense foliage, Venez. (Schäfer 1953b).

**Status and habitat:** Uncommon to fairly common (infrequently seen) in wetter forest, forest borders, and tall second growth, occas. coffee plantations. Can be seen on Cuchilla de San Lorenzo on n slope Santa Marta Mts.; elsewhere inaccessible or threatened by deforestation.

**Range:** 900-2300m. Santa Marta Mts. (*colombiana*); Perijá Mts. (*albicauda*); and ne end of E Andes in Norte de Santander s on e slope to w Meta, above Villavicencio (*mesaeus*). Ne Colombia and n Venez.

**Note:** Does not incl. Bearded Guan (*P. barbata*) of sw Ecuador and nw Peru, sometimes considered a subsp. of *P. argyrotis*.

## 6. ANDEAN GUAN
*Penelope montagnii*          Pl. 6, Map 148

**Identification:** 24″ (61cm). Upper highlands. Throat more feathered than most *Penelope*; *small red dewlap* often not evident in field; bare ocular area dull blue; legs dull red. *Head, neck, and chest grayish; head finely streaked and breast feathers edged* (scaled) *grayish white*; otherwise bronzy brown above; lower back and rump dull chestnut brown; lower breast and underparts rufescent.

**Similar species:** In Andes poss. confused with sim.-sized Variable Chachalaca (4), which has paler head, whitish belly, and mostly chestnut outer tail feathers. In mts. of ne overlaps Band-tailed Guan (5), but latter has more prom. dewlap and facial markings, brighter and whiter feather edging on breast, and rufous tip on tail. Sickle-winged Guan (13) lacks scaly streaking, is distinctly 2-toned below, and has large, bare blue ocular area. Crested Guan (10) looks twice the size.

**Voice:** Apparently calls mainly Feb–Mar (Venez. Andes); sim. to Band-tailed Guan but weaker. A loud honking (R. Ridgely). Unlike other *Penelope*, wing-whirr display a single rattle, not 2-parted (P. Schwartz).

**Behavior:** Much like Band-tailed Guan, perhaps even more arboreal, and mostly at mid-level or higher. Wanders seasonally in search of fruit, at times well out into second growth or to isolated trees away from forest. Small groups of 3-7 when not breeding.

**Breeding:** A downy chick, presum. this sp., 27 Mar, 3500m (Delacour and Amadon 1973); a juv., 11 June, near Bogotá (Olivares 1969a).

**Status and habitat:** Uncommon to locally fairly common in humid forest, forest borders, and tall second growth. Found at higher el. than any other *Penelope* in Colombia and often survives in rather small patches of highland forest where not persecuted.

**Range:** 2200-3400m; rare stragglers higher or lower. Perijá Mts., E Andes (incl. sight recs. in Huila), and C Andes s through e Nariño. Nw Venez. s in Andes to nw Argentina.

## 7. BAUDO GUAN
*Penelope ortoni*          Pl. 6, Map 149

**Identification:** 26″ (66cm). *Small* and plain with rather long tail. Bare ocular area blue; *prom. dewlap red*; legs dull red. Head and upper neck grayish brown; *otherwise mainly rich brown*; feathers of foreneck and breast narrowly edged whitish.

**Similar species:** A small drab guan. Sim.-sized Sickle-winged Guan (13) lacks red dewlap and whitish feather edging on breast and has contrasting rufous lower underparts; at close range note latter's *much larger bare blue ocular area*. Crested Guan (10) is sim. but much larger and more crisply streaked below. Andean Guan (6), normally at higher el., has small dewlap and more rufescent rearparts.

**Behavior:** Single birds seen in w Ecuador perched quietly for long per. in upper part of trees on steep forested slopes (Hilty; F. Vuilleumier).

**Status and habitat:** Perhaps local. Humid and wet forest, esp. in lower foothills. Known from only a small no. of localities.

**Range:** 100-1500m. Spottily from near Panama border (Río Juradó) s on Pacific slope (Baudó Mts.; Dagua and Anchicayá vals.) to Cauca (below Cerro Munchique). W Colombia and w Ecuador.

## 8. SPIX'S GUAN
*Penelope jacquacu*          Pl. 6, Map 150

**Identification:** 35″ (89cm). *Large*. Rather long neck and tail, slight bushy crest. Bare facial skin blue; dewlap and legs coral red. Mainly olive brown; wings and tail glossed green; neck and breast *finely* streaked white (only edges of feathers); *lower breast and abdomen dull chestnut*.

**Similar species:** Only guan in its range. As large as a curassow but more slender and with proportionally smaller head and longer neck. At e base of E Andes may meet sim. Crested Guan (10), which has bushier crest, broader and more extensive white edging on neck and breast, and mostly olive brown (not chestnut) lower underparts.

**Voice:** Very noisy during breeding season (mostly Jan–Apr in ne Venez.); 2-part wing-rattle display (P. Schwartz). "Song" a very loud, raucous crowing, *kerr-ow, kerr-ow, kerrrow, urrrreck, urrrreck, kerrrrow* . . . , reminiscent of distant howling dog; vocal mainly predawn and dusk.

**Behavior:** Single birds or pairs (not groups) are rather wary and keep mainly from forest mid-level to canopy; seldom descend to ground.

**Breeding:** A nest 15 Apr, gallery forest near Carimagua, ne Meta; mostly leaves, about 5m up in tree (S. Furniss). BC ♂, mid-Aug, Vaupés (Olivares and Hernández 1962).

**Status and habitat:** Humid forest, forest borders, slashed clearings with scattered trees, and gallery forest; forest-based but less confined to forest than curassows.

**Range:** To 500m in foothills at e base of Andes. Casanare-Cundinamarca-Meta boundary (Río Upía), ne Meta (sightings Carimagua, 1976—S. Furniss), and e Vichada (El Tuparro—INDERENA) southward. Guyana and s Venez. s to e Bolivia and most of Amazonian Brazil.

### 9. CAUCA GUAN

*Penelope perspicax*      Pl. 6, Map 151

**Identification:** 30″ (76cm). Rather large with short crest. Bare facial skin blue; dewlap and legs coral red. Head, neck, upper back, and breast brownish gray narrowly scaled whitish on mantle, heavily scaled whitish on breast; otherwise *rearparts and tail mainly chestnut.*

**Similar species:** Crested Guan (10) is sim. but somewhat larger, more conspic. streaked (rather than scaled), and rearparts olive brown (not chestnut). Andean Guan (6) differs as follows: tiny dewlap, much smaller size, weaker and grayer streaking on foreparts, *much duller* chestnut on lower back and wings, and tail brown.

**Breeding:** An egg, 3 May, at La Palma in upper Magdalena Val. reputedly of this sp. (Delacour and Amadon 1973).

**Status and habitat:** Uncertain, poss. near extinction (no recent recs.). Formerly humid forest but former range largely deforested. Pacific slope recs. are mostly near low passes, and the sp. is unlikely to be found extensively on Pacific slope.

**Range:** ENDEMIC. 1300-2000m. Definitely only the slopes above mid. Cauca Val. from Quindío area s to Cauca (Cerro Munchique), a few low passes on adj. Pacific slope in Valle and Cauca (at least formerly); poss. head of Magdalena Val. (La Palma, sw of San Agustín).

### 10. CRESTED GUAN

*Penelope purpurascens*      Pl. 6, Ill. 28, Map 152

**Identification:** 36″ (91cm). Large with long neck and tail. Short bushy crest; bare facial skin blue; *large red dewlap* and rosy red legs. Mostly dark olive brown; *neck and breast with conspic. narrow white streaks* (feather edging); mantle

narrowly edged grayish; rump and under tail coverts chestnut.

**Similar species:** As big as a curassow but more slender. Most other *Penelope* within its range look only half its size. Cf. Baudo Guan (7; faint white edging), Andean Guan (6; small dewlap and rufescent rearparts), and Band-tailed Guan (5; frosty facial pattern and tail band); also Spix's (8) and very rare Cauca Guan (9).

**Voice:** "Song" a loud nasal and guttural honking *quonk, quonk, quonk rrrrrrrrrrr* (Hilty); alarm *oo-eek, oo-eek* (Chapman) and various other grunts and whistles. In n Venez. sing mostly Nov–May; double wing-whirring drum in display flight (P. Schwartz).

**Behavior:** A rather wary, mainly arboreal guan, most often seen in pairs in fruiting trees. Walk alertly along branches, at times call very noisily, at other times remarkably quiet and secretive. Feed most actively in dim light of dawn or dusk.

**Breeding:** 5 BC birds, Mar–May, n Colombia (Carriker). Bulky leaf and twig nest in broken stump or well up in tree; about 3 white eggs, (Delacour and Amadon 1973).

**Status and habitat:** Uncommon and local in humid and wet forest and forest borders; occas. drier forest or riparian areas of n Colombia.

**Range:** Mostly below 1000m (once to 1950m). Pacific slope, and e from Gulf of Urabá across most of n Colombia n of Andes to Santa Marta area, s in mid. Magdalena Val. to nw Santander, head of Magdalena Val. (w of San Agustín), and e base of E Andes from Norte de Santander s to n Boyacá. Mexico to w Ecuador and n Venez.

[*Aburria* (Piping-Guans and Wattled Guans): Slender, med.-sized; differ from most *Penelope* in having even more arboreal habits, shorter legs, larger wattle or dewlap and different color patterns; flight display well developed; 1 sp. in lowlands, 1 in highlands, often separated generically.]

### 11. COMMON PIPING-GUAN

*Aburria (Pipile) pipile*      Pl. VIII, Map 153

**Identification:** 27″ (69cm). Unmistakable. Long neck and tail. Base of bill baby blue; tip of bill, *throat, and dewlap cobalt blue; legs red. Mostly black* glossed greenish blue with bare white ocular area; *shaggy white crest and nape; large white wing patch*; wing coverts and chest flecked with white.

**Voice:** Noisy during breeding season; otherwise quiet. "Piping" (hence name) a ser. of about 6 high, clear whistles, gradually ascending in pitch, reminiscent of Scale-backed Antbird (H. Sick), this often followed by wing-whirring flight display of 2 quick wing-claps, then 2 wing-whirring rattles that seem to fan in one direction, than fan back in reverse (rattles faster, drier and higher-pitched than *Penelope*); song and rattle given mainly at dawn (P. Schwartz).

**Behavior:** An attractive sp. found in 2's or 3's; when not breeding in much larger groups. Move with agility among canopy or subcanopy branches, rarely on the ground. Cross clearings with a flurry of wing beats, then a sail. Can usually be seen without difficulty where not persecuted.

**Breeding:** Laying ♀♀, 29 May, Tres Troncos, e Caquetá (Blake 1955); 1 BC ♀, 4 Feb, Macarena Mts. (Olivares 1962); another, 17 Feb, Orinoco region (Cherrie 1916); twig nest in dense canopy vegetation; 3 yellowish white eggs (Delacour and Amadon 1973).

**Status and habitat:** Local. Humid *terra firme* and *várzea* forests, esp. along forest borders and river edges; gallery forest in s llanos.

**Range:** To 500m. E. of Andes from Cundinamarca-Boyacá boundary (Río Guavio) eastward and southward. The Guianas and s Venez. to e Bolivia, w Amazonian Brazil, and n Paraguay.

**Note:** Common Piping-Guan (*A. pipile*) incl. the largely allopatric forms *pipile, cumanensis, grayi, nattereri,* and *cujubi,* some or all of which have been considered separate spp. in the genus *Pipile.* Only *cumanensis* (White-headed Piping-Guan) is found in Colombia.

## 12. WATTLED GUAN
*Aburria aburri*                    Pl. 6, Map 154
**Identification:** 28″ (71cm). Long slender neck and small head. Bill pale blue basally with dark tip; legs pale yellow. *Plumage blackish strongly glossed bronze green; small bare yellow throat patch and long dangling yellow wattle.* Young birds lack the wattle.

**Similar species:** Only rather large blackish cracid of subtropical el.

**Voice:** "Song" a loud, sirenlike *ba-reeeeer-ah* (J. Weske), rising, sustained, then snapping over at end; repeated incessantly. Rarely heard wing-whirr flight display a clap then 2 quick rattles (like Common Piping-Guan), usually given once or twice at dawn or dusk (P. Schwartz). In PN Cueva de los Guácharos most calling Dec–Feb (P. Gertler).

**Behavior:** In 2's or 3's, mainly in forest midlevels to canopy though at various hts. in fruiting trees. Noisy during breeding season and then easily found.

**Breeding:** Ad. with 2 chicks, late Mar, PN Cueva

de los Guácharos (P. Gertler). Nest undescribed; eggs from Antioquia, believed this sp., dirty white, smoother shelled than most cracids (Sclater and Salvin 1879).

**Status and habitat:** Humid and wet forest and adj. tall second growth and borders; almost always in steep mt. terrain. Numerous in PN Cueva de los Guácharos but threatened with loss of habitat over much of Colombian range.

**Range:** 600-2500m (el. limits vary locally, perhaps seasonally). Ne base Santa Marta Mts. (Los Gorros 600m), Perijá Mts., and all 3 Andean ranges, incl. Macarena Mts. Andes of nw Venez. s to s Peru.

[*Chamaepetes*: Small, arboreal, montane guans related to *Aburria* but with proportionally longer legs and no dewlap. Flight display well developed.]

## 13. SICKLE-WINGED GUAN
*Chamaepetes goudotii*              Pl. 6, Map 155
**Identification:** 25″ (64cm). Small, compact, and mostly dark. *Large bare loral and orbital area bright blue;* legs dull pinkish red. Head, neck, upperparts, and upper breast dark olive brown (or foreneck mainly rufescent—*sanctaemarthae*); wings and tail glossed green; *lower breast and abdomen contrasting uniform rufous chestnut* (or darker, more slaty black above—*fagani*).

**Similar species:** Bright blue face, absence of dewlap, small size, and contrasting "2-toned" underparts are the marks. Cf. Andean, Baudo, Band-tailed, and much larger Crested guans (6, 7, 5, 10), all of which have red dewlaps and whitish streaking on neck and breast. Wattled Guan (12) is larger, all bronzy black, and longer-necked.

**Voice:** Usually quiet. Loud alarm a repeated *kée-uck,* when foraging a soft *whéet-ta.* Flight display a single 2-sec wing-rattle (like holding flexible strip in spokes of revolving bicycle wheel) in short (about 20m) downward inclined flight; about 3-6 flights, mostly between same 2 trees at dawn or dusk; displays seen Nov, Finca Merenberg, Huila (Brown), mostly Mar–May in Santa Marta area (Johnson and Hilty 1976).

**Behavior:** Small, rather wary guan usually in pairs or groups of 3-5. Primarily arboreal and usually forest midlevel or higher though also infrequently on ground. Often visit fruiting trees at dawn or dusk; some seasonal el. movements in part of range.

**Breeding:** 3 BC birds, June, C and W Andes (Carriker); 2 ♀♀, each with 1 barely flying juv., 3 June, Santa Marta Mts., 2400m (Hilty);

eggs from Antioquia, reportedly this sp., white, finely-pitted (Sclater and Salvin 1879).
**Status and habitat:** Humid and wet mt. forest, forest borders, tall second growth, and occas. lighter open woodland (coffee plantations). One of the few guans that can still be seen from or near roadsides in several areas, esp. San Lorenzo above Santa Marta, Florencia-Guadalupe road, old Buenaventura road, and Finca Merenberg, Huila.
**Range:** Mostly 1500-3000m; to 500m on Pacific slope in Anchicayá Val. Santa Marta Mts. (*sanctaemarthae*); W and C Andes, and E Andes from Cundinamarca to Cauca (*goudotii*); Pacific slope in Nariño (*fagani*); e slope in Nariño (*tschudii*) and w Caquetá (subsp.?). Not in Perijá Mts. Colombia s in Andes to s Peru and n Bolivia (La Paz).

[*Nothocrax*: From *Crax* by cryptic plumage, smaller size, and nocturnal behavior.]

## 14. NOCTURNAL CURASSOW

*Nothocrax urumutum*     Pl. VIII, Map 156
**Identification:** 26″ (66cm). Small curassow. *Long, expressive black crest of slightly recurved feathers.* Bill reddish orange; large, bare, multicolored ocular area yellowish above, blue in front, slaty below. *Mainly chestnut*; back, wings, and central pair of tail feathers vermiculated with fine wavy black lines; rest of tail black with broad buffy tip.
**Voice:** "Song," at night mostly before midnight or before dawn (moonlight or dark) from a perch high in tree is a soft, hollow, pigeonlike booming or humming *hoo, hoo-hoo, hoo-hoo-hoo,* then a long pause and a guttural hoot (Wetmore); or a 2-pt. *hm-hm-hm̂, hm-hm̂-hm-uh* with a long, deep, downward groan at end; more resonant and louder than booming of related *Crax* (Sick *in* Delacour and Amadon 1973); about once a min.
**Behavior:** Nocturnal when singing. In upper Río Negro heard mid-Oct and late Jan–early Feb. Groups of 3-4 seen on ground under fruit trees at dusk, then flushed to trees (Ruschi 1979).
**Breeding:** Laying ♀, 16 Oct, and large stick nest with 2 white eggs 4m up in nearby viny tree, upper Río Negro (Ruschi 1979).
**Status and habitat:** Humid forest. Numerous in Río Guainía region (P. Schultes) and on Río Vaupés at Caño Tí w of Mitú (B. Lamar). Perhaps more common in blackwater region of Río Orinoco and Negro than s in Amazonia.
**Range:** To about 500m. Spottily e of Andes from w Caquetá (near Florencia, at least formerly) and Río Guaviare (not rec. n to Macarena Mts.) southward. Sw Venez. (Amazonas) to e Peru and w Amazonian Brazil.

[*Crax*: Large, robust, mainly black (♂) or cryptically patterned (some ♀♀); usually crested (some curly), often with colored knobs, wattles, or adornments at base of bill; most terrestrial of family. Sing by humming or whistling (no flight display), often from perch above ground. Nest a small coarse stick and leafy saucer, low to med. ht. in tangle, on stump, or at palm frond base; 2 white eggs. Nests known for Crestless, Northern Helmeted, Great, and Black curassows, none yet from Colombia. Unlike other cracids, do not regurgitate to feed young.]

## 15. CRESTLESS (LESSER RAZOR-BILLED) CURASSOW

*Crax tomentosa*     Pl. VIII, Map 157
**Identification:** 33″ (84cm). *No crest.* Bill red, paler at tip; legs orange red (♂), yellow (♀). Mainly black; mantle and breast glossed blue; *belly, under tail coverts, and broad tail tip chestnut.*
**Similar species:** Only curassow with combination of chestnut belly and chestnut tail tips. ♀ Wattled Curassow (23) has chestnut belly but solid black tail, also curly crest. May contact range of Salvin's Curassow (16) at base of Macarena Mts. and along Ríos Apaporis and Caquetá, but latter has white belly and tail tips. Also see Black and Yellow-knobbed curassows (22, 21), both with white bellies.
**Voice:** "Song" a booming or humming *umm——um-m-um,* 2d ser. after a pause of about 3 sec; in captivity a sharp *cut cut cweer* of annoyance, much like Salvin's and Black curassows (Delacour and Amadon 1973). Like other *Crax*, sings mornings, evenings, moonlight nights, and intermittently during day; vocal much of yr. in Venez. (P. Schwartz).
**Behavior:** Mostly terrestrial but poss. spends more time in trees than most other *Crax*. Calls from an elevated perch or from ground and, like other curassows, rather unsuspicious.
**Breeding:** In Venez. Orincoco, 2 nests with eggs, June (Cherrie 1916).
**Status and habitat:** Humid *terra firme* forest, esp. along small streams; also gallery forest in s llanos. Reported relatively numerous n of Río Caquetá in Amazonas and replaced on s bank by *C. salvini* (Scheuerman 1977).
**Range:** To 500m. E of Andes from s Meta (Río Guayabero at s base of Macarena Mts.; 1 examined on Río Camoa near San Martín—Brown) and extreme ne Meta (sighting, 1976—S. Furniss) e to Río Orinoco (sightings, El Tuparro, e Vichada, 1977—T. O. Lemke; Venez.

side at San Fernando de Atabapo and Yavita) and s to Río Caquetá. Guyana, Venez. s of Orinoco (n of it in Apure), e Colombia, and adj. nw Amazonian Brazil.

**Note:** Placed by some in the genus *Mitu.*

### 16. SALVIN'S CURASSOW
*Crax salvini*                  Pl. VIII, Map 158
**Identification:** 35″ (89cm). Well-developed crest usually carried depressed. Legs and bill reddish orange; *upper mandible deep, compressed, and strongly arched.* Mainly black; mantle and breast glossed bluish; *belly, under tail coverts, and broad tail tip white.*
**Similar species:** In its range the only curassow with combination of white belly and white tail tip. Black Curassow (22) and ♂ Wattled Curassow (23) have solid black tails; nearby note bill differences. Also see Crestless and Razor-billed curassows (15, 17), both of which may contact or slightly overlap range of Salvin's.
**Voice:** Booming or humming "song" a low *cronk cronk cronk,* somewhat different than usual tubalike curassow song (Delacour and Amadon 1973); or *cóohgh, coóóohgh,* repeated for long periods while crouching on branch (Lehmann *in* Delacour and Amadon 1973).
**Behavior:** Presum. typical of the genus.
**Status and habitat:** Humid *terra firme* forest. Few recs. but certainly reg. well away from settled areas. Meets and may be replaced at n border of range by Crestless Curassow and to the e by Razor-billed Curassow.
**Range:** To 600m. E of Andes from s Meta (s base of Macarena Mts. on Río Guayabero) and w Caquetá (sw of Florencia) e to c Amazonas (approx. 71°W) on Río Caquetá and southward. E Colombia, e Ecuador, and ne Peru.
**Note:** Placed by some in the genus *Mitu.*

### 17. RAZOR-BILLED CURASSOW
*Crax mitu*                      Pl. VIII, Map 159
**Identification:** 35″ (89cm). Well-developed crest usually carried depressed. *Legs and bill red,* upper mandible swollen basally and much raised with narrow culmen. Mainly black; mantle glossed bluish; *belly, thighs, and under tail coverts chestnut; broad tail tip white.*
**Similar species:** Only curassow with combination of chestnut belly and white tail tips. In Amazonas meets or overlaps several *Crax* with confusingly sim. patterns. Crestless Curassow (15) has chestnut tail tip, Salvin's (16) a white belly, and both sexes of Wattled (23) a solid black tail (♂ also a white belly); nearby, bill differences of all of above are helpful.
**Voice:** Humming or booming song of ♂, *hm-hm——hm, hm-hm——hm,* last note sharply accented, given after a pause 2-3 times as long

as previous notes (Sick *in* Delacour and Amadon 1973); soft *pweet* of annoyance or alarm (O'Neill 1974).
**Behavior:** Much like other *Crax.* In se Peru pairs, less often groups of 4-5, walk on ground but flush readily to trees when disturbed. ♂ ♂ sing from perch 6-12m up, day or night except heat of day (R. Ridgely).
**Status and habitat:** Humid *terra firme* forest, smaller canopied forest streams, and swampy places in forest, also *várzea* in se Peru (R. Ridgely). Thought to meet or be replaced n of Río Caquetá by Crestless Curassow, and w of approx. 71°W (Amazonas) by Salvin's Curassow (Scheuerman 1977).
**Range:** To 300m. E Amazonas from Pto. Nariño (on Río Amazon) n to s bank of Río Caquetá and w to approx. 71°W (incl. San Martín on Peruvian side of Río Putumayo). Extreme se Colombia, e Peru, e Bolivia, and Amazonian Brazil s of Río Amazon (doubtless n of it near Colombia).
**Note:** Placed by some in the genus *Mitu.*

### 18. NORTHERN HELMETED CURASSOW
*Crax pauxi*                     Pl. VIII, Map 160
**Identification:** 36″ (91cm). *Large fig-shaped bluish gray casque on forehead.* Bill and legs dull red. ♂ and normal phase ♀: mostly black; mantle and breast glossed greenish and bluish and scaled dull black; *belly, under tail coverts, and tail tip white.* Rufous phase ♀ (uncommon): *head and neck blackish, rest of plumage rufous brown finely barred and vermiculated black;* wing coverts with small white tips; belly and under tail coverts white; tail blackish broadly tipped buffy white.
**Voice:** ♂'s booming "song" a low ventriloquial droning (like groan of old tree), 6-10 four-part drones per min. (Schäfer 1953b); alarm a soft repeated *tzsuk.*
**Behavior:** Notably terrestrial, although roosts, nests, sings, and seeks safety in lower branches. Flight, chiefly when pressed, is usually a flurry of wings followed by a long sweeping glide. Pairs or family groups, occas. up to 6 individuals or more are somewhat crepuscular and mod. wary.
**Breeding:** Laying ♀, 7 Apr; BC ♂, 21 June; juv., 11 Aug, Perijá Mts. (Carriker); nest building, Mar, Venez., 4-6m up and as in others of genus; 2 eggs; juvs. with ads. until Oct (Schäfer 1953b).
**Status and habitat:** Cool, humid forest ("cloud forest"), esp. humid ravines with a thick undergrowth of dwarf palms and terrestrial aroids (avoids forest borders).
**Range:** 900-1800m; prob. wanders higher and lower. Perijá Mts. and e slope of E Andes from

se Norte de Santander to n Boyacá; reported by hunters in foothills of sw Arauca. Ne Colombia and n and nw Venez.
**Note:** Placed by some in the genus *Pauxi.*

## 19. GREAT CURASSOW
*Crax rubra*                    Ill. 28, Map 161
**Identification:** 36″ (91cm). Prom. curly crest extending to nape. ♂: *mainly black with base of bill and large knob on upper mandible bright yellow;* abdomen and under tail coverts white (rarely narrow white tail tip). ♀: head, crest, and upper neck finely barred black and white; *otherwise mainly bright chestnut;* tail rufous chestnut with 6-8 conspic. *buffy white bars bordered black; no yellow knob on bill.* Imm. ♂: like ad. but somewhat browner and no yellow knob. Dark and barred phase ♀♀ of C America and Mexico do not occur in Colombia.
**Similar species:** Unmistakable on Pacific coast; in upper Sinú Val. see Blue-billed Curassow (20).
**Voice:** ♂'s "song" a prolonged low booming or humming *oom-m-m,* subdued and ventroloquial (Wetmore 1965a), also a high-pitched descending whistle, *wheep, wheep, wheeu,* or either note singly (Eisenmann).
**Behavior:** Alone, in pairs, or occas. small family groups. Like other *Crax,* mosty terrestrial but roost and seek cover in trees, sometimes ascending to canopy. Unwary where not persecuted.
**Breeding:** 4 BC birds, incl. 2 laying ♀♀, Mar, Chocó and nw Antioquia (Carriker); in Panama nest like others of genus, 3-30m up; 2 eggs, rough-shelled (Wetmore 1965a).
**Status and habitat:** Humid and wet lowland and foothill forest. Persists only in remoter areas and cannot be seen near any roads on Pacific coast. Meets and is presum. replaced by Blue-billed Curassow in upper Sinú region (Haffer 1975).
**Range:** To 300m. Pacific coast from Panama border southward, Gulf of Urabá region (on e side e to lower Río Mulatos) and e to upper Sinú Val. (Quebrada Naín) at n end of W Andes. E Mexico s to w Ecuador.

## 20. BLUE-BILLED CURASSOW
*Crax alberti*                    Pl. VIII, Map 162
**Identification:** 36″ (91cm). Prom. curly crest extending to nape. ♂: mostly glossy black with *base of bill and large knoblike wattles at base of lower mandible bright blue;* belly, thighs, and under tail coverts white; tail tipped white. Normal phase ♀: *mostly black with primaries, lower underparts, and front of thighs bright chestnut;* crest, back, wings (except primaries), tail, and center of breast with *narrow, widely spaced, wavy white*

*lines;* tail broadly tipped white, *base of bill blue* (no wattles); tip yellow. Rare barred phase (only n slope Santa Marta Mts.): sim. but primaries, foreneck, and entire underparts (except belly and under tail coverts) coarsely and thickly barred white.
**Similar species:** Only *Crax* with blue base of bill; ♂ otherwise much like ♂ Great Curassow (19). Striking white-barred ♀ not likely confused.
**Voice:** ♂'s song a low booming or humming like other *Crax* (Delacour and Amadon 1973).
**Behavior:** As in other *Crax.*
**Breeding:** 2 July, chicks with ad., Santa Marta area (Todd and Carriker 1922).
**Status and habitat:** Humid lowland, foothill, and lower mt. forest. Reportedly not common anywhere in Santa Marta region but most numerous (at least formerly) in humid lowlands, esp. Don Diego area (Todd and Carriker 1922). Now quite scarce in Snía. de San Jacinto (Haffer 1975) and doubtless in settled areas elsewhere.
**Range:** ENDEMIC. To 1200m (n slope Santa Marta Mts.). Isolated forests of n Bolívar (Snía. de San Jacinto) and lower Magdalena Val. in sw Magdalena; from upper Sinú Val. (Quimarí) e across n base of W and C Andes (incl. upper Río San Jorge, lower Cauca, and Nechí vals.) to w side of humid mid. Magdalena Val. (Snía. San Lucas) s at least formerly to w of Honda in n Tolima; w, n, and e slopes of Santa Marta Mts. (s on w to Aracataca).

## 21. YELLOW-KNOBBED CURASSOW
*Crax daubentoni*                    Pl. VIII, Map 163
**Identification:** 36″ (91cm). Well-developed curly crest extending to nape. ♂: *glossy black with base of bill, large knob on cere, and large knoblike wattles on lower mandible bright yellow;* belly, thighs, and under tail coverts white; tail tipped white. ♀: sim. but *breast barred white,* crest feathers white basally (seldom visible in field), and bill black.
**Similar species:** Only curassow in its range. ♂ much like Blue-billed Curassow (20), which it may meet in e Santa Marta area, but base of bill and adornments bright yellow (not blue). ♀ lacks chestnut lower underparts and white upperpart barring of ♀ Blue-bill. E of Andes in llanos see Crestless and Black curassows (15, 17), whose ranges may or may not contact that of Yellow-knobbed.
**Voice:** Territorial song, mainly Feb–June in Venez. llanos, a loud, clear, leisurely whistle, *wheeeeeeeeuuuuuuu,* rising slightly, then falling and fading (reminiscent of whistle of falling bomb!).
**Behavior:** ♂♂ scatter on territories during

breeding season but at other times, esp. in drier periods, may gather in loose groups near water. Call and display with raised fanned tail from trees and otherwise also rather arboreal. **Breeding:** Juv., 13 Aug, w slope Perijá Mts., 800m (Carriker); in Venez. Apr–June (early rains); 2 ♀♀, mid-May, had large eggs (Delacour and Amadon 1973); 1 Guárico nest in tree, 5 June; 2 eggs (W. Mader). **Status and habitat:** Known from a few scattered localities in moister gallery forest and wooded hammocks in llanos of Arauca; in the Perijá foothills from pockets of damp woods in vals. and ravines surrounded by drier deciduous woodland. **Range:** 500-1500m. W foothills of Perijá Mts. from Montes de Oca (Carraipía) s to Fonseca; e of Andes from e Norte de Santander s to nw Arauca. Ne Colombia to c Venez. (mainly llanos).

## 22. BLACK CURASSOW
*Crax alector*                  Pl. VIII, Map 164
**Identification:** 38″ (97cm). Very large. Short curly and erect crest extends to nape. ♂: mainly glossy black with *slightly swollen cere and base of bill orange red* (orange yellow—Macarena Mts.); *belly, thighs, and under tail coverts white.* ♀: sim. but crest barred white at base (seldom visible in field). **Similar species:** Short curly crest, lack of distinct adornments on bill, and solid black tail are good marks. Most other curassows in or contacting range (cf. Crestless, 15, Salvin's, 16, Razor-billed, 17, poss. Yellow-knobbed, 21) have white or chestnut tail tips. Also see Wattled Curassow (23). **Voice:** "Song" a deep humming or booming *umm-um . . . umm, um-um,* mainly midnight to early morning, also late evening; *pit pit peer* when annoyed; *peep* or short whistle in alarm. **Behavior:** Usually alone or in pairs on forest floor. Sing from ground or elevated perch; seek safety in lower- or middle-story branches and roost in trees. Occas. accompany Gray-winged Trumpeters when foraging. Complex display involves posturing, wing claps, and booming song. **Breeding:** BC ♀, 9 Jan, Macarena Mts. (Olivares 1962). **Status and habitat:** Floor of humid *terra firme*

forest, tangled forest borders, riverine thickets, and gallery forest. Common (at least formerly) along e base of E Andes; on slopes of Macarena Mts. Gilliard est. 1 bird per 3 acres of forest (Delacour and Amadon 1973). **Range:** Lowlands. E of Andes from nw Meta (to 1300m in foothills above Villavicencio at least formerly) and Macarena Mts. (Río Guayabero) e to e Vichada (Maipures) and s to Río Caquetá (Tres Troncos, e Caquetá). E Colombia, s Venez., the Guianas, and n Amazonian Brazil.

## 23. WATTLED CURASSOW
*Crax globulosa*                Pl. VIII, Map 165
**Identification:** 35″ (89cm). Well-developed curly crest. ♂: *mainly black with base of bill, large knob on cere, and 2 knoblike wattles at base of lower mandible bright red;* belly and under tail coverts white. ♀: sim., but *white replaced by chestnut;* crest barred white at base (seldom visible in field); and *base of bill red but no wattles or knob.* **Similar species:** Best marks for gaudily handsome ♂ are adornments at base of bill and solid black tail; ♀ much like Crestless Curassow (15) but lacks chestnut tail tips. Cf. Salvin's and Razor-billed curassows (16, 17), both of which have white-tipped tail; also Black Curassow (22), which is known to overlap at Tres Troncos on Río Caquetá. **Voice:** "Song" a high-pitched, descending whistle, *wheeeeeeee,* much like that of Yellow-knobbed Curassow (Delcour and Amadon 1973); no booming or humming yet rec. **Behavior:** Apparently somewhat more arboreal than other curassows and does not often descend to the ground. Reported to be best located by its characteristic whistle given from an elevated perch. **Status and habitat:** Apparently local. Drier parts of humid lowland forest (in Peru—the Koepckes), riverine *várzea* border on Río Javarí s of Leticia (Hilty), and near edge of a lake and pond (H. W. Bates). Not well known in much of range. Generally found s of range of Black Curassow. **Range:** To 300m. E of Andes from Río Caquetá (Tres Troncos, e Caquetá) to Leticia. Se Colombia to ne Bolivia and w and c Amazonian Brazil (s of Río Negro).

# WOOD-QUAILS, BOBWHITES: Phasianidae (9)

The majority of the species in this family are Old World in distribution, especially in Asia. Most Colombian species are secretive forest inhabiting wood-quails, far better known by their loud ringing calls than by sight. Only the familiar Crested Bobwhite is found in more open areas and frequently seen. In actions and song it is much like its well-known northern allies. Members of the family are, in general, terrestrial and granivorous; all nest on the ground.

## 1. CRESTED BOBWHITE
*Colinus cristatus*                Ill. 29, Map 166
**Identification:** 8-9″ (20-23cm). *Conspic. pointed crest sandy buff.* ♂: *face and throat buff to whitish*; hindneck black spotted white; upperparts brown spotted and vermiculated black; underparts buff to chestnut with *large white spots on breast and flanks*; belly barred black (or chestnut below with large white spots on belly and flanks—e slope E Andes). ♀: duller, crest brown, throat streaked black.
**Similar species:** Pointed crest and white spotted underparts are the marks. Other Colombian quail are confined to forest.
**Voice:** ♂ a flat *oit, bob-white*, 1st note faint or lacking; call resembles that of Northern Bobwhite (*C. virginianus*), but faster, not as rich and mellow.
**Behavior:** Terrestrial and run rapidly on ground in small coveys or in pairs when breeding. Normally shy and if flushed, fly off a short distance in different directions, then drop down and hide. ♂ less vocal than Northern Bobwhite but can be heard throughout year.
**Breeding:** 8 BC birds, July–Sept, chicks in Feb, Santa Marta area (Carriker; Darlington 1931); broods Apr–July (early wet season) at Carimagua, ne Meta (S. Furniss). Nest on ground; up to 15 eggs.
**Status and habitat:** Fairly common in drier grassland and pastures with brush and thickets.
**Range:** Carib. region from upper Sinú Val. e to Guajira (to 1000m in Santa Marta area), Pacific slope in upper Dagua and upper Patía vals., entire Cauca Val. (to 1800m). Magdalena Val. (to about 2200m) and temperate zone

of E Andes from Boyacá (Lago de Tota, 3100m) to Sabana de Bogotá; lowlands e of Andes s to Macarena Mts. and Río Guaviare, spottily in pockets of savanna or following deforestation to Vaupés and w Putumayo. Guatemala s to w and c Panama; Colombia e to Guianas and nw Brazil.

## 2. MARBLED WOOD-QUAIL
*Odontophorus gujanensis*        Pl. 1, Map 167
**Identification:** 9-11″ (23-28cm). *Bare ocular area orange to red.* Short bushy crest brown to blackish; otherwise *mainly dark brown*; nape, upper back, and foreneck grayish; and entire plumage finely barred and vermiculated buff and black.
**Similar species:** Only wood-quail with bare orange to red facial skin and otherwise more or less uniform plumage. Size and color of several small tinamous but none finely barred throughout; note different shape. Tinamous are small-headed, have longer thinner necks, and look tailless.
**Voice:** A fast, rhythmic, and musical *córocorovado, córocorovado, córocorovado . . .* , mostly at dawn and dusk. Call antiphonal: ♂ gives *córocoro*, ♀ the *vado* (Chapman 1929).
**Behavior:** Small coveys of 5–8 call softly and move more or less single file on forest floor. When alarmed, crouch and hide, or run; fly only when surprised or hard-pressed.
**Breeding:** BC ♂ and 3 laying ♀♀, Mar–May; Mar nest (1 egg) at base of forest tree and chicks, Apr, nw Colombia (Carriker); BC ♀, Feb, Putumayo (Blake 1955). Nest may have leaf and stick roof and side entrance (Sclater and Salvin 1879). Prob. 4 eggs; chicks precocial (Skutch 1947b).
**Status and habitat:** Floor of humid forest, occas. forest edge or tall second growth. Numerous on Río Apaporis (Dugand 1952) and Río Vaupés.
**Range:** To 1200m on e slope E Andes. From Panama border s in n Chocó to Río Truandó, e across humid lowlands n of Andes to lower and mid. Magdalena Val. (s to nw Santander); Snía. de San Jacinto; e base of E Andes and generally from s Meta (Macarena Mts.) and e Guainía southward (no Amazonas recs.). Costa Rica to e Bolivia and Amazonian Brazil.

## 3. RUFOUS-FRONTED WOOD-QUAIL
*Odontophorus erythrops*          Pl. 1, Map 168
**Identification:** 10-11″ (25-28cm). Short crest blackish brown. *Forehead and sides of head chestnut*; otherwise dark brown above finely ver-

29. CRESTED BOBWHITE (♂)

miculated buff; a few inconspic. black spots on wing coverts and back; *throat and chest black with a prom. narrow white crescent across lower throat; rest of underparts chestnut.*
**Similar species:** Only other wood-quail with a white throat collar is rare and poss. extinct Gorgeted Wood-Quail (7), which is spotted white below. See Tacarcuna Wood-Quail (8). Chestnut Wood-Quail (5) lacks white throat collar but is otherwise sim.
**Voice:** Mainly early morning; a rollicking, energetic *chowita, chowita, chowita . . .* , repeated rapidly a doz. times or more and with merry ringing quality; usually 2 or more birds call together.
**Behavior:** Pairs or family-sized groups are terrestrial and when alarmed may "freeze"; if pressed run rapidly, but rarely fly. As with other wood-quail, often travel single file across trails or small forest openings.
**Breeding:** 6 BC birds, Jan–May, nw Colombia and Valle (Carriker); pair with downy chicks, Apr, Anchicayá Val. (Hilty). Costa Rica nest a small excavation at base of spur tree root; leaf and grass lining; 4 unmarked creamy white eggs (Carriker 1910).
**Status and habitat:** Uncommon on floor of humid and wet forest; mostly foothills and lower slopes, local in lowlands.
**Range:** To 1100m (Anchicayá Val.). Pacific slope from Panama border southward, e across n end of W and C Andes to mid. Magdalena Val. in s Bolívar (Snía. San Lucas) and s to n boundary of Caldas. Costa Rica to w Ecuador.
**Note:** Colombian *parambae* is perhaps a separate sp. from C American *melanotis*, which ranges to e Darién (Mt. Pirre and Pto. Obaldia) and poss. nw Colombia (R. Ridgely); *melanotis* has sides of head and throat black and lacks white throat band.

## 4. BLACK-FRONTED WOOD-QUAIL
*Odontophorus atrifrons*          Pl. 1, Map 169
**Identification:** 11-12″ (28-30cm). *Short bushy crest and hindcrown chestnut. Forehead, sides of head, and throat black;* remaining upperparts brown vermiculated buff, grayish, and black becoming pale sandy brown on lower back; breast grayish brown somewhat spotted white; belly cinnamon buff streaked black.
**Similar species:** Only wood-quail with uniform black face and throat. Cf. very rare Gorgeted Wood-Quail (7). At s end of E Andes see Chestnut Wood-Quail (5).
**Voice:** A whistled *bob-white*, much like Santa Marta Antpitta (T. B. Johnson); a rattling call resembling that of Grey-breasted Wood-Rail (Todd and Carriker 1922) is presum. a rhythmically repeated phrase typical of the genus.

**Behavior:** As in other wood-quail.
**Breeding:** 2 BC ♂♂, 1 laying ♀, Aug, 1 imm., July, Perijá Mts. (Carriker).
**Status and habitat:** Fairly common (seldom seen) on floor of humid mt. forest in Santa Marta region. Status uncertain in now largely deforested n end of E Andes.
**Range:** 1200-2800m. Santa Marta and Perijá mts.; n end of E Andes in Norte de Santander (near Cáchira) and e Santander (6°40′N near Molagavita). Ne Colombia and w Venez.

## 5. CHESTNUT WOOD-QUAIL
*Odontophorus hyperythrus*          Pl. 1, Map 170
**Identification:** 10-11″ (25-28cm). *♂: bare area around eye and streak behind eye whitish;* upperparts brown vermiculated black; large black spots on scapulars and some buff and gray markings on nape and wings; *sides of head and underparts rufous chestnut;* breast and belly paler more orange rufous. ♀: sim. but breast and belly grayish brown.
**Similar species:** White on head and solid rufous chestnut underparts (incl. throat) are the marks. Rufous-fronted Wood-Quail (3) lacks the white and has black throat; no known range overlap. See Dark-backed Wood-Quail (6) in sw Nariño.
**Voice:** Like other wood-quail, a long rollicking song, mostly in early morning, a rapidly repeated *orrit-killyit . . .* , or either part separately; alarm a low *peetit, peetit . . .* (Brown); in W Andes above Cali heard Mar–Apr (Miller 1963).
**Behavior:** As in other wood-quail. Shy coveys of 3-9 run rapidly on ground or occas. perch slightly above ground (P. Gertler).
**Breeding:** BC ♂ and laying ♀, May, C Andes (Blake 1955; Carriker).
**Status and habitat:** Uncommon and local on floor of humid mt. forest, occas. denser borders and second growth. Reg. (difficult to see) in PN Cueva de los Guácharos (P. Gertler).
**Range:** ENDEMIC. 1600-2700m. W and C Andes s to Cauca and head of Magdalena Val. in Huila (both slopes).

## 6. DARK-BACKED WOOD-QUAIL
*Odontophorus melanonotus*          Map 171
**Identification:** 10-11″ (25-28cm). *Head and upperparts deep brownish black finely vermiculated rufous;* flight feathers uniform dusky; *throat and upper breast rufous chestnut;* lower underparts blackish brown vermiculated pale rufous; bare ocular area and feet dusky.
**Similar species:** Not known to overlap range of Chestnut Wood-Quail (5), which has rufous sides of head and conspic. bare whitish ocular area. Rufous-fronted Wood-Quail (3) has black throat and chest and narrow white throat band.

**Status and habitat:** Known in Colombia from 1 ♂ at Ricaurte, Nariño (1500m), 27 June 1957 (Fitzpatrick and Willard 1982). Montane forest. In nw Ecuador occurs 1200-1500m.
**Range:** Lower subtropical zone. Sw Colombia and nw Ecuador.

### 7. GORGETED WOOD-QUAIL
*Odontophorus strophium*                      Map 172
**Identification:** 10″ (25cm). Very rare. ♂: short crest and ear coverts blackish brown; eye-stripe, malar area, and chin speckled black and white; *throat, sides of neck, and chest black with narrow white collar across lower throat*; rest of underparts rufous chestnut; *breast boldly spotted white*; upperparts dark brown spotted black and lightly streaked buff on mantle. ♀: sim., but chin and throat white with band of black spots across center of throat.
**Similar species:** Only wood-quail in range with black and white throat bands and white spots on breast. Cf. Rufous-fronted and Black-fronted wood-quails (3, 4).
**Status and habitat:** Floor of humid forest. Formerly known only from 2 "Bogota" specimens and 2 specimens (1915) from a w spur ridge of E Andes w of Bogotá Subía. A recent specimen (ca. 1972) taken in oak forest on the w slope of E Andes near Betulia, Santander, is prob. this sp. but needs confirmation (King 1979). This sp. is endangered as the type area in Cundinamarca is largely deforested, but some suitable forest areas still remain in Santander.
**Range:** ENDEMIC. 1500-1800m. W slope of E Andes at Subía (w of Bogotá), Cundinamarca, and Betulia, Santander.

### 8. TACARCUNA WOOD-QUAIL
*Odontophorus dialeucos*
**Identification:** 9-10″ (23-25cm). Crown and crest black; *broad eyebrow, ocular area, and foreface incl. chin white*; cheeks to sides of neck brown; hindneck buffy; remaining upperparts dark brown vermiculated black; *throat and chest white with a black band across lower throat*; rest of underparts buffy brown vermiculated black.
**Similar species:** White eyebrow and foreface unique in range.
**Behavior:** A little known wood-quail of humid forest floor, found in pairs or small groups, once observed 5m up in small tree; fairly common in extreme e Panama (Wetmore 1965a).

**Status and habitat:** First discovered in Panama in 1963. Recently rec. on slopes of Cerro Tacarcuna in PN Los Katíos, n Chocó (Rodríguez 1982).
**Range:** 1200-1450m in Panama. Extreme nw Chocó, Colombia, and e Darién, Panama.
**Note:** Starred Wood-Quail (*O. stellatus*), of e Ecuador (Río Napo southward) to n Bolivia and w Brazil s of Amazon, might occur in se Colombia. 10″; crown bright rufous chestnut; upper back gray becoming olive brown on lower back; wings brown; wing coverts dotted buff; throat and sides of head gray; rest of underparts rufous chestnut. ♀ has dusky crown. Lowland forest; habits and rollicking call like others of genus.

### 9. TAWNY-FACED QUAIL
*Rhynchortyx cinctus*                    Pl. 1, Map 173
**Identification:** 7-8″ (18-20cm). ♂: *eyebrow and entire sides of head bright tawny orange* with crown and narrow stripe behind eye brown; otherwise brown above mottled gray and buff on wings; *throat and breast gray*; lower underparts buff to whitish. ♀: above like ♂, *head and breast chestnut*; throat and narrow streak behind eye buffy white; *lower underparts white coarsely barred black*.
**Similar species:** Much smaller than wood-quail. ♂ easily told by bright orangish sides of head, ♀ by barred lower underparts.
**Voice:** When disturbed a rapid nervous chirruping rather like Northern Bobwhite, *Colinus virginianus* (Karr 1971).
**Behavior:** A shy terrestrial forest bird that usually "freezes" or runs when disturbed, rarely flies. One of a flock of 8 flushed to a small branch 3m up (Olivares 1957b); apparently often pairs.
**Breeding:** BC ♀, 3 Jan, Punto Muchimbo, Valle; BC ♀, 22 Feb, Río Nuquí, Chocó; 3 BC birds, Apr–May, n Antioquia (Carriker); laying ♀, Mar, and 2 downy young, Apr, e Panama (Wetmore 1965a).
**Status and habitat:** Apparently rather rare and local but because of its small size and secretive habits it may be more common than recs. indicate. Floor of humid forest, rarely forest borders.
**Range:** To 1000m. Pacific coast (no recs. from n boundary of Valle to s Cauca) and e along n base of W and C Andes to mid. Magdalena Val. in s Bolívar (e slope Snía. San Lucas at Volador). Honduras to nw Ecuador.

# LIMPKINS: Aramidae (1)

The Limpkin is a marsh-dwelling bird superficially resembling an ibis but most closely related to cranes (Gruidae) and rails. The single species in the family is confined to warmer parts of the New World. They are usually seen in freshwater swamps or marshes where they feed mainly on large *Pomacea* snails.

## 1. LIMPKIN

*Aramus guarauna*     Pl. 3, Map 174

**Identification:** 24-28" (61-71cm). Ibislike with broad rounded wings, slender neck, long legs, and long *slightly drooped bill*. Plumage *mainly brown with a few inconspic. whitish streaks on head, neck, and upper back*; bill and legs dark.

**Similar species:** Ibises have more decurved and slender bills, bare facial skin, and a smoother more sustained flight (except Green Ibis). See nonbreeding ad. and imm. Glossy Ibis (p 75) and imm. Balck-crowned Night-Heron (p 66).

**Voice:** Often noisy, esp. at dusk or at night; a loud wailing or lamenting *kree-ee-oou* or *carée-oou*, over and over.

**Behavior:** Partially nocturnal though normally abroad by day as well. Probes shallow water or marshy vegetation and when not feeding may perch in low bushes. Flight buoyant with stiff upward jerks of wings. Often alone, but during dry periods several may concentrate at remaining ponds with water and even probe cracks in mud.

**Breeding:** BC ♂, 3 Aug, Cesar Val. (Carriker); Sept–Oct, Guárico, Venez. (Thomas 1979b). In Trinidad Aug–Nov (rainy season); platform nest of twigs and leaves less than 3m up in marsh vegetation; 3-6 eggs cream with brown blotches and spots (ffrench 1973).

**Status and habitat:** Local in swamps, freshwater marshes, marshy river banks, mudflats, and mangroves. Common in PN Salamanca and adj. lower Magdalena Val. In llanos of Venez. most numerous June–Oct (Thomas 1979b).

**Range:** To 400m. Pacific coast (mangroves), e across most of n Colombia n of Andes to Guajira and w base of Perijá Mts.; s in Cauca and Magdalena vals. (Tolima); spottily in Norte de Santander (Cúcuta); and e of Andes in w Meta (near Villavicencio—P. Gertler), ne Meta (1 seen, El Porvenir, Apr 1979—W. McKay), and in w Caquetá. Prob. more widespread e of Andes (rec. just n of Arauca in Venez. and "common" at Limoncocha, Ecuador—Pearson et al., 1977). S Florida and Mexico s to Bolivia, n Argentina, and Uruguay. Greater Antilles.

# TRUMPETERS: Psophiidae (1)

Trumpeters are a small group of terrestrial birds largely confined to Amazonia. Allied to cranes (Gruidae) and rails, they are more rhealike (Rheidae) in shape with long legs, a humped carriage, and short fowllike bill. The feathers of the head and neck are very short, dense, and velvety in appearance. They eat both plant and animal matter including reptiles and amphibians and are known to swim to cross rivers. Their courtship, breeding, and social behavior, and even the significance of their "play" (O'Neill 1974) have not been studied.

## 1. GRAY-WINGED TRUMPETER

*Psophia crepitans*     Ill. 30, Map 175

**Identification:** 19-22" (48-56cm). *Long-legged, hunchbacked bird* with short yellowish bill. *Mainly velvety black with purplish and greenish gloss on lower foreneck; rather lax gray inner wing feathers cover the lower back*; legs bluish gray.

**Voice:** A single note or ser. of 6-8 low, guttural, humming *guum* or *umm* notes, starting quickly, then slowing and falling, *ummumm-umm-umm, umm, umm, umm* (P. Schwartz); often vocal at night or in groups. Loud harsh grunts in alarm.

**Behavior:** A terrestrial and notably social forest bird, usually in groups of 3-15 (occas. 50 or more). Flee by running but when pressed fly laboriously to branches of mid. story or higher. Normally rather wary but as pets become tame and affectionate and are much prized for their habit of "sounding the alarm" at disturbances day or night and for their prowess as snake hunters. Roost in trees and frequently active at night.

**Breeding:** BC ♂, upper Orinoco, Venez., 17 Mar (Friedmann 1948); 8-10 flightless young with 10-12 ads., 21 Apr, Guyana; reported nesting colonies of 5-6 in adj. trees, and twig and leaf nests 4-5m up (Beebe et al. 1917) need confirmation; 1 incubating in hollow tree in Surinam; white eggs (Haverschmidt 1968).

**Status and habitat:** Uncommon on floor of hu-

30. GRAY-WINGED TRUMPETER

mid *terra firme* forest, usually well away from settled areas.

**Range:** To 500m. E of Andes from w Meta (formerly Villavicencio area) and Río Guaviare southward. The Guianas and s Venez. to e Ecuador, ne Peru (s to Río Marañon) and extreme nw Brazil (s to Río Amazon).

**Note:** Pale-winged Trumpeter (*P. leucoptera*) of e Peru, nw Bolivia, and Amazonian Brazil is found n of Amazon in nw Brazil and ne Peru and may occur in extreme e Amazonas or Vaupés (meeting but not overlapping range of Gray-winged). From Gray-winged Trumpeter by distinctly whitish (not gray) secondaries.

# RAILS, GALLINULES, COOTS: Rallidae (28)

This cosmopolitan family is well represented in Colombia, although little is known of the habits of most species. Many are notoriously secretive denizens of marsh, swamp, or damp tall grassland. Some are also crepuscular or nocturnal in habits and are rarely detected except by their calls. From the spotty records, ranges have been assumed, but without doubt some birds are more widespread than present records indicate. "Typical" rails are characterized by narrow, laterally compressed bodies and fairly long bills; crakes are similar but usually have shorter bills; both inhabit damp or marshy areas. By contrast, gallinules and coots are specialized for a more aquatic habit and are excellent swimmers. Coots, with the addition of lobed toes, are also good divers. Most rails are quite omnivorous, a fact that has undoubtedly contributed to their success. The sequence of genera and species follows Olson (1973a).

## 1. SPECKLED CRAKE

*Coturnicops notata*  Map 176
**Identification:** 5.5″ (14cm). Very small. Short bill and dusky legs; eyes orange. Dark olive brown above *streaked with black and spotted white*; the white spots more scalelike on wing coverts and rump; *below blackish streaked white on foreneck and breast and barred with narrow widely spaced white bands across flanks, abdomen, and under tail coverts*; throat white.
**Similar species:** Gray-breasted Crake (6) is quite dark, but upperparts and breast are uniform (not streaked or spotted). Also see Black Rail (see note under 6), which lacks the white streaking on breast.
**Behavior:** Has been taken at night with lights. Apparently very secretive and reluctant to flush.
**Status and habitat:** Very rare. Known from 1 specimen in Colombia and from about 16 in widely scattered localities in S America. Grassy savanna, rice, and alfalfa fields and dense marshy vegetation (Ripley 1977). Apparently not a true marsh rail. Birds from n S America (incl. Colombia) may be migrants from the south.
**Range:** E of Andes in s Meta at s base of Macarena Mts. (Río Guayabero, 400m; Mar). Venez. (Portuguesa—Aug; Mérida—June), Guyana (Sept), Paraguay (Dec) Uruguay, s Brazil (Sept), and s Argentina.

## 2. OCELLATED CRAKE

*Micropygia schomburgkii*  Pl. 7, Map 177
**Identification:** 5.5″ (14cm). Very small mostly yellowish buff rail. Short bill dusky; eyes and legs coral red. Crown and hindneck dusky brown *finely spotted white*; rest of upperparts pale brown with *numerous large white spots rimmed with black; eyebrow, sides of head, and underparts cinnamon buff to yellowish buff*; center of throat and abdomen whitish. Imm.: uniform grayish brown above with some white spotting on neck and shoulders; below creamy white with diffused ochraceous band across breast.
**Similar species:** Most like Yellow-breasted Crake (18) but without latter's blackish upperparts and boldly barred flanks.
**Voice:** Song in Brazil, presumed this sp. a ser. of clear strong *pr-pr-pr*'s, lasting 20-30 sec, ascending at first; a harsh whirring *pirrr* may be an alarm (Sick *in* Ripley 1977).
**Behavior:** Mostly on or near the ground in tall grass. Difficult to flush; 1 captured at night by lantern light (Olivares 1959).
**Breeding:** BC ♂, 18 Mar, Río Guayabero, Ma-

carena Mts. (Olivares 1959). Guyana eggs, buff with fine and coarse light brown spots (Schönwetter).
**Status and habitat:** Apparently local in tall damp grass and grassland, sometimes near marshes or forest borders. Primarily a "grass" rail; not in marshes. Reg. in small nos. at Carimagua, Meta (S. Furniss).
**Range:** To 500m. E of Andes. Known only from s Meta (Río Guayabero, s base of Macarena Mts.) and extreme ne Meta at Carimagua (1976—S. Furniss). Sw Costa Rica; spottily in s and e Venez., Guyana, Fr. Guiana, e Peru, e Bolivia, and c and se Brazil (Mato Grosso southeastward).
**Note:** Placed in the genus *Coturnicops* by Ripley (1977).

## 3. CHESTNUT-HEADED CRAKE

*Anurolimnas castaneiceps*  Pl. 7, Map 178
**Identification:** 8″ (20cm). Short thick bill yellowish green with dark tip; legs dull orange red. *Head, neck, and breast rufous*; hindcrown and back of neck darker; rest of plumage contrasting olive brown. Imm.: duller, rufous replaced by brown to olive brown.
**Similar species:** Uniform Crake (15) is all dull rufous brown without the contrasting upperparts and underparts. Russet-crowned Crake (5), also mostly uniform above and below, has gray cheeks and black (not yellowish green) bill.
**Voice:** Loud chorus, like a wood-rail, often antiphonal, a syncopated *koook to-kok, kook to-kok* . . . with vars. (T. Parker); recalls several "cuckoo clocks" running simultaneously.
**Behavior:** Not well known. Secretive and primarily a "land rail." Walks rather upright like a wood-rail (R. Ridgely).
**Breeding:** BC pair, 2 June, w Caquetá (Carriker).
**Status and habitat:** Uncommon, perhaps also local, in bushes or on floor of humid *terra firme* forest, second growth, and thickets along stream banks; lowlands and foothills.
**Range:** To 1500m. E of Andes, known from w Caquetá, Putumayo, and se Nariño (poss. Amazonas). Se Colombia to e Peru (incl. mouth of Río Curaray).

## 4. BLACK-BANDED CRAKE

*Anurolimnas fasciatus*  Pl. 7, Map 179
**Identification:** 7″ (18cm). Short black bill; greenish legs. *Head, neck, and breast chestnut*; belly, flanks, and crissum orange rufous *widely*

*banded black*; remaining upperparts olive brown. **Similar species:** Rufous-sided Crake (8) shows white down part or all of median underparts and has flanks barred black and white (not broad black and rufous bands). Also see Virginia Rail (10). Other Colombian rails e of Andes with rufous underparts have unbarred flanks.
**Voice:** Often vocal. Song, frequently given simultaneously by both members of a pair (antiphonal?), a low churring rattle much like that of 5, 7, and 8.
**Behavior:** Pairs act much like others of the genus (see Russet-crowned, 5); skulk in tall damp grass. Most vocal in early morning and late evening.
**Breeding:** Bulky, grassy, domed nest with side entrance, June 1981, 1.7m up on vine-covered fallen limb in clearing, Río Javarí, Brazil (Hilty).
**Status and habitat:** Tall wet grass and marshy vegetation along streams and pools. Prob. more widespread than the few recs. indicate.
**Range:** To 500m. W Caquetá (s of Florencia; Tres Esquinas), w Putumayo (sight near Río Putumayo—Brown) and Amazons (Leticia). Se Colombia, Ecuador, e Peru (incl. Pebas in ne) and w Amazonian Brazil (e to Río Purús).
**Note:** Has been placed by some in the genus *Laterallus*.

## 5. RUSSET-CROWNED CRAKE
*Anurolimnas viridis* Pl. 7, Map 180
**Identification:** 6.5″ (16.5cm). Small plain rail. Short bill blue gray tipped dusky; eyes and narrow bare eyering red; legs dull rosy red. *Crown rufous contrasting with gray sides of head*; hindneck and rest of upperparts olive brown; below cinnamon rufous fading to buff on throat and center of belly (no flank bars).
**Similar species:** Easily confused with Uniform Crake (15), which lacks contrasting gray on sides of head, is more uniform rufous brown above and below, and has yellowish green bill. Also see Chestnut-headed Crake (3).
**Voice:** A loose, churring rattle sim. to Rufous-sided but is louder and slower, with individual notes more enunciated (R. Ridgely).
**Behavior:** Furtive and difficult to see. Stays under cover as walks daintily on ground or climbs or runs through grass, thickets, even on low branches, and rarely or never flushes. Most vocal in morning and evening.
**Breeding:** 6 nests in marsh(?), 21 May–10 June, El Centro, Santander (Boggs 1961); spherical grass nest with side entrance, sometimes also ladderlike platform, about 1m up in dense vegetation; 1-3 eggs (Sclater and Salvin 1879).
**Status and habitat:** Brushy manioc patches,

damp grassy or bushy pastures, and overgrown roadsides. Mainly a "grass" rail.
**Range:** To 900m. Lower Cauca Val. at n end C Andes (Valdivia) e to mid. Magdalena Val. in s Bolívar (e slope Snía. San Lucas) and s to ne Antioquia (Remedios) and w Santander (El Centro); e of Andes near Villavicencio, w Meta, and sighting at Pto. Inírida, e Guainía (Sept 1978—Hilty and Robbins). Locally in Guianas and s and e Venez. s through most of Brazil, e Ecuador, and e Peru to Mato Grosso and Rio de Janeiro.
**Note:** Placed by some in the genus *Laterallus*, which it *closely* resembles in voice.

## 6. GRAY-BREASTED CRAKE
*Laterallus exilis* Pl. 7, Map 181
**Identification:** 6″ (15cm). Short bill dusky above, green below; legs yellow brown (or orange red?—Cauca Val.). *Head, neck, and underparts mostly gray; throat whitish; flanks and under tail coverts barred black and white; nape and upper back bright chestnut*; remaining upperparts olive brown; wing coverts obscurely barred white.
**Similar species:** No other Colombian rail with gray underparts has bright chestnut mantle. See Colombian and Paint-billed Crake (19, 20), former also with unbarred flanks. Larger Ash-throated Crake (17) is streaked above.
**Voice:** Call in Panama, reportedly this sp., *dit dit . . . dit dididee-deet*, last part fast and tinkling; in response to playback a louder *dit-deet-deet-dur* (J. Wall recording); also a soft sharp *check* (D. Pearson).
**Behavior:** Very difficult to see unless flushed, then flies weakly a short distance and drops in marsh.
**Breeding:** BC ♀, 8 Feb, Chocó (Carriker); Trinidad nest in July, a grassy sphere with side entrance and near sugar cane root; 3 cream-colored eggs spotted dark brown at larger end (ffrench 1973).
**Status and habitat:** Apparently uncommon and local in marshy lake edges, flooded rice fields, and wet meadows. Usually requires some shallow standing water, occas. away from water but not in dry grass.
**Range:** To 1200m. Scattered recs. in n Chocó (Sautatá; Nuquí), n Córdoba (Montería), Barranquilla area, mid. Cauca Val. (Valle), w slope of E Andes in nw Cundinamarca (below Albán, 1200m), and e of Andes in w Meta (near Villavicencio), w Caquetá, and e Putumayo. Belize s locally to w Ecuador, c Peru, Bolivia, n Brazil, Paraguay, and the Guianas. Trinidad.
**Note:** Black (Crake) Rail (*L. jamaicensis*), known from 2 presumed Colombian specimens ("Bogotá" and "Nouvelle Grenade") may occur in

temperate zone of E. Andes. Breeds in N America; winters from gulf coast of US s an unknown distance. Rec. spottily in C America and reappears as a resident in coastal Peru and in Chile and Argentina. Like Gray-breasted Crake but differs as follows: much darker overall, bill black, and midback spotted white.

## 7. WHITE-THROATED CRAKE
*Laterallus albigularis*                  Pl. 7, Map 182
**Identification:** 6″ (15cm). Small slender rail. Short greenish bill; greenish gray legs; eyes red. Crown, hindneck, and upperparts brown; forehead and *sides of head to sides of breast bright rufous; throat, foreneck, and most of median underparts white* (median breast sometimes rufous); flanks and under tail coverts barred black and white. Imm.: duller above; sides of head to sides of breast gray; belly dark brown very narrowly barred whitish.
**Similar species:** Virginia Rail (10) has streaked back, gray cheeks, and short white eyestripe. Other Colombian rails w of Andes that are predom. rufous below lack flank barring.
**Voice:** Call an abrupt, loose, churring, gradually descending (settling down) but not slowing, *thur'tr'tr'tr'tr'tr'tr'tr'tr*; often answered by another nearby.
**Behavior:** Often heard though very furtive and extremely difficult to see. Runs through grass and is almost imposs. to flush. Pairs may call almost from an observer's feet yet remain invisible.
**Breeding:** 13 BC birds, Dec–Aug, Chocó to Cesar (Carriker); in Antioquia globular grass nests with side entrance, a little above ground or water, in bush or grass; 3-5, pale buffy white eggs sparsely dotted reddish brown (Sclater and Salvin, 1879).
**Status and habitat:** Commonly heard in damp grassy pastures, thickets, ditches, forest clearings, and marshy areas. Does not require standing water and more a "grass rail" than a "marsh rail." Replaced e of Andes by next sp.
**Range:** To about 1600m. Generally w of Andes but not rec. on Pacific coast n of mid. Río San Juan (Sipí, 4°39′N). Nicaragua to w Ecuador.
**Note:** Considered by some a subsp. of next sp.

## 8. RUFOUS-SIDED CRAKE
*Laterallus melanophaius*                  Map 183
**Identification:** 6″ (15cm). Very sim. to White-throated Crake, differing mainly in under tail coverts uniform unbarred rufous brown (not barred black and white).
**Similar species:** Black-banded Crake (4) has entire head and underparts rufous (no white) and entire lower underparts broadly banded black. Also see Virginia Rail (10).

**Voice:** Virtually identical to White-throated Crake.
**Behavior:** As in White-throated Crake.
**Status and habitat:** Damp grassy or marshy areas, often well away from water. Not well known in Colombia.
**Range:** To 500m (prob. higher). E of Andes in w Caquetá, prob. also Putumayo and Amazonas. Venez. (only in n), Guyana, and Surinam locally e of Andes to c Argentina and Uruguay.
**Note:** Does not incl. *L. albigularis* (White-throated Crake) of w of Andes, by some considered a subsp. of this sp.

## 9. CLAPPER RAIL
*Rallus longirostris*                  Map 184
**Identification:** 13″ (33cm). Large grayish brown salt marsh rail. *Rather long bill slightly decurved*; lower mandible yellowish; legs grayish. Above olive streaked grayish; crown and hindneck brown; short eyestripe and throat white; sides of head and foreneck grayish becoming pale ochraceous on lower underparts; *flanks coarsely banded olive brown and white.*
**Similar species:** Large size, faded gray brown plumage, and prom. barred flanks are best marks in salt marsh habitat. Smaller, brighter Virginia Rail (10) has contrasting gray cheeks and is presently known only from freshwater habitats in Colombia.
**Voice:** A loud grating or ticking ser., *kek-kek-kek . . .* , also a snarling note; noisy during breeding season (ffrench 1973).
**Behavior:** Like n birds, flushes at one's feet from brackish marsh, flies with legs dangling and soon drops in; most active at low tide. Preys heavily on fiddler crabs.
**Breeding:** In Trinidad, Apr–Dec, mostly May–June; twig nest among mangroves near water level; 3-7 pale buff eggs spotted and blotched deep purple (ffrench 1973).
**Status and habitat:** Resident in saltwater and brackish water marshes and in mangroves along coasts. Prob. more widespread than the few known localities suggest.
**Range:** Carib. coast in Guajira (Ríohacha, Bahía Portete, Pto. López) and coastal Nariño (2 sightings, 6 Sept 1979, Boca Grande s of Tumaco—Hilty). Coastal s US s to Belize; ne Colombia casually to e Brazil; sw Colombia s on coast to nw Peru.

## 10. VIRGINIA (LESSER) RAIL
*Rallus limicola*                  Map 185
**Identification:** 8″ (20cm). *Med.-sized* with rather long, slender, slightly decurved bill; lower mandible and legs brownish red. Above streaked brown and black; shoulders dull

brownish chestnut; throat and short eyestripe white; *sides of head gray contrasting with cinnamon neck and underparts; flanks black barred white*. Imm. (n subsp. *limicola*): mainly dark brown more or less streaked black above; sides of head gray; throat, center of breast, and belly white; sides and flanks blackish, usually with some barring.

**Similar species:** Rufous-sided Crake (8) has short greenish bill, and sides of head and throat uniform ferruginous; smaller Russet-crowned Crake (5) has unbarred flanks and is not *known* to overlap in range. Also see Clapper Rail (9).

**Voice:** Best known by voice. In Ecuador a rather metallic, clattering *keh-keh-keh kehkehkeh* dropping and weakening and much like n temperate birds (R. Ridgely).

**Behavior:** N birds (*limicola*) are very secretive and adept at hiding in marshy grass. Seldom fly and when flushed soon drop down again.

**Breeding:** Presum. like n birds; grass and reed platform in wet grass or reeds; 7-12 pale buff eggs spotted brown.

**Status and habitat:** Resident in freshwater marshes, reed beds, and wet grassland. Not well known in Colombia.

**Range:** Both slopes of Nariño; on the e near headwaters of Río Putumayo at Sibundoy (2200m), on the w near Túquerres (2500-2600m) in Sapuyes Val. N populations breed from Canada s to Mexico; winter to Guatemala. S populations resident from sw Colombia s to Tierra del Fuego.

## 11. BOGOTA RAIL
*Rallus semiplumbeus*    Pl. 7, Map 186
**Identification:** 10″ (25cm). Med.-sized with *conspic. dull red bill and legs*. Above dull olive brown streaked black; shoulders dull rufous chestnut; *sides of head and underparts gray*, central throat whitish; *flanks black coarsely banded white*.

**Similar species:** From any other Colombian rail with gray underparts by red bill and legs; note restricted range.

**Voice:** A clear, piercing, high-pitched *peeep*, like signal whistle of ground squirrel (*Spermophila*); a short clattering when disturbed.

**Behavior:** Seems less furtive than others of the genus. Reg. comes to edge of rushes and small openings early in morning.

**Status and habitat:** Uncommon to locally fairly common in marshes and reed beds around lakes on Sabana de Bogotá. Easiest to see at Parque La Florida near El Dorado International Airport.

**Range:** ENDEMIC. E Andes from c Boyacá (Lago Tota, 3100m) s to Sabana de Bogotá (2500-2700m).

**Note:** A single specimen of *R. (limicola?) peru-*

*vianus* (Virginia Rail) from an unknown Peruvian locality may be a subsp. of Bogota Rail.

## 12. RUFOUS-NECKED WOOD-RAIL
*Aramides axillaris*    Pl. 7, Map 187
**Identification:** 12″ (30cm). Large. Bill yellowish green; legs coral red. *Head, neck, breast, and sides rufous chestnut*; central throat white; upper back blue gray; *lower back, abdomen, and tail black*; wings olive with rufous primaries. Imm.: sim. but rufous of head, neck, and underparts replaced by gray.

**Similar species:** See Gray-necked and Brown wood-rails (13, 14), both of which have gray heads. Several other Colombian rails (see esp. Uniform Crake, 15) are mostly rufous below but are smaller and lack black rearparts.

**Voice:** Recalls Gray-necked Wood-Rail, a loud incisive *pik-pik-pik*, or *pyok-pyok-pyok*, repeated about 8 times, mostly at dawn and dusk; often antiphonal (ffrench 1973).

**Behavior:** Poorly known. Secretive and difficult to see in mangroves but at low tide may leave them to forage in open on mudflats. Tail cocked.

**Breeding:** In Trinidad, July and Oct.; nest and eggs like Gray-necked Wood-Rail (Belcher and Smooker 1934-37).

**Status and habitat:** Apparently local. Largely or wholly confined to mangroves on Pacific coast; on ne end Santa Marta Mts. rec. on floor of wooded foothill forest. Extent of occurrence inland unknown.

**Range:** Carib. region from Cartagena area very spottily e to ne end (600-1200m) Santa Marta Mts. (near Dibulla). Once on Pacific coast in Chocó (Nuquí). W Mexico and Yucatan s locally to w Ecuador and the Guianas. Trinidad. Coastal in Mid. America.

## 13. GRAY-NECKED WOOD-RAIL
*Aramides cajanea*    Pl. 7, Map 188
**Identification:** 14-15″ (36-38cm). Large. Bill mod. long, yellowish at base, greenish at tip; eyes, bare eyering, and *legs coral red. Head and longish neck gray*; throat paler; crown tinged brown; upperparts olive; *breast and sides cinnamon rufous; rearparts incl. abdomen, rump, and tail black*; primaries rufous chestnut (usually concealed at rest). Imm.: duller; bill and legs dusky.

**Similar species:** Brown Wood-Rail (14), only other Colombian rail nearly as large, is very sim. but differs as follows: less extensive gray on neck; upperparts and underparts nearly uniform dark chestnut brown (not with breast contrasting pale cinnamon); and bill uniform greenish yellow.

**Voice:** Well known for loud vigorous chorus,

given mostly at dawn or dusk, a cackling *kook-kooky, kook-kooky, kook-kooky . . . ko-ko-ko . . .* (J. V. Remsen); also *kook-kak*, or *kré-ko . . .* , and so on with var.; often several in a chorus that gradually winds down with only 1 bird *kré-ko*-ing at end.

**Behavior:** Usually secretive, suspicious, and difficult to see but often heard. Occas. walk in open but seldom far from cover. Single birds, pairs, or small groups but in llanos dry season may concentrate in nos. near pools. Prey heavily on crabs in mangroves. Mostly on ground, at times in bushes. Partially nocturnal; roost above ground.

**Breeding:** 3 BC birds, Apr–June, s Córdoba (Carriker; Haffer 1975); another, Mar, Macarena Mts. (Olivares 1962); a Panama nest, 28 Apr (Stone 1918); breeds July–Sept, Guárico, Venez. (Thomas 1979b); in Trinidad, May–Aug; deep twiggy bowl 1-7m up in vines or bush; 3-7 eggs pale cream spotted and blotched brown (ffrench 1973).

**Status and habitat:** Fairly common in swampy woodland, forested river banks, mangroves, and seasonal pools near gallery woodland in llanos; sometimes some distance from water. Locally to 2000m (near Popayán), twice to 2300m at Finca Merenberg, Huila (sightings—Ridgely and Gaulin 1980) where prob. a wanderer. Only recent Cauca Val. recs. are near Popayán (voice, July 1977—Hilty et al.). Replaced s of Baudó Mts. on Pacific coast by Brown Wood-Rail.

**Range:** To 2300m. Pacific coast s to Baudó Mts.; otherwise generally throughout country (except e Guajira). C Mexico s to n Argentina and Uruguay. Trinidad.

## 14. BROWN WOOD-RAIL

*Aramides wolfi* Pl. 7, Map 189

**Identification:** 13″ (33cm). Much like Gray-necked Wood-Rail; bill greenish yellow. *Mainly dark brown above and below*; head and upper neck gray; throat paler; primaries and rearparts as in Gray-necked Wood-Rail.

**Similar species:** See Gray-necked Wood-Rail (13) and smaller Rufous-necked Wood-Rail (12).

**Voice:** A frequently repeated *kui-co-muí* (Olivares 1957b) is apparently much like that of Gray-necked Wood-Rail.

**Behavior:** Presum. as in Gray-necked Wood-Rail.

**Status and habitat:** Mangroves, forested rivers and streams, swampy woodland, and marshy areas along rivers. Replaces Gray-necked Wood-Rail on Pacific coast s of Baudó Mts.; both are known from Alto del Buey, Baudó Mts.

**Range:** To 100m (900m in Baudó Mts.). Pacific coast from Baudó Mts. southward. W Colombia to nw Peru.

**Note:** Red-winged Wood-Rail (*A. calopterus*) from Río Suno, ne Ecuador, and several e Peru localities may occur in Putumayo and Amazonas, Colombia. Slightly smaller (14″) than Gray-necked Wood-Rail. Olive above, gray below with broad chestnut stripe from sides of head down neck and continuous with chestnut wing coverts and primaries; rearparts black; bill pale green; legs coral red. Believed more a bird of wet places inside forest rather than banks of rivers as in Gray-necked Wood-Rail (J. O'Neill).

## 15. UNIFORM CRAKE

*Amaurolimnas concolor* Pl. 7, Map 190

**Identification:** 8-8.5″ (20-22cm). Rare. Rather small mainly uniform rufous brown rail. Short thick bill yellow green; legs reddish. *Above mostly dull rufous brown; below rufous brown, brighter than upperparts*; throat pale.

**Similar species:** In known range likely confused only with White-throated Crake (7), which has black and white barred flanks and white throat, or larger Rufous-necked Wood-Rail (12), which has gray upper back. May occur e of Andes where it could easily be confused with Russet-crowned Crake (5; gray cheeks and shorter bill) or Chestnut-headed Crake (3; contrasting rufous head and underparts).

**Voice:** In Costa Rica a whistled *toooo* call; "song" 6-9 upslurred whistles, rising then falling, *tooeee, Tooeee, Tooeee, TOOEEE, Tooee, tooee-twee-tui* (Stiles 1981a).

**Behavior:** Apparently extremely secretive, preferring to skulk, hide, or run rather than fly. Probes leaf litter in damp places.

**Breeding:** Nov nest in Costa Rica, leafy cup on stump in swampy forest; 4 pale buff eggs with red brown splotches (Stiles 1981a).

**Status and habitat:** Only 3 definite Colombian localities. Apparently a "land rail" of damp thickets, dense second growth, and leaf litter at the edge of small forest streams or in wet spots.

**Range:** To 100m. Pacific coast where known from Pizarro, Chocó (mouth of Río Baudó), Guapí, Cauca, and Barbacoas, Nariño; also "Bogota." Perhaps e base of E Andes as known from e Ecuador (Napo). S Mexico spottily to w Ecuador, e Bolivia, Amazonian and se Brazil, and Guyana. Jamaica (formerly?).

## 16. SORA

*Porzana carolina* Pl. 7, Map 191

**Identification:** 8-9″ (20-23cm). Rather small and

plump. Legs greenish. *Short thick yellow bill surrounded by black face patch and throat; sides of head and most of underparts gray; flanks barred black and white*; central abdomen and under tail coverts white; above brownish streaked black and white. Imm.: duller and browner, esp. below, no black face, and central throat whitish.
**Similar species:** Best mark is the yellow bill encircled by black. Several other Colombian rails are gray below; see esp. (6, 17, 19, 20).
**Voice:** A distinctive, whinnylike ser. of a doz. or more downscale notes; when disturbed a sharp metallic *kee.*
**Behavior:** Rather furtive but more easily seen than many rails. Walks into openings or at edge of reeds in early morning but not far from cover. Flushes readily, sometimes also swims. Tail cocked.
**Status and habitat:** Uncommon to locally common migrant and winter resident (Oct–Apr, rarely May) to freshwater marshes, rice fields, and wet grassy areas, occas. on mudflats or in brackish water. Requires standing water. A few may oversummer (sighting, 30 July 1978, Parque La Florida, Bogotá—Hilty et al.).
**Range:** To 2600m. Carib. lowlands from near Cartagena s locally to Santa Marta Mts.; mid. and upper Cauca Val.; temperate zone of e and w Nariño (Lago La Cocha, Lago Cumbal), E Andes in Boyacá and Cundinamarca, and lowlands e of Andes in w Caquetá (Florencia area). Breeds from Canada to Mexico; winters from s US to c Peru and Guyana. Trinidad.

## 17. ASH-THROATED CRAKE

*Porzana albicollis*          Pl. 7, Map 192
**Identification:** 9″ (23cm). More slender than Sora. *Short bill greenish yellow*; culmen dusky; legs purplish brown. Crown, hindneck, and upperparts brownish olive; back streaked black; *sides of head, foreneck, and underparts gray*; throat whitish; *flanks barred black and white.*
**Similar species:** Gray-breasted and Paint-billed crakes (6, 20) are smaller and unstreaked above, former also with rufous mantle, latter with red at base of bill and pinkish legs. Also see Sora (16).
**Voice:** Call a sharp *tuk*; song a loud fast ser. (about 18 phrases in 20 sec), vibrating and like a machine-gun, *d'd'd'd'd'd'-ou, d'd'd'd'd'd'-ou . . .* (P. Schwartz recording).
**Behavior:** Flushes readily, flies a short distance dangling legs, then drops down. Occas. skulks partially in open near cover.
**Breeding:** In Guyana Feb–July, peaking in May; woven grassy bowl on ground in grass; 2-3 eggs, pinkish cream to white, finely spotted

brown and lilac at larger end (Beebe et al. 1917).
**Status and habitat:** Local in damp grassy or sedgy areas, rice fields, and drainage ditches, also marshes and marshy lakes. Both a "grass" and a marsh dweller; some seasonal movements poss.; seen Dec–Mar near Carimagua, ne Meta (S. Furniss; Brown); Mar–Sept at Hacienda La Corocora, w Meta (W. McKay); and reported to move to cattails during dry season at Ciénaga Grande (Darlington 1931).
**Range:** To 1000m. Cauca Val. e of Cali (sighting, CIAT Ag. Exp. Station, 5 July 1975—Hilty, D. Zimmerman, J. Abramson), lower Magdalena Val. (Ciénaga; Río Frío), and e of Andes from Arauca to s Meta (Macarena Mts.), and extreme ne Meta. Venez., the Guianas, and e Brazil to se Peru (Madre de Dios), e Bolivia, Paraguay, and c Argentina. Trinidad.

## 18. YELLOW-BREASTED CRAKE

*Poliolimnas flaviventer*          Pl. 7, Map 193
**Identification:** 5.5″ (14cm). *Very small.* Short dusky bill; legs yellow. *Crown and stripe through eye black; short eyebrow white*; hindneck and remaining upperparts buffy brown streaked black and white; wings more ochraceous with dusky and white streaking; *below creamy yellow buff* with whitish throat and *conspic. black and white barred flanks and under tail coverts.*
**Similar species:** In flight or in marsh a tiny, predom. yellowish buff rail with boldly barred flanks. Sim.-sized Ocellated Crake (2) lacks the bold head pattern and flank barring.
**Voice:** Call a hoarse, slightly downscale *zeee-eee-eee-eee*, about 1 note per sec (W. McKay); a loud ringing, almost scraping *clureéoo* (G. B. Reynard recording).
**Behavior:** Walks and climbs through grass and reeds growing in water or through floating vegetation. Not esp. furtive but difficult to see because of small size; flushes easily, dangling legs, and soon drops down. In Panama a few may perch and forage in open in early morning but withdraw to cover later in day (Wetmore 1965a).
**Breeding:** Imm., 7 Feb, upper Río Negro near se Guainía (Friedmann 1948). In Antilles, loosely built nest in water plants; 5 eggs, sparsely spotted (Bond 1961).
**Status and habitat:** Local in freshwater marshes and floating vegetation in choked pools and lagoons. Common seasonally at Hacienda Corocora, w Meta (seen only Mar–early July—W. McKay).
**Range:** To 1000m. N Colombia from lower Río Sinú e spottily to lower and mid. Magdalena Val. (s to San Gil, Santander), and mid. Cauca

Val. (Valle); e of Andes in w Meta (sighting, Feb 1970, Mozambique—F. Gill and A. Stokes; and Hacienda La Corocora—W. McKay). Prob. se Guainía as rec. at Cucuhy on upper Río Negro, Brazil. S Mexico s very spottily to n Argentina and c Brazil. Greater Antilles. Trinidad.

**Note:** Sometimes placed in the genus *Porzana*.

## 19. COLOMBIAN CRAKE

*Neocrex colombianus*          Map 194
**Identification:** 7.5″ (19cm). *Plain unmarked rail.* Bill green with red base and black tip; legs orange to reddish brown. Hindneck, upperparts, and flanks brownish olive; *crown, sides of head, and most of underparts slaty gray;* throat whitish; abdomen and under tail coverts pale buff.

**Similar species:** Gray-breasted Crake (6) has chestnut mantle and barred flanks. Ashthroated Crake and Bogota Rail (17, 11) are both streaked above, latter also with red bill and legs. Also see Paint-billed Crake (20), which replaces Colombian Crake in E Andes and lowlands e of Andes.

**Breeding:** Three birds fluttered against lighted windows in W Andes 9 and 13 Dec and 3 Jan; all near BC and believed resident (Miller 1963); BC ♂, 2 Jan, Acandí, Gulf of Urabá (Carriker).

**Status and habitat:** Rare. Wet grass, pastures, and small marshy areas. Believed to be mainly a "grass" rail (not restricted to water).

**Range:** To 2100m. Scattered recs. across most of n Colombia and s on both slopes of W Andes to Nariño. Acandí, extreme nw Chocó; Santa Marta Mts. (1500-2100m), Snía. de Macuira, e Guajira; W Andes above Cali (1800m); Guapí, sw Cauca (50m) and Barbacoas, w Nariño (50m). C Panama to n and w Colombia and w Ecuador.

**Note:** Considered by some a race of Paint-billed Crake.

## 20. PAINT-BILLED CRAKE

*Neocrex erythrops*          Pl. 7, Map 195
**Identification:** 7.5″ (19cm). Much like Colombian Crake. Bill yellow green, *basal half red;* legs orange to reddish brown. Hindcrown, hindneck, and upperparts brownish olive; *front and sides of head and most of underparts gray;* throat whitish; *flanks, abdomen, and under tail coverts barred black and white.*

**Similar species:** Sim. Gray-breasted Crake (6) has dark bill (no red) and chestnut patch on nape and mantle. Larger Ash-throated Crake (17) also lacks red on bill and is streaked above. Colombian Crake (19) not known to overlap range.

**Voice:** Loud *qur'r'r'rk* and *auuk*, both *very* guttural, buzzy, and froglike; or in ser., *qurrrk' auuk qurrrk' auuk* . . . (P. Schwartz recording).

**Behavior:** Very furtive and hard to see although can be flushed short distances. At Rancho Grande, n Venez. has been attracted to lighted windows in May and June.

**Breeding:** Dec–Feb in Galapagos, grassy nest in clump of vegetation; up to 7 eggs, creamy, heavily-blotched red brown (Harris 1974). Nests found in cornfields in Venez. (Friedmann and Smith 1955).

**Status and habitat:** Apparently local. Wet grassy pastures, marshes, and overgrown grassy and bushy areas. Mainly a "grass and thicket" rail. Reported "common" in ne Venez. in Aug at dirt road puddles (Friedmann and Smith 1950); reported "common" on Sabana de Bogotá (Olivares 1974b).

**Range:** 2500-2600m in E Andes from Boyacá (Laguna de Fúquene) s to Sabana de Bogotá; 300-500m e of Andes in w Meta (near Villavicencio) and Vaupés (Mitú). C Venez., Surinam, Guyana, e Brazil, e Bolivia, ne Argentina, and Paraguay; w Peru. Galapagos.

## 21. BLACKISH RAIL

*Pardirallus nigricans*          Pl. 7, Map 196
**Identification:** 11″ (28cm). *Large dark rail with rather long greenish bill.* Eyes and *legs red.* Dark olive brown above with *head and underparts mostly slate gray;* throat light gray to whitish; center of belly and under tail coverts black. Imm.: sim. but browner esp. on posterior upperparts.

**Similar species:** Only Colombian rail with uniformly dark lower underparts. Other somewhat sim. "long-billed" rails (*Rallus*, 9, 10, 11) are not known to overlap in range. Larger wood-rails (12, 13, 14) have proportionally shorter bills.

**Voice:** A very fast, metallic *tii'd'dit* (recalls a spinetail); also a complaining *keeeeaaa* resembling cry of a small hawk (R. Ward recording in Brazil).

**Behavior:** Usually furtive and not easily seen unless flushed; then flies a short distance and drops in. Occas. walks in open on muddy shore with other water birds or in open near marshy vegetation (Mitchell 1957).

**Breeding:** Aquatic vegetation nest in tall damp grass; 3 pale buff eggs with a few small brown spots (Sclater and Salvin 1879).

**Status and habitat:** Uncommon in marshes, vegetation-choked waterways, flooded rice fields, and tall damp grass. Reg. flushed from Lago de Sonso marshes or rice fields in Valle (Cauca Val. flood plain); also reported from hilly headwaters of Cauca Val.

**Range:** 800-2200m. Cauca Val. from latitude of Medellín s to head of val. (El Tambo w of Popayán); w Nariño. E Ecuador, e Peru, ne Argentina, Paraguay, and e Brazil.
**Note:** Sometimes placed in the genus *Rallus* or *Ortygonax*.

## 22. SPOTTED RAIL
*Pardirallus maculatus*                   Pl. 7, Map 197
**Identification:** 10″ (25cm). Conspic. spotted and barred black and white. Bill rather long, greenish yellow, small red spot at base; legs reddish. *Upperparts, head, neck, and breast black spotted with white; rest of underparts boldly barred black and white*; throat and under tail coverts white; wings with some brownish streaking. Imm.: black replaced by brown; underparts nearly uniform, or with faint whitish barring and spotting.
**Voice:** Reportedly a 4-noted whistle, the 1st high and long, the rest shorter and in rapid succession (Birkenholz and Jenni 1964).
**Behavior:** Secretive and not easily flushed but often leaves cover to feed partially in open in early morning. Runs rapidly, crosses open spaces, even roads occas. In Costa Rica, territories are small and birds occur in locally high densities of 8-9 per 22 hectares (Birkenholz and Jenni 1964).
**Breeding:** 2 young birds in rice field, 15 Dec, Magdalena Val., Tolima (Nicéforo and Olivares, 1964); in Trinidad, June and Aug; open rush nest just above water; 2-7 pale buff eggs marked dark purple mainly at larger end (ffrench 1973).
**Status and habitat:** Fairly common locally in flooded rice fields, marshes, and wet grassy ditches. Numerous e of Cali at CIAT Ag. Exp. Stat. (P. Jennings).
**Range:** Mostly 400-1000m; 2000m near Popayán. Mid. and upper Cauca Val. (Valle and Cauca), mid. Magdalena Val. (Tolima), and e of Andes in w Meta (several sightings Apr–May, Hacienda La Corocora—W. McKay). E Mexico, Belize; Costa Rica locally to Bolivia, n Argentina, and Uruguay. Cuba; Trinidad.
**Note:** Sometimes placed in the genus *Rallus*.

## 23. PURPLE GALLINULE
*Porphyrio martinica*                   Pl. 7, Map 198
**Identification:** 13″ (33cm). *Frontal shield pale blue, thick bill red with yellow tip; legs bright yellow. Very iridescent.* Head, neck, and entire underparts *brilliant bluish purple*; back and wings bronzy green; under tail coverts white. Imm.: brown above; wings bronzy blue; sides of head, *foreneck, and chest buffy white*; throat and lower underparts white; bill dusky; frontal shield and legs as in adult.

**Similar species:** Brilliant ad. easily recognized. Common Gallinule (26) is slaty with red shield and white flank stripe. Imm. from ad. Azure Gallinule (24) by larger size, buff on breast and sides of head and neck, and *bluish frontal shield contrasting with darker bill*; from imm. Azure Gallinule by larger size, unstreaked back and browner (not blackish) rump and tail.
**Voice:** Various guttural notes and reedy cackles similar to Common Gallinule; also a limpkinlike wail.
**Behavior:** Walks over floating vegetation or in marshy vegetation, swims less than Common Gallinule, and usually avoids open water. Often perches on a bush, low branch, or even fence post near water. Flies rather slowly but directly with rapid wing beats and dangling legs; raises legs on longer flights.
**Breeding:** Nests late May–Aug (18 from 27 June to 14 July) in w Meta (W. McKay); 1 nest, early June, w of Bucaramanga in mid. Magdalena Val. (Boggs 1961); 2 on 10 Oct, Santa Marta area (Todd and Carriker 1922). Bulky open grass or rice stem nest a little above water in marsh or rice field; prob. 4-7 eggs (W. McKay), cream to buff spotted brown and pale purple (Wetmore 1965a).
**Status and habitat:** Locally common in freshwater marshes, pools, lagoons, and esp. rice fields. In w Meta, where considered an agricultural pest in rice fields, abundant late Mar–Oct; much smaller nos. remainder of yr. and believed locally migratory (W. McKay).
**Range:** To 1000m throughout; occas. to 2600m on Sabana de Bogotá. Se US and Mexico s to n Argentina (once Chile and Uruguay). W Indies; Trinidad.
**Note:** Sometimes placed in the genus *Porphyrula* or in *Gallinula*.

## 24. AZURE GALLINULE
*Porphyrio (Porphyrula) flavirostris*                   Pl. 7,
Map 199
**Identification:** 10″ (25cm). Small and delicately proportioned; *plumage looks faded*. Bill and frontal shield pale greenish yellow; legs bright yellow. Crown, hindneck, and back pale brownish olive; *back obscurely streaked dusky*; rump and tail dark brown; *shoulders and wing coverts azure blue; sides of head, neck, and breast pale sky blue*; throat, foreneck, center of breast, and entire lower underparts white. Imm.: browner above; sides of head, neck, and breast buffy.
**Similar species:** Should be recognized by distinctive "washed out" appearance and pale azure blue on sides of head, neck, and breast. Cf. imm. Purple Gallinule (23). Imm. also re-

sembles adult Ash-throated Crake (17) but legs bright yellow (not purplish brown).

**Voice:** Usually rather quiet; at times a short trill (J. V. Remsen).

**Behavior:** Skulks in vegetation much more than Purple Gallinule and seldom swims (rarely in open water). Flushes readily and flies a short distance with dangling legs; sometimes perches exposed on marshy or floating vegetation and typically holds wings up momentarily upon alighting.

**Breeding:** In Surinam, dry reedy cup nest in marsh, May–Aug; 4-5 eggs, creamy, thickly dotted red brown (Haverschmidt 1968).

**Status and habitat:** Uncommon and local in freshwater marshes, rice fields, and marshy shores of ponds, lakes, and lagoons. In w Meta only late Mar–mid-July on 2 successive yrs. (W. McKay). Reports of migrants Mar–May to Sabana de Bogotá (J. Hernández; Nicéforo and Olivares 1965).

**Range:** To 500m. E of the Andes from c and w Meta (San Carlos de Guaroa; sightings, Hacienda la Corocora, 1977-78—W. McKay) s through w Caquetá and Amazonas (undoubtedly Putumayo). Prob. n to Arauca (rec. in adj. Apure, Venez.). The Guianas and c and s Venez. spottily s east of Andes to n Argentina and Paraguay.

## 25. SPOT-FLANKED GALLINULE

*Gallinula (Porphyriops) melanops*         Pl. 7, Map 200

**Identification:** 11″ (28cm). *Stout lime green bill;* legs greenish. Foreface and crown blackish, becoming slate gray on sides of head, neck, mantle, and breast; remaining upperparts olive brown; *shoulders chestnut; flanks brownish thickly spotted white;* center of belly and under tail coverts white.

**Similar species:** *Porzana*-like in shape but easily told from Sora (16) or from much larger gallinules (23, 24, 26) by green bill and spotted flanks.

**Voice:** A loud hollow cackling that slows and dies away.

**Behavior:** Scattered individuals swim among floating vegetation along shore and pick at the surface like coots. Seldom walk in marshy vegetation or on land. Patter across surface to get airborne and are normally conspic. and easily seen.

**Breeding:** 2 nests early Feb, Lago de Tota, Boyacá (Borrero 1952b); reed nest roofed over on damp ground near water; 4-8 light brown eggs blotched and spotted red brown (Johnson 1965).

**Status and habitat:** Locally common in marshy ponds and lakes. Easily seen at Parque La Florida near Bogotá.

**Range:** 2500-3100m. E Andes from c Boyacá (Lago Tota) to Sabana de Bogotá. Spottily from e Peru s to c Argentina and Chile; e Brazil s to Uruguay.

## 26. COMMON (MOORHEN) GALLINULE

*Gallinula chloropus*         Ill. 31, Map 201

**Identification:** 13-14″ (33-36cm). *Frontal shield and thick bill red;* tip of bill yellow; greenish legs with red "garters" (hard to see). *Mainly slate gray;* blacker on head and neck; browner on back and wings; *conspic. white stripe on sides and flanks;* "divided" white under tail coverts. Imm.: pale gray to brownish gray, browner above; throat, sides of head, and chest mottled white; throat, sides of head, and chest mottled white; *flank stripe white;* bill dull yellowish brown.

**Similar species:** See Purple Gallinule (23) and the coots (27, 28).

**Voice:** A deep *kuk;* also cackling and clucking.

**Behavior:** Unlike Purple Gallinule, usually seen swimming. Swims along edge of open water, pumps head back and forth like a coot, and seeks cover in marsh vegetation if alarmed. Reluctant to fly, then pattering on surface to get airborne.

**Breeding:** In Panama mostly Dec–Jan (Wetmore 1965a); open reed nest at edge of water. Eggs from Sabana de Bogotá, whitish or grayish spotted dark brown (Olivares 1969a).

**Status and habitat:** Local resident and poss. n migrant (Oct–Apr) in freshwater ponds and marshy lakes. Fairly common in Cauca Val.

**Range:** To 3100m. Carib. region from lower Magdalena Val. (Atlántico) e to w base of Santa Marta Mts., s locally in most of Cauca and Magdalena vals. and to temperate zone of E Andes (c Boyacá at Lago Tota s to Sabana de Bogotá). Virtually worldwide except Australia and New Zealand. In New World breeds from s Canada s locally to n Chile and Argentina. W Indies. N birds migratory.

## 27. AMERICAN COOT

*Fulica americana*         Map 202

**Identification:** 13-14″ (33-36cm). Stocky and rather ducklike in water. *Short thick bill chalky white* (yellowish basally when breeding) with broken dark ring near tip; *small inconspic. frontal shield chestnut. Mostly slate gray,* head and neck blacker; white on sides of under tail coverts. In flight shows white rear border on secondaries. Imm.: paler gray below, throat and foreneck mottled white.

**Similar species:** Much like Slate-colored Coot

31. COMMON (MOORHEN) GALLINULE (left), SLATE-COLORED COOT (right)

(see 28). Also cf. Common Gallinule (26) and Caribbean Coot (see note).

**Voice:** Often noisy; a var. of cackles, clucks, and grating sounds.

**Behavior:** More aquatic than most other rails and usually seen swimming. Dives well, tips up to feed, and walks easily on shore. Rather reluctant to fly, preferring to patter across the surface with great commotion to reach safety. Often in flocks.

**Breeding:** 1 bird, building nest, Mar; 3 pairs with 2-week to 2-month-old chicks, mid-Aug, Sabana de Bogotá (Hilty). Nest a large pile of aquatic vegetation in reeds; eggs light brown marked darker brown (Johnson 1965).

**Status and habitat:** Locally common resident and migrant (larger nos. Oct–Apr) in lakes, ponds, and sloughs bordered by aquatic weeds and rushes. A few present all yr. in Cauca Val. may be oversummering migrants or resident breeders(?).

**Range:** To 1000m in Cauca Val.; 2500-3100m in E Andes from c Boyacá (Lago Tota) s to Sabana de Bogotá; C Andes in PN Puracé (to 3400m) and mts. of Nariño (2000-3000m). Breeds from N America to Nicaragua, and Colombia to n Argentina and c Chile; n birds winter s to W Indies, Panama, and prob. Colombia.

**Note:** Caribbean Coot (*F. caribaea*) of W Indies, s Florida, and casually to N Venez. is unrec. but likely on n Colombian coast. Like American Coot but prom. *large* frontal shield white

like bill (not small chestnut shield), or tinged yellowish.

## 28. SLATE-COLORED COOT

*Fulica ardesiaca*　　　　Ill. 31, Map 203

**Identification:** 16″ (41cm). Very sim. to American Coot but larger and body plumage sometimes lighter slate color contrasting more with blackish head and neck. Bill white (yellowish when breeding) with dark broken ring near tip; frontal shield larger than American Coot and *white* (not chestnut); secondaries *usually entirely slate without white rear border*; legs grayish (not greenish).

**Similar species:** See American Coot (27).

**Breeding:** Late Feb, Laguna La Cocha, e Nariño (Borrero 1952b).

**Status and habitat:** Locally common on lakes and marshes above 2000m. Common at Laguna La Cocha in Feb (Borrero 1952b).

**Range:** 2200-3600m. E and w Nariño (Laguna La Cocha, Sibundoy marshes, Cumbal area) and w Putumayo (Sibundoy Val.). Sw Colombia s in Andes to nw Argentina and n Chile.

**Note:** Regarded by some as a polymorphic race of American Coot (*F. americana*) with both white-shielded and chestnut-shielded color phases. Both white- and chestnut-shielded birds occur from s Colombia to s Peru although one or the other may be absent locally and presumed mixed pairs have been reported (Gill 1964, *Condor* 66:209-211). Only chestnut-shielded birds are found s of Peru.

# FINFOOTS: Heliornithidae (1)

Finfoots are a small pantropical family of aquatic birds related to rails. There is one species each in the New World, Africa, and Asia. They have short legs and lobed toes, swim and dive with ease, and eat a variety of small aquatic life and some seeds. ♂♂ are unique in possessing folds of skin or pockets under their wings where the young can be carried.

## 1. SUNGREBE

*Heliornis fulica*　　　　　　Pl. 7, Map 204

**Identification:** 11-12″ (28-30cm). Grebelike with rather long tail; eyering and short bill dull red (brighter when breeding); feet gaudily banded black and yellow. ♂: crown and hindneck black with *white postocular stripe* bordered below by black stripe through eye; *sides of neck with a bold black and white stripe; remaining upperparts olive brown*; tail blackish narrowly tipped white; foreneck and underparts white; sides tinged buffy. ♀: sim. but cheeks buffy.

**Similar species:** Striped head and long slender body are diagnostic, but when seen quickly (usually is) may look mainly brown. When flushed resembles a small weak-flying brown juv. duck or grebe with broad pale-tipped blackish tail. Bright feet seldom visible.

**Voice:** A deep, hollow ser. of honking notes, *ooh, ooh, ooh, ooh, ooh* (B. Coffee recording); in Mexico described as a sonorous laugh, *eeoó, eeoó, eeoó-eeyéh, eeyéh*, resembling call of some grebes (Alvarez del Toro 1971).

**Behavior:** Rather wary. Swims along shady secluded stream banks, keeping near or under overhanging shoreline vegetation. Dives quickly, swims partly submerged with only head and neck above water. If alarmed, flies with pattering run across water but stays low and seldom flies far.

**Breeding:** BC ♀, 6 Jan, Pacific coast, Valle (Carriker); 2 Panama nests with eggs, June–July (Wetmore 1965a); twig platform lined with leaves in bush about 1m above water; 2 pale cinnamon eggs spotted reddish brown; short (11-day) incubation per. (Alvarez del Toro 1971).

**Status and habitat:** Uncommon and local on freshwater ponds, lagoons, and slow-moving streams, almost always where trees, vines, and vegetation overhang the banks.

**Range:** To 500m, once to 2600m on Sabana de Bogotá. Spottily on Pacific coast. Cauca Val. (now only extreme lower part) and upper Patía Val. Throughout e of Andes; rec. Norte de Santander to w and ne Meta (sightings, Carimagua, 1976—S. Furniss; Brown); Vaupés, w Caquetá, and Amazonas (sightings at Leticia—J. V. Remsen; Hilty). S Mexico to ne Argentina and s Brazil.

# SUNBITTERNS: Eurypygidae (1)

The single species in this family is an elegant and sedate bird of shady forest streams in warmer parts of the New World tropics. Somewhat raillike or heronlike, it has a long slender neck, moderately long legs and tail, and unwebbed toes. The somber colors belie a "sunburst" of color on the flight feathers, which can be seen to advantage during spectacular displays with spread wings, fanned tail, and lowered head.

## 1. SUNBITTERN

*Eurypyga helias*　　　　　　Ill. 32, Map 205

**Identification:** 18-19″ (46-48cm). Bustardlike in proportions but more slender. Small head; rather long straight bill, blackish above and yellow below. *Head black with a long white stripe above and below eyes*; throat and foreneck white; *rest of neck and upperparts brown, everywhere vermiculated and barred with black, gray, and chestnut*; wing coverts spotted white; wings with bright *orange rufous patches* in primaries (conspic. in flight and display); breast brownish finely vermiculated black and fading to plain buffy white on lower underparts; tail vermic-ulated gray and black and crossed by 2 black-bordered chestnut bands; legs orange yellow.

**Voice:** Notably vocal in early morning or late evening; a high, penetrating whistle (pure tone), *wuuuuuuuu*, much like Cinereous Tinamous; often doubled and ventriloquial; when disturbed a high, thin, complaining trill (Hilty); alarm a louder *ka, ka, ka . . .* of 6-8 notes (Ridgely 1976).

**Behavior:** Solitary birds or pairs walk daintily along stream banks or damp places in forest but seldom wade in water. Fly lightly to low branches if disturbed. Usually rather wary but sometimes easily approached. Pick, glean, or

32. SUNBITTERN

jab at small aquatic or nonaquatic animal life from gravel and rocks at water's edge or damp litter on forest floor.

**Breeding:** 2 BC ♂♂, Mar, Chocó (Carriker). In Costa Rica, a nest, 26 Mar, about 7m up in tree near bouldery stream; globular mass of vegetation, moss, and mud with shallow depression; 2 eggs (Skutch 1947a); in Venez. 3 eggs, 10 May–9 July; buffy with a few black, brown, and lilac spots at larger end (Wetmore 1965a).

**Status and habitat:** Local along shady streams, small forested pools, and damp, dense second growth thickets near water; in the llanos also along small faster-flowing gravelly riffles in streams through gallery forest.

**Range:** To 600m (once to 800m, Snía. San Lucas). Pacific coast in n Chocó (lower Atrato, near Panama boundary, and at Guapí, sw Cauca; absent from wettest Pacific coastal belt); e across n base of Andes to lower Cauca Val. (Río Nechí) and mid. Magdalena Val. in s Bolívar (e slope Snía. San Lucas); base of Perijá Mts. at n end (Carraipía); e of Andes from Norte de Santander southward (no recs. in Vichada and Vaupés). S Mexico to w Ecuador, n Argentina, and Uruguay (rarely c Chile).

# JACANAS: Jacanidae (1)

Jacanas are a small family of rather delicately proportioned marsh birds found throughout tropical and warmer subtropical areas of the world. They have exceedingly long toes and nails that enable them to walk over floating vegetation with ease. They are also notable for a leathery frontal shield above the bill and a sharp spur on the carpal joint of the wing. They eat small aquatic plant and animal life. The New World species are polyandrous breeders.

33. WATTLED JACANA (imm. left; ad. right)

## 1. WATTLED JACANA
*Jacana jacana*                    Ill. 33, Map 206

**Identification:** 10″ (25cm). *Bill yellow* with bi-lobed red frontal shield and red lappets; long legs and *very long toes greenish.* Head, neck, and underparts black; *central back and most of closed wing maroon chestnut; flight feathers pale yellow* (prom. in flight). Or mostly uniform black; most of back and closed wing glossed greenish, and sometimes suffused maroon chestnut on wing coverts, back, and rump—*hypomelaena.* Imm. very different: brown above; crown and hindneck blackish; *long white eyestripe and black postocular stripe;* otherwise white below; *flight feathers pale yellow as in ad.;* bill brown; pinkish frontal shield rudimentary or lacking.

**Similar species:** Imm. often mistaken for a rail but none have such boldly striped head and long toes.

**Voice:** Chattering and cackling *kee-kick, kee-kick* . . . as flies over marsh; often noisy.

**Behavior:** Scattered individuals walk on floating vegetation or in shallow water near shore or in nearby grassy areas. Lift and flash yellow wings when disturbed; fly low over marsh with a flurry of quick, stiff wing beats alternating with short glides. In flight usually hold long legs and toes raised. Can swim but rarely do.

**Breeding:** Eggs near Cali, 4 June (Hilty); downy chicks, 20 July, Leticia (J. V. Remsen); copulation, 29 June, 2 downy chicks, 2 Nov, Arauca (J. Jorgenson and W. McKay); chicks 8 Dec, Carimagua, ne Meta (S. Furniss). Nest in pasture or aquatic vegetation; 4 olive brown eggs streaked and scrawled black. Polyandrous ♀♀ (usually) lay for 2 or more ♂♂ that incubate separate clutch in sex role reversal (Osborne and Bourne 1977).

**Status and habitat:** Common. One of most characteristic birds in shallow freshwater pools, marshes, lagoons, and sluggish rivers with floating and emergent vegetation. Nos. fluctuate seasonally at Laguna Carimagua in ne Meta, greatest no. during the dry season, Jan–Mar, fewest in Apr–July (S. Furniss).

**Range:** To 1000m (once to 2600m, Boyacá). From Panama border to w Guajira, s to upper Magdalena Val. (*hypomelaena*); mid. and upper Cauca Val. and poss. e tip Guajira and nw Arauca (*melanopygia*); e of Andes from Norte de Santander to Caquetá and Vaupés (*intermedia*); se Amazonas near Leticia (*peruviana*). W Panama to n Argentina and Uruguay; w Ecuador and nw Peru; rarely c Chile.

**Note:** Considered by some to be conspecific with *J. spinosa* (Northern Jacana) of C America s to c Panama.

# OYSTERCATCHERS: Haematopodidae (1)

Oystercatchers are a small family found on coastlines throughout the world except in arctic regions and oceanic islands. They are rather large stout shorebirds with short necks, moderately

34. AMERICAN OYSTERCATCHER

long legs, and a unique coral-colored, laterally compressed bill with a distinct chisellike tip. The bill is used to pry open oysters and shellfish and chisel limpets from rocks.

## 1. AMERICAN OYSTERCATCHER
*Haematopus palliatus*                    Ill. 34
**Identification:** 16-18″ (41-46cm). Large chunky shorebird with *bright coral red bill*; pale yellow eyes; pink legs. *Head, neck, and chest black*; otherwise dark brown above and white below. In flight shows *conspic. white rump and wing stripe*.
**Voice:** Often very noisy day and night; an insistent piping *wheep*, usually loud.
**Behavior:** Pairs are conspic. but wary; usually keep somewhat apart from other shorebirds.
**Breeding:** As yet unreported in Colombia; 1 nest, 20 Mar, Pacific coast, Panama; a depres-
sion on beach, sometimes lined with shells or pebbles; 3 pale buff eggs evenly spotted grayish brown (Wetmore 1965a).
**Status and habitat:** Rare and local resident on rocky shoreline, sandy beach, or adj. mudflats. On Carib. coast reported only from mouth of Río Magdalena (Isla de Salamanca) and Guajira Peninsula (Ríohacha); few Pacific coast recs.
**Range:** Spottily on Pacific and Carib. coasts. Breeds locally on Pacific coast from Baja Californias to Chile, on Atlantic locally from New Jersey and Mexico to Argentina. W Indies, Dutch Leewards, Trinidad; the Galapagos.

# LAPWINGS, PLOVERS: Charadriidae (10)

Plovers and lapwings are a large, virtually worldwide family that differs from sandpipers in, among other things, having a shorter, thicker, pigeonlike bill and more robust proportions. They favor coastlines and edges of bodies of fresh water, although they wade little. Many are also found in grassy fields and dry savanna. Lapwings differ from other plovers in rounded, spurred wings, and slower more bounding flight. Several Colombian species are arctic breeders that spend most of the year on neotropical wintering grounds.

## 1. SOUTHERN LAPWING
*Vanellus chilensis*                    Ill. 35
**Identification:** 13-14″ (33-36cm). Bold black and white pattern. Bill pinkish with black tip; legs pink. *Mostly brownish gray above*; shoulders bronzy greenish; *long pointed occipital crest, forehead, throat patch, and breast black*; belly white. In flight broad rounded wings mostly black with large white patch on wing coverts; rump white; tail black.
**Similar species:** Superficially like Andean Lapwing (2) but latter lacks black on face, throat, and breast, and is mostly bronzy green (not grayish brown) above.
**Voice:** Very noisy bird, uttering loud, metallic scolding *keek, keek, keek . . .* and other notes at slightest disturbance.
**Behavior:** Single birds, pairs, or loose groups are conspic. standing in bare or grassy pastures. Flight is slow and bounding, usually not long sustained.
**Breeding:** 2 nests, Jan–Feb, Finca Merenberg, Huila (Ridgely and Gaulin 1980); flightless young, Mar–July; 2 nests, May and June, ne Meta (S. Furniss); other nests, June–July, n Arauca (J. Jorgenson); in Venez. May–July (Friedmann and Smith 1950; Thomas 1979b); eggs olive brown, spotted and blotched black, in small ground depression (Sclater and Salvin 1879).
**Status and habitat:** Common in grassland, open
pastures, and damp marshy areas; usually where grass is short. Populations fluctuate seasonally in w Meta (Hacienda La Corocora) with much higher nos. Dec–early Aug (W. McKay).
**Range:** To 2600m (E Andes); to 3100m (sight, PN Puracé). In suitable habitat throughout s to s Cauca (not Nariño); local on Pacific slope, rarely Amazonia. C Panama to Guianas, e and c Brazil; n and e Bolivia to Paraguay, Uruguay, and Tierra del Fuego; Ecuador (2 specimens); Trinidad.

35. SOUTHERN LAPWING

## 2. ANDEAN LAPWING

*Vanellus resplendens*                    Ill. 36

**Identification:** 13″ (33cm). Bold black and white pattern in flight. Bill coral red tipped black, eyes red, legs coral red. No pointed crest. *Head, neck, and breast pale grayish white*; breast somewhat darker; rest of underparts white; *back and wings bronzy green.* In flight broad rounded wings and distal half of tail black; large wing patch and base of tail white.

**Similar species:** Southern Lapwing (1) has crest, grayish upperparts (not bronzy green), and black face and breast.

**Voice:** Noisy. Calls resemble those of Southern Lapwing, a loud shrill gull-like *klee, klee, klee* . . . , or *ka-leék, ka-leék.* . . .

**Behavior:** Upper el. counterpart of Southern Lapwing and with sim. behavior.

**Breeding:** Unreported in Colombia. Nest a ground depression lined with plant matter; 4 olive brown eggs with small dark brown spots (Johnson 1965).

**Status and habitat:** Grassy pastures, open drier country, and shores of lakes and ponds. Largest group is over 300, 13 July 1976, n of Guachucal, Nariño (R. Ridgely). Very sparingly n to Cauca in s C Andes.

**Range:** Mostly 2500-3200m (doubtless higher); to about 4000m in c Ecuador. C Andes from Cauca (PN Puracé) s through mts. of Nariño; casually n in E Andes to Sabana de Bogotá. S Colombia s in Andes to n Argentina and Chile.

## 3. PIED LAPWING

*Hoploxypterus cayanus*                    Ill. 37

**Identification:** 9″ (23cm). Bold and unusual pattern. Bill brown; eyering and legs coral red. Crown sandy brown bordered white; forecrown, sides of head, hindneck, upper mantle, and broad collar across breast black; *scapulars black bordered white forming conspic. band on sides of back*; otherwise mainly sandy brown above and white below. In flight primaries, band on sides of back, and outer half of tail black; most of inner half of wings, rump, and base of tail white.

**Similar species:** Much smaller than Southern Lapwing and with very different distribution of black and white.

**Voice:** A sweet, whistled *wheé-whoo,* given quickly, 1st note higher (Friedmann and Smith 1955). Unlike other American lapwings, rather quiet.

**Behavior:** A charming little bird, usually seen alone or infrequently in small groups. Stands quietly near water or patter runs short distances across sand, then stops with a dip and picks at sand or damp mud. Often rather wary.

**Breeding:** Copulation, 8 Dec, n Arauca (J. Jorgenson); nest, 24 July, on sand bar on Amazon river isl. near Leticia (Hilty); 2-3 olive buff eggs speckled darker brown, more heavily at larger end; in unlined scrape in sand. Eggs covered with sand before leaving.

**Status and habitat:** Uncommon and local. Re-

36. Andean Lapwing

stricted to sandy river banks, sand bars, and freshwater pools. The requirement is sand.
**Range:** To 500m. Spottily distributed throughout e of Andes. The Guianas and Venez. s to e Bolivia, Paraguay, and se Brazil; accidental in nw Argentina.

## 4. BLACK-BELLIED (GRAY) PLOVER
*Pluvialis squatarola*                                    Ill. 38
**Identification:** 12″ (30 cm). Chunky with rather large head and short bill. Nonbreeding plumage: *light grayish brown above inconspic. mottled white*, below white somewhat mottled gray on breast; rump and tail white, tail lightly barred black. Breeding plumage: *sides of face and most of underparts black*; white forehead extends as stripe around sides of head to sides of breast; upperparts heavily marbled black and white. In flight in any plumage shows *white rump, mostly white tail*, white wing stripe and *black axillars* ("armpits"). Molting birds with underparts mottled or blotched black are often seen in Mar.
**Similar species:** See less common Golden Plover (5).
**Voice:** A plaintive, whistled *cleee-er-ree*, lower-pitched than American Golden Plover.
**Behavior:** Usually scattered individuals; not in large flocks. Rather wary.
**Status and habitat:** Fairly common transient and winter resident (chiefly Sept–Mar) to mudflats, beaches, and coastal lagoons, occas. grassy areas inland. A few oversummer; several, 1-2 June (T. B. Johnson); others, June–

Aug, PN Salamanca (P. Donahue), and 23-30 June near Barranquilla and at Manaure, Guajira (A. Sprunt IV).
**Range:** Carib. and Pacific coast; stragglers inland w of Andes to 2600m in C and E Andes. Circumpolar breeder; s in winter to S Hemisphere. In New World from s US s on both coasts to s S America; throughout Old World.

## 5. LESSER (AMERICAN) GOLDEN-PLOVER
*Pluvialis dominica*
**Identification:** 9-11″ (23-28cm). Resembles Black-bellied Plover. Nonbreeding plumage: brownish flecked yellow above, cap darker; below white tinged brown, belly palest. Breeding plumage: brown above thickly spotted and flecked golden yellow; *sides of face and most of underparts black* with narrow white forehead extending as stripe behind cheeks to sides of breast. In flight from above in any plumage uniformly dark.
**Similar species:** Smaller and darker than Black-bellied Plover (4); in flight shows no white above and no black axillars below.
**Voice:** Clear high *queedleet* or *que-e-e-a* (dropping at end), unlike plaintive call of Black-bellied Plover.
**Status and habitat:** Uncommon fall transient, poss. rare winter resident (Sept–Dec) to grassy pastures, less frequently beaches and mudflats (reverse of Black-bellied Plover). Few recs. e of Andes (1 on 27 Dec 1975, Carimagua, ne Meta–S. Furniss; 1 on 3 and 17 Nov 1974

37. PIED LAPWING

near Leticia—J. V. Remsen); only spring recs. are 1 at Buenaventura Bay, 9 Feb 1984 (Hilty, R. Ridgely) and a few in Apr 1977, El Tuparro, e Vichada (T. O. Lemke).

**Range:** To 2600m. E and w of Andes. Breeds in N America and n Asia; in New World migrates chiefly e of Andes to wintering grounds mainly in Argentina, occas. Chile.

## 6. SEMIPALMATED PLOVER
*Charadrius semipalmatus* Ill. 39
**Identification:** 6.5-7.5″ (16-19cm). Small plover with rather large-headed appearance. *Short yellow bill tipped black;* yellow legs. Brown above with white forehead and eyebrow; *white collar on hindneck* continuous with white underparts; narrow black breast band. Nonbreeding plumage: sim. but breast band brown, bill black.
**Similar species:** Easily confused with Collared Plover (see 8); also Thick-billed Plover (10).
**Voice:** A plaintive slurred *chu-reép*, 2d note higher.
**Behavior:** Usually in rather small groups that scatter when feeding.
**Status and habitat:** Common transient and winter resident (mostly Sept–Apr), small nos. all year; sandy beaches and tidal flats, infre-

quently inland (once, Popayán; once, Macuira Hills, Guajira, Jan—Marinkelle 1970).
**Range:** Carib. and Pacific coast. Breeds in n N America; winters from s US s on both coasts to Chile and Argentina; inland in Bolivia. Dutch Leewards; Trinidad.

## 7. [SNOWY PLOVER]
*Charadrius alexandrinus* Ill. 39
**Identification:** 6.5″ (16.5cm). *Slender black bill and blackish legs. Above very pale sandy brown* (darker in nonbreeding garb) with *blackish mark across forecrown* and another on ear coverts; forecrown, sides of head, and underparts white with *smudgy black mark on sides of breast* forming an incomplete breast band. Imm.: black markings replaced by pale brown or lacking.
**Similar species:** Nearest Collared Plover (8) but legs dark (not pale) and breast band incomplete. Much paler than any other small Colombian plover.
**Status and habitat:** Hypothetical. No specimens. Sight recs. at 4 localities on coast of Bolívar (La Boquilla, Punta Canoas, Arroya de Piedra, Lomarena) Oct 1978–May 1979 (Naranjo 1979b). To be expected on Guajira Peninsula; reg. on Venez. coast (Falcón) in

38. Black-bellied (Gray) Plover (non-breeding plumage)

Sept and Oct (Altman and Parrish 1978); and 1 seen 18 Jan, Chichiriviche, Falcón (P. Alden).

**Range:** Carib. coast. Breeds in s and w US, Mexico, W Indies, coastal Peru, Chile, and much of Old World; also on Dutch and Venez. isls. (Curaçao is closest). N New World populations winter locally to s Honduras (accidental to Costa Rica and Panama).

## 8. COLLARED PLOVER
*Charadrius collaris*                    Ill. 39
**Identification:** 5.5-6″ (14-15cm). *Slender bill all black*; legs flesh pink to yellow. Above brown with rather large white patch across forehead; center crown blackish; *hindcrown and nape strongly tinged cinnamon, sometimes forming a distinct cinnamon nuchal collar* (no white collar on hindneck); below white with a black breast band. Imm.: duller with little cinnamon on head.
**Similar species:** Easily confused with Semipalmated Plover (6) but smaller and daintier and has thinner black bill (winter Semipalmated also has black bill), no white nuchal collar, and usually rufous on hindcrown. Thick-billed Plover (10) is larger with decidedly heavy bill and prom. eyestripe. Also see Snowy Plover (7).
**Voice:** Usually silent. When disturbed a short *dreep* or 2-noted *keedup*, 2d syllable lower (K. Kaufman).
**Behavior:** Single birds scatter along sand bars. Not in flocks. Rather confiding.
**Breeding:** No Colombian recs. Downy chick (photo), 27 Jan, below San Carlos, Guainía on Río Negro (Friedmann 1948). May breed in Amazonia late June–Sept (lowest water) on exposed sand bars. In Chile nests on sandy river banks; 2 eggs, cream with numerous black spots and scrawls (Johnson 1965).
**Status and habitat:** Locally common on sand and gravel bars along larger rivers, on mudflats, beaches, and less frequently short grassy fields. Some seasonal movements: in w Meta, scattered birds, Feb–May (W. McKay); in extreme ne Meta, mainly Apr–Aug (S. Furniss); and in Amazonas near Leticia mainly during low water, June–Sept and Dec–Feb (J. V. Remsen).
**Range:** To 1000m (Cauca Val.). Throughout. W Mexico to Chile and n Argentina. Dutch Antilles; Trinidad.

## 9. KILLDEER
*Charadrius vociferus*
**Identification:** 9-11″ (23-28cm). Bill black, narrow eyering red, legs pinkish. Above brown; *rump and basal two-thirds of tail cinnamon orange*; rest of tail black with narrow white tip; fore-head, eyebrow, collar on hindneck, and underparts white; *2 black breast bands.*
**Similar species:** Only Colombian plover with 2 breast bands. Note large size.
**Voice:** Loud, vociferous *kil-dee* or *kil-deéa.*
**Behavior:** Scattered individuals, rarely small loose flocks. Sometimes with other shorebirds but usually not in saline coastal habitats.
**Status and habitat:** Very uncommon and local winter resident (Dec–Mar) to fields, waste places, airports, etc., usually away from water. Most recs. from n part of country s to latitude of Bogotá.
**Range:** To 2600m. Spottily w of Andes. Breeds from s Canada to Mexico, W Indies, and in coastal Peru and nw Chile. N birds winter s to Ecuador, n Colombia, and n Venez.

## 10. THICK-BILLED (WILSON'S) PLOVER
*Charadrius wilsonius*                    Ill. 39
**Identification:** 7-8″ (18-20cm). *Rather long, heavy black bill; legs dusky pink.* ♂: above brown (or strongly tinged rufous on sides of head and nape—resident *cinnamominus*); forehead, broad eyebrow, narrow collar on hindneck, and underparts white; narrow black bar on crown and *single broad black breast band.* ♀: sim. but lacks black on crown; breast band rusty (resident *cinnamominus*) or brown. Nonbreeding ♂ sim. to ♀.
**Similar species:** Larger than Semipalmated or Collared plovers (6, 8) and easily told by long *heavy* black bill. Collared Plover lacks white nuchal collar, Semipalmated has yellow (not dull grayish pink) legs.
**Voice:** Call an emphatic, whistled *phit* or *pheet.*
**Behavior:** Usually scattered individuals or pairs, not in large flocks.
**Breeding:** BC ♀, 10 Feb, imm. ♀, 11 Apr, Córdoba (Carriker). BC ♀, Apr, coastal Bolívar, and display flights with constant calling (Naranjo 1979b). In Trinidad May–June, 2-3 grayish white eggs, heavily spotted dark brown; on bare scrape in pebbly beach or near mudflat (ffrench 1973).
**Status and habitat:** Fairly common to common local resident on pebbly or sandy beaches, seldom mudflats, and rarely inland (1, Macuira Hills, e Guajira, Jan—Marinkelle 1970). Some movement to muddy areas during high water (June–late Aug) in PN Isla de Salamanca— T. B. Johnson. Only n migrants reported (*C. w. wilsonius*) have been 2 on 16 Jan and 1 in Aug near Barranquilla (Naranjo 1979a).
**Range:** Resident on both coasts. Breeds from nw Mexico s to Ecuador and nw Peru on the Pacific, from se US to Surinam and ne Brazil on the Carib. Aruba and Trinidad. N American birds winter s to Ecuador and Bahía, e Brazil.

39. Snowy Plover (upper left), Thick-Billed (Wilson's) Plover (♂ center), Collared Plover (lower left), Semipalmated Plover (right, non-breeding plumage)

## SANDPIPERS, SNIPES, ETC.: Scolopacidae (29)

This large worldwide family of wading birds is closely related to plovers but differs in having, among other things, more slender proportions, longer necks and legs, and longer and sometimes curved or drooping bills. Most are also more gregarious during migration and on their wintering grounds and are more closely confined to water. They occur mainly in the lowlands, some regularly in small numbers to very high elevations as well. Many Colombian species are north temperate or arctic breeders and are for the most part transients or nonbreeding residents; first-year birds of many species oversummer. The migrant species are mainly encountered in their more confusing nonbreeding plumages in Colombia, and identification is often difficult. The five species of snipe are resident; a migratory form of the Common Snipe also reaches Colombia.

### 1. SOLITARY SANDPIPER
*Tringa solitaria*                                  Ill. 40

**Identification:** 7.5″ (19cm). *Decidedly slender* black bill; long *dusky green legs*. Above dark olive finely streaked and spotted white; *conspic. white eyering*; below white lightly streaked dusky on upper breast; center of tail blackish; outer feathers white barred black. In flight note *barred sides of tail, dark rump, and lack of wing stripe*.

**Similar species:** Spotted Sandpiper (4) teeters more, in flight has prom. wing stripe, and flies stiffly with shallow wing beats (not deep, swallowlike strokes). Lesser Yellowlegs (2) has yellow (not dark) legs and a white rump.

**Voice:** Emphatic *peet!* or *peet-weet-weet!* when flushed, higher and sharper than Spotted Sandpiper.

**Behavior:** Usually alone, sometimes 2 or 3 scattered birds, but never flocks. Nods head continually as wades rather deliberately in shallow water along margins of small pools. Flight is rapid but erratic, almost ternlike or swallowlike with deep quick wing strokes.

**Status and habitat:** Transient and winter resident in small nos. early Aug–early Apr; occas. birds return by July (1 on 12 July 1974, Leticia—J. V. Remsen; 1 on 24 July 1978, Leticia, and 28 July 1976 near Buga, Valle—Hilty). All kinds of fresh water incl. rain pools, ponds, and muddy stream banks, esp. near trees or woodland. In Amazonas mostly as fall transient late July–late Oct (J. V. Remsen).

**Range:** To 2600m (1 sighting to 3000m, Represa Neusa n of Bogotá—A. Gast). Throughout. Breeds in n N America; winters from s Mexico to Bolivia and c Argentina.

## 2. LESSER YELLOWLEGS

*Tringa flavipes*                                                    Ill. 40

**Identification:** 10-11″ (25-28cm). *Slender straight black bill; long yellow legs.* Above grayish brown freckled and barred with white; below white lightly streaked and spotted dusky on neck and sides of breast. In flight note *dark wings* (no stripe) and *whitish rump and tail.*

**Similar species:** Easily confused with slightly larger Greater Yellowlegs (see 3). Solitary Sandpiper (1) has dark legs, dark rump, and strong barring on sides of tail. Smaller nonbreeding Stilt Sandpiper (16) has prom. eyestripe, greenish legs, and proportionally longer bill (longer than length of head). Smaller Wilson's Phalarope (p 169), somewhat sim. in flight, is immaculate white below with needlelike bill.

**Voice:** *Yew* or *you-you* (1 or 2 notes), less forceful than Greater Yellowlegs' rhythmic 3-note call.

**Behavior:** Feeds actively, sometimes in flocks, and often loosely assoc. with peeps. Not as wary as Greater Yellowlegs.

**Status and habitat:** Fairly common migrant and winter resident (mostly early Aug–mid-Apr) to tidal flats, lake shores, and freshwater marshes. Scattered individuals oversummer. At PN Isla de Salamanca most numerous during fall passage, Aug–Nov (T. B. Johnson); in w Meta more numerous Dec–mid-Mar (W. McKay).

**Range:** To 2600m (once to 3300 m, 14 Feb 1984, Laguna San Raphael, e Cauca—A. Keith, R. Ridgely). Throughout. Breeds in Canada and Alaska; winters from s US s both inland and on coasts to Chile and Argentina. Dutch and Venez. Isls. Trinidad.

## 3. GREATER YELLOWLEGS

*Tringa melanoleuca*                                                  Ill. 40

**Identification:** 12-14″ (30-36cm). Almost identical to Lesser Yellowlegs in plumage but larger (noticeable when the 2 are together); bill somewhat heavier, *slightly upturned* (not always apparent), *proportionally longer* (longer than length of head instead of about equal to length of head), and *basal half grayish* contrasting with darker distal half (instead of all black).

**Similar species:** See Lesser Yellowlegs (2); in addition to bill and size differences they are easily separated by calls.

40. GREATER YELLOWLEGS (top left), LESSER YELLOWLEGS (top right), SOLITARY SANDPIPER (bottom center)

**Voice:** Loud, ringing 3- or 4-note *teu-teu-teu*, in contrast to softer, characteristically 1- or 2-note call of Lesser Yellowlegs.

**Behavior:** As in Lesser Yellowlegs but partial to coastal habitats and more wary.

**Status and habitat:** Common transient and winter resident (mostly early Aug–early May) on coasts, less numerous inland on lakes and marshes. Small nos. oversummer. Peak nos. in Sept at PN Isla de Salamanca (T. B. Johnson).

**Range:** Carib. and Pacific coasts and inland to 2600m (sighting to 3000m, Represa Neusa, n of Bogotá—A. Gast). Throughout. Breeds in n N America; winters from s US s to Chile and Argentina. Trinidad.

### 4. SPOTTED SANDPIPER

*Actitis macularia*                    Ill. 41

**Identification:** 7-8″ (18-20cm). Bill dull yellowish tipped black; legs dull yellow (color of both varies in nonbreeding birds). Nonbreeding plumage: olive brown above, white below with whitish eyebrow and *dusky smudge on sides of breast*. Breeding plumage: sim. but obscurely barred blackish above and *thickly spotted black below* (large round spots). In flight in any plumage note white wing stripe and *stiff shallow quivering wing beats* interspersed with short glides with wings bowed downward. *Compulsively teeters* as though not well balanced.

**Similar species:** See Solitary Sandpiper (1), which lacks wing stripe, shows barred white outer tail feathers, bobs head more, and teeters less.

**Voice:** A clear *peet* or *peet-weet-weet!* (cf. 1), often the 1st indication of its presence.

**Behavior:** Inconspic. and nonsocial. Individuals scatter uniformly through suitable habitat and do not flock, seldom even loosely assoc. with other peeps.

**Status and habitat:** Very common transient and winter resident to all kinds of coastal and inland waters, mainly early Aug–early May (once 30 May 1978, w Meta—W. McKay). Only summer recs. are 1 on 7 July 1975, Buenaventura Bay (Hilty et al.), and in July at PN Isla de Salamanca (P. Donahue).

**Range:** To 3300m. Throughout, incl. Malpelo Isl. (sight). Breeds in N America; winters from US to Chile, Argentina, and s Brazil. Aruba to Trinidad.

### 5. WILLET

*Catoptrophorus semipalmatus*                    Ill. 42

**Identification:** 14-16″ (36-41cm). *Bold black and white wing pattern* in flight. Nondescript at rest. *Rather long heavy blackish bill*; legs blue gray. Nonbreeding plumage: pale gray above; white below with a dull whitish eyestripe. Breeding plumage: grayish brown above thickly streaked and barred dusky; below white spotted and

41. SPOTTED SANDPIPER (non-breeding plumage)

barred dusky on neck, breast, and sides; *rump white*; tail pale gray. In flight in any plumage note *large size and flashing white wing stripe contrasting with black flight feathers.*
**Similar species:** Larger and grayer than Greater Yellowlegs, with gray legs and heavier bill. In flight bold wing pattern is characteristic.
**Voice:** Loud, shrill flight call *quee-quee-queep.*
**Behavior:** Usually singly or in small loose groups with other shorebirds. Not in large flocks. Teeters and nods less than yellowlegs and walks with bill angled downward. Flight is strong and buoyant with downstroke emphasized.
**Status and habitat:** Common transient and winter resident to both coasts, mainly Sept–Apr. In nos. yr.-round on Pacific coast, smaller nos. oversummer locally on Carib.
**Range:** Both coasts, occas. inland (lowlands). Breeds in N America, the Bahamas, W Indies, and Isla Los Roques off Venez.; winters from s US s mainly on coasts to Peru and s Brazil, occas. to n Chile.

## 6. RUDDY TURNSTONE
*Arenaria interpres* Ill. 42
**Identification:** 8-9″ (20-23cm). Slender pointed black bill, slightly upturned at tip; *short orange legs.* Breeding plumage: *upper back and wings bright rufous chestnut*; head and underparts white; prom. *broad black chest band spreads in complicated patern up onto sides of head*, over shoulders, and onto back; lower back, rump, and most of tail white; tail with subterminal black band. Nonbreeding plumage recognizably sim. but much duller: head and upperparts mainly brown; broad dusky chest band spreads onto sides of neck and lower breast; throat and lower underparts white. In flight in any plumage note boldly striped black, white, and rufous pattern on back, wings, and tail.
**Voice:** A sharp, rather metallic *ut-e-kut.*
**Behavior:** Scattered individuals or loose flocks often associate with other shorebirds. Turn over pebbles and other bits of jetsam. Sometimes perch above beach on larger rocks.
**Status and habitat:** Common transient and winter resident (mainly Sept–May) to pebbly beaches and tidal mudflats. Scattered individuals to large nos. oversummer. "Common" 30 June, PN Isla de Salamanca (T. B. Johnson). Rarely inland.
**Range:** Carib. and Pacific coasts. Circumpolar breeding; N American birds winter s on both coasts of Middle and S America to Chile and Argentina; in Old World s to s Africa and s Asia.
**Note 1:** Sometimes placed in the family Charadriidae. **Note 2:** Surfbird (*Aphriza virgata*), breeding in Alaska and wintering s on Pacific coast to s California and locally to Panama, Ecuador, Peru, and n Chile, is likely on Pacific coast of Colombia. Chunky (9-10″) with fairly

42. WILLET (left and flying), RUDDY TURNSTONE (right)
(both in non-breeding plumage)

short yellow bill tipped black; short legs yellowish or greenish. Nonbreeding plumage: *mainly dark gray* with whitish eyebrow, throat, and belly, latter streaked and spotted gray. Breeding plumage: above blackish streaked gray and brown; below white heavily scalloped white. In flight shows white wing stripe, white rump, and *white tail with black wedge on tip*. Scattered individuals are difficult to see as they feed over dark wave-washed rocks, on reefs or mudflats adj. to rocky areas.

### 7. WANDERING TATTLER
*Heteroscelus incanus*
**Identification:** 10.5-11.2″ (27-28cm). Rather long straight black bill; *short stout legs yellow.* Nonbreeding plumage: *above solid gray* (no pattern in wings and tail in flight) with white line over eye; underparts white shaded grayish on head, neck, breast, and flanks. Breeding plumage: sim. but *underparts closely barred black and white.*
**Similar species:** In nonbreeding plumage (the one likely in Colombia) much like nonbreeding Spotted Sandpiper (4) but larger, more robust, and with heavier bill, gray wash across chest (as opposed to white with dusky smudge at sides), and no wing pattern in flight.
**Voice:** Noisy. A quick *tu-ee-ee-et* is flatter than Greater Yellowlegs.
**Behavior:** Bobs and teeters on wave-washed rocks and often with turnstones, surfbirds, and Spotted Sandpipers.
**Status and habitat:** Known from 2 ♀♀ and a ♂ taken from a flock of about 25 on Malpelo Isl. (500km w of Buenaventura), 8-9 Feb 1937 (Bond and Meyer de Schauensee 1938). As yet unrec. on Pacific Colombian coast but doubtless a casual winter visitant or winter resident to rocky shores and offshore isls.
**Range:** Malpelo Isl. off Pacific coast. Breeds locally in Alaska, the Yukon, and nw British Colombia; winters chiefly on S Pacific isls.; also spottily on rocky Pacific coast from California to Peru; the Cocos and Galapagos Isls.

### 8. [RED KNOT]
*Calidris canutus*
**Identification:** 9″ (23cm). *Stocky and short-necked.* Straight black bill mod. short; legs dull greenish. Nonbreeding plumage: *grayish above* with fairly prom. eyestripe; below white, sometimes obscurely mottled dusky on sides. Breeding plumage: above mottled dusky and buff; *sides of head incl. eyebrow and entire underparts brick red*; belly and rump whitish. In flight in any plumage shows narrow white wing stripe and scaly *pale grayish white rump.*
**Similar species:** Breeding ads. resemble dowitchers but have shorter bills than the long snipelike bills of latter. In difficult nonbreeding garb note large size (nearly as large as Black-bellied Plover), chunky shape, faded gray plumage and lack of strong contrast between back, rump, and tail. Also see Dunlin and Curlew sandpipers (note).
**Behavior:** Scattered individuals occur on tidal flats or coast with Black-bellied Plovers and turnstones; tight flocks in temperate latitudes.
**Status and habitat:** Hypothetical. Prob. rare transient, but few recs. (no specimens): 1 seen in breeding plumage, 13 May 1972, PN Isla de Salamanca (T. B. Johnson); others, presumed this sp., in same area 1974-75 (P. Donahue); 3 seen in breeding plumage, 22 Apr 1979, La Boquilla and Ciénaga de Juan Polo, Bolívar (Naranjo 1979b); 4 nonbreeding plumage birds at Buenaventura Bay, 9 Feb 1984 (R. Ridgely, C. Wilds, Hilty) are only Pacific coast recs. May winter sparingly, although most go further south.
**Range:** Carib. and Pacific coasts. Breeds in circumpolar regions; in S America migrates mainly along Atlantic. Winters on coasts of s US and Mid. America s to Strait of Magellan; in Old World s to s Africa, Asia, Australia, and New Zealand.
**Note 1:** Two other sim. N Hemisphere sandpipers are unrec. but poss. Dunlin (*C. alpina*) winters mostly in s N America but casually s to Panama. There are no S American recs. Nonbreeding birds resemble winter Red Knot but are smaller (7″) and have a rather long bill with stout base and obvious droop at tip; otherwise nondescript gray above and whitish below with gray wash on breast and sides. In flight shows a prom. wing stripe and blackish central rectrices. Breeding plumage birds (very unlikely in Colombia) are bright rusty above, and whitish lightly streaked gray below with a large black belly patch. **Note 2:** Curlew Sandpiper (*C. ferruginea*) of Eurasia is a reg. visitor to e N America and is reported from the Carib., Trinidad, Peru, and Argentina. At rest nonbreeding birds are nondescript and almost exactly like winter Dunlin, but distinctive bill is curved throughout its length (not just at tip). When flushed, shows a conspic. white rump (like White-rumped Sandpiper) and white wing stripe. Brick red breeding ads. are unmistakable but unlikely in Colombia.

### 9. LEAST SANDPIPER
*Calidris minutilla*                                   Ill. 43
**Identification:** 6″ (15cm). *Small peep.* Short thin bill; *legs yellowish or greenish yellow.* Above dark brown edged rufous, below white shaded grayish and streaked brown on breast. Non-

breeding plumage: upperparts grayish brown without rufous; below much duller, markings obscure. In flight shows faint narrow white wing stripe and white on sides of rump.

**Similar species:** Only small peep with yellowish legs (color often difficult to see) and always looks dark-chested (compared to white-chested, nonbreeding Semipalmated and Western sandpipers). See Baird's, Pectoral, Semipalmated, and Western sandpipers (10, 12, 13 14).

**Voice:** A thin *kree-eet*, more drawn out than note of Western Sandpiper (Peterson 1961).

**Behavior:** Alone or in confiding little flocks. Usually assoc. with other shorebirds.

**Status and habitat:** Common transient and fairly common winter resident on both coasts and inland, mainly late July–early Apr. Most common peep inland in wet, muddy, and marshy areas; on coast usually less numerous than Western Sandpiper. Few summer recs. (2, 4, and 30 June 1972, PN Isla de Salamanca—T. B. Johnson; a few in July 1974 in same area— P. Donahue).

**Range:** Both coasts and inland throughout. To 1000m (prob. occas. to temperate zone). Breeds in arctic N America; winters from s US to s S America on both coasts and locally inland s to n Chile and c Brazil. W Indies; Trinidad.

## 10. BAIRD'S SANDPIPER
*Calidris bairdii*

**Identification:** 7″ (18cm). Bill short; legs blackish. *Buffy brown above*, the feathers pale-edged giving a *scaled* appearance (most conspic. in imms.); breast light buffy brown finely and obscurely streaked dark brown; rest of underparts white. In flight shows inconspic. narrow white wing stripe and white on sides of rump. At rest *long wings extend slightly beyond tail.* Wing tips of other peeps (except White-rumped) scarcely reach tail tip.

**Similar species:** Confusing. Approaches White-rumped Sandpiper (11) in size but separable from any plumage of latter by dark center down rump. Larger Pectoral Sandpiper (12) is more striped (not scaled) above and has greenish yellow (not dark) legs; Baird's has buffy head and breast. Other sim. small peeps— Least, Semipalmated, and Western sandpipers—(9, 13, 14) are grayer, esp. in nonbreeding plumages usually seen in Colombia. Spring Sanderling (15) is rusty buff on head and breast, has more prom. wing stripe, and is rarely away from sandy beaches.

**Voice:** Call note *kurrp*, much lower-pitched than Least Sandpiper but not as low-pitched and coarse as Pectoral (K. Kaufman).

**Behavior:** Likely to be seen alone or with other

sandpipers (such as Pectoral) that frequent grassy pools and ponds.

**Status and habitat:** Fall transient in low nos. (late Aug–Oct) and apparently very rare spring transient (no recs.?) to small freshwater pools, flooded rice fields, and grassy borders of lakes.

**Range:** To 3400m (Laguna San Rafael, PN Puracé) w of Andes (no recs. e of Andes). Breeds in Arctic America and e Siberia; in New World, winters chiefly in Andes from Peru southward.

## 11. WHITE-RUMPED SANDPIPER
*Calidris fuscicollis*                               Ill. 43

**Identification:** 7″ (18cm). In any plumage note *all white rump in flight.* Legs dark greenish. Nonbreeding plumage: *uniform grayish above*; white below lightly shaded and streaked grayish on upper breast. Breeding plumage: mottled rufous brown above; white below streaked dusky on breast. In flight white white wing stripe indistinct. At rest *wing tips extend slightly beyond tip of tail* (as in Baird's Sandpiper).

**Similar species:** Only small peep with an all white rump. Larger than Least, Semipalmated, and Western (9, 13, 14); smaller than Pectoral (12). Baird's (10), always more buffy, is scaly-backed in spring (White-rumped is slightly streaked but not scaly).

**Voice:** Call, highest-pitched of Colombian peeps, a thin, metallic, almost scraping *skeet*, often doubled (M. Robbins).

**Status and habitat:** Prob. uncommon spring and fall transient e of Andes, but as yet only 2 fall recs.: 1 (photo) near Leticia, 24 Oct 1974 (Remsen 1977a) and 8 seen at Pto. Inírida airport, Guainía, 18 Sept 1978 (Hilty and M. Robbins). In Surinam, late Aug–early Oct and late Apr–early June (Spaans 1978). Most movement prob. e of the Andes. Presence on Carib. coast of Colombia (there are unconfirmed sight recs.—Naranjo 1979b) will require documentation.

**Range:** To 400m. E of Andes. Breeds in Arctic N America; winters chiefly e of Andes from the Guianas and Venezuela to Tierra del Fuego.

## 12. PECTORAL SANDPIPER
*Calidris melanotos*                                Ill. 43

**Identification:** 8-9″ (20-23cm). *Rather large long-necked peep.* Legs greenish yellow. Above brown heavily streaked black; *head, neck, and breast buffy streaked brown in sharp contrast to white lower underparts.* In flight little or no wing stripe visible; rump whitish on sides with dark center.

**Similar species:** Best distinguished from other peeps by buffy streaked breast sharply cut off from white belly. Larger than other peeps and

streaking somewhat bolder above. In coloration closest to Least Sandpiper (9), but note longer neck, more erect carriage, and much larger size. Also see Baird's Sandpiper (10).
**Voice:** A rough *tr'r'r'k* or *ch'r'r't*, often doubled, grating and coarser than other sandpipers.
**Behavior:** Reg. in small flocks and usually with other shorebirds. Rather snipelike zigzag flight when flushed.
**Status and habitat:** Fairly common fall transient early Aug–mid-Nov (1 on 4 Aug 1975 at Leticia is earliest—J. V. Remsen), and very uncommon or rare spring transient (prob. Mar–May); 1 on 4 Feb 1976, Río Zanza, Macarena Mts. (T. O. Lemke and P. Gertler), and another 16 Feb 1973 near Santa Marta (Hilty, T. B. Johnson, and S. M. Russell) may have been early migrants. Mostly freshwater ponds, lakes, and flooded fields; scarce on coast. No definite summer recs.
**Range:** To 3100m (Lago Tota, Boyacá). Throughout. Breeds in Arctic America and nw Siberia; winters chiefly in s S America.

## 13. SEMIPALMATED SANDPIPER
*Calidris pusilla*
**Identification:** 6-6.5″ (15-16.5cm). Small grayish brown peep. Bill *rather short* and thick; *legs blackish*. Above mottled *grayish* brown; below white, washed buff and indistinctly streaked darker on neck and breast. Nonbreeding plumage: sim. but grayer. In flight shows pale wing stripe and white sides on rump.
**Similar species:** From Least Sandpiper (9) by black legs but often not separable from Western Sandpiper (14). Western usually has a longer bill with droopy tip, and in breeding plumage is rustier on back and scapulars. Grayish nonbreeding plumage Western usually retains rusty edges on scapulars, and birds with either bill droop or rusty scapular edges are prob. Western. But because short-billed ♂ Western may lack droopy bill tip, and in fall plumage may lack rusty scapulars, the reverse is not true for confirming a Semipalmated Sandpiper. Most Semipalmated *are* safely identified by voice and bill measurements (Phillips 1975). In the hand exposed culmen lengths of unsexed birds less than 20mm are Semipalmated, from 20-22mm either bird, 23 or over prob. Western, and over 24 definitely Western.
**Voice:** Call a short *chit-chit*, lower than the usual shrill *cheep* of Western Sandpiper and like a distant ♀ Great-tailed Grackle (Phillips 1975); a short *cherk* or *cher* less thin and sharp than notes of other peeps (Peterson 1963).
**Status and habitat:** Prob. fairly common transient and winter resident, but see identifica-

tion problems above. Recorded early Sept–May on coastal mudflats and beaches, once inland (1, Macuira Hills, e Guajira, Jan—Marinkelle 1970). Thousands, believed this sp., oversummering 26-28 June, Manaure, Guajira (A. Sprunt IV).
**Range:** Carib. and Pacific coasts. Breeds in Arctic America; winters on coasts from Florida to s S America.

## 14. WESTERN SANDPIPER
*Calidris mauri*                                    Ill. 43
**Identification:** 6.2-6.7″ (15.7-17cm). Rather long bill, thick at base, *often droopy at tip; legs blackish*. Breeding plumage: *rusty above*; white below with brownish streaks on neck and upper breast. Nonbreeding plumage: grayer above but *often* rusty on scapulars. In flight like Semipalmated Sandpiper.
**Similar species:** See Semipalmated (13) and Least sandpipers (9).
**Voice:** Usual call a thin *squeep*.
**Status and habitat:** Very common transient and winter resident to tidal mudflats and shallow lagoons on both coasts, rarely inland. Oversummers in nos.
**Range:** Both coasts. Breeds in w Alaska and ne Siberia; winters from s US s on Pacific coast to Peru, on Carib. coast to Surinam and Fr. Guiana.

## 15. SANDERLING
*Calidris alba*                                      Ill. 43
**Identification:** 7.5-8.5″ (19-22cm). Compact thick-set shorebird. *Sturdy black bill and legs.* Nonbreeding plumage: above pale gray; below white; *blackish shoulders and primaries*. Breeding plumage: mostly bright rusty with black mottling on upperparts, head, neck, and breast; lower underparts white. In flight in any plumage shows *prom. broad white wing stripe, wider and larger than any other peep*.
**Similar species:** In winter the palest Colombian shorebird, looking almost white at a distance. Note contrasting black bill and legs and mechanical behavior. Breeding birds are very bright on head, upper back, and breast and are larger and more robust than most other Colombian peeps.
**Voice:** A distinctive short *trick* or *tuit*.
**Behavior:** Mechanical and toylike as it patrols beaches and chases waves. Alone, scattered individuals, or in small or large, solid or mixed shorebird flocks. Confiding.
**Status and habitat:** Fairly common transient and winter resident on sandy beaches of both coasts, rarely inland (Cauca Val.). Only oversummering rec. is several seen at Manaure, Guajira, 26-28 June 1974 (A. Sprunt IV); 5,

Buenaventura Bay, 31 July 1976, may have been early migrants (Hilty, F. Loetscher, N. Loetscher).
**Range:** Carib. and Pacific coasts. Breeds in circumpolar regions; winters on both coasts of US s to s S America; in Old World from s Europe and Asia southward.

### 16. STILT SANDPIPER
*Micropalama himantopus*                Ill. 43
**Identification:** 8-9″ (20-23cm). Slender med.-sized shorebird with dowitcherlike head. Long straight bill, sometimes droops slightly at tip; *long usually greenish legs* (sometimes dull yellowish, rarely bright yellow); slender neck. Nonbreeding plumage: gray above with *narrow white superciliary*; below white faintly streaked gray on sides. Breeding plumage: grayish brown above, *whitish below closely barred dusky; crown and sides of head tinged rusty with narrow white superciliary*. In flight shows whitish rump and tail, no wing stripe.
**Similar species:** Spring ad. has much longer legs than Wandering Tattler (7) and is paler above with white (not all dark) rump. Nonbreeding birds resemble nonbreeding dowitchers (23, 24) but have shorter bills, longer legs, whiter underparts, and slenderer bodies. Dowitchers have stocky short-legged look. Nonbreeders from similar-shaped yellowlegs (2, 3) by almost uniform gray upperparts, usually greenish legs (leg color var. and not always reliable), and different feeding behavior. Bill much heavier than Lesser Yellowlegs and never looks upturned as in Greater Yellowlegs (K. Kaufman).
**Voice:** A single *que*, lower and hoarser than Lesser Yellowlegs; raspy *tri-i-i-ik*.
**Behavior:** Often with dowitchers and feed with sim. sewing-machine motion. Usually scattered individuals or loose flocks. Wade up to belly in water.
**Status and habitat:** Very uncommon transient and rare winter resident both on coast and inland. No oversummer recs.; on Pacific coast of Chocó and Carib. near Ciénaga as early as mid-Sept (Meyer de Schauensee 1950); as late as 29 Mar on Río Arauca (Blake 1961). In Falcón, n Venez., 2 breeding plumage ads. seen 1 Aug 1969 (P. Alden) may have been early fall migrants.
**Range:** Carib. and Pacific coasts and once e of Andes on Río Arauca. Breeds in Arctic America; winters mostly in s S America, a few linger northward.

### 17. BUFF-BREASTED SANDPIPER
*Tryngites subruficollis*
**Identification:** 8″ (20 cm). Small head, long neck,

and erect carriage recall Upland Sandpiper. *Bill short;* legs yellowish. Black above, *feathers broadly edged buff giving a spotted or scaled appearance; below uniform buff; large whitish eyering* imparts an alert wide-eyed look. In flight wings dark above, *mostly white below.*
**Similar species:** Smaller than Upland Sandpiper (19) and entire underparts uniform buff.
**Voice:** A low trilled *pr-r-r-reet*, a sharp *tik* (Wetmore 1965a).
**Behavior:** Very social and almost always in flocks. Tame. Sometimes may "freeze" rather than fly, allowing close approach. Flight is erratic and twisting.
**Status and habitat:** Uncommon fall transient (early Sept–mid-Nov; once in Dec, near Popayán). Spring status uncertain. Rec. in Apr; also Feb sightings near Mozambique (e of Villavicencio), Meta (F. Gill and A. Stokes); flock of about 500, 26 Feb–30 Mar 1977, w Meta at Hacienda La Corocora (W. McKay).
**Range:** To 2600m. Throughout (fall recs. mostly w of Andes). Breeds in w Arctic America; winters mainly in s S America.

### 18. RUFF (♂) REEVE (♀)
*Philomachus pugnax*
**Identification:** ♂ 10-12″ (25-30cm); ♀ 9″ (23cm). Straight, med.-length bill *slightly yellowish at base;* legs dull yellowish. Nonbreeding plumage: above brownish gray, feathers inconspic. pale-edged giving a *slightly scaled appearance;* rump and tail blackish with *large oval white patch on each side of base of tail* (distinctive in flight); below dull whitish with buffy tinge on foreneck and breast. Breeding ♂ ♂ (very unlikely in Colombia) have large erectile neck ruff colored black, white, or chestnut.
**Similar species:** Nonbreeding birds easily confused because of size var. Size and shape nearest Lesser Yellowlegs (2), but plumage browner and bill shorter. Pectoral Sandpiper (12) has more sharply cut off dark breast. Tail pattern in flight is diagnostic, and all birds should be flushed. Cf. Upland Sandpiper (19).
**Behavior:** Most New World recs. are with yellowlegs or dowitchers.
**Status and habitat:** Known from 1 "Bogotá" specimen of indefinite locality. Almost certainly a straggler to Carib. coast and inland.
**Range:** Breeds in n Eurasia; winters from s Europe to Africa and is a reg. but rare visitant to N America and Lesser Antilles. Sight recs. in Trinidad, n Venez. (Falcón), Panama, and Peru.

### 19. UPLAND SANDPIPER
*Bartramia longicauda*                Ill. 44
**Identification:** 11-12″ (28-30cm). *Rather short*

43. Stilt Sandpiper (upper left), Pectoral Sandpiper (upper right), White-rumped Sandpiper (middle left), Sanderling (middle right), Least Sandpiper (lower left), Western Sandpiper (lower right) (all in non-breeding plumage)

bill; *long yellow legs. Small head, long neck,* and longish pointed tail. Eyes large for size of head. Upperparts, head, neck, and breast brown streaked buff; rump and central tail blackish; belly white.

**Similar species:** Best clues are distinctive proportions, size, and lack of pattern in plumage. See smaller Buff-breasted Sandpiper (17), Ruff or Reeve (18), and larger Thick-knee (p 170).

**Voice:** A mellow, slightly trembling *quip-ip-ip-ip* or *que-lee-lee* given quickly; haunting song, not likely given in Colombia, a short rattling followed by a long-drawn, tremulous, reedy wolf whistle.

**Behavior:** Solitary or in small groups and usually not with other shorebirds or near water. Usually seen standing in open fields. Upright stance, stiff movements, and habit of holding wings raised momentarily upon alighting are characteristic. Sometimes rather wary in migration.

**Status and habitat:** Uncommon to fairly common spring and fall transient, early Sept–late Oct and late Feb–mid-May (spring specimens only in Apr) to grassy or burned pastures, airports, rough fields, and other open areas. Flocks of 15-30 near Carimagua, ne Meta, 9-29 Apr 1976 (S. Furniss). Ciénaga Grande is only reported locality on Carib. coast.

**Range:** To 2600m (Sabana de Bogotá). Throughout. E of Andes in Norte de Santander, Meta, e Guainía (sighting, Pto. Inírida, Sept—Hilty and M. Robbins), w Caquetá (Tres Esquinas), Vaupés (Mitú), and Amazonas (Leticia). Breeds in N America; migrates through n S America; winters mostly in s S America.

### 20. WHIMBREL
*Numenius phaeopus*                                          Ill. 45

**Identification:** 16.5-18″ (42-46cm). Long bill (3-4″) *decurved at tip*; legs grayish. Mainly grayish brown mottled buffy white, *dull black and white stripes on crown*; belly whitish. In flight from above shows inconspic. paler area on lower back and rump; otherwise unpatterned.

44. UPLAND SANDPIPER

**Similar species:** Godwit bill turns up, not down. Also see Long-billed Curlew (note).

**Voice:** Musical call, 5-7 short, rapid whistles *ti-ti-ti-ti-ti* (Peterson 1963).

**Behavior:** Scattered individuals on mudflats. In Panama roost in large flocks in mangroves during high tide (Ridgely 1976).

**Status and habitat:** Common transient and winter resident to tidal flats and beaches of both coasts; rare transient inland to flooded fields or river banks. Scattered birds oversummer. Peak nos. late Aug–late Sept at PN Isla de Salamanca (T. B. Johnson).

**Range:** Both coasts. Inland w of Andes to Cauca Val.; once to Sabana de Bogotá (2600m). Once e of Andes in c Meta (Mozambique, Feb 1970—F. Gill and A. Stokes). Breeds in Arctic; winters s on both coasts from s US to s S America; in Old World s to s Africa, Asia, and Australia.

**Note:** Long-billed Curlew (*N. americanus*), breeds in w N America and winters s to Guatemala, rarely to Panama, and may be a rare winter visitor to n Colombia. From Whimbrel by larger size (22-26″), *usually* longer sickle-bill (5-8″), buffier plumage, lack of crown stripes, and in flight by conspic. cinnamon wing linings. Likes grassy fields.

## 21. [HUDSONIAN GODWIT]
*Limosa haemastica*

**Identification:** 14-16″ (36-41cm). *Accidental.* Rather large shorebird. *Long slender bill* (2.6-3.8″) *slightly upturned*; basal half orange, distal half black. Nonbreeding birds are mainly *smooth gray above*, paler below, and with *broad white*

*rump band* separating black lower back and tail. Breeding birds are browner above and *bright reddish chestnut below*. In flight in any plumage shows *blackish primaries*, broad white wing stripe, blackish wing linings, and black tail with white rump band.

**Similar species:** Marbled Godwit (22) is larger, buffier, and lacks the black and white tail pattern.

**Status and habitat:** Hypothetical. No specimens. Sight recs. nw of Barú (Isla Barú) and at edge of Cholón and Barú Ciénagas, Bolívar, 8 Nov 1978 (Naranjo 1979b).

**Range:** Carib. coast on Bolívar. Breeds in Arctic N America and winters in s S America to Tierra del Fuego. Casual migrant in Venez.; unrec. in Panama. Bolivia (sight).

## 22. [MARBLED GODWIT]
*Limosa fedoa*

**Identification:** 17-19″ (43-48cm). Large shorebird. *Long slender bill* (4-5″) *slightly upturned; basal half pink, distal half black*; legs grayish. Mainly rich buffy brown heavily mottled dark brown above; lightly mottled below on breast and sides. In flight from below shows *cinnamon wing linings*; from above essentially unpatterned.

**Similar species:** Distinguished as godwit by slightly upturned bill but see the smaller Hudsonian Godwit (21). Whimbrel (20) has decurved bill. Long-billed Curlew (see note under 20) has sim. cinnamon wing linings but markedly long decurved bill (not upturned).

**Status and habitat:** Hypothetical. One sight rec.

of 2 on mudflats at Pto. Colombia, Atlántico (near Cartagena), 24 Dec 1969 (Easterla and George 1970). A reg. transient and sparse summer and winter visitant in Panama (Ridgely 1976) and to be expected occas. on larger mudflats on either coast of Colombia. No specimens have been taken in Colombia.

**Range:** Breeds in w N America; winters from s US s on both coasts to Panama, rarely on Carib. to Colombia or Pacific to n Chile.

### 23. [LONG-BILLED DOWITCHER]
*Limnodromus scolopaceus*

**Identification:** 11″ (28cm). *Long straight snipe-like bill* (2-3″). Very like Short-billed Dowitcher and prob. not separable in Colombia except by voice. Note longer bill (on average) of this sp. Breeding plumage: darker above; deeper rusty red below; tail predom. black (white bars narrower than black); and *flanks rather irreg. barred* (not spotted). At any season should be flushed in an attempt to make bird call. Also note habitat *preferences*.

**Similar species:** See under Common Dowitcher (24).

**Voice:** Call note a thin incisive *kik!* or *keek!*, usually trebled or more when taking flight. Frequently calls when on the ground (K. Kaufman). Cf. call of Common Dowitcher.

**Status and habitat:** Hypothetical. A 1st-yr. ♂ (MM) from Boquilla near Cartagena, Mar 1979, is, if valid, the only recent rec. (Naranjo 1979b). Old specimens, presum. this sp., have been taken near Medellín but require confirmation in light of newer criteria for separating dowitchers. Normally prefers fresh water along pond margins, ditches, and flooded or grassy fields; usually not brackish or salt water.

**Range:** Poss. migrant w of Andes. Breeds in N America and ne Siberia; winters from California to Panama, a few S American recs. in Colombia, w Ecuador, w Peru, and Argentina.

### 24. COMMON (SHORT-BILLED) DOWITCHER
*Limnodromus griseus*          Ill. 45

**Identification:** 11″ (28cm). *Long straight snipe-like bill* (2.5-2.7″); legs greenish. Breeding plumage: above blackish; back streaked and edged buff; eyebrow white; stripe through eye blackish; below brick red with a few spots on sides and bars on flanks. Nonbreeding plumage: above brownish gray, below white with a few obscure bars on flanks. At all seasons tail whitish, closely and narrowly barred blackish. In flight note *white rump, continuing as white wedge up back*; also *whitish rear edge of inner wing*.

**Similar species:** Dowitchers in general are recognized by their long bills, snipelike appear-

ance, and white rump tapering to a point in midback. Although breeding plumages may be retained into Sept, most dowitchers in Colombia are prob. not safely separated by plumage characteristics alone. This sp. has shorter bill (some overlap), less rusty below (sometimes belly immaculate white), sides and flanks with a few scattered spots (never with definite bars), and tail has white bars broader than black. In nonbreeding plumage the 2 are distinguished only by bill length (perhaps long-billed ♀♀ of 23 recognizable in field) and by *voice* (habitat also helpful but not conclusive). In the hand unsexed birds with exposed culmen less than 56mm are this sp., those greater than 68mm, Long-billed Dowitchers. See also Stilt Sandpiper (16).

**Voice:** Usual flight call a metallic *tu-tu-tu* rather like a yellowlegs and unlike that of Long-billed Dowitcher. Resting or feeding birds almost always silent, in contrast to Long-billed (K. Kaufman).

**Behavior:** Rests on mudflats or feeds by wading up to belly in shallow water and probing with peculiar sewing-machine motion. Submerges head completely at times. Gregarious, sometimes gathering in large flocks and often with other shorebirds.

**Status and habitat:** Fairly common transient and winter resident with nonbreeders present yr.-round; up to 11, late June, PN Isla de Salamanca (T. B. Johnson); and "common," 26-28 June at Manaure, Guajira (A. Sprunt IV). Mostly on tidal mudflats and in shallow brackish or salt water.

**Range:** Carib. and Pacific coasts. Only inland rec. is 1 sighting, believed this sp., near Leticia, 17 Nov 1979 (J. V. Remsen). Breeds in Alaska and Canada; winters from s US to Peru, c Brazil, and the Guianas.

### 25. COMMON SNIPE
*Gallinago gallinago*          Ill. 46

**Identification:** 10.5-11.5″ (27-29cm). *Long slender bill* (2.7″); short greenish legs. Mainly dark brown above; mantle streaked and barred buff; *inconspic. eyebrow and crown stripes whitish*; below whitish *mottled buff and brown on foreneck and breast*; short orange rufous tail (sometimes conspic. in flight); primaries unbarred (hard to see). Resident *paraguaiae* (see note) differs in hand as follows: darker coloration; less barring on flanks and sides; buff instead of white under tail coverts; narrower and whiter (less buff) outer tail feathers; and black bars on axillars narrower than the white ones.

**Similar species:** Very like somewhat larger Noble Snipe (26), which has longer bill and darker, more heavily mottled underparts (by

45. WHIMBREL (top), COMMON (SHORT-BILLED) DOWITCHERS (bottom)

comparison to Common Snipe, much darker below with only central belly white). Other snipes, Giant (local), Cordilleran, and Imperial (27, 28, 29), have heavily barred bellies. Also resembles dowitchers (23, 24) but has brown (not white) rump and lower back, a striped crown, and different behavior and habitat.

**Voice:** Flush with nasal *khatch* (Snyder 1966); in courtship flight, Argentinian and Brazilian birds (*paraguaiae*) "winnow" like those of N America (R. Ridgely); song *chip-a, chip-a, chip-a* in flight.

**Behavior:** Usually "freeze," relying on cryptic coloration. Flush at last moment with zigzag flight, a nasal call, and bill pointed downward.

**Breeding:** Resident *paraguaiae* presumed to breed in Colombia. In Trinidad May–Oct; a depression in ground; 2 buff eggs blotched brown (ffrench 1973).

**Status and habitat:** Fairly common transient and winter resident (*delicata*), late July–late Mar w of Andes in open boggy areas along streams and marshes; to 3900m in Santa Marta Mts.;

to 3500m in E Andes. Status uncertain e of Andes where both migrant and resident forms occur. At Hacienda La Corocora, w Meta, snipes present only Sept–early May (most common Apr–early May) and thought to be mostly migrant forms (W. McKay).

**Range:** Tropical zone (resident *paraguaiae*) e of Andes s to s Meta, Vaupés, and Amazonas (Leticia). N American breeders (*delicata*) winter s to Colombia (throughout w of Andes and e of them s at least to s Meta and Vaupés), e Ecuador, Venez., and the Guianas. Resident forms e of Andes s to Uruguay, w of them in Chile; Trinidad. Also breeds in Europe and Asia (that form sometimes considered a separate sp.).

**Note 1:** Sometimes placed in genus *Capella*. **Note 2:** Resident *paraguaiae* (Paraguayan, or South American Snipe) may be a separate sp.

## 26. NOBLE (PARAMO) SNIPE
*Gallinago nobilis*                              Ill. 46

**Identification:** 12″ (30cm). Very long slender bill (3.2-3.8″). Closely resembles Common Snipe

but larger; *bill proportionally longer*; foreneck and breast darker, tawny buff, and *more heavily streaked and mottled with black*; only central belly uniform white.
**Similar species:** See Common Snipe (25) from which not always safely told in field. Cordilleran Snipe (28) is slightly smaller, and entire underparts narrowly barred incl. belly. Rare Imperial Snipe (29) is barred above and below.
**Voice:** Flushes with nasal grating note. In crepuscular display flight, circles and dives producing a whistling or winnowing sound, presumably with tail. One or more, prob. this sp., displaying, 30 Aug, near shores of Represa Neusa (3000m), n of Bogotá (Hilty and M. Robbins).
**Behavior:** Like other snipes, a close sitter, depending on camouflage for protection. Flush off in zigzag flight.
**Breeding:** 5 BC birds, 23 July–23 Aug, W, C, and E Andes (Carriker). BC ♂, 24 Jan, Malvasá, Cauca, 3200m; a downy young, 16 Sept, Ecuador (Vuilleumier and Ewert 1978). Nest on ground in marshy area; eggs brownish olive spotted several shades of dark brown, esp. at larger end (Sclater and Salvin 1879).
**Status and habitat:** Fairly common locally in marshes, boggy meadows, and wet open areas of temperate and paramo zone. Partially sympatric with Cordilleran Snipe but center of abundance apparently lower.
**Range:** Mostly 2500-3900m (to 2000m near El Tambo, w of Popayán). W, C, and E Andes s through mts. of Nariño. Extreme nw Venez. to s Ecuador.
**Note:** Sometimes placed in the genus *Capella*.

## 27. GIANT SNIPE
*Gallinago undulata*                          Ill. 46
**Identification:** 13.5-14.5″ (34-37cm). *Very large*, but otherwise rather like other snipes. Long bill (4″) rather thick for a snipe. Above dark brown streaked and barred buff, *markings bolder than other snipes*; throat and belly whitish; foreneck streaked and breast and sides finely barred black (white spaces twice width of brown bars). In flight shows *barred primaries* (difficult to see) and black and cinnamon barred rump.
**Similar species:** Only snipe with barred primaries, but this hard to see in field. Known range overlaps only Common Snipe (25), which is considerably smaller, more or less mottled on foreneck and breast (not sharply streaked), and has fewer bars on sides and flanks.
**Voice:** When flushed, a harsh 2-noted *kek-kek* (Haverschmidt 1974b). In Brazil during nocturnal courtship flights, a 3-noted *hó-go, go* or *gá-ga ga*, 1st part loud then fading (vocal?);

also a strong, droning *sch* lasting 4 sec, resembling buzzing bee swarm (Sick *in* Sutton 1981).
**Behavior:** More nocturnal than Common Snipe. Seldom flushes; either squats and freezes or walks slowly away taking long steps (Sick *in* Sutton 1981).
**Breeding:** In Surinam, BC birds, Dec–Feb (Haverschmidt 1974b); eggs (Brazil), rusty brown sparsely spotted rufous and lilac gray (Schönwetter).
**Status and habitat:** Apparently uncommon and local in tall dry grass, damp pastures, and marshy savanna. Seen only 3 times, late Dec–mid-Jan, marshy w shore of Lake Carimagua, ne Meta (S. Furniss).
**Range:** Foothills on e slope W Andes in extreme s Antioquia (at Río Frío near Támesis, 1500m); e of Andes spottily in Meta (prob. also Vichada) and Vaupés (Mitú). Locally in Venez., Guyana, and Surinam; se Brazil, Paraguay, and prob. Uruguay. Río Grande, Argentina (photo).
**Note:** Sometimes placed in the genus *Capella*.

## 28. CORDILLERAN SNIPE
*Gallinago stricklandii*                      Ill. 46
**Identification:** 11″ (28cm). Long bill (3″) heavy for a snipe. Mainly dark brown above; mantle streaked and barred with buff; central crown stripe and eyebrow deep buff; sides of head, throat, and chest brownish buff speckled and streaked with brown; *rest of underparts buffy white irreg. barred dark brown*; no rufous in tail.
**Similar species:** Conspic. darker below than Common and Noble snipes (25, 26, both of which look pale below in flight) and with *entire breast and belly barred* instead of barring confined to sides and flanks. As flushes, tail mottled brown (not orangish). Rare Imperial Snipe (29) is much darker (almost blackish) and heavily barred above and below with thick blackish bars.
**Voice:** In aerial display at dusk, a jetlike whine or winnowing (swelling dramatically as bird passes overhead) accompanied by a loud, rapid, vocal *wic-a, wic-a, wic-a* . . . in dive; display repeated several times as bird circles overhead.
**Behavior:** As in other snipes. Flush with a peculiar whining noise (Vuilleumier).
**Breeding:** Dusk displays mid-Sept and ad. off nest with downy chick, 15 Sept, Páramo de Neusa, Cundinamarca (3400m); frail grass saucer on ground on dry slope far from bog; 2 egg shells, light brown thinly spotted dark brown (Hilty and M. Robbins); another paramo nest, 9 May, near Bogotá (Olivares 1969a); 2 BC birds, Aug–Sept, Norte de Santander and Boyacá (Carriker).

**Status and habitat:** Uncommon (perhaps local) in high boggy meadows and open paramo slopes, esp. grassy areas with *Espeletia*.
**Range:** Mainly 3200-3800m (2100-4200m in Santa Marta Mts.; rec. at lowest el. at end of dry season). The Santa Marta Mts. and E and C Andes s through mts. of Nariño. Andes of Venez. s to Tierra del Fuego.
**Note:** Placed by some in the genus *Chubbia*. The 2 forms, *jamesoni* (Venez. to Bolivia) and *stricklandii* (Chile and Argentina) have sometimes been considered separate sp.

### 29. IMPERIAL (BANDED) SNIPE
*Gallinago imperialis*
**Identification:** 12″ (30cm). *Long bill (3.6″). Above rufous broadly banded black*; throat and chest rufous; foreneck and chest barred black; *rest of underparts boldly barred black and white.*
**Similar species:** Only Colombian snipe with boldy barred upperparts. By comparison with

Cordilleran Snipe (28), darker, more rufescent, throat brighter rufous, and upper and underparts boldly barred and banded (instead of finer barring mainly on underparts).
**Voice:** Vocal at dusk. Song (about 10 sec.) a sequence of rough staccato notes, then a complex ser. of evenly spaced single notes in level circular flight, each song ending in a shallow dive and an audible rush of air (Terborgh and Weske 1972).
**Status and habitat:** In Colombia known from 2 "Bogotá" specimens of uncertain locality, poss. in vicinity of Bogotá. In Peru (1 specimen and several sight recs.) inhabits timberline zone of elfin forest, bogs, and tall grass; the preferred habitat within this zone is unknown.
**Range:** Prob. temperate or paramo zone of E Andes. Peru in Cordillera, Vilcabamba, Cuzco.
**Note:** Sometimes placed in the genus *Chubbia*.

46. GIANT SNIPE (upper left), NOBLE (PARAMO) SNIPE (upper right), COMMON SNIPE (lower left), CORDILLERAN SNIPE (lower right)

# STILTS: Recurvirostridae (1)

Stilts and avocets form a small group of graceful, long-legged, slender-billed waders, widespread locally in both warm and temperate regions of the world. All members of the family are boldy patterned black and white, though often with various shades of buff on the head and neck when breeding. Only one of the three New World species is resident in Colombia.

## 1. BLACK-NECKED STILT

*Himantopus mexicanus*                    Ill. 47

**Identification:** 14-15.5″ (36-39cm). Slim, long-necked shorebird. Extremely long red or pink legs trail far behind in flight; long, thin black bill. *Black above*; rump, wedge up back, and tail white; *forehead and entire underparts white.* In flight *wings solid black above and below.*

**Voice:** Often noisy. Sharp ternlike *yip* or *hip* notes.

**Behavior:** In small excitable flocks; wade actively, probing mud or shallow water. Sometimes sit on ground as if on nest.

**Breeding:** BC pair, 24 Jan, La Raya, lower Río Cauca (Carriker). In Ecuador, small colonies of 4-5 nests, Apr; dry reed stem nest on ground near water (Marchant 1960). In Trinidad May–June; 3-4 olive buff eggs blotched and spotted black (ffrench 1973).

**Status and habitat:** Usually fairly common in saline coastal lagoons and freshwater ponds and marshes, but nos. fluctuate, and birds often move locally. In w Meta at Hacienda La Corocora, present mainly mid-Jan–June (W. McKay); at Carimagua, ne Meta, Dec–late Apr (S. Furniss).

**Range:** Tropical zone of entire Carib. coast, s locally to Cauca and Magdalena vals., and once to temperate zone on Sabana de Bogotá (2600m); e of Andes from Arauca (flock seen, mid-Nov, Arauca, in Arauca—J. Jorgenson and W. McKay), s to Meta, w Caquetá, and once near Leticia (sighting, 9 Aug 1975—J. V. Remsen). Breeds from w and s US s through Mid. America, W Indies, and most of S America. Migratory in the n.

**Note:** Sometimes merged with *H. himantopus* (Black-winged Stilt) of Old World, the enlarged sp. then called Common Stilt.

47. BLACK-NECKED STILT

# PHALAROPES: Phalaropodidae (3)

Phalaropes are dainty sandpiperlike birds with lobed toes and much more pelagic habits outside the breeding season than other shorebirds. They swim readily and take tiny invertebrate life from the water by stirring the surface with a spinning motion of the body. ♀♀ are brighter and larger than ♂♂ and the sex roles are reversed. For a differing taxonomic opinion on this group, see Jehl (1968), who places *Phalaropus* within the Scolopacidae.

## 1. WILSON'S PHALAROPE
*Phalaropus tricolor*
**Identification:** 9″ (23cm). *Black needlelike bill*; greenish yellow legs. Nonbreeding plumage: smooth pale gray above; pure white below with *blurry gray smudge through eye*. Breeding plumage ♀: gray above with reddish chestnut stripe across shoulders and *another across back continuing up sides of neck and becoming blackish behind eye*; below whitish. Breeding plumage ♂: echoes pattern of ♀ but much duller and browner. In flight in any plumage both sexes show *solid gray wings* (no stripe) and white rump and tail.
**Similar species:** Breeding birds distinctive. Winter plumage birds (those likely in Colombia) resemble Stilt Sandpiper (p 161) and Lesser Yellowlegs (p 155), but note needlelike bill and pure white underparts (not grayish on breast or sides). If swimming, behavior is distinctive. Other phalaropes have a wing stripe (see Red Phalarope, 2).
**Voice:** Low nasal *rank*.
**Behavior:** Nervous and very active like other phalaropes but swims less.
**Status and habitat:** Rare fall transient mid-Sept–late Oct; once on n Chocó coast (18 Sept); 1 on 28 Sept 1979, Represa Neusa (3000m) n of Bogotá (sighting, A. Gast and W. McKay); 1 on 1 Oct, Río Medellín, Antioquia; and 1 on 20 Oct near Popayán. Only winter rec. is about 150 on saline ponds near Hotel Irotama, 5-10 Feb 1977 (R. Ridgely); in Panama reported late Aug–late Sept (Ridgely 1976). Much less pelagic than other phalaropes, often occurring inland on freshwater lakes, ponds, and rivers.
**Range:** Pacific coast and inland w of Andes. Breeds in w N America; winters on coast and inland from Peru to Chile and Argentina.
**Note:** All 3 phalaropes are placed in separate genera by some.

## 2. RED PHALAROPE
*Phalaropus fulicarius*
**Identification:** 8″ (20cm). *Rather stout bill yellow tipped black* (or usually black in fall birds); legs yellowish. Nonbreeding plumage: smooth gray above; *white below with black streak through eyes*. Breeding plumage ♀: crown and throat black; sides of head white; upperparts streaked cin-

namon and dusky; neck and *underparts bright brick red*. Breeding plumage ♂: sim. but crown streaked cinnamon and black, underparts much duller. At all seasons shows a *conspic. white wing stripe* and dark center on rump and tail; outer base of tail white.
**Similar species:** Breeding birds unmistakable. Winter birds easily distinguished in flight from Wilson's Phalarope (1) by wing stripe (lacking in Wilson's) and dark (not white) rump and tail, but are much like Sanderlings (p 160) in flight. On the water note phalarope's chunkier shape. Wilson's has longer, more slender neck and long needlelike (not thickish) black bill. See also very sim. winter plumage of Red-necked Phalarope (3).
**Voice:** *Pik*, sim. to but louder and less flat than Northern Phalarope (Stallcup 1976).
**Behavior:** Gregarious in small scattered flocks. Swims buoyantly, dabs with bill, and spins daintily on water. Often distinguishable as a phalarope on these behaviors alone.
**Status and habitat:** Only 3 recs.: 1 a young bird from "US Colombia Seebohm Coll." (Sharpe 1896); another, a ♀, taken 4 Mar 1967 on Río Guëjar at base of Macarena Mts., s Meta (Olivares 1974b). Sight rec. of 1 off Chocó coast at 6°24′N, 70°43′W, 7 Dec 1977 (R.G.B. Brown). The most pelagic of the phalaropes; usually migrates and winters well offshore. The scarcity of recs. is due, in part, to sea-going habits. Uncommon but reg. off Pacific coast of Mid. America, mostly over 5 miles from shore (Jehl 1974).
**Range:** Pacific coast. Accidental in s Meta. Breeds in Arctic; winters at sea in Atlantic. Pacific and Indian oceans, but distribution not well known. Rec. spottily off coasts of Ecuador (once), Peru, Chile (reg. offshore); also Paraguay, Argentina (accidental), and Brazil (Mato Grosso).

## 3. RED-NECKED PHALAROPE
*Phalaropus lobatus*
**Identification:** 7″ (18cm). Nonbreeding birds are dark gray above, almost always with some *pale stripes on back* (some winter birds are very pale above). Crown, hindneck, and stripe through eyes blackish, much more prom. than the Red Phalarope. Breeding plumage ♀: dark

gray above with white throat, large rusty patch on foreneck continues up sides of neck to behind black cheeks; rest of underparts whitish. Breeding plumage ♂: sim. but duller. In flight in any plumage shows wing stripe, dark rump and mostly dark tail.

**Similar species:** From winter Red Phalarope (2) by slightly smaller size, slimmer proportions, needlelike bill (not stout) and more blackish back (usually striped). Wilson's Phalarope (1) has a conspic. white (not dark) rump and tail and lacks a wing stripe.

**Status and habitat:** A previous rec., 2 recent recs., and a no. of sightings are reported by L. G. Naranjo H. (1984a). One ♀ collected 8 Oct 1969 by J. I. Borrero and G. Cataño near Isla de la Muerte, Bahía Málaga n of Bue-

naventura, Valle; a ♂ collected by J. H. Gambon, 3 Jan 1983, about 8 miles off the coast of Valle; 1 ♀ at Punta Soldado in Buenaventura Bay, 23 Jan 1983. Additional sight recs. consist of groups of 5-10 birds approx. 40 miles off the coast of Valle 9 Feb 1983, and 4 groups of 4-41 birds along the e coast of Isla Gorgona (off the coast of Cauca), 6-8 Feb 1983. The Red-necked Phalarope appears to be a reg. winter visitor along the Pacific coast.

**Range:** Migrant and winter visitor along Pacific coast (Valle) and Gorgona Isl. (off the coast of Cauca). Breeds in Arctic; winters at sea in Atlantic, Pacific, and Indian oceans. Irreg. but seasonally numerous in Pacific Panama (Ridgely 1976), s Ecuador (sight), Peru, Chile, and Argentina.

# THICK-KNEES: Burhinidae (1)

Thick-knees are a small family found in most tropical and temperate regions of the world, though they are notably absent from North America, New Zealand, and the Pacific. They are rather robust cursorial birds, somewhat resembling oversized plovers with their fairly long legs and short bills. Their large eyes are well adapted for nocturnal habits. In bright light the eyes are constricted with the upper part cut off by the brow. Most show a preference for rather open dry country and often spend much of the day crouched unobtrusively on the ground. They eat a variety of animal matter.

## 1. DOUBLE-STRIPED THICK-KNEE
*Burhinus bistriatus* Ill. 48

**Identification:** 18″ (46cm). *Large and ploverlike.* Big yellow eyes; short stout bill; fairly long greenish legs. Upperparts, head, and breast dark brown streaked fulvous; throat and belly white; *broad white eyebrow bordered above by a black line.* In flight shows a broad wing stripe and narrow white subterminal band on tail.

**Voice:** Mostly vocal at night; a loud *dit-dit dit-dit*, also *dit dit dit churrrr* given rather fast and often repeated (Brown); a long-continued, reedy *prrrip prrrip prrrip pip pip pip pipipipipi-pipipi*, accelerating (Slud 1964).

**Behavior:** Single birds, pairs, or small loose groups; rather wary. Diurnal or nocturnal though usually most active and noisy at night. Often squat or crouch to avoid detection. Run swiftly for short distances; taxi to take off.

**Breeding:** Apparently dry season. Several young, early Apr–early May, near Carimagua, ne Meta (S. Furniss); 2 BC ♂♂, 14 May, e base Santa Marta Mts. (Carriker); 2 olive buff eggs blotched brown and gray (Freese 1975). ♂ may do most incubating (Dickey and Van Rossem 1938).

**Status and habitat:** Drier savanna and flat open pastureland, with or without scattered trees and shrubs. Uncommon and local w of Andes, fairly common in suitable habitat e of Andes.

**Range:** To 500m. The Carib. coast from Cartagena area e to Guajira, the upper Magdalena Val., and generally e of Andes in the llanos s to s Meta (Macarena Mts.) and the Río Guaviare. S Mexico to Costa Rica; n and e Colombia to Guyana and nw Brazil. Margarita Isl.; Curaçao. Hispaniola.

# SKUAS, JAEGERS: Stercorariidae (3)

Jaegers and skuas are large powerful predatory seabirds, well known for aerial piracy. Jaegers breed in north polar regions, skuas are bipolar breeders, and both are highly migratory on the open sea outside the breeding season. Although resembling gulls, skuas and jaegers have wings that are sharply flexed at the wrist. Jaegers have long falconlike wings, long tails, and elongated central tail feathers; skuas have broader, rounded buteonine wings and short tails. Their flight is swift, and they easily outdistance gulls and terns, harassing them until they give up their food.

48. DOUBLE-STRIPED THICK-KNEE

In the tropics they also take fish and galley refuse from the surface. Adult jaeger plumages are distinctive but are not acquired for several years, and the immature plumages pose special identification problems requiring some comparative experience (for some problems and criteria, see Walter 1962).

### 1. [GREAT SKUA]
*Catharacta skua*
**Identification:** 23″ (58cm). *Large robust seabird with broad wings and wedge-shaped tail. Conspic. white wing patches* on upper and lower wing surfaces. Plumage var., from sooty black to cinnamon to pale grayish brown; darker birds streaked golden buff; neck, hackles, and mantle of all birds usually paler. S Hemisphere birds are grayish or rusty on underparts; s polar form (*maccormicki*) has shortest, stubbiest bill of all.
**Similar species:** Larger and stockier than the jaegers, but cf. dark imm. Pomarine Jaeger (2). Resembles the imm. Herring Gull (p 174) somewhat, but more robust, and note the conspic. white flashes in the broad wings.
**Behavior:** Fly with stiff unhurried wing beats, but leisurely flight is deceptive—they easily overpower gulls and terns. Should be looked for among groups of seabirds.
**Status and habitat:** Hypothetical. Prob. reg. in offshore or pelagic waters of Pacific; status unknown (prob. accidental) in Carib. waters.

No specimens. Unconfirmed sight recs. of "a few" about 5 miles offshore of Punta de la Cruz, Guajira, in Feb 1979, and 1 at La Boquilla, Bolívar, Apr 1979 (Naranjo 1979b), are only recs. Antarctic breeders (*maccormicki*), South Polar Skua, wander or migrate to the equator or beyond and are prob. the most likely form in Colombia. It is uncertain if other forms (either pole) are also transequatorial migrants; in fact, the relationships of the var. forms of skuas (6 forms currently recognized) are uncertain, but it is likely that more than 1 sp. is involved (see Devillers 1977).
**Range:** Carib. coast. Unrec. but almost certain off Pacific coast (rec. Feb–Mar, Sept, and early Nov in Panama—Ridgely 1976). Breeds in n Atlantic, on coasts of s S America, subantarctic isls., and Antarctica. Both n and s forms wander widely.

### 2. [POMARINE JAEGER]
*Stercorarius pomarinus*          Ill. 49
**Identification:** 17″ (43cm). *Largest and heaviest jaeger.* Pointed wings show conspic. white

49. POMARINE JAEGER (light phase)

patches at base of primaries above and below. Tail wedge-shaped with 2 thick twisted feathers *projecting up to 4"* (often broken or missing) beyond tail. Light phase (most common): brownish above with black crown and whitish collar across hindneck; below whitish, usually with narrow dusky breast band and sides more or less barred; cheeks yellowish (pale-headed look at a distance). Dark phase (rare): all sooty brown with pale wing patches. Imm.: like dark phase (or mottled and barred above and below) and virtually no projecting tail feathers.

**Similar species:** Much like Parasitic Jaeger (3), but ads. with full tails are distinctive. Imm. usually not separable from Parasitic even with size comparison, but Pomarine has larger proportions (bill, head, neck, frame) and more primary shafts (outer part) with white (5-8 vs 3-5—Stallcup 1976). Also, very slightly projecting central tail feathers are bluntly rounded or square tipped in Pomarine, more pointed in Parasitic and Long-tailed jaegers (visible only at close range under ideal conditions—K. Kaufman).

**Behavior:** Flight heavier than other jaegers but more buoyant and graceful (less stiff) than Skua; flapping often alternates with short glides. Usually solitary or in pairs but migrate in flocks and reg. assoc. with gulls and terns. Often settle on water.

**Status and habitat:** Hypothetical. Prob. an uncommon winter resident to offshore waters, occas. within sight of land or in bays; poss. irreg. yr.-round. No specimens. Sight recs. as follows: 1 in Cartagena harbor, Feb 1972 (Denham 1972); imms. or subads. seen on 7 dates betw. 3 and 31 July 1974 in Santa Marta harbor with max. of 8 on 3 July (P. Donahue);

1 on 16 Jan. 1978 off Cañaveral, PN Tayrona (J. Hernández); 1 off Chocó coast at 6°24'N 70°43'W on 7 Dec 1977 (R.G.B. Brown). Several recs. off Venez. coast, Dec–Mar, once Sept (Meyer de Schauensee and Phelps 1978).
**Range:** Carib. and prob. Pacific coasts. Breeds in Arctic; winters s at sea, mostly in New World, to Peru on Pacific, Guyana on Carib.

### 3. [PARASITIC JAEGER]
*Stercorarius parasiticus*
**Identification:** 16" (41cm). Both color phases and imm. much like Pomarine Jaeger, but slightly smaller, slimmer, and *short pointed central tail feathers project up to 3" (7.6 cm) beyond tail*. Light phase usually has paler breast band (occas. lacking) than Pomarine.
**Similar species:** Similar in size to Laughing Gull (Pomarine Jaeger is slightly larger). Ads. with full tails are distinctive, but Long-tailed Jaegers often have broken or short tail feathers. By comparison to Pomarine (2), less robust, with smaller head and bill, has only 3-5 white primary shafts, and more agile (less ponderous) flight. For imm. see Pomarine Jaeger (2)
**Status and habitat:** Hypothetical. No specimens but prob. an uncommon transient (mostly winter?) to offshore waters, less frequently coasts. Sight recs. as follows: 2 subads. in Santa Marta harbor, 3 July 1974 (P. Donahue); 1 imm. in Cartagena harbor, 21 Jan 1977 (Gochfeld et al. 1980); and an imm. (believed this sp.) at Manaure, Guajira, 28 June 1974 (A. Sprunt IV). Considered an uncommon but reg. transient and winter resident on both coasts of Panama (Ridgely 1976). Only Venez. rec. a sighting of a subad., 16 Jan 1975, near Tucacas, Falcón (P. Alden).
**Range:** Carib. and undoubtedly Pacific coasts. Breeds in Arctic; migrates s at sea to s S America in the New World.
**Note:** Long-tailed Jaeger (*S. longicaudus*), also unrec., is prob. a rare offshore migrant on both coasts. By comparison with other jaegers, it is smaller (15"), trimmer, has long central tail feathers projecting up to 10" beyond the tail, less white in primaries (3 or less white primary shafts), proportionally smaller bill (but some Parasitics have small bill), and more graceful ternlike flight. Light phase ads. differ from other jaegers by immaculate cheeks, complete white collar on hindneck setting off black cap, paler gray back, no breast band, and usually darker abdomen. In hand, nail on bill is longer than cere over nostril (the reverse of Parasitic) and legs gray (not black).

# GULLS, TERNS: Laridae (27)

Gulls and terns are familiar birds distributed throughout the world's seacoasts and to a lesser extent inland or at sea. They are characterized by predominatly gray and white plumage, gregarious habits, and easy buoyant flight. The majority of the Colombian species breed in the Northern Hemisphere and spend the northern winter offshore or along the coast. Several are Southern Hemisphere migrants and four species breed on offshore or river islands. Gulls are usually larger and heavier than terns and have heavier hooked bills, roundish wings, and rounded tail. They often swim, and when possible subsist by scavenging. Terns, in contrast, have slender pointed bills, pointed wings, and usually forked tails. They dive into the water for prey and seldom swim.

## 1. GRAY GULL

*Larus modestus*                    Ill. 50

**Identification:** 17.5″ (45cm). Bill and feet black. *Mainly dull gray with front of head white* (head pale grayish brown in nonbreeding plumage); flight feathers blackish with *broad white band on trailing edge of secondaries*; tail gray with black subterminal band and white tip. Imm.: more brownish below; no white on head. Juv.: uniform dull brown; wings and tail blackish edged buff; bill and legs like adult.

**Similar species:** Uniformly dull gray plumage of ad. (with or without white front of head) is distinctive. Imm. prob. not reliably separated from other imm. gulls but usually grayer with rump and tail dark (white with dark subterminal band in Franklin's, Laughing, and Ring-billed gulls (5, 4, 2). Imm. Herring Gull (3) is all dark brown (not grayish) and larger.

**Behavior:** Reported to favor sandy beaches where it feeds on sand crabs (*Emerita*) exposed by receding waves (Johnson 1967).

**Status and habitat:** Casual. Wanders to sw coast and offshore isls. To be expected chiefly May–Oct (nonbreeding season in Peru and Chile). In Ecuador largest nos. reported May–Nov.

**Range:** Sw Colombia on Gorgona Isl. and Nariño coast. Breeds in interior deserts of s Peru

and Chile. Ranges n along coast of w S America to s Colombia; accidental in Panama.

**Note:** Band-tailed Gull (*L. belcheri*), a s breeder from coast of n Peru to c Chile and coast of Argentina, prob. wanders n along Pacific coast of Colombia. It has been seen off Pacific Panama in May, Aug, and Dec (Ridgely 1976). Larger than Laughing Gull (20-22″ vs. 15-17″) and mainly white with blackish mantle and broad subterminal black tail band; thick yellow bill with broad red tip and black spot on upper mandible; legs yellow. Nonbreeding and subad. plumage: sim. but bill duller, head dusky, and neck light gray. Imm.: duller and browner than nonbreeding ad. and with tail dusky mottled white; head, neck, and throat often very dusky; bill yellow with black tip. Ad.'s large size and dark mantle is distinctive (no other blackish-backed gulls in Colombia, but see notes 1 and 2 under Herring Gull). Imm. best told by size and bill color.

## 2. [RING-BILLED GULL]

*Larus delawarensis*

**Identification:** 17″ (43cm). Med.-sized. Ad. differs from Herring Gull in *smaller size, yellowish green legs*, and yellow bill *with narrow black ring*. Nonbreeders have brownish mottled heads. Imm.: very like 2d-yr. Herring Gull, but tail all white with a *broad black subterminal band* (not mostly dusky tail); legs pink; bill pinkish tipped black.

**Similar species:** See larger Herring Gull (3). Winter and imm. Laughing Gulls (4) have black bill and legs and are much darker above, usually with dusky wash on neck and breast.

**Status and habitat:** Known from 2 sight recs.; a winter ad., 19 Jan 1978 (P. Alden, Hilty, R. Sides, N. Hill), and 1 subad., 9 Feb 1984 (R. Ridgely, C. Wilds, Hilty), both at Buenaventura Bay. A specimen without data in the Univ. Nacional coll. at Bogotá (formerly labeled *L. atricilla*) may be from Colombia (P. Donahue). Prob. an occas. winter visitant on

50. GRAY GULL

both coasts (numerous Panama recs., Nov–June; Ridgely 1976)

**Range:** Breeds in s Canada and n US; winters from US to Mexico and in W Indies, rarely to Panama, Colombia (twice), and Trinidad. Once (specimen) Tefé, Amazonas, Brazil.

### 3. [HERRING GULL]
*Larus argentatus*

**Identification:** 22-25″ (56-64cm). Large white gull (ad.) with pearly gray back. Nonbreeding plumage: bill yellow with red spot on lower mandible; legs pink. Mainly white with mantle, back, and wings pearl gray; *wing tips black with several white spots near tip and white rear border to entire wings*; head and neck mottled brownish. Breeding plumage (4th yr.): sim. but head and neck all white. 1st-yr. imm.: mottled grayish brown, slightly paler below; dusky flight feathers and tail; legs dusky pink; bill blackish. 2d-yr. imm.: mantle grayer; head, neck, and rump white mottled with brown; tail dusky and underparts whitish; legs pinkish tipped or ringed black. 3d-yr. imm.: recognizably sim. to ad. but with traces of brown above and below and at least vestiges of a dark bar across both mandibles.

**Similar species:** Large size and pink legs of ad. are distinctive. Both imm. and ad. closely resemble smaller Ring-billed Gull (see 2). Also see Lesser Black-backed Gull (note), 1st-yr. imm. of which is usually inseparable from Herring Gull of sim. age.

**Status and habitat:** Very rare though poss. reg. winter visitor in coastal waters. Two sight recs.: a 2d-yr. bird at PN Isla de Salamanca, 20 Jan 1975 (P. Donahue), and at least 3 2d-yr. birds in Cartagena harbor, 21-22 Jan 1977 (Gochfeld et al. 1980). Since all recs. are of imm. birds, specimens or photos are desirable for confirmation of this and all other large dark imm. gulls found in Colombia (see identification problems below).

**Range:** Carib. coast. Breeds in N America and Europe; winters in New World s to Mexico, the W Indies, and other Carib. Isls., rarely Panama and n S America (a few recs. in Venez. and Trinidad).

**Note 1:** Lesser Black-backed Gull (*L. fuscus*) of Eurasia is known from numerous recs. in se US and a smaller no. in W Indies and is poss. in Colombia. Ads. (22″) resemble ad. Herring Gull, but entire back and upper wings blackish (or dark gray—s form); legs greenish to flesh (winter). 1st-yr. imms. are not safely separated in field from Herring Gulls of corresponding age. Older birds are progressively darker-backed than Herring. **Note 2:** Kelp Gull (*L. dominicanus*), breeding coastally and inland in Andes from Peru and se Brazil to Tierra del Fuego, wanders n to Ecuador and may occas. reach sw Nariño coast. Large (21″): ad. all white with *center of back and mantle black*; thick yellow bill has red tip; legs greenish yellow. Only S American gull with black back and wholly white tail.

### 4. LAUGHING GULL
*Larus atricilla*                                    Ill. 51

**Identification:** 15-17″ (38-43cm). Med.-sized gull. Bill and legs blackish (dusky red in breeding plumage). Nonbreeding plumage: *mantle dark gray darkening to black on wing tips*; rear border of wing white; head, underparts, and tail white; *mottled brownish gray on back of head and ear coverts* (not a distinct "half hood" as in Franklin's Gull). Breeding plumage: sim. but head black with conspic. white eyelids. Subad. (2d winter): like nonbreeding ad. but browner above and with black tail band. Imm. (1st winter): mostly dark grayish brown with whitish throat and belly; rear edge of wings, *rump, and tail white; tail with broad black subterminal band.*

**Similar species:** Ad. Franklin's Gull (5) always separable by different wing tip pattern. Nonbreeding and subad. Franklin's also have much more extensive "half hood" (Laughing has some dusky mottling on back of head), but beware of occas. subad. Franklin's with developing hood and white tail (like ad.) and all dark wing tips (like imm.). These are easily confused with nonbreeding Laughing. Imm. always distinguishable from Franklin's by tail pattern; Laughing has black subterminal band entirely across tail but in Franklin's the outermost rectrix on each side entirely white (K. Kaufman).

**Voice:** A strident *ka-ka-ka-ka-ka-ka-kaa-kaa-kaa*; a shorter *ka-wick*.

**Behavior:** The most common winter gull, often in large flocks. Aggressive and opportunistic when foraging.

**Status and habitat:** Common transient and winter resident on both coasts (mostly Sept–mid-May); imms. reg. oversummer, ads. rarely do. Many, late June–Aug, PN Isla de Salamanca (P. Donahue); and common at Manaure, Guajira, late June (A. Sprunt IV); mainly mid-Nov–mid-May in Santa Marta harbor, with peak nos. Feb–Apr (T. B. Johnson).

**Range:** Carib. and Pacific coasts, rarely inland w of Andes (Cauca Val., 1000m; E Andes at Lago Tota, Boyacá, 3100m). Breeds locally on Atlantic and gulf coasts of N America s to Belize; also W Indies, Trinidad, isls. off Venez., and on Pacific Mexico s to Sinaloa. Winters off Carib., Pacific, and Atlantic coasts s to Peru and mouth of Amazon.

51. LAUGHING GULL (non-breeding in flight)

## 5. FRANKLIN'S GULL
*Larus pipixcan*
**Identification:** 14″ (36cm). Much like Laughing Gull. Bill and legs reddish (brightest in breeding season). Nonbreeding plumage: mantle gray, paler than Laughing Gull; *black wing tips narrowly separated from gray mantle by white*; rear border of wings and rest of plumage white with a *dusky "half hood" from midcrown to nape extending down on sides of head to below and behind eye* and incl. ear coverts (hood obscure or lacking in Laughing Gull). Breeding plumage: sim. but head black with conspic. white eyelids. Subad. (2d winter): like nonbreeding ad. but less white separating black wing tips (occas. white absent) and tail with dusky subterminal band. Imm. (1st winter): mainly brownish gray with contrasting white rump and underparts; head whitish with *more or less distinct "half hood"* (like nonbreeding ad.); rump and tail white with *broad black subterminal tail band, outer feather white*.
**Similar species:** See Laughing Gull (4); also Gray-hooded Gull (note).
**Voice:** Shrill *kuk-kuk-kuk*; also a nasal *karr, karr* (Peterson 1961).

**Behavior:** Social and often with Laughing Gull, its closest ally. Flight more graceful and buoyant than Laughing Gull.
**Status and habitat:** Uncommon transient and winter resident (or visitant), rec. early Jan.–May (no fall recs.?). Much of migratory movement (thousands reach Peru) may take place in offshore waters off Colombia's Pacific coast.
**Range:** Pacific coast. Breeds in interior plains of w N America; winters on Pacific coast from Guatemala to n Chile; sight Lake Titicaca, Bolivia, and Peru; on Carib. coast in Panama.
**Note:** Gray-hooded Gull (*L. cirrocephalus*), resident locally in Ecuador and Peru (breeding) and coastal se S America, prob. wanders to Pacific coast (1 sighting in Panama—Ridgely 1976). Breeding ads. resemble Franklin's Gull, but hood pale gray (not black) and primaries mostly black with very large white area at base and small white spot near tip. Nonbreeding birds have white head with grayish hindcrown ("half hood") and a dusky ear spot. 1st-yr. imm.: mostly brown above with paler forecrown and nape, blackish primaries and subterminal tail band, white underparts with brownish sides.

## 6. [LITTLE GULL]
*Larus minutus*
**Identification:** 11" (28cm). *The smallest gull* and a very rare migrant. Nonbreeding ad.: mainly white; back and upperwing pale gray (no black); *underwings blackish gray; dusky cap* and ear patch; tail square; bill black; legs pink. Breeding ad.: similar but head black, bill dark red. Imm. (1st-yr. birds): like nonbreeding ad. but with a black bar along leading edge of upperwing joining the black outer primaries and forming a **W** *pattern in flight; underwings white*; black tip on square tail.
**Similar species:** Sabine's Gull (7) is larger with a distinctly forked tail and the black primaries forming a broad triangle on front of outer wing and a large white triangular area behind. Bonaparte's Gull, which may occur in Colombia (see note under 7) shows a conspic. white triangle on primaries of ad. or a white patch on dark primaries of imm.
**Status and habitat:** Hypothetical. 1st rec. for Colombia and S America is 1 1st-yr. bird seen at Buenaventura harbor, 9 Jan 1983 (R. Ridgely and B. Whitney).
**Range:** Breeds in Eurasia, wintering to the Mediterranean. Has bred irreg. in N. America (Ontario, Michigan, and Wisconsin). Rare but more or less reg. in Great Lakes area and along Atlantic coast.

## 7. SABINE'S GULL
*Xema sabini*
**Identification:** 13-14" (33-36cm). *Small* with *distinctly forked tail* (Swallow-tailed Gull is much larger). Bill black *with yellow tip*; legs black. Nonbreeding plumage: *flashing black, white, and gray wing pattern conspic.*; mantle pale gray with *broad black triangle on front of outer wing and large white triangular area behind*; otherwise all white with dusky smudge on nape. Breeding plumage: sim. but *head slate gray* narrowly bordered behind by black. Imm.: like nonbreeding birds, but mantle and wing coverts to mid-crown brown; white tail has *prom. triangular black wedge on tip*.
**Similar species:** Swallow-tailed Gull (8) is very sim. but *much larger* and with white spot at base of bill in breeding plumage. In nonbreeding plumage has white head with conspic. black eyering. See rare Little Gull (6) and Bonaparte's Gull (note).
**Behavior:** Flight is graceful and ternlike with fairly rapid, continuous flapping; often dips to the surface but does not dive. Less social than many other gulls and usually only scattered individuals or in small groups with other seabirds.
**Status and habitat:** Prob. uncommon to fairly common transient and winter resident. One seen off coast of Valle, 4°11'N 80°13'W, 31 Oct 1977, another off coast of N Chocó, 7°11'N 79°40'W, 7 Dec 1977 (R.G.B. Brown). Rec. as late as 11 May off Bahía Cuevita (5°25'N) on Chocó coast (Murphy 1936). Offshore and pelagic waters; rarely coastal waters where visible from shore.
**Range:** Pacific coast. Breeds in Arctic; winters at sea, in the New World, on Pacific coast from Colombia s to Peru and extreme n Chile (details of winter distribution uncertain but presum. mostly off Peru).
**Note 1:** Bonaparte's Gull (*Larus philadelphia*) is unrec. but likely on Carib. coast. It winters s casually to W Indies, rarely to Panama. A small gull (13"), in winter plumage rather sim. to Sabine's Gull, but most of wing gray with conspic. flashing white (not black) triangle on primaries, which are narrowly bordered black; white head with dark spot behind auriculars. Breeding plumage: head black with white eyelids. Imm.: like nonbreeding ad., but tail crossed by a narrow black subterminal band, more black edging on primaries, and diagonal brownish band on wings; bill black in any plumage. **Note 2:** Black-headed Gull (*L. ridibundus*) of Eurasia is also poss. as it is a rare but reg. visitant to e N America and frequent in the W Indies. Much like Bonaparte's Gull but slightly larger with heavier bill that is red to dull yellowish orange (never black) in all plumages.

## 8. SWALLOW-TAILED GULL
*Creagrus furcatus*
**Identification:** 21-23" (53-58cm). *A very large gull* with flashing black and white wing pattern and *deeply forked tail*. Dark bill tipped paler green or blue when breeding; legs red. Nonbreeding plumage: mainly white; *large conspic. eyering black*; mantle gray; black on outer primaries with *very large white triangle on wings and narrow white stripe on sides of back* (scapulars). Breeding plumage: head slaty with large white spot at base of bill. Imm.: white heavily spotted and streaked dark brown and with black subterminal band on tail; legs, bill, and eyering dark.
**Similar species:** Recalls much smaller Sabine's Gull (7).
**Voice:** Thin harsh scream and a very ungull-like rattle (Harris 1974).
**Behavior:** Mainly nocturnal; forages for fish and squid. Flight undulating.
**Status and habitat:** Feb breeding colony, with nestlings, Malpelo Isl. (Bond and Meyer de Schauensee 1938). No recs. on Pacific coast and status during remainder of yr. on Malpelo

unknown. Rocky isls., seascoasts, and pelagic waters.

**Range:** Breeds on Malpelo Isl. off Pacific Colombia (500km w Buenaventura). Main breeding colony on Galapagos Isls. Migrates or wanders to coasts of Ecuador, s Peru, and n Chile, Pacific Panama (rare), and prob. also Colombia.

## 9. BLACK TERN
*Chlidonias niger*                              Ill. 52

**Identification:** 9-10″ (23-25cm). *Small with slightly notched tail.* Black bill and legs. Nonbreeding ad. and imm.: above gray; head and underparts white with *dusky patch on back of head and smaller patch around eyes and on ear coverts.* Breeding plumage: above gray; *head and underparts black* with white under wing and under tail coverts. Note: confusing birds in molt with pied or blotched black and gray plumage are commonly seen during summer mos.

**Similar species:** Unmistakable in breeding plumage. Yellow-billed and Least terns (18, 19) the only other small Colombian terns, are very different, with deeply forked tails, black primaries, and blackish nape bands (not pied pattern).

**Voice:** A sharp *keep*, or *kee-ip*.

**Behavior:** Gregarious and often in large flocks on wintering grounds. Flight is erratic, fluttery, and nighthawklike with frequent pauses and dips. Swoops to surface but rarely plunges into water.

**Status and habitat:** Common to locally abundant transient and winter resident on both coasts (not inland), but usually greater nos. on Pacific coast. Tens of thousands in offshore and pelagic waters off Chocó in Sept (Murphy 1938). Oversummers in nos. on Pacific coast, less numerous and erratic during n summer on Carib. but also sometimes in large flocks.

**Range:** Carib. and Pacific coasts. Breeds in N America and Europe. N American birds winter from both coasts of Mexico s to Peru (accidental to Chile, nw Argentina, and Surinam).

52. Common Tern (upper left; flying in breeding plumage at upper right), Roseate Tern (upper right; flying in breeding plumage), Gull-billed Tern (lower left), Black Tern (lower right; non-breeding plumage)

## 10. LARGE-BILLED TERN
*Phaetusa simplex*                                    Ill. 53
**Identification:** 15″ (38cm). A *large* tern with a *thick yellow bill*; legs greenish. Crown black; mantle and slightly forked (almost square) tail dark gray; underparts white. In flight bird shows a *conspic. white triangular area on secondaries and wing coverts* contrasting with dusky primaries. Nonbreeding ad. has white mottling on crown. Imm.: sim. but upperparts mottled with brownish, dusky band on wings, and less black on crown.
**Similar species:** Flashing black and white wing pattern and heavy pointed yellow bill are distinctive.
**Voice:** Noisy; *sque-ee* and nasal parrotlike *ink-onk* (Snyder 1966).
**Behavior:** Usually singly or in pairs but gathers in small flocks to rest or roost along river; occas. in much larger concentrations.
**Breeding:** Colonies, often mixed with skimmers and Yellow-billed Terns, breed late July–Sept (low water) on sand bars in Amazon near Leticia; 2 olive brown eggs blotched and spotted darker, on scrape in sand (Hilty). In Orinoco area, Dec–Feb (Cherrie 1916); 1 nest, in Guyana, 9 Nov, on river bank (Davis 1935).
**Status and habitat:** Common along Amazon and larger tributaries close to it; wanders throughout e of Andes, incl. llanos, but very scarce on large blackwater rivers of Orinoco and Río Negro regions. W of Andes both coastal and inland (may breed in lower Magdalena area), but somewhat erratic, sometimes in nos.
**Range:** Larger rivers and estuaries of Carib.; occas. inland to 3100m in E Andes (Sabana de Bogotá n to Lago Tota, Boyacá) and C Andes (Laguna San Rafael, Cauca, 3450m); no Pacific slope rec.; e of Andes in all major river systems. C Panama (rare), n Colombia, and generally e of Andes s to c Argentina; w Ecuador.

## 11. GULL-BILLED TERN
*Sterna (Gelochelidon) nilotica*              Ill. 52
**Identification:** 13-14″ (33-36cm). A *very white tern* with rather broad wings and slightly forked tail. *Thick black gull-like bill*; legs black. Nonbreeding plumage: mostly white with light gray mantle, blackish area in front of eye, and *dusky ear patch*. Breeding plumage: crown and nape jet black; no dusky ear patch. Imm. may have obscure yellow bill tip. Juv. also mottled dark brown on crown and back.
**Similar species:** The palest Colombian tern; at a distance, white and gull-like (note tail only slightly forked). Sandwich Tern (23) has more forked tail and a thin black bill usually tipped yellow (hard to see at distance). Nonbreeding

Sandwich Tern has black hindcrown (nonbreeding Gull-billed has only dusky ear patch).
**Voice:** Call a rasping *jéep* and *ra* note; also *chey-ráck*, repeatedly.
**Behavior:** In flight carries bill directed forward, not downward as do many terns. Flies with smooth easy strokes, more leisurely than other large terns. Swoops to the surface for prey but seldom dives. Takes prey ranging in size from crustaceans to insects, fish, and crabs.
**Status and habitat:** Uncommon transient throughout yr. along Carib.: 1 specimen, a ♂ off Isla de Salamanca, Sept 1969 (Naranjo 1979b). Recent sightings in Jan, Feb, May–Aug, and Nov from Barranquilla e to Manaure, Guajira (T. B. Johnson; Hilty; A. Sprunt IV; Donahue 1974) and 3 seen Oct 1978 off La Boquilla, Bolívar (Naranjo 1979b). Two Pacific coast sightings: 3 on 19 June 1975 (Hilty) and 1 on 4 Feb 1977 (Gochfeld et al. 1980), all at Buenaventura Bay.
**Range:** Carib. and Pacific coasts. Breeds locally on coast of s US, w Mexico, the Bahamas, Virgin Isls., and on Atlantic coast from Guyana to c Argentina; poss. w Ecuador; also much of Old World. N American birds winter s to Peru and the Guianas.

[Several *Sterna* terns and at least 1 *Chlidonias* (Black Tern) have a *portlandica* or subad. plumage broadly equiv. to the imm. plumage of gulls. The plumage is present chiefly during the 1st yr. and is most likely to be seen on or near the wintering grounds where most *Sterna* and *Chlidonias* remain at least during their 1st full summer. In general portlandica plumages resemble those of the respective nonbreeding ads. They are not treated here.]

## 12. CASPIAN TERN
*Sterna (Hydroprogne) caspia*
**Identification:** 21-23″ (53-58cm). Large broad-winged tern with slightly forked tail; *very heavy red bill*; legs blackish. Nonbreeding plumage: mostly white with light gray mantle; blackish edged primaries (most noticeable from below); slightly bushy *crown and nape black streaked with white*. Breeding plumage: crown all black (prob. never seen in Colombia). Imm. has mottled brown back.
**Similar species:** Nonbreeding Royal Tern has white crown (not streaked black and white) and in any plumage is slighter and smaller with more slender orange (not deep red) bill, distinctly pale primaries from below (not blackish edged), and deeply forked tail (Caspian has slight fork). At rest Royal has shorter legs, more squat appearance, and wings reach to tail tips, not well beyond as in Caspian Tern.

**Voice:** A deep raucous croaking *kaah kaah* (Watson 1966).
**Behavior:** Often alone. Flight is strong and gull-like; occas. soars. In flight carries bill pointed downward. Dives into water for prey.
**Status and habitat:** Occas. transient and winter resident (mostly mid-Dec–late May) on coastal lagoons, estuaries, and large rivers near coast. A few oversummer: about 40 seen 30 June 1972 (T. B. Johnson); several 20 June–late July 1974 (P. Donahue); and 1 on 5 June 1980 (Hilty et al.) at PN Isla de Salamanca; also 2-3 at Manaure, Guajira, 27-28 June 1974 (A. Sprunt IV). Most recs. concentrated betw. Cartagena and Santa Marta, esp. at PN Isla de Salamanca.
**Range:** Carib. coast and lower Magdalena River. Breeds in N America, Europe, and Africa. N American birds winter s to Belize, a few to Costa Rica, Panama, n Colombia, and nw Venez.

### 13. COMMON TERN
*Sterna hirundo*                                    Ill. 52
**Identification:** 13-15″ (33-38cm). Slender, med.-sized tern with forked tail. Ad. bill usually orange red and usually tipped black (coral red only when breeding), but bill color var. (often blackish) and unreliable; legs reddish to dull orange. Nonbreeding plumage: mostly white with black hindcrown and nape; mantle light gray; sides of tail edged blackish. In flight *from above outer primaries to bend of wing blackish; from below outer 3-5 primaries broadly tipped black forming a V-shaped area enclosing a wedge of white* (black border on both leading and trailing edge of wing) visible in field. Breeding plumage: sim., but crown and nape solid black, and bend of wing not dusky. In flight at any season note distinct shape (side profile) with wings approx. centered betw. long bill and head and relatively short tail. At rest folded wing reaches to tail.
**Similar species:** Caution. Med.-sized *Sterna* terns are difficult to identify and often not safely separable in nonbreeding season. Comparative experience is mandatory. Common Tern most resembles Arctic Tern (14) but differs as follows: by side profile in flight, longer bill giving more sleek-headed appearance; from above presence of black wedge on outer primaries (lacking in Arctic); from below by generally darker flight feathers (little light passes through) with outer 3-5 primaries more broadly tipped black (Arctic has 8-9 primaries very narrowly tipped black), black-edged tail (not all white), and sides of head without obvious face stripe (Arctic shows clearly defined white facial stripe between black cap and grayish

underparts but this most apparent in breeding season). At rest, wings reach to tail tip (not shorter than tail), and legs longer (best in direct comparison only). Roseate Tern (15) also differs in side profile (wings set forward with long tail trailing behind), as well as longer, much more deeply forked tail (beware of worn or growing feathers), no black edge on tail, and from below outer primaries blackish forming an elongate black wedge on leading edge of wing with an equally long white wedge on trailing edge that gets narrower near tip (no black trailing edge). At rest wings noticeably shorter than tail tips. Also see Sandwich Tern (23).
**Voice:** Seldom vocal in winter; calls var., much like other *Sterna* (Stallcup 1976).
**Behavior:** Gathers in flocks over fish schools or to rest. Flight is buoyant with deep wing strokes and frequent hovering. Dives into water.
**Status and habitat:** Uncommon transient and winter resident on both coasts and on extreme lower Magdalena River (mainly delta area and 30-40km inland), mid-Nov–early Mar. A few oversummer: many seen 27-28 June 1974 at Manaure, Guajira (A. Sprunt IV); scattered individuals 25 June–20 Aug 1974 (P. Donahue) and 1 on 12 Aug 1979 (Hilty et al.) at PN Isla de Salamanca. Usually coastal waters and not far at sea. In winter more tolerant of muddy, low salinity water than other allies (Watson 1966) and the only *Sterna* likely to be found inland other than Yellow-billed Tern.
**Range:** Carib. and Pacific coasts. Breeds locally on coast of s US and e Mexico; also W Indies, isls. of n S America, and on w African coast. New World birds winter s to Peru, Bolivia, Chile (Valdívia), and Argentina; inland recs. in Ecuador, Bolivia, and Brazil.

### 14. ARCTIC TERN
*Sterna paradisaea*
**Identification:** 15″ (38cm). Plumage much like Common Tern and often not safely separable. Comparative experience mandatory. When breeding, told by solid blood red bill (no black tip). At other times differences very subtle. Arctic Tern has *all white tail incl. edge*; and in flight *from above, primaries narrowly edged black on leading edge* (not a broad wedge); *from below all flight feathers translucent admitting much light, and most of primaries* (8-9) *very narrowly tipped black* (not just outer 3-5 with broad black tips). In side profile in flight, wings are positioned far forward (not equidistance from front and back) and bill short, giving a round-headed look. Gray-tinged underparts (hard to see) separated from black crown by a narrow white facial stripe (mainly breeding season). When

perched, wings do not reach to tail tips and tarsus very short (useful mainly in direct comparison—Stallcup 1976).

**Similar species:** See under Common Tern (13). Roseate Tern (15) differs in whiter overall appearance (above and below), long slender bill (sleek head), much longer more deeply forked tail, and outer primaries from below blackish forming an elongated black wedge bordered behind by a white wedge (no black trailing edge on primaries). At rest Roseate's wings much shorter than tail, and legs (tarsus) longer, about like Common Tern.

**Status and habitat:** One rec.: a bird taken about 200km w of Pacific Colombian coast, 4 Oct 1924 (Wetmore 1965a). Highly pelagic and in migration favors cold offshore waters. Unlikely near coast and not expected on Carib.

**Range:** Pacific coast. Breeds in Arctic and migrates to Antarctic waters by moving s along w coast of Africa and Pacific coast of W Hemisphere. N movement is presum. along both coasts of S America, but there are no Carib. recs. Reg. off Ecuador and Peru.

### 15. [ROSEATE TERN]
*Sterna dougallii*                             Ill. 52

**Identification:** 15″ (38cm). *Bill wholly black* (red at base when breeding); feet orange (light red when breeding). Nonbreeding plumage: forecrown white spotted black; rearcrown and nape black; mantle pale gray (paler than Common and Arctic terns); underparts, rump, and *very long forked tail pure white* (tail projects well beyond the closed wing, and no blackish edge on outer tail feathers). In breeding plumage crown and nape all black; breast tinged pinkish.

**Similar species:** See Common and Arctic terns (13, 14). Sandwich Tern (23), also very light-colored, has a slender black bill usually with yellow tip, black legs (not orange or red), and only mod. forked tail.

**Voice:** A raspy *ka-a-ah* and a soft bisyllabic *chuick* or *chivy* suggests Semipalmated Plover and is diagnostic (Peterson 1947) but is seldom heard in winter (R. Ridgely).

**Status and habitat:** Sight recs. (no specimens): a nestling banded near Long Isl., New York, 8 Aug 1969, was recovered 27 Oct 1969 on Gorgona Isl., Colombia (Hays 1971); 4-6 birds seen 14 Jan 1975, PN Isla de Salamanca, and 1 (poss. 2) seen in Cartagena harbor, 21 Jan 1977 (Gochfeld et al., 1980). To be expected occas. on Carib. coast. Accidental on Pacific; usually farther offshore and in deeper, warmer, and clearer water than Common Tern (Watson 1966).

**Range:** Carib. and Pacific coasts. Breeds locally on Atlantic coast of N America, off Belize and Honduras, the Dry Tortugas, the Bahamas, W Indies, Dutch Antilles, and isls. off Venez. coast; also in Old World. Winters at sea mainly in e Carib. and adj. Atlantic coastal waters, a few to n Colombia, n Venez. and rarely e Brazil.

### 16. BRIDLED TERN
*Sterna anaethetus*                            Ill. 55

**Identification:** 14″ (36cm). Slender black bill and black legs. *Grayish brown above*; primaries from above slightly darker; *tail decidedly paler* (looks almost whitish); deeply forked, outer tail feathers white; black cap and stripe through eyes merge on hindcrown; forehead, superciliary (extends well behind eye), and underparts white; collar across hindneck white (very difficult to see in field). In flight longer- and slimmer-winged than Black Tern. Nonbreeding birds are streaked white on crown and back; forecrown white. Imm.: crown and upperparts dark brown streaked and barred white; below white.

**Similar species:** See Sooty Tern (17). Nonbreeding and imm. Black Terns (9) are sim. but smaller with all gray tail.

**Behavior:** Quite wary. Flight perhaps swifter and more buoyant than Sooty Tern. Often rests on water.

**Breeding:** Presum. on Octavia Rocks off n Chocó. In Trinidad and Tobago on cliffs, Apr–July; 1 creamy white egg finely spotted brown; both sexes incubate for about 24-hr. periods (ffrench 1973).

**Status and habitat:** Numerous around Cabo Margo and Octavia Rocks off n Chocó, 11 Sept 1937, where presumed breeding with Brown Noddys (Murphy 1938). Carib. recs. consist of 1 ♂ taken at Cartagena, Oct 1978 (MM); sightings on coast of Bolívar (Naranjo 1979b); 30 seen 3 July 1974 and 35 on 18 July 1974 around big rock in Santa Marta harbor (Gochfeld et al. 1980). To be expected on Carib. mainly as a wanderer. Occurs in coastal and offshore waters, less frequently pelagic waters where partially replaced by Sooty Tern.

**Range:** Carib. and Pacific coasts. Breeds locally on many isls. in tropical oceans incl. the W Indies, and off Mexico, Costa Rica, Colombia, and poss. Panama; also Antilles (Aruba and Curaçao); Trinidad. Ranges widely near coasts and at sea when not breeding.

### 17. SOOTY TERN
*Sterna fuscata*                               Ill. 55

**Identification:** 16″ (41cm). *Mainly black above* and white below; white forehead and eyebrow line just reaching eyes (not a field mark); tail deeply forked, outer feathers white; bill and feet black. Imm.: mainly dusky brown; belly dirty white; upperparts and upper wing coverts barred white, barring lost with wear.

**Similar species:** Ad. resembles ad. Bridled Tern (16) but upperparts blackish (not dark gray), and tail concolor with back (*not decidedly paler*). In hand Bridled has white neck collar and longer white superciliary. Imm. is only all dark, fork-tailed tern. Brown Noddy (25) has long wedge-shaped tail.

**Voice:** Noisy. Loud *kay-rak*, or *wide-a-wake*.

**Behavior:** Pelagic. Often wanders far from breeding colonies. Flight sim. to Bridled Tern, more buoyant than Black Tern. All typically fly rather near surface of water.

**Status and habitat:** Rare. Two recs.: 1 off coast of sw Cauca near Guapí, 14 Jan 1956 (Olivares 1957b); and another on coast of Córdoba near Moñitos, 20 Oct 1978 (Serna 1980). Breeds Jan–Mar on isls. off Venez. coast (Meyer de Schauensee and Phelps 1978) and could be expected later in yr. off Colombia.

**Range:** Pacific and Carib. coasts. Breeds in W Indies, Trinidad, Tobago, isls. off Venez. coast, Dry Tortugas off Florida. Nearly cosmopolitan in tropical and subtropical waters; wanders widely at sea when not breeding.

### 18. YELLOW-BILLED TERN

*Sterna superciliaris*                    Ill. 53

**Identification:** 10″ (25cm). Tiny with slightly forked tail. *Stout yellow bill*, nonbreeders occas. with slight dusky tip; legs dull yellow. Breeding plumage: pale gray above with *4-5 outer primaries blackish forming a narrow wedge on wing tip*; crown, nape, and line through eyes black; forehead and underparts white. Nonbreeding plumage and imm.: head mainly white streaked black on nape and around eyes.

**Similar species:** Very sim. Least Tern (19), mainly a coastal bird, has crisp black-tipped yellow bill when breeding or blackish bill at other seasons (never all yellow). Yellow-billed Tern, by comparison, has a heavier bill, a shorter and less forked tail, proportionally longer wings and larger black wedge on primaries (4-5 vs 2 outer primaries black). Imm. Yellow-billed Tern lacks heavy blackish mot-

53. LARGE-BILLED TERN (center; flying at upper right), LEAST TERN (lower left; flying at upper left), YELLOW-BILLED TERN (lower right; flying at center)

tling on forewing and extensive black on primaries shown by imm. Least Tern.
**Behavior:** Usually single birds, pairs, or small
groups; somewhat less social than larger terns.
Flight is quick with rapid wing beats and frequent hovering. Dives into water for prey.
**Breeding:** Incubating ♀, 30 Mar 1947, mid.
Magdalena Val. in s Bolívar (Simití), 4 BC ♂ ♂,
23 Jan 1948, lower Río Cauca, s Bolívar (Carriker). Several nests among larger colony of
skimmers and Large-billed Terns, 21 July 1976,
Amazon river isl. sand bar near Leticia (Hilty);
1 nest, 11 Aug 1975, same area (J. V. Remsen).
Reported by local residents to nest along Río
Meta near Carimagua (S. Furniss); 2 dark
brown eggs with blackish markings (Davis
1935).
**Status and habitat:** Rivers and freshwater lakes.
Abundance and distribution much like Large-
billed Tern e of Andes but usually less numerous. Not in coastal waters in Colombia,
rarely coastal elsewhere.
**Range:** To 500m. Lower Cauca and mid. Magdalena vals. in s Bolívar and s Cesar; e of Andes in Orinoco and Amazon basins. E Colombia, Venez. and the Guianas s to n
Argentina and Uruguay. Trinidad.

### 19. LEAST TERN
*Sterna albifrons*                                    Ill. 53
**Identification:** 9″ (23cm). *Colombia's smallest tern.*
Much like Yellow-billed Tern but paler gray
above, bill thinner, black loral streak broader,
tail somewhat longer and more deeply forked,
only 2 outer primaries black (instead of 5); *bill
yellow tipped black* (breeding) or blackish (nonbreeding). Imm.: sim., but forewing heavily
mottled blackish and primaries extensively
black from bend of wing to tip.
**Similar species:** See Yellow-billed Tern (18),
also Peruvian Tern (note).
**Voice:** A sharp, repeated *kit*; a harsh, squealing
*zreek-eek* or *zeek*; also a rapid *kitti-kitti-kitti* (Peterson 1961).
**Behavior:** Like Yellow-billed Tern.
**Status and habitat:** Uncommon transient and
winter resident to coastal lagoons and mudflats (rarely inland over fresh water) with var.
nos. erratically yr.-round. In PN Isla de Salamanca most numerous late June–late Aug
(T. B. Johnson); poss. breeding (no nests
found) late June near Manaure, Guajira, and
Barranquilla (A. Sprunt IV). Considered
mainly a fall transient (mid-Aug–late Dec) in
Panama on both coasts and often well offshore
(Ridgely 1976).
**Range:** Carib. coast (prob. also Pacific). Breeds
locally in N America, both coasts s to n C
America, the Carib., isls. off Venez. coast; also

virtually worldwide in warmer regions. New
World birds winter s along Carib. coast to ne
Brazil; on Pacific s to Pacific Panama; Peru
(sight).
**Note 1:** Two ♀ ♀ reported from Macarena Mts.
(Olivares 1962) refer to *S. superciliaris.* **Note
2:** Peruvian Tern (*S. lorata*) breeds on Peruvian coast, disperses along coast to Chile and
Ecuador, and is prob. a wanderer to Colombian waters of sw Nariño and Gorgona Isl.
Closely resembles Least Tern, but in general
rather uniform pale gray (not white) with very
little black on primaries (wings mostly whitish), and bill longer (29-34mm vs 25-31mm),
more slender, and black (extreme base of bill
yellowish when breeding).

### 20. ROYAL TERN
*Sterna maxima*                                       Ill. 54
**Identification:** 19-21″ (48-53cm). Large with
conspic. bushy nuchal crest. *Stout bill reddish
orange to orange*; legs black. Nonbreeding
plumage: mainly white with *black hindcrown
and nape* (sometimes lightly streaked white);
back and wings pale gray; outer primaries
faintly dusky above; tail mod. forked. Breeding plumage: crown solid black (very short
duration and rarely seen in Colombia).
**Similar species:** See Caspian Tern (12), which
never has white forehead. Also Elegant and
Cayenne terns (21, 22).
**Voice:** A shrill *keer*, or *keerlep*, unlike low, raspy
note of Caspian Tern.
**Behavior:** Gull-like in flight with deliberate wing
beats. Usually flies rather high and fishes by
plunging into sea. Dives from greater ht. than
Caspian Tern (Watson 1966).
**Status and habitat:** Fairly common to common
transient and winter resident (mostly Oct–early
May) to coastal lagoons and esp. sandy beaches;
usually within sight of land. Nonbreeders
present yr.-round.
**Range:** Carib. and Pacific coasts. Breeds on both
coasts of s US, Mexico, and isls. off n coast of
S America; also w Africa. Winters s coastally
to Peru and Argentina.

### 21. [ELEGANT TERN]
*Sterna (Thalasseus) elegans*
**Identification:** 16-17″ (41-43cm). Much like
Royal Tern and not always easily separated.
Elegant differs as follows: slightly smaller size,
*decidedly slender yellow to orange yellow bill* (bill
shape like that of Sandwich Tern, not like
thicker bill of Royal), and a *longer* black crest
on rearcrown and nape (never streaked white
as in Royal). Breeding plumage sim. but bill
more orange; cap solid black (sometimes re-

54. SANDWICH TERN (flying), CAYENNE TERN, non-breeding plumage (left),
ROYAL TERN, non-breeding plumage (right)

tained for a time after breeding); and underparts faintly tinged pinkish.
**Similar species:** See Royal Tern (20).
**Status and habitat:** Hypothetical. Only rec. is
1 seen (with broken leg) 3 Mar 1979 in Buenaventura Bay with other terns and gulls
(P. Alden, N. Hill, R. Sides, Hilty, et al.). Believed to be a pelagic migrant and prob. rarely
to coastal waters off Pacific Colombia.
**Range:** Breeds from s California to s Baja California and isls. in Gulf of California; apparently migrates mainly at sea to winter quarters
from coastal Ecuador to c Chile. Scattered
coastal recs. off Pacific Mid. America.

### 22. CAYENNE TERN
*Sterna eurygnatha*                    Ill. 54
**Identification:** 16″ (41cm). Sim. to Sandwich
Tern, but bill *pale lemon yellow* instead of black
or black with yellow tip. In hand underside of
tarsus yellow.
**Similar species:** See Sandwich Tern (23). Cas-
pian and Royal terns, (12, 20) are larger, bulk-
ier, and have heavier orange and reddish bills.
**Behavior:** Like Sandwich Tern.
**Status and habitat:** Uncommon. One specimen
and scattered sight recs.; erratic and in small

nos. On Carib. 2-3 seen 23 May and 2 on 30
June 1972 (T. B. Johnson); several 27-28 June
1974, Manaure, Guajira (A. Sprunt IV); and
2 intermed. Cayenne/Sandwich types with 2
typical Sandwich Terns in Cartagena harbor,
21 Jan. 1977 (Gochfeld et al., 1980). Only Pacific rec. is 1 nearly "typical" Cayenne seen 4
Feb 1977 in Buenaventura Bay (Gochfeld et
al. 1980). Fish in offshore and coastal waters
and roost on sandy beaches and mudflats.
**Range:** Carib. coast from Cartagena eastward;
once on Pacific. Breeds in Dutch Antilles, isls.
off Venez., and coastal Argentina. Ranges along
coast from n Colombia e and s along Carib.
and Atlantic to Argentina.
**Note:** Often regarded as a race of Sandwich
Tern (*S. sandvicensis*), which it may be. Now
known to interbreed with latter on Curaçao
(Ansingh et al. 1960). Apparently bill var. of
the 2 range from pure black and yellow to
pure yellow, although the extreme forms are
the most common.

### 23. SANDWICH TERN
*Sterna sandvicensis*                    Ill. 54
**Identification:** 15-16″ (38-41cm). Med.-sized
with mod. forked tail and *long slender bill with*

*yellow tip* (tip difficult to see at a distance and occas. lacking). Nonbreeding plumage: *mainly white* with black hindcrown and nape; back and wings pale gray; outer primaries edged dusky. Breeding plumage: solid black cap briefly while breeding. Imm.: back and wings mottled with black; primaries and tail dusky gray.

**Similar species:** Cayenne Tern (22) is almost identical, but bill typically pale yellow. Hybrid Sandwich X Cayenne Tern (mainly Curaçao) may have any bill color var. from pure yellow to solid black with yellow tip. Gull-billed Tern (11) has heavier all black bill, less deeply forked tail, and blackish ear coverts (not rearcrown). Also see Common Tern (13). At close range, the only Colombian tern with a yellow tip on black bill.

**Voice:** A grating *kirr-ick*, higher than Gull-bill's *kay-weck* (Peterson 1963).

**Behavior:** Gregarious, esp. with other sp. of terns. Flight is stronger and faster than med.-sized *Sterna* terns but not as heavy and gull-like as large *Sterna*. Dives from considerable hts. and sometimes stays submerged longer than other terns (Watson 1966).

**Status and habitat:** Apparently uncommon transient and winter resident to both coasts (rec. late Dec–late Mar). On Carib.: 1-10 seen on 4 dates between 24 Dec 1974 and 20 Jan 1975 at PN Isla de Salamanca (P. Donahue). On Pacific: an ad. banded by J. Shepard on Cape Hatteras, NC, 8 June 1975 was recovered and released alive near Buenaventura, 29 Mar 1976; 5 seen 4 Feb 1977 (Gochfeld et al. 1980), and 8 seen 3 Mar 1979 (P. Alden, Hilty et al.), all in Buenaventura Bay on Pacific. In Panama oversummers reg., esp. on Pacific coast (Ridgely 1976) and prob. also in Colombia. Coastal or offshore waters, often well offshore. Roosts on sandy beaches and mudflats.

**Range:** Carib. and Pacific coasts. Breeds on coasts of se US, Bahamas, Carib. coast of Mexico to Yucatan, occas. Curaçao and Trinidad; also Europe, N Africa, and se Asia. New World migrants and nonbreeders winter s to coastal Ecuador, Peru, and Uruguay.

**Note:** Placed by some in the genus *Thalasseus*.

## 24. [INCA TERN]

*Larosterna inca*

**Identification:** 16″ (41cm). *Bill and feet coral red*, wattles at base of bill yellow. Bluish slate gray, paler below and blackish on crown; *prom. white moustachial stripe below eye extending back as curving plumes*; outer primaries edged white, inner primaries and secondaries tipped white (forms a *white stripe on rear edge of wing in flight*). Tail

med.-forked. Imm.: browner, plumes inconspic., bill and legs duller.

**Behavior:** Captures small fish by diving from the air; sometimes feeds on refuse.

**Status and habitat:** Hypothetical. First recs. for Colombia are sight recs. of 5 birds at the s tip of Gorgona Isl. by H. Von Prahl, Apr 1983, and by J. E. Orejuela and G. Cantillo at the same place, June 1983 (Naranjo 1984b). Favors rocky coasts and islets.

**Range:** Pacific coast from Gorgona Isl. off the coast of s Colombia, Ecuador (Guayaquil) s to c Chile (Valdivia). Breeds mainly on rocky isls. along Peruvian coast and locally in n Chile (Aconcagua).

## 25. [WHITE (FAIRY) TERN]

*Gygis alba*

**Identification:** 10-13″ (25-33cm). All white with black ring around dark eye; tail forked; bill black, feet black or bluish. Distinctive.

**Behavior:** Flight is light and fluttering; captures small flying fish on the wing (Watson 1966).

**Status and habitat:** Hypothetical. Sight recs. of 4 birds off coast of Chocó, Colombia, 30 Oct 1980, betw. 04°39′N 80°10′W and 04°24′N 80°10′W (R.G.D. Brown).

**Range:** Pelagic waters off Pacific Colombian coast. Tropical oceans. Breeds locally on isls. of s Pacific, incl. Hawaiian, Christmas, and Marquesas isls. Also isls. in s Atlantic off the bulge of Brazil. One Galapagos rec.

**Note:** Sometimes placed in the genus *Anous*.

## 26. BROWN NODDY

*Anous stolidus*                                      Ill. 55

**Identification:** 15-16″ (38-41cm). Med.-sized dark tern; long, slender black bill; black legs. *Entirely dark brown (ridgwayi)* or plain brownish (*stolidus*) with a prom. white cap fading to grayish on midcrown and nape; long wedge-shaped tail, sometimes notched in center. Imm.: darker with grayish forehead and superciliary (no white cap).

**Similar species:** See Black Noddy (26).

**Voice:** Usually silent; when disturbed a deep, hoarse croak, *kaarr*, or short cluck (ffrench 1973).

**Behavior:** Very gregarious and often with other spp. of terns (esp. Sooty Tern) at sea. Flight is strong and fast with steady wing beats, but is erratic, heavier, and less graceful than other med.-sized terns. Swims well and often settles on water. Usually flies close to surface and splashes for small fish (sardines and anchovies) but seldom submerges. Often active at night.

**Breeding:** Many nests, 11 Sept, on Octavia Rocks

off Pacific coast n Chocó (Murphy 1938). Near Trinidad, nest on rocky ledge or shallow depression on ground; 1 pale buff egg spotted darker brown (ffrench 1973).

**Status and habitat:** Breeds on offshore Pacific isls. Primarily pelagic away from breeding grounds. Only Carib. recs. are 4, presum. this sp., seen off Isla Barú, Bolívar, May 1978 (Naranjo 1979b). An imm. was taken near Colombia at Pto. Obaldía, Panama, 10 Aug 1934 (Wetmore 1965a). Likely in offshore or pelagic waters.

**Range:** Both coasts. Breeds on Octavia Rocks off n Chocó and on Gorgona Isl.; wanderer to Malpelo Isl. (*ridgwayi*); sight off Bolívar, breeds on Isla San Andrés (*stolidus*). Locally on isls. from s Florida and Belize to Venez., Curaçao, Trinidad, and Surinam. Also widely known in warmer regions of Atlantic and Pacific. Disperses widely at sea when not breeding.

## 27. BLACK (WHITE-CAPPED) NODDY
*Anous minutus*                                     Ill. 55
**Identification:** 13-14″ (33-36cm). *Long, slender black bill*; legs brown. Dark brownish gray to sooty black with white crown sharply cut off on sides but fading to gray on nape; *slightly*

*forked tail.* Imm.: sim. but browner with blackish primaries, white of crown marked with black or restricted to forehead.

**Similar species:** Very sim. to Brown Noddy (25) and, lacking comparative experience or direct comparison, not always surely identified. Black Noddy has longer, thinner bill and *slightly forked* tail (not wedge-shaped, notched in center). In addition, in direct comparison, Black Noddy is slightly smaller with shorter tail and clearly darker, but *ridgwayi* subsp. of Brown Noddy breeding on Pacific coast is darker (hence is more easily confused) than Carib. *stolidus*.

**Status and habitat:** One rec. and prob. accidental: nonbreeding ad. ♂, 9 Feb 1937 on Malpelo Isl. (Bond and Meyer de Schauensee 1938). May wander to offshore waters of Pacific and Carib. coasts. Even more pelagic than Brown Noddy.

**Range:** Malpelo Isl. (500 km w Buenaventura). Breeds locally on isls. of tropical Pacific, Atlantic, and Carib.; disperses at sea when not breeding. Breeding sites close to Colombia incl. Los Roques isls. off Venez., Cocos Isls. off Costa Rica, and Clipperton Isls. off Pacific Mexico.

**Note:** Merged by some with *Anous tenuirostris* (Lesser Noddy) of the Indian Ocean.

55. Brown Noddy (upper left), Sooty Tern (upper right), Black (White-capped) Noddy (lower left), Bridled Tern (lower right)

# SKIMMERS: Rynchopidae (1)

Skimmers look like large, long-winged terns. Three species are known, one in the Americas, one in tropical Africa, and a third in southeast Asia. All are distinguished by their large, peculiar bills. Both mandibles are laterally compressed and bladelike or knifelike, with the lower one decidedly longer than the upper. The birds fly very low over the water with their bills open and the lower mandibles cutting or "ploughing" the surface. When a small fish or crustacean is contacted, it is quickly snapped up. When not skimming, especially in midday, the birds rest on a sand bar or beach.

## 1. BLACK SKIMMER

*Rynchops nigra*                              Ill. 56

**Identification:** 16-18″ (41-46cm). *Bill bladelike, bright red tipped black, lower mandible longer than upper.* Black above; forehead, trailing edge of wing, and underparts white; tail slightly forked, mostly dark (*cinerascens*—n S America) or white (*niger*—N America; and *intercedens*—s S America). Imm.: like ad. but browner and somewhat streaked above.

**Voice:** Often quiet; a nasal barking *CAaa*, at rest or in flight.

**Behavior:** Gregarious, esp. when breeding. At other times usually in pairs or small groups, sometimes alone. Often loafs on sand bars with gulls and terns. Flies buoyantly.

**Breeding:** 4 BC birds, Jan–Mar, s Bolívar (Car-riker). On Amazon near Leticia, July–early Sept (onset var. with water level) in colonies on river isl. sand bars or river banks (Hilty); several Jan nests in Arauca (J. Jorgenson); 2-3 pale buff eggs blotched dark brown, esp. at larger end. Human predation on eggs poses a threat to many colonies in accessible areas in Amazon (J. V. Remsen). Nesting colony Feb–Mar, Río Guayabero, Meta (Hernández *in* Naranjo 1979b).

**Status and habitat:** Rather irreg. and in small nos. on Carib. and larger rivers w of Andes; seemingly more numerous e of Andes. Rivers, sand bars, and beaches. Some n migrants should occur (as yet unreported).

**Range:** To 500m. Carib. coast and larger rivers e and w of Andes and w to lower Atrato Val.

56. Black Skimmer

(no recs. on Pacific coast or rivers of Pacific drainage). N American birds (*niger*) breed on e and Gulf coasts of US, both coasts of Mexico, and Pacific coast of Guatemala; winter south-ward. S races breed or range over coasts and interior rivers of most of S America; on Pacific coast from Ecuador to Chile.

# PIGEONS, DOVES: Columbidae (32)

This familiar worldwide family is well represented in Colombia, with terrestrial and arboreal species in almost all major habitats. They are typically fast-flying birds with small heads and weak bills. Their plumage is soft, dense, and mostly subdued shades of brown or gray, sometimes with a metallic gloss on the head, neck, or back. Their cooing calls differ in rhythm and tone among the species and are useful in identification. Nests are frail platforms in trees or bushes or on the ground. The young, at first, are fed "pigeon milk" by regurgitation. Pigeons are the largest, heaviest members of the family and have square or rounded tails. Quail-doves are medium-sized, terrestrial, forest inhabiting birds with roundish tails. Ground-doves, the smallest members, are less terrestrial than quail-doves despite their name. They have short squarish tails.

## 1. BAND-TAILED PIGEON
*Columba fasciata*                      Pl. 8, Map 207
**Identification:** 14″ (36cm). Large and robust with broad fan-shaped tail. Bill yellow. Mainly brownish gray; *conspic. white band on hindneck* and metallic bronzy greenish gloss on upper back; head and underparts vinaceous gray; basal half of tail bluish gray, distal half ashy gray with *dusky central band conspic. in flight*.
**Similar species:** Only other large arboreal pigeon of mt. forests is Ruddy Pigeon, which is uniform ruddy brown and is not found in flocks.
**Voice:** A deep mellow cooing *co' oooh, co' oooh*; occas. a grating or croaking *grrrrak*.
**Behavior:** A characteristic bird of high mt. forests. Rather wary; often seen in large fast-flying flocks or perched in treetops. In display ♂♂ fly in wide circles with quick shallow wing beats and short glides (Peeters 1962). Eat mostly acorns and small fruit; arboreal.
**Breeding:** BC ♂, Dec, Boyacá (Olivares 1971), another Feb, Putumayo (Borrero 1952b); 3 BC ♂♂, Jan, Cauca, Apr and July Perijá Mts. (Carriker); 1 nest (eggs), July, W Andes above Cali (Lehmann 1957). Frail stick platform, 2 creamy white eggs (Todd and Carriker 1922).
**Status and habitat:** Common locally in humid mt. forest, clearings with scattered large trees, and even steep scrubby slopes. Shows marked seasonal el. movements, at times occurring far below or above "normal" range. Formerly numerous, now much less so due to loss of habitat.
**Range:** Mainly 2000-3000m (rec. 500-3600m). Santa Marta and Perijá mts., and all 3 Andean ranges. W N America to w Panama; N Venez. s in mts. to nw Argentina; highlands of s Venez. and adj. nw Brazil.

## 2. SCALED PIGEON
*Columba speciosa*                      Pl. 8, Map 208
**Identification:** 12″ (30cm). *Bill red with white tip*; bare eyering red. Mainly reddish chestnut with *decidedly scaled appearance*. Feathers of upper back, neck, and breast with small white central spots and prom. blackish edges; lower underparts buffy to white scaled dark brown.
**Similar species:** Only Colombian pigeon with a white-tipped red bill. In good light scaly appearance unmistakable; in poor light looks blackish. Cf. Pale-vented Pigeon (4).
**Voice:** A low, resonant *ooou, cóok oou, cóok oou, ooOOKoou* in all areas.
**Behavior:** Usually seen perched alone or in pairs in treetops, esp. on exposed bare branches. Occas. small groups. Like other pigeons, visit fruit trees for berries.
**Breeding:** 2 BC ♂♂, May, s Bolívar (Carriker); in Panama several BC birds, Jan–Mar, flying young, June (Wetmore 1968a); Costa Rican nests, Feb–May; flimsy stick platform about 1-18m up; 1 white egg (Skutch 1964c).
**Status and habitat:** Fairly common in humid forest, forest borders, tall second growth, gallery forest, and savanna with scattered trees.
**Range:** To about 1000m (to 1400m—Santa Marta Mts. and e slope E Andes; on Pacific slope mainly coastal plain below 300m). Pacific coast (no w Narino rec.), humid lowlands n of Andes e to mid. Magdalena Val.; Santa Marta Mts.; generally e of Andes (llanos?); No Amazonas rec. S Mexico to w Ecuador, n Argentina, and s Brazil.

## 3. BARE-EYED PIGEON
*Columba corensis*                      Pl. 8, Map 209
**Identification:** 13″ (33cm). Prom. bare blue eyering (like "goggles"); bill and eyes yellow;

legs dull rosy. *Large pale gray pigeon with conspic. white wing patches*; above tinged brownish; hindneck and upper back inconspic. scaled blackish (visible at close range); head and underparts vinaceous becoming white on abdomen.

**Similar species:** Could be confused only with White-winged Dove (11), hypothetical on Colombian mainland.

**Voice:** Four-noted song a distinctive *coooo, chuck-chuk chooouu*, 1st and last note loud and melodious (Freidmann and Smith 1950).

**Behavior:** Alone or in pairs when breeding; at other times in large flocks up to 100 or more. Sometimes flock with Pale-vented Pigeons. Primarily arboreal and often seen perched prom. atop large columnar cactus.

**Breeding:** Poss. dry season; large July and Aug flocks in Guajira (Hilty). In ne Venez. mostly in pairs, Dec–Mar, fledglings, mid-Apr–late July (Friedmann and Smith, 1950). On Curaçao and Bonaire nests in trees, shrubs, and esp. mangroves (Voous 1955).

**Status and habitat:** Common in arid thorn scrub and brushland with columnar cactus in Guajira; absent from more humid n slope of Santa Marta Mts.; local w of them. Fairly common in e half PN Isla de Salamanca.

**Range:** To 200m. Arid lowlands from Barranquilla to w base of Santa Marta Mts.; e base of Santa Marta Mts. and Guajira. Ne Colombia to ne Venez.; Dutch Antilles; Margarita Isl.

### 4. PALE-VENTED PIGEON
*Columba cayennensis*          Pl. 8, Map 210
**Identification:** 12″ (30cm). Bill black; eyes red. *Mainly reddish brown; head and nape contrasting gray*; rump bluish gray; throat, abdomen, and under tail coverts whitish. In flight in good light shows *conspic. rusty shoulders* and upper back.

**Similar species:** Best told by combination of whitish lower underparts and reddish shoulders, but see Scaled Pigeon (2). In nw see Short-billed Pigeon (7), a bird of humid forest.

**Voice:** Usual song a low, mournful cooing (3-8 phrases), *ouu co-woo tu-cooo, tu-coo*, delivered slowly and drowsily.

**Behavior:** Alone, or in pairs, sometimes small to rather large flocks. Perches conspic. in treetops. Displaying ♂♂ fly in wide circles with beating wings held above the back, then sail stiffly with wings held in V. In the lowlands, this and Scaled Pigeon are the only pigeons apt to be seen flying in the open well away from forest.

**Breeding:** 4 BC birds, May–Aug, Cesar, Antioquia, w Caquetá (Carriker); BC ♂, Feb, Meta (Olivares 1962), and June, s Córdoba (Haffer

1975). Panama nests 1st half of yr.; shallow frail twig platform in tangle, spiny palm, etc., a few m up; 1 white egg (Wetmore 1968a).

**Status and habitat:** Fairly common to common in thinner woodland, borders, second growth, mangroves, gallery forest, and open country with scattered trees; dry to humid areas and often near rivers. Not a forest pigeon.

**Range:** To 2100m (usually much lower). Throughout (except e Guajira). S Mexico to n Argentina, Uruguay, and se Brazil.

### 5. RUDDY PIGEON
*Columba subvinacea*          Pls. 8, 9, Map 211
**Identification:** 12″ (30cm). Bill black; eyes and feet dull red. Mainly dark ruddy brown; head, neck, and underparts paler; throat pale cinnamon buff (inconspic. in field); wing linings cinnamon (shows in flight). E of Andes (*purpureotincta* and *ogilvie-granti*) more olivaceous above and grayer below.

**Similar species:** Generally inseparable in field from Plumbeous Pigeon (6), but with comparative experience and under favorable conditions races w of E Andes (*berlepschi, anolaimae*) can sometimes be told from latter by more reddish or ruddy upper and underparts. Races e of Andes are prob. inseparable in field from Plumbeous Pigeon. Plumbeous is darker above with more purplish gloss on shoulders and back, and paler and grayer (not so ruddy) below. Also see Short-billed Pigeon (7; extreme nw only).

**Voice:** Song resembles those of Plumbeous and Short-billed pigeons but is *higher-pitched, faster, and with different rhythm*; a rhythmic *wut woodwoóoo ho*, or (*what do-yoóou know*), 3d syllable emphasized and longer; also a loud purring like other *Columba*.

**Behavior:** Usually alone or in pairs in forest canopy. Less apt to perch in open than Pale-vented or Scaled pigeons.

**Breeding:** 5 BC birds, Apr–June, Perijá Mts., Antioquia, and Huila (Carriker); BC ♂, Aug., Vaupés (Olivares and Hernández 1962); BC ♂, May, Pto. Ayacucho opp. Vichada (Friedmann 1948).

**Status and habitat:** Fairly common in humid forest, older second growth, and along forest borders.

**Range:** To 2800m (usually below 1500m). Humid zones throughout except nw Chocó and Santa Marta areas. Pacific coast s of Río San Juan headwaters (*berlepschi*), upper Sinú Val. (*ruberrima*), Magdalena and Cauca vals. s of 9°N (*anolaimae*), Perijá Mts., Zulia Val. to nw Arauca (*zuliae*), w Meta s to Amazonas (*ogilvie-granti*), and Orinoco and Vaupés (*purpureo-*

*tincta*). Costa Rica to w Panama; e Panama to w Ecuador, e Bolivia, and Amazonian Brazil.

## 6. PLUMBEOUS PIGEON
*Columba plumbea*                    Pl. 9, Map 212
**Identification:** 13″ (33cm). *Much like Ruddy Pigeon.* Dull dark brown above; crown, hindneck, and upperback slightly glossed purplish; below grayish brown; throat pale buff (inconspicuous in field); wing linings gray (sometimes shows in flight). Soft part colors as in Ruddy Pigeon.
**Similar species:** Virtually indistinguishable in field from Ruddy Pigeon (see 5) and usually safely identified only by voice. In extreme nw see Short-billed Pigeon (7), which is not known to overlap in range.
**Voice:** Song sim. to Ruddy Pigeon but lower, slower, decidedly more resonant, with emphasis on 1st and last (not 3d) syllable; w of Andes, *whóo cooks for yoóouu* (or last note slurred *whoo-ou*); e of Andes often shortened to 3 notes (note 2 or 3 omitted). In all songs 1st and esp. last notes are distinctly drawled, last note dropping; also a loud, musical purring like others of genus.
**Behavior:** Solitary or in pairs but gathers in small groups at fruiting trees. Keeps within canopy where difficult to detect unless calling. Does not reg. perch in open.
**Breeding:** 5 BC birds, Apr–July, Perijá Mts. to s Bolívar (Carriker). Nest building, 13 Aug, 11 Sept, and 19 Nov in upper Anchicayá Val. (Hilty).
**Status and habitat:** Fairly common to common in humid forest, forest borders, and advanced second growth. Chiefly foothills and lower highlands on Pacific slope.
**Range:** To 1600m, small nos. to 2100m. Pacific slope from headwaters of Río San Juan (Cerro Tatamá) south; humid lowlands along n base of W and C Andes to mid. Magdalena Val. (s to latitude of Bogotá) e of Andes in Norte de Santander and from e Cundinamarca s along base of Andes to Macarena Mts. and generally from Río Guaviare southward (no recs. in Guainía). W Venez. incl. Perijá Mts. Guianas and s Venez. s to e Bolivia, Paraguay, and se Brazil.

## 7. SHORT-BILLED PIGEON
*Columba nigrirostris*                    Map 213
**Identification:** 10-11″ (25-28cm). Smaller, browner Mid. American ally of Plumbeous Pigeon. Short black bill. Mainly warm umber brown; back, wings, and tail darker and duller olive brown.
**Similar species:** Ruddy Pigeon (5) is slightly

larger and more uniform ruddy (instead of dark olive brown above and lighter below) but they are more reliably told by calls.
**Voice:** Mellow, mournful song, *oh-whit-mo-gó* (Wetmore 1968a) or *ou oo-cu-coóoo*, last note drawn out; also a musical purring.
**Behavior:** Mid. American birds are usually in mid. or upper levels of forest, though occas. descend quite low. Alone or in pairs, less suspicious than Plumbeous and Ruddy pigeons, but like them seldom perch conspic. in open.
**Breeding:** BC ♂, 10 Jan, northernmost Chocó (Carriker). In Costa Rica, nesting Mar and Aug (Skutch 1964c); 1 in nw Panama, June (Wetmore 1968a); flimsy twig platform up to 30m up; 1 white egg.
**Status and habitat:** Humid forest and forest edge. One of the most characteristic lowland forest birds in Mid. America, though barely reaches Colombia.
**Range:** To about 1500m. Extreme nw Colombia near Carib. Panama border (Acandí and e slope of Cerro Tacarcuna). S Mexico to extreme nw Colombia.

## 8. DUSKY PIGEON
*Columba goodsoni*                    Pl. 9, Map 214
**Identification:** 10.5″ (27cm). Bill black; eyes pale gray; narrow eyering and feet dull red. Mainly dark brown tinged vinaceous above; crown slate gray; *throat pearly gray; sides of head and underparts bluish gray* with vinaceous tinge; *abdomen brownish*; wing linings and inner web of flight feathers cinnamon rufous (shows in flight).
**Similar species:** Best told from other dark *Columba* pigeons in Colombia by small size, noticeably "2-toned" underparts (grayish with brown belly), slaty crown and pale throat. In flight watch for flash of cinnamon rufous, brighter and more extensive than in Ruddy Pigeon.
**Voice:** Usual song a brisk, rather high-pitched *hóo-goo-goo* (Haffer 1975); purrs as do other *Columba*.
**Behavior:** Like other forest *Columba*, usually alone or in pairs in canopy, not in flocks.
**Breeding:** 5 BC birds, Jan–May, n Chocó and nw Antioquia (Carriker); BC ♂, Aug, nw Antioquia (Haffer 1975).
**Status and habitat:** Apparently common very locally in wet lowland and hill forest. "Common" near Mutatá, n Antioquia (Haffer 1975), rare in w Valle.
**Range:** To 1000m (usually much lower). W of W Andes from the mid. Atrato Val. (Mutatá) and the Baudó Mts. southward. W Colombia and w Ecuador.

## 9. MOURNING DOVE
*Zenaida macroura*
**Identification:** 11-12″ (28-30cm). A slim, graceful dove with a *long, pointed, white-edged tail.* Pale grayish brown above; nape grayer; underparts a little paler and tinged pinkish buff; throat and belly palest; *small black spot on ear coverts* and a few larger black spots on wings.
**Similar species:** Eared Dove (10) has much shorter, more wedge-shaped tail; at close range 2 black marks visible on sides of head. *Leptotila* doves are chunkier with shorter, rounded tails.
**Behavior:** Much as in Eared Dove.
**Status and habitat:** Known from 1 taken in May 1957, s of Cartago in Cauca Val. (banded as nestling in nw Iowa in 1956). Prob. a rare winter straggler or winter resident to n Colombia.
**Range:** Breeds in N America s locally to c Panama, Bahamas, and the Greater Antilles; a few n birds winter s to Panama; Colombia (once).

## 10. EARED DOVE
*Zenaida auriculata*          Pl. 8, Map 215
**Identification:** 10″ (25cm). Rather uniform dove with prom. *wedge-shaped tail.* Brownish olive above; wing coverts and tertials conspic. spotted black; center crown blue gray; *2 black marks on sides of head*; rest of head and underparts uniform vinaceous pink. In flight outer tail feathers with narrow black subterminal band and *prom. white tips.* Or underparts shaded cinnamon and *outer tail tips dark rusty (stenura; pentheria).*
**Similar species:** When flushed, look superficially like *Leptotila* doves, esp. White-tipped Dove (22), but are smaller, slimmer, and have wedge-shaped (not fan-shaped) tails and white (or rusty) tips on all but central pair of feathers (not mainly corners). At rest black marks on sides of head are diagnostic. In flight resembles a short-tailed Mourning Dove (9).
**Voice:** Low-pitched cooing, *ooo-ah-ooo*, audible only a short distance; also a soft rising *coooo.*
**Behavior:** Gregarious when not breeding. Often congregates in immense flocks in agricultural areas where it becomes destructive to grain crops and is considered an agricultural pest. Feeds mostly on ground; some local or long distance dispersal may occur in response to food levels. Flies swiftly and directly, without sailing, and is often hunted for sport.
**Breeding:** 4 BC birds, Mar–Aug, Cesar to Huila (Carriker). At Carimagua, ne Meta, 1 nest, 3 Jan (S. Furniss); in nw Venez. mainly Apr–Nov; 2 white eggs, on flimsy stick platform (Friedmann and Smith 1950; Thomas 1979b).
**Status and habitat:** Fairly common to locally abundant, mainly in drier open country, fields,

and agricultural areas. Reaches tremendous abundance in mid. Cauca Val. in cropland. Peak flock nos. Mar–July in Venez. llanos (Friedmann and Smith 1950); in Aug in Trinidad (ffrench 1973).
**Range:** 600-3000m, w of W Andes in drier upper Dagua and Patía vals., mid. and upper Cauca Val., and C Andes s to Cauca (*caucae*); 2800-3400m, mts. of Nariño (*vulcania*); 1500-2800m, E Andes (*pentheria*); up to 1750m, Carib. area from Atlántico e to Guajira and s in Magdalena Val. to n Huila, e of Andes s to Meta and Río Guaviare (*stenura*). Colombia e to Guianas, and s locally to Tierra del Fuego. Dutch and Lesser Antilles; Trinidad. Once in Panama.

## 11. [WHITE-WINGED DOVE]
*Zenaida asiatica*
**Identification:** 11″ (28cm). Hypothetical. Bill black; eyes and legs reddish; small bare blue eyering. Mainly grayish brown above with small black spot on ear coverts and purplish gloss on hindneck; flight feathers dusky; *wing coverts mostly white* (conspic. white patch in flight and visible at rest); below buffy gray; tail rounded, outer feathers with narrow subterminal black band and *broad white tips.*
**Similar species:** Easily confused with Bare-eyed Pigeon (3), which is slightly larger and heavier, has yellow (not black) bill, and lacks white tail tipping. At close range latter has prom. blue "goggles" and blackish scaling on hindneck; in flight the 2 are remarkably sim.
**Voice:** Cooing *whoo coo coóo-aah* song.
**Status and habitat:** Hypothetical. Known from 1 sighting of a pair well studied in Guaira Wash, Rodadero (s of Santa Marta), 30 Oct 1972, and a few other sightings, presumed this sp. in same area (S. M. Russell).
**Range:** Sw US s locally to n Costa Rica; locally in sw c Panama; sw Ecuador to n Chile; s Bahamas, Greater Antilles, Isla San Andrés, and Providencia.

## 12. COMMON GROUND-DOVE
*Columbina passerina*          Pl. 8, Map 216
**Identification:** 6.5″ (16.5cm). Tiny square-tailed dove with scaly breast. *Bill pinkish or yellow tipped black.* Grayish or olive brown above, vinaceous gray below; head paler; wing coverts spotted black; *feathers of neck and breast dark centered giving conspic. scaled appearance;* outer tail feathers mostly black narrowly tipped white. In flight base of primaries and under wing coverts rufous. ♀ is duller below.
**Similar species:** In size and shape much like next 2 spp. but always distinguishable from Plain-breasted Ground-Dove (13) by scaly neck

and breast, *pale* bill (not dark), and slightly larger size; from ♀ Ruddy Ground-Dove (14) by chestnut wing flash (not all rufescent brown above), bill color, and scaly underparts. Also see ♀ Blue Ground-Dove (16).

**Voice:** A soft, monotonously repeated *coo-ah* (or *cooah* at distance), with rising inflection, given several times per song.

**Behavior:** Pairs or small groups feed exclusively on the ground, walking and pecking in a jerky toylike manner. If disturbed, flush very suddenly and fly away rapidly. Often rest in low shrub or tree. More wary than Ruddy Ground-Dove.

**Breeding:** 5 BC birds, Aug, Cartagena, 2 in Oct, incl. incubating ♀, Cúcuta (Carriker); 3 nests, Apr–June (Todd and Carriker 1922), and fledged young, late Nov (S. M. Russell), Santa Marta area; 1 nest, 11 Mar (nestlings), near Cúcuta (Brown). Small matlike nest of grass and twigs; on ground or low in shrub; 2 white eggs.

**Status and habitat:** Locally common in arid scrub, waste fields, scrubby grassland, and drier open areas; mainly lowlands.

**Range:** To 2100m. Carib. region from ne Córdoba e to Guajira; Pacific slope in upper Dagua and Patía vals., mid. and upper Cauca Val. (to Popayán) and in most of Magdalena Val. (mainly Bucaramanga southward); E Andes in Boyacá (Tunja, 2200m); e of Andes in Norte de Santander, Vaupés (Mitú), and prob. elsewhere. S US to c Costa Rica; Colombia e to the Guianas, spottily in n and e Brazil; temperate zone in Ecuador. Dutch Antilles, Venez. isls.; Margarita Isl.; Trinidad.

### 13. PLAIN-BREASTED GROUND-DOVE
*Columbina minuta*                    Pl. 8, Map 217
**Identification:** 6″ (15cm). Much like Common Ground-Dove. *Bill blackish.* Above grayish brown, crown and nape paler and more bluish gray; below vinaceous gray; wing coverts with a few obscure blue black spots. In flight flashes *conspic. rufous in primaries*; wing linings rufous. ♀ duller.

**Similar species:** See Common Ground-Dove (12). Dull ♀ Ruddy Ground-Dove (14) often very sim. but larger, and wings (in flight) show more ruddy above (not just in primaries). Also see ♀ Blue Ground-Dove (16).

**Voice:** Usual song, *whoop whoop whoop* . . . , from 5 to 30 times without pausing (Ridgely 1976).

**Behavior:** Much like Common Ground-Dove. Alone or in pairs, though occas. several. ♂♂ display by sailing out from low perches on stiffly spread wings.

**Breeding:** BC ♀, Jan, Macarena Mts. (Olivares 1962); nest (with eggs) near Pto. Inírida, 26

Sept (Hilty); another, mid-Jan, w Meta (W. McKay); incubating ♀, 11 May, Cesar Val. (Carriker); shallow grass and twig nest cup, on ground to 3 m up; 2-3 white eggs (Wetmore 1968a).

**Status and habitat:** Locally common in dry scrub, abandoned fields, brushy borders, and open areas with scattered bushes and trees. Likes brushy ecotone separating woodland and grassland.

**Range:** To 1400m (Ocaña, Santander). Locally in drier parts of n Colombia, upper Río Sucio (Antioquia), s of Barranquilla in Atlántico, and drier Cesar Val. s to Ocaña, Norte de Santander and c Córdoba; mid. and upper Cauca Val.; e of Andes from Norte de Santander s to w Putumayo and Vaupés (Mitú). No Amazonas recs. Se Mexico s locally to the Guianas, c Argentina, and s Brazil; w Peru. Trinidad.

### 14. RUDDY GROUND-DOVE
*Columbina talpacoti*                    Pl. 8, Map 218
**Identification:** 6.5″ (16.5cm). Bill black. ♂: small, mostly *cinnamon rufous dove*, with paler underparts and *contrasting light gray crown*; wing coverts with some black spotting; outer tail feathers black; flight feathers largely rufous. ♀: much duller, esp. below, but back mainly ruddy brown.

**Similar species:** ♂ is distinctive. ♀ easily confused with Plain-breasted Ground-Dove (13). Also see larger ♀ Blue Ground-Dove (16).

**Voice:** ♂'s call a hollow, monotonous *ka-hóo, ka-hóo* . . . (Hilty), or *hoo-whoop, hoo-whoop* . . . , repeated 3-10 times at a slower pace than Plain-breasted Ground-Dove. Usually calls from elevated perch (Ridgely 1976).

**Behavior:** Notably sociable and confiding. Feeds mostly on ground, alone, in pairs, or in groups of var. size. Walks mechanically with short quick steps. Threats and quarrels are often accompanied by flashing a raised wing. Flushes suddenly with an audible wing-whirr and flies away a short distance.

**Breeding:** Nest building, 7 Aug (Hilty); other nests, Apr–June and Oct–Nov, Santa Marta area (Darlington 1931); fledgling, 3 Apr, Cali; nest (with eggs), 6 June, near Buga, Valle (Hilty). 5 BC birds, May–Aug, Cartagena and Cesar (Carriker). Frail shallow nest 1m or more up in bush; 2 white eggs.

**Status and habitat:** Common to abundant in drier open country, fields, farms, lawns, gardens, and populated areas; local in Amazonia where perhaps spreading with deforestation.

**Range:** Usually below 1600m; locally to 2400m in E Andes (sightings, Laguna Fúquene— A. Gast). Drier zones throughout (not Pacific slope s of Juradó, Chocó). S Mexico (occas. s

Texas) s to n Argentina, Paraguay, and Uruguay (sightings); accidental in Chile; nw Peru. Trinidad.

## 15. PICUI GROUND-DOVE

*Columbina picui*                    Map 219

**Identification:** 7″ (18cm). ♂: grayish brown above; forehead and underparts whitish; breast tinged violaceous; wing coverts with purple spotting and prom. *white wing bar; outer feathers of short squarish tail mostly white.* In flight shows conspic. *black primaries and white patch on wing coverts;* under wing coverts black. ♀: sim. but browner below.

**Similar species:** Flashing black and white wing pattern is distinctive. At rest note white wing bar.

**Status and habitat:** Poss. a trans-Amazonian migrant; known only from a ♀ (of a pair) taken 29 Apr 1957, Pto. Nariño, Amazonas. Peruvian specimens and the Colombian bird have all been taken during austral winter. To be expected in village clearings, overgrown weedy fields, thickets, gardens, and parks, mainly late Apr–late Sept.

**Range:** To 100m. Amazonas, Colombia (once). Ne and s Brazil, and n Bolivia s to Uruguay, c Argentina, and n Chile; a few recs. in Peru.

**Note:** Croaking Ground-Dove (*C. cruziana*) of coastal nw Ecuador (Esmeraldas) s to n Chile may be spreading n (sightings, reported this sp., at Barbacoas, Nariño, 1976—D. Gardner and D. Englemann). Like Picui, but primaries black, bill yellow with black tip (not all gray), and no white in wings and tail. Distinctive, froglike, low-pitched call, *kee-wa-wa* (Johnson 1965).

## 16. BLUE GROUND-DOVE

*Claravis pretiosa*              Pl. 8, Map 220

**Identification:** 8.5″ (22cm). ♂: *distinctly bluish gray;* head and underparts paler; wings spotted and flecked black, tail squarish with *outer feathers black.* ♀: buffy brown above, duller below with whitish throat and abdomen; wings with a few chestnut spots and *2 irreg. pale-edged chestnut bands across inner remiges; rump and tail rufous;* outer tail feathers black.

**Similar species:** ♂ unmistakable. ♀ from ♀ Ruddy Ground-Dove (14) by larger size, contrasting rufous rump, black and rufous tail (not all ruddy), and chestnut bands and spotting on wings; from Common Ground-Dove (12) also by lack of spotting or scaling below. Smaller and duller Plain-breasted Ground-Dove (13) lacks chestnut wing markings (has a few dark spots), contrasting rufous rump, and bicolored tail.

**Voice:** ♂'s call a soft, hollow, abrupt *boop* or

*woop,* singly or doubled, or more often several in ser.; somewhat ventriloquial.

**Behavior:** In pairs or infrequently small groups; often rather wary. Feeds on ground, sometimes in shady clearing or roadside, but otherwise keeps in thicker cover than *Columbina* ground-doves, hence less often seen. Most frequently seen as it shoots by in flight, higher above ground than other ground-doves. Calls from a semiconcealed perch, mostly at mid. hts.

**Breeding:** 8 BC birds, Feb–Oct, n Colombia to Chocó (Carriker); nests, May–July, nw Santander (Boggs 1961); frail nest, 1-6 m up in tangle; 2 white eggs (Skutch 1959b, 1964c).

**Status and habitat:** Widespread but local in dry to humid forest edge, shrubby clearings, ranchland, and lighter woodland. Most numerous in Carib. region and scrubby woodland and savanna regions near the Orinoco. Least numerous and very local in wet borders of Pacific lowlands and Amazonia.

**Range:** To 1000m (occas. to 1800m, Munchique area). Throughout except upper Cauca and Magdalena vals.; Amazonia (?). S Mexico s to w Ecuador and nw Peru; e of Andes to n Argentina, Paraguay, and s Brazil. Trinidad.

## 17. MAROON-CHESTED GROUND-DOVE

*Claravis mondetoura*          Pl. 8, Map 221

**Identification:** 8.5″ (22cm). ♂: *mainly dark gray* with whitish foreface and throat; *chest to upper abdomen deep purplish chestnut;* 2 blotchy purplish black wing bars; *outer tail feathers white* (conspic. in flight). ♀: olive brown above; forehead fulvous; 2 blotched purplish black wing bars as in ♂, underparts buffy, browner on chest and flanks; *outer tail feathers blackish broadly tipped white* (show in flight).

**Similar species:** ♂ unmistakable with distinctive maroon chest. ♀ much like ♀ Blue Ground-Dove (16) but lacks the rufous rump and tail and has purple wing bars (not chestnut spots) and broad white tail tips; the 2 spp. should not overlap in range.

**Voice:** Song rather like that of Blue Ground-Dove, a deep resonant *hwoop,* at intervals (Eisenmann).

**Behavior:** Solitary or in pairs. Calls from dense growth in low to midstrata and prob. feeds on ground. Shy and difficult to observe.

**Status and habitat:** Apparently rare and local. A "cloud forest" bird; esp. inside or at edge of forest where there is thick bamboo undergrowth. Only recent recs. are a few sightings from PN Cueva de los Guácharos (P. Gertler). To be looked for in dense bamboo-laden forests above Bucaramanga. Distribution and abundance perhaps closely tied to seeding of bamboo (R. Ridgely).

**Range:** 2000-2600m (prob. also lower). Spottily in E Andes (Norte de Santander; Bogotá area, where it may no longer occur; PN Cueva de los Guácharos), C Andes in Caldas (e of Manizales), and W Andes in Cauca (Munchique area). Se Mexico to w Panama; n Venez. s in mts. to Bolivia.

## 18. BLACK-WINGED GROUND-DOVE

*Metriopelia melanoptera*           Pl. 9, Map 222

**Identification:** 9″ (23cm). Med.-sized, square-tailed dove of Nariño mts. Bare orange patch in front of eyes. ♂: grayish brown above, paler pinkish buff below; *flight feathers, underwings, and tail black; conspic. white patch on shoulder.* ♀: sim. but pale sandy brown below.

**Similar species:** Black tail prevents confusion with Picui Ground-Dove (15), which prob. should not occur at high el. in Colombia.

**Behavior:** Usually in small tight flocks and rather wary. Flush with a characteristic whirring of wings and fly away fast and directly. Feed and rest on the ground and sometimes huddle under a small bush or tussock of taller grass.

**Breeding:** In Chile in groups of 10-20 pairs, often in thick bushes along streams; up to 4900m in the north. Two eggs, usual dove nest (Johnson 1965); 6 nests 2m up in *Polylepis* grove, s Peru, 3900m (Roe and Rees 1979).

**Status and habitat:** Local on open, arid, grassy, or shrubby slopes of temperate and paramo zone.

**Range:** Above 3000m. Mts of Nariño from Pasto southward. Sw Colombia s in Andes to s Argentina and Chile.

## 19. SCALED DOVE

*Scardafella squammata*           Pl. 8, Map 223

**Identification:** 8.5″ (22cm). *Scaly-looking little dove; long pointed tail.* Sandy gray above, whitish below; the feathers above and below edged blackish, giving a scaled appearance; *primaries dusky with cinnamon inner webs* (flashes rufous in flight); outer feathers of long tail black tipped white.

**Similar species:** Easily recognized at rest by scaly appearance; in flight told from other small doves that flash rufous in wings by pointed, white-edged tail.

**Voice:** Usual song a monotonously repeated *too-ca-dóo,* sim. in quality to 2-noted call of its n ally, the Inca Dove (*S. inca*).

**Behavior:** Pairs or small groups and very confiding. Feed on the ground, pecking and shuffling along with their bellies almost scraping the ground. Flush suddenly with a dry rus-

tling whirr of wings and usually fly to nearby tree. Call and loaf in scrubby thickets or small trees.

**Breeding:** Building nest, 2 Mar (Brown), and another, 10 Aug (P. Kaestner), Santa Marta area; in ne Venez., Jan–June and Sept; twiggy cup more substantial than that of most doves; usually 1-2m up (Friedmann and Smith 1950), sometimes on ground (Cherrie 1916), or much higher; 2 white eggs.

**Status and habitat:** Common in arid scrub, around dwellings, and in waste areas with thickets and trees. Most numerous around farm building and settled areas.

**Range:** To 500m. N Colombia from s Magdalena and Santa Marta area e to Guajira; e of Andes from Arauca to the Orinoco, and s to w Meta (where local). Ne Colombia to n Venez. Fr. Guiana; e Brazil to n Argentina and Paraguay.

[*Leptotila:* Plump; uniform above; forehead and belly pale; wing linings rufous; outer tail feathers tipped white. Told by range, subtle difference in head color and tail tipping, and tones of breast and belly. Rather terrestrial.]

## 20. GRAY-CHESTED DOVE

*Leptotila cassinii*           Pl. 9, Map 224

**Identification:** 10″ (25cm). *Red loral line and orbital skin;* pale yellow eye. Above olive brown; crown, sides of head, and neck pale gray *becoming darker gray on breast;* throat and belly whitish; tail grayish with *small white tips on outer feathers.*

**Similar species:** Very sim. and more widespread White-tipped Dove (22) has much more conspic. white tail tips, vinaceous or pinkish brown (not gray) breast, and blue loral and orbital skin. Also see Gray-headed Dove (23). Pallid Dove (24) occurring farther s on Pacific coast, is much paler on head and underparts.

**Voice:** A deep, low-pitched, long-drawn *cooooooh,* longer than notes of Ruddy or Violaceous quail-doves (Willis and Eisenmann 1979) or White-tipped Dove. Sings from 2-5m up.

**Behavior:** A terrestrial dove, usually seen alone, occas. in pairs. Walks quietly away from an observer or flushes to a low perch where it nods head and jerks tail and rearparts upward several times. Heard more often than seen.

**Breeding:** 10 BC birds, Jan–Apr, upper Río Sinú to n Chocó (Carriker). In Panama, Feb–Sept (Eisenmann), a frail mat of twigs in dense tangle, 1-3m up; 2 white eggs (Skutch 1964c).

**Status and habitat:** Uncommon on or near floor of humid forest, at breaks and tangles, overgrown borders, and older second growth

woodland. More a forest bird than White-tipped Dove, which it meets along wooded borders.
**Range:** To 900m (perhaps higher). From Panama border s on Pacific coast to Baudó Mts. (Río Baudó) and e across humid n base of Andes to mid. Magdalena Val. (s to Pto. Berrío, e Antioquia). Se Mexico to n Colombia.

## 21. TOLIMA DOVE
*Leptotila conoveri*                    Pl. 9, Map 225
**Identification:** 10″ (25cm). Eyes white. Dark brown above becoming blue gray on crown; forehead and throat whitish; *sides of neck and upper breast dark vinaceous buff in sharp contrast to buff lower breast and abdomen*; under tail coverts white; tail slaty with *small white tips on outermost feathers*. In flight under wing coverts cinnamon rufous.
**Similar species:** In limited range found only with White-tipped Dove (22), which has white (not deep buff) belly, lacks blue gray crown, and has more broadly white-tipped tail. All other Colombian *Leptotila* doves have whitish bellies.
**Behavior:** Prob. like other *Leptotila*.
**Status and habitat:** Uncertain. Rec. in humid forest and bushy forest borders. Much of the habitat in its known range is now destroyed.
**Range:** ENDEMIC. 1800-2500m. E slope of C Andes from near Ibaque, Tolima (Río Toche), s to headwaters of Magdalena Val. in Huila (Isnos; San Agustín).

## 22. WHITE-TIPPED DOVE
*Leptotila verreauxi*                    Pl. 8, Map 226
**Identification:** 11″ (28cm). Loral line and orbital skin light blue (or red—*decolor*). Above grayish brown; *forehead and underparts pale pinkish gray fading to whitish on throat, abdomen, and under tail coverts*; outer tail feathers blackish, *all but central pair with broad white tip*; under wing coverts cinnamon rufous.
**Similar species:** Best told from other Colombian members of the genus by absence of blue gray on crown and broader white tail tips. Pallid Dove (24; range overlaps on Pacific coast s of Valle) is sim. but smaller, paler-headed (no blue gray), and rufous brown above (more contrast between upper and underparts). Gray-chested Dove (20) has gray (not pale pinkish gray) chest. Also see Gray-headed Dove (23); e of Andes, see Gray-fronted Dove (25).
**Voice:** A deep, drawn out *woob w'wooooo* (Willis and Eisenmann 1979) at short intervals. Reminiscent of sound produced by blowing across top of bottle.
**Behavior:** Typical of the genus. Single birds, or 2's, terrestrial, and rather wary. Walks me-chanically about on ground with much head-nodding as it picks at trifles. When disturbed, walks away quietly or flushes with an audible wing whirring to a nearby low perch where it nervously nods head, dips tail, and often walks along branch a few steps to better concealment.
**Breeding:** 12 Santa Marta nests, Mar–Sept (Todd and Carriker 1922) and thought to peak there July (S. M. Russell); nw Santander, 3 nests, May–June (Boggs 1961); Huila nests, Feb–Oct (Miller 1952). Usual dove platform of twigs and grass, low in bush or tree, occas. on ground; 2 white eggs (Skutch 1964c).
**Status and habitat:** Common in lighter woodland, rather open second growth, tangled borders, plantations, and shady pastures in dry to fairly humid areas. Primarily nonforest.
**Range:** To 2700m (mostly below 2200m). Mid. and upper Cauca Val., upper Dagua and Patía Vals., Pacific coast in sw Cauca s and both slopes of mts. in Nariño (*decolor*); nw Chocó near Panama border e to Guajira and s in Magdalena Val. to s Huila, e of Andes in Norte de Santander, and extreme ne Vichada at Pto. Carreño (*verreauxi*). S Texas and Mexico to w Peru, c Argentina, and Uruguay. Aruba to Trinidad.
**Note:** N and s forms with different orbital skin color are perhaps separate spp.

## 23. GRAY-HEADED DOVE
*Leptotila plumbeiceps*                    Pl. 9, Map 227
**Identification:** 10″ (25cm). Red orbital skin and black loral line; eyes yellowish white. Forehead light gray; *crown and hindneck bluish gray contrasting with olive brown upperparts; cheeks pale buff* (often hard to see in field); underparts whitish with strong pinkish vinaceous tinge on breast; outer tail feathers blackish tipped white; under wing coverts cinnamon.
**Similar species:** From other *Leptotila* by obviously gray crown contrasting with brownish back, no gray on breast, and at close range, buff on cheeks. Most like Gray-fronted Dove (25), but range overlaps only White-tipped Dove (22).
**Voice:** Described as a low, reedy *cwuh-h-h-a* in nw Panama (Wetmore 1968a), and a resonant *hoo-hoo* with quality of White-tipped Dove in sw Panama (Ridgely 1976).
**Behavior:** Much like White-tipped Dove. Has been reported in small loose groups.
**Breeding:** 4 BC birds, Jan, Puracé (Carriker).
**Status and habitat:** Uncommon and at least now local in drier forest, second growth woodland, small woodlots, and tangled borders. Can be seen in remnant woodlots around Lago de Sonso, Buga, and Bosque Castillo se of Cali.

**Range:** Mainly 1000-1800m (to 2600m Puracé). Mid. and upper Cauca Val. from sw Caldas (Chinchina), s to Popayán and Munchique area; Pacific slope in upper Dagua Val. S Mexico to w Panama; w Colombia.

## 24. PALLID DOVE
*Leptotila pallida*                          Pl. 9, Map 228
**Identification:** 10″ (25cm). Eyes pale yellow. *Forehead whitish; crown blue gray becoming dark gray on hindneck and ruddy brown on remaining upperparts;* below whitish; foreneck and breast tinged vinaceous; outer tail feathers black broadly tipped white; under wing coverts cinnamon.
**Similar species:** Shows more contrast between pale head and underparts and dark upperparts than other *Leptotila* and is the only *Leptotila* with ruddy to rufous brown upperparts. Might overlap White-tipped Dove (22) locally on Pacific coast from Cauca s but should normally be the only *Leptotila* inside forest in the "superwet" belt. The white tail tips are almost as large as those of White-tipped Dove. Also see sim.-sized Dusky Pigeon (8), which is gray and brown below (not whitish), lacks white tail tips, and perches in canopy. In n Chocó cf. Gray-chested Dove (20).
**Voice:** A deep, hollow *whoOOou*, much like Gray-fronted Dove.
**Behavior:** Like others of the genus.
**Breeding:** BC ♂, 27 Dec, s Chocó (Carriker).
**Status and habitat:** Fairly common (esp. by voice) in wet forest, older second growth, and borders. Most recs. are from broken hill forest and foothills along tributaries of upper Río San Juan, e of Buenaventura, and Barbacoas, Nariño.
**Range:** To 700-800m. Pacific slope from the upper Río San Juan (on Río Tatamá) southward. W Colombia and w Ecuador.

## 25. GRAY-FRONTED DOVE
*Leptotila rufaxilla*                        Pl. 8, Map 229
**Identification:** 10.5″ (27cm). Bare loral line and orbital skin red; eyes pale yellow. Forecrown grayish white *becoming blue gray on rear crown and buffy brown on nape;* rest of upperparts olive brown; *sides of head and neck pale rufescent buff;* underparts whitish with vinaceous to vinaceous buff tinge on breast; outer tail feathers black tipped white; under wing coverts rufous chestnut.
**Similar species:** The only *Leptotila* in most of wide range. Darker above than White-tipped Dove (22) and with blue gray (not grayish brown) crown; at close range sides of head and neck rufescent buff (not pinkish gray). Calls differ.

**Voice:** More frequently heard than seen. Call a deep, very resonant and abrupt *whooouu,* like blowing across top of a bottle, the sound expanding and contracting quickly; given every 5 sec or so.
**Behavior:** Like White-tipped Dove. Usually seen when it flushes noisily from leaf litter beside a trail, or as it shoots rapidly across small clearings.
**Breeding:** 2 BC ♂♂, June, w Caquetá, and July, Norte de Santander (Carriker); 1 nest, 22 Aug, Leticia; usual dove type nest, 1.3m up at edge of second growth (J. V. Remsen); 2 white eggs (Haverschmidt 1968).
**Status and habitat:** Common in gallery and *várzea* forest, humid second growth, and around shrubby clearings and openings in *terra firme* forest.
**Range:** To 500m. Throughout e of Andes. Guianas and c and s Venez. s to ne Argentina and Uruguay.

[*Geotrygon:* Plumper and shorter-tailed than *Leptotila,* no white tail tips; forest floor; infrequently seen.]

## 26. SAPPHIRE QUAIL-DOVE
*Geotrygon saphirina*                        Pl. 9, Map 230
**Identification:** 8.5″ (22cm). Rather stubby with very short tail. *Crown and nape dark blue in sharp contrast to white forehead and cheeks;* cheeks bordered below by *conspic. bluish black malar line;* hindneck bronzy green becoming *iridescent purplish on back and shoulders;* rump violet blue; remiges dull brownish chestnut; *underparts white* with gray tinge on chest and cinnamon bronze patch on sides of neck; loral line and narrow eyering red; eyes yellow. ♀ duller with olive tinge on upperparts. Or slightly larger and crown pale gray (*saphirina;* see range and note).
**Similar species:** A beautiful and richly colored quail-dove and the only one with a combination of white forehead and underparts and blackish malar. Olive-backed Quail-Dove (29) in poor light has somewhat sim. head pattern but is much darker below. See also Violaceous Quail-Dove (28).
**Voice:** Call on Pacific slope (only Feb, upper Anchicayá Val.) a soft, hollow, dovelike *whot, whoo-oó-oit,* 1st note brief and almost inaudible; last short and rising; weak and repeated at short intervals.
**Behavior:** Usually seen singly but prob. often in separated 2's. Retiring and seems to be strictly terrestrial; walks quietly away from an observer but if frightened, flutters a short distance to ground again. Calls from ground.
**Status and habitat:** Uncommon (at least infrequently seen). Light-flecked floor of humid

and wet forest and advanced second growth. Mostly foothills and lower mts. on Pacific slope; also lowlands e of Andes (see range).
**Range:** To 900m (sightings to 1100m, Anchicayá Val.—Hilty). Pacific slope from extreme upper Atrato Val. (Bagadó, 5°25'N) southward *(purpurata)*; prob. e of Andes in Putumayo and Amazonas *(saphirina)*. W Colombia and nw Ecuador; e Ecuador (n to Limoncocha), e Peru, and extreme w Amazonian Brazil.
**Note:** Pacific slope birds, *purpurata*, may be a separate sp. from Amazonian *saphirina*.

## 27. RUDDY QUAIL-DOVE
*Geotrygon montana*          Pl. 8, Map 231
**Identification:** 9" (23cm). Bill, loral line, and eyering red; eyes reddish or yellowish. ♂: *upperparts and sides of head to below eyes rufous chestnut*; back slightly glossed purple; fairly prom. *narrow cinnamon cheek stripe bordered below by dark chestnut moustachial streak*; rest of underparts cinnamon with vinaceous wash on breast. ♀: duller and darker; *olive brown above*; forehead, sides of head and underparts dull cinnamon or buff with brownish olive tinge on breast and suggestion of darker moustachial streak. Imm.: like ♀ but with a few dark bars and spots on back and wings.
**Similar species:** Cheek stripe and overall ruddy color are ♂'s best marks. ♀ lacks strong facial pattern, and both lack contrasting rufous head and olive back of Russet-crowned Quail-Dove (30) found near Panama border.
**Voice:** A soft, resonant, and moaning *cooo* or *wooo*, repeated at about 3- to 5-sec intervals; sim. to but longer than call of Gray-chested Dove (Hilty); higher-pitched than call of White-throated Quail-Dove (Miller 1963); also cf. call of Lined Quail-Dove (31).
**Behavior:** A shy and unobtrusive forest dove. Chiefly terrestrial, though if surprised, may flush to a low branch. Often on forest floor beneath fruiting trees where it eats fallen seeds and fruit. Flies fast with abrupt, batlike swerving, usually low over ground.
**Breeding:** 9 BC birds, Jan–June, Norte de Santander to Chocó incl. BC ♂ on Mar nest with 2 eggs (Carriker). 2 BC ♂♂, May, Vaupés (Olivares 1964b). In Costa Rica and Panama, Apr–Aug; usual dove nest about 2.5m up in bush or top of stump; 2 buff or cream eggs (Skutch 1949; Willis and Eisenmann 1979).
**Status and habitat:** Locally fairly common on floor of humid forest, second growth, and esp. lighter open or thinned woodland such as coffee plantations. Numerous in humid portions of Santa Marta Mts. up to about 1700m (T. B. Johnson).

**Range:** To 2600m (Sabana de Bogotá). Prob. throughout w of Andes in fairly humid regions. Santa Marta and Perijá mts.; Pacific slope s to Nuquí (Chocó), upper Dagua Val. (at least formerly), and sw Cauca (Guapí); e along humid n base of W and C Andes, upper Cauca Val., and mid. and upper Magdalena Val. (nw Santander; Sabana de Bogotá; San Agustín, Huila); e of Andes in Norte de Santander and from Meta and Guainía (Venez. side of Río Negro) southward. W and s Mexico s to ne Argentina and s Brazil. Greater and Lesser Antilles. Trinidad.

## 28. VIOLACEOUS QUAIL-DOVE
*Geotrygon violacea*          Pl. 8, Map 232
**Identification:** 9.5" (24cm). Bill, loral line, and eyering red; eyes yellow. *Forecrown white* becoming gray on midcrown and *rich reddish chestnut heavily glossed metallic violet on hindcrown, hindneck, and back*; sides of head and underparts grayish white; throat and abdomen white; foreneck and breast washed pinkish vinaceous. ♀ duller with olive brown wings and grayer breast.
**Similar species:** *Only Colombian quail-dove with no moustachial stripe.* ♀ resembles ♀ Ruddy Quail-Dove (27) but is predom. grayish (not cinnamon buff) below, and belly white. See Gray-fronted Dove (25); all *Leptotila* (20-25) have white tail tips.
**Voice:** In Panama a short hollow *coooo*, about 18 per min from 3-15m up; higher in pitch than calls of Ruddy Quail-Dove or Gray-chested Dove (Willis and Eisenmann 1979).
**Behavior:** Walks on ground and eats small fallen fruits, as do other *Geotrygon*. Flight silent unlike that of *Leptotila*.
**Breeding:** 4 BC birds, Mar–June and juv. in July, Perijá Mts. and ne Antioquia (Carriker); barred juv., 25 Sept, Santa Marta (Todd and Carriker 1922). Panama stick nest 2-3m up, July; 2 buff eggs (Willis and Eisenmann 1979).
**Status and habitat:** Rare or very uncommon and local on floor or in undergrowth of humid forest, (esp. younger forest on Barro Colorado Isl., Panama). Doubtless more widespread than the few known localities.
**Range:** To 1650m. N slope of Santa Marta Mts. (to 450m), Perijá Mts. (Carraipía, Hiroca, to 1650m), n end C Andes in upper Río Nechí (280m), and Snía. San Lucas (800m); e of Andes in Macarena Mts. (Pico Renjifo, 1600m). Known from several localities in e Darién, Panama, and likely in adj. nw Colombia. Locally from Nicaragua to e Venez.; Surinam (once); e and se Brazil to Bolivia, n Argentina, and Paraguay.

## 29. OLIVE-BACKED QUAIL-DOVE

*Geotrygon veraguensis*          Pl. 9, Map 233
**Identification:** 9.5″ (24cm). Bare eyering and loral line red; eyes yellow. *Forehead and long broad stripe below eyes white*; otherwise all dark olive brown above glossed purplish on nape and dull green on back; below brownish gray, throat paler; flanks tinged cinnamon-buff; and center of belly white. ♀ even darker and with buffy forehead.
**Similar species:** An all dark quail-dove easily recognized by prom. white forehead and facial stripe, esp. conspic. when head moves in shady forest undergrowth. In flight all dark with cinnamon underwing coverts. In poor light, head pattern resembles that of Sapphire Quail-Dove (see 26).
**Voice:** A low-pitched, mournful *woOOOu*, lasting about a sec and a half and repeated at about 5-sec intervals; recalls that of Ruddy Quail-Dove.
**Behavior:** Terrestrial and sometimes less wary than other quail-doves. Prefers to walk away quietly rather than flush. Slight wing-rattle in flight (Wetmore 1968a). Alone or in separated pairs.
**Breeding:** 7 BC birds, Jan–Apr, ne Antioquia to Chocó (Carriker). A July Canal Zone nest, a flimsy platform about 1.8m up in forest near stream (R. Ridgely; J. Karr).
**Status and habitat:** Uncommon and local in very humid and wet forest and tall second growth. Apparently most numerous in wet ravines in hilly lowlands and lower foothills.
**Range:** To 900m. Pacific coast (missing from less humid forest around Gulf of Urabá) and e around n base of W Andes to lower Cauca Val. (Pto. Valdivia), and n end C Andes (Río Nechí). Costa Rica to nw Ecuador.

## 30. RUSSETT-CROWNED QUAIL-DOVE

*Geotrygon goldmani*          Pl. 9, Map 234
**Identification:** 11″ (28cm). Eyes orange. *Crown and nape rufous chestnut*; rest of upperparts dull brown glossed purple on back; *forehead and broad facial stripe cinnamon buff, the latter bordered below by a narrow black moustachial stripe; throat white*, becoming gray on foreneck and breast; belly buffy white; lower abdomen and flanks brownish.
**Similar species:** Good marks are contrasting crown, cinnamon forehead and facial stripe, and white throat. Likely to overlap in range only with Ruddy Quail-Dove (27) or very different Olive-backed Quail-Dove (29). Also see smaller Violaceous Quail-Dove (28).
**Voice:** In Panama call reported to be a soft hollow cooing sound like that made by blowing across the top of a bottle (Wetmore 1968a).

**Breeding:** A juv., 13 Oct, Río Juradó, Chocó (Meyer de Schauensee 1950).
**Status and habitat:** Few Colombian specimens. Floor and undergrowth of humid forest. In Panama mainly 900-1600m; perhaps also mostly foothills and lower slopes in Colombia (but see range).
**Range:** 100-1600m. Extreme nw Colombia (headwaters of Río Cutí, Cerro Tacarcuna; once in lowlands on Río Juradó, 100m). E Panama.
**Note:** Poss. a race of the *G. linearis* (Lined Quail-Dove) complex (Eisenmann).

## 31. LINED QUAIL-DOVE

*Geotrygon linearis*          Pl. 8, Map 235
**Identification:** 11.5″ (29cm). Large. Loral line and eyering red. *Forecrown* (or whole crown—*infusca*) *cinnamon*; otherwise rich brown above with purplish gloss on upper back; *conspic. gray band from nape extending forward to eye*, sometimes with white spot visible on sides of nape; feathers of sides of neck and extreme upper back scaled black; *throat white bordered by a very long narrow black moustachial streak*; sides of head and underparts pale buff with vinaceous wash on breast that deepens to tawny rufous on abdomen.
**Similar species:** Known range overlaps 2 other *Geotrygon*: the smaller Ruddy Quail-Dove (27) which lacks the striking multihued head pattern; and smaller Olive-backed Quail-Dove (29), which is almost all dark with white foreface (Lined and Olive-backed both recorded at Pto. Valdivia in lower Cauca Val.) Could meet White-throated Quail-Dove (32) in Cauca Val. s of Medellín (at least before deforestation). White-throated differs chiefly in more extensive white throat (to foreneck) and slaty gray crown.
**Voice:** Call a deep, hollow, pigeonlike *ooouk!* at 15- to 20-sec intervals from forest midlevels or higher; recalls low groan of Band-tailed Pigeon. During breeding season quite vocal, often at intervals throughout day.
**Behavior:** Much like other quail-doves, though perhaps more arboreal, esp. when calling.
**Breeding:** 7 BC birds, Apr–Oct, Santa Marta and Perijá mts. and C Andes in Antioquia (Carriker); rather deep twig cup about 4-6m up; 2 eggs, rich cream (ffrench 1973).
**Status and habitat:** Fairly common in humid forest and tall second growth from 1500-2400m on n slope Santa Marta Mts. (T. B. Johnson) and replaced in more open woodland at lower el. in same region by Ruddy Quail-Dove. Apparently rather thinly spread (or local?) elsewhere.

**Range:** 300-2500m. Santa Marta Mts. (*infusca*); Perijá Mts., C Andes s to Medellín on w slope and n boundary of Caldas on e slope; w slope of E Andes in Cundinamarca (1500-2100m) and e slope of E Andes from Norte de Santander s to w Meta (above Villavicencio), Macarena Mts., and Caquetá (*linearis*). N Colombia to n Venez. Trinidad.

**Note:** Some also incl. in this spp. group *G. albifacies* (White-faced Quail-Dove) of Mexico to Nicaragua and *G. chiriquensis* (Rufous-breasted Quail-Dove) of Costa Rica and w Panama.

## 32. WHITE-THROATED QUAIL-DOVE

*Geotrygon frenata*                    Pl. 9, Map 236

**Identification:** 13″ (33cm). Large. Eyes orange. Forehead and sides of head dull buff bordered below by a *long narrow black moustachial line; crown slaty gray*; otherwise dark ruddy brown above; upper back strongly glossed purple and with a few narrow black scallops on sides of neck; *throat and foreneck white*; breast brownish gray becoming sandy brown on lower underparts; center of abdomen whitish.

**Similar species:** A very large dark quail-dove with conspic. white throat. On Pacific slope see Sapphire and Olive-backed quail-doves (26, 29), elsewhere Ruddy Quail-Dove (27); all are smaller and lack contrasting white throat.

**Voice:** Call a sustained *woo*, at well-spaced intervals from mid. story or higher. In W Andes above Cali heard mainly during wet mos., seldom July–Sept (Miller 1963).

**Behavior:** Semiterrestrial. Feeds mostly on ground; flushes readily to low branches where nervously flicks tail up to line of body and spreads it, then often drops to ground and walks away quietly. If disturbed when calling, sits quietly, hidden in foliage, or glides silently down to ground. Usually found singly.

**Breeding:** BC ♂ and juv., 23 Aug, Munchique (Carriker). Jan–July in W Andes; 1 nest, 22 Mar, 2m up in thick tangle; flat platform; 1 pale buff egg (Miller 1963).

**Status and habitat:** Uncommon in humid and wet forest ("cloud forest") and tall second growth.

**Range:** Mainly 1500-2500m (sightings to 900m, Anchicayá Val.—Hilty). Pacific slope from headwaters of Río San Juan (below Cerro Tatamá) southward; locally on e slope of W Andes (above Cali), both slopes of C Andes from Quindío area southward, head of Magdalena Val. (w of San Agustín) and both slopes of Nariño. Andes of Colombia s to nw Argentina.

# PARROTS: Psittacidae (51)

Parrots are an anatomically homogeneous group of birds found in greatest abundance in tropical regions and in temperate Australia. Noisy, social, and with heavy hooked bills and yoke-toed feet, they need little introduction. Most Colombian species are predominantly green but range in size from the tiny sparrow-sized *Forpus* parrotlets to the garishly colored, king-sized macaws. They are most numerous in humid lowlands but can be found in every habitat from sea level to the cold, treeless paramo. They feed on a variety of seeds, fruits, and blossoms. Nests are usually in tree holes, woodpecker holes, or in cavities dug in arboreal termite nests. A few highland species (especially *Bolborhynchus* and some *Aratinga*) nest, or are presumed to nest, in burrows or crevices in high rocky cliffs. The larger *Amazona* and macaws usually mate for life, and pairs often fly together within larger flocks. The stirring sight and sound of these great birds commuting long distances mornings and evenings to favorite feeding and roosting sites is, unfortunately, rapidly being lost to mankind in many parts of Colombia as the destruction of rain forest continues at an accelerating pace.

[*Ara*: Large size, long pointed tail, bare cheeks and facial area; plumage often gaudy.]

## 1. BLUE-AND-YELLOW MACAW

*Ara ararauna*                    Pl. 11, Map 237

**Identification:** 33″ (84cm). Unmistakable. Very long pointed tail; black bill. *Bright cerulean blue above and orange yellow below*, incl. under wings and under tail; forehead green; upper throat black; bare sides of head white with narrow lines of black feathers.

**Voice:** In flight a loud, raucous *raak*, weaker and more nasal than calls of Scarlet and Red-and-green macaws.

**Behavior:** Fly in pairs or 3's, these also maintained in larger flocks that may reach 30 or more in Amazonia. Often commute long distances each morning and evening between roosting and feeding locations, at which time usually noted by call long before they appear in view. Feed quietly, high in canopy. Flight is strong, steady, and leisurely, with long tail streaming behind.

**Breeding:** BC pair, 8 Dec, Magdalena; BC ♂,

14 Feb, Córdoba (Carriker). Cavity nest in large dead palm trunk; 2 eggs (Forshaw 1973).

**Status and habitat:** Fairly common in gallery woodland and humid lowland forest, well away from human activity but almost always near water; doubtless now less numerous w of Andes but many seen w and s of Fundación, Magdalena, Feb 1976 (R. Ridgely). Move seasonally in search of food, sometimes into partially open country.

**Range:** to 500m. Pacific coast from se Panama border (Río Juradó) e across lower Atrato Val. and n of Andes to s Atlántico, w base of Santa Marta Mts. (Aracataca), w base of Perijá Mts. (to 11°N), and s to Nechí drainage and mid. Magdalena Val. (Pto. Berrío); e of Andes from w Caquetá and ne Guainía (sighting Pto. Inírida, Sept 1978—Hilty and M. Robbins) southward. E Panama to n Bolivia, Paraguay, and se Brazil.

## 2. MILITARY MACAW

*Ara militaris*                            Pl. 11, Map 238

**Identification:** 28″ (71cm). Bill blackish; very long pointed tail. *Largely green with red forehead* and blue on lower back and rump; flight feathers edged deep blue, long pointed tail brownish red tipped blue; bare skin of face whitish with narrow lines of black feathers. In flight from below *wings and tail olive yellow.*

**Similiar species:** See very similar Great Green Macaw (3). In poor light yellowish under wing and under tail surfaces much like those of Blue-and-yellow Macaw (1).

**Voice:** A raucous, drawn out *kraaak.*

**Behavior:** Sim. to other large *Ara.* In some regions quite seasonal and has been noted crossing high mt. passes.

**Breeding:** In w Mexico 1 nest reportedly in abandoned Imperial Woodpecker(?) cavity; 2 eggs (Forshaw 1973); may also nest in limestone cliff cavities.

**Status and habitat:** Local. Favors drier deciduous forest, open woodland, and riparian woodland; at least seasonally into humid and wet forest. Fairly common on n slope Santa Marta Mts.; sporadic elsewhere and movements not well known. Seen with some frequency May–early Aug in PN Cueva de los Guácharos where reg. cross E Andes from Huila to w Caquetá (P. Gertler).

**Range:** *Disjunct.* Locally to 2000m or more. N and w base of Santa Marta Mts., Perijá Mts. s on w slope E Andes to Bucaramanga, e slope C Andes, n Antioquia (Remedios), poss. in n base of C Andes to lower Cauca Val.; mid. Cauca Val. (formerly Medellín area) w to w base of W Andes (near Río San Juan headwaters) and s sporadically to Dagua Val. (also sighting presum. this sp., Anchicayá Val., Aug 1975—Hilty); e slope of upper Magdalena Val. (PN Cueva de los Guácharos) e to e base of E Andes from Macarena Mts. to w Putumayo (Pto. Asís—Lehmann 1960a). Locally from w Mexico to Bolivia and nw Argentina.

## 3. GREAT GREEN MACAW

*Ara ambigua*                            Ill. 57, Map 239

**Identification:** 35″ (89cm). *Much like Military Macaw,* differing as follows: *larger size;* general plumage *distinctly paler more yellowish green, esp. on upper wing coverts* (not green); lighter blue lower back and rump; more orange (not brownish red) on basal part of central tail feathers; and bill larger (exposed culmen 65-81mm vs 53-59mm). Best told by range, as

57. Great Green Macaw

they are not known to overlap (potential contact closest in lower Cauca Val.). Bare facial skin can flush to deep pink (R. Ridgely).
**Voice:** Raucous cries; a loud groaning *aa*———*aa* (Slud 1964).
**Behavior:** Much less gregarious than other macaws and usually in pairs or groups up to 4, seldom to 8-10, and not with other large macaws (R. Ridgely).
**Breeding:** Little known. In Costa Rica 1 ♀ with formed egg, Feb (Carriker 1910).
**Status and habitat:** Humid lowland forest and intervening tracts of semiopen country. Favors wetter forest than Military Macaw (Haffer 1975).
**Range:** To 600m (perhaps higher). W of W Andes from Panama border s on Pacific coast to Baudó Mts. (Río Nuquí) and Mutatá, and e to northernmost end of W Andes in upper Sinú Val. (Quimarí and Murrucucú), sw Córdoba. Nicaragua and Costa Rica; nw Colombia and w Ecuador.

## 4. SCARLET MACAW

*Ara macao* Pl. 11, Map 240
**Identification:** 35″ (89cm). Very long pointed tail. Bill whitish above, black below. *Mainly scarlet with yellow median upper wing coverts* (conspic. when perched or in flight from above); flight feathers, rump, and short outer tail feathers blue; bare white skin on sides of head without markings.
**Similar species:** Red-and-green Macaw (5) is even larger, has *green* (not yellow) *upper wing coverts*, deeper, more scarlet (less red) plumage, and up close shows red-feathered lines on bare face.
**Voice:** Flight call a very loud *raaaaah*, harsher and more drawn out than that of Blue-and-yellow Macaw (J. V. Remsen); the coarsest and most grating call of the 3 large Amazonian *Ara* in Colombia.
**Behavior:** Notably gregarious and may flock with other large macaws; otherwise typical of the genus. May roost communally.
**Breeding:** Costa Rica nests, Jan–Apr (R. Ridgely; Hilty); 1 in Nicaragua in Apr (Forshaw 1973); tree cavities 10-25m up.
**Status and habitat:** Gallery forest, river banks, forest openings, and partially cleared lowland forest where there are big trees; also widely in unbroken forest in Amazonia (R. Ridgely). Fairly common e of Andes and persists even near settlements where unmolested. Like most *Ara*, moves seasonally in search of fruit.
**Range:** To 500 m. N lowlands from Cartagena (formerly) e to lower Magdalena Val. (s of Barranquilla); s to se Córdoba and mid. Magdalena Val. sw of Bucaramanga near Chucurí

(7°09′N), Santander; e of Andes from w Meta (formerly near Villavicencio) and Vaupés southward (throughout?). Se Mexico to n Bolivia and Amazonian Brazil.

## 5. RED-AND-GREEN MACAW

*Ara chloroptera* Pl. 11, Map 241
**Identification:** 37″ (94cm). Much like Scarlet Macaw. Bill whitish above, blackish below, proportionally larger than that of Scarlet. *Mainly deep scarlet with green median upper wing coverts* (fairly conspic. when perched and in flight from above); flight feathers, rump, and most of short outer tail feathers blue; bare skin on sides of head white *with narrow lines of red feathers.*
**Similar species:** See Scarlet Macaw (4), which has yellow upper wing coverts.
**Voice:** Flight calls like those of Scarlet Macaw but slightly less raucous and not as hoarse.
**Behavior:** Like other large *Ara.*
**Status and habitat:** Humid lowland forest, gallery forest, savanna with scattered trees, other partially cleared terrain. Still occurs along ne base of Santa Marta Mts., esp. Río Don Diego area, and w and s of Fundación, as well as throughout less settled portions of the llanos and Orinoco region. Local in Amazonia.
**Range:** To 500m. Pacific coast s to Baudó Mts., e in humid regions n of Andes through upper Sinú and lower Cauca vals. (Pto. Valdivia); Santa Marta region, locally in Guajira and nw base of Perijá Mts. (Montes de Oca); throughout e of Andes from Norte de Santander southward. E Panama to n Argentina, Paraguay, and s Brazil.

## 6. CHESTNUT-FRONTED MACAW

*Ara severa* Pl. 11, Map 242
**Identification:** 18″ (46cm). Half the size of large *Ara.* Long pointed tail; bill grayish black. *Plumage mostly green;* crown tinged blue with narrow inconspic. chestnut forehead; bare face whitish; flight feathers bluish above; *underside of wings and tail dull red.*
**Similar species:** Superficially like Red-bellied Macaw (7), but under wings dull reddish (not dull greenish yellow), wing beats slower, flight calls very different; up close bare face is white (not pale yellow) but often *looks yellowish* in low sun.
**Voice:** When perched a liquid or gurgling *kurrit;* in flight a harsher, scratchy *jaiii* or *kwaaa,* macawlike but faster (more conversational), shriller, and without the deep gruffiness of the larger spp.
**Behavior:** Usually in small groups of up to 10-12 birds, sometimes roosting in much larger nos. Active mornings and evenings, also more

often in flight during midday than larger macaws (R. Ridgely).

**Breeding:** 2 BC birds, Mar–May, s Bolívar, s Córdoba (Carriker), BC ♀, 26 Feb, Panama (Wetmore 1968a); nest in cavity, often dead palm, sometimes over water (Haverschmidt 1968; McLoughlin and Burton 1970).

**Status and habitat:** Humid lowlands along forest edges, clearings, and rivers, or flying over unbroken forest; also *várzea* and swampy regions. Enters llanos along gallery forest and in morichales.

**Range:** To 1000m (mostly lowlands). Pacific coast s to Baudó Mts. (Río Baudó), e through upper Río Sinú, formerly throughout Cauca Val. (now only along n base of Andes) and mid. Magdalena Val. s to Antioquia (Pto. Berrío); e of Andes from Norte de Santander southward. E Panama to w Ecuador, n Bolivia, and se Brazil (Bahía).

### 7. RED-BELLIED MACAW
*Ara manilata*                    Pl. 11, Map 243

**Identification:** 20″ (51cm). Long pointed tail; bill black. Mostly green; crown and remiges bluish; *bare face pale yellow; underside of wings and tail dull yellowish*; center of abdomen dull red (difficult to see either perched or in flight).

**Similar species:** See Chestnut-fronted Macaw (6). Best marks are the large bare face (cf. with *Aratinga* parakeets) and dull yellowish under wings.

**Voice:** An unmacawlike, plaintive wailing *choiiiaaa* in flight (J. V. Remsen).

**Behavior:** Less typically macawlike than 6. In flight resembles a large *Aratinga* with its faster wing beats and less steady flight. Shows a strong preference for palm fruits, esp. *Mauritia*, and when approached may cling to underside of palm fronds rather than fly.

**Breeding:** Feb–May or June in Guyana; cavity in dead palm, often over water (McLoughlin and Burton 1970); 2 eggs (Herklots 1961).

**Status and habitat:** Uncommon and local. Favors mixed savanna and forest, savanna with scattered palms (esp. *Mauritia*), and palm swamps in extensively forested areas. Occas. flocks seen in flight mid-June–mid-Nov near Leticia (J. V. Remsen).

**Range:** To 500m. E of Andes from Meta and w Vaupés (San José del Guaviare) s to Putumayo and Amazonas (prob. to e Vichada). Generally e of Andes s to n Bolivia and Amazonian Brazil.

[*Aratinga*: Large parakeets; long pointed greenish tails. Look like miniature *Ara*, but cheeks feathered.]

### 8. BLUE-CROWNED PARAKEET
*Aratinga acuticauda*             Pl. 10, Map 244

**Identification:** 15″ (38cm). Bill pale pinkish above, pale gray below. Orange yellow eyes surrounded by *conspic. bare ocular ring. Forecrown blue; otherwise mainly green*; underside of tail yellowish olive; outer feathers dull reddish near base.

**Similar species:** Note *large size*. Brown-throated Parakeet (12) is smaller and mostly brownish olive below. White-eyed Parakeet (10), wandering to llanos, lacks blue forecrown and flashes conspic. red and yellow under wing coverts in flight.

**Voice:** A loud, rapidly repeated *cheeeah*, unlike harsh grating calls of Brown-throated Parakeet, which is often in same habitat (Friedmann and Smith 1950).

**Behavior:** Pairs or scattered flocks, ocas. to 200 birds. Fond of ripe mangos.

**Breeding:** Believed to be mainly Mar–July near Cantaura, Venez.; flocks during remainder of yr. (Friedmann and Smith 1950). Cavity nester high in trees.

**Status and habitat:** Fairly common in arid scrub and dry woodland in Guajira; near Carimagua, ne Meta; common Mar–July (absent rest of yr.) in gallery woodland (S. Furniss). Reported in nos., mid-Mar, n Vichada at Caño Hato Tigre (Olivares 1974b) and late Sept e of Villavicencio (Nicéforo and Olivares 1966).

**Range:** To 400m. Guajira w to e base of Santa Marta Mts.; e of Andes from Arauca, Arauca (sightings, 1978—W. McKay and J. Jorgenson) s to w Meta (Quenane e of Villavicencio) and e to Carimagua, ne Meta (sighting—S. Furniss), and n Vichada (Hato Caño Tigre). N and e Colombia; w and c Venez.; e and s Brazil to Bolivia and c Argentina.

### 9. SCARLET-FRONTED PARAKEET
*Aratinga wagleri*                Pl. 10, Map 245

**Identification:** 14″ (36cm). Long pointed tail. Bill horn gray; large bare whitish ocular ring. *Plumage green with red forecrown* and a few red spots on sides of neck; *underside of wings and tail yellow olive*.

**Similar species:** Only *Aratinga* w of E Andes with a red forecrown (not conspic. at a distance) and no red on wings. Noisy flocks of rather large, long-tailed parakeets in highlands are likely to be this sp.

**Voice:** Loud, strident *steak!*, singly or in longer ser., irritating with repetition.

**Behavior:** Noisy, gregarious, and almost always in flocks; also roosts in flocks. Groups of up to 300 or more (F. C. Lehmann) infrequently seen today. Eat a var. of fruits and seeds and are occas. destructive to cornfields.

**Breeding:** 11 BC birds, late Dec–early June, Santa Marta and Perijá mts. and Valle (Carriker). Nest colonially in rock cliffs; cavities 6-8m up on cliff in upper Patía Val. were reportedly occupied prior to 10 Apr (Brown); other known sites are above Río Vinagre near Puracé, Cauca, and near Pereira, Risaralda (Lehmann 1960a).

**Status and habitat:** Still fairly common locally in forested or partially forested moist to humid regions in Andes and inter-Andean vals. Formerly more widespread in foothills and lower els. but still occas. wander to mostly deforested floor of Cauca Val.

**Range:** 350-2800m (mainly 900-2500m). Santa Marta and Perijá mts., W and C Andes, and w slope E Andes; once on e slope E Andes in w Caquetá (near Florencia). N Venez. s in mts. to e and w Peru.

### 10. WHITE-EYED PARAKEET

*Aratinga leucophthalmus* Pls. 10, 11, Map 246

**Identification:** 14″ (36cm). Long pointed tail. Orange eyes surrounded by large bare whitish ocular ring (the "white eye"). Mostly green with *bright red lesser under wing coverts bordered behind by bright yellow greater coverts* (flashes conspic. red and yellow in flight); underside of flight feathers and tail dull yellowish olive; neck sometimes with a few red spots. Or with red frontal band (*nicefori*).

**Similar species:** From other *Aratinga* by red and yellow under wing coverts. The name is misleading, as most other Colombian *Aratinga* also have bare whitish ocular rings and appear "white-eyed."

**Voice:** Flight call a loud, grating *geeait* or *jeeee-it* (sometimes given in long ser.), much coarser and raspier than corresponding call of Dusky-headed Parakeet.

**Behavior:** Commonly in flocks of 5-30 feeding in treetops along rivers or at forest edges, also high over forest or partially open country in long distance flight. Flight is swift and rather direct at treetop level or slightly above. Often feed on *Erythrina* blossoms along smaller *várzea* tributaries near Leticia.

**Status and habitat:** Fairly common in *terra firme* and *várzea* borders, esp. along rivers, and in gallery forest and morichales (*Mauritia* palms) in llanos. Local or absent from black water regions of extreme east.

**Range:** To 500m. E of Andes from n Meta s to Putumayo and Amazonas, not Vichada to Vaupés (*callogenys*); from Guaicaramo, Río Guavio on Meta-Casanare border (*nicefori*). The Guianas and e Venez. to n Argentina and Uruguay.

**Note:** Some incl. *A. finschi* (Crimson-fronted

Parakeet) of Nicaragua to w Panama with present sp., treating *A. l. nicefori* (known from 1 specimen) as intermed.

### 11. DUSKY-HEADED PARAKEET

*Aratinga weddellii* Pl. 10, Map 247

**Identification:** 11″ (28cm). Long, pointed tail. Yellowish white eye surrounded by large bare whitish ocular ring. Mainly green, paler yellowish green below; *head dull brownish gray*; flight feathers and tail tip (from above) mostly dull blue; *under wing coverts green.*

**Similar species:** Nondescript; best told by dingy brownish gray head and *lack of conspic. color in wings*; cf. slightly larger White-eyed Parakeet (10), which has red and yellow under wing coverts.

**Voice:** Some flight calls sim. to White-eyed Parakeet but smoother, less grating, and more nasal, *je-eek*; not given in longer ser.

**Behavior:** Usually in small flocks, larger ones of 75-100 at good food sources, and along rivers may come to ground to salt-impregnated soil. Unlike White-eyed Parakeet rarely in flocks high over forest (R. Ridgely).

**Breeding:** Presumed incubating bird, 21 Feb, Pto. Asís, Putumayo; cavity 6m above water in palm stub (Brown); 4 pairs at cavities (dead trees and termitary), 4-13m up in swampy forest edge near Leticia, 9 June–13 Aug (J. V. Remsen; Hilty).

**Status and habitat:** Common in humid *várzea* forest, river edges, and tall swampy second growth. Fond of *Erythrina* blossoms.

**Range:** To 500m. E of Andes from w Caquetá (Belén) to Putumayo and Amazonas. Se Colombia to e Bolivia and Amazonian Brazil.

### 12. BROWN-THROATED PARAKEET

*Aratinga pertinax* Pl. 10, Map 248

**Identification:** 10″ (25cm). Eyes yellow; bill dusky. Green above, usually with bluish tinge on crown; *forehead, sides of head, and breast pale brown to grayish brown, fading to greenish yellow on lower underparts; under wing coverts greenish yellow*; underside of flight feathers dark grayish. Or with large yellowish feathered eyering (*lehmanni*).

**Similar species:** Small *Aratinga* green above, yellowish brown below with yellowish under wing coverts but otherwise *no color in wings*. Often in same habitat as Blue-crowned Parakeet (8).

**Voice:** High-pitched shrill screeching, uttered constantly in flight. When perched, *cheer-cheeedit*, 2d note abruptly terminated (Forshaw 1973).

**Behavior:** Perches in lower trees and scrub and flies fast and low in tight twisting flocks through scrubby semiopen country. Known locally as

"Perico Cara Sucia," or "dirty-faced parakeet."

**Breeding:** Feb–Apr in ne Meta (S. Furniss); pair digging termitary cavity, 3 Mar, w Meta (Brown); also Feb–Apr in ne Venez., usually in termitary 3-7m up; 3-4 eggs (Friedmann and Smith 1950).

**Status and habitat:** Most common parakeet in Carib. lowlands and llanos e Andes. Arid scrub, mangroves, gallery and semiopen savanna woodland, and ranchland. In Santa Marta area some seasonal movement to more humid areas during driest mos., Dec–May (Darlington 1931).

**Range:** To 1000m. Sinú Val. (*griseipecta*); e across Carib. lowlands to Guajira and s in mid. Magdalena Val. to Bucaramanga (Lebrija Val.) and Zulia N., Norte de Santander (*aeruginosa*); e of Andes from Casanare to s Meta, northernmost Vaupés (San José del Guaviare), the Orinoco (*lehmanni*), and ne Guainía (sightings, Pto. Inírida, 1978—Hilty and M. Robbins). Sw Panama to the Guianas and n Brazil.

### 13. GOLDEN-PLUMED PARAKEET
*Leptosittaca branickii*          Pl. 9, Map 249
**Identification:** 14″ (36cm). *Aratinga*-like. Eyes orange; bill pale horn; narrow bare bluish white eyering. Mostly green with *narrow orange frontlet; lores and tuft behind eyes yellow; broad indistinct band across lower breast yellow mixed reddish orange*; underside of long pointed tail dull reddish.

**Similar species:** In treeline habitat likely confused only with macaw-sized Yellow-eared Parrot (14), which has sides of head conspic. yellow (not just a narrow yellow tuft), and lacks the pale breast band.

**Behavior:** Not well known. Usually seen in smaller, chattering flocks.

**Status and habitat:** Rare, local, and doubtless declining. Upper temperate zone forest, elfin woodland, and treeline shrubbery. Occas. seen flying in canyons or over largely deforested nw end of PN Puracé. Recently seen above Santa Rosa de Cabal, Risaralda (J. Orejuela; M. Alberico).

**Range:** 1800-3500m. C Andes from Nevado del Ruiz (Caldas/Tolima) s to e Cauca (Coconuco) and se Nariño (Llorente); once in W Andes at Cerro Munchique. Colombia, s Ecuador, and c Peru.

**Note:** Prob. best incl. in the genus *Aratinga* (R. Ridgely).

### 14. YELLOW-EARED PARROT
*Ognorhynchus icterotis*          Pl. 9, Map 250
**Identification:** 17″ (43cm). Looks like a small macaw. Very thick blackish bill and long pointed tail; large bare ocular area dark grayish. Mostly green with a *broad band of yellow on forehead continuing across cheeks to form plumes on ear coverts and sides of head*; breast and belly lighter greenish yellow; underside of tail dull red.

**Similar species:** Large size and conspic. yellow on sides of head is distinctive. See Golden-plumed Parakeet (13).

**Voice:** Distinctive, nasal, bisyllabic call is gooselike; flock notes at distance resemble a musical, conversational babble.

**Behavior:** Little known. Flocks prob. wander seasonally in search of food. Once fairly common in Moscopán region of sw Huila during Dec–Apr visits; by July 1956 only a single bird observed (Lehmann 1957).

**Breeding:** 2 BC birds (♀ laying) early Mar, Moscopán Huila (Forshaw 1973); nesting colonies in May in holes more than 25m up in Wax Palms on Quindío Trail above Río Tochecito and Río Toche, n Tolima (Chapman 1917).

**Status and habitat:** Rare and endangered. Mt. forest and partially cleared terrain, esp. where there are Wax Palms (*Ceroxylon andiculum*). Only recent sightings known are as follows: flock of 25 on ne slope Cerro Munchique, 16 July 1978 (Hilty et al.); pair over Laguna San Rafael paramo, PN Puracé, 18 May 1976 (R. Ridgely and S. Gaulin); 1 small group, 1975, PN Cueva de los Guácharos (P. Gertler).

**Range:** Mostly 2000-3400m (occas. lower). Formerly widely scattered localities in all 3 Andean ranges but mostly C Andes. One very old rec. (1854) n to Ocaña (1200m), nw Norte de Santander; once in w Nariño at Ricaurte (1400m) in 1958; once to 1300m in upper Patía Val. Colombia and n Ecuador.

[*Pyrrhura*: Slender, med.-sized, fast-flying. *Long, tapering* (but blunt-ended) *maroon tail*. Outer primaries mainly blue above.]

### 15. PAINTED PARAKEET
*Pyrrhura picta*          Pl. 10, Map 251
**Identification:** 8.5″ (22cm). Bill brownish gray; bare ocular ring grayish (or feathered red eyering—*pantchenkoi*). Back, most of wings, and lower underparts green; crown dark brown; narrow frontlet, sides of head, *abdominal patch, rump, and tail maroon*; outer tail feathers green basally; narrow inconspic. nuchal collar blue; throat and chest dusky conspic. scaled buffy white; patch on ear coverts yellowish brown. In flight *point of shoulders red*; under wing coverts green; primaries dusky below; blue above. Or with blue-tinged crown and grayish white patch on ear coverts (*caeruleiceps*).

**Similar species:** In Amazonas easily confused with Maroon-tailed Parakeet (17), which dif-

fers in having red under wing coverts (not just bend of wing), green rump, and all green belly. In E Andes see Flame-winged Parakeet (18). All 3 spp. have scaly breasts.
**Voice:** Flight screams a descending *EE-ee-m* and a single *eek* (Snyder 1966); both calls harsh and forceful.
**Behavior:** As in Santa Marta Parakeet.
**Breeding:** 5 BC birds, Mar–June, Norte de Santander and s Córdoba (Carriker).
**Status and habitat:** Humid forest and forest borders. Specimens w of Andes are mainly from foothills and lower slopes. Not well known in Colombia.
**Range:** 100-1300m, Perijá Mts. (2000m) on Venez. boundary (*pantchenkoi*); e of Casacarás at base of Perijá Mts., base of E Andes near Aguachica, s Cesar (*caeruleiceps*); Sinú Val. from Montería s to Quimarí and Murrucucú in Córdoba (*subandina*); poss. the intervening lowlands in lower Cauca and mid. Magdalena vals.; poss. se Colombia in Amazonas (*luciani* subsp. rec. in nw Brazil and e Peru). Panama (Azuero Pen.), Guianas, w and s Venez., se Ecuador, e Peru, Amazonian Brazil, and n Bolivia.

### 16. SANTA MARTA PARAKEET
*Pyrrhura viridicata*　　　　Pl. 10, Map 252
**Identification:** 10″ (25cm). Bill and bare ocular area grayish. Mostly green *flecked and marked red, yellow, and orange on upper and under wing coverts* and on belly; narrow frontlet red; ear coverts and hindneck brownish. In flight primaries blue and underside of tail dull reddish (green above).
**Similar species:** In restricted range likely confused only with Scarlet-fronted Parakeet (9), which is larger, mostly green (no blue in primaries), lacks the red and orange flash on wing coverts, and has different flight habits.
**Voice:** Screeching calls sim. to Painted Parakeet and other *Pyrrhura*.
**Behavior:** Like most *Pyrrhura*, fly fast in tight twisting groups, often through trees, and constantly utter screechy calls; alight suddenly within tree crown, then typically, pause a few moments before clambering slowly along limbs and uttering soft notes. Flush noisily but sometimes return.
**Breeding:** 4 BC birds and juv., Sept, San Lorenzo (Carriker); pair at cavity 6m up in stub, June (Hilty).
**Status and habitat:** Fairly common in cooler humid mt. forest and forest borders or in flight across intervening clearings. Readily found near San Lorenzo on n slope Santa Marta Mts.
**Range:** ENDEMIC. 2000-2500m (prob. higher). Santa Marta Mts.

### 17. MAROON-TAILED PARAKEET
*Pyrrhura melanura*　　　　Pl. 10, Map 253
**Identification:** 10″ (25cm). Bill grayish; bare ocular area whitish (narrower and grayish—*pacifica*). Mostly green with brown crown; *dusky chest narrowly scaled buffy white* (or *broadly scaled buffy white incl. throat and hindneck—chapmani*); *bend of wing and greater primary coverts bright red*; tail maroon; outer feathers green basally.
**Similar species:** See Painted and Flame-winged parakeets (15, 18). Larger Scarlet-fronted Parakeet (9) is all green with red forecrown.
**Voice:** Loud raucous shrieking (like Painted Parakeet) in flight or as bird flushes.
**Behavior:** Much like Santa Marta Parakeet. Roost communally; do not assoc. with other parakeets; usually in treetops but come low to fruit trees.
**Breeding:** Copulation, Macarena Mts., 25 Jan (Lemke 1977). Nesting, Apr–June, Napo headwaters, Ecuador (Goodfellow 1901); 4 eggs, in captivity (Forshaw 1973).
**Status and habitat:** Found in a wide var. of forested zones from humid lowlands (incl. sandy-belt forest) to wet mt. forest, "cloud forest," forest borders and partially cleared regions. Often fairly common, but distribution patchy; some seasonal movement poss.
**Range:** To 300m (sight to 1400m, Junín, Sept 1979—Hilty) on Pacific slope of Nariño (*pacifica*); upper Magdalena Val. (1600-2800m) from s Tolima to head of val. in Huila (*chapmani*); e of Andes (to 500m) from Macarena Mts. s to Putumayo (*souancei*); Vaupés (San José de Guaviare) to extreme se Guainía (Macacuní) and Amazonas (*melanura*). Colombia and s Venez. to ne Peru and w Amazonian Brazil.

### 18. FLAME-WINGED PARAKEET
*Pyrrhura calliptera*　　　　Pl. 10, Map 254
**Identification:** 9″ (23cm). Bill pale yellowish; narrow bare ocular area whitish. Mostly green with dusky brown crown; throat and breast dark brown indistinctly scaled warm buff; ear coverts, patch on abdomen, and tail maroon; *bend of wing and upper and under wing coverts yellow* often mixed with orange (conspic. in flight).
**Similar species:** Easily recognized in limited range by flashing yellow in wing.
**Voice:** Harsh, far-carrying *screeyr screeyr*, like others of genus (R. Ridgely).
**Behavior:** Usually in small fast-flying bands of 6-14 that act like others of the genus (R. Ridgely; W McKay).
**Breeding:** 5 BC birds, Oct, Lago de Tota, Boyacá (Olivares 1971).
**Status and habitat:** Local. Forest edges and

treeline shrubbery. Habitat within known range much fragmented, but still in nos. where woodland remains; at least 40 seen and heard, 14 Feb 1977, from 2000-3000m in upper Río Cusiana Val., e Boyacá (R. Ridgely); small nos. daily in bushes and ravines or over paramo 3200-3400m, PN Chingaza, Sept–Nov 1979 (W. McKay). **Range:** ENDEMIC. 1700-3400m. Both slopes of E Andes from s Boyacá (Lago de Tota; Ramiriquí s of Tunja) s to sw Cundinamarca (Fusagasugá).

[*Bolborhynchus*: Small; short wedge-shaped tail and blunt bill; highlands.]

## 19. BARRED PARAKEET
*Bolborhynchus lineola*          Pl. 10, Map 255
**Identification:** 7″ (18cm). *Small green parakeet with entire upperparts, sides, and flanks barred black; bend of wing black; tip of short pointed tail black;* bill and legs pale. In flight small size and short pointed tail are best marks (barring very hard to see).
**Similar species:** Sim.-sized *Touit* parrotlets (29-32) have short square tails and different behavior; smaller *Forpus* parrotlets are unbarred, differ in behavior, and are usually found at lower el.
**Voice:** High-pitched musical chattering uttered constantly in flight.
**Behavior:** Feed in treetops in forest or forest edge where quiet, sluggish, and very difficult to see. Most often seen in high flying flocks of up to 150 or more, traveling long distances over forest or partially wooded terrain. Flight very fast, direct, and buzzy.
**Breeding:** BC ♂, 16 Aug, Munchique (Carriker). Others of the genus in Argentina and Chile nest in colonies in burrows excavated in banks or crevices in rocky cliffs (Olrog 1968; Johnson 1965).
**Status and habitat:** Rare and unpredictable in highland forested zones; perhaps somewhat affiliated with bamboo when seeding (R. Ridgely). Most records in W Andes of Valle are May–Aug (Lehmann 1957; Miller 1963; Hilty); perhaps more numerous in Santa Marta Mts. than elsewhere.
**Range:** 1600-2600m (once to 1100m on Pacific slope in Valle, sight 1973—Hilty). Spottily in all 3 Andean ranges: E Andes in Norte de Santander and e Huila (sight, 1978—Hilty); C Andes in s Antioquia and in Caldas; w Andes in Valle and Cauca; Santa Marta Mts. (sightings, n slope below San Lorenzo, 1500-2000m—many observers). S Mexico locally to c Peru.

## 20. RUFOUS-FRONTED PARAKEET
*Bolborhynchus ferrugineifrons*    Pl. 10, Map 256
**Identification:** 8″ (20cm). Dusky bill rather thick and swollen. *Dull green,* lighter on upper tail coverts and tinged olive yellow on throat and chest; *narrow rufous band on forehead and around base of bill;* primaries, underside of wings, and short wedge-shaped tail bluish green.
**Similar species:** Note known range. Barred Parakeet (19) is smaller and barred above and has paler bill.
**Breeding:** BC ♂, mid-Jan (Forshaw 1973). Reported nesting in cliff cavities, Nevado del Ruiz (J. Hernández).
**Status and habitat:** Rare. Known from only a few specimens from cold, scrubby, temperate zone slopes near or above treeline.
**Range:** ENDEMIC. 3000-3800m. C Andes in n Tolima (Nevado del Tolima, 3700m; e slope of Páramo del Ruiz) and ne of Popayán (Malvasá, 3000m). Prob. Nevado del Huila.

[*Forpus*: Tiny and chunky; short wedge-shaped tail; all much alike; ♂♂ with blue in wings.]

## 21. GREEN-RUMPED PARROTLET
*Forpus passerinus*          Map 257
**Identification:** 5″ (13cm). Sparrow-sized parrot. Bill whitish. ♂: *mainly bright green,* paler below and *brightest on rump;* greater upper and under wing coverts violet blue; secondaries pale blue; underside of flight feathers bluish green. ♀: sim. but *forehead and ocular region tinged yellow;* no blue in wings.
**Similar species:** ♂ is only one of genus with bright green instead of blue rump (all have blue in wings). ♀ prob. not separable from ♀ Blue-winged Parrotlet (22) but less yellowish green below.
**Voice:** A high, finchlike *chee chee chee;* when foraging, a soft, chattery *cheet-it.*
**Behavior:** Pairs or small twittering and chattering groups call incessantly but are difficult to locate if perched in foliage. Feed on small berries, fruits, and grass and weed seeds.
**Breeding:** Pair in abandoned hornero nest (presumed nesting), 10 Aug, w Guajira (Hilty); May–June nests, Cúcuta (Nicéforo 1945); 1 nest, Venez. Orinoco, late Apr, 5 eggs and 2 young (Cherrie 1916); 4 BC birds, Oct–Nov, Cúcuta (Carriker). Cavity nest in hollow limb, termitary, hollow stump, etc.
**Status and habitat:** Common in dry or arid scrub, ranchland, and gallery woodland. Replaced w of Santa Marta Mts. by Blue-winged Parrotlet.
**Range:** To 500m. From e and extreme s base of Santa Marta Mts. (sw of Valencia at Camperucho) to Guajira; e of Andes in Zulia Val.,

Norte de Santander. Poss. n Arauca and n Vichada. Guianas, ne Amazonian Brazil, e Venez., and generally n of Orinoco w to ne Colombia. Trinidad; Curaçao and Jamaica.

## 22. BLUE-WINGED PARROTLET
*Forpus xanthopterygius*        Pl. 10, Map 258
**Identification:** 5″ (13cm). Bill pinkish white, base of upper mandible grayish. ♂: mainly green, lighter and more yellowish green below; upper wing coverts and *rump turquoise blue* (or violet blue—*crassirostris*); secondaries blue. ♀: forehead and ocular region sometimes tinged yellowish; no blue in wings; underparts more yellowish green.
**Similar species:** In arid n, ♂ from ♂ Green-rumped Parrotlet (21) by blue instead of green rump; from ♂ Spectacled Parrotlet (23) by range and absence of bluish ocular area (but this often obscure in Spectacled Parrotlet). In se Colombia either sex from Dusky-billed Parrotlet (24) by bill color. ♀ in general not separable from other *Forpus* (except 24) although usually the most yellowish below; note range.
**Voice:** Flight call a high-pitched, chattering *zit-zit-zit-zit* . . . (J. V. Remsen).
**Behavior:** Like other *Forpus*.
**Breeding:** Cavities in hollow limbs, trunks, and old hornero nests in Brazil and Argentina; 3-7 eggs (Forshaw 1973).
**Status and habitat:** Uncommon and rather local in drier open woodland, scrubby pasture land, and riparian woodland in the north; clearings and second growth edge in Amazonas.
**Range:** To 300m. Arid Carib. coastal region from Cartagena e across lower Magdalena Val. to w base of Santa Marta Mts. (*spengeli*); extreme se Colombia near Leticia (*crassirostris*); poss. Putumayo (rec. at Limoncocha, Ecuador). Ne Ecuador, ne Peru, and Amazonian Brazil s to ne Argentina and Paraguay.

## 23. SPECTACLED PARROTLET
*Forpus conspicillatus*        Pl. 10, Map 259
**Identification:** 5″ (13cm). Bill ivory. ♂: mainly green, lighter and more yellowish green below; *ocular region blue* (often inconspic., esp. for *metae*); upper and under wing coverts and rump violet blue; underside of flight feathers bluish green. ♀: *entirely green (no blue)*, brightest, becoming emerald green around eyes, forehead, and rump.
**Similar species:** Only *Forpus* parrotlet in its range, although contact with others is poss. in some areas. ♂ distinguishable from other ♂ *Forpus* by blue around eye; additionally from Green-rumped Parrotlet (21) by rump color and from Dusky-billed Parrotlet (24) by bill

color. ♀ not safely told in field from other ♀ *Forpus* except by range and by attendant ♂, although differs in emerald green (not yellow or greenish yellow) forehead and ocular area.
**Voice:** Chatters and twitters incessantly with little finchlike notes.
**Behavior:** Pairs or small twittery flocks are usually noisy and conspic. Flight is dipping, erratic, and usually not long sustained compared with other parrots; often swoop up to alight on perch. Eat grass and weed seeds, small berries, and fruit, and roost communally; a popular cage bird.
**Breeding:** 2 late Jan nests (Miller 1947), another, 10 Mar (Brown), upper Magdalena Val.; BC pair, 30 Mar, Cali (Miller 1963); BC ♂, Dec, Cali, 4 BC birds, Jan–Mar, s Bolívar (Carriker). Cavity nest in fence post, trunk, limb, or termitarium at almost any ht., often only 1-2m up; usually 4 white eggs.
**Status and habitat:** Most common *Forpus*; often abundant in drier semiopen cultivated areas, ranchland, woodlots, even humid clearings with trees in mts.
**Range:** 200-1800m (occas. to 2600m, Sabana de Bogotá). Coastal sw Nariño near Tumaco (sightings, 1979—Hilty), drier upper Dagua and Patía vals., mid. and upper Cauca Val. n to sw Antioquia (*caucae*). Upper Río Sinú and lower Cauca Val. e to w slope of Perijá Mts., thence s in mid. and upper Magdalena Val. to s Huila (*conspicillatus*): e of Andes from Casanare to Meta; prob. the Río Meta in ne Vichada (*metae*). E Panama, Colombia, and the Río Meta in Venez.

## 24. DUSKY-BILLED PARROTLET
*Forpus sclateri*        Pl. 10, Map 260
**Identification:** 5″ (13cm). *Bill dusky above*, paler below. *Much like Blue-winged Parrotlet*. ♂: mostly green, darker than other *Forpus*; upper wing coverts and rump dark blue; secondaries blue. ♀: dark green above, rump blue green, underparts paler green with forehead and cheeks tinged greenish yellow.
**Similar species:** Either sex from other *Forpus* by dusky bill. See Blue-winged and Spectacled parrotlets (22, 23).
**Voice:** Chattering and twittering calls much like other *Forpus*.
**Behavior:** Typical of the genus. Flocks up to 75 or more at Mitú in Feb (Hilty).
**Status and habitat:** Local. Humid forest edge, clearings with trees, second growth, and along rivers.
**Range:** To 500m. E of Andes from w Caquetá (s of Florencia) and extreme se Guainía (along Río Negro) southward. Fr. Guiana, Guyana, and s Venez. s to n Bolivia and Amazonian Brazil.

[*Brotogeris*: Small; short wedge-shaped tail; lowlands.]

## 25. CANARY-WINGED PARAKEET
*Brotogeris versicolurus*          Pl. 10, Map 261
**Identification:** 9″ (23cm). Pointed tail. Bill yellowish. Mainly dull green with *yellow inner wing coverts*; outer primaries blue; *rest of flight feathers white* (conspic. in flight).
**Similar species:** Only small Colombian parakeet with prom. yellow and white wing patches.
**Voice:** Noisy. Flight call sim. to that of Tui Parakeet, but *screek* notes interspersed with *weechah-weechah* notes lacking in Tui (J. V. Remsen).
**Behavior:** Pairs or small to large flocks fly slightly above to far above canopy and wander widely, esp. along Amazon tributaries and channels. Flight is fairly direct. Call noisily as they fly and roost communally. Large nos. roost in palms in park in Leticia.
**Status and habitat:** Common at Leticia. Although reported by Dugand and Borrero (1946) as common in the Leticia area, the local population was increased by the release of large nos. of caged birds in the early 1960s (M. Tsalickis). Uncommon and widely scattered away from Leticia area. Treetops in forest or second growth edge and river banks.
**Range:** To 300m. S Amazonas along the Amazon and its tributaries. Fr. Guiana, Amazonian Brazil, and e Peru s to n Argentina and Paraguay.

## 26. ORANGE-CHINNED PARAKEET
*Brotogeris jugularis*          Pl. 10, Map 262
**Identification:** 7″ (18cm). *Short pointed tail*; bill dull yellowish. Mainly green with *small orange chin spot* (inconspic. in field) and *large bronzy brown shoulder patch; under wing coverts yellow*; flight feathers bluish green.
**Similar species:** *Forpus* parrotlets are smaller, even shorter-tailed, and lack the brown shoulders and yellow flash under the wing in flight. E of Andes see Cobalt-winged Parakeet (27).
**Voice:** A ser. of quick, raspy, chattering notes in flight.
**Behavior:** Usually in small chattery flocks when not breeding. Fly in quick spurts with frequent direction changes, as buzzy wing beats alternate with short glides. Keep fairly high in trees, eat blossoms and fruit; sometimes destructive to cultivated fruit.
**Breeding:** 7 BC birds, Jan–Mar, n Antioquia and Santa Marta (Carriker). Nest, presum. with young, 10 Mar, Huila (Brown). Cavity nest in dead tree or excavated in termitary, low to high but usually rather high; 1 Panama nest, 8 fledglings (Wetmore 1968a).
**Status and habitat:** Locally common in drier woodland and partially deforested or cultivated areas with trees; less numerous in humid forest canopy and forest edge. Sightings in forested lower Dagua Val. (June 1980—Hilty) may be escaped cage birds or pioneers to recent clearings.
**Range:** To 1000m. Pacific coast s to Baudó Mts., sighting s to Buenaventura (above); e in lowlands n of Andes to Santa Marta region, w base of Perijá Mts., and s to upper Río Nechí and upper Magdalena Val. (Villavieja); e of Andes in Norte de Santander (Zulia Val.) and sw Arauca. S Mexico to c Venez.

## 27. COBALT-WINGED PARAKEET
*Brotogeris cyanoptera*          Pl. 10, Map 263
**Identification:** 8″ (20cm). Short pointed tail. Bill dull yellowish. Mainly green with yellowish forecrown (not prom.) and orange chin spot (hard to see in field); *primaries and under wing coverts cobalt blue* (conspic. in flight); flight feathers bluish green below.
**Similar species:** In flight the flashing blue wings are the mark; at close range note orange chin spot. Tui Parakeet (28) lacks the chin spot and blue primaries and has prom. yellow forehead. *Forpus* parrotlets (22, 23, 24) show some blue in wing (not on primaries) but are *much* smaller. Sapphire-rumped Parrotlet (29) has blue at bend of wing and on rump but tail is short and square.
**Voice:** Like others of the genus, esp. Tui Parakeet.
**Behavior:** Usually in small lively flocks of 10-20 or more, occas. pairs. Feed in treetops or at edge of forest canopy.
**Breeding:** 2 BC ♀♀, early June, w Caquetá (Carriker).
**Status and habitat:** Locally fairly common in canopy of humid second growth, forest edges, river banks, and heavily deforested areas with patches of forest and scattered trees; also in areas with scattered trees in llanos. Numerous in semiopen savanna woodland of ne Guainía.
**Range:** To 500m. E of Andes from w Meta (Villavicencio), ne Meta (Carimagua—S. Furniss), and the Orinoco region southward. S Venez. to e Ecuador, e Peru, n Bolivia, and w Amazonian Brazil e to Río Negro.

## 28. TUI PARAKEET
*Brotogeris sanctithomae*          Pl. 10, Map 264
**Identification:** 6.5″ (16.5cm). Short pointed tail. Bill dull brownish. *Mostly green with prom. yellow forecrown*; rump and underparts lighter more yellowish green.
**Similar species:** Superficially like Cobalt-winged Parakeet (27) but lacks the blue in wings, and yellow forecrown conspic. None of the smaller *Forpus* have yellow forecrowns.

**Voice:** Flight call a high-pitched, dry *screek*, repeated constantly (J. V. Remsen); calls become an incessant, shrill chattering at a distance.
**Behavior:** Noisy chattering flocks visit riverside palms and *Erythrina* trees, where often feed on blossoms. Buzzy, somewhat dipping flight sim. to Orange-chinned Parakeet.
**Breeding:** Near Leticia, pairs at termitarium holes, 28 May and 27 July; begging juv., 21 June (J. V. Remsen).
**Status and habitat:** Common in second growth, *várzea*, and swampy borders, river banks, and on river isls. Abundant on disturbed partially flooded river isls. near Leticia.
**Range:** To 100m. Extreme s Amazonas along Río Amazon. Banks of Amazon and major tributaries from ne Peru to e Brazil; n Bolivia.

[*Touit*: Small and chunky; *short square* tail; often with colorful wing coverts and tail.]

## 29. SAPPHIRE-RUMPED PARROTLET
*Touit purpurata* Pl. 10, Map 265
**Identification:** 7″ (18cm). Yellowish bill gray at base. ♂: *mainly green*, lighter more yellowish green below; *rump violet blue*; scapulars and tertials dull brown (forms a stripe on either side of back); central feathers of *short square tail* green, rest magenta tipped and edged black. ♀: has subterminal green band on outer tail feathers.
**Similar species:** Easily confused. In flight note square tail and blue rump (latter hard to see). Smaller *Forpus* (22, 24) are wedge-tailed and have dipping flight. Tui Parakeet (28) has pointed tail and yellow forehead; Cobalt-winged (27) is larger with blue primaries.
**Voice:** Flight call a nasal, hornlike *hoya* as though from larger parrot (J. V. Remsen).
**Behavior:** Pairs or small flocks fly low over forest canopy or cross rivers and streams at treetop ht. Fly swiftly and directly with fast (but not buzzy) wing beats. Perch quietly in forest canopy where normally overlooked.
**Breeding:** ♀ excavating cavity in dead *várzea* tree, 19 Nov, Leticia (J. V. Remsen); BC ♂, Mar, s Venez. (Forshaw 1973); 1 on 11 Apr at termitarium nest in Surinam (Haverschmidt 1968).
**Status and habitat:** Uncommon (easily overlooked) in humid *terra firme* and *várzea* forests (usually seen as they fly across streams).
**Range:** To 400m. E of Andes from w Caquetá (Tres Esquinas) and extreme se Guainía (along Río Negro) southward (sightings on Río Vaupés, June 1976—R. Ridgely; sightings near Leticia and adj. ne Peru—J. V. Remsen, Hilty). Guianas, s Venez., e Ecuador, ne Peru (sight), and Amazonian Brazil (mainly n of the Amazon).

## 30. SCARLET-SHOULDERED PARROTLET
*Touit huetii* Map 266
**Identification:** 6″ (15cm). Bill yellowish; prom. bare whitish ocular region. Mostly green; forehead black becoming blue on forecheek; upper wing coverts dark blue; *bend of wing, under wing coverts, and axillaries scarlet; primaries black*; under tail coverts yellow; central feathers of *short square tail* green, rest red (or greenish yellow—♀) tipped black.
**Similar species:** Should be recognized by flaming red under wing coverts and small size. Orange-cheeked Parrot (36) in flight shows a conspic. blaze of red on under wings but is *much larger* and has gaudy black and orange head.
**Voice:** Flight call a soft bisyllabic *touit* (O'Neill 1969); a high-pitched *witch-witch* in flight (Snyder 1966).
**Behavior:** In e Peru large flocks climbed silently about in trees and called softly as flew in compact flocks; roost communally (O'Neill 1969).
**Breeding:** BC ♂, early Apr, opp. Vichada at San Fernando de Atabapo, Venez. (Forshaw 1973).
**Status and habitat:** Apparently rare and local. Canopy and at edge of humid lowland forest. Unobtrusive habits may partly account for scarcity of recs.
**Range:** To 400m. Known definitely only from ne base of Macarena Mts. (Río Güejar; Río Guapayá). Almost certainly in extreme ne Guainía at mouth of Río Guaviare (rec. in adj. Venez.). N Guyana, s Venez. (local), e Ecuador, e Peru, and Brazil.

## 31. RED-WINGED PARROTLET
*Touit dilectissima* Pl. 10, Map 267
**Identification:** 6.5″ (16.5cm). Bill dull yellowish; bare ocular region whitish. ♂: mostly green with blue forecrown; blue spot at base of bill and on ear coverts; narrow lores and line below eye red; *upper wing coverts, shoulders, and outer edge of wing red; under wing coverts bright yellow* (flashes red and yellow in flight); primaries partly black; central feathers of short square tail green, rest red tipped black. ♀: sim. but red on wings much reduced or lacking.
**Similar species:** Only small parrot w of Andes with flashing red and yellow (♂) or yellow (♀) wing coverts and short square tail. Barred Parakeet (19) has pointed tail, bars, and no color in wings; Orange-chinned Parakeet (26), a lowland bird, has pointed tail, no wing color, and brown shoulders.
**Voice:** Flight call a high, nasal whining *tuu-eet*,

vaguely 2-noted (unparrotlike) and weak; essentially silent at rest.

**Behavior:** Pairs or groups up to 15 or more perch or climb quietly in canopy, sometimes in mid. story or low inside forest, but do not perch in open or in isolated trees in clearings. Flight is fast, somewhat twisting, and with smooth, rapid wing beats. Compact groups call softly as they fly low over treetops, directly through forest, or infrequently high above it; roost communally in canopy.

**Breeding:** 2 BC ♂ ♂, 10 June, upper Anchicayá Val. (Hilty 1977); in e Panama 1 left an arboreal termitary, 11 Jan and 2 ads. with 3 juvs., 24 July (Ridgely 1976).

**Status and habitat:** Humid and wet forest ("cloud forest") and tall second growth. Mostly foothills and lower highlands, but often wander to adj. lowlands. Sometimes seen from road in Anchicayá Val., Valle, or near Junín, Nariño.

**Range:** 100-1700m (on Pacific slope most numerous 800-1400m). Pacific coast and slope from Baudó Mts. southward; n end E Andes above Ocaña (Norte de Santander-Cesar boundary, now deforested). Locally in Costa Rica; e Panama, w Venez. (Perijá Mts. and Andes), and nw Ecuador.

**Note:** Incl. *T. costaricensis* (Red-fronted Parrotlet) of Costa Rica and w Panama, sometimes considered a separate sp.

## 32. SPOT-WINGED PARROTLET
*Touit stictoptera*            Pl. 10, Map 268
**Identification:** 7″ (18cm). Bill gray, yellowish near tip. ♂: mainly green; foreface yellowish green; *upper wing coverts brown tipped buffy white* (giving spotted appearance); patch on outer median coverts dull orange; underside of flight feathers bluish green; *short square tail* green above, olive yellow below. ♀: sim. but *wing coverts green spotted black*, and lores and forecheeks brighter yellow.

**Similar species:** ♂ shows small orangish wing patch in flight but is otherwise mainly a small green parrot without strong markings. Other *Touit*'s have red, or red and yellow on wings. Also cf. *Forpus* (esp. 23) and Barred Parakeet (19). Orange-chinned Parakeet (26) has brown shoulders but a pointed (not square) tail and yellow under wing coverts.

**Voice:** In flight a harsh repeated *ch-ch-ch* (R. Ridgely).

**Behavior:** Dugand (1945) reported it feeding on berries of mistletoe, *Ficus*, and *Clusia*. In e Ecuador, 2 flocks flew through and just over the canopy (R. Ridgely).

**Status and habitat:** Known definitely from only 3 localities in forested mts. in Colombia (Borrero 1958; Blake 1962); found in Nov. below Fusagasugá (sw Bogotá) but not the following Apr (Dugand 1945). Deforestation may now threaten it.

**Range:** 600-1700m. Known from w slope of C Andes in Cauca (San Andrés); w slope of E Andes in Cundinamarca (near Fusagasugá); and Macarena Mts. (Caño Entrada); prob. e Nariño. Colombia, e Ecuador, and n Peru.

[*Pionites*: Square-tailed; white underparts; squealing calls.]

## 33. BLACK-HEADED PARROT
*Pionites melanocephala*        Pl. 10, Map 269
**Identification:** 9″ (23cm). Bill dusky. Unusal color pattern. *Crown black*; rest of upperparts bright green with *throat and broad collar encircling neck yellow in front, orangy behind; breast and belly white*; flanks, thighs, and under tail coverts yellow (or hindneck, flanks, and thighs deeper apricot—*melanocephala*).

**Similar species:** Only Colombian parrot mostly white below. On s bank of Amazon see White-bellied Parrot (note).

**Voice:** Flight call a distinctive, high-pitched squealing or screeching *cleeeooo-cleeeooo* (J. V. Remsen); when perched a var. of whistles, piping, and slurred notes, some musical, others seemingly electronic, none parrotlike.

**Behavior:** Small flocks of 3-10 fly fast and directly with mod. deep wing beats, usually at or just above canopy ht. Eat fruit in canopy but occas. come quite low; often unsuspicious. Spread wings as they give loud *kleek* calls in treetop display.

**Breeding:** 1 BC ♂, Apr, Pto. Ayacucho on Orinoco (Friedmann 1948); 1 BC ♀, May, w Caquetá (Carriker).

**Status and habitat:** Fairly common in humid *terra firme* forest and forest edge. Quite numerous in blackwater regions of e Guainía and Vaupés.

**Range:** To 500m. E of Andes from w Meta and Vaupés (Mitú) southward (*pallida*); ne Guainía (sightings, Pto. Inírida, 1978—Hilty and M. Robbins) n prob. to e Vichada, as known on Venez. side (*melanocephala*). Guianas and s Venez. to e Ecuador, ne Peru, and n Amazonian Brazil (s to n bank of Amazon).

**Note:** Replaced on s bank of Amazon by *P. leucogaster* (White-bellied Parrot), which differs mainly in crown being apricot instead of black. Latter not likely on n Amazon bank.

## 34. BROWN-HOODED PARROT
*Pionopsitta haematotis*              Map 270
**Identification:** 8.5″ (22cm). Chunky and short-tailed. Bare bluish white ocular ring. *Head dark grayish brown*; otherwise mostly green with *small rosy patch on ear coverts* and sometimes an in-

distinct pinkish collar on foreneck; wing coverts and wing linings blue; *axillaries scarlet* (conspic. from below in flight).
**Similar species:** From Rose-faced or Blue-headed parrots (35, 40) by prom. red axillary patches ("armpits").
**Voice:** Flight calls a quite high-pitched *check-check* or *cheek-cheek* and a thin *tseek* (Ridgely 1976).
**Behavior:** Usually in small groups in forest canopy or in distinctive rapid flight, tossing from side to side, lifting wings above the horizontal (Ridgely 1976).
**Status and habitat:** Humid lowland and foothill forest. Not found in n Chocó by Haffer (1975). Replaced in wetter forest to the s by Rose-faced Parrot.
**Range:** To 600-1200m. Panama boundary s to Río Juradó, w side of Gulf of Urabá at Unguía and e of it in upper Río Sinú, sw Córdoba (Quimarí; Murrucucú). S Mexico to extreme nw Colombia.

## 35. ROSE-FACED PARROT
*Pionopsitta pulchra*          Pl. 9, Map 271
**Identification:** 9″ (23cm). Chunky and short-tailed. Narrow whitish orbital ring; eyes gray. Mostly green with *dusky brown crown* becoming dull yellowish olive on hindneck and on chest, this encircling a *large rosy pink patch on sides of head that extends to ear coverts and sides of throat*; wing coverts and wing linings dark blue; edge of shoulder mixed yellow and orange.
**Similar species:** Rosy face is the mark. Lacks the red collar on foreneck and red axillar patches of Brown-Hooded Parrot (34). Also see Blue-headed Parrot (40).
**Voice:** Flight call a harsh shrieking *skreek-skreek*, resembling corresponding call of Blue-headed Parrot.
**Behavior:** Pairs or groups of var. size, up to 25 or more, perch exposed on high dead branches or more frequently inside canopy or lower, where they climb quietly about in search of fruit. Flight much like Brown-hooded Parrot, with deep wing beats and wings raised above back.
**Breeding:** 3 BC birds, Nov–Dec, Guapí, sw Cauca (Olivares, 1957b); 6 BC birds, Jan–Mar, Chocó (Carriker).
**Status and habitat:** Uncommon and local in wet forest, tall second growth, plantations, and clearings with scattered trees.
**Range:** To 2100m (on slopes of Cerro Tatamá); usually below 1200m. Pacific coast and slope from Mutatá southward. W Colombia and w Ecuador.
**Note:** Considered a race of *P. haematotis* (Brown-hooded Parrot) by Meyer de Schauensee (1966,

1970), but for a different view, see Haffer (1975). A gap of only 100 km separates the 2 and no intergradation is known.

## 36. ORANGE-CHEEKED PARROT
*Pionopsitta barrabandi*          Pl. 10, Map 272
**Identification:** 10″ (25cm). Size and shape of *Pionus*. Bill dusky; narrow bare orbital ring whitish. Mostly green with *black head and large gaudy orange malar patch*; upper chest yellow olive; *shoulders orange; under wing coverts scarlet* (conspic. in flight); primaries blackish.
**Similar species:** Colorful and easily recognized. Flaming red wing linings and orange shoulders prom. in flight. Black-headed Parrot (33) has black crown (not all black head) and mostly white underparts. Also cf. rare Scarlet-shouldered Parrotlet (30), which is half the size and lacks the black head.
**Voice:** Flight call a mushy or reedy *chewit* or *choyet*, somewhat bisyllabic and very distinctive.
**Behavior:** Usually in pairs or small flocks of 3-7 in mid. story or higher. Fly very fast with deep wing beats and slightly twisting or rolling flight, generally at treetop ht. or lower, sometimes skimming low along forest borders.
**Status and habitat:** Uncommon to common locally in humid *terra firme* and *várzea* forest, occas. patches of trees in partially deforested regions. Numerous in lower Río Inírida region in sandy-belt woodland.
**Range:** To 500m. E of Andes from w Caquetá (formerly Florencia), ne Guainía (sightings near Pto. Inírida, 1979—Hilty and M. Robbins), and Vaupés southward. Venez. (s Bolívar and Amazonas), e Ecuador to n Bolivia and w Amazonian Brazil.

## 37. SAFFRON-HEADED PARROT
*Pionopsitta pyrilia*          Pl. 9, Map 273
**Identification:** 9.5″ (24cm). Bill whitish; bare ocular ring whitish rimmed with black. *Head, neck, and shoulders yellow*; outerwise largely green with olive chest; *bend of wing, under wing coverts, and axillaries scarlet* (conspic. in flight).
**Similar species:** Unmistakable. Only Colombian parrot with an all yellow head.
**Voice:** Flight call a reedy *cheweek* much like others of the genus, esp. Orange-cheeked Parrot.
**Behavior:** Small groups fly rapidly through forest canopy or lower along borders, calling loudly like others of genus.
**Breeding:** 4 BC birds, Mar–June, n Antioquia, and 3 juvs., July, Perijá Mts. (Carriker).
**Status and habitat:** Humid and wet lowland forest, tall second growth, and borders. Frequently observed on w side Magdalena Val.

in Caldas (Olivares 1969a) and still in nos. at several localities along n base of Andes. **Range:** To about 1000m (scattered recs. to 1700m). N end of W Andes from upper Río Sinú e across humid n base of Andes to w side of Perijá Mts. (e of Fonseca), s to mid. Magdalena Val. in e Caldas (La Dorada), and formerly below Fusagasugá (sw Bogotá); also e Norte de Santander and se Boyacá. Erratically (wanderer?) s on Pacific coast to Noanamá, Chocó, and Buenaventura (sight rec. Aug 1977; June 1981—Hilty et al.); formerly in C Andes to Medellín (at Santa Elena). E Panama to w Venez.

## 38. RUSTY-FACED PARROT

*Hapalopsittaca amazonina*          Pl. 9, Map 274
**Identification:** 9″ (23cm). Highlands only. Dull; chunky; short-tailed; *Pionus*-sized. Bill pale. Mostly green with olive green breast; *front of head rusty red*; lengthened ear coverts olive with faint yellow shaft streaks; *shoulders extensively dull red; lesser under wing coverts red*; rest of under wing coverts greenish blue; *flight feathers blue black*; tail mostly dull red broadly tipped blue. Or sim. but plumage olive green, forecrown and foreface greenish yellow, rest of crown bluish, and ear coverts unstreaked (*fuertesi*).
**Similar species:** Bronze-winged Parrot (43) is darker and lacks red shoulders; at close range shows whitish throat patch (in flight both show blue black wings and red at base of tail). Also cf. Speckle-faced Parrot (42).
**Voice:** Flight call an undistinctive repeated *chek-chek-chek-chek* . . . (Ridgely and Gaulin 1980).
**Behavior:** Pairs or small groups up to 5 in Merenberg area (w Huila). In flight, by comparison to *Pionus*, appears smaller with proportionally longer tail and shallower wing beats (Ridgely and Gaulin 1980). One group of 7 in forest edge treetops at PN Cueva de los Guácharos (P. Gertler).
**Status and habitat:** Rare and local. Only recent recs. are a few sightings in humid forested highlands in Huila as follows: Finca Merenberg (1976—Ridgely and Gaulin 1980); PN Cueva de los Guácharos (Apr 1976—P. Gertler); also e Cauca on e slope PN Puracé (prob. sight, Apr 1973—G. Tudor et al.); above Santa Rosa de Cabal, Risaralda, 1980 (J. Orejuela; M. Aberico). No recent rec. in n part of E Andes. Prob. endangered.
**Range:** 2000-2700m (E Andes and upper Magdalena Val.); 3100-3600m (C Andes in Caldas). Known only from E Andes in Norte de Santander (Cáchira; Gramalote), w slope in e Santander (Molagavita), and sw of Bogotá above Fusagasugá (*amazonina*); C Andes sw of

Manizales on Caldas-Tolima border (*fuertesi*); and sight recs. in Risaralda, s Huila, and e Cauca. Andes from nw Venez. to Peru.

## 39. SHORT-TAILED PARROT

*Graydidascalus brachyurus*          Pl. 10, Map 275
**Identification:** 9.5″ (24cm). Distinctive *short-tailed* shape in flight. *Bill dusky. Plumage green*; upper tail coverts and underparts slightly paler; *inconspic. maroon frontlet extends back as narrow dusky line fore and aft of red eye.*
**Similar species:** Confusing. In flight a bobtailed all green parrot without markings. At close range the dark "frown" line through eyes is distinctive. Most likely confused with several larger *Amazona* parrots, which have very different flights and usually show a colored patch on wings (sometimes hard to see). Cf. esp. Festive Parrot (46), which has red stripe up back, no color in wings, and typical *Amazona* flight.
**Voice:** One of the noisiest, coarsest-voiced parrots in Amazon basin; flight call a raucous *shreek*; when feeding a slightly trilled, hornlike *fuuuuudle-fuuuuudle* (J. V. Remsen).
**Behavior:** Often in large boisterous flocks of 50 or more that feed in treetops, esp. on *Cecropia* catkins and when available cultivated fruits such as guava (*Psidium*). Fly fast and directly, often quite high, but on approach may roll and twist as though slightly out of control.
**Status and habitat:** Locally common in taller swampy second growth on Amazon river isls., river banks, and *várzea* borders. Not away from river isls. or banks of Amazon and its larger tributaries.
**Range:** To 400m. E of Andes along Río Caquetá, Río Putumayo, and Río Amazon, and their major tributaries from w Caquetá to Amazonas. Rivers from e Colombia, e Ecuador, and e Peru to mouth of Amazon.

[*Pionus*: Med.-sized; dark motley appearance with red vent; deep wing beats raised to horizontal only.]

## 40. BLUE-HEADED PARROT

*Pionus menstruus*          Pl. 11, Map 276
**Identification:** 10″ (25cm). Dusky bill with pinkish base. Bare whitish ocular area. *Head, neck, and chest blue* more or less mixed red on foreneck; ear coverts black; otherwise mainly green with *red under tail coverts* and red base of underside of tail. Imm.: head largely green.
**Similar species:** One of the most familiar lowland parrots and the only one with an all blue head (often hard to see). In flight best told by deep "wing-clapping" wing strokes (wings al-

most touch below); red on base of bill often prom. In Perijá and Santa Marta mts. see Red-billed Parrot (41), on Pacific slope, Rose-faced Parrot (35).

**Voice:** Noisy. Flight call a screeching, high-pitched, and characteristically doubled *kee-wenk, keewenk*; at rest other calls, typically *krrreeeck* (Ridgely 1976).

**Behavior:** Single birds, pairs or raucous flocks of 100 or more (largest groups mainly on Pacific coast). Usually in treetops and like to perch on exposed palm frond spikes or bare branches at times.

**Breeding:** Two nests with young, Feb and Mar, upper Anchicayá Val. (Hilty); in Panama, Jan–May (Willis and Eisenmann 1979). Venez. nest, 13 Mar, with 3 young of different sizes (Cherrie 1916); 1 clutch of 4 (ffrench 1973).

**Status and habitat:** Common in humid and wet lowland forest, second growth, and clearings with scattered trees. Absent or very thinly spread in drier Carib. region and e of Andes in the llanos. Stragglers still appear over now totally deforested middle and upper Cauca Val. (formerly common there).

**Range:** To 1500m (mostly below 1100m). Throughout in humid forest regions e and w of Andes. Costa Rica s to n Bolivia and s central and coastal Brazil.

## 41. RED-BILLED PARROT
*Pionus sordidus*                     Pl. 11, Map 277

**Identification:** 11″ (28cm). *Bill reddish*. Unkempt appearance. Bare whitish ocular ring and pale yellow eyes. Mostly dull green; feathers of head mottled brownish, broadly tipped blue, and usually with some scattered white showing through; throat and chest bluish; *under tail coverts and base of underside of tail red.*

**Similar species:** Much like Blue-headed Parrot (40) but duller, head dingy bluish brown, and bill red (color var. and sometimes hard to see in field). Red-billed Parrot is normally found above the range of Blue-headed. In E Andes see Bronze-winged Parrot (43).

**Voice:** Flight call closely resembles that of Blue-headed Parrot, but 2d syllable different; a harsh, inflected *keeank, keeank*.

**Behavior:** Much like allied Blue-headed Parrot of lowlands. Gather in large "shrieking" flocks, eat fruits and blossoms, and fly with labored but deep and free wing strokes raised just to horizontal.

**Breeding:** 5 BC birds, Feb–Apr, incl. ♂ on nest, 21 Apr, Santa Marta Mts. and w Guajira (Carriker).

**Status and habitat:** Humid forest, second growth, partially deforested areas with scattered tall trees, and lighter woodland over cof-

fee; occas. into drier areas. Fairly common in Santa Marta region.

**Range:** 200-2400m (foothills and lower highlands). Santa Marta and Perijá mts., and locally in E Andes ("Bogotá" skins); sightings at head of Magdalena Val., Huila (PN Cueva de los Guácharos—P. Gertler). N Venez. s in mts. to n Bolivia.

## 42. SPECKLE-FACED (WHITE-CAPPED) PARROT
*Pionus tumultuosus*                  Pl. 11, Map 278

**Identification:** 11″ (28cm). Bill olive yellow; bare ocular ring whitish. *Forecrown whitish* with scattered pink-edged feathers; rest of head dusky violet heavily mottled and speckled white; upperparts green; below dull purplish brown, spotted pinkish on throat; sides and *under wings green; under tail coverts red.*

**Similar species:** Has ragged motley appearance. Rusty-faced Parrot (38) is more uniform dull green, lacks whitish forecrown, and shows red on shoulder and under wing coverts. Bronze-winged Parrot (43) is much darker with deep ultramarine blue primaries and all dark head.

**Voice:** Unlike calls of Bronze-winged and Blue-headed parrots, a smooth *chiank* with laughing quality.

**Behavior:** Highly nomadic. Groups of 10-20 at Finca Merenberg from 15 July–1 Aug perhaps later (Ridgely and Gaulin 1980).

**Status and habitat:** Uncommon and local in humid forest and forest edge. Primarily a temperate zone sp. that wanders seasonally to lower el. Reported "common" in late July, Finca Merenberg, Huila, but not observed prior to that period (Ridgely and Gaulin 1980); 1 pair, late June, e slope of PN Puracé, 7 on 8 Aug, PN Cueva de los Guácharos, 2-3 pairs above Bucaramanga (2400m), June (Hilty).

**Range:** 1600-3000m. Spottily throughout E Andes; C Andes from n Tolima (e side Quindío Mts. at Toche) s through Nariño. Nw Venez. s in Andes to Bolivia.

**Note:** Incl. *P. tumultuosus* (Plum-crowned Parrot) of Peru and Bolivia and *P. seniloides* (White-capped Parrot) of Venez. to Peru (see O'Neill and Parker 1977), sometimes considered separate spp.

## 43. BRONZE-WINGED PARROT
*Pionus chalcopterus*                 Pl. 11, Map 279

**Identification:** 11″ (28cm). Bill yellowish; bare ocular ring buffy. Mostly *dark dusky blue; back bronzed greenish, shoulders brownish, and with large whitish throat patch*; under tail coverts and base of underside of tail red. In flight *primaries and* *under wing coverts deep ultramarine blue*; primaries blue green from below.

**Similar species:** In Perijá Mts. easily confused with Dusky Parrot (44), which lacks whitish throat and is overall duller with plain dull dark brown back (no bronzy green). In Andes see Rusty-faced, Red-billed, and Speckle-faced parrots (38, 41, 42), none of which is as dark.

**Voice:** Flight call sim. to that of Blue-headed Parrot.

**Behavior:** Like most highland parrots, notably nomadic, and usually in flocks. Flight and habits otherwise much like Blue-headed Parrot.

**Breeding:** Mar nest in tree cavity, Perijá Mts. (Yepez 1953); pair feeding young, late May, PN Cueva de los Guácharos (P. Gertler), BC ♀, 21 Mar, Huila (Carriker).

**Status and habitat:** Local in humid highland forest, forest borders, and clearings, or partially deforested terrain with scattered tall trees. Wanders widely though seasonal el. movements not well known.

**Range:** Mostly 1400-2400m (wanderer to 400m on Pacific slope; to 2800m sw of Bogotá). Spottily in all 3 Andean ranges. Nw Venez. (incl. Perijá Mts.) s in mts. to nw Peru.

## 44. DUSKY PARROT
*Pionus fuscus* Map 280

**Identification:** 10" (25cm). Bill dusky yellowish; bare ocular ring buffy. *Very dull and dark.* Brownish, the feathers slightly pale-edged on upperparts, edged dark bluish to plum purple on underparts; head dull slate blue; auriculars blackish bordered behind by a *fringe of white streaks on sides of neck*, sometimes faint white mottling on cheeks; primaries and tail deep ultramarine blue; under wings brilliant purplish blue; *under tail coverts and base of tail red.*

**Similar species:** In flight lacks the contrasting greenish back and brown shoulders of Bronze-winged Parrot (43), thus appearing more uniform. When perched, look for irreg. white markings on sides of neck.

**Voice:** Flight call in Venez., 3-4 rough *craáak* notes, reminiscent of call of Blue-headed Parrot.

**Behavior:** In Surinam and Venez., singly, in pairs, or small flocks in forest canopy, but may drop low to fruiting trees in clearings. Much more a forest bird than allied Blue-headed Parrot.

**Breeding:** BC ♂, 6 Apr, Perijá Mts. (Carriker). Cavity nest, about 12 m up in tall dead tree, Apr, Guyana; 4 young of different sizes (Beebe and Beebe 1910).

**Status and habitat:** Humid foothill and lower highland forest and forest edge. Known from

3 localities in Colombia. Isolated Colombian population deserves further study.

**Range:** 1200-1800m. W slope of Perijá Mts. at Tierra Nueva and Monte Elías (se of Fonseca), and La África (above Casacará). Ne Colombia (isolated population), e Venez., Guianas, and e Brazil.

[*Amazona*: Large; bright green; stiff shallow *wing tip* flight. Familiar talking or "polly" parrots.]

## 45. RED-LORED PARROT
*Amazona autumnalis* Pl. 11, Map 281

**Identification:** 13" (33cm). Bill pale yellow above, dusky below. *Red forehead and lores* (very hard to see in flight); otherwise mainly green; feathers of crown and hindneck broadly edged lavender blue; *sides of head and throat more yellowish green;* wing speculum red (visible in flight); tail broadly tipped yellowish green, outer feathers red at base (*salvini*).

**Similar species:** Easily recognized as an *Amazona* by large size and characteristic "stiff-winged" flight, but at a distance or in flight not easily told from others of the genus except by voice. Narrow red forehead is diagnostic if seen. Note absence of definite yellow on head (cf. 47, 48). In presence of Mealy Parrot (50) smaller size is apparent.

**Voice:** Usually vocal in flight; a very loud, harsh *chikák chikák* or *oorák oorák oorák* (F. Chapman); more shrieking and discordant than other *Amazona* in nw Colombia.

**Behavior:** Perch in treetops. Fly in pairs, or pairs within flocks. Flight and other habits typical of genus. In Panama may roost in large flocks of its own after breeding (R. Ridgely).

**Breeding:** 2 BC ♀♀, Jan, Bolívar, Feb, Chocó (Carriker); BC birds, Dec–Jan, sw Cauca (Olivares 1957b); Panama nests, Feb and Apr in tree cavities (Willis and Eisenmann 1979).

**Status and habitat:** Found in a var. of humid forested or partially forested lowland regions from heavy humid forest to plantations with scattered trees. A few in foothills; absent from dry Carib. region and wettest Pacific coast belt. Common in sw Cauca (Olivares 1957b).

**Range:** To 1000m. Pacific coast from Panama border s to Baudó Mts. and from sw Cauca (Guapí) southward; e n of Andes to lower Magdalena Val. (s Atlántico) and mid. Magdalena Val. (Pto. Berrío, Antioquia). E Mexico to w Venez. (incl. Perijá Mts.) and w Ecuador; nw Brazil.

## 46. FESTIVE PARROT
*Amazona festiva* Pl. 11, Map 282

**Identification:** 14" (36cm). Bill dusky; no bare eyering. Mainly green with *rump and wedge up*

*lower back red*; lores and narrow frontal band dark red; feathers above and behind eye tinged blue; primaries dark blue; *wings otherwise uniform green*; no red or orange patch on secondaries (*festiva*). Or as above but broader, conspic. red band on forehead; sides of head more extensively light blue, outer webs of primaries green (*bodini*).

**Similar species:** Only *Amazona* with red lower back (though red not conspic. even in flight), and the only *Amazona* in its range with no bright color (red or orange) on secondaries.

**Voice:** Flight call a distinctive nasal, and laugh-like *wah-wah*, usually doubled (almost human-like at a distance); large var. of notes and carols when perched (J. V. Remsen; Hilty).

**Behavior:** Much like other *Amazona* parrots but with a decided preference for vicinity of water. Largest flocks (up to about 50) May–June near Leticia (J. V. Remsen). An accomplished talking parrot in captivity.

**Status and habitat:** *Várzea* forest, swampy river isl. second growth, and river banks; gallery forest in llanos. One of the most numerous *Amazona* near Leticia; locally fairly common along Río Casanare (Romero 1978). Few recs. elsewhere.

**Range:** To 500m. Lower Río Casanare (Mochuelito) and undoubtedly lower Río Meta (*bodini*); Río Vaupés near Mitú and the Amazon near Leticia (*festiva*). Nw Guyana, Venez. (lower Río Meta and mid. and lower Orinoco), e Peru, and w Amazonian Brazil.

## 47. YELLOW-CROWNED PARROT
*Amazona ochrocephala*          Pl. 11, Map 283

**Identification:** 14″ (36cm). Pale bill with dusky tip. Mainly green with *yellow central crown patch* (also forehead—*panamensis*); flight feathers tipped blue; *shoulders and patch on secondaries red*; small amount of red at base of tail.

**Similar species:** Only Colombian *Amazona* with yellow crown patch and otherwise all green head. Cf. Orange-winged Parrot (48), which has yellow cheeks as well as crown patch and lacks red shoulders. Larger and more robust Mealy Parrot (50) occas. shows yellow in crown but has prom. bare orbital ring; also lacks red shoulders.

**Voice:** Quite var. but more mellow and musical than other Colombian *Amazona*; most characteristic flight call a doglike *ker-our, ker-our*, or *bow-wow, bow-wow*, usually doubled or several.

**Behavior:** Much like others of the genus. Often kept in cages for its talking ability.

**Breeding:** BC pair, late Dec, Magdalena (Carriker); BC ♂, Jan, ne Meta (MCN). In ne Venez. late Feb–May; cavity nest in termitary, dead

palm stub, etc., often low (Friedmann and Smith 1950; Beebe 1909).

**Status and habitat:** Drier open woodland and humid forest borders in the north; gallery woodland and savanna with scattered trees in the llanos; and swampy or more open areas in Amazonia. Notably local; daily flocks of 500 or more around a lagoon n of Río Apaporis (Dugand 1952).

**Range:** To 500m. N Chocó from Panama border e across most of lowlands n of Andes to w and se base of Santa Marta Mts., w base of Perijá Mts. (Fonseca), and s locally to upper Magdalena Val. in Huila (Villavieja); sightings (P. Gertler) at PN Cueva de los Guácharos (*panamensis*); e base of E Andes in w Caquetá and w Putumayo (*nattereri*); Catatumbo lowlands in Norte de Santander and locally in remaining area e of Andes prob. s to Amazonas (*ochrocephala*). N Honduras and w Panama to e Peru, n Bolivia, and Amazonian Brazil.

**Note:** Formerly incl. *Amazona oratrix* (Yellow-headed Parrot), of se Mexico and Belize, and *A. auropalliata* (Yellow-naped Parrot), of Oaxaca, Mexico to nw Costa Rica, both now considered separate spp.

## 48. ORANGE-WINGED PARROT
*Amazona amazonica*          Pl. 11, Map 284

**Identification:** 13″ (33cm). Pale bill with dusky tip. Mainly green with *yellow crown patch and yellow cheeks separated by blue forehead and lores*; primaries tipped blue black; *wing speculum red orange*; underside of tail mostly dull orange and crossed by green band.

**Similar species:** Yellow cheeks are the mark. Cf. Yellow-crowned Parrot (47), which lacks the yellow cheeks and blue on crown.

**Voice:** A high, shrill, bisyllabic *klee-ak*, often varied to *kleeak, quick-quick*, over and over; also many harsh screeches and whistles. Usually more high-pitched and screeching than other *Amazona* (cf. calls of Red-lored, Yellow-crowned and Mealy parrots).

**Behavior:** Like other *Amazona*. Large nos. roost in remoter mangroves and swamps in PN Salamanca.

**Breeding:** 5 BC birds, Dec–Feb, Magdalena and Bolívar (Carriker). In Trinidad most lay in Mar in palm stub cavity; 2-5 eggs (Nottebohm and Nottebohm 1969).

**Status and habitat:** Locally fairly common. Drier woodland, swampy forest and mangroves in Carib. region, gallery forest and savanna with scattered trees or Moriche Palms (*Mauritia*) e of Andes in llanos; apparently *várzea* or swampy areas in Amazonia.

**Range:** To 500m. N Colombia from Sinú Val.

e to w base of Santa Marta Mts. and s to mid. Magdalena Val. (Pto. Berrío); throughout e of Andes. The Guianas and Venez. s to e Peru, Amazonian Brazil, and ne Bolivia.

## 49. SCALY-NAPED PARROT

*Amazona mercenaria*          Pl. 11, Map 285
**Identification:** 13″ (33cm). Bill dusky with pale area at base of upper mandible. *Mainly green; feathers of hindneck and breast edged black* (not conspic. in field); upper tail coverts pale yellowish green; flight feathers tipped blue; leading edge of wing tipped orange yellow but *usually no red speculum present;* outer tail feathers green with median red band and paler yellowish green tip.
**Similar species:** The only *Amazona* in the highlands. Large size and characteristic "stiff-winged" flight are helpful in identifying this sp. The distinctive tail pattern or scaling on hindneck and breast are hard to see in field.
**Voice:** Flight call reminiscent of that of Mealy Parrot but higher-pitched, shriller, and uttered faster, *ka-lee*, sometimes in long ser.
**Behavior:** As in others of genus. Pairs or multiples of 2 in groups up to about 30 to 40. Often rather wary.
**Breeding:** Pair feeding young, late May, PN Cueva de los Guácharos (P. Gertler); 3 BC birds, Mar–May, Perijá Mts. and sw Huila (Carriker).
**Status and habitat:** Local. Humid highland forest and in flight over partially deforested terrain. Some seasonal el. movement or nomadism in W Andes in Valle; in PN Cueva de los Guácharos, resident but most numerous Dec–Mar (P. Gertler).
**Range:** 1600-3600m (treeline). In most areas well below treeline; once to Villavicencio (about 500m). Santa Marta and Perijá mts. and all 3 Andean ranges; no recs. in E Andes n of Cundinamarca, or in W Andes n of Valle, or in Nariño. Nw Venez. s in mts. to n Bolivia.

## 50. MEALY PARROT

*Amazona farinosa*          Pl. 11, Map 286
**Identification:** 16″ (41cm). *Large bare ocular region whitish;* pale bill tipped dusky. *Mostly green,* occas. with a small spot of yellow on crown; feathers of hindneck and mantle edged bluish appearing as a powdery bloom; *secondaries with red speculum* (visible in flight); *2-toned tail* with basal half dark green, distal half pale yellow green.
**Similar species:** Largest and dullest green *Amazona* and without good marks. Large orbital ring and distinctive flight calls are helpful; at close range note lack of red or yellow on head and 2-toned tail.

**Voice:** Var. but most common flight call a deep, throaty *cho-auk* or *choop*, often doubled or repeated many times; at rest an astonishing repertoire of whistles, clucks, gurgles, and babbles.
**Behavior:** Much like other *Amazona* though generally found in heavier forest.
**Breeding:** Several near BC, sw Cauca, early Jan (Olivares 1957b). Guyana hole nest in palm stub, 3 young (McLoughlin and Burton 1970).
**Status and habitat:** Humid and wet forest and forest borders. On Pacific coast wanders into mts. and upper Anchicayá Val. (to 1100m) Oct–Jan (Hilty); near Leticia, most numerous June–Oct (J. V. Remsen).
**Range:** To 1100m. Pacific coast, humid lowlands n of Andes e to mid. Magdalena Val. (s to Lebrija Val.), Snía. de San Jacinto, Sucre, and entire w base of Perijá Mts. (not on n coast or in Santa Marta region); prob. throughout e of Andes (no recs. in llanos). S Mexico to n Bolivia and s Brazil.

## 51. RED-FAN PARROT

*Deroptyus accipitrinus*          Pl. 11, Map 287
**Identification:** 14″ (36cm). Hawklike. *Long slightly rounded tail. Forecrown buffy white;* rest of crown, sides of head, and throat brown with faint whitish shaft streaks; *feathers of hindneck* (which can be raised in fan-shaped ruff surrounding head) *and entire underparts red broadly edged blue;* back, wings, tail, and under tail coverts green; primaries and underside of tail black.
**Similar species:** A handsome but oddly proportioned parrot that can be recognized by long tail, large head, and peculiar undulating flap-and-glide flight; the distinctive neck ruff is usually held depressed. Perched it is easily taken for a small bird of prey; best mark at rest is prom. whitish forecrown.
**Voice:** Distinctive. Flight call several *chacks* followed by 1-5 high-pitched, almost squealing *tak tak heéya heéya* phrases (McLoughlin and Burton 1976); at a distance only the *heéya* notes audible. At rest a var. of musical and unmusical chatters and whistles.
**Behavior:** Pairs or small groups of 4-7 often perch exposed on dead treetops. Fly low, usually skimming the treetops, a few shallow flaps followed by a short glide with wings held angled slightly downward, tail slightly spread, and head raised (like swimming breast stroke). In Mitú called *Kina-Kina* after call (Lehmann 1957).
**Breeding:** 3 nests, mid-Mar–late Apr in Surinam (Brown; Haverschmidt 1968); 5 Guyana nests, late Jan–late Mar (McLoughlin and

Burton 1976). Cavity nest in dead trunk, limb, or woodpecker hole.

**Status and habitat:** Local. Sandy-belt forest and mixed forest and savanna in blackwater regions of extreme east.

**Range:** To 400m. Extreme e from Vichada (Pto. Carreño) s to Vaupés (Mitú; Río Apaporis); perhaps locally to w Vaupés and s Meta in vicinity of San José del Guaviare. Guianas and s Venez. to e Ecuador, ne Peru (Loreto), and n Amazonian Brazil (both banks of Amazon s to n Mato Grosso).

# CUCKOOS Cuculidae (18)

Cuckoos and their allies are a group of anatomically similar but behaviorally diverse birds found from tropical to temperate regions worldwide. They are slim-bodied, long-tailed birds, and many have inconspicuous and unobtrusive habits. The Colombian species occur in a wide variety of lowland and lower montane habitats and include both terrestrial and arboreal members. Their breeding habits are diverse, often unconventional. Two groups, *Tapera* and *Dromococcyx* are parasitic, while *Crotophaga* are generally communal nesters. In several arboreal species with more conventional breeding habits the nestlings leave the nest well before they are able to fly. Several Colombian species are north or south temperate migrants, and a few others are suspected of being so. Their food is chiefly insects and caterpillars although the larger terrestrial species also eat small vertebrates.

## 1. DWARF CUCKOO
*Coccyzus pumilus*                    Pl. 12, Map 288
**Identification:** 8″ (20cm). Uncuckoolike. *Tail shorter than others of the genus.* Black bill slightly curved; eyes and eyering bright red. Brownish gray above, crown grayer; *throat and chest rufous;* rest of underparts whitish; tail graduated, each feather blackish distally with narrow white tip (most visible from below). Imm.: light brown above with pale gray throat; tail tipping obscure or lacking; eyes brown; eyering yellow.
**Similar species:** Small size, contrasting rufous throat and chest, and short tail may suggest a thrush. Imm. closely resembles Ash-colored Cuckoo (2) but is shorter-tailed, less buffy below, and eye and eyering color differ.
**Voice:** Call a *churr,* or a grating *trrr trrr trrr . . .* at about 1 per sec (Ralph 1975); dawn song a *kööa kööa* (P. Schwartz).
**Behavior:** Sluggish and inconspic. as it peers slowly about in both inner and outer branches at almost any ht. or as it occas. even drops to ground near cover. Usually alone.
**Breeding:** Jan–Aug near Cali but perhaps throughout year. Monogamous and polyandrous mating occurs. Flimsy twig, tendril, and leaf platform 1-7m up, usually in canopy of smaller tree; 2-3 white eggs; young leave 4-11 days prior to full flight (Ralph 1975).
**Status and habitat:** Fairly common (easily overlooked) locally in gallery forest, woodlots, tree-lined or shrubby pastures, parks, and gardens. Favors drier areas but has recently expanded into humid and wet regions in forest clearings (Nicéforo and Olivares 1966; Ralph 1975).
**Range:** To 1000m (small nos. to 2600m). Pacific coast near Buenaventura, Carib. region from Atlántico e to w base of Santa Marta Mts. (Ciénaga), n end Perijá Mts. (Carraipía), mid. Magdalena Val. in s Cesar (8°40′N) and Sabana de Bogotá s to Tolima; e of Andes from Norte de Santander to Arauca (sightings in n Arauca, Nov 1978—W. McKay and J. Jorgenson), Meta (photo—Brown; Carimagua—S. Furniss) and w Caquetá (Florencia). Perhaps e to the Orinoco. Colombia and Venez.

## 2. [ASH-COLORED CUCKOO]
*Coccyzus cinereus*                    Pl. 12, Map 289
**Identification:** 9.5″ (24cm). Tail mod. long and rather square. Black bill slightly curved; eyes and eyering red. Pale brownish gray above, palest on head; *throat and breast buffy gray;* otherwise pearly white below, abdomen tinged buff; ungraduated tail ash brown, the feathers subterminally black with *narrow white tips* (visible from below).
**Similar species:** See imm. Dwarf Cuckoo (1). Larger, longer-tailed Black-billed Cuckoo (3) is not reported e of Andes. Other *Coccyzus* cuckoos show more contrast betw. upper and underparts and have large round terminal tail spots (cf. 5, 7).
**Voice:** In Argentina a sonorous *cow-w cow-w cow cow,* like Yellow-billed Cuckoo but without the usual clucking ending of latter (Wetmore 1926).
**Status and habitat:** Hypothetical. 1 sight rec. at Leticia, 14 July 1975 (B. D. Parmeter, J. Parmeter, G. Bolander). Perhaps a trans-Amazonian migrant from the austral region. Scrubby areas.
**Range:** To 300m. Leticia, Amazonas. Breeds

in e Bolivia, n Argentina, Paraguay, and Uruguay. Accidental in e Peru (sight) and e Brazil.

### 3. BLACK-BILLED CUCKOO
*Coccyzus erythropthalmus*
**Identification:** 11" (28cm). Long graduated tail. Slightly curved black bill; *bare eyering red* (or yellow—imm.), eyes dark. Brownish olive above, white below; throat usually tinged buff; tail feathers becoming dusky subterminally with *narrow white tips* (visible from below). Imm.: tinged buff below and primaries somewhat rufous.
**Similar species:** Yellow-billed Cuckoo (4) has yellow lower mandible (except imm.), rufous primaries, much broader white tail tip spots, and grayish eyering (or yellow in imm.). Also cf. 2, 6, 7, 8.
**Behavior:** Like others of the genus, shy and furtive and seldom away from cover. Rarely or never vocal on wintering ground.
**Status and habitat:** Rare transient and winter resident, rec. early Nov–early Apr. Recs. few and widely scattered but to be expected almost anywhere. Reported mostly in Oct in Panama (Ridgely 1976).
**Range:** To 1600m (prob. higher). W of Andes. Breeds in e N America; winters in w S America mostly from n and w Venez. to n Peru. Accidental in n Argentina, Paraguay, Bolivia, Trinidad.

### 4. YELLOW-BILLED CUCKOO
*Coccyzus americanus* Pl. 12, Map 290
**Identification:** 12" (30cm). Closely resembles Black-billed Cuckoo. Bill black above, *yellow below* (var. in imm.); eyes dark; bare eyering gray (yellow in imm.). Slender. Brownish olive above, white below; long graduated tail, all but central feathers blackish with *broad, spotlike white tips* (visible from below); *primaries rufous* (conspic. in flight).
**Similar species:** See Black-billed Cuckoo (3). Mangrove Cuckoo (6) has prom. black mask, buffy underparts, and lacks the rufous primaries. Also cf. Pearly-breasted, Dark-billed, and Gray-capped cuckoos (5, 7, 8).
**Behavior:** Shy, furtive, and quiet on wintering grounds. Usually within denser cover. Transients sometimes concentrate in nos. temporarily.
**Status and habitat:** Transient and winter resident, mostly mid-Sept–mid-May, a few linger on oversummer (sightings, 3 June near Bogotá; 6 June at Buga, Valle; 10 June, Santa Marta—Hilty; 25 June near Barranquilla—A. Sprunt IV; and once 20 Aug). Fairly common locally, but birds of arid Carib. zones may move seasonally: numerous Sept–Dec in dry

scrub near Santa Marta, thereafter rare or absent (S. M. Russell). At Popayán, Cauca, 7 recs. 8 Oct–22 Nov, and 6 recs. 21 Apr–24 May, none in betw. (Wallace 1958). Large nos. of transients 19-26 Apr at Laguna Fúquene n of Bogotá (A. Gast).
**Range:** To 2600m. W of Andes (no recs. in sw region—see range map); e of them at Villavicencio, Macarena Mts., Vaupés (Mitú, 5-27 Sept), and 6 recs. at Leticia (16 Oct–20 May—J. V. Remsen). Breeds in N America, Mexico, and n W Indies; winters mostly in S America s to Brazil and Argentina; rarely C America.

### 5. PEARLY-BREASTED CUCKOO
*Coccyzus euleri* Pl. 12, Map 291
**Identification:** 10" (25cm). Much like previous 2 sp. Slender and long-tailed; bare eyering gray; bill black above, *chrome yellow below*. Uniform brown above, light pearly gray below; center of belly whitish; underside of graduated tail blackish with *broad spotlike white tips*.
**Similar species:** From Yellow-billed Cuckoo (4) by uniform brown wings (no rufous); from Black-billed (3) by yellow lower mandible, large, round, terminal tail spots (from below), and gray eyering. Also cf. Dark-billed Cuckoo (7).
**Voice:** Song 5-15 (sometimes up to 20 or more) deliberate *kuoup* notes (sounds doubled), 1 per sec or slower, esp. at end; recalls the slow terminal notes of Yellow-billed Cuckoo: less often a short, ascending rattle followed by 4-9 accented notes almost identical to those of Yellow-billed Cuckoo, *tuctuctuctuctuctuc towlp, tówlp, tówlp tówlp*, (P. Schwartz recording). Migrant Yellow-billed Cuckoo is normally silent in Colombia.
**Status and habitat:** Sandy-belt woodland, scrub, and gallery forest. Known from only 2 localities in Colombia. Prob. an austral migrant (R. Ridgely).
**Range:** To 400m. The Carib. coast near Cartagena (22 Jan), and extreme se Guainía along the Río Negro (Macacuní). Very locally in Surinam, Guyana, Venez. (incl. Río Orinoco opp. Vichada), se Peru, e and s Brazil, and n Argentina.

### 6. MANGROVE CUCKOO
*Coccyzus minor* Map 292
**Identification:** 12" (30cm). Slender and long-tailed. *Lower mandible yellow*; bare eyering yellow. Grayish brown above; crown grayish; *broad black mask through eyes and ear coverts*; underparts light to dark buff, palest on throat; tail graduated, all but central feathers dusky with *broad spotlike white tips* (visible from below).
**Similar species:** Dark-billed Cuckoo (7) is smaller with all black bill and grayish band

from lower cheeks to sides of neck. Gray-capped Cuckoo (8) is much darker and more richly colored above and below, and tail black from above. Also see Yellow-billed Cuckoo (4).
**Voice:** A low, grating *ke-ke-ke-ke-ka-ka-ka* (ffrench 1973), slower than Yellow-billed.
**Behavior:** Everywhere skulking and secretive.
**Breeding:** In Trinidad, July and Sept; frail stick and leaf platform 2-3 m above water in mangroves; 3 bluish green eggs (ffrench 1973).
**Status and habitat:** Known only from "Bogotá" skins, presum. from Colombia. Elsewhere in mangroves or thickets near water, much less frequently in lightly wooded or scrubby areas away from water.
**Range:** Presum. Carib. coast. Breeds in W Indies and s Florida, locally in Mid. America, Venez., Trinidad, Dutch Antilles, the Guianas, and ne Brazil.

## 7. DARK-BILLED CUCKOO
*Coccyzus melacoryphus*     Pl. 12, Map 293
**Identification:** 10″ (25cm). Typical *Coccyzus* shape. *Bill black*; bare eyering grayish. Grayish brown above; crown and nape grayish; *black mask through eyes and ear coverts; underparts buff*; narrow band from lower cheeks down sides of neck pale gray; graduated tail bronzy above, blackish below with *large, round, spotlike white tips*.
**Similar species:** See rare Gray-capped and Mangrove cuckoos (8, 6), both of which are more fulvous below, have some yellow on lower mandible and lack the inconspic. gray band on sides of neck. Also cf. other *Coccyzus* (3, 4, 5).
**Voice:** Infrequent song, *cu-cu-cu-cu-cu-kolp, kolp, kulop*, or with last 3-4 notes omitted, recalls that of Yellow-billed Cuckoo (4) but shorter, slower, and weaker; also a dry, rattling *dddddrr*.
**Behavior:** Usually solitary and rather low in leafy vegetation but less secretive than others of the genus, occas. even perching in the open on fence wires, or along thickety borders.
**Breeding:** BC ♂, 24 Oct and 2 laying ♀♀, 1 with pale blue egg, 18 Oct, near Cúcuta, Norte de Santander (Carriker). Aug breeding in Venez. (Thomas 1979b).
**Status and habitat:** Fairly common in humid *terra firme* and *várzea* borders, streamside thickets and mangroves, as well as drier open ranchland with shrubby borders, woodlots, and gallery forest. Perhaps some austral migrants(?) e of Andes (seen only 31 May–4 Oct near Leticia—J. V. Remsen; 7 May–20 Aug at Carimagua, ne Meta—S. Furniss). Yr.-round w of Andes but poss. less numerous during austral summer. No breeding in Jan in upper Magdalena Val. (Miller 1947); return to breed in n Argentina in Sept (Hudson 1920).

**Range:** To 2100m (sightings to 2400m, Laguna Fúquene, late Apr—A. Gast). Prob. throughout, incl. Gorgona Isl. (but see range map). The Guianas and Venez. to w Peru, n Chile, c Argentina, and Uruguay.

## 8. GRAY-CAPPED CUCKOO
*Coccyzus lansbergi*     Pl. 12, Map 294
**Identification:** 10″ (25cm). Typical *Coccyzus* shape. Bill black, small spot of yellow at base of lower mandible. *Rich rufescent brown above with dark gray cap to below eyes; underparts deep rufous buff*, deepest on throat and chest; long graduated *tail black above and below with broad, spotlike white tips* (mainly visible from below).
**Similar species:** Much darker above and below than Mangrove or Dark-billed cuckoos (6, 7). Note slaty cap, blackish tail, and darker fulvous underparts than any other *Coccyzus*.
**Voice:** Faster than most others of the genus: 6-8 rapid, hollow *cu*'s, the last slightly slower, *cucucucucucu-cu*; may be repeated several times in quick succession (P. Schwartz recording).
**Behavior:** Furtive and apparently usually low in thickets.
**Breeding:** BC ♂, 5 May, w Guajira (Carriker). In sw Ecuador 3 flat twig and lichen nests 1-2m up in horizontal branches of a small tree and bushes; 2-3 greenish white eggs. Blackish young leave nest before they can fly (Marchant 1960).
**Status and habitat:** Few recs. Known from thickets and dense shrubbery near water; once at edge of wet forest. In sw Ecuador believed migratory with most breeding during rainy early half of yr. (Marchant 1960).
**Range:** To 600m. Carib. region from near Cartagena (Turbaco) and sw Atlántico (Laguna Luruaco) e to w and ne base Santa Marta Mts. and w Guajira (Los Gorros); mid. Magdalena Val. in s Bolívar (Simití) and Norte de Santander (near Cúcuta, 600m); 1 sight record, 3 Feb 1977, Pacific slope in upper Anchicayá Val., 500m (M. Gochfeld, G. Tudor, and G. S. Keith). Locally in n and w Venez. (to 1400m), sw Ecuador, and n Peru.

## 9. SQUIRREL CUCKOO
*Piaya cayana*     Pl. 12, Map 295
**Identification:** 17″ (43cm). Large and loose-jointed. *Bill and bare orbital ring pale greenish yellow* (or orbital ring red—e of Andes); eyes red. *Chestnut above*; throat and upper breast buff fading to light gray on lower breast and becoming black on abdomen and under tail coverts; *very long graduated tail dark chestnut, the feathers with broad, round, spotlike white tips below*.
**Similar species:** Remarkably like Black-bellied Cuckoo (10), which has gray cap, red bill, yellow loral spot, and blackish lower underparts.

Little Cuckoo (11), a half-sized version of Squirrel Cuckoo, has mostly cinnamon chestnut underparts and a proportionally shorter tail.
**Voice:** Several distinctive calls, none given frequently. Most common a loud dry *chick, kwah,* a loud *geep-kareer,* reminiscent of Great Kiskadee (Ridgely 1976), a loud *stit* or *stit-it* in alarm; song a loud ringing *wheep* repeated 5-8 times (Willis and Eisenmann 1979).
**Behavior:** Often unobtrusive as hops along limbs or up through vine tangles in a series of leaping bounds or squirrellike runs, then sails out across a clearing. Solitary or with mixed flocks, occas. at army ant swarms.
**Breeding:** Nestling, 18 May, fledgling, 25 May, ne Meta (S. Furniss). Copulation, 21 Jan, upper Anchicayá Val. (B. Hilty). Santa Marta nest, 10 July (Todd and Carriker 1922); 2 laying ♀♀, Apr and May, s Córdoba and s Bolívar (Carriker). In Costa Rica, Jan–Oct (Skutch 1966). Frail, unlined platform in fork of bush or tree, 2-3 white eggs. Young leave prior to flying.
**Status and habitat:** Common in dry to wet forest, forest borders, tall second growth, and semiopen areas with trees. In Amazonia partially replaced in *terra firme* forest by Blackbellied Cuckoo.
**Range:** To 2700m. Throughout. W Mexico to n Argentina and Uruguay.

## 10. BLACK-BELLIED CUCKOO
*Piaya melanogaster*                    Pl. 12, Map 296
**Identification:** 15″ (38cm). Much like Squirrel Cuckoo. *Bill red;* bare orbital area blue; *large yellow loral spot.* Rufous chestnut above with *gray cap;* throat and breast orange buff becoming black on abdomen and under tail coverts. Tail as in Squirrel Cuckoo but shorter.
**Similar species:** See Squirrel Cuckoo (9).
**Voice:** Reminscent of Squirrel Cuckoo but harsher and heard far less frequently; a loud *jjit, jjit-jjit-jjit,* and scratchy, descending *yaaaaa* followed by a dry, jaylike rattle.
**Behavior:** Like Squirrel Cuckoo, though mainly in forest canopy, less frequently in low shrubby growth away from forest.
**Breeding:** A BC bird, Apr, upper Orinoco, Venez. (Friedmann 1948).
**Status and habitat:** Uncommon in humid *terra firme* forest incl. sand-belt forest, occas. forest borders, even low, scrubby, savanna woodland in e Guainía.
**Range:** To 500m. E of Andes from s Meta (Macarena Mts.) ne Guainía (sightings, Pto. Inírida, Sept 1978—Hilty and M. Robbins), and Vaupés southward. Guianas and s Venez. s to e Peru, n Bolivia, and w Amazonian Brazil.

## 11. LITTLE CUCKOO
*Piaya minuta*                    Pl. 12, Map 297
**Identification:** 10″ (25cm). A small version of Squirrel Cuckoo. Differs in throat and breast rufous chestnut, *lower underparts buffy gray* (not black), *much smaller with proportionally shorter tail,* and bare red eyering. Imm.: darker, more liver brown with dusky primaries; no white on tail feather tips; and bill dark.
**Voice:** Calls usually given infrequently. Harsh clucking *tchek* or *kek* (ffrench 1973) and a sharp *quienk* (O'Neill 1974); a nasal chattering *aannh anhh-anhh-anhh. . . ,* opening note distinctly separate, rest descending chatter; also a low whistled *tyoooooo* (J. V. Remsen); a weak, hoarse *geep, were,* like a muted Squirrel Cuckoo.
**Behavior:** Furtive and easily overlooked as it peers sluggishly in low, shrubby growth. Drops to ground frequently.
**Breeding:** 3 BC birds, Jan–May, upper Río Sinú and lower Cauca (Carriker). A July nest in Trinidad (ffrench 1973). Deep twig cup in thick shrubbery; 2 white eggs.
**Status and habitat:** Uncommon to fairly common but local. Forest borders, thickets, and shrubby second growth, usually near water. Can reg. be found around Lago de Sonso, Valle.
**Range:** To 1600m. Spottily throughout (few recs. on Pacific coast and none in Nariño) in humid regions. E Panama to the Guianas and s e of Andes to n Bolivia and s c Brazil.

## 12. GREATER ANI
*Crotophaga major*                    Ill. 58, Map 298
**Identification:** 18″ (46cm). *Prom. white eyes* (or brown—imm.). Black bill compressed with arched ridge on basal portion of upper mandible ("*broken nose*" profile). *Sleek, glossy bluish black* with greenish luster on wings and purplish gloss on long rounded tail.
**Similar Species:** Smooth-billed and Groovebilled Ani (13, 14) are smaller with dark eyes and much duller plumage. ♂ Great-tailed Grackle (p 567) has pale eyes, but the shape of bill and tail are different.
**Voice:** Often noisy. Strange electronic noises incl. a guttural gobbling or bubbling *kro-koro* repeated rapidly in a chorus ("pot-boiling" sound), a drawn out reptilian growl, and a variety of croaks, grates, hisses, and whirrs.
**Behavior:** Gregarious in groups of 4-100 or more. Perch low, *normally* near water but occas. with army ants deep in forest or along forest roads away from ants. More wary than other anis. Eat insects, small vertebrates, and other smaller prey.
**Breeding:** 2 BC ♀♀, Dec and Jan, n Antioquia (Carriker). In Trinidad, Aug–Nov, often breed communally (ffrench 1973). In Guyana (Young

58. SMOOTH-BILLED ANI (left), GREATER ANI (center),
GROOVE-BILLED ANI (right)

1925) and Panama nests are bulky, flat, leaf-lined cups on branches overhanging water; 6-7 greenish blue eggs covered with chalky coating. (Wetmore 1968a; Willis and Eisenmann 1979).

**Status and habitat:** Locally common in thickets and trees along rivers, lakes, swamps, edges of marshes, and in mangroves. Esp. numerous in the Amazonian region.

**Range:** Mostly below 500m (occas. wanders to Sabana de Bogotá, 2600m). From Panama border s on Pacific coast to mid. Río San Juan (4°39′N), n of Andes e to w base of Santa Marta Mts., s to lower Cauca Val., locally to upper Magdalena Val., and generally e of Andes (local in llanos). C Panama to n Argentina.

### 13. SMOOTH-BILLED ANI
*Crotophaga ani* Ill. 58, Map 299
**Identification:** 13″ (33cm). Black bill arched and laterally compressed with a *raised hump on the basal half of the upper mandible* forming a distinct notch between the bill and forehead. Eyes dark. Plumage dull black with long loosely connected, rounded tail.

**Similar species:** Often confused with Groove-billed Ani (14) and best identified by voice or by distinct hump on basal half of upper mandible, as opposed to the smooth even arc of the Groove-billed Ani's bill that tapers smoothly from the forehead. Caution: young Smooth-billed Anis often lack a distinct hump on bill. Presence or absence of grooves on bill is best seen in the hand. Also see Greater Ani (12).

**Voice:** A whining, long-drawn *ooeeeck* or *oooo-eeelk* that may be repeated several times, esp. in flight (Eisenmann 1957).

**Behavior:** Gregarious and inevitably in small, loose, unkempt groups that are conspic. and familiar everywhere. Perch in bushes, small trees, on the ground, or lined up in disheveled rows on fences. Flight is weak and barely utilitarian, a few quick flaps and a sail. Called "Garrapateros" by some for frequent assoc. with cattle and occas. habit of picking ticks from the animals.

**Breeding:** Building nest, 28 July, above Cali (S. Gniadek), and 20 Aug and 23 Dec on Pacific slope in Valle; dependent fledgling with 4-5 ads., 6 June, Cali (Hilty). In Trinidad breed yr.-round with May–Oct peak. Nest communally. Large open cup, sometimes with several layers, each with unincubated eggs, usually 2-6m up in shrubbery; normally up to 9 eggs (max. of 29 reported).

**Status and habitat:** Common in brushy pastures, clearings, and more or less open areas. Has greatly profited from deforestation, esp. at higher el. Replaced in swampy areas by Greater Ani, and prefers more humid places than the drier, scrubbier habitat of the Groove-billed.

**Range:** To about 2000m, in smaller nos. to 2700m. Throughout incl. the Guajira peninsula. S Florida; W Indies, and sw Costa Rica to w Ecuador and n Argentina.

### 14. GROOVE-BILLED ANI
*Crotophaga sulcirostris*     Ill. 58, Map 300
**Identification:** 11-12″ (28-30cm). Black bill arched and laterally compressed, *the culmen forming a smooth, unbroken arc with forehead*; upper mandible with inconspic. grooves on the side. Eyes dark. Plumage dull black, somewhat glossier than Smooth-billed Ani. Tail long, rounded, loosely connected.

**Similar species:** See slightly larger Smooth-billed Ani (13).

**Voice:** A dry *swilk* or *hwilk*, usually in ser.; faster series resemble *wicka* calls of flicker (*Colaptes*) of N America (Eisenmann 1957).

**Behavior:** Flies even slower than Smooth-billed Ani, but behavior and disheveled appearance otherwise sim.

**Breeding:** Nest, 22 Oct, Cúcuta (Carriker); 2 nests, July and Sept–Nov in Venez. (Thomas 1979b); 1 on 13 Jan, upper Magdalena Val. (Miller 1947). Apparently communal; build large, open, stick and bowl bowl or use abandoned nest of other birds; each ♀ lays up to 4 blue green eggs with chalky "bloom" that rubs off; up to 18 eggs (Skutch 1959c).

**Status and habitat:** Locally common in drier scrubby areas, thickets, and pastures. Sometimes with Smooth-billed Ani, though latter favors more humid regions.

**Range:** To 500m. Disjunct and local. Carib. region from n Córdoba e to Guajira, s in drier parts of mid. and upper Magdalena Val. to n Huila, extreme sw Nariño near Tumaco, Norte de Santander (Cúcuta region), and extreme e Vichada (along Orinoco). Sw US s to w Peru, rarely n Chile; e of Andes in Venez. Guyana and n Argentina. Aruba to Trinidad.

### 15. STRIPED CUCKOO
*Tapera naevia*     Pl. 12, Map 301
**Identification:** 11-12″ (28-30cm). *Quaillike head with short bushy crest* rufous striped black. Rather long graduated tail; short bill slightly curved. *Above sandy brown streaked buff and blackish*, incl. very long uppertail coverts (over half length of tail); long whitish eyebrow and black "whisker" line; underparts whitish with *narrow black malar stripe*; throat and chest tinged buff. Imm.: darker, more rufescent than ad.; crown and upperparts with pearllike buff spots; scattered buff barring on chest.

**Similar species:** Pheasant Cuckoo (16) is slightly larger, with broader tail, much darker unstreaked upperparts, solid chestnut crown, and spotted throat and chest. Also cf. Pavonine Cuckoo (note under 15).

**Voice:** Often vocal. Most common call a pure, mellow, minor-keyed whistle, 2d note a half-tone higher than the 1st, *wüüü weee*, this sometimes expanded to a 3-, 4-, 5-, or 6-note call with the last 2 notes quicker, next to last a half-tone higher. Notably ventriloquial and far carrying.

**Behavior:** Heard far more than seen. Usually calls from exposed perch on top of low bush, fence post, or low bare limb but otherwise secretive and skulking, and usually alone in dense cover near ground. Raises crest and spreads alula feathers when singing. Runs rapidly on ground, and often stops to posture with crest raises, wing droops, and alula flexes as though afflicted with a nervous tic.

**Breeding:** Parasitic; favors spp. with domed nests such as spinetails, wrens, and *Myiozetetes* flycatchers (N. G. Smith). 2 BC ♀♀, 1 with pale blue egg in oviduct, Apr, s Bolívar (Carriker); Sept in Venez. (Thomas 1979b).

**Status and habitat:** Fairly common in scrubby or open areas with scattered trees, thickets, and bushes. Quite local in forested zones where confined to clearings, bushy regrowth in pastures, and scrub on river isls. (e.g., Amazon river isls. near Leticia).

**Range:** To 1800m. Generally w of Andes except on Pacific coast where rec. only from lower Atrato Val. and w Valle (sightings, lower Dagua and lower Anchicayá vals., 1977-1978—Hilty); e of Andes s to s Meta and Río Guaviare; and the Amazon near Leticia (many voice and sight recs. since 1978 on Isla Corea and adj. banks of the Río Amazon—Hilty, R. Ridgely). S Mexico to sw Ecuador, Bolivia, and c Argentina. Trinidad.

### 16. PHEASANT CUCKOO
*Dromococcyx phasianellus*     Pl. 12, Map 302
**Identification:** 15″ (38cm). *Thin-necked and small-*

headed. *Short, pointed, chestnut crest* bordered by long white postocular streak; *upperparts dark brown*, the feathers pale-edged; *throat and chest tinged buff with a band of dusky spotting across chest*; rest of underparts whitish; *long, wide, graduated (fan-shaped) tail brown*, the feathers pale-tipped, and covered by elongated, plumelike dark brown upper tail coverts, almost as long as the tail.

**Similar species:** See Striped Cuckoo (15) and Pavonine Cuckoo (note).

**Voice:** Resembles short call of Striped Cuckoo. A 3-note, whistled *se-sée-werrrrrrr*, the last note quavering; also a 4-noted, rising *sa, seh, si-see* (Willis and Eisenmann 1979).

**Behavior:** Secretive and infrequently seen but sometimes rather vocal. Usually 1-2m up, occas. higher but always near cover, which it flies to in short undulating flight with tail spread.

**Breeding:** BC ♂, 30 Apr, Snía. San Lucas (Carriker). Parasitic, laying in open nests more than covered nests; 1 egg was long, narrow, and dull white with a wreath of scattered rufous on large end (Naumburg 1930).

**Status and habitat:** Local. Thickets and undergrowth along forest borders or in second growth woodland. Because of secretive habits, prob. more widespread and numerous than the few recs. suggest.

**Range:** To 1300m. W slope Perijá Mts. (Tierra Nueva), mid. Magdalena Val. on e slope Snía. San Lucas (Norosí; Sta. Rosa); e base of Andes from Arauca to Meta (above Villavicencio); numerous sightings at Leticia (Quebrada Tucuchira, 1974-1975—J. V. Remsen). S Mexico locally to n Bolivia, ne Argentina, and se Brazil.

**Note:** Pavonine Cuckoo (*D. pavoninus*), known from nw and s Venez., e across the Guianas, e and s Brazil, e Ecuador, e Peru, and ne Bolivia to Paraguay, may occur in the Perijá region of ne Colombia and in Putumayo (rec. upper Río Napo, Ecuador), poss. extreme e and se Colombia (known from s Amazonas, Venez.). Much like Pheasant Cuckoo but smaller (10-11″), tail shorter, postocular stripe buff, and throat and chest uniform buff (no spotting). Call a whistled *püü, pee, püü-pe-pe*, 1st note lowest, last 2 a half-tone higher (P. Schwartz; A. Altmann).

## 17. RUFOUS-VENTED GROUND-CUCKOO

*Neomorphus geoffroyi*  Pl. 6, Map 303
**Identification:** 18″ (46cm). *Large, terrestrial, forest cuckoo*, in shape reminiscent of Greater Roadrunner (*Geococcyx*). Heavy, slightly decurved bill yellow green; bare blue green skin behind yellow eye. *Above, incl. long tail, bronzy*

brown (or bronzy green—*aequatorialis*) glossed green on wings; flat crest blue black; forehead and underparts brownish buff with a *narrow, broken black band across chest* deepening to rufous on lower underparts.

**Similar species:** Banded Ground-Cuckoo (18), which it prob. meets on mid. Pacific coast, is black below with white barring, not mainly buffy brown.

**Voice:** In Amazonian Brazil loud bill-clapping and a soft dovelike moaning *oooooo-oóp* (R. Ridgely).

**Behavior:** Mainly terrestrial though may perch well up in a tree when flushed (Carriker 1910). Often follows army ants and bands of White-lipped Peccaries. Runs like a roadrunner; notably wary and best detected by its frequent bill-snapping at swarms.

**Breeding:** Not parasitic; ads. with young seen in Brazil (Sick 1962; Willis and Eisenmann 1979). Brazil nest, 1 Sept, 2.5m up in dense swampy second growth; flat stick and leaf platform; 1 yellowish white egg on fresh green leaves (Roth 1981). 5 BC birds, Mar–Apr, n Antioquia to Chocó, incl. laying ♀ from Mutatá with whitish egg (Carriker).

**Status and habitat:** Rare and local. Humid forest in lowlands and foothills.

**Range:** To 1000m. Panama border s on Pacific coast to Baudó Mts., and e along n base of Andes in Córdoba (Quimarí) to upper Río Nechí (*salvini*); e of Andes in w Caquetá and Putumayo (*aequatorialis*). Nicaragua to nw Colombia; se Colombia and Brazil s of the Amazon s to n Bolivia.

**Note 1:** Two other *Neomorphus* cuckoos are poss. in e Colombia. Rufous-winged Ground-Cuckoo (*N. rufipennis*) of Surinam (sight), s Venez. (w to n and c Amazonas—Río Orinoco on Vichada boundary) and adj. n Brazil; undoubtedly occurs in e Vichada and poss. e Guainía. Shape and size of Rufous-vented but with large bare red ocular area; mostly dark bronzy green above; head, neck, and chest glossy purplish blue black; throat paler; lower breast and belly dull grayish brown, inner remiges maroon. **Note 2:** Red-billed Ground-Cuckoo (*N. pucheranii*) of ne Peru (lower Río Napo and Pebas) and both banks of Amazon in w Brazil should be found in Amazonas. Much like Rufous-winged Ground-Cuckoo, but bill red (not greenish yellow with dusky base) and red markings on face. Habits of both much as for Rufous-vented Ground-Cuckoo.

## 18. BANDED GROUND-CUCKOO

*Neomorphus radiolosus*  Pl. 6, Map 304
**Identification:** 18″ (46cm). *Large, terrestrial, for-*

*est cuckoo.* Shape reminiscent of Greater Road-runner (*Geococcyx*). Heavy bill dusky above, yellowish below; large bare blue ocular region. *Prom. crest and hindneck glossy blue black*; upper back and entire underparts black, *the feathers edged buffy white giving a scaled or banded appearance*; wings and lower back *uniform chestnut* and long tail blackish glossed bronzy green.

**Similar species:** See Rufous-vented Ground-Cuckoo (17).

**Behavior:** Presum. as for preceding sp. One was collected following peccaries.

**Status and habitat:** Rare and local. Known from only a few specimens from wet forest, mostly in foothills and lower slopes. Several recs. are from La Costa on slopes w of Cerro Munchique, Cauca.

**Range:** To 1200m (most recs. 700-1200m). Pacific Colombia from lower Río San Juan southward. W Colombia and nw Ecuador.

## HOATZINS: Opisthocomidae (1)

The hoatzin is a peculiar neotropical bird treated by some as most closely allied to galliformes, but recent biochemical and anatomical evidence suggests an affinity to cuckoos. They feed primarily on leaves and shoots of several marsh and swamp plants. To accommodate the dietary bulk, they have a large specialized crop that when filled makes balance and flight difficult, and as a result they often seem awkward and clumsy. The young are hatched largely naked and remain in the nest a long time, eventually acquiring two successive coats of down. At hatching they possess a claw on each wing that permits them to clamber about bushes with a degree of freedom shared only with some cuckoos. When frightened, the young drop into water below the nest and swim or dive to safety, later climbing back to the nest using their claws, bill, and feet. The claws and swimming ability are lost in a few weeks.

MicHel K. 75

59. HOATZIN

## 1. HOATZIN

*Opisthocomus hoazin*          Ill. 59, Map 305
**Identification:** 24-26″ (61-66cm). Unmistakable *prehistoric* appearance. Long-necked, long-tailed, and with *long, frizzled rufous crest. Large bare ocular area bright blue*; eyes red. Mainly bronzy olive above boldly streaked buff on hindneck and mantle; *shoulders and broad tail tip pale buff*; throat and breast buffy white; rest of underparts and *primaries chestnut.*
**Voice:** When disturbed, loud hissing and blowing sounds as if exhaling loudly; also low nasal reedy and guttural notes (Hilty); a harsh, low *ca-cherk*, resembling distant frog chorus when repeated (Friedmann and Smith 1950).
**Behavior:** Sedentary and sluggish in thickets or low to mid. branches near or over water; occas. treetops, esp. when roosting. Form small groups of 2-10 when breeding; larger groups up to 50 or more during nonbreeding periods. Fly weakly, typically a few flaps and glides interspersed with awkward hops and bounds among branches as they peer suspiciously and retreat deeper into swampy habitat.
**Breeding:** Small loose colonies. Frail stick platform 2-8m up over water; 1 Leticia nest, eggs, mid-July (Hilty and R. Bailey); 1 Aug nest (J. V. Remsen). June–Dec (high water) breeding, Venez. Orinoco (Cherrie 1916; Thomas 1979b). Mating poss. indiscriminate and polygamous with all group members participating in incubation and care of young. 2-5 pinkish cream eggs spotted pink, blue, or brown.
**Status and habitat:** Fairly common but local. Vegetation-choked borders of swamps, forested river banks, and oxbow lakes, esp. where giant arums (*Montrichardia* and *Caladium*) are present.
**Range:** To 500m. Throughout e of Andes but no Vichada recs; but prob. occurs in Guianía. The Guianas and e and c Venez. to Bolivia and Amazonian Brazil.

# BARN OWLS: Tytonidae (1)

Barn owls are found virtually worldwide. They are similar to typical owls in most respects but differ externally in having a heart-shaped facial disk and long legs. Mainly nocturnal, they are relentless hunters of small rodents and have proven a great benefit to those engaged in agriculture. They show great fidelity to nest sites, which may be buildings, steeples, or hollow logs.

## 1. BARN OWL

*Tyto alba*          Ill. 60, Map 306
**Identification:** 15″ (38cm). Med.-sized, *light-colored, earless owl with long legs.* Tawny above, mottled with dark gray and dotted black and white; *white to deep buff heart-shaped face* with narrow dusky rim; underparts white to deep buff dotted dusky; eyes blackish. In flight at night whitish under surface of wings and pale body appear ghostlike.
**Similar species:** No other Colombian owl is so pale. See Great Potoo (p 234), wich differs in shape and habits.
**Voice:** A var. of fairly loud hisses, snores, and scraping sounds but does not hoot. Most frequently a rough shriek or hiss; at nest loud bill snapping.
**Behavior:** Mostly nocturnal although occas. abroad at twilight. Often hunts from fence posts or other fairly low perches. A renowned "mouse-catcher," it also takes other small prey.
**Breeding:** Church steeple nest with eggs, 15 Sept, Sabana de Bogotá (Olivares 1969a). In

60. BARN OWL

w Ecuador lowlands, 4 fledglings, 4 July; nest with eggs, 21 July (Vuilleumier). 3-4 white eggs.
**Status and habitat:** Local in semiopen regions and around human habitations where it often roosts and nests. Almost certainly more numerous than scattered recs. suggest. Common along roads in w Meta (W. McKay); reported "numerous" in nw Ecuador (Vuilleumier) and doubtless also occurs in Pac. Nariño.

**Range:** To 3000m. Carib. region (Atlántico; s Magdalena), dry upper Magdalena Val., spottily in all 3 Andean ranges (no recs. w of W Andes), near Cúcuta, Norte de Santander, and e of Andes from Meta (Villavicencio; Macarena Mts.; Carimagua—S. Furniss) s to Caquetá-Putumayo boundary (Tres Esquinas). Virtually worldwide except Arctic and Antarctic regions and some oceanic isls.

# TYPICAL OWLS: Strigidae (22)

Owls are mainly solitary nocturnal birds of prey, although a few species normally hunt by day. They are characterized by large heads, feathered faces forming "facial disks," and large forward-facing eyes. Like other birds of prey, they have hooked bills and strong raptorial feet and claws but with two toes front and rear. The feet are usually feathered. The owls' soft plumage gives them a noiseless flight that is buoyant but not swift. Some have prominent feathered earlike tufts or "horns." Prey, located by both sight and sound, is mainly small mammals, birds, or occasionally snakes and frogs. Some of the smaller species eat mainly large insects. Typically prey is swallowed whole; and bones, fur, and other matter are later regurgitated in the form of pellets. Owls nest in tree holes, abandoned stick nests of other birds, or on the ground. Their eggs are white. Most Colombian owls, as is true elsewhere in humid tropical regions, are very infrequently seen and poorly known.

### 1. VERMICULATED SCREECH-OWL
*Otus guatemalae*            Pl. IX, Map 307
**Identification:** 8″ (20cm). *Small with ear tufts and no conspic. streaks or bars.* Bill and eyes yellow. Dark brown above, vermiculated dusky; wing coverts and scapulars spotted white; underparts light brown becoming whitish on abdomen and *very closely and narrowly vermiculated with wavy dusky brown bars* and with a few inconspic. narrow streaks. Rufous phase: shaded chestnut above and rufous below and appearing more uniform overall; otherwise sim.
**Similar species:** Tropical Screech-Owl (2) has black-rimmed facial disk and much more clearly defined black streaks below (few vermiculations). Rare Rufescent Screech-Owl (3) is conspic. streaked and barred below.
**Voice:** In Panama a short, quavering trill, *ro'o'o'o'o'oh* (unlike long song in Belize), resembles *Otus asio* of N America but is much shorter (Willis and Eisenmann 1979).
**Breeding:** ♀ ready to lay, 19 Mar, e Panama (Wetmore 1968a).
**Status and habitat:** Few recs. Understory to lower midlevels of humid forest and second growth in lowlands and lower mts.
**Range:** To 1000m. Known definitely only from Baudó Mts. (1000m); prob. also Panama border (rec. Cerro Pirre, Cerro Mali, e Darién) and Perijá Mts. (on Venez. slope). Mexico locally to w and n Venez.; e and w Ecuador, e Peru, n Bolivia; s Venez. and adj. n Brazil.
**Note:** Birds from Costa Rica southward

(*O. vermiculatus*) differ in voice and are sometimes considered a separate sp. from n *O. guatemalae.*

### 2. TROPICAL SCREECH-OWL
*Otus choliba*            Pl. IX, Map 308
**Identification:** 9″ (23cm). *Small owl with ears.* Yellow eyes. Grayish to cinnamon brown above with narrow dusky streaks and buffy mottling; large spotted white line on scapulars and wing coverts; flight feathers barred cinnamon brown and dusky; eyebrows and facial disk buffy white *with a conspic. black rim*; underparts whitish to cinnamon *with a few prom. narrow black streaks cross-hatched with very fine dusky lines.*
**Similar species:** By far the most common small owl in Colombia. Rufescent Screech-Owl (3) is sim. below but lacks prom. black facial rim and has brown (not yellow) eyes. Vermiculated Screech-Owl (1) lacks the black facial rim and has almost no definite streaks below. In extreme nw see Bare-shanked Screech-Owl (5).
**Voice:** Most vocal just after dusk or before dawn. Call a short, tremulous, whistled trill, usually followed by 2-3 abrupt accented notes at end, *ououououououou ook! ook!*, with frequent var.; the accented end notes are sometimes omitted.
**Behavior:** Entirely nocturnal and nearly always in pairs. Roosts in a cavity or on a branch at mod. ht.
**Breeding:** 3 BC birds, Jan–July, Magdalena and n Antioquia (Carriker); 2 nests with young, upper Magdalena Val., Jan–Feb (Miller 1947;

1952); 5 Panama nests, Jan–Mar (Wetmore 1968a). Nest in almost any kind of cavity, open rotten fence post, or abandoned bird nest, usually rather low; 1-3 white eggs.

**Status and habitat:** Common in dry to humid regions of lighter open woodland, tall second growth, *terra firme* and *várzea* forest borders, clearings with trees, and residential areas.

**Range:** To 2800m (sightings to 3000m, Represa Neusa, n Bogotá—Hilty and M. Robbins). Throughout e and w of Andes (w of W Andes known only from drier areas of Río Sucio in lower Atrato drainage and in upper Dagua Val.). Costa Rica to n Argentina, Paraguay, and s Brazil.

### 3. RUFESCENT SCREECH-OWL

*Otus ingens*                                      Map 309

**Identification:** 10-11″ (25-28cm). Large screech-owl with *rather small ears and brown eyes*. Sandy brown above, vermiculated blackish; partly concealed whitish to buff collar on hindneck; scapulars and wing coverts spotted white; flight feathers and tail barred dark brown and cinnamon; *facial disk sandy brown, no distinct facial rim*; throat buff finely barred brown; rest of underparts buffy white with a few prom. narrow black streaks cross-hatched sparsely with fine dusky lines.

**Similar species:** Much like Tropical Screech-Owl (2) but larger and has brown eyes and no black facial rim.

**Voice:** Song a fast, *utututututut . . .* , ser. of about 50 *ut* notes in 10 sec; pitch and quality much like that of Tropical Screech-Owl (P. Schwartz recording).

**Behavior:** Little known. An Anchicayá bird roosted alone about 7m up in same pocket of moss against a trunk on 2 consecutive days (Hilty).

**Breeding:** BC ♀ (1 ova 16 mm), 23 Jan, Anchicayá Val., 1250m (Hilty 1977).

**Status and habitat:** Few recs. Apparently rare in humid and wet mt. forest.

**Range:** 1200-1700m (higher ?). W slope Perijá Mts. (1200m) at Hiroca (*venezuelensis*); upper Cauca Valley (El Tambo, 1700m) and Pacific slope (1250m) in Anchicayá Val. (*colombianus*); e slope Andes (subsp.?) in Nariño (2 ♂♂ coll. by Von Sneidern, El Carmen, 1600m, Dec 1970—J. Fitzpatrick). W. Venez. s locally in Andes to n Bolivia.

**Note 1:** The *colombianus* subsp. is apparently a separate sp. (J. Fitzpatrick and J. O'Neill). **Note 2:** A "Bogota" skin (ANSP), originally misidentified, is prob. an undescribed sp. of *Otus* also recently found in Ecuador and Peru (M. Robbins and T. Schulenberg—*fide* J. Fitzpatrick). All 3 of these *Otus* are dark-eyed and closely related.

### 4. TAWNY-BELLIED SCREECH-OWL

*Otus watsonii*                        Pl. IX, Map 310

**Identification:** 9″ (23cm). *Small dark owl with decidedly long ear tufts*. Eyes amber. *Essentially uniform dusky brown above*; crown, "ears," and narrow facial rim blackish; *eyebrows, facial disk, and underparts ochraceous tawny* with some faint blackish vermiculations and a few fairly distinct narrow dark brown streaks on breast.

**Similar species:** Somewhat var. in color but always much darker above and more tawny below than Tropical Screech-Owl (2) and lacks latter's white eyebrow, white spotting on wing coverts and scapulars, and streaking below. Voice quite different.

**Voice:** Call a long (up to 20 sec or more) rapid ser. of low mellow *whoo* notes at about 2 per sec; often begins softly, swells in mid., then gradually fades away becoming very faint at end. May call even before dusk.

**Behavior:** Sim. to Tropical Screech-Owl but mainly an interior forest *Otus*.

**Status and habitat:** Uncommon (perhaps local) in humid *terra firme* and *várzea* forest, occas. at forest borders.

**Range:** To 500m. E of Andes from s Meta (Macarena Mts.) and Vaupés (net capture at El Dorado on Río Vaupés, June 1976—R. Ridgely) southward (*watsonii*). Prob. entire e base of E Andes s to Amazonas and e to Guianía. Surinam and Venez. (s of Orinoco; e base of Andes in Táchira; e side Perijá Mts. at 2000-2100m) e of Andes s to n Bolivia and Amazonian Brazil.

### 5. BARE-SHANKED SCREECH-OWL

*Otus clarkii*                                      Map 311

**Identification:** 9.5″ (24cm). *"Spotted" and with ear tufts*. Eyes yellow. Rufous brown above; crown streaked and back mottled with black; wing coverts and scapulars spotted white; *face cinnamon with no well-defined facial rim; throat and breast buffy brown spotted buffy white* and streaked blackish; rest of underparts buffy white irreg. barred tawny and narrowly streaked black (appears spotted). Most of tarsus bare (not visible in field).

**Similar species:** Note restricted range in Colombia. From other small owls by large (almost squarish) white spots below, rimless cinnamon face, and large-headed appearance (large even for an *Otus*).

**Voice:** Call a rather high, musical, 2-part hooting, *coo, coo-coo-coo* (Wetmore 1968a).

**Breeding:** A nearly grown young, 30 May, Colombia-Panama boundary (Wetmore 1968a).

**Status and habitat:** One Colombian specimen from humid mt. forest. Elsewhere a nocturnal owl of forest, woodland borders, and tree-lined fence rows, 1450-2250m.

**Range:** 1450m on Cerro Tacarcuna, Colombia-

Panama boundary. Costa Rica to extreme nw Colombia.

## 6. WHITE-THROATED SCREECH-OWL

*Otus albogularis*          Pl. IX, Map 312

**Identification:** 10″ (25cm). *Very dark owl with contrasting white throat and scarcely noticeable ear tufts.* Eyes yellow orange. Upperparts, head, and breast dark brown finely speckled white and buff; black rim on facial disk obscure; conspic. narrow white throat; belly and lower underparts tawny buff sparsely streaked dark brown. Juv.: buffy white finely and evenly barred dusky.

**Similar species:** A virtually earless screech-owl, darker than any other Colombian *Otus*. Look for the contrasting white throat and speckled upperparts. Only in mts.

**Voice:** A prolonged ser. of high-pitched, rapidly whistled notes, sometimes continuing uninterrupted for nearly a min, *wu wu wu wu . . .* (Hilty); a ser. of 7-17 clear notes, *hu hu hu . . .* , or longer ser. of 15-32 notes, *ko-ko-koko-koko-koko . . .* (Burton 1973).

**Behavior:** Nocturnal as in others of the genus.

**Breeding:** Needs confirmation. Salmon reports ground nests among ferns or grass; 1 incubating egg in deserted cup nest above ground (Sclater and Salvin 1879).

**Status and habitat:** Rare and local (perhaps overlooked). Known from a no. of widely scattered highland localities; mostly forest borders, open woodland, and semiopen areas with scattered trees.

**Range:** 2000-3000m. All 3 Andean ranges (in W Andes only rec. in Cauca and in E Andes s to Condinamarca). Nw Venez. (where rec. 1300-2100m) to n Bolivia.

## 7. CRESTED OWL

*Lophostrix cristata*          Pl. IX, Map 313

**Identification:** 16″ (41cm). Unmistakable. Large with *prom. white eyebrows continuous with very long, erect, partially white ear tufts.* Upperparts var., dark brown to light buffy brown somewhat mottled rufescent; wing coverts and scapulars with large white spots; primaries barred dark brown and buff; *facial disk rufescent; underparts tawny buff finely barred and vermiculated dusky.*

**Similar species:** Only Colombian owl with combination of unstreaked underparts and such spectacularly long white ear tufts.

**Voice:** Call a low-pitched, notably froglike *k, k, k'k'k'kkrrrrrr* (rapidly accelerates to a purr), at a distance sounds like an accelerating *grrrrrrr*; repeated about once every 5 sec at max. rate (P. Schwartz; Eisenmann). Cf. with sim.-sounding but 2-noted call of Bare-throated Tiger-Heron.

**Behavior:** Strictly nocturnal. Calls from upper part of tall trees but may roost by day (often in pairs) in dense undergrowth or at med. hts., often near streams.

**Breeding:** 4 BC ♂♂, Feb.–May, s Córdoba and n Chocó (Carriker). Hollow tree nests reported in Guyana (*in* Wetmore 1968a); 2 young in loft of Georgetown House, 1925 (Snyder 1966), an unusual site for a forest owl.

**Status and habitat:** Apparently rare and local in humid lowland forest, tall second growth and patches of woodland. No foothill or mt. recs.

**Range:** To 100m (Pacific coast); to 500m (e of Andes). Pacific coast from Panama border s to Nariño (Barbacoas); e along n base of Andes to mid. Magdalena Val. in Santander (El Tambor, 500m, in Lebrija Val.); e of Andes from w Caquetá southward. Locally from s Mexico to Bolivia, Amazonian Brazil, and the Guianas.

## 8. GREAT HORNED OWL

*Bubo virginianus*          Pl. IX, Map 314

**Identification:** 19-22″ (48-56cm). *Largest Colombian owl. Conspic. ear tufts; eyes yellow.* Above dark brown mottled buff and gray; facial disk buffy white rimmed black; *throat white*; rest of underparts closely *barred dark brown and whitish*; chest with a few broad blackish streaks.

**Similar species:** Crested Owl (7) has longer mostly white ear tufts, no prom. barring on underparts, and may meet but is not *known* to overlap in range.

**Voice:** Call usually 4-7 very deep, mellow hoots with considerable carrying power.

**Behavior:** Nocturnal. Roost and nest in tall palms at Carimagua, ne Meta (S. Furniss); prey on a variety of med.-sized animals, e.g., coati, rabbit, and 2 spp. of snipe in the Andes (Lehmann 1946).

**Breeding:** BC ♀, 22 Jan, lower Río Cauca (Carriker); 1 fledged young, 30 Apr, Guárico, Venez. (Mader 1981). Usually uses large abandoned hawk nest in palm or tall tree, occas. on ground or cave entrance; 2 eggs (sometimes more).

**Status and habitat:** Local. Several pairs at Carimagua, ne Meta, 1976 (S. Furniss), and a no. of sight recs. from temperate and paramo regions of C Andes (Lehmann 1946); otherwise recs. widely scattered. Apparently absent from humid lowland forest.

**Range:** To 4000m. Carib. region from lower Río Sinú and lower Río Cauca (s Bolívar) e to Guajira (Ríohacha), the upper Magdalena Val. in Tolima s to its headwaters, C Andes from Nevado del Tolima (nw of Ibaque) s to Nariño; e of Andes from n Arauca (sightings, Nov 1977—W. McKay) and e Vichada (sight,

El Tuparro, Aug 1977—P. Gertler) to Meta (Carimagua; San Martín). N America s to Tierra del Fuego but very local in tropical lowlands.

## 9. SPECTACLED OWL

*Pulsatrix perspicillata*  Pl. IX, Ill. 61, Map 315
**Identification:** 18″ (46cm). Large earless owl. Eyes yellow. Head and underparts dark chocolate brown; *broad eyebrows extending to lores and below eyes* (the "spectacles") *white;* throat white; *chest band dark brown; lower underparts creamy buff.* Juv. very different: *almost entirely buffy white with black face* (somewhat heart-shaped) and brown wings. May require up to 5 yrs. to attain fully ad. plumage.
**Similar species:** Band-bellied Owl (10) has same pattern as ad., but lower underparts barred (not uniform creamy buff). Buff-fronted Owl (22), also superficially sim., is only half the size and confined to high el. Nothing resembles the charming juv.
**Voice:** Most common call a fairly rapid ser. of 6-8 low-pitched, resonant, motmotlike hoots, *boo-boo-boo-boo-boo-boo,* with slight popping quality (Hilty); also a descending ser. of muffled *woof* notes, and occas. a med.-pitched descending whistle (O'Neill 1974). More vocal on moonlit nights.
**Behavior:** Mainly nocturnal, although occas. abroad on cloudy days. Roosts from near eye level to canopy.
**Breeding:** BC ♂, 15 June, w Caquetá (Carriker). Panama nestlings, 9 Sept and 30 Oct (Willis and Eisenmann 1979). Nests in tree holes; 2 white eggs (ffrench 1973).
**Status and habitat:** Fairly common (but infre-

quently seen) in humid lowland forest, second growth, and lighter woodland; also gallery forest in drier areas. Absent from wet Pacific belt between Baudó Mts. and Nariño, but reappears in w Ecuador.
**Range:** To 1000m (most recs. below 500m). Pacific coast from Panama border s to Baudó Mts., e across entire n lowlands n of Andes to w Guajira, s in mid. Magdalena Val. to n Tolima (Honda; Ambalema); once to mid. Cauca Val. s of Cali; e of Andes prob. throughout (rec. from e Norte de Santander, w Meta, w Caquetá, and Vaupés; also Venez. side of Orinoco, and a sighting on Río Javarí, Brazil, s of Leticia, 1979—Hilty). S Mexico to w Ecuador, nw Argentina, Paraguay, and s Brazil. Trinidad.

## 10. BAND-BELLIED OWL

*Pulsatrix melanota*  Map 316
**Identification:** 18″ (46cm). Large earless owl. *Much like Spectacled Owl.* Differs in having lower breast dark brown with a few whitish cross lines (forms a fairly distinct dark band), belly and *rest of underparts white heavily barred rusty brown.*
**Similar species:** See under Spectacled Owl (9).
**Voice:** Several deep muffled hoots in Peru (T. Parker).
**Status and habitat:** Little known; perhaps rare throughout range. Known in Colombia from 1 ad. specimen (FMNH, Chicago) of undetermined sex, locality, or date (E. R. Blake). Humid lowland forest.
**Range:** *Presum.* se Colombia. E Ecuador (to 1000m on upper Río Napo), e Peru, and n Bolivia.

## 11. LEAST PYGMY-OWL

*Glaucidium minutissimum*  Ill. 62, Map 317
**Identification:** 5.5″ (14cm). Small earless owl. Eyes yellow. *Head grayish dotted with white, esp. on crown;* narrow buff nuchal collar terminating on either side of rearcrown in a small oval black spot ("false eyespot"); otherwise essentially uniform brown above, or with a few buffy white spots on shoulders and wings; tail black with *3 visible white bars* and narrow white tip; *underparts white broadly streaked dark rufous on chest and sides.* Imm.: lacks white dots on head.
**Similar species:** Crown of ad. Ferruginous Pygmy-Owl (13) is streaked (not spotted) with white or buff, and tail has more bars. Andean Pygmy-Owl (12), a highland bird, is barred or spotted below (not streaked). Ranges of other *Glaucidium* not known to overlap.
**Voice:** Call in Venez. a short fast ser. of low, staccato *poop*'s, 6-12 in 2 sec on the same pitch or slightly descending (P. Schwartz); faster and

61. SPECTACLED OWL (juv.)

62. ANDEAN PYGMY-OWL (bottom left), FERRUGINOUS PYGMY-OWL (top center),
LEAST PYGMY-OWL (bottom right)

shorter than that of Ferruginous Pygmy-Owl.
**Behavior:** Active by day or night in forest; found
from canopy to mid. story. Flight dipping.
**Status and habitat:** Apparently very local. Humid lowland forest and forest borders; not
well known in Colombia.
**Range:** To 600m. Known from near Panama
boundary at base of Cerro Tacarcuna (Río
Tacarcuna, 600m) and n end of W Andes in
sw Córdoba (Río Verde del Sinú). Spottily from
w Mexico to nw Colombia; e Venez., Guyana,
e and s Brazil, e Peru, and Paraguay.

## 12. ANDEAN PYGMY-OWL
*Glaucidium jardinii*          Ill. 62, Map 318
**Identification:** 6″ (15cm). No ear tufts. Eyes
yellow. Dark brown above; *crown dotted with
buff, and back spotted buff;* semiconcealed cinnamon buff nuchal band terminates on each
side of nape in black oval eyespot ("false eyes");
flight feathers barred buff and white; tail
blackish with about *4 visible white bars and narrow white tip;* underparts white with irreg. brown
band across chest (often broken in middle);
*sides and flanks extensively barred and spotted* and
with a few streaks (streaking not prom.). Rufous phase: mostly rufous below with little
barring and no streaking. Imm.: unspotted
grayish crown (or spots on forecrown only);
sides streaked rather than barred.
**Similar species:** Only pygmy-owl in the high-

lands. From lowland Ferruginous Pygmy-Owl
(13) by dotted rather than finely streaked crown
(hard to see in field), 1 less white tail bar, and
barring and spotting on flanks (Ferruginous
has no barring below). Also see Least Pygmy-Owl (11).
**Voice:** Call in Costa Rica and Colombia a long
ser. of whistled *poop*'s given in couplets (Wolf
1976; Miller 1963). In Peru a long ser. (up to
several min) of evenly spaced *poop*'s (T. Parker) much like that of Ferruginous Pygmy-Owl.
**Behavior:** Abroad by day or by night. Stays in
canopy or forest midlevels.
**Breeding:** BC ♂, late Dec, Boyacá (Olivares
1971).
**Status and habitat:** Known from only a few
scattered localities in humid mt. forest and
forest borders. Prob. often overlooked.
**Range:** 2100-2800m. Perijá Mts. (Cerro Pintado) and locally in the Andes: n Boyacá (Guicán) to e of Bogotá (Choachí) in E Andes; e
of Medellín and Quindío Mts. in C Andes;
above Cali (San Antonio) and sighting at Cerro
Torrá, s Chocó (P. Silverstone) in W Andes.
Costa Rica to w Venez. and s in Andes to Bolivia.

## 13. FERRUGINOUS PYGMY-OWL
*Glaucidium brasilianum*        Ill. 62, Map 319
**Identification:** 6.5″ (16.5cm). No ear tufts. Eyes

yellow. 2 color phases. Either grayish brown or rufous above; *crown narrowly streaked buff or whitish*; oblong black eyespot ("false eye") on each side of back of head; wings with buff or whitish spots; *underparts white broadly streaked rufous or brown*, esp. on sides and flanks; *tail with 5-6 visible whitish bars.* Imm. lacks crown streaks.

**Similar species:** Note range. See Andean (12) and Least pygmy-owls (11).

**Voice:** Call a long ser. (up to several min) of *toot*'s or *poip*'s at rate of about 2.5 per sec; when excited a ser. of short purring or trilling *chir-rup*'s. Calls most often at dusk or before dark, sometimes during day.

**Behavior:** Active day or night and often mobbed by small birds. Responds strongly to whistled imitation of call as do many other birds in regions where it occurs. Flicks tail when agitated.

**Breeding:** Uses tree holes or cavities in termitaries. BC ♂, Mar, Cesar Val. (Carriker); 3 nests and fledglings, Mar–July, ne Venez. (Friedmann and Smith 1955); 1 Apr nest, Guárico, Venez. (Mader 1981). Cavity 3-12m up; 2-5 white eggs (ffrench 1973).

**Status and habitat:** Fairly common to locally common (esp. in drier areas) from dry forest and scrubby semiopen areas with trees and thickets to humid *terra firme* and *várzea* forest borders.

**Range:** Lowlands and foothills to at least 1000m. N Chocó (once); generally from Cartagena area e to Guajira (Ríohacha; Carraipía) and s to s Magdalena; e of Andes from Arauca (sightings, Arauca, 1978—W. McKay and J. Jorgenson) and e Vichada (El Tuparro—INDERENA) s to se Nariño and Leticia. Extreme sw US to n Chile, c Argentina, and Uruguay.

## 14. BURROWING OWL

*Speotyto cunicularia* Ill. 63, Map 320

**Identification:** 9″ (23cm). *Terrestrial earless owl with long legs and short tail.* Eyes yellow. Above rufous brown thickly spotted buff and white; *eyebrows and forehead white*; underparts mostly white with *narrow dusky chest band* (often interrupted in the mid.); breast and sides barred and spotted rufous brown. Imm.: plain buffy white below.

**Voice:** Usually quiet. A repeated *cack* when alarmed. At night a soft *coo-coooo.*

**Behavior:** Diurnal but most active mornings and evenings. Perches on ground, fence post, or other low place during the day. Bows and bobs frequently, esp. when disturbed.

**Breeding:** Colonies up to 10-20 pairs where unmolested. Grown young, 19 Jan, and nest with eggs, 23 Jan, upper Magdalena Val. (Miller

63. BURROWING OWL

1947); juvs. at nest burrows, Mar, c and ne Meta (S. Furniss; Brown). 2-11 white eggs in burrow that birds may dig.

**Status and habitat:** Local in grassland and semiopen arid scrub.

**Range:** To 500m. Cesar Val. (Casacará) e to Guajira Peninsula; arid portions of upper Magdalena Val. in Tolima and Huila; generally e of Andes in llanos s to Río Guaviare and s Meta (Macarena Mts.). Breeds locally in w N America (winters rarely to Panama), s Florida, W Indies, and locally in open parts of S America.

## 15. BLACK-AND-WHITE OWL

*Ciccaba nigrolineata* Pl. IX, Map 321

**Identification:** 16″ (41cm). Med.-sized; no ear tufts. Eyes yellowish brown. *Above sooty black narrowly barred white on upper back; facial disks black*; eyebrows and indistinct band surrounding disks speckled white; *otherwise white below narrowly and evenly barred black*; tail black with several narrow white bars.

**Similar species:** Much darker Black-banded Owl (16) has entire upperparts narrowly banded white (not just upper back), and is black below with narrow white lines (not mostly white with black lines); face does not contrast with underparts. Intermeds. betw. the 2 are known from e Colombia (Blake 1958).

**Voice:** Two very different calls, both much like next sp. (and see note): a high-pitched dry scream, rising, then falling, catlike, and strained as though only air is expelled (Hilty); and a deep, resonant, deliberate *hu, hu, hu, hóo-ah* (last phrase slurred) with var.; a ser. of 9-14 slow *hu-wah*'s and a single loud, deep *boo* at intervals (P. Schwartz recording).

**Behavior:** Nocturnal. In Panama and Venez. birds have been seen hunting near outdoor lights; roosting 10-20m up during day.

**Status and habitat:** Apparently very local in humid forest, forest borders, tall second growth, and clearings with trees, sometimes near habitations.

**Range:** To 1500m (once at 2400m near Cerro Munchique, Cauca). Spottily but prob. throughout w of Andes; e of them s poss. to w Caquetá (presumed contact zone with *C. huhula*). Known definitely from near Tierralta, Córdoba; Atrato, upper Dagua and Patía vals. on Pacific slope, Cauca Val. from near Cali (Ríofrío) to Cerro Munchique, ne base of Santa Marta Mts., Perijá Mts. (above Casacará), Magdalena Val. in s Bolívar and Tolima, and e of Andes in Norte de Santander (n of Cúcuta). S Mexico to c Venez. and nw Peru.

**Note:** May be conspecific with *C. huhula* (Black-banded Owl). Intermeds. from Río Barrero and w Caquetá (Blake 1958).

## 16. BLACK-BANDED OWL

*Ciccaba huhula*     Pl. IX, Map 322

**Identification:** 14″ (36cm). No ear tufts. Eyes yellow to brown. *Entirely black with very narrow white bars* (lines) *above and below* (slightly wider below); eyebrows and margins of facial disks speckled white; tail black with several narrow white bars and broader white tip.

**Similar species:** See allied Black-and-white Owl (15).

**Voice:** As in preceding sp. An ascending catlike scream, *whoeeeruh* followed after a short pause by a loud *booo*; also a deliberate, deep, resonant *hu, hu, hu, HOOO*, with var. (P. Schwartz recording).

**Behavior:** Nocturnal. Calls from mid. hts. to canopy.

**Breeding:** Young bird, 27 Jan, near Villavicencio (Lehmann 1957). BC ♂, Feb, Río Casiquiare, Venez. (Friedmann 1948).

**Status and habitat:** Known from 4 Colombian specimens but prob. often overlooked. Heard reg. on both banks of Río Javarí s of Leticia in July and Aug (J. V. Remsen, Hilty, et al.). Humid *terra firme* and *várzea* forests, forest borders, and trees in clearings.

**Range:** To 500m. E of Andes in w Meta (near Villavicencio) and w Caquetá (near Florencia). Prob. throughout s of Río Guaviare (known from adj. Río Casiquiare, Amazonas, Venez.). Guianas and s Venez. s to e Peru, Bolivia, n Argentina, and Amazonian Brazil.

## 17. RUFOUS-BANDED OWL

*Ciccaba albitarsus*     Pl. IX, Map 323

**Identification:** 14″ (36cm). No ear tufts. Eyes brown. Head and upperparts blackish brown thickly barred and spotted buffy rufous; *eyebrows and loral area buffy white*; throat white; *chest dark brown barred and spotted tawny and whitish* (forms broad indefinite chest band); feathers of rest of underparts edged silvery white and centrally divided with rufous brown, *forming large squarish white spots* (looks "ocellated"). Juv. is uniformly buffy.

**Similar species:** Like Mottled Owl (18), but hindneck and mantle much more boldly mottled and barred, facial markings more prom., and belly "*ocellated*" with silvery white in contrast to dark chest band.

**Voice:** Much like main song of Black-banded and Black-and-white owls; a deep, deliberate, resonant *hu, hu-hu-hu, HOOOa*, repeated at 8- to 11-sec intervals (P. Schwartz recording). Differs from above sp. mainly in rhythm: pause after 1st note, next 3 are quicker, last prolonged and strongly emphasized.

**Behavior:** Nocturnal. One roosted about 4m up along a forest border at Finca Merenberg, Huila (Ridgely and Gaulin 1980).

**Breeding:** Recently fledged bird, 22 June, e Huila (R. Ridgely).

**Status and habitat:** Apparently rare (prob. overlooked). Humid mt. forest and forest borders. Only recent report is from Merenberg (above).

**Range:** 1700-3000m. Spottily in all 3 Andean ranges (in W Andes known only from Cerro Munchique, Cauca, 2000m, C Andes s to Cauca and E Andes in Norte de Santander and Cundinamarca). The Andes from nw Venez. (incl. Perijá Mts.) to w Peru and Bolivia.

## 18. MOTTLED OWL

*Ciccaba virgata*     Pl. IX, Map 324

**Identification:** 13″ (33cm). No ear tufts. *Eyes brown*. Above dark brown mottled with buff and black (appears dusky at a distance); *eyebrows and narrow edge of facial disks buffy white*; flight feathers and tail barred dark brown and buffy gray; *chest buff heavily mottled and streaked dusky brown; lower underparts buffy white broadly streaked dark brown.*

**Similar species:** See Rufous-banded Owl (17). Other *Ciccaba* are barred below.

**Voice:** Most common call a very deep, resonant *whooou*, usually in pairs or triplets or sometimes 5-6 in a row. Also, rarely, a catlike scream.

**Behavior:** Nocturnal. Mid-story to canopy. One of the most vocal large neotropical owls.

**Breeding:** Downy young, 15 Apr, Santa Marta Mts. (Todd and Carriker 1922); 4 BC birds,

Feb–May, and juv., July, Guajira to Córdoba (Carriker). Nest in tree holes or old nests of other birds, 7-8m up; 2 white eggs (ffrench 1973).

**Status and habitat:** Locally fairly common in humid forest, forest borders, and tall second growth.

**Range:** To 2000m. Pacific coast, the humid lowlands n of Andes, Santa Marta and Perijá mts., and s to upper Cauca and Magdalena vals.; e of Andes from w Meta (incl. Macarena Mts.) to w Caquetá and Leticia. W Mexico to w Ecuador, n Argentina, and Paraguay. Trinidad.

## 19. STRIPED OWL

*Rhinoptynx clamator*                Pl. IX, Map 325

**Identification:** 14″ (36cm). Med.-sized owl with *long black ear tufts*. Eyes light brown. Above tawny buff streaked blackish; flight feathers and tail barred dark brown; *facial disks whitish rimmed black*; throat white; *rest of underparts buffy white very boldly striped blackish*. In flight from below shows prom. black "wrist patches." Imm. has cinnamon face.

**Similar species:** Short-eared Owl (21) has tiny ear tufts, yellow eyes, and darker (more tawny) underparts. Stygian Owl (20), occas. in lowlands, has dark face, yellow eyes, and is *much* darker below and without the bold stripes.

**Voice:** In Venez. a loud semiwhistled *wheeyoo*; also a ser. of barking or yapping hoots, *ow, ow, ow* . . . , like bark of a small dog (P. Schwartz recording).

**Breeding:** Nest on ground or low mound; 1 Panama nest, 17 Dec (Wetmore 1968a); 3 Surinam nests, Sept–Oct, 1 in Feb; 2-4 eggs (Haverschmidt 1968).

**Status and habitat:** Nonforest owl. Common locally in open or semiopen grassland or marshy areas with scattered trees and bushes.

**Range:** To 500m (once to 1600m, upper Magdalena Val.). Carib. coast from Atlántico e to Santa Marta region, mid. and upper Magdalena Val. from n Tolima (Honda) s to near San Agustín, Huila (La Candela); e of Andes in Norte de Santander and from Río Casanare to w Meta. Prob. more widespread in llanos. Se Mexico locally to n Argentina and Uruguay.

## 20. STYGIAN OWL

*Asio stygius*                Pl. IX, Map 326

**Identification:** 16-17″ (41-43cm). Dark. *Prom. closely spaced ear tufts enclose pale patch on forehead.* Eyes yellow. Above blackish brown with a few buff spots; *facial disk dusky* narrowly rimmed grayish; *below pale buff; chest blotched sooty brown; rest of underparts with broad herringbone-shaped streaks of sooty brown.*

**Similar species:** Best marks are dark appearance, inward curving and closely spaced ear tufts, yellow eyes in dark face, and blotchy "black and buff" underparts. Cf. Short-eared (21) and Striped owls (19).

**Voice:** A very low and loud *hu* or *hu-hu* (Bond 1961); ♀ a short catlike *miah* (Belize—G. Reynard recording).

**Breeding:** BC ♀, 8 May, Bucaramanga, Santander (Borrero 1955). Nest of palm shreds on ground in Cuba, old bird nests in trees in Mexico (Bond 1942).

**Status and habitat:** Rare and local. Known from a few widely scattered localities in humid mt. forest, forest borders, and in groves of trees on open Sabana de Bogotá (formerly). One specimen from univ. property in Cali; formerly relatively common in C Andes near Puracé; in Popayán 10 were taken from the central plaza as they arrived at night (2200-2300 hr) to prey on roosting Eared Doves (Lehmann 1957). Once from thorn scrub (435m) in upper Magdalena Val. (Miller 1952).

**Range:** Mostly 1700-3000m (occas. much lower). In W Andes known only from e slope in Cauca (El Tambo), also near Cali (once); C Andes s to Nariño and near Villavieja Huila (once); E Andes in Santander and Cundinamarca. Poss. in e Vichada. N Mexico to Nicaragua, Venez. (incl. Perijá Mts.) locally to n Argentina. Greater Antilles.

## 21. SHORT-EARED OWL

*Asio flammeus*                Pl. IX, Map 327

**Identification:** 14″ (36cm). Med.-sized *diurnal owl with inconspic. ear tufts*. Eyes yellow. Almost *entirely tawny buff streaked above and below with dark brown* (darker and more mottled above); wings and tail barred brown; eyebrows and lores white; facial disks buffy becoming black centrally. In flight from above or below shows conspic. black "*wrist patch*" and from above a large pale buff patch at base of remiges. Note diurnal habits and bounding flight.

**Similar species:** Most resembles Striped Owl (19), but ear tufts insignificant, less boldly streaked below, and eyes yellow. Also see much darker Stygian Owl (20).

**Voice:** Usually silent. In nest defense a catlike mewing and a high-pitched *cri cri cri cri* (Borrero 1962). Infrequently a ser. of 6-10 *toot*'s (Burton 1973); near Caracas, Venez., a very harsh, scratchy buzz, *jjjjjjeeeaa* (P. Schwartz recording).

**Behavior:** An open country owl often seen in characteristic springy, mothlike flight on slightly crooked wings, esp. in late afternoon. Alone or small groups; perch on ground, fence post, or other low place.

**Breeding:** Two Sept nests on ground in pas-

tures, Sabana de Bogotá (1 with eggs, 1 with nestlings); young leave before flying; 3 eggs (Borrero 1962; Olivares 1969a).
**Status and habitat:** Local. Pastures, grassland, and paramo. Formerly numerous on Sabana de Bogotá (Olivares 1969a); only early May–early Aug 1976 in ne Meta (S. Furniss); groups of 4-5 in Venez. llanos, June–Sept (Friedmann and Smith 1950).
**Range:** 500-2600m (prob. much higher). Known from upper Cauca Val. (near Popayán), Sabana de Bogotá, and e of Andes in s Meta (sighting, 17 Dec 1976, Lomo del Conejo, Macarena Mts.—T. O. Lemke and P. Gertler) and ne Meta at Carimagua (S. Furniss). Prob. also paramo zone of s Nariño (known from 3300-4000m in n Ecuador). Breeds in N America (winters s to Costa Rica), locally in S America s to Tierra del Fuego and widely in Old World.

**22. BUFF-FRONTED OWL**
*Aegolius harrisii*                    Pl. IX, Map 328
**Identification:** 8″ (20cm). Small with no ear tufts. Eyes greenish yellow. Dark chocolate brown above with conspic. white spots on wings and tail; *forecrown and eyebrows creamy buff; facial disks creamy buff with narrow black rim*; lores to base of bill, small chin patch, and band across chest blackish; *broad nuchal collar and entire underparts creamy yellowish buff*.
**Similar species:** Rich yellow buff forehead, facial disks (rimmed black) and uniform lower underparts are the marks. Nothing really resembles it. Cf. Spectacled Owl (9).
**Voice:** A quavering trill, *tutututututututu*, of 3- or 4-sec. duration, sometimes var. slightly in pitch, or with a brief pause in mid. (J. Vielliard recording).
**Breeding:** Hollow tree nests in Argentina (Olrog 1968).
**Status and habitat:** Very rare and little known; 3 Colombian specimens. Highland clearings and semiopen areas with trees. Reported to edge of paramo (3800m) in Venez. (Meyer de Schauensee and Phelps 1978).
**Range:** 1700-2000m (prob. much higher). Known from "Bogota," upper Cauca Val. (El Tambo w of Popayán), and se Nariño (Llorente, e of Ipiales). To 3100m in arid highlands near Quito, Ecuador. Andes of nw Venez. spottily to Ecuador and Peru; ne Brazil to Uruguay, n Argentina, and nw Paraguay.

# OILBIRDS: Steatornithidae (1)

Oilbirds are closely related to nightjars and, to a lesser extent, to owls. They are notable for their strong hooked bill, rictal bristles, weak feet placed far forward on the body, and long stiff tails. They are also the only nocturnal fruit-eating birds in the world. Oilbirds roost by day in caves and feed at night on fruit that is plucked in flight and swallowed whole; the seeds are later regurgitated. Although capable of navigation by echo location, fruit is apparently located by smell, or in nonaromatic fruit such as palms, by sight (Snow 1976). Two cave breeding sites are now protected by the Colombian natural resources agency, INDERENA, but deforestation near the caves, and at traditional nonbreeding season foraging areas that are often far from the breeding caves, may pose a threat to the security of this unique New World species in Colombia.

**1. OILBIRD**
*Steatornis caripensis*                    Ill. 64, Map 329
**Identification:** 19″ (48cm). Nightjarlike. Heavy hooked bill, prom. rictal bristles, and long pointed wings (spread 3.5′, or 107cm). *Above rufous brown spangled with large black-encircled white spots on wing coverts, outer primaries, and secondaries*; below cinnamon buff with *smaller diamond-shaped white spots on head and underparts*, long graduated tail narrowly barred black. ♂ is grayer than ♀. Eyes reflect bright red.
**Voice:** Often *very noisy*. Var. screams, snarls, and snoring sounds; also in caves a ser. of clicks used to navigate by echo location. Contact call in flight away from caves *karr-karr* or *kuk-kuk* (Snow 1961a).
**Behavior:** Nocturnal and gregarious at colonies and when foraging. Nightly flights of 25km or more from breeding cave or cliff may be covered to reach fruiting trees, usually large-seeded palms, laurels (Lauraceae), or incense (Burseraceae). Migrate seasonally to regions remote from breeding cave, presum. in search of food (F. C. Lehmann).
**Breeding:** Nest on cliffs or in complete darkness in caves. Nest a rim or mound of regur-

64. OILBIRD

gitated seeds on cave ledge; several often close together; 2-4 eggs, white but staining brown, laid at 2- to 6-day intervals. Young fledge in 3-4 mos. (Snow 1961a, 1962a, 1976). Breed Dec–late June in PN Cueva de los Guácharos (P. Gertler), approx. same in PN Puracé (Hilty), and are mostly absent from caves remainder of yr.

**Status and habitat:** Local. Caves in mts. Largest colonies are in PN Cueva de los Guácharos with over 3000-5000 in main caves and about 100 on outside cliffs along Río Suaza (P. Gertler); about 1000 in cave in PN Puracé. Forage in humid mt. forest and adj. lowlands. Recent deforestation has interfered with historic seasonal movements, and starved and exhausted birds are occas. found in agricultural Cauca Val., even in metropolitan downtown Cali. Reported "Guácharo" caves near Florencia appear to be abandoned. In Vaupés birds presumed to breed locally in caves of cerro and tableland region across central Vaupés (Olivares 1964b).

**Range:** To 3000m. Rec. from Santa Marta Mts., all 3 Andean ranges, Macarena Mts., and Vaupés (Soratama). Panama (Canal Zone and Darién); Guianas and Venez. s in mts. to nw Bolivia. Trinidad.

# POTOOS: Nyctibiidae (5)

Potoos are a small New World family of solitary and nocturnal birds. Most are so poorly known they seem more fiction than substance, their gruff or wailing cries ghostly delusions of the dim nocturnal world they inhabit. Potoos resemble nightjars, with their large eyes and mouths and cryptic plumage, but differ from them in, among other things, their more upright perching posture, larger size, and absence of rictal bristles. Potoos rest motionless during the day on a bare branch or stub, where they are exceedingly difficult to detect. Perched in upright but hunched posture, they gradually assume a bitternlike vertical posture if disturbed. Their diet is made up mostly of insects, mainly large night-flying ones captured by sallying to air. Nest sites, as far as known, are depressions or knotholes on branches or stubs where one egg is laid; no nest is built.

## 1. GREAT POTOO

*Nyctibius grandis*     Pl. X, Map 330

**Identification:** 20″ (51cm). *Large and usually whitish.* Eyes dark (reflect glowing orange at night). Above grayish white to brownish, finely vermiculated blackish and buff; shoulders darker; *below whitish* finely barred and vermiculated dusky; breast with a broken band of a few blackish spots; tail grayish white, crossed by 8-9 dusky bars, *each usually sharply bordered black* (esp. in paler birds and diagnostic if seen in field).

**Similar species:** Despite large size (only Long-tailed Potoo is as large) not always easily identified. Very pale or whitish birds are distinctive, brownish ones, in addition to size, are best told by barring and vermiculation below (no striping) and black-bordered tail bands. Cf. Common (3) and Long-tailed potoos (2).

**Voice:** Call a gruff guttural growl, *gra-a-a*, not loud, or sim. harsh, grating *wah-h-h oo-oo-oo*.

**Behavior:** As in Common Potoo, but usually perches on *high* open limbs during day. Calling confined *almost exclusively* to moonlit nights.

**Breeding:** 2 BC ♀♀, Mar, Unguía, Gulf of Urabá (Carriker); 1 presumed nest, early Apr, 10m up in gallery forest edge, Meta (Brown); Guárico, Venez. nest with egg, 6 Apr, another with week-old chick, 16 Apr (W. Mader); white egg with dark markings (Wetmore 1968a).

**Status and habitat:** Humid forest borders and gallery forest, or openings inside forest. Prob. more numerous than the few recs. suggest, esp. e of Andes. Can be found reg. along gallery forest edges in adj. Apure, Venez.

**Range:** To 400m. W of Andes known from lower Atrato Val., Río Esmeraldas (s Córdoba), Cesar Val. near Codazzi and mid. Magdalena Val. (La Dorada, e Caldas); scattered localities throughout e of Andes (w Meta, Macarena Mts., w Putumayo, se Nariño and Leticia). No rec. in Vichada to Vaupés. Se Mexico (sight) and Guatemala to n Bolivia and s Brazil.

## 2. LONG-TAILED POTOO

*Nyctibius aethereus*     Pl. X, Map 331

**Identification:** 20″ (51cm). *Dark with long tail over half total body length.* Mainly deep rufous brown streaked, spotted, and marbled blackish above and below; underparts slightly paler and with a few large blackish spots on mid-breast; prom. black malar; shoulders black (usually concealed); tail rufous buff with about 7-8 broad dark brown bands (about 5-6 bands show below wings).

**Similar species:** General plumage much like Common Potoo (3) but larger with *much longer* strongly graduated tail and fewer and broader tail bands. Great Potoo (1), even brown individuals, are paler and bulk slightly larger, seldom show such a prom. malar, and usually have narrower and distinctly black-rimmed bands across tail.

**Status and habitat:** Little known. Rec. from regions of humid and wet lowland forest.

**Range:** Below 300m. Known from 3 localities: a ♂ and ♀ from s Chocó (Nóvita on Río Tamaná), a sight rec. near Buenaventura, Valle (Borrero 1974), and the extreme e in Vaupés (Cerro de Mitú). Scattered recs. in the Guianas, e Venez., e Ecuador, e Peru, Amazonian and se Brazil, and Paraguay.

**Note:** N forms poss. a separate sp. from *aethereus* of se Brazil and Paraguay, and if so regarded, should be called *N. longicaudatus* (Long-tailed Potoo).

### 3. COMMON POTOO

*Nyctibius griseus*     Pl. X, Map 332
**Identification:** 14-16″ (36-41cm). Eyes yellow (reflect amber or orange at night). *Grayish brown to dark brown* mottled, streaked, and vermiculated throughout with cinnamon, gray, and black; breast sometimes with a few black spots in broken chain across chest; tail with about 8-10 blackish bands.

**Similar species:** Darker birds much like Long-tailed Potoos (2) and prob. barely separable in field, but smaller and with shorter, less graduated, and more narrowly banded tails (about 7-9 vs 5-6 *visible* bands on tail). Great Potoo (1) is twice as large and usually much paler (often whitish), but darker Great Potoos easily confused.

**Voice:** Song, often heard on moonlit nights, is one of the most haunting sounds of the American tropics; a marvelously apparitional ser. of up to 8 melancholy wailing or lamenting phrases, loud at 1st, then dropping in pitch in sliding steps and fading in vol., *BU-OU, BU-ou bu-ou.* . . . In many parts of its vast range the song is attributed to a sloth by rural people.

**Behavior:** By day perches immobile on a dead snag in a tree, usually fairly high but sometimes low and in the open on stubs, even fence posts. Active at night, esp. just after dusk when it assumes a rather prom. exposed perch from which it makes frequent sallies to air for large flying insects.

**Breeding:** 4 BC birds, Apr–May, n Antioquia (Carriker); 2 incubating birds, 13 and 15 Jan, in *Cecropia* trees in Cauca Valley near Cali (Borrero 1970); Costa Rican birds have long (33-day) incubation period, about 47-day fledging time; young fed by regurgitation at

1st (Skutch 1970a); white egg with lilac spots and streaks (ffrench 1973).

**Status and habitat:** Uncommon, perhaps local, in humid and wet forest borders, lighter woodland, woodlots, and gallery forest borders; both *terra firme* and *várzea* in Amazonia. The only potoo likely to be seen w of Andes in Colombia.

**Range:** To 1900m. Spottily throughout, but no definite rec. from Santa Marta, arid Carib. region, or Vichada s to Vaupés. W Mexico to n Argentina, Paraguay, and n Uruguay. Jamaica and Hispaniola.

**Note:** N birds from Mexico to Costa Rica and in the W Indies are larger, have a very different call, and are doubtless a separate sp.

### 4. WHITE-WINGED POTOO

*Nyctibius leucopterus*     Pl. X, Map 333
**Identification:** 15″ (38cm). *Very rare.* Sim. to dark brown individuals of Common Potoo. Mainly dark brown heavily spotted and vermiculated black; *inner wing coverts white with black tips forming a broad whitish bar* on upper surface; wings notched buff; tail dark brown with numerous paler bands.

**Similar species:** From any other potoo by prom. whitish band on wings.

**Range:** Known from "Bogotá" colls.; also w slope of E Andes in Norte de Santander (Las Ventanas, 2000m), and e slope E Andes at Llorente (1800m) in se Nariño (Fitzpatrick and Willard 1982). Also extreme w Venez. (e Táchira at Boca de Monte, 2400m), e Ecuador (Baños, 1820m), Peru, Bolivia (2800m—J. V. Remsen), and e coast of Brazil (Bahía).

### 5. RUFOUS POTOO

*Nyctibius bracteatus*     Pl. X, Map 334
**Identification:** 12″ (30cm). *Smallest potoo. Mostly cinnamon rufous* vermiculated blackish; white spots on back and *larger conspic. black-encircled white spots on shoulders, tertials, and belly*; under tail coverts tipped white; tail faintly barred blackish brown.

**Similar species:** Best told by bright cinnamon plumage and large white spots on shoulders.

**Voice:** Song believed this sp. in se Peru, a lamenting wail resembling that of Common Potoo but weaker, coarser, and shorter, *quaaw-co* (B. Coffee recording).

**Behavior:** One roosted in palm thicket in forest understory, se Peru (T. Parker).

**Status and habitat:** Very rare. Known in Colombia only from "Bogotá" colls. Prob. will be found e of the Andes in Amazonia.

**Range:** "Bogotá" (perhaps e slope E Andes at s end). E Ecuador (Sarayacú, 500m) and e Peru; once in Guyana.

# NIGHTHAWKS, NIGHTJARS: Caprimulgidae (19)

The members of this virtually cosmopolitan family are often better known by their voices than by sight. Many are rarely seen by day unless accidentally flushed from cover. The Colombian species divide naturally into two groups: the nighthawks with long pointed wings and crepuscular habits; and the true nightjars with shorter rounded wings and longer tails. All have small bills, remarkably wide gaping mouths, and conspicuous rictal bristles. The plumage is soft, lax, and always cryptically patterned; some birds are so similar they are difficult to distinguish by plumage pattern alone. The feet are extremely weak, and the birds usually settle directly on the ground or lengthwise on a branch, or at most shuffle only a short distance on foot. Nighthawks forage actively, diving and twisting in aerial pursuit of insects, while nightjars sally from stationary perches, mostly on or near the ground and close to cover. Eggs are laid directly on the ground or in small scrapes in sand.

## 1. SHORT-TAILED (SEMICOLLARED) NIGHTHAWK

*Lurocalis semitorquatus*  Pl. X, Map 335

**Identification:** 8.5″ (22cm). *Very short square tail and long pointed wings.* Above blackish speckled heavily with rufous and buff; throat white; rest of underparts dark brown barred black. Or as above but larger, 10″ (25cm), and belly plain unbarred rufescent (*rufiventris*). In flight looks blackish; sometimes *paler tertials* visible; and *no white band on wing tips*. At rest wing tips extend well beyond tail.

**Similar species:** Short-tailed, almost batlike shape and uniformly dark plumage in flight are the marks. *Chordeiles* are longer-tailed, have white wing bands, and usually hunt over clearings or open country. Band-tailed Nighthawks (6) are smaller, same shape as *Chordeiles*, usually in groups; nearby show a small white band on sides of tail.

**Voice:** Often silent. Usual call 2 brief barks and a hiccup—*tor-ta quírrt*, or *tor quírrt*—or either of latter 2 notes separately (P. Schwartz recording). In se Ecuador a fast *kwa-kwa-kwa-kwa-ko*, then sometimes more *kwa*'s (R. Ridgely).

**Behavior:** Crepuscular. Usually singly or in pairs in treetop flight at forest edge or over small clearings, rarely low over streams with *Chordeiles*. Erratic "gear-changing" flight as in *Chordeiles*. Presum. rest high in forest trees by day.

**Breeding:** Laying ♀, 23 Mar, Perijá Mts. (Carriker).

**Status and habitat:** Uncommon and local. Humid forest and forest borders. S migrants (*nattereri*) reported in n Venez. but not yet in Colombia; differ from resident *semitorquatus* in larger size and different voice, a rising *turreet* (P. Schwartz recording).

**Range:** To 3000m. The Santa Marta region (Río Frío) and e of Andes at San Carlos on se Guainía boundary (*semitorquatus*); Quebrada Tucuchira, w of Leticia, Amazonas (sighting Aug 1979—Hilty et al.), subsp.? Spottily in Perijá Mts. (Hiroca, 1600m, e of Casacarás) and E Andes (Bogotá area; sighting above Mocoa, w Putumayo, 1976—R. Ridgely), the C Andes at Coconuco, Cauca (*rufiventris*). Nicaragua; Panama to w Ecuador, Venez., the Guianas, and s to Bolivia, n Argentina, and se Brazil. Trinidad.

**Note:** Incl. southern *L. nattereri* (Chestnut-bellied Nighthawk), Andean *L. rufiventris* (Rufous-bellied Nighthawk) and northern lowland *L. semitorquatus* (Short-tailed Nighthawk), all perhaps separate spp.

## 2. LEAST NIGHTHAWK

*Chordeiles pusillus*  Pl. X, Map 336

**Identification:** 6″ (15cm). *Smallest nighthawk.* Wings long, slender, and pointed. Tail notched. Grayish brown above, vermiculated black; tail dark brown with several narrow grayish white bands and tip; throat white; rest of underparts whitish closely barred brown, under tail coverts white. In flight shows conspic. *white band across center of primaries and pale trailing edge on secondaries.*

**Similar species:** Virtually a miniature of Lesser Nighthawk (4) but much smaller and with pale-edged secondaries; shows white vent at close range.

**Voice:** Low *churr* and weak nasal *beep* in flight. Song *cur-cur-cur-curry* in Guyana and Venez. (Snyder 1966; P. Schwartz).

**Behavior:** Usually alone or in widely scattered pairs beating back and forth over open country. Buoyant erratic flight sim. to Lesser and Common nighthawks, but wing beats faster. Flies at mod. ht., higher than Lesser Nighthawk, lower than Common.

**Breeding:** BC ♀, 27 Jan, near San Carlos, Guainía (Friedmann 1948).

**Status and habitat:** Open savanna with scattered trees in the llanos and in pockets of scrub and savanna in forested zones of Guainía and Vaupés.

**Range:** To 200m. E of Andes from n c Meta

(Remolino on Río Meta) e to Río Orinoco (Maipures) and s to Vaupés (Sabana del Cubiyú) and se Guainía (San Carlos). E Colombia, s and e Venez., Guyana, and ne and s Brazil.

### 3. SAND-COLORED NIGHTHAWK
*Chordeiles rupestris*　　　　　Pl. X, Map 337
**Identification:** 8.5″ (22cm). *Mostly white below.* Wings long, slender, and pointed; tail more deeply notched than other nighthawks. Above sandy buff speckled and vermiculated black; below white with band of buff and blackish vermiculations on upper breast. In flight *4 outer primaries and trailing edge of all flight feathers black; rest of under wing and patch at base of primaries on upper wing white* (no white bar); tail mostly white with conspic. *black tip*, central feathers and outer web of outer feathers dusky.
**Similar species:** Bold wing pattern and white underparts unique. See larger and bulkier Nacunda Nighthawk (7).
**Voice:** Often quiet. Trilling call and several nasal notes (J. V. Remsen).
**Behavior:** Like other nighthawks, crepuscular and rarely abroad much before dusk. Flight is shifting but not as erratic as Common or Lesser nighthawks; the smoother, deeper, and oddly mechanical flapping resembles that of a tern or shorebird. Forage in loose groups up to 50 or more, low over sand bars or higher over rivers, even swooping around village streetlights. By day rest in driftwood piles and scrubby thickets on sand bars.
**Breeding:** Nest on sand bars during low-water period (prob. July–late Sept in Leticia area). Downy chick, 26 Jan, juv., 20 Jan, Río Guayabero, s Meta (Olivares 1962). Two eggs sandy buff tinged bluish, splotched and scrawled brown; scrape in sand (O'Neill 1974).
**Status and habitat:** Locally fairly common to common on sand bars or over nearby airports and village streets along larger rivers of Amazon, Negro, and Orinoco drainage. Near Leticia present only mid-July–late Sept (J. V. Remsen).
**Range:** To 400m. E of Andes from w Meta (Villavicencio area) and ne Guainía (many seen, Sept 1978, Pto. Inírida—Hilty and M. Robbins) and Vaupés southward. S Venez. to n Bolivia and w Amazonian Brazil.

### 4. LESSER NIGHTHAWK
*Chordeiles acutipennis*　　　　Pls. X and XI,
　　　　　　　　　　　　　　　　Map 338
**Identification:** 8″ (20cm). Wings long, slender, and pointed. Tail fairly long, notched. ♂: above grayish brown mottled and speckled blackish, gray, and buff; throat white, rest of underparts buffy white closely barred dusky; tail grayish, crossed by several narrow bands and more *prom. white band near tip.* In flight primaries blackish with *white band nearer tip than bend of wing.* ♀: sim. but throat and wing bands buffy (look white at distance), and no white tail band. At rest wings reach end of tail (Pauraques and nightjars have broader wings that do not reach end of tail); 5 subspp. rec. in Colombia inseparable in field.
**Similar species:** Very sim. to Common Nighthawk (see 5) but slightly smaller, and white wing band positioned nearer wing tip. ♀ has buff throat and wing bands (both sexes of Common Nighthawk have white), but this is rarely helpful in field. Note flight habits and calls. See smaller Least Nighthhawk (2).
**Voice:** Lacks the nasal *peent* of Common Nighthawk and does not "power dive." Infrequently a "winnowing" call in flight, on the ground a low nasal raillike ser. of *chuck* notes and a long-sustained, toadlike, dribbling trill.
**Behavior:** Both this sp. and Common Nighthawk fly buoyantly with light, easy wing strokes alternating with quicker erratic strokes. Both are crepuscular but are occas. abroad by day as well, feeding over open areas. Lesser flies low, sometimes swerving perilously close to the ground, but on migration normally quite high in loosely assorted groups.
**Breeding:** 7 BC birds, June–July, se base Santa Marta Mts.—*acutipennis* (Carriker); 5 BC birds and courtship display, Jan–Feb. Huila—*crissalis* (Miller 1959). Feb nest on flat-topped boulder, Venez. Orinoco; 2 vinaceous buff eggs marked and dotted grayish (Cherrie 1916).
**Status and habitat:** Uncommon to locally fairly common in a var. of drier, more open lowland habitats. Reported "common" at Hacienda, Corocora in w Meta (W. McKay). The status of the 5 subspp. in Colombia is complicated by the fact that even in the hand some (esp. ♀♀ of *texensis* vs *micromeris*) are difficult to distinguish with certainty. Two resident subspp. *acutipennis* and *crissalis*, are known to breed, the former over much of Colombia, the latter in n Huila. *C. a. micromeris*, rec. in Jan in Magdalena, may be a wanderer from e Panama (where known to breed) or a resident breeder (a BC ♀, 22 Jan 1948, from s Bolívar, and presumed to be *texensis* may be *micromeris*). N migrant *texensis* is rec. Dec–Apr w of E Andes s to sw Cauca. S migrant *aequatorialis* from Ecuador(?) is rec. once in Mar in n Chocó (Unguía) and may prove to be resident in sw Nariño.
**Range:** To 1000m (mainly below 500m). W of E Andes from the Carib. coast southward; e of the Andes in Norte de Santander (Zulia

Val.), nw Meta and e Vichada. Sw US to n Bolivia, Paraguay, and s Brazil. N breeders winter s to nw Colombia.

## 5. COMMON NIGHTHAWK
*Chordeiles minor*

**Identification:** 9″ (23cm). Very sim. to Lesser Nighthawk but slightly larger and *broad white bar about midway between bend and tip of wing.* Throat and wing bar white in both sexes. ♀: no white tail band; throat occas. buff. In the hand, upperparts of either sex coarser than Lesser Nighthawk.

**Similar species:** Migrating nighthawk flocks high overhead are usually this sp. in Colombia but are seldom safely separated from Lesser Nighthawk (4). At closer range, position of wing bar and call is helpful. At rest usually indistinguishable from Lesser but ♀ ♀ and some ♂ Lessers show buff barring or spotting at base of primaries (solid black in Common Nighthawk).

**Voice:** Call a diagnostic nasal *peent* given yr.-round; the "power dive" accompanied by a loud boom is a courtship display given only on temperate breeding grounds.

**Behavior:** Sim. in most respects to Lesser Nighthawk but usually, though not always, flies higher; both fly high overhead in migration.

**Status and habitat:** Uncommon to fairly common fall migrant (many races) late Aug–late Nov, uncommon to rare during n migration Mar–Apr. Nighthawks, presumed this sp., early Feb at Mitú, may have been wintering (Hilty). Breeding in extreme nw poss. but unproven (definite breeding rec. as close as c Panama in May—Wetmore 1968a).

**Range:** To 2600m (Sabana de Bogotá). Throughout. Breeds from Canada to c Panama; winters in S America s to Argentina. Trinidad and Curaçao.

## 6. BAND-TAILED NIGHTHAWK
*Nyctiprogne leucopyga*          Pl. X, Map 339

**Identification:** 7″ (18cm). Long, slender, pointed wings. *Small dark nighthawk* with white band across mid. of tail *(from above shows as small white notch on each side of tail).* Above dusky brown speckled with buff, below closely barred whitish and dark brown with small white patch at sides of throat (inconspic. in field). In flight, wings all dark (no bars); notched tail fairly long.

**Similar species:** Only other Colombian nighthawk with uniformly dark wings (no white bar) is larger and differently proportioned Short-tailed Nighthawk (1). Median white bar on sides of tail diagnostic but hard to see at dusk.

**Voice:** Usually quiet. Occas. a low guttural *qurk.*

**Behavior:** More strictly crepuscular (or nocturnal) than *Chordeiles* nighthawks and rarely or never abroad by day. Feed mostly 1-10m up in groups of var. size (to 30 or more) over rivers and along river banks. Rapid erratic flight, a few quick flutters and a short glide with wings in V, is reminiscent of *Chordeiles,* but unlike them, Band-tailed fly stiff-winged (not bent) with shallow wing strokes (Hilty). Roost in dense thickets by day along rivers or ponds; sometimes huddle in small groups all facing the same direction (Cherrie 1916).

**Breeding:** 9 BC birds, Jan–Mar, sw Amazonas, Venez. (Friedmann 1948). Eggs whitish speckled light and dark gray (Schönwetter).

**Status and habitat:** Locally fairly common along savanna ponds, streams, and larger rivers of the extreme e. Numerous along Río Vaupés at Mitú.

**Range:** To 300m. E of Andes from Río Arauca (Venez. side) e to Orinoco (Maipures) and s to Vaupés and Amazonas (Leticia). Fr. Guiana, Guyana, c and s Venez., and Peru-Brazil boundary (Río Javarí) s of Leticia (sight).

## 7. NACUNDA NIGHTHAWK
*Podager nacunda*          Pl. X, Map 340

**Identification:** 11″ (28cm). Large, robust, and handsomely marked; broad, slightly rounded wings; tail notched. Above buffy brown thickly speckled and vermiculated blackish; broad band on upper breast finely barred and vermiculated brown in sharp contrast to *pure white throat and lower underparts;* tail barred buff and black, broad white tail tip (♂). In flight *black primaries crossed by broad white bar; under wing coverts white.*

**Similar species:** A startlingly large, boldly patterned nighthawk that could scarcely be confused. Sand-colored Nighthawk (3) is petite by comparison, lacks the white wing bands, and flies differently.

**Voice:** Virtually silent when feeding; may flush with low *chuck* or *cluck.*

**Behavior:** Crepuscular and nocturnal. Single birds, pairs, or seasonally in flocks of 100 or more, latter perhaps nonbreeders or migrants. Rest by day on sand bars, salt flats, or grassy pastures and open savanna, usually in loose groups fully exposed all day. Feed along rivers or over open areas, normally flying quite high. Leisurely flight loose and bounding like a large moth and without swerving.

**Breeding:** Believed nesting, 23 Jan, Huila (Miller 1947); 2 BC ♂♂, Mar, June, n Cesar (Carriker); 3 Trinidad nests, Apr; 1-2 eggs, cream blotched and lined rich brown at larger end; laid on ground on dead leaves (ffrench 1973).

**Status and habitat:** Fairly common locally in open areas of dry or humid regions. Some seasonal movements and nos. augmented by s temperate migrants *nacunda*, larger and darker than resident *minor*. Migrants rec. late May in Venez. (Friedmann and Smith 1950) and early July in n Magdalena (Wetmore 1968b). Large flocks only July–late Oct in Meta (S. Furniss; W. McKay) mid-May–late Oct near Leticia (J. V. Remsen; R. Ridgely); flocks Sept–late Nov in Santa Marta area (Darlington 1931). *P. n. nacunda* is resident in Uruguay Sept to Apr with young in Nov (Gore and Gepp 1978).
**Range:** To 500m. Santa Marta region and Guajira, also the dry upper Magdalena Val. (Villavieja, n Huila); e of Andes throughout. Guianas and Venez. to s Argentina and Uruguay.

## 8. PAURAQUE
*Nyctidromus albicollis*          Pl. XI, Map 341
**Identification:** 11″ (28cm). Broad rounded wings and longish rounded tail. ♂: above brownish mottled with buff and blackish; *large buff-encircled black spots on scapulars*; ear coverts chestnut; chin dusky; throat white; rest of underparts finely barred buff and blackish. In flight *dusky primaries crossed by broad white bar; sides of tail mostly white* (conspic. when flushed). ♀: sim. but wing band narrower and buffy, and only outer tip of tail white (not conspic.). At rest wings reach about half the tail length.
**Similar species:** ♂ is larger, darker, and more boldly marked than ♂ White-tailed Nightjar (13). At higher el. see Band-winged Nightjar (12). ♀ from allies by rufous cheeks, rich scapular pattern, size, and wing bands.
**Voice:** Vocal, esp. during breeding season, when loud whistled *coo-wheéeer o* (last *o* note separate but hard to hear at distance); at dusk a longer *coo-coo-coo-cu-wheéeer.*
**Behavior:** Strictly nocturnal and seldom seen by day unless accidentally flushed from a thicket. Sallies to air from ground or favorite low perch for flying insects. Its true nos. are best revealed through its call, often heard during breeding season.
**Breeding:** Song chiefly Dec–Apr. PN Cueva de los Guácharos (P. Gertler); 17 BC birds, Jan–Apr, n Colombia, incl. 2 ♂♂ incubating 1 egg each, Jan and Mar (Carriker). 2 BC birds, Feb and May, Valle (Miller 1963); 1 in Aug, Vaupés (Olivares and Hernández 1962); 2 nests, Apr and May, Santa Marta (Todd and Carriker 1922); 2 more, Mar and May, Orinoco region; 2 vinaceous buff eggs marked vinaceous brown; on ground (Cherrie 1916).
**Status and habitat:** Most common and widespread Colombian nightjar and the one most often flushed from roads at night. Forest borders, second growth woodland, thickets, shrubby areas, and woodlots in fairly dry to humid zones. Replaced at high el. by smaller Band-winged Nightjar.
**Range:** To 2300m. Throughout (mainly moist or humid regions in Carib. and Santa Marta area). S Texas and Mexico to n Argentina and s Brazil.

## 9. OCELLATED POORWILL
*Nyctiphrynus ocellatus*          Ill. 65, Map 342
**Identification:** 8″ (20cm). Rounded wings; rather long rounded tail. *Very dark.* Mostly brownish black, somewhat mottled and vermiculated tawny, esp. on shoulders, and with *2 large round white spots on wing coverts*; narrow white collar across throat; lower breast and belly mottled and barred buff to white. In flight *wings uniformly dark; tail dark with crisp narrow white tip on all feathers (rosenbergi).* Sexes sim. Birds from e Ecuador and prob. e base of Colombian E Andes differ thus: mainly rufescent brown; wing coverts and belly with several barblike black spots; all but central tail feathers tipped white (*ocellatus*).
**Similar species:** Small, very dark, and likely confused only with Blackish Nightjar (16), but not known to overlap in range in Colombia.
**Voice:** Call, *que'e'e'ro*, like a distant Pauraque, often repeated every few sec for 20 times or more in succession (P. Schwartz recording).
**Behavior:** Usually calls from low elevated perch inside forest or at edge, less often high or from ground on trail (T. Parker). Not seen on roads.
**Status and habitat:** Local in humid and wet forested zones where favors small shady openings or more open understory. Most Colombian recs. are from foothills and lower slopes.
**Range:** 50-900m. W side Baudó Mts. (Río Jurubidá, 900m), and Pacific slope in Valle (Dagua Val.) and Nariño (*rosenbergi*). Prob. e slope E Andes (*ocellatus*). Nicaragua (once); nw and e Ecuador, e Peru, n Bolivia, and w Amazonian and s Brazil (s of Amazon) to n Argentina and Paraguay.

## 10. CHUCK-WILL'S-WIDOW
*Caprimulgus carolinensis*
**Identification:** 11.5″ (29cm). Large. Very sim. to Rufous Nightjar and not safely separable in field; differs in slightly larger size and underparts more buff, lacking strong rufescent tones. In the hand ♂ differs in having inner web of 3 lateral tail feathers almost wholly white (not with large subterminal white patches and broad buff tips); also in the hand both sexes have lateral filaments on rictal bristles (lacking in Rufous Nightjar) and throat with

65. Swallow-tailed Nightjar (♂ top, flying; ♀ middle, sitting) Lyre-tailed
Nightjar (♂ middle, flying), Ocellated Poorwill (♂ bottom, sitting)

more dusky mottling (not almost uniform buffy rufous).

**Similar species:** Only other *large* nightjars without wing bands (white or buff) are ♀ Swallow-tailed and Lyre-tailed nightjars, (18, 19), both smaller and found at high el.; ♂♂ of 18 and 19 also lack wing bands, but normally have long tails.

**Voice:** On breeding ground (but not wintering ground) says its name, a distinct, 4-syllabled *chuck-will-wid-ow*, with 1st note weak.

**Status and habitat:** Apparently rare (few recs.) winter resident reported late Nov–mid-Feb (once in June).

**Range:** 1000-2600m. Spottily in all 3 Andean ranges: w Nariño (Ricaurte), near Popayán (e Tambo), Medellín, and near Bogotá (Sabana de Bogotá; Silvania). Breeds in se US; winters in Florida, the Greater Antilles, and Mid. America to w Colombia, once to Venez.

## 11. RUFOUS NIGHTJAR
*Caprimulgus rufus*          Pl. XI, Map 343

**Identification:** 10-11″ (25-28cm). Very *large ruddy* nightjar with *no white in wing*. Above rufescent, streaked, spotted, and vermiculated black; below finely barred and mottled rufous and dusky; throat rufescent buff bordered below by whitish throat collar (no collar on hindneck). In flight shows white on inner web of terminal quarter of 3 outer tail feathers (no white in ♀) and broad buffy tail tip. In the hand, rictal bristles lack lateral filaments (cf. 10).

**Similar species:** Except by voice not safely told in field from Chuck-will's-widow (see 10). ♀ Parauque (8) and Band-winged nightjar (12) have a buff to whitish wing band and look more uniformly barred; at rest Pauraque shows stronger pattern on head and shoulders.

**Voice:** Song, persistently repeated for a short

per. during early breeding season, an energetic rhythmic *chuck, wick-wick-wéeoo*, mid. 2 notes quick, last faint at a distance. Reminiscent of Chuck-will's-widow but faster and higher-pitched; sometimes given from a perch 10-20m above ground (Wetmore 1968a).
**Behavior:** Nocturnal and difficult to locate outside breeding season when usually quiet. Does not sit on roads or enter clearings as frequently as Pauraque (Ridgely 1976).
**Breeding:** BC ♀, 3 May, w Guajira (Carriker); 1 nest, 16 Apr, Santa Marta (Todd and Carriker 1922); 2 creamy white eggs with vague blotches of light brown and dull lilac; on bare ground under thicket in semiopen area.
**Status and habitat:** Infrequently heard or seen. Fairly dry or semiopen humid forest, second growth woodland, and borders. Rec. from a no. of localities within present boundary of PN Tayrona where apparently very uncommon.
**Range:** To 1800m. Santa Marta area and w Guajira s to s Magdalena; e of Andes in w Meta (Villavicencio; Macarena Mts.); prob. e Vichada (on Venez. side of Orinoco); also rec. near Colombian boundary at Pto. Obaldía, Panama. Locally from Costa Rica (once) to n Argentina, Paraguay, and se Brazil.

### 12. BAND-WINGED NIGHTJAR
*Caprimulgus longirostris*      Pl. XI, Map 344
**Identification:** 8.5″ (22cm). Rounded wings and fairly long tail. ♂: *mainly blackish* speckled and dotted rufous; wide *rufous nuchal collar* and narrow white band across lower throat. In flight blackish primaries crossed by *broad white bar; terminal half of all but central tail feathers white.* ♀: sim. but *wing and throat band buffy*; tail barred buff and dusky (no white).
**Similar species:** Both sexes smaller and much darker than Pauraque (8), and ♂ shows much broader white tail tip than ♂ Pauraque; up close note rufous collar on hindneck. Other high el. nightjars *lack bands on wings*; see ♀♀ of Swallow-tailed and Lyre-tailed nightjars (18, 19).
**Voice:** Song a high, thin *seeeeeert*, reminiscent of White-tailed Nightjar; also a high *chee-wit-chee-wit-chee-wit*.
**Behavior:** Strictly nocturnal. Sallies short distances to air from ground or slightly elevated perch for flying insects; sings from low perch shortly after dusk. By day rests on the ground, under a bush or thicket, or on roadcuts; frequently sits on roads at night.
**Breeding:** 10 BC birds, Feb–June, ♀ on 1 egg, 4 July, Perijá Mts. (Carriker). Mar–Apr nests, Santa Marta Mts. (Todd and Carriker 1922); 1 nest, 9 Nov, Páramo de Chuza (W. McKay); A July nest near Bogotá, ♀ with shelled egg

mid-Oct, Boyacá (Olivares 1971); 1 white to pinkish egg with small spots; on ground or bare rock (Sclater and Salvin 1879).
**Status and habitat:** Fairly common and widespread in grassy clearings, open slopes, and woodland borders in the highlands; often near treeline or even above in paramo. Largely replaces Pauraque above 2000m.
**Range:** 1600-3600m (once at sea level in w Nariño; once near Ríohacha, Guajira?). Santa Marta and Perijá Mts. and all 3 Andean ranges (W Andes only in Antioquia and Cauca and E Andes s to Cundinamarca). N Venez. (to 4200m) s in Andes to Bolivia and Chile, s Argentina, Paraguay, and se Brazil.

### 13. WHITE-TAILED NIGHTJAR
*Caprimulgus cayennensis*      Pl. XI, Map 345
**Identification:** 8.5″ (22cm). Rounded wings and fairly long tail. ♂ pale below, ♀ much darker. ♂: brown above, mottled and vermiculated gray, black, and buff; *buffy nuchal collar; entire throat and lower underparts white*; breast finely barred buff and brown. In flight blackish primaries crossed by a *broad white bar; sides of tail white; underside of tail mostly white.* ♀ very different: browner above and barred buff and blackish below incl. throat; *nuchal collar tawny*; primaries crossed by 1 *cinnamon buff* (not white) *band; and no white on tail.*
**Similar species:** Note small size. Pauraque (8) is decidedly larger and grayer with white confined to tail tip. ♀ is only Colombian nightjar with combination of cinnamon wing bar, rufescent nuchal collar, and no white throat band. See ♀ Ladder-tailed Nightjar (17), which is confined to Amazonian riverine habitats.
**Voice:** Call a high, drawn out *spit-cheeeeuua*, 1st note faint, last rising then falling (Hilty); in display a sharp *knock-knock* striking wings together, followed by an audible wing-whirr (P. Schwartz recording).
**Behavior:** Strictly nocturnal. As in Pauraque but less vocal.
**Breeding:** 6 BC birds, Mar–July, Santa Marta and s Bolívar (Carriker); May nest, Venez. Orinoco; 2 pale vinaceous buff eggs marked lilac and rufous brown, more heavily at large end; on ground (Cherrie 1916).
**Status and habitat:** Fairly common. Grassland, scrubby ranch country, and eroded hillsides with scattered bushes and thickets. Common on dry hills between Cali and lower Pichindé Val.
**Range:** To 2100m. Carib. lowlands (below 150m) from Cartagena e to Santa Marta Mts. and Guajira, spottily s to upper Magdalena Val.; Cauca Val. from Antioquia southward; e of Andes from n Arauca to s Meta (Macarena Mts.) and e to e Vichada (El Tuparro—IN-

DERENA). Costa Rica to the Guianas and n Brazil; Aruba to Trinidad; Lesser Antilles.

## 14. SPOT-TAILED NIGHTJAR

*Caprimulgus maculicaudus*      Pl. XI, Map 346
**Identification:** 8" (20cm). Rounded wings. *Small rather buffy nightjar with no white wing band.* Crown and sides of head blackish; conspic. *pale buff eyebrow and narrow rufous nuchal collar;* upperparts buffy brown freckled darker; throat and breast blackish coarsely spotted buff and white; more buff on throat; belly almost uniform tawny; tail with *broad white tip* (or gray—♀) and several pairs of large white spots on underside (not visible in field). In flight ♂ shows dark primaries with *several rufescent wing bars.* **Similar species:** ♂ is only small Colombian nightjar with a white terminal tail band and no white wing band. ♀ resembles ♀ White-tailed (13) and Little Nightjars (15), but head blackish with distinct eyebrow, and dingy throat not sharply set off from obviously spotted (not finely barred) breast. Other sim. ♀♀ occur only at higher el.
**Voice:** Call a thin, high *pit-sweet* or *spit-sweet.*
**Behavior:** As in other *Caprimulgus.*
**Breeding:** 9 BC birds and incubating ♀, Mar, Unguía, nw Antioquia (Carriker); ground nest in open grassy area, w Meta, 29 Feb; 2 buff eggs spotted reddish brown (Brown).
**Status and habitat:** Uncommon in savanna, bushy pastures, and edges of lighter woodland. Ranchland in nw Chocó (Haffer 1975); netted in *Mauritia* palms and over a rice field in w Meta (W. McKay).
**Range:** To 400m. Nw Chocó near base of Snía. del Darién (Sautatá; Titupú), the lower Río Sinú (Lorica) and a few widely scattered localities e of the Andes: w Meta, ne Meta (Carimagua—S. Furniss), w Vaupés (San José del Guaviare), and se Guainía (Macacuní). Sw Mexico locally (not Panama) to n Bolivia and se Brazil.

## 15. LITTLE NIGHTJAR

*Caprimulgus parvulus*      Pl. XI, Map 347
**Identification:** 8" (20cm). Rounded wings. Small, dark nightjar, grayer than allies. ♂: grayish brown above with some black streaking; band of rufous spots on hindneck forms collar; *entire throat pure white sharply set off from sooty brown barring and spotting of rest of underparts.* In flight blackish primaries crossed by *broad white band;* from below tail feathers broadly tipped white; from above only narrow white tip on outer feathers. ♀: sim. but throat buffy; dusky primaries with broken rufous bars and no white in tail.
**Similar species:** ♂ told by small size, large clean-

cut white throat, and small white outer tail tips (from above). ♀ much like ♀ White-tailed Nightjar (13), but throat buff (not barred blackish), tail shorter, and wings have rufous barring (not a single buff band). Also cf. ♀ Spot-tailed Nightjar (14).
**Voice:** Call briefly early in breeding season, 2 short notes and a fast bubbly roll, *píck-you gobble-gobble-gobble,* at short intervals (P. Schwartz recording); late Apr–early May in n Venez. (C. Parrish).
**Behavior:** Sim. to other *Caprimulgus.*
**Breeding:** ♂ incubating 2 eggs on bare ground in thick bush, 22 Oct; BC ♀, 24 Oct, near Cúcuta (Carriker).
**Status and habitat:** Apparently rare. Savanna thickets, shrubby pastures, and lighter deciduous woodland in dry zones; lowlands and hills.
**Range:** To 300m. Known from n base of Santa Marta Mts. (La Tigrera below Minca; e of Santa Marta), Catatumbo lowlands (Cúcuta), and "Bogotá." N Venez.; Brazil s of Amazon to Bolivia, c Argentina, and Uruguay.

## 16. BLACKISH NIGHTJAR

*Caprimulgus nigrescens*      Pl. XI, Map 348
**Identification:** 8" (20cm). Rounded wings. *Small and very dark.* ♂: mostly blackish brown, dotted above and finely barred below with rufous; indistinct pale dotted eyebrow; *narrow white collar across lower throat* (often only small patch on each side of chest). In flight shows a *small white band* (white spot on 3 inner primaries) *across flight feathers and tiny white tip on outer tail feathers.* ♀: all dark except for narrow white band (often incomplete) on lower throat.
**Similar species:** No other nightjar in its range looks so blackish.
**Voice:** A soft, purring *pu'r'r'r'r't* or *qu'r'r'r'r't* repeated 3-5 times in about 4 sec. or more; call a sharp *prek,* like a bubble bursting (P. Schwartz recording). Song in Peru (presum. this sp.) a rapid *chuk, wik-wik-wheéeo,* much like that of Rufous Nightjar (T. Parker). Temperamental, and song not often heard.
**Behavior:** Nocturnal. By day rest on ground under thickets, or exposed on rocks and boulders, often in mid. of rivers. Call from low perch in bush or small tree.
**Breeding:** BC ♂, 8 Jan, Pto. Ayacucho opp. Vichada (Friedmann 1948); 1 egg on ground in open, sparsely vegetated area, 26 Apr, Guyana (Beebe et al. 1917); 1 egg in Apr, another in same place, early Sept, Surinam; egg light pinkish buff blotched dark brown and lilac (Haverschmidt 1968).
**Status and habitat:** In and near openings of humid forest borders, shrubby clearings, or

rocks in bouldery rivers. Very common at edge of savanna woodland mixed with large granite outcrops and cerros in sandy-belt region of Guainía and Vaupés.
**Range:** To 800m (on cerros). E of Andes from w Meta (Villavicencio) to e Vichada s to Vaupés (Mitú; Río Apaporis). Prob. cerros at head of Apaporis. The Guianas and s Venez. locally to n Bolivia and w Amazonian Brazil.

## 17. LADDER-TAILED NIGHTJAR
*Hydropsalis climacocerca*     Pl. XI, Map 349
**Identification:** ♂ 11″ (28cm); ♀ 9″ (23cm). Wings rounded; tip of long tail double-notched. Sexes very different. ♂: sandy buff above, vermiculated and finely streaked blackish; throat whitish merging into finely barred buffy brown breast; lower underparts white. Tail *unusual*: central feathers long, outer pair longest and mostly white, feathers in between shortest. In flight *blackish primaries crossed by broad white band; long tail flashes much white at tip and long white wedges on either side of central feathers*; underside of tail (rarely seen in field) with curving black and white bars. ♀: mostly mottled buffy brown and blackish; throat whitish. In flight primaries crossed by a *narrow cinnamon bar; tail rather long*, no white, and "double notched" tip less evident than in ♂.
**Similar species:** Flashy ♂ unmistakable. ♀ most like ♀ White-tailed Nightjar (13), but tail longer with jagged tip, and habitat usually very different.
**Voice:** Soft, musical *chewit* when flushed.
**Behavior:** Nocturnal. Sally short distances from sand bars or low perches along river edge for flying insects. By day sleep in driftwood piles, cane, and thickets on sand bars or on adjoining river banks.
**Breeding:** 4 nests, 23-24 July, Isla Corea in Río Amazon, w of Leticia; scrape on ground in driftwood, mudflat, or sand shaded by scrub; 2 olive drab eggs speckled darker (Hilty); 1 nest, 14 Dec, and BC birds, Jan–Feb. nw Amazonas, Brazil (Friedmann 1948).
**Status and habitat:** Common on or near sand bars along larger rivers and on river isls.
**Range:** To 400m. Amazon drainage from w Caquetá to Amazonas; doubtless to e Guainía (rec. on boundary in Venez.). The Guianas and Venez. (s of Orinoco) to n Bolivia and Amazonian Brazil.

## 18. SWALLOW-TAILED NIGHTJAR
*Uropsalis segmentata*     Ill. 65, Map 350
**Identification:** ♂ 26″ (66cm); ♀ 9″ (23cm). ♂ unmistakable: *long scissorlike tail over twice body length*; plumage mainly brownish black freckled and barred rufous; narrow white collar

across lower throat. In flight *wings uniformly dark* (no white); outer pair of tail feathers exceedingly long and straight; outer web notched buff, shafts white. ♀: crown black spotted rufous; tail normal, barred blackish and rufous.
**Similar species:** See Lyre-tailed Nightjar (19). Band-winged Nightjar (12) has buff or whitish wing bands.
**Voice:** For brief period in Peru, give pauraque-like *puit-sweeet* (T. Parker); flush with low *churr*.
**Behavior:** Nocturnal. Sally short distances to air from ground or low perch and often sit on roadsides at night. By day roost under a bush, *Espeletia* (Compositae), or on road cut.
**Breeding:** ♀ and nestling, 30 Aug, Zancudo, Caldas (Carriker 1955); ♀ brooding downy chick on ground, 11 Feb, paramo, PN Cueva de los Guácharos (P. Gertler).
**Status and habitat:** Uncommon and local. Open or shrubby slopes, forest edge or treeline clearings, and paramo. Readily found at Chupayal del Perico entrance to PN Puracé. Usually above range of Lyre-tailed.
**Range:** 2500-3500m. C Andes in Antioquia, Caldas (Zancudo), and e Cauca and w Huila (PN Puracé); E Andes in Boyacá (Arcabuca), near Bogotá (Páramo de Choachí; Fómeque), and e Huila (PN Cueva de los Guácharos). Colombia s in Andes to Bolivia.

## 19. LYRE-TAILED NIGHTJAR
*Uropsalis lyra*     Pl. XI, Ill. 65, Map 351
**Identification:** ♂ 30″ (76cm); ♀ 10″ (25cm). ♂ unmistakable: *marvelously long, streaming, lyre-shaped tail nearly 3 times body length*. Mostly brownish black thickly barred and spotted rufous; narrow rufous nuchal collar; usually a narrow white collar on lower throat; spectacularly long outer pair of tail feathers curve gracefully inward in lyre shape with *long white tips*. ♀: sim. but tail normal, blackish barred rufous on all but central pair of feathers; crown grayish lightly streaked black. Primaries notched rufous, no bands (♂ and ♀).
**Similar species:** ♂ Swallow-tailed Nightjar (18) has shorter, straighter, and more rigid scissorlike tail with no white tips. ♀ almost identical to ♀ Swallow-tailed Nightjar but crown spotted and vermiculated black and grayish (not black and rufous); nuchal collar rufous (more or less lacking in latter), and in hand by buffier (less rufous chestnut) mottling above and below, perhaps also by buff (not whitish) throat band.
**Voice:** Advertising call a melodious ser. of 5-9 rolling *wéeou-tee* phrases, each a little higher-pitched and stronger than the preceding (Hilty); courtship song in flight display a rapid

*weep weep weep weepupup*; calls, perched or in flight, incl. *weep weep weep* and rapid *chip-chip-chip* (W. McKay and P. Gertler).

**Behavior:** Nocturnal. ♂♂ at edge of forest clearings sally to air from a low to fairly high open perch, less often from ground, sometimes from roadsides. In courtship at communal aerial lek 1 to several ♂♂ circle and call at or chase 1 to several ♀♀ that join; prob. always display from clearings; 1 or 2 ♂♂ roost crosswise on slender vines at cave entrance at PN Cueva de los Guácharos (P. Gertler and W. McKay).

**Breeding:** Most advertising and courtship songs July, Aug, and Dec, PN Cueva de los Guá-charos (W. McKay and P. Gertler); BC ♂, 18 June, se Antioquia (Carriker).

**Status and habitat:** Local. In or near openings at edge of humid and wet mt. forest; may favor vicinity of cliffs, rocky ravines, and cave entrances. Replaced at higher el. and in more open situations by Swallow-tailed Nightjar.

**Range:** 800-2500m. E slope of W Andes in Valle (♂♂ seen above Pance—D. Bailey; Hilty), C Andes from n Antioquia s to Cauca-Huila border (PN Puracé); E Andes from northernmost Boyacá (e slope on Río Cobugón) and w Santander (Río Carare near Landázuri) s to e Huila (PN Cueva de los Guácharos). Nw Venez. (Mérida) s in Andes to s Peru.

# SWIFTS: Apodidae (15)

Swifts are a worldwide family with the greatest number of species occurring in tropical regions. They superficially resemble swallows but differ in having a more robust body, shorter stiffer tail, and straighter faster flight on swept back wings. The plumage is compact and predominantly shades of brown and black. Swifts represent perhaps the ultimate avian adaptation to an aerial existence, feeding, mating, and some reputedly even sleeping aloft. They alight only when roosting or at their nests, at which time they cling to streamside cliffs or enter hollow trees, holes in cliffs, or man-made equivalents such as chimneys. When at rest they cling to a vertical surface aided by sharp claws. Nests of some birds are semicircular saucers of twigs glued together, whereas those of others are masses of plant floss and feathers glued into a feltlike consistency. The nestling period is very long, but when young swifts leave the nest, they are capable of strong flight. The status and distribution of some Colombian swifts is imperfectly known, and the great similarity of plumages, and plumage change with feather wear and soiling, often makes field identification unreliable.

### 1. WHITE-COLLARED SWIFT

*Streptoprocne zonaris*          Pl. XII, Map 352

**Identification:** 8″ (20cm). *Largest Colombian swift; tail shallowly forked.* Blackish with *conspic. white collar encircling neck* (collar broadest across chest). Imm.: white collar more or less interrupted on sides, sometimes much reduced.

**Similar species:** Large size, distinctly notched tail and distinct white collar diagnostic. See Biscutate Swift (note).

**Voice:** Flight calls incl. thin hisses, squeals, and chittering; sound like *s-ree s-ree s-ree* when a flock suddenly calls at once (Slud 1964).

**Behavior:** Notably gregarious in small to mod.-sized flocks, sometimes hundreds in huge milling groups riding thermals to great hts. on stiff outstretched wings. In level flight fly very fast with deep, steady, and fluid wing beats. Often range very far from roosting site during daily foraging; swoop down mt. valley at tremendous speed with wings producing a loud swooshing sound.

**Breeding:** Nest on *wet* cliffs near water, often even behind waterfalls. Colony with eggs and nestlings, late Feb–early Mar, PN Cueva de los Guácharos (P. Gertler); another colony active 19 Mar, Santa Marta Mts. (Todd and Carriker 1922). Mud and moss nest on ledge; 2 white eggs (Sclater and Salvin 1879).

**Status and habitat:** Common in foothills and mts. and reg. wander up to 50km or more onto adj. lowlands and llanos. Fly over forested, partially open, or completely open terrain. Reports at Leticia (incl. flocks of 100 or more) may or may not refer to this sp. (see note).

**Range:** To 3500m (usually much lower). Throughout w of Andes, e of them along base of foothills and adj. lowlands, Macarena Mts., once on Río Orinoco (Sanariapo, Venez.) and locally around cerros in Vaupés and Guainía (sightings, R. Ridgely, Hilty et al.); the Amazon near Leticia(?). Mexico to n Argentina and s Brazil. Greater Antilles; Trinidad; s Florida (once).

**Note:** Large "white-collared" swifts in Amazonas may be this sp. or Biscutate Swift (*S. biscutata*) of e and se Brazil. The latter, unrec. in Colombia or anywhere nearby, would be difficult to separate in the field, and prob.

overlooked. Differs from White-collared Swift in slightly smaller size (7.5″), white collar on hindneck and chest not joined at sides, and square tail.

[*Cypseloides*: Larger and blacker than *Chaetura*; back, wings, rump, and tail always uniform (no contrast); underparts uniformly dark (or with chestnut or white on throat and chest).]

## 2. CHESTNUT-COLLARED SWIFT

*Cypseloides rutilus*          Pl. XII, Map 353
**Identification:** 5″ (13cm). Blacker and distinctly longer-tailed than most *Chaetura* swifts. ♂: blackish with *broad rufous chestnut collar encircling neck* (often not conspic.), tail square or slightly notched. ♀: collar usually incomplete or lacking, occas. complete. Juv.: partial collar (♂♂) and rufous edgings on some feathers of crown and breast.
**Similar species:** ♂'s collar is diagnostic but usually hard to see except against a dark background or from above. In flight, from most *Chaetura* by proportionally longer tail and narrower wings, and in some cases, more steady (less erratic) flight. ♀ and imm.: much like rare White-chinned Swift (4) but smaller and slightly longer-tailed. Also see Black Swift (note).
**Voice:** High-pitched hoarse chattering, more metallic and buzzy than calls of *Chaetura* swifts (ffrench 1973).
**Behavior:** Single birds or small groups up to a few doz. may fly in unmixed flocks or with flocks of *Chaetura*.
**Breeding:** BC ♂, 1 June, Snía. San Lucas (Carriker). Colombian nests reported by Orton (1871) and Nicéforo and Olivares (1967), in damp shade near water on vertical rock surface of cliff, cave entrance, bridge culvert, etc.; saucer or truncated cone of moss, soft plant material, mud, and poss. saliva; used repeatedly. In Trinidad, mainly May–Aug; 2 broods a season common; 2 white eggs (Snow 1962c; Collins 1968a; ffrench 1973).
**Status and habitat:** Uncommon to fairly common in foothills and mts. Flies mostly over open or partially open terrain, also forest areas, even villages and towns. Although migrants suspected (Miller 1963), no S American specimen is conclusively from a n (i.e., Mexican) population (C. Collins).
**Range:** 800-2500m (sightings to 3300m). PN Puracé—Hilty et al.). All 3 Andean ranges incl. Snía. San Lucas (unrec. in Santa Marta or Perijá Mts.). Mexico locally to Guyana and in Andes s to Bolivia. Trinidad.
**Note 1:** Great Dusky Swift (*C. senex*) of c and s Brazil is unrec. but should be watched for e

of Andes as a poss. trans-Amazonian migrant. Several recent sightings, presum. this sp., near Iquitos, Peru, in June (P. Alden). Very large (7.5″), almost entirely uniform sooty brown with grayish tinge on head and throat and with short *square* tail. **Note 2:** Black Swift (*C. niger*), also unrec., is poss. Breeds in w N America, W Indies poss. s to Costa Rica, and is known from Guyana (specimens and sightings) and Trinidad (sightings). Large (6″), sooty black with frosty white forecrown (visible nearby). ♀♀ sometimes with white barring below; tail shallowly forked. Very difficult to separate conclusively from White-chinned Swift in field, but in the hand, tail longer (48-55 vs 41-48mm). Specimens would be required to confirm presence of either of above in Colombia.

## 3. SPOT-FRONTED SWIFT

*Cypseloides cherriei*          Pl. XII, Map 354
**Identification:** 5″ (13cm). Uniform sooty black, chin whitish (probably not observable in field), large *conspic. white spot on either side of forehead* ("false eyespots"), and a small white spot or streak behind eye; short square tail. Some juvs. have whitish edges to lower breast and body feathers (*C. Collins*).
**Similar species:** Large eyespots prom. in flight. See White-chinned Swift (4).
**Breeding:** Only known nest is 1 from Rancho Grande, n Venez. (900m), July 1976; typical *Cypseloides* nest of moss and ferns on streamside cliff in forest; apparently 1 egg (C. Collins).
**Status and habitat:** Known from 1 specimen near San Gil s of Bucaramanga, Santander (1100m), Jan. In Aragua (Rancho Grande), Venez., prob. a permanent resident with recs. all mos. except Sept and Oct (C. Collins). All recs. are from mt. regions.
**Range:** Santander (once). N Venez. (coastal cordillera) and Costa Rica (Volcán Irazú).

## 4. WHITE-CHINNED SWIFT

*Cypseloides cryptus*          Pl. XII, Map 355
**Identification:** 5.5″ (14cm). *Uniformly dark swift with short square tail.* Sooty black above; dark grayish brown below, usually with inconspic. white chin spot (not discernible in field); chin sometimes buffy in ♂♂. Some ♀♀ with white feather tipping on belly and crissum. Tail proportionally shorter (41-49mm) and tarsus longer (15-16mm) than other *Cypseloides* swifts (Eisenmann and Lehmann 1962).
**Similar species:** Very difficult and prob. seldom safely identified in field. ♀ and imm. Chestnut-collared Swift (2) are slightly smaller and proportionally longer-tailed; in the hand

lack white chin spot. Imm. White-chested Swift (5), when it lacks white on chest, differs only in slightly larger size and slightly forked (not squarish) tail; in the hand lacks white chin. Also see unrec. Black Swift (note under 2) and the larger *Chaetura* swifts (esp. 6, 7, 10).
**Behavior:** Sometimes with flocks of Chestnut-collared or White-collared swifts.
**Status and habitat:** Few recs. Known from Cauca (Jan and Apr) and Córdoba (May) where reported feeding over bare eroded or grassy foothills and lower slopes. Breeding area unknown, but the Cauca birds had enlarged gonads (Eisenmann and Lehmann 1962).
**Range:** 300-1200m. E slope of W Andes in Cauca (Santander on Cali-Popayán road; San José) and n end of W Andes in sw Córdoba (Río Esmeralda). Locally from Belize to Guyana and s in mts. to Peru. Poss. only a migrant to Mid. America.

### 5. WHITE-CHESTED SWIFT
*Cypseloides lemosi*                     Pl. XII, Map 356
**Identification:** 6″ (15cm). *Large.* Uniformly sooty black with *large conspic. white chest patch tapering to a point on breast*; tail slightly forked. In the hand lacks projecting spines on tail. Imm.: usually with a few white feathers on chest, or occas. no white.
**Similar species:** Most likely confused with White-collared Swift (1), which is larger, has proportionally longer and more narrow wings, and *complete* white collar encircling neck (not just chest). Imm. separable from White-chinned Swift (where if present) on chest.
**Behavior:** Has been seen in flocks (20-25) of its own or mixed with White-collared, Chestnut-collared, or White-chinned swifts; mostly 15-25m above ground (Eisenmann and Lehmann 1962).
**Status and habitat:** Apparently very local. Most recs. Feb, Apr, May, and Oct, though presum. resident (Eisenmann and Lehmann 1962). Reported feeding over flat pastures and eroded foothills with coarse grass and scattered scrubby vegetation.
**Range:** ENDEMIC. 1000-1300m. The mid. and upper Cauca Val. between Cali and Popayán (Santander; Río Ovejas; Cerro de los Cristales above Cali).

### 6. CHAPMAN'S (DARK-BREASTED) SWIFT
*Chaetura chapmani*                     Pl. XII, Map 357
**Identification:** 5-5.5″ (13-14cm). Large notably blackish *Chaetura. Above blackish; upper wing surface and back glossed greenish* (fresh plumage) *or bluish* (worn plumage); rump dark brown,

slightly paler than back (weak contrast); *underparts virtually uniform sooty gray,* throat only slightly paler (not contrasting).
**Similar species:** Not easily identified. Compared to other *Chaetura,* darker, glossier, and more uniform above and below (shows little contrast on rump or throat). Chimney (7) and Ashy-tailed swifts (10) are sim. in size but paler overall and with contrasting pale throats and slightly shorter tails. *Cypseloides* swifts are completely uniform above. Also see Vaux's Swift (note under 7).
**Behavior:** Often in mixed swift flocks, esp. with other *Chaetura,* though can be very difficult to separate unless seen well against a dark background or from above.
**Breeding:** 1 Trinidad nest, Apr; shallow half saucer of small twigs glued together with saliva; on vertical concrete wall with nests of Short-tailed Swifts (Collins 1968b).
**Status and habitat:** Transient or breeding resident(?). Not well known. Mar–Apr recs. (*viridipennis*) in Antioquia are of transequatorial migrants (C. Collins); sightings (this subsp.?) from Amazonas, June–July (Hilty et al.) and Aug (J. V. Remsen); and Pichindé in Valle in July above Cali (J. V. Remsen), may be residents or migrants. Due to difficulties of sight identification, further specimen verification is desirable.
**Range:** 100-1600m. Antioquia, Valle (above Cali), and Amazonas (near Leticia). C Panama spottily e to the Guianas; ne and s central Brazil; e Peru. Trinidad. Distribution imperfectly known.

### 7. CHIMNEY SWIFT
*Chaetura pelagica*
**Identification:** 5.5″ (14cm). Mod. large *Chaetura.* Sooty grayish brown above with slightly paler rump (little contrast between rump and back); grayish brown below; *throat distinctly paler, almost whitish;* tail short.
**Similar species:** Most like Chapman's Swift (6) but has decidedly paler, contrasting throat (both show less contrast between rump and back than any others of genus), and usually not as black and glossy above. Also see Vaux's Swift (note).
**Status and habitat:** Few recs. Transient. Once from E Andes (Apr). No fall recs. In Panama believed to be a transient Oct–Nov and early Mar–mid-May, though few recs. (Wetmore 1968a; Ridgely 1976); near Lima, Peru, mostly Oct–late Dec (M. Koepcke *in* O'Neill 1974).
**Range:** Once n of Lago Tota, Boyacá (2500m) in E Andes, also in W Andes. Breeds in e and c N America; migrates through Mid. America, W Indies, Colombia, and Venez.; apparently

winters in w Amazonia (e to Manaus) and Chile (Arica); perhaps w Peru.

**Note:** Six *Chaetura* swifts occur in Colombia, and another, Vaux's Swift (*C. vauxi*), breeds as close as Venez. (n cordilleras) and w Panama and is a poss. vagrant to Colombia. Small (4″) and short-tailed; sooty black above with grayish brown rump (only slight contrast with back); sooty grayish brown below with paler gray throat. Most like 7 (above) but much smaller (at least the race most likely) and blacker above. Short-tailed and Ashy-tailed swifts are even shorter-tailed and both have paler rumps.

## 8. GRAY-RUMPED SWIFT
*Chaetura cinereiventris*        Pl. XII, Map 358
**Identification:** 4.2″ (10.7cm). Rather small. Tail proportionally longer than most *Chaetura*. Glossy black above with *sharply contrasting pale gray rump and upper tail coverts*; dark gray below, *throat paler*; under tail coverts blackish.
**Similar species:** Compared with other *Chaetura*, small, slender, relatively longer-tailed, somewhat paler below, gray rump area larger, and plumage predom. black and gray (no brownish tones). Typical of higher el. than Short-tailed Swift (11). See Chimney (7), Band-rumped (9), and Ashy-tailed swifts (10), also Vaux's Swift (note under 7).
**Voice:** In flight rapid twittering like other *Chaetura*.
**Breeding:** 4 BC birds, Mar–Apr, n Antioquia (Carriker). Nest typical of genus, a semicircular saucer glued with saliva to inner chimney wall or other vertical surface; 4 eggs (Sick 1959).
**Status and habitat:** Fairly common over forested or partially cleared terrain on lower slopes, foothills, and onto adj. hilly lowlands. Prob. common in extreme e Vaupés, since 18 ♂♂ and 25 ♀♀ taken in July on Río Vaupés opp. Tahuapunto, Brazil (Zimmer 1953), also rec. at Yavita-Pimichín just e of Guainía boundary. Sight recs. at El Dorado in c Vaupés, early June 1976 (R. Ridgely).
**Range:** To 1800m. Rather spottily in all 3 Andean ranges, adj. coastal lowlands of Pacific slope (many sightings near Buenaventura—Hilty et al.), and n foothills of W and C Andes in n Antioquia; e base of E Andes in Meta and Caquetá; locally in Vaupés and Guainía. Nicaragua to nw Panama; Colombia e to Guyana; Ecuador, e Peru, w Amazonian Brazil; coastal se Brazil, e Paraguay, and ne Argentina. Trinidad.

## 9. BAND-RUMPED SWIFT
*Chaetura spinicauda*        Pl. XII, Map 359
**Identification:** 4.2″ (10.7cm). Small and *slender*.

Deep black above with *narrow whitish rump band* sharply dividing lower back from upper tail coverts and tail; *throat whitish*; rest of underparts dark grayish brown becoming sooty black on abdomen. In good light from above the whitish rump band is very bright, almost beaconlike.
**Similar species:** Same size, shape, and flight pattern as Gray-rumped Swift (8) but easily told by brighter (whitish not gray) and much narrower rump band (whole rump and tail appear gray in latter).
**Behavior:** Scattered individuals, pairs, or fast flying flocks; often with other swift, esp. preceding sp. Wing beats twittery.
**Breeding:** BC pair, Mar, lower Río Cauca (Carriker); aerial mating and BC birds, Feb–Mar, Panama (Wetmore 1968a); Trinidad pair feeding young, July; tree cavity 10m up (Snow 1962c).
**Status and habitat:** Fairly common over forested or partially cleared terrain.
**Range:** To 1500m. Pacific coast s to Valle, generally across n lowlands to Santa Marta region and Guajira, and s to lower Cauca and mid. Magdalena val. (to Bucaramanga); e of Andes in w Caquetá and w Putumayo; extreme e in Guainía (sighting Pto. Inírida, Sept 1978—Hilty and Robbins) and prob. in Vaupés. Costa Rica s to n Colombia, Venez., Guianas, and n Brazil.

## 10. ASHY-TAILED SWIFT
*Chaetura andrei*        Pl. XII, Map 360
**Identification:** 5.3″ (13.5cm). Fairly large; *tail very short*. Dusky brown above with *contrasting pale brownish gray rump and upper tail coverts* (latter usually completely cover gray tail); *throat pale gray*; rest of underparts dark sooty brown.
**Similar species:** Easily confused. Best marks are fairly large size, short tail, overall smoky or dusky brown color, and contrasting pale rear end (from above) and throat. Shape much like Short-tailed Swift (11) but larger, wings narrower (lacks latter's broad secondaries), throat decidedly pale and flight smoother and steadier. Chimney Swift (7) has proportionally longer tail and lacks the strongly contrasting hind end; otherwise quite sim. Also see Gray-rumped Swift (8).
**Voice:** Usual call a low *chu chu chu chu* followed by a rattling chipper in Paraguay (Wetmore 1926).
**Behavior:** Occurs in mixed swift flocks or flocks of its own, mostly rather low over open terrain. Flight intermed. betw. twittery wing beats of typical *Chaetura* and floppy batlike fluttering of Short-tailed Swift.
**Status and habitat:** Few recs., but prob. reg.

transient or austral winter resident (*meridionalis*): taken 8 Aug at w base of Santa Marta Mts. on Río Frío (Darlington 1931); another near Cartagena, Bolívar, 27 Aug 1942 (Wetmore 1968a); sightings of flocks (this race?) 8 Aug 1977 near Santa Marta, 11 Aug 1979 in PN Isla de Salamanca (Hilty et al.), and 22 Aug 1975 near Leticia (J. V. Remsen).
**Range:** Tropical zone. Known from coastal Bolívar, n Magdalena, and Leticia, Amazonas. C Panama (once in Aug), Venez. (1 migrant, Sept), and Surinam (Aug). Breeds in e and s Brazil, n Paraguay, and ne Argentina (*meridionalis*). N form (*andrei*) may breed in Venez.(?).

## 11. SHORT-TAILED SWIFT
*Chaetura brachyura*          Pl. XII, Map 361
**Identification:** 4″ (10.2cm) *Very short tail.* Sooty black above with *conspic. contrasting ashy gray rump and upper tail coverts* (latter covering tail); below sooty brownish black; throat only slightly paler (no contrast); under tail coverts pale brownish. In the air very stubby with rather long wings, the secondaries decidedly broad and protruding (forms a gap between wings and body).
**Similar species:** Uniformly dark plumage and pale rear end are good marks, but even more helpful are proportions and flight characteristics, esp. the essentially tailless appearance, rather broad wings (due esp. to secondaries), and floppy batlike flight unlike any other *Chaetura*. See Ashy-tailed Swift (10) and larger Chimney Swift (7).
**Voice:** A wheezy twittering *whoyzi-whoyzi-zi-zi-zi-zi-zi* in flight (J. V. Remsen).
**Behavior:** Like other *Chaetura* often in flocks. Typically rather slow flying, a few floppy wing beats alternate with short glides; flies rather high above ground.
**Breeding:** BC ♂, 2 June, Ayacucho, s Cesar (Carriker). In Panama breeding begins with May rains (E. S. Morton); in Trinidad, Apr–Sept; shallow, half-saucer twig nest glued with saliva to sheltered vertical wall of cavity, cave, etc.; 1-7 eggs (Collins 1968a).
**Status and habitat:** Most common swift e of Andes over forested or partially cleared lowlands, also often in drier open country far from mts., a habitat where many other swifts are scarce.
**Range:** To about 800m. Throughout e of Andes; w of Andes known from mid. Magdalena Val. (s Cesar near La Gloria; Casabe, Antioquia 7°N) and Pacific coast at Quibdó (a few seen 10 Mar 1978—Hilty and P. Bailey). Perhaps also locally in Carib. lowlands (presumed sightings, PN Isla de Salamanca). C Panama; Colombia, and generally e of Andes s to e Peru, n Bolivia, and c Brazil.

[*Aeronautes*: Square-tailed edition of *Panyptila* with less white in plumage.]

## 12. [WHITE-TIPPED (MOUNTAIN) SWIFT]
*Aeronautes montivagus*          Pl. XII, Map 362
**Identification:** 5″ (13cm). *Mod. long tail square* or slightly notched (no spines). ♂: mostly sooty black with *conspic. white throat and chest;* white band across lower belly reaches to small white flank tufts; *tertials and tail usually prom. tipped white.* ♀: browner than ♂ and often with paler lower back and rump, duller white on underparts and tertials, and tail usually without white tipping.
**Similar species:** Lesser Swallow-tailed Swift (13) has longer deeply forked tail (usually held closed in a point), no white tail tips (white tips occas. lacking in ♂ White-tipped Swift, usually so in ♀—C. Collins), a complete white collar, and occurs alone or in pairs, rarely groups.
**Voice:** A rather low-pitched, rachetlike ticking or buzzing in flight; often noisy.
**Behavior:** Notably gregarious in small groups of its own or in mixed swift flocks.
**Breeding:** At Rancho Grande, n Venez., mostly Apr–July in holes in buildings (C. Collins). Breeding unproven in Colombia but observed entering holes in canyon above Río Pasto, early Apr (Brown; F. C. Lehmann).
**Status and habitat:** Hypothetical. Numerous sight recs. (no specimens): many birds 6-10 Apr 1968 and June 1981, along canyons of Río Pasto (2500m) about 40km nw of Pasto, and above Imues, Nariño, June 1981 (Brown; Hilty); 10 birds on Pacific slope in Valle at km 72, Old Buenaventura Road (500m), 17 Jan 1978 (P. Alden, Hilty), 8 in same area, 12 Aug 1978 (Hilty); 4-5 e of Bucaramanga (1800m), 11 June 1980 (Hilty and P. Hall); 10 in hills above Villavicencio, 9 Aug 1975; and 1 in Santa Marta Mts., 22 Jan 1983 (R. Ridgely). Poss. resident locally in mts. Not expected in lowlands.
**Range:** 500-2500m. Santa Marta Mts., w slope E Andes in Santander and s slope in Meta; Pacific slope in Valle (Achicayá Val.) and Nariño (Río Pasto; Río Guáitara). Spottily from Venez. (n cordillera; sightings in Andes—P. Alden) s in Andes to Bolivia; tepui highlands of s Venez. and adj. n Brazil.

[*Panyptila*: Slender with long pointed tail; contrasting black and white plumage.]

## 13. LESSER SWALLOW-TAILED SWIFT
*Panyptila cayennensis*          Pl. XII, Map 363
**Identification:** 5″ (13cm). Long deeply forked tail usually held closed in a point. Mostly black with *prom. white throat and chest joining narrow*

*white collar on hindneck*; small white spot on each side of forehead and *larger white patch on sides of lower back and flanks* (behind wing); base of outer tail feathers white (not a field mark). **Similar species:** See White-tipped Swift (12) and much browner and dingier Fork-tailed Palm-Swift (15). **Behavior:** Solitary or in pairs (not flocks) though occas. loosely assoc. with other spp. of swift. Typically flies very high; flight is fast and maneuverable but slightly erratic; wing beats very fast, some coasting. **Breeding:** Remarkable nest a long cylindrical cone of plant down and a few feathers cemented with saliva to tree trunk, or hanging beneath branch, on cliff, etc.; bottom entrance. Used for roosting as well as nesting; 2 eggs. Apr nestlings and an occupied Dec nest sw of Manizales, Caldas (Borrero 1955). **Status and habitat:** Uncommon and local over humid forested or partially forested lowlands and lower mt. slopes. **Range:** To 1400m. Pacific slope in Valle (sight recs.). Antioquia (locality uncertain), w slope C Andes in Caldas (1400m Chinchiná), Vaupés (sightings at Mitú, Feb 1978—Hilty), sightings near Leticia (J. V. Remsen; P. Alden; Hilty) and sightings in ne Guainía (Pto. Inírida, Sept 1978—Hilty and M. Robbins). Doubtless more widespread. S Mexico locally to e Ecuador (common at Limoncocha), se Peru, Amazonian, and se Brazil. Trinidad and Tobago.

### 14. PYGMY SWIFT
*Micropanyptila furcata*  Pl. XII, Map 364
**Identification:** 4" (10.2cm). A miniature of Fork-tailed Palm-Swift. Sooty brown; underparts paler and with center of throat and center of belly whitish; tail deeply forked; *outer base of tail white from above* (can sometimes be seen when banking). **Similar species:** Prob. does not overlap in range(?) with very sim. Fork-tailed Palm-Swift (15), which is larger and paler, esp. below (breast with whitish mottling), but is most safely told by absence of white at base of tail from above. **Behavior:** Pairs or small family groups over treetops and fields in partially open terrain; wing beats somewhat faster than Fork-tailed Palm-Swift (P. Alden). **Status and habitat:** One specimen from for-ested lowlands of ne Norte de Santander, but prob. not as rare as the single rec. suggests. Recently found over a var. of wooded or open regions in a rather wide area of adj. w Venez. (P. Alden; C. Collins). **Range:** To 100m. Norte de Santander (n of Cúcuta at Petrólea); prob. Perijá Mts. Adj. Venez. on humid n Andean slope (sighting to 800m—P. Alden), s Maracaibo Basin, and e base of Perijá Mts. **Note:** Closely related to and perhaps best placed in the genus *Reinarda*.

### 15. FORK-TAILED PALM-SWIFT
*Reinarda squamata*  Pl. XII, Map 365
**Identification:** 5.2" (13.2cm). *Slender-bodied; long deeply forked tail* usually held closed in a point. Dull blackish brown above with slight greenish gloss and paler grayish-edged feathers on back; below dull light brown with *throat and median underparts mottled dingy whitish.* Juv.: buffy edging on back; sides of head tinged buff (C. Collins). **Similar species:** Slender shape, long pointed tail (or forked if open), and dingy brownish plumage are characteristic. See Pygmy Swift (14). **Voice:** A distinctive buzzing or ticking *d-z-z-z-z-z-z-z* and trilling *trrrreeeeee* in flight (Snyder 1966). **Behavior:** Alone or in small loose groups that fan out low over open fields and clearings. Flight is slightly erratic and stiff-winged with rapid, almost vibrating, wing beats. Roosts in, nests in, and usually is closely assoc. with Moriche (*Mauritia*) palms. **Breeding:** Fledgling, 25 Feb, near Leticia (Nicéforo and Olivares 1967); BC ♂, Mitú, Vaupés, May (Olivares 1964b). In Trinidad breeds Apr–June; fishhook-shaped nest of plant fibers and feathers glued under dead hanging Moriche palm frond; nest chamber in hooked part of nest; 3 white eggs (ffrench 1973; Sick 1948a). **Status and habitat:** Common and widespread in open country, and in clearings and towns in forested zones. **Range:** To 500m. E of Andes from Meta and Vichada southward. Prob. Arauca and Casanare (no rec.). The Guianas and Venez. s east of Andes to e Ecuador, ne Peru, Bolivia, and Mato Grosso, Brazil. Trinidad.

# HUMMINGBIRDS: Trochilidae (143)

Hummingbirds are a large exclusively American family. They range from Alaska to Tierra del Fuego but reach their greatest diversity and abundance within a few degrees north and south of the equator. There are more species of hummingbirds in Colombia than in any other country.

They occur in all habitats from sea level to just below snowline, but they are more visually abundant in cooler subtropical and temperate zone elevations of the Andes. Hummingbirds include among their ranks the smallest birds in the world, those with the fewest feathers, the fastest metabolism, and the fastest wing beats (up to 80 per sec.). Many have glittering, iridescent, almost gemlike plumage that is the result of structural interference of light striking the feather rather than of pigments. Consequently, their colors often appear to change with the angle of light and may appear black in poor light. The wings of hummingbirds are uniquely capable of rotating through an angle of 180° allowing them great maneuverability, from stationary hovering to backward flight. Most hummingbirds are predominantly nectivorous, and some high elevation Andean species regularly become torpid at night, lowering their body temperature markedly to conserve energy. Breeding systems are varied. Some hummingbirds, including *Phaethornis*, *Colibri*, and others, are lek-forming. *Glaucis* defend territories for 1 or more ♀♀, but as far as is known, all nesting activities are carried out by the ♀ and all lay two white eggs. *Glaucis*, *Threnetes*, *Phaethornis*, *Eutoxeres* and perhaps *Androdon* suspend fiber nests with a dangling tail from beneath a palm frond or *Heliconia* tip; as far as we know, others, except *Aglaiocercus*, build simple downy cups. In the following descriptions all glittering colors (which often appear black in the field) are indicated, and wing colors are usually not described, as they are brownish black in most cases. Two measurements are given: body length from forehead to tail tip; and bill length. The two combined give the total length.

NOTE: Twenty presumed hybrid hummingbirds are known from Colombia. Most are only known from a single "Bogota" specimen, but some are known from two or more specimens. A few of the following are probably reliable as species (especially 5, 10, and 18), although the chances that any still survive in the wild are small. Curiously, almost no presumed hybrids have been taken by collectors in the present century. Presumed hybrids include 1. Bearded Coquette, *Lophornis insignibaris*, 2. Dusky Coquette, *L. melaniae*, 3. Berlepsch's Emerald, *Chlorostilbon inexpectatus*, 4. Lerch's Woodnymph, *Thalurania lerchi*, 5. Blue-spotted Hummingbird, *Amazilia cyaneotincta*, 6. Dusky Emerald, *A. veneta*, 7. Eliot's Hummingbird, *Amazilia lucida*, 8. *Coeligena purpurea*, 9. *Homophonia lawrencei*, 10. Lilac-spotted Starfrontlet, *Coeligena traviesi*, 11. Olive-throated Sunangel, *Heliangelus squamigularis*, 12. Green-throated Sunangel, *H. speciosus*, 13. Rothschild's Sunangel, *H. rothschildi*, 14. Glistening Sunangel, *H. luminosus*, 15. *Eriocnemis isaacsonii*, 16. Purple-tailed Comet, *Zodalia glyceria*, 17. Purple-tailed Thornbill, *Chalcostigma purpureicauda*, 18. Nehrkorn's Sylph, *Neolesbia nehrkorni*, 19. *Acestrura decorata*, 20. Hartert's Woodstar *Acestrura harterti*.

[*Glaucis*: Med.-sized; resemble *Phaethornis* but *lack* strongly graduated tail and elongated white-tipped central tail feathers.]

## 1. BRONZY HERMIT
*Glaucis aenea*                    Pl. 13, Map 366

**Identification:** 3.2″ (8.1cm). Bill long (1.1-1.2″, or 28-30mm), *decurved*, underside yellow. Resembles more widespread Rufous-breasted Hermit. Above *bronzy to coppery green; crown and cheeks dusky* with short buff mark over eyes; wing coverts and even flight feathers often pale tipped (visible in hand); *below cinnamon rufous*, chin and abdomen paler; tail rounded, central pair of feathers bronzy green, rest cinnamon rufous with very broad black subterminal band (outer half); tail tips white.

**Similar species:** Rufous-breasted Hermit (2), not always easily separated in field, is *decidedly larger*, greener above (no bronzy or coppery shine), incl. crown, and sometimes paler below. Also cf. ranges. See Band-tailed Barbthroat (4).

**Behavior:** Usually singly, low in *Heliconia* thickets or along mossy banks or bushy borders where gleans insects from leaf undersurfaces,

among moss, etc., or probes *Heliconia* flowers. Like allied Rufous-breasted Hermit, its true nos. are better revealed through mist nets.

**Breeding:** June–July nests, w Panama (Worth 1942); May–Aug, Costa Rica; downy cup fastened to underside of *Heliconia* or banana leaf; nest cup sometimes coarse (eggs visible from below); lasting pair bond suspected (as in next sp.), but ♂ does not participate in nesting (Skutch 1972).

**Status and habitat:** Uncommon to fairly common locally in humid and wet forested lowlands in *Heliconia* patches, bushy forest edges, and along creeks or other openings. Mainly coastal lowlands.

**Range:** To 800m. Pacific coast from c Chocó (upper Río Baudó) southward. Nicaragua to w Panama; w Colombia, and nw Ecuador.

**Note:** By some considered conspecific with next sp.

## 2. RUFOUS-BREASTED HERMIT
*Glaucis hirsuta*          Pls. 13, 16, Map 367

**Identification:** 4″ (10.2cm). Bill long (1.3″, or 33mm), *decurved*, underside yellow. Very like Bronzy Hermit. *Above bronzy green, incl. crown* (not coppery bronze with dusky crown); underparts darker more dull rufous. Tail rounded, central pair of feathers bronzy green tipped white, *rest cinnamon rufous with broad black subterminal band and white tip.* ♀: duller more rufous brown below. Imm.: duller throughout with buff edgings.

**Similar species:** See Bronzy Hermit (1) and Band-tailed Barbthroat (4); e of Andes Pale-tailed Barbthroat (3).

**Voice:** Flight call a sharp, high-pitched, rising *veeep* (J. V. Remsen); territorial call in Trinidad a 5-syllabled *chee-chee-CHee-chee-chee*, rising, then falling, often immediately repeated by ♀ in courtship duet (Snow 1973b).

**Behavior:** Usually singly in the undergrowth, esp. around *Heliconia* thickets and in banana plantations. As with *Phaethornis* hermits, occas. pauses momentarily almost in an observer's face before flitting off. ♂ ♂ do not form group leks.

**Breeding:** 7 BC birds, Jan–Oct, n Colombia (Carriker); 1 Leticia nest, 29 Sept (J. V. Remsen); building nest, w Caquetá, 11 June (Hilty); Santa Marta nests May, July, and Oct; fiber and lichen-covered cup with tail, fastened beneath *Heliconia* leaf or palm frond tip 1-3m up (Todd and Carriker 1922; Darlington 1931). In Trinidad 1-3 ♀♀ nest along a stream or roadside area defended by 1 ♂; ♂♂ do not participate in nesting (Snow 1973b).

**Status and habitat:** Uncommon to locally common in undergrowth and thickets (esp. *Heliconia*) of humid forest, *várzea*, forest edges, and second growth woodland.

**Range:** To 1000m (most recs. below 600m). Pacific coast s to upper Río San Juan (Santa Cecilia, 800-900m near Río Tatamá); wooded regions throughout rest of country (formerly in Cauca Val. s to Cali; no recs. in llanos). C Panama to n Bolivia and s Brazil. Trinidad, Tobago, Grenada.

[*Threnetes*: Much like *Phaethornis* but with black throat, less decurved bill, and no elongated central tail feathers.]

## 3. PALE-TAILED BARBTHROAT

*Threnetes leucurus*　　　　　Pl. 16, Map 368

**Identification:** 4″ (10.2cm). Bill long (1.2″, or 30mm.), decurved, underside yellow with black tip. Bronzy green above: patch behind eyes black bordered above by narrow buff line and below by *broad whitish malar; throat black sharply bordered below by rufous buff band on lower throat*; upper breast black fading to grayish white on belly; tail very rounded, central pair of feathers bronzy green, rest with *basal half buffy white and outer half dusky with narrow white tip.* Imm.

and some ♀♀ with duller or grayish throat; most show at least some buff on lower throat.

**Similar species:** Recalls Rufous-breasted Hermit (2) but has strong head pattern, black throat, lacks latter's rufous underparts; base of tail whitish (not rufous). Also cf. Band-tailed Barbthroat (range not known to overlap).

**Voice:** Song in Guyana a brief high *zit-zit-zeri*, var. to *zer-zee-zer-zeri*, given 2-15 times per min; flight call a typical hermitlike *seep* (Snow 1973a).

**Behavior:** Occurs low inside or along borders of forest, esp. in dense thickets and *Heliconia* patches. ♂♂ display from low perches (apparently in loose groups) during breeding season with persistent singing and wagging of slightly fanned tail.

**Breeding:** 1 BC ♂, June, w Caquetá (Carriker); song throughout Feb–Mar, Guyana (Snow 1973a); nest much like that of *Phaethornis*.

**Status and habitat:** Fairly common to locally common in undergrowth of forest, edges, and second growth. May meet trans-Andean representative *T. ruckeri* at e base of E Andes (n of Villavicencio), but contact zone, if any, unknown.

**Range:** To 600m. E base of E Andes from e Cundinamarca, ne Guainía (Pto. Inírida) and Vaupés (Mitú) southward. Guianas and s Venez. to n Bolivia and e Brazil.

## 4. BAND-TAILED BARBTHROAT

*Threnetes ruckeri*　　　　　Pl. 13, Map 369

**Identification:** 4″ (10.2cm). Bill long (1.2″, or 30mm), *decurved,* underside yellow with black tip. Bronzy green above; *black patch behind eye bordered above by short buff streak, below by broader one; throat black*; lower throat, chest, and flanks cinnamon rufous *fading* to grayish on rest of underparts (or flanks also grayish—*ruckeri*); tail as in previous sp. but base of outer tail feathers white (not buff). Imm. has grayish throat.

**Similar species:** From Bronzy (1) and Rufous-breasted hermits (2) by black throat, rufous mainly on chest, and basal half of tail white (not chestnut). From Pale-tailed Barbthroat (3) which it may meet at e base of E Andes, by buffy (not whitish) facial streaks, rufous chest fading to grayish breast (not sharply truncated rufous and gray), paler under tail coverts (not contrasting greenish brown), and less black on tail.

**Voice:** Song a rapid almost trilled ser. lasting about 4-5 sec.; not as squeaky as many hummingbirds (Skutch 1972).

**Behavior:** Sim. to Pale-tailed Barbthroat.

**Breeding:** 12 BC birds, Jan–May, nw Colombia (Carriker); nest a thin loosely-woven rootlet and vegetable hair cup fastened on underside of a *Heliconia*, etc., with cobweb; ♀ incubates head up, facing leaf, like *Phaethornis* (Skutch 1972).

**Status and habitat:** Local in dense thickets and *Heliconia* in young second growth and overgrown forest borders; lowlands, and foothills. Replaced in Amazonia by Pale-tailed Barbthroat.

**Range:** To 1050m (photo, Anchicayá Val.— Hilty). Pacific coast in sw Nariño (*ruckeri*), rest of Pacific coast, lowlands n of Andes e to mid. Magdalena Val. (s to Bucaramanga), n slope Santa Marta Mts. (*darienensis*); e of Andes in Norte de Santander (*venezuelensis*). Perhaps e slope E Andes at n end. Guatemala and Belize to nw Ecuador and w Venez.

[*Phaethornis*: Distinctive; mainly lowlands (except 7); understory; long decurved bill; prom. facial pattern. Two sizes: large with elongated white-tipped central tail feathers (5-12), or small with shorter, buff- or white-tipped central tail feathers (13-16).]

## 5. WHITE-WHISKERED HERMIT
*Phaethornis yaruqui*          Pl. 13, Map 370
**Identification:** 5″ (13cm). Very long decurved bill (1.8″, or 46mm), lower mandible red at base. ♂: *crown coppery bronze*; otherwise dark metallic green above; dusky patch behind eyes bordered above and below by short buff to white streak; underparts dark greenish gray; usually with indistinct *grayish white median line down throat and breast*; under tail coverts whitish; tail blue black; elongated central pair of feathers tipped white. ♀: sim. but facial streaks usually slightly longer and wider; median stripe down underparts sometimes more prom.
**Similar species:** Easily confused with Green Hermit, which has prom. buff throat stripe (not grayish down throat and breast), lacks coppery crown, and in direct comparison longer white tail tips.
**Voice:** Flight call *squeep* as it dashes off; song a raspy *seek*, monotonously repeated 25-54 times a min. from perch 1-1.5m up; lower-pitched than squeaks of Little Hermit (Hilty 1975b).
**Behavior:** The most common Pacific coast *Phaethornis*; usually seen singly as it goes darting by at eye level with a squeak, but occas. hovers momentarily in one's face before dashing off with a flick of the tail. Like most others of the genus a "trap-line forager," visiting widely separated flowers on "rounds" each day; does not stay and defend flowers. ♂♂ sing at group leks, at least some of which are occupied yr.-round (Hilty 1975b). "Song" accompanied by much tail wagging.

**Breeding:** A 20 July nest, upper Anchicayá Val., is only rec.; nest, like others of genus, fastened to underside of *Heliconia*; 1 egg (Hilty); 6 BC birds, Feb–Dec, Chocó to Valle (Carriker).
**Status and habitat:** Common in wet forest undergrowth. Mostly replaced above 1100-1200m by Tawny-bellied Hermit.
**Range:** To 1500m. Pacific coast from lower Atrato Val. (Río Truandó southward. W Colombia and nw Ecuador.

## 6. GREEN HERMIT
*Phaethornis guy*          Pls. 13, 16, Map 371
**Identification:** 5″ (13cm). Very long decurved bill (1.7″, or 43mm), lower mandible mostly red. ♂: *mainly dark green*; rump tinged bluish; cheeks dusky; short line behind eyes, narrow moustachial stripe, and *line down center of throat buff*; breast and belly dark gray (or dark green— *coruscus*), graduated tail black with elongated central pair of feathers tipped white. ♀: underparts grayer and central tail feathers sometimes longer.
**Similar species:** See White-whiskered Hermit (5). Other large green-backed hermits are pale or whitish below. On e slope E Andes, see White-bearded Hermit (9).
**Voice:** Song in sw Costa Rica a double-sounding *kaneek*, nasal, metallic, repeated just over once per sec.
**Behavior:** Sim. to White-whiskered Hermit. Some song leks may contain several doz. birds.
**Breeding:** Two Aug nests near Toqui, w Boyacá (Snow and Snow 1980); BC ♂, May, Snía. San Lucas, s Bolívar (Carriker); Costa Rican nests, Dec–Feb (Skutch 1964b); Trinidad nests, Nov–July, most Jan–Apr (ffrench 1973); cone-shaped plant down lined nest fastened to underside of palm frond, *Heliconia* leaf, fern, etc., is typical of genus; ♂♂ known to visit nest and poss. assist in nest defense (Snow 1974).
**Status and habitat:** Uncommon and local in humid forest undergrowth of foothills and lower highlands. Replaced on Pacific coast by White-whiskered Hermit.
**Range:** 900-2000m. Extreme nw near the Panama boundary (*coruscus*); locally in W Andes s to Cauca; Snía. San Lucas and C Andes s to Valle; w slope of E Andes s to Cundinamarca (*emiliae*); e slope of E Andes from Norte de Santander to Macarena Mts. (*apicalis*). Costa Rica to n Venez. and s in mts. to se Peru.

## 7. TAWNY-BELLIED HERMIT
*Phaethornis syrmatophorus*          Pl. 13, Map 372
**Identification:** 5″ (13cm). Very long decurved bill (1.6″, or 41mm), lower mandible mostly red. Coppery green above with *bright ochra-*

ceous *rump and upper tail coverts*; dusky patch behind eye bordered above and below by buffy white streaks; malar stripe dusky; *underparts bright tawny buff* with whitish line down central throat; graduated tail black broadly tipped bright tawny buff; *elongated central tail feathers mostly white.*

**Similar species:** From any other Colombian hermit by bright ochraceous rump and underparts; central tail feathers flash more white.

**Voice:** Song a high squeaky *tseep* repeated at rate of 2 per sec.

**Behavior:** Much like White-whiskered Hermit. Seems to forage low inside forest more than allies, venturing outside only to cross trails or small clearings. Lek display prob. seasonal.

**Breeding:** 5 BC birds, Mar–Aug, W and C Andes (Carriker), 1 in Dec, Valle (MCN).

**Status and habitat:** Common in humid and wet forest ("cloud forest") undergrowth. The only Colombian *Phaethornis* found *only* in the highlands.

**Range:** 800-2400m (mainly 1100-2100m). W Andes from Río San Juan headwaters (Cerro Tatamá) southward, C Andes s to Huila and both sides of head of Magdalena Val. in Huila. Doubtless also e slope E Andes in Putumayo and doubtless Nariño. Colombia, e Ecuador, and ne Peru.

## 8. LONG-TAILED HERMIT
*Phaethornis superciliosus* Pl. 16, Map 373

**Identification:** 5″ (13cm). Very long decurved bill (1.6″, or 41mm), most of lower mandible yellow. Mostly *dull brown above*; back tinged bronzy green, *rump heavily scaled buff*; dusky patch behind eyes bordered above and below by buffy white streak; malar area dusky; *underparts grayish buff* fading to buff on belly; throat with narrow whitish central stripe; graduated greenish black tail tipped buff to white; *elongated central tail feathers tipped white.*

**Similar species:** Easily confused. Very sim. Sooty-capped Hermit (11) always looks decidedly grayish below (not buffy or buffy brown), shows whiter, more contrasty facial lines, rufous (not buff) rump, and more white on central tail feathers. White-bearded Hermit (9) has much stronger whitish central throat stripe, grayish rump, and grayish underparts (no buffy tones). Also cf. smaller Pale-bellied Hermit (10).

**Voice:** Flight call a high *switch*; on lek a monotonous squeaky *wheeisk* up to 100 times a min. (Snow 1973a; Willis and Eisenmann 1979).

**Behavior:** As in White-whiskered Hermit. ♂♂ hold small territories and wag tail as they sing from favorite perches 1-5m up for many mos. of the yr. Forage by "trap-lining" flowers.

**Breeding:** 12 BC birds, Jan–Apr, n Antioquia

and Perijá Mts. (Carriker). Costa Rica nests, Jan–Aug (Skutch 1964b); Canal Zone nests, May–Sept, early wet season (Wetmore 1968a; Willis and Eisenmann 1979). Cone-shaped nest cup with dangling fiber tail is attached beneath *Heliconia* leaf or palm frond tip as in other *Phaethornis*; ♀ incubates head up, facing leaf.

**Status and habitat:** Uncommon to common in moist and humid forest undergrowth, edges, and second growth woodland. Numerous in Santa Marta area.

**Range:** To 1800m. From Panama boundary e in humid lowlands n of Andes to mid. Magdalena Val. s to Bucaramanga; Santa Marta and Perijá Mts. (1800m); e of Andes from w Meta (Villavicencio), c Vichada (Santa Teresita), and ne Guainía (Pto. Inírida) southward. C Mexico to n Bolivia and e Amazonian Brazil.

## 9. WHITE-BEARDED HERMIT
*Phaethornis hispidus* Pl. 16, Map 374

**Identification:** 5″ (13cm). Long decurved bill (1.3″, or 33mm), lower mandible yellow. Mostly bronzy green above, crown duskier; *rump grayish scaled and fringed whitish*; dusky patch through and behind eyes bordered above and below by *faint* white streak; *underparts gray fading to whitish on belly*; throat tinged brownish with prom. *wide white central throat stripe*, tail bronze green with dark subterminal band and elongated, white-tipped central tail feathers.

**Similar species:** In general from allies by weaker facial lines and much more prom. throat stripe. Sooty-capped Hermit (11) has orange rufous (not grayish) rump and weaker throat stripe. Also cf. Long-tailed (8) and Pale-bellied hermits (10).

**Behavior:** Like other *Phaethornis*. Usually within 2m of ground.

**Breeding:** 3 BC birds, June, w Caquetá (Carriker); nest 1-2 m up under palm frond like Long-tailed Hermit (Ruschi 1973).

**Status and habitat:** Fairly common in undergrowth or borders of gallery forest, second growth woodland, and *várzea.* "Reg." at Carimagua (S. Furniss); "common" at Limoncocha, Ecuador (Pearson et al. 1977).

**Range:** To 900m. Throughout e of Andes s to Amazonas (Pto. Nariño). Undoubtedly in Guainía and Vaupés, but no recs. as yet. W and s Venez. s to se Peru and w Amazonian Brazil.

## 10. PALE-BELLIED HERMIT
*Phaethornis anthophilus* Pl. 16, Map 375

**Identification:** 4.8″ (12.2cm). Bill long (1.5″, or 38mm), somewhat less decurved than most *Phaethornis*; lower mandible yellow. Bronze green above, with dusky crown; *bold black patch through eyes and auricular area* bordered above by narrow white line, *below by broad whitish submalar area* (accentuates black cheeks); central *throat freckled dusky; rest of underparts dingy white*, belly whitest; bronzy green tail with dusky subterminal band and white tips; central feathers elongated and white-tipped but shorter than Long-tailed Hermit.

**Similar species:** Greener above than Sooty-capped (11) and Long-tailed hermits (8). Lacks dark submalar streak and is whiter below than any other *Phaethornis* in its range. Note dusky on throat and crisp head pattern.

**Behavior:** Much like other *Phaethornis*. May forage more often in the open and in clearings adj. to woodland than most hermits (Ridgely 1976).

**Breeding:** 3 BC ♂ ♂, July, Petrólea, Norte de Santander (Carriker).

**Status and habitat:** Uncommon to fairly common in undergrowth of lighter humid woodland, second growth, brushy edges, and plantations in lowlands; favors drier woodland and borders more than other Colombian hermits.

**Range:** To 900m (once to 1500m, Santandercito, Cundinamarca). Carib. region from Río Sinú e to Santa Marta area and w Guajira s to head of Magdalena Val. in sw Huila (La Plata); e of Andes in Norte de Santander. C Panama and Pearl Isls. to c Venez.

## 11. SOOTY-CAPPED HERMIT
*Phaethornis augusti*          Pl. 16, Map 376
**Identification:** 5″ (13cm). Long decurved bill (1.3″, or 33mm), base of lower mandible red. Bronzy green above, crown more dusky; *rump and upper tail coverts conspic. fringed rufous*; blackish patch through and behind eye bordered above and below by *whitish streaks*; submalar area dusky; *underparts buffy gray*, belly paler; median throat stripe white; wedge-shaped bronzy green tail with white tips, very elongated central feathers tipped white.

**Similar species:** Can be difficult to separate from Long-tailed (8) and White-bearded hermits (9). From either by obviously *rufescent* rump; additionally from Long-tailed by whiter and crisper facial lines, more broadly white-tipped tail, and more grayish tone below (latter marks often not wholly diagnostic alone).

**Voice:** Rapid song, *here here zee-zee-zeet*, monotonously repeated at rate of 6 times per 10 sec (P. Schwartz recording).

**Behavior:** Much like Long-tailed Hermit but more often seen along borders and in the open in small clearings.

**Breeding:** 1 BC bird in June, Santa Marta, 1 in Oct, Cúcuta (Carriker). Building nest, 30

Dec (Hilty), and 2 active nests, late Apr, n Venez. (Gilliard 1959). Usual cone-shaped *Phaethornis* nest with dangling tail; all 3 in road culverts.

**Status and habitat:** Uncommon in undergrowth and edges of fairly dry to humid forest, second growth, and in adj. clearings; chiefly foothills.

**Range:** 600-1500m. Santa Marta Mts. (Venez. side of Perijá Mts.), Catatumbo region (Ocaña), and e slope E Andes s to s Meta (Macarena Mts.). Guyana and adj. s Venez.; n and w Venez. and ne Colombia.

## 12. STRAIGHT-BILLED HERMIT
*Phaethornis bourcieri*          Pl. 16, Map 377
**Identification:** 4.8″ (12.2cm). Only Colombian *Phaethornis* with a *virtually straight bill* (1.3″, or 33mm); lower mandible yellowish flesh-color tipped black. Dull bronzy to coppery green above; feathers of rump broadly edged buff; *indistinct* dusky patch through eyes bordered above and below by *faint narrow buff streaks*; underparts grayish buff, abdomen paler; faint buffy white median throat stripe; graduated tail bronze green with elongated central feathers tipped buffy white.

**Similar species:** Easily known by straight bill and overall faded dingy appearance. See note.

**Voice:** Song at Leticia lek a squeaky *tsee tib-it*, about once a sec as it wags tail.

**Behavior:** Sim. to other *Phaethornis*. Leks near Leticia and Mitú were small. Usually keeps inside forest, but occas. feeds at borders or in open clearings.

**Breeding:** Near Pto. Inírida, Guainía, ad. fed 2 weakly flying fledglings, Sept (Hilty); 1 BC ♂, Jan, Río Casiquiare, Venez. (Friedmann 1948).

**Status and habitat:** Common in undergrowth of humid lowland forest. Perhaps mostly replaced s of Amazon by *P. philippi* (see note).

**Range:** To 400m. E of Andes from w Caquetá (s of Florencia), ne Guainía (sightings, Pto. Inírida, Sept 1978—Hilty and M. Robbins), and Vaupés southward. Guianas and s Venez. to e Ecuador, ne Peru, and n Amazonian Brazil (mostly n of Amazon).

**Note:** Needle-billed Hermit (*P. philippi*) of e Peru and w Brazil s of Amazon occurs on s bank near Leticia. Much like Straight-billed Hermit, but rump and underparts bright cinnamon buff (like Tawny-bellied Hermit) and tail tips rufous; bill straight. *Várzea* and *terra firme* forest.

## 13. DUSKY-THROATED HERMIT
*Phaethornis squalidus*          Pl. 16, Map 378
**Identification:** 3.7″ (9.4cm). *Very small*; bill

slightly decurved (1″, or 25mm), base of lower mandible yellowish. Above dull coppery green, crown brownish, *rump fringed rufous*; blackish patch behind eye bordered above and below by long whitish buff streak; *underparts grayish to brownish buff; throat streaked and freckled black*; wedge-shaped bronzy tail, *central feathers slightly elongated* (shorter than previous sp. and white-tipped.

**Similar species:** Almost a miniature of Pale-bellied Hermit (10), but duller more coppery above, rump fringed rufous, and underparts tinged brownish.

**Behavior:** Like others of the genus. Song lek in tangled undergrowth in Venez. Orinoco (Cherrie 1916).

**Breeding:** Typical *Phaethornis* nest fastened beneath palm frond tip (Ruschi 1949).

**Status and habitat:** Not well known in Colombia. Apparently favors undergrowth or thickety borders of humid sandy-belt forest, savanna woodland, and gallery forest.

**Range:** Río Orinoco (100m) in e Vichada (Maipures). Guyana, s Venez., and n Amazonian and se Brazil.

## 14. REDDISH HERMIT
*Phaethornis ruber*     Pl. 16, Map 379

**Identification:** 3.2″ (8.1cm). *Very tiny*; bill slightly decurved (0.9″, or 23mm), lower mandible yellow basally. ♂: above bronzy green; *rump and entire underparts cinnamon rufous with a narrow black band across breast*; dusky patch through and behind eye bordered above and below by buffy streaks; wedge-shaped tail bronzy green with buff tips, central feathers *tipped buffy to white, barely protruding.* ♀: sim. but paler; black band across chest *reduced to indistinct small patch, or lacking.*

**Similar species:** ♂ is only tiny hermit with narrow black band across breast. ♀ almost identical to Gray-chinned Hermit (15) and often not separable in field; but note Gray-chin's slightly greener back, definitely longer white tips on central tail feathers (protrude about 0.5″, or 13mm; feathers of Reddish Hermit barely protrude), and grayish throat patch. Also see Little Hermit (16).

**Voice:** Song in Guyana a high thin *zee,zee,zee,zeezeze*, gradually descending and jumbled at end; 16-18 times per min (Snow 1973a).

**Behavior:** Much like Little Hermit, but flight more weaving and insectlike.

**Breeding:** BC ♂, 2 Jan, Río Orinoco at Pto. Ayacucho, Venez. (Friedmann 1948); s Guyana ♂♂ sang, Feb and Mar (Snow 1973a). Cone-shaped nest a miniature of larger *Phae-*

*thornis* nests; fastened to low palm frond tip (Oniki 1970b).

**Status and habitat:** Common in undergrowth of humid forest, forest borders, second growth woodland, and scrubby areas in lowlands. Perhaps more numerous in savanna and sandy-belt forests than s in Amazonia.

**Range:** To 500m. E of Andes from w Caquetá, ne Guainía (sightings, Pto. Inírida, Sept 1978—Hilty and M. Robbins), and Vaupés (Mitú) southward. Not rec. in Macarena Mts. Guianas and s Venez. to n Bolivia and s Brazil.

## 15. GRAY-CHINNED HERMIT
*Phaethornis griseogularis*     Pl. 16, Map 380

**Identification:** 3.4″ (8.6cm). Bill slightly decurved (0.9″, or 23mm), lower mandible mostly yellow. *Very sim. to ♀ Reddish Hermit. Bronzy green above*, rump and entire underparts cinnamon rufous; *chin and median throat gray*; blackish patch through eyes bordered above and below by a buffy streak; wedge-shaped tail bronze green subterminally black and tipped buff, central tail feathers white-tipped and *protruding only a short distance (about 0.5″, or 13mm) beyond rest of tail.*

**Similar species:** See ♀ Reddish hermit (14), which is mainly a lowland bird. Little Hermit of e of Andes (16) is also very sim. but duller below and throat with dusky and white streaking.

**Behavior:** Much like Reddish Hermit.

**Status and habitat:** Undergrowth of humid forest and forest edges on lower slopes of E Andes. Mainly a hill country bird.

**Range:** 500-1500m. E base of E Andes from Norte de Santander (El Diamente, 1500m) s to w Meta and w Caquetá. Doubtless s along base of Andes. W Venez. (Perijá Mts.) to e Ecuador and ne Peru; se Venez. and adj. nw Brazil (tepuís).

## 16. LITTLE HERMIT
*Phaethornis longuemareus*     Pls. 13, 16, Map 381

**Identification:** 3.6″ (9.1cm). Bill slightly decurved (1.0″, or 25mm), lower mandible mostly yellow. *Color of underparts var.* Above coppery green, crown darker; rump dull rufous, sides of head dusky bordered above and below by a buffy white streak. Below: uniform cinnamon buff with slight gray tinge on breast (*nelsoni*); or throat and breast grayish buff, abdomen cinnamon buff, throat streaked dusky (*subrufescens, striigularis*); or uniform cinnamon buff below with dusky streaks on throat (*artrimentalis*). Wedge-shaped tail bronzy tipped buff, central feathers white-tipped and slightly elongated.

**Similar species:** Only very small hermit w of Andes; note barely protruding white-tipped central tail feathers. E of Andes easily confused with even smaller Gray-chinned (15) and ♀ Reddish hermits (14); told from either by dusky throat streaking, duller underparts, and larger size (flight more darting). Also see Dusky-throated Hermit (13).

**Voice:** Song a constant very high-pitched squeaking (easily overlooked) with much local var.; in Trinidad a high chittering *ee-wee tiddly weet* (Snow 1968).

**Behavior:** Usually seen singly. Gleans from undersurface of large leaves in undergrowth or "trap-lines" understory flowers. Audible whirr of wings often first indication of its presence, but unlike Reddish Hermit, darts rather than weaves beelike as flies. ♂♂ sing at leks during breeding season; in some regions sing yr.-round (Hilty 1975b), uttering tiny squeaks much of day from perch 0.5-2m up.

**Breeding:** 4 BC birds, Mar, May, and Sept, mid. Magdalena Val. (Carriker); 1 bird building nest, 13 July, upper Anchicayá Val. (Hilty); Apr–Aug and Nov–Jan in Costa Rica; cone-shaped little cup with dangling tail, usually fastened beneath low palm frond tip (Skutch 1964b).

**Status and habitat:** Common in undergrowth and edges of humid and wet forest and second growth woodland. Absent from arid portions of Carib. region and from very dry interior valleys.

**Range:** To 1200m. Lower Atrato Val. s to Juradó and Murindó (*nelsoni*); Pacific slope from Baudó Mts. southward (*subrufescens*); Santa Marta region s to lower Cauca Val. (Pto. Valdivia) and mid. Magdalena Val. to Honda (*striigularis*); e of Andes in Meta e to Carimagua (S. Furniss), s to Putumayo (*atrimentalis*); and sightings at Leticia, Amazonas. S Mexico to w Ecuador, e Peru, Amazonian Brazil, and the Guianas. Trinidad.

## 17. TOOTH-BILLED HUMMINGBIRD

*Androdon aequatorialis*          Ill. 66, Map 382

**Identification:** 4" (10.2cm). Bill very long (1.6", or 41mm) and straight, or occas. with strongly hooked bill tip (R. Zusi), black above and pale yellow below. ♂: *forecrown reddish copper;* otherwise bronzy green above, rump reddish copper; *upper tail coverts with conspic. white band;* rounded tail grayish green with darker subterminal band and *broad white tips;* underparts grayish white; *throat and breast broadly streaked blackish* (or heavier streaks extending to belly—Nariño). In the hand has tiny comblike serrations on cutting edge of outer half of bill. ♀: duller, esp. on crown, less streaked below. Imm. like ♀ but nape tinged bluish.

66. Tooth-billed Hummingbird (top), White-tipped Sicklebill (bottom)

**Similar species:** Only Colombian hummer with long straight bill and streaked underparts. Rump band prom. in flight.

**Breeding:** BC ♂, 12 Feb, Buenaventura Road, Valle (MCN).

**Behavior:** Flies fast in upper understory to subcanopy inside forest or occas. at edges. Gleans rapidly back and forth beneath large leaves (i.e., *Ochroma* and *Cecropia*) with bill pointing up and tail flicking up (Hilty). Also at flowers. Near Quibdó 2 birds sang from low perches a short distance apart (P. Bailey). Function of bill serrations unknown, but may facilitate insect gleaning.

**Status and habitat:** Uncommon to rare in humid and wet forest and forest edges in lowlands and foothills.

**Range:** To 1050m (photo, Anchicayá Val.—Hilty). Pacific coast from Panama border southward; humid lowlands along n base of W and C Andes to mid. Magdalena Val. (s to Remedios, Antioquia). E Panama (750-1550m) to w Ecuador.

## 18. WHITE-TIPPED SICKLEBILL

*Eutoxeres aquila*          Ill. 66, Map 383

**Identification:** 4.5" (11.4cm). Unmistakable, with *distinctive sickle-shaped bill* (1" [25mm] chord) bent almost in a 90° arc; lower mandible yellow. Dark shining green above; *heavily streaked sooty and white below;* rounded bronzy green tail *broadly tipped white.* Muscular and heavy-bodied.

**Similar species:** See Buff-tailed Sicklebill (19).
**Voice:** Flight call a "hermitlike" squeak.
**Behavior:** A rather retiring hummingbird of deep shade and dense thickets. Usually seen singly in undergrowth where feeds at *Heliconia* by clinging to flowers and probing curved corollas; also gleans insects from trunks and branches, usually keeping low. Flies with slow audible wing beats and may pause briefly to examine an observer, but unlike *Phaethornis*, usually from a discreet distance in partial concealment. Bill and head held up slightly when perched.
**Breeding:** 3 BC birds, Apr–May, nw Colombia (Carriker); and 1 in Dec, Valle (MCN); loosely woven palm fiber cup (eggs visible from outside) with hanging tail suspended beneath palm frond tip 2.5m up near creek, 17 Sept, Ecuador (Ruschi 1973).
**Status and habitat:** Common (hard to see) in understory of humid and wet forest and older second growth woodland on Pacific coast and slope. Often in or near patches of *Heliconia*: its abundance is better revealed through mist netting. Local and rare in upper Magdalena Val. at PN Cueva de los Guácharos (P. Gertler).
**Range:** To 1400m (Pacific region); 1600-2100m (Magdalena Val.). W of W Andes from Panama boundary southward; n of W Andes in upper Río Sinú Val.; mid. Magdalena Val. in e Caldas (Río Samaná) and w Cundinamarca s to headwaters in s Huila (near San Agustín); e slope E Andes from Cundinamarca southward, perhaps locally to w Amazonas (rec. at mouth of Río Curaray, nw Peru). Costa Rica to nw Peru.

## 19. BUFF-TAILED SICKLEBILL

*Eutoxeres condamini* Map 384
**Identification:** 4.5″ (11.4cm). Sim. to White-tipped Sicklebill (18), but *4 outer tail feathers cinnamon buff tipped white* (not bronzy green tipped white) and underparts streaked sooty and buffy white (not black and white). In the hand note bluish green patch on sides of neck.
**Behavior:** Sim. to White-tipped Sicklebill.
**Status and habitat:** Undergrowth of shady, wooded ravines and forest streams; also sometimes cut-over areas and overgrown clearings; but like previous sp., fond of *Heliconia*. Replaced in foothills and lower highlands on e Andean slope by allied White-tipped Sicklebill. In an area of presumed sympatry in e Ecuador, Buff-tailed reportedly favored more open or disturbed areas, White-tipped denser forest (Norton 1965).
**Range:** To 400m (to 700m in e Ecuador). E base of E Andes in w Caquetá, Putumayo, and prob. w Amazonas (rec. at mouth of Río Cur-

araray, nw Peru). E Colombia and e Ecuador to se Peru and n Bolivia.

## 20. BLUE-FRONTED LANCEBILL

*Doryfera johannae* Pl. 13, Map 385
**Identification:** 3.4″ (8.6cm). Bill long, 1.0-1.2″ (25-30mm), slender, black, and *very straight*. Plumage appears very dark in field. *Forecrown glittering violet*; upperparts dark bronzy green, rump tinged bluish green; *tail rounded*, steely blue black; underparts dark green to bluish black; under tail coverts tinged bluish. ♀: paler than ♂ and with *shining blue green forehead*, grayish green underparts, and *gray-tipped outer tail feathers*.
**Similar species:** Resembles Green-fronted Lancebill (21) but smaller; ♂ much darker with violet frontlet. ♀ told from ♀ Green-fronted Lancebill by smaller size, shorter bill, shining (not glittering) frontlet, and dull (not coppery) rearcrown.
**Voice:** High chittering perched or flying; a quiet *click-clack*, like echo location clicks when flying in dark cave entrance (Snow and Gochfeld 1977).
**Behavior:** Usually alone and rather low at forest openings or thicket borders. Hovers at horizontal or downward projecting tubular flowers without clinging (Hilty). An Ecuador pair made frequent flycatching sallies from top of low tree (Snow and Gochfeld 1977).
**Breeding:** Nest with 1 egg, 15 July, in Ecuador (600m); moss and cobweb cylinder suspended from rock overhang in cave; nest cup at top (Snow and Gochfeld 1977).
**Status and habitat:** Uncommon in humid forest and forest borders, esp. near rocky outcrops, broken terrain, and caves in foothills. Replaced at higher el. by Green-fronted Lancebill.
**Range:** 400-1600m. E base of E Andes from e Cundinamarca (Río Guatiquía) and w Meta (Villavicencio; Pico Renjifo in Macarena Mts.) southward. E Colombia to se Peru; tepuis of Guyana, se Venez. and adj. n Brazil in Roraima.

## 21. GREEN-FRONTED LANCEBILL

*Doryfera ludoviciae* Pl. 13, Map 386
**Identification:** 4″ (10.2cm). Bill very long (1.4″ or 36mm), slender, and straight. Both sexes resemble ♀ Blue-fronted Lancebill but larger, *forecrown glittering green and rearcrown coppery*. Otherwise, metallic green above, more grayish green below; upper tail coverts bluish, tail steely blue black tipped gray. ♀: duller with only frontlet glittering green and rest of crown bronzy. In either sex head often looks dull and brownish, esp. in dim light.
**Similar species:** See Blue-fronted Lancebill (20).

**Behavior:** A prom. "trap-liner" (Snow and Snow 1980), esp. to clumps of pendent flowers with long corollas where it hovers without clinging; often hawks insects in small openings. Flies fast and direct; in lower story, sometimes very low.

**Breeding:** 2 BC birds and laying ♀, July–Aug, C and E Andes (Carriker); a PN Cueva de los Guácharos nest with eggs, 3 Oct, fledged young late Nov and a 2d brood 24 Jan; 3 other nests, Dec–late Jan; fiber and rootlet nest lined with moss, sunk in moss 1.5-20 m up on rocky cave ledge (P. Gertler; Snow and Gochfeld 1977).

**Status and habitat:** Fairly common to locally common in humid and wet forest ravines and borders. Common at PN Cueva de los Guácharos.

**Range:** 1400-2700m (900-2100m on Pacific slope). All 3 Andean ranges. Doubtless also Panama border on Cerro Tacarcuna (on Panama side at 1300m). Costa Rica; e Panama (Darién); nw Venez. s in mts. to Bolivia.

## 22. SCALY-BREASTED HUMMINGBIRD
*Phaeochroa cuvierii*          Pl. 13, Map 387
**Identification:** 4.5″ (11.4cm). Bill rather short (0.7″, or 18mm), noticeably broad at base; most of lower mandible pink to whitish. Above shining green; below grayish buff *thickly spotted green on throat and breast* (giving a scaly appearance); tail bronzy green above, dark olive below; *the outer feathers broadly tipped white* (white corners on tail); under tail coverts dusky scaled whitish.

**Similar species:** A large robust hummingbird with slightly unkempt ♀-like appearance. Easily confused with ♀ White-necked Jacobin (26), which is usually even more scaly below, has all white (not buff) belly, and lacks white tail corners. Both Plumeleteers (73, 74) lack the scaly underparts, have longer tails, and have prom. white under tail coverts.

**Voice:** A rather good singer for a hummingbird, uttering a loud chirping and trilling song of var. no. of syllables, tirelessly repeated, i.e., *tsup sst-sst-sst*, from an exposed usually low perch (Skutch 1964a; Ridgely 1976).

**Behavior:** Probes flowers or flycatches insects from near ground to treetops, mostly in rather open situations. Sometimes perches or clings to feed at flowers. ♂♂ form small singing assemblies during breeding season.

**Breeding:** Mainly wet season, May–Jan, in Costa Rica; downy cup about 2-8m up in small tree in pasture or semiopen (Skutch 1964a).

**Status and habitat:** Uncommon and somewhat local in drier more open areas, esp. woodland borders, gardens, shrubby clearings, and tree-lined pastures.

**Range:** To 200m. Carib. region from Carta-gena to Barranquilla and arid mid. Magdalena Val. (Gamarra, s Cesar). Mexico (sight) and Guatemala to n Colombia.

## 23. GRAY-BREASTED SABREWING
*Campylopterus largipennis*          Pl. 14, Map 388
**Identification:** 5″ (13cm). Bill stout (1.1″, or 28mm) and slightly decurved. Large and dull. Plain shining green above; outer tail feathers bluish black *broadly tipped white* (white corners on tail); cheeks and underparts uniform dull gray; *white spot behind eye prom.*

**Similar species:** ♀ Fork-tailed Woodnymph (47; races e of Andes) is sim. but decidedly smaller, lacks white spot behind eye, and tail corners only narrowly tipped white. ♀ White-vented Plumeleteer (73) has longer tail, very narrow white tips, snowy under tail coverts, and barely overlaps in range.

**Voice:** Song a ser. of 5-10 *soo-eet* notes at about 2 per sec. sung persistently from a rather low perch (J. V. Remsen).

**Behavior:** Usually seen at low or lower-mid. hts. (not canopy). Has habit of perching rather conspic. in open. ♂♂ may assemble in small loose singing assemblies of 2-4 birds or sing solitarily (J. V. Remsen).

**Breeding:** BC ♂, 10 June, w Caquetá (Carriker); ♂♂ sang May–Nov near Leticia (J. V. Remsen); in Brazil tall cup-shaped nest on horizontal branches near waterfalls and low over water (Ruschi 1973).

**Status and habitat:** Uncommon to fairly common in humid second growth woodland, *terra firme* and *várzea* borders, and scrubby clearings, less often inside tall forest.

**Range:** To 400m. E of Andes from s Meta (Macarena Mts.) and se Guainía (San Felipe) southward. Undoubtedly n to e Vichada. The Guianas and s Venez. to Bolivia and Amazonian and e Brazil.

**Note:** Napo Sabrewing (*C. villaviscensio*) of Napo headwaters (to 1500m) e Ecuador may occur in e Nariño or adj. w Putumayo. 4.5″. ♂: crown glittering golden green; otherwise bronze green above; throat and breast glittering violet blue; lower underparts mixed gray and green; tail mostly dark blue. ♀: sim. but gray below; outer tail feathers narrowly tipped white.

## 24. LAZULINE SABREWING
*Campylopterus falcatus*          Pl. 15, Map 389
**Identification:** 4.5″ (11.4cm). *Bill noticeably decurved* (1.1″, or 28mm) *and heavy.* ♂: entirely glittering green above; *throat and breast glittering violet blue* gradually becoming blue green on belly; under tail coverts and *tail rufous chestnut* (from below); 4 central tail feathers mostly dark green or tipped dark green, rest rufous chestnut sometimes tipped blue black. ♀:

shining green above with large white spot behind eye; underparts mostly *plain gray, throat glittering bluish bordered on sides by grayish white malar line*; sides and flanks disked green; central tail feathers mostly green; *tail otherwise as in ♂*.

**Similar species:** Either sex by slightly decurved bill and extensive rufous chestnut in tail. ♀ is only highland hummingbird with grayish underparts and rufous chestnut outer tail feathers.

**Voice:** Song in Venez. a sputtering ser., *chik, it, chik, it, splek, chat, seet, chik, seet, chik, it, chik, it, . . .* with much var. (P. Schwartz recording).

**Behavior:** Forages at low to med. hts., usually in shade or near cover.

**Breeding:** BC ♂ and laying ♀, June, Perijá Mts. (Carriker).

**Status and habitat:** Local in humid forest, forest borders, shady plantations, and gardens on e slope E Andes; little known elsewhere, perhaps fairly common in Perijá Mts.

**Range:** 900-2600m (once to 500m in mid. Magdalena Val.), Perijá Mts. (2000m). E slope E Andes s to Caquetá and w slope spottily to head of Magdalena Val. (San Agustín); nw end of W Andes below Paramillo Mts. (Peque, 1500m). Prob. also n end of C Andes. N Venez. to e Ecuador.

## 25. SANTA MARTA SABREWING

*Campylopterus phainopeplus*

**Identification:** 5″ (13cm). Bill stout (1.0″, or 25mm) and slightly decurved. ♂: *mainly glittering green*; forecrown green; hindcrown and rest of upperparts glittering green; *throat and chest glittering blue; square tail steely blue black*. ♀: shining green above; forecrown and cheeks duller; *below gray with green flanks and under tail coverts*; tail green, outer feathers narrowly tipped gray.

**Similar species:** ♀ recalls ♀ White-vented Plumeleteer (73), mainly a lowland bird, but tail shorter and under tail coverts green (not white).

**Voice:** In flight and display a plaintive double note, *twit-twit* (Todd and Carriker 1922).

**Behavior:** Usually solitary at flowers at low to mod. hts. in shady or partially open areas. Sings from high exposed perch.

**Breeding:** 4 BC birds, Apr–June (Carriker). At high el. and near treeline singing persistently and performing aerial displays, June–July (Todd and Carriker 1922).

**Status and habitat:** Reported fairly common locally in humid forest borders and shady plantations, esp. banana plantations, on s slope Santa Marta Mts. during Feb–May dry season (mainly 1200-1800m), during June–Oct wet season up to snowline (4500m) on open slopes

(Todd and Carriker 1922). Represented in Perijá Mts. and n end of Andes by more widespread ally, Lazuline Sabrewing.

**Range:** ENDEMIC. 1200-4800m. S slope of Santa Marta Mts. (esp. near San Sebastián); n slope only at extreme e end (upper Río Macotama, 1700m). Not rec. from nw on Cuchilla de San Lorenzo.

**Note:** Most of the areas where this sp. occurs *cannot* be visited safely at present.

## 26. WHITE-NECKED JACOBIN

*Florisuga mellivora*                     Pl. 13, Map 390

**Identification:** 4″ (10.2cm . Bill rather short (0.8″ or 20mm), thick, and slightly drooping. ♂: *head, throat, and chest bright shining blue; large white crescent on hindneck*; otherwise shining green above; *upper breast green; lower underparts white; tail mostly white* with black tip. ♀: bronzy green above; cheeks dusky; throat and breast dusky to greenish *scaled white*; lower underparts white; *under tail coverts dusky scaled white*; tail dark green with dusky subterminal band and usually a narrow white tip. Some ♀♀ show small amts. of bluish on head or throat, more white in tail, others (♀♀?) resemble dull ♂♂.

**Similar species:** Dull plumage (phase?) ♀♀ most like Scaly-breasted Hummingbird (22), but underparts more scaly, belly white (not buff), and without latter's prom. white tail corners.

**Voice:** Indistinct *tsitting* and squeaking notes.

**Behavior:** Usually solitary but may congregate at flowering trees. Forages at var. hts., usually fairly high; often seen hovering, sometimes quite high over rivers or trees, for insects. ♂♂ perform striking swooping and diving breeding display with broadly fanned tail.

**Breeding:** Display late Apr, upper Anchicayá Val. (Hilty); 9 BC birds, Feb–May, nw Colombia; 2 in June, 1 in Nov e of Andes (Carriker). 7 Barro Colorado Isl. nests, Jan–July, were downy cups plastered atop broad leaves less than 2.1m up and near forest streams (Willis and Eisenmann 1979).

**Status and habitat:** Uncommon to common in humid and wet forest borders, clearings, and disturbed areas; less often inside forest.

**Range:** To 1600m (usually below 900m). Humid regions throughout (few Cauca Valley recs. and largely absent from arid Carib. and from llanos e of Andes). S Mexico to Bolivia and c Brazil. Trinidad, Tobago.

## 27. BROWN VIOLETEAR

*Colibri delphinae*                       Pl. 13, Map 391

**Identification:** 4.3″ (10.9cm). Bill fairly short (0.7″, or 18mm) and stout. Large and dull. *Mostly dingy brown with a patch of conspic. rufous barring on rump; ear coverts glittering violet* (hard to see); throat dull green bordered on sides by a *dirty white malar streak*; tail dull greenish bronze with a dusky subterminal band.

**Similar species:** Brown (94) and Bronzy incas (93), both usually of higher el., have much longer straight bills and lack the orangish rump (prom. as hovers).

**Voice:** Song a loud ser. of about 7 *chip* notes, given persistently from a high exposed perch in se Venez.; ♂♂ form loose song leks. In Trinidad a ser. of 5 *chip*'s (ffrench 1973).

**Behavior:** Widespread but erratic. Usually seen singly at low flowering shrubs or bushes at forest openings but also in groups with other hummingbirds at flowering trees in canopy. Fond of Immortelle blossoms. Reg. hawks insects, sometimes by perching on rocks in small streams.

**Breeding:** 3 BC birds, Nov, n end E Andes; 2 in Apr, s end C Andes (Carriker); singing Dec–Jan, se Venez. (Hilty). Small downy cup saddled on twig just over 1m up (ffrench 1973).

**Status and habitat:** Rare throughout most of range but seasonally numerous locally (esp. upper Magdalena Val. and Santa Marta Mts.); shrubby clearings, cultivated areas with trees, and humid and wet forest borders.

**Range:** 100-2200m in Santa Marta Mts. Mostly 900-2800m in Andes. Pacific slope from Valle (sightings, upper Anchicayá Val.—Hilty) southward; both slopes of C Andes in Cauca and s Huila (up to 2600m, Totoró, Cauca); spottily on both slopes E Andes; Macarena Mts. Perhaps locally throughout W and C Andes. Guatemala to Bolivia, n and e Brazil, and the Guianas. Trinidad.

## 28. GREEN VIOLETEAR

*Colibri thalassinus*  Pl. 15, Map 392

**Identification:** 3.8″ (9.7cm). Bill sturdy (0.8″, or 20mm), almost straight. Entirely shining green with throat and breast somewhat glittering; *long glittering violet ear patch*; tail bluish green with *conspic. black subterminal band*. Sexes sim.

**Similar species:** Often confused with Sparkling Violetear (29), which is larger with bluish patch on breast (sometimes hard to see) and violet ear patch that extends forward under bill as a narrow "chin strap." Latter usually at higher el.

**Voice:** Song typically a 2-noted ser., *tsip-chup* or *tsup-chip*, etc., with local var. and repeated *ad infinitum* from a high, bare treetop twig; as with Sparkling Violetear, voice ventriloquial.

**Behavior:** A widespread highland hummingbird usually territorial at flowers from low to canopy ht. Often gathers with other spp. at flowering trees, esp. at Immortelle. Sings solitarily or in small loose leks. Indiv. singers not easily seen despite persistent song.

**Breeding:** Early Mar nest, 2 young w Huila (2700m); down and moss cup less than 1 m up (Brown). 6 BC birds, Mar–Aug, C and E Andes and Santa Marta Mts. (Carriker); 1 in Oct, Boyacá (Olivares 1971).

**Status and habitat:** Fairly common to locally common in forest borders, clearings, and highland pastures with trees. Common in Santa Marta Mts.; very local (few recs.) in W Andes. Seasonal movements often marked.

**Range:** 600-2800m (mainly 1400-2200m; reg. down to 600m on e slope E Andes). Santa Marta and Perijá Mts. and all 3 Andean ranges (except Pacific slope and W Andes n of Valle); Macarena Mts. (Pico Renjifo). S Mexico to Bolivia and n Brazil.

## 29. SPARKLING VIOLETEAR

*Colibri coruscans*  Pl. 15, Map 393

**Identification:** 5″ (13cm). Large. Bill sturdy (1.0″, or 25mm) and almost straight. Mostly shining green with *narrow "chin strap" extending back across ear coverts glittering violet blue;* large patch from center of breast to belly *glittering purplish blue*; tail bluish green with conspic. *dark subterminal band*.

**Similar species:** Likely confused only with Green Violetear (see 28).

**Voice:** Song in PN Puracé typically a loud 3-noted ser. *tsip, tsip, tsip*, repeated with only slight pause (J. Silliman); near Bogotá a single, monotonously repeated *tsip*; in Norte de Santander a *tsip* often followed by a gravelly rattle, etc.

**Behavior:** A characteristic bird of semiopen highlands. Highly territorial and vocal; feeds at var. hts., mostly at upright or horizontal flowers; also hawks insects (Snow and Snow 1980). Usually advertises from an exposed bare treetop twig. In display flies up vertically a few m, then sings, closes wings, spreads tail, and plunges back to perch (Dorst 1956).

**Breeding:** 9 BC birds, May–Sept, n end W and C Andes; laying ♀ Jan, Perijá Mts. (Carriker); 3 BC ♂♂, Jan, Boyacá (Olivares 1963); building nest, 14 Aug (Hilty); Oct nest (Olivares 1969a) near Bogotá. Display and song in Mar at Cerro Munchique (Brown), and May at PN Puracé (J. Silliman).

**Status and habitat:** Common in highland forest borders, pastures with scattered trees, and in parks and gardens. The most common hummingbird around Bogotá. Replaced at lower el. (some overlap) by smaller ally, Green Violetear.

**Range:** 1300-3600m (mainly 2100-3100m). Santa Marta Mts., Perijá Mts., and the Andes.

N Venez. s in mts. to w Argentina; tepuís of s Venez. and adj. n Brazil.

## 30. GREEN-BREASTED MANGO
*Anthracothorax prevostii*    Map 394
**Identification:** 4″ (10.2cm). Bill slightly decurved (1″, or 25mm). ♂: shining metallic green above; loral line glittering green, *center of throat and center of breast velvety black narrowing to central stripe on lower breast and belly*, and bordered on either side by glittering green; small leg tufts white (sometimes partially concealed); central tail feathers green, *rest purplish maroon tipped black*. ♀: above metallic green; *below mostly white with narrow median black stripe more or less mixed blue green from chin to belly* and green on sides and flanks; central tail feathers green, rest purplish maroon with blackish subterminal band and *narrow white tip*.
**Similar species:** See Black-throated Mango (31), and cf. ranges.
**Behavior:** Much more local than Black-throated Mango and generally found in more open areas.
**Breeding:** 3 BC ♂♂ and 2 imms. Mar, El Conejo, w Guajira (Carriker).
**Status and habitat:** Locally fairly common in dry shrubby areas, parks, gardens, and cultivated areas with trees; reg. at flowering trees in Pance s of Cali, local in Guajira (Wetmore 1968b).
**Range:** To 1000m. Mid. Cauca Val. (mostly near Cali) and Guajira Peninsula (Snía. de Macuira at Nazaret; se of Fonseca at Conejo). E Mexico to w Panama; n Venez., w Ecuador, and nw Peru. Carib. Isls.

## 31. BLACK-THROATED MANGO
*Anthracothorax nigricollis*    Pl. 13, Map 395
**Identification:** 4″ (10.2cm). Both sexes almost identical to respective sexes of Green-breasted Mango (30) and usually not separable in field, but known ranges overlap only in Cauca Valley (Valle). ♂ differs in having wider black throat and breast stripe (extends to malar area and side of breast), deep blue border on stripe (not bluish green), and glittering purple (not green) loral line. ♀ differs in having solid deep black median stripe (not black mixed blue green) and smaller white tail tips. In the hand ♂ slightly more coppery above, ♀ with more maroon (less purple) tail and white of underparts more extensive (wider white stripes bordering black.).
**Voice:** A sharp, incisive *tsick* or *tiuck* (ffrench 1973); song in Guyana apparently a ser. of about 7 sibilant *hsl* notes (Snyder 1966).
**Behavior:** Well known for habit of hovering ("helicoptering") for aerial insects in open areas

and often found in the vicinity of water. Occas. found in nos. at flowering trees, but otherwise rather solitary and not known to assemble in singing leks. As in Panama (Ridgely 1976). ♀-plumaged birds outnumber ♂♂.
**Breeding:** 3 BC birds, Dec–Jan. Boyacá (Olivares 1963); 2 in Aug, Vaupés (Olivares and Hernández 1962); 7 BC birds, Feb–Oct, n Colombia; 1 in Oct, Caquetá (Carriker).
**Status and habitat:** Uncommon to locally common in forest borders, shrubby clearings, and cultivated areas in fairly dry to humid areas.
**Range:** To 1750m (mainly below 1000m). Throughout, except Guajira peninsula and on Pacific coast where known only from mouth of Río Atrato eastward. W Panama to Bolivia, ne Argentina and s Brazil. Trinidad and Tobago.

## 32. RUBY-TOPAZ HUMMINGBIRD
*Chrysolampis mosquitus*    Pl. 14, Map 396
**Identification:** 3.1″ (7.9cm). Bill short (0.6″, or 15mm) and almost straight. ♂ unmistakable in good light but *usually looks mostly black*. Crown and nape glowing ruby red, feathers of forehead smoothly covering base of bill; *throat and upper breast glittering topaz orange*; otherwise dark olive brown above and below, mantle blacker and continuing up sides of neck to eye; under tail coverts and *tail rufous chestnut*; tail tipped dusky. ♀: dull bronzy to coppery green above; dull *grayish white below*; central tail feathers bronze green, *rest chestnut with broad dusky subterminal band and narrow white tips*. Imm. ♂: like ♀ but with var. amts. of orange and ruby.
**Similar species:** Dingy undistinguished ♀ easily confused; surest mark is chestnut outer tail feathers with dusky band and white tip.
**Voice:** Song in Brazil a loud double-sounding *tliii, tliii, tliii, . . .* repeated from song perch (Ruschi 1973).
**Behavior:** Usually seen alone at flowers at var. hts., sometimes at large flowering trees. In pretty display ♂ revolves rapidly around ♀ and widely fans tail and raises crown feathers.
**Breeding:** 6 BC birds, June–Oct, Zulia Val. and Guajira (Carriker). Tiny down cup nest decorated with lichen and saddled on fork 1-5m up (ffrench 1973).
**Status and habitat:** Uncommon to rare in dry woodland, scrubby areas, gallery forest edges, and gardens. Generally spotty and seasonal in occurrence; migratory movements suspected in Trinidad and Brazil (ffrench 1973; Ruschi 1973).
**Range:** To 1750m. Arid pockets of W Andes in upper Río Sucio (Dabeiba) and in Dagua Val.; Carib. lowlands from Cartagena to Guajira s locally in Cauca Val. to Popayán (at least

formally), and drier parts of Magdalena Val. (s to Villavieja, Huila; sight to Guadalupe— Hilty), also PN Los Katíos in nw Chocó; e of Andes from Norte de Santander (Zulia Val.) s to Meta and Vichada. The Guianas and Venez., c and s Brazil, and ne Bolivia. Aruba to Trinidad.

### 33. VIOLET-HEADED HUMMINGBIRD

*Klais guimeti*                              Pl. 14, Map 397
**Identification:** 3.2" (8.1cm). Small. *Bill short* (0.5", or 13mm) and *straight.* ♂: *head and throat blue violet with conspic. white spot behind eyes;* otherwise shining green above and grayish flecked and glossed green below; green tail more dusky near tip and with tiny whitish tips. ♀: sim. but crown bluish; *entire underparts gray,* sides flecked green; *tail with broad white tips.*
**Similar species:** Either sex best told by small size and *very prom.* spot behind eyes.
**Voice:** A sharp rapid *tsitt*ing or pebbly twitter when foraging; ♂♂ in Costa Rica tirelessly repeat high insectlike *pit-seet* at rate of 2 per 3-sec interval from bare exposed twig 2-10m up.
**Behavior:** Single birds visit low flowering shrubs and bushes at forest edge; sometimes with other hummingbirds at larger bushes and coocas. hawk for aerial insects. Flight somewhat weaving and beelike. ♂♂ form loose singing leks during breeding season, also less often sing solitarily.
**Breeding:** In Costa Rica chiefly Jan–May; mossy cup low, often on vine over stream, sometimes several nests close together (Skutch 1958c).
**Status and habitat:** Known from a few scattered localities on e slope E Andes where apparently rare and local; favors humid forest borders and second growth woodland with openings and shrubby clearings.
**Range:** 400-1450m (to 1800m on Pico Renjifo, Macarena Mts.). E slope E Andes from extreme e Cundinamarca s to Caquetá (Florencia) and se Nariño (Río Churuyaco); prob. n to Arauca and likely near Panama border (rec. at Caña, Panama; 1 seen, 12 July, 1976, Junín, sw Nariño (R. Ridgely). Honduras to w Venez. and s in mts. to n Bolivia.

[*Lophornis:* Tiny; white rump band (shared with *Popelairia*); ♂♂ highly adorned.]

### 34. RUFOUS-CRESTED COQUETTE

*Lophornis delattrei*                        Pl. 13, Map 398
**Identification:** 2.7" (6.9cm). Tiny. Bill short (0.4", or 10mm), straight, red with black tip. ♂ bronzy green with *large wirelike bushy rufous crest and*

conspic. *buffy white rump band;* gorget glittering green; rest of underparts dull bronze green, sometimes with tiny white tuft below gorget; *tail mostly rufous.* ♀ lacks crest: forecrown, throat, and flanks cinnamon; sometimes belly also with cinnamon mottling; otherwise dusky bronze below and green above with *white rump band;* tail cinnamon with broad black subterminal band.
**Similar species:** ♂ Spangled Coquette (35) has broader bushier crest with black spots (not wirelike and all rufous). ♀ barely separable from ♀ Spangled Coquette, but throat more cinnamon (little white) and without black spots (at most a few dusky spots on lower throat) and belly largely bronze green (not cinnamon).
**Behavior:** A nonforest hummer usually seen at low flowering plants around clearings. Typically perches rather high. Flight is beelike and weaving. As with other coquettes and thorntails, the rump band is conspic. in flight.
**Status and habitat:** Rare and local in shrubby clearings, woodland borders, and overgrown roadsides. Most accessible localities of occurrence are sw of Bogotá from Fusagasugá to Ibaque.
**Range:** 600-2000m. Both slopes of Magdalena Val. from latitude of n Tolima (Honda) s to s Huila (PN Cueva de los Guácharos—P. Gertler); e of Andes in Norte de Santander (sw of Cúcuta at La Selva, 1000m) and along e base of Andes from Río Casanare to w Meta (Villavicencio). Locally from se Mexico to n Bolivia.
**Note:** Tufted Coquette (*Lophornis ornata*) of c and w Venez., the Guianas, ne Brazil, and Trinidad prob. also occurs in ne Vichada (at mouth of Río Meta on Venez. side). ♂ from ♂ Rufous-crested Coquette by very long rufous fanlike plumes on sides of neck each tipped with glittering green disks. ♀ from ♀ Rufous-crested by green (not cinnamon) forecrown and bronzy green (not cinnamon) tail with dark subterminal band.

### 35. SPANGLED COQUETTE

*Lophornis stictolopha*                      Pl. 14, Map 399
**Identification:** 2.7" (6.9cm). Tiny. ♂: almost identical to Rufous-crested Coquette (34), but crest feathers much *wider and bushy* (not spiky and wirelike) *and dotted black at tips.* ♀: much like ♀ Rufous-crested, but *throat more or less white thickly dotted rufous and with some black spots and mottling* (not cinnamon with a few dusky marks on lower throat) and belly largely cinnamon (not bronzy green).
**Behavior:** As in Rufous-crested Coquette, but

Spangled usually seen high in canopy of large flowering trees. In e Ecuador sometimes seen with Wire-crested Thorntail, and like latter often in foothills (R. Ridgely).

**Status and habitat:** Rare, very local, and known from only a few widely scattered localities; woodland borders and drier scrubby areas; known definitely only from foothills and mainly below range of Rufous-crested Coquette in Colombia.

**Range:** E slope E Andes in Cundinamarca (Medina 500-600m), poss. n to Arauca (rec. on e slope in Táchira, Venez.), mid. Magdalena Val. (Icononzo, 1300m, near Tolima-Cundinamarca boundary); also "Bogotá" and "Antioquia" without definite locality. W Venez. (up to 1300m) to e Peru.

## 36. FESTIVE COQUETTE

*Lophornis chalybea*   Pl. 14, Map 400

**Identification:** 3″ (7.6cm). Tiny. Bill short (0.6″, or 15mm). ♂ very ornate: gorget and sides of head glittering green; black streak from bill back under eye ends in *large fanlike tuft of long, white-tipped green feathers that cover sides of throat and neck*; frontlet glittering green bordered by black band across forecrown; rest of crown bronze with a few hairlike feathers springing from hindcrown; otherwise green above with *white rump band*; underparts green; chest brownish; tail purplish copper. ♀: like ♂ but lacks glittering frontlet and fanlike neck ruff; *chin whitish buff extending back as broad white moustachial stripe*; throat brownish indistinctly scaled whitish (appears dusky).

**Similar species:** Tiny and dark (either sex); from other Colombian coquettes by absence of rufous on head and tail; ♀ resembles a ♀ thorntail (cf. 37-39) but moustachial stripe buff-tinged and lacks white flank patch.

**Behavior:** As in other Coquettes. Seen mainly at flowering trees.

**Status and habitat:** Not well known in Colombia. Bushy pastures and forest borders like others of genus.

**Range:** 200-600m. E of Andes from extreme e Cundinamarca (Medina), Caquetá (Río Orteguaza; Tres Esquinas), Vaupés (presumed sighting at Mitú, Feb 1978—Hilty) and Río Igará-Paraná, Amazonas; doubtless to Leticia (rec. across Amazon at Benjamin Constant, Brazil). Se Venez. to n Bolivia and n Amazonian and e Brazil.

**Note:** Bearded Coquette (*L. insignibarbis*) and Dusky Coquette (*L. melaeniae*) are each known from a single Colombian specimen, the former a "Bogotá" bird. They are suspected hybrids.

[*Popelairia:* Small and ornate; white rump band (shared with coquettes); white flank patch (shared with woodstars); ♂♂ have ragged spikelike tail feathers, the outer ones elongated and curving outward near tip.]

## 37. WIRE-CRESTED THORNTAIL

*Popelairia popelairii*   Map 401

**Identification:** ♂ 4.5″ (11.4cm); ♀ 3″ (7.5cm). Bill short (0.5″, or 13mm) and straight. ♂: crown and gorget glittering green; long narrow wirelike crest; otherwise coppery green above with *white rump band, central underparts sooty black*; sides brownish with *white flank patch; blue black tail long and forked, outer 3 pairs of feathers pointed and spiky*; shafts of all tail feathers white. ♀ much smaller: coppery green above with *white rump band*; black below with *white malar streak and flank patch*; short tail mostly blue black tipped white.

**Similar species:** ♂ Black-bellied Thorntail (38) lacks spiky crest and has narrow copper band across breast; up close note grayish (not black) outer tail feathers. ♀ almost identical to ♀ Black-bellied, but central underparts black, not black mixed green on breast. Also cf. ♀ Festive Coquette (36).

**Behavior:** Weaves like a bee as it hovers to feed at flowers of canopy and emergent ht. trees, then perches in open on edge of canopy. In e Ecuador and Peru mainly at flowering *Inga* trees in foothills (R. Ridgely).

**Status and habitat:** Rare and not well known in Colombia. Humid forest and forest borders in Ecuador.

**Range:** Apparently e base E Andes from Cundinamarca southward: known from a few localities in extreme e Cundinamarca (Medina 500-600m) and near Villavicencio. E Colombia, e Ecuador (600-1200m), and ne Peru.

## 38. BLACK-BELLIED THORNTAIL

*Popelairia langsdorffi*   Pl. 14, Map 402

**Identification:** 4.8″ (12.2cm); ♀ 2.6″ (6.6cm). Bill short (0.5″, or 13mm) and straight. ♂: much like ♂ Wire-crested Thorntail, but lacks wirelike crest, *gorget bordered below by narrow coppery red band*, and outer 3 pairs of tail feathers gray (not black). ♀ like ♀ Wire-crested Thorntail, but throat more or less mottled black and white, and dusky underparts mixed green on breast.

**Similar species:** See Wire-crested Thorntail (37); Green Thorntail (39) only w of Andes.

**Voice:** In display a rapid ser. of whistles, *ti ti ti ti ti* (Ruschi 1973).

**Behavior:** Most often seen singly at flowering trees at midstory or canopy ht., and like allied

Green Thorntail, fond of flowers of *Inga* spp. In striking display ♂ darts back and forth in front of and over ♀ while rapidly opening and closing the tail and producing a loud cracking sound (Hilty; O'Neill 1974; Ruschi 1973).
**Breeding:** Nest in Brazil a downy cup fastened on horizontal branch up to 10m up (Ruschi 1973).
**Status and habitat:** Thinly spread in humid lowland forest and forest borders.
**Range:** To 300m. Extreme e and s Colombia from Guainía to Amazonas (mouth of Río Guainía; sightings at Mitú, Vaupés, Feb 1978— Hilty; lower Río Igará-Paraná, w Amazonas; prob. Leticia as rec. at Pebas, ne Peru). S Venez. to e Peru. Amazonian, and se Brazil.

### 39. GREEN THORNTAIL
*Popelairia conversii*     Pl. 13, Map 403
**Identification:** ♂ 4″ (10.2cm); ♀ 2.6″ (6.6cm). Bill short (0.4″, or 10mm) and straight. ♂: crown and gorget glittering green; otherwise mostly shining green with *white rump band and white flank patch*; steel blue tail deeply forked, the outer 3 pairs of feathers greatly elongated and pointed (wirelike at tips). ♀ much smaller: green above with *white rump band*; throat and central underparts black; *broad malar stripe and flank patch white*; sides greenish; short, slightly forked tail black with white tip.
**Similar species:** Only Pacific coast hummingbird (either sex) with white rump band; note ♂'s spiky tail. Cf. Purple-throated Woodstar (139), which has flank patches but no rump band.
**Behavior:** Often numerous at large flowering trees. Usually feeds rather high and seems esp. attracted to brushlike inflorescences of var. legumes, esp. *Mimosa* and *Inga*. Flight is weaving and beelike; reg. hovers to glean from the undersurface of larger canopy leaves.
**Breeding:** Courtship display, 10 June, Anchicayá Val. (Hilty).
**Status and habitat:** Uncommon to seasonally common in humid and wet forest, forest edges, and flowering trees in clearings. Apparently most numerous in foothills but some seasonal el. movements suspected (as in C America) and sometimes locally common in lowlands.
**Range:** To 1000m (1 sight to 1400m, Queremal, July–Hilty et al.). Pacific coast from Chocó (Quibdó) southward. Costa Rica to w Ecuador.
**Note:** Racket-tailed Coquette (*Discosura longicauda*) of the Guianas, s Venez. (Amazonas), and n and e Brazil, prob. occurs in e Vichada (rec. at Nericagua, Venez., on Río Orinoco) and Vaupés (known from Tahuapunto, Brazil, on Vaupés border). ♂: like Green Thorntail, but with spatulate tips on outer pair of

tail feathers. ♀ like ♀ of 39 but central throat stripe solid black, and rest of underparts mixed sooty, green, and white.

[*Chlorestes*: Square or slightly rounded tail; much like *Amazilia* and *Lepidopyga*.]

### 40. BLUE-CHINNED SAPPHIRE
*Chlorestes notatus*     Map 404
**Identification:** 3.5″ (8.9cm). Bill straight (0.7″, or 18mm), with lower mandible red tipped black. ♂: shining bronze green above; *glittering green below; chin and upper throat glittering blue*; steel blue tail *square or slightly rounded*. ♀: sim. but underparts grayish white speckled green, glittering on throat and breast.
**Similar species:** Either sex best told from respective sex of Shining-green Hummingbird (51) by square or slightly rounded steel blue tail (not glossed green and distinctly forked); ♀ also by green (not white) belly. Glittering-throated Emerald (64) shows well-defined wedge of white projecting up onto central breast. Also cf. Blue-tailed Emerald (41).
**Voice:** Song in Trinidad a high metallic ser. *sssoo-sssoo-sssoo*, repeated about 3-5 times in 3 sec (ffrench 1973).
**Behavior:** Rather inconspic. hummingbird, usually seen alone, perched at low to mod. hts., often on open twigs in the shade.
**Status and habitat:** Uncommon in humid second growth woodland, shrubby areas, gardens, and *terra firme* and *várzea* forest edges; occurs with some regularity in clearings around Leticia and on Monkey Isl.
**Range:** To 400m. Prob. throughout e of Andes but known only from a few widely scattered localities (Río Orinoco at Maipures; "llanos of Casanare"; Leticia). The Guianas and Venez. to ne Peru, n Amazonian, and se Brazil. Trinidad.

[*Chlorostilbon*: Small; ♂♂ glittering green with forked tails; ♀♀ light grayish below; dusky cheeks and white postocular; members of this genus are difficult to tell apart.]

### 41. BLUE-TAILED EMERALD
*Chlorostilbon mellisugus*     Pls. 13, 14,
Map 405
**Identification:** 3″ (7.6cm). Small. Bill straight (0.5″, or 13mm) and black. ♂: *mostly glittering green*, esp. below; *forked tail steely blue black*. ♀: shining green above; dusky ear coverts bordered above by prom. white streak behind eye (streak occas. lacking); *underparts pale gray*, sides slightly greenish; square or slightly forked tail steely blue black narrowly tipped grayish white.
**Similar species:** Widespread and often con-

fused. ♂ much like larger Steely-vented Hummingbird (69) but lacks latter's pinkish lower mandible, coppery rump, and steel blue upper and under tail coverts. ♂ from other ♂ *Chlorostilbon* (except Red-billed Emerald, 42) by blue black tail; from latter by dark bill. Also cf. larger Shining-green Hummingbird (51). ♀ hardly separable in field from any other *Chlorostilbon*, but see known range, in good light note tail color.

**Voice:** Weak call a slightly metallic *tsip*; song a short chipping twitter.

**Behavior:** Feeds singly at flowers, usually at low or mod. hts.; occas. several gather at flowering trees. Despite small size, flight is straight and darting (not weaving and beelike).

**Breeding:** 5 BC birds, May–Dec, W and C Andes (Carriker; Miller 1963).

**Status and habitat:** Fairly common to common in gardens, cultivated areas, and shrubby or semiopen areas with trees; favors moist to mod. dry areas. Numerous near Cali.

**Range:** Mainly 1000-2200m in W Andes, Cauca Val., and w slope of C Andes s through Nariño; locally to 600m in dry Pacific slope vals. (Dabeiba; Dagua Val.; Guayacana, sw Nariño); once on e slope C Andes in Tolima (Chicoral, 450m); e of Andes (below 500m) throughout (not rec. in Guainía and Vaupés). Costa Rica to w Ecuador, Amazonian Brazil, and the Guianas. Trinidad.

**Note:** Incl. only the dark-billed forms from sw Costa Rica southward but not the n *canivetti* (Fork-tailed Emerald) of w Mexico to n Costa Rica.

### 42. RED-BILLED EMERALD
*Chlorostilbon gibsoni*          Pl. 14, Map 406

**Identification:** 3″ (7.6cm). Bill straight (0.5″, or 13mm), with *lower mandible mostly red* (♂) *or red at base* (♀). ♂: dark bronze green above with no glitter on crown; sides of head and underparts glittering green to golden green (tinged blue—*chrysogaster; nitens*); tail deeply forked, *steely blue black*. ♀: not distinguishable in field from ♀ Blue-tailed Emerald; in the hand, back more coppery and base of outer tail feathers pale gray.

**Similar species:** ♂ from ♂ Blue-tailed Emerald (41) only by red on lower mandible. ♂ from all other *Chlorostilbon* by blue black tail as well as red lower mandible; from ♂ Steely-vented Hummingbird (69) by smaller size, no copper on rump, and under tail coverts green (not blue; hard to see in field). White-chinned Sapphire (53) is larger with broader all red bill with black tip. Shining-green Hummingbird (51) is larger with green central tail feathers and bluish tinged throat and chest. ♀

sometimes from other *Chlorostilbon* ♀♀ (except Blue-tailed Emerald) by blue black tail.

**Behavior:** As with other *Chlorostilbon*, mainly a "trap-liner" of scattered nectar resources.

**Breeding:** In w Cundinamarca (1600m) down cup with lichen on outside, attached to fern leaf (Olivares 1969a); 8 BC birds, Mar–Aug, n Colombia and Huila (Carriker).

**Status and habitat:** Uncommon and local in drier woodland, shrubby semiopen regions, cultivated areas and dry scrub; more numerous in Dec–Apr dry season at PN Tayrona.

**Range:** To 500m from Sinú Val. e to Santa Marta area (*chrysogaster*); Guajira (*nitens*); to 2300m in drier parts of mid. and upper Magdalena Val. and e of Andes in Zuila Val. (*gibsoni*). N Colombia and w Venez.

**Note:** By some considered a race of *C. mellisugus* (Blue-tailed Emerald).

### 43. COPPERY EMERALD
*Chlorostilbon russatus*          Pl. 14, Map 407

**Identification:** 3″ (7.6cm). Bill straight (0.6″, or 15mm) and black. ♂: back shining green; *rump and upper tail coverts coppery green becoming golden copper on tail*; crown and underparts glittering golden green. ♀: coppery green above; whitish gray below with a little green on flanks; tail coppery bronze, all but central pair of feathers with a *dark bronzy purple subterminal band* and *gray tip*. No dusky ear patch or white streak behind eye.

**Similar species:** ♂ in good light from other *Chlorostilbon* by decided *coppery* upperparts and *golden copper* tail; ♀ in good light from allies by coppery sheen above and coppery green (not green) tail from above; cf. esp. 42, 51, and 69.

**Behavior:** Feeds at low to mod. ht. flowers in rather open shrubby areas. Like other *Chlorostilbon* the flight is darting and direct.

**Breeding:** 8 BC birds, May–June, Santa Marta Mts. (Carriker).

**Status and habitat:** Uncommon and local in shrubby forest borders and cultivated areas. In Santa Marta Mts. most often seen in lower half of el. range (Hilty); replaced in Santa Marta lowlands by Red-billed Emerald.

**Range:** 600-2600m. Santa Marta Mts. (600-1700m), Perijá Mts. and E Andes at Laguna de Fúquene, Boyacá (2600m). W Venez. and ne Colombia.

### 44. NARROW-TAILED EMERALD
*Chlorostilbon stenura*          Pl. 14, Map 408

**Identification:** 3″ (7.6cm). Bill straight (0.7″, or 18mm) and black. ♂: *forecrown glittering golden green*; otherwise shining green above; *underparts glittering emerald green; short tail shining*

*bronzy green*, slightly forked, lateral feathers narrow and tapering (not a field mark). ♀: golden green above with dusky ear patch and short white streak behind eye; pale grayish below; *tail green*, all but central pair of feathers with *dark blue black subterminal band and grayish white tip*, outer pair with very broad white tip.
**Similar species:** Doubtfully separable in field from Short-tailed Emerald (45). In field, wings may reach just to tail tips in Narrow-tailed Emerald, slightly beyond in Short-tailed Emerald. In the hand, ♂ Short-tailed Emerald lacks narrowed outer tail feathers and entire crown (not just forecrown) glittering golden green; ♀ by more bronzy brown crown. Also see 41, 42, and 43.
**Behavior:** Sim. to Short-tailed Emerald.
**Breeding:** 6 BC birds, Sept–Nov, Norte de Santander (Carriker).
**Status and habitat:** Poorly known (in part due to field identification problems); shrubby forest borders and disturbed areas.
**Range:** 1000-2300m. E slope E Andes in Norte de Santander (Ocaña s to Pamplona), perhaps s to w Meta. Nw Venez. (1950-3000m) and ne Colombia.

### 45. SHORT-TAILED EMERALD
*Chlorostilbon poortmanni*          Map 409
**Identification:** 3″ (7.6cm). Bill straight (0.7″, or 18mm) and black. ♂: *entire crown and underparts glittering green*; back shining green; short tail shining dark green (or olive green), slightly forked. ♀: shining green above, *more bronzy brown on crown*; dusky ear patch bordered above by short white streak behind eye; below light gray; flanks tinged green; tail short, central pair of feathers shining green, rest paler green with *blue black subterminal band and grayish white tip*.
**Similar species:** Not safely separated in field from Narrow-tailed Emerald (see 44); either sex from other *Chlorostilbon* emeralds by greenish tail.
**Behavior:** Mostly a "trap-liner" of scattered low flowers with horizontal or upright corollas; 0.6-4m up in rather open areas (Snow and Snow 1980).
**Breeding:** BC ♂, 24 June, Norte de Santander (Carriker).
**Status and habitat:** Uncommon in lighter woodland, second growth, shrubby areas, and forest borders. Favors more humid and wooded regions than Red-billed Emerald. In PN Cueva de los Guácharos mostly in advanced second growth woodland or small forest openings (P. Gertler).
**Range:** 500-2800m (most recs. 1000-2400m). W slope E Andes from Santander to Huila

(PN Cueva de los Guácharos—P. Gertler); e slope E Andes s to w Meta at Cubarral (500m) sw of Villavicencio. W Venez. (Andes) and ne Colombia.

### 46. CROWNED WOODNYMPH
*Thalurania colombica*          Pl. 13, Map 410
**Identification:** ♂ 3.8″ (9.7cm); ♀ 3.3″ (8.4cm). Bill (0.9″, or 23mm) is slightly decurved and black. ♂ often looks blackish; *crown glittering green*, sometimes edged behind with purple (or crown glittering purple—*colombica*); back bronze green; mantle and shoulders usually violet; *gorget glittering green in contrast to glittering violet blue lower underparts*; rather long *deeply forked* tail blue black. ♀: smaller; green above; crown bronze; *throat and chest light gray; breast and belly dark gray to grayish green* (2-toned effect); under tail coverts grayish white, tail slightly forked, blue black, *outer feathers broadly tipped white*.
**Similar species:** E of Andes see Fork-tailed Woodnymph (47). ♂ Violet-bellied Hummingbird (48) is consid. smaller with tail rounded, lower mandible reddish, and gorget shining green (not glittering). ♀ from any other by 2-toned underparts.
**Behavior:** A solitary, territorial, and aggressive sp. usually seen in the lower or lower-mid. strata inside forest or along forest borders. Feeds at low flowers and gleans and flycatches insects; not at large flowering trees or in groups.
**Breeding:** 14 BC birds, Feb–Sept, nw Colombia (Carriker). 6 Anchicayá Val. nests (1000m) Jan, Feb, May, June, Aug, and Nov; downy cup saddled on fork or twig 1-8m up (usually low) in tall grass or shrubbery near forest edge or in forest (Hilty); Santa Marta nest, 19 Dec (Todd and Carriker 1922).
**Status and habitat:** Common in humid and wet forest and forest borders in lowlands and foothills, smaller nos. higher. One of the most numerous forest hummingbirds of Pacific coast.
**Range:** To 1900m. Santa Marta and Perijá Mts., E Andes, and humid sections of Magdalena Val. from s Bolívar to sw Huila (*colombica*); lower Cauca Val. w to Atrato Val. and Pacific coast s to Nariño (*fannyi*); slopes above mid. and upper Cauca Val. (800-1900m) from Quindío to Cauca (*subtropicalis*); w slope of mts. in Nariño (*verticeps*). W Mexico to w Ecuador and nw Venez.
**Note:** Some unite all glittering-crowned *colombica* birds (green, blue, and purple crowns) from w Mexico to w Ecuador and w Venez. with the dull-crowned *furcata* of e and s S America. The present arrangement, following Eisenmann, incl. only glittering-crowned

birds in *colombica*. Even more than 2 spp. may be involved.

## 47. FORK-TAILED WOODNYMPH
*Thalurania furcata* Pl. 14, Map 411
**Identification:** ♂ 4″ (10.2cm); ♀ 3.3″ (8.4cm). Bill (1″, or 25mm) slightly decurved. ♂ sim. to Crowned Woodnymph, but *crown bronze green* with no glitter (or frontlet glittering green—Leticia), and no purple on mantle or shoulders. ♀: smaller; shining green above, crown bronze green; *underparts light gray to buffy white* (no broad dark band across lower breast and belly); slightly forked tail blue black, outer feathers tipped white.
**Similar species:** ♀ most like Gray-breasted Sabrewing (23) but much smaller and lacks latter's broad white tail corners (sabrewing has half of outer 3 tail feathers white).
**Behavior:** As in Crowned Woodnymph.
**Breeding:** 2 BC ♂♂, June, w Caquetá (Carriker).
**Status and habitat:** Fairly common in lower levels of humid forest and forest borders in lowlands and foothills, smaller nos. higher. Replaced w of Andes by allied Crowned Woodnymph.
**Range:** To 1800m (Pico Renjifo, Macarena Mts.). Most recs. below 1200m. E of Andes from extreme e Cundinamarca, ne Meta and Río Orinoco region (recs. on Venez. side) south. The Guianas and s and e Venez. to e Bolivia, ne Argentina, and Paraguay.

## 48. VIOLET-BELLIED HUMMINGBIRD
*Damophila julie* Pl. 13, Map 412
**Identification:** 3.2″ (8.1cm). Bill short and straight (0.5″, or 13mm), lower mandible mostly flesh color. ♂: shining green above, *crown and gorget glittering golden green* (or only gorget glittering—*panamensis*); *lower underparts glittering violet blue*; graduated and *distinctly rounded* tail bluish black. ♀: slightly smaller; green above; *light gray below* becoming whitish on belly; sides of throat sometimes spotted green; *rounded tail* like ♂, *outer feathers tipped gray*. Imm. ♂: like adult ♂ but gray below with a few violet blue spots.
**Similar species:** ♂ from ♂ Crowned Woodnymph (46) by smaller size, rounded tail, reddish lower mandible, and no violet on back. Also cf. Sapphire-throated (49) and Sapphire-bellied hummingbirds (50), both with forked tails. ♀ from several sim. *Amazilia* and *Chlorostilbon* ♀♀ and others by unique combination of very rounded tail and pinkish lower mandible.
**Voice:** ♂♂ hiss an insectlike *vieiei veii veii veii* ser. from perches 1-10m up during breeding

season in Panama; alarm note *see see seek* (Willis and Eisenmann 1979).
**Behavior:** Often seen singly at flowers at var. hts., usually rather low either in forest or in clearings.
**Breeding:** 3 BC ♂♂, Feb–May, n Antioquia, s Bolívar (Carriker); 1 Santa Marta nest, Nov (Darlington 1931); 4 Panama nests 2.5-4.2m up in bushes, Mar–July (Willis and Eisenmann 1979).
**Status and habitat:** Fairly common in humid forest, forest borders, second growth woodland, and shrubby or partially open clearings; mainly lowlands and lower foothills.
**Range:** To 1750m (Magdalena Val.); to 600m elsewhere. Lower Atrato Val. e to lower Río Sinú (*panamensis*); Cartagena e to w side of Santa Marta Mts. and s to n end C Andes and mid. Magdalena Val. at Ibaque, n Tolima (*julie*); poss. sw Nariño. C Panama to w Ecuador.

## 49. SAPPHIRE-THROATED HUMMINGBIRD
*Lepidopyga coeruleogularis* Pl. 13, Map 413
**Identification:** 3.5″ (8.9cm). Bill nearly straight (0.7″, or 18mm), base of lower mandible reddish. ♂: shining green above; *gorget, lower cheeks, and chest glittering violet blue*; rest of underparts bright green; tail blackish, *distinctly forked*. ♀: shining green above; *white below with green sides; tail forked* like ♂, central pair of feathers green, rest blue black tipped grayish white.
**Similar species:** ♂ confusingly sim. to ♂ Sapphire-bellied Hummingbird (50) but lacks glittering blue belly; latter also restricted to mangroves. ♀ Blue-chested Hummingbird (65) is much dingier with squarish tail; ♀ Violet-bellied Hummingbird (48) has rounded tail; other ♀ *Amazilia* and *Chlorostilbon* in range are invariably dingy or grayish below (not pure white).
**Behavior:** Feeds mostly alone at low flowers at borders or in partially open areas.
**Breeding:** 1 BC bird, Mar, Chocó; 1 in July, in Petrólea (Carriker); 2 Panama nests, June, in forks about 1 m up in top of dry weeds (Wetmore 1968a).
**Status and habitat:** Uncommon and local in mangrove borders, drier scrubby areas, and lighter woodland edges near sea level. As in Panama (Ridgely 1976), most numerous near mangroves or within a few km of the coast (all recs. less than 100km inland). Seen with some frequency at Los Cocos, PN Salamanca.
**Range:** To 100m. Lower Río Atrato s on Pacific coast to Nuquí, both sides of Gulf of Urabá and (gap?) from Cartagena e through Ciénaga Grande to w base of Santa Marta Mts. W Panama to n Colombia.

## 50. SAPPHIRE-BELLIED HUMMINGBIRD
*Lepidopyga lilliae*
**Identification:** 3.7" (9.4cm). Bill nearly straight (0.7", or 18mm), most of lower mandible reddish. ♀ *unknown*. ♂: shining green above; *entire underparts glittering blue*; gorget more glittering purple; tail distinctly forked, blue black.
**Similar species:** From Sapphire-throated Hummingbird (49) by glittering blue lower breast and belly. ♀ poss. much like ♀ Sapphire-throated Hummingbird.
**Behavior:** Usually seen alone inside mangroves at var. hts.
**Status and habitat:** Rare and local in coastal mangroves and not found with consistency; most recent recs. are on e side of PN Salamanca (T. Johnson; Hilty).
**Range:** ENDEMIC. Restricted to mangroves in the vicinity of Ciénaga Grande (both sides); mouth of Río Ranchería e of Ríohacha, Guajira (2 seen 6 Aug 1974—P. Donahue).
**Note:** Has been regarded as a race of *L. coeruleogularis* in Bds. Wld., 5, but both have been taken at Ciénaga Grande. Poss. an age stage of *L. coeruleogularis* (Meyer de Schauensee 1966).

## 51. SHINING-GREEN HUMMINGBIRD
*Lepidopyga goudoti*          Pl. 14, Map 414
**Identification:** 3.6" (9.1cm). Bill virtually straight (0.7", or 18mm), lower mandible mostly pink (hard to see). ♂: *shining green above; glittering green below*; throat and chest often *strongly* tinged blue; under tail coverts green edged white; *tail forked*, blue black, *central feathers bronze green*; leg tufts white, (not always visible). ♀: shining green above; throat and breast glittering green with *grayish white feather bases showing through everywhere* (gives scaled or spotted effect); belly pure white; tail as in ♂, less forked.
**Similar species:** A very difficult and often confused sp. that resembles many other med. small green hummingbirds. ♂ from all ♂ *Chlorostilbon* (41-45) by decidedly larger size, bluish throat (usually), whitish edges on under tail coverts, and pink on mandible (except Redbilled Emerald); additionally from Blue-tailed (41) and Red-billed emeralds (42) by green central tail feathers; from Steely-vented Hummingbird (69) by greenish and white under tail coverts (not steel blue), green central tail feathers, and no coppery tinge on rump. Also cf. Blue-throated Sapphire (55), which doubtfully overlaps in range and Indigo-capped Hummingbird (68).
**Voice:** Song a thin, waiflike *tsee-dee*, reminiscent of song of Green-bellied Hummingbird but shorter.
**Behavior:** Glean insects by working among branches and twigs and beneath canopy foliage in tree crowns (Miller 1947) or visit flowers at var. hts., sometimes many gathering in argumentative groups at flowering trees.
**Breeding:** BC ♂ July, e Norte de Santander (Carriker); 2 nests, Oct and Feb, Huila; 1 less than 1 m up in small croton plant in semiopen (Miller 1947).
**Status and habitat:** Fairly common to common in dry to moist scrub, open woodland, and shrubby or partially cleared areas with trees. Seasonally common in Santa Marta area and in s Huila.
**Range:** To 1600m. Lower to upper Sinú Val. e through Carib. region to Santa Marta area and w Guajira, drier areas s to head of Magdalena Val. (San Agustín) in Zulia Val., Norte de Santander; PN Los Katíos nw Chocó and Río Munguidó (Río Sucio Val.) at Pavarandó, n Chocó. N Colombia to w Venez.

## 52. RUFOUS-THROATED SAPPHIRE
*Hylocharis sapphirina*          Pl. 14, Map 415
**Identification:** 3.5" (8.9cm). Bill almost straight (0.8", or 20mm), *bright coral red with black tip* (♂), or only lower mandible red (♀). ♂: mostly dark shining green with *rufous chin and glittering blue throat and chest*; under tail coverts chestnut; square tail *coppery chestnut*. ♀: dark shining green above; chin and upper throat pale rufous; rest of underparts white thickly disked glittering blue on lower throat and chest; under tail coverts buff; tail square like ♂, central feathers green, rest coppery chestnut with broad dusky subterminal band and pale tip. Young ♂♂ usually have distinct rufous chin, otherwise with varying amounts of gray and blue mottling below.
**Similar species:** No other Colombian hummingbirds except other *Hylocharis* have such distinctive red bills. ♂ Golden-tailed Sapphire (56) much like ♂ Rufous-throated, but head all blue, no rufous chin, and only lower mandible red. ♀ from ♀ Golden-tailed by rufous on upper throat and blue (not green) disking on throat. ♂ and ♀ White-chinned Sapphires (53) have blue black tails.
**Voice:** In Surinam a high-pitched, sibilant *zzeee* at 8- to 10-sec intervals (T. Davis).
**Behavior:** Much like White-chinned Sapphire. In e Venez. often at flowering trees at woodland borders, where defend smaller bushes or portions of larger flowering trees; feed by hovering without clinging.
**Status and habitat:** Little known in Colombia. In se Venez. and elsewhere in tall humid savanna forest and borders, shrubby clearings, and drier more open areas with scrub and trees.

**Range:** To 300m. Known from e Vaupés (Rio Vaupés opp. Tahuapunto, Brazil) and skins on Indian ornaments from lower Río Igará-Paraná, e Amazonas. Prob. e Guainía. The Guianas and s Venez. to e Ecuador, e Peru, ne Bolivia, ne Argentina, Paraguay, and Amazonian and se Brazil.

### 53. WHITE-CHINNED SAPPHIRE

*Hylocharis cyanus*        Pl. 14, Map 416

**Identification:** 3.5″ (8.9cm). Bill almost straight (0.9″, or 23mm), *bright coral red with black tip* (♂), or only lower mandible red (♀). ♂: mostly dark shining green with *entire head, throat, and upper breast glittering purplish blue;* chin white (usually hard to see); *rump coppery; steel blue tail* almost square. ♀: mostly dark shining green above becoming *coppery on rump;* below grayish white with a few glittering blue spots on sides of throat and green on sides of breast; tail as in ♂, *blue black* tipped gray; under tail coverts gray.

**Similar species:** ♂ from ♂ Golden-tailed Sapphire (56) by blue-black (not coppery chestnut) tail; ♀ from ♀ Golden-tailed or Rufous-throated sapphires (56, 52) by steel blue tail. W of W Andes and in Cauca Val. see Blue-headed Sapphire (54).

**Voice:** Song a high insectlike squeaking, *zeitzeit . . .* varied to *tweeh-chit . . .* , given incessantly from a fairly high open perch under tree crown.

**Behavior:** Hover without clinging as they feed at flowers from near ground to treetops; often congregate and argue at flowering trees. ♂♂ advertise from solitary song perches.

**Breeding:** BC ♂, July, e Norte de Santander (Carriker).

**Status and habitat:** Fairly common in lighter humid woodland, forest borders, and clearings with trees; also follows riparian woodland into drier areas.

**Range:** To 1000m. Santa Marta region (mostly n and e sides), n end of Perijá Mts., and e of Andes in Norte de Santander (Zulia Val.), e Guainía (opp. Río Casiquiare on Río Negro), Vaupés (Mitú; opp. Tahuapunto on Río Vaupés), and s to Leticia. The Guianas and Venez. locally to e Ecuador, e Peru, n Bolivia, and Amazonian and se Brazil.

### 54. BLUE-HEADED SAPPHIRE

*Hylocharis grayi*        Pl. 14, Map 417

**Identification:** 3.5″ (8.9cm). Bill nearly straight (0.8″, or 20mm) and *coral red tipped black* (decidedly duller in ♀). ♂: mostly shining green, underparts more glittering; *entire head and upper throat glittering blue;* slightly forked tail blue black (or entire head and throat glittering blue

becoming blue green on chest; tail dark green—*humboldtii*). ♀: shining green above; *mostly white below with glittering green disks on throat and breast* (looks spotted) and green sides; tail blue black tipped whitish (or median underparts white, green tail tipped gray—*humboldtii*).

**Similar species:** ♂ unique in range but cf. smaller Violet-headed Hummingbird (33). ♀ resembles numerous other ♀ ♀ but can be told by combination of white underparts (not grayish) with green spots, reddish mainly on base of lower mandible, and dark tail. Cf. ♀ Shining-green, Violet-capped, Blue-chested and Purple-chested hummingbirds (51, 57, 65, 66). ♀ Sapphire-throated (49) lacks spotting below.

**Voice:** A loud rapidly repeated *bzeek* by ♀ from song perch may be scolding (Miller 1963); 1 ♂ in Valle steadily repeated a chippy *chu-we-eee* (2d note lowest, last thin and rising) from perches 2-4m up.

**Behavior:** Feeds at flowers at var. hts. and commonly gathers with others in the crown of flowering trees where notably aggressive.

**Breeding:** BC ♂, 26 Dec, e slope W Andes (Miller 1963); another late Mar near Buenaventura (Ralph and Chaplin 1973).

**Status and habitat:** Local. Mainly near coast in humid forest borders, tall second growth woodland and mangroves, or in drier interior val. in scrubby or cultivated areas and lighter woodland borders; fewer recs. from wet foothills and mts. in between. Erratic in most areas with marked seasonal movements.

**Range:** To 2000m (rarely to 2600m). Entire Pacific coast s to sw Nariño (*humboldtii*), upper Dagua Val., and mid. Cauca Val. (Cali and Buga area) s through upper Patía Val. to n Nariño (*grayi*). Extreme se Panama to nw Ecuador.

### 55. BLUE-THROATED SAPPHIRE (GOLDENTAIL)

*Hylocharis eliciae*        Pl. 13, Map 418

**Identification:** 3.5″ (8.9cm). Bill straight (0.6″, or 15mm), coral red with black tip. ♂: green above becoming *coppery on rump and golden bronze to golden green on tail; gorget violet blue;* rest of underparts dull green, center of breast and belly buffy. ♀: sim. but gorget smaller and the feathers edged dusky; bill duller.

**Similar species:** Much like Rufous-tailed Hummingbird (71), but entire bill red except for tip (not just lower mandible), and throat blue. Also see ♂ Sapphire-throated Hummingbird (49), which has longer deeply forked (not squarish) tail.

**Breeding:** Laying ♀, 24 Jan, Panama (Wetmore 1968a).

**Status and habitat:** Known in Colombia from 4 specimens: 1 near Acandí, 1975, and 3 in PN Los Katíos, 1975 and 1977 (Rodríguez 1978), 1 of these taken in a clearing with *Heliconia*; in Mid. America in dry to humid woodland borders and clearings.

**Range:** To 200m. Carib. drainage of Cerro Tacarcuna on Panama boundary (Acandí s to Sautatá). S Mexico to nw Colombia.

**Note:** Known as Blue-throated Goldentail in Mid. America, but Eisenmann suggests Blue-throated Sapphire to avoid confusion with Golden-tailed Sapphire (56), which has an even more "golden" tail.

### 56. GOLDEN-TAILED SAPPHIRE
*Chrysuronia oenone*      Pl. 14, Map 419

**Identification:** 3.7″ (9.4cm). Bill almost straight (0.8″, or 20mm), lower mandible pink with black tip. ♂: mostly shining green, more glittering below; *entire head, throat, and chest glittering blue violet* (or crown blue violet becoming glittery greenish blue on throat and chest— *josephinae*); *tail coverts and tail shining golden copper.* ♀: bronze green above; mostly green below with median line down underparts white (or mostly white below with glittering green spots on throat, chest, and sides—*josephinae*); *upper tail coverts and tail shining golden copper* tipped grayish.

**Similar species:** See Rufous-throated (52) and White-chinned Sapphire (53). ♀ recalls Glittering-throated Emerald (64) but tail golden copper.

**Voice:** Squeaky 2-noted song steadily repeated.

**Behavior:** Most often seen in the canopy of flowering trees where sometimes gathers in nos. (up to 10-20 reported in Venez. by Schäfer and Phelps, 1954).

**Breeding:** 2 BC ♂♂, June, Norte de Santander and w Caquetá (Carriker).

**Status and habitat:** Fairly common in humid forest borders, second growth woodland, and semiopen areas with scattered trees; gallery woodland in w portion of llanos (i.e., around Villavicencio); few recs. in Amazonia.

**Range:** To 1500m. E base of E Andes from Norte de Santander (n of Ocaña) to Meta (incl. Macarena Mts.), w Caquetá (incl. Tres Esquinas), and Putumayo (*oenone*); e Amazonas (*josephinae*). N and w Venez. to n Bolivia and w Amazonian Brazil. Trinidad.

**Note:** Has been placed in genus *Hylocharis*.

### 57. VIOLET-CAPPED HUMMINGBIRD
*Goldmania violiceps*      Pl. 13, Map 420

**Identification:** 3.4″ (8.6cm). Bill short (0.7″, or 18mm), virtually straight, lower mandible pinkish tipped black. ♂: all shining green with

*bright violet crown*; small tuft of long stiff white feathers near vent; slightly forked *tail deep chestnut broadly edged and tipped golden bronze.* ♀: bright green above, mostly white below *with gray to green spotting on throat, green spotting on sides*; under tail coverts green with a white tuft of stiff feathers like ♂, *tail deep chestnut* with broad bronze green edges, broad subterminal bronze band, and white tips.

**Similar species:** Either sex from any other by *chestnut* tail with broad golden bronze edges. Note limited range. At lower el., cf. 55.

**Voice:** ♂♂ a low, rapid, chipping song (Wetmore 1968a).

**Behavior:** Usually low and alone inside forest (R. Ridgely).

**Status and habitat:** Humid forest or at edges. Known primarily from e Panama, it just reaches Colombian boundary. Foothills and lower slopes.

**Range:** 600-1400m (higher?). E slope of Mt. Tacarcuna (Cutí) near Panama boundary. C Panama to extreme nw Colombia.

### 58. PIRRE (RUFOUS-CHEEKED) HUMMINGBIRD
*Goethalsia bella*

**Identification:** 3.5″ (8.9cm). Bill short (0.5″, or 13mm) and straight. ♂: *frontlet, lores, and chin chestnut*; otherwise entirely shining green with conspic. *buff patch on inner secondaries*, small buff patch on flanks; stiff white tuft on under tail coverts; *tail cinnamon buff* tipped black, *central pair of feathers green.* ♀: entirely green above with chestnut lores; below mostly pale cinnamon buff becoming whitish on breast; *wings and tail like* ♂.

**Similar species:** Only hummingbird in nw Chocó with conspic. buff wing patches.

**Status and habitat:** A little-known hummingbird of humid forested foothills and highlands.

**Range:** 600-1650m. Extreme nw Chocó (Alturas de Nique at head of Río Salaquí) on Panama boundary. Nw Colombia and adj. e Darién, Panama (Cerro Sapo and Cerro Pirre region).

**Note:** Shares with Violet-capped Hummingbird (*Goldmania violiceps*) the peculiar stiffened and lengthened central under tail feathers.

### 59. WHITE-TAILED GOLDENTHROAT
*Polytmus guainumbi*      Pl. 14, Map 421

**Identification:** 3.8″ (9.7cm). Bill rather long (1″, or 25mm), decurved, mostly pale reddish. ♂: golden bronzy green above, a little darker on crown; conspic. dusky patch behind eye bordered above and below by *long white streak*; below glittering golden green; under tail coverts white; tail *long, very rounded*, green with white tip and *broad white edges on outer 3 feathers at base* (flashes conspic. white at base of tail in flight). ♀: like ♂ but white to mostly buff below with green spots on throat and breast.

**Similar species:** Green-tailed Goldenthroat (60) smaller, much less bronzy above, and shorter, less rounded tail lacks white on sides at base.

**Voice:** Call a sharp *tsip-tsip*; song a high-pitched, 3-noted squeak, from higher perch (ffrench 1973).

**Behavior:** Usually seen feeding low and alone in grassy or shrubby areas; gleans insects or hovers (does not cling) to feed at small flowers and not at large flowering trees.

**Breeding:** End of wet season, Oct–Nov, sw Guárico, Venez. (Thomas 1979b). An Aug (wet season) nest, Trinidad (ffrench 1973); Feb, Mar, and July nests (both wet and dry mos.) in Surinam (Haverschmidt 1968). Nest low in grass, weeds, or bushes, sometimes over water and usually rather exposed.

**Status and habitat:** Common to locally abundant in damp or marshy grassland, also dry shrubby savanna with or without scattered trees, but favors vicinity of water. Only hummingbird reg. in open savanna and the most common sp. in llanos of Meta (W. McKay; S. Furniss).

**Range:** To 600m. E base of E Andes s to Macarena Mts. and e to Río Orinoco in Vichada. Most recs. from Meta. Colombia e to the Guianas and ne Brazil (n of Amazon); e Brazil, Paraguay, Bolivia, Argentina, and se Peru.

## 60. GREEN-TAILED GOLDENTHROAT
*Polytmus theresiae* Pl. 14, Map 422

**Identification:** 3.5″ (8.9cm). Bill rather long (1″, or 25mm), decurved, lower mandible pink tipped black. ♂: *entirely shining green*, more glittering below; *dusky patch behind eyes bordered above by short white streak behind eye*; spot of white below eye; tail *slightly rounded*, all green with concealed band of *white at extreme base of tail*; under tail coverts white disked green. ♀ like ♂, but underparts white thickly spotted green on throat and breast; tail narrowly tipped white.

**Similar species:** See White-tailed Goldenthroat (59).

**Voice:** A double note, *twit-twit*, and a long whinnying ser. of up to 10 notes, *ting-ting-ting* . . . (Snyder 1966).

**Behavior:** Sim. to White-tailed Goldenthroat.

**Breeding:** Oct–Nov, Guárico, Venez. (Thomas 1979b). Surinam nests, Apr and July–Sept, in low bushes in open savanna (Haverschmidt 1968).

**Status and habitat:** Sandy-belt forest edge and savanna with scattered low to high bushes. Unlike allied White-tailed Goldenthroat, shows no partic. affinity for water.

**Range:** To 300m. E Guainía (Río Guainía) and Vaupés (Mitú). Sight at El Dorado, upper Río Vaupés, June 1976 (R. Ridgely). Doubtless also Vichada (on Venez. side of Orinoco opp. mouth of Río Vichada). The Guianas, s Venez., ne Peru (Loreto), and locally in Amazonian Brazil.

## 61. BUFFY HUMMINGBIRD
*Leucippus fallax* Pl. 14, Map 423

**Identification:** 3.5″ (8.9cm). Bill nearly straight (0.8″, or 20mm), lower mandible yellowish with dusky tip. ♂: very faded dull green above, head tinged grayish brown; *underparts pale cinnamon buff becoming pure white on lower abdomen and on long fluffy under tail coverts*; tail *slightly rounded*, dull green with dusky subterminal band and broad white tip. ♀: even duller.

**Similar species:** Very faded and washed out in appearance. Unique in arid habitat.

**Behavior:** A characteristic hummingbird of arid Guajira. Often at flowers around habitations; mostly solitary and fond of agave and cactus blossoms.

**Status and habitat:** Locally common in very xerophytic vegetation, thorn scrub, and mangrove borders. This and Red-billed Emerald are two of the most common hummingbirds on the Guajira Peninsula.

**Range:** To 800m. Se base of Santa Marta Mts. (Atanquez, Cesar) and e Guajira (Ríohacha) e to Snía. de Macuira. Ne Colombia, n and w Venez. and adj. offshore isls.

## 62. OLIVE-SPOTTED HUMMINGBIRD
*Leucippus chlorocercus*

**Identification:** 3.5″ (8.9cm). Bill almost straight (0.7″, or 18mm) and dusky. *Faded* plumage with white spot behind prom. black eye. Dull brownish green above, greenest across shoulders and upper back; brownish on head and rump; grayish white below, vaguely mottled dusky on breast; *throat with a few inconspic. dull green disks; tail green* (central feathers greenest) *and slightly rounded, outer feathers with dusky subterminal band and grayish white tip.*

**Similar species:** Looks "♀-plumaged" and easily confused. Gray-breasted Sabrewing (23) is much larger; ♀ Fork-tailed Woodnymph (47) and ♀ Blue-chinned Sapphire (40) have bluish tails. Note habitat.

**Voice:** A sharp *seek, seek-seek, seek*, etc., with no apparent pattern, to leisurely sequence of single, paired, or trebled squeaks; sing from bare twig 2-4 m up.

**Behavior:** Solitary birds glean over foliage or

hover without clinging at small flowers at var. hts.; territorial and chase conspecifics; often curious and may hover closely for a moment. **Status and habitat:** Known from 1 BC ♀, 11 Mar 1975, near Pto. Nariño, Amazonas (Romero 1978); common (many sight rec.—Hilty) on Isla Corea in Amazon River nw of Leticia; resident in viny scrub and thinner, young second growth (trees to 7m ht.) on Amazon river isls. **Range:** S Amazonas. E Ecuador (incl. upper Río Napo, 430m), n Peru (incl. Pebas; mouth Río Curaray), and w Amazonian Brazil.

[*Amazilia:* Difficult group; med. size, "typical" hummingbirds; most with base of lower mandible pinkish red; tail square to slightly forked; normally hover without clinging to flowers.]

## 63. VERSICOLORED EMERALD
*Amazilia versicolor*                Pl. 14, Map 424
**Identification:** 3.3″ (8.4cm). Bill straight (0.7″, or 18mm); lower mandible pinkish with dusky tip. Shining green above; *median throat and chest pure white; median lower underparts dull whitish;* sides of throat and chest bordered glittering blue green; sides of breast green; tail dull green, all but central pair of feathers with a dusky subterminal band. Sexes sim.
**Similar species:** Glittering-throated Emerald (64) has green throat, white wedge from belly to midbreast only. ♀♀ of several spp. (40, 47, 53) are somewhat sim. but grayish below (not with central throat and chest pure white).
**Voice:** Song a shrill *ché-ché-ché-ché-fii* interrupted by whistles; in flight display *trrr-i, trrr-i . . . ;* in alarm *trrch* (Ruschi 1973).
**Behavior:** Sim. to other *Amazilia.*
**Breeding:** 1 BC ♂, 23 Feb, upper Orinoco, Venez. (Friedmann 1948). In Brazil, nest 2-6m up on horizontal branch (Ruschi 1973).
**Status and habitat:** Uncommon in drier open woodland, gallery forest, and scrubby savanna, occas. to humid forest borders. Very uncommon at Carimagua, ne Meta (S. Furniss).
**Range:** To 500m. E of Andes from Arauca s to s Meta (Macarena Mts.) and Vaupés (Mitú; Santa Cruz de Waracapurí); doubtless in Vichada and Guainía (many rec. on Venez. bank of Orinoco). Venez., n Amazonian and se Brazil, ne Argentina, and n Bolivia.

## 64. GLITTERING-THROATED EMERALD
*Amazilia fimbriata*                Pl. 14, Map 425
**Identification:** 3.3″ (8.4cm). Bill straight (0.8″, or 20mm), lower mandible pinkish tipped dusky. ♂: shining green above; glittering green

below with *white abdomen penetrating narrowly to median breast* (forms a wedge of white up median underparts); tail slightly forked, central pair of feathers bronze green, rest progressively darker, the outer ones blue black. ♀: sim. but duller; underparts as in ♂ but *median wedge of white continued to throat, which is disked green.*
**Similar species:** Clean white wedge on underparts of ♂ is distinctive. ♀ can be confused with ♀ Blue-chinned Sapphire (40), but lower underparts and center breast white (not disked green). Versicolored Emerald (63) has pure white throat, and rest of underparts much more extensively white. Also cf. ♀ Shining-green Hummingbird (51).
**Voice:** Call in Guyana a soft *dz-dz* like pebbles struck together (Snyder 1966); flight call a loud *peep-peep* running up and down scale (Friedmann and Smith 1955).
**Behavior:** Forage mostly at low to mod. ht. in shrubbery and second growth and often perch conspic. in open. Usually singly, often around habitations.
**Breeding:** Laying ♀, June, w Caquetá (Carriker). May–Nov nests in Venez. Orinoco (Cherrie 1916); 5 nests, Aug–Nov, 1 in Jan, Venez. (Friedmann and Smith 1950, 1955); yr.-round breeding in Surinam (Haverschmidt 1968); nest on fork of shrub or tip of low branch in tree, mostly below 1 m, rarely 3m up.
**Status and habitat:** Common in shrubby second growth, gallery forest borders, and cultivated areas with bushes and trees.
**Range:** To 500m. Throughout e of Andes. The Guianas and Venez. to s Bolivia and s Brazil.
**Note:** Tachira Emerald (*A. distans*), known from 1 Venez. specimen from Burgua, sw Táchira (300m), and a poss. sighting on n slope of Táchira (1974—P. Alden, M. Gochfeld, M. Kleinbaum), could occur in adj. Colombia. Much like Glittering-throated Emerald, but forecrown, foreneck, and chest glittering blue, throat feathers edged white, belly olive gray.

## 65. BLUE-CHESTED HUMMINGBIRD
*Amazilia amabilis*                Pl. 13, Map 426
**Identification:** 3.5″ (8.9cm). Bill straight (0.7″, or 18mm), lower mandible dull pink basally. ♂: *crown glittering green;* otherwise shining green above; *upper throat dusky green; center of lower throat and chest with patch of glittering violet blue* (duller around edge); rest of underparts dingy green becoming grayish brown on lower abdomen; *tail bronzy purple,* slightly forked. ♀: green above, plain grayish below with green spots on throat and breast and usually with an ill-defined band of *glittering bluish spots across*

*chest*; slightly forked tail brownish black tipped grayish.

**Similar species:** Grayish feather edgings on ♂'s underparts give an unkept ♀-like appearance. ♂ Purple-chested Hummingbird (66) is very sim., but gorget shows pronounced *glittering green above the blue patch* (the latter is larger and positioned mainly on chest), crown dull green (not glittering), and tail lacks bronzy purple tone. ♀ Purple-chested lacks the blue chest spotting, has throat and breast white spotted green, and under tail coverts white (not grayish).

**Behavior:** Usually seen singly feeding at low flowers along forest edges; reg. gleans insects from foliage. Less often several concentrate at flowering trees where they argue with other hummingbirds. ♂♂ gather in loose song assemblies during breeding season, usually keeping rather well separated in upper undergrowth (Skutch 1972).

**Breeding:** 14 BC birds, Feb–May, s Bolívar to Chocó (Carriker); 1 in Mar, n Chocó (Haffer 1975). In Costa Rica, nest 2-5m up on horizontal branch (Skutch 1972).

**Status and habitat:** Fairly common in humid and wet forest borders, second growth woodland, and shrubby areas.

**Range:** To 1000m on Pacific coast (net capture—Hilty); to 1400m (Magdalena Val.). Pacific coast and e in humid lowlands n of Andes to mid. Magadalena Val. from s Bolívar s to nw Cundinamarca (Yacopí). Nicaragua to w Ecuador and nw Peru.

**Note:** Birds of sw Costa Rica and sw Panama may be a separate sp. (G. Stiles).

#### 66. PURPLE-CHESTED HUMMINGBIRD
*Amazilia rosenbergi*　　　　Pl. 13, Map 427
**Identification:** 3.5″ (8.9cm). Bill straight (0.7″, or 18mm), with lower mandible pinkish basally. Closely resembles Blue-chested Hummingbird. ♂: shining green above; gorget glittering green; *patch on center of chest glittering violet blue*; otherwise grayish brown below with green spots on sides; under tail coverts white; tail blue black, more bronzy on central feathers, slightly forked. ♀: green above; throat and breast white *thickly spotted green from throat to upper belly*; lower belly grayish; *under tail coverts white*; tail blue black tipped white.
**Similar species:** See Blue-chested Hummingbird (65) and ♀ Blue-headed Sapphire (54).
**Behavior:** Sim. in most respects to Blue-chested Hummingbird. Song leks not reported.
**Status and habitat:** Uncommon in wet forest borders, second growth woodland, and shrubby clearings in the coastal lowlands. Generally less numerous than Blue-chested Hummingbird.

and seemingly confined to wettest coastal belt. Barely enters lower foothills.
**Range:** To 200m (perhaps higher?). Pacific coast from mid. Atrato Val. (Río Uva n of Quibdó) southward. W Colombia and nw Ecuador.

#### 67. ANDEAN EMERALD
*Amazilia franciae*　　　　Pl. 13, Map 428
**Identification:** 3.6″ (9.1cm). Bill straight (0.9″, or 23mm), lower mandible pinkish with dusky tip. ♂: shining green above with glittering *violet blue crown* (or glittering green—*viridiceps*); sides of head and neck glittering green; *entire underparts pure white with green sides and flanks; upper tail coverts coppery*; slightly forked tail bronzy green with indistinct dusky subterminal band and narrow pale tip. ♀: sim., but crown green (not blue).
**Similar species:** Copper upper tail coverts often prom., and the only hummingbird in highlands with pure white median underparts from bill to tail; otherwise resembles a no. of highland ♀♀, but all have some spotting on throat or breast.
**Voice:** Song a rather loud squeaky ser. suggesting song of Bananaquit but less musical (Miller 1963).
**Behavior:** Usually singly, "trap-lining" scattered flowers at var. hts.; occas. congregates at flowering trees; also hawks insects in short sallies near vegetation (Snow and Snow 1980). ♂♂ sing from exposed perches 7-10m up (Miller 1963).
**Breeding:** 2 BC ♀♀, Oct and Dec, absent Apr–Sept, upper Anchicayá Val. (Hilty); 1 BC ♂, Apr, Queremal; 1 in Oct, Popayán (Miller 1963); 4 BC birds, May, W and C Andes (Carriker).
**Status and habitat:** Humid and wet forest edges, second growth, and highland clearings with trees.
**Range:** 1000-2000m (once to 535m? in Magdalena Val.). W Andes (except Nariño), C Andes, head of Magdalena Val. in Huila and w slope E Andes in Cundinamarca (*franciae*); Pacific slope of Nariño (*viridiceps*). Colombia, w Ecuador, and n Peru.

#### 68. INDIGO-CAPPED HUMMINGBIRD
*Amazilia cyanifrons*　　　　Pl. 14, Map 429
**Identification:** 3.6″ (9.1cm). Bill straight (0.7″, or 18mm), lower mandible red basally. ♂: *crown deep intense indigo blue*; otherwise shining green above becoming *coppery bronze on rump*; entirely glittering green below; small leg tufts white; blue black tail slightly forked. ♀: duller.
**Similar species:** ♂ Crowned Woodnymph (46) in zone of overlap has glittering purple crown, purple lower underparts, longer and much

more deeply forked tail, and lacks prom. coppery brown rump. Steely-vented Hummingbird (69) has green (not deep blue) crown; also see Shining-green Hummingbird (51).

**Behavior:** Argue around flowers at var. hts., usually quite high; notably territorial and pugnacious and commonly gather in nos. at flowering trees (up to 18 in 1 tree near Palestina, Huila).

**Breeding:** 6 BC ♂♂, Apr, sw Huila; 4 more, July, Popayán (Carriker). Nest building, Aug, Toqui, w Boyacá (Snow and Snow 1980).

**Status and habitat:** Very uncommon to locally common in open woodland, shrubby clearings, and cultivated areas in foothills and lower highlands. Shows strong seasonal movements.

**Range:** 400-2000m; once (accidental) at sea level sw of Barranquilla in sw Atlántico. Mid. and upper Magdalena Val. from near Toqui, w Boyacá s to sw Huila; upper Cauca Val. near Popayán; e of Andes in Norte de Santander (Ocaña). Colombia and Costa Rica (once!).

### 69. STEELY-VENTED HUMMINGBIRD

*Amazilia saucerottei*      Pl. 14, Map 430

**Identification:** 3.5″ (8.9cm). Bill straight (0.7″, or 18mm), lower mandible pinkish tipped dusky. ♂: shining green above, glittering green below; *upper tail coverts coppery bronze* forming narrow contrasting band (or blue black like tail—*australis*); under tail coverts *steely blue black edged white* (or bronze to grayish edged white—*saucerottei; australis*), slightly forked tail blue black. ♀: sim., but under tail coverts gray to brownish edged white. Santa Marta birds show little coppery bronze on rump.

**Similar species:** See ♂ Shining-green Hummingbird (51) and ♂♂ of several *Chlorostilbon* emeralds (esp. 41, 42, 43). Blue-chinned Sapphire (40) lacks coppery upper tail covert band, has slightly rounded tail, and is not known to overlap in range. Green-bellied Hummingbird (70) has prom. brownish lower back, rump, and upper tail coverts. Also cf. Indigo-capped Hummingbird (68).

**Voice:** An excited "chitting" sometimes becoming a trill, descending and diminishing; a thin "spinking" *peep peep* may be a song (Slud 1964).

**Behavior:** Principally a flower feeder, mostly in lower bushes and shrubbery. Notably pugnacious.

**Breeding:** 4 BC birds, July–Oct, Santa Marta Mts. (Carriker); 5 more, Jan–Sept, C and W Andes; down cup nest fastened to limb 8m up in July (Miller 1963); Apr fledglings, July courtship, Santa Marta (S. M. Russell).

**Status and habitat:** Fairly common in drier scrubby areas, woodland borders, cultivated land, and gardens. Somewhat seasonal, at times

locally very common. In Santa Marta area resident below 600-700m, seasonally higher (Todd and Carriker 1922).

**Range:** To 2000m. Pacific slope in dry upper Sucio (near Dabeiba), upper Dagua, upper Patía, and mid. Cauca Vals. (*saucerottei*); Carib. region from Snía. de San Jacinto e to Guajira, s in drier parts of Magdalena Val. to s Huila (several seen, June 1981, e of Guadalupe— Hilty) and e slope of Andes in Notre de Santander near Ocaña (*warscewiczi*); dry Guáitara Val., Nariño (*australis*). Nicaragua and Costa Rica; Colombia and w Venez.

### 70. GREEN-BELLIED HUMMINGBIRD

*Amazilia viridigaster*      Pl. 14, Map 431

**Identification:** 3.7″ (9.4cm). Bill straight (0.7″, or 18mm), lower mandible mostly pinkish. Above shining green becoming *very brownish buff on lower back, rump, and upper tail coverts*; glittering green below; cinnamon under tail coverts (not conspic.), sligly forked tail coppery purple (usually looks blackish in field).

**Similar species:** A distinctive green hummingbird with a conspic. brownish lower back and rump. In Norte de Santander cf. Steely-vented (69) and Indigo-capped hummingbirds (68), both with much less coppery brown on rump or upper tail coverts.

**Voice:** Song a thin, waiflike *ta-da titi-da; ti* notes higher.

**Behavior:** Like other *Amazilia* usually seen feeding at flowers; commonly gathers in large argumentative groups at flowering trees (up to 15 in *Erythrina* trees in Feb near Villavicencio); rather pugnacious.

**Breeding:** 5 BC birds, Oct. Cúcuta (Carriker); 6 more, Dec–Jan, Boyacá (Olivares 1963); 2 nestlings in Guyana nest, 21 Feb; 3m up in small tree (Snow and Snow 1974).

**Status and habitat:** Uncommon to fairly common at forest edges and in clearings with scattered trees; foothills and lower highlands. Nos. fluctuate with flower abundance.

**Range:** 400-1600m. E slope E Andes from Norte de Santander (sight to 1800m, Pamplona, 1979—Hilty) s to s Meta (Macarena Mts.). W Venez.; s Venez., s Guyana, and adj. n Brazil (Roraima).

### 71. RUFOUS-TAILED HUMMINGBIRD

*Amazilia tzacatl*      Pl. 13, Map 432

**Identification:** 3.6″ (9.1cm). Bill straight (0.8″, or 20mm), *lower mandible pinkish* (sometimes also upper mandible) *tipped black.* ♂: green above with slightly forked *rufous chestnut tail*; throat and chest glittering green *becoming dingy grayish on breast and belly.* ♀: sim. but feathers of throat and chest edged buff to gray.

**Similar species:** A med.-sized hummingbird w of Andes with an all rufous tail is likely this sp. but see Blue-throated Sapphire (55) and Chestnut-bellied Hummingbird (72), both rare. E of Andes see Golden-tailed Sapphire (56), which has blue head. Also cf. Ruby-topaz Hummingbird (32).

**Voice:** Song in Panama a fast ser. of *tsip* notes (about 5) repeated frequently (Eisenmann).

**Behavior:** Feeds at flowers, hawks insects in short sallies, and gleans from foliage, twigs, spider webs, etc. at low to mod. hts. Sometimes several gather at flowering trees where very argumentative and territorial. A characteristic bird of gardens and habitations in many areas.

**Breeding:** 2 Santa Marta nests, 2 Feb (Hilty); nest building, Aug, Toqui, w Boyacá (Snow and Snow 1980); yr.-round breeding in Costa Rica with dry season (Jan–May) peak; nest 0.6-7m up in bush or tree (Skutch 1931).

**Status and habitat:** Common and ecologically tolerant, occurring in a wide spectrum of fairly dry to wet zones, incl. forest edges, lighter open woodland, shrubby clearings, and cultivated areas. Usually more numerous in humid regions; not inside forest.

**Range:** To 1800m. Pacific coast (to about 1200m); rest of Colombia w of Andes s to latitude of Bogotá and e of them in Catatumbo lowlands. Gorgona Isl. E Mexico and w Venez.

### 72. CHESTNUT-BELLIED HUMMINGBIRD
*Amazilia castaneiventris*

**Identification:** 3.3″ (8.4cm). Bill almost straight (0.8″, or 20mm), lower mandible flesh color basally. Shining reddish bronze above becoming grayish buff on rump; throat and breast glittering green; *lower underparts and tail rufous chestnut*; small leg tufts white.

**Similar species:** Like Rufous-tailed Hummingbird but lower underparts chestnut (not dingy grayish).

**Status and habitat:** Little known and with extremely limited range. Rec. definitely only from 2 localities.

**Range:** ENDEMIC. Known from w slope of E Andes in n Boyacá (Soatá, 2045m, above Chicamocha Val.) and s Bolívar at n end Snía. San Lucas (Norosí, 150m).

### 73. WHITE-VENTED PLUMELETEER
*Chalybura buffonii*                    Pl. 13, Map 433

**Identification:** ♂ 4.5″ (11.4cm); ♀ 4.2″ (10.7cm). *Bill black*, mod. long (1″, or 25mm), slightly decurved. ♂: shining green above, glittering green below (or breast and center of belly glittering blue—*caeruleogaster*); *long puffy under tail coverts silky white; blue black tail decidedly long*,

slightly forked. ♀: smaller; green above, grayish below; under tail coverts like ♂'s; tail as in ♂ but *outer feathers broadly tipped whitish* and with a suggestion of a dusky subterminal band.

**Similar species:** Plumelike white under tail coverts and ample tail are good marks for the genus, but the 2 spp. are easily confused. Under favorable conditions both sexes of Bronze-tailed Plumeleteer (74) can be told by pinkish lower mandible, pink (not black) feet, and bronzy copper tail, but none of these marks easy to see. ♀ woodnymphs (46, 47) resemble ♀ White-vented Plumeleteer but are smaller with shorter tails, and under tail coverts not as extensively white; in addition ♀ Crowned Woodnymph (46) looks "2-tone" below. Also cf. Scaly-breasted Hummingbird (22) and ♀ White-necked Jacobin (26).

**Behavior:** Usually seen singly or in pairs in the lower story of woodland or along shady borders, but occas. at large flowering trees with other hummingbirds.

**Breeding:** 11 BC birds, Mar–Oct, n of W Andes e to nw side E Andes (Carriker).

**Status and habitat:** Fairly common in lighter humid woodland, second growth, and open forest borders (usually not inside heavy forest) of lowlands and lower highlands.

**Range:** Locally to 2000m. W of W Andes (to 900m) from Gulf of Urabá s to Anchicayá Val., Valle (perhaps entire Pacific coast), entire Cauca Val. (at least formerly), and head of Magdalena Val. in s Huila (*micans*); Santa Marta region (to 1400m) to w base Perijá Mts. (*aeneicauda*); mid. Magdalena Val. from s Bolívar s to Tolima, and Catatumbo lowlands of Norte de Santander (*buffonii*); e base of E Andes from Río Casanare s to Macarena Mts. (*caeruleogaster*). W Panama to w Ecuador and n Venez.

### 74. BRONZE-TAILED PLUMELETEER
*Chalybura urochrysia*                    Pl. 13, Map 434

**Identification:** ♂ 4.2″ (10.7cm); ♀ 4″ (10.2cm). Bill moderately long (1″, or 25mm), almost straight, *base of lower mandible pale reddish brown to pink. Feet pale pink* (often visible in field). Much like White-vented Plumeleteer. ♂: bronzy green above; green below (blue green near Panama border) becoming gray on belly; under tail coverts pure white (not as long and puffy as previous sp.); *tail bronzy copper*, rather long, slightly forked. ♀: sim. but light gray below becoming whitish on lower belly; tail tipped gray.

**Similar species:** See White-vented Plumeleteer (73).

**Voice:** Presumed song in Costa Rica a hollow *pirp-pirp-pirpirpirp*; calls are a var. of trills or twitters and ticking notes (Slud 1964).

**Behavior:** Sim. to White-vented Plumeleteer but also reg. found in lower story inside forest; not reported at large flowering trees with other hummingbirds in Colombia.

**Breeding:** 5 BC birds, Feb–Apr, Chocó (Carriker).

**Status and habitat:** Uncommon and perhaps local in humid and wet forest and forest borders, esp. where overgrown with *Heliconia* etc. More a forest bird than allied White-vented Plumeleteer.

**Range:** To 900m. Pacific coast and humid lowlands n of Andes e to mid. Magdalena Val. (s to Remedios, Antioquia), also mid. Cauca Val. in Antioquia (Medellín) and upper Patía Val. in Cauca (El Bordo). Nicaragua to sw Ecuador.

### 75. SPECKLED HUMMINGBIRD

*Adelomyia melanogenys* Pl. 14, Map 435
**Identification:** 3.4″ (8.6cm). Bill short (0.5″, or 13mm) and straight. Dull bronzy green above; *blackish cheeks bordered above by a conspic. buffy white postocular streak; below dingy buffy white* (or buff—*cervina*), speckled dusky on throat (speckling hard to see in field); tail bronze brown tipped buff, slightly forked. Sexes sim.

**Similar species:** Duller and browner than most hummingbirds and often mistaken for a ♀ or imm. See larger Brown Violetear (27) and Fawn-breasted Brilliant (81).

**Voice:** A low-pitched pebbly *dit-dik* when foraging.

**Behavior:** Usually alone, occas. pairs in the lower story of forest or low along thick shady borders. Hovers, often clinging or perching, when probing flowers. Does not gather in groups at flowering trees.

**Breeding:** 6 BC birds, May–Dec, W, C and E Andes (Carriker; Miller 1963); 1 nest, late Jan, PN Cueva de los Guácharos (P. Gertler).

**Status and habitat:** One of the most common mid.-el. hummingbirds in humid forest and forest borders throughout mts.

**Range:** 1000-2500m (usually above 1300m). Perijá Mts. and E Andes s at least to Cundinamarca (*melanogenys*); W and C Andes s to near Popayán, Cauca (*cervina*); head of Magdalena Val. in s Huila (*connectens*); mts. of Nariño (*maculata*). N Venez. s in mts. to nw Argentina.

### 76. BLOSSOMCROWN

*Anthocephala floriceps* Pl. 14, Map 436
**Identification:** 3.3″ (8.4cm). Bill short (0.5″, or 13mm) and straight. ♂: *forecrown buffy white, hindcrown rufous chestnut*; otherwise shining green above with a large white spot behind eyes; underparts grayish buff; central tail feathers bronzy green, rest with broad dusky subterminal band and *white tips* (or buff—*floriceps*). ♀: sim. but crown brownish.

**Similar species:** Whitish forecrown prom. in ♂ (like a tiny spot of light), but caution urged as many other spp. often have foreheads dusted with whitish pollen and could be mistaken for this rare sp. ♀ much like Speckled Hummingbird (75) but lacks the black cheeks and white postocular streak.

**Behavior:** Usually seen alone feeding at flowers in lower story. ♂♂ gather in small song leks and "chip" persistently from a fairly low (2-5m) but exposed horizontal perch.

**Breeding:** 2 BC birds, Sept–Oct, Santa Marta Mts. (Carriker).

**Status and habitat:** *Rare* and local in humid forest, lighter woodland, and older second growth.

**Range:** ENDEMIC. Santa Marta Mts. (600-1700m—*floriceps*); Magdalena Val. where known definitely only from e slope C Andes at Río Toche (1200-2300m) n Tolima (*berlepschi*) and at Finca Merenberg, w Huila (once).

### 77. RUFOUS-VENTED WHITETIP

*Urosticte ruficrissa* Map 437
**Identification:** ♂ 3.7″ (9.4cm); ♀ 3.4″ (8.6cm). Bill straight (0.8″, or 20mm). ♂: shining green above with *long white postocular streak*; glittering green below; under tail coverts mostly buff, feathers of upper breast sometimes edged whitish; tail greenish black, deeply *forked*, central pair of feathers *broadly tipped white forming a large oval central spot on tail* (prom. from above, esp. if tail is spread). ♀: shining green above, white to buff below thickly spotted with green disks; under tail coverts buff; tail greenish black and forked, outer feathers broadly tipped white.

**Similar species:** On Pacific slope see Purple-bibbed Whitetip (78). Large white oval spot on tail of ♂ is unique to the genus. ♀ recalls ♀ Booted Racket-tail (see 120). Also see larger ♀♀ of *Heliodoxa* (82, 83).

**Behavior:** Presum. sim. to Purple-bibbed Whitetip. A ♀ was captured in lower story of forest at Merenberg (Ridgely and Gaulin 1980).

**Status and habitat:** Uncommon or local in humid mt. forest. Perhaps more common in Nariño where 7 specimens taken in 1971 at El Carmen (Fitzpatrick and Willard 1982).

**Range:** 1600-2300m. E slope C Andes in s Huila (San Agustín, now deforested; Finca Merenberg) and se Nariño (El Carmen, 1600m). E Colombia and e Ecuador.

**Note:** By some considered a subsp. of smaller Purple-bibbed Whitetip.

## 78. PURPLE-BIBBED WHITETIP

*Urosticte benjamini*      Pl. 15, Map 438
**Identification:** ♂ 3.5″ (8.9cm); ♀ 3.2″ (8.1cm). Bill straight (0.8″, or 20mm). ♂: *green*; very glittering below with large shining purple crescent on chest (hard to see in field); large white postocular spot; greenish black *tail, forked, central pair of feathers mostly white forming a large oval spot* (conspic. from above, esp. if tail is spread). ♀: green above; *white below thickly spotted green*; lores and spot behind eyes white; forked greenish black tail bronzy purple subterminally, outer feathers *broadly tipped white*.
**Similar species:** See Rufous-vented Whitetip (77), ♀ Booted Racket-tail (120), and ♀ Colorful Puffleg (115).
**Behavior:** A solitary forest-based bird that hovers as it gleans over twigs, along branches, and under foliage, or visits small scattered flowers from lower story to subcanopy. Usually keeps in inner part of trees where inconspic. and difficult to see.
**Status and habitat:** Fairly common (by mist net captures but infrequently seen) in humid and wet forest, also forest borders. No seasonal movements noted in upper Anchicayá Val., 900-1100m (Hilty).
**Range:** 700-1500m. Pacific slope from headwaters of Río San Juan (Cerro Tatamá) southward. W Colombia, w Ecuador, and ne Peru.
**Note:** Often considered conspecific with Rufous-vented Whitetip. The taxonomy of this group is uncertain.

## 79. ECUADORIAN PIEDTAIL

*Phlogophilus hemileucurus*      Map 439
**Identification:** 3″ (7.6cm). Bill straight (0.7″, or 18mm). Above shining green; below white thickly spotted green with a band of white across breast extending up on sides of neck; belly white; rounded, dark green tail with *white band at base and broad white terminal band.* Sexes sim.
**Similar species:** Banded tail distinctive. Paletailed Barbthroat (3) has somewhat sim. tail pattern but is otherwise very different and occurs low in thick young second growth. Also cf. ♂ Rufous-vented Whitetip (77), which shows white patch in center of tail, and ♀, which is spotted below.
**Status and habitat:** Known by 3 specimens taken Mar 1971 at Estación de Bombeo Guamués (1000m), w Putumayo (Fitzpatrick and Willard 1982). Humid forested regions in foothills and lower slopes. In Ecuador, mostly 800-1500m; in n Peru in foothills and on lower slopes 400-1000m (T. Parker).
**Range:** Upper tropical zone. E slope E Andes

in Putumayo, poss. Caquetá. E Colombia, e Ecuador and ne Peru.

## 80. JEWELFRONT (GOULD'S JEWELFRONT)

*Polyplancta aurescens*      Pl. 14, Map 440
**Identification:** 4.8″ (12.2cm). Bill almost straight (0.8″, or 20mm). ♂: *mainly shining green* with median forecrown stripe glittering violet; chin black, throat glittering green; *broad breast band orange rufous*; central tail feathers bronze green; *rest chestnut tipped bronze green.* ♀: duller, median crown stripe faint or lacking; throat grayish mixed green; short chestnut malar stripe.
**Similar species:** Either sex easily told by prom. wide rufous band across chest; cf. Rufous-throated Sapphire (52).
**Behavior:** An inconspic. bird of shady forest understory, esp. near creeks and damp places, infrequently higher and rarely at edges (R. Ridgely).
**Status and habitat:** Prob. often overlooked. Inside humid *terra firme* forest incl. sandy-belt regions, less often *várzea* forest.
**Range:** To 400m. Known from w Putumayo (4 specimens, San Antonio Guamuéz—Fitzpatrick and Willard 1982) and Vaupés (specimens opp. Tahuapunto, Brazil; 1 from El Dorado, upper Río Vaupés, June 1976—R. Ridgely; sightings Feb 1978, Mitú—Hilty). Also Amazonas (sight, 1984—Hilty). S. Venez. to e Ecuador (incl. Limoncocha), e Peru (incl. Pebas and mouth of Río Curaray), and w Amazonian Brazil.

[*Heliodoxa*: Montane; large and robust; heavy bill straight or slightly decurved; feathers of forehead grow over upper base of bill giving "*tapered*" look to forecrown; small white spot behind eye.]

## 81. FAWN-BREASTED BRILLIANT

*Heliodoxa rubinoides*      Pl. 16, Map 441
**Identification:** 4.4″ (11.2cm). Bill slightly decurved (0.9″, or 23mm). ♂: shining green above; *cinnamon buff below*, throat and sides of breast disked green; *small topaz rose patch on center of lower throat*; tail coppery green, ample, slightly forked. ♀: sim., but lacks patch on lower throat.
**Similar species:** Rather dull buffy underparts impart ♀-like appearance. Other large highland hummers with brown or buff below lack the contrasting green upperparts. Cf. Bronzy Inca (93), Brown Violetear (27) and Speckled Hummingbird (75).
**Behavior:** Usually seen singly in the lower or mid. story inside forest, occas. along shady

borders. Does not gather in groups at flowering trees.

**Breeding:** 4 BC birds, Jan—May, W Andes above Cali (Miller 1963); eggs in 23 Apr nest, same area (S. Gniadek); BC ♂, May, n end W Andes (Carriker).

**Status and habitat:** Uncommon and local in humid and wet forest ("cloud forest"). Reg. above Cali (Hilty); rare in PN Cueva de los Guácharos (P. Gertler).

**Range:** 1800-2600m (poss. to 1000m in Magdalena Val.). W Andes at n end and in Valle; C Andes and w slope E Andes from Cundinamarca to head of Magdalena Val. Colombia, e and w Ecuador, and ne Peru.

## 82. VIOLET-FRONTED BRILLIANT

*Heliodoxa leadbeateri*       Pl. 15, Map 442

**Identification:** ♂ 5″ (13cm); ♀ 4.3″ (10.9cm). Bill almost straight (0.9″, or 23mm). ♂: *crown glittering violet*; otherwise bronze green above; *gorget and upper breast glittering green*; lower breast and belly dull olive green; *tail rather large and forked*, central feathers bronze green, rest blackish. ♀: forecrown glittering green; otherwise green above, small white spot behind eye; lores and cheeks dusky bordered below by faint white malar streak; below white thickly disked glittering green on throat and breast, shining green on belly; belly tinged buff; tail as in ♂ but narrowly tipped white and less forked.

**Similar species:** Purple-crowned subsp. of ♂ Crowned Woodnymph (46) in E Andes is superficially sim. but smaller, and upper back and lower underparts glittering purple. Also see rare Green-crowned Brilliant (83); ♀ of latter not safely separated in field from ♀ Violet-fronted, but in hand has shining (not glittering) green crown, whiter upper throat (fewer green disks), and decidedly larger white spot behind eye.

**Behavior:** Solitary 1-10m up at flowers inside forest or small openings at forest edge. Frequently flycatches and does not gather in groups at flowering trees.

**Status and habitat:** Uncommon and local in humid and wet forest and forest edges, occas. lighter woodland or second growth. Replaced at lower el. by Green-crowned Brilliant.

**Range:** 1300-2400m. Perijá Mts., e slope E Andes from Norte de Santander s to Meta (Macarena Mts.) and w slope in Santander (Bucaramanga); C Andes at n end (Pto. Valdivia), head of Cauca Val. (near Popayán), and head of Magdalena Val. in s Huila. N Venez. s in mts. to n Bolivia.

## 83. GREEN-CROWNED BRILLIANT

*Heliodoxa jacula*       Pl. 13, Map 443

**Identification:** ♂ 5″ (13cm); ♀ 4.3″ (10.9cm). Bill straight (0.9″, or 23mm). ♂: *mainly green*; crown and most of underparts glittering green; small violet spot on lower throat (not conspic.); *tail rather long and deeply forked, central pair of feathers bronze green, rest blue black.* ♀: green above with dusky lores and cheeks; white spot behind eyes and prom. white malar streak; *underparts white thickly disked green, whitest on throat, belly often tinged buff, tail forked, otherwise like ♂ but narrowly tipped white.*

**Similar species:** ♂ from ♂ Violet-fronted Brilliant (82) by glittering green (not violet) crown. ♀ essentially sim. to ♀ Violet-fronted Brilliant. In W Andes see Empress Brilliant (84), which it may meet in sw Nariño.

**Behavior:** Sim. to Violet-fronted Brilliant.

**Breeding:** 4 BC birds, May, se Antioquia (Carriker).

**Status and habitat:** Very local in humid and wet forest; not well known in Colombia.

**Range:** Presum. 500-1500m (prob. higher). Cerro Tacarcuna on Panama boundary, extreme n end of W and C Andes, e slope C Andes in Caldas (Río Samaná, 1250m) and both slopes of E Andes in Cundinamarca (w slope at Yacopí, 1400m; e slope at Medina, 500-600m). Prob. sw Nariño (rec. at adj. Cachabí, Ecuador, 500m). Costa Rica to w Ecuador.

## 84. EMPRESS BRILLIANT

*Heliodoxa imperatrix*       Pl. 16, Map 444

**Identification:** ♂ 5.5″ (14cm); ♀ 4.8″ (12.2cm). Large. Bill almost straight (1″, or 25mm). Feathers of forehead grow over base of upper mandible even more noticeably than in others of genus. ♂: *mainly dark green*, very glittering below with small rosy violet patch on lower throat (not conspic. in field); *tail long, deeply forked*, blackish green. ♀: entirely shining green above; *white below thickly spotted glittering green over entire underparts*; tail much shorter, less deeply forked, bronze green. Juv. has rufous malar stripe; otherwise like ♀.

**Similar species:** ♂ much like Green-crowned Brilliant (83) but see ranges (perhaps meet in sw Nariño). ♂ Empress Brilliant differs in tail decidedly longer (about 55-70 vs 40-52mm), more deeply forked, and blackish olive (not blue black); also larger size, more "tapered" forehead, and smaller white spot behind eye; ♀ from ♀ Green-crowned Brilliant mainly in larger size, longer more deeply forked tail, and no whitish tail tips (not always present in latter).

**Behavior:** Most often seen at flowers, where usually alone at low to midlevel inside forest, also low at forest edge. May cling momentarily when foraging, but often hovers directly beneath pendent tubular flowers and probes vertically upward. Wing beats slow.

**Breeding:** ♀ building nest (collecting *Ochroma* seeds), 20 Feb; 2nd ♀ building, 14 Mar; downy cup nest plastered atop palm frond 10m up at forest edge, upper Anchicayá Val. (Hilty).

**Status and habitat:** Uncommon to fairly common (perhaps local) in wet forest ("cloud forest") and forest borders of foothills and lower slopes. In Anchicayá Val. most numerous above 900m.

**Range:** 400-1800m. Pacific slope from Río San Juan headwaters (Cerro Tatamá) southward. W Colombia and nw Ecuador.

## 85. BLACK-THROATED BRILLIANT
*Heliodoxa schreibersii*　　　　Map 445

**Identification:** 4.7″ (12cm). Bill straight (0.9″, or 23mm). ♂: shining green above with glittering forecrown; median *underparts black; patch on lower throat glittering purple*, bordered below by broad band of glittering green on breast and down sides; steel blue tail rather long, deeply-forked. ♀: sim., but with *prom. white to rufous malar stripe*; lower underparts gray disked green; central tail feathers greenish.

**Similar species:** Pink-throated Brilliant (86) is mainly green below (no black on throat or breast) and under tail coverts white (not black). ♀ easily told by conspic. white malar.

**Behavior:** A ♀ near Mitú perched and hovered, flycatching, about 2-4m up in shady understory.

**Status and habitat:** K. Von Sneidern collected 13 specimens in w Putumayo, 5 from San Antonio (w of Pto. Asís), 400m, 1969, and 8 from Estación de Bombeo Guamués (near Nariño boundary), 1000 m, 1971 (Fitzpatrick and Willard 1982). Sight rec. of a ♀ about 15km ne of Mitú, Vaupés, 14 Feb 1978 (Hilty and P. Bailey). Interior of tall humid forest at Mitú.

**Range:** To 1000m. W Putumayo and Vaupés (sight rec.); doubtless se Guainía (rec. 40km s on Río Negro, Brazil), prob. also Amazonas. Nw Amazonian Brazil to e Ecuador and e Peru (incl. Pebas and mouth of Río Curaray).

## 86. PINK-THROATED BRILLIANT
*Heliodoxa gularis*　　　　Map 446

**Identification:** 4.5″ (11.4cm). Bill almost straight (1.1″, or 28mm). ♂: *mainly shining green*; median stripe on forecrown glittering green; *patch on lower throat glittering pinkish red*; belly gray contrasting with *white under tail coverts*; leg tufts

white; tail rather long, *forked*, bronzy green. ♀: like ♂ but throat patch smaller, outer tail feathers sometimes narrowly tipped white.

**Similar species:** See Black-throated Brilliant (85). Very rare Blue-tufted Starthroat (138) has longer bill, ♂ mostly glittering blue below, ♀ grayish disked green below.

**Status and habitat:** A specimen (FMNH) was collected by Von Sneidern at Estación de Bombeo Guamués, w Putumayo (near Nariño boundary), 900m, 1971 (Fitzpatrick and Willard 1982). Lower montane forest. This is prob. the 1st authentic rec. for Colombia. The rec. at Leticia, Amazonas, is very suspect. In Ecuador and Peru this sp. occurs on the e slope in the upper tropical or subtropical zone.

**Range:** 900m (prob. higher). E slope of Andes in w Putumayo. (Leticia, Amazonas?). Ne Ecuador and adj. ne Peru (near Lurimaguas, Loreta).

**Note:** Violet-chested Hummingbird (*Sternoclyta cyanopectus*) of n and nw Venez. s to Táchira on Colombian boundary may occur in Norte de Santander. Large (4.5″). ♂ mainly green with glittering green gorget and large *violet patch on breast*; slightly forked bronzy olive tail tipped buffy white. ♀: above like ♂, underparts grayish white thickly spotted green; *belly unspotted rufous buff*; small white malar streak and white postocular spot; slightly forked tail greenish black, narrowly tipped white. Bill noticeably long (1.2″) and *decurved* in both sexes. Humid forest and ravines; foothills to 1900m in Venez.

## 87. FIERY TOPAZ
*Topaza pyra*　　Pl. 14, Ill. 67, Map 447

**Identification:** ♂ 7.5″ (19cm); ♀ 6″ (15cm). Bill rather short for size of bird (1″, or 25mm), thick, slightly decurved; *leg tufts black*. ♂ unmistakable: top and sides of head black; gorget glittering golden green bordered black; otherwise mainly fiery orange red; upper and under tail coverts and central tail feathers golden green, *rest of tail purplish* with 2 long feathers *protruding about 2.5″ (64mm) and crossing near tip; under wing coverts rufous chestnut.* ♀: shining green above; gorget glittering *coppery red* bordered gold; lower underparts glittering green; tail mostly purplish black edged cinnamon, none of feathers appreciably lengthened; *under wing coverts chestnut.* Both sexes *often look blackish* in field and many ♂ ♂ often lack elongated tail feathers; others (juvs.?) with long tails are mostly green.

**Similar species:** Closely resembles Crimson Topaz (see note). ♀ from other hummingbirds by *very large size*, heavy slightly drooping

67. Fiery Topaz (♂)

bill, and in good light coppery red throat (may look black or rufous in poor light); note chestnut wing linings.

**Behavior:** Feed at flowers in forest mid. story or canopy, sometimes much lower inside or at edge of forest; 1 hovered in open 8-15m up at edge for insects near Mitú (Hilty). In e Ecuador a ♀ 1-3m up on dead branch along blackwater creek (R. Ridgely).

**Breeding:** Apr nest low over blackwater stream, e Ecuador (P. Alden), same area ♀ off 2 eggs in cup attached to partially submerged limb, 1 m over stream, Aug (Hilty); nests of related Crimson Topaz in Brazil placed ca. 1 m above small clear streams (Ruschi 1979).

**Status and habitat:** Rare. Humid sandy-belt forest. The few Colombian recs. are from the rocky cerro-dotted, blackwater region of e Vaupés. Elsewhere reported in sim. habitat, esp. in rocky areas near small streams and waterfalls.

**Range:** To 300m. E Vaupés (Río Vaupés opp. Tahuapunto, Brazil; sight at Mitú); prob. e Guainía and the cerros of w Vaupés and e Caquetá. S Venez, nw Brazil (Río Negro), e Ecuador, and adj. n Peru (incl. mouth of Río Curaray).

**Note 1:** Crimson Topaz (*T. pella*) of se Venez., the Guianas, ne Brazil, and e Ecuador (Río Suno) may also occur in Colombia. Very like

Fiery Topaz, either sex can be told by *white* (not black) leg tufts and *outer 3 tail feathers rufous* (no rufous in ♂ Fiery Topaz, only outer web of outer feather rufous in ♀); ♂ also differs in hand in having base of secondaries rufous (both spp. have rufous wing linings). **Note 2:** *T. pyra* is sometimes considered a subsp. of *T. pella*, but the 2 may overlap in e Ecuador (Norton 1965).

### 88. WHITE-TAILED HILLSTAR
*Urochroa bougueri*  Pl. 15, Map 448
**Identification:** 4.5″ (11.4cm). Bill rather long (1.2″, or 30mm) and almost straight. Above coppery green with conspic. *rufous malar; throat and upper breast glittering blue;* belly brownish gray; central pair and outermost tail feathers dusky bronze, *rest white edged dusky bronze.* Or very different: bronzy green above; no rufous malar; central tail feathers bronzy, *rest white edged dusky bronze (leucura).*

**Similar species:** ♂ Mountain Velvetbreast (91) has somewhat sim. tail pattern (flashes much white), but is smaller, and underparts green and black (not blue). Buff-tailed Coronet (103) flashes buff (not white) tail. Also see Collared Inca (96) and *esp.* on Pac. slope, Velvet-purple Coronet (105).

**Behavior:** An attractive hummingbird that probes flowers, usually 2-10m up inside forest or at edges and is often seen flycatching in partially shaded forest openings. Alone or frequently in pairs and often quite confiding.

**Status and habitat:** Fairly common in humid and wet forest ("cloud forest") and shrubby forest borders in highlands. Marked seasonal el. movements in W Andes.

**Range:** Mainly 1500-2500m; to 500m on Pacific slope (photo, Anchicayá Val.—Hilty). Pacific slope from headwaters of Río San Juan (Cerro Tatamá) southward; e slope W Andes in Valle (Pichindé Val.) and prob. elsewhere (*bougueri*); e slope of Andes in Nariño (*leucura*) and sight rec. in Caquetá (7 Sept 1978—Hilty). Colombia, e and w Ecuador, and n Peru.

### 89. [GIANT HUMMINGBIRD]
*Patagona gigas*
**Identification:** 7.5″ (19cm). Bill straight (1.6″, or 41mm) and heavy. Unmistakable. *The largest hummingbird.* Dull olive brown above; dingy cinnamon buff below with *conspic. white rump and under tail coverts;* throat and chest sometimes mottled or spotted white; tail dark olive, *noticeably forked.* Juv. has grayish underparts, sometimes speckled on throat.

**Voice:** Call a high-pitched strained *eeep* at intervals.

**Behavior:** A large conspic. hummingbird that flies and hovers with slow, batlike wing beats. Attracted to agave flowers (Ortiz-Crespo 1974) and to the flowers of *Lobelia* sp. but also hawks many insects.
**Status and habitat:** Hypothetical. One sight rec. at Ipiales, Nariño (2900m), Apr 1978 (D. Bailey). Prob. reg., at least seasonally, in extreme s Nariño. In n Ecuador, chiefly 2000-3000m rarely to 3300m (the el. limits of agave). Favors dry agave-dominated Andean tableland and canyons with shrubs and brush, also hedges near habitations. Breeding not proved in n Ecuador and occurrence there may correspond to flowering season of agave.
**Range:** Extreme s Colombia to Tierra del Fuego (s birds migratory).

## 90. SHINING SUNBEAM

*Aglaeactis cupripennis*          Pl. 16, Map 449
**Identification:** 4.5″ (11.4cm). Bill straight (0.7″, or 18mm). A large mainly cinnamon rufous hummingbird found near treeline. *Crown and center of back blackish olive* gradually becoming glittering rosy violet (hard to see) on lower back and glittering golden green on rump; otherwise *mostly cinnamon rufous* incl. under wing coverts and outer web of outer primary; central tail feathers mostly bronze olive, rest *cinnamon rufous*. ♀: sim. but duller with smaller glittering patch on back.
**Similar species:** Only mostly cinnamon hummingbird in its range.
**Voice:** Sharp *chirp*s in flight; *tseep, tsit-tsit* when foraging (J. Silliman).
**Behavior:** A characteristic timberline hummingbird. Usually conspic., notably aggressive, and strongly intraspecifically territorial (J. Silliman). Habitually clings briefly with wings held vertically in a V as it feeds at low flowers; also reg. flycatches small flying insects. Sometimes glides short distances down slopes on outstretched wings.
**Breeding:** Building nest about 8m up on horizontal branch, 22 Mar, PN Puracé (Brown); July nest 1.3m up in shrub at forest edge, s Ecuador (R. Ridgely). 6 BC birds, Feb–Aug, C and E Andes (Carriker).
**Status and habitat:** Patchy in distribution but locally common in stunted woodland borders, tall brush, and gardens in ecotonal areas between paramo and upper montane forest; sometimes dense clumps of shrubs and short trees in paramo.
**Range:** 2900-3400m (prob. higher). W Andes from Cauca southward; C Andes from Valle southward; E Andes from c Norte de Santan-

der (7°50′N) s to Cundinamarca. Colombia s in Andes to s Peru.

## 91. MOUNTAIN VELVETBREAST

*Lafresnaya lafresnayi*          Pl. 15, Map 450
**Identification:** 3.5″ (8.9cm). Bill strongly *decurved* (1.0″, or 25mm) and slender. ♂: shining green above; throat, chest, and sides glittering green; *center of breast and belly velvety black*; central tail feathers green, *rest white tipped blackish* (or buff tipped blackish—*lafresnayi*). ♀: shining green above; throat and breast *buffy spotted green*; lower underparts buffy white; *tail like* ♂.
**Similar species:** Best marks are decurved bill and large blocks of flashing white on each side of tail. See White-tailed Hillstar (88), Collared Inca (96; white throat), and Velvet-purple Coronet (105). ♀ recalls Buff-tailed Coronet (103), esp. in E and C Andes but lacks latter's conspic. buff under wing coverts, and habits are different.
**Behavior:** ♂ ♂ frequently hold territories, ♀ ♀ most often "trap-line"; both feed mostly low at flowers with long corolla tubes that fit their curved bills (Snow and Snow 1980). Crown often conspic. dusted with pollen.
**Breeding:** Several young birds, May, San Lorenzo (2200m), Santa Marta Mts. (T. B. Johnson); BC ♀, Sept, W Andes (Carriker).
**Status and habitat:** Often common in humid and wet mt. forest, esp. along shrubby forest borders, but shows marked seasonal movements; at San Lorenzo in Santa Marta Mts., abundant Jan–Mar, absent early Aug–late Nov (T. B. Johnson). Generally found at higher el. and less numerous in Andes than in Santa Marta Mts.
**Range:** 1500-3700m (mainly 2000-3000m). Santa Marta Mts. (*liriope*); Perijá Mts., E Andes (s Santander and Cundinamarca), C Andes s to Valle and e slope in sw Huila (*lafresnayi*); W Andes, w slope C Andes from Cauca s to both slopes of Nariño (*saül*). Nw Venez. s in Andes to Peru.

## 92. GREAT SAPPHIREWING

*Pterophanes cyanopterus*          Pl. 16, Ill. 68,
          Map 451
**Identification:** 6.4″ (16.3cm). *Very large*. Bill straight (1.2″, or 30mm) and rather heavy. ♂: *dark shining blue green above and below*, underparts strongly bluish; *upper and under wing coverts and inner webs of primaries shining blue*, long tail (2.7″ or 69mm), *deeply forked*, outer feathers greenish black. ♀: shining green above, forecrown dusky gray; *wing coverts blue* as in ♂ but primaries with much less blue; *under-*

68. Great Sapphirewing (♂ top), Sword-billed Hummingbird (bottom)

*parts cinnamon rufous*; sides and under tail coverts disked green; *deeply forked tail* greenish black edged grayish white.

**Similar species:** Very large size and slow wing beats are distinctive. In both sexes the wings conspic. flash blue when hovering. Only Giant Hummingbird (different habitat) is larger. ♀ recalls ♀ Golden-bellied (98) and ♀ Blue-throated starfrontlets (100) but from either by larger size, shorter heavier bill, bluish shoulders, and deeply forked tail.

**Behavior:** A spectacular hummingbird, usually seen hovering with slow batlike wing beats. Feeds mostly at flowers at low to mod. ht., either by hovering, clinging momentarily, or perching to feed. Usually alone and territorial but frequently attracted to mixed flocks of highland tanagers, flower-piercers, and warblers; may also "trap-line" flowers.

**Breeding:** BC ♂, Feb, Puracé (Carriker).

**Status and habitat:** Fairly common locally in stunted forest borders, shrubby slopes, elfin woodland/paramo ecotone, and to scattered trees and bushes well into paramo.

**Range:** 2600-3600m (usually above 3000m). E Andes in Norte de Santander (w of Cúcuta) and Cundinamarca; C Andes from n Tolima southward. Colombia s in Andes to Bolivia.

[*Coeligena*: Characteristic of highlands; long, straight, almost needlelike bill; most with small white spot behind eye; mostly "trap-line" low to mod. ht. flowers of forest interior or edge, hover at them without clinging.]

## 93. BRONZY INCA
*Coeligena coeligena*                Pl. 15, Map 452

**Identification:** 4.5" (11.4cm). Bill very long (1.4" or 36mm) and straight. Mostly dark purplish bronze above, a little greener on lower back; *throat and chest dingy white spotted and streaked dusky*; rest of underparts dark rufous brown to grayish; under tail coverts edged cinnamon; bronze tail slightly forked.

**Similar species:** Brown Inca (94) is almost completely brown above and below with prom. white patch on each side of chest. Brown Violetear (27) has shorter bill, cinnamon orange rump, and violet cheek patch. Also see rare Black Inca (95).

**Behavior:** "Trap-lines" mostly flowers of the mid. or lower story inside forest, less frequently along borders. Sometimes gathers with violetears and others at canopy of large flowering trees where holds temporary territories. Esp. fond of long tubular red flowers (i.e., *Cavendishia, Fuchsia*, etc.)

**Breeding:** 1 nest 1 m up in sapling inside forest, 19 Jan, Finca Merenberg, Huila (Ridgely and Gaulin 1980); ♀ ready to lay, 9 May, Cundinamarca (Olivares 1969a); 5 BC birds, Mar–Nov, Perijá Mts., E and C Andes (Carriker).

**Status and habitat:** Fairly common to seasonally common in humid and wet montane forest and forest borders. Strong seasonal movements in some areas. Largely replaced on Pacific slope by Brown Inca (the 2 spp. do not normally occur together).

**Range:** 1500–2600m. Perijá Mts., both slopes of E Andes in Norte de Santander and w slope in s Cundinamarca and e Huila, e slope in Nariño (sightings 2-3 June 1981—Hilty et al.), and W and C Andes s to Cauca and sw Huila (few Pacific slope rec.). N Venez. s in mts. to Bolivia.

## 94. BROWN INCA
*Coeligena wilsoni*            Pl. 16, Map 453
**Identification:** 4.3″ (10.9cm). Bill long (1.3″ or 33mm), slender, and straight. Looks mostly dark brown in field. Reddish bronze above becoming more olive on lower back; *mostly dull brown* below with amethyst patch on center throat and *conspic. white patch on each side of chest*; bronze tail slightly forked. ♀ has smaller throat patch.

**Similar species:** See Bronzy Inca (93) and Brown Violetear (27).

**Behavior:** Stays low in forest, often in thick undergrowth where it feeds at tubular flowers, mainly by "trap-lining." Usually alone and apparently does not gather at flowering trees with other hummingbirds. Often remarkably confiding.

**Status and habitat:** Wet montane forest ("cloud forest"), or at thick forest borders. Replaces Bronzy Inca below about 1800m on Pacific slope. Common at 1000-1300m (esp. above Junín, Nariño), generally uncommon at higher or lower el. throughout range.

**Range:** 700–1900m (usually above 1000m). Pacific slope from sources of Río San Juan (Cerro Tatamá) southward. W Colombia and w Ecuador.

## 95. BLACK INCA
*Coeligena prunellei*            Pl. 16, Map 454
**Identification:** 4.3″ (10.9cm). Bill long (1.2″, or 30mm), straight, and slender. Much like Brown Inca. *Mainly black with conspic. white patch on each side of chest*; shoulders glittering blue; small throat patch glittering greenish blue; under tail coverts edged white; tail black and forked; feet rosy red.

**Similar species:** Easily told in range by white pectoral patches.

**Voice:** Rarely an *ick* when feeding (Snow and Snow 1980).

**Behavior:** Mainly a "trap-lining" nectar feeder, but territories occas. defended; lower midlevels to canopy; favors spp. of pendent flowers with long corolla tubes, esp. vines and climbers (Snow and Snow 1980).

**Status and habitat:** Humid montane forest. Status unknown. Found in nos. on Cerro Carare (9km ese of Toqui, Boyacá) below 2400m (Snow and Snow 1980), but these are the only recent recs. An E Andean replacement of Brown Inca.

**Range:** ENDEMIC. 1400-2600m. Known only on w slope E Andes from se Santander (Virolín, 6°05′N) and w Boyacá (Toqui nw of Tunjá) s to w Cundinamarca (nw of Bogotá at Facatativá, Laguna de Pedropalo, Albán, La Vega, Yacopí and Guaduas, latter perhaps at 1000m?).

## 96. COLLARED INCA
*Coeligena torquata*            Pl. 16, Map 455
**Identification:** 4.5″ (11.4cm). Bill long (1.3″, or 33mm), straight, and slender. Large and showy. ♂: mainly black or blackish green with *large triangular white band across lower throat and chest*; central tail feathers greenish black, *rest white tipped black* (or sim. but *general plumage shining green* with glittering green crown and upper throat; tail tipped golden green—*conradi*). In the hand shows glittering violet to blue crown spot. ♀: like ♂ but shining green, upper throat spotted green (or upper throat buff—*conradi*), and belly gray disked green; no crown patch.

**Similar species:** Only Colombian hummingbird with contrasting white throat band and flashing white on tail.

**Behavior:** An active and silent "trap-lining" nectar feeder. Darts and flashes among low forest shrubbery or at edges; hovers at length below pendent flowers with long corollas, esp. vines, climbers, and shrubs such as *Cavendishia*. Attracted to mixed flocks.

**Breeding:** Nest building under ferns on rock cliff, 25 Nov, Finca Merenberg, Huila (Brown); 9 BC birds, Mar–Aug, C and E Andes (Carriker).

**Status and habitat:** Common and widespread in humid and wet montane forest and shrubby forest borders. Mostly replaced below 2200m by Bronzy Inca, but both sometimes sympatric in zones of contact (i.e., Finca Merenberg—Ridgely and Gaulin 1980; Chapman 1917).

**Range:** 1500-3000m (mainly 2200-2700m). All 3 Andean ranges (*torquata*); e slope E Andes in Norte de Santander (*conradi*). Nw Venez. s in Andes to n Bolivia.

**Note:** Lilac-spotted Starfrontlet (*C. traviesi*), known from "Bogotá" specimens, may be a hybrid of *C. torquata* and an unknown sp. 4. 5″; bill 1.3″. Specimens var. ♂: mostly black above, glittering dark green below; frontlet glittering and wing coverts shining bluish green; rump coppery purple; glittering violet spot on green throat; white chest patch; forked tail bronze green. Some birds uniform shining green above, upper tail coverts greenest.

### 97. WHITE-TAILED STARFRONTLET
*Coeligena phalerata*              Pl. 16, Map 456
**Identification:** 4.4″ (11.2cm). Bill long (1.2″, or 30 mm), straight, and slender. ♂: *mainly shining dark green above*, crown glittering green becoming somewhat glittering light blue rearward; *underparts glittering green*; patch on lower throat glittering violet; *under tail coverts and rounded tail pure white*, tail sometimes with dusky tip. ♀: shining green above, crown somewhat glittering; *underparts cinnamon rufous* more or less disked green on sides; tail bronze, outer feathers tipped buff.
**Similar species:** Unmistakable in limited range.
**Voice:** A pebbly twittering when foraging.
**Behavior:** Much like Bronzy and Collared incas. Usually seen darting and flashing among low shrubbery. Notably pugnacious and territorial, although at times believed to "trapline" rather widely spaced flowers (T. B. Johnson).
**Breeding:** 9 BC birds, Feb–Apr (Carriker).
**Status and habitat:** Usually common in humid and wet montane forest and shrubby forest borders. ♂♂ favor small breaks or openings inside forest, ♀♀ more along borders where appear to outnumber ♂♂, but much overlap. Near San Lorenzo (2200m) least numerous during 1st part of wet season, May–Sept (T. B. Johnson). May occupy broader el. range than *Coeligena* allies of Andes.
**Range:** ENDEMIC. 1400-3300m. Santa Marta Mts.

### 98. GOLDEN-BELLIED STARFRONTLET
*Coeligena bonapartei*             Pl. 15, Map 457
**Identification:** 4.3″ (10.9cm). Bill long (1.2″, or 30mm), straight, and slender. ♂: frontlet glittering green, rest of crown black; upper back shining dark green; *rump golden orange*; gorget and breast glittering green; *lower underparts glittering fiery gold*; tail slightly forked, golden bronze; wings dusky (with broad rufous band—*consita*). ♀: shining green above becoming *golden orange on rump; mostly cinnamon below*, breast mixed green, sides of throat spotted green, belly spotted glittering fiery gold; tail bronze, sometimes with buff tips.
**Similar species:** As with Blue-throated Starfrontlet (100) can look very dark in the field. Best marks for either sex are long straight bill and conspic. golden orange rump.
**Behavior:** Hovers for insects or feeds at tubular flowers around outer edge of med. to tall bushes (A. Gast).
**Breeding:** 1 BC ♂, 8 Nov, Cundinamarca, 3000m (MCN).
**Status and habitat:** Uncommon and local in humid forest borders. Not well known in Colombia.
**Range:** 2150-3000m. Perijá Mts. (above Hiroca—*consita*); E Andes from Boyacá (Arcabuca; Leiva) s to Bogotá area near Fusagasugá (*bonapartei*). Andes of nw Venez. (1400-3200m) and ne Colombia.

### 99. DUSKY STARFRONTLET
*Coeligena orina*
**Identification:** 4.3″ (10.9cm). Bill long (1.3″ or 33mm), straight, and slender. ♂: *uniform dark shining green incl. tail*, feathers of crown edged black; spot on throat glittering blue. ♀: unknown.
**Status and habitat:** Rare. Known from 1 specimen. Forest border below open paramo (Carriker 1954). Its only known locality is on e side of PN Las Orquideas.
**Range:** ENDEMIC. Temperate zone (3200m) at n end of W Andes (Páramo de Frontino above Urrao, Antioquia).

### 100. BLUE-THROATED STARFRONTLET
*Coeligena helianthea*             Pl. 15, Map 458
**Identification:** 4.4″ (11.2cm). Bill long (1.3″, or 33mm), straight, and slender. ♂ looks *very black* in the field. Mainly black to greenish black; frontlet glittering green; *upper tail coverts glittering aquamarine*; throat patch glittering violet blue; *belly glittering rose*; slightly forked tail bronzy black. ♀: greenish black above with glittering *aquamarine upper tail coverts; mostly cinnamon below*, sides spotted green, belly spotted glittering rose.
**Similar species:** ♂ is spectacular in very good light, but colors usually difficult to see in field. Blue green rump and rosy belly (either sex) is diagnostic. Golden-bellied Starfrontlet (98) has golden orange rump and belly. Rare Black Inca (95) has white pectoral tufts. Cf. ♀ with ♀ Great Sapphirewing (92).
**Behavior:** As in others of the genus. "Traplines" low flowers and is often attracted to mixed spp. flocks.

**Breeding:** 1 BC ♀, May, Perijá Mts.; 1 in Aug, Santander (Carriker).
**Status and habitat:** Locally fairly common in humid forest, adj. borders, and on shrubby slopes or around hedges and flower gardens near habitations. Often in garden of Simon Bolívar's house (open to public) in Bogotá. Tolerates or will occur in more open or bushier terrain than other *Coeligena* in Colombia.
**Range:** 1900-3300m (mostly 2400-2900m). Perijá Mts. and both slopes from Norte de Santander s to Cundinamarca (Bogotá area). Andes of w Venez. (sw Táchira) and ne Colombia.

### 101. BUFF-WINGED STARFRONTLET
*Coeligena lutetiae*                      Pl. 16, Map 459
**Identification:** 4.4″ (11.2cm). Bill long (1.3″, or 33mm), straight, and slender. ♂: *mostly velvety black above with large cinnamon buff patch on secondaries and tertials* (obvious in flight or at rest); frontlet and underparts dark glittering green; small blue violet spot on throat, slightly forked tail bronzy black. ♀: dark shining green above; frontlet glittering green; *wing patch buff; throat cinnamon* (usually with obscure glittering blue spot); rest of underparts golden green; forked tail bronzy green.
**Similar species:** Only temperate zone hummingbird with a conspic. buff tertial patch. In the Perijá Mts. cf. Golden-bellied Starfrontlet (98), which has rufous wing band.
**Voice:** Flight call a strained, nasal *eernt*, distinctive.
**Behavior:** A dark and attractive hummingbird usually seen singly at eye level or lower near shrubby woodland borders. Chiefly a nectar feeder, either hovering or clinging momentarily to probe flowers. Notably territorial and often perches near the flowers from which it feeds.
**Breeding:** BC ♂, Feb, Puracé (Carriker).
**Status and habitat:** Uncommon (perhaps somewhat patchily distributed) in humid and wet montane forest, shrubby forest borders, and stunted woodland near timberline.
**Range:** 2600-3600m (usually above 3000m). W slope of C Andes from Caldas (e of Manizales) southward through Nariño and on e slope of C Andes in Cauca (PN Puracé). C Colombia s in Andes to e and w Ecuador and n Peru.

### 102. SWORD-BILLED HUMMINGBIRD
*Ensifera ensifera*                     Ill. 68, Map 460
**Identification:** ♂ 5.5″ (14cm); ♀ 5″ (13cm). *Bill enormously long* (about 4″ or 102mm in ♂; 4.7″ or 119mm in ♀), *rather heavy, and slightly upturned*. ♂: head coppery bronze, incl. feathers covering base of bill; otherwise bronze green

above; throat blackish, sides of throat and chest glittering green; rest of underparts shining green; tail forked, bronze green. ♀: above like ♂, below white, throat spotted olive, rest of underparts heavily speckled green; tail edged grayish white.
**Voice:** Call a low guttural *trrr*.
**Behavior:** Usually seen singly in mid. or upper levels of trees. Perches with bill angled sharply upward. Hovers at flowers, characteristically probing upward from below. Favors spp. of *Passiflora* (passion flowers) and *Datura*, which it often "trap-lines" along reg. routes. Also occas. takes insects by hawking.
**Breeding:** 2 BC ♂♂, Feb–Mar, sw Huila (Carriker). In Ecuador mossy cup hung among root fibers, usually high above ground, 1 inside an occupied hut in paramo (Ruschi 1973).
**Status and habitat:** Uncommon and perhaps local in humid and wet montane forest, forest borders, shrubby slopes, and scattered stunted trees or patches of tall brush in temperate forest/paramo ecotone. Abundance apparently correlated with that of spp. of *Passiflora*. In PN Puracé shows some el. movements.
**Range:** 1700-3300m (mainly 2400-3100m). All 3 Andean ranges (in W Andes n to Cerro Tatamá, n Valle; C Andes n to Quindío). The Andes from Venez. to n Bolivia.

[*Boissonneaua*: Heavy-bodied and short-billed; under wing coverts cinnamon or chestnut; often hold up wings in V; lower highlands.]

### 103. BUFF-TAILED CORONET
*Boissonneaua flavescens*          Pl. 15, Map 461
**Identification:** 4.5″ (11.4cm). Bill mod. short (0.7″, or 18mm), straight, and rather thick. Shining green above; crown and gorget glittering green; breast shining green; belly buff thickly disked green; *under wing coverts cinnamon buff* (conspic. in flight); central tail feathers bronze, *rest creamy buff tipped bronze*. Sexes sim.
**Similar species:** Best marks are cinnamon under wing coverts and creamy tail patches. Mountain Velvetbreast (91) is smaller with decurved bill and different underparts and habits. White-tailed Hillstar (88) has white (not creamy buff) patches in tail. Also cf. Velvetpurple Coronet (105).
**Voice:** Song a ser. of rapid sharp *chip*'s from tree crown (Miller 1963); several may sing from adj. treetops (R. Ridgely).
**Behavior:** Territorial at flowers from midlevel to canopy level; also hawks insects in long sallies from high perches (Snow and Snow 1980) and occas. gathers with other hummingbirds at flowering trees where keeps mainly inside

canopy. Typically clings to flowers when feeding, holding wings up in a V; also holds wings up momentarily when alighting as do others of the genus.
**Breeding:** Downy cup 4m up and near branch tip, 30 July, Pichindé Val., 1600m (Hilty); 6 BC birds, Apr–Aug. W, C, and E Andes (Carriker; Miller 1963).
**Status and habitat:** Fairly common in humid and wet montane forest and forest borders. Replaced on Pacific slope by Velvet-purple Coronet, on e slope E Andes at s end by Chestnut-breasted Coronet.
**Range:** 1400-2800m (once to 850m in w Cundinamarca). All 3 Andean ranges (e slope E Andes definitely only at n end). Nw Venez. s in Andes to w Ecuador.

## 104. CHESTNUT-BREASTED CORONET
*Boissonneaua matthewsii*              Map 462
**Identification:** 4.5″ (11.4cm). Bill mod. short (0.7″, or 18mm), straight, and rather thick. ♂: head and gorget glittering green; otherwise green above and *chestnut below*, central tail feathers coppery green, *rest chestnut tipped and edged green.* ♀: sim., but throat green more or less speckled cinnamon buff.
**Similar species:** Chestnut in tail and on most of underparts is diagnostic. See ♀ Long-tailed Sylph (132). Fawn-breasted Brilliant (81) may overlap range, but is cinnamon buff below (not chestnut), tail is green, and gorget glittering topaz rose (not green).
**Behavior:** Much like Buff-tailed Coronet. Notably pugnacious. Several may congregate at flowering trees (R. Ridgely).
**Status and habitat:** Canopy of humid forest and forest edges; few Colombian records.
**Range:** E slope of Andes at s end in Putumayo and e Nariño. S Colombia, e Eucador (1600-2200m), and e Peru.

## 105. VELVET-PURPLE CORONET
*Boissonneaua jardini*              Pl. 15, Map 463
**Identification:** 4.3″ (10.9cm). Bill rather short (0.7″, or 18mm) and straight. Large and very blackish. ♂: mostly glittering bluish green above; head, throat, and chest black (like "hood"); *frontlet, breast, and lower underparts glittering blue to purple*; throat usually with a little purple; *under wing coverts orange rufous* (conspic.); central tail feathers black, *rest white edged and tipped black.* ♀: duller; breast and belly mixed with buff.
**Similar species:** White-tailed Hillstar (88) and Mountain Velvetbreast (91) flash white in tail but lack rufous under wing coverts; Hillstar also has longer thinner bill, green underparts (including frontlet), rufous malar (in west),

and *no black edge* on sides of tail. Buff-tailed Coronet (103) has buff (not white) in tail and is mostly green below.
**Voice:** Song weak whistles and sharp shrill notes, *si siii, si, sii, siii* (Ruschi 1973).
**Behavior:** Rather like Buff-tailed Coronet but mostly at mid. hts. or lower. As with other *Boissonneaua,* holds wings up momentarily upon alighting. In display ♂ circles ♀, alights, sings, and then buzzes from side to side with fanned tail (Ruschi 1973).
**Breeding:** Moss and lichen-covered down cup on horizontal branch or thin fork in Ecuador (Ruschi 1973).
**Status and habitat:** Uncommon and very local in wet mossy forest, forest borders, and brushy clearings in foothills and lower slopes. Most readily found in w Nariño near Junín, 900-1000 m.
**Range:** 350-2200m. Pacific slope from Río San Juan headwaters (Cerro Tatamá) southward. W Colombia and nw Ecuador.

[*Heliangelus:* Straight bill; ♂♂ with glittering gorget and broad light crescent on chest (except 109); ♀♀ with rusty spotted throat and dark-bordered pale crescent on chest (except 109); highlands; hold up wings momentarily upon alighting.]

## 106. ORANGE-THROATED SUNANGEL
*Heliangelus mavors*              Pl. 15, Map 464
**Identification:** 3.7″ (9.4cm). Bill rather short (0.6″, or 15mm) and straight. ♂; shining green above; *frontlet and gorget glittering golden orange* bordered on sides of head and neck with black and *below by a broad buff pectoral band*; narrow breast band green; *rest of underparts buff*, sides heavily spotted green, tail bronze green with pale tips. ♀: sim., but *throat buff* speckled rufous brown.
**Similar species:** Recalls Amethyst-throated Sunangel (107), but either sex by buff (not white) pectoral band; ♂ additionally by orange throat.
**Behavior:** Apparently sim. to Amethyst-throated Sunangel. Raises wings vertically for a moment when alighting.
**Status and habitat:** Humid montane forest borders, shrubby pastures, and open slopes with brush and scattered trees. Little known in Colombia.
**Range:** Upper subtropical and temperate zone. E slope of E Andes at n end (Páramo de Portachuelo and Zumbador, Norte de Santander) s to e Boyacá (1 seen, 14 Feb 1977, e of Lago Tota—R. Ridgely). Andes of nw Venez. (2000-3200m) and adj. ne Colombia.

## 107. AMETHYST-THROATED SUNANGEL

*Heliangelus amethysticollis*        Pl. 15, Map 465
**Identification:** 3.7″ (9.4cm). Bill rather short (0.7″, or 18mm) and straight. ♂: shining green above, crown purplish (or crown dull green—*clarisse*); narrow frontlet blue green (inconspic. in field); *gorget and foreneck glittering rosy amethyst*, bordered on sides of head and neck by black and *below by broad white crescentic chest band*; narrow band across breast glittering green; flanks dull green; rest of underparts grayish buff, central tail feathers bronze green, rest blue black. ♀: sim., but throat rusty, obscurely flecked blackish, sometimes a little rose on lower throat.
**Similar species:** See Orange-throated Sunangel (106).
**Behavior:** Territorial, mostly low (0.6-6m up) near cover inside or at edge of forest. Hawks insects in short sallies from low perch, and often holds wings up when alighting; frequently active around mixed flocks (Snow and Snow 1980; Hilty).
**Breeding:** 11 BC birds, May–Aug, Perijá Mts. and Santander (Carriker).
**Status and habitat:** Fairly common in humid montane forest, forest edges, and brushy second growth; fond of damp bushy ravines.
**Range:** 2000-3000m. Perijá Mts. (*violiceps*); E Andes from Norte de Santander s to latitude of Bogotá (*clarisse*); Páramo de Tamá, se Norte de Santander (*verdiscutatus*). W Venez. s in mts. to n Bolivia.
**Note:** Birds from w Venez. and ne Colombia, *H. clarisse* (Longuemare's Sunangel), are sometimes considered a separate sp. from *H. amethysticollis* (Amethyst-throated Sunangel) of Ecuador and Peru.

## 108. GORGETED SUNANGEL

*Heliangelus strophianus*
**Identification:** 3.7″ (9.4cm). Bill short (0.6″, or 15mm) and straight. *Much like Amethyst-throated Sunangel.* ♂ differs mainly in broader green breast band (lower underparts mostly green); belly mainly grayish buff (not gray); tail longer (44-50 vs 40-44mm), dark steel blue (not bronze green), and perhaps more forked (not more or less square). ♀: practically identical to ♀ Amethyst-throated Hummingbird, but tail dark blue instead of bronzy green, and throat with traces of white. In both sexes feathers of forehead grow over base of bill covering nostrils (nostrils exposed in Amethyst-throated Hummingbird).
**Similar species:** In limited range likely confused only with Purple-throated Woodstar (139) which is smaller, has chestnut sides and

belly band, and prom. white flank patch, ♀ woodstar also has white throat.
**Behavior:** In Ecuador usually seen singly at low flowers and near cover. Like Amethyst-throated Sunangel seems to favor damp bushy ravines. As in others of the genus holds wings up momentarily upon alighting.
**Status and habitat:** Humid and wet montane forest, shrubby forest borders, and thickets in Ecuador.
**Range:** Known from 2 "Bogotá" skins in Colombia, apparently from Nariño. W Ecuador (1200-2800m) n to within 20km of Colombia (San Gabriel).

## 109. TOURMALINE SUNANGEL

*Heliangelus exortis*        Pl. 15, Map 466
**Identification:** 4″ (10.2cm). Bill short (0.6″, or 15mm) and straight. ♂: entirely shining green above, frontlet glittering green; *gorget glittering violet blue; large patch on lower throat rose*; breast glittering green; lower underparts dusky gray disked green; *under tail coverts white* (conspic.); *long ample tail decidedly forked*, central feathers bronze green, rest purplish black. ♀: bronze green above, forecrown glittering green; *throat and under tail coverts white*; breast glittering green becoming buffy white disked green on belly; tail like ♂, shorter and less forked. Juv. ♂: throat white disked violet and rose; some (ad. ♀ or juv.) have *greenish gray* breast.
**Similar species:** ♂ might recall Greenish Puffleg (118) but is larger with shorter bill, colored gorget (not always conspic.), and white under tail coverts. Note the long tail. Pufflegs have prom. leg puffs. ♀ nearest ♀ trainbearers (121, 122) and ♀ Purple-backed Thornbill (123), but tail shorter and less forked, and throat white; 123 has much shorter bill.
**Behavior:** Chiefly a flower feeder, usually clinging momentarily to them with wings outstretched in a V while feeding. Like other *Heliangelus*, also holds wings up, or flicks them up briefly when alighting. Forages rather low in open or shrubby areas or forest borders and perches on outer perimeter or on top of bushes; lower levels to subcanopy inside forest; notably territorial.
**Breeding:** 7 BC birds, Mar–Aug, W and C Andes (Carriker); courtship display July, sw Huila (Ridgely and Gaulin 1980).
**Status and habitat:** Locally fairly common in humid and wet forest borders, bushy forest clearings, shrubby pastures, and hedges. One of the most common hummers at 2400m in w Putumayo.
**Range:** 1500-3400m (usually above 2300m). All

3 Andean ranges; in E Andes only rec. in w Cundinamarca. Colombia, e Ecuador to n Peru.

[*Eriocnemis*: High el. only; straight bill; portions of plumage usually highly metallic and/or glittering; very large white (or black) leg puffs give charming "booted" look.]

## 110. GLOWING PUFFLEG
*Eriocnemis vestitus*          Pl. 15, Map 467
**Identification:** 3.5" (8.9cm). Bill rather short (0.7", or 18mm) and straight. ♂: dark shining green above becoming *glittering metallic emerald green on rump*; mostly glittering green below *with small violet throat spot; under tail coverts glittering violet; large leg puffs white*, forked tail blue black. ♀: shining green above with glittering golden green rump; narrow buff malar; *throat and breast buff thickly disked glittering purple on throat, green on breast*; rest of underparts whitish heavily mixed white and green; *leg puffs white;* tail like ♂, shorter.
**Similar species:** Easily confused. ♂ shares glittering violet under tail coverts with Turquoise-throated (111), Sapphire-vented (112), and Coppery-bellied pufflegs (113) and is almost identical to 111 (see); 112 is larger, decidedly longer-tailed, and has bluish forecrown; 113 has coppery orange (not green) belly. Golden-breasted Puffleg (114) is much larger. ♀ Glowing Puffleg is *only* puffleg showing buff below.
**Behavior:** As its name implies, its rich, breathtaking colors seem to glow in good light. Hovers or clings momentarily at low flowers on the outside of shrubbery. Pugnacious and territorial and does not gather in groups at flowering trees. May raise wings briefly on alighting.
**Breeding:** 3 BC birds, late June, se Antioquia (Carriker).
**Status and habitat:** Fairly common in upper montane forest borders, overgrown highland pastures, and in shrubby ecotonal areas between woodland and paramo. Often readily found near Termales de San Juan in PN Puracé.
**Range:** 2250-3850m (mainly 2700-3500m). W Andes at n end (Paramillo Mts.; Frontino, 3850m), C Andes in Antioquia (Páramo Sonsón) and s Huila to e Nariño; E Andes s to Cundinamarca. Nw Venez. to e Ecuador and n Peru.

## 111. TURQUOISE-THROATED PUFFLEG
*Eriocnemis godini*
**Identification:** 3.6" (9.1cm). Bill straight (0.7", or 18mm). *Very sim. to ♂ Glowing Puffleg.* Dark shining green above, rump glittering green;

underparts glittering green becoming golden green on belly; *diffused central throat spot glittering blue* (usually faint); under tail coverts glittering violet, large leg puffs white, tail forked, blue black. Sexes sim.
**Similar species:** Doubtfully separable in field from ♂ Glowing Puffleg (110) but perhaps slightly larger, more golden green below, and throat spot blue (not violet), more diffused, and fainter (or virtually lacking).
**Status and habitat:** Little known. Perhaps overlooked due to similarity with Glowing Puffleg.
**Range:** Known only from "Bogotá" specimens in Colombia. Poss. s of Pasto in s Nariño. Nw Ecuador at 2100-2300m (Guaillabamba n of Quito but no recent recs.).
**Note:** Not certainly an authentic sp.

## 112. SAPPHIRE-VENTED (LONG-TAILED) PUFFLEG
*Eriocnemis luciani*          Pl. 15, Map 468
**Identification:** 4.5" (11.4cm). Bill straight, slightly longer (0.8", or 20mm) than others of the genus. Almost entirely dark shining green; more glittering and golden green below; *forecrown shining blue;* under tail coverts glittering violet; leg puffs white; *tail blue black, decidedly long* (2.2", or 56mm), *ample, and forked.* Sexes sim.
**Similar species:** Best marks (from other large pufflegs) are long tail and bluish forecrown. Glowing, Turquoise-throated, and Coppery-bellied pufflegs (110, 111, 113) also have violet under tail coverts, but all are much smaller and shorter-tailed.
**Behavior:** On open steppelike grassy slopes feeds at tiny short flowers by alighting directly on the ground. In bushy areas much like Glowing Puffleg.
**Status and habitat:** Open grassy or bushy slopes, ecotonal areas between temperate forest and paramo, also open paramo. Common in Ecuador.
**Range:** 2800-4800m. Sw Nariño from mts. nw of Ipiales southward. S Colombia to nw Peru.
**Note:** Three "Bogotá" specimens, each somewhat different but originally described as *E. isaacsonii*, are now believed to be hybrids of *Eriocnemis* sp. X *Coeligena* sp. (Meyer de Schauensee 1966).

## 113. COPPERY-BELLIED PUFFLEG
*Eriocnemis cupreoventris*          Pl. 15, Map 469
**Identification:** 3.8" (9.7cm). Bill straight (0.7", or 18mm). Shining green above, rump lighter emerald green; throat and breast glittering green *becoming coppery orange on center of lower breast and belly; under tail coverts glittering violet;*

leg puffs white; forked tail, blue black. Sexes sim.

**Similar species:** Much like Glowing (110) and Turquoise-throated pufflegs (111), but orange rufous underparts are conspic. and lacks glittering rump. Also cf. larger Golden-breasted Puffleg (114), which has dull under tail coverts.

**Behavior:** Territorial, esp. around small trees and shrubs with long corolla tubes such as *Cavendishia* and *Palicourea* (Snow and Snow 1980); acts much like Glowing Puffleg as it darts in and out of shrubbery, keeping low and clinging momentarily to flowers to feed.

**Status and habitat:** Temperate forest borders and shrubby slopes, perhaps also inside humid forest.

**Range:** 1950-3000m. Both slopes of E Andes s to latitude of Bogotá. Andes of nw Venez. and ne Colombia.

## 114. GOLDEN-BREASTED PUFFLEG
*Eriocnemis mosquera*          Pl. 15, Map 470
**Identification:** 4.5″ (11.4cm). Bill straight (0.8″, or 20mm). Above shining green, below glittering green becoming *glittering coppery green on sides of neck, breast, and belly; under tail coverts dull brownish* (or shining green—♀), leg puffs white; tail forked, *greenish black*.

**Similar species:** Good marks are the coppery green breast (obvious in good light), large size, *dull* under tail coverts (not violet), and greener (less blue black) tail than allies.

**Behavior:** Usually seen alone hovering or clinging briefly at low flowers on the perimeter of dense bushes in shrubby areas. Active and aggressive and often darts about in and out of shrubbery as it defends territory. As with others of the genus, sometimes holds or flicks up wings momentarily upon alighting.

**Status and habitat:** Common in PN Puracé in stunted montane woodland and adj. borders and bushy clearings; favors elfin woodland thickets and shrubby areas near timberline. Some seasonal el. movement likely.

**Range:** 1200-3600m; usually above 2600m (in PN Puracé chiefly 2900-3300m—J. Silliman). W Andes from Cauca southward, C Andes from Caldas s to Nariño; presum. E Andes ("Bogotá"). Colombia and n Ecuador.

## 115. COLORFUL PUFFLEG
*Eriocnemis mirabilis*          Map 471
**Identification:** 3.2″ (8.1cm). Bill straight (0.6″, or 15mm), fairly short. ♂: frontlet and gorget glittering green; otherwise dark shining green with *glittering blue belly and glittering red and coppery gold under tail coverts; enormously en-*larged *white leg puffs* fringed cinnamon below and behind; tail forked, dark bronzy olive; feet pink. ♀: dark shining green above and on sides; median throat and median underparts white spotted green on throat and breast and *spotted reddish bronze on lower underparts*; tail bronze green tipped and edged blackish; *leg puffs like ♂.*

**Similar species:** ♂ is only puffleg with glittering blue belly and ruby under tail coverts. ♀ recalls ♀ Booted Racket-tail (120), but latter has smaller leg puffs, white underparts spotted green (no reddish belly spots), and tail with prom. white tips. ♀ Glowing Puffleg (110) has glittering rump and strong buff tinge on throat and breast. Also see Andean Emerald (67) and ♀ of 78 and 123.

**Behavior:** Observed feeding at low flowers in a small clearing near forest.

**Status and habitat:** A spectacular but little known puffleg. Rec. from wet forest and adj. forest borders. Discovered in 1967 (Dunning 1970).

**Range:** ENDEMIC. Known from 1 locality on Pacific slope in Cauca (Charguayaco, 2200m, n of Cerro Munchique in PN Munchique).

## 116. EMERALD-BELLIED PUFFLEG
*Eriocnemis alinae*          Pl. 14, Map 472
**Identification:** 3″ (7.6cm). Bill straight (0.6″, or 15mm). *Smallest puffleg.* ♂: above dark shining green, *rump brighter emerald green* (contrasts with back and tail); frontlet and entire underparts incl. under tail coverts glittering emerald green; *large patch on central breast white* spangled with a few green disks: *white leg puffs extraordinarily large*: short shining green tail slightly forked, brighter below. ♀: lacks glittering frontlet.

**Similar species:** Best told by small size, whitish area on center of breast, large leg puffs, and short shining green tail.

**Behavior:** Usually alone in lower story inside forest, less often at edges.

**Status and habitat:** Common in wet montane forest ("cloud forest") on oak-dominated ridges (2300-2500m) in PN Cueva de los Guácharos (P. Gertler); elsewhere local and spotty in distribution, perhaps due to habitat loss. Unlike other Colombian *Eriocnemis* mainly a subtropical and interior forest sp.

**Range:** 2300-2800m (once to 750m? in w Cundinamarca). E Andes from Boyacá (Tunja) spottily on w slope to head of Magdalena Val. in Huila (PN Cueva de los Guácharos—P. Gertler), e slope C Andes in Cauca (PN Puracé—J. Silliman) and w Huila; Pacific slope in Nariño; prob. e slope E Andes at s end. Colombia, se Ecuador, and e Peru.

## 117. BLACK-THIGHED PUFFLEG

*Eriocnemis derbyi*                    Pl. 15, Map 473
**Identification:** 3.8″ (9.7cm). Bill straight (0.8″, or 20mm). ♂: above shining green becoming coppery on rump; *upper tail coverts glittering green* contrasting with black, sharp-pointed, and forked tail; underparts glittering green, brightest on under tail coverts; large leg puffs black. ♀: slightly smaller than ♂, underparts white thickly spotted glittering green; leg puffs mixed black and white.
**Similar species:** ♂ is only puffleg with black leg puffs (often not conspic. in field). Better marks are intensely glittering upper and under tail coverts. ♀ might recall Emerald-bellied Puffleg (116), but latter has distinct white patch on breast and proportionally larger and pure white leg puffs.
**Behavior:** Much like Glowing Puffleg. Very active.
**Breeding:** BC ♂, 9 Feb, Puracé (Carriker).
**Status and habitat:** Uncommon and local in humid forest borders and bushy partially open pastures and ravines; not inside forest. Sometimes in shrubby ravines above Puracé, Cauca.
**Range:** 2500-3600m (usually above 2900m). C Andes from n Tolima (Santa Isabel at 3600m) and w Quindío (Laguneta at 3150m) s to Nariño. C Colombia and n Ecuador.

[*Haplophaedia*: Leg puffs small and inconspic.; plumage duller than allied *Eriocnemis*.]

## 118. GREENISH PUFFLEG

*Haplophaedia aureliae*                Pl. 15, Map 474
**Identification:** 3.6″ (9.1cm). Bill straight (0.8″, or 20mm). ♂: mainly green above and below, *head coppery green*, rump bright coppery bronze; underparts dull and inconspic. scaled grayish *becoming dingy grayish white on lower underparts*; buffy white *leg puffs small* and not obvious in field; tail slightly forked, blue black. ♀: sim., but even duller; underparts more heavily scaled grayish white; leg puffs white, more noticeable. Both sexes show small white spot behind eye.
**Similar species:** A dull and often confused hummingbird that *lacks good field marks*. In good light coppery shine on head and rump and dingy scaling on underparts is helpful; leg puffs are not usually apparent in field. Note habitat and behavior.
**Voice:** Several ♂♂ in loose assembly sang *turseet* about 1 per sec through much of day from high perch, late Nov, Finca Merenberg, Huila (Brown).
**Behavior:** Usually seen singly at small groups of flowers or gleaning from leaves in lower story, infrequently higher, inside forest. Un-

like *Eriocnemis*, rarely clings to feed at flowers and usually does not hold up wings in a V when alighting. Not as active and pugnacious as *Eriocnemis*.
**Breeding:** 5 BC birds, Dec–Mar, nests Mar and Sept, W Andes above Cali; 2-2.6m up in moss ball beneath ferns at forest edge (Miller 1963); nest building, Nov, Finca Merenberg, Huila (Brown). 7 BC ♂♂, May–July, W and C Andes (Carriker).
**Status and habitat:** Fairly common in humid and wet forest, and forest borders, less often into shrubby clearings.
**Range:** 1500-3100m (rarely above 2500m); seasonally to 900m on w slope in Valle. All 3 Andean ranges (n in E Andes to se Santander, poss. Norte de Santander). Colombia s in Andes to Bolivia.

## 119. HOARY PUFFLEG

*Haplophaedia lugens*                  Map 475
**Identification:** 3.6″ (9.1cm). Bill straight (0.7″, or 18mm). *Green above*, more coppery on crown and rump; *dark grayish black below; decidedly scaled grayish white on throat and breast*; small leg puffs whitish (not conspic.); tail almost square, blackish.
**Similar species:** Resembles Greenish Puffleg (118) but is slaty (not green) below and much more heavily scaled.
**Behavior:** Much like Greenish Puffleg. Usually feeds low.
**Status and habitat:** Humid and wet forest ("cloud forest") and forest borders in lower highlands. Can be found along Pasto-Tumaco road above Junín. Occurs below el. of Greenish Puffleg.
**Range:** 1100-1400m (prob. higher and lower). Pacific slope at s end in Nariño. Sw Colombia and nw Ecuador.

## 120. BOOTED RACKET-TAIL

*Ocreatus underwoodii*                 Pl. 14, Map 476
**Identification:** ♂ 4.8″ (12.2cm); ♀ 3″ (7.6cm). Bill short (0.5″, or 13mm) and straight. ♂ unmistakable: mainly shining green, throat and breast glittering green; central tail feathers shining green, rest blue black, outer pair greatly elongated (3.5″, or 8.9cm) with *bare protruding shafts terminating in large blue black rackets; large leg puffs white*. ♀ very different: green above, forecrown tinged coppery; *prom. white spot behind eye;* underparts white thickly spotted green (or plain white with a few green spots on sides of breast—*melananthterus*), under tail coverts buff; tail normal but rather long and forked central feathers green, outer ones blue black *tipped white; small but obvious white leg puffs*.
**Similar species:** ♀ generally the most com-

mon, very small, white-breasted hummingbird in the highlands; most like either spp. of
♀ whitetip (77, 78) but smaller (beelike flight),
bill half the length, throat less spotted, and
has prom. white leg puffs. ♀ sylphs (132, 133)
are larger, mainly cinnamon below, but also
common and with sim. tail pattern. Also see
Andean Emerald (67), ♀ Colorful Puffleg (115),
and ♀ Purple-backed Thornbill (123).
**Voice:** Weak twittering when feeding; distinctive wing hum, sim. to that of coquettes and
woodstars.
**Behavior:** Hover or occas. cling to blossoms as
they feed from upper undergrowth to canopy.
Flight is weaving and beelike. Occur alone at
lower levels inside forest or commonly gather
in nos. with other hummingbirds at canopy
flowering trees, esp. *Inga* spp. and other legumes with brushlike inflorescences.
**Breeding:** 6 BC birds, Feb–Dec, W, C, and E
Andes (Miller 1963; Carriker); downy cup atop
twig (Merizalde de Albuja 1975).
**Status and habitat:** Fairly common to common
in humid and wet forest borders, second growth
woodland, and open, well-lit areas inside forest. At low el. on Pacific slope in Valle rec.
only May and Dec (Hilty).
**Range:** 1500-2500m; rarely to 3100m (to 900m
on Pacific slope). Perijá Mts. and e slope E
Andes in se Norte de Santander (*discifer*); E
Andes from Norte de Santander s to Macarena Mts. (*underwoodii*); W and C Andes incl.
head of Magdalena Val. (*ambiguus*); Pacific slope
of Nariño (*melanantherus*). N Venez. s in mts.
to Bolivia.

[*Lesbia*: Short bill; extraordinarily long, forked
tail (usually held closed).]

## 121. BLACK-TAILED TRAINBEARER

*Lesbia victoriae*      Pl. 16, Ill. 69, Map 477
**Identification:** ♂ to 10″ (25cm); ♀ 5.5″ (14cm).
Bill fairly short (0.6″, or 15mm). ♂ unmistakable: mostly shining green with glittering gorget; lower underparts buff spotted green; *tail
very long* (to 6.5″, or 165mm), *deeply forked, and
black, all but outermost* (longest) *tipped bronze green.*
♀: bronze green above; white to buffy white
below and thickly spotted green; small irreg.
patch of glittering orange on throat (seldom
visible in field); *tail like ♂'s but much shorter* (to
3.5″, or 89mm), partly edged white.
**Similar species:** ♀ might be mistaken for Green-
tailed Trainbearer (122) but much duller,
heavier bodied (different flight), bill longer,
and tail mostly black (not green). Sylphs (132,
133) have mostly metallic violet tails and different habitat.
**Voice:** Song a rattling trill, *ti-ti tr't t'tr tic-tic-tic*

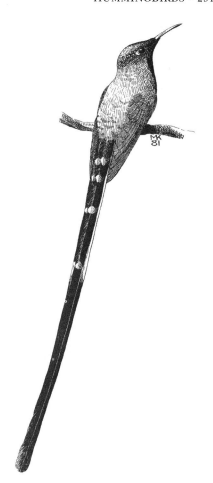

69. BLACK-TAILED TRAINBEARER (♂)

descending at end (B. Coffee recording); call
a high, thin, bell-like *zeeet*; squeaky *chips*'s when
foraging.
**Behavior:** An active, aggressive, territorial
hummingbird. Hovers at flowers from eye level
to tree canopy. In display, ♂ chases or dives
(no arcs) near ♀ with widely spread tail producing a loud, canvas-ripping sound.
**Breeding:** ♂♂ displaying and chasing ♀♀, early
June and Aug, s Nariño, and mid-Sept n of
Bogotá (Hilty). 1 Ecuador nest a wide, open
cup 5.3m up in hotel garden (Greenwalt 1960).
**Status and habitat:** Fairly common locally in
bushy pastures, ravines, and brush near timberline; also hedges, eucalyptus, *Polylepis*
woodland, and occas. open paramo. Favors

drier highlands. Replaced at lower el. by Green-tailed Trainbearer.

**Range:** 2600-4000m. E Andes from Norte de Santander (Pamplona) s to latitude of Bogotá; mts. of Nariño. Colombia s in Andes to s Peru.

## 122. GREEN-TAILED TRAINBEARER

*Lesbia nuna*      Pl. 16, Map 478

**Identification:** ♂ to 6.5″ (16.5cm); ♀ 4.3″ (10.9cm). Bill very short (0.4″, or 10mm). ♂: *bright emerald green with glittering gorget; long tail* (to 4.5″ or 11.4cm), *narrow and deeply forked* (usually held closed), outer pair of feathers dusky, rest bright emerald green. ♀: bright emerald green above; *below white thickly spotted green; tail like ♂'s but shorter* (to 3.5″, 89mm)

**Similar species:** ♂ and ♀ recall respective sexes of Black-tailed Trainbearer (121) but are decidedly smaller, shorter-billed, and much brighter more emerald green; tails mainly green (not just tipped bronze green on all feathers) and appear distinctly narrower in field. ♀ has longer tail than other ♀♀ with sim. underparts (e.g., 77, 78, 110, 120, 123).

**Voice:** A short, high, very buzzy *bzzzt*.

**Behavior:** Active and aggressive like Black-tailed Trainbearer and hovers (usually without clinging) at flowers from below eye level to canopy ht. As with other small-bodied hummingbirds, flight is weaving and beelike (cf. with more darting flight of Black-tailed Trainbearer).

**Breeding:** BC ♂, Jan, Puracé (Carriker).

**Status and habitat:** Fairly common but local in shrubby forest borders, bushy pastures, parks, and open terrain with scattered hedges and patches of second growth woodland. Replaced at higher el. by Black-tailed Trainbearer.

**Range:** 2200-2800m. Both slopes E Andes from Boyacá (Tunja) s to Bogotá area, w slope C Andes in Cauca (e of Popayán), and e slope of Andes in Nariño; poss. also e Huila (net capture, presumed this sp., PN Cueva de los Guácharos—P. Gertler). Nw Venez. (once) s in Andes to n Bolivia.

## 123. PURPLE-BACKED THORNBILL

*Ramphomicron microrhynchum*    Pl. 15, Map 479

**Identification:** 3.2″ (8.1cm). Very small. *Bill extremely short* (0.2″, or 5mm). ♂: *shining purple above with noticeably long, deeply forked, purplish black tail;* gorget glittering golden green tapering to a point on breast; rest of underparts bronzy green. ♀: bronzy green above; *buffy white below, thickly spotted green;* under tail coverts tawny; tail rather long (but shorter than ♂'s), forked, purplish black with *outer feathers tipped white.* Some ♀♀ show white stripe up

center of lower back. Imm. ♂ like ♀ but with var. amts. of purple above.

**Similar species:** Striking ♂ is only Colombian hummingbird with bright purple upperparts. ♀ somewhat resembles several other highland ♀♀, (cf. 77, 78, 110, 115, 120, 122) but can always be told by short thornlike bill and rather long, white-tipped tail.

**Voice:** Alarm *ti, ti ti, ti . . .* , long sustained; song sim. but shrill and weaker (Ruschi 1973).

**Behavior:** Generally at mid. ht. to canopy in trees, often perching exposed on outer perimeter or on top of crown. Several commonly gather with other hummers at flowering trees. Hover at flowers (rarely cling) and often glean over leaves or hawk insects. Flight is weaving and beelike. In display ♂ traces shallow arcs back and forth in front of ♀, this sometimes accompanied by loud cracking or clapping sounds.

**Breeding:** 3 BC birds, May–Aug, W and E Andes (Carriker). ♂♂ displaying, Sept, n of Bogotá (Hilty); downy cup nest (Ruschi 1973).

**Status and habitat:** Widespread but rarely numerous. Humid forest borders and all kinds of more open highland terrain with hedges, woodlots, and scattered trees.

**Range:** 1700-3400m (usually above 2500m). W Andes at n end and in Cauca; C Andes from s Antioquia to e Nariño; E Andes s to Cundinamarca. Nw Venez. s in Andes to e Peru.

## 124. BLACK-BACKED THORNBILL

*Ramphomicron dorsale*    Ill. 70, Map 480

**Identification:** 4″ (10.2cm). Bill extremely short (0.3″, or 8mm). ♂: *head and entire upperparts black,* center of throat glittering greenish gold; breast dusky green; rest of underparts dark gray disked green; *tail long, deeply forked, purplish black.* ♀: bronzy green above; *buffy white below spotted green on throat and flanks;* tail rather long (but shorter than ♂), forked, purplish black, *outer feathers tipped white.*

**Similar species:** ♂ easily told by all black upperparts and short bill. ♀ Tyrian Metaltail (126) shows rufous below.

**Behavior:** Much like Purple-backed Thornbill. Usually in canopy where it often perches exposed on outer perimeter or on top of crown. One to several may gather at flowering trees with other hummingbirds. Feeds by hovering at flowers, occas. gleans over leaves (T. B. Johnson).

**Status and habitat:** Uncommon in humid and wet forest borders at mid. el.; also open bushy slopes near treeline and in paramo up to snowline. Shows strong seasonal el. move-

70. BLACK-BACKED THORNBILL
(♀ top; ♂ bottom)

ments; rec. at San Lorenzo (2200m) only late May–early June (T. B. Johnson).
**Range:** ENDEMIC. 2000-4500m (1 imm. ♂ to 900m). Santa Marta Mts.

## 125. VIRIDIAN METALTAIL
*Metallura williami*          Pl. 15, Map 481
**Identification:** 3.4" (8.6cm). Bill short (0.6", or 15mm), but longer than next sp. ♂: shining dark bronzy green above and below, vague glittering dark green throat patch; tail shining dark bronze green to bronzy dark purple above (depending on light) and deep purplish blue below (or as above but larger [3.6", 9.1cm], with underside of tail shining green—*primolinus; recisa*). ♀: dark bronzy green above; underparts buff heavily disked green; tail like ♂'s above, dark greenish blue below (or shining green below—*primolinus; recisa).*
**Similar species:** Easily confused with much more common and predom. lower el. Tyrian Metaltail (126); both sexes of Viridian are slightly larger with purplish or dark bronzy green tail instead of coppery maroon tail (Tyrian has purplish tail only in Santa Marta and Perijá Mts. where Viridian does not occur). ♀ from ♀ Tyrian by more or less uniformly spotted green and buff underparts (not a solid

rufous throat). Also cf. Black-thighed Puffleg (117).
**Behavior:** Sim. to Tyrian Metaltail.
**Breeding:** BC pair, Feb, Puracé; BC ♂, Aug, n end W Andes (Carriker); ♀ carrying *Espeletia* down, late Mar, PN Puracé (Brown); several nests in loose colony on vines and roots over mt. torrent (3600m), 7 Aug, Mt. Sangay, Ecuador (Moore 1934).
**Status and habitat:** Uncommon and local in shrubby stunted forest borders, hedges, and scattered brush in treeline/paramo ecotone. Fairly common on w slope PN Puracé, 3100-3300m (J. Silliman). Replaces much more common Tyrian Metaltail in more open areas or stunted vegetation and at higher el.
**Range:** 2100-3800m (usually above 2900m). N end W Andes, Páramo Frontino (*recisa*); both slopes C Andes from n Tolima (Nevado del Ruiz) s to Cauca (*williami*); Andes of Nariño (*primolinus*). Colombia s in Andes to s Ecuador.
**Note:** Wetmore (1970) considers *primolinus* of Nariño and Ecuador (incl. *recisa* of W Andes) a separate sp.

## 126. TYRIAN METALTAIL
*Metallura tyrianthina*          Pl. 15, Map 482
**Identification:** ♂ 3.2" (8.1cm); ♀ 3.0" (7.6cm). Bill short (0.4", or 10mm). ♂: *dark coppery green, gorget glittering green, tail shining coppery maroon* (or shining dark purple—*districta*). ♀: dark coppery green above; *cheeks, throat, and upper breast tawny* with a few dark spots; rest of underparts pale whitish buff speckled dusky green on flanks; tail like ♂'s, *tipped buffy white*. Both sexes show white spot behind eye.
**Similar species:** See Viridian Metaltail (125), in Perijá Mts. Perija Metaltail (127).
**Voice:** Song a ser. of weak, unmusical sputtering chips (J. Silliman).
**Behavior:** Rather aggressive little hummingbird, usually seen 1-5m up along shrubby borders. Clings more than hovers when feeding at flowers. Notably tame and territorial around small flowering bushes or clumps of roadside flowers. Sexes often appear segregated locally and in general more ♀♀ than ♂♂ are seen.
**Breeding:** 12 BC birds, Apr–Aug, Perijá Mts., E and C Andes (Carriker); building in cavelike rock niche, July, Cundinamarca; pendent mass of moss and fibers with small nest chamber partially roofed over with moss; ♀ defended nest territory and adj. flowers (Snow 1980).
**Status and habitat:** Often abundant in humid and wet forest borders, overgrown clearings, and in shrubby areas but seldom far from forest; occas. into ecotonal areas between stunted woodland and paramo or at patches of brush

in lower paramo. Shows strong seasonal movements.
**Range:** 1700-3600m (usually above 2400m); to 600m in Santa Marta Mts. Santa Marta Mts. and Perijá Mts. (*districta*) and all 3 Andean ranges (*tyrianthina*). N Venez. s in mts. to Bolivia.

### 127. PERIJA METALTAIL
*Metallura iracunda*
**Identification:** 4" (10.2cm). Bill short (0.4", or 10mm). ♂: mainly coppery greenish black, crown shining green, gorget glittering green; *tail bright shining maroon red to reddish purple*. ♀: dark green above, *buffy below* with a few brown spots, *tail like ♂'s, outer feathers tipped buff*.
**Similar species:** Tail much redder and more glistening than that of decidedly smaller Tyrian Metaltail (126); ♀ has more uniform underparts.
**Status and habitat:** Poorly known and with a restricted range. Rec. from rather open brushy terrain and forest borders.
**Range:** 2800-3100m. Perijá Mts. on summits of Cerro Pintado (e of Valledupar) and Cerro de las Tres Tetas (above Hiroca). Colombia and adj. Venez. (1800-3000m).

[*Chalcostigma*: Large; very short bill and long ample tail; timberline and paramo.]

### 128. BRONZE-TAILED THORNBILL
*Chalcostigma heteropogon*     Pl. 15, Map 483
**Identification:** ♂ 5" (13cm); ♀ 4" (10.2cm). *Bill very short* (0.5", or 13mm) for size of bird. ♂: bronze green above becoming *reddish bronze on rump*; forecrown and *gorget stripe glittering green, gorget tapering to a rosy violet point on chest*; rest of underparts bronze brown, *long, ample tail bronzy and notched*. ♀: like ♂ but throat with glittering green disks, no rosy point, tail shorter.
**Similar species:** A large, long-tailed, dingy bronze hummingbird with a short bill. Coppery red rump conspic., throat stripe flashes in good light. See much smaller Tyrian Metaltail (126).
**Behavior:** A paramo edge bird usually seen singly, feeding at flowers by clinging briefly at each. Hovers with rather slow wing beats. Aggressively defends patches of flowers and does not gather in groups at flowering trees. Has not been noted walking on matted grass as some members of the genus are reported to do.
**Breeding:** BC ♀ and 2 juvs., 21 July, n Santander (Carriker).

**Status and habitat:** Common in patches of stunted woodland and shrubs in upper montane forest/paramo ecotone or in clumps of brush in paramo, esp. around cliffs and rocky outcrops; occas. in adj. lower mt. val.
**Range:** 2900-3500m. E Andes s to s Cundinamarca. Andes of nw Venez. and adj. ne Colombia.

### 129. RAINBOW-BEARDED THORNBILL
*Chalcostigma herrani*     Pl. 15, Map 484
**Identification:** 4.3" (10.9cm). *Bill very short* (0.5", or 13mm). ♂: *slightly crested*, median crown stripe rufous bordered black; otherwise mostly dark bronzy green, rump reddish copper; *narrow, shaggy, beardlike throat stripe green changing to glittering orange and tapering to a fiery red point on breast* and narrowly bordered black; long rounded tail purplish, outer feathers *broadly tipped white*. ♀: sim., but lacks colored beard; underparts buffy brown disked dark green on throat, breast, and sides.
**Similar species:** ♂ is dazzling in good light. White tail tips and large size are good marks for either sex.
**Behavior:** Much like Bronze-tailed Thornbill. Usually seen singly at flowers, often clinging to them to feed. May walk on matted grass and stems foraging for insects, but confirmation needed.
**Breeding:** 2 nests, Sept, Páramo del Tábano (3000m), Nariño; rosy white eggs (Borrero 1952b); nest building, mid-July, in ferns 7m over torrent, Mt. Sangay (4000m), Ecuador (Moore 1934).
**Status and habitat:** Uncommon and local in stunted woodland, adj. shrubby edges, and patches of brush in paramo; 3100m to treeline in PN Puracé (J. Silliman).
**Range:** 2700-3600m. C Andes (Nevado del Quindío on Tolima-Quindío boundary) and W Andes (Munchique area) s through Nariño. Colombia s to s Ecuador and n Peru.
**Note 1:** A specimen of Rufous-capped Thornbill (*C. ruficeps*) from PN Puracé (Schuchmann 1978) is prob. referable to *C. herrani*. Much like latter, esp. ♀, differing as follows: smaller; greener throat patch, no black line bordering rufous crown, and no white tail tips. Andes from s Ecuador to Bolivia. **Note 2:** Blue-mantled Thornbill (*C. stanleyi*), from n Ecuador (30km s of Colombian border in Carchí) to Bolivia is almost certain to be found near timberline in Nariño. ♂ very dull dark bronzy green with dark blue mantle, steel greenish blue tail, and narrow, pointed, glittering green throat stripe becoming violet near tip. ♀: lacks throat stripe.

## 130. BEARDED HELMETCREST

*Oxypogon guerinii*  Ill. 71, Map 485
**Identification:** 4.5″ (11.4cm). Bill very short (0.3″, or 8mm). ♂: olive green above with *long pointed black and white crest and shaggy white beard*, latter with glittering green central stripe (or purplish blue—*cyanolaemus*; or bluish orange—*stübelii*); *sides of head dusky forming a large triangle*; broad buffy white collar encircling neck angles downward onto breast; rest of underparts dingy buff vaguely disked olive; tail long, slightly forked, central pair of feathers bronzy olive, *rest mostly white broadly edged and tipped reddish bronze* (or tail mostly reddish bronze with buffy outer feather—*stübelii*). ♀: like ♂ but duller, *no beard or crest*.
**Similar species:** Large, mostly brownish, and with conspic. dusky triangular patch on sides of head, white collar, and white in tail.
**Voice:** Song a trilled *ti-e-o*, repeated at short intervals (Ruschi 1973).
**Behavior:** Usually seen singly at low flowering bushes or *Espeletia* spp. Also walks on matted grass, sometimes making short hovering jumps for insects (Ruschi 1973). Notably active as it hovers or clings momentarily to probe flowers, then flies off, often considerable distances.
**Breeding:** Laying ♀, 7 Aug, ne Santander (Carriker); 2 nests, mid-Sept, Páramo de Neusa, 3500m (Hilty and M. Robbins); 1 in July, Mérida, Venez. (D. Zimmerman); down cup on rocky cliff, steep bank, near torrent, or in *Espeletia* in paramo. Nest deeper and thicker than those of other hummingbirds and mostly of *Espeletia* down (Ruschi 1973).

71. BEARDED HELMETCREST (♀ left; ♂ right)

**Status and habitat:** Seasonally common in paramo and adj. shrubby mt. vals.; present in open paramo mainly during flowering season of *Espeletia* (Aug–Nov in Venez. and n end E Andes of Colombia). At other times in Venez. reported to be more or less restricted to ecotonal areas betw. *Polylepis* scrub (or other shrubbery) and open paramo (Vuilleumier and Ewert 1978).
**Range:** 3200-5200m. Santa Marta Mts. *cyanolaemus*); E Andes s to s Cundinamarca (*guerinii*); C Andes in nevados of n Tolima and Quindío (*stübelii*). Andes of w Venez. and Colombia.

## 131. MOUNTAIN AVOCETBILL

*Opisthoprora euryptera*  Pl. 15, Map 486
**Identification:** 4″ (10.2cm). *Bill short (0.5″, or 13mm) and upturned at tip*. Robust and heavy-bodied. Above shining green, *crown and sides of head reddish copper*; prom. white spot behind eyes; *throat and breast white streaked dark green*; rest of underparts pale buff becoming cinnamon on belly and spotted green on breast and sides; tail notched, outer feathers dark blue narrowly tipped whitish.
**Similar species:** Only temperate zone hummingbird with *streaky* throat and chest; upturned bill inconspic. except at close range.
**Behavior:** Relatively little known. Usually seen singly, hovering or clinging 1-3m up at tiny tubular flowers in thick shrubbery. Perches low and generally acts more sluggish than pufflegs and other temperate zone hummingbirds.
**Status and habitat:** Rare (infrequently seen) and local in dense upper montane forest and adj. borders or shrubbery along roadsides and roadcuts. Several recent sightings on e slope PN Puracé, 3100-3300m (Hilty), once lower in park (2600m) at Versalles (J. Silliman). Three specimens taken by Von Sneidern near Llorente, se Nariño (e of Ipiales), 3200m, 1974 (Fitzpatrick and Willard 1982).
**Range:** 2600-3600m. W slope C Andes in Caldas (n of Manizales), both slopes in Cauca and e slope in se Nariño. C Colombia, ne Ecuador, and c Peru.

[*Aglaiocercus*: Bill short, straight, and pointed (cf. with even more sharply pointed bills of *Schistes* and *Heliothryx*); ♂'s tail very long, deeply forked, and glittering metallic above; wetter highlands.]

## 132. LONG-TAILED SYLPH

*Aglaiocercus kingi*  Pl. 16, Map 487
**Identification:** ♂ 7″ (18cm); ♀ 3.8″ (9.7cm). Bill short (0.5″, or 13mm). ♂: mostly shining green,

underparts duller: *median crown stripe glittering green*; gorget spot glittering blue (no spot—*caudatus; emmae*); tail graduated, outermost feathers very long (up to 4.5", or 114mm), from above *brilliant shining metallic green or blue green* (or purplish changing to peacock blue on outer half—*kingi; caudatus*), blackish on underside. ♀: shining green above; throat *and chest white lightly spotted green; rest of underparts bright cinnamon*; tail normal, notched, dark blue green, outer feathers tipped white.

**Similar species:** Much like Violet-tailed Sylph (133) but in zone of overlap in W Andes tail brilliant emerald green or blue green (not violet to peacock blue with green tips on feathers); ♀ has green (not glittering blue) crown and spotted chest.

**Behavior:** Favors forest borders and more open areas than Violet-tailed Sylph, and unlike latter, feeds at almost any ht., "trap-lining" or defending territories, and sometimes gathering with other hummingbirds in the canopy of flowering trees along roadsides or in clearings. Hovers or occas. clings to feed at flowers; flycatches from open perches.

**Breeding:** 9 BC birds, Feb–Oct, C and E Andes (Carriker; Olivares 1971); bulky *domed* nest of moss and fiber with *side entrance* and dangling tail; fastened to leafy twig (Ruschi 1973).

**Status and habitat:** Common in humid and wet forest borders, second growth woodland, bushy clearings, and gardens; usually not inside forest. Represented on Pacific slope by forest dwelling Violet-tailed Sylph.

**Range:** 1400-3000m (usually below 2500m). N part E Andes in Norte de Santander (*caudatus*); E Andes from Bucaramanga, Santander to s Cundinamarca (*kingi*); C Andes s to w slope in Cauca, W Andes s to Cauca and w slope Andes of Nariño (*emmae*); head of Magdalena Val. and e slope in Nariño (*mocoa*). N and w Venez. (incl. Perijá Mts.) s in mts. to Bolivia.

**Note:** Incl. *A. emmae* (with *caudatus*), which has been considered a separate sp., the Greentailed Sylph.

## 133. VIOLET-TAILED SYLPH
*Aglaiocercus coelestis*          Pl. 16, Map 488

**Identification:** ♂ 7" (18cm); ♀ 3.8" (9.7cm). Bill short (0.5", or 13mm). ♂ much like ♂ Long-tailed Sylph, but gorget spot slightly more violet (less blue), rump bluer, and *tail mainly brilliant shining metallic violet with blue tips* (instead of emerald green or blue green of Long-tailed Sylph in zone of overlap). ♀: shining green above with *glittering blue crown*; throat white spotted green; *chest unspotted buffy white; rest of underparts cinnamon rufous*; tail normal,

notched, dark blue green, outer feathers tipped white.

**Similar species:** See Long-tailed Sylph (132). ♀ from ♀ of latter by glittering blue crown and immaculate buff white chest.

**Voice:** Song a rapid, double-sounding *tez-it* at 1 per sec for up to several min from understory perch.

**Behavior:** Solitary and usually low inside forest at small clumps of flowers. Mainly a "trapliner" of widely-spaced flowers. Hovers or occas. clings to feed and does not gather at flowering trees.

**Breeding:** ♀ building nest, 6 June, Junín, Nariño, 1100m: suspended side-entrance moss nest with dangling tail much like preceding sp., 6m up, inside forest (Hilty).

**Status and habitat:** Fairly common in wet forest ("cloud forest"), occas. at forest borders; favors very mossy forest.

**Range:** 300-2100m (usually above 900m). Pacific slope from headwaters of Río San Juan (Cerro Tatamá) s to nw Ecuador. Occas. on e slope of W Andes near wet low passes.

**Note:** Has been regarded as conspecific with Long-tailed Sylph; behavior and habitat differ.

## 134. WEDGE-BILLED HUMMINGBIRD
*Schistes geoffroyi*          Pl. 14, Map 489

**Identification:** 3.4" (8.6cm). Bill rather short (0.6", or 15mm), broad at base, and sharp pointed. ♂: bronzy green above, quite coppery on rump; sides of head black bordered above by *white postocular stripe*; gorget glittering green; small violet tuft on sides of chest with *larger white patch below*; rest of underparts bronze green; *tail rounded*, bronze green with *dark blue subterminal band* and whitish tips. Or as above but forecrown glittering, rump not coppery, white patches on sides of chest more or less connected by narrow white line (*albogularis*). ♀: gorget duller and violet tufts smaller. Or *whole throat white*, violet patches mostly replaced by blue (*albogularis*).

**Similar species:** Can be confusing. Good marks are prom. white postocular, white pectoral tufts, and rounded tail. Violet tufts and peculiar bill shape are not conspic. in field.

**Behavior:** Solitary and usually seen inside thicker forest undergrowth and in shady ravines. Feeds at a var. of mostly tubular flowers by hovering, infrequently clinging; prob. "traplines" scattered flowers. Does not gather at flowering trees.

**Status and habitat:** Local in humid and wet montane forest, infrequently at forest borders; favors dense mossy forest ("cloud forest"). Reported "common" at PN Cueva de los Guácharos at 2000m (P. Gertler).

**Range:** 1400-2500m (to 800m on Pacific slope). W slope C Andes, and both slopes W Andes from Valle s to w slope in Nariño (*albogularis*); w slope E Andes s to head of Magdalena Val. (*geoffroyi*), poss. e Nariño. N Venez. s in mts. to Bolivia.

[*Heliothryx*: Much white in plumage, dark auriculars; sharp pointed bill much like *Schistes*.]

### 135. PURPLE-CROWNED FAIRY

*Heliothryx barroti*          Pl. 13, Map 490

**Identification:** ♂ 4.2″ (10.7cm); ♀ 4.5″ (11.4cm). Bill rather short (0.6″, or 15mm). ♂: *glittering violet purple forecrown; black mask through eyes* ends in tiny purple ear tuft and is bordered narrowly below by glittering green across cheeks; otherwise bright shining green above and *pure white below*; tail *long and graduated*, central feathers blackish, *rest white*. ♀ sim., but crown green, no green on cheeks, and central tail feathers shorter than ♂. Imm. has dusky mottling on throat.

**Similar species:** E of Andes see next sp.

**Voice:** Occas. a weak squeak.

**Behavior:** A very active, almost impish hummingbird, darting quickly from flower to flower, repeatedly opening and closing its flashy tail, suddenly flying up to hover momentarily in front of an observer and as quickly darting away. Usually solitary, and feeds from near ground to treetops, but mostly at mid. levels or higher inside forest, lower at edge of forest. Characteristically holds tail cocked up as it hovers (does not cling) at flowers, and often hovers high, in the open like a mango (*Anthracothorax*), as it hawks insects. Does not gather at flowering trees.

**Breeding:** 3 BC ♀♀, Apr–May, Córdoba and n Antioquia (Carriker); 1 nest, Anchicayá Val. (550m), June (Hilty); downy cup with no lichen or moss (Skutch 1961) at var. hts. over streams in forest or near clearings.

**Status and habitat:** Fairly common in humid and wet forest, forest borders, and second growth woodland. Replaced e of Andes by Black-eared Fairy.

**Range:** To 1000m. Pacific coast, humid lowlands along n base of Andes, and mid. Magdalena Val. from s Bolívar s to n Caldas. Se Mexico to w Ecuador.

### 136. BLACK-EARED FAIRY

*Heliothryx aurita*          Map 491

**Identification:** ♂ 4″ (10.2cm); ♀ 4.5″ (11.4cm). Almost identical to Purple-crowned Fairy, but ♂ has glittering green (not purple) crown; ♀

has dusky gray speckling on throat and chest (not immaculate white). Ear tufts blue and purple.

**Similar species:** W of Andes see Purple-crowned Fairy (135).

**Voice:** Song a monosyllablic "*trix* . . ." repeated (Ruschi 1973).

**Behavior:** Much like Purple-crowned Fairy, but stays mostly high inside forest; comes lower at small forest breaks, along shady trails, or at forest edge. In display, ♂ hovers up and down and side to side in front of ♀, then both make a spinning ascent to new perch after which ♂ continues hovering with ear tufts expanded (Ruschi 1973).

**Breeding:** Downy cup nest covered with lichen; usually about 10m up (Ruschi 1973).

**Status and habitat:** Fairly common in humid forest, esp. forested blackwater regions, less frequently along forest borders. Replaced w of Andes by Purple-crowned Fairy.

**Range:** To 800m. E of Andes from s Meta (Macarena Mts.), Río Guaviare, and e Vichada (Maipures) southward. The Guianas and s Venez. to n Bolivia and se Brazil.

**Note:** By some considered a subsp. of Purple-crowned Fairy.

### 137. LONG-BILLED STARTHROAT

*Heliomaster longirostris*          Pl. 13, Map 492

**Identification:** 4″ (10.2cm). Bill *very long* (1.5″, or 38mm) and *straight*. ♂: glittering *pale blue crown*; otherwise bronzy green above, usually with *partly concealed white stripe up lower back; throat glittering violet red bordered on sides by white moustachial streak*; rest of underparts dingy brownish white, green on sides; tail bronzy green, outer feathers broadly tipped white. ♀: crown bronzy like back; throat duller; white moustachial streaks broader.

**Similar species:** A rather dull greenish brown hummingbird with a very long straight bill. Only *Doryfera* (20, 21), and highland *Coeligena* (93-101) have such long straight bills; none have rosy violet throats. Look for diagnostic white stripe up back.

**Voice:** Mostly silent, infrequently low, dry *tsik* notes.

**Behavior:** Usually alone, occas. pairs at med. hts. or higher, but sometimes low at flowering shrubs. Likes to perch near tip of exposed bare twigs. Often hawks tiny insects by extended hovering rather high above ground.

**Breeding:** 4 BC ♂♂, Mar, Sept, and Oct, n Colombia (Carriker); 2 Panama nests, Jan and Apr (Willis and Eisenmann 1979); nest usually on exposed horizontal branch 5-12m up, often in dead tree (Skutch 1972).

**Status and habitat:** Thinly spread and often

erratic. Fairly dry to humid regions in open second growth woodland or partly open terrain with scattered trees and woodlots; sometimes forest borders, but avoids shady forests and is often rare or absent in apparently suitable habitat in forested zones. Nowhere common.

**Range:** To 1500m. Lower Atrato Val. s on Pacific slope to Valle and n of Andes e in humid forest to mid. Magdalena Val. s to latitude of Bogotá, also head of val. in s Huila; mid. Cauca Val. s to Cali (at least formerly); n base Santa Marta Mts. e to w base Perijá Mts.; e of Andes from w Meta and e Vichada (Maipures) spottily s to Leticia (sight—J. V. Remsen). S Mexico to Ecuador, Peru (incl. Pebas), Bolivia, and s Brazil.

## 138. BLUE-TUFTED STARTHROAT

*Heliomaster furcifer*                           Map 493

**Identification:** 5″ (13cm). *Bill long* (1.2″, or 30mm) and *straight*. ♂: shining bronze green above, glittering green to bluish green on crown; *throat glittering violet red; rest of underparts and tuft on sides of neck glittering blue: tail deeply forked*, bronze green. ♀: bronze green above; *whitish below* becoming light gray on sides with a few green spots; white stripe below eye to bill; tail forked, bronze green, outer feathers tipped white.

**Similar species:** ♂ Long-billed Starthroat (137) has blue forecrown and dingy greenish gray breast and belly (not all glittering blue), only a notched tail. From Long-billed Starthroat by plain white throat (no violet rose), whiter underparts.

**Voice:** Song in Brazil a monosyllablic ser. of *triii* or *trrr* notes with little var. (Ruschi 1973).

**Behavior:** In display ♂ drops, then rises in 3 short steps in front of ♀ while singing and expanding neck tufts (Ruschi 1973).

**Status and habitat:** One rec. In Brazil favors cerrado, scrub, and woodland edge; perhaps an austral migrant to Colombia (R. Ridgely).

**Range:** Amazonas (once, Leticia). C and s Brazil, Uruguay, Paraguay, c and w Argentina, and Bolivia.

[Woodstars (*Philodice, Calliphlox, Acestrura, Chaetocercus*): Small; broad white (or cinnamon to buff—♀) pectoral band; white flank patch; bill straight (shortest in *Chaetocercus*). ♂♂ gorgets rosy violet to rose; ♀♀ mostly cinnamon below, no rump band (except *A. heliodor*). Several of these genera are doubtfully distinct, and all prob. best placed in a linear sequence nearest allied *Lophornis* and *Popelairia*.]

## 139. PURPLE-THROATED WOODSTAR

*Philodice mitchellii*                    Pl. 14, Map 494

**Identification:** 3″ (7.6cm). Bill straight (0.6″, or 15mm). ♂: dark bronze green above; *throat glittering rosy violet* (usually looks black in field) bordered below by a *broad white pectoral band* extending well up on sides of neck; rest of underparts dusky bronze; sides chestnut; *large white flank patch behind wing* (conspic. in flight); tail rather long and *deeply forked*, dark bronzy purple. ♀: sim., but throat buffy white speckled dusky, pectoral band faintly indicated, and lower underparts mostly rufous; tail only slightly forked, *rufous* with broad black subterminal band.

**Similar species:** Easily told in range by small size, prom. flank patches, and broad light pectoral band (latter usually faint in ♀). Green Thorntail (39) has white flank patches, also white rump band. No other woodstar is known to occur in W Andes.

**Behavior:** Can be seen at almost any ht., often high when perching, and reg. low to feed at flowering shrubs at forest borders. Solitary or may gather with others at flowering trees. Flight is weaving and beelike (as though floating or suspended in air) and wing hum audible. Congeneric *P. bryantae* (Magenta-throated Woodstar) of Costa Rica has a pendulumlike arcing display accompanied by whistling whines and snaps (Feinsinger 1977).

**Breeding:** 2 near BC ♀♀, Dec, W Andes above Cali (Miller 1963).

**Status and habitat:** Local and erratic in humid and wet forest (esp. "cloud forest"), shrubby forest borders, and small clearings with trees; mainly foothills and lower highlands. Shows strong seasonal movements: in upper Anchicayá Val. (1000m) rec. only Dec and Apr–May but relatively numerous both periods (Hilty).

**Range:** To 1900m. Pacific coast and both slopes of W Andes (highlands on e slope) from Valle s through w Nariño. W Colombia and w Ecuador.

## 140. AMETHYST WOODSTAR

*Calliphlox amethystina*                         Map 495

**Identification:** ♂ 2.6″ (6.6cm); ♀ 2.4″ (6cm). Bill straight (0.5″, or 13mm). General appearance much like Purple-throated Woodstar. ♂: dark bronze green above; *gorget glittering violet red* (often looks black) bordered below by *narrow white pectoral band*; rest of underparts grayish buff, some green on sides; *large white flank patch behind wing* (obvious in flight); tail deeply forked, purplish black. ♀: sim. to ♂ above; throat buffy white with a few glittering green and red spots and bordered white on sides of throat; *white pectoral band* *faintly indicated; otherwise cinnamon below*; tail short, unforked, outer feathers tipped white to buff.

**Similar species:** Unique in range. White flank patches (behind wing) and small size are good marks.

**Behavior:** Usually alone from low shrubbery to canopy but often perches fairly high. Like other small-bodied hummingbirds, flight is beelike with wing beats up to 80 per sec (Greenwalt 1960). In display ♂ arcs back and forth like a pendulum, calls, and produces a presumed mechanical noise (Ruschi 1973).

**Breeding:** Tiny cup saddled on limb 15m up in open tree at forest edge; 2 fledglings, Dec, near Belém, Brazil (R. Ridgely; H. Sick).

**Status and habitat:** Little known in Colombia. Elsewhere in a wide var. of habitats from humid forest borders and forest clearings to scrub and savanna woodland. Often local.

**Range:** Specimens only from "Bogotá." Sightings in ne Guainía (Pto. Inírida, Sept 1978— Hilty and M. Robbins). Poss. in Amazonas (rec. at mouth of Río Curaray, n Peru). The Guianas and c and s Venez. to Bolivia, ne Argentina, and Paraguay; e Brazil.

**Note:** Perhaps best placed in the genus *Philodice*.

### 141. WHITE-BELLIED WOODSTAR

*Acestrura mulsant* Pl. 14, Map 496

**Identification:** ♂ 2.8″ (7cm); ♀ 2.5″ (6.4cm). Bill straight (0.7″, or 18mm), long for size of bird. ♂: shining green above with *large white flank patch* behind wing (conspic. in flight); throat glittering reddish violet, bordered below by *broad white pectoral band* extending up on sides of neck as narrow line behind eye; breast band and flanks green; *belly white*; short, forked tail black, outermost feathers reduced to shafts (not a field mark). ♀: like ♂ above, but with dusky mask through eyes and buffy white postocular streak; throat and indistinct pectoral band buffy white, latter extending well up on sides of neck; *breast and sides cinnamon rufous contrasting with white center of lower breast and belly*; tail square, central feathers green, outer ones cinnamon with broad black subterminal band. Imm. ♂: throat white with or without a few reddish spots.

**Similar species:** ♂ very like ♂ Gorgeted (142) and Rufous-shafted woodstars (143), but belly white. Gorgeted also differs in having gorget elongated on sides and general plumage much darker green. Rufous-shafted has redder gorget and rufous at base of tail. ♀ from ♀ Gorgeted Woodstar by all green rump (no rufous band); ♀ prob. not safely separated in field from ♀ Rufous-shafted, but bill longer and

perhaps center of belly lighter, more whitish; they are not known to overlap in range.

**Behavior:** Usually solitary, hovering insectlike from low to high at flowering shrubs and trees, but may congregate at larger flowering trees. Often perches high on exposed bare twigs or on top of the crown of a bush or tall tree.

**Status and habitat:** Uncommon and local in humid forest borders and highland pastures and cultivated areas with scattered trees and hedges. Mostly nonforest.

**Range:** 1500-2800m (perhaps higher); most recs. above 2200m. C Andes and on both slopes of E Andes from Cundinamarca southward (e slope s to se Nariño). Colombia s in Andes to Bolivia.

**Note 1:** Little Woodstar (*A. bombus*) of e and w Ecuador and n Peru may occur in lowland w Nariño (reported n to Esmeraldas). Like White-bellied Woodstar but smaller, 2.5″ (bill: 0.4″) vs 3″ (bill: 0.7″), and ♂ has buff breast band (not white). **Note 2:** Esmeraldas Woodstar (*A. berlepschi*) of w Ecuador may also occur in sw Nariño (reported n to Esmeraldas). Like Little Woodstar, but ♂ has whitish breast (not buff); ♀ is white below tinged buff on throat (not all cinnamon buff below).

### 142. GORGETED WOODSTAR

*Acestrura heliodor* Pl. 14, Map 497

**Identification:** ♂ 2.5″ (6.4cm); ♀ 2.3″ (5.8cm). *Smallest woodstar.* Bill straight (0.5″, or 13mm) and fairly long for size of bird. ♂: *dark shining green above* (or back blue green, rump blue— *astreans*) with *large white flank patch behind wing* (conspic. in flight); glittering rosy violet gorget *elongated to a point on sides of neck* and bordered below by *broad white pectoral band* continuing up on sides of neck in narrow line to behind eye; breast grayish, sides green, *belly blue green*; black tail forked, central and outer feathers shortest. ♀: dark green above with *narrow rufous rump band* and white flank patches (like ♂); cheeks dusky, postocular streak buffy white; *below mostly uniform cinnamon*; indistinct pectoral band paler and continuing well up on sides of neck; tail unforked, central feathers green, outer ones cinnamon with broad black subterminal band. Presumed imm. ♂: like ad. ♂ but throat white and tail rufous like ♀; others have throat and belly tinged buff.

**Similar species:** ♂ much like ♂ Rufous-shafted Woodstar (143), but gorget flared back to point on sides, plumage *dark* green, and tail lacks rufous (hard to see in field). ♀ from other ♀ woodstars (141, 143) by narrow rufous rump band.

**Behavior:** Much like White-bellied Woodstar,

but favors more wooded regions, often at lower el.

**Breeding:** 2 BC ♀♀, Jan, Santa Marta; 3 BC ♀♀, Oct, Santa Marta Mts. and Boyacá (Carriker; Olivares 1971).

**Status and habitat:** Humid forest, forest borders, shady coffee plantations, and disturbed areas with trees. Mainly highlands, occas. to foothills. Perhaps rare or uncommon (at least seldom seen).

**Range:** 500-2800m (usually above 1200m). Santa Marta Mts. to 800m (*astreans*); 1 rec. on e slope W Andes in Antioquia; w slope C Andes s to Valle and e slope C Andes from Cauca to Nariño; E Andes s to Cundinamarca (*heliodor*). Andes of nw Venez. to nw Ecuador; extreme e Panama (Cerro Pirre) and poss. adj. nw Colombia.

**Note:** *A. harterti* described from C Andes is prob. a hybrid (Meyer de Schauensee 1964).

**143. RUFOUS-SHAFTED WOODSTAR**
*Chaetocercus jourdanii*          Pl. 14, Map 498
**Identification:** 2.8″ (7cm). Bill straight and fairly short (0.4″, or 10mm). Much like Gorgeted Woodstar. ♂ differs in rosier (less violet) gorget that is not elongated to point on sides; upperparts paler and bronzy green (not dark green); and base of outer tail feathers mostly rufous (hard to see in field). ♀ differs from ♀ Gorgeted in having uniformly green upperparts (no rufous rump band) and sides more or less green.

**Similar species:** ♂ has reddest gorget of any Colombian woodstar. Cf. White-bellied Woodstar (141), which is not definitely known to overlap but may meet at s end of range.

**Behavior:** Sim. to that of White-bellied Woodstar.

**Breeding:** BC ♂ and 2 juvs., Nov, Norte de Santander (Carriker).

**Status and habitat:** Not well known. Apparently local in forest borders and disturbed areas. "Numerous" in flowering *Inga* trees over coffee, Nov 1947, s of Cúcuta (Carriker). Perhaps replaced s in E Andes by White-bellied Woodstar.

**Range:** 1400-1800m (prob. higher and lower). Both slopes of E Andes at extreme n end (s Cesar and Norte de Santander to 50km s of Cúcuta). N and w Venez. (900-3000m) incl. Perijá Mts. and ne Colombia.

**Note:** Prob. best placed in the genus *Acestrura*.

# TROGONS, QUETZALS: Trogonidae (13)

Trogons are mostly pan-tropical in distribution. In the New World they reach greatest abundance in humid regions of Central and South America. All are notable for their beautiful, often glossy or metallic colors, the quetzals being especially renowned for their elongated wing and tail coverts. Trogons are characterized by strongly graduated and square-tipped tails (held down), weak feet with two toes forward and two back, and upright posture. They feed on insects and fruit taken on the wing with a swoop and brief hover before falling away to a new perch. Nests are in natural cavities, woodpecker holes, or are excavated in wasp or termite nests or in soft rotten stubs. Young ♂♂ resemble ♀♀ and do not usually acquire definitive adult plumage for more than a year.

**1. CRESTED QUETZAL**
*Pharomachrus antisianus*          Pl. 17, Map 499
**Identification:** 13″ (33cm). ♂: *short crest on forehead* projects over bill; *mostly metallic emerald green* with red lower breast and belly; wing coverts and upper tail coverts elongated, latter projecting about 1″ (2.5cm) beyond tail; *3 outer tail feathers white*, rest black (underside of tail all white at rest); *bill orange yellow.* ♀: head and throat dull brown; otherwise bronzy green above; breast brownish gray, chest washed green, belly red, flanks brownish; *underside of tail black, outer feathers barred black and white on outer web* (rarely some white on inner web); *bill dusky;* no prom. crest; wing coverts and upper tail coverts not elongated.

**Similar species:** ♂ is only quetzal with all white tail from below; ♀ from ♂ or ♀ Golden-headed Quetzal (3) by black and white barring on tail edge from below; also from ♂ of 3 by dull brown head (not green).

**Voice:** Call a loud, deliberate *way-way-wáyo* in PN Cueva de los Guácharos, where most vocal Feb–Apr (P. Gertler); alarm a loud, inflected *ka-ka-ka-ka*, no. of notes var.

**Behavior:** Solitary or in pairs in mid. strata to subcanopy. Most often seen in fruiting trees, esp. those with larger fruits such as *Persea* and *Ocotea*, where they sally out and hover momentarily to pluck fruit. Otherwise often perch quietly and are easily overlooked. Flight undulating.

**Breeding:** 7 BC birds, Feb–June, C Andes and Perijá Mts. (Carriker).
**Status and habitat:** Uncommon. Humid forest, forest edges, and occas. tall second growth woodland. Often with Golden-headed Quetzal, though center of abundance apparently at slightly lower el.
**Range:** 1400-2800m. All 3 Andean ranges (on Pacific slope only sightings, Valle [to 1000m] and Cauca—Hilty), Perijá and Macarena Mts. Nw Venez. s in Andes to Bolivia.

## 2. WHITE-TIPPED QUETZAL
*Pharomachrus fulgidus*          Pl. 17, Map 500
**Identification:** 13″ (33cm). Very sim. to Crested Quetzal (1). ♂ from ♂ Crested by shorter frontal crest, crown golden bronze in contrast to back, and *underside of tail black with only terminal third of outer 3 tail feathers white.* ♀: like ♀ Crested, but crown bronzy green, breast greener, and outer 3 tail feathers tipped white and barred white near tip.
**Similar species:** Only quetzal in its range.
**Voice:** A loud *kirra*, or *kirra, kip*, and when excited *kieer, kip-kip-kip-a*, with var.
**Behavior:** As in Crested Quetzal.
**Breeding:** 4 BC birds, Jan–Apr, Santa Marta Mts. (Carriker). Pairs at cavities, mid-Mar and early Aug, 2000-2200m, Cuchilla de San Lorenzo (Hilty), and late Mar, 1600m (Todd and Carriker 1922); cavity in dead stub or trunk, 4-10m up.
**Status and habitat:** Common in humid forest, forest borders, second growth woodland, and moist ravines in coffee plantations.
**Range:** 1500-2500m. Santa Marta Mts. Colombia and n Venez.

## 3. GOLDEN-HEADED QUETZAL
*Pharomachrus auriceps*          Pl. 17, Map 501
**Identification:** 13″ (33cm). Sim. to Crested Quetzal. ♂ from ♂ Crested (1) by golden bronze (not emerald green) head, shorter crest, and *underside of tail uniformly black (no white).* ♀; from ♀ Crested by *solid black under tail surface.*
**Similar species:** In foothills on e Andean slope see Pavonine Quetzal (4).
**Voice:** Call in Peru a mellow, reedy, somewhat hawklike *wheeeu, we-weeeoo, we-weeeoo* (up to 4 *we-weeeoo* phrases) given deliberately (J. O'-Neill recording); up to 6-7 phrases in Ecuador (R. Ridgely).
**Behavior:** As in Crested Quetzal.
**Breeding:** 4 BC birds, Apr–June, C Andes and Perijá Mts. (Carriker); 7 BC birds, Apr, Cerro Pirre, e Panama (Wetmore 1968a); 2 eggs, grayish blue (Sclater and Salvin 1879).
**Status and habitat:** Uncommon in humid for-

est, forest edges, and occas. second growth woodland. Often with Crested Quetzal; the only quetzal reg. on the Pacific slope.
**Range:** 1400-2700m (to 600m on Pacific slope). Perijá Mts. and all 3 Andean ranges. Nw Venez. s in Andes to n Bolivia.

## 4. PAVONINE QUETZAL
*Pharomachrus pavoninus*          Map 502
**Identification:** 13″ (33cm.) Only quetzal e of Andes. *Bill orange red* (♂); *black with red base* (♀). ♂: metallic emerald green; lower breast and belly red; head tinged golden green; wing coverts and upper tail coverts elongated (latter reach to but rarely beyond tail tip); *underside of tail black.* ♀: like ♂ but duller, breast brownish, underside of tail black, *3 outer feathers notched and barred whitish buff on outer web.*
**Similar species:** ♂ from ♂ Crested or Golden-headed Quetzals (1, 3) by red bill; ♀ from ♀ Golden-headed by red at base of bill and tail barring; from ♀ Crested by red on bill.
**Voice:** Call a loud descending whistle followed by an emphatic *chok* note: *heeeeeear, chok!*; melancholy, slowly repeated about 4-6 times.
**Behavior:** Like other quetzals. Often attracted to a whistled imitation of its call.
**Status and habitat:** Uncommon (perhaps local) in humid *terra firme* forest in lowlands. Replaced in Andes by Golden-headed and Crested quetzals.
**Range:** To 500m (prob. higher). E of Andes from w Caquetá (formerly near Florencia) and Vaupés (Mitú) southward. S Venez. to e Ecuador, n Bolivia, and w Amazonian Brazil.

[In the genus *Trogon* all ♂ ♂ except White-tailed and Violaceous have vermiculated black and white patch on shoulders; these are not mentioned in the following descriptions. Shoulder patches on ♀ ♀ var. and not diagnostic in field.]

## 5. SLATY-TAILED TROGON
*Trogon massena*          Pl. 17, Map 503
**Identification:** 12-13″ (30-33cm). *Orange red bill* and eyering; dark eyes (♂); *lower mandible and base of bill red,* no eyering (♀). ♂: dark metallic bluish green, sides of head and throat black, *lower breast and belly red, underside of tail slaty* (no white). ♀: slaty gray, wings and tail blacker (no vermiculation on wing coverts), belly red, underside of tail slaty or sometimes with faint white notches on outer web of outer feathers and on tip.
**Similar species:** ♂ Blue-tailed Trogon (7) has peacock blue rump and tail; both sexes have

white eyes and no red on bill. Also cf. Black-tailed Trogon (6), which has yellow (not red) on bill.

**Voice:** Song a steady deliberate ser. of *cow* or *cue* notes, lower-pitched and slower than White-tailed Trogon.

**Behavior:** Found singly, in loose pairs, or occas. in families. ♂♂ sometimes gather in loose calling groups (Brown). Like other trogons, sluggish and often perch quietly for long periods, usually in mid. story or higher. Hover-glean fruit and insects. Flight is dipping and headlong.

**Breeding:** 4 BC birds, Feb, Chocó (Carriker). Panama nests (Mar–July) in termitaria (Willis and Eisenmann 1979); 3 bluish white eggs (Skutch 1972).

**Status and habitat:** Common in humid and wet forest and tall second growth; reg. come to forest borders or into clearings with scattered trees. Replaced e of Andes and in n Colombia by allied Black-tailed Trogon, but overlaps it in n Chocó.

**Range:** To 1100m. Pacific coast from Panama border and lower Atrato Val. southward. S Mexico to w Ecuador.

### 6. BLACK-TAILED TROGON
*Trogon melanurus*              Pl. 17, Map 504
**Identification:** 13″ (33cm) or e of Andes 11″ (28cm). Very sim. to Slaty-tailed Trogon (5). ♂: from ♂ Slaty-tailed *by yellow* (not red) *bill and narrow white breast band* separating green chest from red belly. ♀: from ♀ Slaty-tailed by *yellow* (not red) *lower mandible* and some faint vermiculation on shoulders.

**Similar species:** Only trogon e of Andes with all black tail from below (♀ rarely shows faint pale notching on tail edge). Shares red belly with Slaty-tailed, Blue-tailed, Collared, and Blue-crowned trogons (see 5, 7, 9, 12).

**Voice:** A ser. of *waao* notes almost identical to that of Slaty-tailed Trogon, perhaps given faster; also a bubbly purring trill.

**Behavior:** As in Slaty-tailed Trogon.

**Breeding:** 8 BC birds, Jan–May, Guajira to Chocó (Carriker; Haffer 1975); 1 ♀ ready to lay, Mar, e Panama (Wetmore 1968a).

**Status and habitat:** Common in lower Atrato Val. (Haffer 1975) and e of Andes; humid forest, forest edges, and second growth woodland.

**Range:** To 2200m (usually much lower) w of Andes; to 500m e of Andes. Pacific coast s to Baudó Mts. (Río Jurubidá), e in humid lowlands n of Andes to Santa Marta area and w Guajira (Carraipía), s in Magdalena Val. to w Cundinamarca (Fusagasugá) and throughout e of Andes (not yet rec. in Arauca and Vichada). C Panama to n Bolivia and s Brazil.

### 7. BLUE-TAILED TROGON
*Trogon comptus*               Pl. 17, Map 505
**Identification:** 11″ (28cm). Resembles better known Slaty-tailed Trogon. *Eyes white* (both sexes), *bill all yellow*, (♂); *lower mandible yellowish*, rest blackish (♀). ♂: mostly bluish green, *rump and tail purplish blue*; tail with broad, sharply-defined black tip from above, uniform black below; lower breast and belly red. ♀: dark gray with red belly; tail blackish from below.

**Similar species:** ♂ from ♂ Slaty-tailed Trogon (5) by smaller size, white eyes, yellow bill, blue rump and tail, and tail band. ♀ from ♀ Slaty-tailed by white eyes, yellow on bill, and darker gray plumage extending to upper belly. Black-tailed Trogon (6) has white breast band and dark eyes (both sexes).

**Voice:** Sim. to Slaty-tailed and Black-tailed trogons but even slower and lower-pitched (Haffer 1975).

**Behavior:** As in Slaty-tailed Trogon. Calling ♂♂ may gather in loose groups (Haffer 1975) as reported for Slaty-tailed (Brown) and Black-tailed trogons (O'Neill 1974).

**Breeding:** 1 BC ♂, early Mar, n Chocó (Haffer 1975).

**Status and habitat:** Usually less numerous than Slaty-tailed Trogon with which it sometimes occurs. Humid and wet forest and forest borders. Favors foothills and broken hilly terrain. Meets but not known to occur with Black-tailed Trogon along n boundary of range in Colombia and s boundary in w Ecuador.

**Range:** To 1800m. N slope of C Andes (above Pto. Valdivia), around northernmost end of W Andes and from upper Atrato Val. and Baudó Mts. southward on Pacific slope. W Colombia and nw Ecuador.

### 8. WHITE-TAILED TROGON
*Trogon viridis*               Pl. 17, Map 506
**Identification:** 11″ (28cm). *Bill bluish white* (or with dusky upper mandible—♀); *eyering light blue*. ♂: dark greenish black above becoming glossy violet on head, neck, and chest; breast and belly orange yellow; *underside of tail essentially white* (or feathers black broadly tipped white from below—*viridis*). ♀: mostly slaty with *orange yellow* lower breast and belly; underside of tail *mostly white* (or underside of tail slaty black, the feathers *tipped and barred white* on outer web—*viridis*).

**Similar species:** ♂ from all other "yellow-bellied" trogons by white under tail surface; also from Violaceous Trogon (13) by light blue (not yellow) eyering. ♀ (*viridis*) easily confused with ♀ Violaceous but larger, eyering complete and blue (not interrupted white), and never shows whitish chest band.

**Voice:** Song a ser. of brisk *kyoh* or *cow* notes (up to 16 or so), usually *accelerating* (or no acceleration—*chionurus*) and becoming louder near end, sometimes with a few slower *cow's* at end; also a low purr and single *chuck*.
**Behavior:** Much like others of the genus. Usually fairly high and sometimes remarkably confiding. ♂♂ may gather in excited calling groups, perhaps as form of courtship display.
**Breeding:** 8 BC birds, Jan–May, s Bolívar to Chocó; 1 BC ♂, June, w Caquetá (Carriker). In termite nests, Mar–July, Panama (Willis and Eisenmann 1979).
**Status and habitat:** Common in humid and wet forest, forest edges, and esp. younger forest and second growth woodland. Gallery forest in the llanos. With Black-tailed Trogon, the most numerous trogon e of Andes.
**Range:** To 1000m w of Andes; to 1200m e of Andes. Pacific coast, humid lowlands n of Andes to mid. Magdalena Val. and s to Honda, n Tolima (*chionurus*); throughout e of Andes (*viridis*). W Panama to w Ecuador, Bolivia, and s Brazil. Trinidad.

## 9. COLLARED TROGON
*Trogon collaris*                Pl. 17, Map 507
**Identification:** 10″ (25cm). Faint orange red eyering and yellowish bill (♂); prom. *broken whitish eyering*, upper mandible dusky, lower yellowish (♀). ♂: dark glossy green above and on chest; sides of head and throat black; *white band across breast, rest of underparts red*; underside of tail black *narrowly barred* white and with white tips on feathers. ♀: green of ♂ replaced by light coffee brown; red of underparts paler, sometimes pinkish; *tail rufous above with black tip, underside finely vermiculated black and white* (looks grayish at distance), feathers with narrow subterminal black bar and broad white tips (forms 3 bands of white).
**Similar species:** In mts. see Masked Trogon (10); in lowlands e of Andes, Blue-crowned Trogon (12).
**Voice:** A soft, unhurried *cu'du cu-cu-cu-cu-cu-cu-cu* (no. of *cu*'s var.), melancholy; also soft *purr*'s, a descending trill and *churr*'s.
**Behavior:** Like others of genus, but one of the most unsuspicious. Usually mid. story or lower.
**Breeding:** 6 BC birds, Jan–May; begging juv., Apr, W and C Andes (Miller 1963; Carriker); ♀ with nest material, Apr, upper Anchicayá Val. (Hilty); 2 eggs (Wetmore 1968a).
**Status and habitat:** Fairly common to common. Humid and wet forest, second growth woodland and edges; also *várzea* e of Andes. Generally much less numerous e of Andes (lowlands) than w of them (where found mainly in foothills or higher). Occurs locally with

highland ally Masked Trogon at upper end of range.
**Range:** Mainly 400-2000m (rec. to 2700m; to 3100m?). Perijá Mts., all 3 Andean ranges (E Andes from Bogota southward), Baudó Mts., and Macarena Mts.; e of Andes from extreme e Cundinamarca and w Meta s to Putumayo and Amazonas. E Mexico to w Ecuador, n Bolivia, and Amazonian and e Brazil. Trinidad.

## 10. MASKED TROGON
*Trogon personatus*                Pl. 17, Map 508
**Identification:** 10″ (25cm). Resembles Collared Trogon. ♂ from ♂ Collared (9) by bluish tinged head and rump, and underside of tail with *much finer wavy white bars* (or broader white tips and with white barring almost obsolete—*temperatus*, see note), and finer vermiculations on shoulders. ♀ from ♀ Collared by *all yellow bill* (not dusky), sharper black mask and throat, and *underside of tail sharply and narrowly barred black and white* (not vermiculated grayish).
**Similar species:** Narrower tail barring compared to ♂ Collared Trogon makes under tails of all forms of this sp. look mostly slaty with large, "blocky" white tail tips (very unlike Collared Trogon).
**Voice:** A soft, steady ser. of 4-8 *kwa* notes, the pitch somewhat higher than equivalent song of Collared Trogon (R. Ridgely and S. Gaulin 1980); also a descending trill often repeated over and over.
**Behavior:** Sim. to Collared Trogon.
**Breeding:** 12 BC birds, Apr–Aug, Santa Marta and Perijá Mts., W and C Andes (Carriker); cavity nest 3m up, 5 Mar, PN Cueva de los Guácharos; 2 white eggs (P. Gertler).
**Status and habitat:** Fairly common in humid and wet forest, forest edges, and second growth woodland. Occurs locally with Collared Trogon, though usually found at higher el.
**Range:** 700-2100m, Santa Marta Mts. (*sanctaemartae*); 1400-2900m, once to 180m, Perijá Mts., E Andes, and spottily in W Andes (*personatus*), and sighting in Macarena Mts. (25 Sept 1976—T. O. Lemke and P. Gertler); 1000-2500m, once to 3300m in W Andes (*assimilis*); 1900-3600m, E Andes and 2300-3500m C Andes (*temperatus*). Nw Venez. s in Andes to n Bolivia; tepuís of s Venez. and adj. n Brazil and s Guyana.
**Note:** The subsp. *temperatus* of C and E Andes has been considered a separate sp. (Highland Trogon) by Meyer de Schauensee (1964), but definite overlap with other subsp. unproven.

## 11. BLACK-THROATED TROGON
*Trogon rufus*                Pl. 17, Map 509
**Identification:** 10″ (25cm). Bill yellowish green, eyering light blue (♂); upper mandible dusky,

lower yellowish green; prom. *broken eyering white* (♀). ♂: upperparts, head, and chest *dark glossy green*; sides of head and upper throat black; faint white band across breast; *rest of underparts orange yellow; underside of tail narrowly and evenly barred black and white*, large white tips of outer feathers forming 3 bands. ♀: green of ♂ replaced by coffee brown; *white breast band diffused; lower underparts bright yellow*; tail rufous tipped black above, below as in ♂.

**Similar species:** ♂ is only "yellow-bellied" trogon with greenish head and chest (not violet). Cf. White-tailed and Violaceous trogons (8, 13). Other "yellow-bellied" ♀♀ are gray or slaty above and on chest (not brown).

**Voice:** A very slow, evenly spaced ser. of about 2-4 *cuk* notes, about 1 per sec or slower; also a low, churring *trrrr*.

**Behavior:** Like others of the genus. Mid. story or lower, often understory. Confiding; has been noted at army ant swarms.

**Breeding:** 14 BC birds, Feb–May, nw Colombia (Carriker; Haffer 1975); 9 Panama nests, Apr–July (Willis and Eisenmann 1979); cavity 1-4m up; 2 eggs (Skutch 1959a).

**Status and habitat:** Fairly common in humid forest and second growth woodland.

**Range:** To 1100m. Pacific coast and e in humid lowlands n of Andes to mid. Magdalena Val. (s to Honda, n Tolima); e of Andes from s Meta (Macarena Mts.) and Caquetá to Amazonas (prob. also Guainía and Vaupés). Honduras to w Ecuador, e Peru, n Argentina, and se Brazil.

## 12. BLUE-CROWNED TROGON

*Trogon curucui*                     Pl. 17, Map 510
**Identification:** 9.5″ (24cm). Dull yellowish bill, faint yellow orange eyering (♂); upper mandible mostly dusky, lower dull yellowish, *prom. broken white eyering* (♀). ♂: upperparts and chest coppery green with *strong bluish gloss on crown, neck, and tail*; sides of head and throat black; *narrow diffused* (indistinct) *white band across breast*; *belly pinkish red*; underside of tail black, the feathers narrowly barred and tipped white (white bars half as wide as black). ♀: *mostly gray*, pinkish red lower underparts separated from gray breast by faint white band; underside of tail black, *outer webs of feathers notched and tipped white*.

**Similar species:** ♂ from ♂ Collared Trogon (9) by blue crown and faint (not crisp) breast band. ♀ from ♀ Collared by gray (not brown) upperparts and chest; from ♀ Black-tailed (6) by smaller size, broken white eyering, and white notching on tail (from below).

**Voice:** Song much like White-tailed Trogon

but tends to accelerate throughout then stop suddenly (T. Parker); purrs like others of the genus.

**Behavior:** Midlevels or lower and otherwise like other *Trogon*.

**Status and habitat:** Uncommon in humid *terra firme* and *várzea* forest, tall second growth, and at edges.

**Range:** To 500m (prob. higher). E of Andes from s Meta (Macarena Mts.) s to Putumayo and Amazonas. Brazil n of Amazon (Amazonas) and from e Colombia and Brazil s of Amazon to Paraguay and n Argentina.

## 13. VIOLACEOUS TROGON

*Trogon violaceus*                     Pl. 17, Map 511
**Identification:** 9.5″ (24 cm). Bill greenish white, *eyering orange yellow* (♂); upper mandible dusky; *broken white eyering* (♀). ♂: dark shining green to blue green above, *crown, neck, and chest glossy violet blue*; mask and throat black; narrow diffused breast band white; *lower underparts orange yellow; underside of tail black narrowly and evenly barred white*, outer feathers broadly tipped white forming 3 bands. ♀: mostly gray, lower breast and belly yellow, sometimes partially separated from gray breast by indistinct white band; underside of tail black, *outer webs of outer 3 feathers barred and tipped white*.

**Similar species:** ♂ from ♂ Black-throated Trogon (11) by violet blue (not green) crown, neck, and chest; yellow eyering; and absence of vermiculated shoulder patch. Also cf. larger White-tailed Trogon (8).

**Voice:** Song a ser. of up to 15 rather soft *cow* or *cuh* notes, faster (about 2 per sec) and higher-pitched than Slaty-tailed Trogon and steadier and without acceleration of some White-tailed Trogons.

**Behavior:** Like others of the genus. Midlevels or lower.

**Breeding:** 2 BC ♀♀, Mar, s Córdoba (Carriker); Jan young, Panama (Willis and Eisenmann 1979); 10 nests, Feb–June, Costa Rica; all in wasp nests high in trees (Skutch 1972).

**Status and habitat:** A nonforest bird favoring forest borders, shady and lighter second growth woodland, and clearings with scattered trees, humid to dry regions.

**Range:** To 1000m (higher ?). From e side of Gulf of Urabá (Río Tulupa) e across n Colombia to Guajira, Cauca Val. (prior to deforestation s to Popayán), Magdalena Val. (s to Honda, n Tolima), and e of Andes from Norte de Santander (Catatumbo lowlands) s to Amazonas (no recs. in e llanos or Guainía). E Mexico to w Ecuador, n Bolivia, and Amazonian Brazil. Trinidad.

# KINGFISHERS: Alcedinidae (6)

Kingfishers are worldwide in distribution but poorly represented in the New World, with only six of the more than eighty-five species occurring there. They are characterized by short necks, large heads, and often bushy crests. The bills are pointed and disproportionally long and stout, their legs short, their feet weak, and their two front toes joined for more than a third of their length. All New World kingfishers live near water and eat fish taken by diving. Nests are burrows in banks and usually overlook water (except that of the Pygmy Kingfisher); white or buffy white eggs are laid at the end of the unlined burrow.

### 1. RINGED KINGFISHER
*Ceryle torquata*          Ill. 72, Map 512
**Identification:** 15" (38cm). Largest Colombian kingfisher. Ragged crest. ♂: upperparts blue gray, throat and sides of neck white, *rest of underparts rufous chestnut.* ♀: sim. but with *broad blue gray chest band* narrowly bordered below with white; *lower underparts rufous chestnut* as in ♂.
**Similar species:** Smaller Belted Kingfisher (2) lacks the extensive rufous below; ♂ Belted has a single blue gray chest band; ♀ also a narrow rufous band.
**Voice:** Flight call a loud coarse *klek* often repeated; same repeated rapidly in rough rattle in alarm.
**Behavior:** Alone or in pairs and often seen flying high overhead with uneven wing beats and unsteady flight as they commute between watercourses. Spend most of time on perch watching water, then dive, usually without hovering, for fish. On average, hunt from higher perch (5-10m up) than other kingfishers and eat larger fish, mostly in 50-150mm range (J. V. Remsen).
**Breeding:** 1 nest, 16 Feb, PN Isla de Salamanca, and another, 18 Sept, Pto. Inírida (Hilty). In s Amazonas, breed when river lev-

els recede, exposing river banks, mainly June–Sept., and late Nov–Mar, but timing var. (J. V. Remsen). BC ♂, Feb, Antioquia (Carriker); in Venez. Orinoco June–Aug; form loose colonies of 4-5 pairs in favorable areas; colonies over 100 pairs reported (Cherrie 1916).
**Status and habitat:** Common along most bodies of fresh water and in mangroves.
**Range:** Mostly below 500m, (a few to 2600m on Sabana de Bogotá). Throughout. S Texas and Mexico to Tierra del Fuego. Lesser Antilles; Trinidad.

### 2. BELTED KINGFISHER
*Ceryle alcyon*          Ill. 72, Map 513
**Identification:** 12" (30cm). Carib. region. Ragged crest. ♂: upperparts blue gray with white collar almost encircling neck; *below white with a single blue gray chest band.* ♀: sim. but also has *rufous breast band* that extends down on sides and flanks.
**Similar species:** See larger Ringed Kingfisher (1).
**Voice:** A loud wooden rattle in flight or perched, higher-pitched and not as coarse as that of Ringed Kingfisher.
**Behavior:** Usually seen alone in Colombia. Often hovers momentarily before diving. Wing beats

72. BELTED KINGFISHER (♀ left), RINGED KINGFISHER (♀ right)

uneven and flight unsteady as in larger Ringed Kingfisher.

**Status and habitat:** Rare winter visitant and winter resident, late Nov–Feb.; most recs. in or near mangroves on Carib. coast. In Panama, where more widespread, rec. mid-Sept–early Apr (Ridgely 1976); in Venez., Oct–Apr (Meyer de Schauensee and Phelps 1978).

**Range:** Spottily on Carib. coast. Breeds in N America; winters from s US to Panama and W Indies, rarely n S America from Colombia to the Guianas.

### 3. AMAZON KINGFISHER
*Chloroceryle amazona*          Pl. 19, Map 514

**Identification:** 11″ (28cm). Largest *green* kingfisher. ♂: *dark, shiny, oily green above* with narrow white collar on hindneck; below *white* with broad rufous breast band and a few green spots on flanks. ♀: sim. but rufous breast band of ♂ replaced by broken band of green.

**Similar species:** Most likely confused with much smaller Green Kingfisher (4), which has wings conspic. spotted and barred white. Green-and-rufous Kingfisher (5) has no white below and a buffy rufous collar on sides of neck.

**Voice:** In flight or perched a very low-pitched, buzzy *chat*, often repeated; when alarmed a descending ser. of *tew*'s, also used in interspecific encounters (J. V. Remsen).

**Behavior:** Scattered individuals perch in vicinity of water on rather exposed snags. Spend most of time watching water from a perch and rarely hover before diving. Hunt mostly from perches 2-10m up (higher than Green, lower than Ringed Kingfisher); take fish in 37-112mm range (J. V. Remsen). Flight smoother and more direct than Ringed and Belted kingfishers.

**Breeding:** Near Leticia same schedule as Ringed Kingfisher (J. V. Remsen). Aug nestlings, Carimagua, Meta (S. Furniss). 3-4 eggs, at end of burrow to 1.6m long in bank (Skutch 1957).

**Status and habitat:** Common along most bodies of fresh water. Prefer wide, open, and sunlit streams and rivers; with Ringed Kingfisher usually the only kingfisher along open banks of large rivers. Less numerous on smaller shady streams, or on fast-flowing water or stony ripples in foothills.

**Range:** To 1200m. Throughout, except Pacific coast s of Valle (to Río Anchicayá). Mexico to n Argentina; Trinidad and Tobago.

### 4. GREEN KINGFISHER
*Chloroceryle americana*          Pl. 19, Map 515

**Identification:** 7.5″ (19cm). Almost a miniature of Amazon Kingfisher. ♂: dark shining green above with narrow white collar almost encircling neck and *several rows of white spots on wings; outer tail feathers mostly white* (conspic. in flight), below mostly white with a broad chestnut band and green spots on flanks. ♀; sim. but rufous breast band of ♂ replaced by 2 bands of green spots.

**Similar species:** From Amazon Kingfisher (3) by white wing spots, white in tail, smaller size, and brighter green color (not dark oily green). ♀ Amazon has only a single breast band (not 2).

**Voice:** Flight call a low, pebbly *choot*, usually repeated 2-3 times with stuttering or clicking quality; also a descending ser. of *tew*'s sim. to Amazon Kingfisher but much softer and more rapid (J. V. Remsen).

**Behavior:** Scattered individuals perch mostly 1-3m up on branches or twigs near cover along stream banks or lake edges where they watch water for prey; sometimes hover before diving. Eat fish mostly in 30-56mm range (J. V. Remsen). Straight buzzy flight usually very close to water.

**Breeding:** BC ♂, 22 Jan, Chocó (Carriker). In Amazonas presum. same schedule as preceding 2 spp. Fledged young, late Aug, Leticia (J. V. Remsen); in Panama, Jan–Apr, 3-5 eggs, in burrow usually well hidden by overhanging vegetation (Wetmore 1968a).

**Status and habitat:** Fairly common along med.-sized to small streams and edges of lakes and ponds bordered by shrubbery and trees, but usually not streams with completely closed canopy overhead; also mangroves and small nos. along bouldery mt. streams.

**Range:** To 1500m. Throughout. Sw US to Chile and c Argentina.

### 5. GREEN-AND-RUFOUS KINGFISHER
*Chloroceryle inda*          Pl. 19, Map 516

**Identification:** 8.5″ (22cm). A large edition of Pygmy Kingfisher. ♂: dark shining green above, *broad collar on sides of neck, and entire underparts rich orange rufous*; wings and tail lightly speckled white. ♀: sim. but with green and white chest band.

**Similar species:** An all *green and rufous* kingfisher (shows no white below). Pygmy Kingfisher (6) is much smaller and has white belly.

**Voice:** Much like Green Kingfisher. Flight call a low gravelly *zyoot*, sometimes repeated several times; also a descending ser. of *tew*'s in interspecific interactions (J. V. Remsen).

**Behavior:** Usually seen alone. Perches low in shrubbery or concealed on snags inside foliage, usually within 3m of water. Takes fish in 30-76mm range (J. V. Remsen). Flies rather straight, fast (not buzzy), and low over water, infrequently in open.

**Breeding:** 1 BC ♂, 17 Mar, Chocó (Carriker). **Status and habitat:** Often common but very difficult to see. Narrow streams usually covered by closed or partially closed forest canopy; csp. *várzea* streams and adj. flooded forest where water flows under canopy, and not where water meets stream bank as in other kingfishers (J. V. Remsen), also mangroves and less frequently in shrubbery along banks of open streams. **Range:** To 500m. Pacific coast; Carib. coast from the lower Atrato Val. locally to Santa Marta region (prob. entire n lowlands); throughout e of Andes. Nicaragua to w Ecuador, n Bolivia, and s Brazil.

### 6. PYGMY KINGFISHER

*Chloroceryle aenea*          Pl. 19, Map 517
**Identification:** 5″ (13cm). *Sparrow-sized* kingfisher. ♂: dark bronze green above; broad collar on sides of neck, and *underparts rich orange rufous*; belly and under tail coverts white; wings lightly speckled white. ♀: sim. but with band of mixed green and white across breast.
**Similar species:** Green-and-rufous Kingfisher (5) lacks the white belly. Green Kingfisher (4)

is larger, mostly white below, incl. throat, and flashes white in tail in flight.
**Voice:** Flight call a weak clicking *choyt*, sometimes repeated; gravelly and more inflected than corresponding calls of previous 2 spp.; also a descending ser. of *tew* notes, drier, faster, and shorter than the larger sp. (J. V. Remsen).
**Behavior:** An inconspic. little bird usually seen perched low in shrubbery over water. Takes fish in 8-37mm range; reported insect sallies are apparently aborted dives for fish (J. V. Remsen). Flight is fast, buzzy, and difficult to follow; dives without hovering.
**Breeding:** In Trinidad May–Sept; burrow in bank, roots of fallen tree, etc., not necessarily near water; 3-4 eggs (ffrench 1973).
**Status and habitat:** Often common but hard to see. Thicker shrubbery along banks of small wooded streams, forest pools, flooded *várzea* forest, and in mangroves. Perhaps absent from drier regions even in suitable habitat.
**Range:** Mostly below 500m (occas. to 2600m on Sabana de Bogotá). Pacific coast (few recs.), lowlands n of Andes e to Santa Marta area, Sabana de Bogotá and w slope E Andes in Cundinamarca; generally e of Andes. S Mexico to w Ecuador, n Bolivia, and s Brazil. Trinidad.

# MOTMOTS: Momotidae (4)

Motmots are a small, interesting neotropical family, reaching greatest diversity in northern Middle America. Except for the Tody, they are best known for their long, often racket-tipped tails, frequently swung from side to side. The racket tips on the central tail feathers apparently develop as a result of a weak attachment of the feather barbs, which then break off during preening or abrasion. Birds lacking racket tips, or with only one tip, are regularly seen at certain seasons, and some forms east of the Andes never develop them. As a rule motmots are sluggish, inconspicuous birds of forest or lighter woodland. They feed on a variety of invertebrates, small vertebrates, and some fruit and are most active at dawn and in the late afternoon. Nests, as far as known, are unlined burrows; the eggs are white.

### 1. TODY MOTMOT

*Hylomanes momotula*          Pl. 18, Map 518
**Identification:** 7″ (18cm). Chunky and large-headed with no racket tips on short tail. Crown greenish rufous; narrow *black mask through eyes bordered above by short blue eyestripe, below by buffy white stripe*; otherwise dull green above, wedge-shaped tail olive brown; buffy throat bordered laterally by *short white stripe*; rest of underparts dull brownish olive, more greenish on sides, whitish on abdomen.
**Similar species:** The smallest motmot, easily told by striped facial pattern. Dull plumage and sedentary habits recall a puffbird.
**Voice:** Call a loud, resonant *kwa-kwa-kwa-kwa*

. . . in e Panama (Ridgely 1976); also a rapid *Otus*-like, quavering *cooooooo-o-o-oh*, in Belize (Willis *in* Smithe 1966).
**Behavior:** Occurs alone or in pairs in the lower story, often about eye level. As a rule quiet and unobtrusive, sitting motionless except for side to side flicking of tail and sudden darts for prey.
**Breeding:** Laying ♀, 22 Feb, Chocó; BC ♀, May, n Antioquia (Carriker). Prob. burrow like other motmots but unreported (Wetmore 1968a).
**Status and habitat:** Apparently rare: known from only a few scattered localities. Perhaps more common near Panama border as fre-

quently reported in e Darién (R. Ridgeley). Favors humid foothill forest.

**Range:** To 1500m. From Panama boundary s on Pacific coast to Baudó Mts. (Nuquí), and e around northernmost W Andes to lower Cauca Val. (Valdivia). Se Mexico to nw Colombia.

## 2. BROAD-BILLED MOTMOT
*Electron platyrhynchum*        Pl. 18, Map 519
**Identification:** 13″ (33cm). *Head, neck, and upper breast cinnamon rufous*; broad black mask through eyes; spot on breast black; otherwise grass green above, lower underparts and *chin bluish green; tail long, usually ending in a racket tip (or no rackets—pyrrholaemum).*
**Similar species:** Easily confused with Rufous Motmot (3), which is decidedly larger, has rufous of underparts extending to belly (not midbreast), and has smaller breast spot and no blue green on chin (latter hard to see). In general Rufous is longer-tailed and has a proportionally longer, narrower, and more curved bill; calls also differ.
**Voice:** Distinctive call a nasal resonant *oonk* or *quoonk*, singly, in longer ser., or in duet, 1 of pair repeating *ooonk* at about 2-sec intervals, the other joining with faster *kruk* triplets; triplets also given separately. Esp. vocal at dawn and dusk.
**Behavior:** Alone or in pairs at almost all levels but more frequently from mid. to lower story. Sit quietly and unobtrusively on bare horizontal limb, sometimes slowly shifting tail from side to side, then sally suddenly to limbs or foliage for larger prey, much like allied Rufous Motmot but usually harder to see than latter.
**Breeding:** Stub-tailed juv. with 2 ads., Mar, upper Anchicayá Val. (Hilty); unlined bank burrow to 1m long; 3 eggs (Skutch 1971b).
**Status and habitat:** Fairly common in humid and wet forest, and second growth woodland, sometimes near small forest openings; lowlands and foothills.
**Range:** To 1100m. Pacific coast (*platyrhynchum*); humid lowlands n of Andes e to mid. Magdalena Val. and s to Remedios, Antioquia (*colombianum*); e of Andes in s Meta (sighting, 5 Feb 1975), Marcarena Mts.—T. O. Lemke) and w Caquetá s (*pyrrholaemum*), prob. also Amazonas. Honduras to w Ecuador; e Colombia to n Bolivia and w and c Amazonian and s Brazil.
**Note:** The *pyrrholaemum* group (Plain-tailed Motmot) e of Andes does not acquire racket tail tips and is by some considered a separate sp.

## 3. RUFOUS MOTMOT
*Baryphthengus ruficapillus*        Pl. 18, Map 520
**Identification:** 18″ (46cm). *Head, neck, and underparts cinnamon rufous*, broad black mask through eyes; spot on breast black; belly bluish green; remaining upperparts green, *primaries violet blue* (often hard to see); long tail usually with racket tip (or no rackets—*martii*).
**Similar species:** See Broad-billed Motmot (2).
**Voice:** Call often heard well before dawn, an echoing and owllike *oo-doot* or *oot hoot-hoot* (occas. up to 7 notes), often answered by other individuals.
**Behavior:** Solitary or in pairs from upper understory to mid. story, at times into subcanopy, esp. when calling. Perch upright and move abruptly. Prey seized in sudden sally to foliage, limb, or trunk, occas. to ground; sometimes follow army ants. Often swing tail from side to side like a pendulum, esp. when alarmed.
**Breeding:** 2 BC birds, Mar, Chocó (Carriker). 7 Panama nests, holes in gully, Apr–Sept (Willis and Eisenmann 1979); others Feb–Mar (Wetmore 1968a).
**Status and habitat:** Uncommon to fairly common in humid and wet forest and tall second growth woodland in lowlands and foothills. Usually does not tolerate drier woodland and disturbed second growth areas favored by Blue-crowned Motmot.
**Range:** To 1000m. Pacific coast, humid lowlands along n base of Andes and mid. Magdalena Val. s to Honda, n Tolima (*semirufus*); e of Andes from s Meta (Macarena Mts.) to Putumayo (*martii*). Sight recs. e to Vaupés (El Dorado, June 1976—R. Ridgely) and s Amazonas (J. V. Remsen; Hilty). E Nicaragua s to w Ecuador; e Colombia s to Amazonian Brazil and Bolivia. Isolated population (*ruficapillus*) from e Brazil (Goiás) s to s Paraguay and n Argentina.

## 4. BLUE-CROWNED MOTMOT
*Momotus momota*        Pl. 18, Map 521
**Identification:** 16″ (41cm). *Black crown encircled by a band of turquoise deepening to violet on hindcrown; black mask through eyes*; otherwise olive green above; underparts cinnamon; throat and chest tinged olive; small black breast spot; *long tail usually with racket tip.* Or underparts olive green tinged tawny (*microstephanus; momota*). Or larger, 19″ (48 cm), grass green above, olive green below (*aequatorialis*).
**Similar species:** Other motmots have rufous heads or are smaller.
**Voice:** Lowland forms e and w of Andes usu-

ally give a low owllike *hoo-doot*; also a single quavering or tremulous *hrrroo*, sim. to but softer than corresponding call of Rufous Motmot (Ridgely 1976).
**Behavior:** Often in loosely assoc. pairs in the low or mid. part of trees, occas. higher when calling. Sit motionless, or if disturbed slowly swing tail from side to side, but not conspic. despite large size. Sally abruptly to foliage, branches, or ground for prey.
**Breeding:** 2 BC ♀♀, Jan and June, C and W Andes (Carriker); 1 in Feb, Macarena Mts. (Olivares 1962); a Mar nest, Huila (Miller 1963). 3 eggs, often in burrow dug mos. earlier (Skutch 1964d). May roost in burrows (ffrench 1973).
**Status and habitat:** Fairly common (easily overlooked) in humid forest borders, second growth woodland, gallery forest, cultivated areas with thickets, tree-lined borders, and woodlots; not inside tall forest. Local in dry forest in Carib. region.
**Range:** To 1300m (or 1500-3100m—*aequatorialis*). Throughout except Pacific coast s of

6°40′N. Panama boundary s on Pacific coast to Río Napipí and n of Andes in s Córdoba to lower Río Cauca (*conexus*); n Sucre e to w Guajira and s in Magdalena Val. to n Huila (*subrufescens*); Snía. Macuira, e Guajira (*spatha*); Andean highlands above 1500m (*aequatorialis*); e of Andes in Norte de Santander (*osgoodi*) and from Arauca southward (*microstephanus*); e Vichada along Río Orinoco (*momota*). E Mexico to n Argentina and s Brazil. Trinidad.
**Note 1:** *M. aequatorialis* of the Andes of Colombia and e Ecuador and incl. *chlorolaemus* of e Peru is almost surely a separate sp. (Highland Motmot) and was so regarded by Chapman (1923) and presently by Parker et al. (1982) and R. Ridgely. **Note 2:** For discussion on plumage color var. and the synonymizing of *M. m. reconditus* with *M. m. conexus*, see Wetmore (1968a). **Note 3:** The isolated lowland population of *M. m. argenticinctus* of w Ecuador and nw Peru is known n to Esmeraldas and may occur in sw Nariño.

# JACAMARS: Galbulidae (12)

Jacamars are a New World family ranging from southern Mexico to northern Argentina. Although a few are short-tailed and predominantly brown or chestnut, they are best known for their shimmering metallic green plumage, slender tapered bodies, and rather long tails. Most have long slender bills, and in appearance, as well as habit of sallying for flying insects from an open perch, they recall Old World beeeaters (Meropidae). Jacamars are mainly birds of wooded or partially wooded lowlands; only one species is confined to montane forest. As far as known, all nest in burrows dug in banks or in termitaries. The eggs are white. Jacamars are usually grouped with the puffbirds in a suborder of Piciforms (woodpeckers, etc.), but some recent evidence indicates they may actually be more closely related to kingfishers (Sibley and Ahlquist 1972; Haffer 1974).

## 1. WHITE-EARED JACAMAR
*Galbalcyrhynchus leucotis*       Pl. 18, Map 522
**Identification:** 8″ (20cm). Chunky with short square tail. *Large kingfisherlike bill pink with dusky tip. Mostly deep reddish chestnut with conspic. white cheeks*; crown, wings, and tail glossed bronzy black; feet and narrow eyering reddish. In flight looks broad-winged and short-tailed.
**Similar species:** Recalls a small kingfisher. Pink bill (often looks whitish), chestnut plumage, and white cheeks are diagnostic.
**Voice:** Occas. a loud *kyew*, singly or repeated in ser.; also a sharp prolonged rising trill somewhat like a woodcreeper (J. V. Remsen); calls may be given by solitary birds or by several in group concert.
**Behavior:** Single birds, pairs, or groups up to 8, occas. more, perch on open dead limbs in tall treetops and sally to air for insects. Some-

times drop lower along edges. Fly quickly and directly with buzzy wing beats.
**Breeding:** 2 BC ♂♂, 21 June, w Caquetá (Carriker).
**Status and habitat:** Humid *terra firme* or *várzea* forest and second growth woodland, esp. along forest borders overlooking streams and clearings where often common locally.
**Range:** To 500m. E of Andes from s Meta (Macarena Mts.) s to Putumayo and Amazonas. Se Colombia, ne Ecuador, ne Peru, and c Amazonian Brazil.
**Note:** Some consider the southern *G. purusianus* of e c Peru, w Amazonian Brazil, and n Bolivia a subsp. of the northern *G. leucotis*, calling the enlarged sp. Chestnut Jacamar. The contact zone is unknown, and no intermeds. have been found (Haffer 1974).

[*Brachygalba*: Rather small; short-tailed; upperparts brown to blackish brown.]

## 2. BROWN JACAMAR
*Brachygalba lugubris*        Pl. 19, Map 523
**Identification:** 7" (18cm). Bill very long (2", or 51mm) and slender. *Mostly sooty brown*; throat dingy brownish white; *center of lower breast and belly buffy to buffy white*; wings and tail bluish black.
**Similar species:** Pale-headed Jacamar (3) has a mostly ashy white head, white throat, and a chestnut band across white upper belly; otherwise sim.
**Voice:** Call a high descending and insectlike *tick-tick-tick-ti-ti-ti-tit-t-t-t* ending in a stuttering trill.
**Behavior:** Pairs or small families sally into the open from an exposed or partially exposed perch 2-14m up.
**Breeding:** 3 juvs. with ads., late Mar, w Meta (Brown); BC ♂, 28 May, w Caquetá (Carriker).
**Status and habitat:** Local in gallery forest, savanna woodland borders, edges of fields, river banks, and shrubby clearings in forested zones. Not inside forest but often on dead snags at forest or woodland edge and often in regions of extensive humid forest.
**Range:** To 1200m. E of Andes from Meta (Villavicencio; Pto. López; Carimagua—S. Furniss; and ne Guainía (sighting, Pto. Inírida, 1978—Hilty and M. Robbins), s to Putumayo, prob. Amazonas. The Guianas and s Venez. (c Amazonas and Bolívar) s locally to e Bolivia and s Brazil.
**Note:** White-throated Jacamar (*B. albogularis*) of w Amazonian Brazil and extreme ne Peru is known from the Río Javarí about 100km sw of Leticia. Slightly smaller (6") than allied Brown Jacamar; mainly blackish glossed greenish blue; white throat extending onto sides of head and above eye as a superciliary; belly rufous; bill long, slender, and yellow.

## 3. PALE-HEADED JACAMAR
*Brachygalba goeringi*        Pl. 19, Map 524
**Identification:** 7" (18cm). Bill very long (2", or 51mm) and slender. *Head, neck, and upper back pale ashy brown*; rest of upperparts dark brown glossed greenish to bluish black; throat buffy white; chest and sides dark brown, *center of breast and lower underparts white with broad chestnut band across upper belly.* Imm. has whiter throat and buffy nape.
**Similar species:** Recalls Brown Jacamar (2) but head very pale (looks whitish at a distance) in contrast to upperparts and chest.
**Voice:** Call a high thin *weet*, singly or in a ser.

becoming faster, higher in pitch, and ending in a trill, *weet, weet weet t'weet-t'weet-t'weet' ti'ti'ti't't* (Skutch 1968).
**Behavior:** Usually in pairs or small family groups perching on fairly high exposed branches or lower on shrubs, overhanging branches, and roots along stream banks. Sally for flying insects, often in big acrobatic loops (Skutch 1968; Hilty).
**Breeding:** 4 older nestlings, c Venez., 3 May; burrow used as roost after nesting (Skutch 1968).
**Status and habitat:** Local. Gallery forest borders and drier open terrain with bushes, trees, and thickets. Replaced southward in borders of more wooded country by Brown Jacamar (ranges not in contact).
**Range:** To 400m. E of Andes in Arauca and nw Casanare. Perhaps s to Río Meta. Colombia and c Venez.

## 4. DUSKY-BACKED JACAMAR
*Brachygalba salmoni*        Pl. 18, Map 525
**Identification:** 7" (18cm). Bill very long (2", or 51mm) and slender. *Upperparts, chest, and sides dark greenish black*; chest somewhat glossy and crown browner; throat white (or buffy—♀); *belly and center of breast cinnamon.*
**Similar species:** Smaller, shorter-tailed, and much duller than Rufous-tailed Jacamar (9).
**Voice:** A high-pitched insistent *pe-pe-pe-peet* or *pe-peet* or sim. var., often in long ser.
**Behavior:** Separated pairs perch erect and look about alertly from open horizontal branches, usually high and above those used by Rufous-tailed Jacamar. Sally med. to long distances for flying insects and return to same perch.
**Breeding:** 4 BC ♂♂, late Jan–Feb, nw Colombia (Haffer 1975; Carriker).
**Status and habitat:** Fairly common in humid forest borders, second growth with tall trees, openings in forest, or along forested streams; not inside forest.
**Range:** To about 600m. From Panama boundary e through Gulf of Urabá region to n Sucre (Snía. de San Jacinto), n end of W Andes (s Córdoba) and n end of C Andes (Río Nechí). E Panama (e Darién) and nw Colombia.

[*Galbula*: Tail longer and more graduated than *Brachygalba*; plumage metallic.]

## 5. YELLOW-BILLED JACAMAR
*Galbula albirostris*        Pl. 19, Map 526
**Identification:** 7.5" (19cm). Bill rather long; *lower mandible yellow*, upper dusky. Shining metallic bronzy green above, becoming metallic purplish brown on crown; throat white (or buff—

♀); *rest of underparts incl. underside of tail cinnamon rufous*; lores, eyering, and feet yellow. (Or emerald green above, upper mandible yellow tipped dusky—*albirostris*).
**Similar species:** Only jacamar with yellow on bill and mostly rufous underparts. See White-chinned Jacamar (7).
**Voice:** Call a sharp *peek*, sometimes repeated in long rapid ser. by 1 to several birds; song a high-pitched *peea peea-pee-pee-te-t-t-e'e'e'e'e'-e*, ending in a thrill.
**Behavior:** Single birds, loose pairs, or occas. families perch on rather exposed horizontal limbs in the lower or lower mid. story. Like other jacamars, sit erect with alert attitude and look about actively with bill up, then sally for flying insects. Frequently join mixed bird flocks.
**Status and habitat:** Uncommon in humid *terra firme* and *várzea* forest interior, occas. at small forest openings. Much more a bird of forest interior than most jacamars.
**Range:** To 500m. E of Andes from s Meta (Macarena Mts.) s to Putumayo and Amazonas (*chalcocephala*); Mitú, Vaupés (*albirostris*). The Guianas and s Venez. s to e Ecuador, e Peru, and Amazonian Brazil.

## 6. GREEN-TAILED JACAMAR
*Galbula galbula*                   Pl. 19, Map 527
**Identification:** 8″ (20cm). Bill very long (2″, or 51mm) and slender. Upperparts and chest band shining metallic coppery green, throat white (or buff—♀), *lower underparts rufous chestnut*; tail proportionally shorter than others of genus and very rounded at tip, metallic bluish green above, *dusky tinged bluish below*.
**Similar species:** Bronzy Jacamar (10) is darker, more bluish green, with white (not rufous chestnut) belly. Great Jacamar (12) is much larger and has a heavy bill. White-chinned Jacamar (7) has rufous in tail and dark green throat (only chin whitish).
**Voice:** Call a high plaintive *peer*, frequently repeated (Hilty); also a rhythmic *peep-peep* . . . and occas. a rhythmic *daw-dit-dot-dit* (Snyder 1966).
**Behavior:** Sim. to Rufous-tailed Jacamar. Perch and sally at low to mid. levels in shrubby borders.
**Breeding:** BC birds, Feb–Mar, upper Orinoco, Venez. (Friedmann 1948).
**Status and habitat:** Shrubby edges of tall humid forest, gallery forest, and second growth woodland. Favor shrubby areas, esp. along small streams.
**Range:** To 300m. From e Vichada (Maipures) w to ne Meta (Carimagua—S.Furniss); prob. Guainía. The Guianas, s Venez., and n and c Brazil.

## 7. WHITE-CHINNED JACAMAR
*Galbula tombacea*                  Pl. 18, Map 528
**Identification:** 8.5″ (22cm). Bill long (2″, or 51mm) and slender. Upperparts, throat, and breast *dark metallic bronzy green; crown dusky brownish glossed blue on rearcrown; chin spot whitish* (hard to see); belly and underside of tail rufous chestnut. ♀: belly paler ochraceous cinnamon.
**Similar species:** Bronzy Jacamar (10) has white throat and belly; Yellow-billed Jacamar (5) has yellow bill and mostly rufous underparts. See note below.
**Voice:** Call a repeated *keelíp* much like Rufous-tailed Jacamar; song a soft slowly accelerating ser., *pee-pee-pee-pe-pe-pe'pe'pe'pe'e'e'* much like others of the genus.
**Behavior:** Sim. to Rufous-tailed Jacamar. Perches 1-8m up and sallies for flying insects in lower growth and shrubbery near treefalls or other forest openings.
**Status and habitat:** Widespread but seldom numerous. Shrubby gallery forest borders and in Amazonas in cluttered treefall openings or borders of *várzea* forest. Replaces Rufous-tailed Jacamar in w Amazonia n of the Amazon and is itself replaced some distance s of the Amazon by *G. cyanescens* (see note).
**Range:** To 1200m. E of Andes from w Meta (Villavicencio area) and Vaupés (Mitú) southward. E Ecuador, ne Peru, and w Amazonian Brazil (both sides of Amazon).
**Note:** Bluish-fronted Jacamar (*G. cyanescens*) is very sim. to White-chinned Jacamar and is found at the s periphery of its range in w Amazonia s of the Amazon. It is not yet known in Colombia but is reported on lower Río Javarí, ne Peru (sightings as close as Pobre Allegre, July 1975—J. V. Remsen). From White-chinned Jacamar thus: entire crown metallic greenish to bluish, throat sometimes with white freckling.

## 8. COPPERY-CHESTED JACAMAR
*Galbula pastazae*                            Map 529
**Identification:** 9″ (23cm). Bill long (2″ or 51mm). ♂ very sim. to White-chinned Jacamar (7) but crown entirely shining metallic greenish to bluish, bill heavier, tail more coppery, size larger (wing 92-94mm vs 75-80mm; tail 105-110mm vs 83-93mm—Haffer 1974), and *prom. yellowish orange eyering*. ♀ (more distinct) has *dark rufous throat* (lacking in ♀ White-chinned), only upper chest bronzy green; *lower underparts dark rufous* as in ♂ (not pale ochraceous cinnamon as in ♀ White-chinned); eyering less prom.
**Status and habitat:** Known in Colombia from 4 specimens taken in 1971 by Von Sneidern

at El Carmen (1600m), se Nariño (Fitzpatrick and Willard 1982). In Ecuador rec. 1000-2100m, mainly above range of other jacamars. Humid lower montane forest.
**Range:** Upper tropical and subtropical zone. S Nariño, Colombia. E Ecuador.

### 9. RUFOUS-TAILED JACAMAR
*Galbula ruficauda*　　　　　　Pl. 18, Map 530
**Identification:** 9″ (23cm). Bill very long (2″, or 51mm) and slender. *Upperparts and broad breast band shining metallic coppery green, throat white (or buff—♀); rest of underparts and underside of tail rufous chestnut.* Or as above but chin black and 4, instead of 2 central tail feathers green (*melanogenia*).
**Similar species:** Only jacamar in its range with rufous undertail. See Great Jacamar (12).
**Voice:** Call a sharp, inflected *peeup* (Slud 1964); song (some var.) a loud, high, and gradually accelerating *peeo, peeo, peea pee-pee-pee-pe-pe-pe-pe-e-e-e'e'e'e*, ending in a trill.
**Behavior:** Alert and active like most jacamars. Usually in pairs low in shrubbery where they make long sallies from partially exposed perch for flying insects, incl. dragonflies, butterflies, and bees.
**Breeding:** 19 BC birds, Jan-Apr, n and nw Colombia; ♀ incubating 3 eggs, Oct, Norte de Santander (Carriker); early Apr burrow, upper Anchicayá Val. (Hilty); 1 mid-Apr, Santa Marta area (Todd and Carriker 1922); burrow dug in bank or in arboreal termitary; 2-4 white eggs spotted cinnamon (Skutch 1963b, 1968).
**Status and habitat:** Common in shrubby forest borders, second growth thickets, stream banks, and inside forest near treefalls and openings. Fairly dry to wet regions.
**Range:** To 900m on Pacific slope; to 1300m in Magdalena Val. Pacific coast (*melanogenia*); Gulf of Urabá n to 9°N, e to mid. Magdalena Val., s to n Huila and e of Andes in w Arauca and Casanare (*ruficauda*); Carib. lowlands n of 9°N to Santa Marta and w Guajira (*pallens*); e of Andes in Norte de Santander (*brevirostris*). S Mexico to nw Ecuador, n Venez., and the Guianas; Bolivia to se Brazil.
**Note:** Birds from s Mexico to Pacific Colombia and nw Ecuador, *G. melanogenia* (Black-chinned Jacamar), are sometimes given specific rank. Limited hybridization occurs with Rufous-tailed se of Gulf of Urabá (Haffer 1967a, 1975).

### 10. BRONZY JACAMAR
*Galbula leucogastra*　　　　　Pls. 18, 19,
　　　　　　　　　　　　　　　　　Map 531
**Identification:** 8.5″ (22cm). Rather dark. Bill long (2″, or 51mm) and slender. *Upperparts and*

*entire breast metallic bronzy purplish green, crown bluish, throat and belly white* (or both buff—♀), underside of tail dusky, outer feathers edged white (visible from below).
**Similar species:** Only "green" jacamar with white throat and belly. See White-chinned Jacamar (7).
**Behavior:** Pairs or groups of 3-4 perch 2-10m up along sandy-belt forest borders where they look around actively and sally like other jacamars. May sit in open on high perch; more often in shrubby growth at lower ht.
**Status and habitat:** Borders of humid *terra firme* forest and second growth woodland and along river banks. Sight recs. in sandy-belt woodland in ne Guainía (Pto. Inirída, Sept 1978—Hilty and M. Robbins).
**Range:** To 400m. E of Andes from w Putumayo (Pto. Umbría; Río San Miguel) e to Guainía s to Amazonas. The Guianas and s Venez. (s of Río Ventuari in Amazonas) to e Ecuador, e Peru (incl. Pebas), and locally in Amazonian Brazil.

### 11. PARADISE JACAMAR
*Galbula dea*　　　　　　　　　Pl. 19, Map 532
**Identification:** 12″ (30cm). Distinctive streamlined jacamar with *needlelike bill and long stilettolike tail.* Mostly shining metallic blue black with *contrasting white throat*; crown smoky brown; wings glossed bronzy green.
**Similar species:** Usually appears all black at a distance. White throat and shape are diagnostic.
**Voice:** Song a slow, slightly downscale *Peep, Peep, peep, peep, peep, pee, pee pe pe*, weaker and faster at end.
**Behavior:** Alone, in pairs, or in 3's, perched on exposed horizontal bare limbs in upper canopy but occas. lower along borders. Sally in swift agile pursuit of larger flying insects and reg. join canopy flocks.
**Breeding:** Excavating nest in arboreal termitary, 21 May, Río Arené, Peru, w of Leticia (R. Ridgely; D. Gardner).
**Status and habitat:** Often common (easily overlooked) in humid *terra firme* forest and forest borders. Most numerous in sandy-belt forests of Guainía and Vaupés. Behavior and habitat partially convergent with Swallow-winged Puffbird (Burton 1976). The only jacamar normally in the canopy.
**Range:** To 300m. The extreme e from e Guainía (seen n to Pto. Inírida, 1978—Hilty and M. Robbins) w to c Vaupés (sight, El Dorado, 1976—R. Ridgely) and s to Amazonas (w of Pedrera, Río Caquetá; sightings, Leticia—Hilty; P. Alden). The Guianas and s Venez. s to e

Ecuador (Montalvo), e Peru, n Bolivia, and Amazonian Brazil.

### 12. GREAT JACAMAR
*Jacamerops aurea*    Pl. 19, Map 533
**Identification:** 12″ (30cm). Robust. *Bill heavy and slightly decurved.* Shining metallic coppery green above, upper throat green, narrow band on lower throat white (or cinnamon—♀), *rest of underparts bright rufous*, underside of tail blue black.
**Similar species:** Largest jacamar and decidedly heavyset. Note heavy bill and mostly rufous underparts (no dark chest band).
**Voice:** Call, a slow, melancholy *weeeeeee-eeeeer* whistle, raptorlike, infrequent, and at long intervals; rarely other whistles.
**Behavior:** More sluggish than other jacamars and often perches quietly for long periods except for occas. sallies to foliage for prey. Doubtless often overlooked. Alone or in pairs in subcanopy or lower; rarely with forest flocks.
**Breeding:** 5 BC birds, Apr–May, Chocó to s Córdoba (Carriker); BC ♀, Jan, upper Río Negro, Brazil (Friedmann 1948).
**Status and habitat:** Uncommon in humid *terra firme* forest, well-shaded forest borders, and open second growth woodland. Perhaps local.
**Range:** To 900m. Pacific coast s to Río Baudó (Baudó Mts.), humid lowlands n of Andes e to mid. Magdalena Val. (s to Lebrija Val., nw Santander), and e of Andes from s Meta (Macarena Mts.) and se Guainía (Venez. side of Orinoco at San Carlos) southward. Poss. w Nariño as rec. at Río Palabí, nw Ecuador. Costa Rica to n Bolivia and Amazonian Brazil.

# PUFFBIRDS: Bucconidae (22)

Puffbirds are a small New World family occurring from southern Mexico to southern Brazil. Most are rather heavily built with large heads, short necks, short weak legs, and lax plumage. The bill has a cleft hook at the tip but otherwise varies from large and heavy to rather slender and decurved. Puffbirds are lethargic and sit quietly for long periods, then sally for larger invertebrates or small vertebrates, occasionally fruit. Except for *Monasa* and *Hypnelus* most are rather quiet and unobtrusive. Nests as far as known are excavated in arboreal termitaries or burrows in the ground; the eggs are white.

### 1. WHITE-NECKED PUFFBIRD
*Notharchus macrorhynchus*    Pl. 19, Map 534
**Identification:** 10″ (25cm). Bill broad and heavy. Upperparts black with *white forehead* and broad white nuchal collar; sides of head and underparts white with *broad black breast band* and black barring on sides.
**Similar species:** Black-breasted Puffbird (2) is somewhat smaller, lacks white forehead, and has sides of head mostly black with white cheeks. Even smaller Pied Puffbird (3) has narrow white superciliary (no white forehead) and white on tail (from below) and wings. In the extreme e, see Brown-banded Puffbird (note).
**Voice:** Usually quiet. Occas. a minor *purr* that fades and drops (Slud 1964). Rarely heard song a weak ser. of high, thin twitters (Wetmore 1968a).
**Behavior:** Usually perch alone on high open branch in early morning, less exposed later in day. Sit quietly for long periods, then sally to foliage or branches for large prey. Frequently return to original perch to beat prey against the branch before eating it. Occas. drop low near army ants.
**Breeding:** BC ♀, May, s Bolívar (Carriker); 1 ♀ with food at termitary hole 10m up, 19 Sept, Pto. Inírida (Hilty); Panama nests in arboreal termitaries, Jan–July (Willis and Eisenmann 1979).
**Status and habitat:** Fairly common (often overlooked) in humid forest borders, second growth woodland, and scattered trees in clearings.
**Range:** To 500m. Pacific coast sw Cauca (Guapí) southward (missing on wet Pacific coast to north); Gulf of Urabá e across lowlands n of Andes to w Guajira, s in Magdalena Val. to Tolima (Espinal); formerly upper Cauca Val. (El Tambo); e of Andes from Norte de Santander, w Meta and e Vichada (sighting, El Tuparro, 1977—T. O. Lemke), and Guainía s but no recs.in Vaupés or Amazonas. S Mexico to n Bolivia, Paraguay, and s Brazil.
**Note:** Brown-banded Puffbird (*N. ordii*) of s Venez. and nw and e Amazonian Brazil prob. occurs in e Guainía: known from e bank of Río Negro in adj. Venez. (San Carlos) and Brazil (Cucuhy). Like White-necked Puffbird but smaller (8″) with narrow white forehead (not forecrown), narrower black breast band bordered below by broad brown band, more extensive barring on belly, a whitish band across tail (from below), and narrow white tail tip.

## 2. BLACK-BREASTED PUFFBIRD
*Notharchus pectoralis* Pl. 19, Map 535
**Identification:** 8″ (20cm). Heavy bill. Glossy blue black above with *large white cheek patch* extending posteriorly as narrow white nuchal collar; *center of throat white; broad breast band black*; lower underparts white with black barring on flanks.
**Similar species:** See larger White-necked Puffbird (1) and smaller Pied Puffbird (3).
**Voice:** Song a loud ser. of 10 or more *wheet* whistles followed by 3 or so lower *whew* whistles given slower, and ending with a few *wheet-whew* wolf-whistle couplets that gradually fade; rasping *chah-chah-chah-chah* in territorial disputes (Willis and Eisenmann 1979).
**Behavior:** Treetops to midlevels as in White-necked Puffbird, but stays mainly within canopy foliage, much less often on exposed open perches. Drops low at army ant swarms with some frequency.
**Breeding:** 8 BC birds, Mar–May, nw Colombia (Carriker). 6 termitary nests, Mar–July, Panama; 3 eggs (Skutch 1948b; Willis and Eisenmann 1979).
**Status and habitat:** Uncommon in humid and wet forest and second growth woodland, less frequently forest edge. More restricted to forest than preceding sp.
**Range:** To 1000m. Pac. coast and humid lowlands n of Andes e to mid. Magdalena Val. (to s boundary of Santander). C Panama to nw Ecuador.

## 3. PIED PUFFBIRD
*Notharchus tectus* Pl. 19, Map 536
**Identification:** 6″ (15cm). Almost a miniature of White-necked Puffbird. Upperparts bluish black with white spotted crown (visible at close range); *narrow white eyestripe and white patch on secondaries*; underparts white with black chest band and black barring on flanks; *tail broadly tipped white from below.*
**Similar species:** Much smaller than other *Notharchus* puffbirds (1, 2) but this not always obvious at a distance. Eyestripe, black forehead, and white on wings are the marks.
**Voice:** Frequently heard song a long, high-pitched *peed-peed-peed peed-it, peed-it, peed-it, peea, pee, pee, pee*, with var. and usually falling in pitch at end.
**Behavior:** Single birds or separated pairs watch carefully, then sally to foliage or branches for insects, mainly from open perch along woodland border at midlevel to canopy, but also inside canopy where hard to see. More active and sing more than larger *Notharchus*; in humid regions often seen in *Cecropia* trees.
**Breeding:** 5 BC birds, Feb–Aug, Cesar to An-

tioquia (Carriker). Termitary cavity 4m up, June, s Córdoba (Haffer 1975); another in mangroves, Aug, PN Isla de Salamanca (B. Sehl, Hilty).
**Status and habitat:** Uncommon to locally common. Humid and wet forest, forest borders, second growth woodland, and mangroves (common in latter in PN Isla de Salamanca); few recs. e of Andes.
**Range:** To 500m. Pacific coast, the Carib. lowlands (Snía. San Jacinto; PN Isla de Salamanca), and generally s to upper Río Sinú and mid. Magdalena Vals. (Honda, n Tolima); e of Andes in Vaupés (Mitú) and Amazonas (sight, Leticia, 1978—P. Alden). Prob. elsewhere e of Andes. Costa Rica to w Ecuador, e Peru, Amazonian Brazil, and the Guianas.

## 4. CHESTNUT-CAPPED PUFFBIRD
*Bucco macrodactylus* Pl. 19, Map 537
**Identification:** 6″ (15cm). *Crown chestnut*; otherwise brown above faintly speckled ochraceous, inconspic. narrow orange rufous nape band; sides of head black bordered above by narrow white eystripe, below by broad white malar; *buffy beard on chin* and broad black band across chest; *rest of underparts buffy white barred with indistinct fine wavy brown lines*; eyes red.
**Similar species:** Spotted Puffbird (5) has solid brown crown, orange rufous or buff throat, and heavily and coarsely barred and spotted lower underparts.
**Voice:** Usually quiet. Song in e Peru a ser. of abrupt ascending notes ending in a twitter, *pup pup pep pep peep peep pip pip pip piz* (O'Neill 1974); a plaintive ser. of elaenialike *weee-a* notes rising slighty (T. Parker).
**Behavior:** Usually perches alone on low exposed or partially concealed limb 1-5m up, esp. near water or wet areas. As with other puffbirds, sits quietly for long periods. Sallies mostly to foliage for prey.
**Status and habitat:** Uncommon in humid *terra firme* and *várzea* forest borders (esp. along *várzea* river edge), second growth woodland, and wet shrubbery in clearings; locally in gallery forest borders in s llanos.
**Range:** To 500m. E of Andes from w Meta (Villavicencio) and e Vichada (Maipures) southward. S Venez. and w Amazonian Brazil to n Bolivia.

## 5. SPOTTED PUFFBIRD
*Bucco tamatia* Pl. 19, Map 538
**Identification:** 7″ (18cm). *Forecrown orange rufous* becoming brown on hindcrown and upperparts; long white malar stripe bordered above by grayish auriculars, below by large black patch on sides of throat and neck; *throat*

*orange rufous* (or buffy white—*plumentum*) extending as a narrow whitish collar on hindneck; *rest of underparts white very coarsely barred or scaled black*; eyes red.
**Similar species:** See Chestnut-capped Puffbird (4). Collared Puffbird (7) has bright orange bill, no barring below. Also cf. Russetthroated Puffbird (9).
**Voice:** Usually silent. Song a ser. of 10-20 whistled *chyoi* notes (about 2 per sec), then a few at lower pitch and slower, ending with about 4 very inflected *pchooii, pchooii, peejówee* whistles (J. V. Remsen).
**Behavior:** Much like others of the genus. Perches about 2-6m up along or just inside woodland borders.
**Breeding:** 1 ad. with stub-tailed juv., 23 Sept, Pto. Inírida (Hilty). 5 BC birds, Mar–Apr, upper Venez. Orinoco (Friedmann 1948).
**Status and habitat:** Rec. in humid forest borders and sandy savanna woodland along the Orinoco; *várzea* forest and *várzea* borders in Amazonas.
**Range:** To 300m. E Vichada on the Orinoco (Maipures) s to Vaupés near Mitú (*tamatia*); s to Leticia, Amazonas (*pulmentum*). The Guianas and s Venez. to e Ecuador, e Peru, and w and c Amazonian Brazil.

## 6. SOOTY-CAPPED PUFFBIRD
*Bucco noanamae*          Pl. 18, Map 539
**Identification:** 7″ (18cm). Above dusky brown faintly cross-hatched rufescent, *forehead and eyestripe white*, ear coverts grayish, *throat white* extending across sides of neck to form inconspic. whitish gray nuchal collar; *broad black chest band black*, rest of underparts buffy white spotted black on breast and sides; iris red.
**Similar species:** On Pacific coast the only "*brown*" puffbird with a broad black chest band.
**Status and habitat:** Known from only a small no. of specimens from humid and wet forest. Haffer (1975) found 1 in humid forest, another in younger second growth woodland adjoining an abandoned cocoa plantation. Apparently confined to lowlands. Recalls Spotted Puffbird, which it presum. resembles in habits also.
**Range:** ENDEMIC. To 100m. Pacific coast from w side of Gulf of Urabá s to mid. Río San Juan (Noanamá).

## 7. COLLARED PUFFBIRD
*Bucco capensis*          Pl. 19, Map 540
**Identification:** 7.5″ (19cm). *Bill, eyes, and feet bright orange.* Crown and sides of head to below eyes orange rufous; otherwise dark rufous chestnut above, finely barred with wavy lines, narrow buff nuchal collar; *throat white bordered*

*below by black chest band; rest of underparts yellowish buff.*
**Similar species:** Spotted (5) and Chestnut-capped puffbirds (4) have black (not orange) bills, both have black and white on sides of head.
**Voice:** Song a repeated *cua-will, cua-will . . . ,* resembling call of Poorwill (*Caprimulgus*); after playback, *qu'a'a'a'a'al' cua-will* (P. Schwartz recording).
**Behavior:** Usually seen singly in mid. story or subcanopy where it sits quietly and unobtrusively like others of the genus. Sometimes with forest flocks.
**Status and habitat:** Uncommon (prob. often overlooked) in humid *terra firme* forest.
**Range:** To 500m. E of Andes from nw Meta (near Villavicencio) and e Vichada southward. The Guianas and s Venez. to e Ecuador, e Peru, and Amazonian Brazil.

## 8. BARRED PUFFBIRD
*Nystalus radiatus*          Pl. 18, Map 541
**Identification:** 8.5″ (22cm). Bill gray green; eyes yellow. *Cinnamon rufous barred black above,* broad buffy nuchal collar and white throat; sides of face and underparts buff *finely barred black,* most heavily on sides.
**Similar species:** ♀ Fasciated Antshrike (p 379) has chestnut cap, lacks nuchal collar, and is mostly black above narrowly barred buff.
**Voice:** Call a long, slow, wolf-whistle, *phweeeeet-weeeeeuuuu* (about 4-5 sec) repeated about twice a min; ventriloquial, remarkably humanlike, and not often heard.
**Behavior:** Often in separated pairs perched quietly and partially hidden in foliage at midlevel or higher. Occas. lower or may even drop to ground for prey. Sallies at long intervals to foliage or branches for prey.
**Breeding:** BC ♀, May, n Antioquia (Carriker).
**Status and habitat:** Local. Humid and wet forest borders, second growth woodland and overgrown clearings with scattered trees.
**Range:** To 900m. Pacific coast (no recs. between Río Salaquí, n Chocó, and Río Anchicayá, Valle), and humid lowlands n of Andes e to mid. Magdalena Val. s to Tolima (Espinal). C Panama to w Ecuador.

## 9. RUSSET-THROATED PUFFBIRD
*Hypnelus ruficollis*          Pls. 18, 19,
                              Map 542
**Identification:** 8″ (20cm). *Dull brown above* somewhat diffusely spotted and blotched buffy white; narrow white of forehead continues through eyes to form *broad white cheek patch* and narrow whitish nuchal collar; *underparts pale buff,* more cinnamon on lower throat and

with a *single broad black chest band* (or 2 broad black bands on breast—*bicinctus*); eyes yellow to white.

**Similar species:** The only puffbird in dry scrub and deciduous forest. Near the Orinoco, see Spotted Puffbird (5).

**Voice:** Noisy. Song, usually a duet (not antiphonal), a long ser. of very rhythmic *woduk* notes (lasting up to 20 sec.), accelerating and growing louder, then diminishing and usually ending with only 1 bird *woduk*ing; high insectlike *seeeeep* call.

**Behavior:** More conspic. and active than most puffbirds. Single birds, or more usually loose pairs or groups up to 6 or so, perch 1-6m up on open branches or in thorny shrubs and sally short distances to foliage, branches, or the ground. Capture prey with audible bill snap.

**Breeding:** Laying ♀, Apr. Casanare; BC ♂, Oct, Cúcuta (Carriker); Santa Marta nests, May–Aug (4 recs.—S. M. Russell; 1 rec.—Todd and Carriker 1922). 3 eggs, cavity in termitary or abandoned clay oven of *Furnarius*.

**Status and habitat:** Common in arid scrub, deciduous forest, and dry scrubby or waste areas with trees and thickets.

**Range:** To 1200m. Arid Carib. region from Río Sinú (Tierralta) e to Guajira and s to lower Cauca Val. (Tenche) and mid. Magdalena Val. to Pto. Berrío, e Antioquia (*decolor*); e of Andes in Norte de Santander (*coloratus*) and Casanare and Meta (*bicinctus*) prob. to ne Vichada as known in adj. Venez. Rec. from Río Truandó, n Chocó, is prob. an error. N Colombia and w and n Venez. (mostly n of Orinoco).

**Note 1:** Birds from most of Venez. and Colombia e of the Andes, *H. bicinctus* (Two-banded Puffbird), have been considered a separate sp. but the double-banded (*bicinctus*) and single-banded (*ruficollis*) hybridize in Maracaibo region of Venez. and Catatumbo lowlands of Colombia. **Note 2:** *Hypnelus* has been merged with *Bucco* by Cottrell (1968) but is considered closer to *Nystalus* in habitat, behavior, and voice by R. Ridgely.

## 10. WHITE-CHESTED PUFFBIRD
*Malacoptila fusca*          Pl. 19, Map 543
**Identification:** 7″ (18cm). *Bill orange, tip and culmen blackish. Striped all over.* Entire upperparts, throat, and breast dark brown boldly and evenly striped buff; preocular spot white; conspic. white whiskery feathers protrude on sides of upper throat; *narrow crescent-shaped white band across chest* (often not very conspic.). Eyes red.

**Similar species:** From Black-streaked Puffbird

(11) by mostly orange bill (not black) and white crescent on chest. Also see Rufous-necked Puffbird (note).

**Voice:** A high, thin *seeee*, like others of the genus, sometimes lasting up to 2 sec and descending (D. Pearson).

**Behavior:** Much like other *Malacoptila*.

**Status and habitat:** Humid *terra firme* forest and second growth woodland, occas. along woodland borders.

**Range:** To 600m. E of Andes from w Meta (Villavicencio; Macarena Mts.) and se Guainía (Macacuní) southward. The Guianas, s Venez., and w Amazonian Brazil s to e Ecuador and e Peru.

**Note:** Rufous-necked Puffbird (*M. rufa*) of ne Peru and Amazonian Brazil s of the Amazon occurs on s Amazon bank near Leticia (sight recs., lower Río Javarí, 1978-1981, Hilty) and n of it at mouth of Río Curaray, Peru. 7″; mostly brown with prom. rufous cheeks joining rufous nuchal collar; crown gray faintly streaked white; lower throat with narrow white crescent bordered below by black. Pairs in *várzea* forest understory. When disturbed a high plaintive *keeeee*.

## 11. BLACK-STREAKED PUFFBIRD
*Malacoptila fulvogularis*          Pl. 19, Map 544
**Identification:** 7.5″ (19cm). Sim. to White-chested Puffbird (10), but *bill black* (not orange with dusky tip and culmen), throat and most of breast uniform buff (not striped), no narrow white crescent on chest, and in the hand, streaks on crown and mantle narrower and whiter.

**Similar species:** Moustached Puffbird (13) lacks the streaks on upperparts and may not overlap in range.

**Behavior:** Presum. like others of the genus.

**Status and habitat:** Known from only a few scattered localities in Colombia. Humid understory of foothill and lower slope forests in Ecuador and Peru. Prob. replaces Moustached Puffbird geographically at s end of latter's range.

**Range:** About 500-1700m (lower el. uncertain; up to 2100m in e Ecuador). Head of the Magdalena Val. in Huila (El Isno) and e slope of E Andes (known from 2 specimens labeled "Bogotá" and Villavicencio that may have been taken above Villavicencio). S Colombia to Bolivia.

## 12. WHITE-WHISKERED PUFFBIRD
*Malacoptila panamensis*          Pl. 18, Map 545
**Identification:** 7.5″ (19cm). Puffy. Bill dusky above, *yellow green below*; eyes red. Brown to rufescent brown above, lightly dotted paler on

back and wings; sides of head streaked paler (hard to see); white preocular patch and *prom. white moustachial tufts*; throat and upper breast buff to rufescent (or cinnamon rufous—*poliopis*); rest of underparts whitish *streaked dusky.* ♀: grayer above, less rufescent below.

**Similar species:** Easily confused with slightly larger Moustached Puffbird (13), which has base of lower mandible blue gray, sides of head unstreaked (hard to see in field), entire breast cinnamon (not just upper breast), and streaks on lower underparts more diffused (not sharply defined). In the hand, Moustached has longer bill (30-33 vs 27-28mm) and longer tail (70-78 vs 65-67mm; Haffer 1975).

**Voice:** A high, faint *seee* in alarm; in territorial flights var. high-pitched squeaks and a thin *see-it-hee-hee* or sim. phrase rapidly repeated (Willis and Eisenmann 1979).

**Behavior:** Reg. in pairs perched quietly 1-6m up in lower story where very lethargic, almost "stupidly" tame. Watch carefully and at long intervals sally to foliage or to ground for prey, often returning to same perch. Change perches with silent, darting flight. Occas. follow army ants or join forest flocks.

**Breeding:** 9 BC birds, Feb–May, nw Colombia (Carriker); 11 Panama nests, May–Aug, digging burrows, Jan–Oct (Willis and Eisenmann 1979); burrow in bank or sloping ground; collar of sticks at entrance; 2-3 eggs (Skutch 1958b).

**Status and habitat:** Fairly common in humid and wet forest and shady second growth woodland, occas. at borders. Replaced at higher el. by Moustached Puffbird and e of Andes by White-chested Puffbird.

**Range:** To 900m. Pacific coast of Chocó (*chocoana*); Pacific coast of Valle s to Nariño (*poliopis*); w side Gulf of Urabá east in humid lowlands n of Andes to mid. Magdalena Val. and s to Remedios, Antioquia (*panamensis*). S Mexico to w Ecuador.

### 13. MOUSTACHED PUFFBIRD
*Malacoptila mystacalis*          Pl. 18, Map 546
**Identification:** 8″ (20cm). Bill dusky, lower mandible blue gray basally; eyes red. Above brown lightly dotted buff on back and wings; top and *sides of head uniform rufescent brown* with white preocular patch and *prom. white moustachial tufts*; throat and *entire breast cinnamon rufous*; belly whitish obscurely streaked brown.

**Similar species:** See White-whiskered Puffbird (12) and at s end of range in E and C Andes Black-streaked Puffbird (11).

**Voice:** Usually silent. Rarely a high, thin *peeping* sim. to others of the genus.

**Behavior:** Like White-whiskered Puffbird. Perch mostly 2-6m up in forest undergrowth.

**Breeding:** 5 BC birds and 2 juvs., May, C Andes; BC ♀, Aug, Santa Marta Mts. (Carriker). Nearly fledged young in burrow, July, Santa Marta Mts. (Todd and Carriker 1922).

**Status and habitat:** Uncommon in humid and wet forest understory, esp. where dense and cluttered. Replaced at lower el. by White-whiskered Puffbird, to the south by Black-streaked Puffbird.

**Range:** About 800-2100m in Andes (lower el. uncertain and prob. lower on Pacific slope). Pacific slope from sources of Río San Juan (Cerro Tatamá) s to s Nariño; e slope of W Andes in Antioquia; both slopes of C Andes s to Quindío (Salento); the E Andes s to Cundinamarca; and in Macarena Mts. (1200m); Santa Marta Mts. (700-1800m) and Perijá Mts. (1200-1700m). Colombia and w and n Venez.

### 14. LANCEOLATED MONKLET
*Micromonacha lanceolata*          Pl. 18, Map 547
**Identification:** 5.2″ (13.2cm). Rare. Heavy bill; short tail. Dull rufous brown above and on sides of head; *narrow forehead, lores, and area around bill white; underparts white streaked black*; under tail coverts rusty; tail with dusky subterminal band.

**Similar species:** A tiny puffbird with streaked underparts. All nunlets are unstreaked below.

**Behavior:** Not well known. Seen singly perched 3-6m up on exposed shaded bare branches; very confiding.

**Status and habitat:** Few recs. Humid and wet foothills where birds seem to favor shady open borders and second growth woodland, esp. near small openings. Recently found at several localities in the upper Anchicayá Val. and its tributaries.

**Range:** 300-2100m. Pacific slope from headwaters of Río San Juan (below Cerro Tatamá) s to Nariño (Buenavista s of Barbacoas); e of Andes in Macarena Mts. (400m) and se Nariño on Río San Miguel. Costa Rica to e Ecuador, e Peru, and w Amazonian Brazil (upper Río Juruá).

### 15. RUSTY-BREASTED NUNLET
*Nonnula rubecula*          Pl. 19, Map 548
**Identification:** 5.5″ (14cm). Bill dusky, rather long, slender, and slightly decurved. *Brown above and on sides of head* and with slight grayish olive tinge on crown and back; *lores buffy white and narrow eyering white*; throat and breast bright cinnamon becoming white on belly.

**Similar species:** Brown Nunlet (16) is darker, has cinnamon (not whitish) loral area, lacks the white eyering, and has more uniform un-

derparts (no white on belly). No known overlap with Gray-cheeked Nunlet (17).
**Behavior:** Near Leticia birds perched 2-8m up on branches and vines. Sit quietly and watch, then occas. sally short distances to foliage or branches for insects. Prob. often overlooked (Romero 1978; Hilty).
**Status and habitat:** Midlevel to understory in vine-bordered *várzea* forest south of Leticia; rec. mainly from regions of sandy-belt forest in Venez.
**Range:** To 100m. Known only from s Amazonas near Leticia and at Pto. Nariño. Prob. n to e Vaupés (on boundary at Tahuapunto, Brazil) and ne Guainía (on Río Orinoco at San Fernando de Atabapo, Venez.). S. Venez. (Amazonas), ne Peru (incl. mouth Río Curaray), Amazonian and se Brazil, Paraguay, and ne Argentina.

## 16. BROWN NUNLET

*Nonnula brunnea*                    Pl. 18, Map 549
**Identification:** 6″ (15cm). Bluish gray bill rather long, slender, and slightly decurved. *Above and on sides of head uniform brown*; lores and underparts dull cinnamon rufous; belly paler.
**Similar species:** More uniform below than other nunlets (15, 17). Note cinnamon loral spot (not white).
**Behavior:** In e Ecuador reg. with antwren flocks in lower story inside *terra firme* forest (R. Ridgely).
**Status and habitat:** Few Colombian recs. In e Ecuador in humid lowlands from understory to subcanopy of cluttered second growth woodland. Reported "uncommon" at Limoncocha, Ecuador (Pearson et al. 1977).
**Range:** Known definitely only from Río San Miguel, se Nariño, and a few "Bogotá" specimens, the latter prob. from e base of E Andes. E Colombia to e Peru.

## 17. GRAY-CHEEKED NUNLET

*Nonnula frontalis*                    Pl. 18, Map 550
**Identification:** 6″ (15cm). Bill blue gray, rather long, slender, and slightly decurved. Plain brown above tinged rufescent on forecrown; *lores and ocular area gray*; narrow pink eyering; underparts bright cinnamon becoming buffy white on belly (or crown browner; throat and breast buff—*pallescens*).
**Similar species:** Only nunlet w of Andes (but see note below).
**Voice:** In Panama, a plaintive, measured ser., *weeip, weeip, weeip, . . .* up to 20 notes (R. A. Rowlett).
**Behavior:** Spends most of time perched quietly at midlevels or lower (about 3-12m up). occas. sallying to a branch or foliage for insects. Also

joins mixed bird flocks where it sallies more actively. Like other nunlets, perches very upright and is usually tame.
**Breeding:** 4 BC birds, Feb–Apr, nw Colombia (Carriker). Pair with food repeatedly, 23-24 June, Río Verde del Sinú (Hilty).
**Status and habitat:** Fairly common (easily overlooked) in moist to humid second growth woodland, forest borders, and gallery forest, esp. in vine tangles; usually not deep inside unbroken humid forest.
**Range:** To 1000m. Panama border s to Juradó and Mutatá on Pacific (*stulta*); upper Río Sinú e to mid. Magdalena Val. in s Cesar s to Lebrija Val., nw Santander (*frontalis*); Carib. region from Gulf of Urabá to w base Santa Marta Mts. (*pallescens*). C Panama to n Colombia.
**Note:** Rufous-capped Nunlet (*N. ruficapilla*) of e Peru (s of Napo) and w Amazonian Brazil might occur in se Colombia. It does not differ appreciably in field from Gray-cheeked Nunlet (*N. frontalis*) w of Andes, and some consider *frontalis* a race of *ruficapilla*, applying the English name Gray-cheeked Nunlet to all forms.

## 18. WHITE-FACED NUNBIRD

*Hapaloptila castanea*                    Pl. 18, Map 551
**Identification:** 9″ (23cm). Puffy-headed. Bill large, heavy, and black. Crown and sides of head gray; otherwise olive brown above; forehead and *throat white, rest of underparts rufous chestnut*; eyes red.
**Similar species:** Unmistakable in limited range.
**Voice:** Call a ser. of upward inflected single hoots, or *Glaucidium*-like double hoots, sometimes extended into a trill (Miller 1963).
**Behavior:** In nw Ecuador usually in pairs or small groups, not assoc. with other birds; very sluggish, rarely about-faces; heavyset and full-chested with hunched foreward posture more reminiscent of *Malacoptila* than *Monasa* (R. Ridgely).
**Breeding:** ♂ with brood patch, Apr, W Andes above Cali, 1800m (Miller 1963).
**Status and habitat:** Rare and local; known from only a few scattered localities in canopy of humid and wet forest or lower at edge. In Ecuador reg. in small clearings adj. to heavy forest, sometimes perching in open on horizontal limbs about 3m up (R. Ridgely). One stomach contained fruit and insects (Miller 1963). No recent recs. from W Andes (San Antonio area) where Miller's specimens were taken; only recent sight (1980) is 1 above Queremal at Tokio, Valle (S. Rose).
**Range:** 750-2400m. Entire Pacific slope from Frontino at nw end of W Andes southward; locally on e slope of W Andes near lower passes.

W Colombia, w Ecuador, and nw Peru (La Libertad; photo T. Parker).

## 19. BLACK-FRONTED NUNBIRD
*Monasa nigrifrons*          Pl. 18, Map 552
**Identification:** 11″ (28cm). Bill *coral red*, rather slender, and decurved. Entirely dull *slaty black*; black on forehead and chin. Imm. has forehead, chin, throat and sometimes underparts tinged rufous; bill yellowish.
**Similar species:** White-fronted Nunbird (20) is sim. but has white forehead, lores, and chin. Yellow-billed Nunbird (21) has white on shoulder. See Black Nunbird (note).
**Voice:** Noisy. Members of groups often sing in concert; song a rapid rollicking ser. of upward inflected *clerry* or *curry* notes, broken by an occas. downward inflected and trilled *turra* note. Chorus typically sustained for several min and often answered by nearby groups.
**Behavior:** Occur alone, in pairs, or in small groups from lower levels to canopy. Sit quietly, then sally to foliage or the ground, occas. to air for prey. More active than *Bucco* puffbirds and change perches frequently; fly with a few quick wing beats, then a short sail. Also a frequent commensal beneath monkeys, shadowing troops, and taking prey they dislodge. In the evening, less frequently morning, small groups line up on perches and give noisy clamorous concerts (J. V. Remsen; Hilty).
**Breeding:** BC ♀, 7 June, w Caquetá (Carriker). Near Leticia, stub-tailed young with ad., 10 Nov (Brown); in se Peru in dry season; burrow nest excavated in bank or at an angle into level ground; 3 white eggs (O'Neill 1974).
**Status and habitat:** Common along humid forested borders of rivers and streams, swampy river isls., *várzea* borders, and second growth woodland. Replaced in tall forest interior by White-fronted Nunbird.
**Range:** To 500m. E of Andes from w Meta (Villavicencio), w Vaupés (San José del Guaviare), and e Vaupés (Caño Cuduyarí) southward. E Colombia and w Amazonian Brazil s to n Bolivia.
**Note:** Black Nunbird (*M. atra*) of the Guianas, s Venez. (w to Amazonas), and n Brazil, likely occurs in e Vichada and e Guainía (rec. along their entire e boundaries in Venez.). It differs from Black-fronted Nunbird in having shoulders and wing coverts extensively white. Sight recs. of nunbirds on Río Inírida, Guainía (Sept 1978—Hilty) may have been this sp.

## 20. WHITE-FRONTED NUNBIRD
*Monasa morphoeus*     Pl. 18, Ill. 73, Map 553
**Identification:** 10″ (25cm). Bill *orange red*, rather slender, and decurved. *Forehead white*; other-

wise dull black, grayer on back, wing coverts, and belly (or all dark gray with blacker tail; *forehead and chin white—peruana*). Imm. has forehead or forehead and chin cinnamon buff, bill whitish.
**Similar species:** See Black-fronted Nunbird (19).
**Voice:** Much like Black-fronted Nunbird. Gives a noisy rollicking chorus, usually in small groups and mostly in early morning or late evening.
**Behavior:** Like Black-fronted Nunbird, but inside forest (where latter does not occur) in Amazonia and mostly at midlevel to subcanopy hts., rarely low.
**Breeding:** 4 BC birds, Feb–May, n Antioquia (Carriker). Burrow nest excavated on level or sloping ground with low twig and leaf collar around entrance; 3 eggs; nestlings fed by parents and helpers (Skutch 1972).
**Status and habitat:** *Terra firme* forest, occas. forest borders (not along river borders) e of Andes; in nw Colombia also clearings with scattered trees, humid forest edges, and river banks. Fairly common but seldom as numerous as Black-fronted Nunbird, which replaces it in *várzea* and river bank forest e of Andes.
**Range:** To 1100m. Pacific coast s to upper Río San Juan, Chocó, (*pallescens*); e side Gulf of Urabá e to s Córdoba (*fidelis*); lower Cauca Val. (Pto. Valdivia; Nechí) and mid. Magdalena Val. s to Honda, n Tolima (*sclateri*); e of Andes from w Meta and Vaupés (Mitú) to Amazonas (*peruana*), prob. Guainía. Se Honduras to n Bolivia, se Brazil, and sw Venez. (Amazonas).

73. WHITE-FRONTED NUNBIRD
(*pallescens* race)

## 21. YELLOW-BILLED NUNBIRD
*Monasa flavirostris*          Pl. 18, Map 554
**Identification:** 9.5″ (24cm). Bill yellowish white, very slender, pointed, and slightly decurved. Slaty black with *long, conspic. white fringed crescent across shoulders*; under wing coverts white.
**Similar species:** Easily told from other nunbirds in its range by long white shoulder stripe.
**Behavior:** Single birds, pairs, or small groups perch exposed in upper levels of trees along forest or second growth borders or at forest openings. Sit quietly, then sally to air, less frequently to foliage for large arthropods. Usually quiet.
**Status and habitat:** Local. *Terra firme* forest borders, second growth woodland, and overgrown clearings with scattered trees, mainly in or near foothills. Largely replaced inside lowland *terra firme* forest by White-fronted Nunbird, in *várzea* by Black-fronted Nunbird.
**Range:** To 1400m. E base of E Andes from w Meta (Villavicencio) and w Caquetá southward. E Colombia to e Peru (mouth of Río Curaray) and w Amazonian Brazil.

## 22. SWALLOW-WINGED PUFFBIRD
*Chelidoptera tenebrosa*          Pl. 19, Map 555
**Identification:** 6″ (15cm). Plump with short tail and broad wings. Bill broad and short. *Mainly glossy blue black with a white stripe up rump and lower back* (hard to see when perched); *belly cinnamon*; under tail coverts white.
**Similar species:** Plump silhouette recalls a martin or White-browed Purpletuft (p 444) when perched high atop a dead twig. Look for cinnamon belly and white back stripe, in flight the broad-winged almost batlike shape.
**Voice:** Usually silent, occas. a plaintive piping *pi pu* or slight *pit-wit-wit* (Skutch 1948b) or harsh squeaky *tzeet.*
**Behavior:** Single birds or more often pairs or groups of 3-6 perch from ground level on sand banks along rivers to the highest bare twigs in treetops but normally in open near a clearing or open area. Sally for aerial insects with direct fast pursuit and slower undulating return, usually terminated by planing upward to perch (Burton 1976).
**Breeding:** 1 digging burrow, 19 Feb, Mitú (Hilty), and 22 Feb, Meta (Brown). Feb–June nests in Venez. Orinoco (Cherrie 1916); 2 white eggs, in sandy burrow on river banks, road cuts, etc.
**Status and habitat:** Locally common in humid *terra firme* and *várzea* forest borders and along sandy river banks; small nos. along gallery forest borders in the llanos.
**Range:** To 500m. Throughout e of Andes. The Guianas and Venez. to n Bolivia and s Brazil.

# BARBETS: Capitonidae (9)

Barbets are a pan-tropical family reaching the greatest diversity in Africa and se Asia. They are chunky birds with short necks, short legs, and heavy bills surrounded by prominent rictal bristles. The Colombian species are all brightly colored arboreal residents of humid forest. Their calls are variable; some birds are virtually silent, others more vocal, even singing duets. They are usually seen in pairs or small groups, subsist on both fruit and insects, and as far as known nest in tree cavities and lay white eggs. Little is known of their breeding habits in South America.

[*Capito:* Large and robust; stout bill; sexes rather sim.]

## 1. SCARLET-CROWNED BARBET
*Capito aurovirens*          Pl. 21, Map 556
**Identification:** 7.5″ (19cm). Bill dusky, base of lower mandible blue gray; eyes brown (♂) or red (♀). ♂: *crown and nape scarlet; rest of upperparts and sides of head plain olive brown*; throat and upper breast orange; lower underparts dull olive. ♀: sim. but crown and nape frosty white, underparts duller.
**Similar species:** More robust Black-spotted Barbet (6) is black above with yellow and white spots and streaks (not uniform olive brown), always with some black spotting below, and throat is orange or red (see range of Colombian races). Cf. much smaller Lemon-throated Barbet (7).
**Voice:** Often heard call a rapid, rolling, froglike ser., *cruu-cruu-cruu. . .* up to 10 notes and easily overlooked; sometimes several call in concert.
**Behavior:** Pairs or groups, occas. single birds, clamber over twigs and foliage quietly and inconspic. from lower story to canopy, then sit sluggishly for periods. More often away from mixed flocks than in them.
**Breeding:** BC ♂, 21 June, w Caquetá (Carriker).
**Status and habitat:** Common in *várzea* and swampy forest, forest borders, and tall, open

second growth woodland. Occas. into *terra firme* forest where largely replaced by Black-spotted Barbet.
**Range:** To 500m. E of Andes from w Caquetá (near Florencia) and Vaupés (Mitú) southward. E Colombia to e Peru and w Amazonian Brazil.

## 2. SPOT-CROWNED BARBET
*Capito maculicoronatus*          Pl. 21, Map 557
**Identification:** 7" (18cm). Bill blue gray tipped black. ♂: *glossy blue black above*, center of crown spotted white; *upperparts white with broad suffused yellow breast band of varying intensity that is mixed orange in mid*; flanks streaked and spotted black and with scarlet flank patch. ♀: *upperparts, head, throat, and breast glossy blue black*, center crown spotted white; lower underparts white streaked and spotted black on flanks; scarlet patch on flanks.
**Similar species:** Five-colored Barbet (5) has yellowish scapular stripe and yellow spots on wing coverts and tertials. White-mantled Barbet (4) has red forecrown and all white rearcrown and upper mantle. S of Valle on Pacific coast, cf. Orange-fronted Barbet (3; ranges not known to contact).
**Voice:** Usually quiet. A harsh 2-noted "throat-clearing" call (Ridgely 1976); occas. a few guttural croaks.
**Behavior:** Often follow mixed flocks, moving rather deliberately among foliage in upper tree levels. Pairs or small groups, rarely to 10 or more.
**Breeding:** 7 BC birds, Dec–Apr, n Antioquia and Chocó (Carriker; Haffer 1975); poss. nuptial feeding, Mar, Anchicayá Val. (Brown). Excavating 2 nests, Mar; 1 ♂ and 2 ♀♀ at 1 nest (R. Ridgely); fledged young, 2 June (J. Pujals and Eisenmann) in Panama.
**Status and habitat:** Fairly common in humid and wet forest borders, broken hill forest, and second growth woodland. Where range overlaps that of Five-colored Barbet, the 2 apparently do not occur together.
**Range:** To 1000m (usually below 600m). Pacific coast s to Valle (Río Anchicayá) and humid n base of Andes e to mid. Magdalena Val. (s to Remedios, e Antioquia). C Panama to w Colombia.

## 3. ORANGE-FRONTED BARBET
*Capito squamatus*          Pl. 21, Map 558
**Identification:** 7" (18cm). Bill grayish; eyes yellow. ♂: *forecrown orange, rest of crown white*; otherwise glossy blue black above, *tertials broadly edged white*, underparts dingy white tinged yellow on breast; flanks with a few black spots,

thighs black. ♀: like ♂ but upperparts scaled white, throat and breast blue black.
**Similar species:** Five-colored Barbet (5) lacks the orange and white crown and has conspic. V-shaped yellow stripe on back and yellow-spotted wing bar. Also see (2).
**Status and habitat:** Humid and wet forest. Little known in Colombia.
**Range:** To 1500m. S end of Pacific coast in sw Nariño (Ricaurte; La Guayacana). Sw Colombia and w Ecuador.

## 4. WHITE-MANTLED BARBET
*Capito hypoleucus*          Pl. 21, Map 559
**Identification:** 7.5" (19cm). Bill yellowish white basally, bluish at tip. *Forecrown scarlet; hindcrown and mantle mixed black and white* (or tinged yellow); sides of head and rest of upperparts blue black; throat and upper breast white with *diffused buffy breast band*; lower underparts yellowish white, more yellow on flanks. Sexes sim.
**Similar species:** From ♂ Spot-crowned Barbet (2) by pale bill, scarlet forecrown, white rearcrown and mantle, and no streaking on flanks.
**Voice:** Deep croak (E. L. Kerr).
**Breeding:** 10 BC birds, May–Sept, s Bolívar and Antioquia (Carriker).
**Status and habitat:** Little known and apparently rare. Taken in regions of humid forest, mainly in foothills; 8 specimens (1950) are from Botero, 60km ne of Medellín (Carriker), where perhaps once more numerous.
**Range:** ENDEMIC. 200-1500m. Lower Cauca Val. (s to Valdivia), headwaters of Río Nechí, e around n end of C Andes (Snía. San Lucas) and s in mid. Magdalena Val., at least formerly, to n Tolima (Honda) and nw Cundinamarca (Yacopí).

## 5. FIVE-COLORED BARBET
*Capito quinticolor*          Pl. 21, Map 560
**Identification:** 7" (18cm). Bill dusky. ♂: Forehead black; crown and nape crimson; rest of upperparts black with *bold V-shaped yellow stripe on upper back; a broad yellow-spotted wing bar* and yellow-tipped tertials; throat and breast white becoming yellow on belly; flanks mottled black; thighs olive. ♀ sim. above but *streakier*; crown yellowish olive finely streaked black; underparts yellowish *streaked and spotted black except on belly*.
**Similar species:** From other barbets w of Andes (2, 3) by yellow back stripes and yellow-spotted wing bar.
**Behavior:** Clambers among midlevel and upper foliage and branches much like other *Capito*. Alone or in pairs and often with mixed bird flocks.
**Status and habitat:** Wet forest, forest borders,

and tall second growth woodland. Apparently local and confined to coastal lowlands. Seen at several localities near Quibdó but rarely e of Buenaventura (Hilty).
**Range:** ENDEMIC. To 100m. Pacific coast from Quibdó (sightings, Mar 1978—Hilty), and Tadó, Chocó, s to w Nariño (Barbacoas).

## 6. BLACK-SPOTTED BARBET
*Capito niger*                           Pl. 21, Map 561
**Identification:** 7.4″ (19cm). Heavy blackish bill. *Spotted and streaked.* ♂: *forecrown old gold* becoming brownish on hindcrown; sides of head and rest of upperparts black with long gold eyestripe continuing as *broad* V-*shaped gold stripe on upper back*; gold spotted wing bar and yellow tipped tertials; throat orange; rest of underparts bright yellow, flanks spotted black. Or *forecrown and throat red*, rearcrown ochre yellow, eyestripe whitish (*nitidior*); or forecrown orange, rearcrown yellow, *throat red*, eyestripe yellowish (*transilens*). ♀ above like respective subsp. of ♂, but back scaled yellowish; below grayish white tinged yellowish and heavily spotted and streaked black; throat more orangy spotted black. Or uniform red (*transilens; nitidior*).
**Similar species:** From Scarlet-crowned Barbet (1) by streaky upperparts and spotted flanks. Also see much smaller Lemon-throated Barbet (7).
**Voice:** A short ser. of deep, hollow, froglike *ōo-dōōt* notes that seem to fade at end; in some areas a brief pause after 1st note. Ventriloquial and difficult to locate.
**Behavior:** Often heard but infrequently seen. Pairs or small groups hop and scramble through upper limbs of trees and peer at foliage or eat fruit, also occas. drop quite low at fruiting shrubs inside forest or along borders. Often accompany mixed forest flocks.
**Breeding:** BC ♀, 7 June, w Caquetá (Carriker). Pair digging cavity 12m up in dead stub, Feb, Surinam; ♀ digging cavity 8m up in dead stub, Aug, Río Napo, Ecuador (Hilty).
**Status and habitat:** Fairly common (easily overlooked) in humid *terra firme* forest, forest borders, and tall second growth woodland. Occas. into *várzea* forest where mostly replaced by Scarlet-crowned Barbet. Contact zone between red-throated subsp. (*transilens; nitidior*) and orange-throated subsp. (*macintyrei; punctatus*) is unknown.
**Range:** To 1200m. E of Andes in w Meta from Villavicencio to Macarena Mts. (*punctatus*); Río Guayabero, sw Meta s to w Putumayo and se Nariño (*macintyrei*); e Guainía (San Felipe; Macacuní; and sight recs. n to Pto. Inírida, Sept 1978—Hilty and M. Robbins) s to e Vaupés

(*transilens*); se Amazonas at Leticia (*nitidior*). The Guianas and s Venez. s to n Bolivia, w and c Amazonian Brazil.

[*Eubucco:* Smaller green-backed edition of *Capito*; sexes strongly dimorphic.]

## 7. LEMON-THROATED BARBET
*Eubucco richardsoni*                     Pl. 21, Map 562
**Identification:** 6″ (15cm). Stout, sharp-pointed *yellow bill.* ♂: *crown and sides of head deep velvety red; nape band light blue; rest of upperparts bright moss green*; throat yellow; *breast orange* becoming green and white streaked on belly. ♀ very different: *green above with gray green crown; forehead and mask through eyes black surrounded posteriorly by narrow yellow line*; throat pale gray becoming yellowish on breast and yellow green streaked olive on belly; eyes red (♀).
**Similar species:** Much smaller than Scarlet-crowned or Black-spotted barbets (1, 6) and from either by mossy green upperparts. Look for blue nape on ♂, black mask outlined yellow behind on ♀. In foothills see ♀ Red-headed Barbet (8).
**Voice:** A weak ser. of *to-dōōt* notes, like a "small-voiced" Black-spotted Barbet but higher-pitched, less resonant, and faster than latter.
**Behavior:** Usually in pairs, rarely small groups, as they follow bird flocks in forest midlevels or higher. More active than larger *Capito.*
**Status and habitat:** Uncommon inside and at edges of *terra firme* and *várzea* forests; esp. along *várzea* streams.
**Range:** To 1200m. E of Andes from w Meta (above Villavicencio) s to Putumayo and Amazonas (Leticia area). E Colombia to e Peru, Bolivia, and w Amazonian Brazil.

## 8. RED-HEADED BARBET
*Eubucco bourcierii*                      Pl. 21, Map 563
**Identification:** 6.5″ (16.5cm). Stout sharp-pointed *yellow bill.* ♂ unmistakable: *head and neck bright red* with black area around bill and eyes and narrow bluish white nuchal collar; *rest of upperparts grass green*; red throat and upper breast fades to dull yellow on belly; olive streaks on flanks. ♀ very different: dull green above; *forecrown and area around eyes black*; rest of crown greenish yellow; spot above eye and *sides of head sky blue bordered behind by yellow*; throat greenish yellow; chest orangish yellow; lower underparts streaked yellow and olive.
**Similar species:** ♀ resembles ♀ Lemon-throated Barbet (7), but sides of head light blue (not black).
**Voice:** Usually silent.
**Behavior:** Actively clamber among branches and

foliage from low to high but mostly 5-15m up where they often hang to probe dead curled leaves or supplant other birds at fruit trees; occas. flutter to foliage like trogons. One or a pair reg. accompany forest flocks.
**Breeding:** 5 BC birds, Mar–June, W and C Andes (Carriker; Miller 1963); 2 cavity nests, June–early July, Panama (Worth 1938).
**Status and habitat:** Fairly common in humid and wet forest, forest borders, and second growth woodland.
**Range:** Mostly 1200-2400m (to 400m on Pacific slope). Both slopes of W Andes, C Andes at n end (Pto. Valdivia), spottily s on e slope of C Andes to head of Magdalena Val. in Huila, e slope of E Andes in Meta and sighting in Caquetá (Hilty); also in Macarena Mts. Prob. highlands on Panama-Colombia boundary. Costa Rica to w Venez. (Andes) and s in Andes to n Peru.

### 9. TOUCAN BARBET
*Semnornis ramphastinus*  Pl. 21, Map 564
**Identification:** 8″ (20cm). Robust. *Very thick bill yellowish with black band near tip.* Area at base of bill and around eyes, entire crown, and narrow nuchal collar black; broad postocular stripe white; otherwise golden brown above with *yellow rump; sides of head, neck, throat, and*

chest iron gray; breast and center of belly stained red; lower underparts yellowish green.
**Voice:** Song a very loud rhythmic ser. of resonant honking *cuoo*'s, sometimes repeated for several min and often in duet either in or out of synchrony; also a scolding squirrellike chuckle and a soft *quock*. In W Andes above Cali vocal mostly Feb–May (Miller 1963); in w Nariño vocal June–early Sept (yr.-round?). May snap bill loudly when disturbed.
**Behavior:** Single birds or pairs follow mixed flocks where they actively hop along branches from lower midlevels to canopy; often cock tail up and "about-face" on branches; pairs or small groups also move independently of mixed flocks, or sit quietly for period (then inconspic. and easily overlooked).
**Breeding:** 2 BC ♂♂, Feb–May, and juv. in May, W Andes (Miller 1963); tree cavity nest (Lehmann 1957).
**Status and habitat:** Local. Wet forest ("cloud forest") and edges. Unfortunately, a widely sought cage bird, and this together with habitat loss now threatens it in some areas. Common and still easily found in w Nariño in mts. above Junín.
**Range:** 1000-2400m. Both slopes of W Andes (most e slope recs. in Valle) from Valle southward. W Colombia and w Ecuador.

## TOUCANS, ARAÇARIS: Ramphastidae (23)

Toucans are a well-known group of New World birds found from southern Mexico to northern Argentina. They are characterized by enormously large colorful bills, fringed tongues, and a remarkable anatomical structure that allows the tail to be folded flat over the back. In most respects, toucans are ecological counterparts of the Old World hornbills (Bucerotidae), although the two families are not closely related. Toucans are found in almost all kinds of forested regions and feed mostly on fruit supplemented by invertebrate and small vertebrate prey; they also frequently prey on nestlings or eggs of other birds. All nest in tree cavities as far as known, the larger ones in natural cavities at almost any height, the smaller ones often in woodpecker holes. Araçaris (*Pteroglossus*) commonly roost communally in holes as well. The clutch of those species documented is two to four white eggs; the eggs are small for the size of the birds. The systematics of the family, especially the larger *Ramphastos*, is complex. Recent evidence by Haffer (1974), based on bill shape, voice, and distribution, suggests the number of "biological" species is considerably smaller than previously recognized. His treatment is followed here or discussed in footnotes. In the following accounts bill length is included in the total length measurement and also given separately.

### 1. GROOVE-BILLED TOUCANET
*Aulacorhynchus sulcatus*  Pl. 20, Map 565
**Identification:** 14″ (36cm). Bill 2.5-3.5″ (64-89mm). Most of *upper mandible and base and tip of lower mandible yellow*; otherwise black; base of bill bordered white. Mostly bright green, throat bluish gray; ocular area bright blue; tail bluish green (no chestnut tips).
**Similar species:** Emerald Toucanet (3) has

chestnut tail tips, and in Santa Marta Mts. bill mostly black with only ridge yellow. In Perijá Mts. bill of Emerald much like that of Groove-billed, but latter has base of lower mandible yellow (not black). Also cf. 4.
**Voice:** Song a succession of single, nasal *coank* notes, about 2 per sec, much like Emerald Toucanet (Haffer 1974).
**Behavior:** In pairs or small groups from lower

story to canopy. Like other *Aulacorhynchus*, rather active, noisy, and sometimes inquisitive. Often move through the upper levels of forest in single file, "following the leader"; also quietly accompany or "shadow" mixed bird flocks. Omnivorous and often rob bird nests. **Breeding:** BC ♂ and laying ♀, Apr, w Guajira; imm., July Perijá Mts. (Carriker). **Status and habitat:** Common inside or at edges of humid and wet forest, forest borders, and second growth woodland. Sympatric with Emerald Toucanet. **Range:** 600-2000m (usually above 1200m). Santa Marta Mts. and Perijá Mts. from extreme n end s to at least 9°40′N (where it overlaps range of Crimson-rumped Toucanet). N Colombia and n and nw Venez. **Note:** Incl. *A. calorhynchus* (Yellow-billed Toucanet) of the Santa Marta and Perijá mts. and the Merida Andes of Venez., formerly considered a separate sp. but found to hybridize with the red-billed *A. sulcatus* forms in w Venez. (Schwartz 1972a).

## 2. CHESTNUT-TIPPED TOUCANET

*Aulacorhynchus derbianus*        Map 566
**Identification:** 16″ (41cm). Bill 3″ (76mm) and mostly black, *sides of bill at base and distal half of culmen dark red*; base of bill outlined in white. Mostly bright green, throat grayish white; nape and ocular area blue; central tail feathers tipped chestnut (from below).
**Similar species:** Crimson-rumped Toucanet (4) has red rump, bluish breast band (latter not conspic.), and most of upper mandible dark red.
**Voice:** Song a succession of low barking sounds, about 1 per sec; much like Crimson-rumped Toucanet but slower, no growl at end (Schwartz 1972a); *guah gahk hawk gahk . . .* (Haffer 1974). Unlike Groove-billed Toucanet.
**Behavior:** Sim. to others of the genus (see 1).
**Status and habitat:** Known from 1 specimen marked "Colombia" without definite locality. Southward in Andes in humid forest, 600-1600m.
**Range:** Prob. e slope of Andes in Nariño. E Ecuador to n Bolivia; highlands of s Guyana, s Venez., and adj. n Brazil.

## 3. EMERALD TOUCANET

*Aulacorhynchus prasinus*        Pl. 20, Map 567
**Identification:** 13″ (33cm). Bill 2.5-3″ (64-76mm), black with *yellow culmen* (Santa Marta), *or culmen and much of upper mandible also yellow* (Andes); base of bill outlined in white. Mostly bright green, paler below with bluish gray throat (or white—*albivitta*); ocular area blue; *crissum and tail tips* (from below) *chestnut*.

**Similar species:** In Santa Marta and Perijá mts., see Groove-billed Toucanet (1). In the Andes, see Chestnut-tipped and Crimson-rumped toucanets (2, 4).
**Voice:** Song a rapid ser. of short *took* or *churt* notes, about 2-3 per sec.
**Behavior:** Sim. to others of the genus (see 1).
**Breeding:** Tree hole nest, Feb–Mar, PN Cueva de los Guácharos (P. Gertler); poss. courtship feeding, 27 Feb and 12 Apr, Finca Merenberg (Ridgely and Gaulin 1980); 8 BC birds, Jan–June, Santa Marta Mts. and C Andes; Aug imm. Perijá Mts. (Carriker); 3-4 eggs (Skutch 1967).
**Status and habitat:** Common in humid and wet forest, forest edges, and second growth woodland; occas. hedgerows bordering pastures. On average distributed at higher el. than allied Crimson-rumped Toucanet, but both often occur together at mid. el.
**Range:** 1600-3000m (once to 3700m). Cerro Tacarcuna on Panama border (*cognatus*); Santa Marta Mts. (*lautus*); Perijá Mts., E Andes, and e slope C Andes (*albivitta*); w slope C Andes and n end W Andes (*griseigularis*); s portion of W Andes s to Cauca on Pacific slope (*phaeolaemus*). C Mexico to w Venez. and s in Andes to Bolivia.

## 4. CRIMSON-RUMPED TOUCANET

*Aulacorhynchus haematopygus*    Pl. 20, Map 568
**Identification:** 16″ (41cm). Bill 3-3.2″ (76-81mm), *dark red*, most of culmen and central portion of lower mandible black; base of bill outlined in white. Mostly green with *red rump*; bare ocular skin dull dark red; malar patch and diffused breast band blue (both inconspic. in field); *tail tips* (from below) *chestnut*.
**Similar species:** From any other "green" toucanet by red rump; additionally from Emerald (3) or Groove-billed Toucanet (1) by dark red (not yellow) on bill. Also see Chestnut-tipped Toucanet (2).
**Voice:** Song a somewhat nasal, montonously repeated *cua, cua . . .*, about 2 per sec (Hilty); a *gahk, huahk, hoak, gahk . . .*, beginning with bark, ending in growl (Haffer 1974).
**Behavior:** Sim. to others of the genus (see 1).
**Breeding:** 3 BC birds, Mar–May, C Andes (Carriker); 2 BC birds, Apr, W Andes in Valle (Miller 1963).
**Status and habitat:** Common in humid and wet forest, forest borders, and second growth woodland; occas. adj. hedgerows in pastures. Hills and mts., but distribution centered lower than Emerald Toucanet, and both often together at mid. el.
**Range:** 800-2100m; to 300m on Pacific slope. Perijá Mts. (except n part n of 10°N). E Andes

s to latitude of Bogotá, C Andes and W Andes from headwaters of Río San Juan southward. Venez. (Perijá Mts. and Andes at Páramo de Tamá) to w Ecuador.

[*Pteroglossus:* Med.-sized and slender; dark green to blackish above with red rump and long, graduated tail; best told by bill patterns and no. of bands (or lack of) on underparts.]

## 5. COLLARED ARAÇARI
*Pteroglossus torquatus*              Pl. 20, Map 569
**Identification:** 16″ (41cm). Bill 3.5-4.5″ (89-114mm), *most of upper mandible pale yellowish*; culmen, tip, and lower mandible blackish; base of bill outlined in white. *Bare ocular area red.* Dull greenish black above with red rump and inconspic. chestnut nuchal collar; head and throat black; rest of underparts yellow, somewhat stained red; large black spot on breast and *single band mixed black and red across upper belly.*
**Similar species:** Stripe-billed Araçari (6) has distinct black stripe on sides of upper mandible, ocular area bluish slate (not red), and no chestnut collar (hard to see).
**Voice:** Frequently heard call a high-pitched sneezing *ksíyik* (Ridgely 1976), or *pítsek!*, much like call of Stripe-billed Araçari.
**Behavior:** Sim. to others of the genus. See Stripe-billed Araçari.
**Breeding:** 5 BC birds, Jan–May, Cesar to Antioquia (Carriker); Mar–July, Barro Colorado Isl. (Willis and Eisenmann 1979); 3-4 eggs, young fed by parents and helpers (Skutch 1958a).
**Status and habitat:** Common in humid forest and second growth woodland and borders; in Carib. region ranges into moist forest, also riparian woodland in semiarid areas.
**Range:** To 800m. Along Panama boundary (s to Río Juradó) and from e side of Gulf of Urabá eastward n of Andes to Santa Marta area (local in arid Carib.), s to mid. Magdalena Val. (Honda, n Tolima), and e of Andes in Norte de Santander (Zulia Val.). S Mexico to nw Venez.
**Note:** Hybridizes with *P. sanguineus* (Stripe-billed Araçari) along a narrow zone near the Panama boundary and on the e side of the Gulf of Urabá (Haffer 1974). See note under 6.

## 6. STRIPE-BILLED ARAÇARI
*Pteroglossus sanguineus*            Pl. 20, Map 570
**Identification:** 17″ (43cm). Bill 3.5-4.5″ (89-114mm), upper mandible pale yellow with *black culmen and stripe on sides*; lower mandible black. Sim. to Collared Araçari (5), but nape black (no chestnut collar), bare ocular area bluish

slate becoming dark red posteriorly (not all bright red), bill with black stripe on sides of upper mandible, and bill tip yellow (not dusky).
**Voice:** Practically identical to Collared Araçari as well as Chestnut-eared and Many-banded araçaris from e of Andes.
**Behavior:** Like others of the genus, usually in groups, sometimes up to a doz. or more, straggling "single file" across forest openings or clearings and generally keeping in upper levels of trees. Fly with rapid, buzzy wing beats and occas. short glides. Tend to perch in open in early morning, much less so later in day. Fond of *Cecropia* catkins.
**Breeding:** 4 BC birds, Feb–May, Chocó and nw Antioquia (Carriker).
**Status and habitat:** Common in humid and wet forest, second growth woodland, and borders.
**Range:** To 1000m. W of W Andes from near Panama border (e base of Cerro Tacarcuna) and e side of Gulf of Urabá southward. Extreme e Darién, Panama (R. Ridgely), w Colombia, and nw Ecuador.
**Note:** By some considered conspecific with *P. torquatus* (Collared Araçari) because of a narrow hybrid zone in nw Colombia (see Haffer 1974). The enlarged sp. would be called Spot-chested Araçari.

## 7. CHESTNUT-EARED ARAÇARI
*Pteroglossus castanotis*            Pl. 20, Map 571
**Identification:** 18″ (46cm). Bill 4″ (102mm), mostly black with a yellowish brown band on sides of upper mandible broadening and becoming yellow at tip; "teeth" yellow and base of bill outlined in yellow. Mostly dark slaty olive above with red rump and black crown; throat, sides of head, and nuchal collar dark chestnut (looks blackish at distance); *rest of underparts yellow with a single broad band of red across upper belly;* bare ocular area bright blue.
**Similar species:** Only Amazonian araçari in Colombia with a single breast band, but s of Amazon cf. Curl-crested Araçari (see note). Note mostly dark bill; chestnut on head rarely visible.
**Voice:** Call much like Collared and Stripe-billed araçaris; a sharp, inflected *skeéz-up.*
**Behavior:** Sim. to most other *Pteroglossus.* See 6.
**Status and habitat:** Common in humid forest borders, second growth woodland, and *várzea* in Amazonia; gallery forest and savanna woodland in the llanos. The only araçari on swampy Amazon river isls. and mostly replaced in the interior of extensive unbroken forest by sim.-sized Many-banded Araçari.
**Range:** To 500m. From e base of E Andes near n end (headwaters of Río Casanare) and

Vaupés-Amazonas boundary (Río Apaporis) southward. E Colombia to Bolivia, ne Argentina, and s Brazil.
**Note:** Curl-crested Araçari (*P. beauharnaesii*) of e Peru and w Amazonian Brazil s of the Amazon occurs along Río Javarí sw of Leticia (sightings, Pobre Allegre, Peru, 1975—J. V. Remsen; 1979—Hilty), but is not known to cross the Amazon. 15"; black above with red mantle and rump and short curly feathers on crown (like plastic strips); underparts yellow, paler on throat, a single red band across upper belly; bill, almost reverse of most *Pteroglossus*, is black above, white below, with a brownish orange culmen and tip. Mainly *terra firme* forest; pairs or groups; upper stories of forest and at forest edge.

## 8. MANY-BANDED ARAÇARI
*Pteroglossus pluricinctus*                    Pl. 20, Map 572
**Identification:** 17" (43cm). Bill 4-5" (102-127mm) *ivory yellow above with ridge of culmen and lower mandible black*; base of bill outlined in white. Dark slaty green above with red rump; head, neck, and chest black; rest of underparts yellow with *2 black breast bands*, the lower 1 bordered below by red; bare ocular area slaty green to greenish blue.
**Similar species:** Only Colombian araçari with 2 black breast bands. At a distance Lettered Araçari (9) has sim. bill, but no breast bands; Chestnut-eared Araçari (7) has only 1 breast band; and Ivory-billed Araçari (10) has a mostly ivory bill.
**Voice:** Call sim. to those of 5, 6, and 7, a sharp, forceful *kíssit* or *píssit* (Haffer 1974); also a weaker *pítch*, vaguely 2-noted and not as sharp as above call.
**Behavior:** Sim. to other *Pteroglossus*. See 6.
**Breeding:** 1 BC ♂, mid-Jan, Macarena Mts. (Olivares 1962).
**Status and habitat:** Uncommon to fairly common in humid *terra firme* forest, less numerous in *várzea* forest.
**Range:** To 500m. Entire e base of E Andes, and from w Meta (Villavicencio), w Vaupés (San José del Guaviare), and e Vichada (El Tuparro—INDERENA) southward. W and s Venez. s to ne Peru and nw Brazil.

## 9. LETTERED ARAÇARI
*Pteroglossus inscriptus*                    Pl. 20, Map 573
**Identification:** 14.5" (37cm). Bill 2.5-3.5" (64-89mm), upper mandible *pale yellow with black culmen* and row of narrow, vertical black lines on sides near cutting edge; lower mandible black; base of bill outlined in yellow. Dark slaty green above with red rump; head and throat

black; otherwise *pale yellow below (no bands)*; bare ocular area bright blue.
**Similar species:** Only Colombian araçari with no bands on underparts. Vertical lines on bill are diagnostic but difficult to see.
**Voice:** All but silent; very rarely a low *chak*, somewhat oropendolalike, in Bolivia (J. V. Remsen).
**Behavior:** Sim. to other *Pteroglossus*. See 6.
**Breeding:** BC ♂ and ♀, early Mar, Macarena Mts. (Olivares 1962).
**Status and habitat:** Fairly common in humid *terra firme* and *várzea* forests, second growth woodland, and borders; occas. scattered trees in clearings. Found mostly in *várzea* near Leticia, whereas sim.-sized Ivory-billed Araçari occurs mostly inside *terra firme* forest.
**Range:** To 500m. E of Andes from Meta (Villavicencio) and Amazonas southward (no recs. from Orinoco or Río Negro drainage of Guainía and Vaupés). E Colombia to n Bolivia and most of Amazonian Brazil.

## 10. IVORY-BILLED ARAÇARI
*Pteroglossus flavirostris*                    Pl. 20, Map 574
**Identification:** 13" (33cm). Bill 3.1-3.9" (79-99mm), *ivory white* with small black "teeth" and *a diffused brownish stripe on sides of lower mandible* (no white outline on base of bill). Dark olive green above with red rump; crown black (or dark chestnut—♀); throat and neck deep chestnut; *throat bordered below by broad red band, then a broad black band below the red one* (sometimes mixed red on lower border); rest of underparts bright yellow, bare ocular area red behind eye.
**Similar species:** Best marks are mainly ivory bill and black and red breast bands *not* separated by yellow. See Lettered (9) and Many-banded araçaris (8).
**Voice:** Unlike most *Pteroglossus*, a ser. of rapid croaking rattles, about 1 per sec, sometimes becoming yelps or screams, *co-ak . . cro-ak . . coák . . .*, sim. to call of Black-billed Mountain-Toucan but weaker, shorter, and faster (Haffer 1974); also a sharp *kís-sik*, rather like most others of genus (Hilty).
**Behavior:** Sim. to other *Pteroglossus* (see 6).
**Breeding:** BC birds, early Jan and mid-Mar—mid-Apr, w Amazonas, Venez. (Friedmann 1948).
**Status and habitat:** Fairly common in humid *terra firme* forest (incl. sandy-belt forest) and forest borders; gallery forest and savanna woodland in s llanos.
**Range:** To 500m. E of Andes from w Meta (Villavicencio), w Vaupés (San José del Guaviare), and e Guainía (sightings, n to Pto. Inírida, 1978—Hilty and M. Robbins) south-

ward. S Venez. to e Ecuador and ne Peru (n of Amazon) and n Amazonian Brazil.
**Note:** Some consider Brown-mandibled Araçari (*P. mariae*) of s of the Amazon in w Amazonia a race of this sp. *Mariae* differs in lower mandible and bill tip dusky (not mostly ivory).

[*Selenidera:* Homogeneous group; rather small; short bill and tail, yellow ear tufts; mainly black and chestnut plumage. Sexually dimorphic.]

## 11. YELLOW-EARED TOUCANET
*Selenidera spectabilis*      Pl. 20, Map 575
**Identification:** 15″ (38cm). Bill 3-4″ (76-102mm), mostly black with upper portion of upper mandible yellowish green. ♂: back and wings bright olive green; otherwise entirely *black with conspic. yellow tuft on ear coverts* and yellow patch on flanks; under tail coverts red; bare ocular area light green. ♀: chestnut crown and nape; *no yellow ear tufts.*
**Similar species:** Crimson-rumped Toucanet (4) is same size but very different in color.
**Voice:** Call a slowly repeated *krek-ek* (Slud 1964), much like Keel-billed Toucan but weaker, more rhythmic,and usually more distinctly 2-syllabled (Ridgely 1976).
**Behavior:** Alone or in pairs, occas. small groups from understory to canopy but usually rather high. Some seasonal movement to higher el. to breed in Costa Rica (Skutch 1972).
**Breeding:** Laying ♀, 19 Feb, BC ♀, 6 Apr, Chocó (Carriker).
**Status and habitat:** Uncommon to local in humid and wet forest and forest borders. Favors foothill regions and usually absent in lowlands well away from them.
**Range:** To 1500m. Pacific coast s to Río Baudó (perhaps southward); e in humid foothills around n end of W Andes to lower Cauca Val. (Pto. Valdivia). Absent from e side Gulf of Urabá. Honduras to nw Ecuador (Esmeraldas).

## 12. GOLDEN-COLLARED TOUCANET
*Selenidera reinwardtii*      Pl. 20, Map 576
**Identification:** 13″ (33cm). Bill 2-2.5″ (51-64mm), *dark reddish; ridge and distal third black.* ♂: olive green above; tail tipped chestnut; *head and underparts glossy black with conspic. yellow ear tufts and yellow nuchal collar;* flank patch yellow; crissum red; bare ocular area bluish green. ♀: sim., but head and underparts light chestnut, ear tufts bronzy, and bill mostly blackish, dark red basally.
**Similar species:** Tawny-tufted Toucanet (13) has greenish yellow culmen and several vertical black lines and spots on bill.
**Voice:** Call a ser. of low, guttural, froglike ar-

*rowk* notes (*reinwardtii*), about 15 per 10 sec, on both banks of Amazon near Leticia (Brown); low barking growls (*langsdorffii*) in e Peru (J. Brockman and J. Weske).
**Behavior:** Usually alone or in pairs from mid. to upper story, sometimes with mixed bird flocks. Rather inconspic. Often engages in seesawlike movement when calling (as do other members of genus), with each note head thrown forward and down, tail flipped up and over back.
**Status and habitat:** Uncommon in humid *terra firme* forest and forest edges, occas. *várzea.* Replaced in sandy-belt forests of the Orinoco and Río Negro region by next sp.
**Range:** To 500m. E of Andes from s Meta (Macarena Mts.) and Amazonas southward (*reinwardtii*). Prob. n to s Vaupés. E Colombia to e Peru and w Amazonian Brazil.

## 13. TAWNY-TUFTED TOUCANET
*Selenidera nattereri*      Pl. 20, Map 577
**Identification:** 13″ (33cm). Sim. to Golden-collared Toucanet, but bill largely dark red with *distal half of culmen greenish yellow and base and sides of bill with several vertical black lines and spots;* auricular tufts yellow tipped tawny (latter hard to see in field).
**Similar species:** See Golden-collared Toucanet (12); range overlap, if any, unknown.
**Voice:** A ser. of rather low, soft rattles with distinct froglike croaking quality (Amazonas, Venez.—P. Schwartz).
**Behavior:** Apparently sim. to others of the genus.
**Status and habitat:** Humid sandy-belt forest; known from 3 localities in e Vaupés but not well known in Colombia. Replaced s in Amazonia by Golden-collared Toucanet.
**Range:** To 250m. Extreme e in Vaupés (Mitú; Río Papurí; Tahuapunto); prob. to se Guainía (on e bank of Río Negro at San Carlos, Venez.). The Guianas to s Venez., e Colombia, and n Brazil (Río Uaupés and n of Amazon e to the Negro).

[*Andigena:* Highlands; rather large, predom. olive, gray, or blue gray and black; lax almost hairlike plumage, the latter poss. an adaptation to cool damp habitat (Haffer 1974).]

## 14. PLATE-BILLED MOUNTAIN-TOUCAN
*Andigena laminirostris*      Pl. 20, Map 578
**Identification:** 20″ (51cm). Bill 3.5-4″ (89-102mm), band and base of bill black, basal half of lower mandible dark red; otherwise black with a *large raised rectangular yellow plate on basal half of upper mandible. Crown and nape black;*

otherwise olive brown above with yellow rump; tail black tipped chestnut; flank patch yellow; underparts blue gray; crissum red, bare ocular area blue green above eye, yellow below eye forming large yellow patch.

**Similar species:** From Gray-breasted Mountain-Toucan (15) by large rectangular yellow plate on sides of bill. Black-billed Mountain-Toucan (16) has white throat.

**Voice:** In Ecuador, usual call a nasal, whining, querulous *quuuuah, quuuuah* . . . , in a ser., each note rising; resembles that of Gray-breasted Mountain-Toucan; usually does not call from exposed perch as do *Ramphastos* (R. Ridgely). Also a loud, staccato rattle, *t't't't't't*.

**Behavior:** Sim. to others of the genus. Groups may accompany mixed spp. flocks.

**Status and habitat:** Local. Humid and wet mt. forest and forest borders. Not well known in Colombia. Common in nw Ecuador mostly at 1500-2500m (R. Ridgely).

**Range:** 300-3200m (most recs above 1000m). W Nariño s of Patía Val. Sw Colombia and w Ecuador.

## 15. GRAY-BREASTED MOUNTAIN-TOUCAN

*Andigena hypoglauca* Pl. 20, Map 579
**Identification:** 18″ (46cm). Bill 3.5-4″ (89-102mm), with *basal half yellow and a broad vertical black band near base*; culmen and distal half of upper mandible red bordered below with black; distal half of lower mandible black. Crown, nape, and sides of head black; otherwise olive brown above with yellow rump and blackish tail tipped chestnut; *broad collar encircling neck* and entire underparts blue gray; flanks chestnut; crissum red; bare ocular area light blue.

**Similar species:** See Plate-billed Mountain-Toucan (14). Black-billed Mountain-Toucan (16) has white throat.

**Voice:** Call a loud, nasal, slowly rising *kuuuuaat* (lasts 2 sec), repeated for long periods at 4- to 5-sec intervals; sharp contact call, *kik-kik-kik-kik-kik*; also frequent bill rattling (T. Parker and J. O'Neill).

**Behavior:** Usually in pairs or small groups in the upper levels of trees.

**Breeding:** 2 BC ♂♂, 29 Jan, 5 Feb, Puracé (Carriker).

**Status and habitat:** Uncommon and local in humid and wet forest, forest borders, and stunted woodland near treeline. Center of abundance mostly above Black-billed Mountain-Toucan; at sim. el. the 2 do not occur together. Most readily found in Quebrada

Tierra Adentro Canyon at nw end of PN Puracé.

**Range:** 2700-3400m. W slope of C Andes from Caldas border (Nevado del Ruiz) s to w Cauca (w slope PN Puracé) and on e slope of Andes in Nariño. Colombia to e Ecuador and e Peru.

## 16. BLACK-BILLED MOUNTAIN-TOUCAN

*Andigena nigrirostris* Pl. 20, Map 580
**Identification:** 20″ (51cm). Bill 3.7-4.5″ (94-114mm), all black (*nigrirostris*), or black with base of upper mandible red, this extending forward below culmen (*spilorhynchus*), or black with entire base of bill red, extending forward on upper mandible nearly to tip (*occidentalis*). Crown and nape black; otherwise olive brown above with yellow rump; tail black tipped chestnut; *sides of head and throat white*; rest of underparts blue gray; crissum red. Bare ocular area blue in front, yellow behind.

**Similar species:** Only mountain-toucan (*Andigena*) with a white throat. See Gray-breasted Mountain-Toucan (15) and Plate-billed Mountain-Toucan (14).

**Voice:** Song a nasal, mechanical *tu-aát*, repeated a little faster than 1 per sec; last syllable rises, sounds tinny, and with strong harmonics (Hilty); also hollow bill rattles (Haffer 1974).

**Behavior:** Usually in pairs, occas. small groups in upper levels of trees. Rather conspic.

**Breeding:** 4 BC birds, Mar, sw Huila (Carriker).

**Status and habitat:** Fairly common in humid and wet forest and forest borders. Above 2700-3000m mostly replaced by Gray-breasted Mountain-Toucan (the 2 do not occur together). Now increasingly local with habitat destruction.

**Range:** 1600-3200m, to 1200m on Pacific slope and on e slope E Andes. W Andes s to Cauca (*occidentalis*); both slopes C Andes, head of Magdalena Val. in Huila, and e slope of Andes in Putumayo and Nariño (*spilorhynchus*); E Andes s at least to Cundinamarca (*nigrirostris*), w Caquetá (subsp.?). Nw Venez. to ne Ecuador.

[*Ramphastos*: Large and conspic.; mostly black with red under tail coverts, square tail, and enormously large, colored bill. Two groups differing in bill shape, size, and call: smaller "channel-keel-billed" spp., Citron-throated, Yellow-ridged, Keel-billed, and Choco toucans with croaking call; and larger "smooth-billed" spp., Chestnut-mandibled, Black-mandibled, and White-throated toucans with yelping call. Nowhere more than 2 spp. sympatric, usually 1 from each group. Taxonomy often confused by hybridization.]

## 17. CITRON-THROATED TOUCAN
*Ramphastos citreolaemus*         Pl. 20, Map 581
**Identification:** 21″ (53cm). Bill 6-7″ (152-178mm) and *black*; base of lower mandible blue; *base of upper mandible, culmen, and tip yellow.* Mostly black with yellow rump and red crissum; *throat and upper breast pale yellow,* bordered below by inconspic. red band; bare ocular area blue.
**Similar species:** Keel-billed Toucan (19) has a mostly green and orange bill; Chestnut-mandibled Toucan (21) has most of upper mandible yellow (not black).
**Voice:** "Song" a ser. of froglike croaking *creé-op*'s delivered at rate of almost 1 per sec, sounds monosyllabic when given faster (Haffer 1974).
**Behavior:** Sim. to other *Ramphastos* of the channel-keel-billed group. See 19.
**Breeding:** BC ♀, mid-Mar, w Santander (Boggs 1961); BC ♂, Jan, n Antioquia (Carriker).
**Status and habitat:** Humid forest and forest borders. Still fairly common in s Córdoba in 1980 (Hilty).
**Range:** To 900m. N end of W Andes (upper Sinú Val.) e to mid. Magdalena Val. s to n Tolima (Honda); e of Andes in Norte de Santander (Catatumbo lowlands). N Colombia and w Venez. (Maracaibo region).
**Note:** Considered a race of *R. vitellinus* (Channel-billed Toucan) along with *R. culminatus* (Yellow-ridged Toucan) from e of Andes by Haffer (1974). Maracaibo basin populations of this sp. are somewhat intermed. betw. white-breasted *culminatus* and yellow-breasted *citreolaemus.*

## 18. YELLOW-RIDGED TOUCAN
*Ramphastos culminatus*         Pl. 20, Map 582
**Identification:** 19″ (48cm). Bill to 5.6″ (142mm). Sim. to preceding sp., but *throat and chest white* (not yellow), and bird slightly smaller. *Note voice.*
**Similar species:** Almost identical to White-throated (Cuvier's) Toucan (23), but smaller, bill shorter, and call a croak (not a yelp).
**Voice:** Same as Citron-throated Toucan (17).
**Behavior:** Sim. to other *Ramphastos* toucans of the channel-keel-billed group. See 19.
**Breeding:** BC ♀, 9 Feb, Macarena Mts. (Olivares 1962).
**Status and habitat:** Fairly common in canopy of humid forest and forest borders, occas. savanna woodland in the llanos. Greatly outnumbered in Amazonas by White-throated (Cuvier's) Toucan.

**Range:** To 500m. Entire e base of Andes and from s Meta (Macarena Mts.) and e Vichada (El Tuparro—INDERENA) southward. W. Venez. (s slope of Andes to 1700m) and s Venez. s to n Bolivia and w Amazonian Brazil.
**Note:** Considered a race of *R. vitellinus* (Channel-billed Toucan) of e Venez., the Guianas, and e Brazil by Haffer (1974), which it prob. is.

## 19. KEEL-BILLED TOUCAN
*Ramphastos sulfuratus*         Map 583
**Identification:** 19″ (48cm). Bill 5-6″ (127-152mm), *mostly pea green with red tip, broad orange stripe on upper mandible,* and large pale blue area on lower mandible. Mostly black with white rump and red crissum; *throat and chest bright yellow,* bordered narrowly below by red. Bare ocular area greenish.
**Similar species:** Easily told from Citron-throated (17) or Chestnut-mandibled Toucan (21) by mostly green bill with broad orange area on upper mandible. Citron-throated Toucan also has yellow rump.
**Voice:** "Song" a ser. of rapidly repeated, croaking *krik* notes at rate of about 16 per 10 sec, sim. to song of Citron-throated Toucan but much faster (Haffer 1974).
**Behavior:** Usually in pairs or small groups fairly high in trees, but on the average somewhat lower than the larger "smooth-billed" forms of the genus, e.g., see Chestnut-mandibled (Yellow-breasted) Toucan (Haffer 1974). Looks top heavy in flight with long projecting bill. Typical flight is undulating, a few quick flaps, then a glide on set wings; often seems to steadily lose altitude in flight. Calling birds perch exposed in treetops and bob their heads and throw them from side to side with each note.
**Breeding:** Santa Marta nest, 12 May, 2 eggs (Todd and Carriker 1922).
**Status and habitat:** Common in humid forest, second growth and lighter woodland, and borders; riparian woodland in drier coastal areas. Meets Citron-throated Toucan near n base of W Andes (prob. eastward) but apparently does not overlap extensively with it.
**Range:** To 1600m (Santa Marta). From the Panama boundary e across the n lowlands to the Santa Marta area and Perijá Mts. Does not penetrate s into wetter lowlands and foothills near n base of Andes. E Mexico to nw Venez.

## 20. CHOCO TOUCAN
*Ramphastos brevis*         Pl. 20, Map 584
**Identification:** 19″ (48cm). A miniature of Chestnut-mandibled Toucan (21), incl. plum-

age, bill color, and facial skin color; best told by conspic. vocal differences. In the hand separated from Chestnut-mandibled Toucan (R. *swainsonii* of w Colombia) by smaller total bill length (120-156mm vs 157-181mm), narrower width of bill at base (34-38mm vs 38.5-42mm), and narrower width near center of bill (17-21mm vs 23-28mm) (Haffer 1974). In the field may be told, with experience, by smaller size and shorter-billed appearance.

**Similar species:** See Keel-billed (19) and Citron-throated toucans (17), both of which meet but presum. do not overlap the range of Choco Toucan in nw Colombia.

**Voice:** "Song" a ser. of croaks or croaking grunts very sim. to Keel-billed Toucan.

**Behavior:** Apparently like other channel-keel-billed members of genus. See 19.

**Breeding:** BC ♂, 26 Jan, Chocó (Carriker).

**Status and habitat:** Humid and wet forest and forest borders. Broadly sympatric with Chestnut-mandibled Toucan.

**Range:** To 1000m. Pacific Colombia from n Chocó (Río Salaquí and Mutatá) southward. W Colombia and nw Ecuador.

**Note:** Formerly considered a small race of *R. ambiguus* (Black-mandibled Toucan) but here considered a valid sp. (after Haffer 1974).

## 21. CHESTNUT-MANDIBLED TOUCAN

*Ramphastos swainsonii* Pl. 20, Map 585

**Identification:** 24″ (61cm). Bill to 7″ (178mm), *bicolored*; lower mandible and large wedge at base of upper mandible reddish chestnut, otherwise yellow. Mostly black with white rump and red crissum; throat and chest yellow, bordered below by a narrow white line, then a narrow red band. Bare ocular area bright yellow to yellowish green.

**Similar species:** See Choco (20), Citron-throated (17), and Black-mandibled toucans (22).

**Voice:** "Song" a loud, rhythmic, gull-like *keeyós tadáy tadáy* repeated at short intervals, 1st note strongest, last often omitted. A local name *Dios tedé* suggests the call. Jerks bill and tail upward with each call like others of the genus.

**Behavior:** Usually seen in pairs, occas. small groups, fairly high in trees or in canopy. Reportedly stay higher on average than the smaller channel-keel-billed members of the genus (Haffer 1974). Flight and general behavior otherwise like the genus. See 19.

**Breeding:** Feeding young, upper Anchicayá Val., early Apr, and early June; 1 recently fledged juv. with ads. mid-Nov (Hilty); 4 BC birds, Mar–May, nw Colombia (Carriker).

**Status and habitat:** Locally common in humid and wet forest and forest borders. Now nearly

extirpated in much of mid. and upper Magdalena Val.

**Range:** To 2000m. Pacific coast (seldom above 1500m), n base of W and C Andes, s in Cauca Val. to slopes above Popayán (no recent recs. anywhere in mid. or upper Cauca Val.), and s in mid. Magdalena Val. to e Antioquia (Remedios). Honduras to w Ecuador.

**Note:** Sometimes considered a subsp. of *R. ambiguus* (Black-mandibled Toucan), the enlarged sp. becoming *R. ambiguus* (Yellow-breasted Toucan). Zone of integration between *R. swainsonii* and *R. ambiguus*, if any, is unknown.

## 22. BLACK-MANDIBLED TOUCAN

*Ramphastos ambiguus* Map 586

**Identification:** 24″ (61cm). Like preceding sp. but dark reddish chestnut of bill *replaced by black*, and bare ocular area *yellowish green* (*abbreviatus*) or blue (*ambiguus*).

**Similar species:** See Chestnut-mandibled Toucan (21).

**Voice:** Sim. to Chestnut-mandibled Toucan.

**Behavior:** As in other "smooth-billed" members of the genus. See 21.

**Breeding:** 2 BC ♀♀, Mar, sw Huila (Carriker).

**Status and habitat:** Canopy of humid foothill and lower montane forest and forest edge. Meets allied *R. swainsonii* in mid. Magdalena Val. (contact zone unknown) and is replaced by it westward.

**Range:** 100-2400m, Magdalena Val.; 500-2000m, e slope E Andes. Mid. and upper Magdalena Val. (formerly to headwaters in Huila), Perijá Mts., and e of Andes in Catatumbo lowlands (*abbreviatus*); e slope E Andes from Río Casanare and Macarena Mts. southward (*ambiguus*). Colombia and w Venez. to e Peru.

**Note:** Haffer (1974) considers *R. swainsonii* (Chestnut-mandibled Toucan) of C America and w Colombia a subsp. of this sp. See note under 21.

## 23. WHITE-THROATED (INCL. CUVIER'S) TOUCAN

*Ramphastos tucanus* Pl. 20, Map 587

**Identification:** 24″ (61cm). Bill to 7″ (178mm), *black* with base of upper mandible and culmen pale yellow, base of lower mandible light blue. Mostly black with *orange to red rump* and red crissum; throat and chest white, bordered below by narrow band of red. Bare ocular area pale blue. Or as above but black of bill replaced by dark red (*tucanus*); birds south to Caquetá and Amazonas (*cuvieri*) may show traces of dark red in bill.

**Similar species:** Almost identical to Yellow-ridged Toucan (18) but larger and with longer bill. In field best separated by voice.

**Voice:** "Song" a loud ser. of whistled yelps *eeot whe-whe* last syllable sometimes omitted), rhythmic and much like call of Chestnut-mandibled Toucan; differs mainly in last 2 notes being monosyllabic (not more or less bisyllabic).

**Behavior:** Like other smooth-billed members of the genus. See 21.

**Breeding:** BC ♂♂ (*cuvieri*), late Jan, Carimagua, ne Meta (MCN), and Macarena Mts., 7 Feb (Olivares 1962); 5 Guyana nests (*tucanus*) Mar-July, natural cavities 1-18 m up (Bourne 1974).

**Status and habitat:** Fairly common in canopy of humid forest and forest borders.

**Range:** To 1000m. E base of E Andes in Arauca and n Boyacá (*tucanus*); from nw Meta, ne Meta (Carimagua—S. Furniss), and Vaupés southward (*cuvieri*). Prob. Vichada and Guainía. The Guianas and Venez. s to Bolivia and Amazonian Brazil.

**Note:** Incl. *R. tucanus* (Red-billed Toucan) of ne Colombia to the Guianas and se Brazil and *R. cuvieri* (Cuvier's Toucan) of s Colombia to Bolivia and w Amazonian Brazil (after Haffer 1974). They are sometimes considered separate spp.

# WOODPECKERS, PICULETS: Picidae (38)

Woodpeckers are a cosmopolitan group, well represented in Colombia. They occur wherever there are trees and, except for piculets and Old World Wrynecks, usually cling upright on trunks or limbs, using strong, stiff, pointed tail feathers for support. The diminutive piculets, unlike larger woodpeckers, have a soft tail that is not used for support, and in general they resemble a xenops or nuthatches (*Sitta* spp.) in behavior. The bills of larger woodpeckers are strong, tapering, and often chisellike at the tip. The tongue is barbed at the tip and can be greatly extended enabling them to reach bark and wood boring insects. Several species are notably frugivorous; others at least partially specialize in arboreal ant colonies, arboreal termite colonies, or terrestrial ants; and a few regularly sally in to the air. All Colombian woodpeckers hollow out cavities and lay white eggs; a few nest in loose colonies.

[*Picumnus:* Tiny; ♂'s crown dotted yellow to red; ♀'s dotted white (or undotted, ♂), tail not used for support. In all spp., tail is black with inner web of central feathers and edges of tail white to buffy white. Tail not described in following identifications. A difficult genus and the taxonomy not completely understood (see Short 1982).]

## 1. CHESTNUT PICULET

*Picumnus cinnamomeus*          Pl. 23, Map 588

**Identification:** 4″ (10.2cm). *Mostly bright rufous chestnut, forecrown yellowish white*, crown black spotted with yellow in front, white behind (or crown black, only sides and back of crown spotted white—♀); wings brownish.

**Similar species:** Nothing sim. in its range.

**Behavior:** Very active, hitching and creeping over trunks and limbs like a nuthatch (*Sitta* spp.) and hopping through thickets without using the tail for support. Forages at almost all levels, usually in pairs, occas. small family groups and often accompanies mixed spp. flocks. More conspic. than most piculets.

**Breeding:** Laying ♀, Dec, Magdalena; Mar juv., Cesar (Carriker).

**Status and habitat:** Common in arid and semi-

arid scrub, dry forest borders, and mangroves (esp. mangroves of Los Cocos, PN Salamanca). Fond of tangles and thorny woodland.

**Range:** To 300m. Carib. region from n Sucre (Snía. de San Jacinto) e to Guajira and s locally to the lower Cauca Val. (Río Nechí) and mid. Magdalena Val. (Gamarra, Cesar). N Colombia and nw Venez.

## 2. RUFOUS-BREASTED PICULET

*Picumnus rufiventris*          Map 589

**Identification:** 4″ (10.2cm). *Sides of head, nape, and entire underparts rufous*; otherwise olive above with black crown dotted in front with red, behind with white (or all dotted white—♀).

**Similar species:** Only piculet with chestnut underparts in Amazonian region.

**Behavior:** Typical of the genus (see 5). Single birds or pairs, rather low (1-7m up) and often with mixed spp. flocks.

**Status and habitat:** Fairly common in thickety forest borders, second growth woodland, overgrown clearings, and stream banks; also reg. inside *terra firme* and *várzea* forests.

**Range:** To 400m. E of Andes from near Villavicencio (Río Guatiquía) to base of Andes in Putumayo and se Nariño; prob. Amazonas (photo sw of Leticia on Río Cayarú, Peru, 22 July 1978—J. Dunning). E Colombia to n Bolivia and sw Amazonian Brazil.

## 3. PLAIN-BREASTED PICULET

*Picumnus castelnau*                                       Map 590

**Identification:** 3.5″ (9.1cm). *Olive above, faintly scaled yellowish olive*; crown black dotted reddish orange, (or all black—♀); nape and sides of neck finely barred olive and white; inner remiges edged yellowish white; *underparts unmarked whitish* with yellowish tinge on abdomen.

**Similar species:** Only Colombian piculet e of Andes with unmarked whitish underparts. See White-bellied Piculet (note under 4).

**Voice:** In Amazonas a very high, thin, trill, T'E'E'e'e'e'e'e, at 20- to 40-sec intervals; weak, descending slightly, fading at end.

**Behavior:** Inconspic. and sometimes rather deliberate in movements. Solitary or in pairs from subcanopy to lower levels and easily overlooked except for tapping (J. V. Remsen); usually not with mixed flocks.

**Breeding:** ♀ feeding fledgling, 21 June, Amazonas (Remsen 1977a).

**Status and habitat:** Swamp and *várzea* forest, mainly along river banks or on river isls. and esp. in older, more open second growth dominated by *Cecropia* and *Mimosa*. Known in Colombia from 1 ♀, 21 June 1975, Isla Santa Sophia II (Monkey Isl.) and sightings at Quebrada Tucuchira and Monkey Isl. (Remsen 1977a; Hilty).

**Range:** 100m. S Amazonas along the Amazon. Se Colombia and e Ecuador to n Bolivia.

## 4. SCALED PICULET

*Picumnus squamulatus*                          Pl. 23, Map 591

**Identification:** 3.5″ (8.9cm). Crown and nape black, crown dotted orange red (or white—♀), nape dotted white; otherwise *pale brownish above, whitish below and conspic. scaled dusky all over.*

**Similar species:** Looks conspic. scaled above and below, not barred. See Golden-spangled Piculet (7) and Lafresnaye's Piculet (8). Olivaceous Piculet (5) on e and w slope E Andes has scaled throat but uniform breast and smudgy streaks on belly.

**Voice:** Call a very high squeaky *chi-chi-che'e'e'chi*, slightly trilled near end.

**Behavior:** Sim. to others of the genus. Usually seen inspecting tiny twigs and branches from mid. to lower hts. and in thickets.

**Breeding:** BC pair, Jan, Boyacá (Olivares 1963); BC ♂, Oct, Norte de Santander (Carriker); breeding evidence May and Sept, Guárico, Venez. (Thomas 1979b).

**Status and habitat:** Fairly common in drier woodland, gallery forest, scrubby areas, and ranchland with scattered trees.

**Range:** To 1600m. S end of Santa Marta Mts.; e of Andes from Norte de Santander (Zulia Val.) s to s Meta (Macarena Mts.) and e to ne Meta (Carimagua, Meta—S. Furniss), prob. to the Orinoco. Ne Colombia and Venez. n of Orinoco.

**Note:** White-bellied Piculet (*P. spilogaster*) from Apure, Venez. eastward to the Orinoco drainage is known along Río Meta in Venez. and doubtless occurs in adj. Colombia. 3.5″; scarlet forecrown; black hindcrown dotted white; plain olive brown above; white below faintly scaled dusky on sides of neck; tail like other piculets.

## 5. OLIVACEOUS PICULET

*Picumnus olivaceus*                             Pl. 23, Map 592

**Identification:** 3.5″ (8.9cm). Crown black, dotted orange in front, white behind (or all dotted white—♀); otherwise olive above, throat whitish (finely scaled dusky—*olivaceus*), breast brownish olive; rest of underparts *buffy yellow obscurely streaked dusky.*

**Similar species:** Easily confused with Grayish Piculet (6), which has distinctly clean-cut grayish underparts (no dingy scaling or streaking) and is paler and more brownish gray above (hard to see); normally the 2 do not overlap in range.

**Voice:** Call a fine, rapid twitter or trill; also a single sharp, clear note; like other piculets does not drum (Skutch 1969a).

**Behavior:** Actively peck on fine twigs and sticks at low to mid. hts. Recall a nuthatch (*Sitta* spp.) or xenops as they hop in tangles or hitch along limbs. Often with mixed spp. flocks.

**Breeding:** 2 BC birds, May and Sept, Magdalena Val.; 1 in July, n end E Andes (Carriker); a Feb nest, Huila (Miller 1947); holes excavated in soft limb or post 0.1-10m up; cavity used for nesting and roosting (Skutch 1969a).

**Status and habitat:** Uncommon in humid to drier forest borders, lighter woodland, and shrubby clearings; mostly foothills and slopes. Replaced in mid. and upper Cauca Val. by Grayish Piculet.

**Range:** To 1800m (rarely to 2500m). Pacific lowlands, sw Nariño (*harterti*); northernmost Chocó, Unguía (*panamensis*); e slope W Andes at n end and w slope on upper Río San Juan (*antioquensis*); n of Andes from upper Río Sinú e to s Bolívar and n to Snía. San Jacinto, n Sucre (*malleolus*); both slopes C Andes and w slope E Andes (*olivaceus*); e slope E Andes in Norte de Santander (*tachirensis*). Guatemala to w Ecuador and nw Venez. (incl. Perijá Mts.).

## 6. GRAYISH PICULET

*Picumnus granadensis*          Pl. 23, Map 593

**Identification:** 3.5″ (8.9cm). Crown black, dotted yellow in front, white behind (or all dotted white—♀); otherwise pale brownish gray above, *unmarked pale grayish white below.*

**Similar species:** See Olivaceous Piculet (5).

**Voice:** Infrequent call a weak, high-pitched trill on same pitch.

**Behavior:** Sim. to Olivaceous Piculet.

**Breeding:** Copulation, 18 Jan, above Cali (Hilty); pair feeding young, 20 Feb. Pichindé Val., 1600m (S. Gniadek), and 27 Feb, Calima Val., 1700m (Brown); juv. ♂ late July, above Cali (Miller 1963).

**Status and habitat:** Uncommon in dry to humid forest borders, second growth, and lighter woodland. Replaces Olivaceous Piculet geographically in most of Cauca Val. and adj. dry Pacific slope vals.

**Range:** ENDEMIC. 800-2100m; dry Pacific slope vals. incl. the upper Dagua and upper Calima (w to Cisneros) and poss. upper Río Sucio near Frontino; mid. and upper Cauca and upper Patía vals.

## 7. [GOLDEN-SPANGLED PICULET]

*Picumnus exilis*          Pl. 23, Map 594

**Identification:** 3.5″ (8.9cm). Crown black, heavily dotted red on forecrown, white behind (or entire crown black dotted white—♀); otherwise brownish olive above; *mantle and scapular feathers with yellow-encircled dusky bars* (has spotted appearance in field); *underparts dull yellowish white heavily and closely barred blackish throughout.*

**Similar species:** Rather sim. to Lafresnaye's Piculet (8), but upperparts have spotted (not strongly barred) appearance, underparts yellowish (not dull whitish), and ranges may not overlap. Orinoco Piculet (9) has uniform upperparts.

**Behavior:** Alone or with mixed spp. flocks; tap and peck 1-5m up, much like other *Picumnus.*

**Breeding:** Dec–Mar, Venez. (Short 1982); nest hole like others of genus.

**Status and habitat:** Hypothetical. Two sight recs. (no specimens). Sandy-belt forest borders and savanna woodland edges.

**Range:** Orinoco region of ne Guainía (18 and 19 Sept 1978—Hilty and M. Robbins). Doubtless more widespread as known throughout adj. Amazonas, Venez. E Colombia through s and e Venez. to the Guianas and n and e Brazil.

## 8. LAFRESNAYE'S PICULET

*Picumnus lafresnayi*          Pl. 23, Map 595

**Identification:** 3.5″ (8.9cm). Crown dark brown, dotted on forecrown with orange, behind with white (or entire crown dotted white—♀); otherwise *olive green above barred olive yellow;* below yellowish white *broadly barred black* (has banded appearance).

**Similar species:** Only Colombian piculet *barred* above and below. Orinoco Piculet (9) and Bar-breasted Piculet (see note below) have uniform upperparts. Cf. Golden-spangled Piculet (7); also cf. Scaled Piculet (4).

**Behavior:** Sim. to other *Picumnus;* lower levels to canopy.

**Breeding:** In e Ecuador (1000m), 1 nest, mid-Aug, 3.3m up, second growth border near stream; 2 white eggs (Skutch 1948a).

**Status and habitat:** Humid forest borders and second growth woodland. Not well known in Colombia.

**Range:** To 500m (sight to 1400m, w Caquetá, 1981—Hilty). E of Andes from s Meta (Macarena Mts.) and ne Guainía (Pto. Inírida) southward. Most recs. near base of E Andes. E Colombia and e Ecuador (reportedly to 2500m?) to e Peru and Amazonian Brazil (both sides of Amazon e to Río Negro).

**Note 1:** Considered a subsp. of *P. aurifrons* of e Ecuador to Amazonian Brazil s of Río Amazon, by some but a distinct sp. by Short (1982).

**Note 2:** Short (1982) merges *P. borbae,* Bar-breasted Piculet (♂♂ with red-spotted crowns) with *P. aurifrons,* Gold-fronted Piculet (♂♂ with yellow-spotted crowns), calling the enlarged sp. Bar-breasted Piculet (*P. aurifrons*). *P. a. aurifrons* is known from several sightings on s Amazon bank near Leticia (J. V. Remsen et al.; Hilty). 3.5″; crown blackish dotted on forecrown with yellow, behind with white (or entire crown dotted white—♀); plain olive above (sometimes faint yellowish bars on rump); throat whitish; rest of underparts yellowish barred brown on breast and spotted and streaked brown on lower underparts. *Terra firme* and *várzea* forests.

## 9. ORINOCO PICULET

*Picumnus pumilus*          Map 596

**Identification:** 4″ (10.2cm). Forecrown black dotted yellow (buffy white—♀); hindcrown light brown spotted buffy; *upperparts plain olive, below buffy white narrowly and crisply barred black.*

**Similar species:** From Golden-spangled Piculet (7) by plain unmarked upperparts. Scaled Piculet (4) is scaly all over. Lafresnaye's Piculet (8) is barred above.

**Status and habitat:** Presum. savanna and gallery woodland borders and scrubby thickets. Few recs. and little known.

**Range:** To 300m. E Vichada where known from

w bank of Orinoco (Maipures) s to Vaupés (Mitú) and Vaupés-Meta boundary (San José del Guaviare). E Colombia and nw Brazil along Río Uaupés.

**Note:** Considered a subsp. of *P. lafresnayi* (Lafresnaye's Piculet) by Short (1982), but both *P. l. lafresnayi* and *P. pumilis* have been collected at Mitú, Vaupés (Olivares 1955, 1964a).

## 10. SPOT-BREASTED WOODPECKER
*Chrysoptilus punctigula*        Pl. 22, Map 597

**Identification:** 8″ (20cm). *Forecrown black*, hindcrown red; otherwise yellowish olive barred black above; *sides of head white* bordered below by red moustachial streak; throat mottled black and white; breast yellow olive becoming clear yellow on belly, *thinly spotted black on breast and sides.* ♀: sim., but moustache black, only nape red.

**Similar species:** Easily confused with Golden-olive Woodpecker (12), which is uniform above, banded below, and usually found at higher el.

**Voice:** Call a weak, nasal *wha-whe-whe-whe-whe-whe-whe-whe-wha*, rather high-pitched, 1st and last notes slightly lower (J. V. Remsen); also *whew*, a trebled *ta-wick*, and a flickerlike (*Colaptes*) *week-a, week-a* in greeting (Short 1972).

**Behavior:** Singly or in pairs at midlevels or lower, or occas. to ground where they feed on ants.

**Breeding:** 3 BC birds, Jan–May, n Antioquia and Boyacá (Carriker; Olivares 1963); 1 in May, Orinoco opp. Vichada (Friedmann 1948). Fence post nest, 20 Jan, w Meta (W. McKay); pairs excavating, 27 Oct, Santa Marta (Darlington 1931); and 16 Nov, Leticia, latter 3m up over water (Brown).

**Status and habitat:** Nonforest. A sp. of open woodland, borders, cultivated areas with trees, young *várzea*, and mangroves. Most numerous in drier lightly wooded Carib. region.

**Range:** To 1500m. Throughout except Pacific coast s of Buenaventura, Valle and no recs. in Guainía and Vaupés. C Panama to n Bolivia, c Amazonian Brazil and the Guianas.

**Note:** Placed in the genus *Colaptes* by Short (1972) and called Spot-breasted Flicker.

## 11. CRIMSON-MANTLED WOODPECKER
*Piculus rivolii*        Pl. 22, Map 598

**Identification:** 11″ (28cm). *Crown and most of upperparts crimson*, rump yellowish barred black, tail black; *sides of head whitish* bordered below by crimson moustache; *throat and upper breast black scaled white* (or sometimes throat solid black, chest and breast stained red); rest of underparts golden yellow; breast and sides spotted black. ♀: crown and moustachial streak black (not red), throat freckled black and white.

**Similar species:** A striking woodpecker and not likely confused. Golden-olive Woodpecker (12) lacks the crimson mantle.

**Voice:** Rather quiet; occas. a loud flickerlike (*Colaptes*) *kre-ep*, rising slightly (Hilty); also a longer ser. of flickerlike *kick* notes (Short 1970).

**Behavior:** Usually seen singly or in pairs and often accompanying mixed flocks. Probes, pecks, and gleans (usually not tapping), at almost any ht. on mossy and epiphyte-laden surfaces; occas. drops to ground where it feeds on ants (Hilty; Short 1970); or at flowers of *Puya* and *Espeletia* in paramo (W. McKay).

**Breeding:** ♀ presumed incubating, 12 Mar, Cerro Munchique, Cauca (Brown); BC ♂, Feb, Puracé (Carriker).

**Status and habitat:** Fairly common in humid and wet forest (esp. mossy forest), forest edges, clearings with trees, stunted treeline woodland or adj. paramo.

**Range:** 1800-3500m; to 700m on Pacific slope in Cauca. W Andes in Valle and Cauca, C and E Andes. Nw Venez. (incl. Perijá Mts.) s in Andes to n Bolivia.

## 12. GOLDEN-OLIVE WOODPECKER
*Piculus rubiginosus*        Pls. 21, 22, Map 599

**Identification:** 9″ (23cm). Entire crown and nape crimson; otherwise *golden olive above*; rump yellow barred olive; *sides of head white* bordered below by red moustache; throat freckled black and white (or solid black—*gularis*), rest of *underparts banded dark olive and yellowish* (or like above, but center of crown dark gray, only sides of crown and nape crimson—*alleni; rubripileus; michaelis*). ♀ forecrown blackish becoming grayish on top, only nape crimson; moustache black; throat freckled black and white.

**Similar species:** See Spot-breasted Woodpecker (10).

**Voice:** Frequent call a very loud, powerful *geep* or *keer*, somewhat kiskadeelike; also a pecculiar *utzia-deek* (Ridgely 1976).

**Behavior:** Usually singly or in loose pairs from lower mid. story to canopy. Forages mostly by tapping and chiseling on limbs, branches, and vines, much less by climbing trunks or by probing and gleaning along mossy limbs. Often accompanies mixed spp. flocks.

**Breeding:** 12 BC birds, Jan–June, Santa Marta Mts., W and C Andes (Carriker). Digging cavity, Jan, upper Anchicayá Val. (Hilty); cavity 6m up, young, Mar, nw Venez. (Brown).

**Status and habitat:** Fairly common in broken mt. forest, forest borders, second growth woodland, and scattered trees in highland clearings.

**Range:** 900-3100m. W Andes s to Cauca (*pacificus*); Pacific slope in Nariño (*rubripileus*); C Andes s to Cauca and s Huila (*gularis*); Santa Marta Mts. (*alleni*); Perijá Mts. (*meridensis*); w slope E Andes s to se Santander (*palmitae*); e slope E Andes s to Macarena Mts. (*buenavistae*); Río San Miguel, se Nariño (*michaelis*); e slope Andes near Ecuador boundary (*nuchalis*). S Mexico to w Panama; nw Venez. to nw Argentina; Guyana, Trinidad.

### 13. YELLOW-THROATED WOODPECKER
*Piculus flavigula* Pl. 22, Map 600
**Identification:** 8″ (20cm). Slightly crested. Crown and nape crimson; *entire sides of head, foreneck, and throat yellow* (some birds along Río Negro with trace of red moustache); otherwise olive green above, inner webs of primaries rufous; breast and belly whitish heavily scaled dark olive, more spotted on chest. ♀ sim., but crown bronzy olive yellow, only nape red.
**Similar species:** Best mark for either sex is the yellow almost encircling sides of head and neck. Golden-green Woodpecker (15) has sides of head olive with long yellow moustache.
**Voice:** Call is *queea queea*; also a fast *kee kee kee* . . . for 6-8 sec and slowing (P. Schwartz recording).
**Behavior:** Alone or with mixed spp. flocks in forest midlevels or higher. Climbs limbs, branches, and trunks and taps and chisels on bark.
**Breeding:** ♂ digging in stub, 15 Nov, 2m above water, Leticia (Brown).
**Status and habitat:** Fairly common in humid *terra firme* and *várzea* forests.
**Range:** To 500m. E of Andes from s Meta (Macarena Mts.) and Vaupés (Mitú) southward. Doubtless n to se Vichada (rec. on upper Río Orinoco and Río Negro, Venez.). The Guianas and s Venez. to n Peru and n and se Brazil.

### 14. WHITE-THROATED WOODPECKER
*Piculus leucolaemus* Pl. 21, Map 601
**Identification:** 8″ (20cm). *Crown, nape, and moustachial streak crimson*; patch through eyes and upper cheeks olive *bordered below by a broad yellowish stripe*; otherwise golden olive above, remiges rufous broadly tipped dusky; *throat white* somewhat scaled dusky; breast olive coarsely spotted and scaled white becoming barred olive and dirty white on belly; eyes whitish. ♀: lacks red moustache; crown yellowish olive, only nape crimson.
**Similar species:** On Pacific slope see Red-stained Woodpecker (29); in mid. Magdalena Val. Golden-green Woodpecker (15); e of Andes

Yellow-throated (13) and Golden-green woodpeckers.
**Behavior:** Much like Yellow-throated Woodpecker. When excited yellow gape stripe puffed out (G. Tudor).
**Breeding:** ♂ at presumed nest hole 10m up, 7 Mar, upper Anchicayá Val. (Brown); 5 BC birds, Jan–Aug, Antioquia, Valle (Carriker).
**Status and habitat:** Uncommon in humid and wet forest in Pacific slope foothills and lower highlands. Reg. in Anchicayá Val., mainly 800-1000m.
**Range:** 100-1400m. Pacific coast from Baudó Mts. southward; n end of C Andes (Río Nechí) and s in Magdalena Val. to Caldas (Río Samaná) and Yacopí (1400m) nw Cundinamarca. Prob. also e base of E Andes at s end (rec. at adj. Limoncocha, Ecuador). W Colombia to nw Ecuador; e Ecuador to n Bolivia and on both sides of Amazon in w Brazil.
**Note:** Some incl. *P. callopterus* (Stripe-cheeked Woodpecker) of Panama as a race of White-throated Woodpecker, which it prob. is (Short 1972). It is found e to Cerro Pirre, Panama (near Colombian border), and prob. occurs on Colombian side. Differs mainly in having primaries barred rufous and dusky and lower underparts yellower and more evenly barred.

### 15. GOLDEN-GREEN WOODPECKER
*Piculus chrysochloros* Pls. 21, 22
Map 602
**Identification:** 9″ (23cm). Slightly crested. ♂: crown, nape, and moustachial streak red; sides of head dusky and bordered below by a *long narrow yellow streak*; otherwise entirely greenish olive above; primaries rufous basally; below rather *narrowly banded* greenish white and *dark olive*. Or throat plain yellowish buff, rest of underparts barred olive and yellow buff (*aurosus*). ♀ sim., but red of head replaced by olive green. Or crown, nape, and throat golden yellow (*aurosus*) or dull greenish yellow (*xanthochlorus*).
**Similar species:** From White-throated Woodpecker (14) by yellowish throat (*aurosus*) in the mid. Magdalena Val. and by finely barred throat e of Andes.
**Behavior:** Single birds or pairs often follow mixed spp. flocks from forest midlevel to canopy. Mostly glean bark surfaces, esp. for ants, only sporadically tap (Short 1973).
**Breeding:** 2 BC birds, Feb–Mar, Magdalena and Córdoba (Carriker).
**Status and habitat:** Fairly common in humid *terra firme* and *várzea* forests and forest edges. Evidently less numerous in n Colombia than e of the Andes.
**Range:** To 500m. Upper Sinú Val. (Córdoba),

east n of Andes to Santa Marta Mts. and s in mid. Magdalena Val. to Remedios, Antioquia (*aurosus*); e of Andes in Zulia Val., Norte de Santander (*xanthochlorus*); from w Meta (Villavicencio), ne Guainía (sightings, Pto. Inírida, 1978—Hilty and M. Robbins) and Vaupés southward (*capistratus*). E Panama to the Guianas and s to se Bolivia and n Argentina.

[*Celeus*: "Chestnut-colored" (or creamy yellow—19); hammerheaded shape; *bill greenish yellow*; glean bark surfaces or chisel arboreal ant and termite nests.]

### 16. CHESTNUT WOODPECKER
*Celeus elegans*  Pl. 22, Map 603
**Identification:** 11″ (28cm). Hammerheaded with prom. crest. *Entirely chestnut*, decidedly darker on head and underparts; *rump and flanks yellowish buff*; short crimson malar stripe (lacking in ♀). Or with inner web of inner remiges barred black and buff and upper tail coverts as well as rump and flanks yellowish buff (*jumana*).
**Similar species:** Scale-breasted Woodpecker (17) is sim. but smaller and barred black below (or above and below). Ringed Woodpecker (20) is superficially sim., but chest and upper breast black, lower underparts bright yellowish buff, and tail more conspic. barred.
**Voice:** Typical call a raspy, scraping *wháa-jer*, sometimes repeated several times in rapid succession.
**Behavior:** Alone, in pairs, or occas. in loose groups, usually in mid. story, also higher or lower and frequently with mixed flocks. Climbs larger trunks and limbs, gleans from bark surfaces, reg. hammers open arboreal termite nests, and occas. eats fruit (J. V. Remsen).
**Breeding:** Drumming daily, Feb, Mitú (Hilty); Trinidad nests, Apr–May, usually in dead trunk; 3 eggs (ffrench 1973).
**Status and habitat:** Fairly common in humid *terra firme* and *várzea* forests and forest borders; most numerous *Celeus* in Colombia.
**Range:** To 500m. E of Andes from w Meta (Villavicencio and Macarena Mts.) to Caquetá and Amazonas (*citreopygius*); e Vichada (Maipures) to Vaupés (*jumana*). The Guianas and s Venez. to n Bolivia and Amazonian Brazil. Trinidad.

### 17. SCALE-BREASTED WOODPECKER
*Celeus grammicus*  Pl. 22, Map 604
**Identification:** 9″ (23cm). Hammerheaded with short crest. *Mostly chestnut with unbarred yellowish buff rump; shoulders and entire underparts barred and scaled black* (or entirely barred and scaled above and below with more black below—

*grammicus*); short moustachial streak crimson (lacking in ♀); remiges and tail black. Birds from Río Uaupés (Tahuapunto), Brazil, adj. to e Vaupés border are mainly blackish scaled chestnut below and very unlike other subspp.
**Similar species:** See larger Chestnut Woodpecker (16), also Ringed Woodpecker (20).
**Voice:** Commonly a loud, brisk *curry-kuuu*, rather nasal; also a very loud, metallic *Pring-Pring!*, occas. up to 4 notes.
**Behavior:** Rather like Chestnut Woodpecker. Usually in mid. or upper levels, esp. on med.-sized to large trunks and on larger canopy limbs where it taps and gleans on bark surfaces. Sometimes in groups of 3-4 and often with mixed flocks.
**Breeding:** Several BC birds, Mar–Apr, upper Orinoco, Venez. (Friedmann 1948).
**Status and habitat:** Uncommon in humid *terra firme* and *várzea* forests.
**Range:** To 500m. E of Andes from sw Meta (Macarena Mts.) s to w Caquetá (*verreauxii*); e Guainía (prob. e Vichada) s to Leticia on the Amazon (*grammicus*). S Venez. to n Bolivia and w Amazonian Brazil and s of Amazon e to Río Tapajós. Ne Fr. Guiana.

### 18. CINNAMON WOODPECKER
*Celeus loricatus*  Pl. 22, Map 605
**Identification:** 8″ (20cm). Short crest on hindcrown. *Entire head and upperparts bright cinnamon rufous* flecked and barred with black (or sometimes almost uniform); upper throat and moustachial streak crimson (or all cinnamon—♀); *below whitish buff heavily barred and scaled black*; tail coarsely barred buff and black.
**Similar species:** Only mostly "cinnamon" woodpecker w of Andes.
**Voice:** Unwoodpeckerlike call a loud, abrupt, semiwhistled, 4- to 5-note *PHET! phet! phet, phet*, quick and falling in pitch and vol.
**Behavior:** Usually seen singly. Taps and gleans bark surfaces from lower story to canopy but more often high. Away from mixed flocks more than in them.
**Breeding:** 5 BC birds, Jan–Apr, s Bolívar to Antioquia (Carriker).
**Status and habitat:** Uncommon in humid and wet forest, occas. forest borders.
**Range:** To 1500m. Pacific coast; humid lowlands n of Andes e to mid. Magdalena Val. (Lebrija Val., nw Santander); one rec. at sw base of Santa Marta Mts. Nicaragua to w Ecuador.

### 19. CREAM-COLORED WOODPECKER
*Celeus flavus*  Pl. 22, Map 606
**Identification:** 11″ (28cm). Unmistakable. Hammerheaded with short bushy crest on

hindcrown. *Mostly sulphur yellow to creamy buff* with red moustachial stripe (lacking in ♀) and *black tail; wings dusky,* upper coverts edged yellow, inner remiges rufous (or wing coverts brownish edged yellow, remiges brown—*peruvianus*).

**Voice:** Frequently heard call sim. to Chestnut Woodpecker but higher and not as hoarse: a loud sharp *Whéejah,* often doubled or repeated over and over by several birds (J. V. Remsen); also a loud clear *Pueer, pueer, purr, paw,* last 2 notes descending.

**Behavior:** Singly, in pairs, or in groups of 3-4, mostly in mid. story. Primarily break open arboreal ant nests (papery ant nests softer than arboreal termite nests favored by larger Chestnut Woodpecker); often rather noisy (J. V. Remsen). Also eats fruit.

**Breeding:** 3 BC birds, May–June, w Caquetá (Carriker); 1 BC bird, Apr, upper Orinoco Venez. (Friedmann 1948).

**Status and habitat:** Uncommon; mostly *várzea* and swamp forests, swampy second growth woodland, and adj. borders, occas. gallery forest in s llanos.

**Range:** To 700m. E of Andes from w Meta and e Vichada (Maipures) s to Vaupés (*flavus*); w Caquetá to Amazonas (*peruvianus*). The Guianas and Venez. to n Bolivia and Amazonian and se Brazil.

### 20. RINGED WOODPECKER

*Celeus torquatus*          Pl. 22, Map 607

**Identification:** 11″ (28cm). Rare. *Crested head and throat pale cinnamon rufous, rest of upperparts chestnut* more or less barred black; tail chestnut barred and broadly tipped black; moustachial streak crimson (lacking in ♀); *collar encircling neck and broad band across chest and upper breast black;* lower underparts buffy cinnamon barred black.

**Similar species:** Superficially like Chestnut Woodpecker (16) and smaller Scale-breasted Woodpecker (17) but from either by contrasting *pale* cinnamon rufous head and black nuchal collar and breast; also lacks the unbarred yellow rump.

**Voice:** Call a very loud ringing *kuu!kuu!kuu! kuut!* (P. Schwartz recording).

**Behavior:** Little known. One near Leticia was alone on a main trunk near the canopy (J. V. Remsen); in Peru 1 somewhat lower (O'Neill 1974); another with a mixed forest flock stayed mostly 3-9m up on small trunks; others noted much higher (T. Parker).

**Status and habitat:** Rare and perhaps local; humid *terra firme* forest and tall second growth woodland. In Colombia known from 3 specimens (Blake 1962) and a sight rec. near Leticia (Remsen 1976).

**Range:** To 400m. E of Andes in s Meta, Río Guapayá, base of Macarena Mts. (*occidentalis*), and Leticia, Amazonas (sight). The Guianas and s Venez. (incl. Caño Cataniapo and San Fernando de Atabapo opp. Vichada and Guainía, Colombia) to n Bolivia and w and c Brazil; also Bahía, Brazil.

### 21. LINEATED WOODPECKER

*Dryocopus lineatus*          Pl. 22, Map 608

**Identification:** 14″ (36cm). Big with *black bill. Crown, prom. crest, and moustachial streak crimson,* sides of head and upperparts mostly black; 2 white stripes on sides of back *do not join in* V; *narrow white stripe from bill* runs under eye and down sides of neck; throat finely streaked black and white; chest black; rest of underparts barred buff and black. ♀: sim., but forehead and moustachial area black.

**Similar species:** Easily confused with Crimson-crested Woodpecker (34), esp. ♀ of latter; but white stripes do not join on back, bill black, and facial pattern different. ♀ Crimson-crested has very broad (not narrow) facial stripe. At higher el. see Powerful Woodpecker (37).

**Voice:** Usual call a loud flickerlike *(Colaptes) wicka-wicka-wicka* (Eisenmann 1952), and a lower-pitched *kíp-whurrr;* drum a slow roll of about 5-8 taps (cf. *Campephilus*).

**Behavior:** Alone or in pairs at almost any ht. on large trunks and limbs; taps and chisels bark surfaces of both living and dead wood.

**Breeding:** BC bird, Jan, n Chocó (Carriker); 2 in Jan, Santander (Boggs 1961); 2 in Jan–Feb, Macarena Mts. (Olivares 1962). In Costa Rica cavity excavation begins Nov–late Jan; 2-30m up in dead tree (Skutch 1969a).

**Status and habitat:** Widespread in forest borders, plantations, lighter woodland, and clearings with scattered large trees; lowlands and foothills, smaller no. much higher.

**Range:** To 2100m. Throughout. Mexico to nw Peru, n Argentina, Paraguay, and se Brazil.

### 22. ACORN WOODPECKER

*Melanerpes formicivorus*          Ill. 74, Map 609

**Identification:** 9″ (23cm). Mask around white eyes and patch encircling bill black; *forehead yellowish white extending down to lores and joined from below by a broad band of yellowish white on throat;* otherwise black above with black nape band (or no nape band—♀); rump and patch on wing white; breast and sides black streaked white; rest of lower underparts white.

**Similar species:** "Clownlike" face pattern unmistakable. White wing patches prom. in flight.

**Voice:** Noisy, uttering a loud *rack-up* repeat-

74. Acorn Woodpecker (♂ left),
Red-crowned Woodpecker (♂ right)

edly; a more rolling *r-r-rrrack-up* and other throaty calls (Skutch 1969a). Does not drum.
**Behavior:** Rather active; ebullient pairs or gregarious groups of up to 12 usually cling conspic. to high dead stubs. Often flycatch in short aerial sorties; reported storing acorns in Colombia (Miller 1963) and in Panama (Eisenmann 1952), and occas. drop to ground for ants (Brown).
**Breeding:** 6 BC birds, May–June, W and C Andes (Carriker); BC birds and juvs., Sept, Popayán (Miller 1963). Often several "helpers" at nest (Skutch 1969a).
**Status and habitat:** Local. Forest borders, open or lighter woodland, and deforested areas with scattered trees; mainly oak (*Quercus*) woodland.
**Range:** 1400-3300m. Both slopes of W and C Andes to head of Cauca and Magdalena vals. and w slope of E Andes from Norte de Santander (8°N) southward; on Pacific slope s to Cauca. No Nariño recs. W US to Colombia.

## 23. YELLOW-TUFTED WOODPECKER
*Melanerpes cruentatus*        Pl. 22, Ill, 75
                                            Map 610
**Identification:** 8″ (20cm). Eyes yellowish white. *Mostly black with conspic. yellowish white eyering extending backward as a narrow band joining on nape*; center crown crimson (black—♀); *rump white*; center of belly and lower breast red; flanks and under tail coverts barred black and white.

**Similar species:** Only small mostly black woodpecker e of Andes. Usually looks all black at a distance.
**Voice:** Very noisy, uttering a var. of loud raucous *r-r-r-aack-up* calls sim. to those of Acorn Woodpecker.
**Behavior:** Very social and usually in pairs or groups of 3-5, occas. up to 12, less often seen alone. Cling to high dead trunks and stubs where conspic. Omnivorous; often sally to air for insects or eat fruit.
**Breeding:** BC ♂, Mar, Macarena Mts. (Olivares 1962); nest, 29 Mar, nw Meta (Brown). Nesting may be loosely communal with ads. helping at several nests; cavity typically in tall dead stub or trunk (Short 1970).
**Status and habitat:** Common in humid forest or woodland borders and clearings with scattered trees. Apparently requires dead trees or tall dead stubs.
**Range:** To 1200m. E base of E Andes, and from w Meta and e Vichada southward. The Guianas, w Venez. (s base of Andes) and s Venez. to Bolivia and Amazonian Brazil.

## 24. BLACK-CHEEKED WOODPECKER
*Melanerpes pucherani*        Ill. 75, Map 611
**Identification:** 7.5″ (19cm). Wears a mask. ♂: forehead yellow, crown and hindneck red; *broad black mask encircles eyes and continues across cheeks to back*; upperparts black, *mantle finely barred and wings spotted with white; rump white*; small

75. Black-cheeked Woodpecker (♂ left),
Yellow-tufted Woodpecker (♂ right)

*white spot* behind eye; throat and upper breast buffy olive; rest of underparts barred buffy white and black; center of belly red. ♀: forecrown yellow to white; rest of crown black; nape red.
**Similar species:** Golden-naped Woodpecker (25) of Magdalena Val. is superficially sim. but has golden nape, white stripe up back (no barring), and no white spot behind eye.
**Voice:** A churring *cherr*; also a higher *chirrir-ree*, sometimes repeated (Eisenmann 1952).
**Behavior:** Most often alone or in pairs perched high on dead stubs or branches. Notably frugivorous.
**Breeding:** 6 BC birds, Mar–May, nw Colombia (Carriker; Haffer 1975). In Costa Rica and Panama, Dec–Aug, cavity in tall dead stub (Skutch 1969a; Wetmore 1968a; Willis and Eisenmann 1979).
**Status and habitat:** Fairly common in humid and wet forest borders, second growth woodland, and clearings with scattered trees; to a limited extent inside forest. May require dead trees. Lowlands and hill country. Replaced in drier more open areas by next sp.
**Range:** To 400m. Pacific coast and e around northernmost end of W Andes to lower Cauca Val. (n Antioquia). S Mexico to w Ecuador.

## 25. GOLDEN-NAPED WOODPECKER
*Melanerpes chrysauchen*          Map 612
**Identification:** 7.5″ (19cm). Wears a mask. ♂: forehead yellow buff; crown red; *nape golden yellow; broad black mask encircles eyes (no white spot behind eye) and continues across cheeks to back*; upperparts black with *broad white stripe down back and white rump*; wings dotted white; throat and breast dark buff; lower breast and flanks barred black and white; center of belly red. ♀: slightly duller with forecrown black, hindcrown red, nape band yellow.
**Similar species:** A colorful woodpecker resembling Black-cheeked Woodpecker (24) in pattern.
**Voice:** Gives a resonant *churr* much like Black-cheeked Woodpecker; drums occas.
**Behavior:** Sim. to Black-cheeked Woodpecker.
**Breeding:** BC ♂ and laying ♀, Mar, ne Antioquia (Carriker). Begins in Mar in Costa Rica; 3-4 eggs; cavity 5-30m up, also used for communal roosting (Skutch 1969a).
**Status and habitat:** Humid forest, second growth woodland, and borders. Replaced westward in lower Cauca Val. and Pacific coast by Black-cheeked Woodpecker.
**Range:** 400-1400m. Mid. Magdalena Val. from s Bolívar (Snía. San Lucas) s to Honda, n Tolima (*pulcher*). Costa Rica to sw Panama; n Colombia.

**Note:** By some considered specifically distinct from Mid. American *M. chrysauchen* and called *M. pulcher* (Beautiful Woodpecker).

## 26. RED-CROWNED WOODPECKER
*Melanerpes rubricapillus*          Pl. 22, Ill. 74, Map 613
**Identification:** 7″ (18cm). ♂: forehead yellowish white; crown and nape red (or only central crown spot red—*paraguanae*); *rest of upperparts barred black and white*; *sides of head to above eyes and underparts buffy gray*, center of belly red. ♀: crown buffy white, only nape red (or pale orangy brown—*paraguanae*).
**Similar species:** Black-cheeked Woodpecker (24) has black mask and much less barring above.
**Voice:** Noisy with a loud churring *krr-r-r*, and loud *wicka* several times when excited. Drum mostly at start of breeding season (Skutch 1969a).
**Behavior:** A conspic. woodpecker of rather open areas, usually alone or in pairs at med. hts. or lower. Chisels bark surface, inspects broken branch ends, and often eats fruit.
**Breeding:** Jan–Apr, Santa Marta area (S. M. Russell; Todd and Carriker 1922); Mar–June Guárico, Venez. (Thomas 1979b). Cavity hollowed out in large cactus, fence post, and dead or softer living wood, often quite high; 2 eggs.
**Status and habitat:** Common in arid and semiarid scrub, dry woodland, cultivated areas, and mangroves.
**Range:** To 1700m. Gulf of Urabá and upper Sinú Val. e to e base Santa Marta Mts., s to upper Magdalena Val. (San Agustín), and e of Andes in Norte de Santander and e Vichada (*rubricapillus*); Guajira from Ríohacha eastward (*paraguanae*). Sw Costa Rica to Venez. and the Guianas.
**Note:** By some placed in the genus *Centurus*.

## 27. SMOKY-BROWN WOODPECKER
*Veniliornis fumigatus*          Pl. 22, Map 614
**Identification:** 6.5″ (16.5cm). Small. *Entirely uniform smoky brown with red crown* (brown—♀); sometimes a pale patch below the eye; tail dusky; primaries notched dusky and white (underside of wing conspic. barred in flight).
**Similar species:** Best mark is the uniform brownish plumage. Other highland woodpeckers have facial patterns and barred underparts.
**Voice:** A short *chuck*, higher-pitched piping rattle, and during aggression a wheezy, sucking *whicker* (Miller 1962).
**Behavior:** Inconspic. in mid. story, less often from understory to canopy; singly or in pairs and often with mixed flocks. Taps and chisels

on small to large branches, less frequently on trunks.

**Breeding:** Fence post cavity hollowed out, Apr, W Andes above Cali (Miller 1963); Oct nest, upper Anchicayá Val. (Hilty); BC ♂, Jan, Santander (Carriker).

**Status and habitat:** Uncommon (easily overlooked) in humid and wet forest, second growth, lighter woodland, and woodland borders.

**Range:** 1200-2800m; to 600m on Pacific slope (sightings to 3000m, Represa Neusa, E Andes, 1979—A. Gast). Mt. Tacarcuna on Panama border, Santa Marta and Perijá mts., and the Andes. E Mexico to w Ecuador, Venez., and nw Argentina.

### 28. LITTLE WOODPECKER
*Veniliornis passerinus*          Pl. 22, Map 615
**Identification:** 6.5″ (16.5cm). *Small.* ♂: crown and nape red; remaining upperparts yellowish olive, tail blacker; wing coverts inconspic. dotted yellowish; forehead and sides of head brownish olive with an ill-defined whitish moustachial streak, very faint eyebrow; *underparts dirty grayish olive rather finely banded with white*; more spotted on lower throat and breast (or entire underparts banded; *whitish eyebrow and moustachial streak stronger—agilis*). ♀: sim., but crown olive brown faintly dotted whitish, no red.

**Similar species:** Very sim. to *orenocensis* subsp. of Red-stained Woodpecker (29) but even smaller and lacks latter's narrow golden collar; in the hand or nearby, note absence of red staining on shoulders; in direct comparison banding on underparts decidedly fine (not coarse and bold); in se Colombia the *agilis* subsp. also by definite whitish eyebrow and moustache (lacking in 29).

**Voice:** Sim. to Smoky-brown Woodpecker, a high-pitched, dry, wooden rattle; when excited a ser. of *wicka* notes (Hilty); territorial call a short drum then *wi-wi-wi-wi-wi-wi-wi* (Short 1970).

**Behavior:** Alone or in pairs from low to fairly high in trees; sometimes accompanying mixed spp. flocks. Inconspic. as it taps and chisels on bark surface of large or small branches, limbs, and saplings.

**Breeding:** Copulation, 10 Feb, w Meta (W. McKay); prob. wet season, Oct-Mar in se Peru (O'Neill 1974).

**Status and habitat:** Mainly edges of humid *terra firme* and *várzea* forests, borders of swampy lagoons or river banks, or in lighter second growth; also gallery and savanna woodland.

**Range:** To 1200m. E of Andes from e Norte de Santander (El Diamante) and e Vichada s

to Macarena Mts. and Vaupés (*fidelis*); w Putumayo (Rumiyaco, 1200m) and Amazonas (*agilis*). The Guianas and c and s Venez. to Bolivia, n Argentina, and s Brazil.

### 29. RED-STAINED WOODPECKER
*Veniliornis affinis*          Pl. 22, Map 616
**Identification:** 7.5″ (19cm). Bill blackish; red crown speckled with black and bordered behind by a *prom. yellow nuchal collar* extending to sides of neck; remaining upperparts bronzy yellowish olive; wing coverts faintly dotted yellowish and tipped red (latter visible up close in field); forehead and sides of head brownish olive; *underparts coarsely banded dark olive and buffy white* (or with blackish throat—*chocoensis*). ♀: crown smoky brown (no red).

**Similar species:** W of Andes, see White-throated (14) and Red-rumped woodpeckers (30); e of Andes cf. Little (28) and Yellow-throated woodpeckers (13).

**Behavior:** Rather solitary, occas. pairs, in midlevel to canopy branches in e and w Colombia. Has been seen both high and low along forest edge and inside forest in Amazonas.

**Status and habitat:** Humid *terra firme* and *várzea* forests, forest edges, also occas. second growth in Amazonas. Known from only a few recs. w of Andes.

**Range:** To 1000m on Pacific slope; to 500m e of Andes. Pacific slope from w Antioquia (Murindó on Chocó border) s to Valle (*chocoensis*); e of Andes from w Meta (Villavicencio) to Putumayo (*orenocensis*), sight recs. in Vaupés (El Dorado, 1976—R. Ridgely [*orenocensis*?]); Amazonas (Río Calderón—*hilaris*). W Colombia to nw Ecuador; sw Venez. (Amazonas incl. Río Orinoco opp. Vichada) to n Bolivia and Amazonian and se Brazil.

**Note 1:** Incl. the subsp. *chocoensis*, formerly considered a subsp. of *V. cassini* (Golden-collared Woodpecker); also incl. the subsp. *caquetanus* of e of Andes, formerly considered a subsp. of *V. cassini* and now believed a subad.; *V. a. orenocensis* (Short 1974). **Note 2:** Golden-collared Woodpecker of the Guianas, n Brazil, and s Venez. (incl. n and c Amazonas) may also occur in extreme e Colombia. Differs from Red-stained Woodpecker thus: smaller size (6″), no red tipping on wing coverts (usually), and with bolder, more black and white (not olive and white) banding on underparts; yellow collar brighter and more prom. (usually) and bill pale (not blackish).

### 30. RED-RUMPED WOODPECKER
*Veniliornis kirkii*          Pl. 22, Map 617
**Identification:** 6.5″ (16.5cm). Small. Crown red, speckled and mixed black and bordered be-

hind by a *narrow yellow nuchal collar*; remaining upperparts brownish olive (back sometimes washed red) with a *bright red rump* (often concealed by wings); sides of head grayish brown; underparts *evenly banded dirty white and brown*. ♀: crown brownish (no red).

**Similar species:** Only small woodpecker with a red rump. See Smoky-brown (27) and Red-stained Woodpecker (29).

**Voice:** Call a flycatcherlike *keeer* (Slud 1964); also a 2- to 4-note *quee-quee-quee* (ffrench 1973).

**Behavior:** Sim. to Little Woodpecker, and like others of the genus, rather inconspic. and best located by its frequent tapping.

**Breeding:** 3 BC ♀♀, Jan and Sept, Antioquia (Carriker). 3 Trinidad nests, Dec–Apr, 3-7.5m up; 2 eggs (ffrench 1973).

**Status and habitat:** Uncommon in moist to wet forest and second growth or riparian woodlands; common in mangroves of Carib. coast.

**Range:** To 300m on Pacific coast; to 1300m in Magdalena Val. Generally w of Andes (in Cauca Val. s at least formerly to Valle; in Magdalena Val. s to n Huila); e of Andes in Norte de Santander (Catatumbo and Zulia vals.). Poss. also Arauca and n Vichada. No recs. in arid Guajira. Costa Rica to w Ecuador and w and c Venez. (incl. Táchira, Apure, and nw Amazonas).

## 31. SCARLET-BACKED WOODPECKER
*Veniliornis callonotus* Pl. 21, Map 618
**Identification:** 6″ (15cm). Small. ♂: crown black thickly spotted red; *remaining upperparts red*; primaries brown notched white on inner webs; tail black, outer feathers barred buff; sides of head light brown; *underparts uniform buffy white or faintly scaled dusky on breast*. ♀: sim. but crown brownish black.

**Similar species:** Only *small* woodpecker with a scarlet back. At higher el. see larger Crimson-mantled Woodpecker (11). See also Red-rumped Woodpecker (30), which sometimes has red wash on back.

**Status and habitat:** Dry forest and scrub. Known from only a few Colombian recs.

**Range:** To 1000m. Arid Patía Val. in Nariño. Poss. coastal sw Nariño. Sw Colombia to w Ecuador and nw Peru.

## 32. YELLOW-VENTED WOODPECKER
*Veniliornis dignus* Pls. 21, 22
Map 619
**Identification:** 7″ (18cm). Small. ♂: crown and nape red, *cheeks blackish bordered above and below by whitish stripe*; distinct blackish malar; otherwise yellowish olive above with a few faint yellowish dots on shoulders and red stains on mantle; tail black, outer feathers paler and

barred buffy yellow; throat gray; *breast banded pale yellow and dusky; abdomen clear pale yellow.* ♀: sim., but crown slaty, only nape red.

**Similar species:** Good marks are the strong facial pattern and clear yellow belly. See Bar-bellied Woodpecker (33).

**Voice:** Rather quiet; occas. a weak, nasal rattle, high-pitched and much like others of the genus.

**Behavior:** Usually alone or in pairs on midlevel to canopy limbs and smaller branches, seldom understory; reg. with mixed bird flocks. Rather inactive and sometimes taps for long periods of time at 1 spot.

**Breeding:** 5 BC ♂♂, Mar–June, W and C Andes (Carriker; Miller 1963).

**Status and habitat:** Fairly common in humid and wet forest ("cloud forest") and forest edges.

**Range:** 1200-2700m: rarely to 700m. All 3 Andean ranges. In E Andes known on w slope from 1 old rec. in w Cundinamarca (Fusagasugá), on e slope only from w Caquetá (sight, 2100m, Sept, 1978—Hilty and M. Robbins) and e Nariño (Cerro Pax; Río Churuyaco). Nw Venez. s in Andes to Peru.

## 33. BAR-BELLIED WOODPECKER
*Veniliornis nigriceps* Pl. 21, Map 620
**Identification:** 7.5″ (19cm). Only high el. ♂: crown and nape red, *cheeks dusky bordered above and below by a yellowish white stripe*; remaining upperparts yellowish olive with a few inconspic. red stains on mantle; tail blackish, outer feathers paler and barred buffy yellow; *entire underparts evenly banded greenish white and dark olive.* ♀: crown and nape dusky.

**Similar species:** From Yellow-vented Woodpecker (32) by uniformly barred underparts (not unbarred yellow belly) and larger size.

**Behavior:** Much like others of the genus. Taps on bark and probes moss mainly on branches, from lower levels to canopy. Reg. follows mixed flocks, but also found away from them.

**Status and habitat:** Uncommon in humid and wet forest, forest borders, and stunted woodland up to treeline. Only other woodpeckers reaching treeline are Crimson-mantled and rarely the much larger Powerful Woodpecker.

**Range:** 2800-3600m. Both slopes of C Andes from Caldas and n Tolima (Nevado Santa Isabel) s through Nariño; 1 doubtful rec. at n end E Andes in Norte de Santander (Pamplona). C Colombia s in Andes to n Bolivia.

## 34. CRIMSON-CRESTED WOODPECKER
*Campephilus melanoleucos* Pl. 22, Map 621
**Identification:** 14″ (36cm). Large with blackish bill (or bill dusky whitish—*melanoleucos*). ♂: *entire head bright red* with whitish patch at base

of bill and black and white spot on rear cheek; otherwise black above with white stripe on sides of neck continuing down sides of back and *converging to form a* V; throat black; rest of underparts barred buff and black. ♀: sim., but forehead and front of crest black; white neck stripe continues forward as *very broad stripe under eyes to base of bill.*

**Similar species:** ♀ easily confused with ♀ Lineated Woodpecker (21), but stripes meet on back, and white facial stripe broader. Powerful Woodpecker (37) is more robust with jet black bill and white face stripe bordered by black (not partly by red). Also cf. Red-necked Woodpecker (36); in w Nariño, see very sim. Guayaquil Woodpecker (35).

**Voice:** Two typical calls, both reedy and lisping: a vibrating *chis-sic*; and slightly longer *tttt-he-he-he* (Hilty; J. V. Remsen). Often heard drum usually a loud *double rap* occas. trebled. Lacks flickerlike call of Lineated Woodpecker.

**Behavior:** Pairs or groups of up to 5 climb trunks and large limbs from near ground to subcanopy and chisel bark surfaces, esp. on large dead trees and stubs. Flight is strongly undulating. Sometimes in same tree with Lineated Woodpecker.

**Breeding:** 5 BC birds, Dec–May, W and C Andes (Carriker; Miller 1963); 1 Santa Marta nest, early Feb (Hilty). Nest cavity usually high (Kilham 1972); 2 eggs (ffrench 1973).

**Status and habitat:** Fairly common in humid and wet forest, second growth woodland, and borders; sometimes in isolated trees well away from forest; prob. requires presence of large dead trees.

**Range:** To 3100m (mainly below 2000m). Throughout w of E Andes except sw Cauca and Nariño (*malherbii*); e of Andes from Norte de Santander to Amazonas (*melanoleucos*). W Panama to n Argentina and se Brazil.

**Note:** *Campephilus* is placed by some in the genus *Phloeoceastes*.

### 35. GUAYAQUIL WOODPECKER
*Campephilus guayaquilensis*     Pl. 21, Map 622
**Identification:** 14″ (36cm). Bill dark gray, eyes yellow. *Very* sim. to Crimson-crested Woodpecker, but *upperparts brownish black*, primaries brownish, no white patch at base of bill, upper tail coverts barred buff, underparts buffy brown (not brownish white), and more coarsely barred. ♀: like ♀ Crimson-crested, but *upperparts brownish* and entire crown and crest red (not crown and front of crest black), and rump barred as in ♂. Ranges of the 2 prob. meet but are not known to overlap.

**Similar species:** Cf. Lineated (21) and Crimson-bellied woodpeckers (38).

**Behavior:** Sim. to Crimson-crested Woodpecker, which it replaces in sw Cauca and w Nariño. Drum a loud double tap.

**Breeding:** In nw Peru, nest hole 6m up in live *Erythrina*, 1 egg, 1 nestling, 29 May (Williams 1980); and Oct nest, dead tree in clearing (Goodfellow 1902).

**Status and habitat:** Humid to dry forest, forest edges, tall second growth, and mangroves.

**Range:** To 800m (poss. higher). Sw Cauca (Guapí) and w Nariño. Sw Colombia, w Ecuador (to 1500m), and w Peru.

**Note:** Perhaps a subsp. of *C. melanoleucos.*

### 36. RED-NECKED WOODPECKER
*Campephilus rubricollis*     Pl. 22, Map 623
**Identification:** 14″ (36cm). Large. Bill ivory, eyes yellow. Solid black above (no stripes) with *head, pointed crest, neck, and chest crimson; lower underparts rufous chestnut; wing linings rufous chestnut* (prom. in flight). ♀: sim. but forehead white and broad wedge from bill to below eyes white bordered black.

**Similar species:** From any other large woodpecker in its range by rufous chestnut underparts and under wings; also by uniform back.

**Voice:** Call a high-pitched, vibrating *kueop* or *chisup*, sim. to Crimson-crested Woodpecker. Drum a loud double rap like others of the genus.

**Behavior:** Sim. to Crimson-crested Woodpecker. Usually in pairs from lower story to subcanopy.

**Breeding:** 1 BC bird, Apr, upper Orinoco, Venez. (Friedmann 1948). Oval cavity usually high (Haverschmidt 1968).

**Status and habitat:** Humid forest, lighter second growth woodland, and edges, occas. gallery forest. Fairly numerous in sandy-belt woodlands of ne Guainía, fewer in Amazonia.

**Range:** To 600m. E of Andes from w Meta and e Guainía southward. The Guianas and s Venez. to n Bolivia and Amazonian Brazil.

### 37. POWERFUL WOODPECKER
*Campephilus pollens*     Pl. 22, Map 624
**Identification:** 14.5″ (37cm). *Large and robust.* Bill black, eyes yellowish white. Prom. crimson crest (*or all black—*♀); otherwise upperparts, head, throat, and chest black; *white stripe from base of bill* continues down sides of neck to sides of back *converging to form a white* V; primaries narrowly tipped white; *lower back and rump mainly white*; lower underparts barred black and deep buff. Imm. ♂: rump also white.

**Similar species:** ♀ from any other large woodpecker by black head (no red anywhere in plumage) and white lower back; ♂ from ♀ Lineated (21) by more robust shape, converg-

ing (not parallel) white stripes on upper back, and white lower back. Also see ♀ Crimson-crested Woodpecker (34).
**Voice:** Call, unlike others of the genus, a loud peculiar *udd'daa-da-da*, very reedy and strained; drum a loud double rap.
**Behavior:** A large heavily built woodpecker usually found inside mature montane forest where it climbs large trunks and limbs from the understory to subcanopy. Rather wary.
**Breeding:** ♀ digging cavity, early Aug, PN Cueva de los Guácharos (Hilty); 2 BC birds, June and Aug, W Andes (Carriker).
**Status and habitat:** Local; humid and wet forest and forest borders. Occurs with allied Crimson-crested Woodpecker at PN Cueva de los Guácharos.
**Range:** 900-3600m (mostly 1500-3000m). All 3 Andean ranges (to 900m on Pacific slope). No recs. in Baudó Mts.; 1 ♀ seen in Macarena Mts. 21-22 Jan 1976—T. O. Lemke and P. Gertler. Nw Venez. s in Andes to Peru.

## 38. CRIMSON-BELLIED WOODPECKER
*Campephilus haematogaster*     Pl. 21, Map 625
**Identification:** 13″ (33cm). Bill blackish, eyes reddish brown. ♂: entire crown, large pointed crest, and neck red; sides of head and upper throat black with a *broad yellowish white stripe from top of bill to below and behind eyes* and a narrow stripe above and behind eyes; otherwise black above (no stripes) with *dark crimson lower back and rump*; remiges boldly notched white (or buff—*splendens*) on underside (most obvious in flight); *underparts stained crimson and*

*black* (foreneck all black—*haematogaster*). ♀: sim., but neck black, stripe from bill continues down sides of neck, and underparts more heavily mixed black.
**Similar species:** From Red-necked Woodpecker (36), which it doubtfully overlaps, by crimson rump and underparts; from other large woodpeckers by red on rump and lower underparts and absence of white stripes ("suspenders") on back.
**Voice:** Call reportedly a low rattling; drum a double rap (Wetmore 1968a).
**Behavior:** A striking but rather inconspic. sp., usually seen alone, less often in pairs. Customarily low, often in understory where it climbs larger trunks.
**Breeding:** 1 BC ♀, Dec, n Antioquia; 1 BC ♀, May, s Córdoba (Carriker). Digging hole 12m up in large tree, 9 Mar, Pacific slope in Valle (Brown).
**Status and habitat:** Uncommon in humid and wet forest and forest edges. The least numerous "large" woodpecker in Pacific Colombia.
**Range:** To 1100m on Pacific slope (photo—Hilty). W of W Andes, humid lowlands n of Andes e to mid. Magdalena Val., and s to Remedios, Antioquia (*splendens*); e slope of E Andes in Casanare (Río Negro, about 1500m), and prob. rest of e slope (*haematogaster*). W Panama to w Ecuador; e Ecuador (to 2000m) and e Peru.
**Note:** Some consider the form from Panama to w Ecuador, *C. splendens* (Splendid Woodpecker) a separate sp. from birds e of the Andes.

# WOODCREEPERS: Dendrocolaptidae (28)

Woodcreepers are a rather homogeneous group of scansorial bark-foragers found from northern Mexico to Argentina. Closely related to ovenbirds, especially the Philydorinae ovenbirds, they have sometimes been combined into one family (for a review, see Feduccia 1973). Woodcreepers are remarkably uniform in plumage but diverse in bill shape, with bills ranging from short and wedge-shaped to long and sicklelike. Their stiffened tail with projecting spines aids in support during climbing. Several species, notably in the genera *Dendrocincla*, *Dendrocolaptes*, and *Xiphorhynchus*, also often follow army ants. Songs of the various species are unusual lamenting trills or rattles or wailing cries, often helpful in field identification. Nests, as far as known, are in cavities, the eggs are white, and both sexes (except in *Dendrocincla* and *Sittasomus*) help with all aspects of breeding.

## 1. TYRANNINE WOODCREEPER
*Dendrocincla tyrannina*     Pl. 24, Map 626
**Identification:** 10″ (25cm). Largest uniformly plain brown woodcreeper. Tyrantlike blackish bill. *Almost entirely warm brown*, throat paler and with a few indistinct buff shaft streaks on

throat and chest; wings and tail rufous chestnut.
**Similar species:** Only essentially uniform brown woodcreeper at high el. in the Andes. Ruddy Woodcreeper (4) has contrasting ruddy cap; Plain-brown Woodcreeper (2) has grayish

cheeks; and both are smaller, mainly lowland birds.

**Status and habitat:** Rare and local in humid mt. forest. Despite wide range there are few recent recs.

**Range:** Mostly 1900-3000m; to 1500m on Pacific slope. W slope W Andes at n end (near Frontino) and in Risaralda (nw of Cerro Tatamá); e slope in Cauca (Munchique); C Andes in Antioquia (formerly e of Medellín); both slopes in Quindío and n Tolima and e slope in Nariño (Cerro Pax); e slope E Andes in Norte de Santander (Páramo de Tamá) and Boyacá (se of Laguna de Tota); w slope in Santander (above Bucaramanga) and se Huila (Buenavista). Andes from nw Venez. s to Peru.

## 2. PLAIN-BROWN WOODCREEPER

*Dendrocincla fuliginosa*      Pl. 23, Map 627
**Identification:** 8″ (20cm). *Straight blackish bill.* Mostly plain dull brown, wings and tail more rufous chestnut, *cheeks grayish, and usually with an indistinct dusky malar stripe;* throat light brown. Some also show vague paler eyebrow, and throat may be quite pale.

**Similar species:** White-chinned Woodcreeper (3) has darker, more uniformly brown head and distinct white patch on upper throat (but note that some Plain-brown Woodcreepers show decidedly pale throat). Also cf. Ruddy (4), Tyrannine (1), and Cinnamon-throated woodcreepers (10).

**Voice:** Call a loud sharp *squeeeik* (Brown); also a long bubbly or purring rattle (may rise and fall slightly in pitch and vol.) like others of genus and sometimes given more or less continuously for several min, often when over army ants; song a rapid descending whinny of up to 30 notes.

**Behavior:** Reg. follow army ants where found singly or in argumentative groups of up to 12, normally clinging to vertical trunk of mod. size; also alone or in pairs from lower to mid. story with or away from mixed bird flocks. Hitch up trunks or occas. perch crosswise on branches (Willis 1966c).

**Breeding:** 5 BC birds, Jan–Feb, Chocó, 3 in June, w Guajira (Carriker); 5 BC birds, Apr–May, Vaupés (Olivares 1964b). Tree hole or hollow stump nest 1-10m up, 2 eggs (Willis 1972a).

**Status and habitat:** Fairly common in humid or wet forest and tall second growth woodland.

**Range:** To 1500m (usually below 1200m). Throughout. Not in e Guajira or upper Magdalena Val. and no recent recs. in Cauca Val. Honduras s to w Ecuador, n Argentina, and s Brazil. Trinidad.

## 3. WHITE-CHINNED WOODCREEPER

*Dendrocincla merula*      Pl. 23, Map 628
**Identification:** 7″ (18cm). *Bluish gray eyes;* otherwise much like Plain-brown Woodcreeper. Bill shorter, plumage slightly darker brown, little or no gray on cheeks, dark moustachial streak faint or lacking (sides of head more uniform), and *upper throat sharply white.*

**Similar species:** See under Plain-brown Woodcreeper (2).

**Behavior:** A "professional" ant-follower, obtaining most or all food over ant swarms. Cling low over ants on vertical saplings or trunks, then dart to ground for prey; away from swarms, fly rapidly 1-2m up. In general more timid and faster moving than Plain-brown Woodcreeper and work lower on trunks or on vertical saplings (Oniki and Willis 1972; G. Tudor).

**Breeding:** 2 BC birds, May, Vaupés (Olivares 1964b), 2 BC birds, Mar–Apr, upper Orinoco, Venez. (Friedmann 1948).

**Status and habitat:** Uncommon inside humid *terra firme* forest (incl. sandy-belt forest). First rec. in Colombia at Mitú, 1961 (Olivares 1964b).

**Range:** To 500m. Known from s Meta (Macarena Mts.), Vaupés (Mitú), and sightings at Leticia (Hilty et al.). Prob. throughout from s Meta and Guainía southward (rec. at San Carlos, Venez., opp. Guainía, and at Limoncocha, Ecuador). The Guianas and s Venez. to nw Bolivia and Amazonian Brazil.

## 4. RUDDY WOODCREEPER

*Dendrocincla homochroa*      Pl. 23, Map 629
**Identification:** 8″ (20cm). Bill straight, light to dark brown. *Uniform dark rufescent brown, brightest on crown,* and paler, more tawny on throat.

**Similar species:** Only essentially uniform *dark rufous* woodcreeper. Plain-brown Woodcreeper (2) is dull brown with rufous mainly on wings and tail; also gray cheeks and dark malar stripe. Look for the brighter rufous crown and overall warmer brown tone. Also cf. Tyrannine Woodcreeper (1) of highlands.

**Voice:** A short churring or rattling *chu-chu-chuchuchuchu-chut* much like others of the genus (J. Wall recording).

**Behavior:** Rather quiet and retiring and easily overlooked. Reg. follows army ants; usually 1, occas. 2-3, cling low on trunks near swarms. Infrequently seen wandering low in forest away from army ants (Wetmore 1972).

**Breeding:** 2 BC ♀♀, Apr, and laying ♀, May, w Guajira (Carriker). 2 cavity nests in Belize, below 2m up; 3 eggs (Russell 1964).

**Status and habitat:** Few Colombian recs., all from humid forest in hill country and foothills. Usually not in lowland forest.

**Range:** To 800m. Known from extreme n Chocó on Panama border (Unguía), e foothills of Santa Marta Mts. in Guajira (La Cueva; Los Gorros), w slope of Perijá Mts. above Fonseca, and e of Andes on upper Río Arauca. S Mexico to w Venez.

## 5. LONG-TAILED WOODCREEPER
*Deconychura longicauda*          Pl. 23, Map 630
**Identification:** 7.7-8.5″ (19.5-22cm). *Slim appearance* accentuated by slightly longer tail than allies. *Rather short* (1″, or 25mm) *straight bill.* Mostly dull brown with indistinct buff eyestripe and faint short buff streaks on crown; upper throat mostly pale buff; lower throat and *chest with spotlike* buff streaks, with a few narrow buff streaks spreading onto upper breast; wings and tail chestnut. Or sim. but tail slightly shorter and spotlike streaks more obscure and confined to lower throat and chest (*connectens*).
**Similar species:** Easily confused. At a distance shows very little streaking below (esp. e of Andes), then looking like a slender Plain-brown Woodcreeper (2) with a long tail and very short bill; at close range note streaking on crown and chest. Spot-throated Woodcreeper (6) of se Colombia is barely separable in the field but has a chestnut-rufous (not brown) rump contrasting with olive brown back. Straight-billed Woodcreeper (14; Amazonian form) has definite eyebrow and more conspic. streaking. Also cf. other *Xiphorhynchus*, (esp. 16, 17, 18).
**Voice:** In Costa Rica a continuous weak rattle *chih-chih chip-chip-chip-chih-chih* (Slud 1964) much like that of allied *Dendrocincla.*
**Behavior:** One or 2 usually follow mixed flocks. Climb trunks and limbs in lower or mid. levels, occas. higher. Most often seen about eye level.
**Breeding:** 2 BC birds, Jan and Apr, Antioquia (Carriker); 1 cavity nest 9m up in trunk; 3 eggs (Cherrie *in* Wetmore 1972).
**Status and habitat:** Humid *terra firme* and *várzea* forests. Known from only a small no. of localities; apparently uncommon.
**Range:** To 1300m. Nw Colombia from nw Antioquia (Mutatá and e side of Gulf of Urabá) e in humid lowlands to mid. Magdalena Val. s to Lebrija Val. (*longicauda*); e of Andes from extreme se Guainía (San Felipe) and Vaupés (Mitú) southward (*connectens*); poss. also w to base of Andes. Nicaragua to e Peru, ne Bolivia, Amazonian Brazil, and the Guianas.

## 6. SPOT-THROATED WOODCREEPER
*Deconychura stictolaema*          Map 631
**Identification:** 7.5″ (19cm). Very sim. to Long-tailed Woodcreeper (5) but slightly smaller, bill even shorter (0.8″ vs 1″ [20mm vs 25mm]), *rump chestnut rufous* (instead of brown), upper

wing coverts olive brown like the back (instead of tinged rufous), upper throat with small dark spots (instead of uniform buff).
**Status and habitat:** Known in Colombia from 3 specimens (FMNH) collected by Von Sneidern in 1969 at San Antonio, Putumayo (Fitzpatrick and Willard 1982). Undoubtedly more widespread in lowland forests of se Colombia than the recs. indicate.
**Range:** To 400m. W Putumayo (San Antonio, near Pto. Asís) prob. s to Amazonas and e to Guainía. Fr. Guiana, s Venez. (incl. Yavita-Pimichín trail opp. Guainía), ne Peru (incl. mouth of Río Napo), Amazonian Brazil (incl. mouth of Río Putumayo).

## 7. OLIVACEOUS WOODCREEPER
*Sittasomus griseicapillus*          Pl. 23, Map 632
**Identification:** 6.5″ (16.5cm). *Rather short, straight, thin bill. Head, neck, and underparts grayish olive contrasting with rufous lower back, wings, and tail*; mantle olive brown. In flight shows prom. buff wing stripe.
**Similar species:** Only small woodcreeper with a uniform grayish olive head and underparts. Even smaller Wedge-billed Woodcreeper (8) has an eyebrow, chest spotting, and conical bill.
**Voice:** Rather quiet. Song a short (3 sec), fast trill that accelerates and rises, then slows and falls at end; also a long rattling chatter (P. Schwartz recording), and a rising, slightly accelerating *jowe, jowe, jowee jowee, joweet jowee* in Amazonas (Hilty; J. V. Remsen).
**Behavior:** Usually solitary, occas. 1-2 follow mixed flocks. Climb up main trunks or large branches, mostly in more open mid. story and sometimes dart out short distances to air to capture escaping prey.
**Breeding:** 6 BC birds, Mar–June, n Colombia (Carriker); 1 Costa Rica nest in crevice 13m up in palm stub (Skutch 1967).
**Status and habitat:** Uncommon to fairly common in open moist to humid forest, forest edge, *várzea* and second growth woodland. Seems most numerous in Amazonia.
**Range:** To 1000m. Mid. and upper Sinú Val. e to Guajira, w base of Perijá Mts. (e of Valledupar) and s to mid. Magdalena Val. (n boundary of Caldas); e of Andes from s Meta (Macarena Mts.) and Orinoco region southward. Mexico to n Argentina and se Brazil. Trinidad.

## 8. WEDGE-BILLED WOODCREEPER
*Glyphorynchus spirurus*          Pl. 23, Map 633
**Identification:** 5.5″ (14cm). *The smallest woodcreeper. Short, wedge-shaped bill.* Mainly dull brown becoming bright chestnut on rump and tail; *eyebrow* and throat buffy white (or throat

cinnamon—*rufigularis; castelnaudii*); *upper breast with small wedge-shaped buff spots*; lower breast with a few buff shaft streaks. In flight shows prom. buff wing band.

**Similar species:** From all other woodcreepers by small size and stubby bill (cf. Olivaceous Woodcreeper, 7). In highlands easily confused with Fulvous-dotted Treerunner (p 367), which is more uniform rufous above and shows less spotting below. Also see Spotted Barbtail (p 367). Superficially resembles several Xenops (pp 375-376), none of which climb like creepers.

**Voice:** Call a weak sneezing *chief!* or *chief beef!*; song a rapid ser. of chaffy *tiff* notes, usually followed by up to 4 louder sneezing *chief*s.

**Behavior:** Usually alone or in pairs and reg. follows mixed flocks. Taps on bark as it climbs mostly larger trunks in lower or mid. strata. Often flicks wings when agitated.

**Breeding:** 7 BC birds, Jan–Apr, n Colombia (Carriker); 8 more, Feb–Mar, Amazonas (Romero 1978) 16 Panama nests, May–Oct (Willis and Eisenmann 1979). Cavity low in tree or in stump; 2 eggs (Skutch 1969a).

**Status and habitat:** Fairly common to common in humid and wet forest and second growth woodland, occas. trees in clearings.

**Range:** To 2100m (most numerous below about 1200m). E slope Mt. Tacarcuna, Panama border (*pallidulus*); Pacific coast and lower Atrato Val. e to upper Río Sinú (*subrufescens*); mid. Río Sinú e to mid. Magdalena Val. s to w Boyacá and e of Andes from Norte de Santander to nw Arauca (*integratus*); Meta and Vichada s to Putumayo and Vaupés (*rufigularis*); Amazonas (*castelnaudii*). S Mexico to w Ecuador, n Bolivia, and Amazonian and e Brazil.

## 9. LONG-BILLED WOODCREEPER
*Nasica longirostris*          Ill. 76, Map 634
**Identification:** 14″ (36cm). *Small-headed with very long (2.8″, or 71mm), pale, almost straight bill.* Crown and nape blackish streaked white; long eyestripe white; *otherwise bright rufous chestnut above; throat white,* rest of underparts buffy brown with *broad blackish-edged white stripes on breast.*

**Similar species:** Unmistakable. Small head, thin neck and very long, cream-colored bill with slight droop impart an oddly sandpiperlike appearance.

**Voice:** Song a ser. of very loud, eerie, raptorlike whistles, *whoooOOOooo, whoooOOOooo, whoooOOOooo, whoooOOOooo,* each note about 1 sec (sometimes speeded up), and rising and falling in pitch (J. V. Remsen). Unmistakable once learned.

**Behavior:** Usually singly or in pairs and fairly

conspic. on main trunks and large limbs in all strata. Probes *mainly* bromeliad clusters, also cracks and crevices in bark. Reg. follows mixed spp. flocks.

**Breeding:** In e Ecuador, hole 4m up in low tree in small clearing held nestlings, Feb 1980, fed by both parents (R. Ridgely). Imms. Jan and May, Pto. Ayacucho on Orinoco opp. Vichada (Friedmann 1948).

**Status and habitat:** Fairly common in *várzea* forest and swamps or flooded river isls.; much less numerous in *terra firme* forest or forest borders. Generally the *várzea* counterpart of *Campylorhamphus* (J. V. Remsen).

**Range:** To 500m. E of Andes from w Caquetá (Tres Esquinas) and e Vichada (along the Orinoco) southward. Fr. Guiana and s Venez. (s of Orinoco) to Bolivia and Amazonian Brazil.

## 10. CINNAMON-THROATED WOODCREEPER
*Dendrexetastes rufigula*      Pl. 24, Map 635
**Identification:** 10″ (25cm). *Very heavy, straight, pale bill* (looks dull greenish yellow). *Mostly brown above and uniform cinnamon buff below,* brightest on throat; *chest with a few inconspic. narrow and black-edged white streaks* (no barring on underparts); *rump, wings, and tail chestnut.* In this genus the bill is thick and barbetlike.

**Similar species:** Easily confused with Barred Woodcreeper (12), which often looks uniform at a distance in poor light but has black or dark red (not pale) bill and usually different behavior. Plain-brown and White-chinned woodcreepers (2, 3) are smaller and have *thinner* and dark bills; both lack the necklace of streaking on chest.

**Voice:** In Amazonas, a descending trill.

**Behavior:** One or 2 reg. follow mixed spp. flocks in forest, where they climb large trunks at midlevels, hitch along outer canopy limbs, or more often actively hop and clamber about in terminal foliage like a foliage-gleaner (*Philydor*), peering into leaf clusters, hanging upside down, even probing and pecking at fruit.

**Status and habitat:** Uncommon to fairly common in *terra firme* or *várzea* forests, or along forest borders; also taller second growth.

**Range:** To 500m. E of Andes from w Caquetá s to Amazonas (Leticia). Se Colombia to n Bolivia, Amazonian Brazil, and the Guianas (no Venez. recs.).

**Note:** Bar-bellied Woodcreeper (*Hylexetastes stresemanni*) of w Amazonian Brazil and e Peru is known from Río Vaupés at Tahuapunto, Brazil (on Vaupés boundary) and almost certainly occurs in e Vaupés; several sight recs., Feb 1978, Mitú, presumed this sp.—Hilty.

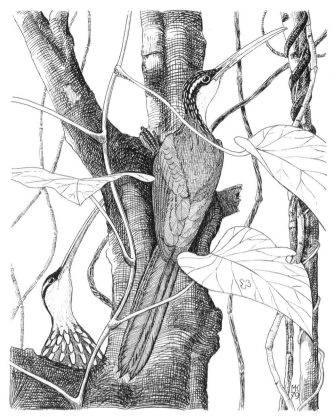

76. LONG-BILLED WOODCREEPER

Large (11″), with *heavy, barbetlike, dark red bill*; mostly plain brown above and below; wings and tail rufous chestnut; throat and breast with a few narrow whitish streaks; lower underparts brownish white *narrowly banded dusky.* Latter perhaps conspecific with *H. perrotii* (Red-billed Woodcreeper) of the Guianas, e Venez., and e Amazonian Brazil e of Ríos Negro and Purús (Zimmer 1934).

## 11. STRONG-BILLED WOODCREEPER
*Xiphocolaptes promeropirhynchus*     Pl. 23,
Map 636

**Identification:** 12″ (30cm). *Very large with long* (1.7-2.1″, or 43-53mm), *heavy, slightly decurved blackish bill* (pale bill—e of Andes). Crown dusky with narrow whitish shaft streaks extending onto upper mantle (or only to nape—*sanctae-martae* and *macarenae*); back brown, lower back, wings, and tail rufous chestnut; sides of head streaked buff and brown with an *indistinct dusky moustachial streak*; throat unstreaked buffy

white; rest of underparts brown, rather narrowly streaked buff, and usually with some fine dusky barring on belly. Or throat slightly streaked brown, breast with *much finer,* less extensive *pale streaks,* belly unbarred (*sanctae-martae*).

**Similar species:** Easily confused with Black-banded Woodcreeper (13), which is slightly smaller, has shorter, straighter, less massive bill, barred lower underparts (bars inconspic. at a distance), and *no dusky malar.* W of the Andes from Buff-throated Woodcreeper (19) by decidedly larger size, and stouter, longer, all blackish (not black above, pale below) bill; e of Andes from very sim. *guttatoides* subsp. of Buff-throated by *slightly* larger size, slightly longer bill, *dusky malar,* and *finer pale streaking* on crown and underparts. Greater Scythebill (25) has longer bill and conspic. white facial streaks.

**Voice:** At dawn or dusk the unmistakable call is a whistled ser. of paired, descending notes, often beginning with a single higher note (Ridgely and Gaulin 1980); a soft catlike *meow*, and var. unmusical lisping notes.

**Behavior:** Singly or more frequently pairs, and sometimes with mixed flocks. Foraging behavior notably versatile; climb trunks and large limbs, rummage among bromeliads and accumulated litter in trees, or in leaf litter on ground (rarely), or follow army ants. In Santa Marta highlands predom. a bromeliad specialist (T. B. Johnson).

**Breeding:** 5 BC birds, Feb–Mar, Córdoba and Huila (Carriker); 1 in May, upper Orinoco, Venez. (Friedmann 1948).

**Status and habitat:** Rare to locally common. Humid and wet forest in lowlands and mts. (incl. "cloud forest"). Much more numerous in Santa Marta highlands (mostly above 2200m) than elsewhere, perhaps due to absence of other large bromeliad and bark foragers.

**Range:** 100-3000m (mostly above 1500m in mts.). Santa Marta Mts. (*sanctaemartae*); Sinú Val. e to Snía. San Lucas in Magdalena Val. (*rostratus*); C Andes s to w slope in Cauca (*virgatus*) base of Perijá Mts. and E Andes from Norte de Santander s to head of Magdalena Val. in s Huila (*promeropirhynchus*); Macarena Mts. s to base of Andes in Caquetá (*macarenae*); e Vichada and e slope Andes, se Nariño (*orenocensis*), Amazonian region(?). S Mexico to w Panama; Colombia, Venez., and the Guianas to n Bolivia and Amazonian Brazil.

## 12. BARRED WOODCREEPER

*Dendrocolaptes certhia*     Pl. 23, Map 637
**Identification:** 10.5″ (27cm). Bill heavy, straight (1.5″, or 38mm), brownish black. *Head, back, and underparts brown, evenly barred dusky*, barring faintest on back; lower back, wings, and tail uniform rufous chestnut. Or as above but *bill dark red*, grayish tinge on throat, and much stronger barring on mantle and shoulders (*radiolatus*).

**Similar species:** Only Colombian Woodcreeper barred above and below (but barring inconspic. except at close range). Strong-billed Woodcreeper (11) has a dusky malar. See Plain-brown (2), White-chinned (3), and Cinnamon-throated woodcreepers (10), all of which also look quite uniform at a distance. Bar-bellied Woodcreeper (note under 10) has even heavier reddish bill and barring only on lower underparts. Black-banded Woodcreeper (13) is streaked on head and mantle.

**Voice:** Song w of Andes a loud ser. of 4-6 lamenting *úreet* notes falling in pitch.

**Behavior:** Frequently follow army ants, keeping mostly 2-10m up over swarms where they cling to or hitch up med.-sized trunks or sally

to air to capture fleeing prey. Away from ants found alone or with forest bird flocks. Often cling motionless to trunks in low or mid. story where inconspic. but may sally rapidly to nearby foliage or trunks for prey; also climb large limbs into canopy (Oniki and Willis 1972; Hilty).

**Breeding:** 2 BC birds, Mar, nw Colombia (Carriker; Haffer 1975); 9 in Apr, upper Orinoco, Venez. (Friedmann 1948). 1 carrying dead leaf, presum. to nest, 20 Feb, Mitú (Hilty).

**Status and habitat:** Uncommon to locally fairly common in humid forest and second growth woodland, less often forest edge and *várzea*.

**Range:** To 900m (once to 1200m). Pacific coast and from Gulf of Urabá e to Snía. San Lucas in mid. Magdalena Val. (*colombianus*); Santa Marta Mts. s to e side of Magdalena Val. in nw Santander (*hyleorus*); e of Andes in Norte de Santander (*punctipectus*); sw Meta and Vaupés to Amazonas (*radiolatus*); e Vichada (*certhia*). S Mexico to nw Ecuador, n Bolivia, Amazonian and e Brazil.

## 13. BLACK-BANDED WOODCREEPER

*Dendrocolaptes picumnus*     Pl. 23, Map 638
**Identification:** 11″ (28cm). Bill heavy, almost straight (1.4″, or 36mm), dusky. Head, upper mantle, and breast brown streaked pale buff; throat buffy white streaked brown; *lower breast to crissum buffy brown evenly barred black*; lower back, wings, and tail rufous chestnut (w of Andes). Or like above but streaking on underpart broader and only on throat and chest (not to lower breast or upper belly); rest of underparts barred more extensively with darker, coarser, and bolder bars, a few birds even with faint barring on back (*validus*).

**Similar species:** A smaller edition of Strong-billed Woodcreeper (11) and not always easily separated in the field. In general less robust, bill shorter, no dark malar, and barring finer and more extensive on lower underparts; in the hand note streaks of both chest and breast are narrower and black-edged (crisper and with more definition); also, all Colombian subspp. have streaked throats (Andean subspp. of Strong-billed have unstreaked throats). Birds from e slope of Andes (*validus*) are much more extensively barred and might be confused with Barred Woodcreeper (12), but head and mantle streaked (not barred).

**Voice:** Song in Venez. a fast, whinnying ser. of about 20 *whin* notes in 4-5 sec, and slowing slightly at end; also a shorter 8- to 10-note whinny in about 2 sec, *chu-we-we-we-we-we-we-we* (P. Schwartz recording).

**Behavior:** Single birds or well-separated pairs climb up trunks and limbs at all hts., but stay in low to mid. strata over army ants where

they drop clumsily to logs or ground for wide size range of prey (Oniki and Willis 1972).
**Breeding:** Tree cavity; 2 eggs, Antioquia (Sclater and Salvin 1879).
**Status and habitat:** Apparently rare; humid forest or forest edge, rarely trees in clearings.
**Range:** 1300-2800m w of Andes; to lowlands e of Andes. Santa Marta Mts. (*seilerni*); Perijá Mts. and all 3 Andean ranges but no Nariño recs. (*multistrigatus*); e base of E Andes from w Meta and w Caquetá to Amazonas (*validus*). Prob. throughout in forested regions e of Andes. S Mexico to w Panama. The Guianas, Venez., Colombia, and e Ecuador to e Bolivia, Amazonian Brazil, Paraguay, and nw Argentina.

## 14. STRAIGHT-BILLED WOODCREEPER
*Xiphorhynchus picus*          Pl. 23, Map 639
**Identification:** 8″ (20cm). *Bill very straight* (1-1.2″, or 25-30mm) and *whitish to pinkish white.* Rufous chestnut above; crown dusky with buffy white streaklike spots extending as buffy streaks onto upper mantle; long whitish eyestripe; *most of sides of head, foreneck, and throat whitish*; large whitish lanceolate spots on chest become narrower streaks on breast (n Colombia). Or as above but darker brown with only a suggestion of whitish postocular streak, throat pale buff, sides of head, foreneck, and chest heavily streaked buffy white, breast lightly streaked buffy white, and lower underparts dull brown (*kienerii?*—Amazonas). Birds from Norte de Santander to Caquetá are intermed. between above forms.
**Similar species:** In n and e Colombia s to Caquetá told by very straight, *pale* bill and broad chalky to creamy white throat and foreneck. From Caquetá to Amazonas easily confused with several allies (see table, p 350), but usually separable by whiter, straighter, more pointed bill, stronger eyestripe, streaks extending onto mantle but not entire back (but cf. Ocellated, 16, which has narrow buff shaft streaks on back that are essentially invisible at a distance), and buffier throat and foreneck. Habitat (not inside forest) is helpful.
**Voice:** Song in Amazonas a ser. of descending whistles, var. in duration, tempo, and intensity (J. V. Remsen), resembling that of Buff-throated (R. Ridgely); also a scolding *deet, deet, deet* (Brown).
**Behavior:** Alone or in pairs and sometimes with mixed flocks. Climb smaller trunks and limbs at low to mid. hts., often at about eye level, and usually rather conspic.
**Breeding:** 4 BC birds, Jan–Oct, w of E Andes (Carriker; Miller 1947); 1 with brood patch, Nov, Santa Marta (S. M. Russell); ♂ with brood

patch, Feb, fledglings, Apr–May, and Aug breeding, Venez. (Friedmann and Smith 1950; Thomas 1979b); 2 nests in May, upper Orinoco, Venez. (Cherrie 1916); 2-3 eggs, in tree cavity or arboreal termitary.
**Status and habitat:** Common and the *only* woodcreeper likely in arid scrub and mangroves in Carib. region. Dry or moist forest and e of Andes in gallery woodland, edges of *terra firme* and *várzea* forests, and young second growth (esp. overgrown pastures, river banks, etc.). In Amazonia usually the only woodcreeper common in young second growth.
**Range:** To 600m. Lower Atrato to upper Sinú vals. (*extimus*); Carib. lowlands n to Cartagena and w base of Perijá Mts., and s to n Huila in upper Magdalena Val. (*dugandi*); Atlántico to Guajira (*picirostris*); Norte de Santander to Meta (*saturatior*); Caquetá region (*borreroi*); Orinoco region (*picus*); rest of se Colombia (*kienerii?*). C Panama, n Colombia and generally e of Andes s to n Bolivia and Amazonian Brazil. Trinidad.
**Note:** The form inhabiting the dry and arid Carib. coast, *X. picirostris*, has been considered a separate sp. (Plain-throated Woodcreeper) by some.

## 15. STRIPED WOODCREEPER
*Xiphorhynchus obsoletus*          Pl. 23, Map 640
**Identification:** 7.8″ (19.8 cm). Bill 0.8″ (20mm) and light brown, lower mandible paler, *but not as pale or as straight as previous sp.* Mostly dull brown, crown darker spotted buff; *mantle, back, and entire underparts to upper belly has conspic. linear buffy white streaks with narrow black margins* (esp. prom. from below); throat pale yellowish buff; rump, wings, and tail chestnut.
**Similar species:** The palest and most heavily streaked of the genus in its range; the streaks (more like stripes) are fairly broad and *decidedly linear* in form, and extend to lower back and upper belly. See esp. buff-throated form of Straight-billed Woodcreeper (14) in Amazonas, which has a weak eyestripe, straighter, paler bill, more rufescent upperparts, and more irreg. streaking (not linear). In the Orinoco region, see Chestnut-rumped Woodcreeper (note under 18). Lineated Woodcreeper (see note under 24) has conspic. linear streaks below but uniform back.
**Behavior:** One or 2 often accompany mixed bird flocks in mid. story of *várzea* forest.
**Breeding:** BC ♂, 27 Apr, Vaupés (Olivares 1964b); ♀ ready to lay, 29 Apr, ne Meta (S. Furniss); several BC birds, Feb–May and Nov, Amazonas, Venez. (Friedmann 1948).
**Status and habitat:** Mainly *várzea* forest and swamps or near water in gallery forest.

IDENTIFICATION TABLE FOR *Xiphlorhynchus* WOODCREEPERS.

| Species No. | English name | Total length (inches) | Bill color | Bill shape | Bill length (inches) | Eye-stripe | Mantle and back | Rump | Throat | Underparts |
|---|---|---|---|---|---|---|---|---|---|---|
| 14 | Straight-billed *a) n Colombia | 8.5 | whitish | straight pointed | 1-1.2 | prom. | a few streaks to upper mantle | — | whitish | more or less streaked to breast |
|  | *b) Amazonas | 8.5 | " | " | " | weak |  | — | pale buff |  |
| 15 | *Striped | 7.8 | Light brown pale below | not as straight as above | 0.8 | none | entire mantle and back striped | chestnut | light yellowish buff | linear streaks |
| 16 | **Ocellated | 8 | dusky | " | 1.1 | " | essentially uniform (faint shaft streaks on mantle) | — | deep buff | vaguely spotted |
| 17 | ***Spix's | 8 | Intermediate; lighter than 16 and 18a darker than 14 and 15 | " | 1 | " | large guttate streaks to mid-back | rump chestnut | upper throat buffy | " |
| 18 | ***Elegant | 8 | dusky | " | 1 | " | larger guttate streaks than 17 (extend to lower back) | rump rufous chestnut | buff | " |
| 18a (note 2) | **Chestnut-rumped | 8.5 | dusky | " | 1 | " | large guttate streaks to lower back | " | rusty buff, darkest of group, vaguely streaked | more streaked than spotted |
| 19 | Buff-throated *a) w of Andes | 9 | dusky above pale below | slightly decurved | 1.2 | " | shaft streaks on mantle | " | unstreaked buff | streaks to breast |
|  | *b) e of Andes (*polystictus*) | 10.5 | dusky above pale below | " | 1.4 | " | " | " | " | " |
|  | (*guttatoides*) | 11 | all pale | " | 1.4 | " | " | " | " | " |

FIELD IDENTIFICATION:   *not too difficult   **very difficult (comparative experience helpful)   ***probably not separable in field from other***

**Range:** To 400m. E of Andes from Arauca and Vichada (Pto. Carreño) southward. The Guianas and c and s Venez. s to ne Bolivia and Amazonian Brazil.

## 16. OCELLATED WOODCREEPER
*Xiphorhynchus ocellatus*   Pl. 23, Map 641
**Identification:** 8″ (20cm). Bill 1.1″ (28mm), *dusky*, and almost straight. Mainly brown, crown and nape dark brown finely dotted buff; mantle with obscure pale buff shaft streaks (*looks virtually uniform* at a distance); upper throat buff; lower throat and upper breast with many small round or drop-shaped buff spots edged dusky (looks somewhat scaled); lower breast with a few obscure pale streaks. Or mantle and belly with narrow but more definite streaks (*napensis*).
**Similar species:** In Amazonas more uniform above than allies (see table, p 350), but easily confused anywhere in range. Upperparts most like Straight-billed (14), but no suggestion of eyebrow, and spots on underparts buff (not whitish) and not as bold. From Spix's (17) and Elegant (18) by much narrower streaks (mere shaft streaks) only on mantle (not broad black-edged droplike streaks extending *at least* to midback); also from Elegant (and to lesser extent Spix's) by decidedly longer bill. Striped Woodcreeper (15) has bold streaks on back and lines of streaks on underparts.
**Voice:** In Amazonas a rapid trill that descends slightly, then ascends for most of duration and accelerates near end (J. V. Remsen); also a whinnying trill, *t'r'r'r'r'a'a'a'eik*, with emphatic squeak at end.
**Behavior:** Solitary or in pairs, climbing trunks from near ground to mid. hts. Like others of the genus, often with bird flocks. May follow army ants.
**Breeding:** BC ♂, 13 May, Vaupés (Olivares 1964b).
**Status and habitat:** Tall second growth and *terra firme* and *várzea* forest, esp. along rivers.
**Range:** To 500m (prob. higher). E of Andes in Vaupés (Mitú) and e Guainía (San Felipe) s to Leticia on Amazon (*ocellatus*); base of Andes in w Caquetá and se Nariño, e prob. to w Amazonas (*napensis*). S Venez. (sw Amazonas) to n Bolivia and w and c Amazonian Brazil.

## 17. SPIX'S WOODCREEPER
*Xiphorhynchus spixii*   Pl. 23, Map 642
**Identification:** 8″ (20cm). Bill (1″, or 25mm), almost straight, rather pale with dusky culmen. Mainly rufescent brown above, crown darker and spotted buff; *mantle to midback with large, drop-shaped, deep buff spots edged with black*, forming spotlike streaks; lower back uniform; upper throat buffy white; lower throat buff;

rest of underparts brown with *large round buff spots* (form vague streaks) *edged with black on foreneck, chest, and breast* and becoming obsolete on belly; rump, wings, and tail chestnut. Or sim. but upper mantle with narrow buff streaks edged dark brown, and spotting on breast less conspic. (*buenaevistae*).
**Similar species:** Very difficult (see table, p 350). Bill intermed. in color betw. several allies (paler than 16, darker than 14, 15) and mantle with broader, buffier, and more spotlike streaking than others of genus (but cf. 18). In Amazonas, Straight-billed Woodcreeper (14) has whiter, more pointed bill, more prom. streaked (not spotted) head, and almost no streaking on mantle. Ocellated (16) has essentially uniform back. Elegant (see 18) doubtfully separable in field. Chestnut-rumped (see note under 18) perhaps by darker more ochre buff throat, chest mainly with lineated streaks (not spotlike streaks), and by rufous rump if visible (overlap in range doubtful). Striped Woodcreeper (15) sim. above (streaks more in spotted lines) but is overall much paler, and underparts have long linear *stripes* (not spotlike streaks).
**Behavior:** Much like Ocellated Woodcreeper. In se Peru climbs trunks, occas. lianas, from near ground to 13m up; usually with forest flocks (S. Parker).
**Status and habitat:** Humid *terra firme* forest.
**Range:** Mainly below 1400m. Head of Magdalena Val. at Moscopán (2400m) and e of Andes in w Meta from Villavicencio to Macarena Mts. (*buenaevistae*); w Caquetá and Vaupés (Mitú) southward (*ornatus*); no Amazonas recs. but known from n Amazon bank in ne Peru and Río Putumayo in nw Brazil. E Colombia to n Bolivia and Amazonian Brazil (s of Amazon except in the nw).

## 18. ELEGANT WOODCREEPER
*Xiphorhynchus elegans*   Map 643
**Identification:** 8″ (20cm). Bill 1″ (25mm), *dusky*, almost straight. Very sim. to Spix's Woodcreeper. Rufescent brown above; crown darker and with buff spots becoming *broad drop-shaped streaks* of buff rimmed black *from mantle to lowermost back*; throat buff; breast with deep buff spots very broadly edged black (form vague streaks); rump, wings, and tail rufous chestnut.
**Similar species:** Doubtfully separable in field from Spix's Woodcreeper (17) but bill darker and streaks on upperparts broader and rounder (more like spots) and extending almost to rump (not just mantle). In the hand, streaks on breast with wider black margins. Also see table (p 350).
**Status and habitat:** Known only from 3 speci-

mens in Colombia, as follows: 2 on 4 and 5 Mar 1975, Río Calderón, Amazonas, about 35km n of Leticia; and 1 subad. ♂, 4 Dec 1976, 1 km nw Duda Cabaña, Macarena Mts., s Meta (Lemke and Gertler 1978). Humid *terra firme* forest.

**Range:** To 500m. S Meta and s Amazonas. E Peru, n Bolivia, and w Amazonian Brazil s of Amazon.

**Note 1:** Poss. a subsp. of *X. spixii* (Spix's Woodcreeper). The identity of all 3 Colombian specimens needs confirmation. **Note 2:** Chestnut-rumped Woodcreeper (*X. pardalotus*) of e Amazonian Brazil, the Guianas, and s Venez. undoubtedly occurs in e Colombia (known from Venez. side of Orinoco at Pto. Ayacucho opp. Vichada and at Cucuhy opp. se Guainía). Very sim. to Spix's Woodcreeper (17) but darker, *throat more rufescent buff and vaguely streaked*, breast more streaked (not droplike spots), and rump rufous chestnut. From Buff-throated Woodcreeper by same; also by smaller size, darker bill, and black-edged streaks on back. Song in Venez. *zut, zut, zut-zut-zut-t't't't,e'e e,* fading at end (P. Schwartz recording).

### 19. BUFF-THROATED WOODCREEPER
*Xiphorhynchus guttatus*    Pl. 23, Map 644
**Identification:** Two types. W of Andes: 9″ (23cm). *Bill rather long, 1.2″* (30mm), heavy, slightly decurved, *blackish above, pale yellowish below*. Mainly brown, crown dusky with drop-shaped buff spots; hindneck, sometimes upper mantle, narrowly streaked buff; *throat buff*; broad black-edged buffy white streaks on upper breast and sides; *lower breast and belly nearly uniform*; rump, wings, and tail rufous chestnut. E of Andes: as above but *much larger*, 10.5-11″ (27-28cm), bill longer 1.4″ (36mm) and dark above, pale below (*polystictus*), or bill *pale above and below* (*guttatoides*).
**Similar species:** From the smaller *Xiphorhynchus* woodcreepers (13-17) by decidedly larger size, longer, heavier bill (most obvious in *guttatoides* subsp. and for comparison, see table, p 350), and broader more flammulated streaks below. Strong-billed Woodcreeper (11) is even larger than *guttatoides* subsp. and more robust with massive bill, finer streaking below, and *dusky malar*. Black-banded Woodcreeper (13) has less streaking on mantle and fine barring on lower underparts (diagnostic if seen). Also cf. Olive-backed Woodcreeper (22).
**Voice:** Alarm a loud slurred *pyewl*, and a repeated loud, slow, *peer peer peer peert* (Willis and Eisenmann 1979); melancholy whistled song starts fast, then descends and slows, *ki, ki, kuee, kuee, whe, whew, whew, whew, whew* (about 3 sec).
**Behavior:** One or 2 follow forest flocks or wander alone from lower story to subcanopy. Climb trunks and limbs, probe bark or epiphytes, and often attend army ants, where 1 to several aggressive individuals may gather and sally to air or nearby foliage for prey. Often noisy mornings and evenings.
**Breeding:** 8 BC birds, Jan–May, n Colombia (Carriker). Mar–May tree-hole nests in Panama; 2 white eggs (Wetmore 1972).
**Status and habitat:** Humid forest, forest borders, tall second growth, and clearings with trees. Widespread and one of the most common woodcreepers in most humid forest zones.
**Range:** To 1100m. Gulf of Urabá region and lower Atrato Val. e to w Guajira, s to lower Cauca Val. and upper Magdalena Val. in s Tolima (*nanus*); Cauca Val. (at least formerly) in Valle (*rosenbergi*); e of Andes in Catatumbo lowlands and nw Arauca (*demonstratus*); Meta and Guainía southward (*guttatoides*); e Vichada (Maipures) on Río Orinoco (*polystictus*). Guatemala to n Bolivia and Amazonian and se Brazil. Trinidad.

### 20. BLACK-STRIPED WOODCREEPER
*Xiphorhynchus lachrymosus*    Pl. 23, Map 645
**Identification:** 9″ (23cm). Bill long, 1.1-1.3″ (28-33mm) (or 1.3-1.5″ [33-38mm]—Pacific coast), slightly decurved, dusky. *Crown and upperparts black broadly streaked buff*; throat buff; *remaining underparts buffy white, the feathers broadly edged black giving a streaked appearance*; lesser wing coverts edged black; rump, wings, and tail rufous chestnut.
**Similar species:** Boldly striped black and buff; upper and underparts are unmistakable. No other woodcreeper resembles it.
**Voice:** Usual call a distinctive ser. of 3-4 very loud descending whistles, *whee, hew, hew*, rather like call of Cinnamon Woodpecker but faster (Ridgely 1976); also a loud *choo-reep*. Song a soft descending trill or whinny of 10-30 *we* notes at about 4 per sec (Willis and Eisenmann 1979).
**Behavior:** Singly or in pairs and more often alone than with mixed flocks. Hitch up trunks and limbs from mid. strata to high canopy, often above other woodcreepers. Frequently check undersides of limbs.
**Breeding:** 7 BC birds, Feb–May, nw Colombia (Carriker); a narrow slit 1.5m up Apr–Jan, Barro Colorado Isl. Panama (Willis and Eisenmann 1979).
**Status and habitat:** Humid and wet forest, forest edge, tall second growth, and mangroves. Uncommon and local on Pacific coast.
**Range:** To 1500m. Pacific coast and e along n base of Andes from upper Sinú Val. to mid. Magdalena Val. (s to Remedios, e Antioquia). E Nicaragua to nw Ecuador.

## 21. SPOTTED WOODCREEPER

*Xiphorhynchus erythropygius*     Pl. 23, Map 646
**Identification:** 9″ (23cm). *Bill rather long* (1.2-1.3″, or 30-33mm) *slightly decurved. Prom. buff eyering.* Mainly olive brown; crown dusky with only a few buff shaft lines; mantle with a few narrow shaft streaks; *throat buff* with small dusky dots (at a distance *crown looks uniform dusky*, throat uniform buff); *rest of underparts with rather large triangular buff spots* (spots smaller and thicker on foreneck and chest); lower back, wings, and tail rufous chestnut.
**Similar species:** Looks definitely "spotted" below (cf. with Buff-throated Woodcreeper, 19, which looks streaked below) and most likely confused with very sim. Olive-backed Woodcreeper (see 22). Spot-crowned Woodcreeper (24) is smaller, thinner-billed, and "streaked" below.
**Voice:** Plaintive song, *d'ddrrear, d'ddrrear, d'ddrrear, whew, whew,* 1st 3 notes drop markedly in pitch, often shortened to only 1st 2 or 3 notes.
**Behavior:** Singly or in pairs and reg. with mixed bird flocks, where it climbs bare or mossy trunks and larger limbs from lower midlevels to forest subcanopy.
**Breeding:** 9 BC birds, Feb–May, nw Colombia (Carriker). Cavity 5m up in dead stump, 12 Sept, upper Anchicayá Val. (Hilty).
**Status and habitat:** Humid and wet forest, forest borders, and occas. lighter woodland. Fairly common in w Valle. Mostly replaced at higher el. by Olive-backed Woodcreeper.
**Range:** To 1500m (once to 2100m in upper Río San Juan); most recs. are from foothills and lower slopes (about 200-1400m). Panama border s on Pacific slope to Nariño, n end of W Andes and e to lower Cauca Val. (Pto. Valdivia, Antioquia) and mid. Magdalena Val. to n boundary of Caldas (Río Samaná). S Mexico to w Ecuador.

## 22. OLIVE-BACKED WOODCREEPER

*Xiphorhynchus triangularis*     Pl. 23, Map 647
**Identification:** 9″ (23cm). Very sim. to Spotted Woodcreeper, differing mainly in a definitely spotted crown and *throat buff boldly scalloped olive brown;* eyering narrow and buffy white (not prom. buff); mantle with shaft streaks or spotlike streaks as in previous sp. (none of above easy to uncritically verify in field). In the hand both spp. definitely "olive-tinged" above.
**Similar species:** See under Spotted Woodcreeper (21), which is a lower el. replacement on Pacific slope.
**Behavior:** Sim. to Spotted Woodcreeper. Mainly 3-13m up larger trunks inside forest (Miller 1963).

**Breeding:** 10 BC birds, Apr–June, W and C Andes; 1 in Sept, E Andes (Carriker; Miller 1963).
**Status and habitat:** Humid and wet forest (esp. "cloud forest"). Fairly common in W Andes.
**Range:** Mainly 1500-2700m, rarely to 800m on Pacific slope (Río Munchique, w Cauca) or to 400m in e Nariño. All 3 Andean ranges (not Santa Marta or Perijá Mts.). N Venez. s in Andes to n Bolivia.

## 23. STREAK-HEADED WOODCREEPER

*Lepidocolaptes souleyetii*     Pl. 23, Map 648
**Identification:** 8″ (20cm); or 7″ (18cm) (Atlántico to Santa Marta area). *Slender, slightly decurved bill* (1″ or 25 mm). *Crown and nape dusky brown finely streaked buffy white;* sometimes upper mantle also finely streaked; *back uniform rufous brown;* rump, wings, and tail rufous; throat buff; rest of underparts light buffy brown broadly striped buffy white and edged dark brown.
**Similar species:** Slender and more delicately proportioned than others in its range. Best marks are the bill, fine streaking on head, and more or less unstreaked back (some indiv. var.). Cf. Straight-billed (14) and Buff-throated woodcreepers (19) and other *Xiphorhynchus* (table, p 350). In highlands, see Spot-crowned Woodcreeper (24).
**Voice:** Song a high-pitched musical trill, descending slightly, *chi-chi-chi-chi . . .* (Skutch 1969a; ffrench 1973).
**Behavior:** Usually alone, climbing trunks and limbs from low (rarely) to high; often hitches along underside of horizontal limbs.
**Breeding:** 3 laying ♀♀, Apr, May, and Oct, n Colombia (Carriker); Jun–July, Venez. (Thomas 1979b; Friedmann and Smith 1950); cavity about 3-25m up; 2 eggs (Skutch 1969a).
**Status and habitat:** Fairly common in drier, relatively open woodland, forest borders, woodlots, lighter second growth, and clearings with scattered trees. Unlike most other woodcreepers (except Straight-billed), not in forest.
**Range:** To 1500m. Pacific coast in lower Atrato Val. (s to Ríos Sucio and Salaquí) and from sw Cauca (Guapí) southward; upper Río Sinú to Santa Marta area, Cauca Val. s to Valle (Cali), and mid. Magdalena Val. to Tolima (Honda); e of Andes from e Norte de Santander to Meta (Villavicencio). S Mexico to w Ecuador, nw Peru, extreme n Brazil, and Guyana.

## 24. SPOT-CROWNED WOODCREEPER

*Lepidocolaptes affinis*     Pl. 23, Map 649
**Identification:** 7.5″ (19cm). Slender slightly de-

curved bill. *Crown and nape dark brown dotted buff; back uniform rufescent brown*; rump, wings, and tail rufous chestnut; *eyestripe white*; throat buffy white; sides of head, foreneck, and underparts brown *broadly streaked white and sharply edged black*. Or streaks shorter, more droplike (*sneiderni*).

**Similar species:** The only med.-sized woodcreeper in the highlands that is distinctly and crisply *streaked* below. Olive-backed Woodcreeper (22) is larger, more robust, and obviously *spotted* below. At lower el. cf. sim. Streakheaded Woodcreeper (23), which is paler, duller, streaked on crown and less "clean-cut" below.

**Voice:** Usually quiet. In Costa Rica, a rapid ser. of weak, melancholy notes very unlike the musical trill of allied Streak-headed Woodcreeper of lowlands (Skutch 1969a).

**Behavior:** Singly or in pairs and almost always with mixed flocks. Climbs mostly branches, less often trunks, from low to high but mainly from midlevels to subcanopy. Probes fissures, cracks, and moss, very often by hitching along the underside of branches.

**Breeding:** 7 BC birds, Apr–July, Perijá Mts.; 5 BC birds, May–Aug, C Andes; 3 BC ♂♂, May–June, n end W Andes (Carriker). July nest, 3 young, and Dec fledgling, Pichindé (1500m), Valle (S. Gniadek); nest, 6 Aug, PN Cueva de los Guácharos (Hilty); cavity 1-8m up; 2-3 eggs (Skutch 1969a).

**Status and habitat:** Common in humid and wet forest ("cloud forest") and in stunted forest nearly to treeline); also forest edges and tall second growth.

**Range:** Mainly 1800-3000m (once to 3400m; rarely to 1200m on Pacific slope or in Santa Marta Mts.). Santa Marta Mts. (*sanctaemartae*); Perijá Mts. and E Andes s to Bogotá (*lacrymiger*); W and C Andes and w slope E Andes from Bogotá s except Nariño (*sneiderni*); Pacific slope in Nariño (*aequatorialis*); e slope in Nariño (*frigidus*). S Mexico to w Panama; n Venez. s in mts. to n Bolivia.

**Note 1:** The *L. lacrymiger* group (Montane Woodcreeper) of S America is sometimes considered specifically distinct from *L. affinis* (Spot-crowned Woodcreeper) of Mid. America. **Note 2:** Lineated Woodcreeper (*L. albolineatus*) of the Guianas, s Venez., Amazonian Brazil, e Ecuador, and Peru may occur in e Colombia (rec. on Orinoco and Yavita-Pimichín area of w Amazonas, Venez.). Much like Spot-crowned Woodcreeper (of Andes) but crown minutely dotted buff (essentially uniform like back at a distance), underparts grayer, stripes more linear and bill slightly shorter (0.9″ vs 1.0″). Striped Woodcreeper (15) has a striped back.

## 25. GREATER SCYTHEBILL

*Campylorhamphus pucheranii*     Pl. 24, Map 650

**Identification:** 11.5″ (29cm). Bill grayish white, stouter, and proportionally shorter (2.2″ chord [56mm]) than other scythebills. Mostly dull rufescent brown; crown and hindneck (sometimes upper mantle) with light buff shaft streaks; throat and breast with dark rusty buff shaft streaks; *broad postocular streak and malar streak white*; rump, wings, and tail chestnut.

**Similar species:** Much larger than any other Colombian scythebill and the only one with a white streak behind and below eyes. Strongbilled Woodcreeper (11) has shorter bill and lacks white facial streaks.

**Behavior:** Much like others of the genus. Mainly mid. story (T. Parker).

**Status and habitat:** Rare and local. Wet mt. forest ("cloud forest"). Known from only a few localities.

**Range:** 900-2500m (prob. higher). W slope of W Andes in Valle and Cauca and occas. on adj. e slope (formerly San Antonio above Cali); upper Magdalena Val. in w Huila (once, Moscopán, 2500m); also "Bogotá." W Colombia, e and w Ecuador, and Peru (mostly 2400-2900m).

## 26. RED-BILLED SCYTHEBILL

*Campylorhamphus trochilirostris*     Pl. 24, Map 651

**Identification:** 9″ (23cm). Bill long (chord 2.3-2.5″ [58-64mm]), *very slender*, sickle-shaped, and reddish. Above brown to rufescent brown; crown dusky, *narrow pale buff streaks on crown*, sides of head, and *upper back; upper throat buffy white*; rest of underparts wood brown broadly streaked light buff on foreneck and breast; wings and tail rufous chestnut.

**Similar species:** Bill proportionally longer (on average) and thinner than any other Colombian scythebill. The only scythebill with a reddish bill w of E Andes; e of Andes best told from Curve-billed Scythebill (28) by streaked mantle. From Brown-billed Scythebill (27) by reddish bill, brighter wings and tail, and perhaps by whitish throat. Also cf. larger, more robust Greater Scythebill (25).

**Voice:** Dawn song in Venez. a fast, sharply ascending, and doubled trill *dedede'e'e'e, dedede'e'e'e'e*; also a rapidly descending trill ending in several slower notes (P. Schwartz recording). Day song in Colombia a descending woodcreeperlike *twee-whee, whew, wheew, whuuew*; alarm *pee-ep* over and over.

**Behavior:** One or 2 wander alone or often join mixed flocks. Climb trunks and limbs and probe crevices in bark, holes in trunks, and arboreal epiphytes, low to subcanopy. Somewhat wary.

**Breeding:** 7 BC birds, Feb–Oct, n Colombia (Carriker); nest in hollow open stump; 1 egg (Sclater and Salvin 1879).
**Status and habitat:** Uncommon and very spottily distributed. Dry to humid forest borders, lighter woodland, disturbed forest, and swampy areas. Mainly lowlands and foothills and replaced in most areas e of Andes by Curve-billed Scythebill. Fairly common in drier parts of Norte de Santander.
**Range:** To 1300m (once to 1700m in nw Cundinamarca). Pacific coast from Panama border s to upper Río Sucio (Dabeiba) and Baudó Mts. and in sw Nariño (no recs. from c Chocó—n Nariño); n end of W and C Andes e across n lowlands to w and e base of Santa Marta Mts.; base of Perijá Mts. s to upper Magdalena Val. (Villavieja, n Huila); e base of E Andes from Norte de Santander to Macarena Mts., prob. to w Putumayo lowlands. C Panama to nw Peru, n Bolivia, n Argentina, Paraguay, and most of Brazil.

### 27. BROWN-BILLED SCYTHEBILL
*Campylorhamphus pusillus*      Pl. 24, Map 652
**Identification:** 8.5″ (22cm). Bill long (chord 2″ [51mm]), sickle-shaped, *brownish*, and usually paler at base. Mostly dark rufescent brown (with olive tinge—*tachirensis*); crown dusky; crown, sides of head, and mantle with narrow buff streaks; *throat and streaks on underparts to upper belly rufescent buff*; rump, wings, and tail chestnut.
**Similar species:** Easily confused. Greater Scythebill (25) is larger with prom. white streak behind and below eyes. Red-billed (26) has whitish upper throat (not deep buff) and longer, thinner, and reddish bill; in the hand Red-billed has lighter buff streaking on underparts. Also cf. Curve-billed Scythebill (28) which it might meet at e base of Andes.
**Voice:** Song a tremulous, almost wailing, *twe-twe-weo-WEO-weo weo-we-we-we-we-we*, louder in mid., and successive songs often more or less connected by soft *twe* and *we* notes; seldom heard.
**Behavior:** One or occas. 2 reg. follow forest flocks. Probe crevices, moss, epiphytes, base of palm fronds, etc. in mid. strata or subcanopy, occas. lower and usually not on bare trunks

and limbs. Like other scythebills, rather wary and often hard to see well.
**Breeding:** 2 BC ♂♂, May, s Huila and June, n end W Andes (Carriker).
**Status and habitat:** Uncommon and local in humid and wet forest (esp. mossy forest), occas. forest borders. Mainly foothills and lower slopes.
**Range:** 300-2100m (once to 50m on Pacific coast); W Andes (mostly Pacific slope) from Antioquia (near Frontino) to w Nariño; w slope C Andes from Valdivia s to Huila (formerly) and e slope in Huila (La Candela); w slope E Andes in Cundinamarca; e slope in Norte de Santander and n Boyacá (*pusillus*); and in Perijá Mts. (*tachirensis*). Prob. more widespread. Costa Rica and w Panama; extreme w Venez. to w Ecuador.

### 28. CURVE-BILLED SCYTHEBILL
*Campylorhamphus procurvoides*      Pl. 24, Map 653
**Identification:** 9″ (23cm). Bill long (chord 1.8-2.2″ [46-56mm]), slender, sickle-shaped, and *reddish*. Essentially sim. to Red-billed Scythebill, but *back virtually uniform* (pale shaft streaks become obsolete on upper mantle), and bill proportionally shorter. In the hand, streaking on throat and breast vaguely "spotted," less decidedly streaked than in Red-billed and Brown-billed scythebills.
**Similar species:** See Red-billed Scythebill (26); other Colombian scythebills are foothill and mt. birds.
**Voice:** At dawn a short (2 sec), 7-9 note ser. *keeea, kee-ke-ke-ke-ke-ke*, high-pitched and bouncy (P. Schwartz recording).
**Behavior:** Much like Red-billed Scythebill.
**Breeding:** BC ♂♂, 9 Feb and 9 Mar, Amazonas, Venez. (Friedmann 1948).
**Status and habitat:** Humid *terra firme* forest. The e representative of Red-billed Scythebill, which it meets along e base of Andes.
**Range:** To 500m. E Norte de Santander, w Meta (Villavicencio area), and w Caquetá (Morelia s of Florencia); prob. e to Guainía, Vaupés, and Amazonas (rec. at Yavita-Pimichín, Venez., opp. se Guainía, and at Tahuapunto, Brazil opp. Vaupés). The Guianas, s Venez. and n Amazonian Brazil (s of Amazon from Ríos Madeira to Tapajós).

# HORNEROS, SPINETAILS, FOLIAGE-GLEANERS, ETC.
## Furnariidae (72)

The ovenbirds and their allies are a heterogeneous group of New World birds, diverse in both appearance and habits. The family reaches greatest diversity in the south temperate New World and numbers gradually decrease northward. Most Colombian species are forest or thicket birds, but some are found in every major terrestrial habitat from the lowlands to paramo. Their food consists mostly of insects or invertebrates taken in a variety of ways, often suggested (though not necessarily correctly) by the English name of the bird, e.g., foliage-gleaner, leaftosser, treehunter. Nests are varied and remarkable, ranging from the hornero's dome-shaped mud nests to the large stick nests of spinetails and thornbirds. Many nest in burrows; xenops and tuftedcheeks hollow out or use existing cavities. Songs are usually short whistles or trills and are seldom musical. Two recent revisions of the family have been proposed (Feduccia 1973; Vaurie 1980), although the more familiar and traditional arrangement is maintained here, with only slight modification.

## 1. STOUT-BILLED CINCLODES

*Cinclodes excelsior*          Pl. 25, Map 654
**Identification:** 8.5″ (22cm). Thrushlike. *Bill noticeably long and heavy* (1″, or 25mm), usually with distinct droop. *Dark brown above*, eyestripe and throat whitish; rest of underparts brownish gray, chest slightly scaled dusky, sides tinged dusky; wing coverts vaguely pale-edged; base of remiges rufous (forms fairly prom. wing stripe in flight) obscurely bordered behind blackish; tail brown edged cinnamon (outer web of outer pair and tip of outer 2 pairs cinnamon).
**Similar species:** See Bar-winged Cinclodes (2).
**Voice:** A ser. of low twittering or stuttering notes in flight; on ground short nasal *druut* and double-sounding *ken-eek*.
**Behavior:** Terrestrial, either alone, in pairs, or several in loose groups. Run rapidly on ground with body held low, then stop abruptly and bob up, often flicking up tail, sometimes wings. Probe mud and habitually dig in soft soil and debris, often flicking aside particles as they dig; less often pick or glean from ground or foliage. Often perch on rocks.
**Status and habitat:** Local; rocky paramo, wet meadows, and rather barren areas with scattered low vegetation; usually near water, or in damp or muddy areas from treeline to snowline. Sometimes with next sp. but usually less numerous.
**Range:** Paramo above 3300m. C Andes from n Tolima (Nevado del Ruiz) spottily s through mts. to Nariño. C Colombia to se Peru.
**Note:** Placed in *Geositta* by Vaurie (1980).

## 2. BAR-WINGED CINCLODES

*Cinclodes fuscus*          Pl. 25, Map 655
**Identification:** 7″ (18cm). Thrushlike. *Bill not noticeably heavy*, lower mandible almost straight, upper slightly curved (0.8″ or 20mm). Mostly dull brown above, paler more grayish brown below; eyestripe whitish; throat whitish obscurely scaled dusky; chest scaled dusky brown; sides tinged brown; wing coverts pale edged; remiges dusky with a *cinnamon patch at base* (forms a conspic. wing stripe in flight); tail brown, *outer 3 pairs of feathers mostly cinnamon*.

**Similar species:** Easily confused with Stout-billed Cinclodes (1), which has longer, heavier, and decidedly decurved bill (greater curvature can be hard to see); also larger size and slightly darker brown upperparts. When flushed, Bar-winged shows *more rufous* in outer tail feathers.
**Voice:** Song a short (about 2 sec), fast, and high-pitched trill, *tetet'i't't't't'i't't't't* that may ascend slightly (P. Schwartz recording); call a sharp *pfip!*, often doubled or trebled.
**Behavior:** Sim. to Stout-billed Cinclodes, but mainly gleans and picks from ground or grass; seldom digs and probes as does its longer-billed ally.
**Breeding:** 7 BC birds, Feb–Sept, Santa Marta and Boyacá (Carriker); 2 BC ♀♀, June, Boyacá (Olivares 1974a); fledged juv., 3 Feb, Santa Marta Mts. (Norton 1975). Nest in rocky outcrop, hole in wall, building, etc., often near stream; 3 white eggs (in Chile—Johnson 1965).
**Status and habitat:** Local. Rocky and poorly vegetated paramo and at least in lower part of range also in wet meadows with short grass. Often near water or muddy places; most numerous at higher el. Much more numerous than Stout-billed Cinclodes, which sometimes occurs with it.
**Range:** 3500-4400m. Santa Marta Mts. and E Andes from n Boyacá to s Cundinamarca; C Andes from Cauca to Nariño. Nw Venez. s in Andes to Tierra del Fuego. S birds migratory.

## 3. PALE-LEGGED HORNERO

*Furnarius leucopus*          Pl. 24, Map 656
**Identification:** 6.5″ (16.5cm). *Long, pale yellowish legs.* Above bright cinnamon rufous (blackish primaries and short rufous wing band prom. in flight); crown brownish gray, with *long white eyestripe*; throat and abdomen white; rest of underparts pale cinnamon, brighter on sides. Bill rather long and slender; *tail short*; eyes dark.
**Similar species:** See Lesser Hornero (4).
**Voice:** Song a loud, explosive ser. of evenly spaced notes that start to ascend, then descend and slow, *teer-teer-teer* . . . ; call a loud *cheeop* (J. V. Remsen; Brown).

**Behavior:** Usually seen singly, walking on wet ground, or hopping through tangled undergrowth, most often near water, where it flips over damp leaves; once at army ant swarm. **Breeding:** 6 BC birds, Jan–July, n Colombia (Carriker); 3 nests in July, river isls. near Leticia (Hilty), 2 in May and Sept (Todd and Carriker 1922); and 1 being built, Aug (Hilty), Santa Marta area; 1 in June, near Atlántico (A. Sprunt IV). Smooth, ovenlike, domed mud nest (about 8-10″ in dia.) saddled over low branch; side entrance spirals inward (right- or left-handed) near bottom; about 2 eggs. **Status and habitat:** Rather common in muddy and wet grassy areas, near piles of floating vegetation, and in tangled brush along streams, rivers, lakes, or temporary pools. In forested or more open brushy terrain. Esp. numerous in dry to humid zones of lower Magdalena River basin e to Santa Marta. **Range:** To 500m. Carib. region from Cartagena e to Santa Marta and w Guajira (*longirostris*); Snía. de San Jacinto and s Magdalena s to upper Río Sinú and mid. Magdalena Val. to Pto. Berrío, Antioquia (*endoecus*); e of Andes in Norte de Santander (sighting near Cúcuta, June 1980—Hilty and P. Hall); along Amazon and its tributaries (*torridus*). Nw Venez., Guyana, and s Colombia to n Bolivia and e Brazil. **Note 1:** The isolated population *F. l. cinnamomeus* in w Ecuador and nw Peru is larger (7″) with a heavier bill, a much wider ochraceous wing bar, a large pale cinnamon spot on inner web of outer primary, and *pale yellow eyes*. Rec. to Pichincha, Ecuador, expanding northward even in humid areas (in clearings), and may reach sw Nariño; prob. a distinct sp. (R. Ridgely), it is less dependent on water. **Note 2:** The *torridus* subsp. has been considered a separate sp., Pale-billed Hornero.

### 4. LESSER HORNERO

*Furnarius minor*          Map 657

**Identification:** 6″ (15cm). Much like Pale-legged Hornero but smaller, and duller cinnamon above; crown brownish gray (browner than 3); *eyestripe buffy* (not white); underparts paler esp. on sides, which are dull buff (not bright cinnamon); and *legs dusky* (not yellowish); bill slightly smaller and blacker. **Behavior:** Much like Pale-legged Hornero. **Status and habitat:** One Colombian rec. (Olivares 1967); several sight recs., presum. this sp., Isla Corea, Amazonas (Hilty, R. Ridgely), and prob. more numerous than the few recs. indicate because of confusion with Pale-legged Hornero. Very young, tangled second growth

and muddy flats along banks of streams, rivers, and river isls. **Range:** Known from Pto. Nariño, Amazonas. Doubtless more widespread in s Amazonas and Putumayo. E Ecuador, ne Peru, and w Amazonian Brazil.

[*Leptasthenura:* Found at high el.; has small stubby bill; strongly graduated tail with central pair of feathers long and pointed.]

### 5. ANDEAN TIT-SPINETAIL

*Leptasthenura andicola*          Pl. 24, Map 658

**Identification:** 6.5″ (16.5cm). Tail long (3.5″ or 8.9cm), 2 *spiky central tail feathers. Crown reddish chestnut streaked black*; eyestripe and chin white; otherwise boldly *streaked dark brown and white above and below*; wings and tail dusky brown; wing coverts and remiges edged rusty (or without rusty edges—*andicola*); outer tail feathers pale-edged. **Similar species:** Many-striped Canastero (30) is chunkier, more sparrowlike and with proportionally shorter tail, rufous patch in wing, and longer bill (not short and stubby). Streak-backed Canastero (29) is unstreaked below and has shorter, rounded tail and longer bill. White-chinned Thistletail (27) is unstreaked. **Voice:** Call a weak, tinkling *téz-dit* or *téz-dit-dit* (P. Schwartz recording); also a high mammallike squeal. **Behavior:** Rather furtive and often flush low for short distance, then quickly drop in. Like chickadees (*Parus*), restlessly examine twigs and foliage from near ground to 3m up in small bushes or keep concealed in taller grass. Sometimes with mixed flocks or small groups of White-throated Tyrannulets (J. Silliman; Hilty). **Breeding:** Nest, Represa Neusa (3400m) n of Bogotá, 15 Sept; thick grass oven concealed on ground in paramo; 2 white eggs (M. Robbins); BC ♂, Sept, Boyacá (Carriker). In Ecuador, Feb nest under eave of thatch-roofed hut (R. Ridgely). **Status and habitat:** Fairly common in damp grassy areas, esp. with scattered shrubs and *Espeletia*, or in *Polylepis* borders; also stunted woodland/paramo ecotone or open paramo. **Range:** 3000-4500m. Santa Marta Mts. (*extima*); E Andes s to at least Cundinamarca (*exterior*); and C Andes from n Tolima (Nevado del Ruiz) s through mts. of Nariño (*andicola*). Nw Venez. s in Andes to n Bolivia.

[*Synallaxis:* Many confusing spp.; tail strongly graduated, double-pointed; lowlands to treeline; usually in thickets near ground; most have 2- to 3-note "song."]

## 6. AZARA'S SPINETAIL

*Synallaxis azarae* Pl. 25, Map 659
**Identification:** 7" (18cm). Mostly dingy olive brown above incl. forecrown; *hindcrown, shoulders, and long tail rufous*; upper throat white; lower throat feathers with black bases (sometimes looks freckled); sides of head and breast gray becoming white on abdomen; sides brownish. Juv.: duller with buffy breast and no black on throat.
**Similar species:** Pale-breasted Spinetail (9) is sim. but has *shorter, brown* (not rufous) tail, and usually occurs at lower el. Only other sim. allies in mts. are Silvery-throated Spinetail (8) of E Andes, and Slaty Spinetail (see 10).
**Voice:** Tirelessly repeated call a loud inflected *pip-squéek!* or *mac-white!*, 2d syllable rising.
**Behavior:** A furtive sp. that skulks in thickets and tangles and is heard far more often than seen. Creeps and hops actively through dense vegetation and seldom rises above 4m up. Usually in pairs.
**Breeding:** 10 BC birds, Jan–Sept, C and E Andes (Carriker). A Mar nest, PN Cueva de los Guácharos (P. Gertler); 3 BC ♂♂, Feb–Mar, and 2 nests with eggs Mar–Apr, W Andes; bulky globular stick nest with long (0.3-0.4m) entry tube; low in tangle; 2 white eggs (Miller 1963).
**Status and habitat:** Common in overgrown clearings, roadsides, and bushy "cloud forest" borders, esp. in bracken fern brakes.
**Range:** 1600-3000m (occas. to 900m on Pacific slope). W and C Andes (*media*) and E Andes (*elegantior*). Nw Venez. s in Andes to n Bolivia.
**Note:** The n subspp. s to n Peru have been considered a separate sp., Elegant Spinetail (*S. elegantior*) by some.

## 7. DUSKY SPINETAIL

*Synallaxis moesta* Pl. 25, Map 660
**Identification:** 6.5" (16.5cm). Bill *rather heavy* for the genus. Mostly *dark grayish olive* incl. forehead; *crown, shoulders, and margins of remiges at base rufous chestnut*; throat black frosted grayish white (feathers black basally); tail rather short, *dark rufous chestnut*; under wing coverts bright cinnamon orange (or sim. but general plumage slaty gray—*brunneicaudalis*).
**Similar species:** Much darker and proportionally shorter-tailed than any other Colombian *Synallaxis* e of Andes except Dark-breasted Spinetail (see 11).
**Breeding:** 2 BC birds, June, w Caquetá (Carriker).
**Status and habitat:** Not well known. Specimens are mostly from undergrowth inside humid forest.
**Range:** 400-1200m. Along e base of E Andes

from s Casanare to nw Meta (*moesta*) southward to Caquetá and Putumayo (*obscura*); se Nariño (*brunneicaudalis*) prob. se to Amazonas. E Colombia, e Ecuador to n Peru.

## 8. SILVERY-THROATED SPINETAIL

*Synallaxis subpudica* Pl. 25, Map 661
**Identification:** 7.5" (19cm). *Very long grayish brown tail* (4.3" or 109mm). Forecrown olive brown; *crown, shoulders, and base of primaries rufous*; otherwise grayish brown, paler below becoming grayish white on abdomen; throat dusky bordered whitish on sides of throat.
**Similar species:** Best mark is the very long grayish brown tail. Azara's Spinetail (6) has shorter rufous tail. Pale-breasted (9) has shorter tail, whitish throat, and is usually at lower el.
**Voice:** A loud chattering or nasal chipping *chi-chi-chi-chi-ti-ti-ti-'i'i*, falling and often answered immediately by another in unsynchronized duet; less vocal than Azara's Spinetail.
**Behavior:** Sim. to Azara's Spinetail though somewhat less furtive.
**Breeding:** 4 BC ♂♂, June–Sept, E Andes (Carriker). Large globular, stick nest with long, tunnellike entrance; 1 egg (Olivares 1969a).
**Status and habitat:** Common in overgrown clearings, thickets, hedgerows, and shrubby forest borders. The most numerous spinetail on the Sabana de Bogotá.
**Range:** ENDEMIC. 1200-3200m (photo 3200m, Represa Neusa—Hilty). N end of E Andes from n Boyacá (about 6°30'N) s to latitude of Bogotá.

## 9. PALE-BREASTED SPINETAIL

*Synallaxis albescens* Pl. 25, Map 662
**Identification:** 6.5" (16.5cm). Forehead, most of upperparts, and mod. long *tail* (3" or 76mm) *grayish brown with rufous crown and shoulders*; throat whitish somewhat speckled black on lower throat; breast light buffy gray; belly whitish.
**Similar species:** W of Andes see Azara's Spinetail (6) and Silvery-throated Spinetail (8); e of Andes, Dark-breasted (11) and Plain-crowned spinetails (12).
**Voice:** Call, incessantly repeated, an emphatic nasal *wáke-up* or *wá-choo*, 1st syllable stronger, 2d falling; call throughout yr.
**Behavior:** Furtive and heard far more often than seen. May call from low exposed perch in early morning but otherwise usually concealed. Creep and hop from near ground to 3m up in tangles and thickets; often in pairs.
**Breeding:** 8 BC birds, Feb–Nov, n Colombia (Carriker); 2 BC ♂♂, Jan, Huila (Miller 1947); June nest (eggs), Cali (Hilty); 1 being built, Apr, Patía Val. (Brown); coarse globular nest

with tubular entrance; semiconcealed in low bush; 3 grayish eggs.

**Status and habitat:** Common in open grassy and "field" habitats with scattered bushes and thickets, overgrown roadsides, and marshy areas. Usually replaced at higher el. by Azara's Spinetail.

**Range:** To 2100m (usually below 1500m). Throughout w of E Andes in suitable habitat except w of W Andes where known only from Gulf of Urabá (Sautatá and Unguía). E of Andes s to Río Guaviare and at Leticia, Amazonas (photo, 21 May, and specimen, 20 June 1975— J. V. Remsen; several sightings—Hilty). Sw Costa Rica to central Argentina. Trinidad.

## 10. SLATY SPINETAIL
*Synallaxis brachyura*          Pl. 25, Map 663

**Identification:** 6.5″ (16.5cm). Mostly *slaty gray incl. forehead; crown, shoulders, and base of flight feathers rufous*; lower back and *tail grayish brown*; throat dusky sometimes with a few faint whitish streaks.

**Similar species:** Only "slaty" spinetail w of the Andes; much darker than either Pale-breasted (9) or Azara's spinetails (6), and latter has much longer rufous tail.

**Voice:** Song a wrenlike, low churring, *chut-chut-churrr*, or gravelly, raillike *turrrrr*, dropping at end. Does not call as incessantly as Pale-breasted Spinetail.

**Behavior:** Sim. to Pale-breasted Spinetail, though often forages higher (to 6m up) and easier to see. Pairs or occas. small family groups.

**Breeding:** 7 BC birds, Apr–Sept, C Andes (Carriker); 5 nests Mar–July, W Andes (S. Gniadek); nest as in others of genus, 0.5-5m up in bush or small tree; 2 eggs, rarely 3 (Skutch 1969a).

**Status and habitat:** Shrubby forest borders, overgrown grassy and bushy clearings, lighter woodland, and coffee groves. Favors more humid areas than Pale-breasted Spinetail. Usually common but easily overlooked.

**Range:** To 2000m (usually more numerous above 1000m). Pacific coast (mostly 0-300m), n base of Andes from upper Río Sinú and Río Nechí s to head of Magdalena Val. in Huila; locally in Cauca Val. to Popayán. Honduras to w Ecuador.

## 11. DARK-BREASTED SPINETAIL
*Synallaxis albigularis*          Map 664

**Identification:** 6.2″ (15.7cm). Forecrown and upperparts mostly olive brown with *rufous crown and shoulders; upper throat whitish*; lower throat black (base of feathers black and when feathers erected throat looks solid black); *sides of head and rest of underparts dark gray* in sharp

contrast to whitish central belly; *short tail* olive brown, feathers pointed and webs frayed.

**Similar species:** Intermed. betw. darker Dusky Spinetail (7) and paler Pale-breasted Spinetail (9). Dusky Spinetail has a longer chestnut (not olive brown) tail, is more robust, and has darker gray (not olive brown) upperparts, dark belly, and noticeably heavier bill. Pale-breasted is *usually* much paler, but light individuals of Dark-breasted Spinetail can look very sim., differing mainly in short tail and all black lower throat (latter hard to see), and then best told by voice. No other spinetail e of Andes is dark gray below.

**Voice:** Often-repeated call a short *dít-dududu?*, 1st note stronger and higher-pitched; often answered by mate.

**Behavior:** Furtive and seldom seen unless calling. Creeps and hops, mostly 0.5-4m up, through tangles. Usually calls from concealment, occas. from semiopen perch. During displays, may raise throat feathers and flash black bases to form solid black throat.

**Breeding:** 1 building nest, 18 June, and 1 nest with young, 24 July, Isla Corea, Leticia; stick and stiff grass-stem nest with tube entrance typical of genus, 1-1.8m up in tangle (Hilty).

**Status and habitat:** Usually common in overgrown clearings, roadsides, bushy forest borders, and tall grass and shrubbery near water.

**Range:** To 1200m. E of Andes from sw Meta (Macarena Mts.) s to Putumayo, se Nariño and Amazonas (Leticia). E Colombia to e Peru and w Amazonian Brazil.

## 12. PLAIN-CROWNED SPINETAIL
*Synallaxis gujanensis*          Pl. 25, Map 665

**Identification:** 6.2″ (15.7cm). *Crown grayish brown*, becoming olive brown on back, with *rufous wings and tail*; underparts dingy white faintly tinged olive on chest; sides and flanks grayish olive.

**Similar species:** Superficially like Rusty-backed Spinetail (25), but latter has crown and upperparts rufous (not just wings and tail).

**Voice:** "Song" a rather coarse, scolding *kew . . . huaa*, with a distinct pause betw. notes; 1st note stronger and higher, as in most *Synallaxis*. Often answered by mate.

**Behavior:** Sim. to others of the genus, but forages lower, often on ground, and usually less than 2m up. Even more secretive and skulking than most other *Synallaxis*.

**Breeding:** Building nest, 30 Aug, Río Javarí, nw Brazil (Hilty); 2 nests, Feb and Nov, ne Meta (S. Furniss); nest sim. to other *Synallaxis*; in shrubbery or low trees; 2-3 eggs; often parasitized by Striped Cuckoo (Haverschmidt 1968).

**Status and habitat:** Shrubby undergrowth in swamp and *várzea* forest, bushy forest borders, and dense young second growth in pastures (not grassy areas). Often numerous but easily overlooked. Very common on swampy Amazonian river isls. and banks of Amazon. **Range:** To 1200m. E of Andes from w Meta (Buenavista above Villavicencio; Los Micos, Macarena Mts.) s to Putumayo and Amazonas. Prob. to Guainía (rec. opp. Río Guaviare in Venez.). The Guianas and s Venez. to n Bolivia and s Brazil.
**Note:** *Synallaxis propinqua* (White-bellied Spinetail) of Fr. Guiana, Amazonian Brazil, e Peru, ne Ecuador, and n Bolivia prob. occurs in Colombia, for it occurs within 50km of border on Ecuador-Peru boundary and at mouth of Río Curaray and Pto. Indiana in n Peru. 6.5"; above grayish brown, lesser wing coverts and tail rufous, throat silvery gray, rest of underparts gray, *center of abdomen white.* Imm.: throat creamy white.

### 13. STRIPE-BREASTED SPINETAIL

*Synallaxis cinnamomea*          Pl. 25, Map 666
**Identification:** 5.5" (14cm). Tail rather short for a *Synallaxis*. Deep rufous brown above, incl. sides of head; shoulders, edges of remiges, and postocular streak dark chestnut; throat black finely streaked white; *breast rufous streaked fulvous,* lighter on belly with fulvous streaks edged rufous brown. Or brown above, breast and belly buff streaked dusky (*aveledoi*).
**Similar species:** Only *Synallaxis* with streaked underparts.
**Voice:** Frequently utters a rather nasal, liquid *churt-wert* or *keep-going,* 1st note higher, 2d lower and rising; also a soft whining *peeeur.*
**Behavior:** Singly or in pairs; skulks in undergrowth, usually close to the ground, but often less furtive than others of the genus.
**Breeding:** 4 BC ♂♂, Nov and June, Norte de Santander (Carriker); yr.-round in Trinidad; nest like others of genus; 2 greenish blue eggs (ffrench 1973); Venez. nests built on ground on a slope (P. Schwartz *in* Vaurie 1980).
**Status and habitat:** Fairly dry to humid forest, second growth, and lighter woodland. In n Venez. also in dry deciduous scrubby woodland.
**Range:** 900-2100m. E slope Norte de Santander, s of Cúcuta (*aveledoi*); both slopes of E Andes s to Bogotá (*cinnamomea*). Ne Colombia, n and nw Venez. (incl. Perijá Mts.). Trinidad.

### 14. RUSTY-HEADED SPINETAIL

*Synallaxis fuscorufa*          Pl. 24, Map 667
**Identification:** 7" (18cm). *Entire head and neck to upper breast orange rufous* (concealed throat spot black); otherwise mostly grayish brown with *rufous wings and long rufous tail.*
**Similar species:** Range overlaps only with very different Streak-capped Spinetail (22).
**Voice:** Call, often tirelessly repeated, a short, nasal *dit-dit-du,* last note lower.
**Behavior:** Pairs or families often accompany mixed flocks. Glean deliberately in shrubs, along small branches, and in viney thickets and brambles, chiefly 0.5-7m up. Less furtive than other *Synallaxis* and often easily seen; sometimes with Streak-capped Spinetail (T. B. Johnson).
**Breeding:** 5 BC birds, Jan–June, and 2 juvs., June–July (Carriker).
**Status and habitat:** Common in humid shrubby forest borders and overgrown clearings, esp. in denser tangles and brambles.
**Range:** ENDEMIC. 900-3000m (mostly above 2000m on Cuchilla de San Lorenzo). Santa Marta Mts.

### 15. RUFOUS SPINETAIL

*Synallaxis unirufa*          Pl. 25, Map 668
**Identification:** 7" (18cm). Entirely *bright rufous chestnut with conspic. black lores;* tail rather long with 2-pointed tip as in other *Synallaxis* (or as above but paler below, forehead and underparts cinnamon and indistinct pale eyebrow— *muñotztebari*). Juv.: paler and no black lores.
**Similar species:** Easily confused with more robust Sepia-brown and Rufous wrens (pp 532-533), both of which have faint barring on wings and tail and usually occur in groups. Note long, thin, 2-pointed tail; shares black lores only with Rufous Wren.
**Voice:** Call a loud, nasal, almost scolding *queeeik,* or *quee-queéeik,* sometimes var. to *quee-quee-quéeik;* recalls Azara's Spinetail. Alarm a low *churr.*
**Behavior:** Pairs or families reg. follow mixed flocks where they hop and clamber, mostly 0.5-4m up, through thick undergrowth. Very furtive if alone, usually much less so when accompanying mixed flocks.
**Breeding:** 2 BC ♂♂, Apr, Perijá Mts. (Carriker); Apr–July, Venez. (Schäfer and Phelps 1954).
**Status and habitat:** Uncommon to fairly common (by voice). Undergrowth of mossy forest, humid and wet forest borders, and tall second growth woodland.
**Range:** 1700-3100m. Perijá Mts. (*muñotztebari*); se Norte de Santander (Páramo de Tamá) on Venez. border (*meridana*); E Andes in Cundinamarca, C Andes and W Andes from upper Río San Juan southward (*unirufa*). Mts. from n Venez. to s Peru.

### 16. RUDDY SPINETAIL
*Synallaxis rutilans* Pl. 25, Map 669
**Identification:** 6″ (15cm). *Dark rufous chestnut above* with dusky gray remiges and tail; *lores and throat black; sides of head and breast dark rufous chestnut* becoming dark olive brown on abdomen (or dark olive brown above with rufous forehead—*dissors*). Tail much shorter than allied Rufous Spinetail.
**Similar species:** Superficially resembles ♀ Blackish Antbird (p 400), but tail longer and throat black.
**Voice:** Call in Venez. a nasal *kít-naaa* resembling that of previous sp.; up to 4 per 5 sec (P. Schwartz recording).
**Behavior:** Hop on or near ground inside forest (G. Tudor).
**Breeding:** 3 BC birds, Apr, Amazonas, Venez. (Friedmann 1948).
**Status and habitat:** Humid *terra firme* forest and second growth woodland. A forest bird like Rufous Spinetail, which replaces it in the mts.
**Range:** To 500m. E of Andes from s Meta (Macarena Mts.), w Caquetá, and Vaupés to Amazonas at Leticia (*caquetensis*); e Guainía and prob. e Vichada (*dissors*). The Guianas and s Venez. to n Bolivia and Amazonian Brazil.
**Note:** Chestnut-throated Spinetail (*S. cherriei*) of e Ecuador, n Peru, and w Brazil may occur in Putumayo, as it has been seen on lower Río Aguarico, ne Ecuador, near Colombian border (R. Ridgely). Resembles brown-backed forms of Ruddy Spinetail, but dull chestnut (not black) throat.

### 17. WHITE-WHISKERED SPINETAIL
*Synallaxis candei* Pl. 24, Map 670
**Identification:** 6.5″ (16.5cm). Unmistakable. Crown grayish brown; otherwise bright rufous above; *sides of head black, bordered below by a broad white whisker stripe that joins on chin*; throat black; postocular streak rufous; breast and sides cinnamon rufous; center of lower underparts white; *tail rufous, distal half dusky.* Or sim., but back brown becoming dusky brown on crown; breast deep rufous; flanks brownish; whisker stripe dotted white, and postocular streak dusky brown like crown (*atrigularis*).
**Voice:** Frequently repeated call a nasal *a-dít-dít-du,* the 1st and last syllables subdued and sometimes dropped or inaudible at a distance.
**Behavior:** Recalls Ruddy Spinetail. Pairs actively hop and forage on the ground or in tangles near ground. Often cocks and lowers tail. Unlike most *Synallaxis*, usually not difficult to see.
**Breeding:** 13 BC birds, Mar–Aug, n Colombia

(Carriker); only rec. nest like others of genus but in tree cavity at ground level (Marinkelle *in* Vaurie 1980).
**Status and habitat:** Arid lowland scrub, thorny woodland, salt flats with scattered bushes, and mangrove borders. Common on Guajira Peninsula; spotty w of Santa Marta Mts. and apparently absent from their nw base.
**Range:** To 300m. Arid Carib. region from n Sucre e to w base of Santa Marta Mts. (*candei*); Cesar Val. and Guajira (*venezuelensis*) and s in drier regions to mid. Magdalena Val. s to Simití (7°58′N), s Bolívar (*atrigularis*). N Colombia and nw Venez. (to 1100m).
**Note:** Placed in the genus *Poecilurus* by some.

### 18. WHITE-BROWED SPINETAIL
*Hellmayrea gularis* Pl. 25, Map 671
**Identification:** 5.2″ (13.2cm). Slender bill black above, yellowish below. *Very short tail (2.2″ or 56mm) rufous.* Rufous brown above, paler more cinnamon brown below (or underparts grayish with brown sides—*brunneidorsalis, cinereiventris*); *eyestripe and upper throat white*; throat bordered dusky all around.
**Similar species:** Rufous Spinetail (15) lacks the white eyestripe and white throat, and has much longer tail. White-chinned Thistletail (27) has much longer tail, white eyering, grayish underparts, and indistinct white chin spot.
**Voice:** Often quiet; an odd, low, nasal whine or trill, *trrrrrrrrrrrr* that descends, and a *chip* (Hilty). Song a high, accelerating, *zit, zit, zit, zit-zit-zit-zit'zit'i'i'i'iii-zit-zit,* last 2 notes slightly higher (P. Schwartz recording).
**Behavior:** Wrenlike as it hops unobtrusively in low tangles and gleans from twigs and bamboo or probes moss; ground to 4m up, infrequently higher. Usually alone, occas. with mixed flocks.
**Status and habitat:** Tangles and dense thickets near humid and wet forest borders and openings; fond of bamboo. Seems most numerous in stunted upper montane forest/paramo ecotone or just below it.
**Range:** 2400-3800m. W Andes at n end and in Cauca, C Andes from s Caldas s to Nariño and E Andes in Boyacá and Cundinamarca (*gularis*); se Norte de Santander, Páramo de Tamá (*cinereiventris*) and Perijá Mts. (*brunneidorsalis*). Nw Venez. to w Ecuador; c Peru.
**Note:** Often placed in the genus *Synallaxis* from which it differs by very short tail (shorter than wing instead of much longer), no rufous wing patch, and voice.

[*Certhiaxis*: Found in lowlands; over or near water in marshes; churring or rattling songs.]

## 19. YELLOW-CHINNED (-THROATED) SPINETAIL

*Certhiaxis cinnamomea*          Pl. 25, Map 672

**Identification:** 6″ (15cm). *Mostly cinnamon rufous above with grayish forecrown* and cheeks and faint whitish eyestripe; *chin yellow* (inconspicuous); rest of underparts white tinged olive on sides; tips of flight feathers dusky.

**Similar species:** Clean-cut appearance much like Red-and-white Spinetail (20) but differs thus: forecrown grayish (not uniform rufous), faint eyestripe, and *lores grayish* (not black).

**Voice:** Call a harsh churring rattle, rising slightly, then settling down, and much like that of *Laterallus* rails of same habitat; also a thin buzzy trill and a sharp *chip.*

**Behavior:** Active and usually in damp places near or over water. Alone or in well-spaced 2's. Hop about, either partially concealed or in open, seldom more than 3m up; sometimes take prey from water surface.

**Breeding:** 2 nests, July–Aug, PN Isla de Salamanca (Hilty); Apr–Sept, Guárico, Venez. (Thomas 1979b); bulky globular stick and grass nest with long entrance tube on side; low in bush or tangle, usually near water; 3-4 white eggs, often parasitized by Striped Cuckoo (ffrench 1973).

**Status and habitat:** Common in marshes, flooded grassy ditches, tangled shore vegetation, and mangrove borders. The requirement is water. Found together with Red-and-white Spinetail in grassy lagoon borders on river isls. near Leticia (J. V. Remsen).

**Range:** To about 500m. Atrato Val. (s to Bagadó se of Quibdó), Río Sinú e to w base of Santa Marta Mts., s to lower Cauca Val., entire Magdalena Val., and e of Andes in n Arauca (sightings, Nov 1978—W. McKay and J. Jorgenson) and Río Amazon near Leticia (photos, 1974-1975—J. V. Remsen). N Colombia and locally throughout e of Andes s to c Argentina. Trinidad.

## 20. RED-AND-WHITE SPINETAIL

*Certhiaxis mustelina*          Pl. 25, Map 673

**Identification:** 6″ (15cm). Closely resembles Yellow-chinned Spinetail. *Bright rufous above incl. forehead; lores black;* underparts white; abdomen tinged buff; tips of flight feathers dusky; bill slender.

**Similar species:** See Yellow-chinned Spinetail (19).

**Voice:** A churring rattle almost indistinguishable from preceding sp.; also a 3-noted *chuk, chuk, chek,* last note slightly higher (J. V. Remsen).

**Behavior:** Apparently sim. to Yellow-chinned Spinetail; the 2 occur together but are not interspecifically territorial (J. V. Remsen). Hop in standing or matted grass or near it on muddy banks at water's edge; to 2m up.

**Status and habitat:** Marshes, and tangled and matted shore vegetation. The requirement is grass near or in water. In Leticia area mostly in grassy lagoon borders on lower end of river isls.

**Range:** To 100m. Banks of Amazon, river isls., and tributaries in s Amazonas (Leticia to Pto. Nariño). Ne Peru and Amazonian Brazil.

[*Cranioleuca*: Mts. or lowlands; tail usually shorter than *Synallaxis*; mostly forest midlevel or higher; act like miniature foliage-gleaners; song typically a chipping trill.]

## 21. CRESTED SPINETAIL

*Cranioleuca subcristata*          Pl. 25, Map 674

**Identification:** 5.5″ (14cm). Short crest usually not evident in field. Olive brown above with *indistinct pale eyestripe and faint blackish streaks on crown; wings and tail rufous;* below light grayish brown, paler on throat; under wing coverts orange cinnamon; lower mandible pale yellow.

**Similar species:** See Ash-browed Spinetail (23). Plain-crowned Spinetail (12) lacks eyestripe and crown streaking and is usually found at much lower el.; in the hand Plain-crown has an all dusky bill.

**Voice:** Song about 3-4 bouncy high notes followed by a short attenuating trill, *pzeep, pzeep, pzeep, pee'pe'pe'e'e'e* (P. Schwartz recording).

**Behavior:** Usually found singly or in pairs creeping and hopping actively over limbs and among foliage from upper understory to subcanopy. Often with mixed spp. flocks.

**Breeding:** Jan–May, Rancho Grande, Venez. (Schäfer and Phelps 1954); pensile, globular nest of grass in tree, entrance hole near bottom (Schwartz *in* Vaurie 1980).

**Status and habitat:** Humid forest and forest borders in mts.; also to lowlands (300m) in nw Arauca.

**Range:** 300-1500m. E slope of E Andes from Norte de Santander s to s Boyacá, incl. Río Arauca and Río Casanare at base of Andes. Colombia to n Venez.

## 22. STREAK-CAPPED SPINETAIL

*Cranioleuca hellmayri*          Pl. 24, Map 675

**Identification:** 6″ (15cm). Much like Crested Spinetail. *Crown chestnut streaked black;* otherwise olive brown above with *whitish eyestripe and rufous wings and tail;* throat dingy whitish; rest of underparts pale grayish olive.

**Similar species:** In its forest habitat occurs only

with very different Rusty-headed Spinetail (14), which has solid orange rufous head.

**Voice:** Call, often monotonously repeated every few seconds, a weak, high-pitched, and squeaky trill, *ti ti'i't'ttttt.*

**Behavior:** Arboreal, mainly from 5m to sub-canopy ht. Pairs, families, or several follow forest flocks where active and restless as they glean from foliage of trees, shrubs, and vines and probe cracks in bark and epiphytes (T. B. Johnson).

**Breeding:** 8 BC birds, Feb–Oct (Carriker); Sept–Nov nests, San Lorenzo; pendulous ball of grass and leaves (T. B. Johnson).

**Status and habitat:** Common in humid forest, forest borders, and tall second growth. Easily found on Cuchilla de San Lorenzo above 1700-1800m.

**Range:** ENDEMIC. 1600-3000m. Santa Marta Mts.

### 23. ASH-BROWED SPINETAIL

*Cranioleuca curtata*          Pl. 25, Map 676

**Identification:** 6″ (15cm). *Crown chestnut, weak eyestripe gray;* otherwise olive brown above with *rufous wings and tail;* below dingy grayish brown with a *suggestion of dusky streaking on breast;* eyes grayish white (e slope Andes).

**Similar species:** Crested Spinetail (21) has plain brownish olive crown more or less streaked black (not solid chestnut) and lacks faint breast streaking. Red-faced Spinetail (24) has sides of head rufous. Known range of Ash-browed does not overlap either of the above but could meet.

**Behavior:** Rather like Red-faced Spinetail. Restless and active as it hops and twists through dense vine tangles and probes along mossy limbs, mostly 2-10m up. Often with mixed flocks, esp. when other furnariids are present.

**Breeding:** 2 BC ♂♂, Apr–May, sw Huila (Carriker).

**Status and habitat:** Uncommon in humid forest and forest edge. Easily overlooked and certainly more numerous than the few scattered recs. suggest.

**Range:** 1000-2500m. W slope of E Andes from se Santander south to head of Magdalena Val. (La Candela; sight, Finca Merenberg, Huila); e slope of E Andes in w Caquetá (sightings above Florencia, 1400m, 1978, 1981—Hilty et al.) and se Nariño (Río San Miguel). S Colombia, e Ecuador, e Peru, and n Bolivia.

### 24. RED-FACED SPINETAIL

*Cranioleuca erythrops*          Pl. 25, Map 677

**Identification:** 5.8″ (14.7cm). *Forecrown and sides of head rufous;* hindcrown and most of upperparts olive brown with *rufous wings and tail;* underparts paler olive brown, becoming light grayish on throat and median underparts and buffy on flanks; tail rather long. Imm. lacks rufous crown but has sides of head tinged rufous, most of underparts tinged orange rufous.

**Similar species:** Often with larger foliage-gleaners, none of which has rufous on sides of head.

**Voice:** Sometimes noisy; song a high-pitched, fast, chattering *seet-seet-seet-se'e'e'e'e'e'e.*

**Behavior:** Active as it hops and twists acrobatically through tangles and along mossy limbs. Usually singly or in pairs from the lower mid. story to canopy; regularly accompanies mixed flocks.

**Breeding:** In W Andes in Valle, 3 nests, Feb–Mar (Miller 1963; Brown); 5 in July–Dec (S. Gniadek). Nest a bulky globular mass of moss and vines fastened near end of drooping branch; small entrance at bottom (Skutch 1967).

**Status and habitat:** Fairly common in humid forest, forest edges, and taller second growth.

**Range:** Mainly 1000-2100m (to 700m on Pacific slope). W Andes s to Nariño and w slope of C Andes from Valdivia at n end to Quindío (Salento). Costa Rica to w Ecuador.

### 25. RUSTY-BACKED SPINETAIL

*Cranioleuca vulpina*          Pl. 25, Map 678

**Identification:** 5.8″ (14.7cm). *Crown and entire upperparts rufous;* back somewhat duller; forehead and *narrow eyestripe dingy white;* sides of head grayish brown with a suggestion of dusky streaking; *underparts brownish buff,* throat paler; eyes yellowish gray.

**Similar species:** Lacks the clean-cut appearance and white underparts of Yellow-chinned and Red-and-white spinetails (19, 20). Yellow-chinned also has grayish forehead; Red-and-white has sharp black lores; and both are found mainly in grass in marshes. In nw Arauca cf. Crested Spinetail (21).

**Voice:** Song, often given simultaneously (not antiphonal) by a pair, a loose, rattly ser. of nasal *kuee* notes gradually descending and changing to *qua* notes (song is 2- to 3-sec duration); sometimes only mutter a few *kuee-kweek's.*

**Behavior:** Pairs peer and glean as they work among vines, tangles, and bushy foliage 1-7m up. Inconspic. but not furtive. Not with mixed flocks.

**Breeding:** Nest building, 10 Dec, ne Meta (Brown); June–July nests in Orinoco region, a mass of grass wedged in sapling or partly submerged brush near or over water; 2 white eggs (Cherrie 1916).

**Status and habitat:** Young second growth thickets and tangled tall grass, bushes, and saplings up on banks of rivers, river isls., or edges of gallery forest. Usually near water but stays higher up in vegetation than spp. of *Synallaxis* or *Certhiaxis* sometimes with it. Common on river isls. near Leticia.
**Range:** To 400m. E of Andes. Known from w and ne Meta (Carimagua—S. Furniss), e Vichada (along Orinoco), and s Amazonas (many sightings—Hilty et al.). C and s Venez. (incl. n bank of Río Arauca), ne Ecuador (Río Aguarico), e Peru, n Bolivia, and most of Brazil. Isla Coiba, Panama.
**Note:** Voice, habitat, and nest site more like *Certhiaxis* than other Colombian *Cranioleuca*.

### 26. SPECKLED SPINETAIL
*Cranioleuca gutturata*          Pl. 25, Map 679
**Identification:** 5.2″ (13.2cm). Eyes whitish. Crown chestnut *and eyestripe buffy*; otherwise olive brown above with rufous chestnut wings and tail; chin spot yellowish; *sides of head and underparts pale buff thickly speckled brown* and becoming uniform dark buff on under tail coverts.
**Similar species:** Only lowland spinetail with speckled underparts. Most likely mistaken for a wren, but no Amazonian sp. are speckled.
**Behavior:** One or 2 reg. accompany *várzea* forest flocks, where they actively hop along branches and viney tangles and poke like wrens into dead leaf clusters and debris from eye level to subcanopy.
**Breeding:** Building nest (getting moss), 20 June, lower Río Javarí, Brazil (Hilty); building nest 3m up small tree in *várzea* clearing, cone-shaped mass of moss 10″ long beneath branch and tapering to entrance hole at bottom, 30 July, Taracoa, Ecuador (R. Ridgely).
**Status and habitat:** *Várzea* forest, small *várzea* openings or borders, and low, poorly drained *terra firme* forest.
**Range:** To 500m. E of Andes from w Caquetá and Putumayo to Amazonas; doubtless to e Vichada (on e bank of Orinoco at Munduapo). Surinam, Fr. Guiana, and s Venez. to n Bolivia and Amazonian Brazil.

[*Schizoeaca*: Found at high el.; resemble *Leptasthenura*, but bill longer, head more wrenlike, and underparts mostly unstreaked; tail strongly graduated, decomposed, and feathers attenuated.]

### 27. WHITE-CHINNED THISTLETAIL
*Schizoeaca fuliginosa*          Pl. 24, Map 680
**Identification:** 7″ (18cm). Tail very long, *the feathers frayed and pointed*; short outer tail feathers scarcely longer than tail coverts. Dark brownish chestnut above with *white eyering and narrow white eyestripe* bordered below by dusky streak through eyes; *chin spot white*; otherwise grayish brown below; eyes dark (imm.?). Or as above but grayish eyestripe, smaller chin spot, and grayer underparts; eyes white (*fuliginosa*).
**Similar species:** Both canasteros (29, 30) have streaked, sparrowlike upperparts and "normal" tails; Andean Tit-Spinetail (5) has stubby bill and is streaked all over. Also cf. Perijá Thistletail (28).
**Voice:** High, sharp, penetrating *tik*, occas. several in ser. Song, resembling that of Streakbacked Canastero but longer, is a high, rattling trill, increasing in tempo and slightly in pitch (Vuilleumier and Ewert 1978).
**Behavior:** Pairs are sometimes retiring as they hop through dense foliage at eye level or lower; hold tail cocked in alarm (Hilty); actively inspect twigs and foliage in bushes and low shrubs at edge of paramo (J. Silliman).
**Breeding:** 3 BC birds, July–Sept, E Andes (Carriker); BC ♂, Aug, and nest of moss, grass, and Frailejón down 13cm up in grass, PN Chingaza; 2 white eggs (W. McKay). 2 BC birds, pairs, and singing ♂♂, late Mar, nw Venez. (Vuilleumier and Ewert 1978).
**Status and habitat:** Dense, shrubby elfin forest borders and tangled tall grass, ferns and bushes in treeline shrubbery. Most numerous near treeline; seldom below 3000m.
**Range:** 2300-3600m. E Andes (*fuliginosa*) and C Andes from s Caldas s to Volcán Chiles, Nariño (*fumigatus*). Nw Venez. s in Andes to n Peru.

### 28. PERIJA THISTLETAIL
*Schizoeaca perijana*          Map 681
**Identification:** 8.3″ (21.1cm). Uniform grayish brown above with *long, pointed, light brown tail feathers and long grayish eyestripe*; wing coverts edged chestnut; chin spot cinnamon buff; rest of underparts grayish brown.
**Similar species:** Only thistletail in Perijá Mts. Cf. White-chinned Thistletail (27).
**Behavior:** Apparently sim. to White-chinned Thistletail, which it replaces in Perijá Mts.
**Breeding:** BC ♂, 2 July, Perijá Mts., Venez., 3000m (Phelps 1977), and 14 July, Cerro Pintado; 1 imm., 6 July (Carriker).
**Status and habitat:** Stunted forest borders and open grassy areas. Described from specimens taken 2 July 1974 in Venez. (Phelps 1977). Carriker took 9 in July 1942, nw slope Cerro Pintado, Colombia.
**Range:** 3000-3400m. Perijá Mts. of Colombia

(Cerro Pintado, s Guajira, 3400m) and adj. Venez.
**Note:** Poss. a subsp. of White-chinned Thistletail.

## 29. STREAK-BACKED CANASTERO
*Asthenes wyatti*                      Pl. 24, Map 682
**Identification:** 6″ (15cm). Streak-backed. Above buffy brown streaked dusky; *flight feathers rufous basally*, blackish distally; *tail very rounded, 4 central feathers dusky, rest dull rufous* (rufous in wings and tail conspic. in flight); narrow buff eyestripe; large *chin spot cinnamon orange*; throat and chest grayish buff faintly speckled and streaked dusky; rest of underparts uniform buff; bill rather long and straight, lower mandible yellow basally.
**Similar species:** Many-striped Canastero (30) is conspic. streaked above and below; thistletails (27, 28) are unstreaked and have longer frayed tails. Also cf. Andean Tit-Spinetail (5).
**Voice:** Two song types: a single insectlike trill; and 3 short insectlike trills; both given in about 1 sec; sometimes sung alternately by adj. birds (Vuilleumier and Ewart 1978).
**Behavior:** Mainly terrestrial. Hop or run rapidly on ground or flush low over grass and quickly dive into cover. Often raise or flick up slightly cocked tail.
**Breeding:** 8 BC birds, Feb–Mar, Santa Marta Mts. (Carriker); 1 in July, Perijá Mts. (Phelps 1977); nest building, Mar, nw Venez. (Vuilleumier and Ewart 1978). *Asthenes* build large, domed, basketlike nests of small sticks and grass (Koepcke 1970).
**Status and habitat:** Locally common in stands of *Espeletia* (Frailejón) and open grassy areas with scattered bushes and shrubs from treeline to snowline; occas. below treeline in open areas. Not found with Many-striped Canastero, except poss. Norte de Santander.
**Range:** 3100-5000m (to 2400m in Santa Marta Mts.). Santa Marta and Perijá mts. (Laguna de Junco, 3500m) and n end of E Andes in n Santander. Nw Venez. and ne Colombia; Ecuador to s Peru.

## 30. MANY-STRIPED CANASTERO
*Asthenes flammulata*                  Pl. 24, Map 683
**Identification:** 6″ (15cm). Crown rufous streaked black; otherwise *dark brown broadly streaked buffy white above and below*; upper throat unstreaked buffy (or orange rufous—*multostriata*); *flight feathers rufous basally*, blackish distally; 4 central tail feathers dusky, *rest dull rufous* (rufous in wings and tail conspic. in flight); tail feathers pointed and somewhat frayed at tip; bill mod. stout.
**Similar species:** See under Streak-backed

Canastero (29). ♀ Plumbeous Sierra-Finch (p 666) is entirely streaked above and below but has conical bill. Also see Andean Tit-Spinetail (5).
**Voice:** Call a soft, plaintive, meowing *peeow*; song is several whining notes followed by a rattle (J. Silliman).
**Behavior:** Partially terrestrial and runs well on ground. Flushes low and usually takes cover quickly in adj. shrubs or forest border. Sings from bushes, sometimes from top; carries tail cocked.
**Breeding:** 2 BC birds, Feb and Sept, C and E Andes (Carriker).
**Status and habitat:** Local. Grassy slopes and brush- and rock-scattered areas at or above treeline, occas. somewhat lower. May overlap range of *A. wyatti* in ne Santander.
**Range:** 2800-4200m. E Andes from Norte de Santander s to s Cundinamarca (*multostriata*); C Andes from Caldas to Cauca (*quindiana*) and Nariño (*flammulata*). N Colombia s in Andes to s Peru.
**Note 1:** Orinoco Softtail (*Thripophaga cherriei*) prob. occurs in e Vichada along the Orinoco (known from Caño Capuana, adj. Venez.). 5″, olive brown above with rufous chestnut wings and tail; *throat bright orange rufous*; eyestripe buff; *sides of head, neck, and most of underparts brown streaked buffy*. **Note 2:** Plain Softtail (*T. fusciceps*) of e Ecuador to Bolivia and w Amazonian Brazil is unrec. but likely in Putumayo (known from Limoncocha, Ecuador). Resembles a *Thylpopsis* tanager in size and shape. Almost *entirely uniform buff*, slightly yellower on throat, and with lower back, wings, and tail rufous; bill mod. short and stout, lower mandible yellowish. Forest edge and second growth.

## 31. PLAIN THORNBIRD
*Phacellodomus rufifrons*            Pl. 25, Map 684
**Identification:** 6.3″ (16cm). *Very plain*. Bill rather stout, lower mandible yellowish. Uniform grayish brown above; indistinct eyestripe and underparts buffy white; paler on throat, browner on flanks; tail rounded.
**Similar species:** A very dull, nondescript bird that might recall a large wren or even a tanager or finch. Note absence of obvious markings and habitat.
**Voice:** Song a bright chippery ser. of *chit* notes delivered loudly and with a mate often enthusiastically joining; speeds then slows; frequently repeated.
**Behavior:** Unlike most Colombian ovenbirds, noisy and conspic. Pairs or families hop about in thickets, bushes, or in the outer edges of spreading crowns of larger trees. Most notable for their remarkable nests (see below).

**Breeding:** BC birds, July–Aug, ne Meta (S. Furniss); July–Nov Guárico, Venez. (Thomas 1979b). Large cylindrical stick nest (often 2m long or more) usually attached to end of drooping branch in isolated tree; multiple chambers may be added; built by family groups, and portions sometimes appropriated by other birds, esp. Troupials; 3 eggs (Skutch 1969b).

**Status and habitat:** Open ranchland with scattered trees, bushes, and weedy thickets.

**Range:** To 500m. E of Andes in Arauca, Casanare, and ne Meta (Carimagua—S. Furniss). Doubtless also n Vichada. N and c Venez., n Peru, ne Bolivia, n Argentina, and s Brazil.

**Note:** Formerly called Rufous-fronted Thornbird (Meyer de Schauensee 1970).

### 32. SPECTACLED PRICKLETAIL

*Siptornis striaticollis*          Pl. 24, Map 685

**Identification:** 4.5″ (11.4cm). Bill thin and warblerlike; *tail short and double-pointed*. Mostly rufescent brown above with chestnut crown and shoulders and rufous tail; *short eyebrow and incomplete eyering white*; underparts pale grayish brown with *sides of head, throat, and chest rather finely streaked buffy white*; under wing coverts cinnamon.

**Similar species:** Easily mistaken for a xenops but lacks white malar. Streaked Xenops (64) has streaked back; all xenops have black bar on wings.

**Voice:** A high-pitched trill (Eley et al. 1979).

**Behavior:** Much like a *Picumnus*. Inconspic. but rather active. Single birds, pairs, or occas. 3-4 follow forest flocks. Creep along outer branches probing moss clumps, dead leaf clusters, and bark, or adopt more xenopslike posture, or sometimes hang upside down like a parid to pick from under leaves. Rarely ever tap on limbs or brace with tail to probe. Mostly 5-15m up, infrequently to subcanopy (Eley et al. 1979).

**Status and habitat:** Rare or local. Humid mossy forest ("cloud forest") and forest edges. Known from only a few localities in Colombia and several recent sightings mostly at PN Cueva de los Guácharos (P. Gertler) and Finca Merenberg.

**Range:** 1650-2400m (to 1300m in Ecuador—R. Ridgely). W slope of E Andes below Bogotá (Fusagasugá), head of Magdalena Val. in Huila, and e slope of E Andes in w Caquetá (sighting above Florencia, 1800m, 9 Sept, 1978—Hilty). S Colombia to e Peru.

### 33. DOUBLE-BANDED GRAYTAIL

*Xenerpestes minlosi*          Pl. 24, Map 686

**Identification:** 4.2″ (10.7cm). Recalls an antwren or parulid warbler. Dark gray above with blackish crown; *long yellowish white eyestripe* and *2 white wing bars*; below creamy white with some grayish mottling on breast and sides of neck; dark gray tail rather rounded; bill thin.

**Similar species:** Might be confused with ♂ Yellow-breasted Antwren (p 396), but latter has solid black cap, white wing edging, white in tail, and mostly bright yellow underparts. Also see Rufous-rumped Antwren (p 398) and Cerulean Warbler (p 576).

**Behavior:** Usually forage at midlevels, sometimes in small groups (to 3 or more) that quite actively search underside of leaves, twigs, even small branches, sometimes hanging upside down or briefly creeping like a xenops; often investigate vine tangles, sometimes with other birds, in same strata as *Herpsilochmus* antwrens (R. Ridgely).

**Breeding:** BC ♂ and imm., 23 Sept, Santander (Carriker). Pair feeding juv., 23 Apr, e Panama (R. Ridgely).

**Status and habitat:** Second growth with scattered large trees (Carriker). Humid forest and forest edge, also deciduous forest. Known from only a few widely scattered localities in Colombia.

**Range:** To 900m. Pacific coast s to lower Río San Juan (Valle-Chocó border) and humid lowlands n of Andes (upper Río Sinú) to mid. Magdalena Val. (nw Santander to w Boyacá near Muzo). E Panama to n Colombia.

### 34. ORANGE-FRONTED PLUSHCROWN

*Metopothrix aurantiacus*          Pl. 24, Map 687

**Identification:** 4.2″ (10.7cm). Warblerlike. Upperparts olive gray, *forehead deep orange brightening to golden yellow on foreface and throat*; rest of underparts pale gray strongly tinged yellow on breast and belly; tail rounded; *legs yellowish orange*; bill thin. Imm. lacks yellow on head.

**Similar species:** Unlike any other furnariid and more likely confused with a warbler, conebill, or small *Thlypopsis* tanager. See Orange-headed Tanager (p 635).

**Behavior:** Small family groups of 2-5 resemble warblers or *Thlypopsis* tanagers as they glean insects from outer foliage and twigs and often hang from leaves; midlevels to canopy where frequently follow mixed flocks (P. Hocking; Hilty).

**Status and habitat:** Most numerous inside or at edge of tall second growth woodland, also *várzea* and *terra firme* forest and edges. Can be found with reg. in Mocoa area.

**Range:** To 500m. E base of Andes from w Putumayo (Mocoa) southward. Se Colombia to e Peru, n Bolivia, and w Amazonian Brazil (Río Purús).

## 35. PEARLED TREERUNNER

*Margarornis squamiger* Pl. 25, Map 688
**Identification:** 6.2″ (15.7cm). Creeperlike. Upperparts *rich rufous chestnut*, browner on crown; *prom. eyestripe and throat white*; sides of neck and rest of underparts olive brown *thickly marked with creamy white teardrop-shaped spots, each narrowly encircled with black*; tail rather long and stiff with protruding spines.
**Similar species:** An exquisitely patterned sp., much brighter, more sharply marked, and usually found above the range of others of its kind. See Fulvous-dotted Treerunner (36), Rusty-winged (37) and Spotted barbtails (38).
**Voice:** Quiet. Infrequently a high thin *tik*; song a ser. of sim. *tik*'s almost trilled, lasting about 1.5 sec.
**Behavior:** Climbs limbs, usually hitching itself along under branches like a creeper, also occas. hanging like a parid, or even hopping and twisting along smaller branches and twigs like a foliage-gleaner. Usually midlevel to canopy; active but unobtrusive; singly, in pairs, or occas. several and habitually with mixed flocks.
**Breeding:** 12 BC birds, Jan–Sept, Perijá Mts., C and E Andes (Carriker), BC ♂, Oct, Boyacá (Olivares 1971). Moss ball nest with side entrance.
**Status and habitat:** Fairly common in humid upper temperate zone forest, forest borders, denser highland hedgerows, and *Polylepis* woodland above treeline. Favors mossy epiphyte-laden trees in stunted temperate forest.
**Range:** 1500-3000m (mainly 2500m to treeline). Perijá Mts., W Andes at n end (Frontino) and in Cauca (Munchique), E and C Andes s to Nariño. W Venez. s in Andes to n Bolivia.
**Note:** Beautiful Treerunner (*M. bellulus*) of e Darién highlands, Panama (Cerro Pirre; Cerro Quía) also surely occurs in adj. Colombia. Like Pearled Treerunner but duller, more brownish above, and spots of underparts reduced in size and no. It may be conspecific with *M. squamiger.*

## 36. FULVOUS-DOTTED TREERUNNER

*Margarornis stellatus* Pl. 25, Map 689
**Identification:** 6″ (15cm). Creeperlike. Uniform rufous chestnut above; *throat whitish bordered below with black, with a few small black-edged white spots spreading onto chest*; otherwise uniform ruddy below; tail stiff with protruding spines; in flight shows a prom. fulvous wing stripe.
**Similar species:** Easily confused with Wedge-billed Woodcreeper (p 345), which has a short eyestripe and is browner above and below, with contrasting rufous tail; creeper also has buff spotted (not white) throat, but this is hard

to see in field. Also see Spotted Barbtail (38) and Pearled Treerunner (35).
**Behavior:** Climbs limbs, sometimes using its tail for support like a woodcreeper, or clambers along without tail support. Quietly pecks and probes mossy branches, twigs, even foliage. Alone, pairs, or often several from lower midlevel to subcanopy where usually seen following mixed flocks.
**Status and habitat:** Fairly common in wet mossy forest ("cloud forest").
**Range:** 1200-2200m (most numerous above 1600m). Pacific slope from headwaters of Río San Juan (Cerro Tatamá) southward and nw end C Andes (Valdivia). W Colombia to nw Ecuador.

## 37. RUSTY-WINGED BARBTAIL

*Premnornis guttuligera* Pl. 25, Map 690
**Identification:** 6″ (15cm). Resembles a small foliage-gleaner. Mostly brown above with *conspic. buffy eyestripe and streaks on hindneck and mantle*; wings and tail rufous, sometimes with faint buffy tipping on wing coverts; *throat buffy white; otherwise sides of head, neck, and rest of underparts brown with broad buff scalloped streaking*. Tail stiff but lacks prom. barbs.
**Similar species:** Lineated Foliage-gleaner (43) is somewhat larger and more finely streaked, incl. crown, and lacks rufous wings. Spotted Barbtail (38) and treerunners (35, 36) are uniform above.
**Behavior:** Hops and twists actively along branches, twigs, and leaves (esp. dead ones) like a foliage-gleaner or *Cranioleuca* spinetail. Seldom creeps or climbs and, unlike allied *Premnoplex*, does not use tail for support; understory to lower mid. story and often with mixed spp. flocks (R. Ridgely; Hilty).
**Breeding:** 3 BC birds, Mar–June, W Andes (Miller 1963; Carriker).
**Status and habitat:** Uncommon to locally common in humid mossy forest; common in PN Cueva de los Guácharos.
**Range:** 1600-2500m (more numerous above 2000m). W Andes at n end (near Frontino) and in Valle; C Andes and E Andes from Norte de Santander southward. Nw Venez. s in mts. to Peru.
**Note:** By some placed in the genus *Premnoplex* or in *Margarornis.*

## 38. SPOTTED BARBTAIL

*Premnoplex brunnescens* Pl. 25, Map 691
**Identification:** 5.2″ (13.2cm). Creeperlike. Uniform gray *brown above*, indistinct buff eyestripe; throat deep buff; rest of *underparts dark brown with numerous drop-shaped buff spots bor-*

dered black; tail brownish black, with stiff protruding spines.

**Similar species:** Considerably darker than others of its kind and the only one with a black tail. Pearled Treerunner (35), found mainly at higher el. and at edges of forest, is larger, mainly rufous above, incl. tail, and has prom. eyestripe. Fulvous-dotted Treerunner (36) lacks eyestripe and has spotting limited to chest; Rusty-winged Barbtail (37) is streaked above. See Wedge-billed Woodcreeper (p 345).

**Voice:** Infrequently heard song a high, thin *eep eep eep ti'ti'ti'titititi*, trilled at end.

**Behavior:** Quiet and unobtrusive as it climbs trunks and limbs like a nuthatch (*Sitta*), hitching itself along mechanically, with or usually without aid of tail for support. Alone or in pairs, 1-6m up in understory; sometimes with mixed flocks, or more often away from them.

**Breeding:** 8 BC birds, Mar–Aug, n Colombia (Carriker); 1 nest with young, Apr, PN Cueva de los Guácharos (P. Gertler); mossy ball nest wedged in crevice between logs, bark, or rocks, and usually low; tubular entrance from bottom to shelf inside; 2 white eggs (Skutch 1967).

**Status and habitat:** Fairly common but easily overlooked in humid and wet mossy forest, occas. along forest borders.

**Range:** 1200-2600m (to 700m on Pacific slope; to 3000m in PN Puracé—J. Silliman). Cerros on Panama border; Santa Marta and Perijá Mts., the Andes and Macarena Mts. Costa Rica to n Venez. and s in Andes to Bolivia.

### 39. BUFFY TUFTEDCHEEK
*Pseudocolaptes lawrencii*     Map 692

**Identification:** 8″ (20cm). Mostly uniform rufous brown above; crown and nape dusky with buff streaks; rump and tail rufous; wings mainly blackish. Wing coverts faintly tipped cinnamon; sides of head blackish with narrow buff eyeline; *throat buffy white continuing back on sides of neck forming prom. tuft;* upper breast buffy white, mottled and scaled dusky brown; rest of underparts fulvous brown, more rufescent on sides and with whitish shaft streaks on lower breast.

**Similar species:** See Streaked Tuftedcheek (40).

**Voice:** Song is several sharp *wit* or *zit* notes followed by a low clear trill that slows and ends with several distinct louder notes (Skutch 1969a); loud metallic *sfink* call.

**Behavior:** Probes and rummages vigorously and noisily in crevices and accumulated debris in bromeliads, often propping itself with its tail or climbing inside them; also clambers along branches to probe moss and other epiphytes from lower midlevel to canopy; habitually with mixed bird flocks.

**Breeding:** Costa Rican nest in woodpecker hole; 10m up in forest opening (Skutch 1969a).

**Status and habitat:** Uncommon in humid and wet mossy forest ("cloud forest"). Replaced at higher el. by Streaked Tuftedcheek.

**Range:** 800-2000m. Pacific slope from Valle (no Chocó recs.) s to Nariño. Costa Rica and w Panama; W Colombia and nw Ecuador.

### 40. STREAKED TUFTEDCHEEK
*Pseudocolaptes boissonneautii*     Pl. 26, Map 693

**Identification:** 8″ (20cm). Not easily told from Buffy Tuftedcheek (39). Differs mainly in having *back with narrow buffy white streaks* (not just crown and nape) *and tufts on cheeks white instead of buffy white;* breast more extensively white (less contrast with throat), and rest of underparts paler and brighter cinnamon. In the hand crown sometimes uniform dusky instead of with pale streaks.

**Voice:** Call a dry *chut;* song 1-2 very sharp notes and a very fast trill that slows, abruptly so at end, *chut, chut ch'iiiii'e'e'e-e-e; chut* notes between songs (P. Schwartz recording).

**Behavior:** Sim. to Buffy Tuftedcheek but seems to be even more of a bromeliad specialist.

**Breeding:** 5 BC ♂♂, July–Aug, n end Andes and Perijá Mts. (Carriker); 1 in Oct, E Andes (Olivares 1971); tree cavity nest; eggs white (Sclater and Salvin 1879).

**Status and habitat:** Fairly common in humid and wet mossy forest and elfin woodland. This is *the* widespread tuftedcheek in Colombia and the one most likely to be seen.

**Range:** 1800-3200m (mostly 2500m to treeline). Perijá Mts. and all 3 Andean ranges. N Venez. s in mts. to n Bolivia.

### 41. CHESTNUT-WINGED HOOKBILL
*Ancistrops strigilatus*     Pl. 24, Map 694

**Identification:** 7.5″ (19cm). *Philydor*-like, but bill heavier. Dark brown above *sharply and rather finely streaked buffy white, with contrasting rufous chestnut wings and tail;* narrow buff eyestripe; sides of head and underparts *yellowish buff somewhat streaked and flammulated dusky,* most heavily on sides of head. Small hook on bill *not* a field mark.

**Similar species:** Striped Foliage-gleaner (42) is darker with plain brown (not rufous) wings, brownish (not pale yellowish buff) underparts, and much less distinct streaking above and below. Chestnut-winged Foliage-gleaner (50) lacks streaking. Also see Rufous-tailed Foliage-gleaner (51).

**Voice:** Call a harsh buzzing *bzzt.*

**Behavior:** One or 2 follow mixed flocks where they hop deliberately along limbs or rummage in vine tangles in upper levels of forest, often

close to trunks. Generally more sluggish than *Philydor* and seem to avoid denser foliage (T. Parker; Hilty).
**Status and habitat:** Uncommon in humid *terra firme* forest, occas. *várzea*.
**Range:** To 500m. E of Andes from s Meta (Macarena Mts.) and w Vaupés (San José del Guaviare) s to Putumayo; Amazonas (sight). E Colombia to se Peru, Bolivia, and w and central Amazonian Brazil (s of Amazon?).

## 42. STRIPED FOLIAGE-GLEANER (WOODHAUNTER)

*Hyloctistes subulatus*  Pl. 26, Map 695
**Identification:** 6.5″ (16.5cm). Bill rather long and slender. *Dark brown above with a few faint shaft streaks on crown; rump and tail chestnut; throat yellowish buff;* rest of underparts dull brownish olive *obscurely streaked buffy on breast.* Or like above but upperparts lighter brown and crown, mantle, sides of head, and throat also streaked buff (*subulatus*).
**Similar species:** Confusing. Generally darker and w of Andes found at lower el. than other sim. allies, but some overlap occurs. W of Andes from Lineated Foliage-gleaner (43) by absence of streaking on mantle and less streaking below; from Streak-capped (61) and Uniform treehunters (62) by smaller size, shorter tail, and mainly unstreaked buffy throat. E of Andes easily confused with Lineated Foliage-gleaner (43), which is much more sharply and extensively streaked below. Also see paler Chestnut-winged Hookbill (41). *Automolus* are decidedly larger and show little or no streaking, (w of Andes see 54, 55).
**Voice:** "Song" in Peru, 2 to 4 clear loud whistles followed by a short, lower-pitched, rattling trill, *tuee-chew tr'r'r'r'r'r'r* (T. Parker); call in Costa Rica and w Colombia a sharp *squirk* (Slud 1964; G. Tudor).
**Behavior:** Active but rather furtive. One or 2 hop and rummage in vine tangles, epiphytes, and leaf accumulations, usually near trunks and from mid. story to near ground. Sometimes follow forest flocks.
**Breeding:** BC ♂ and laying ♀, Feb. Chocó (Carriker).
**Status and habitat:** Uncommon (hard to see) in humid and wet forest in the lowlands and foothills.
**Range:** To 900m. Pacific slope from Baudó Mts. southward (*assimilis*); n Antioquia (Mutatá) and s Córdoba (*cordobae*); e of Andes from s Meta (Macarena Mts.) and Vaupés (Mitú) southward (*subulatus*). Prob. also Guainía (no Amazonas recs.). Nicaragua to s Venez., Amazonian Brazil, and n Bolivia.

[*Syndactyla*: Found in forest understory in mts. Resemble *Anabacerthia* but more heavily streaked above and below. Hard to see.]

## 43. LINEATED FOLIAGE-GLEANER

*Syndactyla subalaris*  Pl. 26, Map 696
**Identification:** 7″ (18cm). Only in highlands. Brown above, *narrowly streaked buffy white on crown and mantle,* streaking most prom. on hindneck; rump and tail dark rufous chestnut; *throat plain buff;* sides of head and *rest of underparts dull brown rather narrowly streaked buffy white* (or crown virtually unstreaked and streaks very narrow below—*striaticollis*).
**Similar species:** See Striped Foliage-gleaner (42). Treehunters (58, 59, 61) are larger, more robust, longer-tailed, and have streaked or scaled throats. Scaly-throated and Montane Foliage-gleaner (44, 45) have conspic. eyerings and fainter streaking.
**Voice:** Song a loud, harsh, rachetlike ser. of about 8 accelerating notes (Miller 1963).
**Behavior:** Active and noisy as it hops along limbs and inspects smaller branches, twigs, and dead leaf clusters in the lower and mid. stories, occas. subcanopy. Alone or in pairs and seen away from flocks as often as in them.
**Breeding:** 5 BC birds, May–July, W and C Andes (Carriker; Miller 1963).
**Status and habitat:** Fairly common in humid forest, occas. forest borders.
**Range:** Mostly 1300-2400m (to 900m on Pacific slope). Cerros on Panama boundary (*tacarcunae*); W Andes and w slope C Andes (*striaticollis*); E Andes and head of Magdalena Val. (*striolata*). Costa Rica to nw Venez. and s in Andes to Peru.

[*Anabacerthia*: Rather small like *Philydor*, but found in mts.; distinctive head patterns; forage in mid. to upper levels; not shy.]

## 44. SCALY-THROATED (SPECTACLED) FOLIAGE-GLEANER

*Anabacerthia variegaticeps*  Pl. 26, Map 697
**Identification:** 7″ (18cm). *Crown dusky with a few faint buff shaft streaks; otherwise rufescent brown above with chestnut tail; large cinnamon eyering and eyestripe form "spectacles";* cheeks and malar dusky, throat buffy white, feathers of lower throat obscurely scaled dusky; remaining underparts pale rufous brown *flammulated cinnamon* on breast; belly paler.
**Similar species:** Montane Foliage-gleaner (45) has whitish (not cinnamon) "spectacles" that are less prom.; underparts almost unstreaked or only faintly with whitish.
**Behavior:** In most respects sim. to Lineated Foliage-gleaner but less vocal and more ar-

boreal, foraging mostly in mid. story or higher and quite active and acrobatic as it hops and flutters along branches, or clings to foliage and fronds, sometimes acting like an overgrown xenops. Reg. with mixed spp. flocks (G. Tudor; Hilty; Slud 1964).
**Status and habitat:** Uncommon and very local; wet forest ("cloud forest").
**Range:** 700-2000m. Pacific slope from c Chocó (below Cerro Tatamá) southward (*temporalis*). Costa Rica and w Panama; once in e Panama highlands; w Colombia to w Ecuador.
**Note:** *Temporalis* subsp. of w Colombia and w Ecuador is very unlike forms of C America and is by some considered a separate sp.

### 45. MONTANE FOLIAGE-GLEANER
*Anabacerthia striaticollis*          Pl. 26, Map 698
**Identification:** 6.5″ (16.5cm). Uniform brown above, slightly dusky on crown; tail rufous; *conspic. eyering and narrow superciliary whitish*; lores and malar area dusky; throat buffy white; *remaining underparts virtually uniform olivaceous buff* with vague buffy white streaking on breast (or finely and definitely streaked—*montana*).
**Similar species:** See Scaly-throated Foliage-gleaner (44). Mostly uniform plumage and whitish "spectacles" are good marks.
**Voice:** Occas. a sharp raspy *chek*; "song" a ser. of same rough *chek* notes, rapid and staccato.
**Behavior:** Hops and twists actively along outer branches, where it gleans from twigs, foliage, and epiphytes, or noisily rustles and pokes dead leaves and hops up vines nearer the trunk. Usually conspic. and easily seen; 1 to several follow mixed flocks mostly from midlevel to subcanopy.
**Breeding:** 7 BC birds, May–June, W and C Andes; 1 in June, Perijá Mts. (Carriker); 1 in Apr, Valle (Miller 1963). 1 nest within broken trunk of thorny *Bactris* palm (Schäfer *in* Vaurie 1980).
**Status and habitat:** Most common foliage-gleaner in mts.; humid and wet forest, occas. borders.
**Range:** 1000-2400m. Santa Marta Mts. (*anxius*); Perijá Mts. and the Andes except Nariño (*striaticollis*); se Nariño (*montana*). N Venez. s in mts. to n Bolivia.

[*Philydor*: Usually seen from midlevel to canopy (except 46 and 47) slender, med.-small (6.5″- 7.5″, or 16.5-19cm); slender bill; active; majority in lowlands.]

### 46. SLATY-WINGED FOLIAGE-GLEANER
*Philydor fuscipennis*          Map 699
**Identification:** 6.5″ (16.5cm). Rufescent brown above, slightly grayer on crown and with *con-trasting brownish slate wings* and bright rufous rump and tail; grayish cheeks bordered above by *long prom. cinnamon buff eyestripe*; throat yellowish buff becoming brownish buff on rest of underparts; central belly more grayish buff.
**Similar species:** Easily recognized in its range by strongly contrasting wings and bold eyestripe.
**Behavior:** In forest understory in Panama (R. Ridgely).
**Breeding:** 8 BC ♂♂, Feb–May, nw Colombia (Carriker). Dependent juv., Apr, Panama (R. Ridgely).
**Status and habitat:** Most common in humid hill forest 500-1000m.
**Range:** To 1200m. From Baudó Mts. n to northernmost end of W Andes and e along n base of Andes to mid. Magdalena Val. (n Santander) s to Río Samaná, n Caldas (*erythronotus*). W Panama to nw Colombia and w Ecuador.
**Note:** *P. fuscipennis* is remarkably like *P. pyrrhodes* (Cinnamon-rumped Foliage-gleaner) of e of Andes and may belong with that sp., as both are understory birds. *P. fuscipennis* was formerly merged with *P. erythrocercus* (Rufousrumped Foliage-gleaner), but the latter is a canopy not an understory sp. (R. Ridgely).

### 47. CINNAMON-RUMPED FOLIAGE-GLEANER
*Philydor pyrrhodes*          Pl. 26, Map 700
**Identification:** 6.5″ (16.5cm). Rufescent brown above with *contrasting slaty wings and bright cinnamon rump and tail*; long eyestripe, sides of head, and *entire underparts bright orange cinnamon*; legs dull yellowish.
**Similar species:** Much brighter and more contrastingly patterned than any other foliagegleaner e of Andes. Could be confused with *erythronotus* race of Slaty-winged Foliage-gleaner (46) or Buff-fronted Foliage-gleaner (49), both of which are hill and mt. birds (not lowlands); from either by much brighter rump and tail and all cinnamon underparts, also yellow legs.
**Voice:** In Peru a loud short trill (T. Parker).
**Behavior:** Actively clambers over or hangs from tips of palm fronds, arums, *Heliconia*, and other larger leaves in open understory, mostly below 5m up, rarely to subcanopy. Singly or in pairs, and often with mixed forest flocks (Pearson 1975; Parker 1979; Hilty).
**Breeding:** 1 BC ♂, 12 Apr, upper Orinoco, Venez. (Friedmann 1948).
**Status and habitat:** Humid *terra firme* and *várzea* forests, esp. open understory with palms and denser vine tangles or at forest edge.
**Range:** To 500m. E of Andes from s Meta (Macarena Mts.) and Vaupés (Mitú) southward.

Prob. n to e Vichada (rec. in adj. Venez.). The Guianas and s Venez. to se Peru and w Amazonian Brazil.

### 48. RUFOUS-RUMPED FOLIAGE-GLEANER
*Philydor erythrocercus*          Map 701
**Identification:** 6.5″ (16.5cm). Plain olivaceous brown above (no contrast); tail rufous; rump only vaguely rufous; *long cinnamon buff eyestripe; underparts pale yellowish buff*, tinged olive on sides.
**Similar species:** Barely separable in field from Rufous-tailed Foliage-gleaner (51), but look for more uniform underparts without vague streaking, also rufous-tinged rump. Both are "yellower" below than other Amazonian *Philydor* allies. Cf. Cinnamon-rumped Foliage-gleaner (47).
**Behavior:** In e Peru pairs or groups peer and clamber actively along slender branches and glean from live or curled dead leaves and in debris in midstory or subcanopy; usually avoid dense foliage and often with mixed flocks (T. Parker).
**Status and habitat:** Widespread in lowland *terra firme* forest in w Amazonia.
**Range:** To 500m. E of Andes from w Meta to se Nariño and undoubtedly s to Amazonas (*subfulvus*). Se Colombia s to n Bolivia and e in Amazonian Brazil to the Guianas.
**Note:** *P. fuscipennis* (incl. *erythronotus*) is merged by some with *P. erythrocercus*.

### 49. BUFF-FRONTED FOLIAGE-GLEANER
*Philydor rufus*          Pl. 26, Map 702
**Identification:** 7.5″ (19cm). *Forehead and long eyestripe cinnamon buff*, dusky line behind eye; crown and hindneck grayish contrasting with brown back; wings and tail rufous; *sides of head and throat bright ochraceous* becoming buffy brown on rest of underparts. Or sim. but crown and back paler grayish brown and underparts more uniform ochraceous (*panerythrus*).
**Similar species:** Buff-throated Foliage-gleaner (55) has whitish throat and lacks bright forehead and rufous wings. Smaller and chunkier Russet Antshrike (p 386) lacks ochraceous forehead and strong facial pattern and has rounded (not pointed) tail feathers.
**Voice:** Two types of *churr*'s, 1 snorting, 1 harsh and croaking, almost froglike (Slud 1964).
**Behavior:** Arboreal and active; hop and twist along branches, glean from foliage on outer portion of limbs or rummage in viny tangles. Usually singly in mixed flocks and easily seen.
**Breeding:** Pair feeding young, 20 June, burrow in bank, upper Anchicayá Val. (Hilty).
**Status and habitat:** Humid and wet forest and

advanced second growth woodland. Perhaps local in Colombia.
**Range:** 900-1800m. Pacific slope from headwaters of Río San Juan (below Cerro Tatamá) to Nariño (*riveti*); lower Cauca Val. (Pto. Valdivia), e slope C Andes s to Caldas (Río Samaná), and w slope E Andes from se Santander to sw Cundinamarca at Fusagasugá (*panerythrus*). Costa Rica and w Panama; mts. of n and s Venez., nw Ecuador, and e Peru to nw Argentina and se Brazil.

### 50. CHESTNUT-WINGED FOLIAGE-GLEANER
*Philydor erythropterus*          Pl. 26, Map 703
**Identification:** 7″ (18cm). Grayish olive above with *contrasting rufous chestnut wings and tail; loral area and throat bright yellowish ochre;* remaining underparts pale buffy gray with yellowish tinge on breast.
**Similar species:** Easily confused with Striped Foliage-gleaner (42), which is larger, streaked buff (esp. above), and differs in behavior (see below). Good marks are the bright orange ochraceous throat and loral area. Also see Rufous-rumped and Rufous-tailed foliage-gleaners (48, 51), both of which lack rufous wings.
**Behavior:** Single birds or pairs follow forest flocks and glean on twigs, foliage, and palm fronds at the ends of limbs (as opposed to *Hyloctistes*, which favors vine tangles or foliage close to trunks) from midlevels to canopy; also frequently hang to inspect curled dead leaves (T. Parker).
**Status and habitat:** Uncommon in *várzea* or partially flooded forest (T. Parker), also sometimes *terra firme* forest.
**Range:** To 500m. E of Andes from w Meta (Villavicencio area) s to Caquetá, Putumayo, and Amazonas (Leticia, 1 taken Aug 1975— J. V. Remsen). S. Venez. (e Amazonas) and e Ecuador to n Bolivia and Amazonian Brazil.

### 51. RUFOUS-TAILED FOLIAGE-GLEANER
*Philydor ruficaudatus*          Pl. 26, Map 704
**Identification:** 6.8″ (17.3cm). *Upperparts incl. wings dull olive contrasting with bright rufous tail; eyestripe and ocular region yellowish buff;* cheeks dusky, vaguely streaked paler; throat yellowish white; remaining underparts dull yellowish olive *indistinctly streaked paler on chest* (hard to see in field).
**Similar species:** See Rufous-rumped Foliage-gleaner (48). Olive-backed Foliage-gleaner (52) has contrasting white throat and no eyestripe. Others (56, 57) are superficially sim. but darker rufescent brown above, not olive, and not so yellowish below.

**Behavior:** Typical of the genus; active as it gleans on live leaves or probes dead curled ones from slender limbs in mid. or upper mid. story (T. Parker).

**Status and habitat:** Rec. from both *várzea* and *terra firme* forest and generally less numerous than *P. erythrocercus*, which it closely resembles.

**Range:** To 500m. E of Andes from w Meta (Villavicencio) to Putumayo and Vaupés and probably Amazonas. The Guianas and s Venez. to n Bolivia and Amazonian Brazil.

[*Automolus*: Resemble *Philydor* but usually larger (7.5″ or 19cm), more robust, and bill heavier; loud 1- to 2-note calls; understory in lowlands.]

## 52. OLIVE-BACKED FOLIAGE-GLEANER

*Automolus infuscatus*          Pl. 26, Map 705

**Identification:** 7.5″ (19cm). Olive brown above with chestnut rump and tail; faint buffy white eyering; *prom. white throat*; underparts grayish white becoming buffy brown on sides, flanks, and under tail coverts; lower mandible yellowish.

**Similar species:** Look for brown head (no eyestripe) and white throat. Easily confused with Crested Foliage-gleaner (53), which has prom. buffy white postocular, slightly more rufescent upperparts, and deeper, stouter bill. Buff-throated Foliage-gleaner (55) has buff throat (e of Andes) and is otherwise buffy brown below.

**Voice:** Alarm a loud nasal *chík-wuk*, rather like a *Synallaxis*; a loud staccato rattle *tu'tu'tu'tu'tu'tu* of var. lengths.

**Behavior:** Typical of the genus. Actively hop and clamber along branches, mostly 1-3m up in sparser undergrowth where they rummage in debris and dead leaves. Usually pairs, occas. several and reg. with mixed forest flocks, esp. those containing antwrens, *Thamnomanes* antbirds, and other furnariids (Hilty; T. Parker).

**Breeding:** BC birds, Nov, Jan, and Apr, Amazonas, Venez. (Friedmann 1948); nest burrow 2m deep (Snethlage *in* Vaurie 1980).

**Status and habitat:** Widespread and common in *várzea* and esp. *terra firme* forest. Meets and overlaps narrowly with *A. dorsalis* at base of e Andes in Caquetá and Putumayo.

**Range:** To 400m. E of Andes from s Meta (Macarena Mts.) and e Guainía (along Río Negro) southward. Surinam, Guyana, and s Venez. to se Peru and Amazonian Brazil.

## 53. CRESTED FOLIAGE-GLEANER

*Automolus dorsalis*          Pl. 26, Map 706

**Identification:** 7.0″ (18cm). No evident crest.

Deep, stout bill. Upperparts incl. wings rufescent brown; rump and tail rufous chestnut; *postocular streak* and faint eyering buffy white; cheeks dusky brown; *prom. white throat*; remaining underparts grayish white becoming buffy brown on flanks; lower mandible yellowish. Some (imm.?) show rufescent eyebrow.

**Similar species:** See very sim. Olive-backed Foliage-gleaner (52).

**Behavior:** Much like Olive-backed Foliage-gleaner.

**Breeding:** BC ♂, June, w Caquetá (Carriker).

**Status and habitat:** Humid foothill forest and adj. mature or secondary *várzea* or along rivers. Predom. a hill country bird and mostly replaced in lowlands away from foothills by Olive-backed Foliage-gleaner.

**Range:** 200-500m (doubtless higher). E base of Andes from w Caquetá (Florencia) southward. E Colombia to Peru (incl. mouth of Río Curaray).

## 54. RUDDY FOLIAGE-GLEANER

*Automolus rubiginosus*          Pl. 26, Map 707

**Identification:** 7.5″ (19cm). Several races. In general, rich ruddy brown above with dark chestnut tail; *throat and chest cinnamon rufous*; remaining underparts buffy brown becoming darker on flanks and under tail coverts. Or darker throughout, above dusky brown, *throat and chest cinnamon rufous*, rest of underparts dark brown and tail black (*nigricauda; saturatus*).

**Similar species:** Essentially a very dark and unmarked foliage-gleaner with contrasting cinnamon throat (all races). The distinctive call is helpful. Very sim. Brown-rumped Foliage-gleaner (57) is paler in center of lower underparts and throat usually more yellow (less cinnamon). Also cf. Uniform Treehunter (62), Ruddy Woodcreeper (p 344), and Tawny-throated Leaftosser (68).

**Voice:** Call e and w of Andes a nasal, whining, and ascending *keeaaah*, often steadily repeated at short intervals.

**Behavior:** Sim. to others of the genus but usually solitary and not with mixed flocks. Active but skulks furtively from 0.1-3m up in undergrowth and very hard to see.

**Breeding:** 8 BC birds, Jan–Oct, n Colombia (Carriker); in s Mexico, burrow 2m deep in bank and 1.2m above stream; nest of rootlets and plant fibers (Rowley 1966).

**Status and habitat:** Humid and wet *terra firme* and *várzea* forests, second growth woodland, and shrubby borders. Mostly foothills w of Andes; also lowlands on Pacific coast where fairly common by voice. In e Peru, where it occurs with Chestnut-crowned Foliage-gleaner, poss. found mostly in *terra firme* forest (T. Parker).

**Range:** To 1800m. Panama border s on Pacific coast to mid. Atrato Val. and n of Andes e to upper Río Nechí (*saturatus*); Baudó Mts. to sw Cauca, perhaps w Nariño (*nigricauda*); Santa Marta Mts. (*rufipectus*); once on w slope E Andes in Cundinamarca (*sasaimae*); e base of Andes in Meta (*cinnamomeigula*), prob. n to Arauca; e base of Andes in Caquetá and Putumayo (*caquetae*), poss. e to w Amazonas. C Mexico spottily to w Ecuador, n Bolivia, extreme nw Brazil, and the Guianas.

## 55. BUFF-THROATED FOLIAGE-GLEANER

*Automolus ochrolaemus*  Pl. 26, Map 708

**Identification:** 7.5″ (19cm). Plain olive brown above with *narrow buff eyering and superciliary*; rump and tail rufous chestnut; *throat whitish (or light buff—turdinus)*; remaining underparts buffy brown; a few vague blurry streaks on chest.

**Similar species:** In Amazonia can be confused with Brown-rumped Foliage-gleaner (57), which lacks the eyestripe and eyering and has an ochraceous orange throat (esp. bright on sides). Chestnut-crowned Foliage-gleaner (56) is darker with conspic. orange eye. Also see 46 and 49. In the hand, note faint chest streaks.

**Voice:** Song a short, unmusical, descending *ke-ke-ka-ka-kakar* mainly morning and evening; alarm a loud descending rattle.

**Behavior:** Like others of the genus, active, poking in debris and dead leaves and hopping and twisting along low branches or through tangles, near ground to 5m up. Alone or sometimes 1 or more with mixed bird flocks.

**Breeding:** 4 BC ♂♂, Mar–Apr, nw Colombia (Carriker; Haffer 1975); nest a burrow dug in bank; 2-3 white eggs (Skutch 1969a).

**Status and habitat:** Widespread in humid *terra firme* and *várzea* forest and second growth woodland. Favors thick tangled undergrowth or dense regrowth around treefalls, creeks, and forest edges.

**Range:** To 1200m. Pacific coast and eastward n of Andes to mid. Magdalena Valley from Aguachica, Cesar, s to Honda, Tolima (*pallidigularis*); e of Andes from w Meta and Vaupés southward (*turdinus*). Poss. ne Vichada. Se Mexico to n Bolivia and Amazonian Brazil.

## 56. CHESTNUT-CROWNED FOLIAGE-GLEANER

*Automolus rufipileatus*  Pl. 26, Map 709

**Identification:** 7.5″ (19cm). *Eyes bright orange yellow. Mainly uniform rufescent brown above* with

slightly contrasting chestnut crown and rufous chestnut rump and tail; underparts brown, more buffy on throat.

**Similar species:** Like Ruddy, Buff-throated, and Brown-rumped foliage-gleaners (54, 55, 57) but appears even more uniform at a distance. Best mark is the conspic. orange yellow eye, but cf. Brown-rumped Foliage-gleaner, which also has red or orange eyes.

**Voice:** Dawn song a loud, nasal, rattling *d'd'd'd'd'd'a*, descending slightly, almost trilled; recalls a *Certhiaxis* spinetail.

**Behavior:** Sim. to other *Automolus*. Pairs or families often follow mixed flocks, esp. those with antbirds and other furnariids, in thick undergrowth along rivers.

**Breeding:** 2 BC ♂♂, June, w Caquetá (Carriker); 2 BC ♂♂, Feb, Amazonas, Venez. (Friedmann 1948).

**Status and habitat:** Tangled undergrowth in *várzea* and river-edge forest and poorly drained second growth woodland. Not inside mature *terra firme* forest.

**Range:** To 500m. E base of E Andes from Río Arauca southward and generally from Meta to Putumayo and Amazonas (photo, Leticia—Hilty). Surinam, Guyana, and Venez. to n Bolivia and Amazonian Brazil.

## 57. BROWN-RUMPED FOLIAGE-GLEANER

*Automolus melanopezus*  Map 710

**Identification:** 8″ (20cm). Eyes red or orange. Rufescent brown above, incl. wings and rump; tail rufous chestnut; *throat ochraceous orange, brighter on sides of throat*; rest of underparts buffy brown, darker on sides and paler in center of lower breast and belly.

**Similar species:** Easily confused with several other *largely uniform* foliage-gleaners. Good marks are eye color (but cf. 56) and bright ochraceous borders (malar area) on throat. Chestnut-crowned (56) and Ruddy foliage-gleaners (54) also look virtually uniform, but former has darker more uniform underparts and contrasting cap, and latter lacks the contrasting rufous chestnut tail. Cf. Buff-throated (55), Rufous-rumped (48), and Rufous-tailed foliage-gleaners (51), latter 2 with different habits.

**Voice:** In se Peru song consists of 2 emphatic notes followed by a fast ser. of harsh notes, *whit-whit-wut-trrrrrrr* (Parker 1982).

**Behavior:** Sim. to others of the genus. One in Peru followed a large furnariid-formicariid flock along banks of forested stream (O'Neill 1974).

**Status and habitat:** Not well known in Colombia. Humid *terra firme* forest and adj. tall second growth in e Ecuador (Pearson et al. 1977). In Amazonian Peru, apparently local, mostly in low-lying forest near water, and often assoc. with bamboo (Parker 1982). Fairly common on upper Río Napo, Ecuador (R. Ridgely). **Range:** To 500m. E of Andes in Putumayo (Pto. Umbría). Se Colombia to e Peru and w Amazonian Brazil.

[*Thripadectes*: Understory of montane forest; large (averaging over 8", or 20cm); robust; bill heavy; most with streaks; more sluggish than previously described foliage-gleaner groups.]

### 58. FLAMMULATED TREEHUNTER
*Thripadectes flammulatus*      Pl. 26, Map 711
**Identification:** 9.5" (24cm). *Blackish above and below*, becoming browner on rump and belly and *boldly striped with buff throughout* (streaks narrower on crown and mantle); wings, rump, and tail uniform chestnut brown.
**Similar species:** A distinctive and strikingly patterned sp. No other Colombian furnariid is so blackish and broadly striped above and below. See Striped Treehunter (59) and much smaller Lineated Foliage-gleaner (43).
**Behavior:** Sim. to other *Thripadectes*, but not often seen.
**Breeding:** BC ♂, June, n end W Andes (Carriker); May, Rancho Grande, Venez. (Schäfer and Phelps 1954); burrow in hillside or earth bank (L. Soderström *in* Vaurie 1980).
**Status and habitat:** Apparently local; undergrowth of humid and wet forest. Seems nowhere numerous. Only 3 mist-net captures in 2 yrs. near San Lorenzo (2200m), Santa Marta Mts. (T. B. Johnson).
**Range:** 1400-3000m (to 800m on Pacific slope of Nariño). Santa Marta Mts. and spottily in all 3 Andean ranges. Nw Venez. s in Andes to w Ecuador.

### 59. STRIPED TREEHUNTER
*Thripadectes holostictus*      Pl. 26, Map 712
**Identification:** 8" (20cm). A smaller edition of Flammulated Treehunter and often not easily told in field. Crown and back blackish narrowly streaked buff; *throat and breast buffy brown, rather diffusely streaked ochraceous buff* (looks yellowish buff below); lower underparts buffy brown with a few pale shaft streaks on upper belly; wings reddish brown; rump and tail dull rufous chestnut. A few birds from C Andes (Quindío area) closely approach size and underpart pattern (more heavily striped even to belly) of Flammulated Treehunter.
**Similar species:** Flammulated Treehunter (58) is larger, usually much blacker, and with broad, crisp, buff streaking against a black ground

color; in Striped Treehunter the streaking is diffused and blurred on a paler brown ground color. Lineated Foliage-gleaner (43) very sim. above but underpart streaking much crisper and thinner and throat plain buffy. Black-billed Treehunter (60) is essentially uniform below.
**Behavior:** Apparently sim. to other *Thripadectes*.
**Breeding:** BC pair, 25 Aug, e Santander (Carriker).
**Status and habitat:** Undergrowth of humid or wet mossy forest. Not well known.
**Range:** 1800-2700m (to 900m on Pacific slope in Cauca). Spottily in all 3 Andean ranges (not rec. n of Cauca in w Andes). Nw Venez. s in Andes to n Bolivia.

### 60. BLACK-BILLED TREEHUNTER
*Thripadectes melanorhynchos*      Map 713
**Identification:** 8" (20cm). Resembles Striped Treehunter above and Streak-capped Treehunter below. Mostly *blackish brown above, crown and back narrowly streaked buff*; wings brown; lower back, rump, and tail rufous chestnut, throat pale yellow ochraceous; feathers of lower throat edged dusky (looks scaled); *rest of underparts uniform ochraceous brown* with a few pale buff shaft lines on chest.
**Similar species:** Only treehunter streaked above and virtually uniform below. See Flammulated (58) and Striped treehunters (59), which are almost identical above but broadly streaked below. Striped Foliage-gleaner (42) has definite streaking on chest and barely overlaps in range. Also cf. Streak-capped Treehunter (61).
**Behavior:** Presum. like others of the genus.
**Status and habitat:** Humid forest; known definitely in Colombia only from 1 locality in mts. In Ecuador seen rarely, inside forest in undergrowth (R. Ridgely).
**Range:** 1200m. E slope of E Andes in Meta (above Villavicencio at Buenavista). E Colombia and e Ecuador (1500-1700m) to s Peru.

### 61. STREAK-CAPPED TREEHUNTER
*Thripadectes virgaticeps*      Pl. 26, Map 714
**Identification:** 8.5" (22cm). *Crown and nape blackish with a few fine white shaft streaks*; back and wings dark rufescent brown to wood brown becoming dark rufous chestnut on rump and tail; *throat and chest cinnamon obscurely streaked brown*, sometimes with a few pale shaft streaks spreading onto upper breast; rest of underparts bright cinnamon washed olive on breast and brownish on sides.
**Similar species:** Not easily told from Uniform Treehunter (62) but larger, brighter cinnamon below (not dark brown), blackish crown always with a few whitish shaft streaks, and

without latter's facial markings. Black-billed Treehunter (60) has prom. streaks on mantle and back.

**Voice:** Raspy, nasal *jwick* alarm or scold; call a hard, low-pitched *ju-dut*, quickly.

**Behavior:** Active but furtive and hard to see as it hops about and probes mossy limbs, tangles, and debris mostly 0.5-5m up in dense undergrowth. Single birds, pairs, or families, and more often away from mixed flocks than in them.

**Breeding:** 7 BC ♂♂, Mar–July, se Antioquia and sw Huila (Carriker); 5 burrows in forested road banks, Apr–Aug (Hilty), and a May juv. (Miller 1963) in W Andes above Cali (1800m).

**Status and habitat:** Fairly common. Undergrowth of humid and wet mossy forest ("cloud forest") and tangled forest borders. Apparently most numerous about 1700-2000m and replaced at lower el. on the Pacific slope by *T. ignobilis.* Reg. in Andes above Cali, and in general the *Thripadectes* most often seen in Colombia.

**Range:** 1200-2500m. Pacific slope from headwaters of Río San Juan southward and on adj. e slope in Valle; e slope C Andes in se Antioquia near Caldas boundary, head of Magdalena Val. (sw Huila) and e slope of Andes in Nariño. N and nw Venez. to e and w Ecuador.

## 62. UNIFORM TREEHUNTER

*Thripadectes ignobilis*      Pl. 26, Map 715

**Identification:** 7.5″ (19cm). Only member of the genus *virtually unstreaked above.* Upperparts, wings, and tail dark rufescent brown; narrow buff eyering and *faint buff postocular streak*; underparts plain dark brown with *buffy streaks on throat* and a few shaft streaks to breast; sides of head with a few pale shaft streaks; bill shorter and thicker than others of the genus.

**Similar species:** A small, dark-plumaged *Thripadectes* lacking strong pattern. Good marks are uniform upperparts, eyering, and postocular. See Streak-capped Treehunter (61), Ruddy Foliage-gleaner (54), and Striped Foliage-gleaner (42). Tawny-throated Leaftosser (68) very different in behavior.

**Behavior:** Actively hops along branches and vine tangles, often poking and rustling debris; usually 1-5m up in cluttered undergrowth, occas. higher. Mostly seen singly and more often away from mixed flocks than in them.

**Status and habitat:** Wet forest in foothills and lower slopes; not found with any regularity but apparently more numerous at lower el.

**Range:** 200-2500m. Pacific slope from n Antioquia (upper Río Sucio) southward. W Colombia to sw Ecuador (El Oro—R. Ridgely).

[*Xenops*: Small; bill straight, or lower mandible upturned; white malar (except 63); broad diagonal cinnamon band on wing.]

## 63. RUFOUS-TAILED XENOPS

*Xenops milleri*      Pl. 25, Map 716

**Identification:** 4″ (10.2cm). Bill straight; *no white malar.* Crown blackish sharply streaked buff and with weak yellowish white eyestripe; *upper back olive brown streaked buffy white*; rump and tail plain rufous; wings blackish; tertials and a broad diagonal band across remiges cinnamon (forms a stripe esp. prom. in flight); *underparts pale olive brown streaked whitish.*

**Similar species:** Only xenops *lacking* a crescentic white malar streak. Solid rufous tail (no black streaks) diagnostic but sometimes difficult to see in field. See Slender-billed Xenops (64).

**Behavior:** Typical of the genus. Sidle along small bare branches and vines, constantly turning from side to side as they search for prey. Normally with canopy or subcanopy mixed flocks containing tanagers, greenlets, and antwrens.

**Status and habitat:** Upper levels of humid *terra firme* forest incl. sandy-belt forest. Only 1 Colombian specimen but several sight recs. Found reg. n of Leticia.

**Range:** To 500m. E of Andes at e base of Macarena Mts., Meta; sightings in Vaupés (El Dorado, June 1976—R. Ridgely) and Amazonas (Leticia—J. V. Remsen; Hilty). Prob. e Guainía (on Venez. side of Río Negro). Fr. Guiana, Surinam, and s Venez. to se Peru and Brazil s of Amazon between Río Purús and Juruá.

## 64. SLENDER-BILLED XENOPS

*Xenops tenuirostris*      Pl. 25, Map 717

**Identification:** 4.2″ (10.7cm). Bill short and pointed, lower mandible slightly upturned at tip. Crown brown finely streaked white; buffy white eyestripe and *conspic. crescentic white streak on lower cheek*; rest of *upperparts cinnamon brown streaked buffy*; remiges dusky, crossed by broad diagonal cinnamon band; tail rufous with 2 longitudinal black stripes; *below grayish olive streaked whitish*; throat whitish.

**Similar species:** Much like Rufous-tailed Xenops (63) but shows white cheek stripe; at close range watch for black in tail. Plain Xenops (66) is unstreaked above. Streaked Xenops (65) is almost identical (prob. not separable in field) but larger, more streaked above, and with thicker and more obviously upturned bill; latter mainly a mt. bird but range overlap poss. at e base of Andes from Caquetá southward.

**Behavior:** Typical of the genus.

**Breeding:** BC ♂, 15 May, Mitú (Olivares 1964b).
**Status and habitat:** Humid forest incl. sandy-belt forest. Known from only 2 definite localities in Colombia.
**Range:** To 500m (to 1000m se Ecuador). E of Andes in w Caquetá (Morelia) and Vaupés (Mitú). Doubtless also e Vichada and e Guainía (on Venez. side of Río Orinoco at Caño Cataniapo, and on Río Negro at San Carlos). Fr. Guiana, Surinam, and s Venez. to nw Bolivia and Amazonian Brazil.

### 65. STREAKED XENOPS
*Xenops rutilans*                    Ill. 77, Map 718
**Identification:** 4.5″ (11.4cm). Bill short, lower mandible decidedly upturned at tip. Brown above, blacker on cap, and streaked pale buff; wings dusky, crossed by broad diagonal cinnamon band; tail rufous with 2 longitudinal black streaks (or almost no black—*phelpsi*); eyebrow buffy white and *conspic. crescentic stripe on lower cheeks white*; throat whitish; *rest of underparts olive brown streaked buffy white*.
**Similar species:** Plain Xenops (66) is unstreaked above and on belly and usually found at lower el. Also see smaller lowland (rarely foothills) Slender-billed Xenops (64), which is prob. inseparable in field, and Spectacled Prickletail (32).
**Voice:** Call a quick descending ser. of shrill *zeet* notes.
**Behavior:** Gleans bare slender twigs, usually by hanging beneath them and hitching along sideways; lower midlevel to canopy. Mostly pairs or 3's that keep rather close together as they follow mixed flocks; most often with flocks

77. STREAKED XENOPS

containing furnariids, flycatchers, and other insectivores.
**Breeding:** Pair excavating cavity 10m up in dead limb, Mar, W Andes in Valle (Brown). BC ♀, Aug, Santander (Carriker).
**Status and habitat:** Fairly common in humid forest and forest edges in the mts. Replaced at lower el. by Plain Xenops.
**Range:** 1500-2800m (mostly below 2400m). Santa Marta Mts. (*phelpsi*); Perijá Mts. and n end of E Andes s to Santander (*perijanus*); E Andes in Cuninamarca and W and C Andes (*heterurus*). Costa Rica s to Argentina and se Brazil.

### 66. PLAIN XENOPS
*Xenops minutus*                    Pl. 25, Map 719
**Identification:** 4.8″ (12.2cm). Bill short, lower mandible decidedly upturned at tip. *Above plain brown* with buffy eyestripe and *conspic. crescentic white streak on lower cheeks*; wings dusky with broad diagonal cinnamon band; tail rufous with 2 longitudinal black streaks; throat whitish; *rest of underparts dull olive brown*, sometimes with a few whitish streaks on chest.
**Similar species:** Differs from all other Colombian *Xenops* by essentially unstreaked upper and underparts. Also cf. Spectacled Prickletail (32).
**Voice:** Note a soft chip, uttered singly or rapidly in a trill; song a very fast chattering trill, accelerating then slowing at end, *dit dit dit-dit 'dt'd'd'd'd'd'd'd'a'a'a'*.
**Behavior:** Sim. to other *Xenops*.
**Breeding:** 10 BC birds, Jan–May, nw Colombia (Carriker); June and Sept nests, Panama (Willis and Eisenmann 1979); cavity excavated in dead stub, 1-10m up; 2 white eggs (Skutch 1969a).
**Status and habitat:** Fairly common in humid and wet forest, forest edge, second growth, and lighter woodland. Replaced at higher el. by Streaked Xenops.
**Range:** To 1800m (stragglers higher). Wooded areas throughout. Se Mexico to ne Argentina and se Brazil.

### 67. GRAY-THROATED LEAFTOSSER (LEAFSCRAPER)
*Sclerurus albigularis*                    Pl. 26, Map 720
**Identification:** 6.5″ (16.5cm). Bill long, rather slender, and straight (lower mandible can look slightly upturned). Above dark brown becoming chestnut on rump; tail black; *throat pale grayish white bordered below by a broad band of cinnamon rufous on chest*; rest of underparts dark grayish brown.
**Similar species:** From any other leaftosser by ashy gray throat (becomes whitish on upper

throat) and fairly distinct cinnamon rufous chest band. In nw Meta and Macarena Mts. see Tawny-throated, Short-billed, and Black-tailed leaftossers (68, 69, 70).
**Voice:** Song in Venez. *tuee, tuee, tuee, tweéep*, each note inflected, sometimes last doubled. In conflict, *chuee-chuee-chueee che'e'e'e'e'e'e'e*, much faster than song (P. Schwartz recording).
**Behavior:** Sim. to other *Sclerurus*. See Tawny-throated Leaftosser.
**Breeding:** 3 burrows excavated in bank, May–Jun, 1600m, Santa Marta Mts.; 2 white eggs (Todd and Carriker 1922).
**Status and habitat:** Floor and undergrowth of humid forest. Not well known in Colombia.
**Range:** 1500-2100m in Santa Marta Mts.; n end of Perijá Mts. (Cerro Alto del Cedro, 450m; Monte Elias, 1800m) and e slope of E Andes in Meta (above Villavicencio, 1200m; Pico Renjifo in Macarena Mts., 1800m). Costa Rica and w Panama; n Venez. s on e slope of Andes spottily to nw Bolivia.

## 68. TAWNY-THROATED LEAFTOSSER (LEAFSCRAPER)
*Sclerurus mexicanus*               Pl. 26, Map 721
**Identification:** 6.0″ (15cm). Bill rather long (1″, or 25mm) and *slightly drooped*. Rich dark brown above becoming brighter and *more rufescent on rump*; tail black; *throat cinnamon rufous* gradually darkening to deep brown on lower underparts.
**Similar species:** See very sim. Short-billed Leaftosser (69). Could be confused with Song Wren (p 540), which has bare blue ocular area, barring on wings and tail, and sometimes whitish streaking on hindneck. Also cf. Ruddy Foliage-gleaner (54).
**Voice:** Song in Costa Rica a descending ser. of sharp *squee* notes (Slud 1964); call a sharp, chipmunklike *chick*.
**Behavior:** Like other *Sclerurus*, a furtive, largely terrestrial forest bird, usually seen when it flushes ahead with a sharp call. Hops (not walks) on ground or logs, noisily tossing aside dead leaves or probing soft earth. Solitary or in well separated 2's, not with mixed flocks.
**Breeding:** 3 BC birds, Apr–May, n Antioquia (Carriker).
**Status and habitat:** Uncommon in moist places in humid and wet forest, mostly in foothills and lower slopes. Poss. local.
**Range:** To 2000m. Pacific coast, w slope of W Andes (e slope in Valle), n end C Andes (incl. Snía. San Lucas), Perijá Mts., and w slope of E Andes in Santander (near Bucaramanga) and e slope in Meta, incl. Macarena Mts. (Pico

Renjifo). Prob. entire e slope E Andes. Se Mexico to n Bolivia and se Brazil.

## 69. SHORT-BILLED LEAFTOSSER (LEAFSCRAPER)
*Sclerurus rufigularis*              Pl. 26, Map 722
**Identification:** 6″ (15cm). *Bill shorter than other leaftossers* (0.6″ vs 1″, or 15mm vs 25mm), and virtually straight. Much like Tawny-throated Leaftosser, differing in that throat is more buffy ochraceous (less cinnamon), and bill markedly shorter and straighter; may also show suggestion of cinnamon rufous eyestripe and cinnamon area around eye.
**Similar species:** Black-tailed Leaftosser (70) differs in noticeably longer bill, whitish throat faintly scaled dusky, and in the hand, slightly less contrasting reddish chestnut rump.
**Behavior:** See Tawny-throated Leaftosser.
**Breeding:** 2 BC birds, May, Vaupés (Olivares 1964b); 2 more, Apr, upper Orinoco, Venez. (Friedmann 1948).
**Status and habitat:** Floor and undergrowth of humid forest, incl. sandy-belt and swampy forests. Not well known in Colombia. Two specimens collected by Von Sneidern at Estación de Bombeo Guamués, w Putumayo (near Nariño boundary), 900m, 1971 (Fitzpatrick and Willard 1982).
**Range:** Mainly below 500m; to 1800m in Macarena Mts. (Pico Renjifo). E of Andes where known from sw Meta, w Caquetá (Río Pescado s of Florencia), w Putumayo, and Vaupés (Mitú). The Guainas, s Venez. (incl. Río Negro), Amazonian Brazil, and n Bolivia.

## 70. BLACK-TAILED LEAFTOSSER (LEAFSCRAPER)
*Sclerurus caudacutus*              Pl. 26, Map 723
**Identification:** 7″ (18cm). Bill rather long and straight, lower mandible slightly upturned at tip. Rich dark brown above becoming rufescent on rump; tail black; *throat white*, the feathers edged brownish (looks faintly scaled); rest of underparts dark brown.
**Similar species:** From any other Amazonian Leaftosser by whitish throat. Could overlap range of Short-billed Leaftosser (69), which has short bill, Tawny-throated Leaftosser (68), which has slightly downcurved bill, and Gray-throated Leaftosser (67), which has chest band.
**Voice:** Song accelerates then slows and fades, *queet, queet queet-queet queet'queet'ke'ke'keke' queet'queet-que-queet*, loud and emphatic (P. Schwartz recording).
**Behavior:** Much like Tawny-throated Leaftosser.
**Status and habitat:** Moist shady forest floor, esp. around fallen logs in humid *terra firme*

forest. Common at Limoncocha, Ecuador (Pearson et al. 1977).

**Range:** To 500m. E of Andes from w Meta (Villavicencio; Macarena Mts.) to Caquetá and se Nariño; once in Vaupés (1 netted, El Dorado, June 1976—R. Ridgely). The Guianas and s Venez. (incl. Río Negro), e Ecuador and e Peru (incl. mouth of Río Curaray), to n Bolivia and Amazonian and se Brazil.

## 71. SCALY-THROATED LEAFTOSSER (LEAFSCRAPER)

*Sclerurus guatemalensis*      Pl. 26, Map 724

**Identification:** 6.5″ (16.5cm). Bill with slight droop. Rich dark brown above becoming blackish on tail (no contrasting rump); *throat white, the feathers edged blackish giving scaly appearance*; chest rufescent brown with suggestion of paler spotting; lower underparts dark brown.

**Similar species:** Only leaftosser w of Andes that lacks a contrasting rufescent rump; throat diagnostic if seen.

**Voice:** Alarm is usual *wheek*; song a descending ser. of accented whistles, about 3 per sec, *whit whit whit peet peet peet pert pert*, often repeated over and over (Willis and Eisenmann 1979).

**Behavior:** See Tawny-throated Leaftosser.

**Breeding:** BC ♂, May, s Córdoba (Carriker); 1 nestling in stream bank burrow, 28 Mar, Barro Colorado Isl. Panama; cup nest of leaf stems (Skutch 1969a).

**Status and habitat:** Damp floor of humid forest. Absent from wettest Pacific coast zone but occurs both n and s of it.

**Range:** To 900m. Pacific coast s to Baudo Mts.

(Río Jurubidá) and e in humid lowlands n of Andes to mid. Magdalena Val. (Snía. de San Lucas; nw of Bucaramanga). May occur in sw Nariño as reported n to Esmeraldas, Ecuador. Se Mexico to n Colombia; nw Ecuador.

## 72. SHARP-TAILED STREAMCREEPER

*Lochmias nematura*      Pl. 26, Map 725

**Identification:** 6″ (15cm). Shape recalls *Sclerurus*. Bill slender and slightly decurved. Uniform rich dark brown above; tail black; sides of head and *underparts dark brown thickly spotted and scaled white*.

**Similar species:** Closely resembles Spotted Barbtail (38) but hops on ground, not up mossy trunks. Posture much like that of a leaftosser.

**Voice:** A ser. of high-pitched trills, all on same pitch, is prob. the song (T. Parker).

**Behavior:** Hops sneakily among dense low tangles, on ground, or on rocks along streams and pecks or flicks leaves. Usually solitary or in well-spaced 2's; flight jerky and erratic, like *Sclerurus* (Wetmore 1972; Hilty).

**Breeding:** Mainly rainy season (May–June) in Rancho Grande, Venez. (Schäfer and Phelps 1954). Brazil nest a densely woven ball of rootlets and plant material in burrow; 2 white eggs (Goeldi 1894).

**Status and habitat:** Uncommon and apparently local; humid mossy forest along streams in mts.

**Range:** 1300-2100m. W Andes at north end and in Valle and Cauca, w slope of C Andes in Valle and both slopes of E Andes in Cundinamarca. Prob. Mt. Tacarcuna (rec. on Panama side). E Panama to Venez. and s to ne Argentina and se Brazil.

# ANTBIRDS: Formicariidae (136)

Antbirds are a large and complex family of neotropical passeriformes. Found from southern Mexico to northern Argentina and Paraguay, they reach greatest diversity and abundance in the vast rain forest of the Amazon basin. They are most closely related to ovenbirds (Furnariidae), differing in tarsal scutellation and in their hooked bill. Except for the terrestrial species, most are sexually dimorphic. They occur in virtually all Colombian habitats from sea level to treeline or above but are much less numerous at higher elevations. Despite their name, relatively few are persistently associated with ants. Those that are, including especially *Percnostola, Myrmeciza, Pithys, Gymnopithys, Rhegmatorhina, Hylophylax, Phaenostictus* and *Phlegopsis*, follow army ants (mainly *Eciton* sp. and *Labidus* sp.) and capture prey flushed by the raiding ant columns on or near the forest floor. Other antbirds occur from the ground to the canopy. Their name is often suggestive (though not necessarily correctly) of their behavior or appearance, e.g., antshrike, antwren, antvireo, fire-eye, bare-eye. The terrestrial members of the family including *Chamaeza, Formicarius, Myrmornis, Pittasoma, Grallaria, Hylopezus, Myrmothera* and *Grallaricula*, are, as a group, the most difficult to observe and among the least known of all South American birds. The calls of many are loud, distinctive, sometimes unusual, and may be the only indication of the bird's presence. Nests are varied, often simple suspended baskets; a few are pensile pouches or are in cavities. Much of what is known about antbirds in life is due to the pioneering studies of E. O. Willis (see, e.g., 1967, 1972c, 1973, and references under species accounts).

## 1. FASCIATED ANTSHRIKE

*Cymbilaimus lineatus*     Pls. 27, XIII, Map 726
**Identification:** 7" (18cm). Heavy hooked bill. Eyes red. ♂: crown black usually with a few fine white bars; rest of *upperparts, wings, and tail black narrowly barred white*; below narrowly barred black and white. ♀: *crown chestnut*; upperparts, wings, and tail black narrowly barred buff; below *buff narrowly barred black*.
**Similar species:** ♂ Undulated Antshrike (2) is *decidedly larger* and more robust, with black throat and faint wavy white barring; ♀ Barred and Lined antshrikes (6, 8) are coarsely (not finely) barred and have yellow eyes. ♀ Undulated Antshrike is *much larger* and rufous barred black above and below (not with underparts buff barred black), *incl. crown*.
**Voice:** Song a steady, repeated ser. of soft, resonant, whistled notes at about 2 per sec, *ouee, ouee, ouee* . . . , ventriloquial; each note falls, then rises in pitch; alarm a nasal *wanyurk* (Eisenmann 1952; C. Munn).
**Behavior:** Usually in pairs in forest midlevels, occas. higher or lower where there are dense vines and leaves. Move slowly and deliberately as they peer for large insects. Easily overlooked unless calling or noted with mixed flocks. Seldom follow army ants (Oniki and Willis 1972).
**Breeding:** 7 BC birds, Mar–May, n and e Antioquia (Carriker); loosely woven cup fastened by rim, 2-8m up; 2 creamy white eggs spotted dark brown and lilac (Wetmore 1972; Skutch 1972).
**Status and habitat:** Uncommon to mod. common in vine-tangled forest borders or openings inside forest; also second growth woodland and dense foliage along streams; less frequently treetops inside forest.
**Range:** To 900m. Humid forested regions throughout except Santa Marta area, drier Carib. region, and llanos e of Andes. Se Honduras to n Bolivia and Amazonian Brazil.

## 2. UNDULATED ANTSHRIKE

*Frederickena unduligera*     Pl. XIII, Map 727
**Identification:** 9" (23cm). *Very large.* Heavy hooked bill. Slightly crested. Eyes red. ♂: *throat and chest uniform black*; otherwise *entirely black with fine wavy grayish white barring and freckling.* ♀: crown chestnut and *upperparts rufescent brown, both barred black*; underparts bright rufous barred black; tail black with narrow gray bars. Subad. ♂: black more or less barred and scaled buff and white throughout or with patches of solid black on throat. In *Frederickena* the tail is rather small and narrow for size of bird.
**Similar species:** See Fasciated Antshrike (1). ♂ Barred and Lined antshrikes (6, 8) are

smaller and more coarsely barred; ♀ Undulated is only Colombian antshrike completely barred rufous and black *above and below (incl.* crown).
**Voice:** Song a steady ser., *uué, uué, uué* . . . , about 11-16 notes, much like Fasciated Antshrike but faster with more notes (latter usually gives 4-6 note song), and higher-pitched (Hilty). In response to playback a loud *chee-chee-chee-chee-chee*, repeated (T. Parker). Not as vocal as smaller *Thamnophilus*.
**Behavior:** A skulker. Single birds or pairs are retiring and very hard to see as they hop from fallen trunk to trunk or in vines and dense stands of saplings; keep mostly 1-3m up.
**Status and habitat:** Uncommon in dense cluttered undergrowth near treefall openings or at edges of humid *terra firme* forest, esp. where there is rank second growth with fallen logs, *Heliconia* and saplings.
**Range:** To 500m. E of Andes from w Caquetá to Putumayo; also Amazonas (no specimens). E Colombia to e Peru and w Amazonian Brazil incl. upper Río Negro.

## 3. GREAT ANTSHRIKE

*Taraba major*     Pls. 27, XIII, Map 728
**Identification:** 8" (20cm). Heavy hooked bill. *Eyes red.* Slightly crested. ♂: *black above* with white tips on wing coverts forming 2 wing bars and portions of a third; *underparts white*; tail black narrowly fringed white (or tail barred white from below—*semifasciatus*). ♀: *rufous brown above, pure white below* tinged brownish on flanks and under tail coverts. Imm. ♀ has gray brown iris and rufous wing coverts.
**Similar species:** A robust and widespread bird easily told by bright red eyes and 2-toned color pattern. See much smaller Black-and-white Antbird (70).
**Voice:** Song by both sexes an accelerated ("bouncing ball") ser. of nasal *cuk* notes, rather drawn out, trogonlike, and usually ending abruptly with a snarled *quaah*.
**Behavior:** Pairs hop and peer deliberately in vine tangles and thickets and usually keep out of sight; mostly 1-5m up. Seldom follow mixed flocks or ant swarms.
**Breeding:** 4 BC birds, Apr–May, nw Colombia (Carriker); open cup nest suspended by rim low in thicket; 2 eggs, cream marked brown and lilac (Skutch 1969a).
**Status and habitat:** Fairly common in dense overgrown clearings and bushy forest borders.
**Range:** To 1400m (occas. to 1800m). Gulf of Urabá s on Pacific coast to Barbacoas, sw Nariño and in Cauca Val. in Valle (*obscurus*); extreme sw Nariño (*transandeanus*); Sinú Val. e to mid. Magdalena Val. s to n Tolima, nw base

of Santa Marta Mts. and e base of E Andes s to Macarena Mts. in Meta (*granadensis*); e Vichada (*semifasciatus*); Caquetá and Putumayo to Amazonas (*melanurus*). Se Mexico to n Argentina, Uruguay, and sw Brazil.

### 4. BLACK-CRESTED ANTSHRIKE

*Sakesphorus canadensis*     Pl. 27, Map 729

**Identification:** 6.2″ (15.7cm). Conspic. crest. ♂: *entire head black* (sometimes mixed white), the black *continuing and narrowing to a point on lower breast*; narrow nuchal collar and rest of underparts white; sides and flanks gray; back rufous brown to brownish black; wings black edged and spotted white forming 2 bars; tail black tipped white. ♀: *crown chestnut*; sides of head whitish speckled black; rest of upperparts bright cinnamon brown; wings like ♂; underparts light buff to cinnamon, whiter on throat and lightly streaked black on breast; tail black tipped white.

**Similar species:** ♂ easily told by conspic. crested black head outlined in white; ♂ Black-backed Antshrike (5) has solid black head, nape, and back. ♀ resembles ♀ Black-backed Antshrike but crown chestnut (not dusky brown) and tail mainly black (not chestnut).

**Voice:** Call by both sexes an accelerating ser. of about 10 *took* notes rising slightly; higher-pitched than Barred Antshrike.

**Behavior:** Pairs or families peer and hop about in thickets and bushes or ascend into subcanopy edges of lighter woodland. Inconspic. but not hard to see and sometimes with mixed flocks.

**Breeding:** 3 BC ♀♀, Aug–Sep, Bolívar (Carriker; MCN); Jan nest, ne Meta (S. Furniss); Jun–Sep, upper Orinoco (Cherrie 1916); thin-walled cup suspended by rim in low fork; 2 white eggs spotted reddish brown.

**Status and habitat:** Fairly common in dry to moist regions in scrub with scattered bushes and trees, lighter woodland, gallery forest, mangroves, and occas. humid forest borders.

**Range:** To 400m. From n Chocó (Río Truandó) and lower Atrato ne in Carib. lowlands to e Guajira, s to mid. Magdalena Val. (near Bucaramanga) and e of Andes to Río Guaviare (locally to Amazonas). The Guianas and Venez. to e Peru (not Ecuador) and n and s Brazil. Trinidad.

### 5. BLACK-BACKED ANTSHRIKE

*Sakesphorus melanonotus*     Pl. 27, Map 730

**Identification:** 6.2″ (15.7cm). ♂: *black above with gray rump*; wing bars and edges of remiges white; upper tail coverts and tips of central tail feathers white; underparts black; sides, flanks, and under tail coverts white. ♀: *crown blackish*; back buffy brown; wings dusky brown,

coverts and inner remiges edged buff; sides of head and underparts buff, sometimes mottled and lightly streaked dusky; *tail chestnut, outer feather edged buffy white.*

**Similar species:** See Black-crested Antshrike (4).

**Voice:** A short throaty roll *rrrrrrrr*; in conflict, *curr-ah* (P. Schwartz recording).

**Behavior:** Pairs are inconspic. as they hop deliberately, 0.1–5m up in dense dry tangles; occas. on ground, and almost continually wag tails downward.

**Breeding:** 7 BC birds, Mar–Oct, n Colombia (Carriker); May–July in Santa Marta area (S. M. Russell; Todd and Carriker 1922); open unlined cup suspended by rim to thorny bush; 2 white eggs marked with purple.

**Status and habitat:** Uncommon (easily overlooked) in thickets in semiarid scrub, dry thorn forest, or riparian woodland in dry zones. Less numerous than Black-crested Antshrike and the 2 are not usually found together. Black-backed usually favors drier vegetation. Most easily found in stream-side thickets and woodland s of Cúcuta.

**Range:** To 400m. Carib. region from Barranquilla e to Guajira and s to upper Cesar Val. and s Magdalena; Zulia Val., e Norte de Santander. Ne Colombia and nw Venez.

### 6. BARRED ANTSHRIKE

*Thamnophilus doliatus*     Pls. 27, XIII, Map 731

**Identification:** 6″ (15cm). Crested. Bill fairly heavy and hooked. Eyes yellow. ♂: crown black; (with concealed white at base—e of Andes s to Meta); *above black rather coarsely barred white, below evenly barred black and white.* ♀ very different: *bright cinnamon rufous above*, sides of head and hindneck buff streaked and mottled black, *underparts uniform cinnamon buff*, paler on throat. Amt. of black barring on underparts of ♂ var. with subsp.

**Similar species:** Very sim. ♂ Lined Antshrike (8) has narrower white bars (appears blacker at distance) but is best told by accompanying ♀, which is barred below (the 2 spp. slightly overlap in range at e base of Andes). ♂ Bar-crested (7), also *very* sim., differs by barred crown, ♀ by barred underparts.

**Voice:** Frequently heard song by both ♂ and ♀ a nasal accelerating *hu, hu hu hu huhuhuuuu-wank*, like "bouncing ball," also a guttural growl, *gurrr*.

**Behavior:** Usually in pairs 1-6m up and well-concealed in foliage. Peer and glean for large arthropods like most other antshirkes; occas. follow army ants.

**Breeding:** 1 BC bird, Apr, Snía. San Lucas; 1 in July, Zulia Val. (Carriker); 2 laying ♀♀,

Jan, upper Magdalena Val. (Miller 1947). In Panama Mar–Aug; loose open cup suspended from low fork; 2 white eggs spotted dark brown or gray (Wetmore 1972).

**Status and habitat:** Common in shrubby forest borders and overgrown clearings and thickets, rarely inside forest. *Mostly* replaced in foothills at e base of Andes by Lined Antshrike and in Cauca Val. and foothills and higher above the Magdalena Val. by Bar-crested Antshrike.

**Range:** Mainly below 800m; to 1500m in w Cundinamarca, to 1400m in se Boyacá. Gulf of Urabá e to w Guajira and s in entire Magdalena Val. to s Huila; e of Andes spottily throughout s to Amazonas. Mexico to w Peru. The Guianas, Venez. s to Bolivia, Argentina, and Paraguay. Trinidad and Tobago.

## 7. BAR-CRESTED ANTSHRIKE

*Thamnophilus multistriatus*  Pls. 27, XIII,
Map 732

**Identification:** 6.2″ (15.7cm). Eyes yellow. ♂: sim. to Barred Antshrike but *crown barred black and white*. ♀ very different: *rufous chestnut above, sides of head and nuchal collar streaked black and white, underparts evenly barred black and white*.

**Similar species:** ♂'s barred crown is diagnostic but hard to see. See Barred Antshrike (6), which appears to overlap in w Cundinamarca and e Boyacá. Range of Lined Antshrike (8) not proved to overlap.

**Voice:** Much like Barred Antshrike but lazier and without marked acceleration at end; typically a 6- to 10-note *dü dü dü du du-du-da'da'*.

**Behavior:** Much like Barred Antshrike though seems to ascend into subcanopy of trees more frequently.

**Breeding:** 6 BC birds, May–June, Antioquia and e Caldas (Carriker); 3 BC ♂♂, Mar–May, near Cali (Miller 1963); white eggs thickly spotted and streaked red brown (Sclater and Salvin 1879).

**Status and habitat:** Fairly common in shrubby borders of dry to humid forest and in clearings, parks and cultivated areas with thickets and trees. Replaced in e Andean foothills by Lined Antshrike and at lower el. (local overlap) elsewhere by Barred Antshrike.

**Range:** 900-2200m. Pacific slope (to 400m) in upper Dagua and upper Patía vals.; e slope W Andes e to w slope of E Andes and s to n Nariño; e slope E Andes in Norte de Santander and n Boyacá. Venez. (Perijá Mts.) and Colombia.

## 8. LINED ANTSHRIKE

*Thamnophilus palliatus*  Pls. 27, XIII,
Map 733

**Identification:** 6″ (15cm). Eyes yellow or whit-ish. ♂: sim. to Barred Antshrike with crown uniform black, but upperparts black with *very narrow white bars; below black narrowly barred white* (not evenly barred black and white). ♀ sim. to Bar-crested Antshrike but darker, more chestnut above, and blacker below (black bars wider than white bars); flanks tinged buffy brown.

**Similar species:** ♂ appears decidedly blacker (esp. on back) than very sim. Barred Antshrike (6); in hand lacks white at base of crown (cf. 6). From ♂ Bar-crested Antshrike (7), which should not overlap in range, by narrower white bars and uniform black crown. ♀ doubtfully separable in field from Bar-crested.

**Voice:** Song a slow, accelerating, "bouncing ball" ser. almost identical to Barred Antshrike; given by both sexes.

**Behavior:** Much like Barred Antshrike.

**Status and habitat:** Low in second growth woodland, viny forest borders and overgrown clearings. Mostly foothills and lower slopes. Usually less numerous and above range of Barred Antshrike which it narrowly overlaps.

**Range:** 100-1200m. E base of E Andes from Catatumbo lowlands (Petrólea) to Macarena Mts. and Nariño. Colombia to n Bolivia and Brazil s of Amazon e to Río Madeira.

## 9. BLACK ANTSHRIKE

*Thamnophilus nigriceps*  Pl. 27, Map 734

**Identification:** 6.0″ (15cm). Slightly crested. Fairly heavy hooked bill; eyes brown. ♂: *entirely black* with white under wing coverts and inner webs of inner flight feathers. ♀: uniform rufous brown above; *head and underparts black streaked buffy white*; breast and sides grayish; belly uniform buffy brown.

**Similar species:** ♂ Slaty Antshrike (16) and Jet Antbird (62) have white on wings and tail; both sexes of Immaculate Antbird (86) have bare blue orbital areas. ♀ easily told by streaking on underparts.

**Voice:** Song a nasal slightly accelerating *kuok, kuok, kuok, kuok-ku-ku-ku-ku* as bird pounds tail downward (recalls song of White-shouldered Antshrike). Calls incl. a hollow nasal *peero*, 1 to several times, a rapid querulous *kuo-lu-lu-lu*, and a nasal growl.

**Behavior:** Pairs are usually easy to see as hop and peer for large arthropods like other *Thamnophilus*, mostly 1-7m up along woodland edges.

**Breeding:** 7 BC birds, Jan–July, Cesar to Córdoba (Carriker).

**Status and habitat:** Common in or near edges of humid forest and lighter woodland, and viny second growth and thickets in clearing. May replace Barred Antshrike in taller growth and more wooded regions.

**Range:** To 600m. From Gulf of Urabá region s in Atrato Val. to 7°10'N, ne in n lowlands to Snía. de San Jacinto, sw base of Santa Marta Mts. (Fundación), w base Perijá Mts., and s to lower Cauca Val. (Tarazá, 7°35'N) and mid. Magdalena Val. in n Tolima (Honda). E Panama and n Colombia.

**Note:** Cocha Antshrike (*Thamnophilus praecox*), known from a single ♀ on Río Lagarto Cocha, ne Ecuador near Río Putumayo, should occur in se Colombia. ♀ very sim. to ♀ White-shouldered Antbird but smaller and without bare ocular area: 6.5"; head, throat, and upper breast black with fine white streaks on forecrown; otherwise tawny ochraceous with a band of cinnamon at base of primaries. ♂ unknown.

### 10. BLACKISH-GRAY ANTSHRIKE

*Thamnophilus nigrocinereus*     Pl. 29, Map 735
**Identification:** 6.5" (16.5cm). Strong hooked bill. ♂: *crown blackish*; back slaty gray somewhat mixed blackish on mantle; concealed interscapular patch white; wings black, the *wing coverts narrowly fringed white* forming several narrow bars, flight feathers edged white; *tail blackish tipped white*; below gray, paler on abdomen. ♀: *crown and sides of head blackish*, grayer on cheeks; rest of upperparts brown; wing coverts narrowly tipped cinnamon rufous; underparts and under wing coverts *cinnamon rufous*.
**Similar species:** ♂ recalls ♂ Slaty and *amazonicus* subsp. of Amazonian Antshrike (16, 17) but is darker (slaty not gray) with much narrower white edging on wings and tail. ♀ nearest ♀ Spot-winged Antbird (74) but crown blacker and lacks round wing spots. See Dusky Antbird (59).
**Voice:** Song a slow bouncing *chook, chook, chook, chuchuchu chu-chu*, low-pitched; calls incl. a low complaining *caw*; and churring growl *urr-r-r-r-r-r-r*.
**Behavior:** Pairs follow bird flocks or wander independently of them, mostly 1-4m up in gallery forest; occas. drop to ground (Brown; S. Furniss).
**Breeding:** BC birds, 15 Jan, ne Meta (MCN), and Mar, upper Orinoco, Venez. (Friedmann 1948).
**Status and habitat:** Humid forest borders and gallery forest. Numerous in gallery woodland of e Meta.
**Range:** To 400m. E of Andes in Meta (Villavicencio; Carimagua), Vichada on Río Orinoco (Maipures) and Guainía (San Felipe; Macacuní). E Colombia, s Venez. (Amazonas), Amazonian Brazil, and Fr. Guiana.
**Note:** One or 2(?) ♂♂ from ne Guainía, presumed this sp., show white-dotted eyering and

large white spot in loral area (photo, Jan 1981— J. Dunning). Albinism may or may not be involved.

### 11. CASTELNAU'S ANTSHRIKE

*Thamnophilus cryptoleucus*     Pl. 29, Map 736
**Identification:** 7" (18cm). *Very heavy hooked bill.* ♂: entirely *shiny black* with grayish flanks and concealed white interscapular patch; *shoulders, bend of wing, and under wing coverts white*; upper wing coverts *fringed white* forming 2 or more prom. bars. In the hand, underside of axillaries and inner web of inner remiges white. ♀ sim. but duller, and shoulders and upper wing coverts black, bend of wing and under wing coverts mixed black and white.
**Similar species:** Black race (*aethiops*) of White-shouldered Antshrike (12) is very sim. to ♂ but lacks the extensively white fringed wing coverts (coverts more dotted) and white shoulders (white on carpal edge only) and bill shorter and even stouter. Other "black" antbirds— White-shouldered (84), Black (61) and Blackish (60)—lack extensive white on wing and have smaller bills. ♀ is only black ♀ *Thamnophilus.*
**Voice:** Song by ♂ and ♀ a *short*, very nasal, resonant ser. of rapidly accelerating notes, *keok, keok, keok-keok'kuk'ku'ku'ku'ku, raa*, growl at end not always given; also (song?) a low, nasal, *káou, káou, káou, káou*, slowly and deliberately; alarm, *káou, raaaaa!* (B. Coffee; Hilty).
**Behavior:** Less vocal than many *Thamnophilus* and very secretive and wary. Single birds or pairs move deliberately 1-6m up through thick undergrowth, occas. follow small bird flocks; pounds tail downward as sings (J. V. Remsen; Hilty).
**Breeding:** BC pair, late Mar, Leticia (Russell and Lamm 1978).
**Status and habitat:** Uncommon resident in dense undergrowth of tall swampy second growth woodland on river isls.
**Range:** To 100m. Known from Isla Santa Sofia III (Monkey Isl.), nw of Leticia. Also on adj. river isls. and n bank of Amazon. Ne Peru from Pebas and Ríos Ucayali and Marañon e to Río Negro in w Amazonian Brazil.
**Note:** Formerly regarded as a subsp. of 10.

### 12. WHITE-SHOULDERED ANTSHRIKE

*Thamnophilus aethiops*     Pl. 29, Map 737
**Identification:** 6.2" (15.7cm). Very heavy hooked bill. Eyes bright dark red (♂) or dark red (♀). ♂: mainly dark gray with blackish crown, wings, and tail (or uniform black—*aethiops*); *carpel edge of wing and small dots on shoulders and wing coverts white*; under wing coverts mixed black and white; no white interscapular patch. ♀: uni-

form dark brownish chestnut above, slightly paler below; tail chestnut brown (or dusky—*aethiops*).

**Similar species:** Easily confused. ♂ (gray races) much like ♂ Spot-winged Antbird (74) but more robust with heavier, all-black bill (not pale lower mandible) and blackish crown. ♂ Blackish-gray Antshrike (10) has narrow wing bars (not rows of spots) and white-tipped tail. Other "black" ♂ antbirds, Blackish, Black, and Jet (60, 61, 62) are smaller with thinner bills and solid wing bars (not spots). Black race much like ♂ Castelnau's and Black-capped Antshrike (see 11; 14). ♀ is only "large" virtually uniform chestnut antbird e of Colombian Andes.

**Voice:** Song a soft, slow, and very nasal *aow, ou, ou, ou*, rather trogonlike, and usually repeated every 4-6 sec; nasal *ahh* call typical of *Thamnophilus* (T. Parker).

**Behavior:** Pairs hop and peer mostly 1-5m up in stands of dense regrowth inside or at edges of forest. Usually not with mixed flocks.

**Status and habitat:** Undergrowth of humid *terra firme* forest, or in dense young second growth at edges or openings inside forest.

**Range:** To 500m. E of the Andes from Macarena Mts. to w Caquetá (*wetmorei*) and Vaupés (Mitú) e to Guainía and prob. e Vichada (*polionotus*); se Nariño (*aethiops*); prob. Amazonas. S Venez. to n Bolivia, Amazonian and e Brazil.

### 13. UNIFORM ANTSHRIKE

*Thamnophilus unicolor*  Pl. 27, Map 738

**Identification:** 6.2″ (15.7cm). Fairly heavy hooked bill. Eyes gray. ♂: almost *entirely uniform slate gray*, primaries inconspic. edged brownish. ♀: dull dark rufescent brown above, brighter on crown; *forehead, sides of head and upper throat gray*, underparts ochraceous brown.

**Similar species:** ♂ is only "slaty" antshrike in most of the forested highlands. In w Cauca see Western Antshrike (29), on e slope of E Andes Plumbeous Antvireo (26). Gray face of ♀ distinctive.

**Voice:** Song heard less often than many others of the genus, a nasal accelerating ser. of "bouncing ball" *na* notes, recalls Great Antshrike but slower, much softer and lacks terminal snarl (Hilty); calls incl. a wrenlike scolding *cha-a-a-a-a*, also a *mew* (Miller 1963).

**Behavior:** Pairs range from understory to subcanopy where more deliberately through foliage or hop up vines like other antshrikes; infrequently follow mixed flocks.

**Breeding:** 6 BC birds, May–June, Antioquia (Carriker); 2 BC birds, Feb–Mar, and 2 dependent juvs. July, Valle (Miller 1963); a Feb juv., Queremal, Valle (Hilty).

**Status and habitat:** Humid and wet forest (esp. "cloud forest"), occas. forest borders; seldom numerous.

**Range:** 1400-2300m, rarely to 2700m (to 900m on Pacific slope). Both slopes of W and C Andes (recs. scattered), w slope of E Andes n to Cundinamarca and e slope in Caquetá (sighting—Hilty) and in Nariño. Colombia, e and w Ecuador, and ne Peru.

### 14. BLACK-CAPPED ANTSHRIKE

*Thamnophilus schistaceus*  Pl. 29, Map 739

**Identification:** 5.7″ (14.5cm). Fairly heavy hooked bill. Eyes dark red. ♂: *crown and nape black*, otherwise slate gray above, gray below. ♀: *crown dull rufous*; rest of upperparts olive brown; *sides of head grayish* with a few faint whitish shaft lines; throat dingy white becoming pale ochraceous olive on rest of underparts; belly paler, more buffy.

**Similar species:** ♂ is only antshrike in Amazonia with black cap and uniform gray plumage (no white on wings or tail). See gray race of White-shouldered Antshrike (12). ♀ barely separable from ♀ Mouse-colored Antshrike but latter with whiter throat and usually with faint buff-dotted wing coverts.

**Voice:** Song near Leticia a very nasal ser. of *ank* notes almost identical to Mouse-colored Antshrike but slightly longer (about 10 vs 6-7 notes) and given faster; hurried double note at end is characteristic of both sp.

**Behavior:** Usually in pairs 1-5m up in denser undergrowth. Peer carefully for arthropods on twigs and foliage like other antshrikes. Not shy but sometimes hard to see because of thick foliage they favor. Often sing persistently.

**Breeding:** 1 nest e Peru, vireolike cup 1 m up in bush; 2 eggs, cream with dark spots (Zimmer 1930).

**Status and habitat:** Fairly common in tall second growth and shrubby forest borders, also often inside *terra firme* or *várzea* forests.

**Range:** To 500m. E of Andes from s Meta (Macarena Mts.) and Vaupés (Mitú) southward. E Colombia to n Bolivia and Amazonian Brazil.

### 15. MOUSE-COLORED ANTSHRIKE

*Thamnophilus murinus*  Pl. 29, Map 740

**Identification:** 5.3″ (13.5cm). Fairly heavy hooked bill. ♂: olive gray above with concealed white interscapular patch and *distinctly brownish tinged primaries*; wing coverts with *small whitish dots on tips* forming 2 dotted bars; underparts light gray, paler on throat, almost white on abdomen and washed olive brown on flanks; tail dusky narrowly tipped white. ♀: olive brown above with *dull chestnut brown crown and wings*, wing coverts with indistinct terminal buffy dots; underparts pale ochraceous olive, *center of throat and abdomen whitish,* flanks washed olive brown; tail dark chestnut brown.

**Similar species:** A dull confusing sp. ♂'s best marks are brownish wings, weakly dotted wing coverts and overall pale gray (not dark gray) appearance. Cf. ♀ with ♀ Black-capped Antshrike (14).

**Voice:** Song a nasal *ank, ank-ank-ank-ank-ank-wánkaa,* double note at end quicker and slightly lower pitched; almost identical to that of Black-capped Antshrike but lazier (not brisk) and usually with fewer notes.

**Behavior:** Usually in pairs that act much like other antshrikes. Peer rather slowly at foliage and small branches, mostly 3-15m up inside forest. Occas. but not reg. with bird flocks, seldom at ant swarms (Oniki and Willis 1972).

**Breeding:** 1 BC ♀, Apr, upper Orinoco, Venez. (Friedmann 1948).

**Status and habitat:** Inside humid *terra firme* forest; most numerous in sandy-belt forests of Guainía and Vaupés and perhaps largely replaced s in Amazonas by Black-capped Antshrike.

**Range:** To 400m. Extreme e from Guainía s to Amazonas. The Guianas and s Venez. to e Ecuador, ne Peru, and n and w Amazonian Brazil.

## 16. SLATY ANTSHRIKE

*Thamnophilus punctatus*     Pl. 29, Map 741

**Identification:** 5.7″ (14.5cm). Fairly heavy hooked bill. ♂: mostly gray above with *black crown;* concealed white interscapular patch; back mixed with black (or mostly black—*interpositus*); *wings and tail black with much white spotting and edging on scapulars, wing coverts, and remiges;* upper tail coverts and *tail tipped white;* below gray, paler than above. ♀: olive brown above with *dull chestnut crown;* wings and tail brown *marked like ♂ but with buff;* (or white—*interpositus*); concealed white interscapular patch; underparts light brownish olive; throat, chest, and abdomen tinged buffy.

**Similar species:** Cf. ♂ Amazonian Antshrike, esp. black-capped subsp. (17). Pearly Antshrike (19) has *larger* spots on wing coverts and large terminal spots on inner remiges (lacking in Slaty). ♀ has bolder wing markings than most other ♀ antbirds and lacks orangish head of ♀ Amazonian Antshrike.

**Voice:** Song w of Andes is 10-30 rapid accelerating whistled *hu* or *du* notes ending in nasal *dwenk;* calls incl. a loud *ank gr-r-r-r-r;* nasal *cah,* and *cah-cah.*

**Behavior:** Often more conspic. than other antshrikes. Pairs move deliberately among twigs and foliage or hop up vines near trunks as they peer and glean in usual antshrike fashion. W of Andes occas. follow mixed flocks or army ant swarms.

**Breeding:** 7 BC birds, Feb–Apr, s Bolívar to Chocó (Haffer 1975; Carriker); mostly Apr–Sept but rec. all mos. except Oct and Nov, Barro Colorado Isl., Panama (Willis and Eisenmann 1979). Usual thin-walled cup attached by rim to fork 1-4m up; 2 white eggs spotted rufous and brown (Skutch 1969a).

**Status and habitat:** Fairly common w of Andes in humid forest, taller second growth woodland and along open forest borders. Not well known e of Andes in Colombia. Amazonian forms favor second growth and scrubbier forest edges where do not usually follow army ants (Oniki and Willis 1972).

**Range:** To 500m. Pacific coast (*atrinucha*); entire lowlands n of Andes, s to upper Magdalena Val. (n Huila), e of Andes in Catatumbo lowlands and e base of Andes in n Boyacá (*subcinereus*); w Meta incl. Macarena Mts. (*interpositus*), perhaps throughout e of Andes; Gorgona Isl. (*gorgonae*). Guatemala to w Ecuador (not e Ecuador), ne Peru, Bolivia, and s Brazil.

## 17. AMAZONIAN ANTSHRIKE

*Thamnophilus amazonicus*     Pl. 29, Map 742

**Identification:** 6″ (15cm), (or 5.7″ [14.5cm]—*cinereiceps*). ♂ of black-capped subsp. (*amazonicus*) almost identical to Slaty Antshrike and best told by voice or by presence of ♀; in hand gray of back mixed with more black. ♂ of gray-headed subsp. (*cinereiceps*) like Slaty Antshrike but *crown uniform gray* (not black). ♀: entire head, throat, and breast orange rufous; lower underparts pale cinnamon (or whitish, sharply defined—*cinereiceps*); wings and tail dusky marked with white like ♂.

**Voice:** Song by both sexes at Mitú a rather rapid trogonlike roll that grows louder and accelerates slightly in mid., then slows and diminishes in vol. at end, about 3.5 sec. Tail trembles (*cinereiceps*) when bird sings.

**Behavior:** Like Slaty Antshrike, rather easy to see. Usually in pairs peering and hopping in foliage or vines, mostly 1-8m up at edge or inside woodland. Sometimes follows mixed flocks, esp. along savanna woodland borders.

**Status and habitat:** From Vichada to Vaupés (*cinereiceps*) fairly common inside or at shrubby edges of sandy-belt forest or savanna woodland or along swampy creeks. In Amazonia (*amazonicus*) more often inside or at vine-tangled edges of *várzea* forest or low lying forest near water.

**Range:** To 500m. E of Andes from Meta (Villavicencio area) s to Amazonas (*amazonicus*); extreme e from Orinoco (Maipures) s to c and w Vaupés (Mitú; San José del Guaviare— *cinereiceps*). The Guianas and s Venez. s to n Bolivia and Amazonian Brazil.

**Note:** *T. cinereiceps* (Gray-capped Antshrike) of the upper Orinoco in Venez., Colombia, and nw Brazil may be a separate sp.

### 18. SPOT-WINGED ANTSHRIKE
*Pygiptila stellaris*      Pl. 29, Map 743
**Identification:** 5.5″ (14cm). *Tail short*. Bill heavy and hooked. ♂: *crown black*; otherwise blue gray, paler below; concealed white interscapular patch; *wing coverts with several rows of terminal white dots*. ♀: light blue gray above; wings brownish, wing coverts unmarked, flight feathers edged rufous; forehead, sides of head, and underparts dull ochraceous.
**Similar species:** A distinctly plump-bodied, short-tailed bird with a very heavy bill; usually high in trees. Shape is best clue. See longer-tailed Mouse-colored Antshrike (15) and Russet Antshrike (23).
**Voice:** Distinctive song a short vibrating trill quickly ending in a ringing whistle, *t-t-t-t-teer!*, repeated 1 to several times, or sometimes continuing for several min at rate of once every 3-4 sec.
**Behavior:** Pairs or occas. several follow mixed flocks in upper midlevels to canopy where they hop along outer branches and peer in foliage. More active than *Thamnophilus* and with more horizontal, short-legged posture.
**Breeding:** Sept nest, 11m up in thick foliage of crown of small tree, se Peru (C. Munn).
**Status and habitat:** Fairly common inside or along edges of humid *várzea* and swamp forest and *terra firme* forest.
**Range:** To 500m. E of Andes from w Caquetá and Vaupés southward. Poss. n to e Vichada. The Guianas and s Venez. to n Bolivia and Amazonian Brazil.

### 19. PEARLY ANTSHRIKE
*Megastictus margaritatus*      Pl. 29, Map 744
**Identification:** 5.5″ (14cm). Eyes gray. ♂: blue gray above, paler below, esp. on throat; no white interscapular patch; wings and tail black, *wing coverts and tips of remiges with bold round white spots*; upper tail coverts and tail broadly tipped white. ♀: olive brown above; orange ochraceous below, paler on throat; wings and tail as in ♂ but *spots buff*. Bill not as heavy as in *Thamnophilus*. Constantly raises and lowers tail.
**Similar species:** A striking and boldly patterned bird that should not be confused. No other antbird has such large wing and tail spots.

See Slaty and Amazonian antshrikes (16, 17).
**Voice:** Song at Mitú about 4-5 soft melancholy *wheet* or *white* whistles given rather slowly.
**Behavior:** Pairs or groups of 3-4 are unobtrusive and often quiet as they hop up through open mid. story branches 4-10m up. Peer and glean like a Slaty Antshrike; wander alone or with forest flocks, esp. those containing other insectivores.
**Status and habitat:** Inside or at edge of tall sandy-belt forest or tall old second growth. Fairly common in Vaupés; few recs. in Amazonas.
**Range:** To 500m. E of Andes from w Caquetá and Vaupés southward. Prob. n to Río Guaviare. S Venez. to e Ecuador, ne Peru, and nw Brazil.
**Note:** Wings proportionally longer than allies and much like those of flycatching *Thamnomanes* antshrikes (T. Schulenberg).

### 20. BLACK BUSHBIRD
*Neoctantes niger*      Pl. 30, Map 745
**Identification:** 6.3″ (16cm). Bill mainly blue gray; *wedge-shaped lower mandible upturned*. ♂: deep black with concealed white interscapular patch; tail rather short. ♀: sim. but *breast and upper belly deep chestnut*.
**Similar species:** A rather stocky and robust "black" antbird easily recognized by peculiar beveled lower mandible. ♀ unlike any other.
**Voice:** Ventriloquial song a semiwhistled *work* or *querk* repeated steadily at rate of about 2 per sec for up to several min without pause; also a fast vibrating *d'd'd'd'd'd'd'd*.
**Behavior:** Usually in pairs hopping deliberately from near ground to 4m up in dense viny tangles, tall saplings around treefalls, or along muddy forest streams. Often peck and chisel fallen rotten logs somewhat like a piculet. Retiring and hard to see.
**Status and habitat:** Uncommon inside or at edge of humid *terra firme* and *várzea* forests, esp. in log-scattered swamps or creek borders and in dense young second growth in openings inside forest or at forest edge. Pairs widely scattered at Mitú, Vaupés.
**Range:** To 400m. E of Andes from e Nariño (Río San Miguel) to Vaupés (Mitú) and Amazonas (Leticia). Se Colombia, e Ecuador, ne Peru, and w Amazonian Brazil.

### 21. RECURVE-BILLED BUSHBIRD
*Clytoctantes alixi*      Pl. 27, Map 746
**Identification:** 6.5″ (16.5cm). *Bill very large, recurved and laterally compressed* with sharp-ridged culmen. Unmistakable. ♂: mainly slaty gray; lores, *throat, and upper breast deep black* ; wing coverts faintly dotted white; concealed inter-

scapular patch white; tail short; legs and feet large and strong. ♀: rufescent brown; forehead, sides of head, and sides of body rufous chestnut; wings and tail dusky; concealed interscapular patch white; bill and legs as in ♂.
**Voice:** Loud call given infrequently (Carriker 1955).
**Behavior:** Secretive in dense growth close to ground; once at an ant swarm with Ocellated Antbird, Rufous-vented Ground-Cuckoo, and Spotted Antbird (Carriker).
**Breeding:** 4 BC birds, Apr–May, s Córdoba to s Bolívar (Carriker).
**Status and habitat:** Dense young second growth, tangled impenetrable thickets, and forest borders in humid areas. Perhaps more numerous than specimens and sight recs. indicate because of secretive habits; 10 specimens are from Snía. San Lucas, s Bolívar (Carriker).
**Range:** 180-1000m. Upper Río Sinú and lower Cauca vals. (Pto. Valdivia) e to mid. Magdalena Val. (Snía. San Lucas and s Cesar) s to e Caldas (Río Samaná). N Colombia and extreme nw Venez. (Perijá Mts. in Zulia).
**Note:** In *Clytoctantes* the hind claw is longer and straighter than in *Neoctantes*, and the bill is much larger.

## 22. SPECKLED ANTSHRIKE
*Xenornis setifrons*　　　　　　Map 747
**Identification:** 6.0″ (15cm). Eyes light gray. Bill mod. heavy and hooked. ♂: crown and upperparts dusky brown *broadly streaked and dappled deep buff; wings with 2 conspic. cinnamon wing bars;* sides of head and underparts dark slaty gray; tail blackish narrowly tipped white. ♀: *above like* ♂; upper throat grayish white edged dusky; rest of underparts light brown, darkest on belly, mottled and streaked buff on breast. In the hand plumage lax and soft.
**Similar species:** Rather "prehistoric looking" ♂ is much darker below than above and unlike any other antbird. ♀ might recall ♀ Dusky Antbird (59) but is conspic. streaked and dappled above and below.
**Behavior:** Little known and apparently secretive; usually in pairs. A peculiar bird, poss. a relict of an older group (Wetmore 1972).
**Status and habitat:** Rare in humid forest. Panama specimens are mainly from forest undergrowth on slopes well above streams in foothills and lower mts.
**Range:** To 600m. Panama border (Cerro Tacarcuna) and Pacific coast to Baudó Mts. Not found in Gulf of Urabá area by Haffer (1975). E Panama and nw Colombia.

## 23. RUSSET ANTSHRIKE
*Thamnistes anabatinus*　　Pl. 27, Map 748
**Identification:** 5.8″ (14.7cm). *Strong hooked bill.*

Brown above; rufescent on crown and *brighter rufous on wings and tail*; concealed interscapular patch orange (lacking in ♀); *eyestripe buff*; throat and breast yellowish buff; sides and abdomen tinged grayish. Rather thickset appearance.
**Similar species:** Easily confused. Good marks are stocky shape and stout bill. Like several foliage-gleaners, esp. Buff-fronted (p 371) but smaller and lacks gray crown and pointed tail feathers of latter. Also see smaller ♀ Plain Antvireo (24), ♀ Spot-winged Antshrike (18), Cinnamon Becard, and other "cinnamon colored" ♀ becards (pp 446-449).
**Voice:** Song a ser. of about 5 plaintive *peeea* notes (T. Parker recording); call a high sibilant *peet-seep*, var. to *peet-se-seet-sip* not often heard but occas. repeated persistently.
**Behavior:** One or 2 often follow mixed flocks in upper levels and crown of forest. Peer and glean actively like foliage-gleaners, mostly in denser foliage and on smaller outer limbs and twigs.
**Breeding:** 4 BC birds, Feb–Apr, Chocó (Carriker). In Costa Rica, vireolike cup high in tree, Apr (Skutch 1969a).
**Status and habitat:** Uncommon to fairly common in humid and wet forest and forest borders. Mainly foothills and lower slopes.
**Range:** To 1500m. Pacific coast and slope and e to upper Sinú Val. (Quimarí); 1 sighting presumed this 28 Feb 1975, PN Tayrona (Brown); e slope E Andes from Macarena Mts. southward. Se Mexico to sw Ecuador, w Venez. (sw Táchira) and e slope of the Andes to s Bolivia.

[*Dysithamnus:* Stocky; resembles small *Thamnophilus* but tail shorter, bill proportionally thinner, and posture less erect; glean foliage (cf. with *Thamnomanes*).]

## 24. PLAIN ANTVIREO
*Dysithamnus mentalis*　　Pl. 28, Map 749
**Identification:** 4.5″ (11.4cm). Bill stout. Tail short. ♂: *dark olive gray to dark gray above,* darker on crown and *esp. on cheeks;* 2 narrow white wing bars; below paler gray, throat and center of belly whitish; concealed white interscapular patch. ♀: *crown chestnut;* upperparts grayish olive to brown; 2 indistinct buffy wing bars; *eyering white and cheeks dusky;* underparts pale grayish olive, whiter on throat and abdomen (or lower underparts tinged yellowish—Perijá Mts. and n end E Andes).
**Similar species:** A large-headed little bird resembling a vireo in shape and behavior. Dusky cheeks a good mark; in ♀ also chestnut crown and eyering. *Thamnomanes* antshrikes (27, 28, 29) are larger, longer-tailed, and perch more

upright; antwrens are smaller, more active, and have thinner bills.

**Voice:** Song an accelerating roll like a "small" *Thamnophilus* but higher-pitched and more subdued; also a soft, nasal *nyoot*, and *choot-nyoo* (Ridgely 1976).

**Behavior:** Pairs or small groups (families?) wander alone or occas. join small antwren and warbler flocks in lower or lower mid. story. Unobtrusive as move sluggishly like vireos, hopping along small branches and gleaning foliage or hovering beneath it.

**Breeding:** 18 BC birds, Apr–May, C Andes and Perijá Mts. (Carriker); 5 BC birds, Mar–July, and 2 dependent young, July and Sept, W Andes above Cali (Miller 1963). Frail open cup attached by rim to low fork in bush; 2 whitish eggs blotched purplish brown (Skutch 1969a).

**Status and habitat:** Fairly common in humid forest; mostly foothills and lower slopes. Replaced at lower el. (below about 1000m) on Pacific slope by Spot-crowned Antvireo.

**Range:** Mostly 600-2200m (to 300m near Panama border). Ne base Santa Marta Mts. in Guajira, Perijá Mts., and the Andes incl. Macarena Mts. and mts. near Panama border. Se Mexico to w Ecuador, n Argentina, and s Brazil.

## 25. SPOT-CROWNED ANTVIREO
*Dysithamnus puncticeps*  Pl. 28, Map 750
**Identification:** 4.5″ (11.4cm). Eyes whitish. ♂: *crown black dotted white*; upperparts dark gray tinged olive; 2 narrow white dotted wing bars; below grayish white *narrowly and faintly streaked dusky on breast*; tail short. ♀: *crown dull rufous streaked and spotted dusky*; upperparts olive brown; 2 narrow buff-dotted wing bars; throat and chest buffy white *faintly streaked dusky*; lower underparts buff tinged olive on sides.

**Similar species:** Both sexes of Plain Antvireo (24) have uniform (not spotted) crown; ♂ also has prom. dusky cheeks, ♀ a *prom. eyering*, whiter wing bars, and no streaking.

**Voice:** Song a soft tremulous roll, accelerating, descending slightly and fading, *hu hu-h-h-h-h-h-u-u-u-u.*

**Behavior:** Much like Plain Antvireo.

**Breeding:** BC ♂, Mar, Chocó (Carriker); nest building, 26 Aug, upper Anchicayá Val. (Hilty). Nests in Apr (1) and July (3) in Panama (Willis and Eisenmann 1979); nest as in Plain Antvireo (Wetmore 1972).

**Status and habitat:** Fairly common in humid and wet forest. Mostly foothills and lower slopes. Replaced at higher el. by Plain Antvireo.

**Range:** To 1000m. Pacific slope (not drier lowlands around Gulf of Urabá), Baudo Mts., and

n base of W Andes to lower Cauca Val. (Pto. Valdivia). Sw Costa Rica to w Ecuador.

## 26. PLUMBEOUS ANTVIREO
*Dysithamnus plumbeus*  Pl. 29, Map 751
**Identification:** 5.2″ (13.2cm). Chunky and short-tailed. ♂: *mostly slaty gray, abdomen paler, throat and chest blackish*; wing coverts blackish with 2 narrow white-dotted wing bars and indistinct white scapular dots; small concealed white interscapular patch. ♀: *crown bright chestnut*; upperparts rufescent brown; sides of head and underparts gray broadly streaked white.

**Similar species:** ♂ Plain Antvireo (24) is much paler below and lacks black on throat and breast. ♂ Dusky Antbird (59) is slimmer and longer-tailed. ♀ should be easily recognized by streaked underparts.

**Voice:** Song 4-5 whistled notes, *wheer, wheer, whuu, were*, last 2-3 notes drop in pitch (P. Schwartz recording).

**Behavior:** Sim. to Plain Antvireo. Pairs or families glean from lower foliage like others of the genus; wander alone or with mixed groups of antwrens, antvireos, etc. (Schäfer and Phelps 1954; P. Schwartz; Hilty).

**Status and habitat:** Undergrowth of humid forest. Few recs.

**Range:** 900-1600m. E slope of E Andes in Meta and doubtless southward (*leucostictus*). N Venez.; e Colombia to e Ecuador; se Brazil.

**Note 1:** Called White-spotted Antvireo (*Dysithamnus plumbeus*) in Meyer de Schauensee (1964) but later incorrectly transferred to *Thamnomanes* (Meyer de Schauensee 1966).

**Note 2:** Birds from se Brazil may be a separate sp., in which case Andean birds, *T. leucostictus*, may be called White-spotted Antvireo.

[*Thamnomanes*: Rather long-tailed and long-winged; perch erect like a flatbill (flycatcher); sally to foliage; ♀♀ more distinct than ♂♂.]

## 27. DUSKY-THROATED ANTSHRIKE
*Thamnomanes ardesiacus*  Pl. 29, Map 752
**Identification:** 5.2″ (13.2cm). Flycatcherlike. ♂: *dark bluish gray, paler on abdomen; throat black*; tail very narrowly tipped white (inconspic. in field); with or without concealed white interscapular patch. ♀: olive brown above, browner on wings and tail; faint whitish eyering; *throat buffy white; breast washed olive; remaining underparts buffy ochraceous.*

**Similar species:** ♂ Cinereous Antshrike (28) lacks dusky throat and has longer tail; ♀ Cinereous has bright cinnamon rufous lower underparts. Also see note.

**Voice:** Song in Peru an ascending ser. of buzzy whistles ending with an emphatic lower note, *zu-zu-zu-zu-zu-zt-zt-zzzt-Bzzz!* (T. Parker); in

Surinam, raspy, rising *jaaw, jay, gee-ge-ge'ge'g'g'*, attenuated at end; calls incl. a sharp double-sounding *skéeap*, and buzzy *juueeer*; lacks loud rattle of Cinereous Antshrike and not as noisy as latter.

**Behavior:** Sit somewhat vertically like flycatchers, although not as vertically as Cinereous Antshrike (28), and sally to foliage 1-5m up in undergrowth. Pairs or small families are normally with mixed antwren and flycatcher flocks, esp. those containing Cinereous Antshrikes; on average stay lower to ground; not as noisy and not as important to mixed flock leadership and cohesion as latter; occas. at army ants.

**Breeding:** In se Peru 7 vireolike nests, Aug–Jan, 0.5-2m up in forks of small saplings, often festooned with a few dead leaves; 2 pinkish white eggs spotted reddish brown (C. Munn).

**Status and habitat:** Common in undergrowth of *terra firme* and *várzea* forests.

**Range:** To 500m. E of Andes from s Meta (Macarena Mts.) and Vaupés, southward; prob. also Guainía. The Guianas and s Venez. to e Ecuador, e Peru (mostly w of Ríos Amazon and Ucayali), and Amazonian Brazil.

**Note:** Incl. *T. saturinus* (Saturnine Antshrike) of ne Peru and w Amazonian Brazil s of the Amazon, by some considered a separate sp.

## 28. CINEREOUS ANTSHRIKE

*Thamnomanes caesius*　　Pl. 29, Map 753

**Identification:** 5.8" (14.7cm). Flycatcherlike. Tail long. ♂: *uniform dark bluish gray*; wings and tail somewhat dusky; concealed white interscapular patch. ♀: dark olive brown above; faint cinnamon eyering; throat grayish white; chest olivaceous gray; *remaining underparts bright cinnamon rufous*, incl. under wing coverts; concealed white interscapular patch.

**Similar species:** See Dusky-throated Antshrike (27). ♂ Black-capped Antshrike (14) has black cap (in Colombia) and dark red (not brown) eyes. Also see note below.

**Voice:** Song, several wheezy whistles accelerating into a rapid bubbly trill fading at end, *wheee, wheee, wheesp wheesp whes whes we we e-e-e-e-u-u-u-r*, about 6 sec; calls incl. 1 to several loud *wert* notes; a *loud* staccato rattle, *wert-wert d'd'd'd'd'd'd!* as bird leads mixed flocks.

**Behavior:** Much like Dusky-throated Antshrike. A nuclear sp. in many mixed flocks of forest midlevels or lower in Amazonia. Sit vertically like flycatchers on slender horizontal perches 3-10m up but move lower over army ants, which they occas. follow. Sally to air or foliage, rarely ground, and often return to same perch after a sally (Oniki and Willis 1972).

**Breeding:** 1 BC bird, Apr, upper Orinoco, Venez. (Friedmann 1948). Six open cup nests 0.5-3.0m up in fern-covered crotches of saplings, Aug–Nov, se Peru; 2 pinkish white eggs blotched reddish brown (C. Munn; Beebe et al. 1917).

**Status and habitat:** Common in humid *terra firme* and *várzea* forests. Apparently replaced s and e of Ríos Amazon and Ucayali in w Amazonia by Bluish-slate Antshrike (see note).

**Range:** To 500m. E of Andes from w Meta (Villavicencio area) and se Vichada (Maipures) southward. The Guianas and s Venez. to e Peru, n Bolivia, and Amazonian Brazil (mostly n of Amazon e of Río Purús).

**Note:** Bluish-slate Antshrike (*T. schistogynus*) of e Peru e and s of Ríos Amazon and Ucayali, n Bolivia, and sw Brazil has been rec. s of Amazon (Río Javarí) near Leticia. Specimens attributed to this sp. are known from n(?) side of Amazon in ne Peru. ♂: almost identical to ♂ Cinereous Antshrike (not separable in field by plumage); ♀ has upperparts, throat, and chest dark bluish gray, slightly paler on throat, and *sharply separated* from bright cinnamon rufous lower underparts. Habits, song, and chirp rattle sim. to Cinereous Antshrike (T. Parker).

## 29. WESTERN ANTSHRIKE

*Thamnomanes occidentalis*　　Map 754

**Identification:** 6" (15cm). Slaty black above, paler below; wings brownish black with *2 white-dotted wing bars*; concealed white interscapular patch. ♀: *crown chestnut*; back chestnut brown; wings and tail dusky. 2 *buff-dotted wing bars* and small white patch on shoulder; *eyebrow, sides of head, and underparts slaty gray with fine whitish shaft streaks*; abdomen olive brown.

**Similar species:** ♂ Uniform Antshrike (13) lacks white on wing; ♀ Uniform Antshrike has distinct gray face and ochraceous brown underparts. Also see Dusky Antbird (59).

**Status and habitat:** Little known; apparently humid and wet forest. There are about 10 specimens incl. those in e Ecuador (T. Schulenberg).

**Range:** 900-1200m. Pacific slope in sw Cauca (Río Munchique; Cocal; La Costa). E slope of Andes in Ecuador (500-1000m; San José, Sarayacú, Zamora); prob. adj. e slope in Colombia and Peru.

**Note:** Called Western Antvireo (*Dysithamnus occidentalis*) by Meyer de Schauensee (1964) but transferred to *Thamnomanes* by Meyer de Schauensee (1966) because of presumed relationship to *T. ardesiacus*. Its true taxonomic placement (sallying *Thamnomanes* or gleaning *Dysithamnus*) is unknown.

[*Myrmotherula*: Small; short tail; rather long thin bill; many spp. ♀♀ confusing. ♂♂ form 3 groups: (1) mostly black and white striped, (2) predom. brown and buff with or without chestnut rump, or (3) mainly gray or black with or without black throat and white-tipped wing coverts.]

## 30. PYGMY ANTWREN
*Myrmotherula brachyura*     Pl. 28, Map 755
**Identification:** 3.2" (8.1cm) (or 2.7" [6.9cm]—*ignota*). Tiny and virtually tailless. ♂: *above black streaked white; rump gray*; 2 white wing bars; primaries edged white; *throat white* bordered by *narrow black malar stripe*; remaining underparts pale yellow with a few black streaks on sides; white interscapular patch. ♀: sim., but crown and sides of head streaked buff (not white).
**Similar species:** See Short-billed Antwren (31) and Yellow-throated Antwren (32). Other small "black-and-white" streaked antwrens lack yellow underparts.
**Voice:** Song a single note (almost a "bouncing ball") repeated and accelerating into a short trill, *chree, chree-chre-chre-che-ee-ee-e'e'e'e*; often heard.
**Behavior:** Single birds or pairs actively hop and flit in foliage from upper understory to subcanopy. Often follow mixed flocks at forest edge.
**Breeding:** BC ♀, Apr, n Antioquia (Carriker). Building nest about 6m up, *várzea*, s of Leticia in Brazil, 29 Aug (Hilty).
**Status and habitat:** Humid and wet forest borders, tall second growth woodland, and in canopy of *terra firme* and *várzea* forests. Rare and local on Pacific slope. Fairly common e of Andes; may be partially replaced in e foothills by Short-billed Antwren.
**Range:** To 900m (photo, Anchicayá Val.—Hilty) on Pacific coast s to Nariño and n of Andes from upper Río Sinú e to upper Río Nechí (*ignota*); to 500m e of Andes from w Meta (Villavicencio area) and Guainía southward (*brachyura*). C Panama to n Bolivia and Amazonian Brazil.
**Note:** The form *ignota* of Panama and w Colombia may be a separate sp. or more closely allied to Short-billed Antwren.

## 31. SHORT-BILLED ANTWREN
*Myrmotherula obscura*     Pl. 28, Map 756
**Identification:** 3.2" (8.1cm). Closely resembles Pygmy Antwren but much less striped with white above (*looks virtually black above or from side* in field) and *moustachial streak very broad and heavy* (not narrow). In the hand bill shorter (less than 11 mm vs greater than 12mm). ♀:

differs in same manner and additionally by *throat and breast washed buffy yellow*, streaks on crown and sides of head *white*.
**Similar species:** Also see Yellow-throated Antwren (32).
**Voice:** Song in Peru sim. to Pygmy Antwren but slower and lower-pitched; also a short *chut-chur* and soft complaining *peer* (T. Parker).
**Behavior:** Much like Pygmy Antwren; in vines and denser foliage in mid. story (T. Parker).
**Breeding:** BC ♂, 19 May, Mitú, Vaupés (Olivares 1964b).
**Status and habitat:** Shrubby forest borders and second growth woodland. Not well known in Colombia.
**Range:** To 500m (prob. higher). E base of E Andes from w Meta (Villavicencio area) to se Nariño and e to Vaupés (Mitú). Prob. s to Amazon (rec. both sides of Amazon in ne Peru). E Colombia to c Peru and w Amazonian Brazil (Tefé).

## 32. YELLOW-THROATED ANTWREN
*Myrmotherula ambigua*     Map 757
**Identification:** 3.4" (8.6cm). Resembles Pygmy Antwren. ♂: black above streaked white on head and neck and pale yellowish on mantle; rump grayish; 2 wing bars and edges of inner remiges yellowish white; tail tipped pale yellow; moustachial streak black; *underparts incl. throat pale yellow* (unstreaked); concealed interscapular patch pale yellow. ♀: like ♂ above; streaks on head and neck brownish yellow; sides of body buffy.
**Similar species:** From either Pygmy or Short-billed antwrens (30, 31) by yellow (not white) throat. ♀ Short-billed antwren (overlap poss. in e Vaupés) has buffy wash on throat but head streaks white (not tawny). In the hand Yellow-throated has longer bill than Pygmy Antwren (about 16mm vs 12mm), and longer tail (21-24mm vs 17-19mm; Meyer de Schauensee 1952).
**Status and habitat:** Known only from white sandy soil forests of upper Río Negro.
**Range:** Extreme e Colombia at mouth of Río Guainía. Prob. e Vaupés as rec. at boundary of Río Vaupés in Brazil. S Venez. from Cerro Duida to confluence of Ríos Casiquiare and Negro, and nw Brazil.

## 33. STREAKED ANTWREN
*Myrmotherula surinamensis*     Pl. 28, Map 758
**Identification:** 3.7" (9.4cm). ♂: *black above streaked white*; rump gray; 2 white wing bars and much *white edging* on shoulders and remiges; underparts incl. throat white streaked black; concealed interscapular patch white. ♀: sim. to ♂ above, but *crown and nape cinnamon rufous*

IDENTIFICATION DIAGRAM FOR MAJOR GROUPS OF COLOMBIAN *Myrmotherula* ANTWRENS. SPECIES WITH AN ASTERISK (*) NOT YET REPORTED IN COLOMBIA.

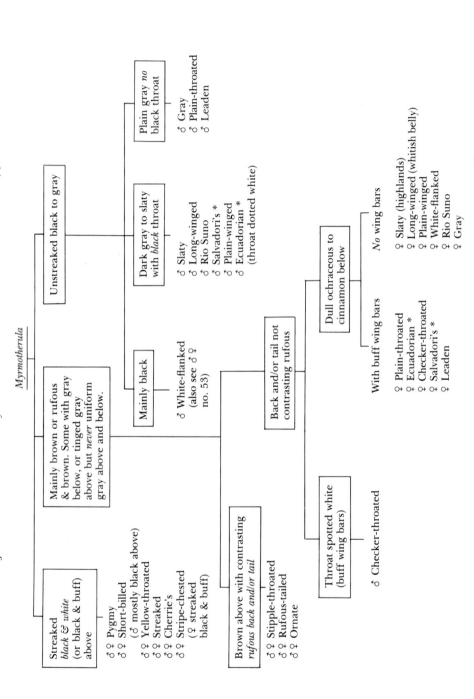

streaked black; sides of head, throat, and breast pale orange ochraceous finely streaked black (or virtually unstreaked pale orange buff—*pacifica*), belly whitish; interscapular patch white.

**Similar species:** Pattern of ♂ recalls a Black-and-white Warbler (p 575) but shape and habits different. Cherrie's Antwren (35) is very sim., and comparative experience needed for separation. Stripe-chested Antwren (34) of e foothills and with little range overlap, has streaks confined to chest (♂) or underparts essentially unstreaked (♀).

**Voice:** Song a bright chipper ser. of notes that accelerate and rise slightly *chi-chi-chi-chi-che'che'che'cheche*; sings incessantly in early morning; call, *cheep derp*.

**Behavior:** Pairs or families hop and flit actively as they glean from twigs and leaves or flutter at foliage in low thickets and shrubbery. Not a forest bird and usually not with mixed flocks but occas. join them in shrubby clearings.

**Breeding:** 1 nest, 5 Mar, Nuquí, Chocó; thin somewhat pensile cup suspended from low fork; 2 white eggs spotted dark (Wetmore 1972); 4 BC birds, Apr–May, n Antioquia (Carriker).

**Status and habitat:** Common in shrubby forest borders, vine-tangled clearings and bushy *várzea* forest borders, esp. along streams or near water. Partially replaced in foothills e of Andes by Stripe-chested Antwren.

**Range:** To 1100m. Pacific coast and e in humid lowlands n of Andes to mid. Magdalena Val. near Bucaramanga, (*pacifica*); e of Andes (to 350m) in Meta (*multostriata*); sightings in Vaupés, Putumayo and Amazonas, prob. *multostriata*. Doubtless e Vichada and Guainía (in adj. Venez.). W Panama to w Ecuador, Venez., the Guianas, e Peru (incl. Pebas and mouth of Río Curaray), and Amazonian Brazil.

### 34. STRIPE-CHESTED ANTWREN

*Myrmotherula longicauda*     Pl. 28, Map 759

**Identification:** 3.7″ (9.4cm). ♂: *black above streaked white*; 2 white wing bars and white edges on remiges; tail broadly tipped and edged white; underparts white *streaked black only on chest, upper breast, and sides (throat* and all of lower underparts unstreaked). ♀: above like ♂, but crown and back black streaked deep buff; throat and breast uniform pale creamy ochraceous, *sharply divided* from white lower underparts. Sides occas. with vague streaks (looks essentially uniform). In the hand no white interscapular patch (both sexes).

**Similar species:** ♂ from ♂ Streaked Antwren (33) by unstreaked throat, lower breast, and belly. ♀ from ♀♀ of 30, 31, and 33 by more or less unstreaked "2-toned" underparts.

**Voice:** Song in Peru a ser. of 8-9 *tee-tur* notes, at short intervals; rather mournful *churr* call; alarm *char-ti-ti-ti-ti* (T. Parker).

**Behavior:** Act like other black-and-white streaked members of the genus, hopping and fluttering 2-5m up in second growth; usually in pairs, not flocks (T. Parker; R. Ridgely).

**Status and habitat:** Common in second growth and vines along streams, clearings and forest borders. Mostly a foothill and hill country bird found above the range of Streaked Antwren.

**Range:** 400-1000m (prob. higher). E base of e Andes in w Putumayo and se Nariño (prob. also w Caquetá). E Colombia to n Bolivia.

### 35. CHERRIE'S ANTWREN

*Myrmotherula cherriei*     Pl. 28, Map 760

**Identification:** 3.7″ (9.4cm). Very like Streaked Antwren. ♂: differs in *underparts much more coarsely streaked with black*, streaks fewer in no. and as wide as the white spaces between (hence looks blacker). No interscapular patch. ♀: differs from *multostriata* race of ♀ Streaked Antwren in having underparts more uniformly buffy cinnamon (♀ Streaked Antwren has white belly) and black streaks coarse as in ♂ (not decidedly narrow and shaftlike).

**Similar species:** See Stripe-chested Antwren (34) of foothills.

**Voice:** Call a soft *pe-choo* lacking nasal quality of corresponding call of Streaked Antwren.

**Behavior:** Sim. to Streaked Antwren but may follow small bird flocks more often.

**Breeding:** Pair building hanging nest from dead limb low over water, 29 Apr, Carimagua, ne Meta (S. Furniss).

**Status and habitat:** Fairly common in shrubbery along borders of gallery forest or tall humid forest, or in savanna woodland with scattered thickets and shrubs. May partially replace Streaked Antwren in savanna regions.

**Range:** To 500m. E of Andes from s Meta (Macarena Mts.) and ne Meta (Carimagua—S. Furniss) e to e Vichada (Maipures), ne Guainía (Pto. Inírida), and se Guainía (opp. Río Casiquiare). E Colombia, s Venez., and nw Brazil in upper Orinoco and upper Río Negro regions.

### 36. PLAIN-THROATED ANTWREN

*Myrmotherula hauxwelli*     Pl. 28, Map 761

**Identification:** 3.8″ (9.7cm). *Tail short.* ♂: mostly uniform gray, paler below; wings slaty with 2 *narrow but distinct white bars; large white spots on tips of inner secondaries;* white tips on upper tail coverts and tail; concealed white interscapular patch. ♀: dull olive brown with dusky wings and tail; wing coverts blackish; 2 *buff wing bars, large buff spots on inner secondaries,* and buff tips on upper tail coverts and tail; *below bright cinnamon rufous*, throat paler.

**Similar species:** ♂ is only small "gray" antwren with prom. white terminal spots on inner remiges. ♀ from any other small Colombian antwren by bright cinnamon rufous underparts and buff wing spots.

**Voice:** Song a very deliberate, penetrating ser. of *chuée* notes increasing in vol. and lasting about 2-3 sec; song rises slightly in pitch.

**Behavior:** Alone or in pairs or small groups (families?). Cling to vertical saplings and small stems from near ground to 2m up in open understory where they glean foliage or drop to ground. Also hop and flutter in tangled *várzea* brush along streams (J. V. Remsen; Hilty).

**Breeding:** Open vireolike nest 0.3m up in sapling fork, Sept, se Peru (C. Munn).

**Status and habitat:** Uncommon in *terra firme* and *várzea* forest undergrowth or in partially flooded stream-side saplings.

**Range:** To 500m. E of Andes from w Meta (Villavicencio area) and Vaupés (Mitú) southward. E Colombia to n Bolivia and Amazonian Brazil w of Río Negro and s of Amazon.

## 37. CHECKER-THROATED ANTWREN
*Myrmotherula fulviventris*      Pl. 28, Map 762
**Identification:** 4.2″ (10.7cm). *Iris pale.* ♂: brownish olive above, slightly grayer on sides of face; wing coverts blackish with 2 buff bars; *throat checkered black and white*; rest of underparts uniform buffy brown. ♀: sim. above; underparts *uniform* dull ochraceous or with a few dusky streaks on throat.

**Similar species:** ♂ easily recognized. ♀ from ♀ White-flanked Antwren (41) by wing bars, more uniform underparts (no white flank tuft), and pale eye (not always conspic.). ♀ Slaty Antwren (42), not in lowlands but overlapping in foothills, lacks wing bars and is tawny (not buff) below.

**Voice:** Song a loud high-pitched *tseek-seek-seek-seek*; territorial ♂ ♂ give squeaky *syip* notes rapidly as they bow back and forth 1 m apart with puffed throats (Willis and Eisenmann 1979); mob with loud *peesk* notes (Wiley 1971).

**Behavior:** Pairs or several often assoc. with mixed flocks, esp. other antwrens, and move restlessly through lower or mid. strata (usually lower than White-flanked Antwren). Frequently examine dead curled leaves (Wiley 1971).

**Breeding:** 6 BC birds, Apr–May, s Bolívar to sw Antioquia; 1 laying ♀, Dec, Valle (Carriker); 58 Panama nests (mainly rainy season), all mos. except Dec, Feb, and Apr; deep pensile pouch of fiber with narrow oval entrance;

about 0.4-2m up at tip of slender twig; 2 white eggs dotted red brown and lilac (Willis and Eisenmann 1979; Skutch 1969a).

**Status and habitat:** Common in humid forest and second growth woodland in lowlands, smaller nos. in foothills.

**Range:** To 2000m (mostly below 1100m). Pacific coast, and e in lowlands n of Andes to mid. Magdalena Val. (s to Remedios, e Antioquia). Honduras to w Ecuador.

## 38. STIPPLE-THROATED ANTWREN
*Myrmotherula haematonota*      Pl. 28, Map 763
**Identification:** 4″ (10.2cm). Eyes usually dark. ♂: grayish brown above with *bright chestnut back* (not rump); *wing coverts black with white-dotted wing bars; throat black, finely dotted white,* sides of head and underparts gray becoming brown on belly. ♀: *sim. to* ♂ *above but wing bars spotted buff*; sides of head and underparts ochraceous buff becoming darker and browner on belly.

**Similar species:** ♂ from ♂ Ornate Antwren (40) by white-dotted (not solid black) throat and brownish instead of grayish upperparts. ♂ Rufous-tailed Antwren (39) has rufous lower back *and tail*, lacks *blackish wing coverts*, and throat uniform or a few vague dark streaks on lower throat. ♀ from ♀ Ornate by uniform throat (not black streaked white); from ♀ Rufous-tailed by brown (not rufous) tail and brownish belly.

**Voice:** Alarm at Mitú an often repeated staccato rattle, *tre'e'e'e'e*.

**Behavior:** Pairs or more often small restless groups travel with mixed flocks containing other antwrens. Examine curled dead leaves, and piles of trash 1-7m up much like Rufous-tailed Antwren.

**Breeding:** BC birds, Apr, Amazonas, Venez. (Friedmann 1948).

**Status and habitat:** Uncommon in humid *terra firme* forest.

**Range:** To 500m. E of Andes from w Caquetá and Vaupés (sightings at Mitú, 1978—Hilty) southward (*pyrrhonota*). Prob. also Guainía and e Vichada. S Venez. to s Peru and w Amazonian Brazil.

**Note 1:** Ecuadorian Antwren (*M. spodionota*) of e slope of Andes in e Ecuador and ne Peru should occur along se base of Colombian Andes. ♂ sim. to ♂ Stipple-throated Antwren (38), but head and back slaty gray, only forehead and upper tail coverts washed olive brown. ♀ olive brown above with 2 buff-spotted wing bars; throat ochraceous buff and rest of underparts olive brown; chest and median breast flammulated ochraceous buff. Both sexes from Stipple-throated, Rufous-tailed, and Ornate antwrens (38, 39, 40) by lack of rufous above. **Note 2:** *M. spodionota* has been considered a race of *M. haematonota* (Stipple-throated Antwren) because presumed intermeds. are known from n Peru, but most Ecuador recs. of *spodionota* are at higher el. (500-1100m). Has also been considered a subsp. of *M. leucophthalma* (White-eyed Antwren) of se Peru, Bolivia, and Brazil.

### 39. RUFOUS-TAILED ANTWREN
*Myrmotherula erythrura* Pl. 28, Map 764
**Identification:** 4.5" (11.4cm). Tail slightly longer than others of the group. ♂: olive brown above with *rufous lower back and tail; wing bars spotted pale buffy white;* forehead, sides of head, and underparts light gray (usually with some vague black speckling on lower throat); abdomen buffy brown. ♀: sim., but throat ochraceous buff; remaining underparts olive buff.
**Similar species:** ♂ or ♀ is only one of its kind with a *rufous tail;* ♂♂ of Stipple-throated and Ornate antwrens (38, 40) also differ in *obvious* black on throat. ♀ most like ♀ Stipple-throated but tail rufous (not brown).
**Voice:** Song a high almost squeaky *seeep-seeep-seeep* in Peru; alarm a short bubbling rattle like that of Stipple-throated Antwren in alarm (T. Parker).
**Behavior:** Pairs follow mixed flocks, esp. with other antwrens, and normally probe curled dead leaves 1-9m up; also restlessly inspect vine tangles.
**Breeding:** Begging juv., 30 Aug, Río Javarí, Brazil, s of Leticia (Hilty).
**Status and habitat:** Uncommon to common in *terra firme* and *várzea* forests.
**Range:** To 500m. E of Andes from s Meta (Macarena Mts.) and Vaupés (Mitú) southward. E Colombia to e Peru and w Amazonian Brazil.

### 40. ORNATE ANTWREN
*Myrmotherula ornata* Pl. 28, Map 765
**Identification:** 4.2" (10.7cm). ♂: *dark gray above with chestnut lower back and rump;* wing coverts black with prom. white-spotted wing bars; *throat black;* breast and belly gray; abdomen and flanks brownish. ♀: olive brown above with *chestnut lower back and rump;* wing coverts black with conspic. white-dotted wing bars; *throat black narrowly streaked white;* remaining underparts dull ochraceous buff tinged olive.
**Similar species:** Rufous rump of this and other small antwrens can be hard to see in field. Cf. much browner ♂ Stipple-throated Antwren (38); ♂ Rufous-tailed Antwren (39) has mostly gray (not black) throat and rufous tail. ♀ from ♀ Stipple-throated or Rufous-tailed by crisp black throat streaked white; also from latter

by olive brown (not rufous) tail; ♀ from sim. ♂♂ of 38 and 39 by ochraceous lower underparts. See Ash-winged Antwren (57).
**Voice:** Infrequently a short emphatic trill (T. Parker).
**Behavior:** Pairs glean small insects in tangles of dead leaves and vines 3-12m up; more often seen in mixed flocks than away from them (Pearson 1977).
**Status and habitat:** Dense vines and tangles in humid *terra firme* forest and older secondary woodland. Common at Limoncocha, Ecuador (Pearson et al. 1977).
**Range:** To 1200m. E of Andes from Meta (w of Villavicencio; Macarena Mts.) to se Nariño; doubtless e to Amazonas. E Colombia to n Bolivia and Amazonian Brazil w of Río Negro and s of Amazon.

### 41. WHITE-FLANKED ANTWREN
*Myrmotherula axillaris* Pl. 28, Map 766
**Identification:** 4" (10.2cm). ♂: *slaty black* with 3 *white-dotted wing bars;* under wing coverts and *long silky flank plumes white;* tail usually narrowly tipped white. ♀ very dull: olive brown to grayish olive above; wings and tail browner with inconspic. buff-dotted wing bars; throat whitish becoming ochraceous on breast and paler on lower underparts; *under wing coverts and long flank plumes white like ♂.*
**Similar species:** Either sex distinguished by protruding white flank plumes (sometimes concealed under wing but watch for wing flicks).
**Voice:** In w Colombia a descending *cheep-doo* or *cheep cheep-doo;* e of Andes *nyaa-whop;* dry rattle alarm at nest *trrrrrr;* song at dawn or in dispute a measured ser. of 6-10 descending whistles, 2 per sec, *pyee, pee, piy, pey, puh, pu* (Willis and Eisenmann 1979; Hilty).
**Behavior:** Pairs or small groups usually follow forest flocks and restlessly flick wings as glean from foliage or small twigs in mid. story or lower. In nw Colombia commonly with Checker-throated and Dot-winged antwrens; e of Andes with other spp.
**Breeding:** 8 BC birds, Jan–May, 1 in Sept, 1 in Dec, n Colombia (Carriker); BC ♂, Mar, nw Santander (Boggs 1961); in Panama, sturdy black filament-lined cup attached by rim to fork 0.2-4m up, always with large overhanging leaf or leaves; 2 eggs (Willis and Eisenmann 1979; Skutch 1969a).
**Status and habitat:** Humid and wet forest and older second growth woodland. One of the most numerous forest antwrens e of Andes.
**Range:** To 900m. Pacific coast and Gulf of Urabá e to lower Cauca Val. and Río Nechí (*albigula*); w base of Santa Marta Mts. to mid. Magdalena Val. (w of Bucaramanga) and e of Andes

throughout (*melaena*) but no Amazonas recs. Honduras to n Bolivia and se Brazil.

## 42. SLATY ANTWREN
*Myrmotherula schisticolor*     Pl. 28, Map 767
**Identification:** 4″ (10.2cm). ♂: slaty gray with throat and breast black (or only throat and foreneck black—*sanctaemartae*); wing coverts blackish, 2 *wing bars dotted white*; under tail coverts mottled with white. ♀ very dull: brownish olive above, back grayer (or more bluish gray—*interior*); wing coverts uniform; throat pale buff occas. with black flecking; rest of underparts brownish buff tinged ochraceous on breast.
**Similar species:** ♂ Long-winged Antwren (43) of e lowlands has white on shoulders, more distinct wing bars (not rows of dots), and paler gray underparts (black throat and chest in sharp contrast to gray). ♀ Long-winged Antwren has buff eyering and white (not buffy brown) belly. Also see ♂ and ♀ White-flanked and Rio Suno antwrens (41, 44), ♂ of latter very sim. but smaller, tail decidedly shorter, wing dots fainter and in the hand, no white mottling on under tail coverts.
**Voice:** Call a nasal whining *yyeeet*; a short *tee-up.*
**Behavior:** Pairs or small groups glean twigs and leaves like warblers in lower story; sometimes with mixed flocks containing antwrens and warblers.
**Breeding:** 7 BC birds, Mar–June, n Antioquia and Perijá Mts. (Carriker); 3 BC ♂♂, Apr, Valle (Miller 1963); frail black fiber cup suspended from low horizontal fork; 2 eggs, white to cream blotched and spotted dark (Skutch 1969a).
**Status and habitat:** Uncommon to fairly common in undergrowth of humid and wet forest and second growth woodland. Normal range is above that of sim. allies.
**Range:** 900–2100m (to 400m on e slope E Andes in Caquetá). Santa Marta and Perijá mts. (*sanctaemartae*); W Andes s to Nariño, both slopes C Andes in Antioquia and w slope in Valle (*schisticolor*); e slope of E Andes and head of Magdalena Val. (*interior*). S Mexico to n Venez. and s Peru.

## 43. LONG-WINGED ANTWREN
*Myrmotherula longipennis*     Pl. 28, Map 768
**Identification:** 4″ (10.2cm). ♂: dark gray, paler gray below with *contrasting black patch on throat and central chest*; wing coverts black fringed white forming 3 narrow white wing bars and white on shoulder; tail blackish with faint white tip. ♀: olive brown above; wing coverts unmarked; narrow cinnamon buff eyering (not conspic.); throat and upper breast yellowish

buff; lower underparts whitish; sides of body grayish olive.
**Similar species:** In foothills see ♂ and ♀ Slaty Antwren (42), in lowlands ♂ and ♀ Rio Suno Antwren (44). ♀ Long-winged Antwren also not easily told from several other ♀ *Myrmotherula* antwrens (cf. esp. 41, 45, 46) but differs by presence of buff eyering and brighter yellowish buff throat and breast more or less contrasting with white belly. ♀ White-flanked Antwren (41) shows white flank patches as flicks wings. S of Amazon see ♀ Salvadori's Antwren (note under 44).
**Voice:** Song in Peru a high, thin, rising *chewey-chewey-chewey-chewee-chewee-che* (T. Parker).
**Behavior:** Pairs or several flutter busily in foliage at midlevels or lower with mixed forest flocks. Reg. hover below leaves to snap off small prey (H. Wiley).
**Breeding:** Several BC birds, Oct–Nov, Amazonas, Venez. (Friedmann 1948). In se Peru 4 open cup nests 2-6m up in forks of leafy saplings, Aug–Nov (C. Munn).
**Status and habitat:** Humid *terra firme* and *várzea* forests. Fairly common at Mitú, Vaupés.
**Range:** To 400m. E of Andes from w Caquetá and se Guainía (San Felipe and Río Negro) southward. The Guianas and s Venez. to se Peru and Amazonian Brazil.

## 44. RIO SUNO ANTWREN
*Myrmotherula sunensis*     Pl. 28, Map 769
**Identification:** 3.6″ (9.1cm). *Tail very short.* ♂: slaty gray; *throat and chest black, the black spreading well onto upper chest; small whitish dots* form *dotted* wing bars; no white tail tips. ♀: olive gray above; wings and tail brownish; underparts ochraceous buff, paler on throat; sides, flanks, and crissum washed olive brown.
**Similar species:** ♂ Long-winged Antwren (43) is very sim. but larger, longer-tailed, usually with distinct wing bars (usually reduced to tiny rows of dots on Rio Suno Antwren), decidedly paler gray (not slaty) underparts, *more extensively black* on throat and chest, and tail narrowly tipped white (some Rio Suno ♂♂ show small white tips also). Cf. ♂ Slaty Antwren (42). S of Amazon see Salvadori's Antwren (below). ♀ hardly separable in field from several other ♀ *Myrmotherula* but esp. cf. ♀ Slaty (42) and ♀ Plain-winged antwrens (whitish eyering, 45); from ♀ Long-winged Antwren (43) by smaller size, absence of eyering and more uniform ochraceous underparts (belly not white).
**Behavior:** Apparently much like Long-winged Antwren.
**Status and habitat:** Humid *terra firme* forest at e base of Andes. Not well known in Colombia but apparently mainly a foothill and hill coun-

try bird overlapping somewhat with lowland White-flanked and highland Slaty antwrens.
**Range:** 400-500m. Known from Río Churuyaco on Nariño-Putumayo boundary near e base of Andes (poss. Amazonas as rec at mouth of Río Curaray, n Peru). Se Colombia to e Peru.
**Note:** Salvadori's Antwren (*M. minor*) of ne Peru (Iquitos eastward), w Amazonian Brazil s of the Amazon, and se Brazil occurs s of Amazon opp. Leticia. ♂ resembles Rio Suno Antwren but black patch on throat smaller (barely reaches chest), tail with subterminal black band and white tip, and wing bars (not dots) broader. ♀ is brownish olive above, wing coverts tipped pale buff, throat whitish faintly scaled dusky, otherwise bright olive buff below. *Várzea* forest midlevels with mixed flocks.

### 45. PLAIN-WINGED ANTWREN
*Myrmotherula behni*                    Map 770
**Identification:** 3.7" (9.4cm). ♂: *uniform dark gray with black throat spreading onto chest*; wing coverts unmarked. ♀: reddish brown above; narrow eyering and *throat whitish*; remaining underparts olivaceous buff; wing coverts unmarked.
**Similar species:** Overlaps only Slaty Antwren (42) in known foothill and mt. range. ♂ like ♂ Slaty but lacks wing bars; ♀ from very sim. ♀ Slaty by more rufescent upperparts and eyering. Range is above several sim. lowland allies that it may meet or overlap in hill country incl.: Long-winged Antwren (43), ♂ with paler plumage, white on shoulders, and wing bars; and ♂ Gray Antwren (46) with wing bars and no black throat.
**Voice:** A med. high trill *kyerrrrrr* (Snyder 1966).
**Status and habitat:** Little known in Colombia. Undergrowth of humid foothill and highland forests.
**Range:** 1300-1800m. Known only from s Meta in Macarena Mts. (Pico Renjifo) and "Bogotá." Tepuis of s Venez. and adj. nw Brazil and Guyana.

### 46. GRAY ANTWREN
*Myrmotherula menetriesii*      Pl. 28, Map 771
**Identification:** 3.7" (9.4cm). ♂: *uniform gray*, paler below; *wing coverts with distinctive subterminal black band and white tip* (coverts look black with 3 white bars at a distance); under tail coverts tipped white; tail narrowly tipped white; throat sometimes with white speckling. ♀: bluish gray above; wings and tail tinged olive brown; wing coverts unmarked; throat whitish; rest of underparts bright buffy ochraceous, sides and belly duller.
**Similar species:** ♂ of this, ♂ of Plain-throated Antwren (36), and ♂ of Leaden Antwren (47)

are only "gray" *Myrmotherula* in Colombia without black throats; Plain-throated ♂ differs in white spots on inner secondaries, tail coverts, and tail tip; Leaden ♂ differs in lacking the black subterminal band on wing coverts and in habitat. ♀ much like ♀♀ of other "gray" *Myrmotherula* antwrens lacking wing bars (42, 44, 45) but paler and grayer above and brighter ochraceous below. Also see ♀ Long-winged (43).
**Voice:** Song a weak, thin, wavering ser. of about 12 *ree* notes that rise in pitch and accelerate slightly.
**Behavior:** Usually in pairs or small groups with bird flocks from lower to upper midlevels. Commonly hop along leafy twigs peering downward or hanging.
**Breeding:** BC pair 15 May, Mitú (Olivares 1964b); 3 BC birds, Apr, Amazonas, Venez. (Friedman 1948); nest at Mitú, 11 Feb, mostly dead leaves wrapped and suspended in fork 4.5m up (Hilty).
**Status and habitat:** Common; humid *terra firme* forest.
**Range:** To 500m. E of Andes from Meta (Villavicencio area), Río Guaviare and e Vichada (Maipures) southward. The Guianas and s Venez. to n Bolivia and Amazonian Brazil.

### 47. [LEADEN ANTWREN]
*Myrmotherula assimilis*
**Identification:** 4.2" (10.7cm). ♂: plain light gray above; paler gray below becoming whitish gray on belly; wing coverts plain gray with 2 white wing bars; tail slaty gray narrowly tipped white. ♀ like ♂ above but wings tinged brownish with *2 buff wing bars*, pale cinnamon below, throat whitish. In the hand both sexes have a large concealed white interscapular patch (lacking in 46).
**Similar species:** ♂ is one of 3 mainly "gray" antwrens found in Colombia with no black on the throat; ♂ Gray Antwren (46) has distinctive subterminal black band on the wing coverts and habitat differs; ♂ Plain-throated Antwren (36) has large white spots on inner secondaries. ♀ is much paler and grayer above than other ♀ antwrens with buff wing bars and cinnamon or ochraceous underparts; see ♀ Plain-throated Antwren (36) with large buff spots on inner secondaries and ♀ Checker-throated Antwren (37) which is brownish olive above (not plain light gray).
**Voice:** Fast descending chippering trill lasting 2-3 sec, given mostly (only?) by ♂.
**Behavior:** In pairs but foraging independently about 3-7m up (R. Ridgely).
**Status and habitat:** Hypothetical. A sight rec. of a pair on Isla Corea, 18 Jan 1983 (R. Ridgely; B. Whitney); there are earlier unconfirmed

sightings in nearby area. Specimen confirmation needed. Apparently restricted to semiopen *várzea* shrub and younger growth on Amazon river isls. Prob. often overlooked in its unusual habitat.

**Range:** Isla Corea, near Leticia, Amazonas. Ne Peru (Nauta; Pto. Indiana) e along Río Amazon to the isls. opp. Santarem, Brazil, n to mid. Río Negro and s on Río Juruá, Río Purús and spottily on Río Madeira to n Beni, Bolivia.

## 48. BANDED ANTBIRD
*Dichrozona cincta*                    Pl. 32, Map 772
**Identification:** 4.2″ (10.7cm). *Bill long and narrow.* Tail very short. ♂: crown and mantle chestnut brown; lower back and rump black crossed by a *white rump band*; wings black, shoulders spotted white; *2 broad buff wing bars* (first bar sometimes white), primaries broadly edged brown; sides of head gray; *underparts white with necklace of black spots across chest*; tail black, outer feathers white. ♀: sim. but shoulder spots and rump band buff, and fewer chest spots.
**Similar species:** Remarkably like Spot-backed Antbird (99), which differs in having black throat, buff-spotted back, no rump band, and different behavior.
**Voice:** In e Peru a long, drawn out, insectlike trill, *pseeyouweeeeeeeeeeeee*, very slightly ascending (O'Neill 1974); also, presum. this sp., a soft rising and accelerting ser. of notes *zee-zee-zee* . . . (T. Parker).
**Behavior:** Recalls a Nightingale Wren as it walks on forest floor and wags tail. Flushes with wagging tail, displaying ribbonlike white on outer feathers (T. Parker).
**Status and habitat:** Uncommon on ground in humid *terra firme* forest. Not well known in Colombia.
**Range:** To 500m. E of Andes from s Meta (Macarena Mts.) and se Guainía (opp. mouth of Río Casiquiare) southward. S Venez. to n Bolivia and nw and c Amazonian Brazil.

[*Herpsilochmus*: Gnatcatcherlike with long tail; crown black (♂) or usually rufous chestnut (♀); most with prom. superciliary. Vines in treetops or lower at edges.]

## 49. SPOT-TAILED ANTWREN
*Herpsilochmus sticturus*              Map 773
**Identification:** 4″ (10.2cm). ♂: crown and nape black; *long broad eyestripe white*; face grizzled whitish and gray; back clear gray (appears unmarked); wings black with *bold white spotting on coverts* (almost like bars), remiges edged white; underparts grayish white (grayest on breast); tail black narrowly tipped white above

and with white spots on center (from above); from below tail grayish with large white spots on tips of feathers (pattern of Yellow-billed Cuckoo). ♀: sim. but crown and nape mainly rufous, underparts dirty buff. Description of ♂ based on *sticturus* subsp. from Venez., and modified by sight rec. of presumed *dugandi* in e Ecuador (R. Ridgely). ♂ of *dugandi* has not been collected.
**Similar species:** See Spot-backed Antwren (50). Both vaguely recall Tropical Gnatcatcher (p 551), but white on wings and tail much more extensive. Other *Herpsilochmus* (51, 52) are mostly yellow below.
**Voice:** In Surinam a short, accelerating ("bouncing ball") roll, *chit, chit chi-chi' chi'chi'i'i'i'*, reminiscent of Pygmy Antwren or an antvireo.
**Behavior:** Resembles Rufous-winged Antwren, and like that sp., when it calls, its tail shivers.
**Status and habitat:** Known definitely from 1 ♀ at Belén, Caquetá (sw Florencia). In ne Ecuador in canopy and subcanopy of *várzea* and to a lesser extent *terra firme* forest; prob. overlooked because it remains so high (R. Ridgely).
**Range:** 400-450m. E of Andes in w Caquetá (*dugandi*), doubtless Putumayo. The Guianas, ne Brazil, s Venez., and e Ecuador.

## 50. SPOT-BACKED ANTWREN
*Herpsilochmus dorsimaculatus*         Pl. 28, Map 774
**Indentification:** 4.5″ (11.4cm). ♂: differs from very sim. Spot-tailed Antwren (subsp. *sticturus*, 49) in slightly larger size; *back spotted and striped black and white* (not appearing uniform gray); and underparts paler, more whitish. ♀: like ♀ Spot-tailed Antwren, but forehead spotted buff, *crown black spotted white*, underparts paler more whitish with lores, sides of neck and breast washed yellowish.
**Behavior:** Single birds (this sp. or 49) accompanied a mixed flock on 2 occas. at Mitú, where they actively gleaned outer foliage and twigs in the upper canopy.
**Status and habitat:** Perhaps rare; humid sandy-belt forest and forest edge. Few Colombian recs.
**Range:** To 250m. Extreme e Colombia in Vaupés on Río Vaupés (opp. Tahuapunto, Brazil; Mitú, sight?) and se Guainía (opp. Caño Casiquiare, Venez.). E Colombia, s Venez., and nw Brazil.

## 51. YELLOW-BREASTED ANTWREN
*Herpsilochmus axillaris*              Pl. 28, Map 775
**Identification:** 4.8″ (12.2cm). Cocks tail. ♂: *crown black* spotted white; *long white eyestripe speckled black*; auriculars black with black and white speckling below eyes; back uniform olive gray;

*wings black with 2 white wing bars and faint gray edgings*; throat white; *remaining underparts clear pale yellow*; sides washed olive; tail mostly black broadly tipped and edged white. ♀: like ♂, but *crown and nape rufous chestnut*, back brownish.

**Similar species:** With bright plumage, more likely mistaken for a warbler than an antwren. Rufous-winged Antwren (52) is rather sim. but both sexes have conspic. rufous primaries. Also cf. Double-banded Graytail (p 366).

**Voice:** Song much like Rufous-winged Antwren but weaker, a slow, bouncy roll as though from a small *Thamnophilus* antshrike.

**Behavior:** Singly, in pairs, or in groups of 3-6 gleaning in denser foliage and vine tangles in canopy or upper forest levels. Usually with mixed flocks; restless, active, almost warbler-like and often difficult to see well.

**Status and habitat:** Very uncommon in humid and wet forest and occas. forest borders on Pacific slope where known from only a few localities. Prob. more numerous on e Andean slope.

**Range:** 900-1800m on Pacific slope from headwaters of Río San Juan (w of Cerro Tatamá) s to w Cauca. Two sight recs. on e slope E Andes: (1 ♂, 7 Sept 1978, ♂ and ♀, 9 June 1981, 1500-1600m, above Florencia, Caquetá—Hilty). Doubtless w Putumayo. W Colombia; e slope of Andes from se Colombia to e Ecuador and e Peru.

## 52. RUFOUS-WINGED ANTWREN

*Herpsilochmus rufimarginatus* Pl. 28, Map 776

**Identification:** 4.5″ (11.4cm). ♂: *crown and narrow stripe through eye black; long eyestripe white*; back gray mixed black in center; wing coverts and inner secondaries black with *2 broad white bars* and edgings; *primaries and most of secondaries bright chestnut*; throat whitish, remaining underparts creamy yellow; tail dark gray broadly tipped white. ♀: sim. but *crown chestnut*, back olive.

**Similar species:** From any other *Herpsilochmus* by bright chestnut remiges. See Yellow-breasted Antwren (51); flashy plumage of both recalls a warbler.

**Voice:** Song in Venez. a smoothly accelerating roll, *ku, ku ku-ku-ku'ku'we' e'e'e'e'djt*, bouncy with rough note at end (P. Schwartz recording).

**Behavior:** Much like Yellow-breasted Antwren. Usually in pairs that follow mixed flocks and glean in foliage like an active vireo or occas. hover-glean; midlevel to canopy.

**Status and habitat:** Apparently local. Vine tangles in open or lighter humid forest and savanna and gallery woodland; wanders away from woodland along bush- and tree-lined borders.

**Range:** 100-1200m. Panama and n end of W Andes from Sinú Valley e to mid. Magdelena Val. (s Bolívar); e slope of e Andes in nw Arauca, w Meta, and e Nariño. E Panama, Venez. (n and s of Orinoco and Perijá Mts.) s locally to e Ecuador, e Peru, n Bolivia to s Brazil.

## 53. DOT-WINGED ANTWREN

*Microrhopias quixensis* Pl. 28, Map 777

**Identification:** 4.5″ (11.4cm) (or 5.0″ [13cm]—*quixensis*). Tail strongly graduated, longer than *Myrmotherula* and often held cocked. ♂: *glossy black with a single broad white wing bar and white-dotted lesser coverts; rounded tail broadly tipped white* (obvious from below); partly concealed white interscapular patch. Or lower back with more white and white tail tips narrower (*quixensis*); birds s of Leticia (s bank of Amazon) have *tail all white from below* due to broader white tips on tail feathers (*intercedens?*). ♀: slaty to black above, head grayer; deep rufous chestnut below; wings, tail, and dorsal patch as in ♂. Or head and throat black—*quixensis*.

**Similar species:** ♂ recalls ♂ White-flanked Antwren (41) but lacks tufts and has conspic. tail spots. Larger ♂ Jet Antbird (62) has 2 white wing bars. Richly colored ♀ unlike any other.

**Voice:** Song a rapid ser. of 5-10 upscale whistles, *pu-peh-pey-pih-pee-pyee*, often alternated in dispute with 2 rough *zhalet* notes; alarm a falsetto *peep* and *chew* and tiny *buzz* (Willis and Eisenmann 1979).

**Behavior:** Pairs or small groups wander alone or with other *Myrmotherula* antwrens both e and w of Andes. Very active as they glean from dense foliage and tangles in forest midlevels or lower. Often slightly spread cocked tail.

**Breeding:** 8 BC birds, Mar–May, nw Colombia (Carriker); 2 Panama nests, Feb; deep, thick-walled cups of dead leaves and fibers suspended by rim 1-7m up; 2 white eggs dotted brown, more heavily at large end (Johnson 1953).

**Status and habitat:** Fairly common w of Andes, less so e of Andes; humid and wet *terra firme* and *várzea* forests, and second growth woodland; often around dense vines and treefalls.

**Range:** To 900m. Pacific coast, humid lowlands n of Andes e to mid. Magdalena Val. s to Remedios, Antioquia (*consobrina*); e of Andes from w Caquetá to se Nariño (*quixensis*), prob. Amazonas as *quixensis* rec. n of Amazon at Pto. Indiana and mouth of Río Curaray in n Peru. Se Mexico to w Ecuador; e Colombia to Bolivia and Amazonian Brazil.

## 54. WHITE-FRINGED ANTWREN

*Formicivora grisea*         Pl. 28, Map 778
**Identification:** 5″ (13cm). ♂: brownish gray above, wings black with a single white bar and white-dotted shoulders; tail blackish, rounded and broadly tipped white; *black sides of head and underparts separated from upperparts by broad white eyestripe continuing down sides of neck and widening on sides and flanks.* ♀: like ♂ above; underparts white to buffy white somewhat mottled dusky on sides of head and breast. Or eyestripe and entire underparts cinnamon rufous (*rufiventris*).
**Similar species:** Unique in the dry scrub it favors.
**Voice:** A single whistled *tu*, followed by a soft trill; also an incisive *tu-ik*, repeated slowly then faster, both calls sometimes merging (ffrench 1973). In Surinam a ser. of up to 20 *chup* notes (T. Davis).
**Behavior:** Pairs stay in thickets and from near ground to a few m up, hopping deliberately and gleaning foliage and small twigs; often with small mixed flocks. May wag tail from side to side and droop wings exposing white underwings. Not secretive.
**Breeding:** 14 BC birds, Jan–Dec (9 in Aug), nw Colombia (Carriker); 7 Santa Marta nests, Apr–Oct (S. M. Russell; Todd and Carriker 1922); thinly woven grass cup suspended by rim from fork; 2 grayish white eggs spotted lilac and blotched brown.
**Status and habitat:** Common in dry woodland borders and arid scrub in n Colombia; savanna woodland borders and pockets of scrub from Río Orinoco to Vaupés.
**Range:** To 1100m. Carib. region from Gulf of Urabá and upper Sinú Val. e to Barranquilla and s to upper Magdalena Val. (*hondae*); Santa Marta area to Guajira (*intermedia*); e of Andes in Catatumbo lowlands (*fumosa*); ne Guainía (Pto. Inírida) to Vaupés (*rufiventris*); sight recs. in n Meta (Apr 1978—W. McKay) and n Vichada. Pearl Isls., Panama; n Colombia to the Guianas, e Amazonian, and se Brazil. Trinidad and Tobago.

## 55. LONG-TAILED ANTBIRD

*Drymophila caudata*         Pl. 28, Map 779
**Identification:** 6″ (15cm). Streaked. ♂: *head and back black streaked white; throat and underparts white streaked black;* lower back and posterior underparts rufous chestnut; narrow broken eyering white; wing coverts black with *2 white wing bars*, remiges olive brown; *long graduated tail* dark olive, blacker subterminally with *broad white tips.* ♀: sim. but streaked black and cinnamon (not black and white), esp. on upperparts.

**Similar species:** More likely mistaken for a wren or furnariid than an antbird. Note streaked foreparts, rufous rearparts, and long white-tipped tail.
**Voice:** Unusual and unantbirdlike song, 2 clear rhythmic notes, then 2 very wheezy phrases, the accented note higher-pitched, *chuet, chuet pa-fjéee-jt, pa-fjéee-jt*; also plaintive *chuep* notes.
**Behavior:** Pairs or small groups, less frequently alone. Hop like wrens in dense bamboo, vines, and shrubbery from understory to subcanopy. Sing frequently and not shy but can be difficult to see.
**Breeding:** 3 BC birds, Apr–June, Santa Marta and n Antioquia (Carriker).
**Status and habitat:** Somewhat local and in var. of habitats from fairly dry to wet. Favors dense vines, tangles, or bamboo at forest borders, around treefalls, or in tall second growth.
**Range:** 1200-2700m. Santa Marta Mts. (to 600m), Perijá Mts. (se of Codazzi) and spottily throughout Andes (E Andes s to se Santander and in e Huila). N Venez. s in mts. to n Bolivia.
**Note:** Striated Antbird (*D. devillei*) from e Ecuador (upper Río Napo), ne Peru (incl. Pebas) and ne Brazil s to n Bolivia may occur in Putumayo or Amazonas. Much like Long-tailed Antbird, it differs in smaller size (5.3″), shorter tail, mostly white underparts with only a few black streaks on sides, and only sides and flanks (not belly) cinnamon rufous. ♀ sim. but upperparts streaked buff and black. In e Peru in bamboo and vine tangles in lowlands and foothills below range of Long-tailed Antbird. Song recalls long-tailed, 1-2 introductory chips, 2-3 wheezes, then 4 rising chips (T. Parker).

[*Terenura*: Small, slender and warblerlike; bill thin; midlevel to canopy.]

## 56. RUFOUS-RUMPED ANTWREN

*Terenura callinota*         Pl. 28, Map 780
**Identification:** 4.2″ (10.7cm). Warblerlike. ♂: *crown black with narrow white eyestripe* and black line through eye; back olive green with concealed chestnut interscapular patch; *rump orange rufous;* bend of shoulder bright yellow; *wing coverts black with 2 broad yellowish white wing bars;* underparts grayish white; belly tinged yellow; tail grayish. ♀: sim. but cap and shoulders olive like back.
**Similar species:** Rufous-winged (52) and Yellow-breasted antwrens (51) are superficially sim. but larger, less slender and lack rufous rump; former also has prom. rufous chestnut primaries. Other "rufous rumped" antwrens (38, 39, 40) are chiefly lowland birds. Also see White-banded Tyrannulet (p 467).
**Voice:** A very high, thin, chipping *ti-ti-ti'ti'i'i'i'i'ti-*

*tzzs, tzzs, tzzs,* as it forages, no. of buzzy notes at end var. (B. Whitney).

**Behavior:** One or more usually follow mixed flocks from forest midlevels to canopy where they very actively glean from terminal foliage and vines like a warbler or cling upside down to leaves like greenlets.

**Status and habitat:** Uncommon (easily overlooked) in humid and wet forest and forest edge. Related Ash-tailed Antwren of Amazonian lowlands not known to overlap or even meet in range.

**Range:** 800–2400m. Pacific slope from Valle (Anchicayá Val.) southward, head of Magdalena Val. in Huila and n on w slope of E Andes to latitude of Bogotá and on e slope in Caquetá (sighting June 1981—Hilty); e Nariño. Guyana, nw Venez. (Perijá Mts.), e and w Ecuador and e Peru.

**Note:** Chestnut-shouldered Antwren (*T. humeralis*) of e Ecuador, e Peru (incl. Pebas), and w Brazil s of the Amazon may occur in se Colombia. ♂: much like Rufous-rumped Antwren but shoulders chestnut, center of belly gray and flanks and under tail coverts tinged yellow. ♀: like ♀ of 56 but crown brownish, throat buffy, and lower underparts olive. Lowlands below range of 56. Song in se Peru sim. to that of 56 but lacks buzzy notes at end (C. Munn).

## 57. ASH-WINGED ANTWREN
*Terenura spodioptila*    Pl. 28, Map 781
**Identification:** 4″ (10.2cm). Warblerlike. ♂: *crown black with narrow white eyestripe* and black line through eye; *upper mantle gray; rest of back chestnut;* wings dark gray with *2 broad white wing bars;* sides of head and underparts *light gray becoming white on abdomen;* tail gray. ♀: crown reddish brown; upper mantle olive; *rest of back chestnut;* wings and tail like ♂; throat and breast tinged ochraceous; lower underparts pale gray becoming white on abdomen.

**Similar species:** ♀ recalls several "rufous-rumped" antwrens, esp. Stipple-throated and Rufous-tailed antwrens (38, 39), but told from any by conspic. white wing bars, eyestripe, and whitish lower underparts. May meet Rufous-rumped Antwren (56) of highlands along e base of Andes; latter differs in yellow lower underparts.

**Voice:** Song a high-pitched rapid ser. of chipping notes accelerating into a trill, sim. to that of several others of the genus (T. Parker; P. Schwartz); high-pitched *see-see-see* call in Brazil (Willis 1977).

**Behavior:** Sim. to Rufous-rumped Antwren and others of the genus.

**Status and habitat:** Humid forest. Few Colombian recs.

**Range:** To 500m. E of Andes where known only from w Caquetá (Morelia s of Florencia) and Vaupés. The Guianas, s Venez. (w to upper Río Negro on Caño Casiquiare and along Orinoco), Amazonian Brazil n of Amazon and s of it at Río Tapajós.

[*Cercomacra:* Gray or black ♂♂ much alike; ♀♀ usually ochraceous to rufous below (except 62); vine tangles in undergrowth or canopy; slimmer and longer-tailed than *Myrmeciza.*]

## 58. GRAY ANTBIRD
*Cercomacra cinerascens*    Pl. 29, Map 782
**Identification:** 6″ (15cm). Eyes brown to gray. ♂: *uniform dark bluish gray* with small white dots on wing coverts (dots sometimes obsolete or lacking); graduated tail blackish with *broad white tips* (mostly visible from below); concealed dorsal patch white (sometimes lacking). ♀: olive brown above, grayer on rump and tail; wing coverts sometimes with small whitish dots; *sides of head, throat, and breast dull ochraceous,* dingier more olive on belly; tail tipped white as in ♂.

**Similar species:** ♂ much like ♂ Dusky Antbird (59) but has prom. white tail tips (very obscure in 59), shows very little white on wing coverts, and habits different. ♀ Dusky may have faint buff-dotted wing bars, is bright cinnamon rufous (not dull ochraceous) below, and *lacks* white tail tips.

**Voice:** Usual song a rising and falling *crookshank . . . ,* repeated several times, often the only clue to the bird's presence and very sim. to song of Jet Antbird; less often a rhythmic *keep-it-up . . .* or sim. var. several times in a ser., repeated song perhaps antiphonal.

**Behavior:** Secretive and usually very difficult to see as they hop and creep through vine-tangled tree crowns in upper levels of forest or tall second growth. Do not follow mixed flocks; single birds or separated pairs.

**Status and habitat:** Fairly common (usually overlooked) in densest treetop vine tangles of humid *terra firme* and *várzea* forests and borders.

**Range:** To 600m. E of Andes from s Meta (Macarena Mts.), Vaupés and Guainía southward. The Guianas and s Venez. to n Bolivia and Amazonian Brazil.

## 59. DUSKY ANTBIRD
*Cercomacra tyrannina*    Pl. 29, Map 783
**Identification:** 5.2″ (13.2cm). ♂: *slate gray,* somewhat paler below, sometimes mottled whitish on belly; wing coverts blackish *narrowly*

but *distinctly edged white* forming 2 bars and fringes on lesser coverts; *tail very narrowly tipped white* (sometimes missing through wear); concealed interscapular patch white. ♀: olive brown above, slightly grayer on crown; wing coverts sometimes narrowly tipped buff; forehead, sides of head, and *underparts bright cinnamon rufous.*

**Similar species:** More common than others with which it is likely confused. See Black (61) and Gray antbirds (58). ♂ Blackish Antbird (60) is larger, longer-tailed, and has different call. ♀ Blackish is deep orange rufous (not paler cinnamon rufous) below. See Blackish-gray Antshrike (10). On Pacific coast see Esmeraldas and Stub-tailed antbirds (76, 77).

**Voice:** ♂ sings a loose, nasal, rattling ser. of *klu* notes, slightly accelerating, as ♀ joins or follows with unsynchronized ser. of 3-4 *jut-ut' jut-ut' jut-ut' jut-ut'* notes; call in sw Córdoba a rough buzzy *dz'z'z'z'z'.*

**Behavior:** Usually in pairs within a few meters of the ground where frequently heard, but retiring and often remain hidden in thickets. Seldom follow army ants or mixed flocks.

**Breeding:** 8 BC birds, Mar–June, n Antioquia and s Córdoba (Carriker); rather deep pendent pouch, suspended from fork or twig in undergrowth; 2 white eggs spotted reddish brown (Skutch 1969a).

**Status and habitat:** Fairly common to common. Shrubby forest borders and thickety clearings in humid zones.

**Range:** To 1800m (rarely to 2100m). Pacific coast, humid lowlands n of Andes, Cauca Val. (formerly to Valle), Magdalena Val. s to latitude of Bogotá, and e of Andes s to w Caquetá and Vaupés (Mitú). Se Mexico to w Ecuador, Amazonian Brazil (n of Amazon), and the Guianas.

## 60. BLACKISH ANTBIRD
*Cercomacra nigrescens*          Pl. 29, Map 784

**Identification:** 6.1″ (15.5cm). Eyes dark. ♂: *dark gray to slaty black* with 2 very narrow white-dotted wing bars; bend of wing and lesser coverts faintly edged white; *tail black* (no white tips), longer than tails of 58, 59, and 61, sim. to 62; concealed interscapular patch white. ♀: *forecrown,* sides of head, and underparts deep *orange rufous,* brightest around the eye; upperparts dull brown to rufescent olive; concealed white interscapular patch.

**Similar species:** Neither sex easily told from Black Antbird (61) unless singing. ♂ looks dark gray to slaty below, ♂ Black Antbird looks black; in the hand Blackish has longer tail (59-63 vs 55-58mm; Meyer de Schauensee 1952). ♀ nearest ♀ Black Antbird but told by rufous

forehead. ♂♂ of Gray and Dusky antbirds (58, 59) have white tail tips (faint in Dusky) and ♀♀ are much paler below (not deep orange rufous). Also see Slate-colored Antbird (73).

**Voice:** Call a loud clear *paal-pte'e'e'e'e'e'r,* 2d phrase higher and trilled (Hilty); very different song (less frequently heard), 5-6 nasal flat *chaa* notes rising steadily (T. Parker), recalls that of ♂ Dusky Antbird.

**Behavior:** Sim. to Dusky Antbird.

**Status and habitat:** Thickets and shrubbery in *várzea* and swampy forest borders, occas. wetter borders of *terra firme* forest and second growth woodland.

**Range:** To 500m. E of Andes in se Nariño; Leticia, Amazonas (no specimens). Se Colombia to n Bolivia, Amazonian Brazil, Surinam, and Fr. Guiana.

## 61. BLACK ANTBIRD
*Cercomacra serva*          Pl. 29, Map 785

**Identification:** 5.8″ (14.7cm). Much like Blackish Antbird. ♂: slaty black, *throat and breast blackest*; bend of wing and edges of lesser coverts narrowly fringed white, 2 narrow white wing bars; tail black (no white tips); concealed interscapular patch white. ♀: olive brown above *incl. forehead*; lores, short eyebrow, sides of head, and *underparts orange rufous.*

**Similar species:** See under Blackish Antbird (60), ♂ and ♀ of which are very sim. to ♂ and ♀ of this sp. ♂ Slate-colored Antbird (73) differs from ♂ in having dots on wing coverts (not wing bars). ♀ of 73 has dotted wing bars and lacks the eyebrow.

**Voice:** Song in Peru a rising ser. of 5-6 slightly bisyllabic *palik* notes given rather quickly, each note "spit out" abruptly; call a harsh low rattle *prt-tututututu,* almost churring; ♀ a dry *whut-tit-tit* (T. Parker).

**Behavior:** Mainly 0.1-1.5m up in dense growth at forest edge (T. Parker).

**Status and habitat:** Very uncommon (few recs.) in vines and dense shrubbery along edges of forest and second growth woodland.

**Range:** To 500m. E of Andes from w Caquetá southward (e to Amazonas?). E Colombia to n Bolivia and sw Amazonian Brazil.

## 62. JET ANTBIRD
*Cercomacra nigricans*          Pl. 29, Map 786

**Identification:** 5.8″ (14.7cm). ♂: *deep black with 2 well-marked wing bars;* bend of wing white (sometimes hard to see) and lesser coverts fringed white; tail much graduated, *broadly tipped white;* concealed interscapular patch white. ♀: slaty above; wings and tail as in ♂ but duller; *throat and chest slaty with distinct fine*

*white streaks*; rest of underparts slaty. Juv. like ♀ but underparts somewhat scaled whitish.
**Similar species:** ♂ is blackest and most boldly marked of the genus. ♀ easily recognized by streaky throat and chest, also by combination of bold wing marks and long white-tipped tail.
**Voice:** Persistently repeated song a guttural *check-wah, check-wah, check-wah, check-wah*; occas. more than 4 phrases. Cf. with very sim. song of Gray Antbird (58).
**Behavior:** Pairs hop and sneak through dense low shrubbery and tangles where they peer for insects. Usually difficult to see though often heard. Rarely at army ants.
**Breeding:** ♂ fed juv., 10 Mar, Quibdó, Chocó (Hilty); Dec juv., Meta (Olivares 1974b); grass nest in low bush, 2 pinkish eggs heavily spotted and lined reddish brown and lilac (Sclater and Salvin 1879).
**Status and habitat:** Locally common in thick shrubbery and vines along forest edges, young second growth, and esp. damp tangles near water. Easily found in PN Tayrona and n end of Lago de Sonso.
**Range:** To 1500m. Pacific coast s to Valle, humid n lowlands e to Santa Marta area, Cauca Val. s to Cali, Magdalena Val. s to c Tolima (Río Coello), and e of Andes from upper Río Arauca to w Caquetá. W Panama to w Ecuador (incl. Esmeraldas), s Peru, ne Brazil, and Venez.

### 63. WHITE-BACKED FIRE-EYE
*Pyriglena leuconota*          Pl. 27, Map 787
**Identification:** 7″ (18cm). *Eyes red.* Looks "small headed"; *bill small and short.* ♂: deep glossy black with semiconcealed white interscapular patch; *tail rather long and ample.* ♀: sim., but *mantle, back, and wings brown.*
**Similar species:** ♂ has red eyes and a bill that seems too small for size of bird. White in back usually not visible. Brown-backed ♀ should be easily distinguished.
**Voice:** Song by ♂ and ♀, a loud, fast, chippering ser. of about 20 *cheep* notes, descending and slowing slightly; reminiscent of song of White-bellied Antbird.
**Behavior:** Usually in pairs, mostly below 3m up in thickets. Like many other antbirds retiring and hard to see. Pound tail downward in alarm (Hilty). Often follow army ants, taking prey from ground and foliage (Oniki and Willis 1972).
**Breeding:** 4 BC ♂♂, Mar–May, sw Huila (Carriker); 2 BC ♂♂, May and June, upper Magdalena Val. (AMNH).
**Status and habitat:** Shrubby overgrown clearings, thickets, forest borders, and less often understory of mature humid forest. Common at PN Cueva de los Guácharos, San Agustín

and other areas in extreme upper Magdalena Val.
**Range:** 400-2700m. Head of Magdalena Val. (Huila) and e slope of E Andes from w Caquetá southward (*castanoptera*). S Colombia, e and w Ecuador, e Peru, n Bolivia, and e Amazonian (s of Amazon) and sw Brazil.
**Note:** Birds from Esmeraldas, w Ecuador, *pacificus*, may be a separate sp. (Pacific Fire-eye) and may occur in w Nariño, Colombia. ♂ differs in longer bill, shorter tail, and more concealed white interscapular patch. ♀ very different: umber brown above, paler on sides of head; semiconcealed white interscapular patch; underparts buffy brown; under tail coverts and tail sooty black.

[*Myrmoborus*: Chunky and short-tailed; long blue gray legs; ♂♂ mostly gray and black; ♀♀ brown, buff and white; undergrowth; songs much alike; pound tail downward.]

### 64. WHITE-BROWED ANTBIRD
*Myrmoborus leucophrys*          Pl. 32, Map 788
**Identification:** 5.4″ (13.7cm). ♂: *forecrown and long eyestripe grayish white; sides of head and throat black;* otherwise plain blue gray; wing coverts unmarked. ♀: *forecrown and long eyestripe bright cinnamon bordered below by black mask;* crown and upperparts russet brown; wing coverts faintly tipped buff; underparts white; sides mottled olive brown.
**Similar species:** ♂ Black-faced Antbird (66) has white wing bars and black face outlined in gray; ♀ of 66 has bold buffy wing bars and white throat in sharp contrast to buffy underparts. Also see Ash-breasted Antbird (65).
**Voice:** Song of ♂ and ♀ a loud rapid ser. *pe'ee'ee'ee'ee'* . . . *eer* of about 30 notes in 3 sec, gradually descending at end; resembles song of Ash-breasted Antbird. Also a rough *huah* and short rattle.
**Behavior:** Pairs drop to ground from a low bush or move 1-4m up in fallen trees or undergrowth where hop and sally short distances for insects. Often cling to vertical stems. Follow army ants when swarm moves through dense young second growth or forest edge thickets, otherwise join mixed flocks or wander alone (Oniki and Willis 1972; Hilty).
**Status and habitat:** Thickets and dense brush along borders of forest, disturbed areas and *várzea*, esp. near wet places or along streams. Replaced inside mature forest by Black-faced Antbird. Fairly common.
**Range:** Mainly below 500m (to 1400m in w Meta and se Boyacá). E base of Andes and generally from Villavicencio and Río Guaviare

southward. The Guianas, nw and s Venez. to n Bolivia, and n and sw Amazonian Brazil.

## 65. ASH-BREASTED ANTBIRD
*Myrmoborus lugubris*                    Pl. 32, Map 789
**Identification:** 5.2" (13.2cm). ♂: above gray, paler on forehead; *sides of head and throat black in strong contrast to pale gray underparts*; center of abdomen whitish. ♀: pale rufous brown above with *black mask through eyes*; wing coverts faintly dotted buff; *underparts white, breast tinged pale gray*, sides tinged brownish. Eyes red (both sexes).
**Similar species:** ♂ resembles ♂ Black-faced Antbird (66) but mostly white (not gray) below and wing coverts unmarked. ♀ like ♀ White-browed Antbird (64) but lacks conspic. cinnamon forehead and eyestripe.
**Voice:** Song resembles that of White-browed Antbird, a loud, rapid, descending ser. of *tew*'s (reminiscent of North American Canyon Wren (*Catherpes mexicanus*); also a buzzy *tew, tew* or *tew, tuw, tuw*, 1st note higher, a sharp *jeet* and a churring rattle (J. V. Remsen).
**Behavior:** Usually alone or in pairs within 1 m of the ground; peck or sally short distances as they cling to vertical *Heliconia* stems or hop on ground; can be hard to see but less wary and more vocal than many antbirds.
**Status and habitat:** Common in *várzea* and swamp forest on Monkey Isl. and adj. Amazonian river isls. near Leticia; rare along tributaries of Amazon. First Colombia rec. 1972 (Russell and Lamm 1978).
**Range:** Amazonian river isls. and banks of Río Amazon. Ne Peru (incl. mouth of Río Curaray; Pto. Indiana) e on both banks of Amazon to w Amazonian Brazil.

## 66. BLACK-FACED ANTBIRD
*Myrmoborus myotherinus*              Pl. 32, Map 790
**Identification:** 5" (13cm). ♂: crown and back gray; *sides of head and throat black* bordered above by narrow grayish white forehead and eyestripe that continues to *grayish white of underparts*; wing coverts *black edged white forming 3 wing bars*; concealed interscapular patch white. ♀: olive brown above with *black mask through eyes* and narrow dull buffy forehead and eyestripe; wing coverts dark brown edged buff forming *3 wing bars; throat white* bordered below by a few black spots; *rest of underparts cinnamon buff*. Eyes red (dull red—♀).
**Similar species:** ♂ from ♂ White-browed and Ash-breasted antbirds (64, 65) by white wing bars; ♀ from ♀ of 65 by buff wing bars and contrasting white throat and buff underparts. Also see Black-tailed Antbird (see note below).
**Voice:** Song a falling and slowing ser. of 12 or

so loud *jeep* notes, harsher at end, lasting about 3 sec; 1 call a sharp, low-pitched *péeap*.
**Behavior:** Like others of the genus in Colombia (64, 65) but found mainly inside humid forest.
**Status and habitat:** Common in humid *terra firme* forest and older second growth woodland; favors dense undergrowth and stands of saplings around treefalls. Replaced in forest edges and *várzea* by White-browed Antbird.
**Range:** To 600m. E of Andes from w Meta (Villavicencio area) and Vaupés (Mitú) southward. S Venez. to n Bolivia and Amazonian Brazil.
**Note:** Black-tailed Antbird (*M. melanurus*) of ne Peru from Ríos Ucayali to Javarí occurs near Leticia on s bank of Amazon (photo, Río Javarí, July 1978—J. Dunning and A. Brash). ♂ mainly dark gray with sides of head and throat black, wings and tail black, 3 white wing bars. ♀ dull brown above, whitish below with buff-tinged band on breast and brownish sides; wing coverts black with 3 white wing bars. Song a loud, clear, fast ser. of descending *tew* notes much like Ash-breasted Antbird (T. Parker). *Terra firme* and *várzea* forests.

## 67. WARBLING ANTBIRD
*Hypocnemis cantator*                    Pl. 28, Map 791
**Identification:** 4.7" (12cm). Tail fairly short. ♂: crown black, median crown line dotted white; *long eyebrow white* bordered below by a black line through eye; *mantle streaked black and white*; wing coverts black broadly tipped and spotted white; remiges, rump, and tail brown; throat to center of belly white *more or less scaled or mottled black on breast* (or throat and breast pale yellow, sides of breast streaked dusky—*flavescens*); *flanks and crissum bright orange rufous*. ♀: sim. but center crown dotted buff; wing coverts tipped buff.
**Similar species:** Warblerlike in appearance. Yellow-browed Antbird (68) has yellow eyestripe, uniform back, and olive flanks. *Herpsilochmus* antwrens (49-52) are mainly *canopy*, not undergrowth, dwellers.
**Voice:** Song a slow, descending, buzzy *tew-zew-zew-tzy-tzzu*, rough at end, up to 8 notes; also a slow wheezy *whew, tew-tew*, 1st note lowest (J. V. Remsen). Song resembles that of Black-chinned Antbird.
**Behavior:** Single birds or pairs wander alone, with small forest flocks, or occas. to army ants. Peer in foliage like gnatwrens and peck or sally to overhead leaves from near ground to about 4m up (Oniki and Willis 1972); occas. much higher, esp. when singing.
**Breeding:** 2 BC ♂♂, June, w Caquetá (Carriker).

**Status and habitat:** Usually common. Vine tangles or clumps of denser vegetation inside or at edges of *terra firme*, *várzea*, or savanna forests, also taller second growth. Favor thickets along creeks or in swampy areas.
**Range:** To 500m. E of Andes from s Meta (Macarena Mts.) s to se Nariño and Leticia, Amazonas (*saturata*); Guainía (Río Macacuní; sightings, Pto. Inírida 1978—Hilty and M. Robbins) and e Vaupés s to Río Apaporis (*flavescens*). The Guianas and s Venez. to n Bolivia and Amazonian Brazil.

## 68. YELLOW-BROWED ANTBIRD
*Hypocnemis hypoxantha*          Pl. 28, Map 792
**Identification:** 4.6″ (11.7cm). Crown black with median stripe spotted white (or yellow—♀); long yellow eyestripe from nostrils bordered below by narrow black line through eyes; otherwise *uniform olive green above*; tail brownish; wing coverts with 2 white-spotted bars; sides of head and *underparts bright yellow* with a black malar and *black streaking on sides of breast; flanks olive*.
**Similar species:** See Warbling Antbird (67). Yellow-throated Antwren (32) is much smaller with predom. streaked upperparts and breast mostly unstreaked. Yellow-browed Tody-Flycatcher (p 481) and *Herpsilochmus* antwrens (49-52) are very different in shape and are forest canopy birds.
**Voice:** One song a fast (2 sec), sharp *queeque-queeet* repeated every 3-4 sec.
**Behavior:** Pairs or small groups are mod. active, hopping and peering in foliage and branches, mostly 1-10m up in lower levels of forest. Occas. with forest flocks and usually less vocal than Warbling Antbird.
**Breeding:** BC ♂, June, w Caquetá (Carriker).
**Status and habitat:** Uncommon to fairly common in humid *terra firme* forest understory, esp. dense saplings around treefalls or in bushy forest borders. More a bird of upland forest than Warbling Antbird.
**Range:** To 500m. E of Andes from w Caquetá (Morelia sw of Florencia) and Vaupés (sightings, Mitú, 1978—Hilty) to Amazonas. E Colombia to e Peru n of Marañon and w Amazonian Brazil.

## 69. BLACK-CHINNED ANTBIRD
*Hypocnemoides melanopogon*     Pl. 28, Map 793
**Identification:** 4.8″ (12.2cm). Chunky with short tail and slender bill. ♂: *dark gray*, slightly paler below with *black throat patch; wing coverts narrowly tipped white forming 3 bars*; tail blackish, *narrowly but conspic. tipped white*. ♀: above like ♂, below whitish, throat mottled gray, chest

sides and flanks clouded gray becoming white on belly.
**Similar species:** ♂ might be mistaken for one of the "gray" *Myrmotherula* antwrens, esp. Longwinged Antwren (43), but is larger, more robust, and tail has prom. terminal white tips. Also see Black-headed and Black-throated antbirds (72, 87). ♀ distinctive but see ♂ Silvered Antbird (75).
**Voice:** Song an accelerating *psheep psheep eep ep-ep-e-e-e'e'e'* *weep-weep-jeep-jeep* slowing, descending slightly and raspy at end; alarm a double sounding *péechup*.
**Behavior:** Like Silvered Antbird restricted to edge of water but Silvered often hops on ground, this sp. hops on logs or low through shrubbery, less frequently on ground; sometimes clings to vetical stems. Usually pairs, occas. noisy groups that are not as shy as sing and call excitedly.
**Breeding:** BC bird, May, Pto. Ayacucho, Venez. opp. Vichada (Friedmann 1948).
**Status and habitat:** Fairly common in swamps and along edges of stagnant backwater creeks in *várzea*, *terra firme*, and gallery forests. Not in well-drained *terra firme* forest. Replaced s of Amazon by *H. maculicauda* (below).
**Range:** To 500m. E of Andes from w Meta (near Villavicencio) ne Meta (S. Furniss) and e Vichada southward (no Amazonas recs.). The Guianas and s Venez. s to ne Peru at mouth of Napo (not Ecuador) and both sides of Amazon in Brazil.
**Note:** Band-tailed Antbird (*H. maculicauda*) of e Peru, n Bolivia, and Amazonian Brazil s of Amazon, occurs s of Amazon opp. Leticia (sight). Both sexes from Black-chinned Antbird as follows: slightly larger size, more extensive white fringing on wing coverts, and tail with a prom. *broad white band at tip* (not just white tips). Song resembles that of Black-chinned Antbird. Swampy riverside forest, flooded backwaters, and *várzea* streams.

## 70. BLACK-AND-WHITE ANTBIRD
*Myrmochanes hemileucus*       Pl. 28, Map 794
**Identification:** 4.8″ (12.2cm). Almost a miniature of Great Antshrike. *Bill long and slender*; tail short. *Black above and pure white below*; rump gray (hard to see); *wing coverts broadly spotted white*; tail narrowly tipped white; semiconcealed interscapular patch white; eyes dark. ♀ differs in white lores and gray (not black) lower mandible.
**Similar species:** Both sexes resemble ♂ Great Antshrike (3) but are half the size and have a slender (not heavy hooked) bill. Also see Black-and-white Tody-Tyrant (p 478).
**Voice:** Often heard song a brief, accelerating

("bouncing ball") *Pip! bip'bip'bip'ip'ip'?*, querulous, odd, and usually answered immed. by a mate with a loud, sharp *bpip!*, singly or several in succession.
**Behavior:** Usually in pairs that are mod. active hopping and fluttering for insects near the ground to 4m up in thickets. Inconspic. but often not as wary as many other thicket-dwelling antbirds.
**Status and habitat:** Local. Scrubby or bushy thickets in early successional vegetation and saplings on seasonally flooded Amazon river isls., rarely on banks of Amazon. First reported in Colombia in 1972 (Russell and Lamm 1978).
**Range:** Known only from Leticia area (Isla Santa Sofia III; Isla Corea, etc.). Río Amazon and its major tributaries (the Río Ucayali and Río Napo) in e Peru and Brazil (s of Amazon on Ríos Purús, Mamoré, and Madeira); n Bolivia.

## 71. BARE-CROWNED ANTBIRD
*Gymnocichla nudiceps*               Pl. 27, Map 795
**Identification:** 6.5″ (16.5cm). ♂: *black with bare, bright blue crown and ocular area*; wing coverts narrowly fringed white; tail narrowly tipped white (sometimes no white tips). ♀: *bare ocular area blue* (not crown); above rufous brown tinged olive; *wing coverts tipped rufous buff*; entire *underparts bright rufous*. Concealed white interscapular patch on both sexes. Imm. ♂ like ad. ♂, but forecrown more or less feathered, only bare ocular area blue, greater wing coverts uniform slaty brown.
**Similar species:** ♂ Immaculate Antbird (86) lacks blue crown and white on wing coverts; ♀ of 86 is dark brown (not rufous). ♀ Chestnut-backed Antbird (79) from ♀ by smaller size, slaty head, and less uniform underparts; both have bare blue oculars.
**Voice:** Song a ser. of about 7–9 loud, rich *cheep* notes, slightly accelerating (recalls Immaculate Antbird); also a loud bubbly rattle, *ji'i'i'i'i'i*; robinlike *skeeip* in alarm.
**Behavior:** A confirmed army ant follower though occas. seen away from them. Pairs or several forage from near ground to 2.5m up at swarms but are retiring and difficult to see; often flee by short hops through undergrowth. Pound tail downward when alarmed, vibrate it when singing.
**Breeding:** 14 BC birds, Jan–June, s Cesar to s Córdoba (Carriker), and ♂ in June, Chocó (Haffer 1975).
**Status and habitat:** Uncommon in dense vine-crowded thickets and bushy second growth in pastures and woodland borders; also dense understory in taller second growth, esp. along streams. Common in s Córdoba.

**Range:** To 400m. Pacific coast s to lower Río San Juan (Pto. Muchimbo), Urabá region, humid lowlands n of Andes locally e to Guajira (Macuira Hills), and s to upper Río Sinú and mid. Magdalena Val. (Nare, se Antioquia). Guatemala and Belize to n Colombia.

## 72. BLACK-HEADED ANTBIRD
*Percnostola rufifrons*               Pl. 30, Map 796
**Identification:** 5.5″ (14cm). Eyes red. Robust with strong bill. ♂: *dark gray with black crown and throat* (neither in strong contrast to rest of plumage); wing coverts blackish with white-fringed lesser coverts and 2 white wing bars; no interscapular patch. ♀ very different: crown rufous brown; back and tail dark grayish olive; *wing coverts blackish tipped buff* forming 3 distinct bars; sides of head cinnamon rufous; underparts throat and upper breast bright cinnamon rufous *sharply divided* from pale buff lower underparts; flanks tinged olive.
**Similar species:** ♂ superficially like Black-chinned Antbird (69) but much larger, heavier-billed, more robust, and crown black. ♀ Slate-colored Antbird (73) has uniform deep cinnamon rufous underparts (not "2-toned") and wing coverts spotted (not sharply fringed buff). ♀ Spot-winged Antbird (74) has uniform orange rufous breast and belly and head is gray (not rufous brown and cinnamon). ♀ Chestnut-tailed Antbird (82) has rather sim. "2-toned" underparts but ranges not known to overlap.
**Voice:** Song a ser. of 6–10 loud whistled *peer* notes on same pitch, a little stronger near end.
**Behavior:** Alone or in pairs from near or on ground to about 2.5m up. Reg. follow army ants but also found away from them. At swarms drop to ground, lunge, toss leaves, or leap vertically to vegetation (Oniki and Willis 1972). Pound tail downward and not as wary as many ant-following antbirds.
**Breeding:** 6 BC birds, Apr–May, Vaupés (Olivares 1964b).
**Status and habitat:** Undergrowth of humid *terra firme* forest, and taller second growth woodland. Found mainly in white sandy soil forests. Fairly common at Mitú.
**Range:** To 250m. Río Negro region of se Guainía (Río Macacuní) s to Vaupés (Mitú; poss. Amazonas. The Guianas, s Venez., and n Brazil (n of Amazon) to ne Peru n of Amazon.
**Note 1:** Song and tail pounding behavior nearer *Myrmeciza* than other Colombian *Percnostola*, and perhaps best placed in the genus *Myrmeciza*. **Note 2:** White-lined Antbird (*Percnostola lophotes*), known from a few localities in e Peru (Loreto to Madre de Dios) may occur in e Colombia. ♂ seen (2d heard) and tape rec.

17 and 20 Feb 1978, low at woodland edge at Mitú (Hilty) may have been this sp. (song recordings believed sim. to birds in se Peru— T. Parker). ♂ of this sp. previously described as *P. macrolopha* (White-lined Antbird), ♀ as *P. lophotes* (Rufous-crested Antbird), but now known to be conspecific (J. P. O'Neill). 6", crested. ♂: slaty with *black crown and black throat and central underparts*; wing coverts black, lesser coverts fringed white; 2 wing bars, bend of wing, and under wing coverts white. ♀ very different: *crown bright cinnamon rufous* becoming duller on back and chestnut on tail; *wing coverts broadly edged bright cinnamon rufous*; sides of head, throat, sides, and flanks ashy gray; central underparts white with bright cinnamon wash on belly. Song 6-8 hollow, nasal, trogonlike *kouk* notes beginning slowly then speeding and falling slightly (T. Parker).

## 73. SLATE-COLORED ANTBIRD

*Percnostola schistacea*          Pl. 30, Map 797
**Identification:** 5.6" (14.2cm). Both sexes *slightly darker* than respective sexes of Spot-winged Antbird. *Bill all black*, legs black. ♂: *entirely uniform dark bluish gray above and below*, 3 rows of small white dots on wing coverts. ♀: *crown dull rufous*, back dark rufescent brown, both with faint pale shaft streaks; *3 rows of cinnamon dots* (larger than ♂) *on wing coverts*; sides of head and underparts bright rufous chestnut; flanks and crissum dark brown.
**Similar species:** ♂ barely separable in field from ♂ Spot-winged Antbird (74) but note shorter all black bill (not rather long and pale below) and darker, uniform leaden plumage (*subplumbea* subsp. of Spot-winged shows little contrast above and below, but *infuscata* subsp. is decidedly paler gray below than above and looks "2-toned"). In the hand bill shorter (16-17 vs 18-20mm) than 74. ♀ from ♀ Spot-winged by dull rufous (not gray) crown and sides of head, perhaps when close, by pale shaft streaks on upperparts. Also cf. ♀ Black-headed (72) and Black-throated antbirds (87).
**Behavior:** Presum. like Spot-winged Antbird.
**Status and habitat:** Not well known. Undergrowth inside humid forest. Near Leticia found near water in low-lying forest and swampy ravines. Perhaps in swampier forest regions than next sp.
**Range:** To 400m. E of the Andes in Putumayo and Amazonas. Se Colombia to e Peru (not rec. in Ecuador) and both sides of Amazon in Brazil.

## 74. SPOT-WINGED ANTBIRD

*Percnostola leucostigma*          Pl. 30, Map 798
**Identification:** 5.7" (14.5cm). Bill rather long,

mod. strong, *dusky above, paler below*. Legs dusky (or pale blue—*infuscata*; or pale pink—e Vichada). ♂: slaty gray above, only slightly paler below (or distinctly paler gray below giving a "2-toned" appearance—*infuscata*); wing coverts blackish with 2 rows of small white dots and a few dots on lesser coverts; primaries tinged brownish. ♀: *crown and sides of head gray* (or with sides of head brownish olive—*infuscata*); back brown becoming dusky on tail; wings dark brown with *3 rows of round buff spots*; upper throat buffy white deepening to *deep orange rufous on rest of underparts*.
**Similar species:** Not easily told from Slate-colored Antbird (see 73). Both sexes of Plumbeous Antbird (83) have bare blue ocular areas and are larger and more robust; also see ♂ and ♀ Black-headed Antbird (72). ♂ White-shouldered Antshrike (12) has heavier all black bill and more white on shoulder. ♀ nearest ♀ Black-throated Antbird (see 87).
**Voice:** In Surinam a soft rising trill (T. Davis). Alarm a frequently repeated *chip-pip*; also a bubbly rattle.
**Behavior:** Usually in pairs. Rather furtive as they hop low through undergrowth, on logs or on ground, or occas. cling to vertical stems. Rarely follow army ants, and unlike Black-headed Antbird, flick tail up.
**Breeding:** BC ♀, June, w Caquetá (Carriker).
**Status and Habitat:** Dense undergrowth or treefalls inside humid *terra firme* forest, also damp places inside forest. Common in white sandy soil forests of Vaupés.
**Range:** To 500m. Entire e base of E Andes to se Nariño (*subplumbea*); Guainía and Vaupés (*infuscata*); e Vichada (subsp.?), Amazonas (*subplumbea*?), The Guianas and s and extreme w Venez. (Táchira) s to e Peru (incl. Pto. Indiana and mouth of Río Curaray—*subplumbea*) and n and c Brazil.

## 75. SILVERED ANTBIRD

*Sclateria naevia*          Pl. 30, Map 799
**Identification:** 6" (15cm). *Bill long* (1" or 25.4cm) *and slender*, tail short. Long legs flesh color. ♂: dark gray above with 2 white-dotted wing bars and white dots on lesser coverts; median underparts white; sides and flanks, sometimes also chest, clouded and flammulated gray (not streaked). ♀: dark brown above with *indistinct cinnamon eyestripe; wing coverts dotted buff; below white*, sides of neck, breast, and flanks washed tawny cinnamon.
**Similar species:** ♂ should not be confused, but see ♀ Black-chinned Antbird (69). ♀ nearest ♀ White-browed Antbird (64) but lacks the black mask. Cf. ♀ with ♀ Black-throated Antbird (87).

**Voice:** Song 1-2 short rising whistled notes becoming a loud ringing and bubbly trill, *weeea-tri-tr-tr'tr'tr'tr'tr'tr'tr'tr'a'a'*, loudest in mid., fading at end, about 4 sec; alarm, sharp *chit* or *chit-it*; bubbly *p'p* as it forages.

**Behavior:** Usually seen alone or in pairs. Hops on ground or leaf litter or low through dense undergrowth, keeping just above or at edge of water in swampy areas. Not furtive and not reported at army ant swarms. Often cocks tail or switches it side to side.

**Breeding:** Eggs buffy gray heavily spotted and blotched reddish brown (Schönwetter).

**Status and habitat:** Locally common near water in dense undergrowth of swampy or *várzea* forests. Shares swampy creek edges with Black-chinned Antbird.

**Range:** To 500m. E of Andes from se Nariño, ne Meta (Carimagua—S. Furniss), and e Vichada southward (*argentata*). The Guianas and s Venez. to e Peru and c Amazonian Brazil.

## 76. ESMERALDAS ANTBIRD

*Sipia rosenbergi* Pl. 29, Map 800

**Identification:** 5.5″ (14cm). Eyes fiery red (♀?). Bill long and mod. heavy; tail rather short. ♂: *mostly uniform blackish slate*; wing coverts black with *2 rows of white dots*; concealed interscapular white. ♀: head and underparts slate gray; throat dotted white, belly brownish; *back and wings rufescent brown*; wing coverts blackish with 2 rows of buffy white dots, lesser coverts dotted white; tail dusky.

**Similar species:** ♂ from ♂ Dull-mantled Antbird (80) by uniform slaty plumage and brighter red eyes; ♀ very like ♀ Dull-mantled but bill longer(?), and tail dusky (not chestnut). Chestnut-backed Antbird (79) has bare blue ocular area. Also see Stub-tailed Antbird (77).

**Voice:** In w Ecuador call is a short ser. of high thin notes (reminiscent of Dull-mantled Antbird), very sharp and insistent, *psee-psee-psee-psée*, sometimes an extra unaccented *psee* at end (R. Ridgely).

**Behavior:** Rather like Dull-mantled and Chestnut-mantled antbirds, which occur in sim. habitat. Single birds or pairs hop on ground, on logs, and through denser undergrowth. Often cling to vertical stems.

**Status and habitat:** Not well known. Wet forest and tall second growth woodland of foothills and lower slopes. Uncommon or rare on steep slopes at 900-1000m in upper Anchicayá Val.

**Range:** 400-1100 (once to 200m). Pacific slope from upper Río San Juan southward. W Colombia to sw Ecuador.

**Note:** Prob. best placed in *Myrmeciza*, which it resembles in behavior.

## 77. STUB-TAILED ANTBIRD

*Sipia berlepschi* Pl. 29, Map 801

**Identification:** 5.2″ (13.2cm). *Tail very short*; bill long and mod. heavy. ♂: *entirely uniform black* with concealed white interscapular patch. ♀: sim. but wing coverts dotted white and *throat and upper breast thickly dotted white*. Eyes reddish brown (both sexes).

**Similar species:** Esmeraldas Antbird (76) is slaty (not black) with fiery red eye. ♂ Immaculate Antbird (86) is larger, longer-tailed, and has bare, bluish white ocular area. ♀ Jet Antbird (62) is very different in shape (long-tailed) and has different habitat; also cf. ♀ of 76.

**Voice:** Song of ♂ a slightly rising ser. of 7-9 *peer* notes increasing in vol.; ♀'s song sim. but higher-pitched. Alarm a high, sharp rattle *tr'rt'rt'it*.

**Behavior:** Pairs wander alone from near ground to 2m up; cling to vertical stems as often as horizontal perches, pound tail downward, and do not skulk as much as some undergrowth antbirds.

**Breeding:** 3 BC birds, Dec, Valle (Carriker).

**Status and habitat:** Apparently local. Undergrowth of wet forest in coastal lowlands and lower foothills. Common near Quibdó. Replaced in foothills and lower slopes by allied Esmeraldas Antbird.

**Range:** To 400m. Pacific coast from upper Atrato Val. (Quibdó) southward. W Colombia and nw Ecuador.

**Note:** Prob. best placed in the genus *Myrmeciza*, which it resembles in behavior and vocalization.

[*Myrmeciza*: Undergrowth; may or may not follow army ants; bill mod. heavy; tail mod. long, pounded down; shorter-tailed and more robust than *Cercomacra*.]

## 78. WHITE-BELLIED ANTBIRD

*Myrmeciza longipes* Pl. 29, Map 802

**Identification:** 5.8″ (14.7cm). *Legs long and flesh colored.* Bill mod. long. ♂: *bright rufous chestnut above; sides of head, throat, and chest black bordered by gray forehead, gray eyestripe, and gray on sides of neck*; breast and belly white; flanks washed cinnamon. Or with gray crown (*panamensis; boucardi*). Or black of throat and chest also bordered gray below (*griseipectus*). ♀: above rufous chestnut; wing coverts usually with subterminal black bar; forehead and eyestripe gray; *cheeks dusky*; underparts white strongly washed ochraceous on breast and sides. Eyes dark red; narrow eyering blue (both sexes).

**Similar species:** Bright rufous chestnut upperparts should distinguish either sex. ♀ from

♀♀ of Bicolored and White-cheeked Antbird (90, 91) by ochraceous breast (not white).

**Voice:** Song a loud ringing crescendo of 15-25 rapid *jeer* notes, falling, trailing off, and ending in a few *cherr* notes on same pitch.

**Behavior:** Pairs or single birds hop on or near the ground and occas. follow army ants (Oniki and Willis 1972). Retiring and usually hard to see.

**Breeding:** 10 BC birds, June–Jan, n Colombia (Carriker); 1 BC ♀, May, upper Orinoco, Venez. (Friedmann 1948).

**Status and habitat:** Fairly common in dense undergrowth or at shrubby borders of dry to moist seasonal woodland and second growth. Easily found in PN Tayrona.

**Range:** To 1700m. N Colombia from e Córdoba and Snía. de San Jacinto e to Guajira (Carraipía) and s to mid. Magdalena Val. in s Bolívar (*panamensis*); rest of Magdalena Val. from Tolima (Honda) to headwaters (*boucardi*); e Norte de Santander and n Arauca (*longipes*); w Meta e to Orinoco (*griseipectus*). C Panama to Venez., Guyana, and nw Brazil.

### 79. CHESTNUT-BACKED ANTBIRD
*Myrmeciza exsul*      Pl. 29, Ill. 78, Map 803

**Identification:** 5″ (13cm). Tail rather short. *Bare ocular region pale blue*; eyes brown. ♂: *back, wings, and tail chestnut brown*; 2 white-dotted wing bars (or no dots—*niglarus*); *head, neck, and underparts slaty black*; flanks and belly warm brown. ♀: like ♂ above but duller and dots on greater wing coverts buffier (or no wing dots—*niglarus*); sides of head and upper throat slaty; chest cinnamon orange becoming buff on breast and brown on belly (or underparts rufous chestnut—*maculifer*).

**Similar species:** Esmeraldas and Dull-mantled antbirds (76, 80) lack the bare ocular area and have red (not brown) eyes. ♂ of 76 is also all slaty above and below.

**Voice:** Persistently whistled song a loud, emphatic, *Cheap Cheer* or *Cheap Cheap, Cheer*, last note lower (Hilty); calls incl. *quit-it*, a rattle, and a nasal *nyaah* (Willis and Oniki 1972).

**Behavior:** Heard far more than seen. Single birds or pairs keep near ground to 2m up in undergrowth. Hop and peer for insects, often cling to vertical stems, and occas. follow army ants. Pound tail downward in alarm.

**Breeding:** 6 BC birds, Feb–Apr, n Antioquia to s Córdoba (Carriker), 1 in Mar, Chocó (Haffer 1975); in Panama Apr–Nov; bulky cup-shaped nest sits loosely on plants or debris near ground; 2 pinkish white eggs heavily blotched reddish brown (Willis and Oniki 1972).

**Status and habitat:** Common in humid and wet forest and second growth woodland in lowlands and foothills, a few higher. Partially replaced in very wet ravines and on steep slopes

78. Chestnut-backed Antbird (top left, ♂ *cassini* race; middle left, ♂ *niglarus* race; botton left, ♀ *niglarus* race), Dull-mantled Antbird (center: ♂ above; ♀ below), Immaculate Antbird (♂ top right)

with tangled treefalls and landslides by Dull-mantled Antbird.

**Range:** To 900m. W shore Gulf of Urabá near Acandí (*niglarus*); n Chocó s to Río Napipí and across s Córdoba e to mid. Magdalena Val. s to Pto. Berrío, Antioquia (*cassini*); rest of Pacific coast (*maculifer*). Nicaragua to w Ecuador.

## 80. DULL-MANTLED ANTBIRD
*Myrmeciza laemosticta*   Pl. 29, Ill. 78, Map 804
**Identification:** 5.5″ (14cm). Eyes dull red. ♂: head and neck slaty; *upper back and wings brown; lower back, rump, and tail chestnut;* wing coverts black, greater wing coverts with a row of *buff dots,* median and lesser wing coverts dotted white; *throat and chest black* (or only throat—*palliata*); rest of underparts slaty gray; flanks and lower belly brown. ♀: sim. but *throat checkered black and white* and all wing coverts with buff dots. Concealed white interscapular patch in both sexes.

**Similar species:** See Chestnut-backed and Esmeraldas antbirds (79, 76), ♀ of latter doubtfully separable in field from ♀ of 80.

**Voice:** Song, unusual for the genus, about 6 measured high, thin notes, *eek, eek, zeet, zeet, eet, eek,* 2d pair lowest, last highest (Anchicayá Val.). Calls incl. a rattle and *chip-ip.*

**Behavior:** Single birds, pairs, or families often cling vertically to stems as hop and peer low in undergrowth but not on ground. Occas. follow army ants. Do not sing as persistently as Chestnut-backed Antbird.

**Breeding:** A stub-tailed young followed 2 ad., 9 June, upper Anchicayá Val. (Hilty); 3 BC birds, May, s Bolívar and se Antioquia (Carriker).

**Status and habitat:** Wet shady ravines and rank growth around treefalls and landslides in humid and wet forest. Fairly common in foothills and lower slopes, fewer on coastal lowlands. Compared to Chestnut-backed Antbird, favors damper shadier ravines.

**Range:** To 1100m. Pacific slope from extreme n end W Andes southward (*nigricauda*); upper Sinú Val. (*bolivari*) e in n foothills of lower Cauca and mid. Magdalena Val. to w Norte de Santander and s to Río Samaná, n Caldas (*palliata*). Costa Rica to nw Ecuador and nw Venez.

## 81. GRAY-BELLIED ANTBIRD
*Myrmeciza pelzelni*
**Identification:** 5″ (13cm). ♂: rufous brown above; *wing coverts and tertials blackish with large terminal buff spots;* lesser coverts with smaller buff dots; sides of head mottled gray and white; *throat to upper breast black; rest of underparts gray;* flanks and lower belly brown. ♀: sim. to ♂ but

*throat and breast white;* feathers of lower breast edged black giving a scaled and streaked appearance. No interscapular patch (either sex).

**Similar species:** ♂ resembles ♂ Black-throated Antbird (87), but sides of head mottled gray and white and wing coverts have large buff spots (not small white dots). ♀ from ♀ Black-throated by white of throat extending to mid-breast, and lower breast streaked and scaled black and white (instead of breast uniform rufous). ♀ from White-cheeked Antbird (91) by boldly spotted wing bars and mottled sides of head. Cf. Wing-banded and ♀ Silvered antbirds (109, 75).

**Status and habitat:** Little known. Specimens are from a region of white sandy-belt forest in upper Río Negro drainage.

**Range:** To 400m. Known only from w bank of Río Guainía opp. mouth of Río Casiquiare. Extreme e Colombia, adj. s Venez. and nw Brazil.

**Note:** This sp. and the next have been placed in the genus *Myrmoderus.*

## 82. CHESTNUT-TAILED ANTBIRD
*Myrmeciza hemimelaena*   Pl. 30, Map 805
**Identification:** 5″ (13cm). Small for genus; short tail. ♂: crown dark gray; remaining upperparts rufescent brown becoming chestnut on tail; wing coverts blackish *conspic. tipped buffy white; sides of head, throat, and breast black;* sides gray; flanks brownish; *center of lower breast and belly white;* concealed white interscapular patch. ♀: above sim. to ♂, but *wing coverts tipped buff;* sides of head gray; *throat and breast cinnamon buff rather sharply defined from buffy white belly;* flanks brownish.

**Similar species:** ♂ most likely confused with Black-throated Antbird (87), but center of lower breast and belly white and tail chestnut (not dusky). ♀ Black-throated Antbird has white (not cinnamon buff) throat and dusky (not chestnut) tail. ♀ from other ♀♀ with rufescent underparts in its range by conspic. buff-spotted wing bars and buffy white belly. Cf. ♀♀ of 27, 28, 60, 61, and 74.

**Voice:** Song in Peru, *chcep, cheep, chee-chew-chew-tu-tu-tu,* starting high and falling rapidly in pitch; also a metallic clinking note, sometimes doubled (T. Parker).

**Behavior:** Pairs keep mostly in dense shaded undergrowth, hop on ground or in interior of low bushes. Usually do not follow army ants (T. Parker).

**Status and habitat:** Little known in Colombia. In Peru most numerous in foothills and lower slopes (to 900m) in drier savanna shrubbery and dense undergrowth of humid forest and tall second growth woodland (T. Parker).

**Range:** To 400m. E base of Andes in w Putumayo (Pto. Umbría). Poss. Amazonas; known on s bank Río Amazon e and w of Leticia (Orosa, ne Peru; São Paulo de Olivença, Brazil). E Colombia to n Bolivia and Amazonian Brazil s of Amazon and in Mato Grosso.

## 83. PLUMBEOUS ANTBIRD
*Myrmeciza hyperythra* Pl. 30, Map 806
**Identification:** 7″ (18cm). *Bare ocular region light blue.* Bill strong. ♂: *uniform slate gray*; wings and tai! blackish; wing coverts with *2 rows of small white spots.* ♀: dark gray above; wing coverts with 2 rows of small white spots and a few buff and white spots on lesser coverts; *underparts bright orange rufous.*
**Similar species:** Slate-colored and Spot-winged (*subplumbea*) antbirds (73, 74) are *much smaller* and *lack bare ocular areas*; ♀♀ of both have slightly larger wing spots. Cf. White-shouldered and Sooty antbirds (84, 85).
**Voice:** Rather loud song a fast, rattly *wo-wu-wh-wr'wr'wr'wr'wr'wr'wr'wr* by ♂ and ♀; or (same?) an accelerating *whir dududu dududu* . . . , slowing and fading at end; in alarm *wut* and bubbly *puok-bubu,* over and over.
**Behavior:** Pairs may perch rather upright or cling to vertical stems, and peer and peck as they hop from near ground to 3m up through *várzea* understory. Usually unsuspicious; seldom at army ant swarms. Pound tail downward.
**Status and habitat:** Inside *várzea* forest, and esp. in or near cluttered areas with saplings and around treefalls. Where occurs with White-shoulded Antbird, favors shady open *várzea* interior near patches of denser growth while latter takes denser shrubbery and vine tangles at edge. Common on s bank of Amazon near Leticia.
**Range:** To 500m. E of Andes from w Caquetá (Tres Esquinas) southward. Prob. Amazonas (rec. at mouth of Río Curaray, n Peru; sightings s of Amazon at Leticia). E Colombia to n Bolivia and Amazonian Brazil s of Amazon.

## 84. WHITE-SHOULDERED ANTBIRD
*Myrmeciza melanoceps* Pl. 30, Map 807
**Identification:** 7″ (18cm). *Bare ocular region blue*; heavy black bill. ♂: *entirely black with bend of wing and shoulder white* (often concealed in field). ♀ very different: entire *head, throat, and chest black*; otherwise *entirely bright cinnamon rufous,* paler below.
**Similar species:** ♂ Sooty Antbird (85) is mostly dark gray with black confined to throat and breast; ♂ Plumbeous Antbird (83) is grayish and has 2 small white-dotted wing bars. ♂ from other "black" antbirds e of Andes by

bare ocular area. Striking ♀ could only be confused with rare Cocha Antshrike (note under 9).
**Voice:** Distinctive often heard song is far-carrying and titmouselike (*Parus*), a whistled *sit-tup peter, peter, peter, peter, peter,* 1st 2 notes brief and faint; loud robinlike *cheeop* call.
**Behavior:** Single birds, pairs, or occas. several, stay in shade and mostly out of sight as hop and peer on low vines and stems from near ground to 2-3m up; occas. at army and swarms or with mixed flocks. Pound tail downward.
**Breeding:** 2 BC birds, June, w Caquetá (Carriker).
**Status and habitat:** *Terra firme* and *várzea* forest undergrowth. Where occurs with Sooty Antbird, usually in lower poorly-drained areas or along streams; replaced on drier ridges and in upland ravines by latter. Also sometimes with Plumbeous Antbird (see 83). Fairly common.
**Range:** To 500m. E of Andes from s Meta (Macarena Mts.) and Amazonas southward, sighting n to Vaupés (Mitú, Feb 1978—Hilty). E Colombia to e c Peru and c Amazonian Brazil.

## 85. SOOTY ANTBIRD
*Myrmeciza fortis* Pl. 30, Map 808
**Identification:** 7.2″ (18.3cm). *Bare ocular region blue.* Bill heavy and black. Slightly crested. ♂: *dull sooty gray; crown, throat, and breast blackish;* bend of wing and part of under wing coverts white. ♀: crown chestnut contrasting with dull rufescent brown upperparts; *sides of head and underparts pale gray.* Imm. ♂ resembles ad. ♀ or with var. amts. of black and dusky gray.
**Similar species:** ♂ much like White-shouldered Antbird (84), which is blacker (hard to see in field), has white patch (often concealed) on shoulder, not just on edge of bend of wing and underwing coverts. ♂ Immaculate Antbird (86) is mainly at higher el. at e base of Andes. Smaller Blackish and Black Antbird (60, 61) usually show white-dotted wing bars. ♀ distinctive, but see ♀ White-lined Antbird (note under 72).
**Voice:** Song much like that of White-shouldered Antbird, but faster and beginning notes rise slightly; a loud, whistled *pi-peeer, peer-peer-peer-peer-peer* (T. Parker); loud alarm rattle and softer *chirr* like many other antbirds.
**Behavior:** A large "professional" army ant follower that perches 0.1-2m up in undergrowth. Often drops to ground over swarms for prey. Pounds tail downward in alarm; usually retiring and hard to see.
**Status and habitat:** Interior of humid *terra firme* forest and advanced second growth woodland, esp. drier ridges and higher ravines;

mostly replaced in lower, damper areas or near streams by White-shouldered Antbird. Seldom with *várzea*-inhabiting Plumbeous Antbird. **Range:** To 500m. E of Andes from w Caquetá and Amazonas southward; sighting n to Vaupés (El Dorado, June 1976—R. Ridgely). E Colombia to se Peru and w Amazonian Brazil (both sides of Amazon).

## 86. IMMACULATE ANTBIRD
*Myrmeciza immaculata* Pl. 27, Ill. 78, Map 809
**Identification:** 7.2″ (18.3cm). *Bare ocular region light blue in front, whitish behind.* Bill heavy and black. ♂: deep black; *bend of wing white* (visible in flight). ♀: *almost uniform chocolate brown*; sides of head, upper throat, and tail dusky; white on wing like ♂. Tail rather long and ample in both sexes.
**Similar species:** Easily recognized w of Andes by large size and bare ocular area. On e slope of E Andes mainly above range of sim. Plumbeous, White-shouldered, and Sooty antbirds (83, 84, 85). ♂ of 84 has more extensive white on shoulders; 83 and 85 are grayer.
**Voice:** Song a fast ser. of 8-10 strong, whistled *peep* notes slowing at end; loud robinlike (*Turdus*) *chirk* call.
**Behavior:** Pairs or families often cling to vertical stems as they hop through undergrowth peering and pecking and keeping out of sight. Reg. over army ant swarms in foothills; much less often at them in highlands where few swarms occur. Pound tail down.
**Breeding:** BC ♂, Mar, Chocó (Carriker); dependent juvs., 21 Feb and 10 Apr, Valle (Hilty); in Costa Rica 1 bulky cup nest near ground; lined with black rootlets; 2 eggs, white heavily marked purplish chestnut (Carriker 1910).
**Status and habitat:** Humid and wet forest, second growth woodland, and bushy borders. Favors steep foothills and ravines. Small nos. in hilly lowlands.
**Range:** 100-1500m on Pacific coast and slope (not Gulf of Urabá region); 400-2000m spottily from e slope of W Andes to w slope of E Andes in Santander and Cundinamarca; e slope of E Andes s to s Meta and Macarena Mts. Costa Rica to w Ecuador and nw Venez.

## 87. BLACK-THROATED ANTBIRD
*Myrmeciza atrothorax* Pl. 30, Map 810
**Identification:** 5.5″ (14cm). Small with slender bill. ♂: *olive brown above*, more dusky on rump and tail; *2 rows of white dots on wing coverts and a few white dots on lesser coverts; throat and central breast black*; sides of head, sides of neck and rest of underparts dark gray; concealed white interscapular patch. ♀: above like ♂ but dots

on shoulders buffy white; sides of head gray; *throat white becoming rufous on breast* and sides; belly white.
**Similar species:** ♂ Black-chinned Antbird (69) is gray (not brown) above. In extreme e see ♂ Gray-bellied Antbird (81). ♀ nearest ♀ Spotwinged Antbird (74) but has white throat. Yapacana Antbird (88) is dark gray (not olive brown) above. Also see ♀ Chestnut-tailed and Slate-colored antbirds (82, 73).
**Voice:** Song a loud high-pitched *pepee pee-pee-pee-pee-peep*, unmusical and slightly upscale at end; noisy sharp *tseerp* in alarm; calls incl. 2 or more *chips* and flat *chip-chip't't't* rattle.
**Behavior:** Noisy pairs or families flick tail up as they hop 0.1-3m up in dense shrubbery and grass. Usually do not cling to vertical stems like most *Myrmeciza*, and seldom follow army ants or bird flocks.
**Breeding:** BC ♂, Jan, upper Río Negro in Brazil (Friedmann 1948).
**Status and habitat:** Grassy and bushy borders of *terra firme, várzea*, and savanna forests, and in young or middle-aged second growth. Perhaps local. Common at Mitú.
**Range:** To 500m. E of Andes where known from w Meta (Villavicencio; Macarena Mts.) e to Vaupés. Prob. Guainía (on Venez. side of Río Negro) s to Amazonas. The Guianas and s Venez. to n Bolivia and Amazonian Brazil.
**Note:** Behavior unlike other *Myrmeciza*. Has been placed in the genera *Myrmophylax* and *Myrmoderus*, neither now recognized.

## 88. YAPACANA ANTBIRD
*Myrmeciza disjuncta*
**Identification:** 5.3″ (13.5cm). ♂: *blackish gray above*; top of head tinged brown; lesser and median wing coverts narrowly tipped white; lores and sides of head *pale gray*; chin white; *throat and breast white suffused with ochraceous buff*, deepest on breast and sides of throat; sides ochraceous buff becoming dark gray on under tail coverts; mid. of abdomen white. Concealed white interscapular patch. Bill black above, pale below. ♀: like ♂ but wing coverts tipped dark ochraceous buff; under tail coverts ochraceous.
**Similar species:** Both sexes nearest ♀ Black-throated Antbird (87), but upperparts dark gray (not brownish). ♀ Spot-winged Antbird (74) also differs in brown back, heavier bill, shorter tail, and more uniform rufous underparts. Cf. ♀ White-fringed Antwren (*rufiventris* subsp., 54).
**Status and habitat:** One rec., a ♀ mist-netted by John S. Dunning near Pto. Inírida, Guainía, Mar 1981. Local(?). Formerly known only from Cerro Yapacana and Pto. Yapacana, upper

Río Orinoco, Amazonas, Venez. Scrubby sandy-belt forest undergrowth.

**Range:** 100m. Ne Guainía (Pto. Inírida). Extreme e Colombia and w central Amazonas, Venez.

#### 89. WHITE-PLUMED ANTBIRD
*Pithys albifrons*                Pl. 32, Map 811
**Identification:** 5″ (13cm). Unmistakable. *Conspic. long white bifurcated tufts on forehead form 2 "horns" and tuft on chin forms a "beard."* Head and lower throat black; back and wings dark blue gray; *nuchal collar, underparts, rump, and tail chestnut;* legs yellow.
**Voice:** Calls *see-see-see* or *tsee*; repeated *churr* over ant swarms is sim. to that of many other ant-followers (Willis 1972d; Ingels 1980).
**Behavior:** A "professional" ant follower and seldom seen away from them. Often the most numerous sp. at swarms, though can be wary and hard to see. Clings to slender vertical saplings and bounces from one to another low over swarms. Darts to the ground, sallies to foliage and branches, and occas. hops on ground for prey.
**Breeding:** BC ♀, Apr, 3 juvs., May, Mitú (Olivares 1964b); 8 BC birds, Mar—Apr, upper Orinoco, Venez. (Friedmann 1948); 2 nests (Guyana; Surinam) sunk in dead leaves 30-40cm up in spiny crown of small palm; 2 rosy white eggs speckled brownish (Willis 1972d; Ingels 1980).
**Status and habitat:** Undergrowth of humid *terra firme* forest and second growth woodland; occas. follow swarms to open forest borders.
**Range:** To 500m. Entire e base of E Andes and generally from Río Guaviare and Vaupés southward; prob. n to Guainía. The Guianas, w Venez. (Táchira), and s Venez. s to e central Peru (w of Ucayali) and w Amazonian Brazil n of Amazon.

#### 90. BICOLORED ANTBIRD
*Gymnopithys bicolor*                Pl. 27, Map 812
**Identification:** 5.7″ (14.5cm). *Bare ocular area dusky;* tail short; legs dusky. Rufous brown above with black malar, lower cheeks, and auriculars; throat and median underparts white; sides of neck and breast brown.
**Similar species:** Essentially "bicolored," brown above, white below, with bare ocular region. Not likely confused in its shady deep forest habitat.
**Voice:** Song a rising, then falling ser. of accelerating and ringing whistles, *whee, whee, whee, whe'we'we'we'we'we,* often followed by nasal snarls; whining *chirrrr* call sim. to that of many other antbirds; also a loud *chip-ip* (Willis 1967).
**Behavior:** A "professional" army ant follower

and infrequently seen away from swarms. Pairs or antisocial groups, occas. up to 20 birds, gather at ant swarms. Active and wary as drop to ground or sally to foliage and branches for prey; often cling to vertical perches. This sp., with Ocellated and Spotted antbirds, compose the "trio" of antbirds most likely to be seen at army ant swarms w of Andes.
**Breeding:** 15 BC birds, Feb–Mar, n Antioquia to Chocó (Carriker; Haffer 1975). In Canal Zone mainly wet season, Apr–Nov; bulky cup within 1m of ground in hollow palm stump or the like; 2 whitish eggs spotted and streaked reddish brown (Willis 1967; Skutch 1969a).
**Status and habitat:** Uncommon to fairly common in undergrowth of humid forest and tall second growth woodland. Replaced e of Andes by next sp.
**Range:** To 900m. Pacific coast in Nariño and Cauca (*aequatorialis*); Valle n to Baudó Mts. (*daguae*); n Chocó to upper Río Sinú (*bicolor*). Río Nechí e to Remedios in mid. Magdalena Val. (*ruficeps*). Honduras to w Ecuador.
**Note:** Some incl. *G. leucaspis* (White-cheeked Antbird) of e of Andes with this sp. The enlarged sp. becomes *G. leucaspis* (Bicolored Antbird).

#### 91. WHITE-CHEEKED ANTBIRD
*Gymnopithys leucaspis*                Pl. 30, Map 813
**Identification:** 5.7″ (14.5cm). Sim. to Bicolored Antbird (only w of Andes), differing as follows: bare ocular area *light blue* (not dusky); legs flesh-colored; malar and lower cheeks white; only rear auricular area black; and sides of neck and breast black.
**Similar species:** Superficially recalls ♀ Silvered Antbird (75), which differs in having buff wing dots, buff sides, longer bill, and swampy creek edge habitat (not shady *terra firme*). Ash-breasted Antbird (65) lacks the bare ocular skin and dusky brown sides and also occurs in different habitat. Cf. ♀ White-bellied Antbird (78).
**Voice:** Repertoire of about 14 vocalizations nearly identical to those of Bicolored Antbird (Willis 1967).
**Behavior:** As in Bicolored Antbird but occurs with a different set of "professional" army ant following antbirds.
**Breeding:** 1 BC bird, May, Vaupés (Olivares 1964b).
**Status and habitat:** Uncommon to fairly common in undergrowth of *terra firme* forest and tall second growth woodland. Mostly replaced s of Amazon by Salvin's Antbird, e of Río Negro and Orinoco by Rufous-throated Antbird (see note).
**Range:** To 450m. E of Andes in Meta and Ca-

quetá (*leucaspis*); Vaupés (*lateralis*) and w Putumayo to Amazonas (*castanea*). Sighting (subsp.?) in ne Guainía (Pto. Inírida, Sept 1978—Hilty and M. Robbins). E Colombia to e Ecuador, e Peru and nw Brazil. **Note 1:** Sometimes merged with *G. bicolor* (Bicolored Antbird). **Note 2:** Rufous-throated Antbird (*G. rufigula*) of s Venez., the Guianas, and n Brazil, occurs along Venez. sides of Ríos Orinoco and Negro and may occur on Colombian side. Brown above with black forehead, large blue ocular area, chestnut throat, and mostly ochraceous underparts. **Note 3:** Salvin's (White-throated) Antbird (*G. salvini*), widespread s of Río Amazon in w Amazonia occurs on s Amazon bank at Leticia. ♂: mainly gray with white eyestripe, black eyeline, white throat and black and white barred tail. ♀: brown above somewhat barred and ocellated black and rufous; crown dusky, forehead, sides of head, and underparts chestnut fading to brown on belly; tail barred chestnut and black. Both this sp. and Rufous-throated follow army ants in well-drained *terra firme* forest (Willis 1968); Salvin's also in open *várzea*.

## 92. CHESTNUT-CRESTED ANTBIRD

*Rhegmatorhina cristata*          Pl. 30, Map 814
**Identification:** 6″ (15cm). Bushy crest often held flat and not prom. in field. *Large, bare, bluish white ocular area (like "goggles") surrounded by black sides of head and upper throat;* rest of head, neck, and underparts deep rufous chestnut becoming brown on flanks and belly; back, wings, and tail olive brown. ♀: sim. but crest shorter, mantle sprinkled with short black bars.
**Similar species:** See Hairy-crested Antbird (93).
**Voice:** Song, *Eeeee, HEEER, you, you, you, you,* 2d note inflected, last notes dropping and fading; chirping little faint song at ant swarms *whreeeeer, wheer-whih!*, or the like, 2d note generally strongest; other chips and churrs much like those of related *Gymnopithys* and *Phlegopsis* (Willis 1969).
**Behavior:** A "professional" ant follower and much like Bicolored Antbird in behavior. Flicks tail upward (Willis 1969).
**Breeding:** BC ♂, Mitú, Vaupés, 16 May (Olivares 1964b).
**Status and habitat:** Undergrowth of humid sandy-belt forest. Reg. in c Vaupés from El Dorado and Mitú eastward.
**Range:** To 250m. Known only from Río Vaupés region (Mitú); sightings El Dorado Lodge, Vaupés, (June 1976—R. Ridgely). Colombia and adj. Río Vaupés (São Jeronimo), nw Brazil.

## 93. HAIRY-CRESTED ANTBIRD

*Rhegmatorhina melanosticta*       Pl. 30, Map 815
**Identification:** 6″ (15cm). *Large, round, bare, bluish white ocular area* (like "goggles") *surrounded by black sides of head and upper throat;* rather bushy and filamentous crest grayish white (often held depressed); otherwise reddish brown above; neck and underparts olive brown. ♀: sim. but mantle, back, and wing coverts with buff-edged black tips giving spotted or scaled appearance; crest as in ♂.
**Similar species:** Crest and large bare ocular ring impart almost prehistoric appearance. Chestnut-crested Antbird (92) has crown, neck, and underparts rufous chestnut (not hoary white crown and olive brown underparts).
**Voice:** Song sim. to pattern of other *Rhegmatorhina*, a loud *heeeeee* followed by several short, whistled notes at a lower pitch or falling in pitch, as *Wheeeeer, whee-whee-whee-ee-ai-aihh!* Var. chirrs and snarls sim. to those of Bicolored Antbird (Willis 1969).
**Behavior:** A "professional" ant-follower, much like Bicolored Antbird in behavior. Pairs or families actively sally to or near ground for prey. Flick tail upward (Willis 1969).
**Breeding:** Nearly grown juv. followed an ad. pair, 20 Oct, e Ecuador; breeding may peak during two rainiest periods, Apr and Oct in w Amazonia (Willis 1969). In se Peru almost unlined cup nest 0.5 m up in hollow top of stump, Oct; 2 pinkish eggs spotted reddish brown (C. Munn).
**Status and habitat:** Undergrowth of humid *terra firme* forest. Known in Colombia from 2 specimens collected by Von Sneidern at San Antonio, Putumayo (e of Pto. Asís), 400m, 1969 (Fitzpatrick and Willard 1982) and sight recs. near Pt. Umbría, Putumayo (Willis 1969).
**Range:** To 400m. W Putumayo at San Antonio and Pto. Umbría. Prob. e along Río Putumayo to Amazonas. Extreme s Colombia s to n Bolivia and w Amazonian Brazil (incl. s bank near Leticia and n bank near mouth of Río Putumayo).

## 94. BLACK-SPOTTED BARE-EYE

*Phlegopsis nigromaculata*         Pl. 27, Map 816
**Identification:** 7.0″ (18cm). *Large area of bare facial skin bright pinkish red. Head, neck, and underparts black; belly brownish;* back and wing coverts olive brown sprinkled with *large, droplike buff-rimmed black spots;* wings chestnut with terminal black spots on tertials; tail chestnut with no black (*nigromaculata*).
**Similar species:** Rare (poss. hybrid) Argus Bare-eye (95) has *small* black-rimmed *buff* spots (not large black spots), a black wing speculum, and

subterminal half of tail black with narrow chestnut tip. ♂ Reddish-winged Bare-eye (96) has back boldly scaled white and 3 large rufous wing bars; ♀ is orange rufous below.
**Voice:** Song a leisurely set of 2 or more loud rough whistles, *zeeeew, zeeeeew, zeeeeew*, each lower-pitched than the preceding (J. V. Remsen); or *heeeee, hergh, hugh*; alarm a buzzy *chirr* and sharp *chac*; much squalling and conversation over ants (Willis 1979).
**Behavior:** Usually pairs or groups of disputing families (up to 22 individuals) low over army ant swarms where they drop to ground or toss leaves for prey. Pairs and families maintain territories and pairs usually stay together (Willis 1979; Oniki 1972). Like many ant-followers, rather wary.
**Breeding:** Nest unknown but in ne Brazil believed to use low cavities in stumps or buttress roots; breed late Aug–early Mar (Willis 1979). In se Peru 2 almost unlined cup nests 0.3 and 0.5m up in hollow tops of tree stumps, Nov; 2 pinkish eggs spotted reddish brown (C. Munn).
**Status and habitat:** Undergrowth of *várzea* forest or tall *várzea* second growth near streams; less common in *terra firme* forest where partially replaced by Reddish-winged Bare-eye (both may occur together).
**Range:** To 500m. E of Andes from s Meta (Macarena Mts.) to Putumayo (*nigromaculata*) and s Amazonas (sightings, no specimen, Leticia—many obs.). E Colombia to n Bolivia and Amazonian Brazil s of Río Amazon.
**Note:** *Phlegopsis* is here placed adj. to *Rhegmatorhina* as both build an open cup nest on a low stump. They are often separated in sequence by *Hylophylax*, which builds a suspended nest and lacks the bare orbital area.

### 95. ARGUS BARE-EYE
*Phlegopsis barringeri*
**Identification:** 7.0″ (18cm). *Large area of bare facial skin red.* ♂: *head and underparts glossy black*; back and wing coverts reddish brown with *small black-rimmed buff spots*; remiges, tail, and under tail coverts largely chestnut; *speculum on primaries and subterminal portion of tail black*; tail tip chestnut. ♀: unknown.
**Similar species:** See very sim. Black-spotted Bare-eye (94).
**Status and habitat:** Presum. undergrowth of humid forest.
**Range:** Known only from the type specimen from Río Rumiyaco, a tributary of Río San Miguel, se Nariño on Ecuadorian boundary.
**Note:** Several birds in the Río Rumiyaco collection, from which this bird is taken (Meyer

de Schauensee 1951b), are birds of the foothills and Andean slopes, not lowlands, and this may be the habitat of this sp. Conversely, it may represent a hybrid betw. *P. nigromaculata* and *P. erythroptera* (Willis 1979).

### 96. REDDISH-WINGED BARE-EYE
*Phlegopsis erythroptera*            Pl. 27, Map 817
**Identification:** 7.2″ (18.3cm). ♂ unmistakable: large, *bare facial area bright red; plumage mostly black with feathers of shoulders and entire back boldly scalloped white;* 2 wing bars and a *very broad speculum across primaries rufous chestnut* (latter forms third bar). ♀ lacks bare facial skin and is very different: rufescent brown above; sides of head and underparts cinnamon rufous; wings and tail black; *3 broad rufous wing bands*; broadest forms a speculum across primaries.
**Similar species:** Good marks for ♀ are the broad wing bands. See Black-spotted Bare-eye (94).
**Behavior:** Sim. to Black-spotted Bare-eye. An army ant-following antbird that usually drops to the ground for food from perches under 1m up (Willis 1969). Rather wary.
**Status and habitat:** Undergrowth of humid *terra firme* forest. Generally less numerous than other smaller ant-following antbirds with which it is found. Mostly replaced in *várzea* forest by Black-spotted Bare-eye.
**Range:** To 500m. E of Andes from w Caquetá (Morelia sw of Florencia) and Vaupés (Mitú) southward. S Venez. to e Ecuador, e Peru, and w Amazonian Brazil.

### 97. OCELLATED ANTBIRD
*Phaenostictus mcleannani*            Pl. 27, Map 818
**Identification:** 8″ (20cm). Unmistakable with *large bare blue ocular region, long tail, and overall spotted appearance*. Olive brown above with large buff-rimmed black spots; crown grayish; *lower cheeks, throat, and chest black; rest of underparts rufous chestnut boldly spotted black.*
**Voice:** Alarm, sharp *wheerrr chirr* (Eisenmann 1952) and loud *chip-ip-ip*. Faint song an ascending, then descending *whee, hu, hee, choo*; loud song a long ser. of high whistles that ascend, then descend, often end in rough *charr* notes, *pee, pee, pee, pee, pee, pee-pe-te'e'e'e'e'pe-peer peer charr* (Willis 1973; Hilty).
**Behavior:** A confirmed army ant-follower and seldom seen away from them. Single birds, pairs, or loose family clans dominate other ant-followers as they perch over swarms and drop to ground or sally for prey. Often jerk tail upward (Willis 1973). Usually wary and suspicious.
**Breeding:** 10 BC birds, Feb–May, nw Colom-

bia (Carriker); in Panama, Apr–Dec; nest unknown but 1 attributed to this sp. was an open cup on ground between buttress roots; 1 egg, heavily speckled (Willis 1973). **Status and habitat:** Humid and wet forest in the lowlands and lower foothills, seldom higher. Least numerous of the 3 habitual "ant-followers" (with Bicolored and Spotted antbirds) on Pacific coast. **Range:** To 900m. Pacific coast and humid forest n of Andes e to lower Cauca Val. (Pto. Valdivia). Se Honduras to nw Ecuador. **Note:** Some merge *Phaenostictus* and *Skutchia* (of e Amazonian Brazil) in the genus *Phlegopsis*. Willis (1979) keeps them separate because of different facial skin color.

## 98. SPOTTED ANTBIRD
*Hylophylax naevioides*          Pl. 32, Map 819
**Identification:** 4.5″ (11.4cm). Chunky with short tail. Legs pinkish. ♂: crown and sides of head dark gray; *back chestnut*; wings blackish with *2 broad chestnut bars* and white spots on scapulars; throat black, *rest of underparts white with a broad necklace of black spots across breast*; tail brownish with broad black subterminal band and buff tip. ♀: sim. above but duller; head brownish; underparts buffy white with less distinct necklace.
**Voice:** Distinctive wheezy song a high, soft, rollicking *peety weety weety weety weety weety weety weety weety weety*, the whole ser. falling slightly in pitch; buzzy *chirr* and sharp *peep* calls (Willis 1972c; Willis and Eisenmann 1979).
**Behavior:** An attractively patterned but rather inconspic. sp. that forages at army ant swarms or independent of them about equally. Individuals or pairs actively hop or cling to low perches and drop to ground or sally to foliage and twigs for prey. Flicks tail up.
**Breeding:** 9 BC birds, Feb–May, nw Colombia (Carriker). In Panama, Apr–Oct; trashy cup nest suspended from low twigs; 2 whitish eggs, streaked, and blotched dark brown and chestnut (Willis 1972c; Willis and Eisenmann 1979).
**Status and habitat:** Undergrowth of humid and wet forest and second growth woodland. Lowlands and foothills. Replaced e of Andes by Spot-backed Antbird.
**Range:** To 900m. Pacific coast and e in humid lowlands n of Andes to mid. Magdalena Val. (s to Pto. Berrío, e Antioquia). Honduras to w Ecuador.

## 99. SPOT-BACKED ANTBIRD
*Hylophylax naevia*          Pl. 32, Map 820
**Identification:** 4.5″ (11.4cm). Much like Spotted Antbird. Chunky with short tail. Legs pinkish. ♂: crown and sides of head dark gray;

mantle, back, and wings black; wing coverts with 3 rows of large whitish spots; *back thickly spotted bright buff*; throat black; rest of underparts white with a *bold necklace of black spots across breast*; tail brownish tipped white. Or like above but crown and back brown (*naevia*). ♀: sim. but throat white; rest of underparts buffy white with a thin necklace of black spots on breast.
**Similar species:** Easily recognized by small size and attractive pattern, but see Dot-backed (see note) and Banded antbirds (48).
**Voice:** Song at Mitú a soft, high-pitched and rhythmic *pée-be, pée-be, PEE-BE, pée-be, pée-be, pée-be, pee-be* closely resembling that of Spotted Antbird; chirring rattle and *peéea* also sim.
**Behavior:** Much like Spotted Antbird but sallies to foliage or ground more and follows ant swarms less.
**Status and habitat:** Undergrowth of humid *terra firme* forest and second growth woodland; also *várzea*. Usually common but inconspic.
**Range:** To 500m. E of Andes from s Meta (Macarena Mts.) s to e Nariño and Amazonas (*theresae*); Vaupés and prob. Guainía (*naevia*). The Guianas and s Venez. to n Bolivia and Amazonian Brazil.
**Note:** Dot-backed Antbird (*H. punctulata*) of s Venez. (Río Ventuari opp. se Guainía, Colombia), nw Amazonian Brazil and ne Peru (incl. Pto. Indiana) is not rec. but likely in Colombia. Closely resembles brown-backed forms of Spot-backed Antbird but *lores and cheeks whitish* (not dark gray) and *entire back and rump black thickly dotted with white* (not central back black with buff dots). ♀: much like ♀ Spot-backed but entire back and rump black dotted as in ♂; white (not slaty gray) streak above black malar.

## 100. SCALE-BACKED ANTBIRD
*Hylophylax poecilonota*          Pl. 28, Map 821
**Identification:** 5″ (13cm). ♂: entire head, mantle, and underparts gray; back and wings black; *scapulars, wing coverts, and back conspic. scalloped white*; tail black with a row of white spots across center and narrow white tip; concealed interscapular patch white. ♀: *head and upper throat bright cinnamon rufous* becoming cinnamon buff on underparts; upper back and remiges dark reddish brown; *scapulars, wing coverts, and center of back black scalloped white*; tail as in ♂ (or top and sides of head rufous brown, breast and belly cinnamon brown—*lepidonota*).
**Similar species:** Only small gray (♂) or rufescent (♀) antbird with prom. white fringing on back.
**Voice:** Song at Mitú up to 10 slow quavering

*preeeeee* whistles, each a half tone higher in pitch than the preceding.
**Behavior:** A faithful attendant at army ant swarms but also commonly forages alone or in pairs about 0.5-3m up in understory away from swarms. Sallies to ground or low foliage, flicks tail up sometimes, and often remarkably unsuspicious.
**Status and habitat:** Open undergrowth in humid *terra firme* forest, less often *várzea*. More numerous in white sand forests of the Orinoco and Negro regions than in Amazonia.
**Range:** To 500m. E of Andes from w Meta (Villavicencio; Macarena Mts.) to Guainía and Vaupés (*duidae*); Caquetá to se Nariño (*lepidonota*) and sightings (subsp.?) near Leticia, Amazonas (Hilty). Prob. in e Vichada (rec. at Munduapo, Venez. on e bank of Orinoco). The Guianas and s Venez. to se Peru and Amazonian Brazil.

## 101. SHORT-TAILED ANTTHRUSH

*Chamaeza campanisona*　　　　Pl. 31, Map 822
**Identification:** 7.5″ (19cm). Thrushlike with short bill and *short cocked tail*. Pale legs strong and rather short. *Plain brown above* with white loral spot and *long prom. white postocular stripe*; throat whitish; remaining underparts buffy white; the feathers edged dusky giving a *streaked and hatched appearance; tail with blackish subterminal band*; narrow white tail tip, sometimes lacking.
**Similar species:** Much like other *Chamaeza* antthrushes (except Barred Antthrush, 104) and most easily told by voice and range. Cf. esp. Striated Antthrush (102) found mainly at lower el. Rufous-tailed Antthrush (103), not *known* to overlap, is more rufescent above, has heavier blackish markings on underparts (esp. dense hatching on chest), and no black band or white tip on tail.
**Voice:** Distinctive song a ventriloquial, trogonlike ser. of about 10 accelerating and rising *woo* notes followed by an abruptly slowing and falling series of *woop* notes; alarm a sharp *quock*.
**Behavior:** Almost completely terrestrial and usually seen singly walking jauntily over the forest floor or on logs and twitching short tail downward. Rarely follows army ants and difficult to see even though sings frequently.
**Status and habitat:** Floor of humid forest, usually with fairly open undergrowth. Foothills and lower slopes.
**Range:** 400-1800m. E slope of E Andes in w Meta (above Villavicencio) and Macarena Mts. Doubtless entire e slope. S Guyana; n and s Venez., the e slope of Andes to n Bolivia; se Brazil to ne Argentina.

## 102. STRIATED ANTTHRUSH

*Chamaeza nobilis*　　　　Pl. 31, Map 823
**Identification:** 9.2″ (23.4cm). A larger edition of Short-tailed Antthrush. Differs mainly in *size*; deeper rufescent upperparts; darker more dusky crown; and *always* lacks white tail tips. In general whiter on throat and belly than Short-tailed and with greater contrast to dark hatching on chest.
**Similar species:** See under Short-tailed Antthrush (101). Range overlap with Rufous-tailed Antthrush (103) unlikely; latter is smaller and much more heavily marked below.
**Voice:** Distinctive song a few whistled *whoo* notes gradually accelerating into a hollow trill, then an abrupt pause and 2-3 lower sliding notes (O'Neill 1974).
**Behavior:** Much like Short-tailed Antthrush and heard far more often than seen.
**Status and habitat:** Floor of humid *terra firme* forest and second growth woodland. Common at Limoncocha, Ecuador (Pearson et al. 1977). Replaced in foothills and higher el. by Short-tailed Antthrush.
**Range:** To 500m. Lowlands e of Andes from s Meta (Macarena Mts.) s to Putumayo; sight rec. in Vaupés (El Dorado, 1976—R. Ridgely); and Amazonas (1984—Hilty; Ridgely). E Colombia to e Peru (incl mouth of Río Curaray) and w Amazonian Brazil s of Río Amazon.

## 103. RUFOUS-TAILED ANTTHRUSH

*Chamaeza ruficauda*　　　　Pl. 31, Map 824
**Identification:** 7.5″ (19cm). Stocky and thrushlike with short bill and *short cocked tail*. Pale legs strong and rather short. Dark rufescent brown above; brighter rufescent on crown, rump, and tail; white loral spot and *long prom. white postocular stripe*; throat white; rest of underparts white faintly tinged buff; the feathers *heavily edged black* giving a streaked and slightly hatched appearance, esp. on breast.
**Similar species:** See Short-tailed Antthrush (101). From any antpitta by postocular stripe and cocked tail. Barred Antthrush (104) is barred (not streaked) below.
**Voice:** Remarkable song a single trogonlike, whistled *cu* repeated rapidly for up to 50 sec *without a pause*; ser. seems to grow stronger and increase slightly in tempo and pitch as it goes along.
**Behavior:** Terrestrial and much like Short-tailed Antthrush.
**Breeding:** BC ♂, 15 May, s Huila (Carriker); May-June, Rancho Grande, Venez. (Schäfer and Phelps 1954).
**Status and habitat:** Floor of humid, mossy, montane forest. Favors wetter forest at higher el. than closely related Short-tailed Ant-

thrush; fairly numerous (by voice) in PN Cueva de los Guácharos.
**Range:** 1600-2600m. Head of Magdalena Val. in Huila and w slope of C Andes in Valle (above Palmira). Doubtless more widespread. Colombia; coastal mts. in n Venez. and se Brazil.

## 104. BARRED ANTTHRUSH
*Chamaeza mollissima*          Pl. 31, Map 825
**Identification:** 8″ (20cm). Chunky and thrushlike with short bill and tail. Very dark uniform dull chestnut brown above with gray lores and *long black and white freckled postocular stripe*; entire underparts densely *barred dark brown and whitish.*
**Similar species:** From any other *Chamaeza* by barred underparts, and any *Grallaria* (both Undulated and Giant antpittas are barred below) by white postocular and cocked tail. *Chamaeza* carry the tail cocked, *Grallaria* carry it depressed. No *Formicarius* is barred below.
**Voice:** Song much like Rufous-tailed Antthrush but not as long (typically 18-22 sec); a rapidly repeated note, no pause but toward end each note increasingly emphasized and slightly louder (R. Ridgely).
**Behavior:** Walks on forest floor pumping its tail, usually held cocked; sings from the ground or low perch, head raised high when singing (R. Ridgely).
**Status and habitat:** Rare and little known throughout its range. Known from a few widely scattered localities in undergrowth of humid forest ("cloud forest").
**Range:** 1400-3100m. Both slopes C Andes from Quindío (w of Ibaque near Quindío Pass) to e Cauca (sw of Popayán; PN Puracé); e slope of W Andes in Valle (above Cali) and Cauca (Munchique); also "Bogotá." Andes from Colombia to n Bolivia.

[*Formicarius*: Terrestrial; walk with cocked tail twitching downward; show little pattern on dark forest floor.]

## 105. RUFOUS-CAPPED ANTTHRUSH
*Formicarius colma*          Pl. 31, Map 826
**Identification:** 7″ (18cm). Raillike with short usually cocked tail. ♂: *crown and nape bright chestnut*; otherwise dark olive above; *forehead, sides of head, throat, and breast black* gradually fading to dark olive gray on lower underparts. ♀: sim. but throat whitish freckled black; belly dull grayish brown.
**Similar species:** Likely confused only with Black-faced Antthrush (106), which lacks chestnut cap and extensive black on breast.
**Voice:** Song a rather slow, quavering trill, *hu-*

*hu-hu-u-uuuuuuuuuuuu* rising in pitch toward the end (lasts about 4 sec); at a distance like a slow, rising glissando.
**Behavior:** Like others of the genus largely terrestrial and usually seen walking delicately over the forest floor, pecking here and there or flicking aside leaves. Often follow army ants keeping mostly at periphery. Hard to see.
**Breeding:** 5 BC birds, Apr, upper Orinoco, Venez. (Friedmann 1948).
**Status and habitat:** Floor of humid *terra firme* forest. Fairly common in sandy-belt forest of Vaupés region. Where occurs with Black-faced Antthrush, found mostly in higher ravines and on drier ridges and replaced in lower poorly drained areas or in *várzea* by latter.
**Range:** To 500m. E of Andes from s Meta (Macarena Mts.), and Guainía southward. The Guianas and s Venez. to se Peru and Brazil except extreme south.

## 106. BLACK-FACED ANTTHRUSH
*Formicarius analis*      Pl. 31, Ill. 79, Map 827
**Identification:** 7″ (18cm). Raillike with short usually cocked tail and rather short legs. Narrow bare blue eyering. *Dark brown above*, more rufescent on rump; *cheeks and throat black*; small loral spot white; sides of neck cinnamon behind black face (or no cinnamon—*connectens*); rest of underparts brownish gray; flanks tinged brown; crissum chestnut; tail blackish.
**Similar species:** E of Andes see Rufous-capped Antthrush (105); w of Andes see Black-headed Antthrush (107), which has all black head, and Rufous-breasted Antthrush (108) which has chestnut cap, breast, and belly.
**Voice:** Distinctive song a loud, emphatic whistle, followed after a brief pause by 2-5 lower-pitched whistles that fall in pitch and slow in tempo, *whe!; wü, wü, wü*; alarm, loud *churlip* over and over, often at dusk.
**Behavior:** Sim. to Rufous-capped Antthrush.
**Breeding:** 16 BC birds, Feb–July, Norte de Santander to Córdoba (Carriker); 3 BC ♂♂, Mar–June, nw Colombia (Haffer 1975); cup of leaves less than 4m up in cavity or hollow stump; 2 white eggs (Skutch 1969a).
**Status and habitat:** *Terra firme* and *várzea* forests and second growth woodland. Replaced in wet forest on Pacific coast by Black-headed Antthrush; e of Andes where occurs with Rufous-capped Antthrush usually in damper areas or in *várzea*. Usually common (by voice).
**Range:** To 1000m. W base Santa Marta Mts. s to Snía. de San Jacinto (*virescens*); Perijá Mts. s to Codazzi (*griseoventris*); Pacific coast s to Río Napipí (*panamensis*); upper Sinú Val. and n of Andes to mid. Magdalena Val. (s to Pto. Berrío, e Antioquia); e of Andes in Norte de

79. Black-headed Antthrush (left), Rufous-breasted Antthrush (center), Black-faced Antthrush (*panamensis* race) (right)

Santander and Arauca (*saturatus*); from Meta and Vaupés southward (*connectens*). Se Mexico to n Bolivia and Amazonian Brazil.

## 107. BLACK-HEADED ANTTHRUSH
*Formicarius nigicapillus*  Ill. 79, Map 828
**Identification:** 6.5″ (16.5cm). Essentially a very dark replica of Black-faced Antthrush. Dark brown above; *entire head, neck, throat and chest sooty black*, fading to slate gray on breast and pale gray on belly; crissum chestnut; tail black.
**Similar species:** Much darker than Black-faced or Rufous-breasted antthrushes (106, 108)
**Voice:** Song resembles that of Rufous-capped Antthrush, but shorter, an eerie, quavering glissando of about 30 notes in 3 sec, sliding upscale and slowing noticeably at the end; ventriloquial.
**Behavior:** Like other *Formicarius*, terrestrial and usually seen alone, occas. in pairs, walking cautiously and deliberately over forest floor with cocked tail. May follow army ants.
**Breeding:** 5 BC birds, Dec–Mar, Chocó and Valle (Carriker).
**Status and habitat:** Uncommon and somewhat local; floor of wet forest and wet second growth woodland. In Anchicayá Val. found only in coastal lowlands and lowest hills below 200m (Hilty), elsewhere reported much higher. Replaced in less humid regions of n Chocó by Black-faced Antthrush (no known range overlap).
**Range:** Locally to 1800m. Pacific coast from w base of Baudó Mts. (Nuquí) southward. Costa Rica to w Ecuador.

## 108. RUFOUS-BREASTED ANTTHRUSH
*Formicarius rufipectus*  Pl. 31, Ill. 79, Map 829
**Identification:** 7.5″ (19cm). A chestnut replica

of Black-faced Antthrush. *Crown and nape dark chestnut*; remaining upperparts dark olive; *lores, sides of head, and throat black; sides of neck and breast chestnut* becoming dark olive on abdomen; crissum chestnut; tail black.
**Similar species:** Both Black-faced and Black-headed Antthrushes (106, 107) lack the chestnut crown and breast. Rufous-crowned Antpitta (111) has cinnamon rufous (not black) throat and carries tail depressed (not cocked).
**Voice:** Song a flat, insipid *üü, üü* whistle (quality of Striped Cuckoo), 2d note on same pitch or a quarter tone higher than 1st; at dawn repeated steadily at 10- to 20-sec intervals.
**Behavior:** As in other *Formicarius* but even harder to see because of dense habitat it occupies.
**Breeding:** BC ♂, 16 June, n Antioquia (Carriker).
**Status and habitat:** *Very local.* Fairly common (by voice) above Junín, w Nariño. Recently reported above Dapa, nw of Cali (P. Jennings). Floor of shorter, dense, second growth woodland. In Costa Rica in damp *Heliconia* thickets in dense young second growth and at forest edge on steep hillsides (B. Whitney).
**Range:** 1100-2200m (once to 3100m on Cerro Munchique). Both slopes of W Andes from extreme n Valle (Pacific slope of Cerro Tatamá) southward and n end of C Andes s on w slope to Valle (above Palmira). Costa Rica to e Peru.

## 109. WING-BANDED ANTBIRD
*Myrmornis torquata*  Pl. 31, Map 830
**Identification:** 6.5″ (16.5cm). Bill long; *tail very short*; legs greenish yellow and short; bare orbital skin blue. ♂: dull chestnut above faintly scaled dusky; *wings blackish with several tawny*

*buff bars and a broader band near tip of remiges; throat and chest black*, bordered all around (incl. behind eye) by an irreg. area of vermiculated black and white (or vermiculations on sides of neck only—*stictoptera*); remaining underparts dark gray; crissum chestnut. ♀: sim., but throat and chest rufous; only cheeks black.

**Similar species:** An oddly proportioned ground-dweller, unlike antthrushes or antpittas and easily told from either by numerous bars and bands on wings.

**Voice:** Song about 12-14 fairly loud *preea* whistles, each a little higher than the previous; when alarmed, a rough *churr*.

**Behavior:** Tame, quiet pairs are mostly terrestrial, keep close together and feed independent of ant swarms. Hop (not walk as do antthrushes) over forest floor tossing leaves like a *Sclerurus* leaftosser (Karr 1971). If alarmed may mount a perch to eye level or higher and flick wings.

**Breeding:** 1 BC ♀, Mar, nw Antioquia, 1 in Apr, s Córdoba (Carriker).

**Status and habitat:** Floor of humid forest. Poss. local; known from only a few widely scattered recs. Specimen taken by Von Sneidern at Estación de Bombeo Guaméz, Putumayo (near Nariño boundary), 900m, 1971 (Fitzpatrick and Willard 1982).

**Range:** Lowlands to 900m. From Panama boundary (se of Mt. Tacarcuna) through upper Sinú Val. to mid. Magdalena Val. in w Boyacá (*stictoptera*); e base of E Andes in w Caquetá (sw of Florencia) and w Putumayo (*torquata*). Se Nicaragua; c and e Panama (to 1060m, e Darién) spottily to e Ecuador, c Brazil, and the Guianas.

**Note:** Birds w of E Andes have been considered a distinct sp., *M. stictoptera* (Buff-banded Antpitta).

[*Pittasoma*: Terrestrial; shape of *Grallaria* but bill more massive.]

## 110. BLACK-CROWNED ANTPITTA
*Pittasoma michleri*

**Identification:** 7.5″ (19cm). A large strikingly patterned and virtually tailless bird with very long legs. ♂: *crown and nape glossy black*; cheeks chestnut; otherwise brown above with 2 rows of inconspic. buff dots on wing coverts; throat mostly black; rest of *underparts white boldly and heavily scalloped black*. ♀: sim., but white of underparts replaced by buff.

**Similar species:** Only Colombian Antpitta with such boldly scalloped underparts.

**Voice:** A sudden, loud, harsh ser. of 10-16 squirrellike *wak* notes in 1-1.5 sec. Song in Costa Rica a long ser. of clear, penetrating *tu*

notes for up to a min or more, starting rapidly, gradually slowing to about 1 per sec (B. Whitney).

**Behavior:** Almost entirely terrestrial. Hop or bound rapidly over the forest floor but occas. sit up on low horizontal perch when disturbed. Usually singly at ant swarms (Karr 1971; Ridgely 1976).

**Breeding:** In Panama a thin-walled cup nest 1m up in low palm (Wetmore 1972); in Canal Zone a recently fledged imm. followed a ♀, 12 July (Karr 1971); 2 pinkish buff eggs blotched dark brown, with spots forming a cap at large end and dotted paler on rest of surface.

**Status and habitat:** Floor of humid forest in lowlands and lower hills. Not well known in Colombia but reported with some reg. in Darién, Panama.

**Range:** To 400m. Nw Colombia near Panama boundary (s to Río Truandó). Costa Rica to nw Colombia

## 111. RUFOUS-CROWNED ANTPITTA
*Pittasoma rufopileatum*          Pl. 31, Map 831

**Identification:** 6.5-7″ (16.5-18cm). Plump and short-tailed with rather heavy bill. *Crown and nape rufous bordered on sides by a broad black eyestripe*; rest of upperparts dark olive brown obscurely streaked black; wing coverts tipped white; throat and sides of head cinnamon orange; underparts pale ochraceous; flanks tinged brownish. Or underparts deep orange rufous with black barring var. from none to heavy on breast and belly (*harterti*). ♀ has eyestripe flecked white (all subsp.).

**Similar species:** A distinctively patterned Pacific coast antpitta easily told by rufous crown and black eyestripe.

**Behavior:** Much like larger Black-crowned Antpitta.

**Breeding:** BC ♂, 19 Feb, Chocó (Carriker).

**Status and habitat:** Floor of wet forest in lowlands and lower mts. Apparently absent from drier, more seasonal forests of n Chocó. Common in sw Cauca (Olivares 1958).

**Range:** To 1100m. Pacific coast from nw base of W Andes (Mutatá) and Baudó Mts. s to s Chocó (*rosenbergi*); sw Cauca and w Nariño (*harterti*). W Colombia to nw Ecuador.

## 112. UNDULATED ANTPITTA
*Grallaria squamigera*          Pl. 30, Map 832

**Identification:** 9″ (23cm). *Large* with notably heavy bill. Olivaceous brown above, *heavily washed gray on crown and mantle*; lores buffy; throat white *bordered on sides by a dusky malar*; sides of head and rest of underparts yellowish fulvous; *feathers edged black giving a rather coarse, wavy barred appearance.*

**Similar species:** Giant Antpitta (113) is even larger, with ground color of underparts cinnamon buff (not yellowish), and no white throat or dusky malar.

**Voice:** Song in Peru a vibrating, *Otus*-like (or froglike) *cocococococococo* on same pitch (T. Parker); in Venez. sim. but rises distinctly at end, e.g. *huhuhuhuhuhuhuhu'hu'hu* (P. Schwartz recording).

**Behavior:** Mostly terrestrial. Hop from dense tangles into openings, grassy areas and open glades with filtered light to feed. Usually alone and rather retiring; flies low and directly (T. Parker).

**Breeding:** BC ♂, Aug, n end W Andes (Carriker).

**Status and habitat:** Undergrowth of humid forest and adj. small openings. Known from only a few widely scattered areas.

**Range:** 2300-3800m. W Andes at n end in Antioquia (Páramo Frontino), in Cauca (Munchique) and Valle (sighting above Cali, 2100m, 1973—Hilty), C Andes from n Tolima (Nevado Santa Isabel) s to Cauca (Coconuco) and E Andes s to latitude of Bogotá (Páramo de Choachí). Nw Venez. s in Andes to n Bolivia.

**Note:** Great Antpitta (*G. excelsa*) of Venez. Andes and Perijá Mts. is also likely on Colombian side of Perijá Mts. Much like Undulated Antpitta, it differs thus: brown back in sharp contrast to gray crown and nape, no moustachial streak, and larger size (10.5″ vs 9″). In Venez. rec. 1700-2300m. Poss. a race of next sp.

## 113. GIANT ANTPITTA
*Grallaria gigantea*          Pl. 30, Map 833

**Identification:** 10.5″ (26.7cm). Much like Undulated Antpitta. Bill decidedly thick and heavy. Olive brown above; hindcrown and nape tinged pale gray; forehead and lores, sides of head, and *entire underparts deep rusty; the feathers of throat and breast edged black giving a rather wavy barred appearance.* Imm. shows a few tawny rufous and black bars on mantle.

**Similar species:** See Undulated Antpitta (112).

**Status and habitat:** A little known bird of the floor of humid highland forest. Few recs.

**Range:** 2300-3000m. Known only from e slope of C Andes at head of Magdalena Val. in Huila (Río Moscopán area). Prob. s Nariño (rec. at El Pun, e Ecuador, 2700m, on Colombian border). S Colombia and e and w Ecuador.

## 114. MOUSTACHED ANTPITTA
*Grallaria alleni*

**Identification:** 7″ (18cm). Very rare and local. *Dark rufescent brown above with slate gray crown*

and nape; sides of head dark brown; *broad white malar* narrowly scaled black; throat russet bordered below by a *white band across chest*; breast olive brown with a few narrow white streaks; belly buffy white; flanks and under tail coverts washed cinnamon.

**Similar species:** Could be easily confused with Scaled Antpitta (115), which has crown and all of upperparts scaled with black but is otherwise quite sim. Brown-banded Antpitta (125) has brown (not slaty) crown and lacks white malar and chest band. Slate-crowned Antpitta (132) is half the size; Bicolored (119) lacks the moustache and has gray breast and belly.

**Status and habitat:** Rec. at only 2 localities. Undergrowth of very humid montane forest.

**Range:** ENDEMIC. Known from the type from w slope of C Andes in Quindío (above Salento on w side of Quindío Mts., at 2100m) and 1 specimen from e Huila (PN Cueva de los Guácharos).

**Note:** Poss. a subsp. of Scaled Antpitta (*G. guatimalensis*). See Hernández and Rodríguez (1979).

## 115. SCALED ANTPITTA
*Grallaria guatimalensis*          Pl. 31, Map 834

**Identification:** 7″ (18cm). Nape gray; crown and rest of upperparts olive brown; *the feathers of all of upperparts scaled blackish*: remiges uniform rufescent brown; throat brown bordered on sides by a buffy malar and below by an indistinct buff crescentic band (or center line of throat and crescentic bar on lower throat white bordered below by a black band—*regulus*); rest of underparts cinnamon tawny with some dusky mottling on chest.

**Similar species:** Blackish scaling on upperparts hard to see in field. See Moustached Antpitta (114) and much smaller Brown-banded Antpitta (125).

**Voice:** Song in Venez. a quavering, *Otus*-like *huhuhuhuhuhuhu hú dudu hu*, much like that of Undulated Antpitta but does not rise perceptibly (P. Schwartz recording).

**Behavior:** Mostly terrestrial. Hops on the ground or logs, or occas. perches on branches in undergrowth. When flushed, flies low and directly for a short distance. Retiring and usually hard to see.

**Breeding:** 2 BC birds, Apr, Perijá Mts. (Carriker); bulky cup nest of sticks and leaves low in shrub; 2 downy black nestlings, 23 Apr, Valle (Miller 1963); 5 Panama nests, Apr–June (Wetmore 1972); blue egg in Mexico (Edwards and Lea 1955).

**Status and habitat:** Apparently local. Floor of humid forest, esp. in ravines and steep vals. Mostly foothills and mts.

**Range:** 300-2000m (mainly below 900m). Baudó Mts. and n Chocó (*chocoensis*); Santa Marta (n slope) and Perijá Mts. s to n boundary of Boyacá (*carmelitae*); E Andes at w base in s Cesar and e base from nw Casanare to w Putumayo (*regulus*); W Andes above Cali (subsp.?). C Mexico to Bolivia, extreme n Brazil, and se Venez.

**Note 1:** Plain-backed Antpitta (*G. haplonota*) of n Venez., 900-2000m) and w Ecuador (Paramba near Colombia boundary) may occur in Pacific Colombia; songs sim. to this sp. in n Venez. have been rec. in w Nariño and w Valle, 900-1200m (Hilty). Recalls Scaled Antpitta 7″, plain olive brown above with dull white loral spot and throat, and obscure whitish line below eye; underparts buffy ochraceous. Song up to 10 low, hollow whistles (like blowing over bottle) that steadily rise then fall. **Note 2:** Variegated Antpitta (*G. varia*) of s Venez. and the Guianas to ne Argentina is known opp. e Guainía on Caño Casiquiare, Venez., and may occur in Colombia. Like Scaled Antpitta but larger (8″) with gray nape, more heavily streaked breast, and white crescent on chest reduced to a small patch. Hollow swelling song *hoo-hoo-hooo-hoooo-HOO' HOO' HOO' ho*, 1st notes faint (T. Davis).

### 116. OCHRE-STRIPED ANTPITTA
*Grallaria dignissima*

**Identification:** 7.5″ (19cm). Rather large and chunky. Rufescent brown above tinged grayish on crown; lores and eyering fulvous; *throat orange ochraceous; rest of underparts white broadly striped orange ochraceous on breast; sides of breast and long flank plumes striped blackish and white.*

**Similar species:** Strikingly patterned. Likely confused only with Thrush-like or Spotted antpittas (129, 127), both of which are smaller and have white (not orange ochraceous) throats.

**Status and habitat:** One Colombian rec., 12 Sept 1966, San Miguel (300m), Putumayo, on Ecuador-Colombia border. The region is humid forest. Poss. along Río Putumayo to w Amazonas as rec. at Lagartacocha, Ecuador on Río Napo, and mouth of Río Curaray, n Peru.

**Range:** Se Colombia, e Ecuador, and adj. ne Peru.

### 117. CHESTNUT-CROWNED ANTPITTA
*Grallaria ruficapilla*        Pl. 31, Map 835

**Identification:** 8″ (20cm). Large. *Crown, nape, and sides of head bright cinnamon rufous in contrast to olive upperparts and snowy white throat;* rest of underparts white broadly streaked and edged blackish and olive.

**Similar species:** The most numerous antpitta in most of the Colombian highlands and easily recognized. Bay-backed Antpitta (121) is un-

streaked below; *Chamaeza* antthrushes (101-104) have a white postocular and lack the cinnamon rufous head.

**Voice:** Often heard song is 3 clear whistles, *wee, wü, woou*, 1st highest, next lowest, last slightly upslurred. An onomatopoeic local name is *Compra pan*.

**Behavior:** Like others of the genus mostly terrestrial. Hop about on or near the ground or run rapidly on the ground. Usually keep concealed in tangled undergrowth but may bound into small openings and grassy clearings, even roadsides to feed in early morning or late evening.

**Breeding:** 10 BC birds, Apr–Sept, n end W Andes, Perijá Mts. (Carriker); 2 BC ♂♂, Mar, Valle (Miller 1963); Antioquia nest a mass of dead leaves, roots, and moss some ht. above ground (Sclater and Salvin 1879).

**Status and habitat:** Widespread and common on the floor of humid forest, forest borders, and second growth woodland.

**Range:** 1200-2800m (usually above 1700m). All 3 Andean ranges and Perijá Mts. N Venez. s in mts. to c Peru.

### 118. SANTA MARTA ANTPITTA
*Grallaria bangsi*        Pl. 31, Map 836

**Identification:** 7″ (18cm). Olive brown above with whitish lores and eyering; *throat bright ochraceous buff; rest of underparts dull white streaked brownish olive;* flanks brownish somewhat streaked white; under wing coverts cinnamon buff.

**Similar species:** The only *large* antpitta in its range that is common. Cf. Scaled Antpitta (115), which prob. overlaps only at lower el.

**Voice:** Frequently heard call a loud, flat, *bob white*, reminiscent of bobwhite's whistle, but not strongly upslurred (T. B. Johnson).

**Behavior:** Terrestrial or on low horizontal perches but less retiring and easier to see than many *Grallaria*.

**Breeding:** 1 BC ♀, Jan, 1 in Sept (Carriker); pin-feathered juv. followed ad., 7 July, San Lorenzo (T. B. Johnson).

**Status and habitat:** Common (by voice) on floor of humid forest and tall second growth. Often enters small open spaces, clearings, or roadsides at forest edge.

**Range:** ENDEMIC. 1200-2400m (usually above 1600m). Santa Marta Mts.

### 119. BICOLORED ANTPITTA
*Grallaria rufocinerea*        Pl. 30, Map 837

**Identification:** 6.5″ (16.5cm). Head, throat, and entire upperparts uniform dark rufous brown; chest to crissum *dark gray* (some birds have throat mixed gray—♀?).

**Similar species:** Chestnut-naped Antpitta (120) is sim. but *much* larger, has crown chestnut in contrast to reddish brown back, and blackish throat. Hooded Antpitta (134) is smaller and has orange head.
**Voice:** A high, clear, whistled *treeeee* or double-sounding *treeeeeaaaa* last part slurred lower, at 2½- to 3-sec intervals. May be answered reg. by a mate.
**Behavior:** As in others of the genus.
**Breeding:** BC ♂, June, se Antioquia (Carriker).
**Status and habitat:** Floor or undergrowth of humid montane forest.
**Range:** ENDEMIC. 2100-3100m. W slope of C Andes in Quindío area (above Salento on w side of Quindío Mts.), e slope C Andes in Antioquia (8 km e of Medellín at Santa Elena; Páramo Sonsón, 20km n of Caldas boundary), e slope C Andes in Cauca (Río Bedón in PN Puracé), and e slope Andes in Nariño (sight, 2 June 1981, ca. 20km e San Francisco at 2450m—Hilty et al).

## 120. CHESTNUT-NAPED ANTPITTA
*Grallaria nuchalis*          Pl. 30, Map 838
**Identification:** 8.5″ (22cm). Big. *Rear crown and nape bright chestnut contrasting with duller rufous brown upperparts; below uniform slate gray; blackish on throat,* facial area, and auriculars.
**Similar species:** See very sim. but much smaller Bicolored Antpitta (119). Smaller Bay-backed Antpitta (121) is mostly white below (not dark gray); no other large highland antpittas (e.g., 114, 115, 117, 124, 125) are gray below.
**Voice:** Song in Peru a clear ser. of *kook* notes followed by a gradually rising ser. of notes that accelerate slightly and become very high and thin at end, *kook, kook, kook-who-who-hu-hu-hu-hu-e-e-e* (T. Parker).
**Behavior:** Sim. to other *Grallaria*. Hard to see. Usually call from slightly elevated and concealed perch at intervals throughout the day (T. Parker).
**Breeding:** BC ♀ and juv., Jan, se Antioquia (Carriker).
**Status and habitat:** Floor and undergrowth of humid forest, esp. in bamboo. Uncommon (infrequently heard or seen) in PN Puracé (J. Silliman; Hilty).
**Range:** 2200-3000m. Both slopes of C Andes s to Cauca (PN Puracé) and w slope of E Andes sw of Bogotá (one 1917 specimen at El Peñon, 2900m but no recent recs.). Andes of Colombia, e and w Ecuador, and n Peru.

## 121. BAY-BACKED (WHITE-BELLIED) ANTPITTA
*Grallaria hypoleuca*          Pl. 30, Map 839
**Identification:** 7″ (18cm). Sides of head and

upperparts chestnut brown, brightest on sides of head; *underparts white with gray tinge on breast and sides;* flanks rufous brown.
**Similar species:** Only Colombian antpitta uniformly whitish below. Bicolored (119) and Chestnut-naped antpittas (120) are dark gray below. Tawny Antpitta (124) is buffy ochraceous below.
**Voice:** Distinctive song 3 clear whistles, 1st longest and a half tone lower than couplet that follows, *puuuh; pü; pü.*
**Behavior:** Much like Chestnut-naped Antpitta.
**Breeding:** 5 BC birds, Mar–Sept, C and E Andes (Carriker).
**Status and habitat:** Thick undergrowth in humid mossy forest borders, second growth, and dense overgrown clearings; inside forest mostly at dense tangles around treefalls or landslides. Common at PN Cueva de los Guácharos.
**Range:** 1500-2100m. Both slopes of C Andes in Antioquia (prob. s to Nariño); w slope of E Andes from se Santander s to head of Magdalena Val. in Huila. Andes of Colombia s to e Ecuador and Peru.
**Note 1:** Does not incl. *G. flavotincta* (Yellow-breasted Antpitta) of the Pacific slope. **Note 2:** Peruvian birds (3 forms) may also be separate spp. (see Meyer de Schauensee 1966).

## 122. YELLOW-BREASTED ANTPITTA
*Grallaria flavotincta*          Map 840
**Identification:** 7″ (18cm). Upperparts *uniform deep rufous brown; throat and breast pale yellow* becoming whitish on lower belly; flanks deep rufous brown.
**Similar species:** Only antpitta in its range with uniform pale yellow throat and breast.
**Voice:** Song is 2- or 3-noted, the 1st so brief it is unnoticed at a distance, the last note a half tone higher than 2d, *puh-püüü, puuh,* quality recalls Bay-backed Antpitta (121) (B. Whitney and R. Ridgely).
**Behavior:** Like others of genus, often heard but difficult to see. Usually calls from concealed perch near ground.
**Breeding:** 4 BC birds, June, n end W Andes (Carriker).
**Status and habitat:** Mossy cloud forest (at 1800m) above Queremal; dense shrubbery and bamboo in understory; favors ravines. Frequently heard but difficult to see (B. Whitney and R. Ridgely).
**Range:** ENDEMIC. 1300-1800m. Pacific slope from n Antioquia (Río Sucio drainage) to Nariño (Ricaurte).
**Note:** Sometimes considered a subsp. of Bay-backed Antipitta (*G. hypoleuca*) but differs in having tail shorter than tarsus (not longer), 10 (not 12) rectrices, and in color (S. Olson); voice also differs.

### 123. RUFOUS ANTPITTA.
*Grallaria rufula*     Pl. 31, Map 841
**Identification:** 5.5″ (14cm). Small. *Entirely uniform rufous chestnut*, a little brighter below and becoming buffy on center of belly. Or center of belly white (*spatiator*). Or uniform olive brown becoming grayish brown on lower underparts (*saltuensis*).
**Similar species:** Most likely confused with larger Tawny Antpitta (124), which is dull brown above and tawny ochraceous below (no rufous or chestnut in plumage). No other unstreaked, highland antpitta (*Grallaria* or *Grallaricula*) is so entirely uniform rufescent.
**Voice:** A ser. of rapid, whistled, *tu* notes, rattling, almost trilled, and rising at end (J. Silliman); usual song a flat 2-noted *tüü, tüük*, repeated at 10-20 sec. intervals.
**Behavior:** Hops on ground like others of the genus; occas. perches in shrubs or bushes, esp. when disturbed.
**Breeding:** 5 BC birds, Mar–May, Perijá and Santa Marta mts. (Carriker).
**Status and habitat:** Undergrowth and ground at edge of dense, humid mt. forest, esp. damp areas and near streams. Partially replaced in more open terrain at higher el. by Tawny Antpitta. Uncommon in most areas.
**Range:** 2400-3600m (to treeline or above). Santa Marta Mts. (*spatiator*); Perijá Mts. (*saltuensis*), and spottily in all 3 Andean ranges (*rufula*). Nw Venez. s in Andes to Bolivia.

### 124. TAWNY ANTPITTA
*Grallaria quitensis*     Pl. 31, Map 842
**Identification:** 7″ (18.0cm). Dull brownish olive above, *large loral spot and narrow eyering buffy white; sides of head and underparts ochraceous buff*; somewhat mottled whitish. Young birds show var. amt. of buff and black barring, mostly on crown, nape, and breast.
**Similar species:** A rather dull antpitta and the most likely one to be found near or above treeline in Colombia. See Rufous (123) and rare Brown-banded antpittas (125). Several other large, unstreaked, highland antpittas (119, 120, 121) are grayish or whitish below (not ochraceous buff).
**Voice:** Frequently heard song a loud, clear whistle, *took, tu tu*, 1st note slightly higher and louder. Calls incl. a single whistle, *cheew* (J. Silliman), and scolding *tsee-er*.
**Behavior:** Runs rapidly or hops on ground and seeks cover in thickets or grass but unlike other *Grallaria*, often unsuspicious and remarkably easy to see, even perching on fence posts, tops of bushes, or other elevated sites to call. Usually solitary, occas. pairs and notably vocal.
**Breeding:** 2 BC birds, Feb, Cauca, 1 in Aug,

Santander (Carriker); June juv., Cundinamarca (Olivares 1967).
**Status and habitat:** Often common in paramo with scattered bushes, shrubs, and Frailejón (*Espeletia*) or in dense thickets at humid temperate forest borders. Most numerous in Nariño.
**Range:** 2200-3700m (usually above 3000m). E Andes from ne Santander s to Cundinamarca, C Andes from Caldas to Nariño, and head of Magdalena Val. in Hulia. Colombia s in mts. to n Peru.

### 125. BROWN-BANDED ANTPITTA
*Grallaria milleri*     Pl. 31, Map 843
**Identification:** 7″ (18cm). Dark brown above, lores, *throat, and center of belly dingy white; broad breast band brown*.
**Similar species:** Dull and easily confused. Moustached Antipitta (114) is larger with brown throat bordered on sides and below by white. Tawny Antpitta (124) is mainly ochraceous buff below with paler mottling and has *no* breast band; also see Scaled, Bicolored, Bay-backed, and Rufous antpittas (115, 119, 121, 123).
**Status and habitat:** Nothing known. All specimens were taken in a region of humid montane forest (now mostly deforested).
**Range:** ENDEMIC. 2700-3100m. Known only from w slope of C Andes in Quindío (Laguneta, above Salento).

[*Hylopezus*: Plump and short-tailed; med.-sized; breast conspic. streaked or spotted; 126 and 127 with prom. eyering; lowlands or foothills; formerly placed in *Grallaria* but eggs heavily spotted (*Grallaria* eggs unmarked bluish green).]

### 126. STREAK-CHESTED ANTPITTA
*Hylopezus perspicillatus*     Ill. 80, Map 844
**Identification:** 5.5″ (14cm). "Pot-bellied" shape. Crown and nape gray; otherwise brownish olive above, back usually with a few buff shaft streaks; wing coverts with 2 rows of buff dots; lores and *large eyering ochraceous*; narrow malar streak black; *below white; chest, upper breast, and sides buff boldly streaked black*. Downy chick mostly rusty rufous, wings like ad.
**Similar species:** Closely resembles Fulvousbellied Antpitta (128), which *lacks the eyering*, dots on wing coverts and the sharply streaked underparts.
**Voice:** Persistently repeated song in s Córdoba a loud, clear, whistled ser. of 5-9 notes, *pay-pee-pee-pee-pay-pay-paaw*, rising slightly, last 3 notes falling; melancholy and ventriloquial. In Panama *deh, dee, dee, dee, dee, deé-eh, deéh-oh, dóh-a*, couplets falling off (Eisenmann 1952).

80. STREAK-CHESTED ANTPITTA (left),
FULVOUS-BELLIED ANTPITTA (right)

**Behavior:** Solitary and heard far more than seen. Hops on ground or logs; also runs or walks readily. Often sings from an open perch 3-9m up inside forest and then not shy. Like Fulvous-bellied Antpitta, often rocks body from side to side and fluffs belly feathers.
**Breeding:** 14 BC birds, Feb–May, nw Colombia (Carriker); Panama nest, July (Willis and Eisenmann 1979); low nests may have been slightly remodeled accumulations of trash or old nests of another sp.; 2 light gray eggs coarsely mottled dark at larger end (Skutch 1969a).
**Status and habitat:** Floor of humid and wet forest, esp. with lighter undergrowth. Local and much less numerous than allied Fulvous-bellied Antpitta.
**Range:** To 1200m. Pacific coast and humid lowlands n of Andes to mid. Magdalena Val. (s to latitude of Bucaramanga). Nicaragua to w Ecuador.

### 127. SPOTTED ANTPITTA

*Hylopezus macularius*      Pl. 31, Map 845
**Identification:** 6″ (15cm). Very like Streak-chested Antpitta. *Crown and nape gray;* otherwise uniform brownish olive above with 2 faint buff-edged wing bars; large loral spot and *prom. eyering buff; throat white* bordered on sides by 2 narrow black malar stripes; *chest and sides buff boldly streaked black*; rest of underparts white.
**Similar species:** Thrush-like Antpitta (129) lacks malars and eyering and has breast streaking diffused (not sharp and confined mostly to

chest). More sim. Fulvous-bellied Antpitta (128) has weak eyering, very diffused streaking below, and is apparently rare in zone of overlap.
**Voice:** Song a deep, hollow, whistle *coo-hoo-yóu-ooo-cyoo-cýoo*, rhythmic (T. Davis), also a thin wooden rattle, *trrrrrr* (Snyder 1966).
**Behavior:** Much like Streak-chested Antpitta. Hops on or near ground, singly or in pairs. Fluffs out throat when singing (T. Davis).
**Status and habitat:** Open understory or floor of humid *terra firme* forest. Not well known in Colombia.
**Range:** To 300m. Known only from Amazonas nw of Leticia (Río Loreto-Yacú). The Guianas, extreme s Venez., Amazonian Brazil, ne Peru (incl. Pto. Indiana), and ne Bolivia.

### 128. FULVOUS-BELLIED ANTPITTA

*Hylopezus fulviventris*   Pl. 31, Ill. 80, Map 846
**Identification:** 6.5″ (16.5cm). Resembles Streak-chested Antpitta. Crown, nape, and sides of head slaty, becoming *dark olive on back and brownish on wings* (no dots on coverts); *throat white* separated on sides by a narrow black malar line; *rest of underparts ochraceous buff diffusely streaked blackish on breast and sides*; center of belly white; lower abdomen and flanks *bright cinnamon rufous.*
**Similar species:** Most like Streak-chested Antpitta (126) but lacks strong eyering, upperparts darker and uniform (incl. wing coverts), and flanks cinnamon rufous. E of Andes see Spotted and Thrush-like antpittas (127, 129).
**Voice:** Song on Pacific coast, a brisk ser. of about 8 (4-12) mellow, whistled notes gradually rising in pitch, last few notes on same pitch and ending abruptly, *oh-oh-ou-oü-oü-üü-üü-üü!*
**Behavior:** Sings persistently even throughout the heat of day. Decoys well but exceedingly difficult to see. Usually singly, running, walking, or hopping with springy bounds over forest floor or on logs; sings mostly from a log or low perch above ground. When perched often sways body from side to side while holding legs and head stationary as do others of the genus.
**Breeding:** 4 BC birds, Mar–May, nw Colombia (Carriker).
**Status and habitat:** Locally common (by voice) in thickets and dense undergrowth in younger second growth woodland and forest borders (not inside tall forest except at large treefalls). Very common on disturbed coastal plain in w Valle, smaller nos. well into foothills and lower slopes. Little known (rare?) e of Andes.
**Range:** To 900m. Upper Sinú Val. to w shore of Gulf of Urabá and s on entire Pacific coast; e base of E Andes from w Caquetá southward. Nicaragua to w and e Ecuador.

## 129. THRUSH-LIKE ANTPITTA

*Myrmothera campanisona*        Pl. 31, Map 847
**Identification:** 6" (15cm). Resembles a tailless thrush. Olive brown above; loral spot buffy white; *underparts white rather diffusely streaked brownish olive on breast and sides* (or breast olivaceous with yellowish white streaks—*modesta*). Amt. of breast streaking var. in all subsp.
**Similar species:** Fulvous-bellied Antpitta (128) has darker, more slaty upperparts, a black malar, bright cinnamon rufous flanks, and more ochraceous abdomen. Also see Spotted Antpitta (127).
**Voice:** Song 5-7 or so low, hollow, resonant whistles, deliberate and increasing in strength, then dropping slightly in pitch and vol. *wuh-wuh-wuH-WUH-Wuh-wu.*
**Behavior:** Single birds or pairs hop on or near the ground, and usually stay in denser forest undergrowth. Like other antpittas, furtive, difficult to see, and *heard far more often* than seen.
**Status and habitat:** Floor and dense undergrowth of humid *terra firme* forest. Usually uncommon and thinly spread.
**Range:** To 600m. E of Andes in w Meta s to Macarena Mts. (*modesta*); Caquetá and w Putumayo e to Vaupés at Mitú (*dissors*); se Nariño (*signata*), Amazonas (subsp.?). The Guianas and s Venez. to e Peru and Amazonian Brazil.

## 130. OCHRE-BREASTED ANTPITTA

*Grallaricula flavirostris*        Pl. 31, Map 848
**Identification:** 4" (10.2cm). Virtually tailless. Olive brown above with grayish tinge on crown and *tawny loral spot and eyering; sides of head and underparts ochraceous* fading to white on belly; lightly streaked dusky on breast and sides.
**Similar species:** Likely confused only with other *Grallaricula.* Cf. Rusty-breasted and Slate-crowned antpittas (131, 132) neither of which has streaks on breast. Fulvous-bellied Antpitta (128) is much larger.
**Voice:** Song in Costa Rica a short ascending ser. of 5-8 mellow whistles, *wu-wu-wu-uu-uu-uu-ueet,* faster at end; pattern reminiscent of Fulvous-bellied Antpitta (B. Whitney).
**Behavior:** Usually alone, perching near ground in undergrowth where active and unsuspicious (almost fearless) but hard to see because of small size and sudden movements. Flit or sally to foliage or briefly to the ground. Rather sedentary.
**Status and habitat:** Apparently local. Fairly open undergrowth of wet mossy forest in foothills and mts. More numerous at higher el.
**Range:** 500-2100m. Pacific slope (also e slope near low passes) from s Chocó (Cerro Tatamá) southward; e base of E Andes from w Meta

(Río Gramalote nw of Villavicencio) to se Nariño (Río San Miguel). Costa Rica to w Ecuador; e Colombia s on e slope of Andes to n Bolivia.

## 131. RUSTY-BREASTED ANTPITTA

*Grallaricula ferrugineipectus*        Pl. 31, Map 849
**Identification:** 4.5" (11.4cm). Virtually tailless. Legs pale pink. Olive brown above with *large buff loral spot and eyering; throat white expanding to larger white crescent on chest; rest of underparts rusty buff*; center of belly and under tail coverts white. Or as above but crown and sides of head deep rufous brown, underparts deeper rufous and white on throat and chest much reduced (*rara*).
**Similar species:** Slate-crowned Antpitta (132) is darker above and below with contrasting slaty crown (not uniform with back). Ochre-breasted Antpitta (130) has dusky streaking on breast and is not yet proved to overlap in range.
**Voice:** Call in Venez. a sad, liquid *quierk* or doubled *quiu, quiu* in alarm; dawn song *twa-twa-twa-twa-twa-twa-cwi-cwi-cwi-cwi-cwi-cwi-cwi, cu-cu; cwi* notes higher and louder, last 2 lower (Schwartz 1957).
**Behavior:** Sim. to Ochre-breasted Antpitta. Drops to forest floor, sallies to foliage, or flycatches (Schwartz 1957).
**Breeding:** Mainly rainy season; 1 nest, 10 Oct. 1800m, Santa Marta Mts. (Todd and Carriker 1922); in n Venez. breeding starts late May; shallow twig cup about 1m up; 2 pale greenish or grayish eggs marked with shades of brown (Schwartz 1957).
**Status and habitat:** Apparently rare and local. Fairly open undergrowth in humid forest.
**Range:** 600-1800m. Santa Marta Mts. (*rara*); e slope E Andes in Norte de Santander and w slope of E Andes in Cundinamarca (*ferrugineipectus*). N and nw Venez. (incl. Perijá Mts.); ne Colombia; n Peru and Bolivia.
**Note:** Birds from Santa Marta Mts. and Perijá Mts., Venez., *G. rara* (Rufous-breasted Antpitta), may be a separate sp.

## 132. SLATE-CROWNED ANTPITTA

*Grallaricula nana*        Pl. 31, Map 850
**Identification:** 4.4" (11.5cm). Resembles Rusty-breasted Antpitta. *Crown and nape slate gray*; rest of upperparts dark umber brown; *large loral spot and prom. eyering ochraceous; underparts deep orange rufous*, paler on throat; narrow indistinct white crescent across chest; center of lower underparts white.
**Similar species:** See Rusty-breasted Antpitta (131). Ochre-breasted Antpitta (130) has dusky streaks on breast.

**Voice:** Song in Venez. a loud fast trill, ascending, then dropping (3 sec), *we'ti'ti'ti'ti'ti'te'tee'too* (P. Schwartz recording); in Peru a very soft ser. of 5-8 *zee's*, same pitch or slightly downscale, ventriloquial, and usually closer than it sounds (T. Parker).
**Behavior:** Like other *Grallaricula* hops on perches in shrubbery in open understory from near ground to about eye level. Sallies to foliage, gleans foliage from perch, or drops momentarily to ground; inconspic. and hard to see.
**Breeding:** BC ♂, June, se Antioquia (Carriker); May, Rancho Grande, Venez. (Schäfer and Phelps 1954).
**Status and habitat:** Humid forest undergrowth.
**Range:** 1900-2100m; to 1300m on Pacific slope. W Andes in Valle and Cauca, head of Magdalena Val. in Huila, and ne end of E Andes (Norte de Santander). N Venez. to e Ecuador and n Peru.

### 133. CRESCENT-FACED ANTPITTA
*Grallaricula lineifrons*
**Identification:** 4.8″ (12.2cm). Rare. Virtually tailless. Crown and sides of head slaty black with a *broad white crescent in front of eyes* and cinnamon patch on sides of neck; remaining upperparts olive tinged yellow; throat white bordered on sides by black malar; *breast and sides broadly streaked cinnamon buff and black*; belly white streaked black.
**Similar species:** No other antpitta has a distinct white facial crescent.
**Status and habitat:** Known from 1 Colombian specimen (J. Silliman) in thick undergrowth of a steep forested canyon and 1 seen in same region by R. Belding (Lehmann et al. 1977). Cold dense elfin woodland.
**Range:** 3000-3200m. W slope of C Andes in Cauca (about 7km e of Puracé and 1 km n of Popayán-Neiva road on s slope of Quebrada Tierra Adentro Canyon; and sight rec. about 2km sw of Laguna San Rafael), at nw end of PN Puracé. Ne Ecuador (1 specimen).

### 134. HOODED ANTPITTA
*Grallaricula cucullata*       Pl. 31, Map 851
**Identification:** 4.5″ (11.4cm). *Bill orange. Entire head and throat bright orange rufous*; otherwise olive brown above and *gray below with narrow white crescent across chest*; center of lower breast and belly white.
**Similar species:** No other small antpitta has a bright orange rufous head. See Rufous-headed Pygmy-Tyrant (p 475) with rufous wings and longer rufous tail.

**Behavior:** Usually alone, hopping from near ground to 1.5m up in undergrowth; often rocks body from side to side while holding head and legs stationary (Gertler 1977) as do some larger antpittas.
**Status and habitat:** Local; undergrowth of humid forest. Common in PN Cueva de los Guácharos at about 2000m (P. Gertler) but known from only a few other localities.
**Range:** 1500-2700m. E slope of W Andes (once above Cali), e slope of C Andes (e of Medellín) and head of Magdalena Val. in Huila. Colombia and nw Venez. (sw Táchira on Río Chiquito).

[*Conopophaga*: Plump and short-tailed; formerly placed in the family Conopophagidae. ♂♂ of most, ♀♀ of some, with silvery postocular stripe ending in tuft. The only other genus in the family, *Corythopis*, has been transferred to the Tyrant Flycatchers.]

### 135. CHESTNUT-CROWNED GNATEATER
*Conopophaga castaneiceps*       Pl. 31, Map 852
**Identification:** 5.2″ (13.2cm). Plump with rather long, pale blue legs. Tail short. ♂: dark grayish olive above with *orange rufous forehead* and *chestnut crown; long prom. postocular stripe white* (ends in tuft); sides of head and underparts dark slate gray; center of abdomen whitish. ♀: olive brown above with *entire head and breast dark orange rufous; long postocular tuft white*; belly and median throat whitish.
**Similar species:** A dark, chunky, almost flycatcherlike bird with long legs; either sex best told by long silvery white postocular stripe.
**Voice:** Call of both sexes a raspy chipping rattle, *chit, chit-it, chit-it-it-it-it* given occas.; alarm a raspy *chek*; in flight wings make a low whirring sound.
**Behavior:** Single birds or separated pairs wait hunched on low horizontal or vertical perches in undergrowth, then sally short distances to ground or foliage for small prey. Change perches frequently and often retiring (Hilty 1975a).
**Breeding:** 6 BC birds, Mar–June, C Andes (Carriker); 1 nest, Feb, upper Anchicayá Val.; concealed bulky cup 0.8 m up in forest (Hilty 1975a).
**Status and habitat:** Apparently local (easily overlooked) in dense undergrowth of humid and wet forest, esp. near treefalls and landslides surrounded with tall saplings. Can be found in Bosque Yotoco, Buga.
**Range:** Mostly 1200-1800m (to 700m on Pacific slope in Valle; to 500m in w Meta). Baudó

Mts., w slope W Andes from n end (Quimirí and Cerro Murrucucú) southward, e slope W Andes in Valle, n end C Andes, head of Magdalena Val. in Huila, and e slope E Andes in Cundinamarca. Colombia to e Ecuador and n Peru.

### 136. CHESTNUT-BELTED GNATEATER
*Conopophaga aurita*                Pl. 31, Map 853
**Identification:** 5″ (13cm). Plump with rather long pale blue legs. Tail short. ♂: crown rufous brown bordered on sides by *prom. silvery white postocular stripe* (ends in tuft); otherwise olive brown above faintly scaled black; *forehead, sides of head, and throat black bordered below by a rufous chest band*; lower breast and belly white; flanks tinged olive. ♀: sim., but lores and *upper throat white*; sides of head, lower throat, and breast rufous.
**Similar species:** Unusual pattern should be easily recognized. Look for silvery postocular and rufous chest band.
**Behavior:** Sim. to Chestnut-crowned Gnateater but occas. follows army ants (Oniki and Willis 1972). Produces a whining sound with wings in threat display (Goodfellow 1901).
**Status and habitat:** Uncommon in undergrowth of humid *terra firme* forest, esp. in denser growth around treefalls.
**Range:** To 500m. E of Andes in w Caquetá and Putumayo. Doubtless e to Vaupés (rec. at Tahuapunto, Brazil opp. Vaupés). The Guianas and e Colombia to e Peru (incl. mouth of Río Curaray) and Amazonian Brazil (not rec. in s Venez.).

## TAPACULOS: Rhinocryptidae (9)

Tapaculos are a New World family mainly of the southern third of South America. A few range northward, mostly in the mountains, as far as Costa Rica. They differ most notably from their antbird allies in having a cocked tail and moveable flap or operculum covering the nostrils. Tapaculos are terrestrial or semiterrestrial insectivores. Many south temperate species are gregarious in open drier country, the Colombian species are all retiring forest inhabitants found alone or in pairs. Nests as far as known, are globular balls in burrows, banks, crevices, or tree cavities and always well-concealed. Most Colombian species belong to the genus *Scytalopus*, a group of wrenlike birds characterized by a rather narrow laterally compressed bill with a high thin culmen. The various species are very difficult to differentiate even in the hand and are hard to glimpse in the field. The number of species within the genus is still uncertain. The name tapaculo is apparently derived from the Spanish "to cover your posterior," a reference to the habit of holding the tail cocked up (Darwin 1845).

### 1. RUSTY-BELTED TAPACULO
*Liosceles thoracicus*                Pl. 41, Map 854
**Identification:** 7.5″ (19cm). With rather long cocked tail recalls an antbird or wren. Dark rufous brown above; head tinged gray; wings brown with 2 fulvous-dotted blackish wing bars; narrow eyebrow and spots on cheeks white; *throat and breast white with a broad rufous chest band* (or chest band narrower, upper half tinged yellowish—*erithacus*); sides streaked and barred grayish; *flanks and abdomen heavily barred brown and white*, barring more rufous and brown posteriorly; eyes yellow.
**Similar species:** White underparts, chest band, and barred flanks are the marks. See much smaller Nightingale Wren (p 539) and Chestnut-belted Gnateater (above).
**Voice:** Song a low, hollow, whistled *woouk . . . wu, wu, wu, wu, wu* (in Putumayo and Amazonas) with quality reminiscent of a pygmy-owl; 1st note followed after 3- or 4-sec pause by slow, slightly descending ser. of 6 or so (occas. up to 12 or more) notes, then ends abruptly.
**Behavior:** Recalls a large wren or antbird as it walks and hops over forest floor picking at leaf litter. Usually seen singly in denser undergrowth and unless singing, likely overlooked. Perches on fallen logs to sing, where bends over, fluffs throat feathers and thrusts head downward with each note.
**Status and habitat:** Undergrowth and floor of *terra firme* forest, esp. in areas of cluttered forest with fallen logs and saplings; also reg. in *várzea* in e Ecuador (R. Ridgely).
**Range:** To 400m. Se Colombia from w Putumayo (Pto. Umbría—*dugandi*) and se Nariño (*erithacus*) e to Amazonas (sightings, Leticia—Hilty). E Ecuador, e Peru, and w Amazonian Brazil.

[*Scytalopus*: Recall holarctic Winter Wren (*T. troglodytes*) in mouselike behavior and cocked tail; hop through mossy tangles and scurry under forest debris; weak flight mostly wing-assisted hops and short flutters; complex geographical var. and secretive habits complicate taxonomy and field observation.]

## 2. ASH-COLORED TAPACULO
*Scytalopus senilis*          Pl. 41, Map 855
**Identification:** 5.7″ (14.5cm). Bill and legs dusky.
♂: dark gray, slightly paler below; *tail decidedly long* (2.4″, or 6cm) *and usually carried cocked up.*
♀: sim. but feathers of back and lower underparts edged brownish. Imm.: cinnamon brown above; ochraceous tawny below with subterminal black bars on tertials, sometimes also on wing coverts.
**Similar species:** Shape sim. to other *Scytalopus*, but tail longer, plumage paler, and ads. have no barring on flanks and lower underparts.
**Voice:** In Peru low *kep* notes and a short low trill sim. to that of Andean Tapaculo (T. Parker).
**Behavior:** In Peru hops 1-3m up, occas. even higher, in bamboo (T. Parker).
**Status and habitat:** Bamboo in wet forest or forest borders, esp. stunted forest near treeline in Peru (T. Parker).
**Range:** 2400-3100m. W slope of C Andes in Caldas (Nevado del Ruiz; El Zancudo); E Andes in Norte de Santander (Páramo de Tamá) and in Cundinamarca (sw of Bogotá at El Peñon). Colombia to n Peru. Prob. also w Venez. in Táchira.
**Note:** Often placed in the genus *Myornis*, being separated from *Scytalopus* mainly on longer tail length. *S. femoralis* is intermed. in tail length betw. this sp. and other *Scytalopus.*

## 3. RUFOUS-VENTED TAPACULO
*Scytalopus femoralis*          Pls. 41, 42, Map 856
**Identification:** 5.5″ (14cm). Bill black, slightly arched; *tail long for the genus* (2″, or 51mm) and usually cocked. Above blackish gray, wings browner; *lower back uniform dark brown*; underparts dark gray; belly sometimes scaled grayish white; flanks and under tail coverts chestnut barred black (or somewhat darker overall with faint bars on rump and bars on flanks and under tail coverts fainter—*nigricans*). *Diagnostic white crown spot often present*, more prevalent in ♂ ♂ than ♀ ♀ and perhaps with greater frequency in Perijá and Santa Marta mts. ♀: sim. but browner above. Juv. mostly scaled dark brown and buff below.
**Similar species:** Birds lacking crown spot easily confused with Nariño Tapaculo (6) and *meridanus* race of Brown-rumped Tapaculo (7) of E and C Andes, but tail longer (2″ vs 1.5″, or 51 vs 38mm), and generally darker than Brown-rumped, esp. below, and with much more prom. barring on lower underparts. Andean Tapaculo (8) at n end of W and C Andes (*canus*) is all gray; elsewhere (*griseicollis*) more sim. but foreparts paler, rearparts unbarred and much brighter.
**Voice:** Song, usually preceded by a few slower

warm-up notes, a hard nasal raillike ser. of notes, *na, da, da-dt-dt-dt-dt-dt* . . . at rate of about 3 per sec for up to 20 sec.
**Behavior:** Typical of the genus.
**Breeding:** ♀ just laid, 24 May, se Antioquia, and 3 BC ♂ ♂, Aug–Oct, Santa Marta Mts. (Carriker); 1 nest Apr, PN Cueva de los Guácharos; mossy ball in narrow vertical crack in cave entrance ceiling with bottom of groove sealed with mud; short 2-3″ entrance runway; egg shells white, 2 nestlings (P. Gertler).
**Status and habitat:** Fairly common (by voice) on or near floor of humid and wet forest and tall second growth woodland in foothills and lower slopes. Generally found at lower el. than most other Colombian *Scytalopus.*
**Range:** 1200-3100m; mostly 300-1500m on Pacific slope. Santa Marta Mts. (*sanctaemartae*), Perijá Mts. (*nigricans*) all 3 Andean ranges (no recs. in W Andes n of Valle) and Macarena Mts. (*confuscus*), e slope E Andes on Río Negro in w Casanare (*atratus*) and se Nariño (*micropterus*). W Venez. s in mts. to nw Bolivia.

## 4. UNICOLORED TAPACULO
*Scytalopus unicolor*          Pls. 41, 42, Map 857
**Identification:** 5.2″ (13.2cm). Wrenlike with short cocked tail and pointed, slightly arched black bill. *Uniform blackish slate.* Imm.: dark brown above; buffy below with rump, flanks and sometimes most of upperparts more or less barred dusky; eyes dark.
**Similar species:** Much darker and shorter-tailed than Ash-colored Tapaculo (2); ad. from all other Colombian *Scytalopus* by *larger size* and uniform blackish plumage without any barring or brown tones (hard to see in dark undergrowth).
**Voice:** In W and E Andes a nasal trill, perhaps to scold, recalls that of Rufous-vented Tapaculo but *much* faster (6 or more notes per sec), higher and of shorter duration; presumed song in Ecuador and Colombia an endlessly repeated *work, work* . . . , about 1 per sec (T. Davis; Hilty).
**Behavior:** Terrestrial or within 1-2m of ground. Hops in dense mossy tangles and forest floor litter.
**Breeding:** 13 BC birds, Feb.–Aug, W and C Andes (Carriker). Oct nest e Ecuador (2550m), ball-shaped mass of moss and pale fibers with small side entrance; inside cavity poss. dug by them; 2 nestlings (Skutch 1972).
**Status and habitat:** Fairly common (by voice) on or near ground in humid and wet mossy forest, dense second growth, and bushy canyons. Essentially a temperate zone bird, thus differing from Rufous-vented Tapaculo, and in most areas found mainly above 2500m (e.g. Cerro Munchique).

**Range:** 1700-3300m. All 3 Andean ranges (*latrans*). Not Santa Marta or Perijá Mts. W Venez. s in Andes to Bolivia.

## 5. PALE-THROATED TAPACULO
*Scytalopus panamensis*                   Pl. 41, Map 858
**Identification:** 4.5″ (11.4cm). Sooty black above with *conspic. grayish white eyebrow*; below gray, throat decidedly paler; lower breast and belly mottled pale gray; lower back, flanks, belly, and crissum cinnamon brown barred black. ♀: sim. but back browner.
**Similar species:** Much like others of the genus but easily told by whitish eyestripe; looks decidedly 2-toned below (light gray throat and chest, dark chestnut belly).
**Voice:** Song a piping ser., *tseety-seety seety seety* . . . (Wetmore 1972), presum. much like others of the genus.
**Behavior:** Sim. to other *Scytalopus*.
**Status and habitat:** Reported common on a high ridge of Cerro Tacarcuna, e Darién, Panama (Wetmore 1972).
**Range:** 1100-1500m. Cerro Tacarcuna on Colombia-Panama boundary. Extreme nw Colombia and adj. e Panama (Cerro Mali; Cerro Tacarcuna).
**Note:** *S. vicinior* (Nariño Tapaculo) is sometimes merged with this sp.

## 6. NARINO TAPACULO
*Scytalopus vicinior*                   Pl. 41, Map 859
**Identification:** 4.7″ (12cm). Wrenlike with short cocked tail. *Crown sooty black*; mantle browner becoming dark chestnut brown on back; sides of head, throat, and chest dusky gray becoming lighter gray on belly and mottled whitish on center of belly; *rump, flanks, and crissum cinnamon brown barred black.* ♀: sim. but brighter brown above and paler gray below. Juv.: like ♀ but darker brown above and entire underparts cinnamon brown barred black.
**Similar species:** Much like Rufous-vented Tapaculo (3) and prob. not safely told in field unless latter's crown spot present, but tail shorter (about 1.5″ vs 2″, or 38 vs 51mm). In the hand, from Brown-rumped Tapaculo (7) by darker crown (dusky not brownish). ♀ Narino with brown crown prob. inseparable from 7 but ranges not known to overlap. Also see Andean Tapaculo (8).
**Behavior:** Presum. as in other *Scytalopus*. Voice unknown.
**Status and habitat:** Little known. Rec. in undergrowth of cooler mossy forest. Prob. partially sympatric in montane forest with Rufous-vented and/or Unicolored tapaculos but should occur below range of Andean Tapaculo.
**Range:** 450-3700m. Known definitely from w

slope of W Andes in Cordillera de Paramillo (3700m), Río Sucio in w Antioquia (450m) and w Nariño at Ricaurte; w slope of C Andes in Quindío Mts. E Panama in se Darién (Cerro Pirre), w Colombia, and nw Ecuador (Paramba in Imbabura).
**Note:** Treated as a subsp. of Pale-throated Tapaculo by Meyer de Schauensee (1964, 1966, 1970) and others but as a distinct sp. by Wetmore (1972) and Ridgely (1976).

## 7. BROWN-RUMPED TAPACULO
*Scytalopus latebricola*                   Pl. 42, Map 860
**Identification:** 5″ (13cm). Wrenlike with rather short cocked tail. *Above dark brownish gray*, wings browner, *underparts paler and grayer* and often frosted whitish on lower breast and belly; *rump, flanks, and crissum cinnamon rufous indistinctly barred black* (or paler overall with very faint dark bars—*latebricola*). ♀: sim. but browner above. Imm.: entirely brown more or less barred dusky throughout except on wings and tail.
**Similar species:** See very sim. Rufous-vented Tapaculo (3); *griseicollis* subsp. of Andean (8) is also sim. but *lacks barring* and has much brighter, more contrasting foreparts and rearparts. Narino (6) is almost identical but not known to overlap in range.
**Voice:** In Venez. a short fast trill *c'e'e'e'e'et*, and a long (about 15 sec) rattly trill, *ti'ti'ti'ti'ti* . . . , slowing at end (P. Schwartz recording); harsh alarm near Caracas a loud rhythmic *ka kík-kík-ka ka*, (A. Altman and Hilty).
**Behavior:** Like other *Scytalopus*.
**Breeding:** 2 BC birds, Feb–Mar, Santa Marta Mts., 4 more, May–June, Perijá Mts., 4 more, July–Sept, E Andes (Carriker).
**Status and habitat:** Dense thickets, tangled undergrowth, or floor of humid and wet forest and tall second growth woodland. Fairly common (voice and mist nets) in Santa Marta Mts. (T. B. Johnson) and in PN Cueva de los Guácharos (P. Gertler).
**Range:** 1200-3600m. Santa Marta Mts. (*latebricola*); Perijá Mts., E Andes and e slope of C Andes (*meridanus*); head of Magdalena Val. (*spillmani*). N and w Venez. s in Andes to Ecuador.

## 8. ANDEAN TAPACULO
*Scytalopus magellanicus*                   Pls. 41, 42
Map 861
**Identification:** 4.5″ (11.4cm). Wrenlike with *short* cocked tail. Bill blackish, somewhat thinner than other *Scytalopus. Head and forepart of body pale silvery gray above and below; lower back, rump, and flanks unbarred bright rufous brown*; wings and tail rufous brown (*griseicollis*). Or entirely dark gray, underparts slightly paler;

esp. throat and breast (*canus*). Imm.: entirely cinnamon buff barred black except on wings and tail; barring faint on breast.

**Similar species:** The *griseicollis* subsp. differs from other Colombian *Scytalopus* in distinctly "divided" foreparts and rearparts, and lack of barring. The *canus* form much like Unicolored Tapaculo (4) but somewhat paler (dark gray not blackish) and smaller (4.5″ vs 5.2″, or 11.4 vs 13cm); tail shorter.

**Voice:** Song (or scold) in Peru a short (1.5 sec), fast, almost froglike trill, *tttttttt*, much like Ash-colored Tapaculo but lower-pitched (T. Parker); also a measured ser. of double whistles, *ty-ook, ty-ook, ty-ook* . . . in Peru (Zimmer 1930), Argentina (Short 1969a), and in Nariño, Colombia.

**Behavior:** As in others of the genus.

**Breeding:** 2 imm., Aug, Páramo Frontino (Carriker). In Chile, nests on steep slopes above mt. streams; large root-fiber and moss nest lined with horsehair, at end of tunnel (about 0.6m) into thick vegetation; 3 large white eggs (Johnson 1965).

**Status and habitat:** Not well known in Colombia. Dense lower growth and thickets in stunted forest to treeline; often near streams. Apparently mostly above el. of other Colombian *Scytalopus*.

**Range:** Mostly 3700-3800m in W and C Andes; 2500-3200m in E Andes near Bogotá. N portion of W Andes (Paramillo Mts.; Páramo Frontino), C Andes on Caldas-Tolima border e of Manizales (*canus*); E Andes in Cundinamarca and s Boyacá (*griseicollis*); e slope C Andes in Huila (PN Puracé), both slopes of Nariño (subsp.?). W Venez. s in Andes to Tierra del Fuego.

**9. OCELLATED TAPACULO**
*Acropternis orthonyx*          Ill. 81, Map 862
**Identification:** 9″ (23cm). Unmistakable. High-

lands. ♂: *forehead, sides of head, and throat cinnamon rufous*; rump and upper and under tail coverts chestnut; rest of body plumage and wing coverts chestnut to tawny *thickly spotted with drop-shaped, black-encircled, white spots*; remiges and tail dark brown. Bill black with a high culmen flattened on top; hindclaw very long (1″ or 25mm) and straight.

**Voice:** In Venez. a loud jaylike *queeow*, singly, or up to 40 in 75 sec (P. Schwartz recording); in Peru a whistled *weeeoou* rising slightly, then falling, sometimes followed by up to 4 *tu* notes (T. Schulenberg).

**Behavior:** In Peru seen singly, in pairs, and poss. a family of 3. Run on ground or hop 0.1-2m up in bamboo. Reacted strongly to imitation of whistle (T. Schulenberg).

**Status and habitat:** Little known. Floor or undergrowth of humid forest (esp. in bamboo?).

**Range:** 2700-3000m. Spotty. Known from both slopes of C Andes in Antioquia (e of Medellín; Paramo Sonsón); w slope in Caldas-Quindío area and in Cauca (Coconuco); w slope of E Andes w of Bogotá (El Peñon near Fusagasugá). Nw Venez. (2250-3300m but mainly above 3000m) s in Andes to Peru.

81. OCELLATED TAPACULO

# MANAKINS: Pipridae (25)

Manakins are a New World family found in warmer humid regions from s Mexico to n Argentina and Paraguay. Almost half of all the species breed in Colombia. For the most part they are a rather homogeneous group of small forest birds characterized by short bills, short tails, chunky shape, large eyes, and the middle toe partially joined to an adjacent toe. Movements are typically sudden, and unlike most passerines, they do not hop. ♂ ♂ of *Pipra* and *Manacus* and a few others are bright and contrastingly patterned, while the ♀ ♀ are dull greenish. Many *Pipra* and *Manacus* are well known for their remarkable displays, often performed at a communal lek. There ♂ ♂ advertise and perform an often complex repertoire of stereotyped movements accompanied by bizarre mechanical as well as vocal sounds. In a few genera such as *Sapayoa* and *Schiffornis* there is no elaborate display, no sexual dimorphism, and no bright patterns; these species may not belong in the Pipridae. As far as known, no manakins form lasting pair bonds (*Piprites* is suspected of doing so) and the ♀ ♀ perform all nesting activities. Nests are mostly pendent cups fastened to a forked branch. Food is mainly berries plucked in hovering flight; smaller numbers of insects are eaten and the young are fed mostly insects at first.

## 1. GOLDEN-HEADED MANAKIN
*Pipra erythrocephala*        Pl. 32, Map 863
**Identification:** 3.6″ (9.1cm). *Eyes white* (ad. ♂), gray (ad. ♀), darker in imm. Bill yellowish white; legs usually pale or flesh. ♂: glossy black; *top and sides of head shining golden yellow*; thighs red and white (hard to see in field). ♀: dingy olive green above, paler below becoming yellowish white on lower underparts.
**Similar species:** ♀ much duller and dingier than ♀ Blue-crowned Manakin (5) and lacks the contrast between crown, back, and rump of ♀ Blue-rumped Manakin (4). ♀ White-crowned Manakin (3) has distinctly gray head and bright red eye. ♀ Red-capped Manakin (2) very sim. but slightly larger (tail longer), legs brownish, ranges meet but do not overlap.
**Voice:** Displaying ♂♂ are noisy, uttering sharp, dry, chipping and trilling notes. Advertising call a clear *pu*; when more excited a trill and final note added, *pu-prrrrrr-pt*; when very excited, *pir-pir-prrrrrrrrr-pt-pt* (Snow 1962b).
**Behavior:** ♂♂ gather in permanent groups of 6-12, each occupying horizontal perches a few m apart and about 5-12m up. Most conspic. display a swift swooping flight to display perch, accompanied by a rapid ser. of *kew* calls, a sharp buzz, and sometimes a rapid backward slide along the perch (Snow 1962b). Visit fruiting trees from understory to canopy.
**Breeding:** 19 BC birds, Jan–Oct, nw Colombia (Carriker; Haffer 1975); nest with eggs, 23 May, s Bolívar, laying ♀, 21 June, e Guajira (Carriker). Thinly woven cup fastened to horizontal fork about 1-10m up; 2 pale greenish yellow eggs thickly spotted and streaked brown in wreath at large end (Snow 1962b).
**Status and habitat:** Upper understory to mid. story of humid forest and esp. open second growth woodland. Most numerous in sandy-belt forest of the Orinoco and Negro drainage, local elsewhere. Replaced in wettest Pac. forests by Red-capped Manakin.
**Range:** To 500m. Pacific coast s to mid. Atrato Val. (Río Napipí and Murrí), e in humid lowlands n of Andes to lower and mid. Magdalena Val. (s to Honda, n Tolima), n base Santa Marta Mts., Sniá. de San Jacinto, Perijá Mts., and e of Andes throughout. E Panama to ne Peru, Brazil (n of Amazon), and the Guianas. Trinidad.
**Note:** Some merge *P. rubrocapilla* (Red-headed Manakin) of s of Amazon with Golden-headed Manakin calling the enlarged complex Flame-headed Manakin; *rubrocapilla* differs in red (instead of yellow) head. *Várzea* forest; call unlike allied Golden-headed Manakin, a high *peet-jeeeek*, last note slightly buzzy (D. Snow recording).

## 2. RED-CAPPED MANAKIN
*Pipra mentalis*        Pl. 32, Map 864
**Identification:** 4″ (10.2cm). Eyes white (♂), or brown (♀ and imm.). Legs dull brown. ♂: velvety black; *top and sides of head and nape bright red*; thighs bright yellow; under wing coverts pale yellow. ♀: olive green above, paler and more greenish yellow below.
**Similar species:** ♀ much like ♀ Golden-headed Manakin (see 1) but ranges not known to overlap. ♀ Golden-collared Manakin (12) is larger and has orange legs. ♀ Blue-crowned Manakin (5) is grass green (not olive) above.
**Voice:** Displaying ♂♂ call vigorously. A short high *psit* often repeated; a high thin drawn-out *pit-peeeeeEEEEaaa-psick*, sliding down, last note sharp; also a loud mechanical wing buzz, "bronx cheer."
**Behavior:** ♂♂ gather in loose groups 5-15m up in forest. Each ♂, on or near horizontal display perch that is separated from a neighbor's perches by 6-35m, performs several stereotyped display movements, incl. darting back and forth, rapid "about faces," leg stretching, and sliding (sidling) up and down branches, all accompanied by mechanical wing snaps and vocal noises. In C America display mainly in dry season, Dec–May or even July (Skutch 1969a).
**Breeding:** 10 BC birds, Dec–Mar, Pacific coast (Carriker; Haffer 1975). In Costa Rica mainly Feb–May, sometimes to July; shallow cup attached to horizontal fork 1.5-3m up; 2 grayish buff eggs heavily mottled brown in wreath around larger end (Skutch 1969a).
**Status and habitat:** Fairly common to locally common in humid and wet forest and second growth woodland in lowlands and lower foothills. Occas. hybrids with parapatric ally Golden-headed Manakin are known in e Panama (Haffer 1975).
**Range:** To 900m (rarely above 400-500m). Pacific coast from mid. Atrato Val. (Río Uva and Mutatá) southward. Se Mexico to e Panama; nw Colombia to nw Ecuador.

## 3. WHITE-CROWNED MANAKIN
*Pipra pipra*        Pl. 32, Map 865
**Identification:** 4″ (10.2cm). *Eyes red* (brighter in ♀). Legs purplish pink. ♂: glossy black; *crown and nape white* (white extends to upper

back—*unica*). ♀: *crown and nape gray contrasting with bright olive green upperparts* (back duller olive green—*pipra*); below paler olive green and washed yellowish on belly. Imm.: like ♀ but slightly grayer below.

**Similar species:** ♀ is only manakin with contrasting gray cap and bright red eye (both fairly prom. in field).

**Voice:** On Pacific slope a thin, cicadalike *shre-e-e-e-e*, slightly trilled, repeated at 15- to 20-sec intervals; e of Andes in Vaupés sim. but repeated at about 30-sec. intervals.

**Behavior:** E of Andes territorial ♂♂ are usually rather thinly spread and more audible than visible to rivals. Pacific slope in Valle, lek ♂♂ more concentrated perhaps due to terrain (Hilty). ♂♂ hold territories about 45m across and advertise from 4-5 perches about 3-9m up, usually by sitting quietly and calling. The few displays are a simple quick to-and-fro flight betw. perches, an "about face," a shallow **S**-curve swooping flight, and in presence of ♀ a slow flapping butterflylike flight (Snow 1961b). ♀♀ are usually seen in understory.

**Breeding:** 14 BC birds, Mar–May, C Andes, Antioquia to Huila (Carriker).

**Status and habitat:** Humid forest. Common in sandy-belt forest of Orinoco and Negro drainage, much less numerous s into Amazonia; local on Pacific slope.

**Range:** Pacific slope in Valle and Cauca, 600-1200m (*minima*); n end of W Andes in s Córdoba, Murrucucú, 1200m (*bolivari*); Magdalena Val., Caldas to Huila, 1600m (*unica*); e slope C Andes at n boundary of Caldas, base and slope of E Andes (to 1400m) from Norte de Santander to se Nariño, and Macarena Mts. (*coracina*); Guainía (photo, Pto. Inírida, 1978—Hilty) s to Vaupés and n Amazonas (*pipra*); sighting (subsp.?) near Leticia, s Amazonas (Hilty). Costa Rica to e Eucador, ne Peru, Amazonian and se Brazil, and the Guianas.

### 4. BLUE-RUMPED MANAKIN
*Pipra isidorei*          Pl. 32, Map 866

**Identification:** 3″ (7.6cm). Tiny. ♂: deep black; *crown and nape milky white; rump and upper tail coverts pale azure blue*; bill and legs dark. ♀: above grass green, *crown more yellowish; rump paler emerald green contrasting with brownish tail*; dingy grayish yellow below, more yellowish on belly.

**Similar species:** ♂ most like ♂ Blue-crowned Manakin (5), but crown white (not blue) and rump bluish white (often hidden); ♂ White-crowned Mankin (3) is larger, lacks the pale rump, and has dark red eye. ♀ *much like* ♀ Blue-crowned Manakin (5) and perhaps not usually separable in field, but crown has yel-

lowish tinge. Also cf. ♀ Golden-headed Manakin (1).

**Behavior:** Most visible at forest edge when it often comes to feed at fruiting trees (e.g. *Miconia*) with other manakins, etc. (R. Ridgely).

**Status and habitat:** Little known in Colombia where taken in a region of humid foothill forest; in e Ecuador locally quite common, esp. 700-1100m in the southeast; perhaps partially replaces White-crowned Manakin in e Andean slope foothills though the 2 have been found sympatric in 1 area in Ecuador (R. Ridgely).

**Range:** 500-1200m. Known only from w Meta (Acacías; above Villavicencio). Prob. locally s on e slope. Colombia, e Ecuador, and ne Peru.

### 5. BLUE-CROWNED MANAKIN
*Pipra coronata*          Pl. 32, Map 867

**Identification:** 3.5″ (8.9cm). ♂: velvety black; *crown bright blue* (belly and under tail coverts tinged greenish blue—*carbonata*); bill and legs blackish; eyes dark red. ♀: *above bright grass green*, below paler, more grayish on throat and *pale yellowish on belly*; bill, eyes, and legs dark. Imm. ♂: like ♀ but crown blue.

**Similar species:** Cf. White-crowned (3) and Blue-rumped manakins (4); for ♀ also cf. ♀ Golden-headed and ♀ Red-capped (1, 2).

**Voice:** E of Andes often heard advertising call a low, slightly hoarse, *thó-wiik*, sometimes preceded by a sharp note, e.g., *hist thó-wiik*. W of Andes birds presum. sound sim. to those in Panama, a semimusical trill, *treereereeree*, by both sexes, and at display grounds located in forest lower growth. ♂♂ also utter several harsher vocalizations but do not snap wings. ♂'s advertising call e of Andes very sim. to that of Dwarf Tyrant-Manakin (cf. 21).

**Behavior:** Not as noisy and conspic. as some *Pipra*. Displaying ♂♂ form leks but individuals within lek scatter over a wide area. Call from 1 of several slender advertising perches 2-5m up (occas. to 9m up). No mechanical sounds; displays are mostly back-and-forth flights betw. advertising perches; at intervals a short looping flight or level zigzag flight (Skutch 1969a). Sometimes join forest bird flocks.

**Breeding:** 7 BC birds, Jan–May, Chocó and s Córdoba (Carriker; Haffer 1975); nest as in others of genus but usually lower, 0.6-1.5m up; 2 whitish or pale gray eggs heavily mottled brown, esp. at larger end (Skutch 1969a).

**Status and habitat:** Uncommon to locally common in humid and wet forest and second growth woodland in lowlands and hills. Quite numerous in sandy-belt forests of Vaupés.

**Range:** To 1400m. Pacific coast, e in humid

lowlands n of Andes to lower Cauca Val. (Pto. Valdivia) and mid. Magdalena Val. s to Remedios, e Antioquia (*minuscula*); e of Andes from s Meta (Macarena Mts.) to Caquetá (*caquetae*); se Nariño, Guainía, and Vaupés s to Amazonas (*carbonata*). Costa Rica to nw Ecuador, n Bolivia, and n Amazonia Brazil.
**Note:** Poss. more than 1 sp. involved, as advertising calls of Panamanian and Amazonian populations appear to differ (R. Ridgely).

## 6. WIRE-TAILED MANAKIN
*Pipra filicauda*　　　　　　　Pl. 32, Map 868
**Identification:** 4.2″ (10.7cm). *Eyes white.* ♂ gaudy and unmistakable: *crown, nape, and edge of upper back scarlet;* rest of upperparts velvety black; inner remiges with a white patch on inner webs (visible in flight); *forehead, sides of head, and entire underparts golden yellow;* shafts of tail feathers project as long wirelike filaments about 2″ (51mm) beyond tail (look closely to see in field). ♀: dark olive green above, paler below becoming yellow in center of belly; tail filaments as in ♂ but shorter.
**Similar species:** ♀ from allies by relatively large size, *white eyes,* and yellowish belly. Tail filaments relatively easy to see if bird nearby.
**Voice:** Advertising call at 20-sec intervals or so a clear nasal whistle, *eeeeeeeeeea,* descending slightly (Hilty); also a *klok* and *kloop* apparently made by the wings (Schwartz and Snow 1978).
**Behavior:** Quiet and easily overlooked except for call. ♂ ♂ form leks; perch mainly 1-8m up in forest or woodland. Individuals often widely scattered, each with several display perches. Mostly silent displays incl. lateral side-jumps, short flights, often slow and butterflylike, and swoop-in flights accompanied by a *klok* on landing; also side-to-side pivoting with head low, feathers of upper back and sides erected like fan, and raised tail filaments brushing ♀'s face and throat (Snow and Schwartz 1978; Hilty). ♀ ♀ usually seen in lower story; either sex at almost any ht. incl. canopy when at fruiting trees.
**Breeding:** ♀ with begging young, 8 Nov, Leticia (J. V. Remsen); BC ♂, July, e Norte de Santander (Carriker); in n Venez. mainly Apr–July; cup nest usually below 2m up in small trees beside stream (Schwartz and Snow 1978); excess material hanging below nest aids concealment (Sick 1967).
**Status and habitat:** Local. Gallery forest, second growth, and lighter open woodland, even plantationlike areas and in Amazonas mainly *várzea* forest; in all habitats often near streams.
**Range:** To 500m. E of Andes from Catatumbo lowlands s to Amazonas. N Venez. s to e Ecuador, ne Peru, and w Amazonian Brazil.
**Note:** Formerly placed in the genus *Teleonema*.

## 7. LANCE-TAILED MANAKIN
*Chiroxiphia lanceolata*　　　　Pl. 32, Map 869
**Identification:** 5″ (13cm). *Legs orange;* spiky central tail feathers project more in ♂. ♂: sooty black with *slightly crested red crown* and *light blue back.* ♀: olive green above, sometimes with a little red on crown; underparts paler, dingy and becoming whitish on belly. Imm. ♂: like ♀ but crown red.
**Similar species:** ♀ resembles a ♀ *Manacus* but is paler below and can always be told by projecting tail spikes. See ♀ White-bearded (11) and ♀ Golden-collared manakins (12).
**Voice:** Often heard calls are unusual, mellow, easily imitated whistles, *curry-ho,* or *toe-curry-ho* var. to *toe-whee-o,* a single *kow,* and nasal snarl. No mechanical sounds.
**Behavior:** Well known by calls but can be discouragingly difficult to see. ♂ ♂ gather in small groups in upper understory or midlevels during breeding season and participate in communal lek displays (as opposed to displays where ♂ ♂ are noncooperative rivals, i.e., *Pipra* and *Manacus*) where 2 (usually) or more ♂ ♂ take an equal part in a joint performance incl. side-by-side calling, jumping up and down and short to-and-fro flights.
**Breeding:** 3 BC birds, June, s Bolívar and Guajira (Carriker); ♀ building nest, 4 Mar, PN Tayrona (Brown); small cup attached to horizontal fork and partially covered outside with dry leaves (Todd and Carriker 1922); 2 Panama nests, Aug and Sept, latter 1m up; 2 cream to brownish white eggs spotted reddish brown and lilac in wreath around larger end (Hallinan 1924).
**Status and habitat:** Locally common in dry to fairly humid regions in tall to scrubby woodland, usually with fairly open understory.
**Range:** To 850m. Carib. region from mouth of Río Sinú e to Santa Marta region, w Guajira and Snía. Macuira at e tip; e of Andes in Norte de Santander. Sw Costa Rica to n Venez.

## 8. BLUE-BACKED MANAKIN
*Chiroxiphia pareola*　　　　　　　Map 870
**Identification:** 5.5″ (14cm). *Legs orange* (♂); *flesh yellow* (♀). ♂: Like ♂ Lance-tailed Manakin, but back darker blue and tail normal (no protruding tail spikes). ♀: olive green above, paler below becoming pale yellowish to pale greenish on belly; tail normal.
**Similar species:** ♀ resembles ♀ Black Manakin (15) but chunkier, shorter-tailed, and legs yellow (not dusky gray); from ♀ White-bearded Manakin (11) by yellow (not bright orange) legs and larger size. Much larger than any ♀ *Pipra.*
**Voice:** Characteristic call note a rolling *churrrrr-chup* or *whee-wher,* sometimes *coo-ee;* ♂ ♂ dur-

ing jump display, a vibrant twanging or buzzing *arrrrr* . . . , ending in sharp *zeek-eek* (Snow 1963).

**Behavior:** Much like Lance-tailed Manakin; ♂♂ participate in true communal displays (♂♂ prob. being rivals but cooperate) with close coordination betw. pairs of ♂♂, 1 presum. dominant at each display perch, which is a horizontal or sloping branch or vine near ground with surrounding leaves plucked off. ♂♂ call alone or synchronously in pairs while perched side-by-side, sometimes alternately jumping up and down or cartwheeling over each other in rapid succession. Precopulatory display, always by a single ♂, a bounding flight to-and-fro across a perch (Snow 1963). Sally for fruit from understory to lower canopy.

**Breeding:** Mar copulation, Tobago (Snow 1963). In Brazil, typical manakin nest slung from horizontal fork near ground (Pinto 1953).

**Status and habitat:** Poorly known in Colombia. Prob. local in humid forest and second growth woodland in foothills of upper tropical zone. *Várzea* forest in Amazonian Brazil and in foothills up to subtropical forest (1700m) in Bolivia (R. Ridgely).

**Range:** To 500m (prob. higher). E of Andes in s Meta (1 ♂ seen, 7 Aug 1975, Caño Yarmales, Macarena Mts.—T. O. Lemke and P. Gertler), w Caquetá, w Putumayo (Pto. Umbría), se Nariño, and Amazonas. The Guianas and s Venez. to n Bolivia and Amazonian and se Brazil. Tobago.

## 9. GOLDEN-WINGED MANAKIN

*Masius chrysopterus*          Pl. 32, Map 871

**Identification:** 4.3″ (10.9cm). Legs purplish pink. ♂: *mostly black; the feathers of forecrown golden yellow, erect and curling forward over bill in flattish crest;* rest of central crown golden yellow, the feathers quill-like, deformed, and brown to reddish brown (or orange—*chrysopterus;* or orange red—*pax*) on hindcrown and nape; elongated black feathers on sides of crown project backward forming small horns (hard to see in field); narrow throat and larger patch on upper chest pale yellow; *inner webs of primaries bright yellow* (flash conspic. in flight). ♀: above olive, paler below with center of *throat and expanded patch on chest pale greenish yellow; legs as in* ♂. Imm. ♂ like ♀ but soon acquires yellowish crest and crown.

**Similar species:** Ornate ♂ unmistakable. Chest pattern of greenish ♀ is duller echo of ♂.

**Voice:** Infrequent call a low, nasal grunt, *nurrt.* No mechanical or other vocal sounds known.

**Behavior:** Quiet and unobtrusive. Solitary ♂♂ fly silently through understory to mid. story; occas. join forest flocks and may briefly go to fruiting trees in canopy. No display known but

♂♂ occas. chase ♀♀ through lower forest levels and flash yellow in wings as they go.

**Breeding:** ♀ off nest, 22 June, upper Anchicayá Val. (1000m); very thin-walled rootlet and moss cup suspended from horizontal fork 2.3m up over stream; 2 eggs, cream spotted brownish in broad band over center and large end (Hilty); 2 BC birds, May–July, Antioquia (Carriker).

**Status and habitat:** Uncommon to locally fairly common in wet mossy forest ("cloud forest") and tall second growth woodland, occas. forest borders.

**Range:** 1200-2300m in Andes; to 600m on Pacific slope. Pacific slope in Cauca and Nariño (*coronulatus*); Pacific slope in Valle n to headwaters of Río San Juan and e to both slopes of C Andes in Antioquia (*bellus*); w slope E Andes in Cundinamarca s to head of Magdalena Val. in s Huila (*chrysopterus*); e slope E Andes in Nariño (*pax*). Andes of nw Venez. s to n Peru.

## 10. WHITE-RUFFED MANAKIN

*Corapipo leucorrhoa*          Pl. 32, Map 872

**Identification:** 3.7″ (9.4cm). Eyes and legs dark. ♂: *glossy blue black; throat white,* feathers at sides of throat and neck lengthened to form ruff; under tail coverts sometimes tipped white. ♀: olive green, paler below; *throat and sides of head grayish;* belly pale yellowish.

**Similar species:** ♀ much like ♀ Red-capped Manakin (2), but throat distinctly gray and upperparts brighter. ♀ Golden-collared (12) and White-bearded manakins (11) have orange legs; ♀ Golden-headed Manakin (1) has pale yellow (not dark) bill and is more dingy above and below. Also cf. ♀ White-crowned Manakin (3).

**Voice:** Call a high, thin, insectlike *s-e-e-e-e-e-t,* slightly trilled; in flight display a twangy *seet't't-u u u.*

**Behavior:** Forest midlevels or lower. Singly, in 2's, or in small groups incl. both sexes and imms. In C America wander widely and move up or down in el. during nonbreeding per. ♂♂ (*altera* incl. those of nw Colombia) gather in small leks, usually near an old fallen log around which displays are centered. ♂♂ alternately fly toward log in slow bouncing and fluttering flight with puffed out plumage and ruff spread (like a bouncing black and white ball!), or fly swiftly and directly at log as they give dull wing-snap and sometimes a few shrill cries (Skutch 1967). Displays of *leucorrhoa* (most of Colombia) presum. sim.

**Breeding:** 8 BC birds, May–Oct, n Colombia (Carriker); shallow cup nest, bottom partly covered with leaf fragments and suspended from horizontal fork 7m up; 2 dull white eggs

heavily marked brown, esp. in wreath at larger end (Skutch 1967).
**Status and habitat:** Apparently uncommon and local in humid forest in foothills and on lower slopes.
**Range:** 200-1500m (el. of some highland recs. uncertain). Pacific slope s to Baudó Mts. (*altera*); Pacific slope in Valle (Dagua Valley), humid n base of Andes to mid. Magdalena Val. and s to n Tolima (Honda); poss. the Cauca Val. to Cali (formerly); n end Perijá Mts. (Montes de Oca) and e of Andes in Norte de Santander and nw Arauca (*leucorrhoa*). Se Honduras to w Venez.
**Note 1:** *Altera* of Mid. America and nw Colombia has the outer primary much reduced and by some is considered a separate sp. from *leucorrhoa* (White-bibbed Manakin) of e Colombia and w Venez. **Note 2:** White-throated Manakin (*C. gutturalis*) of s Venez. (c Amazonas e), the Guianas, and n Brazil (Roraima and Amapá) may occur in e Guainía. ♂: shiny blue black with white throat projected to point on breast. ♀: olive above, throat and belly white, broad breast band and sides olive. Forest midlevels in hill country; high, wiry *tse'e'e'e'e'e*.

## 11. WHITE-BEARDED MANAKIN

*Manacus manacus*     Pl. 32, Map 873
**Identification:** 4″ (10.2cm). *Legs orange.* ♂ mainly black and white; crown black; *broad collar encircling neck and entire underparts white*; belly tinged gray; feathers of throat lengthened to form a short beard; back, wings, and tail black; rump dark gray (or white parts of plumage tinged yellowish—*flaveolus*). ♀: above dull olive green, pale grayish on throat, pale greenish yellow below.
**Similar species:** ♀ like ♀ Golden-collared Manakin (12) and doubtfully separable in field but paler below and throat light grayish (not yellowish olive).
**Voice:** Usual call a slightly trilled *peerr*; in display *chwee*, an excited *pee-you* (Snow 1962d), and vigorous, firecrackerlike snaps and "bronx-cheer" rolls produced mechanically with wings.
**Behavior:** One of the noisiest and best known lek-forming manakins. ♂♂ gather in groups, sometimes up to 60 or more. Display all yr. but abate somewhat during per. of molt. Each ♂ "owns" a small "court" on the forest floor where the ground is cleared of leaves and debris. Six different displays are performed below eye level on 2 or more vertical saplings in the court and are dazzling for speed and energy. They incl.: to-and-fro jumps betw. saplings with wing-snapping jumps to ground and back, sliding down the pole (sapling), and "fanning" with wings. Calling, snapping, and

display reaches a frenzy at the approach of a ♀. Mating promiscuous (Snow 1962d). Away from lek sally rapidly for fruit or insects in understory.
**Breeding:** 6 BC birds, July–Aug, Santander and e Norte de Santander (Carriker); 1 Santa Marta nest, May (Todd and Carriker 1922); building nest, Jan, w Meta (Hilty); typical manakin nest a flimsy shallow cup suspended from low fork, often near stream; 2 eggs, dull white with brown streaks mainly at larger end (Snow 1962d).
**Status and habitat:** Locally common in second growth or gallery woodland and forest borders in lowlands and foothills. Common in PN Tayrona and in Meta, less numerous southward.
**Range:** To 1900m (usually below 1000m). N Colombia from mouth of Río Sinú e to Guajira and s to lower Cauca (Pto. Valdivia) and mid. Magdalena vals. (*abditivus*); Bucaramanga to s Tolima (*flaveolus*); sw Cauca to sw Nariño (*bangsi*); e of Andes throughout (*interior*). The Guianas and Venez. s to n Bolivia, ne Argentina, Paraguay, and s Brazil; w Ecuador; Trinidad.
**Note:** Hybrids with *M. vitellinus* are known from Caucasia, lower Cauca Val. where Golden-collared ♂♂ occupied 1 end of a lek, White-bearded ♂♂ the other, and hybrids the mid. (Haffer 1967a); sim. hybrids near Guapí, sw Cauca (Olivares 1958).

## 12. GOLDEN-COLLARED MANAKIN

*Manacus vitellinus*     Pl. 32, Map 874
**Identification:** 4″ (10.2cm). *Legs orange.* ♂: crown black; *throat and broad collar encircling neck golden yellow*; throat feathers lengthened forming a short beard; otherwise olive below; back, wings, and tail black; rump olive. ♀: dull olive green above, paler more yellowish olive below.
**Similar species:** See White-bearded Manakin (11). ♀ from other ♀ manakins in range (except White-bearded, 11, and Lance-tailed manakins, 7) by orange legs; from ♀ Lance-tailed (ranges may meet in lower Río Sinú) by slightly smaller size (chunkier and shorter-tailed), no projecting tail spikes, and by slightly yellower lower underparts.
**Voice:** Mechanical and vocal sounds sim. to White-bearded Manakin. Most common calls a clear *chée-pooh* and a slightly trilled *peerr*. Loud wing-snaps and "cloth ripping" sounds in display.
**Behavior:** Essentially sim. to White-bearded Manakin and like it found in vigorous noisy groups (usually less than 20 ♂♂) in undergrowth. Apparently lacks "fanning" display (Snow 1962b). Displays all yr. on Pacific slope.
**Breeding:** 24 BC birds, Feb–May, Chocó and

n Antioquia (Haffer 1975; Carriker); ♀ with dependent fledgling, 8 Sept, upper Anchicayá Val. (Hilty). Panama nest typical manakin style 0.6-1.5m up and usually less than 100m from display area; eggs as in White-bearded Manakin (Chapman 1935).

**Status and habitat:** Very common in humid and wet second growth woodland and thickety forest borders in lowlands and foothills.

**Range:** To 1200m. Pacific coast s to sw Cauca (Guapí), prob. w Nariño; Gulf of Urabá to lower Río Cauca and upper Río Nechi; formerly upper Cauca Val. Costa Rica to w Colombia.

## 13. STRIPED MANAKIN
*Machaeropterus regulus* Pl. 32, Map 875
**Identification:** 3.5″ (8.9cm). *Tiny.* ♂: olive green above with *red crown and nape;* throat whitish; otherwise *striped reddish chestnut and white below;* breast sometimes stained crimson; inner remiges stiffened and enlarged, the tips white; underside of tail white; eyes and legs reddish brown. ♀: olive green above, much paler below becoming sulphur yellow on belly and under tail coverts; *sides and flanks faintly streaked darker; flanks smudged rufous;* tail white below.

**Similar species:** Marks of ♀ are streaking on sides, pale yellow belly, and rufous tinge on flanks.

**Voice:** In Vaupés advertising call a fast ser. of hummingbirdlike "chips" followed by a short sneezing buzz, *whit whit whit whit skeéezz,* less often a short sneezing *tease-zip* (Hilty); in display a mechanical wing rattling.

**Behavior:** Weak calls and inconspic. habits attract little attention. Alone or in 2's in understory or lower mid. story. Displays may involve 2 ♂♂ perched close together, but a true communal display not yet demonstrated. Regional var. also suspected. In nw Colombia ♂♂ repeatedly make a short vertical jump from a horizontal branch as they raise vibrating wings and make insectlike buzz (Haffer 1967b); in ne Ecuador in presence of a ♀, ♂ made sharp buzzing sounds as it revolved rapidly around a slender horizontal twig, clinging to it with feet (Skutch 1969a). In Brazil 2 ♂♂ perch together, then 1 flips to hanging position and rapidly rotates to and fro. An accompanying whirr may be from modified secondaries (Sick 1967). Sallies rapidly for berries and insects like many manakins.

**Breeding:** 12 BC birds, May–Aug, n Antioquia, s Bolívar (Carriker).

**Status and habitat:** Very local. Humid forest, forest borders, and second growth woodland from lowlands to lower mt. slopes. Replaced on Pacific slope from Valle (Queremal area)

s by Club-winged Manakin (Haffer 1967b).

**Range:** To 1500m. Both slopes of W Andes s to Valle (to Bosque Yotoco, 1500m); n end of C Andes and s in mid. Magdalena Val. to latitude of Bogotá; e base of Andes from n Norte de Santander s and generally from s Meta (Macarena Mts.) and Vaupés (Mitú) southward. N Venez. (incl. Perijá Mts.) s to n Bolivia and w and c Amazonian and se Brazil.

## 14. CLUB-WINGED MANAKIN
*Allocotopterus deliciosus* Pl. 32, Map 876
**Identification:** 4″ (10.2cm). Legs flesh color. ♂: *mainly chestnut;* rump and abdomen blackish; *forecrown scarlet;* wings black with *white on inner webs of inner remiges,* latter also have peculiarly thickened shafts bent near tip giving the secondaries a curly appearance; bend of wing yellow; under wing coverts and outer tail feathers white; bill black. ♀: olive green above; *inner remiges white on inner webs;* throat white; *sides of face washed cinnamon;* otherwise pale yellowish olive becoming pale yellow on belly; *under wing coverts white.* Imm. ♂ like ♀, less cinnamon.

**Similar species:** ♀ is only ♀ manakin with white on wings (sometimes hard to see in field). Also note cinnamon wash on sides of face, yellow belly, and restricted range.

**Voice:** ♂'s advertising call (apparently a mechanical wing sound) an unusual insectlike or "electronic" buzz preceded by 2 dry tipping sounds, *tip-tip buuuuuu,* repeated 2-3 times a min; occas. a high-pitched, vocal *kee! kee! kee!*

**Behavior:** Usually alone in lower or mid. strata of forest, occas. with mixed flocks. ♂♂ call and display throughout yr. in loose groups ("exploded arenas"), where they perch 1-9m up (usually midlevels) and within hearing distance of neighbors. Simple, mostly rear-oriented display: 2 quick wing flicks creating a black and white flash posteriorly and presum. the *tip* notes, immediately followed by a downward rotation of wings when they give dull *buuuuuu.* ♂♂ frequently "about face" on horizontal display perches or jump from 1 to another (Willis 1966b; Hilty).

**Breeding:** Near Queremal (1400m) a deep, mossy, pensile cup nest less than 1m up in bush, 22 Mar and a few m from a ♂'s display site. Two brownish white eggs speckled brown (Willis 1966b).

**Status and habitat:** Very local. Wet mossy forest ("cloud forest") and second growth woodland. Display groups are usually in a more open area of forest or near break or large old treefall. ♀♀ and imms. infrequently seen but mist nets reveal large "floating" populations.

**Range:** 400-1900m. Pacific slope of W Andes

from Valle (Queremal) southward. W Colombia and nw Ecuador.

**Note:** Poss. congeneric with more wide ranging and allopatric *Machaeropterus*.

### 15. BLACK MANAKIN
*Xenopipo atronitens* Pl. 32, Map 877

**Identification:** 5″ (13cm). *Flycatcherlike.* Tail long for a manakin; legs dark. ♂: *uniform glossy blue black;* wings and tail brownish black; under wing coverts dark; *bill rather heavy; pale bluish horn.* ♀: dark grayish olive above (darker and duller than other "green" manakins); throat tinged grayish; otherwise dull yellowish olive below; wings and tail tinged brownish.

**Similar species:** Proportionally longer tail and larger size than most manakins recalls a flycatcher, tanager, or even small finch. Note "wide-eyed" manakinlike eyes and habitat. ♀ like ♀ Blue-backed Manakin (8), but legs dark (not yellow). Green Manakin (16) is much brighter green above.

**Voice:** Occas. call a rather loud sharp *skee! kep-kep-kep-kep,* sometimes 1st rough note omitted.

**Behavior:** Uncharacteristic of family. Usually alone or 2-3 with mixed spp. flocks; low to midlevel in scrubby woodland. Display limited chiefly to calling and chasing rivals with no special perch or display area (Sick 1967).

**Status and habitat:** Fairly common in scrubby savanna forest, savanna woodland, and woodland borders in sandy-belt region of extreme east; locally w in pockets of scrub in table mt. region of Vaupés; also gallery forest.

**Range:** To 300m. Ne Guainía (photos, Pto. Inírida, 1978–Hilty) s to Vaupés (Mitú) and w to c Meta (Mozambique). Prob. also e Vichada. The Guianas and s Venez. to se Peru and Brazil.

### 16. GREEN MANAKIN
*Chloropipo holochlora* Pls. 32, 33,
Map 878

**Identification:** 4.8″ (12.2cm). Legs grayish to brown; bill black above, pale below. Above *dull olive green;* throat and breast grayish olive *contrasting with yellowish belly* (or brighter grass green above—*holochlora*). Sexes sim.

**Similar species:** Easily confused and best told from sim. plumaged ♀♀ of other manakins by large size and proportionally longer tail; additionally from ♀ Blue-crowned Manakin (5) by duller upperparts (*litae*) and e of Andes by grayish olive (not grass green) breast. Also see even larger Broad-billed Manakin (23).

**Behavior:** Solitary in forest understory. Not well known.

**Breeding:** 1 BC ♀, Mar, n Chocó (Haffer 1975); 1 in May, n Antioquia (Carriker).

**Status and habitat:** Undergrowth of humid and wet forest in lowlands and lower slopes. Poss. more common than the few recs. indicate.

**Range:** To 900m (to 1300m on e slope E Andes, Macarena Mts. and Panama border). Entire Pacific slope (*litae*); e of Andes from w Meta (Villavicencio) s to se Nariño (*holochlora*), e limits of range uncertain. E Panama to nw Ecuador; e Colombia to e Peru.

### 17. YELLOW-HEADED MANAKIN
*Chloropipo flavicapilla* Pl. 32, Map 879

**Identification:** 5″ (13cm). Bill pale; *eyes red or orange.* ♂: *above yellowish olive; crown, broad flattish crest, and hindneck bright golden yellow;* below yellowish olive becoming pale yellow on belly; legs dark. ♀: sim. but duller; crown dull yellow but distinctly brighter than the back; throat and breast dull olive; legs pinkish flesh. *Under wing coverts white* in both sexes. Imm. ♂ like ♀.

**Similar species:** Dull, confusing ♀ best told by crown distinctly yellower than the back, large size (for manakin), and piprid shape (large wide-eyed look, rounded head, and bill). Up close note red or orange eyes, in flight the white under wings.

**Behavior:** Quiet and infrequently seen (prob. often overlooked). Usually solitary 1-8m up in forest. Occas. with mixed forest flocks.

**Breeding:** ♀ feeding dependent juv., May; ♀ with large brood patch, Sept, W Andes above Cali (Miller 1963). BC ♀, Mar, sw Huila (Carriker).

**Status and habitat:** Uncommon (perhaps local) in humid forest and tall second growth woodland. Can be found in Bosque Yotoco and upper Pichindé Val.

**Range:** ENDEMIC. 1200-2400m. Spottily on both slopes of W Andes (Valle and Cauca), w slope C Andes in Antioquia, and head of Magdalena Val. in Huila, perhaps also e slope E Andes at s end. Ecuador (Mapoto?).

### 18. CINNAMON MANAKIN
*Neopipo cinnamomea* Pl. 32, Map 880

**Identification:** 3.5″ (8.9cm). *Tiny.* Short narrow bill light brown; legs light brown. *Crown dark gray; semiconcealed median crown stripe yellow* (or orange rufous—♀); back grayish brown gradually becoming bright *cinnamon rufous on rump and tail; wings rufous;* throat pale buff; *rest of underparts cinnamon.*

**Similar species:** Remarkably like Ruddy-tailed Flycatcher (p 489), but bill much narrower and crown with median yellow stripe (not always visible). Note manakinlike shape with large eyes, large rounded head, and slightly hunched posture. Flycatcher perches erect, frequently flicks wings up.

**Status and habitat:** Little known in Colombia. Taken in a region of sandy-belt forest.

**Range:** To 300m. Known only from Río Guainía (opp. mouth of Casiquiare), se Guainía. The Guianas and s Venez. to e Ecuador (upper Río Napo), e Peru, and w Amazonian Brazil.

## 19. YELLOW-CROWNED MANAKIN

*Heterocercus flavivertex*          Pl. 32, Map 881

**Identification:** 5.6″ (14.2cm). Large and robust. ♂: olive green above with *semiconcealed yellow crown stripe*; cheeks blackish; *throat silky white* with feathers at sides of throat lengthened to form a ruff and bordered narrowly below with olive; *rest of underparts rich chestnut*, belly paler. ♀: sim. but no yellow crown stripe; throat and ruff light gray; underparts paler cinnamon.

**Similar species:** ♂ unmistakable. ♀ from other large "olive" manakins by dusky cheeks, chestnut wash on breast, and obvious "ruff." Also cf. White-crested Spadebill (p 487).

**Behavior:** Acts like a manakin but looks more like a flycatcher. Usually alone in understory where pauses to peer, then moves on a short distance. Sometimes with small mixed flocks (Hilty). Solitary displays in related *H. linteatus* (see note) incl. loud advertising calls with throat patch spread laterally and chases between rivals (Sick 1967).

**Breeding:** BC ♀, mid-Dec, e of Mitú, Vaupés (Olivares 1955).

**Status and habitat:** Not well known. Sandy-belt and gallery forests. Fairly common in shrubby stream borders in gallery forest at Carimagua, ne Meta (S. Furniss).

**Range:** To 300m. Extreme e from e Vichada s to Vaupés (near Mitú) and w to ne Meta (Carimagua—S. Furniss). S Venez. (Amazonas) and adj. nw Brazil.

**Note 1:** By some considered conspecific with *H. linteatus* (Flame-crowned Manakin), which replaces it in ne Peru (n bank of Amazon at Pto. Indiana) and Amazonian Brazil s of the Amazon. *H. linteatus* may occur in Amazonas, Colombia. Both sexes differ from *H. flavivertex* by darker olive gray upperparts (not olive green); ♂ additionally by black crown with orange scarlet median stripe. **Note 2:** Orange-crowned Manakin (*H. aurantiivertex*) of e Ecuador and n Peru may occur in Putumayo (known from Limoncocha, Ecuador). From Yellow-crowned Manakin thus: orange crown stripe (not yellow) and *uniform* cinnamon breast and belly (not darker chestnut on breast forming a band). ♀ like 19 but underparts paler.

## 20. SAFFRON-CRESTED TYRANT-MANAKIN

*Neopelma chrysocephalum*          Pl. 32, Map 882

**Identification:** 5″ (13cm). Flycatcherlike. Bill and tail rather long for a manakin; *eyes yellowish white to orange.* Above olive green; wings and tail tinged brownish; crown and sides of head olive gray; *wide semiconcealed central crown stripe yellow* (or orange rufous posteriorly) forms a slight flattish crest at rear of head (yellow usually visible but can be hard to see); throat grayish white; breast clouded olive; *rest of underparts contrasting pale yellow.*

**Similar species:** Easily mistaken for a flycatcher, but note chunky shape, less erect posture, and at close range the prom. orangish to yellowish eyes. Absence of wing bars separates it from many flycatchers. See Greenish and Forest elaenias (pp 462 and 461).

**Voice:** Loud, *very nasal* song in Surinam may recall an insect more than a bird; a twangy, jew's-harp-like,     *jewee-jewEE-JEWEE-JEwee-jewee,* occas. shortened to 3 notes, often sung persistently at short intervals, but ventriloquial; loud sharp alarm, *kwip,* 1-3 times, nasal call a softer *chip* (Hilty; Davis 1949a).

**Behavior:** Usually solitary in lower more open parts of sandy scrub or woodland. Active and partially insectivorous, sallying short distance to air or to foliage. Simple displays are solitary (no communal display area) with ♂ ♂ well separated but prob. within hearing distance. Each ♂ performs a short upward jump with raised and spread crest as it gives twanging call. No special perch used; display from 3-20m up (Davis 1949a; Snow 1961b).

**Breeding:** 7 BC birds, May, Vaupés (Olivares 1964b).

**Status and habitat:** Not well known. Eastward found primarily in sandy savanna woodland.

**Range:** To 200m. Known only from Vaupés (Caño Cubiyú near Mitú). Also rec. at San Carlos on Venez. side of Río Negro opp. se Guainía. The Guianas, s Venez. (Amazonas), and nw Brazil.

## 21. DWARF TYRANT-MANAKIN

*Tyranneutes stolzmanni*          Pl. 32, Map 883

**Identification:** 3.5″ (8.9cm). *Very tiny and stubby. Eyes yellowish white.* Above dull olive; throat and breast pale grayish olive; breast slightly darker and very obscurely streaked whitish (hard to see in field); belly pale yellowish; bill black above, pale below. Sexes sim.

**Similar species:** Looks like a tiny flycatcher or like its name, a *tiny* manakin. From sim.-sized Double-banded Pygmy-Tyrant (p 477) and White-eyed Tody-Tyrant (p 480) by lack of wing markings; from ♀ ♀ of other "typical" manakins by very small size and pale eye. Also cf. Helmeted Pygmy-Tyrant (p 477).

**Voice:** Advertising call a loud, slightly twangy and hoarse *tjur-heet* tirelessly repeated at short intervals. More emphatic, coarser, and with stronger emphasis on 2d syllable than otherwise very sim. call of Blue-crowned Manakin (5).

**Behavior:** Noisy but frustratingly difficult to see. Solitary ♂♂, usually within hearing distance of each other, call steadily from perches 2-15m up. When excited, erect short frontal crest. Allied *T. virescens* (Tiny Tyrant-Manakin) of the Guianas performs a slow floating display flight (body held vertical) from perch to perch (Snow 1961b).

**Breeding:** BC ♂, May, Vaupés (Olivares 1964b), and Mar, Macarena Mts. (Olivares 1962).

**Status and habitat:** Fairly common (need to know call) in humid *terra firme* forest. The most common manakin in sandy-belt forests near Mitú, Vaupés. Also *várzea* forest in e Ecuador (R. Ridgely).

**Range:** To 400m. E of Andes from w Meta (Villavicencio) and Vaupés (Mitú) southward. Prob. n to Vichada (on Venez. side of Orinoco). S Venez. s to n Bolivia and Amazonian Brazil (not e of Río Negro on n bank of Amazon).

## 22. WING-BARRED MANAKIN
*Piprites chloris*                Pl. 32, Map 884

**Identification:** 5.5″ (14cm). *Vireolike. Bright olive green above with strong gray tinge on hindcrown, nape, and ear coverts*; wings and tail dusky; *2 yellowish wing bars,* upper one indistinct; inner remiges tipped yellowish; forehead and lores yellowish; *prom. eyering bright yellow*; underparts light yellowish green becoming yellow on belly (or upper throat and under tail coverts light yellow, breast gray, belly whitish—*chlorion*). Sexes sim.

**Similar species:** May recall a Yellow-throated Vireo (p 555) or a flycatcher, but plump proportions, large round head, and big eye are typically piprid. Bill is short even for a manakin; note yellow face and eyering. Vireo (above) has more prom. *white* (not yellowish) wing bars.

**Voice:** Song, given at infrequent intervals, a loud, brisk, slightly nasal, *kuep kuep kuep kuep kue-di-le kuep?* or sim. var., with quality of shorebird such as plover or godwit (T. Parker); easily recognized once learned. Responds to taped playback.

**Behavior:** Heard far more than seen. Solitary or 2's (pairs?) often follow mixed flocks in forest midlevels or higher and act like flycatchers or vireos (or even becards). Unlike other manakins, ads. apparently eat mainly insects.

**Breeding:** BC ♂, May, se Antioquia (Carriker).

**Status and habitat:** Uncommon and perhaps local in humid forest and sandy-belt woodlands. Often at forest edge and in Andes to lower subtropical zone.

**Range:** To 1500m. Perijá Mts. *(perijanus)*; nw end C Andes (Pto. Valdivia) and mid. Magdalena Val. s to n boundary of Caldas (Río Samaná); e of Andes from w Meta to se Nariño *(antioquiae)*; Vaupés and Guainía *(chlorion)*; se tip of Guainía near Macacuní *(tschudii)*. The Guianas and Venez. s to n Bolivia, ne Argentina, Paraguay, and se Brazil.

## 23. BROAD-BILLED MANAKIN
*Sapayoa aenigma*                Pl. 33, Map 885

**Identification:** 6″ (15cm). *Flycatcherlike. Bill broad and flat; tail long for a manakin.* Dark oily green above; concealed yellow crown stripe (♂ only); wings and tail dusky with olive green edgings; *underparts dingy yellowish* strongly washed olive on breast and sides.

**Similar species:** Resembles a flycatcher or tanager and prob. often overlooked. Broad bill and long tail (as well as rictal bristles) very unlike many otherwise sim. plumaged ♀ manakins. Cf. Thrush-like (25) and Green manakins (16, *litae* subsp.). Size and proportions recall Olivaceous or Eyering flatbills (pp 485 and 484), but Broad-billed lacks the eyering and yellow wing edgings of either. Also cf. Carmiol's Tanager (p 627), which has larger heavier bill, and ♀ Tawny-crested Tanager (p 631), which is brownish.

**Voice:** Resembles that of Blue-crowned Manakin (J. Karr *in* Wetmore 1972).

**Behavior:** Usually alone or in mixed forest flocks, almost always of mixed antwren-type flocks (R. Ridgely). Peers like *Schiffornis* in lower or mid. strata, than sallies to air or to foliage for insects or fruit like a flycatcher.

**Breeding:** 14 BC birds, Feb–Apr, Chocó and nw Antioquia (Carriker; Haffer 1975).

**Status and habitat:** Not well known in Colombia. Humid and wet forest from lowlands to lower slopes. Perhaps local.

**Range:** To 1100m. Pacific coast from Panama border to Nariño; n of Andes e to upper Sinú Val. (Murrucucú) and mid. Magdalena Val. (Snía. San Lucas). C Panama to nw Ecuador.

**Note:** Poss. better placed with the Tyrannidae or Cotingidae and called Broad-billed Sapayoa.

## 24. GREATER MANAKIN
*Schiffornis major*                Pl. 33, Map 886

**Identification:** 6″ (15cm). Head color var. Head and back rufous, usually with var. amts. of gray on sides of head and rarely on crown (or head gray and back brown—*duidae*) *becoming bright cinnamon on rump and tail*; primaries blackish; throat buffy gray; breast rusty; belly pale cinnamon; bill and legs dark; *eyes large.* Sexes sim.

**Similar species:** Like Thrush-like Manakin (25), but overall brighter, more cinnamon rufous, rump and tail much brighter, belly cinnamon (not brown or olive brown), and head often with some gray (or all gray—*duidae*).

**Voice:** Song recalls Thrush-like Manakin (25) but is longer; loud slurred whistles are deliberate and syncopated, *toweeou, tweeEET, teeu-dewEET, tweeEET . . . teeu . . . dewEET . . . teeu . . . dewEET*, last 2 phrases coming after pauses of about 2-3 sec; most vocal at dawn and dusk (Hilty; J. Fitzpatrick).

**Behavior:** As in Thrush-like Manakin.

**Status and habitat:** First rec. in Colombia is 1 BC ♂, 28 Feb 1975, on Río Calderon about 50km n of Leticia (Romero 1978). Also known from numerous sight recs. since that date. Uncommon (by voice) in *várzea* forest and shrubby *várzea* borders on both banks of Amazon w of Leticia.

**Range:** To 100m. S Amazonas (*major*). Prob. more widespread (*duidae* subsp. taken at San Fernando de Atabapo on Venez. side of Orinoco). S Venez. s through w and c Amazonian Brazil to e Ecuador, e Peru, and ne Bolivia.

**Note 1:** The var. in head color of *major* subsp. has no apparent relationship to age, sex, season, or locality (Zimmer 1936). **Note 2:** Family placement of *Schiffornis* is uncertain; perhaps Cotingidae or Tyrannidae.

## 25. THRUSH-LIKE MANAKIN

*Schiffornis turdinus*          Pl. 33, Map 887
**Identification:** 6.5″ (16.5cm). *Mainly brown or grayish olive brown.* Some races tinged olive, or with crown slightly darker. *Large dark eyes*; bill and legs dark.

**Similar species:** A confusing bird that resembles a short-tailed dull brown thrush. Recognized by stocky proportion, relatively long tail (for a manakin), large eye ("wide-eyed" appearance), and lack of distinct markings. See Broad-billed and Greater manakins (23, 24).

**Voice:** Distinctive call usually given only at long intervals, often a min. or more apart. Call var. geographically, usually accompanied by subspecific difference, but always recognizable: typically a clear, sweet 3- or 4-note whistle, halting slightly, then with sharp upward inflection at end; e.g., on Pacific slope *eee, cre-EEK*; (*rosenbergi*); in e Guainía (*amazonus*) a more deliberate mellow *pee-ree-rét* (Hilty); in Panama-Colombia border highlands (*acrolophites*), described as *twick-sweet-twee* given very slowly with 2-sec interval betw. notes (Wetmore 1972). In Venez. sim. vocal differences betw. races are documented (P. Schwartz).

**Behavior:** Solitary and retiring understory bird, occas. heard but not often seen. Best told by voice but the call is difficult to track down. Often clings 1-2m up on vertical stems or saplings where peers slowly about with very wide-eyed look (Ridgely 1976).

**Breeding:** 6 BC birds, Jan–June, n Colombia (Carriker), 1 in Apr, Vaupés (Olivares 1964b); Costa Rica nests are bulky leafy cups lined with skeletal leaves and fine rootlets; 0.5-1.5m up in palm stump or lodged against palm trunk. 2 pale buff eggs marked with dark brown and lilac gray in wreath at larger end (Skutch 1969a).

**Status and habitat:** Fairly common and widespread (based on voice) in humid and wet forest and tall second growth woodland in lowlands and foothills.

**Range:** To 1400m (higher on Panama side of Mt. Tacarcuna). Throughout in more *humid wooded areas* incl. Guajira (not yet rec. in Amazonas). Se Mexico to w and e Ecuador, e Peru, Bolivia, and Brazil.

**Note 1:** More than 1 sp. may be involved betw. highland and lowland forms in Panama and nw Colombia. **Note 2:** *Schiffornis* is perhaps not a manakin.

# COCKS-OF-THE-ROCK: Rupicolidae (2)

The two species in this family are of uncertain affinity. They are placed in a family of their own, Rupicolidae, or in the Cotingidae by various authors with little consistency (e.g., Meyer de Schauensee 1966; Snow 1973). The bill is fowllike, the legs and toes are strong, and both sexes have a permanently erect disklike crest (much larger in the ♂). Despite bright colors (♂ ♂), they are often difficult to observe away from display grounds as they are rather shy and may live in rugged mt. ravines or remote hilly lowlands. ♂ ♂ display at traditional communal leks for much of year; the ♀ ♀ perform all nesting activities.

## 1. GUIANAN COCK-OF-THE-ROCK

*Rupicola rupicola*      Pl. 33, Map 888

**Identification:** 12.5″ (32cm). Eyes orange (♂); yellowish white (♀). ♂ unmistakable: *brilliant orange; permanently erect disklike crest with maroon subterminal band* (resembles Roman helmet) largely conceals bill; wings blackish; white wing speculum visible in flight; inner remiges broad, truncate, and tipped orange; the outer webs lengthened into long springy orange filaments; long orange upper tail coverts cover over half of short blackish tail; tip of tail orange. ♀: olive brown tinged orange on rump and tail; crest very small.

**Similar species:** Dull ♀ told by size, chunky shape, and small crest.

**Voice:** Rather quiet, though noisy near display area. Most common call a loud, distinctive *kreeayouu*, at or away from display arena (Hilty); also away from lek or at long intervals on it *keeow* and *waaow*; during aggressive interactions low wavering caws, gabbling and var. rough notes. ♀ rarely a high plaintive *kiuoow* or *kawee* (Gilliard 1962b).

**Behavior:** Most easily located by voice, esp. when near a display arena. Polygamous ♂♂ spend much of each day at a communal lek, either in direct combative display and bill snapping above arena, or in static posturing on the ground (Gilliard 1962a). Otherwise usually in mid. strata of forest or to canopy in fruiting trees; rarely at army ants (Oniki and Willis 1972). Flight strong and direct. Forms leks containing up to 40-50 ♂♂ or more in Guyana and Surinam; sim. concentrations as yet unreported in e Colombia.

**Breeding:** 2 nests with nearly grown nestling in rocky cave niches, May, near Mitú (Olivares 1964b); 4 Guyana nests, Feb–Apr, 2-4m up at cave entrance and less than 200m from lek; mud cup plastered to vertical rock wall; 2 eggs, no pair bond (Gilliard 1962b).

**Status and habitat:** Local near rocky outcrops and isolated cerros in sandy-belt forest. Small nos. turn up in cage trade, esp. in Villavicencio.

**Range:** To 300m. Extreme e from se Vichada s through cerros and table mts. of Guainía to Vaupés (Mitú) and Río Apaporis on the Caquetá boundary. The Guianas, s Venez., and n Brazil.

## 2. ANDEAN COCK-OF-THE-ROCK

*Rupicola peruviana*      Pl. 33, Map 889

**Identification:** 12.5″ (32cm). Eyes orange (♂); bluish white (♀). Bill and legs orange yellow. ♂ unmistakable: *deep* scarlet (*sanguinolenta*) or bright orange red (*aequatorialis*); *permanently erect disklike crest nearly covers bill*; wings and tail black; *shinglelike pearly gray inner remiges long and wide.* ♀: mainly dark reddish brown; inner remiges grayish brown; *crest small.* Or as above but mainly orangish brown, head cinnamon brown (*aequatorialis*).

**Similar species:** Dark ♀ told by large size, chunky shape, and small crest.

**Voice:** Rather quiet except on lek. Display with loud stuttering squawk and piglike squeals and grunts (Hilty). Away from lek a loud querulous *uankk* by ♂ or ♀ as fly through forest or when disturbed (R. Ridgely).

**Behavior:** Polygamous ♂♂ spend much of each day during long breeding season at communal lek in mid. strata or subcanopy of forest (not on ground as in *R. rupicola*). Wary but enter more exposed trees at forest edge or in clearings in early morning and late evening where they sally like trogons for fruit. Ad. mostly frugivorous, young fed much animal matter at first (C. Benalcazar). Flight strong and swift.

**Breeding:** 7 nests, Feb–July. ♂♂ displaying, Jan–Sept, Pichindé Val., Valle (C. Benalcazar); 3 nests, Feb–June, PN Cueva de los Guácharos (P. Gertler); mud cup plastered to cave entrance or rocky outcrop in forested ravine, very close to far (1 km or more) from lek; 2 eggs.

**Status and habitat:** Locally fairly common in steep, humid and wet forested ravines, usually close to streams; rocky outcrops required for breeding. Accessible colonies (but not easy to see) at La Reserva de los Gallos de Monte in Pichindé (above Cali), along Río Hacha above Florencia and Río Guiza below Ricuarte, Nariño. As in Guianan Cock-of-the-Rock, often sought for cage bird trade.

**Range:** Mostly 1400-2400m; to 500m on Pacific slope and on e slope W Andes (*sanguinolenta*); C and E Andes (*aequatorialis*). W Venez. (Táchira) s in Andes to Bolivia.

# COTINGAS: Cotingidae (41)

Cotingas are a very heterogeneous group of New World birds found from the southwestern border of the US to northern Argentina. They reach greatest diversity in the equatorial latitudes of northern South America. Most closely allied to tyrant flycatchers and to manakins, several genera, notably the controversial *Attila, Pseudattila, Casiornis, Laniocerca,* and *Rhytipterna,* have recently been transferred to the tyrant flycatchers (Meyer de Schauensee 1970). Almost half the cotingid genera are monotypic; others are so distinct that their relationship, if any, to other genera within the family is in doubt. As a group they are essentially arboreal, forest or forest edge dwellers, almost all of which eat some fruit. Otherwise they share few anatomical or behavioral characteristics and include some of the most interesting, beautiful, and bizarre birds to be found in the American tropics. Breeding, as far as known, is monogamous, or in some lek-forming species, polygamous. Much recent information on the remarkable breeding and mating systems of some of the cotingas and their complex relationships with fruiting trees has been accumulated by A. F. Skutch, D. W. Snow, and B. K. Snow (see Snow 1976 and references under species accounts). The classification of the Cotingidae follows Snow (1973) with some modifications.

## 1. BLACK-NECKED RED-COTINGA
*Phoenicircus nigricollis*          Pl. 33, Map 890
**Identification:** 9.5″ (24cm). Brilliant ♂ slightly crested: *crown scarlet;* throat, sides of head, back, and wings black; *lower back and tail scarlet;* tail tipped black; *rest of underparts scarlet;* bill orange; eyes dark. ♀: *crown and tail dull maroon red;* otherwise olive brown above; tail narrowly tipped brownish; throat olive brown; *rest of underparts pale rosy crimson.*
**Similar species:** ♂ recalls overgrown Masked Crimson Tanager (p 624), but neck all black (not red) and short plushy crest usually evident, even extending partly over bill. ♀'s best marks are large size, dark crimson cap, and rosy underparts.
**Voice:** A loud crowlike *(Corvus) qua-a-a* from canopy near Leticia.
**Behavior:** Rather jaylike. One ♂ in canopy of fruiting tree (Brown); a ♀ in midstrata of mature forest (Hilty). In extreme ne Ecuador several ♂♂ were 8-10m up in same area of understory for several days; noisy but shy, strongly reminiscent of *Rupicola* (R. Ridgely). Believed to have some form of communal display (Olalla 1943).
**Status and habitat:** Apparently rare in humid *terra firme* forest. Not well known.
**Range:** To 400m. E of Andes: known from w Caquetá, w Putumayo (s of Mocoa), Vaupés (1 ♂ seen June 1976—R. Ridgely) and Amazonas; undoubtedly Guainía. S Venez. (Río Negro), e Ecuador, ne Peru, and w Amazonian Brazil (w of the Río Negro and Xingú).
**Note:** United toes, plumage, and communal display suggest this sp. may be a manakin (Snow 1973).

## 2. SHRIKE-LIKE COTINGA
*Laniisoma elegans*          Pl. 34, Map 891
**Identification:** 7″ (18cm). Bill slightly hooked, flesh color below. ♂: olive green above; *crown and nape black; underparts golden yellow with a few scalelike black bars on sides of throat, breast, and flanks;* eyes dark red. ♀: sim. but crown green like back. Imm.: ochraceous buff above

with a few black spots, wing coverts dusky tipped ochraceous.
**Similar species:** The smaller ♀ Barred Becard (17) is paler yellow below, has a conspic. rufous wing patch, and is usually at higher el. Also cf. Sharpbill (p 455).
**Voice:** Persistent call a very high sibilant *siiiiiiiiieeeee,* insectlike and easily overlooked (T. Parker).
**Behavior:** In Peru usually solitary, sluggish, and overlooked (need to know voice) in forest canopy (T. Parker).
**Status and habitat:** Apparently rare and local in humid lowland and foothill forest. Doubtless more widespread than single Colombian rec. In Venez. 200-500m (Meyer de Schauensee and Phelps 1978); in Peru to 1800m (Thoresen 1974).
**Range:** Known only in the foothills of E Andes 700m) in northernmost Boyacá (Fátima). Surely more widespread on e slope (rec. at 500m, sw Táchira, Venez., and at 600m on upper Río Napo, Ecuador). Spottily from nw Venez. s in w Amazonia to nw Bolivia; se Brazil.

## 3. RED-CRESTED COTINGA
*Ampelion rubrocristatus*          Pl. 34, Map 892
**Identification:** 9″ (23cm). Short swollen bill chalky white with black tip; eyes bright red. *Mainly gray; head, wings, and tail blackish;* long chestnut maroon crest usually laid flat (hence hard to see), rarely splayed out in spectacular fan shape; large white spot on inner web of all but central tail feathers forms *prom. subterminal white band* (visible from below at rest, above or below in flight); rump and somtimes lower back striped white; belly and under tail coverts mixed white. Imm.: crest reduced or lacking, upperparts streaked white, underparts yellowish white streaked gray.
**Similar species:** Imm. resembles Chestnut-crested Cotinga (4) but less yellow below, lacks chestnut shoulders, and always shows white subterminal tail band.
**Voice:** Often quiet. Occas. a peculiar froglike

trill or chatter, *trrrrrrrr*, perched or in flight (Hilty).

**Behavior:** Generally solitary as they perch in tall treetops or lower in tops of large bushes and nervously turn head and look around. Usually take fruit while perched; occas. sally to air for insects.

**Breeding:** 11 BC birds, Feb–Aug, Santa Marta and n end of C and E Andes (Carriker). Ecuador nest, Oct, 5m up (R. Ridgely). Bolivia nest 1.6m up in small tree; small twig and lichen cup stained red apparently from berries; 1 feathered nestling (Vuilleumier 1969a).

**Status and habitat:** Fairly common in humid forest, forest borders, and semiopen parklike areas with scattered trees and bushes.

**Range:** 2200-3700m (mainly 2700 to treeline). Santa Marta and Perijá Mts. and all 3 Andean ranges. W Venez. s in Andes to n Bolivia.

### 4. CHESTNUT-CRESTED COTINGA

*Ampelion rufaxilla*                Pl. 34, Map 893

**Identification:** 9″ (23cm). Highlands. Short curved bill bluish gray. Olive gray above streaked dusky; wings and tail blackish; *shoulders chestnut*; forecrown gray becoming black on center crown; long crest tipped chestnut (usually held flat, occas. erected like a fan); *throat, sides of head, and nuchal collar cinnamon*; chest olive gray; *rest of underparts pale yellow broadly streaked blackish*. Eyes bright red.

**Similar species:** See imm. Red-crested Cotinga (3).

**Voice:** Rather silent. In Peru and Bolivia, *trrrrrrrr*, much like that of Red-crested Cotinga (Taczanowski 1884; R. Ridgely).

**Behavior:** Sim. to 3. Usually rather high, often on an exposed perch in the canopy; found singly or in pairs and generally not closely assoc. with other birds. Reg. sally to air (R. Ridgely).

**Breeding:** 2 BC birds, Mar–Apr, sw Huila (Carriker). In se Peru, shallow open cup nest of twigs and lichen, 12m up in tree crown at edge of cloud forest (2000m); on 6 Dec 1 greenish blue egg (incomplete?) heavily marked and spotted dusky (T. Schulenberg *in* Snow 1982).

**Status and habitat:** Rare and local. Tall well-developed and humid subtropical forest, less often temperate forest; often at forest borders.

**Range:** 1900-2700m (mainly above 2300m). C Andes s to Quindío, and in sw Huila (Moscopán); W Andes in Valle (San Antonio) and Cauca (Munchique). Not rec. in Nariño. Colombia; Peru to nw Bolivia (no Ecuador recs.).

### 5. GREEN-AND-BLACK FRUITEATER

*Pipreola riefferii*                Pl. 34, Map 894

**Identification:** 8″ (20cm). *Bill and legs orange red; eyes dark.* ♂: *whole head, throat, and upper breast glossy greenish black bordered on front and sides by a narrow yellow band*; rest of upperparts dark moss green; tertials blackish tipped white; *breast and belly yellow mixed greenish on sides.* ♀: sim. but head and upper breast green like back; lower breast and belly *streaked* green and yellow.

**Similar species:** ♂ or ♀ Barred Fruiteater (6) is barred below with yellow spots on wings and black tail band. ♂ Black-chested Fruiteater (7) is smaller, *lacks* the white on tertials and yellow border on hood, and has greenish legs and pale eyes. ♀ from ♀ Black-chested by dark eyes, larger size, duller green plumage, and orange red legs.

**Voice:** Often heard call a very high sibilant *ti-ti-ti-ti-ti-* . . . ser. (up to 5 sec) dying away and descending slightly.

**Behavior:** Pairs or loose family groups of 3-6 perch quietly or hop lethargically from understory to midlevel and sometimes follow bird flocks. Eat fruit while perched or in clumsy hover. Notably unsuspicious.

**Breeding:** 12 BC birds, Feb–July, W and C Andes (Miller 1963; Carriker); 2 nests, Mar and July, above Cali; black, rootlet-lined moss cup 1-2m up in forest or at edge; 2 eggs, cream with wreath of fine red brown dots on larger end, fewer elsewhere (Miller 1963).

**Status and habitat:** Common in humid mossy forest ("cloud forest"), forest borders, second growth woodland, and occas. small patches of trees away from forest. Most common Colombian fruiteater. Partially replaced at higher el. by Barred Fruiteater; below about 1500m on Pacific slope by Orange-breasted Fruiteater.

**Range:** 1500-2700m (to 900m on Pacific slope). All 3 Andean ranges. N Venez. (incl. Perijá Mts.) s through mts. to n Peru.

### 6. BARRED FRUITEATER

*Pipreola arcuata*                Pl. 34, Map 895

**Identification:** 8.5″ (22cm). Large. Typical fruiteater shape. Bill, legs, and eyes orange red. ♂: head, throat, and chest glossy black; *rest of underparts pale yellow closely barred black*; above olive green; *wing coverts, inner remiges, and tertials black with large yellowish subterminal spots* and black tips; upper tail coverts narrowly barred yellow and black; *broad subterminal black bar* and narrow white tip on tail. ♀: sim. but crown green (no black hood) and entire underparts barred.

**Similar species:** From Green-and-black Fruit-

eater (5) by heavy barring below, large wing spots, and black band near tip of tail. Cf. Black-chested Fruiteater (7).
**Voice:** An extremely high, thin, almost hissing *se-e-e-e-e-e-a-a-a-a-* (about 2.5 sec) sim. to Orange-breasted Fruiteater, but longer and descending in Cauca.
**Behavior:** Solitary or in pairs in mid. story or lower. Like other *Pipreola*, notably unsuspicious.
**Breeding:** BC ♂, 4 May, Perijá Mts. (Carriker).
**Status and habitat:** Uncommon in humid and wet forest and bushy forest borders. Generally above range of Green-and-black Fruiteater and not as numerous.
**Range:** 1500-3100m (mainly above 2200m; rarely to 900m on Pacific slope). Known from W Andes in Cauca (Munchique area), both slopes of C Andes from Quindío and n Tolima to Cauca; Perijá Mts., and e slope E Andes from Norte de Santander to se Boyacá. Nw Venez. s in Andes to n Bolivia.

### 7. BLACK-CHESTED FRUITEATER
*Pipreola lubomirskii*     Pl. 34, Map 896
**Identification:** 6.7″ (17cm). Bill red (dusky orange, ♀); *legs olive, eyes white.* ♂: *head to center of breast shiny black*; upperparts grass green (*no white spots on tertials*); sides and flanks mixed green and yellow (may show black line on sides of chest to flanks); median breast and belly yellow. ♀: upperparts, head, throat, and upper breast grass green; lower underparts streaked green and yellow.
**Similar species:** See larger Green-and-black Fruiteater (5).
**Behavior:** Much like Green-and-black Fruiteater.
**Breeding:** BC ♂, 25 Mar, sw Huila (Carriker).
**Status and habitat:** Rare and local. Humid montane forest ("cloud forest"). Not well known in Colombia. Recent recs. (♀ specimen and sightings) are from PN Cueva de los Guácharos (P. Gertler; Hilty).
**Range:** 1600-2100m. Known from 3 localities at head of Magdalena Val. in Huila (e and sw of San Agustín); se Nariño. Prob. w Caquetá and Putumayo. S Colombia, e Ecuador, and ne Peru.
**Note:** Has been considered a subsp. of Golden-breasted Fruiteater. See note under 9.

### 8. ORANGE-BREASTED FRUITEATER
*Pipreola jucunda*     Pl. 34, Map 897
**Identification:** 7″ (18cm). Bill red orange; legs gray green; *eyes yellowish white.* ♂: *entire head and throat shiny black*; rest of upperparts grass green; *lower throat to center of breast yellow orange*

extending narrowly across sides of neck in a line to behind ear coverts and bordered below by black; center of breast and belly yellow; sides and narrow band (often incomplete) across center of breast green. ♀: upperparts, head, and throat grass green; rest of underparts streaked green and yellow; no white spots on wings.
**Similar species:** ♂ from any other *Pipreola* in Colombia by broad orangish patch across upper breast. ♀ easily confused with ♀ Green-and-black Fruiteater (5) but smaller, more extensively yellow below (streaks extend almost to throat) no white tertial tips, and legs gray green (not orange).
**Voice:** An extremely high-pitched (higher than Green-and-black Fruiteater), thin, hissing *se-e-e-e-e-e-e-e-e-e* (about 2-2.5 sec), easily overlooked; high *eeest* at short intervals.
**Behavior:** Usually alone or in scattered pairs. Perches quietly in lower to mid. story, sometimes joins but rarely follows mixed flocks. Lethargic and remarkably tame; eats berries with clumsy hover or from perch like others of genus.
**Status and habitat:** Fairly common to common in wet mossy forest ("cloud forest"), mainly in narrow belt of most intensely foggy forest in upper tropical zone. Easily found above Junín, Nariño.
**Range:** 900-1400m (mainly 1100-1300m). Pacific slope from s Chocó (n limits of range uncertain) s to w Ecuador.
**Note:** Has been considered a subsp. of Golden-breasted Fruiteater. See note under 9.

### 9. GOLDEN-BREASTED FRUITEATER
*Pipreola aureopectus*     Pl. 34, Map 898
**Identification:** 6.7″ (17cm). Typical fruiteater shape. Bill red orange; legs gray green; eyes yellowish white. ♂: grass green above, sometimes faintly tinged bluish; *inner remiges tipped white*; chin and lores blackish; *throat and breast golden yellow* (yellow extends in narrow line up behind ear coverts—*decora*), *fading to lemon yellow on belly*; sides and flanks mixed green and yellow. ♀ uniformly green above; inner remiges tipped white; *throat yellow streaked green*; rest of underparts *green streaked yellow*; bill dusky.
**Similar species:** ♂ is only Colombian fruiteater uniformly green above and yellow below, ♀ the only one entirely streaked below.
**Voice:** Sim. to Orange-breasted Fruiteater, a very high thin *se-e-e-e-e-e-e-e-e-e*, about 2 sec.
**Behavior:** Much like Orange-breasted Fruiteater but more often seen in mid. story, less often understory.

**Breeding:** 18 BC birds, Jan-June, 1 in Sept, n Colombia (Carriker).
**Status and habitat:** Common in Santa Marta Mts. in humid forest, forest borders, and second growth woodland. Prob. fairly common in Perijá Mts. (14 specimens) but apparently very uncommon to rare (or local) in Andes.
**Range:** 1300-2300m (usually above 1700m). Santa Marta Mts. (*decora*); Perijá Mts. s in E Andes to s Norte de Santander, n end C Andes (Valdivia) and W Andes at n end s of Frontino, Antioquia (*aureopectus*); spottily s to Nariño (Concordia, Antioquia; Cerro Munchique, Cauca; s of Barbacoas at 300-400m, Nariño— subsp.?). Nw and n Venez. and Colombia.
**Note:** Nos. 7, 8, and 9 (along with Masked Fruiteater, *P. pulchra*, of Peru) have been treated as a single sp. They are linked by the unique combination of red bill, white eyes and gray green legs, but 7 and 8 are believed to overlap in sw Colombia.

### 10. [FIERY-THROATED FRUITEATER]
*Pipreola chlorolepidota*     Pl. 34, Map 899
**Identification:** 4.8″ (12.2cm). Smallest *Pipreola*. Bill orange red tipped black; legs orange; eyes grayish white. ♂: *grass green above; inner remiges tipped white;* lores dusky; *throat orange becoming scarlet on breast;* rest of underparts deep green; center of belly yellowish. ♀: sim. above; most of *underparts rather coarsely scaled green and yellow,* throat yellower, breast greener; bill duller.
**Similar species:** Decidedly smaller than other *Pipreola*. ♀ recalls a manakin (esp. a *Chloropipo*, p 436), but note white-tipped inner remiges, scaled underparts, and behavior.
**Behavior:** In Peru often follow mixed flocks through forest canopy or subcanopy, or along edges, and to fruiting trees (T. Parker).
**Status and habitat:** Hypothetical. No specimens. Humid forested foothills.
**Range:** Upper tropical zone. Known only from w Caquetá (sight). E Colombia, e Ecuador (800-1000m in se—R. Ridgely), and e Peru (mainly 300-900m—T. Parker).

### 11. SCALED FRUITEATER
*Ampelioides tschudii*     Pl. 34, Map 900
**Identification:** 8″ (20cm). Even plumper than *Pipreola*, and tail shorter. Eyes pale yellow. ♂: *top and sides of head to below eyes black;* lores and stripe from base of bill to below eye yellowish white and joining *yellow nuchal collar; above black conspicuously scaled olive yellow;* wings black, remiges tipped olive; greater coverts greenish yellow forming a broad band; *throat white mottled dusky; rest of underparts yellowish white broadly*

scaled olive; tail olive, outer feathers black tipped buff; bill and legs gray brown. ♀: sim., but crown olive green, and upperparts more olivaceous (broader olive borders on feathers).
**Similar species:** Plump shape, white throat, and scaly appearance are the marks.
**Voice:** Territorial song a loud raptorlike whistle, rising in pitch and vol., then fading, *wheeeEEEEEaaa,* given Dec–early Apr in upper Anchicayá Val. (Hilty); sometimes over and over at short intervals (T. Parker).
**Behavior:** Solitary, in pairs, or less often groups of 3-4; hop deliberately along moss- and bromeliad-covered limbs in mid. story to canopy where they frequently follow bird flocks. More active and wary than *Pipreola* and harder to see.
**Breeding:** 3 BC birds, July, and imm., Aug, Perijá Mts. and n end E Andes (Carriker).
**Status and habitat:** Uncommon and local in humid and wet forest ("cloud forest").
**Range:** 650-2700m. Pacific slope of W Andes, Perijá Mts. (2400-2700m), e slope E Andes at n end in Norte de Santander (650m, 73°04′W) and in Macarena Mts. and w slope in Huila. Nw Venez. s in Andes to n Bolivia.

### 12. WHITE-BROWED PURPLETUFT
*Iodopleura isabellae*     Pl. 33, Map 901
**Identification:** 4.7″ (12cm). Tiny cotinga with stubby bill and tail. Above brownish black; *band across rump, crescent in front of eyes, and postocular stripe white;* throat, stripe down center of underparts, and under tail coverts white; sides and flanks dark brown somewhat barred; pectoral tufts silky violet (or white—♀) and rarely visible in field.
**Similar species:** Unique, but on tall treetop perch recalls a Swallow-winged Puffbird (p 320). Note white head markings and white stripe down underparts.
**Voice:** Usually quiet. Rarely a high weak *jee-jee-jee,* or thin, wiry *eeeeE* over and over.
**Behavior:** Pairs or small groups of 3-5 perch on bare twigs in tops of tallest canopy trees. Sit quietly or occas. sally for insects. Drop lower, esp. at forest edge to eat fruit.
**Breeding:** 3 birds attending, 2 observed building tiny hummingbirdlike cup of fine fibers, spider webs, and mossy material, well-camouflaged atop horizontal branch, 16m up, Nov 1977, Belém, Brazil (R. Ridgely).
**Status and habitat:** Uncommon (prob. often overlooked) in humid *terra firme* and *várzea* forests and forest edge; lowlands.
**Range:** To 500m. E of Andes from w Meta (near Villavicencio), w Vaupés (San José del Guaviare), and se Guainía (Macacuní) south-

ward. Sighting near Pto. Inírida, ne Guainía (Sept 1978—Hilty and M. Robbins). S Venez. s to n Bolivia and Amazonian Brazil.

## 13. OLIVACEOUS PIHA
*Lipaugus cryptolophus*          Pl. 33, Map 902
**Identification:** 10″ (25cm). *Thrushlike.* Large dark eyes. *Olive green above; yellow olive below becoming brighter and yellower on belly;* bend of wing and under wing coverts sulphur yellow. Concealed black crown patch rarely visible in field.
**Similar species:** See Dusky Piha (14). Chunkier than a *Turdus* thrush and with shorter heavier bill. Also see Gray-tailed Piha (see note).
**Behavior:** Rather inactive; perch erect and alone in more open midlevel or lower in forest. Occas. follow bird flocks. Peer sluggishly and then flutter to foliage for insects or lunge and hover to pluck fruit.
**Status and habitat:** Uncommon to fairly common but local. Humid and wet mossy forest and forest edge. Usually at lower el. than larger ally, Dusky Piha. Reg. in PN Cueva de los Guácharos.
**Range:** 900-2300m. Pacific slope of Valle (sightings above Queremal, 1800m, Aug 1976—Hilty), Cauca, and Nariño; head of Magdalena Val. in s Huila. Prob. e slope E Andes. Colombia, e and w Ecuador, and Peru.
**Note:** Gray-tailed Piha (*Lipaugus subalaris*) of humid foothill forest (mostly 800-1000m) in e Ecuador and e Peru doubtless occurs on e Colombian slope. 10″, gray eyering; upperparts and wings bright olive green; *rump and tail gray;* upper throat whitish, lower throat and chest dull olive gray with pale shaft streaks and *becoming plain gray from center of breast to lower underparts;* bend of wing and under wing coverts yellow.

## 14. DUSKY PIHA
*Lipaugus fuscocinereus*          Pl. 33, Map 903
**Identification:** 13″ (33cm). *Large* with decidedly long tail (6″, or 15cm). Short thick bill slightly decurved. *Plumage entirely gray;* wings slightly darker; lower underparts and tail tinged brownish.
**Similar species:** Olivaceous Piha (13) is distinctly smaller and greenish (not gray) above and below. Band-tailed Pigeon (p 187) is shorter-tailed and has pale bill and nape band.
**Voice:** Recalls Screaming Piha, a loud whistled *whee-a-wheeee* or *whee-a-wheeee-a wheeeea,* usually answered by others of the lek.
**Behavior:** Rather inactive and sluggish in forest canopy or subcanopy but may sometimes sit out in open on canopy branches and fly back and forth between trees while calling.

Occas. accompanies bird flocks; takes fruit with a trogonlike lunge and brief flutter.
**Status and habitat:** Apparently uncommon and local in humid mt. forest. Recent observations are above Bucaramanga, in PN Cueva de los Guácharos and above Mocoa in w Putumayo.
**Range:** 2000-3000m. N end of W Andes (Cordillera de Paramillo), spottily in C Andes (most recs. at head of Magdalena Val.), both slopes E Andes from Norte de Santander to Cundinamarca; sightings on e slope in w Putumayo (R. Ridgely; Hilty; M. Robbins). Colombia, e Ecuador, and n Peru.
**Note:** *Lipaugus* has been placed in the Tyrannidae by some.

## 15. SCREAMING PIHA
*Lipaugus vociferans*          Pl. 34, Map 904
**Identification:** 10-11″ (25-28cm). *Thrush-sized all gray bird,* slightly paler on throat and belly; bill and legs dusky; eyes grayish. Imm. sim. but tinged rufous on upper wing coverts and tail tip.
**Similar species:** May not always be safely separable in field from Grayish Mourner except by voice. Mourner (p 507) is somewhat smaller, less robust, and more uniformly gray below; in the hand Mourner is faintly greenish.
**Voice:** One of *the* sounds of the Amazon basin. Loud advertising call a whip-cracking and ringing *cree-CREE-o* or *wee-WEE-u,* usually preceded by about 4 low gurgling notes, sometimes a single *weéeeoo* in warm up (cf. with very different calls of Grayish Mourner). ♂♂ call much of day and yr.-round.
**Behavior:** Groups of 3-8 or so ♂♂ form well-separated leks in mid. story of forest. Calling birds maintain small territories and do not form forest pair bonds (Snow 1961). Usually not with forest flocks and even when calling can be difficult to see. Ads. eat mostly fruit taken with trogonlike fluttering hover.
**Breeding:** Perhaps prolonged but little known; 3 BC ♂♂, Aug, Mitú, Vaupés (Olivares and Hernández 1962). In e Peru all dry season (May–Oct) birds had enlarged gonads (O'Neill 1974). Sept nest in Brazil, 7m up in small tree, a tiny stick platform entirely concealed by incubating bird (E. Willis *in* Snow 1982).
**Status and habitat:** Common and widespread in humid *terra firme* and *várzea* forests in lowlands; smaller nos. in foothills.
**Range:** To 600m. E of Andes from w Meta (near Villavicencio) and ne Guainía (calling birds, Pto. Inírida—Hilty) southward. Prob. e Vichada (rec. on Venez. boundary). The Guianas and s Venez. s to n Bolivia and Amazonian and se Brazil.

## 16. RUFOUS PIHA
*Lipaugus unirufus*     Pl. 35, Map 905
**Identification:** 9.5" (24cm). *Uniform cinnamon brown*, slightly brighter on crown and paler almost buffy on throat; bill blackish.
**Similar species:** Easily confused with somewhat smaller Rufous Mourner (p 508) but more robust (appears broader-shouldered), head rounder (mourner looks "flat-headed"), bill heavier, and wings and crown uniform or slightly brighter than back (not duller). At rest piha tends to sit more erect (mourner more horizontal), sometimes with slightly cocked or raised tail. Both more easily told by calls. Cinnamon Becard (20) is much smaller and paler below.
**Voice:** Birds in scattered leks give a loud startling whistle, *quir-a* or 3-noted *peehéar-wit*; occas. a single *quir* followed by several low buzzy *cla* notes, at Quibdó (Hilty). Also a loud rattling *trrt-trrt-trrt-trrt*; calls are ventriloquial and usually given only at long intervals or in response to another noise.
**Behavior:** Often inconspic. as they sit alone and quiet, peering about in forest midlevels to canopy, less often lower story. When foraging, more active and sometimes join forest flocks.
**Breeding:** 9 BC birds, Jan–May, s Bolívar to Chocó (Carriker). In Costa Rica ♂♂ advertise from territories, and no lasting pair bond formed. Very frail, flat platform of tendrils usually 5-10m up; 1 smoky gray egg heavily mottled brown. Incubation and nestling per. very long (nearly 30 days each); nest torn apart when empty (Skutch 1969a).
**Status and habitat:** Uncommon to fairly common in old humid and wet forest in lowlands, sparingly into foothills. Represented e of Andes by gray-plumaged Screaming Piha.
**Range:** To 1000m. Pacific coast and e along humid n base of Andes to mid. Magdalena Val. (s to Remedios, e Antioquia); isolated population in Snía. de Macuira, e Guajira. S Mexico to w Ecuador.

## 17. BARRED BECARD
*Pachyramphus versicolor*     Pl. 35, Map 906
**Identification:** 5" (13cm). Highlands. ♂: above glossy black; wing coverts and secondaries broadly edged white; rump and tail gray; tail narrowly tipped white; *lores, eyering, sides of head, throat, and chest greenish yellow*; rest of underparts grayish white and *entire underparts finely barred dusky*. ♀: crown and nape slaty; back olive green; wings dusky; *wing coverts and edges of outer secondaries cinnamon rufous*; innermost remiges edged ochraceous; eyering

yellow; *lores, sides of head, and underparts dull yellow* becoming whitish on belly and *obscurely barred dusky*.
**Similar species:** Either sex by chunky shape, stout bill, and barred underparts (latter inconspic. at a distance). ♀'s best mark is bright, contrasting rufous on wings.
**Voice:** ♂♂ sing a soft melodious *we-pe-pi-pi-pi-pi*, rising then falling (Hilty) or *treedididee*? (R. Ridgely).
**Behavior:** Pairs reg. follow mixed flocks in low to upper midlevels of forest and lighter woodland. Usually a little more active than other *Pachyramphus* as they flit at foliage or hop along branches like vireos.
**Breeding:** BC ♂, June, Antioquia (Carriker). Nestlings, May and Oct, W Andes above Cali (S. Gniadek); large globular moss and vine ball with entrance near bottom; 2-3m up (Skutch 1967); 1 Costa Rican egg, white spotted and lined cinnamon and brown at large end (Wetmore 1972).
**Status and habitat:** Uncommon to fairly common in humid montane forest, forest borders, and lighter woodland.
**Range:** Mainly 1600-2600m (once to 400m in Magdalena Val.). W Andes (not rec. n of Valle), C Andes and E Andes from ne Boyacá and se Santander to se Nariño (Río Churuyaco). Costa Rica to w Venez. and s in Andes to n Bolivia.

## 18. CINEREOUS BECARD
*Pachyramphus rufus*     Pl. 35, Map 907
**Identification:** 5" (13cm). ♂: mainly pearl gray above; tail darker; *cap shiny black; lores and forehead white*; wings blackish; coverts and inner remiges *narrowly edged white*; below white tinged gray on breast. ♀: bright cinnamon rufous above; crown more chestnut; *lores white; underparts whitish* tinged buff on chest. Juv. ♂: like ♀ but crown blackish.
**Similar species:** When in pairs, combination of gray ♂ and rufous ♀ unique. ♂ Black-and-white Becard (23) is confusingly sim., but tail black broadly tipped white (not solid gray) and wings blacker and more extensively bordered white. ♂♂ of White-winged (21) and Black-capped becards (22), also superficially sim., are blacker above, show more white in wings, and have white tail tips. ♀ most like Cinnamon Becard (20) but smaller and with white (not gray) lores; ♀ whiter below than other "rufous" becards; ♀ One-colored Becard (24) is obviously larger.
**Voice:** Song, *twee, twee twee-twee-tweetwee'-ti'ti'ti'ti'ti*, rising, accelerating, and like a woodcreeper; also *twee-twee-twee-tweedo* (P. Schwartz recording).

**Behavior:** Alone or in pairs from low scrub to mid. or subcanopy of trees. Rarely with bird flocks.

**Breeding:** 6 BC birds, Apr–Oct, n Colombia (Carriker); 1 in Feb, Santander (Boggs 1961); large grass and leaf ball with side entrance; usually high; 2-5 vinaceous brown eggs with dark spots often in ring at large end (Haverschmidt 1968).

**Status and habitat:** Uncommon and local in lighter woodland, second growth, or groves of trees; often in cultivated areas. Favors drier regions.

**Range:** To 1500m. Guajira and Santa Marta area spottily s to mid. Cauca Val. (Valle) and upper Magdalena Val. (n Huila); e of Andes known only from Norte de Santander and sight recs. at Leticia (15 and 20 June 1975—J. V. Remsen). Prob. Arauca and Vichada. C Panama to e Ecuador, ne Peru, Amazonian Brazil, and the Guianas.

**Note:** White-naped Xenopsaris (*Xenopsaris albinucha*) of Venez., n Bolivia, n Argentina, Paraguay, and e Brazil, may occur in n Arauca and Vichada. ♂ like Cinereous Becard but smaller (5″), with broad nuchal collar, white (not gray) underparts, and brownish wings. ♀ has crown mixed brown and belly tinged yellow. Thickets and borders in ranchland or along rivers and in reeds.

### 19. CHESTNUT-CROWNED BECARD

*Pachyramphus castaneus*        Pl. 35, Map 908

**Identification:** 5.5″ (14cm). Amazonian lookalike of Cinnamon Becard. Crown chestnut *bordered by gray band from eyes to nape and encircling rearcrown; supraloral line buffy*; otherwise cinnamon rufous above; primaries dusky; below pale cinnamon; bill blackish.

**Similar species:** Easily confused with Cinnamon Becard (20) but should not overlap (may meet) in range. Cinnamon has well defined blackish lores and no gray band on crown.

**Voice:** At Leticia a soft, thin *teeeer, tee-tee* (1-4 tee notes), much like song of Cinnamon Becard but shorter.

**Behavior:** As in Cinnamon Becard. Often stays high.

**Breeding:** 2 BC birds and juv., May, Vaupés (Olivares 1964b); 2 July nests, canopy (35m) of tall *várzea* emergent, e Ecuador; large messy ball with entrance facing down; wedged in crotch, not suspended (R Ridgely).

**Status and habitat:** Uncommon (prob. often overlooked) in humid forest borders, second growth woodland, and clearings with scattered trees; *terra firme* or *várzea* forests.

**Range:** To 500m. E of Andes from Macarena

Mts. (Río Dudita) and Vaupés (Mitú) southward. N Venez., Colombia, and e Ecuador (to 900m) to ne Argentina, Paraguay, and e Brazil.

**Note:** Green-backed Becard (*Pachyramphus viridis*) of Guyana, Venez. and e Ecuador to n Argentina prob. occurs in upper tropical zone hills of e Nariño and w Putumayo. 6″; forehead and lores white; *cap glossy black; back bright olive green;* wing coverts black edged greenish yellow; sides of head and throat yellowish; *chest band greenish yellow;* center of throat, lower breast, and belly white. ♀: cap like back, *wings mostly chestnut.*

### 20. CINNAMON BECARD

*Pachyramphus cinnamomeus*     Pl. 35, Map 909

**Identification:** 5.5″ (14cm). Chestnut rufous above, *darkest on crown; lores slaty black bordered above by buffy white supraloral line;* underparts pale cinnamon; throat whitish (or underparts whitish washed cinnamon—*magdalenae*); bill black above, paler below.

**Similar species:** Easily confused with ♀ ♀ of several less common becards. ♀ One-colored (24) is slightly larger, has crown uniform with back, no distinct supraloral stripe, and is frequently inside forest. Also cf. Chestnut-crowned (19) and ♀ Cinereous becards (18).

**Voice:** Often heard song a sweet, mellow *tee-dear-dear-dear* falling, trailing off and often given briskly.

**Behavior:** Alone, in pairs, or less frequently in loose groups (colonies?); alternates active sallying to foliage, or visits to fruiting trees with periods of sluggishness. Rather sedentary and usually in midlevels of trees. Often nods head.

**Breeding:** 12 BC birds, Jan–Oct, n Colombia (Carriker; Haffer 1975); building nest, 3 Mar, Buenaventura (Hilty and P. Alden) and Apr–May in nw Santander (Boggs 1961). Large trashy ball nest with side entrance is typical of genus; usually rather high and near end of branch where conspic.; 3 olive gray eggs spotted and streaked olive brown around larger end (West 1976b).

**Status and habitat:** Common in humid forest borders, second growth, and lighter woodland and clearings. Replaced in Amazonia by Chestnut-crowned Becard.

**Range:** To 1300m. Lower Magdalena Val. and n Sucre s to 9°N (*magdalenae*); Pacific coast, humid lowlands n of Andes e to e Guajira (Snía. de Macuira) and s to mid. Magdalena Val. (Honda, n Tolima), and mid. Cauca Val. in s Antioquia; e of Andes from Catatumbo lowlands to w Meta at Villavicencio (*cinnamomeus*). Se Mexico to sw Ecuador and w Venez.

## 21. WHITE-WINGED BECARD

*Pachyramphus polychopterus*  Pl. 35, Map 910
**Identification:** 5.5″ (14cm). ♂: *crown black* glossed blue; mantle black; rump gray (gray nuchal collar—*dorsalis*); underparts light to dark gray; wings black; *wing coverts and scapulars broadly edged white; tail graduated, black with broad white tips* (or all black above and below with only wing coverts and tail tips edged white—*niger; tenebrosus*). ♀: light olive brown above; *crown browner; broken eyering white;* wings dusky with broad cinnamon buff edgings on scapulars, coverts, and remiges; tail black tipped cinnamon buff; underparts light yellow.
**Similar species:** Easily confused ♂ is only "black-and-white" becard with solid black cap and upper back and no white or gray lores (see 18, 22, 23). ♀, dullest of the 4, has dull brown (not bright chestnut) crown and lacks the white eyebrow of ♀ Black-capped Becard.
**Voice:** Song a soft, sweet *teeur, tur-tur-tur-turtu-tur?* with var.; also a weak, mellow *tu tu tu tu* sometimes falling slightly. Both sexes sing.
**Behavior:** Single birds or pairs move rather deliberately as they follow bird flocks in wooded regions or away from them in more open areas. Usually midlevel or lower, occas. to subcanopy. Peer and flutter in foliage and eat small berries.
**Breeding:** 6 BC birds, May–Aug, n Colombia (Carriker); building nest, 1 Mar, upper Calima Val., Valle (Brown); and mid-June near Leticia (J. V. Remsen); nest like other *Pachyramphus* (see 20); 3-4 pale gray eggs mottled brown; only ♀ incubates (Skutch 1969a).
**Status and habitat:** Common in moist to wet forest borders, second growth, lighter woodland, and clearings; also *várzea* second growth. The most common and most widespread Colombian Becard.
**Range:** To 2700m (rarely above 2000m) throughout. N Colombia s to upper Río Sinú and Gamarra, Cesar (*cinereiventris*); Pacific slope and foothills to sw Nariño and e to w slope E Andes in Cundinamarca (*dorsalis*); e of Andes from Norte de Santander s, prob. to Guainía (*tristis*); w Meta to Vaupés (*niger*); w Caquetá to se Nariño and Amazonas (*tenebrosus*). Guatemala s to n Argentina and Uruguay.

## 22. BLACK-CAPPED BECARD

*Pachyramphus marginatus*  Pl. 35, Map 911
**Identification:** 5.2″ (13.2cm). ♂: crown black glossed blue; *back mixed black and gray;* lower back gray; tail black, strongly graduated and outer feathers tipped white; wings black with broad white edges on scapulars, coverts, and remiges; *gray supraloral stripe meets over bill;* sides of head, nape and, underparts light gray. ♀:

crown bright chestnut; otherwise pale olive brown above; wings dusky with broad cinnamon buff edges on scapulars, wing covers, and remiges; tail black tipped cinnamon buff; supraloral stripe white, sides of head and underparts pale yellow washed olive on breast and sides.
**Similar species:** ♂ is only "black-and-white" becard with back mixed or streaked black and gray (not solid black or solid gray); nearby note gray (not white) supraloral. ♀ like ♀ Black-and-white Becard (23) but lacks the sharp black margin bordering crown. Also see White-winged Becard (21).
**Behavior:** Like other becards, peer and flutter short distances for fruit and insects in mid-level to canopy of forest and second growth and often with mixed flocks.
**Breeding:** BC ♂, 22 Apr, upper Orinoco, Venez. (Friedmann 1948); May breeding, n Venez. (Schäfer and Phelps 1954).
**Status and habitat:** Inside humid forest and tall second growth woodland in lowlands, mostly replaced at forest edges and in lighter woodland by White-winged Becard.
**Range:** To 500m. E of Andes from s Meta (Macarena Mts.) and se Guainía (Macacuní) southward. Sight recs. to ne Guainía (Pto. Inírida, 1978—Hilty and M. Robbins). The Guianas and Venez. s to n Bolivia and Amazonian and se Brazil.

## 23. BLACK-AND-WHITE BECARD

*Pachyramphus albogriseus*  Pl. 35, Map 912
**Identification:** 5.2″ (13.2cm). ♂: crown black glossed bluish and in sharp contrast to *light gray hindneck and back; narrow white supraloral streak* joins over bill; wings black; wing coverts and remiges edged white; sides of head and underparts light gray; graduated *black tail broadly tipped white.* ♀: *crown rufous chestnut crisply bordered black all around and with narrow white eyebrow and broken white eyering;* otherwise pale olive brown above; wings dusky with cinnamon buff wing bars and edgings on remiges; sides of head light gray becoming whitish on throat and light olive yellow on underparts; graduated dusky tail broadly edged cinnamon buff.
**Similar species:** ♂ from other confusing "black-and-white" becards (but see ♂ of 18) by solid gray back (not solid black, or mixed black or gray); also from Black-capped Becard (22) by white (not gray) supraloral. ♀ has the most strongly patterned head of allies (see 21, 22).
**Voice:** From Venez. to Peru a sweet, mellow *chu-u-ree,* occas. varied to *cheer, chew-a-weet* (P. Schwartz recording; T. Parker).
**Behavior:** Like Black-capped Becard occurs

mainly inside forest at midlevels where often follows mixed flocks.

**Status and habitat:** Humid foothill and lower montane forests, prob. also into dry tropical forest (common in latter virtually down to sea level in w Ecuador and nw Peru (R. Ridgely; T. Parker).

**Range:** 900-2300m (100-2700m in Ecuador). Sw slope Santa Marta Mts., e slope E Andes from n Norte de Santander (Convención 1400m) to n Boyacá (Río Cobugón 2300m) and se Nariño (Río San Miguel). N and w Venez. (incl. Perijá Mts.) s to e and w Ecuador and nw Peru.

### 24. ONE-COLORED BECARD

*Platypsaris homochrous*  Pl. 35, Map 913

**Identification:** 6.5″ (16.5cm). ♂: *entirely blackish slate*; crown, wings, and tail darker; bill black. ♀ and imm.: *uniform cinnamon rufous above*; primaries dusky edged cinnamon; below cinnamon buff; paler almost whitish on throat and center of belly.

**Similar species:** ♂ is only all black becard w of Andes. ♀ much like Cinnamon Becard (20) but lacks latter's short supraloral, and upperparts more uniform. ♀ Cinereous Becard (18) is decidedly smaller and whiter below. Also see Rufous Mourner (p 508).

**Voice:** A loud, sharp, chattering *ske-e-et'et'it'IT, tseer, tsrip*, or sim. var. at Quibdó and Aracataca.

**Behavior:** Usually in pairs that forage from midlevels to subcanopy of forest edges or lighter woodland, sometimes also inside forest. Often pumps head like a *Myiarchus* and raises crown feathers giving head a distinctive bushy-crested but still rounded look. Sometimes accompanies mixed flocks.

**Breeding:** 13 BC birds, Jan–May, n Colombia (Carriker); Nest sim. to *Pachyramphus* (see 20) but see note below. Eggs brown faintly spotted darker around large end (Sclater and Salvin 1879).

**Status and habitat:** Common in dry to moist forest, gallery woodland, and edges on w base and ne base of Santa Marta Mts. (Todd and Carriker 1922); not reported on n slope; uncommon and local in superwet Pacific coast region (Hilty), but very numerous in w Ecuador lowlands, even in disturbed partially opened arid woodland or xeric scrub at sw end of range (R. Ridgely). Its Amazonian representative is Pink-throated Becard.

**Range:** To 900m (Baudó Mts.). Pacific coast s to s Chocó (lower Río San Juan) and n of Andes e to Santa Marta region, and base of Perijá Mts. s to mid. Magdalena Val. (Reme-

dios?). C Panama to w Venez., w Ecuador (incl. Esmeraldas), and nw Peru.

**Note 1:** Sometimes merged with *P. aglaiae* (Rose-throated Becard) of Mid. America. **Note 2:** *Platypsaris* has been merged with *Pachyramphus* (Snow 1973), but nest differences (*Platypsaris* apparently build suspended rather than supported nests in a horizontal or vertical crotch) as well as vocal and minor morphological differences suggest retention in *Platypsaris*.

### 25. PINK-THROATED BECARD

*Platypsaris minor*  Pl. 33, Map 914

**Identification:** 6.5″ (16.5cm). ♂: *black above: slaty gray below with rose red patch on throat* (hard to see in field); bill blackish. ♀: *crown, nape, and upper mantle slate gray* becoming rufous on lower back and tail; narrow supraloral spot, *sides of head, neck, and entire underparts pale cinnamon*; wings rufous; primaries blackish.

**Similar species:** ♂ unique. ♀ from Chestnut-crowned Becard (19) by grayish crown and upper back. Also see Citron-bellied Attila (p 506).

**Voice:** Often quiet. Call a clear, rising whistle, *tyoooeee*, also a soft grosbeaklike *(Pheucticus) pik* (J. V. Remsen).

**Behavior:** One or 2 often follow mixed flocks of mid. story to subcanopy of tall forests and along edges. Sally to air or foliage for insects; also partially frugivorous; bobs head as do most becards.

**Status and habitat:** Uncommon to fairly common in humid *terra firme* forest and forest borders, less frequently *várzea* forest.

**Range:** To 500m. E of Andes from w Meta (near Villavicencio) and Vaupés s to Amazonas. The Guianas and s Venez. to n Bolivia and Amazonian Brazil.

### 26. BLACK-TAILED TITYRA

*Tityra cayana*  Pl. 35, Map 915

**Identification:** 8″ (20cm). ♂: *crown, sides of head, wings, and entire tail black*; otherwise pale silvery white above; white below; *bare ocular area, facial skin, and bill red; bill tip black.* ♀: sim. but darker gray, crown brownish, back and breast lightly streaked black.

**Similar species:** Shares red face with Masked Tityra (27), but latter has only forehead and foreface black (not entire crown) and tail tipped white. ♀ Masked lacks streaking on breast. Also cf. Black-crowned Tityra (28).

**Voice:** A soft, nasal, double-noted croaking (J. V. Remsen).

**Behavior:** Pairs or small loose groups, less often solitary; perch high and frequently exposed. Fly rapidly and directly; and like other tityras, they act aggressive and are almost never with other birds. Mostly frugivorous.

**Breeding:** 3 BC birds, June, w Caquetá (Carriker); 2 Meta nests, Mar (Brown); 3 Leticia nests, July (Hilty), 1 in Nov (J. V. Remsen); cavity in stub or woodpecker hole (usually high) lined with leaves and small twigs.

**Status and habitat:** Fairly common in a wide var. of humid habitats but most often along forest borders, tall open second growth along rivers, or in clearings with scattered trees. Lowlands and foothills.

**Range:** To 500m (perhaps higher). Throughout e of Andes. The Guianas and Venez. s to ne Argentina and Paraguay.

## 27. MASKED TITYRA

*Tityra semifasciata*                    Pl. 35, Map 916

**Identification:** 8″ (20cm). ♂: mainly white; upperparts tinged pearly gray; wings and most of tail black; *base and tail tip white; bare ocular area, facial skin, and bill red;* bill tip black; *forehead and narrow area surrounding bare face black.* ♀: sim., but crown brown and back smudged and streaked brown.

**Similar species:** See Black-tailed Tityra (26). ♂ Black-crowned Tityra (28) has solid black cap (to nape) and no red; ♀ has feathered rusty face (no bare red skin).

**Voice:** Recalls Black-tailed Tityra. Peculiar nasal croaking or clicking and an unusual dry *kuert* or *quert* sometimes doubled.

**Behavior:** Widespread and conspic. tityra found almost wherever there are a few tall trees. Strictly arboreal and usually perches high; alone, in pairs, or with several. Mostly frugivorous but also seeks invertebrate prey with clumsy leaps and flutters. Flies strongly and often seen crossing clearings.

**Breeding:** 11 BC birds, Jan–May, nw Colombia (Carriker); building or occupying holes, Feb, Mar, Apr, and Aug, upper Anchicayá Val. (Hilty); nest as in previous sp.; 2 dark buff eggs heavily marked brown and black; ♀ incubates (Skutch 1969a).

**Status and habitat:** Common. Forest borders and clearings with scattered trees in moist to wet zones; prob. also reg. in canopy of forest (easily overlooked). Largely replaced in n Amazonia by Black-tailed Tityra.

**Range:** To 1700m (mostly below 1200m). Throughout w of Andes (no recs. in mid. and upper Cauca Val.); e of Andes only rec. near Villavicencio, Meta; perhaps Amazonas as rec. n of Amazon in ne Peru. N Mexico s to n Bolivia and Amazonian Brazil.

## 28. BLACK-CROWNED TITYRA

*Tityra inquisitor*                       Pl. 35, Map 917

**Identification:** 7″ (18cm). Bill black above, blue gray below. ♂: crown to eyes black (or cheeks and ear coverts also black—*erythrogenys*); otherwise mostly white tinged pearly on back; primaries and distal half of tail black (or tail largely black—*erythrogenys; buckleyi*). ♀: sim., but *forehead buff becoming rusty on cheeks;* back brownish streaked dusky.

**Similar species:** Only tityra with a solid black cap and lacking bare red face and red bill. Note ♀'s buff forehead and rusty cheeks.

**Voice:** Resembles other tityras but drier and less grunty (Ridgely 1976); froglike grunting, *zick*ing and *squick*ing notes (Slud 1964).

**Behavior:** Sim. to Masked Tityra.

**Breeding:** Like other *Tityra.* 2 BC ♂♂, May, s Cesar, July, Norte de Santander (Carriker); breeds May, July, and Aug in sw Guárico, Venez. (Thomas 1979b).

**Status and habitat:** Fairly common to common e of Andes; much less numerous and local w of Andes. Habitat as in Masked Tityra, the 2 often even nesting in same tree. Coexistence may be due to size differences.

**Range:** To 800m. Pacific coast, entire lowlands n of Andes, Magdalena Val. s to Villavieja, n Huila (*albitorques*); e of Andes in Norte de Santander and the llanos (*erythrogenys*); Caquetá and Putumayo s to Amazonas (*buckleyi*). E Mexico to w Ecuador, ne Argentina, and se Brazil.

## 29. PURPLE-THROATED COTINGA

*Porphyrolaema porphyrolaema*  Pl. 35, Map 918

**Identification:** 6.5″ (16.5cm). Short black bill and small head. ♂: *black above;* feathers of back and upper tail coverts bordered white; wing coverts tipped white forming a single bar; tertials edged white; *throat rosy purple; rest of underparts white;* center of chest stained purple. ♀ very different: *brown above scaled buffy white;* forehead barred cinnamon buff; *throat cinnamon rufous; rest of underparts narrowly barred buff and black.* Imm. ♂: like ♀; gradually acquires ad. plumage.

**Similar species:** ♂ might recall Rose-breasted Grosbeak (p 646), but throat purplish (not rose red) and bill much smaller. ♀ most like ♀ Plum-throated (31) and Spangled cotingas (32) but smaller and distinctly barred below.

**Voice:** A high, plaintive, complaining *preeeeeer,* over and over from treetop where bird is easily overlooked; much like call of Dusky-capped Flycatcher.

**Behavior:** Alone from midlevel to forest canopy; occas. several gather at fruiting trees.

**Status and habitat:** Uncertain. Most Colombian recs. are from *várzea* forest or *várzea* edge. Prob. more common than the few recs. indicate but apparently more numerous in e Ecuador than eastward in Amazonian Colombia.

**Range:** To 500m. E of Andes from w Caquetá (s of Florencia) and Amazonas (several sightings at Leticia). Se Colombia to e Peru and w Amazonian Brazil.

### 30. BLUE COTINGA
*Cotinga nattererii*                    Map 919
**Identification:** 7″ (18cm). Dovelike shape; small black bill. ♂: *shining turquoise blue* with dark purple throat and purple patch on center of belly; wings black with blue edgings; tail black, enlongated blue upper tail coverts cover most of black tail from above. ♀ very different: dark brown above scaled whitish and faintly tinged blue; *below buffy more or less scaled and spotted dark brown throughout* except on throat; cinnamon on lower abdomen and *under wing coverts* (conspic. in flight).
**Similar species:** ♂ is unmistakable but can look black against the sky or in poor light. ♀ shows more contrast between upper and underparts than others of the genus (none overlap in range). Her best marks are plump, small-headed silhouette and scaly appearance.
**Voice:** Silent vocally. Wings of ♂ whistle in flight (Willis and Eisenmann 1979).
**Behavior:** Often perches high and exposed on bare branch above canopy where erect dovelike posture is characteristic. Several may gather at fruiting trees, but otherwise are solitary and sluggish, remaining quietly perched for long periods. Ad. diet is almost wholly fruit taken by brief fluttering hover.
**Breeding:** 14 BC birds, Jan–Apr, s Bolívar to Chocó (Carriker); 3 Panama nests, Feb–Mar (1 in same crotch as previous yr.); on horizontal canopy limb about 30m up; all nesting activities apparently by ♀; nestlings 1st covered by white down. Empty nests torn apart as in Rufous Piha (Skutch 1969a).
**Status and habitat:** Uncommon (usually overlooked) in humid and wet lowland forest or second growth woodland with scattered primary trees; small nos. in foothills and lower highlands.
**Range:** To 1000m. Pacific coast and humid lowlands along n base of Andes to mid. Magdalena Val. (to Muzo, sw Boyacá). C Panama to w Venez. and nw Ecuador (very rare).

### 31. PLUM-THROATED COTINGA
*Cotinga maynana*               Pl. 34, Map 920
**Identification:** 7.5″ (19cm). Both sexes usually with dark eyes (yellow?). An Amazonian replica of Blue Cotinga. ♂: *shining turquoise blue; upper throat plum purple*; primaries black; inner webs white; wing converts and remiges broadly edged blue; tail blue above, black below. ♀ very different: above grayish brown scaled pale buff; below grayish buff; the breast and belly

feathers dark centered giving a *scaled and dappled appearance; abdomen, under tail coverts, and under wing converts cinnamon* (latter conspic. in flight).
**Similar species:** ♂, often confused with ♂ Spangled Cotinga (32), is decidedly smaller, has smaller throat patch, and has more uniformly blue plumage (lacks the numerous black patches that always show on ♂ Spangled). ♀ much like ♀ Spangled, but underparts distinctly dappled (♀ Spangled more uniform) and *rather bright cinnamon* on abdomen, crissum, and under wing coverts (spangled only faintly tinged buff on these parts).
**Voice:** Apparently silent vocally but ♂'s wings whistle in normal flight (Hilty) and much more loudly in display as ♂ leaves high perch, angles slightly downward, then straight out over open space (often water) for about 40m, brakes suddenly with loud whistling "whirr," and returns to perch. ♀'s wings not known to whistle (J. V. Remsen).
**Behavior:** As in Blue Cotinga.
**Breeding:** 2 BC ♂♂, May and June, w Caquetá (Carriker).
**Status and habitat:** Uncommon to fairly common in humid *terra firme* and *várzea* forests of Amazonian drainage; fewer in Vaupés drainage.
**Range:** To 500 m. E of Andes from w Caquetá (Morelia and Vaupés (Mitú) southward. Se Colombia to n Bolivia and w Amazonian Brazil.

### 32. SPANGLED COTINGA
*Cotinga cayana*               Pl. 34, Map 921
**Identification:** 8″ (20cm). Much like Plum-throated Cotinga. Small black bill. ♂: *brilliant shining (enamellike) turquoise blue mixed with black giving a slightly patchy appearance; throat and upper chest bright reddish purple*; wings black with blue edgings on coverts and remiges; tail all black. ♀ very different: dark brown above, the feathers edged paler giving a scaled appearance; below sim. but paler and grayer; throat uniform grayish; *under wing coverts dull* (not bright) *cinnamon brown* (cf. with other ♀ *Cotinga*). Imm. ♂ like ♀ or mottled and pied blue and plum.
**Similar species:** See Plum-throated Cotinga (31). ♀ more uniform below (less spotted or scaled) than other cotingas.
**Voice:** Faint wing-whistles in normal flight; no whistling flight display described.
**Behavior:** Much like Blue Cotinga.
**Breeding:** 3 BC ♂♂, May–June, w Caquetá (Carriker). ♀ on low branch of isolated tree was apparently brooding a downy white young; with no visible nest; 24 Feb, Villavicencio, Meta (Nicéforo 1947).

**Status and habitat:** Uncommon in humid *terra firme* and *várzea* forests in Amazonia where outnumbered by Plum-throated Cotinga, but n in sandy-belt forests of Vaupés and Guainía gradually replaces Plum-throated completely. Small nos. into gallery forest and savanna woodland. **Range:** To 500m. Throughout e of Andes (not reported in Putumayo or most of llanos). The Guianas, w Venez. (Táchira), and s Venez. s to n Bolivia and Amazonian Brazil.

## 33. PURPLE-BREASTED COTINGA
*Cotinga cotinga*                      Pl. 34, Map 922
**Identification:** 7.5″ (19cm). Dovelike shape with small black bill. ♂ unmistakable: upperparts, lower breast, and belly deep violet blue; *throat to mid belly dark wine purple*; wings and tail black. ♀ very different: dark brown above with buffy white feather edgings; light brown below with crisp buffy white feather edgings giving an *entirely scaled appearance; under wing coverts dull cinnamon.*
**Similar species:** ♀ prob. not safely told in field from ♀ Plum-throated Cotinga (31), but range overlap minimal (e of Mitú). Under favorable conditions shows distinctly scaled throat (not more or less uniform) and decidedly bolder crisper scaling below (not diffused dappling) and *lacks* cinnamon on lower abdomen and crissum. Cf. larger Spangled Cotinga (32).
**Voice:** ♂'s wings whirr in normal flight. No vocal sound rec.
**Behavior:** Sim. to others of the genus. Often takes a prom. treetop perch for a while, otherwise sits somewhat lower and unmoving for long periods in a screen of foliage.
**Status and habitat:** One specimen and sight recs. 19km e of Mitú (Santa Cruz de Waracapurí); sight recs. of 2 ♂♂, 21 and 22 Sept 1978, 40km s of Pto. Inírida, Guainía (Hilty and M. Robbins). Humid sandy-belt forest and second growth in blackwater regions. Reported "common" e of Mitú (Olivares 1955) and doubtless more numerous than the few recs. suggest.
**Range:** To 250m. Extreme ne Guainía (sight) s to Vaupés (Mitú). Prob. e Vichada. The Guianas, s Venez., and n Brazil.

## 34. POMPADOUR COTINGA
*Xipholena punicea*                      Pl. 34, Map 923
**Identification:** 8″ (20cm). *Eyes white.* ♂ unmistakable: *entirely deep glossy wine red with white flight feathers*; long stiff pointed wing coverts project down over flight feathers at rest. ♀: entirely grayish tinged brown and becoming buffy white on abdomen; *wing coverts and remiges heavily edged white*; under tail coverts white.

**Similar species:** Gorgeous ♂ cannot be confused even in flight when rapidly fanned white wings twinkle transparently against dark foliage. Good marks for ♀ are plump silhouette and white eyes.
**Voice:** Usually silent. On occas. utters a loud, ventriloquial, froglike, rattling croak (Beebe 1924) or gurgling notes (Haverschmidt 1968).
**Behavior:** Usually in canopy and frequently takes a prom. exposed treetop stub perch as do other *Xipholena* and *Cotinga*. Alone or when at fruiting trees may gather in groups. In undulating flight, wings fanned then closed briefly (Hilty). Silent display apparently involves ritualized chasing between ♂♂ in treetops, but unlike other group-displaying cotingas, the site may shift over a wide area rather than remain fixed at 1 locality (Snow 1971b).
**Breeding:** A ♀ carried hairlike nest material, 18 Sept, Pto. Inírida (Hilty); 1 Guyana nest, 6 Mar, about 20m up in bamboo at clearing edge; frail open nest of curly wood tendrils; 1 blunt, greenish gray egg, spotted and blotched drab, denser at large end; incubating ♀ completely conceals small nest (Beebe 1924).
**Status and habitat:** Fairly common in sandy-belt forest, and savanna and gallery woodland in ne Guainía.
**Range:** To 200m. Extreme ne Guainía (sightings) to se Guainía (San Felipe) and Vaupés (Mitú); once (♂) on Río Arauca. The Guianas, s Venez. (incl. Río Orinoco opp. n Vichada), and nw Brazil.

## 35. WHITE (BLACK-TIPPED) COTINGA
*Carpodectes hopkei*                      Ill. 82, Map 924
**Identification:** 9.5″ (24cm). *Pigeonlike.* Small black bill; *red eyes.* ♂: *white*; outer primaries narrowly tipped black and in younger birds the central tail feathers also black-tipped (both markings very inconspic. in field). ♀: grayish brown above; wings and tail brownish black; wing coverts and inner remiges edged white; throat and breast pale gray becoming white on abdomen. In flight wings broad and rounded.
**Voice:** No vocal sound known. A seldom heard call of 2-6 rapid *chue* or *chee* notes (oriolelike) is reported for allied *C. nitidus* of C America (Slud 1964). Latter's swooping display flight (♂) apparently silent (Skutch 1970b).
**Behavior:** Usually perch high, either in a screen of canopy foliage or prom. in open for shorter periods, esp. in early morning. Flap slowly with broad-winged, bounding flight like fruitcrow, as they fly from treetop to treetop. Single birds, pairs, or infrequently groups of 3-7 are sluggish but more active than *Cotinga*

82. White (Black-tipped) Cotinga (♀ left; ♂ right)

and usually more conspic. Often at *Cecropia* trees.

**Breeding:** 5 BC birds incl. laying ♀, Jan–Mar, Chocó (Carriker).

**Status and habitat:** Locally fairly common in humid and wet lowland and lower foothill forest or in second growth with scattered tall trees; also mangroves. Rarely far into foothills. Can reg. be seen n of km 100 on Cali-Buenaventura highway.

**Range:** To 1450m (rarely above 300m). Pacific coast from Panama border (Río Juradó) and upper Atrato Val. southward. E Panama (se Darién) to nw Ecuador.

**Note:** Sometimes merged with *C. nitidus* (Snowy Cotinga) of C America.

## 36. BARE-NECKED FRUITCROW

*Gymnoderus foetidus*     Pl. XIII, Map 925

**Identification:** ♂ 13.5″ (34cm); ♀ 12″ (30cm). ♂: *mainly black; wings silvery gray above and black below* (visible in flight); outer tail feathers gray. At close range, crown, hindneck and chin black, the feathers short, dense, and plushlike; *bare cobalt blue to white neck and throat skin* hangs in curious folds and lappets; bill blue gray tipped black; eyes red. ♀: more slaty and upper wing surface like back (not silvery). Juv.: gray, heavily vermiculated dusky below. In flight ad. ♂ shows flashing black and silver wing pattern.

**Similar species:** Chunky shape accentuated by thin bare neck and small head is diagnostic. Vulturine in appearance at close range.

**Voice:** No known vocalization.

**Behavior:** Alone or in groups of var. sizes, up to 20 or more. Eat mostly fruit, some insects, in canopy. Most often seen flying very high across rivers or other large open spaces (Hilty).

Loosely composed high-flying flocks may represent local migratory or wandering movements (J. V. Remsen). Reported wandering during longest dry season (Aug–Oct) in Surinam (Haverschmidt 1968).

**Breeding:** In Mato Grosso, small cryptic nest (in contrast to *Querula purpurata*) a few lichens and tendrils on horizontal branch 5-9m up; ♀ completely covers nest when incubating; 1 egg; no ♂ present at nests (Berault 1970).

**Status and habitat:** Often common along edges of large rivers (esp. in *Cecropia*), river isls. and borders of *várzea* and *terra firme* forests of Amazonia. Apparently much less numerous in sandy-belt forests of Vaupés and Guainía.

**Range:** To 500m. E of Andes from w Meta (Villavicencio) and Orinoco region (Mataveni, se Vichada) southward. The Guainas and s Venez. s to n Bolivia and Amazonian Brazil.

## 37. PURPLE-THROATED FRUITCROW

*Querula purpurata*     Pl. 33, Map 926

**Identification:** ♂ 11-12″ (28-30cm); ♀ 10-11″ (25-28cm). Chunky and short-legged. ♂: entirely black with slightly iridescent *purplish red throat* (fanned into broad gorget in display). ♀ and imm.: lack throat patch. In flight, shows broad rounded wings and short tail.

**Similar species:** ♂'s purple throat often hard to see. Behavior, distinctive silhouette, and calls are characteristic.

**Voice:** Noisy. Low, mellow whistles incl. *oo-waa*, a more drawn out, rising *wooooo* (Snow 1971a), *wheeooowhoo* (mid. *ooo* sliding lower, then rising), and other var. as well as harsher notes.

**Behavior:** Normally travel in small restless groups of 3-6 or so, attracting attention to themselves with repeated calls and swooping

flight as they bound into view. Perch well up in trees but often bold, curious, and easy to see. Frequently vibrate tail, esp. when excited. Pluck fruit in air with agile, trogonlike hover.
**Breeding:** 8 BC birds, Feb–May, ♀ on Mar nest, nw Colombia (Carriker). Dependent young with 2 or more ads., July, Buenaventura, 2 ads. building nest, June, Leticia (Hilty); 2 Guyana nests, Jan–early Apr, attended by communal groups of 3-4 ads.; stick- and vegetable-lined flattish nests 10-20m up or more, fairly conspic. in partially isolated tree; 1 dark olive egg thickly marked dark brown; long 32- to 33-day fledging period despite mostly insect diet (Snow 1971a).
**Status and habitat:** Common in humid forest and second growth woodland; favor broken forest, borders, and forest openings. Lowlands and foothills.
**Range:** To 1200m. Pacific coast, e in humid lowlands n of Andes into lower Cauca and mid. Magdalena Vals. (s to n boundary of Caldas); e of Andes from s Meta (Macarena Mts.) and Vaupés (sight El Dorado, 1976— R. Ridgely) southward. Costa Rica to w Ecuador, n Bolivia, and Amazonian Brazil.

## 38. RED-RUFFED FRUITCROW

*Pyroderus scutatus* Pl. XIII, Map 927
**Identification:** ♂ 17″ (43cm); ♀ 15″ (38cm). Black with feathers of *throat, chest, and sides of neck stiff, crimped, and shiny reddish orange*; breast with some chestnut mottling (or breast and upper belly solid chestnut—*occidentalis*); under wing coverts rufous brown; heavy bill silvery gray.
**Similar species:** Should be easily recognized at rest but on Pacific slope see Long-wattled Umbrellabird (40), which has sim. broad-winged shape in flight.
**Voice:** Usually silent. ♂♂ display on lek with low resonant booming, typically a 3-noted *umm-umm-umm* sounds like blowing across bottletop, repeated after long pauses (T. Parker) or upon arrival of other ♂♂ and ♀♀ at lek (P. Schwartz).
**Behavior:** ♂♂ hold small advertising territories at communal lek (Olalla 1943; P. Schwartz) and raise throat and breast feathers to form a ruff in display. Away from lek usually solitary or in pairs in midlevels or higher in trees; often at fruiting trees. Bounding flight.
**Breeding:** 4 BC birds, Apr–May, Perijá Mts. and n end W Andes (Carriker). Small, frail, stick platform located high; eggs (apparently 2 or more?) pale buff blotched and spotted shades of reddish brown and lilac, mostly at larger end (Sclater and Salvin 1879).
**Status and habitat:** Local in humid and wet forest (esp. "cloud forest"), forest borders, and

clearings with scattered trees. Now increasingly rare with habitat loss though often readily seen in W Andes above Queremal.
**Range:** 1600-2700m (sighting to 2900m, PN Farallones—F. C. Lehmann; once to 600m on Pacific slope in Cauca). W Andes and w slope C Andes (*occidentalis*); Perijá Mts., E Andes and e slope C Andes (*granadensis*). Guyana, se and w Venez., and the Andes to s Peru; ne Argentina, Paraguay, and se Brazil.

## 39. AMAZONIAN UMBRELLABIRD

*Cephalopterus ornatus* Pl. XIII, Map 928
**Identification:** ♂ 20″ (51cm); ♀ 18″ (46cm). *Bluish white eyes in both sexes*; heavy black bill. ♂: *black glossed bluish and with peculiar "umbrella-shaped" crest* (with white feather shafts); *wide flat pendent wattle* 3-4″ in length hanging from lower throat (wattle feathered in front, bare behind, and often not conspic. in field). ♀: crest less exaggerated and wattle shorter. In flight wings broad, tail short, and spiky crest erect.
**Similar species:** Woodpeckerlike (or even like a jay) in flight but *shows no white* and crest more prom. (woodpeckers hold crest flat in flight).
**Voice:** Normally silent. Displaying ♂♂ spread crest and utter a low prolonged *boooo*; resembles bellow of distant cattle (Taczanowski 1884).
**Behavior:** Single birds, pairs, or groups up to 6 or so move with big jaylike hops through rather open canopy and subcanopy limbs, or occas. sit for short periods in the open. Alert, rather wary, and most often seen in undulating flight as they cross rivers.
**Breeding:** BC ♂ and ♀, Mar, Macarena Mts. (Olivares 1962). In Peru, frail nest of long sticks 3m up in sapling (T. Parker); in Brazil, sim. flattish twig nest fairly high; 1(?) khaki brown egg with dark brown and lilac marks and spots (Sick 1951).
**Status and habitat:** Uncommon. Borders of large rivers and lakes, river isls., and broken *terra firme* or *várzea* forests. Often in *Cecropia* along large rivers. Usually *not* far inside unbroken lowland forest. Lowlands and foothills.
**Range:** To 1200m. E base of Andes from w Boyacá (Río Casanare) s and generally from w Meta and Vaupés (Mitú) southward. Sight rec. n to El Tuparro, Vichada, 1977 (T. O. Lemke). Guyana and s Venez. to Peru, n Bolivia, and Amazonian Brazil.
**Note:** Capuchinbird (*Perissocephalus tricolor*) of the Guianas, n Amazonian Brazil, and s Venez. will almost certainly be found in Colombia in se Guainía as it has been rec. at the mouth of Río Casiquiare near the east boundary and the upper Río Negro to the south. Large (14″), *bare blue gray crown and sides of head*; otherwise

cinnamon brown darkening to rufous brown on lower back and chestnut on lower underparts; wings and tail blackish; *under wing coverts white*. Local in small dispersed leks in canopy. Has 2 far-carrying calls, 1 a calflike *moo*, the other a growling *grrraaaaooooooooo* (Snow 1961), the latter like a distant chain saw.

## 40. LONG-WATTLED UMBRELLABIRD

*Cephalopterus penduliger*      Pl. XIII, Map 929
**Identification:** ♂ 20″ (51cm). ♀ 18″ (46cm). *Eyes brown* in both sexes. ♂: sim. to Amazonian Umbrellabird but crest not as well developed, crest feathers with black (not white) shafts and *wattle much longer* (11-13″, or 28-33cm), round and completely feathered; underwings sometimes mottled whitish. ♀ and imm.: wattle shorter or almost lacking.
**Similar species:** Imm. and ♀ recall Red-ruffed Fruitcrow (38), esp. in flight, but crest almost always visible. At rest fruitcrow's fiery red throat usually obvious.
**Voice:** Usually silent. In display ♂ ♂ jump from branch to branch with spread crest, and wattle and throat distended as they utter a prolonged grunt (Goodfellow 1901).
**Behavior:** Usually alone perched in canopy, sometimes on an exposed bare limb for short per. but shy (?) and hard to approach. Flight is strong, slightly undulating, and woodpeckerlike; sometimes can be seen in flight crossing large steep valleys. Wattle can be lengthened or shortened at will and is held drawn up close to chest in flight. Rare in upper Anchicayá and adj. Río Verde vals., Valle (about 6 sightings in 15 mos., 1972-73—Hilty).
**Status and habitat:** Rare and local. Humid and wet mt. forest ("cloud forest"), forest borders, and isolated trees in clearings.
**Range:** 700-1800m. Pacific slope in Valle (sightings, Anchicayá Val.), Cauca, and Nariño. W Colombia and nw Ecuador.

## 41. BEARDED BELLBIRD

*Procnias averano*
**Identification:** 11″ (28cm). Perijá Mts. ♂: *mainly grayish white with brown head and black wings*; bare throat with numerous short black mosslike wattles giving an unkempt bearded appearance. ♀ and imm.: olive green above, head more dusky; *underparts streaked dull yellowish and green*; bare throat gray with a few fine pale feathers.
**Similar species:** ♂ unmistakable. ♀ recalls ♀ Golden-breasted Fruiteater (9) but is twice the size and much darker.
**Voice:** In Venez. 3 main calls (only 1st 2 in Trinidad): advertising call a remarkably loud dull *bock* at intervals of a few sec (can be heard nearly 2km away); a ser. of "hammer-on-an-

vil" calls, *tonk, tonk, tonk . . . ,*" repeated 1-2.5 times a sec; a more musical *kering-kerong* at intervals. ♀ ♀ apparently silent. In Trinidad vocal yr.-round except Oct molt (Snow 1970); in n Venez. call mainly Jan—July (P. Schwartz).
**Behavior:** Polygamous ♂ ♂ spend most of each day calling on permanent territories, either advertising from exposed perches above canopy or giving other calls and ritualized displays lower in canopy or mid. story. Ventriloquial and difficult to locate. Ad. and young eat almost wholly fruit, mainly large protein rich drupes of Lauraceae and Burseraceae. Large seeds regurgitated.
**Breeding:** In Trinidad Apr–July, a few Oct–Nov; all nest activities by ♀; inconspic. twig platform 3-15m up; 1 light tan egg mottled brown; long 33-day fledging period (Snow 1970).
**Status and habitat:** Humid forest; status unknown.
**Range:** 150-600m. Known only from Montes de Oca region at n end of Perijá Mts. Perhaps mid. Magdalena Val. n of Río Sogamosa in nw Santander (Wyatt 1871). Ne Colombia to Guyana and ne Brazil. Trinidad.
**Note:** The Sharpbill (*Oxyruncus cristatus*) (Ill. 83) of Costa Rica, Panama, se Venez., Guyana, Surinam, Peru, Brazil, and Paraguay occurs on Cerro Tacarcuna, e Panama, and likely occurs in nw Colombia. 6″; plump and sharpbilled; eyes orange. Mostly olive green above; sides of crown black; central crown usually with concealed red orange patch; below yellowish white *thickly spotted black*. Active as they search large limbs and terminal foliage in canopy and subcanopy for insects or visit fruit trees; occas. hang upside down like parids and reg. with mixed canopy flocks. Song a high, drawn-out buzzy trill, *zeeeeeeeeeuuuuu'-u'u'u'u'u'*, coarse and slightly descending (T. Davis). Found in foothills and lower montane forest.

83. SHARPBILL

# FLYCATCHERS: Tyrannidae (183)

The tyrant flycatchers are the largest strictly New World family of birds. They are found from the arctic to Tierra del Fuego but reach the greatest diversity and abundance in warmer tropical regions. Most north and south temperate breeders are migratory, and many occur in Colombia as nonbreeding residents during the north and south temperate winters. Flycatchers occur in every Colombian habitat from the seacoast to snowline and are extremely diverse in behavior and appearance. Unlike most north temperate migrants, which are predominantly arboreal and sally for insects on their breeding grounds, those of tropical and south temperate latitudes include terrestrial species, some of which run rapidly on the ground, and arboreal species that sally to air or to foliage, glean foliage like vireos, or eat mostly fruit. Field identification of the many similar species can be very difficult, and some knowledge of shapes, and voice and habits of the genera is essential. Breeding systems and ♂ participation at the nest vary, but monogamy predominates. In a few genera, including *Oncostoma*, *Lophotriccus*, *Pipromorpha*, and possibly *Laniocera* and *Cnipodectes*, ♂ ♂ remain on display leks much of the time and breeding is polygamous. Nest sites range from the ground or on buttress roots to the canopy; nest shape varies from simple open cups and closed domes to the elaborate suspended nests of *Onychorhynchus*, *Rhynchocyclus*, and others. A few, notably *Myiarchus*, are cavity nesters; *Legatus* pirates nests from other birds. The present classification follows Traylor (1977).

## 1. SOOTY-HEADED (SOOTY-CRESTED) TYRANNULET

*Phyllomyias griseiceps*  Pl. 36, Map 930

**Identification:** 4" (10.2cm). Short bill. Slight bushy crest. *Cap dusky* (or da1k olive gray— *griseiceps*); short white eyebrow bordered below by dusky line through eye and smudge on cheeks; otherwise olive above, wings darker, remiges edged whitish (*no wing bars*); throat grayish white; *rest of underparts pale yellow* with olive wash on chest rather sharply demarked from yellow belly.

**Similar species:** Shape of *Zimmerius* and *Tyrannulus* (see 7-9, 16) but told by distinct dark cap, short eyebrow, and lack of wing bars (*Zimmerius* lack bars but have crisp yellow, not white, edgings on wing coverts and remiges). Also cf. Southern Beardless-Tyrannulet (12).

**Voice:** Song a bright rhythmic *whit, wheet-wheet-wheeu*, frequently (Hilty); also a slightly trilled *tee'p'p'pip*, over and over (P. Schwartz recording).

**Behavior:** Usually alone in midlevel to canopy foliage where sallies or flutters short distances up to underside of leaves, or gleans and flits like a kinglet (*Regulus*). Often calls from an exposed perch on top of foliage.

**Breeding:** Pair bringing insects to 2 (3?) young in small lichen-encrusted cup on crotch of small, partially shaded dead branch 13m up, nw Ecuador, Feb (R. Ridgely).

**Status and habitat:** Often common (easily overlooked). Drier woodlots, shrubby tree-scattered semiopen terrain, and humid forest borders.

**Range:** Recs. widely scattered (see range map). Extreme nw Chocó (Río Juradó) e to Santa Marta region and s to upper Magdalena Val.

(*cristatus*); mid. and upper Cauca Val. (*caucae*); sight recs., 1980 (Hilty), Río Verde del Sinú (subsp.?); also undoubtedly e Norte de Santander (*cristatus*) and sw Nariño (*griseiceps*). E Panama, w Ecuador; n and s Venez., Guyana; nw and e Brazil; n and c Peru.

## 2. PLUMBEOUS-CROWNED TYRANNULET

*Phyllomyias plumbeiceps*  Pl. 36, Map 931

**Identification:** 4.6" (11.7cm). *Short bill. Crown and nape dark gray; white eyebrow* bordered below by dusky streak through eye; sides of head whitish; *dusky black crescent on ear coverts* faintly rimmed whitish; otherwise olive green above; wings dusky with *2 prom. yellow wing bars* and yellow edgings; throat whitish; remaining underparts yellow; chest and sides washed olive.

**Similar species:** See Marble-faced and Variegated bristle-tyrants (52, 54). Not easily told from Ashy-headed Tyrannulet (6), which differs mainly by yellowish (not whitish) throat and faint streaking on breast; also perhaps by more blue gray crown, and more greenish yellow sides of head. Sooty-headed Tyrannulet (1) lacks auricular crescent and wing bars.

**Behavior:** Often with bird flocks in forest mid. story. Flashes up 1 wing and then the other. Sallies mostly short distances to foliage.

**Status and habitat:** Uncommon in humid and wet mossy forest. Perhaps somewhat local.

**Range:** 1300-2200m. Both slopes of W Andes from Valle southward, w slope C Andes, w slope E Andes in Cundinamarca (below Bogotá), and head of Magdalena Val. No Nariño recs. Colombia and e Ecuador s in Andes to s Peru.

**Note:** By some placed in the genus *Oreotriccus*.

## 3. ROUGH-LEGGED TYRANNULET
*Phyllomyias burmeisteri*
**Identification:** 4.5″ (11.4cm). Olive above with *dark gray cap and sharp white eyebrow distinctly broadest over lores and on forehead*; narrow line through eye dusky; cheeks grizzled gray and white (not conspic.); wings dusky with yellowish white edgings and *2 yellowish wing bars; throat whitish*; rest of underparts pale yellow with some indistinct olive streaking and mottling on breast; eyes whitish.
**Similar species:** Much like Slender-footed and Yellow-crowned tyrannulets (8,16) though not definitely known to overlap in range. From either by slightly larger size, sharper whiter eyestripe distinctly narrowed over and behind eye, gray and white flecked cheeks, and definite yellow wing bars; from latter by white throat. In the hand no yellow crown patch and bill thicker (but not broad) and longer.
**Voice:** In w Caquetá a buzzy *t'e'eeeszip*, at 5-sec intervals or less (Hilty); in Brazil a rather sim. insectlike *zeeeeup, zeeeeup* . . . (W. Belton recording). In Costa Rica, where perhaps a different sp., excited insistent *psss psss psss* (Slud 1964).
**Behavior:** Active as it flits up to foliage, changes perches often, then pauses to cock head and peer. One or 2 stay midlevel to well up in trees; posture rather horizontal like *Zimmerius*, but tail level with body or only slightly cocked. Occas. flicks up a wing as do *Leptopogon* and some others.
**Status and habitat:** Few recs. Humid forest borders and clearings.
**Range:** Foothills and lower slopes. E slope E Andes in Meta (once, Buenavista, 1250m) and w Caquetá (2 seen above Florencia, 600m, 12 June 1981—Hilty). Spotty. Costa Rica and w Panama; Venez., e Colombia, sw and se Ecuador, se Peru, e Bolivia to n Argentina, and se Brazil.
**Note 1:** Often placed in the genus *Acrochordopus*. **Note 2:** *P. zeledoni* (Zeledon's Tyrannulet) of Costa Rica and Panama has been considered distinct from the S American forms. **Note 3:** Birds of Venez. and Colombia to Peru have been lumped with Mid. American birds, *P. zeledoni* (White-fronted Tyrannulet). **Note 4:** Birds of e Bolivia to se Brazil have been considered a distinct sp., *P. burmeisteri* (Rough-legged Tyrannulet).

## 4. BLACK-CAPPED TYRANNULET
*Phyllomyias nigrocapillus*          Pl. 36, Map 932
**Identification:** 4.5″ (11.4cm). Short bill. *Black cap with prom. white eyebrow*; otherwise dark olive above; *wings black with 2 yellowish white wing bars*; inner remiges edged yellowish white;

throat grayish; *rest of underparts pale yellow*; breast washed olive. Or as above but cap dark brown, eyebrow and entire underparts pale yellow *(flavimentum)*.
**Similar species:** See Tawny-rumped Tyrannulet (5). White-banded tyrannulet (34) is white below and has gray (not black) crown. Brown-capped Vireo (p 557) lacks wing bars.
**Voice:** Call a clear, high *peeeeep*, unflycatcherlike, often persistently repeated.
**Behavior:** Active and warblerlike as it hops and gleans in foliage from lower midlevel to canopy; 1 or 2 often accompany mixed flocks. Carries tail slightly up at times.
**Breeding:** 6 BC birds, Mar–Nov, Santa Marta, n end C and E Andes (Carriker).
**Status and habitat:** Uncommon to fairly common in clearings, open woodland, and humid forest borders. Often into stunted forest up to treeline (in PN Puracé mainly 3000-3300m—J. Silliman).
**Range:** 1600-3400m (usually above 2400m). Santa Marta Mts. *(flavimentum)*; E Andes from n Norte de Santander s to Cundinamarca, C Andes (incl. once, 950m, Snía. San Lucas), and W Andes in Antioquia, Valle, and Cauca *(nigrocapillus)*. Nw Venez. s in Andes to c Peru.
**Note:** Sometimes placed in the genus *Tyranniscus*.

## 5. TAWNY-RUMPED TYRANNULET
*Phyllomyias uropygialis*          Pl. 36, Map 933
**Identification:** 4.4″ (11.2cm). Short bill. *Cap dusky brown; narrow forehead and eyebrow white*; upperparts olive brown shading to *tawny on rump and upper tail coverts*; tail dusky; *wings black with 2 pale buff wing bars* and pale buff edgings; sides of head grayish; throat and chest pale gray; chest and sides washed brownish; lower underparts yellowish white.
**Similar species:** Resembles Black-capped Tyrannulet (4), but rump tawny, wing bars buffy, and lower underparts paler yellow (almost white). Also see White-tailed and White-banded flycatchers (32, 34).
**Behavior:** Like a Black-capped Tyrannulet. Active and warblerlike as it follows canopy or midlevel bird flocks in forest or at edges (T. Parker).
**Status and habitat:** Humid forest and shrubby forest borders. Not well known in Colombia. Recs. spotty.
**Range:** 1500-2600m (to 3100m in Venez.). E Andes in Santander (Angostura), Cundinamarca (e and s of Bogotá at Choachí and Une), and Meta (above Villavicencio at Caños Negros); W Andes in Cauca and Nariño. Nw Venez. s spottily in Andes to Bolivia.

## 6. ASHY-HEADED TYRANNULET
*Phyllomyias cinereiceps*          Pl. 36, Map 934
**Identification:** 4″ (10.2cm). Short bill; dark red eyes. *Pale olive green above with contrasting blue gray crown*; narrow lores and eyering white; sides of head pale greenish yellow with *prom. black crescent on ear coverts*; wings dusky; *2 yellowish white wing bars* and yellowish white edgings; below bright yellow flammulated olive on throat and breast (*looks faintly and finely streaked*).
**Similar species:** Plumage pattern much like that of bristle-tyrants (52, 54), Plumbeous-crowned Tyrannulet (2), and larger Slaty-capped Flycatcher (48). From all by distinctly blue gray (not dark gray or dusky) cap, greenish yellow (not grayish or whitish) sides of head surrounding crescent, and cleaner yellow underparts (no. 2 has whitish throat).
**Behavior:** One or 2 often join canopy or upper level forest flocks. Sit upright or slightly hunched and look about alertly, then change perches quickly or flit to foliage; occas. cling briefly to leaves.
**Status and habitat:** Apparently local. Wet mossy forest. Common from 1900-2300m in PN Cueva de los Guácharos (P. Gertler; Hilty); few recs. elsewhere.
**Range:** 1800-2700m. Spotty. W Andes in Cauca (incl. once to 400m?, upper Patía Val., Cauca), C Andes s to head to Magdalena Val. in Huila and w slope E Andes from Santander (near Bucaramanga, 850m) s to near Bogotá (Santandercito). Andes of Colombia, e and w Ecuador, and Peru.
**Note:** By some placed in the genus *Tyranniscus.*

[*Zimmerius*: Stubby pointed bill; short eyebrow; wing coverts and remiges crisply edged yellow (no distinct wing bars). Longish narrow tail slightly cocked up; characteristically perch on top of leaves, esp. *Cecropia.*]

## 7. PALTRY TYRANNULET
*Zimmerius vilissimus*          Pl. 36, Map 935
**Identification:** 4.7″ (12cm) (or 4″ [10.2cm]—*parvus*). Eyes dark (or pale—*parvus*). *Slaty cap* contrasts with olive back; *forehead and short eyestripe white; wings dusky with sharp yellow edgings* (no bars); bend of shoulder yellow (usually concealed); below light gray; sides and lower belly tinged yellow.
**Similar species:** Golden-faced Tyrannulet (9) has crown concolor with back and short yellowish eyestripe (yellow not obvious at a distance); otherwise sim. Good marks for both are crisp yellow wing edging and grayish white underparts (most other forest-based tyran-

nulets in range are yellowish below and also have wing bars).
**Voice:** In Panama, and prob. extreme nw Colombia, a heavy *chee-yíp* or *vireo*; a fast *pier-he-he-he-he* (Willis and Eisemann 1979); at dawn a short *beef, beer* rather like Golden-faced Tyrannulet.
**Behavior:** Singly or in pairs, either alone or occas. with mixed flocks. Glean, sally short distances, and flutter in outer foliage from understory to canopy; often eat small berries.
**Breeding:** 5 BC birds, Mar–Nov, Perijá Mts. and n end E Andes (Carriker); in Costa Rica late Jan–Sept. Domed nest with side entrance; usually fastened to or in tuft of hanging moss; 2 white eggs speckled or blotched cinnamon (Skutch 1960).
**Status and habitat:** Fairly common in humid forest, forest borders, lighter woodland, and clearings with scattered trees in Santa Marta highlands.
**Range:** To 100m in extreme nw Chocó (Río Juradó; Acandí) near Panama border (*parvus*); 1500-2400m in Santa Marta and Perijá mts.; 1200-2300m at n end of E Andes s to Pamplona, Norte de Santander (*tamae*). Se Mexico to nw Colombia; nc Colombia to nw and n Venez.
**Note 1:** Sometimes placed in the genus *Tyranniscus.* **Note 2:** More than 1 sp. may be involved.

## 8. SLENDER-FOOTED TYRANNULET
*Zimmerius gracilipes*          Pl. 36, Map 936
**Identification:** 4″ (10.2cm). Tiny bill; eyes pale. *Grayish crown contrasts with olive back; short eyestripe dull white*; lores blackish; wings blackish; *inner remiges crisply edged yellow*; wing coverts faintly edged yellow (weak wing bars); throat dingy white becoming light yellowish olive on breast and clear pale yellow on belly. Narrow tail usually slightly cocked up.
**Similar species:** Easily confused. Yellow-crowned Tyrannulet (16) has dusky cap, semiconcealed yellow crown patch (usually not visible), definite whitish wing bars, and dark eyes (hard to see). Also see Rough-legged (3) and Red-billed tyrannulets (note). In e Andean foothills may meet Golden-faced Tyrannulet (see 9).
**Voice:** Call a soft inflected *what?* (J. V. Remsen).
**Behavior:** Inconspic. and hard to see. Alone or in pairs, sometimes in bird flocks, and usually in outer canopy foliage of large trees. Gleans and flutters in leaves like others of the genus.
**Breeding:** ♀ ready to lay, Amazonas, 14 June (J. V. Remsen). Rounded dome nest with side

entrance; 2 dull white eggs spotted chestnut and lilac at larger end (Beebe et al. 1917).
**Status and habitat:** Fairly common (usually overlooked) in humid *terra firme* and *várzea* forests, forest borders, and clearings with scattered trees.
**Range:** To 500m. E of Andes from w Putumayo (Pto. Umbría) and e Vichada (Maipures) southward. The Guianas and s Venez. to n Bolivia and Amazonian Brazil.
**Note 1:** Sometimes placed in the genus *Tyranniscus*. **Note 2:** Red-billed Tyrannulet (*Z. cinereicapillus*) of ne Ecuador (Napo-Pastaza) and e Peru may occur in se Colombia. A little larger (5″) than Slender-footed Tyrannulet; above olive with gray tinged crown and nape, below plain whitish yellow, throat whitish, wings dusky, wing coverts and inner remiges sharply edged yellow (weak bars), lower mandible dull reddish flesh (inconspic.). Tall forest canopy where easily overlooked.

## 9. GOLDEN-FACED TYRANNULET
*Zimmerius viridiflavus* Pl. 36, Map 937
**Identification:** 4.3″ (10.9cm). Tiny bill; eyes dark. Olive above incl. crown; *narrow forehead and short eyebrow golden yellow*; wings dusky; *wing coverts and inner remiges sharply edged yellow* (weak wing bars) below grayish white; abdomen and under tail coverts tinged yellow.
**Similar species:** Dull and nondescript. The yellow eyebrow and wing edgings (no distinct bars) are the marks. See under Paltry Tyrannulet (7).
**Voice:** One of *the* characteristic calls in the canopy of highland forest; a querulous, inflected *hueer?* and at dawn *teer-tif*, distinctive once learned; also a plaintive *chu-de-de'e'e*, and high-pitched *peer, pear, ptrtititi* dropping; in aerial chase (display?) a loud mechanical wing flutter.
**Behavior:** Perky and active as it hops and flits in outer canopy foliage. Alone or with mixed flocks. Often perches exposed on outer perimeter of tree crown. Like others of genus, usually carries tail "half-cocked."
**Breeding:** 13 BC birds, Mar–Dec, W, C, and E Andes (Carriker; Miller 1963); 1 nest, June, W Andes (S. Gniadek); building nest, Sept, above Florencia, Apr, June, and Nov nests in Anchicayá Val. (1000m); dome-shaped ball nest with side entrance; tucked in hanging moss 8-12m up (Hilty).
**Status and habitat:** Common in humid and wet forest, forest borders, and tall trees in clearings in foothills and lower highlands.
**Range:** 300-2400m (occas. to 100m but not in lowlands; rarely to 2700m). Santa Marta and

Perijá Mts. and all 3 Andean ranges. Nw Venez. s in Andes to Peru.
**Note:** Often placed in the genus *Tyranniscus*.

## 10. WHITE-LORED TYRANNULET
*Ornithion inerme* Pl. 36, Map 938
**Identification:** 3.6″ (9.1cm). *Tiny with very short tail. Short thick bill.* Olive above with *gray crown; prom. narrow white eyeline from nostril to rear edge of eye* and white lower eyelid (forms "spectacles"); wings dusky with faint yellowish edgings and *2 rows of large white spots forming spotlike wing bars* (like wing spots of an antbird); throat grayish white becoming olive yellow on chest and yellow on center of belly.
**Similar species:** Easily recognized by small size and distinctive "white-spotted" wing bars.
**Voice:** In se Peru sings from treetop perch often over wooded swamps; a repetitious, high-pitched *whee-whee-whee-whee-whee* (Parker 1982).
**Behavior:** Actively hop and glean like vireos in foliage from very high in forest canopy to mid. story; often with bird flocks.
**Status and habitat:** Few recs. Humid forest, scrubby sandy-belt forest, gallery forest, and woodland borders; also *várzea* forest (R. Ridgely). Replaced w of Andes by next sp.
**Range:** To 300m. Known from w Putumayo (Pto. Umbría), e Vichada (Maipures), and ne Guainía (sighting, Sept 1978, Pto. Inírida—Hilty). Prob. more widespread. The Guianas and e and s Venez. southward e of Andes to Bolivia and n Argentina.

## 11. BROWN-CAPPED TYRANNULET
*Ornithion brunneicapillum* Pl. 36, Map 939
**Identification:** 3.3″ (8.4cm). *Tiny with very short tail. Short thick bill.* Olive green above with *dark brown cap; sharp white eyebrow extends to behind eye*; wings dusky with weak greenish yellow edgings (no bars); *underparts bright yellow*; throat and breast with faint olive tinge.
**Similar species:** Told by tiny size, brown cap, and eyestripe.
**Voice:** Distinctive: 4-6 fast, piping, downscale whistles, *pee, pih-pey-peh-püh*; also a high *peep* (Eisenmann 1952).
**Behavior:** Active and vireolike as they hop among terminal twigs and foliage in canopy, less often to lower story. Often accompanies forest bird flocks.
**Breeding:** 2 BC birds, Jan–Feb, Chocó and n Antioquia (Carriker). In Panama, building nest, 12m up in semiopen woodland, Aug; untidy flat saucer on small fork (Wetmore 1972); July nest 3.5m up in small tree, w Ecuador; pair feeding 2 nestlings (R. Ridgely).
**Status and habitat:** Uncommon in canopy of humid lowland and foothill forest, forest bor-

ders, and second growth woodland. Several recent sightings in PN Tayrona.
**Range:** To 600m(?). Pacific coast, e north of Andes in humid lowlands to mid. Magdalena Val. (s to Pto. Berrío, e Antioquia); humid n foothills of Santa Marta Mts. Costa Rica to nw Ecuador and n and w Venez. (incl. Perijá Mts.).
**Note:** Often merged with *O. semiflavum* (Yellow-bellied Tyrannulet) of s Mexico to n Costa Rica.

## 12. SOUTHERN BEARDLESS-TYRANNULET

*Camptostoma obsoletum*          Pl. 36, Map 940
**Identification:** 3.8″ (9.7cm). Small. *Distinct peaked crest and "sleepy-eyed" look.* Bill dusky above, orange yellow below. Brownish olive above with *noticeably darker brown cap* (or crown like back— *bogotensis*); weak eyering and *narrow eyebrow whitish,* wings dark brown; wing edgings and *2 wing bars dull white;* throat grayish white; *otherwise very pale yellow below* with light olive wash on chest (or throat and breast light olive yellow, rest of underparts yellow—*olivaceum*). Young birds have buffy wing bars.
**Similar species:** Cap darker, crest bushier, and wing bars whiter than others of sim. plumage. The small-eyed, peaked-headed appearance is distinctive once learned. Cf. with Mouse-colored and Slender-billed tyrannulets (13, 37). Pale-tipped Tyrannulet (38) has dusky tail and pale eyes; Sooty-headed Tyrannulet (1) a dusky head.
**Voice:** Loud but plaintive and descending *plee-plee-pee-pee-pee* or sim. var.; also melancholy *to-rée* (usually doubled or trebled).
**Behavior:** Single birds or pairs peer and glean like vireos on twigs and foliage 2-10m up; also flutter to leaves, occas. sally short distances to air within tree. Confiding and appealing as carry tail slightly cocked up and call frequently.
**Breeding:** 6 BC birds, Jan–June, n Colombia and Valle (Carriker; Miller 1963); BC birds Jan–Mar, ne Meta (S. Furniss). Globular nest with side entrance; 1-4m up in shrub or tree, often near wasp's nest; 2 white eggs spotted lilac and reddish brown, mainly at larger end (Marchant 1960).
**Status and habitat:** Fairly common; tolerates a wide var. of habitats from dry scrubby to humid and wet shrubby regions, clearings, and gardens.
**Range:** To 2000m (mainly below 1200m). Throughout (except Pacific coast lowlands from Juradó, nw Chocó southward; and Guajira). W of Andes (*caucae*); Arauca and Boyacá (*napaeum*), w Meta (*bogotensis*), w Caquetá to Amazonas (*olivaceum*). Sw Costa Rica to n Argentina and se Brazil.

## 13. MOUSE-COLORED TYRANNULET

*Phaeomyias murina*          Pl. 36, Map 941
**Identification:** 5″ (13cm). Very plain and nondescript. Bill blackish above, pale below. Grayish brown to *plain dull brown* above with *dingy white eyestripe;* wings dusky with edgings and *2 wing bars pale buff;* throat whitish becoming dull grayish on breast and dirty white faintly tinged yellow on belly.
**Similar species:** Easily confused. Brownish with weak eyestripe and buffy bars. Southern Beardless (12) is perkier, more crested, and with whitish bars and cleaner pale yellow belly. Scrub Flycatcher (14) has stubbier black bill and erect posture. Also cf. Fuscous Flycatcher (118) and smaller Slender-billed Tyrannulet (37).
**Voice:** Call a weak *czert,* often followed by brief rattle (Hilty); harsh, fast, chattering *jejejejeje-jew,* varied to *jejejejéw* (R. Ridgely); dawn song several clear, rising *pip* notes followed by a jumbled chatter (J. Fitzpatrick).
**Behavior:** Inconspic. as it gleans and flutters in foliage, 2-8m up. Alone or in pairs. Does not follow mixed flocks as there are few in the more open areas it prefers.
**Breeding:** 14 BC birds, May–Oct, Santa Marta and Cúcuta (Carriker). Feeding juv., Jan; brood patches June–Sept, Santa Marta (S. M. Russell); July fledging, ne Meta (S. Furniss); building nest, June, Valle (Hilty). Small, grassy, feather-lined cup, to 6m up in tree fork (Haverschmidt 1972b; Cherrie 1916). Two eggs, pale cream or white (Marchant 1960).
**Status and habitat:** Common in drier scrubby or shrubby areas, lighter woodland borders, parks, and gardens. Local in Amazonia.
**Range:** To 1000m, once to 1700m. W of W Andes only in upper Dagua and upper Patía vals.; Cartagena e to w Guajira and s in Cauca Val. to Cauca and in Magdalena Val. to n Huila; spottily throughout e of Andes. W Panama to nw Argentina, Paraguay, and se Brazil. Trinidad.

## 14. SCRUB FLYCATCHER

*Sublegatus arenarum*          Pl. 37, Map 942
**Identification:** 6″ (15cm). Resembles a miniature *Myiarchus.* Slight crest. *Short black bill* (wider at base than *Elaenia*). Grayish brown above; whitish supraloral stripe and narrow grayish eyering (broken in front); wings dusky; edgings and *2 prom. wing bars grayish white; throat and breast gray in sharp contrast to pale yellow lower underparts.*
**Similar species:** *Myiarchus* have longer bills and lack the supraloral and wing bars. Resembles several elaenias (17, 20, 25) but none with such distinctly "divided" (gray and yellow) underparts; also told by short black bill and supra-

loral (in the hand no crown patch). Cf. Short-billed Flycatcher (15).
**Voice:** Rather quiet. Call a plaintive *chee*, sometimes doubled; also *chee, teeateea*, and clear high *peew-wit* near Santa Marta.
**Behavior:** Inconspic. and rather sluggish as they sit upright with tail down, in thicket, low scrub, or shade of smaller tree (occas. fully exposed in open). Sally short distances to air or pick at foliage, occas. at fruiting shrub; alone or in pairs.
**Breeding:** Stub-tailed young, Aug, Santa Marta (Hilty); BC ♂, Jan, ne Meta (S. Furniss); 1 in Mar, s Bolívar (Carriker). Venez. Orinoco nest, Apr (Cherrie 1916). Simple cup 2-6m up; 2 creamy white eggs with wreath of dark brown at larger end (ffrench 1973).
**Status and habitat:** Fairly common resident in dry scrub, deciduous thorn woodland, and mangroves. One s temperate migrant (*brevirostris*) taken 4 Oct 1960 at Mitú (Olivares 1964a).
**Range:** To 500m. From n Sucre (Snía. de San Jacinto) e to Guajira and s in Magdalena Val. to Simití (8°N), s Bolívar (*atrirostris*); e of Andes in e Meta (*orinocensis*); and nw Meta at Villavicencio. Costa Rica, Panama, n Colombia, Venez. to the coastal Guianas. Trinidad. Austral breeders migrate n to e Peru and Amazonian Brazil, rarely (?) to e Colombia.
**Note:** For taxonomy of *Sublegatus* followed here see Traylor (1982).

## 15. SHORT-BILLED FLYCATCHER
*Sublegatus modestus*                     Map 943
**Identification:** Sim. to Scrub Flycatcher (14), but *wing bars dull gray and indistinct; throat and breast darker* ashy gray blending into yellowish *white belly*.
**Similar species:** Cf. Southern Beardless and Mouse-colored tyrannulets (12, 13), Fuscous Flycatcher (118), and Small-billed Elaenia (23); none with such distinctly "divided" underparts.
**Behavior:** Sim. to Scrub Flycatcher.
**Status and habitat:** Local in gallery forest borders and semiopen savanna woodland or pockets of scrub in humid forested zones.
**Range:** To 500m. E of Andes in Meta (Villavicencio) and w Putumayo (Pto. Umbría). Doubtless e Vaupés (rec. near e boundary, Río Vaupés, Brazil. No Amazonas recs. E Colombia to e Peru, nw Bolivia and e to c and e Venez., the Guianas, and ne Brazil.
**Note:** For taxonomy followed here see Traylor (1982).

[*Tyrannulus*: Shape of *Zimmerius*, but told from it or allied *Phyllomyias* by yellow crown patch; plumper than *Zimmerius*.]

## 16. YELLOW-CROWNED TYRANNULET
*Tyrannulus elatus*               Pl. 36, Map 944
**Identification:** 4" (10.2cm). Tiny and plump; stubby bill. Olive brown above with *dusky cap, sometimes with large semiconcealed yellow crown stripe* showing; short grayish eyebrow bordered below by dark line through eye; *2 white wing bars* and whitish edgings; *throat and sides of head light gray*; rest of underparts dull yellow with olive tinge on breast and sides. Juv. lacks yellow crown patch.
**Similar species:** In plumage a miniature of Forest Elaenia (17) but plumper and bill stubbier. If diagnostic crown patch is concealed (usually), then much like Slender-footed Tyrannulet (8), but latter has crisp yellow (not white) edgings, no distinct wing bars, and slimmer shape. Also cf. Sooty-headed Tyrannulet (1; no wing bars), Rough-legged Tyrannulet and Southern Beardless-Tyrannulet (3, 12), and Forest Elaenia (17).
**Voice:** Distinctive call, persistently uttered even during the heat of the day, a brief whistled (little "wolf-whistle") *pree teer* or *wee wheer*.
**Behavior:** Often heard, though inconspic. and sometimes hard to see. Sits alone at mod. ht. in foliage or in tops of smaller trees, flits short distances to foliage or takes small berries. Not with mixed flocks and unlike *Zimmerius* and *Phyllomyias*, does not carry tail cocked up.
**Breeding:** 11 BC birds, Jan–Sept, nw Colombia, 2 in June, w Caquetá (Carriker); fledglings, July, Aug nest, fine shallow cup 10m up, Panama (Eisenmann); a Mar nest, 8m up on horizontal branch, 2 nestlings, Panama (R. Ridgely).
**Status and habitat:** Common (need to know call) in lighter woodland, forest borders, shrubby clearings, and gardens; also canopy of *várzea* forest. Mod. dry to humid regions.
**Range:** To 1000m. Throughout w and e of Andes. W Panama to nw Ecuador, n Bolivia, and Amazonian Brazil.

[*Myiopagis*: Smaller and somewhat darker-capped than *Elaenia*; bill smaller than *Tolmomyias*. Semiconcealed crown patch yellow or white.]

## 17. FOREST ELAENIA
*Myiopagis gaimardii*            Pl. 37, Map 945
**Identification:** 5" (13cm). Eyes dark; base of lower mandible pale. Above greenish olive; crown slightly darker and slatier and with a usually concealed whitish to pale yellow crown patch (or *bright yellow—macilvainii*); indistinct white eyebrow and eyering; wings dark brown with *greenish yellow edgings and 2 conspic. yellowish wing bars*; throat grayish white; other-

wise pale yellowish below with a suggestion of olive or olive streaking on chest.
**Similar species:** Often confused. Greenish Elaenia (19) lacks the prom. wing bars and shows more contrast in underparts (grayer throat and chest). Also easily mistaken for a *Tolmomyias*, all of which have broader, flatter bills (87-90).
**Voice:** A sharp emphatic *pitchweet* (Eisenmann) or *pill-dweet* (J. Fitzpatrick), or *chuwéep*, last half rising and usually with a long pause betw. repetitions.
**Behavior:** Often with mixed flocks in canopy or at forest edge and usually difficult to see. Perch-gleans among twigs and foliage and eats small berries. Sometimes cocks tail slightly.
**Breeding:** 8 BC birds, Mar–Sept, Córdoba to Guajira, n Colombia (Carriker); building nest, Feb, Panama (Wetmore 1972). Cup 3-5m up; sim. to that of Yellow-bellied Elaenia but smaller and unlined; 2 eggs, pale cream marked deep red brown and lavender at larger end (ffrench 1973).
**Status and habitat:** Fairly common (essential to know voice or otherwise usually overlooked) in humid forest, forest edge, tall second growth, and gallery woodland; frequently along rivers. Fewer recs. e of Andes, but prob. overlooked (common at Limoncocha, Ecuador— R. Ridgely).
**Range:** To 600m(?). Carib. lowlands from upper Río Sinú e to w and s base of Santa Marta Mts. and se Guajira (*macilvainii*); n side of Santa Marta and e of Andes from Norte de Santander and Arauca to Putumayo (*bogotensis*); Vichada to Vaupés (Mitú) and prob. Amazonas (*guianensis*). A rec. of *gaimardii* from Meta is poss. a s migrant. C Panama to n Bolivia and se Brazil. Trinidad.

## 18. GRAY ELAENIA
*Myiopagis caniceps*          Pl. 37, Map 946
**Identification:** 5″ (13cm). Slight crest. ♂: *blue gray above*; darker on crown and with concealed white crown patch; *wings black with prom. white edgings and 2 white wing bars*; below white; breast tinged light gray. ♀: olive green above with dark gray crown and concealed pale yellow crown patch; *wings black like ♂ but markings pale yellow* (instead of white); *throat and chest gray*; lower underparts pale greenish yellow (or white—*parambae*).
**Similar species:** ♂ much grayer than other small Colombian flycatchers and superficially nearer several ♂ becards, esp. Cinereous Becard (p 446) but slimmer and smaller-headed. ♀ much like Forest Elaenia (17), but wings blacker and throat and chest grayer in stronger contrast to lower underparts.

**Behavior:** Single birds or pairs act like other *Myiopagis* in outer canopy foliage; may cock tail up.
**Status and habitat:** Few recs., but easily overlooked. Treetops in dry to humid forest and forest edge. In e Panama mainly a foothill bird (500-1000m).
**Range:** To 300m (sight recs. to 900m). Pacific coast from Panama border s to Valle-Chocó border (*parambae*) and sightings in Valle (upper Anchicayá Val. 1973—Hilty); e of Andes in e Guainía (mouth of Río Guainía); also Río Vaupés, Brazil on Vaupés border (*cinerea*). E Panama to w Ecuador; w Venez. (Perijá region); s Venez. and Fr. Guiana s spottily e of Andes to Bolivia, Paraguay, and s Brazil.

## 19. GREENISH ELAENIA
*Myiopagis viridicata*          Pl. 37, Map 947
**Identification:** 5.2″ (13.2cm). Eyes dark; base of lower mandible pinkish. Above greenish olive with *semiconcealed crown patch golden yellow*; sides of head tinged grayish; indistinct eyebrow whitish; wings edged yellowish green; *wing bars obscure or lacking; grayish throat merging into olive gray chest is set off from pale yellow lower breast and belly.*
**Similar species:** Drab and easily confused. Forest Elaenia (17), more a forest bird (both can occur together), has definite wing bars, less contrasting underparts, and e of Andes, a whitish crown patch. Also see *Tolmomyias* (87, 88), both with flat bills, and in the extreme e, Yellow-crowned Elaenia (note below) and Saffron-crested Tyrant-Manakin (p 437).
**Voice:** Usual call a buzzy *cheerip* (Ridgely 1976) or *screechit* (E. S. Morton), more slurred and less emphatic than Forest Elaenia's distinctly 2-syllable call. In Costa Rica, dawn song *peer-pee, peer-pee, peer-peer-pee*, persistently repeated (Skutch 1960).
**Behavior:** Perch-gleans on foliage and twigs at midlevels in shady open woodland; partly frugivorous. Inconspic. and undistinguished. Tends to perch more vertically than Forest Elaenia and rarely if ever cocks tail up like latter (R. Ridgely).
**Breeding:** 6 BC birds, Mar–Aug, Guajira to s Bolívar (Carriker); 1 in Nov, Cundinamarca (MCN); small loosely woven cup in crotch about 6m up; 2 eggs, whitish blotched and marked lilac and brown, most heavily at larger end (Rowley 1962).
**Status and habitat:** Locally fairly common (easily overlooked) in lighter woodland, gallery forest, and clearings with trees; prefers drier areas.
**Range:** To 1300m. Generally w of Andes except Pacific coast (definitely w of W Andes

only in drier Dagua and Patía vals.); e of Andes in Norte de Santander (El Diamante), ne Meta (Carimagua—S. Furniss), and e Nariño. Prob. throughout e of Andes. Mexico to n Argentina and se Brazil (in Venez. both n and s of Orinoco).

**Note:** Yellow-crowned Elaenia (*M. flavivertex*) of the Guianas, e and s Venez., Amazonian Brazil, and e Peru, prob. occurs in extreme e and se Colombia (at San Fernando de Atabapo, Venez. opp. e Vichada). 5.4"; olive green above; more olive brown on crown; semiconcealed bright yellow crown patch; wings dusky with 2 pale yellowish green wing bars and wing edgings; throat and breast pale brownish olive; belly pale buffy yellow. Very sim. Forest Elaenia (17) is slightly smaller with grayer throat, faint streaky breast, and white crown patch (in area of overlap). Greenish Elaenia (19) lacks the wing bars. Understory of *várzea* and swampy forests; loud, startling *wecheche-e-e-e-e-e*, *e* at irreg. intervals.

## 20. YELLOW-BELLIED ELAENIA
*Elaenia flavogaster*                    Pl. 37, Map 948
**Identification:** 6.5" (16.5cm). Small-headed; short round bill. *Conspic. bushy crest usually raised and parted in center to expose white crown patch.* Olive brown above; wing edgings and 2 prom. wing bars whitish; faint whitish eyering; pale gray throat merges into grayish olive chest and sides; *lower underparts light yellow.* Imm.: browner above; wing bars buff; no white in crown.

**Similar species:** *The most familiar elaenia in Colombia.* Easily recognized by bushy crest (slightly parted and almost always showing white at base) and yellow belly. See Lesser Elaenia (25) and e of Andes Large and Small-billed elaenias (21, 23).

**Voice:** Noisy. Most common call a slightly hoarse *breeeer*; also a hoarse, buzzy *dreer-tree* often repeated rapidly and with mate joining enthusiastically (Hilty); dawn song a buzzy *we-do, we-do* (Skutch 1960).

**Behavior:** Lively, garrulous, and easily aroused to a state of rather confused noisy excitement. Browse in shrubbery for berries and insects, occas. sally short distances. Singly or in pairs; gather in groups at fruiting shrubs.

**Breeding:** May–Sept nests, nw Santander (Boggs 1961); nest in upper Dagua Val., June (Hilty); 1 in Patía Val. Nov; ♀ ready to lay in Feb, above Cali (Miller 1963); feather-lined grass cup adorned with bark and lichen; 2 eggs, pale salmon with reddish brown spots around larger end (Skutch 1960; Sclater and Salvin 1879).

**Status and habitat:** Common in dry to humid semiopen shrubby areas, woodland borders, gardens, and parks. Sometimes scarce or absent in seemingly suitable areas in extensively forested zones.

**Range:** To 2100m (usually below 1700m). Virtually throughout, but no recs. in nw Pacific lowlands or in Amazonas. S Mexico to n Argentina and se Brazil. Trinidad; Lesser Antilles.

## 21. LARGE ELAENIA
*Elaenia spectabilis*
**Identification:** 7" (18cm). Resembles Yellow-bellied Elaenia but larger and with *3 wide wing bars* (all 3 well marked); *darker grayish olive above; throat and breast darker gray in sharper contrast to pale yellow belly;* crest decidedly smaller and little or no white at base.

**Similar species:** See Small-billed Elaenia (23) and even larger Mottle-backed (29) and Brownish elaenias (24); also Short-crested Flycatcher (153).

**Voice:** Most common call a soft, somewhat manakinlike *weeoo* (R. Ridgely).

**Behavior:** Usually solitary. Perch-gleans and browses, mostly exposed and 1-8m up in foliage of bushes and other shrubbery.

**Status and habitat:** An austral migrant to shrubby clearings, gardens, forest borders, and along streams and rivers. Early June–late Aug near Leticia where reg. in small nos. (J. V. Remsen; Hilty). First rec. in Colombia July 1965 (Olivares 1967).

**Range:** To 100m. Se Colombia in Amazonas (Leticia; Pto. Nariño). Poss. n to Vaupés. Spottily in e Ecuador (sight—Ridgely), e Peru, Brazil, Bolivia, and n Argentina.

## 22. WHITE-CRESTED ELAENIA
*Elaenia albiceps*
**Identification:** 5.8" (14.7cm). Slight crest. Dark olive above with *partially concealed creamy white crown patch*; 2 yellowish white wing bars; indistinct buff eyering; *underparts almost uniformly light gray tinged olive*; belly white; sides of breast darker olive; flanks and under tail coverts tinged buffy yellow. S migrants (*chilensis*) differs in outermost primary longer than 5th, instead of shorter (Meyer de Schauensee 1950).

**Similar species:** Prob. not safely told in the field from several other highland elaenias, but it is the grayest below and the only one with a white belly. Most like Lesser Elaenia (25) but more uniform below and without any pale yellow in center of belly, and wing bars tinged yellow. Sierran Elaenia (28) is almost identical, but entire underparts have a distinct yellowish wash. Mountain Elaenia (27) has smooth, round, uncrested head, is greener above, yellower below, and usually has yellowish wing bars and edgings; in the hand lacks concealed white crown patch.

**Breeding:** In Chile, well built cup lined with feathers or thistle down; in bush or fork of small tree; 2-3 creamy white eggs with a few red spots (Johnson 1965).

**Status and habitat:** Resident and/or perhaps austral migrant. Apparently bushy areas, partially wooded terrain and stunted forest borders. Sight recs. at s end of PN Puracé (Aug) and elsewhere require specimen confirmation.

**Range:** 2100m to treeline on both slopes of Andes in s Nariño (*griseogularis*). Once (s migrant?) in E Andes w of Bogotá (La Mesa, 1300m). Colombia to Tierra del Fuego. S breeders migratory.

**Note:** A specimen, reportedly *E. a. griseogularis*, from Caño Cubiyú, Vaupés (Nicéforo and Olivares 1976a), may be austral migrant *chilensis* or another sp.

### 23. SMALL-BILLED ELAENIA
*Elaenia parvirostris*          Pl. 37, Map 949
**Identification:** 5.8″ (14.7cm). Slight crest. *Bill not obviously smaller than others of the genus.* Olivaceous above with semiconcealed white crown patch; 2 prom. white wing bars; a 3d (upper) small one and white wing edgings; *prom. white eyering* (looks "wide-eyed"); throat and breast light gray *becoming white on lower underparts.*

**Similar species:** The eyering and whitish belly are the marks. Lesser Elaenia (25) lacks conspic. eyering and has center of belly tinged yellowish (but this not conspic.). Yellow-bellied Elaenia (20) is more obviously bushy crested (shows white at base of crest) and belly pale yellow. Large Elaenia (21) is bigger and has 3 distinct wing bars and belly tinged pale yellow.

**Voice:** Call, *chéee-oh* at intervals; song, *chit chit cheea-oh-weet* in Brazil (W. Belton recording).

**Behavior:** Perches low along borders and in shrubbery areas. Usually solitary, quiet, and inconspic. in Colombia.

**Status and habitat:** Uncommon to fairly common austral migrant early Apr–late Oct (most recs. late May–late Aug) to shrubbery clearings, gardens, and woodland borders e of Andes. Numerous in young successional growth on Amazonian river isls.

**Range:** To 1800m (Pico Renjifo, Macarena Mts.). Throughout e of Andes; w of them in Santa Marta area and E Andes from Santander s to head of Magdalena Val. Breeds in e Bolivia, Argentina, Paraguay, Uraguay, and se Brazil; winters n (austral winter) to n S America e of Andes. Trinidad.

### 24. [BROWNISH ELAENIA]
*Elaenia pelzelni*
**Identification:** 7.5″ (19cm). Thrushlike. Bill very short. Head rounded; small concealed white crown patch (lacking—♀). *Dull dark brown above;* 2 obscure grayish wing bars; throat and chest pale brown, palest on throat; sides and flanks light brown; *remaining underparts dull dingy white.*

**Similar species:** Very large mainly brownish elaenia with dull white lower underparts. Might recall a thrush (esp. Black-billed Thrush, (p 547) more than an elaenia. Also see Large and Mottle-backed elaenias (21, 29).

**Behavior:** Rather wary as wander around 1-10m up in edges of shrubbery and patches of second growth.

**Status and habitat:** Hypothetical. No specimens: 4 seen 24 Aug 1979 in scrub and young shrubby second growth on Isla Corea (Amazonian river isl.), Colombia, about 45km nw Leticia (Hilty). Perhaps undertakes local or seasonal movements.

**Range:** To 100m. Río Amazon near Leticia. Ne Peru (mouth of Río Curaray); w and c Amazonian Brazil from Río Juruá e to Río Tapajós; n Bolivia.

### 25. LESSER ELAENIA
*Elaenia chiriquensis*          Pl. 37, Map 950
**Identification:** 5.5″ (14cm). Closely resembles several other elaenias. *Slight crest with partly concealed white crown patch.* Grayish brown above with narrow whitish eyering and *2 whitish wing bars* and edgings; throat grayish merging into olive of upper breast, sides, and flanks; *center of lower breast and belly whitish faintly tinged yellow* (or brownish olive above, crown darker, breast tinged brown—*brachyptera*). Imm.: browner above incl. wing bars, no white in crown.

**Similar species:** Easily confused and some comparative experience helpful. Sierran Elaenia (28) has yellowish white (not white) wing bars, more extensive *yellowish underparts,* and is overall slightly darker, browner, and dingier. Mountain Elaenia (27) is definitely dingier, has very round uncrested head (never white in crown), more uniformly yellowish olive underparts, and different call. Yellow-bellied Elaenia (20) is slightly larger, crest more conspic. and usually slightly parted, and underparts more contrasting. Small-billed Elaenia (23) is almost identical, but eyering more prom. Also see White-crested Elaenia (22).

**Voice:** Var. of calls, all softer and more plaintive (less hoarse) than Yellow-bellied Elaenia's; a burry *chibu* or *jwebu,* a soft *weeb* or *beebzb* repeated, also a burry *freeee* or *feee* (Ridgely 1976). Dawn song a rapid endlessly repeated *a we d' de de* often given in flight (Skutch 1960).

**Behavior:** More subdued than Yellow-bellied Elaenia but otherwise sim.
**Breeding:** 16 BC birds, Mar–July, Santa Marta and Perijá Mts. and sw Huila (Carriker). Small feather-lined cup usually 1-4m up in bush or tree; 2 eggs (rarely 1), dull white with spots of brown in a wreath at larger end; ♀ may sing while incubating (Skutch 1960).
**Status and habitat:** Uncommon to fairly common in mt. pastures, cultivated land, and other open areas with shrubbery and scattered trees. Most numerous in lower highlands (1400-2100m). Reported fairly common Apr–early May (migrants?) e of Andes at Carimagua, ne Meta (S. Furniss). C American populations migratory(?) or undergo local movements; austral populations migratory, and both(?) may occur in Colombia at opp. seasons.
**Range:** To 2200m (mostly foothills or higher). Santa Marta and Perijá mts., E and C Andes, W Andes in Valle and Cauca, poss. Antioquia; e of Andes in Meta, w Caquetá, and e Nariño (*albivertex*); w Nariño (*brachyptera*). Costa Rica to nw Argentina and s Brazil.

### 26. RUFOUS-CROWNED ELAENIA
*Elaenia ruficeps*     Pl. 37, Map 951
**Identification:** 5.7″ (14.5cm). Slight crest with *semiconcealed rufous crown patch usually visible on rearcrown* (sometimes hard to see). Dark olive brown above, darkest on crown; faint eyering, wing edgings, and *2 distinct wing bars dirty white*; throat whitish shading to grayish on breast and pale yellowish white on belly; throat and breast *faintly streaked* grayish.
**Similar species:** Only elaenia with rufous crown patch and a suggestion of streaking below; a little darker than others with which it might be confused. Lesser Elaenia (25) is grayer above, whiter below. Also cf. Small-billed (23) and Plain-crested elaenias (note).
**Behavior:** Pairs wander 1-8m up in scrubby woodland; perch-glean or flutter up to foliage in bushes for insects or visit fruiting shrubs; 1 to several, sometimes with other birds.
**Breeding:** BC ♂♂, 26 Apr, Mitú, Vaupés, 15 Feb, Macarena Mts. (Olivares 1962, 1964b).
**Status and habitat:** Common in scrub and bushes in savanna and borders of sandy-belt woodland in the extreme east (Pto. Inírida) and prob. in scattered pockets of sim. habitat to the southeast.
**Range:** To 500m. E of Andes from se base of Macarena Mts. locally e to Orinoco (sightings, Pto. Inírida, Sept 1978—Hilty and M. Robbins), se Guainía (opp. Casiquiare), and Vaupés (Mitú). E Colombia, s Venez., the Guianas, and n and c Brazil.
**Note:** Plain-crested Elaenia (*E. cristata*), of

Venez., Guianas, ne and se Brazil, and se Peru, is widespread in Orinoco region, Venez., and should be found in e Vichada and Guainía. Almost identical to Small-billed Elaenia but crest more prom., no white coronal patch, eyering fainter, and belly more strongly tinged yellow. Specimen confirmation required. Scattered low bushes and scrub in savanna.

### 27. MOUNTAIN ELAENIA
*Elaenia frantzii*     Pl. 37, Map 952
**Identification:** 5.5″ (14cm). *Head very round; uncrested.* Brownish olive above (no concealed white crown patch), narrow yellowish eyering; 2 distinct *yellowish wing bars; inner remiges edged pale yellow* (in the hand outer web of innermost tertial largely whitish); *underparts almost uniform pale yellowish olive*, slightly paler on throat and becoming pale yellow on belly.
**Similar species:** See White-crested and Lesser elaenias (22, 25). Sierran Elaenia (28) has brownish crest, concealed white crown patch, more prom. eyering (broken in front) and more yellowish throat; in the hand innermost tertial tipped buff, not white.
**Voice:** A plaintive whistled *peeeeerr*, drawn out, and a shorter whistled *peeee-oo* or *twee-oo* (Ridgely 1976); at dawn a repeated *d' weet, d' weet . . .* (Skutch 1967).
**Behavior:** Sim. to Yellow-bellied Elaenia but less animated, more horizontal posture, and seems even more frugivorous, often concentrating in nos. at fruiting shrubs. Reg. seasonal movements likely, some apparently in response to fruit abundance (Skutch 1967; Wolf 1976).
**Breeding:** 16 BC birds, Mar–Nov, W, C, and E Andes (Carriker; MCN). Young in Aug nest, W Andes above Cali (Miller 1963). Small, firm, moss-covered cup usually lined with a few feathers; 2-17m up in var. of trees and locations; 2 dull white or pale buff eggs with brown spots forming a wreath at larger end (Skutch 1967).
**Status and habitat:** Fairly common to common in highland pastures, clearings, and cultivated areas with bushes and trees. In W Andes above Cali reported only Jan–Aug (Miller 1963).
**Range:** Mostly 1600-2500m (rec. 1500-3000m in Andes; 900-3600m in Santa Marta Mts.). Santa Marta and Perijá mts. and all 3 Adean ranges s to s Cauca (not Nariño). Guatemala to w Venez.

### 28. SIERRAN ELAENIA
*Elaenia pallatangae*     Pl. 37, Map 953
**Identification:** 5.8″ (14.7cm). Small brownish crest and *concealed white crown patch.* Dark olive above; crown slightly darker; prom. yellowish

white eyering interrupted in front; wings dusky brown with *2 broad yellowish white wing bars* and small pale buff spot on innermost tertial; chin grayish; *throat yellowish;* chest and sides yellowish clouded brownish; rest of underparts pale yellowish.
**Similar species:** Mountain Elaenia (27) is nearest but has round head (not slightly crested), less prom. eyering, olive tinged throat, and no white in crown. In general yellower on throat than breast, and yellower on belly than any of the 4 other *Elaenia* spp. (22, 23, 25, 27) in the Colombian highlands.
**Breeding:** 6 BC birds, Jan–Aug, Cauca (Carriker). Cup nest 1m up in fork of bush in Peru; 2 white eggs with dark spots at larger end (Taczanowski 1886).
**Status and habitat:** Bushy highland pastures and woodland borders. Known from a rather large no. of specimen localities.
**Range:** 1600-2500m. W Andes from Valle southward, and C Andes from Quindío (near Ibaque) s to both slopes of Nariño. S Colombia s in Andes to n Bolivia.

## 29. MOTTLE-BACKED ELAENIA
*Elaenia gigas*                     Pl. 37, Map 954
**Identification:** 7.5″ (19cm). *Large.* Prom. dark bifurcated crest ("horned") with usually exposed white crown patch. Olive brown above; *feathers of back somewhat pale-edged giving a spotted or mottled appearance;* wing edgings and 2 wing bars whitish; throat whitish; *foreneck and chest washed brownish;* sides faintly streaked brownish; *remaining underparts clear pale yellow* (obscurely streaked yellowish on breast).
**Similar species:** Should be easily recognized by unique (among *Elaenia*) Harpy Eaglelike crest. Also yellower and more mottled and dingy below than other large, lower el. elaenias with which it might be confused. Brownish Elaenia (24) is browner, lacks mottling on back, and has dull white abdomen (not pale yellow). Also see Large Elaenia (21) and somewhat smaller Yellow-bellied Elaenia (20).
**Voice:** A loud *wurdít* or *purdíp* in e Ecuador (R. Ridgely) or *wher-cheer*, burry at end in Peru (J. Fitzpatrick).
**Behavior:** Mostly 3-20m up where forages like other elaenias. Crest often held erect with white patch showing conspic. betw. 2 "horns" (J. Fitzpatrick). More vocal in morning when they perch prom. in top of shrub or small tree isolated in clearing (R. Ridgely).
**Status and habitat:** Few recs. Shrubby forest clearings, pastures, and forest borders, esp. in foothills.
**Range:** 250-600m (almost certainly higher). Meta (near Villavicencio; Macarena Mts.) to w

Caquetá and Vaupés (Mitú). Mostly e base of E Andes from Colombia to nw Bolivia.

## 30. SLATY ELAENIA
*Elaenia strepera*
**Identification:** 6.3″ (16cm). Bill wider than other *Elaenia.* Slight crest with semiconcealed white crown patch. ♂: *differs from all other elaenias by distinctive dark gray plumage with contrasting white belly;* wings and tail dusky brown; edgings and 2 indistinct wing bars dull gray; faint whitish eyering. ♀: sim. but tinged olive and narrow wing bars buffy. Imm.: like ♀ but throat whitish, breast faintly streaked dusky, and belly tinged yellowish. Wings long for the genus.
**Behavior:** Rather swallowlike as they sally from open perches in clearings or from forest treetops as they follow canopy bird flocks in migration in se Peru (J. Fitzpatrick).
**Status and habitat:** Austral migrant to brushy pastures, shrubby clearings, forest borders, and forest treetops. Rec. Aug and Sept in Venez. (Meyer de Schauensee and Phelps 1978); 14 Oct 1974 at Leticia (J. V. Remsen).
**Range:** To 500m. E of Andes. Known from s Meta (base of Macarena Mts.), and Amazonas (Leticia). Breeds in s Bolivia and nw Argentina; migrates n as far as n Venez.

[*Mecocerculus*: Highlands; sim. plumage but shape, size, posture, and behavior differ among the spp. Most common sp., *M. leucophrys*, least typical of genus (perhaps not a *Mecocerculus*).]

## 31. WHITE-THROATED TYRANNULET
*Mecocerculus leucophrys*          Pl. 36, Map 955
**Identification:** 5.8″ (14.7cm). *Decidedly long tail. Short bill.* Dark russet brown above with *2 conspic. buff wing bars;* remiges edged buffy; dull whitish eyestripe; *large puffy white throat* contrasts with light brownish breast; lower underparts white tinged yellow (or as above but olive brown, wing bars buffy white, center of breast gray—*montensis, setophagoides*).
**Similar species:** Everywhere told by puffy white throat and long tail. Cf. other *Mecocerculus* (all with shorter tail, duller throat, and different posture).
**Voice:** Call a frequently repeated *pit* or *peet* (typically 1-3 notes), distinctive; seldom heard song a soft complex warble (J. Silliman).
**Behavior:** One of *the* characteristic temperate zone woodland birds. Groups of 3-5, often with mixed flocks, actively work over bushes and trees as they hop through them, sally very short distances, or examine branch ends and glean foliage like chickadees (*Parus* sp.). Perch upright; tail held loose and depressed (J. Silliman).

**Breeding:** 17 BC birds, Feb–Aug, Santa Marta and Perijá mts., E and C Andes (Carriker), and 2 in Jan, Boyacá (Olivares 1974a). Adults feeding juvs., 24 Mar, PN Puracé; building cup nest 2m up in small tree, 9 Mar, n Venez. (Brown).
**Status and habitat:** Common and widespread in stunted humid mt. forest, bushy pastures, and cut over woodland.
**Range:** Mostly 2600-3400m (treeline); rec. 1900-3800m in Andes; 1500-3600m in Santa Marta Mts. Santa Marta Mts. (*montensis*); Perijá Mts. and E Andes (*setophagoides*); C and W Andes (*notatus*); s Cauca and mts. of Nariño (*rufomarginatus*). N Venez. s in mts. to nw Argentina; tepuis of s Venez. and adj. n Brazil.

## 32. WHITE-TAILED TYRANNULET
*Mecocerculus poecilocercus*          Pl. 36, Map 956
**Identification:** 4.1" (10.4cm). *Warblerlike shape*, rather short tail. *Crown gray contrasting with olive green back; upper tail coverts pale yellow* (often hard to see); tail grayish *outer feathers largely white on inner web* (from below when perched, tail looks all white with gray edge); narrow white eyebrow; *wing coverts dusky with 2 conspic. yellowish white wing bars*; small area ("speculum") at base of inner remiges black; inner remiges edged yellowish; underparts light gray becoming white on belly (latter sometimes tinged yellowish).
**Similar species:** See White-banded (34) and Sulphur-bellied tyrannulets (33).
**Voice:** An occas. wheezy *wee, weez-weez-weez* when foraging.
**Behavior:** Active and somewhat warblerlike with horizontal posture (in contrast to upright posture of White-throated Tyrannulet). Perchgleans or sally-gleans from foliage in canopy or subcanopy; 1's or 2's, and often with mixed flocks.
**Breeding:** 2 BC ♂♂, Aug–Sept, Santander (Carriker).
**Status and habitat:** Uncommon in humid mt. forest and forest edge. Center of abundance at lower el. than sim. White-banded Tyrannulet.
**Range:** 1600-2700m (mostly 2000-2400m). All 3 Andean ranges (W Andes n to Cauca; C Andes n to Caldas; E Andes from Norte de Santander s to Cundinamarca). Colombia s in Andes to Peru.

## 33. SULPHUR-BELLIED TYRANNULET
*Mecocerculus minor*          Pl. 36, Map 957
**Identification:** 4.7" (12cm). Proportions sim. to White-banded Tyrannulet; bill slightly thicker. *Crown gray contrasting with olive green upperparts*; wings and tail brownish; wing edgings and *2 broad wing bars buff*; small black area ("speculum") at base of inner remiges (best seen in the hand); narrow white eyestripe; *underparts mostly clear soft yellow*; throat whitish; breast and sides tinged olivaceous.
**Similar species:** Contrasting crown, wing bars, and sulphur yellow underparts are good marks. No other *Mecocerculus* (31, 32, 34) is so extensively yellow below.
**Behavior:** Essentially like White-tailed Tyrannulet. Pairs or groups of 3 (families?) follow mixed flocks at midlevels or lower along forest edge.
**Status and habitat:** Borders of humid forest and tall second growth. Perhaps local. Found with some frequency on e slope in e Nariño.
**Range:** 1600-2400m. E slope E Andes from Norte de Santander (Páramo de Tamá on Venez. border) to Boyacá (Río Negro); head of the Magdalena Val. in Huila (Isnos to PN Cueva de los Guácharos); e slope of E Andes in e Nariño (sightings, Sept 1978, June 1981—Hilty). Nw Venez. (Táchira) s in Andes to se Ecuador and Peru.

## 34. WHITE-BANDED TYRANNULET
*Mecocerculus stictopterus*          Pl. 36, M 958
**Identification:** 5" (13cm). Bill thin. Tail longer than that of White-tailed Tyrannulet. Brownish olive above with contrasting gray crown; *long broad white eyebrow* bordered below by dark line through eye; *wing coverts black with 2 broad white wing bars*; remiges edged yellowish buff with black area ("speculum") at base (best seen in the hand); throat and breast light gray; lower underparts white; flanks tinged yellow; tail grayish below.
**Similar species:** From White-tailed Tyrannulet (32) by longer tail (most apparent in direct comparison), bolder eyebrow and wing bars, browner back and uniform rump and tail (no yellowish rump, no white in tail). Sulphur-bellied Tyrannulet (33) is mostly yellowish below. Also see Black-capped Tyrannulet (4).
**Voice:** High-pitched, sibilant *zeeet tu*; longer ser. *zeeeeet, zeeeeet . . .*; dawn song a slightly rasping *zeeeeet titititi*, last part trilled (P. Schwartz recording); loud descending *skee! dr'e'e'e'e*, as forage in PN Puracé.
**Behavior:** Resembles that of White-tailed Tyrannulet but more often lower, from tops of smaller trees to subcanopy. Usually with mixed flocks (J. Silliman). Posture somewhat horizontal (not upright as in White-throated Tyrannulet).
**Breeding:** 2 BC birds, Jan and Aug, C Andes (Carriker); 2 ad. fed juv., Dec, PN Puracé (J. Silliman).
**Status and habitat:** Fairly common in humid

and wet forest (mossy forest), stunted forest, and at edges. Generally at somewhat higher el. than White-tailed and Sulphur-bellied tyrannulets.
**Range:** 1800-3600m (mostly 2500-3300m). W Andes from Cauca (Cerro Munchique) southward; C Andes; E Andes from Santander (Bucaramanga) to Cundinamarca. Andes of nw Venez. s in mts. to n Bolivia.

### 35. [RIVER TYRANNULET]
*Serpophaga hypoleuca*          Pl. 38, Map 959
**Identification:** 4.2″ (10.7cm). Slender. Resembles a gnatcatcher. *Crown black,* slightly crested (or· virtually no crest—*venezuelana*); upperparts brownish gray; wings and *long narrow tail* dusky (no wing bars); outer tail feathers vaguely pale-edged; *underparts white* with light gray wash on breast.
**Similar species:** Tropical Gnatcatcher (p 551) is paler and grayer and carries white-tipped black tail cocked up.
**Behavior:** Pairs actively hop and glean about 1-5m up in small bushes or flit short distances to air, then fly off some distance to new sites. At rest perch fairly upright, occas. flick tail.
**Breeding:** Pair feeding juv., 24 July, Leticia (Hilty).
**Status and habitat:** Hypothetical. No specimens. Frequent sightings since 1974—many observers. Sparse early successional scrub and small trees on sand or mud bars on Amazon river isls., occas. banks of the Amazon. Sparsely wooded savanna near Río Meta in Venez. (Meyer de Schauensee and Phelps 1978).
**Range:** To 300m. S Amazonas along the Amazon (*hypoleuca*). Doubtless n Vichada along Río Meta (*venezuelana*). C Venez. (banks of Ríos Orinoco, Apure, and Meta); ne Ecuador (Río Napo), e Peru (incl. Pto. Indiana; mouth of Río Curaray), Brazil along banks of Amazon, and n Bolivia.

### 36. TORRENT TYRANNULET
*Serpophaga cinerea*          Ill. 84, Map 960
**Identification:** 4.4″ (11.2cm). Mt. streams. *Mostly pale gray,* paler below; center of belly white; *crown and sides of head black* with small concealed white crown stripe; *wings and tail black;* wings narrowly edged white.
**Similar species:** Not likely confused. Shares its mt. torrent habitat only with dipper, Black Phoebe, and Torrent Duck.
**Voice:** Loud, sharp, frequently repeated *chip* audible above stream noise. Song a duet of repeated *chip*'s; at dawn same but slower (Skutch 1960).
**Behavior:** Spritely and alert. Pairs patrol small sections of rocky streams and are usually seen

84. TORRENT TYRANNULET

sitting on a boulder in the mid. of the stream or on a branch overhanging the water. Sally to surface of rocks or to vegetation along river bank for flying insects; often flick tail upward.
**Breeding:** 4 BC birds, Sept, W and E Andes (Carriker); in Costa Rica begin in Mar; moss-covered and feather-lined cup 1-4m up on branch over water; 2 pale buff eggs, unmarked (Skutch 1960).
**Status and habitat:** Common along swift boulder-filled mt. streams. Mostly 900-2400m and in decreasing nos. down to base of foothills (where river gradient decreases), a few wander nearly to treeline.
**Range:** 100-3200m. Santa Marta and Perijá Mts. and all 3 Andean ranges. Costa Rica and w Panama; nw Venez. s in Andes to n Bolivia.

### 37. SLENDER-BILLED TYRANNULET
*Inezia tenuirostris*          Pl. 36, Map 961
**Identification:** 3.7″ 9.4cm). *Tiny* and nondescript; bill short and slender. Dull grayish brown above; narrow eyering and *short eyestripe whitish;* wing edgings and *2 wing bars dull whitish; below dingy grayish white; lower breast and abdomen tinged yellow;* outer web of outer tail feather pale (best seen in the hand).
**Similar species:** Confusing. Small size and thin bill are helpful. Southern Beardless-Tyrannulet (12) is larger and otherwise differs mainly in head shape (more crested; smaller "sleepy-looking" eye), thicker bill, and voice.
**Voice:** Frequently heard song a long, dry, chipping trill fading at end (Hilty); also whistled *teer-TEER-Teer-teer-teer,* rising then falling (J. Fitzpatrick).
**Behavior:** Gleans like a vireo from outer foliage and twigs 1-5m up in shrubs and trees (not thickets). Rather tame, sedentary, and often alone. Tail cocked up slightly like Southern Beardless-Tyrannulet.
**Status and habitat:** Dry thorn woodland, arid

scrub, and scrubby cattleland. Easily seen at w base of Santa Marta Mts. (esp. Hotel Irotama grounds) and on Guajira Peninsula. **Range:** To 300m (prob. higher). Santa Marta region (not humid n slope) and Guajira. Ne Colombia and nw Venez.

### 38. PALE-TIPPED TYRANNULET
*Inezia subflava*                    Pl. 36, Map 962
**Identification:** 4.7″ (12cm). Typical small tyrannulet. Sturdy black bill. Olivaceous brown above with *prom. white supraloral stripe;* faint white eyering and dusky lores; white wing edgings and *2 bold white wing bars; dusky tail tipped and edged dull whitish* (not always conspic.); upper throat whitish; rest of underparts pale yellow (or breast and sides washed olive—*obscura*); eyes straw yellow to dark.
**Similar species:** Look for white "spectacles," sharp white wing bars, and *blackish* tail tipped and edged white. See Southern Beardless-Tyrannulet, and Mouse-colored, and Slender-billed tyrannulets (12, 13, 37).
**Voice:** Often noisy. Most common calls, *teep tee'r'r,* last note falling, and clear *peep, pe-de-de* (often up to a doz. or more *de's* rapidly); also in Guainía a loud, penetrating *cher-dup,* over and over.
**Behavior:** Single birds or pairs hop about with tail slightly cocked, perch-glean from twigs and foliage, mostly in shrubbery up to more open midlevels of larger trees; usually advertises its presence by loud calls and shows decided fondness for vicinity of water or low-lying, even swampy areas in dry to humid zones.
**Breeding:** 11 BC birds, Jan–Aug, Cesar to Antioquia (Carriker); 2 nestlings, 26 Sept, Pto. Inírida; very thin cup suspended from crotch 2.5m up in isolated sapling (Hilty and M. Robbins); nest often high; eggs white (Haverschmidt 1968).
**Status and habitat:** Fairly common in lighter woodland, gallery forest, and *streamside* shrubbery; also semiopen country with patches of scrub, thorny bushes, or scattered trees; drier regions but locally in moist and humid woodland borders. Very common at Pto. Inírida, ne Guainía.
**Range:** To 400m. Lower Magdalena Val. e to w Guajira and Cesar Val. (*intermedia*); e of Andes in Vaupés and Guainía (*obscura*), prob. Vichada. Poss. n Arauca (*caudata*). Colombia to the Guianas and n and c Amazonian Brazil.

### 39. [LESSER WAGTAIL-TYRANT]
*Stigmatura napensis*               Pl. 38, Map 963
**Identification:** 5.2″ (13.2cm). Short bill. *Long graduated tail.* Grayish olive above; eyestripe and weak eyering pale yellow; wing edgings

and *2 prom. wing bars whitish;* underparts yellowish white; breast tinged olive; *tail blackish; all but central feathers broadly tipped white;* the outer feathers also white basally.
**Similar species:** Easily told in limited habitat by "spectacles," wing bars and rounded, white-tipped tail often cocked up.
**Voice:** A loud, clear, whistled *weéert?,* and *weeeEE!;* and a harsh scolding rattle, *sque'e'e'e,* descending slightly.
**Behavior:** Loosely assoc. pairs glean and browse actively in foliage or make short aerial sallies as they hop 1-5m up in scrub or grass. Constantly jerk tail to an angle above back, sometimes also slightly spread tail. Usually do not remain long in open.
**Breeding:** Distraction displays and persistent calling 23 July, Leticia (Hilty).
**Status and habitat:** Hypothetical. First sight recs. are 1 on 6 July 1974 on an Amazon river isl. (J. V. Remsen), and 1 on Colombian bank of Amazon 17 July 1975 (Hilty; D. Zimmerman) both nw of Leticia. Locally common (many sightings) breeding(?) resident of thin to dense early successional bushes, saplings, and vines on sandy Amazon river isls. and in grass and bushes on river banks. Most Colombian recs. are from Isla Corea.
**Range:** To 100m. The Río Amazon, Amazonas (*napensis*). Amazonian Brazil to ne Peru (incl. mouth of Río Curaray).

### 40. TUFTED TIT-TYRANT
*Anairetes parulus*                 Pl. 38, Map 964
**Identification:** 4.3″ (10.9cm). Short thin bill; *long, thin, wispy black crest curling forward* (often hard to see). *Eyes white.* Crown and sides of head black with white supraloral streak and white spot below eye; *otherwise dark brownish gray above;* 2 white wing bars and white edgings on tail feathers; *throat and breast whitish prom. streaked black;* belly pale yellow.
**Similar species:** Recurved hairlike crest diagnostic but not easy to see. Agile Tit-Tyrant (41) is larger with decidedly long tail, broad white superciliary, and streaks *above* and below.
**Voice:** Call a rapid atonal trill, diminishing (J. Silliman); a soft plaintive *pee-de-dit* (1st note lower); song loud for so small a bird, *chew, wit tititi wit,* sometimes abbreviated.
**Behavior:** Alone or in 2's, rarely several. Perch inside rather dense temperate shrubbery where inconspic. Flit and glean in dense foliage and frequently call as forage. Unlike next sp. not regularly with bird flocks.
**Breeding:** BC ♂, 31 Jan, Puracé (Carriker). In Chile, small cup in shrub or bamboo near stream or small opening; lined with thistle down

and feathers; 2-3 cream colored eggs unspotted (Johnson 1965).
**Status and habitat:** Uncommon to fairly common (easily overlooked) in semiopen bushy hillsides, patches of treeline shrubbery, and dense stunted forest borders.
**Range:** 2100-3600m (mostly 3000-3400m). S end of C Andes from Cauca (PN Puracé) s through Nariño. S Colombia to Tierra del Fuego and isls. in Strait of Magellan.

## 41. AGILE TIT-TYRANT
*Anairetes agilis* Pl. 38, Map 965
**Identification:** 5″ (13cm). Very short bill. *Decidedly long tail* notched at tip and narrowly edged white. Flattened blackish crest (protrudes slightly on rearcrown; *long white eyestripe; back and wings brown streaked dusky; throat, breast, and sides whitish heavily streaked dark brown*; belly pale yellow.
**Similar species:** See Tufted Tit-Tyrant (40).
**Voice:** Most common call a flat trill, *pti'i'i'i'i'i*, recalls Cinnamon Flycatcher but weaker and shorter (Hilty).
**Behavior:** Pairs or groups of 3-5 persistently accompany treeline bird flocks. Rapidly glean foliage like chickadees (*Parus* sp.) mostly 1-6m up near tip of branches (seldom sally). Rather confiding (J. Silliman).
**Breeding:** BC ♀, 2 Feb, Puracé (Carriker).
**Status and habitat:** Common in more open, stunted, temperate forest, forest borders, bamboo, and treeline brush. At lower el. perhaps only a wanderer.
**Range:** 1800-3400m (mainly 2700-3400m). E slope of E Andes from s Boyacá (Rondón) to s Cundinamarca; head of Magdalena Val. and both slopes of C Andes at s end from Cauca (PN Puracé) s through Nariño. Colombia and n Ecuador.
**Note:** Sometimes placed in the genus *Uromyias*.

## 42. BEARDED TACHURI
*Polystictus pectoralis* Pl. 38, Map 966
**Identification:** 3.8″ (9.7cm). Short black bill. ♂: short, flat crest dusky gray; elongated feathers with hidden white bases; faint white supraloral streak; otherwise light rufous brown above; wings and tail dark brown; *2 cinnamon wing bars* and broad cinnamon edgings; *upper throat and cheeks mottled black and white*; lower throat whitish *becoming cinnamon on breast and sides*; center of lower underparts white. ♀: lacks black on throat; underparts more extensively cinnamon.
**Similar species:** Might recall a dull Ruddy-breasted Seedeater (p 663), but crest, dusky throat (♂), and thin bill are diagnostic. Also cf. Tawny-crowned Pygmy-Tyrant (44) of dry lowlands.

**Voice:** Infrequent weak *feee* (R. Ridgely).
**Behavior:** In Brazil favor tall grass where reg. with flocks of seedeaters (esp. Plumbeous Seedeater), *Coryphaspiza, Cistothorus*, etc. Cling to tall grass stems, sally to stems (not ground) for insects, and frequently change perches. Appear slender as perch quite upright with long tail straight down (R. Ridgely). Flush with rapid undulating flight to low perch in top of weeds (Wetmore 1926).
**Breeding:** ♀ ready to lay, 24 June, and fledged juv., 25 June, ne Meta (S. Furniss).
**Status and habitat:** Very local resident. Fairly common in open savanna with scattered bushes and tall clumped grass (*Andropogon* sp.) and weeds in ne Meta (S. Furniss).
**Range:** 150-2600m. W Andes in dry upper Dagua Val. (above Dagua, 1400m), once in Suba Marshes (2600m) of Sabana de Bogotá (*bogotensis*); e of Andes in nw and ne Meta (Carimagua—S. Furniss) (*brevipennis*). Doubtless adj. Vichada and Arauca. Spottily in Surinam, Guyana, Venez., Bolivia, Uruguay, Paraguay, Argentina, and n Brazil.

## 43. SUBTROPICAL DORADITO
*Pseudocolopteryx acutipennis* Pl. 38, Map 967
**Identification:** 4.6″ (11.7cm). Slender warbler-like black bill. *Uniform olive above* with dark brown flight feathers; *entire underparts bright golden yellow*. In the hand inner primaries attenuated. Some birds (♀?) show dull cinnamon wing bars; buffy patch on cheeks and even a buff postocular streak. Imm. has lower mandible yellow.
**Similar species:** Only small Colombian flycatcher in highlands with essentially uniform upperparts and all bright yellow below. Shape of Yellow Tyrannulet (only lowlands) but bill narrower and underparts much brighter yellow.
**Behavior:** Acts like a tit-tyrant as it perch-gleans at tips of grass. Keeps rather low and usually quiet (T. Parker).
**Status and habitat:** Few recs. Wet grassy areas, marsh grass, and shrubbery in semiopen regions. Birds from Colombia to Peru may be austral migrants (Olrog 1963).
**Range:** 1500-1900m (to 2600m in Ecuador). N end of C Andes near Medellín and in Quindío Mts. (Salento); perhaps E Andes ("Bogotá" specimen; 1 sight rec. 25 Feb 1984 at La Florida Park near Bogotá (R. Ridgely). Colombia s locally to nw Argentina and Paraguay.

## 44. TAWNY-CROWNED PYGMY-TYRANT
*Euscarthmus meloryphus* Pl. 36, Map 968
**Identification:** 4″ (10.2cm). *Short thin bill*; lower mandible yellow. Tail slightly rounded. *Plain brown above* with semiconcealed rufous crown

patch; wings dark brown *faintly edged cinnamon buff* (weak wing bars); *lores and cheeks cinnamon buff*; cinnamon eyering faint or usually lacking; underparts dirty white; breast washed olive brown forming indistinct band; belly pale creamy yellow.

**Similar species:** Scrub Greenlet (p 559) is even plainer with pale bill, olive tinged upperparts, and no buff on lores or cheeks. Smaller Slender-billed Tyrannulet (37) has 2 wing bars and a short eyestripe. Also cf. 42.

**Voice:** Song a gravelly chattering or twittering *plítick* or *pli-plíterick* or sim. var. over and over.

**Behavior:** Restless and active as it hops like a vireo in thickets and weeds mostly within 1m of ground. Perch-gleans from leaves (does not sally) or hops on ground and picks at leaves; usually remains hidden (J. Fitzpatrick; Hilty).

**Breeding:** 4 BC ♂♂, Oct–Nov, near Cúcuta, Norte de Santander (Carriker). In sw Ecuador 20 nests, Feb–May (after rains); thin dry cup suspended 0.5-1.7m up in bush; 2 yellowish white eggs with lilac and buff spots, usually visible through nest (Marchant 1960).

**Status and habitat:** Thickets, weeds or bushes in dry pastures, woodland borders, and scrubby semiarid areas. Locally common; esp. s of Cúcuta. Weedy areas are usually preferred habitat.

**Range:** To 1000m. Santa Marta region and w Guajira s through drier parts of Magdalena Val. to Huila (Villavieja; sight Guadalupe—Hilty); e of Andes in Norte de Santander (Cúcuta). N Venez.; sw Ecuador, w Peru, n and s Bolivia; n Argentina to se Brazil.

### 45. STREAK-NECKED FLYCATCHER
*Mionectes striaticollis*     Pl. 37, Map 969
**Identification:** 5″ (13cm). Slender and small-headed. Fairly long narrow bill. Olive green above; *crown and nape dark gray* (or olive—*viridiceps*), wings dusky narrowly edged olive yellow (no distinct wing bars), *small but prom. white spot behind eye* (less prom. than in Olive-striped Flycatcher); *throat, chest, and sides of head olive gray finely streaked yellowish white*; breast and sides olive flammulated yellow; center of belly yellow.

**Similar species:** See Olive-striped Flycatcher (46), a lower el. replacement.

**Voice:** Usually silent. Song, Jan–May in W Andes in Valle, a thin wiry ser. of alternating upward and downward inflected units, each with 2 elements; also a wing rattle, presum. produced by attenuated 9th primary (Miller 1963).

**Behavior:** Sim. to Olive-striped Flycatcher's, though it occurs from understory to subcanopy.

**Breeding:** 4 BC ♂♂, Jan–Apr, W Andes above

Cali; (Miller 1963). Eggs white (Sclater and Salvin 1879).

**Status and habitat:** Uncommon to common (infrequently seen and nos. better revealed through mist netting) in humid and wet mossy forest, forest borders, and taller second growth.

**Range:** 1600-2700m. C Andes; E Andes in Cundinamarca (Fusagasugá, Choachí) and Huila (*columbianus*) and sight recs. in e Nariño (many observers); W Andes (*selvae*) and Pacific slope sw Nariño (*viridiceps*). Colombia s in Andes through e and w Ecuador to n Bolivia.

### 46. OLIVE-STRIPED FLYCATCHER
*Mionectes olivaceus*     Pl. 37, Map 970
**Identification:** 5″ (13cm). Very sim. to olive-crowned form of Streak-necked Flycatcher. *Crown, sides of head, and upperparts dark greenish olive; prom. small whitish spot behind eye*; underparts olive becoming yellow on center of lower belly; *throat, breast, and sides flammulated and streaked yellow*.

**Similar species:** Streak-necked Flycatcher (45) has dark gray crown (except w Nariño) and decided grayish appearance to sides of head and throat and with very fine, narrow whitish streaking (not broader, blurrier, and yellowish), and more extensive yellow on belly.

**Voice:** Essentially silent. Below Junín, Nariño, an exceedingly high, thin, wiry *zeeeeee* at 4- to 6-sec intervals.

**Behavior:** Solitary or occas. with mixed flocks briefly and almost always seems timid and nervous. Mainly frugivorous, taking small berries in undergrowth with a quick fluttering hover; also hover-gleans under foliage or clings momentarily to leaves. Frequently nods head and flicks wings anxiously (or flashes up 1 like *Leptopogon*, etc.).

**Breeding:** 2 BC ♂♂, 21 Apr, 4 imms., July, Perijá Mts. (Carriker). Panama nest 7 Feb (Wetmore 1972); 2 nests in Trinidad, believed this sp., globular with side entrance (no dangling tail), suspended from roots; 3 white eggs (Belcher and Smooker 1937). Confirmation needed.

**Status and habitat:** Usually very common (but inconspic. and infrequently seen) in humid and wet forest, forest borders, and tall second growth, esp. damp shady undergrowth in ravines. Mist netting reveals true nos. Replaced at higher el. by Streak-necked Flycatcher.

**Range:** To 1800m (mostly foothills and lower slopes; once to 2400m in Norte de Santander). Cerro Tacarcuna on Panama boundary, Pacific coast and slope, foothills along n base of W and C Andes to mid. Magdalena Val. s to Cundinamarca; mid. Cauca Val. (Yotoco, Valle); Santa Marta and Perijá Mts.; e slope E Andes s to Meta (incl. Macarena Mts.) and a sighting in w Caquetá (Florencia road, June 1981—Hilty). Costa Rica to n Venez. and s in hills and mts. to s Peru.

### 47. OCHRE-BELLIED FLYCATCHER

*Mionectes oleaginea*          Pl. 36, Map 971
**Identification:** 5″ (13cm). Rather slender and small-headed. Bill narrow, lower mandible pinkish basally. Greenish olive to grayish olive above; wings and tail brownish with narrow ochraceous edgings and 2 indistinct ochraceous buff wing bars; *sides of head and throat olive gray;* chest tinged olive; *rest of underparts dull orangish buff.*
**Similar species:** Note the thin bill, "burnt orange" lower underparts, and wing raising habit. Cf. smaller Ruddy-tailed Flycatcher (98). ♀ Dusky-throated and ♀ Cinereous antshrikes (pp 387, 388) have heavier bills and lack indistinct wing bars and wing-lifting habit.
**Voice:** Song, given on display grounds, a var. ser. of spaced chirps and twitters alternating with several rapid *choo* or *pitchóo* sneezes; calls from slender horizontal perches 2-6m up as continually flashes up 1 wing or the other and raises short crest (Willis et al. 1978).
**Behavior:** Solitary and inconspic. except when singing (on dispersed lek). Occas. joins mixed flocks; sallies up short distances to foliage, usually to hover-glean fruit, also insects. Mostly 1-10m up.
**Breeding:** 6 BC birds, Apr–June, Cesar to Antioquia (Carriker), 1 in Feb, n Chocó (Haffer 1975); pyriform-shaped side entrance nest usually moss-covered; suspended from root or vine or under stream bank; 2-3 white eggs (Wetmore 1972); ♀ alone attends nest (Skutch 1960).
**Status and habitat:** Common in humid forest, second growth woodland, and along borders, often along forest streams. Very numerous in sandy-belt forests of the extreme east.
**Range:** To 1700m (mostly lowlands and hill country w of Andes). Pacific coast s to Río Napipí, n Chocó, and in sw Nariño (not wet belt from c Chocó to s Cauca); generally n of Andes to Santa Marta and c Guajira, s to mid. Cauca Val. (Cali) and upper mid. Magdalena Val. (s Huila); e of Andes throughout. S Mexico to w Ecuador, n Bolivia and Amazoian and e Brazil.
**Note 1:** Often placed in the genus *Pipromorpha.*
**Note 2:** McConnell's Flycatcher (*M. macconnelli*), a sibling Amazonian ally widely distributed from the Guianas and e and s Venez. to e Peru and n Bolivia, may be found in sandy-belt forest of the extreme east. Almost identical to Ochre-bellied Flycatcher but lacks wing

bars (occas. individuals show wing bars); in the hand a blackish (not yellow) gape. *Terra firme* forest; cf. Ochre-bellied, which is generally not in *terra firme* forest where sympatric with *macconnelli* (Willis et al. 1978).

[*Leptopogon:* Dark cheek patch; narrow bill; erect posture.]

### 48. SLATY-CAPPED FLYCATCHER

*Leptopogon superciliaris*          Pl. 36, Map 972
**Identification:** 5.5″ (14cm). Bill longer and narrower than *Pogonotriccus;* tail longish. Olive green above with *slaty crown;* eyebrow and area in front of and below eye grizzled gray and white ("salt and pepper") and bordered behind by a *black crescentic patch on ear coverts* (no white border behind); wings dusky with yellow edgings and 2 yellow "spotted" (or *cinnamontransandinus; superciliaris*) *wing bars;* throat pale gray; breast yellowish olive; lower underparts pale yellow.
**Similar species:** Larger than the bristle-tyrants (52-54) and with no whitish border behind black ear patch. Also see Sepia-capped Flycatcher (49) and Plumbeous-crowned and Ashy-headed tyrannulets, (2, 6).
**Voice:** Infrequently a sharp, emphatic *skeet'de'e'e'er!* (Hilty) or sim. *hit chú* (Skutch 1967).
**Behavior:** As with *Pogonotriccus, Mionectes,* etc., frequently flicks up a wing when at rest. Perches upright in lower to mid. story, sallies up short to med. distances to foliage, and changes perches frequently; 1 or 2 normally accompany forest bird flocks.
**Breeding:** 6 BC birds, Apr–Oct, Perijás, C and E Andes (Carriker); 1 in Dec, Valle (MCN); in Anchicayá Val., building nest in Feb; 2 pairs with dependent fledglings, early Apr (Hilty). Semiglobular nest with side entrance, sometimes visor, suspended from log, root, or edge of earth bank; 2 white eggs (Skutch 1967; Belcher and Smooker 1937).
**Status and habitat:** Fairly common in humid and wet forest and second growth woodland, less often forest borders. Foothills and lower slopes.
**Range:** 120-2100m (usually above 600m except Pacific slope and e slope of Andes). W Andes in Cauca and Nariño (*transandinus*); rest of Andes incl. Perijá and Macarena Mts. and base of Andes in nw Meta (*poliocephalus*); e base of Andes in w Caquetá (*superciliaris*). Perhaps occas. lowlands e of Andes as rec. in Venez. (tepuis?) near se Guainía and in n Peru (mouth of Río Curaray). Costa Rica to Venez., w and e Ecuador and s to n Bolivia. Trinidad.

## 49. SEPIA-CAPPED FLYCATCHER

*Leptopogon amaurocephalus*    Pl. 36, Map 973
**Identification:** 5.5″ (14cm). Bill longer and narrower than *Pogonotriccus*; tail longish. Olive above with *brown cap* and brown tail; *cheeks mottled buff; patch on posterior ear coverts brown*; wings dusky with yellowish buff edgings and *2 broad cinnamon wing bars*; throat grayish merging into olive of breast and sides; lower underparts pale yellow.
**Similar species:** Slaty-capped Flycatcher (48), chiefly a mt. bird (may meet in foothills), has slaty cap, yellow wing bars (or cinnamon bars—w Caquetá), and sides of head grizzled grayish (not buff).
**Voice:** Rather quiet. A low *pree-ee-ee-ee* in Panama (Wetmore 1972).
**Behavior:** Sim. to Slaty-capped Flycatcher. Pairs, usually in low or mid. forest strata; often in mixed flocks.
**Breeding:** 5 BC birds, Jan–May, Cesar and n Antioquia (Carriker); nest like Slaty-capped Flycatcher; in Mexico a round side-entrance ball suspended from roots, beneath logs, or under stream bank; 1-3 white eggs (Moore 1944).
**Status and habitat:** Understory of more open moist and humid forest and lighter second growth woodland, esp. along creeks; lowlands and hill country; fairly common in PN Tayrona. Uncommon in extensive humid forest and perhaps less numerous e of Andes.
**Range:** To 600m. N Colombia from upper Sinú Val. e to Santa Marta region, s in mid. Magdalena Val. to se Tolima (Chicoral), entire e base of E Andes from Norte de Santander and Macarena Mts. southward; e to ne Meta (Pto. Gaitán; Carimagua—S Furniss). S Mexico to n Argentina and se Brazil.

## 50. RUFOUS-BREASTED FLYCATCHER

*Leptopogon rufipectus*    Pl. 36, Map 974
**Identification:** 5.2″ (13.2cm). Bill rather long and narrow; tail longish. Olive green above with *dark gray cap*; wings dusky; tail dark brown; *2 rufous buff wing bars* and ochraceous edgings; *lores, cheeks, throat, and chest rufous*; obscure dusky crescent on ear coverts; lower underparts pale yellow.
**Similar species:** Easily confused with Handsome Flycatcher (see 104) but larger; throat and breast much deeper rufous (not buff).
**Behavior:** Like all *Leptopogon*, often flashes up a wing over back when at rest; 1 or 2 commonly follow mixed flocks in the mid. story or lower.
**Breeding:** BC ♂, mid-Oct, e Boyacá (Olivares 1971).
**Status and habitat:** Fairly common to common

in humid mossy forest. In C Andes much of habitat in its range now destroyed but easily found in E Andes at PN Cueva de los Guácharos (P. Gertler) and Finca Merenberg (Brown).
**Range:** 1600-2700m (most numerous 1900-2400m). Both slopes of C Andes, w slope of E Andes from Cundinamarca (3 old recs.) s to head of Magdalena Val. and e slope E Andes from Norte de Santander (55km nw of Cúcuta) and Boyacá (Río Cusiano) s to w Caquetá (sightings 1600m, Sept 1978—Hilty). Extreme w Venez. (sw Táchira) s in Andes to ne Ecuador.

## 51. RUFOUS-BROWED TYRANNULET

*Phylloscartes superciliaris*    Pl. 36, Map 975
**Identification:** 4.5″ (11.4cm). Slender; bill thinner and tail longer than allies. *Crown slaty gray*, narrow inconspic. *frontal band and superciliary dark rufous* (extends to behind eye); *spot at upper base of bill and auriculars white*; latter encircled by dusky band that is continuous with *dusky moustache*; otherwise dull olive above; wings and tail dusky brown; inner remiges and tail edged yellowish green; underparts white clouded gray on chest; belly tinged yellow.
**Similar species:** Acts like a gnatcatcher or *Odontorchilus* wren and should be easily recognized by bold head pattern, whitish cheeks, and behavior.
**Voice:** Vocal. In Costa Rica a lively, arresting *wiss wreewreewreewreewree* and *wree titititi*; also single *whiss* (Slud 1964) or sharp *screech* (Ridgely 1976).
**Behavior:** Active and gnatcatcherlike; gleans or flits to foliage in mid. or upper levels of trees. Often with mixed flocks; tail carried loose, slightly cocked, frequently flicks up a wing like *Leptopogon*.
**Status and habitat:** Known from 1 definite locality (5 specimens) in Colombia. In C America mainly forest and forest edges of humid foothills and lower montane slopes. Very local throughout known range.
**Range:** Se Santander (1700m) on Río Virolín (6°07′N); also "Bogota," without precise locality. Prob. Chocó-Panama border (rec. 600-1100m on Cerro Tacarcuna). Locally from Coast Rica to nw Venez. (Perijá Mts.).
**Note:** Yellow-green Tyrannulet (*Phylloscartes flavovirens*) of c and e Panama has been seen near Colombian border (R. Ridgely) and is poss. in nw Chocó. 4.2″. Rather long slender bill. *Prom. white eyering*; uniform olive green above and yellow below; wings dusky with *edgings and 2 wing bars bright yellow*. Cf. closely 12, 16, 17, 87, and 88.

[*Pogonotriccus*: Miniature of *Leptopogon* but more active and bill shorter; bold dark ear patch, except 53 with prom. white eyering; forest midlevels to canopy.]

## 52. MARBLE-FACED BRISTLE-TYRANT
*Pogonotriccus ophthalmicus*     Pl. 36, Map 976
**Identification:** 4.6″ (11.7cm). Slender. Bill rather narrow and *blackish*. Crown and nape dusky gray; face and *sides of head grizzled gray and white* and with *white-rimmed black crescent on ear coverts*; narrow inconspic. white eyering; otherwise olive green above; wings dusky; wing edgings and *2 wing bars pale yellow*; throat pale gray; breast yellowish olive; belly bright yellow.
**Similar species:** Easily confused. Plumbeous-crowned Tyrannulet (2) lacks grizzled facial area, has prom. white eyebrow, whitish (not gray) throat, and stubbier bill. Also see Variegated Bristle-Tyrant (54), Slaty-capped Flycatcher (48), and Ashy-headed Tyrannulet (6), all of which have sim. head patterns.
**Voice:** Song a brief, squeaky, unmusical *eskeek e' ti'ti'ti'ti'ti'ti*.
**Behavior:** Fairly active as they perch upright and sally short distances to snap prey from foliage and twigs, usually without a brief hover; 1 to several normally follow bird flocks in canopy or subcanopy. Often flick a wing up when perched as do *Leptopogon* and several other small tyrannids.
**Breeding:** Pair building mossy cup about 18m up on small forked branch, 7 June, W Andes above Cali (Hilty).
**Status and habitat:** Fairly common in humid and wet forest ("cloud forest") in W Andes from 1600–2100m. "Rare" at Finca Merenberg, Huila (2300m) at upper limit of range (Ridgely and Gaulin 1980).
**Range:** 1400-2400m (to 600m on Pacific slope). W Andes from extreme n Valle (Cerro Tatamá) southward, both slopes of C Andes from n Tolima (Quindío Mts.) to head of Magdalena Val.; se Nariño (Cerro Pax). N Venez. s in mts. to w Ecuador and nw Bolivia.
**Note 1:** Placed in the genus *Phylloscartes* by Traylor (1977). **Note 2:** Ecuadorean Bristle-Tyrant (*P. gualaquizae*) of subtropical zone on e slope of Andes in Ecuador, Peru and Bolivia, may occur on adj. Colombian slope in e Nariño and w Putumayo. Ecuadorean much like Variegated Bristle-Tyrant, but wing bars pale yellow.

## 53. SPECTACLED BRISTLE-TYRANT
*Pogonotriccus orbitalis*     Map 977
**Identification:** 4.2″ (10.7cm). Slender. Bill black above, pale below. Crown dark gray; otherwise olive green above with *conspic. white eyering*; 2 distinct yellowish white wing bars and secondaries edged yellowish white; underparts yellow.
**Similar species:** Distinguished from allies by prom. white eyering, *lack* of blackish pattern on sides of head, and rather small size. Cf. 48, 52, 54.
**Behavior:** Much like others of the genus.
**Status and habitat:** Known in Colombia from 5 specimens (FMNH) taken mid-Mar 1971 at Estación de Bombeo Guamués (900m) in Putumayo. Lower montane forest. May be fairly common locally in foothills or higher.
**Range:** Upper tropical zone. E slope of Andes in sw Putumayo. Se Colombia and e slope of Ecuador to n Bolivia.

## 54. VARIEGATED BRISTLE-TYRANT
*Pogonotriccus poecilotis*     Pl. 36, Map 978
**Identification:** 4.5″ (11.4cm). Much like Marble-faced Bristle-Tyrant (52), *but wing bars wider and bright cinnamon* (not yellow), and *lower mandible orange yellow* (not dark).
**Similar species:** Readily told from other sim. allies, Plumbeous-crowned (2) and Ashy-headed tyrannulets (6), by broad cinnamon wing bars and orange yellow lower mandible. Also see Slaty-capped Flycatcher (48), which is larger with "spotted" wing bars and blackish bill. Also cf. 33.
**Voice:** Clear, thin *whee-see* on 1 pitch (Miller 1963).
**Behavior:** Sim. to Marble-faced Bristle-Tyrant and sometimes found with it. Lower mid. story to subcanopy.
**Breeding:** 5 BC birds, Mar–May, C Andes (Carriker). July nest, dependent fledglings, Oct, above Cali (S. Gniadek).
**Status and habitat:** Fairly common in humid and wet forest ("cloud forest").
**Range:** 1500-2300m. W Andes (not Antioquia), C Andes, and head of Magdalena Val. in Huila; Perijá Mts. and E Andes from Norte de Santander (50km nw of Cúcuta) and se Santander to sw Cundinamarca. Nw Venez. s in Andes to nw Ecuador and s Peru.
**Note:** Placed in the genus *Phylloscartes* by Traylor (1977).

## 55. YELLOW TYRANNULET
*Capsiempis flaveola*     Pl. 36, Map 979
**Identification:** 4.5″ (11.4cm). Slender; rather long-tailed. *Yellowish olive above*; wings dusky with yellow edgings and *2 yellow wing bars; long eyestripe yellow* (or whitish—*leucophrys*); faint yellowish to whitish eyering broken by dusky lores and smudge behind eye; *entire underparts yellow*. Tail often slightly cocked.

**Similar species:** Yellowish green upperparts, the eyebrow, and yellow underparts are best marks. Yellow-breasted Flycatcher (90) lacks eyestripe; Southern Beardless, Slender-billed, and Pale-tipped tyrannulets (12, 37, 38) are not as yellow below. See Subtropical Doradito (43) a mt. bird.
**Voice:** Soft conversational notes, *pee-tee*, or *pee-teetee*, etc.; rolling quality.
**Behavior:** Usually in chattery pairs or groups of 3-4. Perch-glean in foliage 1-8m up like vireos, occas. hover-glean and frequently eat small berries. Sometimes sit rather quietly.
**Breeding:** 3 BC birds, Apr–May, s Bolívar, n Antioquia (Carriker). Yr.-round in Costa Rica; open cup with some green moss outside; 3-7m up in small tree or shrub; 2 white eggs (Skutch 1960).
**Status and habitat:** Shrubby clearings, thickets, and in tangled borders of dry to humid woodland; gallery woodland in llanos.
**Range:** To 500m. Carib. lowlands from Snía. de San Jacinto in n Sucre to n base W Andes (sight recs. upper Río Sinú), and drier parts of mid. Magdalena Val. to Giradot, sw Cundinamarca (*leucophrys*); e of Andes s to Meta and Vichada, in pockets of scrub to Vaupés (*cerula*), locally to Río San Miguel in e Nariño (*flaveola*). Nicaragua to the Guianas and s east of Andes to e Bolivia, ne Argentina, and Paraguay.
**Note:** Placed in the genus *Phylloscartes* by Traylor (1977).

## 56. BRONZE-OLIVE PYGMY-TYRANT

*Pseudotriccus pelzelni* Pl. 38, Map 980
**Identification:** 4.4″ (11.2cm). Small dark flycatcher. Weak crest. Eyes dark red; legs ochre. *Dark brownish olive above*; crown dusky obscurely streaked olive; wings and tail dusky *edged cinnamon brown; throat buffy white*; otherwise olive brown below; *center of belly pale creamy yellow* (or mainly dull dark olive above, paler below, crest as above—*pelzelni*).
**Similar species:** Best marks are more or less uniform dark appearance, cinnamon wing edgings, and creamy throat and belly. No other small flycatcher in its range is as dark below. See Orange-crested Flycatcher (103). Also cf. dark imm. and ♀ Golden-winged and Golden-collared manakins (pp 433, 434).
**Voice:** Song about 4-6 sharp, explosive, wheezy *piff* notes, 1 per sec.
**Behavior:** Usually alone 1-5m up in understory where it very actively flutters and leaps short distances to foliage, usually snapping off prey without hovering. Often continually snaps bill in short bursts when foraging or alarmed as

do others of the genus; does not follow mixed flocks. Wings whirr audibly, somewhat like manakin's, as flies from perch to perch in undergrowth.
**Breeding:** BC ♂, May, sw Huila (Carriker).
**Status and habitat:** Understory of humid and wet forest ("cloud forest"), occas. dense forest borders. In Peru (apparently also Colombia) replaced at higher el. by next sp. (Weske 1972).
**Range:** 700-2500m (mostly below 2000m). Highlands along Panama border (Cerro Tacarcuna), e to n end C Andes (Valdivia) and s on Pacific slope in Cauca and Nariño (*annectens*); Pacific slope in Cauca and Nariño (*berlepschi*); head of Magdalena Val. (sw of San Agustín) and e slope of E Andes in w Meta (1200m), prob. southward (*pelzelni*). E Panama to w Ecuador; e Colombia to s Peru.

## 57. RUFOUS-HEADED PYGMY-TYRANT

*Pseudotriccus ruficeps* Pl. 38, Map 981
**Identification:** 4.3″ (10.9cm). Plump with rather short tail. Bill black above; yellowish below. *Entire head and throat orange rufous*; otherwise mostly olive with *rufous wings, tail, and thighs*; center of belly yellowish.
**Similar species:** No other Colombian flycatcher resembles it (nearest is Rufous-crowned Tody-Tyrant, 65). See Hooded Antpitta (p 425)
**Voice:** Song a bright, high-pitched, fast trill, descending slightly then rising, with snap at end, *teeeeeaaaaaeeeeee-ip*; often bill snaps loudly.
**Behavior:** Wrenlike and inconspic. and usually hard to see. Single birds or pairs strike at foliage in short sallies from inside dense undergrowth; mostly 0.1-3m up, occas. hop on ground.
**Status and habitat:** Uncommon to locally fairly common in undergrowth of dense wet forest ("cloud forest") and bushy forest borders. Upper el. ally of Bronze-olive Pygmy-Tyrant.
**Range:** Mostly 1400-2800m (to 400m in se Nariño; to 3600m, Nevado Santa Isabel, Tolima). W Andes (Valle southward), C Andes (except Antioquia), head of Magdalena Val. in Huila, w slope of E Andes in sw Cundinamarca, and e slope E Andes in se Nariño. Colombia s in Andes to nw Bolivia.

## 58. RINGED ANTPIPIT

*Corythopis torquata* Pl. 33, Map 982
**Identification:** 5.5″ (14cm). *Recalls an ovenbird or waterthrush*. Bill strong, dusky above, yellowish below; long legs flesh pink. Dark olive brown above; crown slightly grayish; *throat pure white*; rest of underparts whitish with a *bold necklace of black streaks across chest* (coalescing

at top to form chest band); under tail coverts brownish.

**Similar species:** Spotted Antpitta (p 423) is superficially sim. but virtually tailless. Also cf. Spot-backed Antbird (p 414) and Banded Antbird (p 396).

**Voice:** A whistled *peeeur-prayer*, both notes slurred downward, 1st higher; snaps bill emphatically when disturbed or flushed, reg. also when foraging (J. Fitzpatrick), the way the bird is most often found.

**Behavior:** Bobs head and wags tail as it walks, like a Spotted Sandpiper, a few springy steps then a pause, on forest floor or perches rather exposed up to eye level in undergrowth. Alone or separated pairs and occas. at army ants. Not shy but unobtrusive.

**Breeding:** BC ♂ 16 May, Mitú, Vaupés (Olivares, 1964b), several more in Apr, upper Orinoco (Friedmann 1948). Mossy oven nest on forest floor, ne Brazil; 2 pinkish eggs with darker mottling (Oniki and Willis 1980).

**Status and habitat:** Infrequently seen. On or near ground in humid *terra firme* forest, sometimes also damp places along streams or in broad, dry, temporary creek beds.

**Range:** To 500m. E of Andes from e base Macarena Mts. to Putumayo, se Nariño (Río San Miguel) and e to Vaupés (Mitú; Caño Cubiyú; Caño Negro); prob. Vichada to Amazonas. The Guianas and s Venez. s to n Bolivia and Amazonian Brazil.

**Note:** Earlier placed in the *Conopophagidae*.

## 59. SHORT-TAILED PYGMY-TYRANT

*Myiornis ecaudatus*                    Pl. 36, Map 983

**Identification:** 2.7″ (6.9cm). The smallest tyrannid. *Practically tailless*. Bright green above with *contrasting black crown* (or gray—*miserabilis*); sides of head gray with *prom. white lores and eyering* ("spectacles"); wings blackish edged yellow (no distinct bars); *underparts white*; sides tinged grayish; under tail coverts yellow (sides tinged yellowish olive, flanks yellowish—*miserabilis*). ♀: cap grayer and duller.

**Similar species:** E of Andes cf. Slate-headed Tody-Flycatcher (78), which is larger, longer-tailed, and has conspic. yellow wing bars and *very* different behavior. Black-capped Pacific form could recall Black-headed Tody Flycatcher (73) in both appearance and behavior, but latter is more yellow below, lacks white spectacles, and has longer tail.

**Voice:** Pacific birds utter a weak, high-pitched *eeeek* or *creek* remarkably like a cricket or small tree frog, and repeated 2-20 times, sometimes faster and faster; e of Andes at Pto. Inírida, 2-3 chirplike squeaks sim. to twisting a well-rosined bird squeaker.

**Behavior:** A difficult bird to see because of small size, sudden movements, and *easily overlooked voice*. Sits quietly 2-18m up, then darts out to underside of foliage or to new perch, occas. sallies a short distance to air. Movements are mechanical, buzzy, and insectlike. Sometimes remarkably unsuspicious.

**Breeding:** 6 BC birds, Feb–May, s Córdoba to n Antioquia (Carriker); 1 dependent fledgling, Anchicayá Val. Mar (Hilty). Rather large moss-covered fibrous ball with side entrance; suspended from twig 1-6m up; 2 white eggs with brownish or cinnamon spots in a wreath at larger end and scattered elsewhere (Wetmore 1972).

**Status and habitat:** Fairly common (usually overlooked) in lower levels of humid and wet forest and at open forest borders.

**Range:** To 900m on Pacific slope; to 500m e of Andes. Panama border e to upper Río Nechí and s on Pacific coast to Nariño (*atricapillus*); e of Andes known from w Meta (Villavicencio), e base of Macarena Mts. (*miserabilis*) and ne Guainía (sightings, Sept. 1978—Hilty). Costa Rica s to n Bolivia, Amazonian Brazil, and the Guianas. Trinidad.

**Note:** Some consider the black-capped *M. atricapillus* (Black-capped Pygmy-Tyrant) of Costa Rica to w Ecuador a separate sp. from gray-capped birds e of Andes.

## 60. SCALE-CRESTED PYGMY-TYRANT

*Lophotriccus pileatus*                   Pl. 36, Map 984

**Identification:** 3.8″ (9.7cm). Tiny. *Yellowish eyes* and broad ample crest of *rufous-edged black feathers*. Crest usually carried depressed but evident nonetheless (elevated and spread crest gives very fierce appearance to such a tiny bird). Olive green above; wings and tail dusky; wing edgings and 2 indistinct wing bars yellowish; *throat and breast dull white* (or pale yellow—*santaluciae*) *rather finely and obscurely streaked olive*; belly pale yellow.

**Similar species:** The crest and *streaky* breast are diagnostic. Distinctive call usually betrays its presence.

**Voice:** Call, loud for so small a bird, a metallic ser. of *preet, pic,* or *trik* notes, sometimes slightly accelerating and rising in pitch; like slowly winding a watch. Trachae abnormally large (Slud 1964).

**Behavior:** Solitary and prob. lek-forming ("exploded lek") in forest understory where advertises its presence by persistent calling throughtout day. ♂♂ remain at well dispersed calling areas much of yr.; perhaps no lasting pair bond formed (Skutch 1967). Leap and flutter short distances to foliage for prey.

**Breeding:** 5 BC ♂♂ Mar–June, Perijá Mts., W

and C Andes (Carriker). Pensile globular nest with side entrance, visor and long, thin, dangling tail; attached to twig 4m up; apparently only ♀ attends nest (Skutch 1967).

**Status and habitat:** Fairly common to common in humid and wet forest and tall second growth (easily overlooked except by voice). Foothills and lower slopes; a highland ally of next sp.

**Range:** 300-2300m (mostly below 1500m), once at sea level in w Cauca. Perijá Mts. (*santaluciae*), E Andes (*squamaecrista*), W and C Andes (*hesperius*). Costa Rica to n Venez. and s in mts. to s Peru.

## 61. DOUBLE-BANDED PYGMY-TYRANT
*Lophotriccus vitiosus* Map 985

**Identification:** 3.8″ (9.7cm). Tiny. *Yellowish white eyes and crest of rather narrow black feathers broadly scalloped gray.* Crest normally held depressed but still apparent. Pale olive green above; wings and tail dusky; wing edgings and 2 fairly prom. *wing bars yellowish;* innermost tertial with pale edge (easily seen in hand); bend of wing yellow (usually concealed); sides of head grayish; underparts yellowish white; throat, breast, and sides indistinctly streaked grayish olive; breast and sides tinged olive; olive-edged tail rather short (shorter than 62 or 72).

**Similar species:** See Helmeted Pygmy-Tyrant (62), which is *very* sim. Also White-eyed Tody-Tyrant (72).

**Voice:** A buzzy trill, *tr'E'E'E'E'E'* or *turrrrrrrrr*, sometimes 3-4 in a ser., bentbill-like but much louder, less nasal, and a little slower (Hilty; T. Parker).

**Behavior:** Dart up short distances to underside of foliage and snap prey without hovering; 1-8m up in forest. Seldom join mixed flocks. Solitary and prob. lek-forming as are others of the genus.

**Breeding:** A Surinam nest, 13 Sept (Haverschmidt 1968); 1 nest building, 29 Aug, Río Javarí, nw Brazil; pensile globular nest (about 0.6m total length) with downward facing side entrance near bottom; visor and short dangling tail; suspended 4m up (J. Dazenbaker and Hilty).

**Status and habitat:** Undergrowth or slightly higher in open *terra firme* or *várzea* forests and tall second growth woodland and esp. in edge situations, forest openings, etc. Occurs mostly s of range of Helmeted Pygmy-Tyrant (may overlap in Vaupés, Guainía, and se Amazonas) and prob. less often in forests of white sand belt.

**Range:** To 500m. E of Andes from s Meta (Macarena Mts.) and extreme e Guainía (Río Guainía) southward. The Guianas; se Colombia to e Peru and Amazonian Brazil.

## 62. HELMETED PYGMY-TYRANT
*Lophotriccus galeatus* Pl. 36, Map 986

**Identification:** 3.9″ (9.9cm). Very sim. to Double-banded Pygmy-Tyrant, but *crest not as full or broad* (feathers longer, narrower, and scalloped grayish olive); *no distinct* wing bars (*yellowish green* wing covert edgings form 2 weak wing bars); inner remiges edged yellowish green; pale edge nearly absent on innermost tertial (this most evident in the hand); underparts whiter giving more defintion to streaking; belly white; flanks tinged yellow; olive-edged tail longer than in Double-banded Pygmy-Tyrant (41-46mm vs 34-36mm), slightly shorter than tail of White-eyed Tody-Tyrant (41-46mm vs 48-51mm).

**Similar species:** See Double-banded Pygmy-Tyrant (61). Also White-eyed Tody-Tyrant (72).

**Voice:** Sim. to Scale-crested Pygmy-Tyrant, a loud accelerating ser. of 4-10 *pic* or *trik* notes, slightly rising; also 2-3 quick *pik*'s followed by a short, rising, warbled phrase.

**Behavior:** Much like Double-banded Pygmy-Tyrant but on average perches higher, usually mid. story or slightly lower.

**Breeding:** 3 BC birds, Feb–Apr, sw Amazonas, Venez. (Friedmann 1948). Pendent nest reportedly resembles that of *Todirostrum*; eggs white (Haverschmidt 1968).

**Status and habitat:** Common inside sandy-belt forest and tall savanna woodland of the extreme east; less often forest edges or swampy woodland.

**Range:** To 400m. E of Andes from e Vichada (Maipures) s to e Vaupés (Mitú); once to Amazonas (sight and tape recording, Leticia, June 1981—Hilty). The Guianas and e and s Venez. to e Colombia and n and e Brazil.

**Note:** Sometimes placed in the genus *Colopteryx*.

## 63. PALE-EYED PYGMY-TYRANT
*Atalotriccus pilaris* Pl. 36, Map 987

**Identification:** 3.5″ (8.9cm). Tiny. Bill shorter, narrower, and more pointed than *Todirostrum*. *Conspic. yellow or white eye* (or dark—juv.). Pale olive above (or crown brownish gray contrasting with back—*griseiceps*); lores and narrow eyering whitish; cheeks tinged buff; wings dusky; wing edgings and *2 prom. wing bars greenish yellow; underparts dingy white; throat and breast indistinctly streaked brownish;* flanks and under tail coverts tinged yellow. In the hand peculiar wing diagnostic; outer 4 primaries greatly reduced in length and width (J. Fitzpatrick).

**Similar species:** See Pearly-vented Tody-Tyrant (70). White-eyed Tody-Tyrant (72) has forehead and sides of head grayish (instead of white lores and eyering and buff tinge on cheeks) and olive wash on underparts. Dull obscurely streaked underparts rule out most other small flycatchers except 61 and 62, both forest birds.

**Voice:** Usual calls are fairly long dry trills, *trrrrr* and *trrreeet*, sometimes *tit, tit trrrrrtreeeeet* (Ridgely 1976); loud for size of bird.

**Behavior:** Often in pairs that actively glean on foliage or flit up at it, usually about eye level. Inconspic.

**Breeding:** 6 BC birds, Mar–Apr, Perijá Mts. and Guajira; 2 laying ♀♀, Oct, Cúcuta (Carriker); 1 BC ♂, Jan, Huila (Miller 1947); dependent fledglings, May and July, ne Meta (S. Furniss) and Aug, Ríohacha (Hilty). Pensile nest about 0.3m long, side entrance, 25 June, Caicara, Venez. (G. Cherrie notes).

**Status and habitat:** Common in arid scrub, dry thickets, and deciduous woodland.

**Range:** To 2000m (mainly below 800m). Carib. lowlands from n Sucre (Snía. de San Jacinto) to Guajira, and Perijá Mts., s in drier parts of mid. and upper Magdalena Val. to s Huila (La Plata); e of Andes from Zulia Val., Norte de Santander, to Macarena Mts., Meta (*pilaris*), and e to Orinoco in Vichada (*griseiceps*). W Panama to Guyana.

[*Poecilotriccus*: From *Todirostrum* by shorter, narrower, more pointed bill; short tail not cocked up.]

## 64. BLACK-AND-WHITE TODY-TYRANT

*Poecilotriccus capitale*               Pl. 38, Map 988

**Identification:** 3.7″ (9.4cm). Bill rather long and flat, (black above, orangish below in ♂). ♂ unmistakable: *mostly glossy black with white lores and eyering; center of throat and breast white; abdomen white* with yellow tinge on flanks; bend of wing and edges of inner remiges yellow. ♀ very different: olive green above with *chestnut crown and buffy eyering*; bend of wing and edge of tertials pale yellow; *throat white; sides of head and entire breast gray*; belly white tinged yellow on sides.

**Similar species:** ♀ recalls Rufous-crowned Tody-Tyrant (65) of highlands but lacks latter's head markings and bright yellow belly.

**Behavior:** In Peru peer 0.5-3m up in dense foliage of shrubbery and sally-glean short distances upward to foliage (T. Parker).

**Status and habitat:** Dense taller second growth (where regrowth is 2-3 yrs. old or more). Not a well-known bird; perhaps rare or local. In Peru, esp. in hill country or foothills of upper tropical zone (T. Parker).

**Range:** To 500m. E of Andes in w Putumayo (Pto. Umbría) and se Nariño (Río Churuyaco). Se Colombia, e Ecuador, ne Peru e to Río Javarí (sight), and w Amazonian Brazil.

**Note:** Often placed in the genus *Todirostrum* and called Black-and-white Tody-Flycatcher.

## 65. RUFOUS-CROWNED TODY-TYRANT

*Poecilotriccus ruficeps*               Pl. 38, Map 989

**Identification:** 3.8″ (9.7cm). Plump with puffy head and rather long bill, fairly broad at base. *Rufous crown* bordered behind by black band and then a gray band on nape; otherwise olive green above; wings blackish with *2 yellow wing bars* and yellowish edgings; *supraloral spot, cheeks, and throat white or rufous buff; eye, mark behind eye, and malar streak black* (or no malar streak—*rufigenis*); *chest white separated from bright yellow lower underparts by narrow diffused olive band* across upper breast.

**Similar species:** Easily told by rufous crown, prom. facial pattern, and "divided" underparts. Pattern most like ♀ Black-and-white Tody-Tyrant (lowlands only). Also cf. Rufous-headed Pygmy-Tyrant (57), which has solid rufous head and throat.

**Voice:** Call a short, pebbly stutter, *patreer-pít*, last note sometimes omitted, or several stutters given in succession, or with other var.; weak and easily overlooked.

**Behavior:** Alone or pairs, occas. several (families?); sit or hop 1-3m up in dense thickets and dart at underside of foliage or to new perch. Often keep concealed and difficult to see, occas. in open at edge of foliage.

**Breeding:** 4 BC birds, Mar–Sept, C and E Andes (Carriker).

**Status and habitat:** Uncommon to locally common in overgrown bushy pastures, hedgerows, and shrubby forest borders. The key is bushes.

**Range:** 1600-2700m (rarely down to 1000m). W and C Andes s to Cauca and head of Magdalena Val. (*melanomystax*); Andes of w Nariño (*rufigenis*); E Andes from Norte de Santander s to se Nariño (*ruficeps*). Nw Venez. s in Andes to n Peru.

## 66. SOUTHERN BENTBILL

*Oncostoma olivaceum*               Pl. 36, Map 990

**Identification:** 3.6″ (9.1cm). Distinguished by *rather thick bill peculiarly bent downward. Eyes usually pale yellow.* Olive above with 2 greenish yellow wing bars and edgings on inner remiges; *throat and breast olive yellow* becoming pale yellowish on belly; breast often faintly streaked darker.

**Similar species:** The Northern Bentbill (67) is very sim., but throat and chest are grayish white streaked gray.

**Voice:** Persistently given call a weak, toadlike, purring trill, *prrrrrrr* or *gurrrrrr*, very nasal and not at all like a bird. Easily overlooked.

**Behavior:** Perches motionless in thick lower

growth, occas. darting off a short distance to new perch or up at foliage. Usually unnoticed unless calling. Thought to call and display on dispersed leks; otherwise solitary and silent (Skutch 1960; Willis 1972c).

**Breeding:** 14 BC birds, Feb–June, Cesar to n Antioquia (Carriker); 1 Apr nest (Skutch 1960), another in Aug (Wetmore 1972), c Panama; small roundish nest with visor and side entrance near top; suspended from branch 1-4m up; 2 white eggs with small blotches and scrawls mostly at large end (Skutch 1960).

**Status and habitat:** Locally fairly common in thickets and undergrowth in forest borders or second growth and lighter woodland (moist to humid regions). Numerous in PN Tayrona.

**Range:** To 1000m. From Panama border and mid. Atrato Val. (s to Quibdó) e across lowlands n of Andes to w and n base of Santa Marta Mts. and Cesar Val. s in Magdalena Val. to n Cundinamarca (Pto. Salgar). C Panama to n Colombia.

**Note:** Often merged with *O. cinereigulare* (Northern Bentbill) of s Mexico to w Panama, calling it Bentbill, but a recent rec. (if valid) indicates overlap of range (see 67).

### 67. NORTHERN BENTBILL
*Oncostoma cinereigulare*

**Identification:** 3.5-4″ (8.9-10.2cm). Iris pale. Resembles Southern Bentbill (66) and with the same *peculiar bent downward bill*, but sides of head grayish, *throat and chest grayish white streaked gray*, rest of underparts pale yellow, flanks washed olive. Adults usually have a grayish cap; otherwise olive green above. Imm. has olive cap.

**Status and habitat:** One specimen (MUNB), Apr 1965, nw Antioquia near Chigorodó, 7°41′N, 76°40′W (Romero and Rodríguez 1980), reportedly this sp. This rec., if valid, is 400-600km e of previous Panama recs.; the intervening territory is occupied by Southern Bentbill. Lower thicker vegetation in second growth woodland and forest borders.

**Range:** Disjunct(?). Nw Colombia (nw Antioquia). S Mexico to w Panama (poss. c Panama).

[*Hemitriccus*: Compared to *Todirostrum*, bill narrower, shorter, and more pointed; plumage duller; tail not cocked up. Low wing noise in flight is characteristic (as also of *Lophotriccus*, *Myiornis*, even a few *Todirostrum*—J. Fitzpatrick).]

### 68. STRIPE-NECKED TODY-TYRANT
*Hemitriccus striaticollis*

**Identification:** 4.3″ (10.9cm). Eyes white. Crown dull brown *contrasting* with plain olive back; *lores and weak eyering white*; wing coverts olive

like back (no wing bars or wing edgings); throat white *distinctly streaked* blackish, the streaks continuing onto green tinged chest; rest of underparts bright yellow.

**Similar species:** See very sim. Johannes' and also Spotted tody-flycatchers (69, 77).

**Behavior:** Fairly easy to see as it perches at low or mid. levels, often in open. Posture rather upright, like other *Hemitriccus* and unlike Spotted Tody-Flycatcher (R. Ridgely).

**Status and habitat:** Three specimens and a few sight recs. Low shrubby growth near wet woodland in ne Meta (S. Furniss). Gallery forest in Brazil (R. Ridgely).

**Range:** To 400m. Known from w Meta and ne Meta at Carimagua (specimens and sightings 1975—S. Furniss). Isolated populations(?) in e Colombia and n Peru. Extreme se Peru, n Bolivia, and n Mato Grosso to ne Brazil.

**Note:** 68-72 sometimes placed in the genus *Idioptilon*.

### 69. JOHANNES' TODY-TYRANT
*Hemitriccus johannis*      Map 991

**Identification:** Very sim. to Stripe-necked Tody-Tyrant (68), but *crown and back uniform olive* (no contrast); *faint lores and eyering dull buff* (sometimes a whitish supraloral mark); wing coverts edged yellow forming *faint wing bars*; throat usually tinged yellow and streaks on throat and breast duller and blurry (not crisp and clean-cut); lower underparts yellow with sides of breast and flanks washed greenish olive.

**Similar species:** Very sim. Spotted Tody-Flycatcher (77) has inner remiges sharply edged yellow, dusky blackish forecrown contrasting with gray rearcrown and bright olive back, and *crisp spotlike streaks* on throat and breast (not dull and blurry). No known range overlap with 68.

**Status and habitat:** Known from one specimen in Colombia at San Antonio, Putumayo (Traylor 1982) and another at Pto. Nariño, Amazonas (Nicéforo and Olivares 1976a).

**Range:** To 400m. W Putumayo to se Amazonas (Río Amazon). Se Colombia, e Peru, w Amazonas, Brazil to n Beni, Bolivia.

### 70. PEARLY-VENTED TODY-TYRANT
*Hemitriccus margaritaceiventer* Pl. 36, Map 992

**Identification:** 4″ (10.2cm). Bill rather long and flat. Plumage drab. Eyes orange yellow (or yellowish brown—imm.). Plain brown above (or grayish olive—*septentrionalis*); crown slightly darker; *lores and narrow eyering white*; wings dusky brown with buffy white edgings; *2 conspic. buffy white bars*; throat and breast dull white *obscurely streaked buffy brown*; lower underparts *pure silky white*.

**Similar species:** From very sim. Pale-eyed Pygmy-Tyrant (63) by browner upperparts, larger size, longer bill, more streaking below, and pure white abdomen (no yellow tinge). **Voice:** Calls frequently. Loud, sharp *tuk, tuk, quéek, quéek*, or 1-2 more *quéek*'s each higher-pitched than the preceding; also a sharp note followed by a rapid descending trill *tick't'r'r'r'r*; a brief nasal trill, and a soft mechanical frog-like buzz (J. Fitzpatrick; P. Schwartz recording). **Behavior:** Hops deliberately among small twigs and foliage, perch-gleans or flits up to leaves, or sallies to air, mostly eye level to the crown of small trees. Does not cock tail up like *Todirostrum*. **Breeding:** 5 BC birds, Apr–June, Santa Marta (Carriker), 2 in Jan, Huila (Miller 1947); 8 nests, May–June, Santa Marta area; globular nest with side entrance near top is suspended from drooping twig; 1-3 dull white eggs sparsely speckled rusty at large end (Todd and Carriker 1922). **Status and habitat:** Fairly common in thickets, arid scrub, and drier deciduous woodland, occas. moist woodland borders. **Range:** To 1100m. Carib. lowlands from Santa Marta area to Guajira and s in Magdalena Val. to Santander (*impiger*), mid. and upper Magdalena Val. from Tolima to n Huila (*septentrionalis*). N Colombia and Venez. locally to Paraguay and se Brazil.

### 71. BLACK-THROATED TODY-TYRANT

*Hemitriccus granadensis*         Pl. 36, Map 993

**Identification:** 4.2″ (10.7cm). Looks bare-faced. Bill rather flat; eyes dark. Dark olive above; inner remiges edged yellowish; *ocular area, lores, and sides of forehead whitish* (or *buff—lehmanni*) and bordered below by *black throat and black lower cheeks*; lower throat whitish deepening to gray or grayish brown on breast; belly white; bend of wing yellow (usually not visible in field). **Similar species:** Easily recognized by large pale ocular area and black throat (no wing bars). **Voice:** One or 2 short gravelly stutters, *dut't't, dut't't*; a more nasal froglike *tip-buuuuu*, and sharp *pik, peet peet*; also a low wing sound in flight as in others of the genus. **Behavior:** Rather quiet and unobtrusive as it perches alone about 2-8m up. Hops deliberately, then darts out in buzzy direct flight (like a *Myiornis*) to foliage or new perch. Sometimes in mixed flocks. **Breeding:** 5 BC birds, Mar—July, Santa Marta and Perijá Mts., W Andes (Carriker; Miller 1963). **Status and habitat:** Uncommon in humid forest ("cloud forest"), forest borders, and tall second growth woodland.

**Range:** 1500-2800m, rarely to 3100m. Santa Marta Mts. (*lehmanni*); Perijá Mts. and E Andes s to w Santander (*andinus*); E Andes from Boyacá southward, W and C Andes (*granadensis*). N Venez. s in mts. to n Bolivia.

### 72. WHITE-EYED TODY-TYRANT

*Hemitriccus zosterops*         Pl. 36, Map 994

**Identification:** 4.4″ (11.2cm). *Pale yellow eyes.* Bill slightly broadened at base but not long or broad like *Todirostrum*. Olive green above; more grayish on forehead and sides of head; *narrow white eyering; 2 fairly prom. pale yellow wing bars*; inner remiges edged greenish yellow; innermost with pale edge; throat grayish lightly streaked paler; *breast olive flammulated with yellow*; sides and flanks tinged olive; center of belly clear pale yellow. **Similar species:** From Double-banded and Helmeted pygmy-tyrants (61, 62) by smooth, uniform, uncrested head (both of above have shaggy scalloped crest usually flattened), narrow eyering, larger size, and slightly broader and longer bill; tail longer than Double-banded; (48-51mm vs 34-36mm) wing bars *much brighter* than Helmeted. Also cf. Pale-eyed Pygmy-Tyrant (63) a scrub bird. **Voice:** In e Peru, frequent loud call a pair or triplet of loud, staccato notes with nasal piping quality, uttered at 5- to 10-sec intervals for long periods; also soft, short trill followed by a single note, *ddddd dueet* (J. Fitzpatrick; T. Parker). Also *kwedíp; kwedíp; kwedíp . . .* (R. Ridgely). **Behavior:** Solitary or in pairs in midlevels inside tall forest, rarely down to eye level. Flits up to underside of leaves like other *Hemitriccus* (J. Fitzpatrick). **Status and habitat:** Humid open *terra firme* forest. Not well known in Colombia. **Range:** To 500m E of Andes in w Caquetá and Vaupés (Caño Cubiyú and Caño Negro, both near Mitú); prob. southward. Fr. Guiana, Surinam, and s Venez. (s of Río Ventuari, Amazonas) s to n Bolivia, most of Amazonian and e Brazil.

[*Todirostrum*: Tiny and pert; rather long narrow flat bill; cocked tail; most with bold pattern.]

### 73. BLACK-HEADED TODY-FLYCATCHER

*Todirostrum nigriceps*         Pl. 36, Map 995

**Identification:** 3.5″ (8.9cm). Rather long flat bill; short tail; *dark eyes. Crown, nape, and sides of head to below eyes glossy black contrasting sharply with bright olive green back and white throat*; wings and tail black; 2 yellow wing bars and yellow-ish wing edgings; breast and lower underparts bright yellow.

**Similar species:** Common Tody-Flycatcher (76) is larger with white eyes and grayish hindcrown that merges into olive back (not sharply contrasting).
**Voice:** Call a loud (louder than Common Tody-Flycatcher) bright *peep*, singly or doubled and normally as part of brisk ser. of up to 10-12 notes.
**Behavior:** As in Common Tody-Flycatcher but normally from midlevels to canopy (not low) where keeps inside the outer perimeter of foliage and easily overlooked except for loud call.
**Breeding:** 1 BC ♂ Feb, n Antioquia, 1 in May, Cesar (Carriker); 2 Santa Marta nests June, one 3m up; pendent fiber ball with downy lining; 1 white egg sparsely spotted yellowish brown and rust at large end (Hilty; Todd and Carriker 1922). Panama nest 10m up, forest edge, Aug (R. Ridgely).
**Status and habitat:** Moist to wet forest borders, second growth woodland, and clearings with tall trees. Fairly common locally in the north, rare on Pacific slope. Common in PN Tayrona and along sw base of Santa Marta Mts.
**Range:** To 600m. Spotty. Pacific slope in upper Anchicyá Val. (sightings, 800-1100m); Gulf of Urabá region, e north of Andes to Santa Marta area, and s in mid. Magdalena Val. to e Caldas (La Dorado); foothills at e base of E Andes from n Boyacá (La Ceiba) s to Cundinamarca (Medina). Costa Rica to e and w Ecuador and nw Venez.

## 74. YELLOW-BROWED TODY-FLYCATCHER
*Todirostrum chrysocrotaphum*    Pl. 36, Map 996
**Identification:** 3.4″ (8.6cm). Rather long flat bill; short cocked tail; pale eyes. *Crown, nape, and sides of head to below eyes black* contrasting with olive green upperparts; small white loral streak *broader and yellow behind eye*; wings black; 2 yellow bars and yellow edgings; chin white; rest of underparts yellow with *necklace of black streaks across chest and on sides of throat.*
**Similar species:** Recalls Common Tody-Flycatcher (76), but cap black, throat white, and necklace prom. Black-headed Tody-Flycatcher (73), no known range overlap, differs in solid black head to below eyes and no necklace. Cf. much duller Spotted Tody-Flycatcher (77).
**Voice:** In w Caquetá a loud monosyllabled *pip*, often 8-10 in ser. (much like Black-headed) and unlike double-sounding *chevík* of *T. pictum* in the Guianas (see note 1 below).
**Behavior:** Alone or in 2's from scrub to lower canopy but more often high where small size and habit of keeping in foliage make it incon-

spic. Flutters about with tail cocked up as do others of the genus.
**Breeding:** Building nest 4-5m up in second growth, June, Florencia (Hilty). July nest, 35m up in forest emergent tree, e Ecuador (R. Ridgely).
**Status and habitat:** Uncommon (easily overlooked) in tall humid *terra firme* and *várzea* borders, advanced second growth, and shrubby areas with tall trees.
**Range:** To 500m. Generally from w Meta (Villavicencio) and Guainía southward (*guttatum*). S Venez. to n Bolivia and Amazonian Brazil.
**Note 1:** Does not incl. *T. pictum* (Painted Tody-Flycatcher) of the Guianas, s Venez. and n Brazil, which lacks the yellow eyebrow and is sometimes merged with *T. chrysocrotaphum.* **Note 2:** *T. pictum* may occur in extreme se corner of Guainía (rec. at São Gabriel, upper Río Negro, Brazil).

## 75. GOLDEN-WINGED TODY-FLYCATCHER
*Todirostrum calopterum*    Pl. 36, Map 997
**Identification:** 3.8″ (9.7cm). Recalls Black-headed Tody-Flycatcher. *Upperparts olive contrasting with black head and white throat*; shoulder patch chestnut bordered below by a *wide yellow wing band*; rest of wings and tail black; inner remiges edged pale yellow; breast and lower underparts bright yellow. Eyes dark brown.
**Similar species:** Common Tody-Flycatcher (76) lacks the chestnut shoulders, wing band, and sharply contrasting crown and back, and has longer bill more rounded at tip. Yellow-browed (74) has bold yellow postocular and black necklace. Black-headed (73) lacks chestnut shoulders.
**Voice:** In se Peru a mechanical *tsk-t-t-t-t-t*, rapid, descending, repeated at 5- to 10-sec intervals (J. Fitzpatrick); note like Common Tody-Flycatcher (T. Parker).
**Behavior:** Peer about in dense low growth at forest edge, then sally-glean short distances upward to foliage (T. Parker).
**Status and habitat:** Few recs. Low in dense bushy pastures and shrubby forest clearings at Limoncocha, (D. Tallman). In Peru mainly in hill country, 300-1000m (T. Parker).
**Range:** 350-450m. E of Andes in w Putumayo (Río Guineo near Pto. Umbría) and se Nariño (Río Churuyaco). Se Colombia, e Ecuador, and e Peru.

## 76. COMMON TODY-FLYCATCHER
*Todirostrum cinereum*    Pl. 36, Map 998
**Identification:** 3.8″ (9.7cm). Tiny with cocked tail and *conspic. whitish eyes*; rather long flat bill. *Sides of head and forecrown black becoming slate gray on nape and olive on back and rump*; wings

black with yellow edgings; graduated black tail broadly tipped white; *underparts bright yellow* (or throat white—*sclateri*).

**Similar species:** See Black-headed Tody-Flycatcher (73); e of Andes, Yellow-browed and Golden-winged tody-flycatchers (74, 75). Subtropical Doradito (43) has different shape and lacks blackish forecrown.

**Voice:** Rather vocal. Call a bright single or doubled *teet*; also trilled *te'e'e'eet!* like Tropical Kingbird but usually repeated several times quickly (Tropical gives single trill).

**Behavior:** Flutters and hops with tail up, stopping to look overhead here and there in rather dense foliage from shrub to treetop hts.; makes quick darts at undersides of leaves, occas. sallies at flying prey; usually in pairs. In a common display hitches sideways along perch with tail cocked and shivering over back (J. Fitzpatrick).

**Breeding:** 3 nests, Apr–June, Cali; 3 more, Jan–Apr, Anchicayá Val. (Hilty); 1 in Mar, Calima Val., Valle (Brown); 1 in Aug, ne Meta (S. Furniss). Pendent nest trashy and globular with side entrance and usually a hanging tail; 1-5m up, rarely to 20m up; 2-3 white eggs.

**Status and habitat:** Common in shrubby areas, thickets, gardens, and into overgrown clearings in forested areas. Not arid regions and sometimes uncommon in apparently suitable area within forested regions. Perhaps replaced in most of Amazonian region by Spotted Tody Flycatcher (J. Fitzpatrick).

**Range:** Lowlands and in decreasing nos. to 1900m. Pacific slope and coast from sw Cauca (Guapí) to Nariño (*sclateri*), otherwise generally w of Andes (except Guajira) and e of Andes s to their base in Putumayo (*cinereum*), poss. e to ne Guianía at mouth of Río Guaviare (rec. in adj. Venez.). S Mexico to nw Peru, Bolivia, and se Brazil (except most of Amazonia).

### 77. SPOTTED TODY-FLYCATCHER

*Todirostrum maculatum*      Pl. 36, Map 999

**Identification:** 3.8″ (9.7cm). Rather long flat bill; prom. yellowish orange eyes. Forecrown blackish *shading to gray on hindcrown and bright olive green on upperparts*; wings and tail dusky brown; inner remiges and wing coverts edged yellowish green (no distinct bars); loral spot white; throat whitish *narrowly and sharply streaked blackish*; otherwise yellow below; chest and sides washed olive and with a few vague streaks becoming blurry on sides.

**Similar species:** Very like Johannes' Tody-Tyrant (69) and not easily separated in the field. Tody-Flycatcher has gray crown in contrast to olive back; also streaking on throat and upper

chest crisp, narrow, and almost dotlike (not broad, blurred and merging with wash on chest), and sharp yellow wing edgings (faint in 69). Bill shape differences and tody-tyrant's faint buff eyering best compared in the hand. Stripe-necked Tody-Tyrant (68), even more sim. than 69, is not known to overlap in range. It differs in brownish crown, faint white eyering, and no yellow edging on inner remiges.

**Voice:** Loud *PEEP*, singly or doubled and always uttered as part of ser. of 4-10. Pairs commonly syncopate their ser. of notes in a duet (J. Fitzpatrick).

**Behavior:** More difficult to see than Common Tody-Flycatcher (76) and generally less animated. Flits to underside of foliage, mostly 1-5m up in thickets; usually pairs.

**Breeding:** Stub-tailed young with ads., 22 Aug, Leticia (Hilty); nest as in Common Tody-Flycatcher; usually near wasp's nest and less than 3m up; 2 white eggs with red dots in Surinam (Haverschmidt 1968).

**Status and habitat:** Common. Shrubby second growth and in thickets with scattered trees in pastures and clearings; also brush along *várzea* forest stream borders and young second growth on Amazonian river isls. or banks of Amazon. Occurs se of preceding sp.

**Range:** To 500m. E of Andes from w Caquetá (Tres Esquinas) s to Amazonas (Leticia). The Guianas, e and s Venez., Amazonian Brazil, e Peru, and n Bolivia. Trinidad.

### 78. SLATE-HEADED TODY-FLYCATCHER

*Todirostrum sylvia*      Pl. 36, Map 1000

**Identification:** 3.7″ (9.4cm). Fairly long flat bill; eyes dark. Olive green above with *slate gray head; loral stripe and eyering* (broken in front) *white*; wings blackish with yellow wing edgings and *2 conspic. yellow wing bars; throat and belly white*; breast and sides smudged pale gray. Imm.: top of head olive green like back; throat and breast faintly washed olive; eyes whitish to dark.

**Similar species:** See Short-tailed and Pale-eyed pygmy-tyrants (59, 63).

**Voice:** Easily overlooked. Call a soft gravelly *trup* or *tuk grrrt*, last note slightly rolled (both rather like Rusty-fronted Tody-Flycatcher); also a longer, nasal, froglike trill sim. to Southern Bentbill and Pale-eyed Pygmy-Tyrant.

**Behavior:** Often tame but keeps concealed in dense thickets and difficult to see. Hops about and gleans or flits at foliage, mostly 0.1-4m up.

**Breeding:** 7 BC birds, Jan–Aug, Cartagena and n Antioquia (Carriker). Pendent, pear-shaped nest with side entrance sim. to Common Tody-Flycatcher; low in thicket; 1 nest in Mar, Costa

Rica (Brown), 1 in June, Venez., Orinoco, 2 creamy white eggs dotted and spotted brown at larger end (Cherrie 1916; Skutch 1960). **Status and habitat:** Fairly common in dense thickets and vine-tangled young second growth along forest borders, gallery forest, woodlots, etc.; dry to humid regions. **Range:** To 1100m. Upper Río Sinú ne to Santa Marta region, s in Cauca Val. to Cali, and in Magdalena Val. to n Huila; Pacific slope in mid. Dagua Val. (Cisneros, 300m) and e of Andes s to w Meta (Villavicencio) and e Vichada (Maipures). S Mexico to the Guianas and ne Brazil.
**Note:** Berlepsch's Tody-Flycatcher (*Todirostrum hypospodium*), known only from 1 "Bogota" specimen is poss. a dark var. of *T. sylvia*.

## 79. RUSTY-FRONTED TODY-FLYCATCHER

*Todirostrum latirostre*          Pl. 36, Map 1001
**Identification:** 3.7″ (9.4cm). Nondescript for a *Todirostrum*. Bill rather long and flat (but shorter than Common Tody-Flycatcher; eyes dark. *Forehead and face rusty buff*; crown brownish gray becoming olive on upperparts; wings dusky with 2 more or less distinct ochraceous wing bars and yellow edgings; *underparts dull grayish white*; breast and sides tinged olive; tail slightly shorter than others of the genus.
**Similar species:** Easily confused. Best told from other small thicket-dwelling tody-flycatchers and pygmy-tyrants by rusty buff on forehead and around eyes and dull unstreaked underparts. Cf. Double-banded and Pale-eyed pygmy-tyrants (61, 63).
**Voice:** Froglike call a short, dry, low-pitched *chup, trrrr trrrr* slightly trilled and gravelly; or sim. var., but 1 or more trills is characteristic.
**Behavior:** Hops about very low (0.1-3m up) in dense thickets where notably difficult to see and would seldom be detected except for occas. weak call. Sallies short distances up to foliage after looking about carefully.
**Breeding:** 3 BC birds, June, w Caquetá (Carriker).
**Status and habitat:** Uncommon to fairly common in dense second growth thickets and overgrown tangles in pastures, riverbanks, and *terra firme* or *várzea* borders. Common (by voice) around Leticia.
**Range:** To 500m. E of Andes from w Caquetá (Florencia) and Vaupés (near Mitú) southward. Se Colombia to n Bolivia, Amazonian and s Brazil, and Paraguay.

## 80. BROWNISH FLYCATCHER

*Cnipodectes subbrunneus*          Pl. 39, Map 1002
**Identification:** ♂ 7″ (18cm); ♀ 5.5″ (14cm).

*Rather long tail.* Broad bill black above, pale below; prom. rictal bristles; eyes light orange. *Mainly dull brown*, rump and tail rufescent brown; small buff loral spot; wing coverts and flight feathers with narrow buff edes; throat light brown (paler than underparts); center of belly yellowish buff. Ad. ♂ has peculiarly twisted outer primaries with thickened shafts.
**Similar species:** Resembles Royal Flycatcher (96), but head rounded (not "hammer-headed"). From Thrush-like Manakin (p 439) by longer more rufescent tail, buff wing bars and edgings, and yellowish tinge on belly; also by peculiar wing-lifting habit.
**Voice:** Persistent call all through the day both e and w of Andes, a sharp, emphatic, whistle, *KUEER!* or *KUEER! KUEER!*, less often a trebled *KUHEER! KUHEER-QUER*, all var. often preceded by 1-2 loud bill snaps. Can produce a very audible *pr'r'r'r'r'r* in flight with wings.
**Behavior:** Usually seen singly, perhaps in scattered leks, in well shaded open understory of forest or taller second growth. Often rather unsuspicious. Has habit of raising a wing over the back in casual, almost stretching, motion.
**Breeding:** 11 BC birds, Jan–Apr, n Antioquia to Chocó, 1 in June, w Caquetá (Carriker). Unfinished Mar nest, Barro Colorado Isl., a long (1 m) cylindrical mass of dangling fibers with side entrance; attached to aerial root 2m up. Shape resembled nest of Royal Flycatcher but bulkier, material more homogeneous (Skutch *in* Wetmore 1972).
**Status and habitat:** Uncommon in open humid forest and old second growth, sometimes near small streams.
**Range:** To 1200m (to 400m e of Andes). Pacific coast and e north of Andes in humid lowlands to mid. Magdalena Val. (s to Remedios, e Antioquia); e of Andes from s Meta (Macarena Mts.) s to se Nariño and Amazonas (sightings). C Panama to w and e Ecuador, ne Peru, and Amazonian Brazil.

## 81. RUFOUS-TAILED FLATBILL

*Ramphotrigon ruficauda*          Pl. 37, Map 1003
**Identification:** 6.3″ (16cm), Large-headed; bill flat and fairly broad (not as wide as *Rhynchocyclus*); lower mandible pale basally. Olive above with *bright rufous rump and tail; 2 broad rufous wing bars and all of remiges broadly edged bright rufous*; narrow whitish eyering; throat grayish; rest of underparts pale yellow obscurely streaked olive; heaviest on breast and sides; crissum cinnamon.
**Similar species:** Should be unmistakable with rufous wing bars, edgings, and tail. See much smaller Ruddy-tailed Flycatcher (98).
**Voice:** Plaintive, mournful whistle (followed by

a low note, *whooooo, wot*, flutelike quality (T. Parker); sometimes only a single *wheeeer* rather like Dusky-capped Flycatcher.

**Behavior:** Sluggish but usually more active than allied *Rhynchocyclus*. Single birds or pairs perch mainly 3-12m up in shady mid. story. Sit quietly, then dart to leaf or branch or flutter momentarily before falling away to new perch. More often seen away from bird flocks than in them.

**Status and habitat:** Humid *terra firme* and *várzea* forests; most common in sandy woodlands as at Mitú.

**Range:** To 600m. E of Andes from w Meta (Villavicencio), w Vaupés (San José del Guaviare), and se Guainía southward. The Guianas and s Venez. s to n Bolivia and Amazonian Brazil.

## 82. DUSKY-TAILED FLATBILL
*Ramphotrigon fuscicauda*
**Identification:** 6.5″ (16.5cm). Bill as in 81. Above brownish olive, crown somewhat darker; lores and narrow eyering whitish; *wings and tail dusky*; inner remiges edged buffy yellow, *2 cinnamon wing bars*; underparts dull yellow streaked dusky.

**Similar species:** From any other "flatbill" by combination of cinnamon wing bars and lack of eyestripe. Rufous-tailed Flatbill (81) has bright rufous rump and tail and mostly rufous wings. Smaller Large-headed Flatbill (83) has narrow whitish eyestripe and is less distinctly streaked below. Olivaceous Flatbill (85) has yellowish (not cinnamon) wing bars and broader bill.

**Voice:** Call a loud drawn-out *peeeeeewEEP*, slowly slurring downscale with upward inflection at end (J. Fitzpatrick).

**Status and habitat:** One specimen 30 Oct 1969 is only rec. Low to mid. story vine tangles in swampy forest in Peru (J. Fitzpatrick).

**Range:** 300m. Sw Putumayo (San Antonio on Río Guamués). Se Colombia, ne Ecuador (lower Río Suno), e Peru, and Bolivia.

## 83. LARGE-HEADED FLATBILL
*Ramphotrigon megacephala*     Pl. 37, Map 1004
**Identification:** 5.2″ (13.2cm). *Small flatbill* with heavy-headed appearance; bill dusky, lower mandible pale at base. Olive above with slightly contrasting brownish crown; *short narrow yellowish white eyestripe and white eyering*; wings dusky brown with *2 prom. cinnamon buff bars* and yellowish edgings; throat yellow olive; breast olive tinged yellow; *both vaguely streaked paler*; belly clear yellow.

**Similar species:** Smaller than other flatbills (81, 82, 85, 86); from 85-86 by prom. cinnamon

buff wing bars, short eyestripe, and contrasting crown and back. See Roraiman Flycatcher (106; narrower bill, faint supraloral stripe).

**Voice:** In Peru, 2 mournful whistles slurred together *wheee, whew* (inhale, exhale), 1st note higher and ventriloquial (T. Parker).

**Behavior:** In Peru perch rather exposed, 2-6m up, usually in bamboo. Typically avoid dense foliage but sit motionless and difficult to see. Sally-glean short distances forward and upward to branches and foliage (T. Parker).

**Status and habitat:** Known from only a few Colombian localities, all close to or in foothills. In Peru in bamboo patches and nearby-cluttered understory (O'Neill 1974).

**Range:** To 500m. E of Andes from s Meta (Río Dudita and Río Guapayá in Macarena Mts.) to w Putumayo (Pto. Umbría). Prob. to nw Arauca (on upper Río Arauca, Venez.) and e to Vaupés and Amazonas. Venez. s to e Peru, n Argentina, w Amazonian and se Brazil, and Paraguay.

[*Rhynchocyclus*: Large-headed; very broad flat bill and dull plumage; large size (compared to *Tolmomyias*; forest.]

## 84. EYE-RINGED FLATBILL
*Rhynchocyclus brevirostris*     Pl. 37, Map 1005
**Identification:** 6″ (15cm). Broad flat bill with pale lower mandible. Very sim. to Olivaceous Flatbill (85) but somewhat darker above and below; *throat, breast, and sides more or less unstreaked yellowish olive* (more uniform and darker than Olivaceous Flatbill); wings with inconspic. tawny olive edgings (instead of broad yellow bars and edgings); *wider, more conspic. white eyering*. Also *note ranges*.

**Voice:** Often rather quiet. In Costa Rica a buzzy rising *bzzeeeep* (recalls a *Tolmomyias*); also a quick sibilant *toost* or *whust*, harsh and burry (Hilty; Slud 1964).

**Behavior:** Sim. to Olivaceous Flatbill.

**Breeding:** 3 BC birds, Mar, Chocó (Haffer 1975). Nest sim. to Olivaceous Flatbill's; 2 pale reddish brown eggs mottled dark red brown, esp. in a wreath at larger end; nests used as dormitories yr. round (Skutch 1960).

**Status and habitat:** Forest, less often forest borders. In e Panama and on Panama-Colombia border occurs chiefly in highlands (above 600m) and above range of Olivaceous Flatbill; however, Olivaceous does not enter the very wet lowland forests of Pacific Colombia and here the Eye-ringed Flatbill occurs in lowlands (where the abundantly wet forest may offer sim. ecological conditions to montane forest elsewhere) as well as the lower highlands (Haffer 1975).

**Range:** Disjunct. About 700-1500m on Panama border (Cerro Tacarcuna) and lowlands up to 1100m (sightings, Valle—Hilty) on Pacific slope from mid. Atrato Val. (Mutatá; Río Uva) southward. S Mexico to nw Ecuador.

## 85. OLIVACEOUS FLATBILL

*Rhynchocyclus olivaceus*      Pl. 37, Map 1006
**Identification:** 5.8″ (14.7cm). *Broad flat bill* black above, flesh color below. Upperparts dark olive; wings with broad yellowish edgings and *fairly prom. yellowish wing bars*; indistinct whitish eyering (large eye); *throat and breast yellowish gray obscurely streaked olive*; lower underparts yellowish white, palest on belly.
**Similar species:** See Eye-ringed and Large-headed flatbills (84, 83).
**Voice:** Call a loud, sharp, whistled *skreeek* sim. to Gray-crowned Flycatcher but hoarser and lower-pitched (J. V. Remsen). In n Venz. 5-7 nasal, upslurred notes, *tree-tree-tree-e-e-e*, ascending and faster at end (J. Fitzpatrick).
**Behavior:** Lethargic and usually acts a little dazed. Alone or in forest bird flocks; sits quietly, looking about in mid. story or lower. Perches very erect, turns head slowly, darts quickly to foliage or a twig, then drops away to a new perch (seldom sallies to air).
**Breeding:** 15 BC birds, Feb–Jun, n Colombia (Carriker; Haffer 1975). Bulky pear-shaped nest usually with downward projecting entrance spout at side of bottom (shape of *Tolmomyias* nest but larger and coarser material); 2-7m up, often used as dormitory (Skutch 1960).
**Status and habitat:** Uncommon in humid forest, older second growth woodland, and *várzea*. Does not enter superwet belt on Pacific coast s of Panama border.
**Range:** To 600m. Panama border s on Pacific to Río Napipí, n Chocó, e across lowlands to mid. Magdalena Val. near Bucaramanga; Snía. San Jacinto, n Sucre, n and ne base of Santa Marta Mts., and n end Perijá Mts.; e of Andes from Norte de Santander and Arauca to se Nariño and Amazonas (Leticia). Panama to n Bolivia, Amazonian and e Brazil, and the Guianas.

## 86. FULVOUS-BREASTED FLATBILL

*Rhynchocyclus fulvipectus*      Pl. 37, Map 1007
**Identification:** 6″ (15cm). Large-headed; broad flat bill; lower mandible pale. Olive green above; wings and tail brownish; wing coverts edged rufous (no distinct bars); remiges edged tawny buff; *throat and breast tawny ochraceous contrasting with streaky yellowish buff belly*.
**Similar species:** From other flatbills (84, 85) by combination of very weak eyering, tawny

to rufous wing edgings, and very different underparts.
**Behavior:** Sim. to Olivaceous Flatbill. Joins bird flocks in understory where sits quietly 1-4m up and looks about for long periods, then sallies med. distances to foliage (may hover-glean) and goes on to different perch.
**Breeding:** BC ♂, May, n end W Andes (Carriker). Nest sim. to others of the genus (T. Parker). Eggs from Antioquia reportedly white with a few reddish spots near large end (Sclater and Salvin 1879).
**Status and habitat:** Uncommon in humid and wet forest, second growth woodland, and shrubby borders. Sometimes in more bushy areas than other flatbills.
**Range:** 750-2100m (sight recs. to 200m) on Pacific slope from n end of W Andes (Frontino, Antioquia) s to Nariño; 1900-2300m on w slope of E Andes s to head of Magdalena Val.; prob. e slope of E Andes as known from adj. sw Táchira, Venez. (1800m), and ne Ecuador (1500m). Venez. s in Andes to n Bolivia.

[*Tolmomyias*: Members of this genus are difficult to identify; fairly broad flat bill; crisp yellow wing bars and wing edgings. All *Tolmomyias* songs follow sim. temporal pattern, differ primarily in quality of notes (J. Fitzpatrick).]

## 87. YELLOW-OLIVE FLYCATCHER

*Tolmomyias sulphurescens*      Pl. 37, Map 1008
**Identification:** 5.6″ (14.2cm). Rather heavy-headed; *flattish bill black above, pale below; eyes pale.* Bright olive green above, crown grayish (or grayish olive crown—*exortivus*) with whitish loral streak and narrow eyering; wings dusky with *yellow edgings and 2 more or less distinct yellowish bars* (no pale speculum at base of primaries); underparts olive yellow, becoming sulphur yellow on lower underparts (or slightly grayer on throat and breast—*asemus*).
**Similar species:** See Yellow-margined and Gray-crowned flycatchers (88, 89). Forest and Greenish elaenias (17, 19) have roundish (not flat) bills, dull wing edgings (Greenish also lacks wing bars), and more slender appearance; in the hand concealed yellow crown stripes.
**Voice:** Calls resemble Yellow-margined Flycatcher's but more staccato, less penetrating; usually 1-2 (occas. up to 6) high-pitched, emphatic, and slightly lispy *pipt* or *tsipt* notes (Hilty); in longer sequences always a longer pause betw. 1st and 2d notes, and final note or 2 emphasized more than others, *tsip . . . tsip tsip TSIP* (J. Fitzpatrick).
**Behavior:** Moves deliberately in midlevels or lower canopy. Flits or leaps at foliage, chases disturbed insects, and occas. eats small berries.

**Breeding:** 7 BC birds, Jan–June, n Colombia (Carriker); 1 in Nov, Tolima (MCN); 1 in Dec, Valle (Hilty); building nest, Jan, upper Magdalena Val. (Miller 1947). Retort-shaped bag of hairlike fibers has downward facing entrance tube at bottom side; often suspended in open over road or stream; about 2-7m up; 2-3 creamy white eggs with slight rufous tinge and brown speckles. Nest also used as dormitory (Skutch 1960).

**Status and habitat:** Uncommon to fairly common in a var. of fairly dry to humid habitats, incl. open woodland, gallery woodland, forest borders, shady plantations, and semiopen areas with scattered trees and woodlots. Quite numerous in taller moist woodland of Santa Marta region.

**Range:** To 1800m (most recs. below 1200m). N Sucre (Snía. San Jacinto) to Santa Marta region, w Guajira, and Cesar Val. (*exortivus*); Gulf of Urabá to sw Córdoba (*flavo-olivaceus*); Pacific coast s to sw Cauca, upper Cauca Val., and head of Magdalena Val. (*asemus*); Magdalena Val. from Santander to n Huila and e of Andes from Norte de Santander to w Caquetá and ne Meta (Carimagua—S. Furniss), prob. to Orinoco (*confusus*). S Mexico to n Argentina, Paraguay, and se Brazil. Trinidad.

## 88. YELLOW-MARGINED FLYCATCHER
*Tolmomyias assimilis*      Map 1009
**Identification:** 5″ (13cm). *Very sim.* to Yellow-olive Flycatcher and often not easily distinguished even in the hand. Smaller with slightly darker gray crown contrasting more with back; white eyering (broken in front); usually *lacks whitish lores* of Yellow-olive; no definite wing bars; wings more broadly edged yellowish (hard to see in field); and throat and breast grayer, contrasting more with yellow lower underparts. Overall has somewhat crisper, clean-cut plumage pattern. Told up close by *definitive whitish wing speculum* produced by wider edge of pale yellow on 3 primaries just below the primary wing coverts. In the hand note 10th (outer) primary longer than the 4th (the reverse in Yellow-olive).
**Similar species:** See under Yellow-olive Flycatcher (87).
**Voice:** Common call a ser. of 3-5 sim. notes, rather harsh, buzzy, and given deliberately but emphatically, *zhweek, zhweek, zhweek,* or *tsish, tsish, tsish, tsish,* followed by a pause of several min. before repeated again (Ridgely 1976), and often with slight pause after 1st note of ser. (J. Fitzpatrick).
**Behavior:** A little more active and spritely than Yellow-olive Flycatcher. Usually amid foliage in mid. and upper levels, sometimes accom-

panying small mixed flocks (Willis 1972c). Occas. cocks tail up slightly.
**Breeding:** BC pair, May, s Córdoba (Carriker); 1 nest building in Apr, Panama (Wetmore 1972).
**Status and habitat:** Fairly common in humid forest and forest edge. Much more a forest bird than Yellow-olive Flycatcher. Seems most numerous e of Andes.
**Range:** To 800m. Gulf of Urabá e in humid lowlands to lower Cauca Val. (Pto. Valdivia) and s on Pacific coast to Nariño; e of Andes from s Meta (Macarena Mts.) and e Vichada (Maipures) southward (Amazonas?) Costa Rica to w Ecuador, n Bolivia, and Amazonian Brazil.

## 89. GRAY-CROWNED FLYCATCHER
*Tolmomyias poliocephalus*      Pl. 37, Map 1010
**Identification:** 4.6″ (11.7cm). Sim. to Yellow-olive Flycatcher but *decidedly smaller; crown and nape dark gray in sharp contrast to bright olive green back*; and bill black, only base of lower mandible pale; eyes usually pale.
**Similar species:** Differs from Yellow-margined Flycatcher (88) by slightly smaller size and more or less distinct wing bars (like Yellow-olive), but positively separated in field from Yellow-margined only where size comparison poss. (J. Fitzpatrick) or by voice; up close or in the hand by absence of (or faint) pale wing speculum.
**Voice:** In Amazonas a somewhat wheezy, high-pitched whistle *fweeee!* (rising inflection); also a ser. of 5-15 low, soft, inflected whistles, *pchoi-pchoi-pchoi . . .* (J. V. Remsen); also in Venez., *feee, feeea . . .* up to 3 *feeea's* (P. Schwartz recording).
**Behavior:** Movements less deliberate than Yellow-olive Flycatcher. Forages amid foliage, mostly at midlevels, occas. higher or lower, and often with small insectivorous bird flocks.
**Breeding:** Amazonas nests, 25 Jan (Hilty) and 4 and 24 June (J. V. Remsen); all in *várzea* (last only 2m above water). Pendent pouch much like Yellow-olive Flycatcher's, 2-25m up, often near wasp's nest; 2 eggs, creamy white with small reddish spots and blotches (Haverschmidt 1968).
**Status and habitat:** Uncommon in humid *terra firme* forest, *várzea*, and borders.
**Range:** To 500m. E of Andes from s Meta (Macarena Mts.), w Vaupés (San José del Guaviare), and e Vichada (Maipures) southward. The Guianas and s Venez. s to n Bolivia and Amazonian and se Brazil.

## 90. YELLOW-BREASTED FLYCATCHER
*Tolmomyias flaviventris*      Pl. 37, Map 1011
**Identification:** 4.8″ (12.2cm). Stouter than others

of the genus; broad flat bill. *Bright yellow olive above*, brighter and yellower on forehead; *lores and eyering ochre yellow*; wings dusky with 2 yellow wing bars and broad yellowish edgings; *underparts mainly yellow with golden tinge on throat and breast* (or dingy olive green above, paler yellow below, chest washed brownish olive, lacks ochre lores—*viridiceps*).

**Similar species:** From all others of the genus by entirely yellow underparts and crown concolor with back. Yellow Tyrannulet (55) has yellow eyestripe, narrow bill, and more slender, delicate proportions.

**Voice:** A loud, shrill, and emphatic but deliberately spaced *surreep . . . surreep, surreep* (J. Fitzpatrick).

**Behavior:** Usually alone or 2's from eye-level to midlevel or higher in borders, shrubby places, and stream sides. Forages amid leaves like others of the genus.

**Breeding:** 4 BC birds, Mar–June, Guajira and s Bolívar (Carriker); 19 Santa Marta nests, Apr–June; retort-shaped nest as in Yellow-olive Flycatcher, suspended from slender branch usually near wasp's nest; 2-3 creamy white eggs with a few dark brown spots at larger end (Todd and Carriker 1922).

**Status and habitat:** Fairly common to locally common in drier seasonal woodland, shrubby areas, and gallery woodland, a few in humid forest borders (thinly spread in Amazonia).

**Range:** To 500m (prob. occas. higher). Carib. lowlands from Sinú Val. e to Guajira and s in Magdalena Val. to Simití, s Bolívar (*aurulentus*); e of Andes from Norte de Santander s to Río Guaviare (*collingwoodi*); w Caquetá and Putumayo to Amazonas (*viridiceps*). The Guianas and Venez. to n Bolivia and Amazonian and se Brazil.

[*Platyrinchus*: Tiny and chunky; exceptionally broad flat bill and short tail; movements sudden; inconspic. in understory. Usually *do not* join mixed flocks.]

### 91. WHITE-CRESTED SPADEBILL

*Platyrinchus platyrhynchos*  Pl. 36, Map 1012
**Identification:** 4.5″ (11.4cm). Stubby with broad flat bill and short tail. *Crown and sides of head slate gray* with semiconcealed white crown streak; otherwise tawny brown above; *throat white; rest of underparts bright cinnamon buff*; paler on abdomen; lower mandible yellow.

**Similar species:** See White-throated Spadebill (92).

**Voice:** Sharp *skip!* or *pip!* like note of *Sclerurus* but weaker and repeated at 3- to 5-sec intervals (Hilty); also a very brief mechanical-sounding buzz, quickly rising up, then falling downscale, much lower-pitched and more na-

sal than song of Golden-crowned Spadebill (J. Fitzpatrick).

**Behavior:** Not as difficult to see as most other spadebills. Alone from a little below eye level to lower midlevel.

**Breeding:** BC ♂, May, Vaupés (Olivares 1964b).

**Status and habitat:** Open lower levels of humid sandy-belt forest near Mitú. Few recs. in Colombia.

**Range:** To 300m. E Guainía (Victorino, Venez. at Guainía boundary) and e Vaupés (Mitú), prob. e Vichada. Surinam, Guyana, and s Venez. s to e Ecuador, n Bolivia, and Amazonian Brazil.

### 92. WHITE-THROATED SPADEBILL

*Platyrinchus mystaceus*  Pl. 36, Map 1013
**Identification:** 3.7″ (9.4cm). Tiny with *broad black bill* and stubby tail. *Strong face pattern.* Olive brown above with usually concealed yellow crown stripe (small or lacking—♀); *loral streak, eyering, and line drooping behind eye buffy yellow*; cheek spot buffy yellow bordered in front by *brown patch below eye, behind by brown crescent; throat white*; breast and sides washed brown and becoming pale yellowish on belly.

**Similar species:** Should not be confused in foothill and mt. habitat. Golden-crowned Spadebill (93), superficially sim., has pale yellow (not white) throat, conspic. black-bordered cinnamon crown, and more contrasting face pattern. Yellow-throated Spadebill (95) has entire head cinnamon, no face pattern, and is mostly yellow below.

**Voice:** Usually rather quiet; a short sharp *squeep!* (Hilty); song a high thin buzzy trill *pe'e'e'e'e'e'e'e'e'e'e't*, rising slightly, then dropping (P. Schwartz recording).

**Behavior:** Very hard to see as perches alone and quietly for long periods, usually well below eye level in undergrowth, then suddenly darts short to med. distance to underside of foliage for prey or flits off to a new perch. Nos. better revealed through mist netting.

**Breeding:** 4 BC birds, May–July, n Colombia (Carriker); 1 in Dec, Río Calima, Valle (MCN). In Costa Rica, compact cup of light-colored fibers with fine black filament lining, about 1m up in crotch; 2 yellowish white eggs with faint rufous wreath at large end (Skutch *in* Wetmore 1972).

**Status and habitat:** Uncommon to fairly common (infrequently seen) in undergrowth of humid and wet forest and tall second growth. Formerly on floor of now deforested Cauca Val. from Valle (Palmira) to Cauca headwaters. Rarely overlaps range of lowland ally, Golden-crowned Spadebill.

**Range:** Mostly 900-2000m (occas. lower on Pacific slope). W of Andes (recs. widely scattered in E Andes), incl. Santa Marta and Perijá mts.; e slope of E Andes from headwaters of Río Casanare s to s Meta and Macarena Mts. (doubtless southward). E Costa Rica to ne Argentina and se Brazil.

### 93. GOLDEN-CROWNED SPADEBILL
*Platyrinchus coronatus*            Pl. 36, Map 1014
**Identification:** 3.4″ (8.6cm). Tiny with broad flat bill and stubby tail. *Strong face pattern.* Olive above with *broad orange rufous crown* bordered black; partially concealed central crown stripe yellow (or lacking—♀); *lores, eyering, and line drooping behind eye pale yellow*; cheeks yellowish bordered in front by *black patch below eye and behind by black crescent from eye; underparts light yellow* with olive wash on breast and sides. Birds w of Andes are brighter yellow below.
**Similar species:** W of Andes see White-throated Spadebill (92); e of Andes Cinnamon-crested Spadebill (94), which lacks prom. facial pattern.
**Voice:** Song a weak, insectlike, buzzing trill, *se'e'e'e'e'e'r'r'r'e'e'e* descending slightly, then ascending; barely audible (J. Fitzpatrick); w of Andes faint notes sometimes added *pip! . . . se'e'e'e'e'a'a'a'e'e'e 'pip 'pip!* as sings at dawn from perch 6-10m up.
**Behavior:** Much like White-throated Spadebill. Single birds, pairs, or families perch mostly 0.5-4m up in open understory where dart short to long distances to foliage for small prey.
**Breeding:** 5 BC birds, Jan–Apr, nw Colombia (Carriker; Haffer 1975); pair feeding Aug fledgling s of Leticia (Hilty). Hummingbird-like cup but bulkier, 1-2m up in sapling crotch; 2-3 whitish or creamy buff eggs blotched var. shades of brown (Skutch 1960).
**Status and habitat:** Uncommon to fairly common in humid forest; on s Amazon bank at Leticia more numerous in open *várzea* than *terra firme* forest.
**Range:** To 900m w of Andes; to 400m e of Andes. Pacific coast and from Gulf of Urabá along humid n base of Andes to mid. Magdalena Val. (to nw Santander); e of Andes in w Caquetá and se Nariño. Prob. se Guainía (at El Carmen, Venez. opp. Guainía) to Amazonas. Honduras to w Ecuador, e Peru, n Bolivia, Amazonian Brazil and the Guianas.

### 94. CINNAMON-CRESTED SPADEBILL
*Platyrinchus saturatus*            Map 1015
**Identification:** 3.7″ (9.4cm). Tiny with broad flat bill, stubby tail, and *without prom. facial pattern.* Dark rufescent brown above with *large partially concealed cinnamon orange crown patch* (small patch—♀); lores, eyering, and throat

white; breast and sides washed olive brown fading to yellowish on lower underparts.
**Similar species:** White-crested Spadebill (91) is larger with slaty (not brownish) crown and bright orange buff breast and sides. Golden-crowned Spadebill (93) has conspic. facial pattern and black-bordered crown patch.
**Behavior:** In ne Venez. and Guyana single birds seen low in undergrowth, and apparently loosely assoc. with bird flocks (G. Tudor).
**Status and habitat:** Few recs. Humid forest. Colombian recs. are from sandy-belt forest.
**Range:** To 300m. Extreme e in Vaupés (Caño Cubiyú; Caño Negro; netted at El Dorado—J. Dunning). The Guianas, s Venez. ne Peru (inc. Pto. Indiana), and Amazonian Brazil.

### 95. YELLOW-THROATED SPADEBILL
*Platyrinchus flavigularis*            Pl. 36, Map 1016
**Identification:** 4″ (10.2cm). Small with broad flat bill (lower mandible bright yellow), short tail, and *no prom. facial pattern.* Olive above with *contrasting cinnamon brown head*; usually concealed crown patch white, the feathers tipped black (not visible in field); *below pale yellow*, brightest on throat and with a smudgy olivaceous breast band.
**Similar species:** Only highland spadebill without a prom. facial pattern.
**Behavior:** Like other *Platyrinchus.*
**Breeding:** 5 BC birds, Apr–June, Perijá Mts. (Carriker).
**Status and habitat:** Apparently rare in Andes in undergrowth of humid montane forest. Carriker took 9 in Perijá Mts. where perhaps more numerous.
**Range:** 1800-2300m. Perijá Mts.; w slope E Andes in nw Cundinamarca (Albán) and head of Magdalena Val. in sw Huila. Nw Venez. s in Andes to ne Ecuador, n and c Peru.

### 96. ROYAL FLYCATCHER
*Onychorhynchus coronatus*            Pl. 39, Map 1017
**Identification:** 6.5″ (16.5cm). Rather nondescript except on rare occas. when spectacular crest is raised. Closed crest projecting over hindcrown and long wide bill give prom. *hammerheaded* appearance. Fully expanded crest a full semicircle fan of shiny vermilion (or yellow—♀) tipped steel blue. Upperparts warm brown; *rump and tail cinnamon* (paler on rump); wing coverts conspic. dotted buff; underparts yellowish buff, throat paler, chest tinged brown and lightly barred dusky. Birds e of Andes (*castelnaui*) have proportionally shorter bill and tail, cinnamon rufous rump, rufous chestnut tail, and more heavily barred underparts; ♀ has orange crest.
**Similar species:** See Brownish Flycatcher (80).

**Voice:** Usually rather quiet. Call a low-pitched jacamarlike *sur-líp*, sometimes over and over.
**Behavior:** Solitary birds are inconspic. as sally med. distances to foliage without hovering; alone or less often in or beneath forest flocks; mainly understory rarely to subcanopy. Function of remarkable crest uncertain as seldom seen expanded. Under natural conditions has been seen raised when preening, once in courtship as ♂ turned head from side to side, fanned tail, and quivered wings (Skutch 1960), and in apparent agnostic display betw. 2 ♂♂ (Hilty and M. Robbins).
**Breeding:** 5 BC birds, Feb–May, n Colombia (Carriker). Long (1-2m), slender, loose (not woven), pensile nest has side entrance to shallow nest chamber; attached to slender branch or vine 2.5-6m up over shady stream; 2 eggs, dark reddish brown at larger end, paler at small end; nestlings barred (Skutch 1960).
**Status and habitat:** Uncommon in shaded lower levels of moist and humid forest, forest borders, and older second growth, esp. near streams; also *várzea* forest in Amazonas. Apparently absent from wet belt of Pacific lowlands and swampy regions of lower Atrato and lower Magdalena vals.
**Range:** To 1200m. From upper Río Sinú e across n lowlands to Santa Marta region, w base of Perijá Mts., and s in mid. Magdalena Val. to San Vicente, w Santander, and e of Andes in Norte de Santander, nw Arauca, and n Boyacá (*fraterculus*); generally from s Meta and Guainía to Amazonia (*castelnaui*). S Mexico to Panama, Venez. and the Guianas s to Bolivia and Brazil.
**Note:** Birds from Mexico to nw Venez. may be a separate sp. *O. mexicanus* (Northern Royal-Flycatcher), from those e of the Andes *O. coronatus* (Amazonian Royal-Flycatcher).

## 97. ORNATE FLYCATCHER
*Myiotriccus ornatus*                  Pl. 37, Map 1018
**Identification:** 4.5″ (11.4cm). Chunky and short-tailed. Bold pattern unmistakable. *Head blackish* with concealed yellow crown stripe and *conspic. white crescent-shaped spot in front of eyes* ("false eyespots"); back dark olive; *rump golden yellow*; wings and tail black, latter extensively cinnamon at base (or all cinnamon—*phoenicurus*); throat grayish becoming olive on breast and *golden yellow on lower underparts.*
**Voice:** Call a high-pitched, penetrating *peet*, often repeated; occas. about 6 quick almost squeaky *skeep* notes, run together.
**Behavior:** Single birds or occas. pairs or family groups reg. join mixed flocks. Actively sally med. to long distances in acrobatic loops and often return to same perch, mostly in open understory to subcanopy, also dart up short

distances to foliage. Movements sudden, flight buzzy.
**Breeding:** 2 BC ♂♂, May, C Andes (Carriker); Mar nest, Anchicayá Val.; 1 nestling in moss and fine rootlet cup, well-concealed 1.3m up on steep earth bank (Hilty).
**Status and habitat:** Fairly common to common locally in very humid and wet forest ("cloud forest"), old second growth, and forest borders. Poss. local.
**Range:** 600-2300m (to 400m on Pacific slope). Pacific slope from Río Atrato headwaters (Bagadó) s to Nariño (*stellatus*); both slopes C Andes in Antioquia and e slope in Caldas (w of Honda), w slope of E Andes from se Santander (Río Virolín) to sw Cundinamarca (*ornatus*); e slope of E Andes from w Caquetá (above Florencia) southward (*phoenicurus*). Colombia to w Ecuador and se Peru.

## 98. RUDDY-TAILED FLYCATCHER
*Terenotriccus erythrurus*             Pl. 36, Map 1019
**Identification:** 4.3″ (10.9cm). Small and perky with slight crest and short bill. *Head and back olive gray; rump and tail bright cinnamon rufous*; wings dusky heavily edged rufous (look mostly rufous at a distance); narrow white eyering; throat whitish; otherwise mostly cinnamon below; legs pale yellow.
**Similar species:** Color pattern remarkably like Cinnamon Manakin (p 436), but posture and shape very different. Manakin lacks eyering, has a round head (no crest), perches more horizontally (not upright), and has narrow and rounded (not broad) bill. Manakin's crown stripe (lacking in flycatcher) usually concealed. Also see Ochre-bellied Flycatcher (47).
**Voice:** In Panama a short, high-pitched, double whistle *tsee, peet* and faint *pe-e-e-eet* (Willis and Eisenmann 1979); sim. e of Andes in Colombia or a single *peeeeea*, falling at end.
**Behavior:** Usually solitary or occas. well separated 2's, and sometimes in mixed flocks. Characteristically perch rather quietly from eye level to midforest ht., then move suddenly to a new perch; take mostly small insects by flitting abruptly to foliage or to air but do not return to same perch. At rest often flick up both wings at once.
**Breeding:** 13 BC birds, Feb–Aug, nw Colombia (Carriker; Haffer 1975); Panama nest a pear-shaped pouch of dark fibers and leaf fragments with entrance, often covered by visor, on side near bottom; suspended from vine or twig 2-6m up; 2 white eggs blotched dark brown mostly around larger end (Skutch 1960).
**Status and habitat:** Fairly common in understory of humid forest and tall second growth; mostly lowlands. Seemingly much less nu-

merous in wet Pacific coastal belt than elsewhere.
**Range:** To 900m. Pacific coast to Nariño and n base of W and C Andes to e and n base of Santa Marta Mts., and s in Magdalena Val. to latitude of Bucaramanga, Santander; e base of E Andes from n Boyacá to se Nariño and generally from w Meta and Guainía southward. S Mexico to n Bolivia and c Brazil.

### 99. TAWNY-BREASTED FLYCATCHER
*Myiobius villosus*       Pl. 37, Map 1020
**Identification:** 5.8″ (14.7cm). Much like better known Sulphur-rumped Flycatcher. *Conspic. yellow rump and rounded black tail*; otherwise very dark olive brown above with semiconcealed yellow (or cinnamon—♀) crown patch; *below mostly tawny brown*; throat whitish; center of belly yellowish.
**Similar species:** See Black-tailed and Sulphur-rumped flycatchers (100, 101).
**Voice:** Sharp explosive *espít!* much like Sulphur-rumped Flycatcher's.
**Behavior:** Sim. to Sulphur-rumped Flycatcher.
**Status and habitat:** Uncommon in undergrowth and lower levels of humid and wet mt. forest, esp. stream sides and usually not far from water. Apparently a montane replacement of Sulphur-rumped Flycatcher (the 2 may overlap at lower el.).
**Range:** Mostly 800-2100m. Pacific slope from nw Antioquia (Frontino) southward; Perijá Mts. (Tierra Nueva) and e slope of E Andes at Arauca-Casanare border (Río Negro). E Panama (Cerro Tacarcuna near Colombian border) to nw Ecuador; nw Venez. s on e Andean slope to nw Bolivia.

### 100. BLACK-TAILED FLYCATCHER
*Myiobius atricaudus*       Pl. 37., Map 1021
**Identification:** 5″ (13cm). Much like Sulphur-rumped Flycatcher. (esp. *barbatus* of e of Andes, which it does not overlap in range). Olive above with concealed yellow crown patch (faint or lacking—♀); *bright yellow rump and rounded blackish tail*; faint whitish eyering; throat yellowish white; *breast washed buffy olive*; lower underparts yellow.
**Similar species:** Meets *aureatus* race of Sulphur-rumped Flycatcher (101) w of Andes from which it differs by fainter eyering and much duller underparts (chest tinged buffy olive *not bright tawny ochraceous* on chest and sides). Tawny-breasted Flycatcher (99) is larger, much darker above, and is mostly tawny below (Black-tailed completely lacks tawny below.)
**Behavior:** Much like Sulphur-rumped Flycatcher but somewhat less acrobatic, not dropping wings and fanning tail as much, and

perching "normally" more often (R. Ridgely). Also differ in habitat, nest site location, and egg color.
**Breeding:** 6 BC ♂♂, Feb–July, n Colombia (Carriker), 1 in Feb, Valle (MCN). On Barro Colorado Isl., June–July (8 nests); sim. to nest of Sulphur-rumped Flycatcher, but all suspended over water; 2 dull peach eggs with faint wreath of darker marks at larger end (Gross 1961).
**Status and habitat:** Dry to moist woodland, shrubby thickets, second growth, and humid forest borders, esp. near water. Normally replaced inside humid forest by better known Sulphur-rumped Flycatcher.
**Range:** To 1400m. Pacific slope near Panama border Río Juradó) and locally s in dry vals. (upper Río Sucio; upper Río Calima, Valle,; once in wet lower Río Calima, Valle,; sw Nariño; Gulf of Urabá e to s base Santa Marta Mts. and w base of Perijá Mts. and s to mid. Cauca Val. (near Cali) and mid. Magdalena Val. (Pto. Berrío, e Antioquia). Perhaps e of Andes in Putumayo and Amazonas (at Limoncocha, Ecuador, and Pto. Indiana, ne Peru). Costa Rica to nw Peru; e Ecuador, e Peru, and Brazil s of Amazon.

### 101. SUPHUR-RUMPED FLYCATCHER
*Myiobius barbatus*       Pl. 37, Map 1022
**Identification:** 5″ (13cm). *Conspic. yellow rump and rounded black tail*; otherwise olive green above with concealed yellow crown patch (♂ only); distinct white eyering; below yellow with *bright tawny wash on upper breast and sides* (or throat yellowish white, chest pale olivaceous, belly yellow—*barbatus*); rictal bristles prom.
**Similar species:** Birds w of E Andes easily confused with Tawny-breasted Flycatcher (99) but smaller, paler olive above, and much more yellow below incl. throat (tawny wash restricted to chest or upper breast, not spreading over most of underparts). The 2 spp. are separated, in part, by el. Also see Black-tailed Flycatcher (100).
**Voice:** Rather quiet. Usual call a low sharp *psit* or *pit* (Skutch 1960).
**Behavior:** Remarkably animated and redstart-like, almost constantly fanning and closing tail, drooping wings, and pivoting and posturing on perch. Perches horizontally on twigs 3-15m up or clings momentarily on sides of trunks and sallies acrobatically to air, occas. to foliage; 1 or 2 reg. accompany mixed flocks.
**Breeding:** 25 BC birds, Feb–May, nw Colombia (Carriker; Haffer 1975). Closed bell-shaped nest with side entrance at bottom; attached to branch 2-14m up, often over stream; 2 white eggs speckled dark brown (Skutch 1960).
**Status and habitat:** Usually common in open

understory of humid lowland forest, smaller nos. in foothills and lower slopes. Replaced in highlands by Tawny-breasted Flycatcher, in seasonal dry or moist woodland by Black-tailed Flycatcher. **Range:** To 1000m. W of W Andes from Gulf of Urabá to Nariño (*aureatus*); humid lowlands n of Andes e to Snía. San Lucas and nw Santander (Río Lebrija) in mid. Magdalena Val. (*semiflavus*); e of Andes from w Meta (Macarena Mts.) and se Guainía southward (*barbatus*); sight recs. n to ne Guainía (Hilty and M. Robbins). Se Mexico to w Ecuador; e of Andes from the Guianas and s Venez. to e Peru and se Brazil. **Note:** *M. sulphureipygius* (Sulphur-rumped Flycatcher) of Mexico to w Ecuador and *M. barbatus* (Whiskered Flycatcher) e of the Andes are sometimes considered separate spp.

## 102. FLAVESCENT FLYCATCHER
*Myiophobus flavicans*          Pl. 37, Map 1023
**Identification:** 5″ (13cm). Shape and posture suggest an *Empidonax*. Olive above with concealed golden crown patch (♂ only); wings and tail dusky brown; *2 prom. buffy wing bars; distinct narrow yellow eyering* broken in front by dark lores; faint yellowish supraloral stripe (not conspic. in field); *underparts rather bright yellow*, duller on throat; *tinged olivaceous on breast and sides.* **Similar species:** Yellow eyering and buff bars are good marks. Wing bars buffier and underparts much yellower than any migrant *Empidonax*. See Orange-crested and Handsome flycatchers (103, 104). **Behavior:** Pairs or families perch erect in lower or mid. story where quiet and inconspic. Sally short distances to air, occas. to foliage. Usually do not join mixed flocks. **Breeding:** 3 BC birds, June, Perijá Mts.; 1 in Mar, sw Huila (Carriker); 2 in Oct, Boyacá (Olivares 1971); 1 nestling in cup nest; twigs, tiny vines, and feather lining; late Feb, PN Cueva de los Guácharos (P. Gertler). **Status and habitat:** Fairly common in humid and wet forest borders (esp. mossy forest), less numerous inside forest. **Range:** Mostly 1500-2700m (to 1200m on Pac slope). Perijá Mts. and all 3 Andean ranges (not rec. n of Valle in W Andes). N Venez. s in mts. to c Peru.

## 103. ORANGE-CRESTED FLYCATCHER
*Myiophobus phoenicomitra*      Pl. 37, Map 1024
**Identification:** 5″ (13cm). Resembles Flavescent Flycatcher. *Dark olive above* with concealed cinnamon rufous crown patch (some-

times lacking in ♀); throat and belly *pale yellow*; entire breast and sides greenish olive. **Similar species:** Differs from Flavescent Flycatcher (102) by much darker and greener upperparts, no pale loral stripe, eyering faint or absent, and paler yellow underparts with yellow wash restricted mainly to throat and central abdomen. In the hand told by usually cinnamon rufous (not golden) crown patch. Also see Bronze-olive Pygmy-Tyrant (56). **Voice:** Call 3 buzzing chips, each higher than preceding, last loudest, *bzip, bzip, bZIP.* **Behavior:** Like Flavescent Flycatcher rather quiet, unobtrusive, and easily overlooked but usually perch lower. Pairs or families sally to air 2-6m up in open understory. Sedentary; usually not with mixed flocks. **Breeding:** BC ♂, 22 Mar, upper Anchicayá Val., 1 with slightly enlarged testis and heavy molt mid-June (Hilty). **Status and habitat:** Humid and wet forest ("lower el. cloud forest"); prob. foothills and lower slopes (few recs.). **Range:** To 1100m. Pacific slope from s Chocó (above Novita near Valle border) s to Anchicayá Val. in Valle (*litae*); sight rec. near Junín, w Nariño (1976—R. Ridgely). W Colombia and nw Ecuador (Esmeraldas); e Ecuador and e Peru. **Note:** Olive-chested Flycatcher (*Myiophobus cryptoxanthus*) of e Ecuador (below San José) and ne Peru (n to mouth of Río Curaray) could occur in se Colombia. 4.8″. Above brown with concealed yellow crown patch (reduced in ♀), 2 buffy white wing bars; mainly yellow below, throat whitish, upper breast washed and lower breast streaked grayish olive, tail grayish brown.

## 104. HANDSOME FLYCATCHER
*Myiophobus pulcher*            Pl. 37, Map 1025
**Identification:** 4.5″ (11.4cm). Shape recalls *Empidonax*, but posture less erect, and head rounded. Highlands. *Cap to eyes olive gray* contrasting with olive brown to dull olive upperparts; concealed cinnamon orange crown patch (sometimes lacking in ♀); wings and tail dusky; edges of inner remiges and *2 prom. wing bars pale cinnamon*; tertials often with a pale spot; *throat and chest orange buff contrasting with creamy sulphur yellow lower underparts*; or throat and chest paler and merging into underparts; wing bars buffy—*pulcher*). **Similar species:** Resembles Rufous-breasted Flycatcher (50) but considerably smaller and shorter-tailed, lacks rufous on sides of head, crown lighter gray, and proportions and behavior different (Rufous-breasted more erect and peweelike with longer bill and habit of flicking a wing up when at rest). From other

*Myiophobus* (102, 103, 105) by contrasting gray cap and distinctive orangish throat and chest. **Behavior:** Pairs or up to 4 or more reg. follow mixed flocks from upper understory to subcanopy. Flit actively to foliage, seldom sally to air. **Breeding:** 4 BC birds, Feb–Aug, W, C, and E Andes (Carriker). **Status and habitat:** Fairly common to common locally inside wet mossy forest ("cloud forest"), less often at edges. **Range:** Spotty. Mostly 1800-2600m; on Pacific slope 1500-2200m, rarely (or locally) to 800m (w Cauca). Pacific slope in Valle and Cauca (*pulcher*—specimens only from Cauca); e slope W Andes in Valle (sightings, 1977-79—Hilty), both slopes of mid. and upper Magdalena Val. (Santander, se of Bucaramanga; Quindío Mts., n Tolima; Cundinamarca s to head of val.—*bellus*); sight recs. on e slope of E Andes in w Caquetá (Sept 1978—Hilty; M. Robbins) and w Putumayo (July 1976—R. Ridgely). Colombia, e and w Ecuador s to se Peru.

## 105. BRAN-COLORED FLYCATCHER

*Myiophobus fasciatus*          Pl. 37, Map 1026
**Identification:** 4.5″ (11.4cm). Bill and shape suggests an *Empidonax*. *Cinnamon to reddish brown above* (or dull brown—*crypterythrus*) with usually concealed yellow crown stripe (faint in ♀); wings and tail dusky; wing edgings and 2 con*spic. wing bars buffy*; underparts dull buffy white (or dull white—*crypterythrus*); *breast and sides indistinctly streaked brown* (blurry streaks). **Similar species:** Recalls a small *Empidonax*, but upperparts reddish brown and always shows some streaking below. Imm. Vermilion Flycatcher (120) is larger, darker, and lacks wing bars. Also see Tawny-rumped Tyrannulet (5). **Voice:** Call, low *wheesp*; song a quick *whee seety seety* (Wetmore 1972); at dawn in w Ecuador a wheezy, *wisk, wee-wee-wee*, rather quickly (Hilty). Most common song (Venez. and Brazil) a slow, clear, musical trill, descending slightly (J. Fitzpatrick). **Behavior:** Alone or in 2's, usually perched rather low and inconspic. in bushy growth or edges of pastures. Sallies aerially, or perch-gleans from foliage; occas. at small fruiting shrubs and trees. **Breeding:** 3 BC birds, Aug–Oct, n end W, C, and E Andes (Carriker); 1 in Jan, Boyacá (Olivares 1963). In Costa Rica, Mar–Apr (Skutch 1960). Woven cup fastened by rim to low horizontal fork; 2 eggs, cream with a few rusty spots at larger end (Sclater and Salvin 1879). **Status and habitat:** Local. Brushy overgrown fields, forest edges, shrubby areas, or thickets along fence rows in dry or humid regions.

Spreads into shrubby regrowth following deforestation and now in such formerly forested regions as lower parts of PN Cueva de los Guácharos (P. Gertler) and tributaries of Río Anchicayá. **Range:** 600-2000m (to 2600m in E Andes). Santa Marta region, all 3 Andean ranges, and mid. and upper Cauca, Dagua, Patía, and Magdalena vals.; e base of Andes from Norte de Santander to w Caquetá (*fasciatus*); no Meta recs.; humid Pacific slope Nariño (*crypterythrus*). Sw Costa Rica locally to n Chile, n Argentina, and s Brazil.

## 106. RORAIMAN FLYCATCHER

*Myiophobus roraimae*
**Identification:** 5.2″ (13.2cm). *Empidonax*-like. Brown above with concealed cinnamon orange crown patch (small in ♀); wings and tail dusky brown; edges of inner remiges and 2 *broad wing bars rufous buff*; faint yellowish eyering; throat yellowish white; rest of underparts washed yellow; chest and sides tinged grayish olive. **Similar species:** Much like Flavescent Flycatcher (102; no known range overlap); in range most easily confused with Euler's Flycatcher (117). From latter by richer brown upperparts, rufescent buff (not whitish to buff) wing bars and edgings, shorter tail, and no eyering (or faint one). Also see Fuscous Flycatcher (118; prom. eyestripe) and Traill's Flycatcher (116). **Behavior:** In Peru usually 1-4m up in understory near edge of tall dense foothill forest mostly 500-1000m (T. Parker). **Status and habitat:** Known from only 2 localities; edge or inside dense scrubby sandy-belt woodland or taller sandy-belt forest. At least in portions of range (Guyana, Venez. and Peru) found in mossy highland forest. **Range:** To 250m. E Vaupés (Caño Cubiyú; Caño Negro, both near Mitú). Sw Guyana, s Venez. (tepuis from 900-2000m), extreme nw Brazil (550m), c Peru. **Note:** Perhaps more than 1 sp. involved, as known range disjunct and habitats differ markedly.

## 107. BLACK-BILLED FLYCATCHER

*Aphanotriccus audax*          Pl. 37, Map 1027
**Identification:** 5.2″ (13.2cm). Slender. *All black bill* a little long and heavy for size of bird. Greenish olive above, crown tinged gray; wings and tail darker; *2 buffy yellow wing bars* (rear bar more prom.); *narrow white supraloral stripe* and faint white eyering; whitish throat and clear, pale yellow belly separated by broad indistinct olive green wash on breast.

**Similar species:** Plumage recalls an *Empidonax*, shape nearer that of *Leptopogon* (e.g. 49) or a small elaenia. *Empidonax* lack the *all black* bill, supraloral stripe, and breast band (Euler's may show *faint* supraloral and faint breast band). Forest and Greenish elaenias (17, 19) also lack supraloral stripe, are much paler below, and usually high (not in undergrowth).

**Voice:** Song at intervals or on approach of an observer, a loud wheezy *bee BEE, be-be-be-bez* or shorter fainter *bee beez bez baw*.

**Behavior:** *Empidonax*-like, though does not perch as erectly (Wetmore 1972). Usually in pairs 1-4m up where they sally or flutter short distances to foliage and continue to different perch. Rather sedentary and more often independent of mixed flocks than in them.

**Breeding:** 4 BC ♂♂, Mar–Apr, s Córdoba to s Bolívar (Carriker); A juv. followed 2 ads., 22 June, sw Córdoba (Hilty).

**Status and habitat:** Undergrowth near creeks or swampy areas inside humid forest; lowlands and foothills (most recs. from latter). Fairly common in Río Verde del Sinú.

**Range:** 100-600m. Gulf of Urabá area (from Panama border e to upper Río Sinú, sw Córdoba), e in humid lowlands at n base of Andes to extreme lower Cauca and mid. Magdalena Val. (Snía. San Lucas) and sw base of Perijá Mts. (Casacará); also Snía. San Jacinto, n Sucre. E Panama and n Colombia.

**Note:** Has been placed in genus *Praedo*.

## 108. CINNAMON FLYCATCHER
*Pyrrhomyias cinnamomea*   Pl. 37, Map 1028
**Identification:** 5″ (13cm). Olive brown above with narrow cinnamon rump band and blackish tail (or *entirely rufous above*, tail dusky broadly edged rufous, rump paler—*assimilis*); concealed crown patch yellow; wings dusky with *bright cinnamon wing bars*; a cinnamon patch on inner remiges; and rufous edgings; *underparts entirely cinnamon.*.

**Similar species:** Unique. Only small mostly rufous flycatcher in highlands. Cf. much larger Cliff Flycatcher (141).

**Voice:** Most common call a dull, low-pitched, flat, rattle, *pti-i-i-i-i* spit out rather suddenly (J. Silliman); also a stuttering *pit, pit-pit-pit-pit* when disturbed.

**Behavior:** A conspic. and charming little bird that is remarkably confiding. Pairs perch alert and erect 3-15m up, energetically sally short distances to air, occas. to foliage, and usually return to same perch. Highly sedentary; join but do not follow mixed flocks.

**Breeding:** 9 BC birds, Mar–July, Santa Marta to Antioquia (Carriker). Prob. yr.-round at San Lorenzo, Santa Marta Mts. but more activity

in Aug–Feb wet season (T. B. Johnson); 5 nests, Jan–June, PN Cueva de los Guácharos (P. Gertler), begging juv., 5 June, W Andes in Valle (Hilty). Moss cup on rock ledge, crevice in rock or bark, fallen log, etc.; usually 1-3m up; 2 white eggs blotched reddish brown (P. Gertler; Ewert 1975).

**Status and habitat:** One of the most common highland flycatchers in humid and wet forest borders, small forest openings, and esp. forest-bordered road cuts.

**Range:** 600-3100m (mostly 1500-2700m). Santa Marta Mts. (*assimilis*); Perijá Mts., the Andes and Macarena Mts. (*pyrrhoptera*). N Venez. s in mts. to nw Argentina.

## 109. TUFTED FLYCATCHER
*Mitrephanes phaeocercus*   Pl. 37, Map 1029
**Identification:** 5″ (13cm). *Conspic. pointed crest.* Olive above, crest duskier; wings and tail dusky; *2 narrow ochraceous wing bars*; prom. loral spot and *eyering whitish; throat and breast buffy ochraceous becoming bright yellow on lower underparts.*

**Similar species:** Only prom. crested *little* flycatcher in w Colombia. Creamy ochraceous throat and breast a good mark.

**Voice:** Frequently repeats a spirited bubbly ser. of 4-7 *pee* or *pik* notes as flicks tail; call reminiscent of that of Greater Pewee but faster, weaker, and not as sharp.

**Behavior:** A perky and confiding little flycatcher, peweelike in behavior. Perch erect and conspic. on open low or mid. level twig or branch and sally to air, often several times in quick succession, and usually return to same perch. Habitually flick or quiver tail on alighting.

**Breeding:** 1 BC ♂, Feb, Chocó (Carriker); 2 Costa Rican nests, Apr and June; shallow open moss and lichen cup on vine or limb, 6-15m up; 2 eggs, dull white with a conspic. wreath of brownish blotches around thicker end (Skutch 1967).

**Status and habitat:** Fairly common in humid and wet forest borders, shrubby clearings, and treefalls; foothills and lower slopes.

**Range:** 100-1200m. Panama border (Mt. Tacarcuna) and lower Atrato Val. (Baudó Mts.) s on Pacific slope to w Nariño. W Mexico to w Ecuador.

**Note:** By some considered conspecific with *M. olivaceus* (Olive Flycatcher) of e Ecuador to Bolivia.

## 110. OLIVE-SIDED FLYCATCHER
*Contopus borealis*
**Identification:** 7″ (18cm). Rather stout large-headed flycatcher with decided crest and short tail. Mainly dark grayish olive with weak gray-

ish white wing bars; *white throat and white median underparts contrast with dark olive sides and flanks*; *large white tuft behind wing sometimes protrudes* (or is hidden by closed wing).

**Similar species:** Resembles an overgrown woodpewee but stouter, shorter-tailed, and with fainter wing bars and darker sides. Look for the tuft protruding behind wing.

**Voice:** Occas. a loud, whistled *hic-three-beers* in spring migration; or loud *prip-prip-prip* like Greater Pewee.

**Behavior:** Perches on a high exposed dead branch or snag from which it sallies long distances for flying insects and usually returns to same favorite perch.

**Status and habitat:** Fairly common migrant and winter resident, late Aug–late May (once, early June, Santa Marta Mts.—T. B. Johnson) to forest borders and semiopen areas; mostly foothills and highlands, once to edge of Páramo de Neusa, Sept (Hilty and M. Robbins).

**Range:** To 3300m. Santa Marta and Perijá mts. and the Andes, rarely lowlands w or e of Andes. Breeds in n and w N America; winters chiefly in n and w S America from Venez. s in mts. to se Peru and n Bolivia (sight)

### 111. EASTERN WOOD-PEWEE
*Contopus virens*

**Identification:** 6″ (15cm). Slight crest. Bill dark above, yellowish below, tip dusky. Dark grayish olive above; wings and tail dusky with 2 distinct light gray wing bars (no eyering); below whitish; breast and sides tinged grayish olive; belly sometimes with faint yellowish wash (esp. young birds).

**Similar species:** Dull, easily confused, and often not safely separated from Western and Tropical pewees (112, 113) in field. Voice is helpful if heard. *Empidonax* (115-117) are smaller, proportionally shorter-winged, have longer tarsi (always 14.5mm or larger vs 14.5mm or less), and may show eyering (often faint, sometimes lacking). Also see Olive-sided Flycatcher (110).

**Voice:** Plaintive song *pee-a-wee*, or *pee-weé*, or downslurred *pee-ur*. Sings more than Western Pewee and often heard during both migrations.

**Behavior:** Perches erect and alone at midlevels or lower; makes long sallies, often returning to same perch.

**Status and habitat:** Prob. common transient and winter resident (var. races rec. Sept–late Apr) but sight identifications usually uncertain. Forest borders, clearings with scattered trees, and lighter woodland.

**Range:** Most recs. below 1700m (a few higher). E and w of Andes. Breeds in e N America;

winters mainly in n and w S America from Venez. s to Peru; rarely winters n to Costa Rica.

**Note:** *C. sordidulus* (Western Wood-Pewee) often merged with this sp.

### 112. WESTERN WOOD-PEWEE
*Contopus sordidulus*

**Identification:** 6″ (15cm). Very sim. to Eastern Wood-Pewee and, unless calling, generally not safely distinguished in the field (sometimes not even in the hand). Plumages of both vary seasonally and with age; worn individuals of the 2 spp. are essentially inseparable. In fresh plumage Western is slightly browner and darker (less gray and never olive), more extensively dark below (broad chest band often not interrupted; under wing coverts darker); bill sometimes mostly or entirely dark (Eastern always has all but tip of lower mandible dull yellowish or pinkish); and concealed centers of feathers of under tail coverts dark (not uniformly pale). Young birds of both spp. show fairly distinct pale wing bars. Wing formulas sim.

**Similar species:** Also see Tropical Pewee (113).

**Voice:** Common call a harsh or hoarse nasal *peeyee* or *peeeer* (Peterson 1961), or a descending *phear* (Phillips et al. 1964); latter resembles the more plaintive blurred *pee-ur* of Eastern Wood-Pewee, but neither call heard frequently on wintering grounds.

**Behavior:** Sim. to Eastern Wood-Pewee but usually silent.

**Status and habitat:** Uncertain due to identification problems. Believed to be common transient and winter resident mid-Aug–mid-May (specimens early Oct–mid-May). Common Sept transient (based on voice) in W Andes (Miller 1963). One July specimen, Sasaima, Cundinamarca (Nicéforo and Olivares 1975).

**Range:** To 2600m. W of Andes, and e of them from w Meta to se Nariño. Breeds in w N America s in mts. to Honduras (poss. Costa Rica); winters in n and w S America s to Bolivia; also e Panama.

**Note:** Four BC specimens of *C. sordidulus*, at Nuquí, Chocó (Meyer de Schauensee 1952), are *C. cinereus* (S. Olson).

### 113. TROPICAL PEWEE
*Contopus cinereus*                    Pl. 37, Map 1030

**Identification:** 5.5″ (14cm). Very sim. to Eastern and Western wood-pewees and sometimes not safely distinguished in field except by voice. In general, smaller, trimmer, tail proportionally longer, upperparts (esp. crown) darker, belly usually tinged yellowish, and *loral area usually with pale grayish or whitish spot* (not conspic., but a diagnostic mark at close range); aside from loral spot can be definitely told in field only by voice. In the hand Tropical's 10th (outermost) primary is shorter than 6th, and wing shorter than the wood-pewee's (65-77mm vs 77-91mm—Ridgely 1976). Also cf. Euler's Flycatcher (117) and other *Empidonax* (115, 116).

**Voice:** Call a soft, short, slightly trilled *tirrip* or *treeee* or sim. var. At dawn a repeated ser. of *weet's* var. to a low *we-ye*, sometimes warbled (Skutch 1960).

**Behavior:** Like other pewees but may perch lower. Easily overlooked.

**Breeding:** 4 BC birds, Feb, Chocó; 2 in Apr, Santa Marta (Carriker); lichen-covered cup nest 3-14m up on fairly exposed horizontal branch or in more upright fork; 3 dull white eggs spotted brown and lilac, mostly at larger end (Skutch 1960).

**Status and habitat:** Fairly common resident in forest edges and shrubby clearings in humid areas; edges of gallery woodland in drier areas. Easily found in PN Tayrona.

**Range:** To ca. 1000m (wanders higher). Pacific coast in Chocó (Nuquí); Santa Marta region spottily s to mid. Magdalena Val. (occas. 1800-2600m in E Andes; Norte de Santander; se Santander; Sabana de Bogotá) and along e base of E Andes s to w Caquetá (s of Florencia). S Mexico locally to n Argentina, Paraguay, and s Brazil.

**Note:** Blackish Pewee (*C. nigrescens*) of the upper tropical zone in e Ecuador and ne Peru should occur on adj. e Andean slope in Colombia. Has plumage of Greater Pewee but shape of Tropical Pewee (not prom. crested). 5″; all *dark* gray with black cap (no white anywhere in ad.). Imm. with 2 whitish wing bars. Forest canopy to midlevel at edges. Call in Peru a *pip-pip-pip* ser., sharper than Greater Pewee's (T. Parker).

### 114. GREATER PEWEE
*Contopus fumigatus*                    Ill. 85

**Identification:** 6.7″ (17cm). *Prom. crest. Uniform dark slate gray*, somewhat paler below, esp. on belly, and with yellowish lower mandible.

**Similar species:** Most like Olive-sided Flycatcher (110) but entirely dark slaty gray; crest a good mark in any light.

**Voice:** A bright, spirited *pip-pip-pip*, often persistently repeated from prom. lookout. Dawn song (quality of Olive-sided Flycatcher), *wheer, wheerit* or *peer-peerEET*, emphatic (J. Fitzpatrick).

**Behavior:** Sits erect and alert on an exposed dead snag or stick like an Olive-sided Flycatcher but usually at lower ht., infrequently

85. Greater Pewee

to canopy, very rarely to emergent treetops; sallies med. to long distance and usually returns to same perch. Solitary except when breeding.

**Breeding:** 9 BC birds, Mar–July, 1 in Nov, W, C, and E Andes, Perijá Mts. (Carriker; Miller 1963); 1 building nest in June, Anchicayá Val. (Hilty); nestlings, 12 Oct, e Ecuador; open moss and lichen cup saddled on horizontal branch, often rather high (Skutch 1967).

**Status and habitat:** Fairly common resident in humid and wet forest borders (often "cloud forest" edges), and clearings with scattered trees.

**Range:** 300-3000m (mostly 1500-2500m but commonly to 500m on Pacific slope). Perijá Mts. and the Andes. Costa Rica and w Panama; n Venez. s in Andes to nw Argentina.

**Note:** Does not incl. migratory *C. pertinax* (Coues' Flycatcher) of sw US to Nicaragua, often merged with this sp. but which has different voice.

### 115. ACADIAN FLYCATCHER
*Empidonax virescens*

**Identification:** 5.5″ (14cm). Rather flat bill, lower mandible yellowish. Dull *olive green above* with 2 whitish wing bars and whitish eyering (latter usually faint); *throat usually white*; rest of underparts whitish, breast tinged olive, belly sometimes with yellowish wash. Fall birds often decidedly yellowish below, even on throat.

**Similar species:** *Empidonax* flycatchers are difficult to separate in the field except by voice, and unfortunately they are mostly silent on the wintering grounds. Dull and worn Acadians closely resemble Traill's Flycatcher but are usually greener above and yellower below. In the hand Acadian has difference betw. longest and 6th primary (5th from outside) of more than 6mm, Traill's *usually* less than 6mm, and both have outer edge of 6th primary normal (not emarginate or cut out toward tip). Yellow-bellied Flycatcher (see note), poss. in nw Colombia, has difference betw. longest and 6th primary *usually* less than 5mm, and the outer edge of 6th primary var. but often somewhat emarginate near tip. Wing chord (not flat) of Acadian is 67-81mm, of Traill's, 64-78mm, and of Yellow-bellied, 62-70mm (Phillips et al. 1966). Also see Euler's Flycatcher (117) and other complications under Traill's Flycatcher.

**Voice:** Often heard call a sharp, rising *fweep!*; song seldom heard in Colombia an abrupt *spit-chee!* (Peterson 1947).

**Behavior:** Keeps within understory of more wooded regions. Sallies short distances for flying insects or to foliage. Typically inconspic.; in Panama even reported followiing ant swarms (Willis 1966a).

**Status and habitat:** Common winter resident late Aug–Apr to understory of humid forest and second growth or cut-over woodland.

**Range:** To 2700m. W of Andes and e of them at base of E Andes. Breeds in e N America; winters from Costa Rica to Venez. and e and w Ecuador.

**Note:** Yellow-bellied Flycatcher (*E. flaviventris*), breeding in n N America and wintering s to w Panama (rarely e Panama) is poss. in nw Colombia. Sim. to and easily confused with Acadian Flycatcher, but usually yellower below, esp. throat; olive "vest" more extensive, and bill smaller. Specimen confirmation would be required.

## 116. TRAILL'S FLYCATCHER

*Empidonax traillii*
Includes Alder (*E. alnorum*) and Willow (*E. traillii*) Flycatchers.
**Identification:** 5.4″ (13.7cm). Sim. to Acadian Flycatcher, but upperparts slightly darker, more brownish (esp. *E. t. brewsteri* of w N America), and less greenish than Acadian. Fall birds sometimes difficult to distinguish even in the hand. Imm.: browner with buffy wing bars and sometimes buffy wash on flanks.

**Similar species:** For the most part inseparable

from Acadian Flycatcher in the field except by voice. See under Acadian and Euler's flycatchers (115, 117).

**Voice:** Usual call in Colombia a short dry *whit* or *pit*. The song types (the main basis for separation of the siblings *alnorum* and *traillii*) are seldom heard in Colombia but differ as follows: a burry, semiwhistled *fee-zwee-o* or *we-bee-o* represents *E. alnorum*, the more northern breeder, and a 2-noted *fitz-bew* is *E. traillii*, the more s and w breeder. Perhaps both sing more in spring passage; *E. traillii* sings reg. on wintering ground in Panama (R. Ridgely).

**Behavior:** Inconspic. and quiet but usually more in the open than Acadian Flycatcher.

**Status and habitat:** Prob. fairly common migrant and winter resident, but status uncertain due to field identification problems. In addition to confusion with Acadian Flycatcher, Traill's is now known to represent 2 closely related sibling spp. (above) distinguishable solely on the basis of vocalizations (the latter thus essentially inseparable in Colombia under most circumstances). It is possible that most of those wintering in Colombia represent *E. alnorum* (Alder Flycatcher), while those of Mid. America and poss. extreme nw Colombia are *E. traillii* (Willow Flycatcher). In general, both forms favor thickety bushy pastures and shrubbery in clearings and more open areas, while Acadian tends to be found mostly in forest or woodland.

**Range:** Mostly below 1000m (to 2600m Sabana de Bogotá). W of Andes (most recs.) and e of them at base of Andes. Breeds in N America; winters from s Mexico to n Argentina.

## 117. EULER'S FLYCATCHER

*Empidonax euleri*          Pl. 37, Map 1031
**Identification:** 5.2″ (13.2cm). Rather flat bill dark above, pale below. Olive brown above, wings darker with 2 grayish wing bars; whitish eyering; throat pale grayish white becoming light brownish olive on breast; belly light yellow (*lawrencei*). Or as above but wing bars dull buff and belly white tinged yellow (*bolivianus*).

**Similar species:** In addition to voice (most reliable), told from n migrant *Empidonax* (115, 116) by buffier wing bars (esp. *bolivianus*), darker and greener back (or crown and back mostly rusty brown in s migrant *argentinus*, which may occur in Colombia), and crisp black band between wing bar and pale edges on primaries; in the hand by more rounded wing (J. Fitzpatrick).

**Voice:** Usual call *peer, peeer-wheer* (R. Ridgely); in Peru a burry *bzeeer*, 1-3 times (T. Parker). Song in Trinidad and Venez. a rather loud, slightly hoarse ser., the 1st note loudest and

prolonged, followed after a slight pause by several quick diminishing notes, *quée, di-di-di-di* (ffrench 1973; P. Schwartz recording).
**Behavior:** Usually alone and perched low. Sallies for flying insects but seldom returns to same perch as do pewees; frequently flicks tail (ffrench 1973).
**Breeding:** In Trinidad (*E. e. lawrencei*) May–July; soft, black, fiber-lined cup in fork or over knothole about 1-2m up; 2-3 eggs, cream with reddish brown spots and blotches, chiefly at larger end (ffrench 1973).
**Status and habitat:** Low to midlevels in second growth woodland, esp. near or at edges (T. Parker). Also swampy woodland. Not well known in Colombia.
**Range:** To 500m. E of Andes in Zulia Val., Norte de Santander (Petrólea), and Arauca to w Caquetá (*lawrencei*); once as migrant near La Javilla, Zulia Val. (*bolivianus*). Prob. range of resident *bolivianus*, based on extralimital recs. near s and e Colombian boundary, could extend from Guainía to Amazonas and w Putumayo. Surinam (once) and Venez. s east of Andes to c Argentina and Paraguay. Trinidad; Grenada.

### 118. FUSCOUS FLYCATCHER
*Cnemotriccus fuscatus*          Pl. 37, Map 1032
**Identification:** 5.5″ (14cm). Slight crest. *Somewhat peweelike* (usually erect posture), but tail longer and bill narrower and blackish (only base of lower mandible pale). Grayish brown to slightly rufescent brown above with *2 broad buff wing bars and long conspic. whitish eyebrow*; tail long (2.5″) and dark brown; throat grayish white; otherwise whitish below with light brown wash on breast and sometimes yellowish tinge on belly.
**Similar species:** Mouse-colored Tyrannulet (13) has whitish (not bright buff) wing bars, less pronounced eyestripe, and much less erect posture. Euler's Flycatcher (117) lacks the eyestripe and has prom. eyering. Also see Tropical Pewee (113).
**Voice:** Song, *chip-weeti-weeti-weetiyee, chip-weety-weety-weety-teepip*, or *chewy-chewit-cheepeer* (jumbled clear notes); dawn song an excited ser. of clear high notes, *p-pit-pit-PEEDit* (J. Fitzpatrick).
**Behavior:** Rather quiet and inconspic. Flycatches from low perches, often to ground, and generally remains in or near brushy undergrowth where difficult to see.
**Breeding:** 3 BC birds, Mar–Oct, Santa Marta and Cúcuta (Carriker); black fiber-lined twig and bark cup about 3m up in small crotch; 3 white eggs with black markings, chiefly around larger end (ffrench 1973).

**Status and habitat:** Drier deciduous forest borders, shrubby second growth, humid forest borders, and overgrown clearings.
**Range:** To 900m. Carib. lowlands from n Córdoba to w Guajira and s to mid. Magdalena Val. in sw Cundinamarca (Giradot); e of Andes from Norte de Santander to Amazonas (Pto. Nariño). No Caquetá or Putumayo recs. The Guianas and Venez. s locally e of Andes to nw Argentina and Paraguay. Trinidad.

### 119. BLACK PHOEBE
*Sayornis nigricans*          Ill. 86, Map 1033
**Identification:** 7.5″ (19cm). Unmistakable. *Entirely sooty black with white belly*; upper wing coverts and inner remiges broadly edged white; outer tail feathers with some white edging.
**Voice:** A bright rising *peeert* and other shrill notes as flicks tail up.
**Behavior:** A confiding bird often seen perched on boulders in streams, or on buildings, utility lines, or other exposed places near water. Sallies short distances, usually near water surface or ground and returns to same perch.
**Breeding:** BC pair, Apr, Santa Marta (Carriker); 2 nests in July, Cundinamarca (Borrero et al. 1962). Cup nest of mud pellets and grass on rocky ledge, crevice, under bridge, or eave and usually in vicinity of water; 2 white eggs.
**Status and habitat:** Fairly common resident along most perennial streams in hills and mts., occas. shores of ponds and lakes; mainly foothills and mts. Usually not in lowlands where rivers lack steep gradients. Once on Río Truandó (100m).
**Range:** 100-2800m. Santa Marta and Perijá Mts., all 3 Andean ranges and Macarena Mts. W N America s in mts. to nw Argentina.
**Note:** Birds from e Panama highlands and S

86. BLACK PHOEBE

America, *S. latirostris* (White-winged Phoebe), may be a separate sp.

## 120. VERMILION FLYCATCHER
*Pyrocephalus rubinus*          Pl. 37, Map 1034
**Identification:** 5.5″ (14cm). Slight crest. ♂: *crown and entire underparts bright scarlet*; stripe through eye, rearcrown, and entire upperparts sooty brown. ♀ very different: dark ashy brown above; throat and breast white *narrowly and indistinctly streaked dusky; lower underparts pinkish salmon*; center of abdomen often white. Or white below, more or less heavily streaked dusky (no pink tinge on lower underparts) with pale yellow crissum (*rubinus*). Imm. like ♀, but abdomen often yellowish.
**Similar species:** ♂ unmistakable. ♀ has erect posture, slight crest, streaks on breast, and rosy or yellowish wash on lower underparts. See Bran-colored Flycatcher (105) and imm. Riverside Tyrant (135).
**Voice:** Call a soft plaintive ser. of 3-4 slightly trilled notes. In display flies up, then sings a ser. of tinkling notes as it flutters down.
**Behavior:** An unsuspicious bird usually seen perched prom. on lower outer branches of a tree, or on bushes, fences, or utility wires. Sallies to air or to ground for insects.
**Breeding:** 2 incubating ♀♀, Apr, Cesar (Carriker). Eggs in Dagua Val. nest, Feb (Brown). In ne Meta 2 nesting attempts, Jan and Mar (S. Furniss); in mid. Cauca Val., chiefly Dec–Apr, with some activity all yr. (Borrero 1972a); open lichen and grass cup suspended or saddled in low crotch; 2-3 white eggs with large red brown spots.
**Status and habitat:** Common resident locally in drier open country with trees and scrubby vegetation, esp. in parklike areas, hotel grounds, etc. Austral migrant to se Colombia; at Leticia rec. 16 June–22 Sept (Hilty; J. V. Remsen).
**Range:** To 2600m. Cauca, Dagua, and Patía vals., Pacific coast in Valle and Nariño, mid. and upper Magdalena Val. incl. Sabana de Bogotá (*piurae*); Carib. lowlands near Barranquilla (once), w base of Santa Marta Mts. (sightings, Hotel Irotama) e to Guajira and s to Cesar Val.; e of Andes in Norte de Santander, n Arauca (sightings, 1978—W. McKay and J. Jorgenson) and ne Meta (Carimagua—S. Furniss) (*saturatus*); w Caquetá, Vaupés (Mitú), and Leticia (s temperate breeding *rubinus*). Sw US to Nicaragua; Panama (twice); Colombia and Venez. locally to n Chile and s Argentina. Galapagos Isls.

[*Ochthoeca*: Highlands (except 126); short thin bill; chunky shape; narrow tail; typically have long eyebrow.]

## 121. BROWN-BACKED CHAT-TYRANT
*Ochthoeca fumicolor*          Pl. 38, Map 1035
**Identification:** 6″ (15cm). Flat-headed; short thin bill. Warm brown above with *long broad whitish eyebrow*; wings and tail blackish with *2 rufous wing bars* (lower bar more prom.); throat grayish; *rest of underparts cinnamon buff* becoming white on center of abdomen (or deeper rufescent above and below with buffy eyestripe—*ferruginae*).
**Similar species:** Crowned Chat-Tyrant (124) is smaller, browner, lacks prom. wing bars, and is grayish (not cinnamon buff) below. Rufous-breasted Chat-Tyrant (122) has white belly.
**Voice:** Several calls though often quiet; a loud, abrupt, clear whistle, *kleeeip*, perched or in flight; a softer *tee-oo* when countercalling and *pw-pw-pw* in flight (Smith and Vuilleumier 1971).
**Behavior:** Takes a prom. perch on top or sides of low shrubs and bushes, sallies to air or ground, or occas. picks prey from foliage. Usually alone or in well separated pairs; flicks tail in alarm.
**Breeding:** 16 BC birds, Feb–Sept, C and E Andes (Carriker); 2 in Dec, Boyacá (Olivares 1963). Building nest, 18 Mar, *Polylepis* woodland, 4000m, Venez.; fur-lined cup a little above ground in *Espeletia* (Vuilleumier and Ewert 1978); eggs from Antioquia, white with a few rusty spots (Sclater and Salvin 1879).
**Status and habitat:** Common in a wide var. of fairly open habitats, incl. esp. stunted trees and bushes bordering clearings and in scattered thickets near treeline; *Polylepis* above treeline; wander to *Espeletia* in open paramo.
**Range:** 2500-3600m (once to 1800m). E Andes s to s Cundinamarca (*fumicolor*); n end of W and C Andes in Antioquia (*ferruginea*); s end W Andes, C Andes from Caldas southward and both slopes of Nariño (*brunneifrons*). Nw Venez. s in Andes to n Bolivia.

## 122. RUFOUS-BREASTED CHAT-TYRANT
*Ochthoeca rufipectoralis*          Pl. 38, Map 1036
**Identification:** 5″ (13cm). Chunky with narrow tail and short thin bill. Brown above, crown darker, *long broad white eyebrow*; wings blackish with *1 broad cinnamon wing bar*; throat gray bordered below by a *broad orange rufous chest band* contrasting with white lower breast and belly; tail dark brown, outer feathers narrowly edged white.
**Similar species:** Eyebrow and breast band distinctive. Larger Brown-backed Chat-Tyrant (121) is mostly cinnamon buff below.
**Voice:** Song an abrupt *ch-brrr, ch-brrr, ch-brrr*; also several clucking notes (J. Silliman), a faint

*cleeoo* and a rapid ser. of *pt* notes ending with 2 *cleeoo* notes (Smith and Vuilleumier 1971).
**Behavior:** Unobtrusive in pairs in upper mid. level to canopy, either alone or accompanying mixed flocks; sally to air within canopy or hawk from foliage.
**Breeding:** 11 BC birds, Jan–Sept, Perijá Mts. and Andes (Carriker). Moss cup on rock ledge sheltered by stunted trees (Todd and Carriker 1922).
**Status and habitat:** Locally fairly common in humid forest near openings, forest borders, occas. stunted forest and shrubby slopes near treeline. Generally much more a forest bird than previous sp.
**Range:** 2000-3600m (mostly 2600-3100m). Perijá Mts., Santa Marta Mts., and all 3 Andean ranges. Extreme w Venez. s in Andes to n Bolivia.

## 123. SLATY-BACKED CHAT-TYRANT
*Ochthoeca cinnamomeiventris* Pl. 38, Map 1037
**Identification:** 4.8″ (12.2cm). Unmistakable. Chunky; short thin bill. *Mostly slaty black with very short white eyebrow* ("false eyespots"); *lower breast and belly deep chestnut;* no wing bars.
**Voice:** Loud often-heard call a high, burry whistle, *sweeeeeea,* rising slightly then falling (Hilty); also a high-pitched *chew* (J. Silliman).
**Behavior:** Alone or in separated 2's, perched low inside forest or in denser vegetation on slopes near streams. Often perches partially exposed though easily overlooked except for persistent calls audible even above rushing torrents. Normally sally short to med. distance in loops to air; may or may not return to same perch.
**Breeding:** 7 BC birds, Jan–Aug, Andes (Carriker), 1 in Oct, Boyacá (Olivares 1971); 1 nest, Feb, Finca Merenberg (Ridgely and Gaulin 1980); 3 in Feb, PN Cueva de los Guácharos; mossy cup on rocky cliff or boulder in river (P. Gertler). Eggs from Antioquia white with large reddish spots mostly at large end (Sclater and Salvin 1879).
**Status and habitat:** Fairly common at or near small forest openings, forest borders, or in dense shrubby or brushy slopes and *always in vicinity* of rushing mt. streams. The key is dense brush near streams; occas. a short distance inside humid forest.
**Range:** 1600-3000m (once to 900m on Pacific slope). All 3 Andean ranges. Nw Venez. s in Andes to n Bolivia.

## 124. CROWNED CHAT-TYRANT
*Ochthoeca frontalis* Pl. 38, Map 1038
**Identification:** 5″ (13cm). Chunky; short thin bill. *Uniform dark brown above,* head darker; *forehead and long eyebrow white* (or yellow

forehead and white eyebrow—*frontalis*); *entire underparts gray;* under tail coverts cinnamon; pale wing bars faint or lacking.
**Similar species:** See Brown-backed Chat-Tyrant (121).
**Voice:** A distinctive *ti-tirrrr,* but usually quiet.
**Behavior:** Shy and unobtrusive. Usually hidden 1-3m up in undergrowth where flits more to mossy limbs and trunks than to foliage.
**Status and habitat:** Uncommon (easily overlooked) in stunted forest, denser forest borders, and scrubby thickets; 2600-3600m. Seems to occur mainly in first 100-200m el. zone of elfin forest below treeline.
**Range:** 2300-3600m. Once to 1300m at Sasaima, Cundinamarca. E Andes in s Norte de Santander and Cundinamarca (*albidiadema*); W Andes at n end (Páramo Frontino) and C Andes from nevados on Caldas-Tolima border s through Nariño (*frontalis*). Colombia s in Andes to n Bolivia.

## 125. YELLOW-BELLIED CHAT-TYRANT
*Ochthoeca diadema* Pl. 38, Map 1039
**Identification:** 4.7″ (12cm). Chunky; short thin bill. Mostly dark olive above with *prom. yellow forehead and long yellow eyebrow;* wings and tail dusky; 2 rufescent wing bars (or wing bars obscure—*jesupi* and *diadema*); underparts olive yellow; brighter on throat and belly.
**Similar species:** Only *small* Colombian tyrannid with a long conspic. yellow eyestripe. The smaller Golden-faced Tyrannulet (9) has a shorter yellow eyestripe and crisp yellow wing edgings.
**Voice:** Call a long buzzy trill that sags a little in mid.
**Behavior:** Separated pairs capture prey in foliage or near ground; keep mostly 0.1-4m up in denser undergrowth. Not esp. wary but usually within cover inside forest. Sometimes join mixed flocks.
**Breeding:** 3 BC ♂♂, Jan and Oct, Santa Marta Mts. and Boyacá (Carriker). Four creamy white eggs, apparently in moss cup in bank (Sclater and Salvin 1879), but reports of nest type are conflicting.
**Status and habitat:** Uncommon to fairly common locally in very humid forest ("cloud forest") and shrubby forest borders. On n slope Santa Marta Mts. mostly 1900-2300m (T. B. Johnson); in PN Cueva de los Guácharos in oak-dominated mossy forest well above 2000m (P. Gertler); not in bamboo.
**Range:** 1700-3100m (mostly 1800-3100m). Santa Marta Mts. (*jesupi*); Perijá Mts. (*rubelula*); E Andes from Norte de Santander southward (*diadema*); C and W Andes s to both slopes of Nariño (*gratiosa*); not rec. n of Valle in W Andes. Nw Venez. s in Andes to n Peru.

## 126. DRAB WATER-TYRANT

*Ochthoeca littoralis*      Pl. 38, Map 1040
**Identification:** 5.2″ (13.2cm). Nondescript but always on large river banks. Mainly pale sandy brown; crown brown; *wings and tail dusky brown; rump very pale brown; narrow eyebrow and chin whitish with dark line through eye;* center of belly yellowish white.
**Similar species:** Along Amazon see Little Ground-Tyrant (134).
**Voice:** Call a weak, whistled *fwoit* or *fweet* (J. V. Remsen); in frequent display with outstretched wings, pairs duet, with warbled *wee-chidle-chee* over and over (J. Fitzpatrick).
**Behavior:** Single birds or pairs flush inconspic. ahead of boats and fly along edge of river or perch on exposed roots on steep cut river banks, sometimes on sand bars; usually fly and perch within a few ft. of water. Sally to air or ground for insects.
**Breeding:** In e Peru, open cup of grass stems and mud placed close to river edge during dry season (O'Neill 1974).
**Status and habitat:** Common but thinly spread along steep eroded banks of larger rivers, esp. where snags, exposed roots, and driftwood are present (not grassy river banks or smaller rivers).
**Range:** To 500m. E of Andes from w Meta and Vaupés (Mitú) southward; sight recs. n to Pto. Inírida, ne Guainía (1978—Hilty and M. Robbins). Prob. to e Vichada. The Guianas and s Venez. s to n Bolivia and Amazonian Brazil.
**Note:** Habitat and distribution unlike other *Ochthoeca*, and perhaps better placed in monotypic *Ochthornis*.

## 127. STREAK-THROATED BUSH-TYRANT

*Myiotheretes striaticollis*      Pl. 38, Map 1041
**Identification:** 9″ (23cm). Large. Dull brown above; wings and tail dusky; *inner webs of remiges and all but central pair of tail feathers cinnamon tipped black* (in flight wings and tail show large blocks of cinnamon; *throat white sharply streaked black;* rest of underparts and under wing coverts cinnamon rufous.
**Similar species:** Santa Marta Bush-Tyrant (130) is smaller with less prom. throat streaks, mostly dusky tail, and olive wash on breast. Also see Red-rumped Bush-Tyrant (128).
**Voice:** Call a loud, clear, humanlike whistle rising slightly in pitch *peeeeeee* (J. Silliman).
**Behavior:** Usually alone or in well-spaced 2's. Hunt from exposed elevated perches, esp. utility wires, rocks, or bushes where they scan about and sally long distances in swooping aerial forays or drop to ground for insects. Often return to same perch.

**Breeding:** 9 BC birds, Jan–June, Perijá and Santa Marta mts., C Andes (Carriker).
**Status and habitat:** Fairly common in open pastures or cleared areas with scattered trees and bushes, landslide areas, even highland gardens. Usually not in very wet or very arid highlands. Replaced in forest by Smoky Bush-Tyrant, in dense low treeline shrubbery by Red-rumped Bush-Tyrant.
**Range:** 1500-3600m (mostly 2400-3400m). Santa Marta and Perijá Mts. and all 3 Andean ranges (recs. spotty in E and W Andes). Nw Venez. s in Andes to nw Argentina.

## 128. RED-RUMPED BUSH-TYRANT

*Myiotheretes erythropygius*      Pl. 38, Map 1042
**Identification:** 9″ (23cm). Large. Relatively small bill. *Crown light gray; forehead grizzled whitish;* otherwise dark brownish gray above with *rufous rump;* wings and tail blackish brown; *wings with a white patch on secondaries; all outer tail feathers rufous tipped dusky;* throat white streaked gray; *rest of underparts gray* becoming rufous on lower abdomen.
**Similar species:** At rest pale crown and gray breast are diagnostic. In flight look for white wing patch and rufous rump. Unlike Streak-throated Bush-Tyrant (see 127), rather sleek and elegant.
**Voice:** Call in Peru a short whistle sim. to Streak-throated Bush-Tyrant but slightly blurry (T. Parker).
**Behavior:** In Peru single birds or separated pairs perch in tops of low bushes and shrubs; forage on ground or drop to ground from low perch, sometimes rather wary (T. Parker); in Ecuador reg. up to 4000m in patches of *Polylepis* and foraging out into paramo and grasslands, quite in open, perching on fences, boulders, and wires, sallying to air as well as dropping to ground (R. Ridgely).
**Breeding:** 6 BC birds, Mar, 2 in Sept, Santa Marta Mts. (Carriker).
**Status and habitat:** Not well known in Colombia. Prob. *Polylepis* and adj. shrubs and open areas much as in n Ecuador. Perhaps usually above el. of Streak-throated Bush-Tyrant.
**Range:** 3100-3900m. Santa Marta Mts., 3100-3600m, E Andes in Norte de Santander (Chitagá, s of Pamplona ca. 3200m); southernmost Cundinamarca at Laguna Chisaca, 3900m (*orinomus*); extreme s Nariño on Volcán Cumbal, 3800m (*erythropygius*). Colombia s in Andes to nw Bolivia.

## 129. SMOKY BUSH-TYRANT

*Myiotheretes fumigatus*      Pl. 38, Map 1043
**Identification:** 8″ (20cm). Rather large, dark,

and nondescript. Looks like a thrush. *Uniformly dark brown* with whitish mottling on throat; closed wing and tail dusky; *base of flight feathers cinnamon on inner webs* (shows as prom. broad stripe in flight); upper wing coverts faintly edged buffy; under wing coverts cinnamon.

**Similar species:** Large uniformly dark highland flycatcher with whitish on throat and a cinnamon flash in wings. See other *Myiotheretes* (127, 128, 130).

**Voice:** Call in Peru a soft, slightly descending whistle much like that of Streak-throated Bush-Tyrant (T. Parker).

**Behavior:** Single birds, pairs, or families often follow mixed flocks. Perch exposed above or on outer perimeter of foliage or on open limbs inside canopy; hawk from foliage; hover-glean or less frequently sally to air, seldom to ground (T. Parker; Hilty).

**Breeding:** 3 BC birds, July–Aug, Perijá Mts. and n end E Andes (Carriker); 1 in Nov, Cundinamarca (MCN).

**Status and habitat:** Uncommon to fairly common locally in humid forest and forest edge; usually well below treeline. Replaced in open areas by Streak-throated Bush-Tyrant, in thick shrubbery near treeline by Red-rumped Bush-Tyrant.

**Range:** 1800-3600m (mainly 2400-3000m). Perijá Mts., E Andes (local), C Andes, and W Andes from Cauca south. Nw Venez. s in Andes to c Peru.

## 130. SANTA MARTA BUSH-TYRANT

*Myiotheretes pernix*      Pl. 38, Map 1044

**Identification:** 8.3″ (21cm). Much like Streak-throated Bush-Tyrant (see 127) but smaller and darker below; *tail largely black, only outer web of outer feather edged rufous*; throat whitish diffusely streaked dusky; breast and sides washed olive; and lower underparts ferruginous; lores whitish. In flight shows prom. cinnamon flight feathers as in Streak-throated Bush-Tyrant (127).

**Behavior:** Usually alone perched exposed on top of bush or smaller tree. Feeds by long sweeping aerial sallies, rarely sallies within tree crown. Occas. joins mixed flocks briefly (T. B. Johnson).

**Status and habitat:** Uncommon in shrubby forest and second growth borders, road cuts, and overgrown hillsides. In general at lower el. and in more bushy or wooded areas on Cuchilla de San Lorenzo than 127 (T. B. Johnson).

**Range:** ENDEMIC. 2100-2900m. Santa Marta Mts.

## 131. BLACK-BILLED SHRIKE-TYRANT

*Agriornis montana*      Pl. 38, Map 1045

**Identification:** 9.5″ (24cm). Large and unflycatcherlike. Black bill rather long and heavy. Mostly dark grayish brown with *buffy loral streak and white throat narrowly streaked blackish*; lower abdomen whitish; *outer tail feathers white* (conspic. in flight).

**Similar species:** When perched, most likely mistaken for a large furnariid, esp. a cinclodes (p 356) or for a bush-tyrant (see 127-130); latter are sim. in shape although different in color. In flight easily recognized by prom. white outer tail feathers sim. in pattern to those of a meadowlark.

**Voice:** Frequently heard call a loud, clear whistle, *weee-cheeer*, rising then falling (Hilty); also a loud whistled *pyuk* (Smith and Vuilleumier 1971).

**Behavior:** Sits exposed atop a rock, house, or small bush when singing but drops to ground or near ground to feed and then inconspic. until it flies, often a long distance. Eats seeds, insects, even small vertebrates incl. birds and mice. Runs well and sometimes pumps tail up and down.

**Breeding:** Carrying food, 18 Aug, Ecuador (F. Vuilleumier); stick and dry grass nest, sometimes lined with wool; on ground or vegetation in paramo, low bush near stream, or in mud wall or tile roof; 2-3 eggs, cream spotted reddish (Johnson 1965).

**Status and habitat:** Uncommon and somewhat local, though a highly visible sp. where it occurs. Drier open terrain and rocky slopes with scattered scrubby vegetation, in tree-bordered pastures, around dwellings, even in villages.

**Range:** 2800-3600m (treeline or above). S Nariño from Pasto region southward. S Colombia s in Andes to c Chile and Argentina.

## 132. PLAIN-CAPPED GROUND-TYRANT

*Muscisaxicola alpina*      Pl. 38, Map 1046

**Identification:** 7.5″ (19cm). Thrushlike. *Bill thin and short; legs long*. Grayish brown above; crown tinged rufous; whitish below with light grayish brown wash on breast; *supraloral and broad eyebrow white*; small spot below eye white; lores and malar area dusky; *notched tail blackish; outer feather narrowly edged white*.

**Similar species:** Spot-billed Ground-Tyrant (133) is smaller with different proportions, yellow at base of lower mandible (often hard to see), no rufous tinge on crown, and is usually at lower el.

**Voice:** A weak plaintive note; usually quiet (Rhoads 1912).

**Behavior:** Pairs or occas. small loose groups perch erect on ground, rock, or atop low bush.

Feed on ground with short robinlike run or bouncy run hop, then stop suddenly and stand erect; sometimes sally to ground from low perch; often flick tail.

**Breeding:** 5 BC birds, Sept–Dec, Boyacá, 3300-4000m (Olivares 1974a; Carriker); 1 in Aug, Ecuador, 3900m (F. Vuilleumier). In Chile, sparsely lined grass and root nest in hole or crevice under rock; 4 white eggs with a few reddish spots (Johnson 1965).

**Status and habitat:** Uncommon in paramo in stands of *Espeletia* or areas characterized by rocky soil and low impoverished vegetation from treeline to snowline (J. Silliman).

**Range:** 3300-4200m. N part of E Andes from Boyacá to extreme s Cundinamarca (*quesadae*); C Andes from Caldas-Tolima border (Nevado del Ruiz) spottily s to PN Puracé in Cauca (*columbiana*); prob. Nariño. Colombia s in Andes to c Chile and Argentina.

### 133. SPOT-BILLED GROUND-TYRANT
*Muscisaxicola maculirostris*     Pl. 38, Map 1047

**Identification:** 5.7″ (14.5cm). *Pipitlike. Thin black bill* with small inconspic. yellow spot on base of lower mandible. Pale sandy brown above; upper wing coverts edged paler; *dark line through eye* bordered above by narrow white eyebrow; *underparts white with buff tinge on breast and abdomen*; tail black narrowly edged white. In flight wings noticeably pointed.

**Similar species:** Much like Plain-capped Ground-Tyrant (132) but decidedly smaller, slimmer, shorter-legged, with longer bill and more buffy underparts, and usually at lower el. Proportions and behavior recall a pipit, not a thrush (as in preceding sp.).

**Voice:** A short undistinctive *tek*, repeated. In aerial display (lacking in 131), a ser. of *tk* notes and a clear *whee-oo*, the former given in fluttery climb with dangling legs, the latter in dive (Smith and Vuilleumier 1971).

**Behavior:** Terrestrial in scattered pairs. Run rapidly on ground with body held low and horizontal. At rest stand fairly erect. Fly low and slightly bounding like a horned lark.

**Breeding:** Prob. June–July, Ecuador (Smith and Vuilleumier 1971). In Chile, open cup exposed or partially concealed on ground, esp. near bush, grass tuft, or rock; 2-3 whitish eggs (Johnson 1965).

**Status and habitat:** Uncommon and local on open sparsely vegetated slopes with or without scattered shrubs, also shores of high lagoons. Prefer more xeric steppelike land at lower el. than preceding sp.

**Range:** 2600-3200m (prob. higher). E Andes from c Boyacá (Lago Tota) s to Sabana de Bogotá (Mosquera). Prob. Nariño. Colombia

s in Andes to c Chile and Argentina. S breeders migratory.

### 134. [LITTLE GROUND-TYRANT]
*Muscisaxicola fluviatilis*     Pl. 38, Map 1048

**Identification:** 5.5″ (14cm). *Pipitlike.* Bill thin. Grayish brown above, head browner; wings brown with 2 indistinct buff bars and buff edgings; *tail black edged white*; underparts whitish; upper breast and sides of throat tinged sandy buff.

**Similar species:** Drab Water-Tyrant (126) has *distinct* short whitish eyebrow, no white edge on browner tail, less extensive white on belly, and different behavior (usually does not run on ground).

**Voice:** Usually quiet. Occas. a single, high-pitched, weak *peep* with rising inflection (J. Fitzpatrick).

**Behavior:** Mostly terrestrial and much like allied Spot-billed Ground-Tyrant of highlands.

**Status and habitat:** Hypothetical. Known only from sight recs. w of Leticia on Isla Corea, Colombia (11 Aug 1975—J. V. Remsen; 24 July 1978, 24 Aug 1979—Hilty). Bare or sparsely vegetated sand bars on Amazonian river isls. or river banks.

**Range:** To 100m. Amazon river isls. near Leticia, Amazonas. Prob. adj. n and s banks of river. Large rivers of extreme se Colombia, e Peru, n Bolivia, and sw Amazonian Brazil.

### 135. RIVERSIDE TYRANT
*Knipolegus orenocensis*     Pl. 38, Map 1049

**Identification:** 6″ (15cm). Slightly rounded tail; *stout silvery blue bill;* eyes dark red. ♂: *entirely blackish slate;* head blackest; slight crest. ♀: like ♂ but dark brownish gray. Imm.: brownish gray; center of belly grayish white. Subad. ♂♂ often mottled with black.

**Similar species:** Erect posture and hint of crest suggests a phoebe. ♂ Amazonian Black-Tyrant (137) is smaller and all glossy black (but bill also silvery blue). Imm. resembles ♀ Vermilion Flycatcher (120) but lacks streaks and the tinge of salmon below.

**Voice:** Call a soft stuttering *pit-weet* or *pit-pit-weet,* suggesting dawn song of Tropical Kingbird.

**Behavior:** Single birds or pairs perch 0.5-2m up in grass or shrubs where sally to grass or drop to ground. Usually fairly conspic. though can be wary and hard to approach. Often flick tail up.

**Breeding:** BC birds, Mar, ne Meta (S. Furniss). Apr juv., Orinoco (Cherrie 1916).

**Status and habitat:** Few recs. Specimens, Feb 1976 at Carimagua, ne Meta (S. Furniss); sight recs. as follows: Dec 1976 at same locality

(Brown), and 1-4 birds on 6 separate dates (Jan, July, Aug), 1977-1979 on Isla Corea, near Leticia (Hilty et al.). Apparently local in seasonally flooded and scrubby young second growth, grass and bushes on river isls., river banks, and edges of lakes. Favors much more open areas than allied Amazonian Black-Tyrant.

**Range:** To 300m. Ne Meta and Amazon river isls. near Leticia. Undoubtedly ne Vichada. Spottily in c Venezuela (lower Río Meta and along Río Orinoco from mouth to confluence with Río Meta); ne Peru; c Brazil s of Amazon.

### 136. RUFOUS-TAILED TYRANT
*Knipolegus poecilurus*          Pl. 37, Map 1050
**Identification:** 5.5-6″ (14-15cm). *Red eyes.* Brownish gray above; *wings darker with 2 dull buffy gray wing bars;* inner remiges edged cinnamon; underparts cinnamon buff, upper throat and breast washed grayish; *crissum pale cinnamon; tail dusky, all but central feathers broadly edged cinnamon rufous* (conspic. in flight). Tail slightly cocked at times.

**Similar species:** Only Colombian flycatcher with a red eye and rufous edging on tail (sometimes held up slightly). Shape and behavior (but not color) might recall ♀ Vermilion Flycatcher (120).

**Behavior:** Phoebelike. Lifts tail, then lowers it slowly as perches on shrubs, lower part of trees, or on fence wires, infrequently higher at edge of forest. Sallies for passing insects or drops to ground. Alone or in pairs.

**Breeding:** 12 BC birds, Mar–Sept, Perijá Mts. and Andes (Carriker; Miller 1963).

**Status and habitat:** Local in mountainous semi-open terrain. Shrubby hedgerows, woodland borders, bushes, and scattered trees in pastures. Often near but not in forest.

**Range:** Mostly 1600-3100m (mainly below 2000m). Perijá Mts. and all 3 Andean ranges (W Andes from Valle south; recs. scattered in E and C Andes). N and nw Venez. s in mts. to n Bolivia; tepuis of s Venez. and adj. n Brazil.

### 137. AMAZONIAN BLACK-TYRANT
*Knipolegus poecilocercus*          Pl. 38, Map 1051
**Identification:** 5.2″ (13.2cm). Chunky with slight crest; eyes dark (not red); bill silvery blue. ♂ a small version of Riverside Tyrant; *mainly glossy black,* primaries tinged brownish, outer 3 very short, narrow, and pointed (not a field mark). ♀: dull olive brown above; wings browner; *wing bars and wing edgings pale dull buff;* loral region and underparts creamy buffy white; *lower throat and breast washed brownish gray and streaked darker* forming a broad dark band across breast; primaries as in ♂; *upper tail coverts and inner margins of tail feathers broadly edged rufous.*

**Similar species:** ♂ Riverside Tyrant (135) is larger, heavier, duller black, and occurs in open or shrubby areas (not along shady forest streams). ♂ Black Manakin (p 436), has different-shaped bill and head, latter more rounded, with proportionally larger eye. Good marks for dull ♀ are rufous edgings on rump and tail and streaks on breast.

**Voice:** A distinctive low clicking noise, very froglike (J. V. Remsen).

**Behavior:** Usually alone. In Brazil invariably seen inside shady, dank woodland (unlike Riverside Tyrant), near water usually, perching at or below eye level, and frequently in seasonally flooded areas. Sallies or flits to foliage or to water surface of small woodland pools, etc., for insects. Usually silent; sudden movements rather manakinlike (R. Ridgely).

**Breeding:** ♀ building in July; untidy ball nest (side entrance?) of moss and grass in branch fork, 1m up at edge of forested stream, Río Javarí, nw Brazil (Hilty).

**Status and habitat:** Two specimens: Dec 1971, c Meta at Mozambique (C. D. Fisher), and 17 Mar, 20km s of Pto. Carreño, Vichada (Romero 1977). Interior of swamp, *várzea,* or lowlying forests, or at edge of wooded creeks or pools.

**Range:** To 350m. C Meta and e Vichada. Prob. locally from Arauca to Vichada (known from several adj. Venez. localities). Four sight recs., 27-30 Oct 1974 and 6 June 1975, near Leticia, Amazonas (J. V. Remsen). Locally in Guyana, c Venez., Amazonian Brazil, and ne Peru.

### 138. PIED WATER-TYRANT
*Fluvicola pica*          Ill. 87, Map 1052
**Identification:** 5″ (13cm). *Small black and white flycatcher,* distinctive in its marshy habitat. White with rear crown and mid. of back black; wings and tail black; edges of inner remiges and tip of tail white. Imm.: much duller but with suggestion of adult pattern.

**Voice:** Call a very nasal, buzzy *zhreeeoo.*

**Behavior:** Scattered individuals glean from foliage and leaves on or near the ground or in emergent vegetation over water; rarely sally to air. Frequently flick tail downward. Usually tame and conspic.

**Breeding:** Building nest, 6 June, Lago de Sonso, Valle (Hilty); several Aug nests (Todd and Carriker 1922), 1 in Mar (Brown), Santa Marta area; Apr–Sept Guárico, Venez. (Thomas 1979b). Oval ball nest of dried grass, plant down, and leaves with feather lining and side entrance; at end of branch or small bush, often

87. Pied Water-Tyrant

88. White-headed Marsh-Tyrant
(♀ top; ♂ bottom)

low over water; 2-3 white eggs with a few brown spots at larger end (ffrench 1973).
**Status and habitat:** Locally common around freshwater marshes and ponds.
**Range:** To 1000m (Cauca Val.). Throughout w of Andes except Pacific region (s in lower Atrato Val. to Río Sucio); e of Andes s to s Meta and Río Guaviare (*pica*). C Panama to n Argentina, Uruguay, and s Brazil.
**Note:** Southern *F. p. albiventer*, n to ne Peru (Pebas), may be a distinct sp. (Black-backed Water-Tyrant) and may occur in se Colombia as an austral migrant. Differs in having all black back with only narrow rump band white and narrower white edges on inner remiges and tail.

### 139. WHITE-HEADED MARSH-TYRANT
*Arundinicola leucocephala*     Ill. 88, Map 1053
**Identification:** 5″ (13cm). Slightly crested. ♂ unmistakable: blackish brown with *entire head and upper chest white*; lower mandible yellow. ♀ very different: pale grayish brown above, wings and tail darker; *forecrown, sides of head, and underparts white*; breast with a few indistinct grayish streaks.
**Similar species:** ♀ most likely confused with imm. Pied Water-Tyrant (138), but latter retains pied pattern of ad., though much duller and browner and often perches on the ground.
**Voice:** Usually quiet. Call a high-pitched *tzeek* (ffrench 1973).
**Behavior:** Conspic. and almost always seen perching upright on the top of vegetation or on a low snag over water. Sallies aerially, usually close to perch and not to ground. More ♂♂ are seen than ♀♀.

**Breeding:** 3 BC birds, Jan–Mar, n Colombia (Carriker); Aug and Nov, Venez. (Thomas 1979b); ball nest like that of Pied Water-Tyrant but with "porch" concealing entrance; 2-4 creamy white eggs (ffrench 1973).
**Status and habitat:** Locally fairly common around freshwater marshes, ponds, and river banks. Spotty along the Río Amazon.
**Range:** To 500m. N Colombia from lower Atrato Val. (Río Sucio) e to Santa Marta area (Guajira?), s in Magdalena Val. to n Huila (Villavieja); e of Andes in Arauca (sightings near Arauca 1978—W. McKay and J. Jorgenson), Meta, Vaupés (Río Apaporis), and Amazonas (many sight recs., Leticia). N Colombia to the Guianas and e of Andes to Bolivia, Uruguay, and se Brazil. Trinidad.
**Note:** Sometimes placed in the genus *Fluvicola*.

### 140. LONG-TAILED TYRANT
*Colonia colonus*     Ill. 89, Map 1054
**Identification:** ♂ 10″ (25cm); ♀ 8″ (20cm). Unmistakable. Central pair of tail feathers *greatly elongated* (up to 5″, 13cm, beyond rest of tail) in ♂♂; shorter in ♀♀ and molting ♂♂. *Brownish black with conspic. white forehead and eyebrow*; crown grizzled and streaked grayish white and

89. LONG-TAILED TYRANT

black; center of back and rump white (rump only—*fuscicapilla*).
**Voice:** Most common call a soft, rising, *wheet*, often repeated (resembles 1 call of Barn Swallow) as flicks tail up; also *twee-ta-twee-ta-twee* . . . softly.
**Behavior:** Usually 1 pair, occas. single birds perch conspic. on exposed dead snags or trunks, sally short to med. distances to air, and faithfully return to same perch. Confiding, sedentary, and seldom far from their favorite snags.
**Breeding:** 5 BC birds, Jan–May, s Bolívar to Córdoba (Carriker). Cavity at mod. ht. in dead stub or burned trunk in or at edge of clearing; 1 upper Anchicayá Val. nest June (Hilty); white eggs (Schönwetter 1968).
**Status and habitat:** Common in small clearings, forest borders, or other openings in humid forested regions; presence of an exposed dead stub or dead tree is the requirement.
**Range:** To 1800m (usually below 1200m). Humid forested regions throughout w of Andes except Carib. and Santa Marta area (*leuconota*); e of Andes from Casanare-Cundinamarca boundary and nw Meta s to se Nariño (*fuscicapilla*); perhaps to w Amazonas (rec. at mouth of Río Curaray, Peru). Honduras to w Ecuador, Peru, ne Argentina, Paraguay, and se Brazil.
**Note:** Yellow-browed Tyrant (*Satrapa icterophrys*), an austral migrant to Venez., should occur in open areas with bushes, around pools, or along rivers e of Andes in Colombia. 6.3";

olive green above with broad yellow eyebrow and blackish mask through eyes; underparts bright yellow; wings and slightly notched tail blackish; 2 grayish wing bars, inner remiges edged yellowish, outer tail feather mostly white; bill decidedly thin and short.

## 141. CLIFF FLYCATCHER
*Hirundinea ferruginea*          Pl. 38, Map 1055
**Identification:** 7.2" (18.3cm). Unmistakable in cliff habitat. Bill rather long and wide at base; *wings long and swallowlike.* Sooty brown above *with large rufous patch at base of remiges* (shows as wing stripe in flight); forecrown, sides of head, and upper throat mottled black and white; *otherwise deep ferruginous below;* tail slightly rounded, dark brown with inner web of all but central feathers largely rufous (or forecrown and entire tail sooty brown—*ferruginea*).
**Similar species:** See larger and paler Streakthroated Bush-Tyrant (127) and smaller Cinnamon Flycatcher (108).
**Voice:** High-pitched, rapid, twittering and chattering calls, *killy, killy* . . . or *ka-leé, ka-leé* . . ., and other var., recall a kestrel.
**Behavior:** Single birds, pairs, or families perch on exposed rock faces, cliffs, or hanging cliff vegetation overlooking large open spaces. Conspic. as chatter noisily and sally long distances in buoyant, swallowlike flight. Often "about face" on perch.
**Breeding:** Pair at grassy cup nest 10-12m up on rock road cut, w Meta, 29 Jan (Hilty and P. Alden).
**Status and habitat:** Local. Cliffs, rocky canyons, and road cuts, mostly in foothills and on isolated quartzite cerros and mesas dotting Vaupés and Guainía.
**Range:** To 1500m (prob. higher). Perijá Mts. and e slope of E Andes from n Boyacá s to Meta and Macarena Mts. (*sclateri*); cerros of Guainía and Vaupés s to Río Apaporis (*ferruginea*). The Guianas and Venez. s locally to n Argentina, Uruguay, and e Brazil.

## 142. CATTLE TYRANT
*Machetornis rixosus*          Pl. 39, Map 1056
**Identification:** 7.5" (19cm). Kingbirdlike with *red eyes and long legs.* Mainly pale *olive brown* above, crown grayer and with usually concealed fiery orange crest (♂ only); *narrow dusky line through eye,* wings, and tail brownish, tail pale edged; *underparts bright yellow* incl. under wing coverts.
**Similar species:** Tropical Kingbird (180) is olive above with grayer head and only lower underparts yellow; usually not on ground.
**Voice:** High-pitched squeaky calls resemble

those of other kingbirds. At dawn a trilled whistle *swee see dee* (Wetmore 1926) like Tropical Kingbird's but higher.

**Behavior:** Pairs or small family groups are mostly terrestrial when feeding; otherwise sit on top of low bushes or lower branches of trees. Run well, follow and perch on backs of cattle, occas. sally to air from perch.

**Breeding:** Building nest, 4 Mar, Meta (Brown); juvs., July, lower Río Sinú (Haffer 1975); BC ♂, 30 May, Bolívar, and 19 May, Cesar Val. (Carriker); June–Aug, Guárico, Venez. (Thomas 1979b). Appropriates abandoned thornbird nests (Skutch 1959b) or builds bulky grass ball well above ground. Three creamy buff eggs heavily marked shades of chestnut (Naumburg 1930).

**Status and habitat:** Fairly common to common in drier semiopen country, savanna, and pastureland with scattered trees and bushes; occas. sandy beaches. A ground-foraging kingbird.

**Range:** To 500m (to 800m, Santa Marta Mts.) Carib. lowlands from upper Río Sinú to Guajira and s to s Bolívar; e of Andes from Norte de Santander to s Meta and Vichada. Once on Pacific at Buenaventura (photo, 3 Mar 1979—Hilty). N and e Colombia to Venez.; e and c Brazil to n Argentina and Uruguay. S birds migratory.

## 143. BRIGHT-RUMPED ATTILA

*Attila spadiceus*                Pl. 33, Map 1057

**Identification:** 7.5″ (19cm). *Myiarchus*-like. Bill heavy, straight, decidedly hooked at tip; eyes pale; head rather large. Color var. but *always has 2 wing bars, and rump contrasting with back.* Olive green above; *rump yellow to bright buff*; wings and tail brownish; 2 grayish wing bars; underparts olive fading to whitish on belly; throat and breast clouded and streaked yellow and white. Or bright cinnamon rufous above; *rump and tail cinnamon orange*; wings rufous brown with 2 rufous bars; underparts cinnamon, often paler on belly. Or occas. any color in between.

**Similar species:** From Cinnamon Attila (145) by *contrasting* rump and back, presence of *wing bars*, and breast almost always darker and in contrast to belly (less evident in very cinnamon individuals). Larger and more robust Dull-capped Attila (144) has gray crown in contrast to back; also *white eyes.* Also see Citron-bellied Attila (note).

**Voice:** Heard far more often than seen. Main song a loud, emphatic, whistled *whéetit, whéetit, whéetit, whéetit, wheeuu* (Slud 1964) often alternated with *weed-we-two, weed-we-two, weed-we-two, we're took* (Willis and Eisenmann 1979),

swelling, rising, then sliding off at end. There are var., esp. at dawn, but *wheetit* ("beat-it") or *weed-we-two* phrases are usually characteristic. Alarm a sharp *di-di-dit.*

**Behavior:** Sings persistently, often from fairly high perch in foliage where difficult to locate. Solitary, sluggish, and sometimes with mixed flocks. Forages at almost any ht. (predom. midlevels) by sallying short distances then hover-gleaning from foliage and twigs for insects and fruit.

**Breeding:** BC pair, Feb, Antioquia (Carriker); 1 nest, Mar, Valle-Chocó border (Brown); 2 in Mar–Apr, Costa Rica (Skutch 1971c). Cup nest rather low, wedged in crotch, mossy rock outcrop, tree cavity, etc.; 3-4 pale buff eggs coarsely marked reddish brown, esp. at larger end.

**Status and habitat:** Fairly common in humid and wet forest, forest borders, and esp. tall denser second growth woodland, also clearings with tall trees. Most numerous w of Andes.

**Range:** To 2100m (usually below 1500m). Pacific coast, and n of Andes to Santa Marta Mts. and s in Magdalena Val. to Pto. Berrío, e Antioquia; e of Andes in s Meta (Macarena Mts.), Vaupés (Mitú), and w Caquetá; Amazonas (no specimens; prob. also Arauca and Vichada (in adj. Venez.). Mexico to w Ecuador, n Bolivia, and se Brazil. Trinidad.

**Note:** Citron-bellied Attila (*A. citriniventris*) of humid forest in s Venez., nw Brazil, ne Peru, and e Ecuador, doubtless occurs in se Guainía and poss. e Vaupés, Colombia. Much like rufous phase of Bright-rumped Attila but lacks wing bars, and entire head gray incl. crown, nape, sides of head, and throat; center of belly washed yellow; base half of lower mandible pinkish as in Bright-rumped Attila. Song a slightly ascending, attilalike *cuee-cuee-cuee-cuee-cuee-cuée-cuu*, last note lower (P. Schwartz recording).

## 144. DULL-CAPPED ATTILA

*Attila bolivianus*                Pl. 33, Map 1058

**Identification:** 8.5″ (22cm). Bill heavy, straight, and decidedly hooked at tip; *eyes white. Crown dull brownish gray*; back and wings rufous brown; flight feathers blackish; *rump and tail cinnamon rufous*; underparts cinnamon rufous; chin grayish; belly more tawny; throat and chest sometimes faintly streaked dusky.

**Similar species:** From Bright-rumped or Cinnamon attilas (143, 145) by white eyes and contrasting gray-tinged crown. Also see Citron-bellied Attila (note under 143).

**Voice:** Main song much like Bright-rumped Attila's, an emphatic rising ser., last note sliding lower, but each note *single* (not double-sounding), *wheet, wheet, wheet, wheet, wheet, weeu* (Hilty) or *whee-whee-whee wée-per, wée-per, wée-per wheu* (T. Parker); also a loud rapid, staccato ser. *tu-tu-tu-tu-tu*.

**Behavior:** Like Bright-rumped Attila, sings persistently, but wary and difficult to locate. Solitary in lower or mid. strata and usually partially concealed in foliage; sluggish.

**Breeding:** June nest 1.3m above water in *várzea* forest, Leticia: rusty moss cup (color of bird's plumage) at base of epiphyte on trunk; 2 white eggs blotched reddish brown (J. V. Remsen).

**Status and habitat:** Local. Fairly common on swampy river isls., *várzea* forest, and *várzea* borders on and near Isla Santa Sophia III ("Monkey Isl."), Amazonas. First Colombia rec., 12 Oct 1974 (J. V. Remsen).

**Range:** To 100m. Extreme se Colombia in Amazonas (w of Leticia). E Peru, n Bolivia, and sw Amazonian Brazil.

### 145. CINNAMON ATTILA

*Attila cinnamomeus*          Pl. 33, Map 1059

**Identification:** 8″ (20cm). Bill heavy, straight, and decidedly hooked at tip. *Mainly cinnamon rufous*, slightly paler on rump, throat, and belly; *primaries blackish*, tertials and wing coverts dusky with conspic. rufous edgings (but no wing bars).

**Similar species:** Bright-rumped Attila (143) always has wing bars and contrasting rump. Dull-capped Attila (144) has grayish crown and white eyes. Also see Citron-bellied (note under 143) and Ochraceous attilas (146).

**Voice:** A loud, clear, somewhat drowsy whistle, *tuu-tueeeeeer*, over and over; song, *weary weary weary weer-ry*, recalling Bright-rumped Attila's.

**Behavior:** Rather like Bright-rumped Attila but usually easier to see, often rather unsuspicious as perch lethargically in forest midlevels or lower with tail down and peer about slowly.

**Breeding:** In Surinam, cup of sticks and finer material in crevice in tree crotch, wedged at base of bromeliad, etc.; 3 eggs salmon pink with purplish spots and reddish brown markings (Haverschmidt 1968).

**Status and habitat:** Swampy palm groves, *várzea* forest, and *várzea* and lake borders. Apparently uncommon and local (only a few Colombian specimens).

**Range:** To 500m. E of Andes from Meta (Río Ocoa se of Villavicencio and Vaupés (Mitú) s to Amazonas. Prob. e Guainía and e Vichada (on Venez. side of Orinoco at San Fernando de Atabapo). The Guianas and e and s Venez. to e Ecuador, e Peru, n Bolivia, and Amazonian Brazil.

### 146. OCHRACEOUS ATTILA

*Attila torridus*

**Identification:** 8.5″ (22cm). A "yellowish" edition of Cinnamon Attila, differing as follows: mainly *cinnamon yellow* above, 2 distinct cinnamon wing bars, underparts *tawny yellow*, rump and belly saffron yellow. Eyes reddish brown; bill dusky.

**Similar species:** Rufous individuals of Bright-rumped Attila (143) are rather sim. but look cinnamon rufous rather than yellowish and have pale eyes. Also see Rufous Mourner (149).

**Status and habitat:** Known in Colombia from 1 ♂ taken 13 Mar 1958, Candelilla, Río Míra, Nariño (Blake 1959).

**Range:** 100m. Lowlands of sw Nariño. Sw Colombia, w Ecuador (to 900m), and nw Peru.

**Note:** Has been considered a subsp. of Cinnamon Attila.

### 147. GRAYISH MOURNER

*Rhytipterna simplex*          Pl. 34, Map 1060

**Identification:** 8″ (20cm). Bill rounded, slight hook at tip. Dark red eyes. Rear crown with suggestion of crest. *Plain gray*, slightly paler below; wings and tail tinged brownish; abdomen faintly tinged yellowish green (not obvious in the field). Imm.(?) may have narrow fulvous edges on wings and tail.

**Similar species:** Usually not safely told from Screaming Piha (p 445) in the field except by voice. Latter is larger, more robust, and lacks greenish yellow cast on abdomen. Also see Cinereous Mourner (150).

**Voice:** Song a loud and very rapid rising yodel (to 24 syllables) ending in a sharp note, *kolu-lulululu . . . whik* (N. Howe *in* Snyder 1966).

**Behavior:** Single birds, pairs, or families perch quietly and inconspic. in subcanopy foliage, then hover-glean from leaves after a long sally, less often short sally. Often with forest flocks (J. Fitzpatrick).

**Breeding:** BC ♂, Aug, Vaupés (Olivares and Hernández 1962).

**Status and habitat:** Uncommon (easily overlooked unless calling) in humid *terra firme* forest.

**Range:** To 500m. E of Andes from w Meta (near Villavicencio; Macarena Mts.) and Vaupés (Mitú) southward. Prob. n to e Vichada (on Venez. side of Orinoco). The Guianas and s Venez. to n Bolivia and Amazonian and se Brazil.

### 148. PALE-BELLIED MOURNER

*Rhytipterna immunda*

**Identification:** 7.5″ (19cm). *Myiarchus*-like. *Pale eyes.* Grayish brown above becoming browner on upper tail coverts and tail, *2 indistinct gray-*

*ish wing bars*; primaries and outer tail feathers edged rufous; throat and breast gray becoming pale dirty yellow on lower underparts; belly tinged rusty. ♀: primaries and tail edged whitish.

**Similar species:** Much like a *Myiarchus* but grayer, esp. above, head rounded and dovelike (not slightly crested), eyes pale, wing bars more prom., and belly tinged rusty. "Short-legged" horizontal posture unlike more erect stance of *Myiarchus*.

**Voice:** Dawn song in Surinam a loud, clear, whistled *peer-REEP, chuueer*; also a single *pueeeer* rather like Dusky-capped Flycatcher (W. Lanyon recording).

**Behavior:** Single birds or separated pairs, low to fairly high in bushes or trees of open sandy savanna scrub and borders where perch quietly, hidden in foliage. Peer about very slowly like other mourners, occas. sally short distances to foliage (Hilty; W. Lanyon).

**Status and habitat:** Known only from mouth of Río Guainía and 1 sight rec. 23 Sept 1978 on lower Río Inírida, ne Guainía (Hilty). Apparently confined to sandy-belt scrub and adj. savanna woodland borders in Surinam (W. Lanyon) and elsewhere.

**Range:** To 250m. E Guainía near the Orinoco (San Felipe; Río Inírida). Fr. Guiana, Surinam, e Colombia, and n and e Amazonian Brazil.

### 149. RUFOUS MOURNER

*Rhytipterna holerythra*        Pl. 35, Map 1061
**Identification:** 8″ (20cm). Bill blackish, hooked at tip. *Mainly rufous*, lower underparts and under tail coverts paler, more cinnamon.

**Similar species:** Confusing. Much like Rufous Piha (p 446) but appears somewhat "flat-headed"; also slightly smaller, slimmer, throat and breast more uniform rufous, and in good light, crown and wing coverts somewhat duller and darker than back (uniform in Piha). Also note behaviorial differences (see discussion under Rufous Piha). Speckled Mourner (151) has rufous spotting on dusky wing coverts and usually shows fine grayish scaling on breast (hard to see in dim light). All 3 are easily separated by voice. Also see Cinnamon Becard (p 447) and ♀ One-colored Becard (p 449); in sw Nariño Ochraceous Attila (146), which is yellowish with black primaries and 2 rufous wing bars.

**Voice:** Call a clear, slow, lamenting *wheeeep, deeeur* rising and falling (a leisurely "wolf whistle").

**Behavior:** Inconspic. Alone or in pairs perched low to high but usually sing from high perch. Sit quietly, then flutter short distances to foliage or dart after prey.

**Breeding:** 9 BC birds, Feb–May, n Antioquia to Chocó (Carriker); may nest in hole in bank (F. Vuilleumier).

**Status and habitat:** Uncommon (sometimes local) in humid and wet forest and tall second growth woodland. Least numerous in wet forest belt south of c Chocó. Replaced e of Andes by Grayish Mourner.

**Range:** To 1000m. Pacific Colombia and e in humid zone n of Andes (not Carib. region) to mid. Magdalena Val. (s to Bucaramanga and n boundary of Caldas). Guatemala to nw Ecuador.

### 150. CINEREOUS MOURNER

*Laniocera hypopyrrha*        Pl. 34, Map 1062
**Identification:** 8″ (20cm). Somewhat thrush-like; bill rounded, slightly hooked at tip. *Mainly gray*, slightly paler below; wings darker with *2 rows of large orange rufous spots forming conspic. wing bars*; tail tips and tuft at sides of chest orange rufous (latter often concealed); sometimes a few black-tipped buff feathers on breast. ♀ has pale yellowish pectoral tufts. Imm.: largely rufous spotted black below; pectoral tufts mixed yellow and rufous.

**Similar species:** No other mainly gray mourner or piha has boldly spotted orange rufous wing bars.

**Voice:** Song, 10-15 very high, thin, singsong *seea-weh* phrases, delivered drowsily from ravine woodland, and repeated tirelessly, even during the heat of the day. Song very sim. to Speckled Mourner's (see 151): ventriloquial and easily passed off as an insect or amphibian at a distance.

**Behavior:** Inconspic. ♂♂ sing from open perches in forest midlevels in loosely composed leks. Feed like an *Attila* on insects and berries in mid. or lower story.

**Status and habitat:** Fairly common in humid sandy-belt forest and more extensive savanna woodland of the extreme east (e.g. near Pto. Inírida). Apparently much less numerous in Amazonia (few recs).

**Range:** To 500m. E base of E Andes from extreme sw Casanare and ne Guainía (sight, Pto. Inírida, Sept 1978—Hilty) southward. The Guianas and s Venez. to n Bolivia and Amazonian Brazil.

### 151. SPECKLED MOURNER

*Laniocera rufescens*        Pl. 35, Map 1063
**Identification:** 8″ (20cm). Bill roundish, slightly hooked at tip. *Dull cinnamon rufous*, underparts slightly paler and *usually with indistinct fine gray scalloping on chest*; wing coverts dusky *tipped with large cinnamon spots forming 2 or 3 dull wing bars*; yellow pectoral tufts usually hid-

den by wings. ♀: sim., but tufts (if present) orange ochraceous. Imm.: like ♀ but markings on wings and underparts more prom.
**Similar species:** Rufous Mourner (149) and Rufous Piha (p 446) are usually separable by their more uniform brown plumage and absence of wing spots, pectoral tufts, and scaly markings on breast. Piha also larger.
**Voice:** Song a ringing, ventriloquial, *tlee-yee, tlee-yee* . . . , up to 10-15 couplet phrases in a ser. and given persistently throughout day (R. Ridgely). Much like song of Cinereous Mourner.
**Behavior:** Perch alone and inconspic. in vines and branches 10-20m up. ♂ ♂ sing persistently for yrs. at traditional song sites (Willis and Eisenmann 1979). Like other *Laniocera* peer sluggishly and sally short distances to foliage.
**Breeding:** 4 BC birds, May, s Bolívar (Carriker).
**Status and habitat:** Ravines and streams in humid and wet forest and tall second growth. Most Colombian recs. are from foothills. Replaced e of Andes by Cinereous Mourner.
**Range:** To 1000m. Pacific Colombia, and e in humid lowlands n of Andes to mid. Magdalena Val. (Río Ite; Remedios, e Antioquia). Guatemala to nw Ecuador.

## 152. SIRYSTES
*Sirystes sibilator*     Pl. 39, Map 1064
**Identification:** 7-7.5″ (18-19cm). Distinctive black, gray, and white pattern. Slightly crested. *Cap black* becoming slate gray on sides of head; *wings black* edged gray (or with 2 broad white bars and broad white edgings—*albogriseus*); *rather long square tail black* (with white tip—*albogriseus*); *otherwise mainly pale gray with white rump and lower underparts.*
**Similar species:** From any sim. flycatcher or becard by contrasting white rump. Cf. Crowned Slaty-Flycatcher (174), which is browner above, and Cinereous and Black-and-white becards (pp 446; 448), which show more contrast; also imm. Fork-tailed Flycatcher and Eastern Kingbird (178, 179).
**Voice:** Loud noisy whistles from treetop; e of Andes *wheer whít-it* or *wheer whít* or var.; also noisy chattering (P. Schwartz recording); in Panama brisk *Myiarchus*-like ser. of loud *prip* or *hrip* notes, often accelerating into chatter (R. A. Rowlett recording).
**Behavior:** Behavior and proportions recall a *Myiarchus*. Pairs perch in treetops, follow mixed flocks in forest canopy, and sally for insects or small fruits.
**Breeding:** 3 BC birds, Feb, sw Córdoba and n Chocó (Carriker). In Panama examining cavities and apparently gathering nest material near ground, Feb (Wetmore 1972).

**Status and habitat:** Local in humid forest, tall second growth, and gallery forest. "Common" at Limoncocha, Ecuador (Pearson et al. 1977) near Putumayo boundary but few Colombian recs.
**Range:** To 500m. N Chocó (Juradó) s to Baudó Mts. (Nuquí) and e to mid. and upper Río Sinú (*albogriseus*); e of Andes in w Meta (e of Villavicencio; Macarena Mts.) (*albocinereus*); sight recs., n Arauca (14 Dec 1977—W. McKay) and Leticia, Amazonas (J. V. Remsen). E Panama; nw Venez. (s Táchira), s Surinam; most of Amazonian Brazil, e Ecuador, and e Peru s to ne Argentina and Paraguay.
**Note:** Birds from Panama, w Colombia, and w Ecuador differ in plumage and voice (usually silent) and are perhaps a different sp. (R. Ridgely).

[*Myiarchus*: Members of this genus notoriously difficult to distinguish; all slightly crested; very minor differences in appearance; voice usually diagnostic.]

## 153. SHORT-CRESTED FLYCATCHER
*Myiarchus ferox*     Map 1065
**Identification:** 7.2″ (18.3cm). Slightly crested; *bill black.* Brownish olive above, head somewhat darker; wings and tail dark brown (*no rufous in tail*); throat and breast pale gray; lower underparts pale yellow; 2 indistinct dull gray wing bars. Juv. has narrow rufous edgings on wings and tail.
**Similar species:** Virtually indistinguishable in field from Venezuelan and Panama flycatchers (154, 155), but ranges, as now understood, do not overlap. Swainson's Flycatcher (159) is larger, decidedly duller (looks faded), and lower mandible pale (reddish brown to flesh color). Also see Dusky-capped Flycatcher (161).
**Voice:** Most common call a short, soft, purring (or rolling) trill, *turrrt* or *prrrt* (Hilty), also a descending trill of about 6 notes, sim. to but more prolonged than that of Southern Beardless Flycatcher (J. V. Remsen). No whistled notes (Lanyon 1978).
**Behavior:** Alone or in pairs about 1-10m up in well-lit foliage of bushes and trees. Often nods head. Typically sallies out and hover-gleans from foliage; much less often sallies to air or to ground. Unobtrusive habits and weak calls usually do not attract much attention.
**Breeding:** 9 BC birds, May, Venez. (Lanyon 1978). Cavity usually lined with cast off snake skin; 2 creamy white eggs with band of reddish spots around larger end (Haverschmidt 1968).
**Status and habitat:** Fairly common resident in humid forest borders, shrubby clearings, and semiopen areas with bushes and trees.

**Range:** To 500m. E of Andes. The Guianas and most of Venez. southward e of Andes to n Argentina, Uruguay, and se Brazil. Austral birds not migratory (Lanyon 1978).

## 154. VENEZUELAN FLYCATCHER
*Myiarchus venezuelensis*          Pl. 39, Map 1066
**Identification:** 7.3″ (18.5cm). Not safely separated in field from Short-crested or Panama flycatchers except by voice (and usually by range). Differs from both by narrow rufous edges to outer webs of primaries and tail (from above). Imm. has broader rufous edges. In the hand ads. in fresh plumage are darker above than Panama Flycatcher, paler than (or sim. to) Short-crested Flycatcher, and have outer web of outer tail feather noticeably paler than inner web. Bill black; mouth lining orange.
**Similar species:** Best told from Panama Flycatcher (155) by voice (both overlap from n Sucre to Guajira). Brown-crested Flycatcher (158) is larger, heavier-billed, has base of lower mandible pale, and more rufous in tail (esp. below), but more easily told by voice. Great Crested Flycatcher (160) has more rufous on tail (looks entirely rufous from below) and different voice.
**Voice:** Dawn song consists solely of plaintive whistles (no *huit* notes) at intervals of several sec. Repeated rasp whistles and *wheer-r-r* to intruding conspecifics, latter much like that of Dusky-capped Flycatcher. No purring trill as in Short-crested Flycatcher (Lanyon 1978).
**Behavior:** Much like Short-crested Flycatcher.
**Breeding:** Laying ♀, 19 Oct, Cúcuta (Carriker); several BC birds and dependent juv. with ad., May, Venez. (Lanyon 1978).
**Status and habitat:** Deciduous woodland and drier scrubby ranchland with scattered trees and brushy borders (upper el. limits need documentation).
**Range:** To ca. 500m. Carib. lowlands from n Sucre (Sincelejo; Snía. de San Jacinto) e to Guajira; e of Andes in Norte de Santander (Cúcuta). N Colombia and n Venez. Tobago.
**Note:** Formerly considered a race of *M. ferox* (Short-crested Flycatcher).

## 155. PANAMA FLYCATCHER
*Myiarchus panamensis*          Map 1067
**Identification:** 7.5″ (19cm). Essentially indistinguishable in field from Short-crested and Venezuelan flycatchers (see 153, 154) except by voice. In the hand paler and more olivaceous on back. Imm., as in many other imm. *Myiarchus*, has inconspic. rufous edgings on wings and tail (underside of tail dusky).
**Similar species:** Brown-crested Flycatcher (158)

is larger, wings and tail narrowly edged rufous, base of lower mandible pale, and voice different. Great Crested Flycatcher (160) has rufous wing edgings, much rufous in tail (mostly rufous from below), and different voice.
**Voice:** Softer and not as sharp as Brown-crested or Great Crested flycatchers'. Most common call a short whistle in pairs or in rapid ser. (Lanyon 1978). Dawn song a fast, whistled *tseéedew* or *wheedeedew*; also semiwhistled twittering *tee, deedeedeedeedeedee* with var., and soft, clear, whistled *whee* and *prrrt* notes (Ridgely 1976).
**Behavior:** Much like Short-crested Flycatcher.
**Breeding:** Nestlings in mangroves near Buenaventura, 24 Mar; 1 with brood patch, 31 Mar (Ralph and Chaplin 1973). Mostly cavities, occas. open cup under eave; 2 pale greenish white eggs heavily marked dark brown (Wetmore 1972).
**Status and habitat:** Apparently fairly common in drier semiopen and scrubby areas, clearings, brushy borders, lighter woodland, and mangroves; lowlands and foothills.
**Range:** To 600m. Pacific coast (s to Tumaco, Nariño), generally n of Andes (Guajira?), and s in Magdalena Val. to n Huila (Villavieja). Sw Costa Rica to nw Venez.
**Note:** Until recently considered a race of *M. ferox* (Short-crested Flycatcher). Separation is based on vocal differences (Lanyon 1978).

## 156. APICAL FLYCATCHER
*Myiarchus apicalis*          Pl. 39, Map 1068
**Identification:** 7.5″ (19cm). Tail distinctive: *slightly rounded with outer web of outermost feather and tip of all but central pair whitish* (esp. prom. from below in field); *head sooty gray* (darker than back) with rather bushy crest; throat and chest dingy gray; otherwise much like others of the genus.
**Similar species:** From any other *Myiarchus* by rather broad whitish tail tips; head and throat darker and crest bushier than most.
**Behavior:** Sim. to other *Myiarchus* (see 153).
**Breeding:** Young in cavity 5m up; isolated stump in pasture, 14 Aug, Bosque Yotoco, Valle (Hilty); BC ♂, Jan, and ♀ at fence post hole near stream-side woods, Huila (Miller 1947). Several BC ♂♂, Jan–Apr, Colombia (Lanyon 1978).
**Status and habitat:** Locally fairly common in forest and lighter woodland borders, scrubby areas, patches of woodland, and stream-side trees and brush. Most numerous in dry to arid inter-Andean vals., a few in mod. humid areas.
**Range:** ENDEMIC. 400-2300m (mainly below 1700m). Pacific slope in upper Dagua and Patía vals., spottily in mid. and upper Cauca Val.

(no recs. n of Valle), and mid. and upper Magdalena Val. from Santander (San Gil) and Boyacá (Soatá) to headwaters in Huila.

## 157. PALE-EDGED FLYCATCHER

*Myiarchus cephalotes*    Pl. 39, Map 1069
**Identification:** 8" (20cm). Bill black. Brownish olive above, head slightly browner (not dusky); edges of secondaries and *2 rather prom. wide wing bars grayish to buffy white; outer web of outermost tail feather buffy white* (white does not extend quite to tip); below much like others of the genus.
**Similar species:** Apical Flycatcher (156) has prom. pale spotlike tail tips (most obvious from below), darker head and throat and slightly less distinct wing bars, and occurs mostly in the drier vals. From any other *Myiarchus* by white edge on tail and more prom. wing bars.
**Voice:** Call (and dawn song—Lanyon 1978) a loud clear *pip* or *piup* repeated over and over (recalls note of Greater Pewee); day song a spirited but plaintive whistled *wheep, pip-peer-peer-peer*, 2d note briefest.
**Behavior:** Much like others of the genus (see 153). Perches rather low, often quite in open.
**Breeding:** 6 BC birds, Feb–July, W and C Andes (Carriker). 2 nests, Mar–Apr, PN Cueva de los Guácharos; trashy cups under eave (P. Gertler).
**Status and habitat:** Uncommon to locally common in humid forest borders, clearings with scattered bushes and trees, and in or near patches of lighter woodland. Easily found in PN Cueva de los Guácharos.
**Range:** 1500-2400m (rarely to 2700m). All 3 Andean ranges from Norte de Santander and Antioquia s through Nariño (few recs. Pacific slope or in E Andes). Mts. of n Venez. Colombia s in Andes to n Bolivia.

## 158. BROWN-CRESTED (WIED'S CRESTED) FLYCATCHER

*Myiarchus tyrannulus*    Pl. 39, Map 1070
**Identification:** 8" (20cm). Bill black, lower mandible often pinkish at base. Crown dull brown, contrasting slightly with grayish olive back; 2 dull grayish white wing bars; primaries edged rufous; inner webs of *outer tail feathers broadly margined rufous* (underside of tail shows much rufous); below like other *Myiarchus* but slightly paler.
**Similar species:** Very sim. to Great Crested Flycatcher (160) but less rufous on tail, esp. from below, underparts paler, and voice (best clue) different. Also see Venezuelan and Panama flycatchers (154, 155).
**Voice:** Often noisy. Call a short, slightly rough *whip* or *hurrip*, sometimes repeated in harsh

ser. (Hilty); no whistled notes (Lanyon 1978) and without strong rising inflection of Great Crested.
**Behavior:** Much like other *Myiarchus* (see 153) but noisier.
**Breeding:** 4 BC ♂♂, Feb–June, Guajira and Gulf of Urabá (Carriker); mainly cavities; often lined with cast off snake skin. 2-3 creamy white eggs heavily marked dark purple and lavender, esp. at larger end (ffrench 1973).
**Status and habitat:** Common in arid and drier semiopen areas, deciduous woodland, thorn scrub, and mangroves.
**Range:** To ca. 1000m. Carib. lowlands from Río Sinú (Snía. de Abibe) e to Guajira; e of Andes from Norte de Santander (Río Zulia) to Meta and Vichada. Sw US to nw Costa Rica; n Colombia; n Venez. and the Guianas s to c Argentina and se Brazil (except w Amazonia). Dutch and Venez. isls.; Trinidad.

## 159. SWAINSON'S FLYCATCHER

*Myiarchus swainsoni*
**Identification:** 7.7-8.2" (19.5-21cm). Migrant races (*ferocior* and *swainsoni*) differ from all others of the genus by light brown upper mandible and *flesh pink to orangish lower mandible*. In general the *dullest, plainest* S American *Myiarchus*. Dark olive brown above with sooty cap, no rufous in wings and tail (imm. may show some rufous edgings); wing coverts pale-edged but no distinct wing bars; below like others of the genus (*swainsoni*). Or very pale olive brown above (looks faded and washed out in field), dull below (*ferocior*).
**Similar species:** Pinkish lower mandible (*whole mandible looks pale*) is the best mark; *ferocior* subsp. can also be told by very faded dull plumage, esp. upperparts and head.
**Voice:** A plaintive whistled *phweeee*, reminiscent of Dusky-capped Flycatcher (Hilty); a rapid ser. of short whistles (Lanyon 1978); most distinctive call on breeding grounds a short, soft *whoo* or *poo* (R. Ridgely).
**Behavior:** One to several wander alone or more often with mixed flocks in forest subcanopy or edge and are quite frugivorous.
**Status and habitat:** Apparently an uncommon austral migrant, May–Aug (prob. Mar–Oct), to humid forest borders, shrubby clearings, and shrubbery along borders of lakes, streams, and *várzea* forest.
**Range:** Lowlands e of Andes. Rec. in w Caquetá (Florencia), Amazonas (near Leticia), once to temperate zone on Sabana de Bogotá (2600m). Fr. Guiana, Guyana, and Venez. (migrant and resident) e of Andes to c Argentina, Uruguay, and s Brazil. S breeders (*ferocior* and *swainsoni*)

migrate n across Amazonia to e Colombia and Venez.

**Note:** The race *phaeonotus*, resident in e and s Venez., undoubtedly occurs in e Guainía (rec. at 3 localities close to boundary). From migrant *swainsoni* by all black bill and much darker head. Best told from Short-crested Flycatcher by voice, from Dusky-capped Flycatcher by larger size.

**160. GREAT CRESTED FLYCATCHER**
*Myiarchus crinitus*
**Identification:** 8″ (20cm). Resembles Brown-crested Flycatcher (158) but darker, upperparts slightly tinged olive (*crown not distinctly brown*); *more rufous in tail* (whole underside appears rufous); primaries edged rufous; throat and breast darker gray and belly deeper yellow (not pale whitish yellow). Voice always diagnostic.
**Similar species:** See Venezuelan and Panama flycatchers (154, 155), e of Andes Short-crested Flycatcher (153), none of which shows rufous in tail.
**Voice:** Distinctive upward inflected *wheeeep* often heard on wintering ground; throaty rolling ser. of *prrrip* notes (commonly heard on temperate breeding grounds) seldom given in Colombia.
**Behavior:** Ofen at fruiting trees and shrubs on wintering grounds.
**Status and habitat:** Uncommon winter resident, mid-Oct–early May, to humid forest borders, shrubby clearings, and second growth, occas. canopy of undisturbed forest.
**Range:** To 1100m. W of Andes; prob. a few e of Andes except the extreme se. Breeds in e N America; winters from s Florida and Texas to Colombia, e Ecuador (few recs.), and w Venez. (casual).

**161. DUSKY-CAPPED (OLIVACEOUS) FLYCATCHER**
*Myiarchus tuberculifer*     Pl. 39, Map 1071
**Identification:** 6.5″ (16.5cm). Differs from other Colombian *Myiarchus* by *small size, blackish or dusky brown cap, decidedly darker than brownish olive to grayish olive back*; primaries very narrowly edged rufescent (not a field mark); *no rufous in tail*. Voice diagnostic.
**Similar species:** Small size and dark cap are characteristic. See other *Myiarchus*.
**Voice:** Most frequent call a plaintive, drawn-out whistle, *peeeeeeer*, dropping slightly; also a soft, brief *whit*. Sometimes a rapid ser. of short whistles (Lanyon 1978).
**Behavior:** Much like other *Myiarchus* (see 153) but frequently range up to subcanopy.
**Breeding:** BC ♂, Apr, Perijá Mts., and Aug,

Cesar (Carriker); 1 fence post nest, Jan, w Meta (W. McKay). Near Popayán Apr–Aug (Lanyon 1978). Cavity, broken stub, bird box, etc., lined with soft fine material; 2-4 dull white eggs heavily blotched dark brown, esp. in wreath at larger end (Wetmore 1972).
**Status and habitat:** Fairly common in humid and wet forest borders, at openings inside forest, and in second growth woodland, coffee plantations, and wooded areas near streams.
**Range:** To 1800m (once to 2400m in extreme s Nariño). Throughout. Sw US to nw Argentina, Paraguay, and se Brazil. Trinidad. Most, if not all, S American populations are nonmigratory (Lanyon 1978).

**162. GREAT KISKADEE**
*Pitangus sulphuratus*     Pl. 39, Map 1072
**Identification:** 8.5″ (22cm). Broad-shouldered and short-tailed; heavy black bill. *Black crown encircled by broad white band*; concealed crown patch yellow; sides of head black; small yellow malar mark; otherwise *brown above, wings and tail edged rufous* (or wings narrowly edged rufous, tail brown—e of Andes); throat white; rest of underparts bright yellow.
**Similar species:** From Boat-billed Flycatcher (164) by brown (not olive) back, more rufous in wings (and tail—w of Andes), and less massive bill. Lesser Kiskadee (163) is smaller, decidedly slimmer, and with proportionally longer and more slender bill.
**Voice:** A var. of loud exuberant calls, most distinctive the *kis-ka-deé!*, hence its name; this often shortened to *ka-deé*.
**Behavior:** A noisy and irascible bird that is conspic. throughout its range. Alone or in pairs (not groups) and often perches rather low. Aggressive and notably opportunistic when feeding, eating everything from small vertebrates and fish to more usual insect and fruit fare.
**Breeding:** Feb nest with young, Santa Marta (Hilty); others, Apr–May (Todd and Carriker 1922); 2 pairs building nest, Mar, Leticia (Hilty); 1 in May, ne Meta (S. Furniss); Mar–Sept, Guárico, Venez. (Thomas 1979b). Large untidy dome nest of grass has side entrance (a few open cups reported—Smith 1962); usually wedged high and exposed in crotch, utility pole brace, etc.; 2-4 eggs cream with a few dark reddish brown markings at larger end (ffrench 1973).
**Status and habitat:** Usually common around habitations, clearings, and cultivated areas with trees, esp. near water. Sometimes uncommon in suitable areas within forested zones. One of the most common birds of residential areas and boulevards in Cali.

**Range:** To 1500m. Throughout except w of W Andes. Carib. coast from n Sucre (Snía. San Jacinto) to Guajira (*rufipennis*); Río Sinú region, Cauca Val., and mid. and upper Magdalena Val. (*caucensis*); e of Andes s to Meta and Vaupés (*trinitatis*); w Caquetá to Amazonas (*sulphuratus*). S Texas and Mexico to c Argentina. Trinidad.

### 163. LESSER KISKADEE
*Pitangus lictor*          Pl. 39, Map 1073
**Identification:** 7″ (18cm). Very sim. to Great Kiskadee (esp. brown-tailed forms e of Andes). Best told by smaller size, *more slender body* (lacks Great Kiskadee's robust, broad-shouldered look), proportionally *longer and much narrower bill*, and very faint rufous edgings on wings and tail. Habitat helpful and calls diagnostic.
**Similar species:** See White-bearded Flycatcher (note under 169); also Rusty-margined and Social flycatchers (165, 166).
**Voice:** Unlike Great Kiskadee, a wheezy sneezing *queé-be* or *dree, dear-wr*, 1st note strongest and rising, 2d (and 3d) lower. Mutual display with fluttering wings and *wip wip wip you* (Willis 1962).
**Behavior:** Usually seen in pairs or families perched low (seldom over 2m up) over water. Sally to vegetation or surface of water, occas. drop to ground along shore, and unlike Great Kiskadee not pugnacious and aggressive.
**Breeding:** 2 BC ♂♂, July, Cesar (Carriker); 2 nests, 25 June, Caquetá (Hilty). Open cup of coarse material on stump or low shrub over water; 2-3 creamy white eggs spotted violet at larger end (Haverschmidt 1968; Willis and Eisenmann 1979).
**Status and habitat:** Bushy vegetation, dead snags and stubs along shores of lakes, pools, lagoons, sluggish streams, and mangroves. Common in Amazonia, less numerous in n Colombia. Shares its specialized habitat with Great Kiskadee but is not found along more open, less vegetated banks of larger and faster flowing rivers where latter also occurs.
**Range:** To 500m. Panama border (s to Río Truandó), e across Carib. lowlands to w Guajira and s in Magdalena Val. to Remedios, Antioquia; throughout e of Andes. Panama to n Bolivia and s Brazil.

### 164. BOAT-BILLED FLYCATCHER
*Megarhynchus pitangua*          Pl. 39, Map 1074
**Identification:** 9″ (23cm). Kiskadeelike with *conspic. large, broad black bill*. Crown and sides of head blackish; concealed yellow crown stripe; broad white eyebrow extends to and almost meets on nape; otherwise *olive brown above*;

wings and tail very inconspic. edged rufous (or no rufous tail edges—*mexicanus*); throat white; remaining underparts bright yellow.
**Similar species:** See Great and Lesser kiskadees (162, 163) and note voice difference.
**Voice:** Noisy with several harsh calls, most frequently a distinctive nasal, mocking *nya-nya-nya-nya* as bobs head.
**Behavior:** Rather var. in actions but usually perches fairly high and partially within canopy and foliage where less conspic. than most other "kiskadee types." Eats a var. of insects, other invertebrates, small vertebrates, and fruit.
**Breeding:** 3 BC ♂♂, June–Aug, Guajira and Cesar (Carriker); 1 in Jan, Huila (Miller 1947). Building nests July and Oct (J. V. Remsen); incubating in Aug, Leticia (P. Kaestner). Nest, unlike many allies, a shallow open cup; 6-30m up; 2-3 whitish eggs thickly speckled brown and pale lilac (Skutch 1951).
**Status and habitat:** Fairly common in forest borders, woodland borders, lighter second growth, clearings with scattered trees, and in drier areas in riparian woodland. Less numerous than Great Kiskadee and prefers more wooded surroundings.
**Range:** To 1400m. Nw Chocó s to Río Juradó (*mexicanus*); the Carib. lowlands to Guajira, s in Magdalena Val. to Huila; throughout e of Andes (*pitanga*). Mexico to w Ecuador, ne Argentina, Paraguay, and se Brazil. Trinidad.

[*Myiozetetes*: Short-billed miniatures of kiskadee; basic pattern incl. dark cheeks, white throat, and yellow underparts; white eyestripe does not encircle crown.]

### 165. RUSTY-MARGINED FLYCATCHER
*Myiozetetes cayanensis*          Pl. 39, Map 1075
**Identification:** 6.5″ (16.5cm). Stubby black bill. *Upperparts brown contrasting with black median crown stripe* and sides of head, long eyebrow white (does not meet on nape); semiconcealed crown patch golden orange; flight feathers narrowly (or conspic.—*rufipennis*) edged rufous; throat white; otherwise bright yellow below. Imm.: sim. but shows rufous edging on tail.
**Similar species:** From confusingly sim. Social Flycatcher (166) by brown (not olive) back contrasting with black (not brownish gray) central crown, absence of buffy wing edgings or wing bars, and different voice. Note: w of E Andes rufous wing edges are difficult to see and imm. Social Flycatcher may also show sim. rusty edgings; but e of Andes easily distinguished from Social by the *conspic.* rufous in the wing. Also cf. Lesser Kiskadee (163; longer

bill), White-ringed (169), and White-bearded flycatchers (note under 169).

**Voice:** Noisy. Thin plaintive *peeeeea*; when excited *too-eeéet* and rapid rolling ser. of *q-wit* notes; also *tis-u* over and over (Hilty), and *chew . . . chew-chewit* (J. Fitzpatrick).

**Behavior:** Much like Social Flycatcher but a little less vocal, less common around residential areas, and more often sallies over water.

**Breeding:** Juv. and laying ♀, n Huila, Jan (Miller 1947); building nest, Mar (2), Aug (1), and Nov (1), fledglings, early June, Anchicayá Val.; building nest, early June, Buga, Valle (Hilty); nestlings, May, w Meta (W. McKay). Bulky dome nest of dried grass with side entrance; conspic. near end of branch.

**Status and habitat:** Common and widespread in forest borders, clearings, and most semi-open habitats, esp. near water. In absence of Social Flycatcher, often in residential or cultivated areas, in its presence mostly away from vicinity of buildings; in upper Amazonia apparently replaced by Social and/or Gray-capped flycatchers.

**Range:** To 1500m, rarely to 2100m. W of E Andes (*hellmayri*); e of E Andes from Norte de Santander to Tres Esquinas, w Caquetá, and Mitú, Vaupés (*rufipennis*). W Panama to w and e Ecuador, Venez., the Guianas, n, e, and se Brazil, and across Mato Grosso to e Bolivia and s Peru (sight).

### 166. SOCIAL (VERMILLION-CROWNED) FLYCATCHER

*Myiozetetes similis*  Pl. 39, Map 1076

**Identification:** 6.5″ (16.5cm). Short black bill. *Olive above*; wing coverts and *inner remiges edged grayish white to buffy white; center crown brownish gray* (little contrast with olive back) with semi-concealed vermilion crown patch; long eyebrow white (does not meet on nape); sides of head blackish; throat white, rest of underparts bright yellow. Imm.: no crown patch, and wings and tail narrowly edged rufous.

**Similar species:** See Rusty-margined and Gray-capped flycatchers (165, 167). Also White-bearded Flycatcher (note under 169) and Lesser Kiskadee (163).

**Voice:** A var. of rather loud, unmusical calls, most of which are unlike Rusty-margined Flycatcher's; e of Andes *tchew* or *techedew*, and *tititchew* (J. V. Remsen); w of Andes a corresponding *cre-u*, a ser. of *chur*'s, a slightly trilled *triiu*.

**Behavior:** Pairs or family groups are lively, excitable, often noisy. Sally to foliage or to air from perches at mid. hts., or sometimes much higher or lower. Also gather around fruiting trees and shrubs; small berries taken in quick hover.

**Breeding:** Building nest, Jan, Leticia (Hilty); 1 nest, Mar (Darlington 1931); 13 in Apr, Santa Marta area (Todd and Carriker 1922); breeding in most areas believed protracted (J. Fitzpatrick). Domed grass nest with side entrance wedged in fork of branch, often over water or near bee, wasp, or stinging ant nest (occas. in cavities that are filled with grass that protrudes from hole—J. Fitzpatrick). Usually 3 eggs whitish finely spotted shades of brown, mostly at larger end (Wetmore 1972).

**Status and habitat:** Common in shrubby clearing, gardens, residential areas, and forest borders. More often around dwellings than Rusty-margined Flycatcher.

**Range:** Mainly below 900m (to 1200m on e slope E Andes). Carib. lowlands from Río Sinú e to Guajira, entire Magdalena Val., Norte de Santander and generally e of Andes (llanos?). Mexico to ne Argentina and se Brazil.

### 167. GRAY-CAPPED FLYCATCHER

*Myiozetetes granadensis*  Pl. 39, Map 1077

**Identification:** 6.5″ (16.5cm). Resembles Social Flycatcher, but head different. *Crown and nape gray* with blackish mask across eyes and ear coverts; *narrow white forehead extends back as short eyestripe just to eyes*; concealed crown stripe scarlet (reduced or absent in ♀); otherwise olive above and yellow below with white throat. Imm.: crown tinged olive, wings and tail with buffy edgings.

**Similar species:** Mostly gray head and short eyestripe are the marks. Rusty-margined and Social flycatchers (165, 166) have bolder black-and-white heads. Larger Sulphury Flycatcher and Tropical Kingbird (176, 180) lack the narrow white forehead and have different shape.

**Voice:** A sharp strong *kip!* or *kip kip kip-it!* with var.; recalls that of Social Flycatcher but sharper and more emphatic.

**Behavior:** Like Social Flycatcher but more often alone and frequently perches lower.

**Breeding:** Mar nest, Buenaventura (Hilty). In Panama, Feb–May (dry season); domed grass nest with side entrance like others of the genus (Wetmore 1972); 2-3 white eggs speckled and blotched lilac and brown, mostly in ring at large end (Skutch 1960).

**Status and habitat:** Fairly common in overgrown forest borders, shrubby clearings, and second growth with scattered taller trees in humid and wet areas. Widely overlaps range of Social Flycatcher but favors more humid regions, is absent from drier regions of Carib. where latter is common, is not found in residential areas favored by latter, and is usually not as numerous.

**Range:** To 800m. Pacific coast, the humid lowlands n of Andes e to lower Magdalena Val.

(s to se side Snía. San Lucas); e of Andes from w Meta and Vaupés (Mitú) southward. Honduras to nw Peru, e Bolivia, and w Amazonian Brazil.

## 168. LEMON-BROWED FLYCATCHER
*Conopias cinchoneti*     Pl. 39, Map 1078
**Identification:** 6.3″ (16cm). Upperparts and sides of head olive green; wings and tail browner; *forehead bright yellow and continuing as a broad yellow eyestripe that almost joins on nape; entire underparts bright yellow.*
**Similar species:** Shape of *Myiozetetes*, but bill longer and otherwise easily told by long, broad, yellow eyestripe and all yellow underparts (no white throat). Also see Yellow-browed Tyrant (note under 140).
**Voice:** Peculiar high, quavering *ptreeer* or *ptreeer-ptreeer-ptreeer* is distinctive and recalls that of White-ringed Flycatcher w of Andes.
**Behavior:** Single birds, pairs, or families perch exposed on small twigs or stand on leaves on top of canopy where change perches frequently, bob heads, and utter complaining calls. Sally short distances to foliage or pluck fruit with a quick hover. Often follow forest flocks containing tanagers and other treetop birds.
**Status and habitat:** Notably local in steep, humid, and wet mt. forest, forest borders, small forest openings, and in isolated trees in clearings. Predom. a bird of "cloud forest" and "cloud forest clearings."
**Range:** Mostly 900-2100m (to 400m on Pacific slope, Anchicayá Val.—Hilty). Perijá Mts. (rec. on Venez. side) and spottily in all 3 Andean ranges. Nw Venez. s in Andes to c Peru.

## 169. WHITE-RINGED FLYCATCHER
*Conopias parva*     Pl. 39, Map 1079
**Identification:** 6.5″ (16.5cm). Easily confused. *Bill rather long.* Black crown *completely encircled by a broad white band;* concealed crown patch yellow; sides of head black; otherwise olive brown above, wings and tail browner; *underparts bright yellow* (or throat white—*albovittatus*).
**Similar species:** Microhabitat (high in tree, often perching on top of leaves) is best clue. White-throated race much like Rusty-margined and Social flycatchers (165, 166), but bill decidedly longer, wings lack buffy or rufous edgings, and broad eyestripe completely encircles head. Both kiskadees (162, 163) have even longer heavier bills, rufous edgings on wings, and different habits.
**Voice:** Calls of *albovittatus* a rattling or whirring trill (Skutch 1972) and a short note followed by a rattly trill, *qua-tre'e'e'e'e'e*; call of *parvus*, unlike w subsp., a rapid, querulous, almost

trilled *queelele* or *cue-le-le* (Hilty), or *weedle-de weedle-de-wee* (ffrench *in* Snyder 1966).
**Behavior:** Like Lemon-browed Flycatcher, stays high and usually actively flutters and sallies in canopy foliage; alone, pairs, or families.
**Breeding:** Hole or crevice nest usually high and stuffed with grass. Two eggs, glossy cream streaked and blotched forming an unbroken ring at larger end (Haverschmidt 1968).
**Status and habitat:** Uncommon in humid and wet forest, forest borders, tall second growth, and scattered trees in forest clearings; mostly lowlands. On Pacific slope replaced in mts. by Lemon-browed Flycatcher.
**Range:** To 900m. Pacific coast (*albovittatus*); extreme e Colombia in Vaupés (Mitú) and e Guainía (*parvus*). Costa Rica to nw Ecuador; the Guianas, s Venez., extreme e Colombia, and adj. n Brazil.
**Note 1:** Perhaps 2 spp. involved. **Note 2:** White-bearded Flycatcher (*C. inornatus*) of c Venez. should be found in Colombia in Arauca and Vichada, as taken at El Amparo, Apure, opp. Río Arauca and sighted at Maipures on Orinoco (Cherrie 1916). All but identical to Rusty-margined Flycatcher (*Myiozetetes cayanensis*), but long white eyestripe extends to and just meets on nape, rusty wing edgings barely evident (not conspic.), and in the hand lacks concealed crown stripe. Often placed in the genus *Myiozetetes*, but see Thomas (1979a). Gallery forest, trees around haciendas, and ranchland with ponds, scattered shrubs, and trees.

## 170. SULPHUR-BELLIED FLYCATCHER
*Myiodynastes luteiventris*
**Identification:** 8″ (20cm). Much like more numerous resident race of Streaked Flycatcher, but lower *underparts clear sulphur yellow* (not whitish or tinged dull yellow); *wing edgings white* instead of rufous (migrant race of Streaked Flycatcher has white wing edgings); *eyebrow whitish* (not dull yellow); *dusky moustachial streak joins narrowly across chin* (instead of chin white).
**Similar species:** Cf. migrant race of Streaked Flycatcher (171), also Golden-crowned (172) and Variegated flycatchers (175).
**Voice:** Usually rather quiet on migration and on wintering grounds; call an emphatic *squéez-ick* like a small squeeze toy.
**Behavior:** As in Streaked Flycatcher.
**Status and habitat:** Uncommon or rare transient. Rec. Oct (most recs.) and Mar–Apr, mostly in lighter open woodland and forest borders. Only a few Colombian recs.
**Range:** 400-2600m. Spottily w of Andes; e of them near Florencia, Caquetá. Breeds from sw US (Arizona) s to Costa Rica; winters mainly in e Peru and Bolivia.

## 171. STREAKED FLYCATCHER

*Myiodynastes maculatus* Pl. 39, Map 1080
**Identification:** 8.5″ (22cm). Bill black, *base of lower mandible pink.* Mainly brown streaked dusky above; concealed yellow crown patch; *forehead and broad eyebrow dull whitish yellow;* broad blackish band through eyes bordered below by white submalar streak; prom. wide dusky moustachial streak; wings dusky with rufous edges; *rump and tail rufous;* underparts white (or faintly tinged dingy yellow) *broadly streaked dusky on breast and sides.* S migrants (*solitarius*) are darker above with blacker streaks, and entire underparts, incl. throat, white broadly and sharply streaked black; tail black narrowly edged rufous (not all rufous); no rufous in wings.
**Similar species:** A large, heavily-streaked flycatcher with rufous tail (or rufous-edged tail—s migrant), yellowish eyebrow, and no yellow below. Cf. Sulphur-bellied Flycatcher (170). S migrants from latter by broader and crisper black streaking below, white chin, and blackish tail only narrowly edged rufous. Also see Piratic and esp. Variegated flycatchers (173, 175).
**Voice:** Often noisy. Loud *dit* call (singly or repeated); harsh *eéchup* (Ridgely 1976); at dawn and dusk a squeaky and slightly musical *wheet-siddle-whít* (J. V. Remsen).
**Behavior:** Spends much time in mid. or upper levels of trees but also sometimes quite low. Alone or in pairs and rather inconspic. except when calling. Captures large insects by short sallies to foliage or branches; often highly frugivorous.
**Breeding:** 6 BC birds, Mar–June, and juv. in July, n Colombia (Carriker); 2 BC birds, Jan, Huila (Miller 1947); late Dec–Aug in Panama; cavity or woodpecker hole filled with twigs and finer material, occas. open cup in palm, under eave, etc.; 2-3 whitish eggs heavily marked red or lilac (Skutch 1960; ffrench 1973).
**Status and habitat:** Fairly common resident in lighter second growth woodland, moist and humid forest borders, clearings with scattered trees, and open young *várzea* woodland (mostly river isls.). Rare or absent from excessively wet belt on Pacific coast. S migrants, May–July and Dec, e of Andes, once in C Andes at PN Puracé, 3000m.
**Range:** To 1500m (resident forms). Prob. throughout but no recs. from Chocó s on Pacific coast; no recs. in llanos e of Andes. E Mexico to c Argentina and se Brazil. Nonbreeding n Mid. American birds winter s to Panama and n S America; s breeders (*solitarius*) from s Peru and se Brazil to c Argentina winter n east of Andes to n S America.

## 172. GOLDEN-CROWNED FLYCATCHER

*Myiodynastes chrysocephalus* Pl. 39, Map 1081
**Identification:** 8″ (20cm). Bold head pattern recalls a kiskadee, but duller and with dusky malar. Crown grayish brown; usually concealed golden crown patch; dusky band through eyes bordered above by *long white eyestripe; lower cheeks and throat buff separated by long dusky moustachial stripe;* otherwise grayish olive brown above; *wings and tail prom. edged rufous;* pale yellow below; *chest and sides clouded and obscurely streaked olive.*
**Similar species:** Recalls both Boat-billed and Sulphur-bellied flycatchers (164, 170) but from either by buffy throat, moustachial streak, and cloudy chest streaking as well as mt. forest habitat.
**Voice:** Noisy, often persistently repeating its loud, forceful *kíss-u* call from treetop.
**Behavior:** Single birds or separated pairs often nod as sit erect but slightly hunched, usually high and exposed or partially so on bare limb near foliage. Attract attention with their loud angry calls; flutter and hawk insects or fruit in tree crown and noisily join mixed flocks.
**Breeding:** 16 BC birds, May–July, Santa Marta and Perijá Mts. and Andes (Carriker); Aug nestlings in Santa Marta Mts.; Aug eggs in Valle, and Jan and June in Venez.; mossy cup on cliff, in crevice, rocky road cut, hole in bank or tree cavity; 2 eggs, dull cream finely spotted reddish brown (Hilty).
**Status and habitat:** Common in humid and wet forest, usually near breaks or borders in steep mts. "Cloud forest" ally of Streaked Flycatcher.
**Range:** 900-2400m; to 400m on Pacific slope in Valle. Santa Marta Mts., Perijá Mts., the Andes, and Macarena Mts. E Panama and n Venez. s in mts. to Bolivia.

## 173. PIRATIC FLYCATCHER

*Legatus leucophaius* Pl. 39, Map 1082
**Identification:** 6″ (15cm). Much like Variegated Flycatcher but smaller, *back uniform and darker brown, rump and tail with virtually no rufous edging* (compared to broad rufous edges), wing coverts and inner remiges vaguely pale edged (not crisply white edged), and *bill proportionally stubbier* and all black.
**Similar species:** See Variegated Flycatcher (175), also larger and much more robust Sulphur-bellied and Streaked flycatchers (170, 171).
**Voice:** Song a loud, clear, downslurred whistle, *tee-u* normally followed after a pause by a short rising trill *de-di-di-di-di;* calls persistently throughout the day.
**Behavior:** Usually alone, perched high, often

on a bare exposed twig or branch where it tirelessly repeats its song. Ad. almost wholly frugivorous (Morton 1977).

**Breeding:** Usurps domed or pendent nests of var. birds (caciques, oropendolas, orioles, becards, *Tolmomyias* flycatchers, and others) for its own use by constant harassing of rightful owners. Most oropendola or cacique colonies have a pair of these birds. 9 BC birds, Apr, s Bolívar and Huila (Carriker). Mar and Aug breeding, Guárico, Venez. (Thomas 1979b). 2-3 gray brown eggs with dark brown scrawls (Wetmore 1972). Eggs of appropriated nest always thrown out.

**Status and habitat:** Fairly common locally in lighter humid woodland, forest borders, and clearings with scattered tall trees.

**Range:** To 1700m (near San Agustín, Huila). Throughout in suitable habitat. Se Mexico to n Argentina and se Brazil. Mid. American birds apparently migrate to S America during nonbreeding season (late Sept–early Jan in Panama); s birds migrate n in austral winter.

## 174. CROWNED SLATY-FLYCATCHER

*Empidonomus aurantioatrocristatus*      Pl. 39, Map 1083

**Identification:** 7″ (18cm). Dull and undistinguished. Bill short. *Smoky brown above with black crown* and concealed chrome yellow crown patch; wing coverts and inner remiges vaguely pale edged; *eyebrow, sides of head and neck, and entire underparts gray;* belly paler and washed yellowish on under tail coverts.

**Similar species:** Shape recalls a *Myiarchus* but otherwise a rather dark confusing flycatcher; note black crown, brown upperparts, gray underparts, and absence of strong markings. Birds in worn plumage are even duller. Slaty Elaenia (30) is more uniformly gray with contrasting white belly and no black crown. Also see Sirystes (152) and ♀ Riverside Tyrant (135).

**Voice:** Usually silent on nonbreeding grounds. In Paraguay ♂♂ give a low whistling *pree-ee-ee-er* and a series of squeaky notes, presum. a song (Wetmore 1926).

**Behavior:** Usually solitary and lethargic. Perch exposed in tops of shrubs or small to mod. ht. trees where sally like kingbirds.

**Status and habitat:** Uncommon migrant and austral winter resident in Amazonas (prob. Mar–Sept) to *terra firme* and *várzea* forest borders and bushy pastures with scattered trees.

**Range:** To 400m. E of Andes; known from Putumayo (Pto. Asís, 30 June), Vaupés (El Dorado sightings early June—R. Ridgely), and Leticia. Breeds in e Brazil (s of Amazon), Paraguay, Uruguay, and Argentina; trans-Amazonian migrants reach n Bolivia, ne Peru, Colombia, s Venez. and n Brazil.

## 175. VARIEGATED FLYCATCHER

*Empidonomus varius*      Pl. 39, Map 1084

**Identification:** 7″ (18cm). Larger edition of more widespread Piratic Flycatcher. *Lower mandible pale at base.* Head blackish brown with usually concealed yellow crown patch; long white eyebrow almost joins on nape; broad dusky line through eye and brownish moustachial streak separated by long white submalar streak; *back brown, vaguely (but decidedly) streaked paler;* wings dusky with sharp white edgings; rump and tail dark brown, *both conspic. edged rufous;* throat dirty white; rest of underparts yellowish white; breast and sides clouded and rather distinctly streaked dusky.

**Similar species:** From smaller Piratic Flycatcher (173) by rufous edging on rump and tail, paler back with suggestion of streaking, and proportionally longer bill pale at lower base (not all black). Sulphur-bellied and Streaked flycatchers (170, 171) are larger, more robust, and sharply streaked below.

**Voice:** Usually rather quiet; a harsh *chee-chee-chu*, last note prolonged; also gives a high, thin, nasal *zreee* or *zreeetee* (Snyder 1966).

**Behavior:** Usually alone and typically perched lower than Piratic Flycatcher, either exposed on small bushes or in outer perimeter of lower and mid. part of trees, occas. prom. on top. Sallies in air or flutters to foliage for insects and small fruit.

**Status and habitat:** Uncommon to fairly common austral migrant (*varius*); forest borders, lighter woodland, and clearings with bushes and scattered trees; mainly Mar–Aug. Breeding (?); 2 seen 18 Feb 1984 may have been residents (R. Ridgely, Hilty). See range.

**Range:** To 500m. E of Andes throughout. The Guianas and Venez. s east of Andes to c Argentina and Uruguay. S breeders (*varius*) reach e Colombia, Venez., the Guianas, and Trinidad during austral winter; *rufinus*, resident in Venez. and elsewhere, is unrec. in Colombia but likely (rec. along Orinoco); streaking below more clouded, less distinct than *varius*.

## 176. SULPHURY FLYCATCHER

*Tyrannopsis sulphurea*      Pl. 39, Map 1085

**Identification:** 8″ (20cm). Resembles Tropical Kingbird but smaller with *shorter square tail.* Crown dusky gray with concealed orange yellow crown patch; blackish mask through eyes spreads over sides of head; *otherwise olive brown above,* wings and tail darker; *center of throat white;* sides of throat grayish; rest of underparts bright yellow; *chest (esp. at sides) obscurely* *streaked and washed gray*; sides of breast and flanks tinged olivaceous; *bill rather short and stubby*.

**Similar species:** See Tropical and White-throated kingbirds (180, 183). From either by darker face and upperparts, chunkier shape, square tail, short bill, and grayish streaking at sides of chest. Dusky-chested Flycatcher (177) is much smaller and darker, esp. on head, and throat and chest streaked.

**Voice:** Often noisy with harsh squealing calls, *jweez* or *jweez-z jweez* (ffrench 1973), very unlike Tropical Kingbird.

**Behavior:** Single birds, pairs, or families are conspic., vocal, and almost always seen sitting in the tops of Moriche Palms. Sally aerially and chase passing insects; also eat fruit.

**Breeding:** ♀ ♀ ready to lay, Feb and Apr, Carimagua, ne Meta, (S. Furniss). Cup nest of sticks in crown of Moriche Palm; 2 creamy buff eggs, blotched brown and pale violet (ffrench 1973).

**Status and habitat:** Local in savanna, pastures, and even towns where there are Moriche (*Mauritia*) palms; also forest edges.

**Range:** To 400m. E of Andes. Known from e and w Meta (Carimagua; Villavicencio), Vaupés (sightings, Mitú, 1978—Hilty) and Amazonas (sightings in Leticia—J. V. Remsen; Hilty). The Guianas and s Venez. locally to e Ecuador, e Peru, and Amazonian Brazil. Trinidad.

#### 177. DUSKY-CHESTED FLYCATCHER
*Tyrannopsis luteiventris*          Pl. 39, Map 1086
**Identification:** 5.5-6″ (14-15cm). Darker miniature of Sulphury Flycatcher. *Entire head and upperparts dark brown*; concealed orange crown stripe (♂ only); sides of head vaguely streaked gray; *throat whitish streaked dusky*; rest of underparts bright yellow; *chest and upper breast strongly shaded olive and obscurely streaked dark olive*; bill stubby; tail square.

**Similar species:** Shape resembles *Myiozetetes* but otherwise most like Sulphury Flycatcher (see 176).

**Voice:** Frequent call a nasal, meowing *neeow*, and soft *neea*; when excited a rapid *neea-ne-wít!*

**Behavior:** Usually pairs, infrequently single birds, perch erect 3-20m up, typically high in trees or treetops, and on small bare twigs or on top of leaves where fully exposed like *Conopias* flycatchers. Sally short distances to foliage, less often to air, and reg. at fruiting trees where hover-glean small berries; not seen to join mixed flocks. Often flick up tail as call, esp. as alight, sometimes jerk up head and tail.

**Breeding:** BC ♂, May, Vaupés (Olivares 1964b).

**Status and habitat:** Shrubby edges or high in canopy of *terra firme* and *várzea* forests, high shrubbery at forest edges, or clearings with scattered bushes and trees. Not well known in Colombia. Poss. a migrant, but 3 sightings were of pairs at Leticia, late June–July (Remsen 1977b).

**Range:** To 250m. E of Andes: rec. in w Putumayo (Cuhimbé). Vaupés (Mitú) and s Amazonas (sight). Surinam; se Venez., e Ecuador, e Peru, and w Amazonian Brazil (e to Río Negro and Tapajós).

**Note:** By some placed in the genus *Myiozetetes*.

#### 178. FORK-TAILED FLYCATCHER
*Tyrannus savana*          Ill. 90
**Identification:** ♂ 15″ (38cm); ♀ 11″ (28cm). *Very long deeply forked tail* (shorter in ♀). *Crown, nape, and sides of head to below eyes black*; back light gray, wings darker; tail black, *underparts entirely white*. Imm. and molting ads. lack the long outer tail feathers; imm. also with brownish cap.

**Similar species:** Imm. and molting ad. resemble Sirystes (see 152).

**Voice:** Weak *tic* notes; twittering flight song.

**Behavior:** Scattered individuals or small or large flocks. Typically perch in open on fence or top of bush or smaller trees; migrants may

90. FORK-TAILED FLYCATCHER

turn up almost anywhere, even in forest tree-tops, and often gather in flocks of hundreds or thousands to roost. Sally aerially or drop to ground for insects or congregate at fruiting trees in season.

**Breeding:** BC ♂, 2 laying ♀♀, May, w Guajira (Carriker); 2 BC ♂♂, Jan, Huila (Miller 1947); ♀ incubating, 14 Feb 1960, top of fence post s of Cali (photo—Brown); Feb juv. in Cauca (Meyer de Schauensee 1948); nests with eggs near Medellín (Sclater and Salvin 1879). Shallow plant material cup 1-10m up; 3 glossy white eggs irreg. marked chocolate and lilac (Wetmore 1972).

**Status and habitat:** Drier scrubby nonforest regions and ranchland w of Andes (nos. fluctuate seasonally); e of Andes in both open country and in clearings or along rivers in forested zones. Birds w of Andes may be resident with nos. augmented by post-breeding Mid. American birds. Birds e of Andes may be mostly austral migrants but movements need documentation as some Mid. American migrants presum. also winter widely e of Andes (many recs. of *monachus* in Meta and Vichada). In ne Meta, present only early Nov–mid-July, with peak nos. (at colonial roost) Nov–Mar (S. Furniss); at Leticia largest flocks Mar (Hilty) and Sept (J. V. Remsen); large *northward* moving flocks, mid-Sept, ne Guainía (Hilty and M. Robbins) and huge flocks of short-tailed birds in w Meta in Apr (W. McKay).

**Range:** To 2600m. Throughout. S Mexico to c Argentina and Paraguay. The s race (*savana*) migrates n east of Andes to Colombia (spottily w of Andes), Venez., the Guianas, and Trinidad. Mid. American birds (*monachus*) are thought to migrate into n S America; perhaps also resident in Cauca and Magdalena vals.; *sanctaemartae* is apparently resident in Carib. lowlands of Colombia from Río Sinú to Guajira.

**Note 1:** By some placed in the genus *Muscivora* where it becomes *M. tyrannus*. **Note 2:** In the hand s migrants (*savana*) can be told from other races by much darker gray back. In addition, the var. races are distinguished by the degree of emargination of outer primaries: outer primaries notched near tip, *savana*; deeply notched, *monachus*; or nearly normal, *sanctaemartae* (Meyer de Schauensee 1964).

## 179. EASTERN KINGBIRD

*Tyrannus tyrannus*

**Identification:** 8.5″ (22cm). *Head to below eyes, and entire upperparts blackish*; concealed fiery orange crown stripe; *underparts white*; tail (fan-like in flight) black with *conspic. white terminal band*.

**Similar species:** Gray Kingbird (181) is gray above (not black) and lacks tail band; Sirystes (152) has gray throat and chest, white rump, and lacks tail band.

**Voice:** Usually silent in migration and on wintering grounds.

**Behavior:** Migrate in groups of var. size, infrequently alone. Perch high on outer perimeter of tree and fly off abruptly in compact flocks that sometimes wheel and change direction erratically, like waxwings.

**Status and habitat:** Fairly common transient in open woodland, forest edges, parks, and pastures with scattered trees (but can occur almost anywhere), early Sept–late Oct, and early Mar–early May (latest is 1 seen Santa Marta, 1 June 1980—Hilty et al.). Most recs. are w of Andes, few e of Andes; sightings, 28 Sept 1974 Leticia—J. V. Remsen; 11 and 23 Oct, Hacienda La Corocora, w Meta—W. McKay and B. Lamar); small nos. on 19, 20 Feb 1984, Leticia (R. Ridgely, Hilty).

**Range:** To 2600m. Throughout but mainly near the Andes. Breeds in N America; winters from w Amazonia s to s Bolivia and c Argentina; wanders e to Venez., Guyana, and Mato Grosso, Brazil.

## 180. TROPICAL KINGBIRD

*Tyrannus melancholicus*          Pl. 39, Map 1087

**Identification:** 8.5″ (22cm). Head gray with dusky mask through eyes; concealed orange crown patch; *back grayish olive*; wings and slightly forked tail dusky brown; *throat pale gray*; lower underparts yellow with *strong olive wash on breast*. Learn thoroughly the *gestalt* (shape, habits, etc.) of this widespread bird.

**Similar species:** Sulphury Flycatcher (176), only e of Andes, is sim. with shorter square tail, darker head, browner back, white throat set off by lightly streaked chest. In Amazonia see White-throated Kingbird (183), in sw Nariño, Snowy-throated Kingbird (182).

**Voice:** Usual call a high trilled *tre'e'e'eip*. More elaborate dawn song is several short *pip*'s followed by a rising twitter (Eisenmann). Rather vocal and one of the 1st morning bird sounds.

**Behavior:** Perches conspic. in open on tops of trees, wires or other exposed places, usually at mid. hts. Sallies for insects at almost any ht., occas. even to the ground or water; sometimes pursues flying insects in agile swooping flight. Notably pugnacious.

**Breeding:** Eggs, Feb, Popayán (Brown); several nests, Apr–May, Santa Marta area (Todd and Carriker 1922); building nest, Aug, Anchicayá Val. (Hilty), and Nov, ne Meta (S. Furniss). Rather frail cup usually saddled in fork about 5-15m up; 2-3 creamy white eggs boldly spot-

ted and streaked reddish brown (ffrench 1973). **Status and habitat:** One of the most common and conspic. Colombian birds in open or semiopen country with trees, in residential areas, and in clearings and river edges of forested zones. Nos. in Amazonas, *esp.* along Río Amazon, greatly augmented by s migrants, May–Sept (J. V. Remsen; Hilty). **Range:** To 2700m. Throughout. Breeds from s Mexico to c Argentina. Dutch Leeward Isls., Trinidad.
**Note:** Does not incl. *T. couchii* (Couch's Kingbird) of Texas to c Mexico.

## 181. GRAY KINGBIRD
*Tyrannus dominicensis* Pl. 39, Map 1088
**Identification:** 9″ (23cm). Bull-headed with *thick black bill.* Gray above with narrow dusky mask through eyes and concealed orange crown stripe; wings and tail dusky brown; tail slightly forked; *underparts white* with grayish tinge on chest.
**Similar species:** Slightly smaller Tropical Kingbird (180) is olive above and mostly yellow below; Eastern Kingbird (179) is blackish above.
**Voice:** A rolling throaty *pe-cheer-ry* (Peterson 1947).
**Behavior:** Usually conspic. whether alone or in loose flocks. Perches in open on bushes, fences, or utility wires. Sallies for insects in typical flycatcher fashion and notably frugivorous seasonally.
**Breeding:** BC ♀♀, 11 Mar, Cesar Val., 16 May, El Bahía, e Guajira, and BC ♂, 7 May, Santa Marta (Carriker). Apr nest, sw Guárico, Venez. (Thomas 1979b).
**Status and habitat:** Locally fairly common winter resident in drier open or semiopen areas and in towns, early Sept–late Apr (rarely early May). May breed sparingly in Carib. region but only oversummering rec. is 1 seen 27-29 June 1974, Manaure, Guajira (A. Sprunt IV). Nos. peak in Santa Marta region mid-Sept–mid-Oct (T. B. Johnson).
**Range:** Carib. lowlands from lower Sinú Val. e to Guajira, s in Magdalena Val. to Huila (to 2600m in Cundinamarca; 2 sight recs. to 3000m, Sept 1979, Represa Neusa—A. Gast); e of Andes in Meta and nw Vichada (sighting Apr 1980—P. A. Silverstone); once on Pacific coast to mid. Río San Juan; small nos. at Buenaventura (1st rec. 19 Jan 1978, photo—Hilty). Breeds in coastal se US, W Indies, isls. off Venez., and c llanos of Venez.; winters in s W Indies, Panama, n Colombia, Venez. (s to nw Amazonas), and the Guianas.

## 182. SNOWY-THROATED KINGBIRD
*Tyrannus niveigularis* Pl. 39, Map 1089
**Identification:** 7.5″ (19cm). Resembles more numerous Tropical Kingbird. Pale gray above becoming olive on lower back and rump; semiconcealed crown stripe yellow; narrow blackish forehead and *dusky mask through eyes;* wings dusky, inner remiges edged whitish; tail black, *square tipped; lower cheeks and throat puffy white,* shading to light gray on chest and yellow on lower underparts.
**Similar species:** From Tropical Kingbird (180) by smaller size, grayish upperparts, definite gray (not olive) chest, square tail, and prom. puffy white throat.
**Voice:** A thin twittering (Marchant 1960).
**Behavior:** Much like others of the genus. Perches on top of bushes but usually less prom. exposed than Tropical Kingbird. Hawks berries and sallies for insects (T. Parker).
**Breeding:** In sw Ecuador late Feb–mid-May (rainy season); thin twig, stem, and lichen cup about 2-8m up in bush or small isolated tree; 3-4 eggs, rarely 2, yellowish white blotched brown and lavender (Marchant 1960).
**Status and habitat:** Drier semiopen country with scattered bushes and small trees, acacia in washes, etc., or clearings in humid forested regions. Not well known in Colombia.
**Range:** To 1200m; extreme sw Nariño (Ricaurte). Sw Colombia to nw Peru.

## 183. [WHITE-THROATED KINGBIRD]
*Tyrannus albogularis* Pl. 39, Map 1090
**Identification:** 8.3″ (21cm). Very sim. to Tropical Kingbird but slightly smaller and with much *paler gray head and whitish crown contrasting more with dark mask through eyes; throat and lower cheeks pure white* (instead of pale gray) rather sharply set off from yellow underparts; chest only faintly tinged olive, back slightly paler and greener; tail less forked, and bill slightly smaller and shorter.
**Similar species:** In field best told from Tropical Kingbird (180) by pure white throat, *whitish* (not gray) *crown,* more contrasting black mask, and crisper separation between white throat and yellow underparts (*virtually lacks* olive tinge on chest). *All* marks (not just throat) should be carefully checked as the 2 spp. are not easily separated and occas. Tropical Kingbirds can look *very* "white-throated" (but not "white-crowned").
**Voice:** Apparently less vocal than Tropical Kingbird. In Bolivia calls are sim. to those of Tropical Kingbird but higher and thinner (J. V. Remsen).
**Behavior:** Much like Tropical Kingbird but on

average perches lower, usually within 3-4m of ground near Leticia (J. V. Remsen; Hilty). In Brazil when breeding perches higher and often closely assoc. with *Mauritia* palm swamps, where often with Sulphury Flycatcher (R. Ridgely).
**Status and habitat:** Hypothetical. Known only from sight recs.; the 1st on 21 May 1974 near Leticia (J. V. Remsen), with a no. of recent sightings May–late Aug in same area, where

presum. an austral migrant. Smaller trees, bushes, and grass along rivers, or river channels and lagoons on river isls., rarely far from water.
**Range:** To 100m. S Amazonas (near Leticia). Spottily in sw Surinam (breeds?), w Guyana, se Venez., Amazonian and se Brazil, e Peru, and Bolivia. Breeds primarily in Brazil s of Amazon.

# LARKS: Alaudidae (1)

The Horned Lark is the only American member of this Old World group. Widespread in north temperate regions, it reappears as an isolated population in the highlands of Colombia's Eastern Andes.

## 1. HORNED LARK
*Eremophila alpestris*          Ill. 91. Map 1091
**Identification:** 6″ (15cm). Brownish with "sparrowlike" streaked back; black stripe and "horns" above *white forehead and eyebrow; yellow throat bordered on sides with black;* black crescent on chest; otherwise whitish below; tail black narrowly edged white. In the hand note elongated, nearly straight hind nail.
**Similar species:** Paramo Pipit (p 553), Grassland Yellow-Finch (p 665), and Stripe-tailed Yellow-Finch (p 665) all lack the prom. facial pattern. In flight only Stripe-tailed Yellow-Finch shows white in tail like the lark.
**Behavior:** Largely terrestrial. Alone, in pairs, or small groups; flush close at hand and fly off with slightly undulating flight. Walk or run on ground; eat insects and seeds.
**Status and habitat:** Local in barren fields and

91. HORNED LARK

short grass pastures. Can sometimes be seen in open grassy fields between El Dorado International Airport and Bogotá.
**Range:** 2500-3000m (prob. higher). Sabana de Bogotá and adj. plateaus in Cundinamarca and Boyacá. Holarctic and s in N America to Baja California and mts. of s Mexico.

# SWALLOWS, MARTINS: Hirundinidae (18)

Swallows are a beloved family of virtually cosmopolitan distribution. Characterized by streamlined bodies, long pointed wings, and wide gapes, they are graceful and accomplished in flight and spend much of their time in the air. Unlike swifts, the flight is more buoyant and maneuverable and they frequently perch on wires, branches, or roofs. Resident species and north and south temperate migrants occur in Colombia from the lowlands to above treeline. Most are gregarious at least seasonally, and some, especially martins, gather in large roosting and feeding flocks. Nests of the resident species are placed in cavities or holes and contrary to most north temperate breeders, few make use of man-made structures.

## 1. TREE SWALLOW
*Tachycineta bicolor*
**Identification:** 5″ (13cm). *Steely blue to greenish black above;* wings and slightly forked tail blue black; *underparts snowy white.* Imm.: dark brown above, whitish below, sometimes with an incomplete smudgy brown breast band.
**Similar species:** Much like Blue-and-white

Swallow (9), mainly of highlands, but under tail coverts immaculate white (not black). More dingy imm. easily confused with Bank Swallow (16) and migrant races of Rough-winged Swallow (15). See also very rare Violet-green Swallow (2).
**Status and habitat:** Rare winter visitant, usually in flocks. Once in Nariño highlands in Feb

(Lago La Cocha, 2800 m). Sight recs. as follows: 50-100 at PN Isla de Salamanca, 29 Jan 1975—P. Donahue; 20 at PN Salamanca, 6 Feb 1977—R. Ridgely; 10 near Ríohacha, Guajira, 5 Feb 1978—P. Alden, Hilty, et al.
**Range:** Mainly Carib. coast. Breeds in N America; winters from s US to Honduras, occas. Panama (several recs.) and n S America (at least 2 Venez. recs. at Chichiriviche, Falcón, 25 Feb 1972 and 15 Jan 1976—P. Alden and R. Sides).
**Note:** By some placed in the genus *Iridoprocne*.

## 2. [VIOLET-GREEN SWALLOW]
*Tachycineta thalassina*
**Identification:** 5-5.5″ (13-14cm). Dark metallic green above glossed violet on rump; immaculate white below extending up and behind eye; *large patch of white on either side of rump.*
**Similar species:** Tree Swallow (1) lacks the white rump patches and white behind the eye. Also cf. Mangrove Swallow (note under 3).
**Status and habitat:** Hypothetical. Accidental. Only rec. for Colombia (or S America) is 2 seen flying with swifts above San Lorenzo ridge on Santa Marta Mts. (2200m), 22 Jan 1983 (B. Whitney and R. Ridgely).
**Range:** Breeds w N America; winters Mexico to Honduras, sometimes to Costa Rica and Panama.

## 3. WHITE-WINGED SWALLOW
*Tachycineta albiventer*          Pl. 40, Map 1092
**Identification:** 5.5″ (14cm). Shining bluish green above; *rump and underparts immaculate white; inner remiges and upper wing coverts broadly edged white* forming a conspic. white patch on inner wing at rest or in flight.
**Similar species:** Only Colombian swallow with white patches in wing.
**Voice:** Usual call a trilled *zweeed* (J. V. Remsen).
**Behavior:** Pairs or small groups perch prom. over water on partially submerged sticks or branches. Fly leisurely and rather directly, usually skimming low over lakes and rivers. Often with White-banded Swallows e of Andes.
**Breeding:** Nestlings, Jan and Feb, Macarena Mts. (Olivares 1962). Feb nest upper Magdalena Val. (Miller 1947); and 1 in Jan, mouth of Río Cauca (Carriker); Feb–Apr nests in Venez. Orinoco; nest often over water in hole in stub, eave, crevice between boulders, cliff, etc.; 4 white eggs (Cherrie 1916).
**Status and habitat:** Fairly common along larger rivers and lakes; wanders away from water over grassy airstrips and pastures. Widely sympatric with White-banded Swallow (*Atti-*

*córa fasciata*) but differs in flight habits and preference for more open expanses of water where flies well away from rocks, river banks, and forest vegetation.
**Range:** To 500m. From lower Atrato Val. e across n Colombia n of Andes, entire Magdalena Val., and throughout e of Andes. The Guianas and Venez. to n Argentina and Paraguay.
**Note:** Mangrove Swallow (*T. albilinea*) of Mexico to e Panama (*albilinea*) and w coast of Peru (*stolzmanni*) is poss. on either coast of Colombia. Glossy greenish to blue above (fresh plumage greener becoming blue with wear), white rump, white supraloral stripe, no white in wings, and immaculate white underparts (or smaller size, much smaller bill, no white supraloral stripe, and breast and rump tinged grayish—*stolzmanni*). The form *stolzmanni* is perhaps a separate sp. (Wetmore).

## 4. BROWN-CHESTED MARTIN
*Phaeoprogne tapera*          Pl. 40, Map 1093
**Identification:** 7″ (18cm). Large; tail slightly forked. Dull grayish brown above; white below with *smudgy brown chest band* (or with dusky droplike spots below chest band—austral migrant, *fusca*); under tail coverts long, silky white, and *usually protruding on sides and visible from above.*
**Similar species:** Like Bank Swallow (16) but decidedly larger and with steadier martinlike flight. Note conspic. white edges on basal portion of tail that are formed by silky under tail coverts, and indistinct (not sharp) edges of chest band. No other brownish imm. swallow has an unbroken chest band and white throat. Cf. imm. Gray-breasted Martin (7).
**Voice:** Rich gurgling sim. to that of Purple Martin (J. V. Remsen); also a flat weak *chu, chu* (Wetmore 1926).
**Behavior:** Pairs or groups rest on driftwood or scatter in flight over savanna. Sometimes hundreds loaf in tops of tall bare trees near water.
**Breeding:** BC ♂, 2 Mar, upper Río Sinú; another, 5 May, lower Río Cauca; BC ♀, 14 Mar, Norosí, s Bolívar, all *tapera* subsp. (Carriker). Cavities, incl. arboreal termite nest (Haverschmidt 1968), but usually in abandoned hornero nests (Naumburg 1930). Not a colonial breeder. Location of known BC birds coincides with range of Pale-legged Hornero.
**Status and habitat:** Fairly common in clearings, along river banks, and sand bars, or over savanna; usually near water. Resident and undoubtedly breeds (*tapera*); 8 scattered recs. from Vaupés to Carib. coast (Cartagena) of austral migrant (*fusca*), 26 Apr–4 Nov. Partially sympatric with allied Gray-breasted Martin, which

forages mainly over vegetation rather than water.

**Range:** To 1600m (San Agustín, Huila); austral migrants to 3000m in E Andes. N Colombia from Sinú Val. eastward, entire Magdalena Val., and generally e of Andes. The Guianas and Venez. (resident) to c Argentina and Paraguay. Austral migrants reach Panama.

## 5. PURPLE MARTIN
*Progne subis* Pl. 40

**Identification:** 7.5″ (19cm). ♂: entirely glossy blue black. ♀ and imm.: *forehead frosty grayish*; otherwise brown above with slight purple gloss on head and wings; throat and breast dingy grayish brown; *sides of neck and nape grayish contrasting with dark cheeks*; lower underparts white, lightly to heavily streaked and smudged brown.

**Similar species:** ♀-plumaged birds from either sex of Gray-breasted Martin (7) by gray forecrown (forecrown occas. dark), paler area on sides of neck and nape, and darker more heavily streaked underparts (Gray-breasted virtually lacks streaks). Also see Southern (6) and Snowy-bellied martins (note).

**Status and habitat:** Transient and winter resident, rec. late Aug–Dec in E Andes; 1 sight rec. of ♂, presumed this sp., 8 Feb 1977, Fundación, Magdalena (R. Ridgely). In Panama uncommon to locally common early Aug–late Sept and rare mid-Feb–mid-Mar. In Venez. and Trinidad Sept–Apr. Usually in open areas.

**Range:** To 3100m. The E Andes from s Boyacá (Lago Tota) to Sabana de Bogotá. Breeds in N America; migrates (recs. spotty) through Mid. America; winters locally from n S America s to n Bolivia and se Brazil.

**Note:** Snowy-bellied (Caribbean) Martin (*P. dominicensis*) breeds in w Mexico and the W Indies s to Tobago and should be watched for in Colombia. Nonbreeding range unknown but absent Oct–Jan in Tobago (ffrench 1973) when presum. in continental S America. Ad. ♂: glossy blue black with sharply defined white belly. ♀ and imm.: like Gray-breasted Martin but with rather sharply demarcated white belly.

## 6. [SOUTHERN MARTIN]
*Progne modesta* Pl. 40

**Identification:** 6.5″ (16.5cm). ♂: sim. to ♂ Purple Martin (not safely separable in the field) but slightly smaller and tail longer and more deeply forked. ♀ and imm.: sooty blackish above; *dusky brown below incl. belly*; underparts sometimes with a few pale edgings. Many ad. ♀♀ are almost uniformly dark below.

**Similar species:** ♀ much darker below than any other ♀ martin in Colombia (cf. esp. 7 and ♀-plumaged of 5, which have whitish bellies). Both sexes of Gray-breasted Martin (7) are *paler* below.

**Status and habitat:** Hypothetical. Austral migrant, prob. Apr–Sept. Only rec. is a flock of ca. 25 seen 14 July 1975 at Leticia (J. V. Remsen et al.). Also reported from sightings on Brazilian side of Río Vaupés, as well as e and c Panama and is abundant around Iquitos, Peru during austral winter mos. (R. Ridgely). Most likely along rivers or near water.

**Range:** Breeds in w Peru and n Chile (*murphyi*) and from Bolivia and Argentina to Uruguay (*elegans*). Migratory s forms are known mainly n to nw Brazil and e Peru, sightings to Panama. The resident Galapagos Isls. form (*modesta*) may be a separate sp.

## 7. GRAY-BREASTED MARTIN
*Progne chalybea* Pl. 40, Map 1094

**Identification:** 6.8″ (17.3cm). ♂: *glossy steel blue above incl. forehead*; throat, breast, and sides grayish brown; rest of underparts dull white. ♀: sim. but much duller, upperparts brownish glossed blue. Imm.: entirely sooty brown above and very dingy light brown below, belly paler.

**Similar species:** See Purple Martin (5). Imm. resembles Brown-chested Martin (4) but lacks latter's distinct chest band and whitish throat.

**Voice:** Rich gurgling and bubbling sim. to Purple Martin.

**Breeding:** BC ♂, July, e Norte de Santander (Carriker); 1 in Mar, w Santander (Boggs 1961); entering palm stub holes mid-Mar, Venez. (Brown). Loose stick and stem cup in natural cavity, eave, or pipe. Would prob. use artificial bird boxes if available (ffrench 1973).

**Status and habitat:** Very much a bird of towns and inhabited areas where often locally abundant. Absent over extensively forested areas though appears with clearing. One of the largest colonies is resident in Buenaventura. S breeders (*domestica*), which differ in larger size, are known from Venez. (May and Oct) and Surinam but not yet Colombia.

**Range:** To 1200m. Locally throughout but few recs. in e llanos (*chalybea*). S Texas (casual) and Mexico to c Argentina. Extreme n and s populations partially migratory but movements little known.

## 8. BROWN-BELLIED SWALLOW
*Notiochelidon murina* Pl. 40, Map 1095

**Identification:** 5.5″ (14cm). Large and dark. Blackish above with strong green gloss on back; *underparts sooty grayish brown*; under tail coverts black; tail forked. Imm.: sooty brown above; grayish white below; *throat dark brown*.

**Similar species:** The common large dark swallow of the temperate zone. Often looks blackish in the field.
**Behavior:** Flies in rather small, loose, low-flying groups, nearer the ground and less erratic than Blue-and-white Swallow. Usually quiet and less vocal than other Colombian swallows.
**Breeding:** 6 BC birds, Jan–Aug, C and E Andes (Carriker). Small colonies in cavities in cliffs, road cuts, or in eaves. BC ♂, Aug, and ad. building nest, Sept–Oct, PN Chingaza (W. McKay).
**Status and habitat:** Open terrain in highlands.
**Range:** 2100-3500m (mostly 2500m up to treeline). Santa Marta and Perijá mts., E Andes s to Cundinamarca, C Andes, and extreme n end W Andes. Nw Venez. s in Andes to Bolivia.

### 9. BLUE-AND-WHITE SWALLOW
*Notiochelidon cyanoleuca*      Pl. 40, Map 1096
**Identification:** 5″ (13cm). *Dark glossy blue above; immaculate white below; under tail coverts black;* tail slightly forked. S migrants (*patagonica*) are slightly larger; wing linings gray (not blackish); and less black on under tail coverts. Imm.: brownish with blue gloss on upperparts; lower throat and chest pale buff.
**Similar species:** See Tree (1) and Pale-footed swallows (10).
**Voice:** A thin, rapid, often repeated *chit-chit* (J. Silliman); song a ser. of jumbled buzzes and squeaks (B. Coffee recording).
**Behavior:** *The* conspic. mid. el. swallow. Pairs or small families fly erratically, often rather high above ground. Frequently roost in houses where remarkably confiding.
**Breeding:** Several Mar–Apr nests, PN Cueva de los Guácharos (P. Gertler). In Cauca Val. and W Andes in Valle, Feb–July (many recs.); some activity perhaps all yr. (Miller 1963). Singly or colonially as space permits in eaves, crevices, cliffs, drain pipes, or holes dug in soft banks; 2-4 eggs (usually 3 or 4), white.
**Status and habitat:** Common and familiar highland resident in small forest clearings, around habitations, and in villages and towns. Undoubtedly spreading with deforestation. Austral migrant *patagonica* reported early May–early Oct, mainly in lowlands (common July–Aug at Hacienda La Corocora, w Meta—W. McKay).
**Range:** To 3000m (resident birds mainly foothills to 2500m). Santa Marta, Perijá, and Macarena mts., the Andes, and e of them from Meta (e to Carimagua) to Putumayo (*cyanoleuca*). Breeds from Costa Rica to Tierra del Fuego. Austral migrants casual n to Nicaragua, Honduras, and s Mexico.

### 10. PALE-FOOTED SWALLOW
*Notiochelidon flavipes*      Pl. 40, Map 1097
**Identification:** 4.8″ (12.2cm). Rare and local. Tail forked. Upperparts shiny steely blue black; *throat pinkish buff in contrast to white breast and belly; sides and flanks sooty brown;* under tail coverts dark steel blue; feet pinkish flesh as in others of this genus (not a field mark).
**Similar species:** Easily overlooked. Much like imm. Blue-and-white Swallow (9) but bluish (not brown) above, throat deeper pinkish buff, and sides and flanks dusky. From ad. Blue-and-white Swallow by smaller size, blackish sides, and faster more direct flight; cinnamon throat not always visible.
**Voice:** Call a musical *threeép* and distinctive buzzy *bzeet.*
**Behavior:** Small flocks of 10-15, infrequently up to 50, fly rapidly and low over forest canopy or through open parts of forest; perch on dead branches of tall trees. Occas. with Blue-and-white Swallows, which favor more open areas (Parker and O'Neill 1980).
**Status and habitat:** Known from 3 specimens from C Andes in Colombia and a sight rec. of a pair at the sw (Palaterá) entrance to PN Puracé, 12 Feb 1984 (R. Ridgely, Hilty). In Peru "common" very locally (2600-3000m) over forest and forest edge, once to treeline; usually just above range of Blue-and-white Swallow (Parker and O'Neill 1980).
**Range:** W slope of C Andes near Manizales (Laguneta, Caldas, 3000m) and the adj. e slope near Ibaque (Toche, Tolima, 2200m) and Nariño near Ecuador boundary (La Victoria, 2000m). E. Ecuador (Sangay area), c Peru, and n Bolivia.

### 11. WHITE-BANDED SWALLOW
*Atticora fasciata*      Pl. 40, Map 1098
**Identification:** 6″ (15cm). Unmistakable. Long deeply forked tail (often held closed in point). Entirely glossy blue black with *conspic. white breast band;* thighs white (hard to see in field).
**Voice:** A fine buzzy *z-z-z-z-ee-eep* (Snyder 1966).
**Behavior:** Pairs or small groups fly low over water or in small clearings in lowlands and foothills. Often perch on large boulders or on snags along rivers, sometimes with White-winged Swallow. Flight erratic and usually nearer rocks or shore vegetation than latter.
**Breeding:** Usually small colonies. Dig holes in river banks; at holes, Feb, Vaupés (Hilty); and Mar, Meta (Brown); ♀ ready to lay, Feb, Macarena Mts. (Olivares 1962).
**Status and habitat:** Uncommon to locally common along clear or blackwater rivers, and in small clearings in foothills. In blackwater regions of Vaupés prefer vicinity of rocky rapids

and falls on larger rivers. Rare or only common very locally along large muddy rivers such as the Amazon.
**Range:** To 1400m (sight, w Caquetá). E of Andes from w Meta (Villavicencio) and Guainía and Vaupés southward. The Guianas and s Venez. to nw Bolivia and Amazonian Brazil.

## 12. BLACK-COLLARED SWALLOW
*Atticora melanoleuca*          Pl. 40, Map 1099
**Identification:** 5.5″ (14cm). *Long deeply forked tail* (usually held closed in point). Glossy blue black above; *immaculate white below with narrow black breast band* and black under tail coverts.
**Similar species:** Superficially like Bank Swallow (16), but tail deeply forked, upperparts shiny blue black, and with more crisp clean cut appearance. Also see imm. Barn Swallow (17).
**Behavior:** Much like White-banded Swallow but seldom far from larger lowland rivers. At times flies higher than White-banded Swallow, sometimes quite high over rivers or adj. forest and with other swallows.
**Breeding:** Feb–Mar nests, crevices in large rocks in Orinoco region; dry grass and feather nest usually about 2m above water; white eggs (Cherrie 1916); Feb nest in bank of Río Casiquiare, Venez., 3 eggs (Friedmann 1948).
**Status and habitat:** Locally fairly common along larger forested blackwater rivers near rocky outcrops, rapids, and waterfalls.
**Range:** To 250m. The extreme e from e Vichada (sightings, Maipures, Apr 1977—T. O. Lemke) and Guainía (sightings, Pto. Inírida, Sept 1978—Hilty and M. Robbins) s to Vaupés (Mitú). The Guianas and s Venez. to ne Argentina (Iguazú).

## 13. WHITE-THIGHED SWALLOW
*Neochelidon tibialis*          Pl. 40, Map 1100
**Identification:** 4″ (10.2cm). Tiny and batlike. Tail mod. forked. *Entirely chocolate brown*; rump and underparts slightly paler and gray tinged; *thighs white* (sometimes visible when perched). Or larger (7″, or 13cm), rump and underparts paler (*griseiventris*).
**Similar species:** Only very small all dark brown swallow in the lowlands. Sympatric with Rough-winged Swallow (15) from which it differs in having dark plumage, small size, more twisting flight at low ht., and tendency to fly in small forest openings, even among trees.
**Voice:** Call a soft slightly trilled *pe'e'e'd*.
**Behavior:** Pairs or families are confiding as fly rather low and buoyantly with erratic batlike movements, more in circles than in lines. Often perch together on low to high bare twigs or branches.

**Breeding:** 6 BC birds, Mar–May, Chocó and s Bolívar (Carriker). Copulation, Jan, Valle (Hilty); dry grass nest in hole in bank (Sclater and Salvin 1879) or in dead trees (Ridgely 1976).
**Status and habitat:** Locally fairly common in small forest clearings, roadsides, or over streams in forested humid or wet lowlands and hills. In upper Anchicayá Val. (1000m) only Apr and July–Nov (Hilty).
**Range:** To 1000m. Pacific coast and e along n base of Andes to mid. Magdalena Val. s to El Centro sw of Bucaramanga (*minima*); e of Andes known from Macarena Mts., w Caquetá, se Nariño, and Vaupés (*griseiventris*). C Panama to nw Ecuador and locally e of Andes to s Peru and Amazonian and se Brazil.

## 14. TAWNY-HEADED SWALLOW
*Alopochelidon fucata*          Pl. 40, Map 1101
**Identification:** 4.7″ (12cm). Tail slightly forked. Much like Rough-winged Swallow but *decidedly smaller*, cap blacker, *no pale rump*, and *eyebrow and broad nuchal collar deep tawny rufous* merging into cinnamon buff throat and chest (looks "tawny-faced").
**Similar species:** See under Southern Rough-winged Swallow (15).
**Behavior:** In Brazil, when breeding seen in pairs favoring open areas, esp. near water (ponds, marshes, streams). Flight low and swoopy; seldom very numerous or with other swallows (R. Ridgely).
**Status and habitat:** Presum. known from 3 ♂♂ and 1 ♀, 28 Apr, from foothills at e base of E Andes at La Colorada on Río Casanare, Arauca. Resident or austral migrant(?). Open terrain 460-1600m in Venez. (Meyer de Schauensee and Phelps 1978).
**Range:** Ca. 600m. Ne Colombia. Mts. of n and s Venez. (definitely breeds) and adj. n Brazil; e Peru s to c Argentina and Paraguay.

## 15. SOUTHERN ROUGH-WINGED SWALLOW
*Stelgidopteryx ruficollis*          Pl. 40
**Identification:** 5.3″ (13.5cm). Tail notched. Sandy brown above, crown darker; *rump whitish to pale buffy gray; throat cinnamon buff*; breast and sides light grayish brown fading to yellowish white on center of belly.
**Similar species:** Only brownish swallow in Colombia with a pale rump. N and austral migrants (both as yet unrec.) have dark rumps and resemble Bank Swallow (16) but never show a white throat. Also see Tawny-headed Swallow (14).
**Behavior:** Single birds, pairs, or small groups are found throughout in open areas. Flight is

somewhat erratic but more in lines than in circles and at mod. ht. but usually lower than Blue-and-white Swallows. Perch on wires or tops of bare trees.

**Breeding:** 4 BC birds, Jan–Mar, Chocó and n Antioquia (Carriker); 1 digging burrow, 3 July (S. Gniadek); and others nesting, Feb–July, W Andes above Cali; in arid upper Magdalena Val., Mar–June (Miller 1963); 1 Santa Marta nest, 12 June (Todd and Carriker 1922); 1 ♀ with shelled egg, 26 Apr, ne Meta (S. Furniss); nest in holes in banks; 4 white eggs.

**Status and habitat:** Common resident in open terrain or clearings in forested zones. The migratory n temperate sp. *S. serripennis* is unrec. but should occur. It is a fairly common transient and winter resident early Sept–mid-Mar in Panama (Ridgely 1976).

**Range:** To ca. 2200m (occas. higher, 1 sighting to 3600m, PN Puracé—J. Silliman). Throughout. Pacific slope e to C Andes (*uropygialis*); n Colombia from Río Atrato to Santa Marta area s in Magdalena Val. to s Huila and e of Andes s to Meta (*aequalis*); w Caquetá and ne Guainía southward (*ruficollis*). Breeds from Costa Rica to n Argentina and Uruguay. N temperate breeding Northern Rough-winged Swallow winters from W Indies to s Panama and prob. n S America. Austral birds from s portion of range of form *ruficollis* also migratory (extent unknown). Some Mid. American races may be migratory.

**Note:** Recent studies in Costa Rica indicate 2 spp. (*S. serripennis/ruficollis*) involved (Stiles 1981b).

### 16. BANK SWALLOW
*Riparia riparia* Pl. 40
**Identification:** 5″ (13cm). A miniature of Brown-chested Martin. Upperparts and *band across chest grayish brown*; throat and rest of underparts white.

**Similar species:** From Brown-chested Martin (4) by smaller size, more sharply defined breast band, quicker wing beats, and more erratic flight. Martin usually shows definite protruding white under tail coverts visible on sides of tail, even from above. First-yr. Barn Swallow (17) can be very sim. but is larger and glossy above. Also see Black-collared Swallow (12). Southern Rough-winged Swallow (15) has cinnamon throat and pale rump.

**Status and habitat:** Sporadically common fall transient, early Sept–mid-Oct; in spring reported only Feb: twice, incl. a flock of 150 at Pivijay, Magdalena, 8 Feb 1977—and 5 or more migrating n at Buenaventura harbor, 5 May 1976; in Panama, fairly common early Sept–late Oct and uncommon early Mar–early May;

small nos. of recent wintering recs., with Barn Swallows, in Panama (R. Ridgely).

**Range:** To 3000m. Spottily throughout. Breeds in N Hemisphere and locally in tropical portions of the Old World. In New World winters in S America s to Tierra del Fuego.

### 17. BARN SWALLOW
*Hirundo rustica* Pl. 40
**Identification:** 6″ (15cm). *Long deeply forked tail.* Shining steel blue above with chestnut forehead; throat chestnut, partially separated from *cinnamon underparts* by narrow incomplete dusky line across chest; inner webs of tail feathers *white near tip.* Imm.: sim. but duller, tail much shorter (but still with white markings), and underparts buffy to whitish, sometimes with incomplete dusky band on chest (cf. Bank Swallow).

**Similar species:** Fork-tailed ad. with rusty underparts are distinctive, but see Cliff Swallow (18). Imm. easily confused with Bank Swallow (16) but larger, always with pale forehead, usually with white markings in tail (hard to see), and upperparts somewhat glossy.

**Behavior:** Can occur almost anywhere but usually in open terrain where may be seen singly or in flocks, sometimes numbering in the hundreds. Flies low, usually coursing back and forth in zigzag lines.

**Status and habitat:** Common transient and locally common winter resident, mainly mid-Aug–early May; 4 seen 15 June 1978, at Hacienda La Corocora, w Meta (W. McKay), and 4 on 29 June 1974, at Manaure, Guajira (A. Sprunt IV), may have been summering. Noted only as transient mid-Sept–mid-Nov at Leticia (J. V. Remsen). Wintering concentrations often assoc. with sugar cane fields (R. Ridgely).

**Range:** To 2800m. Throughout. Breeds in N America, Europe, Asia, and N Africa; N American birds winter locally throughout S America; also Aruba to Trinidad.

### 18. CLIFF SWALLOW
*Petrochelidon pyrrhonota*
**Identification:** 5.5″ (14cm). Square tail. Mainly dull dark blue above with *prom. cinnamon buff rump; forehead buffy white*; nuchal collar grayish and back with a few narrow whitish streaks; *sides of head and throat dark chestnut*; patch on chest black; breast grayish fading to white on lower underparts.

**Similar species:** From Barn Swallow (17) by prom. buffy rump, whitish forehead, and square tail (tail of imm. and molting ad. Barn Swallow often very short and nearly square). See Cave Swallow (note).

**Behavior:** Often with Barn Swallows.
**Status and habitat:** Uncommon and sporadic fall transient early Sept–mid-Oct (several seen in Nov in ne Meta—S. Furniss). Largest reported flock, 500-1000 moving s along Represa Neusa shores n of Bogotá, 13 Sept 1979 (A. Gast). Less reported as spring transient (all recs. Apr or May) and only 1 specimen (San Gil, Oct 15). Spring sightings as follows: 4, 5, and 30 Apr, Hacienda La Corocora, w Meta, and 11-19 Apr, El Porvenir, Meta (W. McKay); 200-300 each day, 28-30 Apr, in ne Meta at Carimagua (S. Furniss); 50 + n at Buenaventura harbor, 5 May 1976; a few now winter, usually with Barn Swallows in Panama (R. Ridgely).
**Range:** To 3000m. Spottily throughout. Breeds in N America; winters mostly in s S America.
**Note:** Cave Swallow (*P. fulva*), breeding locally in sw US, Mexico, and W Indies, and resident in w Ecuador and Peru, is unrec. but poss. (2 recent Panama sightings). Wintering range of n populations unknown. Very like Cliff Swallow but forehead chestnut (not whitish), sides of head and throat pale buff (not chestnut), and at close range, lacks Cliff Swallow's black patch on lower throat.

# CROWS, JAYS: Corvidae (7)

Members of this varied family are found virtually worldwide but reach their greatest development in north temperate regions. Only jays are found in Colombia and South America; no typical crows (*Corvus*) occur south of Nicaragua. Jays are noisy and active, but because several Colombian species are rare and local they are infrequently seen and comprise a relatively small portion of the avifauna. They are essentially omnivorous and arboreal. Most normally wander in groups at various heights through open woodland. Jays, as far as known, build large twiggy cup nests in shrubs or trees. With the exception of the Green Jay (see Alvarez 1975) the habits and nesting of jays in Colombia are poorly known. Many jays that have been studied elsewhere are notable for their complex social organization.

## 1. COLLARED JAY
*Cyanolyca viridicyana*            Pl. 12, Map 1102
**Identification:** 13.5″ (34cm) (or 12″ [30 cm]—*armillata*). Mostly *dark blue* (or *dark purplish blue*—*armillata*); crown somewhat paler blue; *forehead and mask through eyes black and continuing narrowly down sides of neck to form a collar across lower throat*; throat bright blue; rather long tail black below.
**Similar species:** See under Turquoise Jay (2).
**Voice:** Vocal with large repertoire; alarm is *schree*, flock-social call a sharp, staccato, upward inflected *reek!*; also a soft *croooh*, a chatter, and an unjaylike *peep*, recalling a baby chick (Hardy 1967).
**Behavior:** Usually in small, loose, vocal groups; act like other jays as peer and hop in mid. to upper forest levels.
**Breeding:** 4 BC birds, June–Sept, W and E Andes (Carriker); 1 in Oct, Boyacá (Olivares 1971).
**Status and habitat:** Uncommon to rare in humid forest, forest edges, and older second growth, esp. with bamboo and tree ferns. Most reg. encountered in e Nariño (above Mocoa) where perhaps fairly common.
**Range:** 1600-3100m. N end of W Andes in Antioquia, entire C Andes s to the e slope of Nariño (*quindiuna*); E Andes s to Cundinamarca (*armillata*). Nw Venez. s on e slope of Andes to nw Bolivia.

## 2. TURQUOISE JAY
*Cyanolyca turcosa*            Pl. 12, Map 1103
**Identification:** 12.5″ (32cm). *Much like Collared Jay.* Mostly turquoise blue; head and throat *light milky blue*; forehead and mask through eyes black and continuing narrowly down sides of neck to form a narrow collar across lower throat; underside of tail black.
**Similar species:** Differs from Collared Jay (1) in having lighter plumage, shorter tail, and crown *very pale, almost whitish* (not light blue). Also by paler milky blue throat (like crown) separated from contrasting darker blue green underparts by *narrower* black band across lower throat.
**Behavior:** Much like Collared Jay.
**Status and habitat:** Humid forest and forest edge up into elfin woodland at treeline. In Ecuador common on both slopes, greatly outnumbering Collared; there ranging into rather degraded forest; on w Ecuadorian slope also overlaps with Beautiful Jay at 1500-2000m, but not seen to flock with that sp. (R. Ridgely). Not well known in Colombia.
**Range:** 2600-3000m (prob. lower and higher). Both slopes of Andes in Nariño; prob. n to extreme s end PN Puracé in Cauca. S Colombia, e and w Ecuador, and ne Peru.
**Note:** Considered a subsp. of Collared Jay by some.

### 3. BEAUTIFUL JAY
*Cyanolyca pulchra*          Pl. 12, Map 1104
**Identification:** 11″ (28cm). *Forehead and mask black; crown milky blue* deepening to violet blue on mantle, wings, and tail; back violet blue tinged brown; below purplish blue; breast tinged brown.
**Similar species:** Turquoise Jay (2) has black band across lower throat and is more uniform blue.
**Voice:** Calls incl. guttural smacking and clicking notes and a loud inflected *chewp*, often doubled.
**Behavior:** Single birds or pairs hop, peer, and fly short distances between lower and midlevel branches; inconspic. but often vocal. Like many other jays may bounce up and down as call.
**Status and habitat:** Rare and local in wet mossy forest ("cloud forest"), forest edge, and taller second growth. Not well known.
**Range:** 900-2300m. Pacific slope from headwaters of Río San Juan (Cerro Tatamá, Valle) southward. W Colombia and nw Ecuador.

### 4. VIOLACEOUS JAY
*Cyanocorax violaceus*          Pl. 12, Map 1105
**Identification:** 13″ (33cm). Slightly crested. Usually looks dull in field. *Head, throat, and upper breast black;* nuchal band milky white deepening to *dull violet blue on rest of plumage;* underparts paler and tinged grayish.
**Similar species:** The only jay in most of its range. In the Orinoco and Río Negro region see Azure-naped Jay (5).
**Voice:** Noisy as they bounce up and down and scream with loud raspy *peeough!*, falling in pitch, less often a sharp *clop-clop-clop-clop.*
**Behavior:** Families or groups up to 8-10 troop noisily about in midlevel branches. Bold, inquisitive, and mob readily.
**Breeding:** BC ♂, Jan, Macarena Mts. (Olivares 1962); 2 begging young, July, Venez. llanos (Hardy 1969a); in Orinoco area 1 bulky Apr nest 9m up; 5 bluish white eggs thickly speckled several shades of brown (Cherrie 1916).
**Status and habitat:** Locally common in humid *terra firme* and *várzea* forest edges, second growth woodland, and gallery forest.
**Range:** To 1100m (sight to 1350m). E of Andes throughout. Guyana and c and s Venez. to e Ecuador, e Peru, and Amazonian Brazil.

### 5. AZURE-NAPED JAY
*Cyanocorax heilprini*          Pl. 12, Map 1106
**Identification:** 13″ (33cm). Forecrown with short stiff crest; eyes whitish yellow. *Forehead, sides of head, throat, and chest black;* short malar streak cobalt blue; hindcrown bluish white becoming sky blue on nape; rest of upperparts grayish blue tinged violet brown; below dull violet fad-

ing to whitish on lower underparts; *tail tipped white,* more conspic. on underside.
**Similar species:** From Violaceous Jay by white tail tips, less black on crown, and white belly.
**Voice:** Resembles that of Violaceous Jay (Borrero 1960a).
**Breeding:** 2 imms., Mar–Apr, Amazonas, Venez. (Friedmann 1948).
**Status and habitat:** Local in sandy-belt forest edge, second growth, and thinner savanna woodland.
**Range:** To 250m. Extreme e Guainía (opp. mouth of Río Casiquiare) and e Vaupés (near Mitú). Prob. n to se Vichada. W Amazonas, Venez., and nw Brazil along Río Negro.

### 6. BLACK-CHESTED JAY
*Cyanocorax affinis*          Pl. 12, Map 1107
**Identification:** 13″ (33cm). Eyes yellow (ad.). Crown, sides of head, throat, and upper breast black; spot above and below eye and short malar bright blue; nape and upperparts violet brown; wings and tail dark blue; *lower underparts and broad tail tips white to creamy white.*
**Similar species:** Only jay in range with white lower underparts and white tail tips.
**Voice:** Most common call a loud *kyoop!*, 1-3 times in succession (Hardy 1969b); also var. guttural clicks and rattles.
**Behavior:** Groups up to about 6 individuals are conspic. roaming through mid. and upper branches, occas. lower; mob noisily.
**Breeding:** 5 BC birds, Jan–May, n Colombia (Carriker); 2 in Jan and 2 groups dependent young, Jan–Feb, Huila (Miller 1947); nest building near Barranquilla and Mutatá, n Antioquia, Mar (Brown); 11 Santa Marta nests, Apr–May, 3-5 buffy eggs (Todd and Carriker 1922).
**Status and habitat:** Common in dry to humid forests of n Colombia, also wet forest zones on Pacific; favors forest edge, second growth, and open thinned woodland; perhaps local on Pacific coast.
**Range:** To 2200m. Pacific coast s to Valle (Anchicayá Val.), the lowlands n of Andes to Santa Marta region, locally to e Guajira, s in Cauca Val. to Medellín, and in Magdalena Val. to s Tolima; e Norte de Santander (Zulia Val. and Catatumbo lowlands). Costa Rica to w Venez.

### 7. GREEN JAY
*Cyanocorax yncas*          Pl. 12, Map 1108
**Identification:** 12.5″ (32cm). Unmistakable. Eyes yellow. Short stiff frontal crest and area at base of bill blue; otherwise *sides of head, throat, and chest black; rest of underparts bright yellow;* crown and nape bluish white (or blue—*cyanodorsalis*); upperparts and tail bright green; *outer tail feathers yellow.*

**Similar species:** Only green and yellow jay in Colombia.

**Voice:** Noisy with loud discordant calls, often trebled, commonly *quin-gun-gun*, hence local name "Quinquin" (J. Silliman); also a trebled *clee-op*, dry ticking, and *jeer* among others (Hardy 1969a).

**Behavior:** Travel on permanent territories in active, conspic. groups of 3-9 at all levels in forest; sometimes rather bold and inquisitive.

**Breeding:** 5 BC birds, Apr–Aug, n end W Andes and Perijá Mts. (Carriker). Begins in Mar in Antioquia; shallow, loosely woven basket 4-10m up; 4 bluish white eggs densely blotched brownish; each flock has a breeding pair and "helpers" (Alvarez 1975).

**Status and habitat:** Common *very locally* in humid and wet forest, forest edge, tall second growth, and trees in clearings.

**Range:** 1200-2800m (once to 3000m); to 900m in Pacific Cauca. Perijá Mts. to e slope E Andes near Cúcuta (*andicola*); southward on e slope to Cundinamarca (*cyanodorsalis*); w slope E Andes, C Andes, and W Andes s to Valle (*galeata*); W Andes in Cauca, w slope C Andes in Cauca and e slope of Andes in Nariño (*yncas*). Se Texas to Honduras; n Venez. to n Bolivia.

**Note:** Birds of s US and Mid. America are perhaps a separate sp. from Andean forms.

## DIPPERS: Cinclidae (1)

Dippers are a small discontinuously distributed family with two species in the Old World and two or perhaps three species in the New World. Believed to be allied to wrens, or possibly Old World thrushes, they are the only truly aquatic passeriform birds. In addition to large feet, chunky shape, dense plumage, and musty odor, they have a thick downy plumage, an exceptionally large oil gland, a moveable nostril covering, and a very well developed nictitating membrane. Dippers are virtually restricted to colder fast-moving mt. streams where they feed on a variety of aquatic life.

### 1. WHITE-CAPPED DIPPER
*Cinclus leucocephalus*                    Ill. 92
**Identification:** 6" (15cm). Unmistakable. Chunky with short tail. Mostly brownish black with *crown, center of back, and underparts white* (or brownish gray with only crown and throat white—*rivularis*).

**Voice:** Song a prolonged loud trill; flight call a sharp *zeet*.

**Behavior:** Single birds or loosely assoc. pairs bob up and down at water's edge on boulders in mt. torrents as they patrol a section of a stream. Fly low and rapidly up stream or down with buzzy wing beats. Not definitely known to swim under water as do dippers of N and Mid. America.

**Breeding:** 5 BC birds, Feb–Sept, Santa Marta Mts. and n end W and C Andes (Carriker). Juvs., Dec and Apr, PN Puracé (J. Silliman); 2 nests, Mar, nw Venez. (Vuilleumier and Ewert 1978); 1 in Sept, e Ecuador (Skutch 1972); mossy domed nest in streamside crevice; 2 eggs.

**Status and habitat:** Fairly common. Restricted to rushing mt. streams with boulders.

**Range:** 100-3900m (foothills to lower paramo). Santa Marta Mts. (*rivularis*); Perijá Mts. and all 3 Andean ranges (*leuconotus*). W Venez. s in Andes to Bolivia.

**Note:** This or allied *C. mexicanus* (American Dipper) or an undescribed form is poss. in the highlands on Panama boundary as there is an unconfirmed sight rec. of a dipper in e Darién, Panama (Ridgely 1976).

92. WHITE-CAPPED DIPPER

## WRENS: Troglodytidae (31)

Wrens are a well-known and essentially New World family with only one species in the Old World. They attain the greatest diversity in Central and South America. Many are gifted songsters, especially members of the genera *Cyphorhinus* and *Thryothorus*. Mated pairs of the latter often sing duets, many of them precisely antiphonal. Wrens are rather small, chunky, and thin-billed birds, often with short cocked tails. Plumage is usually various shades of brown, often with gray or white below and with barring on the wings and tail. Although active and insectivorous, the skulking habits of some species make them difficult to observe. Most build domed nests with side entrances, and a few regularly nest in cavities; "dummy" nests are often built and sometimes used as dormitories; *Donacobius* builds a deep, bulky open cup nest. Breeding systems are monogamous or polygamous and in some *Camphylorhynchus*, and perhaps others, "helpers" may assist with nesting.

## 1. BLACK-CAPPED DONACOBIUS

*Donacobius atricapillus*      Pl. 41, Ill. 93, Map 1109

**Identification:** 8.5″ (22cm). Slender with long tail. *Eyes bright yellow. Top and sides of head black becoming dark chocolate brown* on rest of upperparts; white patch at base of primaries (conspic. in flight); and *broad white tail tips*; rump and *entire underparts creamy buff*; usually finely barred on sides; concealed bare orange patch on sides of neck.

**Similar species:** In n Colombia see Bicolored Wren (2); unmistakable in Amazonia.

**Voice:** Has a large repertoire; most common calls incl. a loud *poyp-poyp-poyp-poyp* . . . ; a harsh *jeeeeah*, often doubled; and descending whistled notes *zeeeoo-zeeeoo* (J. V. Remsen). Also duets (below).

**Behavior:** Single birds or pairs are noisy, conspic. and usually perch exposed in marshy grass or on low stubs near water. In display pairs sit side by side or one a little above the other, bobbing heads, wagging partly spread tails from side to side asynchronously and calling antiphonally, the 1st uttering a rough *jeeer*, the 2d a musical *kueéea*.

**Breeding:** 2 BC birds, July–Aug, n Colombia (Carriker); in Amazonas, 2 nests in July (Hilty); 1 in Aug (J. V. Remsen); Venez. nests, May–June; deep bulky cup in tall grass near or over water; 3 eggs densely mottled reddish brown (Skutch 1968).

**Status and habitat:** Locally common in tall grass and marshy vegetation bordering pools, lakes and rivers, or in wet pastures.

**Range:** To 500m. Panama border s to upper Atrato Val. (sighting s of Quibdó, 10 Mar 1978—Hilty and P. Bailey), n of Andes to w base of Santa Marta Mts., s to lower Cauca and mid. Magdalena vals. (Honda, n Tolima); e of Andes from Arauca and w Vaupés (San José del Guaviare) to Putumayo and Amazonas. E Panama to the Guianas and s to n Bolivia, ne Argentina, and Paraguay.

**Note:** Usually placed in the family Mimidae, but vocalizations and behavior are sim. to cer-

93. Tropical Mockingbird (left), Black-capped Donacobius (right)

tain wrens. Studies of the osteology and pterylosis confirm this (Wetmore, Pasquier, and Olson). Formerly Black-capped Mockingthrush.

## 2. BICOLORED WREN

*Campylorhynchus griseus*        Pl. 42, Map 1110
**Identification:** 8″ (20cm). Large Colombian wren. Crown, nape, and streak through eye blackish brown with *prom. white eyebrow and underparts*; otherwise uniform rufous brown above; tail blackish; outer feathers barred and tipped white. Or 9″ (23cm); like above but upperparts brownish black; outer tail feathers distally white tipped black (*bicolor; zimmeri*).
**Similar species:** Told by large size, white eyestripe, and white underparts. Cf. Black-capped Donacobius (1), which lacks eyestripe and has pale eyes.
**Voice:** Often noisy; var. calls incl. a loud *awk-chook* and guttural *óok-a-chuk*; pairs singing duets combine the phrases uttering a rapidly repeated *óh-chuck, awk-a-chuck*; scold with loud, harsh *rud* notes.
**Behavior:** Pairs hop deliberately, peering and pecking along limbs and palm fronds at almost any ht.; pause occas. to perch upright side by side and sing a duet. Inquisitive and scold noisily.
**Breeding:** Feb–July nests, Santa Marta, Barranquilla (S. M. Russell; Brown; Todd and Carriker 1922); 1 BC ♂, Mar, ne Meta (S. Furniss); Apr–July nests, Orinoco region (Cherrie 1916). Often appropriates larger abandoned nest of other spp. such as *Pitangus* and *Myiozetetes*; 3-5 buff to cinnamon eggs thickly speckled brown.
**Status and habitat:** Common in arid and semiarid regions with cactus and scrub, esp. near habitations and villages and locally into moist open woodland and edges.
**Range:** To 1700m in Santa Marta Mts.; to 2100m in Magdalena Val., upper Río Sinú e to Guajira and s to mid. Magdalena Val. in nw Santander (*albicilius*); w slope E Andes in Santander and Boyacá (*bicolor*); upper Magdalena Val. in Tolima and Huila (*zimmeri*); e of Andes s to Villavicencio, Meta (*minor*) and e to El Tuparro (INDERENA) on Orinoco (*pallidus?*). Colombia to Guyana and n Brazil.

## 3. WHITE-HEADED WREN

*Campylorhynchus albobrunneus*        Pl. 41, Map 1111
**Identification:** 7.5″ (19cm). Large and unmistakable. Brownish black above with *entire head and underparts white*. Or var. with traces of pale bars above; head more or less stained dusky; underparts dusky mixed white and gray

(*aenigmaticus*). Latter a poss. hybrid with Bandbacked Wren, *C. zonatus.*
**Voice:** Frequent call a very raspy, guttural *cawk*, often repeated; song a guttural, scraping *tooda-dick, tadick*, or sim. phrase repeated several times by 1 or pair.
**Behavior:** Pairs or more often groups of 3-10 clamber about limbs, epiphytes, and foliage, and with tail up and swinging; usually at midlevels or higher, rarely to ground. May follow forest flocks but usually independent of them.
**Breeding:** 6 BC birds, Feb–May, nw Colombia (Carriker); Feb nest, nw Colombia (Haffer 1975); copulation, Dec, upper Anchicayá Val. (Hilty).
**Status and habitat:** Somewhat local (dispersed colonies?) in wet forest borders, forest openings, and clearings with scattered trees. Replaced in moist and drier forests to the ne and s by allied *C. zonatus.*
**Range:** To 1500m. Northernmost end of W Andes in upper Sinú Val., Pac. coast s to Valle (*harterti*); w Cauca(?); sw Nariño (*aenigmaticus*). C Panama to sw Colombia.

## 4. BAND-BACKED WREN

*Campylorhynchus zonatus*        Pl. 41, Map 1112
**Identification:** 7″ (18cm). Recalls Stripe-backed Wren. Crown brownish gray spotted black; narrow eyestripe buffy white; otherwise *back, wings, and tail boldly banded black and buffy white*; rump tinged cinnamon; *throat to upper breast white conspic. spotted black*; rest of underparts pale cinnamon barred black on sides. Juv.: unspotted black crown; back streaked or spotted brown and underparts dingy white mottled gray; wings and tail like ad.
**Similar species:** Only Colombian wren boldly barred on mantle. See Stripe-backed Wren (6).
**Voice:** Song in Colombia a rapid raspy *zwittook-to-zueer* or sim. var. repeated up to 6 times or more, often as duet.
**Behavior:** Pairs or groups of 3-12 are noisy and conspic. as they actively hop and clamber over limbs, vine-covered trunks, or palm fronds, usually rather high but occas. low.
**Breeding:** 3 BC birds, Apr–July, n Colombia (Carriker); Apr–June nests, 1 building nest in Nov, nw Santander (Boggs 1961); Mar nest, Barranquilla 10m up in *Acacia* (Brown); large globular nest with side entrance; 5 white eggs, sometimes with brown specks around larger end; nest helpers usually present (Skutch 1960).
**Status and habitat:** Locally fairly common in dry and moist forest borders or clearings with tall trees. Apparently does not occur together with Bicolored or Stripe-backed wrens; replaced in wet forest by White-headed Wren.
**Range:** To 1600m. N Colombia from w side of

Gulf of Urabá and upper Río Sinú to sw base of Santa Marta Mts. and upper Cesar Val. s spottily in Magdalena Val. to latitude of Bogotá. E Mexico to nw Panama; n Colombia; nw Ecuador. **Note:** Poss. hybrids with *C. albobrunneus* (White-headed Wren) known from zone of contact on sw Colombia-nw Ecuador border (Haffer 1975).

## 5. THRUSH-LIKE WREN

*Campylorhynchus turdinus*    Pl. 41, Map 1113
**Identification:** 8″ (20cm). Thrushlike. *Dull grayish brown above* vaguely scaled lighter (appears uniform in field); weak eyestripe whitish; *underparts white heavily spotted dusky except on throat* (rows of spots form streaks on chest); under tail coverts pale rufous barred blackish.
**Similar species:** Large wren, uniform grayish above, spotted below, and most likely mistaken for a juv. thrush.
**Voice:** Frequently given song a *very loud*, rhythmic, staccato duet, *chooka-cookcook, chooka-cookcook* . . . , recalls an oropendola; loud rough *jiff* scold (J. V. Remsen; Hilty).
**Behavior:** Families or groups of 3-8 peer and hop deliberately among large, epiphyte-laden limbs or in dense vines 7-35m up; independent of forest flocks and usually heard before seen.
**Breeding:** 3 Leticia nests, June, July, and Oct, were 12-15m up; 3-4 birds assoc. with each nest suggesting "helpers" or communal nesting (J. V. Remsen; Hilty); 2 BC ♂♂, May and June, w Caquetá (Carriker).
**Status and habitat:** Locally common in humid *terra firme* and *várzea* forests; usually at forest edges and in scattered trees in clearings around habitations.
**Range:** To 500m. E of Andes from Meta (Villavicencio; Macarena Mts.), w Caquetá and Amazonas (Leticia) southward. E Colombia to n Bolivia and Amazonian Brazil s of the Amazon e and s to Espírito Santo.

## 6. STRIPE-BACKED WREN

*Campylorhynchus nuchalis*    Pl. 42, Map 1114
**Identification:** 7″ (18cm). Resembles Band-backed Wren. Crown buffy brown spotted black; faint buffy nuchal collar; eyestripe white; otherwise *back broadly striped black and white; wings and tail broadly banded and notched white; underparts white thickly spotted dusky*. Eyes yellowish white.
**Similar species:** Only Colombian wren striped above and spotted below. See Band-backed Wren (4).
**Voice:** Song in Venez. and Colombia, sometimes by 2 or more birds in unison, a scratchy

and rapidly repeated *zhewít-here*, or *arrowak-gero-kíck* or sim. var.; also loud, harsh, guttural, and chucking notes.
**Behavior:** Much like Band-backed Wren but almost always in families or groups of 3-10, several of which form loosely assoc. colonies.
**Breeding:** BC pair, May, s Bolívar, 2 imms., June, Cesar (Carriker); breed Apr–Sept, Gúrico, Venez. (Thomas 1979b). Apparently appropriates large abandoned nests of other birds such as *Pitangus* or *Myiozetetes*; 4 white eggs (Cherrie 1916).
**Status and habitat:** Locally common; dry, moist, and occas. humid woodland borders, gallery forest, and scattered trees in cultivated areas. Apparently does not occur together with congeners Bicolored or Band-backed wrens.
**Range:** To 800m. Carib. region from lower Río Sinú to w Guajira and Perijá foothills s to mid. Magdalena Val. (Gamarra, s Cesar); e of Andes near Arauca in Arauca (sightings, Nov 1977—W. McKay). N Colombia and Venez. e to Orinoco delta.

## 7. GRAY-MANTLED WREN

*Odontorchilus branickii*    Pl. 42, Map 1115
**Identification:** 5″ (13cm). Gnatcatcherlike. *Dull bluish gray above*; crown tinged brownish; sides of head and faint eyestripe whitish; *below white tinged buffy; long cocked tail gray barred black; outer feathers barred white*; under tail coverts barred black and white.
**Similar species:** Best marks are shape, behavior, and barring on long *cocked* tail. Cf. Double-banded Graytail (p 366).
**Voice:** Usually silent, occas. a thin, weak *si-si-si-si* when foraging.
**Behavior:** An arboreal and active bird usually seen accompanying mixed flocks in the canopy or subcanopy. Recalls a gnatcatcher as cocks tail and hops along larger mossy limbs, seldom into terminal foliage; inconspic.
**Status and habitat:** Rare and local in humid and wet forest and forest edges; known from only a few localities in Colombia.
**Range:** 800-1100m on Pacific slope in Anchicayá drainage; perhaps to w Nariño (in nw Ecuador at Parambá, 1100m); 1650-2300m in upper Magdalena Val. (sw of San Agustín; sighting, Finca Merenberg), and e slope of E Andes in w Caquetá (sighting above Florencia, 1200-1400m, Sept 1978, June 1981—Hilty et al.). Colombia s to nw and e Ecuador, e Peru, n Bolivia.

## 8. RUFOUS WREN

*Cinnycerthia unirufa*    Pls. 41, 42, Map 1116
**Identification:** 7″ (18cm). *Uniform bright cinnamon rufous*; lores dusky; wings and tail *very*

*obscurely* barred black (or sim. but duller rufous brown—*unirufa*). Eyes reddish brown (or white or gray—*chakei*). Occas. birds have buffy white forecrown patch.
**Similar species:** Very sim. Sepia-brown Wren (9) has more distinct black barring on wings and tail, often a whitish forehead (ad.?), no dusky lores, and different voice. Rufous Spinetail (p 360) has longer double-pointed tail, more conspic. black lores, and no barring.
**Voice:** Scold a *tsip* or *sshssh*; song a loud, clear, flutey duet, *wuh, tódaly-tódaly-tódaly-woo*, 3 repeated phrases in mid. typical (J. Silliman), sometimes simply a rolling *tódaly-tódaly-tódaly* . . . repeated rapidly up to 15 times or more (T. Davis recording).
**Behavior:** Families or groups (occas. a doz. or more) follow mixed flocks or forage independent of them; usually keep close to ground in thick cover. Curious and frequently mob noisily.
**Breeding:** 5 BC birds, June–Aug, Perijá Mts., C and E Andes (Carriker). Juv., PN Puracé, Mar (J. Silliman; Brown).
**Status and habitat:** Fairly common in humid mossy forest, forest borders, and dense tangles, esp. with bamboo. Sometimes even in brush and pockets of stunted woodland above normal treeline.
**Range:** 2200-3800m. Perijá Mts. (*chakei*); both slopes of E Andes s to Cundinamarca (*unirufa*); C Andes and both slopes of Nariño and n end W Andes (*unibrunnea*). Nw Venez. s in Andes to e and w Ecuador and n Peru.

### 9. SEPIA-BROWN WREN
*Cinnycerthia peruana*     Pl. 41, Map 1117
**Identification:** 6.5" (16.5cm). *Rufous brown*, paler on throat and breast; *wings and tail narrowly but distinctly barred black*. Some ad. birds have buffy white forecrown patch. Juv. duller, throat grayish.
**Similar species:** See Rufous Wren (8) and Rufous Spinetail (p 360).
**Voice:** Soft low *wurt* notes when foraging. Song a rich melodious *bubububububu, qua-keep, qua-keep, qua-keep, wa-téer-cup, tututututututu* . . . , and so on, var. (T. Parker recording).
**Behavior:** Families or groups up to 10 or more actively hop and peer among mossy tangles and foliage from near ground to 6m up like allied Rufous Wren. Often conspic. and reg. with mixed flocks.
**Breeding:** 5 BC birds, June–Aug, W, C, and E Andes (Carriker).
**Status and habitat:** Fairly common in wet mossy forest ("cloud forest"), tangled forest borders, and second growth, esp. with bamboo.
**Range:** 1500-3100m; to 900m on Pacific slope

in Cauca. W slope of E Andes from se Santander to Cundinamarca; C Andes (n half), w slope W Andes (locally) and both slopes in Nariño. Colombia s in Andes to n Bolivia.

### 10. SEDGE WREN (GRASS WREN)
*Cistothorus platensis*     Pl. 42, Map 1118
**Identification:** 4" (10.2cm). Tiny with cocked tail. Crown brown; *short eyestripe buffy; mantle streaked black and buffy white*; wings and stubby tail rufescent barred black; underparts pale buff; sides, flanks, and under tail coverts buffy cinnamon (or crown streaked dusky, eyestripe inconspic. or lacking, underparts whitish, flanks cinnamon buff—*alticola*). *Buffy cinnamon flanks* prom. in flight.
**Similar species:** Very sim. Apolinar's Marsh-Wren (11) is larger with gray (not buffy) eyestripe, coarser tail barring, and much duller flanks; note range of 11.
**Voice:** Somewhat var. song a bright, complicated ser. of trills, churrs, and *seet* notes, characteristically beginning with an insectlike buzz, then several piping notes, ending in a buzz (J. Silliman; Hilty); in Venez. a ser. of about 5 phrases, each on a different pitch, *tu-tu-tu-tu, tee-tee-tee, ter-ter-ter, tsee-ee-ee-ee*, etc. (P. Schwartz recording).
**Behavior:** Often sings from an exposed perch but otherwise creeps and hops on or near ground in tall sedgy grass or wet tangles at base of a bush where difficult to observe or flush. Usually in small loose colonies.
**Breeding:** 10 BC birds, Feb–Aug, Santa Marta Mts., W and E Andes (Carriker); 4 more, June–July, ne Meta (S. Furniss); large ball-like grassy nest concealed on or near ground in tall grass; 4-6 white eggs (Johnson 1967).
**Status and habitat:** Locally common in marshy or sedgy areas or other open areas with grass. Most numerous above 3000m or in paramo. Considered the most abundant sp. in PN Chingaza (W. McKay).
**Range:** 2400-4000m (locally to 1400m in Andes; 150-175m in ne Meta). Perijá Mts. (Venez. side) and Santa Marta Mts. (*alticola*); E Andes s to Cundinamarca (*tamae*); C Andes in n Tolima (*tolimae*); s end C Andes and W Andes (Cauca southward) and both slopes of Nariño (*aequatorialis*); e of Andes in s Meta (1 sighting 20 Feb 1976 near El Pueblo, Macarena—T. O. Lemke and P. Gertler) and ne Meta (Carimagua, poss. new subsp.—S. Furniss). E N America s to w Panama; Colombia, Venez., and Guyana s in Andes to Tierra del Fuego.
**Note:** More than 1 sp. prob. involved. Songs of Colombian birds differ from those of N American populations and tail longer (40-46mm vs 32-41mm).

## 11. APOLINAR'S MARSH-WREN
*Cistothorus apolinari*          Pl. 42, Map 1119
**Identification:** 5″ (13cm). Much like Sedge
Wren. Crown uniform olive brown; *eyestripe
grayish*; mantle streaked black and buffy white;
wings and *short tail* rufescent barred black;
*underparts whitish with dull buff on sides and flanks.*
**Similar species:** See smaller Sedge Wren (10).
**Voice:** Song an energetic bubbly ser. of 1-3 or
so rather low-pitched, rhythmic *toe-a-twée*
phrases interrupted by short gravelly churrs;
scold with low *churr.*
**Behavior:** Usually sings or scolds from a semi-
exposed perch but is otherwise secretive in tall
cattails and very difficult to observe or flush.
Like Sedge Wren, may form loose colonies.
**Breeding:** BC ♂♂, Mar and late Aug, Bogotá
(Borrero 1953); colonies with fledglings, Oct,
Laguna Chisacá, Cundinamarca (Olivares
1969a).
**Status and habitat:** Fairly common very locally
in tall cattails bordering lakes and lagoons; less
numerous in tall bullrushes. Most accessible
colony on Sabana de Bogotá is at Parque La
Florida.
**Range:** ENDEMIC. 2500-4000m. N portion of
E Andes in n Boyacá (Guicán) and in Cun-
dinamarca from Sabaná de Bogotá s to Pá-
ramo de Sumapaz.

## 12. SOOTY-HEADED WREN
*Thryothorus spadix*          Pl. 41, Map 1120
**Identification:** 6″ (15cm). *Crown sooty becoming
black on sides of head and throat*; narrow streaks
on ear coverts white; *otherwise largely chestnut,*
brighter on breast and duller brown on lower
underparts; tail barred black.
**Similar species:** Mostly rufous with a black head
and throat. Other Pacific slope wrens have
white or grayish white throats.
**Voice:** Most common calls a sad *tee-dooo*, or
*chur-dóo, chur-dáw*, 2d and 4th notes lower;
duet, much like others of the genus, is loud,
vigorous, and somewhat var.
**Behavior:** Pairs stay in dense undergrowth and
thickets and like other *Thryothorus* are difficult
to glimpse.
**Breeding:** 8 BC birds, Apr–Sept, C and E Andes (Carriker); building nest, Mar and Dec;
eggs, Sept, Anchicayá Val; bulky side entrance
ball of leaves and coarse material about 1 m
up in *Heliconia* thicket; 2 white eggs with small
reddish spots around larger end (Hilty).
**Status and habitat:** Common in undergrowth
of wet mossy forest ("cloud forest"), occas. forest borders. Replaced in thickets along forest
borders and in second growth or stream sides
by Bay-headed Wren.
**Range:** Mostly 800-1800m (sightings to 400m,

Anchicayá Val.—Hilty). Pacific slope from up-
per Río San Juan s to Cauca; sight to s Nariño
(Junín, 1976—R. Ridgely); n end of C Andes
(Valdivia) e to mid. Magdalena Val. (Snía. San
Lucas; Bucaramanga) s to n boundary of Cal-
das. E. Panama (Cerro Tacarcuna; Cerro Quía),
Colombia; poss. nw Ecuador.
**Note:** By some considered a race of *T. atro-
gularis* (Black-throated Wren) of Nicaragua to
w Panama; the songs differ markedly.

## 13. BLACK-BELLIED WREN
*Thryothorus fasciatoventris*          Pl. 41, Map 1121
**Identification:** 6″ (15cm). Upperparts rufous
chestnut; wings and tail barred black; narrow
whitish superciliary; *ear coverts and narrow mask
through eyes black; throat and upper breast white;
lower breast and belly black narrowly barred white.*
Juv.: duller with grayish throat and chest; lower
underparts brownish more or less barred paler.
**Similar species:** Large wren easily told by pure
white throat and chest contrasting with black
lower underparts.
**Voice:** Often antiphonal. Rich liquid duet one
of the most pleasing of genus; typically, a repeated ser. of low slurred phrases, e.g., *cheerful, whip-por-warble* short calls incl. *jeer-whoop*
(like Coraya Wren), *bubu-whoop*, and so on.
**Behavior:** Skulks in dense wet thickets, frequently near streams, and even more difficult
to glimpse than most members of the genus.
**Breeding:** 5 BC birds, May–July, n Colombia
(Carriker); BC ♀, Mar, nw Santander (Boggs
1961). Building nest in Feb, lower Anchicayá
Val. (Hilty 1977).
**Status and habitat:** Uncommon to common in
dense stream-bordered thickets and young
second growth in pastures or woodland edges.
Most common nonforest wren in overgrown
clearings in s Córdoba and nw Antioquia.
**Range:** To 1000m (Cauca Val.); to 200m on
Pacific coast. Pacific coast s to Valle, humid
lowlands n of Andes e to sw base of Santa
Marta Mts., s to lower Cauca Val. (Valdivia)
and Magdalena Val. to n Tolima (Honda).
Costa Rica to Colombia.

## 14. PLAIN-TAILED WREN
*Thryothorus euophrys*          Pl. 41, Map 1122
**Identification:** 6.5″ (16.5cm). *Crown grayish brown*
bordered on sides by black; otherwise rufous
above, *wings and tail unbarred*; long eyestripe
white, stripe through eyes black; ear coverts
streaked black and white; upper throat white
with broad black submalar; *lower throat, foreneck, and breast white heavily streaked and spotted
black*; rest of underparts brownish buff.
**Similar species:** Large wren superficially like
Moustached Wren (15). Look for unbarred

wings and tail, spots and streaks on breast, and *contrasting* crown.
**Voice:** Liquid duet resembles that of Moustached and Coraya wrens.
**Behavior:** Sim. to Moustached Wren.
**Status and habitat:** Not well known in Colombia. In Peru, tangled forest borders and cut over areas in or near dense bamboo thickets (T. Parker).
**Range:** 2200-2600m (poss. somewhat lower). Extreme s Nariño on Ecuador border (Mayasquer w of Volcán Chiles). Andes of s Colombia, e and w Ecuador, and n Peru.

### 15. MOUSTACHED WREN

*Thryothorus genibarbis*        Pl. 42, Map 1123
**Identification:** 6″ (15cm). *Crown to upper mantle brownish gray*; rest of back, wings, and tail rufous chestnut; tail barred black (or olive barred black—*macrurus*); long superciliary white; sides of head gray streaked white and *bordered below by prom. white malar and black submalar streak*; throat white becoming grayish on chest and *buffy brown on rest of underparts.*
**Similar species:** Best marks are 2-toned upperparts, prom. black and white malar stripes and dingy underparts; meets Coraya Wren (16) in e foothills; latter is slightly smaller and lacks malar streaks.
**Voice:** Song an exceptionally rich, mellow, ser.of liquid whistles, usually in duet, *to-wit-to-wéebo*, or *chuwee boo-bop, chuweebo*, or sim. var.; most common call a sudden low *wéebop.*
**Behavior:** A gifted songster that usually skulks furtively in dense thickets and is very difficult to see. Pairs are heard far more often than seen.
**Breeding:** 7 BC birds, Apr–June, 1 in Nov, Perijá Mts. and Andes (Carriker); fiber ball nest with side entrance; 0.3 m up in grass and ferns, n Venez. (Beebe 1949).
**Status and habitat:** Fairly common in dense tangles of vines, saplings, and ferns in forest borders or treefalls, or shrubby thickets in clearings, less frequently inside forest. Replaced in most of w Amazonian lowlands by Coraya Wren.
**Range:** 1000-2800m (usually 1200-2400m). W slope W Andes s to Cauca, and in upper Cauca Val. (*saltuensis*); w Nariño (*yananchae*); C Andes s to Valle and head of Magdalena Val., w slope E Andes from Santander s to Meta (*macrurus*); e slope E Andes from Norte de Santander south (*amaurogaster*); Perijá Mts. (subsp?). N Venez. s through Andes to n Bolivia and most of Brazil s of Amazon.

### 16. CORAYA WREN

*Thryothorus coraya*        Pl. 42, Map 1124
**Identification:** 6″ (15cm). Crown and nape dusky

brown becoming uniform chestnut on rest of upperparts; tail pale brown barred black; sides of head black with *narrow eyestripe, eyering, and streaks on ear coverts white*; broad decurved streak on lower cheeks solid black (no moustachial streak); throat white becoming gray on chest and *reddish brown on lower underparts.*
**Similar species:** Buff-breasted Wren (23) lacks extensive black on lower cheeks and has most of underparts bright buff. Moustached Wren (15) occurs at higher el.
**Voice:** Var. repertoire. Distinctive call a loud, rolling (inhaled) *jeeer jeeer*, often followed by rapid, staccato *wop-wop-wop-wop*, less often *chut-chut-chut-chut híst-or-ee*; alarm a complaining *cut-cut-cooo.* Duet recalls many others of the genus; less rich and mellow than that of Moustached Wren.
**Behavior:** Sim. to Moustached Wren. Pairs or families hop and peer in dense bushes or on ground. Sometimes join mixed flocks or hop up vine tangles with Gray Antbird and others in mid. strata of forest edge.
**Status and habitat:** Often common in undergrowth at edge or inside *terra firme* and *várzea* forests, taller second growth, or river edge.
**Range:** To 500m. E of Andes from s Meta (Macarena Mts.), and e Guainía (Pto. Inírida; Macacuní) southward. S Venez. to se Peru and n and c Amazonian Brazil.

### 17. RUFOUS-BREASTED WREN

*Thryothorus rutilus*        Pl. 42, Map 1125
**Identification:** 5.5″ (14cm). Uniform brown above, more rufous on crown; tail broadly barred dusky (wings unbarred); narrow superciliary white; *sides of head and throat speckled black and white in sharp contrast to bright orange rufous breast* (breast spotted with black—*laetus*); center of belly grayish white; flanks tinged cinnamon.
**Similar species:** Only Colombian wren with speckled face and throat and contrasting bright rufous breast. See Spot-breasted (18) and Stripe-throated wrens (20).
**Voice:** Distinctive call *chip-reeez*, rising in an arc (Slud 1964). Vigorous musical song, usually antiphonal, resembles Buff-breasted Wren's and is not as rich as that of many other *Thryothorus*; typically several rather short rollicking phrases repeated rapidly (often twice), e.g., *eer-tosee-towhep* or *sweer-ta-owheer ta-here*, and many other var.
**Behavior:** Pairs or small families are sometimes less furtive and forage somewhat higher than others of the genus. Usually 1-10m up where examine curled dead leaves or hop up vines near trunks. Often in same habitat as Rufous-and-white and Buff-breasted wrens.
**Breeding:** 6 BC birds, Apr–June, Santa Marta

to w Guajira (Carriker); 1 in Dec, Boyacá (Olivares 1963); 2 pairs with begging juvs., Aug, PN Tayrona (Hilty); ball-like nest, typical of the genus, 1-5m up in vine tangles; 2-3 white eggs spotted brown, more heavily at large end (Skutch 1960).

**Status and habitat:** Fairly common in scrubby thickets, viny tangles, and borders of seasonal dry and moist forest or lighter woodland, esp. in foothills.

**Range:** To 1900m. Base of Santa Marta and Perijá mts. and w Guajira (*laetus*); w slope E Andes s to Bucaramanga (*interior*); e slope E Andes in Norte de Santander (*rutilus*); e slope E Andes from Arauca to nw Meta (*hypospodius*). Costa Rica to c Panama; ne Colombia to n Venez.

**Note:** Some incl. *T. maculipectus* (Spot-breasted Wren) with this sp.

### 18. SPOT-BREASTED WREN

*Thryothorus maculipectus*   Pl. 42, Map 1126

**Identification:** 5″ (13cm). Uniform plain brown above; more rufous on crown; tail broadly barred dusky (wings unbarred); narrow superciliary white; *sides of head and underparts white heavily barred and spotted black*; flanks and under tail coverts brownish buff.

**Similar species:** Spotted and barred underparts distinctive in range. Rufous-breasted Wren (17) is not known to overlap in range.

**Voice:** Call in Mexico, an ascending trill, *pleet* (Davis 1972); var. song, usually antiphonal, a repetitious ser. of *swee-purpiyou* phrases (Peterson and Chalif 1973).

**Behavior:** Much like Rufous-breasted Wren.

**Status and habitat:** Thickets, tangles, and vines at forest borders and in lighter woodland. Not well known in Colombia; 5 ♂♂ (1946-48) are from Sasaima (Olivares 1969a).

**Range:** 1300-2000m. W slope of C Andes in Valle (above Palmira at Miraflores, 2000m) and w slope of E Andes in Cundinamarca (Sasaima; La Mesa; La Vega). Mexico to n Costa Rica; c Colombia; arid foothills and slopes of sw Ecuador and n Peru.

**Note:** By some considered conspecific with *T. rutilus* (Rufous-breasted Wren).

### 19. BAY WREN

*Thryothorus nigricapillus*   Pl. 41, Map 1127

**Identification:** 5.8″ (14.7cm). *Crown and sides of head mostly black*; narrow eyestripe, malar, and a few streaks on ear coverts white; otherwise *bright rufous chestnut above*; wings and tail barred black; *throat and entire underparts barred black and white*; flanks and belly tinged rufous (or as above but throat white, unbarred—*connectens*).

**Similar species:** Only Pacific slope wren barred black and white below.

**Voice:** Very vocal; distinctive calls incl. a stuttering *sst-sst-churrr*, an accelerating crescendo-like *sssssssch-wower* (Slud 1964), and a loud, incisive, ringing *hist-o-whíp*. Large and var. repertoire of mostly antiphonal songs are among the most vigorous and energetic of the genus; typically a loud, ringing, whistled phrase repeated several times, then sometimes abruptly changed to a very different phrase.

**Behavior:** A lively and vocal wren fond of rank thickets near watercourses. Pairs are sometimes inquisitive, though usually remain partially concealed and difficult to see.

**Breeding:** 14 BC birds, Jan–May, Chocó and nw Antioquia (Carriker; Haffer 1975); Feb, July, and Aug, nests Anchicayá Val. (Hilty). Nest, usual coarse ball, 1-5m up in thicket or shrub; 3 white eggs speckled cinnamon, more heavily at large end (Carriker 1910).

**Status and habitat:** Common in undergrowth around openings and borders in humid and wet forest and second growth, esp. *Heliconia* thickets near water. Replaced inside forest in foothills by Sooty-headed Wren.

**Range:** To 1800m (few above 1400m). Panama border e to n end of C Andes (Río Nechí), the mid. Magdalena Val. s to s Bolívar, and the Pacific coast in Chocó (*schottii*); Pacific coast from Valle to Nariño (*connectens*). Nicaragua to w Ecuador.

### 20. STRIPE-THROATED WREN

*Thryothorus leucopogon*   Pl. 41, Map 1128

**Identification:** 5″ (13cm). Plain brown above; wings and tail barred black, narrow superciliary white; *sides of head and throat streaked black and white*; rest of underparts pale cinnamon brown. Eyes yellow.

**Similar species:** Buff-breasted Wren (23) is rather sim. but has unstreaked white throat. Also cf. Bay Wren (19) and White-breasted Wood-Wren (26).

**Behavior:** Not well known in Colombia. Presum. much like Stripe-breasted Wren of C America, which hops and peers from near ground to lower midlevels and is less furtive than some wrens.

**Breeding:** 8 BC birds, Apr, Chocó and nw Antioquia (Carriker); 1 in Apr, Chocó (Haffer 1975); 1 globular nest of allied *T. thoracicus* over branch 5-6m up with downward facing entrance; 2-3 white eggs (Skutch 1972).

**Status and habitat:** Undergrowth of humid and wet forest borders. Mostly lowlands.

**Range:** To 900m. Pacific coast (no Valle or Cauca recs); w side of Gulf of Urabá to n end of W Andes in Córdoba (Murrucucú), prob. to mid. Magdalena Val. E Panama to w Ecuador.

**Note 1:** By some considered a subsp. of *T. thoracicus* (Stripe-breasted Wren) of Nicaragua to c Panama. **Note 2:** Gray Wren (*T. griseus*), from e bank Río Javarí to upper Río Purús, w Brazil, occurs near s Amazon bank opp. Leticia. 5″; grayish brown above, gray below, faint whitish eyebrow, under tail coverts with faint dusky bars, *broad* but *very short* tail with a few black bars. *Várzea* forest vine tangles, eye level to subcanopy; shy. Song reminiscent of Stripe-breasted Wren (above), a rhythmic *tor-chílip, tor-chílip* . . . , or *fidle-dip, fiddle-dip* . . . , or *chur-dúrt, chur-dúrt* . . . , 5-8 melodic phrases in ser., typically growing stronger as it goes along; many single phrases.

### 21. RUFOUS-AND-WHITE WREN
*Thryothorus rufalbus*     Pl. 42, Map 1129
**Identification:** 6″ (15cm). *Bright rufous above with prom. white superciliary*; wings and tail barred black; sides of head white streaked black; *underparts white*; sides and flanks tinged brown; under tail coverts barred with black. Or rufous brown above with darker crown (*minlosi*).
**Similar species:** A big, bright rufous wren with white median underparts. See Buff-breasted Wren (23); in the mts. Niceforo's (22) and Moustached wrens (15).
**Voice:** Unusual songs are very melodic though unlike others of the genus; a common var. (among many) is 4 or 5 low-pitched, slow, mellow, bouncing whistles preceded and followed by a higher note, *weeee, boo boo boo boo whít*; occas. also sings antiphonally.
**Behavior:** Rather restrained and deliberate in actions. Individuals or pairs hop on ground or poke and peer in thick foliage 1-6m up, where usually furtive and hard to see but often heard.
**Breeding:** 13 BC birds, May–Oct, and Oct nest, n Colombia (Carriker). BC birds, Apr–May (S. Furniss), and building nest, Dec (Brown), ne Meta; Aug nest PN Tayrona (Hilty); elbow-shaped globular nest, entrance near top.
**Status and habitat:** Often common in undergrowth and tangles of lighter, drier deciduous woodland or along streamsides in drier foothills; locally to more humid areas with open woodland; gallery forest in llanos.
**Range:** To 1400m. Cartagena to Santa Marta Mts. (*cumanensis*); Perijá Mts. s to nw base E Andes at Gamarra, Cesar; e of Andes from Norte de Santander s to Macarena Mts. (*minlosi*), sight e to Vichada (1977, El Tuparro—P. Gertler). Se Mexico to w and w c Venez.

### 22. NICEFORO'S WREN
*Thryothorus nicefori*     Map 1130
**Identification:** 6″ (15cm). *Resembles Rufous-and-white Wren but with 2-toned back.* Crown and upper back *olive brown*; lower back, rump, wings, and tail *rufous brown*; wings and tail barred black; sharp white superciliary; cheeks white streaked black; *below white*; sides and flanks pale grayish brown; crissum barred black.
**Similar species:** See Rufous-and-white Wren (21).
**Behavior:** Not well known but presum. much like 21.
**Status and habitat:** Known from a few specimens from a region of lighter woodland and coffee plantations.
**Range:** ENDEMIC. W slope of E Andes on Río Fonce (1100m) at San Gil, Santander.
**Note:** Poss. a subsp. of *T. rufalbus* (Rufous-and-white Wren); see Paynter (1959).

### 23. BUFF–BREASTED WREN
*Thryothorus leucotis*     Pl. 42, Map 1131
**Identification:** 5.5″ (14cm). Reddish brown above with *prom. white eyestripe*; wings and tail barred black; sides of head white streaked dusky; *throat white; breast buff becoming cinnamon buff on belly* (or center of belly whitish, sides cinnamon buff—*venezuelanus*); under tail coverts uniform deep cinnamon.
**Similar species:** Recalls an overgrown House Wren (24) but brighter buff below and cheek stripes prom. Rufous-and-white Wren (21) is larger with all white median underparts and barred crissum. In Amazonia widely sympatric with Coraya Wren (16) from which it differs by buffy breast (not whitish) and sides of head streaked black (instead of with droopy black cheek mark), also by voice and habitat.
**Voice:** Distinctive call a very rapid, incisive *chit-cho*, or *chit, cho-cho*; loud, rollicking, antiphonal song resembles that of many other *Thryothorus* wrens, typically a repetitious musical *amelia-choke, amelia-choke* . . . or *chee-bur-EE-chee* . . . , or sim. var., usually antiphonal; simpler songs often repeated many times, complex ones less repetitive.
**Behavior:** Active but like others of the genus hard to see. Usually in pairs 0.2-4m up in undergrowth, sometimes on the ground.
**Breeding:** 6 BC birds, Aug–Oct, Cartagena and Cúcuta, Jan nest, mouth of Río Cauca (Carriker); May nest, Santa Marta (Todd and Carriker 1922), July and Aug (Hilty); 2 BC ♂♂, Jan and Apr (S. Furniss); building nest, Dec (Brown), ne Meta; globular nest, entrance near top; 2-3 white eggs, spotted brown and lilac, esp. at larger end.
**Status and habitat:** Common in bushy thickets along forest borders, streams, and clearings from regions of drier woodland to humid forest, *várzea*, and mangroves; often near water.
**Range:** To 600m. Panama border and Gulf of

Urabá (*galbraithii*); Sinú Val. to w base Santa Marta Mts. s to lower Cauca Val. and upper Magdalena Val. in n Huila (*leucotis*); n and e base Santa Marta Mts. to c Guajira (*venezuelanus*); Snía. Macuira, e Guajira (*collinus*); e Norte de Santander (*zuliensis*); Arauca and Vichada to s Meta (*bogotensis*); Caquetá to Amazonas near Leticia (*peruanus*); C Panama to e central Peru and Amazonian Brazil.

## 24. HOUSE WREN

*Troglodytes aedon*          Pl. 42, Map 1132
**Identification:** 4.5″ (11.4cm). Brown to grayish brown above with indistinct dusky barring on wings and tail; *weak eyestripe buffy white*; below more or less buff to pinkish buff, usually paler on throat and belly; under tail coverts uniform or barred.
**Similar species:** A small brown and buff wren *lacking* prom. field marks. See Mountain Wren (25).
**Voice:** Song a spirited bubbling or gurgling warble much like n populations. Its pleasing song is heard yr.-round.
**Behavior:** A cheerful and energetic little bird often found in the company of man. Cocks its tail as actively hops along fence-rows or in shrubbery, occas. higher in a tree.
**Breeding:** Apparently yr.-round in many areas (Miller 1963); building nest in paramo (3300m), Sept, Represa Neusa (Hilty), and Apr (2200m), Nariño (Brown); globular nest in cranny, a building, low shrubbery, or even on ground.
**Status and habitat:** Common in almost all kinds of semiopen areas and in clearings in extensively forested areas, esp. near human habitation.
**Range:** To 3400m (lowlands to treeline or above). Throughout (sometimes absent from extensively forested areas). S Canada s to all of S America.
**Note:** Incl. the *T. musculus* group (Tropical House Wren), sometimes considered specifically distinct.

## 25. MOUNTAIN WREN

*Troglodytes solstitialis*          Pl. 42, Map 1133
**Identification:** 4.2″ (10.7cm). A *smaller* and *rufous* edition of House Wren. Bright rufous brown above with wings and tail barred black; *prom. eyestripe buff; underparts pale to deep buff* (darkest at head of Magdalena Valley and in Nariño); under tail coverts buffy white barred black.
**Similar species:** Ruddier than House Wren (24) with broader and much more buffy eyestripe, smaller size, and different habitat.
**Voice:** Infrequent song a high-pitched, short trill, descending in pitch and fading, *tee-de-d-d-d-dt*; scold a hissing buzz (J. Silliman).

**Behavior:** Pairs or families of 3-5 hop actively along larger trunks, mossy limbs or in vine tangles in mid. story or lower into undergrowth; often with mixed flocks but inconspic.
**Breeding:** 7 BC birds, Mar–Sept, Santa Marta and Perijá mts. and Andes (Carriker); nests, Aug and Nov, and juv. in May, PN Puracé (J. Silliman; Hilty); building nest, Mar, Finca Merenberg, Huila (Ridgely and Gaulin 1980); 2 white eggs (Sclater and Salvin 1879); nest as in 24.
**Status and habitat:** Uncommon to common (higher el.) in humid and wet forest, forest borders, and stunted woodland up to treeline.
**Range:** 1500-3600m (to 1100m in Pacific Nariño); Santa Marta Mts. (to 4500m); Perijá Mts. and all 3 Andean ranges. Nw Venez. s in Andes to nw Argentina.

## 26. WHITE-BREASTED WOOD-WREN

*Henicorhina leucosticta*          Pl. 42, Map 1134
**Identification:** 4″ (10.2cm). *Tiny with very short, usually cocked tail.* Bright chestnut above; wings and tail barred black; crown blackish brown (or chestnut like back—*inornata*) with *long white superciliary*; sides of head streaked black and white; *below mostly white*; sides of breast grayish; flanks rufous brown. Imm.: breast grayish.
**Similar species:** Closely resembles Gray-breasted Wood-Wren (27) but mostly white (not gray) below, slightly smaller, and tail shorter.
**Voice:** Energetic songs richer, shorter, and more var. than those of Gray-breasted Wood-Wren; common var. incl. *cheery-cheery-chéee* (nw Venez.), *we-per-chee, purty-choo* or *geear-hurry hurry* or *sKEEET, purty-purty-purty*, and so on; also rattly trills; *chut* call and *churr* scold.
**Behavior:** A perky and often inquisitive little bird, seen alone or in pairs hopping on fallen logs or in thicker cover on or near the forest floor; not always easy to see but will usually come out to look over observers with patience. Sometimes follows army ants.
**Breeding:** 13 BC birds, Jan–June, Chocó; 1 early July, Perijá Mts. (Carriker). In Costa Rica, Feb–May; globular nest with side entrance; concealed close to ground; 2 white eggs. Dormitory nests also built (Skutch 1960).
**Status and habitat:** Undergrowth of humid and wet forest, esp. in damp ravines and tangles around treefalls or logs; seems to favor hill country w of the Andes and usually below range of Gray-breasted Wood-Wren, though sometimes both occur together; mostly lowlands e of Andes.
**Range:** To 1000m. Upper Río Sinú and Atrato Val. s on Pacific coast to Baudó Mts. (*darienensis*); upper Río San Juan to Nariño (*inor-*

*nata*); headwaters (formerly) of Dagua Val. (1200-1600m) in Valle (*eucharis*); Cauca Val. s to Valle, mid. Magdalena Val. from Snía. San Lucas s to w Cundinamarca (*albilateralis*); e of Andes from Meta and Vaupés southward (*hauxwelli*). S Mexico to w Ecuador, ne Peru, n Brazil, Surinam, and Fr. Guiana.

## 27. GRAY-BREASTED WOOD-WREN
*Henicorhina leucophrys*　　Pl. 42, Map 1135
**Identification:** 4.5″ (11.4cm). Small with *short, usually cocked tail*. Mostly reddish brown above, crown usually tinged olive (or crown rufous brown like back—*brunneiceps*); *prom. white superciliary*; wings and tail lightly barred black; sides of head streaked black and white; *below mostly gray*, throat usually paler (or below grayish white—*anachoreta*), upper throat sometimes checkered gray and white; flanks and abdomen tinged brown.
**Similar species:** Closely resembles White-breasted Wood-Wren (26) but gray below, tail slightly longer, and usually at higher el. (limited range overlap).
**Voice:** Sings yr.-round. Song has much longer phrases and is not as rich as that of White-breasted Wood-Wren; typically a fast *chee-rooeechée-cheewéecheerooéechee* or sim. var. (Ridgely 1976) except in w Cauca and w Nariño where sings a remarkably different fife-like ser. of tinkling notes in many patterns and is perhaps a different sp. (Hilty). Call 1 or more gravelly *churr*'s.
**Behavior:** Like White-breasted Wood-Wren. Sedentary but inquisitive and always seems to be poking through dark tangles where it is heard more often than seen.
**Breeding:** 1 BC ♂, Apr, juv. in June, Perijá Mts. (Carriker); in e Huila, Dec–May (P. Gertler); in W Andes above Cali, 1 nest in Mar (Miller 1963), 2 in May, 5 in June (S. Gniadek). Globular nest with downward facing entrance; concealed low in undergrowth; 2 white eggs (Skutch 1960).
**Status and habitat:** Common in damp, mossy undergrowth of humid and wet forest ("cloud forest"), and lighter woodland with tangles and treefalls.
**Range:** Mainly 1000-2900m (to 400m on Pacific slope). Santa Marta Mts., 600-2100m (*bangsi*), 1800-3600m (*anachoreta*); w slope W Andes s to w Nariño (*brunneiceps*); e slope W Andes (Valle s) e to w slope E Andes (Santander s) and e slope Nariño (*leucophrys*); upper Atrato Val. (subsp.); Snía. de Darién (subsp.); Baudó Mts. (subsp.); Perijá Mts. (subsp.); e slope E Andes from Norte de Santander to Meta; Macarena Mts. and w Caquetá (*tamae*). Mexico to n Venez. and s in Andes to n Bolivia.

## 28. NIGHTINGALE WREN
*Microcerculus marginatus*　　Pl. 42, Map 1136
**Identification:** 4.5″ (11.4cm). Bill rather long and slender. *Tail short, often cocked up. Uniform dark brown above*; wings and tail unbarred; *throat to upper belly white*; sides, flanks, and abdomen brown, sometimes lightly scaled. Presumed juvs. are uniformly dark brown, paler or whitish on throat; birds believed older have median underparts grayish to white scaled or mottled dusky, the scaling gradually being lost with increasing age.
**Similar species:** Superficially resembles unrelated Rusty-belted Tapaculo (p 426) and Banded Antbird (p 396). Tapaculo is larger with longer tail and rusty chest band; antbird has necklace, wing bars, and white rump band but shares teetering habit and both otherwise act sim. Also see ♀ Silvered Antbird (p 405) and White-breasted Wood-Wren (26). Scaled imm. recalls Spot-breasted Wren (see 18; both at La Vega, w Cundinamarca).
**Voice:** Heard far more than seen. Unusual and unforgettable song a long, very slow ser. of pure-toned whistles (up to 10 or more), each about a half tone lower than the preceding and given at progressively longer intervals (last few notes separated by pauses of 10 sec or more); in a common var. the pauses are briefer and the notes almost at random pitch but usually end with a few slow descending notes. Song. sim. both e and w of Andes, incl. Amazonia.
**Behavior:** A very furtive, inconspic. bird that is frequently heard but seldom seen. Walks on or near forest floor and almost constantly teeters its rear end.
**Breeding:** 14 BC birds, Mar–July, 1 in Dec, Chocó to Perijá Mts. (Carriker); 1 building nest, 15 Feb, upper Anchicayá Val. (Hilty); white eggs (Schönwetter).
**Status and habitat:** Locally fairly common (based on voice) in undergrowth of humid and wet forest, esp. in wooded foothill ravines.
**Range:** To 1200m (prob. higher); mainly 600-1200m in Santa Marta Mts. Pacific coast, n of Andes in humid regions to Santa Marta foothills, base of Perijá Mts. in Guajira, and s to lower Cauca and mid. Magdalena vals. (to La Vega, Cundinamarca); e of Andes in Norte de Santander (Cúcuta) and from w Meta and Vaupés (Mitú) southward. Se Mexico to w Ecuador, n Bolivia, Amazonian Brazil, and Venez.
**Note 1:** Birds from se Mexico to c Costa Rica (*philomela*) have a different song from birds of s Costa Rica to n Amazonia and are almost surely a separate sp. (G. Stiles). Birds e of the Andes (*marginatus*) have also been considered a distinct sp. by some, although the song in

Colombia is sim. to birds w of the Andes. Birds from se Peru, ne Bolivia and parts of Amazonian Brazil (*bolivianus?*) sing yet another song and are prob. also a different sp. **Note 2:** Wingbanded Wren (*Microcerculus bambla*) of the Guianas, n Brazil (incl. junction of Río Uaupés and upper Río Negro), s Venez. (150-1500m), e Ecuador (500-1000m), and e Peru (sight) may occur in Colombia on e slope of E Andes in Putumayo and Nariño, poss. e Guainía. Dark wood brown, grayer below; wings and tail blackish with a single large white wing bar; behavior as in Nightingale Wren; eerie song a single high, thin, long sustained glissando falling slightly, *ee-ee-ee-ee-ee-ee-ee-ee-ee-eu-eu-eu*.

## 29. CHESTNUT-BREASTED WREN

*Cyphorhinus thoracicus*          Pl. 41, Map 1137

**Identification:** 6″ (15cm). Bill thick for a wren, *culmen arched. Dark wood brown above*; wings and tail unbarred dusky; crown and lores blackish, the feathers somewhat stiff and erect; *cheeks, sides of neck, throat, and breast orange chestnut*; flanks and belly dark brown.

**Similar species:** Shape and habits bring to mind a tapaculo or antbird, but note bright orange chestnut underparts. Also see Song Wren (30), a lowland bird, and Tawny-throated Leaftosser (p 379).

**Voice:** Raspy *churr* call usually repeated several times; haunting flutelike song (much var. in pattern) a ser. of 2-4 minor key notes, about 1 per sec or slower, that ascend, descend, or alternate in pitch in half tone steps and may be repeated over and over for several min, e.g., *here-see, here-see* . . . (*here* note higher). Like Nightingale Wren, not forgotten once learned.

**Behavior:** Furtive and difficult to see and often does not sing persistently, so hard to locate. Pairs or families hop on ground or on logs and peck or poke under leaves or in debris. Sometimes active beneath mixed flocks.

**Breeding:** 2 BC birds, June, n end C Andes (Carriker), 1 in Mar and grown juv., Apr, W Andes above Cali (Miller 1963); in same area building nest in Sept and 2 juvs. with ad. in Dec (S. Gniadek).

**Status and habitat:** Often common (infrequently seen) in undergrowth of mossy forest ("cloud forest"), esp. in tangles.

**Range:** 1300-2600m (to 700m on Pacific slope in Cauca). Both slopes of W Andes in Valle and Cauca, and C Andes s to c Tolima. Prob. e slope E Andes at s end. Andes of Colombia, e Ecuador, and Peru.

## 30. SONG WREN

*Cyphorhinus phaeocephalus*          Pl. 41, Map 1138

**Identification:** 5″ (13cm). Bill thick for a wren, *culmen arched*. Mostly dark reddish brown with *sides of head, throat, and chest rufous chestnut; conspic. bare blue ocular area*; wings and tail barred black. Or upper belly grayish, throat sometimes with var. amts. of white (*lawrencii*).

**Similar species:** Several antbirds have sim. bare blue ocular areas but lack barring on wings and bright rufous chestnut on throat; cf. Chestnut-backed Antbird (p 407). Tawny-throated Leaftosser (p 377) lacks bare ocular area. In highlands see Chestnut-breasted Wren (29).

**Voice:** Unusual song a distinctive ser. of guttural *churr*'s and "pot boiling" sounds interrupted by rather loud, exceptionally melodic (fifelike) whistles that may vary enormously in pitch, e.g., *ong cutta cutta, whong cutta cutta glut, WHOO HEE*, etc. (Willis and Eisenmann 1979); *churr*'s continually when disturbed.

**Behavior:** Often wary and difficult to glimpse. Pairs or families hop on or near ground or on logs, poking under fallen leaves; occas. follow army ants or join mixed flocks.

**Breeding:** 4 BC birds, Mar–May, n Antioquia to s Bolívar (Carriker). In Costa Rica 2 retort-shaped nests in Feb, saddled over small branches, 1-2.5m up; tubular entrance on side; white eggs, speckled brown around larger end; sleep in dormitory nests (Skutch 1960).

**Status and habitat:** Fairly common in undergrowth of humid and wet forest and tall second growth.

**Range:** To 1000m (usually much lower). Panama border s to Baudó Mts. (*chocoanus*); w side Gulf of Urabá to upper Atrato Val. (*lawrencii*); headwaters of Río San Juan s to Nariño (*phaeocephalus*); Sinú Val. e in humid lowlands n of Andes to mid. Magdalena Val. s to Remedios, e Antioquia (*propinquus*). Honduras to w Ecuador.

**Note:** Poss. conspecific with *C. arada* (Musician Wren).

## 31. MUSICIAN WREN

*Cyphorhinus arada*          Pl. 42, Map 1139

**Identification:** 5″ (13cm). Sim. to Song Wren but more olive brown above; throat and breast *as well as forecrown and eyebrow* brighter, more orange rufous. Bare blue ocular area smaller than in Song Wren (R. Ridgely).

**Similar species:** More likely mistaken for an antbird or tapaculo than a wren. Note peculiar bill shape, bare blue ocular area, and barring on wings and tail.

**Voice:** Flutelike song with *churr*'s resembles that of Song Wren but even more elaborate with numerous characteristic *hée-hoo* phrases (1st note at least an octave higher than 2d).

**Behavior:** As in Song Wren and like it has habit

of coming in to look over an observer quickly, then moving off, all the while churring. **Breeding:** Laying ♀, May, s Bolívar (Carriker); July, Guyana nest sim. in shape to that of Song Wren; 2 dull white eggs (Beebe et al. 1917). **Status and habitat:** Fairly common on ground or in undergrowth of humid *terra firme* forest. **Range:** To 500m. E of Andes in Vaupés (Mitú) and w Caquetá (*transfluvialis*); Putumayo and

Nariño (*salvini*) to Amazonas (subsp.). Guianas and e Venez. to n Bolivia and Amazonian Brazil. **Note:** Birds from the Guianas, e Venez. and n Brazil e of Río Negro (*arada*) are sometimes considered a separate sp.; alternately all forms from Honduras (see previous sp.) to the Guianas and n Bolivia are considered a single sp. by some.

# MOCKINGBIRDS, THRASHERS: Mimidae (2)

Mockingbirds and thrashers are a small New World family related to thrushes and wrens. Famed for their songs and in the case of some mockingbirds for their powers of vocal mimicry, most are otherwise rather undistinguished. They are slender, long-tailed birds, usually found in shrubby areas or woodland, often in the vicinity of man. The family is mostly insectivorous but fruit is occas. eaten. Nests are usually bulky open cups. No typical thrashers (*Toxostoma*) occur in Colombia, none being found s of Mexico.

## 1. GRAY CATBIRD

*Dumetella carolinensis*

**Identification:** 8″ (20cm). *Mainly slate gray with black cap* and rather long blackish tail; *crissum chestnut.*

**Status and habitat:** One old rec. on 23 Mar at Ciénaga, Magdalena. Recent recs. as follows: 1 on 6 Jan 1978 in PN Katíos, nw Chocó, and 1 sight rec. 35km further nw near Panama border; another sight rec. 26 Jan 1975 near Acandí, Chocó (Rodríguez 1980). No other S American recs. Skulks in thickets. Poss. a regular winter visitor in small nos. to extreme nw Colombia.

**Range:** Breeds in N America; winters from s US to Canal Zone, Panama, and W Indies.

## 2. TROPICAL MOCKINGBIRD

*Mimus gilvus*                           Ill. 93, Map 1140

**Identification:** 10″ (25cm). Slender and long-tailed. *Pale grayish brown above* with narrow dusky mask and *prom. chalky white eyestripe*; wings blackish; coverts edged white (no white patches in wing); tail blackish broadly tipped white; below dull white. Imm. sim. but browner above, buffier below.

**Voice:** Song a long rambling ser. of notes and phrases, some repeated several times, others

not; reminiscent of Northern Mockingbird (*M. polyglottos*) but huskier, and unlike it, does not mimic other birds.

**Behavior:** A conspic. bird of mostly open or urban areas, notably aggressive around nest sites. Often feeds on the ground, and like Northern Mockingbird, frequently "wing-lifts."

**Breeding:** 11 BC birds, Jan–June, Santa Marta and Huila (Carriker); juvs., Apr, May, June, ne Meta (S. Furniss); 1 nest 28 July, W Andes above Cali (S. Gniadek); in Venez. Jan–Sept; twiggy bowl low in bush or shrub; 3 eggs (Friedmann and Smith 1950), pale greenish blue with rusty spots at larger end (Sclater and Salvin 1879).

**Status and habitat:** Common in towns, ranchland, and other drier open areas with scattered shrubbery; also arid scrub and cactus.

**Range:** To 2600m (Sabana de Bogotá); usually much lower. Generally w of Andes in nonforested regions (no Nariño recs.; Pacific coast?), and e of them s to Meta (Macarena Mts.) and e Vichada (El Tuparro—INDERENA). S Mexico to Honduras; introduced in Panama; Colombia to the Guianas, n and se Brazil; most of Carib. isls.

**Note:** Mayr and Short (1970) consider this sp. conspecific with *M. polyglottos* (Northern Mockingbird).

# THRUSHES, SOLITAIRES: Turdidae (26)

Thrushes form a large nearly cosmopolitan family most numerous in temperate regions of the Old World and most closely related to Old World warblers (Sylvidae) and Old World flycatchers (Muscicapidae). Some are among the finest songbirds in the world. Thrushes eat a variety of animal matter and fruit, often taken on the ground; some are highly frugivorous seasonally. The various species of *Turdus* are the largest and best known Colombian thrushes, while *Catharus* and

*Myadestes* are mostly shy woodland dwellers less often seen but often notable for their beautiful, flutelike songs. Colombian species, as far as known, build open cup nests either in bushes or trees, or in the case of *Catharus* and *Myadestes* on or near the ground.

## 1. ANDEAN SOLITAIRE

*Myadestes ralloides*          Pl. 43, Map 1141

**Identification:** 7″ (18cm). Short bill dusky above, yellow below. *Upperparts brown* becoming rufescent on rump; *entire head and underparts leaden gray*; white band at base of primaries visible in flight; *tail dark brown, outer feathers tipped white*, outermost with long white wedge on inner web. Juv. mostly rufescent brown heavily spotted ochraceous, crown and underparts more dusky, tail as in adult.

**Similar species:** Dull, mostly warm brown above, gray below; white tail tips often conspic. See next sp.

**Voice:** Its beautiful, lilting song of pipelike purity is usually the 1st indication of its presence; the clear liquid phrases are given deliberately and with frequent pause, *lee-day . . . lur-lur . . . see-see . . . eee-ooo, eee-oh-lay . . . lur-lur-lur*, and so on.

**Behavior:** A rather shy unobtrusive bird that sits motionless and erect among a screen of foliage in the mid. story or lower. Often slips away quietly at an observer's presence and would doubtless often be overlooked but for its frequent song heard throughout the yr.

**Breeding:** 8 BC birds, Mar–Aug, Perijá Mts. and W Andes (Carriker; Miller 1963). Mar nest, W Andes above Cali (Miller 1963); 1 in July, same area (S. Gniadek); 1 in Mar, e Huila (P. Gertler); 3 more, Mar–Apr, Popayán (Wallace 1965); moss cup on bank or log; 2 dull white eggs speckled reddish brown at larger end.

**Status and habitat:** Common in humid and wet forest ("cloud forest") and taller second growth woodland.

**Range:** 1200–2700m; to 800m on Pacific slope. Perijá Mts., all 3 Andean ranges and Macarena Mts. Nw Venez. s in Andes to n Bolivia.

## 2. VARIED SOLITAIRE

*Myadestes coloratus*

**Identification:** 7″ (18cm). Only found near Panama boundary. Like Andean Solitaire (1), but bill and legs *orange, forehead and face black*, and tail gray (no white tips).

**Status and habitat:** Recently rec. on slope of Cerro Tacarcuna in PN Los Katíos, in Chocó (Rodríguez 1982). Moist mt. forest and forest borders.

**Range:** Above 800m (Panama). Extreme nw Chocó, Colombia and e Darién (Cerros Tacarcuna, Pirre, and Quía), Panama.

**Note:** Some merge *M. coloratus* of e Panama

and *M. melanops* (Black-faced Solitaire) of Costa Rica and w Panama with *M. ralloides*.

## 3. RUFOUS-BROWN SOLITAIRE

*Myadestes leucogenys*          Pl. 43, Map 1142

**Identification:** 8.1″ (20.6cm). Rare. Bill short, rather wide at base, black above, *yellow below*; eyes light brown. Upperparts, head, throat, sides of neck, and upper breast rufous brown becoming *pale gray on lower breast and upper belly*; lower belly ochraceous tawny; *under tail coverts bright ochraceous orange*; wing linings ochraceous orange; tail cinnamon brown, outer feathers paler and all but central pair *tipped ochraceous*.

**Similar species:** No other rufous brown "thrush" has pale gray belly and *bright* ochraceous orange under tail coverts. See Andean Solitaire (1).

**Status and habitat:** No specimens. Only rec. is a bird netted and photographed by J. Dunning, 15 Aug 1977 at Yatacué (550m), upper Anchicayá Val. Wet upper tropical zone forest.

**Range:** 550m. Pacific slope in Valle. W Guyana, se Venez., w Colombia, nw Ecuador (1000m), and c Peru; se Brazil.

## 4. BLACK SOLITAIRE

*Entomodestes coracinus*          Pl. 43, Map 1143

**Identification:** 9″ (23cm). Unmistakable. Bill black above, orange below; eyes red. Tail rather long. *Jet black with white cheeks, white pectoral tufts, and large white outer tail tips*; inner webs of inner remiges white (prom. in flight).

**Voice:** A high-pitched, slightly buzzy *tszeeeeeeee*, weak and easily overlooked.

**Behavior:** Individuals or pairs occur alone from understory to subcanopy, may follow forest flocks, and occas. gather in groups of 3-4 at fruiting trees and shrubs. Can be inordinately wary and difficult to see and usually is only glimpsed as flies rapidly ("frightened dash") across small forest openings.

**Status and habitat:** Local in wet mossy forest ("cloud forest"), forest edges, and tall second growth. Fairly common above Junín in Nariño, decidedly less numerous northward. In upper Anchicayá Val. (1050m), Valle, rec. only May–June and Oct–Nov; elevational or local movements likely (Hilty 1977).

**Range:** 400-1900m. Pacific slope from Río San Juan headwaters (below Cerro Tatamá) southward. W Colombia and nw Ecuador.

## 5. ORANGE-BILLED NIGHTINGALE-THRUSH

*Catharus aurantiirostris*     Pl. 43, Map 1144
**Identification:** 6.5″ (16.5cm). *Bill and legs bright orange*; narrow eyering orange. *Warm brown above, light gray below fading to white on throat and belly* (or crown and sides of head gray, upperparts tinged olive—*phaeopleurus*).
**Similar species:** Told from other brown-backed Colombian thrushes by orange bill, eyering, and legs.
**Voice:** A poor singer for a nightingale-thrush; short jumbled songs are mostly squeaky unmusical warbles; at San Agustín *wa-trípsee-spít-wachee*, or sim. var.; scold with nasal *waa-a-a-a*. Song types vary geographically.
**Behavior:** Often sings tirelessly from a concealed perch in low dense thickets where difficult to see. Hops on or near ground to feed, sometimes onto trail or small opening.
**Breeding:** 10 BC birds, Apr–July, 1 in Nov, Santa Marta and Perijá mts., C and E Andes (Carriker); Mar–May nests, Popayán; bulky cup of moss and grass low in shrub or thicket; 2 pale blue eggs, somewhat spotted brownish (Wallace 1965).
**Status and habitat:** Locally common in shrubby pastures, fence-rows, forest borders, and lighter woodland (esp. shady coffee plantations); moist to humid regions.
**Range:** 600–2200m. Santa Marta Mts. (*sierrae*); Perijá Mts. and e slope E Andes in Norte de Santander (*aurantiirostris*); w slope E Andes in Santander (*inornatus*); e slope E Andes in s Boyacá and head of Magdalena Val. (*insignis*); mid. and upper Cauca Val. (Valle southward), upper Dagua and Patía vals. s to w Nariño (*phaeopleurus*). N Mexico to w Panama; n and w Venez.; Trinidad.
**Note:** Incl. *C. griseiceps* (Gray-headed Nightingale-Thrush) of sw Costa Rica, w Panama, and w Colombia, formerly considered a separate sp. from brown-headed birds of rest of range.

## 6. SLATY-BACKED NIGHTINGALE-THRUSH

*Catharus fuscater*     Pl. 43, Map 1145
**Identification:** 7″ (18cm). *Bill and legs orange; eyes white. Dark slate gray above*; head blackish with narrow orange eyering; *below grayish olive*, throat paler; center of breast and abdomen pale yellow (fades to whitish in specimens). Or crown, sides of head, and chin blackish; throat, breast, and sides dark gray (*sanctaemartae*).
**Similar species:** ♂ Pale-eyed Thrush (13) is larger, entirely lustrous black, and bill and legs yellow (not orange). Orange-billed Night-

ingale-Thrush (5) is warm brown above with dark eye.
**Voice:** Song in Santa Marta Mts. a haunting, ethereal, 2-3 noted flutelike phrase, *eer-lee*, or *ur-eee-lee* like distant rusty gate; call a catlike *meow*.
**Behavior:** A shy denizen of forest undergrowth and usually near ground. Singing birds drift further and further away as an observer approaches and are *difficult to see*.
**Breeding:** 11 BC birds, Apr–Sept, Santa Marta and Perijá mts., n end W Andes (Carriker). Costa Rican cup nest low in bush; pale blue eggs thickly spotted and blotched rufous chestnut (Carriker 1910).
**Status and habitat:** Fairly common (seldom seen) in humid and wet mossy forest.
**Range:** 600–2800m. N end W Andes (*opertaneus*); Santa Marta Mts. (*sanctaemartae*); Perijá Mts. and both slopes E Andes s to Santander (*fuscater*), and Boyacá (e of Laguna de Tota), and most of Magdalena Val. to s Huila (PN Cueva de los Guácharos—P. Gertler). Doubtless entire e slope E Andes; perhaps Pacific slope sw Nariño (subsp?). Costa Rica to nw Venez.; e and w Ecuador s in Andes to n Bolivia.

## 7. SPOTTED NIGHTINGALE-THRUSH

*Catharus dryas*     Pl. 43, Map 1146
**Identification:** 7″ (18cm). *Bill and legs red orange.* Mainly olive above; crown and sides of *head jet black* with narrow orange eyering; *below apricot yellow* (fades to whitish in specimens) *spotted dusky on throat and breast*; flanks grayish; under tail coverts white.
**Similar species:** Most like Slaty-backed Nightingale-Thrush (6) but yellow below with spots.
**Voice:** Rich, liquid song *cholo-chu . . . ee-o . . . tuEE-o . . . lur-we, clo-EE-o*, and other short whistled phrases, occas. odd guttural note; many phrases strongly reminiscent of Wood Thrush of N America (P. Schwartz recording); often bill clacks loudly (T. Parker).
**Behavior:** Shy, in undergrowth or on forest floor where it hops on ground and picks at leaves with typical thrush mannerisms (T. Parker). Sometimes attracted to whistled imitations of its calls.
**Status and habitat:** Not well known in Colombia. Undergrowth in mossy forest, esp. in damp ravines and along forest streams. A few seen in PN Cueva de los Guácharos (P. Gertler).
**Range:** 700–2100m. Head of Magdalena Val. in Huila, and e slope of E Andes from n Boyacá (Fátima) to s Meta (Macarena Mts.). Doubtless the entire e slope. Sw Mexico to

Honduras; Andes from nw Venez. to e and w Ecuador and s to nw Argentina.

## 8. VEERY
*Catharus fuscescens*

**Identification:** 7″ (18cm). *Uniform rufescent brown above*; white below, chest and sides of neck heavily washed buff; *very lightly speckled brown on chest*. Legs pale brown.

**Similar species:** Swainson's (10) and Gray-cheeked thrushes (9) are usually olive brown above (no rufescent tones) with more distinct and more extensive spotting below. Swainson's also has buffy eyering.

**Behavior:** Sim. to other migrant thrushes. Follows army ants at times in migration (Willis 1966e).

**Status and habitat:** Very uncommon fall migrant (4 Sept–23 Oct) on ground or low in undergrowth in forest, forest edges, open woodland, and second growth; only spring rec. is 1 seen 2 Mar 1976, Macarena Mts. (T. Lemke and P. Gertler).

**Range:** To 2300m. Carib. region from Atlántico (s of Barranquilla) to Santa Marta Mts., e slope of E Andes in Norte de Santander (Pamplona), and once in Macarena Mts. (sight). Breeds in N America; transient in Mid. America and W Indies, winters from n S America (Oct–Apr) in Guyana) to Amazonian Brazil, Bolivia (once), Peru (sight), and Chile (Arica); no Ecuador recs.

## 9. GRAY-CHEEKED THRUSH
*Catharus minimus*

**Identification:** 7″ (18cm). Uniform dull olive brown above, cheeks grayish with no distinct eyering; below white, chest tinged grayish buff, sides more gray; dusky spots on chest and breast.

**Similar species:** On the average, darker than Swainson's Thrush (10) but not always easily separated; Gray-cheeked has grayish (not buffy) cheeks and lacks prom. buffy eyering (1 race of Swainson's may lack eyering in fall; Eisenmann). Also see Veery (8).

**Behavior:** Much like more numerous Swainson's Thrush but usually seen in damp low tangles or on ground.

**Status and habitat:** Apparently uncommon migrant (early Oct–early May) in forested or lightly wooded regions. Always greatly outnumbered by next sp.

**Range:** To 2600m. Throughout e and w of Andes. Breeds in N America and ne Siberia; winters mostly in n S America (to 3000m in Venez.) s to Ecuador, n Peru, and Brazil n of Amazon. Trinidad, Curaçao.

## 10. SWAINSON'S THRUSH
*Catharus ustulatus*

**Identification:** 7″ (18cm). Uniform brownish olive above (some birds almost russet); *cheeks and usually prom. eyering buffy*; below white; chest and sides buff liberally speckled dusky.

**Similar species:** See Gray-cheeked Thrush (9) and Veery (8). One race of Swainson's is grayer with less prom. eyering (eyering reportedly often absent in fall) and is easily confused with Gray-cheek; in hand, wing averages shorter (88-105 vs 97-109mm) than latter.

**Behavior:** Timid and usually seen singly near thick cover; sometimes accompanies mixed flocks. Mostly mid. story or lower, but well above ground; in migration very frugivorous, sometimes concentrating in large nos. near fruiting trees and shrubs. Sings weakly in late Mar and Apr.

**Status and habitat:** Most common migrant thrush; transient and winter resident, early Oct–late Apr, to forest, lighter woodland, and second growth. Its true nos. (esp. during local migratory build-ups) are better revealed through mist netting.

**Range:** To 2700m (sighting to 3000m, PN Chingaza 1979—W. McKay). Throughout e and w of Andes. Breeds in N America; winters mainly in S America s to n Argentina and w Brazil, a few in Costa Rica and Panama, rarely s Mexico(?).

## 11. WOOD THRUSH
*Hylocichla mustelina*

**Identification:** 7.5-8″ (19-20cm). Brown above becoming *bright rusty on crown and nape*, underparts white *boldly spotted black throughout*.

**Similar species:** Readily distinguished from 8, 9, and 10 by contrasting rufous crown and large round spots below.

**Status and habitat:** Accidental: 1 rec. on 6 Dec 1975, PN Katíos, nw Chocó at e base of Snía. del Darién (Rodríguez 1980). Reported early Oct–mid Apr in w and c Panama (Ridgely 1976).

**Range:** Breeds in e N America; winters from Mexico to Canal Zone, Panama, and Curaçao. Accidental to Guyana and Colombia.

## 12. YELLOW-LEGGED THRUSH
*Platycichla flavipes*  Pl. 43, Map 1147

**Identification:** 8.5″ (22cm). *Bill and legs bright yellow* (bill dusky with yellow ridge—♀). ♂: *mostly black with narrow yellow eyering*; back and rump slaty gray; *belly gray*. ♀: brownish olive above with *narrow yellow eyering*; below pale brownish buff; *throat streaked dusky; center of belly buffy white*. Eyes dark (both sexes).

**Similar species:** ♂ from ♂ Pale-eyed Thrush

(13) by dark eyes and grayish back and belly; ♀ from ♀ Pale-eyed by streaked throat, duller (less rufous brown) upperparts, and buffy white (not gray) belly. See larger Glossy-black (15) and Black-hooded thrushes (16).
**Voice:** Song a rambling, semimusical ser. with many *sweet to-weeea-speet*, and *swet to-weeea* phrases interspersed (P. Schwartz recording); mimicking reported in Trinidad (ffrench 1973) and se Brazil (T. Parker; R. Ridgely).
**Behavior:** Alone or in pairs from bushes and lower midlevels to canopy and like many neotropical thrushes, rather timid. Usually sings from treetops.
**Breeding:** 4 BC birds, and laying ♀, June, Norte de Santander (Carriker); Sept and Dec juvs., Norte de Santander (Nicéforo and Olivares 1976b). Trinidad nests, Mar–July; shallow, moss-covered, partially mud cup on bank or rock face; 2 eggs pale blue to greenish blue marked with reddish brown (ffrench 1973).
**Status and habitat:** Fairly common in forest borders, lighter woodland (esp. coffee plantations) and second growth; foothills and higher. Perhaps partially migratory.
**Range:** 600-1800m. Santa Marta Mts. and e slope of E Andes in Norte de Santander. Ne Colombia to Guyana, and adj. n Brazil; e Brazil to ne Argentina. Trinidad.

## 13. PALE-EYED THRUSH
*Platycichla leucops*　　　　Pl. 43, Map 1148
**Identification:** 8″ (20cm). ♂: *bill and legs yellow; eyes bluish white* (no distinct eyering); *otherwise entirely lustrous black.* ♀: dark brown above; sides of head and underparts paler brown becoming *grayish buff on lower breast and belly*; sides tinged rufescent; under wing coverts cinnamon rufous; bill and eyes dark, narrow yellow eyering; legs dull yellowish brown. Imm. ♂: dark brown, blacker above, esp. on wings and tail; conspic. buff spotting on wing coverts and underparts; eyes pale blue (R. Ridgely).
**Similar species:** ♂ is only all black Colombian thrush with white eyes; ♀ is darker than ♀ Yellow-legged Thrush (12), lacks streaking on throat, and has belly grayish (not buffy white). Also see Glossy-black Thrush (15).
**Voice:** Song a disjointed, somewhat musical ser., *wheero-weet, chup-e, ez-t, e-ta, ti't, eez, cheur-ez-weet* . . . , quite var. and with many very high thin notes (P. Schwartz recording).
**Behavior:** Very wary and usually difficult to see; singly or in pairs in lower or mid. story, less often subcanopy. Not with mixed forest flocks (Hilty) but sometimes aggregate with other spp. at fruiting trees in canopy; sing from canopy (R. Ridgely).
**Breeding:** BC ♂, May, Huila (Carriker). Pair

with food, June, Anchicayá Val.; stub-tailed juv., June, n Venez. (Hilty).
**Status and habitat:** Uncommon (easily overlooked) and poss. also local in humid and wet forest (esp. mossy forest) and taller, denser, second growth woodland.
**Range:** 1300-2000m; to 900m on Pacific slope in Valle. Both slopes W Andes in Valle, upper Magdalena Val. in Huila, e slope of E Andes in Meta and in Macarena Mts. N Venez. s through Andes (e and w Ecuador) to Bolivia; tepuis of s Venez., n Brazil, and Guyana.

## 14. GREAT THRUSH
*Turdus fuscater*　　　　Pl. 43, Map 1149
**Identification:** 13″ (33cm). *Large. Bill and legs orange. Uniform dark grayish brown above with narrow orange eyering*; wings and tail darker, underparts paler (or more olive brown throughout—*gigas*; or lower breast and belly whitish—*opertaneus*). ♀♀(?) and younger birds may lack orange eyering. Juv.: paler, mottled with black and buff.
**Similar species:** Noticeably larger and sootier (not black) than other "black" thrushes. Flight silhouette can bring to mind a small accipiter.
**Voice:** Noisy. Calls incl. a robinlike *sée-ert*, a loud *kuet-kuet-kuet-kuet*, and waxwinglike *eeeee* (Hilty); also a loud *chee-yop* (often in flight) ending in choked off squeak (J. Silliman). Seldom heard song a var. ser. of 1-3 robinlike phrases followed by a high, nearly inaudible note (B. Coffee recording).
**Breeding:** 7 BC birds, Jan–Aug, Perijá Mts. and Andes (Carriker); 2 fledglings, Jan, e Boyacá (Borrero 1955); carrying food n of Bogotá, Sept (Hilty); family groups, May, PN Puracé (J. Silliman); 1 nest Apr, nw Venez.; very large bulky cup low in shrub; 2 eggs pale greenish blue, spotted darker, chiefly at larger end (Sclater and Salvin 1879).
**Behavior:** Conspic. and familiar above 2000m *throughout the highlands.* Single birds, pairs, or families hop on ground, esp. in grassy pastures, drop to ground from low bush or visit fruiting trees.
**Status and habitat:** Very common in open, "cultivated" highlands with hedgerows, short grassy pastures, and brushy slopes; sometimes in isolated patches of brush or *Polylepis* far above treeline.
**Range:** 1400-4100m (seldom below 2000m). Santa Marta Mts. (*cacozelus*); Perijá Mts. (*clarus*); E Andes from Norte de Santander s at least to Cundinamarca (*gigas*); n part of W Andes in Antioquia (*opertaneus*); rest of W Andes, entire C Andes to both slopes in Nariño (*quindio*). Nw Venez. s in Andes to Bolivia.

## 15. GLOSSY-BLACK THRUSH
*Turdus serranus*                   Pl. 43. M 1150
**Identification:** 10″ (25cm). ♂: bill and legs orange yellow; otherwise *uniform lustrous black with narrow orange eyering and dark eye.* ♀: plain brown to olivaceous brown above, tail slightly darker; *narrow yellowish eyering*; buffy brown below; under wing coverts ochraceous; bill and legs dull yellowish brown; eyes dark.
**Similar species:** Great Thrush (14) is obviously larger and much dingier than ♂ Glossy-black; ♀ from smaller ♀ Yellow-legged Thrush (12) by unstreaked throat and darker (not buffy white) belly; from ♀ Pale-eyed Thrush (13) by more prom. eyering and brownish (not grayish) belly. Also see ♀ Black-hooded Thrush (16).
**Voice:** Song a *very fast* warbled *tee-do-dede-dodéet* or *e-te-je'te-o-ét*, shrill, rising slightly, and often monotonously repeated at short intervals (P. Schwartz recording; Hilty).
**Behavior:** Like many thrushes, shy and inconspic. Single birds or pairs in mid. story to canopy; ♂♂ sing persistently (Feb–late July in W Andes) from treetops, there often exposed and seen more than ♀♀. Usually not with mixed flocks.
**Breeding:** 5 BC birds, Mar–Aug, Perijá Mts. and C Andes (Carriker). In W Andes above Cali, Apr nest (Miller 1963), building nest, May, nest with eggs, July, stub-tailed fledgling, Oct, older fledglings, Nov (S. Gniadek); mossy cup low in vine tangle; 2 pale blue eggs spotted purple and light brown.
**Status and habitat:** Fairly common in humid forest, forest edge, and older second growth woodland (not open areas); can be seen in remaining woodlots and patches of forest above Cali.
**Range:** 1400-2800m (sightings to 1000m, Sept–Oct, Anchicayá Valley). Perijá Mts. and all 3 Andean ranges (e slope E Andes only reported in Norte de Santander). N Venez. s in Andes (both e and w Ecuador) to n Bolivia and nw Argentina.

## 16. BLACK-HOODED THRUSH
*Turdus olivater*                   Pl. 43, Map 1151
**Identification:** 9″ (23cm). ♂: bill yellow, legs dull yellow; *entire head and upper breast black* (forms hood); narrow yellow eyering; otherwise olive brown above and *sandy buff below with blackish tail* (or sim. but lower underparts light brownish olive—*sanctaemartae*; or head and throat black, chest pale brown, rest of underparts sandy buff—*caucae*). ♀ like ♂ but black replaced by brown giving faint indication of ♂'s hood; bill dusky, legs yellowish brown (bill yellow—*caucae*).

**Similar species:** ♂'s black hood distinctive; easily confused ♀ is paler and buffier below than ♀ *Platycichla* or Glossy-black Thrush (12, 13, 15); look for ♀'s *subtle brownish hood.* Also see Clay-colored Thrush (23), mainly a lowland bird, and Pale-breasted Thrush (18).
**Voice:** Song a *Turdus*-like, full-bodied caroling; *too-doo, too-dee*, and *chur-dee* phrases often separated by high thin *ee'ee* notes (P. Schwartz recording).
**Behavior:** Like other *Turdus* but less wary than most; lower story to canopy.
**Breeding:** 14 BC birds, Jan–June, 2 juvs., July, Santa Marta and Perijá mts. (Carriker); 1 Santa Marta nest, May; mud and moss cup; eggs like White-necked Thrush's but larger and more heavily marked (Todd and Carriker 1922).
**Status and habitat:** Fairly common in Santa Marta Mts. in humid forest, forest borders, and lighter woodland (esp. coffee); no recent recs. in sw Colombia.
**Range:** 1200-2300m. Santa Marta Mts. (*sanctaemartae*); Perijá Mts. and e slope of E Andes in Norte de Santander (*olivater*); sw slope of C Andes at headwaters of Patía Val. (La Sierra, 2000m) and Cauca Val. headwaters at Urubamba s of Popayán (*caucae*). Colombia to n Venez.; tepuis of s Venez. and adj. Brazil and Guyana.

## 17. CHESTNUT-BELLIED THRUSH
*Turdus fulviventris*                   Pl. 43, Map 1152
**Identification:** 10″ (25cm). Bill yellow; narrow eyering orange. *Head and upper throat black*, throat somewhat streaked gray; otherwise dark gray above with blackish tail; *chest pale gray; breast and upper belly orange rufous*; under tail coverts grayish. ♀ sim. but throat dusky gray mottled paler.
**Similar species:** Only Colombian thrush with bright orange rufous breast; bears a remarkable resemblance to N American Robin (*T. migratorius*).
**Voice:** Song a notably var. ser. of choppy phrases, somewhat *Turdus*-like but with many trills and buzzes, *che'e'e-chert chee-rt-ee e'r'r', chuwurt, titi, t't't, eet* . . . (P. Schwartz recording); call a wooden *peent.*
**Behavior:** Sim. to its n ally *T. migratorius* but usually in more forested regions. Occurs at almost all hts. from ground, where often hops into small openings or along roadsides, to the canopy where sings and eats fruit.
**Breeding:** BC ♂ and juv., June, w Putumayo (Lehmann 1960a); 8 BC birds, Apr–Aug, and 2 juvs., July, Perijá Mts. (Carriker).
**Status and habitat:** Common in w Putumayo in mossy forest ("cloud forest") and forest edge, esp. on steep hillsides; also tall second growth

and shrubby disturbed areas. Not well known elsewhere in Colombia.

**Range:** 1700-2300m. Perijá Mts. and spottily on both slopes of E Andes at n end, head of Magdalena Val. and e slope of Andes in Putumayo and e Nariño. Nw Venez. s in Andes to Peru.

## 18. PALE-BREASTED THRUSH

*Turdus leucomelas*                    Pl. 43, Map 1153

**Identification:** 9.5″ (24cm). *Pale olive brown above contrasting with gray head and nape*; ear coverts finely streaked whitish; throat white streaked dark brown; breast and sides pale buffy gray; *center of belly and crissum white*; under wing coverts cinnamon rufous; bill yellowish brown.

**Similar species:** From Black-billed Thrush (19) and other brownish thrushes by contrast between head and back, also by decided *olive* tinge to back; bill paler than 19 and throat streaks more contrasty. White-necked Thrush (25) has a streaked throat but can always be told by white crescent on lower throat (prom. if seen but as with many shyer neotropical *Turdus*, often faces away). Also see Pale-vented Thrush (22).

**Voice:** Song a pleasant carol reminiscent of American Robin (*T. migratorius*), the phrases *hereit, hereit, tuweeee* or *tuwee, tuwee* are prom.; alarm *zit*, usually doubled, sometimes trebled; and guttural *quwaak*.

**Behavior:** Like more common Black-billed Thrush but favors more wooded regions.

**Breeding:** 3 BC birds, June–Aug, n Colombia (Carriker); BC birds, Jan, Feb, and Apr; young in May, ne Meta (S. Furniss); building nest, Mar, Santa Marta region (Brown); in July, Guárico, Venez. (Thomas 1979b); Surinam all yr.; moss and rootlet cup in shrub, tree, or on building; 2-3 eggs, bluish green spotted reddish brown (Haverschmidt 1968).

**Status and habitat:** Drier open woodland, gallery forest, plantations, and gardens (but usually with some heavier cover nearby); forest edge in more humid regions. Seldom very numerous though fairly common in Santa Marta foothills near Minca.

**Range:** To 1600m. Santa Marta region, Snía. Macuira, Guajira, Perijá Mts. (2000m) and s to lower Cauca and upper Magdalena vals.; e of Andes s to s Meta (Macarena Mts.) and Río Vichada. Ne Colombia, Venez., and the Guianas s to ne Argentina and Paraguay (no Ecuador recs.).

## 19. BLACK-BILLED THRUSH

*Turdus ignobilis*                    Pl. 43, Map 1154

**Identification:** 9.5″ (24cm). *Dingy with black bill. Uniform dark dull brown to dull olive brown above*;

throat white streaked dusky, gradually becoming pale olive brown on breast; center of belly and under tail coverts white; under wing coverts pale buff (or throat white sharply streaked dusky with narrow whitish band across lower throat; breast paler and grayer—*debilis*).

**Similar species:** One of the dullest and dingiest Colombian thrushes; often confusing. The *debilis* subsp. most like White-necked Thrush (25) but grayer, lacks strong contrast between upper and underparts (White-necked is brown above, grayish below), throat *much* less boldly streaked black, white band at base of throat smaller and less conspic., and under wing coverts pale buff (not gray). At close range White-necked has inconspic. red eyering. Also see Pale-breasted (18) and Pale-vented thrushes (22); w of W Andes White-throated Thrush (26).

**Voice:** Uninspired caroling song is *Turdus*-like but subdued, often introduced by a *wert* note and with *your-your-we* phrases frequently inserted.

**Behavior:** Widespread and conspic. in settled areas where it is the Colombian replacement of the American Robin (*T. migratorius*) of temperate N America. Individuals or pairs hop on ground, lawns, etc., in open areas; up in bushes or trees in less open areas.

**Breeding:** 8 BC birds, Dec–Aug, W and C Andes (Carriker); 10 nests Feb–May (Miller 1963; Wallace 1965); 2 nests, Aug and Oct, mid. and upper Cauca Val. (Hilty; S. Gniadek). Coarse cup, usually with mud, low in bush, tree or stump; 2 blue eggs heavily marked brown.

**Status and habitat:** Common in clearings, parks, gardens, and lighter woodland, occas. humid forest or forest edge. Replaced in Carib. region by *T. grayi*.

**Range:** To 2800m (mainly 900-2100m w of E Andes). Cauca Val. from Quindío s to Cauca and cleared or drier vals. on Pacific slope from n Antioquia s to Cauca (*goodfellowi*); w slope C Andes in Antioquia and Caldas and Magdalena Val. from Santander to s Huila (*ignobilis*); e slope of E Andes in Norte de Santander and Boyacá, and spottily e of Andes throughout to s Amazonas (*debilis*). Colombia to Surinam and s to n Bolivia and Amazonian Brazil.

## 20. LAWRENCE'S THRUSH

*Turdus lawrencii*                    Map 1155

**Identification:** 9″ (23cm). *Bill bright yellow* (♂); or dusky (♀ and imm.). Uniform dark grayish brown above, wings and tail dusky; dull brown to olivaceous brown below, paler than back; throat buffy white streaked black; *belly and* *under tail coverts white*; under wing coverts cinnamon.

**Similar species:** Most like Bare-eyed Thrush (24), but no bare ocular area, and known range in Colombia does not overlap. ♂ from other Colombian *Turdus* by combination of bright yellow bill and white crissum, but *best known by song*. ♀ from Black-billed Thrush (19; *debilis* race) by lack of white crescent beneath streaked throat; ♀ in the hand from Pale-vented Thrush (22) by heavier and blacker streaks on throat, dusky (not brown) tail, and no russet tinge above.

**Voice:** An astoundingly *accomplished mimic, surpassing any other New World sp.*; loud, deliberate ser. of vocal imitations, with short interval pauses, often continues uninterrupted for 30 min or more, only occas. incl. nonmimic phrases (see J. D. Frisch, Bird Songs from Brazil).

**Behavior:** ♂♂ sing from high perch in tall forest canopy or subcanopy where extremely difficult to detect, even when singing; occas. with mixed flocks (Hilty). Typically feeds in damp leaf litter on ground but *usually noted* in canopy on one of its regular song perches (T. Parker).

**Status and habitat:** Known from 1 specimen near Leticia taken in 1976 (Morales 1979) and 2 specimens from San Antonio (near Pto. Asís), w Putumayo, 400m (Fitzpatrick and Willard 1982). Several widely scattered birds seen near Mitú in humid *terra firme* forest (1978—Hilty). Poss. local. In se Peru, in *várzea* forest, or near streams in *terra firme* forest (T. Parker).

**Range:** To 400m. W Putumayo s to Amazonas (confluence of Caño Cabinas and Río Amacayacú nw of Leticia), and Vaupés (sight). S. Venez., ne and w Amazonian Brazil, e Ecuador, and e Peru (incl. Pebas).

## 21. COCOA THRUSH

*Turdus fumigatus*                        Map 1156

**Identification:** 9″ (23cm). Bill brown. *Mostly uniform rufous brown*, paler below; throat buffy white streaked dark brown; center of abdomen white; *under tail coverts dull cinnamon brown*.

**Similar species:** Much more rufescent above and below than any other Colombian *Turdus*. See Pale-vented Thrush (22).

**Voice:** Song a ser. of loud, musical, mostly rapidly repeated phrases with much var.; also a rapid *wee-a-wee-a-wee-a* . . . descending slightly; alarm a harsh *kik-ik-ik-ik*; sings mostly when breeding in Trinidad (ffrench 1973).

**Behavior:** Pairs are usually seen hopping on ground or in lower forest levels, occas. quite high. Inconspic. and somewhat retiring.

**Breeding:** BC pair, Aug, e Norte de Santander (Carriker). Yr.-round in Trinidad; bulky plant

and mud cup up to 5m up on trunk, stump, or niche in bank; 2-4 eggs, pale greenish blue marked with pale reddish brown (Snow and Snow 1963).

**Status and habitat:** Lighter woodland, gallery forest, and humid *terra firme* and *várzea* forests.

**Range:** 100-1400m. E of Andes in Norte de Santander at Palogordo (s of Cúcuta) and Petrólea (*aquilonalis*). The Guianas and n and e Venez. to Amazonian se Brazil and e Bolivia; many Carib. isls.

**Note:** By some considered conspecific with *T. obsoletus* (Pale-vented Thrush) of Costa Rica to w Ecuador and from se Colombia to the upper Río Negro drainage; birds from the latter region (*T. o. hauxwelli*) are of uncertain affinity.

## 22. PALE-VENTED THRUSH

*Turdus obsoletus*              Pl. 43, Map 1157

**Identification:** 9″ (23cm). Bill blackish. *Mostly uniform russet brown to warm brown* above and below, slightly duller below with *contrasting white belly and under tail coverts* (or under tail coverts white tinged buffy—*orinocensis*); throat lightly streaked dusky; under wing coverts cinnamon ochraceous.

**Similar species:** Much less rufescent than Cocoa Thrush (21) and with white or white tinged buff (not dull cinnamon brown) under tail coverts. Black-billed Thrush (19) is duller and grayer, lacks bright under wing coverts (usually conspic. in flight), and sings infrequently. Also see ♀ Lawrence's and Pale-breasted thrushes (20, 18).

**Voice:** In Panama, song resembles that of Clay-colored Thrush but faster, less rich and interspersed with *chrrr*'s and squeaky notes (Ridgely 1976).

**Behavior:** A timid and inconspic. thrush of the forest interior. Keeps mainly in midlevels or a little higher, usually alone, sometimes accompanying mixed flocks.

**Breeding:** Apr nest, W Andes above Cali; 2 eggs (S. Gniadek).

**Status and habitat:** Uncommon and perhaps local in humid and wet forest, gallery forest, and occas. forest edge; foothills and lower slopes in Andes; in lowlands only e of Andes.

**Range:** To 1900m w of Andes; below 500m e of Andes. W shore of Gulf of Urabá, Panama border (*obsoletus*); Pacific slope from Valle southward (*parambanus*); mid. Cauca Val. in Valle and upper Patía Val. in Cauca (*colombianus*); upper Magdalena Val. (subsp.?); e of Andes from Arauca s to Macarena Mts., e to Vichada (Río Orinoco) and prob. e Guainía (*orinocensis*); Vaupés (Mitú) s to Amazonas and

undoubtedly Putumayo (*hauxwelli*). Costa Rica to w Ecuador; Venez. (Amazonas and llanos), e Peru, w Amazonian Brazil, and n Bolivia.
**Note:** Taxonomy follows Meyer de Schauensee and Phelps (1978) in treating *orinocensis* as a subsp. of *T. obsoletus*, although described by Zimmer and Phelps (1955) as a subsp. of *T. fumigatus* (Cocoa Thrush) and not differentiated earlier from *hauxwelli*. The classification of the var. thrush populations assigned to *T. obsoletus* or to *T. fumigatus*, following Meyer de Schauensee (1966, modified in 1978) is tentative. *T. hauxwelli* may be a separate sp.

## 23. CLAY-COLORED THRUSH
*Turdus grayi*                     Pl. 43, Map 1158
**Identification:** 9.5″ (24cm). *Bill yellow olive.* Dull olive brown above; *virtually uniform pale buffy brown below* with inconspic. dusky streaks on throat. Imm.: sim. but faintly spotted below, wing coverts spotted buff. Bill dusky.
**Similar species:** Pale-breasted Thrush (18) has gray head contrasting with olive brown upperparts; very sim. ♀ Black-hooded Thrush (16) is darker with dusky (not yellowish green) bill and is mainly a highland bird.
**Voice:** Song, often heard even through the heat of the day, a pleasant caroling much like American Robin (*T. migratorius*) but smoother and mellower (Slud 1964); most characteristic call a peculiar ascending, nasal, *quierre.*
**Behavior:** Much like its well-known n relative, the American Robin, though only infrequently seen on ground and less conspic.
**Breeding:** 5 BC birds, Mar–May, n Colombia (Carriker). In c Panama mainly dry season Dec–late Apr (Morton 1971). Cup nest of mud and plant material, usually rather low; 3 greenish blue eggs heavily marked shades of brown (Skutch 1960).
**Status and habitat:** Uncommon to fairly common in cultivated areas with scattered trees, around habitations, or in open thinned woodland and forest edge; favors drier and more semiopen zones. Rare or absent on n side Santa Marta Mts.
**Range:** To 300m. Gulf of Urabá to e tip of Guajira (Snía. de Macuira) s to lower Cauca and mid. Magdalena vals. in s Bolívar. S Texas to n Colombia.

## 24. BARE-EYED THRUSH
*Turdus nudigenis*                Pl. 43, Map 1159
**Identification:** 9.5″ (24cm). Bill olive yellow. Brownish olive above with *large bare orange yellow ocular area*; below brownish olive, paler than above; throat white streaked dusky; center of belly and under tail coverts white. In worn plumage much grayer.

**Similar species:** From any other *Turdus* by conspic. bare ocular area. Likely in same habitat as 18 and 19.
**Voice:** Very melodious song a pleasing *Turdus*-like carol; call a distinctive, nasal, catlike *meow.*
**Behavior:** Mostly arboreal though occas. on ground, hopping as do other *Turdus.* Often in flowering or fruiting trees but seldom in groups.
**Breeding:** 1 BC ♀, Aug, ne Meta (S. Furniss); 1 in May, Boyacá, 1500m (Olivares 1963; July–Sept breeding Guárico, Venez. (Thomas 1979b); in Orinoco, May–June; nest is usual *Turdus* cup of mud and plant material; 2-3 pale greenish blue eggs speckled and blotched reddish (Cherrie 1916).
**Status and habitat:** Gallery forest borders and semiopen areas with scattered groves of trees, occas. lawns and gardens. Seldom numerous.
**Range:** To 1600m. E Norte de Santander (Catatumbo lowlands), e slope E Andes in Boyacá (to 1500m), Cundinamarca (Choachí, 1600m), and Meta; lowlands e of Andes from Arauca to s Meta (Macarena Mts.) and Río Orinoco (Maipures). E Colombia e to the Guianas and ne Amazonian Brazil; ne Peru. Trinidad; Tobago; Lesser Antilles.

## 25. WHITE-NECKED THRUSH
*Turdus albicollis*               Pl. 43, Map 1160
**Identification:** 9″ (23cm). Bill dark. Dark brown above; *throat white boldly streaked dark brown; white continuing below streaks as a prom. crescent-shaped band across lower throat and upper chest;* breast and sides pale grayish brown, center of belly and under tail coverts white; under wing coverts gray. Very narrow eyering red.
**Similar species:** See Black-billed Thrush (19), esp. *debilis* subsp. e of Andes, which is dingier, lacks boldly marked throat (black streaks less distinct and white patch smaller) and shows less contrast between upper and underparts. Also cf. 18, 20-24, all of which overlap in portions of range.
**Voice:** E of Andes, *Turdus*-like song a simple, monotonously repeated ser. of *paired* phrases, *two-e-o, two-ee,* melancholy, lazy and var. only slightly in pitch but remarkably rich and pleasing; alarm at Mitú a rough *jjig-wig,* or *jjig-wig-wig.*
**Behavior:** Rather secretive and hard to see, remaining in forest undergrowth, or sometimes to forest midlevels. Reg. on forest floor where may follow army ants. Usually single birds or pairs, and commonly sought as a cage bird for its pleasing song.
**Breeding:** BC ♂, June, Norte de Santander (Carriker). Yr.-round in Trinidad, Mar–June

peak; nest as in other *Turdus*; 2-3 pale greenish blue eggs marked shades of brown (Todd and Carriker 1922; Snow and Snow 1963).
**Status and habitat:** Fairly common (easily overlooked but for song) in humid *terra firme* and *várzea* forests, sometimes forest edge.
**Range:** Santa Marta and Perijá mts. (to 1500m); w slope E Andes at n end, Guamalito, Norte de Santander (1500m); e of Andes (to 1000m) from Norte de Santander and Vichada s to Vaupés and se Nariño; Amazonas (no specimens). Generally e of Andes to ne Argentina, Paraguay, and se Brazil.
**Note:** Some incl. *T. assimilis* (White-throated Thrush) of Mid. America to w Ecuador with this sp.

## 26. WHITE-THROATED THRUSH

*Turdus assimilis* Map 1161
**Identification:** 9″ (23cm). Bill yellowish. Sim. to White-necked Thrush, but breast and sides duller, darker brown (not pale grayish brown), and ranges do not overlap.
**Similar species:** Only robin-sized thrush in its range with a prom. white crescent on throat. Cf. 19, 22, and 23.
**Voice:** Song a loud and exceptionally melodic, robinlike caroling. Also a distinctive short, guttural, or nasal *enk* or *urrrk*, almost froglike in quality, and a scratchy *dzee-yoo* (Ridgely 1976).
**Behavior:** Sim. in many respects to White-necked Thrush; but unlike it, much less secretive, often easily seen, and reg. rises up into fruiting trees, or to sing.
**Breeding:** 4 BC birds, Mar–Apr, Chocó (Carriker).
**Status and habitat:** Fairly common in humid and wet forest edges, taller second growth, clearings, and cultivated areas.
**Range:** To 900m. W of W Andes from Panama border and lower Atrato Val. (e to Mutatá, Antioquia) southward (*daguae*). N Mexico to nw Ecuador.
**Note:** By some merged with *T. albicollis* (White-necked Thrush) of Santa Marta area and e of Andes, but calls and song differ. Birds from Darién, Panama to nw Ecuador *T. daguae* (Dagua Thrush) have also been considered a separate sp.

# GNATCATCHERS, GNATWRENS, OLD WORLD WARBLERS: Sylviidae (5)

Gnatcatchers and gnatwrens are the only Neotropical members of this large Old World family, but their taxonomic position is still in doubt. The gnatwrens were formerly placed with the antbirds, while the gnatcatchers have usually been placed with Old World warblers (Sylviidae). Some have placed both American genera in the family Polioptilidae or have placed them in the subfamily Polioptilinae including them with thrushes (Turdinae), Old World warblers (Sylviinae), and others in the enlarged family Muscicapidae. Gnatcatchers are spritely, warblerlike birds of middle and upper level foliage in lighter woodland and shrubs. Gnatwrens, in contrast, are found in lower foliage, often inside forest, and are less conspicuous. Nests of all three American genera are, as far as known, small well-formed cups. All are insectivorous.

## 1. COLLARED GNATWREN

*Microbates collaris* Pl. 42, Map 1162
**Identification:** 4.2″ (10.7cm). Wrenlike with *long bill; short tail usually cocked*. Uniform warm brown above; long white eyestripe; sides of head white with *black stripe behind eye and long black malar stripe; underparts white crossed by broad black chest band*; flanks tinged grayish brown.
**Similar species:** Easily recognized by long bill, boldly striped head pattern, and black chest band. See Banded Antbird (p 396); in foothills at e base of E Andes next sp.
**Voice:** Song a high, thin, drawn out *eeeeea* repeated every 4-5 sec for long periods (at a distance like song of Slaty-capped Shrike-Vireo); harsh *jipp* scold.
**Behavior:** A perky and animated little bird that constantly wags its cocked tail and is often curious but can still be difficult to see. Sallies to ground, flits to foliage, or stretches its neck to pick from leaves or poke curled dead ones as works through lower vines and tangles in undergrowth. Pairs or families and sometimes with mixed flocks (Hilty; Oniki and Willis 1972).
**Breeding:** At Manaus, Brazil, a bulky cup nest of dead leaves near forest floor; 2 white eggs with a few dark spots (Oniki and Willis 1979).
**Status and habitat:** Low in humid *terra firme* forest, occas. forest edge. Common at Mitú, Vaupés. May meet allied *M. cinereiventris* in hills at base of Andes.
**Range:** To 500m. E of Andes from w Caquetá (Florencia) and Vaupés (Mitú) s to w Putumayo and Amazonas (Leticia). Rec. on e

boundary of Guainía (Victorina). Fr. Guiana, Surinam, s Venez. (s of Río Ventuari, Amazonas), and n Brazil.

## 2. HALF-COLLARED (TAWNY-FACED) GNATWREN

*Microbates cinereiventris*      Pl. 42, Map 1163
**Identification:** 4″ (10.2cm). Wrenlike. Long slender bill; *stubby tail usually cocked up.* Warm brown above; *sides of head and neck bright cinnamon* (with black postocular streak—*cinereiventris*); throat white bordered on sides by *black malar*; rest of underparts gray with *broken collar of short black streaks across chest*; abdomen tinged brownish.
**Similar species:** In dim light of forest undergrowth can be confused with several wrens, esp. Nightingale Wren (p 539) but from any by partial black chest collar. Long-billed Gnatwren (3) is usually higher in undergrowth. At e base of E Andes see Collared Gnatwren (1).
**Voice:** Song a high, thin, drawn out *teeeeea*, repeated over and over, sometimes preceded by a few rough nasal *jik, jik, jik* scolds; also a rapid chatter.
**Behavior:** Sim. to Collared Gnatwren e of Andes but seems more difficult to see.
**Breeding:** 11 BC birds, Dec–May, n Antioquia to n Chocó (Carriker); ad. with food, 10 Apr, upper Anchicayá Val. (Hilty); bulky plant material cup low in undergrowth, Apr, Costa Rica; 2 white eggs with reddish and dark brown dots, more at larger end (Kiff 1977).
**Status and habitat:** Fairly common to common (easily overlooked) in humid and wet forest.
**Range:** To 900m (sightings to 1000m Anchicayá Val.—Hilty). W side of Gulf of Urabá (*semitorquatus*); entire Pacific coast (*cinereiventris*); upper Sinú e in humid lowlands n of Andes to Río Nechi (*albapiculus*); mid. Magdalena Val. from Snía. San Lucas, s Bolívar s to Pto. Berrío, e Antioquia (*magdalenae*); e base of Andes near Mámbita, e Cundinamarca (*unicus*); w Putumayo and se Nariño (*hormotus*). Nicaragua to w Ecuador; e Colombia to s Peru (incl. mouth of Río Curaray).
**Note:** For revision of subsp. see Olson (1980a).

## 3. LONG-BILLED GNATWREN

*Ramphocaenus melanurus*      Pl. 42, Map 1164
**Identification:** 5″ (13cm). *Very long, thin, straight bill; longish* tail usually cocked up. Light brown above with rufescent tinge on crown; sides of head and neck strongly washed cinnamon; *underparts buffy white*, throat whiter with faint dusky streaks extending onto chest; narrow graduated tail blackish, outer feathers tipped white.

**Similar species:** Easily told by extraordinarily long bill and animated blackish tail. No wren has such a *long* bill.
**Voice:** Song in s Córdoba a loud antbirdlike *wheit-wheit-wheit-wheit-wheit-wheit*, often preceded by *chert, chert-sweet,* or *skee-er,* or other phrases; also a slowly rising trill, *tic-tic-tre-e-e-e-e-e* (Valle), and rapid vibrating *tre-ee-ee-ee-ee-ee-* on 1 pitch.
**Behavior:** A droll bird with perpetually wagging and uptilted tail. Pairs or families call back and forth and extend their necks to peck prey from leaves as actively work through vine tangles and dense foliage 2-10m up. Sometimes follow mixed flocks.
**Breeding:** 12 BC birds, Dec–July, nw Colombia (Carriker); 1 in Sept, Bolívar (MCN); 2 Venez. nests, June, low in dense tangles; grassy cup with hairlike, black fiber lining; 2 white eggs spotted reddish brown mostly at larger end (Skutch 1968).
**Status and habitat:** Fairly common (common, s Córdoba) in moist to humid forest borders, lighter woodland, and shrubby areas; inside *terra firme* and *várzea* forests and usually near tangled openings.
**Range:** To 1500m (once to 2700m? above Medellín). Upper Río Sinú e to w Guajira, s in Cauca Val. to Valle (Miraflores; sight—Pichindé), and s in Magdalena Val. to latitude of Bogotá; w of W Andes in n Antioquia (Río Sucio) and lower Río Calima, Valle; e base of E Andes from Norte de Santander to w Meta and Macarena Mts.; perhaps locally to Río Orinoco and sightings (Hilty) near Leticia, Amazonas. S Mexico to nw Ecuador (Esmeraldas), the Guianas, and Venez. s to ne Peru and Bolivia, Amazonian and e Brazil.

## 4. TROPICAL GNATCATCHER

*Polioptila plumbea*      Pl. 42, Map 1165
**Identification:** 4.5″ (11.4cm). Slender with thin bill and long cocked tail. ♂: *crown and nape to eyes glossy black* (with white eyebrow—*bilineata*); otherwise blue gray above; remiges blackish, *inner ones edged white;* tail black, outer feathers white (tail all white from below); *cheeks, sides of head, and underparts white with gray tinge on breast and sides.* ♀: sim. but no black cap.
**Similar species:** ♀ not unlike Bicolored Conebill (p 589) but more spritely with longer, white-edged tail usually held cocked up. Hooded Tanager (p 633) is more robust, with spectacles, yellow legs, and different behavior. Also see Slate-throated Gnatcatcher (5) and very sim. Guianan Gnatcatcher (see note below).
**Voice:** Frequent call a petulant mewing *meaa;* song a clear, high-pitched, rhythmic *peet, peet,*

*peet peeti peeti, ti'ti'pee, pee pee* or sim. var., usually rising then falling slightly in pitch.
**Behavior:** A saucy little bird with a constantly twitching tail. Pairs glean from terminal twigs or leaves by working along upper limbs of smaller trees (esp. dry areas) or in canopy in humid forested areas and are often notably fearless. Reg. follow insectivorous bird flocks.
**Breeding:** 10 BC birds, Mar–Oct, n Colombia (Carriker); sw Ecuador nests, Feb–Apr (Marchant 1960); Orinoco area, fledgling, 20 June (Cherrie 1916). Dainty moss and lichen cup nest saddled on limb about 2-8m up; 2-3 white eggs speckled with brown.
**Status and habitat:** Widespread in lighter, drier woodland, scrubby areas, and arid scrub; less numerous in humid forest borders, incl. *várzea*.
**Range:** To 1600m. Pacific coast (mainly mangroves), upper Sinú Val. n across Carib. lowlands to w base Santa Marta Mts. s to s Bolívar (*bilineata*); Dagua and upper Patía vals., poss. Cauca Val. in Antioquia and Valle (*daguae*); drier mid. and upper Magdalena Val. s to Huila (*anteocularis*); Guajira, upper Cesar Val., and e of Andes from Norte de Santander s to ne Meta, (Carimagua—S. Furniss; *plumbiceps*); e Vichada (Maipures) and ne Guainía (sightings Pto. Inírida—Hilty and M. Robbins). Prob. locally throughout e of Andes (sight, Monkey Isl., Amazonas, May 1976—R. Ridgely; mouth of Río Javarí, Brazil, Aug 1979—Hilty et al; and Limoncocha, Ecuador). Se Mexico to w Peru, e Ecuador, n Amazonian and se Brazil, and the Guianas.
**Note:** Guianan Gnatcatcher (*P. guianensis*) of the Guianas, s Venez. s of Río Ventuari, adj. ne Brazil (upper Río Negro) and s Brazil, may occur in e Guainía, Colombia (rec. in Venez. opp. mouth of Río Guainía). ♂: very like ♀ Tropical Gnatcatcher but *cheeks, lower throat, and breast gray*, inner remiges edged gray (not

white), and with prom. *white eyering.* ♀: facial area paler with indistinct whitish postocular streak.

### 5. SLATE-THROATED GNATCATCHER
*Polioptila schistaceigula*          Pl. 42, Map 1166
**Identification:** 4″ (10.2cm). Slender and spritely with long cocked tail. *Upperparts blackish slate*; sides of head gray; lores and eyering whitish; *throat and breast gray; lower breast to vent white*; under tail coverts and tail blackish. Birds from n Antioquia (Valdivia), Valle, and nw Ecuador have sides of head, throat, and chest much lighter, med. to pale gray with some white mottling on throat, whitish mottling on sides of head, and faint whitish eyebrow (undescribed subsp.? age or sexual difference?).
**Similar species:** Blackish upperparts will distinguish it from Tropical Gnatcatcher (4). Pale birds recall Gray-mantled Wren (p 532), which is also notably arboreal. Latter differs most obviously in white bars on underside of tail and uniform white underparts.
**Voice:** Call a nasal mewing much like that of Tropical Gnatcatcher.
**Behavior:** Sim. to Tropical Gnatcatcher but mainly midlevel or lower in trees and less confiding. Normally follows bird flocks., esp. mixed tanager and honeycreeper flocks.
**Status and habitat:** Wet forest, forest edges, and tall second growth woodland. Seldom numerous and poss. local.
**Range:** To 1000m; to 500m (sightings) in Anchicayá Val. Pacific coast from c Chocó (sighting, Quibdó Mar 1978—Hilty) to Valle, northernmost end of W Andes to lower Cauca and mid. Magdalena vals. (se of Barrancabermeja, w Santander). One questionable rec. from e base of E Andes in Cundinamarca (Mámbita). C Panama to nw Ecuador.

# PIPITS, WAGTAILS: Motacillidae (2)

In the New World two species of wagtails breed in Alaska and one also in Greenland; otherwise only pipits occur in the Americas. Pipits are trim, slender-bodied, terrestrial birds with long hind claws and thin bills. One Colombian species inhabits the cold treeless paramo, the other the tropical grasslands east of the Andes. Both have a flight display and are mainly insectivorous.

### 1. YELLOWISH PIPIT
*Anthus lutescens*          Ill. 94, Map 1167
**Identification:** 5.2″ (13.2cm). Slender with sparrowlike streaked back. *Bill thin*, dusky above, pale below. *Above buffy brown streaked dusky*; narrow eyering and *underparts yellowish white streaked dark brown on breast*; notched tail blackish; *outer feathers white* (conspic. in flight).

Legs pale. Birds in very worn plumage lack yellow tinge below.
**Similar species:** From any sparrow-plumaged finch by thin bill and white outer tail feathers; Paramo Pipit (2) is only at or above treeline.
**Voice:** Flight song a ser. of *tsit*'s as bird ascends, then a longer slurred *zeeeeeeeeu* as bird glides earthward (Friedmann and Smith 1950); also

94. YELLOWISH PIPIT (left), PARAMO PIPIT (right)

sings from ground, a shorter *tsisirrit* (Ridgely 1976).

**Behavior:** Loosely colonial; walks or runs through grass, crouches if alarmed, and difficult to see unless flushed. Flight is swooping.

**Breeding:** 1 BC ♂, 26 Feb, ne Meta (S. Furniss); Dec nest, n Arauca; 2 eggs (W. McKay and S. Jorgenson). Ovenlike nest in short grass, June, Venez.; 5 nestlings (Friedmann and Smith 1955).

**Status and habitat:** Locally common in short grass, fields, and lagoon borders.

**Range:** To 500m. E of Andes from n Arauca (sightings Nov 1977—W. McKay) and Casanare to s Meta (Macarena Mts.) and e to ne Vichada (El Delirio). Locally in Pacific Panama and e of Andes from Venez. and Guyana to n Argentina; w of Andes in coastal Peru and n Chile.

## 2. PARAMO PIPIT
*Anthus bogotensis*          Ill. 94, Map 1168

**Identification:** 6″ (15cm). Slender with sparrowlike back. *Thin bill* dusky above, pale below. Cinnamon brown above streaked buff and black; narrow whitish eyering; *underparts buffy white with a few dusky spots across chest and sides;*

notched tail dusky, outer feather mostly buff (looks whitish in flight); legs pale.

**Similar species:** ♀ Plumbeous Sierra-Finch (p 666) is much more heavily streaked below and has a thick bill; also see Grassland (p 665) and Stripe-tailed yellow-finches (p 665). Yellowish Pipit (1) is a lowland bird.

**Voice:** Thin *pit-sit* flight call; skylarking song as bird flies into air, then slowly floats earthward is a musical and exhuberant *sweet-sweet-sweet-sweez-twe e'e'e'e'e'e'e sr'r'r'r, tsee, tseez-tseez* at Páramo Neusa.

**Behavior:** Like Yellowish Pipit. Single birds, scattered pairs, or loose groups of 4-5 hide in grass, then flush off with a few weak notes.

**Breeding:** 9 BC birds, Aug–Oct, E Andes (Carriker); May juv., Laguna de Chisacá, Cundinamarca (Olivares 1969a). Display flights, mid-Sept, Represa Neusa (Hilty); believed breeding, late Mar, nw Venez. (Vuilleumier and Ewert 1978).

**Status and habitat:** Locally common in grassy pastures, fields, and paramo (with or without *Espeletia* sp.).

**Range:** 3100-3600m. E Andes s to s Cundinamarca; n end C Andes s through mts. to Nariño (gap? from s Antioquia to n Cauca). Nw Venez. s in Andes to nw Argentina.

# WAXWINGS: Bombycillidae (1)

The three species of waxwings breed and are found mainly in temperate regions of North America and Eurasia. They eat fruit and some insects and are noted for their sleek well groomed plumage and waxlike red feather tips on the secondaries, hence the name.

## 1. CEDAR WAXWING
*Bombycilla cedrorum*

**Identification:** 7″ (18cm). *Sleek with pointed crest.*

*Mostly soft cinnamon brown with crisp black mask* outlined in white; throat black; underparts paler *becoming yellow on belly*; wings grayish with

waxy red tips on secondaries; tail gray with broad *yellow tip.*
**Voice:** Call a high sibilant *eeeeee*, slightly tremulous.
**Behavior:** In temperate latitudes gregarious in compact flocks, often large, at fruiting trees and shrubs. More likely straggling small groups to Colombia.
**Status and habitat:** Accidental. Once at Nuquí,

Chocó (Feb), and recent sighting of 1 ad. on Bajo Calima road near Buenaventura, Valle, 5 Jan 1983 (R. Ridgely). May be an irreg. visitor to Pacific coast.
**Range:** Breeds in N America; winters in decreasing nos. irreg. s to c Panama and Greater Antilles; once to Venez. (Cerro Pejochaina, 1650m, Perijá Mts.).

# VIREOS, PEPPERSHRIKES, SHRIKE-VIREOS: Vireonidae (17)

Vireos are a small family of New World nine-primaried oscines notable for their dull plumage and sluggish behavior (except greenlets). All are arboreal and eat insects, some are also highly frugivorous at least seasonally. There are four distinct groups in Colombia: peppershrikes (*Cyclarhis*) with chunky shapes and heavy, hooked bills; shrike-vireos (*Vireolanius*), which resemble peppershrikes in shape but have bright blue, green, and yellow plumage; typical vireos of the genus *Vireo*, smaller than peppershrikes or shrike-vireos, duller in plumage, and with a rather thick but not hooked bill, and usually with a superciliary or eyering; and greenlets (*Hylophilus*), the smallest members of the family, with slender, pointed bills and active warblerlike habits. Vireos live in forest or drier scrub, build open cup nests suspended by the rim from a fork, and except for the genus *Vireo*, are nonmigratory.

### 1. RUFOUS-BROWED PEPPERSHRIKE
*Cyclarhis gujanensis*          Pl. 46, Map 1169
**Identification:** 5.5-6″ (14-15cm). Bull-headed; *shrikelike bill yellowish brown*, paler at base. Upperparts olive green; crown gray; forehead and *broad eyebrow rufous chestnut*; cheeks and upper throat light gray *becoming yellow on lower throat and breast*; lower underparts whitish; legs pinkish; eyes orange.
**Similar species:** Easily confused with Black-billed Peppershrike (2), which is mostly gray below and has black bill and olive cheeks and crown.
**Voice:** Monotonously repeated song a musical whistled phrase; each individual usually has 2-6 song types (J. Barlow), typically a somewhat oriolelike *we're waiting to hear you* or *D'you wash every week*, given hurriedly (Skutch 1967). There are regional dialects.
**Behavior:** Heard far more often than seen. Sings most of yr. but sluggish, arboreal, and usually in foliage where hard to see. Paired yr.-round. Reg. with mixed bird flocks when at forest edges.
**Breeding:** 6 BC birds, Mar–Oct, n Colombia (Carriker) and 4 in Aug, Nov, and Feb, ne Meta (S. Furniss); May nest, Venez. Orinoco (Cherrie 1916); June nest, w Panama (Worth 1938). Thin-walled grassy cup usually high; 2-3 pinkish white eggs spotted and blotched brown (ffrench 1973).
**Status and habitat:** Fairly common in dry and

moist woodland borders, scrubby areas, and clearings with trees.
**Range:** To 1800m (usually below 1500m). Carib. lowlands from n Sucre e to Guajira, s to upper Magdalena Val. (San Agustín area), and e of Andes from Norte de Santander (Zulia Valley) s to Meta (Macarena Mts), and sightings in w Caquetá and w Putumayo (Hilty); e Vichada to Vaupés; sw Nariño. Se Mexico to c Argentina (absent from most of Amazonia). Trinidad.
**Note:** Peppershrikes have been placed in a separate family, Cyclarhidae, by some.

### 2. BLACK-BILLED PEPPERSHRIKE
*Cyclarhis nigrirostris*          Pl. 46, Map 1170
**Identification:** 6-6.5″ (15-16.5cm). Bull-headed; *shrikelike bill.* Resembles Rufous-browed Peppershrike but slightly larger with *black bill*; olive tinged crown and cheeks; dusky chestnut lores and frontlet; *light gray underparts* with olive wash on foreneck and chest; center of belly whitish (or all gray—*atrirostris*).
**Voice:** Song much like Rufous-browed Peppershrike's but decidedly richer and more melodious (usually), and apparently with less var., also *remarkably* sim. to some songs of Slate-colored Grosbeak; typically a rather fast, loud, oriolelike whistle *teetoo-tooa-chéwit* or warbled *come right here RIGHT now*.
**Behavior:** Single birds or pairs hop and peer deliberately in foliage and outer branches from

midforest to canopy. Sing frequently but usually hard to see; unlike previous sp., reg. follow mixed flocks.
**Breeding:** 10 BC birds, May–July, 1 in Oct, Andes (Carriker); singing, Mar–Aug, W Andes (Miller 1963; Brown).
**Status and habitat:** Uncommon to locally fairly common in humid and wet forest (incl. "cloud forest") and forest edges. Not in clearings and shrubby areas favored by allied *C. gujanensis* and usually at higher el. and in more humid zones.
**Range:** 1600-2700m (usually below 2400m). W Andes s to Cauca, C Andes, head of Magdalena Val. in Huila, and e slope E Andes in Norte de Santander and w slope from Boyacá s to Cundinamarca (latitude of Bogotá) prob. southward (*nigrirostris*); Pacific slope in Nariño (*atrirostris*). Colombia and e and w Ecuador.

### 3. YELLOW-BROWED SHRIKE-VIREO
*Vireolanius eximius*          Pl. 46, Map 1171
**Identification:** 5.5″ (14cm). Large-headed and chunky; *shrikelike black bill.* Crown and nape blue; *otherwise bright grass green above; prom. eyestripe, spot below eye, and throat yellow*; rest of underparts pale yellowish green.
**Similar species:** ♀ (Green Honeycreeper (p 596) is slimmer and *all* green; Slaty-capped Shrike-Vireo (4; no known range overlap) is darker above, has slaty crown, and is bright yellow below. Also cf. small chlorophonias (pp 600-601) of highlands.
**Voice:** Unknown. Related Green Shrike-Vireo (*V. pulchellus*) of Mid. America s to c Panama has a loud 3-noted *peea, peea, peea,* tirelessly repeated even during the heat of the day, reminiscent of call of Tufted Titmouse (*Parus*) of N America.
**Breeding:** 5 BC birds, May–June, s Bolívar and n Antioquia (Carriker). A Green Shrike-Vireo in Panama built a mossy vireolike cup, 14m up (Willis and Eisenmann 1979).
**Status and habitat:** Humid forest and tall second growth woodland in lowlands and foothills. Most recs. in *foothills.*
**Range:** 100-800m (to 1500m, Perijá Mts). From Panama border and Gulf of Urabá eastward n of Andes to mid. Magdalena Val. (Snía. de San Lucas) s to n boundary of Caldas; PN Tayrona (sightings, Feb 1977—R. Ridgely); Perijá Mts. and e base of E Andes from Norte de Santander s to n Boyacá. E Panama (Darién) to Colombia and nw Venez.
**Note 1:** Sometimes merged with the *V. pulchellus* (Green Shrike-Vireo) of Mid. America, which has a green crown and no eyestripe; no intergrades are known. **Note 2:** S. Olson does not consider *mutabalis* a valid subsp. **Note 3:**

Sometimes placed in the genus *Smaragdolanius.* **Note 4:** Shrike-Vireos have been placed in a separate family, Vireolaniidae, by some.

### 4. SLATY-CAPPED SHRIKE-VIREO
*Vireolanius leucotis*          Pl. 46, Map 1172
**Identification:** 5.5-6″ (14-15cm). Large-headed and chunky; *shrikelike bill* black above, pale below. Eyes lime green, *legs pinkish flesh.* Crown and sides of head slate gray; rest of upperparts olive green; *broad eyebrow, spot below eye, spot at base of lower mandible, and entire underparts bright yellow*; sides and flanks tinged olive green. Or with whitish cheek stripe (*leucotis*).
**Similar species:** Face pattern distinctive. See Yellow-browed Shrike-Vireo (3).
**Voice:** W of Andes a single monotonously repeated *eear* or *deear,* about 1 per sec, sometimes for long periods without a break; rarely a soft *whit.*
**Behavior:** Pairs or occas. 3-4 hop and peer deliberately on limbs, twigs, and foliage, rarely even hang from leaves, as persistently follow forest flocks in mid. story to canopy, infrequently lower. Sing tirelessly even when foraging, but *difficult* to see.
**Status and habitat:** Fairly common (need to know call) in wet forest (incl. mossy forest) and forest borders in foothills and lower highlands on Pacific slope; *leucotis* subsp. prob. in *lowlands* of Amazonia (as elsewhere) but thus far reported only at base of Andes.
**Range:** 300-2100m (seldom above 1800m). Pacific slope from upper Río San Juan (Cerro Tatamá) southward (*mikettae*); e base of E Andes in se Nariño (*leucotis*). W Colombia and w Ecuador; e of Andes from the Guianas and s Venez. s to e Ecuador, e Peru, n Bolivia, and Amazonian Brazil.

### 5. YELLOW-THROATED VIREO
*Vireo flavifrons*
**Identification:** 5.5″ (14cm). Bright olive green above; lower back and rump gray; *conspic. yellow lores and eyering* ("spectacles"); wings and tail blackish; wings with white edgings and *2 prom. white wing bars; throat and breast bright yellow;* rest of underparts white.
**Similar species:** Yellow spectacles, wing bars, and clean-cut appearance. Easily recognized.
**Voice:** Sings occas. on wintering grounds; pleasing, well-separated phrases resemble those of Solitary Vireo (*Vireo solitarius*) but shorter, richer, and distinctly husky (J. Barlow).
**Behavior:** Single birds follow mixed flocks or wander alone, slowly hop and peer low to fairly high in trees.
**Status and habitat:** Uncommon migrant and winter resident, early Dec–late Mar to forest

borders, second growth, and lighter woodland in n Colombia; a few s into Andes.
**Range:** To ca. 1600m (once to 2700m near Medellín). Santa Marta region, Guajira, and s to n portion of all 3 Andean ranges (to Norte de Santander in E Andes; to Quindío Mts., Tolima, in C Andes; to Pacific slope of Valle in W Andes, sighting 900m, 10 Mar 1976—Brown; several sightings, Pichindé Val., 1500m, Jan–Feb 1984—Hilty et al.); once e of Andes to Vaupés. Breeds in e N America; winters from e Mexico to n Venez.

## 6. PHILADELPHIA VIREO
*Vireo philadelphicus*
**Identification:** 4.7″ (12cm). Dull olive green above with *grayish tinge on head*; whitish eye-stripe bordered below by narrow dark streak through eyes; *underparts pale yellow*, brightest on chest (amt. of yellow var.).
**Similar species:** Brown-capped Vireo (9) can look very sim. but usually has obviously *brown* crown, decidedly brighter, crisper facial pattern, and browner (less olive) back. Red-eyed Vireo (8) is larger with more prom. head stripes and yellow only on sides and under tail coverts. Also cf. Tennessee Warbler (p 575).
**Status and habitat:** Three recs.; 2 in nw Chocó (Oct and Nov) and 1 in Bogotá (Nov). Fairly common foothill and highland winter resident (Oct–early Apr) in Panama, less numerous in lowlands (Ridgely 1976), and prob. overlooked in nw Colombia.
**Range:** Breeds in N America; winters in large nos. to w Panama (but not rec. e of Canal Zone), casual to Colombia w of Andes.

## 7. BLACK-WHISKERED VIREO
*Vireo altiloquus*
**Identification:** 5.5″ (14cm). Much like Red-eyed Vireo but with slightly larger bill and *narrow black malar streak*. Olive green above; crown shaded grayish to brownish gray; whitish eye-stripe bordered below by dusky line through eyes; underparts whitish tinged yellowish olive on flanks. Imm. is buffier and duller with brownish malar streak.
**Similar species:** Dusky "whisker" mark is diagnostic but some molting, even wet, Red-eyed Vireos may appear to show a faint whisker stripe.
**Voice:** Extent of singing in Colombia, if any, unknown. Song resembles Red-eyed Vireo's; 1-4 (usually 3) notes, strongly accented, *whip-Tom KELLY* (Snyder 1966).
**Status and habitat:** Uncommon to rare n temperate transient (winter resident?), mid-Aug–late Sept and mid-Mar–mid-Apr to lighter woodland, forest borders, and disturbed areas;

1 seen 25 June 1974 in Santa Marta area (A. Sprunt IV) is only "summer" rec.; 1 on 13 Nov 1971 at Bogotá (T. B. Johnson) may have been wintering.
**Range:** To 1200m (prob. higher). Santa Marta region s to n end of E Andes (Bucaramanga and Cúcuta); once e of Andes at Pto. Inírida, Guainía (24 Sept 1978—Hilty and M. Robbins), once to Bogotá (sight). Breeds in s Florida, the W Indies, Netherlands Antilles, and isls. off n Venez.; winters to ne Colombia, ne Peru, n Brazil (s to s bank of Amazon in c Amazonia) and Guyana, rarely Panama.

## 8. RED-EYED VIREO
*Vireo olivaceus*    Pl. 46, Map 1173
**Identification:** 5.5″ (14cm). Eyes red (resident subspp.?). Above dull olive green; *crown and nape gray; eyestripe white bordered above by black line and below by dusky streak through eye*; underparts white, usually with faint yellow tinge on sides (esp. fall and imm. birds). Or sim. but head stripes less distinct (sometimes almost absent), and sides, flanks, and under tail coverts greenish yellow (*flavoviridis*).
**Similar species:** Philadelphia and Brown-capped vireos (6, 9) are smaller and duller with less distinct eyestripes with no black borders. Caution: *flavoviridis* form of Red-eyed Vireo sometimes shows only vague head-striping; then looks much like Philadelphia (R. Ridgely). The 3 groups of Red-eyed Vireos (each sometimes considered a separate sp.) differ in the hand as follows: *olivaceus* has the longest wing with the outermost (9th) primary usually longer than the 6th, and always longer than the 5th; *chivi* has outermost usually shorter than 5th, always shorter than 6th; *flavoviridis* is intermed., the outermost usually shorter than the 6th, sometimes equal to 6th, or occas. as short as 5th (Zimmer 1941). Additionally *flavoviridis* can be told by brighter olive green upperparts, duller head markings (lacks the crisp pattern of *olivaceus*), and much more yellow on sides and vent. Also cf. Black-whiskered Vireo (7).
**Voice:** N American breeders (*olivaceus*) apparently silent on wintering grounds, even in migration. On temperate breeding grounds typically a ser. of rather abrupt 3-4 note phrases more or less continuous with only short intervening pauses. Resident birds typically sing 2-noted phrases with longer pauses between phrases (J. Barlow). Extent of singing in *flavoviridis* unknown; Miller (1952) reported half-vol. singing in Mar; song in Mid. America resembles *olivaceus* but faster, less var., individual phrases shorter, and intervening pauses longer.

**Behavior:** Found low to fairly high in shrubby clearings and forest borders and often with bird flocks. Notably frugivorous, migrants reported to be almost totally so.
**Breeding:** 3 nests, May and June, Santa Marta (Hilty; Todd and Carriker 1922); 2 nests June, upper Venez. Orinoco (Cherrie 1916). Typical suspended fiber cup; 2 white eggs spotted blackish mostly at larger end. Panama birds (*flavoviridis*) breed Feb–Aug, perhaps e to extreme nw Colombia.
**Status and habitat:** Common resident (*vividior, caucae*); n temperate migrant (*olivaceus*) mid-Sept–mid-May; s temperate migrant (*chivi*) Apr–Aug; transient (and perhaps winter resident?) early Mar–Apr and July–late Dec from lower Mid. America (*flavoviridis*); prob. transient Nov and ? from s Texas and n Mid. America (*forreri*). Status and seasonal movements of the var. forms warrant investigation.
**Range:** To 3600m (resident birds to about 1500m). Throughout e and w of Andes; *vividior* resident in Carib. lowlands and e of Andes; *caucae* resident on Pacific coast and in Cauca, Dagua, and Patía vals.; *chivi* migrant e of Andes; others throughout. Breeds in N America (*olivaceus* group incl. S American *vividior*), s Texas to c Panama (*flavoviridis* group) and most of S America (*chivi* group incl. *caucae*). N American breeders winter mostly in Amazon basin; Mid. American breeders to S America.
**Note:** S temperate *chivi* group (Chivi Vireo) and Mid. American *flavoviridis* group (Yellowgreen Vireo) are sometimes considered separate spp.

## 9. BROWN-CAPPED VIREO
*Vireo leucophrys*                    Pl. 46, Map 1174
**Identification:** 4.7" (12cm). Olive brown above with *distinct brown crown and white lores and eyestripe*; throat whitish; rest of underparts pale yellow to buffy yellow.
**Similar species:** Only *Vireo* with a brown cap. Smaller and yellower below than Red-eyed Vireo. Several greenlets (*Hylophilus* spp. 11, 14, 16) have brown crowns, but all are slender-billed and more active.
**Voice:** Song a musical warbled *witweetchur wetweetchur witwéet*, rising at end. Recalls Warbling Vireo (*V. gilvus*). Call 1-4 well-separated, buzzy *zreeee* notes like a *Tolmomyias*.
**Behavior:** Familiar highland bird usually seen in mid. or upper story with mixed flocks.
**Breeding:** 13 BC birds, Mar–July, Santa Marta and Perijá mts. and Andes (Carriker; Miller 1963).
**Status and habitat:** Common in humid and wet

forest (incl. "cloud forest"), forest borders, and tall second growth woodland.
**Range:** 1400-2800m (seldom above 2500m); on Pacific slope to 1200m. Santa Marta and Perijá mts. and all 3 Andean ranges. Costa Rica and w Panama; n Venez. s in mts. to nw Bolivia.
**Note:** Often merged with the *V. gilvus* group (Warbling Vireo) of temperate N America s to Nicaragua.

[*Hylophilus*: Small and warblerlike; slender, pointed bill usually looks pale; much alike in appearance; often cling upside down from leaves; 2 prom. groups: mainly forest canopy-inhabiting *semibrunneus/hypoxanthus/decurtatus* group (except 16), and scrub-inhabiting *aurantiifrons/flavipes* group. The genus needs revision; perhaps 2 genera involved.]

## 10. LEMON-CHESTED GREENLET
*Hylophilus thoracicus*              Pl. 46, Map 1175
**Identification:** 5" (13cm). Bill light brown above, pale below. Legs flesh colored; *eyes light yellow*. Bright olive green above with *grayish nape*; underparts grayish white with a *distinct broad yellow pectoral band*.
**Similar species:** Dusky-capped Greenlet (14) is mostly yellow below and dull brown above. Other greenlets in range, Tawny-crowned (16) and Brown-headed (11) almost completely lack yellow below.
**Voice:** Song in Peru a rolling *seeerr, seeerr, seeerr, seeerr*, reminiscent of "T-Kettle" song of Carolina Wren (*Thryothorus*) of N America (T. Parker); high-pitched buzzy *chips* when foraging.
**Behavior:** Restless and active like other greenlets. Often follows bird flocks from lower mid. level to canopy (T. Parker; Hilty).
**Status and habitat:** No recs. from a *definite* Colombian locality. Elsewhere in humid *terra firme* and *várzea* forests and forest borders. Fairly common in *várzea* and *várzea* borders on Río Javarí s of Leticia.
**Range:** Known only from "Bogotá" specimens. Doubtless se Colombia as it is known from Brazil side of Río Vaupés adj. to e Vaupés, and from several localities on Peru and Brazil side of Río Javarí s of Leticia (sightings J. V. Remsen; Hilty et al.). The Guianas, se Venez., e Peru, n Bolivia, and Amazonian and se Brazil.
**Note 1:** Birds of se Brazil (perhaps elsewhere) may be a separate sp. (R. Ridgely). **Note 2:** Gray-chested Greenlet, *H. semicinereus* of Fr. Guiana, s Venez. and Amazonian Brazil may occur in ne Guainía (rec. on Orinoco at San Fernando de Atabapo, Venez.). A bird photographed by John Dunning at Villavicencio,

w Meta has tentatively been identified as this sp. Bill and eyes pale. Olive green above with *gray nape*, underparts gray, lower breast washed olive, center of belly whitish; eyes yellowish white. In e Amazonian Brazil in mid. and upper forest levels; song reminiscent of Scrub Greenlet but weaker and faster, more a repetition of a single slurred note (R. Ridgely). **Note 3:** Buff-cheeked Greenlet *H. muscicapinus* of the Guianas, Venez., and Amazonian Brazil may also occur in e Vichada (rec. on Orinoco at Pto. Ayacucho) or se Guainía (rec. on upper Río Negro, Brazil). Forehead, sides of head, throat, and breast bright buff; rear crown gray otherwise olive green above and white on belly.

## 11. BROWN-HEADED GREENLET
*Hylophilus brunneiceps*          Pl. 46, Map 1176
**Identification:** 4.5″ (11.4cm). *Drab and nondescript.* Bill and legs light brown; eyes dark. Olive above with *light brown crown and yellowish wing edgings*; sides of head mixed brown and buff; *throat and chest brownish buff in weak contrast to pale gray belly and lower underparts.*
**Similar species:** Much like Tawny-crowned Greenlet (16) but lacks latter's contrasting forecrown, pale eye, and faintly yellowish streaked underparts. Good marks are weakly contrasting underparts and yellowish wing edgings. Also cf. Lemon-chested Greenlet (10).
**Status and habitat:** Apparently confined to sandy-belt forest and blackwater regions of the extreme east. Little known.
**Range:** To 400m. Known only from extreme se Guainía (mouth of Río Guainía) and on Río Vaupés opp. Brazilian border. S. Venez., e Colombia, nw Brazil (Río Negro/Río Uaupés region) and n Amazonian Brazil s to the lower Río Negro.

## 12. RUFOUS-NAPED GREENLET
*Hylophilus semibrunneus*          Pl. 46, Map 1177
**Identification:** 5″ (13cm). Bill rather heavy for a greenlet, dark above, yellowish below. *Crown, rear cheeks, and nape rufous* becoming rufous brown on upper back and olive on rest of upperparts; *lores, lower cheeks, and throat whitish to grayish white* and separated from olive buff underparts by a *wash of rufous on chest* forming an obscure rufescent pectoral band.
**Similar species:** Tawny-crowned Greenlet (16), an understory bird, has rufous forecrown (not entire crown and nape), lacks the pectoral band, and wings and tail always russet brown, not olive (prob. no range overlap). Golden-fronted Greenlet (13) differs in orange yellow forehead (can be hard to see) less extensive rufous on head (does not extend to rear cheeks or

upper back), and more uniform underparts (no pectoral band). See ♀ Plain Antvireo (p 386).
**Voice:** Weak musical song a vireolike, warbled *wacheera-ditit*, rising in pitch.
**Behavior:** Single birds, pairs or families, peer and glean actively in outer foliage from mid-forest levels to subcanopy; often with bird flocks. Do not hang from leaves as frequently as Tawny-crowned Greenlet.
**Breeding:** 5 BC birds, Mar–July, Perijá Mts. and C Andes (Carriker), 1 in Apr (Miller 1963), stub-tailed juv. with ad., Mar (Hilty), W Andes above Cali.
**Status and habitat:** Uncommon or rare and local inside more open humid and wet forest, at forest borders, and in taller second growth woodland. More recs. (specimens and sightings) from Valle in W Andes than elsewhere.
**Range:** 1000-2100m. Spottily on both slopes of W Andes from Antioquia s to Valle; w slope C Andes in Valle, e slope in n Caldas and head of Magdalena Val. in Huila; w slope E Andes in Santander and Cundinamarca and e slope in Norte de Santander (2100m); Perijá Mts. (e of Casacará, 1600m). W Venez. (down to 450m) s to e Ecuador.

## 13. GOLDEN-FRONTED GREENLET
*Hylophilus aurantiifrons*          Pl. 46, Map 1178
**Identification:** 4.5″ (11.4cm). Rather pale. *Eyes dark*, with narrow pale gray eyering. Bill dark above, pinkish below, slightly heavier than that of other greenlets. Forehead dull orange yellow but this often hard to see (or pale dirty yellow—*saturatus*) becoming *light rufescent brown on crown*; upperparts light olive green; throat whitish otherwise *clear light yellow below more or less washed buffy on breast.*
**Similar species:** Most like Tawny-crowned Greenlet (16), which may or may not overlap in range. From it by greenish (not brownish) upperparts, dark (not pale) eyes, and *more uniform* and light yellowish underparts. Also cf. Scrub (15) and Rufous-naped greenlets (12; range overlap uncertain).
**Voice:** Often heard song in Santa Marta foothills, a short warbled phrase, *de-whichy-de-whéeter*, semimusical and given quickly; recalls a N American parulid.
**Behavior:** Single birds, pairs, or 3-4 glean and flutter actively in foliage of bushes and trees; occas. follow mixed flocks, and like other *Hylophilus*, often cling upside down from leaves. Mostly midlevels or lower.
**Breeding:** BC ♂ and juv., Aug, Cesar (Carriker). In Trinidad Apr–Oct; deep, leaf, stem, and grass cup suspended from lateral fork or vine 1.6-10m up; 3 white eggs sparsely dotted

brown; often parasitized by Shiny Cowbird (ffrench 1973).

**Status and habitat:** Uncommon to fairly common in dry scrubby areas and borders of dry forest, smaller nos. to borders of moist and humid woodland.

**Range:** To 700m (prob. higher). Upper Río Sinú e across Carib. lowlands to Santa Marta region and Cesar Val., prob. Guajira (*aurantiifrons*); e base E Andes in w Arauca and Casanare (*saturatus*). C Panama to extreme e Venez. Trinidad.

## 14. DUSKY-CAPPED GREENLET
*Hylophilus hypoxanthus*        Map 1179

**Identification:** 4.5″ (11.4cm). Bill dusky above, pale below. Eyes dark. *Crown brown, darker on forecrown*; mantle brownish olive (or sepia brown—*fuscicapillus*), becoming olive green on rump and tail; *throat grayish white; rest of underparts bright olive yellow with ochraceous stain on breast.*

**Similar species:** Only Amazonian greenlet with mostly yellowish underparts. Cf. Tawny-crowned (16) and Lemon-chested greenlets (10).

**Voice:** Song in e Peru and Ecuador a bright, quick *which-ey, wheeee-weet*, last note sometimes dropped, or *perswitchitwee*, or sim., reminiscent of a N American parulid (T. Parker; R. Ridgely).

**Behavior:** Sim. to that of Lesser/Gray-chested group of *Hylophilus*, active and noisy with flocks in canopy and mid. strata, not shrubbery at edge (R. Ridgely).

**Breeding:** BC ♂, May, Vaupés (Olivares 1964b).

**Status and habitat:** Few recs. (prob. overlooked). Upper levels of lowland *terra firme* forest.

**Range:** To 400m. E of Andes from se Guainía (mouth of Río Guainía) to Mitú in Vaupés (*hypoxanthus*); Pto. Umbría in w Putumayo, and prob. (but no specimens) to s Amazonas (*fuscicapillus*). Sw Venez. to e Ecuador, e Peru (incl. Pebas, ne Loreto), n Bolivia, and Amazonian Brazil.

## 15. SCRUB GREENLET
*Hylophilus flavipes*        Pl. 46, Map 1180

**Identification:** 4.5″ (11.4cm). Very plain. *Bill and legs flesh color* (dark in imm.); eyes whitish. Olive green to brownish olive above, slightly darker on crown; throat dull whitish; otherwise dull yellowish below, palest on abdomen and with buff wash on breast.

**Similar species:** Often found in same habitat as Golden-fronted Greenlet (13) but much duller and without yellowish orange forecrown. Also note song difference.

**Voice:** Frequently heard song a rapid, very penetrating ser. of *peeree, peeree, peeree* . . . notes, up to 15 or more.

**Behavior:** Rather deliberate for a greenlet, peering in foliage, gleaning from leaves, or clinging upside down from leaves mostly 1-6m up. When perched sit rather upright. Single birds, pairs, or families infrequently follow bird flocks.

**Breeding:** 7 BC birds, Mar–May, Cesar and sw Huila (Carriker), 2 in Oct, ne Meta (S. Furniss); deep, fine, grass cup slung from twigs ca. 3m up; 3 white eggs lightly spotted brown (ffrench 1973).

**Status and habitat:** Common in arid scrub, drier scrubby areas, and lighter woodland, a few into more humid shrubbery.

**Range:** To ca. 1000m. E side of Gulf of Urabá and mid. Sinú Val. (sw Córdoba) e across Carib. lowlands to Guajira, s in drier parts of Magdalena Val. to Huila and e of Andes from Norte de Santander to Meta; prob. to Vichada. Sw Costa Rica to Venez. Tobago. Margarita Isl.

**Note:** Olivaceous Greenlet (*H. olivaceus*) of subtropical zone on e Andean slope from ne Ecuador (1000-2500m) to Peru may occur on adj. Colombian slope. Resembles Scrub Greenlet (no overlap) but slightly larger (5″). Dull olive above, forehead tinged yellowish, underparts yellowish olive, yellower on belly and under tail coverts, under wing coverts and axillaries light yellow; bill pinkish, eyes whitish, legs pale flesh. Humid lower subtropical forest.

## 16. TAWNY-CROWNED GREENLET
*Hylophilus ochraceiceps*        Pl. 46, Map 1181

**Identification:** 4.5″ (11.4cm). *Eyes yellowish white* (all subsp.). *Forecrown dull rufous*, brightest at base of bill; otherwise olive above; *wings and tail cinnamon brown*; throat light gray; rest of underparts light olive sometimes obscurely streaked yellowish. Or *forecrown tawny yellow*, crown tawny, back sometimes brownish, and breast and sides olive yellow (*bulunensis*).

**Similar species:** Much like ♀ Plain Antvireo (p 386) and often with it; latter differs in *white eyering*, more contrasting rufous crown, narrow buff wing bars, heavier hooked bill, and more sluggish behavior (does not cling to underside of leaves). Dusky-capped Greenlet (14) of e of Andes is much brighter olive yellow below and has whiter throat. Also see Brownheaded Greenlet (11) e of Andes, Lesser Greenlet (17) w of Andes, and Golden-fronted Greenlet (13) in the north. Several ♀ antwrens (*Myrmotherula*) are superficially sim. but have heavier bills; see esp. ♀ Long-winged (p 394) and ♀ Slaty antwrens (p 394).

**Voice:** Unusual for a greenlet; usually a harsh nasal *nya, nya* constantly repeated; also a slightly descending whistle (Ridgely 1976). In Peru, a very high, thin, wispy *eeeee-it eeeee-it* (T. Parker). Apparently no true song (Skutch 1960).

**Behavior:** Unlike many other greenlets, almost always seen in small groups, often with antwrens, antvireos, ant-tanagers, and others, and typically found *inside* forest in *lower* growth. Lively and active as it flits in foliage and clings upside down to leaves from eye level to mid. story.

**Breeding:** BC pairs, Feb, nw Antioquia (Carriker). In Costa Rica, Mar–May; sturdy fiber cup partially covered with moss and suspended from horizontal fork 2-7m up; 2 eggs; both sexes care for young (Skutch 1960).

**Status and habitat:** Uncommon in humid forest and taller second growth woodland in lowlands and foothills.

**Range:** To 800m (to 1550m in Panama). Pacific coast from Panama southward (*bulunensis*); e of Andes from s Meta (Macarena Mts.) and se Guainía (mouth of Río Guainía) southward (*ferrugineifrons*). Prob. e Vichada. Se Mexico to w Ecuador, n Bolivia, Amazonian Brazil, and s Venez.

## 17. LESSER GREENLET

*Hylophilus decurtatus*                    Pl. 46, Map 1182

**Identification:** 3.7-4″ (9.4-10.2cm). *Small, plump, and short-tailed* (shape unlike other Colombian *Hylophilus*). Bill rather long and dusky. Head dull olive with *whitish eyering; otherwise bright yellowish green above*; underparts grayish white with greenish yellow wash on sides of breast and flanks.

**Similar species:** Plump shape and rather large head suggest an antwren (*Myrmotherula* sp.), but none are yellowish green above (or any other shade of green above). Plumage sim. to Tennessee Warbler (p 575), but shape and long bill quite different.

**Voice:** Call in Panama a rapid musical phrase resembling that of Red-eyed Vireo but even more monotonously repeated, *deedereét* or *itsacheét* (Ridgely 1976).

**Behavior:** Small family clans are active and warblerlike. Commonly forage in mid. story to subcanopy, higher than Tawny-crowned Greenlets, and with mixed insectivorous flocks, less often independent of them.

**Breeding:** BC ♀, May, s Córdoba (Carriker). Apr Costa Rican nest in isolated tree near woodland; deep, open, leafy cup bound with fibers and spider web; attached by rim 4.6m up; 2 white eggs spotted and blotched pale brown chiefly at large end (Skutch 1960).

**Status and habitat:** Fairly common in humid forest, tall second growth woodland, and borders in lowlands and foothills.

**Range:** To 300m (Pacific slope); to 500m (Magdalena Val.). Pacific coast from Panama border s to Dagua Val., Valle, and e in humid lowlands along n base of Andes to mid. Magdalena Val. s to Lebrija Val. w Santander (*darienensis*) Pacific coast w Cauca (subsp.?); sw Nariño (*minor*). S Mexico to Panama (to 1500m), w Ecuador and nw Peru.

**Note:** Some consider *H. minor* (incl. *darienensis*) of extreme e Panama to nw Peru a separate sp. from Gray-headed birds of Mid. America.

# OROPENDOLAS, AMERICAN ORIOLES, BLACKBIRDS: Icteridae (37)

This heterogeneous family, confined to the Americas, has the greatest number of species in tropical latitudes. They are characterized by rather long, conical, pointed bills and many also have predominantly black plumage. The sexes are usually similar, though ♂♂ are often larger. Icterids occur from seashore to treeline but mainly in open or cleared areas with scattered trees rather than inside forest. Orioles are accomplished songsters, while others, such as the oropendolas and caciques, are noted for their marvelously complex and often bizarre vocalizations. Breeding is solitary or colonial, and the colonial species are often polygamous as are the parasitic cowbirds. Some species weave exquisite pouches or long stockinglike bags that may be seen hanging from the branch tips of tall isolated trees. Breeding colonies of caciques and oropendolas present one of the most fascinating spectacles of the American tropics and may involve complex ecological interrelationships with other organisms, though further documentation is needed (see Smith 1968). Some icterids have profited from man's activities and are now conspicuous birds in settled areas; sadly, others have suffered heavily with settlement.

## 1. SHINY COWBIRD
*Molothrus bonariensis*  Pl. 44, Map 1183
**Identification:** 8.5″ (22cm). *Bill short and conical; eyes dark* (both sexes). ♂: *entirely glossy purplish black.* ♀: dull grayish brown above, much paler below; faint, short, grayish white eyebrow. Imm.: sim. to ♀, but feather edges brownish buff above, yellow buff below; imm. ♂ obscurely streaked dusky.
**Similar species:** ♂ most easily told by distinctive small-headed and rather thick-chested shape and in flight by shallow wing beats. Carib Grackle (18) has short tail and white eyes; Bronze-brown Cowbird (2) is smaller, brownish, shorter-tailed, and red-eyed. ♀ recalls Grayish Saltator (p 644), but bill more pointed and conical, and lacks white throat and black whisker. In sw Nariño see Scrub Blackbird (under 17).
**Voice:** ♂'s song a musical liquid warbling sometimes interspersed with harsher notes, and usually accompanied by puffing up neck feathers.
**Behavior:** Like other cowbirds, walks with tail held slightly cocked. Often forages on the ground in open places, alone, or more frequently in small loose groups; large groups unusual except at roosts. Shows no special preference for cattle. Flight is slightly swooping; in display ♂ angles upward with rapid, shallow, wing-tip flight.
**Breeding:** A brood parasite; mating promiscuous. Breeding mid-Feb–July, Andes above Cali (Miller 1963); fledgling fed by Carib Grackle, mid-July, ne Meta (S. Furniss); ♀ about to lay, Dec, Santander (Boggs 1961), and Oct, Valle (MCN). Lay in nests of spp. mostly smaller than itself, poss. up to 5 eggs per yr. Eggs whitish, markings var. (ffrench 1973).
**Status and habitat:** Common in cultivated areas, pastures, and forest clearings. Occupies a broad spectrum of habitats from dry to humid to wet regions with almost equal frequency.
**Range:** To 2000m. Throughout. Extreme e Panama to c Chile and s Argentina. Lesser Antilles. Trinidad and Tobago.

## 2. BRONZE-BROWN COWBIRD
*Molothrus armenti*  Pl. 44, Map 1184
**Identification:** 8″ (20cm). Short conical bill. Eyes red (both sexes). Shiny *bronzy brown;* wings and tail blue black, slightly glossy; neck ruff usually prom. ♀: slightly duller, ruff less conspic.
**Similar species:** From Shiny Cowbird (1) by slightly smaller size (looks shorter-tailed), ruff, obviously *brownish* cast to body, and at close range, red eyes. ♀ Shiny Cowbird is brownish

gray, much paler than this sp. See Bronzed Cowbird (below).
**Voice:** Give *eez-eez-dzlee* or sim. unmusical phrase as ruffs head and expands neck ruff.
**Behavior:** Usually forages alone on ground where walks with tail slightly cocked. Apparently shows no preference for cattle. Loaf alone or in small groups.
**Status and habitat:** Uncommon to fairly common (though apparently known from only 4 specimens, 2 prior to 1967) in dry scrub or open roadsides with scattered bushes in w half of PN Isla de Salamanca. Sightings throughout yr. (Hilty; P. Donahue; J. Hernández et al.). Previous reports from Leticia (Friedmann 1957) are surely erroneous. It is now known that this Carib. sp. was mixed with Leticia cage bird shipments being quarantined at Barranquilla prior to export.
**Range:** ENDEMIC. Dry tropical zone ner Carib. coast in Atlántico (Cartagena) and nw Magdalena (PN Isla de Salamanca).
**Note:** Perhaps conspecific with *M. aeneus* (Bronzed Cowbird) of sw US to e Panama. Latter is essentially bronzy black (not bronze brown), and is apparently spreading e with deforestation into e Panama. Bronzed is unrec. but poss. in extreme nw Colombia.

## 3. GIANT COWBIRD
*Scaphidura oryzivora*  Pl. 44, Map 1185
**Identification:** ♂ 14″ (36cm); ♀ 11″ (28cm). Long tail; relatively small-headed and flat-headed appearance. Bill stout with small black frontal shield; eyes red (throughout?). ♂: entirely glossy purplish black; *ruff prom.* ♀: smaller, brownish black, ruff lacking. Imm.: like ♀ but sometimes yellowish and eyes whitish (mimic host); feathers pale-edged. In flight shows rather long tail, wedge-shaped body (barrel-chested), and rapid, slightly undulating flight, a few flaps, then wings closed tightly.
**Similar species:** ♂ is almost as large as Great-tailed Grackle (19) but bill shorter and stouter, ruff conspic., and tail flat, rounded, and shorter. ♀ by distinctive cowbird silhouette and intermed. size, considerably larger than Shiny Cowbird, smaller than ♀ Great-tailed Grackle; nearby, frontal shield diagnostic.
**Voice:** Usually silent. Occas. in flight a var. of slightly grating *quick, zrip, crick, ek,* or *uk* notes (Slud 1964), also a strident whistle *tew-tew-hee,* last note higher (ffrench 1973).
**Behavior:** Seen alone, in pairs, or in groups of 3-20 (infrequently more) perched high in a tree near a cacique or oropendola colony, or flying in a direct line high over trees. Feed

mostly on the ground, on river banks, or in other semiopen areas. Walk and strut with tail up. Occas. with cattle.

**Breeding:** A brood parasite; lays only in cacique and oropendola colonies as far as known. BC ♀ and 2 BC ♂♂, May, Cesar Val. (Carriker). Up to 6 eggs in 1 nest (ffrench 1973); egg color, shape, and size vary; only bluish eggs in cacique nests, only white ones in *Psarocolius* nests (Haverschmidt 1968). Also see Smith (1968).

**Status and habitat:** Widespread but local in humid lowlands wherever caciques and oropendolas breed. When not breeding, disperse widely, sometimes far from known host colonies. Formerly widespread in Cauca Val. (no extant host colonies) but now only a straggler there.

**Range:** To 2200m. Throughout (only a straggler to many areas) except arid e Guajira and ne llanos (?). Se Mexico to w Ecuador, ne Argentina, and s Brazil. Trinidad and Tobago.

## 4. BAND-TAILED OROPENDOLA
*Ocyalus latirostris*     Pl. 45, Map 1186

**Identification:** ♂ 13″ (33cm); ♀ 9″ (23cm). Eyes blue; *bill short*; small rounded frontal shield and upper mandible black, tip and lower mandible yellowish white. Plumage velvety black; crown and upper mantle chestnut (hard to see in field); tail yellow, *central pair of tail feathers and broad terminal tail band black forming an inverted T.*

**Similar species:** Easily confused with sim.-sized Yellow-rumped Cacique (12) but lacks yellow on inner remiges, and all tail feathers tipped black (Cacique's outer tail feathers all yellow).

**Voice:** A var. of harsh and grating sounds, some reminiscent of Solitary Black Cacique (J. V. Remsen).

**Behavior:** Alone or more frequently in flocks of var. size, commonly assoc. with other caciques and oropendolas, esp. Yellow-rumped Cacique. Usually stays in mid. or upper levels of trees.

**Breeding:** BC ♂ mid-June, Quebrada Tucuchira w of Leticia (J. V. Remsen).

**Status and habitat:** Known only from Isla Santa Sofia III (Monkey Isl.), and adj. n bank of Amazon at Quebrada Tucuchira (Remsen 1977a) and Quebrada Arara, July 1975 (Hilty et al.). *Várzea* forest edge, *Cecropia* trees along rivers and on river isls. More a bird of floodplain areas and river borders than allied *Cacicus cela.*

**Range:** To 100m. Extreme se Colombia on

banks of the Amazon. E Ecuador (no recent recs.?), e Peru, and w Amazonian Brazil.
**Note:** *Ocyalus* is merged into *Psarocolius* by some.

## 5. CHESTNUT-HEADED OROPENDOLA
*Zarhynchus wagleri*     Pl. 44, Map 1187

**Identification:** ♂ 14″ (36cm); ♀ 11″ (28cm). Small; bill ivory to greenish yellow with dusky tip; eyes blue (gray—♀). *Head and neck chestnut*; otherwise mostly black becoming deep chestnut on rump and belly; tail yellow, central pair of tail feathers black. ♂♂ have a few long hairlike crest feathers on hindcrown.

**Similar species:** *Much smaller* than any other oropendola w of the Andes. Russet-backed Oropendola (8) lacks chestnut head (this sometimes hard to see) and has yellow forehead. Also cf. Crested Oropendola (6).

**Voice:** Both sexes, esp. displaying ♂♂, give a var. of loud croaks and gurgling notes, the latter musical and suggesting dripping water *plup, plup, plup, plup-loo-upoo* (Ridgely 1976).

**Behavior:** Noisy and conspic., esp. around nesting colonies, which are occas. quite large. Actively hop and scramble among branches and peer in mid. to upper strata foliage. Fly faster and with quicker wing beats than larger oropendolas. Away from breeding colonies often seen in flocks.

**Breeding:** 6 BC birds, Feb–May, s Córdoba and Chocó (Carriker). Panama colonies of 25-50, occas. to 100 pairs; long socklike nests suspended fairly high in isolated or partly isolated tree, built by ♀; 2 pale blue eggs splotched brownish black (Chapman 1928). Often parasitized by Giant Cowbird.

**Status and habitat:** Fairly common in humid and wet forest, tall second growth, and clearings in lowlands and lower foothills. Often with 1 or more spp. of larger oropendolas.

**Range:** To 1000m (mainly below 300-400m). Pacific coast and humid lowlands n of Andes e to mid. Magdalena Val. (s to Remedios, e Antioquia). Se Mexico to w Ecuador.

**Note 1:** *Zarhynchus* is sometimes merged with *Psarocolius*. **Note 2:** Casqued Oropendola (*Clypicterus oseryi*) of e Peru (n to Pebas) and e Ecuador (n to Limoncocha) may occur in adj. Putumayo or Amazonas, Colombia. Much like Chestnut-headed Oropendola but bill shorter and frontal shield swollen forming a knob on forehead and throat; breast olive yellow. Trees along lake and river borders or high inside humid forest. Most common call a long, loud rising *sqwaaaoook*; also a *Psarocolius*-like water dropping call and other caciquelike notes (T. Parker).

# PLATES

## Notes Facing Plates

ABBREVIATED plate notes discuss all species resident in Colombia except those illustrated by line drawings in the text. Migrant species are mentioned if space permits. The notes condense identification points detailed in the text but should be used in conjunction with the text and range maps. Symbols (♂, ♀) are used when the plumage of sexes differ. Letters modifying numbers (1a, 2a, etc.) denote other plumage differences, e.g., age or color phase. Immature refers to plumage(s) succeeding natal down and preceding adult plumage. Juvenal is restricted to the first plumage following natal down. If space permits, ranges are noted, E (east of Andes), W (Andes westward), N (n of Andes), SE (Amazonia), SW (w Nariño), Andes (E, C, W cordilleras), Mts. (Andes, plus Perijá and Santa Marta mts.). A dividing line on the plates indicates two different size scales; otherwise all birds on a plate are drawn to scale.

# PLATE I RAPTORS

**1. Osprey** *Pandion haliaetus* p 90 Map 78
N migrant (some individuals present yr.-round). *White head with black postocular stripe*; narrow bent wings; black wrist. All el.; usually near water.

**2. Black Vulture** p 88 Map 75
*Coragyps atratus*
Widespread. Broad wings, *short fanned tail* (almost tailless); *white base* of primaries; flap-and-glide flight. Settled areas.

**3. Carunculated Caracara** p 114 Map 127
*Phalcoboenus carunculatus*
Andes (Cauca S). Bold black and white pattern. Páramo. Cf. 8

**Vultures** *Cathartes* Small-headed; long wings held in V; longish tail.

**4. Turkey** *C. aura* Upper Wing p 87 Map 72
Two-toned wings as in 5, but *primary quills all dark from above; head reddish* (dusky, imm.). N. migrants lack white band across nape.

**5. Lesser Yellow-headed** p 87 Map 73
*C. burrovianus*  5a Upper Wing
N; E. *Whitish primary quills from above*; mostly *yellow* head (dark, imm.). Usually confined to wet savanna and marshes. Soars low.

**6. Greater Yellow-headed** p 88 Map 74
*C. melambrotus*  6a Upper Wing
E. Larger, *much blacker* than 4 or 5; flight feathers show less contrast; from below *inner primaries blackish*; head *deep yellow* (dusky, imm.). Flight rather heavy, less tilting. Forest.

**7. Yellow-headed Caracara** p 115 Map 129
*Milvago chimachima*
Widespread. Slighter than 8, but flight pattern sim. *Pale head and underparts*. See Pl.4

**8. Crested Caracara** p 115 Map 128
*Polyborus plancus*  8a. Imm.
Robust. Bare red face, *bushy crest, thighs and lower underparts black*. Less numerous than 7. Imm. brownish, streaky below.

**Caracaras** *Daptrius* Mostly glossy black; long full tail, bare yellow, orange or red facial skin and legs. Glide but no soaring. Forested zones.

**9. Black** *D. ater* p 114 Map 125
E. *White band on tail coverts; conspic. orange face.*

**10. Red-throated** *D. americanus* p 114 Map 126
*Belly and crissum white*; bare dark red facial skin; bicolored bill. Social, very noisy; upper levels inside forest. Cf. *Crax*.

# PLATE II RAPTORS

**Hawks** *Buteo* Typically rather chunky with broad wings and med. length fanned tail. Usually soar, esp. larger spp., for prolonged periods and to considerable hts. Most dominant Accipitrine group numerically and visually in open to partially wooded terrain.

**1. Zone-tailed** p 109 Map 118
*B. albonotatus*
Imm. (Ad., Pl.III)
Shape and tilting flight mimics Turkey Vulture. *Long 2-toned wings*, small head. Imm. *dappled white below*, flight feathers paler than ad. Cf. 2a.

**2. Short-tailed** p 107 Map 113
*B. brachyurus* 2a Dark Phase
Typical chunky buteo shape. Dark phase (rare): *all black with whitish flight feathers*. More common light phase mostly white below, flight feathers *tipped dusky; dark hood*. *White forehead* and narrow tail bands in both phases. Imm. recalls respective ad. Light phase often streaky on head and neck; dark phase spotted with white below.

**3. White-throated** *B. albigula* p 107 Map 114
Andes. Shaped like 2. All plumages streaky below, esp. chest and flanks. Note *dark hood, barred thighs*. Imm. much like 6a (see text).

**4. White-rumped** *B. leucorrhous* p 106 Map 111
Subtropical forests. Small, short-winged. *White rump*, bold tail bands, *contrasting white wing linings* (cf. 2a); rufous barred thighs. Imm. mottled above, streaked below; barred primaries (see text).

**5. Gray** *B. nitidus* p 105 Map 109
Ad. Gray plumage contrasting with *black and white tail bands*; close gray barring below (cf. 7). Imm. very different (see text); has diagnostic *pale patches at base of primaries* from above. Cf. 6a and 7a. Also Pls.4,5.

**6. Broad-winged** *B. platypterus* p 106 Map 112
6a Imm.
N migrant. Ad. (Pl.5); chunky; banded tail, *rusty-barred underparts, white wing linings*. Imm. confusing, but note *prom. streaky effect below* (cf. 5 imm. and 7a).

**7. Roadside** *B. magnirostris* p 106 Map 110
7a Imm.
Common, smallish hawk. Ad. (Pl.5): *grayish above* with brownish tinge; *chest unbarred; rufous patch in primaries* (from above). Imm. streaky breast, a few *coarse bars on sides and belly*.

**8. Hook-billed Kite** p 91 Map 80
*Chondrohierax uncinatus*
Notably var. See Plates III, V, 4. In all plumages note *rangy shape, longish tail, heavy hooked bill, greenish white eyes*, and *orange supraloral spot. Boldly barred flight feathers* in normal phase ad.

**9. Double-toothed Kite** p 94 Map 86
*Harpagus bidentatus* 9a Imm.
Small. Short broad wings and longish tail recall *Accipiter* but often soars. *Rear edge of wing angles inward* (not shown on plate); *throat stripe and protruding puffy white undertail coverts* (visible even from above) diagnostic. See Pl.5. Imm. dusky above; below whitish, usually streaked; *throat stripe*.

**10. Sharp-shinned Hawk** p 97 Map 91
*Accipiter striatus*
Higher el. Slim-bodied, long-tailed; rather short-winged in flight. Usually in cover, infrequently soars. *Solid rufous thighs*. See Pl.5.

*Exploruma Camp*

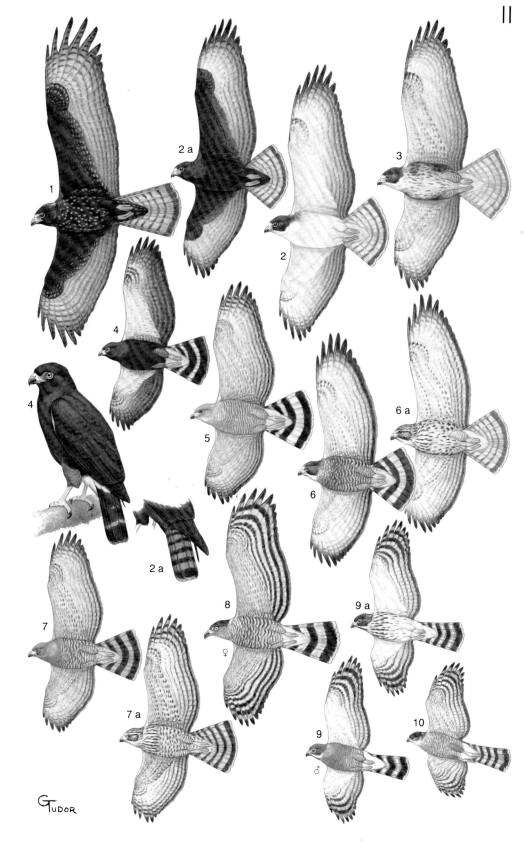

GTUDOR

# PLATE III RAPTORS

**1. Crane Hawk** p 95 Map 88
*Geranospiza caerulescens*
N; E. Lanky, loose-jointed; dark bluish gray; *long reddish-orange legs*; long tail. *White crescent on primaries* (in flight from below). At rest easily confused (see text). Imm. brownish but *under wings and tail much like ad.*; below heavily streaked; lower underparts mottled and banded paler. Also Pl.4.

**2. Hook-billed Kite** p 91 Map 80
*Chondrohierax uncinatus* 2a Black Phase Ad.
Lanky wings, long narrow tail. Complex plumage var. (text). All plumages by heavy conspic. *hooked bill, supraloral spot, and light eyes*. Rare black phase almost uniformly dark below; 1 broad tail band. See Plates II, V, 4.

**3. Zone-tailed Hawk** p 109 Map 118
*Buteo albonotatus*
Two-toned wings held in V and tilting flight recall Turkey Vulture. Cf. differently shaped black-hawks (Pl.IV), dark-phase Short-tailed Hawk (Pl.II). Imm., Pl.II.

**4. Slate-colored Hawk** p 100 Map 96
*Leucopternis schistacea* Imm.
SE. Bluish slate. *Red orange cere and legs*. Imm. closely barred wing-linings and lower underparts; sometimes 2 tail bands. Ad. (Pl.4) chunky, sluggish, Amazonian backwaters.

**5. Slender-billed Kite** p 94 Map 85
*Helicolestes hamatus* Imm.
E. Chunky, slate gray, *2 narrow bands on very short square tail; reddish cere and legs; whitish eyes* (cf. 6, red eyes). Ad. (Pl.4) lacks tail bands. Swampy woodland.

**6. Snail Kite** *Rostrhamus sociabilis* p 93 Map 84
6a Imm.
Much like 5, but longer wings and tail impart lankier shape. All plumages by *thin hooked bill, red cere and legs, white tail base*. ♀ like 6a, less streaky below. Also see Pl.4.

**7. Gray-headed Kite** p 90 Map 79
*Leptodon cayanensis* Dark Phase Imm.
Var. Usually head and upperparts dark; heavily streaked below; primaries barred. Note small head, long tail, blunt wing tips. Ad. and light phase imm., Pl.V.

**Harriers** *Circus*

**8. Cinereous** *C. cinereus* p 96 Map 89
Typical harrier. ♂ nearest ♂ N Harrier (see text); ♀ like other ♀ Colombian harriers, but both told by bold *rufous and white barring on lower underparts*. Imm. buff to rufous nape.

**9. Long-winged** *C. buffoni* p 97 Map 90
9a Dark Phase Imm.
Typical harrier. Plumage complicated and var., but all show *white rump, gray primaries barred dusky above*. Light phase ad. blackish above (brownish, ♀), paler below with *contrasting chest band*. Dark phase ad. sim., but *body blackish* (see text). Imms. recall respective ad. phases but streaked below; dark phase imm., *rufous thighs*, rufous barred crissum. Cf. ranges of other harriers.

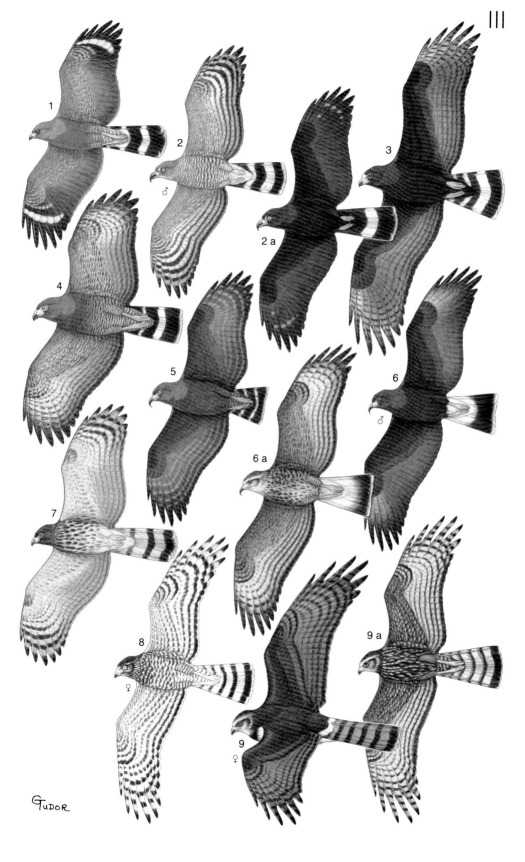

III

GUDOR

# PLATE IV RAPTORS

NOTE: Mostly large, rugged hawks with broad wings and short tails. Reg. soar for extended periods.

### 1. Black-chested Buzzard-Eagle p 104 Map 107
*Geranoaëtus melanoleucus*  Imm.
Longer, more wedge-shaped tail than ad. Long, broad wings, primaries decidedly longer than 7. Older birds gradually acquire more black on chest and assume stub-tailed shape of ad. Ad., Pl.VII.

### 2. White-tailed Hawk p 108 Map 115
*Buteo albicaudatus* 2a Imm.
Large, broad-winged. Light phase: slaty above, *rufous shoulders*, white wing linings contrast with dark flight feathers; *blackish head ("hood") and tail band (cf.* light phase Short-tailed Hawk, Pl.II). For Dark phase (scarce; mainly e of Andes), see text. Imm. var., but tail often whitish, shoulders tinged rufous (esp. older birds); *wing linings darker than flight feathers.*

### 3. Savanna Hawk p 103 Map 105
*Heterospizias meridionalis*  Imm.
For body size *the longest-winged* Colombian raptor. Heavily mottled black and buff; *rufous tinged* shoulders and thighs; ranch habitat. Ad. mostly rufous; small tail (Pl.4).

### 4. Black-collared Hawk p 104 Map 106
*Busarellus nigricollis*  Imm.
N; E. Large wings, short fanned tail. Ad. (Pl.4) rufous with whitish head. Imm. confusing, heavily mottled, *usually traces of black collar,* older birds with traces of rufous. All plumages show *blackish outer primaries.* Always near water.

### Black-Hawks *Buteogallus*

### 5. Common *B. anthracinus* p 102 Map 102
Ad.: *single median tail band*; base of bill, cere, and lores bright yellow (cf. 6, larger, less yellow on bill, basal half of tail white). Imm. much like imm. of 6 but *fewer tail bands,* sides usually darker; from imm. of 3 by chunkier, shorter-winged shape, no rufous. Mainly coastal.

### 6. Great *B. urubitinga* p 102 Map 103
6a Imm.
Larger ally of 5. *Entire basal half of tail white;* tail longer, legs longer, base of bill black (or sometimes gray). Cf. 7. Likes vicinity of water but more inland than 5. Voices differ.

### 7. Solitary Eagle p 103 Map 104
*Harpyhaliaetus solitarius*
Apparently confined to hills and mts. Rare. Very large; broader- and longer-winged than 5 or 6; *nearly tailless flight profile; slate gray* (not blackish) plumage; median tail band. Also see text. Imm. underparts extensively blotched black (esp. chest and thighs); short tail lacks distinct barring, becomes blacker distally. Cf. Imm. of 1, 5, 6, and *Oroaetus* (Pl.VI).

IV

1
imm

2

2 a
imm

3
imm

4
imm

5

6

5

6

6 a
imm

7

Gꭲᴜᴅᴏʀ

# PLATE V RAPTORS

NOTE: In general med. to large, forest-dwelling raptors; most with longish tail, blackish upperparts, pure white underparts. Soar reg. (except 2) but tend to perch inconspic. inside forest.

**Hawks** *Leucopternis*

**1. White Hawk** *L. albicollis* p 101 Map 101
Am. of black on shoulder and back var. (see text), but *underparts always immaculate; tail white with broad subterminal band.* Imm. may show streaked crown (cf.6), otherwise like ad., incl. tail.

**2. Black-faced** *L. melanops* p 101 Map 100
SE (rare). Small size, *streaked* crown, *black tail with white median band* (reverse of 1), faint white tail tip; *orange* cere (not gray as 1). Dense river edge(?); not known to soar (unlike 1).

**3. Hook-billed Kite** p. 91 Map 80
*Chondrohierax uncinatus* Juv.
Light phase juv. *Bill and facial markings as in ad.;* blackish crown, *pale* collar, faint scalelike bars below (usually), rangy shape. See Plates II, III, 4.

**4. Gray-headed Kite** p 90 Map 79
*Leptodon cayanensis* 4a Light Phase Imm.
Sleek ad. distinctive (no phases). *Blackish wing linings,* boldly *barred* primaries, contrasting *smooth gray* head, rounded wings, longish tail (bands less distinct above). 4a much like 5 and often confused (see text). Note shape, yellow lores, heavier banding on primaries. Dark phase imm., Pl.III.

**5. Black-and-white Hawk-Eagle** p 111 Map 121
*Spizastur melanoleucus*
Rare. Smallish eagle (usually smaller than 6). Wings not as elliptical (butterfly-shaped) as 6 (or 3, Pl.VI); tail shorter than 4 and 6. Note short black crest, *red orange cere, black lores, nearly immaculate underparts* (cf. 6); more eaglelike proportions than 4a, stronger legs feathered to toes.

**6. Ornate Hawk-Eagle** p 112 Map 123
*Spizaetus ornatus*
Imm. Rather like 4a, 5 (also imm. 4 and 5, Pl.VI). Wings very elliptical and bluntly rounded (like butterfly wing); legs feathered to toes; *thighs barred, wing linings spotted* (more prom. in older birds), cere yellow, lores pale, long crest blackish in older birds (also see text).

V

1

1

2

3

4

4 a

4 a

4

5

5

6

6

GTUDOR

# PLATE VI RAPTORS

**1. Collared Forest-Falcon** p 118 Map 135
*Micrastur semitorquatus* Dark Phase
Incl. to show shape of genus. Small rounded wings,
rather long tail. Does not soar. Imm., Pl.4; ad., Pl.5.

**Hawk-Eagles** *Spizaetus* Large, lanky forest-based
eagles with *uniquely oval-shaped wings*; long rounded
tail, legs feathered to toes, bill deeper and heavier
than *Spizastur*; projecting aquiline head in flight; wings
and tail broadly banded in ads.

**2. Ornate** *S. ornatus* p 112 Map 123
Ad. Distinctive; sides of head and neck *rufous*, black
malar stripe, *coarsely barred wing linings and lower
underparts* (but see text for sim. but smaller Gray-bellied Hawk, (Pl.5). Wings *decidedly narrow and indented at base* (effect of butterfly wings). Imm. (Pl.V):
head and underparts white, all show *barred thighs and
flanks*; less barring on wing linings than ad.

**3. Black** *S. tyrannus* p 112 Map 122
3a Imm.
Shape much like 2, wings narrower, even more constricted at base(?); crest short and bushy. Ad.: prom.
banding on flight feathers (appears *checkered* at distance); black body. Imm. much darker than imm. of 2;
pale eyebrow, *blackish* cheeks; *sides and flanks
blackish*.

**4. Black-and-chestnut Eagle** p 113 Map 124
*Oroaetus isidori* Early Imm.
Subtropical and temperate zone. Ad. description, Pl.VII.
Wings not obviously oval-shaped as in *Spizaetus*. Imm.:
youngest birds *rather pale, mottled dirty brownish*; older
ones progressively darker; all stages apparently retain
*pale primary patch* (from below), *streaky chest*. Third-
yr. birds show significant amts. of black and chestnut.

**5. Crested Eagle** p 110 Map 119
*Morphnus guianensis* 5a Banded Phase
Very large and broad-winged; body rather slender,
longish legs unfeathered. Ad.: gray head and chest,
unmarked wing linings and lower underparts. Rare
banded phase: darker head and chest; *coarsely barred
below*. Imm.: youngest birds, like youngest of 6a, are
*white-headed*; wing linings barred and mottled; numerous tail bands; older stages attain grayish head,
white wing linings. *Single-pointed* crest (all ages).

**6. Harpy Eagle** *Harpia harpyja* p 111 Map 120
6a Early Imm.
Immense, powerful eagle (esp. ♀). Ad.: *Black chest
band, barred thighs, heavily black-mottled wing linings*; up close divided crest, huge bill and tarsi. Imm.:
youngest stage much like corresponding plumage of
5 but always shows divided crest; all but youngest *show
dark chest band* and dark crest.

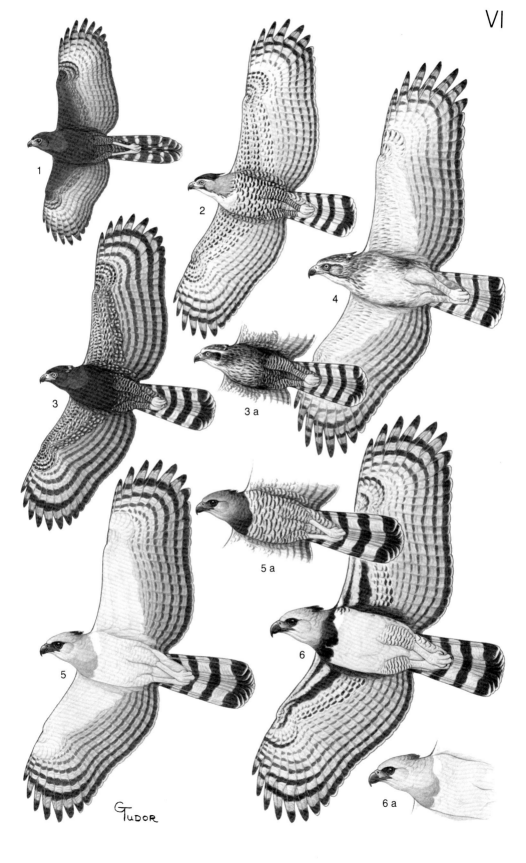

G. TUDOR

# PLATE VII RAPTORS

**1. Black-chested Buzzard-Eagle** p 104 Map 107
*Geranoaetus melanoleucus*
Ad. Large eagle of open temperate zone or higher. Long *extremely broad* wings; short wedge-shaped, fanned tail (no bars) *barely protruding behind wings*; blackish above, *contrasting silvery gray shoulder patches*; dark head and chest. Imm., see text and Pl.IV.

**2. Black-and-chestnut Eagle** p 113 Map 124
*Oroaetus isidori*
Subtropical and temperate zone. Ad.: *projecting aquiline head plumes*; breast chestnut streaked black; wing linings chestnut, *darker than flight feathers*. Note *large pale areas on outer primaries*, broad black *terminal band on longish tail*. Imm., Pl.VI. Scarce.

**3. Red-backed Hawk** *Buteo polyosoma* p 108 Map 116
C Andes (higher el.; s migrant?). Ad. var., at least 5 color phases; but *all have white tail with broad black subterminal band*. Several phases have rufous backs (only ♀♀?), otherwise vary from gray above and white below to slaty black above and below (see text). Imm. has light and dark phase; older light phase birds show rufous on back. Conclusive field identification is complicated by presence of VARIABLE HAWK *B. poecilochrous* s migrant; all 5 color phases of Red-backed are believed duplicated in latter (see text).

**4. Barred Hawk** *Leucopternis princeps* p 100 Map 98
Andean foothills and lower el. Med.-large, broad-winged hawk; plumage recalls 1 (no range overlap). Note longer tail with prom. white band, *uniformly dark upperparts*, dark head and chest. Also Pl.4.

**5. Black-shouldered Kite** p 93 Map 83
*Elanus caeruleus*   Imm.
Graceful, med.-sized kite of open country in lowlands. Ad. pearly white; *black shoulders*; black underwrist patch; often hovers for extended periods. Imm. sim. but *tinged and streaked brownish* above and on chest; *retains contrasting shoulders*.

**6. Plumbeous Kite** *Ictinia plumbea* p 95 Map 87
6a Imm.
Resident and migrant. Widespread common kite of forested zones. *Long obliquely-pointed wings*. Ad. has *rufous at base of primaries from below*, orange red legs, white bands on black tail from below. At rest (Pl.4), *short orange red legs*; wing tips beyond tail. Notably social. MISSISSIPPI *I. mississippiensis* N migrant: much like 6 and usually not safely told in field (see text).

**7. Bat Falcon** *Falcon rufigularis* p 119 Map 139
Small dark falcon. All dark head forms black hood (cf. 10); *broad blackish vest covers entire breast*; white barring fine. Characteristically perches high on stubs at forest edge. Cf. rare Orange-breasted Falcon (Pl.5), larger, with less black below, coarser barring.

**8. Pearl Kite** *Gampsonyx swainsonii* p 92 Map 82
N, E. A tiny kite of open zones. Blackish above, mostly white below, contrasting *rufous thighs; white on rear wing edge* in flight. The smallest Colombian raptor; often perches on high wires. Pl.5.

**9. Peregrine Falcon** *Falco peregrinus* p 120 Map 142
Imm.
N migrant (S migrant?). A large dashing falcon, most often seen in flight. *Black cap and sideburns; bluish* back. Imm. brownish above, heavily streaked below; pale eyebrow.

**10. Aplomado Falcon** *Falco femoralis* p 120 Map 141
Imm.
Open drier zones. Slender falcon, longer-tailed and *much paler* than allies. Note *white "sweatband," black "sideburns,"* narrow black vest. Imm. darker above, breast more heavily streaked, lower underparts paler, buffy. Pl.5.

**11. Merlin** *Falco columbarius* p 119 Map 138
W (n migrant). Another *small* compact falcon, decidedly scarce. ♂ *bluish* above; imm. and ♀ *brown* above; streaked underparts. *Lacks* obvious facial pattern (cf. larger 9).

**12. American Kestrel** p 119 Map 137
*Falco sparverius*
Common small falcon of open country. Both sexes told by *rufous back and tail*. The 3 subsp. differ markedly in color and pattern of underparts. Pl.5.

VII

# PLATE VIII CURASSOWS

NOTE: Med. to large cracids; plumage predom. black (except 7). None easily found.

**Curassows** *Crax* White or chestnut belly and tail tips; usually have curly crest, colored knobs, etc. at base of bill.

**1. Yellow-knobbed** *C. daubentoni* p 129 Map 163
NE (drier hills). White belly and *tail tips*. ♂ has yellow knobs and cere. ♀ has white eyes, white scaled breast, no yellow adornments.

**2. Blue-billed** *C. alberti* p 129 Map 162
N. ♂ has *blue* cere and wattles. Normal phase ♀ has chestnut belly, blue cere (no wattles), narrowly barred upperparts and tail. Rare barred ♀ (Santa Marta Mts.) heavily scaled white below. GREAT *C. rubra* NW: white belly and yellow knob on upper surface of bill. For ♀, see text.

**3. Northern Helmeted** *C. pauxi* p 128 Map 160
NE (humid Mts.). *Reddish* bill and legs; *fig-shaped grayish casque on forehead*. ♂ and normal ♀ have *white belly and tail tips*. Rare rufous phase ♀ vermiculated rufescent and black from chest to rump.

**4. Common Piping-Guan** p 125 Map 153
*Aburria pipile*
SE. *Large white* wing patches, *shaggy white* crest, *blue facial skin* and dewlap.

**5. Black Curassow** *Crax alector* p 130 Map 164
E. Swollen cere (no knobs) orange red (or yellow in Macarena); *white belly; tail all black*.

**6. Wattled Curassow** *Crax globulosa* p 130 Map 165
SE. ♂ *bright red knobs around bill*, white belly. ♀: red cere (no knobs); *chestnut belly. Tail all black* (both sexes).

**7. Nocturnal Curassow** p 127 Map 156
*Nothocrax urumutum*
SE. Med.-sized cracid with tinamoulike pattern. Mainly *chestnut; buff tail tips, red bill*, curly black crest, bare slate- and *yellow*-colored ocular region. Vocal from well up in trees at night.

**Curassows** *Crax*

**8. Crestless (Lesser Razor-billed)** p 127 Map 157
*C. tomentosa*
SE. *Chestnut belly and tail tips*; thickish red bill; no crest. Sexes nearly alike.

**9. Salvin's** *C. salvini* p 128 Map 158
SE. *White belly and tail tips*; compressed, arched reddish bill. Sexes alike.

**10. Razor-billed** *C. mitu* p 128 Map 159
SE. *Chestnut belly, white tail tips*; compressed, arched reddish bill (razor-bill); crested. Sexes alike.

## VIII

PRALL

# PLATE IX OWLS

**1. Spectacled Owl** p 228 Map 315
*Pulsatrix perspicillata*
Large, earless. Chocolate brown above; *white facial markings, deep brown chest band,* uniform buff underparts. BAND-BELLIED *P. melanota* SE: differs in *brown band* lower on breast; *rusty barred belly.*

**Owls** *Ciccaba* Med.-sized, earless.

**2. Mottled** *C. virgata* p 231 Map 324
Heavily mottled brownish above, more *streaky below.* Pale outline on dark facial disks; *eyes brown.* Notably vocal.

**3. Rufous-banded** *C. albitarsus* p 231 Map 323
Rare highland ally of 2. Differs in *coarser* markings on hindneck and mantle, bolder facial disk outline, decidedly *rufous* chest band, and *very spotty lower underparts.*

**4. Black-and-white** *C. nigrolineata* p 230* Map 321
Only Colombian owl with white underparts *uniformly lined* black. Note *contrasting black face.* Cf. 5.

**5. Black-banded** *C. huhula* p 231 Map 322
SE. *Blackish above and below; narrow white lines* (faint above).

**6. Crested** *Lophostrix cristata* p 227 Map 313
*Long white ear tufts* impart commanding appearance if erect but may be laid back horizontally along sides of head. Note *unstreaked underparts;* voice (hard to locate).

**7. Striped Owl** *Rhinoptynx clamator* p 232 Map 325
Widespread owl of grasslands, open country. Prom. ears, dark eyes, *sharp black outline* around whitish face, *bold black stripes* on buff-white underparts (cf. 8, 9).

**Owls** *Asio*

**8. Short-eared** *A. flammeus* p 232 Map 327
Very local in open zones. Diurnal; usually seen on the wing. Like 7, but *markings much subdued,* ears inconspic.; yellow eyes in blackish orbits.

**9. Stygian** *A. stygius* p 232 Map 326
Local. Overall *dark appearance;* prom., *closely spaced* ears; *pale* forehead; heavy herringbone streaks below; yellow eyes.

**10. Great Horned Owl** p 227 Map 314
*Bubo virginianus*
Largest Colombian owl. Mostly nonforest zones. *Widely spaced ears;* white throat, closely barred underparts. BURROWING OWL *Speotyto cunicularia* N, E: mainly terrestrial in drier zones (see text).

**Screech-Owls** *Otus* Small; short ear tufts; most easily separated by voice.

**11. Vermiculated** *O. guatemalae* p 225 Map 307
NW (elsewhere?). *Virtually uniform.* Lacks rim on facial disk; almost *no streaks* below.

**12. Tropical** *O. choliba* p 225 Map 308
Most common, most widespread *Otus.* Well-defined *black facial rim; crisp black streaks and faint cross hatching* over pale underparts. Yellow eyes. Often heard (learn voice). RUFESCENT *O. ingens* Andes: much like smaller 12; lacks black facial rim; brown eyes. For BARE-SHANKED *O. clarkii* NW, see text.

**13. Tawny-bellied** *O. watsonii* p 226 Map 310
E. *Dark, esp. above.* Facial rim not prom.; underparts ochraceous tawny, only faintly streaked and vermiculated.

**14. White-throated** *O. albogularis* p 227 Map 312
Higher el.; rare. Very dark; *contrasting white throat;* rather speckled above, ears rudimentary.

**15. Buff-fronted Owl** *Aegolius harrisii* p 233 Map 328
Cold semiopen highlands; rare. Small; contrasting black and rich buff pattern.

## IX

Gwynne

# PLATE X NIGHTHAWKS and POTOOS

NOTE: Nighthawks have narrow pointed wings, hunt in sustained stiff-winged flight, usually high above ground (except 5).

**1. Nacunda Nighthawk** p 238 Map 340
*Podager nacunda*
N, E. *Quite large*; heavy bodied; white wing band; *white wing linings and belly*; short tail. Bounding flight.

**Nighthawks** *Chordeiles* Open zones, sand bars. Crepuscular. ♀ ♀ of some with buffy throat, buff wing band, less white in tail.

**2. Sand-colored** *C. rupestris* p 237 Map 337
E. Flashing black and white wing pattern: *no wing bands*. Much smaller, paler, longer-tailed than 1. Mechanical flight (no "gear-changing"). Vincinity of water.

**3. Lesser** *C. acutipennis* p 237 Map 338
Resident and n migrant subsp. (see text). Med.-sized (cf. 4); prom. white (buff ♀) wing band *near tip*. COMMON *C. minor* N migrant: differs in having wing band placed *midway to tip* (see text).

**4. Least** *C. pusillus* p 236 Map 336
E. Smaller version of 3. Note *white vent, pale trailing edge on secondaries*. Savannas near Orinoco.

**5. Band-tailed Nighthawk** p 238 Map 339
*Nyctiprogne leucopyga*
E. Small, *uniformly dark; no wing bands*. From above shows only small white notch on mid-tail edge (hard to see). Groups flutter low over water at dusk.

**6. Short-tailed Nighthawk** p 236 Map 335
*Lurocalis semitorquatus*
Mts; E. *All dark, short-tailed*; batlike flight. Forest canopy and forest edge. Normally flies over tree canopy. Local. Two rather different races (see text).

**Potoos** *Nyctibius* Nocturnal, solitary; cryptic as they sit erect and motionless. Eyes reflect orangish to yellow at night. Note vocalizations. Several spp. poorly known.

**7. Great** *N. grandis* p 234 Map 330
Very large and robust; *usually whitish* (some var.); no dusky malar. Tail bar pattern diagnostic if seen (see text). Gruff voice *on moolit nights*.

**8. Long-tailed** *N. aethereus* p 234 Map 331
Very rare. Almost as large as 7; pattern most like 11 but tail proportionally longer, more graduated than any other.

**9. White-winged** *N. leucopterus* p 235 Map 333
Subtropics. *Whitish median wing coverts* form contrasting bar. Rare.

**10. Rufous** *N. bracteatus* p 235 Map 334
Another rare potoo. *Small, rufous; white shoulder spots*.

**11. Common** *N. griseus* p 235 Map 332
Most common, most widespread. Med-sized, and lacks strong markings. Cf. 7, 8, and 9 (see text). Haunting call *on moonlit nights*.

X

# PLATE XI NIGHTJARS

NOTE: Confusing group, esp. at rest when key marks often cannot be seen. If in doubt flush these birds. Look for presence or absence of white wing bands, white in tail, and white on throat in ♂♂; these markings usually buff or lacking in ♀♀. In the hand undertail pattern of ♂♂ usually distinctive. Learn the voices.

### 1. Lesser Nighthawk p 237 Map 338
*Chordeiles acutipennis*
May sit on ground. Unlike *Caprimulgus*, wing tips of *Chordeiles* reach end of tail. Note strong coarse barring on underparts (shared with Common and Least nighthawks, Pl.X).

### 2. Ladder-tailed Nightjar p 243 Map 349
*Hydropsalis Climacocerca*
Common, Amazonian sandbars, river edges. ♂: white wing band; *long tail with white slash on both sides* (not edge) as flushes. ♀ virtually without markings; note narrow *cinnamon band* on primaries, *pointed tips on longish tail* (cf. ♀ of 4).

### 3. Pauraque *Nyctidromus albicollis* p 239 Map 341
Most common, most widespread nightjar and the one whose eyes are most likely seen shining on roads at night at lower el. *Prom. buff and black* scapular markings. ♂: white wing band (buff, ♀); shows white most of length of tail as it flushes. ♀: faint white outer tail tips.

### Nightjars *Caprimulgus*

### 4. White-tailed *C. cayennensis* p 241 Map 345
*Small* nightjar of drier open country; prom. *buff nuchal collar.* ♂: white wing band (cinnamon, ♀), edge and underside of tail white. ♀: no white on throat or tail.

### 5. Band-winged *C. longirostris* p 241 Map 344
Subropical, temperate zone. Smaller and darker than 3 and found at *higher el.* ♂: large white wing bands and outer tail patch; rufous nuchal collar. ♀: *buff wing bands*, all dark tail (cf. ♀ of 10).

### 6. Little *C. parvulus* p 242 Map 347
N (scarce). Despite name, about same size as 4, 5, 7, and 8. Dark and short-tailed. ♂: conspic. *white throat diagnostic*; note white wing bands, tiny white tail tip. ♀: throat buff; *several rufous wing bars* (cf. longer-tailed ♀ of 4).

### 7. Spot-tailed *C. maculicaudus* p 242 Map 346
NW; llanos in E. A *small, notably, dark nightjar lacking a prom. wing band* (has several rufescent bars). Note pale eyebrow, spotty underparts, white tail tip (gray, ♀). Cattle country.

### 8. Blackish *C. nigrescens* p 242 Map 348
E. The *darkest Colombian nightjar.* ♂: partial white wing band; tiny white outer tail tip. ♀ *all blackish.* Common on rocky blackwater rivers. OCELLATED POORWILL *Nyctiphrynus ocellatus* W, SE(?): very dark; 2 large white shoulder spots: *dark wings: broad white band* on tail tip.

### 9. Rufous *C. rufus* p 240 Map 343
N, NE. *Large very ruddy nightjar with no white or buff wing bands*; no pattern on shoulders (cf. 3). ♂ has white on underside of tail (not a field mark). CHUCK-WILL'S WIDOW *C. carolinensis* N migrant: slightly larger than 9 but not safely separated in field (see text).

### 10. Lyre-tailed Nightjar *Uropsalis lyra* p 243 Map 351
Andes. Dark highland nightjar *lacking* wing bands. ♂ with streaming ribbonlike white-tipped tail is unmistakable. ♀ essentially without strong markings; primaries crossed by several small rufous bars (cf. ♀ of 5). SWALLOW-TAILED *U. segmentata* E, C Andes: ♂ has *rigid scissorlike tail* slightly shorter than ♂ of 10; ♀ virtually identical to ♀ of 10 (see text). Occurs at higher el. than 10 (slight overlap).

XI

# PLATE XII SWIFTS

NOTE: Many swifts are among the most difficult birds to identify in the field. Thoroughly learn plumages, flight patterns, habits, and el. of more common spp. (1, 2, 5, 6, 9, and 13) before attempting others shown here. *CAUTION.* Several additional spp. described in text may also occur in Colombia.

### 1. White-collared Swift p 244 Map 352
*Streptoprocne zonaris*
W (usually near mts.) *Largest. Broad white collar*, slightly notched tail. Almost always in flocks.

**Swifts** *Cypseloides* Larger and blacker than *Chaetura*; back, wings, rump, and tail always uniform (no contrast); underparts more or less uniform (or with chestnut or white on throat and chest).

### 2. Chestnut-collared *C. rutilus* p 245 Map 353
Mts. Blackish; rather *long-tailed.* ♂ has chestnut collar often not easily seen. Stronger, steadier flight than *Chaetura.* ♀ shows little or no chestnut.

### 3. White-chinned *C. cryptus* p 245 Map 355
W (rare). *Uniformly blackish; short square* tail. Prob. not safely told from several allies (see text). In hand (field?) white chin diagnostic.

### 4. Spot-fronted *C. cherriei* p 245 Map 354
Santander (once; status?). White supraloral spot and postocular diagnostic (hard to see).

### 5. Band-rumped Swift p 247 Map 359
*Chaetura spinicauda*
Small slender swift with speedy, veering flight. From all others by *narrow whitish* rump band; tail blackish, throat quite pale.

### 6. Gray-rumped p 247 Map 358
*Chaetura cinereiventris*
*Obviously gray* rump and upper tail coverts (cf. narrow band of 5) contrast with black back. Smaller, longer-tailed than most *Chaetura*; no brown in plumage.

### 7. White-chested Swift p 246 Map 356
*Cypseloides lemosi*
Cauca Val. (status uncertain). Large blackish swift; *prom. white patch on chest.* Imm. may completely lack white, then much like ♀ of 2 and others.

**Swifts** *Chaetura* Small; many spp. very difficult to separate in field; all with contrasting pale rump and/or tail; some with pale throat; flight usually twittery.

### 8. Chapman's *C. chapmani* p 246 Map 357
Scarce (status?). Glossiest and most uniform plumage of the genus. *Glossy blackish above*; brown rump does not contrast strongly; essentially uniform sooty gray below; throat vaguely paler (cf. larger *Cypseloides*). CHIMNEY *C. pelagica* N migrant: sooty grayish brown, rump paler; contrasting whitish throat. Few recs.

### 9. Short-tailed *C. brachyura* p 248 Map 361
N, E (mainly over forested zones). Common. Tail is very short but best marks are *broad secondaries* indented near body, and peculiar *floppy flight* (not twittery); conspic. *pale rear end* from above.

### 10. Ashy-tailed *C. andrei* p 247 Map 360
N (S migrant). Larger and shorter-tailed than most *Chaetura*. Rump and upper tail coverts light brownish gray, throat decidedly pale. Cf. sim. Chimney Swift. Often flies low over open zones.

### 11. White-tipped Swift p 248 Map 362
*Aeronautes montivagus*
Local. Streamlined fast flier much like 12 but *square-tailed* (or slightly notched); *usually with white tail tip from above;* ♀ *usually without* white tips. Both sexes *lack* white hind collar of 12. *Notably social* (unlike 12).

### 12. Lesser Swallow-tailed Swift p 248 Map 363
*Panyptila cayennensis*
Much like 11. Long deeply forked tail usually held closed in a point; complete white collar across hindneck; solitary or in pairs, *not* flocks.

### 13. Fork-tailed Palm-Swift p 249 Map 365
*Reinarda squamata*
E. A *dingy brown, point-tailed* swift (forked tail held closed) low over open areas with scattered palms; whitish median underparts, buzzy eratic flight; *slender* profile.

### 14. Pygmy Swift p 249 Map 364
*Micropanyptila furcata*
NE (rare). Like 13 but decidedly smaller, less white below; white at base of outer tail feathers may be visible as twists and turns; faster wing beats than 13.

XII

# PLATE XIII  ANTSHRIKES and LARGE COTINGAS

NOTE: ♂ antshrikes with black-and-white plumage.

**1. Undulated Antshrike** p 379 Map 727
*Frederickena unduligera*
SE. Large and robust. ♂: fine wavy barring; *solid black throat and chest* (cf. 3). ♀: rufous barred black *above and below.* Undergrowth.

**2. Great Antshrike** *Taraba major* p 379 Map 728
♂ black and white. ♀ chestnut and white, Red eyes (both sexes). Widespread.

**3. Fasciated Antshrike** p 379 Map 726
*Cymbilaimus lineatus*
Red eyes. ♂ finely barred; *solid black cap* (cf. 1). ♀, crown unbarred (cf. ♀ of 1). Well up in vines in forest.

**Antshrikes** *Thamnophilus* Slight or no range overlap between 4, 5, and 6.

**4. Barred** *T. doliatus* p 380 Map 731
Yellow eyes. ♂ coarsely barred (except crown). ♀ rufous and buff; sides of head freckled; *unbarred below.* Widespread.

**5. Bar-crested** *T. multistriatus* p 381 Map 732
C vals. ♂ much like 4, crown barred (see text). ♀ rufous above, *barred black and white below.*

**6. Lined** *T. palliatus* p 381 Map 733
E base Andes. ♂ finely barred, appearing *blacker* than allies. ♀ slightly darker than ♀ of 5 (see text).

**7. Red-ruffed Fruitcrow** p 454 Map 927
*Pyroderus scutatus*
Andes (spotty). Large, mostly black. *Red crinkled throat feathers.* W subsp. extensively chestnut below.

**8. Bare-necked Fruitcrow** p 453 Map 925
*Gymnoderus foetidus*
SE. Vulturine appearance when perched. ♂ black; *silvery gray upper wing surface* flashes in flight. ♀ all dull blackish. High over Amazonian rivers.

**Umbrellabirds** *Cephalopterus*

**9. Amazonian** *C. ornatus* p 454 Map 928
Quite large, black; woodpeckerlike in flight. ♂ has exaggerated permanently erect crest; wattle usually inconspic. ♀ has smaller crest, no wattle. Perches high; favors Amazonian river edges and river isls.

**10. Long-wattled** *C. penduliger* p 455 Map 929
Pacific slope cloud forest. Much like 9. ♂: wattle considerably longer than 9. ♀ has no wattle. Wary, infrequently seen.

# PLATE 1 TINAMOUS and WOODQUAILS

**1. Highland Tinamou** p 42 Map 5
*Nothocercus bonapartei*
Andes. Rufescent; *slaty* crown, *bright cinnamon* throat (cf. 9).

**Tinamous** *Tinamus* Med. to large, mostly lowlands.

**2. Gray** *T. tao* p 41 Map 1
Large; *grayish*; freckled sides of head; obscure neck stripe; throat white. Mostly hills.

**3. Great** *T. major* p 42 Map 3
Large; *olive brown* back, *grayish brown* underparts; crown chestnut (most subsp); whitish throat and belly.

**Tinamous** *Crypturellus* Small, mostly lowlands.

**4. Brown** *C. obsoletus* p 44 Map 10
"Bogota." Like ruddiest races of 5 but larger, throat gray, *flanks definitely barred* (cf. 1 and 9).

**5. Little** *C. soui* p 43 Map 9
Small; common. Var. but whitish throat and essentially unbarred plumage holds (6 is larger). ♀ darker, richer than ♂. CHOCO *C. kerriae* Baudó: differs in slaty sides of head, darker plumage, red legs, strong flank barring.

**6. Undulated** *C. undulatus* p 44 Map 11
SE. Uniform grayish brown, paler below and *without obvious markings* (faint bars on rear flanks and crissum). Distinct call (see text). GRAY-LEGGED *C. duidae* S Macarena: ♂ like 6 but breast rufous; ♀ has barred rearparts.

**7. Red-legged** *C. erythropus* p 45 Map 13
N. Complex var. *Pinkish* legs diagnostic in its range; typically barred above, stronger in ♀.

**8. Variegated** *C. variegatus* p 46 Map 15
E. *Black* head, *rufous* neck, *boldly barred* upperparts.

**9. Tawny-breasted Tinamou** p 43 Map 6
*Nothocercus julius*
Andes. Like 1 but slightly smaller; *cap chestnut, throat white.* Ranges to higher el.

**10. White-throated** *Tinamus guttatus* p 42 Map 4
E. Med.-sized. Slaty-crown, white throat, *rearparts spotted and speckled buffy white.* Cf. 3, which is barred black.

**11. Barred Tinamou** p 46 Map 16
*Crypturelllus casiquiare*
Orinoco. Small; *boldly barred* above; foreneck and breast gray. Cf. 8.

**12. Marbled Wood-Quail** p 131 Map 167
*Odontophorus gujanensis*
NW, E. *Bare reddish ocular area; no strong plumage pattern.*

**13. Berlepsch's Tinamou** p 43 Map 8
*Crypturellus berlepschi*
W. *Very dark;* head blackish; *dark red* legs, red mandible. Lacks barring or spottings.

**14. Cinereous Tinamou** p 43 Map 7
*Crypturellus cinereus*
E. *Uniform grayish brown* (no markings or contrast); dull orange legs.

**15. Tawny-faced Quail** p 133 Map 173
*Rhynchortyx cinctus*
NW. Small. ♂ has *orange* on head; *gray* breast. ♀ has white eyestripe and throat, barred belly.

**Wood-Quails** *Odontophorus*

**16. Chestnut** *O. hyperythrus* p 132 Map 170
Andes. ♂: *white spectacles,* rufous foreface and underparts. ♀ has lower underparts grayish brown. GORGETED *O. strophium* Cundinamarca: white speckled eyebrow and malar, black throat, rufous breast *spotted white.* Rare.

**17. Black-fronted** *O. atrifrons* p 132 Map 169
NE. Only wood-quail in range. *Black face,* otherwise unpatterned.

**18. Rufous-fronted** *O. erythrops* p 131 Map 168
Andes. *Chestnut face and underparts;* narrow white crescent in black throat. DARK-BACKED *O. melanonotus* SW Nariño: brownish black; rufous throat.

# PLATE 2 HERONS

NOTE: See text ills. 9, 10, 11

**1. Yellow-crowned Night-Heron** p 67 Map 35
*Nyctanassa violacea*
Coastal. Ad. gray; striped head. Imm. much like imm.
2 (see text).

**2. Black-crowned Night-Heron** p 66 Map 34
*Nycticorax nycticorax*
W. Gray wings, black of back more extensive than 3;
*all white* underparts. Imm. well spotted above, thicker
bill than 1.

**3. Boat-billed Heron** p 70 Map 43
*Cochlearius cochlearius*
*Massive bill; extraordinarily large eyes; pale wings* (except NW), *rusty belly*; broad white forehead, less black
above (cf. ad. 2). Imm. cinnamon above.

**4. Capped Heron** *Pilherodius pileatus* p 66 Map 33
*Blue* face, *black* cap. Most have *strong creamy buff
wash on neck and breast.* Chunky.

**Tiger-Herons** *Tigrisoma* Juvs. broadly banded and all
much alike; older birds nearer respective ad.
plumage.

**5. Fasciated** *T. fasciatum* p 67 Map 37
Rivers in forested hills. Slaty back and neck finely barred
buff; black cap. BARE-THROATED *T. mexicanum* NW: bare
yellow throat (all plumages).

**6. Rufescent** *T. lineatum* p 67 Map 36
6a Juv.
Ad. has *reddish chestnut* head and neck. Juv. and
imm. stages much like 5 (see text). Widespread.

**7. Pinnated Bittern** *Botaurus pinnatus* p 69 Map 42
From imm. *Tigrisoma* by *streaked mantle and wings.*
Note dusky cap, fine buffy barred neck. *Black* flight
feathers.

**8. Stripe-backed Bittern** p 68 Map 40
*Ixobrychus involucris*
Seldom seen. *Ochraceous* appearance; black cap,
striped back, buff-tipped wings.

**9. Striated Heron** *Butorides striatus* p 65 Map 29
9a Imm.
Small, common. *Gray foreparts.* Imm. streaky foreneck. GREEN *B. virescens* (p 64) N migrant: *maroon*
foreneck. Imm. like 9, foreparts less gray.

**10. Zigzag Heron** *Zebrilus undulatus* p 68 Map 39
10a Imm.
E. Small, dark, forest heron. Finely barred above; vermiculated below. Imm. sides of neck uniform rufous.
Rarely seen.

**11. Least Bittern** *Ixobrychus exilis* p 69 Map 41
Back black (♂), or chestnut (♀); rufous on head and
neck; pale shoulders in flight; no buff wing tips,

**12. Whistling Heron** *Syrigma sibilatrix* p 66 Map 32
E, llanos. Striking *black, blue, and pink face and bill;*
yellowish neck and shoulders. *White rump and tail* in
flight.

**13. Tricolored Heron** p 64 Map 27
*Hydranassa tricolor*
Coastal. Contrasting *white* belly and wing linings. Long
bill, thin neck (cf. 14).

**14. Agami Heron** *Agamia agami* p 65 Map 30
14a Imm.
*Chestnut* neck and lower underparts; *very long* bill. Imm.
dark brown, streaked white below. Forests.

## PLATE 3 LIMPKIN, IBISES, and DUCKS

**1. Limpkin** *Aramus guarauna* p 134 Map 174
Ibislike, but bill thicker and straighter. *Heavily spotted* neck and mantle. Stiff, up-flicked wing stroke.

**2. Glossy Ibis** *Plegadis falcinellus* p 75 Map 53
2a Imm.
Bronzy maroon color diagnostic. Facial skin always slaty; longer-legged than allies. Nonbreeders and imm. streaky white on head and neck.

**3. Scarlet Ibis** *Eudocimus ruber* p 74 Map 52
Juv.
Scarlet ad. unmistakable. Juv. has white lower underparts like juv. White Ibis. Older birds have pink patches.

**4. Buff-necked Ibis** *Theristicus caudatus* p 72 Map 47
Rich buff neck; *bold* wing pattern.

**5. Green Ibis** p 73 Map 49
*Mesembrinibis cayennensis*
Dark greenish bill and legs; slaty face. Favors woodland.

**6. Whispering Ibis** *Phimosus infuscatus* p 73 Map 50
N, E. Bare *pinkish* legs and face. Small size, shorter tail. Social (unlike 5).

**7. Sharp-tailed Ibis** *Cercibus oxycerca* p 72 Map 48
E. *Large*, long-tailed; pinkish legs and facial skin; *orange* throat.

**8. Orinoco Goose** *Neochen jubata* p 80 Map 61
E. *Creamy white* foreparts, *chestnut* body; white wing band (flight). Erect posture.

**9. Masked Duck** *Oxyura dominica* p 86 Map 71
N, E. Small, retiring. ♂: *black foreface.* ♀ and nonbreeding ♂: *two head stripes, white wing patch* in flight. RUDDY *O. jamaicensis* Resident, Mts.: ♂: black head; ♀ *single* head stripe, *dark* wings.

**10. Brazilian Duck** p 84 Map 67
*Amazonetta brasiliensis*
E. Small; *pale* sides of head and neck, contrasting wing pattern. ♂: red bill. ♀: head spots. Llanos.

**11. Blue-winged Teal** *Anas discors* p 82 Map 64
N migrant. ♂: white crescent on face. ♀: mottled brown; blue wing patch (as in Cinnamon Teal). CINNAMON *A. cyanoptera* Mainly resident: breeding ♂ distinctive. ♀ and nonbreeding ♂ like ♀ of 11 (see text).

**12. Speckled Teal** *Anas flavirostris* p 80 Map 62
Andes. Foreparts usually *prom. spotted; blue gray* bill.

**13. White-cheeked Pintail** p 81 Map 63
*Anas bahamensis*
Carib. coast. Red on bill; *white cheeks*, pointed tail.

**14. Torrent Duck** *Merganetta armata* p 83 Map 65
Mountain torrents in Andes. *Unique* but inconspicuous when in water. Imm. whitish below.

**Whistling-Ducks** *Dendrocygna*

**15. Black-bellied** *D. autumnalis* p 79 Map 60
N, E. *Rosy* bill (dark, imm.) Black belly; *black* and *white wing pattern.*

**16. White-faced** *D. viduata* p 79 Map 59
N, E. *White face* diagnostic. *All dark* wings.

**17. Fulvous** *D. bicolor* p 79 Map 58
N, E. Mostly cinnamon brown; *gray* bill, *white band* across base of tail; *all dark* wings.

## 3

# PLATE 4 RAPTORS

**1. Yellow-headed Caracara** p 115 Map 129
*Milvago chimachima* 1a Imm.
Creamy head and underparts; whitish wing patches in flight. Imm. recalls imm. of 7. Note slighter build, weaker blue gray feet; wing patches. Pl.I.

**2. Plumbeous Kite** *Ictinia plumbea* p 95 Map 87
Short-legged; long pointed wings reach beyond tail; note orange legs, rufous in wings, white tail bands from below. Pl.VII.

**3. Semiplumbeous Hawk** p 101 Map 99
*Leucopternis semiplumbea*
NW. *White underparts and under wings*; yellow eyes (cf. 4).

**4. Plumbeous Hawk** p 100 Map 97
*Leucopternis plumbea*
NW. *All slaty* forest hawk with *white under wings*, orange cere and legs, single tail band.

**5. Gray Hawk** *Buteo nitidus* p 105 Map 109
Imm. Buffy underparts more obviously *spotted* than streaked. In flight a *light patch on primaries* from above (less prom. than 1a). Plates II, 5.

**6. Slate-colored Hawk** p 100 Map 96
*Leucopternis schistacea*
Chunky *gray* unsuspicuous hawk of Amazonian backwaters. *Red orange cere, orbit and legs*; yellow eyes; 1 tail band. Pl.III.

**7. Crane Hawk** p 95 Map 88
*Geranospiza caerulescens*
Acrobatic hawk of open or forested zones. *Long orange legs*, long double-banded tail; dark cere, dark red eyes. *White crescent on underside* of primaries. Pl.III.

**8. Collared Forest-Falcon** p 118 Map 135
*Micrastur semitorquatus*
Imm. *Buff to tawny collar and underparts.* Am. of *coarse barring* var.; long tail. Ad., Plates VI, 5.

**9. Snail Kite** *Rostrhamus sociabilis* p 93 Map 84
9a Imm.
Marsh dweller with scimitarlike bill. ♂: *large white base* on square tail; orange or red soft parts. ♀ and imm. mottled brownish; tail like ♂. Pl.III.

**10. Slender-billed Kite** p 94 Map 85
*Helicolestes hamatus*
Swamp dweller; bill like 9. *Pale eyes, all dark tail* (sexes sim.). Imm. Pl.III.

**11. Hook-billed Kite** p 91 Map 80
*Chondrohierax uncinatus*
11a Black Phase
*Heavy hooked bill, pale supraloral* spot, and *pale* eyes impart peculiar appearance. Note short legs. ♂♂ usually gray, ♀♀ usually brownish. Rare melanistic birds blackish (both sexes). Plates II, III. Imm., Pl.V.

**12. Barred Hawk** p 100 Map 98
*Leucopternis princeps*
Robust, broad-winged. *Black head and chest* contrast with light underparts. Soars over wetter foothills and mts. Pl.VII.

**13. Harris' [Bay-winged] Hawk** p 105 Map 108
*Parabuteo unicinctus*
Drier open country. Blackish brown. *Chestnut* shoulders; and thighs; *white base and tip* on tail.

**14. Savanna Hawk** p 103 Map 105
*Heterospizias meridionalis*
Sluggish, long-legged hawk of ranchland. *All cinnamon rufous; very long wings*, short black tail. Pl.IV.

**15. Black-collared Hawk** p 104 Map 106
*Busarellus nigricollis*
Mostly *rufous fishing hawk with creamy white head*, black collar, black flight feathers. Pl.IV.

4

# PLATE 5 RAPTORS

**Falcons** *Falco*

**1. Bat** *F. rufigularis* p 119 Map 139
Common. Very dark. *Fine white* barring on *extensively black* breast (cf. larger 2). Pl.VII.

**2. Orange-breasted** *F. deiroleucus* p 120 Map 140
Rare (spotty). Black on breast less extensive, *barring coarser* than on 1, *and buffy*. Note large feet; large size.

**3. Aplomado** *F. femoralis* p 120 Map 141
Paler and longer-tailed than 1 and 2; *light bluish back, white head band, narrow sideburns*. Drier zones. Pl.VII.

**4. American Kestrel** *F. sparverius* p 119 Map 137
Small. Note sideburns; rufous back and tail. Pl.VII.

**5. Pearl Kite** *Campsonyx swainsonii* p 92 M 82
*Tiny*, mainly open country kite. *Blackish above, black cap*, contrasting *rufous* thighs. Pl.VII.

**Hawks** *Buteo*

**6. Gray** *B. nitidus* p 105 Map 109
*Obviously gray; entirely barred below*; contrasting black and white tail. Note *narrow white inner band*. Imm., Plates II, 4.

**7. Roadside** *B. magnirostris* p 106 Map 110
Can look as gray above as 6 but *chest unbarred, ru-fous in primaries*; tail bands uniform. Most common Colombian raptor. Imm., Pl.II.

**8. Broad-winged** *B. platypterus* p 106 Map 112
N migrant. *Brown above* (cf. 6, 7); *rusty* bars below, incl. chest. Imm, Pl.II.

**9. Double-toothed Kite** p 94 Map 86
*Harpagus bidentatus*
Rather small. *Prom. throat stripe*; puffy white under tail coverts; contrasting gray head. Pl.II (flight).

**Hawks** *Accipiter* Short rounded wings, long tail; long legs and dashing habits; ♀♀ usually much larger than ♂♂; most have dark-capped appearance; very little bare facial skin (cf. *Micrastur*). Mainly bird predators.

**10. Bicolored** *A. bicolor* p 99 Map 94
10a Imm.
*Never barred below*. Ad. light to dark gray below; rufous thighs. Imm. var., whitish to rufous below, usually with pale collar; thighs often darker.

**11. Sharp-shinned** *A. striatus* p 97 Map 91
11a Light Phase 11b Dark Phase Imm.
Ad. var. Almost clear breasted (white or melanistic) to heavily barred rufous below; thighs usually rufous. Imm. heavily streaked below (see text). Pl.II (flight). For COOPER'S *A. cooperi* N migrant (accidental), see text.

**12. Gray-bellied** *A. poliogaster* p 99 Map 95
12a Imm.
Rare. Resembles 10 but larger; underparts *lighter gray, cheeks darker*, no rufous thighs. Cf. 15. Imm. resembles much larger Ornate Hawk-Eagle.

**13. Tiny** *A. superciliosus* p 98 Map 93
13a Imm.
Tiny forest hawk. Finely barred gray underparts (cf. *Micrastur*). Rufous phase: rufescent above; rusty barring. For imm., see text. SEMICOLLARED *A. collaris* Mts.: from 13 by larger size, pale hindcollar, mottled cheeks.

**Forest-Falcons** *Micrastur* Slender round-headed forest hawks; short rounded wings, long graduated (rounded) tail; bare lores and bare orbital skin surrounding eyes; long bare yellow legs; notably stealthy but often vocal.

**14. Collared** *M. semitorquatus* p 118 Map 135
Light Phase
Largest of genus. *Green facial skin*. White collar and underparts; *prom. black crescent below eyes*. Tawny and dark phase darker below respectively. Imm. Pls.4,Ad., Pl.VI.

**15. Slaty-backed** *M. mirandollei* p 117 Map 134
Confusing. Ad.: uniform gray cheeks, yellow facial skin, clear white breast (cf. 12, 14). Imm. scaled or streaked below (*not* barred).

**16. Lined** *M. gilvicollis* p 117 Map 132
E. Like more common 17. Lacks rufous phase; note *white eyes, red orange facial skin*; tail (see text). Imm. essentially like imm. of 17.

**17. Barred** *M. ruficollis* p 116 Map 131
17a Imm.
W. *Yellow* facial skin, finely barred underparts, narrow white tail bars (cf. *Accipiter*). Rufous phase: upperparts, throat and chest cinnamon rufous. Imm.: pale collar and *narrow, widely-spaced bars* typical; less often uniform deep buff below. PLUMBEOUS *M. plumbeus* SW: resembles normal phase 17, but tail with only 1 white band.

5

# PLATE 6 CHACHALACAS, GUANS, and GROUND-CUCKOOS

**1. Wattled Guan** *Aburria aburri* p 126 Map 154
Subtropics. Large, blackish; *yellow* legs; long slender neck.

**Ground-Cuckoos** *Neomorphus* Shy, terrestrial, forest cuckoos; Raise and lower crest and tail. Shape of N American Roadrunner.

**2. Rufous-vented** *N. geoffroyi salvini* p 222 Map 303
NW, SE. *Brownish;* black chest band. SE subsp. has greenish tail.

**3. Banded** *N. radiolosus* p 222 Map 304
W. Glossy *blue black; scaled* below.

**4. Sickle-winged Guan** p 126 Map 155
*Chamaepetes g. goudotii*
Mts. Small; prom. *bare blue face; rufous* belly. Common.

**Guans** *Penelope* Med.-to-large forest guans. Red dewlap, scaly foreparts. All spp. remarkably sim. (cf. ranges).

**5. Cauca** *P. perspicax* p 125 Map 151
Perhaps extinct. Much like 6 but *smaller;* browner above; *chestnut brown rearparts.* Some overlap with 12.

**6. Crested** *P. purpurascens* p 125 Map 152
W. Only *very large Penelope* in most of range.

**7. Chestnut-winged Chachalaca** p 121 Map 144
*Ortalis garrula*
N. *Rufous head and primaries; whitish* belly. GRAY-HEADED *O. cinereiceps* N Choco: *gray* head, rufous primaries; grayish brown belly.

**8. Baudo Guan** *Penelope ortoni* p 124 Map 149
Pacific. *Small* and short-legged; blackish; little evident crest. Cf. range 6.

**Chachalacas** *Ortalis.*

**9. Variable** *O. motmot columbiana* p 123 Map 146
W. Gray-headed; *spotted* chest; *rufous* outer tail feathers. E race: head and neck dark brown, but chest spotting holds.

**10. Rufous-vented** *O. ruficauda* p 122 Map 145
N. *Dark gray* foreparts; *rufous* crissum; wings uniform; tail tipped white or chestnut (see text).

**Guans** *Penelope*

**11. Band-tailed** *P. argyrotis* p 123 Map 147
NE. Smaller. *Frosty white* eyebrow and sides of head; prom. red dewlap; *pale tipped* tail.

**12. Andean** *P. montagnii* p 124 Map 148
Widespread, Mts. *Small. Grayish streaking* on face and foreparts; red dewlap rudimentary.

**13. Spix's** *P. jacquacu* p 124 Map 150
E. Only *Penelope* in range. Cf. 6 (see text) in E Andes.

# PLATE 7 RAILS and SUNGREBE

**1. Blackish Rail** *Pardirallus nigricans* p 142 Map 196
W. Med.-large. *Slaty* head and underparts; long *greenish yellow* bill; *red* legs.

**Wood-Rails** *Aramides* Large; longish bill; rufous primaries, *black* rearparts; coral legs.

**2. Brown** *A. wolfi* p 140 Map 189
Pacific. *Dark brown.*

**3. Gray-necked** *A. cajanea* p 139 Map 188
Widespread. Gray head and neck. Imm. duller.

**4. Rufous-necked** *A. axillaris* p 139 Map 187
Mainly coastal. Deep *rufous* head and foreneck (grayish, imm.). Smaller than 2 or 3.

**5. Spotted Rail** *Pardirallus maculatus* p 143 Map 197
W. *Densely spotted and barred*; brown wings; red legs.

**6. Bogota Rail** *Rallus semiplumbeus* p 139 Map 186
E Andes. *Gray* foreparts; *reddish bill and legs*; rufous shoulders.

**Crakes** *Porzana*.

**7. Sora** *P. carolina* p 140 Map 191
N migrant. *Black* face surrounds *yellow* bill; dark gray foreparts. Imm. duller, no black face.

**8. Ash-throated** *P. albicollis* p 141 Map 192
Med.-sized. *Streaked brown back; gray below;* dusky legs; greenish yellow bill brighter than shown.

**9. Yellow-breasted Crake** p 141 Map 193
*Poliolimnas flaviventer*
Tiny. *Yellow buff foreparts*; bold flank bars and eyestripe. Note *yellow* legs.

**10. Ocellated Crake** p 136 Map 177
*Micropygia schomburgkii*
Tiny. *Ochraceous* below; *white ocelli on upperparts; coral red* legs (redder than shown). Rare.

**11. Paint-billed Crake** *Neocrex erythrops* p 142 Map 195
E. *Uniform brown* above; *barred* flanks, red legs; *red* on bill. COLOMBIAN *N. columbianus* Replaces 11 in W: differs in unbarred brownish buff flanks.

**Crakes** *Laterallus*

**12. Gray-breasted** *L. exilis* p 137 Map 181
Gray underparts paler than 11; nape to upper back *chestnut.* Legs dusky yellow (or reddish?).

**13. White-throated** *L. albigularis* p 138 Map 182
W. Rufous below; *barred flanks and crissum;* whitish throat. RUFOUS-SIDED *L. melanophaius* E: like 13, but *crissum uniform rufous.*

**Gallinules** *Porphyrio*

**14. Azure** *P. flavirostris* p 143 Map 199
E. *Bill, frontal shield and legs yellow; azure* foreparts. Imm. like 15a but smaller, back more streaked, *rump blackish.*

**15. Purple** *P. martinica* p 143 Map 198
15a Imm.
Ad. mostly bright *bluish purple;* yellow-tipped *red* bill. Imm. buff and white below; yellow legs; blue wash on wings; *contrasting* frontal shield and bill (cf. 14).

**16. Spot-flanked** *Gallinula melanops* p 144 Map 200
E Andes. *Flank* spots, *lime green* bill, *chestnut* shoulders. Cootlike habits.

**17. Russet-crowned Crake** p 137 Map 180
*Anurolimnas viridis*
Thickets. Gray cheeks, *no barring* on rufous underparts; Note *rosy* legs, *blue gray* bill.

**18. Sungrebe** *Heliornis fulica* p 146 Map 204
Grebelike or ducklike. *Mainly brown;* bold head and neck stripes. Usually seen swimming away. ♂ has *white* cheeks.

**19. Uniform Crake** p 140 Map 190
*Amaurolimnas concolor*
Pacific (elsewhere?). Dull brown above, rufescent below. Note *absence* of barring.

**Crakes** *Anurolimnas*

**20. Chestnut-headed** *A. castaneiceps* p 136 Map 178
SE. Contrasting rufous foreparts (cf.19). Forest.

**21. Black-banded** *A. fasciatus* p 136 Map 179
SE. Rufous foreparts; *bold black and buff barring.*

PLATE 8 PIGEONS

**Pigeons** *Columba* Large, arboreal, high-flying. Voices distinctive.

**1. Bare-eyed** *C. corensis* p 187 Map 209
Arid N. Large and pale; *white wing patches*; bare blue "goggles."

**2. Pale-vented** *C. cayennensis* p 188 Map 210
Widespread. *Reddish shoulders and mantle*; white abdomen; *black bill*. In flight cf. 3.

**3. Scaled** *C. speciosa* p 187 Map 208
*Neck and underparts scaled; reddish shoulders and mantle; red bill* with white tip.

**4. Ruddy** p 188 Map 211
*C. subvinacea purpureotincta*
E. Dark olive above, vinaceous below (but see races in W, Pl.9). In good light slightly ruddy. Black bill. (cf. 7, Pl.9).

**5. Band-tailed** *C. fasciata* p 187 Map 207
Highlands. *White neck band; 2-toned* tail; *yellow* bill.

**6. Scaled Dove** p 193 Map 223
*Scardafella squammata*
Dry N. *Heavily scaled*; long, narrow, white-edged tail; *rufous* in primaries.

**Ground-Doves** *Columbina* Small; short tail, rufous in primaries.

**7. Common** *C. passerina* p 190 Map 216
Widespread. *Scaly* neck and breast; base of bill *pinkish or yellow*.

**8. Ruddy** *C. talpacoti* p 191 Map 218
Distinctive. *Mainly rufous* with *gray cap*. ♀ duller, back and *entire wings rufous* unlike 9; *pale head*.

**9. Plain-breasted** *C. minuta* p 191 Map 217
*Bill black* (cf. 7); *no scales or spots on neck*. ♀ much like ♀ of 8 but smaller, rufous only on primaries. PICUI *C. picui* Amazonas: *black primaries and white wing patch*; whitish below.

**10. Eared Dove** *Zenaida auriculata* p 190 Map 215
Widespread. Note wing spots, *2 marks on cheeks*; wedge-shaped tail tipped white (or rusty). MOURNING *Z. macroura* Accidental: longer tail than 10, tips always white; *single* black cheek mark.

**Ground-Doves** *Claravis* Larger, longer-tailed, *less numerous* than *Columbina*.

**11. Blue** *C. pretiosa* p 192 Map 220
♂ all blue gray. ♀: two chestnut bands on primaries; *rufous rump and tail*. Both ♂ and ♀ have black outer tail.

**12. Maroon-chested** *C. mondetoura* p 192 Map 221
Mts. Rare. ♂: *maroon breast; white outer tail feathers*. ♀ like ♀ of 11 but no rufous; *tail tipped white*.

**Doves** *Leptotila* (also Pl.9).

**13. White-tipped** *L. verreauxi* p 194 Map 226
Most widespread of genus. *Lacks blue gray tone on crown*; broad white tail tips; orbital skin blue (red in Nariño). Mainly nonforest.

**14. Gray-fronted** *L. rufaxilla* p 195 Map 229
E. Only *Leptotila* in most of range. From 13 by *blue gray crown*; *buff* on cheeks; darker above; voice differs.

**Quail-Doves** *Geotrygon* (also Pl.9).

**15. Ruddy** *G. montana* p 196 Map 231
Widespread. Cinnamon cheek stripe (faint, ♀). ♂ mainly rufous chestnut. ♀ and imm. olive brown above, cinnamon below; little rufous in wings.

**16. Violaceous** *G. violacea* p 196 Map 232
Local. *No moustachial stripe* (cf. *Leptotila*); whitish forehead; violet and reddish chestnut above. ♀: grayish below; belly white.

**17. Lined** *G. linearis* p 197 Map 235
Mainly mts. Large. *Cinnamon* forecrown; *gray nape* band on multicolored head; buff tones below. Note range.

## PLATE 9 PARROTS and PIGEONS

**Parrots** *Pionopsitta* Square-tailed. Flight like *Pionus* but more rapid, wings raised above horizontal.

**1. Rose-faced** *P. pulchra* p 210 Map 271
Pacific. *Black-rimmed rose face; no* red on foreneck or axillaries. BROWN-HOODED *P. haematotis* NW: brownish head with rosy earpatch and forecollar; *red axillaries.*

**2. Saffron-headed** *P. pyrilia* p 210 Map 273
W (local). *Yellow* head; *red* blaze under the wing.

**3. Rusty-faced Parrot** p 211 Map 274
*Hapalopsittaca a. amazonina*
3a *H. a. fuertesi*
Highlands. Mainly green. All races by *red on shoulder and underwing coverts,* and tail (cf. 9, 11, Pl.11).

**4. Golden-plumed Parakeet** p 203 Map 249
*Leptosittaca branickii*
Treeline. Rather large; *long narrow tail;* yellow eyestreak; blurry orange breast band if nearby.

**5. Yellow-eared Parrot** p 203 Map 250
*Ognorhynchus icterotis*
*Upper el. Size of small macaw. Yellow face.* Long narrow tail.

**Pigeons** *Columba* See Pl.8.

**6. Ruddy** *C. subvinacea berlepschi* p 188 Map 211
W. Dark ruddy brown forest pigeon. From sim. 7 by ruddier tones, less contrast above and below. Often inseparable. E subsp. on Pl.8. SHORT-BILLED *C. nigrirostris* (p 189) NW Chocó: from 6 by voice.

**7. Plumbeous** *C. plumbea* p 189 Map 212
Darker brown above, grayer below than 6. Best told by voice.

**8. Dusky** *C. goodsoni* p 189 Map 214
Pacific. Small; treetops. Note *slaty crown, gray head, 2-toned* underparts.

**9. Black-winged Ground-Dove** p 193 Map 222
*Metriopelia melanoptera*
Nariño. *Blackish* flight feathers. Nearby bare orange ocular ring.

**Doves** *Leptotila*

**10. Gray-chested** *L. cassinii* p 193 Map 224
NW. *Red* orbital skin; *decidedly grayish* chest (cf. 13, Pl.8).

**11. Tolima** *L. conoveri* p 194 Map 225
Tolima and Huila. *Blue gray* crown; *buff* underparts, incl. belly.

**12. Gray-headed** *L. plumbeiceps* p 194 Map 227
Cauca Val. *obviously gray crown and hindneck;* vinaceous wash on breast.

**13. Pallid** *L. pallida* p 195 Map 228
Pacific. Rather dark above; contrasting *whitish head and underparts.* Back and wings ruddy. Cf. 15, Pl.8.

**Quail-Doves** *Geotrygon* Plump; short-tailed; terrestrial, inside forest.

**14. Sapphire** *G. saphirina purpurata.* p 195 Map 230
Pacific. Head pattern recalls 15. Note *white underparts,* in good light colorful upperparts. Subsp. in SE(?) has crown pale gray.

**15. Olive-backed** *G. veraguensis* p 197 Map 233
W. Bold head pattern, otherwise dark (cf. 14). ♀: buffy forehead.

**16. White-throated** *G. frenata* p 198 Map 236
Upper el. Large and dark. Contrasting *white throat;* gray crown and chest.

**17. Russet-crowned** *G. goldmani* p 197 Map 234
NW. Large. *Cinnamon rufous* head.

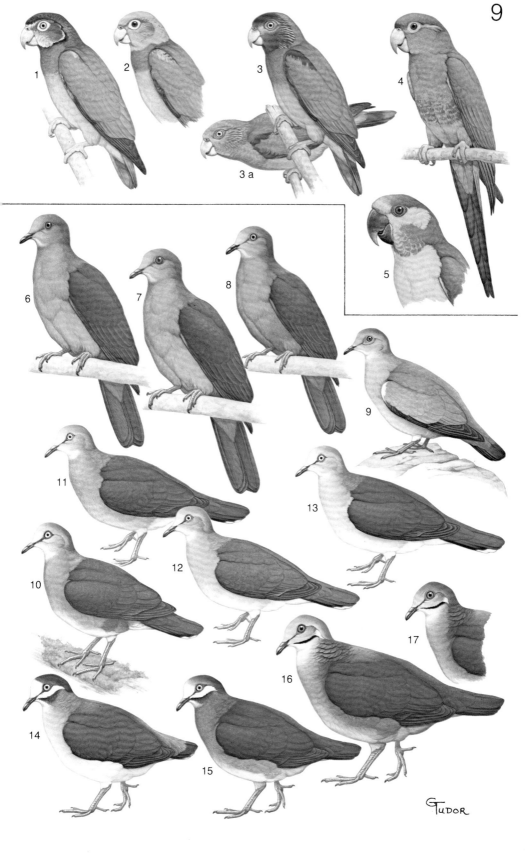

9

## PLATE 10  SMALLER PARROTS

**Parakeets** *Aratinga*

**1. Brown-throated** *A. pertinax* p 202 Map 248
N, E. *Bright green* above; *brownish* foreparts; *yellow* underwings. N race *lacks* yellow eyering.

**2. Dusky-headed** *A. weddellii* p 202 Map 247
SE. Lacks strong marks. Dull brownish gray head; *no* color in wings, etc.

**3. Blue-crowned** *A. acuticauda* p 201 Map 244
N, E. *Forecrown light blue; no* red on wings; base of tail tinged red unlike 4 and 5.

**4. White-eyed** *A. leucophthalmus* p 202 Map 246
SE. Green. *Red and yellow* underwing coverts. Juv. all green; pale bill.

**5. Scarlet-fronted** *A. wagleri* p 201 Map 245
Highlands. *Red* forecrown. *No red* on wings.

**Parrotlets** *Forpus*

**6. Blue-winged** *F. xanthopterygius* p 206 Map 258
N, SE. ♂ bright green; blue rump; blue on wings (like all ♂ *Forpus*). ♀ has no blue in wings; like ♀ of Green-rumped Parrotlet (see text) but more yellowish green below; less yellow on face. Both sexes from 8 by pale (not dusky) maxilla.

**7. Spectacled** *F. conspicillatus* p 206 Map 259
W. ♂: blue around eye; blue rump. ♀: no yellow on head (see text).

**8. Dusky-billed** *F. sclateri* p 206 Map 260
E. *Maxilla dusky*, otherwise ♂ and ♀ much like respective sexes of 6.

**Parakeets** *Pyrrhura* Tail dull crimson; primaries blue.

**9. Maroon-tailed** *P. melanura* p 204 Map 253
S. Note racial var. (see text). Green lower underparts and rump; red underwing coverts; scaling on chest less prom. than in 10 (but see *chapmani* race).

**10. Painted** *P. picta* p 203 Map 251
N. Note racial var. (see text). Most *lack* pale auriculars and have *brownish* crown; *red rump and belly*; red wrist; *heavy V-shaped* scales.

**11. Flame-winged** *P. calliptera* p 204 Map 254
E Andes. *Extensive yellow* on wings.

**12. Santa Marta** *P. viridicata* p 204 Map 252
Only *Pyrrhura* in range. Red and orange on wing.

**Parakeets** *Bolborhynchus*

**13. Rufous-fronted** *B. ferrugineifrons* p 205 Map 256
C Andes. Uniform green; *rufous* around dusky bill. Rare.

**14. Barred** *B. lineola* p 205 Map 255
Highlands. Barring diagnostic if seen. Note voice, small size, high-flying flocks (see text).

**15. Orange-chinned Parakeet** p 207 Map 262
*Brotogeris jugularis*
W. *Brownish* shoulders; *yellow* underwing coverts. Up close chin spot.

**16. Canary-winged Parakeet** p 207 Map 261
*Brotogeris versicolurus*
SE. *Yellow and white* wing patches.

**Parrotlets** *Touit*

**17. Sapphire-rumped** *T. purpurata* p 208 Map 265
SE. *Dark blue* rump; *short square* tail. Fast flight (no dipping).

**18. Spot-winged** *T. stictoptera* p 209 Map 268
Rare. Mainly green. ♂: pale spots on dusky wings; orange wing patch. ♀: green wing coverts spotted black.

**19. Red-winged** *T. dilectissima* p 208 Map 267
W (local). Red and yellow underwing coverts.

**20. Short-tailed Parrot** p 211 Map 275
*Graydidascalus brachyurus*
SE. *Rivers. Short-tailed. No color* on wings (cf. 15. Pl.11). Maroon frown line. Noisy.

**21. Cobalt-winged Parakeet** p 207 Map 263
*Brotogeris cyanoptera*
SE. *Blue* flight feathers. *Orange* chin spot.

**22. Tui Parakeet** p 207 Map 264
*Brotogeris sanctithomae*
SE. *Yellow forecrown; no* blue on wings (cf. 21).

**23. Orange-cheeked Parrot** p 210 Map 272
*Pionopsitta barrabandi*
E. Gaudy. *Scarlet* underwing coverts; *orange* moustachial patch. Note flight (see text).

**24. Black-headed Parrot** p 209 Map 269
*Pionites m. melanocephala*
E. *Black* cap; *mostly white* below; squealing flight call.

10

PLATE 11 MACAWS and LARGER PARROTS

**Macaws** *Ara*

**1. Blue-and-yellow** *A. ararauna* p 198 Map 237
N, E. Unmistakable. Note blue flight feathers as in 2, 3, and 4.

**2. Red-and-green** *A. chloroptera* p 200 Map 241
Much like 3, but median upper wing coverts *green.* Note facial lines; deeper red plumage.

**3. Scarlet** *A. macao* p 200 Map 240
*Yellow* median upper wing coverts (cf. 2). *Unlined* face.

**4. Military** *A. militaris* p 199 Map 238
Large, green; red forecrown; blue primaries and yellowish underwings (cf. 1). GREAT GREEN *A. ambiguua* NW: much like 4, no range overlap.

**5. Chestnut-fronted** *A. severa* p 200 Map 242
NW, E. *Chestnut* frontlet; white facial skin. In flight *red underwings* and undertail.

**6. Red-bellied** *A. manilata* p 201 Map 243
*Yellowish underwings and tail;* red belly; yellowish facial skin.

**7. White-eyed Parakeet** p 202 Map 246
*Aratinga leucophthalmus*
*Red and yellow* under wing coverts; flight feathers and tail *dull yellowish* from below.

**8. Red-fan Parrot** p 215 Map 287
*Deroptyus accipitrinus*
E. Hawklike. *Whitish forecrown;* long tail. Expressive fan-like ruff frequently raised. Odd flight.

**Parrots** *Pionus.* Red crissum; deep *under-the-body* wing beats.

**9. Bronze-winged** *P. chalcopterus* p 212 Map 279
Highlands. Dark. *Greenish* back, *brown* shoulders; *ultramarine* flight feathers. Note yellow bill. Local

**10. Red-billed** *P. sordidus* p 212 Map 277
Highlands. *Red* bill (usually); much duller than 11; mottled head.

**11. Speckle-faced** *P. tumultuosus* p 212 Map 278
Highlands. *White* forehead, *heavily mottled* head; *green* wings (cf. 3, Pl.9).

**12. Blue-headed** *P. menstruus* p 211 Map 276
Widespread. *Blue* head, green body; *pink* on bill.

**Parrots** *Amazona*

**13. Scaly-naped** *A. mercenaria* p 215 Map 285
Andes. Usually *no red* on wings; *pale-tipped* tail. If nearby *black scaled* hindneck and breast

**14. Orange-winged** *A. amazonica* p 214 Map 284
N, E. *Yellow cheeks;* yellow and blue on crown (cf. 16); red orange wing speculum. Common.

**15. Festive** *A festiva* p 213 Map 282
*No red* on wings; red patch on lower back (difficult to see); *narrow maroon* frontlet (SE); or *distinct red forehead* (NE).

**16. Yellow-crowned** p 214 Map 283
*A. o. ochrocephala*
N, E. *Crown patch yellow; bend of wing and wing speculum* red (cf. 14); small bare orbital ring (cf. 17).

**17. Mealy** *A. farinosa* p 215 Map 286
Largest *Amazona.* Lacks good marks. Note *2-toned* tail, *large bare ocular ring.* Yellow crown patch present or absent.

**18. Red-lored** *A. autumnalis* p 213 Map 281
W. *Red* frontlet; *red* wing speculum; lavender edges on crown and hindneck.

11

G TUDOR

# PLATE 12 CUCKOOS and JAYS

## Cuckoos *Coccyzus*

**1. Yellow-billed** *C. americanus* p 217 Map 290
N migrant. *Rufous primaries,* whitish underparts; yellow eyering, lower mandible (often dusky, imm.). BLACK-BILLED *C. erythropthalmus* N migrant: *lacks rufous primaries; black bill, red eyering, small tail spots.* MANGROVE *C. minor* N. much like 1 but larger, buff below, no rufous in wings; broad blackish mask.

**2. Dark-billed** *C. melacoryphus* p 218 Map 293
Ad. *lacks rufous primaries. Buff below; black bill,* contrasting auriculars.

**3. Gray-capped** *C. lansbergi* p 218 Map 294
W. *Dark gray cap.* Much darker above and below than other *Coccyzus.* Rare.

**4. Pearly-breasted** *C. euleri* p 217 Map 291
N, E. Much like 1 but no rufous in wings. Rare.

**5. Dwarf** *C. pumilus* p 216 Map 288
Smallest *Coccyzus. Rufous throat;* small white tips on rather short tail.

**6. Striped Cuckoo** *Tapera naevia* p 221 Map 301
Widespread. *Quaillike* head, expressive crest. *Striped above;* black whisker mark. Imm. rather spotted above; faint barring below.

**Cuckoos** *Dromococcyx* Hunch-backed; long wide tail, flat pointed crest; spotted uppertail coverts nearly as long as tail; suspicious and retiring.

**7. Pavonine** *D. pavoninus* p 222
SE. *Unspotted* fulvous neck and breast. Cf. larger 8. Hypothetical.

**8. Pheasant** *D. phasianellus* p 221 Map 302
NE; SE. Scaly above; *speckled* neck and chest. Tail much longer and broader than 7. Note *chestnut* cap.

**9. Little Cuckoo** *Piaya minuta* p 219 Map 297
Much smaller, shorter-tailed than 10. *Red* eyering; *dark* lower underparts.

**10. Squirrel Cuckoo** *Piaya cayana* p 218 Map 295
Bill and orbital ring greenish yellow; (or orbital ring red, e of Andes); lower underparts mostly light gray (cf. 12).

**11. Ash-colored Cuckoo** p 216 Map 289
*Coccyzus cinereus*
SE. Small. *Cinereous* plumage; *black* bill; *red* eyering; faint tail tips. Austral migrant? Hypothetical.

**12. Black-bellied Cuckoo** p 219 Map 296
*Piaya melanogaster*
SE. *Red* bill, blue, and yellow facial skin. *Gray* cap; *black* belly.

NOTE: Compare ranges of Colombian jays: in most areas only 1 sp. occurs. (Maps 1102-1108).

## Jays *Cyanolyca*

**13. Beautiful** *C. pulchra* p 528 Map 1104
Pacific. Mostly violet blue; *milky white* crown; *no* chest band.

**14. Turquoise** *C. turcosa* p 527 Map 1103
S. Quite like 15. Note *whiter* crown; lighter, more azure plumage; *narrower* chest band.

**15. Collared** *C. viridicyana* p 527 Map 1102
An all "*blue*" jay. Crown and throat not as pale as 14; temperate zones.

## Jays *Cyanocorax*

**16. Black-chested** *C. affinis* p 528 Map 1107
W. *White* lower underparts; *white* tail band. Only jay in most of its range.

**17. Green** *C. yncas* p 528 Map 1108
Highlands. Green and yellow; *yellow* outer tail.

**18. Violaceous** *C. violaceus* p 528 Map 1105
E. Foreparts black; nape pale; body duller violet blue than shown (cf. 19).

**19. Azure-naped** *C. heilprini* p 528 Map 1106
Orinoco. Foreparts black; *abdomen and tail band white.* Note *yellow* eyes; blue malar.

12

PLATE 13 HUMMINGBIRDS

**1. Purple-chested** p 273 Map 427
*Amazilia rosenbergi*
W. Plumage brighter than 9. ♂ *glittering green* upper throat; crown *not* glittering. ♀ green discs on *white* breast; *white* crissum.

**2. Violet-capped** *Goldmania violiceps* p 270 Map 420
NW. Chestnut tail (cf. 13). PIRRE HUMMINGBIRD *Goethalsia bella* NW: buff wing patches; cinnamon outer tail.

**3. Blue-throated Sapphire** p 269 Map 418
*Hylocharis eliciae*
NW. *Red* bill, *blue* throat, *coppery* rump, squarish tail.

**4. Sapphire-throated** p 267 Map 413
*Lepidopyga coeruleogularis*
N. Forked tail. ♂: *bright blue gorget and chest.* ♀: snowy white underparts. SAPPHIRE-BELLIED *L. lilliae* N: ♂ has *glittering blue belly* (cf. 14); ♀ unknown.

**5. Crowned Woodnymph** p 266 Map 410
*Thalurania colombica*
W. ♂: dark; *emerald gorget, violet shoulders and belly*; forked tail. ♀: *2-toned* below; gray tail tips. In E see 24 (Pl.14).

**6. Blue-tailed Emerald** p 264 Map 405
*Chlorostilbon mellisugus*
W. Small. ♂ all glittery green, *short black bill*; forked steely tail. For ♀, see text. (See 10, Pl.14.)

**7. White-necked Jacobin** p 259 Map 390
*Florisuga mellivora*
*White nape and belly*; tail mostly white. ♀ like ♂, or underparts scaly, incl. crissum; tiny white tail tips.

**8. Scaly-breasted** *Phaeochroa cuvierii* p 258 Map 387
N. Large. Scaly below; dusky vent; large white tail corners (cf. ♀ of 7).

**9. Blue-chested** *Amazilia amabilis* p 272 Map 426
W. ♂: dingy; blue chest, glittery crown. ♀: green spots on *grayish* breast.

**10. Violet-bellied** *Damophila julie* p 267 Map 412
NW. *Rounded* tail. ♂: violet belly. ♀: pinkish lower mandible.

**Plumeleteers** *Chalybura*

**11. White-vented** *C. buffonii* p 275 Map 433
W. *Silky white crissum*; black bill, blue black tail tipped white.

**12. Bronze-tailed** *C. urochrysia* p 275 Map 434
W. Much like 11. *Pinkish feet and lower mandible*; bronze copper tail.

**13. Rufous-tailed Hummingbird** p 274 Map 432
*Amazilia tzacatl*
W. *Red* bill; *rufous* tail, *dingy* lower underparts. CHESTNUT-BELLIED *A. castaneiventris* E, C Andes: *rufous belly and tail*

**14. Andean Emerald** p 273 Map 428
*Amazilia franciae*
Andes. *Crown bluish* (green, ♀); upper tail coverts *coppery*; immaculate median underparts.

**15. Purple-crowned Fairy** p 297 Map 490
*Heliothryx barroti*
W. *Immaculate* underparts; white outer tail. BLACK-EARED *H. aurita* E: much like 15 (no overlap).

**16. Black-throated Mango** p 261 Map 395
*Anthracothorax nigricollis*
♂: mostly *black* below, maroon in tail. ♀ black median breast stripe. GREEN-BREASTED *A. prevostii*. Local. Mainly green below, *black confined to throat*. ♀ like ♀ of 16.

**17. Rufous-crested Coquette** p 262 Map 398
*Lophornis delattrei*
♂: *wirelike rufous crest*, pale rump band, mostly rufous tail. ♀ much like ♀ of 1 (Pl.14).

**18. Blue-fronted Lancebill** p 257 Map 385
*Doryfera johannae*
E. Long straight bill; *dark* plumage. ♂: violet frontlet. ♀: grayish below, gray tail tips, *blue green* forecrown.

**19. Long-billed Starthroat** p 297 Map 492
*Heliomaster longirostris*
W. Long bill; blue crown (♂), magenta throat, white back stripe. BLUE-TUFTED *H. furcifer* SE (rare): ♂ much like ♂ of 19 but crown green, *breast glittery blue*. ♀ whiter below.

**20. Green-fronted Lancebill** p 257 Map 386
*Doryfera ludoviciae*
W. *Paler* than 18. ♂ green frontlet, coppery rearcrown. ♀ like ♀ of 18.

**21. Green Thorntail** p 264 Map 403
*Popelairia conversii*
W. *White rump band* diagnostic in range (both sexes).

**22. Green-crowned Brilliant** p 278 Map 443
*Heliodoxa jacula*
W. ♂ glittery above; long deeply forked tail (but cf. 22, Pl.16). For ♀ see text.

**23. Brown Violetear** *Colibri delphinae* p 259 Map 391
W. Brown. *Orangish* rump, glittery ear pitch.

**Hermits** *Phaethornis*

**24. Little** *P. longuemareus* p 255 Map 381
Underparts var. Small size unique in W; in E throat *streaked dusky* unlike 9 and 10 (Pl.16). See 8, Pl.16.

**25. Green** *P. guy* p 252 Map 371
Subtropics. Dark below, *crown dark green* (cf. 26), buff throat stripe. See 2, Pl.16.

**26. White-whiskered** *P. yaruqui* p 252 Map 370
W. Dark below; *coppery crown*; gray throat stripe.

**27. Tawny-bellied** *P. syrmatophorus* p 252 Map 372
Subtropics. *Ochre rump and underparts*; long white tail tips.

**28. Band-tailed Barbthroat** p 251 Map 369
*Threnetes ruckeri*
W. *Black throat, white tail base.*

**Hermits** *Glaucis*

**29. Rufous-breasted** *G. hirsuta* p 250 Map 367
N, E. Larger than 30; *chestnut* in tail. Crown and upperparts green. See 11, Pl.16.

**30. Bronzy** *G. aenea* p 250 Map 366
W. Bronzy or coppery green above; *crown dusky* (cf. 29).

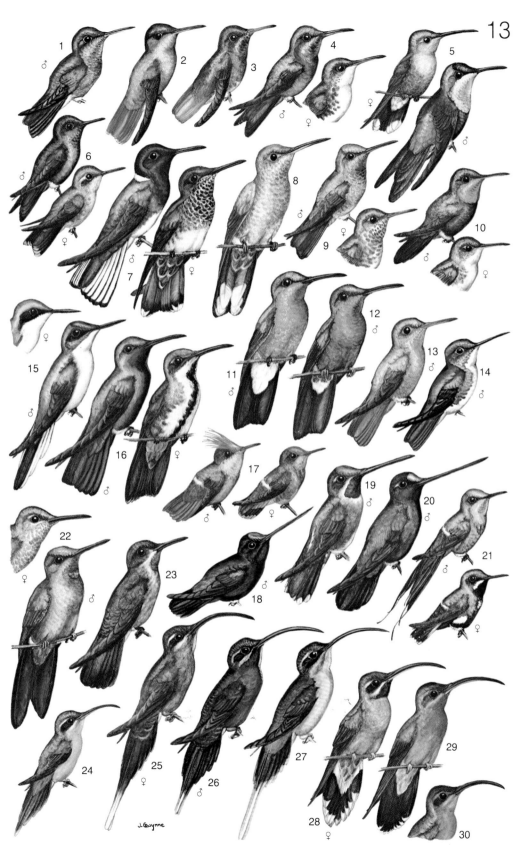

13

PLATE 14 HUMMINGBIRDS

**1. Spangled Coquette** p 262 Map 399
*Lophornis stictolopha*
E Andes. ♂: *bushy black-dotted* crest; rufous tail. ♀: rufous forecrown, thickly spotted throat (cf. 17, Pl.13).

**2. Emerald-bellied Puffleg** p 289 Map 472
*Eriocnemis alinae*
S. *White chest patch*; enormous leg puffs.

**3. Purple-throated Woodstar** p 298 Map 494
*Philodice mitchellii*
W Andes. *Whitish flank patch; no rump band.* ♂: solid green breast (buff, ♀). Cf. 7, 9. For AMETHYST WOOD-STAR *Calliphlox amethystina* E: see text.

**4. Festive Coquette** p 263 Map 400
*Lophornis chalybea*
SE. ♂ fanlike ruff, glittering frontlet. ♀ like ♀ of 5.

**5. Black-bellied Thorntail** p 263 Map 402
*Popelairia langsdorffi*
SE. ♂ *no* crest; thin copper chest band. ♀ white malar, green and black median underparts. WIRE-CRESTED *P. popelairia* E: ♂ like 5 but spiky crest; no chest band. For ♀, see text.

**6. Booted Racket-tail** p 290 Map 476
*Ocreatus underwoodii*
Andes. ♀ spotty below; white tail tips.

**7. White-bellied Woodstar** p 299 Map 496
*Acestrura mulsant*
E, C Andes. ♂: *white belly.* For ♀ see text.

**8. Rufous-shafted Woodstar** p 300 Map 498
*Chaetocercus jourdanii*
E Andes. ♂: *redder* gorget than allies. ♀ *lacks* rufous rump band (cf. ♀ of 9).

**9. Gorgeted Woodstar** p 299 Map 497
*Acestrura heliodor*
Mts. ♂ *much darker* than 7 or 8; *flared* gorget. For ♀, see text.

**Emeralds** *Chlorostilbon.* For ♀♀ see text.

**10. Blue-tailed** *C. mellisugus* p 264 Map 405
W. ♂ *all glittery green, short black bill,* forked steely tail.

**11. Narrow-tailed** *C. stenura* p 265 Map 408
E Andes. ♂ short *bronzy green* tail (cf. 10). SHORT-TAILED *C. poortmanni* E Andes: like 11, tail shorter (see text).

**Emeralds** *Amazilia*

**12. Versicolored** *A. versicolor* p 272 Map 424
E. *White median underparts, bluish submalar.*

**13. Glittering-throated** *A. fimbriata* p 272 Map 425
E. ♂: *white wedge* up breast; green tail. ♀ duller; white throat spotted green.

**14. Coppery Emerald** p 265 Map 407
*Chlorostilbon russatus*
NE. *Very coppery above incl. tail.* For ♀ see text.

**15. Red-billed Emerald** p 265 Map 406
*Chlorostilbon gibsoni*
N. ♂ like ♂ of 10 but *bill red.* For ♀ see text.

**16. Shining-green Hummingbird** p 268 Map 414
*Lepidopyga goudoti*
N. Forked tail centrally green. ♂: *bluish throat,* pink lower mandible base. ♀ spotty below; belly white. BLUE-CHINNED SAPPHIRE *Chlorestes notatus* E: nearest 16 (see text).

**17. Wedge-billed hummingbird** p 296 Map 489
*Schistes geoffroyi*
Andes. *White pectoral band;* dark subterminal tail band.

**18. Speckled Hummingbird** p 276 Map 435
*Adelomyia melanogenys*
Andes. Brown. *Dusky cheeks, buff* tail tips.

**19. Blossomcrown** p 276 Map 436
*Anthocephala floriceps*
Mts. ♂ *pale* forehead (see CAUTION in text), *rufous* hindcrown, buff tail tips. For ♀, see text.

**20. Green-bellied Hummingbird** p 274 Map 431
*Amazilia viridigaster*
E Andes. *Brownish* lower back and rump; tail purplish.

**21. Blue-headed Sapphire** p 269 Map 417
*Hylocharis grayi*
W Andes. ♂: *blue head and red bill.* ♀ gray below.

**22. Steely-vented Hummingbird** p 274 Map 430
*Amazilia saucerottei*
W. *Larger* than 10. *Dull coppery rump;* scaled crissum.

**23. Indigo-capped Hummingbird** p 273 Map 429
*Amazilia cyanifrons*
E Andes. ♂: *indigo cap, brown rump.* ♀ duller.

**24. Fork-tailed Woodnymph** p 267 Map 411
*Thalurania furcata*
E. ♂: *emerald gorget, purple belly,* deeply forked tail. ♀: *gray* underparts and tail tips. See 5, Pl.13.

**25. Golden-tailed Sapphire** p 270 Map 419
*Chrysuronia oenone*
E. *Coppery* tail. ♂: *blue* head. ♀ spotty below.

**Sapphires** *Hylocharis* ♂ bill bright red

**26. Rufous-throated** *H. sapphirina* p 268 Map 415
E. *Rufous* chin, *rufous* tail. ♂: violet throat.

**27. White-chinned** *H. cyanus* p 269 Map 416
N, E. *Copper rump.* ♂: *violet* head. ♀ gray below.

**28. Buffy Hummingbird** p 271 Map 423
*Leucippus fallax*
NE (arid). Faded; buff below. OLIVE-SPOTTED *L. chlorocercus* SE (river isls.): dingy; mantle greenish; dusky subterminal tail band.

**29. Ruby-topaz Hummingbird** p 261 Map 396
*Chrysolampis mosquitus*
N. *Rufous in* tail (reduced, ♀). ♂: glowing foreparts often look black. ♀ *coppery* above, gray below.

**30. Violet-headed Hummingbird** p 262 Map 397
*Klais guimeti*
NW. *Small. Eyespot;* white tail tips. ♂ *violet* head.

**Goldenthroats** *Polytmus* Brighter green than most other genera.

**31. Green-tailed** *P. theresiae* p 271 Map 422
E. Smaller, greener than 32. ♂: green tail lacks white at base. ♀: mottled white underparts.

**32. White-tailed** *P. guainumbi* p 270 Map 421
E. Golden above; stronger facial pattern than 31; reddish bill. ♂: white tail base and tip. ♀ white below.

**33. Fiery Topaz** *Topaza pyra* p 279 Map 447
SE. Large. *Rufous wing linings and tail.*

**34. Jewelfront** *Polyplancta aurescens* p 277 Map 440
SE. *Rufous pectoral band;* chestnut in tail.

**35. Gray-breasted Sabrewing** p 258 Map 388
*Campylopterus largipennis*
SE. Gray below; *broad white* tail tips.

1 ♂
2 ♂
3 ♂ ♀
4 ♂
5 ♂ ♀
6 ♂ ♀
7 ♀ ♂
8 ♀ ♂
9 ♂
10 ♀ ♂
11 ♂
12
13 ♂
14 ♂
15 ♂
16 ♂
17 ♂
18
19 ♂
20
21 ♂
22 ♂
23 ♂
24 ♂ ♀
25 ♂
26 ♂
27 ♂ ♀
28 ♂
29 ♂ ♀
30 ♂ ♀
31 ♂
32 ♂
33 ♀
34 ♂
35
G TUDOR

## PLATE 15 HUMMINGBIRDS

**Pufflegs** *Eriocnemis*

**1. Golden-breasted** *E. mosquera* p 289 Map 470
W, C Andes. Golden green breast; dull vent (cf. 7).

**2. Black-thighed** *E. derbyi* p 290 Map 473
C Andes. *Glittering* upper and under tail coverts; *black*
leg puffs.

**3. Tyrian Metaltail** p 293 Map 482
*Metallura tyrianthina*
Mts. Small. ♂ coppery maroon tail (dark purple, N). ♀
*rufous* throat spotted green. For PERIJÁ *M. iracunda*
Perijá Mts.: see text.

**4. Bronze-tailed Thornbill** p 294 Map 483
*Chalcostigma heteropogon*
E Andes. Large; *short bill; reddish bronze rump.*

**5. Purple-backed Thornbill** p 292 Map 479
*Ramphomicron microrhynchum*
Andes. Tiny bill. ♂ *purple back.* ♀ spotted below; long
white-tipped tail. BLACK-BACKED *R. dorsale* Santa
Marta: ♂ hood and upperparts black; for ♀ see text.

**6. Coppery-bellied Puffleg** p 288 Map 469
*Eriocnemis cupreoventris*
E Andes. *Coppery orange belly.*

**7. Glowing Puffleg** p 288 Map 467
*Eriocnemis vestitus*
Andes. *Glittering green rump.* ♂: *blue* throat spot, violet crissum (shared with others). ♀ speckled below;
*buff* malar. TURQUOISE-THROATED *E. godini* S: more
golden below; throat spot fainter than 7. COLORFUL *E.
mirabilis* W: enormous puffed legs. ♂: *blue belly, ruby*
crissum; ♀ spotted below; *all dark tail.*

**8. Violet-fronted Brilliant** p 278 Map 442
*Heliodoxa leadbeateri*
E Andes. ♂ violet crown; glittering green gorget. ♀
inseparable from ♀ of 22 on Pl.13.

**9. Viridian Metaltail** *Metallura williami* p 293 Map 481
W, C Andes. ♂ uniform dark bronzy green (tail pur-
plish in some lights). ♀ buff with green spots below.
Cf. more common, smaller 3.

**10. Rainbow-bearded Thornbill** p 294 Map 484
*Chalcostigma herrani*
C Andes. Colorful beard (lacking, ♀); *reddish copper
rump; big white* tail tips.

**11. Sapphire-vented Puffleg** p 288 Map 468
*Eriocnemis luciani*
S. *Obviously long* tail; large leg puffs.

**Violetears** *Colibri*

**12. Green** *C. thalassinus* p 260 Map 392
Mts. Dark subterminal tail band.

**13. Sparkling** *C. coruscans* p 260 Map 393
Mts. Larger than 12; dark chin strap, *bluish* breast.

**14. Purple-bibbed Whitetip** p 277 Map 438
*Urosticte benjamini*
W. ♂: *purple chest spot*, white postocular, *large white
central tail spot.* ♀ spotted below; white tail tips. RUFOUS-
VENTED *U. ruficrissa*: larger than 14; ♂ lacks purple; ♀:
buffy vent. ECUADORIAN PIEDTAIL *Phlogophilus hemileucurus* E: banded tail; white chest band.

**15. Mountain Avocetbill** p 295 Map 486
*Opisthoprora euryptera*
C Andes. *Reddish copper* head; *streaks.* Note bill
shape.

**16. Greenish Puffleg** p 290 Map 474
*Haplophaedia aureliae*
Andes. *Coppery* tinged head; dingy belly; *small* leg
puffs. HOARY *H. lugens* SW: *Slaty underparts frosted white;
small* leg puffs.

**17. Mountain Velvetbreast** p 281 Map 450
*Lafresnaya lafresnayi*
Mts. Decurved bill; *white to buffy* outer tail. ♀ buff
spotted green below.

**18. Lazuline Sabrewing** p 258 Map 389
*Campylopterus falcatus*
W. Decurved bill; *chestnut* outer tail. ♂: *violet blue*
throat and breast. ♀ *gray* below. For SANTA MARTA *C.
phainopeplus*, see text.

**19. Velvet-purple Coronet** p 286 Map 463
*Boissonneaua jardini*
W. *Black hood; orangish* wing linings; *white outer tail.*
CHESTNUT-BREASTED *B. matthewsii* E: *chestnut* breast
and outer tail.

**Sunangels** *Heliangelus* Short bill.

**20. Tourmaline** *H. exortis* p 287 Map 466
Andes. ♂: rosy throat spot, white crissum; forked tail.
♀: white throat and crissum.

**21. Orange-throated** *H. mavors* p 286 Map 464
E Andes. ♂ *orange* gorget; *buff* chest crescent. ♀:
buff throat flecked brown.

**22. Amethyst-throated** p 287 Map 465
*H. amethysticollis*
E Andes. ♂: amethyst gorget; white chest crescent.
♀: rusty throat flecked black. GORGETED *H. strophianus*
SW: ♂ broader green breast band than 22 (see text).

**23. Buff-tailed Coronet** p 285 Map 461
*Boissonneaua flavescens*
Andes. Spotty belly; *cinnamon* wing linings and *buff*
outer tail.

**24. White-tailed Hillstar** p 280 Map 448
*Urochroa bougueri*
Andes. Long bill, *blue* throat; *white* outer tail. W subsp.
has rufous malar.

**25. Bronzy Inca** *Coeligena coeligena* p 282 Map 452
Andes. *Looks reddish brown;* whitish throat and chest
obscurely streaked.

**Starfrontlets** *Coeligena*

**26. Golden-bellied** p 284 Map 457
*C. b. bonapartei*
*26a C. b. consita* ♀
E Andes. ♂: *golden orange* rump; *fiery gold belly.*
26a: Rufous wing band (Perijá). ♀: *cinnamon* underparts. DUSKY *C. orina* W Andes: ♂ uniformly dark; blue
throat spot; ♀ unknown.

**27. Blue-throated** *C. helianthea* p 284 Map 458
E Andes. *Aquamarine rump.* ♂ *blackish;* violet blue
throat. ♀: *cinnamon* underparts.

## 15

# PLATE 16 HUMMINGBIRDS

**Hermits** *Phaethornis*

**1. Pale-bellied** p 253 Map 375
*P. anthophilus*
N. Whitish submaler; *no* throat stripe; *greenish back
and rump*, whitish underparts (cf. 5).

**2. Green** *P. guy* p 252 Map 371
Subtropics. Dark below, *crown dark green* (cf. 26, Pl.13),
buff throat stripe.

**3. White-bearded** *P. hispidus* p 253 Map 374
E. *Prom.* throat stripe; *grayish* below (no contrast).

**4. Sooty-capped** *P. augusti* p 254 Map 376
NE. *Rufous rump, bold facial lines;* longer white tail
than 1 or 3.

**5. Long-tailed** *P. superciliosus* p 253 Map 373
*Buff facial stripes and rump;* buff tinge below.

**6. Straight-billed** *P. bourcieri* p 254 Map 371
SE. *Straight bill,* dull plumage.

**7. Dusky-throated** *P. squalidus* p 254 Map 378
E. Small. *Dusky* throat, grayish breast, *faint* rufous rump.

**8. Little** *P. Longuemareus* p 255 Map 381
Underparts var. Small size unique in W; in E throat
streaked dusky unlike 9 and 10. See 24, Pl.13.

**9. Gray-chinned** *P. griseogularis* p 255 Map 380
E. Greenish back, cf. 8; ♀ of 10.

**10. Reddish** *P. ruber* p 255 Map 379
E. Tiny. *Rufous below.* ♀ paler; *pectoral band* reduced or lacking.

**11. Rufous-breasted Hermit** p 250 Map 367
*Glaucis hirsuta*
N, E. *Chestnut in tail; green crown and upperparts;*
rufous below. See 29, Pl.13.

**12. Pale-tailed Barbthroat** p 251 Map 368
*Threnetes leucurus*
E. Strong face and throat pattern; *base of tail and tips
white* (cf. 28, Pl.13).

**Sylphs** *Aglaiocercus*

**13. Long-tailed** *A. kingi* p 295 Map 487
Andes. ♂ metallic *blue green* tail; no throat spot. ♀
*green* crown; *no pectoral band* (cf. ♀ of 14).

**14. Violet-tailed** *A. coelestis* p 296 Map 488
W. ♂ shimmering *metallic violet* tail and gorget spot.
♀: *blue* forecrown; *white chest divides underparts.*

**15. Black Inca** *Coeligena prunellei* p 283 Map 454
E Andes. Black; *white pectoral tufts.* Local.

**16. Great Sapphirewing** p 281 Map 451
*Pterophanes cyanopterus*
Andes. Large; batlike flight. ♂: *sapphire shoulders.* ♀:
*rufous* underparts.

**17. Shining Sunbeam** p 281 Map 449
*Aglaeactis cupripennis*
Andes (treeline). Large; *rufous. Brilliant* lower back.

**18. Green-tailed Trainbearer** p 292 Map 478
*Lesbia nuna*
E, C Andes. *Bright* green. ♂ narrow green tail usually
closed. ♀ spotted below; tail narrower, shorter than
20.

**19. Collared Inca** *Coeligena torquata* p 283 Map 455
Andes. *Showy chest and tail.* ♀ duller.

**20. Black-tailed Trainbearer** p 291 Map 477
*Lesbia victoriae*
Larger, *much longer-tailed* than 18; *tail mainly black.*
♀ spotty below, shorter tail.

**Brilliants** *Heliodoxa*

**21. Fawn-breasted** *H. rubinoides* p 277 Map 441
Andes. *Buff below, no contrast under tail;* lilac throat
spot. BLACK-THROATED *H. schreibersii* SE: ♂ has black
underparts; ♀ has *rufous to white* malar. PINK-THROATED
*H. gularis* SE: mostly green; reddish throat patch.

**22. Empress,** *H. imperatrix* p 278 Map 444
W. Quite large. ♂: *deeply forked blackish tail.* ♀ spotty
below, much like 22 (on Pl.13).

**23. Brown Inca** *Coeligena wilsoni* p 283 Map 453
Pacific. Brown. *White pectoral tufts.*

**Starfrontlets** *Coeligena*

**24. Buff-winged** *C. lutetiae* p 285 Map 459
Andes. *Buff wing patch.* ♂ blackish above; ♀ greenish.

**25. White-tailed** *C. phalerata* p 284 Map 456
Santa Marta Mts. ♂ has *white tail;* ♀ *rufous below.*

16

# PLATE 17 TROGONS

**Quetzals** *Pharomachrus* Larger, heavier than *Trogon*; rather wedge-tailed, slight bushy crest. Emerald upperparts, incl. elongated scapulars and upper tail coverts; red belly. Sexes differ. Highlands (except Pavonine).

**1. Golden-headed** *P. auriceps* p 301 Map 501
Andes. *Black undertail.* ♂: golden bronze head (cf. 2).
PAVONINE *P. pavoninus* SE: red bill (red on base, ♀).

**2. Crested** *P. antisianus* p 300 Map 499
Andes. Bushy frontal crest. ♂: *immaculate white undertail*, emerald head. ♀: *barred* undertail, dull brown head (cf. ♀ of 1).

**Trogons** *Trogon*

**3. Slaty-tailed** *T. massena* p 301 Map 503
Pacific. Large. *Orange red* bill, *dark* eyes (cf. 4). ♂ has *no* white chest band. ♀: undertail sometimes faintly barred.

**4. Blue-tailed** *T. comptus* p 302 Map 505
Pacific. *Yellow bill* (lower mandible, ♀); *white eyes*, blue rump in ♂ (cf. 3).

**5. Blue-crowned** *T. curucui* p 304 Map 510
SE. ♂ bluish crown, blurry chest band; plumage often dull (cf. 11). ♀ grayish. Note *broken* eyering, *whitish* chest.

**6. White-tipped Quetzal** p 301 Map 500
*Pharomachrus fulgidus*
Santa Marta Mts. ♂: contrasting head, *partially white* undertail. ♀ much like ♀ of 2 (no range overlap).

**Trogons** *Trogon*

**7. White-tailed** *T. viridis* p 302 Map 506
Large. *Bluish* bill, *complete blue eyering in both sexes.* ♂ mostly *white* undertail. ♀ much like ♀ of 8 (see).

**8. Violaceous** *T. violaceus* p 304 Map 511
♂: *yellow eyering*, barred undertail, narrow chest band.
♀ from ♀ of 7 by indistinct breast band, *broken* (feathered) eyering, smaller size.

**9. Black-tailed** *T. melanurus* p 302 Map 504
N, E. *Yellow* mandible, dark eyes (both sexes); *narrow white* chest band (♂ only). *Slaty undertail* like 3 and 4.

**10. Masked** *T. personatus* p 303 Map 508
Andes. ♂ from ♂ of 11 by *much finer tail barring* (bars often not discernible in field); ♀ by *black mask, all yellow bill.*

**11. Collared** *T. collaris* p 303 Map 507
♂ *coarse* tail barring. ♀ indistinct mask, vermiculated undertail, yellow on bill (cf. 10).

**12. Black-throated** *T. rufus* p 303 Map 509
Coarse tail barring. ♂ *greenish*; well-defined mask, blue eyering. ♀ *brown and yellow.*

PLATE 18 JACAMARS, PUFFBIRDS and MOTMOTS

**1. Dusky-backed Jacamar** p 310 Map 525
*Brachygalba salmoni*
NW. Small; short dark tail.

**Jacamars** *Galbula* Tail longer, more graduated than *Brachygalba*; plumage metallic. ♀ buff throat (except 17, Pl.19).

**2. Rufous-tailed** *G. ruficauda* p 312 Map 530
W, NE. *Rufous undertail* unique in range.

**3. White-chinned** *G. tombacea* p 311 Map 528
SE. Lacks conspic. throat patch; brownish crown glossed blue; ♂ deep rufous lower underparts.

**4. Bronzy** *G. leucogastra* p 312 Map 531
E. Greenish above; bronzy breast "divides" *white* (or *buff* ♀) throat and belly. Scarce. See 14 on Pl.19 for ♂.

**5. White-eared Jacamar** p 309 Map 522
*Galbalcyrhynchus leucotis*
SE. Kingfisherlike. Chestnut. Note *pink bill, white cheeks.*

**6. Sooty-capped Puffbird** p 315 Map 539
*Bucco noanamae*
Pacific. *Broad chest band;* coarsely *spotted or barred* lower underparts.

**7. Russet-throated Puffbird** p 315 Map 542
*Hypnelus ruficollis*
N, E. Unique in range. Single chest band in N; double-banded in E (see 9, Pl.19).

**8. Barred Puffbird** *Nystalus radiatus* p 315 Map 541
W. Finely barred black. Note heavy bill; stolid upright posture (cf. ♀ Fasciated Antshrike).

**Nunlets** *Nonnula*

**9. Gray-cheeked** *N. frontalis* p 318 Map 550
W. Only nunlet in range. Note gray face; pink eyering.

**10. Brown** *N. brunnea* p 318 Map 549
E. Cinnamon loral area and pink eyering; more uniform below than 8 on Pl.19.

**11. Tody Motmot** p 307 Map 518
*Hylomanes momotula*
NW. Chunky; greenish. Striped facial pattern.

**12. Lanceolated Monklet** p 317 Map 547
*Micromonacha lanceolata*
Local. *Small. Spotlike streaking* below; white around bill and eyes.

**Puffbirds** *Malacoptila*

**13. White-whiskered** p 316 Map 545
*M. p. panamensis*
13a *M. p. chocoana*
W. Bill *yellowish green* below; rufous (or light buff) wash *confined* to chest; *extensively streaked* below (cf. 14).

**14. Moustached** *M. mystacalis* p 317 Map 546
Upper el. Bill blue gray below; breast *extensively* rufous; *weak streaking confined to abdomen* (cf. 13).

**15. Blue-crowned Motmot** p 308 Map 521
*Momotus momota*
Large. Greenish above; *long* racket-tipped tail.

**16. Broad-billed Motmot** p 308 Map 519
*Electron platyrhynchum*
Much like larger 17 but *rufous only to midbreast.* Note larger breast spot, shorter tail, chunkier shape.

**17. Rufous Motmot** p 308 Map 520
*Baryphthengus ruficapillus*
Quite large. Mostly rufous below; small breast spot. "Leaner" appearance, and bill different shape than 16.

**Nunbirds** *Monasa*

**18. Yellow-billed** *M. flavirostris* p 320 Map 554
E. *Yellow* bill; *white shoulders.*

**19. Black-fronted** *M. nigrifrons* p 319 Map 552
SE. Entirely black; *coral red* bill. Cf. habitat with 20.

**20. White-fronted** *M. morphoeus* p 319 Map 553
W, SE. *White* area around *coral red* bill. Forest (cf. 19).

**21. White-faced Nunbird** p 318 Map 551
*Hapaloptila castanea*
Pacific (subtropics). *Gray* cap; *white* around bill; *cinnamon rufous* below. Rare.

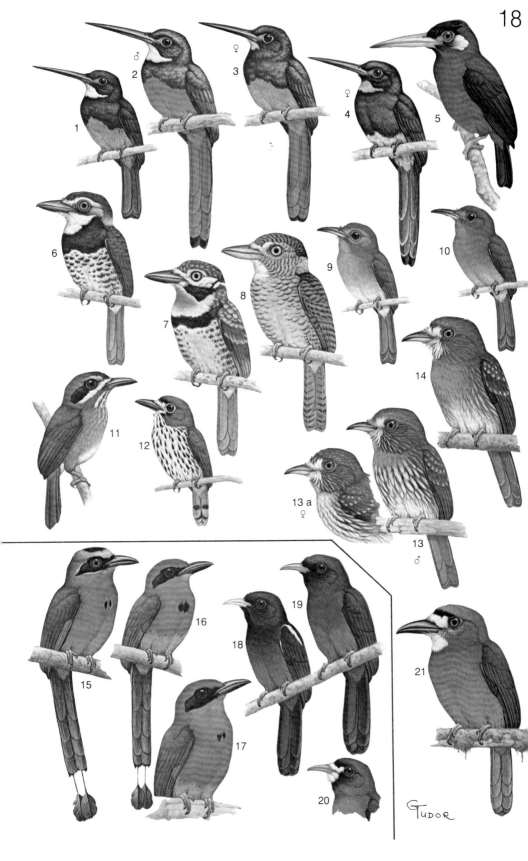

# PLATE 19 PUFFBIRDS, JACAMARS and KINGFISHERS

**1. Swallow-winged Puffbird** p 320 Map 555
*Chelidoptera tenebrosa*
E. Rufous belly; *white rump*. Takes off from treetops, sallies in open.

**Puffbirds** *Notharchus* Bold black and white; perch high.

**2. White-necked** *N. macrorhynchus* p 313 Map 534
Large. *white* forehead; broad nuchal collar (cf. 4).

**3. Black-breasted** *N. pectoralis* p 314 Map 535
Pacific. *White cheeks; no* white on forehead or over eyes.

**4. Pied** *N. tectus* p 314 Map 536
W; SE. Small. *Narrow superciliary; white on wings* and *undertail.* Glossy crown nearby.

**5. Russet-throated Puffbird** p 315 Map 542
*Hypnelus ruficollis bicinctus*
*Double breast band* (Casanare and Meta); single band in N (7, Pl.18).

**Puffbirds** *Malacoptila.* Subdued plumage; understory.

**6. Black-streaked** *M. fulvogularis* p 316 Map 544
E. *Black* bill. Streaked above and below. *Throat and chest uniform buff.* Rare.

**7. White-chested** *M. fusca* p 316 Map 543
E. *Orange* bill. Heavily streaked *above and below.* White chest crescent may not show.

**8. Rusty-breasted Nunlet** p 317 Map 548
*Nonnula rubecula*
SE. *Whitish* lores and eyering; rufous breast *contrasts* with pale belly.

**Puffbirds** *Bucco*

**9. Spotted** *B. tamatia* p 314 Map 538
E. Cinnamon rufous throat; *broad black malar bar; coarse spotlike bars* below.

**10. Chestnut-capped** p 314 Map 537
*B. macrodactylus*
E. *Chestnut crown; black chest band "divides"* white throat and chest. Faint barring on breast.

**11. Collared** *B. capensis* p 315 Map 540
SE. *Orange* bill. *Rufous* head, black chest band.

**Jacamars** *Brachygalba* Small; rather short-tailed (cf. *Galbula*).

**12. Pale-headed** *B. goeringi* p 310 Map 524
E. Mostly *ashy white* head and throat.

**13. Brown** *B. lugubris* p 310 Map 523
SE. Brownish, *incl.* head; *contrasting* belly.

**Jacamars** *Galbula* ♀ differ from ♂ in having buff (not white) throat.

**14. Bronzy** *G. leucogastra* p 312 Map 531
E. Greenish above; bronzy breast "divides" white throat and belly. Scarce. See 4 on Pl.18 for ♀.

**15. Green-tailed** *G. galbula* p 311 Map 527
E. Rufous lower underparts; *blackish* undertail.

**16. Yellow-billed** *G. a. albirostris* p 310 Map 526
16a *G. a. chalcocephala*
SE. *Yellow* on bill, rufous below, *incl.* undertail.

**17. Paradise** *G. dea* p 312 Map 532
E. *Blackish.* Pointed at *both* ends. Prom. *white throat.* Canopy.

**18. Great Jacamar** *Jacamerops aurea* p 313 Map 533
NW; E. Much larger, heavier. Note *long thick* slightly arched bill. Rufous underparts *lack* chest band.

**Kingfishers** *Chloroceryle.* ♀♀ have green chest band.

**19. Amazon** *C. amazona* p 306 Map 514
Dark oily green; essentially no white in wings or tail. ♀: rufous replaced by single green band.

**20. Green** *C. americana* p 306 Map 515
*Small.* Green; *white spotted* wings; flashes *white* in tail as flies.

**21. Pygmy** *C. aenea* p 307 Map 517
*Tiny.* Deep rufous below; *white belly.*

**22. Green-and-rufous** *C. inda* p 306 Map 516
NW, N, E. Larger. All *deep rufous below, incl.* belly. ♀: has chest band.

J. GWYNNE

## PLATE 20 TOUCANS

**1. Yellow-eared Toucanet** p 327 Map 575
*Selenidera spectabilis*
NW. No other toucanet in range.

**Toucanets** *Aulacorhynchus* Smaller, predom. green; subtropics; do not perch in open.

**2. Groove-billed** *A. sulcatus* p 323 Map 565
N. Bill extensively yellow; no chestnut tail tips.

**3. Emerald** *A. prasinus albivitta* p 324 Map 567
3a *A. p. lautus* (Santa Marta)
Bill black, *maxilla extensively yellow; chestnut* tail tips, rump uniform (cf. 4). 3a: bill black, *ridge yellow.*

**4. Crimson-rumped** *A. haematopygus* p 324 Map 568
Bill mainly *dark red;* rump *red.* CHESTNUT-TIPPED *A. derbianus:* base and outer half bill dark red; *bare bluish* ocular area.

**Araçaris** *Pteroglossus* Crimson *rump.* Note bill pattern and belly bands (or lack of). Lowlands.

**5. Stripe-billed** *P. sanguineus* p 325 Map 570
W. *Yellow* bill tip; bare *bluish slate* ocular area.

**6. Collared** *P. torquatus* p 325 Map 569
N. Maxilla *mostly yellow,* tip *dusky;* bare *red* ocular area.

**7. Many-banded** *P. pluricinctus* p 326 Map 572    *11-1⁰ smaller*
SE. *Two* belly bands; bill *ivory above, black below.*

**8. Chestnut-eared** *P. castanotis* p 325 Map 571    *Nov. 10*
SE. *Single belly band* diagnostic in Amazonia.

**9. Lettered** *P. inscriptus* p 326 Map 573
SE. *No belly bands.* Bill nearest 7.

**10. Ivory-billed** *P. flavirostris* p 326 Map 574
E. Brownish smudge on *ivory bill. Fused* red and black belly bands.

**Toucanets** *Selenidera* Golden ear tufts (except ♀ of 1). ♂ black foreparts. Infrequently seen.

**11. Golden-collared** *S. reinwardtii* p 327 Map 576
SE. Black tip on *deep red* bill. ♂ black and yellow; ♀ rufous.

**12. Tawny-tufted** *S. nattereri* p 327 Map 577
Much like 11 (no range overlap). Note *spotted* bill.

**13. Black-billed Mountain-Toucan** p 328 Map 580
*Andigena nigrirostris*
Andes. *Black* bill; *white* throat.

**Toucans** *Ramphastos* Large size; enormous colorful bill. Note voice (croak or yelp), color of bill, bib, rump. Often sit in open.

**14. Choco** *R. brevis* p 329 Map 584
W. Miniature of 15; told by voice (see text).

**15. Chestnut-mandibled** *R. swainsonii* p 330 Map 585
W. Bicolored *chestnut and yellow* bill; *yellow* bib; white rump. BLACK-MANDIBLED *R. ambiguus:* like 15 (incl. voice), but bill black (not chestnut). KEEL-BILLED *R. sulfuratus* N: red and orange on *pea green* bill; *yellow* bib, *white* rump.

**16. Gray-breasted Mountain-Toucan** p 328 Map 579
*Andigena hypoglauca*
C Andes. Recalls 13 and 20. Note *black bands on orangish bill.*

**Toucans** *Ramphastos*

**17. Citron-throated** *R. citreolaemus* p 329 Map 581
N. Mostly *black* bill; *yellow* rump.

✓ **18. Yellow-ridged** *R. culminatus* p 329 Map 582
Best told from 19 by call (see text).

**19. White-throated** *R. tucanus* p 330 Map 587
Larger than 18, bill proportionally larger, but reliably told only by voice.

**20. Plate-billed Mountain-Toucan** p 327 Map 578
*Andigena laminirostris*
SW. Yellow "plate" on side of blackish bill. Cf. 13 and 16.

# PLATE 21 BARBETS and WOODPECKERS

**1. Guayaquil Woodpecker** p 342 Map 622
*Campephilus guayaquilensis*
SW. Primaries brownish. ♂: *no white* at base of bill. ♀: *entire* crown and crest red (cf. 19, Pl.22).

**Woodpeckers** *Veniliornis* Smaller, more compact than *Piculus*. Markings usually more subdued.

**2. Bar-bellied** *V. nigriceps* p 341 Map 620
Temperate zone. Facial pattern like more common 3; *entire* underparts narrowly barred.

**3. Yellow-vented** *V. dignus* p 341 Map 619
Subtropics. *White lines border black cheeks; unmarked* yellow belly. See 11, Pl.22.

**4. Scarlet-backed** *V. callonotus* p 341 Map 618
SW. *Scarlet* upperparts; often *nearly uniform* below.

**Woodpeckers** *Piculus* Amazonian spp. (and subsp. of 5) on Pl.22.

**5. Golden-green** *P. chrysochloros* p 335 Map 602
N, E. Narrowly *barred or banded* underparts; *narrow yellow streak* below olive cheeks; golden yellow throat. ♀ *golden yellow* crown and nape.

**6. White-throated** *P. leucolaemus* p 335 Map 601
W. *Throat white,* underparts *coarsely scaled.* Narrow yellow streak below cheeks as in 5.

**7. Golden-olive** *P. rubiginosus* p 334 Map 599
Subtropics. *White sides of head;* uniform above, narrowly barred or banded below. See 7, Pl.22.

**8. Crimson-bellied Woodpecker** p 343 Map 625
*Campephilus haematogaster*
Larger, Dark red lower back; red stains on underparts; *2* white head stripes (cf. 1; also 18-21, Pl.22).

**Barbets** *Capito*

**9. Spot-crowned** *C. maculicoronatus* p 321 Map 557
W. Broad white crown stripe dotted black; red and black on flanks; wings uniform black. ♀ has black hood like 10.

**10. Orange-fronted** *C. squamatus* p 321 Map 558
SW. Red orange (yellow, ♀) forehead; white crown stripe; *white edged* tertials. ♂ mostly white below.

**11. White-mantled** *C. hypoleucus* p 321 Map 559
Pale bill, red forecrown; mostly white (or yellowish) back; white underparts. Rare.

**12. Black-spotted** p 322 Map 561
*C. niger punctatus* 12a *C. n. transilens*
Two kinds. Races near E base Andes orange-throated. Races in extreme E (12a) red throated. All told by *heavy black and yellow* streaks and spots.

**13. Five-colored** *C. quinticolor* p 321 Map 560
Pacific. Yellow V on back; *yellow spots on wings.* ♂ has red crown. ♀ *spotted* below.

**14. Toucan Barbet** p 323 Map 564
*Semnornis ramphastinus*
SW. Multicolored. Note *gray* on foreparts; *yellow* rump. Thick "ringed" bill and expressive tail.

**15. Scarlet-crowned Barbet** p 320 Map 556
*Capito aurovirens*
SE. Buttery orange breast. ♂ has red crown; ♀, frosty crown.

**Barbets** *Eubucco* Smaller than *Capito;* thinner more sharp-pointed bill. Less vocal.

**16. Red-headed** *E. bourcierii* p 322 Map 563
♀ mostly olive green. Note *yellow* bill; *blue* and black face; *streaky* flanks.

**17. Lemon-throated** *E. richardsoni* p 322 Map 562
Mossy green back; *streaky* flanks. ♂: velvety red crown. ♀: *black* cheeks, ochre line across chest.

LB McQUEEN

## PLATE 22 WOODPECKERS

**Woodpeckers** Celeus Chestnut-colored (yellowish, 5); crested, greenish yellow bill; glean bark surface, chisel arboreal ant and termite nests.

**1. Chestnut** C. elegans p 336 Map 603
E. Large, dark; essentially *unbarred; yellow* rump.

**2. Scale-breasted** C. grammicus p 336 Map 604
E. Smaller than 1; coarsely barred *above and below* (or bars above confined to shoulders, W Amazonian subsp).

**3. Cinnamon** C. loricatus p 336 Map 605
W. Unique in range.

**4. Ringed** C. torquatus p 337 Map 607
E. *Black collar and foreparts;* yellow belly barred black; *lacks* yellow rump.

**5. Cream-colored** C. flavus p 336 Map 606
SE. *Buffy yellow.* Amt. of brown on wings var.

**6. Spot-breasted Woodpecker** p 334 Map 597
Chrysoptilus punctigula
Lowlands. *White* sides of head; *barred* above; *spotted* below (cf. 7).

**Woodpeckers** Piculus

**7. Golden-olive** P. rubiginosus p 334 Map 599
Mts. *White* sides of head; *uniform* above, *barred* below.

**8. Golden-green Woodpecker** p 335 Map 602
P. chrysochloros 8a ♀ n subsp.
N, E. Finely barred below; *long yellow streak* below olive cheeks. 8a: see also Pl.21.

**9. Yellow-throated** P. flavigula p 335 Map 600
SE. *Sides of head yellow to nape; coarsely scaled* below.

**10. Crimson-mantled** P. rivolii p 334 Map 598
Andes. *Crimson* upperparts.

**Woodpeckers** Veniliornis Smaller, more compact than Piculus. Markings usually more subdued.

**11. Yellow-vented** V. dignus p 341 Map 619
Andes. Two white lines border black cheeks; *unmarked yellow* belly. Also illus. on Pl.21.

**12. Smoky-brown** V. fumigatus p 339 Map 614
Andes. *Uniform brown;* pale cheeks; barred primaries.

**13. Red-rumped** V. kirkii p 340 Map 617
W. *Red rump;* yellow nuchal collar.

**14. Little** V. passerinus p 340 Map 615
E. *Lacks* yellow nuchal collar (cf. 15). Faint white moustachial streak. Definite *whitish eyebrow and moustache* in Amazonia.

**15. Red-stained** V. affinis p 340 Map 616
W, SE. *Yellow nuchal collar;* tiny red dots on lesser upper wing coverts (inconspic.).

**Woodpeckers** Melanerpes Predom. black (except 16); white lower back and rump.

**16. Red-crowned** M. rubricapillus p 339 Map 613
Black-and-white barring above.

**17. Yellow-tufted** M. cruentatus p 338 Map 610
E. Only small black woodpecker in range. For ACORN M. formicivorus, BLACK-CHEEKED M. pucherani, and GOLDEN-NAPED M. chrysauchen, see text.

**18. Lineated Woodpecker** p 337 Map 608
Dryocopus lineatus
Narrow white cheek stripe (cf. 19); white "suspenders" *do not* meet on back; *dusky bill.*

**Woodpeckers** Campephilus

**19. Crimson-crested** C. melanoleucos p 341 Map 621
Scapular stripes *meet* on back; pale bill. ♂: *solid red* head, white cheek spot, white around bill. ♀: *broad white cheek stripe;* black forehead.

**20. Powerful** C. pollens p 342 Map 624
Andes. Scapular stripes *meet;* rump *white.* ♂ head sim. to ♀ of 18 and 19. ♀ *entirely* black and white (no red).

**21. Red-necked** C. rubricollis p 342 Map 623
SE. Head, neck and chest largely crimson; *wing linings and belly cinnamon rufous.*

# PLATE 23  PICULETS and WOODCREEPERS

**Piculets** *Picumnus* ♀ ♀ have white-dotted (or uniform) crown.

**1. Chestnut** *P. cinnamomeus* p 331 Map 588
Arid N. Rufous chestnut. RUFOUS-BREASTED *P. rufiventris* SE: below like 1. PLAIN-BREASTED *P. castelnau* SE: plain whitish below.

**2. Olivaceous** *P. olivaceus* p 332 Map 592
W. Lower underparts *vaguely streaked* (cf. 4).

**3. Scaled** *P. squamulatus* p 332 Map 591
E. Pale. Scaled *above and below*.

**4. Grayish** *P. granadensis* p 333 Map 593
W. *Unstreaked grayish white* underparts.

**5. Lafresnaye's** *P. lafresnayi* p 333 Map 595
SE. Barred *above and below; whitish* below

**6. Golden-spangled** *P. exilis* p 333 Map 594
E. Spotted above, yellowish below (cf. 5). ORINOCO, *P. pumilus* E: below like 5; above *unmarked*.

**7. Olivaceous Woodcreeper** p 345 Map 632
*Sittasomus griseicapillus*
Small. Thin bill, grayish olive foreparts.

**8. Wedge-billed Woodcreeper** p 345 Map 633
*Glyphorynchus spirurus*
Short wedge-shaped bill; buff eyebrow (cf. 26, Pl.25).

**9. Long-tailed Woodcreeper** p 345 Map 630
*Deconychura longicauda*
Slender. Short straight bill. *Little evident streaking* below. SE subsp. even less streaked.

**Woodcreepers** *Dendrocincla* Uniform plumage, straight bill.

**10. White-chinned** *D. merula* p 344 Map 628
SE. Bluish white eyes (cf. 11). *Whitish chin*.

**11. Plain-brown** *D. fuliginosa* p 344 Map 627
Only common member of genus. *Grayish* cheeks, faint dusky malar (cf. 10).

**12. Ruddy** *D. homochroa* p 344 Map 629
N. Dark rufous; throat tawnier, crown brighter.

**Woodcreepers** *Lepidocolaptes* Smaller, more slender than *Xiphorhynchus*. Pale bill thinner, decurved; back unstreaked.

**13. Streak-headed** *L. souleyetii* p 353 Map 648
Pale. *Profuse linelike* streaks.

**14. Spot-crowned** *L. affinis* p 353 Map 649
Mts. Spotted crown; bold *spotlike streaks* below.

**Woodcreepers** *Xiphorhynchus* Larger, more robust than *Lepidocolaptes*; bill heavier, straighter but note variation (e.g., cf. 16 with 19).

**15. Ocellated** *X. ocellatus* p 351 Map 641
E. Dusky bill; *essentially unstreaked* mantle and breast; spotted hood.

**16. Buff-throated** *X. guttatus* p 352 Map 644
Two kinds. W subsp.: long dark bill; streaked to upper mantle and mid-breast. E subsp.: larger, streaked to lower back and lower breast.

**17. Spix's** *X. spixii buenaevistae* p 351 Map 642
E. Spotlike streaks to mantle and lower breast. SE subsp. more streaked below (cf. 15, 18, 19). ELEGANT, *X. elegans* SE: like 17, but back more *spotted*; spots go *to rump*.

**18. Striped** *X. obsoletus* p 349 Map 640
E. Paler; linear stripes above and below. Swamps.

**19. Straight-billed** *X. picus* p 349 Map 639
Marked racial var. *Straight whitish bill*. In N foreparts *heavily streaked whitish*. In SE darker, buffier, eyebrow weaker (cf. 15).

**Woodcreepers** *Dendrocolaptes* Large, robust; stout bill.

**20. Barred** *D. certhia* p 348 Map 637
In W *bill dusky; barred below*, faintly above. In SE *bill reddish*; heavier barring above.

**21. Black-banded** *D. picumnus* p 348 Map 638
Large. Much like 22 but *lacks dusky malar*; bill smaller, straighter. *Streaked and barred below* (bars faint).

**22. Strong-billed** p 347 Map 636
*Xiphocolaptes promeropirhynchus*
Very large. Heavy slightly decurved bill. Subsp. vary but *dusky malar, unstreaked throat* holds. Belly streaked or barred.

**Woodcreepers** *Xiphorhynchus*

**23. Black-striped** *X. lachrymosus* p 352 Map 645
NW. Heavily striped *blackish foreparts*.

**24. Spotted** *X. erythropygius* p 353 Map 646
W. Crown and throat more or less uniform (cf. 25). *Spotted* below.

**25. Olive-backed** *X. triangularis* p 353 Map 647
Higher el. than 24. *Spotted* crown, *scalloped* throat.

GTUDOR

# PLATE 24 WOODCREEPERS and FURNARIIDS (SPINTAILS etc.)

**1. Tyrannine Woodcreeper** p. 343 Map 626
*Dendrocincla tyrannina*
Highlands. Larger than 11 on Pl.23; uniform warm brown.

**Scythebills** *Campylorhamphus* Distinctive sickle-shaped bill; most with sim. plumage; told by bill color, bill length, body size, voice, and range.

**2. Greater** *C. pucheranii* p 354 Map 650
Temperate zone. Large. *Strong* facial pattern; *chalky* bill.

**3. Brown-billed** *C. pusillus* p 355 Map 652
W. *Pale brownish* bill; deep buff throat; streaking deeper buff than 4.

**4. Red-billed** *C. trochilirostris* p 354 Map 651
N, E. Decidedly *reddish* bill (but cf. 5); whitish throat.

**5. Curve-billed** *C. procurvoides* p 355 Map 653
SE. Quite like 4 and bill *reddish*; mantle *more or less unstreaked.*

**6. Cinnamon-throated Woodcreeper** p 346 Map 635
*Dendrexetastes rufigula*
SE. *Heavy greenish yellow bill; unpatterned* brownish plumage. Look for the necklace. Often acts like a foliage-gleaner.

**7. Andean Tit-Spinetail** p 357 Map 658
*Leptasthenura andicola*
Páramo. *Heavily streaked; long* double-spiked tail; *stubby* bill. N races have rusty-edged wings.

**Canasteros** *Asthenes* High el.; streaked sparrowlike back; rounded unfrayed graduated tail; heavier bill than *Leptasthenura* or *Schizoeaca*. Partly terrestrial.

**8. Many-striped** *A. flammulata* p 365 Map 683
Paramo. Heavily streaked like 7. Rufous in wings and rounded tail like 9. Most races lack chin spot.

**9. Streak-backed** *A. wyatti* p 365 Map 682
NE (Paramo). Streaked above; *rufous in wings* (broad band) *and tail* (cf. 8).

**10. White-chinned Thistletail** p 364 Map 680
*Schizoeaca fuliginosa*
*Unstreaked.* Iron gray below; *white eyes* (or dark, Nariño) and *eyering; long* frayed tail.

**11. Spectacled Prickletail** p 366 Map 685
*Siptornis striaticollis*
S, Mts. Large *eyebrow spot*; freckled throat, chestnut cap.

**12. Double-banded Graytail** p 366 Map 686
*Xenerpestes minlosi*
NW. Warblerlike shape and habits. White eyestripe and wing bars.

**13. Chestnut-winged Hookbill** p 368 Map 694
*Ancistrops strigilatus*
SE. Heavy *yellow buff streaking* above, obscure below. Rufous wings and tail.

**14. Rusty-headed Spinetail** p 360 Map 667
*Synallaxis fuscorufa*
Santa Marta. Rufous head and foreparts.

**15. Streak-capped Spinetail** p 362 Map 675
*Cranioleuca hellmayri*
Santa Marta. Dingy. Note *dull eyebrow, dark streaked* cap.

**16. Pale-legged Hornero** p 356 Map 656
*Furnarius leucopus*
N, SE. Partially terrestrial. *Bright cinnamon rufous* above; *contrasting* cap; eyestripe, *short* tail.

**17. White-whiskered Spinetail** p 361 Map 670
*Synallaxis c. candei* 17a *S. c. atrigularis*
Bold head pattern. *Bright* cinnamon rufous back in arid N. Brown back in Magdalena Val.

**18. Orange-fronted Plushcrown** p 366 Map 687
*Metopothrix aurantiacus*  Red legs
SE. Recalls a conebill. Orange forecrown, yellow throat.

Seen in trees by Cane farm, Explorama

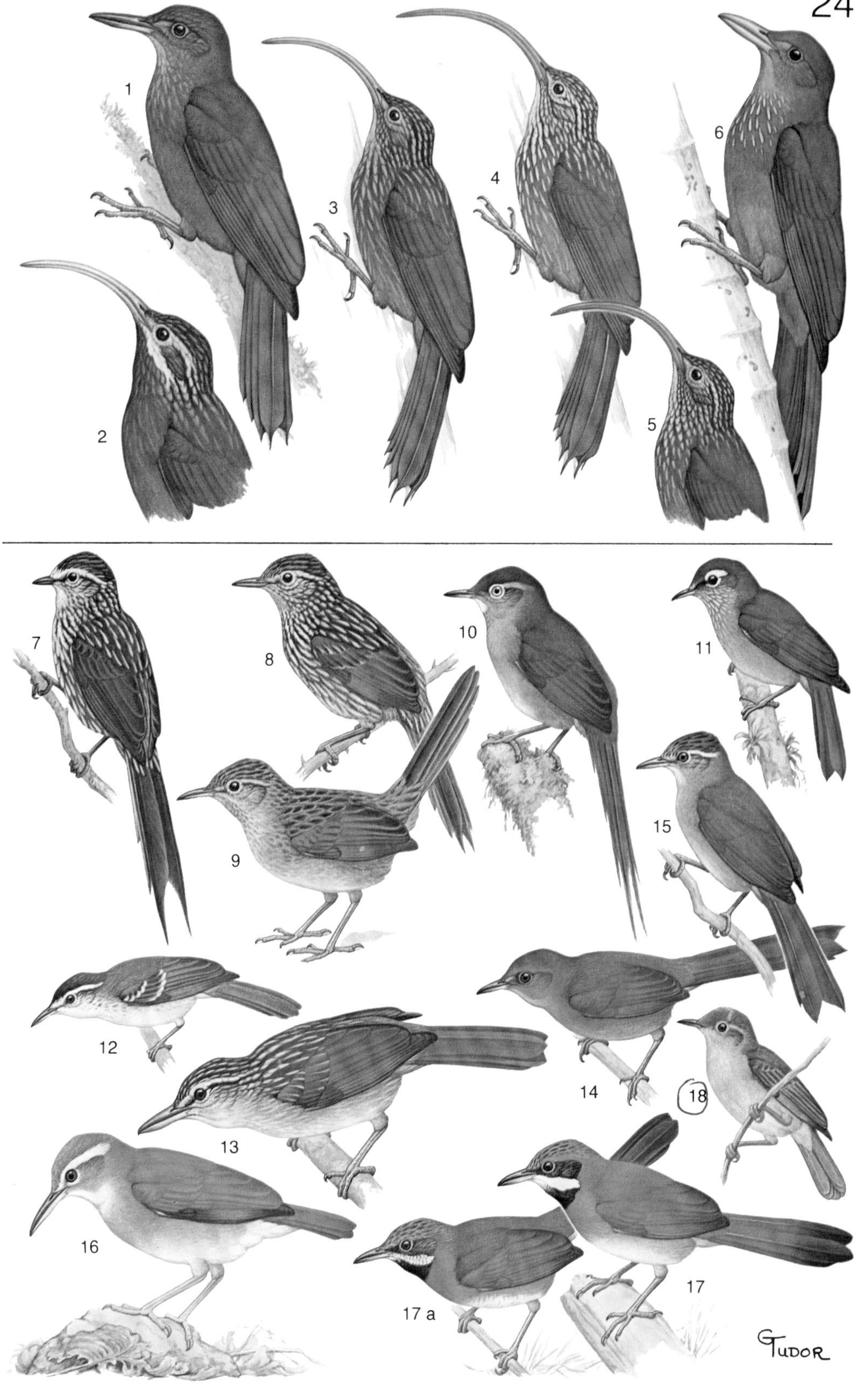
1
2
3
4
5
6
7
8
9
10
11
12
13
14
15
16
17
17 a
18
GTUDOR

PLATE 25 FURNARIIDS (SPINETAILS etc.)

## 24

**Cinclodes** *Cinclodes* Terrestrial. Strong eyebrow and rufous wing band. Paramo to snowline.

**1. Bar-winged** *C. fuscus* p 356 Map 655
Most common. Bill thinner than 2; lower mandible straight; outer tail extensively rufous.

**2. Stout-billed** *C. excelsior* p 356 Map 654
Bill *decidedly decurved* (incl. lower mandible).

**3. White-browed Spinetail** p 361 Map 671
*Hellmayrea gularis*
Treeline. *White* eyebrow and throat; short tail.

**Spinetails** *Synallaxis*

**4. Rufous** *S. unirufa* p 360 Map 668
Bright rufous; black lores; long tail (cf. Rufous Wren). Perijá race has eyestripe, paler underparts.

**5. Stripe-breasted** *S. cinnamomea* p 360 Map 666
NE. Rufous postocular; *streaked* underparts.

**6. Azara's** *S. azarae* p 358 Map 659
Subtropics. Long rufous tail (cf. 10). Common.

**7. Slaty** *S. brachyura* p 359 Map 663
W. *Slaty* (incl. tail); cap and shoulders rufous.

**8. Dusky** *S. moesta* p 358 Map 660
E. Very dark. Rufous cap, shoulders, *and tail*. Heavy bill.

**9. Silvery-throated** *S. subpudica* p 358 Map 661
E Andes. Grayish tail decidedly *longer* than 10.

**10. Pale-breasted** *S. albescens* p 358 Map 662
Widespread. Grayish brown tail. Note call.

**11. Plain-crowned** *S. gujanensis* p 359 Map 665
SE. *Brownish* head; rufous shoulders *and wings*.

**12. Ruddy** *S. rutilans* p 361 Map 669
SE. Dull, dark rufous; *throat and tail black*.

**13. Plain Thornbird** p 365 Map 684
*Phacellodomus rufifrons*
E. *Very plain*. No obvious marks. Note thickish bill, rounded tail, social habits.

**Spinetails** *Certhiaxis*

**14. Yellow-chinned** *C. cinnamomea* p 362 Map 672
N, SE. *Bright rufous* above, immaculate below; *grayish* forehead and lores.

**15. Red-and-white Spinetail** p 362 Map 673
*C. mustelina*
SE. Like 14 but larger, *forehead concolor* with upperparts; sharp *black* lores.

**Spinetails** *Cranioleuca*

**16. Crested** *C. subcristata* p 362 Map 674
NE. *Dull faintly streaked cap*; grayish brown eyebrow; pale mandible; dark eyes (cf. 18).

**17. Rusty-backed** *C. vulpina* p 363 Map 678
SE. *Dingier* below than 14 and 15. Note different habitat, streaking on cheeks.

**18. Ash-browed** *C. curtata* p 363 Map 676
Eyestripe *gray*; obscure streaks on chest; eyes white (E slope) or dark(?).

**19. Red-faced** *C. erythrops* p 363 Map 677
W, highlands. Head *mostly rufous*.

**20. Speckled** *C. gutturata* p 364 Map 679
SE. Unlike any other. Cf. wrens.

**21. Orinoco Softtail** p 365 (Note 1)
*Thripophaga cherriei*
Orinoco. Orange chin; linear *buff* streaks.

**Xenops** *Xenops*

**22. Plain** *X. minutus* p 376 Map 719
Back *unstreaked; white* malar. Widespread. STREAKED *X. rutilans*. Highlands. Back and underparts to belly streaked.

**23. Slender-billed** *X. tenuirostris* p 375 Map 717
SE. Streaked *above and below*. White malar.

**24. Rufous-tailed** *X. milleri* p 375 Map 716
SE. Rather like 23 but *lacks* white malar; *no black* in tail.

**Treerunners** *Margarornis*

**25. Pearled** *M. squamiger* p 367 Map 688
Temperate zone. *Rich rufous* above; eyestripe, throat, and *ocelli creamy white*.

**26. Fulvous-dotted** *M. stellatus* p 367 Map 689
Pacific. Fulvous eyestripe and underparts; *white throat* bordered below by necklace of black-edged white spots.

**27. Spotted Barbtail** p 367 Map 691
*Premnoplex brunnescens*
*Dark brown* (cf. 28); profuse *deep buff* spotting. Unobtrusive.

**28. Rusty-winged Barbtail** p 367 Map 690
*Premnornis guttuligera*
*Streaked above and below*; contrasting rufous tail. Cf. larger foliage-gleaners.

PLATE 26 FURNARIIDS

## 25

**1. Streaked Tuftedcheek** p 368 Map 693
*Pseudocolaptes boissonneautii*
Throat and *cheek tufts* buffy white; *back streaked*. BUFFY
*P. lawrencii* Pacific: quite like 1 but lower el; back *more
or less unstreaked* (see text).

**Treehunters** *Thripadectes*

**2. Streak-capped** *T. virgaticeps* p 374 Map 714
*Fine* streaking; crown blackish; breast cinnamon.

**3. Striped** *T. holostictus* p 374 Map 712
Smaller than 4, *brownish* (not black) streaking less prom.
BLACK-BILLED *T. melanorhynchus* W Meta: above like
3, below most like 2 (nearly uniform ochraceous brown
below).

**4. Flammulated** *T. flammulatus* p 374 Map 711
Large. Bold *black and buff* streaking (cf. 3).

**Foliage-gleaners** *Anabacerthia*

**5. Scaly-throated** *A. variegaticeps* p 369 Map 697
Pacific. *Cinnamon spectacles*; breast *flammulated* cinnamon.

**6. Montane** *A. s. striaticollis* p 370 Map 698
Widespread. *Buff spectacles* over dusky cheeks; essentially unstreaked. SE subsp. faintly streaked below.

**7. Lineated Foliage-gleaner** p 369 Map 696
*Syndactyla subalaris*
Profuse *narrow* streaks; throat *unstreaked* (cf. 18; also
larger treehunters).

**8. Uniform Treehunter** p 375 Map 715
*Thripadectes ignobilis*
Pacific. Much like 2 but smaller, virtually *unstreaked*
above; *faint* fulvous eyering and postocular. Very dark.

**Foliage-gleaners** *Philydor* Midlevel to canopy; prom.
eyebrow.

**9. Buff-fronted** *P. rufus* p 371 Map 702
*Eyebrow* and throat bright buff; *rufous* wings. Pacific
race has grayer crown; less ochraceous below.

**10. Cinnamon-rumped** *P. pyrrhodes* p 370 Map 700
SE. *Bright cinnamon* rump, tail and underparts; *contrasting slaty* wings; yellow legs. SLATY-WINGED *P. erythronotus* W: much like 10; legs *dusky* (no range overlap).

**11. Rufous-tailed** *P. ruficaudatus* p 371 Map 704
SE. Yellow buff eyestripe; whitish throat; *faint chest*
streaks; lacks rufous on wings. RUFOUS-RUMPED *P. erythrocercus* SE: most like 11, but no streaking below.

**12. Chestnut-winged** *P. erythropterus* p 371 Map 703
SE. Like 11, but *wings rufous*; back grayer, throat more
ochraceous.

**Foliage-gleaners** *Automolus* Understory; rufous tail;
most with little or no facial pattern.

**13. Crested** *A. dorsalis* p 372 Map 706
SE. Whitish throat and postocular (cf. 16).

**14. Chestnut-crowned** *A. rufipileatus* p 373 Map 709
SE. *Orange yellow* eyes. Slightly contrasting crown and
tail.

**15. Buff-throated** *A. ochrolaemus* p 373 Map 708
Widespread. *Buff eyering and eyestripe*; light buff throat.

**16. Olive-backed** *A. infuscatus* p 372 Map 705
E. *White throat*; weak eyering. Common.

**17. Ruddy** *A. rubiginosus* p 372 Map 707
*Very dark*. Look for contrasting cinnamon throat. Voice
diagnostic.

**18. Striped Foliage-gleaner** p 369 Map 695
*Hyloctistes subulatus*
W, SE. Rather small; *throat and mantle streaked* (throat
unstreaked yellow buff, mantle unstreaked, Pacific
slope).

**Leaftossers** *Sclerurus* Most spp. very sim. and
confusing. Bill shape and throat color helpful.

**19. Gray-throated** *S. albigularis* p 376 Map 720
N, E. Ashy throat; broad *rufous* chest band.

**20. Tawny-throated** *S. mexicanus* p 377 Map 721
Widespread. Bright cinnamon rufous throat; rather long
drooped bill (cf. 24).

**21. Black-tailed** *S. caudacutus* p 377 Map 723
SE. Faintly scaled *whitish* throat, otherwise dark brown,
dull rufescent rump.

**22. Sharp-tailed Streamcreeper** p 378 Map 725
*Lochmias nematura*
Along Andean streams. Recalls *Sclerurus*. Dense white
spotting below.

**Leaftossers** *Sclerurus*

**23. Scaly-throated** *S. guatemalensis* p 378 Map 724
W. *Lacks* contrasting rump; *scaled* throat.

**24. Short-billed** *S. rufigularis* p 377 Map 722
SE. *Short straight* bill; buff throat (cf. 20).

## 26

# PLATE 27 ANTSHRIKES, ANTBIRDS, etc.

**Antshrikes** *Thamnophilus*

**1. Lined** *T. palliatus* p 381 Map 733
E. ♀ rich chestnut above; black bars wider than white.
♂ barred black and white (Pl.XIII).

**2. Bar-crested** *T. multistriatus* p 381 Map 732
W. ♀ not safely told from 1 (no range overlap) but
whiter below, white bars wider than black. ♂, Pl.XIII.

**3. Black-backed Antshrike** p 380 Map 730
*Sakesphorus melanonotus*
♂ black *above and below*; white sides and *abdomen*.
♀: *black* crown, *chestnut* tail; buff wing edgings (cf.
7).

**4. Black Antshrike** p 381 Map 734
*Thamnophilus nigriceps*
NW. ♂ black; white wing-linings. ♀: *streaked head and
underparts.* SPECKLED ANTSHRIKE *Xenornis setifrons* NW:
brown *crown, upperparts* streaked buff; 2 cinnamon
wing bars; below dark gray. ♀ browner below. Rare.

**5. Fasciated Antshrike** p 379 Map 726
*Cymbilaimus lineatus*
Finely barred above and below. Cap black (♂), chest-
nut (♀). See Pl.XIII.

**6. Barred Antshrike** p 380 Map 731
*Thamnophilus doliatus*
♂: coarse bars; white in crown. ♀ *unbarred* below (cf.
1 and 2). See Pl.XIII.

**7. Black-crested Antshrike** p 380 Map 729
*Sakesphorus canadensis*
N,E. *Brown* back; *white* wing edgings. ♂ black "hood"
and chest bordered white. ♀ *chestnut* crown, *dusky*
tail, (cf. ♀ of 3).

**8. Russet Antshrike** p 386 Map 748
*Thamnistes anabatinus*
W. Stocky; heavy bill. Note *pale eyebrow*, rather *short,
rufous* tail (cf. foliage-gleaners).

**9. Uniform Antshrike** p 383 Map 738
*Thamnophilus unicolor*
Andes. Pale gray eyes. ♂ uniform dark gray, ♀ *con-
trasting gray* face.

**10. Great Antshrike** *Taraba major* p 379 Map 728
Large. ♀ rufous chestnut above, immaculate below;
red eyes. ♂, Pl.XIII.

**11. Bicolored Antbird** p 411 Map 812
*Gymnopithys bicolor*
W. *White median underparts*; bare dusky blue ocular
arera; black cheeks. See White-cheeked Antbird (Pl.30).

**12. Bare-crowned Antbird** p 404 Map 795
*Gymnocichla nudiceps*
W. ♂: bare pale blue forehead and face. ♀: bare ocu-
lar area; rich rufous below; rufous-tipped wing coverts.

**13. Immaculate Antbird** p 410 Map 809
*Myrmeciza immaculata*
Andes. *Bare bluish white* ocular area. ♂ black. ♀ *dark
brown.*

**14. Recurve-billed Bushbird** p 385 Map 746
*Clytoctantes alixi*
N base Andes. Note bill. ♂ black. ♀ rich rufous below.

**Bare-eyes** *Phlegopsis* Large robust antbirds; *bare red
facial skin* (all ♂♂; some ♀♀). ♂♂ have head and
underparts black. Follow army ants.

**15. Reddish-winged** *P. erythroptera* p 413 Map 817
SE. ♂: *rufous* wing bars and wing band; scaled back.
♀: *buff wing bars and primary band*; rich rufous below.

**16. Black-spotted** *P. nigromaculata* p 412 Map 816
SE. *Black spots* rimmed buff; tail *chestnut* (no black).
ARGUS *P. barringeri* Nariño: Differs from 16 by *spots buff*
rimmed black; blackish subterminal tail band. ♀ unknown.

**17. White-backed Fire-eye** p 401 Map 787
*Pyriglena leuconota*
E Andes. Red eyes, small bill, long tail. ♂ black. ♀:
brown back.

**18. Ocellated Antbird** p 413 Map 818
*Phaenostictus mcleannani*
W. Unique. Blue facial skin, pink legs. Note *orange
rufous collar; spotted* appearance.

## 27

TUDOR

# PLATE 28 ANTBIRDS, ANTWRENS, etc.

**1. Scale-backed Antbird** p 414 Map 821
*Hylophylax poecilonota*
E. White scaled wings and back; tail spots. ♂ gray.
♀: cinnamon rufous head and foreparts.

**2. Black-and-white Antbird** p 403 Map 794
*Myrmochanes hemileucus*
Amazonas. Glossy black above, immaculate below.
*Long, slender* bill, gray rump.

**3. Dot-winged Antwren** p 397 Map 777
*Microrhopias quixensis consobrina*
3a *M. q. quixensis.*
*Single broad* white bar; *bold tail tips.* ♀ of larger SE
race (3a) has black throat.

**4. Yellow-browed Antbird** p 403 Map 792
*Hypocnemis hypoxantha*
SE. *Uniform olive green* back. Yellow eyebrow and underparts; sides *streaked.*

**5. Black-chinned Antbird** p 403 Map 793
*Hypocnemoides melanopogon*
E. Fringed wings; tail tipping (faint, ♀). ♂: black throat.
♀ clouded below.

**6. Slaty Antwren** p 394 Map 767
*Myrmotherula schisticolor*
Highlands. ♂: black throat and breast. ♀: gray back.

**7. Yellow-breasted Antwren** p 396 Map 775
*Herpsilochmus axillaris*
W. Grayish olive above, light yellow below; dotted crown; white eyebrow. ♀: chestnut crown.

**8. Rufous-rumped Antwren** p 398 Map 780
*Terenura callinota*
Andes. Slender. Black cap, *rufous* rump; thin bill.

**Antwrens** *Myrmotherula.* See table, p 390

**9. Long-winged** *M. longipennis* p 394 Map 768
E. Larger than 10, tail longer; white tail tip.

**10. Rio Suno** *M. sunensis* p 394 Map 769
SE. Smaller, very short tail (no white tips); darker than 9, black of throat more extensive.

**11. Checker-throated** *M. fulviventris* p 392 Map 762
W. ♀-plumaged; buff wing spots. ♂ checkered throat.

**Antwrens** *Herpsilochmus* White eyebrow and spots and edges on wings and tail.

**12. Rufous-winged** *H. rufimarginatus* p 397 Map 776
W. Only *Herpsilochmus* with rufous on wings.

**13. Spot-backed** *H. dorsimaculatus* p 396 Map 774
E. Black and white markings on back. ♂: crown black spotted white. SPOT-TAILED *H. sticturus* E. ♂ has gray back; ♀ rufous crown.

**14. Ash-winged Antwren** p 399 Map 781
*Terenura spodioptila*
E. *Chestnut* back; whitish eyebrow and wing-bars; *light gray* below. ♂: *black cap.*

**Antwrens** *Myrmotherula* See table, p 390

**15. Pygmy** *M. brachyura* p 389 Map 755
Streaked above. ♂: white throat. ♀: sides of head buff.
YELLOW-THROATED *M. ambigua* E. ♂ like 15, but throat yellow; for ♀, see text.

**16. Plain-throated** *M. hauxwelli* p 391 Map 761
SE. *Spots on tertials;* tail tip white (buff, ♀). ♂: no black on throat. ♀ *orange rufous* below.

**17. Rufous-tailed** *M. erythrura* p 393 Map 764
SE. Brownish above; *rufous back and tail.* ♀ buff below.

**18. Stipple-throated** *M. haematonota* p 392 Map 763
SE. Brownish above, *chestnut back.* ♂ has checkered throat.

**19. Short-billed** *M. obscura* p 389 Map 756
E. Much like 15 but blacker above; malar thicker.

**20. Ornate** *M. ornata* p 393 Map 765
Chestnut back. ♂: *gray head, black* throat. ♀: checkered throat.

**21. Streaked** *M. surinamensis* p 389 Map 758
♂ entirely streaked. ♀ has rufous streaked crown; W race, unstreaked orange buff head and foreparts.

**22. Stripe-chested** *M. longicauda* p 391 Map 759
SE. ♂: streaks below *confined to chest* (cf. 21). ♀: *unstreaked ochraceous chest,* white belly.

**23. White-flanked** *M. axillaris* p 393 Map 766
*White flank plumes.* ♂ very blackish.

**24. Gray** *M. menetriesii* p 395 Map 771
E. ♂ has *no black* on throat; white-edged wing coverts. PLAIN-WINGED *M. behni* SE: ♂ like 24, but throat black, wings unmarked.

**25. Cherrie's** *M. cherriei* p 391 Map 760
E. ♂ coarser underpart streaking than 21. ♀ more streaked than 21.

**26. White-fringed Antwren** p 398 Map 778
*Formicivora grisea intermedia*
26a *F. g. rufiventris*
N (dry). ♂: *white eyebrow and stripe on sides; black breast.* ♀: white eyebrow, freckled chest; E subsp. cinnamon below.

**Antvireos** *Dysithamnus* More robust than *Myrmotherula.*

**27. Plain** *D. mentalis* p 386 Map 749
♂: pale below; *dusky cheeks.* ♀: *chestnut* crown, *white eyering.* ♀ of NE subsp. yellowish below.

**28. Spot-crowned** *D. puncticeps* p 387 Map 750
W. ♂: black crown *dotted white.* ♀: streaky rufous crown, faint breast streaks.

**29. Long-tailed Antbird** p 398 Map 779
*Drymophila caudata*
W. Wrenlike. *Streaked* foreparts; *rufous* rearparts; *spots on long* tail.

**30. Warbling Antbird** p 402 Map 791
*Hypocnemis cantator*
SE. *Streaked.* White eyebrow; *rufous flanks.* More common than 4.

## 28

# PLATE 29 ANTSHRIKES and ANTBIRDS

**1. Pearly Antshrike** p 385 Map 744
*Megastictus margaritatus* 1a ♀
E. Wing and tail spots *large and round*. ♀: spots buff; underparts *ochraceous*.

**Antshrikes** *Thamnophilus*

**2. Slaty** *T. punctatus* p 384 Map 741
♂: *prom.* wing and tail markings; crown *black*. ♀: dull chestnut crown.

**3. Amazonian** *T. amazonicus* p 384 Map 742
♂ of Orinoco race like 2 but *lacks* black cap. Amazonian race from 2 by voice. ♀: *orangish* head and foreparts.

**4. Mouse-colored** *T. murinus* p 383 Map 740
E. Weak buff wing dots; *brownish primaries*. ♀ drab; rufescent crown.

**5. White-shouldered** *T. aethiops* p 382 Map 737
E. Heavy bill; wings *dotted* white. Nariño subsp. blackish. ♀ uniform brownish chestnut.

**6. Blackish-gray** *T. nigrocinereus* p 382 Map 735
E. Very dark. Narrow white margins on coverts and wings (cf. 2 and 5). ♀ like ♀ of 9, but crown blackish; no wing spots.

**7. Spot-winged Antshrike** p 385 Map 743
*Pygiptila stellaris*
SE. Short-tailed; heavy bill. ♀ has rufous in wings. Canopy.

**8. Black-capped Antshrike** p 383 Map 739
*Thamnophilus schistaceus*
SE. *Uniform* gray with *black* crown. ♀ much like ♀ of 4 but *no wing dots*.

**9. Castelnau's Antshrike** p 382 Map 736
*Thamnophilus cryptoleucus*
Amazonas. *Large; very heavy bill. Glossy black;* extensive white on wings. ♀ duller.

**Antbirds** *Cercomacra*

**10. Jet** *C. nigricans* p 400 Map 786
♂: white wing coverts, *bold white tail tips*. ♀: *throat finely streaked white*.

**11. Black** *C. serva* p 400 Map 785
SE. *Blacker* than 13; narrow white margins on wing coverts; thin bill. ♀ like 13, but forehead *not rufous*.

**12. Dusky** *C. tyrannina* p 399 Map 783
♂: white wing covert margins; faint tail tips (usually). ♀ olive brown above; *pale* rufous below.

**13. Blackish** *C. nigrescens* p 400 Map 784
SE. ♂ wing coverts margined white. *Voice* distinctive (see text). ♀ *bright rufous forehead* and underparts.

**14. Gray** *C. cinerascens* p 399 Map 782
E ♂: *large tail spots;* faint wing dots. For ♀, see text. Only member of genus in forest canopy.

**Antshrikes** *Thamnomanes* Forest lower story; *erect posture*; distinctive voices.

**15. Dusky-throated** *T. ardesiacus* p 387 Map 752
E. ♂ has dusky throat. ♀ abdomen much duller than ♀ of 16.

**16. Cinereous** *T. caesius* p 388 Map 753
SE. ♂ entirely gray. ♀ has *contrasting rich rufous* abdomen. WESTERN *T. occidentalis* W Cauca: white-dotted wing bars (buff, ♀); ♂ slaty; ♀ has chestnut cap, faint streaks below.

**17. Plumbeous Antvireo** p 387 Map 751
*Dysithamnus plumbeus*
E Andes. Short-tailed. ♂: *blackish* throat. ♀: rusty crown, *gray and white streaked* underparts.

**18. Chestnut-backed Antbird** p 407 Map 803
*Myrmeciza exsul*
W. *Bare bluish ocular area;* dark eyes. ♂ has *rich brown* rearparts. ♀: head slaty; *rufous* underparts.

**Antbirds** *Sipia*

**19. Stub-tailed** *S. berlepschi* p 406 Map 801
W. *Stubby tail;* large bill. ♀ densely spotted white below.

**20. Esmeraldas** *S. rosenbergi* p 406 Map 800
W. *Fire red eyes.* ♂ blackish slate; *wing dots.* ♀ like ♀ of 22, but *tail dusky*.

**21. White-bellied Antbird** p 406 Map 802
*Myrmeciza longipes*
N, E. ♂ and ♀ *bright rufous* above; white belly.

**22. Dull-mantled Antbird** p 408 Map 804
*Myrmeciza laemosticta*
W. Dull red eyes (*no bare ocular area*); ♂: chestnut rearparts *and tail.* ♀: checkered throat (cf. ♀ of 20). GRAY-BELLIED *M. pelzelni* Guainía: ♂ recalls ♂ of 2 (Pl. 30), but sides of head freckled, wing spots *buff;* ♀ has white throat and chest.

PLATE 30 ANTBIRDS, ANTPITTAS, etc.

## 29

**1. Black-headed Antbird** p 404 Map 796
*Percnostola rufifrons*
E. ♂ *crown and throat* black; wing coverts margined
white. ♀ much like ♀ of 4; wing coverts *margined* buff.

**2. Black-throated Antbird** p 410 Map 810
*Myrmeciza atrothorax*
SE. *Small. Brown* above; wings dotted white. ♂: extensive black throat. ♀: *white throat, rufous* breast.

**3. Chestnut-tailed Antbird** p 408 Map 805
*Myrmeciza hemimelaena*
Putumayo. ♂: black foreparts *contrast sharply* with white
belly. ♀: throat and breast *cinnamon buff.*

**Antbirds** *Percnostola*

**4. Slate-colored** *P. schistacea* p 405 Map 797
SE. *Darker* than ♂ and ♀ of 5; *tiny* wing dots. ♂ from
5a ♂ by shorter all black bill (not *pale* below). ♀: rufous crown; *buff* wing dots (cf. ♀ of 1); rufous chestnut
below.

**5. Spot-winged** p 405 Map 798
*P. leucostigma infuscata*
5a *P. l. subplumbea*
E. ♂ *2-toned;* dark gray above, lighter below; *prom.*
wing spots. ♀: gray sides of head, *rufous* underparts.
Amazonian race (5a) darker, wing spots smaller; rather
long bill dusky above *pale* below (cf. 4).

**6. Silvered Antbird** *Sclateria naevia* p 405 Map 799
E. Long bill; pinkish legs. ♂ *white* below. ♀: median
underparts *white;* sides rusty. *Swampy* places.

**Antbirds** *Myrmeciza* Bill mod. heavy; tail mod. long,
pounded down; shorter-tailed and more robust than
*Cercomacra.* Undergrowth; may follow army ants.

**7. Plumbeous** *M. hyperythra* p 409 Map 806
SE. *Large. Bare facial skin;* prom. wing spots. ♀ *rufous*
below.

**8. Sooty** *M. fortis* p 409 Map 808
SE. Large. *Bare facial skin.* ♂: *blackish* crown and
breast; primaries tinged brown. ♀: chestnut crown; gray
foreparts.

**9. White-shouldered** *M. melanoceps* p 409 Map 807
SE. *Bare facial skin.* ♂ black; *white* under wrist. ♀ unmistakable (but see Cocha Antshrike, Note, p 382).

**10. White-cheeked Antbird** p 411 Map 813
*Gymnopithys leucaspis*
SE. *White median underparts.* Note bare bluish ocular
area; *blackish* sides.

**Antbirds** *Rhegmatorhina* Bare *whitish* ("goggle-like")
ocular area surrounded by *black* face. Follow army
ants; poorly known.

**11. Hairy-crested** *R. melanosticta* p 412 Map 815
SE. Bushy *ash-colored* crown; *light* olive brown below.
♀: mantle barred.

**12. Chestnut-crested** *R. cristata* p 412 Map 814
Vaupés. *Rufous head and underparts.* ♀: mantle barred.

**13. Black Bushbird** *Neoctantes niger* p 385 Map 745
SE. Chisellike upturned bill. ♂ entirely black. ♀ has
deep chestnut breast. Rare.

**Antpittas** *Grallaria* Plump, long-legged; very short tail
carried depressed. Terrestrial, usually hop (can run
well).

**14. Giant** *G. gigantea* p 419 Map 833
C Andes. Very large. *Deep ferrugineous barred black*
below. Rarely encountered.

**15. Undulated** *G. squamigera* p 418 Map 832
Andes. Large. *Ochraceous barred black* below; white
throat, black whisker (cf. 14).

**16. Bay-backed** *G. hypoleuca* p 421 Map 839
C, E Andes. Only Colombian antpitta *whitish* below.
YELLOW-BREASTED G. *flavotincta* W: like 16 but yellow below.

**17. Chestnut-naped** *G. nuchalis* p 421 Map 838
C, E Andes. *Blackish* throat, *iron gray* underparts.

**18. Bicolored** *G. rufocinerea* p 420 Map 837
C Andes. Smaller than 17; *rufous* throat, *iron gray* below.

## 30

# PLATE 31 ANTTHRUSHES, ANTPITTAS, GNATEATERS, etc.

**1. Brown-banded Antpitta** p 422 Map 843
*Grallaria milleri*
W. Quindío. Brown breast band. Rare.

**Antthrushes** *Chamaeza* Walk usually with cocked tail; plumper than *Formicarius*; long postocular stripe.

**2. Barred** *C. mollissima* p 416 Map 825
C, W Andes. *Densely barred* below; barred postocular.

**3. Striated** *C. nobilis* p 415 Map 823
SE. *Larger, more contrasty* below than 4 and 5.

**4. Short-tailed** *C. campanisona* p 415 Map 822
E Andes. Streaked below; *dusky subterminal* tail band, white tips. *Distinctive* voice (see text).

**5. Rufous-tailed** *C. ruficauda* p 415 Map 824
E, C Andes (local). More heavily marked below than 4; no white tail tips. *Voice* (see text).

**Antpittas** *Grallaria* Terrestrial, retiring. Note voices.

**6. Tawny** *G. quitensis* p 422 Map 842
E, C Andes, paramo. Ochraceous below, *contrasting* white throat; *buff* eyering.

**7. Rufous** *G. rufula* p 422 Map 841
Highlands. *Small; uniform* rufous chestnut.

**8. Chestnut-crowned** *G. ruficapilla* p 420 Map 835
Highlands. Large; *rufous* head; white throat; sharply streaked below. Common.

**9. Rufous-crowned Antpitta** p 418 Map 831
*Pittasoma rufopileatum*
Pacific. *Rufous* head, *black* eyestripe. ♀ has white in eyestripe. BLACK-CROWNED *P. michleri* NW: black crown; *bold scallops* below.

**10. Scaled Antpitta** p 419 Map 834
*Grallaria guatimalensis*
W. Rather uniform; faintly scaled above. Note dark throat, buff malar. MOUSTACHED *G. alleni* W. Quindío: like 10, crown and nape grayer; *no* scales. Rare.

**Antpittas** *Grallaricula* Smaller than *Grallaria*; less terrestrial.

**11. Rusty-breasted** p 424 Map 849
*G. ferrugineipectus*
NE. Crown concolor with back (cf. 15); ochre breast band.

**12. Ochre-breasted** *G. flavirostris* p 424 Map 848
E, W Andes. Lightly *streaked* below; gray tinged crown.

**13. Spotted Antpitta** p 423 Map 845
*Hylopezus macularius*
E. Bold necklace and eyering; gray crown. OCHRE-STRIPED *Grallaria dignissima* Putumayo: most like 13. Larger, throat ochraceous, more extensively streaked below.

**14. Thrush-like Antpitta** p 424 Map 847
*Myrmothera campanisona*
E. Common (voice). *Dull white* below; blurry *breast streaks*.

**15. Slate-crowned Antpitta** p 424 Map 850
*Grallaricula nana*
Andes. Much like 11. Crown *slaty; deeper* rusty below. CRESCENT-FACED *G. lineifrons* Puracé: *white crescent* on face; *streaked* cinnamon and black below. Rare.

**16. Hooded Antpitta** p 425 Map 851
*Grallaricula cucullata*
W, C Andes. Orange-rufous head; gray below.

**17. Santa Marta Antpitta** p 420 Map 836
*Grallaria bangsi*
Buff orange throat; narrow streaks below. Only *Grallaria* in range.

**Gnateaters** *Conopophaga* Silvery white postocular tuft.

**18. Chestnut-belted** *C. aurita* p 426 Map 853
SE. ♂: black face and throat; rusty chest. ♀: black replaced by rufous.

**19. Chestnut-crowned** p 425 Map 852
*C. castaneiceps*
Andes. Blue legs. ♂: chestnut cap; dark gray below. ♀: cinnamon rufous head and chest.

**20. Fulvous-bellied Antpitta** p 423 Map 846
*Hylopezus fulviventris*
Pacific; SE base Andes. Blurry necklace; eyering *weak or lacking*; flanks and abdomen *bright cinnamon rufous*. STREAK-CHESTED *H. perspicillatus* W: from 20 by *prom.* eyering (like 13), *buff-dotted wing coverts*, *bold* breast streaks, and *white* flanks and abdomen.

**Antthrushes** *Formicarius* Walk raillike with twitching tail.

**21. Black-faced** *F. analis* p 416 Map 827
N, E. Black face and throat; *grayish* below. Common. BLACK-HEADED *F. nigricapillus* Pacific: like 21, but *entire* head to upper breast sooty black.

**22. Rufous-capped** *F. colma* p 416 Map 826
E. *Chestnut* crown; *sides of head to breast* black.

**23. Rufous-breasted** *F. rufipectus* p 417 Map 829
C, W Andes (local). *Extensively* chestnut below; cap chestnut.

**24. Wing-banded Antbird** p 417 Map 830
*Myrmornis torquata*
N, E. Distinctive. Black throat (rufous, ♀); *buff wing bars and band*. Long bill, *stubby* tail.

GUDOR

PLATE 32 ANTBIRDS and MANAKINS

**Antbirds** *Myrmoborus* Prom. eyebrow. ♂♂ have black throat.

**1. White-browed** *M. leucophrys* p 401 Map 788
E. ♂: *broad white* eyebrow; *no wing bars.* ♀: cinnamon eyebrow; all white below.

**2. Black-faced** *M. myotherinus* p 402 Map 790
E. ♂ from ♂ of 1 by *wing bars,* gray eyebrow, pale underparts. ♀ tawny below with contrasting throat; buff wing bars.

**3. Ash-breasted** *M. lugubris* p 402 Map 789
Amazonas. ♂ has whitish underparts. ♀ like ♀ of 1 but no eyebrow.

**Antbirds** *Hylophylax*

**4. Spot-backed** *H. naevia* p 414 Map 774
SE. Ornate. ♂: black throat, necklace, spotted back (cf. 6). ♀: necklace less prom.; buff wash below.

**5. Spotted** *H. naevioides* p 414 Map 819
W. Unique in range. ♂: gray head, bold necklace, rufous bars. ♀: brownish head; below like 4.

**6. Banded Antbird** *Dichrozona cincta* p 396 Map 772
SE. Wrenlike shape. Long bill, stubby tail. Note necklace, wing bars, white rump band (buff, ♀).

**7. White-plumed Antbird** p 411 Map 811
*Pithys albifrons*
E. White *plumes.* Chestnut collar and underparts.

**8. Lance-tailed Manakin** p 432 Map 869
*Chiroxiphia lanceolata*
N. ♂, ♀, and imm. have spiky central tail feathers and dull orange legs. Imm. like ♀ but cap red. BLUE-BACKED *C. pareola* SE: like 8 but no tail spikes.

**9. Wire-tailed Manakin** *Pipra filicauda* p 432 Map 868
E. Wirelike tail filaments in both sexes. ♀: belly yellowish; *eyes white.*

**10. White-bearded Manakin** p 434 Map 873
*Manacus manacus*
♂ black-and-white. ♀ has orange legs (cf. 19, text).

**11. Golden-winged Manakin** p 433 Map 871
*Masius chrysopterus*
Subtropics. ♂: *yellow* under wing coverts and inner webs of primaries; ♀: yellow *chin and throat patch;* pinkish purple legs. Imm. like ♀ but *flat-headed.*

**Manakins** *Pipra* Bright ♂♂ distinctive. ♀♀ dull greenish, difficult. Imm. intermed.

**12. Red-capped** *P. mentalis* p 430 Map 864
W. ♀ like 13, but eyes and legs brownish (no range overlap).

**13. Golden-headed** *P. erythrocephala* p 430 Map 863
N, E. ♀ has *pale* eyes; brownish legs.

**14. White-crowned** *P. pipra* p 430 Map 865
♀: contrasting *gray* crown; *red* eyes.

**15. Club-winged Manakin** p 435 Map 876
*Allocotopterus deliciosus*
Pacific. ♀: *cinnamon* face smudge; *white wing linings;* light yellow belly.

**16. Blue-crowned Manakin** p 431 Map 867
*Pipra coronata*
♀ *green* above; yellow tinged belly. Dark soft parts.

**17. Blue-rumped Manakin** p 431 Map 866
*Pipra isidorei*
E. ♀ like ♀ of 16, crown tinged yellow.

**18. Black Manakin** p 436 Map 877
*Xenopipo atronitens*
E. Longer tail than *Pipra.* ♀ drab, *dark grayish olive* (see text).

**19. Golden-collared Manakin** p 434 Map 874
*Manacus vitellinus*
W. Orange legs. ♀ not separable from 10 (see text).

**20. Striped Manakin** p 435 Map 875
*Machaeropterus regulus*
E, W (local). ♂: red cap; candy cane underparts. ♀: *rufous* blush on flanks; *faint* chest streaks.

**21. White-ruffed Manakin** p 433 Map 872
*Corapipo leucorrhoa*
N. ♀: *grayish* throat and sides of head; *dark* soft parts.

**22. Dwarf Tyrant-Manakin** p 437 Map 883
*Tyranneutes stolzmanni*
SE. Found by voice. Tiny; pale eyes; no wing markings (see text).

**23. Cinnamon Manakin** p 436 Map 880
*Neopipo cinnamomea*
E. Like Ruddy-tailed Flycatcher but rarer (Pl.36). Note *crown stripe, shape, posture,* thin bill.

**24. Wing-barred Manakin** p 438 Map 884
*Piprites chloris*
N, SE. *Yellowish* foreface; *yellow* eyering; *single* wing bar; flycatcherlike manner.

**Manakins** *Chloropipo* Large; longish tail.

**25. Yellow-headed** *C. flavicapilla* p 436 Map 879
Subtropics. *Head and underparts yellowish* (crown bright yellow, ♂). Note orange eyes, white wing linings.

**26. Green** *C. h. holochlora* p 436 Map 878
E. *Darker, greener;* yellow belly; lower mandible pale. Pacific subsp., Pl.33.

**27. Yellow-crowned Manakin** p 437 Map 881
*Heterocercus flavivertex*
E. ♂: white throat and ruff, chestnut underparts. ♀: throat grayish, belly fulvous.

**28. Saffron-crested Tyrant-Manakin** p 437 Map 882
*Neopelma chrysocephalum*
E. *Grayish olive.* Note red eyes, *yellowish* belly, *dark crown* (usually with yellow at rear).

GUDOR

# PLATE 33 COTINGAS, MANAKINS, ATTILAS, etc.

**Pihas** *Lipaugus*

**1. Dusky** *L. fuscocinereus* p 445 Map 903
Andes (local). Quite large, long tailed; *gray*.

**2. Olivaceous** *L. cryptolophus* p 445 Map 902
Subtropics. Greenish. Under wing coverts and belly
*yellowish*.

**3. Purple-throated Fruitcrow** p 453 Map 926
*Querula purpurata*
Common, noisy. Fanlike magenta throat (all black, ♀).

**4. Black-necked Red-Cotinga** p 441 Map 890
*Phoenicircus nigricollis*
SE. ♀: dark red cap and tail; rosy underparts. Rare.

**Cock-of-the-Rocks** *Rupicola*

**5. Andean** *R. peruviana aequatorialis* p 440 Map 889
5a *R. peruviana sanguinolenta*
Andes. ♂ orange red (deep scarlet, W Andes). ♀ gallinelike shape, small crest, white eyes.

**6. Guianan** *R. rupicola* p 440 Map 888
E. ♀ *brownish; small crest, white eyes.*

**7. Pink-throated Becard** p 449 Map 914
*Platypsaris minor*
SE. ♂ slaty; pink throat collar. Buffy ♀ has *gray cap,
rufous* wings.

**Manakins** *Schiffornis* Larger, dull.

**8. Greater** *S. major* p 438 Map 886
Amazonas. Found by voice. Cinnamon; *gray* face, short
bill.

**9. Thrush-like** *S. turdinus* p 439 Map 887
Dull brown. Lacks obvious marks. Note large eye, voice.

**10. Green Manakin** p 436 Map 878
*Chloropipo holochlora litae*
Pacific. *Dull* greenish olive; *light yellow* belly; bill pale
below. See Pl.32 for E subsp.

**11. Broad-billed Manakin** p 438 Map 885
*Sapayoa aenigma*
Pacific. Large; longer-tailed than 10. Looks like a fly-
catcher.

**12. White-browed Purpletuft** p 444 Map 901
*Iodopleura isabellae*
SE. White on face, rump, median underparts. Treetops
(cf. Swallow-winged Puffbird).

**Attilas** *Attila* Straight hooked bill; contrasting rump;
erect posture, drooped tail.

**13. Dull-capped** *A. bolivianus* p 506 Map 1058
SE. *Grayish crown, whitish eyes.* (Cf.14, incl. *voice*).

**14. Bright-rumped** *A. spadiceus* p 506 Map 1057
Var. Plumage shown is most widespread. Note *wing
bars, contrasting rump.*

**15. Cinnamon** *A. cinnamomeus* p 507 Map 1059
SE. Much like cinnamon forms of 14 but *lacks* wing
bars, little contrast on rump and belly; voice. OCHRA-
CEOUS *A. torridus* SW: like 15 but *yellowish above and
below; distinct wing bars.*

**16. Ringed Antpipit** p 475 Map 982
*Corythopis torquata*
SE. Mostly terrestrial, teetering and walking like sand-
piper. *White* throat, *necklace, pink* legs. Forest.

GTUDOR

PLATE 34 COTINGAS and MOURNERS

**1. Pompadour Cotinga** p 452 Map 923
*Xipholena punicea*
E. ♂ wine red with white wings. ♀ *uniform* gray; *white* wing edgings, *white* eyes. Imm. intermediate.

**Cotingas** *Cotinga* ♂♂ some shade of blue; plum-colored throat. ♀♀ scaly and brown. Treetops.

**2. Purple-breasted** *C. cotinga* p 452 Map 922
E. ♂ deep blue; throat to breast purple. ♀ uniformly scaled *above and below* (cf. 3, 4).

**3. Spangled** *C. cayana* p 451 Map 921
E. ♂ has black mottling on enamel blue plumage; throat patch larger than 4. ♀ like 2 and 4 but nearly uniform below.

**4. Plum-throated** *C. maynana* p 451 Map 920
SE. ♂ shining turquoise; small throat patch. ♀ less scaled than 2 (little range overlap) but *more* scaled below than 3 and best told from both by *cinnamon* on lower abdomen and under tail coverts.

**5. Red-crested Cotinga** p 441 Map 892
*Ampelion rubrocristatus*
Mts. *Pale bill*, white streaked lower back; *white* under-tail band. Crest may be inconspic. Imm. more streaked below.

**6. Cinereous Mourner** p 508 Map 1062
*Laniocerca hypopyrrha*
E. *Orange* spotted wing bars. Imm. var. amt. of rufous orange spotting below. Note voice. Scarce.

**7. Grayish Mourner** p 507 Map 1060
*Rhytipterna simplex*
SE. Smaller, less robust than 8; greenish yellow tinged abdomen. Canopy; note voice.

**8. Screaming Piha** p 445 Map 904
*Lipaugus vociferans*
SE. Loud often heard Amazonian voice. Larger, more common than 7; usually perches lower.

**9. Chestnut-crested Cotinga** p 442 Map 893
*Ampelion rufaxilla*
Andes. *Cinnamon* throat, sides of head, and *collar*; streaked below. Scarce.

**10. Scaled Fruiteater** p 444 Map 900
*Ampelioides tschudii*
Andes. *Scaly.* Whitish line below eye to hind collar. ♂ has *black cap*; ♀, black malar.

**Fruiteaters** *Pipreola* Highlands; plump, short-tailed, moss green or grass green above; bill (sometimes legs) orange red; bill of ♀ often duller.

**11. Barred** *P. arcuata* p 442 Map 895
Andes. ♂ barred below; *prom. spots* on wing coverts and tertials. ♀ *lacks* hood, all barred below.

**12. Green-and-black** *P. riefferii* p 442 Map 894
Mts. ♂: hood bordered yellow. ♀: dark eyes, orange legs, white tertial edges (cf. 17). Most common.

**13. Shrike-like Cotinga** p 441 Map 891
*Laniisoma elegans*
NE (once). Black cap (green like back, ♀). *Golden* underparts *weakly* scaled along sides.

**Fruiteaters** *Pipreola*

**14. Fiery-throated** *P. chlorolepidota* p 444 Map 899
SE (once). Manakin-sized. *Cherry* throat.

**15. Golden-breasted** *P. aureopectus* p 443 Map 898
W (spotty). ♂ *uniform* yellow below. ♀ *entirely* streaked below, throat mainly yellow.

**16. Orange-breasted** *P. jucunda* p 443 Map 897
Pacific. ♂ has *broad orange chest* patch. ♀ like ♀ of 12 but *no tertial tips*; gray legs (see text).

**17. Black-chested** *P. lubomirskii* p 443 Map 896
Mts. Recalls 12. Note *white eyes, gray legs, lack* of tertial spots. ♂ *no* yellow collar. Does not overlap range of 16.

## 34

# PLATE 35 BECARDS etc.

**1. White-winged Becard** p 448 Map 910
*Pachyramphus polychopterus*
Widespread. ♂ *solid black* lores, cap, and back (or plumage all blackish, SE). ♀: *dull brown* crown.

**2. Black-and-white Becard** p 448 Map 912
*Pachyramphus albogriseus*
N, E slope. ♂: *solid gray back; white* lores. ♀: *chestnut crown bordered black.*

**3. One-colored Becard** p 449 Map 913
*Platypsaris homochrous*
N. ♂ uniform blackish. ♀ like 6 but *no supraloral line.*

**Becards** *Pachyramphus* Compact shape; thickish bill, slightly rounded tail; lethargic.

**4. Barred** *P. versicolor* p 446 Map 906
Upper el. Both sexes *lightly barred* below. ♂: *yellow* tinged face. ♀: *rufous* in wings; gray cap.

**5. Cinereous** *P. rufus* p 446 Map 907
W. ♂ paler than allies; *less white on wings; no tail spots;* white lores. ♀ cinnamon; white lores; very pale below.

**6. Cinnamon** *P. cinnamomeus* p 447 Map 909
W. Sexes sim. *Slaty* lores; *buff* supraloral line.

**7. Black-capped** *P. marginatus* p 448 Map 911
E. ♂: *black-and-gray back;* gray lores. ♀: chestnut crown *lacks black border* (cf. ♀ of 2).

**8. Chestnut-crowned** *P. castaneus* p 447 Map 908
SE. Sexes sim. Like 6 but with *gray nape band.*

**9. Speckled Mourner** p 508 Map 1063
*Laniocera rufescens*
W. *Buff-tipped* wing coverts; *faint dusky* markings on breast. Look for yellowish pectoral tufts.

**10. Rufous Mourner** p 508 Map 1061
*Rhytipterna holerythra*
W. Uniform rufous. Cf. larger 11 (see text).

**11. Rufous Piha** *Lipaugus unirufus* p 446 Map 905
W. Uniform rufous. Larger than 10 (see text).

**12. Purple-throated Cotinga** p 450 Map 918
*Porphyrolaema porphyrolaema*
SE. ♂ black above, 1 white wing bar; *white* below, *purple* throat. ♀ distinctly *barred* brown below (not scaly), throat rufous.

**Tityras** *Tityra* Thick-set; heavy bill. ♂♂ white with black on wings, head and tail. ♀♀ brownish on back.

**13. Black-tailed** *T. cayana* p 449 Map 915
E. ♂: *bare red face; entire crown black* (cf. ♂ of 14). ♀: *streaks* on breast.

**14. Masked** *T. semifasciata* p 450 Map 916
W. ♂: *bare red face;* black *only* around foreface. ♀ duller; *no* streaks below.

**15. Black-crowned** *T. inquisitor* p 450 Map 917
♂: *black bill and crown. No* red. ♀: buff forehead, chestnut cheeks (caution: cheeks can look red at distance).

## 35

Gwynne

# PLATE 36 TYRANT FLYCATCHERS

**1. Short-tailed Pygmy-Tyrant** p 476 Map 983
*Myiornis ecaudatus* la. E. subsp. Smallest of all. Rudimentary tail; spectacles, black cap (gray cap, ♀; ♂ and ♀ of la).

**Spadebills** *Platyrinchus*
**2. White-crested** *P. platyrhynchos* p 487 Map 1012
E. *Gray head lacks pattern; cinnamon below.*
**3. Golden-crowned** *P. coronatus* p 488 Map 1014
Orange crown *bordered black; strong* facial pattern.
**4. White-throated** *P. mystaceus* p 487 Map 1013
Mts. *Strong facial pattern; no black on crown.*
**5. Yellow-throated** *P. flavigularis* p 488 Map 1016
Mts. *Cinnamon brown head; no facial pattern.*
**6. White-eyed Tody-Tyrant** p 480 Map 994
*Hemitriccus zosterops*
SE. *No crest. Bold wing bars; narrow eye ring.*

**Tody-Flycatchers** *Todirostrum* Long flat bill; narrow tail.
**7. Rusty-fronted** *T. latirostre* p 483 Map 1001
SE. *Rusty foreface; grayish crown.*
**8. Golden-winged** *T. calopterum* p 481 Map 997
SE. Head like 10; golden wing patch, chestnut shoulders.
**9. Common** *T. cinereum* p 481 Map 998
White eyes; *entirely yellow below.*
**10. Black-headed** *T. nigriceps* p 480 Map 995
W. *White throat, contrasting black head.*
**11. Yellow-browed** p 481 Map 996
*T. chrysocrotaphum*
SE. *Black cap, necklace; yellow postocular.*
**12. Spotted** *T. maculatum* p 482 Map 999
SE. *Gray crown; crisp narrow streaking.*
**13. Slate-headed** *T. sylvia* p 482 Map 1000
*Gray foreparts; spectacles; golden wing bars.*

**Tody-Tyrants** *Hemitriccus*
**14. Black-throated** *H. granadensis* p 480 Map 993
Mts. *Whitish face; black throat; no wing bars.*
**15. Pearly-vented** p 479 Map 992
*H. margaritaceiventer*
N. Long bill. Larger than 16; *brownish above.*
**16. Pale-eyed Pygmy-Tyrant** p 477 Map 987
*Atalotriccus pilaris*
N, E. Tiny; *olive back; streaky chest.*

**Pygmy-Tyrants** *Lophotriccus* Crested.
**17. Helmeted** *L. galeatus* p 477 Map 986
E. Grayish crest feathers; no distinct wing bars. DOUBLE-BANDED *L. vitiosus* SE: like 17, but *obvious* wing bars (see text).
**18. Scale-crested** *L. pileatus* p 476 Map 984
W. *Rufous scaled crest; faint chest streaks.*
**19. Southern Bentbill** p 478 Map 990
*Oncostoma olivaceum*
N. Thick, "bent" bill; pale eyes; voice. For NORTHERN *O. cinereigulare* NW (once), see text.
**20. Tawny-crowned Pygmy-Tyrant** p 470 Map 968
*Euscarthmus meloryphus*
N. Dull brown; orange in crest. Voice.
**21. Mouse-colored Tyrannulet** p 460 Map 941
*Phaeomyias murina*
Brownish; dingy eyestripe; *pale buff* bars.
**22. Southern Beardless-Tyrannulet** p 460 Map 940
*Camptostoma obsoletum*
Obvious crest darker than back; wing bars.

**Tyrannulets** *Inezia*
**23. Slender-billed** *I. tenuirostris* p 468 Map 961
N. Tiny; crown and back concolor; voice.
**24. Pale-tipped** *I. subflava* p 469 Map 962
N, E. *Strong* wing bars; *dusky tail edged* white.
**25. Black-capped Tyrannulet** p 457 Map 932
*Phyllomyias nigrocapillus*
Mts. Black or brown crown; light yellow below.
**26. Tawny-rumped Tyrannulet** p 457 Map 933
*Phyllomyias uropygialis*
Mts. (rare). *Buff tinged* wing bars; *tawny* rump.
**27. White-throated Tyrannulet** p 466 Map 955
*Mecocerculus leucophrys*
Temperate zone. *Puffy white throat; longish tail.*

**Tyrannulets** *Ornithion* Tiny; short tail.
**28. Brown-capped** *O. brunneicapillum* p 459 Map 939
W. Dark brown cap; short white eyebrow.
**29. White-lored** *O. inerme* p 459 Map 938
E. *White-spotted* wing bars.
**30. Yellow Tyrannulet** p 474 Map 979
*Capsiempis flaveola*
W, E (part). Yellow eyebrow and underparts.
**31. Rufous-browed Tyrannulet** p 473 Map 975
*Phylloscartes superciliaris*
W. *Slaty* cap; rufous brow; cheeks *outlined black.*
**32. Golden-faced Tyrannulet** p 459 Map 937
*Zimmerius viridiflavus*
Mts. *Yellow* eyebrow and wing edgings. Canopy. Common.
**33. Paltry Tyrannulet** p 458 Map 935
*Zimmerius vilissimus*
N. *Slaty* cap; white spectacles; *yellow* wing edges.
**34. Plumbeous-crowned Tyrannulet** p 456 Map 931
*Phyllomyias plumbeiceps*
Andes. Short bill; *cleaner* white face (cf. 35, 42, 44).
**35. Marble-faced Bristle-Tyrant** p 474 Map 976
*Pogonotriccus ophthalmicus*
Andes. "Grizzled" face; longer bill than 34.
**36. Slender-footed Tyrannulet** p 458 Map 936
*Zimmerius gracilipes*
SE. *Grayish* crown; crisp yellow wing edgings.
**37. Yellow-crowned Tyrannulet** p 461 Map 944
*Tyrannulus elatus*
Stubby bill; gray sides of head and throat.
**38. Sooty-headed Tyrannulet** p 456 Map 930
*Phyllomyias griseiceps*
W. Dusky cap, *no definite* bars; voice.

**Tyrannulets** *Mecocerculus*
**39. White-tailed** *M. poecilocercus* p 467 Map 956
Andes. Small; yellowish rump; white undertail.
**40. White-banded** *M. stictopterus* p 467 Map 958
Andes. Larger than 39; dark rump and undertail.
**41. Sulphur-bellied** *M. minor* p 467 Map 957
E Andes. Buff bars; sulphury underparts.
**42. Variegated Bristle-Tyrant** p 474 Map 978
*Pogonotriccus poecilotis*
Andes. *Cinnamon* wing bars; *orange* mandible. SPECTACLED *P. orbitalis* S: *white eyering; no* dusky facial crescent.
**43. Ochre-bellied Flycatcher** p 472 Map 971
*Mionectes oleaginea*
Olive above, *burnt orange* abdomen; *flicks* wings.
**44. Ashy-headed Tyrannulet** p 458 Map 934
*Phyllomyias cinereiceps*
Andes. Stubby bill; *blue gray* cap; *faint* chest streaks (cf. 34, 35).

*Continued*

## 36

**Flycatchers** *Leptopogon* Larger than *Pogonotriccus.*

**45. Rufous-breasted** *L. rufipectus* p 473 Map 974
Andes. *Rufous* throat and breast. Cf. 17 on Pl.37.

**46. Slaty-capped** *L. superciliaris* p 472 Map 972
W. *Slaty* cap, dingy face (cf. smaller 35).

**47. Sepia-capped** *L. amaurocephalus* p 473 Map 973
N, E. *Sepia* cap; *buff* bars.

**48. Ruddy-tailed Flycatcher** p 489 Map 1019
*Terenotriccus erythrurus*
Small. Eyering, *crest*, *ruddy* tail. Cf. 23 (Pl.32).

# PLATE 37 TYRANT FLYCATCHERS

**1. Cinnamon Flycatcher** p 493 Map 1028
*Pyrrhomyias cinnamomea*
Mts. Small, mostly cinnamon. Common.

**2. Tufted Flycatcher** p 493 Map 1029
*Mitrephanes phaeocercus*
W. Small; *prom. pointed* crest; tawny chest.

**3. Ornate Flycatcher** p 489 Map 1018
*Myiotriccus ornatus*
W. *Black* head; *eyespots*; *yellow* rump and belly.

**Flycatchers** *Mionectes*

**4. Olive-striped** *M. olivaceus* p 471 Map 970
W. Thin bill; *eyespot*, *narrowly streaked* underparts.

**5. Streak-necked** *M. striaticollis.* p 474 Map 969
W. Head and throat *grayer* than 4; *streaking finer.*

**6. Vermilion Flycatcher** p 498 Map 1034
*Pyrocephalus rubinus*
♀: streaky chest, *rosy* belly. *No rose* in SE.

**7. Black-billed Flycatcher** p 492 Map 1027
*Aphanotriccus audax*
NW. *Narrow white* supraloral; broad breast band.

**Flycatchers** *Myiobius* Yellow rump; active.

**8. Tawny-breasted** *M. villosus* p 490 Map 1020
W. Larger, darker above, *tawnier below* than allies.

**9. Sulphur-rumped** *M. barbatus* p 490 Map 1022
*Palest*; distinct eyering (see text).

**10. Black-tailed** *M. atricaudus* p 490 Map 1021
W. Duller below than 9, weaker eyering (see text).

**11. Orange-crested Flycatcher** p 491 Map 1024
*Myiophobus phoenicomitra*
W. *Dark olive* above; *faint* eyering; cinnamon bars.

**12. Rufous-tailed Tyrant** p 503 Map 1050
*Knipolegus poecilurus*
Andes. *Red* eyes; expressive *rufous-edged* tail.

**13. Tropical Pewee** p 494 Map 1030
*Contopus cinereus*
Smaller than allies; pale loral spot; voice (see text).

**14. Euler's Flycatcher** p 496 Map 1031
*Empidonax euleri*
E. Buffier wing bars (see text). For ACADIAN *E. virescens*, and TRAILL'S *E. traillii*, N migrants, see text.

**15. Fuscous Flycatcher** p 497 Map 1032
*Cnemotriccus fuscatus*
N, E. *Brownish*; *long* eyestripe; *long* tail.

**Flycatchers** *Myiophobus*

**16. Flavescent** *M. flavicans* p 491 Map 1023
W. Yellower below, eyering stronger than 11.

**17. Handsome** *M. pulcher* p 491 Map 1025
Andes. Gray cap; *orangish* throat and chest.

**18. Bran-colored** *M. fasciatus* p 492 Map 1026
W. *Reddish brown* (except Nariño); *always streaked* below.

**Flycatchers** *Tolmomyias.* Wide flat bill.

**19. Yellow-olive** *T. sulphurescens* p 485 Map 1008
Larger; crown *grayish*; spectacles; eyes *pale.* YELLOW-MARGINED *T. assimilis* N, E: like 19 (see text).

**20. Gray-crowned** *T. poliocephalus* p 486 Map 1010
SE. Smallest, *grayest* crowned; bill blackish.

— **21. Yellow-breasted** *T. flaviventris* p 486 Map 1011
N, E. *Orange* supraloral; *bright olive* above.

**22. Olivaceous Flatbill** p 485 Map 1006
*Rhynchocyclus olivaceus*
N, E. Wide bill; *weak* eyering; *definite* streaks below.

**Flatbills** *Ramphotrigon* Bill *fairly* wide.

**23. Large-headed** *R. megacephala* p 484 Map 1004
SE. Small; *buff* wing bars; *short* eyestripe. DUSKY-TAILED *R. fuscicauda* SE: large; cinnamon wing bars; narrow eyering.

**24. Rufous-tailed** *R. ruficauda* p 483 Map 1003
SE. *Rufous* wings and tail.

**25. Scrub Flycatcher** p 460 Map 942
*Sublegatus arenarum*
Supraloral streak; short bill; *sharply divided* gray and yellow underparts. Cf. *Myiarchus.* SHORT-BILLED *S. modestus* SE: wing bars indistinct; *darker* gray breast blends into yellowish *white* belly.

**Elaenias** *Myiopagis* Smaller than *Elaenia.*

**26. Greenish** *M. viridicata* p 462 Map 947
Lacks obvious wing bars; *yellow* crown patch.

**27. Forest** *M. gaimardii* p 461 Map 945
N, E. *Prom.* wingbars; narrow bill (cf. 19).

**28. Gray** *M. caniceps* p 462 Map 946
♂ gray; *strong* markings on black wings. For ♀, see text.

**Flatbills** *Rhynchocyclus* Wide flat bill.

**29. Eye-ringed** *R. brevirostris* p 484 Map 1005
W. *Prom.* eyering; *unstreaked* below.

**30. Fulvous-breasted** *R. fulvipectus* p 485 Map 1007
Andes. *Rufous* wing edgings; *fulvous* breast.

**Elaenias** *Elaenia* Confusing. Usually crested; semiconcealed crown patch; small bill.

**31. Yellow-bellied** *E. flavogaster* p 463 Map 948
Large; *bushy* crest, *light yellow* belly. Common. LARGE *E. spectabilis* SE: Larger than 31; *3 prom.* wing bars. BROWNISH *E. pelzelni* SE: larger still; *brownish.*

**32. Lesser** *E. chiriquensis* p 464 Map 950
Lacks strong contrast; *weak* eyering; *white* in crest.

**33. Small-billed** *E. parvirostris* p 464 Map 949
S migrant. *Large* eyering; *whitish* belly (cf. 32).

**34. Rufous-crowned** *E. ruficeps* p 465 Map 951
E. *Rufous* crown patch; *vague* breast streaks.

**35. Sierran** *E. pallatangae* p 465 Map 953
Andes. *Yellow tinged* throat and belly (see text). WHITE-CRESTED *E. albiceps* Mts.: *grayer* than allies; belly *whitish.*

**36. Mountain** *E. frantzii.* p 465 Map 952
Mts. *Uncrested*; *yellowish tinged* wing bars and underparts.

**37. Mottle-backed** *E. gigas* p 466 Map 954
E. Large; *bifurcated* crest; back mottled. SLATY *E. strepera* S migrant: *slaty*; white belly.

# PLATE 38 TYRANT FLYCATCHERS

**1. River Tyrannulet** p 468 Map 959
*Serpophaga hypoleuca*
SE. Black crown; grayish white. River edges. TORRENT
*S. cinerea* Mts.: whitish; black cap, wings, and tail
(Ill. 83). Streams.

**2. Lesser Wagtail-Tyrant** p 469 Map 963
*Stigmatura napensis*
SE. *Large white* tail spots; *yellowish* below. Rivers.

**3. Drab Water-Tyrant** p 500 Map 1040
*Ochthoeca littoralis*
E. *Sandy brown; pale* rump; dark eyeline. Rivers.

**Tyrants** *Knipolegus*

**4. Amazonian Black-Tyrant** p 503 Map 1051
*K. poecilocercus*
E. Smaller than 5. *Glossy* black. For ♀ see text.

**5. Riverside Tyrant** *K. orenocensis* p 502 Map 1049
E. *Dull blackish;* open areas Cf. 4. For ♀ see text.

**6. Subtropical Doradito** p 470 Map 967
*Pseudocolopteryx acutipennis*
C Andes (migrant?). *Uniform* above; *bright yellow* below.

**7. Bearded Tachuri** p 470 Map 966
*Polystictus pectoralis*
Local. Flat crest; *cinnamon* breast. ♂: black *mottled* throat.

**8. Little Ground-Tyrant** p 502 Map 1048
*Muscisaxicola fluviatilis*
SE. *Walks* on sand bars; black tail *edged white*.

**Tit-Tyrants** *Anairetes* Tiny bill; streaked. Temperate zone.

**9. Agile** *A. agilis* p 470 Map 965
Andes. Eyeline; *long* tail; *flat* crest.

**10. Tufted** *A. parulus* p 469 Map 964
Andes. *Tiny; curled* crest; white eyes.

**Tody-Tyrants** *Poecilotriccus* Bill shorter than Todirostrum.

**11. Black-and-white** *P. capitale* p 478 Map 988
SE. ♂ unique. ♀ has *chestnut* cap; *olive* back.

**12. Rufous-crowned** *P. r. ruficeps* p 478 Map 989
Andes. Ornate. Note *rufous* cap; *black facial lines.*

**Pygmy-Tyrants** *Pseudotriccus* Often bill snap.

**13. Rufous-headed** *P. ruficeps* p 475 Map 981
Andes. *Rufous* head, wings, and tail. *Tiny.*

**14. Bronze-olive** *P. pelzelni* p 475 Map 980
Andes. *Dark; creamy* belly, *red* eyes.

**Chat-Tyrants** *Ochthoeca*

**15. Slaty-backed** p 499 Map 1037
*O. cinnamomeiventris*
Andean rivers. *Eyespots; chestnut* belly.

**16. Yellow-bellied** *O. diadema* p 499 Map 1039
Subtropics. *Yellow* eyestripe; *yellowish* below.

**17. Crowned** *O. frontalis* p 499 Map 1038
Temperate zone. Long eyestripe, *gray* below; *no* wing bars.

**18. Rufous-breasted** p 498 Map 1036
*O. rufipectoralis*
Andes. Long eyestripe; *rufous* chest.

**19. Brown-backed** *O. fumicolor* p 498 Map 1035
Treeline. Eyestripe; *rufous* wing bars, underparts.

**Bush-Tyrants** *Myiotheretes* Rufous wing band in flight.

**20. Smoky** *M. fumigatus* p 500 Map 1043
Temperate Andes. *Very dark.*

**21. Santa Marta** *M. pernix* p 501 Map 1044
*Smaller* than 22; tail *edged* cinnamon.

**22. Streak-throated** *M. striaticollis* p 500 Map 1041
Mts. More common than 21; tail *mostly cinnamon.*

**23. Cliff Flycatcher** p 505 Map 1055
*Hirundinea ferruginea*
E. Cliffs. *Ferrugineous* underparts and wing stripe.

**24. Black-billed Shrike-Tyrant** p 501 Map 1045
*Agriornis montana*
Mts., S. Dark; sides of tail *extensively white.*

**Ground-Tyrants** *Muscisaxicola*

**25. Spot-billed** *M. maculirostris* p 502 Map 1047
Páramo. Small; slender; pipitlike habits; *faint* bill spot

**26. Plain-capped** M. *alpina* p 501 Map 1046
Andes. Grayer, much larger than 25; *brownish* cap.

**27. Red-rumped Bush-Tyrant** p 500 Map 1042
*Myiotheretes erythropygius*
Mts., S. Frosty gray foreparts; *white* wing spot.

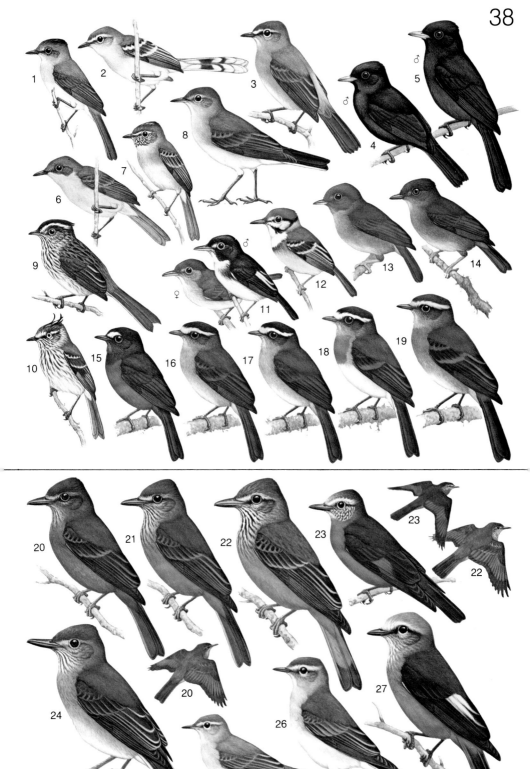

## 38

# PLATE 39 TYRANT FLYCATCHERS

**1. Cattle Tyrant** *Machetornis rixosus* p 505 Map 1056
N, E. *Light* brown above; *all yellow* below; *terrestrial.*

**2. Royal Flycatcher** p 488 Map 1017
*Onychorhynchus coronatus*
N, E. Hammerheaded. Pale rump, rufous tail.

**3. Brownish Flycatcher** p 483 Map 1002
*Cnipodectes subbrunneus*
NW, E. *Dark* brown; *longish* rufescent tail.

**Flycatchers** *Myiarchus* Difficult. Note voice and range.

**4. Pale-edged** *M. cephalotes* p 511 Map 1069
Andes. Obvious *pale-edged* tail.

**5. Apical** *M. apicalis* p 510 Map 1068
W. *Sooty* head; tail broadly *pale-tipped.*

**Kingbirds** Tyrannus

**6. Snowy-throated** *T. niveigularis* p 520 Map 1089
SW. *Snowy white* throat. Drier zones.

**7. Gray** *T. dominicensis* p 520 Map 1088
Heavy-billed. *Gray* above, *whitish* below; mask. EASTERN
*T. tyrannus* N migrant: blackish above; white tail band.

**8. Tropical** *T. melancholicus* p 519 Map 1087
Olive wash on chest. Throat *gray to whitish* (cf. 6, 9).

**9. White-throated** *T. albogularis* p 520 Map 1090
SE. Pale-headed; *white* throat *meets* yellow breast.

**Flycatchers** *Tyrannopsis*

**10. Sulphury** *T. sulphurea* p 517 Map 1085
E. *Blackish* face; large white throat, *streaky chest.*
Chunky shape; short bill. Moriche Palms.

**11. Dusky-chested** *T. luteiventris* p 518 Map 1086
SE. Smaller, darker than allies. Obscure streaking on throat and chest.

**Flycatchers** *Conopias* Longer bill, less common than *Myiozetetes.* Yellow throat (in most).

**12. Lemon-browed** *C. cinchoneti* p 515 Map 1078
Andes. Olive above; *yellow ring encircles* crown.

**13. White-ringed** *C. parva* p 515 Map 1079
13a. Pacific subsp.
E. White ring encircles crown; yellow throat. Pacific subsp.: throat white. Perches high in tree.

**Flycatchers** *Myiozetetes* Short bill; *white* throat.

**14. Social** *M. similis* p 514 Map 1076
N, E. Crown more or less *concolor* with back; *olive* above; dusky olive cheeks (cf. 16).

**15. Gray-capped** *M. granadensis* p 514 Map 1077
*Gray* crown; *white forehead,* short eyebrow.

**16. Rusty-margined** *M. cayanensis* p 513 Map 1075
Black crown *contrasts* with olive brown back; blackish cheeks (cf. 14). Less rufous in wings w of E Andes.

**Flycatchers** *Myiodynastes*

**17. Streaked** *M. maculatus* p 516 Map 1080
Heavily streaked; *faintly yellowish* eyebrow; *no yellow* below. SULPHUR-BELLIED *M. luteiventris* N migrant: much like 17 (see text).

**18. Golden-crowned** p 516 Map 1081
*M. chrysocephalus*
Mts. Head pattern recalls kiskadee. Note *malar, buff* throat, *blurry* chest streaks.

**19. Boat-billed Flycatcher** p 513 Map 1074
*Megarhynchus pitangua*
N, E. Bill obviously larger than 20; culmen curved. *No rufous* in wings; back olive.

**Kiskadees** *Pitangus*

**20. Great** *P. sulphuratus* p 512 Map 1072
Heavy bill; brown back; *rufous-edged* wings.

**21. Lesser** *P. lictor* p 513 Map 1073
N, E. Smaller than 20; *slender* bill. Likes water.

**22. Piratic Flycatcher** p 516 Map 1082
*Legatus leucophaius*
Stubby bill; *uniform* back; *no rufous* in tail.

**Flycatchers** *Empidonomus*

**23. Variegated** *E. varius* p 517 Map 1084
Back *mottled; rufous* in tail; bill larger than 22.

**24. Crowned Slaty-** p 517 Map 1083
*E. aurantioatrocristatus*
SE (S migrant). *Dusky* crown; *gray* below.

**25. Sirystes** *Sirystes sibilator* p 509 Map 1064
NW, E. Black crown; contrasting *white* rump.

**Flycatchers** *Myiarchus* Difficult. Note voice and range.

**26. Brown-crested** *M. tyrannulus* p 511 Map 1070
N, NE. Brownish crown; *rufous* on tail (see text). GREAT
CRESTED *M. crinitus* N migrant: *bright, contrasty* below; tail very rufous.

**27. Venezuelan** *M. venezuelensis* p 510 Map 1066
N, E. *Almost no rufous* in tail. PANAMA *M. panamensis*
NW, SHORT-CRESTED *M. ferox* E, from 27 by voice and range. SWAINSON'S *M. swainsoni* SE, s migrant: palest; dullest; bill mostly pink below.

**28. Dusky-capped** *M. tuberculifer* p 512 Map 1071
Smallest; *dusky* cap; no rufous in tail.

39

# PLATE 40 SWALLOWS

**1. White-thighed Swallow** p 525 Map 1100
*Neochelidon tibialis griseiventris* Ia *E. t. minima*
W. Tiny. Dark brown, rump and underparts *paler; white
leg puffs* (at rest). Ia: smaller; rump and underparts
nearly like back.

**2. Blue-and-white Swallow** p 524 Map 1096
*Notiochelidon cyanoleuca*
Widespread in Mts. Ad. and imm. Snowy below; black
crissum. Imm. brownish above; *brownish wash* on throat
and chest.

**3. Barn Swallow** *Hirundo rustica* p 526
N migrant. Imm.: rump dark; tail length var. Look for
*white* in tail. Ad.: *forked* tail; rusty below. Cliff *Petrochelidon pyrrhonota* N migrant: *buff* rump; whitish forehead.

**Swallows** *Notiochelidon*

**4. Pale-footed** *N. flavipes* p 524 Map 1097
C Andes. Recalls imm. of 2. Note *cinnamon* throat,
*blackish* sides (see text). Rare.

**5. Brown-bellied** *N. murina* p 523 Map 1095
Temperate zone. Larger. Dark above *and below.*

**6. Tawny-headed Swallow** p 525 Map 1101
*Alopochelidon fucata*
NE. *Rufous* eyebrow and collar; *dark* rump (cf. 9).

**Swallows** *Atticora* Deeply forked tail.

**7. Black-collared** *A. melanoleuca* p 525 Map 1099
E. White below; *black chest band.* Black water rapids.

**8. White-banded** *A. fasciata* p 524 Map 1098
E. *White* chest band. Often along rivers.

**9. Southern Rough-winged Swallow** p 525
*Stelgidopteryx ruficollis*
Brownish above; *pale* rump.

**10. Bank Swallow** *Riparia riparia* p 526
N migrant. Brown above; *chest* band (cf. larger 13).

**11. White-winged Swallow** p 522 Map 1092
*Tachycineta albiventer*
N, E. *White wing patches;* usually over water. Tree T.
*bicolor:* ad. much like 2 but *entirely* white below; imm.,
see text.

**12. Southern Martin** *Progne modesta* p 523
SE. ♂ much like ♂ of 15 (see text). ♀ only ♀ martin
almost *entirely dark* below.

**13. Brown-chested Martin** p 522 Map 1093
*Phaeoprogne t. tapera* 13a *P. t. fusca*
N, E. Brown *chest band; puffy white* crissum. Favors
water. 13a: S migrant; *spotted chest band.*

**Martins** *Progne*

**14. Gray-breasted** *P. chalybea* p 523 Map 1094
Mostly *grayish below;* forehead *never* pale.

**15. Purple** *P. subis* p 523
N migrant. ♂ *glossy blue black* (cf. ♂ of 12). ♀: *gray*
forehead and patch on sides of neck. Few recs.

## 40

LEMcQUEEN

# PLATE 41 TAPACULOS and WRENS

**Tapaculos** *Scytalopus* Confusing group of higher el. Taxonomy and no. of spp. uncertain.

**1. Pale-throated** *S. panamensis* p 428 Map 858
W. Pale gray throat; *white* eyebrow.

**2. Andean** *S. magellanicus canus* p 428 Map 861
C Andes. Like 6 but *smaller*, dark gray. *Griseicollis* subsp. on Pl.42.

**3. Narino** *S. vicinior* p 428 Map 859
W Andes. Like 4 (range overlap?), but back *browner*, tail *shorter*.

**4. Rufous-vented** p 427 Map 856
*S. femoralis confusus*
Lower el. than most allies. *Rusty brown* rump and flank barring. *White crown spot* on some (see 2, Pl.42).

**5. Rufous Wren** *Cinnycerthia unirufa* p 532 Map 1116
Andes. Dull rufous brown; *faint* barring; *blackish* lores. Brighter *unirufa* subsp. (E Andes) on Pl.42. Some individuals show whitish foreheads.

**6. Unicolored Tapaculo** p 427 Map 857
*Scytalopus unicolor*
Andes. *Uniform* blackish slate; *no barring* (see Pl.42).

**7. Ash-colored Tapaculo** p 427 Map 855
*Scytalopus senilis*
E, C Andes. *Paler* below; *long* tail; *no bars*. OCELLATED *Acropternis orthonyx*: large; *rufous* with *silvery spots*. Andes. (see text ill.).

**8. Sepia-brown Wren** p 533 Map 1117
*Cinnycerthia peruana*
Andes. Even duller than *unibrunnea* subsp. of 5; *barring distinct*; lores less black. Some ads. have white foreheads.

**9. Rusty-belted Tapaculo** p 426 Map 854
*Liosceles thoracicus*
SE. *White* underparts; barred flanks; *long* tail.

**Wrens** *Cyphorhinus* High arched culmen.

**10. Chestnut-breasted** *C. thoracicus* p 540 Map 1137
Andes. *Chestnut* underparts; wings unbarred.

**11. Song** *C. phaeocephalus* p 540 Map 1138
W. *Bare ocular patch*; chestnut below; barring.

**Wrens** *Thryothorus* Eyebrow; striped cheeks (usually).

**12. Stripe-throated** *T. leucopogon* p 536 Map 1128
W. Pale. *Streaked* throat; *buffy brown* underparts.

**13. Bay** *T. nigricapillus* p 536 Map 1127
W. Dense *black and white bands* below.

**14. Sooty-headed** *T. spadix* p 534 Map 1120
Pacific. *Black* face and throat; *weak* eyestripe.

**15. Plain-tailed** *T. euophrys* p 534 Map 1122
SW. Large; unbarred. *Gray* crown, *spotted* breast.

**Wrens** *Campylorhynchus*

**16. Band-backed** *C. zonatus* p 531 Map 1112
N. *Banded* back. Cf. 7 on Pl.42.

**17. White-headed** *C. albobrunneus* p 531 Map 1111
Pacific. As shown or amt. of white var. (see text).

**18. Black-bellied Wren** p 534 Map 1121
*Thryothorus fasciatoventris*
NW. *Black* cheeks; *white* throat and chest.

**19. Thrush-like** p 532 Map 1113
*Campylorhynchus turdinus*
SE. Thickly *spotted* below. None sim. in range.

**20. Black-capped Donacobius** p 530 Map 1109
*Donacobius atricapillus*
N, E. Marshy areas. *Yellow* eyes. *Creamy buff* below; *white* tail tips.

# PLATE 42 TAPACULOS, WRENS, and GNATWRENS

## 41

**Tapaculos** *Scytalopus* See Pl.41.

**1. Unicolored** *S. unicolor* p 427 Map 857
Andes. *Uniform* blackish slate; *no barring* (see Pl.41).

**2. Rufous-vented** . p 427 Map 856
*S. femoralis nigricans*
Lower el. than most allies. Slightly darker, barring a bit weaker than *confusus* subsp. (Pl.41). Some have *white crown spot*.

**3. Brown-rumped** *S. latebricola* p 428 Map 860
3a Juv.
E, C Andes. *Slightly paler gray than 2*; rump and flanks lighter rusty.

**4. Andean** *S. magellanicus griseicollis* p 428 Map 861
Andes. "Divided" *gray* foreparts, *rufous* posterior. *Canus* subsp., Pl.41.

**5. Rufous Wren** p 532 Map 1116
*Cinnycerthia u. unirufa*
Andes. Bright rufous; barring *obscure*; lores *blackish*. Some ads. have white foreheads. Duller *unibrunnea* subsp., Pl.41.

**Wrens** *Campylorhynchus*

**6. Bicolored** *C. griseus* p 531 Map 1110
N. Large. *White eyebrow* and underparts.

**7. Stripe-backed** *C. nuchalis* p 532 Map 1114
N. Mantle *striped*. Cf. 16 on Pl.41.

**Wrens** *Thryothorus*

**8. Rufous-breasted** *T. rutilus* p 535 Map 1125
N, E. *Orange rufous* breast; *black and white speckled* face.

**9. Moustached** *T. genibarbis* p 535 Map 1123
Andes. Large. *Brownish gray* crown; *black* submalar; dull below.

**10. Coraya** *T. coraya* p 535 Map 1124
E. *Extensive black* on lower cheeks; dull below (cf. 12).

**11. Rufous-and-white** *T. rufalbus* p 537 Map 1129
N, E. Bright rufous above (except *minlosi* subsp. in E); white below; *barred crissum*. NICEFORO'S *T. nicefori* Santander: from 11 by *contrasting olive brown* crown.

**12. Buff-breasted** *T. leucotis* p 537 Map 1131
N, E. Buffy breast. Lighter, warmer brown above than allies.

**Wood-Wrens** *Henicorhina* Streaked cheeks; *very short* tail.

**13. Gray-breasted** *H. leucophrys* p 539 Map 1135
Mts. *Gray* throat and breast.

**14. White-breasted** *H. leucosticta* p 538 Map 1134
Lowlands. *White* throat and breast.

**Wrens** *Troglodytes*. Small; eyestripe; cheeks unmarked.

**15. Mountain** *T. solstitialis* p 538 Map 1133
Andes. Brighter rufous than 16; *buff* eyestripe. Shorter tail.

**16. House** *T. aedon* p 538 Map 1132
Widespread. *Plain; weak eyebrow*.

**17. Spot-breasted Wren** p 536 Map 1126
*Thryothorus maculipectus*
C, E Andes. *Scaled and spotted* below.

**18. Sedge (Grass) Wren** p 533 Map 1118
*Cistothorus platensis*
Streaked mantle; most subsp. with *buff* eyestripe.

**19. Apolinar's Marsh-Wren** p 534 Map 1119
*Cistothorus apolinari*
E Andes. Larger than 18; *gray* eyestripe.

**20. Nightingale Wren** p 539 Map 1136
*Microcerculus marginatus* 20a Imm.
Long bill; short tail; *throat to upper belly* white. Found by voice. Imm. scaled dusky below (see text).

**21. Half-collared Gnatwren** p 551 Map 1163
*Microbates cinereiventris*
W. Long bill; *rusty* face; *necklace*; cocks wagging tail.

**22. Gray-mantled Wren** p 532 Map 1115
*Odontorchilus branickii*
Local. Gnatcatcherlike. *Barred* tail; *weak eyebrow*.

**23. Slate-throated Gnatcatcher** p 552 Map 1166
*Polioptila schistaceigula*
W, E slope. *Slaty; white* belly. Wagging tail.

**24. Collared Gnatwren** p 550 Map 1162
*Microbates collaris*
E. Long bill; *black* facial lines; *black collar*.

**25. Long-billed Gnatwren** p 551 Map 1164
*Ramphocaenus melanurus*
Brownish; *long* bill; cocked long tail.

**26. Tropical Gnatcatcher** p 551 Map 1165
*Polioptila plumbea* 26a *P. p. bilineata*
♂: black cap. ♀: black tail edged white. 26a: N, Pacific coast. White eyebrow in ♂.

**27. Musician Wren** p 540 Map 1139
*Cyphorhinus arada*
E. Chestnut below; *bare blue ocular ring*.

# PLATE 43 THRUSHES

## 42

**1. Yellow-legged Thrush** p 544 Map 1147
*Platycichla flavipes*
N. ♂: *yellow* soft parts; *grayish* back and belly. ♀:
eyering; pale throat and lower belly (see text).

**2. Glossy-black Thrush** p 546 Map 1150
*Turdus serranus*
Subtropical *forests*. ♂: *orange* bill and legs. ♀: yellowish *bill and eyering*, throat dark.

**3. Great Thrush** *Turdus fuscater* p 545 Map 1149
Temperate zone. *Much larger* than allies. Grayish brown
to blackish.

**4. Pale-eyed** *Platycichla leucops* p 545 Map 1148
Andes. ♂: glossy black; *white* eyes. ♀: *dark*; narrow
yellow eyering (cf. 2).

**Thrushes** *Turdus*

**5. Bare-eyed** *T. nudigenis* p 549 Map 1159
E. Warm buffy brown. *Bare eyering*. LAWRENCE'S *T.
lawrencii* SE, scarce; ♂ has yellow bill; for ♀, see text.
Note voice.

**6. Pale-vented** *T. obsoletus* p 548 Map 1157
Russet brown; white lower belly. COCOA *T. fumigatus*
NE: like 6 but *much more rufous brown*.

**7. Black-hooded** *T. olivater* p 546 Map 1151
N. ♂: *black hood*. ♀: hood *faintly* indicated.

**8. Black-billed** *T. ignobilis* p 547 Map 1154
8a *T. i. debilis*
W. Dull, lacking good marks. *White belly*. 8a: E of Andes. Throat distinctly streaked, *narrow* white crescent
on lower throat. Cf. 9. Settled areas.

**9. White-necked** *T. albicollis* p 549 Map 1160
E. Throat *sharply streaked, prom.* white crescent on
lower throat; yellow eyering. WHITE-THROATED *T. assimilis*
Pacific: like 9 but darker below. No range overlap.

**10. Clay-colored** *T. grayi* p 549 Map 1158
N. *Yellowish* bill; *uniform* buffy brown.

**Nightingale-Thrushes** *Catharus* Resident spp. have
orange bill and legs. For n migrants VEERY
(*C. fuscescens*), GRAY-CHEEKED (*C. minimus*), SWAINSON'S
(*C. ustulatus*), see text.

**11. Orange-billed** *C. aurantiirostris* p 543 Map 1144
Mts. Brown back; *gray* below; orange *soft parts*.

**12. Spotted** *C. dryas* p 543 Map 1146
Andes. *Black* cap, *yellowish* underparts; *spots*. Scarce.

**13. Chestnut-bellied Thrush** p 546 Map 1152
*Turdus fulviventris*
E Andes. *Rufous* belly unique. ♀ duller.

**14. Pale-breasted** p 547 Map 1153
*Turdus leucomelas*
N, E. Contrasting *gray* head and *olive* tinged back.

**15. Slaty-backed Nightingale-Thrush**
p 543 Map 1145
*Catharus fuscater*
Mts. Slaty with sooty head; *white* eyes. Undergrowth.

**Solitaires** *Myadestes* Shy, arboreal; *erect* posture;
short legs.

**16. Andean** *M. ralloides* p 542 Map 1141
Andes. Often heard. Iron gray; *brown* back.

**17. Rufous-brown** *M. leucogenys* p 542 Map 1142
Pacific (once). *Uniform* russet brown; *ochraceous* crissum; *yellow* lower mandible.

**18. Black Solitaire** p 542 Map 1143
*Entomodestes coracinus*
Pacific. *White* cheeks; *white* in wings and tail.

John C. Yrizarry

PLATE 44 ICTERIDS

## Orioles *Icterus*

**1. Yellow-tailed** *I. mesomelas* p 572 Map 1213
NW. Yellow outer tail feathers.

**2. Yellow-backed** *I. chrysater* p 572 Map 1212
W (mainly mts.). Large and sleek. *Yellow back; solid* black wings.

**3. Orange-crowned** *I. auricapillus* p 570 Map 1208
N. Orange forecrown. For imm., see text. Also for OR-CHARD *I. spurius*, BALTIMORE *I. galbula*, n. migrants, see text.

**4. Troupial** *Icterus icterus* p 570 Map 1209
N, E. *Shaggy black* hood; *white* scapular patch; *bare blue ocular area.* Subsp. in Arauca has mainly yellow back.

**5. Yellow Oriole** *Icterus nigrogularis* p 571 Map 1211
N, E Lemony yellow; *single white* wing bar. Imm. much duller, white in wing reduced or nearly lacking.

**6. Yellow-billed Cacique** p 567 Map 1199
*Amblycercus holosericeus*
W. White eyes; yellowish white bill; skulks. Occurs only at high el. in parts of range.

## Caciques *Cacicus*

**7. Scarlet-rumped** *C. uropygialis* p 565 Map 1196
W. Scarlet rump less extensive than 6 (Pl.45); no overlap.

**8. Yellow-rumped** *C. cela* p 565 Map 1194
N, E. Yellow on wings, rump, and crissum *less extensive* than E subsp. (see Pl.45). Base of tail yellow.

**9. Chestnut-headed Oropendola** p 562 Map 1187
*Zarhynchus wagleri*
NW. *Much smaller* than allies. Chestnut head.

**10. Black Oropendola** p 564 Map 1191
*Gymnostinops guatimozinus*
NW. Blackish. *Bare pale* cheeks; *yellow and black* bill. CHESTNUT-MANTLED *G. cassini* NW (rare): like 10, but back, wings, and flanks *bright chestnut.*

**11. Crested Oropendola** p 563 Map 1188
*Psarocolius decumanus*
Only large Colombian oropendola with *all white* bill.

**12. Yellow-hooded Blackbird** p 569 Map 1205
*Agelaius icterocephalus*
♀ brownish; yellow hood faintly indicated. Marshes.

**13. Velvet-fronted Grackle** p 568 Map 1204
*Lampropsar tanagrinus*
SE. Short bill; rather long roundish tail; plumage *lacks* gloss. *Várzea.*

**14. Carib Grackle** *Quiscalus lugubris* p 567 Map 1200
N, NE. *White* eyes; *short,* wedge-shaped tail. Note longish bill. ♀ sooty brownish. Settled areas.

**15. Red-breasted Blackbird** p 573 Map 1215
*Leistes militaris*
♀ heavily streaked; *pinkish* stain on breast. Imm. usually *lacks* pinkish or red. EASTERN MEADOWLARK *Sturnella magna* E (W local): has white tail patches. For BOBOLINK *Dolichonyx oryzivorus* N migrant, see text.

## Cowbirds *Molothrus*

**16. Shiny** *M. bonariensis* p 561 Map 1183
♂: *glossy* plumage reflects purple; *dark* eyes; shorter tail than 14. ♀: pointed conical bill; faint eyebrow.

**17. Bronze-brown** *M. armenti* p 561 Map 1184
N coast. *Red* eyes; head, back, and underparts *bronze brown.*

**18. Giant** *Scaphidura oryzivora* p 561 Map 1185
*Long flat* tail, neck *ruff,* and *short* bill give *small-headed, hunch-backed* appearance. Eyes red. ♀ much smaller, lacks ruff. Juv., pale eyes and bill (like hosts).

44

Gwynne

# PLATE 45 ICTERIDS

**Oropendolas** *Psarocolius*. Large icterids. Central pair of tail feathers black, rest yellow (tail all yellow below); ♂♂ much larger than ♀♀. Cheeks feathered (cf. *Gymnostinops*).

**1. Green** *P. viridis* p 563 Map 1189
E. Mainly *dark olive; pea green bill* tipped red.

**2. Russet-backed** p 563 Map 1190
*P. a. angustifrons* 2a *P. a. sincipitalis*
E. Bill *black*; dull *olive brown*. 2a: W. Forehead, eyebrow, and bill *bright yellow*; back, rump, and flanks *bright chestnut*.

**3. Olive Oropendola** p 564 Map 1193
*Gymnostinops yuracares*
E. *Yellow olive* foreparts, *chestnut* rearparts; bare pink cheek patch. Black bill tipped red.

**4. Oriole Blackbird** p 572 Map 1214
*Gymnomystax mexicanus*
E. Yellow head and underparts. Open areas.

**5. Orange-backed Troupial** p 571 Map 1210
*Icterus jamacaii*
SE. *Brilliant orange*, unmistakable in range. Vicinity of water.

**6. Red-rumped Cacique** p 565 Map 1195
*Cacicus haemorrhous*
E. *Scarlet* rump. See 7 on Pl.44; no overlap.

**7. Band-tailed Oropendola** p 562 Map 1186
*Ocyalus latirostris*
Amazonas. Recalls 11. *Central tail feathers* and terminal tail band black. *No* yellow on wings or rump. Maxilla mostly *black*.

**8. Red-bellied Grackle** p 568 Map 1202
*Hypopyrrhus pyrohypogaster*
C, E Andes (local). *Red* belly; white eyes. Social; forest.

**9. Mountain Cacique** p 566 Map 1197
*Cacicus leucoramphus*
Andes. Yellow shoulders and rump; *tail black*. Higher el. than 11.

**10. Mountain Grackle** p 568 Map 1203
*Macroagelaius subalaris*
E Andes (rare). *Wing linings and axillary tufts chestnut* (inconspic.); rather long bill. Cf. 18 on Pl.44.

**11. Yellow-rumped Cacique** p 565 Map 1194
*Cacicus c. cela*
E. Yellow *on wings*; rump, crissum, and *entire base of tail* yellow. Cf. W subsp. (8, Pl.44).

**Orioles** *Icterus*

**12. Epaulet** *I. cayanensis* p 569 Map 1206
Leticia. Yellow *shoulders*.

**13. Moriche** *I. chrysocephalus* p 569 Map 1207
SE. Yellow crown, shoulders, and rump.

**14. Solitary Black Cacique** p 566 Map 1198
*Cacicus solitarius*
E. Dark eyes (all ages, both sexes?); pale bill. Low near water. Note voice. Cf. 6 on Pl.44.

45

# PLATE 46 VIREOS and WOOD WARBLERS

**1. Rufous-browed Peppershrike** p 554 Map 1169
*Cyclarhis gujanensis*
W. Crown and cheeks gray; *underparts yellow; broad rufous eyebrow.*

**Shrike-Vireos** *Vireolanius* Heavy hooked bill.

**2. Slaty-capped** V. *leucotis* p 555 Map 1172
W, SE. Contrasting gray crown; *yellow eyebrow* and underparts. SE subsp. has *white cheek stripe.*

**3. Yellow-browed** V. *eximius* p 555 Map 1171
N. Bright green above. *Blue* crown; *yellow eyestripe and throat; greenish breast.*

**Vireos** *Vireo* See n migrants in text, pp.555-556.

**4. Red-eyed** V. *olivaceus* p 556 Map 1175
*Gray* crown; *white* eyestripe. See text for subspp.

**5. Brown-capped** V. *leucophrys* p 557 Map 1174
W. *Brown* cap, whitish eyebrow; *yellowish* below.

**Greenlets** *Hylophilus* Small, active, often pale-billed.

**6. Tawny-crowned** H. *ochraceiceps* p 559 Map 1181
E. *White* eyes; *brownish* above with *contrasting rufous* forecrown (or *tawny yellow*, Pacific coast).

**7. Brown-headed** H. *brunneiceps* p 558 Map 1176
E. *Brownish* crown; *yellowish* wing edgings; *buff* chest.

**8. Lesser** H. *decurtatus* p 560 Map 1182
W. *Plumper* than allies; *whitish* eyering and belly.

**9. Lemon-chested** H. *thoracicus* p 557 Map 1175
SE. *Yellow chest band;* contrasting cap and back.

**10. Black-billed Peppershrike** p 554 Map 1170
*Cyclarhis nigrirostris*
Andes. *Bill black;* mostly *gray* below; sides of neck and broken chest band yellowish. Peppershrike bill.

**11. Golden-fronted Greenlet** p 558 Map 1178
*Hylophilus aurantiifrons*
N. *Light rufous brown* crown; *yellowish* below; *dark* eyes.

**12. Scrub Greenlet** p 559 Map 1180
*Hylophilus flavipes*
N, NE. *Pale bill; white* eyes. Crown slightly darker than back.

**13. Rufous-naped Greenlet** p 558 Map 1177
*Hylophilus semibrunneus*
Andes. Crown and nape *rufous; whitish* below; obscure chest band.

**14. White-lored Warbler** p 586 Map 1231
*Basileuterus conspicillatus*
Santa Marta. Mts. Like 17 but *white eyering* and supraloral stripe.

**15. Yellow Warbler** p 576 Map 1218
*Dendroica petechia peruvianus*
15a D. p. *erithachorides*
Pacific coast (15a: Caribbean coast). ♂ of all resident subspp. (confined to coast) have chestnut on head. N migrants *lack* chestnut.

**16. Tropical Parula** *Parula pitiayumi* p 575 Map 1217
W. *Blackish* face, *white* wing bars; *orange yellow* chest.

NOTE: For n migrant wood warblers, see text.

**Warblers** *Basileuterus*

**17. Russet-crowned** B. *coronatus* p 586 Map 1230
Andes. *Gray* head; *orange crown stripe* bordered black.

**18. Gray-throated** B. *cinereicollis* p 587 Map 1232
NE. *Gray* from face to mid-breast; *yellow* coronal patch.

**19. Rufous-capped** B. *rufifrons* p 587 Map 1233
N. *Chestnut* crown; white eyestripe.

**20. Black-crested** B. *nigrocristatus* p 586 Map 1229
E, C Andes. *Broad crown stripe and lores black.*

**21. Flavescent** B. *flaveolus* p 585 Map 1226
NE. *Crown and upperparts uniform;* short yellowish eyestripe; yellowish legs. Low el.

**22. Citrine** B. *luteoviridis* p 585 Map 1227
Andes. Duller than 21; face duskier, legs dark. Cf. *Hemispingus.* PALE-LEGGED B. *signatus* E Andes (once).

**23. Golden-crowned** B. *culicivorus* p 584 Map 1224
Mts. *Upperparts grayish;* eyebrow *whitish; dusky* eyeline (cf. 24).

**24. Golden-bellied** B. *chrysogaster* p 584 Map 1225
SW. *Obviously olive* above; faint eyebrow; *no dusky line* through eyes (cf. 23).

**25. Masked Yellowthroat** p 581 Map 1219
*Geothlypis aequinoctialis*
♂: *small black* mask; *gray* crown; ♀: sides of head olive. OLIVE-CROWNED G. *semiflava* W: ♂ has *large black mask; olive* crown; ♀, olive head. COMMON G. *trichas* N migrant.

**Warblers** *Basileuterus*

**26. Buff-rumped** B. *fulvicauda* p 588 Map 1236
W. *Buff* rump and base of tail. Near water.

**27. Three-striped** B. *tristriatus* p 587 Map 1234
Andes. *Black and buff* crown stripes; *dingy* below.

**28. Santa Marta** B. *basilicus* p 588 Map 1235
Upper el. *Black and white* head.

PLATE 47 HONEYCREEPERS and REDSTARTS

## 46

**Redstarts (Whitestarts)** *Myioborus* White outer tail feathers.

**1. Golden-fronted** *M. ornatus* p 583 Map 1221
Andes. *Foreface* and underparts yellow (see text).

**2. Yellow-crowned** *M. flavivertex* p 584 Map 1223
Santa Marta Mts. *Yellow* crown patch.

**3. Slate-throated** *M. miniatus* p 583 Map 1220
Mts. Slaty *throat and chest.*

**4. Spectacled** *M. melanocephalus* p 584 Map 1222
Mts. S. Center crown *mostly chestnut.* Facial pattern var.; most typical shown.

**5. Scarlet-thighed Dacnis** p 598 Map 1266
*Dacnis venusta*
W. ♀: *bluish tinged* head and rump; *unstreaked buff* below.

**6. Green Honeycreeper** p 596 Map 1260
*Chlorophanes spiza*
♀: rather long *sharp pointed yellow* bill.

**Honeycreepers** *Cyanerpes* Long slightly decurved bill.

**7. Red-legged** *C. cyaneus* p 596 Map 1259
*Red legs, yellow* wing linings (both sexes).

**8. Purple** *C. caeruleus* p 595 Map 1257
♂: *lemon yellow* legs. ♀: *cinnamon buff* face and throat.
SHINING *C. lucidus:* ♂ very like ♂ of 8 (see text); ♀: crown grayish, little cinnamon on face.

**9. Short-billed** *C. nitidus* p 595 Map 1256
SE. *Bill shorter* than allies. ♂: black on throat spreads to chest (cf. 8); legs pinkish. ♀: no cinnamon on face.

**Dacnis** *Dacnis* Sharp pointed bill rather short.

**10. Blue** *D. cayana* p 597 Map 1262
♂: black lores and throat (cf. *Pseudodacnis*). ♀ green; *contrasting gray blue* head. Pacific subsp., Pl.48.

**11. Black-faced** *D. lineata* p 597 Map 1263
E. Turquoise; black mask; white belly. For ♀, see text. W subsp., Pl. 48.

**12. White-bellied** *D. albiventris* p 599 Map 1268
SE (rare). ♀ greenish above, yellowish below.

**13. Yellow-bellied** *D. flaviventer* p 598 Map 1265
♀ rather like 11 but obscurely mottled olive on breast and *eyes red* (both sexes).

**14. Scarlet-breasted** *D. berlepschi* p 599 Map 1267
SW. ♀ mainly brown; *reddish orange wash* on breast.

**15. Bananaquit** *Coereba flaveola* p 591 Map 1245
Settled areas. *White* eyestripe and wing spot; *yellow* rump.

**Conebills** *Conirostrum.* Pointed conical bills.

**16. Bicolored** *C. bicolor* p 589 Map 1239
16a Imm.
N, mangroves. Imm. *yellow wash* on face and underparts.

**17. Chestnut-vented** *C. speciosum* p 589 Map 1237
SE. ♂ small; *chestnut vent.* ♀ like ♀ of 18 but *greenish* above, *less buff* below.

**18. White-eared** *C. leucogenys* p 589 Map 1238
N. ♂: black cap; *white cheeks.* ♀: *whitish* rump; yellowish buff face and underparts.

**19. Capped** *C. albifrons* p 591 Map 1243
Andes. ♂ in W has dark blue cap (see Pl.48).
♀: *contrasting bluish* head and olive upperparts (cf. ♀ of 10).

**20. Blue-backed** *C. sitticolor* p 590 Map 1240
Andes. Blue back; deep rufous below.

**Flower-Piercers** *Diglossa* Bill slightly upturned, hooked at tip.

**21. Rusty** *D. sittoides* p 594 Map 1255
Mts. ♂ *cinnamon* below. ♀ lacks good marks; look for *obscure* breast streaking.

**22. White-sided** *D. albilatera* p 594 Map 1254
Mts. *Conspic. white* flank tufts (both sexes).

**23. Chestnut-bellied** *D. gloriosissima* p 593 Map 1250
W Andes. *Chestnut* belly; gray shoulders.

**24. Black** *D. h. humeralis* p 593 Map 1252
24a *D. h. aterrima*
E Andes. Slightly smaller and duller than 25; rump *grayish.* 24a: C Andes. *Uniform* black incl. shoulders.

**25. Glossy** *D. lafresnayii* p 593 Map 1251
E, C Andes (see 24). All glossy black; *grayish* shoulders.

**26. Bluish** *D. caerulescens* p 591 Map 1246
Andes. *Dull grayish blue;* black lores; *thin* bill.

**27. Masked** *D. cyanea* p 592 Map 1247
Andes. Larger; bright blue; *fire red* eyes; *mask.*

**28. Indigo** *D. indigotica* p 592 Map 1249
Pacific. Brilliant deep blue; *fire red* eye. DEEP-BLUE *D. glauca* E slope: like 28, but eyes *golden yellow.*

2
3
4
♂
5
♀
1
♂
6
♀
♂
7
♀
♂
8
♀
♂
9
♂
14
♂
10
♀
♂
11
♀
♂
12
♂
13
15
16
16 a
♂
17
♂
18
♀
♂
19
♀
0
♂
21
♀
♂
22
♀
23
28
W. TRIMM
24
25
24 a
26
27

# PLATE 48 HONEYCREEPERS and TANAGERS

## 47

**1. Scarlet-and-white Tanager** p 634 Map 1373
*Erythrothlypis salmoni*
♀: scarlet of ♂ replaced by *olive green*. Juv. duller than ♀, flanks olive. Imm. ♂ pied olive and scarlet.

**2. Yellow-collared Chlorophonia** p 601 Map 1271
*Chlorophonia flavirostris*
*Orange bill and legs; white eyes.* ♂: *yellow collar.* ♀ dull green, yellowish belly.

**3. Giant Conebill** *Oreomanes fraseri* p 591 Map 1244
S. *Polylepis.* White cheeks; *chestnut* underparts.

**4. Golden-collared Honeycreeper** p 597 Map 1261
*Iridophanes pulcherrima*
Andes (local). Longish bill. ♂: *blue on wings; black mantle* (cf. 13, Pl.49). ♀: narrow collar; blue green wing edgings.

**Conebills** *Conirostrum*

**5. Cinereous** *C. cinereum* p 590 Map 1242
Andes. Pale buff eyeline and white *L-shaped wing patch.*

**6. Rufous-browed** *C. rufum* p 590 Map 1241
E Andes. Rufous face and underparts. Scrub.

**7. Capped** *C. albifrons* p 591 Map 1243
W Andes. Glossy dark blue cap. E subsp. and ♀, Pl. 47.

**8. Black-faced Dacnis** p 597 Map 1263
*Dacnis lineata*
W. ♂ turquoise and black; *yellow belly.* E subsp. and ♀, Pl.47.

**9. Turquoise Dacnis-Tanager** p 606 Map 1288
*Pseudodacnis hartlaubi*
Andes (very rare). ♂: *black throat; turquoise eyering* and belly (cf. 8). For ♀, see text.

**Dacnis** *Dacnis*

**10. Blue** *D. cayana* p 599 Map 1262
W. Deeper, more purplish blue than E subsp. (Pl.47). ♀ greenish; *contrasting blue gray* head.

**11. Viridian** *D. viguieri* p 598 Map 1264
NW. ♂ aquamarine; *yellow eyes; lacks black throat.* ♀ light olive; black lores, wings and tail.

**Tanagers** *Tangara* Brightly patterned; mainly subtropical.

**12. Blue-browed** *T. cyanotis* p 612 Map 1306
Mts. SE. *Blue eyebrow;* black head and back.

**13. Golden-naped** *T. ruficervix* p 614 Map 1311
Andes. *Mainly blue;* top of head purplish black. Small *golden buff nape band.*

**14. Metallic-green** *T. labradorides* p 612 Map 1307
Andes. Usually looks dull and faded. *Straw-colored eyebrow;* black *coronal stripe.*

**15. Golden-eared** *T. chrysotis* p 612 Map 1304
E Slope. *Lime green;* golden eyestripe, *coppery* cheeks, *chestnut* median underparts.

**16. Saffron-crowned** p 611 Map 1303
*T. xanthocephala*
Andes. *Turquoise blue; silky golden head,* black face (cf. 26).

**17. Scrub** *T. vitriolina* p 616 Map 1317
W. *Rufous* cap, black mask. Deforested areas.

**18. Rufous-throated** *T. rufigula* p 610 Map 1300
Pacific slope. *Black* head; scaled or spotted *above and below;* rufous throat.

**19. Blue-whiskered** *T. johannae* p 609 Map 1297
Pacific lowlands. Apple green; *forepart of head black.* Look for the blue whisker patch.

**20. Emerald** *T. florida* p 609 Map 1296
Pacific. *Emerald green; black rectangle on head,* yellow crown. ♀ duller, crown green.

**21. Gray-and-gold** *T. palmeri* p 614 Map 1313
Pacific. Larger; plumper. *Pearly gray;* well-defined *black face mask;* black mottling on mantle and chest.

**22. Plain-colored** *T. inornata* p 615 Map 1314
NW. Sleek gray plumage; *white* belly.

**23. Golden-hooded** *T. larvata* p 613 Map 1309
W. Contrasting gold head; black back and chest; *white belly* (cf. 11, 19, Pl.49).

**Tanagers** *Chlorochrysa* Thinner bill, heavier legs than *Tangara.* Cloud Forest.

**24. Glistening-green** *C. phoenicotis* p 607 Map 1290
W slope. "Glistening" green. ♀ duller.

**25. Orange-eared** *C. calliparaea* p 607 Map 1289
E slope. "Glistening" green; *black* throat, *orange* rump. ♀ duller, throat *gray.*

**26. Multicolored** *C. nitidissima* p 607 Map 1291
W, C Andes. ♂: *mostly yellow* head; *yellow* mantle. ♀ and imm. duller; *mantle green.*

PLATE 49 TANAGERS

## 48

**Chlorophonias** *Chlorophonia.* Plump; short-tailed; green.

**1. Chestnut-breasted** *C. pyrrhophrys* p 601 Map 1272
Andes. Purplish blue crown bordered black (bordered maroon, ♀). ♂ lacks yellow collar (cf. 2, Pl.48).

**2. Blue-naped** *C. cyanea* p 600 Map 1270
Mts. ♂ only Colombian chlorophonia *with blue rump;* belly uniform yellow. ♀: *green* crown and *blue* nape.

**3. Swallow-Tanager** *Tersina viridis* p 600 Map 1269
W, NE. ♂ turquoise; black mask and throat; barred flanks. ♀ grass green; barred flanks. Erect posture.

**Tanagers** *Tangara*

**4. Golden** *T. arthus* p 610 Map 1301
Andes. *Rich golden yellow;* black patch on cheeks.

**5. Flame-faced** *T. parzudakii* p 612 Map 1305
Andes. *Silvery opaline* rump and underparts; *flame red face.* Cf. 6. Pacific subsp. smaller, face color less intense.

**6. Saffron-crowned** p 611 Map 1303
*T. xanthocephala* See 16 on Pl.48.

**7. Blue-and-black** *T. vassorii* p 616 Map 1320
Andes. Shining dark blue; black wings. Only *Tangara* in temperate zone.

**8. Silver-throated** *T. icterocephala* p 611 Map 1302
Pacific. Mainly bright yellow; *white throat;* narrow malar line. ♀ and imm. much duller.

**9. Black-capped** *T. heinei* p 617 Map 1321
Subtropics. *black crown; aquamarine face and throat.* ♀: dusky green crown; face and underparts much duller than ♂; faint chest streaking.

**10. Beryl-spangled** *T. nigroviridis* p 616 Map 1319
Andes. *Shining opaline crown;* black mask and back; *spotted underparts.*

**11. Blue-necked** *T. cyanicollis* p 613 Map 1308
Andes. *Solid black back and underparts;* turquoise blue head; burnished gold shoulders. Nonforest.

**12. Burnished-buff** *T. cayana* p 616 Map 1318
E. *Straw-colored;* coppery crown, blackish cheeks. ♀ duller. Open areas.

**13. Black-headed** *T. cyanoptera* p 617 Map 1322
Mts. Opaline; black head, wings and tail (cf. 4, Pl.48). ♀ much like 9 but crown grayish.

**14. Rufous-winged** *T. lavinia* p 615 Map 1316
Pacific. Brighter than allied 17, little range overlap. *Golden mantle, rufous primaries.*

**15. Turquoise** *T. mexicana* p 614 Map 1312
E. Blackish; dark blue face and breast; *clear yellow belly,* flanks mottled black. Nonforest.

**16. Speckled** *T. guttata* p 610 Map 1298
E, C Andes. *Spotted above and below;* yellow on face; white underparts.

**17. Bay-headed** *T. gyrola* p 615 Map 1315
Widespread. *Mainly green; brick red head;* underparts mainly blue. NE subsp. largely green below. Cf. 14.

**18. Green-and-gold** *T. schrankii* p 609 Map 1295
E. Emerald green. Large black *cheek patch;* yellow rump and median underparts.

**19. Masked** *T. nigrocincta* p 613 Map 1310
E. Pale, faded lavender blue head; black back and chest; *white belly* (cf. 11).

**20. Yellow-bellied** *T. xanthogastra* p 610 Map 1299
SE. *Speckled* underpart. Recalls 16 but underparts green, belly yellow.

**21. Opal-crowned** *T. callophrys* p 608 Map 1293
SE. Very dark; *prom. opal eyebrow.*

**22. Paradise** *T. chilensis* p 608 Map 1294
SE. *Turquoise below.* Note *apple green face; scarlet rump* in SE; scarlet and yellow rump in NE.

**23. Opal-rumped** *T. velia* p 608 Map 1292
SE. *Looks blackish.* Opal rump; *deep chestnut* belly.

49

# PLATE 50 MOUNTAIN TANAGERS and ALLIES

**1. Grass-green** *Chlorornis riefferii* p 640 Map 1392
Andean Subtropics. Large, *green; orange* bill and legs;
*chestnut face.*

**2. Hooded Mountain-Tanager** p 620 Map 1330
*Buthraupis montana*
Andes. Entire head black; back dull blue. Large. *Red
eyes.*

**3. White-capped Tanagar** p 635 Map 1377
*Sericossypha albocristata*
E, C Andes (local). Black with *white* cap. Social; loud
shrieking cries.

**4. Buff-breasted Mountain-Tanager** p 622 Map 1337
*Dubusia taeniata*
Mts. *Frosty blue eyebrow;* black hood and throat in
Andes; buff throat in Santa Marta.

**Mountain-Tanagers** *Buthraupis*

**5. Masked** *B. wetmorei* p 620 Map 1331
C Andes (rare). Rather mustard yellow. Note *bright
yellow eyebrow and rump.* Yellow of underparts ex-
*tends nearly to chin.*

**6. Black-chested** *B. eximia* p 620 Map 1332
C Andes. *Blue* crown; *rich mossy green back* (cf. 2).
Scarce.

**Mountain-Tanagers** *Anisognathus.* Smaller than
*Buthraupis.*

**7. Black-cheeked** *A. melanogenys* p 618 Map 1326
Santa Marta Mts. Closely allied to 8 but range overlaps
only 4.

**8. Lacrimose** *A. lacrymosus* p 619 Map 1327
Andes. Common. Dull dusty blue above; *orange yellow below. Yellow spots* (tears) on sides of head.

**9. Scarlet-bellied** *A. igniventris* p 618 Map 1325
E, C Andes. *Sky blue rump patch* in flight.

**10. Black-chinned** *A. notabilis* p 619 Map 1329
Pacific slope. Recalls much more common 11 but *back
contrasting yellow olive;* less blue in wings; bill longer.

**11. Blue-winged** *A. flavinucha* p 619 Map 1328
Andes. Yellow crown stripe; blue in wings. Back black
in C, W Andes.

**12. Moss-backed Tanager** p 621 Map 1335
*Bangsia edwardsi*
Pacific slope. *Dull blue* sides of head; *yellow* chest
patch. Cloud Forest.

**Tanagers** *Iridosornis* Smaller than *Buthraupis* or
*Anisognathus.* Less social; usually keep under cover.

**13. Purplish-mantled** p 617 Map 1323
*I. porphyrocephala*
Pacific slope. Rich blue; *yellow* throat; buff lower un-
derparts.

**14. Golden-crowned** *I. rufivertex* p 618 Map 1324
Andes, temperate zone. *Intense purplish blue plumage;* golden crown patch; chestnut vent.

**Tanagers** *Bangsia* Chunky; rather short-tailed. Cloud
forest of lower subtropics.

**15. Black-and-gold** p 621 Map 1334
*B. melanochlamys*
Pacific. Blackish; median underparts *golden yellow.*
Poorly known.

**16. Golden-chested** *B. rothschildi* p 621 Map 1333
Pacific. Navy blue; like 15 but yellow confined to *chest*
and *abdomen.* Fairly common within narrow el. band.

**17. Gold-ringed** *B. aureocincta* p 622 Map 1336
Pacific. Prom. *yellow ring* encircling face. Poorly known.

GTUDOR

# PLATE 51 TANAGERS

**Tanagers** *Thraupis*

**1. Blue-gray** *T. episcopus* p 622 Map 1338
Widespread. Light gray head *contrasts* with *darker* back. Most subspp. E of Andes have *white* shoulder patch.

**2. Glaucous** *T. glaucocolpa* p 623 Map 1339
N (dry). Grayish head *concolor* with back; contrasting *white belly*; *dark spot* at base of *greenish edged* primaries.

**3. Palm** *T. palmarum* p 623 Map 1340
Dull grayish olive; yellowish forecrown; *rear half of wing black* (2-toned effect).

**4. Blue-capped** *T. cyanocephala* p 623 Map 1341
Andes. *Blue* head; *bright olive* back; gray underparts. Mainly nonforest.

**Tanagers** *Piranga*

**5. Hepatic** *P. flava* p 625 Map 1348
Mts. Dusky bill; lores grayish (both sexes). SUMMER *P. rubra* N migrant: bill *yellowish* (both sexes); brighter red than 5. SCARLET *P. olivacea* N migrant.

**6. White-winged** *P. leucoptera* p 626 Map 1349
Andes (local). Small. Black wings with white wing bars (both sexes).

**7. Red-hooded** *P. rubriceps* p 627 Map 1350
Andes (local). *Bright red hood* extending to mid-breast. ♀: red extends to chest.

**8. Red-crowned Ant-Tanager** p 628 Map 1354
*Habia rubica*
N, SE. ♂: scarlet crown stripe *bordered black*. ♀: semiconcealed tawny yellow crown stripe *bordered black*; throat slightly brighter than rest of underparts.

**9. Silver-beaked** p 624 Map 1342
*Ramphocelus carbo*
E. ♂ blackish; swollen *white* lower mandible. ♀: mandible duller; underparts reddish brown.

**10. Crimson-backed Tanager** p 624 Map 1343
*Ramphocelus dimidiatus*
W. ♂ *white mandible* like 9; rump and lower underparts *bright red*. ♀ like ♀ of 9, but rump and belly brighter red.

**Ant-Tanagers** *Habia*

**11. Red-throated** *H. fuscicauda* p 628 Map 1355
NW. Dull; contrasting *rosy red* throat. ♀: *ochre yellow* throat (cf. 8).

**12. Crested** *H. cristata* p 629 Map 1357
W Andes. Cardinallike. Prom. *scarlet crest and foreparts*; gray sides. SOOTY *H. gutturalis* N: scarlet crest; *sides of head black*; rosy throat; ♀ duller; throat pinkish white.

**13. Red-shouldered Tanager** p 630 Map 1362
*Tachyphonus phoenicius*
E. Small. White wing linings; red at bend of wing usually concealed. ♀: slightly contrasting *grayish* head, *dull white* throat. Scrubby savannas.

**14. Masked Crimson Tanager** p 624 Map 1344
*Ramphocelus nigrogularis*
SE. *Rich velvety red*; black back and belly (cf. 20). Near water.

**Tanagers** *Tachyphonus* ♂♂ are black with white wing linings and var. amts. of white on shoulder.

**15. Fulvous-crested** *T. surinamus* p 630 Map 1361
E. ♂: *crown and rump buffy yellow* (but not throat); tawny flank patches (not always visible). ♀ olive above, *crown tinged gray*; prom. yellow *spectacles*.

**16. Flame-crested** *T. cristatus* p 630 Map 1360
SE. ♂ from 15 by *buffy yellow throat patch*; rear of crest scarlet or orange in most races. ♀ warm *rufous brown*; ochraceous below.

**Tanagers** *Ramphocelus*

**17. Lemon-rumped** *R. icteronotus* p 625 Map 1346
Pacific. ♀ brownish above; pale *yellow* rump and underparts. Imm. ♂ like ♀; older birds mottled with black.

**18. Flame-rumped** *R. flammigerus* p 624 Map 1345
W. ♂ like ♂ of 17, but rump *flame scarlet*. ♀ (shown) like ♀ of 17 but *rump and chest stained orange*. Hybrids of 17 and 18 are intermed.

**19. Fulvous Shrike-Tanager** p 629 Map 1358
*Lanio fulvus*
SE. ♂: black head, contrasting tawny yellow back and underparts. ♀ very like ♀ of 16 but rump darker rufous, throat tinged brownish; bill heavier, hooked.

**20. Vermilion Tanager** p 625 Map 1347
*Calochaetes coccineus*
SE. *Black mask and throat*; back and underparts *scarlet* (cf. 14 and ♂ Scarlet Tanager). Cloud forest.

## 51

# PLATE 52 TANAGERS

**1. Ochre-breasted Tanager** p 627 Map 1353
*Chlorothraupis stolzmanni*
Pacific. Dingy; lacks obvious marks. *Heavy dusky bill*; ochraceous buff underparts; robust appearance.

**2. White-shouldered Tanager** p 621 Map 1363
*Tachyphonus luctuosus*
♂: prom. white shoulders. ♀: gray head, olive back, whitish throat, ochre yellow underparts (cf. larger ♀ of 8).

**3. Yellow-backed Tanager** p 634 Map 1372
*Hemithraupis flavicollis albigularis*
NW. ♂: throat white spotted black; sides of throat and rump yellow; underparts white. ♀ brownish olive above, yellow below, belly and narrow eyering white. (Yellow-throated subsp. 13, Pl.53).

**Tanagers** *Chlorothraupis* Robust; dingy; heavy slightly hooked bill; often noisy; humid forest understory; act somewhat like ant-tanagers.

**4. Lemon-browed** *C. olivacea* p 627 Map 1352
Pacific. Yellow *spectacles*; thick blackish bill; mainly dull olive green.

**5. Carmiol's** *C. carmioli* p 627 Map 1351
NW, SE. No. obvious marks. Robust, dull olive green, heavy dusky bill. No overlap with 1.

**6. Tawny-crested Tanager** p 631 Map 1364
*Tachyphonus delatrii*
Pacific. ♂: cinnamon orange to yellow crest. ♀ uniform dark brown.

**7. Scarlet-browed Tanager** p 632 Map 1365
*Heterospingus xanthopygius*
W. *White pectoral tufts*. ♂ black; *red "horns"*; yellow rump. ♀ *gray; yellow* rump.

**8. Gray-headed Tanager** p 632 Map 1367
*Eucometis penicillata*
W, SE. Slightly crested *gray* head and throat; rich butter yellow underparts.

**9. White-lined Tanager** p 629 Map 1359
*Tachyphonus rufus*
♂ entirely black; white wing linings show in flight. ♀ all rufous. Semiopen areas.

**10. Dusky-faced Tanager** p 632 Map 1368
*Mitrospingus cassinii*
Pacific. Black face, white eyes; yellowish crown stripe. Streamside shrubbery.

**11. Rosy Thrush-Tanager** p 633 Map 1369
*Rhodinocichla rosea*
NE. ♂ rosy pink below. ♀: cinnamon rufous underparts.

**Bush-Tanagers** *Chlorospingus*

**12. Dusky-bellied** *C. semifuscus* p 638 Map 1384
Pacific slope. Foreparts *dark gray; prom.* pale yellow eyes with white spot behind in some races.

**13. Yellow-green** *C. flavovirens* p 636 Map 1380
Pacific (1 locality). Lores and ear coverts dusky; otherwise essentially without marks.

**14. Pirre** *C. inornatus* p 636
Darien highlands, Panama (not yet rec. in Colombia). Like 16 but *head to below eyes blackish*; faint dusky spots on throat.

**15. Yellow-throated** *C. flavigularis* p 637 Map 1381
Andes. Rather var.; *throat, bright yellow*. (cf. 3, 4, Pl.54).

**16. Tacarcuna** *C. tacarcunae* p 636 Map 1379
NW, Cerro Tacarcuna. Crown *concolor* with back; *mostly yellow below*; eyes white.

PLATE 53 TANAGERS and ALLIES

## 52

**Euphonias** *Euphonia* Plump; short bill and tail. Sexes differ, both difficult. For most ♀ ♀, see text.

**1. Thick-billed** *E. laniirostris* p 604 Map 1281
♂ only blue-backed Euphonia in Colombia with *yellow throat*. ♀: olive upperparts, yellow below, buff tinge on breast.

**2. Orange-bellied** *E. xanthogaster* p 602 Map 1274
♂: yellow cap extends *well behind eyes*. No obvious orange on belly. ♀: *gray nape*; buffy gray below. Both sexes of NE subsp. have *chestnut* foreheads. TAWNY-CAPPED *E. anneae* NW: ♂ from ♂ of 2 by rufous crown. PURPLE-THROATED *E. chlorotica* E: ♂ nearly identical to ♂ of 2 but brighter, more lemon yellow. ♀ resembles ♀ of 1. Cf. 4.

**3. Velvet-fronted** *E. concinna* p 603 Map 1277
Magdalena Val. ♂ from ♂ of 2 by *narrow black forehead* and smaller yellow cap *confined to forecrown*. ♀ nearest 2.

**4. Trinidad** *E. trinitatis* p 603 Map 1279
N (Carib). ♂ smaller; lighter yellow than ♂ of 2 (range overlap unlikely).

**5. White-vented** *E. minuta* p 603 Map 1276
NW, SE. *White* abdomen and crissum (both sexes).

**6. Blue-hooded** *E. musica* p 601 Map 1273
Andes. *Blue crown and nape.* ♂: yellow rump. ♀: narrow rufous frontlet.

**7. Orange-crowned** *E. saturata* p 603 Map 1278
W Andes. ♂: *entire crown* and lower underparts burnt orange. ♀ much like ♀ of 1.

**8. Rufous-bellied** *E. rufiventris* p 605 Map 1283
SE. ♂: lower underparts *deep rufous; no yellow* on crown. ♀: partial breast band; *tawny rufous* crissum. PLUMBEOUS *E. plumbea* E: ♂ like ♂ of 8 but steel gray above; underparts yellow.

**9. Fulvous-vented** *E. fulvicrissa* p 605 Map 1282
NW. *Tawny crissum* in both sexes.

**10. Golden-bellied** *E. chrysopasta* p 605 Map 1285
SE. Olive upperparts tinged gray blue; *whitish loral spot* (both sexes).

**11. Bronze-green** *E. mesochrysa* p 605 Map 1284
E Andes (scarce). *Bronzy green; yellow* forehead; deep orange yellow (gray, ♀) abdomen.

**Tanagers** *Hemithraupis* Thin pointed bill.

**12. Guira** *H. guira* p 633 Map 1371
W (spotty). ♂: *black face outlined yellow*; orange rufous chest and rump. ♀: yellowish eyestripe, eyering, and rump.

**13. Yellow-backed** *H. flavicollis* p 634 Map 1372
NW, SE. ♂: yellow throat and rump; white underparts. ♀ like ♀ of 12 but lacks eyestripe; eyering whitish. N subsp. Pl.52.

**14. Hooded Tanager** p 633 Map 1370
*Nemosia pileata*
N, SE. *Yellow eyes and legs* (both sexes); *mantle gray blue*; white loral line. ♂: *black cap.*

**15. Fulvous-headed Tanager** p 635 Map 1374
*Thlypopsis fulviceps*
NE. ♂: head and throat *rufous chestnut*. ♀: throat buffy white. ORANGE-HEADED *T. sordida* SE: *head orange rufous*, contrasting dark gray upperparts, light gray underparts.

**Bush-Tanagers** *Chlorospingus*

**16. Common** *C. ophthalmicus* p 636 Map 1378
Andes. Notably var. NE subsp. *head dusky*, prom. *white postocular spot*; spotted throat. See other subspp., Pl.54.

**17. Ash-throated** *C. c. canigularis* p 637 Map 1383
Andes. Crown *usually grayer* than 16; breast band; unspotted throat; no white postocular spot (see Pl.54).

**18. Gray-hooded Bush-Tanager** p 638 Map 1386
*Cnemoscopus rubrirostris*
Andes. *Gray hood, pink* bill. Wags tail downward.

**19. Rufous-chested Tanager** p 635 Map 1376
*Thlypopsis ornata*
C Andes. *Head and underparts orange rufous*; belly white.

**Hemispingus** *Hemispingus.*

**20. Oleaginous** *H. frontalis* p 639 Map 1389
Andes. *Dingy yellow olive; obscure yellowish* eyestripe.

**21. Superciliaried** *H. superciliaris* p 639 Map 1388
E, C Andes. *White eyestripe*; blackish cheeks; bright yellow below.

**22. Black-capped** *H. atropileus* p 638 Map 1387
Andes. Black head; *white eyebrows* reach nape; ochraceous yellow throat and breast. (Note: plumage not quite as green as shown.)

**23. Black-eared** *H. melanotis* p 639 Map 1390
Andes. *Gray above, cinnamon buff* below; *black cheeks.*

**24. Black-headed** *H. verticalis* p 640 Map 1391
Andes. Small; grayish. Black head with pale ashy brown crown stripe.

**25. Fawn-breasted Tanager** p 606 Map 1287
*Pipraeidea melanonota*
Andes. *Bright blue crown*, black mask, creamy buff below. ♀ duller.

**26. Rufous-crested Tanager** p 632 Map 1366
*Creurgops verticalis*
Andes. Dull blue gray above; rufous below. ♂: rufous crest.

**27. Plush-capped Finch** p 641 Map 1395
*Catamblyrhynchus diadema*
Mts. Plushy *golden yellow* crown; *chestnut* underparts. Short, thick bill. Bamboo.

# PLATE 54 BUSH-TANAGERS, BRUSH-FINCHES, etc,

## 53

**Bush-Tanagers** *Chlorospingus*

**1a. Common** . Andes p 636 Map 1378
*C. ophthalmicus nigriceps*
1b *C. o. flavopectus*. E Andes
1a: notably var. Dusky head, yellowish white eyes;
speckled throat; broad breast band. Some subspp. in
NE have prom. postocular spot (Pl.53). 1b: much like
2 (ranges overlap). Note yellowish eyes, *dusky cheeks*.

**2. Ash-throated** *C. canigularis* p 637 Map 1383
Andes. *Gray* head, *dark* eyes, yellowish chest band
(Pl.53).

**3. Short-billed** *C. parvirostris* p 637 Map 1382
Andes. *Mustard yellow* of throat *confined to sides*;
darker gray chest than 4. Mainly higher el. than 4.

**4. Yellow-throated** *C. f. flavigularis* p 637 Map 1381
Andes. *Solid yellow* throat; *pale gray* lores; chest lighter
than 3.

**Brush-Finches** *Atlapetes*

**5. Dusky-headed** *A. fuscoolivaceus* p 650 Map 1419
Upper Magdalena Val. Sooty head, dark upperparts,
*narrow dark malar*. OLIVE-HEADED *A. flaviceps* Magdalena Val. (rare): like 5, but *head yellowish olive*; no malar line.

**6. Yellow-throated** *A. gutturalis* p 648 Map 1414
Andes. Black head, *white coronal stripe; yellow throat*.

**7. Santa Marta** *A. melanocephalus* p 649 Map 1417
Santa Marta Mts. Black head; *silvery gray* cheek patch.

**8. Tricolored** *A. tricolor* p 650 Map 1418
Pacific. *Dark. Brownish gold* crown stripe; yellow underparts.

**9. Rufous-naped** *A. rufinucha* p 649 Map 1416
Andes. Smaller. Crown and nape *rufous; entire* underparts yellow. *White wing spot* (some subsp.). Chin and
forehead black in NE.

**10. Moustached** *A. albofrenatus* p 650 Map 1421
E Andes. Rufous crown; *olive* upperparts; *white* throat
(see Pl.55).

**11. Pale-naped** *A. pallidinucha* p 649 Map 1415
E, C Andes. Rather like several allies but occurs at
higher el. *Bicolored* cinnamon orange crown stripe
fades to white behind. Brighter NE subsp., Pl.55.

**12. White-rimmed** *A. leucopis* p 651 Map 1422
C Andes (s end). *Very dark;* chestnut cap; *white around
eyes*.

**13. Olive Finch** p 648 Map 1412
*Lysurus castaneiceps*
Pacific; E Andes. Chestnut crown; *gray* face. Dark like
12.

**14. Slaty Brush-Finch** p 651 Map 1424
*Atlapetes s. schistaceus*
Andes. Chestnut crown; *white throat and wing spot*;
narrow malar stripe. Blacker NE subsp. without white
wing spot but with *brighter rufous* crown (Pl.55).

**15. Tanager-Finch** p 648 Map 1413
*Oreothraupis arremonops*
Pacific. Striped head; *bright ferruginous* underparts.
On or near ground.

**16. Black-backed Bush-Tanager** p 638 Map 1385
*Urothraupis stolzmanni*
C Andes. *Mainly black; white throat,* mottled breast.
Cf. larger 14.

**17. Stripe-headed Brush-Finch** p 652 Map 1426
*Atlapetes torquatus assimilis*
Mts. *Gray and black striped head; white* underparts.
NE subsp. with *black chest band*, Pl.55.

**18. Black-headed Brush-Finch** p 652 Map 1427
*Atlapetes a. atricapillus*
Andes (local). *Head to below eyes black* (some indi-
viduals with small white markings on head).

TUDOR

PLATE 55 LARGER FINCHES

**1. Red-capped Cardinal** p 647 Map 1410
*Paroaria gularis*
E. Red head (buff, imm.). Near water.

**2. Vermilion Cardinal** p 646 Map 1407
*Cardinalis phoeniceus*
Guajira. Long red crest in both sexes.

**3. Slaty Grosbeak** *Pitylus grossus* p 645 Map 1404
W, SE. Slaty; *large red bill.*

**4. Black-winged Saltator** p 644 Map 1400
*Saltator atripennis*
Andes. *Black hood;* white eyebrow and ear spots; black wings.

**5. Yellow Grosbeak** p 647 Map 1409
*Pheucticus chrysopeplus*
Mts. ♂: golden yellow head and underparts in all subspp.; back var. (see text). ♀ duller; upperparts streaked blackish.

**6. Black-backed Grosbeak** p 646 Map 1408
*Pheucticus aureoventris*
6a *P. a. crissalis*
♂: black hood and back. ♀: pattern of ♂ faintly indicated; brownish, mottled. 6a: S subsp., *yellow rump;* more yellow below; ♀ has yellow eyebrow. For ROSE-BREASTED *P. ludovicianus* N migrant, see text.

**7. Yellow-green Grosbeak** p 645 Map 1405
*Caryothraustes canadensis*
E. Yellow olive; small mask. YELLOW-SHOULDERED *C.humeralis* SE: gray crown and underparts; black stripe through eyes; scaly throat.

**Saltators** *Saltator*

**8. Streaked** *S. albicollis* p 645 Map 1403
W. *Bright olive green* above; *streaked* below.

**9. Grayish** *S. coerulescens* p 644 Map 1401
N, E. Obviously *gray* above (all subspp.); short eyebrow

**10. Buff-throated** *S. maximus* p 643 Map 1399
*Bright olive green* above; head grayish; *unstreaked* below, *black border on buff* lower throat.

**11. Orinocan** *S. orenocensis* p 644 Map 1402
NE. Head, *broad sideburns* black; long eyebrow; *cinnamon buff* below.

**12. Orange-billed Sparrow** p 653 Map 1430
*Arremon aurantiirostris*
W, SE. *Bright orange bill;* striped head.

**13. Rufous-collared Sparrow** p 668 Map 1469
*Zonotrichia capensis*
Mts. Common. Striped head, pert crest, rusty nape. Juv. *very fine* streaking.

**Sparrows** *Arremonops*

**14. Black-striped** *A. conirostris* p 653 Map 1428
W. Gray and olive; *black head stripes.*

**15. Tocuyo** *A. tocuyensis* p 653 Map 1429
Guajira. Smaller than 14; head stripes *whitish clay.*

**16. Pectoral Sparrow** p 654 Map 1432
*Arremon taciturnus*
16a *A. t. taciturnus*
E. *Boldly striped head;* partial black chest band; *yellow shoulders.* 16a: (Orinoco) chest band complete, bill all black; ♀♀ all subspp. duller, buffy below.

**17. Golden-winged Sparrow** p 654 Map 1431
*Arremon schlegeli*
N. *Orange yellow bill; black hood, yellow* shoulders.

**Brush-Finches** *Atlapetes*

**18. Pale-naped** *A. p. pallidinucha* p 649 Map 1415
E, C Andes (E subsp. shown). Darker form on Pl.54. Note bicolored crown stripe.

**19. Moustached** *A. albofrenatus.* p 650 Map 1421
E Andes. Rufous crown, *olive* upperparts; *white* throat (Venez. subsp. shown—see Pl.54 for Colombian subsp. with white throat and narrow black forehead).

**20. Slaty** *A. schistaceus* p 651 Map 1424
Andes. *Rufous* crown; *white* throat; *narrow* malar stripe. Subsp. shown occurs in Perijá Mts. and n end E Andes. More widespread subspp. (paler; chestnut crown; wing spot), Pl.54.

**21. Chestnut-capped** p 652 Map 1425
*A. brunneinucha*
Mts. (not Santa Marta). Dark olive back; black forehead, *puffy white* throat, *black* chest band.

**22. Stripe-headed** *A. torquatus* p 652 Map 1426
Mts. Underparts like 21 (but Andean subsp., Pl.54, lacks chest band); *gray and black head stripes.*

**23. Ochre-breasted** *A. semirufus* p 651 Map 1423
E Andes. Head and underparts *rich orange rufous.*

**24. Black-faced Tanager** p 641 Map 1394
*Schistochlamys melanopis*
E; (local in W). Ad.: gray; *black foreface and throat.* Imm. olive green. Not a finch.

**Grosbeaks** *Cyanocompsa*

**25. Blue-black** *C. cyanoides* p 642 Map 1397
♂: culmen straight; blue areas in E subsp. very bright (except rump). ♀ deep brown *above and below.*

**26. Ultramarine** *C. brissonii* p 643 Map 1398
W. Much like respective sexes of 25. Bill more swollen. ♂: rump much brighter. ♀ sandy brown obviously paler below. Nonforest sp. BLUE *Guiraca caerulea* N migrant: bright rusty wing bars (both sexes). For INDIGO BUNTING *Passerina cyanea* N migrant, see text.

PLATE 56 FINCHES

## 55

**Seed-Finches** *Oryzoborus* Thick bill; culmen straight.

**1. Large-billed** *O. crassirostris* p 658 Map 1443
W, NE. ♂: thick white bill; white wing spot (usually). ♀: bill dusky (thicker than 2). GREAT-BILLED *O. maximiliani* SW, SE (scarce): ♂ has massive white bill (black, SE); larger than 1; ♀ has dusky bill (all subspp.).

**2. Lesser** *O. angolensis* p 658 Map 1442
White wing linings. ♂ black (W); dark brown belly (Magdalena Val.); chestnut belly (E). ♀ cinnamon brown below. BLUE SEEDEATER *Amaurospiza concolor* SW: ♂ indigo blue, blackish foreface; ♀ *bright* cinnamon brown

**3. Blue-back Grassquit** p 664 Map 1458
*Volatinia jacarina*
♂ small; glossy. ♀ only very small finch *streaked below* (but see under 12).

**Grassquits** *Tiaris* Resemble *Sporophila* but bill thinner, more pointed and conical. ♀♀ dingy olive (see text).

**4. Yellow-faced** *T. olivacea* p 655 Map 1435
Mts. ♂: blackish foreparts; *yellow face pattern*. ♀ and imm. olive; faint face pattern.

**5. Black-faced** *T. bicolor* p 655 Map 1434
N. ♂ has back face and underparts.

**6. Sooty** *T. fuliginosa* p 654 Map 1433
W. ♂ sooty black; belly grayish brown.

**7. White-naped Seedeater** p 657 Map 1440
*Dolospingus fringilloides*
E. Larger than *Sporophila*. ♂: large conical pale bill; *single broad wing band*. ♀ brown, whitish lower belly (cf. ♀ of 2).

**Seedeaters** *Sporophila* Bill very thick, short; *culmen curved*; ♂♂ usually distinctive, ♀♀ *very sim.*, usually dull brownish above, paler below, yellowish or whitish on belly. Young ♂♂ resemble ♀♀, gradually assume ad. ♂ plumage.

**8. Lined** *S. lineola* p 661 Map 1449
E. ♂: rump, malar patch, *coronal line white*. VARIABLE *S. americana* Pacific, SE: ♂ black and white (see text); SE subsp. has *white wing bars*. DOUBLE-COLLARED *S. caerulescens* SE: ♂ brownish gray above, white below; black *chin and chest band*.

**9. Lesson's** *S. bouvronides* p 662 Map 1450
E. ♂ like 8 but *no coronal stripe*.

**10. Black-and-white** *S. luctuosa* p 662 Map 1451
Mts. ♂: hood and upperparts black; *wing spot; white* belly.

**11. Yellow-bellied** *S. nigricollis* p 662 Map 1452
♂ black on head and chest, back olive (cf. 10); abdomen yellowish (usually).

**12. Ruddy-breasted** *S. minuta* p 663 Map 1455
W, NE. ♂ brownish gray; rump and underparts rufous. TUMACO *S. insulata* SW: like 12, but ♂ with white in wings and tail base (rump not rufous). CHESTNUT-THROATED *S. telasco* SW: ♂ paler than 12; chestnut upper throat; *white wing patch* and underparts; narrow white rump band (not rufous).

**13. Gray** *S. intermedia* p 659 Map 1446
W, NE. *Much paler*, less contrasty than 14; no white on neck. W race nearer 14 but *never show wing bar*.

**14. Slate-colored** *S. schistacea* p 659 Map 1445
W, NE. ♂ *slate* gray; white neck spot; *wing bar* (sometimes); *contrasting belly*, but see W races of 13.

**15. Plumbeous** *S. plumbea* p 660 Map 1447
E. Recalls 14. Bill *blackish*, white below eyes.

**16. Dull-colored Grassquit** p 655 Map 1436
*Tiaris obscura*
W. Ad. ♂ like ♀. Pointed *bicolored* bill. Flocks.

**17. Chestnut-bellied** p 664 Map 1456
*Sporophila castaneiventris*
SE. ♂ *bright blue gray*; *chestnut* median underparts.

**Seedeaters** *Catamenia* Upper el.; culmen curved, bill pale and stubby, tail proportionally longer than *Sporophila*; crissum usually chestnut.

**18. Paramo** *C. homochroa* p 656 Map 1437
Yellow (or pinkish?) bill. ♂ *slaty*; blackish foreface. ♀ dark brown, streaked above (and below imm.).

**19. Plain-colored** *C. inornata* p 656 Map 1438
E, C Andes. Brownish pink bill. ♂ much *lighter gray* than 18; back more distinctly streaked. ♀ paler, buffier than 18, *streaking* more prom. BAND-TAILED *C. analis*: gray, chestnut under tail coverts; *white band across tail* from below; ♀ brown, streaked above and below; tail like ♂ but less conspic. Mts. (see text ill.).

**20. Plumbeous Sierra-Finch** p 666 Map 1464
*Phrygilus unicolor*
Paramo. Conical *black* bill. ♂ lead gray. ♀ *coarsely streaked* all over.

**21. Slaty Finch** *Haplospiza rustica* p 666 Map 1463
Mt. forest. ♂ slaty gray (darker than 20). ♀ dark brown, *obscurely* streaked below. Thin sharp-pointed bill.

**22. Pileated Finch** p 647 Map 1411
*Coryphospingus pileatus*
N. Gray; white eyering. ♂ black crown conceals *scarlet* crest. ♀: *white lores*.

**23. Wedge-tailed Grass-Finch** p 667 Map 1465
*Emberizoides herbicola*
Long tail (recalls *Synallaxis*); white eyering.

**Sparrows** *Ammodramus* Nondescript. Ad. streaked above, plain below; juvs. faintly streaked below. Open country, mostly solitary.

**24. Grassland** *A. humeralis* p 668 Map 1468
*Yellow* lores; *white eyering*, crisp black streaking. GRASS-HOPPER *A. savannarum* Cauca Val.: like 24, but *buff coronal stripe*; buff below.

**25. Yellow-browed** *A. aurifrons* p 667 Map 1467
E. *Yellow eyebrow and eyering*; duller streaks than 24.

**26. Dickcissel** *Spiza americana* p 642 Map 1396
N migrant. *Rusty* shoulders, streaked back, *yellow* eyestripe and chest. Breeding plumage (see text).

**27. Saffron Finch** *Sicalis flaveola* p 665 Map 1461
27a Imm.
N, E. ♂ yellow; *orange crown*; ♀ duller, juv. *streaked below*. Imm. *yellow collar* and crissim.

**Yellow-Finches** *Sicalis* Mainly yellow; some yellow on underparts; thick stubby bill; open country; social.

**28. Orange-fronted** *S. columbiana* p 666 Map 1462
E. Smaller than 27. ♂: orange *forecrown*. ♀ streaked above but *unstreaked below*.

*Continued*

## 56

**29. Stripe-tailed** *S. citrina* p 665 Map 1460
Mts. ♂: Crown, sides of head *uniform*, but forecrown brighter; white undertail spots. ♀: streaked breast; tail spots smaller.

**30. Grassland** *S. luteola* p 665 Map 1459
W. ♂: lores and ocular area bright yellow; crown finely streaked. ♀ *unstreaked below* (cf. 29).

**31. Lesser Goldfinch** *Spinus psaltria* p 670 Map 1474
W. *White* wing band, *no yellow* on crown (both sexes).

**Siskins** *Spinus* Small, arboreal; yellow or red patch on black wing. Duller ♀♀ often have pattern of ♂♂ faintly indicated. Sometimes put in genus *Carduelis*.

**32. Yellow-bellied** *S. xanthogaster* p 670 Map 1473
Andes. ♂: black hood and upperparts. ♀ much duller.

**33. Andean** *S. spinescens* p 669 Map 1470
Andes. ♂: black cap. ♀: *whitish* vent and crissum.

**34. Hooded** *S. magellanicus* p 669 Map 1472
C. Andes. ♂ has black head and throat. For ♀, see text.

**35. Red** *S. cucullatus* p 669 Map 1471
NE. ♀ has salmon red blush on flanks (cf. *Pyrocephalus*).

## 6. CRESTED OROPENDOLA

*Psarocolius decumanus*      Pl. 44, Map 1188
**Identification:** ♂ 17″ (43cm); ♀ 13″ (33cm).
*Large white bill.* Eyes bluish. *Glossy black;* rump
and crissum dark chestnut; crest of narrow
hairlike black feathers often inconspic.; central tail feathers black, rest bright yellow.
**Similar species:** *Only* large all black oropendola with a *white* bill. In the nw see much smaller
Chestnut-headed Oropendola (5).
**Voice:** At Leticia ♂ ♂ fall forward as sing a loud
rapid *st-st-e-e-E-E-E-E'WOO! chif, chif, chif, chif;*
peculiar 1st ser. like a rusty hinge, the last 4
wing rustling as regain balance; call a low *choke*.
**Behavior:** More solitary than other *Psarocolius*
oropendolas but individuals or small groups
are often with large mixed cacique and oropendola flocks. Usually in upper strata or canopy, peering about.
**Breeding:** Building nest, 25 Jan, Leticia (Hilty);
25 Feb, Macarena Mts. (Olivares 1962); and
mid-Apr in Santander (Boggs 1961). Frequently nest near other oropendolas though
apparently in separate trees and usually in
smaller colonies. Trinidad 1-2 pale green or
gray eggs with blackish spots or lines (Tashian
1957). Each colony has a dominant ♂ surrounded by subordinates holding territories
in nearby trees; mating promiscuous (Drury
1962).
**Status and habitat:** Locally fairly common in
humid forest, forest borders, and partially
cleared areas in the lowlands and foothills.
Now virtually exterminated in Cauca Val., mid.
and upper Magdalena Val., and the Santa
Marta area.
**Range:** To 2600m (usually below 1000). Formerly throughout except Pacific coast, where
only in lower Atrato Val. s to Río Salaquí near
Panama border. Recs. are spotty e of E Andes.
W Panama to n Argentina and se Brazil. Trinidad.

## 7. GREEN OROPENDOLA

*Psarocolius viridis*      Pl. 45, Map 1189
**Identification :** ♂ 17″ (43cm); ♀ 14.5″ (37cm).
Prom. frontal shield and bill pale yellowish,
bill tipped reddish orange. Eyes pale blue. Pale
olive green; rump and lower underparts
chestnut; flight feathers dusky; central tail
feathers black, rest yellow; inconspic. crest of
hairlike feathers on hindcrown.
**Similar species:** Olive Oropendola (11) is confusingly sim. but much more yellowish, has
prom. bare pink cheeks, and a black bill with
red tip. Also see Russet-backed Oropendola
(8).
**Voice:** In Venez. displaying ♂ ♂ squeal a rapid,

liquid *E-E-E-e-e-e D'D'CLOCK, agoogoo,* the
1st a spring stretching, then dull sticks, last
mellow hoots; call *chuwert,* or *chut-ut,* scratchy
*queea* and other notes (P. Schwartz recording).
**Behavior:** As in other oropendolas. Gregarious
and usually fairly high in canopy and forest
edges, peering in foliage.
**Breeding:** Sim. to Crested Oropendola. Feeding at colony Mar–Apr, ne Meta (S. Furniss);
eggs white with reddish and purplish lines and
spots (Haverschmidt 1968).
**Status and habitat:** Sandy-belt forest and gallery forest of Orinoco and Negro region; near
Leticia mainly *várzea* forest and river edges
along south bank tributaries of the Amazon.
Apparently nowhere very numerous in Colombia. Sometimes with Olive Oropendola.
**Range:** To 300m. E Vichada (El Tuparro—
INDERENA) s to Vaupés (lower Río Apaporis) and w to Meta (Carimagua—S. Furniss);
sight recs. in Macarena Mts. (Aug 1975, and
Oct 1976—T. O. Lemke). Prob. s to Amazonas. The Guianas and s Venez. to e Ecuador, ne Peru, and n Brazil.

## 8. RUSSET-BACKED OROPENDOLA

*Psarocolius angustifrons*      Pl. 45, Map 1190
**Identification:** 18.5″ (47cm); ♀ 14″ (36cm). *Bill
yellowish* (or *black—angustifrons*); no frontal
shield; eyes light blue. *Forehead yellow* (or forehead and *eyebrow yellow—sincipitalis*); head and
upper back olivaceous deepening to chestnut
on back and rump; underparts olivaceous to
chestnut; wings dusky; central and outer pair
of tail feathers dusky, rest bright yellow. Or
entirely dull olivaceoeus brown, head (incl.
forehead) and throat olive, central pair of tail
feathers dusky, rest bright yellow tipped olive
(*angustifrons*).
**Similar species:** E of Andes the only large dingy
oropendola with a black bill; west of Andes
from Chestnut-headed Oropendola (5) by
larger size, (esp. ♂) and yellow forehead (or
yellow forehead and eyebrow). Crested Oropendola (6) is all black with a chalky white bill.
Also see (9).
**Voice:** ♂'s song w of Andes in Anchicayá Val.
a liquid *Whoop-KE-chot!;* e of Andes at Leticia
a very different *wooEEL-tii-oop!;* but in both
like water dropping into a pool and given as
♂ falls forward raising wings and crest; low
*chuweep,* and *chuck* and other calls.
**Behavior:** Widespread and esp. numerous in
Amazonia. Often roost in immense flocks on
Amazonian river isls., groups streaming in from
afar at dusk. Fly with steady, rowing, crowlike
(*Corvus*) wing beats. Peer in folige in mid. or

upper strata of trees and loosely gregarious at all times.

**Breeding:** Colonial, usually groups of 5-10 nests, mating promiscuous; some colonies with a few Yellow-rumped Cacique nests. Like other oropendola and cacique colonies, the large conspic. nests are usually located in an isolated or partly isolated tree where they form a familiar sight to travelers. In Amazonia may breed much of year; 5 Leticia colonies, late Oct–late Apr; 2 colonies, early Sept–late Feb, Pto. Asís. Ad. fed juv., 29 June, W Andes above Cali (S. Gniadek); Apr colony, upper Anchicayá Val. Eggs from Antioquia, pale pinkish lightly spotted and blotched reddish brown, mostly at larger end (Sclater and Salvin 1879).

**Status and habitat:** Local on Pacific slope in humid and wet forest borders and in clearings with scattered trees in foothills and lower mts. Common in Amazonia in second growth and *Cecropia* trees along rivers, in *várzea* forest edges, and on swampy river isls. Apparently largely replaced in *terra firme* forest in Amazonia by Green and Olive oropendolas.

**Range:** Mostly 400-2400m w of Andes; also lowlands e of Andes. W and C Andes s to Nariño (*salmoni*); w slope of E Andes from Santander s to head of Magdalena Val. (*sincipitalis*); Perijá Mts. and e slope E Andes from Cundinamarca to Caquetá (*neglectus*); e of Andes from Meta and Vaupés to Amazonas (*angustifrons*). N and w Venez. s to e and w Ecuador, n Bolivia, and w Amazonian Brazil.

**Note:** Songs, plumages, and soft part colors of birds e and w of Andes differ and more than 1 sp. prob. involved.

## 9. BLACK OROPENDOLA

*Gymnostinops guatimozinus*    Pl. 44, Map 1191
**Identification:** ♂ 19″ (48cm); ♀ 16″ (41cm). *Bare cheek patch bluish and pink; bill black tipped yellow,* frontal shield black; eyes brown. Mainly black; shoulders, lower back, rump, and under tail coverts dark chestnut; tail yellow with central pair of feathers black; narrow filiform black crest.

**Similar species:** Much like Chestnut-mantled Oropendola (10). No other oropendolas in the nw have conspic. bare cheeks and bicolored black and yellow bill.

**Voice:** Song of ♂ a loud resonant *skol-l-l-l-l-wool!* rather like others of the genus; low *cruk* call.

**Behavior:** Pairs, 3's, or small to large flocks stream out long distances from colonies. Peer and clamber about in upper forest levels like other oropendolas.

**Breeding:** 3 BC ♂♂, Apr, s Córdoba (Carriker). Large active colony, late June, upper Río

Verde de Sinú (Hilty), eggs pale pinkish white sparsely spotted with large red brown spots (Sclater and Salvin 1879).

**Status and habitat:** Humid forest and forest edge, common in Río Verde del Sinú, sw Córdoba; prob. not as numerous e in less humid forest.

**Range:** To 800m. N Chocó s along Panama border to Río Salaquí, upper Río Sucio, and e along n base of W and C Andes to mid. Magdalena Val. (Remedios, Antioquia), and s (at least formerly) to n Caldas (sight—A. Dugand). E Panama and nw Colombia.

**Note:** *Gymnostinops* is sometimes considered congeneric with *Psarocolius.*

## 10. CHESTNUT-MANTLED OROPENDOLA

*Gymnostinops cassini*    Map 1192
**Identification:** ♂ 18″ (46cm); ♀ 16″ (41cm). Sim. to Black Oropendola, but *most of back, entire closed wing, and flanks bright chestnut*; bill longer and wider than Black Oropendola. In the hand bare pink patch at base of bill is smaller and narrow white line shows at base of bill.

**Similar species:** See under Black Oropendola (9).

**Status and habitat:** Uncertain. Known from 3 specimens in the humid lowlands of n Chocó. May hybridize with *G. guatimozinus;* an intermed. specimen is known from the Río Salaquí on the border between the 2 spp.'s ranges (see Haffer 1975).

**Range:** ENDEMIC. N Chocó where known only from Río Truandó near Panama boundary and upper Río Baudó-Atrato watershed divide.

**Note:** Meyer de Schauensee (1966) suggested that *G. guatimozinus, G. cassini* and poss. *G. montezuma* (Montezuma Oropendola of e Mexico to c Panama) as well as *G. bifasciatus* (Para Oropendola of lower Amazonian Brazil) should be regarded conspecific under the name *G. bifasciatus.*

## 11. OLIVE OROPENDOLA

*Gymnostinops yuracares*    Pl. 45, Map 1193
**Identification:** ♂ 20″ (51cm); ♀ 16″ (41cm). *Conspic. bare pink cheek patch; bill black tipped red;* bill expanded onto forehead as frontal shield. Eyes yellowish brown. *Body distinctly bicolored,* front half bright yellow olive, rear portion incl. wings bright chestnut; central tail feathers olive, rest bright yellow.

**Similar species:** Often confused with Green Oropendola (see 7). Russet-backed Oropendola (8) in Amazonia is uniformly dingy olive, lacks the prom. bicolored body and has black bill and bare cheek patches.

**Voice:** In Peru and Colombia liquid gurgling song *stek-ek-ek-ek-ek-eh-o'o'gloop!* resembles that of Crested Oropendola; nasal *raap* and *whrup* calls (M. Koepcke recording).

**Behavior:** Sim. to Green Oropendola and often with it.

**Status and habitat:** Common in humid *terra firme* forest (usually not *várzea*) and clearings with scattered trees. Broadly sympatric with slightly smaller Green Oropendola and apparently replaced in *várzea* and esp. river edge habitats by Russet-backed Oropendola in Amazonia.

**Range:** To 500m. E of Andes from w Meta (sight, e of San Martín, Mar 1960—Brown), Macarena Mts. and Vaupés southward; sight recs. to ne Guainía at Pto. Inírida, Sept 1978—Hilty and M. Robbins. The Guianas (common), s Venez. and e Ecuador (rare) s to n Bolivia; Amazonian Brazil.

## 12. YELLOW-RUMPED CACIQUE

*Cacicus cela*      Pls. 44, 45, Map 1194

**Identification:** ♂ 11″ (28cm); ♀ 9.5″ (24cm). Bill pale greenish white. Eyes bluish white. Mainly *black with yellow patch on inner wing; lower back, rump, base of tail* and *under tail coverts yellow*. Or yellow patch on inner wing coverts and base of tail considerably larger (*cela*).

**Similar species:** See Band-tailed Oropendola (4). All oropendolas have yellow only on tail (not on wings, rump, and under tail coverts). Mountain Cacique (15), a mt. bird, differs in having tail all black and rounded (not square) and black vent.

**Voice:** Flight call a loud liquid *schweeooo* (J. V. Remsen); a downscale *skeek, weer, wrup*, or just last 2 notes and other harsh to melodious calls as forages; birds e of Andes are excellent mimics, but birds w of Andes not known to mimic (Santa Marta birds?).

**Behavior:** Sim. to oropendolas and often with them though generally more active and bolder. Forages at almost any ht., reg. descending quite low at forest edges and in second growth.

**Breeding:** Nests colonially with oropendolas, or more frequently in separate smaller colonies nearby, mostly in isolated trees in clearing or occas. forest edge. Nests shorter than oropendola nests, more oblong in shape, and placed much closer together, very often touching; often near wasp nests. 9 BC birds, Jan–June, n Colombia (Carriker); 3 colonies, late Oct–early Mar, and dependent fledgling, 26 Jan, near Leticia. In Orinoco area, colonies of 6-75 nests, Apr–June (Cherrie 1916). Two bluish white eggs spotted chestnut and brown.

**Status and habitat:** Humid lowlands in almost all kinds of wooded or partially wooded habitats, occas. even in towns and settled areas. Common in Amazonia, esp. in *várzea* and swampy situations, somewhat less numerous at borders or inside *terra firme* forest.

**Range:** To 600m. From n Chocó to w and se base of Santa Marta Mts. and s in Magdalena Val. to Espinal, Tolima (*vitellinus*); n base of Santa Marta Mts., w Guajira, and e of Andes throughout (*cela*). W Panama to n Bolivia and Amazonian Brazil.

**Note:** Vocal differences between e *cela* and w *vitellinus* suggest 2 spp. may be involved.

## 13. RED-RUMPED CACIQUE

*Cacicus haemorrhous*      Pl. 45, Map 1195

**Identification:** ♂ 10″ (25cm); ♀ 8″ (20cm). Bill pale yellowish white; eyes bluish white. *Glossy black; lower back and rump scarlet*; tail square.

**Similar species:** Sim. to Solitary Black and Yellow-billed caciques (16, 17), but lower back and rump red (often hidden).

**Voice:** Flight call a reedy *shoewip*; when foraging a var. of odd notes, whistles, and a guttural *quack*.

**Behavior:** Gregarious around breeding colonies and often also away from them. Frequently with mixed spp. flocks in mid. to upper levels inside forest or at forest edges.

**Breeding:** Unlike Yellow-rumped Cacique, uses mainly trees at forest edge; 2 Surinam colonies of about 20 and 30 nests, early Mar, both in isolated trees at forest edge; only ♀ builds (Brown); 2 white eggs with reddish and purplish dots and blotches (Haverschmidt 1968).

**Status and habitat:** Uncommon to very uncommon (much more numerous e in the Guianas). Humid forest and forest borders, rarely *várzea* forest. Widely sympatric in Amazonian forests with Yellow-rumped Cacique from which it separates most conspic. by habitat. Both are replaced in *várzea* understory and dense growth near water by the Solitary Black Cacique.

**Range:** To 500m. E of Andes from s Meta (Macarena Mts.) and Vaupés (Mitú) southward. The Guianas, s Venez., and e Ecuador s to n Bolivia, ne Argentina, Paraguay, and s Brazil.

## 14. SCARLET-RUMPED CACIQUE

*Cacicus uropygialis*      Pl. 44, Map 1196

**Identification:** ♂ 11.5″ (29cm); ♀ 10″ (25cm). Bill greenish white; eyes bluish white. Slightly crested. *Deep black; rump scarlet*; tail slightly rounded. Or smaller (♂ 10″, or 25 cm; ♀ 8.5″, or 22cm) and rump orangish red (*pacificus*).

**Similar species:** Only cacique with a red rump w of the Andes (rump often concealed except in flight). Replaced e of Andes by allied *C. haemorrhous*, which has bluish glossed plumage, square tail, and red extending to lower back.

**Voice:** Most common call (*pacificus*) of large vocabulary, a nasal *kuok*, in flight or perched. Calls of more montane *uropygialis* unknown.

**Behavior:** One to several follow mixed flocks or travel independent of them; hop along branches and peer at foliage at almost any ht., most often at midlevels. Call frequently while foraging or in flight.

**Breeding:** Nest alone, occas. 2-3 nests together; 7 BC birds, Jan–May, Chocó to Córdoba (Carriker; Haffer 1975). Mar nest, 1 building nest, 19 Aug, upper Anchicayá Val. (Hilty); 1 active, Mar–May, PN Cueva de los Guácharos (P. Gertler). Nest as in Yellow-rumped Cacique; 2 eggs, white marked with a few brown or blackish spots and scrawls; only ♀ builds (Skutch 1972).

**Status and habitat:** Fairly common (*pacificus*) in humid and wet forest, forest borders, and second growth woodland in lowlands and foothills on Pacific coast. Highland *uropygialis* little known.

**Range:** To 1000m (mainly below 700m) on Pacific coast and n end of W Andes (upper Sinú Val.) to Pto. Valdivia in lower Cauca Val. (*pacificus*); 1500-2300m (once to 1000m) in W Andes s to Valle, C Andes s to Quindío, w slope E Andes in Cundinamarca (at least formerly at Fusagasugá) s to head of Magdalena Val. in s Huila, e slope E Andes in s Norte de Santander and sight (R. Ridgely) in w Putumayo (*uropygialis*). E Panama to w Ecuador, w Venez. and s in Andes to e Ecuador and ne Peru.

**Note:** The smaller *pacificus* subsp. (Pacific Cacique) may be specifically distinct but strict sympatry with *uropygialis* subsp. (of lower highlands) unproved. Both occur at headwaters of Río San Juan, *pacificus* at lower el.

## 15. MOUNTAIN CACIQUE
*Cacicus leucoramphus*          Pl. 45, Map 1197

**Identification:** ♂ 11″ (28cm); ♀ 10″ (25cm). Bill and eyes bluish white. Glossy black; *shoulder patch, lower back, and rump bright yellow*; tail rounded and all black. Juv. birds have blackish bill with pale tip.

**Similar species:** Yellow-rumped Cacique (12) of lower el. has vent and base of tail yellow. They may or may not contact in range.

**Voice:** A var. of calls when foraging, most frequently a nasal, gull-like *key*, and *ca*, both often repeated; also a more jaylike *krek*.

**Behavior:** One or 2 often accompany mixed

flocks, and esp. groups of Hooded Mountain-Tanagers, in mid. to upper strata of forest. Normally noisy and conspic. Apparently breed solitarily.

**Breeding:** 3 BC ♂♂, Feb–July, Andes (Carriker).

**Status and habitat:** Uncommon and somewhat local in humid to wet highland forest, less often at forest edges. Favor tall mt. forest, and usually not in short or stunted forest at very high el. Most easily found in mts. above Mocoa in w Putumayo and e Nariño.

**Range:** 1700-3200m. Spottily (at least now) in all 3 Andean ranges. W Venez. (Táchira) s in Andes to n Bolivia.

## 16. SOLITARY BLACK CACIQUE
*Cacicus solitarius*          Pl. 45, Map 1198

**Identification:** ♂ 11″ (28cm); ♀ 9.5″ (24cm). *Bill pale greenish white; eyes dark* (or pale in some, age, or sex?). *Entirely black*, slightly crested.

**Similar species:** Like Red-rumped Cacique (13), which often has red rump hidden, but habitat different. Also see Ecuadorean Black Cacique (note below).

**Voice:** A large and var. repertoire of bizarre sounds. Most common call a forceful, nasal, and exhaling *WHEEEAH* sim. to 1 call of Black-capped Donacobius; also a squeaky, accordionlike ser. of ascending notes (J. V. Remsen), a loud resounding *Tsonk!* usually repeated several times, a nasal squishing or mocking *naaaaah*, and a strange ser. of "electronic" sounds, apparently the main song.

**Behavior:** Solitary or less often seen in pairs; skulk, mostly low in edges of dense second growth along rivers, sometimes higher in denser vegetation.

**Breeding:** Solitary. Nest, sim. to that of Yellow-rumped Cacique, reportedly about 9m up over stream or pond in Mato Grosso, Brazil; 2 eggs, vinaceous white sparsely dotted and blotched darker (Naumburg 1930).

**Status and habitat:** Uncommon to fairly common in rank second growth and grass along borders of rivers and lakes, also low in swampy river isl. forest and *várzea* borders; much less often well inside second growth woodland where usually in mid. story.

**Range:** To 400m (once to 1400m, Miraflores, Boyacá). Entire e base of E Andes and from s Meta (Macarena Mts.) s to Amazonas. E limits of Colombian range uncertain. W Venez. (s base of Andes) s to ne Argentina, Paraguay, and w Uruguay.

**Note:** Ecuadorian Black Cacique (*Cacicus sclateri*) is unrec. but poss. in s Colombia. Known only from e Ecuador (as close as Limoncocha).

Resembles Solitary Black Cacique but smaller (♂ 8.5″, ♀ 8″), brownish tinge on wings, and eyes pale blue. Well up inside tall second growth woodland. Pairs, not flocks.

## 17. YELLOW-BILLED CACIQUE
*Amblycercus holosericeus*　　Pl. 44, Map 1199
**Identification:** ♂ 10″ (25cm); ♀ 9″ (23cm). Eyes white to light yellow; bill yellowish white (or deep yellow—*flavirostris*). Plumage entirely dull black.
**Similar species:** Scarlet-rumped Cacique (14) has red rump (often hidden) and different habitat. Solitary Black Cacique (16) of Amazonian lowlands should not overlap in range but is very sim., differing in dark eye (always?), and more greenish tinge to pale bill.
**Voice:** Heard far more than seen. ♂ gives ser. of clear whistles, often doubled, *whew-whew, whew-whew . . .*, answered at once by *wheeee, churrrr* from ♀ (Skutch 1954; Willis and Eisenmann 1979); also a var. of liquid whistles and long churrs incl. a loud whistled *pur-wee-pew*, a sweet *wreeeeeoo*, a harsher *queeyoo*, and a ducklike ser. of quacking notes (Ridgely 1976).
**Behavior:** Furtive and difficult to see. Solitary birds or pairs skulk in dense understory or second growth thickets, often near the ground. Sometimes follow mixed flocks; 1 followed army ants in s Mexico.
**Breeding:** BC ♂, June, Perijá Mts. (Carriker); Jan–June, Costa Rica; 2 nests in overgrown cane fields surrounded by low thickets; bulky vine and cane leaf cup 1m up; 1-2 pale blue eggs with a wreath of black spots at larger end (Skutch 1954).
**Status and habitat:** Humid forest borders and second growth with thickets from the lowlands to highlands. In Peru where found only in highlands, confined to *Chusquea* bamboo (T. Parker), perhaps also in sim. habitat in temperate zone of E Andes in Colombia.
**Range:** To 1800m on Pacific slope from nw end W Andes (Río Sucio) to Nariño (*flavirostris*); to 1200m (mainly below 600m) from nw Chocó (Río Juradó) to Sinú Val. and Cartagena (*holosericeus*); 1500-3300m in Santa Marta Mts., Perijá Mts., E Andes in Norte de Santander, w Cundinamarca, and s Huila, C Andes in Caldas and Tolima (*australis*). E Mexico to n Venez.; se Ecuador to n Bolivia.
**Note 1:** Sometimes placed in the genus *Cacicus* but osteological characters of skull differ (A. Rea) as well as voice and behavior. **Note 2:** Scrub Blackbird (*Dives warszewiczi*) of w Peru and w Ecuador is spreading n with deforestation and may soon reach Nariño. ♀″, glossy

blue black, ♀ slightly smaller, and duller. Much like Shiny Cowbird (see 1) but a little larger, bill decidedly longer, tail longer, and with var. melodic song. Opened-up areas.

## 18. CARIB GRACKLE
*Quiscalus lugubris*　　Pl. 44, Map 1200
**Identification:** ♂ 10.5″ (27cm); ♀ 8.5″ (22cm). *Eyes pale yellow* (both sexes), bill black, somewhat slender and decurved; *tail wedge-shaped.* ♂: entirely black with slight purplish gloss. ♀: dark sooty brown, throat paler. Juv.: like ♀ but eyes dark.
**Similar species:** From Shiny Cowbird (1) by pale eyes, grackle bill, and wedge-shaped tail.
**Voice:** As in other grackles has a var. of calls, most common a loud strident *queek, queek, queek, queek*, reminiscent of 1 call of Great-tailed Grackle.
**Behavior:** Gregarious. Scavenges on the ground where walks jauntily, ♂♂ often giving a var. of displays sim. to those of Great-tailed Grackle. Roosts in large noisy flocks in trees, often in parks in towns.
**Breeding:** Colonial or solitary. Colony of 200-300 birds at breeding-roosting site yr.-round, Carimagua, ne Meta; more begging young in Oct (S. Furniss). Coarse open cup of mud, dead leaves, and dry grass low to high above ground; 2-4 greenish white eggs spotted blackish brown (ffrench 1973).
**Status and habitat:** Fairly common in the llanos in drier ranchland, cultivated areas with trees, and in towns, occas. along gallery forest borders. May be spreading with settlement.
**Range:** To 600m. E of Andes s to s Meta. N and c Venez. the Guianas, and ne Brazil. Trinidad; Lesser Antilles.

## 19. GREAT-TAILED GRACKLE
*Quiscalus mexicanus*　　Map 1201
**Identification:** ♂ 18″ (46cm); ♀ 13″ (33cm). *Long stout bill; eyes yellow* (♂), yellowish brown (♀). ♂: glossy purplish black; *tail long and wedge-shaped* forming a trough or keel when spread. ♀: brown above; eyebrow and throat pale buff; rest of underparts buffy brown; tail shorter, less obviously wedge-shaped than in ♂. First-yr. birds like ♀ but eyes dark.
**Similar species:** Flat-headed and long-tailed profile distinctive in either sex. ♂ Giant Cowbird has flat tail, shorter bill, dark eyes, and normally shows neck ruff. Also cf. much smaller Shiny Cowbird (1).
**Voice:** Noisy. Both sexes have a var. of calls, incl. a dull rough *chak*, a sharper ser. of *krit* or *quit* notes given rapidly; ♂ also a shrill quavering *kuueeeeeee*, drawn out.

**Behavior:** Loosely gregarious though also seen alone. Roost and nest colonially in trees but forage mostly on ground, esp. in vicinity of water where they scavenge anything edible. Thrive in coastal towns and settled areas where they generally act bold and aggressive. ♂♂ strut and swagger as walk about, and frequently display, esp. a threat, signaled by stretching tall with bill pointed up.

**Breeding:** Colonies in trees in parks, around human habitations, along rivers, or in bushes, and marshy vegetation; deep cup of mud and coarse vegetation; 2-3 eggs, bright blue to pale blue gray dotted and scrawled black and brown (Skutch 1954).

**Status and habitat:** Common along both coasts in mangroves, estuaries, and semiopen areas with scattered trees; esp. numerous in towns where congregates in parks, waterfronts, and dooryards.

**Range:** Carib. coast and on Pacific coast s to sw Cauca (Guapí) and prob. Nariño. Sw US to nw Peru.

**Note:** Formerly placed in the genus *Cassidix*.

## 20. RED-BELLIED GRACKLE

*Hypopyrrhus pyrohypogaster*    Pl. 45, Map 1202
**Identification:** ♂ 12″ (30cm); ♀ 10.5″ (27cm). *Unmistakable.* Conical and pointed black bill; yellowish white eyes. Black with *bright red belly and under tail coverts*; black thighs. In the hand feathers of entire head, nape, and throat narrow and thickened with shiny shafts.

**Behavior:** Usually in small, active, noisy groups in canopy of trees at forest edge (P. Gertler). Alone when breeding, at other seasons in groups of 6-8 (Sclater and Salvin 1879). Sometimes with mixed flocks, or with oropendolas; hop and clamber about in outer foliage, occas. even clinging upside down.

**Breeding:** Solitary. 9 BC birds, Mar–Aug, n end W and C Andes (Carriker); nestlings, May, se Huila (Lehmann 1961). Cup nest of large dead leaves and sticks loosely placed in fork of small tree; eggs greenish gray spotted and streaked lilac and dark brown (Sclater and Salvin 1879).

**Status and habitat:** Rare and local. Humid forest canopy and borders in foothills and mts. Formerly known from a no. of localities around Medellín and hills above lower Cauca Val., now almost all completely deforested. Most recent sightings are from PN Cueva de los Guácharos (P. Gertler; R. Ridgely), above Pto. Valdivia on Río Cauca (Willis 1972b), or above Florencia in w Caquetá.

**Range:** ENDEMIC. 1200-2700m (poss. lower). N half of W Andes s to extreme n Valle (Cerro Tatamá), n half of C Andes s to n Tolima

(Nevado del Tolima; Río Toche), head of Magdalena Val. in e and s Huila, and e slope of E Andes in w Caquetá.

## 21. MOUNTAIN GRACKLE

*Macroagelaius subalaris*    Pl. 45, Map 1203
**Identification:** ♂ 12″ (30cm); ♀ 11″ (28cm). Conical black bill. Long tail slightly rounded; eyes dark. Entirely dull bluish black with *chestnut wing linings and axillaries.*

**Similar species:** Much like Giant Cowbird (3) but bill shorter, plumage not as shiny, and lacks neck ruff; nearby note areas of chestnut. Also see Red-bellied Grackle (20).

**Breeding:** 5 BC birds, Sept, Norte de Santander (Carriker).

**Status and habitat:** Little known although reported common (formerly?) around Aguadita (1950m) above Fusagasugá (Olivares 1969a). Most recs. are from Norte de Santander and e Santander, esp. n and e of Bucaramanga where much forest still remains.

**Range:** ENDEMIC. 1950-3100m. Both slopes of E Andes in Norte de Santander and w slope from ne Santander (Cachirí; Páramo de Santurbán) s locally to sw Cundinamarca (Fusagasugá).

**Note:** Some consider *M. imthurni* (Golden-tufted Grackle) of the tepui highlands of s Venez., adj. Guyana, and n Brazil, a subsp. of this sp. but see Meyer de Schauensee (1951a). It wanders in canopy of forest or at forest edges in small tight flocks, members calling *kur-a-leek* noisily (like rusty gates), esp. in flight.

## 22. VELVET-FRONTED GRACKLE

*Lampropsar tanagrinus*    Pl. 44, Map 1204
**Identification:** ♂ 8.5″ (22cm); ♀ 7.5″ (19cm). *Very short bill* conical and pointed; *eyes dark; tail rather long, slightly rounded.* Entirely black with slight bluish gloss above. In the hand the forecrown feathers are very short, dense and plushlike.

**Similar species:** Shape much like Shiny Cowbird (1) and easily confused with it, though bill much stubbier (not always obvious in field) and tail proportionally longer. Other good clues are different habitat and calls.

**Voice:** A gracklelike (*Quiscalus*) *chack* or crackling note; a higher semiwhistled *cheziit*; groups often call in flight or as alight. Semimusical song at dusk from roost in *várzea* clearing, a rapid, gurgling *puk, chur-cal-a wík!* var. to *chuk, chuk, churcal-a-wík!*

**Behavior:** Usually in small active groups of 6-20 birds trooping about, noisily or quietly, at all hts. but frequently rather low. Settle low in shrubs and trees along lake borders or from eye level to lower canopy ht. over *várzea* forest streams where peer at leaflets and terminal twigs and peck branch tips, even flowers, then fly off in a group after a few min. Sometimes on or near ground inside *várzea* forest or in open marsh vegetation.

**Breeding:** One nest over water along a small creek, 28 Mar, Guyana (Myers *in* Snyder 1966).

**Status and habitat:** Uncommon to fairly common in *várzea* borders, along *várzea* streams, and in marshy lake edges in Amazonia; always near forest.

**Range:** To 400m. E of Andes from w Caquetá s and e to Amazonas. Prob. e to Orinoco (on Venez. side opp. Maipures, e Vichada). Guyana and s Venez. s to n Bolivia and w Amazonian Brazil.

**Note:** Perhaps better placed in *Macroagelaius*, which it recalls in shape and vocalizations, i.e., *M. imthurni* (Golden-tufted Grackle). See note under 21.

## 23. YELLOW-HOODED BLACKBIRD

*Agelaius icterocephalus*       Pl. 44, Map 1205

**Identification:** ♂ 7″ (18cm); ♀ 6.5″ (16.5cm). Conical, pointed bill. ♂: black with *yellow hood and black lores.* ♀: dull brownish olive above obscurely streaked dusky; *eyebrow and throat yellow; facial area and crown dingy yellow*; rest of underparts olive yellow, more brownish on belly.

**Similar species:** ♂ unmistakable. ♀ recalls ♂'s pattern but much duller.

**Voice:** Labored, unmusical song (like rusty hinge), *took, TOOWEEEEZ*, 1st note faint, 2d loud and rasping, or sometimes followed by short musical *te-tiddle-de-de-do-dee*, down then up.

**Behavior:** Notably gregarious even when breeding, and usually in small loose flocks.

**Breeding:** Loose colonies in marshes. 5 BC birds, May–July, n Colombia (Carriker); Cali juvs., Feb (Brown); 1 juv., Jan, Sabana de Bogotá (Olivares 1969a). Aug–Nov, Guárico, Venez. (Thomas 1979b). Grass and weed cup slung between reeds or tall grass; 3-4 pale blue eggs dotted and scrawled black (ffrench 1973).

**Status and habitat:** Common in freshwater marshes, flooded wetlands, and river banks, esp. in open country. Uncommon in lower Atrato Val. near its w range limit (Haffer 1975). At Carimagua, ne Meta, present only late Dec–30 Apr (S. Furniss).

**Range:** To 2600m (Sabana de Bogotá). From lower Atrato Val. e to Santa Marta region, s to mid. Cauca Val. (Valle), and upper Magdalena Val. (to s Tolima); e of Andes s to s Meta and Vichada; s Amazonas along the Amazon. The Guianas and Venez. s to ne Peru and n and w Amazonian Brazil. Trinidad.

**Note:** Pale-eyed Blackbird (*A. xanthophthalmus*) of e Peru and e Ecuador n to Limoncocha may occur in Putumayo, Colombia. Small (8″), entirely dull black, thin pointed bill, slightly rounded tail, *orange white eyes*. Juv.: brownish with some pale yellow edging on breast (T. Parker). Reed beds, marshes, and shrubs along lake borders; songs incl. a loud *spee, tu-tu-tu-tu-tu-tu*, a higher-pitched *swit-swit-swit-swit-swit-swit-chew!*, a staccato trill, a ringing, cardinal-like *tuew tuew tuew* . . . and *chew-it, chew-it, chew-it* . . . , some of which resemble songs of Black-capped Donacobius; also a smacking *tsuck*.

## 24. EPAULET ORIOLE

*Icterus cayanensis*       Pl. 45, Map 1206

**Identification:** 8″ (20cm). Entirely black with *yellow to tawny yellow shoulders.*

**Similar species:** Moriche Oriole (25) also has crown, rump, and thighs yellow, as well as shoulders. See note.

**Voice:** Call in Bolivia a rich *oint* or nasal descending *whoaank* (J. V. Remsen); song resembles that of Moriche Oriole (T. Parker).

**Behavior:** Pairs move with mixed flocks in forest canopy or more often forest edges and second growth, even out in brushy fields in Peru (T. Parker).

**Status and habitat:** Uncertain. Known only from Leticia. Elsewhere widely sought as a cage bird and this perhaps the source of the Colombian bird. Confirmation of a natural or introduced breeding population, or presence as cage bird from distant source needed.

**Range:** Amazonas (Leticia). The Guianas and Amazonian and se Brazil to e Peru, n Bolivia, n Argentina, Paraguay, and Uruguay.

**Note:** Specimens intermed. betw. Epaulet and Moriche orioles containing var. amts. of yellow on rump and thighs are known from Surinam (Haverschmidt 1968), Fr. Guiana, and on Amazon in Brazil (Blake 1968). The 2 may be conspecific.

## 25. MORICHE ORIOLE

*Icterus chrysocephalus*       Pl. 45, Map 1207

**Identification:** 8.5″ (22cm). Black with *crown, nape, shoulders, rump, and thighs yellow.*

**Similar species:** A mostly black oriole with conspic. yellow crown and other yellow markings. See Epaulet Oriole (24).

**Voice:** Typical song at Mitú a slow, sweet, whistled *swéet tuew twéet tuew wheew swéet*, 1st, 3d, and last note rising, and repeated monotonously over and over, occas. with var.

**Behavior:** Singly or in pairs, usually rather high along forest borders, trees in clearings, palms along rivers, or in open areas with flowering trees. Follow mixed flocks in forest canopy.

**Breeding:** BC ♂, 22 Feb, ne Meta (S. Furniss). In Guyana, Feb–June; thin oriolelike woven basket fastened beneath palm frond; 1-2 creamy white eggs spotted and marked shades of brown, mostly at larger end (Beebe 1917). **Status and habitat:** Found in a var. of mostly "edge" habitats, esp. where there are Moriche Palms (*Mauritia*) for nesting; also borders of humid *terra firme* and *várzea* forests (esp. in s Amazonas). Seldom very numerous. **Range:** To 500m. E of Andes from w Meta (Villavicencio) and s Vichada southward (only sight recs. in Amazonas). The Guianas and c and s Venez. s to e Ecuador, ne Peru, and n and w Amazonian Brazil. Trinidad. **Note:** Hybridizes with Epaulet Oriole (see 24), which replaces it eastward and southward in Amazonia.

## 26. ORCHARD ORIOLE
*Icterus spurius*

**Identification:** 6″ (15cm). ♂: mostly black with *breast, belly, rump, and patch on shoulder chestnut*; wings heavily edged pale brown. ♀: olive green above; wings dusky olive with *2 white bars*; below greenish yellow. First-yr. ♂: like ♀ but *with black bib*.
**Similar species:** ♂ from any other Colombian oriole by chestnut (not yellow or orange) color. ♀ nearest imm. Yellow Oriole but smaller and greener, esp. above, and with 2 (not 1) wing bars. Also see ♀ Northern Oriole (31).
**Behavior:** Usually found around flowering trees or shrubbery, alone, or in 2's or 3's, rarely larger groups as in C America (Ridgely 1976). Usually silent in Colombia.
**Status and habitat:** Uncommon to rare winter resident early Aug–early May in light woodland, clearings, or semiopen areas.
**Range:** To 500m. From Panama border e across Carib. lowlands to Santa Marta region (prob. also Guajira); e of Andes in Catatumbo lowlands and s to w Meta (Villavicencio); 20 at Lago de Sonso (1000 m), Valle, 17 Feb 1984 (R. Ridgely, Hilty). Breeds from e and c US to c Mexico; winters from s Mexico to nw Venez.

## 27. ORANGE-CROWNED ORIOLE
*Icterus auricapillus*  Pl. 44, Map 1208

**Identification:** 7.5″ (19cm). *Forecrown and sides of head orange* (sometimes entire crown orange); narrow forehead, ocular area, bib, *upper back, wings, and tail black*; hindcrown, rump, shoulders, and lower underparts yellow. Juv.: dull olive above; head yellowish olive; wings and tail dusky with pale yellow edgings; underparts dull yellow, sometimes marked dusky on lower throat.
**Similar species:** Orange forecrown diagnostic

and conspic., but amt. of orange var. Yellow Oriole (30) lacks orange crown, has a yellow back, and always shows at least 1 white wing bar, sometimes also white wing edgings. Also see Yellow-backed and Yellow-tailed orioles (32, 33).
**Voice:** Song in Venez. a loud, musical, whistled *werr, chéet-your-kurr*; also a musical but slower and longer rambling ser.; call a complaining burry *wheea* and sharp *ze'e't* (P. Schwartz recording).
**Behavior:** Much like Yellow Oriole but more often found in humid and heavily wooded regions.
**Breeding:** 6 BC birds, Jan–Sept, w Guajira to n Antioquia (Carriker); 3 nests, Apr–June, Santa Marta (Todd and Carriker 1922); June nests, nw Santander (Boggs 1961); usual *Icterus* type nest suspended from palm frond or leaves; eggs sim. to Yellow Oriole.
**Status and habitat:** Dry to humid (seasonal) forest, lighter woodland, and cultivated areas with trees. More often humid regions.
**Range:** To 800m. From Gulf of Urabá e across Carib. region to Santa Marta area, w Guajira and s to upper Magdalena Val. (Villavieja, n Huila); e of Andes in Catatumbo lowlands and nw Arauca; poss. s to w Meta (presumed sightings). E Panama to n Venez. n of the Orinoco.

## 28. TROUPIAL
*Icterus icterus*  Pl. 44, Map 1209

**Identification:** 9″ (23cm). Rather heavy conical bill bluish gray; *yellow eyes surrounded by large bare blue ocular area. Entire head and upper breast black*, the feathers shaggy and pointed; upper back, wings, and tail black; *broad white scapular patch and broad white edgings on inner remiges*; nuchal collar, shoulders, rump, and lower underparts bright orange yellow. Or as above but upper back yellow crossed by black band (*metae*).
**Similar species:** Strikingly patterned and unmistakable in its range.
**Voice:** Song in c Venez. a loud, pleasing *taaw-chéer, taaw-chéer . . .*, up to 9 times, or *cheer-toe, cheer-toe . . .*, sometimes *taaw-chu-chéera* or sim. phrases.
**Behavior:** Pairs or family groups. Often on giant cactus, esp. when in fruit. Highly esteemed as a cage bird for its beauty and marvelously rich song.
**Breeding:** 6 BC birds, Mar–July, upper Cesar Val. and w Guajira (Carriker); June–Sept, Guárico, Venez. (Thomas 1979b). Appropriates abandoned nests of thornbird, Great Kiskadee, caciques, other orioles, etc.; 3 white eggs tinged pinkish buff and thickly spotted

and marked brown around larger end (Cherrie 1916).

**Status and habitat:** Arid scrub and dry woodland; gallery forest and ranchland in n Arauca.

**Range:** To 700m (mainly below 400m). Guajira s along se base of Santa Marta Mts. to Valencia (*ridgwayi*); e of Andes in n Arauca (*metae*) prob. n Vichada (*icterus*). N and c Venez.; Trinidad; Aruba, Curaçao, and Margarita. Introduced to Puerto Rico and St. Thomas.

**Note:** Orange-backed Troupial (*I. jamacaii*) incl. Amazonian *croconotus* is sometimes merged with the Troupial, but voice, habitat, and plumage differ.

### 29. ORANGE-BACKED TROUPIAL

*Icterus jamacaii*      Pl. 45, Map 1210

**Identification:** 8.5" (22cm). Conical bill black, base of mandible blue gray; *eyes yellow orange surrounded by bare blue ocular area; brilliant orange yellow with forehead, sides of head, throat, and chest black*; wings and tail black, lesser wing coverts yellow; *small white patch* on inner remiges.

**Similar species:** The only mainly "orange" oriole in se Colombia.

**Voice:** Song at Leticia, a loud, rich, leisurely *túee-turk, túee-turk, túee* or sim. ser. (no. of phrases var.), last note often rises. Recalls songs of 28 but even richer and phrasing differs.

**Behavior:** In Amazonia, pairs or occas. families keep fairly high in forest edges or in irreg. second growth in clearings. A favorite cage bird.

**Breeding:** At Leticia, 3 nests, late July–Aug (J. V. Remsen); Sept–Oct at Limoncocha, Ecuador (Pearson 1974). Renovates abandoned nests of Great Kiskadee, caciques, other orioles, etc.

**Status and habitat:** Edges of humid *várzea* forest, swampy lagoons, and marshy ponds in clearings (usually not in *terra firme* regions). Fairly common near Leticia.

**Range:** To 250m. E of Andes in w Putumayo (Pto. Asís) and Amazonas, Leticia (*croconotus*). S Guyana, Amazonian Colombia, Peru, and Bolivia to Brazil and Paraguay.

**Note:** By some merged with Troupial of n Colombia and Venez.

### 30. YELLOW ORIOLE

*Icterus nigrogularis*      Pl. 44, Map 1211

**Identification:** 8.5" (22cm). Mainly *lemon yellow* with black ocular region, bib, wings, and tail; distinct but *narrow white wing bar* and whitish edgings on inner flight feathers. Imm.: much duller, sometimes lacking black bib and lores, but almost always with white wing bar (wing bar sometimes faintly indicated).

**Similar species:** Much like Yellow-backed Oriole (32) but less robust, more *lemony*, and in any plumage shows a single white wing bar however faint. The 2 normally do not share the same habitat, Yellow being mainly in dry areas, Yellow-backed in mts. Other Colombian orioles have black on the back.

**Voice:** Rather infrequent song a detached ser. of short musical phrases, *tur-a-leet, tur-sweet, twur . . . tweet, tweet*, and so on (Hilty); in Venez. *swéet, weet-weet-weet-péit-tear*, or sim.; dawn song has added harsh and high-pitched notes (P. Schwartz recording).

**Behavior:** Roam about in pairs or 3's, occas. singly. Hop and peer in foliage, or visit flowering trees; eye level to canopy.

**Breeding:** 5 BC birds, Jan–July, Cesar to n Antioquia (Carriker). Most of long dry season in Santa Marta area; 3 nests, late Nov–early Dec, 1, late Mar (Hilty), and 17, Apr–May (Todd and Carriker 1922). Several building nest, Nov–Feb, others Dec–May, Carimagua, ne Meta (S. Furniss). Usual *Icterus* type pendent nest, sometimes quite low; 2-3 eggs, white to bluish white scrawled purplish black, chiefly around larger end (Todd and Carriker 1922).

**Status and habitat:** Common in arid scrub, dry woodland, shrubby areas, and gardens; not extensively into humid zones. Most common oriole in Santa Marta area, and even in mangroves.

**Range:** To 300m. Lower Sinú Val. e across Carib. lowlands to Guajira and s in drier parts of lower and mid. Magdalena Val. to Pto. Berrío, Santander; e of Andes s to s Meta and e Vichada (El Tuparro—INDERENA). N Colombia to n Venez., the Guianas, and n Brazil. Aruba to Trinidad.

### 31. NORTHERN (BALTIMORE) ORIOLE

*Icterus galbula*

**Identification:** 7" (18cm). ♂: *entire head, neck, and most of upperparts black*; rump, outer tip of tail, shoulders, and lower underparts orange; broad *white wing bar and prom. white wing edgings*. ♀: brownish olive above; yellowish orange below with *bright orange wash on breast*; wings dusky with *2 white bars*.

**Similar species:** ♂ is only Colombian oriole with entirely black head, neck, and upper back. Cf. Troupial (28). Most other Colombian orioles are mainly yellow and black. ♀ from allies by white wing bars and orange wash on breast. ♀ Orchard Oriole (26) is greener above, more yellow green below, and lacks the orange wash.

**Behavior:** Usually singly. Like other orioles often at flowering trees. Rarely sings on wintering grounds.

**Status and habitat:** Uncommon to rare winter

resident, mid-Oct–early May, to forest edge, lighter woodland, and more open areas of irreg. second growth. Most often seen in hills in coffee belt of Santa Marta region. **Range:** To 1600m. From Panama border e across the Carib. lowlands to Santa Marta and Perijá mts. (Guajira?); s in Cauca Val. to Valle (many recs.—U. Alvarez, P. Silverstone); e of Andes in Catatumbo lowlands, once to w Meta. Breeds in N America; winters in small nos. in s US, mainly Mexico to Panama, a few to nw Venez.

### 32. YELLOW-BACKED ORIOLE

*Icterus chrysater*                Pl. 44, Map 1212
**Identification:** 8.5″ (22cm). Mostly *golden yellow* with black forehead, ocular area, bib, wings, and tail. Black bib sometimes faintly outlined with brownish orange.
**Similar species:** Sleek and clean-cut. Only other oriole with an *all yellow back* is Yellow Oriole (see 30).·Normally the only oriole in the Andes.
**Voice:** A superb songster. Song typically 5-10 very loud, rich, musical whistles of much var.; e.g., at Merenberg, *wheer-hee who-hee who-hee ha-heet, wita-wita-wita*; sometimes more detached, jerky ser. of *weet's* and *jur-keet's*; call, a musical *chert*.
**Behavior:** Pairs or groups up to 10 act like other orioles as hop along branches, check flowers, and occas. sing loudly.
**Breeding:** 6 BC birds, Feb–Oct, n Colombia (Carriker); nestlings and ♀ ready to lay, Jan, e Boyacá (Borrero and Olivares 1955); juvs. with ad., late Feb–early May, e Huila (P. Gertler); usual *Icterus* type nest; 2 eggs, sim. to Yellow Oriole (Olivares 1969a); 5 birds at nest under construction, Feb, Panama (Willis and Eisenmann 1979).
**Status and habitat:** Widespread in humid regions, esp. in highlands. Forest borders, lighter woodland, clearings, and shrubby slopes. Unreported in Santa Marta Mts. by Todd and Carriker (1922) but now widespread there, esp. in the coffee belt (about 1200-1700m), which they prob. invaded when the area opened.
**Range:** 50-2700m (to 2100m in Santa Marta Mts.). Generally w of Andes (except arid Guajira) s to Nariño, and upper Cauca and Magdalena vals.; e slope of E Andes s to Meta and Macarena Mts. Se Mexico to Colombia and n Venez. (no Costa Rican recs.).
**Note:** For revision of subspp., see Olson (1981d).

### 33. YELLOW-TAILED ORIOLE

*Icterus mesomelas*                Pl. 44, Map 1213
**Identification:** 9″ (23cm). *Mainly bright yellow;*

ocular area, bib, upper back, wings, and tail black; *shoulders, outer tail feathers, and entire under surface of tail yellow. No* white on wing.
**Similar species:** Only Colombian oriole with conspic. all yellow outer tail feathers. Yellow-backed Oriole (32) has yellow (not black) back. Also see Yellow (30) and Orange-crowned orioles (27).
**Voice:** Distinctive call a loud whistled *pik-drup* or *pik, pik-drup* often repeated several times; song a rich ser. of whistled *chuck, chuck-yeaow* phrases 1 to several times per song.
**Behavior:** Sim. to other orioles. Pairs or families usually forage fairly high. Has habit of jerking tail up and down when flying giving the impression of labored flight.
**Breeding:** 5 BC birds, Jan–Apr, s Córdoba, n Antioquia (Carriker); 1 in Nov, nw Santander, June eggs (Boggs 1961); 2 nests, Nov, Santa Marta (Darlington 1931). Usual *Icterus* type nest 2-4m up; in Guatemala, 3 white eggs tinged blue with dark brown blotches around large end, finer dots elsewhere (Skutch 1954).
**Status and habitat:** Fairly common in humid and wet forest borders and second growth. Prefers riparian woodland, river borders, and swampy or wetter growth. Replaced in arid scrub and dry woodland in Carib. region by Yellow Oriole.
**Range:** To 1600m (to 200m on Pacific coast). Pacific coast, humid lowlands n of Andes to mid. Magdalena Val., s to Cundinamarca, and n locally to Santa Marta area and Guajira; e of Andes in Catatumbo lowlands. Se Mexico to nw Peru and w Venez.

### 34. ORIOLE BLACKBIRD

*Gymnomystax mexicanus*                Pl. 45, Map 1214
**Identification:** 12″ (30cm). Oriolelike. Bill rather heavy and pointed. *Mostly golden yellow with black back, wings, and tail;* black lores and ocular area; short black malar. Imm.: sim. but cap black.
**Similar species:** As the name implies, looks like an oriole, esp. in flight. Note large size, absence of bib, and different habits.
**Voice:** Song pattern var. with the population; typically 1-4 wheezy and extremely discordant buzzes, *zzzzweeeek*, often preceded and/or followed by 1 or more short grating *grt* notes.
**Behavior:** Pairs or small loose flocks, occas. single birds, perch in marshes, walk on ground in grassy pastures, on river banks, etc., and roost and loaf in trees or other elevated perches. Usually conspic.
**Breeding:** Two imms., late Mar, Meta (Brown); a stub-tailed juv. Isla. Corea, on Río Amazon, late July (Hilty); thick-walled grass and weed cup 6m up in tree, May, Orinoco region; pale

blue eggs marked brown at larger end (Cherrie 1916).

**Status and habitat:** Common in ranchland and edges of marshes, lagoons, and gallery woodland in the llanos; mainly open river edge, marshes, and tall grass and young second growth on river isls. in Amazonia.

**Range:** To 400m. Throughout e of Andes (no recs. in Guainía, Vaupés, or Caquetá). Fr. Guiana, Guyana, and n and c Venez. s to e Ecuador, ne Peru, and n Amazonian Brazil.

## 35. RED-BREASTED BLACKBIRD
*Leistes militaris*                Pl. 44, Map 1215
**Identification:** 7.5″ (19cm). ♂ unmistakable: *mainly black with red throat and breast.* In fresh plumage feathers of back and wings heavily edged pale brown, this largely disappearing with wear. ♀ sparrowlike: *broadly streaked dark brown and buff above*; tail narrowly barred; crown stripe, eyebrow, and underparts buffy; *breast lightly stained pinkish*; sides streaked dark brown. Imm.: like ♀ but paler, no red.

**Similar species:** See ♀ and nonbreeding ♂ Bobolink (37). Cf. ♀ Eastern Meadowlark (36).

**Voice:** Song var. geographically. At Lago Calima, Valle, a weak note and an insectlike buzz, *chert-zeeeeee-e-e-e*, in ne Meta 2 song types in same area, *zit zit . . . toweeeezzzz*, and *kéet; . . . dear*, last note lower (Brown). In Trinidad a flight display with song (latter as in Valle) is reported (ffrench 1973).

**Behavior:** Somewhat like a meadowlark. Mainly a ground-dweller in open grassy pastures though more often seen when perched on a post or shrub. Singly, in pairs, or loosely gregarious in suitable habitat, and often in small loose flocks (♂♂, ♀♀, and imms.) when not breeding.

**Breeding:** 15 BC birds, Jan–Apr, n Antioquia (Carriker); 1 in June, Huila (Lehmann 1961). Apr eggs, nw Santander (Boggs 1961); pairs and song, Mar, e Meta (Brown). Grassy cup nest on ground, sometimes with entrance tunnel; 2-4 eggs, deep cream heavily blotched pale reddish brown; often parasitized by Shiny Cowbird (ffrench 1973). ♂♂ poss. polygamous (Haverschmidt 1968).

**Status and habitat:** Open country. Grassland, pastures, and rice fields; spreading with deforestation (Haffer 1975; Hilty 1977). First rec. near Cali, Apr 1956 (Lehmann 1957). On Pacific slope, 1st rec. at Quibdó, Chocó, Feb 1978 (Hilty); at Guapí, Cauca, 26-30 Jan 1983 (Ridgely).

**Range:** To 1600m. Pacific coast from lower Atrato Val. (Turbo; Mutatá) spottily s to Cauca (no w Nariño recs.); e north of Andes to w base of Santa Marta Mts. (Ciénaga), e Guajira

and s locally to Cauca Val. in Valle and upper Magdalena Val. to Huila (La Plata Vieja, Mar 1961—Lehmann and Brown); e of Andes s to s Meta and clearings in w Putumayo (sightings, Pto. Asís, Sept 1978—Hilty and M. Robbins). Sw Costa Rica (where a recent invader) to e Ecuador and Peru, Venez. (mostly n of Orinoco), the Guianas, and ne Brazil (n Maranhão). Trinidad.

**Note 1:** Has been placed in the genus *Sturnella*.

**Note 2:** Sightings of "red-breasted" blackbirds near Barbacoas, Nariño (D. Gardner et al.), may be this sp. or Peruvian Red-breasted Meadowlark (*Sturnella bellicosa*) of w Ecuador (n to Esmeraldas) to Argentina and Falkland Isl. Latter, unrec. in Colombia, differs as follows: slightly larger size, 8″, heavier bill, and white (not red) underwings, white thighs, and a red superciliary becoming white behind eye. ♀ by larger size, heavier bill, underparts mostly whitish speckled black on breast and suffused pinkish on belly.

## 36. EASTERN MEADOWLARK
*Sturnella magna*                Ill. 95, Map 1216
**Identification:** 9.5″ (24cm). Chunky with short square tail. Long pointed bill slopes smoothly to forehead. Above heavily streaked blackish and buff; crown striped black and white; *below bright yellow with broad black V across breast.* Flashes *white outer tail feathers* in flight; often flicks them nervously when walking.

**Similar species:** Tail pattern of Black-billed Shrike-Tyrant (p 501) sim. but bird otherwise rather different. Also cf. ♀ Red-breasted Blackbird, and nonbreeding ♂ Bobolink (35, 37).

95. EASTERN MEADOWLARK

**Voice:** Songs near Bogotá resemble those of N American birds but are flatter, more warbled, and usually contain more than 4 slurred whistles. Near treeline in w Venez. at dawn a whistled *chewa-cheea, chewa-chorra.*

**Behavior:** Mainly terrestrial in grassland. Walks jerkily on the ground, and may crouch to avoid detection, but not a "close sitter" as are many open country birds. Sings mainly from a conspic. elevated perch such as post or small bush. A few quick wing flutters alternate with short stiff sails in flight.

**Breeding:** 17 BC birds, Jan–Nov, Santa Marta to n end E Andes (Carriker); 1 in Oct, NP Chingaza, (W. McKay); 2 in Jan, Boyacá (Olivares 1974a); and 1 in June, Huila (Lehmann 1961). Dome-shaped nest on ground; 2 eggs (Olivares 1969a).

**Status and habitat:** Common resident in grassland and damp savanna from lower paramo and treeline ecotone downward. Somewhat local but now spreading with deforestation. First reached sw Huila (1900m), 1958 (Lehmann 1960a).

**Range:** To 3500m (E Andes). Sw slope of Santa Marta Mts. (to 2700m) s to w base of E Andes (near Aguachica), highlands of E Andes s to head of Magdalena Valley at San Agustín (formerly s in E Andes only to Bogotá); e slope C Andes in PN Puracé; e of Andes s to s Meta (incl. sightings in Macarena Mts., 1975-77—T. O. Lemke) and e to Orinoco. E N America, locally to Venez., the Guianas, and n Brazil.

## 37. BOBOLINK
*Dolichonyx oryzivorus*

**Identification:** 7" (18cm). Rather stout conical bill. Tail graduated and spiky. ♀ and nonbreeding ♂: *sparrowlike with upperparts buffy brown streaked blackish, crown broadly striped dark brown and buff, underparts yellowish buff* with a few fine dusky streaks on upper breast and sides. Breeding plumage ♂ (seldom seen in Colombia) *mostly white above and black below*: rich buff patch on back of head and nape; scapulars, lower back, and rump white; otherwise black. In fresh breeding plumage, black feathers almost completely obscured by long buffy tips that are lost with wear. Full breeding color usually acquired by May.

**Similar species:** ♀ Red-breasted Blackbird (35) has less prom. head stripings, pinkish wash on breast, and up close, finely barred tail (no spiky tips). Grassland Yellow-Finch (p 665) is quite yellow below. Wedge-tailed Grass-Finch (p 667) is gray below with much longer tail.

**Voice:** Flight call a clear *pink* (Peterson 1963); several giving full song in Panama in spring passage (R. Ridgely).

**Behavior:** Gregarious though only occas. in large flocks during fall (southward) passage. Often in large flocks during northward movement.

**Status and habitat:** Common very locally as transient, early Sept–late Nov, and early Mar–mid-May to marshes, rice fields, and grassy pastures; notably erratic. Many near Ciénaga Grande, Magdalena, early Sept–mid-Oct (Todd and Carriker 1922); up to 70-80 daily, late Apr, ne Meta (S. Furniss); var. nos., 4 Mar–17 May, at Hacienda La Corocora, w Meta (W. McKay).

**Range:** To 2600m (Sabana de Bogotá). Santa Marta area and s in Magdalena Val. to n Huila; e of Andes from e Arauca, s Meta (Macarena Mts.), and e Vichada (El Tuparro–INDERENA) s to e Nariño and Vaupés (Caño Cubiyú; Río Apaporis). Breeds in N America; winters in c and s S America. Transient mainly through W Indies and e of Andes in n S America; a few reach Mid. America and Galapagos Isls.

# WOOD WARBLERS: Parulidae (50)

Wood Warblers are an active and often colorfully patterned group of New World insectivores characterized by, among other things, small size, delicate proportions, slender bill, and rictal bristles. They are anatomically closest to some tanagers and emberizine finches. The genera *Conirostrum* and *Coereba* of the Coerebidae (Honeycreepers) are included in the Parulidae by some, though both are of uncertain affinity. More than half the parulids occurring in Colombia breed in temperate North America east of the Rockies and occur in Colombia as transients or nonbreeding residents during the northern winter. They occur in a variety of lightly wooded or shrubby areas but few are regularly found inside tall rain forest; only one resident species (Buff-rumped Warbler) occurs in Amazonian Colombia. The resident species belong mainly to three genera: the yellow-throats (*Geothlypis*) resembling their northern counterparts; the redstarts (*Myioborus*), an arboreal and active group of highland species, and the *Basileuterus*, a large group, many of which have striped heads and are found on or near the ground. Many *Basileuterus* differ little from tanagers of the genus *Hemispingus*. Species of *Geothlypis* and *Myioborus* build open cup nests, those of *Basileuterus*, as far as known, domed nests with side entrances. The sequence is generally that of Lowery and Monroe *in* Peters (1968).

## 1. BLACK-AND-WHITE WARBLER
*Mniotilta varia*
**Identification:** 5″ (13cm). ♂: *streaked black and white above and below, and with white lower underparts*; cheeks black. ♀ and imm.: sim. but cheeks whitish and much less streaky (whiter) below.
**Similar species:** Breeding Black-poll Warbler (18) has solid black (not streaked) crown.
**Behavior:** Single birds normally follow mixed flocks; creep over larger bare (not mossy) branches and limbs from lower story to subcanopy.
**Status and habitat:** Uncommon to fairly common migrant and winter resident, late Aug–early Apr, to forest, lighter woodland, and borders.
**Range:** To 2000m (prob. occas. higher). W of Andes and e base of them s to Macarena Mts. Breeds in e N America; winter from s US to n Venez, w Ecuador (rare), and nw Peru (sight). W Indies.

## 2. GOLDEN-WINGED WARBLER
*Vermivora chrysoptera*
**Identification:** 4.5″ (11.4cm). ♂: gray above with yellow forecrown and *large yellow patch on wing coverts*; sides of head and underparts white, *black face stripe and black throat.* ♀: black of face and throat replaced by gray; crown duller, back tinged olive.
**Similar species:** ♂ is unmistakable; duller ♀ and imms. always show enough of ♂'s pattern for recognition.
**Behavior:** Most likely found accompanying mixed flocks; gleans from foliage actively at all levels.
**Status and habitat:** Transient and winter resident, early Sept–late Mar, to forest, lighter woodland, and borders; mostly foothills and lower slopes. Fairly common in W Andes, less numerous eastward.
**Range:** To 2700m (mostly 500-2000m). W of Andes s to Cauca and Huila, and on e slope E Andes s to Meta (Villavicencio). Breeds in e N America; winters from Guatemala to Colombia and n Venez.

## 3. BLUE-WINGED WARBLER
*Vermivora pinus*
**Identification:** 4.5″ (11.4m). *Most of head and entire underparts bright yellow with short black line through eye*; hindcrown and upperparts olive green; wings grayish with *2 bold white wing bars.* ♀ duller.

**Similar species:** Wing bars and black eyeline distinctive. See imm. Yellow Warbler (6).
**Status and habitat:** One rec., 21 Mar, n slope of Santa Marta Mts. (600-1200m).
**Range:** Breeds in e US; winters from s Mexico to Nicaragua, rarely to e Panama and n Colombia.

## 4. TENNESSEE WARBLER
*Vermivora peregrina*
**Identification:** 4.5″ (11.4). Breeding plumage: crown gray in contrast to bright greenish olive upperparts; eyebrow and underparts white with dusky streak through eyes. ♀ is tinged olive on crown. Nonbreeding plumage: *greenish above with distinct yellowish eyebrow* and sometimes a faint whitish wing bar; dingy yellowish below with *white under tail coverts.* Many are in breeding plumage by midwinter. Nonbreeding plumage birds perhaps all 1st-yr. birds.
**Similar species:** Dull nonbreeding plumage birds are vireolike and easily confused; good marks are slender pointed bill, eyestripe, and white under tail coverts.
**Behavior:** Like Golden-winged Warbler.
**Status and habitat:** Migrant and winter resident, early Oct–early May (sighting 10 May, Finca Merenberg is latest–Ridgely and Gaulin 1980) in most forested or wooded areas; favors lighter open woodland, esp. coffee zone; mostly foothills and highlands. Common in Santa Marta Mts., thinly spread s in Andes in forested regions.
**Range:** To 2600m. W of Andes and on e slope in Meta. Breeds in n N America; winters mainly Guatemala to n Venez., a few s to n Ecuador.

## 5. TROPICAL PARULA
*Parula pitiayumi*          Pl. 46, Map 1217
**Identification:** 4″ (10.2cm). Mostly blue gray above with *small black mask; triangular olive patch on mantle* and 2 white wing bars; *deep yellow below* with tawny wash on chest; lower underparts white.
**Similar species:** Cf. Yellow-throated Warbler (10).
**Voice** Song a fast, buzzy, umusical trill with numerous var., typically *tsee tsee tsee zeeeeeeeerrrip.*
**Behavior:** Single birds or pairs work through subcanopy foliage, sometimes lower in bushes; not as restless as *Dendroica* warblers. Sings persistently.
**Breeding:** 11 BC birds, Jan–Oct. n Colombia and W Andes above Cali (Carriker; Miller 1963); begging juv. in June, Valle (S. Gni-

adek); dome-shaped, moss nest with side entrance; high above ground in epiphytes; 2 white eggs marked chestnut (ffrench 1973).

**Status and habitat:** Common in forest borders and lighter woodland; *mostly* foothills and highlands.

**Range:** To 2600m. Santa Marta Mts., Perijá Mts., all 3 Andean ranges; scattered lowland recs. n of Andes and on Pacific coast from Chocó (Nuquí) s to Nariño. S Texas to nw Peru, n Argentina, and Uruguay. Trinidad and Tobago.

**Note:** Northern Parula (*P. americana*) is likely in n Colombia. Breeds in e N America; winters from e Mexico to Costa Rica, s Florida, W Indies, casually to isls. off n S America (Los Roques; Curaçao). No continental S American recs. Much like Tropical Parula, but black mask confined to forehead and lores, prom. broken white eyering, broader wing bars, and narrow chestnut band across chest (faint ♀; lacking or gray smudge on sides of chest, imm.). Several recs., Isla San Andrés.

## 6. YELLOW WARBLER

*Dendroica petechia*          Pl. 46, Map 1218

**Identification:** 4.5″ (11.4cm). ♂: *mainly canary yellow*; upperparts more yellowish olive; wings and *tail dusky heavily edged yellow; breast and sides with rusty streaks* (sometimes faint). Birds from the Carib. mangroves (*erithachorides* and *chrysendeta*) have whole head to chest rufous chestnut. Birds from Pacific coast (*jubaris* and *peruviana*) have crown chestnut; sides of head and throat tinged rusty. ♀ and imm. duller, more olive above, dingier below with rusty breast streaking virtually or completely lacking; mangrove forms lack chestnut on head or chest.

**Similar species:** ♀ and imm. easily confused with imm. Bicolored Conebill (p 589); from other sim. appearing "yellowish" warblers by yellow tail edging; see esp. imm. Tennessee Warbler (4).

**Voice:** Songs of all resident forms more or less sim. to n migratory birds, typically several bright, fast *tseet* notes ending in an emphatic *seécha* at end. Loud *tsip* call.

**Behavior:** An active and conspic. bird, gleaning from foliage and shrubbery at almost all hts.

**Breeding:** 13 BC birds, Jan–Feb, coastal Chocó, 3 in May, Guajira (Carriker), 1 in Mar, Buenaventura (Ralph and Chaplin 1973).

**Status and habitat:** Migratory forms are fairly common transients and winter residents, late Aug-early May, in all kinds of drier semiopen areas, esp. along tree-lined streams; mostly below 1000m. Resident forms restricted to vicinity of mangroves where locally common, but usually not found with Bicolored Conebill (they apparently exclude each other).

**Range:** To 2000m (sight recs. higher). W of Andes and along e base of them s to Macarena Mts. (sighting e to Carimagua, ne Meta— S. Furniss; 1 ♀, 24 Feb 1984, Isla Corea, Amazonas—Hilty, R. Ridgely). Breeds in N America and Mexico; winters (migratory forms) from Mexico to Peru, Bolivia (once), n Brazil, and the Guianas. Resident forms (in or near mangroves) from Cartagena e to Guajira and Pacific coast from Nuquí, Chocó s to s Nariño. Pacific coast nw Mexico to Peru, Carib. coast Mexico to Venez. and locally in W Indies.

**Note:** Incl. the *D. aestiva* group (Yellow Warbler) of temperate N America to w Mexico (all migratory), the *D. petechia* group (Golden Warbler) of the Florida keys, W Indies, Cozumel Isl., and Cocos and Galapagos Isls., and the *D. erithachorides* group (Mangrove Warbler) of coastal Mid. and S America s to nw Peru and Venez. and in Pearl Isls., all sometimes considered separate spp.

## 7. CHESTNUT-SIDED WARBLER

*Dendroica pensylvanica*

**Identification:** 4.5″ (11.4cm). Rare. Nonbreeding plumage: *bright yellowish green above*; crown dull yellow and sides of head whitish; wings dusky with *2 yellowish white wing bars*; most of *underparts white with var. amts. of chestnut on sides.* Imm.: crown like the back; sides of head grayish with *white eyering*; underparts white; *no chestnut on sides.* Breeding adult has *yellow crown*, black streaked back, and vertical black streak below eye connected to *broad chestnut streak on sides and flanks.*

**Similar species:** Imm. is brighter green above and whiter below than other imm. migratory warblers.

**Status and habitat:** Three recs.: 1 in Tolima (Oct); 1 in Santander (Nov); 1 in Cauca Val. (Nov) s of Cali (Orejuela et al. 1980).

**Range:** Breeds in e N America; winters from Guatemala to c Panama, stragglers to Colombia and n Venez.

## 8. CERULEAN WARBLER

*Dendroica cerulea*

**Identification:** 4.5″ (11.4cm). ♂: *dull cerulean blue above*; wings duskier with *2 white wing bars; back streaked black; below white with narrow black collar across chest* and dusky streaking on sides. ♀ and imm.: dingy olive green above with *blue gray tinge on crown; narrow whitish eyestripe and 2 white wing bars*; dull white below faintly tinged or streaked buffy on sides.

**Similar species:** Dull ♀ and imm. easily con-

fused with imms. of other migrant warblers, esp. Tennessee (4), Bay-breasted (19), and Black-poll (18); also see Double-banded Graytail (p 366). The bluish tinge on crown, eyestripe, and buff sides are good marks for ♀.
**Behavior:** Scattered individuals follow forest flocks, and usually keep high in foliage. Occas. sing a short buzzy *zree-zree-zree-zree-zreeeeet* prior to spring migration.
**Status and habitat:** Uncommon fall transient (Oct) and very uncommon winter resident and spring transient (mostly to Mar); forest and woodland borders in foothills and lower slopes. Most winter s of Colombia.
**Range:** 500-2000m. W of Andes; once e of Andes in w Meta (Guamal). Breeds in e US; winters in Andes from Venez. to n Bolivia.

### 9. BLACK-THROATED BLUE WARBLER
*Dendroica caerulescens*
**Identification:** 5″ (13cm). Only warbler with a white spot at base of primaries. ♂ unique: dull blue above with *prom. white spot on primaries; forehead, sides of head, throat, and sides black*; breast and belly white. ♀: brownish olive above with narrow white eyestripe and *prom. white spot at base of primaries like ♂*; dull yellowish brown to buffy below.
**Status and habitat:** Four recs. Prob. casual in n Colombia; 1 in Dec on n slope of Santa Marta Mts. (Cuchilla de San Lorenzo, 1500 m), and 3 in Jan in forested val. se of Titujura, extreme e Guajira.
**Range:** To 1500m. Santa Marta Mts. and Guajira. Breeds in e N America; winters mostly in Greater Antilles, a few to Lesser Antilles and straggles to Mid. and n S America.

### 10. [YELLOW-THROATED WARBLER]
*Dendroica dominica*
**Identification:** 5″ (13cm). Sexes sim. *Gray above with white eyestripe and 2 white wing bars*; cheeks and sides of throat black bordered behind by *large white patch on neck; throat and chest yellow*; lower underparts white, streaked black on side.
**Similar species:** Most like Blackburnian Warbler (14) but back unstreaked and lacks orange or yellowish head stripes.
**Status and habitat:** Hypothetical. Known from a sighting 23 Dec 1969 at Barranquilla (Easterla and George 1970); another seen, 9 and 11 Oct 1971, s of Santa Marta in Guaira Wash (Russell 1980). No other S American recs.
**Range:** N Colombia. Breeds in e US and part of Bahamas; winters from Florida and Texas to Nicaragua and Greater Antilles, stragglers to Panama, the Lesser Antilles and n Colombia.

### 11. TOWNSEND'S WARBLER
*Dendroica townsendi*
**Identification:** 5″ (13cm). ♀ and nonbreeding ♂: olive green above lightly streaked dusky on crown and back; 2 white wing bars; sides of head incl. eyestripe yellow, *enclosing distinct dusky cheek patch; throat and breast yellow*; throat (♂♂ only), chest, and sides streaked dusky. Imm.: duller with streaking obscure below. Breeding ♂: crisper with black crown; black cheeks and solid black throat and chest.
**Similar species:** See Black-throated Green-Warbler (12).
**Status and habitat:** Accidental: 1 ♀ specimen, mid-Jan in xerophytic vegetation of Snía. Macuira, Guajira, is only S American rec. (Marinkelle 1970).
**Range:** N Colombia. Breeds in nw N America; winters from w US to Nicaragua, casually to w Panama.

### 12. BLACK-THROATED GREEN WARBLER
*Dendroica virens*
**Identification:** 5″ (13cm). Nonbreeding plumage: olive green above, wings duskier with 2 white wing bars; *sides of head incl. eyestripe yellow; cheeks usually faintly outlined olive; below whitish with var. amts. of blackish on chest and sides* (imm. flecked black mainly on sides). Breeding ♂: brighter and sharper with solid black throat and chest.
**Similar species:** ♀ and imm. Townsend's Warbler (11) have crown faintly streaked, dusky olive cheeks (instead of cheeks with only a tinge of olive), and throat and breast usually yellow (not whitish).
**Status and habitat:** Prob. casual: 1 specimen, 12 Apr, n slope of Santa Marta Mts. (Cincinati, 1600m), and numerous sight recs., early Dec–late Mar, Santa Marta Mts. (many observers); 2 sightings in E Andes near Bogotá (Nov—Hilty; late Jan—P. Donahue).
**Range:** N Colombia. Breeds in e N America; winters mostly Mexico to c Panama (common in w highlands) and in W Indies; straggling to n Colombia and Venez. (several recent recs. in n Cordillera).

### 13. PRAIRIE WARBLER
*Dendroica discolor*
**Identification:** 4.5″ (11.4cm). *Very rare.* ♂: olive above with a few chestnut streaks on back and 2 dull whitish wing bars; *sides of head and underparts yellow with bold black streaks on sides of head and continuing along sides.* ♀: black face pattern subdued and no chestnut on back. Imm.: even duller with whitish eyering; *grayish sides of head and whitish throat*; black confined

to obscure streaking on sides; wing bars faint. Often flicks up tail.

**Similar species:** Imm. recalls imm. Magnolia Warbler (15); latter differs in yellow rump, white tail patches, and definite white wing bars.

**Status and habitat:** One ♀ specimen, 28 Aug 1977, near coast of Córdoba at Moñitos (Serna and Rodríguez 1979) is only continental S American rec.

**Range:** Breeds in e US; winters chiefly in Florida and isls. in Carib., small nos. from Yucatan to Nicaragua (chiefly offshore isls.), sightings to Costa Rica (specimen from Cocos Isl.); poss. Aruba.

## 14. BLACKBURNIAN WARBLER
*Dendroica fusca*

**Identification:** 5″ (13cm). Breeding plumage ♂: mostly black above with white stripes on back and *large white patch on wing coverts; small crown patch, eyestripe turning down behind ear coverts, and throat and chest fiery orange;* lower breast and belly white; sides streaked black. Nonbreeding plumage and imm.: dull olive green above with 2 white wing bars and white back striping (lacking in imm.); *facial pattern and underparts much duller* than breeding ♂; fiery orange replaced by pale yellowish orange or whitish.

**Similar species:** Best told in any plumage by distinctive head pattern.

**Behavior:** Usually single birds follow mixed flocks in mid. or upper levels; conspic.

**Status and habitat:** Very common and widespread transient and winter resident, early Sept–early May (latest date is 1 seen, 5 May, 600m, Anchicayá Val.—R. Ridgely and S. Gaulin) wherever there is forest or patches of woodland. The most common wintering warbler in the Colombian Andes.

**Range:** To 3600m (mainly 600-2500m). Generally w of Andes and on e slope E Andes; once to ne Meta (1 seen Oct, Carimagua—S. Furniss). Breeds in e N America; winters chiefly from n Venez. s in Andes to n Bolivia; small nos. overwinter in C America.

## 15. MAGNOLIA WARBLER
*Dendroica magnolia*

**Identification:** 5″ (13cm). Nonbreeding plumage: dull olive above with grayish head and white spectacles; 2 white wing bars; *dull yellow rump and broad band on either side of tail white;* below yellow streaked dusky on sides. Breeding plumage: much brighter with small black mask; short white stripe over eye; mantle blackish; large white patch on wing coverts; *bright yellow below, heavily streaked black* (except throat).

**Similar species:** In any plumage the combination of yellow rump and broad white bands on tail is distinctive.

**Status and habitat:** Rare. Only recs. are a specimen in Dec from Boyacá, and 3 seen at PN Tayrona, 3 Feb 1977 (R. Ridgely); 1 ♀, 23 Mar 1976, Ríohacha, another, 26 Mar 1976, Sevilla, Magdalena (T. Davis, K. Overman, A. Maley). Several Isla San Andrés recs.

**Range:** Breeds in N America; winters mostly from Mexico to c Panama (a few sight recs. in e Panama) and W Indies; stragglers to Colombia.

## 16. YELLOW-RUMPED (MYRTLE) WARBLER
*Dendroica coronata*

**Identification:** 5-5.5″ (13-14cm). Nonbreeding plumage: *dull brownish above with dusky streaks on back*; 2 white wing bars and *conspic. yellow rump*; throat white; rest of underparts dingy white, brownish wash on chest and sides and *usually conspic. yellow patch on sides.* Breeding plumage ♂: much brighter, more *blue gray above*; back streaked black; crown and sides of head blackish with yellow crown patch; white below with *black chest and sides; yellow patch on sides; wing bars and rump as in nonbreeding plumage.* ♀ duller.

**Similar species:** Yellow rump and yellow patch at sides of chest should be diagnostic in any plumage. Also see Magnolia and Cape May warblers (15, 17).

**Status and habitat:** One specimen from Ciénaga, Magdalena, 23 Mar; and a sight rec., 24 Feb 1972, on Cuchilla de San Lorenzo, n slope of Santa Marta Mts. (S. M. Russell, T. B. Johnson).

**Range:** Breeds in n N America; winters from c US to Panama; straggler to n Colombia and Venez.

## 17. [CAPE MAY WARBLER]
*Dendroica tigrina*

**Identification:** 5″ (13cm). Nonbreeding plumage. ♂: olive green to grayish green above; rump yellow; crown blackish; *patch of chestnut on sides of head*; sides of neck yellowish; 2 white wing bars; underparts dingy white to pale yellow, *lightly to heavily streaked dusky throughout.* ♀: like ♂ but duller; top and sides of head olive; *patch on sides of neck yellowish* (often indistinct). Imm.: like ♀ but even duller; underparts with less or no yellow and only a faint tinge of yellow on sides of neck. Breeding ♂: much brighter yellowish green above and *bright yellow below boldly streaked black;* white wing coverts (forms large patch). Breeding ♀: brighter yellow than non-breeders with *prom. yellow neck patch.*

**Similar species:** Imm. and ♀ easily confused with several other imm. migrant warblers, esp. Yellow-rumped (16; larger, browner, and streaked above), Magnolia (15; white tail patches), and Blackburnian warblers (14; lacks yellowish rump and only sides streaked).

**Status and habitat:** Hypothetical. Known from sight recs.: 2 seen 3 Feb 1977, PN Tayrona (R. Ridgely). There are a few recs. from Isla San Andrés, and Providencia where prob. reg. May be casual on Colombian mainland as there are several recent sight recs. in Panama and specimens from Los Roques and La Orchila Isl. off Venez. Coast; There are several sight recs. in Venez. incl. ♂ ♂ in Jan in Caracas, and Mar in Portuguesa (P. Alden, M. Goodwin and R. Arbib).

**Range:** Breeds in n N America; winters chiefly in W Indies, small nos. from Florida and Yucatan to Costa Rica and n S America.

**Note:** Palm Warbler (*D. palmarum*) of n N America, winters casually to Costa Rica and Panama and may occur in Colombia. Rec. on Isla Providencia; sightings on Isla San Andrés. 5-5.6". Sexes sim. Nonbreeding plumage: brownish above with *yellowish olive rump;* back indistinctly streaked dusky; weak yellowish white eyestripe; underparts dull whitish, somewhat streaked brown on chest and with *bright yellow under tail coverts* (some forms mostly pale yellow below). Breeding plumage: sim. but with chestnut cap and stronger pale eyestripe. *Wags tail constantly,* feeds on ground. Cf. Northern and Louisiana waterthrushes (22, 23).

## 18. BLACKPOLL WARBLER
*Dendroica striata*

**Identification:** 5" (13cm). Mostly e of Andes. Nonbreeding plumage: dull olive gray above narrowly streaked blackish on crown and back; wings duskier with 2 white bars; *below dingy white tinged olive,* sometimes with faint dusky streaking on sides; *under tail coverts white; legs pale yellowish.* Breeding plumage ♂: solid black crown and black malar enclose white cheeks; otherwise grayish olive streaked black above; 2 white wing bars; white below streaked black on sides. Breeding ♀ much as in nonbreeding plumage but brighter and more sharply streaked below.

**Similar species:** Nonbreeding birds much like Bay-breasted Warbler (19) and not always easily separated in field; from latter by white crissum (usually more buff in Bay-breasted), pale (not blackish) legs, usually more *distinctly olive* underparts, and more breast streaking (Bay-

breasted usually whitish below, a few tinged buff, generally no streaks and *virtually all* show a trace of bay on flanks).

**Status and habitat:** Fairly common transient and winter resident, early Sept–late Apr, e of Andes and taken at numerous places in Santa Marta region; otherwise *rare* w of Andes. Wooded areas, often in canopy.

**Range:** To 2600m. Throughout (mainly e of Andes). Breeds in n N America; winters mostly e of Andes s to Peru, the Guianas, and n Brazil (rarely Argentina or Chile); migrates through W Indies, straggler to Mid. America.

## 19. BAY-BREASTED WARBLER
*Dendroica castanea*

**Identification:** 5" (13cm). W of Andes. Nonbreeding plumage: very like nonbreeding Black-poll Warbler, differing in usually buff tinged underparts incl. under tail coverts (not olive tinge with white under tail coverts); *blackish legs;* and *often traces of chestnut on sides* (most adults). Breeding plumage ♂ very different: *crown, throat, chest, and sides chestnut;* sides of head black bordered behind by *large buffy neck patch;* 2 white wing bars; lower underparts white. Breeding ♀ much duller.

**Similar species:** See nonbreeding Black-poll Warbler (18). Easily recognized breeding plumage ♂ is rarely seen in Colombia.

**Behavior:** Single birds reg. follow bird flocks; feed high or low and are often quite frugivorous.

**Status and habitat:** Common in forest edges, second growth, and lighter woodland, late Oct–late Apr. Most numerous on Pacific coast.

**Range:** To 1200m (usually below 700m). Gulf of Urabá region e to Santa Marta area, Pacific coast s to Valle, Cauca Val. s to Cauca, and mid. Magdalena Val. s to Tolima (Honda); e base of Andes s to sw Meta (Guamal). Breeds in n N America; winters mostly from Panama to n Venez., once to ne Ecuador.

## 20. AMERICAN REDSTART
*Setophaga ruticilla*

**Identification:** 4.5" (11.4cm). ♂: *mostly black* with white belly and *bright orange patch on wings, sides of chest, and sides and base of tail.* ♀ and imm.: grayish brown above, *head grayer with white spectacles;* underparts whitish; patches on wings, sides of chest, and tail like breeding ♂ *but pale yellow* (those of 1st-yr. ♂ orangish).

**Similar species:** Wing and tail pattern unique.

**Behavior:** An extremely active bird, constantly fanning its tail and drooping its wings; sallies short distances or gleans in lower story or near ground. Often with mixed flocks of insectivores.

**Status and habitat:** Fairly common transient and winter resident (rec. 24 Aug–1 May); forest edges, lighter woodland, and shrubby areas. **Range:** To 2800m (mostly below 1500m). W of Andes and e of them s to Caquetá and Vaupés (Sabana de Cubiyú). Breeds in n N America; winters from Florida, W Indies, and Mexico to Peru, n Amazonian Brazil, and the Guianas.

### 21. OVENBIRD
*Seiurus aurocapillus*
**Identification:** 5″ (13cm). Olive above with *conspic. white eyering and dull orange crown patch bordered black on sides*; white below *heavily streaked black on breast and sides*. Imm.: crown duller.
**Similar species:** Both waterthrushes (22, 23) have prom. eyestripe (no eyering) and lack orange crown patch.
**Behavior:** Walks on ground in forest or shrubby thickets. Solitary, quiet, and easily overlooked.
**Status and habitat:** One specimen, 4 Oct, e of Santa Marta, and several sight recs., Jan–Feb, in Santa Marta area (Hilty; T. B. Johnson; S. M. Russell; J. Lupke; R. Ridgely).
**Range:** Breeds in e N America; winters from Florida and Mexico to w Panama and W Indies; small nos. to n Colombia and n Venez.

### 22. NORTHERN WATERTHRUSH
*Seiurus noveboracensis*
**Identification:** 5″ (13cm). Dull olive brown above with *prom. creamy to yellowish eyestripe*; underparts yellowish white (to almost white—*notabilis*) heavily streaked dark brown *incl. throat*.
**Similar species:** See much less numerous Louisiana Waterthrush (23). Also Ovenbird (21).
**Behavior:** Fond of watercourses or damp areas where walks on ground and constantly bobs rear end; frequently heard call a loud *chink*. Holds wintering territories (Schwartz 1964).
**Status and habitat:** Common transient and winter resident (rec. 8 Sept–30 Apr). Sluggish streams, pools, and mangroves on wintering grounds but can occur almost anywhere in migration. Highest rec. el. are 1 seen 19-26 Apr 1979, 2600m, Laguna Fúquene (A. Gast) and 3 at Lago Tota, 3000m, 15 Feb 1977 (R. Ridgely).
**Range:** To 2000m (sight to 3000m). Throughout. Breeds in n N America; winters from Florida, W Indies, and Mexico to ne Peru, the Guianas, and nw Brazil (Río Parú).

### 23. LOUISIANA WATERTHRUSH
*Seiurus motacilla*
**Identification:** 5.3″ (13.5cm). Much like Northern Waterthrush, but *eyestripe always pure white* (Northern's occas. dull white); throat unstreaked white with only dusky moustachial

streak on sides (Northern has central throat dotted white) and often with a *buffy wash on flanks*; also slightly bigger and bill larger.
**Similar species:** See Northern Waterthrush (22) and Ovenbird (21).
**Behavior:** As in Northern Waterthrush. In Panama reported to favor running rather than quiet water (Ridgely 1976).
**Status and habitat:** Rare transient and winter resident; rec. early Nov–Feb, mostly in Santa Marta area. One seen Dagua Val. Valle, 4 Feb 1977—G. Tudor et al.
**Range:** Known from Santa Marta area (to 1700m), Villavicencio (500m), Meta, and Dagua Val., Valle. Breeds in e US; winters from W Indies and Mexico to Panama; a few to n Colombia and Venez.

### 24. PROTHONOTARY WARBLER
*Protonotaria citrea*
**Identification:** 5″ (13cm). ♂: *entire head and underparts bright orange yellow* with white belly and under tail coverts; back olive; *wings uniform blue gray*; tail blue gray with some white. ♀: duller, less orange.
**Similar species:** Golden head and blue gray wings diagnostic. See Blue-winged, Yellow, and ♀ Hooded warblers (3, 6, 31).
**Status and habitat:** Common winter resident, rec. 26 Aug–5 Apr, in mangroves (where very numerous), moist woodland, tree-lined streams, and arid scrub; often, though not necessarily always, near water. Mainly Carib. region, rarely to Andes. Only wet season (Aug–Dec) resident in Santa Marta arid scrub (Russell 1980).
**Range:** To 1000m (once to 3300m, Santa Marta Mts.—Carriker). From Panama boundary e across drier Carib. lowlands to Guajira, s to mid. Cauca Val. (Cali), to upper Magdalena Val. (Villavieja, Huila), and e of Andes in Catatumbo lowlands; once on Pacific coast (Nuquí, Chocó—Carriker). Breeds in e US; winters from Mexico to n Colombia and Venez.; straggler to Ecuador and Surinam.

### 25. COMMON YELLOWTHROAT
*Geothlypis trichas*                                    Ill. 96
**Identification:** 4.5″ (11.4cm). ♂: olive above with *broad black mask across forehead to cheeks and bordered above by white to pale gray band*; throat and breast yellow becoming *white on belly*. ♀: head mostly olive (no black mask); *throat light yellow*; rest of underparts dull whitish strongly tinged brown, esp. on flanks.
**Similar species:** Both sexes of other yellowthroats (26, 27) are entirely yellow below and ♂♂ also lack white or pale gray border above black mask.
**Status and habitat:** Prob. more numerous than

96. Olive-crowned Yellowthroat (♂ left), Masked Yellowthroat (♂ center),
Common Yellowthroat (♂ right)

the few recs. indicate. Taken in Snía. Macuira, Guajira, mid-Jan; Santa Marta Mts. at 4500m in paramo, 21 Apr; and at 1600m on n slope, 11 Oct; Baudó Mts, Chocó, 16 June; mist netted on Isla Punta Arenas, Buenaventura Bay, 27 Mar. Secretive in tall damp grass or marshes.
**Range:** Known from Pacific coast, Santa Marta Mts., and Guajira. Breeds in N America s to Mexico; winters s US to W Indies and Panama; a few reach n Colombia and Venez.

### 26. OLIVE-CROWNED YELLOWTHROAT
*Geothlypis semiflava*                              Ill. 95
**Identification:** 5.2″ (13.2cm). ♂: *broad black mask across front half of crown and sides of head and neck* (black more extensive than Masked Yellowthroat); *otherwise olive green above incl. rear crown* (no gray on crown); *underparts entirely yellow*; sides olive green. ♀: sim. but lacks black mask; forecrown and sides of head *yellowish olive*; hindcrown like back.
**Similar species:** See Common Yellowthroat (25), and *very* sim. but allopatric Masked Yellowthroat (27).
**Voice:** Seldom heard musical song, a somewhat *Sporophila*-like *t'tseet-soup-si-si-chu-chew ti'ti'tweer-ter, teer* with rambling and var. ending in Costa Rica (B. Whitney recording); call a hoarse *chuck* much like other yellowthroats.
**Behavior:** Skulks in taller damp grass but may be attracted briefly to look over an observer; sometimes sings from exposed position.
**Breeding:** 10 BC birds, Jan–Feb, Chocó (Carriker). Grassy cup nest concealed low in grass clump, 12 Apr, upper Anchicayá Val.; 1 white egg with a few dark reddish brown spots around larger end (Hilty).

**Status and habitat:** Common but somewhat local on Pacific slope in tall grass and bushes in pastures, small clearings, and roadsides; favors damp areas or vicinity of water.
**Range:** To 1800m. Pacific coast from Baudó Mts. southward; Cauca Val. near Cali. Honduras to nw Panama; w Colombia to w Ecuador.

### 27. MASKED YELLOWTHROAT
*Geothlypis aequinoctialis*          Pl. 46, Ill. 96
                                        Map 1219.
**Identification:** 5.2″ (13.2cm). Resembles preceding 2 spp. ♂: *black mask across forehead and sides of head* (black less extensive than in Olive-crowned Yellowthroat); *crown gray*; rest of upperparts olive green; *underparts bright yellow*; sides of body olive green. ♀: sim. but no black mask (sides of head olive); *crown tinged gray*.
**Similar species:** See Common Yellowthroat (25). Olive-crowned Yellowthroat (26) of Pacific coast and mid. Cauca Val. in Valle, is not known to overlap; ♂ differs in having *front half* of crown black (not just forehead), rest of crown *olive* (not gray), and black less extensive on sides of head; ♀ perhaps in field by olive (not gray) tinge to crown.
**Voice:** In Venez. a sweet warbled *tee-chee-chee teecheweet teecheweet* (P. Schwartz recording).
**Behavior:** As in other yellowthroats.
**Breeding:** 8 BC birds, Jan–May, Córdoba to n Antioquia (Carriker), several in Aug, ne Meta (S. Furniss). Deep, grassy, cup placed low; 2 white eggs marked brown and lilac (ffrench 1973).
**Status and habitat:** Wet fields, pastures, and marshes with tall grass, bushes, and thickets.

Common in w and ne Meta (W. McKay; S. Furniss).

**Range:** To 500m. Rio Sinú (Tierralta) e to lower Cauca Val. (mouth of Río Cauca) and mid. and upper Magdalena Val. (Pto. Berrío, Santander; Villavieja, n Huila); e of Andes from Norte de Santander (Zulia Val.) s to Meta (Macarena Mts.) and e to Meta-Vichada boundary (Carimagua—S. Furniss). Prob. e to Orinoco. The Guianas and Venez. locally s to w Ecuador, e and w Peru, n Argentina, and Uruguay.

**Note:** Some merge *G. chiriquensis* (Chiriquí Yellowthroat) of sw Costa Rica and sw Panama with the present sp.

## 28. KENTUCKY WARBLER
*Oporornis formosus*

**Identification:** 5″ (13cm). ♂: bright olive green above with *black forehead; conspic. yellow "spectacles" and black "sideburns" extending below eye onto sides of neck;* bright yellow below. ♀: black on face and neck reduced; imm. has most of black replaced by olive; both otherwise sim. to ♂.

**Similar species:** See the yellowthroats (25, 26, 27), all of which favor grassy or shrubby areas (not woodland). Imm. most like Canada Warbler (32) but olive green (not gray) above.

**Behavior:** Inconspic. and unobtrusive on or near ground in woodland or forest undergrowth; often follows army ants.

**Status and habitat:** Rare. Known only from a few recs., early Oct–late Jan in the Santa Marta area; dry to humid forest and light woodland, occas. deciduous scrub (but not after leaves drop).

**Range:** To 200m. Santa Marta area. Breeds in e N America; winters from s Mexico to Panama, smaller nos. to n Colombia and w Venez.

**Note:** Some place 28, 29, and 30 in the genus *Geothlypis.*

## 29. CONNECTICUT WARBLER
*Oporornis agilis*

**Identification:** 5.5″ (14cm). All plumages have *unbroken white eyering.* ♂: olive green above with entire head, throat, and chest gray forming hood; crown sometimes with faint brownish tinge; lower underparts yellow, under tail coverts reach nearly to tip of tail. ♀: sim. but hood paler with more obvious brownish tinge. Nonbreeding ♀ and imm.: duller with whitish throat and suggestion of grayish brown hood.

**Similar species:** Often not safely separable from much more numerous Mourning Warbler (30) found mainly in mts. w of Andes. Ad. ♂ Connecticut usually told from ad. ♂ Mourning by complete eyering, brown tinged hood, and

longer under tail coverts. Ad. ♀ and imm. Connecticut *cannot* be told with certainty from ♀ and imm. Mourning on basis of eyering alone (a very few Mourning have complete eyerings). In the hand Connecticut's wing averages longer (64-77 vs 55-67mm) and can *always* be told by wing minus tail equal to 19 mm or more (Lanyon and Bull 1967).

**Status and habitat:** Few recs. Apparently a rare transient (Oct and late Apr) and rare winter resident, Dec and Jan in w and c Meta—Hilty; D. Fisher; T. B. Johnson). Poss. often overlooked (many Venez. recs., Oct–May, to 4200m, Meyer de Schauensee and Phelps 1978).

**Range:** Known from base of Santa Marta Mts., and e of Andes in Meta and Vichada (Maipures). Breeds in n central N America; apparently migrates se across W Indies; winters from ne Colombia and n Venez. to n Brazil; se Peru (once).

## 30. MOURNING WARBLER
*Oporornis philadelphia*

**Identification:** 5″ (13cm). Sim. to preceding sp. ♂: olive green above with gray head and *blackish throat and chest* (blackish feathers are gray edged giving a scaly effect that disappears with wear); rest of underparts yellow; *no eyering.* ♀ and imm.: duller with pale gray or brownish tinged hood (no black on throat or chest); imm. *typically* shows a broken white eyering, ♀ *typically* lacks eyering but there is much var. (a few even have complete eyering).

**Similar species:** Ad. ♂ easily told by black bib and lack of eyering; all imms. or ♀♀ lacking eyerings or with broken eyering separable from Connecticut (always complete eyering). Also see note. Those with complete eyerings separable from Connecticut (29) only in hand.

**Behavior:** Skulks in grass like others of the genus but normally not too hard to see.

**Status and habitat:** Uncommon transient and winter resident, mid-Oct–late Apr, in grass and low bushes in clearings or shrubby borders.

**Range:** To 3000m (PN Chingaza—W. McKay). W of Andes and e of them in Meta and w Caquetá. Breeds in n N America; winters from Nicaragua to n Ecuador.

**Note:** Macgillivray's Warbler (*O. tolmiei*) breeds in w N America and winters to w Panama (rarely to Canal Zone), and should be watched for in nw Colombia. Ad. ♂ like ♂ Mourning but with broken eyering. ♀ and imm. separable from Mourning only in hand; wing minus tail 2-10mm vs 10-18mm (Lanyon and Bull 1967).

## 31. [HOODED WARBLER]

*Wilsonia citrina*

**Identification:** 5″ (13cm). ♂: *black crown; sides of neck, throat, and chest surrounds bright yellow forehead and face*; otherwise olive green above and yellow below; white in tail. ♀: has suggestion of ♂'s hood with olive on crown, sides of neck, and wash on sides of chest, which partially encloses yellow face; underparts yellow, otherwise like ♂.

**Similar species:** ♂ unmistakable; ♀ most like Prothonotary Warbler (24) but lacks all yellow head and white belly.

**Status and habitat:** Hypothetical. Several sightings (no specimens) of at least 2 ♂♂ at Cañaveral, PN Tayrona, 29 Nov 1972 (S. M. Russell, and G. Tufts), 29 Jan and 8-9 Feb 1973 (Hilty, S. M. Russell, and J. Lupke). Prob. casual.

**Range:** Santa Marta area. Breeds in e US; winters from s Mexico to c Panama, casually to n Colombia and extreme nw Venez.

## 32. CANADA WARBLER

*Wilsonia canadensis*

**Identification:** 5″ (13cm). ♂: uniform *gray* above conspic. *yellow spectacles*; forehead and short mark below eye black; underparts bright yellow with *crisp black necklace across chest*. ♀ and imm.: slightly duller, but *usually with traces of black necklace on chest* (lacking in some imms.); no black on face.

**Similar species:** Look for the necklace; imms. without it can be told by yellow spectacles and uniform gray upperparts.

**Behavior:** Usually 1-10m up in thicker foliage; often with mixed flocks.

**Status and habitat:** Common transient and winter resident, rec. 29 Sept–5 May (latter a sighting in Anchicayá Val.–R. Ridgely); forested areas, esp. inside shrubby borders in foothills and mts., less numerous in lowlands.

**Range:** To 2600m. All 3 Andean ranges and e of them in w Meta and Caquetá; no Carib. coast recs.; once in Santa Marta Mts. (sight, San Lorenzo, Feb 1981—P. Jennings). Breeds in e N America; winters from Colombia and Venez. (mostly mts.) to c Peru; also tepuis of s Venez. and n Brazil.

## 33. SLATE-THROATED REDSTART (WHITESTART)

*Myioborus miniatus*          Pl. 47, Map 1220

**Identification:** 5″ (13cm). *Upperparts, head, throat, and chest slate gray*; small chestnut crown patch (sometimes concealed); *breast and belly bright yellow*; under tail coverts and *conspic. outer tail feathers white*.

**Similar species:** Golden-fronted Redstart (34) has foreface and entire underparts yellow. Also see Spectacled (35) and Yellow-crowned redstarts (36).

**Voice:** Often heard song a weak, colorless *chueet-chueet-chueet-chueet-chuee*, lacking inspiration.

**Behavior:** Like other redstarts, conspic., extremely active, and constantly posturing like a butterfly with drooped wings and fanned tail as it acrobatically sallies short distances, hops along high or low branches, or clings momentarily to vines or trunks. Usually pairs or families and often with mixed flocks.

**Breeding:** 7 BC birds, Mar–Nov, Perijá Mts., n end C and E Andes (Carriker); 10 nests, late Dec–July, upper Anchicayá Val. (Hilty); breeding in W Andes above Cali, Jan–July (Miller 1963); and 6 nests there, June–July (S. Gniadek; Hilty); 1 nest, early Apr, PN Cueva de los Guácharos (P. Gertler). Open moss cup sunk into side of steep bank; 1-3 white eggs, dotted brown, esp. at larger end (Skutch 1954).

**Status and habitat:** Very common in forest, lighter woodland, and edges; foothills and mts. Overlaps with and is eventually replaced at higher el. (usually above 2400m) by *M. ornatus*.

**Range:** 500-2700m. Santa Marta and Perijá mts., the Andes, and Macarena Mts. N Mexico (rarely sw US) to Guyana, n Brazil (highlands only), and Andes s to Bolivia.

## 34. GOLDEN-FRONTED REDSTART (WHITESTART)

*Myioborus ornatus*          Pl. 47, Map 1221

**Identification:** 5.5″ (14cm). *Forepart of head and entire underparts bright yellow; foreface tinged orange*, rear part of head blackish; small crescent on ear coverts white; back and wings olivaceous gray; *tail black, outer feathers conspic. white*. Or sim. but no orange tinge and sides of head white (*ornatus*).

**Similar species:** Spectacled Redstart (35) has spectacles and mostly dark head. Also see Slate-throated Redstart (33).

**Voice:** Song (*ornatus*) a high-pitched, rambling *pit it, t'chit, tswit tsweet, pits-whew! sits sweet iit . . .*, for up to 15 sec; *tsip* while foraging.

**Behavior:** Generally like Slate-throated Redstart but frequently in small flocks of its own or nuclear in mixed spp. flocks. Flit and sally actively from low to high, keeping near periphery of trees and bushes, and often very confiding.

**Breeding:** May juvs. with ads., PN Puracé (J. Silliman); Nov juvs., Cundinamarca (Olivares 1969a); BC ♂, July, Santander (Carriker); open cup nest lined with finer fibers;

eggs white spotted red brown, esp. at larger end (Sclater and Salvin 1879).
**Status and habitat:** Common in forest, forest edges and stunted woodland near treeline. Overlaps and is eventually replaced by *M. miniatus* at lower el.
**Range:** 1800-3400m (treeline), usually above 2400m. E Andes s to Bogotá (*ornatus*); E Andes in w Caquetá (sight); W and C Andes s to s Cauca (*chrysops*); n Nariño(?). Nw Venez. s in Andes to s Colombia.

### 35. SPECTACLED REDSTART (WHITESTART)

*Myioborus melanocephalus*              Pl. 47, Map 1222

**Identification:** 5.7″ (14.5cm). Head pattern var. Slate gray above, head blacker; *typically forehead, loral streak, and eyering yellow and most of crown rufous*; or entire forecrown and ocular region yellow with center of crown rufous; or any var. in between; otherwise bright yellow below; under tail coverts white; *conspic. white outer tail feathers.*
**Similar species:** See Slate-throated and Golden-fronted redstarts (33, 34)
**Voice:** Song in Peru, a somewhat squeaky *zeet-de-de-zeet, zeet-de-de-zeet* . . . more or less continuously for up to 20 sec (J. O'Neill recording). Constantly utters a high-pitched *tsip*.
**Behavior:** Like Golden-fronted Redstart.
**Status and habitat:** Forest, woodland, and borders; replaced n in Andes by Golden-fronted Redstart. Fairly common in e central Nariño.
**Range:** 2000-3300m. Both slopes of Nariño from latitude of Pasto southward. Prob. also w Putumayo. S Colombia to n Bolivia.

### 36. YELLOW-CROWNED REDSTART (WHITESTART)

*Myioborus flavivertex*         Pl. 47, Map 1223

**Identification:** 5.5″ (14cm). Found only in Santa Marta Mts. Top and sides of head black with *conspic. yellow central crown patch*; otherwise olive green above; narrow forehead and lores yellowish; *underparts bright yellow*; tail black with *conspic. white outer feathers.*
**Similar species:** Slate-throated Redstart (33) has dark gray throat and chest, and no yellow crown spot.
**Voice:** Call, sharp *chip*; song a weak sibilant ser. of phrases reminiscent of Slate-throated Redstart.
**Behavior:** Conspic. as continually wags tail downward and flits and flutters in foliage; rarely sallies to air or postures with wings and tail spread as does Slate-throated Redstart. Follows mixed flocks from upper understory to subcanopy.

**Breeding:** One cup nest, 20 May, 2000m; bulky and on ground(?); 2 white eggs, speckled reddish brown (Todd and Carriker 1922).
**Status and habitat:** Common in humid forest, lighter woodland, and edges. Overlaps with *M. miniatus* at lower el. and often in mixed flocks with it.
**Range:** ENDEMIC. 1500-3000m; mostly above 2000m. Santa Marta Mts.

### 37. GOLDEN-CROWNED WARBLER

*Basileuterus culicivorus*              Pl. 46, Map 1224

**Identification:** 5″ (13cm). *Grayish olive above;* orange to yellow central crown stripe bordered on sides by broad black stripe; *eyebrow whitish to yellowish white; dusky line through eyes;* cheeks olivaceous; *entire underparts bright yellow*; legs pale dull yellow; bill dark.
**Similar species:** Very sim. to Golden-bellied and Three-striped warblers (see 38, 48), but brighter and cleaner cut than either. Citrine Warbler (40), usually at higher el., lacks black and orange crown stripes; Russet-crowned Warbler (43) is obviously gray on sides of head and throat. Also cf. Flavescent Warbler (39).
**Voice:** Song in Anchicayá Val. a husky, buzzy, *tweez, tweez, tuwezz,* upscale, or *tweez tweez twezz-e-e-e-e-e;* no. of notes var. but rise at end characteristic.
**Behavior:** Pairs, families, or occas. solitary birds chatter as restlessly glean from foliage near ground or in lower story; often follow bird flocks. More subdued and skulking than Three-striped Warbler.
**Breeding:** 8 BC birds, Mar–June, Perijá Mts. and n end E Andes (Carriker); pair fed Mar fledgling, upper Anchicayá Val. (Hilty); nest, in Trinidad, a grass or fiber dome low on bank; 2-4 white eggs marked reddish brown mainly at larger end (ffrench 1973).
**Status and habitat:** Fairly common in moist to wet forest, older second growth, and lighter woodland with undergrowth; foothills and lower slopes.
**Range:** 300-2000m (usually below 1500m). Santa Marta Mts. (300-1200m), Perijá Mts. (1300-1600m), Pacific slope in Valle, upper Patía Val., slopes above Cauca Val.; e slope C Andes at n end; w slope E Andes in s Cesar and Santander, and e slope of E Andes s to Meta (Macarena Mts.). W Mexico to w Panama; n Venez. to s Colombia; highlands s Venez. and adj. Guyana and n Brazil; e Brazil to Uruguay, Argentina, and Bolivia.

### 38. GOLDEN-BELLIED WARBLER

*Basileuterus chrysogaster*         Pl. 46, Map 1225

**Identification:** 5″ (13cm). *Olive green above;* median crown stripe orange broadly bordered

on sides and forehead with black; *indistinct eyebrow yellowish olive*; lores dusky; sides of head olivaceous; *throat and median underparts yellow*; sides, flanks, and under tail coverts clouded olive; legs pale brown.
**Similar species:** Very sim. Golden-crowned Warbler (37) has *distinct blackish line* through eye, whitish eyestripe (not yellowish olive), and looks grayish above (not olive) and brighter and more extensively yellow below. Russet-crowned Warbler (43) has entire sides of head and upper throat gray. Also see Three-striped Warbler (48).
**Behavior:** Sim. to Golden-crowned Warbler.
**Status and habitat:** Undergrowth of humid and wet forest and shrubby forest edges in foothills and on lower slopes. Not well known in Colombia.
**Range:** 300-1000m. Pacific slope in w Cauca (below Cerro Munchique) and w Nariño (*chlorophrys*). Sw Colombia and w Ecuador; e Andean slope of c and s Peru.
**Note:** May or may not be conspecific with *B. bivittatus* (Two-banded Warbler) of highlands of s Venez., Guyana, and n Brazil, and se Peru to nw Argentina.

### 39. FLAVESCENT WARBLER
*Basileuterus flaveolus*          Pl. 46, Map 1226
**Identification:** 5.5″ (14cm). Much like Citrine Warbler but brighter. Bright olive green above (incl. crown) with narrow yellow eyebrow and blackish lores; sides of head yellowish becoming olive green on ear coverts; bright yellow below; breast tinged olive; *bill pale; legs pale yellowish*; tail rounded.
**Similar species:** Look for the yellowish face, pale bill and legs; Citrine Warbler (40) is usually at *much* higher el. Golden-crowned Warbler (37) has orangish to yellow coronal stripe and black crown stripes. Also see Three-striped Warbler (48) and duller and darker Superciliaried Hemispingus (p 639).
**Voice:** Song in Venez., a thin high *ee-ee-due-ee-ee chew-chew*, var. to *ee-ee-titi chew-chew*, or *ee-a-ee-a dee-e chew-chew* given quickly (P. Schwartz recording).
**Behavior:** Alone or in pairs walking or hopping on ground or near it; often flicks and slightly spreads tail.
**Breeding:** 3 BC ♂♂ and incubating ♀, late Oct, near Cúcuta, Norte de Santander; covered nest of leaves and fibers on ground with side entrance, 3 eggs (Carriker).
**Status and habitat:** Undergrowth of dry or moist forest, or in shrubby or thorny thickets, and woodland borders. Uncommon.
**Range:** 200-1000m. Drier parts of Zulia Val. (w and s of Cúcuta), Norte de Santander. Poss.

Cauca Valley(?). N and w Venez.; ne Bolivia; Paraguay; e Brazil.

### 40. CITRINE WARBLER
*Basileuterus luteoviridis*          Pl. 46, Map 1227
**Identification:** 5.7″ (14.5cm). Dull olive above; *eyebrow yellow* (or yellowish white—*quindianus*); lores dusky, sides of head olive green; underparts yellow heavily tinged olive on breast and sides; legs pale brownish; bill black. Or eyebrow and throat whitish, lower underparts paler yellow (*richardsoni*).
**Similar species:** Sim. to more contrasty Superciliaried Hemispingus (p 639), which is slightly larger and darker with *narrower* white eyestripe, dark olive to blackish forecrown, and brighter yellow underparts. Also cf. Oleaginous Hemispingus (p 639), Black-crested, Three-striped, and Flavescent warblers (42, 48, 39); also very rare 41.
**Voice:** Song a fast, high-pitched *trit trit chet chet seewit-seewit-seewit-tri'i'i'e'e'E'E'e'e'u'u* in C Andes (Hilty); also a complex duet, 1 giving a rapid chatter, the other a ser. of squeaks and high notes, in Venez. (P. Schwartz recording).
**Behavior:** Pairs or 2-4 glean actively in lower story and often follow bird flocks, esp. those with tanagers, small flycatchers, and other warblers.
**Breeding:** 3 BC birds, Sept–Oct, n end C and E Andes (Carriker) 1 in Oct, Boyacá (Olivares 1971).
**Status and habitat:** Common in thick undergrowth of humid and wet forest, dwarf forest, and dense borders, esp. near treeline.
**Range:** 1700-3400m, mostly above 2500m (recs. spotty in W and C Andes). E Andes s to e Nariño (*luteoviridis*); C Andes in Antioquia (n of Medellín) s to Cauca (*quindianus*); W Andes at n end (Frontino) and in Munchique area, Cauca (*richardsoni*). Nw Venez. s in Andes to n Bolivia.
**Note:** Pacific slope birds, *B. richardsoni* (Richardson's Warbler) have been considered a separate sp. by some.

### 41. PALE-LEGGED WARBLER
*Basileuterus signatus*          Map 1228
**Identification:** 5.5″ (14cm). Very sim. to *luteoviridis* race of Citrine Warbler. Differs mainly in *smaller size, brighter underparts* (less olive on breast and sides), weaker eyestripe, yellow eyelids, and *yellowish flesh legs* (not brownish). Bill black.
**Similar species:** Flavescent Warbler (39) has a pale (not black) bill, occurs at lower el., and ranges not known to overlap.
**Breeding:** 1 BC ♂, June, Páramo de Guasca, Cundinamarca (Borrero and Hernández 1958,

where called *B. luteoviridis* but subsequently identified as *B. signatus* by Meyer de Schauensee 1959).

**Status and habitat:** A ♂ near treeline (3400m) at edge of Páramo de Guasca is only Colombian rec. Poss. a wanderer(?) or an isolated n Andean population (see breeding and range). Its occurrence in Colombia is anomalous.

**Range:** Páramo de Guasca (ne of Bogotá), Cundinamarca. Subtropical zone from c Peru to nw Argentina.

### 42. BLACK-CRESTED WARBLER
*Basileuterus nigrocristatus*  Pl. 46, Map 1229
**Identification:** 5.7″ (14.5cm). Olive green above with *broad black crown stripe bordered on sides by bright yellow eyebrow; short black line through eye;* throat bright yellow gradually shading to olivaceous yellow on lower underparts.

**Similar species:** See Citrine Warbler (40).

**Voice:** Call a *loud* sharp *chit;* song, given yr.-round, a few sharp notes accelerating into a rattly trill, *tuk-tuk-ti-ti'ti'ti'ti'ti'r'r'r* (J. Silliman).

**Behavior:** Active but inconspic., usually keeping low in denser thickets or bamboo; 1 or 2 reg. accompany bird flocks containing tanagers, finches, flower-piercers, and other warblers.

**Breeding:** 4 BC birds, May–July, Perijá Mts. and C Andes (Carriker); 3 feathered nestlings, Oct, PN Puracé, 2500m (J. Silliman); a juv., June, Cundinamarca (Olivares 1969a). Grassy nest on bank or mound of moss on ground; eggs thickly spotted and blotched red brown (Sclater and Salvin 1879; J. Silliman).

**Status and habitat:** Fairly common to common in denser undergrowth of humid forest, dwarf forest, shrubby edges, and brushland near timberline.

**Range:** Mostly 2600-3400m (to 1300m in sw Nariño). Perijá Mts. and all 3 Andean ranges (recs. widely scattered in E and W Andes) s through both slopes of Nariño. N Venez. s through Andes to n Peru.

### 43. RUSSET-CROWNED WARBLER
*Basileuterus coronatus*  Pl. 46, Map 1230
**Identification:** 6″ (15cm). Olive above with broad *orange rufous crown stripe bordered on sides by black stripes* continuing to nape; *long black line through eye; otherwise eyestripe, entire sides of head, and neck continuing around nape gray;* throat paler gray; rest of underparts yellow; breast and sides tinged olive.

**Similar species:** No sim. warbler in its range has so much gray on head (gray encircles neck). Gray-throated Warbler (45) also lacks black eyeline, has smaller yellow (not rufous) crown

stripe, and gray reaches midbreast. Smaller Golden-crowned Warbler (37) has no gray at all below.

**Voice:** Antiphonal song in C Andes consisted of a fast stuttering ser. of notes, ending in a "burr" or fast trill, which in one bird falls at the end, and in the other remains the same or rises (Brown). In Venez. on 2 separate occas. antiphonal pairs were collected and it was determined that the ♂ rises at the end and the ♀ falls at the end (P. Schwartz).

**Behavior:** Pairs or families are active but often hard to see. Hop (sometimes like *Cranioleuca spinetail*) in tangles and vines, esp. around large trunks, in lower or mid. story, occas. on ground. Follow bird flocks, esp. those with other warblers.

**Breeding:** 6 BC birds, May–June, W and C Andes (Carriker); 3 more, Feb–July, W Andes (Miller 1963); and 1 in Oct, Boyacá (Olivares 1971); fledglings with ads., May, June, Sept, and Oct, Valle (S. Gniadek). Nest (prob. domed type of genus) in a bank; white eggs spotted cinnamon (Sclater and Salvin 1879).

**Status and habitat:** Fairly common in humid forest, older second growth woodland, and at forest edges.

**Range:** 1400-3100m in the Andes (no recs. n of Boyacá in E Andes) s to Cauca on w slope (*regulus*); Pacific slope of Nariño (*elatus*). Nw Venez. s in Andes to w Peru and n Bolivia.

### 44. WHITE-LORED WARBLER
*Basileuterus conspicillatus*  Pl. 46, Map 1231
**Identification:** 5.6″ (14.2cm). *Olive green above* with narrow orange yellow coronal stripe bordered on sides by *black stripes* extending to nape; sides of head to nape gray; supraloral stripe and *eyering white;* stripe through eye dusky; *throat pale gray;* rest of underparts yellow; sides of breast and flanks washed olive.

**Similar species:** Golden-crowned Warbler (37) has bright yellow (not gray) throat and is grayer above. Russet-crowned and Gray-throated warblers (43, 45) do not occur in Santa Marta Mts.

**Behavior:** Sim. to 43.

**Breeding:** 7 BC birds, Apr–June (Carriker); domed nest on ground in earth bank or tree roots; 3-4 white eggs spotted chestnut brown (Todd and Carriker 1922).

**Status and habitat:** Rather common in humid forest, forest edges, and older second growth.

**Range:** ENDEMIC. 750-2200m in Santa Marta Mts.

**Note:** Prob. a subsp. of *B. coronatus* and often so considered.

## 45. GRAY-THROATED WARBLER

*Basileuterus cinereicollis*     Pl. 46, Map 1232

**Identification:** 5.7″ (14.5cm). Dark olive green above, *partially concealed yellow crown patch enclosed by indistinct blackish stripes; forehead, eyebrow, and sides of head to upper breast gray;* throat grayish white; lower breast and belly yellow, sides washed olive.

**Similar species:** Much like ♀ Mourning Warbler (30) but with darker crown, yellow coronal stripe (usually visible), and paler throat. Also see Russet-crowned Warbler (43).

**Behavior:** Not well known. Presum. sim. to Russet-crowned Warbler; it is not known if the 2 are ever sympatric.

**Breeding:** 7 BC ♂♂, Mar–June, Perijá Mts. (Carriker).

**Status and habitat:** Humid forest and forest edge. May now be rare in much of range due to habitat loss.

**Range:** 800-1800m. N end of Perijá Mts. s on both slopes of E Andes to latitude of Bogotá (to Fusagasugá). Nw Venez. (to 2100m) and ne Colombia.

## 46. RUFOUS-CAPPED WARBLER

*Basileuterus rufifrons*     Pl. 46, Map 1233

**Identification:** 5″ (13cm). Olive green above; *crown and ear coverts rufous chestnut, separated by long white eyestripe;* dusky lores bordered below by whitish malar area; bright yellow below.

**Similar species:** The rufous chestnut crown and ear coverts are the marks.

**Voice:** Song, near La Plata, Huila a fast, energetic, *tis-tis weecha weecha beécher,* some var. but emphatic *beecher* or *reécha* ending characteristic; recalls Chestnut-sided or Yellow warblers.

**Behavior:** Solitary or in loosely assoc. pairs, usually low in thickets and shrubbery; rather sedentary. Often cocks tail in pert attitude.

**Breeding:** 10 BC birds, Mar–May, and juv. in July, Santa Marta to Huila (Carriker); 1 in Nov, Cundinamarca (MCN). Oven-shaped nest concealed on ground near a rock, log, or bush; 1-3 white eggs, finely speckled cinnamon, mostly at larger end (Skutch 1967).

**Status and habitat:** Tangles and thickets in moist woodland, second growth, and coffee plantations. Common in w Huila, and near watercourses even in arid zones elsewhere in upper Magdalena Val.; less numerous in Santa Marta area.

**Range:** To 1900m. Snía. de San Jacinto, Santa Marta area e to Guajira, (Manaure), Perijá Mts. and s in Magdalena Val. to s Huila. S Mexico to n Venez.

**Note:** Some consider *B. delattrii* (Chestnut-capped Warbler) of s Mexico and Guatemala a separate sp.

## 47. PIRRE WARBLER

*Basileuterus ignotus*

**Identification:** 5.2″ (13.2cm). Grayish green above with *chestnut crown* and *pale greenish yellow forehead and eyestripe;* sides of head mixed greenish yellow and dusky; underparts creamy yellow.

**Similar species:** Only warbler in its limited range with a chestnut crown.

**Status and habitat:** Recently rec. in PN Los Katíos in n Chocó on the slopes of Cerro Tacarcuna opp. Panama border (J. Hernández and J. V. Rodríguez).

**Range:** Extreme nw Colombia and highlands of E Darién (Cerro Pirre, Cerro Tacarcuna) in Panama.

**Note:** *B. ignotus* is considered by some to be a subsp. of *B. melanogenys* (Black-cheeked Warbler) of Costa Rica and Panama.

## 48. THREE-STRIPED WARBLER

*Basileuterus tristriatus*     Pl. 46, Map 1234

**Identification:** 5″ (13cm). *Long buffy coronal stripe and superciliary separated by black stripe on sides of crown;* cheeks dusky with indistinct buffy patch below eye; otherwise dull olive above; dull whitish yellow below tinged olive on breast and sides. Or coronal stripe dull orange; sides of head olive; dusky on ear coverts reduced to line through eye (*tacarcunae*).

**Similar species:** Russet-crowned Warbler (43) has sides of head and throat gray; Golden-crowned and Golden-bellied warblers (37, 38) have yellow to orange crown stripes and are brighter yellow below.

**Voice:** Incessant call a high-pitched, husky *cheewéep;* squeaky song an unmusical, agitated twittering ending in a chatter of 2 or 3 notes.

**Behavior:** Pairs or small groups sweep ebulliently through lower story, actively and acrobatically gleaning from foliage and chattering noisily; often in mixed flocks, esp. with bush-tanagers.

**Breeding:** 11 BC birds, May–July, Perijá Mts., W and C Andes (Carriker); eggs, 29 Apr, PN Cueva de los Guácharos (P. Gertler); begging juv., upper Anchicayá Val., 18 Apr (Hilty). Jan–July, W Andes above Cali (Miller); in same area 2 nests, May and June, dependent juvs., Sept and early Oct; cup nest (domed?) on ground; 2 eggs (S. Gniadek).

**Status and habitat:** Common in undergrowth

of humid and wet forest, and older second growth; foothills and mts.
**Range:** 300-2500m. Cerro Tacarcuna on Panama border (*tacarcunae*); Snía. Macuira, e Guajira, Perijá Mts. and all 3 Andean ranges (*auricularis*). Not Santa Marta or Macarena Mts. Costa Rica to n Venez. and s in Andes to Bolivia.

### 49. SANTA MARTA WARBLER
*Basileuterus basilicus*          Pl. 46, Map 1235
**Identification:** 6″ (15cm). Unmistakable in range. Olive green above; *entire head black with white crown stripe; long white superciliary; white crescent on ear coverts and white spot below eye;* throat white dotted blackish; rest of underparts yellow, clouded olive on sides. Juv.: much duller; head mostly buffy gray; markings only vaguely outlined.
**Behavior:** Pairs or groups of 3-5 glean 1-4m up in dense thickets and shrubs, recall a *Hemispingus* (e.g., *superciliaris*) in actions, and usually keep out of sight; often accompany mixed flocks containing furnariids, tanagers, and warblers; (T. B. Johnson, Hilty).
**Breeding:** BC ♂, Mar, 3 juvs., Sept (Carriker). begging juv., Aug, San Lorenzo (Hilty).
**Status and habitat:** Uncommon to fairly common (often hard to see) in dense shrubby forest borders, esp. with bamboo, inside well-developed to stunted forest, and on dense brush-covered (chaparrallike) slopes; humid zones.
**Range:** ENDEMIC. 2100-3000m (usually above 2300m—(T. B. Johnson). Santa Marta Mts.
**Note:** Formerly placed in the genus *Hemispingus*; some now believe it allied to *B. tristriatus* (Three-striped Warbler).

### 50. BUFF-RUMPED WARBLER
*Basileuterus fulvicauda*          Pl. 46, Map 1236
**Identification:** 5.7″ (14.5cm). Behaves like a waterthrush. Brownish olive above, crown grayer; *rump and basal two-thirds of tail bright yellowish buff;* eyestripe and underparts pale buffy white; throat and abdomen whitish.
**Similar species:** The contrasting rump is the mark. Waterthrushes (22, 23) are streaked below.
**Voice:** Very loud song an accelerating crescendo of *tsue* notes, ending with a few slower

distinct *chew*'s, easily heard above the sound of rushing streams.
**Behavior:** Much like a waterthrush. Terrestrial. Hops, rarely walks, at edge of puddles or streams, and sweeps broadly fanned tail from side to side (does not bob like waterthrush). Repeatedly flushes ahead short distances with a loud *chip*. Sings from ground or log.
**Breeding:** 4 BC birds, Feb–Apr, n Antioquia to Chocó (Carriker). Grass and rootlet, oven nest 8 Apr, on bank near stream, upper Anchicayá Val.; 2 dull white eggs speckled rusty with a dense ring at larger end (Hilty).
**Status and habitat:** Common along forest streams, shady roadside puddles adj. to forest, occas. damp areas on ground inside forest but seldom far from water.
**Range:** To 1000m. Pacific coast, and from Gulf of Urabá e to mid. Magdalena Val. s to s Huila (La Plata); e of Andes from w Meta (Macarena Mts.) southward. Honduras to nw Peru; e Colombia and w Brazil to e Ecuador and se Peru.
**Note 1:** May be conspecific with *B. rivularis* (River Warbler) of c and s Amazonas, Venez., the Guianas, and e Brazil to Paraguay, ne Argentina, and Bolivia. River Warbler differs chiefly in upperparts, being uniform brownish olive with *no contrasting buff* on rump or tail. Both forms may meet or integrade in extreme e Colombia from the Orinoco to Río Vaupés. **Note 2:** Some place *B. rivularis* and *B. fulvicauda* in the genus *Phaeothlypis*. **Note 3:** Rose-breasted Chat (*Granatellus pelzelni*) of s Venez., Guyana, Surinam, n Amazonian and e Brazil, and n Bolivia should occur in e Colombia along the Orinoco and in e Guainía (taken at Munduapo opp. Río Vichada, and upper Río Negro region of Brazil). ♂: slaty blue above, head black with *broad white postocular stripe,* throat white bordered narrowly below by black, otherwise *rosy pink below,* sides white. ♀: pale slaty blue above, forehead, sides of head, throat and most of underparts cinnamon buff, *crissum rosy pink.* Low or high in tangled forest borders or streamsides, or high inside dry to humid forest. Quite active, often postures with raised fanned tail; alone or pairs. Nasal *tank* call reminiscent of waterthrush; song, in Surinam, a clear, unhurried, *wheat, wheat, wheat, wheat, wheat, wheat.*

# HONEYCREEPERS: Coerebidae (32)

Honeycreepers are a heterogeneous and artificial family, many of whom are obviously related to tanagers, others to wood warblers, and some without apparent close affinities. In current practice (see Storer *in* Peters, 1970) the coerebid genera *Dacnis, Chlorophanes, Cyanerpes,* and *Iridophanes* are placed in the subfamily Thraupinae within the enlarged family Emberizidae. Others with less certain affinities, including *Oreomanes* and *Diglossa*, are included with Thraupinae as *Genera Incertae Sedis*. The remaining genera, *Conirostrum* and *Coereba*, are transferred to the Parulidae. Because of some uncertainty regarding the allocation of certain genera, we here maintain for convenience the older arrangement, recognizing the need for realignment of many genera. Nevertheless, the sequence of genera and species is generally that of Paynter and Storer *in* Peters (1968, 1970).

## 1. CHESTNUT-VENTED CONEBILL

*Conirostrum speciosum*        Pl. 47, Map 1237

**Identification:** 4″ (10.2cm). ♂: *mainly dark bluish gray*, slightly paler below; small white wing speculum; shoulder blackish (not prom. in field); *under tail coverts chestnut*. ♀ very different: *crown bluish gray; back olive green*; wings and tail brownish with yellow green edgings; lores, sides of head, and underparts buffy white becoming white on center of belly and buff on crissum; sides washed light gray.

**Similar species:** ♂ most like Bicolored Conebill (3) but more uniform blue gray and vent chestnut. ♀ is better told by attendant ♂; from ♀ White-eared Conebill (2) by greenish back; from imm. Bicolored Conebill by greenish back and no yellow tinge on throat. Also see Tennessee Warbler (p 575) and ♀ Blue Dacnis (26).

**Voice:** Song in Brazil a thin leisurely *tidée, tidée, tidée, tidée, tidue'ít* (W. Belton recording).

**Behavior:** Like other *Conirostrum* usually in pairs or small active groups, infrequently alone. Gleans from small terminal foliage in upper levels or canopy, esp. of *Mimosa* or other trees of sim. leaf-type. Sometimes with mixed flocks.

**Status and habitat:** Rare or perhaps often overlooked. *Várzea* forest borders and swampy river isls. in Amazonia. May also occur in gallery forest and deciduous woodland in ne Vichada (rec. opp. mouth of Río Meta in Venez.).

**Range:** To 100m (prob. higher). Known only from "Bogota" and sight recs. on the Amazon, s Amazonas (Monkey Isl., July 1976; Aug 1978—Hilty). The Guianas, c Venez., and e Ecuador (lower Río Suno) locally to n Argentina, Paraguay, and s Brazil.

## 2. WHITE-EARED CONEBILL

*Conirostrum leucogenys*        Pl. 47, Map 1238

**Identification:** 4″ (10.2cm). Small sharp-pointed bill. ♂: mainly dark bluish gray above with *black crown; conspic. white ear patch* and white rump (some Santa Marta birds with small white patch at base of primaries); below light bluish gray; under tail coverts chestnut. ♀ very different: dull bluish gray above with *white rump; eyebrow, sides of head, and entire underparts pale yellowish buff*; breast darker.

**Similar species:** ♂'s black crown and white ear patch unique. ♀ (usually with ♂) recalls ♂

Bicolored Conebill (3), but brighter below, rump white, and bill thinner. Also see ♀ Chestnut-vented Conebill (1).

**Behavior:** Small active groups, less often single birds or pairs, restlessly glean terminal foliage, probe leaf axiles near branch tips, or check flowers from mid. to upper levels; sometimes hang paridlike.

**Breeding:** 3 BC ♂♂, Jan, Apr, and May, Magdalena to s Bolívar (Carriker); building nest, Jan, Huila (Miller 1947).

**Status and habitat:** Uncommon to fairly common locally in drier open woodland, woodland borders, plantations, and gallery forest; trees in humid forest clearings in upper Sinú Valley.

**Range:** 50–600m. Carib. lowlands from upper Sinú Val. e to w and s base of Santa Marta Mts. (Tucurinca; Fundación; Valencia; sighting near Río Frio, May 1982—Hilty et al.), w base of Perijá Mts., in Cesar Val., and s locally to upper Magdalena Val. (Villavieja, n Huila; sight to Garzón, 1976—R. Ridgely); Catatumbo lowlands in Norte de Santander. E Panama to n Venez.

## 3. BICOLORED CONEBILL

*Conirostrum bicolor*        Pl. 47, Map 1239

**Identification:** 4″ (10.2cm). *Dull. Eyes dark red; legs pale purplish pink.* Light grayish blue above, dingy grayish white below, sometimes with buffy tinge. Imm.: dull grayish olive above (older birds tinged bluish); underparts dull grayish white *tinged yellow on throat*. ♂♂ may breed in partial imm. plumage (Haverschmidt 1968).

**Similar species:** Only in mangroves in n Colombia. Imm. much like imm. Yellow Warbler (p 576), but *legs pale*, bill heavier, and yellow largely confined to throat. Also see ♀ White-eared Conebill (2) and in Amazonia ♀ Hooded Tanager (p 633) and Chestnut-vented Conebill (1).

**Voice:** Song a rapid, high chatter, colorless and on 1 pitch; call a sibilant squeaky *tsik*, also *pitsik* and *few-it-sip*.

**Behavior:** Pairs or small active groups glean from foliage and twigs in mangroves and keep in mid. or upper levels. Sometimes probe tight clusters of small leaves.

**Breeding:** 3 BC ♂♂, May, ne Guajira (Carriker); 2 ads. feeding fledgling, 2 Feb, PN Salamanca (Hilty); small, compact, deep cup of grass mixed with feathers, 0.3-4m up in mangrove crotch; 2 pale buff eggs with dark brown blotches mainly at larger end; often parasitized by Shiny Cowbird (ffrench 1973).

**Status and habitat:** Common in mangroves, rarely away from them to Magdalena river delta forest. Easily seen in mangroves of PN Isla de Salamanca where it replaces mangrove race of Yellow Warbler. Small nos. found along river bank second growth or on swampy river isls. in Amazonas.

**Range:** To 100m. Cartagena; Magdalena delta e to Ciénaga Grande and coast of e Guajira. N Colombia and n Venez. locally along coast to mouth of Amazon and coastal se Brazil; both banks of Amazon to ne Peru (Río Curaray). First rec. on Río Amazon in Colombia, Feb 1984 (Hilty, R. Ridgely).

### 4. BLUE-BACKED CONEBILL
*Conirostrum sitticolor*     Pl. 47, Map 1240
**Identification:** 4.7″ (12cm). Brightest conebill. Mainly black with *blue mantle: breast and lower underparts deep cinnamon rufous*. Sexes sim.
**Similar species:** Resembles a small tanager and in poor light can look blackish. See Plush-capped Finch (p 641), which has yellow forecrown; in W Andes see Chestnut-bellied Flower-piercer (14).
**Voice:** Much liker other conebills; a high-pitched, complex, chattery ser. of thin notes.
**Behavior:** Even more active and restless than the tanagers, warblers, and brush-finches it usually accompanies. Mainly insectivorous, foraging rapidly like parids through the outer part of thick foliage of bushes and lower tree crowns with quick probing and gleaning motions. Pairs or several together (J. Silliman).
**Breeding:** 2 BC birds, Feb and July, C Andes (Carriker).
**Status and habitat:** Common in dense temperate forest borders and shrubbery, esp. stunted or elfin forest near treeline. Less numerous at lower el.
**Range:** 2600-3700m. Prob. throughout in all 3 Andean ranges, but no recs. s of Cundinamarca in E Andes, and rec. only in Antioquia and Cauca in W Andes. W Venez. (incl. Perijá Mts.) s in Andes to n Bolivia.

### 5. RUFOUS-BROWED CONEBILL
*Conirostrum rufum*     Pl. 48, Map 1241
**Identification:** 5″ (13cm). Above dark gray, wings and tail blacker; *forehead, sides of head to above eyes, and entire underparts deep rufous*. Sexes sim. Juv. duller.
**Similar species:** ♂ Rusty Flower-piercer (19)

is much paler below with blackish face mask and hooked bill.
**Voice:** A high-pitched complicated ser. of squeaky notes given very fast; resembles song of Blue-backed Conebill.
**Behavior:** Much like Blue-backed Conebill though favors more open bushy hillsides and more apt to be seen in pairs rather than groups. Sometimes with mixed bird flocks.
**Breeding:** 6 BC birds, Feb—Sept, Santa Marta and E Andes (Carriker); 2 ads. fed Aug fledgling, Represa Neusa (Hilty).
**Status and habitat:** Uncommon to fairly common in bushy or shrubby areas (not in forest) or in stunted trees up to treeline. Easily found on slopes above Represa Neusa, Cundinamarca, less numerous in mts. above Bogotá. Reported "rare" in Santa Marta Mts. (Todd and Carriker 1922).
**Range:** ENDEMIC. 2650-3300m. Santa Marta Mts. (2700-3350m) and n end E Andes in Norte de Santander (Páramo de Guerrero w of Salazar) s to Cundinamarca (Bogotá area).

### 6. CINEREOUS CONEBILL
*Conirostrum cinereum*     Pl. 48, Map 1242
**Identification:** 4.7″ (12cm). Sharp pointed bill. Dull grayish brown above incl. cheeks; crown darker with narrow forehead and *long eyebrow buffy white*; underparts *pale cinnamon buff*; *conspic.* L-shaped white patch on wing (formed by broad wing bar and patch at base of primaries). Sexes sim.
**Similar species:** Looks "hen-plumaged." Good marks are the long eyestripe and patch on wings. See ♂ Rusty Flower-piercer (19).
**Voice:** Common foraging call a fine, 2-noted, *tsip-tsip* (J. Silliman); song a rapid jumble of twittering phrases, virtually indistinguishable from song of Carbonated Flower-piercer (Moynihan 1963).
**Behavior:** Active, nervous, and often with mixed flocks. Pairs glean in foliage near tips of dense bushes, shrubs, and stunted trees (J. Silliman). ♂ sings from perches in center of established territories (Moynihan 1963).
**Breeding:** 2 BC ♂♂, Feb. Puracé (Carriker); song in Mar, PN Puracé (Brown); territorial dispute and display, May, Ecuador (Moynihan 1963). In n Chile, a woven cup of fibers and vegetable down, lined with horsehair; 3 pale grayish blue eggs thickly dotted purplish gray (Johnson 1967).
**Status and habitat:** Uncommon in bushy temperate woodland borders, patches of dense stunted shrubbery, and in fields with scattered shrubs and trees, often near treeline.
**Range:** 3100-3600m (sightings at 2600m, e of Popayán—Hilty et al.). C Andes from Cauca

(PN Puracé area) s through Nariño. S Colombia s in Andes to n Chile.

## 7. CAPPED CONEBILL
*Conirostrum albifrons*     Pls. 47, 48, Map 1243
**Identification** 5″ (13cm). ♂ : *cap white* (or *dark glossy blue—atrocyaneum*); otherwise dull black glossed violaceous on shoulders and rump. ♀ very different: *crown pale grayish blue; rest of upperparts olive green;* throat and upper breast gray tinged blue; otherwise pale yellowish green below.
**Similar species:** ♂ unmistakable. ♀ much like ♀ Blue Dacnis (26) of lower el., but upperparts much duller. Also cf. Tennessee Warbler (p 575).
**Behavior:** One or 2, occas. several, follow mixed flocks in the canopy, usually well inside forest (J. Silliman). Actively hop and twist side to side along branches like warblers as glean foliage; also reg. probe leaf axiles and stem tips like other conebills. Habitually wags tail up and down.
**Breeding:** 9 BC birds, Mar–Sept, W, C, and E Andes (Carriker).
**Status and habitat:** Often common. Humid and usually mossy forest, occas. forest edges, most numerous 2100-2600m.
**Range:** 1800-3000m. W Andes from Antioquia (Frontino) s to w slope in Nariño (*atrocyaneum*); C Andes s to Cauca and w Huila and e slope in Nariño (*centralandium*); w slope E Andes s to Cundinamarca (*albifrons*). N Venez. s in mts. to n Bolivia.

## 8. GIANT CONEBILL
*Oreomanes fraseri*     Pl. 48, Map 1244
**Identification:** 6.5″ (16.5cm). Nariño only. Fairly long bill straight and pointed. *Gray above and chestnut below; eyestripe chestnut; large ear patch white.* Juv.: sim. but more white on sides of head; breast streaked and spotted.
**Similar species:** Unmistakable in restricted habitat.
**Voice:** In Peru ♂ ♂ sing a high-pitched plaintive *ssit, ssit, ssit,* or *seet, sseet, sseet,* monotonously repeated (George 1964); soft high *seep* in e Ecuador when foraging.
**Behavior:** Unobtrusive as they actively clamber over trunks and branches of *Polylepis* like a nuthatch, and scale off thin, curly, cinnamon-colored bark (color of conebill's underparts). Usually alone or in pairs, occas. families.
**Breeding:** In Ecuador, cup nest of dry grass and moss, horsehair lining; 2.6m up in open shrub; 2 eggs (Goodfellow 1901).
**Status and habitat:** Not well known in Colombia. Confined to *Polylepis* groves at or above treeline.

**Range:** 3000-4500m. Mts. of s Nariño ("Pasto"). Prob. only higher slopes of Volcán Cumbal and Chiles, perhaps Volcán Galeras(?). S Colombia s in Andes to w Bolivia.

## 9. BANANAQUIT
*Coereba flaveola*     Pl. 47, Map 1245
**Identification:** 4″ (10.2cm). Warblerlike. *Short thin bill distinctly decurved.* Above dusky gray to dusky brown; *blackish on crown and sides of head; long white eyestripe and small white wing speculum;* throat pale gray; *rest of underparts and rump yellow.*
**Similar species:** Widespread. Striped head, spot on wings, and sharp curved bill are the marks.
**Voice:** Song a short, high-pitched ser. of unmusical, hissing chips and buzzes, often incessantly repeated. Much geographical var. in song pattern.
**Behavior:** A very active, energetic little bird seen alone or in loose pairs at almost any ht. above ground where it probes flowers for nectar and eats small berries. Often becomes very tame, taking sugar from bowls in country hotels.
**Breeding:** 5 BC birds, May–June, Bolívar (Carriker), and Apr, Aug, Oct, Nov, ne Meta (S. Furniss); Feb copulation, July fledgling, Anchicayá Val. (Hilty); yr.-round breeding, W Andes above Cali (Miller 1963). Build "dummy" or dormitory nests; oval grassy ball with side entrance; 2-3 buffy white eggs, thickly dotted reddish brown, esp. at larger end (Sclater and Salvin 1879).
**Status and habitat:** Common in gardens, plantations, lighter woodland, shrubby areas, and mangroves; usually scarce or absent in very arid zones or extensive areas of humid forest.
**Range:** To 1500m, smaller nos. to 2000m. Throughout (no Amazonas recs.). Se Mexico to ne Argentina. S Florida (rare), W Indies (except Cuba) to Trinidad.

[*Diglossa*: Placed in Thraupinae of Emberizidae in Check-list of Birds of the World, 13 (Paynter and Storer in Peters 1970). Slightly upturned bill, upper mandible longer and sharply hooked at tip, lower mandible sharp-pointed; downward facing, U-shaped tongue with brush tip. Partially nectivorous; montane; several usually sympatric. Scientific nomenclature follows Vuilleumier (1969b) with amendments (Vuilleumier; Graves 1982).]

## 10. BLUISH FLOWER-PIERCER
*Diglossa caerulescens*     Pl. 47, Map 1246
**Identification:** 5.6″ (14.2cm). *Thin bill, not decidedly upturned as in most Diglossa;* eyes reddish orange. *Dull dark blue to bluish gray, paler be-*

low; center of belly grayish; narrow forehead and chin black, ♀: duller. Juv.: base of lower mandible yellow.

**Similar species:** Dull and looks blackish in poor light, then easily confused with several "black" flower-piercers (15, 16, 18) as well as larger Masked Flower-piercer (11). At close range note thin warblerlike bill (not obviously upturned).

**Behavior:** Usually singly or in pairs, restless, and often with mixed flocks. Like other *Diglossa*, punctures flower corollas for nectar at almost any ht. but more often at midlevels. Also occas. eats berries, insects, and small flowers. Reported to like plants of the genus *Clusia* (F. Vuilleumier).

**Breeding:** 8 BC birds, June–Aug, Perijá Mts. and Andes (Carriker); open, dry grass and moss cup in bush; eggs pale greenish blue blotched and spotted reddish brown mainly at large end (Sclater and Salvin 1879).

**Status and habitat:** Uncommon to fairly common in humid montane forest borders incl. a var. of second growth types; esp. elfin forest (F. Vuilleumier). Like other mid. el. *Diglossa*, more closely tied to forest than those of higher el. Often with Masked, and Deep-blue, occas. White-sided flower-piercers.

**Range:** 1700-3100m (mainly 2100-2700m; once to 250m, Río Bojabá, Arauca). Perijá Mts. and all 3 Andean ranges. N Venez. s in mts. to n Bolivia.

## 11. MASKED FLOWER-PIERCER
*Diglossa cyanea*　　　　Pl. 47, Map 1247
**Identification:** 6″ (15cm). Fairly long bill only slightly upturned and hooked at tip; *eyes fire red. Deep rich blue with forehead, sides of head to behind eye, and upper throat black forming a mask.* ♀: slightly duller.

**Similar species:** Tanagerlike but bill proportionally longer and thinner. Indigo Flower-piercer (13) is decidedly smaller, black on face more restricted, and usually at lower el. Bluish Flower-piercer (10) is duller, smaller, and lacks the black mask. See Blue-and-black Tanager (p 616).

**Voice:** Song, given yr.-round, 2 stuttering *zeet zee* notes followed by a rapid tinkling and twittering (about 3 sec) that drops in pitch and accelerates. First 2 notes lacking in other *Diglossa* songs (J. Silliman; P. Schwartz).

**Behavior:** Solitary or singly with bird flocks. Sluggish and more frugivorous than smaller flower-piercers; usually in treetops (higher than other *Diglossa*), though occas. quite low (J. Silliman; Hilty).

**Breeding:** 9 BC birds, June–Sept, Andes (Carriker). Display and prob. nesting, May, Ec-

uador (Moynihan 1963). A nest and eggs from Antioquia much like preceding sp. but nest feather-lined, eggs slightly larger (Sclater and Salvin 1879).

**Status and habitat:** Fairly common in humid forest and forest borders. Some seasonal and el. fluctuation in nos., e.g., in PN Puracé sometimes numerous well above 3000m (J. Silliman). Only forest-based *Diglossa* in upper temperate zone.

**Range:** 1800-3600m (mostly 2200-3000m). All 3 Andean ranges. N and w Venez. (incl. Perijá Mts.) s in mts. to n Bolivia.

## 12. DEEP-BLUE FLOWER-PIERCER
*Diglossa glauca*　　　　Map 1248
**Identification:** 4.5-5″ (11.4-13cm). Small. Bill short, strongly hooked at tip; *eyes brilliant golden yellow. Bright deep blue*; narrow forehead and lores black (shows little black in field).

**Similar species:** From any other flower-piercer in range by prom. yellow eyes.

**Voice:** A high-pitched, pure *keeeee*, mechanical or amphibianlike, often doubled; also *ti-ti-dweeee*; song a high thin ser. of chips and squeaks, dropping, accelerating, and very jumbled at end.

**Behavior:** Active and nervous, almost constantly fidgeting and wing flicking. Alone or 1 or 2 with mixed flocks; pierce flowers or away from them in vines and on mossy limbs from lower midlevel to subcanopy.

**Status and habitat:** Fairly common to common in humid and wet forest (esp. mossy forest) and forest borders. Center of abundance at lower el. than other e slope *Diglossa* but in higher part of range reg. with Bluish and Masked flower-piercers. Represented on wet Pacific slope at sim. or even lower el. by next sp.

**Range:** 1400-2300m. E slope E Andes from w Caquetá (sightings above Florencia, Sept 1978, June 1981–Hilty et al.) s through w Putumayo and e Nariño. Colombia s on e slope of Andes to n Bolivia.

## 13. INDIGO FLOWER-PIERCER
*Diglossa indigotica*　　　　Pl. 47, Map 1249
**Identification:** 4.5″ (11.4cm). *Very small.* Bill short, upturned and strongly hooked at tip; *eyes fire red. Bright shining indigo blue*; remiges blackish edged greenish blue (edging hard to see in field); lores and narrow eyering black.

**Similar species:** A miniature of Masked Flower-piercer (11) but usually at much lower el. and black confined to lores and eyering (not forehead and sides of head to behind eye).

**Voice:** Usually quiet. Occas. a high, thin *chip*; also a deliberate *squik, squik, squik, squik.*

**Behavior:** As in Deep-blue Flower-piercer. Persistently follows mixed flocks; mid. strata or higher.
**Breeding:** Building in June, upper Anchicayá Val. (Hilty).
**Status and habitat:** Local in wet mossy forest ("cloud forest"), forest edges, and tall second growth. Mainly 1000-1300m in upper Anchicayá Val., Valle; common 1100-1400m in w Nariño. Represented on e slope E Andes by more widespread *D. glauca*.
**Range:** 700-2200m. Pacific slope from headwaters of Río San Juan (Cerro Tatamá) southward. W Colombia and w Ecuador.

## 14. CHESTNUT-BELLIED FLOWER-PIERCER

*Diglossa gloriosissima*          Pl. 47, Map 1250
**Identification:** 6″ (15cm). Bill upturned and sharply hooked at tip; eyes dark. Mainly glossy black; *breast and belly chestnut rufous*; shoulder patch blue gray; rump faintly tinged slaty (not a field mark).
**Similar species:** Black-throated Flower-piercer (17), which overlaps range of n population, has chestnut malar stripe and blue gray rump. Cf. s population with Blue-backed Conebill (4).
**Behavior:** Presum. as in Glossy Flower-piercer.
**Status and habitat:** Known from 2 widely separated localities in W Andes in shrubbery and elfin forest near treeline. Little known.
**Range:** ENDEMIC. 3000-3750m. N end W Andes in Antioquia (Paramillo, Páramo Frontino) and mts. of w Cauca (Cerro Munchique, 3000m). To be looked for in PN Farallones above Cali and other isolated high peaks in W Andes.
**Note:** Treated as a subsp. of Glossy Flower-piercer (*D. lafresnayii*) by some.

## 15. GLOSSY FLOWER-PIERCER

*Diglossa lafresnayii*          Pl. 47, Map 1251
**Identification:** 6″ (15cm). Bill upturned and sharply hooked at tip. *Glossy black with bluish gray shoulders* and dark eyes.
**Similar species:** Easily confused with var. subspp. of Black Flower-piercer (16), and at n end of E Andes barely separable in field, if at all, from *humeralis* subsp. of latter, but averages slightly larger and glossier (but fully ad. individuals of latter almost as glossy), and rump uniform with back, not dark gray (hard to see in field). In C Andes *aterrima* subsp. of Black Flower-piercer differs in uniformly black plumage (no blue gray shoulders), slightly smaller size, and perhaps less glossy luster.
**Voice:** Song a fast, high-pitched, musical warble of accented high notes and lower phrases,

sometimes lasting 15 sec or more (J. Silliman), slower and less jumbled (phrases more distinct) than other flower-piercers or Cinereous Conebill (Moynihan 1963).
**Behavior:** Often sings from top of shrub but otherwise rather furtive as hops quickly and secretively through thick vegetation, occas. popping into view momentarily or flycatching actively. Keeps low as follows bird flocks, crosses open spaces quickly, and dives into dense cover (J. Silliman). Pierces corollas or eats insects (F. Vuilleumier).
**Breeding:** 4 BC birds, Feb–July, C Andes (Carriker); late Mar fledgling, Bogotá (Brown); gray juvs., Aug, Ecuador (Moynihan 1963).
**Status and habitat:** Common in shrubby thickets and brushland near treeline; in forest borders, bushy pastures, and flower gardens at lower el. Often found with Black Flower-piercer.
**Range:** 2000-3700m (usually above 2700m). E Andes s to latitude of Bogotá, C Andes from se Antioquia, Caldas, and Tolima (Nevado del Ruiz area) s through mts. of Nariño. Nw Venez. s in Andes to extreme nw Peru.

## 16. BLACK FLOWER-PIERCER

*Diglossa humeralis*          Pl. 47, Map 1252
**Identification:** 5.7″ (14.5cm). Bill upturned and sharply hooked at tip. *3 subspp.*: entirely dull black or when fully ad. glossy black (*aterrima*); or black with dark gray rump (*nocticolor*); or dull black with dark gray rump and small blue gray shoulder patch (rarely with chestnut vent near Bogotá—*humeralis*). Imm.: grayish brown, indistinctly streaked dusky above and below as are some ♀♀ of *aterrima*; plumages and molt in need of thorough study (F. Vuilleumier).
**Similar species:** See Glossy Flower-piercer (15). Black-throated and Chestnut-bellied flower-piercers (17, 14) have chestnut underparts. Also cf. Bluish Flower-piercer (10).
**Voice:** Song a rapid sputtering ser. of squeaky trills and twitters (J. Silliman), faster than song of Glossy Flower-piercer but otherwise sim. (F. Vuilleumier); also virtually indistinguishable from song of Cinereous Conebill (Moynihan 1963).
**Behavior:** Much like Glossy Flower-piercer but less often with mixed flocks (J. Silliman); like latter holds individual territories during nonbreeding season; pairs are highly territorial when breeding (F. Vuilleumier).
**Breeding:** 15 BC birds, Feb–Sept, Perijá and Santa Marta mts., C and E Andes (Carriker). May fledglings in 2 successive yrs., Ecuador (Moynihan 1963); rootlet and moss cup suspended from swordlike aloe leaf less than 1m

up; 2 blue eggs speckled rufous (near Quito; Goodfellow 1901).

**Status and habitat:** Fairly common in shrubby areas, brushland, and dwarf forest borders up to treeline. As with previous sp., mainly nonforest.

**Range:** 2200-3400m (sightings to 4000m in *Polylepis* shrubbery on Nevado del Ruiz—F. Vuilleumier). Santa Marta and Perijá mts. (*nocticolor*); E Andes from Norte de Santander s to latitude of Bogotá (*humeralis*); C Andes in Caldas and Tolima (Nevado del Ruiz region) s (gap?) through PN Puracé (w slope only) to Nariño, and s end of W Andes from Cauca (Munchique area) s except for gap in Patía Val. (*aterrima*). W Venez. s in mts. to extreme nw Peru.

**Note:** By some considered a subsp. of *D. carbonaria* (Carbonated Flower-piercer), along with the next sp.

## 17. BLACK-THROATED FLOWER-PIERCER

*Diglossa brunneiventris* Map 1253

**Identification:** 6″ (15cm). Bill upturned and strongly hooked at tip. Black above with blue gray rump and shoulders; *central throat black; rest of underparts chestnut incl. broad malar stripes connected to sides of breast.* Imm.: brown above, buff below, and indistinctly streaked throughout; upper wing coverts edged buffy; broad buffy white malar stripe.

**Similar species:** See Chestnut-bellied Flower-piercer (14), which overlaps in range at n end of W Andes.

**Voice:** In Peru, song of *brunneiventris* essentially indistinguishable from that of Black Flower-piercer (F. Vuilleumier).

**Behavior:** Presum. much like Glossy Flower-piercer. Punctures flowers in Peru (F. Vuilleumier).

**Breeding:** 6 BC ♂♂ and 3 imms., July–Aug, n end W and C Andes (Carriker). Ground nest of related *D. gloriosa* in sw Venez.; deep cup of grass, moss, and *Espeletia* down (Vuilleumier and Ewert 1978).

**Status and habitat:** Not well known in Colombia. Taken from shrubland and scrubby woodland. Habitat apparently sim. to Black Flower-piercer's, which it replaces in its disjunct range.

**Range:** 2000-3900m. Two isolated colonies (*vuilleumieri*). N end of C Andes in high mts. around Medellín (Angelópolis; Santa Elena; Hacienda Zulaiba) and at n end of W Andes (Paramillo Mts.; Páramo Frontino 3700-3900m). Colombia; Peru (except extreme nw) s in Andes to n Bolivia.

**Note 1:** Formerly considered a subsp. of *D.*

*carbonaria* (Carbonated Flower-piercer) along with *D. humeralis* (Black Flower-piercer), and *D. gloriosa* of Venezuela. **Note 2:** *Vuilleumieri* subsp. follows Graves (1981).

## 18. WHITE-SIDED FLOWER-PIERCER

*Diglossa albilatera* Pl. 47, Map 1254

**Identification:** 5.2″ (13.2cm). Bill slightly upturned (visible in field) and hooked at tip. ♂: blackish slate to slate gray; *partly concealed white patch at sides of body and white under wing coverts.* ♀ very different: olive brown above, buffy to buffy brown below; *semiconcealed white patch and white under wing coverts as in* ♂. Imm.: like ♀ but obscurely streaked darker on breast.

**Similar species:** Either sex by white patches under wings (watch for wing flicks); at least some white almost always visible.

**Voice:** Song a high-pitched, flat trill, about 1.5 sec, usually preceded by 2 faint notes (trill much like that of Cinnamon Flycatcher but longer and faster); unlike songs of *brunneiventris*, *lafresnayi*, *caerulescens* complex (Hilty; F. Vuilleumier).

**Behavior:** Restless, active, and frequently flicks wings as it punctures flowers at midlevel or lower, esp. those of trees (F. Vuilleumier). Often in pairs and more frequently away from bird flocks than in them.

**Breeding:** 17 BC birds, Apr–Aug, Santa Marta and Perijá mts., C and E Andes (Carriker); Feb fledglings, PN Puracé (J. Silliman); moss, grass, and lichen cup about 1m up in bamboo, 20 Oct, Ecuador (Skutch 1954). Eggs from Antioquia greenish blue thickly marked reddish brown around larger end (Sclater and Salvin 1879).

**Status and habitat:** Uncommon to locally common in forest borders, shrubby second growth, and gardens, occas. inside forest.

**Range:** 1600-3100m (usually below 2800m). Santa Marta and Perijá mts. and all 3 Andean ranges. N Venez. s in mts. to n Peru.

## 19. RUSTY FLOWER-PIERCER

*Diglossa sittoides* Pl. 47, Map 1255

**Identification:** 5″ (13cm). Bill upturned and prom. hooked at tip. ♂: *above uniform bluish gray;* forehead and sides of head blackish (or forehead and sides of head like upperparts—*hyperythra*); *underparts pale cinnamon.* ♀: pale brownish olive above and *dingy pale buff below, indistinctly streaked dusky on breast.*

**Similar species:** ♂ distinctive; cf. with larger Fawn-breasted Tanager (p 606). ♀ resembles ♀ and imm. White-sided Flower-piercer (18) but lacks the white patches under wings.

**Behavior:** Much like White-sided Flower-piercer

but seldom with bird flocks. Punctures flowers and sometimes actively flycatches.

**Breeding:** 4 BC birds, May–Aug, Perijá Mts., W and C Andes (Carriker), 1 in Apr, Valle (Miller 1963). In Costa Rica allied *D. plumbea* (Slaty Flower-piercer) builds bulky open moss, leaf, and fine fiber nest; usually 1-4m up; 2 light blue eggs speckled brownish (Skutch 1954).

**Status and habitat:** *Local.* Uncommon to fairly common in forest borders, bushy pastures, and in gardens around habitations.

**Range:** Mainly 1700-2800m (rarely to 600m) in Santa Marta Mts.; 1500-3400m (usually below 2400m) in Andes. Santa Marta Mts. (*hyperythra*); Perijá Mts. (*coelestis?*); the Andes (*dorbignyi*). N Venez. s in mts. to nw Argentina.

**Note:** Sometimes merged with *D. baritula* (Cinnamon Flower-piercer) of n Mid. America and *D. plumbea* (Slaty Flower-piercer) of Costa Rica and Panama.

[*Cyanerpes*: Bill decurved; ♂♂ purplish blue, legs bright red to yellow; ♀♀ some shade of green, underparts streaked, legs dull (except 23); forest or woodland.]

## 20. SHORT-BILLED HONEYCREEPER

*Cyanerpes nitidus*  Pl. 47, Map 1256

**Identification:** 4.2″ (10.7cm). *Bill short* (0.4″, or 10mm), slightly decurved; *legs reddish pink* (♂), pale pink (♀). ♂: *mainly bright purplish blue; lores, throat, center of chest, and upper breast black;* wings and tail black; *under wing coverts black.* ♀: grass green above; lores dusky; *ocular region green;* spot of blue below eye; *throat and center of underparts buffy yellow;* breast and sides green streaked white; under wing coverts yellowish white.

**Similar species:** ♂ from ♂ Purple Honeycreeper (21) by *pink legs,* lighter blue (less purplish) plumage, decidedly shorter bill, and black on throat spreading onto upper breast (not sharply cut off at throat). Also cf. Red-legged Honeycreeper (23; amt. of range overlap uncertain). ♀ much like ♀ Purple Honeycreeper (21) but latter has longer bill, cinnamon forehead and loral area, and sides of head mostly rufous (not green), and legs greenish gray (not pale pink).

**Behavior:** Unlike other *Cyanerpes,* usually in *pairs,* generally accompanying large mixed flocks high in forest canopy, or at forest edges, sometimes lower in canopy (Hilty; R. Ridgely).

**Status and habitat:** Tall humid lowland forest and forest edges. Far less numerous than allies.

**Range:** To 400m. E of Andes from w Caquetá and se Guainía (mouth of Río Guainía) south-ward. S Venez. (s of Orinoco) to e Ecuador, ne Peru, and nw Amazonian Brazil.

## 21. PURPLE HONEYCREEPER

*Cyanerpes caeruleus*  Pl. 47, Map 1257

**Identification:** 4.5″ (11.4cm). Bill long (0.7″, or 18mm), slender and decurved. *Legs bright lemon yellow* (♂) or greenish gray (♀). ♂: mainly purplish blue; paler on crown and sides of head; *lores, throat, wings and tail black;* the black of throat terminating squarely on lower throat; *under wing coverts black.* ♀: grass green above; *forehead, lores, and sides of head cinnamon buff; throat deep buff;* sides of head faintly streaked with white; long blue malar stripe; rest of underparts *broadly streaked* blue green and buffy yellow; center of belly yellow; *under wing coverts dull yellowish white.*

**Similar species:** See Short-billed Honeycreeper (20). ♀ Red-legged Honeycreeper (23) lacks the cinnamon buff area on forehead, face, and throat and has underparts obscurely streaked greenish and white and under wing coverts yellow. In nw Chocó cf. Shining Honeycreeper (22).

**Voice:** High lisping *zzree* notes.

**Behavior:** Usually in canopy though sometimes comes quite low in forest interior or along forest edges in shrubby areas. Small groups or with mixed spp. flocks. Drink nectar from flowers, glean from foliage like warblers, flutter and sally to air, or eat fruit.

**Breeding:** 3 BC birds in Mar, Chocó, 2 in June and July, Zulia basin and w Caquetá (Carriker); 1 in Mar, Chocó (Haffer 1975). Nest a small moss cup lined with rootlets; rather low; prob. 2 white eggs spotted dark brown (ffrench 1973).

**Status and habitat:** Uncommon to locally common in humid and wet forest, forest edge, and shrubby areas. Geographical and el. shifts in population occur seasonally. Partially replaced in drier less wooded areas by Red-legged Honeycreeper, but both often occur together in regions of overlap.

**Range:** To 1400m (usually below 800m). Pacific coast, humid lowlands n of Andes to mid. Magdalena Val. s to Honda, n Tolima; n base of Santa Marta Mts. and base of Perijá Mts.; e of Andes from Norte de Santander to Meta and Guainía southward. Extreme e Panama to the Guianas and s to w Ecuador, n Bolivia, and Amazonian Brazil. Trinidad.

## 22. SHINING HONEYCREEPER

*Cyanerpes lucidus*  Map 1258

**Identification:** 4.5″ (11.4cm). Bill slender and decurved, intermed. in length (0.6″, or 15mm) betw. preceding 2 spp. *Legs bright lemon yellow* (♂); greenish (♀). ♂: mainly purplish blue, paler on crown and sides of head; lores, throat, wings, and tail black, the black of throat *spreading onto chest and rounded across bottom*; under wing coverts black. ♀: grass green above; *crown and sides of head strongly tinged bluish gray*; narrow blue malar stripe; throat buffy; rest of underparts buffy white, *streaked blue on breast* and washed green on sides; under wing coverts dull yellowish white.

**Similar species:** ♂ not always safely separated from ♂ Purple Honeycreeper (21), but black of throat more extensive and rounded (not squared off) on bottom, bill slightly shorter, and plumage darker (apparent in direct comparison); much easier ♀ lacks extensive buffy area on sides of head of ♀ Purple; grayish crown contrasts with back, breast streaked with blue (not green), and median underparts whitish (not yellow). Also see Red-legged Honeycreeper (23).

**Voice:** Call in Belize a high cricketlike *zee*, continuously repeated (Russell 1964); a hard metallic *click* or *tick* (Skutch 1972).

**Behavior:** Like Purple Honeycreeper.

**Breeding:** A Costa Rica nest in June, 2 others with fledged young, Sept and Oct; nest a shallow, manakinlike cup attached by rim to horizontal twig; fairly high; 2 eggs, dark (Skutch 1972).

**Status and habitat:** A Mid. American sp.; not well known in Colombia. Meets more s ally *C. caeruleus* (Purple Honeycreeper) along Panama boundary but sympatric breeding unproved. *C. caeruleus* also known from 2 localities just inside Panama border (Wetmore and Galindo 1972).

**Range:** To 100m. Extreme nw Chocó on Panama border (Río Jurádo). Se Mexico to nw Colombia.

## 23. RED-LEGGED HONEYCREEPER

*Cyanerpes cyaneus* Pl. 47. Map 1259

**Identification:** 5" (13cm). Bill long (0.7" or 18mm), slender and decurved. *Legs bright red* (♂); *dull reddish* (♀). ♂: bright purplish blue, crown contrasting pale azure; mantle and central back, wings and tail black; *under wing coverts bright yellow*. ♀: dull green above, *yellowish green streaked dusky below, throat and vague eyebrow greenish white.* After breeding, ♂ molts into an "eclipse" plumage that resembles ♀ except for black back, wings and tail. Or similar but larger (6", or 15cm) and darker (*gigas*, Gorgona Isl.).

**Similar species:** ♂ from other "blue" honeycreepers by red legs and bright *yellow* underwings. ♀ from all other ♀ *Cyanerpes* honeycreepers by reddish legs and bright yellow under wing coverts (e of Andes see ♀ Short-

billed [20] with pinkish legs, yellowish white under wing coverts and buffy yellow throat); most other ♀♀ also have buff throats.

**Voice:** Dawn song a ser. of weak unmusical *tsip* and *chaa* notes repeated for up to 20 min. (Skutch 1954); high wheezy *shree* call.

**Behavior:** Active and restless. Typically seen in groups, or with mixed spp. flocks, infrequently alone. Forages in canopy or a little lower for nectar, fruit, and insects, the latter often caught in the air.

**Breeding:** 11 BC birds, Jan–June, s Bolívar to Chocó (Carriker); thin-walled fiber cup suspended by rim from twig 3-15m up in tree or bush; 2 white eggs speckled light brown mostly around larger end (Skutch 1954).

**Status and habitat:** Locally or seasonally very common in forest borders, second growth shrubbery, clearings, and lighter woodland. Often found in drier areas than Purple Honeycreeper.

**Range:** To 1100m. Pacific coast (Baudó Mts. southward), upper Sinú Val., Guajira, and Santa Marta region s to lower Cauca? and mid. Magdalena val. (Bucaramanga); e of Andes in Norte de Santander (Zulia Val.), w Meta, Guainía, and Vaupés (Mitú); perhaps southward. S Mexico to w Ecuador, n Bolivia, and s Brazil.

## 24. GREEN HONEYCREEPER

*Chlorophanes spiza* Pl. 47, Map 1260

**Identification:** 5.5" (14cm). *Sharp, pointed bill bright yellow with black on culmen* (duller in ♀), stouter and not as decurved as *Cyanerpes*. ♂: *glistening emerald green to bluish green; top and sides of head black;* eyes red. ♀ very different; *mostly dull green, paler below;* throat and center of belly yellowish; eyes dark.

**Similar species:** ♂ unmistakable. Easily confused ♀'s best mark is *bill shape.* Dull imm. Bay-headed (p 615) and Rufous-winged tanagers (p 615) much like ♀ but have heavier, blunter, dark bills and less uniformly green plumage (usually traces of pattern on head or wings). Glistening-green Tanager (p 607) much brighter with black bill. Also see ♀ Blue Dacnis (26).

**Voice:** Lisping chips.

**Behavior:** Restless but not as active as *Cyanerpes* honeycreepers. Usually singly or in pairs in forest midlevels to canopy where eat fruit, sally to air for insects, and drink nectar; commonly follow mixed tanager-honeycreeper flocks.

**Breeding:** 6 BC birds, Feb–Aug, C Andes (Carriker), 1 in Feb, Santander (Boggs 1961); shallow, leaf, fiber, and horsehair cup fastened to fork with cobweb, 3-12m up; 2 white eggs with

wreath of brown spots at larger end (Skutch 1962b).
**Status and habitat:** Fairly common in humid forest, forest borders, and second growth woodland in lowlands and foothills, smaller nos. into highlands.
**Range:** To 2300m. Pacific coast from lower Atrato Val. southward, and generally e through Andes to e slope of E Andes; Perijá Mts. (not Santa Marta); e of Andes throughout from Norte de Santander southward (llanos?). Se Mexico to w Ecuador, Bolivia, and s Brazil.

### 25. GOLDEN-COLLARED HONEYCREEPER
*Iridophanes pulcherrima*      Pl. 48, Map 1261
**Identification:** 5″ (13cm). *Tangara*-like. Bill like *Chlorophanes* but shorter, less decurved. Eyes dark red. ♂: entire head, throat, and upperparts black; *lower back and rump pale shining opalescent; narrow nuchal collar orange yellow;* shoulders blue, remiges and tail with purplish blue edgings; breast and lower underparts shining opalescent. ♀: olive green above; rump brassy; *wing coverts and inner remiges edged pale bluish green;* underparts yellowish buff; breast and sides tinged greenish; *faint golden nuchal collar.* Imm. ♂ like ♀, older birds mottled with black.
**Similar species:** ♂ recalls Black-headed Tanager (p 617), but mantle black and collar conspic. (*known* ranges do not overlap). ♀ by shape, wing edgings, and faint nuchal collar. Cf. ♀ Green Honeycreeper (24) and imm. Black-capped Tanager (p 617), latter usually at higher el.
**Voice:** High lisping and buzzy *czee* call, sometimes doubled.
**Behavior:** Sim. to Green Honeycreeper. Often feeds in *Cecropia*.
**Breeding:** Fledgling, 30 Mar, Queremal, Valle; imm., 16 June, Anchicayá Val. (Hilty 1977).
**Status and habitat:** Rare and local, though perhaps reg. in upper tropical zone on e slope E Andes at s end (common 1300-1600m in e Ecuador—R. Ridgely). Very humid forest, forest edges, and tall second growth woodland, esp. near clearings or at breaks in forest. Sight recs. as follows: 3 above Quermal, Valle (Hilty 1977); 1 ♂ near Cueva de los Guácharos, 1900m, 6 Aug 1978, several above Florencia, w Caquetá, 1400-1500m, Sept 1978, June 1981, and w Putumayo, 1600m, June 1981 (Hilty et al.); 2 above Junin, w Nariño, 1300m, 12 July 1976 (R. Ridgely). Also known from "Bogotá" skins and a specimen (MCN) reportedly from Dagua Val. (F. C. Lehmann).
**Range:** 1000-1900m Pacific slope in Valle and Nariño (sight), head of Magdalena Val. in Huila

(sight), and e slope E Andes in Caquetá and Nariño (sight). S Colombia s in Andes to e and w Ecuador and Peru.
**Note:** By some placed in the genus *Tangara* (Thraupidae) and near *T. cyanoptera* (Black-headed Tanager). Behavior intermed. betw. *Tangara* and *Chlorophanes*.

### 26. BLUE DACNIS
*Dacnis cayana*      Pls. 47, 48, Map 1262
**Identification:** 5″ (13cm). Conical bill short, straight, and pointed. ♂: mostly blue to rich cobalt blue (or turquoise blue—*cayana; glaucogularis*); lores, throat, mantle, and tail black; wings broadly edged blue; eyes reddish brown. ♀: *bright green above,* paler below with *bluish gray head;* throat grayish. Legs flesh pink (both sexes).
**Similar species:** ♂ Turquoise Dacnis-Tanager (p 606) has banditlike black mask across sides of head and shorter heavier bill. See Black-faced Dacnis (27), also with mask across face as well as bold yellow eyes. ♂ Viridian Dacnis (28) of nw only, is obviously green with yellow eyes, ♀ lacks bluish head of ♀ Blue Dacnis. In the highlands see ♀ Capped Conebill (7).
**Behavior:** Occur alone, or in pairs, seldom in groups but otherwise much like *Cyanerpes* in actions. Actively glean insects from twigs and foliage from lower levels to canopy and often at fruiting trees and shrubs. A reg. member of mixed tanager and honeycreeper flocks.
**Breeding:** 9 BC birds, Jan–Sept, n Colombia (Carriker), 2 in Jan, Santander (Boggs 1961); 1 in Apr, Gulf of Urabá (Haffer 1975); Panama nest, 15m up in forest, July (R. Ridgely); deep nest cup of fine fibers and plant down suspended between terminal forks about 6-8m up; 2 whitish eggs with dark markings (Skutch 1962b).
**Status and habitat:** Fairly common in humid forest borders, second growth woodland, and shrubby clearings, esp. where flowering and fruiting trees are present; lowlands and foothills, occas. wander higher.
**Range:** To 1000m. Throughout. Baudó Mts. and Mutatá s to Nariño (*baudoana*); Río Juradó and w side of Gulf of Urabá (*ultramarina*); e side of Gulf of Urabá to w Guajira (*napaea*); lower Cauca and lower and mid. Magdalena vals. (*coerebicolor*); e of Andes from Arauca to Vaupés (*cayana*); Caquetá and Putumayo (*glaucogularis*); Amazonas (subsp.). Nicaragua to w Ecuador, ne Argentina, Paraguay, and s Brazil. Trinidad.

### 27. BLACK-FACED DACNIS
*Dacnis lineata*      Pls. 47, 48, Map 1263
**Identification:** 4.5″ (11.4cm). Bill sort, thin,

and very pointed. *Eyes bright yellow.* ♂: mostly *bright turquoise blue*; broad *black mask from bill across sides of head* continues to hindneck and upper back; wings and tail black; upper half of folded wing turquoise; center of belly and under tail coverts white (or yellow—*egregia*). ♀ very different: above dull brownish olive, below sim. but much paler, becoming *buffy white on abdomen*; under wing coverts white (or under wing coverts and belly yellowish, sometimes a faint bluish tinge above—*egregia*).

**Similar species:** Striking ♂ likely confused only with ♂ Turquoise Dacnis-Tanager (p 606), which has a black chin and lacks yellow or white belly. Nondescript ♀ best known by the accompanying ♂. Good marks are the thin dacnislike bill and buffy white (or yellow—*egregia*) belly. ♀ Yellow-bellied Dacnis (29) has prom. red eye; otherwise sim. Also cf. ♂ to ♂ Blue Dacnis (26).

**Behavior:** Pairs or several glean in canopy and subcanopy foliage, sometimes hanging to examine underside of leaves. Follow mixed flocks high in forest or at edges; loaf in treetops.

**Breeding:** 3 BC birds, May–Sept, s Bolívar (Carriker); 2 in Dec, Santander (Boggs 1961).

**Status and habitat:** Uncommon in humid *terra firme* and *várzea* forests, forest edges, and second growth. Habitat much as in *D. cayana* though more confined to forest. Spec. collected w of Garzón, s Huila, Mar 10, 1961 (Lehmann and Brown).

**Range:** To 1200m. N end of W Andes (upper Río Sinú) e to Río Nechí and mid. and upper Magdalena Val. s to s Huila (*egregia*); e of Andes from w Meta (Villavicencio) and sw Guainía (San Felipe; Macacuní) southward (*lineata*). The Guianas, w Venez. (sw Táchira) and s Venez. to n Bolivia and Amazonian Brazil; w Ecuador.

**Note:** The *aequatorialis* subsp. of w Ecuador may occur in sw Nariño (rec. n to Esmeraldas). Sim. to *egregia* subsp., but ♂ greenish blue and center of belly richer yellow; ♀ sim. to *egregia* but throat and foreneck grayer.

### 28. VIRIDIAN DACNIS
*Dacnis viguieri*          Pl. 48, Map 1264

**Identification:** 4.5″ (11.4cm). Bill short, conical, and pointed; *eyes yellow* (♀?). ♂: mostly bright *greenish blue* var. to green or blue green with light; rump pale blue; *lores, triangular patch on upper back, and tail black*; wings mostly green contrasting with black primaries. ♀: dull pale olive green above; *lores and tail black; outer primaries black* edged greenish; underparts light yellowish green becoming light yellow on under tail coverts.

**Similar species:** Blue green ♂, usually seen from below, resembles ♂ Blue Dacnis (26) from distance but lacks black throat. ♀ recalls ♀ Green Honeycreeper (24) but is smaller, with black primaries and short bill; ♀ Black-faced Dacnis (27—*egregia*) has yellowish belly and under wing coverts.

**Behavior:** Sim. to other Dacnis.

**Status and habitat:** Canopy of humid forest and forest edge in lowlands and foothills. Small nos. in upper Río Verde del Sinú, sw Córdoba (Hilty); perhaps more numerous in hill country.

**Range:** 50–600m. The extreme nw on both sides of Gulf of Urabá (Río Tulupa on e side), upper Río Sinú Val. (incl. Quimarí), and rivers near Panama boundary (Río Juradó; Río Salaquí). Extreme se Panama and nw Colombia.

### 29. YELLOW-BELLIED DACNIS
*Dacnis flaviventer*          Pl. 47, Map 1265

**Identification:** 5″ (13cm). Short conical bill. *Eyes red.* ♂ *mainly yellow and black*; cap dull green (not conspic.; sides of head, mantle, wings, and tail black; *scapulars, sides of back, rump, and entire underparts bright yellow; central throat black*. ♀ very different: pale brownish olive above, wings and tail somewhat darker; below dingy yellowish buff obscurely mottled olive on breasts and sides. Juv. ♂ like ♀.

**Similar species:** ♂ might bring to mind a Bananaquit (9), but head pattern different and no white wing spot. Note prom. yellow scapular bands connecting with lower back. ♀ very like ♀ Black-faced Dacnis (27) but eyes red.

**Voice:** Call a high, buzzy, and coarse *zreet*.

**Behavior:** Much like Blue Dacnis but more often seen away from mixed flocks than in them.

**Breeding:** BC pair, June, w Caquetá (Carriker).

**Status and habitat:** Uncommon to locally common in *terra firme* and *várzea* edges, along rivers, and in nearby scattered trees and irreg. second growth.

**Range:** To 400m. E of Andes from w Caquetá and Vaupés (Mitú) southward (sighting n to c Meta needs confirmation). S Venez. (n to San Fernando de Atabapo on Orinoco) to n Bolivia and Amazonian Brazil.

### 30. SCARLET-THIGHED DACNIS
*Dacnis venusta*          Pl. 47, Map 1266

**Identification:** 4.8″ (12.2cm). Bill short and pointed. Eyes red (♂ ♀). ♂ mostly *turquoise blue above and black below*; crown, sides of head, center stripe of mantle, scapulars, and lower back turquoise blue; forehead, lores, center of throat, sides of mantle, *wings, tail, and entire underparts black*; thighs scarlet (often hidden). ♀ very different: sides of head and *upperparts dull bluish green*, tinged dusky on back, wings,

and tail; *rump and cheeks distinctly bluish; underparts mostly buffy brown*, paler on throat, yellowish buff on belly.
**Similar species:** ♂ might be confused with Blue-necked Tanager (p 613), but latter has all black back and silvery green shoulders. ♀ is the only coerebid with combination of bluish rump and unstreaked buffy underparts. See ♀ Blue Dacnis (26) and White-eared Conebill (2).
**Behavior:** Even more restless than Blue Dacnis, almost warblerlike in actions. Occurs from lower shrubbery to subcanopy, singly, in pairs, or occas. in small groups, and frequently with mixed tanager and honeycreeper flocks (though not so persistently as Blue Dacnis). Eats small berries (esp. *Miconia*) and insects.
**Breeding:** Not well known. BC ♂, 26 Jan, Chocó (Carriker). Panama fledgling, 18 July (Willis and Eisenmann 1979); 1 Costa Rican nest, 9 May; cryptic and very shallow, frail cup of tendrils, rootlets, and bits of fern and grass, suspended by cobweb to 2 branches, about 17m up; 2 young (Skutch 1962b).
**Status and habitat:** Uncommon to fairly common (somewhat erratic) in humid and wet forest borders and second growth woodland in the lowlands; broken hillside forest and shrubby edges in foothills or higher. Most numerous in lower foothills (about 150-600m); wanders higher.
**Range:** To 1000m. Pacific coast (sight to 1100m, Anchicayá Val.) and along n base of Andes e to mid. Magdalena Val. (s to Remedios, Antioquia). Costa Rica to w Ecuador.

### 31. SCARLET-BREASTED DACNIS
*Dacnis berlepschi*      Pl. 47, Map 1267
**Identification:** 4.6″ (11.7cm). Short pointed bill. Eyes yellow. ♂ unmistakable: *entire upperparts, head, throat, and chest brilliant violaceous blue*; forehead and mask blackish; *back and wing coverts profusely streaked light silvery blue*; wings and tail black; wings with blue edgings; *lower breast flame scarlet* fading to orange buff on lower underparts. ♀: above brown, below buffy brown; *breast heavily washed reddish orange*.
**Similar species:** ♂ recalls Blue-backed Conebill (4) of higher el. but is much brighter and

streaked. ♀ from allies by reddish orange wash on breast, and yellow eyes.
**Status and habitat:** Uncommon or rare. Wet forest edges ("cloud forest") and tall second growth in w Nariño foothills. Not well known.
**Range:** 200-800m (sightings to 1200m near Junín—R. Ridgely; Hilty). Extreme sw Nariño (Río Guiza Val.; La Guayacana). Sw Colombia and nw Ecuador.

### 32. WHITE-BELLIED DACNIS
*Dacnis albiventris*      Pl. 47, Map 1268
**Identification:** 4.6″ (11.7cm). Black bill very short, pointed, and conebill-like; eyes yellow (♂;♀?). ♂: *mostly bright purplish blue with small black mask from forehead to ear coverts; center of lower breast to under tail coverts white*; flanks gray; wings and tail black heavily edged purplish blue; under wing coverts white. ♀ very different: olive green above, distinctly brighter green on rump; throat grayish white; *rest of underparts greenish yellow*; center of belly yellowish.
**Similar species:** Hooded Tanager (p 633) is larger, more robust, and has entire underparts white. Turquoise Tanager (p 614) is mainly blue above, center of belly yellow (whitish-bellied subsp. not known to overlap). Bicolored (3) and Chestnut-vented conebills (1) lack the black mask and contrasting white belly. ♀ is more contrasty with greener upperparts and yellower underparts than allied ♀♀ such as Black-faced and Yellow-bellied dacnis (27, 29).
**Behavior:** Upper strata and canopy of forest. In Brazil an ad. ♂ and an imm. followed a small mixed flock about 10m up (Sick 1960). Bill shape suggests foraging habits nearer *Conirostrum* than *Dacnis*.
**Status and habitat:** Very rare. Known only from a few widely scattered localities in humid lowland forest.
**Range:** To 400m. E of Andes where known from w Putumayo (Pto. Umbría), an indefinite locality in Meta ("llanos del Meta") and "Bogotá." S. Venez. (Río Negro; Cerro Duida), e Ecuador, ne Peru, and Amazonian Brazil (se Pará).

# SWALLOW-TANAGERS: Tersinidae (1)

The single member of this South American family resembles a tanager but differs in, among other things, longer swallowlike wings, broad flat bill, and short weak tarsi. These differences have apparently resulted from a shift toward aerial insect feeding and ingestion of larger fruits and away from more typical tanagerlike gleaning and searching of branches and foliage. They also differ from tanagers in hole-nesting habits, gregarious behavior, and migratory movements. In spite of these differences, recent electrophoretic evidence from egg proteins (Sibley 1973) suggests they are closely related to tanagers and probably best placed near the genera *Tangara* and *Thraupis*.

## 1. SWALLOW-TANAGER
*Tersina viridis*          Pl. 49, Map 1269
**Identification:** 6" (15cm). Broad flat bill. ♂ : *mostly turquoise with forehead, mask, and throat black*; wings and tail black with broad blue edgings; center of belly white; *flanks barred black*. ♀ : *mostly bright grass green* with forehead, mask, and throat grayish brown; lower underparts pale yellow *with broad green barring on flanks*; wings and tail black edged green.
**Similar species:** ♂ bears some resemblance to ♂ Blue (p 451) or Plum-throated cotingas (p 451), ♀ to several "green" tanagers but has bars on flanks.
**Voice:** ♂'s squeaky twittering song resembles that of Blue-gray Tanager; high thin *tsee* call.
**Behavior:** Markedly gregarious, esp. when not breeding. Flight is strong and rather swallowlike. Perch high or low but often on more open branches within a tree. Eat fruit or insects, latter by sallying short distance to air.
**Breeding:** 6 BC birds, Apr–May, and 3 juvs., July, Perijá and Santa Marta mts., n end E Andes (Carriker); BC ♀, Apr, ne Meta (S. Furniss); Feb nest, w Meta (Brown), 2 Santa Marta nests, May–June; singly or in loose colonies as space permits in holes in buildings, bridges, walls, or cavity dug by ♀ in bank or road cut; 2-3 white eggs (Todd and Carriker 1922; Schäfer 1953a).
**Status and habitat:** Fairly common Jan–Aug in Santa Marta hill country, elsewhere *notably* erratic, though with some reg. e of Andes. Moist forest, lighter woodland and edges, and gallery forest. Seasonal movements need study; may breed locally on slopes above Cauca and Magdalena vals.; mostly absent from Pacific slope, rare in Cauca Val.
**Range:** 50-1600m (occas. to 2100m). Prob. throughout, but recs. very spotty w of Andes. E of Andes to e Vichada (El Tuparro—INDERENA) and s to w Caquetá and Vaupés. E Panama to ne Argentina, Paraguay, and s Brazil.

# TANAGERS Thraupidae (127)

Tanagers are a large and varied group of New World birds closely related to finches, honeycreepers, and wood warblers. In current practice (Paynter and Storer *in* Peters, 1970), the tanagers, including several genera previously placed in the Coerebidae, are treated as a subfamily Thraupinae of the Emberizidae (see discussion under Honeycreepers and Finches). But because of uncertain affinities of some genera the older arrangement is temporarily maintained here. There are, however, essentially no taxonomic characters that precisely define the limits of the family, and many species are remarkably finchlike, others warblerlike. Typical tanagers reach their greatest diversity in the New World tropics; only four species, all migratory, breed in temperate latitudes. Most tanagers feed on fruit supplemented by varying quantities of insects; chlorophonias and euphonias are almost wholly frugivorous, many eating mainly mistletoe berries and acting as dispersal agents for the seeds of the plants. With some notable exceptions, most Colombian tanagers are poor songsters; some have almost no song at all. Nests vary from open cups built by most species to mossy globular balls of chlorophonias and euphonias.

[*Chlorophonia*: Plumper and shorter-tailed than *Euphonia*; bill short and rather broad; predom. bright green; frugivorous; stomach rudimentary; treetops.]

## 1. BLUE-NAPED CHLOROPHONIA
*Chlorophonia cyanea*          Pl. 49, Map 1270
**Identification:** 4.2" (10.7cm). Chunky. ♂ : *entire head throat, and chest bright green*; ocular region blue; back and rump bright blue; wings and tail green; breast and *lower underparts bright yellow* (or as above but forehead yellow, only nuchal collar and rump blue, back green—*psittacina*). ♀ : like respective ♂ but duller; back green; *only nuchal collar blue* (rump also blue—*psittacina*); breast and lower underparts dull greenish yellow.
**Similar species:** Other ♂ chlorophonias (2, 3) have yellow (not blue) rumps. ♀ most like ♀ Chestnut-breasted Chlorophonia but crown green (not purplish blue). ♀ Yellow-collared Chlorophonia has orange bill and legs (not dusky).
**Voice:** Nasal *peent* and short rattle.
**Behavior:** Pairs or small groups usually stay in upper levels of trees; only occas. join mixed flocks. Sluggish and mostly frugivorous.
**Breeding:** 10 BC birds, Apr–May, Santa Marta

and Perijá mts., W and C Andes (Carriker); 2 in Apr and May (Miller 1963), building nest, Jan and June, and 4 begging juvs., May and July (S. Gniadek) in W Andes above Cali; 3 Santa Marta nests, May, in vertical bank or cliff; grassy oval ball with side entrance; 3 white eggs sprinkled chestnut (Todd and Carriker 1922).

**Status and habitat:** Uncommon in humid forest, forest borders and clearings with scattered trees. Most numerous in Santa Marta Mts.

**Range:** 600-2100m (usually above 1400m in Andes). Santa Marta Mts. (*psittacina*); Perijá Mts., and mid. Magdalena Val. from Snía. San Lucas to head of val. (*longipennis*); spottily on Pacific slope of W Andes s to Valle and on e slope in Valle (*intensa*). Guyana, Venez., and in Andes to ne Argentina; se Brazil, Paraguay.

## 2. YELLOW-COLLARED CHLOROPHONIA

*Chlorophonia flavirostris* Pl. 48, Map 1271

**Identification:** 4″ (10.2cm). *Eyes white with yellow eyering. Bill and legs orange.* ♂: upperparts, head, throat and chest bright green; *broad collar on hindneck yellow; rump yellow;* breast and lower underparts yellow separated from chest by a very narrow (sometimes broken) chestnut band. ♀ and imm.: mostly uniform grass green, center of breast and belly yellowish.

**Similar species:** ♂ Chestnut-breasted Chlorophonia (3) lacks yellow collar and has blue crown. Best marks for dull ♀ and imm. are small size, yellow eyering, and dull orange legs and bill.

**Voice:** Most common call a soft *pek*; more plaintive *peeeeeee* perched or in flight; brief song a slow rattling buzz followed by 1 to several soft whistles.

**Behavior:** Pairs or groups up to 30, rarely to 80, wander alone or with mixed flocks over steep forested hillsides. Usually well up in trees or in treetop foliage where not easy to see; mostly frugivorous, esp. mistletoe and *Miconia* berries. Bright ♂♂ always outnumbered by duller ♀♀ and imms.

**Breeding:** June pairs believed nesting, upper Anchicayá Val. (Hilty).

**Status and habitat:** Few specimens (Hilty 1977) but fairly common in wet forest (lower el. "cloud forest") and forest borders; foothills and lower slopes. Easily overlooked except for frequent soft calls.

**Range:** 100-1900m. Pacific slope in Valle (Río Anchicayá and Río Digua drainage) and s Nariño (La Guayacana, 250m; sightings above Junín). W Colombia to nw Ecuador.

## 3. CHESTNUT-BREASTED CHLOROPHONIA

*Chlorophonia pyrrhophrys* Pl. 49, Map 1272

**Identification:** 4.6″ (11.7cm). Chunky. ♂: upperparts, throat, and chest green; crown and nape *purplish blue* bordered on front and sides with black; *rump yellow;* lower underparts yellow separated from chest by narrow band mixed chestnut and black; *chestnut median stripe from breast to crissum.* ♀: upperparts, throat, and chest green; *crown blue; nape blue with chestnut border;* breast and belly dull yellow.

**Similar species:** See other chlorophonias (1, 2) and Blue-hooded Euphonia (4).

**Voice:** Song a long rambling chatter suggesting that of a *Spinus* (Miller 1963); *tut tut tut too-dée too-dée . . .* , or *na-deár, na-deár . . . to-d'leép*, with var.; nasal *near* notes often predom. (Schwartz recording).

**Behavior:** Usually in pairs from midlevel to canopy.

**Breeding:** 2 BC ♂♂, Feb and Apr, W Andes above Cali (Miller 1963); BC ♂ and imm., May, Perijá Mts. (Carriker). Mar nest in Venez. a grass and moss ball with side entrance, 6m up on roadcut bank, montane forest (R. Ridgely).

**Status and habitat:** Uncommon and somewhat local; humid forest, forest borders, and disturbed areas, even pastures with isolated trees.

**Range:** 1400-2700m (once to 3600m). Perijá Mts. (3300m); E and C Andes (few recs.), e slope W Andes and Pacific slope in Antioquia, Valle, and Nariño. Nw Venez. s in Andes to Ecuador and c Peru.

[*Euphonia*: Short thick bill, short tail; ♂♂ (except 4, 15, 16, 17) with "standard" yellow and blue black pattern are best told by differences in cap, throat, and vent; ♀♀ dull olive, usually difficult to tell apart. Frugivorous; stomach rudimentary; nest a side entrance ball.]

## 4. BLUE-HOODED EUPHONIA

*Euphonia musica* Pl. 53, Map 1273

**Identification:** 4.5″ (11.4cm). ♂: glossy purplish black above with *contrasting turquoise blue crown and nape* and *bright yellow rump;* forehead, sides of head, and throat black; remaining underparts yellow (or rump and underparts ochraceous yellow—*intermedia*). ♀: olive green above with rufous forehead and *turquoise blue crown and nape;* below olive yellow.

**Similar species:** ♀ from ♀ Chestnut-breasted Chlorophonia (3) by rufous forehead, brighter blue cap, and duller more uniform underparts. ♂ unlike any other.

**Voice:** Song of rapid twitters and trills up to

30 sec or more is conebill-like; calls incl. soft *cheer* and *deeer deeer deeer dee* (P. Schwartz recording).

**Behavior:** Pairs or less frequently small, rather quiet groups in the mid. or upper level of trees; often with forest flocks.

**Breeding:** 7 BC birds, Jan–May, Cauca and Huila (Carriker); 5 in Dec–Jan, Boyacá (Olivares 1963); BC ♀, Jan (Miller 1963); building nest in Apr (S. Gniadek), W Andes above Cali; nest in May, PN Cueva de los Guácharos (P. Gertler); globular grass and moss ball with side entrance; 2 eggs, cream marked brown and black mainly at large end (ffrench 1973).

**Status and habitat:** Uncommon to locally fairly common; forest borders, second growth woodland, and disturbed areas.

**Range:** 1400-2100m (sighting to 2600m, Puracé, Cauca—Hilty). Both slopes E Andes from Norte de Santander s at least to Cundinamarca (*intermedia*); C Andes, and W Andes in Valle and Cauca (*pelzelni* X *intermedia*); undoubtedly in Nariño (*pelzelni?*). W Mexico to n Argentina and se Brazil; W Indies.

**Note:** Incl. *E. musica* (Antillean Euphonia) of W Indies, *E. elegantissima* (Blue-hooded Euphonia) of Mid. America, and *E. cyanocephala* (Golden-rumped Euphonia) of S America. Prob. more than 1 sp. involved.

## 5. ORANGE-BELLIED EUPHONIA

*Euphonia xanthogaster*     Pl. 53, Map 1274

**Identification:** 4.3″ (10.9cm). Widespread. ♂ has standard euphonia pattern: steel blue above with blue black sides of head, throat, and breast; *forehead and crown to behind eyes ochraceous yellow* (or chestnut—*badissima*); *lower underparts yellow*; small white band on inner remiges and large white spot on inner web of outer pair of tail feathers. ♀: *forehead dull yellow* (or chestnut—*badissima*); *nape gray*; otherwise olive above; *mostly buffy gray below*, washed yellowish olive on sides.

**Similar species:** ♂ almost identical to ♂ Purple-throated Euphonia (11), but forecrown ochraceous orange or chestnut (not lemon yellow). In hand throat blue black (not deep purple) and only outer pair (not outer 2 pairs) of tail feathers with white. In n Colombia cf. Trinidad Euphonia (10); also see 7, 8, 9, 12, and 13. Good marks for ♀ are gray nape and buffy gray underparts.

**Voice:** Frequently repeated call *dee, dee deet*, last note higher; a nasal *nay, nay* and gravelly *chee-chee*; song a rambling disconnected *deeu deeu . . . deet deet deet . . . jew jew . . . chu chu chut . . . jew jew . . . .*

**Behavior:** Pairs or small families reg. follow mixed flocks of other frugivors. Eat mostly fruit, esp. mistletoe; upper understory to canopy, often low at forest edge to fruiting bushes.

**Breeding:** 8 BC birds, May–July, Perijá Mts. and C Andes in n Antioquia and Caldas (Carriker); 1 in Mar, Chocó (Haffer 1975); 5 in Feb–Apr, W Andes; Valle (Miller 1963); 7 nests, Nov–Apr, in Anchicayá Val. at 1000m (Hilty). Usual side entrance globular mossy ball a few m above ground.

**Status and habitat:** Humid and wet forest, second growth woodland, and borders. The most common euphonia in the Colombian Andes.

**Range:** To 2600m; ca. 20-350m in Pacific coast lowlands from Baudó Mts. southward (*chocoensis*); 350-2600m on both slopes of W Andes s to Nariño, both slopes C Andes s to Quindío region and w slope in Cauca, w slope E Andes in Santander (*oressinoma*); 1300-2100m, Perijá Mts. and e base E Andes from Norte de Santander to Boyacá (*badissima*); w slope E Andes in Norte de Santander and s Cesar (*oressinoma* X *badissima*); 100-1800m, E Andes in Cundinamarca s to sw Huila and e of Andes from w Meta, Guainía and Vaupés to Putumayo (*brevirostris*); Amazonas (*dilutior*). E Panama to nw Peru, Guyana, Bolivia, and se Brazil.

**Note:** For revision of the subspp. of *E. xanthogaster* see Olson (1981c).

## 6. TAWNY-CAPPED EUPHONIA

*Euphonia anneae*     Map 1275

**Identification:** 4.5″ (11.4cm). ♂: *entire crown rufous chestnut*; otherwise upperparts, sides of head, and throat glossy steel blue; lower underparts tawny yellow; under tail coverts white. ♀: dark olive above with *rufous forecrown*; yellowish olive below with entire median underparts grayish.

**Similar species:** ♂ is only Colombian euphonia in its range with wholly chestnut cap (but see *badissima* subsp. of 5). ♀ from ♀ Fulvous-vented Euphonia (13) by gray on central underparts. ♀ White-vented (7) and Thick-billed euphonias (12) lack rufous forecrown.

**Voice:** Calls incl. a rather harsh, unmusical, and usually doubled *enk*, a catlike *mya* and trilling and chattering (Slud 1964).

**Behavior:** Sim. to Orange-bellied Euphonia.

**Status and habitat:** Humid forest, second growth woodland, and borders. Not well known in Colombia. Replaced in most of Colombian hill country by allied Orange-bellied Euphonia.

**Range:** Known in Colombia only from hills (prob. to 1500m) w of Gulf of Urabá along Panama boundary. Costa Rica to extreme nw Colombia.

## 7. WHITE-VENTED EUPHONIA
*Euphonia minuta*          Pl. 53, Map 1276
**Identification:** 4″ (10.2cm). ♂ has usual euphonia pattern: upperparts, sides of head, throat, and chest steely blue black; *only forehead yellow* (extends just to eyes); lower underparts yellow; *abdomen and under tail coverts white.* ♀: uniform olive above; throat grayish; breast olivaceous yellow; *center of abdomen and under tail coverts white to grayish white.*
**Similar species:** Either sex from any other euphonia in Colombia by white abdomen and under tail coverts.
**Voice:** Usual call a single, sharp *peet* rather like several other euphonias.
**Behavior:** Sim. to Fulvous-vented Euphonia and w of Andes often with it (Hilty); e of Andes often with small flocks of other treetop euphonias (J. V. Remsen).
**Breeding:** In Costa Rica, late Mar–Aug; nest 5-7m up; side entrance, globular mossy ball in epiphytes or on mossy limb; 3 white eggs heavily blotched and spotted brown (Skutch 1972).
**Status and habitat:** Fairly common in humid and wet forest, second growth woodland, and forest borders.
**Range:** To 1000m. Pacific coast (usually below 500m), e in humid lowlands n of Andes to mid. Magdalena Val. (s to Remedios, e Antioquia), and e of Andes from w Meta (Villavicencio) and Vaupés (Mitú) southward. Prob. entire e base of E Andes (in adj. s Táchira, Venez.). Se Mexico to n Bolivia and Amazonian Brazil.

## 8. VELVET-FRONTED EUPHONIA
*Euphonia concinna*          Pl. 53, Map 1277
**Identification:** 3.8″ (9.7cm). ♂ has usual euphonia pattern, but *forehead black and only a yellow patch on forecrown;* otherwise upperparts, sides of head, throat, and chest steely blue black, back glossed purplish; lower underparts yellow tinged ochraceous; no white in tail. ♀: dull olive; grayer on nape; *narrow, dull yellow forehead; underparts dull yellow* (sometimes with faint orangish tinge); center of belly brightest.
**Similar species:** ♂ is only Colombian euphonia with a black forehead and with yellow confined to patch on forecrown. Very sim. ♂ Orange-bellied Euphonia (5) has entire forehead and forecrown yellow; ♀ much like ♀ Orangebellied Euphonia but duller, lacks distinct gray nape, and has yellowish (not grayish) tinge on underparts. Also see larger ♀ Thick-billed Euphonia (12).
**Behavior:** Much like other euphonias and may

occur with Orange-bellied Euphonia at mistletoe in canopy of large roadside trees.
**Breeding:** 3 BC birds, Jan–Apr, upper Magdalena Val. (Miller 1947; Carriker).
**Status and habitat:** Canopy of open drier woodland, hedgerows, and trees bordering streams. Uncommon and greatly outnumbered by Orange-bellied Euphonia, which occurs in same area.
**Range:** ENDEMIC. 200-1000m (to 1800m in w Cundinamarca). Dry mid. and upper Magdalena Val. from n Tolima (Honda) to sw Huila (La Plata).

## 9. ORANGE-CROWNED EUPHONIA
*Euphonia saturata*          Pl. 53, Map 1278
**Identification:** 4.2″ (10.7cm). ♂: *entire crown to nape orange yellow;* otherwise glossy purplish black on upperparts, sides of head, throat, and chest; *entire lower underparts deep orange.* ♀: bright olive green above with dull yellowish forehead; below olive yellow; brighter and yellower on belly.
**Similar species:** Distinctive ♂ is only Colombian euphonia with whole crown orange yellow. ♀ is smaller but otherwise prob. not safely separable in field from ♀ Thick-billed Euphonia (12). Also see ♀ Orange-bellied Euphonia (5).
**Voice:** Distinctive, high *pee-deet*, reminiscent of Trinidad Euphonia.
**Behavior:** Alone or in pairs that keep well up in trees or in treetops in rather open areas; in w Nariño with mixed tanager-honeycreeper flocks on steep forested slopes at 900m el.
**Status and habitat:** Uncommon and local; fairly dry to wet forest borders, woodlots, parks, and tree-lined streams; occurs in a wide var. of semiopen areas or even clearings in forest or inside broken hillside forest but nowhere numerous.
**Range:** 700-1300m. Both slopes of W Andes and adj. Cauca Val. from Valle (Dagua Val. and Buga area) s to w Nariño. W Colombia, w Ecuador, and nw Peru.

## 10. TRINIDAD EUPHONIA
*Euphonia trinitatis*          Pl. 53, Map 1279
**Identification:** 3.8″ (9.7cm). ♂ has usual euphonia pattern: upperparts, sides of head, and throat steely blue black with forecrown to behind eyes bright yellow; *underparts bright yellow;* 2 (sometimes 3) outer tail feathers with large white spot on inner web. ♀: pale olive green above; *throat, sides, and under tail coverts bright greenish yellow; center of breast and belly grayish white.*

**Similar species:** ♂ much like Orange-bellied Euphonia (5) but smaller and brighter yellow, esp. cap. In hand, 2-3 vs 1 pair of outer tail feathers with white spot. Near the Orinoco region may meet Purple-throated Euphonia (see 11). Easier ♀ lacks gray nape of Orange-bellied and has central underparts gray bordered bright greenish yellow on sides (not dull buffy gray throughout). Also see larger ♀ Thick-billed Euphonia (12).

**Voice:** Distinctive, often-heard call a thin, penetrating *dee-dee*, higher-pitched than corresponding call of Orange-bellied Euphonia.

**Behavior:** Pairs wander alone, usually well up in trees; occas. join mixed flocks. Mostly frugivorous but also hop along limbs and twigs gleaning insects.

**Breeding:** 3 BC birds, Mar, Cesar (Carriker); 1 juv. in July, Santa Marta (S. M. Russell); 1 nest, 17 Apr, Venez. Orinoco (Cherrie 1916); nest like others of genus; 2-12m up; 4 eggs, cream marked brown (ffrench 1973).

**Status and habitat:** Common in drier open woodland borders, cultivated areas and scrub, locally into more humid regions. Meets or narrowly overlaps range of Orange-bellied Euphonia along s border of range.

**Range:** To 1100m. Carib. region from Atlántico (w of Barranquilla) to Guajira and s to mid. Magdalena Val. (Remedios, e Antioquia). Poss. Vichada along Orinoco. N Colombia to Venez. and Trinidad.

**Note:** Sometimes considered a subsp. of *E. chlorotica* (Purple-throated Euphonia), but both have been taken at Caicara, Río Orinoco, Venez.

## 11. PURPLE-THROATED EUPHONIA
*Euphonia chlorotica*                    Map 1280

**Identification:** 3.8" (9.7cm). ♂ has standard euphonia pattern: upperparts, sides of head, throat, and chest glossy, steel blue black; *forecrown to eyes lemon yellow*; lower underparts bright yellow; inner web of outer 2 pairs of tail feathers white. ♀: bright olive green above with *dull yellowish forehead*, dull yellow below, palest on belly.

**Similar species:** ♂ hardly separable from Orange-bellied Euphonia (5) in field but brighter and more lemon yellow; in hand, 2 vs 1 pair of outer tail feathers with white. In Orinoco may overlap Trinidad Euphonia (10) where ♂♂ best distinguished by accompanying ♀, which differs from ♀ Trinidad most obviously by *yellowish forehead* and yellowish (no greenish tinge) underparts. ♀ very like ♀ Thick-billed Euphonia (12) but smaller, yellower below, and bill less massive. ♀ Orange-bellied Euphonia (5) from ♀ by duller olive (less green) back,

gray nape, and buffy gray (not yellowish) underparts.

**Voice:** Most common call a clear, high, whistled *pee-pee*; also *pee pee pay*.

**Behavior:** Much like Orange-bellied Euphonia.

**Breeding:** 3 BC birds, 19 Apr, Río Casanare (Carriker 1955), 1 BC ♂, 21 Apr, ne Meta (S. Furniss).

**Status and habitat:** Treetops in gallery forest and humid *várzea* and *terra firme* forests, often lower at forest borders.

**Range:** To 500m. E of Andes from Casanare (Río Casanare), Meta (incl. Carimagua—S. Furniss), and Orinoco region; poss. to Amazonas (?). The Guianas and Venez. (Táchira, Apure, and s of Orinoco) to n Bolivia, n Argentina, Paraguay, and Amazonian Brazil (incl. n bank of Amazon in Amazonas). Not rec. in Ecuador.

## 12. THICK-BILLED EUPHONIA
*Euphonia laniirostris*          Pl. 53, Map 1281

**Identification:** 4.3" (10.9cm). Bill *thicker* than other euphonias, but this hard to see in field. ♂: upperparts glossy steel blue; forecrown yellow; *entire underparts incl. throat and chest bright yellow*; large white spot on inner web of outer 2 pairs of tail feathers. ♀: olive green above, *yellow below* washed olive on breast.

**Similar species:** ♂ is only dark-backed Colombian euphonia with *entirely yellow* underparts (throat not black). Easily confused ♀ lacks yellowish forehead of ♀ Purple-throated Euphonia (11) and had brighter yellow throat. ♀ Trinidad Euphonia (10) is slightly smaller with gray median underparts; ♀ Orange-bellied Euphonia (5) has gray nape and mostly buffy gray underparts with contrasting yellow olive sides.

**Voice:** Usual calls a sweet *chweet* or *wheep* and clear *peet-peet* (Ridgely 1976); both sexes are excellent mimics, esp. of alarm and contact notes of many spp. (Morton 1976b; Remsen 1976)

**Behavior:** Solitary, in pairs, or occas. small groups. Mostly midlevel or higher in trees and often with mixed flocks, esp. other euphonias.

**Breeding:** 8 BC birds, Apr–July, Perijá Mts. to Córdoba (Carriker; Haffer 1975); 1 in Nov, Cundinamarca (MCN); building nest, Dec, Santander (Boggs 1961); 2 nests, Dec and Jan, Caldas (Borrero 1955); dome nest typical of genus; 2-4 white eggs thickly speckled reddish brown (Todd and Carriker 1922).

**Status and habitat:** Widespread and usually common. Woodlots, clearings with trees, forest borders, and second growth woodland in

dry to humid zones. Favors more open areas with trees.
**Range:** To 1800m (usually below 1100m). Throughout (on Pacific coast rec. only at Mutatá, n Chocó, and Río San Juan headwaters but reappears in nw Ecuador). No recs. in llanos (?). Costa Rica to w Peru, n Bolivia, and Amazonian Brazil.

## 13. FULVOUS-VENTED EUPHONIA
*Euphonia fulvicrissa*          Pl. 53, Map 1282
**Identification:** 4.2″ (10.7cm). ♂: upperparts, throat, and chest steely blue black with yellow forecrown and yellow lower underparts; *center of belly and under tail coverts tawny.* ♀: olive green above with *rufous forecrown;* yellowish olive below; *under tail coverts and center of belly tawny.*
**Similar species:** ♂ and ♀ much like respective sex of many other euphonias in Colombia but told from any by tawny lower belly.
**Voice:** Call a dull rattle, *de-e-e,* often doubled.
**Behavior:** Pairs normally keep in treetops but reg. come down low at forest edge and in disturbed areas. Like other euphonias, often with mixed flocks containing other frugivors.
**Breeding:** 13 BC birds, Jan–July, Norte de Santander to Chocó (Carriker); 2 in Apr, nw Antioquia (Haffer 1975).
**Status and habitat:** Humid and wet forest, forest borders, and shrubby second growth woodland; fairly common in lowlands and foothills.
**Range:** To 1000m (usually below 500m). Pacific coast and humid lowlands along n base of Andes e to mid. Magdalena Val. (s to Remedios and Bucaramanga); e base of E Andes in Norte de Santander (Bellavista, 650m). C Panama to nw Ecuador.

## 14. RUFOUS-BELLIED EUPHONIA
*Euphonia rufiventris*          Pl. 53, Map 1283
**Identification:** 4.5″ (11.4cm). ♂ *lacks yellow on head;* entire upperparts, head, throat, and chest glossy steel blue; *lower breast and belly orange rufous;* no white in tail. ♀: olive above with gray nape; *underparts pale gray with greenish yellow sides and incomplete greenish yellow breast band; under tail coverts tawny rufous.*
**Similar species:** ♂, along with ♂ of Plumbeous Euphonia (see 17), are only dark-backed Colombian euphonias with *no yellow* on crown. Best marks for ♀ are incomplete breast band and rufous wash on vent. ♀ from ♀ Golden-bellied Euphonia (16) by absence of whitish loral spot. Also see ♀ Orange-bellied Euphonia (5) and ♀ Purple-throated Euphonia (11).

**Voice:** Call a low, buzzy, 4-noted *bz-bz-bz-bz* (J. V. Remsen) much like that of Fulvous-vented Euphonia.
**Behavior:** Single birds or pairs are often around epiphytes in canopy but sometimes lower at forest edge. Reg. follow forest flocks but seldom with other euphonias.
**Status and habitat:** Uncommon in humid *várzea* and *terra firme* forests and forest edges.
**Range:** To 500m. E of Andes from s Meta (Macarena Mts.) and e Guainía (Río Guainía-Río Negro region) southward. Prob. to se Vichada. S Venez. to n Bolivia and w Amazonian Brazil.

## 15. BRONZE-GREEN EUPHONIA
*Euphonia mesochrysa*          Pl. 53, Map 1284
**Identification:** 3.8″ (9.7cm). ♂ looks "♀-plumaged": *bronzy olive above; nape tinged blue gray; forehead yellow;* throat, chest, and sides yellowish olive; *center of lower breast, belly, and under tail coverts deep orange yellow.* ♀: bronzy olive above, incl. forehead; *throat, chest, and sides slightly paler; more yellowish olive; center of lower breast and belly gray;* under tail coverts yellowish.
**Similar species:** A confusing and prob. often overlooked sp. ♂ recalls both sexes of Golden-bellied Euphonia (16) but lacks whitish lores and chin and has intense orange yellow lower underparts. ♀ differs from Rufous-bellied Euphonia (14) chiefly in smaller size and yellow olive (not gray) throat. ♂ from ♀ Orange-bellied Euphonia (5) by brighter, bronze-tinged upperparts, deep yellow vent, and no gray tinge on underparts; ♀ from ♀ of 5 by buffy wash on throat and breast. Also see 11.
**Behavior:** A ♂ with a mixed flock ranged from mid. to canopy ht. along a forested roadside (Hilty).
**Status and habitat:** Not well known in Colombia. Humid foothill and lower montane forest.
**Range:** 500-2300m. Known from e slope of C Andes at head of Magdalena Val. (El Isno, 1700m; La Candela, 2300m), e base of E Andes in w Meta (Villavicencio), and a sight rec. in w Caquetá (1400m; 7 Sept 1978—Hilty). Andes from Colombia to Perú (incl. ne lowlands e to mouth of Río Curaray) and n Bolivia.

## 16. GOLDEN-BELLIED EUPHONIA
*Euphonia chrysopasta*          Pl. 53, Map 1285
**Identification:** 4.5″ (11.4cm). ♂ looks "♀ plumaged": *glossy bronze green above, back tinged gray;* crown and nape bluish gray; upper tail coverts greenish yellow; *large loral spot grayish white;*

chin whitish; otherwise dull golden yellow below, somewhat mottled dusky olive on breast and sides. ♀: sim. to ♂, but underparts pale gray; flanks and under tail coverts olive yellow.

**Similar species:** Best mark for either sex is the large whitish loral patch. See Bronze-green Euphonia (15).

**Voice:** Notes incl. *chit-weéep*, last rising, at short intervals, and sharp *sit!* (P. Schwartz recording); jumbled song of *chit*'s, *sit*'s, *weep*'s, and other notes sputters on much like Mid. American *E. gouldi* (Olive-backed Euphonia); spreads and wags tail, sometimes even pumps body like latter as it sings.

**Behavior:** Pairs often follow frugivor flocks in upper levels of trees but come low at forest edge; seldom with mixed euphonia flocks.

**Breeding:** Pair building side entrance ball nest 10m up in epiphytes, Limoncocha, Ecuador, 25 Aug (Hilty).

**Status and habitat:** Canopy of humid *terra firme* and *várzea* forest edges and trees in clearings and pastures; less frequently treetops inside tall forest. In most of the se Colombian lowlands the least numerous euphonia.

**Range:** To 1200m. E of Andes from w Meta (above Villavicencio), Río Guaviare, and e Vichada southward. The Guianas and s Venez. to n Bolivia and Amazonian Brazil.

## 17. [PLUMBEOUS EUPHONIA]

*Euphonia plumbea*          Map 1286

**Identification:** 3.6″ (9.1cm). ♂ has *no yellow* on head; *entire upperparts, head, throat, and chest glossy dark blue gray*; lower underparts bright yellow orange. ♀: crown, nape, and mantle dark gray; otherwise dark olive green above; primaries and tail dusky; *sides of head and throat pale gray*; rest of underparts dull yellowish olive; much brighter yellow on belly.

**Similar species:** ♂ most like Rufous-bellied Euphonia (14) in pattern but dark blue gray (not steel blue) above and yellowish (not deep rufous) below. ♀ somewhat like ♂ Golden-bellied Euphonia (16) but lacks white loral patch and has gray chest and throat.

**Voice:** High-pitched penetrating call *wee-pee-pee*, slightly nasal, frequently repeated.

**Behavior:** Like other euphonias usually in pairs or small chattery groups in mid. or upper levels of trees; sometimes with mixed flocks.

**Status and habitat:** Hypothetical. Common in sandy-belt forest edges, esp. around edges of large flat granite outcrops; also savanna woodland and semiopen savanna with scattered trees and bushes of ne Guainía. No Colombian specimens.

**Range:** Ca. 100m. Ne Guainía (sight recs., Pto.

Inírida area, Sept 1978—Hilty and M. Robbins). Surinam, Guyana, s Venez. (incl. several localities on e bank of Río Orinoco and Río Negro opp. Colombia) and n Brazil n of Amazon.

[*Pipraeidea*: Like *Tangara* but bill shorter, wider, and swallowlike; wings longer; often more aerial.]

## 18. FAWN-BREASTED TANAGER

*Pipraeidea melanonota*          Pl. 53, Map 1287

**Identification:** 6″ (15cm). Eyes red. *Crown and nape bright pale blue with broad black mask through eyes*; otherwise dull dusky blue above with pale blue lower back and rump; wings and tail edged blue; *entire underparts fawn buff*. ♀: sim. but duller, esp. on crown.

**Similar species:** Easily recognized. Much smaller Rusty Flower-piercer (p 594) lacks the contrasting head pattern and fire red eye. Also cf. 99 and 123, both in different habitat.

**Voice:** Song a squeaky unmusical ser. of notes, not heard often.

**Behavior:** Reminiscent of a swallow-tanager though not social. Single bird or pairs are usually alone as glean from twigs and limbs, sally for flying insects, or visit trees and shrubs for fruit. Forage from shrub to treetop ht., and rarely join mixed flocks. Flight swifter than that of related *Tangara*.

**Breeding:** 2 BC ♂♂, Mar and July, Huila and Valle (Carriker; Miller 1963); building in Mar, PN Cueva de los Guácharos (P. Gertler).

**Status and habitat:** Uncommon to fairly common (but often thinly spread) in bushy pastures, cultivated areas, gardens, and other *nonforest* habitats; very small nos. into clearings or at forest borders in forested zones.

**Range:** 1400-3000m; to 900m on Pacific slope. All 3 Andean ranges (recs. scattered; Pacific slope only in Valle and Nariño). N and s Venez.; Andes s to Bolivia; n Argentina to s Brazil.

## 19. TURQUOISE DACNIS-TANAGER

*Pseudodacnis hartlaubi*          Pl. 48, Map 1288

**Identification:** 4.5″ (11.4cm). *Eyes yellowish.* ♂ is turquoise and black: *throat and mask through eyes black; crown, nape, and eyering turquoise*; otherwise black above with turquoise shoulders, scapulars, and rump; underparts turquoise. ♀ very different: dull brown above; wing coverts and inner secondaries edged pale tawny buff; below grayish buff becoming yellowish white on center of breast and belly. Bill like *Tangara*.

**Similar species:** ♂ remarkably like Black-faced Dacnis (p 597), which is brighter turquoise, lacks eyering and black throat, and has white or yellow belly and thinner bill. ♂ Blue Dacnis (p 597) is deeper blue (subspp. w of E Andes) and lacks the broad black mask through and behind eyes. ♀, best known by attendant ♂, is very sim. to ♀ Black-faced Dacnis, but back brown (not olive), inner secondaries more prom. edged buff, underparts buffier, and prob. found mainly at higher el. (cf. ranges).

**Behavior:** A ♂ at Bosque Yotoco perched quietly on a high exposed bare limb and followed a mixed tanager-honeycreeper flock in subcanopy where hopped sluggishly on a mossy branch and at a bromeliad. Movements suggest a *Tangara* more than a Dacnis.

**Breeding:** 1 BC ♂, nw Bogotá, 8 Aug; fruit in stomach (ICN).

**Status and habitat:** Very rare and local. Humid forest borders and clearings with scattered trees. Recent sight recs. are from Río Bogotá below Tequendama Falls, formerly a region of extensive lower montane "cloud forest" (Munves 1975), and Bosque Yotoco, Valle, Aug 1979 (Hilty, J. Danzenbaker, et al.).

**Range:** ENDEMIC. 300-2200m. Known from Pacific slope foothills of lower Dagua Val. (Cisneros, 300m), near Dagua Val. headwaters (Las Pavas, 1300m; La Cumbre, 1700m), w slope C Andes in Quindío (Calarcá, 1500m), and w slope E Andes in Cundinamarca (Río Bogotá, 1700-2200m; Laguna de Pedropalo, 30km nw Bogotá, 2000m).

**Note:** Has been placed in the genus *Dacnis*.

[*Chlorochrysa*: Resemble allied *Tangara*, and usually with them; differ in voice, behavior, heavier tarsus, and longer, proportionally thinner bill.]

## 20. ORANGE-EARED TANAGER

*Chlorochrysa calliparaea*     Pl. 48, Map 1289

**Identification:** 5″ (13cm). ♂: *shining, metallic, emerald green above* with small orange crown spot and orange rump band; *throat black with prom. burnt orange spot on sides of neck*; otherwise emerald green below becoming blue green on lower underparts; black bases to green body feathers show through here and there giving slightly mottled appearance. ♀: sim. but duller with grayish throat and smaller burnt orange neck patch.

**Similar species:** Only small green tanager in its range with a prom. black (or gray—♀) throat. Look for the burnt orange patch on side of neck.

**Voice:** High-pitched wheezy *seeep*.

**Behavior:** Much like Glistening-green Tanager.

**Status and habitat:** Fairly common on steep, humid, forested slopes or at forest edges in w

Caquetá and w Putumayo (esp. above Mocoa). Few Magdalena Val. recs.

**Range:** 900-1800m (1600-1800m in Magdalena Val.). W slope of E Andes in Cundinamarca (at least formerly) s to head of Magdalena Val. (San Agustín area); e slope of E Andes in w Caquetá and w Putumayo (sightings, many obs.). E Colombia to n Bolivia.

## 21. GLISTENING-GREEN TANAGER

*Chlorochrysa phoenicotis*     Pl. 48, Map 1290

**Identification:** 5″ (13cm). *Almost entirely brilliant, glistening, emerald green*; small tuft behind eye shining gray tipped orange; *wing coverts shining gray*; inner webs of primaries and tail feathers black (inconspic. in field); bill black; legs steel gray. ♀: duller.

**Similar species:** ♀ Green Honeycreeper (p 596) is duller with sharp-pointed yellowish bill. Imm. Bay-headed Tanager (46) is largely green but much duller; imm. Multicolored Tanager (22) is mostly *dull* green; ♀ Multicolored is also mostly green but usually shows some face pattern.

**Voice:** Most common call a high, *lisping* 3- or 4-noted *czee, czee, czee*, var. to *ee-see-seez-seez*, weak but distinctive once learned.

**Behavior:** Single birds, pairs, or families follow flocks containing *Tangara* in upper forest levels where actively run along limbs and glean in outer foliage or cling upside down to terminal leaves; less often glean twigs or visit fruiting trees. Faster-moving and less frugivorous than most *Tangara* and usually do not peer head down along limbs like many of latter.

**Breeding:** 2 BC birds, June, n end C Andes (Carriker). Begging juv., 6 Sept, w Nariño; 3 breeding recs., Apr–June, Anchicayá Val. (1100m), cup nest hollowed in moss on side of limb, mid. strata (Hilty).

**Status and habitat:** Fairly common (easily overlooked). Upper understory to subcanopy of very wet mossy forest ("cloud forest"), forest edges, and tall second growth. Does not occur with *C. nitidissima*, which replaces it on e slope and locally at higher el. on Pacific slope. In Valle, most readily seen above Queremal at Tokio; common above Junín, Nariño.

**Range:** 700-2400m (mainly 1000-2200m). Pacific slope from Río San Juan headwaters (below Cerro Tatamá) southward; nw end of C Andes (2400m) in n Antioquia. W Colombia to nw Ecuador.

## 22. MULTICOLORED TANAGER

*Chlorochrysa nitidissima*     Pl. 48, Map 1291

**Identification:** 5″ (13cm). Harlequin patterned. ♂: *forepart of head and throat bright yel-*

*low*; center of throat golden orange; black patch on ear coverts bordered behind by chestnut; otherwise glistening emerald green above with *large triangular lemon yellow patch on back*; rump, breast, and belly glistening blue with center of lower breast and belly black. ♀: sim. but duller with back yellowish green (no yellow patch) and breast and belly green; black ear patch prom. on mainly yellow head. Imm.: mostly dull green.

**Similar species:** Ads. look mostly dark green in poor light, then easily confused with Saffron-crowned Tanager (34), which has short black mask through eyes and black (not yellow) throat. ♂'s yellow patch on back is best mark but not always easily seen. Cf. imm. to Glistening-green Tanager (21) and ♀ Green Honeycreeper (p 596).

**Voice:** Call, 1 to several wheezing *ceeet* notes sim. to Orange-eared Tanager.

**Behavior:** Much like Glistening-green Tanager, and like it, habitually gleans from outer foliage by clinging to leaves (Multicolored often clings to palm frond tips) or by peering along outer limbs (does not look under limbs like many *Tangara*) of upper understory to subcanopy.

**Breeding:** Stub-tailed juv. with 2 ads., 1 Nov, grown juv., 8 Jan, W Andes above Cali (Hilty).

**Status and habitat:** Humid to wet mossy forest ("cloud forest"), tall second growth woodland, and borders. Still fairly numerous in remnant patches of forest above Cali.

**Range:** ENDEMIC. 1400-2000m (to 900m on Pacific slope in Cauca). W slope of C Andes in Quindío and e slope in Caldas; e slope of W Andes above Cauca Val. from sw Antioquia to Cauca; very locally on Pacific slope from headwaters of Río San Juan s to w Cauca.

[*Tangara*: Large genus; remarkable for bright colors and diverse color patterns; no true song; many spp. (up to 9 or more) often sympatric; all partially frugivorous; food plants predom. spp. of Melastomataceae (esp. *Miconia* and *Cecropia*; greatest diversity in Andean subtropics and replaced at higher el. by larger *Anisognathus*, *Iridosornis*, and *Buthraupis*. Fewer spp. in forested lowlands where favored "edge" habitat is scarce.]

### 23. OPAL-RUMPED TANAGER
*Tangara velia*　　　　　Pl. 49, Map 1292
**Identification:** 5.5" (14cm). *Black above with opalescent lower back and rump*; wings heavily edged purplish blue; forehead, sides of head, and entire underparts purplish blue; *center of belly and under tail coverts chestnut* (though often look blackish in poor light).

**Similar species:** Much like Opal-crowned Tanager (24) but lacks broad opal forecrown and eyebrow, and under tail coverts chestnut (not black).

**Voice:** Weak chipping as forage.

**Behavior:** Peer "head down" under limbs like many *Tangara* or check epiphytes and debris in canopy or subcanopy, esp. on large limbs; may drop lower to small fruiting trees. Usually in pairs or small groups with the next sp., or with canopy flocks of var. types.

**Breeding:** Begging juv. with 3 ads., 18 Sept, ne Guainía (Hilty).

**Status and habitat:** Humid *terra firme* forest and forest edges, occas. taller irreg. second growth or treetops in clearings. Uncommon but usually more numerous than next sp.

**Range:** To 500m. E of Andes from w Meta (Villavicencio), Río Guaviare, and e Vichada (El Tuparro—INDERENA) southward. S Venez. to se Peru, n Bolivia, and Amazonian and se Brazil.

### 24. OPAL-CROWNED TANAGER
*Tangara callophrys*　　　　　Pl. 49, Map 1293
**Identification:** 5.8" (14.7cm). Much like Opal-rumped Tanager. *Broad opal forecrown and eyebrow*; otherwise black above with opalescent lower back and rump; wings heavily edged blue; narrow forehead and sides of head shining purplish blue; *center of belly and under tail coverts black*.

**Similar species:** See Opal-rumped Tanager (23) and like the latter looks very dark at a distance. The opal eyebrow is the mark.

**Voice:** High-pitched *zit* call usually repeated 2-4 times quickly; much like notes of Turquoise Tanager.

**Behavior:** As in preceding sp.

**Status and habitat:** Humid *terra firme* forest and forest edge. Less numerous than previous sp.

**Range:** To 500m. E of Andes in w Caquetá (Morelia) and Putumayo; perhaps to e Amazonas (rec. at mouth of Napo in adj. Perú). E Colombia to se Peru and Amazonian Brazil s of Amazon.

### 25. PARADISE TANAGER
*Tangara chilensis*　　　　　Pl. 49, Map 1294
**Identification:** 6" (15cm). Gorgeous, multicolored pattern unmistakable. *Crown and sides of head scaly green* with black eyering; otherwise black above with *scarlet rump* (or upper rump scarlet, lower rump yellowish orange—*coelicolor*); throat violet becoming *turquoise on rest of underparts*; center of belly and under tail coverts black.

**Voice:** High *czit* call, singly or in rapid ser.

**Behavior:** Chipping groups of 4-10 are often "nuclear" in treetop forest flocks; also wander alone in monospecific flocks or are accompanied by smaller nos. of Green-and-gold Tangaras. Like many *Tangara*, visit fruiting trees and shrubs and hop along bare canopy or subcanopy limbs peering underneath them; also peer at foliage or check bromeliads.
**Breeding:** In Brazil, cup nest 5-20m up; 2-4 greenish white eggs heavily spotted brown and black (Ruschi 1979).
**Status and habitat:** Common in humid *terra firme* and *várzea* forests, forest borders, and treetops in clearings.
**Range:** To 500m (once to 1500m on w? slope E Andes, Huila; sighting, w Caquetá, 1100m—Hilty). W Meta (Villavicencio; e base Macarena Mts.) to Vaupés and e Guainía, poss. se Vichada (*coelicolor*); Caquetá, Putumayo, and Amazonas (*chilensis*). The Guianas and s Venez. to n Bolivia and Amazonian Brazil.

### 26. GREEN-AND-GOLD TANAGER
*Tangara schrankii*          Pl. 49, Map 1295
**Identification:** 5.5″ (14cm). Mostly green and yellow. *Forecrown ocular region and area behind eye black*; crown yellow (green—♀); back golden green streaked green; *rump bright yellow*; wings and tail mostly black; *throat and sides grass green; otherwise golden yellow below.*
**Similar species:** Only small predom. "green-and-yellow" tanager *without* spots e of Andes. See Yellow-bellied Tanager (30). Allied (and very sim.) Emerald Tanager only occurs w of Andes.
**Behavior:** Often accompanies groups of Paradise Tanagers or other canopy flocks of var. types that contain Paradise Tanagers. Usually peer in dense foliage and on outer limbs more than latter, but like them, spend less time "head down" beneath limbs than many highland allies.
**Status and habitat:** Canopy of humid *terra firme* and *várzea* forests, forest borders, and occas. trees in clearings. Usually less numerous than Paradise Tanager.
**Range:** To ca. 500m. E of Andes from w Caquetá and e Vaupés southward. Poss. also e Guainía. S Venez. to n Bolivia and w Amazonian Brazil.
**Note:** A subsp. (*anchicayae*) described from the Anchicayá Val. and erroneously assigned to this sp. (Lehmann 1957) is referable to *T. florida* (Haffer 1975).

### 27. EMERALD TANAGER
*Tangara florida*          Pl. 48, Map 1296
**Identification:** 5″ (13cm). ♂: *mostly bright emerald green with yellow crown*; patch encircling bill black; *square patch on ear coverts black*; back streaked black; rump and belly yellow; wings and tail black; wings heavily edged green. ♀: sim. but duller and *no yellow crown*.
**Similar species:** Essentially an emerald and black tanager. Recalls Blue-whiskered Tanager (28), but latter has mostly black head and throat and conspic. blue whisker.
**Voice:** Raspy *jree* or *dzreee* call penetrating and even burrier than notes of Golden and Silver-throated tanagers.
**Behavior:** Much like Golden and Silver-throated tanagers and often with them but, on average, searches mossier, often completely moss-jacketed limbs. Center of abundance at lower el. than above spp.
**Breeding:** 2 nests and 2 stub-tailed juvs., Jan–Apr, upper Anchicayá Val.; mossy cup on epiphyte- and moss-covered limb 8 and 12m up; 2 eggs (Hilty).
**Status and habitat:** Somewhat local; wet mossy forest and forest edges in foothills and lower slopes (in Valle most numerous 500-1000m el.); stragglers to edge of coastal plain.
**Range:** 100-1100m. Pacific slope from sources of Río San Juan (Cerro Tatamá) s to sw Nariño. Costa Rica to nw Ecuador.

### 28. BLUE-WHISKERED TANAGER
*Tangara johannae*          Pl. 48, Map 1297
**Identification:** 5.2″ (13.2cm). *Throat and forepart of head black* narrowly bordered blue and with *conspic. broad blue malar stripe*; otherwise mostly golden green above; back streaked black; rump yellow; wings mostly black with *broad blue edgings; underparts bright apple green.*
**Similar species:** Likely confused only with Emerald Tanager (27). Look for the short blue malar stripe and mostly black head.
**Voice:** Shrill buzzy *tzzeee*, higher-pitched than allies that occur with it.
**Behavior:** Search "head down" much like Golden and Silver-throated tanagers, but center of abundance lower, even below that of Emerald Tanager, and more often in second growth than latter. Usually seen accompanying mixed flocks that contain several other spp. of tanagers, honeycreepers, and dacnis.
**Breeding:** 1 carrying food to cup nest; high mossy limb; 19 Jan, lower Dagua Val. (Hilty).
**Status and habitat:** Uncommon in wet forest borders and second growth woodland in coastal lowlands and lower foothills. The least numerous Pacific lowland *Tangara*.
**Range:** To 700m. Pacific coast from n Antioquia (Mutatá) and c Chocó (Río Baudó) s to Nariño. W Colombia and nw Ecuador.

## 29. SPECKLED TANAGER

*Tangara guttata*    Pl. 49, Map 1298
**Identification:** 5.2″ (13.2cm). *Spotted above and below.* Green spotted black above; lores black; inconspic. eyestripe and orbital area yellowish; wings black heavily edged blue; *underparts white spotted black*; center of belly unspotted; flanks and crissum yellow green.
**Similar species:** Easily confused with lowland Yellow-bellied Tanager (30), which overlaps it in foothills and is mostly green (not white) below with yellow (not white) belly. Also see Beryl-spangled Tanager (50) of mostly higher el.
**Voice:** Call a ser. of weak twittering chips, sometimes almost trilled; recalls notes of Masked Tanager.
**Behavior:** Much like Rufous-throated Tanager though not so much a canopy dweller and also occas. peers "head down" under bare outer limbs in the manner of many *Tangara*.
**Breeding:** 4 BC birds, May–June, Norte de Santander to n Antioquia (Carriker). Small, fibrous, open cup 3-8m up at woodland edge or in clearing; 2 white eggs heavily mottled brown (Skutch 1954).
**Status and habitat:** Fairly common in humid forest borders and trees and shrubs in clearings.
**Range:** 1000-1800m. E slope of E Andes s to s Meta, Macarena Mts., and w Caquetá (sightings above Florencia, 1975, 1978—Hilty); lower Cauca Val. (Valdivia) e around n end C Andes (Snía. San Lucas) and s on slopes above Magdalena Val. to latitude of Bogotá. Costa Rica to extreme e Panamá; w Venez. (incl. Perijá Mts.) to e Colombia; tepui highlands of s Venez. and n Brazil. Trinidad.
**Note 1:** Dotted Tanager (*T. varia*) of Fr. Guiana, Surinam, s Venez. and Brazil on Río Negro and Tapajóz, should occur in e Colombia (rec. on Venez. side of Orinoco and Negro). ♂: mainly bright green; mantle and breast *faintly* speckled black (looks essentially uniform); wings and tail greenish blue. ♀: less blue on wings; belly greenish yellow. Cf. more heavily speckled 30. **Note 2:** Spotted Tanager (*T. punctata*) of the Guianas, s Venez., ne Brazil, and e Ecuador to n Bolivia, may occur on e slope of Colombian Andes s of range of Speckled Tanager. Differs from latter thus: foreface tinged blue (not yellow), wings edged green (not blue), sides of breast greenish yellow.

## 30. YELLOW-BELLIED TANAGER

*Tangara xanthogastra*    Pl. 49, Map 1299
**Identification:** 4.8″ (12.2cm). Spotted. *Mostly grass green; upperparts, throat, and breast spotted black*; center of belly bright yellow (unspotted); wings black heavily edged blue; no yellowish ocular region.
**Similar species:** See Speckled Tanager (29).
**Behavior:** Sim. to Speckled Tanager.
**Breeding:** BC birds, early Jan, nw Brazil (Friedmann 1948).
**Status and habitat:** Uncommon in humid forest, forest borders, and second growth woodland. Mostly replaced at higher el. by Speckled Tanager.
**Range:** To 600m (prob. higher). E of Andes from w Meta (Villavicencio area) and Vaupés southward. S Venez., nw Brazil (s at least to lower Río Javarí) and e Colombia to n Bolivia.

## 31. RUFOUS-THROATED TANAGER

*Tangara rufigula*    Pl. 48, Map 1300
**Identification:** 4.7″ (12cm). Spotted. *Head black with rufous throat; otherwise black above, the feathers heavily scaled golden green* (looks spotted); lower back and rump mostly unspotted opalescent golden green; wings and tail black edged silvery green; *breast and sides greenish white spotted black*; center of belly white; under tail coverts buff.
**Similar species:** Looks dark-headed; rufous throat often hard to see. Black-capped Tanager (52) of higher el. has streaky silvery green throat and cheeks and is more or less unspotted. Beryl-spangled Tanager (50) lacks the black head (mask only) and is much blacker.
**Voice:** Excited bursts of ticking and twittering, *tic-ti-ti-ti* . . . , esp. as 1 or several closely follow each other across clearings.
**Behavior:** Pacific slope equivalent of Speckled Tanager. Twittering pairs or small groups glean foliage on outer twigs, sometimes even hang from leaves, then fly off to fruit trees. Do not peer "head down" beneath limbs. At rest often perch in open on top of canopy. In poss. display (courtship?) 1 often chases a mate, virtually holding to tail, as both twitter excitedly and fly back and forth across small clearings.
**Breeding:** 2 nests, Aug, Sept, upper Anchicayá Val.; moss cups, 1 in hanging epiphytes; 10-18m up (Hilty).
**Status and habitat:** Fairly common to common in upper levels of wet forest ("cloud forest"), forest edges, and second growth; favors broken or irreg. forest and small openings on steep slopes.
**Range:** 400-2100m. Pacific slope from sources of Río San Juan (below Cerro Tatamá) southward. W Colombia and nw Ecuador.

## 32. GOLDEN TANAGER

*Tangara arthus*    Pl. 49, Map 1301
**Identification:** 5″ (13cm). *Mostly bright golden*

*yellow*; area surrounding bill and *large square patch on ear coverts black*; upper back streaked black; *wings and tail black*; wings heavily edged golden yellow. Or as above but deep golden yellow (*occidentalis*), or brownish yellow (*sclateri*).

**Similar species:** Likely confused only with paler Silver-throated Tanager (33), which has silvery white throat and black malar.

**Voice:** Call *seet*, not as buzzy as that of Silver-throated and Emerald tanagers.

**Behavior:** Typical of the group of *Tangara* that forage by peering "head down" along midlevel to canopy limbs. When not at fruiting trees and shrubs, customarily check bare or partly mossy branches and limbs (usually not twigs) for insects as follow forest flocks that contain several other spp. of tanagers. Single birds or pairs, sometimes several, but not in groups of their own.

**Breeding:** 10 BC birds, Apr–Sept, W and C Andes and Perijá Mts. (Miller 1963; Carriker). Begging juvs., July and Aug, w above Cali (S. Gniadek); building nest, July, Sept, and Oct, and juvs. in May, Anchicayá Val. (Hilty).

**Status and habitat:** Common in humid and wet forest ("cloud forest") and forest borders in W Andes; less numerous in upper Magdalena Val. and E Andes. More a forest dweller than many *Tangara*.

**Range:** 700-2500m (usually above 1000m). W Andes and w slope C Andes (*occidentalis*); Perijá Mts., e slope C Andes, w slope E Andes from Cundinamarca to Huila (*aurulenta*); w slope E Andes (1800m) at La Palmita, s Cesar (*palmitae*); e slope E Andes in Norte de Santander (subsp.?); both slopes E Andes in Santander and Boyacá, and Macarena Mts. (*sclateri*); rest of e slope E Andes (subsp.?). N Venez. s in mts. to Bolivia.

## 33. SILVER-THROATED TANAGER

*Tangara icterocephala*        Pl. 49, Map 1302

**Identification:** 5.2″ (13.2cm). *Mostly bright yellow*; upper back streaked black; *throat silvery greenish white bordered on sides by long, narrow black malar*; wings and tail black edged green. ♀ and esp. imm.: duller.

**Similar species:** See Golden Tanager (32). Dingy imms. can be confusing but usually show, at least faintly, the ad. markings.

**Voice:** Call a buzzy *schreet*, or *bzzeet*, harsher than Emerald or Golden tanagers.

**Behavior:** Much like Golden and Emerald tanagers and sometimes with both of them but usually more numerous in mixed flocks, with up to 12-15 noisy individuals in some flocks. Spurt energetically along limbs habitually

peering beneath them; occas. hang from moss tufts or check bromeliads; usually fairly high, sometimes down to eye level inside forest.

**Breeding:** BC pair, June, n end C Andes (Carriker). Nests or carrying food, Feb and Oct, dependent juv., June, upper Anchicayá Val. (Hilty); mossy cup nest 2-11m up; 2 eggs, white to grayish white heavily mottled brown (Skutch 1954).

**Status and habitat:** Common in wet forest, forest borders, and second growth woodland. Much less numerous and somewhat local above 1200m, where greatly outnumbered by allied Golden Tanager.

**Range:** 400-2100m. Entire Pacific slope and w slope C Andes at n end (Valdivia). Costa Rica to nw Ecuador.

## 34. SAFFRON-CROWNED TANAGER

*Tangara xanthocephala*        Pls. 48, 49,
                               Map 1303

**Identification:** 5.2″ (13.2cm). *Head golden yellow with small black mask and throat*; narrow nuchal collar black; *otherwise almost entirely opalescent blue to turquoise green* depending on the light; back streaked black; wings and tail black edged blue green; center of belly and under tail coverts cinnamon buff.

**Similar species:** Can be confused with Multicolored (22) and Flame-faced tanagers (36), esp. in poor light of cloud forests where all 3 are usually seen. All have much yellow on head; Multicolored lacks the black mask and throat; Flame-faced has red foreface and silvery green shoulders and rump.

**Behavior:** Much like Golden Tanager but often work further out and on smaller branches and limbs than latter, sometimes even on twigs in the open; rarely leafy terminal areas. Generally less inside forest, more along borders or in tall second growth, and more frugivorous than Golden and Silver-throated tanagers; center of abundance at higher el. than above spp.

**Breeding:** 2 BC ♂♂, July, Perijá Mts.; 1 in June, n end W Andes (Carriker); 4 BC birds, Mar–May, W Andes above Cali (Miller 1963).

**Status and habitat:** Fairly common in mossy forest ("cloud forest"), forest edges, and second growth. Most numerous in upper half of el. range where often with Flame-faced, Metallic-green, Golden-naped, and Beryl-spangled tanagers.

**Range:** 1300-2400m (once to 3100m). Perijá Mts., all 3 Andean ranges (on e slope reported only in Norte de Santander and w Putumayo) and Macarena Mts. Nw Venez. s in Andes to n Bolivia.

## 35. GOLDEN-EARED TANAGER
*Tangara chrysotis*            Pl. 48, Map 1304
**Identification:** 5.5" (14cm). *Mostly lime green* var. to opalescent green to blue with the light; patch from below eye to ear coverts *coppery gold*; center of crown, lores, and patch on lower cheeks black; *broad forehead and eyestripe shining straw yellow*; back black finely streaked green; wings and tail black heavily edged blue green; *center of lower breast to under tail coverts cinnamon rufous*.
**Similar species:** Superficially like Metallic-green Tanager (38) but more boldly marked, and with conspic. cinnamon rufous lower underparts (not cinnamon buff).
**Behavior:** As in Golden Tanager and often with it in mixed flocks or groups at fruiting trees and shrubs. Sometimes also peers in outer foliage.
**Status and habitat:** Humid and wet forest and forest edges. Fairly common on e slope E Andes (many sightings, Caquetá and Putumayo), less numerous but reg. (as at Finca Merenberg) in upper Magdalena Val. where rec. only above 1700m.
**Range:** 1100-2400m (el. range based on sight recs.). Upper Magdalena Val. in Huila; e slope of E Andes from w Caquetá southward. E Colombia s in mts. to n Bolivia.

## 36. FLAME-FACED TANAGER
*Tangara parzudakii*            Pl. 49, Map 1305
**Identification:** 5.8" (14.7cm). Lores, ocular area, throat, and broad bar extending back to ear coverts black; *forehead and sides of head red changing to silky golden yellow on hindcrown and nape*; upper back black; *lower back and rump, shoulders, and underparts shining opalescent silvery green*; center of belly and under tail coverts cinnamon buff. Or smaller (5.5", or 14cm) with orange red forecrown and cheeks (*lunigera*).
**Similar species:** Stunning and unmistakable in good light; in poor light see Saffron-crowned (34) and Multicolored tanagers (22).
**Voice:** Call *seeet* like Golden Tanager.
**Behavior:** Much like Golden Tanager but favors mossier limbs; peers beneath limbs, habitually checking lichen tufts (*Usnea*) and hanging moss clumps, only infrequently peers or gleans in outer foliage. Even more a forest dweller than Golden Tanager, which is often with it.
**Breeding:** BC ♂, Mar, sw Huila (Carriker). Mar, ♀ ready to lay, Cundinamarca (Olivares 1969a); Feb courtship feeding, Finca Merenberg (Ridgely and Gaulin 1980); begging Mar juv., PN Cueva de los Guácharos (P. Gertler); pair building nest, 5 June, w Nariño, 1100m (Hilty).
**Status and habitat:** Mossy forest ("cloud forest"), less often forest borders. In most areas except extreme sw Colombia, fairly common only above 1800m.
**Range:** 1000-2500m (rarely to 700m, Pacific slope in Cauca). Pacific slope from Río San Juan headwaters (Cerro Tatamá) southward (*lunigera*); mid. and upper Magdalena Val. from w Cundinamarca to headwaters in Huila and e slope E Andes from w Caquetá (sighting—Hilty), w Putumayo, and e Nariño southward (*parzudakii*). Prob. entire e slope. Nw Venez. (s Táchira) s to e Ecuador and e Peru.

## 37. BLUE-BROWED TANAGER
*Tangara cyanotis*            Pl. 48, Map 1306
**Identification:** 4.8" (12.2cm). *Mostly black above with long, conspic. bluish green eyebrow*; shoulders, rump, and underparts shining silvery bluish green to silvery green depending on the light; center of belly and under tail coverts cinnamon buff.
**Similar species:** Beryl-spangled Tanager (50) lacks eyestripe and black crown and is spotted below. Also see Black-capped Tanager (52).
**Status and habitat:** Canopy of humid and wet mossy forest and forest edge. Fairly common at PN Cueva de los Guácharos (P. Gertler) but not well known elsewhere.
**Range:** 1600-2200m. Head of Magdalena Val. in Huila (no recs. on w side) and e slope of E Andes in w Putumayo and e Nariño (sighting—many observers). E Colombia s in Andes to nw Bolivia.

## 38. METALLIC-GREEN TANAGER
*Tangara labradorides*            Pl. 48, Map 1307
**Identification:** 5" (13cm). Mostly shining silvery green to silvery blue depending on the light; *forehead and broad eyestripe bright opalescent green to straw gold; mask through eyes and center of crown and nape black*; scapulars, wings, and tail black edged green; wing coverts mainly blue; center of belly and under tail coverts cinnamon buff.
**Similar species:** A confusing sp. that can look very different depending upon the light but usually looks pale and washed out. Best marks are eyestripe, mask, and black stripe down center of crown. See Beryl-spangled (50) and Black-capped tanagers (52).
**Voice:** Call a high coarse *jitt*; ticking twitter in flight.
**Behavior:** Recalls Rufous-throated and Speckled tanagers. Works actively along smaller limbs and peers at small twigs and outer foliage, sometimes fluttering or hanging acrobatically; infrequently peers "head down" like Golden

Tanager and allies. Pairs or groups visit fruiting trees or shrubs, esp. *Miconia*, even more persistently than many other *Tangara*.

**Breeding:** 14 BC birds, Mar–July, W Andes and n end C Andes (Carriker; Miller 1963); 1 nest in July, stub-tailed juvs. in June, Aug, and Nov, W Andes above Cali (S. Gniadek).

**Status and habitat:** Humid forest, second growth woodland, borders, and bushy pastures; favors edges. Most numerous in W Andes, where frequently with 32, 34, 42, 50, and 52.

**Range:** 1300-2400m (to 900m on Pacific slope in Cauca; once to 500m, e Cundinamarca). W Andes and C Andes s to Nariño, w slope E Andes in Cundinamarca and Huila; e base of E Andes on Cundinamarca-Casanare border. Colombia s in Andes to Peru.

### 39. BLUE-NECKED TANAGER

*Tangara cyanicollis*          Pl. 49, Map 1308

**Identification:** 5″ (13cm). *Mostly black with contrasting turquoise blue head becoming purplish* on throat; lores black; shoulders and rump glistening silvery green to burnished gold depending on the light; primaries and tail edged blue green. Imm.: much duller, often mostly brown; older birds mottled black but still with brownish head.

**Similar species:** Distinctive in most areas, but on e Andean slope confusingly sim. to Masked Tanager (41), which has paler head, greenish cheeks (hard to see), and white instead of black belly. ♂ Scarlet-thighed Dacnis (p 598) is superficially sim. but has blue back and black on throat; also cf. Golden-hooded Tanager (40).

**Voice:** Weak chips and a *seep*.

**Behavior:** A nonforest bird of bushy pastures and open situations with trees and brush. Single birds, pairs, or families loaf at var. hts. in trees or sally clumsily to air or hop in foliage, then fly off to fruiting trees and shrubs. Seldom peer "head down" along limbs; sometimes follow flocks containing other *Tangara* along forest borders.

**Breeding:** 7 BC birds, June–Aug, C and E Andes (Carriker); 6 breeding recs., Jan–Aug (2 nests in Feb), Anchicayá Val.; mossy cup at mod. ht. in tree in clearing (Hilty).

**Status and habitat:** Common and widespread in var. kinds of open areas with bushes and trees or at forest edges.

**Range:** Mostly 900-2400m (to 400m on Pacific slope in Valle). All 3 Andean ranges. N Venez. (incl. Perijá Mts.) s in mts. to n Bolivia; s Brazil.

### 40. GOLDEN-HOODED TANAGER

*Tangara larvata*          Pl. 48, Map 1309

**Identification:** 5″ (13cm). *Head mostly metallic*

gold with small black mask surrounded by blue foreface*; upperparts black with glistening pale blue wing coverts and rump; wings edged blue; *chest, upper breast, and sides black* becoming blue on flanks; *center of lower breast to crissum white*.

**Similar species:** Pattern superficially like that of Blue-necked Tanager (39), which has all turquoise blue head and black (not white) belly. Also see Gray-and-gold Tanager (44).

**Voice:** Weak *tsip*'s often repeated rapidly, esp. in flight.

**Behavior:** Sim. to Blue-necked Tanager but usually loafs in treetops. Like other "open situation" *Tangara*, seems more frugivorous than forest-based allies. Rarely peers under limbs.

**Breeding:** 4 BC birds and 2 imms., May, s Bolívar (Carriker); 2 BC ♂♂, Mar and Apr, nw Colombia (Haffer 1975); 5 nests, late Jan–May, upper Anchicayá Val. (Hilty).

**Status and habitat:** Common in clearings, bushy pastures, and sometimes along forest borders, occas. short distances into forest canopy.

**Range:** To 1800m (usually below 1100m). Pacific coast and humid lowlands n of Andes e to mid. Magdalena Val. (s to Honda, n Tolima). Se Mexico to w Ecuador.

**Note:** Perhaps conspecific with *T. nigrocincta* (Masked Tanager) of e of Andes and so treated by many.

### 41. MASKED TANAGER

*Tangara nigrocincta*          Pl. 49, Map 1310

**Identification:** 5″ (13cm). Has faded, "*washed out*" appearance. Head mostly faded lavender blue with small *black mask and pale greenish cheeks*; upperparts largely black with bright blue wing coverts and rump; *wings broadly edged light green*.; chest, breast, and sides black; flanks blue; *center of lower belly to crissum white*. ♀: duller, black on breast edged grayish blue; flanks tinged greenish.

**Similar species:** See Blue-necked (39) and Turquoise tanagers (43).

**Voice:** Sim. to Golden-hooded Tanager.

**Behavior:** As in Golden-hooded Tanager.

**Breeding:** 2 BC birds, Jan, nw Brazil near Vaupés border (Friedmann 1948).

**Status and habitat:** Clearings, overgrown pastures, and shrubby forest borders, stragglers into upper canopy of tall forest. Spotty and far less numerous than allied Golden-hooded Tanager of w of Andes.

**Range:** To 1400m. E of Andes from w Meta (Villavicencio) and e Vichada (El Tuparro—INDERENA) southward locally. Guyana and s Venez. to n Bolivia and c Amazonian Brazil.

**Note:** Often merged with Golden-hooded Tanager.

## 42. GOLDEN-NAPED TANAGER

*Tangara ruficervix* Pl. 48, Map 1311

**Identification:** 5″ (13cm). *Mostly turquoise blue; crown, foreface, and nape black, small band across hindcrown golden buff* bordered above and below by violet (latter not a field mark); wings and tail black edged blue; *center of belly buffy white* becoming cinnamon buff on under tail coverts.

**Similar species:** An almost all blue tanager with black on head and small gold spot on nape (latter its best mark). See duller Black-capped Tanager (52).

**Behavior:** A "head down" branch searcher like Golden Tanager, though also reg. searches in foliage and more frequently found alone or in pairs away from mixed flocks. Usually stays fairly high, takes a var. of fruit, incl. berries of *Miconia* shrubs. Its most common assoc. in W Andes are Metallic-green and Beryl-spangled tanagers.

**Breeding:** 5 BC birds, Mar–June, C Andes from n Antioquia to Huila (Carriker); building nest Apr (S. Gniadek); 2 BC birds, Feb, and dependent juv., Sept (Miller 1963) in W Andes above Cali.

**Status and habitat:** Fairly common in humid and wet forest borders, second growth of var. ages, and trees and bushes in clearings; also inside tall forest where usually in canopy or near openings.

**Range:** 1500-2400m (to 1100m in w Nariño). W and C Andes and w slope of E Andes n to Cundinamarca; perhaps e Andean slope at s end. Colombia s in Andes to e and w Ecuador, e Peru, and n Bolivia.

## 43. TURQUOISE TANAGER

*Tangara mexicana* Pl. 49, Map 1312

**Identification:** 5.2″ (13.2cm). At a distance looks black with yellow belly. *Mostly black above* with blue rump and silvery blue shoulders; forecrown, sides of head, and underparts purplish blue with spangled black; esp. on sides and flanks; *center of belly to crissum clear yellow* (or *yellowish white—media*).

**Similar species:** Masked Tanager (41) has a very faded blue head; Opal-rumped Tanager (23), mostly a forest bird, lacks the yellow lower underparts.

**Voice:** Very high-pitched, thin *tic* call often rapidly repeated or trilled; higher-pitched than many *Tangara*.

**Behavior:** Usually in twittering groups of 3-6 that visit fruiting trees and shrubs or move about, normally quite high, examining the undersurfaces of small twigs. Loaf in tops of tall trees; rarely with mixed flocks.

**Breeding:** Building nest, 19 Feb, Mitú (Hilty);

nest, 14 Oct, Leticia (J. V. Remsen); small open cup fairly high; 3 grayish green eggs marked brown (ffrench 1973). Several "helpers" may also feed young (Snow and Collins 1962).

**Status and habitat:** Usually fairly common in forest borders, second growth woodland, and treetops in clearings and pastures.

**Range:** To 500m. E of Andes from w Meta (Villavicencio area) to Putumayo and Amazonas (*bolivianus*); e Vichada (Maipures), and ne Guainía (*media*). The Guianas and s Venez. to n Bolivia and Amazonian and se Brazil. Trinidad.

## 44. GRAY-AND-GOLD TANAGER

*Tangara palmeri* Pl. 48, Map 1313

**Identification:** 5.8″ (14.7cm). Large, robust *Tangara. Mostly light gray above and whitish below with short black mask;* wings and tail black edged gray, a sprinkling of black spots mixed silvery green across mantle continues on sides of neck and as *necklace of black spots* mixed gold across chest.

**Similar species:** An unusually patterned tanager, larger than most *Tangara*. Looks mostly gray and black in the field; gold on chest hard to see. See Golden-hooded Tanager (40).

**Voice:** Unlike other *Tangara* has a var. of musical calls and staccato notes; most common *chup, chup-sweeeeet* (last note rising) or any of above singly or over and over; also greet or fly off with rapid excited ser. of *chup*'s, *sweeet*'s and other notes.

**Behavior:** Unique among Colombian *Tangara*. Noisy and excitable pairs or groups of 3-8 are "nuclear" in canopy tanager and honeycreeper flocks but fly rapidly and tend to leave flock behind. At rest often perch exposed on top of foliage in canopy. More frugivorous than any other *Tangara* in w Colombia, but also sally short distances to air or flutter and hop in treetop foliage or along branches (do not peer "head down" along branches); rarely drop low to fruiting shrubs like many other *Tangara*.

**Breeding:** Perhaps yr.-round; 1 nest, July, 1 in Aug, 2 in Dec, building nest in Jan, another in Feb, and feeding fledgling in Apr, upper Anchicayá Val. (Hilty).

**Status and habitat:** Fairly common on steep hillsides in wet forest and forest edges; mostly foothills and lower slopes, less numerous on coastal plain.

**Range:** To 1100m (mostly above 300m). Pacific coast from nw Antioquia (Mutatá) and the mid. San Juan (Río Sipí) to sw Nariño; prob. along Panama border. Extreme e Panama (Darién) to nw Ecuador.

## 45. PLAIN-COLORED TANAGER

*Tangara inornata*          Pl. 48, Map 1314

**Identification:** 4.8″ (12.2cm). Dull and uniform for a *Tangara*. *Mostly plain gray*; underparts paler becoming *white on belly*; lores and ocular area dusky; wings and tail dusky black with usually concealed blue lesser wing coverts.

**Similar species:** In poor light Blue-gray and Palm tanagers (69, 71) can look grayish; both are larger and lack the white belly. Palm also has rear half of wing black.

**Voice:** A low trebled *tst* when feeding.

**Behavior:** Often in groups of 3 or more; peer underneath rather open bare limbs like many *Tangara* (see under Golden Tanager), and flutter or sally for aerial insects. Often at fruit trees, esp. *Cecropia*; join mixed tanager and honeycreeper flocks or forage independent of them.

**Breeding:** 5 BC birds, Jan–May, lower Cauca Val. to n Chocó (Carriker) and 1 in Apr, nw Chocó (Haffer 1975); Canal Zone nests, Apr–Aug (Brown; Eisenmann 1952; Skutch 1954); open cup nest fairly high; 2 white eggs speckled dark.

**Status and habitat:** Clearings with trees, lighter second growth woodland, and humid forest edges. Mostly lowlands, smaller nos. into foothills of humid zones.

**Range:** To 1200m. Pacific coast in n Chocó (Urabá region; Río Juradó) s to Quibdó area (sighting at Yuto, Mar 1978—Hilty and P. Bailey) and Buenaventura (J. Pujals, Aug 1980) and e in humid lowlands along n base of Andes to mid. Magdalena Val. (s to n Caldas). Costa Rica to n Colombia.

## 46. BAY-HEADED TANAGER

*Tangara gyrola*          Pl. 49, Map 1315

**Identification:** 5.5″ (14cm). *Head brick red; rest of upperparts grass green* with blue rump; *lower throat, breast, and belly turquoise*; center of belly and crissum green (or *all grass green except head—toddi*); narrow yellow nuchal collar (or no collar—*deleticia*). Imm.: much duller, but *usually* with traces of brownish chestnut, or with darker head faintly indicated.

**Similar species:** On Pacific slope easily confused with mostly lower el. Rufous-winged Tanager (47), which has shining golden yellow mantle and rufous wings; imm. of the 2 spp. often difficult, but latter usually with some rufous on wings, both usually accompany ads.

**Voice:** Call a buzzy *seeaaweee*, mid. part slurred lower; a coarse *shree* like Emerald Tanager and others is often heard in flight.

**Behavior:** If not at fruiting trees and shrubs will usually be seen in midlevels or higher, peering "head down" beneath mostly live bare limbs (rarely mossy limbs or on outer twigs) in fashion of many *Tangara* (see Golden Tanager) but at more deliberate pace. Single birds, pairs, or families, and often with mixed flocks.

**Breeding:** 13 BC birds, Apr–Sept, n end C Andes and Perijá Mts. (Carriker). Begging juv., Aug, older juvs. with ads., Nov and Mar, upper Anchicayá Val. (Hilty); open mossy cup 3-8m up; 2 white eggs speckled brown (Skutch 1954).

**Status and habitat:** Humid and wet forest, forest borders, and lighter second growth woodland, sometimes trees in clearings. Lowlands to mts. except Pacific coast where only in higher foothills and above (Pacific lowlands occupied by allied Rufous-winged Tanager, but they overlap narrowly between about 500-1000m).

**Range:** To 2100m (500-2100m on Pacific slope). W and C Andes, humid hills n of them from s Córdoba (Quimarí) to s Bolívar, Perijá Mts., and w slope E Andes (*deleticia*); w slope Andes in Nariño (*nupera*); Santa Marta Mts. and e slope E Andes in Norte de Santander and n Boyacá (*toddi*); e slope E Andes from Meta s to se Nariño and in Macarena Mts. (*catharinae*); Putumayo and Guainía spottily s to Amazonas (sighting—Hilty) on the Amazon (*parva*). Costa Rica to w Ecuador, n Bolivia, and Amazonian Brazil.

## 47. RUFOUS-WINGED TANAGER

*Tangara lavinia*          Pl. 49, Map 1316

**Identification:** 5.2″ (13.2cm). *Head and most of wings bright brick red*; otherwise bright grass green above and below with *shining golden yellow mantle* and blue line down center of breast and belly. ♀ and imm.: duller, esp. imm., but usually with some chestnut on head and wings.

**Similar species:** Resembles better-known Bay-headed Tanager (46) but brighter, and latter never has rufous on wings. Dull imms. can look much like imm. Bay-headed but usually show traces of reddish chestnut on wings. Also cf. ♀ Green Honeycreeper (p 596).

**Voice:** Call a weak *tst*; "song" a weak lispy *seetsir, tsirtsir, tsirtsir*, high-pitched (Slud 1964).

**Behavior:** Rather sim. to Bay-headed Tanager and sometimes with it, though more active (less methodical as search limbs), often noisier, sometimes *tst*ing constantly, and frequently comes low to fruiting shrubs.

**Breeding:** 1 BC ♂, Mar, nw Chocó (Haffer 1975); building nest, July, w Valle (Hilty).

**Status and habitat:** Fairly common in humid and wet forest, second growth woodland, and borders; mostly coastal lowlands and foothills below 500m, stragglers higher where gradually replaced by Bay-headed Tanager.

**Range:** To 700m (sightings to 1000m, Anchicayá Val.—Hilty). Entire Pacific coast and Gorgona Isl. Guatemala to nw Ecuador.

## 48. SCRUB TANAGER
*Tangara vitriolina*  Pl. 48, Map 1317
**Identification:** 5.5″ (14cm). Dull-plumaged. *Crown rufous; sides of head black forming a mask; otherwise mostly grayish green to silvery green* depending upon the light; underparts paler, becoming whitish on belly; wings and tail dusky broadly edged pale green.
**Similar species:** Rufous cap and black mask are the marks. Does not overlap sim. Burnished-buff Tanager.
**Voice:** Shrill buzzy *ziit* note.
**Behavior:** Single birds or pairs peer somewhat like vireos, from low bush to treetop ht. in foliage and shrubbery, mostly for insects. Occas. at fruiting trees or shrubs. Not with mixed flocks, being mainly in "open situations" where few form.
**Breeding:** 4 BC birds, June–Aug, n end W and C Andes (Carriker); 2 in Jan, upper Magdalena Val. (Miller 1947); 2 in Mar near Cali, Nov in upper Patía Val. (Miller 1963); carrying food, 17 Aug, Queremal, Valle (P. Kaestner); open cup nest; 2 pale greenish eggs spotted and blotched darker (Sclater and Salvin 1879).
**Status and habitat:** Common in drier scrubby or cultivated areas, overgrown pastures, wasteland, and even around habitations; follows deforestation into wetter zones (Hilty 1977). Replaced e of Andes by Burnished-buff Tanager.
**Range:** 500-2200m (once reportedly to 3000m). Interior Andean vals. incl. the mid. and upper Magdalena, Cauca, Dagua, and Patía, and s through c Nariño. Recently spreading into cleared humid areas on Pacific slope. Colombia and nw Ecuador.
**Note:** Poss. a race of *T. cayana* (Burnished-buff Tanager).

## 49. BURNISHED-BUFF TANAGER
*Tangara cayana*  Pl. 49, Map 1318
**Identification:** 5.5″ (14cm). *Crown coppery rufous; sides of head black forming a mask; otherwise shining straw gold to pale greenish yellow above* depending on the light; wings and tail dusky broadly edged greenish blue; underparts pale yellowish buff tinged greenish blue on throat and foreneck. ♀: much duller.
**Similar species:** A "straw-colored" tanager of open scrubby country, easily recognized by black mask and coppery rufous crown.
**Voice:** Call a buzzy *tzit*; "song" a buzzy ser. of more or less sim. thin *sizza* notes (Snyder 1966; Hilty).

**Behavior:** Sim. to Scrub Tanager but occas. in small groups.
**Breeding:** BC birds, Mar, Aug, and Nov, and May juv., ne Meta (S. Furniss); 1 BC bird, Apr, Vaupés (Olivares 1964b); breeding, Dec–Apr in Orinoco area; open cup nest rather low in scrubby oak in savanna; 2 soiled white eggs finely speckled dark, esp. at larger end (Cherrie 1916).
**Status and habitat:** Fairly common in drier, open situations, ranchland, gallery and savanna woodland borders, and scrubby wasteland. Replaced w of Andes by closely allied Scrub Tanager.
**Range:** To 500m. E of Andes s to s Meta (Macarena Mts.) and Vichada, locally to Vaupés (Sabana de Cubiyú). The Guianas, Venez. and locally in e Peru, Amazonian Brazil, Bolivia, nw Argentina, and Paraguay.

## 50. BERYL-SPANGLED TANAGER
*Tangara nigroviridis*  Pl. 49, Map 1319
**Identification:** 5″ (13cm). *Looks dappled. Black mask through eyes;* head otherwise bluish opal to greenish opal depending on the light; nape somewhat spotted black; *upper back black;* rump greenish blue; wings and tail black edged greenish blue; *underparts black heavily spotted bluish to greenish opal;* throat bluer.
**Similar species:** A dark, *heavily spotted* tanager often confused with Black-capped (52) and Metallic-green tanagers (38). Former has black cap, latter lacks the spotted underparts.
**Voice:** Chips like many other *Tangara.*
**Behavior:** Much like Silver-throated and Golden tanagers but customarily peers underneath very small, bare, terminal twigs (not larger branches or limbs), sometimes moss tufts on twigs or even ends of bare weeds or sim. in clearings near forest; pairs or up to 12 or more with mixed flocks; low to fairly high, but mostly midlevels when inside forest. Notably frugivorous.
**Breeding:** 10 BC birds, May–July, n end W and C Andes and Perijá Mts. (Carriker); 3 BC ♂♂, Mar–July (Miller 1963), and Nov fledgling (S. Gniadek) in W Andes above Cali.
**Status and habitat:** Common in mossy forest, second growth woodland, edges, and clearings with trees. Often with Golden, Saffron-crowned, Flame-faced, Metallic-green, and Golden-naped tanagers.
**Range:** 900-3000m (mostly 1500-2600m). Perijá Mts., all 3 Andean ranges, and Macarena Mts. N Venez. s in mts. to n Bolivia.

## 51. BLUE-AND-BLACK TANAGER
*Tangara vassorii*  Pl. 49, Map 1320
**Identification:** 5.5″ (14cm). *Mostly shining deep*

*blue; lores, wings, and rather short tail black*; shoulders and single broad wing bar blue.
**Similar species:** Recalls Masked Flower-piercer (p 592) but has black wings and tail and lacks the latter's bright red eye.
**Voice:** Chipping notes; "song," rarely heard, a ser. of high-pitched *wheedly* notes starting slowly, ending in trill (J. Silliman).
**Behavior:** Pairs or lively groups of up to 6 often follow mixed flocks, esp. to fruiting trees and shrubs. Hop and flutter in foliage like Rufous-throated Tanager and allies but also occas. peer head down a few times on limbs before moving on rapidly.
**Breeding:** 9 BC birds, Feb–Aug, C Andes in Cauca, E Andes in Santander (Carriker); fledglings, May, PN Puracé (J. Silliman); 2 nests, June, and begging young, Jan, Pichindé Val. (S. Gniadek).
**Status and habitat:** Fairly common in humid forest borders and overgrown pastures. Only *Tangara* reg. found in the temperate zone and usually with *Iridosornis*, or *Anisognathus* tanagers, and conebills rather than other *Tangara*. Some seasonal el. movements suspected (J. Silliman).
**Range:** 1900-3400m (mostly 2400-2900m). All 3 Andean ranges. Pacific slope only at n end in Antioquia, and in Cauca. Nw Venez. s in Andes to n Bolivia.

## 52. BLACK-CAPPED TANAGER
*Tangara heinei*          Pl. 49, Map 1321
**Identification:** 5.2″ (13.2cm). *Crown and nape black*; rest of upperparts shining silvery blue to bluish gray depending on the light; wings and tail darker; *sides of head, throat, and chest glistening pale green to silvery green*; feathers of chest black-edged giving a scaly appearance; rest of underparts grayish. ♀: *crown dusky green; rest of upperparts shining light green*; primaries dusky edged blue green; below like ♂ but much paler and greener; chest and breast mottled dusky. Even duller imm. mostly dingy light green but usually with pattern of ♀ faintly indicated.
**Similar species:** See Beryl-spangled Tanager (50). ♀ most like ♀ Black-headed Tanager (see 53).
**Behavior:** Sim. to Blue-and-black Tanager but usually seen singly or in pairs and more often peers under branches.
**Breeding:** 15 BC birds, Jan–Sept, Santa Marta and Perijá mts., n end of Andes (Carriker); building nest, Jan, PN Cueva de los Guácharos (P. Gertler); Apr nest with young, W Andes above Cali (S. Gniadek); 1 carrying food, 9 Aug, Santa Marta Mts.; 1 building and 1 nest, Aug, Pamplona, Norte de Santander; grassy

cup decorated with moss; 2-3m up; 1 dull blue egg heavily blotched and spotted reddish brown (Hilty).
**Status and habitat:** Uncommon to locally fairly common in forest borders, bushy pastures, and clearings with scattered trees, usually not inside forest. One of the least numerous *Tangara* in W Andes.
**Range:** 700-2700m (mostly 1500-2200m). Santa Marta and Perijá mts., all 3 Andean ranges s to Nariño. N Venez. s in mts. to Ecuador and ne Peru.

## 53. BLACK-HEADED TANAGER
*Tangara cyanoptera*          Pl. 49, Map 1322
**Identification:** 5″ (13cm). ♂: *head and throat black*; otherwise entirely *opalescent to straw yellow* depending on the light (sometimes tinged greenish); *black wings and tail*; primaries edged blue. ♀: *crown grayish*; back dingy green becoming *greenish yellow on rump; sides of head and throat light gray tinged green*, becoming pale yellow green on belly and flanks; wings dusky, primaries *edged pale green*.
**Similar species:** Dingy ♀ confusing and much like ♀ Black-capped Tanager (52), but crown grayish (not dusky green), sides of head light gray tinged green (not shining green), and rump contrasting yellowish (not more or less uniform shining green above).
**Behavior:** Pairs hop and flutter on outer branches and foliage, usually high, alone or with mixed flocks. Seldom peer underneath branches like many *Tangara*.
**Breeding:** 9 BC birds, Mar–June, Santa Marta and Perijá mts. to Norte de Santander (Carriker).
**Status and habitat:** Common in moist to humid forest borders, lighter woodland, and tall second growth in Santa Marta Mts., esp. in foothills and coffee zone.
**Range:** 600-2000m (stragglers lower). Santa Marta and Perijá mts. and both slopes of n end of E Andes in Norte de Santander. Mts. of Guyana, Venez. and nw Brazil.

[*Iridosornis*: Rich blue plumage with yellow on head or throat; larger than *Tangara*, bill proportionally shorter and thicker; *only* in highlands.]

## 54. PURPLISH-MANTLED TANAGER
*Iridosornis porphyrocephala*          Pl. 50, Map 1323
**Identification:** 6″ (15cm). Unmistakable in its range. *Mainly rich purplish blue* becoming bluer on lower back (can look greenish in some lights) with *contrasting bright yellow throat*; foreface blackish; center of belly buffy becoming *chestnut on under tail coverts.*

**Similar species:** See Yellow-throated Tanager (note).
**Voice:** A high-pitched, slightly raspy trill; also (song?) a high, buzzy, downscale *seeeer*, repeated over and over.
**Behavior:** Single birds, pairs, or families follow mixed tanager flocks or forage alone, 2-10m up inside or at edge of forest and usually keep mostly out of sight in shrubbery. Hop and peer in dense foliage for berries and insects but do not gather at fruiting trees with other frugivores.
**Breeding:** 9 BC birds, May–June, n end W and C Andes (Carriker). Begging young with 2 ads. July, Cerro Munchique (Hilty).
**Status and habitat:** Uncommon to fairly common locally in mossy forest ("cloud forest"), forest borders, and second growth woodland; occas. less humid areas.
**Range:** Mainly 1500-2200m (rarely 750m in w Cauca; to 2700m above Medellín). Pacific slope and locally on adj. e slope near low passes; both slopes of C Andes in Antioquia (at least formerly). W Colombia to w and se Ecuador.
**Note:** Yellow-throated Tanager (*I. analis*) of montane se Ecuador to se Peru may occur in w Putumayo. A sight rec. in w Putumayo, 1800m, 2 Sept 1978 (Hilty), was this or the above sp. (neither previously reported on e slope). Differs from Purplish-mantled Tanager thus: more extensive yellow throat reaching upper breast, and tawny buff more extensive on lower underparts. Specimen confirmation needed.

## 55. GOLDEN-CROWNED TANAGER
*Iridosornis rufivertex*      Pl. 50, Map 1324
**Identification:** 7" (18cm). *Entire head, neck, and throat deep black surrounding large, round, golden crown patch*; otherwise mainly deep, intense *purplish blue*; wings and tail black heavily edged purplish blue; lower belly and under tail coverts chestnut (or purplish blue—*caeruleoventris*).
**Similar species:** A stunning sp. but in poor light looks blackish; also remarkably like Plush-capped Finch (p 641); latter has rusty (not dark blue) underparts.
**Voice:** Usually quiet; occas. high thin *seeeep*.
**Behavior:** Pairs or groups up to 4 are characteristic members of temperate zone tanager and finch flocks. Peer and skulk mostly 0.5-5m up in dense vegetation, then fly rapidly across open spaces and dive quickly into center of thicket; partly frugivorous (J. Silliman; Hilty).
**Breeding:** 12 BC birds, Feb–Aug, C and n end E Andes (Carriker); 1 juv., May, Cundinamarca (Olivares 1969a); begging juv., July, PN Puracé (J. Silliman).

**Status and habitat:** Fairly common in thick bushes and borders of low, dense, mossy forest, esp. stunted treeline vegetation. Readily found in PN Puracé.
**Range:** 2300-3800m (mostly above 2600m). Both slopes of E Andes from s Norte de Santander and ne Santander southward and on e slope in Nariño (*rufivertex*); n end of C Andes and n end of W Andes in Antioquia (*caeruleoventris*); spottily in rest of W and C Andes and in Nariño (*ignicapillus*). Nw Venez. s in Andes to e and w Ecuador and n Peru.

[*Anisognathus*: Larger than *Iridosornis*; more arboreal; yellow to red on some or all of underparts; highlands only.]

## 56. SCARLET-BELLIED MOUNTAIN-TANAGER
*Anisognathus igniventris*      Pl. 50, Map 1325
**Identification:** 7.5" (19cm). *Unmistakable.* One of Colombia's flashiest tanagers. *Mostly deep black with scarlet* (or orange red) *lower breast and belly*; triangular patch on ear coverts scarlet; *shoulders and rump sky blue* (latter visible mainly in flight); crissum scarlet and black (or all black—*erythrotus*). An esp. showy bird in flight.
**Voice:** Frequent song a tinkling, bell-like jumble of notes, poured out rapidly in a repetitive rising and falling pattern like cranking an old engine; usually sings from concealment.
**Behavior:** Pairs or loose groups, occas. up to 15 or more, slip quietly along hedgerows, bounding from the interior of 1 dense thicket or tree to the next with short undulating flights, or join mixed tanager and finch flocks along forest borders. Sit relatively immobile or hop jaylike up through foliage; predom. frugivorous (Hilty; J. Silliman).
**Breeding:** 6 BC birds, Feb, Cauca, 2 in July, Santander (Carriker); 3 in late Dec. Boyacá (Olivares 1974a); 1 in Nov, Cundinamarca (MCN).
**Status and habitat:** Usually common in hedgerows, clearings and pastures with scattered trees or bushes, and in patches of remnant dwarf forest and shrubs near treeline, less often inside forest where meets *A. lacrymosus*.
**Range:** 2400-3400m (usually above 2600m). E Andes s to Bogotá area, Cundinamarca (*lunulatus*); C Andes from Caldas (Nevados e of Manizales) s to Nariño (*erythrotus*). Nw Venez. s in Andes to Bolivia.

## 57. SANTA MARTA (BLACK-CHEEKED) MOUNTAIN-TANAGER
*Anisognathus melanogenys*      Pl. 50, Map 1326
**Identification:** 7.3" (18.5cm). *Crown and nape blue, sides of head black* with small yellow spot below eye; remaining upperparts dull gray

blue; *entire underparts golden yellow*; thighs black.
**Similar species:** Santa Marta Brush-Finch (p 649) has wholly black head with silver cheeks.
**Behavior:** Pairs or groups of 3-6 are conspic. as they run and hop rapidly along branches and in foliage from 2m to canopy, mostly sub-canopy or lower. Often with mixed flocks and at fruiting trees and shrubs (T. B. Johnson).
**Breeding:** 8 BC birds, Jan–June, se slope Santa Marta Mts. (2200-3200m), 2 in Sept, San Lorenzo (Carriker); 1 BC ♀, June; 1 building open cup nest 14m up, Oct, San Lorenzo (T. B. Johnson).
**Status and habitat:** Common in mossy forest borders, second growth woodland, and overgrown pastures, less frequently inside forest. Populations shift lower during June–Sept wet season (T. B. Johnson). Occupies a broader spectrum of habitats than Lacrimose Mountain-Tanager, its Andean representative.
**Range:** ENDEMIC. 1600-3200m. Santa Marta Mts.
**Note:** Merged with *A. lacrymosus* (Lacrimose Mountain-Tanager) by some.

## 58. LACRIMOSE MOUNTAIN-TANAGER
*Anisognathus lacrymosus*      Pl. 50, Map 1327
**Identification:** 7.3″ (18.5cm). *Slaty above, blacker on crown and sides of head*; small spot below eye and *larger patch behind ear coverts yellow*; rump dark blue; wings and tail inconspic. edged purplish blue; *entire underparts deep mustard yellow* (or as above but forehead, sides of head and neck yellowish olive, crown and back dull grayish blue—*pallididorsalis*).
**Similar species:** Easily recognized highland tanager. Mainly slaty above and mustard yellow below with conspic. patch behind ear coverts.
**Voice:** Call a high thin *seeek* (J. Silliman); song in Nariño sputtering, high *ee-chut-chut-ee, ee-chut-chut-ee . . .* excitedly.
**Behavior:** Pairs or several are conspic. members of mixed flocks containing flycatchers, finches, and other tanagers. Hop and peer deliberately in foliage, pluck fruit, and occas. sally clumsily for flying insects; eye level to subcanopy.
**Breeding:** 12 BC birds, Feb–Aug, Perijá Mts., W and C Andes (Carriker); May nest, begging juv., July, PN Puracé (J. Silliman).
**Status and habitat:** Common in humid forest and forest borders, esp. stunted mossy forest of temperate zone to treeline/paramo ecotone. More a forest bird than allied Scarlet-bellied Mountain-Tanager.
**Range:** 2000-3800m (mostly above 2600m). N end of W Andes (Paramillo Mts.; Frontino) and C Andes s to Quindío (*olivaceiceps*); e slope

W Andes in Valle and both slopes in Cauca (*intensus*); C Andes from Cauca and Huila s to e and w Nariño (*palpebrosus*); Perijá Mts. (*pallididorsalis*); n end E Andes in Norte de Santander and Boyacá (*tamae*). Nw Venez. s in Andes to s Peru.

## 59. BLUE-WINGED MOUNTAIN-TANAGER
*Anisognathus flavinucha*      Pl. 50, Map 1328
**Identification:** 7.5″ (19cm). Forehead and *sides of head black; broad stripe from crown to nape and entire underparts bright golden yellow*; otherwise mainly black above with blue shoulder patch; flight feathers and tail *broadly edged bright turquoise blue* (*antioquiae*). Or bright cobalt blue (*cyanoptera*). Or like *antioquiae* but back and rump moss green (*victorini*); or back and rump mixed black and green (*baezae*).
**Similar species:** On Pacific slope easily confused with Black-chinned Mountain-Tanager (60), which differs in slimmer shape, more oriolelike bill, *bright yellow olive* (not black) back contrasting with head, and yellow stripe only on rearcrown (not entire crown). Blue-winged shows brighter and broader wing edgings, but this hard to see in field.
**Voice:** An undistinctive *seeet*; also slightly buzzy ticking, chipping, and trilled notes, none loud.
**Behavior:** Pairs or groups of 3-10 hop rather actively among outer limbs or in terminal foliage, where pluck fruit and peer for insects; wander alone or join mixed flocks; generally conspic., midlevels to canopy.
**Breeding:** 17 BC birds, May–Sept, n end of W and C Andes (Carriker); 3 BC birds, Mar (Miller 1963); Nov fledgling, W Andes above Cali (S. Gniadek); June nestlings, Bosque Yotoco, Valle (Hilty).
**Status and habitat:** Common in humid forest, forest edges, and taller second growth woodland. The most common and most widespread mountain-tanager in Colombia, and found at lower el. than most of its allies.
**Range:** 1400-2600m (once to 3300m?; locally to 1200m on Pacific slope). N end W Andes (Paramillo Mts.) both slopes of C Andes in Antioquia, and s on e slope to Tolima (*antioquiae*); rest of W Andes to Nariño and w slope of C Andes from Quindío southward (*cyanoptera*); w slope E Andes in Santander, both slopes in Cundinamarca and head of Magdalena Val. in Huila (*victorini*); e slope of Andes in Nariño (*baezae*). N Venez. s in mts. to n Bolivia.

## 60. BLACK-CHINNED MOUNTAIN-TANAGER
*Anisognathus notabilis*      Pl. 50, Map 1329
**Identification:** 7.3″ (18.5cm). Looks "black-headed" and oriolelike. Bill rather pointed.

Entire forecrown, sides of head, and chin black; *stripe down center of rearcrown and entire underparts bright golden yellow; back and rump bright yellow olive*; wings and tail black; wing coverts edged violet blue; primaries and tail faintly edged deep purplish blue.

**Similar species:** Resembles better known Blue-winged Mountain-Tanager but from it or any other bird in its range by entire back pale yellowish olive *contrasting sharply with black head*. See Yellow-backed Oriole (p 572).

**Voice:** High thin *tic* notes.

**Behavior:** Often in groups of up to 5-6; sit sluggishly and rather erect like orioles, then briskly run-hop along branches and peer at foliage or for fruit like allied Blue-winged Mountain-Tanager.

**Status and habitat:** Uncommon and very local; mid. and upper levels of wet mossy forest and forest edges. Most readily found on w slopes below Cerro Munchique, Cauca, above Queremal, Valle, or above Junín, Nariño.

**Range:** 900-2200m (once to 300m in w Nariño). Pacific slope from headwaters of Río San Juan, Chocó (w side of Cerro Tatamá) southward. W Colombia and w Ecuador.

[*Buthraupis*: Largest and most robust of the mountain-tanagers; chunkier shape than *Anisognathus*; bill relatively small compared to body size; mostly temperate zone and treeline.]

## 61. HOODED MOUNTAIN-TANAGER

*Buthraupis montana*  Pl. 50, Map 1330

**Identification:** 9.0″ (23cm). Very large. *Eyes bright red. Head and throat black, remaining upperparts glistening deep blue*; wings and tail broadly edged deep blue; *rest of underparts golden yellow*; narrow band from sides of rump to thighs blue; thighs black.

**Similar species:** Easily recognized by large size, black head, all blue upperparts, and red eye. Cf. Black-chested and Lacrimose mountain-tanagers (63, 58).

**Voice:** Frequent contact call a high-pitched, thin *tseep* (J. Silliman); often in flight a thin, trilled *ti'ti'ti'ti' ti*.

**Behavior:** Usually in conspic. groups of 3-10 roaming long distances along steep forested slopes or canyons, members often crossing considerable gaps with each flight, stragglers then hurrying to keep up. Hop up through outer canopy limbs and foliage and eat mostly fruit. Also frequently accompany mixed flocks or are accompanied by Mountain Caciques.

**Breeding:** 6 BC birds, Jan–Sept, Perijá Mts. and W and C Andes (Carriker).

**Status and habitat:** Fairly common in humid and wet forest and forest borders, sometimes

into second growth woodland and partially cleared areas, though seldom far from taller woodland.

**Range:** 2200-3300m (once to 1100m on Pacific slope). Perijá Mts. and all 3 Andean ranges Nw Venez. s in Andes to n Bolivia.

## 62. MASKED MOUNTAIN-TANAGER

*Buthraupis wetmorei*  Pl. 50, Map 1331

**Identification:** 8.0″ (20cm). *Crown and nape yellowish olive* becoming olive green on back and *yellowish on rump; sides of head (to above eyes), upper throat, and sides of throat black forming a broad drooping disklike mask*; forehead and narrow line over mask dull yellow (brighter than crown); *rest of underparts bright mustard yellow*; sides and flanks (sometimes belly) mixed dusky olive; wings and tail black; shoulders and 1 wing bar shiny blue.

**Similar species:** Much "yellower" above than any of its highland allies; *yellow rump* prom. in flight. Black-chested Mountain-Tanager (63) differs in blue crown, all black throat and chest, moss green back and wing edgings. Buff-breasted Mountain-Tanager (68) has black head and long silvery-blue eyebrow.

**Behavior:** Not well known. Single birds with mixed flocks in PN Puracé perched in or on top of scrubby trees near treeline; moved rather heavily, once sallied clumsily for a flying insect. Reminiscent of Black-chested Mountain-Tanager, and with it in 1 mixed tanager-finch flock.

**Breeding:** BC ♀, 28 Feb, Páramo Puracé (Carriker).

**Status and habitat:** Apparently rare and local; stunted mossy ("elfin") forest and dense, wet, "chaparrallike" brushland near treeline. Known in Colombia from 2 specimens and 2 sight recs. as follows: specimen from Puracé, Cauca, and from Páramo de Puracé, near Laguna San Rafael; 1 seen on Popayán-Neiva Rd. (km 143), PN Puracé, July 1976 (Hilty and F. Loetscher), 1 seen on Coconuco Rd. (km 35), PN Puracé, June 1980 (Hilty et al).

**Range:** 3300-3450m (sight to 3000m). Both slopes of C Andes in e Cauca (PN Puracé). S Colombia; se Ecuador (to 3600m); n Peru.

## 63. bLACK-CHESTED MOUNTAIN-TANAGER

*Buthraupis eximia*  Pl. 50, Map 1332

**Identification:** 8.5″ (22cm). Large. *Crown and nape shiny cornflower blue; back moss green (or with blue rump—eximia)*; wings and tail black with blue lesser wing coverts (often partly hidden) and green-edged secondaries; *sides of head, throat, and chest black*; rest of underparts bright yellow.

**Similar species:** Only large mountain-tanager with a blue cap and mossy green back. See Hooded and rare Masked mountain-tanagers (61, 62).

**Behavior:** Pairs or usually groups of 3-6, either alone or with mixed flocks, move rather heavily and quietly through the upper part of trees, hopping through foliage or along mossy limbs pecking here and there. Not as conspic. as Hooded Mountain-Tanager.

**Status and habitat:** Uncommon and apparently local; shorter mossy forest, forest borders, and elfin woodland. Reg. found on e slope of PN Puracé near Termales de San Juan, and at both s entrances to park.

**Range:** 2000-3800m (mostly 2800-3400m). N end of W Andes (Paramillo Mt.), C Andes from Quindío Mts. (Santa Isabel) s to Cauca and PN Puracé (*zimmeri*); E Andes from Norte de Santander (near Pamplona) s to Cundinamarca (*eximia*); e slope of Andes in Nariño near Laguna La Cocha (*chloronota*). Extreme nw Venez. (Táchira) to s Ecuador and n Peru.

[*Bangsia*: Small, shorter-tailed editions of *Buthraupis* that occur at lower el. in very wet, mossy forest; note restricted ranges.]

### 64. GOLDEN-CHESTED TANAGER
*Bangsia rothschildi*          Pl. 50, Map 1333
**Identification:** 6.2″ (15.7cm). Mostly dark navy blue with *large, bright, golden yellow patch on chest and yellow under tail coverts*; bill all black.
**Similar species:** Black-and-gold Tanager (65) differs mainly in blackish plumage and the golden yellow chest patch continuing as a broad yellow median stripe to belly. See Moss-backed Tanager (66).
**Voice:** Infrequently, a shrill, high-pitched *kjeee*; rarely heard song a buzzy, insectlike *tiz-ez-ez-ez-ez-ez-ez*, up to 10 times a min.
**Behavior:** One or 2 usually follow mixed flocks containing other tanagers and frugivors. Suggest barbets as "about face" on open branches with tail cocked and head low but more like vireos as hop sluggishly and peer along branches and into other foliage; lower midlevel to subcanopy.
**Breeding:** 1 with nest material, 24 June, upper Anchicayá Val. (Hilty 1977). Nest of related Blue-and-gold Tanager (*Bangsia arcaei*) of w Panama is a euphonialike large clump of moss with side entrance on hanging branch 10m up at edge of cloud forest; parents bringing fruit, 4 July, 1982 (R. Ridgely).
**Status and habitat:** Wet forest and forest borders of foothills and lower slopes. Fairly common and readily seen in foothills (300-500m) along Old Buenaventura Road. Replaced above

1000-1100m in Valle by allied Moss-backed Tanager.
**Range:** 250-1100m. Pacific slope from headwaters of Río Atrato southward. W Colombia and nw Ecuador.

### 65. BLACK-AND-GOLD TANAGER
*Bangsia melanochlamys*          Pl. 50. Map 1334
**Identification:** 6.2″ (15.7cm). Rather like previous sp. *Almost entirely dull black with golden yellow patch on chest extending as broad yellow median stripe to lower belly*; upper wing coverts and upper tail coverts dull blue; bill black.
**Similar species:** See Golden-chested Tanager.
**Breeding:** 11 BC birds, June 1948, above and se of Valdivia, nw end C Andes (Carriker).
**Status and habitat:** Humid and wet forest. One of Colombia's least known tanagers. Apparently fairly common (at least formerly) on saddle between Cauca and Nechí drainage near Las Ventanas (above Valdivia, 1600-2450m) in "cloud forest" with heavy undergrowth (Carriker). Area is largely deforested now.
**Range:** ENDEMIC. 1300-2450m. W and n slope of C Andes at nw end (La Frijolera; and Las Ventanas above Valdivia) and w slope of W Andes near headwaters of Río San Juan (slopes of Cerro Tatamá at La Silva and Río Jamarraya).

### 66. MOSS-BACKED TANAGER
*Bangsia edwardsi*          Pl. 50. Map 1335
**Identification:** 6.2″ (15.7cm). Bill *yellowish flesh color below*, mostly dusky above (looks "pale" in field). Throat, foreface, and center of crown black; *sides of head and sides of crown blue; otherwise moss green above*; wings and tail dusky green; wing coverts tinged blue; *large patch on chest golden yellow*; rest of underparts mostly olive green; median underparts more yellow green.
**Similar species:** Gold-ringed Tanager (67) has sides of head blackish encircled by a conspic. yellow ring. Both have prom. yellow chest patches.
**Voice:** Song in Nariño a bubbly, rattling trill *tr'e'e'E'E'e'e'r tr'e'e'E'E'e'e'r . . .*, for up to a min. without interruption from prom. perch.
**Behavior:** A rather lethargic, almost unsuspicious tanager, usually seen singly or in pairs, and frequently with mixed flocks in the mid. or lower levels of forest, occas. to subcanopy. Peer heavily at branches or foliage mostly for fruit; once at army ants (Hilty 1974). Likes to perch prom. in open for several min. on bare stubs or tips of palm frond spikes that overlook forested hillsides.
**Breeding:** Stub-tailed young with ad., 24 Jan, upper Anchicayá Val. (Hilty).
**Status and habitat:** Common locally in wet and

mossy forest or at forest edges, infrequently trees in small clearings. Easily found in "cloud forests" at Tokío above Queremal, Valle, and above Junín, Nariño; rarely down into foothills.
**Range:** 400-2100m (*mainly above* 900m in Nariño and 1200m in Valle). Pacific slope from the Dagua Val. (Valle) southward. W Colombia and nw Ecuador.

### 67. GOLD-RINGED TANAGER
*Bangsia aureocincta*          Pl. 50, Map 1336
**Identification:** 6.2" (15.7cm). Resembles Moss-backed Tanager. ♂: head, throat, and sides of breast black; *conspic. bright yellow ring starts above eye, encircles ear coverts, and goes forward to base of bill*; otherwise mostly moss green above; wings dusky blue; *large golden yellow patch on chest*; rest of underparts yellowish olive; darker on sides and flanks; bill dark above, pale below. ♀ sim. but black replaced with dark olive green.
**Similar species:** ♂ looks "black-headed" with big yellow ring. See Moss-backed Tanager (66). Golden-chested and Black-and-gold tanagers (64, 65) also superficially sim., both lack yellow ring on sides of head.
**Status and habitat:** A very little known bird. Taken in wet mossy forest, it may replace *B. edwardsi* n of the Dagua Val.
**Range:** ENDEMIC. 2000-2200m. Known only from headwaters of Río San Juan (Cerro Tatamá) s to northernmost Valle (Novita Trail 2150m).

### 68. BUFF-BREASTED MOUNTAIN-TANAGER
*Dubusia taeniata*          Pl. 50, Map 1337
**Identification:** 7.5" (19cm). *Head, throat, and upper mantle black; feathers of forehead and superciliary tipped silvery blue* forming a long frosty eyestripe; back dark blue; wings and tail black; upper wing coverts broadly edged silvery blue; greater wing coverts and remiges edged dark blue; *band across chest buff*; breast and belly bright yellow; under tail coverts buff (or as above but midcrown dark blue and midthroat as well as chest buff—*carrikeri*).
**Similar species:** Superficially like several mountain-tanagers but from any by long "frosted" eyestripe. Buffy chest a good mark if close.
**Voice:** Call (or song?), sometimes repeated persistently, a *very loud*, whistled *pheeeee-bay*, 2d note lower, or slurred lower; brings to mind a chickadee (*Parus*) of temperate N America but louder.
**Behavior:** More often heard than seen. Single birds or pairs follow mixed flocks or wander alone, often apparently moving over large

areas. Peer and hop rather deliberately at almost any ht. but generally fairly low and partially concealed in denser foliage; now and then sit stolidly on a bushtop for a few moments, or take berries from fruiting trees (J. Silliman; Hilty).
**Breeding:** 8 BC birds, Feb–Sept, Santa Marta Mts., E and C Andes (Carriker); 2 in late Dec, Boyacá (Olivares 1974a).
**Status and habitat:** Uncommon in humid forest (usually mossy) and forest borders, occas. patches of brush and denser second growth.
**Range:** 2400-3600m (seldom below 2600m). Santa Marta Mts. (*carrikeri*); E ad C Andes to both slopes of Nariño, W Andes in Cauca (*taeniata*). Nw Venez. (incl. Perijá Mts.) s in Andes to c Peru.
**Notes:** Sometimes placed in the genus *Delothraupis*.

### 69. BLUE-GRAY TANAGER
*Thraupis episcopus*          Pl. 51, Map 1338
**Identification:** 6.5" (16.5cm). Head, neck, and underparts pale blue gray *contrasting* with darker and bluer upper back; wings and tail edged bluish, shoulders light to dark blue (or *shoulders and wing bar white* to bluish white—*leucoptera; mediana; coelestis*).
**Similar species:** *Head always paler than back.* Duller Palm Tanager (71) is sim. in many respects but has rear half of wing black. In Carib. region cf. very sim. Glaucous Tanager (70).
**Voice:** Call a dry, slightly strained *tsuup*, sometimes followed by a few twittering notes; song a var. ser. of squeaky twitters much like Palm Tanager.
**Behavior:** The noisy and energetic "Azulejo" as it is widely known, is one of Colombia's most familiar birds in settled areas. It is sociable, found in pairs or small groups, and when foraging, notably versatile as peers head down along branches, scans foliage, flycatches, and visits fruiting and flowering trees, or feeders with fruit. Usually stays well up in trees or shrubbery and sometimes with Palm Tanagers.
**Breeding:** 6 Santa Marta nests, Apr–May (Todd and Carriker 1922); nest with young, 4 Mar, Meta (Brown); BC birds, Apr, Aug, and Oct, ne Meta (S. Furniss); building nest near Cali, 11 May (S. Gniadek), and 13 Oct, upper Anchicayá Val. (Hilty); thick, deep, cup nest; 2-3 bluish white eggs heavily streaked and spotted darker.
**Status and habitat:** Common in a broad spectrum of essentially nonforest habitats incl. all kinds of settled areas, plantations, city parks, var. stages of second growth and forest edges from dry to very wet regions.
**Range:** To 2600m (usually below 2000m). Sw

Cauca and w Nariño (*quaesita*); rest of Colombia w of Andes incl. Santa Marta, and e base of Andes in Norte de Santander and nw Arauca (*cana*); e of Andes in w Casanare and Meta (*leucoptera*); e Vichada along Orinoco (*nesophila*); Vaupés and undoubtedly Guainía (*mediana*); Caquetá s to Amazonas (*coelestis*). E Mexico to w Peru, n Bolivia, and Amazonian Brazil. Trinidad and Tobago. Introduced into s Florida.

## 70. GLAUCOUS TANAGER
*Thraupis glaucocolpa*          Pl. 51, Map 1339
**Identification:** 6.5″ (16.5cm). Much like Blue-gray Tanager, but differs in having *darker gray head uniform with back* (instead of head paler), primary coverts dark blue forming a *dark spot at base of primaries*, remiges edged greenish turquoise instead of dark blue (hard to see in field), and most of underparts tinged greenish blue with a contrasting *white belly* (amount of contrast varies).
**Voice:** Calls and song essentially sim. to Blue-gray Tanager.
**Behavior:** Much like Blue-gray Tanager but favors drier areas. Both may occur together in dry parts of Carib. region.
**Breeding:** 3 BC birds, Apr–July, Cesar Val. and w Guajira (Carriker); breeds in Aug, Guárico, Venez. (Thomas 1979b); building in unfinished thornbird nest, 22 July, Venez. (Skutch 1969b).
**Status and habitat:** Gallery woodland, deciduous woodland and dry to arid scrubby areas, gardens, and plantations; much less numerous than Blue-gray Tanager.
**Range:** To 500m (once to 750m). Carib. region from Cartagena e to Santa Marta area and Guajira. Colombia and n Venez.
**Note:** Formerly placed with *T. sayaca* (Sayaca Tanager) of s S America.

## 71. PALM TANAGER
*Thraupis palmarum*          Pl. 51, Map 1340
**Identification:** 6.5″ (16.5cm). *Mostly grayish olive*, darker and dingier on back and glossed violaceous or bluish in some lights; *forecrown, lower underparts, and wing coverts strongly tinged yellowish; terminal half of closed wing black* (conspic. in flight or at rest), forming a large black triangle.
**Similar species:** Shape and behavior much like Blue-gray Tanager (69) and often with it, but in any light can be told by black rear half of wings. Also see Glaucous Tanager (70).
**Voice:** Squeaky song and calls resemble those of Blue-gray Tanager.
**Behavior:** Sim. to Blue-gray Tanager but less an urban bird and often even in treetops well

inside forest. Reg. clings to tips of palm fronds, or hangs upside down beneath the tip.
**Breeding:** BC ♀♀, Feb and Aug, ne Meta (S. Furniss); a BC ♂, Mar, n Chocó (Haffer 1975); 4 nests in upper Anchicayá Val., Dec–July; 1 in PN Tayrona, 4 Aug; 1 at Pto. Inírida, 18 Sept (Hilty). Open cup next often at base of palm fronds or in a cavity.
**Status and habitat:** Common in populated areas, shrubby clearings, forest edges; less often in humid forest; fairly dry to wet regions.
**Range:** To 2100m (sight rec. to 2600m, Bogotá—P. Gertler). Throughout (except Guajira?). Nicaragua to n Bolivia, Paraguay, and se Brazil. Trinidad.

## 72. BLUE-CAPPED TANAGER
*Thraupis cyanocephala*          Pl. 51, Map 1341
**Identification:** 7.5″ (19cm). *Head cobalt blue* with black lores and forehead; *otherwise bright yellowish olive above*; throat and underparts blue gray; thighs, under tail coverts, and under wing coverts golden yellow (or thighs olive yellow—*annectens*).
**Similar species:** No other Colombian tanager resembles it. Blue head and yellow under tail coverts are good marks. See note below.
**Voice:** An occas. high, insignificant *sit*; squeaky song resembles Blue-gray Tanager's.
**Behavior:** Pairs or less frequently groups of 3-8 wander alone or join mixed flocks. Usually in mid. levels of trees or higher but lower to fruiting shrubs.
**Breeding:** 13 BC birds, Apr, Perijá and Santa Marta mts., 5 in May–Sept, n end W Andes, 5 in June–July, C and E Andes (Carriker); open cup nest 8m up in crotch of limb; 2 pale greenish blue eggs marked sepia (ffrench 1973).
**Status and habitat:** Fairly common in shrubby forest borders, patches of second growth woodland, overgrown pastures, and highland hedges.
**Range:** 1400-3000m (seldom below 1800m). Santa Marta Mts. (*margaritae*); Perijá Mts. and both slopes E Andes s to Meta (*auricrissa*); C and W Andes s to both slopes of Nariño and in w Putumayo (*annectens*). N Venez. s in mts. to n Bolivia.
**Note:** Blue-and-yellow Tanager (*T. bonariensis*) of Andes from Ecuador to n Argentina and in se Brazil is common n to Quito and may occur in drier scrubby highlands of extreme s Nariño. From Blue-capped Tanager by *orange yellow lower back and underparts* and black wings and tail margined blue. ♀ is duller and buffy below.

[*Ramphocelus*: Nonforest; rich velvety plumage, crown feathers plushy; expanded white lower mandible (esp. prom. in ♂♂).]

## 73. SILVER-BEAKED TANAGER
*Ramphocelus carbo*          Pl. 51, Map 1342
**Identification:** 7″ (18cm). Broad lower mandible *silvery white.* ♂ looks mostly black with contrasting white bill; deep *velvety black above* slightly glossed maroon; *throat and upper breast dark crimson becoming deep black on lower underparts.* Or blackish maroon above, brighter crimson below (*venezuelensis*). ♀: *dull reddish brown above; brighter and redder on rump*; underparts maroon brown; bill blackish.
**Similar species:** ♂ unmistakable. ♀ can be confused with a no. of "brownish" ♀ tanagers and finches but usually shows paler lower mandible and a reddish wash below. Does not overlap range of Crimson-backed Tanager (74).
**Voice:** Noisy. Common call a loud *chink*; also a more musical *zweep* (J. V. Remsen); dawn song (in Trinidad) a ser. of 2- to 5-syllabled phrases, *kick-wick* or *che-wa*, deliberate, thrushlike but thinner and often followed by a creaky *weer* (ffrench 1973).
**Behavior:** Usually in conspic. and boisterous groups of its own trooping noisily about in undergrowth along forest borders or in gardens and clearings. Peers in foliage for fruit and insects. Duller ♀ ♀ and imms. outnumber ad ♂ ♂.
**Breeding:** Jan–Mar nests, ne Meta (S. Furniss); 2 BC birds, Mar, Macarena Mts. (Olivares 1962); a dependent young with ♀, 30 May, Leticia (J. V. Remsen). Two blue eggs with dark spots.
**Status and habitat:** Common in shrubby clearings and forest borders. Replaced w of Andes by *R. dimidiatus.*
**Range:** To 1200m. E of Andes in Arauca and Casanare (*venezuelensis*); e Cundinamarca, w and e Meta (*unicolor*); Vichada and Caquetá southward (*carbo*). The Guianas and Venez. to Bolivia, Paraguay, and se Brazil. Trinidad.

## 74. CRIMSON-BACKED TANAGER
*Ramphocelus dimidiatus*          Pl. 51, Map 1343
**Identification:** 7″ (18cm). ♂ has *lower mandible gleaming silvery white*; head, mantle, throat, and chest deep maroon red, becoming *bright crimson on lower back, rump, and lower underparts; wings and tail black*; thighs and center of belly black. ♀: like ♂ but much duller, almost blackish on throat and chest, but retains red rump and red lower underparts; bill blackish.
**Similar species:** ♂ unmistakable. ♀ Flame-rumped Tanager (76) has contrasting reddish orange (not red) rump and is partly yellow below. ♀ also rather like ♀ ♀ of Red-crowned (87) and Red-throated ant-tanagers (88) but rump and belly red.
**Voice:** Much like previous sp. Dawn song in

Panama *sweet you-do sweet you-do you-do* (Skutch 1954).
**Behavior:** Sim. to Silver-beaked Tanager.
**Breeding:** 14 BC birds, Apr–Aug, Santa Marta s to Huila (Carriker); BC birds, Nov–Dec, nw Santander (Boggs 1961); dependent juvs. with ad., Feb, PN Tayrona (Brown); Santa Marta nests in May, low cup, 2 blue eggs finely spotted dark (Todd and Carriker 1922).
**Status and habitat:** Shrubby clearings, cultivated areas, and forest borders. Common in more humid areas of n Colombia, somewhat less numerous in inter-Andean vals. Uncommon and very local s into c Chocó.
**Range:** To 1500m. Generally w of E Andes except Pacific coast where only in Chocó and Dagua and Anchicayá Val.; e of Andes in Norte de Santander (Catatumbo lowlands). W Panama to w Venez.

## 75. MASKED CRIMSON TANAGER
*Ramphocelus nigrogularis*          Pl. 51, Map 1344
**Identification:** 7.5″ (19cm). Base of lower mandible gleaming silvery white. *Head and most of underparts brilliant crimson scarlet with black mask from forehead and throat to behind eyes*; otherwise black above with *scarlet lower back and rump*; belly black. ♀ duller.
**Similar species:** Unmistakable in range. Vermilion Tanager (78), a foothill and mt. bird, is remarkably sim. (lacks black mantle and belly), but range overlap unlikely.
**Voice:** Call an undistinctive, sharp *tchi*; song a weak but sweet *whee-chu* repeated over and over (J. V. Remsen).
**Behavior:** Chattering pairs or groups of 3-12 troop about from eye level to subcanopy along forest borders, sometimes with Silver-beaked Tanagers; often high at *Erythrina* flowers along river banks.
**Breeding:** 2 BC ♂ ♂, June, w Caquetá (Carriker).
**Status and habitat:** Fairly common in *várzea* forest borders and streamside shrubbery; seldom far from water.
**Range:** To 500m. E of Andes from s Meta (Macarena Mts.) to Putumayo and Amazonas. E Colombia to se Peru and Amazonian Brazil.

## 76. FLAME-RUMPED TANAGER
*Ramphocelus flammigerus*          Pl. 51, Map 1345
**Identification:** 7.5″ (19cm). ♂ unmistakable. velvety black with *flame scarlet lower back and rump* (var. to reddish orange to orange in zone of hybridization on Pacific slope); bill pale bluish with black tip. ♀: *dark brown above with reddish orange rump*; below pale yellow with *diffused reddish orange chest band*. Imm. ♂: like ♀, older imms. extensively mottled black.

**Similar species:** ♀ Lemon-rumped Tanager (77) is paler, more grayish brown above with yellow (not orangish) rump, and lacks the orangish wash on chest. See Crimson-backed Tanager (74).
**Voice:** Sim. to Lemon-rumped Tanager.
**Behavior:** As in Lemon-rumped Tanager.
**Breeding:** 4 BC ♂♂, July, near Popayán, Cauca (Carriker). Cup nest low in weeds, 26 Feb, upper Calima Val., Valle (1800m); 2 bluish white eggs with wreath of dark spots at large end (Brown).
**Status and habitat:** Fairly common in overgrown pastures, shrubby areas, and forest borders. Replaced at lower el. on Pacific slope by *R. icteronotus* but hybridizes with it in a narrow zone (above 800m) where deforestation has allowed the populations to contact (Sibley 1958). "Orange-rumped" hybrids are frequent above 800m, virtually unknown below 800m where birds are essentially all "lemon-rumped."
**Range:** ENDEMIC. 800-2000m. Both slopes of Cauca Val. s to Cauca, adj. Pacific slope from Río San Juan headwaters (Cerro Tatamá) s to Valle, and the upper Río Patía drainage.
**Note:** Prob. this sp. should be merged with the next.

## 77. LEMON-RUMPED (YELLOW-RUMPED) TANAGER

*Ramphocelus icteronotus* Pl. 51, Map 1346
**Identification:** 7.5″ (19cm). ♂ unmistakable: velvety black with *brilliant lemon yellow lower back and rump*; bill pale bluish with black tip. ♀: grayish brown above with *rump and entire underparts clear pale yellow*; throat whitish; bill like ♂. Imm. ♂: like ♀; older birds mottled black.
**Similar species:** See ♀ Flame-rumped Tanager (76).
**Voice:** Much like Flame-rumped Tanager. Common calls *pssst*, or nasal *nyeck* and *cheeick* (Eisenmann).
**Behavior:** Noisy, conspic., and usually in small fussing groups in thickets or shrubbery or in smaller fruiting trees and shrubs. ♂♂ often sit in open with wings drooped and rump exposed. "♀-plumaged" birds usually outnumber ♂♂.
**Breeding:** 11 BC birds, Feb–May, s Bolívar to Gulf of Urabá (Carriker). Pacific slope breeding, early Dec–mid-Apr (1 BC ♂, Haffer 1975; 7 nests, Anchicayá Val.—B. Hilty; S. Hilty; BC ♂, 1 nest, Guapí, Cauca—Olivares 1958). Open cup nest in low bush; 2 blue eggs speckled dark.
**Status and habitat:** One of the most common and most characteristic Pacific coast birds in

overgrown clearings and shrubby forest borders. Hybridizes with Flame-rumped Tanager above 800m.
**Range:** To 2100m (rarely above 1400m). Pacific coast and e along n base of Andes to mid. Magdalena Val. (s to Ibaque, n Tolima) W Panama to w Ecuador.
**Note:** Perhaps a subsp. of *R. flammigerus* (Flame-rumped Tanager).

## 78. VERMILION TANAGER

*Calochaetes coccineus* Pl. 51, Map 1347
**Identification:** 6.7″ (17cm). *Mostly brilliant scarlet with small black mask and throat* (latter rounded off on center of chest); *wings and tail black*; bill blackish. ♀ slightly duller.
**Similar species:** Much like Masked Crimson Tanager (75) but *lacks* black mantle and belly; ranges may meet in hills at base of Andes, but preferred habitats differ markedly.
**Breeding:** BC ♀, June, w Caquetá (Carriker).
**Status and habitat:** Rare. Known definitely only from or above Churuyaco (600m) on Nariño-Putumayo boundary, 1 bird presum. this sp., from s of Florencia (Pto. Venicia, 320m), Caquetá (Carriker), and another locality of uncertain el. above Florencia, Caquetá. Prob. well into "cloud forest" of the subtropical zone (wet mossy forest to 2000m in Peru—T. Parker).
**Range:** 320-600m (doubtless higher). E base and slope of E Andes in w Caquetá and se Nariño. Colombia to s Peru.

## 79. HEPATIC TANAGER

*Piranga flava* Ill. 51, Map 1348
**Identification:** 7″ (18cm). *Bill blackish above, bluish to horn color below.* ♂: mainly dark crimson red (or brick red—Santa Marta), brighter below; *lores grayish.* ♀: olive above, *yellow* below, tinged olive. Both sexes lack dusky cheeks of N American forms.
**Similar species:** ♂ Summer Tanager (80) is brighter and rosier, ♀ Summer Tanager is greener above, brighter yellow below. The mainly blackish bill of the Hepatic Tanager is not always a distinguishing mark as the pale bill of the Summer Tanager darkens on its wintering ground.
**Voice:** Alarm *chup* (Miller 1963); call in Panama is a distinctive *chup-chitup*, and song a ser. of sweet rising and falling phrases (R. Ridgely 1976). Voice of Colombian birds needs confirmation.
**Behavior:** Single birds or pairs are usually seen alone in the upper part of tall trees; rather unobtrusive as they peer heavily at foliage and twigs.
**Breeding:** 11 BC birds, June–Nov, Santa Marta Mts., n end E Andes in Norte de Santander,

C Andes in Cauca (Carriker), 3 BC birds, Mar–Apr, W Andes above Cali (Miller 1963); frail flat nest sometimes rather low; 2 eggs (Todd and Carriker 1922), greenish spotted brown (ffrench 1973).

**Status and habitat:** Rather open woodland, tall second growth, and forest borders or trees in clearings (rarely inside mossy forest); seldom very numerous.

**Range:** 1500-2200m in the Andes. Santa Marta and Perijá mts. (200-2200m), w slope E Andes in Norte de Santander; n end of C Andes in Río Nechí drainage, both Andean slopes above the Cauca Val. and Pacific slope from Valle to w Nariño (upper Patía Val.). Sw US to w Peru, Uruguay, Paraguay, and the Guianas. Trinidad. N birds migratory (none reach S America).

### 80. SUMMER TANAGER
*Piranga rubra*

**Identification:** 7″ (18cm). *Bill whitish in ♂; pale yellowish in ♀* (but darker in both sexes on wintering grounds). ♂: *all rosy red*, darker above; wings and tail dusky. Ad. ♂ remains red all yr. ♀: olive above, wings and tail dusky, clear yellow below. First-yr. imm. ♂ like ♀; molting subadults mottled red and yellow.

**Similar species:** See Hapatic Tanager (79). In hand, outermost primary equal to next 2, not shorter as in Hepatic Tanager (Meyer de Schauensee and Phelps 1978).

**Voice:** Staccato *Stic-a-tup* call often heard in Colombia, song rarely heard.

**Behavior:** Single birds wander alone or follow mixed flocks. Stay mostly inside or in shade of rather open tree canopy where peer, and often sally to foliage or to air for insects; occas. at fruiting trees.

**Status and habitat:** Fairly common transient and winter resident, early Oct–late Apr; in shrubby clearings, forest borders, and open or thinned woodland (e.g., coffee zone). More numerous in mts. than lowlands.

**Range:** To about 2700m (once to treeline in ne Boyacá). Throughout (most recs. w of Andes). Breeds from US to n Mexico; winters from Mexico to n Bolivia, Amazonian Brazil, and Surinam (twice).

### 81. SCARLET TANAGER
*Piranga olivacea*

**Identification:** 6.3″ (16cm). Unmistakable breeding plumage ♂ seen only in spring migration: *bright scarlet with jet black wings and tail.* Nonbreeding ♂ like ♀, but *wings and tail black.* Molting ♂ mottled red and green. ♀: olive

green above; wings and tail dusky; below greenish yellow. Imm. ♂ like ♀ but cheeks dusky. Bill pale in both sexes.

**Similar species:** ♀ most like ♀ Summer and Hepatic tanagers (80, 79) but smaller with obviously darker wings; underparts dingier. ♀ White-winged Tanager (82) has 2 white wing bars.

**Voice:** Occas. call a low *chip-burr.*

**Behavior:** Usually solitary and at almost any ht. in trees. In spring migration sometimes in loosely assoc. groups.

**Status and habitat:** Uncommon transient and winter resident, 12 Oct–early May (former a sight rec., upper Anchicayá Val.—Hilty); forest, forest edge, and second growth woodland; during migration also in more open woodland, parks, and gardens. Spotty and far less numerous than Summer Tanager.

**Range:** To 2600m (1 sighting to 3000m, 8 Apr 1979, Represa Neusa, Cundinamarca—A. Gast). W of Andes and along e base of Andes (incl. Macarena Mts.). Breeds in e N America; winters from Panama and w S America to nw Bolivia.

### 82. WHITE-WINGED TANAGER
*Piranga leucoptera*    Pl. 51, Map 1349

**Identification:** 5.7″ (14.5cm). ♂: *scarlet with black lores, wings, and tail; 2 broad white wing bars.* ♀: olive yellow above, brighter on crown; *below dull deep yellow; lores, wings, and tail blackish; 2 white wing bars.*

**Similar species:** Only Colombian tanager with bold white wing bars.

**Voice:** Distinctive call, *pit-seet* or *pit-seet-seet,* the *seet* notes musical and rising, also var. sharp *weet* and *chip* notes often rapidly repeated; song, thin, wiry *e-sée-se-whEET.*

**Behavior:** Pairs or small chipping groups travel alone or follow mixed flocks; usually in treetops where peer and flutter in outer twigs and foliage, and glean from leaves as do some *Tangara* (e.g., Rufous-throated Tanager).

**Breeding:** 4 BC birds, Apr–May, Perijá Mts., C Andes in se Antioquia (Carriker). May–June and Nov–Dec in n Venez. (Schäfer and Phelps 1954).

**Status and habitat:** Uncommon and very local; humid forest and forest edges.

**Range:** 1500-2200m (to 600m on Pacific slope). Pacific slope in n Valle (w slope of Cerro Tatamá), and w Nariño, both slopes of C Andes in Caldas-Tolima-Valle area (Río Samaná; Nevado de Quindío; above Palmira); Perijá Mts. and both slopes of E Andes at n end (Norte de Santander; s Cesar) and w slope in Cundinamarca. E Mexico to w Panama; n and s Venez. and adj. nw Brazil; the Andes to n Bolivia.

## 83. RED-HOODED TANAGER
*Piranga rubriceps*          Pl. 51, Map 1350
**Identification:** 7.5″ (19cm). *Unmistakable. Entire head to central breast bright scarlet*; otherwise yellowish olive above and *bright yellow below; wings black*; wing coverts yellow; tail dusky. ♀: sim. but scarlet extends only to chest.
**Behavior:** Pairs or groups of 3-5 hop and peer sluggishly along limbs or in foliage in mid. or upper story; generally independent of mixed flocks.
**Breeding:** BC ♀, Sept, n end W Andes (Carriker).
**Status and habitat:** Humid and wet forest and forest borders. Apparently rare and local over much of Colombian range. Most readily found above Mocoa in w Putumayo—e Nariño area. In PN Cueva de los Guácharos rec. only Feb–May (P. Gertler).
**Range:** 1700-3000m. Spottily from e slope of W Andes (on w slope near low passes), to w slope of E Andes (at least formerly n to Soatá, Boyacá), and e slope of E Andes in Putumayo and Nariño. Colombia s in Andes to e Ecuador and n Peru.

## 84. CARMIOL'S TANAGER
*Chlorothraupis carmioli*          Pl. 52, Map 1351
**Identification:** 6.7″ (17cm). Heavy blackish bill. *Entirely dingy olive green*; slightly paler and yellower below, esp. on throat.
**Similar species:** A dull and confusing bird with a restricted range in Colombia. ♀ Red-crowned Ant-Tanager (87) is much browner with tawny yellow crown stripe, Lemon-browed Tanager (85) has conspic. yellow "spectacles," Broad-billed Manakin (p 438) is more uniformly dull yellow below (lacks contrasting throat) and is not in noisy conspecific groups.
**Voice:** An incessant succession of unpleasant, heavy, chattering squeaks, *skwick, squeak, squirr,* a metallic trebled *wrss* and a hurried *eep-eep-eep-eep* (Slud 1964).
**Behavior:** Sim. to Ochre-breasted Tanager.
**Status and habitat:** Undergrowth of humid forest and forest borders, mostly in foothills above 400m. Not well known in Colombia. Replaced in hills along Pacific slope by Ochre-breasted Tanager.
**Range:** Tropical zone at extreme se base of Andes in e Nariño-w Putumayo border (Río Churuyaco, a tributary of Río San Miguel), n to w Caquetá (sighting above Florencia, 800m, June 1981—Hilty). Doubtless in extreme nw Chocó as known on adj. Cerro Tacarcuna,

Panama. Nicaragua to extreme e Panama; e base of Andes from Colombia to n Bolivia.

## 85. LEMON-BROWED TANAGER
*Chlorothraupis olivacea*          Pl. 52, Map 1352
**Identification:** 6.7″ (17cm). Heavy blackish bill. Sim. to Carmiol's Tanager but darker olive and with *bright yellow lores and eyering forming conspic. "spectacles."*
**Similar species:** See Ochre-breasted and Carmiol's tanagers (86, 84).
**Voice:** Like others of the genus, chatters incessantly, *cheat, cheat, turee, turee,* and so on; also *jee-ut* and *eep* and other notes.
**Behavior:** Much like Ochre-breasted Tanager and often in groups of 3 or more but also frequently alone or in pairs.
**Breeding:** 15 BC birds, Mar–June, n Antioquia to Chocó (Carriker; Haffer 1975).
**Status and habitat:** Fairly common in undergrowth of humid and wet forest, forest borders, and advanced second growth woodland; mostly on coastal plain and in foothills. Apparently not found with Ochre-breasted Tanager, although their ranges may interdigitate locally in the Pacific foothills.
**Range:** To 1500m (rarely above 400m). Pacific coast and n base of Andes e to mid. Magdalena Val. (s to Remedios, e Antioquia). Extreme e Panama to nw Ecuador.
**Note:** Sometimes considered a subsp. of *C. carmioli* (Carmiol's Tanager); if so the enlarged sp. may be called Olive Tanager.

## 86. OCHRE-BREASTED TANAGER
*Chlorothraupis stolzmanni*          Pl. 52, Map 1353
**Identification::** 7.3″ (18.5cm). *Strong dusky bill.* Dark olive above, *dull ochraceous buff below;* sides of throat, breast and belly olive.
**Similar species:** A very robust tanager almost completely devoid of marks; Lemon-browed Tanager (85) has yellow "spectacles"; ♀ Tawny-crested Tanager (97) is smaller and brown (not olive); may also recall a finch, or a ♀ ant-tanager (see 87).
**Voice:** Dawn song, yr.-round in Anchicayá Val., a fast ser. *geegeegee wit'er wit'er tututu, weep, TWEER-TWEER-TWEER, eep'eep k' eep eep eep TWEER-TWEER-TWEER jeep-jeep TWEER* and so on in uninterrupted stream for half hour or more from canopy perch; unmusical, *eep*'s nearly to upper limit of human hearing; each bird sings different repertoire; when foraging, chatters incessantly with rough *jeep-jeep-jeep-jeep*; mobs loudly with *jee'ut* and other notes.
**Behavior:** Noisy groups of 5-15 move rapidly through understory in groups of their own or are joined by other spp. Hop heavily and peer in foliage, rummage dead leap piles, and leap

and sally awkwardly for insects and fruit, sometimes even frogs and lizards; occas. to subcanopy.

**Breeding:** 4 nests, mid-Jan–mid-Feb, stub-tailed fledgling, 9 Apr, upper Achicayá Val. (1000m); rough cup 2-5m up; 1-2 white eggs with dense ring of reddish brown spots mostly at larger end (Hilty).

**Status and habitat:** Common inside wet forest, rarely forest borders; in foothills and lower slopes. Replaced in lower foothills and coastal lowlands by Lemon-browed Tanager.

**Range:** 200-2100m (mostly 400-1500m). Pacific slope from Río San Juan headwaters (Cerro Tatamá) southward. W Colombia and w Ecuador.

## 87. RED-CROWNED ANT-TANAGER

*Habia rubica*                    Pl. 51, Map 1354

**Identification:** 7″ (18cm). Bill blackish. ♂: *dull rosy red to brownish red*, paler below and brighter on throat; *center crown scarlet bordered laterally by a narrow black line.* ♀: *olive brown above* with *tawny yellow central crown stripe*; central underparts pale grayish buff, throat lighter and tinged yellowish; sides of body olivaceous brown.

**Similar species:** Often confused with very sim. Red-throated Ant-Tanager (88). ♂ Red-throated has brighter, redder throat, lacks the black border on red crown stripe, and is overall less rosy. ♀ Red-throated has conspic. ochre yellow throat (its best mark); also lacks tawny yellow crown patch and is browner (not olive). Calls differ.

**Voice:** Usual mobbing call a rapid chatter of several to many staccato *chat, chat . . .* , notes softer than raspy calls of Red-throated; clear sweet dawn songs vary; e of Andes calls differ and incl. short chattering often 1-noted *chij*'s, and indistinct day songs *cree-chree* var. to *chee-cher, chur-chee, chereeher* in boundary disputes near Umbría, Putumayo (Willis 1972b).

**Behavior:** Pairs or families mob noisily in or out of forest flocks w of Andes; seldom away from wandering flocks of antbirds (*Thamnomanes, Myrmotherula*, etc.) e of Andes; peer carefully and hop or sally 2-10m up for arthropods and berries; outside of Mid. America rec. at army ants only in Trinidad. Very territorial and fuss at borders (Willis 1972b; ffrench 1973).

**Breeding:** 4 BC birds, June, Guajira (Carriker); Costa Rica nests, Feb–June; shallow cup fastened by rim 2-4m up; 2-3 bluish white eggs spotted and blotched dark (Skutch 1954).

**Status and habitat:** Undergrowth of humid forest and second growth woodland, esp. near openings or disturbances in forest.

**Range:** To 600m. Sw Guajira, Perijá Mts., entire e base of Andes and from s Meta (Macarena Mts.) and Vaupés to Amazonas (photo, El Dorado 1976—R. Ridgely; sightings, Mitú (1978) and Leticia (1973)—Hilty). C Mexico to Bolivia, ne Argentina, and se Brazil.

## 88. RED-THROATED ANT-TANAGER

*Habia fuscicauda*                    Pl. 51, Map 1355

**Identification:** 7.5″ (19cm). ♂: mostly dull dark rosy red; browner on tail and *much brighter red on throat*; central crown stripe scarlet (no black border). ♀: brownish olive above and below with *contrasting ochre yellow throat* (no crown stripe).

**Similar species:** See Red-crowned Ant-Tanager (87), which has not yet been shown to overlap in range.

**Voice:** In Mexico to Panama, harsh nasal scolds *waaj, waaj, waaj*; also a sharp *scaicait* note; day song in Panama usually 3 clear, sweet, whistles, rising and falling in a triplet sequence *wheh-cherk-wuh, wher-cherk-weh, whuk chee*; dawn song in Panama a more regular ser. of 12-15 mellow but repetitive whistles, e.g., *week, perk, cher*, over and over, 6 or 7 songs per min (Willis 1972b).

**Behavior:** Small groups follow army ant swarms or sometimes join or are joined by mixed flocks away from ant swarms; typically appear briefly to scold an observer, then flee.

**Breeding:** Prob. early rainy season, late Apr–July in Panama; leafy cup low in bush; 2 white eggs (Willis 1972b).

**Status and habitat::** Drier Carib. forests. Found with reg. in forested or densely overgrown parts of Snía. de San Jacinto (Haffer 1975). Much of presumed former range w to mouth of Sinú now deforested.

**Range:** To 200m. Carib. lowlands from Snía. de San Jacinto to Atlántico, also undoubtedly extreme n Chocó as reported from Pto.Obaldía, Panama near Colombian border. C Mexico to n Colombia.

## 89. SOOTY ANT-TANAGER

*Habia gutturalis*                    Map 1356

**Identification:** 7.5″ (19cm). ♂: *mostly dark gray with conspic. scarlet crest; sides of crown to sides of throat black*; center of throat rosy red becoming duller and darker on chest. ♀: sim. but duller, throat whitish tinged pink.

**Similar species:** Easily recognized; crest and gray plumage are the marks.

**Voice:** A fast alarm chatter *chak-cha-cha-cha-cha-cha* of 5-15 notes resembles that of Red-crowned Ant-Tanager; *chak* notes when foraging; dawn song, most musical of the ant-tanagers, is commonly 2-3 rich whistles repeated over and over, *pong, peh, wheee*, or more complex *wheh, hee, whereeheh, wher'erer*; apparently no day song (Willis 1972b).

**Behavior:** Pairs or families of 2-4 follow army ant swarms or join mixed flocks; scan and frequently sally to foliage for prey, mostly 4-10m up, or drop to ground for prey over ant swarms. Noisy like other ant-tanagers but wary away from mixed flocks (Willis 1972b).

**Breeding:** 9 BC birds, Feb–May, s Bolívar to s Córdoba (Carriker); juv. with 2 ads., 9 May, Remedios, e Antioquia (Willis 1972b); deep coarse cup low in undergrowth; eggs grayish white heavily mottled darker, esp. at larger end (Sclater and Salvin 1879).

**Status and habitat:** Humid forest, forest borders, and second growth woodland; perhaps mainly along streams and landslides in extensive unbroken forest; mainly restricted to foothills.

**Range:** ENDEMIC. 100-1100m. N end of W Andes (upper Sinú Val.) e along n base of Andes to both sides of mid. Magdalena Val. (s to Honda, n Tolima).

## 90. CRESTED ANT-TANAGER

*Habia cristata*          Pl. 51, Map 1357

**Identification:** 7.5″ (19cm). Resembles a cardinal. *Long prom. crest scarlet. Sides of head and upperparts dark crimson; throat and breast bright scarlet*; lower underparts grayish stained red. ♀: sim. but crest shorter. Bill black in both sexes. Imm.: much duller, tinged cinnamon above and below.

**Similar species:** Easily recognized though crest is often depressed forming only a scarlet streak on crown and projecting slightly behind head.

**Voice:** Mobs with loud, shrill *chi-veek!*, repeated 2-4 times; contact calls are *chip* or a sharp ser. of *chee* notes; dawn song 3-4 unmusical, monotonous *che'ik* notes given up to 12 times a min (Willis 1966a).

**Behavior:** Rather like other ant-tanagers. Noisy pairs or families of 2-5 hop up vines or saplings or up through bushes and flutter to foliage or peck prey on nearby leaves and twigs. Keep mostly 1-8m up inside concealing foliage; often joins mixed forest flocks (Willis 1966a). Up to 10 at 1 army ant swarm (Gochfeld and Tudor 1978).

**Breeding:** Precopulatory displays and song, late Mar (Willis 1966a).

**Status and habitat:** Fairly common in forest lower story, or dense second growth of steep ravines or landslides above rushing mt. streams. Most easily found along Río Pichindé above Cali or along Río Digua w of Quermal, Valle.

May be partially replaced at lower el. by Dusky-faced and Tawny-crested tanagers.

**Range:** ENDEMIC. 700-1800m. Pacific slope and locally on adj. e slope of W Andes from n Antioquia (Peque, Paramillo Mts.) to Cauca.

## 91. FULVOUS SHRIKE-TANAGER

*Lanio fulvus*          Pl. 51, Map 1358

**Identification:** 6.5″ (16.5cm). Bill heavy and shrikelike. ♂ unmistakable; *entire head, throat, wings, and tail black*; center of breast chestnut; *otherwise ochre yellow above and below* becoming rufous brown on rump and lower underparts; small concealed white patch on lesser wing coverts. ♀: rufous brown above; more rufous on rump and tail; *throat brownish buff; underparts deep ochraceous buff* becoming rufescent on lower underparts.

**Similar species:** ♀ from very sim. ♀ Flame-crested Tanager (93) by heavy hooked bill; in good light rump richer rufous and throat browner (not ochraceous). ♀ Dusky-throated Antshrike (p 387) is smaller and duller with whitish throat and more ochraceous lower underparts.

**Voice:** Rather noisy, as give high-pitched, sharp *skeep!*, short rattles, and other notes. In Surinam a *very* loud *chew!* (T. Davis).

**Behavior:** Single birds or separated pairs wait rather upright on perch and usually look upward, then rapidly sally like flycatchers to foliage; in mixed spp. flocks of forest subcanopy or higher, or sit below flocks and take prey dislodged from above.

**Status and habitat:** Uncommon (or often overlooked) in humid *terra firme* forest, occas. forest edges.

**Range:** To 500m. E base of Andes from Arauca to Putumayo and e to Amazonas. Prob. from Río Guaviare southward (rec. on Orinoco opp. Guainía). The Guianas, s Venez., and w Venez. (Táchira) s to e Ecuador, ne Peru, and Amazonian Brazil n of the Amazon.

**Note:** Replaced s of Amazon by White-winged Shrike-Tanager (*L. versicolor*) of n Bolivia, e Peru, and Amazonian Brazil to s bank of Amazon. ♂: like above but center of forehead yellowish, rump yellow (not rufous brown), throat dusky olive, rest of underparts entirely bright yellow and shoulders more extensively white. ♀: barely separable from ♀ Fulvous Shrike-Tanager, but center of belly yellow.

## 92. WHITE-LINED TANAGER

*Tachyphonus rufus*          Pl. 52, Map 1359

**Identification:** 7″ (18cm). Pointed bill pale bluish. ♂: *lustrous black with white under wing coverts* (normally visible only in flight). ♀ very different: *uniform rufous*, slightly paler below.

**Similar species:** ♂ often confused with smaller White-shouldered Tanager (96), a *forest* bird (not shrubby clearings) that *almost always* shows white shoulders when perched. ♀ resembles a Rufous Mourner (p 508), also only in forest, and several ♀ becards, but from any by pointed bluish bill. In the area of overlap with Red-shouldered Tanager (95) in the Orinoco area ♂ ♂ best distinguished by larger size and attendant ♀ ♀ (if present).

**Voice:** Usually quiet. Song a repetitious musical *cheeru* or *cheep-chooi*, 1st syllable stronger (ffrench 1973).

**Behavior:** Almost always in pairs; stay fairly low and perch in open only briefly; often seen as one follows its mate in low flight across an opening.

**Breeding:** 3 BC birds, May, s Bolívar, 2 in Oct, Cúcuta, Norte de Santander (Carriker); breed, Feb–Mar, W Andes above Cali, late Nov, Patía Val. (Miller 1963; Brown), Mar–May in Orinoco area (Cherrie 1916); coarse cup in low bush; 2 pale rufous eggs spotted brown.

**Status and habitat:** Common in shrubby clearings or forest edges and cultivated areas with thickets; mainly humid areas.

**Range:** To 2700m (usually below 1500m). Virtually throughout w of Andes (except very arid regions); e of Andes rec. in nw Meta and sw Caquetá (Morelia). Costa Rica to nw Ecuador, Peru, ne Argentina, and s Brazil.

### 93. FLAME-CRESTED TANAGER
*Tachyphonus cristatus*          Pl. 51, Map 1360
**Identification:** 6.5″ (16.5cm). ♂: mostly black with *broad flat crest flame scarlet* (or orange— *fallax*); front and sides of crown yellowish buff; *chin to center of throat, straw yellow*; rump straw yellow; lesser upper wing coverts and under wing coverts white. ♀: *warm rufous brown above*; rich ochraceous below, throat paler, almost whitish, crissum darkest; narrow eyering buffy.

**Similar species:** ♂ Fulvous-crested Tanager (94) *lacks* yellowish throat spot, shows *more* white under the wings (pectoral tufts often prom.), and in Amazonia also by fulvous (not scarlet) crest. ♀ in forest canopy can be very difficult to identify; best marks are shape, posture, and uniform upper and underparts. Cf. ♀ Fulvous-crested (94), which has "spectacles" and olive upperparts, also ♀ White-shouldered Tanager (96) and several *Thamnomanes* antshrikes (pp 387-388).

**Voice:** Thin *seeep* notes as forage.

**Behavior:** Pairs or families follow mixed flocks, esp. flocks with other tanagers, in upper forest levels; active as glean and flutter in foliage or visit fruiting trees; perch rather upright.

**Breeding:** BC ♂, 25 Jan, Macarena Mts. (Olivares 1962).

**Status and habitat:** Fairly common (easily overlooked) in humid *terra firme* forest and forest edge at clearings.

**Range:** To 500m. E of Andes from w Meta (Villavicencio area) and se Guainía s to Putumayo and Amazonas (*cristatellus*); e Vichada and prob. n Guainía (*orinocensis*); se Nariño (*fallax*). The Guianas and s Venez. to e Ecuador, e central Peru, Amazonian and se Brazil.

### 94. FULVOUS-CRESTED TANAGER
*Tachyphonus surinamus*          Pl. 51, Map 1361
**Identification:** 6.5″ (16.5cm). ♂: mostly glossy blue black with *central crown stripe and rump deep straw yellow*; lesser upper wing coverts; under wing coverts and *pectoral tuft white*; flanks tawny rufous. ♀: *crown and sides of head gray with yellowish tinge around the eye* (forms "spectacles"); *otherwise olive green above*; throat buffy white; rest of underparts ochraceous, deepest on abdomen.

**Similar species:** ♂ closely resembles ♂ Flame-crested Tanager (see 93). In Orinoco region see ♂ Red-shouldered Tanager (95). ♀ from White-shouldered Tanager (96) by eyering, gray of head less sharply defined, and underparts paler and more uniform (not yellow with crisp white throat); also see ♀ Flame-crested Tanager (93) and therein.

**Voice:** High, weak *steep* notes and buzzy rattles as forage.

**Behavior:** Pairs or families often follow mixed flocks in forest midlevels or higher where peck and hover-glean mostly for insects. Also at fruiting trees and bushes; once over army ants (Oniki and Willis 1972). Often low at shrubby forest edges and in bushes at edges of granite outcrops.

**Status and habitat:** Uncommon to fairly common in humid *terra firme* forest and edges, and esp. sandy forest and scrubbier sandy woodland from Vaupés northward.

**Range:** To 500m. E of Andes from w Meta (Villavicencio) and Guainía southward. The Guianas and s Venez. to se Peru and Amazonian Brazil.

### 95. RED-SHOULDERED TANAGER
*Tachyphonus phoenicius*          Pl. 51, Map 1362
**Identification:** 6.2″ (15.7cm). ♂: *glossy black with small point of shoulder scarlet*, lesser *under wing coverts white* (both scarlet and white normally concealed when perched). ♀: above grayish brown, wings browner; *crown and sides of head dark gray and lores and ocular area dusky* giving "hooded" look; *throat dull white*, more or less sharply defined from sides of head and chest; rest of underparts grayish white; bill rather short and thick, pale below.

**Similar species:** ♂ is only black tanager with red shoulders. But since the red shoulders can be hard to see even in flight, it is difficult to distinguish from ♂ White-lined Tanager (92) except by smaller size and attendant ♀♀ (if present). Best marks for confusing and chunkier ♀ are contrasting whitish throat and dusky loral area.

**Voice:** Weak high-pitched *tsit* notes.

**Behavior:** Single birds, pairs or several flutter and perch-glean 1-6m up in foliage of savanna bushes, or often follow mixed flocks at woodland edges; rather insectivorous.

**Breeding:** BC ♂, 21 Feb, Macarena Mts. (Olivares 1959), 3 in Mar–Apr, upper Orinoco, Venez. (Friedmann 1948); cup nests in Surinam, on ground or in grass near bushes; 2 grayish eggs with dark brown spots and blotches, large end wholly brown (Haverschmidt 1968).

**Status and habitat:** Sandy savanna woodland edges, and open savanna with scattered high bushes, thickets, and patches of woodland. Common in Pto. Inírida area of ne Guainía and prob. w and s near granite outcrops and in scrubby woodland-savanna borders to the Río Guayabero, Meta.

**Range:** To 400m. Along the Río Orinoco and Río Negro drainage of e Vichada and Guainía and locally s in pockets of savanna and scrub to Vaupés and s Meta (s end of Macarena Mts.). Spottily in the Guianas, s Venez., e Ecuador (sight), e Peru, and Amazonian Brazil.

**Note:** Yellow-crested Tanager (*T. rufiventer*) of e Peru s of the Río Marañon to nw Bolivia and upper Río Juruá, w Brazil, occurs n to s bank of Amazon near Leticia (sightings, both sides Río Javarí, 1979-81—Hilty et al.). 6″; bill slender. ♂: black above with yellow crown patch and buffy orange rump; chin to center of throat buffy white; *narrow pectoral band black*; rest of underparts tawny; sides and flanks black; under wing coverts white. ♀: yellowish olive above; rump ochraceous, sides of head grayish; throat white; otherwise ochre yellow below, deeper on crissum. Follow mixed flocks in *terra firme* or *várzea* subcanopy.

## 96. WHITE-SHOULDERED TANAGER

*Tachyphonus luctuosus*          Pl. 52, Map 1363

**Identification:** 5.2″ (13.2cm). ♂: glossy black with conspic. white shoulder patch (always visible); under wing coverts white. ♀: *crown and sides of head gray*, sharply defined from yellowish green upperparts; *throat grayish white; otherwise bright light yellow below*; breast tinged olive; under wing coverts white.

**Similar species:** Larger ♂ White-lined Tanager (92) of open areas, shows little or no white on closed wing. ♀ like a small edition of Gray-

headed Tanager (100) but has paler throat and is usually more arboreal. Cf. ♀ Fulvouscrested Tanager (94), also ♀ Blue Dacnis (p 597).

**Voice:** Frequently heard but insignificant calls are unmusical *tshirrup*'s and squeaky, repeated *tswee*'s (ffrench 1973).

**Behavior:** Pairs or families usually follow mixed forest flocks; perch-glean and flutter in foliage from upper understory to subcanopy, more often midlevels or higher; also sometimes at fruiting trees.

**Breeding:** 8 BC birds, Feb–Aug, Cesar to s Córdoba (Carriker); 1 in Apr, nw Antioquia, Haffer (1975); 1 in Feb, nw Santander (Boggs 1961); in Trinidad, fairly deep, grassy cup within a few ft. of ground; 3 eggs, buff or cream marked reddish brown to blackish brown (ffrench 1973).

**Status and habitat:** Humid and wet forest borders, second growth woodland, and inside forest, esp. near small openings, vine tangles, or where foliage is fairly dense. Mostly lowlands and foothills.

**Range:** To 2200m (usually below 1000m). Humid forested regions virtually throughout; no recs. from e Guainía to n Amazonas; s Amazonas (sight). Honduras to w Ecuador, n Bolivia, Amazonian Brazil, Surinam and Fr. Guiana. Trinidad.

## 97. TAWNY-CRESTED TANAGER

*Tachyphonus delatrii*          Pl. 52, Map 1364

**Identification:** 5.5″ (14cm). ♂ unmistakable: black with prom., close-cropped, cinnamon orange to yellow crest (like Roman helmet). ♀: *entirely dark brown*, upperparts slightly tinged olive.

**Similar species:** Almost wholly chocolate brown ♀ much darker than any other tanager in range. Cf. larger Dusky-faced Tanager (101).

**Voice:** Most common call a loud, sharp, smacking *chit* or *tswik* (Slud 1964), repeated constantly when foraging.

**Behavior:** Very noisy and conspic. in active, fast-moving flocks of 4-20 or more; flutter and hop acrobatically, usually 1-6m up and at forest edge, where they peck at prey, sally to foliage, and eat berries at small fruiting bushes. Sometimes join or are joined by a few other spp., esp. other tanagers, but often travel independently of mixed flocks.

**Breeding:** 18 BC birds, Feb–May, n Antioquia to Chocó (Carriker); 1 in Mar, Chocó (Haffer 1975); 1 in Feb, Valle (MCN).

**Status and habitat:** Common and conspic. in humid and wet second growth woodland and shrubby forest borders, less numerous inside forest.

**Range:** To 1500m (usually below 800m on Pacific slope). Pacific coast except Urabá region; humid lowlands along n base of Andes e to mid. Magdalena Val. s to e Antioquia (Remedios). Gorgona Isl. Nicaragua to nw Ecuador.

## 98. SCARLET-BROWED TANAGER
*Heterospingus xanthopygius*    Pl. 52, Map 1365
**Identification:** 7" (18cm). Bill rather heavy and hooked at tip. ♂: *mostly black* with narrow white line above eye and *conspic. broad red stripe behind eye* (forms raised tuft on each side of head); *shoulders and rump yellow*; pectoral tufts white; lower underparts slaty gray. ♀: *dark gray above, slightly paler below*; yellow rump and white pectoral tufts.
**Similar species:** ♂ Lemon-rumped Tanager (77) lacks the red postocular tufts, yellow shoulders, and white pectoral tufts; best mark for sooty gray ♀ is yellow rump (see 77).
**Voice:** Frequently heard call a loud, forceful *chip*; song a squeaky twittering *cheero-bitty, cheero-bitty, cherro-pit-sup* at Quibdó.
**Behavior:** One or 2 follow mixed tanager and honeycreeper flocks in the canopy or subcanopy and often perch exposed on treetops. Sally awkwardly and flutter and perch-glean in foliage like a *Tachyphonus*, or fly off to fruiting trees chipping loudly.
**Breeding:** 7 BC birds, Mar–May, n Antioquia to Chocó (Carriker); 1 building nest, 12 Dec, upper Anchicayá Val.; pair with begging juv., 19 Jan, lower Dagua Val. (Hilty).
**Status and habitat:** Fairly common in humid and wet forest, second growth woodland, and edges in lowlands and foothills, a few higher.
**Range:** To 1100m. Pacific coast except the drier seasonal forests of Urabá region; e along humid n base of Andes to mid. Magdalena Val. and spottily s to latitude of Bogotá (Cachipay, Cundinamarca). Extreme se Panama to w Ecuador.
**Note:** Sulphur-rumped Tanager (*H. rubrifrons*) of Costa Rica to extreme ne Panama may occur in adj. n Chocó (rec. at Obaldía on Carib. near Colombia). Both sexes indistinguishable in field from ♀ Scarlet-browed Tanager (sometimes regarded as a "hen-feathered" race of latter) but are smaller, 6" vs 7" with wing 78-82 vs 88-92mm and tail 57-60 vs 65-70mm.

## 99. RUFOUS-CRESTED TANAGER
*Creurgops verticalis*    Pl. 53, Map 1366
**Identification:** 6.5" (16.5cm). ♂: *bluish gray above with broad flat cinnamon rufous crest* narrowly bordered black (crest not conspic. in field), *entire underparts cinnamon rufous*. ♀: sim. but no rufous crest and underparts paler cinnamon.
**Similar species:** Black-eared Hemispingus (123)

has black mask and lacks rufous crown stripe; also see smaller ♂ Rusty Flower-Piercer (p 594)
**Behavior:** One or 2 reg. follow mixed flocks in the canopy or subcanopy; hop along bare or mossy outer limbs into foliage, probing, pecking, and often gleaning in leaves; rarely at fruiting trees (Hilty), also often flycatch opportunistically (R. Ridgely).
**Breeding:** 2 BC ♂♂, June, n end W Andes (s of Frontino); 1 in June, se Antioquia and 1 in Mar, s Huila, latter 2 in C Andes (Carriker).
**Status and habitat:** Humid mossy forest ("cloud forest") and forest borders. Apparently much more common in upper Magdalena Val. than in C and W Andes.
**Range:** 1600-2700m. W and C Andes (spotty), head of the Magdalena Val. in Huila, and both slopes of Andes in Nariño. Colombia s in Andes to e Ecuador and s Peru.

## 100. GRAY-HEADED TANAGER
*Eucometis penicillata*    Pl. 52, Map 1367
**Identification:** 7" (18cm). Weak crest. *Entire head gray*, throat slightly paler with contrasting olive green upperparts and *bright deep yellow underparts*.
**Similar species:** Remarkably like ♀ White-shouldered Tanager (96) but considerably larger, brighter, and mainly in undergrowth (not upper forest levels).
**Voice:** Alarm *schip* in Amazonia (Hilty); in Panama a sharp *chip* and high *stet*, and a high *sweezie tsweezie tsweezie*; song a musical sputter, *eat eat meat chop, 'safurry chew, 'safurry chew*, or the like (Willis and Eisenmann 1979).
**Behavior:** Pairs or small groups of 3-4 reg. follow army ants or forage 1-10m up in forest for insects away from ant swarms.
**Breeding:** 6 BC ♂♂, Feb–June, Santa Marta and w Guajira to Córdoba (Carriker). Barro Colorado Isl. nests, Apr–Sept (Willis and Eisenmann 1979); loose cup in thick undergrowth; 2 gray eggs heavily marked brown and blackish (Stone 1918).
**Status and habitat:** Uncommon. Usually low in humid second growth woodland and forest w of Andes; usually *várzea* forest e of Andes.
**Range:** To 1700m in Santa Marta Mts. and Cundinamarca (mostly below 600m). From Panama border e to Santa Marta Mts., and w Guajira s (formerly) in Cauca Val. to Cali, in Magdalena Val. to La Plata, Huila, and e of Andes from Norte de Santander to sw Caquetá and Amazonas. Prob. e Vichada (rec. on Venez. side of Orinoco). Se Mexico to Bolivia and se Brazil.

## 101. DUSKY-FACED TANAGER
*Mitrospingus cassinii*    Pl. 52, Map 1368
**Identification:** 7" (18cm). *Eyes grayish white*.

Crown yellowish; *broad blackish mask from forehead and upper throat across sides of head*; otherwise dark charcoal gray above and olive yellow below.

**Similar species:** At a distance looks dark with oily yellow underparts. Mask and pale eye are good marks. See 97.

**Voice:** Noisy. Chatters a low *chet-ut* or sim. gravelly note incessantly.

**Behavior:** A thicket sp. Troop about in active noisy mobs of up to 15 but seldom with other spp.; act like ant-tanagers or Tawny-crested Tanagers but less frugivorous than latter and usually lower and in denser foliage where harder to see.

**Breeding:** 12 BC birds, Feb–May, n Antioquia to Chocó (Carriker; Haffer 1975); 1 stub-tailed juv. with 2 ads., Sept, upper Anchicayá Val. (Hilty); a bulky cup in undergrowth near a stream in Costa Rica held 2 fledglings fed by at least 3 or 4 birds (Skutch 1972).

**Status and habitat:** Common in *streamside* thickets; also shrubby forest borders, second growth woodland, and occas. at openings inside humid and wet forest but everywhere favors vicinity of streams.

**Range:** To 1100m (net capture, upper Anchicayá Val.); mainly below 800m. Pacific coast and e around n end of W Andes to lower Cauca Val. (Río Nechí drainage). Costa Rica to nw Ecuador.

### 102. ROSY THRUSH-TANAGER

*Rhodinocichla rosea*     Pl. 52, Map 1369

**Identification:** 8″ (20cm). ♂: dark grayish black above with *long rosy red eyestripe* (or eyestripe whitish behind eye—*beebei*); *underparts mostly bright rose red*; flanks and sides of belly brownish. ♀: sim. but rose red replaced by cinnamon rufous.

**Voice:** An excellent songster; in Panama a loud, rich, ringing *cho-oh chowee* or *wheeo-cheehoh*, reminiscent of Black-bellied Wren (Ridgely 1976); in Venez. *chee-a-wee, cle-oh, chee-a-wee, cle-oh* with var. (P. Schwartz recording).

**Behavior:** A lovely bird with a beautiful song but shy and usually frustratingly difficult even to glimpse in its tangled thicket habitat. Single birds or pairs are partially terrestrial and often hop on ground and flick aside leaves and litter.

**Breeding:** 6 BC birds, Mar–July, Perijá Mts., w Guajira, and n end E Andes in Norte de Santander (Carriker); shallow cup nest of sticks and leaves, 16 Apr, Costa Rica; 1 m up in dense tangle; 2 white eggs with black scrawls and spots (Skutch 1962c).

**Status and habitat:** Thickets or ground in dry to humid areas. Second growth, lighter woodland, and dense dry scrub; mostly foothills

and lower slopes. Reportedly "not rare" in Cundinamarca (Olivares 1969a).

**Range:** 500-1700m. W slope of E Andes in Cundinamarca, and e Tolima n to Norte de Santander, ne base of Santa Marta Mts. (*harterti*); n end Perijá Mts. (*beebei*), and w slope of Santa Marta Mts. (sighting below San Pedro, 4 Feb 1972—S. M. Russell; J. Lupke; Hilty). W Mexico; Costa Rica to n Venez.

### 103. HOODED TANAGER

*Nemosia pileata*     Pl. 53, Map 1370

**Identification:** 5″ (13cm). *Eyes and legs yellow.* ♂: *crown, sides of head, and sides of neck extending to sides of chest black*; nape and rest of upperparts blue gray; *lores and underparts white.* ♀: sim. but duller, lacks black hood over head; sides of throat and breast tinged buff. Imm. ♂: like ♀ and may breed.

**Similar species:** More likely mistaken (esp. ♀) for a conebill than another tanager. Bicolored Conebill (p 589) lacks black hood and has dingy grayish-buff underparts. ♀ from ♀ White-eared Conebill (p 589) by sharp white lores and whiter underparts. Also see differently proportioned Tropical Gnatcatcher (p 551).

**Voice:** Rapid *tic* and *chip* notes.

**Behavior:** Pairs or groups of 3-6 search foliage and terminal twigs like vireos in the upper part of trees; seldom eat fruit. Often seen foraging in *Cecropia* and *Mimosa* trees and in most areas attracts attention to itself with outbursts of chipping and twittering (J. V. Remsen; Hilty).

**Breeding:** Pair building nest, 18 July, Leticia (J. V. Remsen); 6 BC birds, Mar–June, Cesar and s Bolívar (Carriker).

**Status and habitat:** Fairly dry to humid forest borders, shrubby clearings, and lighter open woodland. Common in Amazonia in *várzea* borders and on swampy river isls. Uncommon and thinly spread in Carib. region.

**Range:** To 500m. Carib. region from Río Sinú e to sw and se base of Santa Marta Mts. and s to mid. Magdalena Val. (n end C Andes at e base Snía. San Lucas); e of Andes in Amazonas (Leticia area). The Guianas and Venez. to ne Peru, Bolivia, ne Argentina, Paraguay, and Amazonian Brazil.

### 104. GUIRA TANAGER

*Hemithraupis guira*     Pl. 53, Map 1371

**Identification:** 5″ (13cm). Sharp-pointed yellowish bill. ♂: *black mask and throat outlined all around with bright yellow*; otherwise olive green above with orange rufous rump; *center of breast dark orange rufous*; sides and lower underparts yellowish green. ♀: bright olive above with *dull yellow eyestripe and eyering*; rump yellowish; wings and tail edged yellow; sides of head and

underparts yellowish green; flanks tinged gray.
**Similar species:** *Shape* of Green Honey-creeper, but ♂ otherwise unmistakable. Dull warblerlike ♀ easily confused. ♀ Yellow Warbler (p 576) is yellower above and lacks an eyering or eyestripe (side of head wholly yellow); ♀ Yellow-backed Tanager (105) is duller above, with olive (not gray) flanks; also has whitish (not yellow) eyering; no eyestripe.
**Voice:** Song an unmusical ser. of high squeaky phrases reminiscent of Bananaquit.
**Behavior:** Pairs or several follow mixed flocks in canopy or edge of forest. Flutter and glean in outer foliage like warblers or a dacnis.
**Breeding:** 2 BC ♂♂, June, n end C Andes at Valdivia and n end E Andes, Norte de Santander (Carriker).
**Status and habitat:** Apparently very uncommon and very local; fairly dry to humid forest, second growth, and taller open woodland. Perhaps formerly more widespread in Cauca and Magdalena vals. Found reg. in Bosque Yotoco, Valle.
**Range:** 100-2000m (mainly below 1500m). Pacific slope in Valle (♂ seen, Anchicayá Val. 500m, 1977—Hilty et al.), lower and mid. Cauca Val. (Río Nechí and Pto. Valdivia to Valle) and mid. and upper Magdalena Val. (nw Santander to Huila); e of Andes known definitely only from Nórte de Santander (Guamilito in the n; Río Cobugon near Boyacá boundary), Amazonas (near Leticia), and w Putumayo (sight). Spottily throughout S America to w Ecuador, n Argentina, and Paraguay.

### 105. YELLOW-BACKED TANAGER
*Hemithraupis flavicollis*   Pls. 52, 53, Map 1372
**Identification:** 5″ (13cm). Bill sharp-pointed, pinkish below. ♂: *black above with yellow lower back and rump*; small white wing speculum (patch on shoulder also yellow—*peruana*); *throat and chest bright yellow*; breast and belly white with gray sides; under tail coverts yellow (or center of throat white barred and spotted black—*albigularis*). ♀: *brownish olive above*; tinged yellow on rump; narrow white eyering; sides of head and underparts bright yellow; *flanks olive* (or belly whitish—*albigularis*).
**Similar species:** ♂ easily recognized; ♀ very like ♀ Guira Tanager (See 104).
**Voice:** High thin *tseep* notes.
**Behavior:** Pairs or groups actively glean like warblers or dacnis (but seldom flutter or hover) in outer canopy foliage and often follow mixed forest flocks containing other treetop tanagers and honeycreepers; also eat small berries.
**Breeding:** 10 BC birds, Apr–June, s Bolívar to s Córdoba (Carriker) and 1 in Jan, nw Santander (Boggs 1961).

**Status and habitat:** Humid *terra firme* and *várzea* forests, forest edges, second growth, and lighter woodland. Fairly common (easily overlooked) e of Andes.
**Range:** To 1000m. Nw Chocó (Río Juradó) near Panamá border (*ornata*); upper Río Sinú (Quimarí) e along humid n base of Andes to mid. Magdalena Val. s to Santander (Bucaramanga) and s Bolívar (*albigularis*); w Meta s to Putumayo and s Amazonas (*peruana*); ne Guainía (sightings, Pto. Inírida, Sept 1978—Hilty and M. Robbins), prob. se Vichada to e Vaupés (*aurigularis*). E Panama to n Bolivia and se Brazil.
**Note:** Black-and-yellow Tanager (*Chrysothlypis chrysomelus*) of Costa Rica to e Panamá undoubtedly occurs in nw Colombia as it has been rec. on the Panamá-Colombian boundary (R. Ridgely). ♂ largely *bright yellow* with *black wings, tail, and back*; eyes dark surrounded by black eyering; ♀ greenish olive above, wings duller with yellow green edgings, mainly bright yellow below.

### 106. SCARLET-AND-WHITE TANAGER
*Erythrothlypis salmoni*   Pl. 48, Map 1373
**Identification:** 5″ (13cm). Warblerlike; thin bill. ♂ unmistakable: *entire upperparts, head, throat, chest, and median stripe down breast bright scarlet*; sides of breast and belly white. ♀ very different: dull *olive green* above; remiges edged yellowish green; throat and breast grayish buff becoming *dull white on sides and lower underparts*. Imm ♂: like ♀. Subad. ♂: often mottled red, white, and olive green (may breed).
**Similar species:** ♀ looks like a greenlet or "fall plumage" migrant warbler but has longer bill and whitish on sides and lower underparts. As a rule ♀ can be told by presence of 1 or more attendant adult ♂♂.
**Voice:** Call a weak sibilant *chip* or *sciip* when foraging or in flight; apparently no song.
**Behavior:** Pairs or more often families or groups of 3-6 wander alone or with mixed flocks containing other canopy tanagers. Active and spritely as glean in outer foliage, hang from leaves, and hover at leaf tips or in front of arrilate fruits, e.g., *Tovomitopsis* (Guttif.), picking out the seeds. Also often at *Miconia* and other fruiting shrubs and trees; shrubbery to upper canopy.
**Breeding:** 1 BC ♂, 12 Feb, w Valle (MCN); stub-tailed fledglings followed ads. (poss. also "helpers") 18 Apr and 31 May, upper Anchicayá Val. (Hilty).
**Status and habitat:** Fairly common in tall second growth woodland, broken wet foothill forest, forest edges, dense scrub on knife ridges and steep canyons.
**Range:** To 1100m. Pacific coast n to Baudó

Mts., Quibdó, Mutatá, around northernmost end of W Andes and e along n base of Andes to mid. Magdalena Val. (s to Remedios, e Antioquia). W Colombia to w Ecuador.

[*Thlypopsis*: Small and active; stubby bill; orange rufous head; none overlap in range.]

## 107. FULVOUS-HEADED TANAGER
*Thlypopsis fulviceps*          Pl. 53, Map 1374
**Identification:** 5″ (13cm). Bill short. *Entire head rufous chestnut*, throat paler; *otherwise dark gray above and light gray below* becoming whitish on center of belly. ♀: sim. but throat pale buff, almost whitish.
**Similar species:** Easily told within range by rufous chestnut head sharply separated from gray body.
**Behavior:** One or 2 birds, occas. several, often wander with mixed canopy flocks; restlessly search mostly small outer limbs and foliage or drop lower to fruiting trees. Unlike other 2 Colombian *Thlypopsis* reg. found inside forest in mid. to upper levels.
**Breeding:** 3 BC ♂♂, Nov, Norte de Santander, 1 in Apr, Perijá Mts. (Carriker).
**Status and habitat:** Not well known in Colombia. Humid forest, shrubby forest edges, and second growth woodland, occas. mt. bamboo (*Chusquea* spp.)
**Range:** 1700-2300m (prob. also lower). Perijá Mts. (e of Codazzi) s to n end of E Andes (e slope in Norte de Santander at Pamplona; w slope in s Cesar at La Palmita, w of Ocaña). Mts. from n Venez. to extreme ne Colombia.

## 108. ORANGE-HEADED TANAGER
*Thlypopsis sordida*          Map 1375
**Identification:** 5.5″ (14cm). Bill short. *Entire head orange rufous becoming yellow on throat*; otherwise gray tinged brown above and *pale gray below; median underparts whitish*.
**Similar species:** Unique in range.
**Voice:** Thin high *tseet* notes frequently repeated.
**Behavior:** Single birds or pairs, occas. families, glean restlessly like warblers (but seldom hover or flutter) in foliage, mostly for insects; usually low to mid. levels, sometimes high.
**Status and habitat:** At least locally common in young second growth, shrubby areas, parks, and gardens, mainly *along rivers* or in opened up areas. Common in town and outskirts of Leticia and in early successional shrubbery on Amazonian river isls.
**Range:** To 400m. E of Andes in se Nariño (Río San Miguel) and Amazonas (along Amazon). Prob. more widespread along edges of larger Amazonian tributaries, esp. Río Putumayo. Ne Venez.; e Colombia, e Ecuador, and w Amazonian Brazil to Bolivia, n Argentina, and Paraguay.

## 109. RUFOUS-CHESTED TANAGER
*Thlypopsis ornata*          Pl. 53, Map 1376
**Identification:** 5″ (13cm). Bill short. *Entire head and underparts orange rufous*; center of lower breast and belly white; *upperparts wings and tail gray*.
**Similar species:** Rufous-crested Tanager (99), a forest bird, is all blue gray above with only center crown stripe rufous (not whole head).
**Behavior:** Sim. to Orange-headed Tanager, as is voice.
**Status and habitat:** Fairly common very locally in patches of scrubby second growth woodland and dense shrubbery, esp. on steep slopes and canyons above rivers. Doubtless more widespread formerly as little shrub or wooded habitat now remains in its known range. Most easily seen along Río Cauca at junction of Coconuco Road with Popayán-Neiva Road.
**Range:** 2000-3400m. W slope of C Andes at s end (betw. Popayán and PN Puracé in Cauca). Both slopes of Andes in Ecuador and Peru.

## 110. WHITE-CAPPED TANAGER
*Sericossypha albocristata*          Pl. 50, Map 1377
**Identification:** 9″ (23cm). Spectacular and unmistakable. Velvety black with *snow white crown and lores, and crimson throat and chest*; wings and tail blue black. ♀: sim. but throat and chest darker, more plum color. Imm.: no red on throat.
**Voice:** Constantly repeats a very loud *peeeaap!*, sometimes followed by 1 or 2 sharp shrieking *keep* notes; 1st note reminiscent of greatly amplified baby chicken peeping.
**Behavior:** Wide-ranging, wandering flocks of 5-20 move loudly through treetops or perch on tops of bushes and smaller trees and are usually heard long before they are seen. Flock members peer, posture, and cock their tails like jays as hop and leap boldly through trees, then rapidly fly on; not with mixed flocks (J. Silliman).
**Status and habitat:** Uncommon and erratic; humid forest and forest borders. Some movements perhaps seasonal: rec. only Jan–late Apr in PN Cueva de los Guácharos (P. Gertler) and June (R. Ridgely). Can be found most easily in mts. above Florencia, Caquetá, and near e Nariño-w Putumayo border (above 2000m); with less certainty in Quebrada Tierra Adentro Canyon or canyon of Río Bedón in PN Puracé.
**Range:** 1600-3200m. Caldas-Tolima area of C Andes (sight—J. Orejuela) s to w slope in Cauca, both sides of upper Magdalena Val. in Huila, and e slope of E Andes in Norte de Santander (Páramo de Tamá) and w Meta (Manzanares)

s to e slope in Putumayo and Nariño. Nw Venez. (Táchira) s in Andes to Peru. **Note:** Systematic position of *Sericossypha* not certain. Perhaps related to Icteridae.

[*Chlorospingus*: Rather chunky; bill stouter than *Hemispingus*; many with pale eyes; yellow on throat or with olive yellow breast band (except 113 and 117); usually "nuclear" in mixed flocks.]

### 111. COMMON BUSH-TANAGER
*Chlorospingus ophthalmicus*            Pls. 53, 54,
Map 1378
**Identification:** 5.8″ (14.7cm). Eyes yellow (in Magdalena Val. and e slope of Andes; elsewhere?). *Crown and sides of head brownish black to black contrasting with olive green upperparts;* faint or no white spot behind eye (or *prom. white spot behind eye—ponsi; jacqueti; eminens*); throat white finely *speckled* brown; *broad greenish yellow band across chest;* rest of underparts white tinged yellowish olive on sides and under tail coverts. Or *top and sides of head gray; broad dusky black band below eyes; and unspotted throat (flavopectus).*
**Similar species:** Racial var. complex and confusing. Can usually be told from other Colombian *Chlorospingus* (several also have pale eyes) by dusky head and white spot, if present, behind eyes; nearby the throat spots are diagnostic (except *C. o. flavopectus*). Shares its breast band only with Ash-throated Bush-Tanager (116); the 2 are easily confused in se Santander s to w Cundinamarca (where unspotted throat, gray cap, and breast band common to both) but Common differs in yellow (not dark) eyes with dusky band below them
**Voice:** Song, in Peru, *chip-chip-chip-chidip-chidip-chidip-chidip-chew-chew-chew* (O'Neill); *chep* call and trills much like others of the genus.
**Behavior:** As in Yellow-throated Bush-Tanager.
**Breeding:** 8 BC birds, Apr–June, Perijá Mts. and n end E Andes (Carriker); 4 in Oct, e Boyacá (Olivares 1971). Bulky cup nest embedded in moss from ground (on bank) to 16m up; 2 white eggs spotted cinnamon and brown mostly at larger end (Skutch 1967).
**Status and habitat:** Humid and wet forest (esp. mossy forest), edges, and overgrown clearings. Common in upper Magdalena Val. and on adj. e slope of E Andes.
**Range:** 1400-2700m. E slope W Andes at n end (sw of Medellín) and C Andes in Antioquia (*exitelus*); C Andes from Caldas s on the w to Valle, on the e to head of Magdalena Val. in Huila (*nigriceps*); Perijá Mts. (*ponsi*); n end E Andes s on w slope to c Santander and on e

slope of E Andes to s Boyacá (*jacqueti* and *eminens*); w slope Santander at La Pica (*trudis*); w slope E Andes in s Santander and w Cundinamarca (*flavopectus*); Macarena Mts. (*macarenae*); e Andean slope from w Caquetá to w Putumayo and e Nariño (subsp.?). C Mexico to e Panama; nw Venez. s in Andes to nw Argentina.

### 112. TACARCUNA BUSH-TANAGER
*Chlorospingus tacarcunae*            Pl. 52, Map 1379
**Identification:** 5.5″ (14cm). *Eyes yellowish white.* Mostly olive green above; crown and sides of head browner (not in sharp contrast to back); *throat and chest yellow;* lower underparts more olive yellow. No white spot behind eyes.
**Similar species:** Only bush-tanager in its range.
**Behavior:** Small groups wander in lower stratas of forest much like Common Bush-Tanager (Ridgely 1976).
**Status and habitat:** Humid forest; not well known.
**Range:** 1100-1500m. E slope of Mt. Tacarcuna on Panama boundary. E Panama to extreme nw Colombia.
**Note 1:** Poss. a subsp. of *C. ophthalmicus* (Common Bush-Tanager). **Note 2:** Pirre Bush-Tanager (*Chlorospingus inornatus*) of e Darién, Panama (Cerro Pirre; Cerro Sapo) may be found on Colombian side of border. Resembles Tacarcuna Bush-Tanager, but *crown and sides of head blackish;* underparts mostly yellow spotted dusky on throat; iris yellowish. Rec. 850-1700m in Panama. Also perhaps only a race of *C. ophthalmicus.*

### 113. YELLOW-GREEN BUSH-TANAGER
*Chlorospingus flavovirens*            Pl. 52, Map 1380
**Identification:** 6″ (15cm). Very local. Eyes brown. *Dull olive green above;* ear coverts more dusky; *below olive yellow,* brighter on throat; center of abdomen and under tail coverts dull oily yellow.
**Similar species:** Very drab and essentially without distinctive marks. Known to occur definitely only with 1 other bush tanager, Yellow-throated (114), which has contrasting yellow throat, but see Dusky-bellied Bush-Tanager (117) at slightly higher el. Not known to overlap any *Hemispingus* (but see 122). Cf. Ochre-breasted Tanager (86).
**Voice:** Call a loud husky *chut* repeated often; coarser and more raspy than notes of other *Chlorospingus.*
**Behavior:** Pairs or groups of 3-4 call persistently as they hop up epiphyte-laden trunks or along large moss-jacketed limbs in the mid. strata or subcanopy, usually foraging higher

than allied Yellow-throated Bush-Tanager. Often with mixed flocks; eats much fruit.
**Breeding:** 2 nests, 14 Mar and 7 Apr; 1 building nest, 23 Aug, and 1 BC ♂, 10 Oct, upper Anchicayá Val. (Hilty 1977). Mossy cup nests 5 and 7m up in mossy tree crotch and in base of palm fronds.
**Status and habitat:** Wet mossy forest ("cloud forest"), forest edges, and adj. tall trees in clearings. Known from only a single ridge on e side of upper Anchicayá Val., where relatively common.
**Range:** 950-1050m. Pacific slope in upper Anchicáy Val., Valle ("Alto Yunda," 3°32'N, 76°48'W). W Colombia; w Ecuador.

### 114. YELLOW-THROATED BUSH-TANAGER
*Chlorospingus flavigularis*        Pls. 52, 54,
                                        Map 1381
**Identification:** 6″ (15cm). Eyes light yellowish brown. Yellowish olive green above; *loral area gray; throat yellow* (or only chin and *sides of throat yellow*—*marginatus*); otherwise light gray below; sides and under tail coverts tinged olive.
**Similar species:** In *area of overlap* with Short-billed Bush-Tanager (115) best told by brighter all yellow throat (not mustard yellow flaring on sides only). Other Colombian *Chlorospingus* lack contrasting yellow throats.
**Voice:** Song a short weak *chit, twee-twee-twee-twit*, thin and high; *chip*'s incessantly when foraging.
**Behavior:** Noisy, active pairs or groups of 3-5 are "nuclear" in mixed forest flocks. Flutter and hop along smaller branches as perch-glean insects and fruit from understory to subcanopy, more often high only to fruiting trees. Sometimes unsuspicious.
**Breeding:** 7 BC birds, June, n end C Andes (Carriker), 1 in Oct, e Boyacá (Olivares 1971); 1 nest, 10 Feb, carrying food, 15 Apr, building nest, 16 Sept, upper Anchicayá Val.; cup nest embedded in moss, 5m up (Hilty).
**Status and habitat:** Common in humid and wet forest, second growth woodland, and shrubby edges. Foothills and lower slopes and generally below range of other Colombian *Chlorospingus*; the only one likely below 700m.
**Range:** 300-1400m (to 2000m in PN Cueva de los Guácharos—P. Gertler). Pacific slope from Valle to Nariño (*marginatus*); upper Sinú and lower Cauca Val. (above Pto. Valdivia) e to mid. Magdalena Val. (n boundary of Caldas), s to head of val. in Huila, and e slope E Andes from Boyacá south (*flavigularis*). W Panama; Colombia s in Andes to e and w Ecuador, e Peru, and n Bolivia.

### 115. SHORT-BILLED BUSH-TANAGER
*Chlorospingus parvirostris*        Pl. 54, Map 1382
**Identification:** 5.8″ (14.7cm). *Eyes gray to white.* Dingy olive green above; *sides of throat mustard yellow* (feathers flare backward and downward shieldlike below eyes); *underparts grayish brown*; central throat paler.
**Similar species:** From Yellow-throated Bush-Tanager (114; *flavigularis* subsp.) by yellow of throat deeper and confined to sides of throat; olive (not gray) loral area; and underparts somewhat darker and dingier.
**Voice:** Call *tsip* almost incessantly like others of the genus.
**Behavior:** Sim. to Yellow-throated Bush-Tanager.
**Status and habitat:** Common in lower and mid. story of mossy forest and shrubby forest edges. Generally found above range of Yellow-throated Bush-Tanager, below range of Common Bush-Tanager (some overlap with both), and with Ashy-throated Bush-Tanager, which replaces it in canopy and vines.
**Range:** 1400-2100m (poss. lower; once to 2500m, PN Puracé—J. Silliman). Head of Magdalena Val. in Huila and e slope of E Andes from e Cundinamarca southward. Colombia s in Andes to nw Bolivia.

### 116. ASH-THROATED BUSH-TANAGER
*Chlorospingus canigularis*        Pls. 53, 54,
                                        Map 1383
**Identification:** 5.5″ (14cm). Dark eyes. Mainly bright olive green above; head gray, ear coverts darker; below grayish white, sides yellowish olive, *light yellow band across chest*; under tail coverts greenish yellow.
**Similar species:** From any other *Chlorospingus* except Common Bush-Tanager (111) by breast band. From latter by paler head, unspotted throat, and absence of white postocular spot (but *cf.* much more sim. *flavopectus* subsp. of latter in w Cundinamarca and Boyacá where overlap).
**Voice:** Chips and thin twitters much like others of the genus.
**Behavior:** Small groups actively explore foliage, bare or mossy limbs, and esp. vine tangles near ground to treetops, but unlike most other *Chlorospingus* more often in canopy or subcanopy. Usually joined by other spp.
**Breeding:** 4 BC birds, Sept, C Andes, se Antioquia, 1 in May, n end W Andes (Carriker); 2 in Mar–Apr, W Andes above Cali (Miller 1963).
**Status and habitat:** Fairly common in humid forest and vine-tangled forest borders, esp. above steep mt. streams.
**Range:** 1200-2600m. W slope W Andes and e

slope from Valle southward, C Andes in Quindío area (Salento) s to head of Magdalena Val. in Huila and n on w slope of E Andes to n Boyacá; e slope in Norte de Santander. Costa Rica; extreme nw Venez. (Táchira); e and sw Ecuador; n Peru.

## 117. DUSKY-BELLIED BUSH-TANAGER
*Chlorospingus semifuscus*          Pl. 52, Map 1384
**Identification:** 6.0″ (15cm). *Eyes pale yellow. Small white spot behind eye* (at least in *livingstoni*). Dark olive above, more brownish gray on top and sides of head; *underparts dark gray*, sides and under tail coverts tinged olive (or brownish gray below paler than back; center of belly gray—*semifuscus*).
**Similar species:** A *very dark* bush-tanager with rather prom. pale yellow eyes with a small white spot behind. Should be easily recognized. Cf. 113 and 114.
**Voice:** A *very* high-pitched *chip*, and thin penetrating trill.
**Behavior:** Sim. to Yellow-throated Bush-Tanager, which it largely replaces above 1200m on Pacific slope. Mostly mid. story.
**Status and habitat:** Common in wet mossy forest ("cloud forest") and forest borders. Easily found on w slope of Cerro Munchique near upper limit of el. range
**Range:** 1200-2400m (to 900m in w Cauca). Pacific slope from headwaters of Río San Juan (Cerro Tatamá) s to w Cauca (*livingstoni*); Pacific slope of Nariño (*semifuscus*). W Colombia and n Ecuador (w slope).

## 118. BLACK-BACKED BUSH-TANAGER
*Urothraupis stolzmanni*          Pl. 54, Map 1385
**Identification:** 6″ (15cm). *Sides of head and entire upperparts black; throat white*; breast and belly gray mottled with white; flanks and under tail coverts dark gray.
**Similar species:** Longer-tailed than *Chlorospingus* and most likely mistaken for an *Atlapetes*, esp. Slaty Brush-Finch (p 651), which has chestnut crown, black malar, and white wing spot.
**Voice:** A few high weak chipping and trilling notes when foraging.
**Behavior:** Groups of 3-9 hop actively, perch-glean, or stretch to peer above and below leaves; also work foliage and denser vegetation like parids, gleaning, probing, and occas. hanging briefly near branch tip. Wander alone or with mixed flocks and can be difficult to see owing to habit of keeping low in thick bushes and trees (J. Silliman; Hilty).
**Breeding:** BC ♂, 13 Feb, e Cauca (Carriker).
**Status and habitat:** Thick wet forest borders and stunted woodland up to treeline, esp. where

there are many dense bushes and shrubs. Common locally on e and sw slope of PN Puracé.
**Range:** 3000-3600m. C Andes from nevados on Caldas-Tolima border (about 5°N) s to e Cauca (PN Puracé). Prob. s to e Nariño. C Colombia; e Ecuador.
**Note:** Most like *Hemispingus* in behavior but by some placed in Fringillidae next to *Lysurus*.

## 119. GRAY-HOODED BUSH-TANAGER
*Cnemoscopus rubrirostris*          Pl. 53, Map 1386
**Identification:** 6″ (15cm). *Bill pinkish. Entire head, throat, and chest gray*; throat and chest paler; otherwise olive green above and *bright yellow below*.
**Similar species:** Easily recognized in highland habitat by pink bill, gray hood, and habit of constantly wagging tail up and down. ♀ Capped Conebill (p 591) also wags tail, but bill dark and cap blue (not dark gray).
**Behavior:** Pairs or several join mixed forest flocks in canopy or subcanopy, occas. lower, but are not "nuclear" in flocks. Hop or crawl along limbs into foliage as wag tail, often teeter posterior body up and down, and generally bring to mind large *Basileuterus* warblers; less frugivorous than *Chlorospingus*.
**Breeding:** 3 BC birds, July–Aug, n end W and C Andes (Carriker).
**Status and habitat:** Fairly common in tall mossy forest or occas. at forest edge.
**Range:** 2000-3300m (mostly 2400-2700m). All 3 Andean ranges (but recs. scattered). Andes from Nw Venez. to e Peru.

[*Hemispingus*: Not as robust as *Chlorospingus*; bill thin; resemble *Basileuterus* (Parulidae) in behavior, plumage, and shape.]

## 120. BLACK-CAPPED HEMISPINGUS
*Hemispingus atropileus*          Pl. 53, Map 1387
**Identification:** 6.5″ (16.5cm). *Crown and sides of head black with long buffy white eyestripe from nostril to nape*; rest of upperparts greenish olive; throat and breast ochraceous yellow becoming yellow olive on lower underparts.
**Similar species:** Easily confused with *nigrifrons* subsp. of Superciliaried Hemispingus (121) of C Andes, which has blackish forecrown (not entire crown, nape, and sides of head) and is bright yellow (not ochraceous) on throat and breast. Also see Black-crested Warbler (p 586)
**Behavior:** Pairs or small groups are active and warblerlike, gleaning through denser foliage of bushes and bamboo, or from near ground to lower midlevels in taller trees; a nuclear sp. in temperate zone mixed flocks containing warblers, brush-finches, and other tanagers.

**Breeding:** 2 BC birds, Sept, n end W Andes; 2 in Aug, W Andes, Cauca; 1 in Feb, C Andes, Cauca (Carriker); 1 BC ♂, Dec, PN Chingaza (W. McKay).
**Status and habitat:** Humid and wet forest, and dwarf forest, esp. at dense borders where mixed with bamboo (*Chusquea*). Common in higher el. of range.
**Range:** 1800-3600m (mostly above 2400m). All 3 Andean ranges. Andes from nw Venez. to w Ecuador and n Bolivia.

## 121. SUPERCILIARIED HEMISPINGUS
*Hemispingus superciliaris*     Pl. 53, Map 1388
**Identification:** 5.5″ (14cm). Bill thin. *Forecrown gray* (or blackish—*nigrifrons*); otherwise olive above with *rather prom. white eyestripe*; cheeks dusky, *underparts bright* yellow.
**Similar species:** Very sim. to Citrine Warbler (p 585) but brighter below, forecrown gray to blackish (not olive), bill heavier and eyestripe whiter and *much* longer; *nigrifrons* subsp. easily confused with Black-capped Hemispingus (see 120). Oleaginous Hemispingus (122), usually at lower el., is dingier with oily yellow eyestripe, and no gray or black on forecrown.
**Behavior:** Recalls previous sp. Several usually assoc. with mixed flocks. Actively hop and glean in foliage like *Basileuterus* warblers, mostly 1-5m up in thicker shrubbery, less often to canopy of trees on steep hillsides.
**Breeding:** 3 BC birds, Feb–July, C Andes at n end and in e Cauca (Carriker).
**Status and habitat:** Humid forest with heavy undergrowth, bushy forest borders, and second growth. Common in w Santander, mainly 2100-2300m; less reg. encountered elsewhere.
**Range:** 2100-3300m. E slope E Andes in n Boyacá (Güicán), w slope in Santander (sightings 1980–Hilty) and both slopes in Cundinamarca (*superciliaris*); C Andes from ne end in Antioquia s to Chiles, Nariño (*nigrifrons*). Nw Venez. s in Andes to w Ecuador and n Bolivia.

## 122. OLEAGINOUS HEMISPINGUS
*Hemispingus frontalis*     Pl. 53, Map 1389
**Identification:** 5.5″ (14cm). Bill thin. Dull olive above with *weak yellowish eyestripe*; primaries and tail edged brownish; *underparts dingy yellowish tinged olive*, esp. on sides and lower underparts.
**Similar species:** Appear mostly dingy yellowish olive in field. Weak eyestripe is the mark. See Citrine Warbler (p 585), and Superciliaried Hemispingus (121). Very rare Yellow-green Bush-Tanager (113) lacks eyestripe and has heavier bill.

**Behavior:** One or 2 follow or are often nuclear in mixed flocks in bushes and lower shrubbery inside forest. Like others of the genus actively glean in foliage like *Basileuterus* warblers and are often found with the latter
**Breeding:** 5 BC birds, June–Nov, Perijá Mts. and n end C and E Andes (Carriker); 2 in Oct, e Boyacá (Olivares 1971).
**Status and habitat:** Undergrowth of humid forest and vine tangles, less often shrubby forest borders. More a forest dweller than previous 2 spp. and though often fairly common, seen much less often.
**Range:** 1500-2700m (most numerous 1900-2400m). Perijá Mts. and E and C Andes s to s Huila (e Nariño?), W Andes at n end in Antioquia (Frontino), and in Cauca. N Venez. s in Andes to e Ecuador and e Peru.

## 123. BLACK-EARED HEMISPINGUS
*Hemispingus melanotis*     Pl. 53, Map 1390
**Identification:** 6″ (15cm). Bill thin. *Crown and mantle gray* becoming olive on lower back; wings and tail grayish; remiges edged buffy; *broad black mask across eyes and cheeks* usually bordered above by narrow white supraloral streak merging into an indistinct pale gray eyestripe (or no eyestripe, and sides of head dusky—*ochraceus*); *underparts cinnamon buff*; center of belly whitish.
**Similar species:** See Rufous-crested Tanager (99); also recalls Fawn-breasted Tanager (18) but lacks blue crown and rump and is mainly a forest bird (not clearings).
**Behavior:** Single birds or pairs are usually seen in dense forest undergrowth to lower mid. levels; often with mixed flocks, esp. those containing other *Hemispingus*, and often Plush-capped Finch; peer and peck actively among twigs and foliage.
**Breeding:** 1 BC ♂, 7 Sept, Cundinamarca (Olivares 1969a).
**Status and habitat:** In many localities rare and local. Humid forest and shrubbery at forest edge, esp. in dense vine-crowded hillsides with *Chusquea* bamboo and *Dryopteris* tree ferns. Fairly common above Bucaramanga (1700-2000 m), w Santander (Hilty and P. Hall); other recent recs. at Finca Merenberg (Ridgely and Gaulin 1980), PN Puracé (J. Silliman) and upper Río Cusiana, Boyacá (R. Ridgely).
**Range:** 1700-2900m. E Andes on w slope in Santander and both slopes in Cundinamarca, both slopes of C Andes s to Quindío area, e slope C Andes in Huila, e slope of Andes in Nariño (*melanotis*); Pacific slope of Nariño (*ochraceus*). Nw Venez. (sw Táchira) s in Andes to w Ecuador and n Bolivia.

### 124. BLACK-HEADED HEMISPINGUS

*Hemispingus verticalis*          Pl. 53, Map 1391
**Identification:** 5.5″ (14cm). *Eyes whitish*; bill thin. Color suggests an *Atlapetes*. *Head and throat black with long light gray central crown stripe* extending to nape; *otherwise gray above*; wings and tail darker; *light gray below*; center of belly whitish.
**Similar species:** Looks more like a warbler or small finch than a tanager. Black on sides of head is rounded off behind giving impression of a large black disk on each side of head.
**Behavior:** Single birds or pairs, occas. several, follow mixed flocks; actively work over outer foliage or *walk* on leaves and twigs, mostly in tops of thick bushes and smaller trees; eat insects and fruit.
**Breeding:** BC ♂ and 2 imms. 10 Sept, n end W Andes in Antioquia (Carriker).
**Status and habitat:** Uncommon and local. Dense wet temperate forest, elfin woodland, and shrubby forest edges near or at treeline. In PN Puracé best seen at Coconuco entrance or e of Termales de San Juan.
**Range:** 3000-3600m. E Andes in Cundinamarca (doubtless n to se Norte de Santander), C Andes s to Nariño, and n end W Andes (Páramo Frontino). Nw Venez. (Páramo de Tamá in sw Táchira) s in Andes to Ecuador and n Peru.

### 125. GRASS-GREEN TANAGER

*Chlorornis riefferii*          Pl. 50, Map 1392
**Identification:** 8″ (20cm). Unmistakable. Robust. *Bright grass green with orange red bill and legs*; mask, center of abdomen, and under tail coverts chestnut.
**Voice:** Contact call a dry leathery *neck*, distinctive once learned; also a stuttering *du-du-du* and longer whinny, *dut-du-u-u-u-u-u-u* fading in vol.

**Behavior:** A big, usually conspic. highland tanager, customarily seen in pairs or groups of 3-6, with mixed flocks or independent of them. Mostly midlevels but also higher or lower. Fly rather heavily from branch to branch peering like big vireos at foliage or occas. even hanging or fluttering clumsily from leaves for fruit and insects.
**Breeding:** 10 BC birds, Feb–Sept, W and C Andes (Carriker); 1 in Oct, e Boyacá (Olivares 1971); 1 Antioquia nest a large moss and fern bowl; 1 gray egg freckled lilac (Sclater and Salvin 1879).
**Status and habitat:** Common but somewhat local; mossy forest ("cloud forest") and forest edges, occas. into tall second growth. Readily found on upper slopes of Cerro Munchique, Cauca, or at Tokio (1800m) above Queremal, Valle.
**Range:** 1700-3300m (mostly 2400-2700m, locally numerous lower). W and C Andes, and E Andes from Boyacá southward. Colombia s in Andes to n Bolivia.

### 126. MAGPIE TANAGER

*Cissopis Leveriana*          Ill. 97, Map 1393
**Identification:** 11″ (28cm). Unmistakable. *Eyes yellow. Glossy blue black hood* covering entire head, upper mantle, and underparts to point on center of breast; the feathers pointed forming a serrated edge with *white back and white lower underparts; wings and long graduated tail black*; wings edged white; *tail broadly tipped white*.
**Voice:** Occas. heard song a loud, unmusical ser. of jerky whistles and trills (J. V. Remsen); call a loud *check*.
**Behavior:** Noisy and conspic. pairs or families bring to mind jays in appearance and behavior as they call and fly from tree to tree in clear-

97. Magpie Tanager

ings. Inside forest usually in canopy, where may follow mixed flocks.

**Status and habitat:** Fairly common to common in forest borders, or in irreg. second growth mixed with scattered tall trees in clearings, occas. inside tall, humid, *terra firme* forest.

**Range:** To 1400m. Throughout e of Andes in forested zones or in gallery forest. The Guianas and Venez. to n Bolivia, Paraguay, and Amazonian and se Brazil.

## 127. BLACK-FACED TANAGER
*Schistochlamys melanopis*     Pl. 55, Map 1394

**Identification:** 7″ (18cm). Eyes dark red. Bill short and thick, blue gray tipped black. *Forehead, sides of head, throat, and chest black; otherwise entirely gray*; underparts paler gray becoming whitish on belly. Imm.: *olive green above*; paler milky olive below; center of belly and under tail coverts pale yellow; wings edged brownish; tail rounded (not ads.), sometimes narrowly tipped whitish.

**Similar species:** Ads. easily recognized. Imm. likely mistaken for a finch, esp. a saltator, but is essentially uniform above and below; look for yellowish belly and rounded tail.

**Voice:** Song, in Surinam, a weak rambling *whatsur-wheer, wheer-ta-wheét-ta* over and over

(T. Davis); sim. finchlike warble in Meta and Putumayo.

**Behavior:** Single birds or scattered pairs perch in tall grass or in, or on top of bushes in rather open country.

**Breeding:** 5 BC birds, Apr–May, Perijá Mts., s Bolívar and Huila; 3 BC ♂♂, June, w Caquetá (Carriker); 1 BC ♂, Mar, Macarena Mts. (Olivares 1962); 2 BC ♂♂, Jan and Apr, ne Meta (S. Furniss). In Surinam, open grass cup in shrub in grassland; 2 grayish white eggs thickly streaked and blotched dark brown (Haverschmidt 1975b).

**Status and habitat:** Uncommon to fairly common e of Andes in grassland with scattered bushes and trees or along borders of savanna woodland; very local w of Andes. Sparingly in pastures of Pichindé Val. (1300–1400m) above Cali.

**Range:** To 1700m. Mid. and upper Cauca Val. (Valle; Cauca), n slope Santa Marta Mts., Perijá Mts., mid. Magdalena Val. (s Bolívar; ne Santander and se Antioquia) to head of val. in Huila (San Agustín); e of Andes generally s to Meta, spottily to Putumayo (sighting Pto. Asís, Mar 1960–Brown) and Vaupés (Mitú). The Guianas and Venez. locally to e Peru (not yet Ecuador), n Bolivia, and Brazil.

# PLUSH-CAPPED FINCHES: Catamblyrhynchidae (1)

The systematic position of this rather widespread but local Andean highland bird is uncertain. It has been placed with the tanagers, the finches, and retained as a monotypic family between them. The name is derived from the stiff plushy forecrown feathers. The food is apparently small insects and some plant material. The nesting biology is undescribed.

## 1. PLUSH-CAPPED FINCH
*Catamblyrhynchus diadema*     Pl. 53, Map 1395

**Identification:** 5.5″ (14cm). Short black bill thick and swollen. *Forecrown deep yellow*, the feathers short, stiff, and plushlike; lores, hindcrown, and nape black; *rest of upperparts dark bluish gray* incl. graduated tail; *underparts chestnut*. Imm.: grayish olive above, paler below tinged rufescent; older birds show suggestion of yellow on forecrown.

**Similar species:** Easily confused with Goldencrowned Tanager (p 618); at a distance both look dark with yellow crown patch but Finch is chestnut below. Also cf. Blue-backed Conebill (p 590).

**Voice:** Soft high *chip*'s when foraging; infrequent song, in Peru, a monotone of unmusical *chip*'s and twitters, 15–60 sec in length; reminiscent of song of several *Hemispingus* tanagers (T. Parker).

**Behavior:** One or 2, occas. several, follow mixed flocks containing tanagers and finches, and are seldom seen away from them. Mostly a bamboo specialist (*Chusquea* spp.), that hops up the curving stalks, or clings upside down like a parid, and peers at the foliage and stems, mainly 1–6m up. Occas. in ferns and other foliage.

**Breeding:** 2 BC ♂♂, 23 June and 1 July, Perijá Mts.; 1 BC ♂, 26 June, Páramo Sonsón, se Antioquia (Carriker); 1 juv. with ads., 21 Dec, w of Caracas, Venez. (Hilty et al. 1979).

**Status and habitat:** Uncommon and local in bamboo in mossy highland forest, forest borders, and elfin woodland.

**Range:** 2100–3300m (treeline); usually above 2600m. Santa Marta Mts., Perijá Mts. and spottily in all 3 Andean ranges (W Andes from Valle southward). N Venez. s in mts. to w Peru and nw Argentina.

# FINCHES: Fringillidae (83)

Finches form a very large nearly cosmopolitan family (none are native to Australia). Most species have short, thick bills primarily adapted for seed-eating. A few, especially the saltators, are largely frugivorous. They are otherwise quite variable in size and plumage. Many are found in shrubby or open habitats, and only a few occur in tall woodland or rain forest. Most Colombian finches are residents; a small number of species are regular temperate zone migrants from the north or south. Songs range from rich pleasant whistles and warbles to thin unmusical trills and buzzes. Most Colombian species, as far as known, build open cup nests; *Tiaris* and *Arremon* build globular side-entrance nests, and *Sicalis* often use crevices and holes. Recent proposals (in Peters 1968, 1970) split the traditional Fringillidae into two families, the Fringillidae containing, in the New World, the subfamily Carduelinae (siskins), and the Emberizidae containing the rest of the American finches as well as the tanagers and some others. The Emberizidae would contain four subfamilies: Emberizinae (buntings and American sparrows), Catamblyrhynchinae (plush-capped finches), Cardinalinae (cardinals, grosbeaks, saltators, and others), and Thraupinae (tanagers including many genera formerly placed in the Coerebidae). Because the taxonomy of several genera is still disputed, the traditional A.O.U. Checklist is followed here although the order is generally that of Bds. Wld. 13 (Paynter and Storer *in* Peters 1970), the genus *Atlapetes* that of Paynter (1978).

## 1. DICKCISSEL

*Spiza americana*          Pl. 56, Map 1396

**Identification:** 6″ (15cm). Sparrowlike. Breeding plumage ♂: head grayish with *yellow eyestripe*; otherwise light brown above streaked dusky; *shoulders rufous*; throat white with narrow black malar connected to V-*shaped black bib on chest*; breast yellow fading to whitish on belly. Nonbreeding ♂: duller with less yellow; bib reduced or lacking. ♀: like nonbreeding ♂ but eyestripe weaker; dingy white below, breast tinged yellow; dusky malar line leads to indistinct streaking on sides.

**Similar species:** Best marks for ♀ and winter ♂ are rusty shoulders, sparrowlike appearance, and habit of gathering in flocks. See Bobolink (p 574), Grassland (77), and Yellow-browed sparrows (76).

**Behavior:** Small groups or concentrated in dense flocks of several hundred to several thousand in favorable feeding areas. Occas. with Bobolinks.

**Status and habitat:** Locally common winter resident (rec. mid-Sept–very early May) but erratic in many places; open country and agricultural areas, esp. rice fields.

**Range:** To 1600m. From Panama boundary e across n lowlands to e Guajira, and s to mid. Magdalena Val. in Santander (s of Bucaramanga); e of Andes from se Boyacá to s Meta (Macarena Mts.). Breeds in e and c N America; winters mostly from Panama to the Guianas and n Brazil; a few remain in e US.

**Note:** Behavior and morphology perhaps nearer Icteridae than Fringillidae.

## 2. INDIGO BUNTING

*Passerina cyanea*

**Identification:** 5″ (13cm). Rare. Small thick bill.

Breeding plumage ♂: *entirely brilliant deep blue*, darker on head. Nonbreeding ♂: like ♀ but *with traces of blue in wings and tail*. ♀ and imm. very nondescript: plain brown above, buffy white below with a few *indistinct brownish streaks on breast*; ♀ ♀ may show a tinge of blue on wing coverts and tail; very young birds faint whitish wing bars.

**Similar species:** ♂ like a miniature of Blue (5), Blue-black (3), or Ultramarine grosbeaks (4) but much brighter (Blue also has rusty wing bars). Confusing ♀ most like ♀ Blue-black Grassquit (67) but paler, bill much thicker, and breast streaking always suffused (not crisp). ♀ Pileated Finch (19) is grayer and has white eyering.

**Status and habitat:** Winter vagrant: 3 specimen recs., Jan–Mar: twice from n Chocó (Sautatá; Río Uva) and once near sw base of Santa Marta Mts. (El Difícil, Magdalena); 2 sight recs.: 1 ♂, 25 Apr 1972, PN Tayrona, another, 9 May 1972, PN Isla de Salamanca (T. B. Johnson).

**Range:** Breeds in e and c N America; winters from Mexico, Florida, and W Indies to Panama, rarely n Colombia and nw Venez.

## 3. BLUE-BLACK GROSBEAK

*Cyanocompsa cyanoides*          Pl. 55, Map 1397

**Identification:** 6.3″ (16cm). *Very heavy black bill* (not swollen). ♂: *deep blue black*; forehead, eyebrow, and area at base of bill brighter blue (or forehead, eyebrow, and chin much lighter and brighter blue—*rothschildii*). ♀: uniform *deep cocoa brown*.

**Similar species:** See Ultramarine and Blue grosbeaks (4, 5).

**Voice:** Rich, whistled song in Anchicayá Val. *weép-e-aa pee-e-u wegeeahere-see*, introductory phrases slower, rest fast, jumbled, and downscale; sharp metallic *chink* or *chink-chink* call notes.

**Behavior:** Pairs stay in thick undergrowth and near the ground where they are often heard but hard to see.

**Breeding:** 12 BC birds, Feb–Oct, w Guajira to Chocó (Carriker); 3 in Feb–Apr, nw Colombia (Haffer 1975); 1 in May, Vaupés (Olivares 1964b); building nest, Feb, Mitú (Hilty); 1 Santa Marta nest with eggs, July (Todd and Carriker 1922). Frail cup nest of fine twigs in low crotch of bush; 2 bluish white eggs with wreath of reddish brown dots at larger end (Stone 1918; Skutch 1954).

**Status and habitat:** Usually common in undergrowth of humid and wet forest, forest edge, and second growth. Replaced in drier thickets and scrub by Ultramarine Grosbeak.

**Range:** To 1400m. Pacific coast, forested lowlands n of Andes s to Remedios, Antioquia in mid. Magdalena Val., and n to Santa Marta and Perijá Mts. (*cyanoides*); e of Andes in Norte de Santander and from w Meta (Villavicencio), ne Guainía (Pto. Inírida), and e Vaupés (*rothschildii*) southward. S Mexico to nw Peru, n Bolivia, and Amazonian Brazil.

**Note:** Placed in the genus *Passerina* by some.

### 4. ULTRAMARINE GROSBEAK
*Cyanocompsa brissonii*        Pl. 55, Map 1398

**Identification:** 6″ (15cm). Very heavy black bill (slightly swollen). ♂: very sim. to ♂ Blue-black Grosbeak (3) but slightly smaller, *rump paler and brighter than back* (not uniform with back), and bill somewhat curved and swollen. ♀: resembles ♀ Blue-black Grosbeak but slightly smaller and *pale sandy brown* (not rich dark brown) with *underparts obviously paler than upperparts*.

**Voice:** Song recalls Blue-black Grosbeak's but higher-pitched and faster; a flat warbled *wee-se-weep wee-so-weeep wee see wee-so-weeep* without latter's 2 slow introductory phrases (P. Schwartz recording); sharp, metallic *pik* call unlike that of Blue-black Grosbeak.

**Behavior:** A thicket dweller but less retiring than Blue-black Grosbeak and normally not too difficult to see. Alone, in pairs, or 3's.

**Status and habitat:** Local. Common in semiarid scrub, cane, and riverine thickets and scrubby borders in agricultural areas. Esp. numerous in Dagua Val. above Loboguerrero. Replaced in humid forest by Blue-black Grosbeak.

**Range:** 300-1600m. Pacific slope in drier parts of upper Dagua Val. (mostly above Cisneros), upper Patía Val. and mid. Cauca Val. in Valle (Cali, Palmira, and Buga area). Spottily in n Venez., e Brazil, and Mato Grosso, Paraguay, Argentina, and e Bolivia.

**Note 1:** Formerly *Cyanocompsa cyanea.* **Note 2:** Sometimes placed in the genus *Passerina.*

### 5. BLUE GROSBEAK
*Guiraca caerulea*

**Identification:** 6.5″ (16.5cm). Breeding plumage ♂: *deep blue with 2 rusty wing bars*; wings and tail edged blackish. Nonbreeding ♂: feathers blue basally and broadly edged brown giving overall brown appearance (like ♀), but some blue usually shows through; retains wing bars. ♀: brown above, buffy brown below; wings and tail duskier; *2 broad rusty wing bars.*

**Similar species:** In any plumage look for the wing bars, lacking in other "blue" grosbeaks (3, 4) and Indigo Bunting (2).

**Status and habitat:** Two recs. Winter vagrant: 1 specimen, taken by Carriker, 4 Apr 1942, Perijá Mts. (1600m) se of Codazzi, Cesar; 1 ♂ seen 18 Apr 1973, e of Buenaventura (Gochfeld et al. 1974).

**Range:** Breeds from s US to Costa Rica; winters to Panama, rarely n Colombia and ne Ecuador (once e of Limoncocha).

**Note:** Sometimes placed in the genus *Passerina.*

[*Saltator*: Large; heavy bill; usually with *white superciliary* and dark malar; *olive green* or *grayish* back. Arboreal; frugivorous; favor lighter woodland, edges, or shrubs.]

### 6. BUFF-THROATED SALTATOR
*Saltator maximus*        Pl. 55, Map 1399

**Identification:** 7.8″ (19.8cm). *Bright olive green above*; sides of head and *most of underparts gray; short eyebrow* and chin white; *lower throat buff* (often not very noticeable) *bordered on sides by broad black malar stripe*; center of belly and under tail coverts cinnamon buff.

**Similar species:** Grayish Saltator (8) is gray above (not olive green) and lacks buff throat. Streaked Saltator (10) is streaked below.

**Voice:** Song a long ser. of sweet, *Turdus*-like, caroled phrases with much repetition, *cheetelewert, weete-wert, sweetle-e-er, e-te-were.* . . .

**Behavior:** Usually seen singly or in pairs, sometimes with mixed flocks. Rather wary and may keep partially hidden in lower levels, sometimes high to sing or to visit fruiting trees.

**Breeding:** 10 BC birds, Jan–June, Norte de Santander to s Córdoba (Carriker); 3 in Feb–Mar, nw Colombia (Haffer 1975); 2 BC ♀♀, Jan, ne Meta (S. Furniss); June nest with eggs, nw Santander (Boggs 1961); Santa Marta nest in Aug; coarse twig, leaf, and weed cup; 2 pale blue eggs with ring of marks around larger end (Todd and Carriker 1922).

**Status and habitat:** Common in partially wooded zones with irregular second growth, along bushy forest edges, and in lighter woodland

in humid and wet zones. Replaced in drier, scrubbier areas by Streaked Saltator.
**Range:** To 1700m. Throughout except dry parts of Cauca and Magdalena vals. and arid n coast. Mexico to nw Peru, n Bolivia, and s Brazil.

## 7. BLACK-WINGED SALTATOR
*Saltator atripennis*                Pl. 55, Map 1400
**Identification:** 8″ (20cm). *Crown and sides of head black* (forms a hood) *with broad white eyebrow and large white spot on ear coverts;* otherwise olive green above with *black wings and tail;* throat white; rest of underparts grayish white; under tail coverts buffy.
**Similar species:** Easily told by bold head pattern and black wings and tail.
**Voice:** Song a loud, exuberant, and rapidly downscale *twee twaa, toou, toweer, tweeeeear;* loud *tsink,* and descending *cheeeer* calls. In w Nariño a very different *cheeeeeeer, tr-e-e-e-e,* descending, then quavering and upscale.
**Behavior:** Harder to see than most Colombian saltators. Wander alone or chase each other in noisy groups; often with mixed flocks where take mostly fruit from midlevels to canopy.
**Breeding:** 6 BC birds, May–July, C Andes (Carriker), 1 in Mar, W Andes above Cali (Miller 1963); building bulky cup nest low in pasture bush, 13 Apr, upper Anchicayá Val. (Hilty).
**Status and habitat:** Fairly common in humid or wet forest and forest borders, older second growth woodlands, and woodlots. Favors wetter and more mature woods than previous sp. and is sometimes found in canopy well inside forest.
**Range:** 800-2200m (to 400m on Pacific slope). Both slopes of W Andes (on w slope n to headwaters of Río San Juan), w slope of C Andes, e slope C Andes on Snía. San Lucas and n boundary of Caldas, and w slope of E Andes in Cundinamarca. Colombia and w Ecuador.

## 8. GRAYISH SALTATOR
*Saltator coerulescens*                Pl. 55, Map 1401
**Identification:** 8″ (20cm). Nondescript. *Dull gray above* with faint olive tinge (or dark gray— *azarae*); *short eyebrow white; median throat white bordered on sides by broad black malar stripe; gray below,* buffy tinge on flanks, abdomen, and under tail coverts.
**Similar species:** *Only* Colombian saltator with an *obviously gray* (not olive) back. ♀ Shiny Cowbird (p 561) has more pointed bill and lacks white throat and black malar.
**Voice:** Musical and rather disconnected song in n Colombia, *wheer, cheer, pe-chéer, po-chéer, whitwhit-sit-wheet* or sim.; greet with loud, presum. antiphonal, *d'wicker, d'wicker, d'wicker,*

*d'weeter;* in Amazonas, most common song a sweet and leisurely whistled *chúrk, churk-churk-churk chalk-weéeer;* call a loud nasal *chink.*
**Behavior:** Wanders in pairs or small noisy groups in bushy or disturbed areas, and normally rather conspic.
**Breeding:** BC ♂, 5 June, Guajira, and 7 Apr, upper Río Sinú (Carriker); carrying food, 7 Aug (Hilty), and nests found Apr–May in Santa Marta area; bulky stick and grassy cup; 2 pale blue eggs with fine black lines at larger end (Todd and Carriker 1922).
**Status and habitat:** Common in drier scrub and deciduous woodland in n Colombia; dry to humid second growth thickets and bushy pastures elsewhere.
**Range:** To 1300m. Lower Atrato Val. and upper Río Sinú & across Carib. lowlands to Guajira and s in Magdalena Val. to nw Cundinamarca (*plumbeus*); e of Andes in Norte de Santander and Arauca (*brewsteri*); Meta s to Putumayo and Amazonas (*azarae*). N Colombia and e of Andes s to n Argentina and Uruguay.

## 9. ORINOCAN SALTATOR
*Saltator orenocensis*                Pl. 55, Map 1402
**Identification:** 7.5″ (19cm). *Gray above with long conspic. white eyestripe; sides of head, neck, and sides of throat black;* center of throat and small spot at base of bill white; otherwise bright *cinnamon buff below;* tail blackish.
**Similar species:** Nothing really sim. Good marks are black on sides of head, long eyestripe, and buffy underparts.
**Voice:** Song, several deliberate *cheert* notes followed by a high almost squeaky, *pit-cher-each-er pitch-a pit-cher-each-er . . .* then sometimes more *cheert*'s.
**Behavior:** Quieter than other saltators. Pairs or sometimes groups of 3-4 occur in lower growth to canopies of smaller trees. Usually in areas much too open to occur with mixed flocks.
**Breeding:** In Venez. Orinoco, 2 loose, grassy, cup nests, 10 May and 15 June, 2-5m up in cane and low bushes; 2 greenish blue eggs spotted and lined black around larger end (Cherrie 1916); May breeding, Guárico, Venez. (Thomas 1979b).
**Status and habitat:** Fairly common in dry to moist gallery forest, deciduous woodland, and semiopen arid scrub. Often in tall rank grassy and weedy areas where mixed with brush and scattered taller trees.
**Range:** To 500m. Guajira Peninsula from Ríohacha eastward (straggles to e base of Santa Marta Mts.); e of Andes in n Arauca (1 seen near Arauca, Nov 1978—W. McKay); prob. n

Vichada. N Colombia and n Venez. (n of Orinoco).

**Note:** Masked Saltator (*S. cinctus*) of foothills and slopes (2000-3000m) of e Ecuador (near Macas, Zamora) and ne Peru may occur on adj. e slope in s Colombia. Unmistakable. 9″; bill red, iris pale; head blackish; otherwise dark gray with white lower throat, chest, belly, and crissum; very rounded blackish tail; outer feathers broadly tipped white. Fond of *Chusquea* bamboo; shy (see O'Neill and Schulenberg 1979).

### 10. STREAKED SALTATOR
*Saltator albicollis*         Pl. 55, Map 1403

**Identification:** 7.5″ (19cm). *Olive green above*; head, rump, and tail grayer; *short white eyebrow; white below broadly streaked dark olive*; median throat and belly unstreaked (or gray above tinged olive on upper back—*flavidicollis*).

**Similar species:** Only Colombian saltator streaked below. Buff-throated Saltator (6) is sim. above but very different below.

**Voice:** Often heard musical song a lazy, whistled *o-chúck, chuk-weéeaar*, or repeated *chuckwéear* with var.; call *quik*.

**Behavior:** Sings from exposed perches in morning but otherwise near or in thickets and often hidden. Alone, pairs, or in 3's and like others of the genus, almost wholly frugivorous.

**Breeding:** Near Cali, 1 nest, Jan (Skutch 1954); 1 in May, w Santander (Boggs 1961); BC ♂ ♂, Apr and Sept, Cali; and 3 in Jan, upper Magdalena Val. (Miller 1963; 1947). Cup nest 1-7m up in shrub or small tree; 2 eggs (Skutch 1954), pale greenish blue with a band of black lines around larger end (Sclater and Salvin 1879).

**Status and habitat:** Common in drier shrubby areas, pastures, gardens, lighter woodland, and dry scrub. A sp. that has profited from deforestation and now occurs virtually throughout in drier or opened up areas.

**Range:** To 2000m, rarely to 2700m. From Cartagena to Guajira and s to both slopes of E Andes in Norte de Santander (*perstriatus*); upper Patía Val. and sw Nariño (*flavidicollis*); rest of Colombia w of Andes from n Sucre southward and from drier vals. on Pacific slope (upper Río Sucio and upper Río Dagua) e to e slope E Andes in s Boyacá (*striatipectus*). Costa Rica to n Venez. and w Peru.

### 11. SLATY (SLATE-COLORED) GROSBEAK
*Pitylus grossus*         Pl. 55, Map 1404

**Identification:** 7.5″ (19cm). *Heavy coral red bill.* ♂: *mostly dark bluish slate*; small white throat;

facial area and border around throat black. ♀: sim. but slightly paler below and no black on head or around throat.

**Similar species:** The red bill is the mark. White throat often not obvious.

**Voice:** "Loud song" much like that of a peppershrike, a loud, rich, whistled *whíchit-cheecheer, tur-chéeit,* or *preetuur, püü-tréeit,* or other var.; usually 2-3 or more song types alternated by each individual; "faint song" a weak version of preceding song; calls incl. a cardinallike *peek* and nasal whines.

**Behavior:** Single birds or pairs are sedentary and, except for occas. song or call, attract little attention to themselves. Mostly in mid. or upper level of forest, less often low inside forest or at edge; often join mixed forest flocks.

**Breeding:** 4 BC birds, Mar–Apr, n Chocó (Carriker; Haffer 1975); 1 in May, s Córdoba; 1 in Sept, Santander (Carriker).

**Status and habitat:** Fairly common in humid and wet forest, tall second growth, and borders.

**Range:** To 1200m. Pacific slope, humid lowlands n of Andes e to mid. Magdalena Val. and s to Honda, n Tolima; e of Andes from w Meta (Villavicencio area; Macarena Mts.) and Vaupés (Mitú) southward; prob. n to Guainía. E Nicaragua to w Ecuador, n Bolivia, Amazonian Brazil, and the Guianas.

### 12. YELLOW-GREEN GROSBEAK
*Caryothraustes canadensis*         Pl. 55, Map 1405

**Identification:** 6.5″ (16.5cm). Bill heavy. *Bright yellow olive above; facial area and upper throat black* bordered yellow; *underparts yellow* with faint olive tinge on sides of breast.

**Similar species:** Should be easily recognized by mostly yellow olive plumage and small black mask. See rare Yellow-shouldered Grosbeak (13), which has gray crown and underparts.

**Voice:** Call, buzzy *bzzit*, and loud, often-repeated *teach-yerp*.

**Behavior:** Troop about in noisy pairs or flocks, calling loudly, from mid. story to forest crown. Usually independent of mixed flocks.

**Breeding:** 5 BC birds, Feb–Apr, upper Orinoco, Venez. and upper Negro, Brazil (Friedmann 1948). Pair building coarse nest at base of palm frond 7-8m up in forest, Feb, Mitú (Hilty).

**Status and habitat:** Humid forest, occas. forest edge or bushy clearings. Common at Mitú.

**Range:** To 250m. Extreme e in Guainía (Río Guainía; sightings at Pto. Inírida) and Vaupés. Prob. also nw Chocó in foothills on Panama boundary. E Panama; extreme e Colombia, s Venez., the Guianas, and n and e Brazil (incl. upper Río Negro).

**Note:** Some incl. *C. poliogaster* (Black-faced Grosbeak) of Mid. America as a subsp. of *C. canadensis*.

## 13. YELLOW-SHOULDERED GROSBEAK

*Caryothraustes humeralis*  Map 1406
**Identification:** 6.5″ (16.5cm). Heavy blackish bill. Yellowish olive green above; *crown plumbeous gray with broad black stripe through eye; malar area and throat barred dusky and white* and separated by dusky submalar stripe; *rest of underparts gray except for bright yellow under tail coverts*; bend of shoulder and under wings coverts bright yellow.
**Similar species:** Yellow-green Grosbeak (12) lacks the gray crown and underparts and has small black facial area (not stripe through eye) and solid black throat.
**Behavior:** Single birds or pairs are reg. seen in mixed tanager and honeycreeper flocks; often perch on high exposed branches for considerable periods (R. Ridgely); tanagerlike (T. Parker).
**Status and habitat:** Canopy of semihumid and humid hill forest in Ecuador (R. Ridgely) and Peru (T. Parker). Nothing known in Colombia.
**Range:** Known only from "Bogotá" skins in Colombia. Presum. e slope of E Andes in Caquetá, and Putumayo. E Ecuador (Sarayacú, 700m; upper Río Napo), to se Peru, n Bolivia, and sw Amazonian Brazil (upper Río Purús).

## 14. VERMILION CARDINAL

*Cardinalis phoeniceus*  Pl. 55, Map 1407
**Identification:** 8″ (20cm). Unmistakable in arid scrub. *Long pointed crest;* stout pointed bill, pale gray above, yellowish below. ♂: *entirely bright rosy red;* back, wings, and tail edged dusky. ♀: *head pale gray with long rosy red crest;* upperparts pale brownish gray; *below ochraceous buff;* throat whiter; chin black; tail tinged vermilion.
**Voice:** Song a loud whistled *cheer, o-weet, toweet toweet toweet* or *cheer, cheer, heera tower, tower;* call a loud *chip* (P. Schwartz); song and call much like Northern Cardinal (*C. cardinalis*).
**Behavior:** Generally in pairs. Can be shy and hard to see.
**Breeding:** 4 BC ♂♂, May–June, ne base Santa Marta Mts. to Guajira (Carriker).
**Status and habitat:** Arid scrub, esp. in thorny thickets. Common from Ríohacha eastward.
**Range:** To ca. 300m. Arid Guajira peninsula and from ne base of Santa Marta Mts. (Distracción). Ne Colombia and adj. nw Venez.

## 15. ROSE-BREASTED GROSBEAK

*Pheucticus ludovicianus*
**Identification:** 7.5″ (19cm). Heavy chalky white bill. Breeding plumage ♂ (prior to migration): *upperparts, head, and throat black;* 2 large white wing patches, white rump, and white in tail; below white with *rosy chest extending to point on midbreast.* Nonbreeding birds sim. but mottled brownish above; head with a few buffy streaks, underparts flecked brown and with only traces of rose. ♀ and imm.: mostly brown above streaked blackish; *narrow buffy white coronal stripe, eyebrow, and wing bars;* cheeks brown; below buffy white *finely* streaked brown.
**Similar species:** Nonbreeding ♂ always shows some pink on chest. Look for robust shape, head stripes, and brownish cheeks on ♀ and imm.
**Voice:** Call a high metallic *kik.*
**Behavior:** Solitary, or esp. in migration, in small wandering groups of its own. Usually feeds fairly high in trees and independently of mixed flocks.
**Status and habitat:** Uncommon fall transient and common winter resident and spring transient (mid-Oct–late Apr; mainly Dec onward) to forest borders, second growth, and lighter woodland; dry to humid areas.
**Range:** To 3800m. Throughout w of Andes; rec. e of Andes from n Arauca (2 seen, 4-10 Nov 1977—W. McKay) to se Nariño, and ne Meta (Carimagua—S. Furniss). Breeds in N America; winters from Mexico to Venez., Ecuador, n Peru, and Fr. Guiana.

## 16. BLACK-BACKED GROSBEAK

*Pheucticus aureoventris*  Pl. 55, Map 1408
**Identification:** 8.5″ (22cm). Heavy blackish bill. ♂: *entire upperparts, head, throat, and chest black; rest of underparts yellow;* large white patch at base of primaries; white on wing coverts; yellow patch on shoulders and yellow spots on rump (or throat yellow mixed black, chest and rump yellow—*crissalis*). ♀: sim. but browner and somewhat mottled buff above; 2 dull white wing bars; below mostly yellow; throat and chest mottled black (or like ♂ but duller and with eyebrow yellow—*crissalis*).
**Similar species:** Black hood and yellow lower underparts are diagnostic. In flight mostly black above with flashing white patch in wings. See Yellow Grosbeak (17); also Masked and Black-chested mountain-tanagers (p 620).
**Voice:** Rich mellow song and sharp *keek* call resemble those of other *Pheucticus.*
**Behavior:** Alone or in pairs, except at fruiting shrubs where several may gather. Feeds at almost any ht. but usually sings from higher perch within tree. Normally conspic.
**Breeding:** BC ♂, 25 Jan, Cauca (Carriker).
**Status and habitat:** Usually fairly common (though in small nos.) in woodland borders,

cultivated areas with trees and hedgerows, and low shrubby growth on steep hillsides.
**Range:** 1700-3000m. E Andes (rec. s to Cundinamarca), C Andes in Cauca and s Huila (*uropygialis*); mts. of Nariño (*crissalis*). Nw Venez. s in Andes to Argentina.

## 17. YELLOW GROSBEAK
*Pheucticus chrysopeplus*          Pl. 55, Map 1409
**Identification:** 8″ (20cm). Very heavy dusky bill. ♂: *mostly golden yellow; wings black with large white patch at base of primaries* and white spots on tips of inner remiges; back streaked black (or back mostly black—*chrysogaster*); *tail black*, outer feathers edged white near tip. ♀: duller with head and back heavily streaked blackish; wings and tail brownish marked as in ♂. Looks like an oriole in flight.
**Similar species:** Black-backed Grosbeak (16) has entire head and upperparts black (or brown—♀) instead of mostly yellow. Cf. Yellow-backed Oriole (p 572).
**Voice:** Call a high metallic *eek*; song a mellow liquid ser. of deliberate phrases reminiscent of a *Thraupis* tanager or *Turdus* thrush but richer and smoother. Each bird typically has a large no. of song types.
**Behavior:** Sluggish, almost dazed at times. Alone or in pairs, low to high but usually fairly high when singing; often perches in open.
**Breeding:** 8 BC birds, Apr–July, Perijá and Santa Marta mts. (Carriker). In dry w Ecuador, Feb–May; loose, shallow, twiggy cup 3-4m up in bush or smaller tree; 2-4 deep blue green eggs blotched and marked brown (Marchant 1960).
**Status and habitat:** Humid forest or forest borders, bushy clearings, and cultivated areas. Uncommon to fairly common in Santa Marta Mts.
**Range:** 1700-2800m. Perijá and Santa Marta mts. (*laubmanni*); mts. of s Nariño, s of Pasto (*chrysogaster*). W Mexico to Guatemala; Costa Rica and w Panama; n Venez. to n Colombia; extreme s Colombia to Peru.
**Note:** Some consider birds from n Venez. to Peru, *P. chrysogaster* (Golden-bellied Grosbeak), those from Costa Rica to w Panama, *P. tibialis* (Black-thighed Grosbeak), and those from Mexico and Guatemala, *P. chrysopeplus* (Yellow Grosbeak) as separate spp.

## 18. RED-CAPPED CARDINAL
*Paroaria gularis*          Pl. 55, Map 1410
**Identification:** 7″ (18cm). Unmistakable. Eyes white. *Glossy blue black above; entire head and upper throat scarlet*; lores and large triangular patch on lower throat black extending onto chest; *rest of underparts white* (or entire head,

throat, and central chest coming to a point on breast scarlet, broad band across sides of head black—*nigrogenis*). Imm.: scarlet on head replaced by buffy brown.
**Voice:** Song a clear, sweet, *suweet-chú*, repeated at short intervals (P. Schwartz recording); call a soft *chuép*.
**Behavior:** Pairs or families inspect bare sticks and twigs over water or 0.5-8m up in shrubbery at the edge of water. Flies low over water.
**Breeding:** BC ♂, 18 June, w Caquetá (Carriker). Begging juvs., 14 June, Leticia (J. V. Remsen); June–Sept breeding Guárico, Venez. (Thomas 1979b); upper Orinoco nests, 5 June and 6 Aug; thin, neat, rootlet cup low over water in marsh; 2-3 greenish white eggs with brown and mauve patches (Cherrie 1916).
**Status and habitat:** Common; marshes, shrubby lake and stream banks, and edges of *várzea* forest streams, esp. where there are partially submergd sticks and dead bushes that protrude or where bare shoreline is exposed.
**Range:** To 500m. From Arauca to n Meta and e Vichada (*nigrogenis*); s Meta (Macarena Mts.) and Río Guaviare southward (*gularis*). The Guianas and Venez. to n Bolivia and Amazonian Brazil. Trinidad.

## 19. PILEATED FINCH
*Coryphospingus pileatus*          Pl. 56, Map 1411
**Identification:** 5″ (13cm). ♂: *gray above with narrow white eyering; center of crown black concealing long scarlet crown stripe* (sometimes partially exposed); flight feathers and tail dusky; underparts whitish; sides pale gray. ♀: brownish gray above, crown browner; *lores and narrow eyering white*; underparts white, breast and sides tinged and very obscurely streaked gray.
**Similar species:** ♀ is rather nondescript, but nothing really resembles it. Look for white lores and eyering. Most ♀ seedeaters and grassquits are much browner; seedeaters also have obviously thicker bills.
**Voice:** Song in Venez. a deliberate ser. of flat, almost vireolike phrases, *tslip tslip tsweet, tslip tslip tsweet* (P. Schwartz recording).
**Behavior:** Alone, in pairs, or occas. loose groups; stays near ground or on it in dry scrub and thickets. Unobtrusive and easily overlooked.
**Breeding:** BC ♂, 7 June, Guajira (Carriker); nesting Mar–July, 1 nest, late Oct, Rodadero near Santa Marta (S. M. Russell).
**Status and habitat:** Common in arid scrub and arid open thorny woodland.
**Range:** To 450m. Guajira peninsula w to ne and s base of Santa Marta Mts; nw end at Rodadero near Santa Marta; upper Magdalena Val. (s Tolima and n Huila). Ne Colombia to n Venez.; e Brazil.

**Note:** Crimson Finch (*Rhodospingus cruentus*) of w Ecuador and w Peru may occur in coastal sw Nariño (rec. n to Esmeraldas, Ecuador near Nariño border). Small, 4.5″. ♂: *black above* or black scaled gray in fresh plumage; *center of crown scarlet; underparts pinkish red fading to pinkish brown on belly*; under wing coverts and patch at base of remiges white (prom. in flight). ♀: brown above, yellowish brown below becoming browner on sides; *under wing coverts white.* Dry scrub to moist or humid areas; up to 350m.

## 20. OLIVE FINCH
*Lysurus castaneiceps*              Pl. 54, Map 1412
**Identification:** 6″ (15cm). *Crown and nape chestnut; eyebrow, sides of head, throat, and chest gray;* otherwise entirely dull olive green; tail dusky olive.
**Similar species:** Sooty-faced Finch (21) has a conspic. white moustachial streak and ranges do not overlap. White-rimmed Brush-Finch (31) is larger, usually at *higher el.,* black (not olive) above and with a conspic. white eyering. Other brush-finches with chestnut caps are white, yellow, or gray below (not olive with gray throat).
**Status and habitat:** Rare and local. Ground or undergrowth in humid and wet forest.
**Range:** 700-2200m. Pacific slope s to nw Ecuador (no recs. Valle or Nariño); e slope of E Andes in se Nariño, prob. w Caquetá. Colombia, nw and e Ecuador; se Peru.

## 21. SOOTY-FACED FINCH
*Lysurus crassirostris*
**Identification:** 7″ (18cm). Only in mts. near Panama border. Mainly dark olive green; crown chestnut; sides of head and throat blackish with *prom. white moustachial streak*; center of breast and belly yellow. Juv.: dull brown above with paler brown cap; sides of head and throat dusky with indistinct moustachial streak; greenish brown below.
**Similar species:** None quite like it in its restricted range. Chestnut-capped Brush-Finch has a white throat and black chest band. Olive Finch (20) does not overlap in range.
**Voice:** Call a sharp thin whistled *pu-peee* while hidden in thick undergrowth (Ridgely 1976).
**Behavior:** Often in pairs or small groups on or near the ground in thick undergrowth of ravines or near streams; can sometimes be lured into open by imitation of its call (Ridgely 1976).
**Status and habitat:** Recently rec. in PN Los Katíos in n Chocó on slopes of Cerro Tacarcuna near Panama border (Rodríguez 1982).
**Range:** 1500-3100m in Panama. Extreme nw Colombia, Panama, and Costa Rica.

**Note:** *L. crassirostris* is considered a subsp. of Olive Finch (*L. castaneiceps*) by some.

## 22. TANAGER-FINCH
*Oreothraupis arremonops*         Pl. 54, Map 1413
**Identification:** 8″ (20cm). *Head and upper throat black with broad silver gray coronal stripe and eyestripes reaching to nape; otherwise ferruginous above and below,* much brighter on breast; center of lower breast and belly gray; tail blackish. Juv.: duller, mainly brownish with ferruginous back; black wings and tail; and faint head pattern.
**Similar species:** Handsome and easily recognized by boldly striped head and mostly ferruginous plumage.
**Voice:** Call, often steadily repeated at 2- to 3-sec intervals, a soft, froglike whistle, *wert,* easily imitated and easily overlooked; when foraging, sharp *tsip* and thinner *sink.*
**Behavior:** Brings to mind an *Atlapetes.* Pairs, families, or more often groups of 3-6 hop sluggishly near ground, on mossy logs, even on ground in thick undergrowth where peer and peck at foliage, stems, and fruit. Shy and inconspic. though can sometimes be lured into open with a whistled imitation of its call (Hilty). Scratches among ground litter (Carriker 1959).
**Breeding:** 1 dependent juv. followed 2 ads., June, w Cauca (Hilty and M. Isler). BC ♂, 8 June, Antioquia (Carriker).
**Status and habitat:** Infrequently seen though at least fairly common locally by voice; undergrowth of wet mossy forest ("cloud forest"); occas. forest borders. Reg. found on w slope Cerro Munchique.
**Range:** 1700-2300m (sightings to 2500m on Cerro Munchique, 1979—Hilty). Pacific slope at n end (Frontino, Antioquia) southward (most recs. in Cauca; none in Valle or Nariño). W Colombia and nw Ecuador.
**Note:** Taxonomic placement uncertain. Has been placed in Thraupidae, or incl. in the genus *Atlapetes.*

## 23. YELLOW-THROATED BRUSH-FINCH
*Atlapetes gutturalis*            Pl. 54, Map 1414
**Identification:** 7″ (18cm). Dusky gray above; *head black with white median crown stripe; throat bright yellow*; rest of underparts white; flanks and crissum washed brownish olive.
**Similar species:** Pale-naped Brush-Finch (24) has forepart of crown stripe orange to yellow and underparts all yellow (much brighter on throat). Also cf. 25, 27, and 30.
**Voice:** Weak, thin song a slow *o see me, o see, I'm weary, pity me* in Costa Rica (Skutch 1967), not heard often.
**Behavior:** Pairs or small families may skulk but are active and often readily seen. Peer and

hop in thick foliage, then flutter weakly to nearby thicket. Mostly 1-10m up and on ground less than some *Atlapetes*.
**Breeding:** 7 BC birds, May–June, W and C Andes (Carriker). In W Andes above Cali, 1 nest, 3 Mar (Hilty), 2 BC ♂♂, Mar–Apr, begging young, Mar and Sept (Miller 1963), begging young, June and Aug (S. Gniadek). Bulky grass cup low in weeds or bush; 2-3 white eggs (Skutch 1967).
**Status and habitat:** Fairly common in bushy forest borders and overgrown pastures or roadside thickets.
**Range:** 1500-2200m (once to 2600m; once to 800m at Remedios, e Antioquia). W Andes (s to Cerro Munchique, Cauca), C Andes and w slope of E Andes from Cundinamarca to head of Magdalena Val. S Mexico to Colombia.
**Note:** Merged with *A. albinucha* (White-naped Brush-Finch) of s Mexico by Paynter (1978).

### 24. PALE-NAPED BRUSH-FINCH
*Atlapetes pallidinucha*   Pls. 54, 55, Map 1415
**Identification:** 7″ (18cm). Gray tinged olive above; sides of head and neck black (forms a broad mask); *wide central crown orange to yellow on forecrown and fading to white on hindcrown*; throat bright yellow; rest of underparts dull olive yellow; flanks and crissum olive. Or sim. but back dark gray (*papallactae*).
**Similar species:** Moustached Brush-Finch (30) has all rufous crown and white moustache; Yellow-throated Brush-Finch (23) is usually found at lower el.
**Voice:** Song a weak, very high-pitched ser. of trills and sibilant notes (J. Silliman).
**Behavior:** Pairs or families hop on or near ground or peer in foliage and eat berries; mostly below 3m up. Regularly follow mixed flocks; skulk less than some *Atlapetes* and usually easy to see, sometimes even curious.
**Breeding:** 8 BC birds, Feb–Sept, C and E Andes (Carriker). Begging young, Mar, PN Puracé (Brown).
**Status and habitat:** Common in bushy forest borders, stunted shrubby second growth, dwarf forest, and brush up to treeline. Often with Slaty Brush-Finch, var. mountain-tanagers and flower-piercers.
**Range:** 2400-3600m (most numerous above 3000m). E Andes s to Cundinamarca (*pallidinucha*); C Andes from se Antioquia s through Nariño (*papallactae*). Extreme nw Venez. s to e and w Ecuador and n Peru.

### 25. RUFOUS-NAPED BRUSH-FINCH
*Atlapetes rufinucha*   Pl. 54, Map 1416
**Identification:** 6.5″ (16.5cm). *Crown and nape rufous chestnut*; sides of head black (forming a

mask); otherwise *slate gray above with white spot at base of primaries* (spot small or lacking—*simplex; phelpsi; spodionotus*); *bright yellow below*; shaded olive on flanks and crissum. Or forehead and upper throat black (*phelpsi*).
**Similar species:** Moustached Brush-Finch (30) is olive green (not slate gray) above and ads. have white throat (yellowish in imm.). Dusky-headed Brush-Finch (28) lacks rufous chestnut cap, white wing spot, and is much duller and dingier. Also cf. 27 and 29.
**Voice:** Fast, complicated, energetic song (about 2-3 sec) usually has 3-4 distinct parts, *t't't't't't'ut, weet-weet-weet-tu-tu-few-few-few*; with var.; the beginning trill is usually characteristic.
**Behavior:** Less shy and more arboreal than many *Atlapetes* (Paynter 1978), though also often hops on or near ground, sometimes partially in the open at the edge of pastures. Pairs or loose groups up to 6; not reg. with mixed flocks.
**Breeding:** 14 BC birds, Jan–June, and 2 juvs., Aug, Perijá Mts. and C Andes (Carriker). Sclater and Salvin (1879) report pale buff eggs speckled reddish brown chiefly around larger end.
**Status and habitat:** Bushy forest borders, second growth, overgrown pasture and roadside thickets. Common locally in headwaters of Cauca Val. (e of Popayán; Cerro Munchique).
**Range:** Spotty. 1600-2700m (to 3700m in Nariño). Perijá Mts. (*phelpsi*); E Andes in Boyacá from Soatá s to Lago de Fúquene at border of Cundinamarca (*simplex*); both slopes of C Andes in Antioquia (*elaeoprorus*); e slope W Andes in Valle and Cauca and w slope C Andes near Popayán (*caucae*); Andes of Nariño (*spodionotus*). Nw Venez. s in Andes to Peru and n Bolivia.

### 26. SANTA MARTA BRUSH-FINCH
*Atlapetes melanocephalus*   Pl. 54, Map 1417
**Identification:** 6.7″ (17cm). Santa Marta Mts. *Head and upper throat black with conspic. silvery gray cheek patch*; otherwise slate gray above; *yellow below*, shaded olive on flanks and crissum.
**Similar species:** Should not be confused. Look for the silvery cheeks. See Santa Marta Mountain-Tanager (p 618).
**Voice:** Loud, cascading song of chipping and twittering notes.
**Behavior:** A very active and conspic. thicket dweller, mainly 1-10m up. Pairs or groups of 3-7 are nuclear in mixed flocks and usually the most numerous sp. (T. B. Johnson).
**Breeding:** 6 BC birds, Jan–Apr, Cincinati (1500m) on nw slope, and Río Guatapurí (3200m) on se slope (Carriker). Fledglings and

ads., Nov–June, San Lorenzo (T. B. Johnson). Reported domed nest (Todd and Carriker 1922) needs confirmation.

**Status and habitat:** *Very common* in humid, shrubby, forest borders, and overgrown bushy pastures. Not inside mature forest.

**Range:** ENDEMIC. 1500-3200m (rarely to 600m). Santa Marta Mts.

## 27. TRICOLORED BRUSH-FINCH

*Atlapetes tricolor*          Pl. 54, Map 1418

**Identification:** 7″ (18cm). *Center of crown dark gold to brownish gold; sides of head black;* rest of upperparts dusky olive to blackish; *throat and median underparts yellow;* sides and under tail coverts olive.

**Similar species:** Appears very dark in field and not really like any other *Atlapetes* in range. Dusky-faced Tanager (p 632) is superficially sim. but has white eye, black throat, and is mainly a lowland bird with different habits.

**Voice:** Song a semiwhistled *seeuwee, swee swit-swit-swit,* or more complicated var. usually ending in 3-4 sim. notes. At dawn in w Nariño, excited finchlike *EEeu-tsit-tsit-tsueet,* or *EEeu-tsit tsit-tsit-t't't't't't-eet,* 1st note downslurred.

**Behavior:** A rather arboreal brush-finch and less of a skulker than some. Pairs or family groups peer and flutter or peck like ant-tanagers among foliage and dense mossy branches, mostly 1-10m up; often independent of mixed flocks (Hilty; Willis 1972b).

**Breeding:** In upper Anchicayá Val. (1000m) building nest, Nov, Feb, and May; 1 nest with eggs, 12 Apr; thin coarse cup near ground in rotten stump; 1 dull white egg densely spotted dusky throughout (Hilty). Begging juv., 19 June, w Ecuador (Paynter 1978).

**Status and habitat:** Fairly common in wet mossy forest ("cloud forest") borders, second growth, shrubby clearings, and openings inside forest. Poss. somewhat local.

**Range:** 800-2000m (to 300m in w Nariño). Pacific slope from headwaters of Río San Juan (Cerro Tatamá) southward (*crassus,* perhaps other subsp.?). One rec. on e slope of W Andes in Valle (San Antonio) may be erroneous. W Colombia, w Ecuador; e Peru.

## 28. DUSKY-HEADED BRUSH-FINCH

*Atlapetes fuscoolivaceus*       Pl. 54, Map 1419

**Identification:** 7″ (18cm). Only in upper Magdalena Val. *Head and indistinct malar stripe brownish black,* otherwise dark dull olive above, wings and tail duskier; *underparts bright yellow;* flanks shaded olive.

**Similar species:** See very rare Olive-headed Brush-Finch (29).

**Voice:** Distinctly 3-parted song, a very rapid, chippy, *ti-ti-ti-ti-ti-ti, tch-tch-tch-tch, chew-chew-chew,* slower and lower-pitched at end.

**Behavior:** Pairs or small groups are arboreal and active (recall Santa Marta Brush-Finch), hopping, peering, and pecking rapidly as search through thickets; mostly 0.5-6m up; less skulking than many *Atlapetes*.

**Breeding:** 7 BC birds, Feb–Apr, s Huila (Carriker).

**Status and habitat:** Common in bushy overgrown pastures, woodlots, second growth, and shrubby forest borders, less numerous inside forest where usually near tangled openings. Easily found near San Agustín and in PN Cueva de los Guácharos, Huila.

**Range:** ENDEMIC. 1600-2400m. Head of Magdalena Val. in Huila from PN Cueva de los Guácharos on the e (P. Gertler) to Río Moscopán (incl. Finca Merenberg) on the west.

## 29. OLIVE-HEADED BRUSH-FINCH

*Atlapetes flaviceps*               Map 1420

**Identification:** 7″ (18cm). Rare. *Dark olive above; head yellowish olive,* crown and lower auriculars somewhat darker; *eyering and lores conspic. yellow* extending back as faint superciliary; underparts deep yellow tinged olive on sides, flanks, and crissum.

**Similar species:** Dusky-headed Brush-Finch (28) has sooty (not yellowish olive) head, indistinct malar, and lacks the bold yellow eyering and lores; otherwise rather sim.; range overlap unproved but poss.

**Status and habitat:** Apparently very rare. Known from only 2 specimens taken over 65 yrs. ago and 3 birds netted and photographed 18-19 Dec 1967 by J. Dunning. Habitat apparently sim. to 28. Perhaps a lower el. replacement of closely allied Dusky-headed Brush-Finch.

**Range:** ENDEMIC. 1300-2100m. E slope of C Andes in a deep val. of Nevado de Tolima (2050-2150m at Toche and Río Toche) in n Tolima, and photos in n Huila below La Plata Vieja, Río de la Plata Val. (about 1300m).

## 30. MOUSTACHED BRUSH-FINCH

*Atlapetes albofrenatus*     Pls. 54, 55, Map 1421

**Identification:** 7″ (18cm). *Crown and nape rufous chestnut;* forehead and sides of head and neck black with white moustachial streak (not always separated from throat); otherwise olive green above; *throat white; rest of underparts yellow,* flanks and crissum shaded olive.

**Similar species:** Pretty and easily recognized by rufous chestnut cap, white throat, and yellow underparts. See Pale-naped and Rufous-naped brush-finches (24, 25).

**Voice:** Call, thin high-pitched *eeespe,* sometimes

trebled (Hilty); song in Venez., *czeet, czeet, czeet, czeet, tsu-tsu-tsu-tsu-tsu*, last notes a rattling ser. (P. Schwartz recording).
**Behavior:** Most like Tricolored Brush-Finch. Often well above ground, rather active, and not shy. Sometimes follows bird flocks.
**Breeding:** Imm., Jan, Boyacá (Borrero and Olivares 1955), juv., Aug, Perijá Mts. (Carriker).
**Status and habitat:** Fairly common. Tolerates a wide range of habitats from drier scrubby brushland to moist oak woodland to very humid forest and forest borders.
**Range:** 1000-2500m (mostly above 1600m). Both slopes of E Andes from Norte de Santander s to latitude of Bogotá (Fusagasugá). Nw Venez. to ne Colombia.

## 31. WHITE-RIMMED BRUSH-FINCH
*Atlapetes leucopis*                    Pl. 54, Map 1422
**Identification:** 7″ (18cm). Very dark. *Crown and nape rufous chestnut*; sides of head black with *large conspic. white eyering continuing behind as a short streak*; otherwise black above, lower back tinged olive; dark olive green below; throat dusky green.
**Similar species:** Slaty Brush-Finch (33) has white throat and malar streak and lacks eyering and postocular streak. See Olive Finch and Rufous-naped Brush-Finch (20, 25).
**Voice:** Song in PN Puracé, a soft chipping warble; begins with *twoo-twoo* . . . and ends with 4 or 5 musical chips (J. Silliman).
**Behavior:** Usually seen alone or in pairs very low in dense undergrowth. Notably secretive and skulking but sometimes curious and will come out to look over a patient observer. Frequently with mixed tanager, warbler, and finch flocks (J. Silliman; Hilty).
**Status and habitat:** Perhaps local (hard to see). Heavy undergrowth in very humid forest (esp. stunted high el. forest), dense forest borders and second growth brush on e side of PN Puracé above the Río Bedón, and above El Isnos. Not well known. Most specimens from se Nariño on Ecuador border (7, La Victoria; 4, Cerro Pax).
**Range:** 2300-3000m. E slope of C Andes at head of Magdalena Val. in Huila (La Plata; PN Puracé; and 1 sight rec., PN Cueva de los Guácharos—P. Gertler); e slope of Andes in Nariño (La Victoria; Cerro Pax) and w Putumayo (3 seen above Mocoa, km 120 at 2100-2200m, 1978, 1981—Hilty). E Ecuador.

## 32. OCHRE-BREASTED BRUSH-FINCH
*Atlapetes semirufus*                 Pl. 55, Map 1423
**Identification:** 6.5″ (16.5cm). Back, wings, and tail olive green; *entire head, neck, and underparts*

*orange rufous*; center of belly yellow; flanks and under tail coverts olive. Or sim. but back dark olive tinged gray (*zimmeri*).
**Similar species:** Not likely confused in limited range.
**Voice:** Song in Venez., *wheet, peet, p'tsu-tsu-tsu* var. to *eeet, wheet, sweet-sweet-sweet* (P. Schwartz recording).
**Behavior:** Alone, in pairs, or in families; hops on or near ground, where flicks leaves, or skulks in denser undergrowth, though normally not too difficult to see. Usually independent of mixed flocks.
**Breeding:** 5 BC birds, Nov, Norte de Santander (Carriker); 1 juv., Jan, e Boyacá (Olivares 1963).
**Status and habitat:** Humid shrubby forest borders, brushy second growth, and woodlots with thickets. Local (though perhaps formerly more widespread and numerous). In Cundinamarca taken only e and s of Bogotá (most recently at Une).
**Range:** 1600-3500m (mostly above 2500m). E slope of E Andes in Norte de Santander and upper Río Casanare, ne Boyacá (*zimmeri*); w slope E Andes in Boyacá (*majusculus*); e slope E Andes in s Boyacá and Cundinamarca s to Une, se of Bogotá (*semirufus*). N Venez. to ne Colombia.

## 33. SLATY BRUSH-FINCH
*Atlapetes schistaceus*           Pls. 54, 55, Map 1424
**Identification:** 7.0″ (18cm). *Crown chestnut; otherwise slate gray above*, blacker on head; *small white wing speculum; broad white moustachial streak* narrowly bordered black below; median throat and belly whitish *rest of underparts gray* (or blacker above, crown rufous chestnut, no white wing speculum, dark slaty gray below, paler on throat—*fumidus; tamae*).
**Similar species:** A mostly uniform dark gray finch with chestnut cap and white malar; likely confused only with less well known White-rimmed Brush-Finch (31).
**Voice:** Song in PN Puracé an energetic and complicated ser. of high-pitched squeaks and trills, usually ending in a distinctive *chewy-chewy-chewy* or *t'chew, t'chew, t'chew* (J. Silliman).
**Behavior:** A rather arboreal *Atlapetes* that reg. ascends well up in denser, smaller trees by hopping up through branches. Pairs or small groups are active and conspic., almost like tanagers, and common members of temperate zone mixed flocks.
**Breeding:** 16 BC birds, Apr–Sept, Perijá Mts. and n end of all 3 Andes (Carriker); 1 in Nov, Cundinamarca (MCN). Begging juvs., Apr and June, PN Puracé (J. Silliman).
**Status and habitat:** Common in bushes and

shrubs at forest edge, undergrowth of humid forest, and stunted mossy forest and brushland up to treeline.

**Range:** 1900-3700m (most numerous 2500-3300m). Perijá Mts. (*fumidus*); n end E Andes in s Norte de Santander, ne Santander, and e slope in n Boyacá (*tamae*); sw Boyacá and Cundinamarca s in E Andes, C and W Andes s to Nariño (*schistaceus*). Nw Venez. s in Andes to s Peru.

**Note:** White-winged Brush-Finch (*A. leucopterus*) of n Ecuador to n Peru may occur in s Nariño. Smallest *Atlapetes* (6″); crown rufous, sides of head black with white spot in front of eyes; above dark gray, wings and tail dusky, white wing speculum; underparts white. In n Ecuador favors dry scrubby highlands to 2900m.

## 34. CHESTNUT-CAPPED BRUSH-FINCH

*Atlapetes brunneinucha*     Pl. 55, Map 1425

**Identification:** 7.5″ (19cm). Crown chestnut narrowly edged bright cinnamon on sides; *forehead and sides of head black* with 3 small white spots across forehead (inconspic.); otherwise dark olive above; *puffy white throat bordered below by narrow black chest band*; rest of underparts grayish white; sides olive.

**Similar species:** Several *Atlapetes* have chestnut or rufous chestnut crowns, but none also have the mostly white underparts and black chest band of this attractive bird.

**Voice:** Call a high, almost inaudible *seeeep*; song in W Andes in Valle, 3-4 thin, squeaky notes (2d often lowest) followed by a thin trill, *tseee, tep, wee-teeeeeeee* (Hilty); in Venez., *peetee-zeeer, peetee-súueet* (P. Schwartz recording).

**Behavior:** Semiterrestrial and a notorious skulker that is easily overlooked but is curious and may hop up and puff out throat at a quiet observer. Single birds or pairs are quiet as they hop on ground or low in undergrowth and flick leaves with bill. Occas. join, but do not follow, bird flocks.

**Breeding:** 9 BC birds, Mar–Aug, Perijá Mts. and n end of all 3 Andes (Carriker); 3 BC birds and 3-mo.-old juv., Mar, W Andes above Cali (Miller 1963); 1 nest, 3 Mar, Queremal, Valle (Hilty); begging juv., June, 3 nests July–Aug, Pichindé Val. (S. Gniadek). Coarse bulky cup low in bush in forest; 1-2 eggs, pale bluish white (Carriker 1910).

**Status and habitat:** Usually common (but infrequently seen) in undergrowth of humid and wet forest; foothills and mts.

**Range:** 800-3000m (rarely above 2500m). Perijá Mts., the Andes, and Baudó and Macarena mts.; doubtless the mts. on Panama border (but not Santa Marta). Mexico to w Ecuador and s Peru.

## 35. STRIPE-HEADED BRUSH-FINCH

*Atlapetes torquatus*     Plates 54, 55, Map 1426

**Identification:** 7.5″ (19cm). Crown, nape, and sides of head black with *long gray median crown stripe and superciliary* reaching to nape; rest of upperparts olive green, tail darker; *below white*, sides shaded gray, flanks olive (or with black chest band—*perijanus; basilicus*).

**Similar species:** Black-headed Brush-Finch (36) has solid black head or at most some traces of gray (but not gray striped crown). Black-striped Sparrow (37) occurs at lower el.

**Voice:** Song a thin, weak, 5-noted phrase sometimes repeated several times, *twee-eet? twee-o-whew* in PN Puracé (J. Silliman); in Venez., *zuzeet, ah-z-teee* with var. as it rambles without clear break (P. Schwartz recording).

**Behavior:** Semiterrestrial. Single birds or pairs skulk in dense undergrowth and on or near ground where usually hard to see. Hop on ground, flicking leaves like Chestnut-crowned Brush-Finch.

**Breeding:** 15 BC birds, Feb–Aug, Perijá and Santa Marta mts. and Andes (Carriker). In Costa Rica, bulky cup low in bushes or vines; 2 white eggs (Skutch 1954).

**Status and habitat:** Uncommon to fairly common (often overlooked) in undergrowth of humid forest borders and thickety second growth up to treeline.

**Range:** 1700-3600m (most numerous ca. 2500-3100m). Santa Marta Mts. (*basilicus*); Perijá Mts. and e slope of E Andes in s Norte de Santander (*perijanus*); E Andes in Cundinamarca, C Andes, w slope W Andes at n end (Páramo Frontino), e slope W Andes in Cauca (Cerro Munchique), and the mts. of Nariño (*assimilis*). Costa Rica and w Panama; n Venez. s in mts. to w Peru and nw Argentina.

**Note:** Incl. *A. costaricensis* (Gray-striped Brush-Finch) of Costa Rica and w Panama, sometimes treated as a separate sp. (See Paynter 1978).

## 36. BLACK-HEADED BRUSH-FINCH

*Atlapetes atricapillus*     Pl. 54, Map 1427

**Identification:** 7.5″ (19cm). *Crown, nape, and sides of head to below eyes black*; otherwise olive green above; *throat and median underparts white*; sides gray; flanks and under tail coverts olive (or with vague traces of gray coronal and postocular stripes—*tacarcunae*).

**Similar species:** See Stripe-headed Brush-Finch (35) and Black-striped Sparrow (37).

**Voice:** Call a high penetrating *tsit*; thin weak song a high-pitched, short, *tsit*ing trill, almost insectlike (Slud 1964).

**Behavior:** Single birds or pairs skulk, mostly 1-3m up in undergrowth, and are difficult to see but curious and may hop up to look at an

observer. Usually do not follow mixed flocks.
**Breeding:** BC pair and juv., 20 May; 3 BC birds, late May and June, n end C Andes (Carriker). In Costa Rica, bulky cup nest 1-6m up in bush or vines; 2 white eggs (Skutch 1954).
**Status and habitat:** Uncommon and local in humid and wet forest, bushy forest borders, and dense old second growth. Not well known in most of Colombia.
**Range:** Spotty. 700-1500m; 500-1000m on Pacific slope. W slope of E Andes (Santander and Cundinamarca), e slope of C Andes in Caldas and Tolima, w slope at n end (Pto. Valdivia), n of W Andes in upper Sinú Val. and Pacific slope (*atricapillus*); Cerro Tacarcuna on Panama boundary (*tacarcunae*). Poss. n end W Andes. Sw Costa Rica to Colombia.
**Note:** Incl. the form *tacarcunae* of e Panama but not *costaricensis* of Costa Rica and w Panama. See taxonomy of these in Paynter (1978).

### 37. BLACK-STRIPED SPARROW
*Arremonops conirostris*          Pl. 55, Map 1428
**Identification:** 6.5″ (16.5cm) (or smaller 6″ [15cm]—*inexpectatus*). Head and nape gray with 2 black crown stripes and *narrow black stripe through eyes to nape*; rest of *upperparts olive green*; bend of wing yellow (often not obvious); below light gray, sides darker gray. Or darker more brownish olive above (*umbrinus*).
**Similar species:** See Tocuyo Sparrow (38).
**Voice:** Most birds sing 2 to several song types; typically a few slow spaced notes, then a ser. like a 1-cylinder engine starting up, e.g., in PN Tayrona, *wélop; wélop; te-tutututututututu-te* (Hilty), or near Melgar, Tolima, *chort-tea, tua, wepepepe, chóiter, chóiter, chóiter . . .*, up to 10 or more notes (B. Coffee recording); 1 call a sharp *ho-weéet* (Ridgely 1976). See note for song of *A. c. inexpectatus*.
**Behavior:** A rather shy semiterrestrial bird usually seen alone or in separated pairs. Hops on ground or in thickets or ascends a few meters up in bushes, esp. to sing. Distinctive song most often heard in early morning.
**Breeding:** 11 BC birds, May–Oct, Norte de Santander and n Antioquia, May nest with eggs, n Caldas (Carriker); 4 BC ♂ ♂, Oct–Dec, a May nest (Boggs 1961); 4 nests, Apr–May, Santa Marta (Todd and Carriker 1922). Open leafy cup near ground to 2m up; 2 white eggs (Stone 1918).
**Status and habitat:** Fairly common in dry to humid regions in bushy clearings, shrubby woodland borders, and cultivated areas with thickets. Replaced in arid Guajira by Tocuyo Sparrow.
**Range:** To 1600m. Pacific coast in n Chocó (lower Atrato Val. s to Sautatá) and from sw Cauca southward (*striaticeps*); Carib. lowlands

from Río Sinú region e to w Guajira, s in Magdalena Val. to Tolima, and e of Andes from Arauca to s Meta (Macarena Mts.), w Vaupés (San José del Guaviare), and ne Vichada (*conirostris*); Zulia Val. in e Norte de Santander (*umbrinus*); arid upper Magdalena Val. in Huila (*inexpectatus*). Honduras to w Ecuador, extreme n Brazil, and e Venez.
**Note:** The *inexpectatus* subsp. may be a distinct sp. (S. Olson) Song very different, at dusk near Altamira, Huila, *tsu'leép, tsuk-tsuk-tsuk-tsuk* (Hilty).

### 38. TOCUYO SPARROW
*Arremonops tocuyensis*          Pl. 55, Map 1429
**Identification:** 5″ (13cm). A smaller paler edition of Black-striped Sparrow. Differs mainly in *small size*, upperparts paler, more brownish gray (less olive), and *central crown stripe and superciliary paler, whitish tinged clay* (not obviously gray).
**Voice:** Songs in Venez. are thin, sweet *tit, tit'ti'ti'ti', tsuee tsuee*, or *sweeu, sweeu, eeee, tu'tu'tu'tu'* (*eeee* very high-pitched; chatter at end like House Wren); after playback *tuwey, tuwey, eeee, we'we'we'we'we'* (P. Schwartz recording).
**Behavior:** Like better known Black-striped Sparrow but prefers arid regions.
**Status and habitat:** Uncommon to fairly common (shy and inconspic.) on ground or in thickets in low, arid, deciduous woodland, and scrubby areas. Replaces Black-striped Sparrow in arid Guajira; both overlap in dry-arid transition w of Ríohacha.
**Range:** To 200m. Guajira Peninsula from lower Río Ranchería Val. and Ríohacha area eastward. Ne Colombia and nw Venez. (to 1100m).

### 39. ORANGE-BILLED SPARROW
*Arremon aurantiirostris*          Pl. 55, Map 1430
**Identification:** 6″ (15cm). *Bill bright orange*. Head *mostly black* with narrow gray central crown stripe and white eyestripe; rest of upperparts olive green; bend of wing yellow (sometimes concealed); *below white with black chest band*; sides, flanks, and lower belly brownish olive. Imm.: much duller, bill brown, chest band fainter.
**Similar species:** W of Andes could be confused only with Golden-winged Sparrow (40), a dry country bird with solid black head and yellow shoulders. May meet Pectoral Sparrow (41) along e base of Andes s of s Meta.
**Voice:** Song a *very high*, squeaky *t'sue-e-te t'sue-ee-sweet-eet* or sim. var., repeated at 10- to 15-sec intervals. Very high thin *sip* call.
**Behavior:** As in Pectoral Sparrow.
**Breeding:** 15 BC birds, Jan–May, s Bolívar to Chocó and Valle (Carriker); 3 in Feb–Apr, nw Colombia (Haffer 1975); bulky roofed nest

with broad side entrance on ground; 2 white eggs speckled brown (Skutch 1954).

**Status and habitat:** Fairly common (easily overlooked) in open undergrowth of humid and wet forest and older second growth.

**Range:** To 1000m (once to 1800m, Cerro Munchique, Cauca). Pacific coast, e along n base of W and C Andes and s in mid. Magdalena Val. to latitude of Bogotá (Chicoral, Tolima); e base of Andes in w Putumayo. S Mexico to w Ecuador and nw and ne Peru.

## 40. GOLDEN-WINGED SPARROW

*Arremon schlegeli*          Pl. 55, Map 1431

**Identification:** 6″ (15cm). *Bill orange yellow. Crown and sides of head continuing onto sides of neck and chest black*; mantle gray becoming olive on lower back; *shoulders yellow*; rest of wing and tail dark gray; *underparts white*, shaded gray on flanks. Imm.: black bill.

**Similar species:** A handsome bird easily told by yellow shoulders and contrasting black hood and yellow bill.

**Voice:** Song a high, sibilant *zeut, zeut, zeut, zeee*, repeated at short intervals (P. Schwartz recording).

**Behavior:** Sim. to Pectoral Sparrow but forages over a wider range of hts., sometimes well up in bushes and smaller trees.

**Breeding:** 8 BC birds, Apr–Sept, Perijá and Santa Marta mts., n end E Andes in Norte de Santander (Carriker).

**Status and habitat:** Uncommon to fairly common in dry to moist deciduous woodland, scrubby clearings, and thickets. Replaced in humid forest w of Andes by preceding sp., e of Andes by next sp.

**Range:** To 1300m. Carib. area from s of Cartagena (Snía. de San Jacinto) e to Guajira and w slope of Perijá Mts., locally s to drier parts of mid. Magdalena Val. in c Santander (San Gil) and Boyacá (Soatá). N Colombia and n Venez.

## 41. PECTORAL SPARROW

*Arremon taciturnus*          Pl. 55, Map 1432

**Identification:** 6″ (15cm). ♂: *head black with gray coronal stripe and long white eyestripe reaching to nape*; back bright yellow olive; *shoulders yellow*; rest of wings and tail dusky; *below white with black patch on sides of breast*; bill black above, yellow below (or complete black chest band, bill black—*taciturnus*). ♀: buffy below with suggestion of ♂'s black pattern.

**Similar species:** Orange-billed Sparrow (39) has bright orange bill, less contrast between back and wings, and much less extensive yellow on shoulders. Also see Black-striped Sparrow (37).

**Voice:** Song, an *extremely high*, thin, *spit, tseeee tseeee tseeee*, last 3 notes hissing and buzzy, almost to upper limit of hearing. Sharp *tsip* call like others of genus.

**Behavior:** An unobtrusive, semiterrestrial bird of shady woodland interior, found alone or in separated pairs. Hops and scratches on ground or perches a little above it; often sings from a log. Retiring but not a skulker like *Atlapetes*.

**Breeding:** Apr juv., Boyacá (Olivares 1963). Feeding young, 20 Sept, Pto. Inírida (Hilty); ♀ ready to lay, Apr, upper Orinoco (Cherrie 1916). Grassy, leafy, ball nest with side entrance low in shrub or palm base; 2 whitish eggs finely spotted brown and purple (Haverschmidt 1968).

**Status and habitat:** Fairly common (*hard to see*) in open undergrowth of humid forest and tall second growth woodland.

**Range:** To 600m (once 1400m, e Boyacá). E base of Andes s to Macarena Mts. (*axillaris*); extreme e from Orinoco region s to Pto. Inírida, ne Guainía, and Mitú, Vaupés (*taciturnus*). The Guianas, Venez., and ne and e Amazonian Brazil; se Peru to n Argentina.

## 42. SOOTY GRASSQUIT

*Tiaris fuliginosa*          Pl. 56, Map 1433

**Identification:** 4.5″ (11.4cm). Bill dusky. ♂: *entirely dull sooty black with olive tinge*; center of belly grayish brown. ♀: dull olive brown above, slightly brighter below paling to whitish cream on center of belly.

**Similar species:** Subad. ♂ Blue-black Grassquit (67) may be mixed olive and blackish or largely blue black with scattered olive feathers but always looks glossy (not dull sooty). Larger ♂ Lesser Seed-Finch (51) has heavier bill and conspic. white under wing coverts. ♀ is darker than ♀ Black-faced Grassquit (43), esp. below, but prob. not safely distinguished in field except with ♂. Dull-colored Grassquit (45) is paler with a grayish area around eye, pale (not dusky) lower mandible, and whitish or gray brown (not creamy) belly.

**Voice:** Song a thin, high and wiry *ezz-uda-lee*, given quickly and run together (P. Schwartz recording); call *chee*.

**Behavior:** In n Venez. seen singly or in pairs and small loose groups from near ground in grass to midlevel in trees at woodland edge.

**Breeding:** May and July–Dec, Trinidad; globular grass nest with side entrance, ground level to 10m up, usually low; 2-3 white eggs marked rich brown (ffrench 1973).

**Status and habitat:** Not well known in Colombia. Apparently local or seasonal in dry grassy scrub, along borders of moist to humid woodland or at grassy openings in lighter woodland .

**Range:** To 1000m(?). Upper Magdalena and upper Patía vals. (doubtless elsewhere at least seasonally). Locally in n and s Venez. (incl. Perijá Mts.), Guyana, and e Brazil. Trinidad.

### 43. BLACK-FACED GRASSQUIT
*Tiaris bicolor*                   Pl. 56, Map 1434
**Identification:** 4″ (10.2cm). Bill dusky above, dull yellow below. ♂: dull olive above; *fore-crown, sides of head, throat, and breast sooty black* shading to gray on belly; flanks tinged olive. ♀: pale olive gray, paler below becoming whitish on center of belly.
**Similar species:** ♂ like Yellow-faced Grassquit (44) but lacks yellow face pattern. ♀ doubtfully separable in field from ♀ Sooty Grassquit but smaller, overall much grayer (not brown) with center of belly whitish (not buffy cream), and usually in different habitat. Also see other ♀ *Sporophila* (all with heavier, less pointed bills).
**Voice:** Song a weak buzzing *tsee-tsee-tsee-seeseesee* sometimes given in short display flight with rapid vibrating wings in Curaçao (Voous 1955).
**Behavior:** Usually alone or in pairs below eye level in thickets.
**Breeding:** 1 BC ♂, July, s base Santa Marta Mts. (Carriker). Breeds Jan and Aug–Nov, Tobago; grassy dome-shaped nest with side entrance; usually low, occas. high; 2-3 whitish eggs marked pale red brown at larger end (ffrench 1973).
**Status and habitat:** Uncommon and local in arid scrub, low, thorny, deciduous woodland, and dry grassland with scattered bushes.
**Range:** To 1300m. Guajira Peninsula w to se base of Santa Marta Mts. (Camperucho); w slope of E Andes at n end (Norte de Santander to Soatá, Boyacá) s to upper Magdalena Valley. N Colombia to n Venez. Dutch Antilles, Trinidad, Tobago, W Indies.

### 44. YELLOW-FACED GRASSQUIT
*Tiaris olivacea*                  Pl. 56, Map 1435
**Identification:** 4″ (10.2cm). Dull olive above with blackish forecrown and sides of head; *eyebrow, eyering, and throat bright deep yellow*; breast black becoming grayish olive on rest of underparts. ♀ and imm. ♂: sim. but dull olive replaces black on head and breast; *yellow markings faintly indicated.*
**Similar species:** Facial pattern is diagnostic but often faint in ♀♀ and imms.
**Voice:** Song a weak buzzy trill *tttttt-tee*, almost insectlike.
**Behavior:** Usually in pairs, less often in small loose groups or with other seedeaters and Blue-black Grassquits. Eats seeds from ground or

by clinging to stems. Flight is short and buzzy.
**Breeding:** 7 BC birds, May–Aug, n Antioquia; 2 in June, w Caquetá (Carriker). Building nest, Aug, e Huila, June and Aug, upper Anchicayá Val. (Hilty); nesting in W Andes above Cali, Feb–July, perhaps yr.-round (Miller 1963); 1 nest in June, fledgling, Aug, Pichindé Val. (S. Gniadek). Grassy globular nest with side entrance, low in grass or small bush; white eggs spotted brown at larger end (Sclater and Salvin 1879).
**Status and habitat:** Common in semiopen country, grassy and bushy pastures and roadside shrubbery in foothills or higher, rarely lowlands.
**Range:** 600-2300m (to 300m on Pacific slope, Valle). W, C, and E Andes, and e of Andes in w Caquetá (near Florencia, 300m). Not Carib. region or Santa Marta. E Mexico to w Venez. Greater Antilles.

### 45. DULL-COLORED GRASSQUIT
*Tiaris obscura*                   Pl. 56, Map 1436
**Identification:** 4.5″ (11.4cm). Bill more slender than *Sporophila*, almost conical; *upper mandible dark, lower yellowish.* Sexes sim. Grayish brown above, wings browner; slightly grayish around eyes (hard to see); below brownish gray shading to whitish on center of belly (or underparts uniform grayish brown—*haplochroma*); under tail coverts tinged rusty brown.
**Similar species:** Confusing and easily overlooked. The key is the slender 2-toned bill. Esp. watch flocks of uniformly hen-plumaged seedeaters; in other seedeater and grassquit flocks there are almost always a few ad.-plumaged ♂♂ present.
**Voice:** Song in Peru a trilling *zerisleree-zerisleree* (Koepcke 1970).
**Behavior:** Usually in small solid flocks, seldom mixed with other seedeaters or seed-finches. Like other seedeaters, stays rather low.
**Breeding:** 8 BC birds, June–Sept, Santa Marta and Perijá mts., n end C and E Andes (Carriker).
**Status and habitat:** Uncommon and local. Woodland borders, forest clearings, and shrubby areas. More of a woodland edge bird than other *Tiaris* or *Sporophila*.
**Range:** Mainly below 1600m. Perijá Mts. and n and e slope of Santa Marta Mts. (*haplochroma*); lower Cauca Val. (above Pto. Valdivia) and Pacific coast from Valle (Dagua Val.) to Nariño; both slopes above mid. Magdalena Val. (to 2100m) from Santander to Cundinamarca (*obscura*). Prob. more widespread. Nw Venez. locally to nw Peru and nw Argentina.
**Note:** Often placed in *Sporophila* where called Dull-colored Seedeater.

## 46. PARAMO SEEDEATER

*Catamenia homochroa* Pl. 56, Ill. 98, Map 1437
**Identification:** 4.7" (12cm). Thick stubby bill yellowish (much brighter in ♂), more slender, and pointed than other *Catamenia* (this not obvious in field). ♂: *dark slate gray,* inconspic. streaked blackish on mantle; *foreface blackish; under tail coverts chestnut.* ♀: above dark olive brown *streaked dusky;* underparts buffy brown with a few inconspic. dusky streaks; *under tail coverts chestnut* (or throat grayish brown streaked dusky—*oreophila*).
**Similar species:** Dark ♂ distinctive. ♀ easily confused with Plain-colored Seedeater (see 47) but decidedly darker and browner.
**Behavior:** Usually feeds low in thick shrubbery or by hopping on ground near cover; alone, pairs, or in small flocks and often with mixed

98. PARAMO SEEDEATER (♂ top),
BAND-TAILED SEEDEATER
(♂ middle; ♀ bottom)

flocks of tanagers, flower-piercers, and brush-finches.
**Breeding:** 6 BC birds, July, Perijá Mts. and n end C Andes (Carriker).
**Status and habitat:** Fairly common in dense stunted forest, thick forest borders, and brush near or above treeline (not open grassy fields—cf. Plain-colored Seedeater, 47).
**Range:** 2800-3800m. Santa Marta Mts. (2200-3300—*oreophila*); Perijá Mts. (Cerro Pintado, 3400m) and locally in all 3 Andean ranges (*homochroa*). Nw Venez. s in Andes to n Bolivia; highlands of s Venez. and ne Brazil.
**Note:** Incl. *C. oreophila* (Santa Marta Seedeater) now considered a subsp. of *C. homochroa* (Meyer de Schauensee 1970). Ad. ♂ of *oreophila* unknown. Only 6 known specimens.

## 47. PLAIN-COLORED SEEDEATER

*Catamenia inornata* Pl. 56, Map 1438
**Identification:** 5" (13cm). *Stubby bill pinkish orange.* ♂: dull *brownish gray streaked dusky on back;* underparts pale gray becoming grayish buff on belly; *under tail coverts chestnut.* ♀: brownish buff streaked dusky above, pale yellowish buff below; *faintly streaked dusky on throat and chest; under tail coverts washed chestnut.* Imm.: pale buffy brown streaked above and below with dusky.
**Similar species:** ♂ resembles ♀ Paramo Seedeater (46), but upperparts grayer (not decidedly brown) and bill duller and pinkish (not yellow). The 2 usually are not found in the same habitat. ♀ is much paler and buffier below than ♀ Paramo Seedeater (46) and usually faintly streaked below (more prom. in imm.). Also see Band-tailed Seedeater (48).
**Voice:** Somewhat var. (poss. geographical dialects); typical song (Cundinamarca; Nariño) 2-3 musical notes then 2-4 slow buzzes, *chittita zree, bzzz, bree* (inhale, exhale, inhale).
**Behavior:** The most common high el. seedeater. Separated pairs when breeding but otherwise usually in flocks of its own of var. size, sometimes quite large. Feeds mostly on ground in open or in short grass.
**Breeding:** 8 BC birds, late Jan–early Feb, PN Puracé; 3 in late July–early Aug, Santander; 3 in Sept, Boyacá (Carriker); Apr juvs., PN Puracé (J. Silliman); Aug juvs., Pasto; singing ♂♂, Páramo Neusa, Aug–Sept (Hilty). 1 BC ♂, Aug, PN Chingaza (W. McKay).
**Status and habitat:** Common in open grassland, paramo, pastures, and fence-rows with or without scattered shrubs and hedges. Sometimes also shrubby areas, but favors much more open areas and seen more often than forest-based ally, Paramo Seedeater.
**Range:** 2200-3800m (usually above 2700m). E

Andes from Norte de Santander and C Andes from Caldas s through Nariño. Nw Venez. s in Andes to nw Argentina and n Chile (sight).

## 48. BAND-TAILED SEEDEATER
*Catamenia analis*          Ill. 98, Map 1439
**Identification:** 4.8″ (12.2cm). Thick stubby bill pale yellowish white. ♂: *plain gray*, paler below with *chestnut under tail coverts*; tail blackish with a *broad white band across center of inner webs of all but central feathers* (visible from underside or in flight). ♀: grayish brown streaked dusky above (sparrow back); buffy white streaked dusky below; tail as in ♂ but spots smaller; no chestnut on crissum. Imm. ♂: like ♀; may show small white wing speculum.
**Similar species:** Unstreaked ♂ easily recognized by conspic. white band in tail (not visible from above when perched). If in doubt flush the bird. ♀ can be confused with ♀ and esp. imm. Plain-colored Seedeater (47; latter obviously streaked above and below) but *always* shows white in tail. ♀ Paramo Seedeater (46) is darker above, buffy brown below (not buffy white), and lacks white in tail.
**Voice:** Song a faint note and flat, buzzy trill, *tic bzzzzzz.*
**Behavior:** Usually alone or in scattered pairs; feeds low in grass or hops on ground. Sings from top of bush or other low exposed perch; flight undulating.
**Breeding:** Persistently singing ♂♂, Aug–Sept, Páramo Neusa (Hilty); 2 juvs., Feb and Mar, e slope Santa Marta Mts. (Carriker).
**Status and habitat:** Fairly common to common locally in open grassy areas with shrubs and scattered trees; temperate zone to paramo. Apparently quite local in C Andes (no recs. in PN Puracé).
**Range:** Santa Marta Mts. (2700-4600m), E Andes (2600-3200m) in Boyacá and Cundinamarca; generally in C Andes from Caldas (Nevado del Ruiz area) s through Nariño. Colombia s in Andes to c Argentina and Chile.

## 49. [WHITE-NAPED SEEDEATER]
*Dolospingus fringilloides*     Pl. 56, Ill. 100, Map 1440
**Identification:** 5.2″ (13.2cm). *Large pale bill conical and sharp pointed.* Tail rather long. ♂: upperparts, head, and upper throat black with *1 large broad white wing bar and 1 narrow small bar*; small white patch on nape (usually concealed in field) and whitish patch on rump; below white with *narrow white line extending up on sides of neck almost to nape.* ♀: cinnamon brown above and below, paler on throat; center of lower breast, and belly buffy white.
**Similar species:** ♂ most like ♂ Variable Seed-

eater (57; *murallae* subsp.) but larger, bill shape and color different (much heavier, more conical, very sharply pointed, and *pale*), and only 1 conspic. wing bar. Confusing ♀ looks like a ♀ *Sporophila* but larger; ♀ Lesser Seed-Finch (51) lacks the whitish on lower underparts; ♀ Blue-black Grosbeak (3) has even heavier black (not pale) bill.
**Voice:** Song a loud, fast *ne-ne-ne te-te-te ge-ge-ge-jüi jüi jjü, tu-e tu-e tu-e, tu-ée tu-ée tu-ée* or sim. var., the triplets, each on different pitch, apparently being characteristic.
**Behavior:** One ♂ seen from near ground to 4m up in thickets. More wary and less easily observed than a *Sporophila*; responsive to taped playback.
**Status and habitat:** Hypothetical. One sight rec. (with voice recording), 21 Feb 1978, s of Mitú, Vaupés (Hilty). At Mitú, in a dense arum-filled opening in very open, scrubby, sandy-belt (white sand) forest.
**Range:** To 250m. E Vaupés (Mitú), doubtless e Guainía. Sw Amazonas, Venez. (near Cerros Yapacana and Duida), and upper Río Negro of Brazil on Río Xie (15km w of se tip of Guainía, Colombia).

## 50. BLUE SEEDEATER
*Amaurospiza concolor*          Map 1441
**Identification:** 5″ (13cm). Sw Nariño. Bill dusky. ♂: *uniform dark indigo blue*, slightly brighter on forehead and eyebrow; *lores, ocular area, and chin blackish* (hard to see in field); under wing coverts white. ♀: *fairly bright cinnamon brown*, paler below; under wing coverts dark. Some birds (imm. ♂♂?) are dark rufous brown.
**Similar species:** ♂ recalls ♂ Blue-black Grassquit (67) but is larger, bluer, and bill obviously heavier. Indigo Bunting (2), a rare winter visitant, is brighter blue. ♂ Slaty Finch (72), usually at higher el., is dark gray with thinner pointed bill. Caution is urged in separating ♀, which is brighter and more uniform than other ♀ seedeaters; it is most like ♀ Lesser Seed-Finch (51) in coloration but lacks latter's almost grotesquely heavy bill and white under wing coverts.
**Voice:** Song by ♂ in nw Ecuador a short, warbled, *sweet sweet sweet sa-wéet*, weak and colorless.
**Behavior:** Poorly known. Usually singly or in pairs (not flocks) within 1-2m of ground, occas. somewhat higher.
**Status and habitat:** Rare and local. Shrubby forest borders and roadside second growth on humid forested slopes in nw Ecuador 1200-1800m. In w Panama shows a strong affinity for bamboo.
**Range:** 1100-1200m. Pacific slope in Nariño

(Ricaurte; San Pablo). S Mexico to c Panama; sw Colombia and nw Ecuador.

[*Oryzoborus*: Much like *Sporophila* (perhaps best treated as such, see note); differs in large size, thicker more massive bill and *virtually straight* culmen. ♀♀ are richer brown than *Sporophila* and always with white wing linings.]

## 51. LESSER SEED-FINCH
*Oryzoborus angolensis*        Pl. 56, Map 1442
**Identification:** 5" (13cm). *Very heavy black bill.*
♂: glossy black; *under wing linings and small wing speculum white.* Some birds in Santa Marta area have chestnut on belly. Or as above but *breast to under tail coverts deep chestnut* (*angolensis*); or breast and belly chocolate brown (*theobromae*). ♀: brown above, cinnamon brown below, *white under wing linings as in* ♂.
**Similar species:** See Large-billed and Great-billed seed-finches (52, 53). ♀ from other ♀ *Sporophila* with which often assoc. by larger size, darker coloration, and white wing linings.
**Voice:** Song a long sweet ser. of whistles changing about midway to faster warbles and twitters that gradually fade, the 1st part like an Indigo Bunting, *techu, techu chu chi, techu chu chi . . .* and so on.
**Behavior:** Usually singly or in pairs but unlike Large-billed Seed-Finch, sometimes also with other seedeaters and grassquits though rarely as numerous. Gleans grass seeds by clinging to stems or by dropping to ground.
**Breeding:** 5 BC birds, May–Oct, Santander and Antioquia, 1 in June, w Caquetá (Carriker); 2 BC birds, Feb, w Santander (Boggs 1961), Aug and Nov, ne Meta (S. Furniss). Thin grass cup low in bush; 2 greenish white eggs thickly spotted brown, esp. at larger end (Sclater and Salvin 1879).
**Status and habitat:** Fairly common in shrubby and grassy forest or woodland borders, around woodlots, or in clearings; humid zones.
**Range:** To 1600m. Pacific coast s to Valle (Cauca?), humid lowlands n of Andes, lower Cauca Val., mid. Magdalena Val. s to Caldas, and Santa Marta area (*ochrogyne*); w Nariño (*aethiops*); upper Magdalena Val. s to s Huila (*theobromae*); e of Andes throughout (*angolensis*). Se Mexico to ne Argentina and se Brazil. Trinidad.
**Note 1:** Some consider *O. funereus* (Thick-billed Seed-Finch) of Mid. America, Colombia w of E Andes, and w Ecuador, distinct from the *O. angolensis* group (Chestnut-bellied Seed-Finch) e of Andes. Intermeds. with mixed black and chestnut bellies are known from Santa Marta area (Meyer de Schauensee 1966) and upper Magdalena Val. (Olson, 1981a). **Note 2:** Some

suggest placing *Oryzoborus* in *Sporophila*. Hybrids between the 2 genera are not uncommon in Brazil (Sick 1963; Olson, 1981b).

## 52. LARGE-BILLED SEED-FINCH
*Oryzoborus crassirostris*        Pl. 56, Map 1443
**Identification:** 5.5-5.8" (14-14.7cm). *Thick, massive bill chalky white* (♂) *or dark brown* (♀). ♂: *glossy black* with white wing speculum; *under wing coverts and bend of wing white* (conspic. in flight); tail rather long. ♀: brown above, richer buffy brown below; under wing coverts white.
**Similar species:** Closely resembles white-billed form of Great-billed Seed-Finch (53), but ♂ of latter has inconspic. or no wing speculum, and under wing coverts are white mixed black. Smaller ♂ Lesser Seed-Finch (51) has black (not whitish) bill and e of Andes a chestnut belly. More difficult ♀ is larger and deeper buff below than ♀ Lesser Seed-Finch and has proportionally heavier bill.
**Voice:** Song a notably rich, mellow, whistled *twee teer, d'd'd'd twée-teer, twée-teer, twéet-ear, du-weet, du-weet*; also *chut-eet, wheet-wheet-wheet* and other var. (P. Schwartz recording in Venez. of subad. ♂ excited by a caged bird.)
**Behavior:** Less social than seedeaters and usually seen singly or in pairs. Small flock in Mar in lower Atrato Val. (Haffer 1975).
**Breeding:** 1 BC ♂, Mar, n Antioquia (Carriker); juv., May, 2 fledglings, Aug, Vaupés (Olivares 1964b; Olivares and Hernández 1962); stem and grass nest low in bush; 2-3 grayish brown eggs blotched and lined dark brown and lilac (Sclater and Salvin 1879).
**Status and habitat:** Locally fairly common in tall grass and brush near water, and riparian woodland, and borders of second growth woodland. Not in open grassy areas favored by seedeaters and grassquits. Fairly numerous in w Meta at Hacienda La Corocora (W. McKay).
**Range:** To 1000m. N of Andes in upper Sinú and Nechí drainage to mid. Magdalena Val. in s Cesar (Gamarra) and s in Cauca Val. to Medellín; n base Santa Marta Mts. (sighting, PN Tayrona, Aug 1978—Hilty); upper Patía Val. (sightings Apr 1968—Brown; F. C. Lehmann); e of Andes in Norte de Santander (sighting Cúcuta area, June 1980—Hilty and P. Hall) s to Meta (e to Carimagua—S. Furniss) and Vaupés (Mitú). Prob. locally s to Río Amazon (rec. at Pebas, n Peru). N Colombia e to the Guianas and s to the Amazon and ne Peru. Trinidad.

## 53. GREAT-BILLED SEED-FINCH
*Oryzoborus maximiliani*        Ill. 99, Map 1444
**Identification:** ♂ sim. to Large-billed Seed-Finch

99. Great-billed Seed-Finch

(52), but *white wing speculum inconspic. or lacking*; under wing coverts white mixed black; bill yellowish white; ♀ not distinguishable in the field from 52 (*occidentalis*). Or ♂ much larger (6.5″, or 16.5cm) and longer-tailed (65-71mm vs 53-59mm) than 52 with *enormous blackish horn bill*; no visible wing speculum, under wing coverts white; ♀ larger, and with more massive bill than 52 (*gigantirostris*).
**Similar species:** Also see smaller Lesser Seed-Finch (51).
**Breeding:** 1 BC ♂, Jan, sw Cauca (Olivares 1958); 3 nests with eggs, May–June, nw Santander (Boggs 1961).
**Status and habitat:** Very common at Guapí, sw Cauca where it frequents rice plantations and bushes along the river (R. Ridgely; Olivares 1958). At Limoncocha, e Ecuador, it is uncommon in trees and shrubs along the lake edge (Pearson et al. 1977).
**Range:** To 1700m. Pacific Cauca and Nariño (Guayacana); upper Cauca Val. (El Tambo) but no recent recs.; Magdalena Val. in Cundinamarca (La Vega, Sasaima) n to El Centro, Santander (*occidentalis*); e of Andes in Putumayo (*gigantirostris*). Nicaragua to w Panama; e Venez., Guyana and Fr. Guiana, e Ecuador, ne Peru, n Bolivia, and c and e Brazil.
**Note:** Taxonomy follows Meyer de Schauensee (1970) but more work is needed. The black-billed birds from Putumayo, Colombia to Bolivia may be a separate sp. and the Pacific coast birds may be a subsp. of Large-billed Seed-Finch. Both subsp. have been considered subspp. of Large-billed Seed-Finch.

## 54. SLATE-COLORED SEEDEATER
*Sporophila schistacea*          Pl. 56, Map 1445
**Identification:** 4.5″ (11.4cm). *Bill yellow* (♂);

grayish (♀); culmen straight or only slightly curved. ♂: *mostly slate gray*, blacker on wings and tail (blackish around base of bill—*longipennis*); *small white patch on sides of neck* (sometimes not obvious in field) and white wing speculum; some *also with faint to prom.* narrow white wing bar; center of breast and belly white. ♀: olive brown above, paler brownish buff below.
**Similar species:** Like Gray Seedeater (55) but much darker, with *white neck patch*, and with more contrast between dark flanks and white of central underparts; birds with wing bar easily told. ♂ Plumbeous Seedeater (56) has blackish bill. Other "gray" seedeaters are at higher el. ♀ doubtfully separable from ♀ Gray Seedeater and other more or less dark-billed ♀ seedeaters.
**Voice:** Song a very high, sibilant, rapid *zit, zit, ze'z'z'z'z'ze-ze-ze-tuwe-tuwe-tuwe* or sim.; loud vigorous, parulidlike, and much less musical and less var. than song of Gray Seedeater (P. Schwartz recording).
**Behavior:** Scattered individuals, pairs, or less often small loose groups. Frequently perch quite high in trees or bamboo.
**Breeding:** 2 BC ♂♂, Sept, Río Porce, e Antioquia (Carriker). June nests, mid. Orinoco (Caicara); thin-walled rootlet and horsehair cup 2-4m up in small tree or spiny palm; 3 grayish white eggs dotted and blotched darker (Cherrie 1916). Confirmation desirable.
**Status and habitat:** Sporadic. Populations shift from time to time, sometimes common, then disappearing completely. Apparently wanders to burned seedling areas in forest, or thickets and borders of forest and second growth of var. ages. Sometimes a short distance inside tall humid forest.
**Range:** Spotty. To 2000m. Pacific slope from Río San Juan headwaters to Nariño (*incerta*); sw Córdoba (Quimarí) e to mid. Magdalena Val. in Norte de Santander (Las Ventanas) s to e Antioquia (Remedios; Río Porce), Cauca Val. in s Antioquia (Medellín), and sight recs. in Valle (*schistacea*) (Hilty et al.); e of Andes in Macarena Mts. (*longipennis*). Perhaps elsewhere e of Andes (rec. on Río Napo near Peru boundary). S Mexico to w Ecuador, n Bolivia, the Guianas, and ne Brazil.

## 55. GRAY SEEDEATER
*Sporophila intermedia*          Pl. 56, Map 1446
**Identification:** 4.5″ (11.4cm). ♂: sim. to Slate-colored Seedeater but *paler, more bluish gray* (not slate gray), *no white patch on sides of neck*, bill a little more swollen with curved culmen, and never with white wing bar (often lacking in Slate-colored). ♀: sim. to and prob. insep-

arable in field from Slate-colored Seedeater.
**Similar species:** See Slate-colored Seedeater (54); in hand separated from latter by greater depth of upper mandible (4.5mm vs 3mm), shorter wing (less than 60mm vs 60mm or longer), longer tarsus (15mm or more vs 14mm or less; Meyer de Schauensee 1952). Also see Plumbeous Seedeater (56).
**Voice:** Song a spirited ser. of musical twitters, chips, and trills usually beginning, *chu chu chu-wee* . . . , much richer, more var., and lower-pitched than that of Slate-colored Seedeater.
**Behavior:** Much less a bird of woodland or shrubby borders than Slate-colored Seedeater. Pairs or small loose groups often flock with other seedeaters and grassquits.
**Breeding:** 5 BC birds, Nov, Cúcuta; 2 in May, s Bolívar; 2 in Apr, Huila (Carriker); 2 in Jan and 1 in May, W Andes above Cali (Miller 1963); 1 in June, upper Río Sinú (Haffer 1975); 1 in Jan and May nest, w Santander (Boggs 1961). Thin cup 2-7m up in bush or small tree; 2-3 eggs, creamy, marked dark brown (ffrench 1973).
**Status and habitat:** Usually common in open grassy and bushy areas, less numerous along forest borders and in overgrown clearings. This is *the* "gray" seedeater most likely to be seen in most of lowland Colombia.
**Range:** To 2300m. Pacific coast only from s Chocó (lower Río San Juan) to Valle; otherwise w of Andes throughout except e Guajira; e of Andes s to w Meta (Villavicencio) and ne Guainía (Pto. Inírida). Colombia, Venez. and Guyana.
**Note:** A blackish race (*anchicayae*) described from the Anchicayá Val. and erroneously attributed to this sp. (Miller 1960) is *S. americana* (Variable Seedeater).

## 56. PLUMBEOUS SEEDEATER
*Sporophila plumbea*          Pl. 56, Map 1447
**Identification:** 4.3″ (10.9cm). *Bill blackish.* ♂: bluish gray above, lighter below; distinct *small white spot below eye*; chin, malar area, and center of lower breast to crissum white; wings and tail blackish, feathers edged gray; small wing speculum and usually concealed edge of shoulder white. ♀: light brown above; *small light gray spot below eye*; sides of head and underparts yellowish buff; wings darker edged brownish buff. Imm. ♂: like ♀ but with white wing speculum.
**Similar species:** ♂ is only "gray" seedeater in Colombia with a dark bill (see Slate-colored, 54, and Gray seedeaters, 55), also Pileated Finch (19). ♀ poss. separable from other dark-billed ♀ *Sporophila* by light gray area below eye.
**Voice:** Song in Venez. a long ser. of loud, vig-

orous, clear phrases, *queet ut, heet ut-ut, heet uh, chut-et, chue-et, tu'et tu'et, cheet cheet, s'few s'few s'few, wáit-ter, wáit-ter, queet, ut,* with var. in sequence (P. Schwartz recording).
**Breeding:** 5 BC ♂ ♂, May–June, Santa Marta Mts. and s Bolívar (Carriker), 2 in June–July, ne Meta (S. Furniss).
**Status and habitat:** Savanna, usually near damp places or water, or at edges of marshes; reg. in ne Meta (S. Furniss).
**Range:** To 1500m. Se base of Santa Marta Mts. (Cesar Val.) and n end of C Andes (Snía. San Lucas); e of E Andes from Río Casanare to s Meta (Macarena Mts.) and e to n Vichada (Remolino), prob. to ne Guainía. Ne Colombia, Venez. (incl. Perijá Mts. and Amazonas), and the Guianas; s Peru and n Bolivia to Paraguay and s Brazil.

## 57. VARIABLE SEEDEATER
*Sporophila americana*          Ill. 100, Map 1448
**Identification:** 4.3″ (10.9cm). Bill blackish, culmen curved. ♂: *glossy black above* with small white wing speculum; *rump white* sometimes mixed gray; lower *throat and band continuing up behind ear coverts white*; upper throat and *broad breast band black*; rest of underparts white mottled gray and black on sides. Or all white below with narrow black chest band (*ophthalmica*); or 4.7″ (12cm); black chest band narrow; interrupted or lacking and *narrow white wing bar* on median coverts; indistinct or lacking on greater coverts (*murallae*). ♀: dull olive brown above, paler more buffy brown below becoming yellowish buff on belly.
**Similar species:** ♂ is only boldly patterned "black-and-white" seedeater on Pacific coast. E of Andes easily confused with Double-collared Seedeater (62), which is grayish brown above, lacks wings bars, and has chin and upper throat black. Lesson's and Lined seedeaters (59, 58) have entire head and throat black and conspic. white malar. Also see White-naped Seedeater (49). ♀ not usually safely separable from other dark-billed ♀ seedeaters in field but lower underparts "yellower."
**Voice:** Song in Panama a musical *chee-a, chee-a, chee-aweet, o-wee, tweet o-wee toche tiche* (Gross 1952); song sim. e of Andes.
**Behavior:** Pairs or small flocks, often with other seedeaters and grassquits, cling to grass stems and eat seeds.
**Breeding:** 4 BC birds, Dec–Mar, Chocó and nw Antioquia, 3 in June, w Caquetá (Carriker); 1 in Mar, nw Chocó (Haffer 1975); 1 in Apr, Anchicayá Val., Valle (Miller 1960); 1 in Jan, Cauca; 1 in June, Putumayo (Olivares 1958; 1966). In Panama, May–Oct; neat grass and rootlet cup near ground to 8m up in grass,

100. Variable Seedeater (*hicksii* race) (top) (♀ left; ♂ right), Double-collared Seedeater (♂ bottom left), Variable Seedeater (*murallae* race) (♂ bottom center), White-naped Seedeater (♂ bottom right)

bush, or small tree; 2 eggs, pale gray speckled and blotched dark gray and brown (Gross 1952).

**Status and habitat:** Grassy and shrubby areas, and overgrown pastures, roadsides, and forest borders. Common on Pacific slope and e of Andes at Leticia.

**Range:** To 1200m. Pacific coast from both sides of Gulf of Urabá s to Valle (*hicksii*); Pacific coast from Valle (Los Cisneros) to Nariño (*ophthalmica*); e of Andes from w Caquetá to Putumayo (*murallae*); sight recs. n to Meta (Caño Duda, Macarena Mts., Dec 1975—T. Lemke and P. Gertler), Vaupés (Mitú, Feb 1978—Hilty), and s to Amazonas (Leticia—J. V. Remsen). Se Mexico to the Guianas, Amazonian Brazil, and e and w Peru. Tobago and Chacachacare Isl. (not Trinidad).

**Note:** Some consider the form *S. aurita* (Variable Seedeater) of C America and w Colombia to w Peru a separate sp. from *S. americana* (Wing-barred Seedeater) e of Andes.

## 58. LINED SEEDEATER
*Sporophila lineola*          Pl. 56, Map 1449

**Identification:** 4.5″ (11.4cm). Bill blackish (♂), *dull yellow* (♀). ♂: upperparts, head, and throat black; *narrow crown stripe* (sometimes only faintly

indicated) and *broad malar patch white*; rump and lower underparts white; wing speculum white (prom. stripe in flight). ♀: olive brown above, buffy below; center of belly whitish.

**Similar species:** Lesson's Seedeater (59) is very sim., but ♂'s crown is solid black, and flanks, sides, and sometimes chest more or less mottled black. ♀ is indistinguishable in field from ♀ Lesson's but differs from dark-billed ♀ *Sporophila* in having pale yellow bill.

**Voice:** Song in Venez. several short, spaced, whistles followed by a rattle, *dit dit dit-drdrdrdr*, very different from Lesson's Seedeater (P. Schwartz 1975).

**Behavior:** Near Leticia seen singly or more often in loose flocks clinging or perching on grass stems (not a ground forager).

**Status and habitat:** Uncommon and local. Seasonal resident (not known to breed in Colombia or Venez.) to grassy clearings with bushes and trees or in marshes bordering lakes and rivers. At Leticia absent late June or July–early Nov (J. V. Remsen), which is their period of occurrence in Venez. (Schwartz 1975); 1 late flock to 24 July at Leticia (Hilty); 1 ♂ to 22 Aug (P. Kaestner). Present at Carimagua, Meta, only late Apr–late June with peak flocks of 100 or more in late May (S. Furniss); seen at Hacienda Corocora, Meta, only Mar and Oct (W. McKay).

**Range:** To 400m. E of Andes where known from w and ne Meta w Caquetá, Vaupés (sighting, El Dorado, June 1976—R. Ridgely) and Amazonas. The Guianas and Venez. to n Argentina, Paraguay, and se Brazil. Breeding range, not fully established, prob. incl. se Brazil and ne Amazonia.

## 59. LESSON'S SEEDEATER
*Sporophila bouvronides*      Pl. 56, Map 1450
**Identification:** 4.5″ (11.4cm). ♂: sim. to ♂ Lined Seedeater, but crown black with *no white central stripe*; flanks, sides, and even chest more or less mottled black. ♀: indistinguishable from ♀ Lined Seedeater. Some ♂♂ in ♀ plumage (hen-type)) are sexually mature and known to breed.

**Similar species:** Other "black-and-white" ♂ seedeaters (except 58) lack the broad white malar patch. ♀ of this sp. and of Lined Seedeater are only ♀ Colombian *Sporophila* with combination of yellow bill and unstreaked back, but the 2 cannot be separated in the field.

**Voice:** Common song in Venez. an often repeated loud rattle *didididididee* or faster rolling trill *krrrrrrrrrre* sometimes followed by 1 or several *chirp* notes (Schwartz 1975).

**Behavior:** Sim. to Lined Seedeater.

**Breeding:** Laying ♀, BC ♀, BC ♂, and imm., 4–8 Nov, s of Cúcuta; 2 BC ♂♂, 29 Apr, Snía. San Lucas; BC ♂, 8 June, Ayacucho, Cesar; BC ♂, 10 Aug, Cartagena (Carriker); 3 birds not in BC, May, Vaupés (Olivares 1964b); 6 birds not in BC, 12–15 June, w Meta (W. McKay); 2 BC birds, July, n Venez. (Schwartz 1975; Friedmann and Smith 1950). Trinidad nests June–Aug; frail grass and black, fiber-lined cup near ground to 10m up; 2–3 whitish eggs marked with brown or blackish brown (ffrench 1973).

**Status and habitat:** Apparently rather uncommon and local. BC birds (seasonal residents) rec. Apr–Nov mainly north of 7°N. Recs. from further s prob. mostly transients. At Hacienda Corocora, w Meta reported only in June (W. McKay).

**Range:** To 600m (once to 1000m—Río Lebrija, Santander). Carib. region from Cartagena e to w base of Santa Marta Mts., and s in Magdalena Val. to nw Santander; e of Andes in Norte de Santander, w Meta (Villavicencio to Macarena Mts.), Vaupés (Mitú), and Amazonas (Leticia, nonbreeding flock of 20 seen 15 Jan 1983—R. Ridgely). Colombia, n Venez. and the Guianas spottily to ne Peru and Amazonian Brazil. Unlike Lined Seedeater, not found s of Amazonia.

**Note:** In Venez., populations of both Lesson's and Lined Seedeaters are present only June or July–Nov or Dec, at which time both spp. sing (only Lesson's known to breed) distinctly different songs and appear to behave as separate spp. However, songs of the Lined from São Paulo, Brazil, are nearly identical to Lesson's from Venez. (Schwartz 1975). Lesson's has been considered a subsp. of Lined Seedeater.

## 60. BLACK-AND-WHITE SEEDEATER
*Sporophila luctuosa*      Pl. 56, Map 1451
**Identification:** 4.5″ (11.4cm). Bill bluish white, darker below (♂) or blackish (♀). ♂: *glossy black with white lower breast, belly and under tail coverts; prom. white wing speculum.* ♀: olive brown above, buffy brown below with yellowish tinge on abdomen.

**Similar species:** Most likely confused with Yellow-bellied Seedeater (61; ranges overlap in mts.), which lacks the conspic. wing speculum and is olive (not black) above. Variable Seedeater (57), a lower el. bird, has black breast band and white on sides of neck. ♀ doubtfully separable in field from other dark-billed ♀ *Sporophila.*

**Voice:** Song, *chaaw, cheee, childledee-chea-chea-chea* var. to *jaaaw, geee, chutchutchut-jeet,* 1st 2 notes raspy like a grackle or *Agelaius* blackbird, rest melodious (P. Schwartz recording).

**Behavior:** Usually in pairs or small flocks of its own sp. in grass or lower shrubbery. Generally a less familiar bird than its lowland counterpart, the Yellow-bellied Seedeater.

**Breeding:** 3 BC ♂♂, Sept, E Andes in Santander and Boyacá; 2 juvs., Apr, n Antioquia (Carriker).

**Status and habitat:** Uncommon to locally fairly common in grassy and bushy areas, pastures, and roadside shrubbery in mts., rarely in lowlands. Lowland Chocó recs. are prob. from Baudó Mts.

**Range:** Mostly 1500–2500m (rec. 100–3200m). Santa Marta and Baudó mts., w slope W Andes in Antioquia and e slope in Cauca, C Andes s to Cauca (sight), w slope E Andes from Santander to Cundinamarca, and e base of Andes in Meta (incl. Macarena Mts.) and w Caquetá, prob. w Putumayo. Nw Venez. s mostly in mts. to n Bolivia.

## 61. YELLOW-BELLIED SEEDEATER
*Sporophila nigricollis*      Pl. 56, Map 1452
**Identification:** 4.5″ (11.4cm). Bill pale blue (♂); or dark (♀). *Crown, sides of head, throat, and chest black* (forms hood); otherwise *dark olive* above and pale yellowish to whitish below; some

birds have small white wing speculum. ♀: olive brown above, more buffy below.

**Similar species:** The name is misleading as even the brightest ♂♂ are very pale yellow below, duller ones are whitish. Better marks are the black hood and olive upperparts, which set it apart from all other Colombian seedeaters. See Black-and-white Seedeater (60). ♀ doubtfully separable from other dark-billed ♀ *Sporophila*.

**Voice:** Song in W Andes a short musical *tsu tsu tsu chew-seesee-héet*, or *tsu tsu tsu tswidle we's hére* or sim. var., last note typically higher.

**Behavior:** Pairs hold territories when breeding but otherwise are seen in small family groups or flocks, often with other seedeaters and grassquits.

**Breeding:** 4 BC birds, Aug–Sept, n Antioquia; 1 in May, s Bolívar (Carriker). Eggs in Dec and fledglings in Jan (Miller 1963); begging juv., July (S. Gniadek), W Andes above Cali; July nest, Santa Marta (Todd and Carriker 1922). Deep, thin, meshlike grassy cup usually low in bush or small tree; 2 eggs, occas. 3, pale greenish to buff, thickly spotted brown (ffrench 1973). Also see Alderton (1961).

**Status and habitat:** Common, esp. w of Andes, in grassy or shrubby clearings, cultivated areas, and borders of forest and lighter woodland. No Amazonas recs.

**Range:** To 2300m. Throughout except the drier regions n of Andes, and Amazonia (?). Sw Costa Rica to n Bolivia, and se Brazil. Trinidad. Lesser Antilles.

### 62. DOUBLE-COLLARED SEEDEATER
*Sporophila caerulescens*　　Ill. 100, Map 1453
**Identification:** 4.5″ (11.4cm). *Bill pinkish yellow.* ♂: *brownish gray above;* forehead and cheeks blackish with *white malar stripe;* small white spot below eye; *upper throat black bordered below by a white band on lower throat and black chest collar;* rest of underparts white. ♀: pale brownish gray above; throat and breast buff becoming paler on lower underparts; center of belly whitish. Some birds (young ♂♂?) have lower throat and malar buffy white faintly indicating adult ♂ pattern.

**Similar species:** ♂ easily confused with Variable Seedeater (see 57). ♀ might be told from dark-billed *Sporophila* by paler bill.

**Voice:** Song in Brazil a pleasing, buntinglike *te-ee-chéwte-chéwte-su-gewe'e'e'e'e*, trill sometimes omitted or var. (W. Belton recording).

**Behavior:** Near Leticia in small flocks of its own or accompanying other seedeaters. Eats seeds by gleaning from grass stems, not on ground as do many other *Sporophila* (J. V. Remsen).

**Status and habitat:** Known only from sight recs.

and a photo at Leticia but prob. a reg. trans-Amazonian migrant in small nos. to w Amazonia. Sightings, 5-6 Aug, 3 Nov 1974, 7 and 11 Aug 1975 (Remsen and Hunn 1979) and 20 July 1978 (photo, J. Faust). Semiopen grassy or shrubby areas. Seen along border of airstrip and s edge of town at Leticia.

**Range:** S Amazonas (Leticia). Breeds from e and c Brazil to Uruguay, Paraguay, c Argentina, and Bolivia. Some s breeders apparently migrate n into Amazonian Peru (June–Aug) and Colombia.

### 63. TUMACO SEEDEATER
*Sporophila insulata*　　　　　Map 1454
**Identification:** 4″ (10.2cm). Small. Bill blackish (♂), or pale yellowish (♀). ♂: brownish gray above; *narrow rump band and underparts rufous;* wings and tail blackish with *white at base of flight feathers and tail.* Imm. ♂: sim. but belly largely buffy white. ♀: pale olive brown above, vaguely streaked darker; *rump and crown grayish; wings with white as in ♂;* underparts yellowish buff becoming dirty white on belly.

**Similar species:** *Much like* Ruddy-breasted Seedeater (64), but rump patch smaller (forms a band) and white at base of tail. ♀ differs from other Colombian *Sporophila*, except Chestnut-throated Seedeater (66), by vague streaks on back; from latter by gray rump and crown.

**Behavior:** Little known but presum. like Ruddy-breasted Seedeater.

**Status and habitat:** Uncertain. Apparently taken in open grassy and shrubby areas on Tumaco Isl., which is now heavily settled.

**Range:** ENDEMIC. Known only from Tumaco Isl.

### 64. RUDDY-BREASTED SEEDEATER
*Sporophila minuta*　　　　Pl. 56, Map 1455
**Identification:** 4″ (10.2cm). ♂: brownish gray above; wings and tail darker with small white patch at base of primaries (more conspic. in flight); *rump and underparts light cinnamon rufous.* ♀: buffy brown above; wings and tail dark brown; wing coverts and primaries pale edged; *underparts buff to pale dull cinnamon.*

**Similar species:** Chestnut-bellied Seedeater (65), only e of Andes, is bright gray (not brownish) with a rich chestnut stripe down central underparts (not entire underparts pale rufous) and no rump patch. Also see Tumaco Seedeater (63). ♀ is *decidedly smaller* and *buffier* than other dark-billed ♀ *Sporophila* (except 63) but best known by attendant ♂.

**Voice:** Song var. At Laguna de Sonso a lively pleasing *seet-seet, chew-two, peet, wheet, spit'witchew, pit-wit;* at Mutatá, nw Antioquia, a fast musical *zeet zeet, tu-we-tee, zu, tu-we-tee, ee zee* . . . , paired notes at beginning usually characteristic, ending var.

**Behavior:** Pairs when breeding, otherwise usually in flocks, often with other seedeaters and grassquits. A stem-gleaner on small grass seeds.

**Breeding:** 4 BC birds, Apr, May, and Sept, n Antioquia, s Bolívar, Santander (Carriker); BC ♂, Oct, many nests, Apr–July; 1 in Nov, Santander (Boggs 1961); coarse grassy cup, notable for stiff grass projecting from rim, is low in grass or 2m or more up in bush or small tree; 2 white eggs spotted several shades of reddish brown (ffrench 1973).

**Status and habitat:** Common in open grassy fields and weedy roadsides. Resident in Cauca Val. in nos. yr.-round with no seasonal movements yet noticed such as reported in Panama (Karr 1971).

**Range:** To 1000m, small nos. to 2300m. W of Andes except Pacific coast, e of Andes s to s Caquetá and Vaupés. W Mexico to nw Ecuador, e Bolivia, and n Argentina; not w and c Amazonian region.

## 65. CHESTNUT-BELLIED SEEDEATER

*Sporophila castaneiventris*          Pl. 56, Map 1456

**Identification:** 4″ (10.2cm). Bill dusky. ♂: bright *blue* gray; wings and tail edged dusky; *median stripe down underparts from chin to tail rich chestnut*. ♀: olive brown, more rufous on rump; throat and central underparts pale ochraceous.

**Similar species:** Pretty ♂ easily recognized but cf. Ruddy-breasted Seedeater (64) of more open zones (limited range overlap). ♀ is smaller than other dark-billed *Sporophila* (except Ruddy-breasted) and more buffy ochraceous below.

**Voice:** Short song a ser. of sweet notes on var. pitches (J. V. Remsen); sharp *chéeoo* call.

**Behavior:** Often in small loose flocks, esp. with other seedeaters, seed-finches, and grassquits. A stem-gleaner on grass seeds but also forages by hopping on ground occas.

**Breeding:** 6 BC birds, June, w Caquetá (Carriker). ♀ building nest in tall grass, 24 July, Leticia (Hilty); grassy cup nest, sometimes decorated with plant down on rim, low in bush; 2-3 white eggs, thickly spotted brown, lilac, and with irreg. black lines (Beebe et al. 1917).

**Status and habitat:** Common throughout Amazonia in grassy and bushy clearings, marsh grass, river banks, even in parks in town.

**Range:** To 500m. E of Andes from n Meta (Pto. López), and ne Guainía (Pto. Inírida) southward. The Guianas and sw Amazonas, Venez., to n Bolivia and Amazonian Brazil.

## 66. CHESTNUT-THROATED SEEDEATER

*Sporophila telasco*          Map 1457

**Identification:** 4″ (10.2cm). Bill blackish (♂), or pale yellowish (♀). ♂: dull gray above vaguely streaked dusky on crown and mantle; *rump whitish*; wings and tail dusky; *patch of white at base of primaries* (like a wing band); inner remiges edged white; *upper throat chestnut* (often not obvious); *rest of underparts white*. ♀: pale brown above *streaked dusky on crown and back*; wings and tail as in ♂; below white tinged buffy with *obscure streaking on breast and sides*.

**Similar species:** Rather pale, washed out ♂ is only Colombian seedeater with a chestnut throat and white underparts, but better marks (esp. in flight) are whitish rump and wing band. Only other ♀ *Sporophila* streaked above is Tumaco Seedeater, which has gray crown and rump.

**Voice:** Call in Peru a fine *zeeteep* and *cheep*; song a warbling *tsee-chey-wee-chey-wee-chey* . . . sometimes in flight (Koepcke 1970).

**Behavior:** A stem-gleaner for grass seeds and like other *Sporophila* gathers in sizable flocks; wary at Boca Grande.

**Breeding:** In w Ecuador, Mar–June; grassy cup less than 1m up in bush or weeds; 2-3 eggs, pale blue with black spots, blotches, and scrawls, mainly at larger end; incubates only 9-10 days (Marchant 1960).

**Status and habitat:** Fairly common (large flocks) in tall grass with scattered bushes and low trees on Boca Grande (sightings 4 Sept 1979, Hilty); 8 seen at Guapí, Cauca, 28 Jan 1983 (R. Ridgely).

**Range:** Isla Gorgona; sight recs. in sw Nariño and sw Cauca. Sw Colombia to extreme nw Chile.

## 67. BLUE-BLACK GRASSQUIT

*Volatinia jacarina*          Pl. 56, Map 1458

**Identification:** 4″ (10.2cm). Short pointed bill smaller than *Sporophila*. ♂: *uniform glossy blue black*, concealed white spot at bend of wings (usually visible in flight). ♀: olive brown above, wings and tail darker brown; below brownish buff becoming whiter on center of belly; *chest and sides streaked dusky*. Imm. ♂: like ♀ but blacker. Subad. ♂: mottled brownish and black.

**Similar species:** ♂ Lesser Seed-Finch (51) is all black w of Andes but is *much larger* and has heavier bill and entirely white under wing coverts. Also cf. Sooty Grassquit (42). ♀ is the only *very small* "seedeater" in the *lowlands* with distinctly *streaked* underparts. See ♀ Slaty Finch (72), of highlands only.

**Voice:** From a low perch ♂ tirelessly utters an explosive, wheezy *duézz-uu*, usually accompanied by a short vertical jump with spread tail; sings all yr.

**Behavior:** A familiar open country bird seen singly, in pairs, or occas. in small loose flocks with other seedeaters eating grass seeds. The jump display is reportedly used in pair formation and in maintaining territories (Alderton 1963).

**Breeding:** 2 BC ♂♂, Aug, ne Meta (S. Furniss); BC ♀, Aug, Perijá Mts. (Carriker); many nests, Apr–June, 1 in Jan, w Santander (Boggs 1961); Feb nest, n Huila; thin, deep, cup low in grass (Miller 1952); 1-3 eggs (Alderton 1963), pale bluish white spotted reddish brown in Antioquia (Sclater and Salvin 1879).

**Status and habitat:** Common to *abundant* in grassy and weedy clearings and in waste areas, weedy pastures, and other open country; mainly lowlands.

**Range:** To 2200m. Throughout (sometimes absent from suitable areas in extensively forested areas). S Mexico to w Peru, n Chile, Argentina, and s Brazil. Trinidad to Grenada.

## 68. GRASSLAND YELLOW-FINCH

*Sicalis luteola* Pl. 56, Map 1459

**Identification:** 5" (13cm). Much like Stripe-tailed Yellow-Finch. ♂: pale olive above, *streaked dusky on crown and back*; rump plain yellowish olive; wings and tail dark brown edged paler; *lores and ocular area bright yellow*; sides of head olive yellow; underparts bright yellow tinged olive on breast and sides. ♀: sim. but paler yellow below and breast and sides washed brownish olive (*no streaks*). Imm.: like ♀ but even paler and faintly streaked on throat and breast.

**Similar species:** Often confused with Stripe-tailed Yellow-Finch (69) but more conspic. streaked above *incl. crown* (uniform in Stripe-tailed) and with prom. yellow ocular area. ♀ Stripe-tailed is streaked below.

**Voice:** In Panama ♂ sings a thin buzzy trill on perch, a more melodious song in flight (Ridgely 1976); pipitlike *seep* or *tsip-seep* call in flight.

**Behavior:** As in Stripe-tailed Yellow-Finch.

**Breeding:** Perhaps loosely colonial. BC ♂, Feb, Cauca (Carriker); BC bird, May; juv., Jan, Bogotá (Borrero and Hernández 1958; Olivares 1969a). Grassy cup in tall marsh grass bordering pond; 3 pale bluish green eggs speckled brown (Cherrie 1916).

**Status and habitat:** Local; grassland, grain fields, and edges of marshes. Common from w Meta (W. McKay) to ne Vichada; locally common from Sabana de Bogotá n in E Andes; very local and erratic in Cauca Val.; common in c Nariño on dry grassy slopes or cultivated areas with bushes.

**Range:** 50-3300m. Lower Magdalena Val. in Atlántico (sw of Barranquilla), Cauca Val. in Valle and Cauca (1000-2900m), adj. Pacific slope in Valle (Queremal), upper Magdalena Val. in Tolima and n Huila (200-500m), and e of Andes from w Meta to ne Vichada on Río Meta (*luteola*); E Andes from Norte de Santander s to Bogotá (2300-2600m) and mts. of Nariño (2200-3300m) from El Tablón to Cumbal (*bogotensis*). S Mexico locally to s Chile and c Argentina. Introduced to Lesser Antilles.

**Note:** The largely temperate zone race *bogotensis* (Montane Yellow-Finch) may be a separate sp.

## 69. STRIPE-TAILED YELLOW-FINCH

*Sicalis citrina* Pl. 56, Map 1460

**Identification:** 4.7" (12cm). ♂: mantle olive green streaked dusky; *forecrown and rump yellow green* (unstreaked); wings and tail dark brown; *inner web of outer 2 tail feathers with large white spot near tip* (usually visible in flight or from below); underparts bright yellow. ♀: sim. but duller and crown streaked dusky; throat and breast dull yellow *indistinctly streaked dusky*; belly brighter yellow.

**Similar species:** Whitish tail spots diagnostic if seen (often hard to see even from below). See Grassland Yellow-Finch (68).

**Voice:** Song in n Venez. a musical *chu'u'u'u'u'u'u'u, zew-tew-tew-you*, chattery notes or trill at end on different pitch, perched or in fluttering display flight.

**Behavior:** Pairs when breeding but in small loose flocks at other times. Feed in grass or on ground.

**Breeding:** Copulation in July (Hilty); juv., Aug, Bogotá (Olivares 1969a); BC ♂, June, n end E Andes (Carriker).

**Status and habitat:** Common locally in open grassland, cultivated areas, and wet swales and edges of marshes.

**Range:** Disjunct. 600-2800m. Santa Marta Mts. (600-2200m), C Andes in Antioquia (2200m on e slope Barro Blanco e of Medellín), head of Magdalena Val. in s Huila (Belén, 2300m); E Andes on Sabana de Bogotá (2500-2800m) and w slope at n end in Norte de Santander (Guamilito, 950m). Colombia spottily e to Surinam and n and e Brazil; c Peru; nw Argentina.

## 70. SAFFRON FINCH

*Sicalis flaveola* Pl. 56, Map 1461

**Identification:** 5.5" (14cm). Mostly bright yellow. ♂: olive yellow above faintly streaked dusky on back; *forecrown bright orange becoming golden* *yellow on rest of head and underparts.* ♀ like ♂ but duller and less orange on crown. Imm.: sparrowlike; head gray; grayish brown above with yellow olive tinge on mantle and rump; crown and back streaked dusky; *below grayish white* with a few dark shaft streaks; under tail coverts yellow; older imms. have *a pale yellow band on nape and chest.*

**Similar species:** ♂ is brightest of the yellow-finches. See Grassland, Stripe-tailed, and Orange-fronted yellow-finches (68, 69, 71).

**Voice:** A repetitive but musical song *sit-seet sit-seet chitada-chitada-chitada-cheet-seet* with var. (P. Schwartz recording).

**Behavior:** The most familiar Colombian *Sicalis*. Pairs or loose flocks, sometimes numbering several doz. birds, usually feed on the ground but otherwise perch in shrubbery or low in trees. A popular cage bird.

**Breeding:** 2 BC ♂♂ and 2 imms., May, Cesar and n Antioquia (Carriker). Nest in cavities or abandoned nests of other birds, e.g., thornbirds, woodpeckers, orioles; 3 late May nests, Venez. Orinoco (Cherrie 1916); 1 in June, c Venez. (P. Schwartz); July–Nov, Guárico, Venez. (Thomas 1979b). 1(?)-4 pale bluish white eggs thickly spotted brown, most at large end.

**Status and habitat:** Fairly common to common in savanna with scattered bushes and trees; lighter woodland borders, lawns, and gardens.

**Range::** To 1000m. Carib. region from Córdoba e to Guajira and s to lower Cauca Val. (to Medellín); e of Andes from Arauca (at boundary on Venez. side) to Meta (s to Macarena Mts.) and e Vichada. Introduced to Cali area (prior to 1971) and at Buenaventura (photo, Mar 1978—Hilty), prob. through escaped cage birds. Locally throughout S America s to c Argentina. Trinidad. Introduced in Panama and Jamaica.

## 71. ORANGE-FRONTED YELLOW-FINCH

*Sicalis columbiana*                    Pl. 56, Map 1462

**Identification:** 4.5″ (11.4cm). ♂: uniform bright yellow olive above; *forecrown rufescent orange;* lores dusky; underparts golden yellow tinged olive on sides of breast and flanks. ♀: pale brownish gray above, vaguely streaked dusky on back; *below dingy white* (no streaks) with buff tinge on breast and flanks.

**Similar species:** ♂ is much like ♂ Saffron Finch (70) but smaller, darker above, lores dusky, and burnt orange on head darker and confined to forehead (not golden orange yellow on most of crown). ♀ like ♀ Saffron but smaller and completely unstreaked below.

**Behavior:** Pairs or small flocks usually feed on the ground; sometimes with Saffron Finches.

**Breeding:** Building nest, Feb–May ne Meta, fledglings, Apr–July (S. Furniss); 3 nests, June, upper Venez. Orinoco; in hollow limb, hole in bank, or crevice in rock wall; grassy cup nest; 4 pale blue eggs speckled brown at larger end (Cherrie 1916).

**Status and habitat:** Common near water holes, along river banks, and around habitations, in grassland and ranch country.

**Range:** To 400m. C and ne Meta (Pto. Gaitán; Carimagua—S. Furniss) e to Río Orinoco at Maipures, Vichada. E Colombia and e Venez.; locally in e Peru; e Amazonian and se Brazil.

## 72. SLATY FINCH

*Haplospiza rustica*                    Pl. 56, Map 1463

**Identification:** 5″ (13cm). *Conical, pointed bill rather slender for a finch.* ♂: *dark slaty gray*, slightly paler below; wings black narrowly edged gray. ♀: olive brown above, lighter and buffier below and becoming pale yellowish on lower belly; *throat and breast vaguely streaked dusky;* flight feathers edged rufous.

**Similar species:** A good mark for either sex is the slender pointed bill. White-sided Flowerpiercer (p 594) is same size and color but has thin bill and white under wings (watch for wing flicks). Larger and paler Plumbeous Sierra-Finch (73) is found at higher el., smaller Blue-black Grassquit (67) occurs lower.

**Voice:** Song in Peru a fast, complicated burst of high chips, buzzes, and trills, sometimes ending in a descending buzzy trill; like several *Conirostrum* but faster and higher-pitched (T. Parker).

**Behavior:** Not well known. A nervous active bird usually seen from eye level to subcanopy ht. gleaning from small twigs and leaves. Occurs alone, in pairs or often with mixed flocks. In Costa Rica (though not yet elsewhere) reported in flocks in grassy pastures near forest (Stiles and Hespenhide 1972).

**Status and habitat:** Rare and local in humid forest, forest borders, and shrubby clearings.

**Range:** 1200-2500m (once to 2700m, sighting, Cerro Munchique—Hilty et al.). Santa Marta Mts. (San Lorenzo, 2000-2200m, 11 Feb 1972—S. M. Russell and T. B. Johnson; also netted 8 June and 31 Aug 1972—T. B. Johnson), Perijá Mts., and spottily in all 3 Andean ranges (not rec. n of Valle in W Andes or at n end C Andes). S Mexico; Costa Rica to Venez., and s in Andes to nw Bolivia.

## 73. PLUMBEOUS SIERRA-FINCH

*Phrygilus unicolor*                    Pl. 56, Map 1464

**Identification:** 6″ (15cm). Rather large, high mt. finch. Blackish bill *sharply pointed and con-*

ical. Sexes very different. ♂: *entirely leaden gray*, slightly paler below; wings and tail darker; legs pinkish; faint pale eyering. ♀ sparrow-like: brown above and dingy white below, *heavily and boldly streaked with dusky throughout*; edges of wing coverts and wash on chest and sides buff; foreface buff with small whitish spot above the eye.

**Similar species:** ♂ from other "gray" highland finches (46, 47, 48) by larger size and sharp pointed black bill (not stubby pink or yellow bill). Cf. ♂ Slaty Finch (72); also 54 and 55, mainly lowland birds. Heavily striped ♀ looks like an overgrown sparrow. Imm. Rufous-collared Sparrow (78) has fine (not coarse) streaks below, and ad. head pattern usually faintly indicated. ♀♀ of 46-48 (also ♂ of 47) are much smaller and duller.

**Voice:** Call a high thin *tsip* (J. Silliman); song from low perch or in flight in E Andes a short dull buzz then a chipping rattle.

**Behavior:** Well-scattered pairs or loose flocks walk on the ground; wait for a close approach before flushing, then fly off and drop quickly to cover and hide, or less frequently stop exposed on a low bush or rock. Not shy.

**Breeding:** 12 BC birds, late July–early Oct, E Andes; 1 in early Mar, C Andes (Carriker); 1 in Aug, PN Chingaza (W. McKay).

**Status and habitat:** Fairly common in shrubby pastures, fields and meadows, esp. along small rivulets and drainage ditches in paramo, occas. up to snowline.

**Range:** 2700-4500m in Santa Marta Mts., 3000-3800m in E Andes s to Cundinamarca and C Andes from Caldas/Tolima area s through Nariño. Nw Venez. s in Andes to Tierra del Fuego.

## 74. WEDGE-TAILED GRASS-FINCH

*Emberizoides herbicola*          Pl. 56, Map 1465
**Identification:** 7.5" (19cm). Bill black above, yellow below. *Very long tail strongly graduated and pointed.* Brown to grayish brown above heavily streaked blackish; wings tinged olive; bend of wing yellow (sometimes concealed); *lores and conspic. eyering white*; below dull white, breast and sides tinged brownish. Imm.: tinged yellowish below.

**Similar species:** Sparrowlike but none have such an obvious eyering and long tail; note bicolored bill. See ♀ Dickcissel (1) and Bobolink (p 574).

**Voice:** Song in Meta a slightly buzzy *tit-tit, zurreéeet*, in Cauca Val. a sim. *pit-it't't't't't't*, 1st notes faint. In Panama also sing a 2d song type, a musical *tleedeé, tleedeé, tleedeé* with var. (Ridgely 1976).

**Behavior:** May perch on fence or bush to sing, esp. at dawn, but otherwise usually in or near tall grass, where furtive, and hard to flush. Alone or in pairs. Runs well on the ground.

**Breeding:** 22 BC birds, May–June, Santa Marta and s Bolívar; 1 in Sept, n Antioquia; 2 juvs., July and Aug, Perijá Mts. (Carriker); BC birds, Jan, June and Oct, ne Meta (S. Furniss). Pair feeding young, Pto. Inírida airstrip, Sept (Hilty).

**Status and habitat:** Local and seldom very numerous. Taller grassland with or without scattered bushes. Most easily found in savannas e of the Andes; very spotty w of Andes.

**Range:** To 1800m. Santa Marta and Perijá Mts., Cauca and Magdalena vals., and grasslands e of the Andes s to s Meta (Macarena Mts.), in pockets of savanna s to Vaupés (Sabana del Cubiyú). Costa Rica locally to ne Argentina and se Brazil.

## 75. GRASSHOPPER SPARROW

*Ammodramus savannarum*          Map 1466
**Identification:** 4.8" (12.2cm). Flat-headed. *Crown dusky with narrow buff median line and buffy yellow superciliary*; upperparts otherwise streaked blackish and buff; sides of head and *underparts pale buff*, brighter on breast, fading to whitish on center of belly. Imm.: sim. but with a few dusky streaks on breast. Tail narrow and short.

**Similar species:** Grassland sparrow (77) lacks the distinct coronal stripe and superciliary, is less buff below, and tail not so pointed.

**Voice:** Song resembles 1 song type of those of N American birds, a weak buzzy trill, *pít-sip tzzzzzzzzz*, 1st notes faint.

**Behavior:** May sing from an open perch but otherwise stays on ground in taller grass and is difficult to flush. Usually dives quickly into cover after a short dipping flight.

**Status and habitat:** Local in grassland. Can be found most easily in grassy pastures on ICA experimental station sw of Palmira.

**Range:** 1000m. Mid. Cauca Val. near Cali, Yumbo, and Palmira (*caucae*), in Valle. Breeds in N America and locally from s Mexico and Greater Antilles to w Colombia and Ecuador. N birds migrate to Mid. America (accidental s to Pannama and W Indies; none to S America).

## 76. YELLOW-BROWED SPARROW

*Ammodramus aurifrons*          Pl. 56, Map 1467
**Identification:** 5" (13cm). Grayish brown above streaked dusky (no chestnut edging); inner remiges edged dull rufescent brown; bend of wing yellow (usually concealed); *short eyebrow, narrow eyering, and wash at base of lower bill yellow*; below whitish tinged pale grayish buff on breast and sides.

**Similar species:** See *very sim.* Grassland Sparrow (77).

**Voice:** Monotonously repeated song, even through the heat of the day, a high insectlike buzz, *tic, zzzzzz, zzzzzz,* 1st note faint.

**Behavior:** Assertive and conspic. Hops or runs on ground, short grass, lawns, river banks, etc. to feed (rarely up in bushes) but takes a prom. perch on fence post or low bush to sing. Alone or in loosely spaced 2's.

**Breeding:** 3 BC ♂ ♂, June; BC ♂ and juv., May, in Caquetá (Carriker). Begging young, Feb, Mitú (Hilty), Sept, Leticia, and ad. with food, Aug, Leticia (J. V. Remsen).

**Status and habitat:** Common and widespead in open grassy areas with bushes; in towns, clearings, airstrips, and waste areas, esp. within forested zones where it replaces next sp.

**Range:** To 500m. E of Andes in Norte de Santander, e base of Andes and generally from c Meta and the Orinoco region southward. Venez. and e Colombia to n Bolivia and Amazonian Brazil.

**Note:** Often placed in the genus *Myospiza.*

## 77. GRASSLAND SPARROW

*Ammodramus humeralis*          Pl. 56, Map 1468

**Identification:** 5″ (13cm). Local. Dull grayish brown streaked blackish above; the feathers with *narrow chestnut edges* (visible at close range); bend of wing yellow (usually concealed); *inner remiges edged chestnut; lores yellow; narrow eyering white;* cheeks brownish gray, underparts whitish tinged light buffy gray on breast and sides.

**Similar species:** Easily confused with Yellow-browed Sparrow (76). Grassland has only lores yellow, streaking blacker above (most obvious on crown), streaks edged chestnut (faint in worn plumage), inner remiges edged chestnut, (diagnostic but sometimes hard to see) usually narrow white eyering (yellowish or lacking in 76), and with sides of head and neck grayish (not brownish) giving appearance of "grayer" underparts. Also see Grasshopper Sparrow (75).

**Voice:** Song in Meta a high wiry *tii he-he heeee* (Brown); in c Venez. a high, thin *j-EE-ee geee,* 1st note lowest, last slightly trilled, alternating with *j-EE kitjiiii* (P. Schwartz recording).

**Behavior:** Sings from grass clump, shrub, or fence mostly in early morning or evening but otherwise inconspic. Runs rapidly on ground between tall grass tufts, flushes a short distance, then drops in.

**Breeding:** 24 BC birds, Apr–July, Perijá and Santa Marta mts. and C Andes (Carriker); 2 nests, May and Aug, ne Meta, low in grass (S. Furniss). Two Venez. Orinoco nests, May, reportedly this sp., on ground at base of tall grass clump; 1 an open grass cup, the other a grassy sphere with side entrance; 2-3 white eggs (Cherrie 1916); open cup nest in Surinam (Haverschmidt 1968).

**Status and habitat:** Spotty. Tall grass, esp. where grass grows in clumps and with or without scattered bushes. Common at Carimagua, ne Meta (S. Furniss).

**Range:** To 1000m. Cauca Val. in Valle (Cali; Yumbo), Guajira peninsula, Santa Marta and Perijá mts., Cesar Val., and s in Magdalena Val. to s Huila (La Plata); e of Andes s to s Meta (n end of Macarena Mts.) and w Vaupés (San José del Guaviare). Venez., the Guianas, and e Brazil to Uruguay, c Argentina, and se Peru.

**Note:** Often placed in the genus *Myospiza.*

## 78. RUFOUS-COLLARED SPARROW

*Zonotrichia capensis*          Pl. 55, Map 1469

**Identification:** 5.5″ (14cm). Slightly crested. *Head gray with 2 black crown stripes,* a narrow stripe behind eye, and short black malar; *rufous collar across nape and sides of neck;* rest of upperparts brown streaked black on back; throat white bordered below by *blackish patch on each side of chest;* rest of underparts light gray. Imm.: much duller, crown streaked brown and dusky like back; rufous collar faint or lacking; *underparts dingy white finely streaked dusky.*

**Similar species:** Ads. are easily recognized by gray and black striped heads and rufous collar. Streaky imms., often with ads., can usually be told by shape and habits.

**Voice:** Many geographical dialects but everywhere familiar and easily recognized, typically 1 or 2 long slurred whistles with or without a trill at the end, *tee-teooo, e'e'e'e'e* (2d note slurred lower), or *teeeo-teeeee,* etc.

**Behavior:** A friendly and well-known bird seen on the ground or in bushes and hedgerows throughout the cultivated highlands.

**Breeding:** 3 BC birds, Mar–Sept, Santa Marta Mts.; 7 BC ♂ ♂, Apr–July; 2 laying ♀ ♀, May and June, Perijá Mts. (Carriker). In W Andes in Valle breeds all yr., peaking mid-Jan and mid-June at beginning of drier periods (Miller 1961); neat cup nest on ground; 2-3 pale greenish blue eggs speckled and blotched brown (Skutch 1967).

**Status and habitat:** Common almost everywhere in the mts., in agricultural areas, and open areas with bushes and scattered trees; often numerous in parks and on lawns in towns. Uncommon and very local in Río Orinoco-Negro lowlands. Not reported from Baudó Mts., or mts. on Panama boundary.

**Range:** 1000-3700m in Andes. Snía. de Macuira in Guajira (250m), Santa Marta Mts. (850-

3400m), Perijá Mts. (1500-3500m), the Andes and Macarena Mts.; 150-300m in e Guianía locally in pockets of savanna to Vaupés (Sabana del Cubiyú). S Mexico to Tierra del Fuego (mainly in mts.).

## 79. ANDEAN SISKIN

*Spinus spinescens*          Pl. 56, Map 1470

**Identification:** 4.5″ (11.4cm). ♂: olive green above with *black cap*; wings black with *broad yellow band across base of primaries* (esp. prom. in flight); tail black, outer feathers yellow at base (or all black—*nigricauda*); below olive yellow becoming bright yellow on lower underparts. ♀: duller with *center of belly and under tail coverts whitish*.

**Similar species:** ♂ is only Colombian siskin with black cap. ♀ almost inseparable from ♀ Hooded Siskin in field (81; may overlap in C Andes) but has whitish vent area (not pale grayish yellow), more olive (less yellowish) rump, and sides of head vaguely greener (less grayish). Lesser Goldfinch (83) has white wing bands.

**Voice:** Goldfinchlike *tswee*'s in dipping flight. Song a lively, rambling ser. typical of the genus.

**Behavior:** Usually in little flocks well up in trees along rather open borders or feeding nearer ground in weedy patches or in paramo where often at *Espeletia*. Sometimes with mixed flocks.

**Breeding:** Begging young, Mar, PN Puracé (Brown); building nest, June, W Andes above Cali (S. Gniadek); 2 BC birds, Aug, n end W Andes (Carriker); 1 in Aug, PN Chingaza (W. McKay).

**Status and habitat:** Locally and periodically fairly common in woodland borders, open areas with scattered trees, or paramo. Wanders widely.

**Range:** 1800-3700m (sightings to 1500m, Pichindé Val., Valle—Hilty et al.). Santa Marta Mts., 1800-2000m (*capitaneus*); Perijá Mts., E Andes, s end C Andes in Cauca (Popayán; PN Puracé), and Putumayo, and e slope W Andes in Valle (*spinescens*); n end W Andes in Antioquia (Paramillo Mts.; Páramo Frontino), n end C Andes from n Antioquia (Valdivia) s to s Caldas/n Tolima region (*nigricauda*). Undoubtedly in Nariño, as rec. in Carchí, n Ecuador (photo—R. Ridgely). N Venez., Colombia, and n Ecuador.

## 80. RED SISKIN

*Spinus cucullatus*          Pl. 56, Map 1471

**Identification:** 4″ (10.2cm). ♂ unmistakable: *mostly salmon red with black hood; wings black with broad salmon red band across base of flight feathers*;

inner remiges edged white; tail black. ♀: light brown above; wings and tail dusky; *rump, 2 wing bars, and larger patch at base of primaries salmon*; underparts grayish white with *salmon wash on sides of breast* (traces of salmon sometimes also on neck and breast).

**Similar species:** ♀ vaguely recalls ♀ Vermilion Flycatcher (p 498) but much smaller and with red on wings and rump.

**Voice:** Call a raspy *jut-jut*; song a long, rambling, and very complicated ser. of semimusical twitters, trills, and chatters (P. Schwartz recording).

**Behavior:** Small groups perch in tall grass or low bushes.

**Breeding:** 2 BC ♂♂, 24 and 30 Oct, sw of Cucutá (Carriker).

**Status and habitat:** Open grassy areas with bushes and low trees; favors drier areas. Status uncertain, perhaps threatened because of popularity as a cage bird. Now very local though can still be found in small nos. in both Venez. and Colombia (1 small flock seen in 1978 in e Norte de Santander—D. Bailey and P. Bailey).

**Range:** To 1000m (sighting to 1700m, Nov 1947—Carriker). Norte de Santander (s of Cúcuta). Ne Colombia and Venez.; Trinidad (formerly).

## 81. HOODED SISKIN

*Spinus magellanicus*          Pl. 56, Map 1472

**Identification:** 4.5″ (11.4cm). ♂: *entire head and throat black*; back olive yellow becoming bright yellow on rump; *wings black with broad yellow band across base of flight feathers*; tail black; notched yellow at base; underparts bright yellow. ♀: dull olive above (no black head) *becoming yellowish on rump*; wings and tail dusky brown; marked as in ♂; underparts light gray tinged yellowish buff; sides of head tinged grayish.

**Similar species:** Gaudy ♂ can hardly be confused. ♀ much like ♀ Andean Siskin (see 79).

**Voice:** A thin *tseet, tseet-weet, tseet, tseet-weet . . .*, much like others of the genus (J. O'Neill recording).

**Behavior:** Pairs or small flocks feed at all hts. from ground to treetop; dipping flight like other *Spinus*.

**Status and habitat:** Open or cultivated highland areas with hedgerows and scattered groves of trees. Fairly common in s Nariño; very local and erratic n in Andes.

**Range:** 2300-3000m (sightings to 3300m s of Pasto—Hilty). C Andes of Caldas-Quindío region s to Nariño; e of Andes on Río Meta (200m) in ne Vichada (specimens?; rec. on Venez. side in Apure). S Guyana, s Venez.

(100-1300m); c Colombia s in Andes to s Argentina.

## 82. YELLOW-BELLIED SISKIN

*Spinus xanthogaster*                    Pl. 56, Map 1473
**Identification:** 4.5″ (11.4cm). ♂: mostly black with *bright yellow lower breast and belly; patch of yellow at base of flight feathers* (conspic. yellow band in flight) and at base of tail. ♀: olive green above (incl. rump); wings and tail as in ♂; below dull olive; *lower breast and belly yellow* (faintly suggests pattern of ♂); center of belly white. Bill blackish (both sexes).
**Similar species:** ♂ Lesser Goldfinch (83) is all yellow below (lacks the hood) and has a *white* (not yellow) wing stripe. ♀ much like ♀ Andean (79) and Hooded siskins (81) but darker above, rump uniform with upperparts, throat and breast darker olive, belly yellower, and bill heavier and darker.
**Voice:** Song rather like others of the genus.
**Behavior:** Wanders in small chattering flocks in highland clearings; feeds at almost any ht. but generally well up in trees and more a woodland bird than next sp.
**Breeding:** 1 BC ♂, Sept, n end W Andes (Carriker); building nest, Mar, 4m up in cypress; BC ♂, Sept, W Andes above Cali; 2 speckled eggs (Miller 1963).
**Status and habitat:** Fairly common locally but erratic; forest borders, and highland pastures or clearings with trees.
**Range:** 1000-3000m (usually above 1400m). The Andes (except Nariño). Costa Rica to w Panama; nw Venez. (incl. Perijá Mts.) to w Ecuador; Peru; n Bolivia.

## 83. LESSER (DARK-BACKED) GOLDFINCH

*Spinus psaltria*                    Pl. 56, Map 1474
**Identification:** 4″ (10.2cm). ♂: glossy black above incl. sides of head; *bright yellow below; white patch at base of flight feathers* (band in flight), and white on inner remiges and on tail. ♀: olive above, sometimes with traces of dusky on back; wings dusky with *white patches as in* ♂; below dull yellow.
**Similar species:** All other Colombian siskins have a yellow (not white) wing band. Several ♂ euphonias are superficially sim. but have small yellow caps.
**Voice:** Song a rambling, musical ser. of notes and twitterings that rise and fall; not always well-connected.
**Behavior:** Wanders in pairs or small flocks at any ht. from ground to treetop; often feeds in weedy roadsides, on ground, or in thickety waste areas, then flushes off in dipping flight with musical *peee-ee* notes.
**Breeding:** 10 BC birds, May–Oct, Perijá and Santa Marta mts., n end C and E Andes (Carriker); fledglings, Mar (Brown), May (S. Gniadek); and nests with eggs, May, July, Dec, and Jan, W Andes above Cali (Miller 1963); dependent juv. and nest with young, Aug, Norte de Santander (Hilty). Compact thick-walled cup 1-8m up; 2-3 white eggs.
**Status and habitat:** Common in semiopen and cultivated areas with bushy borders, hedges, groves of trees, or other mostly deforested areas in foothills and mts.
**Range:** 200-3100m (usually above 1000m). Throughout (except lowlands e of Andes). W US to Venez. and n Peru.

# WEAVER FINCHES: Ploceidae (1)

The weaver finches comprise a large, predominantly Old World family reaching greatest diversity in northern Africa and western Asia. Most are notably gregarious; several build large elaborate colonial nests. A few species have been introduced widely about the world, either intentionally or otherwise, but none so successfully as the House Sparrow, now an economic pest virtually throughout the civilized world. For review of spread in South America see Smith (1980).

## 1. HOUSE SPARROW

*Passer domesticus*                    Map 1475
**Identification:** 6″ (15cm). Restricted to vicinity of man. Stocky. ♂: crown and nape gray; lores black; *cheeks and sides of neck white* bordered behind by chestnut; otherwise streaked brown and black above with 1 white wing bar and *gray rump; throat and chest with black bib*; rest of underparts grayish white. ♀ nondescript: pale grayish brown above, back streaked dusky; 1 indistinct whitish wing bar; eyestripe and underparts dingy white to buffy white.
**Similar species:** No sim. native sp. is likely in the habitat of this bird. ♂ has black bib and white cheeks; ♀ a weak wing bar and superciliary.
**Status and habitat:** No specimens. A recent arrival; 1st rec. (photo) 3 Mar 1979 at Buenaventura (P. Alden, R. Sides, and Hilty); 6 birds incl. ♀ feeding fledgling. Several doz. in Aug

1979 (Hilty et al.). Large flock at Guapí, Cauca, 26-30 Jan 1983 (R. Ridgely). A noisy, gregarious pest almost always found near human dwellings.

**Range:** W Valle and Cauca; w Nariño (Tumaco?). Will doubtless spread. Europe, Asia, and n Africa, and introduced virtually worldwide. Widespread in e and s S America, w Peru; w Ecuador. In Mid. America s to Guatemala.

## PLATE CREDITS

GUY TUDOR: I-VII, XI, XII, 1-12, 14-18, 23-34, 36-39, 41, 42, 48, 50, 54

JOHN GWYNNE: IX, 13, 19, 22, 35, 45, 49, 52, line drawings in text

H. WAYNE TRIMM: 20, 46, 47, 51, 53, 55, 56

MICHEL KLEINBAUM: X, XII, line drawings in text

LARRY McQUEEN: 21, 40

JOHN YRIZARRY: 43, 44

PIETER PRALL: VIII

## CORRIGENDA

On plate 10 the birds numbered 17, 18, and 19 are ♂♂.

On plate 11, the bird numbered 11 is *P. tumultuosus seniloides*. This should also be noted in Appendix C, p. 689.

On plate 20, the bird numbered 2 is *A. sulcatus calorhynchus*.

On plate 38, the bird numbered 12 is *P. ruficeps melanomystax*. This should also be noted in Appendix C, p. 695.

On plate 52, the bird numbered 15 is the lowland subspecies, *C. flavigularis marginatus*.

On plate 55 the bird numbered 13a is immature.

# APPENDIX A

# Finding Birds in Colombia

Despite the great diversity of birdlife in Colombia many of the more interesting species cannot be found readily without considerable knowledge of habitats and localities. This is especially true in light of rapid deforestation in many accessible parts of the Andes. In addition, the remarkably complex topography of Colombia often produces rapid changes in the composition and distribution of birds within very short distances, and this can also complicate bird finding. The following sections discuss a few of the more accessible areas that we have found to be productive. *One note of caution.* Several potentially productive areas may no longer be visited safely. These include central and eastern Guajira, the south slope of the Santa Marta Mountains, the Macarena Mountains, the Mocoa area, the Volcán Cumbal-Chiles area, the Baudó Mountains, the northern Chocó-Antioquia border, Serranía de San Lucas, and the city of Bogotá and its immediate surroundings. Anyone contemplating a visit to these areas should seek local assistance and the advice of INDERENA.

## SANTA MARTA REGION

The picturesque seaport of Santa Marta is situated amidst dry scrub at the northeastern base of the Santa Marta Mountains. Accommodations are least expensive in Santa Marta and south of town in Rodadero, although the hotels farther south, such as the Irotama, offer a more convenient base from which to explore this diverse region. In the dry scrub look for Blue-tailed Emerald, Steely-vented Hummingbird, Russet-throated Puffbird, Pale-legged Hornero, White-fringed Antwren, Black-crested Antshrike, Slender-billed Tyrannulet, *Myiarchus*, Bicolored Wren, Yellow Oriole, Grayish Saltator, and Pileated Finch.

Tayrona National Park is a major point of interest for those wishing to explore a gradient of tropical zone forests from dry to humid. The best humid zone can be reached thirty minutes east of Santa Marta on the road to Ríohacha—watch for the paved and well-marked Cañaveral entrance on the left. Just inside the entrance and on trails radiating from the vicinity of the restaurant and parking lot ahead, one may see King Vulture, Military Macaw, Pale-bellied and Long-tailed hermits, White-chinned Sapphire, White-bearded and Lance-tailed manakins, a multitude of small flycatchers, Rufous-and-white Wren, Red-legged Honeycreeper, and Yellow-tailed or Orange-crowned orioles. White-bellied Antbirds sing loudly from the woodland undergrowth.

To see birds typical of the Guajira desert scrub, such as Bare-eyed Pigeon, Blue-crowned Parakeet, White-whiskered Spinetail, Orinocan Saltator, Vermilion Cardinal, Tocuyo Sparrow, and Black-faced Grassquit, one must drive much farther east toward Ríohacha. The first patch of desert scrub is on the left near km 130, a second near km 140. Ríohacha is still twenty kilometers beyond.

The Santa Marta Mountains harbor twelve endemic species of birds, and eleven of these can be seen by exploring the Minca road, which begins on the right immediately past the police checkpoint east of Santa Marta. A four-wheel drive is helpful on this road, and essential during the September–December wet period. Allow three hours to reach the INDERENA experimental station of San Lorenzo and plan to concentrate most of your time along the forested road below the station and at patches of roadside woodland above the station to the end of the road at the second telecommunication tower. In the lower zone, 1700-2000m, look for Streak-capped Spinetail, Santa Marta Antpitta, Yellow-crowned Redstart, Santa Marta Mountain-Tanager, and Santa Marta Brush-Finch. White-rumped Hawk also occurs in this zone. Higher elevations are better for Black-and-chestnut Eagle, Sickle-winged Guan, White-tailed Starfrontlet, Rusty-headed Spinetail, Brown-rumped Tapaculo, Santa Marta Warbler, and Santa Marta Parakeet. Andean Condor is occasionally overhead in either zone.

Salamanca National Park, another area of interest, is a mixture of mangroves, tidal pools, and desert scrub one hour west of Santa Marta on the road to Barranquilla. Most of the park lies on a long, narrow strip of sand that separates Ciénega Grande Lake from the Caribbean. To reach the park, follow the coastal highway south from Santa Marta and bear west through Ciénaga. Shortly after crossing the large coastal bridge, you will see a sign marking the entrance to the park. At dawn in the desert scrub at the east end of the park, watch for Bare-eyed Pigeons and Chestnut-winged Chachalacas perched atop the tall cactus. At the Los Cocos headquarters near the west end of the park a long boardwalk winds for a kilometer or more through tidal flats and mangroves. The mangrove forests along the boardwalk are a good place to see Pied Puffbird, Chestnut Piculet, Red-rumped Woodpecker, Scrub Flycatcher, and Bicolored Conebill. Waders, raptors, swallows, and other species often abound on the tidal flats. Opposite Los Cocos and a half kilometer east, scan the marshes for Northern Screamer and White-faced Whistling-Duck.

The long bumpy road south along the western base of the Santa Marta Mountains is poorly maintained, and the region is heavily deforested. Nevertheless, it is a good place to see several species that are rare or do not occur elsewhere in the Santa Marta region. These include Greater Ani, Pale-legged Hornero (very common), One-colored Becard, Lesser Kiskadee, Band-backed Wren, and Black-capped Donacobius. In the extensive marshes between Fundación and Pivijay, Northern Screamers and occasionally Red-and-green Macaws can be seen in numbers.

### BOGOTÁ

Most visitors eventually pass through Bogotá, the nation's capital. Although the region is now largely deforested, many interesting birds can still be found in small tracts of woodland near the city. *Caution* is advised, however, as thieves are a potential problem in many areas in or near Bogotá. In general those who use hired green and white tourist taxis at major hotels or seek buses with knowledgeable local drivers will not encounter problems.

Parque La Florida is a small, pleasant little marsh very near the El Dorado International airport. At dawn it is an excellent locality to look for Least Bittern, Masked Duck, Bogotá Rail, Spot-flanked Gallinule, Noble Snipe, Apolinar's Marsh-Wren, Band-tailed Seedeater, and yellow-finches.

For a half day or more, the Choachí road provides a good introduction to temperate zone birds of the Eastern Andes. About thirty minutes eastward above Bogotá and near the first pass (where one can safely watch birds) one may find Glowing and Coppery-bellied pufflegs, Black-tailed Trainbearer, Bronze-tailed Thornbill, Bearded Helmet-crest, Rufous-browed Conebill, and a variety of tanagers and finches. Farther on, the road crosses a small paramo.

### CALI

Cali is the best base from which to explore southwestern Colombia, and most visitors to this part of Colombia will begin their birding here. Additional details on this region can be obtained in M. Gochfeld and G. Tudor (1974, *Birding* 6:101-115).

*Pichindé Valley*

Less than one hour southwest of Cali, this is the best place to look for the Andean Cock-of-the-Rock. At the Cali water treatment plant entrance, bear uphill off Avenida Circumvalación and onto the road to the statue of Christ (El Christo Rey). The road climbs steadily for several kilometers with a fine view of Cali, then crosses a deep valley and climbs through a zone of well-kept vacation homes. Shortly beyond the first river crossing (rushing torrent) keep left, cross the river again, and then generally bear right at several forks. Several kilometers ahead watch for a white building on the left with the words Casa Blanca on the side. From here upward the road parallels the Cock-of-the-Rock Reserve (Reserva de los Gallos de Monte) in the forested valley below. From the road or in the forest below watch for Crested and Golden-headed quetzals, Red-headed Barbet, Red-faced Spinetail, Sooty-headed and Golden-faced tyrannulets, Glossy-black Thrush, Blue-naped Chlorophonia, and Fawn-breasted, Multicolored, Golden, Metallic-green, Golden-naped, and Bay-headed tanagers.

At least three forest trails penetrate to the river; the first two enter inconspicuously just below the first house on the left beyond Casa Blanca. Here look for White-tailed Hillstar, Bronzy Inca, Booted Racket-tail, Grayish Piculet, Spotted Barbtail, Slaty, Antwren, Black-billed Peppershrike, and Rufous-naped Greenlet; nearer the river Torrent Duck, White-capped Dipper, and Ash-throated Bush-Tanager. The best areas for the Cock-of-the-Rock, as well as Crested Ant-Tanagers, are where these trails intersect the river, or farther up the road where a short trail angles to the river, which is now close to the road. The road continues to a small store, then turns sharply left. There is some habitat beyond the store.

*Kilometer 18 ("El 18")*

Eighteen kilometers above Cali on the road to Buenaventura the highway crosses a low pass over the Western Andes at about 1800m. Turn right onto an inconspicuous gravel road between two restaurants at "El 18" and continue a half kilometer or more beyond to the small woodland that borders both sides of the road. The habitat is limited, but many interesting birds may be found here, including Buff-tailed Coronet, Greenish Puffleg, Blue-crowned Motmot, several foliage-gleaners, Streak-capped Treehunter, Green-and-black Fruiteater, Handsome Flycatcher, Russet-crowned Warbler, Multicolored, Saffron-crowned, Metallic-green, Golden-naped, and Beryl-spangled tanagers, and Blue-winged Mountain-Tanager. Chestnut-crowned Antpitta and Chestnut-breasted Wren are frequently heard. Retracing back down the main highway toward Cali, take the narrow road to the left (marked San Antonio) near km 16. The road climbs rapidly through a settled area of fine weekend homes. At the first fork, about two kilometers ahead, the main or left branch continues several kilometers through forest to a telecommunications tower at 2100m. At the right branch of this fork it is possible to walk ahead a few meters and scramble up the steep right bank (house on left) and onto a fine, though slippery forest trail. Birds are similar to those at "El 18" although in the forest Wedge-billed Hummingbird, Uniform Antshrike, or even an Undulated Antpitta could be encountered.

*The Old Buenaventura Road*

This is probably one of the best areas in the world for seeing a rich diversity of tropical birds, many of which occur only in the narrow belt of wet forest from extreme eastern Panama to northwestern Ecuador. To reach it from Cali, bear left off the paved road to Buenaventura at km 21. The best areas, however, are at least two and a half hours away and more easily reached from Buenaventura by bearing right at the checkpoint outside of town. Leave early from the raucous port city of Buenaventura and look for birds along the lower section between km 80 and 115 during the morning hours. Most of the roadside habitat is varying stages of second growth mixed with taller trees where a large number of birds can always be found. A sampling could include, Scaled Pigeon, Blue-headed and Mealy parrots, Streaked Antwren, Jet, Chestnut-backed, and Immaculate antbirds, Fulvous-bellied Antpitta (voice), White-ringed Flycatcher, Bay Wren, Scarlet-rumped Cacique, Purple Honeycreeper, and Scarlet-browed, Dusky-faced, and Tawny-crowned tanagers. At the confluence of the Río Aguaclara with the Río Anchicayá the road gradually winds upward into the foothills and through an ever unfolding panorama of steep, forest-clad slopes, cascading waterfalls, and cloud-filled valleys. Some of Colombia's most exciting birds can be found in this zone, especially between km 60 and 76. A sampling might include, Barred Hawk, Beautiful Parrot, White-whiskered Hermit, Empress Brilliant, Blue-tailed Trogon, Brown-billed Scythebill, Long-tailed Tyrant, Lemon-browned Flycatcher, Slaty-capped Shrike-Vireo, Scarlet-thighed Dacnis, Yellow-collared Chlorophonia, and many other tanagers, especially Rufous-throated, Gray-and-gold, Golden-chested, Ochre-breasted, and Scarlet-and-white. At the tiny town of Danubio a bridge across the Río Anchicayá gives access to the new hydroelectric plant far up the Anchicayá Valley. Permission can be obtained from the CVC (Corporación Autónoma del Cauca) in Cali to enter this road and secure overnight accommodations. Birds are much like those along the main road, although Long-wattled Umbrellabird (rare) has been seen here. The remainder of the Old Buenaventura Road, from Danubio to Queremal and to the junction with the New (paved) Buenaventura Road, is mostly deforested (the fine cloud forest above Queremal at Tokio is now off limits to visitors).

Limited habitat also exists along the lower section of the New Buenaventura Road. Leaving Buenaventura, bear left onto the gravel road at km 100. The habitat is similar to the lower section of the Old Road but along the first kilometer or two several interesting species are regular, including Semiplumbeous Hawk, Choco and Chestnut-mandibled toucans, Pied Puffbird, Blue Cotinga, White Cotinga, Slate-throated Gnatcatcher, and Blue-whiskered Tanager. Less likely are Saffron-headed Parrot and Five-colored Barbet.

*Laguna de Sonso*

Laguna de Sonso, an old oxbow of the Cauca River, provides a fine introduction to birdlife of the rural farmland and aquatic habitats of the Cauca Valley. It is easily visited in a day from Cali, and is only minutes from the splendid Hotel Guadalajara in Buga. From Buga proceed west about three or four kilometers on the paved highway to Buenaventura. Where the highway swings southward with a fine elevated view of hyacinth-choked marshland and small pools of open water, watch for Cocoi Heron, Pinnated Bittern (rare), Buff-necked Ibis (rare), Whispering Ibis, Horned Screamer, Black-bellied and Fulvous whistling-ducks, Snail Kite, Yellow-breasted Crake, Pale-breasted Spinetail, and Pied Water-Tyrant. Less than one kilometer ahead and just before crossing the Cauca River bridge, a small, elevated dirt road on the left leads to several haciendas. In the viny thickets or *Tillandsia*-draped trees along this road Spectacled Parrotlet, Dwarf, Dark-billed, Little, and Striped cuckoos, Jet Antbird, Cinereous Becard, Sooty-capped, Southern Beardless-, Golden-faced, and Mouse-colored tyrannulets, Spot-breasted Woodpecker, Crimson-backed Tanager and a variety of seedeaters and seed-finches should be seen; less commonly Apical Flycatcher and Orange-crowned Euphonia. The first left, a dusty track that is muddy and slippery in wet weather, leads to a private ranch house. Ask permission if you want to walk ahead to the lake. Bear right (south) from the house and be sure to close all gates.

The south end of the lake can be reached by crossing the Cauca River bridge on the main highway, and turning left at the first gravel road, which leads to the small village of Yotoco. At the far side of town a narrow road winds left a kilometer or so to the Cauca River. Cross the river on the ferry and continue by foot in either direction along the elevated dikes.

### POPAYAN TO PARQUE NACIONAL PURACÉ AND SAN AGUSTÍN

From the pleasant colonial town of Popayán with its springlike climate and fine hotel, travelers are less than two hours from the high, shrub-scattered slopes and wet paramos of Puracé Park. This, perhaps Colombia's most scenic park, straddles the backbone of the Central Andes at elevations of 2500-4700m. Seven active volcanos are often snow-covered. From Popayán (km 200), the road climbs steadily eastward, passing the tiny town of Puracé. Some distance beyond at km 153 watch for a panorama of cliffs on the left where Andean Condors roost (arrive early) and Black-chested Buzzard-Eagle is occasionally seen. At km 152 a right fork off the main Popayán-Neiva road doubles back sharply and climbs for about one and a half kilometers where an inconspicuous left fork then leads to Pilimbalá, the park headquarters. The shrubbery surrounding the restaurant, cabins, and thermal baths at Pilimbalá is home to Shining Sunbeam, Golden-breasted Puffleg, Purple-backed Thornbill, several flower-piercers, Tufted Tit-Tyrant, Scarlet-bellied Mountain-Tanager, Pale-naped Brush-Finch, and other birds. Higher on the boggy slopes in the valley behind, Noble Snipe, Andean Tit-Spinetail, Tawny Antpitta, Plain-colored Seedeater, and Plumbeous Sierra-Finch can be found. An ill-marked trail (ask for a guide) goes to the cinder cone of Volcán Puracé, 4700m, an eight-hour round trip from Pilimbalá.

Returning to the main Popayán-Neiva road, bear right and continue eastward through mixed temperate forest/paramo ecotone to the mist-shrouded and bamboo-dominated forests on the eastern slope of the park. Best areas here are between km 141 and 144, especially along the roadside near the trailhead to the Termales de San Juan. A new hotel is being built here at the time of this writing. On the river look for Torrent Duck, and along the roadside for mixed flocks that contain Glowing Puffleg, Mountain Avocetbill (rare), Agile Tit-Tyrant, numerous tanagers, Plush-capped Finch, and Slaty Brush-Finch. Those with additional time can visit the oilbird cave about ten kilometers beyond, or Finca Merenberg, a private farm with lovely subtropical forest. Merenberg, owned by Gunther Buch, lies one and a half hours ahead. Visitors are welcome.

An even more spectacular portion of the park can be visited by following the Coconuco road at the junction at km 172 on the Popayán-Neiva Road. This road ascends a broad verdant valley to Coconuco, crosses a bleak highland paramo near Paletará, and finally enters the southwestern end of the park at 3000m. The road beyond winds through an exotic highland world of misty bamboo, giant grasses, and stunted, bromeliad-encrusted trees. Here, in one of the wildest and most scenic sections of the park, virtually all of the birds characteristic of temperate forests in the Central Andes can be seen, including Buff-breasted and Black-chested mountain-tanagers, Black-headed Hemispingus, and the rare Masked Mountain-Tanager. Presently the road ends about ten kilometers inside the park, but eventually it should connect with an adjoining road from San Agustín and Isnos in the Magdalena Valley. This latter road, though seldom traveled, is equally scenic; we have found Andean Guan, Swallow-tailed Nightjar, Black-billed Mountain-Toucan, and White-rimmed Brush-Finch there. When the last link between these two roads is completed, a journey from Popayán to San Agustín should require less than five hours. For more information on Puracé Park see S. Hilty and J. Silliman (1983, *American Birds* 37:247-256).

There is limited habitat around rural San Agustín, but the archeological park there is a great treasure, there are fine accommodations, and the woodlands inside the park harbor many birds. Those of particular interest include Shining-green Hummingbird, Booted Rac-ket-tail, White-backed Fire-eye, and the endemic Dusky-headed Brush-Finch and Bar-crested Antshrike.

### POPAYAN TO CERRO MUNCHIQUE AND PARQUE NACIONAL MUNCHIQUE

From Popayán it is two long and dusty hours through uninspiring bare hills to either of these fine areas of wet upper subtropical forest on the Pacific slope. Leave Popayán at the Mobil service station; the road is paved for the first eight kilometers. About thirty minutes west of town the road forks, the left one leading to Tambo and eventually to Cerro Munchique and beyond; the right or main fork continues straight ahead and with a second right fork farther on, leads to Uribe (km 18), Romelia, and Parque Nacional Munchique (km post 41).

Near the base of Cerro Munchique, ca. km 52-53, a narrow but well maintained gravel track (gate or cattle guard at entrance) on the right leads to the telecommunications tower atop the mountain. Early in the morning there is a marvelous panorama of clouds and forest from the tower, and in the forest just below some of the following should be seen: Collared Inca, Sword-billed Hummingbird, Tourmaline Sun-angel, Chestnut-crowned Antpitta, Red-crested Cotinga, Yellow-bel-lied and Rufous-breasted chat-tyrants, Rufous-headed Pygmy-Tyrant, White-banded Tyrannulet, Capped Conebill, Hooded Mountain-Tan-ager, Gray-hooded Bush-Tanager, Grass-green Tanager, and Rufous-naped Brush-finch. Returning to the main road continue ahead one kilometer to the pass or slightly beyond, where several of the above species as well as Long-tailed Antbird and Barred Fruiteater occur. In mixed flocks farther down the road Rufous Spinetail, Pearled Treerunner, Sepia-brown Wren, Citrine Warbler, Dusky-bellied Bush-Tanager, Tanager-Finch, and many others may be found. The road continues through good habitat for ten kilometers below the pass, eventually ending at a tiny, unappealing settlement.

Birds of Munchique National Park are similar to those of the Cerro Munchique area (above), which lies just to the south. Many species can be seen near the INDERENA headquarters at the park entrance. This is the only known locality of the rare Colorful Puffleg and a kilometer or so beyond the headquarters is an excellent place to look for the Tanager-Finch. Both areas are, unfortunately, often foggy and rainy, so arrive early. On clear days one can see the Pacific Ocean and Gorgona Island from the pass just behind the park headquarters.

*Caution.* Travelers should be advised that at the present writing, 1984, guerrilla activity and bandits have been reported in both of the above areas. On Cerro Munchique, birding should be confined to the telecommunications tower road and the pass or immediately below.

At the National Park, visitors should stay near the headquaters and should always consult with INDERENA personnel upon arrival.

### FLORENCIA

For visitors based in the Magdalena Valley at San Agustín or Garzón, the long winding road over the eastern cordillera provides a dramatic cross-section of Andean species, as one descends into the Amazonian lowlands at Florencia. Along this road, forest is still extensive at higher elevations but fragmented at lower elevations. In the higher zones watch for Andean Guan, Black-billed Mountain-Toucan, Barred Becard, Golden-crowned Tanager, and Short-billed Bush-Tanager, as well as an occasional Black-and-chestnut Eagle. At lower elevations, between km 52 and 56, where the road is close to the Río Hacha, mixed flocks may contain Ash-breasted Spinetail, Yellow-breasted Antwren, Gray-mantled Wren, Golden-collared Honeycreeper, and many small tanagers including Paradise and Golden-cheeked. Andean Cock-of-the-Rocks can be heard in the ravine below, though are often troublesome to see unless they ascend into a fruiting tree. Less regularly seen in this zone are Solitary Eagle and small groups of Red-bellied Grackles, the latter often with mixed flocks. In the foothills, lower still, forest is patchy and limited near the road, but this is a good region for species of Amazonian affinity such as Variable (Speckled) Chachalaca, Gray-chinned Hermit, Black-spotted Barbet, Lettered Aracari, Stripe-chested Antwren, Amazonian Umbrellabird, Golden-browed Tody-Flycatcher, Rufous-tailed Flatbill, and Silver-beaked Tanager. Squirrel Monkeys are relatively common in woodland, even along the roadside. The lowlands around Florencia are now entirely deforested and devoted to cattle production. The birder will find little of interest beyond Florencia by road.

### PASTO TO MOCOA

For those with time, the long road from Pasto to Mocoa offers excellent highland birding. Accommodations are available at Laguna La Cocha and at Mocoa, and a long two-hour drive either way reaches a twenty-five-kilometer section of undisturbed forest at 1800-2300m. Birds of this region include Dusky Piha, Sulphur-bellied Tyrannulet, Turquoise Jay, Chestnut-bellied Thrush, Deep-blue Flower-piercer, Orange-eared, Flame-faced, Beryl-spangled, Blue-browed, and White-capped tanagers, and White-rimmed Brush-Finch. At the Nariño-Putumayo border the road narrows to a one-way series of switchbacks as it drops down the eastern wall of the Andes to Mocoa. This steep section is definitely not for the faint-of-heart or those in a hurry. From the bottom, it is about one hour through largely deforested foothills to a junction in the road. The left branch leads to Mocoa, ten kilometers away, the main branch, straight ahead, continues to Puerto Asís, where overland connections can be made to the Río San Miguel and Ecuador, or to the Amazon via boats that ply the Río Putumayo and Río Amazon to Leticia. The latter trip is an adventure of nearly two weeks.

### PASTO TO TUMACO AND BARBACOAS

The only access by road to Colombia's spectacular avifauna in southwestern Nariño is the long dusty trip from Pasto west through Túquerres and Ricaurte to Junín. It is about five hours to Ricaurte, two more to Junín. Leaving the Pasto-Ipiales road at Imues, the road climbs through picturesque wheat fields to Túquerres, then crosses a long, dry altiplano and finally descends gradually to Ricaurte. There are no accommodations beyond Ricaurte (best hotels on west side of town) until one reaches Tumaco or Barbacoas. The best roadside birding is still two hours ahead in the forested hills above Junín. Between 1100-1300m look for Red-winged Parrotlet, Purple-bibbed Whitetip, Velvet-purple Coronet, Hoary Puffleg, Toucan Barbet (common), Rufous-breasted Antthrush, Black Solitaire, Indigo Flowerpiercer, Rufous-throated and Moss-backed tanagers. Excellent forest continues well below Junín (no accommodations) on the road to Barbacoas or the main road to Tumaco. Below Junín look for Orange-fronted Barbet and Scarlet-breasted Dacnis; Velvet-purple Coronet is more common here as well. From Junín it is four hours to Tumaco, mostly through cleared or partially cleared humid lowlands. Vast mangrove forests line the coast and islands near Tumaco. It is about two and a half hours from Junín to Barbacoas.

### LETICIA

Colombia's main port on the Amazon is comfortable, convenient, and rich in birdlife. There is daily jet service from Bogotá, three modern hotels, and excellent guide service available, especially through Turamazonas operated by Mike Tsalickis. A minimum of two days should be spent at Monkey Island Lodge located on an Amazon river island about three hours northwest of Leticia by boat. On the island an assortment of oropendolas, parrots, parakeets, and other species can easily be found, as well as Undulated Tinamou (common voice), Hoatzin, Long-billed Woodcreeper, Castelnau's Antshrike, and Ash-breasted Antbird. From the lodge full day or half day trips can be planned to the Rio Cayarú on the Peruvian bank, to sand bars and scrub on Isla

Corea, or to Quebrada Tucuchira and other streams and forest trails on the north bank of the Amazon where many birds will be seen. A sampling would include up to five species of macaws, ten of parrots and parakeets, four aracaris, and five nightjars, as well as herons, sungrebes, terns, skimmers, and a multitude of smaller birds.

For those based in Leticia and on a smaller budget the long road north of town and its several branches offer many possibilities. Trails leave the road in many places (inquire) and give access to good *terra firme* forest. From trails at km 6, 7, or 10, a sampling of species might include Pavonine Quetzal, Rufous-tailed Xenops, Chestnut-winged Hookbill, Black Bushbird, Reddish-winged Bare-eye, Short-billed Honeycreeper, and Paradise Tanager. A similar road, the Incer Road, runs east of Leticia into Brazil and has a fine branch running north.

Longer trips of several days to a week or more can also be arranged to points farther up the Amazon, e.g., Amacayacú National Park, or to the Rio Javarí, Rio Putumayo, and elsewhere. Near the tiny Indian village of Pobre Allegre or farther up the Rio Javarí, an astonishing variety of birds can be seen. There is daily ferry service between Leticia and Benjamin Constant, Leticia's sister city on the Brazilian bank. More details on Leticia can be found in Remsen (1978).

OTHER AREAS

There are many other excellent areas in Colombia that are not discussed above because access is difficult and time-consuming, accommodations often lacking, and/or special preparations are required. Some are poorly explored ornithologically, and we hope that travelers with the interest and a certain spirit of adventure will wish to investigate further.

# APPENDIX B

# Birds of Isla San Andrés and Isla Providencia

Isla San Andrés and Providencia are two Colombian islands located in the western Caribbean. San Andrés lies about 200 kilometers east of Nicaragua, Providencia about 100 kilometers north of San Andrés. San Andrés is a small, 13 x 4 kilometer sand and limestone island rising to a height of about 100m. Its vegetation is predominantly coconut palm groves, with scattered mangroves, bushy pastures, and some areas of native trees. Providencia is smaller, 5 x 8 kilometers, volcanic, and has steep hills rising to 380m. Most of Providencia is deforested and devoted to ranching. The resident and migrant avifauna of the islands are treated in Bond (1961), the migrants of San Andrés by Paulson et al. (1969), and the residents and some migrants of both islands by Russell et al. (1979). Sixteen resident land bird species and seventy-six migrant species have been recorded (incl. sight records) on the islands. Two species, the Green Heron and Yellow Warbler, are represented by both resident and migrant forms.

### NONRESIDENT SPECIES

Pied-billed Grebe
Audubon's (Dusky-backed) Shearwater
Red-footed Booby
Brown Booby
Magnificent Frigatebird
Great Blue Heron
Great (Common) Egret
Snowy Egret
Little Blue Heron
Tricolored Heron
Green Heron
Cattle Egret
Black-crowned Night-Heron
Yellow-crowned Night-Heron
Glossy Ibis
Blue-winged Teal
Ring-necked Duck
Lesser Scaup
Osprey
Merlin
American Kestrel
Sora
Common Gallinule
Purple Gallinule
American Coot
Black-bellied Plover
Semipalmated Plover
Killdeer
Ruddy Turnstone

Solitary Sandpiper
Lesser Yellowlegs
Greater Yellowlegs
Spotted Sandpiper
Willet
Least Sandpiper
Semipalmated Sandpiper
Western Sandpiper
Sanderling
Whimbrel
Laughing Gull
Sooty Tern
Tern (*Sterna* sp.)
Royal Tern
Belted Kingfisher
Common Nighthawk
Yellow-bellied Sapsucker
Eastern Kingbird
Eastern Wood-Pewee
Bank Swallow
Barn Swallow
Cliff Swallow
Gray Catbird
Black-and-white Warbler
Tennessee Warbler
Parula Warbler
Yellow Warbler
Chestnut-sided Warbler
Black-throated Blue Warbler

Black-throated Green Warbler
Cape May Warbler
Magnolia Warbler
Yellow-rumped (Myrtle) Warbler
Palm Warbler
Black-poll Warbler
Bay-breasted Warbler
American Redstart
Ovenbird
Northern Waterthrush

Louisiana Waterthrush
Worm-eating Warbler
Prothonotary Warbler
Common Yellowthroat
Kentucky Warbler
Hooded Warbler
Dickcissel
Indigo Bunting
Rose-breasted Grosbeak

### RESIDENT SPECIES
(c = common; u = uncommon; r = rare; SA = San Andrés only)

Green Heron
White-crowned Pigeon c
White-winged Dove c
Caribbean Dove u, SA
Mangrove Cuckoo r
Smooth-billed Ani
Green-breasted Mango
Caribbean Elaenia c

St. Andrew Mockingbird (ENDEMIC) SA
San Andrés Vireo (ENDEMIC) c
Thick-billed Vireo c
Black-whiskered Vireo u
Bananaquit c
Yellow Warbler c
Jamaican Oriole c, SA
Black-faced Grassquit c

# APPENDIX C

## Subspecies Illustrated

### PLATE I

1. *P. haliaetus carolinensis*
2. *C. atratus brasiliensis*
3. *P. carunculatus*
4. *C. aura ruficollis*
5. *C. burrovianus*
6. *C. melambrotus*
7. *M. chimachima cordatus*
8. *P. plancus cheriway*
9. *D. ater*
10. *D. a. americanus*

### PLATE II

1. *B. albonotatus*
2. *B. b. brachyurus*
3. *B. albigula*
4. *B. leucorrhous*
5. *B. n. nitidus*
6. *B. p. platypterus*
7. *B. m. magnirostris*
8. *C. u. uncinatus*
9. *H. b. bidentatus*
10. *A. striatus ventralis*

### PLATE III

1. *G. c. caerulescens*
2. *C. u. uncinatus*
3. *B. albonotatus*
4. *L. schistacea*
5. *H. hamatus*
6. *R. s. sociabilis*
7. *L. cayanensis*
8. *C. cinereus*
9. *C. buffoni*

### PLATE IV

1. *G. melanoleucus australis*
2. *B. albicaudatus colonus*
3. *H. meridionalis.*
4. *B. n. nigricollis*
5. *B. a. anthracinus*
6. *B. u. urubitinga*
7. *H. s. solitarius*

### PLATE V

1. *L. a. albicollis*
2. *L. melanops*
3. *C. u. uncinatus*
4. *L. cayanensis*

5. *S. melanoleucus*
6. *S. o. ornatus*

### PLATE VI

1. *M. s. semitorquatus*
2. *S. o. ornatus*
3. *S. tyrannus serus*
4. *O. isidori*
5. *M. guianensis*
6. *H. harpyja*

### PLATE VII

1. *G. melanoleucus australis*
2. *O. isidori*
3. *B. p. polyosoma*
4. *L. princeps*
5. *E. caeruleus*
6. *I. plumbea*
7. *F. r. rufigularis*
8. *G. swainsonii leonae*
9. *F. peregrinus anatum*
10. *F. f. femoralis*
11. *F. c. columbarius*
12. *F. sparverius isabellinus*

### PLATE VIII

1. *C. daubentoni*
2. *C. alberti*
3. *C. p. pauxi*
4. *A. pipile cumanensis*
5. *C. alector erythrognatha*
6. *C. globulosa*
7. *N. urumutum*
8. *C. tomentosa*
9. *C. salvini*
10. *C. mitu tuberosa*

### PLATE IX

1. *P. p. perspicillata*
2. *C. v. virgata*
3. *C. albitarsus*
4. *C. nigrolineata*
5. *C. h. huhula*
6. *L. c. cristata*
7. *R. c. clamator*
8. *A. flammeus bogotensis*
9. *A. stygius robustus*
10. *B. virginianus elutus*
11. *O. guatemalae vermiculatus*

12. *O. choliba crucigerus*
13. *O. w. watsonii*
14. *O. a. albogularis*
15. *A. h. harrisii*

## PLATE X

1. *P. nacunda minor*
2. *C. r. rupestris*
3. *C. a. acutipennis*
4. *C. pusillus septentrionalis*
5. *N. leucopyga exigua*
6. *L. s. semitorquatus*
7. *N. grandis*
8. *N. aethereus longicaudatus*
9. *N. leucopterus maculosus*
10. *N. bracteatus*
11. *N. griseus panamensis*

## PLATE XI

1. *C. a. acutipennis*
2. *H. c. climacocerca*
3. *N. a. albicollis*
4. *C. c. cayennensis*
5. *C. longirostris ruficervix*
6. *C. parvulus heterurus*
7. *C. maculicaudus*
8. *C. n. nigrescens*
9. *C. rufus minimus*
10. *U. l. lyra*

## PLATE XII

1. *S. zonaris albicincta*
2. *C. rutilus brunnitorques*
3. *C. cryptus*
4. *C. cherriei*
5. *C. spinicauda aethalea*
6. *C. cinereiventris sclateri*
7. *C. lemosi*
8. *C. chapmani viridipennis*
9. *C. b. brachyura*
10. *C. andrei meridionalis*
11. *A. montivagus*
12. *P. c. cayennensis*
13. *R. squamata semota*
14. *M. furcata*

## PLATE XIII

1. *F. unduligera fulva*
2. *T. major granadensis*
3. *C. lineatus intermedius*
4. *T. doliatus fraterculus*
5. *T. m. multistriatus*
6. *T. palliatus tenuifasciatus*
7. *P. scutatus occidentalis*
8. *G. foetidus*

9. *C. ornatus*
10. *C. penduliger*

## PLATE 1

1. *N. b. bonapartei*
2. *T. tao septentrionalis*
3. *T. major peruvianus*
4. *C. obsoletus castaneus*
5. *C. soui caucae*
6. *C. undulatus yapura*
7. *C. erythropus cursitans*
8. *C. v. variegatus*
9. *N. julius*
10. *T. guttatus*
11. *C. casiquiare*
12. *O. gujanensis marmoratus*
13. *C. berlepschi*
14. *C. c. cinereus*
15. *R. cinctus australis*
16. *O. hyperythrus*
17. *O. a. atrifrons*
18. *O. erythrops parambae*

## PLATE 2

1. *N. violacea cayennensis*
2. *N. nycticorax hoactli*
3. *C. c. cochlearius*
4. *P. pileatus*
5. *T. fasciatum salmoni*
6. *T. l. lineatum*
7. *B. pinnatus*
8. *I. involucris*
9. *B. s. striatus*
10. *Z. undulatus*
11. *I. exilis erythromelas*
12. *S. sibilatrix fostersmithi*
13. *H. tricolor ruficollis*
14. *A. agami*

## PLATE 3

1. *A. g. guarauna*
2. *P. f. falcinellus*
3. *E. ruber*
4. *T. c. caudatus*
5. *M. cayennensis*
6. *P. infuscatus berlepschi*
7. *C. oxycerca*
8. *N. jubata*
9. *O. dominica*
10. *A. brasiliensis*
11. *A. d. discors*
12. *A. flavirostris altipetens*
13. *A. b. bahamensis*
14. *M. armata colombiana*
15. *D. autumnalis discolor*
16. *D. viduata*
17. *D. bicolor*

PLATE 4

1. *M. chimachima cordatus*
2. *I. plumbea*
3. *L. semiplumbea*
4. *L. plumbea*
5. *B. n. nitidus*
6. *L. schistacea*
7. *G. c. caerulescens*
8. *M. s. semitorquatus*
9. *R. s. sociabilis*
10. *H. hamatus*
11. *C. u. uncinatus*
12. *L. princeps*
13. *P. u. unicinctus*
14. *H. meridionalis*
15. *B. n. nigricollis*

PLATE 5

1. *F. r. rufigularis*
2. *F. deiroleucus*
3. *F. f. femoralis*
4. *F. sparverius isabellinus*
5. *G. swainsonii leonae*
6. *B. n. nitidus*
7. *B. m. magnirostris*
8. *B. p. platypterus*
9. *H. b. bidentatus*
10. *A. b. bicolor*
11. *A. striatus ventralis*
12. *A. poliogaster*
13. *A. s. superciliosus*
14. *M. s. semitorquatus*
15. *M. mirandollei*
16. *M. gilvicollis*
17. *M. ruficollis zonothorax*

PLATE 6

1. *A. aburri*
2. *N. geoffroyi salvini*
3. *N. radiolosus*
4. *C. g. goudotii*
5. *P. perspicax*
6. *P. purpurascens aequatorialis*
7. *O. g. garrula*
8. *P. ortoni*
9. *O. motmot columbiana*
10. *O. r. ruficauda*
11. *P. argyrotis colombiana*
12. *P. m. montagnii*
13. *P. jacquacu orienticola*

PLATE 7

1. *P. nigricans caucae*
2. *A. wolfi*
3. *A. c. cajanea*

4. *A. axillaris*
5. *P. m. maculatus*
6. *R. semiplumbeus*
7. *P. carolina*
8. *P albicollis typhoeca*
9. *P. f. flaviventer*
10. *M. s. schomburgkii*
11. *N. erythrops olivascens*
12. *L. exilis*
13. *L. a. albigularis*
14. *P. flavirostris*
15. *P. martinica*
16. *G. melanops bogotensis*
17. *A. v. viridis*
18. *H. fulica*
19. *A. concolor castaneus*
20. *A. castaneiceps*
21. *A. fasciatus*

PLATE 8

1. *C. corensis*
2. *C. cayennensis pallidicrissa*
3. *C. speciosa*
4. *C. subvinacea purpureotincta*
5. *C. fasciata albilinea*
6. *S. squammata ridgwayi*
7. *C. passerina albivitta*
8. *C. talpacoti rufipennis*
9. *C. m. minuta*
10. *Z. auriculata stenura*
11. *C. pretiosa*
12. *C. m. mondetoura*
13. *L. v. verreauxi*
14. *L. rufaxilla dubusi*
15. *G. m. montana*
16. *G. violacea albiventer*
17. *G. l. linearis*

PLATE 9

1. *P. pulchra*
2. *P. pyrilia*
3. *H. a. amazonina*
3a. *H. a. fuertesi*
4. *L. branickii*
5. *O. icterotis*
6. *C. subvinacea berlepschi*
7. *C. plumbea chapmani*
8. *C. goodsoni*
9. *M. melanoptera saturatior*
10. *L. c. cassinii*
11. *L. conoveri*
12. *L. plumbeiceps*
13. *L. pallida*
14. *G. saphirina purpurata*
15. *G. veraguensis*
16. *G. frenata bourcieri*
17. *G. g. goldmani*

## PLATE 10

1. A. pertinax aeruginosa
2. A. weddellii
3. A. acuticauda haemorrhous
4. A. l. leucophthalmus
5. A. wagleri transilis
6. F. xanthopterygius spengeli
7. F. c. conspicillatus
8. F. s. sclateri
9. P. melanura souancei
10. P. picta caeruleiceps
11. P. calliptera
12. P. viridicata
13. B. ferrugineifrons
14. B. lineola tigrinus
15. B. jugularis exsul
16. B. v. versicolurus
17. T. purpurata viridiceps
18. T. stictoptera
19. T. d. dilectissima
20. G. brachyurus
21. B. c. cyanoptera
22. B. s. sanctithomae
23. P. barrabandi
24. P. m. melanocephala

## PLATE 11

1. A. ararauna
2. A. chloroptera
3. A. macao
4. A. m. militaris
5. A. severa castaneifrons
6. A. manilata
7. A. l. leucophthalmus
8. D. a. accipitrinus
9. P. chalcopterus
10. P. s. sordidus
11. P. tumultuosus
12. P. m. menstruus
13. A. mercenaria canipalliata
14. A. a. amazonica
15. A. f. festiva
16. A. o. ochrocephala
17. A. farinosa chapmani
18. A. autumnalis salvini

## PLATE 12

1. C. a. americanus
2. C. melacoryphus
3. C. lansbergi
4. C. euleri
5. C. pumilus
6. T. n. naevia
7. D. p. pavoninus
8. D. phasianellus rufigularis
9. P. m. minuta

10. P. cayana mehleri
11. C. cinereus
12. P. melanogaster ochracea
13. C. pulchra
14. C. turcosa
15. C. viridicyana armillata
16. C. a. affinis
17. C. yncas cyanodorsalis
18. C. v. violaceus
19. C. heilprini

## PLATE 13

1. A. rosenbergi
2. G. violiceps
3. H. e. eliciae
4. L. coeruleogularis confinis
5. T. c. colombica
6. C. mellisugus pumilus
7. F. m. mellivora
8. P. cuvierii berlepschi
9. A. a. amabilis
10. D. julie panamensis
11. C. buffoni micans
12. C. urochrysia incognita
13. A. t. tzacatl
14. A. f. franciae
15. H. b. barroti
16. A. nigricollis
17. L. delattrei lessoni
18. D. j. johannae
19. H. l. longirostris
20. D. ludoviciae rectirostris
21. P. conversii
22. H. j. jacula
23. C. delphinae
24. P. longuemareus nelsoni
25. P. guy coruscus
26. P. yaruqui sanctijohannis
27. P. s. syrmatophorus
28. T. ruckeri darienensis
29. G. hirsuta affinus
30. G. aenea

## PLATE 14

1. L. stictolopha
2. E. a. alinae
3. P. mitchellii
4. L. chalybea verreauxii
5. P. langsdorffi melanosternon
6. O. underwoodii ambiguus
7. A. mulsant
8. C. jourdanii andinus
9. A. h. heliodor
10. C. mellisugus caribaeus
11. C. s. stenura
12. A. versicolor milleri
13. A. fimbriata apicalis

14. *C. russatus*
15. *C. g. gibsoni*
16. *L. goudoti luminosa*
17. *S. g. geoffroyi*
18. *A. melanogenys connectens*
19. *A. f. floriceps*
20. *A. v. viridigaster*
21. *H. g. grayi*
22. *A. saucerottei warscewiczi*
23. *A. c. cyanifrons*
24. *T. furcata simoni*
25. *C. o. oenone*
26. *H. sapphirina*
27. *H. cyanus viridiventris*
28. *L. fallax cervina*
29. *C. mosquitus*
30. *K. g. guimeti*
31. *P. theresiae leucorrhous*
32. *P. g. guainumbi*
33. *T. pyra*
34. *P. aurescens*
35. *C. largipennis aequatorialis*

## PLATE 15

1. *E. mosquera*
2. *E. d. derbyi*
3. *M. t. tyrianthina*
4. *C. heteropogon*
5. *R. m. microrhynchum*
6. *E. cupreoventris*
7. *E. v. vestitus*
8. *H. leadbeateri parvula*
9. *M. w. williami*
10. *C. h. herrani*
11. *E. l. luciani*
12. *C. thalassinus cyanotis*
13. *C. c. coruscans*
14. *U. b. benjamini*
15. *O. euryptera*
16. *H. aureliae caucensis*
17. *L. lafresnayi liriope*
18. *C. falcatus*
19. *B. jardini*
20. *H. exortis*
21. *H. mavors*
22. *H. amethysticollis clarisse*
23. *B. f. flavescens*
24. *U. b. bougueri*
25. *C. coeligena ferruginea*
26. *C. b. bonapartei*
26a. *C. bonapartei consita*
27. *C. helianthea tamae*

## PLATE 16

1. *P. a. anthophilus*
2. *P. guy apicalis*
3. *P. hispidus*

4. *P. augusti vicarius*
5. *P. superciliosus insolitus*
6. *P. b. bourcieri*
7. *P. squalidus rupurumii*
8. *P. longuemareus striigularis*
9. *P. g. griseogularis*
10. *P. ruber nigricinctus*
11. *G. h. hirsuta*
12. *T. leucurus cervinicauda*
13. *A. kingi emmae*
14. *A. c. coelestis*
15. *C. prunellei*
16. *P. cyanopterus caeruleus*
17. *A. c. cupripennis*
18. *L. nuna gouldii*
19. *C. t. torquata*
20. *L. v. victoriae*
21. *H. rubinoides aequatorialis*
22. *H. imperatrix*
23. *C. wilsoni*
24. *C. lutetiae*
25. *C. phalerata*

## PLATE 17

1. *P. a. auriceps*
2. *P. antisianus*
3. *T. massena australis*
4. *T. comptus*
5. *T. curucui peruvianus*
6. *P. fulgidus festatus*
7. *T. v. viridis*
8. *T. violaceus crissalis*
9. *T. melanurus eumorphus*
10. *T. p. personatus*
11. *T. collaris exoptatus*
12. *T. rufus sulphureus*

## PLATE 18

1. *B. s. salmoni*
2. *G. r. ruficauda*
3. *G. t. tombacea*
4. *G. leucogastra chalcothorax*
5. *G. leucotis*
6. *B. noanamae*
7. *H. ruficollis decolor*
8. *N. radiatus*
9. *N. f. frontalis*
10. *N. brunnea*
11. *H. momotula obscurus*
12. *M. l. lanceolata*
13a. *M. panamensis chocoana*
14. *M. m. mystacalis*
15. *M. momota subrufescens*
16. *E. p. platyrhynchum*
17. *B. ruficapillus semirufus*
18. *M. flavirostris*
19. *M. n. nigrifrons*

20. *M. morphoeus peruana*
21. *H. castanea*

PLATE 19

1. *C. t. tenebrosa*
2. *N. macrorhynchus hyperrhynchus*
3. *N. pectoralis*
4. *N. tectus subtectus*
5. *H. ruficollis bicinctus*
6. *M. fulvogularis substriata*
7. *M. f. fusca*
8. *N. r. rubecula*
9. *B. t. tamatia*
10. *B. m. macrodactylus*
11. *B. c. capensis*
12. *B. goeringi*
13. *B. lugubris fulviventris*
14. *G. l. leucogastra*
15. *G. galbula*
16. *G. a. albirostris*
16a. *G. albirostris chalcocephala*
17. *G. dea brunneiceps*
18. *J. a. aurea*
19. *C. a. amazona*
20. *C. a. americana*
21. *C. a. aenea*
22. *C. inda*

PLATE 20

1. *S. spectabilis*
2. *A. sulcatus calorhynchus*
3. *A. prasinus albivitta*
3a. *A. prasinus lautus*
4. *A. h. haematopygus*
5. *P. sanguineus*
6. *P. torquatus nuchalis*
7. *P. pluricinctus*
8. *P. c. castanotis*
9. *P. inscriptus humboldti*
10. *P. f. flavirostris*
11. *S. r. reinwardtii*
12. *S. nattereri*
13. *A. n. nigrirostris*
14. *R. brevis*
15. *R. swainsonii*
16. *A. h. hypoglauca*
17. *R. citreolaemus*
18. *R. culminatus*
19. *R. tucanus cuvieri*
20. *A. laminirostris*

PLATE 21

1. *C. guayaquilensis*
2. *V. nigriceps equifasciatus*
3. *V. d. dignus*
4. *V. callonotus*

5. *P. chrysochloros aurosus*
6. *P. leucolaemus litae*
7. *P. rubiginosus pacificus*
8. *C. haematogaster splendens*
9. *C. maculicoronatus rubrilateralis*
10. *C. squamatus*
11. *C. hypoleucus*
12. *C. niger punctatus*
12a. *C. niger transilens*
13. *C. quinticolor*
14. *S. r. ramphastinus*
15. *C. aurovirens*
16. *E. b bourcierii*
17. *E. r. richardsoni*

PLATE 22

1. *C. elegans citreopygius*
2. *C. grammicus verreauxii*
3. *C. l. loricatus*
4. *C. torquatus occidentalis*
5. *C. f. flavus*
6. *C. punctigula punctipectus*
7. *P. rubiginosus alleni*
8. *P. chrysochloros capistratus*
8a. *P. chrysochloros xanthochlorus*
9. *P. flavigula magnus*
10. *P. r. rivolii*
11. *V. d. dignus*
12. *V. f. fumigatus*
13. *V. kirkii cecilii*
14. *V. passerinus fidelis*
15. *V. affinis orenocensis*
16. *M. r. rubricapillus*
17. *M. c. cruentatus*
18. *D. l. lineatus*
19. *C. m. melanoleucos*
20. *C. p. pollens*
21. *C. r. rubricollis*

PLATE 23

1. *P. c. cinnamomeus*
2. *P. o. olivaceus*
3. *P. squamulatus rohli*
4. *P. granadensis*
5. *P. lafresnayi*
6. *P. exilis undulatus*
7. *S. griseicapillus levis*
8. *G. spirurus rufigularis*
9. *D. longicauda connectens*
10. *D. merula bartletti*
11. *D. fuliginosa phaeochroa*
12. *D. homochroa meridionalis*
13. *L. souleyetii littoralis*
14. *L. affinis lacrymiger*
15. *X. o. ocellatus*
16. *X. guttatus nanus*
17. *X. spixii buenaevistae*

18. *X. obsoletus notatus*
19. *X. p. picus*
20. *D. certhia radiolatus*
21. *D. picumnus seilerni*
22. *X. promeropirhynchus virgatus*
23. *X. l. lachrymosus*
24. *X. erythropygius aequatorialis*
25. *X. t. triangularis*

PLATE 24

1. *D. t. tyrannina*
2. *C. pucheranii*
3. *C. p. pusillus*
4. *C. trochilirostris venezuelensis*
5. *C. procurvoides sanus*
6. *D. rufigula devillei*
7. *L. a. andicola*
8. *A. f. flammulata*
9. *A. w. wyatti*
10. *S. f. fuliginosa*
11. *S. striaticollis*
12. *X. minlosi umbraticus*
13. *A. s. strigilatus*
14. *S. fuscorufa*
15. *C. hellmayri*
16. *F. leucopus longirostris*
17. *P. c. candei*
17a. *P. candei atrigularis*
18. *M. aurantiacus*

PLATE 25

1. *C. fuscus oreobates*
2. *C. e. excelsior*
3. *S. g. gularis*
4. *S. u. unirufa*
5. *S. c. cinnamomea*
6. *S. azarae media*
7. *S. b. brachyura*
8. *S. m. moesta*
9. *S. subpudica*
10. *S. albescens insignis*
11. *S. gujanensis columbiana*
12. *S. rutilans dissors*
13. *P. rufifrons inornatus*
14. *C. cinnamomea fuscifrons*
15. *C. mustelina*
16. *C. s. subcristata*
17. *C. vulpina alopecias*
18. *C. c. curtata*
19. *C. e. erythrops*
20. *C. gutturata peruviana*
21. *T. cherriei*
22. *X. minutus ruficaudus*
23. *X. tenuirostris acutirostris*
24. *X. m. milleri*
25. *M. squamiger perlata*
26. *M. stellatus*

27. *P. b. brunnescens*
28. *P. guttuligera*

PLATE 26

1. *P. b. boissonneautii*
2. *T. virgaticeps sclateri*
3. *T. h. holostictus*
4. *T. f. flammulatus*
5. *A. variegaticeps temporalis*
6. *A. s. striaticollis*
7. *S. subalaris striolata*
8. *T. ignobilis*
9. *P. rufus riveti*
10. *P. pyrrhodes*
11. *P. ruficaudatus*
12. *P. e. erythropterus*
13. *A. dorsalis*
14. *A. rufipileatus consobrinus*
15. *A. ochrolaemus turdinus*
16. *A. i. infuscatus*
17. *A. rubiginosus nigricauda*
18. *H. s. subulatus*
19. *S. a. albigularis*
20. *S. mexicanus andinus*
21. *S. caudacutus brunneus*
22. *L. nematura sororia*
23. *S. guatemalensis salvini*
24. *S. rufigularis fulvigularis*

PLATE 27

1. *T. palliatus tenuifasciatus*
2. *T. multistriatus brachyurus*
3. *S. melanonotus*
4. *T. n. nigriceps*
5. *C. lineatus intermedius*
6. *T. doliatus fraterculus*
7. *S. canadensis intermedius*
8. *T. anabatinus intermedius*
9. *T. unicolor grandior*
10. *T. major granadensis*
11. *G. bicolor daguae*
12. *G. nudiceps sanctamartae*
13. *M. immaculata berlepschi*
14. *C. alixi*
15. *P. e. erythroptera*
16. *P. n. nigromaculata*
17. *P. leuconota castanoptera*
18. *P. mcleannani chocoanus*

PLATE 28

1. *H. poecilonota duidae*
2. *M. hemileucus*
3. *M. quixensis consobrina*
3a. *M. q. quixensis*
4. *H. h. hypoxantha*
5. *H. melanopogon occidentalis*

6. *M. s. schisticolor*
7. *H. axillaris senex*
8. *T. c. callinota*
9. *M. l. longipennis*
10. *M. s. sunensis*
11. *M. f. fulviventris*
12. *H. rufimarginatus frater*
13. *H. dorsimaculatus*
14. *T. spodioptila signata*
15. *M. b. brachyura*
16. *M. hauxwelli suffusa*
17. *M. e. erythrura*
18. *M. haematonota pyrrhonota*
19. *M. obscura*
20. *M. ornata saturata*
21. *M. surinamensis pacifica*
22. *M. longicauda soderstromi*
23. *M. axillaris melaena*
24. *M. menetriesii cinereiventris*
25. *M. cherriei*
26. *F. grisea intermedia*
26a. *F. grisea rufiventris*
27. *D. mentalis extremus*
28. *D. puncticeps intensus*
29. *D. c. caudata*
30. *H. cantator flavescens*

PLATE 29

1. *M. margaritatus*
2. *T. punctatus subcinereus*
3. *T. amazonicus cinereiceps*
4. *T. m. murinus*
5. *T. aethiops polionotus*
6. *T. nigrocinereus cinereoniger*
7. *P. stellaris occipitalis*
8. *T. schistaceus capitalis*
9. *T. cryptoleucus*
10. *C. n. nigricans*
11. *C. s. serva*
12. *C. t. tyrannina*
13. *C. nigrescens aequatorialis*
14. *C. c. cinerascens*
15. *T. a. ardesiacus*
16. *T. caesius glaucus*
17. *D. plumbeus leucostictus*
18. *M. exsul maculifer*
19. *S. berlepschi*
20. *S. rosenbergi*
21. *M. longipes panamensis*
22. *M. laemosticta palliata*

PLATE 30

1. *P. rufifrons minor*
2. *M. atrothorax metae*
3. *M. h. hemimelaena*
4. *P. schistacea*
5. *P. leucostigma infuscata*

5a. *P. leucostigma subplumbea*
6. *S. naevia argentata*
7. *M. hyperythra*
8. *M. f. fortis*
9. *M. melanoceps*
10. *G. leucaspis castanea*
11. *R. m. melanosticta*
12. *R. cristata*
13. *N. niger*
14. *G. gigantea lehmanni*
15. *G. s. squamigera*
16. *G. hypoleuca castanea*
17. *G. nuchalis ruficeps*
18. *G. rufocinerea*

PLATE 31

1. *G. milleri*
2. *C. m. mollissima*
3. *C. nobilis rubida*
4. *C. campanisona columbiana*
5. *C. ruficauda turdina*
6. *G. q. quitensis*
7. *G. r. rufula*
8. *G. r. ruficapilla*
9. *P. rufopileatum harterti*
10. *G. guatimalensis carmelitae*
11. *G. f. ferrugineipectus*
12. *G. f. flavirostris*
13. *H. macularius diversa*
14. *M. campanisona dissors*
15. *G. nana occidentalis*
16. *G. c. cucullata*
17. *G. bangsi*
18. *C. aurita inexpectata*
19. *C. c. castaneiceps*
20. *H. fulviventris barbacoae*
21. *F. analis connectens*
22. *F. colma nigrifrons*
23. *F. rufipectus carrikeri*
24. *M. t. torquata*

PLATE 32

1. *M. leucophrys erythrophrys*
2. *M. myotherinus elegans*
3. *M. lugubris berlepschi*
4. *H. naevia consobrina*
5. *H. n. naevioides*
6. *D. cincta*
7. *P. albifrons peruviana*
8. *C. lanceolata*
9. *P. filicauda*
10. *M. manacus interior*
11. *M. c. chrysopterus*
12. *P. mentalis minor*
13. *P. e. erythrocephala*
14. *P. pipra coracina*
15. *A. deliciosus*

16. *P. coronata minuscula*
17. *P. i. isidorei*
18. *X. atronitens*
19. *M. vitellinus viridiventris*
20. *M. regulus antioquiae*
21. *C. l. leucorrhoa*
22. *T. stolzmanni*
23. *N. c. cinnamomea*
24. *P. chloris chlorion*
25. *C. flavicapilla*
26. *C. h. holochlora*
27. *H. flavivertex*
28. *N. chrysocephalum*

## PLATE 33

1. *L. fuscocinereus*
2. *L. cryptolophus mindoensis*
3. *Q. purpurata*
4. *P. nigricollis*
5. *R. peruviana aequatorialis*
5a. *R. peruviana sanguinolenta*
6. *R. rupicola*
7. *P. minor*
8. *S. m. major*
9. *S. turdinus amazonus*
10. *C. holochlora litae*
11. *S. aenigma*
12. *I. isabellae*
13. *A. b. bolivianus*
14. *A. s. spadiceus*
15. *A. cinnamomeus*
16. *C. torquata sarayacuensis*

## PLATE 34

1. *X. punicea*
2. *C. cotinga*
3. *C. cayana*
4. *C. maynana*
5. *A. rubrocristatus*
6. *L. hypopyrrha*
7. *R. simplex frederici*
8. *L. v. vociferans*
9. *A. rufaxilla antioquiae*
10. *A. tschudii*
11. *P. a. arcuata*
12. *P. riefferii occidentalis*
13. *L. elegans venezuelensis*
14. *P. chlorolepidota*
15. *P. aureopectus decora*
16. *P. jucunda*
17. *P. lubomirskii*

## PLATE 35

1. *P. polychopterus dorsalis*
2. *P. a. albogriseus*
3. *P. h. homochrous*

4. *P. v. versicolor*
5. *P. rufus*
6. *P. c. cinnamomeus*
7. *P. marginatus nanus*
8. *P. castaneus saturatus*
9. *L. r. rufescens*
10. *R. h. holerythra*
11. *L. u. unirufus*
12. *P. p. porphyrolaema*
13. *T. c. cayana*
14. *T. semifasciata columbiana*
15. *T. inquisitor albitorques*

## PLATE 36

1. *M. ecaudatus atricapillus*
1a. *M. ecaudatus miserabilis*
2. *P. platyrhynchos griseiceps*
3. *P. c. coronatus*
4. *P. mystaceus neglectus*
5. *P. f. flavigularis*
6. *H. z. zosterops*
7. *T. latirostre caniceps*
8. *T. c. calopterum*
9. *T. c. cinereum*
10. *T. nigriceps*
11. *T. chrysocrotaphum guttatum*
12. *T. maculatum signatum*
13. *T. sylvia griseolum*
14. *H. granadensis andinus*
15. *H. margaritaceiventer impiger*
16. *A. p. pilaris*
17. *L. galeatus*
18. *L. pileatus hesperius*
19. *O. o. olivaceum*
20. *E. meloryphus paulus*
21. *P. murina incomta*
22. *C. obsoletum caucae*
23. *I. tenuirostris*
24. *I. subflava intermedia*
25. *P. n. nigrocapillus*
26. *P. uropygialis*
27. *M. leucophrys setophagoides*
28. *O. brunneicapillum dilutum*
29. *O. inerme*
30. *C. flaveola cerula*
31. *P. superciliaris palloris*
32. *P. viridiflavus chrysops*
33. *Z. vilissimus tamae*
34. *P. plumbeiceps*
35. *P. o. ophthalmicus*
36. *Z. g. gracilipes*
37. *T. e. elatus*
38. *P. griseiceps cristatus*
39. *M. poecilocercus*
40. *M. s. stictopterus*
41. *M. minor*
42. *P. p. poecilotis*
43. *M. oleaginea chloronota*

44. *P. cinereiceps*
45. *L. rufipectus*
46. *L. superciliaris poliocephalus*
47. *L. amaurocephalus diversus*
48. *T. erythrurus signatus*

PLATE 37

1. *P. cinnamomea pyrrhoptera*
2. *M. phaeocercus berlepschi*
3. *M. o. ornatus*
4. *M. olivaceus hederaceus*
5. *M. striaticollis columbianus*
6. *P. rubinus piurae*
7. *A. audax*
8. *M. v. villosus*
9. *M. barbatus aureatus*
10. *M. a. atricaudus*
11. *M. phoenicomitra litae*
12. *K. p. poecilurus*
13. *C. cinereus bogotensis*
14. *E. euleri lawrencei*
15. *C. fuscatus cabanisi*
16. *M. f. flavicans*
17. *M. pulcher bellus*
18. *M. f. fasciatus*
19. *T. sulphurescens confusus*
20. *T. p. poliocephalus*
21. *T. flaviventris collingwoodi*
22. *R. olivaceus flavus*
23. *R. megacephala pectoralis*
24. *R. ruficauda*
25. *S. arenarum atrirostris*
26. *M. viridicata accola*
27. *M. g. gaimardii*
28. *M. caniceps cinerea*
29. *R. brevirostris pacificus*
30. *R. fulvipectus*
31. *E. f. flavogaster*
32. *E. chiriquensis albivertex*
33. *E. parvirostris*
34. *E. ruficeps*
35. *E. p. pallatangae*
36. *E. frantzii pudica*
37. *E. gigas*

PLATE 38

1. *S. h. hypoleuca*
2. *S. n. napensis*
3. *O. littoralis*
4. *K. poecilocercus*
5. *K. o. orenocensis*
6. *P. acutipennis*
7. *P. pectoralis brevipennis*
8. *M. fluviatilis*
9. *A. agilis*
10. *A. parulus aequatorialis*
11. *P. capitale*

12. *P. ruficeps melanomystax*
13. *P. ruficeps*
14. *P. pelzelni annectens*
15. *O. c. cinnamomeiventris*
16. *O. diadema gratiosa*
17. *O. f. frontalis*
18. *O. rufipectoralis obfuscata*
19. *O. fumicolor brunneifrons*
20. *M. f. fumigatus*
21. *M. pernix*
22. *M. s. striaticollis*
23. *H. ferruginea sclateri*
23a. *H. f. ferruginea*
24. *A. montana solitaria*
25. *M. maculirostris niceforoi*
26. *M. alpina columbiana*
27. *M. erythropygius orinomus*

PLATE 39

1. *M. rixosus flavigularis*
2. *O. coronatus fraterculus*
3. *C. subbrunneus panamensis*
4. *M. cephalotes caucae*
5. *M. apicalis*
6. *T. niveigularis*
7. *T. d. dominicensis*
8. *T. m. melancholicus*
9. *T. albogularis*
10. *T. sulphurea*
11. *T. l. luteiventris*
12. *C. cinchoneti icterophrys*
13. *C. p. parva*
13a. *C. parva albovittatus*
14. *M. similis columbianus*
15. *M. granadensis occidentalis*
16. *M. cayanensis rufipennis*
17. *M. maculatus nobilis*
18. *M. chrysocephalus intermedius*
19. *M. p. pitangua*
20. *P. sulphuratus caucensis*
21. *P. l. lictor*
22. *L. l. leucophaius*
23. *E. v. varius*
24. *E. a. aurantioatrocristatus*
25. *S. sibilator albocinereus*
26. *M. t. tyrannulus*
27. *M. venezuelensis*
28. *M. tuberculifer brunneiceps*

PLATE 40

1. *N. tibialis griseiventris*
1a. *N. tibialis minima*
2. *N. c. cyanoleuca*
3. *H. rustica erythrogaster*
4. *N. flavipes*
5. *N. m. murina*
6. *A. fucata*

7. *A. melanoleuca*
8. *A. fasciata*
9. *S. ruficollis uropygialis*
10. *R. r. riparia*
11. *T. albiventer*
12. *P. modesta elegans*
13. *P. t. tapera*
13a. *P. tapera fusca*
14. *P. c. chalybea*
15. *P. s. subis*

PLATE 41

1. *S. panamensis*
2. *S. magellanicus canus*
3. *S. vicinior*
4. *S. femoralis confusus*
5. *C. unirufa unibrunnea*
6. *S. unicolor latrans*
7. *S. senilis*
8. *C. peruana olivascens*
9. *L. thoracicus erithacus*
10. *T. thoracicus dichrous*
11. *C. p. phaeocephalus*
12. *T. leucopogon*
13. *T. nigricapillus connectens*
14. *T. spadix*
15. *T. e. euophrys*
16. *C. zonatus brevirostris*
17. *C. albobrunneus harterti*
18. *T. f. fasciatoventris*
19. *C. turdinus hypostictus*
20. *D. a. atricapillus*

PLATE 42

1. *S. unicolor latrans*
2. *S. femoralis nigricans*
3. *S. latebricola meridanus*
4. *S. magellanicus griseicollis*
5. *C. u. unirufa*
6. *C. griseus minor*
7. *C. nuchalis pardus*
8. *T. rutilus interior*
9. *T. genibarbis saltuensis*
10. *T. coraya caurensis*
11. *T. rufalbus cumanensis*
12. *T. leucotis bogotensis*
13. *H. l. leucophrys*
14. *H. leucosticta hauxwelli*
15. *T. solstitialis solitarius*
16. *T. aedon albicans*
17. *T. maculipectus columbianus*
18. *C. platensis tamae*
19. *C. apolinari*
20. *M. marginatus taeniatus*
20a. *M. marginatus squamulatus (imm.?)*
21. *M. c. cinereiventris*
22. *O. b. branickii*

23. *P. schistaceigula*
24. *M. c. collaris*
25. *R. melanurus trinitatis*
26. *P. plumbea daguae*
26a. *P. plumbea bilineata*
27. *C. arada salvini*

PLATE 43

1. *P. flavipes venezuelensis*
2. *T. serranus fuscobrunneus*
3. *T. fuscater quindio*
4. *P. leucops*
5. *T. n. nudigenis*
6. *T. obsoletus colombianus*
7. *T. olivater sanctaemartae*
8. *T. ignobilis goodfellowi*
8a. *T. ignobilis debilis*
9. *T. albicollis berlepschi*
10. *T. grayi incomptus*
11. *C. aurantiirostris phaeopleurus*
12. *C. dryas maculatus*
13. *T. fulviventris*
14. *T. leucomelas albiventer*
15. *C. fuscater sanctaemartae*
16. *M. ralloides plumbeiceps*
17. *M. leucogenys chubbi*
18. *E. coracinus*

PLATE 44

1. *I. mesomelas carrikeri*
2. *I. chrysater giraudii*
3. *I. auricapillus*
4. *I. icterus ridgwayi*
5. *I. n. nigrogularis*
6. *A. holosericeus australis*
7. *C. uropygialis pacificus*
8. *C. cela vitellinus*
9. *Z. wagleri ridgwayi*
10. *G. guatimozinus*
11. *P. decumanus melanterus*
12. *A. i. icterocephalus*
13. *L. t. tanagrinus*
14. *Q. l. lugubris*
15. *L. m. militaris*
16. *M. bonariensis cabanisii*
17. *M. armenti*
18. *S. o. oryzivora*

PLATE 45

1. *P. viridis*
2. *P. a. angustifrons*
2a. *P. angustifrons sincipitalis*
3. *G. y. yuracares*
4. *G. mexicanus*
5. *I. jamacaii croconotus*
6. *C. h. haemorrhous*

7. *O. latirostris*
8. *H. pyrohypogaster*
9. *C. l. leucoramphus*
10. *M. subalaris*
11. *C. c. cela*
12. *I. cayanensis*
13. *I. chrysocephalus*
14. *C. solitarius*

PLATE 46

1. *C. gujanensis canticus*
2. *V. leucotis mikettae*
3. *V. eximius*
4. *V. olivaceus vividior*
5. *V. leucophrys mirandae*
6. *H. ochraceiceps ferrugineifrons*
7. *H. b. brunneiceps*
8. *H. decurtatus darienensis*
9. *H. thoracicus aemulus*
10. *C. n. nigrirostris*
11. *H. aurantiifrons saturatus*
12. *H. f. flavipes*
13. *H. semibrunneus*
14. *B. conspicillatus*
15. *D. petechia peruviana*
15a. *D. petechia erithachorides*
16. *P. pitiayumi elegans*
17. *B. coronatus regulus*
18. *B. c. cinereicollis*
19. *B. rufifrons mesochrysus*
20. *B. nigrocristatus*
21. *B. flaveolus*
22. *B. l. luteoviridis*
23. *B. culicivorus austerus*
24. *B. chrysogaster chlorophrys*
25. *G. a. aequinoctialis*
26. *B. fulvicauda semicervinus*
27. *B. tristriatus auricularis*
28. *B. basilicus*

PLATE 47

1. *M. o. ornatus*
2. *M. flavivertex*
3. *M. miniatus ballux*
4. *M. melanocephalus ruficoronatus*
5. *D. venusta fuliginata*
6. *C. s. spiza*
7. *C. cyaneus dispar*
8. *C. c. caeruleus*
9. *C. n. nitidus*
10. *D. c. cayana*
11. *D. l. lineata*
12. *D. albiventris*
13. *D. flaviventer*
14. *D. berlepschi*
15. *C. flaveola columbiana*
16. *C. b. bicolor*

17. *C. speciosum amazonum*
18. *C. l. leucogenys*
19. *C. albifrons centralandium*
20. *C. s. sitticolor*
21. *D. sittoides dorbignyi*
22. *D. a. albilatera*
23. *D. gloriosissima*
24. *D. h. humeralis*
25. *D. lafresnayii*
26. *D. humeralis aterrima*
27. *D. caerulescens saturata*
28. *D. c. cyanea*
29. *D. indigotica*

PLATE 48

1. *E. salmoni*
2. *C. flavirostris minima*
3. *O. f. fraseri*
4. *I. p. pulcherrima*
5. *C. cinereum fraseri*
6. *C. rufum*
7. *C. albifrons atrocyaneum*
8. *D. lineata egregia*
9. *P. hartlaubi*
10. *D. cayana baudoana*
11. *D. viguieri*
12. *T. cyanotis lutleyi*
13. *T. r. ruficervix*
14. *T. l. labradorides*
15. *T. chrysotis*
16. *T. xanthocephala venusta*
17. *T. vitriolina*
18. *T. rufigula*
19. *T. johannae*
20. *T. florida auriceps*
21. *T. palmeri*
22. *T. i. inornata*
23. *T. larvata fanny*
24. *C. phoenicotis*
25. *C. calliparea bourcieri*
26. *C. nitidissima*

PLATE 49

1. *C. pyrrhophrys*
2. *C. cyanea longipennis*
3. *T. viridis occidentalis*
4. *T. arthus occidentalis*
5. *T. p. parzudakii*
6. *T. xanthocephala venusta*
7. *T. v. vassorii*
8. *T. i. icterocephala*
9. *T. heinei*
10. *T. n. nigroviridis*
11. *T. cyanicollis hannahiae*
12. *T. c. cayana*
13. *T. c. cyanoptera*
14. *T. l. lavinia*

15. *T. mexicana media*
16. *T. guttata bogotensis*
17. *T. gyrola deleticia*
18. *T. s. schrankii*
19. *T. nigrocincta*
20. *T. x. xanthogastra*
21. *T. callophrys*
22. *T. chilensis coelicolor*
23. *T. velia iridina*

PLATE 50

1. *C. r. riefferii*
2. *B. montana cucullata*
3. *S. albocristata*
4. *D. t. taeniata*
5. *B. wetmorei*
6. *B. eximia zimmeri*
7. *A. melanogenys*
8. *A. lacrymosus palpebrosus*
9. *A. igniventris erythrotus*
10. *A. notabilis*
11. *A. flavinucha baezae*
12. *B. edwardsi*
13. *I. porphyrocephala*
14. *I. rufiventer ignicapillus*
15. *B. melanochlamys*
16. *B. rothschildi*
17. *B. aureocincta*

PLATE 51

1. *T. episcopus cana*
2. *T. glaucocolpa*
3. *T. palmarum melanoptera*
4. *T. cyanocephala auricrissa*
5. *P. flava faceta*
6. *P. leucoptera venezuelae*
7. *P. rubriceps*
8. *H. rubica coccinea*
9. *R. carbo venezuelensis*
10. *R. d. dimidiatus*
11. *H. fuscicauda erythrolaema*
12. *H. cristata*
13. *T. phoenicius*
14. *R. nigrogularis*
15. *T. surinamus brevipes*
16. *T. cristatus fallax*
17. *R. icteronotus*
18. *R. flammigerus*
19. *L. fulvus peruvianus*
20. *C. coccineus*

PLATE 52

1. *C. stolzmanni dugandi*
2. *T. luctuosus panamensis*
3. *H. flavicollis albigularis*
4. *C. olivacea*

5. *C. carmioli frenata*
6. *T. d. delattrii*
7. *H. xanthopygius*
8. *E. penicillata cristata*
9. *T. rufus*
10. *M. c. cassinii*
11. *R. rosea harterti*
12. *C. semifuscus livingstoni*
13. *C. flavovirens*
14. *C. inornatus*
15. *C. flavigularis marginatus*
16. *C. tacarcunae*

PLATE 53

1. *E. laniirostris crassirostris*
2. *E. xanthogaster chocoensis*
3. *E. concinna*
4. *E. trinitatus*
5. *E. m. minuta*
6. *E. musica intermedia*
7. *E. saturata*
8. *E. rufiventris*
9. *E. fulvicrissa omissa*
10. *E. chrysopasta nitida*
11. *E. m. mesochrysa*
12. *H. guira nigrigula*
13. *H. flavicollis aurigularis*
14. *N. pileata hypoleuca*
15. *T. f. fulviceps*
16. *C. ophthalmicus jacqueti*
17. *C. c. canigularis*
18. *C. r. rubrirostris*
19. *T. ornata*
20. *H. f. frontalis*
21. *H. superciliaris nigrifrons*
22. *H. a. atropileus*
23. *H. m. melanotis*
24. *H. verticalis*
25. *P. melanonota venezuelensis*
26. *C. verticalis*
27. *C. d. diadema*

PLATE 54

1a. *C. ophthalmicus nigriceps*
1b. *C. ophthalmicus flavopectus*
2. *C. canigularis conspicillatus*
3. *C. parvirostris huallagae*
4. *C. f. flavigularis*
5. *A. fuscoolivaceus*
6. *A. g. gutturalis*
7. *A. melanocephalus*
8. *A. tricolor crassus*
9. *A. rufinucha caucae*
10. *A. a. albofrenatus*
11. *A. pallidinucha papallactae*
12. *A. leucopis*
13. *L. castaneiceps*

14. *A. s. schistaceus*
15. *O. arremonops*
16. *U. stolzmanni*
17. *A. torquatus assimilis*
18. *A. a. atricapillus*

## PLATE 55

1. *P. gularis nigrogenis*
2. *C. phoeniceus*
3. *P. g. grossus*
4. *S. a. atripennis*
5. *P. chrysopeplus laubmanni*
6. *P. aureoventris uropygialis*
6a. *P. aureoventris crissalis*
7. *C. c. canadensis*
8. *S. albicollis perstriatus*
9. *S. coerulescens plumbeus*
10. *S. m. maximus*
11. *S. orenocensis rufescens*
12. *A. aurantiirostris occidentalis*
13. *Z. capensis costaricensis*
14. *A. c. conirostris*
15. *A. tocuyensis*
16. *A. taciturnus axillaris*
16a. *A. t. taciturnus*
17. *A. s. schlegeli*
18. *A. p. pallidinucha*
19. *A. albofrenatus meridae*
20. *A. schistaceus tamae*
21. *A. brunneinucha frontalis*
22. *A. torquatus basilicus*
23. *A. s. semirufus*
24. *S. melanopis aterrima*
25. *C. c. cyanoides*
26. *C. brissonii caucae*

## PLATE 56

1. *O. c. crassirostris*
2. *O. a. angolensis*
3. *V. jacarina splendens*
4. *T. olivacea dissita*
5. *T. bicolor omissa*
6. *T. fuliginosa fumosa*
7. *D. fringilloides*
8. *S. l. lineola*
9. *S. bouvronides*
10. *S. luctuosa*
11. *S. n. nigricollis*
12. *S. m. minuta*
13. *S. i. intermedia*
14. *S. schistacea longipennis*
15. *S. plumbea whiteleyana*
16. *T. o. obscura*
17. *S. c. castaneiventris*
18. *C. h. homochroa*
19. *C. inornata minor*
20. *P. unicolor geospizopsis*
21. *H. r. rustica*
22. *C. pileatus brevicaudus*
23. *E. herbicola sphenurus*
24. *A. h. humeralis*
25. *A. aurifrons apurensis*
26. *S. americana*
27. *S. f. flaveola*
28. *S. c. columbiana*
29. *S. citrina browni*
30. *S. l. luteola*
31. *S. psaltria columbianus*
32. *S. x. xanthogaster*
33. *S. s. spinescens*
34. *S. magellanicus capitalis*
35. *S. cucullatus*

# LITERATURE CITED

Alderton, C. C. 1961. The breeding cycle of the Yellow-bellied Seedeater in Panama. *Condor* 63:390-398.

———. 1963. The breeding behavior of the Blue-black Grassquit. *Condor* 65:154-162.

Alexander, W. B. 1963. *Birds of the Ocean*. N.Y.: Putnam's Sons.

Alpin, O. V. 1894. On the birds of Uruguay. *Ibis* (ser. 6), 6:149-215.

Altman, A., & C. Parish. 1978. Sight records of Wilson's Phalarope, Ruff, and other shorebirds from Venezuela. *American Birds* 32:309-310.

Alvarez, H. 1975. The social system of the Green Jay in Colombia. *The Living Bird* 14:5-43.

Alvarez del Toro, M. 1971. On the biology of the American Finfoot in southern Mexico. *The Living Bird* 10:79-88.

Ansingh, F. H., H. J. Koelers, P. A. Van der Weft, & K. H. Voous. 1960. The breeding of the Cayenne or Yellow-billed Tern in Curaçao in 1958. *Ardea* 48:51-65.

Bangs, O., & T. E. Penard. 1918. Notes on a collection of Surinam birds. *Bull. Mus. Comp. Zool., Harvard* 62:25-93.

Barlow, J. C., & R. D. James. 1975. Aspects of the biology of the Chestnut-sided Shrike-Vireo. *Wilson Bull.* 87:320-334.

Beebe, M. B., & W. Beebe. 1910. *Our Search for a Wilderness*. London: Constable.

Beebe, W. 1909. Birds of northeastern Venezuela. *Zoologica* 1:67-114.

———. 1924. The rarest nests in the tallest grass stems. *Bull. N.Y. Zool. Soc.* 27:114-117.

———. 1925. Life History of Variegated Tinamou *C. variegatus*. *Zoologica* 6:195-227.

———. 1947. Avian migration at Rancho Grande in north central Venezuela. *Ibis* 32:153-168.

———. 1949. *High Jungle*. N.Y.: Duell, Sloan and Pearce.

———. 1950. Home life of the Bat Falcon, *Falco albigularis albigularis* Daudin. *Zoologica* 35:69-86.

Beebe, W., G. I. Hartley, & P. G. Howes. 1917. *Tropical Wild Life in British Guiana*. N.Y. Zool. Soc., N.Y.

Belcher, C., & G. D. Smooker. 1934-37. Birds of the colony of Trinidad and Tobago (6 parts). *Ibis* (13) 4:572-595 et seq.

Berault, E. 1970. The nesting of *Gymnoderus foetidus*. *Ibis* 112:256.

Birkenholz, D. E., & D. E. Jenni. 1964. Observations on the Spotted Rail and Pinnated Bittern in Costa Rica. *Auk* 81:558-559.

Blake, E. R. 1950. Birds of the Acary Mts. of southern British Guiana. *Fieldianna: Zool.* (Chicago) 32:419-474.

———. 1953. *Birds of Mexico*. Chicago: Univ. of Chicago Press.

———. 1955. A collection of Colombian game birds. *Fieldiana Zool.* (Chicago) 37:9-23.

———. 1956. A collection of Panamanian nests and eggs. *Condor* 58:386-388.

———. 1958. Birds of Volcan de Chiriqui, Panama. *Fieldiana Zool.* (Chicago) 36:499-577.

———. 1959. New and rare Colombian birds. *Lozania (Acta Zool. Colombiana)* 11:1-10.

———. 1961. Notes on a collection of birds from northeastern Colombia. *Fieldiana Zool.* (Chicago) 44:25-44.

———. 1962. Birds of the Sierra Macarena, eastern Colombia. *Fieldiana Zool.* (Chicago) 44:69-112.

———. 1968. Family Icteridae. Pp. 138-202 in *Check List of Birds of the World*, ed. J. L. Peters. Vol. 14. Cambridge, Mass.: Harvard Univ. Press.

———. 1977. *Manual of Neotropical Birds*. Vol. 1. Chicago: Univ. of Chicago Press.

Blydenstein, J. 1967. Tropical savanna vegetation of the llanos of Colombia. *Ecology* 48:1-15.

Boggs, G. O. 1961. Notas sobre las aves de "El Centro" en el valle medio del Río Magdalena, Colombia. *Noved. Colombianas* 1:401-423.

Bond, J. 1942. Notes on the Devil Owl. *Auk* 59:308-309.

———. 1961. *Birds of the West Indies*. Boston: Houghton Mifflin Co.

Bond, J., & R. Meyer de Schauensee. 1938. Ecological results of the George Vanderbilt South Pacific Expedition of 1937. Part 2. The birds of Malpelo Island, Colombia. *Proc. Acad. Nat. Sci. Philadelphia* 90:155-157.

Borrero, J. I. 1947. Aves occasionales en la Sabana de Bogotá y las lagunas de Fúquene y Tota. *Caldasia* 4:495-498.

———. 1952a. Algunas aves raras en la Sabana de Bogotá. *Lozania (Acta Zool. Colombiana)* 1:7-12.

———. 1952b. Apuntes sobre aves Colombianas. *Lozania (Acta Zool. Colombiana)* 3:1-12.

———. 1953. Status actual de *Zenaida auriculata* y *Leptotila plumbeiceps* en el Dept. de Caldas y *Cistothorus apolinari* en la region de Bogotá. *Lozania (Acta Zool. Colombiana)* 6:1-6.

———. 1955. Apuntes sobre aves Colombianas. *Lozania (Acta Zool. Colombiana)* 9:1-15.

———. 1958. Apuntes sobre aves Colombianas. *Caldasia* 8:252-294.

———. 1960a. Notas sobre aves de la Amazonia

y Ornioquia Colombianas. *Caldasia* 8:485-514.
———. 1960b. Notas sobre *Schizoeaca fuliginosa* y descripción de una nueva subespecie. *Noved. Colombianas* 1:238-242.
———. 1961. Notas sobre aves Colombianas. *Noved. Colombianas* 1:427-429.
———. 1962. Notas varias sobre *Asio flammeus bogotensis. Rev. Biol. Trop.* 10:45-59.
———. 1970. A photographic study of the potoo in Colombia. *The Living Bird* 9:257-263.
———. 1972a. Historia natural del titiribí. *Pyrocephalus rubinus* (Aves, Tyrannidae) en Colombia, con notas sobre su distribución. *Mitt. Inst. Colombo-Alemán Investig. Cient.* 6:113-133.
———. 1972b. *Aves de Caza Colombianas.* Universidad del Valle. Depto. de Biol., Cali, 79pp.
———. 1974. Notes on the structure of the upper eyelid of Potoos (*Nyctibius*). *Condor* 76:210-240.
———. 1975. Notas sobre el comportamiento reproductivo del Colibri *Amazilia tzacatl. Ardeola* 21:933-943.
———. 1981. Una nueva ave marina para Colombia: el Petrel del Cabo (*Daption capense*). *Rupicola* 1(5):4.
Borrero, J. I., & J. Hernández C. 1958. Apuntas sobre aves Colombianas. *Caldasia* 8:252-294.
———. 1961. Notas sobre aves de Colombia y descripción de una nueva subespecie de *Forpus conspicillatus. Noved. Colombianas* 1:430-445.
Borrero, J. I., & A. Olivares. 1955. Avifauna de la región de Soatá, Dept. Boyacá, Colombia. *Caldasia* 7:52-86.
Borrero, J. I., A. Olivares, & J. Hernández C. 1962. Notas sobre aves de Colombia. *Caldasia* 8:585-601.
Bourne, G. R. 1974. The Red-billed Toucan in Guyana. *The Living Bird.* 12:99-126.
Brown, L., & D. Amadon. 1968. *Eagles, Hawks, and Falcons of the World.* Vols. 1 and 2. N.Y.: McGraw-Hill.
Brown, R.G.B. 1980. Flight characteristics of Madeiran Petrel. *Brit. Birds* 73:263-264.
Buchanan, M. 1971. *Ciccaba virgata* in Trinidad. *Ibis* 113:105-106.
Burton, J. A. 1973. *Owls of the World* N.Y.: E. P. Dutton.
Burton, P. J. 1976. Feeding behavior in the Paradise Jacamar and the Swallow-wing. *The Living Bird* 15:223-238.
Carriker, M. A., Jr. 1910. An annotated list of the birds of Costa Rica, including Cocos Island. *Ann. Carnegie Mus.* 6:314-915.
———. 1954. Additions to the avifauna of Colombia. *Noved. Colombianas* 1:14-19.
———. 1955. Notes on the occurrence and distribution of certain species of Colombian birds. *Noved. Colombianas* 2:48-64.

———. 1959. New records of rare birds from Nariño and Cauca and notes on others. *Noved. Colombianas* 1:196-199.
Chapman, F. M. 1914. Diagnosis of apparently new Colombian birds, II. *Bull. Amer. Mus. Nat. Hist.* 33:167-192.
———. 1917. The distribution of bird life in Colombia. *Bull. Amer. Mus. Nat. Hist.* 36:1-169.
———. 1923. The distribution of the motmots of the genus *Momotus. Bull. Amer. Mus. Nat. Hist.* 48:26-59.
———. 1927. Description of new birds from northwestern Peru and western Colombia. *Amer. Mus. Novit.* 250:1-7.
———. 1928. The nesting habits of Wagler's Oropendola (*Zarhynchus wagleri*) on Barro Colorado Island, Canal Zone. *Bull. Amer. Mus. Nat. Hist.* 58:123-166.
———. 1929. *My Tropical Air Castle.* N.Y.: Appleton and Co.
———. 1935. The courtship of Gould's Manakin (*Manacus vitellinus vitellinus*) on Barro Colorado Island, Canal Zone. *Bull. Amer. Mus. Nat. Hist.* 68:471-525.
———. 1938. *Life in an Air Castle.* N.Y.: Appleton and Co.
Cherrie, G. K. 1916. A contribution to the ornithology of the Orinoco region. *Brooklyn Inst. Arts and Sci. Mus. Bull.* 2:133-374.
Chipley, R. M. 1976. The impact of migrant warblers on resident passerines in a subtropical Colombian woodland. *The Living Bird* 15:119-141.
Collins, C. T. 1968a. The comparative biology of two species of swifts in Trinidad, West Indies. *Bull. Florida State Mus.* 11:257-320.
———. 1968b. Notes on the biology of Chapman's Swift *Chaetura chapmani. Amer. Mus. Novit.* 2320:1-15.
Cottrell, G. W. 1968. The genera of puffbirds (Bucconidae). *Breviora* 285:1-5.
Darlington, P. J., Jr. 1931. Notes on the birds of the Río Frío (near Santa Marta), Magdalena, Colombia. *Bull. Mus. Comp. Zool., Harvard* 71:349-421.
Darwin, C. R. 1845. *The Voyage of the Beagle.* Reprint ed., 1955, London: J. M. Dent and Sons.
Davis, T.A.W. 1935. Some nesting notes from the savannas of the Rupununi district, British Guiana. *Ibis* 5:530-537.
———. 1949a. Field notes on the Orange-crested Manakin *Neopelma chrysocephalum. Ibis* 91:349-350.
———. 1949b. Communal display of the Black-chinned Antcreeper *Hypocnemoides melanopogon. Ibis* 91:351.
———. 1949c. Display of the White-throated Manakin *Corapipo gutturalis. Ibis* 91:146-147.

————. 1958. The displays and nests of three forest hummingbirds. *Ibis* 100:31-39.

Davis, W. E., Jr., P. K. Donahue, & E. G. Perkins. 1980. Observations of the behavior of the Zigzag Heron. *Condor* 82:460-461.

Delacour, J. 1954, 1956, 1959. *The Waterfowl of the World*. Vols. 1, 2, & 3. London: Country Life Ltd.

Delacour, J. & D. Amadon. 1973. *Curassows and Related Birds* N.Y.: Amer. Mus. Nat. Hist.

Denham, R. 1972. Quetzalitis, pt. 1. *Linnaean News-letter*, 16, no. 7.

Devillers, P. 1977. The skuas of the North American Pacific coast. *Auk* 94:417-429.

Dickey, D. R., & A. J. Van Rossem. 1938. The birds of El Salvador. *Field Mus. Nat. Hist. Publ., Zool. Ser.* 23:1-609.

Donahue, P. K. 1974. Gull-billed Tern in Caribbean South America. *Auk* 91:845.

————. 1977. Reddish Egret and Herring Gull in Caribbean Colombia. *Amer. Birds* 31:286.

Dorst, J. 1956. Étude biologique des trochilides des hauts plateaux pérouviens. *L'Oiseau* 26:165-193.

————. 1957. Birds of the Puya stands of Peru. *Ibis* 99:594-599.

————. 1963a. Note sur la nidification et le comportement acoustique du jeune *Asthenes wyatti punensis* au Pérou. *L'Oiseau* 33:1-6.

————. 1963b. Quelques adaptations écologiques des oiseaux de hautes Andes péruviennes. *Proc. 13th Intern. Ornithol. Congr.*, 658-665.

Drury, W. H. Jr. 1962. Breeding activities, especially nest building of the Yellowtail (*Ostinops decumanus*) in Trinidad, West Indies. *Zoologica* 47:39-58.

Dugand, A. 1945. Notas ornithologicas Colombianas, I. *Caldasia* 3:337-341.

————. 1947. Aves del Departamento del Atlántico, Colombia. *Caldasia* 4:499-648.

————. 1952. Algunas aves del Río Apaporis. *Lozania (Acta Zool. Colombiana)* 4:1-12.

Dugand, A., & J. I. Borrero. 1946. Aves de la ribera Colombiana del Amazonas. *Caldasia* 4:131-167.

————. 1948. Aves de la confluencia del Caquetá y Orteguaza (base aerea de Tres Esquinas), Colombia. *Caldasia* 5:115-156.

Dunning, J. S. 1970. *Portraits of Tropical Birds*. Wynnewood, Pa.: Livingston Pub. Co.

————. 1981. *South American Land Birds, a Photographic Guide to Identification*. Newton Square, Pa.: Harrowood.

Easterla, D. A., & W. George. 1970. Marbled Godwit and Yellow-throated Warbler in Colombia, South America. *Condor* 73:473.

Edwards, E. P. 1967. Nests of the Common Bush-Tanager and the Scaled Antpitta. *Condor* 69:605.

Edwards, E. P., & R. B. Lea. 1955. Birds of Monserrate, Chiapas. *Condor* 57:45-46.

Eisenmann, E. 1952. Annotated list of the birds of Barro Colorado Island, Panama Canal Zone. *Smiths. Misc. Coll.* Vol. 117, no. 5, 62 pp.

————. 1953. The nest of the Long-billed Gnatwren (*Ramphocaenus rufiventris*). *Auk* 70:368-369.

————. 1955. The species of Middle American birds. *Trans. Linn. Soc.* 7:1-128.

————. 1957. Notes on the birds of the province of Bocas del Toro, Panama. *Condor* 59:247-262.

————. 1962. Notes on some neotropical vireos in Panama. *Condor* 64:505-508.

————. 1971. Range expansion and population increase in North and Middle America of the White-tailed Kite (*Elanus leucurus*). *Amer. Birds* 25:529-536.

Eisenmann, E., & F. C. Lehmann. 1962. A new species of swift of the genus *Cypseloides* from Colombia. *Amer. Mus. Novit.* 2117:1-16.

Eley, J. W., G. R. Graves, T. A. Parker III, & D. Hunter, 1979. Notes on *Siptornis striaticollis* (Furnariidae) in Peru. *Condor* 81:319.

Ellis, D. H., & R. L. Glinski. 1980. Some unusual records for the Peregrine and Pallid Falcons in South America. *Condor* 82:350-351.

Ellis, H. R. 1952. Nesting behavior of a Purple-throated Fruit crow. *Wilson Bull.* 64:98-100.

Ewert, D. 1975. Notes on the nests of four avian species from the coastal cordillera of Venezuela. *Wilson Bull.* 87:105-106.

Feduccia, A. 1973. *Evolutionary Trends in the Neotropical Ovenbirds and Woodhewers*. Ornithol. Monogr., no. 13. Amer. Ornithol. Union.

Feinsinger, P. 1977. Notes on the hummingbirds of Monteverde, Cordillera de Tilarán, Costa Rica. *Wilson Bull.* 89:159-164.

ffrench, R. P. 1973. *A Guide to the Birds of Trinidad and Tobago*. Wynnewood, Pa.: Livingston.

ffrench, R. P. & F. Haverschmidt. 1970. The Scarlet Ibis in Surinam and Trinidad. *The Living Bird* 9:147-165.

Fitzpatrick, J. W. & D. E. Willard. 1982. Twenty-one bird species new or little known from the Republic of Colombia. *Bull. Brit. Ornithol. Club* 102:153-158.

Forshaw, J. M. 1973. *Parrots of the World*. Garden City, N.Y.: Doubleday.

Foster, M. S., & N. K. Johnson. 1974. Notes on birds of Costa Rica. *Wilson Bull.* 86:58-63.

Fowler, J. M., & J. B. Cope. 1964. Notes on the Harpy Eagle in British Guiana. *Auk* 81:257-273.

Freese, C. H. 1975. Notes on the nesting of the

Double-striped Thick-knee (*Burhinus bistriatus*) in Costa Rica. *Condor* 77:353.

Friedmann, H. 1948. Birds collected by the National Geographic Society's Expeditions to northern Brazil and southern Venezuela. *Proc. U.S. Nat. Mus.* 97:373-569.

———. 1957. The rediscovery of *Tangavius armenti* (Cabanis) *Auk* 74:497-498.

Friedmann, H, & F. D. Smith. 1950. A contribution to the ornithology of northeastern Venezuela. *Proc. U.S. Nat. Mus.* 100:411-538.

———. 1955. A further contribution to the ornithology of northeastern Venezuela. *Proc. U.S. Nat. Mus.* 104:463-524.

Frisch, S., & J. D. Frisch. 1964. *Aves Brasileiras.* S. Paulo, Brazil: Irmãos Vitale S/A.

Fuertes, L. A. 1914. Impressions of the voices of tropical birds. *Bird Lore* 16:161-169.

George, W. G. 1964. Rarely seen songbirds of Peru's high Andes. *Nat. Hist.* 73:26-29.

Gertler, P. E. 1977. Hooded Antpitta (*Grallaricula cucullata*) in the Eastern Andes of Colombia. *Condor* 79:389.

Gill, F. B., F. J. Stokes, & C. C. Stokes. 1974. Observations on the Horned Screamer. *Wilson Bull.* 86:43-50.

Gilliard, E. T. 1958. *Living Birds of the World.* Garden City, N.Y.: Doubleday.

———. 1959. Notes on some birds of northern Venezuela. *Amer. Mus. Novit.* 1927:1-33.

———. 1962. Strange courtship of the Cock-of-the-Rock. *Natl. Geogr. Mag.* 121:134-140.

———. 1962. On the breeding behavior of the Cock-of-the-Rock (Aves, *Rupicola rupicola*). *Bull. Amer. Mus. Nat. Hist.* 124:31-68.

Gochfeld, M. 1979. Nest description and plumage variation of the Sepia-brown Wren *Cinnycerthia peruana*. *Bull. Brit. Ornithol. Club* 99:45-47.

Gochfeld, M., R. Gochfeld, M. Kleinbaum, & G. Tudor. 1974. Sight record of a Blue Grosbeak (*Guiraca caerulea*) in Colombia. *Amer. Birds* 28:958.

Gochfeld, M., S. Keith, & P. Donahue. 1980. Records of rare or previously unrecorded birds from Colombia. *Bull. Brit. Ornithol. Club* 100:196-201.

Gochfeld, M., & G. Tudor. 1978. Ant-following birds in South American subtropical forests. *Wilson Bull.* 90:139-141.

Goeldi, E. A. 1894. Nesting of *Lochmias nematura* and *Phibalura flavirostris*. *Ibis* (ser. 6), 6:484-494.

Goodfellow, W. 1901. Results of an ornithological journey through Colombia and Ecuador. *Ibis* 1901:300-319, 458-480, 699-715.

———. 1902. Results of an ornithological journey through Colombia and Ecuador. *Ibis* 1902:56-67, 207-233.

Goodwin, D. 1976. *Crows of the World.* Ithaca, N.Y.: Cornell Univ. Press.

———. 1977. *Pigeons and Doves of the World.* Ithaca, N.Y.: Cornell Univ. Press.

Gore, M.E.J., & A.R.M. Gepp. 1978. *Las Aves del Uruguay.* S. A. Montevideo: Mosca Hnos.

Grant, P. J., R. F. Scott, & D.I.M. Wallace. 1971. Further notes on the "portlandica" plumage phase of terns. *Brit. Birds* 64:19-22.

Graves, G. 1980. A new subspecies of *Diglossa (carbonaria) brunneiventris*. *Bull. Brit. Ornithol. Club* 100:230-232.

———. 1982. Speciation in the Carbonated Flower-Piercer (*Diglossa carbonaria*) complex of the Andes. *Condor* 84:1-14.

Greenwalt, C. H. 1960. *Hummingbirds.* Garden City, N.Y.: Doubleday and Co.

Gross, A. O. 1950. Nesting of the Streaked Flycatcher in Panama. *Wilson Bull.*. 62:183-193.

———. 1952. Nesting of Hick's Seedeater at Barro Colorado Island, Canal Zone. *Auk* 69:433-446.

———. 1961. Nesting of the Black-tailed Flycatcher on Barro Colorado Island. *Wilson Bull.* 76:248-266.

Haffer, J. 1959. Notas sobre las aves de la región de Urabá. *Lozania (Acta Zool. Colombiana)* 12:1-49.

———. 1961. Notas sobre la avifauna de la península de la Guajira. *Noved. Colombianas* 1:374-396.

———. 1967a. Speciation in Colombian forest birds west of the Andes. *Amer. Mus. Novit.* 2294:1-57.

———. 1967b. On birds from the northern Chocó region, NW Colombia. *Veröff. Zool. Staatssammlung, München* 11:123-149.

———. 1967c. Some allopatric species pairs of birds in northwestern Colombia. *Auk* 84:343-365.

———. 1974. Avian speciation in tropical South America. *Publ. Nuttall Ornithol. Club*, no. 14. Cambridge, Mass.

———. 1975. *Avifauna of Northwestern Colombia, South America.* Bonner Zool. Monog., no. 7. Bonn.

Hainsworth, F. R. 1977. Foraging efficiency and parental care in *Colibri coruscans*. *Condor* 79:69-75.

Hallinan, T. 1924. Notes on Panama birds. *Auk* 41:304-326.

Hancock, J., & H. Elliott. 1978. *Herons of the World.* N.Y.: Harper & Row.

Hardy, J. W. 1967. The puzzling vocal repertoire of the South American Collared Jay *(Cyanolyca viridicyana merida)*. *Condor* 69:513-521.

———. 1969a. A taxonomic revision of the New World Jays. *Condor* 71:360-375.

———. 1969b. *Habits and Habitats of Certain South*

*American Jays*. Contributions in science. Los Angeles County Museum 165:1-16.

———. 1975. *Voices of Neotropical Birds*. 12″ LP records. Gainesville, Fla.: ARA.

———. 1980. *Voices of New World Nightbirds. Owls, Nightjars and their allies*. 12″ LP record. Gainesville, Fla.: ARA.

Harris, M. 1974. *A Field Guide to the Birds of the Galapagos*. N.Y.: Taplinger.

Harrison, E. N., & L. F. Kiff. 1977. The nest and egg of the Black Solitary Eagle. *Condor* 79:132-133.

Haverschmidt, F. 1951. Notes of *Icterus nigrogularis* and *I. chrysocephalus* in Surinam. *Wilson Bull*. 63:45-47.

———. 1955. Notes on the life history of *Todirostrum maculatum* in Surinam. *Auk* 72:325-331.

———. 1958. Notes on the breeding habits of *Panyptila cayennensis*. *Auk* 75:120-129.

———. 1962. Notes on the feeding habits and food of some hawks of Surinam. *Condor* 64:154-158.

———. 1966. The eggs of the Giant Cowbird. *Bull. Brit. Ornithol. Club* 86:144-147.

———. 1967. Additional notes on the eggs of the Giant Cowbird. *Bull. Brit. Ornithol. Club* 87:136-137.

———. 1968. *Birds of Surinam*. Edinburgh and London: Oliver & Boyd.

———. 1970a. Notes on the life history of the Mouse-colored Flycatcher in Surinam. *Condor* 72:374-375.

———. 1970b. Notes on the Snail Kite in Surinam. *Auk* 87:580-584.

———. 1971. Notes on the life history of the Rusty-margined Flycatcher in Surinam. *Wilson Bull*. 83:124-128.

———. 1972a. Notes on the Yellow-billed Tern *Sterna superciliaris*. *Bull. Brit. Ornithol. Club* 92:93-95.

———. 1972b. Bird records from Surinam. *Bull. Brit. Ornithol. Club* 92:49-53.

———. 1972c. Further evidence of the "portlandica" plumage phase of terns. *Brit. Birds* 65:117-119.

———. 1974a. Notes on the life history of the Yellow-breasted Flycatcher in Surinam. *Wilson Bull*. 86:215-220.

———. 1974b. The occurrence of the Giant Snipe *Gallinago undulatus* in Surinam. *Bull. Brit. Ornithol. Club* 94:132-134.

———. 1975a. The Plain-breasted Ground-Dove in Surinam. *Condor* 77:355.

———. 1975b. More bird records from Surinam. *Bull. Brit. Ornithol. Club* 95:74-77.

Hays, H. 1971. Roseate Tern, *Sterna dougallii* banded on Atlantic coast recovered on Pacific. *Bird Banding* 42:295.

Hellmayr, C. E. 1924-1949. Catalogue of birds of the Americas. *Field Mus. Nat. Hist. Publ., Zool*. (ser. 13), pts. 1-11.

Herklots, G.A.C. 1961. *The Birds of Trinidad and Tobago*. London: Collins.

Hernández, C., J., & J. V. Rodríguez M. 1979. Dos nuevos taxa del género *Grallaria* (Aves: Formicariidae) del alto Valle del Magdalena (Colombia). *Caldasia* 12:573-580.

Hilty, S. L. 1974. Notes on birds at swarms of army ants in the highlands of Colombia. *Wilson Bull*. 86:479-481.

———. 1975a. Notes on a nest and behavior of the Chestnut-crowned Gnateater. *Condor* 77:513-514.

———. 1975b. Year-round attendance of White-whiskered and Little Hermits *Phaethornis* spp. at singing assemblies in Colombia. *Ibis* 117:382-384.

———. 1977. *Chlorospingus flavovirens* rediscovered, with notes on other Pacific Colombian and Cauca Valley birds. *Auk* 94:44-49.

Hilty, S. L., & W. L. Brown 1983. Range extensions of Colombian birds as indicated by the M. A. Carriker Jr. collection at the National Museum of Natural History, Smithsonian Institution. *Bull. Brit. Ornithol. Club* 103:5-17.

Hilty, S. L., T. A. Parker III, & J. Silliman. 1979. Observations on Plush-capped Finches in the Andes with a description of the juvenal and immature plumages. *Wilson Bull*. 91:145-148.

Holdridge, L. R. 1967. *Life zone ecology*. San Jose, Costa Rica: Trop. Sci. Cent.

Howell, T. R. 1957. Birds of a second growth rain forest area of Nicaragua. *Condor* 59:73-111.

Hudson, W. H. 1920. *Birds of La Plata*. 2 vols. London & Toronto: Dent & Sons.

Humphrey, P. S., D. Bridge, P. W. Reynolds, & R. T. Peterson. 1970. *Birds of Isla Grande (Tierra del Fuego)*. Lawrence. Kans.: Univ. of Kansas Mus. Nat. Hist.

Ingels, J. 1980. A nest of the White-plumed Antbird (*Pithys albifrons*) in Surinam. *Auk* 97:407-408.

Jehl, J. R. Jr. 1968. Relationships of the Charadriidae (shorebirds): A taxonomic study based on color pattern of the downy young. *Mems. San Diego Soc. Nat. Hist*. 3:1-54.

———. 1973. The distribution of marine birds in Chilean waters in winter. *Auk* 90:119-135.

———. 1974. The near-shore avifauna of the Middle American west coast. *Auk* 91:681-699.

Jenni, D. A., R. D. Gambs, & B. J. Betts. 1974. Acoustic behavior of the Northern Jacana. *The Living Bird* 13:193-210.

Jenny, J. P., F. Ortiz, & M. D. Arnold. 1981.

First nesting record of the Peregrine Falcon in Ecuador. *Condor* 83:387.

Johnson, A. W. 1965, 1967. The birds of Chile and adjacent regions of Argentina, Bolivia and Peru. Vols. 1 & 2. Buenos Aires: Platt Estab. Gráficos.

Johnson, R. A. 1953. Breeding notes on two Panamerican antbirds. *Auk* 70:496.

Johnson, T. B., & S. L. Hilty. 1976. Notes on the Sickle-winged Guan in Colombia. *Auk* 93:194-195.

Kahl, M. P. 1971. Observations on the Jabiru and Maguari Storks in Argentina. *Condor* 73:220-229.

Karr, J. P. 1971. Ecological, behavioral and distributional notes on some central Panama birds. *Condor* 73:107-111.

Kiff, L. F. 1975. Notes on southwestern Costa Rica birds. *Condor* 77:101.

———. 1977. The nest, eggs, and relationships of the Half-collared Gnatwren *(Microbates cinereiventris)*. *Condor* 79:261-262.

Kilham, L. 1972. Habits of the Crimson-crested Woodpecker in Panama. *Wilson Bull.* 84:28-47.

King, W. B. 1967. *Seabirds of the Tropical Pacific Ocean*. Wash. D.C.: Smiths. Inst. Press.

——— (compiler). 1979. *Endangered Birds of the World*. ICBP Bird Red Data Book. Vol. 2, Aves. Wash. D.C.: Smiths. Inst. Press.

Koepcke, M. 1970. *The Birds of the Department of Lima, Peru*. Wynnewood, Pa.: Livingston.

Lamm, D. W. 1948. Notes on birds of the states of Pernambuco and Paraiba, Brazil. *Auk* 65:261-283.

Lancaster, D. A. 1964. Life History of the Boucard (Slaty-breasted) Tinamou in British Honduras. *Condor* 66:165-181, 253-276.

———. 1970. Breeding behavior of the Cattle Egret in Colombia. *The Living Bird* 9:167-194.

Lanyon, W. E. 1975. Evidence of an incomplete prealternate molt in some South American *Myiarchus* Flycatchers. *Condor* 77:511.

———. 1978. Revision of the *Myiarchus* flycatchers of South America. *Bull. Amer. Mus. Nat. Hist.* 161:427-628.

Lanyon, W. E., & J. Bull. 1967. Identification of Connecticut Mourning, and MacGillivray's Warblers. *Bird Banding* 38:187-194.

Lapham, H. 1970. Nesting behavior *Ortalis ruficauda*. *Bol. Soc. Venezolana Cienc. Nat.* 28:291-329.

Laughlin, R. M. 1952. A nesting of the Double-toothed Kite in Panama. *Condor* 54:137-139.

Lehmann V., F. C. 1943. El genero *Morphnus*. *Caldasia* 2:165-179.

———. 1946. Two new birds from the Andes of Colombia. *Auk* 63:218-223.

———. 1957. Contribuciónes al estudio de la fauna de Colombia XII. *Noved. Colombianas* 3:101-156.

———. 1959a. Observations of the Cattle Egret in Colombia. *Condor* 61:265-269.

———. 1959b. Contribuciónes al estudio de la fauna de Colombia XIV. Nuevas observaciónes sobre *Oroaëtus isidori* (Des Murs). *Noved. Colombianas* 1:169-195

———. 1960a. Contribuciónes al estudio de la fauna de Colombia XV. *Noved. Colombianas* 1:256-276.

———. 1960b. Hallazgo de una colonía de *Ardea cocoi* Linneo, en el Valle del Cauca. *Noved. Colombianas* 1:276-279.

———. 1961. Notas generales. *Noved. Colombianas* 1:523-526.

———. 1970. Avifauna in Colombia *in* the Avifauna of Northern Latin America (Symposium). *Smithsonian Contributions to Zool.*, no. 26.

Lehmann V., F. C., & J. Haffer. 1960. Notas sobre *Buteo albigula* Philippi. *Noved. Colombianas* 1:242-255.

Lehmann V., F. C., J. R. Silliman, & E. Eisenmann. 1977. Rediscovery of the Crescent-faced Antpitta in Colombia. *Condor* 79:387-388.

Lemke, T. O. 1977. Copulation observed in Maroon-tailed parakeets in Meta, Colombia. *Auk* 94:773.

Lemke, T. O., & Paul Gertler. 1978. Recent observations on the birds of the Sierra de la Macarena, Colombia. *Condor* 80:453-455.

Lowe, C. 1977. Note on sight record of Northern Bentbill in Canal Zone. *Toucan* 4(6):3.

Lowe-McConnell, R. H. 1967. Notes on the nesting of the Boatbill *Cochlearius cochlearius*. *Ibis* 109:179.

Mader, W. J. 1975a. Extra adults at Harris' Hawk nests. *Condor* 77:482-485.

———. 1975b. Biology of Harris' Hawk in southern Arizona. *The Living Bird* 14:113-155.

———. 1979. First nest description for the genus *Micrastur* (Forest-Falcons). *Condor* 81:320.

———. 1981. Notes on nesting raptors in the llanos of Venezuela. *Condor* 83:48-51.

Marchant, S. 1960. The breeding of some southwestern Ecuadorian birds (2 pts.). *Ibis* 102:349-382, 584-599.

Marinkelle, C. J. 1970. Birds of the Serranía de Macuira, Guajira Peninsula, Colombia. *Mitt. Inst. Colombo-Alemán Investig. Cient.* 4:15-34.

Marshall, J. T., Jr. 1967. Parallel variation in North and Middle American screech-owls. *Western Found. Vert. Zool. Monogr.*, no. 1.

Massey, B. W., & J. L. Atwood, 1978. Plumages of the Least Tern. *Bird Banding* 49:360-371.

Mayr, E., & L. L. Short. 1970. Species taxa of North American birds. *Publ. Nuttall Ornithol. Club*, no. 9. Cambridge, Mass.

McKay, W. D. 1980. Nest and young of the Highland Tinamou in southern Colombia. *Condor* 82:107.

McLoughlin, E., & P.J.K. Burton. 1970. Field notes on the breeding and diet of some South American parrots. *Foreign Birds* 36:169-171, 210-213.

———. 1976. Notes on the Hawk-headed Parrot *Deroptyus accipitrinus*. *Bull. Brit. Ornithol. Club* 92:68-72.

McNeil, R. 1982. Winter resident repeats and returns of austral and boreal migrant birds in Venezuela. *J. Field Ornithol.*, 53(2):125-132.

McNeil, R., & A. Martinez. 1968. Notes on the nesting of the Short-tailed Pygmy-Tyrant (*Myiornis ecaudatus*) in northeastern Venezuela. *Condor* 70:181-182.

Meganck, R. 1975. Colombia's National Parks: An analysis of management problems and perceived values. Ph.D. diss., Oregon State Univ.

Merizalde de Albuya, C. 1975. Reproducción en cinco especies de aves del occidente del Ecuador. *Rev. Univ. Catolica* 3:167-183.

Meyer de Schauensee, R. 1948-1952. The birds of the Republic of Colombia. *Caldasia* (pts. 1-5), nos. 22-26: 251-1212.

———. 1951b. Colombian zoological survey. Part IX. A new species of antbird (*Phlegopsis*) from Colombia. *Not. Naturae* (Philadelphia) 241:1-3.

———. 1952. The status of *Sporophila lineola* (Lined Seedeater) and *S. bouvronides* (Lesson's Seedeater). *Proc. Acad. Nat. Sci. Philadelphia* 104:175-181.

———. 1959. Additions to the birds of the Republic of Colombia. *Proc. Acad. Nat. Sci. Philadelphia* 111:53-75.

———. 1964. *The birds of Colombia*. Narbeth, Pa.: Livingston Press.

———. 1966. *The Species of Birds of South America with Their Distribution*. Narbeth, Pa.: Livingston Press.

———. 1970. *A Guide to the Birds of South America*. Narbeth, Pa.: Livingston Press.

Meyer de Schauensee, R., & W. H. Phelps, Jr. 1978. *A Guide to the Birds of Venezuela*. Princeton, N.J.: Princeton Univ. Press.

Miller, A. H. 1947. The tropical avifauna of the upper Magdalena Valley, Colombia. *Auk* 64:351-381.

———. 1952. Supplemental data on the tropical avifauna of the arid upper Magdalena Valley of Colombia. *Auk* 69:450-457.

———. 1959. A new race of nighthawk from the upper Magdalena Valley of Colombia. *Proc. Biol. Soc. Wash.* 72:155-158.

———. 1960. A blackish race of the Gray Seedeater of northern South America. *Condor* 62:121-123.

———. 1961. Molt cycles in equatorial Andean Sparrows. *Condor* 63:143-161.

———. 1963. Seasonal activity and ecology of the avifauna of an American equatorial cloud forest. *Univ. Calif. Publ. Zool.* 66:1-74.

Miller, A. H. & V. D. Miller. 1968. The behavioral ecology and breeding biology of the Andean Sparrow *Zonotrichia capensis*. *Caldasia* 10:83-154.

Mitchell, M. H. 1957. *Observations on Birds of Southeastern Brazil*. Toronto, Ont.: Univ. Toronto Press.

Mock, D. W. 1975. Social behavior of the Boatbilled Heron. *The Living Bird* 14:185-214.

Moffett, G. M., Jr. 1970. A study of nesting Torrent Ducks in the Andes. *The Living Bird* 9:5-27.

Moore, R. T. 1934. The Mt. Sangay labyrinth and its fauna. *Auk* 51:141-156.

———. 1944. Nesting of the Brown-capped *Leptopogon* in Mexico. *Condor* 46:6-8.

Morales, S., J, E. 1979. Primero registro para Colombia de *Turdus lawrencii* Coues (Aves: Turdidae). *Lozania (Acta Zool. Colombiana)* 29:2-4.

Morrison, A. 1939. The birds of the Dept. of Huancavelia, Peru. *Ibis* (14) 3:453.

Morton, E. S. 1971. Nest predation affecting the breeding season of the Clay-colored Robin, a tropical song bird. *Science* 171:920-921.

———. 1976a. The adaptive significance of dull coloration in Yellow Warblers. *Condor* 78:423.

———. 1976b. Vocal mimicry in the Thick-billed Euphonia. *Wilson Bull.*. 88:485-487.

———. 1977. Intratropical migration in the Yellow-green Vireo and Piratic Flycatcher. *Auk* 94:97-106.

Moynihan, M. 1963. Interspecific relations between some Andean birds. *Ibis* 105:327-339.

Muir, A., & A. L. Butler. 1925. The nesting of *Nyctibius griseus* in Trinidad. *Ibis* (12) 1:654-659.

Munves, J. 1975. Birds of a highland clearing in Cundinamarca, Colombia. *Auk* 92:307-321.

Murphy, R. C. 1936. *Oceanic Birds of South America*. 2 vols. N.Y.: Amer. Mus. Nat. Hist.

———. 1938. Dark Skies. *Nat. Hist.* 41:165-178.

———. 1941. The Askoy Expedition of the American Museum of Natural Histoy in the eastern tropical Pacific. *Science* 94:57-58.

———. 1951. Populations of the Wedge-tailed Shearwater (*Puffinus pacificus*). *Amer. Mus. Novit.* 1512:1-21.

Naranjo, L. G. 1979a. Primer registro de *Cha-*

*radrius wilsonia wilsonia* ord. para Colombia. *Lozania (Acta Zool. Colombiana)* 30:6-7.

———. 1979b. Las aves marinas del Caribe Colombiano. Diss., Fundación Univ. de Bogotá, Jorge Tadez Lozano.

———. 1984a. El Phalaropo Norteño *Lobipes lobatus* (Aves: Phalaropodidae) en Colombia. *Lozania (Acta Zool. Colombiana)*. In press.

———. 1984b. Apuntes sobre la avifauna de la Isla Gorgona. In *La Isla Gorgona*, ed. for the Banco Popular y la Universidad del Valle.

Naumburg, E. M. B. 1930. The Birds of Matto Grosso, Brazil. *Bull. Amer. Mus. Nat. Hist.* 60:1-432.

Nelson, J. B. 1975. Breeding biology of Frigatebirds—a comparative review. *The Living Bird* 14:113-155.

Nicéforo M., H. 1945. Notas sobre aves de Colombia I. *Caldasia* 3:367-395.

———. 1947. Notas sobre aves de Colombia II. *Caldasia* 4:317-377.

Nicéforo M., H., & A. Olivares. 1964. Adiciónes a la avifauna Colombiana, I (Tinamidae-Falconidae). *Bol. Inst. La Salle* 204:5-27.

———. 1965. Adiciónes a la avifauna Colombiana, II (Cracidae-Rynchopidae). *Bol. Soc. Venezolana Cienc. Nat.* 26:36-58.

———. 1966. Adiciónes a la avifauna Colombiana, III (Columbidae-Caprimulgidae). *Bol. Soc. Venezolana Cienc. Nat.* 110:370-393.

———. 1967. Adiciónes a la avifauna Colombiana, IV (Apodidae-Picidae). *Hornero* 10:403-435.

———. 1968. Adiciónes a la avifauna Colombiana, V (Dendrocolaptidae-Cotingidae). *Bol. Inst. La Salle* 208:271-291.

———. 1975. Adiciónes a la avifauna Colombiana, VI (Tyrannidae-Bombicillidae). Entraga A. *Lozania (Acta Zool. Colombiana)* 19:1-16.

———. 1976a. Adiciónes a la avifauna Colombiana, VI (Tyrannidae-Bombicillidae). Entraga B. *Lozania (Acta Zool. Colombiana)* 20:19-34.

———. 1976b. Adiciónes a la avifauna Colombiana, VI (Tyrannidae-Bombicillidae). Entraga C. *Lozania (Acta Zool. Comombiana)* 21:1-15.

Norton, D. W. 1965. Notes on some non-passerine birds from eastern Ecuador. *Breviora* 230:1-11.

Norton, D. W., G. Orcés V., & E. Sutter. 1972. Notes on rare and previously unreported birds from Ecuador. *Auk* 89:889-894.

Norton, W. J. E. 1975. Notes on the birds of the Sierra Nevada de Santa Marta, Colombia. *Bull. Brit. Ornithol. Club* 95:109-115.

Nottebohm, F., & M. Nottebohm. 1969. The parrots of Bush Bush. *Amimal Kingdom* 72:19-23.

Olalla, A. M. 1943. Algunas observaçoes sobre a biologia das aves e mamiferos sul-Americanos. *Pap. Avuls. Dept. Zool. São Paulo* 3:229-236.

Olivares, A. 1955. Algunas aves de la Comisaría del Vaupés (Colombia). *Caldasia* 7:259-275.

———. 1957a. Aves de la costa del Pacifico, Municipio de Guapí, Cauca, Colombia, I. *Caldasia* 7:359-381.

———. 1957b. Aves de la costa del Pacifico, Municipio de Guapí, Cauca Colombia, II. *Caldasia* 8:33-93.

———. 1958. Aves de la costa del Pacifico, Municipio de Guapí, Cauca, Colombia, III. *Caldasia* 8:217-251.

———. 1959. Cinco aves que aparentemente no habian sido registradas en Colombia. *Lozania (Acta Zool. Colombiana)* 12:51-56.

———. 1962. Aves de la región sur de la Sierra de la Macarena, Meta, Colombia. *Rev. Acad. Colombiana Cienc. Exactas, Fisicas Nat.* 11:305-344.

———. 1963. Notas sobre aves de los Andes Orientales en Boyacá. *Bol. Soc. Venezolana Cienc. Nat.* 25:91-125.

———. 1964a. Adiciónes a las aves de la Comisaría del Vaupés (Colombia), I. *Rev. Acad. Colombiana Cienc. Exactas, Fisicas Nat.* 12:163-173.

———. 1964b. Adiciónes a las aves de la Comisaría del Vaupés (Colombia), II. *Caldasia* 9:150-184.

———. 1965. Avifaunae Colombiensis Notulae. No. I. Dos aves nuevas para Colombia. *Hornero* 10:273-275.

———. 1966. Algunas aves de Puerto Asís, Comisaría Del Putumayo, Colombia. *Caldasia* 9:379-393.

———. 1967. Avifaunae Colombiensis Notulae. No. II. Seis nuevas aves para Colombia y apuntaciónes sobre sesenta especies y subespecies registradas anteriormente. *Caldasia* 10:39-58.

———. 1969a. *Aves de Cundinamarca.* Bogotá: Univ. Nac. Colombia.

———. 1969b. Aves de las Comisaría del Vichada y Guainía, Colombia, coleccionadas por el Dr. C. J. Marinkelle. *Bol. Soc. Venezolana Cienc. Nat.* 28:179-200.

———. 1971. Aves de la ladera oriental de los Andes Orientales, Alto Río Cusiana, Boyacá, Colombia. *Caldasia* 11:203-226.

———. 1974a. Aves de la Sierra Nevada del Cocuy, Colombia. *Rev. Acad. Colombiana Cienc. Exactas, Fisicas Nat.* 54:39-48.

———. 1974b. Aves de la Orinoquia Colombiana. *Inst. Cienc. Nat. Ornithología Univ. Nac. Colombia.* 127 pp.

Olivares, A., & J. Hernández C. 1962. Aves de la Comisaría del Vaupés (Colombia). *Rev. de Biol. Trop., Univ. Costa Rica* 10:61-90.

Olrog, C. C. 1963. *Lista y distribución de las aves Argentinas.* Tucuman: Opera Lilloana IX.

———. 1968. *Las Aves Sudamericanas.* Vol. 1. Fundación, Argentina: Instituto "Miguel Lillo."

Olson, S. L. 1973a. A classification of the Rallidae. *Wilson Bull.* 85:381-416.

———. 1973b. A study of the neotropical rail *Anurolimnas castaneiceps* (Aves: Rallidae) with a description of a new subspecies. *Proc. Biol. Soc. Wash.* 86:403-412.

———. 1980a. Revision of the Tawny-faced Antwren *Microbates cinereiventris* (Aves: Passeriformes). *Proc. Biol. Soc. Wash.* 93:68-74.

———. 1980b. Geographic variation in the Yellow Warblers (*Dendroica petechia*: Parulidae) of the Pacific coast of Middle and South America. *Proc. Biol. Soc. Wash.* 93:473-481.

———. 1981a. Interaction between the two subspecies groups of the seed-finch *Sporophila angolensis* in the Magdalena Valley, Colombia. *Auk* 98:379-381.

———. 1981b. A revision of the subspecies of *Sporophila ("oryzoborus") angolensis* (Aves: Emberizinae). *Proc. Biol. Soc. Wash.* 94:43-51.

———. 1981c. A revision of the northern forms of *Euphonia xanthogaster* (Aves: Thraupidae). *Proc. Biol. Soc. Wash.* 94:101-106.

———. 1981d. Systematic notes on certain oscines from Panama and adjacent areas (Aves: Passeriformes). *Proc. Biol. Soc. Wash.* 94:363-373.

———. Geographic variation in *Chlorospingus ophthalmicus* in Colombia and Venezuela (Aves: Thraupidae). In press.

O'Neill, J. P. 1969. Distributional notes on the birds of Peru, including twelve species previously unreported from the republic. *Occas. Papers Mus. Zool., Louisiana State Univ.* 37:1-11.

———. 1974. The Birds of Balta, a Peruvian dry tropical forest locality, with an analysis of their origins and ecological relationships. Ph.D. diss., Louisiana State Univ.

O'Neill, J. P., & T. A. Parker III. 1977. Taxonomy and range of *Pionus "seniloides"* in Peru. *Condor* 79:274.

O'Neill, J. P. & D. L. Pearson. 1974. Estudio preliminar de las aves de Yarinacocha Departamento de Loreto, Peru. *Publ. Mus. Hist. Nat. Javiér Prado. Ser. A. (Zool.)* 25:1-13.

O'Neill, J. P., & T. S. Schulenberg. 1979. Notes on the Masked Saltator, *Saltator cinctus* in Peru. *Auk* 96:610-613.

Oniki, Y. 1970a. Roosting behavior of three species of woodcreepers (Dendrocolaptidae) in Brazil. *Condor* 72:233.

———. 1970b. Nesting behavior of Reddish Hermits (*Phaethornis ruber*). *Auk* 87:720-728.

———. 1972. Studies of the guild of ant-following birds at Belém, Brazil. *Acta Amazonica* 2:59-79.

———. 1975. The behavior and ecology of Slaty Antshrikes (*Thamnophilus punctatus*) on Barro Colorado Island, Panama Canal Zone. *An. Acad. Bras. Ciénc.* 47:477-515.

Oniki, Y. & E. O. Willis. 1972. Studies of ant-following birds north of the eastern Amazon. *Acta Amazonica* 2:127-151.

———. 1979. A nest of the Collared Gnatwren (*Microbates collaris*). *Condor* 81:101-102.

———. 1980. A nest of the Ringed Antpipit (*Corythopis torquata*). *Wilson Bull.* 92:126-127.

Orejuela, J. E., R. J. Raitt, & H. Alvarez. 1980. Differential use by North American migrants of three types of Colombian forests. Pp. 253-264 in *Migrant Birds in the Neotropics: Ecology, Behavior, Distribution and Conservation*, ed. A. Keast & E. S. Morton. Wash. D.C.: Smiths. Inst. Press.

Ortiz-Crespo, F. I. 1974. The Giant Hummingbird, *Patagona gigas*, in Ecuador. *Ibis* 116:347-359.

Orton, J. 1871. Notes on birds in the museum of Vassar College. *Amer. Natur.* 4:711-717.

Osborne, D. R., & G. R. Bourne. 1977. Breeding behavior and food habits of the Wattled Jacana. *Condor* 79:98-105.

Osgood, W. H., & B. Conover. 1922. Game birds from northwestern Venezuela. *Field Mus. Nat. Hist. Zool.* 12:19-41.

Oure, O. T. 1976. A second breeding colony of Waved Albatrosses *Diomedea irrorata*. *Ibis* 118:419-420.

Palmer, R. S. 1962. *Handbook of North American Birds.* Vol. 1. New Haven and London: Yale Univ. Press.

Parker, T. A., III. 1979. An introduction to foliage-gleaner identification. *Continental Birds* 1:32-37.

———. 1982. Observations of some unusual rainforest and marsh birds in southeastern Peru. *Wilson Bull.*, 94(4):477-493.

Parker, T. A., III, & J. P. O'Neill. 1980. Notes on little known birds of the upper Urubamba Valley, southern Peru. *Auk* 97:167-176.

Parker, T. A., III, & S. A. Parker. 1980. Rediscovery of *Xenerpestes singularis* (Furnariidae). *Auk* 97:203-204.

Parker, T. A., III, S. A. Parker, & M. A. Plenge.

1978. *A Checklist of Peruvian Birds.* Tucson, Ariz.

———. 1982. *An Annotated Checklist of Peruvian Birds.* Vermillion, S. Dak.: Buteo Books.

Parkes, K. C. 1975. Birds of the Sierra Nevada de Santa Marta, Colombia: Corrections and clarifications. *Bull. Brit. Ornithol. Club* 95:173-175.

Paulson, D. R., G. H. Orians, & C. F. Leck. 1969. Notes on birds of Isla San Andrés. *Auk* 86:755-758.

Payne, R. B. 1974. Species limits and variation of the New World Green Herons *Butorides virescens* and Striated Herons *Butorides striatus. Bull. Brit. Ornithol. Club* 94:81-88.

Paynter, R. A., Jr. 1959. *Check-list of Birds of the World.* Vol. 9. Cambridge, Mass.: Harvard Univ. Press.

———. 1978. Biology and evolution of the avian genus *Atlapetes* (Emberizinae). *Bull. Mus. Comp. Zool.* 148:323-369.

Paynter, R. A., Jr. & M. A. Traylor. 1981. *Ornithological Gazetteer of Colombia.* Cambridge, Mass.: Mus. Comp. Zool., Harvard.

Pearson, D. L. 1972. Un estudio de las aves de Limoncocha, Provincia de Napo, Ecuador. *Bol. Inform. Cient. Nac. Quito* 13:335-346.

———. 1974. Use of abandoned cacique nests by nesting Troupials (*Icterus icterus*): Precursor to parasitism? *Wilson Bull.* 86:290-291.

———. 1975. Range extensions and new records for bird species in Ecuador, Peru and Bolivia. *Condor* 77:96-99.

———. 1977. Ecological relationships of small antbirds in Amazonian bird communities. *Auk* 94:283-292.

Pearson, D. L., D. Tallman, & E. Tallman. 1977. *The Birds of Limoncocha, Napo Province, Ecuador.* Quito: Inst. Linguistico de Verano.

Peeters, H. J. 1962. Nuptial behavior of the Band-tailed Pigeon in the San Francisco Bay area. *Condor* 64:445-469.

Peters, J. L. 1931-1970. *Check-list of Birds of the World.* Vols. 1-15. Cambridge, Mass.: Harvard Univ. Press.

Peters, J. L. & J. A. Griswold, Jr. 1943. Birds of the Harvard Peruvian Expedition. *Bull. Mus. Comp. Zool.* 92:281-328.

Peterson, R. T. 1947. *A Field Guide to the Birds East of the Rockies.* Boston: Houghton Mifflin Co.

———. 1961. *A Field Guide to Western Birds.* Boston: Houghton Mifflin Co.

———. 1963. *A Field Guide to the Birds of Texas.* Boston: Houghton Mifflin Co.

———. 1980. *A Field Guide to the Birds East of the Rockies.* 4th ed. Boston: Houghton Mifflin Co.

Peterson, R. T., & E. L. Chalif. 1973. *A Field Guide to Mexican Birds and Adjacent Central America.* Boston: Houghton Mifflin Co.

Phelps, K. D. 1953. *Aves Venezolanus.* Caracas: Creole Petroleum Corp.

Phelps, W. H., Jr. 1977. Una nueva especies y dos nuevas subespecies de aves (Psittacidae, Furnariidae) de la Sierra de Perijá cerca de la divisoria Colombo-Venezolana. *Bol. Soc. Venezolana Cienc. Nat.* 33:43-53.

Phillips, A. R. 1975. Semipalmated Sandpiper: Identification, migrations, summer and winter ranges. *Amer. Birds* 29:799-806.

Phillips, A. R., J. Marshall & G. Monson. 1964. *The Birds of Arizona.* Tucson, Ariz.: Univ. of Arizona Press.

Phillips, A. R., M. A. Howe, & W. E. Lanyon. 1966. Identification of the flycatchers of eastern North America, with special emphasis on the genus *Empidonax. Bird Banding* 37:133-171.

Phillips, J. C. 1926. *The Natural History of the Ducks.* Vol. 4. Boston.

Pinto, O. 1953. Sobre a coleçao Carlos Estavao de peles, ninhos e ovos das aves de Belém (Para). *Pap. av. Dept. Zool. S. Paulo, XI* 13:111-222.

Ralph, C. P. 1975. Life style of *Coccyzus pumilus*, a tropical Cuckoo. *Condor* 77:60-72.

Ralph, C. P., & S. J. Chaplin. 1973. Some birds of Isla Punta Arenas, Pacific coast, Colombia. *Condor.* 75:357-359.

Ramo, C. & B. Busto. 1982. Notes on the breeding of the Chestnut-bellied Heron (*Agamia agami*) in Venezuela. *Auk* 99:784.

Remsen, J. V., Jr. 1976. Observations of vocal mimicry in the Thick-billed Euphonia. *Wilson Bull.* 88:487-488.

———. 1977a. Five bird species new to Colombia. *Auk* 94:363.

———. 1977b. A third locality in Colombia for the Dusky-chested Flycatcher *Tyrannopsis luteiventris. Bull. Brit. Ornithol. Club* 97:93-94.

———. 1978. Birding the Amazon at Leticia. *Birding* 10.

Remsen, J. V., Jr., & E. S. Hunn. 1979. First record of *Sporophila caerulescens* from Colombia: A probable long distance migrant from southern South America. *Bull. Brit. Ornithol. Club* 99:24-26.

Remsen, J. V., Jr., J. S. Luther, & D. Roberson. 1976. A Ringed Woodpecker *Celeus torquatus* in Colombia. *Bull. Brit. Ornithol. Club* 96:40.

Rettig, N. 1977. In quest of the snatcher. *Audubon Mag.* 79:26-49.

Rhoads, S. N. 1912. Birds of the páramo of central Ecuador. *Auk* 29:141-149.

Ridgely, R. S. 1976. *A Guide to the Birds of Pan-*

*ama.* Princeton, N.J.: Princeton Univ. Press.
———. 1980. Notes on some rare or previously unrecorded birds in Ecuador. *Amer. Birds* 34:242-248.

Ridgely, R. S., & S. J. C. Gaulin. 1980. The birds of Finca Merenberg, Huila Department, Colombia. *Condor* 82:379-391.

Ridgway, R. 1901-1950. Birds of North and Middle America. *U.S. Nat. Mus. Bull.*, no. 50, pts. 1-11.

Ripley, S. D. 1977. *Rails of the World.* Boston: D. E. Godine.

Robbins, C. S., B. Brunn, & H. S. Zim. 1966. *Birds of North America.* N.Y.: Golden Press.

Rodríguez, J. V. 1978. *Hylocharis eliciae* (Trochilidae) en Colombia. *Caldasia* 12:359-361.

———. 1980. Notas sobre *Dumetella carolinensis* (Linnaeus) y primer registro de *Hylocichla mustelina* (Gmelin) (Aves: Mimidae y Turdidae) en Colombia. *Lozania (Acta Zool. Colombiana)* 30:7-8.

———. 1982. *Aves del Parque Nacional Los Katíos.* Bogotá: INDERENA, 328 pp.

Roe, N. A., & W. E. Rees. 1979. Notes on puna avifauna of Ayangaro Province, Dept. of Puno, southern Peru. *Auk* 96:475-482.

Romero, Z. H. 1977. Primer registro de cuatro aves para Colombia. *Lozania (Acta Zool. Colombiana)* 26:1-4.

———. 1978. Primer registro de doce aves para Colombia. *Lozania (Acta Zool. Colombiana)* 26:1-8.

———. 1980. Una nueva subespecies Colombiana de *Campylorhamphus pusillus* (Aves-Dendrocolaptidae). *Lozania (Acta Zool. Colombiana)* 31:1-4.

Romero, Z. H., & J. V. Rodríguez. 1980. Hallazgo de *Oncostoma cinereigulare* (Sclater) (Aves: Tyrannidae) en Colombia. *Lozania (Acta Zool. Colombiana)* 31:5-6.

Roth, P. 1981. A nest of the Rufous-vented Ground-Cuckoo (*Neomorphus geoffroyi*). *Condor* 83:388.

Rowley, J. S. 1962. Nesting of the birds of Morelos, Mexico. *Condor* 64:253-271.

———. 1966. Breeding records of birds of the Sierra Madre del Sur. Oaxaca, Mexico. *Proc. West. Found. Vert. Zool.* 1:107-204.

Rowley, J. S. & R. T. Orr. 1965. Nesting and feeding habits of the White-collared Swift. *Condor* 67:449-456.

Ruschi, A. 1949. Observaçöes sobre Trochilideos: O acasalamento e a parada nupcial; ovos ou trochilideos, etc. *Bol. Mus. Biol. M. Leitão* 7:61.

———. 1961. Algunas observaçöes sobre: *Phaethornis yaruqui yaruqui* (Bourcier), *Colibri co-*

*ruscans coruscans* (Gould), etc. *Bol. Mus. Biol. M. Leitão* 27:1-21.

———. 1973. *Beija-flores (Hummingbirds). Museu de Biologia "Prof. Mello Leitão."* Brazil: Santa Teresa, 172 pp.

———. 1979. *Aves do Brasil.* São Paulo, Brazil: Editora Rios Ltd.

Russell, S. M. 1964. A distributional study of the birds of British Honduras. *Ornithol. Monogr.*, no. 1. Amer. Ornithol. Union.

———. 1980. Distribution and abundance of North American migrants in lowlands of northern Colombia. Pp. 249-252 in *Migrant Birds in the Neotropics: Ecology, Behavior, Distribution, and Conservation*, ed. A. Keast & E. S. Morton. Wash. D.C.: Smiths. Inst. Press.

Russell, S. M., & D. W. Lamm. 1978. Species of Formicariidae new to Colombia. *Auk* 95:421.

Russell, S. M., J. C. Barlow, & D. W. Lamm. 1979. Status of some birds on Isla San Andrés and Isla Providencia, Colombia. *Condor* 81:98-100.

Schäfer, E. 1953a. Contribution to the life history of the Swallow-Tanager. *Auk* 70:403-460.

———. 1953b. Estudio bioecológico comparativo sobre algunos Cracidae del norte y centro Venezuela. *Bol. Soc. Venezolana Cienc. Nat.* 15.90-63.

———. 1954. Zur biologie des Steisshuhnes *Nothocercus bonapartei. J. Ornithol. Berlin* 95:219-232.

Schäfer, E. & W. H. Phelps. 1954. Las aves del Parque Nacional "Henri Pittier" (Rancho Grande) y sus funciónes ecologicas. *Bol. Soc. Venezolana Cienc. Nat.* 16:1-167.

Scheuerman, R. G. 1977. Hallazgos del Paují *Crax mitu* (Aves-Cracidae) al norte del Río Amazonas y notas sobre su distribución. *Lozania (Acta Zool. Colombiana)* 22:1-8.

Schönwetter, M. 1963-1974. *Handbuch der oologie.* Berlin: Akademie-Verlag.

Schuchmann, K. L. 1978. Notes on the Rufouscapped Thornbill *Chalcostigma ruficeps*, a new hummingbird species for Colombia. *Bull. Brit. Ornithol. Club* 98:115-116.

Schwartz, P. 1957. Observaciónes sobre *Grallaricula ferrugineipectus. Bol. Soc. Venezolana Cienc. Nat.* 18:42-62.

———. 1964. The Northern Waterthrush in Venezuela. *The Living Bird* 3:169-184.

———. 1968. Notes on two neotropical nightjars, *Caprimulgus anthonyi* and *C. parvulus. Condor* 70:223-227.

———. 1972a. On the taxonomic rank of the Yellow-billed Toucanet. *Bol. Soc. Venezolana Cienc. Nat.* 29:459-476.

———. 1972b. *Micrastur gilvicollis*, a valid species sympatric with *M. ruficollis* in Amazonia. *Condor* 74:399-415.

———. 1975. Solved and unsolved problems in the *Sporophila lineola bouvronides* complex. *Ann. Carnegie Mus.* 45:277-285.

Schwartz, P. & D. W. Snow. 1978. Display and related behavior of the Wire-tailed Manakin. *The Living Bird* 17:51-78.

Schwerdtfeger, W. Ed. 1976. *World Survey of Climatology.* Vol. 12, *The Climate of Central and South America.* Amsterdam: Elsevier Scient. Pub. Co.

Sclater, P. L., & O. Salvin. 1879. On the birds collected by T. K. Salmon in the state of Antioquia, United States of Colombia. *Proc. Zool. Soc. London.* 1879:486-550.

Serna D., M. A. 1980. *Catálogo de Aves Museo de Historia Natural.* Medellín, Colombia: Colegio de San José.

———. 1984. *Avifauna Parcial de la Guajira.* Medellín, Colombia: Colegio de San José.

Serna D., M. A., & J. V. Rodríguez. 1979. Una nueva parulida registrada por primera vez en Colombia: *Dendroica discolor discolor* (Aves: Parulidae). *Lozania (Acta Zool. Colombiana)* 29:1-2.

Sharpe, R. B. et al. 1888-1898. *Catalogue of birds of the British Museum.* Vols. 1-27. London.

Short, L. L. 1969a. Observations on three sympatric species of tapaculos (*Rhinocryptidae*) in Argentina. *Ibis* 111:239-240.

———. 1969b. An apparent agnostic display of Whistling Herons (*Syrigma sibilatrix*). *Wilson Bull.* 81:330-331.

———. 1970. Notes on the habits of some Argentine and Peruvian Woodpeckers. *Amer. Mus. Novit.* 2413:1-37.

———. 1972. Systematics and behavior of South American Flickers (Aves, Colaptes). *Bull. Amer. Mus. Nat. Hist.* 149:3-109.

———. 1973. The Green-barred Flicker and Golden-green Woodpecker of South America. *The Living Bird* 12:51-54.

———. 1974. Relationship of *Veniliornis* "cassini" chocoensis and *V.* "cassini" caqetensis with *V. affinis. Auk* 91:631-634.

———. 1975. A zoogeographic analysis of the South American Chaco avifauna. *Bull. Amer. Mus. Nat. Hist.* 154:165-352.

———. 1982. *Woodpeckers of the World.* Greenville, Del. Delaware Mus. Nat. Hist.

Short, L. L. & J. J. Morony, Jr. 1969. Notes on some birds of central Peru. *Bull. Brit. Ornithol. Club* 89:112-115.

Sibley, C. G. 1958. Hybridization in some Colombian tanagers, avian genus *Ramphocelus. Proc. Amer. Philos. Soc.* 102:448-453.

———. 1973. The relationships of the Swallow-Tanager *Tersina viridis. Bull. Brit. Ornithol. Club* 93:2.

Sibley, C. G., & J. E. Ahlquist, 1972. A comparative study of the egg white proteins of non-posserine birds. *Bull. Peabody Mus. Nat. Hist.* 39:1-276.

———. 1973. The relationships of the Hoatzin. *Auk* 90:1-13.

Sick, H. 1948a. The nesting of *Reinarda squamata* (Cassin). *Auk* 65:169-173.

———. 1948b. The nesting of *Chaetura andrei meridionalis. Auk* 65:515-520.

———. 1951. An egg of the Umbrellabird. *Wilson Bull.* 63:338-339.

———. 1959. Notes on the biology of two Brazilian Swifts *Chaetura andrei* and *Chaetura cinereiventris. Auk* 76:470-477.

———. 1960. The honeycreeper *Dacnis albiventris* in Brazil. *Condor* 62:66-67.

———. 1962. Escravismo em aves brasileiras. *Arq. Mus. Nac. Rio de Janeiro.* 52:185-192.

———. 1963. Hybridization in certain Brazilian Fringillidae (*Sporophila* and *Oryzoborus*). *Proc. 13th Intern. Ornithol. Congr.* Pp. 161-170.

———. 1967. Courtship behavior in Manakins (Pipridae), a review. *The Living Bird* 6:5-22.

Skutch, A. F. 1930. The habits and nesting activities of the Northern Tody-Flycatcher in Panama. *Auk* 47:313-322.

———. 1931. The life history of Rieffer's Hummingbird (*Amazilia tzacatl tzacatl*) in Panama and Honduras. *Auk* 48:481-500.

———. 1940. Social and sleeping habits of Central American wrens. *Auk* 57:293-312.

———. 1945a. Incubation and nesting periods of Central American birds. *Auk* 62:8-37.

———. 1945b. Life history of the Allied Woodhewer. *Condor* 47:85-94.

———. 1945c. On the habits and nest of the antthrush *Formicarius analis. Wilson Bull.* 57:122-128.

———. 1945d. Studies of Central American redstarts. *Wilson Bull.* 57:217-242.

———. 1946. Life histories of two Panamanian antbirds. *Condor* 48:16-28.

———. 1947a. A nest of the Sunbittern in Costa Rica. *Wilson Bull.* 59:38.

———. 1947b. Life history of the Marbled Wood-Quail. *Condor* 49:217-232.

———. 1948a. Life history of the Olivaceous Piculet and related forms (*Picumnus aurifrons*). *Ibis* 90:433-449.

———. 1948b. Life history notes on puffbirds. *Wilson Bull.* 60:81-97.

———. 1949. Life history of the Ruddy Quail-Dove. *Condor* 51:3-19.

———. 1951. Life history of the Boat-billed Flycatcher. *Auk* 68:30-49.

———. 1952a. Life history of the Chestnut-tailed Automolus. *Condor* 54:93-100.

———. 1952b. Life history of the Blue-and-white Swallow. *Auk* 69:392-406.

———. 1954. *Life Histories of Central American Birds*. Vol. 1. Pacific Coast Avifauna no. 31.

———. 1956. A nesting of the Collared Trogon. *Auk* 73:354-366.

———. 1957. Life history of the Amazon Kingfisher. *Condor* 59:217-229.

———. 1958a. Roosting and nesting of Aracari Toucans. *Condor* 60:201-219.

———. 1958b. Life history of the White-whiskered Softwing (*Malacoptila panamensis*). *Ibis* 100:209-231.

———. 1958c. Life history of the Violet-headed Hummingbird. *Wilson Bull.* 70:5-19.

———. 1959a. Life history of the Black-throated Trogon. *Wilson Bull.* 71:5-18.

———. 1959b. Life history of the Blue Ground-Dove. *Condor* 61:65-74.

———. 1959c. Life history of the Groove-billed Ani. *Auk* 76:281-317.

———. 1960. *Life Histories of Central American Birds*. Vol. 2. Pacific Coast Avifauna no. 34.

———. 1961. The Purple-capped Fairy Hummingbird. *Audubon* 63:8-9, 13.

———. 1962a. Life history of the White-tailed Trogon (*Trogon viridis*). *Ibis* 104:301-313.

———. 1962b. Life histories of honeycreepers. *Condor* 64:92-116.

———. 1962c. On the habits of the Queo (*Rhodinocichla rosea*). *Auk* 79:633-639.

———. 1963a. Life history of the Little Tinamou. *Condor* 65:224-231.

———. 1963b. Life history of the Rufous-tailed Jacamar (*Galbula ruficauda*) in Costa Rica. *Ibis* 105:354-368.

———. 1963c. Habits of Chestnut-winged Chacalaca. *Wilson Bull.* 75:262-269.

———. 1964a. Life history of the Scaly-breasted Hummingbird. *Condor* 66:186-198.

———. 1964b. Life histories of Hermit Hummingbirds. *Auk* 81:5-25.

———. 1964c. Life histories of Central American pigeons. *Wilson Bull.* 76:211-247.

———. 1964d. Life history of the Blue Diademed (crowned) Motmot. *Ibis* 106:321-332.

———. 1965. Life history notes on two tropical American Kites. *Condor* 67:235-246.

———. 1966. Life histories of three tropical Cuckoos. *Wilson Bull.* 78:139-165.

———. 1967. Life histories of Central American highland birds. *Publ. Nuttall Ornithol. Club*, no. 7. Cambridge, Mass.

———. 1968. The nesting of some Venezuelan birds. *Condor* 70:66-82.

———. 1969a. *Life Histories of Central American Birds*. Vol. 3. Pacific Coast Avifauna no. 35.

———. 1969b. A study of the Rufous-fronted Thornbird and associated birds. *Wilson Bull.* 81:5-43, 123-139.

———. 1970a. Life history of the Common Potoo. *The Living Bird* 9:265-280.

———. 1970b. The display of the Yellow-billed Cotinga (*Carpodectes antoniae*). *Ibis* 112:115-116.

———. 1971a. Life history of the Keel-billed Toucan. *Auk* 88:381-424.

———. 1971b. Life history of the Broad-billed Motmot, with notes on the Rufous Motmot. *Wilson Bull.* 83:74-94.

———. 1971c. Life history of the Bright-rumped Attila (*Attila spadiceus*). *Ibis* 113:316-322.

———. 1971d. *A Naturalist in Costa Rica*. Gainesville, Fla.: Univ. of Florida Press.

———. 1972. Studies of tropical American birds. *Publ. Nuttall Ornithol. Club*, no. 10. Cambridge, Mass.

———. 1973. *The Life of the Hummingbird*. N.Y.: Crown Pub..

Slud, P. 1958. Observations on the Nightingale Wren in Costa Rica. *Condor* 60:243-251.

———. 1960. The birds of Finca "La Selva" Costa Rica. A Tropical Wet Forest locality. *Bull. Amer. Mus. Nat. Hist.* 121:55-148.

———. 1964. The birds of Costa Rica: distribution and ecology. *Bull. Amer. Mus. Nat. Hist.* 128:1-430.

Smith, N. G. 1968. The advantage of being parasitized. *Nature* 219:690-694.

Smith, N.J.H. 1980. Further advances of House Sparrows into the Brazilian Amazon. *Condor* 82:109-111.

Smith, W. J. 1962. The nest of *Pitangus lictor*. *Auk* 79:108-111.

———. 1967. Displays of Vermilion Flycatcher (*Pyrocephalus rubinus*). *Condor* 69:601-605.

———. 1971. Behavior of *Muscisaxicola* and related genera. *Bull. Mus. Comp. Zool.* 141:233-268.

Smith, W. J., & F. Vuilleumier. 1971. Evolutionary relationships of some South American ground-tyrants. *Bull. Mus. Comp. Zool.* 141:181-232.

Smithe, F. B. 1966. *The Birds of Tikal*. Garden City, N.Y.: Amer. Mus. Nat. Hist.

Snow, B. K. 1961. Notes on the behavior of three *Cotingidae*. *Auk* 78:150-161.

———. 1970. A field study of the Bearded Bellbird in Trinidad. *Ibis* 112:299-329.

———. 1973a. The behavior and ecology of Hermit Hummingbirds in the Kanaku mountains, Guyana. *Wilson Bull.* 85:163-177.

———. 1973b. Social organization of the Hairy Hermit (*Glaucis hirsuta*). *Ardea* 61:94-105.

Snow, B. K. 1974. Lek behavior and breeding of the Guy's Hermit Hummingbird *Phaethornis guy. Ibis* 116:278-297.

———. 1980. The nest and territoriality of a female Tyrian Metaltail. *Wilson Bull.* 92:508-509.

Snow, B. K., & D. W. Snow. 1971. The feeding ecology of tanagers and honeycreepers in Trinidad. *Auk* 88:291-322.

———. 1974. Breeding of the Green-bellied Hummingbird. *Auk* 91:626.

———. 1979. The Ochre-bellied Flycatcher and the evolution of lek behavior. *Condor* 81:286-292.

Snow, B. K., & M. Gochfeld. 1977. Field notes on the nests of the Green-fronted Lancebill *Doryfera ludoviciae* and the Blue-fronted Lancebill *Doryfera johannae. Bull. Brit. Ornithol. Club* 97:121-125.

Snow, D. W. 1961a. Natural history of the Oilbird *Steatornis caripensis* in Trinidad, W.I. General behavior and breeding habits. *Zoologica* 46:27-47.

———. 1961b. The displays of the manakins *Pipra pipra* and *Tyranneutes virescens. Ibis* 103:110-113.

———. 1962a. Natural history of the Oilbird *Steatornis caripensis* in Trinidad W.I. II. Population, breeding, ecology, and food. *Zoologica* 47:199-221.

———. 1962b. A field study of the Golden-headed Manakin *Pipra erythrocephala* in Trinidad. *Zoologica* 47:183-198.

———. 1962c. Notes on the biology of some Trinidad swifts. *Zoologica* 47:129-139.

———. 1962d. A field study of the Black and White Manakin. *Manacus manacus* in Trinidad. *Zoologica* 47:65-104.

———. 1963. The display of the Blue-backed Manakin *Chiroxiphia pareola* in Tobago, West Indies. *Zoologica* 48:167-176.

———. 1968. The singing assemblies of Little Hermits. *The Living Bird* 7:47-55.

———. 1971a. Observations on the Purple-throated Fruit-crow in Guyana. *The Living Bird* 10:5-17.

———. 1971b. Display of the Pompadour Cotinga *Xipholena punicea. Ibis* 113:102-104.

———. 1973. The classification of the Cotingidae. *Breviora* 409:1-27.

———. 1976. *The Web of Adaptation: Bird Studies in the American Tropics* N.Y.: Quadrangle, Times Book Co.

———. 1982. *The Cotingas.* Ithaca, N.Y.: Cornell Univ. Press.

Snow, D. W., & C. T. Collins. 1962. Social and breeding behavior of the Mexican Tanager. *Condor* 64:161.

Snow, D. W., & B. K. Snow. 1963. Breeding and annual cycle of three Trinidad thrushes. *Wilson Bull.* 75:27-41.

———. 1973. The breeding of the Hairy Hermit (*Glaucus hirsuta*) in Trinidad. *Ardea* 61:106-122.

———. 1980. Relationships between hummingbirds and flowers in the Andes of Colombia. *Bull. Brit. Mus. Nat. Hist.* 38:105-139.

Snyder, D. E. 1966. *The Birds of Guyana.* Salem, Mass.: Peabody Mus.

Spaans, A. L. 1978. Status and numerical fluctuations of some North American waders along the Surinam coast. *Wilson Bull.* 90:60-83.

Sprunt, A., IV. 1976. A new Colombian site for the American Flamingo (*Phoenicopterus ruber*). *Stinapa* 11:34-39.

Stallcup, R. W. 1976. Pelagic birds of Monterey Bay, California. *Western Birds* 7:113-136.

Stiles, F. G. 1975. Ecology, flowering phenology, and hummingbird pollination of some Costa Rican *Heliconia* species. *Ecology* 56:285-301.

———. 1978. Possible specialization for hummingbird-hunting in the Tiny Hawk. *Auk* 95:550-553.

———. 1981a. Notes on the Uniform Crake in Costa Rica. *Wilson Bull.* 93:107-108.

———. 1981b. Taxonomy of Rough-winged Swallows (*Stelgidopteryx;* Hirundinidae) in southern Central America. *Auk* 98:282-293.

Stiles, F. G., & H. Hespenhide. 1972. Observations on two rare Costa Rican finches. *Condor* 74:99-101.

Stone, W. 1918. Birds of the Panama Canal Zone, with special reference to a collection made by Lindsey L. Jewell. *Proc. Acad. Nat. Sci. Philadelphia* 70:239-280.

Storer, R. W. 1969. The behavior of the Horned Grebe in spring. *Condor* 71:180-205.

Strauch, J. G., Jr. 1975. Observations at a nest of the Black-and-white Hawk-Eagle. *Condor* 77-512.

Sutton, G. M. 1981. On aerial and ground displays of the world's snipes. *Wilson Bull.* 93:457-477.

Taczanowski, M. L. 1884-1886. *Ornithologie du Perou.* 3 vols. Berlin: R. Friedlander & John.

Tashian, R. E. 1952. Some birds from the Palenque region of northeast Chiapas, Mexico. *Auk* 69:60-66.

———. 1957. Nesting behavior of the Crested Oropendola (*Psarocolius decumanus*) in northern Trinidad, British West Indies. *Zoologica* 42:87-98.

Terborgh, J. 1971. Distribution on environmental gradients: theory and a preliminary interpretation of distributional patterns in the avifauna of the Cordillera Vilcabamba, Peru. *Ecology* 52:23-40.

Terborgh, J. & J. S. Walker. 1975. The role of competition in the distribution of Andean birds. *Ecology* 56:562-576.

Terborgh, J., & J. S. Weske. 1972. Rediscovery of the Imperial Snipe in Peru. *Auk* 89:497-505.

Thayer, J. E., & O. Bangs. 1905. The vertebrata of Gorgona Island, Colombia. IV, Aves. *Bull. Mus. Comp. Zool., Harvard* 46:91-98.

Thomas, B. T. 1977. Hooding and other techniques for holding and handling nestling storks. *North Amer. Bird Bander* 2:47-49.

———. 1979a. Behavior and breeding of the White-bearded Flycatcher (*Conopias inornata*). *Auk* 96:767-775.

———. 1979b. The birds of a ranch in the Venezuelan llanos, Pp. 213-232 in *Vertebrate ecology of the northern neotropics*, ed. J. F. Eisenberg. Wash. D.C.: Smiths. Inst. Press.

———. 1981. Jabiru nest, nest building, and quintuplets. *Condor* 83:84-85.

Thoresen, A. C. 1974. First Shrike-like Cotinga record for Peru. *Auk* 91:840.

Todd, F. S., N. B. Gall, & J.R.V. Oosten. 1972. El "Voce del Monte." *Avicul. Mag.* 78:79-83.

Todd, W.E.C., & M. A. Carriker, Jr. 1922. The birds of the Santa Marta region of Colombia: A study in altitudinal distribution. *Ann. Carnegie Mus.*, vol. 14.

Torres, B. A. 1975. Registro de una nueva especie para la avifauna de Colombia y algunos datos sobre comportamiento en cautiverio. *Caldasia* 11:151-154.

Traylor, M. A. 1952. Birds of the Marcapata Valley, Peru. *Fieldiana: Zool.* (Chicago) 34:17-19.

———. 1977. A classification of the Tyrant Flycatchers (Tyrannidae). *Bull. Mus. Comp. Zool.* 148:129-184.

———. 1982. Notes on Tyrant Flycatchers (Aves: Tyrannidae). *Fieldiana, Zool.* (Chicago), new ser., 13:1-22.

Tuck, L. M. 1972. *The Snipes: A Study of the Genus "Capella."* Canadian Wildlife Serv. Monogr. Ser. 5. Ottawa, Canada.

Vaurie, C. 1971. *Classification of the Ovenbirds (Furnariidae).* London: Witherby.

———. 1980. Taxonomy and geographical distribution of the Furnariidae (Aves, Passeriformes). *Bull. Amer. Mus. Nat. Hist.* 166:1-357.

Vaurie, C., & P. Schwartz. 1972. Morphology and vocalizations of *Synallaxis unirufa* and *Synallaxis castanea* with comments on other *Synallaxis. Amer. Mus. Novit.* 2482:1-13.

Von Sneidern, K. 1954. Notas sobre algunas aves del Museo de la Universidad del Cauca, Popayán, Colombia. *Noved. Colombianas* 1:3-14.

———. 1955. Notas ornitológicas sobre la colección del Museo de Historia Natual de la Universidad del Cauca. *Noved. Colombianas* 2:35-44.

Voous, K. H. 1955. *De vogels van de Nederlandse Antillen.* Curaçao: Nat. Werkgroep.

———. 1957. *The Birds of Aruba, Curaçao and Bonaire—Studies Fauna Curaçao Caribbean Islands* 7, no. 29. The Hague: Martinus Nighoff.

Vuilleumier, F. 1969a. Field notes on some birds from the Bolivian Andes. *Ibis* lll:599-608.

———. 1969b. Systematics and evolution in *Diglossa* (Aves, Coerebidae). *Amer. Mus. Novit.* 2381:1-44.

———. 1970a. Insular biography in continental regions. 1. The northern Andes of South America. *Amer. Naturalist* 104:373-388.

———. 1970b. L'organisation sociale des bandes vagabondes d'oiseaux dans les Andes du Perou central. *Revue Suisse de Zoologie* 77:209-235.

Vuilleumier, F., & D. N. Ewert. 1978. The distribution of birds in Venezuelan páramos. *Bull. Amer. Mus. Nat. Hist.* 162:51-90.

Wallace, G. J. 1958. Notes on North American migrants in Colombia. *Auk* 75:177-182.

———. 1965. Studies on neotropical thrushes in Colombia. *Publ. Mus. Mich. State Univ. Biol. Ser.* 3:1-47.

Walter, H. 1962. Vergleichende untersuchungin an den raubmowen *Stercorarius parasiticus* und *longicaudus. J. für Ornithol.* 103:166-179.

Watson, G. D. 1966. *Seabirds of the Tropical Atlantic Ocean.* Wash. D.C.: Smiths. Inst. Press.

Wattel, J. 1973. Geographical differentiation in the genus *Accipiter. Publ. Nuttall Ornithol. Club,* no. 13. Cambridge, Mass.

Weller, W. M. 1975. Ecology and behavior of the South Georgia Pintail *Anas georgica. Ibis* 117:217-231.

Weske, J. S. 1972. The distribution of the avifauna in the Apurimac Valley of Peru with respect to environmental gradients, habitats and related species. Ph.D. diss. Univ. of Oklahoma.

West, S. 1976a. Observations on the Yelloweared Toucanet. *Auk* 93:381-382.

———. 1976b. First description of the eggs of the Cinnamon Becard. *Condor* 78:422-423.

Wetmore, A. 1926. Observations on the birds of Argentina, Paraguay, Uruguay and Chile. *Bull. U.S. Nat. Mus.* 133:1-448.

Wetmore, A. 1939. Observations on the birds of northern Venezuela. *Proc. U.S. Nat. Mus.* 87:173-260.

———. 1965a. *Birds of the Republic of Panama. Part 1. Tinamidae (Tinamous) to Rynchopidae (Skimmers).* Wash. D.C.: Smiths. Inst. Press.

———. 1965b. Additions to the list of birds from the Republic of Colombia. *L'Oiseau* 35:156-162.

———. 1968a. *Birds of the Republic of Panama. Part 2. Columbidae (Pigeons) to Picidae (Woodpeckers).* Wash. D.C.: Smiths. Inst. Press.

———. 1968b. Additions to the list of birds recorded from Colombia. *Wilson Bull.* 80:325-326.

———. 1970. Descriptions of additional forms of birds from Panama and Colombia. *Proc. Biol. Soc. Wash.* 82:767-776.

———. 1972. *Birds of the Republic of Panama. Part 3. Passeriformes: Dendrocolaptidae (Woodcreepers) to Oxyruncidae (Sharpbills).* Wash. D.C.: Smiths. Inst. Press.

Wetmore, A. & P. Galindo. 1972. Additions to the birds recorded in Panama. *Proc. Biol. Soc. Wash.* 85:309-312.

Wetmore, A., R. Pasquier, & S. Olson. *Birds of the Republic of Panama. Part 4. Passeriformes: suborder Passeres, Hirundinidae (Swallows) to Fringillidae (Finches).* Wash. D.C.: Smiths. Inst. Press. 1984.

Wiley, R. H. 1971. Cooperative roles of mixed species flocks of antwrens (Formicariidae). *Auk* 88:881-892.

Williams, M. D. 1980. First description of the nest, eggs and nestling of the Guayaquil Woodpecker (*Campephilus [Phloeoceastes] guayaquilensis*). *Wilson Bull.* 92:506-508.

Willis, E. O. 1960a. Voice, courtship and territorial behavior of ant-tanagers in British Honduras. *Condor* 62:73-87.

———. 1960b. Red-crowned Ant-Tanagers, Tawny-crowned Greenlets and forest flocks. *Wilson Bull.* 72:105-106.

———. 1961. A study of nesting ant-tanagers in British Honduras. *Condor* 63:479-503.

———. 1962. Another Nest of *Pitangus lictor.* *Auk* 79:111.

———. 1963. Is the Zone-tailed Hawk a mimic of the Turkey Vulture? *Condor* 65:313-317.

———. 1966a. Ecology and behavior of the Crested ant-tanager. *Condor* 68:56-71.

———. 1966b. Notes on a display and nest of the Club-winged Manakin. *Auk* 83:475-476.

———. 1966c. Interspecific competition and the foraging behavior of Plain-brown Woodcreepers. *Ecology* 74:667-672.

———. 1966d. Competitive exclusion and birds at fruiting trees in western Colombia. *Auk* 83:479-480.

———. 1966e. The role of migrant birds at swarms of army ants. *The Living Bird* 5:187-231.

———. 1967. The behavior of Bicolored Antbirds. *Univ. Calif. Publ. Zool.* 79:1-127.

———. 1968. Studies of the behavior of Lunulated and Salvin's Antbirds. *Condor* 70:128-148.

———. 1969. On the behavior of five species of *Rhegmatorhina*, ant-following antbirds of the Amazon basin. *Wilson Bull.* 81:363-395.

———. 1972a. The behavior of the Plain-brown Woodcreeper *Dendrocincla fuliginosa.* *Wilson Bull.* 81:377-420.

———. 1972b. Taxonomy, Ecology and behavior of the Sooty Ant-Tanager (*Habia gutturalis*) and other ant-tanagers. *Amer. Mus. Novit.* 2480:1-38.

———. 1972c. *The Behavior of Spotted Antbirds.* Ornithol. Monogr., no. 10. Amer. Ornithol. Union.

———. 1972d. Breeding of the White-plumed Antbird (*Pithys albifrons*). *Auk* 89:192.

———. 1973. *The Behavior of Ocellated Antbirds.* Smiths. Contrib. Zool. 144:1-57.

———. 1977. Lista preliminar das aves da parte noroeste e áreas vizinhas da Reserva Ducke, Amazonas, Brasil. *Rev. Brasil Biol.* 37:585-601.

———. 1979. Comportamento e ecologia da Mãe-de-Taoca, *Phlegopsis nigromaculata* (D'orbigny and Lafresnaye) (Aves, Formicariidae). *Rev. Brasil Biol.* 39:117-159.

Willis, E. O., & E. Eisenmann. 1979. A revised list of birds of Barro Colorado Isl. Panama. *Smiths. Contrib. Zool.* 291:1-31.

Willis, E. O., & Y. Oniki. 1972. Ecology and nesting behavior of the Chestnut-backed Antbird (*Myrmeciza exsul*). *Condor* 74:76-98.

Willis, E. O., D. Wechsler, & Y. Oniki. 1978. On the behavior and nesting of McConnell's Flycatcher (*Pipromorpha macconnelli*): does female rejection lead to male promiscuity? *Auk* 95:1-8.

Wolf, L. L. 1970. The impact of seasonal flowering on the biology of some tropical hummingbirds. *Condor* 71:1-14.

———. 1976. Avifauna of the Cerro de la Muerte region of Costa Rica. *Amer. Mus. Novit.* 2606:1-37.

Worth, C. B. 1938. Nesting of Salvin's Barbet. *Auk* 55:535-536.

———. 1939a. Cedar Waxwings and other birds in Panama. *Bird Lore* 1939:279-280.

———. 1939b. Nesting of some Panamanian birds. *Auk* 56:306-310.

———. 1942. Notes on the hummingbirds at Chiriqui, Panama. *Auk* 59:364-365.

Wyatt, C. W. 1871. Notes on some of the birds of the United States of Colombia [sic]. *Ibis* 1871:113-131, 319-335, 373-384.

Yepez, G. 1953. Estudio sobre la region de Perijá y sus habitantes, XI. El Indio y las aves. *Publ. Univ. Zulia*, pp. 221-223.

Young, C. G. 1925. Notes on the nests and eggs of some British Guiana birds. *Ibis* (12) 1:465-475.

———. 1928. A contribution to the ornithology of the coastland of British Guiana. *Ibis* (12) 4:748-781.

———. 1929. A contribution to the ornithology of the coastland of British Guiana. *Ibis* (12) 5:1-38, 221-261.

Zahl, P. A. 1950. Search for the Scarlet Ibis in Venezuela. *Natl. Geogr. Mag.* 97:633-661.

Zapata, A.R.P. 1965. Hallazgo de un nido de *Syrigma sibilatrix*. *Hornero* 10:279-280.

Zimmer, J. T. 1930. Birds of the Marshall Field Peruvian expedition 1922-1923. *Field Mus. Nat. Hist. Zool.* 17(7):233-480.

———. 1931-1955. Studies of Peruvian birds, 1-66. *Amer. Mus. Novit.*

Zimmer, J. T., & W. H. Phelps. 1955. Three new subspecies of birds from Venezuela. *Amer. Mus. Novit.* 1709:1-6.

Zonfrillo, B. 1977. Re-discovery of the Andean Condor (*Vultur gryphys*) in Venezuela. *Bull. Brit. Ornithol. Club* 97:17-18.

RANGE MAPS

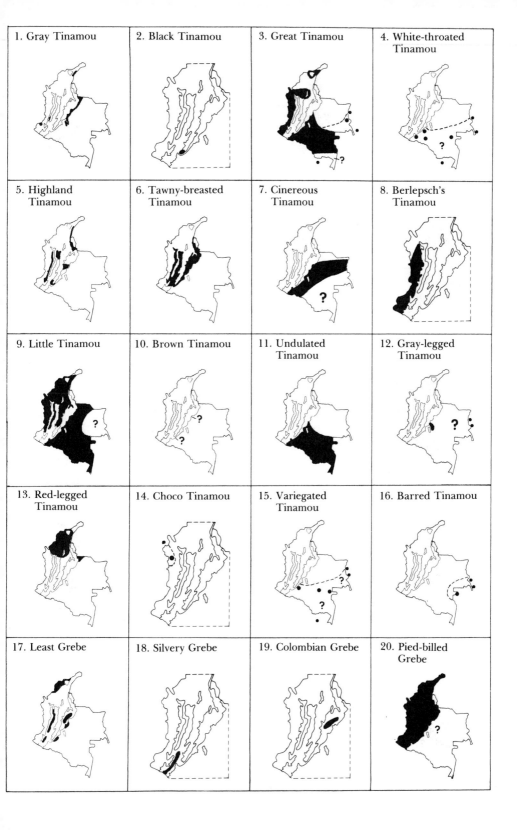

| 1. Gray Tinamou | 2. Black Tinamou | 3. Great Tinamou | 4. White-throated Tinamou |
| 5. Highland Tinamou | 6. Tawny-breasted Tinamou | 7. Cinereous Tinamou | 8. Berlepsch's Tinamou |
| 9. Little Tinamou | 10. Brown Tinamou | 11. Undulated Tinamou | 12. Gray-legged Tinamou |
| 13. Red-legged Tinamou | 14. Choco Tinamou | 15. Variegated Tinamou | 16. Barred Tinamou |
| 17. Least Grebe | 18. Silvery Grebe | 19. Colombian Grebe | 20. Pied-billed Grebe |

| 21. Great Blue Heron | 22. Cocoi Heron | 23. Great Egret | 24. Snowy Egret |
| 25. Little Blue Heron | 26. Reddish Egret | 27. Tricolored Heron | 28. Green Heron |
| 29. Striated Heron | 30. Agami Heron | 31. Cattle Egret | 32. Whistling Heron |
| 33. Capped Heron | 34. Black-crowned Night-Heron | 35. Yellow-crowned Night-Heron | 36. Rufescent Tiger-Heron |
| 37. Fasciated Tiger-Heron | 38. Bare-throated Tiger-Heron | 39. Zigzag Heron | 40. Stripe-backed Bittern |

41. Least Bittern
42. Pinnated Bittern
43. Boat-billed Heron
44. Wood Stork
45. Maguari Stork
46. Jabiru
47. Buff-necked Ibis
48. Sharp-tailed Ibis
49. Green Ibis
50. Whispering Ibis
51. White Ibis
52. Scarlet Ibis
53. Glossy Ibis
54. Roseate Spoonbill
55. Greater Flamingo
56. Horned Screamer
57. Northern Screamer
58. Fulvous Whistling Duck
59. White-faced Whistling Duck
60. Black-bellied Whistling Duck

| 61. Orinoco Goose | 62. Speckled Teal | 63. White-cheeked Pintail | 64. Blue-winged Teal |
|---|---|---|---|
| 65. Torrent Duck | 66. Southern Pochard | 67. Brazilian Duck | 68. Comb Duck |
| 69. Muscovy Duck | 70. Ruddy Duck | 71. Masked Duck | 72. Turkey Vulture |
| 73. Lesser Yellow-headed Vulture | 74. Greater Yellow-headed Vulture | 75. Black Vulture | 76. King Vulture |
| 77. Andean Condor | 78. Osprey | 79. Gray-headed Kite | 80. Hook-billed Kite |

| 81. American Swallow-tailed Kite | 82. Pearl Kite | 83. Black-shouldered Kite | 84. Snail Kite |
| 85. Slender-billed Kite | 86. Double-toothed Kite | 87. Plumbeous Kite | 88. Crane Hawk |
| 89. Cinereous Harrier | 90. Long-winged Harrier | 91. Sharp-shinned Hawk | 92. Semicollared Hawk |
| 93. Tiny Hawk | 94. Bicolored Hawk | 95. Gray-bellied Hawk | 96. Slate-colored Hawk |
| 97. Plumbeous Hawk | 98. Barred Hawk | 99. Semiplumbeous Hawk | 100. Black-faced Hawk |

| 101. White Hawk | 102. Common Black-Hawk | 103. Great Black-Hawk | 104. Solitary Eagle |
| 105. Savanna Hawk | 106. Black-collared Hawk | 107. Black-chested Buzzard-Eagle | 108. Harris' (Bay-winged) Hawk |
| 109. Gray Hawk | 110. Roadside Hawk | 111. White-rumped Hawk | 112. Broad-winged Hawk |
| 113. Short-tailed Hawk | 114. White-throated Hawk | 115. White-tailed Hawk | 116. Red-backed Hawk |
| 117. Variable Hawk | 118. Zone-tailed Hawk | 119. Crested Eagle | 120. Harpy Eagle |

| 121. Black-and-white Hawk-Eagle | 122. Black Hawk-Eagle | 123. Ornate Hawk-Eagle | 124. Black-and-chestnut Eagle |
|---|---|---|---|
| 125. Black Caracara | 126. Red-throated Caracara | 127. Carunculated Caracara | 128. Crested Caracara |
| 129. Yellow-headed Caracara | 130. Laughing Falcon | 131. Barred Forest-Falcon | 132. Lined Forest-Falcon |
| 133. Plumbeous Forest-Falcon | 134. Slaty-backed Forest-Falcon | 135. Collared Forest-Falcon | 136. Buckley's Forest-Falcon |
| 137. American Kestrel | 138. Merlin | 139. Bat Falcon | 140. Orange-breasted Falcon |

| 141. Aplomado Falcon | 142. Peregrine Falcon | 143. Gray-headed Chachalaca | 144. Chestnut-winged Chachalaca |
|---|---|---|---|
| 145. Rufous-vented Chachalaca | 146. Variable Chachalaca | 147. Band-tailed Guan | 148. Andean Guan |
| 149. Baudo Guan | 150. Spix's Guan | 151. Cauca Guan | 152. Crested Guan |
| 153. Common Piping Guan | 154. Wattled Guan | 155. Sickle-winged Guan | 156. Nocturnal Curassow |
| 157. Crestless Curassow | 158. Salvin's Curassow | 159. Razor-billed Curassow | 160. Northern Helmeted Curassow |

| | | | |
|---|---|---|---|
| 161. Great Curassow | 162. Blue-billed Curassow | 163. Yellow-knobbed Curassow | 164. Black Curassow |
| 165. Wattled Curassow | 166. Crested Bobwhite | 167. Marbled Wood-Quail | 168. Rufous-fronted Wood-Quail |
| 169. Black-fronted Wood-Quail | 170. Chestnut Wood-Quail | 171. Dark-backed Wood-Quail | 172. Gorgeted Wood-Quail |
| 173. Tawny-faced Quail | 174. Limpkin | 175. Gray-winged Trumpeter | 176. Speckled Crake |
| 177. Ocellated Crake | 178. Chestnut-headed Crake | 179. Black-banded Crake | 180. Russet-crowned Crake |

| 181. Gray-breasted Crake | 182. White-throated Crake | 183. Rufous-sided Crake | 184. Clapper Rail |
|---|---|---|---|
| 185. Virginia (Lesser) Rail | 186. Bogota Rail | 187. Rufous-necked Wood-Rail | 188. Gray-necked Wood-Rail |
| 189. Brown Wood-Rail | 190. Uniform Crake | 191. Sora Crake | 192. Ash-throated Crake |
| 193. Yellow-breasted Crake | 194. Colombian Crake | 195. Paint-billed Crake | 196. Blackish Rail |
| 197. Spotted Rail | 198. Purple Gallinule | 199. Azure Gallinule | 200. Spot-flanked Gallinule |

| 201. Common Gallinule | 202. American Coot | 203. Slate-colored Coot | 204. Sungrebe |
|---|---|---|---|
| 205. Sunbittern | 206. Wattled Jacana | 207. Band-tailed Pigeon | 208. Scaled Pigeon |
| 209. Bare-eyed Pigeon | 210. Pale-vented Pigeon | 211. Ruddy Pigeon | 212. Plumbeous Pigeon |
| 213. Short-billed Pigeon | 214. Dusky Pigeon | 215. Eared Dove | 216. Common Ground-Dove |
| 217. Plain-breasted Ground-Dove | 218. Ruddy Ground-Dove | 219. Picui Ground-Dove | 220. Blue Ground-Dove |

| 221. Maroon-chested Ground-Dove | 222. Black-winged Ground-Dove | 223. Scaled Dove | 224. Gray-chested Dove |
|---|---|---|---|
| 225. Tolima Dove | 226. White-tipped Dove | 227. Gray-headed Dove | 228. Pallid Dove |
| 229. Gray-fronted Dove | 230. Sapphire Quail-Dove | 231. Ruddy Quail-Dove | 232. Violaceous Quail-Dove |
| 233. Olive-backed Quail-Dove | 234. Russet-crowned Quail-Dove | 235. Lined Quail-Dove | 236. White-throated Quail-Dove |
| 237. Blue-and-yellow Macaw | 238. Military Macaw | 239. Great Green Macaw | 240. Scarlet Macaw |

241. Red-and-green Macaw

242. Chestnut-fronted Macaw

243. Red-bellied Macaw

244. Blue-crowned Parakeet

245. Scarlet-fronted Parakeet

246. White-eyed Parakeet

247. Dusky-headed Parakeet

248. Brown-throated Parakeet

249. Golden-plumed Parakeet

250. Yellow-eared Parrot

251. Painted Parakeet

252. Santa Marta Parakeet

253. Maroon-tailed Parakeet

254. Flame-winged Parakeet

255. Barred Parakeet

256. Rufous-fronted Parakeet

257. Green-rumped Parrotlet

258. Blue-winged Parrotlet

259. Spectacled Parrotlet

260. Dusky-billed Parrotlet

| | | | |
|---|---|---|---|
| 261. Canary-winged Parakeet | 262. Orange-chinned Parakeet | 263. Cobalt-winged Parakeet | 264. Tui Parakeet |
| 265. Sapphire-rumped Parrotlet | 266. Scarlet-shouldered Parrotlet | 267. Red-winged Parrotlet | 268. Spot-winged Parrotlet |
| 269. Black-headed Parrot | 270. Brown-hooded Parrot | 271. Rose-faced Parrot | 272. Orange-cheeked Parrot |
| 273. Saffron-headed Parrot | 274. Rusty-faced Parrot | 275. Short-tailed Parrot | 276. Blue-headed Parrot |
| 277. Red-billed Parrot | 278. Speckle-faced Parrot | 279. Bronze-winged Parrot | 280. Dusky Parrot |

| 281. Red-lored Parrot | 282. Festive Parrot | 283. Yellow-crowned Parrot | 284. Orange-winged Parrot |
|---|---|---|---|
| 285. Scaly-naped Parrot | 286. Mealy Parrot | 287. Red-fan Parrot | 288. Dwarf Cuckoo |
| 289. Ash-colored Cuckoo | 290. Yellow-billed Cuckoo | 291. Pearly-breasted Cuckoo | 292. Mangrove Cuckoo |
| 293. Dark-billed Cuckoo | 294. Gray-capped Cuckoo | 295. Squirrel Cuckoo | 296. Black-bellied Cuckoo |
| 297. Little Cuckoo | 298. Greater Ani | 299. Smooth-billed Ani | 300. Groove-billed Ani |

| 301. Striped Cuckoo | 302. Pheasant Cuckoo | 303. Rufous-vented Ground-Cuckoo | 304. Banded Ground-Cuckoo |
|---|---|---|---|
| 305. Hoatzin | 306. Barn Owl | 307. Vermiculated Screech-Owl | 308. Tropical Screech-Owl |
| 309. Rufescent Screech-Owl | 310. Tawny-bellied Screech-Owl | 311. Bare-shanked Screech-Owl | 312. White-throated Screech-Owl |
| 313. Crested Owl | 314. Great Horned Owl | 315. Spectacled Owl | 316. Band-bellied Owl |
| 317. Least Pygmy-Owl | 318. Andean Pygmy-Owl | 319. Ferruginous Pygmy-Owl | 320. Burrowing Owl |

321. Black-and-white Owl
322. Black-banded Owl
323. Rufous-banded Owl
324. Mottled Owl
325. Striped Owl
326. Stygian Owl
327. Short-eared Owl
328. Buff-fronted Owl
329. Oilbird
330. Great Potoo
331. Long-tailed Potoo
332. Common Potoo
333. White-winged Potoo
334. Rufous Potoo
335. Short-tailed Nighthawk
336. Least Nighthawk
337. Sand-colored Nighthawk
338. Lesser Nighthawk
339. Band-tailed Nighthawk
340. Nacunda Nighthawk

| 341. Pauraque | 342. Ocellated Poorwill | 343. Rufous Nightjar | 344. Band-winged Nightjar |
|---|---|---|---|
| 345. White-tailed Nightjar | 346. Spot-tailed Nightjar | 347. Little Nightjar | 348. Blackish Nightjar |
| 349. Ladder-tailed Nightjar | 350. Swallow-tailed Nightjar | 351. Lyre-tailed Nightjar | 352. White-collared Swift |
| 353. Chestnut-collared Swift | 354. Spot-fronted Swift | 355. White-chinned Swift | 356. White-chested Swift |
| 357. Chapman's Swift | 358. Gray-rumped Swift | 359. Band-rumped Swift | 360. Ashy-tailed Swift |

| 361. Short-tailed Swift | 362. White-tipped Swift | 363. Lesser Swallow-tailed Swift | 364. Pygmy Swift |
|---|---|---|---|
| 365. Fork-tailed Palm-Swift | 366. Bronzy Hermit | 367. Rufous-breasted Hermit | 368. Pale-tailed Barbthroat |
| 369. Band-tailed Barbthroat | 370. White-whiskered Hermit | 371. Green Hermit | 372. Tawny-bellied Hermit |
| 373. Long-tailed Hermit | 374. White-bearded Hermit | 375. Pale-bellied Hermit | 376. Sooty-capped Hermit |
| 377. Straight-billed Hermit | 378. Dusky-throated Hermit | 379. Reddish Hermit | 380. Gray-chinned Hermit |

| 381. Little Hermit | 382. Tooth-billed Hummingbird | 383. White-tipped Sicklebill | 384. Buff-tailed Sicklebill |
| 385. Blue-fronted Lancebill | 386. Green-fronted Lancebill | 387. Scaly-breasted Hummingbird | 388. Gray-breasted Sabrewing |
| 389. Lazuline Sabrewing | 390. White-necked Jacobin | 391. Brown Violetear | 392. Green Violetear |
| 393. Sparkling Violetear | 394. Green-breasted Mango | 395. Black-throated Mango | 396. Ruby-topaz Hummingbird |
| 397. Violet-headed Hummingbird | 398. Rufous crested Coquette | 399. Spangled Coquette | 400. Festive Coquette |

| 401. Wire-crested Thorntail | 402. Black-bellied Thorntail | 403. Green Thorntail | 404. Blue-chinned Sapphire |
|---|---|---|---|
| 405. Blue-tailed Emerald | 406. Red-billed Emerald | 407. Coppery Emerald | 408. Narrow-tailed Emerald |
| 409. Short-tailed Emerald | 410. Crowned Woodnymph | 411. Fork-tailed Woodnymph | 412. Violet-bellied Hummingbird |
| 413. Sapphire-throated Hummingbird | 414. Shining-green Hummingbird | 415. Rufous-throated Sapphire | 416. White-chinned Sapphire |
| 417. Blue-headed Sapphire | 418. Blue-throated Sapphire (Goldentail) | 419. Golden-tailed Sapphire | 420. Violet-capped Hummingbird |

421. White-tailed Goldenthroat

422. Green-tailed Goldenthroat

423. Buffy Hummingbird

424. Versicolored Emerald

425. Glittering-throated Emerald

426. Blue-chested Hummingbird

427. Purple-chested Hummingbird

428. Andean Emerald

429. Indigo-capped Hummingbird

430. Steely-vented Hummingbird

431. Green-bellied Hummingbird

432. Rufous-tailed Hummingbird

433. White-vented Plumeleteer

434. Bronze-tailed Plumeleteer

435. Speckled Hummingbird

436. Blossomcrown

437. Rufous-vented Whitetip

438. Purple-bibbed Whitetip

439. Ecuadorian Piedtail

440. Jewelfront

| 441. Fawn-breasted Brilliant | 442. Violet-fronted Brilliant | 443. Green-crowned Brilliant | 444. Empress Brilliant |
|---|---|---|---|
| 445. Black-throated Brilliant | 446. Pink-throated Brilliant | 447. Fiery Topaz | 448. White-tailed Hillstar |
| 449. Shining Sunbeam | 450. Mountain Velvetbreast | 451. Great Sapphirewing | 452. Bronzy Inca |
| 453. Brown Inca | 454. Black Inca | 455. Collared Inca | 456. White-tailed Starfrontlet |
| 457. Golden-bellied Starfrontlet | 458. Blue-throated Starfrontlet | 459. Buff-winged Starfrontlet | 460. Sword-billed Hummingbird |

| 461. Buff-tailed Coronet | 462. Chestnut-breasted Coronet | 463. Velvet-purple Coronet | 464. Orange-throated Sunangel |
|---|---|---|---|
| 465. Amethyst-throated Sunangel | 466. Tourmaline Sunangel | 467. Glowing Puffleg | 468. Sapphire-vented Puffleg |
| 469. Coppery-bellied Puffleg | 470. Golden-breasted Puffleg | 471. Colorful Puffleg | 472. Emerald-bellied Puffleg |
| 473. Black-thighed Puffleg | 474. Greenish Puffleg | 475. Hoary Puffleg | 476. Booted Racket-tail |
| 477. Black-tailed Trainbearer | 478. Green-tailed Trainbearer | 479. Purple-backed Thornbill | 480. Black-backed Thornbill |

481. Viridian Metaltail

482. Tyrian Metaltail

483. Bronze-tailed Thornbill

484. Rainbow-bearded Thornbill

485. Bearded Helmetcrest

486. Mountain Avocetbill

487. Long-tailed Sylph

488. Violet-tailed Sylph

489. Wedge-billed Hummingbird

490. Purple-crowned Fairy

491. Black-eared Fairy

492. Long-billed Starthroat

493. Blue-tufted Starthroat

494. Purple-throated Woodstar

495. Amethyst Woodstar

496. White-bellied Woodstar

497. Gorgeted Woodstar

498. Rufous-shafted Woodstar

499. Crested Quetzal

500. White-tipped Quetzal

| | | | |
|---|---|---|---|
| 501. Golden-headed Quetzal | 502. Pavonine Quetzal | 503. Slaty-tailed Trogon | 504. Black-tailed Trogon |
| 505. Blue-tailed Trogon | 506. White-tailed Trogon | 507. Collared Trogon | 508. Masked Trogon |
| 509. Black-throated Trogon | 510. Blue-crowned Trogon | 511. Violaceous Trogon | 512. Ringed Kingfisher |
| 513. Belted Kingfisher | 514. Amazon Kingfisher | 515. Green Kingfisher | 516. Green-and-rufous Kingfisher |
| 517. Pygmy Kingfisher | 518. Tody Motmot | 519. Broad-billed Motmot | 520. Rufous Motmot |

| 521. Blue-crowned Motmot | 522. White-eared Jacamar | 523. Brown Jacamar | 524. Pale-headed Jacamar |
|---|---|---|---|
| 525. Dusky-backed Jacamar | 526. Yellow-billed Jacamar | 527. Green-tailed Jacamar | 528. White-chinned Jacamar |
| 529. Coppery-chested Jacamar | 530. Rufous-tailed Jacamar | 531. Bronzy Jacamar | 532. Paradise Jacamar |
| 533. Great Jacamar | 534. White-necked Puffbird | 535. Black-breasted Puffbird | 536. Pied Puffbird |
| 537. Chestnut-capped Puffbird | 538. Spotted Puffbird | 539. Sooty-capped Puffbird | 540. Collared Puffbird |

| 541. Barred Puffbird | 542. Russet-throated Puffbird | 543. White-chested Puffbird | 544. Black-streaked Puffbird |
| 545. White-whiskered Puffbird | 546. Moustached Puffbird | 547. Lanceolated Monklct | 548. Rusty-breasted Nunlet |
| 549. Brown Nunlet | 550. Gray-cheeked Nunlet | 551. White-faced Nunbird | 552. Black-fronted Nunbird |
| 553. White-fronted Nunbird | 554. Yellow-billed Nunbird | 555. Swallow-winged Puffbird | 556. Scarlet-crowned Barbet |
| 557. Spot-crowned Barbet | 558. Orange-fronted Barbet | 559. White-mantled Barbet | 560. Five-colored Barbet |

| | | | |
|---|---|---|---|
| 561. Black-spotted Barbet | 562. Lemon-throated Barbet | 563. Red-headed Barbet | 564. Toucan Barbet |
| 565. Groove-billed Toucanet | 566. Chestnut-tipped Toucanet | 567. Emerald Toucanet | 568. Crimson-rumped Toucanet |
| 569. Collared Araçari | 570. Stripe-billed Araçari | 571. Chestnut-eared Araçari | 572. Many-banded Araçari |
| 573. Lettered Araçari | 574. Ivory-billed Araçari | 575. Yellow-eared Toucanet | 576. Golden-collared Toucanet |
| 577. Tawny-tufted Toucanet | 578. Plate-billed Mountain-Toucan | 579. Gray-breasted Mountain-Toucan | 580. Black-billed Mountain-Toucan |

| 581. Citron-throated Toucan | 582. Yellow-ridged Toucan | 583. Keel-billed Toucan | 584. Choco Toucan |
|---|---|---|---|
| 585. Chestnut-mandibled Toucan | 586. Black-mandibled Toucan | 587. White-throated Toucan | 588. Chestnut Piculet |
| 589. Rufous-breasted Piculet | 590. Plain-breasted Piculet | 591. Scaled Piculet | 592. Olivaceous Piculet |
| 593. Grayish Piculet | 594. Golden-spangled Piculet | 595. Lafresnaye's Piculet | 596. Orinoco Piculet |
| 597. Spot-breasted Woodpecker | 598. Crimson-mantled Woodpecker | 599. Golden-olive Woodpecker | 600. Yellow-throated Woodpecker |

| 601. White-throated Woodpecker | 602. Golden-green Woodpecker | 603. Chestnut Woodpecker | 604. Scale-breasted Woodpecker |
|---|---|---|---|
| 605. Cinnamon Woodpecker | 606. Cream-colored Woodpecker | 607. Ringed Woodpecker | 608. Lineated Woodpecker |
| 609. Acorn Woodpecker | 610. Yellow-tufted Woodpecker | 611. Black-cheeked Woodpecker | 612. Golden-naped Woodpecker |
| 613. Red-crowned Woodpecker | 614. Smoky-brown Woodpecker | 615. Little Woodpecker | 616. Red-stained Woodpecker |
| 617. Red-rumped Woodpecker | 618. Scarlet-backed Woodpecker | 619. Yellow-vented Woodpecker | 620. Bar-bellied Woodpecker |

| 621. Crimson-crested Woodpecker | 622. Guayaquil Woodpecker | 623. Red-necked Woodpecker | 624. Powerful Woodpecker |
|---|---|---|---|
| 625. Crimson-bellied Woodpecker | 626. Tyrannine Woodcreeper | 627. Plain-brown Woodcreeper | 628. White-chinned Woodcreeper |
| 629. Ruddy Woodcreeper | 630. Long-tailed Woodcreeper | 631. Spot-throated Woodcreeper | 632. Olivaceous Woodcreeper |
| 633. Wedge-billed Woodcreeper | 634. Long-billed Woodcreeper | 635. Cinnamon-throated Woodcreeper | 636. Strong-billed Woodcreeper |
| 637. Barred Woodcreeper | 638. Black-banded Woodcreeper | 639. Straight-billed Woodcreeper | 640. Striped Woodcreeper |

| | | | |
|---|---|---|---|
| 641. Ocellated Woodcreeper | 642. Spix's Woodcreeper | 643. Elegant Woodcreeper | 644. Buff-throated Woodcreeper |
| 645. Black-striped Woodcreeper | 646. Spotted Woodcreeper | 647. Olive-backed Woodcreeper | 648. Streak-headed Woodcreeper |
| 649. Spot-crowned Woodcreeper | 650. Greater Scythebill | 651. Red-billed Scythebill | 652. Brown-billed Scythebill |
| 653. Curve-billed Scythebill | 654. Stout-billed Cinclodes | 655. Bar-winged Cinclodes | 656. Pale-legged Hornero |
| 657. Lesser Hornero | 658. Andean Tit-Spinetail | 659. Azara's Spinetail | 660. Dusky Spinetail |

| 661. Silvery-throated Spinetail | 662. Pale-breasted Spinetail | 663. Slaty Spinetail | 664. Dark-breasted Spinetail |
|---|---|---|---|
| 665. Plain-crowned Spinetail | 666. Stripe-breasted Spinetail | 667. Rusty-headed Spinetail | 668. Rufous Spinetail |
| 669. Ruddy Spinetail | 670. White-whiskered Spinetail | 671. White-browed Spinetail | 672. Yellow-chinned Spinetail |
| 673. Red-and-white Spinetail | 674. Crested Spinetail | 675. Streak-capped Spinetail | 676. Ash-browed Spinetail |
| 677. Red-faced Spinetail | 678. Rusty-backed Spinetail | 679. Speckled Spinetail | 680. White-chinned Thistletail |

| 681. Perija Thistletail | 682. Streak-backed Canastero | 683. Many-striped Canastero | 684. Plain Thornbird |
|---|---|---|---|
| 685. Spectacled Prickletail | 686. Double-banded Graytail | 687. Orange-fronted Plushcrown | 688. Pearled Treerunner |
| 689. Fulvous-dotted Treerunner | 690. Rusty-winged Barbtail | 691. Spotted Barbtail | 692. Buffy Tuftedcheek |
| 693. Streaked Tuftedcheek | 694. Chestnut-winged Hookbill | 695. Striped Foliage-gleaner | 696. Lineated Foliage-gleaner |
| 697. Scaly-throated Foliage-gleaner | 698. Montane Foliage-gleaner | 699. Slaty-winged Foliage-gleaner | 700. Cinnamon-rumped Foliage-gleaner |

| 701. Rufous-rumped Foliage-gleaner | 702. Buff-fronted Foliage-gleaner | 703. Chestnut-winged Foliage-gleaner | 704. Rufous-tailed Foliage-gleaner |
|---|---|---|---|
| 705. Olive-backed Foliage-gleaner | 706. Crested Foliage-gleaner | 707. Ruddy Foliage-gleaner | 708. Buff-throated Foliage-gleaner |
| 709. Chestnut-crowned Foliage-gleaner | 710. Brown-rumped Foliage-gleaner | 711. Flammulated Treehunter | 712. Striped Treehunter |
| 713. Black-billed Treehunter | 714. Streak-capped Treehunter | 715. Uniform Treehunter | 716. Rufous-tailed Xenops |
| 717. Slender-billed Xenops | 718. Streaked Xenops | 719. Plain Xenops | 720. Gray-throated Leaftosser |

721. Tawny-throated Leaftosser

722. Short-billed Leaftosser

723. Black-tailed Leaftosser

724. Scaly-throated Leaftosser

725. Sharp-tailed Streamcreeper

726. Fasciated Antshrike

727. Undulated Antshrike

728. Great Antshrike

729. Black-crested Antshrike

730. Black-backed Antshrike

731. Barred Antshrike

732. Bar-crested Antshrike

733. Lined Antshrike

734. Black Antshrike

735. Blackish-gray Antshrike

736. Castelnau's Antshrike

737. White-shouldered Antshrike

738. Uniform Antshrike

739. Black-capped Antshrike

740. Mouse-colored Antshrike

| 741. Slaty Antshrike | 742. Amazonian Antshrike | 743. Spot-winged Antshrike | 744. Pearly Antshrike |
|---|---|---|---|
| 745. Black Bushbird | 746. Recurve-billed Bushbird | 747. Speckled Antshrike | 748. Russet Antshrike |
| 749. Plain Antvireo | 750. Spot-crowned Antvireo | 751. Plumbeous Antvireo | 752. Dusky-throated Antshrike |
| 753. Cinereous Antshrike | 754. Western Antshrike | 755. Pygmy Antwren | 756. Short-billed Antwren |
| 757. Yellow-throated Antwren | 758. Streaked Antwren | 759. Stripe-chested Antwren | 760. Cherrie's Antwren |

| | | | |
|---|---|---|---|
| 761. Plain-throated Antwren | 762. Checker-throated Antwren | 763. Stipple-throated Antwren | 764. Rufous-tailed Antwren |
| 765. Ornate Antwren | 766. White-flanked Antwren | 767. Slaty Antwren | 768. Long-winged Antwren |
| 769. Rio Suno Antwren | 770. Plain-winged Antwren | 771. Gray Antwren | 772. Banded Antbird |
| 773. Spot-tailed Antwren | 774. Spot-backed Antwren | 775. Yellow-breasted Antwren | 776. Rufous-winged Antwren |
| 777. Dot-winged Antwren | 778. White-fringed Antwren | 779. Long-tailed Antbird | 780. Rufous-rumped Antwren |

| 781. Ash-winged Antwren | 782. Gray Antbird | 783. Dusky Antbird | 784. Blackish Antbird |
|---|---|---|---|
| 785. Black Antbird | 786. Jet Antbird | 787. White-backed Fire-eye | 788. White-browed Antbird |
| 789. Ash-breasted Antbird | 790. Black-faced Antbird | 791. Warbling Antbird | 792. Yellow-browed Antbird |
| 793. Black-chinned Antbird | 794. Black-and-white Antbird | 795. Bare-crowned Antbird | 796. Black-headed Antbird |
| 797. Slate-colored Antbird | 798. Spot-winged Antbird | 799. Silvered Antbird | 800. Esmeraldas Antbird |

| 801. Stub-tailed Antbird | 802. White-bellied Antbird | 803. Chestnut-backed Antbird | 804. Dull-mantled Antbird |
|---|---|---|---|
| 805. Chestnut-tailed Antbird | 806. Plumbeous Antbird | 807. White-shouldered Antbird | 808. Sooty Antbird |
| 809. Immaculate Antbird | 810. Black-throated Antbird | 811. White-plumed Antbird | 812. Bicolored Antbird |
| 813. White-cheeked Antbird | 814. Chestnut-crested Antbird | 815. Hairy-crested Antbird | 816. Black-spotted Bare-eye |
| 817. Reddish-winged Bare-eye | 818. Ocellated Antbird | 819. Spotted Antbird | 820. Spot-backed Antbird |

| | | | |
|---|---|---|---|
| 821. Scale-backed Antbird | 822. Short-tailed Antthrush | 823. Striated Antthrush | 824. Rufous-tailed Antthrush |
| 825. Barred Antthrush | 826. Rufous-capped Antthrush | 827. Black-faced Antthrush | 828. Black-headed Antthrush |
| 829. Rufous-breasted Antthrush | 830. Wing-banded Antbird | 831. Rufous-crowned Antpitta | 832. Undulated Antpitta |
| 833. Giant Antpitta | 834. Scaled Antpitta | 835. Chestnut-crowned Antpitta | 836. Santa Marta Antpitta |
| 837. Bicolored Antpitta | 838. Chestnut-naped Antpitta | 839. Bay-backed Antpitta | 840. Yellow-breasted Antpitta |

| 841. Rufous Antpitta | 842. Tawny Antpitta | 843. Brown-banded Antpitta | 844. Streak-chested Antpitta |
|---|---|---|---|
| 845. Spotted Antpitta | 846. Fulvous-bellied Antpitta | 847. Thrush-like Antpitta | 848. Ochre-breasted Antpitta |
| 849. Rusty-breasted Antpitta | 850. Slate-crowned Antpitta | 851. Hooded Antpitta | 852. Chestnut-crowned Gnateater |
| 853. Chestnut-belted Gnateater | 854. Rusty-belted Tapaculo | 855. Ash-colored Tapaculo | 856. Rufous-vented Tapaculo |
| 857. Unicolored Tapaculo | 858. Pale-throated Tapaculo | 859. Narino Tapaculo | 860. Brown-rumped Tapaculo |

861. Andean Tapaculo

862. Ocellated Tapaculo

863. Golden-headed Manakin

864. Red-capped Manakin

865. White-crowned Manakin

866. Blue-rumped Manakin

867. Blue-crowned Manakin

868. Wire-tailed Manakin

869. Lance-tailed Manakin

870. Blue-backed Manakin

871. Golden-winged Manakin

872. White-ruffed Manakin

873. White-bearded Manakin

874. Golden-collared Manakin

875. Striped Manakin

876. Club-winged Manakin

877. Black Manakin

878. Green Manakin

879. Yellow-headed Manakin

880. Cinnamon Manakin

| 881. Yellow-crowned Manakin | 882. Saffron-crested Tyrant-Manakin | 883. Dwarf Tyrant-Manakin | 884. Wing-barred Manakin |
|---|---|---|---|
| 885. Broad-billed Manakin | 886. Greater Manakin | 887. Thrush-like Manakin | 888. Guianan Cock-of-the-Rock |
| 889. Andean Cock-of-the-Rock | 890. Black-necked Red-Cotinga | 891. Shrike-like Cotinga | 892. Red-crested Cotinga |
| 893. Chestnut-crested Cotinga | 894. Green-and-black Fruiteater | 895. Barred Fruiteater | 896. Black-chested Fruiteater |
| 897. Orange-breasted Fruiteater | 898. Golden-breasted Fruiteater | 899. Fiery-throated Fruiteater | 900. Scaled Fruiteater |

| 901. White-browed Purpletuft | 902. Olivaceous Piha | 903. Dusky Piha | 904. Screaming Piha |
|---|---|---|---|
| 905. Rufous Piha | 906. Barred Becard | 907. Cinereous Becard | 908. Chestnut-crowned Becard |
| 909. Cinnamon Becard | 910. White-winged Becard | 911. Black-capped Becard | 912. Black-and-white Becard |
| 913. One-colored Becard | 914. Pink-throated Becard | 915. Black-tailed Tityra | 916. Masked Tityra |
| 917. Black-crowned Tityra | 918. Purple-throated Cotinga | 919. Blue Cotinga | 920. Plum-throated Cotinga |

| 921. Spangled Cotinga | 922. Purple-breasted Cotinga | 923. Pompadour Cotinga | 924. White Cotinga |
|---|---|---|---|
| 925. Bare-necked Fruitcrow | 926. Purple-throated Fruitcrow | 927. Red-ruffed Fruitcrow | 928. Amazonian Umbrellabird |
| 929. Long-wattled Umbrellabird | 930. Sooty-headed Tyrannulet | 931. Plumbeous-crowned Tyrannulet | 932. Black-capped Tyrannulet |
| 933. Tawny-rumped Tyrannulet | 934. Ashy-headed Tyrannulet | 935. Paltry Tyrannulet | 936. Slender-footed Tyrannulet |
| 937. Golden-faced Tyrannulet | 938. White-lored Tyrannulet | 939. Brown-capped Tyrannulet | 940. Southern Beardless-Tyrannulet |

| 941. Mouse-colored Tyrannulet | 942. Scrub Flycatcher | 943. Short-billed Flycatcher | 944. Yellow-crowned Tyrannulet |
| 945. Forest Elaenia | 946. Gray Elaenia | 947. Greenish Elaenia | 948. Yellow-bellied Elaenia |
| 949. Small-billed Elaenia | 950. Lesser Elaenia | 951. Rufous-crowned Elaenia | 952. Mountain Elaenia |
| 953. Sierran Elaenia | 954. Mottle-backed Elaenia | 955. White-throated Tyrannulet | 956. White-tailed Tyrannulet |
| 957. Sulphur-bellied Tyrannulet | 958. White-banded Tyrannulet | 959. River Tyrannulet | 960. Torrent Tyrannulet |

961. Slender-billed Tyrannulet

962. Pale-tipped Tyrannulet

963. Lesser Wagtail-Tyrant

964. Tufted Tit-Tyrant

965. Agile Tit-Tyrant

966. Bearded Tachuri

967. Subtropical Doradito

968. Tawny-crowned Pygmy-Tyrant

969. Streak-necked Flycatcher

970. Olive-striped Flycatcher

971. Ochre-bellied Flycatcher

972. Slaty-capped Flycatcher

973. Sepia-capped Flycatcher

974. Rufous-breasted Flycatcher

975. Rufous-browed Tyrannulet

976. Marble-faced Bristle-Tyrant

977. Spectacled Bristle-Tyrant

978. Variegated Bristle-Tyrant

979. Yellow Tyrannulet

980. Bronze-olive Pygmy-Tyrant

| 981. Rufous-headed Pygmy-Tyrant | 982. Ringed Antpipit | 983. Short-tailed Pygmy-Tyrant | 984. Scale-crested Pygmy-Tyrant |
|---|---|---|---|
| 985. Double-banded Pygmy-Tyrant | 986. Helmeted Pygmy-Tyrant | 987. Pale-eyed Pygmy-Tyrant | 988. Black-and-white Tody-Tyrant |
| 989. Rufous-crowned Tody-Tyrant | 990. Southern Bentbill | 991. Johannes' Tody-Tyrant | 992. Pearly-vented Tody-Tyrant |
| 993. Black-throated Tody-Tyrant | 994. White-eyed Tody-Tyrant | 995. Black-headed Tody-Flycatcher | 996. Yellow-browed Tody-Flycatcher |
| 997. Golden-winged Tody-Flycatcher | 998. Common Tody-Flycatcher | 999. Spotted Tody-Flycatcher | 1000. Slate-headed Tody-Flycatcher |

| 1001. Rusty-fronted Tody-Flycatcher | 1002. Brownish Flycatcher | 1003. Rufous-tailed Flatbill | 1004. Large-headed Flatbill |
| 1005. Eye-ringed Flatbill | 1006. Olivaceous Flatbill | 1007. Fulvous-breasted Flatbill | 1008. Yellow-olive Flycatcher |
| 1009. Yellow-margined Flycatcher | 1010. Gray-crowned Flycatcher | 1011. Yellow-breasted Flycatcher | 1012. White-crested Spadebill |
| 1013. White-throated Spadebill | 1014. Golden-crowned Spadebill | 1015. Cinnamon-crested Spadebill | 1016. Yellow-throated Spadebill |
| 1017. Royal Flycatcher | 1018. Ornate Flycatcher | 1019. Ruddy-tailed Flycatcher | 1020. Tawny-breasted Flycatcher |

| 1021. Black-tailed Flycatcher | 1022. Sulphur-rumped Flycatcher | 1023. Flavescent Flycatcher | 1024. Orange-crested Flycatcher |
| 1025. Handsome Flycatcher | 1026. Bran-colored Flycatcher | 1027. Black-billed Flycatcher | 1028. Cinnamon Flycatcher |
| 1029. Tufted Flycatcher | 1030. Tropical Pewee | 1031. Euler's Flycatcher | 1032. Fuscous Flycatcher |
| 1033. Black Phoebe | 1034. Vermilion Flycatcher | 1035. Brown-backed Chat-Tyrant | 1036. Rufous-breasted Chat-Tyrant |
| 1037. Slaty-backed Chat-Tyrant | 1038. Crowned Chat-Tyrant | 1039. Yellow-bellied Chat-Tyrant | 1040. Drab Water-Tyrant |

| 1041. Streak- throated Bush-Tyrant | 1042. Red-rumped Bush-Tyrant | 1043. Smoky Bush-Tyrant | 1044. Santa Marta Bush-Tyrant |
|---|---|---|---|
| 1045. Black-billed Shrike-Tyrant | 1046. Plain-capped Ground-Tyrant | 1047. Spot-billed Ground-Tyrant | 1048. Little Ground-Tyrant |
| 1049. Riverside Tyrant | 1050. Rufous-tailed Tyrant | 1051. Amazonian Black-Tyrant | 1052. Pied Water-Tyrant |
| 1053. White-headed Marsh-Tyrant | 1054. Long-tailed Tyrant | 1055. Cliff Flycatcher | 1056. Cattle Tyrant |
| 1057. Bright-rumped Attila | 1058. Dull-capped Attila | 1059. Cinnamon Attila | 1060. Grayish Mourner |

| 1061. Rufous Mourner | 1062. Cinereous Mourner | 1063. Speckled Mourner | 1064. Sirystes |
|---|---|---|---|
| 1065. Short-crested Flycatcher | 1066. Venezuelan Flycatcher | 1067. Panama Flycatcher | 1068. Apical Flycatcher |
| 1069. Pale-edged Flycatcher | 1070. Brown-crested Flycatcher | 1071. Dusky-capped Flycatcher | 1072. Great Kiskadee |
| 1073. Lesser Kiskadee | 1074. Boat-billed Flycatcher | 1075. Rusty-margined Flycatcher | 1076. Social Flycatcher |
| 1077. Gray-capped Flycatcher | 1078. Lemon-browed Flycatcher | 1079. White-ringed Flycatcher | 1080. Streaked Flycatcher |

| 1081. Golden-crowned Flycatcher | 1082. Piratic Flycatcher | 1083. Crowned Slaty-Flycatcher | 1084. Variegated Flycatcher |
|---|---|---|---|
| 1085. Sulphury Flycatcher | 1086. Dusky-chested Flycatcher | 1087. Tropical Kingbird | 1088. Gray Kingbird |
| 1089. Snowy-throated Kingbird | 1090. White-throated Kingbird | 1091. Horned Lark | 1092. White-winged Swallow |
| 1093. Brown-chested Martin | 1094. Gray-breasted Martin | 1095. Brown-bellied Swallow | 1096. Blue-and-white Swallow |
| 1097. Pale-footed Swallow | 1098. White-banded Swallow | 1099. Black-collared Swallow | 1100. White-thighed Swallow |

| | | | |
|---|---|---|---|
| 1101. Tawny-headed Swallow | 1102. Collared Jay | 1103. Turquoise Jay | 1104. Beautiful Jay |
| 1105. Violaceous Jay | 1106. Azure-naped Jay | 1107. Black-chested Jay | 1108. Green Jay |
| 1109. Black-capped Donacobius | 1110. Bicolored Wren | 1111. White-headed Wren | 1112. Band-backed Wren |
| 1113. Thrush-like Wren | 1114. Stripe-backed Wren | 1115. Gray-mantled Wren | 1116. Rufous Wren |
| 1117. Sepia-brown Wren | 1118. Sedge Wren | 1119. Apolinar's Marsh-Wren | 1120. Sooty-headed Wren |

| | | | |
|---|---|---|---|
| 1121. Black-bellied Wren | 1122. Plain-tailed Wren | 1123. Moustached Wren | 1124. Coraya Wren |
| 1125. Rufous-breasted Wren | 1126. Spot-breasted Wren | 1127. Bay Wren | 1128. Stripe-throated Wren |
| 1129. Rufous-and-white Wren | 1130. Niceforo's Wren | 1131. Buff-breasted Wren | 1132. House Wren |
| 1133. Mountain Wren | 1134. White-breasted Wood-Wren | 1135. Gray-breasted Wood-Wren | 1136. Nightingale Wren |
| 1137. Chestnut-breasted Wren | 1138. Song Wren | 1139. Musician Wren | 1140. Tropical Mockingbird |

| 1141. Andean Solitaire | 1142. Rufous-brown Solitaire | 1143. Black Solitaire | 1144. Orange-billed Nightingale-Thrush |
|---|---|---|---|
| 1145. Slaty-backed Nightingale-Thrush | 1146. Spotted Nightingale-Thrush | 1147. Yellow-legged Thrush | 1148. Pale-eyed Thrush |
| 1149. Great Thrush | 1150. Glossy-black Thrush | 1151. Black-hooded Thrush | 1152. Chestnut-bellied Thrush |
| 1153. Pale-breasted Thrush | 1154. Black-billed Thrush | 1155. Lawrence's Thrush | 1156. Cocoa Thrush |
| 1157. Pale-vented Thrush | 1158. Clay-colored Thrush | 1159. Bare-eyed Thrush | 1160. White-necked Thrush |

| | | | |
|---|---|---|---|
| 1161. White-throated Thrush | 1162. Collared Gnatwren | 1163. Half-collared Gnatwren | 1164. Long-billed Gnatwren |
| 1165. Tropical Gnatcatcher | 1166. Slate-throated Gnatcatcher | 1167. Yellowish Pipit | 1168. Paramo Pipit |
| 1169. Rufous-browed Peppershrike | 1170. Black-billed Peppershrike | 1171. Yellow-browed Shrike-Vireo | 1172. Slaty-capped Shrike-Vireo |
| 1173. Red-eyed Vireo | 1174. Brown-capped Vireo | 1175. Lemon-chested Greenlet | 1176. Brown-headed Greenlet |
| 1177. Rufous-naped Greenlet | 1178. Golden-fronted Greenlet | 1179. Dusky-capped Greenlet | 1180. Scrub Greenlet |

| 1181. Tawny-crowned Greenlet | 1182. Lesser Greenlet | 1183. Shiny Cowbird | 1184. Bronze-brown Cowbird |
|---|---|---|---|
| 1185. Giant Cowbird | 1186. Band-tailed Oropendola | 1187. Chestnut-headed Oropendola | 1188. Crested Oropendola |
| 1189. Green Oropendola | 1190. Russet-backed Oropendola | 1191. Black Oropendola | 1192. Chestnut-mantled Oropendola |
| 1193. Olive Oropendola | 1194. Yellow-rumped Cacique | 1195. Red-rumped Cacique | 1196. Scarlet-rumped Cacique |
| 1197. Mountain Cacique | 1198. Solitary Black Cacique | 1199. Yellow-billed Cacique | 1200. Carib Grackle |

| 1201. Great-tailed Grackle | 1202. Red-bellied Grackle | 1203. Mountain Grackle | 1204. Velvet-fronted Grackle |
|---|---|---|---|
| 1205. Yellow-hooded Blackbird | 1206. Epaulet Oriole | 1207. Moriche Oriole | 1208. Orange-crowned Oriole |
| 1209. Troupial | 1210. Orange-backed Troupial | 1211. Yellow Oriole | 1212. Yellow-backed Oriole |
| 1213. Yellow-tailed Oriole | 1214. Oriole Blackbird | 1215. Red-breasted Blackbird | 1216. Eastern Meadowlark |
| 1217. Tropical Parula | 1218. Yellow Warbler (resid. subsp.) | 1219. Masked Yellowthroat | 1220. Slate-throated Redstart |

| 1221. Golden-fronted Redstart | 1222. Spectacled Redstart | 1223. Yellow-crowned Redstart | 1224. Golden-crowned Warbler |
|---|---|---|---|
| 1225. Golden-bellied Warbler | 1226. Flavescent Warbler | 1227. Citrine Warbler | 1228. Pale-legged Warbler |
| 1229. Black-crested Warbler | 1230. Russet-crowned Warbler | 1231. White-lored Warbler | 1232. Gray-throated Warbler |
| 1233. Rufous-capped Warbler | 1234. Three-striped Warbler | 1235. Santa Marta Warbler | 1236. Buff-rumped Warbler |
| 1237. Chestnut-vented Conebill | 1238. White-eared Conebill | 1239. Bicolored Conebill | 1240. Blue-backed Conebill |

| 1241. Rufous-browed Conebill | 1242. Cinereous Conebill | 1243. Capped Conebill | 1244. Giant Conebill |
|---|---|---|---|
| 1245. Bananaquit | 1246. Bluish Flower-piercer | 1247. Masked Flower-piercer | 1248. Deep-blue Flower-piercer |
| 1249. Indigo Flower-piercer | 1250. Chestnut-bellied Flower-piercer | 1251. Glossy Flower-piercer | 1252. Black Flower-piercer |
| 1253. Black-throated Flower-piercer | 1254. White-sided Flower-piercer | 1255. Rusty Flower-piercer | 1256. Short-billed Honeycreeper |
| 1257. Purple Honeycreeper | 1258. Shining Honeycreeper | 1259. Red-legged Honeycreeper | 1260. Green Honeycreeper |

| 1261. Golden-collared Honeycreeper | 1262. Blue Dacnis | 1263. Black-faced Dacnis | 1264. Viridian Dacnis |
| 1265. Yellow-bellied Dacnis | 1266. Scarlet-thighed Dacnis | 1267. Scarlet-breasted Dacnis | 1268. White-bellied Dacnis |
| 1269. Swallow-Tanager | 1270. Blue-naped Chlorophonia | 1271. Yellow-collared Chlorophonia | 1272. Chestnut-breasted Chlorophonia |
| 1273. Blue-hooded Euphonia | 1274. Orange-bellied Euphonia | 1275. Tawny-capped Euphonia | 1276. White-vented Euphonia |
| 1277. Velvet-fronted Euphonia | 1278. Orange-crowned Euphonia | 1279. Trinidad Euphonia | 1280. Purple-throated Euphonia |

| | | | |
|---|---|---|---|
| 1281. Thick-billed Euphonia | 1282. Fulvous-vented Euphonia | 1283. Rufous-bellied Euphonia | 1284. Bronze-green Euphonia |
| 1285. Golden-bellied Euphonia | 1286. Plumbeous Euphonia | 1287. Fawn-breasted Tanager | 1288. Turquoise Dacnis-Tanager |
| 1289. Orange-eared Tanager | 1290. Glistening-green Tanager | 1291. Multicolored Tanager | 1292. Opal-rumped Tanager |
| 1293. Opal-crowned Tanager | 1294. Paradise Tanager | 1295. Green-and-gold Tanager | 1296. Emerald Tanager |
| 1297. Blue-whiskered Tanager | 1298. Speckled Tanager | 1299. Yellow-bellied Tanager | 1300. Rufous-throated Tanager |

| 1301. Golden Tanager | 1302. Silver-throated Tanager | 1303. Saffron-crowned Tanager | 1304. Golden-eared Tanager |
|---|---|---|---|
| 1305. Flame-faced Tanager | 1306. Blue-browed Tanager | 1307. Metallic-green Tanager | 1308. Blue-necked Tanager |
| 1309. Golden-hooded Tanager | 1310. Masked Tanager | 1311. Golden-naped Tanager | 1312. Turquoise Tanager |
| 1313. Gray-and-gold Tanager | 1314. Plain-colored Tanager | 1315. Bay-headed Tanager | 1316. Rufous-winged Tanager |
| 1317. Scrub Tanager | 1318. Burnished-buff Tanager | 1319. Beryl-spangled Tanager | 1320. Blue-and-black Tanager |

| 1321. Black-capped Tanager | 1322. Black-headed Tanager | 1323. Purplish-mantled Tanager | 1324. Golden-crowned Tanager |
|---|---|---|---|
| 1325. Scarlet-bellied Mountain-Tanager | 1326. Santa Marta Mounain-Tanager | 1327. Lacrimose Mountain-Tanager | 1328. Blue-winged Mountain-Tanager |
| 1329. Black-chinned Mountain-Tanager | 1330. Hooded Mountain-Tanager | 1331. Masked Mountain-Tanager | 1332. Black-chested Mountain-Tanager |
| 1333. Golden-chested Tanager | 1334. Black-and-gold Tanager | 1335. Moss-backed Tanager | 1336. Gold-ringed Tanager |
| 1337. Buff-breasted Mountain-Tanager | 1338. Blue-gray Tanager | 1339. Glaucous Tanager | 1340. Palm Tanager |

| 1341. Blue-capped Tanager | 1342. Silver-beaked Tanager | 1343. Crimson-backed Tanager | 1344. Masked Crimson Tanager |
|---|---|---|---|
| 1345. Flame-rumped Tanager | 1346. Lemon-rumped Tanager | 1347. Vermilion Tanager | 1348. Hepatic Tanager |
| 1349. White-winged Tanager | 1350. Red-hooded Tanager | 1351. Carmiol's Tanager | 1352. Lemon-browed Tanager |
| 1353. Ochre-breasted Tanager | 1354. Red-crowned Ant-Tanager | 1355. Red-throated Ant-Tanager | 1356. Sooty Ant-Tanager |
| 1357. Crested Ant-Tanager | 1358. Fulvous Shrike-Tanager | 1359. White-lined Tanager | 1360. Flame-crested Tanager |

1361. Fulvous-crested Tanager

1362. Red-shouldered Tanager

1363. White-shouldered Tanager

1364. Tawny-crested Tanager

1365. Scarlet-browed Tanager

1366. Rufous-crested Tanager

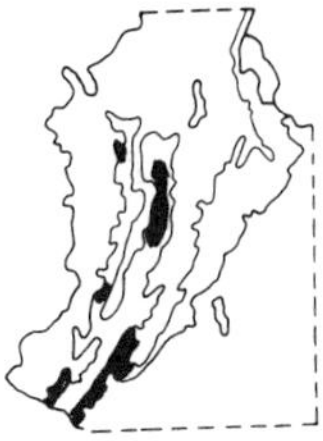

1367. Gray-headed Tanager

1368. Dusky-faced Tanager

1369. Rosy Thrush-Tanager

1370. Hooded Tanager

1371. Guira Tanager

1372. Yellow-backed Tanager

1373. Scarlet-and-white Tanager

1374. Fulvous-headed Tanager

1375. Orange-headed Tanager

1376. Rufous-chested Tanager

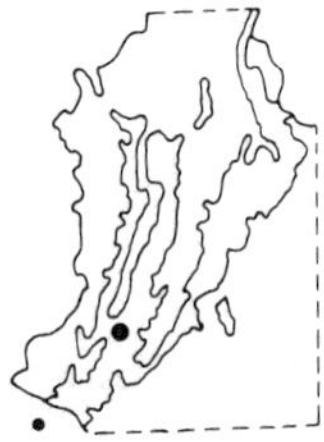

1377. White-capped Tanager

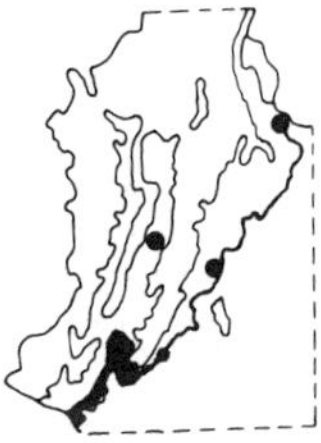

1378. Common Bush-Tanager

1379. Tacarcuna Bush-Tanager

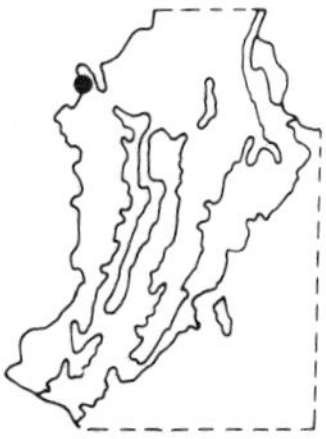

1380. Yellow-green Bush-Tanager

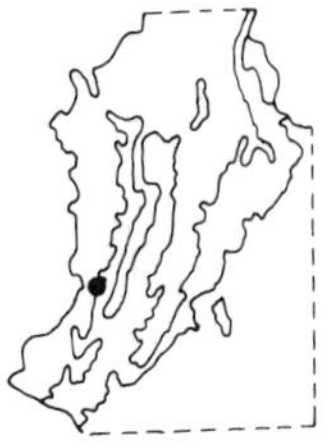

| 1381. Yellow-throated Bush-Tanager | 1382. Short-billed Bush-Tanager | 1383. Ash-throated Bush-Tanager | 1384. Dusky-bellied Bush-Tanager |
|---|---|---|---|
| 1385. Black-backed Bush-Tanager | 1386. Gray-hooded Bush-Tanager | 1387. Black-capped Hemispingus | 1388. Superciliaried Hemispingus |
| 1389. Oleaginous Hemispingus | 1390. Black-eared Hemispingus | 1391. Black-headed Hemispingus | 1392. Grass-green Tanager |
| 1393. Magpie Tanager | 1394. Black-faced Tanager | 1395. Plush-capped Finch | 1396. Dickcissel |
| 1397. Blue-black Grosbeak | 1398. Ultramarine Grosbeak | 1399. Buff-throated Saltator | 1400. Black-winged Saltator |

| 1401. Grayish Saltator | 1402. Orinocan Saltator | 1403. Streaked Saltator | 1404. Slaty Grosbeak |
|---|---|---|---|
| 1405. Yellow-green Grosbeak | 1406. Yellow-shouldered Grosbeak | 1407. Vermilion Cardinal | 1408. Black-backed Grosbeak |
| 1409. Yellow Grosbeak | 1410. Red-capped Cardinal | 1411. Pileated Finch | 1412. Olive Finch |
| 1413. Tanager-Finch | 1414. Yellow-throated Brush-Finch | 1415. Pale-naped Brush-Finch | 1416. Rufous-naped Brush-Finch |
| 1417. Santa Marta Brush-Finch | 1418. Tricolored Brush-Finch | 1419. Dusky-headed Brush-Finch | 1420. Olive-headed Brush-Finch |

| 1421. Moustached Brush-Finch | 1422. White-rimmed Brush-Finch | 1423. Ochre-breasted Brush-Finch | 1424. Slaty Brush-Finch |
| 1425. Chestnut-capped Brush-Finch | 1426. Stripe-headed Brush-Finch | 1427. Black-headed Brush-Finch | 1428. Black-striped Sparrow |
| 1429. Tocuyo Sparrow | 1430. Orange-billed Sparrow | 1431. Golden-winged Sparrow | 1432. Pectoral Sparrow |
| 1433. Sooty Grassquit | 1434. Black-faced Grassquit | 1435. Yellow-faced Grassquit | 1436. Dull-colored Grassquit |
| 1437. Paramo Seedeater | 1438. Plain-colored Seedeater | 1439. Band-tailed Seedeater | 1440. White-naped Seedeater |

| 1441. Blue Seedeater | 1442. Lesser Seed-Finch | 1443. Large-billed Seed-Finch | 1444. Great-billed Seed-Finch |
| 1445. Slate-colored Seedeater | 1446. Gray Seedeater | 1447. Plumbeous Seedeater | 1448. Variable Seedeater |
| 1449. Lined Seedeater | 1450. Lesson's Seedeater | 1451. Black-and-white Seedeater | 1452. Yellow-bellied Seedeater |
| 1453. Double-collared Seedeater | 1454. Tumaco Seedeater | 1455. Ruddy-breasted Seedeater | 1456. Chestnut-bellied Seedeater |
| 1457. Chestnut-throated Seedeater | 1458. Blue-black Grassquit | 1459. Grassland Yellow-Finch | 1460. Stripe-tailed Yellow-Finch |

| 1461. Saffron Finch | 1462. Orange-fronted Yellow-Finch | 1463. Slaty Finch | 1464. Plumbeous Sierra-Finch |
|---|---|---|---|
| 1465. Wedge-tailed Grass-Finch | 1466. Grasshopper Sparrow | 1467. Yellow-browed Sparrow | 1468. Grassland Sparrow |
| 1469. Rufous-collared Sparrow | 1470. Andean Siskin | 1471. Red Siskin | 1472. Hooded Siskin |
| 1473. Yellow-bellied Siskin | 1474. Lesser Goldfinch | 1475. House Sparrow | |

# INDEX TO ENGLISH NAMES

ca 140 Tanagers

# INDEX TO GENERA AND SPECIES

*Library of Congress Cataloging in Publication Data*

Hilty, Steven L.
  A guide to the birds of Colombia.

  Bibliography: p.
  Includes indexes.
    1. Birds—Colombia—Identification.  I. Brown,
William, 1910-    .  II. Title.
QL689.C7H55  1985        598.29861        84-18211
ISBN 0-691-08371-1 (alk. paper)
ISBN 0-691-08372-X (pbk.)